RACEHORSES OF 2017

Price £79.00

A TIMEFORM PUBLICATION

CONTENTS

The age, weight and distance tables, for use in applying the ratings in races involving horses of different ages, appear at the end of the book

Compiled and produced by

Geoff Greetham (Publishing Editor), Paul Muncaster (Managing Editor), John Ingles (Senior Editor, Editor for pedigrees and 'Top Horses Abroad'), Chris Williams (Editor & Handicapper), David Johnson, Pat Jupp, Matt Gardner, Simon Baker, Simon Walker, Billy Nash, Mark Milligan (Handicappers), Phil Turner, Nic Doggett, Ben Fearnley, Adam Houghton (Essays), Kristian Hilliam, Jake Price, Rory King (noteforms), Sally Wright (pedigree updates), David Holdsworth, Wendy Muncaster, Rachel Todd, Chris Wright, Ivan Gardiner, Michael Williamson (Production)

ISBN 978-0-9933900-9-8

TIMEFORM CHAMPIONS IN EUROPE 2017

HORSE OF THE YEAR
BEST THREE-YEAR-OLD FILLY

ENABLE

BEST TWO-YEAR-OLD COLT RATED AT 123

U S NAVY FLAG

BEST TWO-YEAR-OLD FILLY RATED AT 118p

CLEMMIE

BEST THREE-YEAR-OLD MALES RATED AT 136

BATTAASH & CRACKSMAN

BEST OLDER HORSE RATED AT 132

CLOTH OF STARS

BEST OLDER FEMALE RATED AT 130

MARSHA

BEST SPRINTER RATED AT 136

BATTAASH

BEST MILER RATED AT 129

RIBCHESTER

BEST MIDDLE-DISTANCE HORSE RATED AT 136

CRACKSMAN

BEST STAYER RATED AT 128

ORDER OF ST GEORGE

BEST PERFORMANCES IN A HANDICAP IN BRITAIN

ACCIDENTAL AGENT

ran to 120 when winning totescoop6 Challenge Cup at Ascot

SIR DANCEALOT

ran to 120 when runner-up in Wreake Handicap at Leicester

BEST PERFORMANCES ON ALL-WEATHER IN BRITAIN

DECORATED KNIGHT & ARAB SPRING

ran to 119 when first and second in Betway Winter Derby Trial Stakes at Lingfield

JUDDMONTE

Racehorses of 2017

Introduction

'There are *known knowns*, things we know we know. We also know there are *known unknowns*, which is to say we know there are some things we do not know. Then there are also *unknown unknowns*—the ones we don't know that we don't know.' Donald Rumsfeld's idiosyncratic summing-up of American policy in Iraq has a more general application. The existence of so many 'unknown unknowns' attests to the infinite possibilities in life which, in the end, is often shaped by events over which an individual has no control. The 'unknown unknowns' are also part of the intrigue of following a sport like horse racing. The start of each year or season offers the fascinating possibility that a transformational horse (or horses) will emerge. The 2017 racing year provides a perfect illustration. A number of performers, whose names meant little to most of the sport's followers at the turn of the year, emerged to leave an indelible mark. The middle-distance filly **Enable** made a very late, unheralded appearance as a two-year-old, winning a fillies maiden on the tapeta at Newcastle, but she blossomed into the best of her sex trained in Britain since Pebbles over thirty years ago. It would be hard for any filly to better the achievements in a single season of Enable who won five successive Group 1s including the King George VI and Queen Elizabeth Stakes and the Prix de l'Arc de Triomphe, a double achieved previously in the same season by just six colts, including three of the middle-distance 'greats', Ribot, Mill Reef and Dancing Brave (the last-named owned by Enable's highly successful owner-breeder Khalid Abdullah who has now had five winners of the Arc). Enable, whose wide-ranging essay includes a justification of the under-attack weight-for-age scale in horse racing, is only the sixth filly to have been Timeform Horse of the Year (Pebbles was one of the others). Enable was ridden to all her Group 1 wins by Frankie Dettori, for whom she was a record fifth Arc winner. The debt that racing owes to the charismatic Dettori is one of the subjects covered in the essay on Enable's stablemate **Cracksman** (who also ran just once at two) whose brilliant victory in the Champion Stakes provided the seventh British Champions' Day with its defining moment. The essay explains, however, why richly-endowed British Champions' Day, optimistically promoted as 'the day that champions are crowned', is not the be-all and end-all. Becoming a champion racehorse can never be dependent on producing a performance on just one specific day. In common with Enable, another of the 'unknown unknowns' the tip-top sprinter **Battaash** didn't appear on British Champions' Day. He established himself as the best sprinter trained in Britain since Dayjur, and the highest-rated gelding in the history of the *Racehorses* series, with scintillating performances in the King George Stakes at the Qatar Goodwood Festival and in the Prix de l'Abbaye on Arc weekend (when he sported new 'golden' shoes). It must be a long time since there has been a group of sprinters to match those who graced the British turf in the latest season and Battaash's

Enable crowned a magnificent year by winning Europe's richest race, the Prix de l'Arc de Triomphe, in which her success also made Frankie Dettori the first jockey to ride the winner of the great race five times—Enable also became the first filly to win both the King George VI and Queen Elizabeth Stakes and the Prix de l'Arc in the same year, a feat achieved previously only by the colts Ribot (1956), Ballymoss (1958), Mill Reef (1971), Dancing Brave (1986), Lammtarra (1995) and Dylan Thomas (2007); the selecting of a Horse of the Year in **Racehorses** *began in the 'sixties and Enable is just the sixth filly to have been awarded the title, following Allez France (1974), Habibti (1983), Pebbles (1985), Zarkava (2008) and Treve (2013)*

transformation from two (when he was gelded) to three couldn't possibly have been predicted from his racecourse appearances as a juvenile, and even his trainer had no real inkling either, stating at the start of the season that it was his ambition to 'try to find a listed race for him.'

Among the 'known knowns' at the start of the latest season was that Coolmore and its racing arm Ballydoyle, the dominant force in European racing in the first part of the century, was going to have a major say in the destination of the biggest prizes, particularly the classics. The pages of this edition are replete with the achievements of the horses owned by the Coolmore partners, of their trainer Aidan O'Brien and of the phenomenal Coolmore stallion Galileo, the last-named topping the combined sires' table for Britain and Ireland for the ninth time, with his progeny winning a scarcely believable forty-six European pattern races, as discussed in the essay on dual classic winner **Winter**, another of those who went into the new season as virtually an 'unknown unknown'. Winter went on to win the Coronation Stakes and the Nassau at Goodwood, with her stablemates **Roly Poly** and **Hydrangea** filling the places behind her at Royal Ascot as they had done in the Irish One Thousand Guineas. Aidan O'Brien has now had the one, two, three in a European Group 1 on no fewer than eighteen occasions, something he also achieved in the latest season in the Moyglare Stud Stakes (with **Happily**, Magical and September) and in the Dewhurst (in which **U S Navy Flag** led home a one, two, three, four).

Happily went on to beat the colts in the Prix Jean-Luc Lagardere at Chantilly on Arc day but she wasn't the best of the Ballydoyle two-year-old fillies, that palm going to the Cheveley Park winner **Clemmie** who looks a potential classic winner from another fine crop of juvenile fillies for the Coolmore partners. Their latest batch of three-year-old fillies accounted for almost half of Aidan O'Brien's record haul of worldwide Group/Grade 1s, with Roly Poly (whose essay illustrates that it wasn't all plain sailing for Ballydoyle) winning three of them, one more than Hydrangea who equalled the existing trainers' record for O'Brien when winning the Fillies' And Mares' Stakes, which would have been a certainty to draw the biggest headline on British Champions' Day but for Cracksman's performance. **Saxon Warrior** lived up to his name when getting the better of Qatar Racing's **Roaring Lion** in a strong Racing Post Trophy, the last Group 1 of the year in Britain, a victory which took Aidan O'Brien past the world record for Group/Grade 1s on the Flat in a calendar year set fourteen years earlier by American trainer Bobby Frankel (the redoubtable **Highland Reel** finally took O'Brien's total to twenty-eight when winning the Hong Kong Vase).

Saxon Warrior is by Japanese triple crown winner Deep Impact, who is among a number of stallions—with Commonwealth Cup winner **Caravaggio** set to join them—being used by Coolmore as a cross for its large band of Sadler's Wells and Galileo broodmares (U S Navy Flag and his sister Roly Poly—both out of the Galileo mare Misty For Me—are by American stallion War Front). Trainer-breeder Jim Bolger was a key supporter of Galileo, giving the stallion a vital boost in his early days, and the essay on **Verbal Dexterity**, the Bolger-trained winner of the National Stakes on Irish Champions' Weekend before coming fourth in the Racing Post Trophy, illustrates how he is not afraid of ploughing a lone furrow. Also in the classic mix among the Ballydoyle colts is **Gustav Klimt** whose two-year-old season ended prematurely when he was withdrawn, after suffering a stone bruise, from the National Stakes, for which he was odds on.

The National Stakes had been among the races won by **Churchill** who went on to complete the Anglo-Irish Two Thousand Guineas double in the latest season (his essay contains further details about the classic record of his

Saxon Warrior provided Aidan O'Brien with his eighth winner of the Racing Post Trophy (a race that started life as the Timeform Gold Cup in 1961 when it was the most valuable two-year-old event ever staged in Europe and only the King George VI and Queen Elizabeth Stakes, the Derby, the St Leger and the Two Thousand Guineas carried more money); the latest Racing Post Trophy was particularly significant for the fact that Saxon Warrior's victory brought Aidan O'Brien's total of Group/Grade 1 victories for the year to twenty-six, passing a record held by American trainer Bobby Frankel (O'Brien eventually reached twenty-eight for the year)

trainer, whose career is also examined in Highland Reel's essay). **Capri** also landed a classic double for the stable (Irish Derby and Doncaster St Leger) in a year when Ballydoyle won all the colts' classics in Britain and Ireland, 40/1 outsider **Wings of Eagles** winning the Derby (his wide-ranging essay looks at ITV's first year viewing figures since taking over terrestrial racing coverage) and **Order of St George** taking the Irish St Leger for the second time. The essay on Order of St George reflects on the fact that Royal Ascot's oldest race, the Gold Cup (in which Order of St George was just beaten by the very popular **Big Orange**), seemed in terminal decline in the mid-'eighties. Staying events are an attractive feature of British racing and a raft of measures, outlined in the essay on Goodwood Cup winner **Stradivarius**, makes the future for stayers look a lot brighter than it once did. As well as facing Order of St George again, the Cup horses will have to beat another O'Brien-trained stayer, **Rekindling**, who put Aidan O'Brien's son Joseph on the international map when he triumphed in the Melbourne Cup.

The Derby at Epsom has proved to be the sport's greatest invention, emerging not from any marketing department, or as part of any grand design, but from the toss of a coin at a party held at a country house near Epsom in 1779—the race may not be so dominant as it once was, but it remains a major objective each year for European racing's 'superpowers'; Coolmore's racing arm Ballydoyle has had the winner four times in the last six years, 40/1 outsider Wings of Eagles springing a surprise in the latest edition at the expense of stablemate and joint second favourite Cliffs of Moher and the favourite Cracksman

Coolmore/Ballydoyle's fortunes have contrasted sharply in recent years with those of European racing's other major 'superpower', Darley/Godolphin. The various different ownership combinations used by the Coolmore partners mean their prize money is divided up into smaller units for the purposes of the end-of-season owners' tables in *Racehorses* (the *Racing Post* tables, which decide the 'official' championship, treat the Coolmore partners as completely separate entities). Combining all the prize money won by the Coolmore partners would have made them the season's leading owners in Britain, but that title went again, by a large margin, to Godolphin (for the fifth time in six years and for the twelfth time overall). The summer resignation of Sheikh Mohammed's long-standing adviser John Ferguson, the circumstances of which are touched on in the essay on **Thunder Snow**, was one of the year's most surprising news stories. One of the policies that had been abandoned under Ferguson's watch was the automatic transfer to its in-house stables of horses purchased by Godolphin from other stables. Horses like **Ribchester**, the year's leading miler, **Barney Roy** and **Harry Angel**, the last-named the season's top six-furlong horse (his essay covers the transformation in recent times of the sprinting scene), were among the in-training purchases who did particularly well for Godolphin in the latest season after being left with their original trainers. The essay on St James's Palace Stakes winner Barney Roy outlines how Ferguson's departure signalled an end to the Darley/Godolphin boycott of the progeny of stallions based at Coolmore, some of the duels at the yearling sales in the latter part of the year evoking memories of the battles between the Maktoums and Coolmore at the height of the bloodstock boom in the 'eighties. Ribchester, who had also done well for Godolphin as a three-year-old, won a further three Group 1s as a four-year-old and he would probably have added a fourth but for a puzzling defeat in the Sussex Stakes, run in a morass, at the hands of 20/1-shot **Here Comes When**.

Ribchester's achievements helped his trainer Richard Fahey to finish in third place in the trainers' table in Britain for the second year running, again behind only Aidan O'Brien and John Gosden, the latter's domestic earnings being a record for a British-based trainer (Gosden also headed the table for earnings on foreign soil by a British trainer, as detailed in the essay on Enable). Richard Fahey, who was runner-up to John Gosden in the trainers' championship in 2015, tops the growing list of northern-based trainers on the Flat who sit at racing's top table nowadays. Fahey and long-standing Middleham trainer Mark Johnston run two of the biggest and busiest yards in the country (Johnston's latest achievements, which include becoming only the third trainer to reach 4,000 winners in Britain, are outlined in the entry on **Elarqam**). Fahey and Johnston are backed up by the likes of David O'Meara (see the essay on **Suedois**), Kevin Ryan (whose troubled season is touched on in the entry on **Brando**) and Karl Burke. The key to the success of the last-named was a batch of two-year-olds which included the Fillies' Mile winner **Laurens**, the first winner of that race to be trained in the North. French-bred Laurens seems likely to tackle the Oaks at Chantilly, rather than at Epsom, as she is eligible for bonuses in France on top of any prize money (the Prix de Diane is the richest fillies race in Europe anyway). Burke won the Group 1 Prix Morny at Deauville with another of his two-year-olds **Unfortunately**, whose essay applauds the belated introduction of unanimity in the rules across Europe governing interference in races (France and Germany are coming into line with Britain and Ireland).

Uniformity of raceday rules around the world is a prerequisite to horse racing becoming a truly global sport, the greatest barrier to which remains North America's permissive approach to raceday medication, a thorny topic to which this Annual returns in the extended entry on Breeders' Cup Turf winner **Talismanic** which points out that any sport which is a betting medium has to be particularly mindful of not allowing anything to undermine public confidence. The International Federation of Horseracing Authorities has taken a small step by banning horses disqualified for a drugs violation from the official end-of-year racehorse rankings but it should be doing more, including threatening the removal of drug-associated races from the international pattern (the published results of such races—including those at the Breeders' Cup—should at least be accompanied by some sort of symbol to distinguish them from 'clean' races). Talismanic is trained by Andre Fabre, a long-time opponent of raceday medication, and none of his five Breeders' Cup winners have run on lasix (nearly all the domestic runners in the thirteen Breeders' Cup races were on it, as was Ballydoyle's sizeable team). A number of British challengers, among them Ribchester, **Decorated Knight** (who won three Group 1s including Ireland's most important all-aged middle-distance event the Irish Champion Stakes) and **Nezwaah** (who also won a Group 1 in Ireland, the Pretty Polly Stakes), raced 'clean' at the Breeders' Cup, as would late-withdrawal **Ulysses** (whose essay highlights a good year for ten-times champion trainer Sir Michael Stoute).

Ulysses won both the Eclipse at Sandown (holding off Barney Roy by a nose) and York's big all-aged weight-for-age middle-distance event the International which had prize money of £1m for the first time. York's richly-endowed Ebor meeting puts in the shade the prize money on offer at Doncaster's St Leger meeting, which follows fairly shortly afterwards (it is

Weighing room colleagues form a guard of honour on British Champions' Day for champion jockey Silvestre de Sousa; the curtain comes down on the 'official' championship nowadays at Ascot's big end-of-season fixture but de Sousa would still have won the title if it had been decided over the full calendar year, as ideally it should be

one of the topics in the essay on Doncaster Cup winner **Desert Skyline** which also highlights the continuing injustice of the ban on geldings in some of the top weight-for-age events, particularly the classics). Desert Skyline was partnered in the Doncaster Cup by Silvestre de Sousa, whose only booked ride on British Champions' Day was on the same horse. The presentation to de Sousa of his award for winning the 'official' jockeys' championship (which now finishes on Champions' Day) required his presence, though the essay on Desert Skyline—which reiterates that all championships should run from January 1st to December 31st—points out that the two protagonists for the apprentices' title (which came down to the last day) went to ride at Catterick instead, with the presentation being made at the everyday North Yorkshire track afterwards.

'Top Horses Abroad', at the end of this Annual, provides the usual extensive coverage—country by country—of the most significant events around the world, but racing in France, where there were nearly five hundred British-trained runners on the Flat in 2017 (earning, according to IRB figures, £8,218,532 of the worldwide overseas earnings of £23,202,749 by British trainers), continues to be an integral part of *Racehorses*, along with racing in Ireland where there were nearly two hundred British runners on the Flat (Dubai is number three with over a hundred and fifty). Horse racing in Britain, Ireland and France is interwoven, which has led to understandable concerns over Britain's impending withdrawal from the European Union which now seems increasingly likely to impinge on the ease of movement and open borders that the sport has become used to. Customs controls would lead inevitably to hold-ups—not to mention extra red-tape and form filling—which could well have an effect on the competitiveness of European racing (as well as creating difficulties for the breeding industry) as the number of overseas challengers in each of the three countries inevitably declines. For the moment, the top French, German and Irish horses—even if they have not run in Britain—are covered individually in the A to Z, with the major performers given the same treatment as the principal British-trained horses.

Among the French performers with extended entries in this edition are the runner-up to Enable in the Prix de l'Arc **Cloth of Stars**, whose essay looks at Andre Fabre's Arc record and also reflects on the close family connection between Cloth of Stars and Arc third Ulysses. **Al Wukair** and **Brametot** both carried the Al Shaqab colours with distinction, the former's essay outlining an embarrassing story that appeared about the finances of Al Shaqab's British arm, while Brametot's Poule d'Essai des Poulains/Prix du Jockey Club double helped to lift the gloom from the Jean-Claude Rouget stable after it was hit by an outbreak of the same equine herpes virus that struck Kevin Ryan's yard (2017 Horse of the Year Almanzor was among the horses affected and was said by his trainer afterwards to be 'no longer the same horse'). The fillies classics in France were won by outsiders **Precieuse** and **Senga** in a far from vintage year for French fillies and mares (none made the Arc field). There wasn't a single Group 1 winner among the latest crop of French two-year-olds, **Olmedo** and **Polydream** filling the runner-up spot behind Happily and the Godolphin-owned British-trained **Wild Illusion** (whose essay recounts Charlie Appleby's good season) in the Lagardere and Marcel Boussac respectively. The last two Group 1s for two-year-olds in France—staged at Saint-Cloud—were abandoned when protesters blocked access to the paddock, a story covered in the essay on Olmedo. **Zarak** finally fulfilled the early promise of his career, giving his owner the Aga Khan a fourth win in the Grand Prix de Saint-Cloud (the essay looks at the stud record of Zarak's illustrious dam Zarkava).

From further afield, there are extended entries on **Arrogate**, the American-trained Dubai World Cup winner whose dramatic decline afterwards was not easy to explain, American speedball **Lady Aurelia**, who won for the second time at Royal Ascot, and Australia's queen of the turf **Winx** who might or might not have the Royal meeting on her agenda in 2018. Arrogate won the first Pegasus World Cup before his triumph at Meydan, and Australia saw the inaugural running of a new sprint in the same vein, The Everest, which is one of the subjects discussed in the essay on **Limato** who, given the limited opportunities over his ideal trip of seven furlongs in Europe, might be tackling North American targets in the next season. The colours carried by Limato are similar to the kit worn by Plymouth Argyle, the football club which Limato's owner supports. Among other notable horses with links to football clubs are **Beat The Bank**, one of the growing band of runners for Leicester City's owner Vichai Srivaddhanaprabha, and the Champions Sprint winner **Librisa Breeze** who races for Brighton & Hove Albion's owner Tony Bloom.

The year was a busy and sometimes awkward one for British racing's administrators. Top of the list of embarrassing moments were two cases of mistaken identities, the first one coming at Yarmouth in July when 50/1 juvenile winner Mandarin Princess turned out to be a three-year-old stablemate, an error not spotted until after the runners had weighed in. Both horses were bay fillies and had been scanned to confirm their identity when entering the racecourse stables and they became muddled during the afternoon. Trainer Charlie McBride was fined £1,500 and 'Mandarin Princess' (actually Millie's Kiss) was disqualified subsequently by an independent BHA disciplinary panel. Changes to raceday checks were introduced shortly afterwards but the same thing happened in mid-January 2018 when two horses trained by Ivan Furtado—Scribner Creek (who was placed) and African Trader—were mixed up when running at Southwell. Worryingly, the BHA's beefed-up checks were found wanting on this occasion with the muddle only coming to light when a sample taken from Scribner Creek in a routine post-race test was subsequently found not to match the profile of the horse. Without the test, the error would have gone unnoticed. Under the rules, it is the trainer who is responsible for ensuring that the correct horse runs in the right race and Furtado was fined £2,000, while those responsible for 'procedural failings' on the day escaped scot free (it came to light that the two horses were among half a dozen sent by a new owner and had been mistakenly mixed up when they first arrived at Furtado's stable).

The zero-tolerance stance of so many of the rules of racing also applies—or so it seemed—to the sport's anti-doping rules. However, in two cases in 2017 involving banned substances found in post-race samples, one involving jumps trainer Philip Hobbs and the other East Ilsley-based Hughie Morrison, the principle of a trainer's strict liability—the BHA has never had to prove intent or involvement—was undermined when both trainers were effectively exonerated by an independent BHA disciplinary panel which used its limited discretion to rule, that, on the balance of probabilities, neither had been involved in administering the substances which was the work of 'person or persons unknown' (Morrison's assertion that another trainer had doped his filly Our Little Sister, when she finished last at Wolverhampton in January, because of a dispute with a third party, was dismissed as 'ludicrous' by the panel). A trainer has always been held responsible for any illegal substance found in his horses unless he can actually prove that it was administered by someone outside his control. The BHA announced that it would review its anti-doping rules after the two decisions, with chief executive Nick Rust saying 'We need to ensure that our rules are clear about what zero-tolerance means, and the obligations on those responsible for horses and the penalties when the rules are broken.' 'Beyond reasonable doubt' has always been the guiding principle for conviction in a court of law, and society in general has come to the view that it is worse to put an innocent person in jail than to allow a guilty one to walk free. The BHA, it seems, might disagree.

In another high profile corruption case—in which investigations took nearly three years to complete, and which did not finally come before an independent panel until August—Malton trainer John Wainwright and professional gambler John Wright were cleared of charges brought by the BHA alleging they had 'stopped' Blazeofenchantment in a handicap at Southwell in June 2014. The jockey who rode Blazeofenchantment, Adam Carter, claimed he was told by Wainwright to 'miss the break and not be in the first four'. However, Carter subsequently withdrew the allegations when the case first came before the panel in July. He claimed to have been told by his own employer, trainer Bryan Smart, that he would get more lenient treatment if he admitted he had stopped the horse, an accusation subsequently labelled 'disgraceful' by the panel which ruled Carter to be an 'unreliable witness'. The BHA pursued the case even after Carter, their main witness, had withdrawn his allegations, and their decision astonished John Wainwright's solicitors, who said 'The BHA would do well to remember that as a regulator its job is not to secure a conviction at all costs but rather to ensure that a fair outcome is reached.' Among other disciplinary cases, trainer David Evans escaped a ban after being charged with conduct prejudicial to racing over betting on one of his own horses, while failing to notify the Racing Calendar office of a non-runner (Evans was fined £3,140 for betting on Black Dave at Wolverhampton in January 2015 before the eventual withdrawal from the same race of stablemate Tango Sky which he knew would not be running). Two jockeys, Graham Gibbons and Dale Swift, received bans

John Ferguson, for so long a stalwart of the Godolphin operation, resigned from his position as chief executive in June, saying that internal divisions had made his position untenable; Fred Done, the supremo at bookmakers Betfred, announced that the company was withdrawing from sponsorship of races from July 2018 (estimated to be worth £6m a year to racing)

after testing positive for cocaine (Gibbons had tried to use another jockey's sample when tested at a meeting at Kempton in December 2016). Another jockey Robert Havlin, who was backed by his employer John Gosden, failed to persuade the BHA's disciplinary panel in August not to reciprocate the remainder of a six-month drugs ban for cocaine and other substances incurred in France which Havlin maintained were obtained from a contaminated sample.

With no legal challenge to the Government's levy reforms received by the November deadline, the sport's leaders were able to celebrate their success in extending the betting levy for the first time to offshore operators. The then-chancellor George Osborne first announced the proposed change in his budget in March 2014 but legislation was delayed by the General Election which has led to the life of the Levy Board being extended again—this time to 2019 when a new Racing Authority (advised by a liaison group including bookmakers) is set to take over spending the money raised from the levy, which is expected to be around £90m a year under the revised scheme (the sport also receives around £140m of income from media rights, including the pictures transmitted to Britain's 8,650 betting shops, which each pay, on average, around £35,000 a year). As a result of the revised levy, the BHA announced that prize money would reach a record £160m in 2018, much of the £17m increase (from 2017) being used to boost racing at the grassroots through increased prize money, and appearance money down to the first eight in some low-grade races. The 'authorised betting partner' policy, adopted to put pressure on bookmakers to contribute a proportion of their offshore profits, lapsed with the new legislation, but the bad feeling it created has had its ramifications.

Betfred's exclusive deal to operate pools betting—stemming from its original purchase of the Tote in 2011—expires in July 2018 and the majority of Britain's racecourses have decided to operate their own on-course pool betting. Betfred says that the on-course tote business is loss-making and it has twice raised the take-out—now standing at just under twenty per cent—during its six-year tenure. As a result of the racecourses' decision, however, Betfred is ending its £6m sponsorship of British racing once its exclusive pools deal expires. The move will affect more than six hundred races, though Betfred-owned Chelmsford and Ascot, whose in-house betting operation remains with

A number of senior jockeys announced their retirement, among them Steve Drowne, who ended his twenty-seven-year career on a high by riding Met By Moonlight to victory in the last race of the year; and Jimmy Fortune, who enjoyed his best years with the John Gosden stable for which he won the St Leger on Lucarno

Betfred, will not be affected (off-course pools betting will continue to be run by Betfred under the totepool banner, with deals already in place with fellow operators).

Racing's new-found wealth ended the year under some threat from Government restrictions on the stakes allowed on fixed-odds betting terminals which reportedly contribute more towards betting shop profits than the traditional forms of gambling. With horse racing's levy and the media rights deals heavily dependent on the number of betting shops, any large-scale closures, predicted if the maximum stake on the machines is cut drastically, look set to affect racing's income, with prize money likely to bear the brunt. There would also be job losses through the shop closures, however, and the Treasury would lose tax receipts, but, if the worst fears are realised, bookmakers should reflect that they have been on the back foot on the issue of problem gambling since FOBTs went into betting shops. The machines have been labelled 'the crack cocaine of gambling', with a low maximum stake seen as an imperative by vociferous campaigners who have targeted them, though the same groups have not so far called for similar controls on how much an individual can stake on a horse race, or how many tickets can be purchased for the state-sponsored lottery and its associated scratchcards, for example. Whatever changes are eventually made to the stakes permitted on FOBTs, the looming 'crisis' has at least highlighted how much racing has indirectly become dependent on the profits generated by gaming machines on the High Street. The BHA made a submission as part of the government consultation process in which it acknowledged that its business model is linked to the number of betting shops and it warned of the impact that a reduction in FOBT stakes would have on racing. 'It's not for us to interfere in government policy,' said Nick Rust, 'but we have asked government to consider what it has said publicly, which is that it will consider any impact on British racing of any changes to betting policy.'

Racing mourned the loss in 2017 of racing characters past and present, including retired Derby-winning trainers Peter Walwyn and Geoff Wragg, retired northern trainer Patrick Haslam who saddled a winner at every track in Britain during his career, and current trainer David 'Dandy' Nicholls, known as the 'sprint king', who died after a long illness aged sixty-one in June. The essay on **Sovereign Debt**, which Nicholls used to train, contains details of his career (the essay also outlines proposals for reforms to All-Weather Championships' Day). Racing's unsung heroes, who do so much to keep the show on the road, rarely make the headlines but two exceptions, in the saddest of circumstances, were Stephen Yarborough, the first stalls handler to be killed on a racecourse—in a freak occurrence at Haydock in July—since stalls were introduced over half a century ago, and groom Ken Dooley, kicked by a horse and fatally injured in an accident in the racecourse stables at Kempton in October. Another who would not be widely known, the chief executive of the firm that supplies catering to the Jockey Club racecourses, Richard Cousins, died with other family members when their chartered sea plane crashed near Sydney while on holiday.

The season's retirements included one of France's top trainers Criquette Head-Maarek (whose career is summarised in the French section of 'Top Horses Abroad') and a number of jockeys, including Jimmy Fortune who bowed out with third place on Nathra in the Sun Chariot Stakes at Newmarket, riding for John Gosden for whom he enjoyed classic success on Lucarno in the 2007 St Leger and other big-race wins on the likes of Raven's Pass, Oasis Dream, Nannina and Dar Re Mi. Ted Durcan, who rode Light Shift the dam of Ulysses to victory in the Oaks, decided to hang up his saddle at the start of 2018; a long association with the Maktoum family gave him a St Leger winner, Mastery, in the Godolphin colours. Steve Drowne, who takes on a new role as a stipendiary steward, timed his retirement perfectly, going out with victory on Met By Moonlight in the last Flat race of the year (at Lingfield); Drowne rode winners on every course in Britain and reached a hundred winners in a calendar year three times. Martin Lane, who is moving to Fiji, announced his retirement after riding Crown Walk to victory in the Godolphin colours at Chelmsford in December, while George Baker, badly injured in a fall at St Moritz in 2016, decided to call it a day in the autumn, after not riding since his accident. The ranks of the female jockeys were depleted when Cathy Gannon announced in July that she was hanging up her boots after losing a prolonged fight to return from injuries received in an incident in the stalls at Lingfield in May 2016. Another top female jockey Hayley Turner came out of retirement during the year to ride in France—where female jockeys now get an allowance—though her comeback was temporarily halted when the BHA suspended her for having a betting account. The baton once held by Turner and Gannon is now firmly in the hands, in Britain at least, of Josephine Gordon, who achieved the rare feat for a champion apprentice of going on to ride 100 winners in her first season after losing her claim. She won 106 races in 2017, beating Hayley Turner's record for a female jockey of exactly 100. Gordon achieved her first pattern victory on Koropick in the Chipchase Stakes at Newcastle in July, riding for her principal employer Hugo Palmer. John Gosden and Saeed bin Suroor were others who put up Gordon on their horses. She rode for both at Royal Ascot, finishing runner-up in the Wokingham on Steady Pace for bin Suroor (no woman has ridden a winner at the Royal meeting since Gay Kelleway in 1987).

Also among the familiar names to disappear from the racing scene in 2017 was that of Ballymacoll Stud, an Irish stud with strong British connections, which has been wound down in a further sign of the decline of those traditional English owner-breeders with twenty or thirty mares who, for so long, were

The curtain came down on historic Ballymacoll Stud whose broodmare band produced so many good winners for the Sobell and Weinstock families, including that of Troy in the 1979 Derby which was the first of two wins in the race for Sobell/Weinstock home breds, his performance producing the fastest timefigure recorded by any horse in the **Racehorses** *era (1.79 fast, equivalent to a timerating of 145); the inset picture shows long-serving stud manager Peter Reynolds with Group 1 winner and prolific broodmare Islington in the sale-ring at Newmarket on the day the last of the Ballymacoll mares were sold*

the backbone of the sport. Ballymacoll's pale blue, white and yellow check cap has been carried to victory by numerous Group 1 winners in Europe and North America over the years, including by the Derby winners Troy and North Light who gave the Weinstock and Sobell families their finest moments as owner-breeders over the last half century. The Ballymacoll dispersal was completed over the year, with the stud itself sold in June and the final batch of mares coming under the hammer at the December Sales. Even the sale of the top sprinting mare **Marsha** for a record 6,000,000 guineas on the same day couldn't overshadow the poignant moment when long-serving Ballymacoll manager Peter Reynolds took the top-level winner Islington (who bred eleven foals for Ballymacoll, all of them fillies) on a turn of the sale-ring before she was sold.

'Life goes on, but history and legacy remain,' was how Peter Reynolds summed up the demise of Ballymacoll. It couldn't have been put better and brought to mind a letter received at Timeform from a long-standing subscriber, John Feeney, a couple of months before the final act in the Ballymacoll dispersal. After saying how much pleasure he got from his extensive set of Timeform Annuals, John Feeney wrote: 'I know Timeform's "reason to be" is primarily to provide the best information with which punters can make a profit, but I don't know of another profit-making organisation that every year leaves in its wake such a fabulous reference archive. It is quite breathtaking and a phenomenal feat to maintain the standard each year. Timeform has given to racing something unique and very special.' It is for the reader to judge whether this edition, which deals individually with 11,522 horses, lives up to that very high praise.

March 2018

THE TIMEFORM 'TOP HUNDRED'

Here are listed the 'Top 100' two-year-olds, three-year-olds and older horses in the annual. Fillies and mares are denoted by (f).

2 YEAR OLDS

123 U S Navy Flag
121p Bolt d'Oro
120p Good Magic
120p Roaring Lion
120p Saxon Warrior
119 Verbal Dexterity
118p Clemmie (f)
117p Expert Eye
117 Unfortunately
116 Fleet Review
116 Happily (f)
116 Mendelssohn
116 Olmedo
116 Sands of Mali
115 Magical (f)
115 Masar
115 Sioux Nation
114p September (f)
114p The Pentagon
113p Sacred Life
113p Wild Illusion (f)
113 Beckford
112p Elarqam
112p Erasmus
112p Gustav Klimt
112p Nelson
112 Havana Grey
112 Invincible Army
112 Laurens (f)
112 Santry
112 Seahenge
111p Ghaiyyath
111p Wells Farhh Go
111 Chilean
111 Heartache (f)
111 James Garfield
111 Shabaaby
111 Woodmax
110p Barraquero
110p Magic Lily (f)
110 Different League (f)
110 Threading (f)
109p Polydream (f)
109 Cardsharp
109 Mission Impassible (f)
109 Nyaleti (f)
108p Delano Roosevelt
108p Gabr
108p Kew Gardens
108p Luminate (f)
108p Speak In Colours
108 Declarationofpeace
108 Happy Like A Fool (f)
108 Hey Gaman
108 Mythical Magic
108 Purser
108 Warm The Voice
108 Zonza (f)
107p Hey Jonesy
107p Kenya
107 Ellthea (f)
107 Headway
107 Murillo
107 Nebo
107 Rajasinghe
107 Sound And Silence
107 Stage Magic
107 Threeandfourpence
106p Altyn Orda (f)
106p Liquid Amber (f)
106p Mildenberger
106p Wootton
106 Alpha Centauri (f)
106 Bengali Boys
106 Corinthia Knight
106 Dream Today
106 Frozen Angel
106 Red Mist
106 Zyzzyva
105p Gavota (f)
105p Glorious Journey
105p Never Back Down
105p Spud
105p With You (f)
105 Abel Handy
105 Actress (f)
105 Beatbox Rhythm
105 Brother Bear
105 Enjazaat
105 Juliet Capulet (f)
105 Madeline (f)
105 Take Me With You (f)
105 Tangled
105 Tip Two Win
104p I Can Fly (f)
104p Laugh A Minute
104p Mcmunigal
104p Mutaaqeb
104 Capla Temptress (f)
104 Now You're Talking (f)
104 Romanised
104 Rufus King
104 Zaman

3 YEAR OLDS

136 Battaash
136 Cracksman
134 Enable (f)
133 Lady Aurelia (f)
132 Harry Angel
128 West Coast
126 Barney Roy
126 Caravaggio
126 Churchill
125 Beat The Bank
124 Al Wukair
124 Always Dreaming
124 Blue Point
124 Brametot
124 Capri
124 Ice Breeze
124 Wings of Eagles
124 Winter (f)
123p Crystal Ocean
123 Cliffs of Moher
123 Hydrangea (f)
123 Inns of Court
123 Le Brivido
123 Rekindling
123 Stradivarius
122 Eminent
122 Lancaster Bomber
122 Thunder Snow
122 Waldgeist
121 Benbatl
121 Mirage Dancer
121 Roly Poly (f)
121 Windstoss
120 Accidental Agent
120 Hit The Bid
120 Orderofthegarter
120 Sir Dancealot
120 War Decree
120 Wuheida (f)
119 Best Solution
119 Colomano
119 D'bai
119 Defoe
119 Raheen House
119 Taj Mahal
119 Trais Fluors
118p Buthela
118 Desert Skyline
118 Monarchs Glen
118 Mount Moriah
118 Recoletos
118 Rhododendron (f)
118 Sobetsu (f)
118 Son of Rest
117 Call To Mind
117 Dream Castle
117 Dream of Dreams
117 Fas
117 Frankuus
117 Leshlaa
117 Permian
117 Shakeel
117 Spirit of Valor
117 Venice Beach
116 Bound For Nowhere

116 Century Dream
116 Coronet (f)
116 Douglas Macarthur
116 Euginio
116 Khafoo Shememi
116 Khalidi
116 Precieuse (f)
116 Salouen
116 Second Thought
116 Top Score
115 Born To Be Alive
115 Count Octave
115 Delectation (f)
115 Face The Facts
115 Forest Ranger
115 Koropick
115 La Coronel (f)
115 Mac Mahon
115 Parfait
115 Plumatic
115 Rusumaat
115 The Grape Escape
114p Game Starter
114p Weekender
114 Bay of Poets
114 Best of Days
114 Daban (f)
114 Dabyah (f)
114 Sea of Grace (f)
114 Senga (f)
114 Sir John Lavery
114 Time To Study
113p Emmaus
113p Sharja Bridge
113 Alexios Komnenos
113 Glastonbury Song
113 Gulliver
113 Hochfeld
113 Intelligence Cross
113 Law And Order
113 Rivet
113 Ronald R
113 Sutter County

OLDER HORSES

135 Arrogate
134 Winx (f)
133 Gun Runner
132 Cloth of Stars
130 Marsha (f)
130 Ulysses
130 World Approval
129 Collected
129 Ertijaal
129 Ribchester
128 Highland Reel
128 Kitasan Black
128 Order of St George
127 Limato
127 Satono Diamond
126 Idaho
126 Jack Hobbs
126 Mr Stunning
125 Decorated Knight
125 Dschingis Secret
125 Librisa Breeze
125 Mutakayyef
125 Taareef
125 Talismanic
125 The Tin Man
124 Brando
124 Guignol
124 Poet's Word
124 Signs of Blessing
124 Tasleet
124 Time Warp
124 Zarak
123 Deauville
123 Hawkbill
123 Heshem
123 Iquitos
123 North America
123 Persuasive (f)
123 Profitable
123 Silverwave
123 Vazirabad
122 Aclaim
122 Bateel (f)
122 Beauty Generation
122 Big Orange
122 Johannes Vermeer
122 Quiet Reflection (f)
122 Scottish
121 Desert Encounter
121 Erupt
121 Here Comes When
121 Laugh Aloud (f)
121 Massaat
121 Minding (f)
121 Mustashry
121 Muthmir
121 One Foot In Heaven
121 Postponed
121 Prize Money
121 Seventh Heaven (f)
121 Suedois
120p Lord Glitters
120 Ballet Concerto
120 Chemical Charge
120 Dal Harraild
120 Dartmouth
120 Folkswood
120 Full Drago
120 Jimmy Two Times
120 Karar
120 Marmelo
120 Mekhtaal
120 My Dream Boat
120 Nezwaah (f)
120 Queen's Trust (f)
120 Somehow (f)
120 Take Cover
120 Vivlos (f)
120 Zelzal
120§ Frontiersman
119p Gibbs Hill
119 Algometer
119 Arab Spring
119 Donjuan Triumphant
119 Emotionless
119 Ennaadd
119 Home of The Brave
119 Lightning Spear
119 Long On Value
119 Mondialiste
119 Moonlight Magic
119 Palace Prince
119 Secret Number
119 Sheikhzayedroad
119 Success Days
119 The Right Man
119 Tiberian
119 Time Test
119 Zhukova (f)
119 Zonderland

PROMISING HORSES

Selected horses with a p or P are listed under their trainers for 2017.

CHARLIE APPLEBY
Al Hajar (IRE) 2 b.c 101p
Arabian Gift (IRE) 2 br.f 90p
Bow Street 2 ch.c 93p
Brundtland (IRE) 2 b. or br.c 82p
Cross Counter 2 b.c 89p
Crown Walk 2 ch.f 83p
Dathanna (IRE) 2 b.f 89p
Dream Warrior 2 b.c 91p
Espadrille 2 b.f 78p
Flag Festival 2 gr.g 56p
Flora Sandes (USA) 2 b.f 84p
Folk Tale (IRE) 2 ch.g 95p
Ghaiyyath (IRE) 2 b.c 111p
Ghostwatch (IRE) 2 b.c 82p
Glorious Journey 2 b.c 105p
Hadith (IRE) 2 b. or br.f 102p
Imperial Past 2 b.c 75p
Ispolini 2 b.c 90p
Jazirat (IRE) 2 b.g 72p
Key Victory (IRE) 2 b.c 103p
Light Up Dubai 2 b.c 64p
Loxley (IRE) 2 b.c 100p
Lunar Maria 2 b.f 64p
Magic Lily 2 ch.f 110p
Murasaki 2 b.f 58p
Native Appeal (IRE) 2 b.c 84p
Piccola Collina (IRE) 2 b.f 62p
Poetic Charm 2 b.f 94p
Setting Sail 2 b.c 85p
Silverbook 2 b.c 85p
Soliloquy 2 b.f 83p
Suhayl Moon (IRE) 2 b.f 65p
Swiss Knight 2 b.c 91p
Symbolization (IRE) 2 b.c 100p
Wild Illusion 2 b.f 113p

RALPH BECKETT
Akvavera 2 ch.f 79p
Arcadian Cat (USA) 2 b.f 76p
Breath Caught 2 b.c 90p
Cecchini (IRE) 2 br.f 89p
Ceilidhs Dream 2 b.f 71p
Cross My Mind (IRE) 2 b.f 60p
Diocles of Rome (IRE) 2 b.c 64p
Fresh Terms 2 b.f 60p
Gilded Hour (IRE) 2 b.f 73p
Kinaesthesia 2 b.f 84p
Occupy (USA) 2 b.c 87p
Podemos (GER) 2 b.c 84p
Respectable 2 b.f 78p
Rose Tinted Spirit 2 b.c 65p
Silver Crescent 2 b.g 69p
Smart Dart 2 b.f 54p
Victory Chime (IRE) 2 b.g 74p

ROGER CHARLTON
Antagonist 2 b.c 68p
Breathless Times 2 b.c 80p
Buffer Zone 2 br.c 93p
Extra Elusive 2 ch.c 90P
Gavota 2 b.f 105p
Herculean 2 ch.c 95P
Low Profile 2 ch.g 69p
Universal Command 2 b.g 72p

ED DUNLOP
Amplification (USA) 2 b.g 80p
Dubai Frame 2 b.c 65p
Global Art 2 b.c 79p
Global Giant 2 b.c 90p
Global Humor (USA) 2 b.c 83p
Grandscape 2 b.c 77p
Hazarfan 2 b.c 73p
Muraadef 2 b.g 62p
Qawamees (IRE) 2 b.c 89p
Tajarrob (IRE) 2 b.f 60P
Vision Clear (GER) 2 b.g 64p

DAVID ELSWORTH
Amandine 2 b.f 77p
Galloway Hills 2 b.c 63P
Morning Has Broken (IRE) 2 ch.f 65p

RICHARD FAHEY
Aljady (FR) 2 b.c 79p
Arctic Treasure (IRE) 2 b.g 63p
Brisk Tempo (FR) 2 b.g 76p
Chingachgook 2 b.c 76p
Crown of Cortez 2 ch.g 78p
Dubai Acclaim (IRE) 2 b.c 70p
Fool For You (IRE) 2 b.f 74p
Gabrial The Saint (IRE) 2 ch.g 84p
Grise Lightning (FR) 2 gr.f 69p
Knowing Glance (IRE) 2 b.g 72p
Lady Noorah 2 ch.f 71p
Sempre Presto (IRE) 2 b.f 62p
Sugar Coating 2 b.f 68p
The Navigator 2 br. or gr.g 74p
Zip Along (IRE) 2 b.f 68p

JOHN GOSDEN
Aim of Artemis (IRE) 2 ch.f 95p
Antonian 2 b.c 79p
Bold Reason (GER) 2 b.c 89p
Cassini (IRE) 2 b.c 78p
Ceramist 2 b.f 75p
Chloris 2 b.f 65p
Corelli (USA) 2 b.c 88p
Court House (IRE) 2 b.c 81p
Crossed Baton 2 b.c 85p
Culpability (USA) 2 b.c 58p
Daltrey 2 b.c 72p
Doswell (USA) 2 br.g 87p
Elhafei (USA) 2 br.c 69P
Emaraaty 2 b.c 100p
Fennaan (IRE) 2 br.c 89p
First Eleven 2 b.c 79p
Gaudi (IRE) 2 b.c 77p
George Villiers (IRE) 2 b.c 79p
Glencadam Master 2 gr.c 88p
Graffiti Master 2 b.c 101p
Gumriyah 2 b.f 81p
Hameem 2 br.f 66p
Highgarden 2 b.f 86p
Hipster Boy 2 b.c 82p
Holy Heart (IRE) 2 b.g 76p
Il Primo Sole 2 b.c 100p
Jamih 2 ch.c 60p
Kings Shield (USA) 2 b.c 86p

Main Street 2 b.c 89p
Military Law 2 b.c 85p
Msayyan (IRE) 2 b.c 87p
Nassya 2 b.f 65P
Natch 2 b.c 77p
Nawassi 2 b.f 81p
Petit Palais 2 ch.c 64p
Photographer 2 b.c 88p
Pioneer Spirit 2 b.f 83p
Qayes 2 b.c 65p
Rhode Island (IRE) 2 ch.c 67p
Roaring Lion (USA) 2 gr. or ro.c 120p
Rococo 2 b.f 57p
Scottish Jig (USA) 2 ch.f 64P
Sevenna Star (IRE) 2 b.c 89p
Sophie Gray (IRE) 2 b.f 55p
Stealth 2 b.c 61p
Stream Song 2 gr.f 95p
Stylehunter 2 ch.c 80p
Verandah 2 b.f 92p
Wissahickon (USA) 2 ch.c 88p
Without Parole 2 b.c 93p

WILLIAM HAGGAS

Allieyf 2 b.c 73p
Al Muffrih (IRE) 2 b.c 87P
Beauty Filly 2 b.f 84p
Beshaayir 2 b.f 87p
Cavatina 2 b.f 82p
Cosmic Love 2 ch.f 80p
Dramatic Queen (USA) 2 ch.f 80p
Dutch Desire 2 b.f 51p
Final Treat (IRE) 2 b.f 82p
French Heroine 2 b.f 54p
Give And Take 2 b.f 86p
Hateel (IRE) 2 b.f 61p
Humbolt Current 2 b.c 83p
Istanbul Sultan (IRE) 2 gr.g 80p
Jahaafel (FR) 2 gr.c 54p
Mashaheer 2 b.g 67p
Move Swiftly 2 b.f 87P
My Lord And Master (IRE) 2 ch.c 92p
Nicklaus 2 ch.g 75p
Pretty Baby (IRE) 2 b.f 84p
Reiffa (IRE) 2 b.f 76p
Sir Commander (IRE) 2 b.c 71p
Society Power (IRE) 2 b.c 88p
Talaaqy (IRE) 2 b.f 78p
Tallow (IRE) 2 b.f 85p
Three Weeks (USA) 2 gr. or ro.c 84p
Yajooll 2 b.c 52p
Young Rascal (FR) 2 b.c 83p

RICHARD HANNON

Accessor (IRE) 2 b.c 84p
All Out 2 b.f 90p
Birthright 2 b.c 72p
Bullingdon 2 b.c 86p
Doctor Jazz (IRE) 2 b.c 62p
Don Pepe (IRE) 2 b.c 61p
Gendarme (IRE) 2 b.c 73p
Heidi 2 b.f 51p
Maaward (IRE) 2 b.c 83p
Maghaweer (IRE) 2 ch.c 89p
Mushtaq (IRE) 2 b.g 85p
No More Thrills 2 ch.f 61p
Oliver Reed (IRE) 2 b.c 81p
On A Roll 2 b.f 58p
Orange Suit (IRE) 2 b.c 94p
Point Hope (IRE) 2 b.f 72p
Qaysar (FR) 2 b.c 97p
Rajaam (IRE) 2 b.c 81p
Red Starlight 2 br.f 80p
Sergio Leone (IRE) 2 b.c 77p
Vitamin (IRE) 2 b.f 84p

MARK JOHNSTON

Alhawdaj (USA) 2 ch.f 54p
Angelina d'Or (GER) 2 ch.f 78p
Austrian School (IRE) 2 b.c 83p
Baghdad (FR) 2 b.c 83p
Communique (IRE) 2 ch.c 83p
Dalileo (IRE) 2 b.c 78p
Danzay (IRE) 2 b.c 73p
Elarqam 2 b.c 112p
Elegiac 2 b.c 90p
Footsteps Forever (IRE) 2 ch.f 78p
King's Proctor (IRE) 2 b.c 91p
Lucky Deal 2 ch.c 88p
Lynwood Gold (IRE) 2 ro.c 97p
Mildenberger 2 b.c 106p
Rampant Lion (IRE) 2 ch.g 63p
Ready To Impress (USA) 2 b.g 76p
Sea Youmzain (IRE) 2 b.f 74p
Showroom (FR) 2 b.c 88p
Tight Lines 2 b.f 78p

AIDAN O'BRIEN, IRELAND

Amedeo Modigliani (IRE) 2 b.c 98p
Bye Bye Baby (IRE) 2 b.f 100p
Clemmie (IRE) 2 b.f 118p
Delano Roosevelt (IRE) 2 b.c 108p
Family Tree 2 ch.c 88p
Giuseppe Garibaldi (IRE) 2 b.c 98p
Gustav Klimt (IRE) 2 b.c 112p
I Can Fly 2 b.f 104p
James Cook (IRE) 2 b.c 93p
Kenya (IRE) 2 b.c 107p
Kew Gardens (IRE) 2 b.c 108p
Nelson (IRE) 2 b.c 112p
Sarrocchi (IRE) 2 b.f 88p
Saxon Warrior (JPN) 2 b.c 120p
September (IRE) 2 b.f 114p
Snowflakes (IRE) 2 br. or gr.f 91p
The Pentagon (IRE) 2 b.c 114p

JAMIE OSBORNE

La La Land (IRE) 2 br.c 84p
Lush Life (IRE) 2 b.f 79p
Mr Reckless (IRE) 2 gr.c 80p
Rusper (IRE) 2 b.g 87p
Voyager Blue 2 br.c 82p
Arabic Culture (USA) 3 b. or br.g 75P

HUGO PALMER

Breaking Records (IRE) 2 b.c 60p
Burford Brown 2 br.c 59p
Corrosive (USA) 2 b.c 88p
Dukhan 2 br.c 86p
Employer (IRE) 2 b.c 73p
Expensive Liaison (IRE) 2 b.f 76p
Fajjaj (IRE) 2 ch.c 99p
Gododdin 2 b.c 69p
Hedonism (IRE) 2 b.f 52p
Labrega 2 b.f 69p
Momentarily 2 b.f 74p
Morning Beauty 2 ch.f 65p
Mystic Meg 2 b.f 77p
Never Back Down (IRE) 2 b.c 105p

Rashdan (FR) 2 b.c 69p
Silver Quartz 2 gr.c 81p
Strange Society (IRE) 2 br.c 80p
Sudona 2 b.f 58p
Temur Khan 2 br.c 61P
Tenedos 2 b.c 88p
The Revenant 2 ch.c 92p
White Mocha (USA) 2 ch.c 98p

SIR MARK PRESCOTT BT

Codicil 2 b.f 85p
Isle of Avalon (IRE) 2 b.f 63p
On The Warpath 2 ch.c 99p
Rude Awakening 2 b.g 67p
Special Mission 2 b.f 57p
Trouble And Strife (IRE) 2 br.f 52p
True North (IRE) 2 b.g 65p
Twister (IRE) 2 ch.g 66p
White Guard 2 b.c 63p

KEVIN RYAN

Alkhawaneej Boy (IRE) 2 b.c 86p
Commander Han (FR) 2 ch.c 75p
Elnadim Star (IRE) 2 ch.f 84p
Finisher (USA) 2 br.g 63p
Gold Stone 2 b.f 70p
Hey Jonesy (IRE) 2 b.c 107p
How Bizarre 2 ch.g 64p
Jungle Room (USA) 2 b.g 63p
Kings Full (IRE) 2 b.g 77P
Knighted (IRE) 2 b.g 75p
Morning Wonder (IRE) 2 ch.c 87p
New Show (IRE) 2 ch.c 84p
Real Gent 2 gr.c 90p
Vj Day (USA) 2 b.g 71p

DAVID SIMCOCK

Azezati (IRE) 2 ch.f 68p
Birch Grove (IRE) 2 b.f 70p
Come On Tier (FR) 2 b.c 91p
Court of Justice (FR) 2 b.c 80p
Courtside (FR) 2 ch.g 74p
Ejtyah 2 b.f 79P
Encryption (IRE) 2 b.g 60p
Exec Chef (IRE) 2 ch.g 70p
Forward Thinker 2 ch.f 73p
Highbrow 2 b.c 90p
Highland Sky (IRE) 2 b.g 65p
Kaaba Stone (IRE) 2 b.f 76p
Lady of Shalott 2 b.f 81p
Maverick Officer 2 b.g 86p
Mrs Sippy (USA) 2 b.f 89p
Nice Shot (IRE) 2 b.c 88p
Qayed (CAN) 2 b.c 77p
Raid (IRE) 2 b.c 92p
Sarshampla (IRE) 2 b.f 81p
Supernova 2 b.c 81p
Teppal (FR) 2 b.f 93p
Walk On Walter (IRE) 2 b.g 76p
Worship (IRE) 2 b.f 80p

SIR MICHAEL STOUTE

Allante (IRE) 2 b.f 71p
Baritone (IRE) 2 b.c 65P
Comrade In Arms (USA) 2 b.g 73p
Crystal Hope 2 ch.f 71p
Crystal Moonlight 2 ch.f 60p
Desert Diamond 2 b.f 70p
Elector 2 b.c 80P
Eqtidaar (IRE) 2 b.c 91p
Expert Eye 2 b.c 117p
Gabr 2 ch.c 108p
Garden Oasis 2 b.c 60p
Georgian Manor (IRE) 2 br.g 73p
Glitterdust 2 b.f 69p
Hazarfiya 2 b.f 70P
Herdwick 2 b.c 78p
Homeopathic 2 b.f 78p
Ledham (IRE) 2 b.c 72P
Lunar Corona 2 br.f 63p
Private View 2 b.f 60p
Qaroun 2 b.c 84p
Radio Source (IRE) 2 ch.c 87p
Rapier (USA) 2 ch.g 68P
Red Striker (IRE) 2 b.c 63p
Regal Reality 2 b.c 83p
Sun Maiden 2 b.f 61P
Tahreek 2 b.c 70P
Urbino 2 b.c 61P
Veracious 2 b.f 97p
Whitehall 2 b.g 61p

SAEED BIN SUROOR

Autumn Snow 2 b.f 51p
Bedouin's Story 2 b.c 71p
Caring Touch (USA) 2 b.f 84p
Deyaarna (USA) 2 b.c 83p
Kaser (IRE) 2 b.c 80p
Laieth 2 b.c 84p
Moqarrab (USA) 2 b.c 87p
Returning Glory 2 b.c 78p
Ulster (IRE) 2 gr. or ro.c 80p
Wajaaha (IRE) 2 b.c 70p
Welsh Lord 2 gr.c 74p
Winter Lightning (IRE) 2 b.f 85p

ROGER VARIAN

Ace Ventura 2 b.c 81p
Adams Park 2 b.g 82p
Altyn Orda (IRE) 2 ch.f 106p
Augenblick (IRE) 2 b.f 79p
Flavius Titus 2 ch.c 93p
Game Player (IRE) 2 gr.c 78p
Hermosita 2 b.f 80p
Ibraz 2 b.c 72p
Imaginative (IRE) 2 b.c 65p
Jamil (IRE) 2 b.c 82p
Jurz (IRE) 2 ch.c 67p
Kawasir (USA) 2 ch.c 71p
Knightly Spirit 2 br.c 74p
Lady Momoka (IRE) 2 b.f 69p
Lashabeeh (IRE) 2 gr.c 78p
Laugh A Minute 2 b.c 104p
Masaarr (USA) 2 ch.c 101p
Monadee 2 b.g 85p
Noble Expression 2 b.c 85p
Pilaster 2 b.f 63p
Profound (IRE) 2 b.c 80p
Qazyna (IRE) 2 b.f 76p
Queen of Desire (IRE) 2 b.f 61p
Realpolitik (IRE) 2 b.f 76p
Sam Gold (IRE) 2 b.c 89p
Sary Arqa 2 ch.f 60P
Sharja Silk 2 b.c 74p
Sooda (USA) 2 b.f 60p
Talas (IRE) 2 b.g 78p
Watheeqa (USA) 2 b.f 67p
Willie John 2 b.c 87P
Zamandas (IRE) 2 b.c 66p

2017 STATISTICS

The following tables cover Jan 1-Dec 31. The prize money statistics, compiled by *Timeform*, relate to first-three prize money and win money. Win money was traditionally used to decide the trainers' championship until, in 1994, the BHB and the National Trainers' Federation established a championship decided by total prize money as determined by *Racing Post*. In 2007, 2008 and 2009 the trainers' and owners' championships were decided over the turf season (March-November) but, in 2010, the championship was changed to run from November to November (ending with the November Handicap meeting). In 2016 the trainers' championships reverted to Jan 1-Dec 31, while the owners' championship was brought in line with the dates for the jockeys' championship. The jockeys' championship has traditionally been decided by the number of winners ridden during the year, though between 1997 and 2014 the Jockeys' Association recognised a championship that ran for the turf season (March-November). Since 2015 the 'title' has been decided over a shorter period, starting on Two Thousand Guineas day and ending on British Champions' Day at Ascot in October.

			Indiv'l	*Races*			*Stakes*
	OWNERS (1,2,3 earnings)	*Horses*	*Wnrs*	*Won*	*Runs*	*%*	*£*
1	Godolphin	264	138	192	768	25.0	6,285,003
2	Mr D. Smith, Mrs J. Magnier, Mr M. Tabor	20	8	10	38	26.3	3,576,197
3	Mr Hamdan Al Maktoum	229	100	138	734	18.8	2,815,295
4	Mr K. Abdullah	90	38	58	287	20.2	2,088,684
5	Mr M. Tabor, D. Smith & Mrs John Magnier	14	9	11	36	30.6	1,800,136
6	Mrs John Magnier,Mr M.Tabor & Mr D.Smith	19	4	6	42	14.3	1,769,166
7	Cheveley Park Stud	95	39	55	325	16.9	1,571,127
8	Sheikh Hamdan Bin Mohammed Al Maktoum	57	34	60	363	16.5	1,404,080
9	Flaxman Stables Ireland Ltd	10	4	7	44	15.9	1,252,826
10	Mr A. E. Oppenheimer	13	7	10	39	25.6	1,098,843
11	Al Shaqab Racing	82	47	56	306	18.3	1,082,183
12	Qatar Racing Limited	73	25	37	252	14.7	1,080,522

Note: Godolphin won the official owners' championship (with £5,514,437)

			Indiv'l	*Races*			*Stakes*
	OWNERS (win money, £2m+)	*Horses*	*Wnrs*	*Won*	*Runs*	*%*	*£*
1	Godolphin	264	138	192	768	25	3,551,322
2	Mr D. Smith, Mrs J. Magnier, Mr M. Tabor	20	8	10	38	26	2,945,450

			Indiv'l	*Races*			*Stakes*
	TRAINERS (1,2,3 earnings)	*Horses*	*Wnrs*	*Won*	*Runs*	*%*	*£*
1	Aidan O'Brien, Ireland	75	26	32	165	19.4	8,336,375
2	John Gosden	225	103	138	690	20.0	6,188,845
3	Richard Fahey	298	142	200	1,748	11.4	4,262,096
4	Sir Michael Stoute	135	57	82	438	18.7	3,856,639
5	Mark Johnston	217	116	215	1,379	15.6	3,568,123
6	Richard Hannon	268	136	194	1,354	14.3	2,986,683
7	William Haggas	160	107	158	590	26.8	2,704,085

8 Andrew Balding	160	67	93	677	13.7	2,576,593
9 Charlie Appleby	140	80	106	378	28.0	2,163,247
10 Roger Varian	162	75	109	558	19.5	1,915,308
11 David O'Meara	174	69	109	1,078	10.1	1,694,122
12 David Simcock	129	47	64	515	12.4	1,545,732

TRAINER (win money, £2m+)	*Horses*	*Indiv'l Wnrs*	*Races Won*	*Runs*	*%*	*Stakes £*
1 Aidan O'Brien, Ireland	75	26	32	165	19.4	5,564,955
2 John Gosden	225	103	138	690	20.0	4,562,081
3 Richard Fahey	298	142	200	1,748	11.4	2,504,737
4 Mark Johnston	217	116	215	1,379	15.6	2,423,007
5 Sir Michael Stoute	135	57	82	438	18.7	2,372,062

TRAINERS (with 100+ winners)	*Horses*	*Indiv'l Wnrs*	*Races Won*	*2nd*	*3rd*	*Runs*	*%*
1 Mark Johnston	217	116	215	187	166	1,379	15.6
2 Richard Fahey	298	142	200	220	219	1,748	11.4
3 Richard Hannon	268	136	194	177	165	1,354	14.3
4 William Haggas	160	107	158	78	77	590	26.8
5 John Gosden	225	103	138	91	102	690	20.0
6 Roger Varian	162	75	109	113	90	558	19.5
7 David O'Meara	174	69	109	125	132	1,078	10.1
8 Charlie Appleby	140	80	106	63	48	378	28.0

JOCKEYS (by winners)	*1st*	*2nd*	*3rd*	*Unpl*	*Mts*	*%*
1 Silvestre de Sousa	206	157	148	569	1080	19.1
2 Luke Morris	177	157	192	984	1510	11.7
3 Jim Crowley	161	118	83	493	855	18.8
4 Adam Kirby	146	128	102	529	905	16.1
5 Joe Fanning	140	112	100	497	849	16.5
6 Ryan Moore	137	82	48	305	572	24.0
7 P. J. McDonald	128	119	100	540	887	14.4
8 Oisin Murphy	127	122	112	494	855	14.9
9 Daniel Tudhope	122	103	89	421	735	16.6
10 James Doyle	110	69	73	250	502	21.9
11 Josephine Gordon	106	121	99	588	914	11.6
12 Richard Kingscote	100	82	71	429	682	14.7

Note: Silvestre de Sousa won the Stobart-sponsored jockeys' championship (with 155 wins)

JOCKEYS (1,2,3 earnings)	*Races Won*	*Rides*	*%*	*Stakes £*
1 Ryan Moore	137	572	24.0	8,152,042
2 Jim Crowley	161	855	18.8	5,247,474
3 Frankie Dettori	63	257	24.5	4,874,588
4 James Doyle	110	502	21.9	3,339,306
5 Andrea Atzeni	95	504	18.8	3,180,995
6 William Buick	81	368	22.0	3,010,113
7 Oisin Murphy	127	855	14.9	2,560,950
8 Silvestre De Sousa	206	1080	19.1	2,322,809
9 Adam Kirby	146	905	16.1	2,107,198
10 P. J. McDonald	128	887	14.4	1,855,120
11 Luke Morris	177	1510	11.7	1,755,873
12 Daniel Tudhope	122	735	16.6	1,612,845

JOCKEYS (win money, £3m+)	Races Won	Rides	%	Stakes £
1 Ryan Moore	137	572	24.0	5,752,168
2 Frankie Dettori	63	257	24.5	3,729,936
3 Jim Crowley	161	855	18.8	3,179,038

APPRENTICES (by winners)	1st	2nd	3rd	Unpl	Mts	%
1 Kieran Shoemark	65	56	70	339	530	12.3
2 David Egan	61	68	73	310	512	11.9
3 Hollie Doyle	59	62	57	338	516	11.4

Note: David Egan won the Stobart-sponsored apprentice championship (with 53 wins)

SIRES OF WINNERS (1,2,3 earnings)	Races Won	Runs	%	Stakes £
1 Galileo (by Sadler's Wells)	63	478	13.2	7,256,654
2 Dark Angel (by Acclamation)	142	1219	11.6	3,536,107
3 Dubawi (by Dubai Millennium)	128	602	21.3	2,921,597
4 Frankel (by Galileo)	46	210	21.9	2,085,379
5 Kodiac (by Danehill)	161	1301	12.4	2,039,308
6 Iffraaj (by Zafonic)	71	588	12.1	1,984,229
7 Acclamation (by Royal Applause)	111	1075	10.3	1,953,797
8 Sea The Stars (by Cape Cross)	50	273	18.3	1,843,306
9 Nathaniel (by Galileo)	48	303	15.8	1,700,064
10 Exceed And Excel (by Danehill)	126	1033	12.2	1,656,629
11 Invincible Spirit (by Green Desert)	96	847	11.3	1,550,497
12 Pivotal (by Polar Falcon)	76	554	13.7	1,306,939

SIRES OF WINNERS (win money £1m+)	Horses	Indiv'l Wnrs	Races Won	Stakes £
1 Galileo (by Sadler's Wells)	137	46	63	4,649,882
2 Dark Angel (by Acclamation)	214	95	142	2,524,739
3 Dubawi (by Dubai Millennium)	164	90	128	1,567,477
4 Nathaniel (by Galileo)	85	31	48	1,479,587
5 Frankel (by Galileo)	69	32	46	1,379,433
6 Acclamation (by Royal Applause)	176	77	111	1,215,595
7 Kodiac (by Danehill)	228	107	161	1,187,093
8 Exceed And Excel (by Danehill)	191	86	126	1,093,399
9 Iffraaj (by Zafonic)	110	41	71	1,067,659
10 Pour Moi (by Montjeu)	30	11	14	1,007,242

LEADING HORSES (1,2,3 earnings)	Races Won	Runs	Stakes £
1 Ulysses 4 ch.c Galileo – Light Shift	3	5	1,215,462
2 Enable 3 b.f Nathaniel – Concentric	4	5	1,169,717
3 Cracksman 3 b.c Frankel – Rhadegunda	3	4	1,039,612
4 Ribchester 4 b.c Iffraaj – Mujarah	2	4	1,036,749
5 Wings of Eagles 3 b.c Pour Moi – Ysoldina	1	2	937,663
6 Winter 3 gr.f Galileo – Laddies Poker Two	3	3	867,663
7 Highland Reel 5 b.h Galileo – Hveger	2	4	865,027
8 Persuasive 4 gr.f Dark Angel – Choose Me	1	2	677,560
9 Churchill 3 b.c Galileo – Meow	1	4	638,350
10 Harry Angel 3 b.c Dark Angel – Beatrix Potter	3	6	617,395
11 Here Comes When 7 br.g Danehill Dancer – Quad's Melody	2	4	595,836
12 Barney Roy 3 b.c Excelebration – Alina	2	6	583,466

EXPLANATORY NOTES

'Racehorses of 2017' deals individually, in alphabetical sequence, with every horse that ran on the Flat in Britain in 2017, plus a good number of overseas-trained horses and horses that ran abroad for British trainers. For each of these horses is given (1) its age, colour and sex followed by the name of its sire, its dam and the sire of the dam, with highest Timeform Annual rating where the information is available, (2) its breeding, and for most horses, where this information has not been given in a previous Racehorses Annual, a family outline, (3) a form summary giving its Timeform rating at the end of the previous year, followed by an abbreviated summary of all its performances during the past year and the date of its last run, (4) a Timeform rating, or ratings, of its merit in 2017 (which appears in the margin), (5) a Timeform commentary on its racing or general characteristics as a racehorse, with some suggestions, perhaps, regarding its prospects for 2018, and (6) the name of its trainer when it last ran. For each two-year-old the foaling date is also given.

TIMEFORM RATINGS

The Timeform Rating is a measure of the *best* form a horse displayed in the year, expressed in pounds. Without going into complexities, the scale used for Timeform ratings represents around 4 lb a length at five furlongs, 3.5 lb a length at six furlongs, 3 lb a length at seven furlongs, 2.5 lb a length at a mile, 2 lb a length at a mile and a quarter, over 1.5 lb a length at a mile and a half and over 1 lb a length at two miles, though the precise poundage will depend on circumstances, not least the conversion from times to margins used officially in each instance. When a horse has raced on turf and on an artificial surface and its form on one is significantly different from the other, the two ratings are given, the one for artificial surfaces set out below the turf preceded by 'a'. Some of the ratings may be different from those in the final issue of the 2017 Timeform Black Book series. The 'Racehorses Annual' figure is the definitive Timeform Rating.

The following may be attached to, or appear instead of, a rating:-

- p likely to improve.
- P capable of *much* better form.
- \+ the horse may be better than we have rated it.
- d the horse appears to have deteriorated, and might no longer be capable of running to the rating given.
- § unreliable (for temperamental or other reasons).
- §§ so temperamentally unsatisfactory as not to be worth a rating.
- ? the horse's rating is suspect. If used without a rating the symbol implies that the horse can't be assessed with confidence, or, if used in the in-season Timeform publications, that the horse is out of form.

RATINGS AND WEIGHT-FOR-AGE

The ratings in this book embrace all the horses in training it is possible to weigh up, ranging from tip-top performers, with ratings from 130 upwards, through categories such as high-class, very smart, smart, useful, fairly useful, fair and modest, down to the poorest, rated around the 20 mark. All the ratings are at weight-for-age, so that equal ratings mean horses of equal merit: the Timeform handicap is really not a single handicap, but four handicaps side by side: one for two-year-olds, one for three-year-olds, one for four-year-olds and one for older horses. Thus, a three-year-old rated, for argument's sake, at 117 is deemed to be identical in point of 'merit' with a four-year-old also rated at 117:

but for them to have equal chances in, say, a mile race in May, the three-year-old would need to be receiving 9 lb from the four-year-old, the weight difference specified by the Age, Weight and Distance Tables at the end of the book.

USING THE RATINGS

A. Horses of the Same Age

If the horses all carry the same weight there are no adjustments to be made, and the horses with the highest ratings have the best chances. If the horses carry different weights, jot down their ratings, and to the rating of each horse add one point for every pound the horse is set to carry less than 10 st, or subtract one point for every pound it has to carry more than 10 st.

B. Horses of Different Ages

Treat each horse separately, and compare the weight it has to carry with the weight for age prescribed for it in the tables, according to the age of the horse, the distance of the race and the time of the year. Then, add one point to the rating for each pound the horse has to carry less than the weight given in the tables: or, subtract one point from the rating for every pound it has to carry more than the weight prescribed by the tables.

For the purposes of rating calculations it should, in general, be assumed that any allowance a rider is able to claim is nullified by his or her inexperience.

It should be borne in mind that ratings are constantly changing as performances are re-evaluated, and more up-to-date information, which can be found on Timeform's website and in the Black Books, should be referred to when assessing a horse's chance in all races.

WEIGHING UP A RACE

The ratings tell you which horses in a race are most favoured by the weights; but the commentaries should also be studied carefully to see if there is any reason—suitability of going and distance among the most important points to consider—why the horse might be expected not to run up to its rating or indeed, with a lightly raced or inexperienced horse, might improve on it. The quality of jockeyship is also an important factor when deciding between horses with similar chances. In setting out the various characteristics, requirements and peculiarities of each horse in its commentary, we have expressed ourselves in as critical a manner as possible and where real conclusions are not to be drawn, we have been content to state the facts.

THE FORM SUMMARIES

The distance of each race is given in furlongs, fractional distances being expressed in the decimal notation to the nearest tenth of a furlong. The prefix 'a' signifies a race on an artificial surface (except for 'f' for fibresand, 'p' for polytrack and 't' for tapeta).

The going is symbolised as follows: f=firm (turf) or fast (artificial surface); m=good to firm, or standard to fast (artificial surface); g=good (turf) or standard (artificial surface); d=good to soft/dead, or standard to slow (artificial surface); s=soft (turf) or slow, sloppy, muddy or wet (artificial surface); v=heavy.

Placings are indicated up to sixth place, by superior figures, an asterisk denoting a win; and superior letters are used to convey what happened to the horse if it failed to complete or was disqualified: F–fell; pu–pulled up; ur–unseated rider; bd–brought down; rr–refused to race; su–slipped up; ro–ran out; co–carried out; d–disqualified

Where sale prices are considered relevant F denotes the price as a foal, Y the price as a yearling, 2-y-o as a two-year-old, and so on. These are given in guineas unless prefixed by $ (American dollars) ¥ (Japanese yen) € (euros) or £ (pounds sterling).

RACEHORSES OF 2017

Horse *Commentary* *Rating*

AARDWOLF (USA) 3 b.g. Cape Cross (IRE) 129 – Desert Gazelle (USA) 95 (Smart Strike (CAN) 121) [2017 91: 7.5m^{2} 7m* 7g 7m 7.2g^{6} 8.3s^{5} 7g p7g t12.4s^{6} 11.8s^{3} 10v^{5} Oct 23] lengthy gelding: fairly useful handicapper: won at Doncaster (by ½ length from Gallipoli) in May: stays 1¼m: acts on good to firm and heavy going: usually leads: sold to join Warren Greatrex 22,000 gns in October. *Mark Johnston* **94**

ABAAD (IRE) 3 ch.g. Bated Breath 125 – Condition (Deploy 131) [2017 p8g^{6} p10g^{4} 9m^{3} p10g^{4} Oct 12] fair form in maidens: left Roger Charlton after second start: should stay 1¼m+: tried in blinkers. *Mohamed Moubarak* **78**

ABAMANOVA (IRE) 2 b.f. (Mar 31) Camacho 118 – Abama Lady (CAN) (Mr Greeley (USA) 122) [2017 5m^{3} 5g* 5.8v 6g Nov 3] fourth foal: closely related to 2 winners by Holy Roman Emperor, including 5f-1m winner Geno, and half-sister to 1¼m winner The Big Cat (by Footstepsinthesand): dam unraced: fairly useful form: won maiden at Bellewstown (by 4 lengths from Daliyah) in August: best effort at 5f. *W. McCreery, Ireland* **84**

ABANDON SHIP (IRE) 2 gr.c. (Jan 31) Mastercraftsman (IRE) 129 – No Explaining (IRE) 80 (Azamour (IRE) 130) [2017 7m 8d^{2} 8d^{pu} Sep 7] tall colt: fair form when second in minor event at Newmarket in August: fatally injured next time. *Paul Cole* **76**

ABAREEQ 4 ch.g. Haatef (USA) 117 – Hafawa (IRE) 105 (Intikhab (USA) 135) [2017 84§, a96§: p10g* t8.6g p12g* p10d^{5} t12.4s 10.1g 9m^{4} p10s 10.1m p9.4f p12g^{3} Dec 23] good-topped gelding: fairly useful handicapper on turf, useful on all-weather: won at Kempton (by 1½ lengths from Getback In Paris) and Lingfield (by 2½ lengths from Gawdawpalin) in March: stays 1½m: acts on polytrack, tapeta and good to firm going: tried in cheekpieces. *Mark Johnston* **92** **a106**

ABATEMENT 3 b.g. Bated Breath 125 – Iwunder (IRE) 73 (King's Best (USA) 132) [2017 62: p7g* 7g p7d^{3} p8g^{2} 8g^{4} 8m^{4} Aug 25] tall gelding: fairly useful performer: won maiden at Lingfield in January: placed in handicaps at Kempton in May and June: stays 1m: acts on polytrack and good to firm going: sold 18,000 gns in October, sent to USA. *Roger Charlton* **87** **a92**

ABDON 4 b.g. Cacique (IRE) 124 – Kinnaird (IRE) 113 (Dr Devious (IRE) 127) [2017 118: 9m^{4} 9.9g^{6} 9.9g 9.9g p10s^{2} 10s^{2} Oct 28] tall gelding: smart handicapper: second at Chelmsford (½ length behind Petite Jack) in September and Newbury (1¼ lengths behind Century Dream) in October: stays 10.5f: acts on polytrack and any turf going: tried in cheekpieces: sometimes slowly away, often races prominently: sold 50,000 gns in October. *Sir Michael Stoute* **113**

ABEL HANDY (IRE) 2 b.c. (Mar 3) Arcano (IRE) 122 – Belle Isle 46 (Pastoral Pursuits 127) [2017 5d* 5.4g^{2} 5d* 5m^{2} 5m* Oct 13] €7,000Y, resold £9,000Y, £16,000 2-y-o: strong, compact colt: first foal: dam well beaten both starts: useful performer: won maiden at Nottingham in June, minor event at Thirsk (by 1¾ lengths from Rossall) in August and Cornwallis Stakes at Newmarket (by neck from Sound And Silence) in October: likely to prove best at 5f: acts on good to firm and good to soft going: usually leads, often travels strongly. *Declan Carroll* **105**

ABE LINCOLN (USA) 4 b.c. Discreet Cat (USA) 127 – Truly Blushed (USA) (Yes It's True (USA) 116) [2017 111p: 8m 7.9m p8s^{3} Dec 14] angular colt: useful handicapper: third at Chelmsford (2 lengths behind Mutawathea) in December: stays 1m: acts on polytrack and good to soft going: in cheekpieces 3 of last 4 starts: tongue tied in 2017. *Jeremy Noseda* **104**

ABEL TASMAN 3 b.g. Mount Nelson 125 – Helena Molony (IRE) 105 (Sadler's Wells (USA) 132) [2017 p10g^{3} 10g 10d 11.4m^{3} p12g^{2} p11g^{2} Oct 24] 80,000Y: good-topped gelding: seventh foal: half-brother to 3 winners, including 7f-1¼m winner Dance of Heroes (by Danehill Dancer) and 1¼m winner Red Hand (by Mr Greeley): dam, 1¼m winner who stayed 1¾m, sister to Derby winner High Chaparral: fairly useful maiden: second in handicaps at Kempton in October: stays 1½m: acts on polytrack and good to firm going: sometimes slowly away, usually races nearer last than first, often travels strongly. *Ed Walker* **81**

ABERDONIAN 3 b.g. Royal Applause 124 – Delaware Dancer (IRE) 68 (Danehill Dancer (IRE) 117) [2017 –: t6m 7g^{5} 7g^{6} Jun 12] modest maiden: stays 7f. *Jeremy Gask* **52**

Ballymacoll Stud's "Abingdon"

ABERTILLERY 5 b.g. Shamardal (USA) 129 – Nantyglo 101 (Mark of Esteem (IRE) 137) **45**
[2017 a60: p7d p12g p12g Apr 11] modest maiden at best, little impact in 2017 (including over hurdles): stays 7f: tried in headgear: usually races towards rear. *Michael Blanshard*

ABIENTO (IRE) 3 b.g. Requinto (IRE) 109 – Nose One's Way (IRE) 57 (Revoque (IRE) 122) [2017 81: t7.1g 7g⁴ 6.1d⁴ 6d⁴ 6s² 6.1m* 6s³ 6.1m⁶ Oct 16] sturdy gelding: fairly useful handicapper: won at Windsor (by 1¼ lengths from Himself) in August: left Richard Fahey after third start: stays 6f: acts on soft and good to firm going: tried in hood: sold 10,000 gns in November, sent to Spain. *Ed Walker* **84**

ABINGDON (USA) 4 b.f. Street Cry (IRE) 130 – Justlookdontouch (IRE) (Galileo (IRE) 134) [2017 109: 12g* 11.8m² 12.4g³ 11.9d⁶ p10.7g³ Sep 29] rangy filly: smart performer: won listed race at Pontefract (by 10 lengths from Lucy The Painter) in June: placed in Lancashire Oaks at Haydock (½ length behind The Black Princess) in July, Prix de Pomone at Deauville (1¾ lengths behind Bateel) in August and Diamond Stakes at Dundalk (3¼ lengths behind War Decree) in September: stays 12.5f: acts on polytrack and firm going: sold 1,050,000 gns in December, sent to USA. *Sir Michael Stoute* **110**

A BIT OF A TOUCH (IRE) 2 b.g. (Apr 14) Arcano (IRE) 122 – La Vita E Bella (IRE) 105 (Definite Article 121) [2017 7.4g⁶ 7v⁵ 8.2v⁵ Sep 30] modest form in minor events: dead. *Richard Fahey* **60**

A BIT OF GINGER 3 b.f. Camacho 118 – Hel's Angel (IRE) 86 (Pyrus (USA) 106) [2017 –: p8g² 7g⁴ 8g t8.6g⁵ 7.2m t8s 7m 6m Jul 19] modest maiden: stays 1m: acts on polytrack: in headgear last 2 starts. *Ann Duffield* **61**

ABJAR 3 b.g. Nathaniel (IRE) 129 – Kinnaird (IRE) 113 (Dr Devious (IRE) 127) [2017 p8g⁶ t10.2s² t12.2g* t12.2g² Sep 9] 525,000Y: half-brother to several winners, including very smart winner up to 11.6f Berkshire (2-y-o 7f/1m winner, by Mount Nelson) and smart winner up to 10.4f Abdon (2-y-o 1m winner, by Cacique): dam winner up to 1¼m (2-y-o 6f-1m winner), including Prix de l'Opera: fairly useful form: won maiden at Wolverhampton in August: stays 1½m: remains with potential. *Sir Michael Stoute* **91 p**

ABLAZE 3 ch.f. Arcano (IRE) 122 – Angry Bark (USA) 62 (Woodman (USA) 126) [2017 –: p8g p10g 11.6d* 11.6s^2 16.3d^5 11.9d^3 p13.3d p12g Nov 1] leggy, close-coupled filly: fair performer: won seller at Lingfield in July: seems to stay 16.5f: acts on soft going: in cheekpieces last 2 starts. *Laura Mongan* **65**

ABLE JACK 4 b.g. Iffraaj 127 – Solva 110 (Singspiel (IRE) 133) [2017 88: 7d^6 t7.1g^4 Dec 6] useful-looking gelding: fairly useful handicapper: stays 7f: acts on good to firm going: usually wears headgear: often travels strongly. *Stuart Williams* **80**

ABOUT GLORY 3 b.g. Nayef (USA) 129 – Lemon Rock 78 (Green Desert (USA) 127) [2017 –: 10m 10s 9g 9.9g* 10d 9.9v^5 p12g^3 t14g^4 Oct 27] sturdy gelding: fair handicapper: won at Brighton in June: stays 1¾m: acts on polytrack, tapeta and heavy going: in blinkers last 5 starts: has joined John David Riches. *Richard Hannon* **70**

ABOVE NORMAL 3 b.g. Street Cry (IRE) 130 – Saoirse Abu (USA) 112 (Mr Greeley (USA) 122) [2017 12g* 11.8g^4 11s a7f^2 a9.7f^5 Dec 29] fourth foal: half-brother to smart winner up to 1½m Ennistown (2-y-o 1m winner, by Authorized) and a winner abroad by Shamardal: dam 2-y-o 6f/7f winner (including Phoenix Stakes and Moyglare Stud Stakes): fairly useful performer: won maiden at Pontefract in April: second in handicap at Jebel Ali in December: left Saeed bin Suroor after third start: stays 1½m: acts on sand: tried in cheekpieces. *S. Seemar, UAE* **91**

ABOVE THE REST (IRE) 6 b.g. Excellent Art 125 – Aspasias Tizzy (USA) 85 (Tiznow (USA) 133) [2017 110: 6m^4 7m 7.6g^4 7m^4 7g* 7d 7g Aug 25] good-topped gelding: smart handicapper: won Bunbury Cup at Newmarket (by ½ length from Sir Dancealot) in July: best at 7f: acts on soft and good to firm going: wears hood: usually races prominently. *David Barron* **113**

A BOY NAMED SUE 4 b.g. Monsieur Bond (IRE) 120 – Elusive Sue (USA) 83 (Elusive Quality (USA)) [2017 54: t8g^4 t7.1d t8d^2 t8g^3 p8g 9m May 5] modest maiden: stays 1m: acts on tapeta and good to firm going: wears headgear. *Peter Niven* **59**

ABRAJ DUBAI (USA) 3 b.f. Street Cry (IRE) 130 – Pulitzer (USA) (Bernardini (USA) 132) [2017 f7.1g* f7.1g Dec 11] 10,000 3-y-o: first foal: dam unraced half-sister to top-class winner up to 1½m Fantastic Light: fairly useful form when won maiden at Southwell (by 8 lengths from Charlie's Dreamer) on debut in November: well held in handicap there next time. *David O'Meara* **89**

ABSOLUTE ANGEL 6 b.m. Primo Valentino (IRE) 116 – Send Me An Angel (IRE) 75 (Lycius (USA) 124) [2017 t10.2d^5 t10.2g^6 8g t16.3s^6 14d Jul 25] lengthy mare: fifth foal: half-sister to 12.5f-1¾m winner Jonny Delta (by Sulamani): dam 1¼m-1¾m winner: won bumper in 2015: modest maiden on Flat: tried in cheekpieces. *Peter Niven* **59**

ABSOLUTE BLAST (IRE) 5 b.m. Kodiac 112 – Perfect Fun 87 (Marju (IRE) 127) [2017 88: t9.5g* p8d* t8.6g^2 p10m^3 p10g* p10g^2 8.5m^2 8s^3 9m^6 a9.9g^3 p10.7g^2 9.9m^3 Oct 29] good-topped mare: useful performer: won handicaps at Wolverhampton and Kempton, both in January, and listed race on latter course (by neck from Linguistic) in April: placed most starts after, including when 2¼ lengths second to War Decree in Diamond Stakes at Dundalk: left Iain Jardine after third outing: stays 10.7f: acts on polytrack, tapeta, soft and good to firm going: strong traveller. *Archie Watson* **108**

bet365 Bunbury Cup (Heritage Handicap), Newmarket—
Above The Rest comes out on top under 5-lb claimer Clifford Lee; three-year-old Sir Dancealot (stars on sleeves) finishes strongly to edge Godolphin's Steady Pace for second

totescoop6 Challenge Cup (Heritage Handicap), Ascot—Accidental Agent looks a pattern performer in the making as he beats the grey Lord Glitters and Raising Sand (stars on sleeves)

ABSOLUTE CHAMPION (USA) 5 b.g. Henrythenavigator (USA) 131 – Alegendinmyownmind (Cape Cross (IRE) 129) [2017 5m* 6g5 5m3 5g p6s Oct 24] fairly useful performer at 3 yrs for Jamie Osborne: won handicap at Riffa in January: returned to Britain for final outing: stays 6f: acts on polytrack and good to firm going: sold 1,500 gns in October. *George Peckham* **82**

ABSOLUTELY AWESOME 3 ch.g. Choisir (AUS) 126 – Milton of Campsie 83 (Medicean 128) [2017 59: t5g3 t5.1g* p5s3 p5g f5g6 t5.1g Nov 29] fair handicapper: won at Wolverhampton in May: left Scott Dixon after first start: raced only at 5f: acts on polytrack and tapeta. *John Butler* **72**

ABSOLUTELY SO (IRE) 7 b.g. Acclamation 118 – Week End (Selkirk (USA) 129) [2017 113: 6g p6g4 7m2 7.2s* 7m Oct 13] rather leggy gelding: smart performer: won John of Gaunt Stakes at Haydock (by ½ length from Jallota) in June: second in listed race there (neck behind Oh This Is Us) in May: stays 7f: acts on polytrack, good to firm and heavy going: races freely. *Andrew Balding* **111**

ABSTRACTION (IRE) 7 b.h. Majestic Missile (IRE) 118 – Bronze Queen (IRE) (Invincible Spirit (IRE) 121) [2017 107, a92: 5m3 p5g3 5m6 5.2m p5s Sep 30] useful handicapper: third in listed race at Cork (2½ lengths behind Hit The Bid) in June: left Miss Natalia Lupini after third start: best at 5f: acts on polytrack, good to firm and good to soft going: tried in blinkers: front runner/races prominently. *J. S. Moore* **97**

ABU DHABI DOO 2 ch.f. (Feb 25) Red Jazz (USA) 125 – No Nightmare (USA) 51 (Lion Heart (USA) 124) [2017 5m 5s 7d6 6d6 Jul 22] £6,000Y: good-quartered filly: fourth foal: half-sister to 5f/6f winner Dreams of Reality (by Bushranger) and UAE 6f winner Mabrouka (by Sir Prancealot): dam maiden half-sister to useful 2-y-o 5f/6f winner Rabatash: no form: tried in visor. *K. R. Burke* **–**

ABUSHAMAH (IRE) 6 b.g. Nayef (USA) 129 – Adaala (USA) 108 (Sahm (USA) 112) [2017 90: t7.1d6 8m6 8m 8.3g5 8s 8.5m5 8.2s3 8m3 8g3 8d2 8d5 8d3 8m 9v2 10g Sep 27] rangy gelding: fairly useful handicapper: placed 6 times in 2017, including twice at Haydock in June: best up to 9f: acts on good to firm and heavy going: has worn headgear, including in 2017: often races freely. *Ruth Carr* **84**

ACADIAN ANGEL (IRE) 3 b.f. Dark Angel (IRE) 113 – Bon Ton Roulet 63 (Hawk Wing (USA) 136) [2017 t7.1g2 6g* 6.9g3 8m5 6g2 7m* 7d 7d6 Sep 12] €15,000 2-y-o: stocky filly: fifth foal: half-sister to 7f winners Glanely (by Exceed And Excel) and Jeremos (by Jeremy): dam, maiden (stayed 1¼m), half-sister to Lowther Stakes winner Infamous Angel: fairly useful performer: won maiden at Pontefract in April and handicap at Doncaster (by short head from Totally Magic) in July: stays 7f: acts on good to firm going. *John Quinn* **84**

ACAPULCO (USA) 4 ch.f. Scat Daddy (USA) 120 – Global Finance (USA) (End Sweep (USA)) [2017 116: 5g* May 14] big, powerful filly: smart performer at best: left Wesley Ward, won listed race at the Curragh (by ½ length from Ardhoomey) in May: reportedly suffered setback following month: stayed 6f: acted on polytrack and firm going: often in headgear/tongue tie: in foal to Galileo. *Aidan O'Brien, Ireland* **108**

ACCENTO 3 b.g. Elusive Quality (USA) – Azameera (IRE) 96 (Azamour (IRE) 130) [2017 73: p8g May 2] fair form in maidens at 2 yrs, well held sole outing in 2017. *Hugo Palmer* **–**

ACCESSION (IRE) 8 b.g. Acclamation 118 – Pivotal's Princess (IRE) 107 (Pivotal 124) [2017 108: 7m^5 7m t7.1s 7g* 7g^6 7d Sep 30] strong, sturdy gelding: useful handicapper: won at Newmarket (by 2¼ lengths from War Glory) in August: stays 1m: acts on polytrack and any turf going: has worn headgear: front runner/races prominently. *Charlie Fellowes* **105**

ACCESSOR (IRE) 2 b.c. (Apr 18) Exceed And Excel (AUS) 126 – Amarette (GER) 107 (Monsun (GER) 124) [2017 p8g 7g* Oct 17] €140,000Y: closely related to 2 winners abroad by Tiger Hill, including useful German 1¼m winner Ametrin, and half-brother to 2 winners in Germany, including smart 1¼m-1½m winner Amazona (by Dubawi): dam, German winner up to 11f (2-y-o 7f winner), including Preis der Diana, half-sister to dam of Melbourne Cup winner Almandin: fairly useful form: won maiden at Leicester (by ½ length from Ostilio) in October: will prove suited by 1m+: open to further improvement. *Richard Hannon* **84 p**

ACCIDENTAL AGENT 3 b.c. Delegator 125 – Roodle 90 (Xaar 132) [2017 94: 6m^5 7m p7g* 7g^2 7s* 8s^4 p8d Nov 22] good-bodied colt: very smart handicapper: won at Kempton (by 1¾ lengths from Leontes) in September and Ascot (Challenge Cup, by ½ length from Lord Glitters) in October: stays 1m: acts on polytrack, soft and good to firm going: often starts slowly/races in rear, usually responds generously to pressure. *Eve Johnson Houghton* **120**

ACCLAIM THE NATION (IRE) 4 b.g. Acclamation 118 – Dani Ridge (IRE) 92 (Indian Ridge 123) [2017 77: 5m* 5s^6 May 20] fairly useful handicapper: won at Doncaster (by neck from Bashiba) in April: best form at 5f: acts on good to firm and good to soft going: usually races close up. *Eric Alston* **82**

ACCOMPLICE 3 b.f. Sakhee's Secret 128 – Witness 71 (Efisio 120) [2017 p8g^4 p8g p7g 7.1m 9d^3 8.3d^2 8s* 8.1s p8g 8.2v^6 Sep 25] rather unfurnished filly: half-sister to several winners, including 1¼m winner Testimonio (by Cacique): dam 7f winner: fair handicapper: won at Bath in August: stays 9f: acts on soft going. *Michael Blanshard* **77**

ACCURATE 4 b.g. Zoffany (IRE) 121 – More Respect (IRE) (Spectrum (IRE) 126) [2017 8.2s p8s 8m 7s t7.2g t9.5g p10s p10s Nov 17] useful performer when trained in France, well below that level in 2017: stays 7.5f: acts on polytrack: in cheekpieces last 2 starts. *Ian Williams* **66**

ACE MASTER 9 ch.g. Ballet Master (USA) 92 – Ace Maite (Komaite (USA)) [2017 79: 6.1s 5d^5 8.3v^5 5g f5g 8.3g f7.1g^3 f6.1g^4 f8.1g Dec 22] plain gelding: fairly useful handicapper at best, below form in 2017: has won at 1m, probably best at shorter: acts on all-weather, good to firm and heavy going: wears headgear. *Roy Bowring* **50 a68**

ACE OF SPADES (USA) 2 br.c. (Mar 24) Street Cry (IRE) 130 – Force One (Dansili 127) [2017 p6g p6g^5 5v^2 Oct 16] fair form: best effort when fifth in minor event at Kempton (3¼ lengths behind Sergio Leone) in October. *George Scott* **65**

ACE VENTURA 2 b.c. (Apr 13) Mayson 124 – Ventura Highway (Machiavellian (USA) 123) [2017 8g^5 8v* Oct 4] 88,000Y: good-topped colt: half-brother to 3 winners, including smart winner up to 11.5f Alessandro Volta (2-y-o 9f winner, by Montjeu) and 2-y-o 6f winner (stayed 9f) Dylanesque (by Royal Applause): dam unraced half-sister to very smart 1m-10.4f winner Poet: fairly useful form: won minor event at Salisbury (by head from Mandalayan) in October: open to further improvement. *Roger Varian* **81 p**

ACHIANNA (USA) 2 ch.f. (Mar 31) Gemologist (USA) 119 – Adoradancer (USA) (Danzig Connection (USA)) [2017 6v^4 6g 6s^5 Sep 8] $12,000Y, resold £26,000Y: half-sister to several winners abroad, including US Grade 2 7f winner Saint Anddan (by A P Indy): dam, US 8.5f winner, half-sister to US Grade 3 8.5f winner Luftikus: modest form on last of 3 starts in minor events. *Rod Millman* **55**

ACID TEST 3 b.g. Bated Breath 125 – Cresta Gold 107 (Halling (USA) 133) [2017 8g 8.3m May 7] no form in 2 maidens. *Jedd O'Keeffe* **–**

ACKER BILK (IRE) 3 ch.g. Rip Van Winkle (IRE) 134 – Portentous (Selkirk (USA) 129) [2017 8.1g t8g^4 t8g^3 t12.4d^4 Dec 16] fair form: left David Lanigan after first start: stays 12.5f: acts on tapeta. *Keith Dalgleish* **69**

ACLAIM (IRE) 4 b.c. Acclamation 118 – Aris (IRE) 94 (Danroad (AUS) 112) [2017 121: 8s^6 6m 7g^6 6.5g^2 7g* 7d* Oct 1] **122**

The opportunity to train on the historic estate at Manton was one that proved too good to miss for Martyn Meade, who is moving into the same yard where Peter Chapple-Hyam trained Rodrigo de Triano to win the Two Thousand Guineas and

Dr Devious to win the Derby in 1992, and where John Gosden later became the sixth trainer to send out a British classic winner from Manton when Lahan won the One Thousand Guineas in 2000, having taken over from Chapple-Hyam only four months previously. Manton has been the base for George Baker and Brian Meehan in more recent times, that pair having leased their respective yards from Paul Clarke following his purchase from the Sangster family in 2015. Meehan is set to remain but Meade is now the owner of 'a major part' of the estate, including the yard Baker vacated to set up at Robins Farm in the latest season. Meade should be ready to start from Manton in the 2018 Flat season after switching from the fifty-box yard at Sefton Lodge in Newmarket into which he moved only in 2014 (he has also acquired Snailwell Stud in Newmarket with the aim of 'making the circle from training to breeding'). Meade had, incidentally, also originally been based in Wiltshire when sending out his first winner over jumps in 1972 when operating at the grass roots of the game. Indeed, he did not train at all for lengthy periods between 1998 and 2013 as he focused on his business and commercial interests (he now takes more of a back seat as chairman at private investment group Hadleigh Partners). It is only since the move to Sefton Lodge that Meade, who describes himself as 'a man who needs a challenge', has turned his hand to training again, with the emphasis on training better horses ('I don't just want to train handicappers, we are looking for potential Group horses'). Meade's first three seasons at Sefton Lodge told a story of year-on-year progression, his total earnings in 2016 amounting to more than the combined total of his first two seasons at Newmarket. The one thing still missing was a Group 1 winner, the trainer making it plain at the beginning of 2017 that it was his aim to get that first top-level winner on the board.

Eminent looked the most likely to deliver that triumph after an impressive return to action in the Craven Stakes at Newmarket, his victory over the previous year's Racing Post Trophy winner Rivet identifying Eminent as a leading contender for the Two Thousand Guineas. He was sent off third favourite in a hotly-anticipated renewal of the classic, in which the fact that he was an undefeated son of Frankel ensured he received plenty of media attention. Eminent managed only sixth behind Churchill, shaping as if needing a stiffer test of stamina. His next start was in the Derby in which he acquitted himself well, keeping on to finish a length and three quarters fourth to Wings of Eagles. Though victory at the highest level continued to elude Eminent with defeats in the Coral-Eclipse at Sandown and the Irish Champion Stakes at Leopardstown coming either side of a pillar-to-post success in the Group 2 Prix Guillaume d'Ornano at Deauville in mid-August, Eminent still looks the type to do well as a four-year-old in Meade's first year at Manton.

In the end, the distinction of becoming the trainer's first Group 1 winner belonged to the four-year-old Aclaim, who won the Prix de la Foret on Arc day at Chantilly. Aclaim had given Meade his biggest success as a trainer up to that point when completing a hat-trick in the Group 2 Challenge Stakes at Newmarket on his final start in 2016. He made his seasonal reappearance, and debut in Group 1 company, in the Lockinge Stakes at Newbury in May. Aclaim had proved his ability to handle testing conditions when winning a listed race at Newbury as a three-year-old, but that victory had come over seven furlongs, and the combination of soft ground and the extra furlong appeared to stretch Aclaim in the Lockinge, trailing in thirteen lengths sixth of eight behind Ribchester.

Aclaim shaped with more promise when dropped back to six furlongs for the Diamond Jubilee Stakes at Royal Ascot, suffering trouble in running before keeping on well to be beaten just four lengths behind The Tin Man. Aclaim finished with plenty of running left in him and was stepped back up to seven furlongs for the Lennox Stakes at Goodwood in early-August, Frankie Dettori back in the saddle for the first time since the Challenge Stakes. Aclaim never really got the room he needed in a typically muddling race for the track and did well under the circumstances to finish just a length and a quarter behind Breton Rock in sixth. It was France next for the Prix Maurice de Gheest at Deauville in which Aclaim recorded a career-best effort under Olivier Peslier, starting at 37/1 and staying on strongly to finish half a length second to fellow British raider Brando. A second Group 2 victory followed in the Park Stakes at Doncaster in mid-September when, in a good renewal that involved three previous winners at the level and others with plenty of solid pattern form, Aclaim was a comfortable winner by three quarters of a length from Nathra, with Home of The Brave a length further back in third and Spirit of Valor completing the frame just a short head behind.

The Park Stakes was the first time Aclaim had been ridden by Oisin Murphy in what became a landmark season for the jockey, though one that was also not without its low points. One such occasion came on Dark Red at the Qatar Goodwood Festival, the same day that Aclaim ran in the Lennox Stakes. Murphy produced Dark Red to lead entering the final furlong, but his mount hung badly left on the run to the line, bumping and carrying the runner-up Fabricate, owned by the Queen, with him in the process, while also badly hampering Ryan Moore's mount Garcia. The drama did not stop there, however, and events at the resulting stewards' inquiry provoked almost as much debate on social media as the panel's decision to reverse the placings. After Fabricate's jockey Adam Kirby had given his account and claimed that Dark Red's interference cost him the race (there was a head between first and second), Murphy put forward his case in front of the television cameras, telling the stewards 'I believe I did everything in my power to keep the horse straight.' The cutting response of Ryan Moore, who has ridden often for Fabricate's owner, gained plenty of attention. 'He handled the horse well, but he's just not strong enough to keep it straight,' interrupted Moore. Some felt that Moore was implying that Murphy could have done no more and was not at fault for the interference, though the majority interpreted the comment as a light-hearted put down which nonetheless incriminated Murphy. The stewards certainly adjudged Murphy to be at fault, with Dark Red being thrown out and the jockey receiving an eight-day ban for careless riding, following one of the most memorable televised stewards' inquiries in Britain since that into the 2015 St Leger when Simple Verse was disqualified only for the BHA's disciplinary panel to subsequently reinstate her (the first televised inquiry was into the Nassau Stakes at Goodwood in 2010).

With the previous year's winner Limato missing due to the expected very soft ground, Aclaim was presented with perhaps his best chance of gaining that elusive Group 1 victory in the Prix de la Foret on Arc day, sent off second favourite in a ten-strong field. Karar had chased home Limato twelve months earlier and was back attempting to go one better under French champion jockey Pierre-Charles Boudot, with Aclaim's Prix Maurice de Gheest conqueror Brando also prominent in betting headed by the 2016 Prix Jean Prat winner Zelzal, who had nonetheless failed to reproduce his best form in two previous starts in the latest season. Ridden once again by Oisin Murphy, Aclaim never gave his supporters the slightest cause for concern during the race. He tracked the pace set by Karar and, once switched

Alan Wood Plumbing And Heating Park Stakes, Doncaster—Aclaim registers his second Group 2 success; Nathra (right), Home of The Brave (left) and Spirit of Valor (blinkers) complete the frame

Qatar Prix de la Foret, Chantilly—Aclaim makes the most of 2016 winner Limato's absence to provide trainer Martyn Meade and jockey Oisin Murphy with their first Group 1 successes, beating fellow British raider So Beloved (right) and the 2016 runner-up Karar (left)

out of the leader's slipstream over a furlong out, stayed on well to score with more in hand than the three quarters of a length winning margin, the David O'Meara-trained So Beloved finishing strongly to overhaul Karar and secure a one, two for the British raiders. Aclaim did not even have to be at his very best to provide both trainer Martyn Meade and jockey Oisin Murphy with their first Group 1 successes—Murphy doubled his tally when riding Blond Me to win the E.P. Taylor Stakes at Woodbine two weeks later—while Aclaim's victory also meant that each of the six Group 1 races on Arc day had been won by British and Irish trainers, the first time that has happened (there is more in the essay on Enable). Aclaim's Prix de la Foret victory crowned a fine weekend for his stable which had won the Cambridgeshire the previous day with 50/1-shot Dolphin Vista. That emotional day for connections at Chantilly proved to be Aclaim's swansong and he will be standing at the National Stud in 2018, at a fee of £12,500.

Aclaim (IRE) (b.c. 2013)	Acclamation (b 1999)	Royal Applause (b 1993)	Waajib
			Flying Melody
		Princess Athena (b 1985)	Ahonoora
			Shopping Wise
	Aris (IRE) (b 2008)	Danroad (b 1999)	Danehill
			Strawberry Girl
		Cumbres (b 1993)	Kahyasi
			Floripedes

Aclaim's pedigree was covered in *Racehorses of 2016* and, to summarise, he is by Acclamation and the first foal out of Aris, who is by the New Zealand-raced Danehill stallion Danroad. Aris won a seven-furlong maiden from seven starts in Ireland for Paddy Prendergast and was also placed as a two-year-old in the listed Flame of Tara Stakes at the Curragh. Aris is out of Cumbres, who has produced five winners, including the Irish One Thousand Guineas winner Again (by another son of Danehill in Danehill Dancer), while Cumbres herself is a half-sister to Montjeu, both out of the stoutly-bred Floripedes, who won the Prix de Lutece over fifteen furlongs and also appears in the extended pedigree of the King's Stand and Abbaye winner Goldream (great grandam) and the Two Thousand Guineas winner Galileo Gold (great great grandam). A yearling half-sister to Aclaim by Slade Power was entered in the latest Newmarket October Sales Book 1 but was withdrawn. A pair of half-brothers to Aclaim, a three-year-old by Dark Angel named Bere Island and a two-year-old by Dawn Approach named Accept, are both unraced. A lengthy colt, Aclaim was a winner at a mile, but proved best at around seven furlongs and, as a Group 1 and dual Group 2 winner at that trip, he should prove popular with breeders. He acted on polytrack, good to firm and heavy going, and often wore a tongue tie, though he did so less frequently in his four-year-old season. *Martyn Meade*

ACLIMATISE 3 b.g. Acclamation 118 – Favourita 103 (Diktat 126) [2017 t7.1g 8m^2 8g* Jul 18] 32,000Y: fifth foal: half-brother to 1m winners Authoritarian (by Authorized) and Tammuz (by Tamayuz): dam, 2-y-o 7f winner who stayed 1¼m, half-sister to smart 1½m winner Time Zone: fairly useful form: won maiden at Thirsk (by length from Spinnaka) in July: stays 1m. *Mark Johnston* **85**

ACQUIRER (IRE) 2 b.g. (Mar 16) Zoffany (IRE) 121 – See Emily Play (IRE) 63 (Galileo (IRE) 134) [2017 8d Oct 27] 55,000F, 130,000Y: second foal: half-brother to 1m winner See The Master (by Dutch Art): dam lightly-raced sister to useful winner around 1¼m Snowmane: 50/1, considerate introduction when ninth in minor event at Newbury in October: should improve. *Richard Hughes* **51 p**

ACROMATIC (IRE) 2 br.g. (Apr 15) Poet's Voice 126 – Natalisa (IRE) 85 (Green Desert (USA) 127) [2017 5m 6g^4 5.9s 5.9v p5g t5d Nov 4] modest form: best effort when fourth in minor event at Thirsk in June: in headgear last 3 starts. *John Quinn* **50**

ACROSS DUBAI 3 b.g. Cape Cross (IRE) 129 – Saadiah (IRE) (Dubai Destination (USA) 127) [2017 94p: 8m* 10.5m* 12d^5 9.9g^6 Sep 2] sturdy gelding: useful handicapper: won at Yarmouth (awarded race) in May and Haydock (by length from Carigrad with plenty in hand) in July: stays 1¼m: acts on polytrack and good to firm going: strong traveller: gelded after final start. *William Haggas* **107**

ACROSS THE STARS (IRE) 4 b.g. Sea The Stars (IRE) 140 – Victoria Cross (IRE) 101 (Mark of Esteem (IRE) 137) [2017 118: 12s^5 12m 11.4m 12.3v^2 11m 12s Oct 28] tall gelding: smart performer at 3 yrs, not quite at that level in 2017: second in listed race at Chester (½ length behind Duretto) in September: stays 1½m: acts on polytrack, good to firm and heavy going: tried in hood: sometimes slowly away: temperament under suspicion. *Sir Michael Stoute* **108**

ACRUX 4 b.g. Dansili 127 – Ikat (IRE) 100 (Pivotal 124) [2017 84: 8.3m p7s 6.1g 7g^2 7g t8g^6 t7.1d^4 t8g^3 t7.1g^3 t8.6g p7s t7.1g^6 Dec 6] fairly useful handicapper: second at Doncaster in August: left David Lanigan after third start: has won at 9.5f, usually races at shorter: acts on tapeta: wears hood: often races towards rear/travels strongly. *David O'Meara* **82**

ACTRESS (IRE) 2 b.f. (Jan 12) Declaration of War (USA) 128 – Nasty Storm (USA) 118 (Gulch (USA)) [2017 6m^2 5g* 6s^2 6m^6 5m^2 6.3f* 6m^3 6d Aug 24] $250,000Y: tall filly: has scope: half-sister to Italian 7.5f/1m winner A Touch Wild (by Touch Gold): dam US winner up to 8.5f (2-y-o 5.5f winner), including Grade 2 contests: useful performer: won maiden at the Curragh in May and Anglesey Stakes there (by 1¾ lengths from Theobald) in July: third in Phoenix Stakes at same course (2 lengths behind Sioux Nation) in August: stays 6.5f: acts on firm and soft going: usually races prominently. *Aidan O'Brien, Ireland* **105**

ACT SWIFTLY (IRE) 3 b.g. Requinto (IRE) 109 – Silk Point (IRE) (Barathea (IRE) 127) [2017 8.1d^6 11.6g^6 p12s t14g Jul 17] no form, including in handicap: tried in blinkers. *J. S. Moore* **–**

ACTUALISATION 3 b.g. Exceed And Excel (AUS) 126 – Eluding 84 (Street Cry (IRE) 130) [2017 72: 7.5m^{pu} Apr 19] fair maiden at 2 yrs: pulled up sole outing in 2017: stayed 1m: acted on firm and soft going: tried in visor: usually raced prominently: dead. *John Quinn* **–**

ADAMANT (GER) 3 gr.g. Dalakhani (IRE) 133 – Attima 95 (Zafonic (USA) 130) [2017 84p: 9.9m* Apr 30] fairly useful form: won handicap at Salisbury (by neck from Elas Ruby) on sole outing in 2017: will stay 1½m: capable of further progress. *Sir Michael Stoute* **92 p**

ADA MISOBEL (IRE) 4 b.f. Alfred Nobel (IRE) 110 – Startarette (USA) (Dixieland Band (USA)) [2017 62: t7.1g^6 f8d 8.3g p8d May 29] modest at best, no form in 2017: left Garry Moss to rejoin former trainer after first start: wears headgear: often races freely. *Roy Bowring* **–**

ADAM'S ALE 8 b.g. Ishiguru (USA) 114 – Aqua 51 (Mister Baileys 123) [2017 87: 6s* 5m 6d 7g^6 6g^5 5v 6s^2 f6.1g Dec 4] fairly useful handicapper: won at Haydock (by 3 lengths from Rantan) in June: stays 6f: acts on good to firm and heavy going: wears headgear. *Marjorie Fife* **88**

ADAMS PARK 2 b.g. (Feb 15) Mastercraftsman (IRE) 129 – Ile Deserte (Green Desert (USA) 127) [2017 7g^3 8g^3 8d^4 9d^4 Oct 11] 130,000Y: sixth foal: half-brother to 3 winners, including useful 2-y-o 6f winner St Barths (by Cadeaux Genereux) and 17f winner Havisham (by Mount Nelson): dam unraced half-sister to St Leger winner Kingston Hill (by Mastercraftsman): fairly useful form: third in maiden at Goodwood in August: should stay 9f: remains with potential. *Roger Varian* **82 p**

ADDEYBB (IRE) 3 ch.g. Pivotal 124 – Bush Cat (USA) 93 (Kingmambo (USA) 125) **110 p**
[2017 7s^4 8m* 8g* 9.9v^3 9d* Sep 29] 200,000Y: strong gelding: half-brother to several winners, including useful winner up to 11f Blue Tiger's Eye (2-y-o 7f winner, by Motivator) and 2-y-o 1m winner Meer Kat (by Red Ransom): dam 2-y-o 7f winner who stayed 11.4f: smart performer: won maiden at Haydock in June, and handicaps at Ascot (by neck from Juanito Chico) in July and Newmarket (by ½ length from Afaak) in September: stays 1¼m: acts on good to firm and heavy going: will go on improving. *William Haggas*

ADDICTED TO YOU (IRE) 3 ch.g. Medicean 128 – Adalawa (IRE) (Barathea (IRE) **94**
127) [2017 82p: p12g* p14g^3 11.2s^4 13.1s^2 15.9m* 15d^{pu} 16g^2 Aug 12] fairly useful performer: won maiden at Lingfield in March and handicap at Catterick in July: second in handicaps at Hamilton in July and Newmarket in August: stays 2m: acts on polytrack, soft and good to firm going: usually races prominently. *Mark Johnston*

A DEFINITE DIAMOND 4 ch.f. Assertive 121 – By Definition (IRE) 54 (Definite **–**
Article 121) [2017 p8g 6.1d 6m 5.1m 8g 8g Aug 17] leggy filly: no form: has worn headgear, including final start: tried in tongue tie. *Grace Harris*

ADHERENCE 4 b.g. Sir Percy 129 – Straight Laced 68 (Refuse To Bend (IRE) 128) **65**
[2017 66: 12g 14g 14v* 14d^6 12.1v^6 15.9s^4 13.1v* Oct 12] fair handicapper: won at Wetherby in June and Ayr in October: stays 1¾m: acts on good to firm and heavy going: has worn cheekpieces, including last 2 starts: has joined Kenneth Slack. *Tony Coyle*

ADIATOR 9 b.m. Needwood Blade 117 – Retaliator 80 (Rudimentary (USA) 118) [2017 **–**
61: t8.6g 7g Apr 26] fair at best, well held both starts in 2017: stays 7f: acts on good to firm and heavy going: usually wears cheekpieces: has worn tongue tie. *Neville Bycroft*

ADJACENT 3 b.g. Teofilo (IRE) 126 – Local Spirit (USA) 101 (Lion Cavern (USA) 117) **66 p**
[2017 10g^6 Jul 24] angular gelding: seventh foal: half-brother to 3 winners, including smart winner up to 1½m Al Saham (2-y-o 7f winner, by Authorized) and useful 6f-1¼m winner Active Spirit (by Pivotal): dam temperamental 1¼m winner: 11/4, shaped as if in need of experience when sixth in maiden at Windsor: will improve. *Charlie Appleby*

ADJECTIVE 4 b.f. Dansili 127 – Binche (USA) 51 (Woodman (USA) 126) [2017 11.5m* **81**
12s Jul 22] sister to 2 winners, including very smart French/US 7f (including at 2 yrs) to 9.5f winner Proviso, and half-sister to 2 winners, including high-class 1m-1¼m (Prince of Wales's Stakes) winner Byword (by Peintre Celebre): dam ran twice: fairly useful performer: ran 3 times for A. Fabre at 3 yrs: won handicap at Yarmouth in May: should stay 1½m: acts on good to firm going. *James Fanshawe*

ADJUTANT 2 b.c. (Feb 24) Champs Elysees 124 – Jubilee 66 (Selkirk (USA) 129) [2017 **62 p**
8g Sep 7] half-brother to 3 winners, including smart winner up to 7f Professor (2-y-o 6f winner, by Byron) and 1m winner (stays 1¼m) Breanski (by Delegator): dam maiden (stayed 1¼m): 50/1, considerately handled when seventh in minor event at Haydock: will improve. *David O'Meara*

AD LIBITUM 2 b.g. (May 2) Elusive Quality (USA) – Sarmad (USA) 56 (Dynaformer **53**
(USA)) [2017 p8g^6 t8.6g Nov 25] modest form on first of 2 starts in minor events. *Hugo Palmer*

ADMIRABLE ART (IRE) 7 b.g. Excellent Art 125 – Demi Voix (Halling (USA) 133) **80**
[2017 70, a60: t8.6m t9.5g* p7g^4 8m^5 8.1d* 8.1g^4 8m Aug 9] angular gelding: fairly useful **a74**
handicapper: won at Wolverhampton in February and Chepstow (by 1¾ lengths from Spirit of Belle) in June: stays 9.5f: acts on polytrack, tapeta, good to firm and heavy going: has worn cheekpieces, including in 2017. *Tony Carroll*

ADMIRAL ROOKE (IRE) 2 b.g. (Mar 25) Rock of Gibraltar (IRE) 133 – Qenaa 84 **66**
(Royal Applause 124) [2017 t6g 5.5s^4 5s 6d^3 7.4d 5.9v 8s^4 Oct 3] fair maiden: stays 1m. *Michael Dods*

ADMIRAL SPICE (IRE) 2 gr.g. (Apr 28) Lethal Force (IRE) 128 – Rustam (Dansili 127) **66**
[2017 5m 6g 6f 6.1s t7.1g^4 t8s^3 t7.1g^2 Oct 10] tall, lengthy gelding: fair maiden: stays 1m: acts on tapeta: in cheekpieces last 3 starts: front runner/races prominently. *Tom Dascombe*

ADMIRAL'S SUNSET 4 b.f. Mount Nelson 125 – Early Evening 84 (Daylami (IRE) **89**
138) [2017 81: 13d* 14d 11.2s^4 13.3g p11g Oct 4] tall, good-topped filly: fairly useful handicapper: won at Bath in May: stays 13.5f: acts on polytrack, good to firm and heavy going: usually races prominently: sold 21,000 gns in November. *Hughie Morrison*

ADMIRALTY ARCH 3 b.c. Archipenko (USA) 127 – Aldeburgh Music (IRE) (In The **86 d**
Wings 128) [2017 89: p7.5g^4 p8g* p8g p6.5g p7.5g p12.4f 9.9d Jul 15] good-topped colt: fairly useful performer: won claimer at Cagnes-sur-Mer in January: left Richard Hughes and well below form after second start: stays 1m: acts on polytrack, soft and good to firm going: often in headgear. *Cedric Boutin, France*

ADMIRED 2 gr.f. (Feb 2) Oasis Dream 129 – Souviens Toi 107 (Dalakhani (IRE) 133) [2017 7m 7g^4 p7g^3 Oct 18] 150,000F, £140,000Y: first foal: dam Italian 9f-11f winner: fair form: best effort when third in minor event at Kempton (2 lengths behind Revalue) in October. *Sir Michael Stoute* **73**

ADMISSIBLE 2 b.g. (Apr 9) Excelebration (IRE) 133 – Admirable Spirit 92 (Invincible Spirit (IRE) 121) [2017 t6.1g Jun 7] 80/1, very green when well held in minor event at Wolverhampton. *Richard Hughes* –

ADRAKHAN (FR) 6 b.g. Martaline 118 – Annee de La Femme (IRE) (Common Grounds 118) [2017 47: t16.3d^5 t16.3g 16g^6 15.9m^5 14g^3 14m* 12.5g^6 14g^4 16m* t12.4g 15.9s^3 13.9v^5 14v^2 Nov 7] modest handicapper: won at Redcar in June and Musselburgh in August: stays 2m: acts on good to firm and heavy going: tried in tongue tie. *Wilf Storey* **56 a42**

ADULATE 2 b.c. (Mar 26) Acclamation 118 – Paradise Sea (USA) (Stormy Atlantic (USA)) [2017 7g 6.1g^5 7d^3 7g p5g^6 5.1m Oct 16] rather unfurnished colt: fair maiden: stays 7f: acts on polytrack and good to soft going: in headgear last 4 starts: front runner/races prominently. *Hugo Palmer* **66**

ADVENTUREMAN 5 b.g. Kyllachy 129 – Constitute (USA) 85 (Gone West (USA)) [2017 66: t7.1d t8d^6 8.3g^4 8m 9m^2 8g^2 10.2d 8s^4 7.4m 8.9m 8m^2 8d 10.9m^4 t10.2s p10g^6 Oct 5] fair handicapper: stays 9f: acts on polytrack, soft and good to firm going: usually wears headgear: front runner/races prominently. *Ruth Carr* **71 a59**

ADVENTURE ZONE (IRE) 4 b.g. Elnadim (USA) 128 – Eliza Doolittle 67 (Royal Applause 124) [2017 58, a69: p8g^5 f8g 6g* 7d^2 7g^2 7g^6 6s^3 6g* 5.5g^2 6.7s^4 6g^3 6d 6s Oct 26] angular gelding: modest handicapper: left Lee Carter after second start: won at Mulheim in April and July: left H. Grewe after next outing: stays 9f: acts on polytrack, fibresand and good to firm going: wears headgear. *J-V. Toux, France* **64**

AD VITAM (IRE) 9 ch.g. Ad Valorem (USA) 125 – Love Sonnet (Singspiel (IRE) 133) [2017 69: t7.1g^2 6g 8.2g^6 t6d 7m t7.1g^5 t7.2g Dec 13] angular gelding: fair handicapper: best up to 1m: acts on all-weather, good to firm and good to soft going: wears headgear/tongue tie. *Suzzanne France* **69**

AEGEAN BOUNTY (IRE) 3 b.f. Bahamian Bounty 116 – Royal Consort (IRE) (Green Desert (USA) 127) [2017 p7g Nov 1] €6,500Y, resold 7,000Y: sixth foal: half-sister to 2-y-o 8.6f winner Jimmy The Lollipop (by Amadeus Wolf) and 7f winner Big Chill (by Acclamation): dam unraced half-sister to Gimcrack Stakes winner Carrowkeel: 66/1, well held in maiden at Kempton. *John Bridger* –

AEGEAN BOY 4 b.g. Paco Boy (IRE) 129 – Anosti 92 (Act One 124) [2017 56: p5g p6g p6s Dec 7] maiden, no form in 2017: has worn tongue tie, including final start. *John Bridger* –

AEGEAN LEGEND 2 b.g. (Apr 24) Mayson 124 – Aegean Mystery (Dr Fong (USA) 128) [2017 5s^3 7v^5 Sep 9] fourth foal: dam unraced: fair form on second of 2 starts in minor events: remains with potential. *John Bridger* **68 p**

AEGEAN SECRET 3 b.g. Equiano (FR) 127 – Aegean Mystery (Dr Fong (USA) 128) [2017 –: 6.1m^6 7m Jun 17] no form: tried in visor. *John Bridger* –

AELIUS 3 ch.g. Sepoy (AUS) 129 – Syvilla 97 (Nayef (USA) 129) [2017 70: 7g 8.3g 7.2g^3 8m^6 10.2g* 9.8d^5 12g Aug 19] fair handicapper: won at Nottingham in July: stays 1¼m: best form on good going: tried in tongue tie: often races towards rear/lazily. *Michael Easterby* **74**

AEOLUS 6 b.g. Araafa (IRE) 128 – Bright Moll 88 (Mind Games 121) [2017 114: 6m^6 6m^2 t6s^4 6d^2 7g 6v 6d^5 Oct 27] small gelding: smart performer: second in minor event at Haydock (neck behind Mythmaker) in May and Stewards' Cup (Handicap) at Goodwood (¾ length behind Lancelot du Lac) in August: stays 7f: acts on tapeta, good to firm and heavy going: has worn cheekpieces. *Ed Walker* **112**

AFAAK 3 b.c. Oasis Dream 129 – Ghanaati (USA) 122 (Giant's Causeway (USA) 132) [2017 7m^4 8g* 8d* 8m 8g^4 8s^4 9d^2 Sep 29] rangy colt: third foal: half-brother to 1m winner (stays 1¼m) Almuhalab (by Dansili) and useful 7f/1m winner Alnashama (by Dubawi): dam, won 1000 Guineas and Coronation Stakes (also 7f winner at 2 yrs), half-sister to high-class 1m-1½m winner Mawatheeq: useful performer: won maiden at Thirsk in May and handicap at Doncaster (by ¾ length from Mountain Angel) in June: resumed progress when second in handicap at Newmarket (½ length behind Addeybb) in September: stays 9f: acts on soft and good to firm going. *Charles Hills* **108**

AFANDEM (IRE) 3 b.g. Vale of York (IRE) 117 – Al Mahmeyah 78 (Teofilo (IRE) 126) [2017 105: 5.5g t5g 6g 5d 5.4d 5v Sep 9] neat gelding: useful handicapper: largely out of form in 2017: stays 6f: acts on soft and good to firm going: tried in blinkers. *Hugo Palmer* **98**

A FEW GOOD MEN 2 b.g. (Feb 25) Compton Place 125 – Slap And Tickle (IRE) 56 **66 p**
(Exceed And Excel (AUS) 126) [2017 t5.1d^{4} f5g* Dec 29] 10,000F, 17,000 2-y-o: first foal: dam maiden (best efforts at 5f): fair form: won minor event at Southwell (by short head from Magic Pulse) in December: in cheekpieces first start: open to further improvement. *Jose Santos*

AFFAIR 3 b.f. Sakhee's Secret 128 – Supatov (USA) 57 (Johannesburg (USA) 127) [2017 **63**
62: p12g^{6} p10g^{5} t12.2g p12g 11.6g* 11.6d 10g^{4} 14d* 11.6m^{3} 14.1d^{6} 11.9s^{4} 14v* p15.8g Dec 6] modest performer: won seller at Lingfield in June, and handicaps at Bath in August and Redcar in November: stays 1¾m: acts on good to firm and heavy going: front runner/races prominently, often freely. *Hughie Morrison*

AFFECTIONATE LADY (IRE) 6 b.m. Dandy Man (IRE) 123 – Agouti (Pennekamp **–**
(USA) 130) [2017 63: t8s May 23] modest handicapper, below form sole outing in 2017: stays 9f: acts on polytrack, tapeta, good to firm and heavy going: wears headgear: tried in tongue tie: usually races nearer last than first. *Paul Collins*

AFFINA (IRE) 2 b.f. (May 5) Kodiac 112 – Epistoliere (IRE) (Alzao (USA) 117) [2017 **85**
6.9g^{4} 7d* 7.2d* 7m^{4} Aug 26] €65,000F, 70,000Y: closely related to 2 winners, including 1¼m winner Right To Rule (by Rock of Gibraltar), and half-sister to several winners, including smart winner up to 21.7f Simenon (2-y-o 7f/1m winner, by Marju): dam French maiden (stayed 1¼m): fairly useful form: won minor events at Thirsk in July and Ayr in August: will stay 1m+. *Simon Crisford*

AFFLUENCE (IRE) 2 b.c. (Feb 28) Thewayyouare (USA) 117 – Castalian Spring (IRE) **63**
45 (Oasis Dream 129) [2017 7s^{5} 8m^{4} 7s t8.6g 7d Oct 30] sturdy colt: modest maiden. *Martin Smith*

AFFORDABILITY 3 b.g. Bushranger (IRE) 119 – Munaa's Dream (Oasis Dream 129) **47**
[2017 61: t5g^{5} Jan 11] modest maiden, below form sole outing in 2017: stays 6f: acts on tapeta: tried in cheekpieces. *Daniel Loughnane*

AFJAAN (IRE) 5 b.g. Henrythenavigator (USA) 131 – Elusive Galaxy (IRE) 98 (Elusive **116**
City (USA) 117) [2017 110p: 7m* p7s^{pu} Sep 30] smart handicapper: won at Haydock (by 1¾ lengths from Oh This Is Us) in April: stayed 1m: acted on polytrack, tapeta and good to firm going: often raced towards rear/travelled strongly: dead. *William Haggas*

AFKAR (IRE) 9 b.g. Invincible Spirit (IRE) 121 – Indienne (IRE) 69 (Indian Ridge 123) **60**
[2017 73d: p7d^{2} t8g^{3} p8d^{6} Feb 8] strong gelding: modest handicapper nowadays: stays 1m: acts on all-weather, soft and good to firm going: usually wears headgear: front runner/races prominently. *Ivan Furtado*

AFONSO DE SOUSA (USA) 7 br.g. Henrythenavigator (USA) 131 – Mien (USA) **94**
(Nureyev (USA) 131) [2017 95, a109: p12g^{3} p12g* 8.1m^{4} 10.1m t12.2g^{5} 12g t12.2g^{6} t9.5d Dec 16] fairly useful handicapper: won at Lingfield (by 1¼ lengths from Silver Quay) in February: stays 1½m: acts on polytrack and good to firm going: has worn headgear. *Michael Appleby*

AFRICAN 3 b.c. Dubawi (IRE) 129 – Pink Symphony 109 (Montjeu (IRE) 137) [2017 –: **80**
10d 10m* 9.9m^{4} t9.5g^{5} Aug 18] fairly useful handicapper: won at Windsor (by ¾ length from Prosecution) in June: left Aidan O'Brien after first start: stays 1¼m: acts on good to firm going: usually races nearer last than first: sent to Qatar. *Charlie Fellowes*

AFRICAN BEAT (IRE) 3 b.f. Cape Cross (IRE) 129 – Rythmic 88 (Dubai Destination **82**
(USA) 127) [2017 85: p8g^{3} p10g^{3} t12.2g^{2} 14g^{3} t12.2g^{4} Aug 14] fairly useful handicapper: in frame all 5 starts in 2017: left John Gosden after second one: stays 1¾m: acts on polytrack and tapeta. *Richard Hughes*

AFRICAN BLESSING 4 ch.g. Mount Nelson 125 – Bella Beguine 78 (Komaite (USA)) **78**
[2017 81p: f6d 6g^{4} 7m* 6.9g^{5} 7.8g 7d^{4} 7d^{5} 7d* 7m^{5} p7g^{6} p8d^{2} p8g^{4} p8g^{4} p7s^{5} f6.1g^{4} Dec 1] workmanlike gelding: fair performer: won handicap at Doncaster in April and seller at Leicester in August: left David Barron after eighth start: stays 1m: acts on polytrack, fibresand, good to firm and good to soft going: usually races close up. *Charlie Wallis*

AFRICAN FRIEND (IRE) 4 b.g. Equiano (FR) 127 – Fontanally Springs (IRE) 100 **87**
(Namid 128) [2017 65p: 5.1g* 5g^{3} 6s 5d^{2} 5g Oct 18] fairly useful performer: won maiden at Windsor in July: second in handicap at Sandown in September: best form at 5f: acts on good to soft going: slowly away last 2 starts: sold to join Marjorie Fife 14,000 gns in November. *Henry Candy*

AFRICAN GIRL 3 b.f. Equiano (FR) 127 – Tychy 102 (Suave Dancer (USA) 136) [2017 **52**
–: p7g^{4} t6g 7g 6g^{4} 6g^{3} 5.2m^{5} Aug 17] modest maiden: stays 6f. *Lydia Pearce*

AFRICAN GREY 3 gr.g. Kheleyf (USA) 116 – Elbow Beach 76 (Choisir (AUS) 126) [2017 54p: t7.1g* t7.1g4 10.2m 7.8v t7.1d Nov 4] modest handicapper: won at Newcastle (apprentice) in March: went wrong way after: left David Barron after third start: stays 7f: acts on tapeta: has worn headgear, including in 2017: sometimes slowly away. *Martin Todhunter* **64**

AFRICAN QUEST 3 b.f. Air Quest 105 – Pursuit of Purpose 45 (Dansili 127) [2017 7d6 8g 8.1m6 7m4 8s3 11.9d4 p10g Oct 12] rather unfurnished filly: first foal: dam maiden: poor maiden. *Gary Moore* **47**

AFRICAN SHOWGIRL 4 ch.f. Showcasing 117 – Georgie The Fourth (IRE) 79 (Cadeaux Genereux 131) [2017 70: 8s f8.1g5 p8g p10s f8.1g Dec 21] workmanlike filly: fair handicapper, below form in 2017: stays 1m: acts on fibresand and good to soft going. *Ivan Furtado* **54**

AFRICAN TRADER (USA) 4 b.g. Lonhro (AUS) 128 – Nasaieb (IRE) 89 (Fairy King (USA)) [2017 64: 7g6 8.2g4 8g Jul 17] fair maiden: stays 1m: best form on good going: has worn tongue tie. *Daniel Loughnane* **65**

AFTERBURNER 3 b.g. Kyllachy 129 – Singed (Zamindar (USA) 116) [2017 p7s 8.3v 8.3g5 10d t12.4g Oct 10] close-coupled gelding: modest form: tried in visor: sent to the Netherlands. *Hugo Palmer* **63**

AFTERTHISONE 2 ch.g. (Feb 28) Pastoral Pursuits 127 – Mandolin Wind (Haafhd 129) [2017 5g p5g5 5m p7d p7g 8.1s p8grr t9.5g f8.1g Dec 11] small gelding: no form: tried in hood/tongue tie: temperamental. *Robin Dickin* **– §**

AFTER TONIIGHT (FR) 7 b.g. Lando (GER) 128 – Affair (FR) (Montjeu (IRE) 137) [2017 t12.4g2 t12.4g3 Feb 17] bumper winner: fair form when placed in 2 maidens: likely to stay beyond 1½m: remains with potential. *Gillian Boanas* **77 p**

AGAINST THE ODDS 4 b.g. Champs Elysees 124 – Generous Diana 90 (Generous (IRE) 139) [2017 92: p16g 12s3 May 18] compact gelding: fairly useful handicapper: third at Newmarket in May: stays 16.5f: acts on polytrack, tapeta and good to firm going: tried in cheekpieces/tongue tie. *Paul Cole* **90**

AGAR'S PLOUGH 2 ch.g. (Apr 24) Dutch Art 126 – Cloud's End 87 (Dubawi (IRE) 129) [2017 7m 7v2 7g5 8.3g5 Nov 1] fair form in minor events/maiden: best effort at 7f. *Ed Dunlop* **76**

AGATHONIA (USA) 3 b.f. Street Cry (IRE) 130 – Regency Romance (Diktat 126) [2017 76: p12g* 10.9d 11.9g3 11.9g4 14.9d5 13.9d6 10.9s2 10.9s2 12.4s3 11.9s4 Dec 10] useful performer: won maiden at Lingfield (by 7 lengths from Physicist) in April: left Charlie Appleby after next start: placed 3 times in autumn, twice behind Ostana at Hanover, beaten neck in both listed race and Grosser Preis der Mehl-Mulhens-Stiftung: effective at 11f to 15f: acts on polytrack and soft going: in cheekpieces first 2 outings. *H-A. Pantall, France* **106**

AGENT ERROR (IRE) 2 b.f. (Jan 29) Iffraaj 127 – Oasis Sunset (IRE) 82 (Oasis Dream 129) [2017 6s 6d 6v Sep 29] 100,000Y: fourth foal: half-sister to useful 7f/1m winner Sunset Dream (by Acclamation): dam, 2-y-o 7f winner, half-sister to Cheveley Park Stakes winner Seazun: modest form. *David Simcock* **60**

AGENT MURPHY 6 b.h. Cape Cross (IRE) 129 – Raskutani (Dansili 127) [2017 101: 13.3d6 11.4m6 11.6g4 18d Sep 23] good-quartered horse: smart performer in 2015, lightly raced and below that level since: stays 1¾m: acts on firm and soft going. *Brian Meehan* **101**

AGENT OF FORTUNE 2 ch.f. (Mar 19) Kheleyf (USA) 116 – Royal Bloom (IRE) 52 (Royal Applause 124) [2017 6g5 6d5 p6g6 p6g3 7g Oct 16] 800Y: rather leggy filly: fourth foal: dam maiden half-sister to very smart winner up to 7f (best at 5f) Masamah: modest maiden: stays 6f: acts on polytrack: in hood last 4 starts: sometimes slowly away, often races towards rear. *Christine Dunnett* **56**

AGE OF ELEGANCE (IRE) 5 b.m. Makfi 130 – Elegant Pride (Beat Hollow 126) [2017 87: 12g5 10m t12.4s 10f* 10.3g3 Jul 15] rather leggy mare: fairly useful handicapper: won at Wetherby in June: stays 12.5f: acts on polytrack, tapeta and any turf going: usually wears cheekpieces: usually races close up. *Roger Fell* **82**

AGE OF WISDOM (IRE) 4 ch.g. Pivotal 124 – Learned Friend (GER) (Seeking The Gold (USA)) [2017 14d p16g3 14.2v p16d p16s3 16s Oct 15] good-topped gelding: fairly useful handicapper: won maiden in 2016 when trained by A. Fabre: third at Kempton in July and September: stays 2m: acts on polytrack and soft going: in cheekpieces last 2 starts. *Gary Moore* **82**

AGNETHE (IRE) 3 b.f. Requinto (IRE) 109 – Abbasharjah (GER) (Tiger Hill (IRE) 127) **67**
[2017 p7g^6 8m^5 6m^3 6g^2 6g^5 5.2s^2 5.2m^4 p7d p6g^5 Oct 25] 38,000Y: fourth foal: half-sister to useful German 1¼m winner Amona (by Aussie Rules): dam unraced sister/half-sister to smart German performers up to 1m Abbashiva and Abbadjinn: fair maiden: stays 6f: acts on soft and good to firm going. *Paul D'Arcy*

AGREEMENT (IRE) 7 b.g. Galileo (IRE) 134 – Cozzene's Angel (USA) (Cozzene **–**
(USA)) [2017 60: t16.5g^6 Apr 25] lengthy gelding: modest handicapper, below form sole outing on Flat in 2017: stays 2¼m: acts on heavy going: wears headgear: usually races prominently. *Nikki Evans*

AGROTERA (IRE) 2 ch.f. (Jan 11) Mastercraftsman (IRE) 129 – Lombatina (FR) **58 p**
(King's Best (USA) 132) [2017 7d^6 Nov 4] second foal: dam, French 2-y-o 6f winner, out of sister to Samum and Schiaparelli and to dam of Sea The Moon, all Deutsches Derby winners: 16/1, shaped as if in need of experience when sixth in minor event at Newmarket: better to come. *Ed Walker*

AGUEROOO (IRE) 4 b.g. Monsieur Bond (IRE) 120 – Vision of Peace (IRE) (Invincible **81**
Spirit (IRE) 121) [2017 101: p6.5g^6 p7d p6m^5 t6g^6 t6g^5 5.5g^5 5.9g^3 5g^5 5m^5 5d f6.1g p6g^6 **a91**
Dec 21] fairly useful handicapper: left Richard Hannon after third start: stays 6f: acts on all-weather and good to firm going: wears headgear. *Ollie Pears*

AHEAD OF TIME 3 b.g. Dream Ahead (USA) 133 – Malladore (IRE) (Lawman (FR) **68**
121) [2017 68p: p8d^6 p7g^3 Mar 3] attractive gelding: fair form in minor event/maidens: sent to UAE. *David Simcock*

AHFAD 2 br.g. (Feb 7) Dick Turpin (IRE) 127 – Big Moza 68 (Pastoral Pursuits 127) [2017 **54**
7m 7s 7.6s t9.5g^3 t8s Nov 30] well-made gelding: modest maiden: best effort at 9.5f: acts on tapeta. *Stuart Williams*

AHLAN BIL ZAIN (FR) 3 b.c. Elusive City (USA) 117 – Fall View (Pivotal 124) [2017 **89**
85p: 10.1g 8v^4 7g 8f^3 t8.6g^4 p8d^3 p8g^4 Oct 13] fairly useful handicapper: stays 8.5f: acts on polytrack and tapeta: sold 30,000 gns in October. *David Simcock*

AHUNDREDNOTOUT 3 ch.g. Mount Nelson 125 – Forest Express (AUS) (Kaaptive **68**
Edition (NZ)) [2017 –: 7d 8.3s^3 p7g^3 t5.1g* p6g Oct 27] fair performer: won maiden at Wolverhampton in October: stays 7f: acts on tapeta. *J. J. Feane, Ireland*

AIGUILLE ROUGE (FR) 3 ch.f. Falco (USA) 122 – Avanguardia (GER) 97 (Choisir **82**
(AUS) 126) [2017 p9.9g^5 10.7s^2 7.5d^3 10.4d^4 10g^5 Oct 17] fourth foal: half-sister to French 2-y-o 7f-9.5f winner Danza de La Barre (by Turtle Bowl) and high-class but temperamental hurdler Labaik (by Montmartre): dam French 5.5f winner: fairly useful maiden: left D. & P. Prod'homme after fourth start: best effort at 1¼m: fair form over hurdles, won 2 of first 3 starts. *Gary Moore*

AIMEZ LA VIE (IRE) 3 br.f. Arcano (IRE) 122 – La Vita E Bella (IRE) 105 (Definite **94**
Article 121) [2017 76: 7g^2 7.2g* 7f 7d* 7d^5 7.2s* 8m Oct 25] compact filly: fairly useful performer: won maiden at Musselburgh in May, then handicaps at Thirsk in July and Musselburgh (by head from Raselasad) in October: stays 7f: acts on soft and good to firm going: sold 65,000 gns later in October, sent to Saudi Arabia. *Richard Fahey*

AIM OF ARTEMIS (IRE) 2 ch.f. (Feb 6) Leroidesanimaux (BRZ) 127 – Justlookdontouch **95 p**
(IRE) (Galileo (IRE) 134) [2017 6s^3 7d* Sep 12] third foal: half-sister to smart 1¼m-1½m winner Abingdon (by Street Cry) and 1¼m winner Superioritycomplex (by Hard Spun): dam unraced close relative/half-sister to very smart 1¼m-1½m performers Islington and Mountain High: useful form: won minor event at Leicester (by ½ length from Shepherd Market) in September: will stay at least 1m: sold 1,000,000 gns in December: open to further improvement. *Sir Michael Stoute*

AIM TO PLEASE (FR) 4 b.f. Excellent Art 125 – Midnight Flash (IRE) (Anabaa Blue **105**
122) [2017 114: 8g 9m^3 8m^5 10.3d^6 9d Aug 27] lengthy, angular filly: useful performer: third in Dahlia Stakes at Newmarket (7¾ lengths behind Somehow) in May: left Francois Doumen after third start: stays 9f: acts on good to firm and good to soft going: tried in hood: often races in rear. *K. R. Burke*

AINNE 2 ch.f. (May 1) Cityscape 127 – Ayun (USA) 99 (Swain (IRE) 134) [2017 8.1g^5 p7g **55**
p8g^4 Dec 23] 20,000Y: closely related to smart/unreliable 11.5f-16.4f winner Akmal (by Selkirk) and half-sister to several winners, including 2-y-o 9f winner Aazif (by Nayef), stayed 1¾m, and 1½m/13f winner Elrasheed (by Red Ransom): dam 1m-1¼m winner: modest form when fourth at Lingfield on last of 3 starts in minor events: will stay 1¼m. *Sylvester Kirk*

AIRMAX (GER) 2 br.c. (Feb 17) Maxios 123 – Artica (GER) (Pentire 132) [2017 7s6 8d6 Oct 27] fair form in maiden/minor event. *Ralph Beckett* **72**

AIR MINISTRY (IRE) 3 b.g. High Chaparral (IRE) 132 – Hadarama (IRE) 86 (Sinndar (IRE) 134) [2017 10.3g 11.5m5 10.2g 13m5 13f5 7.8g Aug 30] fair maiden: left Michael Bell after fifth start: stays 13f: acts on good to firm going: wears headgear: sometimes slowly away, often races towards rear. *Denis Hogan, Ireland* **67**

AIR OF YORK (IRE) 5 b.g. Vale of York (IRE) 117 – State Secret (Green Desert (USA) 127) [2017 85: p8g t7.1m t7.1g3 7g5 8m4 p7g2 t7.2g* 6d6 6.1v 5d 6.1s4 7.1g 7v4 5.7s* 7s4 t7.2m t6.1g6 Dec 18] smallish gelding: fair handicapper nowadays: won at Wolverhampton in June and Bath in October: stays 7.5f: acts on all-weather and any turf going: usually wears headgear. *John Flint* **75**

AIR PILOT 8 b.g. Zamindar (USA) 116 – Countess Sybil (IRE) 73 (Dr Devious (IRE) 127) [2017 118: 10d* 12m 10g5 9.9g 10d2 Nov 4] compact gelding: smart performer: won Alleged Stakes at Naas (by head from Success Days) in April: second in listed race at Newmarket (neck behind Permission) in November: stays 1½m, usually races at shorter: acts on soft and good to firm going: tried in blinkers. *Ralph Beckett* **116**

AIRPLANE (IRE) 2 b.g. (Feb 20) Pour Moi (IRE) 125 – Abyssinie (IRE) (Danehill Dancer (IRE) 117) [2017 7g 8g5 8g5 8g Sep 27] modest form: will be suited by further than 1m. *Tim Easterby* **59**

AIR RAID 2 b.c. (Feb 24) Raven's Pass (USA) 133 – Siren Sound 80 (Singspiel (IRE) 133) [2017 7v* 7g4 Oct 14] €60,000F: half-brother to several winners, including useful 7f winner Excellent Sounds (by Exceed And Excel) and 1¼m-1½m winner (stays 16.5f) Siren's Cove (by Sir Percy): dam 7f winner: fair form: won minor event at Thirsk (by ¾ length from Qianlong) in September. *Jedd O'Keeffe* **79**

AIRSHOW 2 ch.g. (Apr 12) Showcasing 117 – Belle des Airs (IRE) 92 (Dr Fong (USA) 128) [2017 5g3 5m 6.1m2 6.1m2 5.1m6 7.4v3 p6g3 6s* Oct 28] fair performer: won nursery at Newbury in October: stays 6f: acts on soft and good to firm going: usually wears hood: races prominently. *Rod Millman* **78**

AIRTON 4 b.g. Champs Elysees 124 – Fly In Style (Hernando (FR) 127) [2017 74, a84: 12m 12g2 12g t12.4s* 13.4d 12g3 12.1s5 t12.4g t16.3g Nov 15] rather light-framed gelding: fairly useful handicapper: won at Newcastle in July: should stay 1¾m+: acts on tapeta and good to firm going: tried in hood: often races towards rear. *James Bethell* **88**

AIRWAY 3 b.g. Poet's Voice 126 – Air Kiss (Red Ransom (USA)) [2017 10.2s3 p10g* p11g Oct 11] sixth foal: half-brother to 1¾m/2m winner Always Summer (by Flatter) and a winner in USA by Broken Vow: dam unraced half-sister to very smart performers Craigsteel (best at 1½m-1¾m) and Invermark (stayed 2½m): fairly useful form: won maiden at Chelmsford (by ¾ length from Ennjaaz) in September: will stay 1½m: sold 6,000 gns in November. *James Fanshawe* **85**

AISLIN MOON (IRE) 2 b.f. (Mar 7) Sleeping Indian 122 – Shamrock Lady (IRE) 88 (Orpen (USA) 116) [2017 5f 5s 6v Oct 23] sturdy filly: third foal: half-sister to 6f-1m winner El Principe (by Strategic Prince): dam winner up to 7f (2-y-o 6f winner): poor form in minor events. *Les Eyre* **49**

AIYA (IRE) 2 ch.c. (Mar 19) Declaration of War (USA) 128 – Flamingo Sea (USA) (Woodman (USA) 126) [2017 6s 6g p8g4 Nov 18] €140,000Y, 250,000 2-y-o: useful-looking colt: half-brother to several winners, including very smart/ungenuine winner up to 1½m (Irish Derby) Frozen Fire (2-y-o 7f winner, by Montjeu) and useful performer up to 1¾m Sir Walter Scott (2-y-o 7f winner, by Galileo): dam German 1m winner: fair form when fourth in minor event at Lingfield (in hood, 2¾ lengths behind Rusper) on last of 3 starts: likely to progress further. *Andrew Balding* **69 p**

A J COOK (IRE) 7 b.g. Mujadil (USA) 119 – Undertone (IRE) 84 (Noverre (USA) 125) [2017 57: t5g 6m3 6g 5g t5g 6g4 5s 6g3 6d Sep 2] modest handicapper: stays 6f: acts on good to firm and heavy going: has worn headgear, including in 2017: has worn tongue tie. *Ron Barr* **58**

AJMAN KING (IRE) 3 ch.c. Lope de Vega (IRE) 125 – Third Dimension (FR) (Suave Dancer (USA) 136) [2017 88p: 9.9s2 10.1v* 10.2d* Oct 27] useful performer: won maiden at Epsom and handicap at Doncaster (easily by 3¼ lengths from Society Red) in October: will stay 1½m: acts on heavy going: will go on improving. *Roger Varian* **106 p**

Darley Prix Jean Romanet, Deauville—Ajman Princess makes the breakthrough at Group 1 level in first-time cheekpieces; Siyoushake (left) gets the better of a bunched finish for second, with Left Hand and Smart Call (spotted cap) completing the frame

AJMAN PRINCESS (IRE) 4 b.f. Teofilo (IRE) 126 – Reem Three 103 (Mark of Esteem (IRE) 137) [2017 104: p10g* 12f* 11.8s^3 11.8m^3 10.3d^2 9.9g* 11.9d Sep 10] good-topped filly: smart performer: won maiden at Lingfield in March, listed race at Goodwood (by 5 lengths from Elysian Fields) in May and Prix Jean Romanet at Deauville (by 1¼ lengths from Siyoushake) in August: placed in between in Pinnacle Stakes and Lancashire Oaks (1½ lengths third to The Black Princess), both at Haydock, and listed race at York: below form in Prix Vermeille at Chantilly final outing: effective at 1¼m to 1½m: acts on polytrack, firm and soft going: tried in hood, wore cheekpieces last 2 starts. *Roger Varian* **117**

AJWAN 2 b.f. (Mar 3) Helmet (AUS) 127 – Rock Ace (IRE) 82 (Verglas (IRE) 118) [2017 5s^2 5.9v^2 Jun 8] £27,000Y: third foal: half-sister to French 6.5f winner Sing Something (by Paco Boy): dam, 2-y-o 6f winner, half-sister to smart 6f/7f winner Laddies Poker Two, herself dam of 1000 Guineas winner Winter: fair form when runner-up in maiden at Thirsk and minor event at Carlisle. *Richard Fahey* **77**

AKAMANTO (IRE) 3 b.c. Cape Cross (IRE) 129 – Allofus (IRE) (Celtic Swing 138) [2017 p10g^5 11m 11.6d^5 11.9d 10.1d^5 10g* 10g^4 8.9s 10d^4 Oct 20] good-topped colt: fair performer: won seller at Leicester in August (left Richard Hannon after): stays 1¼m: acts on good to firm going. *R. Mike Smith* **77**

AKAVIT (IRE) 5 b.g. Vale of York (IRE) 117 – Along Came Molly (Dr Fong (USA) 128) [2017 –: t12.4d 17.2f^2 16.2m* 16m^4 16d^2 16.3m* 18g* 20.6v Aug 2] compact gelding: fairly useful handicapper: won at Chepstow in May, and at Lingfield and Pontefract (by 2¼ lengths from La Fritillaire) in June: stays 2¼m: acts on polytrack, tapeta, firm and good to soft going: has worn headgear: front runner. *Ed de Giles* **81**

AKDAAR 3 b.g. Dubawi (IRE) 129 – Min Banat Alreeh (IRE) (Oasis Dream 129) [2017 7m^5 7g^4 a8.4g* Dec 20] fair form: left Roger Varian, won maiden at Doha in December: stays 8.5f: acts on dirt. *Jassim Mohammed G. Jahromi, Qatar* **77**

AKHLAAQ 3 b.g. New Approach (IRE) 132 – Misheer 109 (Oasis Dream 129) [2017 87p: 6m^4 7m^4 Jun 17] good-topped gelding: fairly useful form: stays 7f: races freely. *Owen Burrows* **91**

AKINSPIRIT (IRE) 13 b.g. Invincible Spirit (IRE) 121 – Akebia (USA) (Trempolino (USA) 135) [2017 51§: t12.2g p12g Mar 8] veteran handicapper, no show both starts in 2017: stays 1¾m: acts on polytrack, good to firm and good to soft going: wears headgear/ tongue tie: temperamental. *Nikki Evans* **– §**

AKKADIAN EMPIRE 3 b.g. Arabian Gleam 122 – Floral Beauty 85 (Shamardal (USA) 129) [2017 74: p12g^3 11.9d 8.3m^6 8.3g^4 10g^2 10d 8.9s Sep 16] fair maiden: left Mick Channon after first start: stays 1¼m: acts on good to firm going: in hood last 5 starts. *Iain Jardine* **78**

AKULA (IRE) 10 ch.g. Soviet Star (USA) 128 – Danielli (IRE) 79 (Danehill (USA) 126) [2017 t12.2m Oct 28] workmanlike gelding: maiden, well held sole outing on Flat in 2017: stays 16.5f: acts on tapeta, soft and good to firm going: fair hurdler. *Barry Leavy* **–**

AKUNA MATTATTA (IRE) 3 b.g. Approve (IRE) 112 – Akuna Magic (IRE) (Whipper (USA) 126) [2017 p6g p5g^5 p7g p8d 6.1g^{ur} t5.1m^{rr} Oct 28] good-topped gelding: no form: unseated at start/refused to race last 2 outings: one to avoid. *Ralph Smith* **– §**

AKVAVERA 2 ch.f. (May 1) Leroidesanimaux (BRZ) 127 – Akdarena 113 (Hernando (FR) 127) [2017 7f^2 7d^2 7.4g* Sep 2] fourth foal: dam winner up to 1¼m (2-y-o 8.5f winner), including Blue Wind Stakes: fair form: won minor event at Beverley (by 1½ lengths from Frolic) in September: will stay 1m: remains with potential. *Ralph Beckett* **79 p**

ALAADEL 4 ch.g. Dubawi (IRE) 129 – Infallible 114 (Pivotal 124) [2017 6v* 7.1v^{5} p6d 6v^{2} 6s^{2} 7d^{4} 6d* Oct 27] fourth foal: brother to smart 1m-10.5f winner Intimation and half-brother to smart 6f winner Intrinsic (by Oasis Dream) and high-class 1m-1¼m winner Mutakayyef (by Sea The Stars): dam 7f winner (at 2 yrs, and Nell Gwyn Stakes): fairly useful performer: won maiden at Doncaster in May and handicap at Newbury (by ½ length from Baron Bolt) in October: stays 6f: acts on heavy going: in blinkers last 3 starts: in tongue tie last 4: strong traveller, seems suited by hold-up tactics: sold to join Stuart Williams 90,000 gns later in October. *William Haggas* **94**

ALABANZA 2 b.c. (Apr 8) Big Bad Bob (IRE) 118 – Tahfeez (IRE) 61 (Alhaarth (IRE) 126) [2017 t6g Nov 23] 28/1, well held in minor event at Newcastle. *Keith Dalgleish* **–**

ALABASTER 3 gr.g. Archipenko (USA) 127 – Alvarita 104 (Selkirk (USA) 129) [2017 p8g^{5} p8d^{4} p11d* p14g* 14m^{2} p14s* Jun 22] 100,000Y: half-brother to several winners, including winner up to 1¼m Alla Speranza (2-y-o 8.5f winner, by Sir Percy), 11f/1½m winner Altesse and 1¼m-1¾m winner Alcaeus (all useful, latter 2 by Hernando): dam, 1m-10.5f winner, out of dual Champion Stakes winner Alborada: fairly useful performer: won maiden at Kempton in February and handicaps at Chelmsford in May/June (by 1¼ lengths from Cray in latter): will stay 2m: acts on polytrack and good to firm going: in headgear last 2 starts: remains with potential. *Sir Mark Prescott Bt* **93 p**

ALACRITAS 2 gr.f. (Jan 31) Leroidesanimaux (BRZ) 127 – Albaraka 91 (Selkirk (USA) 129) [2017 6g t7.1g p7g Oct 18] second foal: half-sister to useful 1¼m winner Oasis Charm (by Oasis Dream): dam, 8.6f winner who stayed 11f, half-sister to smart winner up to 1¼m Algonquin out of dual Champion Stakes winner Alborada: little impact in maidens/minor event: type to do better in handicaps. *David Simcock* **– p**

ALADDIN SANE (IRE) 3 b.g. Teofilo (IRE) 126 – Aqua Aura (USA) 86 (Distorted Humor (USA) 117) [2017 8.3g 10d^{6} 8.2d^{6} 8g Jul 17] little impact in maidens/handicap. *Brian Meehan* **–**

A L'ANGLAISE 4 b.f. Invincible Spirit (IRE) 121 – Alabelle 89 (Galileo (IRE) 134) [2017 t9.5g^{4} t10.2d Mar 2] first foal: dam, 1½m winner, closely related to Derby runner-up Dragon Dancer: fairly useful handicapper: won at Chantilly in 2016 on final start for A. Fabre: will be suited by 1½m: acts on polytrack and tapeta. *Rae Guest* **88**

AL ASEF 2 br.c. (Feb 8) Kyllachy 129 – Hot Reply (Notnowcato 128) [2017 6.1d^{3} 6d^{6} t5.1g* Dec 2] 27,000Y, €90,000 2-y-o: first foal: dam twice-raced half-sister to high-class sprinter Krypton Factor (by Kyllachy): fairly useful form: won minor event at Wolverhampton (by 3¼ lengths from Midsummer Knight) in December: best effort at 5f. *Marco Botti* **94**

ALASKA (IRE) 2 b.c. (Feb 17) Kodiac 112 – Sunny Hollow 64 (Beat Hollow 126) [2017 5v^{4} 5g^{3} 6g^{2} 6m* 6.1g^{3} 6m^{4} 6v^{2} 6.1g t6.1g^{4} 6.1d Oct 4] sturdy colt: fair performer: won maiden at Brighton in June: stays 6f: acts on good to firm and heavy going: temperament under suspicion. *Sylvester Kirk* **76**

ALASKAN BAY (IRE) 2 b.f. (May 14) Kodiac 112 – Party Appeal (USA) (Mr Greeley (USA) 122) [2017 5.1m 5g t5.1g^{5} t6.1g^{2} p5s^{4} Dec 7] 6,000Y: third foal: dam, French maiden (placed at 9.5f), half-sister to useful dam of smart 2-y-o sprinter Zebedee: modest maiden: best effort at 6f: acts on tapeta. *Rae Guest* **61**

ALASKAN BEAUTY (IRE) 2 b.f. (Apr 29) Kodiac 112 – My American Beauty 93 (Wolfhound (USA) 126) [2017 5m 5d^{3} 6d 5d 5s t5d Nov 4] €31,000Y: closely related to 7f/1m winner Outback Ruler (by Aussie Rules) and half-sister to several winners, including 6f winner Hee Haw (by Sleeping Indian): dam 5f and (at 2 yrs) 6f winner: modest maiden: best effort at 5f: acts on good to soft going. *Tim Easterby* **55**

ALASKAN STAR (IRE) 2 b.g. (May 10) Kodiac 112 – Lightwood Lady (IRE) 84 (Anabaa (USA) 130) [2017 5m^{6} 5g 6g 5m 5.1s p7g Sep 27] modest maiden: best effort at 5f: acts on good to firm going: in cheekpieces last 3 starts: sent to Spain. *Amanda Perrett* **60**

ALBA DEL SOLE (IRE) 2 b.f. (Apr 11) Dandy Man (IRE) 123 – Winterwell (USA) 89 (First Defence (USA) 119) [2017 5g^{4} 5d^{3} p6g^{3} p6d^{3} p6s^{3} Dec 1] 28,000 2-y-o: first foal: dam, maiden (stayed 7f), half-sister to useful 1m winner Enforce: fair maiden: stays 6f: acts on polytrack and good to soft going. *John Gosden* **70**

ALBA POWER (IRE) 2 b.c. (Mar 7) Fast Company (IRE) 126 – Shehila (IRE) (Zamindar (USA) 116) [2017 6f^{6} 6m* 6g^{5} 7d^{3} 6d^{4} 6.5g^{3} 7s^{2} 8s^{4} Oct 19] €35,000F, £110,000Y: sturdy colt: first foal: dam ran once in France: useful performer: won minor event at Yarmouth in June: placed after in listed race at Ascot, valuable event at Doncaster (2 lengths third of 22 to Laugh A Minute) and Prix Thomas Bryon at Saint-Cloud (6 lengths second to Sacred Life): stays 7f: acts on soft and good to firm going. *Hugo Palmer* **99**

AL BARG (IRE) 2 b.g. (Mar 28) Acclamation 118 – Miss Hawai (FR) (Peintre Celebre (USA) 137) [2017 7g^2 6.1g* 7m Aug 25] 50,000F, €135,000Y: well-made gelding: brother to 5.3f/6f winner Endeavour and half-brother to 2 winners, including smart 1m-1¼m winner (stayed 1½m) Beach Bunny (by High Chaparral), herself dam of smart 6f/7f performer Naadirr: dam unraced half-sister to 1000 Guineas winner Miss France: fairly useful form: won minor event at Windsor (by 1¼ lengths from Time For Wine) in July: stays 7f. *Richard Hannon* **84**

ALBARINO 2 b.g. (Mar 17) Equiano (FR) 127 – Cocabana 69 (Captain Rio 122) [2017 5g 5g 6g t6g t6g t5d 6m^3 Dec 26] poor maiden: left Kevin Ryan before final outing. *S. Postiglione, Italy* **45**

ALBERT BOY (IRE) 4 ch.g. Falco (USA) 122 – Trumbaka (IRE) 115 (In The Wings 128) [2017 73, a67: f8g f8d^4 11.9m* 11.9v^5 11.8d* 11.5s^2 11.6m^5 11.9d 11.8g^3 12d 11.5m^3 f12.1g Aug 28] fair handicapper on turf, modest on all-weather: won at Brighton and Leicester (apprentice) in May: stays 1½m: acts on tapeta, good to firm and heavy going: tried in headgear: front runner/races prominently. *Scott Dixon* **68** **a50**

ALBERTO 7 b.g. Bertolini (USA) 125 – Al Awaalah 52 (Mukaddamah (USA) 125) [2017 –: p7g^{pu} Jan 19] lengthy, angular gelding: little form: often wore headgear: dead. *Lisa Williamson* **–**

ALBERT'S BACK 3 b.g. Champs Elysees 124 – Neath 72 (Rainbow Quest (USA) 134) [2017 10.3g^6 f8g^6 f8.1g^3 14m 12v Sep 30] fair maiden on Flat: won both starts in juvenile hurdles. *Michael Easterby* **78**

ALBERT STREET (IRE) 2 b.c. (Mar 31) Acclamation 118 – Chroussa (IRE) 86 (Holy Roman Emperor (IRE) 125) [2017 5m^4 5g^2 5.9s^5 5s Sep 20] fair form: left Bryan Smart after second start. *Michael Dods* **71**

ALBISHR (IRE) 2 b.c. (Mar 3) Clodovil (IRE) 116 – Casual Remark (IRE) 67 (Trans Island 119) [2017 7m* 7g^2 8g^2 7g^6 10m p8g^2 Dec 20] €38,000F, €38,000Y: lengthy colt: brother to 7f-8.6f winner Big Sylv, closely related to a winner in Italy by Exceed And Excel and half-brother to 2 winners, including useful 1m-1½m winner Remarkable Lady (by Zoffany): dam lightly raced half-sister to dam of smart performer up to 1m Tupi: useful performer: won minor event at Haydock in June: second in listed race at Salisbury (nose behind Mildenberger) in August: left Richard Hannon after fifth start: stays 1m: acts on good to firm going: front runner. *Simon Dow* **99**

ALBIZU CAMPOS 3 b.g. Mastercraftsman (IRE) 129 – Lolita Lebron (IRE) 85 (Royal Applause 124) [2017 –: f8m t7.1g^3 6g 7.5f 8g 5.9s^4 7m 7d Jul 28] smallish gelding: modest maiden: stays 7f: acts on tapeta: often wears headgear. *Lawrence Mullaney* **50**

ALBIZZIA 3 b.f. Archipenko (USA) 127 – Altitude 88 (Green Desert (USA) 127) [2017 8.3g^4 Apr 7] fourth foal: half-sister to 1m winner (stayed 11.5f) Alegra (by Galileo) and 1¼m-1¾m winner Hope Is High (by Sir Percy): dam, 1½m winner, half-sister to dual Champion Stakes winner Alborada: 6/1, fourth in maiden at Leicester (5 lengths behind Zamfir) on debut: capable of better. *Ralph Beckett* **66 p**

ALCATRAZ (IRE) 5 b.g. Camacho 118 – Spring Opera (IRE) 82 (Sadler's Wells (USA) 132) [2017 89: p12g^2 p11g^2 p11g^4 p12g^6 10f^2 12s^2 12v 10.5g^5 11.9s p8g^5 Dec 22] lengthy gelding: fairly useful handicapper: runner-up 4 times in 2017: left George Baker after ninth start: stays 1½m: acts on polytrack and any turf going: often wears headgear/tongue tie: often starts slowly/races towards rear. *Richard John O'Brien, Ireland* **86**

ALDBURY LASS (IRE) 2 b.f. (Jan 27) Dark Angel (IRE) 113 – Heeby Jeeby (Lawman (FR) 121) [2017 6d 8d p6s Dec 1] €15,000Y, £16,000 2-y-o: second foal: dam once-raced half-sister to US Grade 2 9f winner Devious Boy and 6f/7f winner Against The Grain (both smart): no form: left Julia Feilden after first start. *Robert Eddery* **–**

ALDEBURGH 8 b.g. Oasis Dream 129 – Orford Ness 107 (Selkirk (USA) 129) [2017 88: p11g^2 9.9g^4 Apr 15] fairly useful handicapper: second at Kempton in April: stays 1½m: acts on polytrack, tapeta and good to firm going. *Nigel Twiston-Davies* **87**

AL DESTOOR 7 ch.g. Teofilo (IRE) 126 – In A Silent Way (IRE) 102 (Desert Prince (IRE) 130) [2017 92: t10.2g^4 10.3s* 12.1g^2 10.2d^3 10.2s^6 10.3v^2 11.9s Nov 11] useful handicapper: won at Chester (by 5 lengths from Lorelina) in June: placed 3 times after: stays 1½m: acts on tapeta, snow, good to firm and heavy going: has worn hood: wears tongue tie. *Jennie Candlish* **97**

ALDRETH 6 b.g. Champs Elysees 124 – Rowan Flower (IRE) 67 (Ashkalani (IRE) 128) [2017 77, a84: p16g* p16d^2 t16.3g^3 p16g* t16.5g Mar 27] fairly useful handicapper: won at Chelmsford in January and March: stays 17f: acts on polytrack, tapeta and any turf going: wears headgear: races prominently, often travels strongly. *Michael Easterby* **94**

ALDRIN (FR) 4 b.g. New Approach (IRE) 132 – Trip To The Moon 111 (Fasliyev (USA) **70**
120) [2017 77p: 7.6g^5 May 27] fair form in maidens: wears tongue tie: won over hurdles in August. *David Pipe*

ALEEF (IRE) 4 b.c. Kodiac 112 – Okba (USA) (Diesis 133) [2017 103: 5m 5.6g p5s 5v^5 **92**
p5g p6s^4 p6g* Dec 21] fairly useful handicapper: won at Chelmsford (by ½ length from Envisaging) in December: stays 6f: acts on polytrack, soft and good to firm going: wears hood: in tongue tie last 2 starts: usually leads. *David O'Meara*

ALEJANDRO (IRE) 8 b.g. Dark Angel (IRE) 113 – Carallia (IRE) 101 (Common **95**
Grounds 118) [2017 92: t7.1g p8d* p8g^3 p8g 8m 8.5f* 8m^6 8m 9m^6 7.6v 8g^5 p7s^3 t9.5g p7g^6 t7.2d^4 Dec 16] compact gelding: useful handicapper: won at Kempton in February and Beverley (by neck from Palmerston) in May: stays 8.5f: acts on polytrack, tapeta, firm and good to soft going: tried in headgear: front runner/races prominently. *David Loughnane*

ALEMARATALYOUM (IRE) 3 ch.c. Lope de Vega (IRE) 125 – Heart of Ice (IRE) **85**
(Montjeu (IRE) 137) [2017 67p: t7.1g* p8g^6 8.1d 7g^2 7d* t7.2g^4 7d^3 8.2d^4 8.1s* 8.1g Oct 9] sturdy colt: fairly useful performer: won minor event at Newcastle in March, and handicaps at Yarmouth in July and Chepstow (by 1¼ lengths from House of Commons) in September: stays 1m: acts on tapeta and soft going: sold 19,000 gns in November. *Ed Dunlop*

ALEXANDER M (IRE) 3 gr.c. Mastercraftsman (IRE) 129 – Naomh Geileis (USA) 95 **107**
(Grand Slam (USA) 120) [2017 –: p8g^4 p12d^4 f12d^2 9.9f^2 10.2g^3 10.2f^3 9.9d^2 10.2m* 10.3d^5 10.3s* 9.9g^3 10.3g* 9.8g^4 10.3v* 10.3v* Sep 30] quite lengthy, slightly-built colt: useful performer: won minor event at Doncaster in June, and 4 handicaps at Chester in August/September: stays 10.5f: acts on any turf going: front runner/races prominently, usually travels strongly: sent to Saudi Arabia. *Mark Johnston*

ALEXANDRAKOLLONTAI (IRE) 7 b.m. Amadeus Wolf 122 – Story (Observatory **90**
(USA) 131) [2017 91: 8m 8g t8g^2 9.2s 8m^4 8.3s 8g 8g* 7.2m 9.8g^6 8s 8s^5 t8g^5 8m^3 t8d^2 t10.2g t7.1d Dec 16] smallish, strong mare: fairly useful handicapper: won at Redcar in July: placed at Newmarket in October and Newcastle in November: stays 1m: acts on polytrack, tapeta, good to firm and heavy going: wears headgear. *Alistair Whillans*

ALEXIOS KOMNENOS (IRE) 3 b.c. Choisir (AUS) 126 – Alexiade (IRE) 76 **113**
(Montjeu (IRE) 137) [2017 108p: 8g^3 8g* 8d^6 Sep 9] smart performer: won Desmond Stakes at Leopardstown (by 1½ lengths from Music Box) in August: stays 1m: acts on good to firm and good to soft going. *J. A. Stack, Ireland*

ALFA MCGUIRE (IRE) 2 b.c. (Feb 28) Lord Shanakill (USA) 121 – Watsdaplan (IRE) **89**
(Verglas (IRE) 118) [2017 5.9g^5 7.4m* 7s^3 7.4m* 6.5g 8d Oct 28] £11,000Y: second foal: half-brother to 1m winner Helovaplan (by Helmet): dam unraced half-sister to smart US Grade 1 9.5f winner Watsdachances: fairly useful performer: won minor events at Beverley in July and August (by 5 lengths from Book of Dreams): stays 7.5f: acts on soft and good to firm going: often races prominently. *Bryan Smart*

ALFA QUEEN (IRE) 3 b.f. Intikhab (USA) 135 – Insaaf 100 (Averti (IRE) 117) [2017 **79**
10s^4 t9.5g^2 t9.5g^4 t12.4g^3 t12.4g^2 Oct 20] fifth foal: half-sister to winner up to 6f Fear Or Favour (2-y-o 5.7f winner, by Haatef): dam, winner up to 1m (2-y-o 6f winner), half-sister to smart sprinter Priceless: fair maiden: stays 12.5f: acts on tapeta. *Iain Jardine*

ALFARQAD (USA) 2 b.c. (May 6) War Front (USA) 119 – Love And Pride (USA) 120 **77 p**
(A P Indy (USA) 131) [2017 7m^3 7g^4 Oct 16] $1,300,000Y: second foal: half-brother to a winner in USA by Distorted Humor: dam US Grade 1 8.5f/9f winner: fair form when in frame in minor events at Newbury and Yarmouth: remains with potential. *Owen Burrows*

ALFARRIS (FR) 3 b.g. Shamardal (USA) 129 – Rose Et Noire (IRE) (Dansili 127) [2017 **98**
66p: p8g* p10s^2 12g^4 10.2g* p11g^4 Sep 27] well-made gelding: useful performer: won maiden at Chelmsford in May and handicap at Doncaster in August: stays 11f: acts on polytrack, best turf form on good going: in headgear last 2 starts. *William Haggas*

ALF GUINEAS (IRE) 4 b.f. Sea The Stars (IRE) 140 – Sayyedati Storm (USA) 52 (Storm **94**
Cat (USA)) [2017 83: p10g* 12f 10.2g May 31] fairly useful performer: won handicap at Chelmsford in April: disappointing both starts after: stays 1¼m: acts on polytrack and tapeta. *John Gosden*

ALFIE'S ANGEL (IRE) 3 b.g. Dark Angel (IRE) 113 – Penolva (IRE) 65 (Galileo (IRE) **80**
134) [2017 72: 6g* 6.9d^6 6g^6 6d* 6s^6 6s t7.1g t8g t7.1g Nov 3] fairly useful handicapper: won at Pontefract in June and Ayr (by 1½ lengths from Jacob's Pillow) in August: below form after: seems best at 6f: acts on heavy going: tried in cheekpieces: sold £8,500 in November. *Bryan Smart*

ALFOLK (IRE) 3 b.g. Invincible Spirit (IRE) 121 – Elmaam 86 (Nayef (USA) 129) [2017 t7.1m^{6} f8g^{5} p10g t7.1g^{6} t6m p5g Mar 25] modest maiden: usually wears hood: sometimes slowly away, often races in rear/freely. *David Simcock* **55**

ALFONSO MANANA (IRE) 3 ch.g. Dutch Art 126 – Chance For Romance 81 (Entrepreneur 123) [2017 72p: t6m^{2} t5d^{2} p6d^{3} p5m^{3} t5s^{5} 6g^{6} 6g^{3} 7d t6.1g* 6.1v^{6} p7g Aug 31] sturdy gelding: fair performer: won claimer at Wolverhampton in June: stays 6f: acts on polytrack and tapeta: wears headgear. *James Given* **73**

ALFRED HUTCHINSON 9 ch.g. Monsieur Bond (IRE) 120 – Chez Cherie 108 (Wolfhound (USA) 126) [2017 108: p8g* p8g^{3} p8f^{6} p8g 8m p7g^{4} p7s p7g p8g^{2} Dec 31] good-topped gelding: useful performer: won minor event at Lingfield in January: placed in handicaps there in February and December: stays 9.5f, generally races over shorter: acts on polytrack and any turf going: wears headgear: usually races towards rear. *David O'Meara* **104**

ALFRED RICHARDSON 3 ch.g. Dapper – Vera Richardson (IRE) (Dutch Art 126) [2017 58: t8g^{4} 8m* 8d^{3} 8.5m* 9.8m^{5} 10v^{5} Sep 21] fairly useful handicapper: won at Pontefract in April and Beverley in June: stays 8.5f: acts on tapeta and good to firm going. *John Davies* **82**

AL FUJAIRAH 2 b.c. (Apr 30) Showcasing 117 – First Term 64 (Acclamation 118) [2017 6f^{5} 6g^{6} Jun 10] fair form in minor events: dead. *Richard Hannon* **72**

ALGAITH (USA) 5 b.g. Dubawi (IRE) 129 – Atayeb (USA) 81 (Rahy (USA) 115) [2017 108: 8f^{4} 8.3g^{4} May 31] strong, attractive gelding: useful performer, lightly raced last 2 seasons: stays 8.5f: acts on polytrack, tapeta and firm going. *Owen Burrows* **106**

AL GALAYEL (IRE) 3 b.g. Zoffany (IRE) 121 – Glympse (IRE) 59 (Spectrum (IRE) 126) [2017 8.3g p8g^{5} t8g* p8g* Nov 17] 85,000F, 200,000Y: half-brother to several winners, including useful 2-y-o 7f winner Whipper's Boy (by Whipper) and 10.4f winner Glance My Way (by Rock of Gibraltar): dam maiden: useful form: won maiden at Newcastle and handicap at Lingfield in November: will stay 1¼m: open to further improvement. *Luca Cumani* **98 p**

ALGAM (IRE) 2 b.c. (Mar 30) Kodiac 112 – Evangeline (Sadler's Wells (USA) 132) [2017 7d^{2} 6g^{6} 7d* p8s^{2} 6v^{2} 8d^{4} Oct 27] 150,000F, 200,000Y: angular colt: closely related to 3 winners, including useful 2-y-o 5f/6f (Lowther Stakes) winner Infamous Angel (by Exceed And Excel) and 2-y-o 1m winner East Texas Red (by Danehill Dancer): dam unraced: fairly useful performer: won minor event at Leicester in August: second in similar events at Chelmsford in September and Salisbury in October: stays 1m: acts on polytrack and heavy going: tried in blinkers. *Richard Hannon* **90**

ALGHABRAH (IRE) 2 b.f. (Mar 20) Tamayuz 126 – Asheerah 98 (Shamardal (USA) 129) [2017 8.1v^{2} Oct 22] third foal: half-sister to very smart winner up to 1m (including Irish 2000 Guineas) Awtaad (2-y-o 7f winner, by Cape Cross) and useful 2-y-o 7f winner Aneen (by Lawman): dam 7f winner who stayed 1¼m: 16/1, shaped very well when 1¾ lengths second of 18 to Contingent in maiden at Leopardstown, clear of rest: will improve. *Kevin Prendergast, Ireland* **89 p**

ALGOMETER 4 gr.c. Archipenko (USA) 127 – Albanova 119 (Alzao (USA) 117) [2017 119: 9.9m^{2} 12g^{3} 10.3g Jul 29] tall colt: smart performer: second in Brigadier Gerard Stakes at Sandown (1¼ lengths behind Autocratic) in May and third in Princess of Wales's Stakes at Newmarket (4½ lengths behind Hawkbill) in July: stays 1½m: acts on soft and good to firm going: often races towards rear. *David Simcock* **119**

AL HAJAR (IRE) 2 b.c. (Jan 22) Dark Angel (IRE) 113 – Warshah (IRE) (Shamardal (USA) 129) [2017 7d^{2} 7m^{4} 7g* 7d* Oct 28] 220,000Y: second foal: brother to 7f/1m winner Volition: dam unraced half-sister to smart winner up to 12.3f Mickdaam and Prix de l'Opera winner Kinnaird: useful form: won maiden at Redcar in September and nursery at Doncaster (in cheekpieces, by 3½ lengths from Zap) in October: raced only at 7f: will go on improving. *Charlie Appleby* **101 p**

ALHAJJAJ 4 gr.g. Cacique (IRE) 124 – Strawberry Morn (CAN) (Travelling Victor (CAN)) [2017 p8g^{4} f8g^{5} t9.5g* Feb 15] fair form: won maiden at Wolverhampton (by 2 lengths from Ms Gillard) in February: stays 9.5f: wears hood. *Andrew Balding* **76**

AL HAMDANY (IRE) 3 b.g. Kodiac 112 – Easy Times (Nayef (USA) 129) [2017 100: 9m^{6} 10.3d^{5} 10s 10.2d p11s^{5} p11g^{2} 10.2d^{5} p12g* t12.2g^{2} p12g^{2} Dec 31] rather unfurnished gelding: useful handicapper: won at Kempton (by short head from Flight of Fantasy) in November: second at Wolverhampton and Lingfield in December: stays 1½m: acts on polytrack, tapeta and heavy going: tried in cheekpieces: often races towards rear. *Marco Botti* **105**

AL HARETH (IRE) 2 b.c. (Apr 6) Take Charge Indy (USA) 123 – Pure Symmetry (USA) (Storm Cat (USA)) [2017 p7g p7d a6f a7f^ur a7f Dec 29] modest maiden: left George Peckham after second start: stays 7f: usually in cheekpieces: in tongue tie last 3 starts. *A. bin Harmash, UAE* **62**

ALHAWDAJ (USA) 2 ch.f. (Feb 8) Speightstown (USA) 124 – Baragah (USA) (Awesome Again (CAN) 133) [2017 t6s Sep 19] first foal: dam, US 7f/1m winner, out of very smart US Grade 1 9f/1¼m winner Golden Apples: 11/1, 6¾ lengths ninth of 13 to Peace Trail in minor event at Newcastle: should progress. *Mark Johnston* **54 p**

AL HAWRAA 4 b.f. Iffraaj 127 – Kashoof 83 (Green Desert (USA) 127) [2017 71: t8g⁵ 8.3m 8g 9.2d* 12.5v³ Oct 16] fair handicapper: won at Hamilton in September: stays 9f: acts on good to firm and good to soft going. *Kevin Ryan* **70**

ALI BIN NAYEF 5 b.g. Nayef (USA) 129 – Maimoona (IRE) 96 (Pivotal 124) [2017 62: p15.8g p12d³ p12g² p12d⁶ t12.2m p12g⁶ t13.9g⁴ 12g 11g p12g Nov 1] modest handicapper: left Michael Wigham after seventh start: stays 1½m: acts on polytrack and tapeta: tried in blinkers. *John Joseph Hanlon, Ireland* **58**

ALICE SPRINGS (IRE) 4 ch.f. Galileo (IRE) 134 – Aleagueoftheirown (IRE) 107 (Danehill Dancer (IRE) 117) [2017 122: 7d² Apr 9] big, attractive filly: very smart at 3 yrs: second in Gladness Stakes at Naas (½ length behind Diamond Fields) on sole outing in 2017: stayed 1m: acted on firm and good to soft going: tried in hood: usually travelled strongly: stud. *Aidan O'Brien, Ireland* **110**

ALIDARA (IRE) 5 ch.m. Manduro (GER) 135 – Artisia (IRE) (Peintre Celebre (USA) 137) [2017 –: f11.1g^pu May 8] no form in maidens: in hood last 2 starts. *Emma Owen* **–**

ALIENTO 2 ch.f. (Apr 23) Bated Breath 125 – Scarlet Royal 43 (Red Ransom (USA)) [2017 6g 6d 6g Aug 21] fifth foal: half-sister to 3 winners, including 2-y-o 6f winner Momalorka (later successful up to 1¼m in Qatar, by Dutch Art) and 5f-7f winner Baron Bolt (by Kheleyf), both useful: dam lightly raced: little impact in minor events: type to do better in handicaps. *Ollie Pears* **– p**

ALIFAX 2 gr.c. (Apr 22) Mayson 124 – Scrupulous 70 (Dansili 127) [2017 6d 6m⁵ p7s² 7d* 7m⁶ 7v³ 8g 7s³ 7v Oct 1] compact colt: fair performer: won maiden at Chester in June: stays 7f: acts on polytrack, good to firm and heavy going: often races prominently. *Jamie Osborne* **75**

ALINSTANTE 4 b.f. Archipenko (USA) 127 – Algarade 92 (Green Desert (USA) 127) [2017 100: t12.2m³ Jan 16] useful handicapper: third at Wolverhampton (2¼ lengths behind Hot Beat) in January: stays 1½m: acts on polytrack and good to firm going: has worn cheekpieces, including sole outing in 2017. *Sir Mark Prescott Bt* **96**

ALI THE HUNTER (IRE) 4 ch.f. Papal Bull 128 – Polish Spring (IRE) 104 (Polish Precedent (USA) 131) [2017 p10g Sep 26] eighth foal: dam winner up to 8.5f (2-y-o 6f winner), including in USA: poor form in bumpers: 66/1, well held in maiden at Lingfield. *Johnny Farrelly* **–**

ALIZETI (IRE) 2 b.f. (Mar 25) Dutch Art 126 – Ushindi (IRE) 73 (Montjeu (IRE) 137) [2017 7d⁴ Nov 4] 32,000Y: half-sister to several winners, including useful 2-y-o winners Mon Cadeaux (6f, by Cadeaux Genereux) and Territory (7f, by Acclamation): dam 1½m winner: 16/1, considerate introduction when fourth in minor event at Newmarket (7¼ lengths behind Nawassi): will be suited by 1m+: will improve. *Henry Candy* **59 p**

ALJADY (FR) 2 b.c. (Apr 14) Bated Breath 125 – No Truth (IRE) 64 (Galileo (IRE) 134) [2017 6d* Oct 30] first foal: dam, 1½m winner, out of Lancashire Oaks winner State Crystal: 8/1, won minor event at Redcar (by ½ length from Scenic River) on debut: will be suited by 7f+: sure to go on to better things. *Richard Fahey* **79 p**

AL JAWZA 3 b.f. Nathaniel (IRE) 129 – Mosqueras Romance 109 (Rock of Gibraltar (IRE) 133) [2017 t7.1g⁶ p8g⁶ 8.3g⁶ 10.2f 11.6d Jul 19] €170,000Y: second foal: dam 1m winner: fair maiden: should stay 1¼m. *Richard Hannon* **68**

AL JAZI (IRE) 4 b.f. Canford Cliffs (IRE) 133 – Rainbow Crossing 88 (Cape Cross (IRE) 129) [2017 110: 6g* 6m 7s* Aug 4] sturdy filly: smart performer: won listed race at Maisons-Laffitte (by nose from City Money) in April and Oak Tree Stakes at Goodwood (by 1¼ lengths from Eternally) in August: effective at 6f to 9f: acts on polytrack, firm and soft going. *Francois Rohaut, France* **110**

ALJAZZI 4 b.f. Shamardal (USA) 129 – Nouriya 108 (Danehill Dancer (IRE) 117) [2017 106: p8g* 9m⁵ 8m² 8g* 8g 8f Nov 4] angular filly: smart performer: won listed race at Kempton (by 1½ lengths from Materialistic) in April and Atalanta Stakes at Sandown (by **117**

3 lengths from Nathra) in September: second in Duke of Cambridge Stakes at Royal Ascot (¾ length behind Qemah) in June: stays 1m: acts on polytrack, firm and good to soft going: wears hood. *Marco Botti*

AL JELLABY 2 b.c. (Mar 22) Exceed And Excel (AUS) 126 – Dolphina (USA) 83 (Kingmambo (USA) 125) [2017 7d^3 7g^3 8d* Sep 7] €110,000Y: tall colt: fourth foal: half-brother to 1m winner (including at 2 yrs) Cajoled (by High Chaparral): dam, 1¼m winner, out of US Grade 3 8.5f winner Sea of Showers, herself half-sister to high-class US performers Aldebaran (best at 7f/1m) and Good Journey (miler): fairly useful form: won minor event at Salisbury (by neck from White Mocha) in September: stays 1m. *Clive Cox* **85**

ALJEZEERA 3 b.f. Frankel 147 – Dynaforce (USA) 118 (Dynaformer (USA)) [2017 86P: 10s^3 11.9d^3 14.5d^2 14.1g* Oct 16] tall filly: has plenty of scope: useful performer: won listed race at Yarmouth (by 1¾ lengths from Capricious Cantor) in October: second in Park Hill Stakes at Doncaster (½ length behind Alyssa) month before: stays 14.5f: acts on soft and good to firm going. *Luca Cumani* **109**

ALJULJALAH (USA) 4 b.f. Exchange Rate (USA) 111 – Ruler's Charm (USA) (Cape Town (USA) 125) [2017 102: 7d^4 7.2m^2 p7g* p7s^5 8g a8f^4 Dec 29] lengthy filly: useful performer: won minor event at Chelmsford (by ¾ length from Bumptious) in August: second in handicap at Haydock (neck behind Excellent Sounds) time before: left Roger Varian after fourth start: stays 1m: acts on polytrack and good to firm going. *S. bin Ghadayer, UAE* **105**

ALKASHAAF (USA) 3 b.g. More Than Ready (USA) 120 – Abby Road (IRE) 99 (Danehill (USA) 126) [2017 79: t7.1g^3 t7.1g^3 p6g^4 t6d* t6g 7m 8f t7.2g t8d p6g^2 t7.2g Dec 13] sturdy gelding: fairly useful handicapper: won at Newcastle (by ¾ length from Jack Flash) in February: left Archie Watson after tenth start: stays 7f: acts on polytrack and tapeta: usually wears headgear/tongue tie. *Daniel Loughnane* **85**

ALKETIOS (GR) 6 b.g. Kavafi (IRE) 111 – Mazea (IRE) (Montjeu (IRE) 137) [2017 56: 8g^5 p8s^4 8g^4 8s Sep 4] good-bodied gelding: modest handicapper nowadays: stays 1m: acts on polytrack and good to firm going: tried in tongue tie: sometimes slowly away: ungenuine. *Chris Gordon* **61 §**

AL KHAFJI 4 ch.g. New Approach (IRE) 132 – Wadaat 102 (Diktat 126) [2017 80: p10g p8g^6 10.3g^6 11.6m^5 14g 10m Jun 17] angular gelding: fair handicapper nowadays: stays 1¼m: acts on polytrack: in headgear last 5 starts. *Jeremy Gask* **73**

ALKHALIFA (IRE) 2 gr.c. (Apr 26) Kodiac 112 – Bridal Path 75 (Groom Dancer (USA) 128) [2017 6m^3 6v* 6g^3 7g 6g^4 Oct 13] 110,000Y: compact colt: seventh foal: half-brother to 3 winners, including winner up to 7f The McGregornator (2-y-o 5f winner, by Bushranger) and 7f-8.6f winner Icy Blue (by Iceman): dam, 2-y-o 5f winner, closely related to smart winner up to 1¼m Cupid's Glory: fairly useful performer: won minor event at Newbury (by ½ length from Oliver Reed) in July: should stay 7f: acts on heavy going: tried in cheekpieces. *Brian Meehan* **83**

AL KHAN (IRE) 8 b.g. Elnadim (USA) 128 – Popolo (IRE) 66 (Fasliyev (USA) 120) [2017 97: f7g t7.1g^3 p7g^6 t7.1g^5 p7g 7.6d 8g^5 7g 7.4m^2 t7.2g^5 7.2s^6 7s p7g^4 Nov 21] lengthy gelding: useful handicapper: third at Newcastle (½ length behind Flaming Spear) in January: raced mainly around 7f: acts on all-weather, soft and good to firm going: wears headgear: tried in tongue tie: often races towards rear. *Kevin Ryan* **97**

ALKHAWANEEJ BOY (IRE) 2 b.c. (Mar 8) Elzaam (AUS) 115 – Kaplinsky (IRE) 75 (Fath (USA) 116) [2017 7v^4 7v* Sep 25] €22,000F, £10,000Y, 35,000 2-y-o: third foal: half-brother to 5f/5.5f (including at 2 yrs) winner Powerallied (by Camacho): dam 7f winner: fairly useful form: won minor event at Leicester (by 6 lengths from Porth Swtan) in September: will stay 1m: likely to progress further. *Kevin Ryan* **86 p**

ALKHOR 4 b.g. Exceed And Excel (AUS) 126 – Ruse 66 (Diktat 126) [2017 92: p6g* 6m^3 p6g^3 6.1g^3 7g^6 6g 5.5g^2 7d 5d* 5g 5.5g^6 p6.5g p6.5g p7.5g Dec 26] tall gelding: useful performer at best: won handicaps at Lingfield (by length from Salvatore Fury) in April and, having left Richard Hannon after fourth start, Vichy in August: well below form subsequently: stays 6f: acts on polytrack and good to firm going: usually races prominently. *Julien Phelippon, France* **95 d**

AL KOUT 3 gr.g. Oasis Dream 129 – Honorlina (FR) (Linamix (FR) 127) [2017 t9.5g* p10s Dec 8] fair form: won maiden at Wolverhampton (by 1¼ lengths from Majboor) on debut: towards rear in handicap month later. *Heather Main* **79**

ALL ABOUT THE PACE 3 ch.f. Sixties Icon 125 – Phoebe Woodstock (IRE) 76 (Grand Lodge (USA) 125) [2017 57: t9.5g^3 t12.2g^4 p12g^4 t14g Jul 17] modest maiden: stays 1½m: acts on polytrack and tapeta. *Mark Usher* **57**

ALLANTE (IRE) 2 b.f. (Jan 31) Pivotal 124 – Have Faith (IRE) 87 (Machiavellian (USA) 123) [2017 p7g t7.2g^2 Dec 5] 90,000Y: half-sister to several winners, including 7f/1m winner Believe It (by Rip Van Winkle) and 6.5f-1m winner Faithful One (by Dubawi): dam 2-y-o 7f winner: fair form when second in minor event at Wolverhampton (neck behind Point Hope) on second of 2 starts: open to further improvement. *Sir Michael Stoute* **71 p**

ALL DOLLED UP (IRE) 5 b.m. Aussie Rules (USA) 123 – All On Sugar (GER) (Red Ransom (USA)) [2017 58: t12.2g Jan 9] modest maiden at best: no form in 2017, including over hurdles: stays 1m: best form on good going: has worn headgear/tongue tie. *Sarah-Jayne Davies* **–**

ALLEE BLEUE (IRE) 7 ch.g. Mount Nelson 125 – Murrieta 57 (Docksider (USA) 124) [2017 p16s^2 Sep 8] fairly useful maiden: placed twice in France for M. Delzangles in 2013: second in handicap at Kempton on only outing on Flat since: stays 2m: acts on polytrack and good to soft going: useful hurdler. *Philip Hobbs* **80**

ALLEGHENY BAY (IRE) 3 b.g. Power 117 – Allegheny Creek (IRE) (Teofilo (IRE) 126) [2017 –p: p6m^2 p7g^2 p10g^5 t7.1f^4 p6f^2 p6g^2 p7g^5 7g^3 May 30] workmanlike gelding: fair maiden: best at 6f/7f: acts on polytrack: front runner. *J. S. Moore* **66**

ALLEGIANT (USA) 2 b.g. (Mar 7) City Zip (USA) 112 – Preferential (Dansili 127) [2017 p8g Dec 20] 20/1, held back by inexperience when well held in minor event at Kempton. *Roger Charlton* **–**

ALLEGRAMENTE 2 b.f. (Feb 2) Dansili 127 – Allegretto (IRE) 118 (Galileo (IRE) 134) [2017 7d Aug 5] compact filly: fourth foal: sister to 1½m winner Alla Breve and half-sister to useful 1¾m winner (stayed 2m) Baihas (by Nayef): dam 1½m-2m winner (including Goodwood Cup and Prix Royal-Oak) who stayed 2½m: 12/1, very green when well held in minor event at Newmarket. *Sir Michael Stoute* **–**

ALLEN'S FOLLY 4 b.f. Captain Gerrard (IRE) 113 – Rabarama (Xaar 132) [2017 48: f5g^6 f5g t6m f6g t6m^5 t5.1g t6g 6g 5.7s Aug 9] maiden: no form in 2017: tried in blinkers. *Peter Hiatt* **–**

ALLEZ HENRI (IRE) 6 b.g. Footstepsinthesand 120 – Macotte (FR) (Nicolotte 118) [2017 p9.9g p9.9g^2 p9.9g^4 p9.4g^3 p10g^3 10.4g 10m p9.4g^2 p9.4g 9.9s^4 Oct 14] useful performer: placed 4 times in 2017, including in Easter Classic AW Middle Distance Championships Stakes at Lingfield (2¼ lengths third to Convey) in April: stays 1¼m: acts on polytrack and soft going: usually wears cheekpieces. *D. & P. Prod'homme, France* **105**

ALL FOR NOTHING (IRE) 4 b.g. Bushranger (IRE) 119 – Allofus (IRE) (Celtic Swing 138) [2017 55: 12g^6 13.1s^6 11g 9.9g* 12.1g* 10.9m^2 12.9v Sep 8] fair performer: won claimer at Ballinrobe in July and handicap at Catterick (amateur) in August: left Kevin Prendergast after fourth start: stays 13f: acts on soft and good to firm going: in visor/tongue tie last 4 starts: usually races towards rear. *John McConnell, Ireland* **70**

ALL FOR THE BEST (IRE) 5 b.g. Rip Van Winkle (IRE) 134 – Alleluia 117 (Caerleon (USA) 132) [2017 80: t16.5g^2 17.1d^2 16s Aug 17] fairly useful handicapper: second at Pontefract in June: stays 17f: acts on polytrack, tapeta, firm and good to soft going: wears headgear: in tongue tie last 3 starts. *Robert Stephens* **81**

ALLFREDANDNOBELL (IRE) 4 b.g. Alfred Nobel (IRE) 110 – Its In The Air (IRE) (Whipper (USA) 126) [2017 61: t12.4g 15.9s^5 13.9v^4 Oct 21] modest maiden: stays 1¼m: acts on good to soft going: tried in cheekpieces: winning hurdler. *Micky Hammond* **50**

ALLIED 2 ch.c. (Apr 7) Dawn Approach (IRE) 132 – Mambo Halo (USA) (Southern Halo (USA)) [2017 8d Oct 27] 20/1, very green when well held in minor event at Newbury. *Sir Michael Stoute* **–**

ALLIEYF 2 b.c. (Feb 12) New Approach (IRE) 132 – Sajjhaa 121 (King's Best (USA) 132) [2017 8.3v^5 Nov 8] first foal: dam 1m-10.4f winner, including Dubai Duty Free: 17/2, shaped with promise when fifth in maiden at Nottingham (3¼ lengths behind Kinaesthesia) on debut, very slowly away and not knocked about: sure to progress. *William Haggas* **73 p**

ALLIGATOR 3 ch.g. Sepoy (AUS) 129 – See You Later 98 (Emarati (USA) 74) [2017 62§: t9.5g p7m t8.6g^4 Dec 13] compact gelding: modest maiden: stays 8.5f: acts on polytrack and tapeta: has worn headgear, including final start. *Tony Carroll* **51**

ALL MY LOVE (IRE) 5 b.m. Lord Shanakill (USA) 121 – Afilla (Dansili 127) [2017 83: t12.2g^2 11.6g^2 11.6m^4 p11g 11.8d 12.1s* 12g^2 Nov 3] leggy mare: fairly useful handicapper: won at Catterick (by 4½ lengths from Desert Cross) in October: stays 1½m: acts on tapeta, good to firm and heavy going: winning hurdler. *Pam Sly* **87**

ALLNITE (IRE) 2 b.g. (Feb 16) Arcano (IRE) 122 – Paint The Town (IRE) 74 (Sadler's Wells (USA) 132) [2017 7g^5 7.4s Sep 20] well held in minor events. *Tom Dascombe* **–**

ALLOFMELOVESALLOFU 3 ch.g. Sakhee's Secret 128 – La Palma (Sinndar (IRE) 134) [2017 p7g 7m p7s^6 8s 7.1g Aug 28] modest maiden: best effort at 7f. *Ken Cunningham-Brown* **59**

ALL OR NOTHIN (IRE) 8 b.g. Majestic Missile (IRE) 118 – Lady Peculiar (CAN) (Sunshine Forever (USA)) [2017 44: p7g^2 p7g* p7d f7m^6 f6d^2 t6g^5 f6.1g^4 6s 7s^4 6s^4 6.1g f6.1g^2 p7g p7g Dec 21] well-made gelding: modest handicapper nowadays: won at Chelmsford in January: stays 7f: acts on polytrack, fibresand, good to firm and heavy going: has worn headgear/tongue tie: often races prominently. *Paddy Butler* **58**

ALL OUT 2 b.f. (Mar 30) Acclamation 118 – Time Over 76 (Mark of Esteem (IRE) 137) [2017 5d* 6.1m* 6g^3 Nov 3] rather unfurnished filly: sixth foal: half-sister to 3 winners, including smart winner up to 1½m Repeater (2-y-o 7f/1m winner, by Montjeu), stays 2¼m, and 1½m/13f winner Late Shipment (by Authorized): dam 1m winner: fairly useful form: won maiden at Nottingham (by neck from Little Boy Blue) and minor event at Windsor (by neck from Global Tango) in October: third in listed race at Newmarket (3¼ lengths behind Alwasmiya) following month: stays 6f: remains with potential. *Richard Hannon* **90 p**

ALLUMAGE 5 b.m. Montjeu (IRE) 137 – Alaia (IRE) 88 (Sinndar (IRE) 134) [2017 p10g^6 12m 12g^4 Jul 14] rather leggy mare: fairly useful handicapper, missed 2016: stays 1½m: acts on polytrack, best turf form on good going: has worn hood. *Sylvester Kirk* **85**

ALLURINGLY (USA) 3 b.f. Fastnet Rock (AUS) 127 – All For Glory (USA) (Giant's Causeway (USA) 132) [2017 70p: 9g* 11.3m^2 12m^3 12m^6 12f^6 9.5d* 11.9d^5 10s 9.5s^5 8g Oct 7] strong, rangy filly: third foal: half-sister to useful 2-y-o 6f winner Toogoodtobetrue (by Oasis Dream): dam unraced half-sister to Wonder of Wonders out of All Too Beautiful (both runner-up in Oaks), latter sister to Galileo and half-sister to Sea The Stars: useful performer: won maiden at Tipperary in April and listed race at Gowran (by neck from Making Light) in August: placed in listed Cheshire Oaks at Chester (1¾ lengths behind Enable) in May and Oaks at Epsom (11 lengths behind Enable) in June: stayed 1½m: acted on good to firm and good to soft going: tried in visor: usually raced towards rear: retired, visits Galileo. *Aidan O'Brien, Ireland* **107**

ALLUX BOY (IRE) 3 b.g. Iffraaj 127 – Ms Victoria (IRE) 90 (Fasliyev (USA) 120) [2017 73: 8m 7d 7g 6.1g^4 6g Aug 10] fair performer at 2 yrs, below that level in 2017: stays 6f: acts on good to firm and good to soft going: tried in tongue tie: usually races close up. *Nigel Tinkler* **59**

ALL YOU (IRE) 5 b.g. Siyouni (FR) 122 – Diamond Light (USA) 70 (Fantastic Light (USA) 134) [2017 82, a73: t10.2g t9.5m^6 t8.6m t8.6g^2 t8.6g^3 8g 9.9m 7.5f^5 9.9m^2 8.5d 9.9m^3 11.9m^5 Jul 7] fair handicapper: stays 1¼m: acts on tapeta and good to firm going: wears headgear. *David O'Meara* **76**

ALMAGEST 9 br.g. Galileo (IRE) 134 – Arabesque 100 (Zafonic (USA) 130) [2017 18g Jun 25] strong gelding: useful at best, well held sole outing (wore tongue tie) on Flat since 2014: stays 2m: acts on good to firm and good to soft going: has worn headgear, including last 5 starts. *Robert Stephens* **–**

ALMANACK 7 b.g. Haatef (USA) 117 – Openness (Grand Lodge (USA) 125) [2017 73: p8g f8g^4 p8d^2 p7g^5 7m* 8m^3 7.6s p8s Dec 15] lengthy gelding: fair handicapper: won at Salisbury (amateur) in April: stays 8.5f: acts on polytrack, tapeta and good to firm going: has worn cheekpieces/tongue tie: inconsistent. *Mark Pattinson* **72**

ALMANE (IRE) 2 ch.g. (Feb 6) Sir Prancealot (IRE) 111 – Red Rosanna 82 (Bertolini (USA) 125) [2017 5g^4 5m* t5s^6 Jun 1] €18,000Y: third foal: half-brother to 5f winner Frank The Barber (by Zebedee): dam, 5f winner (including at 2 yrs), half-sister to smart sprinter Rose Blossom: fairly useful form: won minor event at Beverley (by length from Emilia James) in April: raced only at 5f. *Richard Fahey* **84**

AL MANSOR (IRE) 3 gr.c. Dark Angel (IRE) 113 – Atullia (GER) (Tertullian (USA) 115) [2017 71: p8g^3 t7.1g 8s 7m^4 a8.4s^4 8.4s^5 7g 6.5d a10.4g Dec 28] fair maiden: left Richard Hannon after fourth start: stays 1m: acts on polytrack and good to firm going: tried in blinkers: front runner/races prominently, often freely. *P. & F. Montfort, France* **71**

ALMANZOR (FR) 4 b.c. Wootton Bassett 119 – Darkova (FR) (Maria's Mon (USA) 121) [2017 133: 9.9g^5 Aug 15] lengthy colt: top-class performer at 3 yrs when wins included Prix du Jockey Club at Chantilly, Irish Champion Stakes at Leopardstown and Champion Stakes at Ascot: disappointing when equal-fifth of 6 behind First Sitting in Prix Gontaut-Biron at Deauville on only outing in 2017, slowly away: would probably have stayed 1½m: acted on good to firm and good to soft going: had a good turn of foot: to stand at Haras d'Etreham, France, fee €35,000. *Jean-Claude Rouget, France* **108**

AL MAYDA (USA) 3 ch.f. Distorted Humor (USA) 117 – Ms Margaret H (USA) (Point **82**
Given (USA) 134) [2017 73p: 10g* 10.2g^{5} 10.1s 10m Oct 13] rather unfurnished filly: fairly useful performer: won maiden at Windsor (by ½ length from Fujaira Prince) in July: stays 1¼m: acts on polytrack: in hood last 2 starts: wears tongue tie: front runner/races prominently. *Hugo Palmer*

ALMERITA MOON (IRE) 3 b.f. Henrythenavigator (USA) 131 – Moonboat (Starcraft **–**
(NZ) 128) [2017 t8.6g Mar 23] first foal: dam unraced half-sister to temperamental 1000 Guineas runner-up Starscope: 18/1, well held in maiden at Wolverhampton: sent to Greece. *Marco Botti*

ALMONER 5 b.m. Oasis Dream 129 – Alumni 100 (Selkirk (USA) 129) [2017 75: p7g* **89**
Jan 11] 45,000 3-y-o: sister to very smart 5f-1¼m winner Dux Scholar (2-y-o 1m winner) and half-sister to 3 winners, including useful 2-y-o 1m winner Cambridge (by Rail Link): dam 11.4f winner: fairly useful form: won maiden at Kempton (by length from Angel of Darkness) on sole start in 2017: stays 7f. *Tracey Collins, Ireland*

ALMOQATEL (IRE) 5 b.g. Clodovil (IRE) 116 – Majestic Night (IRE) (Mujadil (USA) **33**
119) [2017 8d 6s 7d Sep 18] sturdy gelding: poor handicapper: trained on reappearance only by Natalie Lloyd-Beavis: stays 1m: acts on polytrack and firm going: has worn headgear. *Tony Newcombe*

ALMOREB (IRE) 3 b.c. Raven's Pass (USA) 133 – Macadamia (IRE) 115 (Classic **103**
Cliche (IRE) 128) [2017 –p: 7s* 8g^{4} 7m^{6} 8s* t8.6g^{2} p8g* 8g^{3} 9.9v^{2} Oct 4] strong colt: useful performer: won maiden at Newbury in May, and handicaps at Sandown in July and Chelmsford (dead-heated) in August: third in handicap at Sandown (3 lengths behind The Grape Escape) in September: stays 8.5f: acts on polytrack, tapeta and soft going. *Richard Hannon*

ALMOST GEMINI (IRE) 8 gr.g. Dylan Thomas (IRE) 132 – Streetcar (IRE) 69 (In The **79**
Wings 128) [2017 75: 15.9m^{6} 17.2s^{3} 17.1g^{2} 17.1v^{3} Sep 21] rangy gelding: fair handicapper: stays 2¼m: acts on polytrack, good to firm and heavy going: wears headgear. *Kenneth Slack*

AL MUFFRIH (IRE) 2 b.c. (May 8) Sea The Stars (IRE) 140 – Scarlet And Gold (IRE) **87 P**
(Peintre Celebre (USA) 137) [2017 8m^{3} Oct 25] 260,000Y: lengthy, attractive colt: third foal: dam, French 10.5f winner, half-sister to Prix du Jockey Club winner Le Havre and smart winner up to 1¾m Astronereus (by Sea The Stars): 9/2, plenty of promise when third in minor event at Newmarket (3 lengths behind Knight To Behold) on debut: will stay at least 1¼m: open to considerable improvement. *William Haggas*

ALMUNTHER (IRE) 4 b.g. Invincible Spirit (IRE) 121 – Adaala (USA) 108 (Sahm **67**
(USA) 112) [2017 7m^{4} 7g 8m^{5} 10g 9.9v^{3} 10d^{2} Oct 20] fair maiden: likely to stay 1½m: acts on good to soft going: in tongue tie last 2 starts: usually races prominently. *Micky Hammond*

AL MUSTASHAR (IRE) 2 b.g. (Apr 23) Shamardal (USA) 129 – Dresden Doll (USA) **63**
78 (Elusive Quality (USA)) [2017 6g^{6} p7g Oct 18] modest form in minor events. *Saeed bin Suroor*

ALMUTAMARRED (USA) 5 ch.g. Street Cry (IRE) 130 – Sortita (GER) 98 (Monsun **68**
(GER) 124) [2017 62, a78: t10.2s 12.1s^{3} 11.6g t12.2g t12.2g t16.5g t12.4g t14d Dec 27] deep-chested gelding: fair handicapper: left David Brown after third start: stays 12.5f: acts on fibresand, tapeta and soft going: often in headgear in 2017: sometimes slowly away, usually races in rear. *James Unett*

ALNAAS 3 b.f. Dansili 127 – Hedaaya (IRE) 92 (Indian Ridge 123) [2017 7g^{2} p7g* 8m^{4} **85 p**
May 26] third foal: half-sister to useful 7f (including at 2 yrs) winner Tamadhor (by Arcano) and 1m winner Madroos (by Teofilo): dam, 8.5f winner, half-sister to smart 2-y-o 6f winner (stayed 1m) Memory, herself dam of smart winner up to 1¾m Call To Mind: fairly useful form: won maiden at Chelmsford (by 1½ lengths from Isabel's On It) in May: should stay 1m: wears tongue tie: remains with potential. *John Gosden*

AL NAFOORAH 3 b.f. Bated Breath 125 – Cat O' Nine Tails 84 (Motivator 131) [2017 **94**
71: t8.6g^{2} 8.3g^{2} 8.3d^{2} 8g^{2} 8f* 8.1g^{4} 8.3d* 8g 8g* 8d^{6} 8m^{2} Oct 25] angular filly: fairly useful handicapper: won at Wetherby in June, Nottingham in July and Sandown in September: second at Newmarket in October: stays 8.5f: acts on polytrack, tapeta, firm and good to soft going. *Ed Dunlop*

ALNASHAMA 5 b.g. Dubawi (IRE) 129 – Ghanaati (USA) 122 (Giant's Causeway **96**
(USA) 132) [2017 94: 7m^{3} p8d^{3} 8m^{5} 8m^{5} Jul 7] useful handicapper: third at Doncaster (1¼ lengths behind Aardwolf) and Kempton (1¼ lengths behind Ripoll) in May: stays 8.5f: acts on polytrack, tapeta, good to firm and good to soft going: often races prominently. *Charles Hills*

ALNASL (IRE) 3 b.f. Tamayuz 126 – Arwaah (IRE) 106 (Dalakhani (IRE) 133) [2017 –p: 8.5m^3 9.9m* 9.9m 10d 8.2g 10m^3 10d^2 10v^4 t9.5g* 8.9m* t9.5g^4 8.5g* t8.6g^4 Oct 7] tall, rather leggy filly: fairly useful performer: won maiden at Brighton in May, and handicaps at Wolverhampton, Musselburgh and Epsom (by 3½ lengths from Traveller) in August/September: stays 1¼m: acts on tapeta, good to firm and good to soft going: wears hood: front runner/races prominently, often travels strongly: sold 40,000 gns in October, sent to Saudi Arabia. *Archie Watson* **85**

AL NEKSH 4 b.g. Zoffany (IRE) 121 – Mount Crystal (IRE) 80 (Montjeu (IRE) 137) [2017 98: 10.3d^2 10d^6 11.9g^4 10.2d^3 10m Sep 23] strong, attractive gelding: useful handicapper: placed at York (5 lengths behind Master Carpenter) in May and Doncaster (length behind Euginio) in September: stays 1¼m: acts on good to firm and good to soft going: tried in cheekpieces: sold 15,000 gns in October, sent to USA. *William Haggas* **99**

ALNIYAT 3 ch.f. Sepoy (AUS) 129 – Agata Laguna (IRE) (Elnadim (USA) 128) [2017 –: 7d May 12] well held in 2 maidens. *Ed Dunlop* **–**

ALOUJA (IRE) 3 ch.f. Raven's Pass (USA) 133 – Artisti (Cape Cross (IRE) 129) [2017 78: 8.3g^3 8f^3 7g^2 7g t7.2g^5 t8g^4 Sep 22] sturdy filly: fairly useful maiden: stays 8.5f: acts on firm going: in cheekpieces last 2 starts: tried in tongue tie: often races prominently. *Hugo Palmer* **81**

AL OZZDI 2 b.g. (Mar 8) Acclamation 118 – Zibeling (IRE) (Cape Cross (IRE) 129) [2017 7m 7m* 8d^4 p8g^5 Sep 9] neat gelding: fair form: won minor event at Brighton in August: stays 1m: in tongue tie last 3 starts. *Simon Crisford* **72**

ALPHABET 3 b.f. Lawman (FR) 121 – Applauded (IRE) 83 (Royal Applause 124) [2017 78: 6v* 5.8g^4 6g^5 6f 6s^3 5m^3 5f^6 7s 5s 5s^2 6s^2 5d 5.8v^5 6s Oct 21] 440,000Y: sturdy filly: closely related to 2-y-o 6f winner Amnesia (later 8.5f winner in USA, by Invincible Spirit) and half-sister to 3 winners, including 2-y-o 6f winner Mirage (later useful 1m winner in USA, by Oasis Dream): dam, 2-y-o 7f winner, half-sister to Irish 2000 Guineas winner Power: smart performer: won maiden at Naas (by 5½ lengths from Ma Fee Heela) in March: second in Flying Five Stakes at the Curragh (length behind Caravaggio) and Renaissance Stakes at Naas (2¾ lengths behind Quiet Reflection) in September: stayed 6f: acted on heavy going: usually wore tongue tie: raced prominently: retired, visits Galileo. *Aidan O'Brien, Ireland* **112**

ALPHABETICAL ORDER 9 b.g. Alflora (IRE) 120 – Lady Turk (FR) (Baby Turk 120) [2017 82: 11.9m 14.5s^3 13.1s 11.9s^6 12.1g^2 12.1m^4 Aug 27] fairly useful handicapper: second at Beverley in August: stays 2m: acts on heavy going: tried in hood. *David O'Meara* **86**

ALPHA CENTAURI (IRE) 2 gr.f. (Feb 28) Mastercraftsman (IRE) 129 – Alpha Lupi (IRE) (Rahy (USA) 115) [2017 6m* 6s* 6m^2 7s^5 Sep 10] good-quartered filly: sixth foal: closely related to French 7f winner Elitiste (by Danehill Dancer) and half-sister to useful 2-y-o 7f winner Tenth Star (later 8.5f winner in USA, by Dansili): dam, unraced, out of Poule d'Essai des Pouliches and Prix de Diane winner East of The Moon: useful form: won maiden (by 2½ lengths from Actress) and listed race (by 5 lengths from Actress) in May, both at Naas: second in Albany Stakes at Royal Ascot (neck behind Different League) in June: should stay 7f+. *Mrs J. Harrington, Ireland* **106**

ALPHA DELPHINI 6 b.g. Captain Gerrard (IRE) 113 – Easy To Imagine (USA) (Cozzene (USA)) [2017 116: 5m 5f^3 5f^6 5m 5s^2 5g 5g 5v* 5v* Oct 16] strong gelding: smart performer: won minor events at Beverley (by neck from Line of Reason) in September and Musselburgh (by length from Ornate) in October: third in Temple Stakes at Haydock (¾ length behind Priceless) in May: best form at 5f: acts on any turf going: wears headgear. *Bryan Smart* **116**

ALPHA TAURI (USA) 11 b.g. Aldebaran (USA) 126 – Seven Moons (JPN) (Sunday Silence (USA)) [2017 37§, a74§: f7g^5 f8s* f8g^2 f7m^3 f8.1g* 7.6d 7g f7.1g f5g f7.1g Dec 11] smallish, sturdy gelding: fairly useful handicapper: won at Southwell in January and May (by 4½ lengths from Muqarred): stays 1m: most effective on fibresand: has worn headgear/tongue tie: usually races prominently: unreliable. *Charles Smith* **– §** **a84 §**

ALPINE DREAM (IRE) 4 b.f. Dream Ahead (USA) 133 – Infamous Angel 101 (Exceed And Excel (AUS) 126) [2017 80: 6g^6 7m^3 7g^4 7.6s* 8g^5 7m^2 7.6d^4 7.2m^2 7.2m^5 7d t7.1g^5 t8g Nov 24] strong filly: fairly useful handicapper: won at Chester in June: second at York in July and Musselburgh in August: stays 7.5f: acts on soft and good to firm going: wears headgear. *Tim Easterby* **82**

ALPINE PEAK (USA) 2 gr.c. (Jan 29) Mizzen Mast (USA) 121 – Affectionately (Galileo (IRE) 134) [2017 t8.6m^6 p8g^3 t8.6d^5 Dec 9] fair form in minor events. *Roger Varian* **75**

AL QAHWA (IRE) 4 b.g. Fast Company (IRE) 126 – Cappuccino (IRE) (Mujadil (USA) 119) [2017 99: 6s* 6g t6s 6g^{2} 6d 6g 6s^{2} 6g 6d Oct 27] neat gelding: useful handicapper: won at York (by neck from Muntadab) in May: second there (2 lengths behind Flying Pursuit) in July and at the Curragh (1¼ lengths behind Ice Age) in September: best at 6f: acts on heavy going: in headgear last 4 starts. *David O'Meara* **105**

ALQALSAR (IRE) 3 ch.c. Bahamian Bounty 116 – With Colour (Rainbow Quest (USA) 134) [2017 8m^{5} 7s^{2} 8.3m^{2} Jun 15] good-bodied colt: fair form: second twice from 3 starts in maidens. *Brian Meehan* **79**

ALQAMAR 3 b.g. Dubawi (IRE) 129 – Moonsail 82 (Monsun (GER) 124) [2017 74: 11.9d* 14m 12s^{2} 14.1d^{5} p12g Nov 8] well-made gelding: useful handicapper: won at York (by 5 lengths from Lester Kris) in May: stays 1¾m: acts on soft and good to firm going: in headgear in 2017: temperament under suspicion. *Charlie Appleby* **100**

ALRAHAAL (IRE) 2 ch.c. (Mar 31) Raven's Pass (USA) 133 – Loose Julie (IRE) (Cape Cross (IRE) 129) [2017 6g^{2} 6g^{4} Aug 1] 45,000F, 60,000Y: fourth foal: half-brother to 3 winners, including useful winner up to 6f Banaadeer (2-y-o 5f winner, by Tamayuz) and useful winner up to 1m Storm Ahead (2-y-o 7f winner, by Iffraaj): dam unraced: fairly useful form: better effort when fourth in maiden at Goodwood (¾ length behind Thechildren'strust) in August. *Marcus Tregoning* **82**

AL REEH (IRE) 3 br.c. Invincible Spirit (IRE) 121 – Dffra (IRE) 64 (Refuse To Bend (IRE) 128) [2017 85: p7d^{4} p7s Jul 25] fairly useful handicapper: stays 7f: acts on polytrack and good to firm going. *Marco Botti* **83**

ALRIGHT DAVE 2 ch.g. (Apr 18) Frozen Power (IRE) 108 – Crazy Hazy (IRE) (Sakhee's Secret 128) [2017 t7.2m Oct 31] 80/1, well held in minor event at Wolverhampton. *Ronald Harris* **–**

AL SAIL (FR) 3 b.g. Kendargent (FR) 112 – Golden Lily (FR) (Dolphin Street (FR) 125) [2017 70p: p6g^{2} p6g^{2} p6.5g^{4} 5.5d* 5g^{5} Aug 7] fairly useful performer: won maiden at Dieppe in July: left Richard Hannon after second start: stays 6f: acts on polytrack and good to soft going. *Julien Phelippon, France* **85**

ALSHAN FAJER 7 ch.g. Lemon Drop Kid (USA) 131 – Illuminise (IRE) 109 (Grand Lodge (USA) 125) [2017 83: f12g^{5} f12d^{5} p15.8g p12g f12.1g^{4} p11d t12.2g^{6} Jul 17] workmanlike gelding: fairly useful handicapper at best, on downgrade in 2017: stays 1¾m: acts on polytrack and good to firm going: tried in visor/tongue tie: often races towards rear. *J. R. Jenkins* **70**

ALSHIBAA (IRE) 3 br.g. New Approach (IRE) 132 – Amjaad (Dansili 127) [2017 72p: 9.8g^{6} 8.2g* Jun 27] fairly useful handicapper: won at Leicester (by neck from Duchess of Fife) in June: should prove as effective at 1¼m: acts on tapeta and good to firm going: sold 17,000 gns in July, hurdling in USA. *William Haggas* **80**

AL'S MEMORY (IRE) 8 b.g. Red Clubs (IRE) 125 – Consensus (IRE) 91 (Common Grounds 118) [2017 71: 7.1g^{4} 8g t7.2g^{3} t7.2g^{5} p8s Dec 8] small, sturdy gelding: fair handicapper: stays 8.5f: acts on polytrack, tapeta and any turf going: tried in visor: front runner/races prominently. *David Evans* **63**

ALSVINDER 4 b.c. Footstepsinthesand 120 – Notting Hill (BRZ) (Jules (USA) 110) **69 +**
[2017 88: 5m p5s^{2} 5d 5g^{4} 5m p5d* p5g^{2} t5.1g* p5g^{3} Dec 12] fair handicapper on turf, **a103**
useful on all-weather: won at Chelmsford in September and Wolverhampton (by 1½ lengths from Landing Night) in November: raced only at 5f: acts on polytrack and tapeta: tried in hood: usually leads. *David O'Meara*

ALTAAYIL (IRE) 6 br.g. Sea The Stars (IRE) 140 – Alleluia 117 (Caerleon (USA) 132) [2017 12g^{2} 16d^{2} Oct 6] useful handicapper: second at Epsom (¾ length behind C'est No Mour) in September and Ascot (neck behind Dominating) in October: stays 2m: acts on tapeta and soft going. *Gary Moore* **98**

ALTAIRA 6 b.g. Dubawi (IRE) 129 – Peach Pearl (Invincible Spirit (IRE) 121) [2017 61: p7d^{6} p7d^{5} p8d p8g^{2} 7.1g^{6} 8g 10.2d* 11.9d 8v Oct 19] modest handicapper: won at Bath in August: stays 11.5f: acts on polytrack and good to soft going: often in headgear in 2017: signs of temperament. *Tony Carroll* **58**

ALTERED METHOD (IRE) 2 ch.g. (Feb 13) Dawn Approach (IRE) 132 – Swift Action (IRE) 87 (Invincible Spirit (IRE) 121) [2017 6s t7.1d Oct 24] no form in 2 minor events. *Hugo Palmer* **–**

ALTERNATE ROUTE 3 b.g. New Approach (IRE) 132 – Almamia 78 (Hernando (FR) 127) [2017 p7s p8s p10g 11.5m p16g^3 16s^2 p15.8g* p16d^6 t16.5g^3 p12g^2 Dec 20] €27,000Y: fifth foal: half-brother to 11.5f winner (stayed 1¾m) Aloha (by With Approval) and useful 2-y-o 6f winner Alamode (by Sir Percy): dam lightly-raced half-sister to smart winner up to 1¼m Algonquin out of dual Champion Stakes winner Alborada: fairly useful handicapper: won at Lingfield in September: stays 2m: acts on polytrack and soft going: wears headgear: front runner/races prominently, usually travels strongly. *Sir Mark Prescott Bt* **81**

ALTERNATIVE FACT 2 b.c. (Feb 28) Dalakhani (IRE) 133 – O Fourlunda 71 (Halling (USA) 133) [2017 7d^2 8s* 8s^2 Oct 19] 35,000Y: seventh foal: half-brother to 7f winner Four Poets (by Poet's Voice) and a winner in Norway by Green Desert: dam maiden half-sister to very smart winner up to 11f Blue Monday: useful form: won minor event at Salisbury (by 6 lengths from Deyaarna) in September: further improvement when 5 lengths second to Wootton in listed race at Deauville: should stay at least 1¼m. *Ed Dunlop* **96**

ALTHAROOS (IRE) 7 br.g. Sakhee (USA) 136 – Thamara (USA) (Street Cry (IRE) 130) [2017 87: 8.5m^3 9.9d^6 Jun 10] good-topped, attractive gelding: fairly useful handicapper: stayed 1¼m: acted on any turf going: tried in cheekpieces: sometimes slowly away, often raced towards rear: dead. *Micky Hammond* **82**

ALTIKO TOMMY (IRE) 3 b.g. Kodiac 112 – Altishaan (Darshaan 133) [2017 66: p7g* t7.1g^6 p7g^3 p8d 7m 8s p8g^4 Nov 1] compact gelding: fair handicapper: won at Lingfield in March: stays 1m: acts on polytrack, tapeta and good to firm going: tried in blinkers. *George Baker* **72**

ALTON BAY (IRE) 9 b.g. Pushkin (IRE) 116 – Miss Chapman (IRE) 72 (Imperial Ballet (IRE) 110) [2017 92: 16v^4 12g^2 15g^5 16s f12.1g Dec 21] fairly useful handicapper: second in minor event at Bellewstown in July: stays 2¼m: acts on good to firm going: has worn tongue tie. *Peter Fahey, Ireland* **85**

ALTRA VITA 2 b.f. (Jan 29) Animal Kingdom (USA) 129 – Alma Mater 102 (Sadler's Wells (USA) 132) [2017 p7g t7.1g^5 t8.6g Nov 29] fourth foal: half-sister to useful 1m-1¼m winners Alumna (by Mr Greeley) and Aleator (by Blame): dam, 1½m/12.5f winner, half-sister to dual Champion Stakes winner Alborada: no form in minor events. *Sir Mark Prescott Bt* **–**

ALTYN ALQA 3 b.f. High Chaparral (IRE) 132 – Albanka (USA) (Giant's Causeway (USA) 132) [2017 p11g Mar 29] first foal: dam once-raced half-sister to 1000 Guineas winner Sleepytime and high-class miler Ali-Royal: 4/1, well held in maiden at Kempton. *Clive Cox* **–**

ALTYN ORDA (IRE) 2 ch.f. (Jan 30) Kyllachy 129 – Albanka (USA) (Giant's Causeway (USA) 132) [2017 7g^2 7d^2 7m* Oct 13] rather unfurnished filly: second foal: dam once-raced half-sister to 1000 Guineas winner Sleepytime and high-class miler Ali-Royal: useful form: won Oh So Sharp Stakes at Newmarket (by neck from Gavota) in October: will be suited by 1m: open to further improvement. *Roger Varian* **106 p**

ALWAHSH (IRE) 3 b.c. Dubawi (IRE) 129 – Gile Na Greine (IRE) 117 (Galileo (IRE) 134) [2017 64p: 8m^2 10g^4 8.3m* 8d 9.9v^4 9.9g^5 10.3g^3 Oct 14] strong, compact colt: useful performer: won maiden at Nottingham (by 7 lengths from Alqalsar) in June: stays 1¼m: acts on good to firm going: tried in cheekpieces: sold 260,000 gns in November, sent to Saudi Arabia. *William Haggas* **95**

ALWASMIYA 2 b.f. (Feb 23) Kyllachy 129 – Miss Bunter 79 (Bahamian Bounty 116) [2017 t6s^4 6.1d* 6g* Nov 3] £42,000Y, €110,000 2-y-o: first foal: dam, 5f/6f winner, half-sister to smart 5f winner Dutch Masterpiece: useful form: won minor event at Nottingham (by 1½ lengths from Ocala) in October and listed race at Newmarket (by 3 lengths from Izzy Bizu) in November: raced only at 6f: will go on improving. *Simon Crisford* **101 p**

ALWAYS AMAZING 3 ch.g. Kyllachy 129 – Amazed 58 (Clantime 101) [2017 t6.1g* 5m^3 5m Aug 26] 65,000Y: half-brother to several winners, including 5f-7f winner Stunned (by Shamardal) and useful 5f/6f winner (including at 2 yrs) Dazed And Amazed (by Averti), both useful: dam sprint maiden: fairly useful form: won maiden at Wolverhampton (by 1½ lengths from World Power) in June: stays 6f. *Robert Cowell* **87**

ALWAYSANDFOREVER (IRE) 3 b.f. Teofilo (IRE) 126 – Deep Winter 94 (Pivotal 124) [2017 80p: 9.9s* Sep 4] useful form: off 12 months, won maiden at Brighton (by 14 lengths from sole rival Sugardrop) on sole outing in 2017: will go on improving. *Luca Cumani* **95 p**

ALWAYS DREAMING (USA) 3 b.c. Bodemeister (USA) 129 – Above Perfection (USA) (In Excess (IRE) 116) [2017 a8.2f* a9f* a9f* a10s* a9.5f a9f³ a10f Aug 26] $350,000Y: half-brother to several winners, including smart US Grade 1 2-y-o 7f winner Hot Dixie Chick (by Dixie Union): dam US winner up to 7f (2-y-o 5.5f winner), including Grade 3 6f event: improved into a high-class performer, winning maiden at Tampa Bay in January, optional claimer at Gulfstream in March, Florida Derby at Gulfstream (by 5 lengths from State of Honor) in April and Kentucky Derby at Churchill Downs (by 2¾ lengths from Lookin At Lee) in May: 5¼ lengths third to Good Samaritan in Grade 2 Jim Dandy Stakes at Saratoga in July: below form in Travers Stakes on last-named course final outing: stays 1¼m: acts on dirt (effective in wet conditions). *Todd A. Pletcher, USA* **124**

ALWAYS RESOLUTE 6 b.g. Refuse To Bend (IRE) 128 – Mad Annie (USA) (Anabaa (USA) 130) [2017 89: 14.1s⁴ 14s³ 16.3g t12.4g⁴ Dec 6] workmanlike gelding: fairly useful handicapper: third at Haydock in September: stays 17.5f: acts on soft and good to firm going: often races towards rear. *Brian Ellison* **85**

ALWAYS THANKFUL 3 b.f. Showcasing 117 – Thankful 55 (Diesis 133) [2017 74p: 6g² 6.1m⁴ 7m 7s* 8g* 8g 7g² p7g t8g⁴ Nov 24] sturdy filly: fairly useful handicapper: won at Yarmouth in June and Haydock in August: stays 1m: acts on tapeta, soft and good to firm going: in cheekpieces last 4 starts. *Ismail Mohammed* **81**

AL WUKAIR (IRE) 3 b.c. Dream Ahead (USA) 133 – Macheera (IRE) (Machiavellian (USA) 123) [2017 7g* 8m³ 8g² 8d* 8s Oct 21] **124**

Until an embarrassing story appeared in *The Guardian* right at the end of 2017 about its financial problems, the latest season had been a quieter year for Al Shaqab Racing's British arm. Its best horse, the Two Thousand Guineas winner Galileo Gold, was retired after a lacklustre display on his reappearance in the Lockinge Stakes, after which it came to light that he had suffered a soft tissue injury. Another of Al Shaqab's leading lights Mehmas—who competed in many of the top juvenile races during 2016—had already gone to stud at the end of the previous season. On the face of it, this would have been bad news for Al Shaqab's British retained rider Frankie Dettori, whose on-going contract is believed, incidentally, to have been affected in the aftermath of the revelations that several of Al Shaqab's trainers in Britain had been chasing bills that had remained unpaid for months, a situation apparently caused by a financial review and reorganisation within Al Shaqab according to a statement issued by its management. There was some speculation that budgets for the organisation had been used to fund expensive transactions in France where Al Shaqab Racing has apparently decided to concentrate its efforts from now on (it will seemingly have fewer than a dozen two-year-olds in training in Britain in 2018). One of those 'expensive transactions' in France had involved acquiring a significant stake in Brametot just before he won the Poule d'Essai des Poulains (he went on to win the Prix du Jockey Club as well).

Frankie Dettori's opportunities for Al Shaqab in Britain may have been a little more limited than expected but, through another established partnership with John Gosden, he still managed to win six Group 1 races in Britain and Ireland in the most recent season, four of those on Enable, on whom he also won the Arc. Gregory Benoist had become Al Shaqab's retained rider in France at the beginning of 2015 and has partnered most of the operation's Group 1 winners since, including Jemayel (Prix Saint-Alary), Zelzal (Prix Jean Prat), Qemah (Coronation Stakes and Prix Rothschild) and Mekhtaal (Prix d'Ispahan), the principal exception being Treve, whose regular partner was veteran Thierry Jarnet (though Dettori rode her in the 2013 Prix Vermeille). Benoist rode the Andre Fabre-trained Al Wukair on five of his seven career starts, but it was Dettori who was on board for the colt's Group 1 success in the Prix Jacques le Marois, a ride Benoist missed through injury, though Fabre was quick to mention Al Wukair's regular rider after the race: 'I would like to say a word about Gregory Benoist. He had ridden the horse wonderfully in the past and I wish him a quick recovery'. Benoist was back riding soon afterwards and on Al Wukair on his final start in the Queen Elizabeth II Stakes at Ascot, though the pair could manage only seventh behind Persuasive, ridden by Dettori.

Al Wukair will begin his stallion career at Haras de Bouquetot in Normandy, one of five new Group 1-winning additions to the growing roster of stallions at the stud (owned by the brother of the Emir of Qatar, Sheikh Joaan, whose horses race

Prix du Haras de Fresnay-le-Buffard - Jacques le Marois, Deauville—Al Wukair comes between Inns of Court (white cap) and Thunder Snow (cheekpieces) to snatch the honours, taking Andre Fabre level with Francois Boutin as the leading trainer in the race on seven victories

under the Al Shaqab banner). Joining Al Wukair will be Brametot, Zelzal, Joe Hirsch Turf Classic winner Ectot and Sussex Stakes/Queen Anne winner Toronado, who is being transferred after spending his first three seasons at Newmarket's National Stud. The most expensive sire at Haras de Bouquetot is the 2015 champion two-year-old Shalaa (€27,500), who joined the roster in 2016 and is part of a rapidly developing breeding operation that also includes four-times Group 1 winner Olympic Glory and fellow top-level scorers Planteur and Style Vendome, as well as a band of over one hundred broodmares (including dual Arc winner Treve). Given its current trajectory, Haras de Bouquetot seems likely to grow further, too, with the likes of Galileo Gold and Mehmas (both currently at Tally Ho Stud in Ireland) possibly on course to follow Toronado at some point. The influx of stallions isn't a big surprise given the words of Benoit Jeffroy (manager of Haras de Bouquetot and bloodstock advisor to the Al Shaqab operation) at the beginning of 2017: 'The farm was half asleep when Sheikh Joaan bought it in 2012. In the middle was the main house with a barn of thirty boxes and about forty hectares which were developed, and then the rest needed to be fenced. We built two barns with twenty-five boxes and a foaling unit. Planteur and Style Vendome were our first stallions here in 2014—we started in the lunge ring and the office was only a piece of wood. All the stallions we stand have raced for us but, in the future, if there's a good opportunity and we think we might need a new horse, we may invest in one from outside. We have seven stallion boxes at the moment but next year we are going to double the stallion yard in size.'

Al Wukair won both of his starts as a two-year-old, a maiden at Saint-Cloud over seven furlongs and a listed race at Deauville over a mile, and he confirmed himself the leading French-trained Two Thousand Guineas contender when winning the Prix Djebel at Maisons-Laffitte on his reappearance. The Prix Djebel has been a good Guineas trial in recent times (for both Newmarket and Longchamp), with Ribchester second past the post in the 2016 renewal before finishing third at Newmarket while, before that, Style Vendome and Make Believe used the Djebel as a successful platform to Poule d'Essai des Poulains success. The last Djebel winner to follow up in the Two Thousand Guineas was Makfi in 2010, though French Fifteen came within a neck of the same feat in 2012 (beaten at Newmarket by Camelot). The most recent Prix Djebel also looked key form heading into the Guineas, with Al Wukair landing the odds against the previous year's Prix Jean-Luc Lagardere winner National Defense. Al Wukair was value for more than the length winning margin, idling after hitting the front inside the final furlong. Al Wukair was dropped out in the Djebel, but the same tactics didn't suit him in the Guineas itself and he found himself too far back to land a serious blow, finishing well in third, a length and a neck behind Churchill and Barney Roy. Al Wukair was expected to step up in trip for the Prix du Jockey Club on his next start (over a trip he was far from certain to stay), but he missed the race due to a setback and was next seen, down in grade, in the Group 3 Prix Messidor at Maisons-Laffitte. Al Wukair was beaten at odds on by the improving four-year-old Taareef, who had already upset Zelzal (also owned by Al Shaqab Racing) on his reappearance in the Prix Bertrand du Breuil.

Taareef was at shorter odds than Al Wukair when the pair re-opposed in the Prix du Haras de Fresnay-le-Buffard - Jacques le Marois at Deauville next time but it was Godolphin's Thunder Snow who was favourite in the six-runner line-up. Thunder Snow had dominated a similarly small field in the Prix Jean Prat on his previous start, matching his placed efforts in the Irish Two Thousand Guineas and St James's Palace Stakes. Thunder Snow's jockey Christophe Soumillon attempted to do the same in the Jacques le Marois and the tactics almost worked, Thunder Snow leading until the final seventy-five yards and looking the likeliest winner before first Al Wukair's stablemate Inns of Court and then Al Wukair himself struck the front, snatching the race by a short head. After his breakthrough Group 1 success, which gave his trainer Andre Fabre a record-equalling seventh win in the Jacques le Marois, Al Wukair was seen out just once more, when below form in first-time cheekpieces, on the softest ground he'd faced, when trying to become the third French-trained winner of the Queen Elizabeth II Stakes since 2014, following Charm Spirit and Solow, whose victories preceded that of Minding in 2016.

Al Wukair (IRE) (b.c. 2014)	Dream Ahead (USA) (b or br 2008)	Diktat (br 1995)	Warning
			Arvola
		Land of Dreams (b 1995)	Cadeaux Genereux
			Sahara Star
	Macheera (IRE) (b 2004)	Machiavellian (b 1987)	Mr Prospector
			Coup de Folie
		Caerlina (b 1988)	Caerleon
			Dinalina

Al Wukair is the first Group 1 winner for his sire Dream Ahead, who stood at Ballylinch Stud from 2012 until 2016 before making a timely move to Haras de Grandcamp in France ahead of the 2017 covering season. Al Wukair is the joint-fourth most expensive Dream Ahead colt to go through the sale-ring as a yearling to date, making 200,000 guineas at the Newmarket October Sales Book 1 in 2015. Al Wukair's dam Macheera won a newcomers race at Saint-Cloud over a mile as a two-year-old and is a half-sister to several winners including La Nuit Rose, who finished third in both the Poule d'Essai des Pouliches and the Irish One Thousand Guineas in 1998. Al Wukair's grandam Caerlina did even better, finishing third in the Poule d'Essai des Pouliches and winning the Prix de Diane in 1991. Though she herself is out of a Prix de Diane winner, Macheera's progeny have possessed more speed than stamina, none yet raced beyond a mile, her two previous winners being Witches Brew (by Duke of Marmalade), who won at seven furlongs and was listed placed in Ireland, and the fairly useful handicapper Ballyorban (by Cape Cross), who did his winning at six and seven furlongs. Al Wukair's year-younger brother Dream Today won the Convivial Maiden at York on his debut for Mark Johnston in the most recent season and went on to finish second in the Autumn Stakes at Newmarket behind Ghaiyyath. An attractive colt, tall and lengthy if a little finely made, Al Wukair looked in superb shape (immaculately turned out) on both his starts in Britain. He stayed a mile and acted on good to firm and good to soft going. He will stand his first season at Haras de Bouquetot at a fee of €8,000. *A. Fabre, France*

AL YARMOUK 3 b.c. Holy Roman Emperor (IRE) 125 – Disco Volante 105 (Sadler's Wells (USA) 132) [2017 77p: p8m^2 7g 9g^3 7g 6g 5.5g^6 8.5g^4 9.9g^5 Nov 30] fair form: in cheekpieces, second in maiden at Lingfield (head behind Revolutionary War) in January: left John Gosden after: stays 9f. *Jassim Mohammed Ghazali, Qatar* **76**

DFS Park Hill Stakes, Doncaster—Alyssa gives trainer Ralph Beckett a second consecutive victory in the race after Simple Verse in 2016, with a pair of three-year-olds Aljezeera (second right) and Melodic Motion (left) dead-heating for second

ALYSSA 4 b.f. Sir Percy 129 – Almiranta 63 (Galileo (IRE) 134) [2017 105: 13.9g 16.2m³ 14.5d* 12s Oct 21] angular filly: useful performer: won Park Hill Stakes at Doncaster (by ½ length from dead-heaters Aljezeera and Melodic Motion) in September: stays 2m: acts on tapeta, good to firm and good to soft going: front runner/races prominently. *Ralph Beckett* **109**

AL ZAMAN (IRE) 3 b.c. Cacique (IRE) 124 – Flowers of Spring (IRE) 112 (Celtic Swing 138) [2017 89p: t12.2g* 12.3m⁵ 11.9f⁵ 10.3s 12g² 12v⁶ t12.4g⁴ Oct 19] fairly useful performer: won maiden at Wolverhampton in April: second in handicap at Goodwood in August: stays 12.5f: acts on tapeta: in headgear last 5 starts: wears tongue tie: sometimes slowly away. *Simon Crisford* **93**

AMABILIS 3 b.f. Champs Elysees 124 – Pure Joy (Zamindar (USA) 116) [2017 92: p8g* 8g 8s* 8d Sep 29] compact filly: smart handicapper: won at Chelmsford (by 3¾ lengths from Illaunmore) in June and Ascot (by 3½ lengths from Havre de Paix) in September: stays 1m: acts on polytrack, firm and soft going: often races in rear: sent to USA. *Ralph Beckett* **112**

AMADEUS (IRE) 2 gr.c. (Feb 10) Fastnet Rock (AUS) 127 – Alegra 92 (Galileo (IRE) 134) [2017 t6g t7.1g f7.1g p7g Dec 28] poor form: bred to be suited by 1¼m+: tried in blinkers. *Richard Fahey* **41**

AMADEUS ROX (FR) 3 b.g. Falco (USA) 122 – Vittoria Vetra (Danehill Dancer (IRE) 117) [2017 55: p12f³ 12.1g⁴ 14g³ 11.8g⁵ Jul 8] fair maiden: barely stays 1¾m: acts on polytrack, best turf form on good going: tried in cheekpieces. *Alan King* **65**

AMAJARI (FR) 3 b.c. Lonhro (AUS) 128 – Angalia (IRE) (High Chaparral (IRE) 132) [2017 8.1m p12g Nov 17] well held in maidens. *Gary Moore* **–**

AMANDINE 2 b.f. (Jan 20) Shamardal (USA) 129 – Kissable (IRE) 112 (Danehill Dancer (IRE) 117) [2017 6g 6g³ p7d² Aug 16] first foal: dam, 2-y-o 7f winner, later 1½m winner in USA, out of smart sister to St Leger winner Brian Boru and to dam of Derby/Arc winner Workforce: fair form: best effort when second in minor event at Kempton (1¾ lengths behind Quargent) in August: will stay 1m: likely to progress further. *David Elsworth* **77 p**

AMANTO (GER) 7 b.g. Medicean 128 – Amore (GER) (Lando (GER) 128) [2017 72: p13g* p15.8g² p15.8g* 16m⁶ 13m² Jun 24] fairly useful handicapper: won at Lingfield in February and April: stays easy 2m: acts on polytrack and soft going: has worn headgear: in tongue tie in 2017. *Ali Stronge* **83**

AMARETTO 2 b.c. (Feb 2) Kyllachy 129 – Dan Loose Daughter (Sakhee (USA) 136) [2017 7m 7g⁶ 6d Sep 6] 32,000F, 60,000Y: good-quartered colt: second foal: half-brother to 7f winner Domitilla (by Cape Cross): dam useful Italian 1¼m winner (including at 2 yrs): modest form in minor events/maiden: type to do better in handicaps. *Jim Boyle* **56 p**

AMARONE RED (IRE) 2 ch.f. (Apr 3) Harbour Watch (IRE) 121 – Lisa's Strong (IRE) (Kalanisi (IRE) 132) [2017 6g 6.1m⁵ 7g⁶ 8.1s Sep 14] €40,000F: second foal: dam, useful Italian 9f-1½m winner, half-sister to useful 2-y-o 5f winner Faithfilly: little impact in minor events/nursery: tried in cheekpieces. *Tom Dascombe* **–**

AMAZEMENT (GER) 4 ch.g. Lope de Vega (IRE) 125 – Aglow 90 (Spinning World (USA) 130) [2017 97: p8d^3 t9.5g* t9.5g* 9.8m Apr 20] useful handicapper: won at Wolverhampton in February and March (by 1½ lengths from Bunbury): stays 9.5f: acts on tapeta and good to firm going. *James Tate* **101**

AMAZING ALICE 2 b.f. (Feb 27) Sayif (IRE) 122 – Dot Hill (Refuse To Bend (IRE) 128) [2017 5m 6d p6g^2 6.1s^5 p6s* t6.1g* p6s^2 t6.1g* p7s^3 p6d^2 6g Oct 7] 20,000Y: compact filly: fourth foal: half-sister to useful 5f (including at 2 yrs) winner Union Rose (by Stimulation): dam unraced half-sister to smart sprinter Taajub: fairly useful performer: won minor events at Chelmsford in June and Wolverhampton in July/August: second in nursery at Chelmsford in September: stays 7f: acts on polytrack and tapeta: wears cheekpieces: front runner/races prominently. *Archie Watson* **85**

AMAZING AMAYA 2 b.f. (May 12) New Approach (IRE) 132 – Faslen (USA) 92 (Fasliyev (USA) 120) [2017 6s 5d t6.1d Dec 27] 50,000Y: fifth foal: sister to 2-y-o 6f winner Star Citizen and half-sister to useful 6f-1¼m winner Don't Be (by Cape Cross) and 1m winner Samphire Coast (by Fastnet Rock): dam French 2-y-o 4.5f/5.5f winner: no form in minor events/maiden. *Derek Shaw* **–**

AMAZING GRAZING (IRE) 3 b.g. Intense Focus (USA) 117 – North Light Rose (USA) (North Light (IRE) 126) [2017 8v^3 11.2d^5 10.2v t7.1g* p7s^4 Dec 17] rather unfurnished gelding: fair performer: left Brian Ellison, won maiden at Newcastle in September on only start for David O'Meara: stays 11f: acts on tapeta and good to soft going: tried in eyeshields: often races prominently. *Richard Guest* **68**

AMAZING MICHELE (FR) 2 gr.f. (May 13) Mastercraftsman (IRE) 129 – Holy Freud (USA) (Freud (USA) 113) [2017 7g^4 8g^3 8s* 8v 8d Oct 27] €52,000Y: half-sister to several winners, including useful 2-y-o 6f winner Holy Cat (by Kitten's Joy): dam, unraced, close relative to smart US Grade 3 9f winner Wishful Tomcat: fair performer: won minor event at Haydock in September: will stay 1¼m: acts on soft going. *Richard Fahey* **74**

AMAZING RED (IRE) 4 b.g. Teofilo (IRE) 126 – Artisia (IRE) (Peintre Celebre (USA) 137) [2017 89p: t12.2g^3 12.1m^6 14g 12d* 11.9g 11.9g^2 14v^4 Sep 30] useful-looking gelding: useful handicapper: won at Newmarket (by ¾ length from Stamford Raffles) in August: placed at Wolverhampton in April and Doncaster in September: stays 1¾m: acts on tapeta and heavy going: often races towards rear. *Ed Dunlop* **99**

AMAZING ROCK (SWI) 2 ch.g. (May 19) Rock of Gibraltar (IRE) 133 – Adalawa (IRE) (Barathea (IRE) 127) [2017 7s^5 7.2m^6 t8s t8.6g^6 8.2g^4 Oct 17] modest maiden: stays 8.5f. *Mark Johnston* **61**

AMAZING STEPS (IRE) 3 b.c. Footstepsinthesand 120 – Fiordiligi (Mozart (IRE) 131) [2017 10m 11.2d^4 Jul 8] fair form in maidens: sent to Qatar. *Charlie Fellowes* **71**

AMAZOUR (IRE) 5 b.g. Azamour (IRE) 130 – Choose Me (IRE) 109 (Choisir (AUS) 126) [2017 84, a112: p6g t7.1g^4 p7g 6m^3 6m t6s 6.5g* 7s Oct 7] angular gelding: useful handicapper: won at Doncaster (by short head from Muntadab) in September: stays 1m, usually races over shorter: acts on polytrack, tapeta, firm and soft going: in cheekpieces last 2 starts: sometimes slowly away, often races towards rear. *Ismail Mohammed* **107**

AMBER FLUSH 8 b.m. Sir Harry Lewis (USA) 127 – Sari Rose (FR) (Vertical Speed (FR) 120) [2017 –: t13.9f f16g Feb 10] good-topped mare: maiden on Flat, well held in handicaps in 2017: tried in cheekpieces/tongue tie: sometimes slowly away, often races towards rear/lazily: won over hurdles in July. *Clare Ellam* **–**

AMBERINE 3 b.f. Equiano (FR) 127 – Crimson Fern (IRE) 104 (Titus Livius (FR) 115) [2017 –: 5.7m^6 5.7d Aug 19] little sign of ability. *Malcolm Saunders* **–**

AMBER MISCHIEF 3 ch.f. Mayson 124 – Grand Lucre 73 (Grand Slam (USA) 120) [2017 p6f 7v Sep 25] sixth foal: half-sister to a winner in Hong Kong by Kyllachy: dam 7f winner: no form. *Adam West* **–**

AMBER MORNING 3 b.f. Nathaniel (IRE) 129 – Amber Queen (IRE) 92 (Cadeaux Genereux 131) [2017 10s p12d p12g Jul 5] tall filly: fifth foal: half-sister to 9f/1¼m winner (stayed 1½m) Diddy Eric (by Oratorio) and useful winner up to 1¼m Mountain Rescue (2-y-o 6f winner, by High Chaparral): dam, 7f winner, half-sister to smart winner up to 1m Spinning Queen: well held in maidens. *Roger Charlton* **–**

AMBER MYSTIQUE 4 ch.f. Sakhee (USA) 136 – Dame de Noche 102 (Lion Cavern (USA) 117) [2017 74: t8.6g^6 t8g^2 t9.5m^2 7d^3 8m 10.2d^3 10s Jul 11] quite well-made filly: fairly useful handicapper: placed 4 times in 2017: trained by Richard Fahey second/third starts: stays 9.5f: acts on polytrack, tapeta and good to soft going: sold £8,000 in August, sent to Greece. *Kristin Stubbs* **80**

AMBIENT (IRE) 2 b.g. (Apr 2) Born To Sea (IRE) 117 – Undulant Way 83 (Hurricane Run (IRE) 134) [2017 7.6s^2 7d^5 t7.1s^2 Nov 30] good-topped gelding: fair form: best effort when second in minor event at Newcastle (neck behind Strange Society) in November: bred to stay 1m. *Roger Varian* **79**

AMBITIOUS BOY 8 bl.g. Striking Ambition 122 – Cherished Love (IRE) (Tomba 119) [2017 60, a66: t5.1m^6 t6f^6 t6m t6.1g^4 5.7m 5.7s^6 t6.1m^6 t6.1g Dec 13] modest handicapper nowadays: stays 7f: acts on polytrack, tapeta and good to firm going: has worn cheekpieces, including often in 2017: sometimes slowly away, held up. *John O'Shea* **51**

AMBITIOUS ICARUS 8 b.g. Striking Ambition 122 – Nesting Box (Grand Lodge (USA) 125) [2017 82: t5g* t6g^4 t5d^4 6m^5 5.1m 5m^5 6s^3 5d 6.1m^6 5.5f^2 p7s 6g^2 t5g* 6s^3 5g^3 5g^4 t5g^3 t5d^3 5.7s^3 5g^4 t5g^5 6v^3 Nov 7] tall, leggy gelding: fair handicapper nowadays: won at Newcastle in March and July: stays 6f: acts on all-weather, good to firm and heavy going: wears headgear: sometimes slowly away, usually races towards rear. *Richard Guest* **72**

AMBITIOUS ROSIE 6 b.m. Striking Ambition 122 – Cerulean Rose 78 (Bluegrass Prince (IRE) 110) [2017 38: f12s p11d p10d Feb 23] maiden: no form in 2017: has worn headgear, including final start. *Tony Carroll* **–**

AMBROSIA 3 b.f. Frankel 147 – Pearling (USA) (Storm Cat (USA)) [2017 68p: 8g^2 p8g^2 8v^2 7s^3 t8s* Nov 30] fair performer: won maiden at Newcastle in November: left Roger Varian after fourth start: stays 1m: acts on tapeta, good to firm and heavy going: in headgear last 3 starts. *Roger Charlton* **74**

AMBUSCADE 4 b.f. Dick Turpin (IRE) 127 – Tarqua (IRE) (King Charlemagne (USA) 120) [2017 43: p7g p10s f11.1g Dec 29] little form. *Neil Mulholland* **–**

AMEDEO MODIGLIANI (IRE) 2 b.c. (Apr 8) Galileo (IRE) 134 – Gooseberry Fool 96 (Danehill Dancer (IRE) 117) [2017 7g^3 8.3v* Aug 5] 750,000Y: first foal: dam, 2-y-o 7f winner, closely related to Poule d'Essai des Poulains winner Aussie Rules out of very smart winner up to 1¼m Last Second: useful form: 2/9, confirmed debut promise when won maiden at Galway impressively by 5½ lengths from Crecerelle, quickening to lead final 1f: bred to stay 1¼m+: exciting prospect. *Aidan O'Brien, Ireland* **98 p**

AMELIA DREAM 3 ch.f. Kyllachy 129 – Lady Scarlett (Woodman (USA) 126) [2017 70: 8m 9.9f^4 9.9m^4 11.6d^3 p12g^5 11.8g* 12v^2 14.4s^4 11.6d^3 13.4g^3 14s 14.4v p12g Oct 13] rather unfurnished filly: fair handicapper: won at Leicester in July: stays 14.5f: acts on any turf going. *Mick Channon* **79**

AMENHOTEPTHETHIRD 2 b.c. (Jan 27) Motivator 131 – Autumn Wealth (IRE) 108 (Cadeaux Genereux 131) [2017 7m 8d 9.9s 8s p8g Dec 20] no form in minor events/maiden. *Mark Gillard* **–**

AMENTA (IRE) 3 b.f. Roderic O'Connor (IRE) 119 – Pale Light (USA) (Lemon Drop Kid (USA) 131) [2017 53: 7.1s^2 p7d^4 p6g^5 p8g Dec 30] modest maiden: left Roger Charlton after second start: best effort at 7f: acts on soft going: in tongue tie last 2 starts. *John Berry* **63**

AMERICAN CRAFTSMAN (IRE) 3 gr.g. Mastercraftsman (IRE) 129 – Quiet Mouse (USA) (Quiet American (USA)) [2017 –: 8m^3 8g^6 9.9g^5 12.1m* 11.6d^5 12g^5 12.5m^6 Sep 8] fair handicapper: won at Beverley in May: left Roger Fell after fifth start: stays 1½m: acts on good to firm going: often wears cheekpieces: won over hurdles in October. *Jedd O'Keeffe* **67**

AMERICAN ENDEAVOUR (USA) 2 ch.f. (Feb 3) Distorted Humor (USA) 117 – Crazy Party (USA) (A P Indy (USA) 131) [2017 p7g p7g^3 t7.2g* Dec 5] $70,000Y, $125,000 2-y-o: second foal: dam, US 2-y-o 8.5f winner, out of half-sister to high-class US Grade 1 9f winner Dare And Go: fair form: won minor event at Wolverhampton (by neck from Lady Noorah) in December: raced only at 7f. *Marco Botti* **72**

AMERICAN HISTORY (USA) 3 b.g. High Chaparral (IRE) 132 – Spinning Time (USA) (Giant's Causeway (USA) 132) [2017 77: p10g^2 11.9d^2 12d^5 9.9d* p12g^6 11.8s p10g Nov 2] close-coupled gelding: fair handicapper: won at Brighton in August: left John Gosden after first start: stays 1½m: acts on polytrack and good to soft going: wears headgear: front runner/races prominently: temperament under suspicion. *William Muir* **78**

AMERICAN HUSTLE (IRE) 5 b.m. Jeremy (USA) 122 – Love In May (IRE) 80 (City On A Hill (USA) 114) [2017 70: 7.6s^6 7f 9.9f t8s^3 t8g^3 p12g^6 Dec 6] big, strong mare: fair maiden: left Brian Ellison after fifth start: stays 1m: acts on tapeta and soft going: has worn headgear, including in 2017: tried in tongue tie. *Mark Fahey, Ireland* **65**

AMERICAN PATRIOT (USA) 4 b.c. War Front (USA) 119 – Life Well Lived (USA) (Tiznow (USA) 133) [2017 8.5f* 8f* 8f 8d^6 8f Oct 7] well-made colt: second foal: half-brother to smart winner up to 11f Muqtaser (2-y-o 1m winner, by Distorted Humor): dam, **116**

US 8.5f winner, sister to Dubai World Cup winner Well Armed: smart performer: won optional claimer at Gulfstream in February and Maker's Mile Stakes at Keeneland (by neck from Heart To Heart) in April: below form after, including in Queen Anne Stakes at Royal Ascot: stayed 1¼m: acted on firm going: wore blinkers: to stand at Darley Stud in Japan, fee ¥1,500,000. *Todd A. Pletcher, USA*

AMERICAN PATROL (IRE) 3 ch.g. Rio de La Plata (USA) 121 – Gutter Press (IRE) 51 (Raise A Grand (IRE) 114) [2017 55: t7.1m* p8g 12d f8.1g f8.1g Nov 28] well-made gelding: modest handicapper: won at Wolverhampton in January: stays 7f: acts on tapeta. *Neil Mulholland* **63**

AMERICAN RUBY (USA) 2 b.f. (Apr 13) Data Link (USA) 121 – Fifth Avenue Doll (USA) (Marquetry (USA) 121) [2017 7.4g^{6} 7.2d 8g^{5} t7.1g Sep 12] 23,000Y: half-sister to several winners, including very smart 9.5f-14.6f (St Leger) winner Arctic Cosmos (by North Light) and 7f winner (stayed 11f) Street Duel (by Street Cry): dam US 5.5f-8.5f (including at 2 yrs) winner: no form: left Mark Johnston after third start. *Roger Fell* **–**

AMHERST ROCK 3 ch.g. Exceed And Excel (AUS) 126 – Frigid (Indian Ridge 123) [2017 –: t7.2g 6v Nov 7] little form: in tongue tie last 2 starts: often races freely. *Luke McJannet* **–**

AMIIRAH 2 b.f. (Mar 10) Helmet (AUS) 127 – Aalya (IRE) 65 (Peintre Celebre (USA) 137) [2017 5m p6d 7g p8g t9.5g Nov 20] well-grown filly: fourth foal: half-sister to 7f-1½m winner Play Nicely (by Naaqoos) and a winner in Qatar by Kheleyf: dam maiden (stayed 1¾m): no form: tried in blinkers. *John Gallagher* **–**

AMITIE WALTZ (FR) 5 b.g. Sinndar (IRE) 134 – Lia Waltz (FR) (Linamix (FR) 127) [2017 t9.5g^{5} f8g^{2} Apr 18] placed in bumper/novice hurdle for Dan Skelton: fairly useful form when second in maiden at Southwell (short head behind Passcode) on second of 2 starts on Flat. *Richard Hughes* **82**

AMITY ISLAND 2 ch.c. (Mar 9) Harbour Watch (IRE) 121 – Mylington Light (Mount Nelson 125) [2017 t7.1g f7.1g^{3} f7.1g^{3} Nov 28] modest form: best effort when third in claimer at Southwell (7½ lengths behind Powerful Society) in November: likely to stay 1m. *Ollie Pears* **54**

AMLAD (IRE) 3 ch.g. Lope de Vega (IRE) 125 – Pietra Dura 96 (Cadeaux Genereux 131) [2017 83: p10g^{3} 9.9m* 12g* 11.4m^{2} 12v 12g^{4} t12.4g^{2} 12g Sep 28] sturdy gelding: useful performer: won maiden at Beverley in April and handicap at Newmarket in June: second in handicaps at Windsor in July and Newcastle in September: stays 12.5f: acts on polytrack, tapeta and good to firm going. *Ed Dunlop* **97**

A MOMENTOFMADNESS 4 b.g. Elnadim (USA) 128 – Royal Blush 68 (Royal Applause 124) [2017 94: p5g* 5f^{2} 5m^{4} p5s^{3} 5g^{3} 5g^{2} 5.4d^{4} 5.6g^{6} 5s^{5} Oct 7] strong gelding: useful handicapper: won at Kempton in April: in frame next 6 starts: stays 6f: acts on polytrack, firm and soft going: often wears hood: front runner/races prominently: consistent. *Charles Hills* **104**

AMONG ANGELS 5 b.g. Acclamation 118 – Love Action (IRE) 80 (Motivator 131) [2017 84: f7g^{5} f6g^{2} f6g t6d^{5} f7m* f8m f6g f7g^{3} 6m p7d p7s Jun 14] good-quartered gelding: fairly useful handicapper: won at Southwell (by length from Vroom) in February: below form after: stays 7f: acts on fibresand, tapeta and soft going: usually wears headgear: signs of temperament. *Daniel Loughnane* **84**

AMOOD (IRE) 6 ch.g. Elnadim (USA) 128 – Amanah (USA) 100 (Mr Prospector (USA)) [2017 85: t7.1d t7.1s 8m 7g t7.1s^{3} 6s^{3} 6m^{5} t8g^{2} 7.4f t7.1g^{4} 6g^{2} 7.1g^{3} 6g^{3} 6v Oct 4] fairly useful handicapper: second at Newcastle in June: left Simon West after eleventh start: has form at 1¼m, races over shorter nowadays: acts on polytrack, tapeta, good to firm and good to soft going: usually wears headgear: has worn tongue tie: not one to rely on. *Archie Watson* **77 §** **a90 §**

AMOR INVICTO (IRE) 4 b.g. Holy Roman Emperor (IRE) 125 – Love In The Mist (USA) 69 (Silver Hawk (USA) 123) [2017 69: t8.6m^{5} t9.5g Jan 26] good-topped gelding: fair maiden: stays 8.5f: acts on polytrack and tapeta: in blinkers last 4 starts: sent to Denmark. *Daniel Kubler* **65**

AMOURICE (IRE) 2 b.f. (Mar 30) Authorized (IRE) 133 – Amancaya (GER) (Dai Jin 123) [2017 6g^{4} 6g 7d^{2} 7d^{2} Aug 19] €18,000Y: well-made filly: third foal: half-sister to Danish 9f winner French Warrior (by Soldier of Fortune): dam, German 11f winner, half-sister to smart stayer Askar Tau: fairly useful form: second in nursery at Newmarket in August: best effort at 7f: in hood last 2 starts: awkward ride. *Jane Chapple-Hyam* **85**

AMPLIFICATION (USA) 2 b.g. (Apr 22) Lonhro (AUS) 128 – Our Drama Queen (IRE) 76 (Danehill Dancer (IRE) 117) [2017 7g^{3} 7d* Oct 27] $17,000Y, £210,000 2-y-o: third foal: half-brother to 2-y-o 8.6f winner More Drama (by Thewayyouare): dam, 7f **80 p**

winner, half-sister to St Leger/Gold Cup winner Leading Light: fairly useful form: won maiden at Doncaster (by short head from Epic Fantasy) in October: will stay at least 1m: likely to progress further. *Ed Dunlop*

AMY BLAIR 4 b.g. Captain Gerrard (IRE) 113 – Shalad'or 97 (Golden Heights 82) [2017 64: f7g 8.3m^5 8.3m^2 8g 9.2g* 8.3s^4 8.3g* 10.3g 9.2g* 8.3s 9.2s Aug 24] fair handicapper: won at Hamilton in June and twice in July: stays 9f: acts on good to firm and heavy going: wears hood: front runner. *Keith Dalgleish* **79**

ANAAKEED 2 ch.f. (Feb 20) Dubawi (IRE) 129 – Daymooma 104 (Pivotal 124) [2017 8d^5 Oct 24] first foal: dam 9f/1¼m winner: 7/1, fifth in minor event at Yarmouth in October: open to improvement. *Owen Burrows* **60 p**

ANASTAZIA 5 br.m. Kyllachy 129 – Meddle (Diktat 126) [2017 78: p7g^2 8m* 8m^4 8m^4 7d^3 9.1g^4 7g^5 p7g 8g p8g^3 f8.1g^6 Nov 16] fair handicapper: won at Yarmouth in May: stays 8.5f: acts on polytrack, tapeta, soft and good to firm going: has worn headgear, including in 2017. *Paul D'Arcy* **75**

ANCIENT ASTRONAUT 4 b.g. Kodiac 112 – Tatora (Selkirk (USA) 129) [2017 80: 6g* 6s^2 6m 6.1g^3 7s^3 6d^6 t5g Oct 10] rather leggy gelding: fairly useful handicapper: won at Thirsk in April: placed at Newmarket (apprentice) in May and Nottingham in July: stays 6f: acts on heavy going: wears headgear: sold 6,500 gns in November. *John Quinn* **84**

ANCIENT FOE 3 b.g. Shamardal (USA) 129 – Pearl Dance (USA) 102 (Nureyev (USA) 131) [2017 7.6d^6 p8s^3 p8s^4 Aug 9] brother to useful 1m winner Born In Bombay (later successful in Hong Kong) and half-brother to several winners, including smart French winner up to 1¼m Sparkling Beam (2-y-o 1m winner, by Nayef): dam 2-y-o 6f winner who stayed 1m: fairly useful form: best effort when third in maiden at Chelmsford (1½ lengths behind High End) in July. *Andrew Balding* **81**

ANCIENT LONGING 3 b.f. Nathaniel (IRE) 129 – Longing To Dance 98 (Danehill Dancer (IRE) 117) [2017 9.9s^5 12d^4 9.9d^4 9.9d Sep 20] fifth foal: closely related to smart 1m-1¼m winner Be My Gal (by Galileo) and half-sister to 6f/7f winner Foreign Diplomat (by Oasis Dream): dam, maiden (should have stayed 7f), half-sister to dam of high-class performer up to 1m Dutch Art: fair form: barely stays 1½m. *Roger Charlton* **76**

ANDALUSITE 4 br.f. Equiano (FR) 127 – Kammaan 85 (Diktat 126) [2017 66: p5g^5 p6g 5.3g^3 8m* 8f^4 p8s^2 7d 7d* 7d^3 7m^3 7m 8d* p8g p8g Oct 18] fair performer: won minor event in April and handicaps in July and September, all at Brighton: stays 1m: acts on polytrack, good to firm and good to soft going: wears headgear: front runner/races prominently. *John Gallagher* **72 a65**

ANDANOTHERONE (IRE) 4 b.f. Kodiac 112 – Itsanothergirl 77 (Reprimand 122) [2017 68: p7g^5 t8.6g^5 p8g^3 Feb 28] modest maiden: stays 1m: acts on polytrack and good to soft going. *Denis Quinn* **61**

ANDASTRA (GER) 4 b.f. Kamsin (GER) 124 – Arpista (GER) (Chief Singer 131) [2017 t8.6g^4 t9.5g Mar 18] fairly useful form: better effort in 2017 when fourth in minor event at Wolverhampton (3½ lengths behind Third Time Lucky) in February: stays 8.5f: sent to France. *Ralph Beckett* **92**

ANDOK (IRE) 3 b.g. Elzaam (AUS) 115 – My Causeway Dream (IRE) 62 (Giant's Causeway (USA) 132) [2017 92: 8m^5 10s 8d^5 8v^3 10v^3 10m^4 10.2d t10.2g^2 t9.5d^2 Dec 16] rather leggy gelding: fairly useful handicapper: second at Newcastle in November and Wolverhampton in December: stays 1¼m: acts on tapeta, good to firm and heavy going. *Richard Fahey* **91**

ANDRASSY AVENUE (USA) 3 b.g. Street Cry (IRE) 130 – Suez 109 (Green Desert (USA) 127) [2017 83p: p11g^5 Apr 12] fairly useful form: in blinkers, fifth in handicap at Kempton on sole outing in 2017: stayed 11f: dead. *Charlie Appleby* **80**

ANDYS GIRL (IRE) 4 gr.f. Clodovil (IRE) 116 – Fishy (Irish River (FR) 131) [2017 66: t6g^4 t6d^4 Nov 4] modest maiden: stays 6f: acts on tapeta: often races towards rear. *Brian Ellison* **64**

ANEEDH 7 b.g. Lucky Story (USA) 128 – Seed Al Maha (USA) (Seeking The Gold (USA)) [2017 67, a60: 14v^3 12.1m^6 13.9v t12.4d Dec 16] attractive gelding: fair handicapper, well below form in 2017: stays 14.5f, effective at much shorter: acts on polytrack, good to firm and good to soft going: wears headgear. *Clive Mulhall* **46**

ANFAASS (IRE) 3 ro.c. Vale of York (IRE) 117 – Webcast (IRE) 77 (Verglas (IRE) 118) [2017 84: 7m 7g 7s^5 6g^3 7m 6.1m p6g Nov 2] lengthy colt: fair handicapper: stays 6f: acts on polytrack and good to firm going: tried in cheekpieces. *George Margarson* **78**

AN FEAR CIUIN (IRE) 6 b.g. Galileo (IRE) 134 – Potion 98 (Pivotal 124) [2017 86: f12g^{6} f16g^{6} 16m Jun 17] fairly useful handicapper, well below best in 2017: left Richard Ford after second start: wears headgear: front runner/races prominently: fair hurdler. *R. Mike Smith* **–**

ANGEL CARLOTTA (IRE) 2 b.f. (May 5) Camelot 128 – Stravina (GER) (Platini (GER) 126) [2017 7g 7g Oct 14] €80,000Y: half-sister to several winners abroad, including useful German 1m winners Scoville (by Sholokhov) and Skagen (by Dashing Blade): dam German 1m/8.5f winner: well held in maiden/minor event. *Nigel Tinkler* **–**

ANGEL DOWN 3 b.g. Kyllachy 129 – Falling Angel 86 (Kylian (USA)) [2017 82: p7g^{6} p7d 7d* 8d^{3} 8.1m* 8g Sep 15] fairly useful handicapper: won at Newmarket (by ½ length from Patchwork) in June and Windsor (by 2 lengths from Repercussion) in August: stays 1m: acts on polytrack, good to firm and good to soft going: sold 22,000 gns in November. *Henry Candy* **91**

ANGEL FORCE (IRE) 2 ch.f. (Feb 20) Lethal Force (IRE) 128 – Indian Angel (Indian Ridge 123) [2017 5m 5m^{4} 5m^{5} 6m^{6} 6m^{4} 5g* 5d^{2} 5m^{5} 5.1v^{5} 5m Oct 13] €19,000F, £33,000Y: fourth foal: dam unraced half-sister to useful 5f winner Verne Castle out of Nunthorpe Stakes winner Lochangel: fairly useful performer: won nursery at York in July: best form at 5f: acts on good to firm and good to soft going: wears hood: front runner/races prominently. *David C. Griffiths* **86**

ANGEL GABRIAL (IRE) 8 b.g. Hurricane Run (IRE) 134 – Causeway Song (USA) (Giant's Causeway (USA) 132) [2017 107: 14g^{4} 18.6m 14g^{6} 14g 15.9d^{5} 16.1f^{2} 16.3g^{2} 16d^{5} 15.9g^{3} 14.4v^{3} 16.3g Oct 14] good-topped gelding: useful handicapper: stays 2¼m: acts on polytrack, firm and good to soft going. *Richard Fahey* **99**

ANGELICAL EVE (IRE) 3 gr.f. Dark Angel (IRE) 113 – First Lady (IRE) (Indian Ridge 123) [2017 –: p6g^{6} 7.1g 6s p7g^{5} p7g Oct 25] no form: in cheekpieces last 2 starts. *George Baker* **–**

ANGELICAL (IRE) 4 b.f. Dark Angel (IRE) 113 – Ladylishandra (IRE) 82 (Mujadil (USA) 119) [2017 68: 10g* 10d^{3} 11.8d^{4} 10.2d^{4} 10d^{3} 10d^{4} 11.5m^{4} 10g^{2} 10.5v Sep 29] fair handicapper: won at Leicester in April: stays 1¼m: acts on soft and good to firm going: has worn cheekpieces, including in 2017. *Daniel Loughnane* **68**

ANGELIC LORD (IRE) 5 b.g. Dark Angel (IRE) 113 – Divine Design (IRE) 77 (Barathea (IRE) 127) [2017 102: t7.1g p7g^{6} Mar 3] rangy, attractive gelding: smart performer at best: stayed 7f: acted on good to firm and good to soft going: tried in headgear: dead. *Tom Dascombe* **94**

ANGELINA D'OR (GER) 2 ch.f. (Mar 18) Casamento (IRE) 118 – Ange Doree (FR) (Sinyar (IRE)) [2017 t8.6g^{4} t8g^{2} p8s^{3} Dec 15] 4,500Y: third foal: half-sister to 2m winner Golden Jeffrey (by Soldier Hollow): dam Swiss 1m-1½m winner: fair form when in frame in minor events/maiden: will stay 9f+: remains with potential. *Mark Johnston* **78 p**

ANGEL IN DISGUISE (IRE) 3 b.f. Vale of York (IRE) 117 – Meynell 78 (Sakhee (USA) 136) [2017 47: 8.3g May 12] little form. *Philip McBride* **–**

ANGEL IN THE SNOW 4 ch.g. Haafhd 129 – Chilly Filly (IRE) 99 (Montjeu (IRE) 137) [2017 62: 14m^{6} 12.1s^{2} 15.9v^{5} t12.4g^{3} t12.4d^{2} t12.2m^{3} p16s^{6} t14d Dec 27] modest maiden: stays 12.5f: acts on tapeta and soft going: tried in cheekpieces. *Brian Ellison* **58**

ANGEL ISLINGTON (IRE) 2 gr.f. (Feb 3) Dark Angel (IRE) 113 – Doregan (IRE) (Bahhare (USA) 122) [2017 6.1m^{5} 6.1d^{4} p6d^{2} 6.1s^{3} Aug 6] €60,000F, 65,000 2-y-o: half-sister to several winners, including 2-y-o 7f winners Mocenigo (by Refuse To Bend), later successful in Hong Kong, and First Up (by Rip Van Winkle), stays 1¼m: dam, Italian 1½m winner, also successful over hurdles: fair form: raced only at 6f. *Andrew Balding* **76**

ANGELITO 8 ch.g. Primo Valentino (IRE) 116 – Supreme Angel 85 (Beveled (USA)) [2017 65: t6g 5.7d 5.7f^{3} 5.7s^{3} Sep 17] sturdy gelding: modest handicapper nowadays: stays 6f: acts on polytrack, firm and soft going: usually slowly away, often races in rear: signs of temperament. *Tony Newcombe* **58**

ANGEL MEADOW 3 b.f. Mayson 124 – Memo (Groom Dancer (USA) 128) [2017 85: 5s 6d^{5} 6g 6s^{6} Aug 9] fairly useful handicapper: stays 6f: acts on soft going: tried in hood. *Micky Hammond* **81**

ANGEL OF DARKNESS 3 b.f. Dark Angel (IRE) 113 – Chelsea Morning (USA) 80 (Giant's Causeway (USA) 132) [2017 67: p7g^{2} p6g* p7g^{2} 6g* 7m^{2} 6m^{4} 6d 6.1m^{2} 7d^{3} 6s^{6} Sep 16] fairly useful handicapper: won at Lingfield in April and Goodwood in June: placed on 5 other occasions: stays 7f: acts on polytrack, good to firm and good to soft going. *Charles Hills* **91**

ANGEL OF LIGHT (IRE) 5 b.m. Dark Angel (IRE) 113 – Riymaisa (IRE) (Traditionally –
(USA) 117) [2017 –: f8g Jan 5] maiden: well held in handicap sole start in 2017. *Jo Hughes*

ANGEL OF ROME (IRE) 3 gr.f. Mastercraftsman (IRE) 129 – Bright Sapphire (IRE) **71**
55 (Galileo (IRE) 134) [2017 64: t8.6g^3 p8g p12g^6 11.4m 10v^6 Aug 3] fair maiden: best effort at 8.5f: acts on tapeta: tried in blinkers. *Richard Hughes*

ANGEL OF THE SOUTH (IRE) 2 gr.f. (Mar 2) Dark Angel (IRE) 113 – Oeuvre d'Art **79**
(IRE) 100 (Marju (IRE) 127) [2017 5m^2 5m 6.1m^2 6.1m^3 7m 6d 6d p5s^2 t6.1d* Dec 27] £170,000Y: good-quartered filly: second foal: half-sister to 7f winner Dark Destroyer (by Helmet): dam, Italian winner up to 7.5f (2-y-o 6f winner), stayed 11f: fair performer: won minor event at Wolverhampton in December: stays 6f: acts on tapeta and good to firm going: sometimes slowly away. *Dean Ivory*

ANGELOU 3 b.f. Poet's Voice 126 – Quiz Show 82 (Primo Dominie 121) [2017 t6d^6 5g^5 **43**
Jul 18] 36,000Y: half-sister to several winners, including Scandinavian winner up to 1m Better Built (2-y-o 6f winner, by Xaar) and 2-y-o 5f winner Right Answer (by Lujain), both useful: dam, 7f winner, half-sister to very smart sprinter Mind Games: poor form in 2 maidens. *David O'Meara*

ANGEL PALANAS 3 b.g. Mayson 124 – Scottish Exile (IRE) 75 (Ashkalani (IRE) 128) **67**
[2017 68: 6.1d 5d^3 6g 5g^4 5g^3 5d^2 t5s^4 5v^3 5g^4 5s^2 f5g Dec 19] compact gelding: fair maiden: stays 6f: acts on tapeta and soft going: wears cheekpieces. *K. R. Burke*

ANGEL'S ACCLAIM (IRE) 3 gr.f. Dark Angel (IRE) 113 – Miss Otis 78 (Danetime **78**
(IRE) 121) [2017 58p: t5s^4 6g^4 7.2s^4 t7.1d* Aug 10] fair performer: won handicap at Newcastle in August: stays 7f: acts on tapeta and soft going: tried in cheekpieces: often races towards rear. *Kevin Ryan*

ANGEL'S GLORY 2 b.f. (Mar 1) Invincible Spirit (IRE) 121 – Dutch Diamond 83 **78**
(Dutch Art 126) [2017 6v^3 7m^4 Oct 13] 115,000F, 300,000Y: compact filly: second foal: half-sister to 6f winner Edged In Blue (by Acclamation): dam, 8.6f winner, half-sister to very smart 6f-1m winner Toylsome: fair form when in frame in maidens at Haydock and Newmarket. *Roger Varian*

ANGEL'S QUEST (FR) 3 b.f. Dark Angel (IRE) 113 – Lilac Charm (IRE) (Marju (IRE) **83**
127) [2017 76p: 9.9m^5 t7.2g^3 8m^2 8.1m^5 8g 6.1m* Aug 13] fairly useful performer: won maiden at Windsor in August: second in handicap at Newmarket in June: stays 1m: acts on tapeta and good to firm going: usually races close up. *Richard Hughes*

ANGEL'S WHISPER (IRE) 2 gr.f. (Apr 25) Dark Angel (IRE) 113 – Tasheyaat 86 **69**
(Sakhee (USA) 136) [2017 6.1m^2 5s p6g^4 Oct 12] €38,000F, €57,000Y, £85,000 2-y-o: third foal: dam, 1¼m winner, out of half-sister to 2000 Guineas/Champion Stakes winner Haafhd: fair form when second at Windsor (2¼ lengths behind Lamya) on first of 3 starts in minor events. *Jeremy Noseda*

ANGIE B (IRE) 2 b.f. (Feb 5) Acclamation 118 – Musical Peace (IRE) 80 (Oratorio (IRE) **45**
128) [2017 6d 7m 6d^4 6d^3 t7.1g 6g Sep 27] €26,000F, 3,000 2-y-o: first foal: dam, 9.5f winner, half-sister to very smart 1¼m-1¾m winner Pugin: poor maiden: tried in cheekpieces. *John Wainwright*

ANGINOLA (IRE) 8 b.m. Kodiac 112 – Lady Montekin (Montekin 125) [2017 48: 11.2v –
Sep 18] angular mare: modest handicapper, well held sole outing on Flat in 2017: stays 1½m: acts on polytrack, good to firm and heavy going: wears headgear: winning hurdler. *Julia Brooke*

ANGRYWHITEPYJAMAS (IRE) 4 b.g. Manduro (GER) 135 – Ornellaia (IRE) 56 **89**
(Mujadil (USA) 119) [2017 79: p10s* 10g^5 t12.2g^6 10.2d 10d Oct 23] lengthy gelding: fairly useful handicapper: won at Chelmsford (by 4½ lengths from Classic Villager) in June: stays 1¼m: acts on polytrack and tapeta: front runner/races prominently. *William Muir*

ANIERES BOY 5 b.g. Kheleyf (USA) 116 – Place Morny (IRE) (Cadeaux Genereux 131) –
[2017 64: f6g Jan 2] modest handicapper, well held sole start in 2017: stays 6f: acts on polytrack and good to firm going: tried in headgear/tongue tie: often starts slowly. *Oliver Greenall*

ANIF (IRE) 3 b.g. Cape Cross (IRE) 129 – Cadenza (FR) (Dansili 127) [2017 8m^5 8d* 8m^3 **82**
8.3g p8s^5 Dec 17] fourth foal: half-brother to French/Spanish 7.5f-10.5f winner Mungamis (by Medicean) and French 11.5f winner Ladheeda (by Halling): dam once-raced half-sister to smart winner up to 1½m Kandidate: fairly useful performer: won maiden at Ripon (by 1¼ lengths from Liquid Gold) in June: left Charles Hills after fourth start: stays 1m: acts on good to soft going: tried in tongue tie. *Jean-Rene Auvray*

ANNABELLA 4 b.f. Approve (IRE) 112 – Ashlinn (IRE) 86 (Ashkalani (IRE) 128) [2017 **41**
–: p7m p7g p8g p8s p8g^5 Dec 28] poor maiden. *Tim McCarthy*

ANNA BRIGGS 2 b.f. (Feb 16) Havana Gold (IRE) 118 – Netta (IRE) 86 (Barathea (IRE) 127) [2017 p6d 6.1g Jul 24] 8,500Y: lengthy, rather unfurnished filly: third foal: half-sister to 5f winner Naivasha (by Captain Gerrard): dam, 7f winner, sister to useful winner up to 1¾m Pepperwood: little impact in minor events. *Michael Blanshard* –

ANNA MEDICI 3 b.f. Sir Percy 129 – Florentia 75 (Medicean 128) [2017 t6g p6d^{6} t7.1g t8.6g^{3} p7s* 7m* t7.2g* p8g^{4} t8d^{5} p8s* f8.1g^{2} p10g^{4} Dec 21] third foal: sister to 2-y-o 6f-7.5f winner Flora Medici and half-sister to useful winner up to 1¼m Cote d'Azur (2-y-o 7f winner, by Champs Elysees): dam, 1m-9.7f winner, half-sister to useful winner up to 7f Flying Officer: fair handicapper: won at Chelmsford (apprentice) in July, Yarmouth/ Wolverhampton (apprentice) in August and Chelmsford again in November: left Sir Mark Prescott Bt after eleventh start: will probably stay further than 1¼m: acts on all-weather and good to firm going: in cheekpieces last 3 starts. *Mike Murphy* 77

ANNA NERIUM 2 ch.f. (Apr 17) Dubawi (IRE) 129 – Anna Oleanda (IRE) (Old Vic 136) [2017 6.5g^{6} 6g^{3} 7d* 6g* 7m Oct 13] close-coupled filly: sister to smart 2-y-o 6f/7f winner Piping Rock and useful 1m winner Alkawn and half-sister to several winners, including useful winner up to 9.5f Middle Club (2-y-o 7f/1m winner, by Fantastic Light): dam German 1¼m/10.5f winner: useful performer: won minor event at Newmarket in July and Dick Poole Fillies' Stakes at Salisbury (by neck from Eirene) in September: stays 7f: acts on good to soft going. *Richard Hannon* 97

ANNA'S LEGACY 4 b.f. Shirocco (GER) 129 – Gargoyle Girl 75 (Be My Chief (USA) 122) [2017 10d^{6} 12g 9.2s^{5} 12.1v Sep 5] sixth foal: half-sister to 1¾m winner Lady Gargoyle (by Lucky Story) and 13f/14.6f winner Braes of Lochalsh (by Tiger Hill): dam, 11f-2m winner, also won over hurdles/fences: no form: tried in hood. *Jim Goldie* –

ANNE'S VALENTINO 7 b.m. Primo Valentino (IRE) 116 – Annie's Gift (IRE) (Presenting 120) [2017 15.9s Oct 10] fair at best, well held (after long absence) sole outing in 2017: stays 16.5f: acts on good to firm and heavy going. *Rebecca Menzies* –

ANNIE FIOR (IRE) 3 ch.f. Finsceal Fior (IRE) – Annamanamoux (USA) (Leroidesanimaux (BRZ) 127) [2017 79p: p7f p8g^{6} t8.6g 10g^{4} 10.2d^{3} 8v p7g^{4} p5g Oct 20] fairly useful handicapper: third at Bath in August: left Denis Coakley after fifth start: stays 1¼m: acts on polytrack and good to soft going: has worn hood, including in 2017: often races freely. *Thomas P. O'Connor, Ireland* 86

ANNIE SALTS 4 b.f. Zebedee 113 – Dazzling View (USA) (Distant View (USA) 126) [2017 69: p5m^{2} t5.1g* p5g^{5} t5.1g^{4} f5d t5.1g* 5g^{6} 5m^{4} 5.2m* 5.2d^{3} p5g^{3} p5g^{5} t5.1g p5m^{3} Nov 25] compact filly: fair handicapper: won at Wolverhampton in February/April and Yarmouth in August: raced mainly at 5f: acts on polytrack, tapeta and good to firm going: wears hood: tried in tongue tie. *Chris Dwyer* 78

ANNOUSHKA 4 b.f. Proclamation (IRE) 130 – Anapola (GER) (Polish Precedent (USA) 131) [2017 64: 8.1m 8m 11.8g^{2} 11.5m 12.1d^{4} 11.5g Oct 16] modest maiden: stays 1½m: acts on good to soft going: often in headgear/tongue tie: usually leads/races freely. *Mrs Ilka Gansera-Leveque* 58

ANN WITHOUT AN E 2 b.f. (Mar 24) Rip Van Winkle (IRE) 134 – Visanilla (FR) 107 (Danehill (USA) 126) [2017 7v^{3} 7d^{5} 8g^{6} 6.9v^{4} 7s^{6} Oct 15] neat filly: half-sister to French 8.5f winner Veleza (by Dalakhani) and a winner in Hong Kong by Azamour: dam, French 1¼m/10.5f winner, closely related to Prix de la Foret winner Varenar and half-sister to dam of very smart French stayer Vazirabad: fair maiden: stays 7f: acts on heavy going: usually slowly away/races towards rear. *Mick Channon* 72

ANONYMOUS JOHN (IRE) 5 gr.g. Baltic King 120 – Helibel (IRE) 73 (Pivotal 124) [2017 81, a97: p7g p6g^{4} p6g^{4} t7.1g* 7d^{6} p7d^{3} 6m 7m p7d p7g t7.2d Dec 26] fairly useful handicapper: won at Wolverhampton in April: stays 7f: acts on all-weather and any turf going: tried in visor. *Dominic Ffrench Davis* 81

ANOTHER ANGEL (IRE) 3 b.g. Dark Angel (IRE) 113 – Kermana (IRE) (Selkirk (USA) 129) [2017 76: 5g Aug 16] fair form at 2 yrs: well held sole outing in 2017. *Antony Brittain* –

ANOTHER BATT (IRE) 2 ch.g. (Apr 21) Windsor Knot (IRE) 118 – Mrs Batt (IRE) 66 (Medecis 119) [2017 5.8m^{5} 6g^{2} 5d* 5f 6s* 6g^{3} 7d^{2} 7d^{3} 6g* Sep 3] neat gelding: second foal: half-brother to 5f winner Nora Batt (by Art Connoisseur): dam 7f/1m winner: useful performer: won minor events at Ripon in June and Ayr in July, and Group 3 Trakya Trophy at Veliefendi (by 1½ lengths from Armondo) in September: placed in listed events at Newbury (2) and Ascot in between: left John W. Nicholson after second start: stays 7f: acts on soft going: usually races close up: consistent. *George Scott* 100

ANOTHER BOY 4 ch.g. Paco Boy (IRE) 129 – Kurtanella 86 (Pastoral Pursuits 127) [2017 80: 7s^4 7d 7g^4 7d* 7g^3 7.1s 7d^3 Oct 6] compact gelding: fairly useful handicapper: won at Sandown (by ½ length from Bengal Lancer) in July: stays 7f: acts on heavy going: usually wears headgear: front runner/races prominently. *Ralph Beckett* **82**

ANOTHER DAY OF SUN (IRE) 2 ch.g. (Mar 2) Camacho 118 – Sunblush (UAE) 57 (Timber Country (USA) 124) [2017 6m 6g* 6d^6 6d^3 7s^6 t6.1g^3 t7.2g^5 t6g^3 p6d^4 t7.1g^6 Oct 20] fair performer: won minor event at Thirsk in June: stays 6f: acts on tapeta: tried in visor: sold 9,000 gns, sent to Spain. *Mick Channon* **78**

ANOTHER DESPERADO (IRE) 4 b.g. Approve (IRE) 112 – Kind Regards (IRE) 113 (Unfuwain (USA) 131) [2017 –: 5m^4 May 8] no form: tried in cheekpieces. *Rebecca Bastiman* **–**

ANOTHER ECLIPSE (IRE) 3 b.g. Lope de Vega (IRE) 125 – Black Dahlia 100 (Dansili 127) [2017 78: 9g^2 10.5d^3 9.9g* 10.2d^2 10.1m^3 10.2d^2 Sep 14] useful performer: won maiden at Brighton in July: placed other 5 starts in 2017: stays 10.5f: acts on tapeta and good to soft going: tried in blinkers. *David Simcock* **99**

ANOTHER GO (IRE) 4 gr.g. Strategic Prince 114 – Golden Rose (GER) 102 (Winged Love (IRE) 121) [2017 95: 10.3g 11.2v^5 9.2v^5 Sep 5] rather narrow gelding: useful handicapper at 3 yrs, little impact in 2017: stays 1¼m: best form on heavy going. *Sally Haynes* **–**

ANOTHER SITUATION (USA) 2 ch.f. (Jan 11) Trappe Shot (USA) 123 – Return The Jewel (USA) (Broken Vow (USA) 117) [2017 p5g Sep 25] $30,000Y: third foal: half-sister to 2-y-o 5.3f/6f winner Monks Stand (by More Than Ready): dam US 6.5f-9f winner: 12/1, well held in minor event at Kempton. *Richard Guest* **–**

ANOTHER TOUCH 4 b.g. Arcano (IRE) 122 – Alsalwa (IRE) 102 (Nayef (USA) 129) [2017 105: 8g 8m^2 7.9d^4 8.3g* 8m 10.3m 8s* Jul 30] smallish gelding: smart performer: won handicap at Nottingham (by 2½ lengths from Kaspersky) in May and listed race at Pontefract (by neck from Custom Cut) in July: seems to stay 10.5f: acts on good to firm and heavy going. *Richard Fahey* **111**

ANOTHER WISE KID (IRE) 9 b.g. Whipper (USA) 126 – Romancing 79 (Dr Devious (IRE) 127) [2017 96, a81: 6g 5m 6d^5 6s^3 6g Jul 28] leggy gelding: useful handicapper, below best in 2017: stays 6f: acts on polytrack, good to firm and heavy going: tried in cheekpieces. *Paul Midgley* **87**

ANSAAB 9 b.g. Cape Cross (IRE) 129 – Dawn Raid (IRE) 94 (Docksider (USA) 124) [2017 94: t8g f11g^5 p10g* Feb 9] fairly useful handicapper nowadays: won at Lingfield (amateur, by 1¼ lengths from Starboard) in February: stays 1½m: acts on polytrack, good to firm and good to soft going: tried in cheekpieces: has worn tongue tie, including last 4 starts. *Marjorie Fife* **84**

ANTAGONIST 2 b.c. (Mar 26) Dansili 127 – Melodramatic (IRE) 101 (Sadler's Wells (USA) 132) [2017 7g^6 7v^4 p7g Sep 27] fifth foal: half-brother to smart 1¼m/11f winner Almodovar (by Sea The Stars): dam, 1m winner, closely related to high-class winner up to 7f Tante Rose: fair form in minor events: still unexposed. *Roger Charlton* **68 p**

ANTIQUARIUM (IRE) 5 b.g. New Approach (IRE) 132 – Antillia 82 (Red Ransom (USA)) [2017 114: t16.5m* Jan 16] rangy gelding: smart performer: won minor event at Wolverhampton (by 1¾ lengths from Famous Kid) on sole start in 2017: stayed 16.5f: acted on tapeta and firm going: dead. *Charlie Appleby* **115**

ANTON CHIGURH 8 b.g. Oasis Dream 129 – Barathiki 81 (Barathea (IRE) 127) [2017 71, a81: f8g^2 f8s^4 f8m t9.5g^5 p10g^2 10g^4 10.1g^6 10.2g t14g^6 f11.1g Dec 21] tall gelding: fair handicapper at best in 2017: left Tom Dascombe after fifth start: stays 9.5f: acts on all-weather and heavy going: has worn headgear, including last 2 starts. *Nikki Evans* **69 a78 d**

ANTON DOLIN (IRE) 9 ch.g. Danehill Dancer (IRE) 117 – Ski For Gold 76 (Shirley Heights 130) [2017 t16.5m t13.9g^5 t16.5g^4 t12.2g^2 t12.2g t12.2g Dec 13] compact gelding: modest handicapper nowadays: stays 16.5f: acts on polytrack, tapeta and any turf going: wears headgear: modest hurdler. *Michael Mullineaux* **59**

ANTONIAN 2 b.c. (Feb 7) Intello (GER) 129 – Highest 99 (Dynaformer (USA)) [2017 t8.6d^4 t8.6d* Dec 27] second foal: dam, 12.4f winner, half-sister to winner up to 10.3f Wasan and US Grade 2 1½m winner Olaya, both smart: fair form: won minor event at Wolverhampton (by 2½ lengths from Danzay) in December: will go on improving. *John Gosden* **79 p**

ANY JOY (IRE) 4 b.f. Zoffany (IRE) 121 – For Joy (Singspiel (IRE) 133) [2017 –: t8.6g^6 t7.1g Mar 27] no form: tried in cheekpieces. *Ben Haslam* **–**

ANY LITTLE RHYME 2 b.f. (Mar 8) Shamardal (USA) 129 – Free Verse 102 (Danehill Dancer (IRE) 117) [2017 6d5 p6s4 Dec 1] second foal: sister to useful winner up to 1¼m Frontispiece (2-y-o 7f winner): dam, 6f/7f winner (including at 2 yrs), sister to useful performer up to 1¼m Quadrille: fair form in maiden/minor event: will be suited by 7f+: remains capable of better. *Michael Bell* **68 p**

ANYTHINGTODAY (IRE) 3 b.g. Zoffany (IRE) 121 – Corking (IRE) 63 (Montjeu (IRE) 137) [2017 86: 10d 9.9m4 10m2 10d* 10.2s* 10g3 9.9m2 12s 10m3 10.3g Oct 14] sturdy gelding: smart handicapper: won at Newmarket (by ½ length from Pacify) in July and Bath (by 2½ lengths from Mikmak) in August: placed at Newmarket, Goodwood and Newbury after: stays 1¼m: acts on tapeta, soft and good to firm going: wears cheekpieces: often races towards rear, usually travels strongly: sold to join David O'Meara 100,000 gns in October. *Hugo Palmer* **110**

ANYTHINGWITHAPULSE (IRE) 2 br.f. (Mar 6) Dragon Pulse (IRE) 114 – Mahatta (IRE) 66 (Halling (USA) 133) [2017 t6.1g Jun 7] €10,000Y: first foal: dam, lightly raced, out of half-sister to high-class miler Muhtathir: 100/1, well held in minor event at Wolverhampton. *Daniel Loughnane* **–**

AONEDAMPROOFING 2 b.g. (Feb 16) Westlake 100 – Pinball (IRE) 63 (Namid 128) [2017 t6g t7.2g p6g5 Dec 12] no form: in hood last 2 starts. *Lisa Williamson* **–**

APACHE BLAZE 2 b.f. (Mar 13) Champs Elysees 124 – Polar Circle (USA) 92 (Royal Academy (USA) 130) [2017 p7g p8g6 Dec 20] 27,000Y: fifth foal: half-sister to Italian 7f winner Illegal Action (by Smart Strike): dam, 2-y-o 5f/6f winner, later 8.5f winner in USA, sister to smart winner up to 7f Fokine: modest form in minor events. *Michael Appleby* **64**

APALIS (FR) 5 gr.m. Mastercraftsman (IRE) 129 – Parcimonie (Nombre Premier 114) [2017 t10.2s 10s5 16m 14v4 f12.1g t16.3d* Dec 16] fair handicapper: won 3 times for J. M. Lefebvre in 2016: also won at Newcastle in December: stays 16.5f: acts on tapeta, viscoride and good to soft going: in tongue tie last 3 starts. *Michael Easterby* **65 a71**

APEX KING (IRE) 3 b.g. Kodiac 112 – Rainbowskia (FR) (Rainbow Quest (USA) 134) [2017 97: 9m5 11.6d5 10d5 Sep 23] sturdy gelding: useful performer: unproven beyond 7f: acts on good to firm and good to soft going. *Ed Dunlop* **94**

APEX PREDATOR (IRE) 2 b.c. (Apr 18) Acclamation 118 – Key Girl (IRE) 48 (Key of Luck (USA) 126) [2017 7d p7s6 Sep 8] lengthy, rather unfurnished colt: fair form in maiden/minor event. *Seamus Durack* **68**

APHAEA 2 b.f. (Mar 6) Farhh 131 – Wood Chorus 97 (Singspiel (IRE) 133) [2017 7v6 7.9g 7v Oct 21] 16,000Y: good-topped filly: sixth foal: closely related to 1¼m winner Allergic Reaction (by Kyllachy) and half-sister to useful 1m-1¼m winner Sands Chorus (by Footstepsinthesand) and 2-y-o 7f winner Woodukheleyfit (by Kheleyf): dam, 1¼m winner, half-sister to smart performers Polar Ben (at 7f/1m) and Franklins Gardens (stayer): little impact in minor events. *Michael Easterby* **–**

APPEARED 5 b.g. Dubawi (IRE) 129 – Appearance (Galileo (IRE) 134) [2017 103: 12m* 12m2 12d5 11.9g Aug 25] good sort: smart handicapper: won at Ascot (by 4½ lengths from Batts Rock) in May: second in Duke of Edinburgh Stakes at Royal Ascot (2¼ lengths behind Rare Rhythm) in June: stays 1½m: acts on polytrack, tapeta and good to firm going: tried in cheekpieces. *Roger Varian* **111**

APPEASE 8 b.g. Oasis Dream 129 – Penchee 107 (Grand Lodge (USA) 125) [2017 57: p8g t8.6g3 10.1m6 8m* 8d4 Sep 18] modest handicapper: won at Yarmouth in August: left E. Sheehy after second start: stayed 1¼m: acted on polytrack, tapeta and good to firm going: sometimes wore headgear: tried in tongue tie: dead. *Julia Feilden* **59**

APPENZELLER (USA) 2 gr.g. (May 26) Mizzen Mast (USA) 121 – Uforia (USA) (Zilzal (USA) 137) [2017 7.1s6 6g 6.1m5 Oct 16] good-topped gelding: fair form in maiden at Newbury on second of 3 starts: tried in hood. *Richard Hughes* **67**

APPHIA (IRE) 3 b.f. High Chaparral (IRE) 132 – Mixed Blessing 108 (Lujain (USA) 119) [2017 10d2 9.9m* 12m5 12s4 12d6 13.4g4 12d* Sep 29] 100,000Y: good-topped filly: fourth foal: closely related to 2-y-o 1m winner Century (by Montjeu), later successful up to 1½m in Australia, and half-sister to French 9f (including at 2 yrs) winner Privy Garden (by Oasis Dream): dam 2-y-o 6f winner, including Princess Margaret Stakes: useful performer: won maiden at Goodwood (dead-heated with Hadeeqa) in May and Princess Royal Stakes at Newmarket (by ½ length from Pleasant Surprise) in September: stays 13.5f: acts on soft and good to firm going: tried in cheekpieces: front runner/races prominently: sold 500,000 gns in December. *Hugo Palmer* **109**

APPLE ANNI (IRE) 2 b.f. (Feb 18) Fast Company (IRE) 126 – Common Cause 87 (Polish Patriot (USA) 128) [2017 7d^{3} 7.4s* 6s 7s^{4} 9s 8d Nov 4] €20,000Y: half-sister to several winners, including useful 5f-9f winner (including at 2 yrs) Wovoka (by Mujadil) and 2-y-o 1m winner Letham Island (by Trans Island): dam 11.5f/1½m winner: fair performer: won minor event at Beverley in September: should stay at least 1m: acts on soft going. *Mick Channon* **77**

APPLEBERRY (IRE) 5 b.m. Approve (IRE) 112 – Passage To India (IRE) 74 (Indian Ridge 123) [2017 87: f6d^{3} 5.5g^{4} 6v 7d^{4} 5d^{4} 5g f5g f8.1g f6.1g t7.2g Dec 13] good-topped mare: fairly useful handicapper, below form in 2017: stays 6f: acts on soft going: often wears headgear: signs of temperament. *Michael Appleby* **77**

APPOINTED 3 b.f. Delegator 125 – Celestial Harmony (Polish Precedent (USA) 131) [2017 86: 10.3g^{2} 10.3m^{6} 10.3g* 12d^{5} 7.9g 9.9g^{3} 10.5s^{6} 10g Oct 7] useful handicapper: won at York (by ¾ length from Fengate) in July: stays 10.5f: acts on soft and good to firm going: often races prominently. *Tim Easterby* **98**

APPRECIATING 3 b.f. New Approach (IRE) 132 – Star Value (IRE) (Danehill Dancer (IRE) 117) [2017 t6d^{5} t8.6g^{5} Mar 11] 3,000 2-y-o: second foal: dam unraced half-sister to smart French 1¼m-15f winner Shemima out of Prix de Diane winner Shemaka: modest form in maidens. *Kevin Ryan* **62**

APPROACHING MENACE 2 b.f. (Mar 10) Cityscape 127 – Candle 98 (Dansili 127) [2017 t8.6d Dec 9] fourth foal: dam, 1¼m-1½m winner, also won over hurdles, half-sister to useful stayer Colloquial: 50/1, well held in minor event at Wolverhampton. *Amy Murphy* **–**

APPY DAYS (IRE) 7 b.m. King's Theatre (IRE) 128 – A-To-Z (IRE) 101 (Ahonoora 122) [2017 p12g^{3} p12g^{2} Feb 24] sister to 1½m-1¾m winner Royal Alphabet and 1½m/13f winner Queen Alphabet, and closely related/half-sister to 2 winners, including smart 7f-1¼m winner Red Spell (2-y-o 1m winner, by Soviet Star): dam 6f (at 2 yrs)/7f (Nell Gwyn Stakes) winner: bumper/hurdle winner: fair form when placed in maidens at Lingfield: will stay beyond 1½m. *Ian Williams* **73**

APRES MIDI (IRE) 4 b.f. Galileo (IRE) 134 – Rose Bonheur 110 (Danehill Dancer (IRE) 117) [2017 86: 10.2f^{3} 11.4d^{3} 10g^{6} 12g 10g* 9.2s Aug 24] rather leggy filly: fairly useful handicapper: won at Windsor (by short head from X Rated) in July: stays 1¼m: acts on good to firm going: often races prominently. *K. R. Burke* **84**

APRICOT SKY 7 ch.g. Pastoral Pursuits 127 – Miss Apricot 48 (Indian Ridge 123) [2017 90: 5m 5d^{4} 5d 5g 5s 6s^{3} 5v* 5g t5g^{4} f5g^{4} Dec 19] lengthy gelding: fairly useful performer: won claimer at Catterick (by 1¾ lengths from Desert Ace) in October: left Brian Ellison after third start: stays 6f: acts on polytrack, good to firm and heavy going: has worn cheekpieces, including last 5 starts: front runner/races prominently. *Michael Dods* **81**

APROVADO (IRE) 5 b.g. Approve (IRE) 112 – Aldburgh (Bluebird (USA) 125) [2017 88: t5d t6d^{3} t5d^{2} t6g* t5s 5m^{2} 6d^{3} 5.1d 5g^{2} 6d^{5} 6d 6v t5g^{6} Oct 10] fairly useful handicapper: won at Newcastle (by ¾ length from Burtonwood) in March: stays 6f: acts on tapeta, soft and good to firm going: usually wears headgear: usually leads. *Michael Dods* **91**

AQABAH (USA) 2 b.c. (Feb 8) Exchange Rate (USA) 111 – Fast Tip (USA) (Najran (USA)) [2017 5m* 6d^{4} 6f^{5} 7g 7g^{3} 7s^{4} Oct 4] $180,000Y, $550,000 2-y-o: lengthy, attractive colt: first foal: dam, US 5.5f-1m (minor stakes) winner, sister to smart US Grade 2 9f winner Muny: useful performer: won minor event at Ascot in May: fifth in Coventry Stakes at Royal Ascot (1¼ lengths behind Rajasinghe) in June: best effort at 6f: acts on firm going: tried in hood. *Charlie Appleby* **103**

AQSHION STATIONS 3 b.g. Aqlaam 125 – Shersha (IRE) 105 (Priolo (USA) 127) [2017 60: p7m 10.2g 8v^{5} 7.1g Aug 28] maiden: no form in 2017: left William Jarvis after first start: tried in hood. *Richard Price* **–**

AQUA ARDENS (GER) 9 b.g. Nayef (USA) 129 – Arduinna (GER) (Winged Love (IRE) 121) [2017 87: f7g^{2} f8m p7g Mar 17] workmanlike gelding: fairly useful handicapper: stays 8.5f: acts on all-weather, firm and soft going: often wears cheekpieces/tongue tie. *George Baker* **79**

AQUADABRA (IRE) 2 b.f. (May 10) Born To Sea (IRE) 117 – Amazing Win (IRE) 70 (Marju (IRE) 127) [2017 t5.1g^{3} 5m^{3} 5.1m^{3} 6m^{3} 5s^{4} 5f^{2} 5f* 5g^{4} 5d^{6} 5g^{5} 5d 6g 5.1m^{2} p5g^{4} Oct 18] 18,000Y: leggy filly: third foal: half-sister to a winner abroad by Sixties Icon: dam 5.3f/6f winner: fair performer: won nursery at Bath in July: stays 6f: acts on firm going. *Mick Channon* **72**

AQUA LIBRE 4 b.f. Aqlaam 125 – Be Free 60 (Selkirk (USA) 129) [2017 92: p8g p7g p7g^3 7m 8s^4 7d^6 7g^5 t9.5g^5 10s^6 12.1d 9.9v 7s Oct 10] good-topped filly: fairly useful handicapper, below form in 2017: left Philip McBride after seventh start: stays 1m: acts on polytrack, tapeta, firm and good to soft going: in cheekpieces last 2 starts: has worn tongue tie, including final start: often starts slowly. *Jennie Candlish* **73**

AQUAMARINA 3 b.f. Kheleyf (USA) 116 – Reeling N' Rocking (IRE) 82 (Mr Greeley (USA) 122) [2017 t7.1g* 8d p7g p7g Oct 26] 1,200Y: fifth foal: half-sister to 1m winner Conan's Rock (by Shamardal) and 1¼m winner Rock Lobster (by Bahamian Bounty): dam, 7f winner, half-sister to useful 6f winner Entrap: fair form: won maiden at Newcastle in March: stays 7f. *Robyn Brisland* **77**

ARABELA DAWN (IRE) 3 b.f. Delegator 125 – Arabela (IRE) 68 (Medicean 128) [2017 –: 6g^6 7m 8v Oct 12] little form. *John Quinn* **–**

ARABELLA ROSE 3 b.f. Monsieur Bond (IRE) 120 – Moorhouse Girl 71 (Makbul 104) [2017 t7.1g^4 t6g^5 t5g Mar 3] second foal: dam, maiden (raced around 5f), half-sister to very smart 5f winner Moorhouse Lad: modest form on second of 3 starts in maidens. *Ivan Furtado* **56**

ARABELLAS FORTUNE 2 b.f. (Mar 2) Haafhd 129 – Finellas Fortune 65 (Elmaamul (USA) 125) [2017 6s 7.4g Aug 16] first foal: dam staying maiden: well beaten in 2 minor events. *James Ewart* **–**

ARABIAN GIFT (IRE) 2 br.f. (Mar 15) Dubawi (IRE) 129 – Gift Range (IRE) 106 (Spectrum (IRE) 126) [2017 7m^2 Jun 18] 525,000Y: fifth foal: sister to 1½m-2m winner Christmas Hamper and half-sister to a winner in Italy by Cape Cross: dam, 1m winner, sister to 2000 Guineas/King George VI & Queen Elizabeth Stakes winner Golan and Dante Stakes winner/Derby runner-up Tartan Bearer: 2/1, shaped very well when second in minor event at Doncaster (¾ length behind Quivery) on debut: sure to progress. *Charlie Appleby* **90 p**

ARABIAN HOPE (USA) 3 b.f. Distorted Humor (USA) 117 – Achieving (USA) (Bernardini (USA) 132) [2017 74p: p7g* p8g* 7.9m* 8m^3 8g 8g* 8g Oct 7] smart performer: won maiden at Kempton in April, handicap at Chelmsford (by length from Mystique Moon) later same month, listed race at York (by head from Golden Stunner) in June and Istanbul Trophy at Veliefendi (by 1½ lengths from Cheri Cheri Lady) in September: third in Falmouth Stakes at Newmarket (1¾ lengths behind Roly Poly) in July: stays 1m: acts on polytrack and good to firm going: wears hood: usually races prominently. *Saeed bin Suroor* **112**

ARABIAN JAZZ (IRE) 2 b.f. (Mar 25) Red Jazz (USA) 125 – Queen of Rap (IRE) 87 (Alhaarth (IRE) 126) [2017 p5g^{ur} 5g^2 6g^3 7.4m^2 7m 7.4d^4 7.2m* Sep 8] €11,000Y: second foal: half-sister to useful Italian/Australian winner up to 1¾m Ancient King (2-y-o 7.5f/1m winner, by Ramonti): dam 7.5f winner: fair performer: won minor event at Musselburgh in September: stays 7.5f: acts on good to firm and good to soft going: usually races prominently. *Michael Bell* **72**

ARABIAN OASIS 5 b.g. Oasis Dream 129 – Love Divine 120 (Diesis 133) [2017 –: t16.5g^4 t10.2s 12.1m Jul 19] fairly useful at best, just modest form in 2017: stays 9.5f: acts on tapeta: has worn headgear, including last 2 starts: signs of temperament: sold £1,200 in November. *Philip Kirby* **61**

ARABIAN SEA (USA) 2 b.f. (Apr 24) Point of Entry (USA) 128 – Galanty Show 76 (Danehill (USA) 126) [2017 8s p8g Oct 13] half-sister to 5f/6f winner Chatshow (by Distant View) and a winner in USA by Mizzen Mast: dam 6f winner: little impact in minor event/maiden. *Roger Charlton* **–**

ARABIC CULTURE (USA) 3 b.g. Lonhro (AUS) 128 – Kydd Gloves (USA) 99 (Dubai Millennium 140) [2017 8.3m^4 Jun 15] fifth foal: half-brother to 3 winners, including 1m winners Tactfully (at 2 yrs, by Discreet Cat) and Al Jamal (including at 2 yrs, by Authorized): dam 1m-10.4f winner: 7/2, very green when fourth in maiden at Nottingham (8 lengths behind Alwahsh) on debut: open to significant improvement. *Saeed bin Suroor* **75 P**

ARAB MOON 3 b.g. Elnadim (USA) 128 – Albeed 80 (Tiger Hill (IRE) 127) [2017 56: p11g* p12g* 9.9f^5 p11g* 13d^3 p12s* p11s^2 12m Oct 13] close-coupled gelding: useful handicapper: won at Kempton in April, Lingfield in May, and Kempton again in June and August: stays 13f: acts on polytrack, firm and good to soft going: usually races nearer last than first, often travels strongly. *William Knight* **100**

ARAB SPRING (IRE) 7 b.h. Monsun (GER) 124 – Spring Symphony (IRE) 94 (Darshaan 133) [2017 119: p10g^2 11.9g Feb 25] attractive horse: smart performer: second in listed race at Lingfield (short head behind Decorated Knight) in February: below form in H. H. The **119**

Emirs Trophy at Doha only subsequent outing: stays 1½m: acts on polytrack, firm and good to soft going: often races prominently/travels strongly: sold 100,000 gns in July. *Sir Michael Stoute*

ARACHINA (IRE) 2 ch.f. (Apr 4) Arakan (USA) 123 – Tibouchina (IRE) 77 (Daylami (IRE) 138) [2017 7m 6.1g 7d^{5} p6g p7g^{3} p6g Nov 1] €11,000Y: compact filly: seventh foal: half-sister to useful Italian/Australian winner up to 10.5f Wish Come True (2-y-o 8.5f/9f winner, by Aussie Rules) and winner up to 1¼m Viking Hoard (2-y-o 1m winner, by Vale of York): dam won around 1½m: modest maiden: best effort at 7f: acts on polytrack: in visor last 4 starts. *Harry Dunlop* **60**

ARAGON KNIGHT 4 b.g. Kheleyf (USA) 116 – Midnight Allure 85 (Aragon 118) [2017 78: t5.1g p6g^{3} t6g p6g p6s Sep 8] workmanlike gelding: fair handicapper: left Heather Main after fourth start: stays 6f: acts on polytrack and good to soft going: has worn headgear, including last 2 starts: front runner/races prominently. *Daniel Steele* **73**

ARAHAT (USA) 2 b.f. (Mar 28) Temple City (USA) – Perfect Rah (USA) (Perfect Soul (IRE) 122) [2017 t8g Dec 6] $30,000Y: fourth foal: half-sister to a winner in USA by Tale of Ekati: dam lightly-raced half-sister to smart US Grade 3 7f winner Tasteyville: 12/1, well held in maiden at Newcastle. *John Gosden* **–**

ARAMIST (IRE) 7 gr.g. Aussie Rules (USA) 123 – Mistic Sun (Dashing Blade 117) [2017 86: 16d^{6} 16.3g^{4} 14g^{3} 14.1s 16.3d Sep 10] compact gelding: fair handicapper nowadays: stays 16.5f: acts on tapeta, good to firm and heavy going: tried in cheekpieces: often races towards rear. *Sally Haynes* **77**

ARAWAK (USA) 2 b.c. (Feb 24) Uncle Mo (USA) 127 – Spicy Teddy (USA) (Spanish Steps (USA)) [2017 a5s* 6f a6.5f^{5} 7g^{3} a8.5s^{6} 8s^{5} p8f* Dec 7] $200,000Y: big, strong colt: first foal: dam US maiden half-sister to smart US Grade 1 1m-1¼m winner Sir Bear: fairly useful performer: won maiden at Belmont in May and optional claimer at Turfway in December: twelfth behind Rajasinghe in Coventry Stakes at Royal Ascot on second outing: stays 8.5f: acts on dirt and polytrack: in blinkers first 3 starts: has worn tongue tie. *Wesley A. Ward, USA* **94**

ARBALET (IRE) 2 gr.c. (Apr 21) Dark Angel (IRE) 113 – Miss Beatrix (IRE) 106 (Danehill Dancer (IRE) 117) [2017 6m^{2} 6g^{2} 7m* 7g^{3} 8m^{6} Oct 14] €370,000F: strong colt: seventh foal: half-brother to useful French winner up to 1m Jally (2-y-o 5.5f winner, by Tamayuz) and a winner in Turkey by Azamour: dam 2-y-o 7f winner, including Moyglare Stud Stakes: useful performer: won minor event at Redcar in July: third in Solario Stakes at Sandown (3¼ lengths behind Masar) in September: should stay 1m: acts on good to firm going: often starts slowly. *Hugo Palmer* **101**

ARCADIAN CAT (USA) 2 b.f. (Feb 7) Kitten's Joy (USA) 128 – Calissa (IRE) 81 (Danehill Dancer (IRE) 117) [2017 8s^{3} Oct 28] $130,000Y: first foal: dam, 1m winner, out of smart French/US winner up to 11f Mauralakana: 14/1, shaped well when third in minor event at Newbury (3½ lengths behind Highgarden) on debut: sure to progress. *Ralph Beckett* **76 p**

ARCADIAN SEA (IRE) 3 b.g. Born To Sea (IRE) 117 – Drombeg Dawn (IRE) 94 (Orpen (USA) 116) [2017 –: p10g^{4} p8s 11.4m^{6} t14g^{3} 14s^{3} 12g^{3} f12.1g^{6} p10d* p10g^{4} p10s Dec 7] angular gelding: fair handicapper: won at Chelmsford in September: stays 1¾m: acts on polytrack and tapeta: tried in hood. *William Jarvis* **67**

ARCANADA (IRE) 4 ch.g. Arcano (IRE) 122 – Bond Deal (IRE) 104 (Pivotal 124) [2017 113: 7g 8g^{4} 7.9m^{2} 8g 7s p8g* Nov 18] well-made gelding: smart handicapper: won at Lingfield (by length from Sacred Act) in November: stays 1m: acts on polytrack, tapeta, good to firm and good to soft going: tried in cheekpieces: front runner/races prominently. *Tom Dascombe* **117**

ARCANE DANCER (IRE) 4 b.f. Arcano (IRE) 122 – La Reine Mambo (USA) (High Yield (USA) 121) [2017 70: f8g^{4} 7.5f^{2} 7.4m^{4} 7.6s^{5} 8.5m^{3} 8.3d^{3} 7.4d* 8s 8g 9.9m 8.5v t6g t7.2g Nov 7] quite good-topped filly: fair handicapper: won at Beverley in July: stays 8.5f: acts on fibresand, tapeta and any turf going: wears headgear. *Lawrence Mullaney* **68**

ARCANISTA (IRE) 4 ch.f. Arcano (IRE) 122 – Cattiva Generosa 109 (Cadeaux Genereux 131) [2017 70: p7g f7g t8.6g^{4} p8g^{2} t9.5m p7g p6f^{4} t8.6g 9.1d 5.9s^{2} p7g^{3} 6s^{4} 6.1g* 7d p6g^{2} p6g^{5} p6g^{6} Dec 20] lengthy filly: fair handicapper: won at Windsor (amateur) in October: left Richard Hughes after eighth start: stays 7f: acts on polytrack and soft going: wears headgear: has worn tongue tie: usually races prominently. *Chris Dwyer* **68**

ARCAVALLO (IRE) 2 ch.c. (Mar 24) Arcano (IRE) 122 – Pashmina (IRE) (Barathea (IRE) 127) [2017 6m 5.9g^{2} 6d^{2} 5s* 5g* 6g^{2} Oct 7] 10,000Y: third foal: dam unraced half-sister to smart 5f winner Monsieur Joe: fairly useful performer: won minor events at Beverley (twice) in August: stays 6f: acts on soft going: front runner/races prominently, often travels strongly. *Michael Dods* **86**

ARCHANGEL RAPHAEL (IRE) 5 b.g. Montjeu (IRE) 137 – La Sylvia (IRE) 102 (Oasis Dream 129) [2017 92: p12g^5 p11g^6 p11g^3 9.9g p8g 11.2g^5 11.6d^6 11.2s^6 p15.8g^3 12s Oct 28] strong gelding: fair handicapper nowadays: stays 2m: acts on polytrack and good to firm going: usually wears headgear: tried in tongue tie. *Amanda Perrett* **77**

ARCHER'S ARROW (USA) 3 b.c. Lonhro (AUS) 128 – Midnight Music (IRE) 106 (Dubawi (IRE) 129) [2017 81: p8g* p7g^2 p7d t6g p8s^2 p7d^6 Oct 6] fairly useful performer: won maiden at Kempton in April: second in handicaps at Lingfield later same month and Kempton (apprentice) in September: stays 1m: acts on polytrack and tapeta: tried in headgear. *Saeed bin Suroor* **86**

ARCHETYPE (FR) 3 b.c. Le Havre (IRE) 124 – Angel Rose (IRE) (Definite Article 121) [2017 8m^4 p8s* 9.9m^2 9.9m* 9.9v 8g* 8d* p8d^5 Nov 22] €60,000 2-y-o: rangy colt: brother to 7f winner (stays 1½m) Jupiter Custos and half-brother to several winners, including useful 2-y-o 7f winner Kay Es Jay (by Xaar), later 6f winner in USA, and 2-y-o 8.6f winner Encore Encore (by Royal Applause): dam Swedish 2-y-o 1m winner: smart performer: won maiden at Chelmsford in May, handicaps (2) at Sandown in July/September and minor event at Maisons-Laffitte (by 7 lengths) later in September: fifth to Second Thought in listed race at Kempton final outing: stays 1¼m: acts on polytrack, good to firm and good to soft going: front runner/races prominently, often travels strongly. *Simon Crisford* **110**

ARCH GOLD (USA) 2 b.c. (Mar 14) Arch (USA) 127 – Trepidation (USA) (Seeking The Gold (USA)) [2017 6s^3 t8.6m^4 Oct 31] fair form when fourth in minor event on second of 2 starts. *Mark Johnston* **68**

ARCHIBALD LEITCH 2 b.g. (Mar 1) Archipenko (USA) 127 – Aubrietia 104 (Dutch Art 126) [2017 7s p7g^6 p7g Nov 2] rather leggy gelding: no form. *David Evans* **–**

ARCHIBELLE 3 b.f. Archipenko (USA) 127 – Cloud Hill (Danehill (USA) 126) [2017 t10.2g t8d^6 t12.4g^3 12m^2 10m^3 13.1s^4 11.1g^6 12.3d^5 14m 14s t12.4d^3 t12.4d Dec 16] closely related to a winner in Greece by Dubai Destination and half-sister to 3 winners, including useful winner up to 9.4f Dubawi Star (2-y-o 7f winner, by Dubawi) and 1¼m-1½m winner Mista Rossa (by Red Ransom): dam unraced half-sister to St Leger runner-up High And Low: fair maiden: stays 1½m: acts on good to firm going: temperamental. *R. Mike Smith* **67 §**

ARCHIE (IRE) 5 b.g. Fast Company (IRE) 126 – Winnifred (Green Desert (USA) 127) [2017 97: 8.3g 8m^3 7m^5 8m 8d 8g^5 9d p8g p8g^2 Oct 25] fairly useful handicapper: stays 1m: acts on polytrack, firm and good to soft going: has worn hood: sometimes slowly away, usually races in rear. *Tom Clover* **94**

ARCHIE MCKELLAR 2 b.c. (Apr 10) Archipenko (USA) 127 – Desert Berry 74 (Green Desert (USA) 127) [2017 7g^3 7s^3 p7g* 7s^4 Oct 28] £25,000Y: second foal: brother to 5f (including at 2 yrs) winner Rose Berry: dam 1m winner: useful form: won minor event at Kempton in October: best effort when fourth (1¾ lengths behind Nebo) in Horris Hill Stakes at Newbury: raced only at 7f. *Ralph Beckett* **101**

ARCHIE PERKINS (IRE) 2 b.g. (Apr 28) Arcano (IRE) 122 – Sidney Girl (Azamour (IRE) 130) [2017 5f 5g 6g^4 6.1s^4 6d 7.2m^5 7.2m^6 t7.1g^2 t8s* Sep 19] fair performer: won nursery at Newcastle in September: stays 1m: acts on tapeta and good to firm going. *Nigel Tinkler* **70**

ARCHIE'S ADVICE 6 b.g. Archipenko (USA) 127 – Flylowflylong (IRE) 74 (Danetime (IRE) 121) [2017 83§: 10m^4 8.3m^6 11.1g^6 9.2s^6 8.3m^5 10d 8.3s^3 9s 9.2s 15s^5 Oct 3] fairly useful handicapper: third at Hamilton in August: stays 1¼m: acts on polytrack, tapeta, soft and good to firm going: has worn cheekpieces, including in 2017: often starts slowly, usually races nearer last than first: not straightforward (carries head awkwardly) and isn't one to trust. *Keith Dalgleish* **80 §**

ARCHIE STEVENS 7 b.g. Pastoral Pursuits 127 – Miss Wells (IRE) (Sadler's Wells (USA) 132) [2017 79: f5g^5 t5g^5 t5.1g^3 f5g^2 f5g^2 t5.1g^3 t5.1g^6 t5.1g^5 5m p6g^4 t5.1g 5.3m^2 5m^4 6g 5m t5d p5g^3 t5.1m^6 f5g* f5g^2 f5g^3 Dec 21] fair handicapper: won at Southwell in December: left David Evans after fifth start: raced mainly around 5f: acts on all-weather, soft and good to firm going: tried in cheekpieces/tongue tie: front runner/races prominently. *Clare Ellam* **74**

ARCHIMEDES (IRE) 4 b.g. Invincible Spirit (IRE) 121 – Waveband 102 (Exceed And Excel (AUS) 126) [2017 73: f5g f5s* f5g^6 f5m^5 5g 5m^3 5d 6.1m 5f^5 5m^3 5f* 5d^5 5d 5m 5m^5 p5g 5g Oct 18] compact gelding: fair handicapper: won at Southwell in January and Bath in July: best at 5f: acts on fibresand and firm going: wears headgear/tongue tie. *David C. Griffiths* **77**

ARCHIMENTO 4 ch.g. Archipenko (USA) 127 – Caribana 77 (Hernando (FR) 127) **77**
[2017 85: p8g^6 10g 9.9s^4 11.6d^4 11.2s p10s^2 p12g Oct 18] sturdy gelding: fair maiden: left Ed Dunlop after second start: stays 1¼m: acts on polytrack and soft going: in tongue tie last 5 starts. *Philip Hide*

ARCHIPELIGO 6 b.g. Archipenko (USA) 127 – Red Slew (Red Ransom (USA)) [2017 **78**
79: t8d t8g 12g t12.2g t12.2g 9.2g^2 t10.2s* t10.2s t10.2s^6 9d^2 11.1d^5 9.2g^2 t10.2g* 10g^5 10m t9.5g^5 t12.4s^5 t8d^5 t12.2g t10.2g^5 t10.2g t9.5g^4 t9.5g* Dec 18] fair handicapper: won at Newcastle in June and July (lady riders event) and Wolverhampton (amateur) in December: stays 12.5f, raced mainly at shorter: acts on tapeta, soft and good to firm going: often wears headgear. *Iain Jardine*

ARCHIPENTURA 5 b.m. Archipenko (USA) 127 – Bookiesindex Girl (IRE) 66 (Rakti **40**
130) [2017 –: f6g p7d Feb 16] lengthy mare: poor maiden. *J. R. Jenkins*

ARCHIPPOS 4 b.g. Archipenko (USA) 127 – Sparkling Clear 48 (Efisio 120) [2017 86: **90**
10.3g* 12.3d^4 11.9s^5 11.8v^3 16.3g^5 Oct 14] fairly useful handicapper: won at Doncaster (by ¾ length from Hail Clodius) in April: third at Haydock in September: stays 16.5f: acts on heavy going. *Philip Kirby*

ARCHI'S AFFAIRE 3 ch.g. Archipenko (USA) 127 – Affaire d'Amour 100 (Hernando **99**
(FR) 127) [2017 52: t5s 9.2g* 9v* 11.1g^2 11.1d* 12.1s^4 14s Sep 9] useful handicapper: won at Hamilton and Carlisle in June, and again at Hamilton (by 3¼ lengths from Detailed) in July: stays 1½m: acts on heavy going. *Michael Dods*

ARCHITECTURE (IRE) 4 b.f. Zoffany (IRE) 121 – Brigayev (ITY) (Fasliyev (USA) **110**
120) [2017 114: 11m^4 10m^3 12s Oct 28] good-topped filly: smart performer: made frame in Legacy Cup at Newbury (length behind Desert Encounter) in September and listed race at Newmarket at October: stays 1½m: acts on soft and good to firm going. *Hugo Palmer*

ARCH VILLAIN (IRE) 8 b.g. Arch (USA) 127 – Barzah (IRE) 98 (Darshaan 133) [2017 **108**
108: 13.9m^4 16g Sep 28] tall gelding: useful performer: fourth in Ebor at York (3¼ lengths behind Nakeeta) in August: stays 2m: acts on polytrack, good to firm and good to soft going: often wears headgear. *Amanda Perrett*

ARC ROYAL 3 ch.g. Arcano (IRE) 122 – Royal Blush 68 (Royal Applause 124) [2017 88: **86**
6g^5 7.5m^3 7.6m 7.2f^4 7.2s^3 7.6d 7.6d 7g^6 p5g Dec 15] fairly useful handicapper: third at Beverley in April: left Tom Dascombe after eighth start: stays 7.5f: acts on firm going: tried in headgear: usually races prominently. *Richard John O'Brien, Ireland*

ARCTIC ANGEL (IRE) 4 b.g. Dark Angel (IRE) 113 – Charlene Lacy (IRE) 77 (Pips **77**
Pride 117) [2017 77p: p6g^2 6.1m t6.1g^4 Jul 11] fair maiden: second in handicap at Kempton (head behind Deeds Not Words) in May: raced only at 6f: acted on polytrack and tapeta: wore hood in 2017: dead. *James Fanshawe*

ARCTIC FLOWER (IRE) 4 gr.f. Roderic O'Connor (IRE) 119 – Just In Love (FR) **72**
(Highest Honor (FR) 124) [2017 56: p8s 7m^3 7d^4 7s* 7s* 7.6s* 7.6d* 8.1m^6 7.6s 8.1m Oct 16] short-backed filly: fair handicapper: won 4 times at Lingfield in July/August: stays 7.5f: acts on polytrack, soft and good to firm going: front runner. *John Bridger*

ARCTIC SEA 3 b.c. Oasis Dream 129 – Rainbow Dancing 108 (Rainbow Quest (USA) **83**
134) [2017 75: t8g^3 p7g^3 p8g* 8.1m* p11g 8f^2 p11g^4 Aug 30] strong, compact colt: fairly useful handicapper: won at Kempton in April and Chepstow in May: second at Bath in July: likely to stay 1½m: acts on polytrack and firm going: sometimes slowly away. *Paul Cole*

ARCTIC TREASURE (IRE) 2 b.g. (Apr 27) Iffraaj 127 – Street Star (USA) 91 (Street **63 p**
Cry (IRE) 130) [2017 6g^5 6m 5s t7.1g^5 Oct 10] 7,000F, 9,000 2-y-o: fourth foal: brother to 7f winner Free Running: dam, 2-y-o 6f winner, half-sister to smart winners up to 1¾m Shrewd Idea and Alva Glen (latter temperamental): modest form: will be suited by 1m: remains with potential. *Richard Fahey*

ARDAD (IRE) 3 b.c. Kodiac 112 – Good Clodora (IRE) 64 (Red Clubs (IRE) 125) [2017 **102**
107: 5s^4 5m^5 5s Aug 4] good-topped colt: useful performer: won 3 times at 2 yrs, including Windsor Castle Stakes at Royal Ascot and Flying Childers Stakes at Doncaster: below best in 2017: best form at 5f: acted on firm and good to soft going: to stand at Overbury Stud, near Tewkesbury, Gloucestershire, fee £6,500 Oct 1st. *John Gosden*

ARDAMIR (FR) 5 b.g. Deportivo 116 – Kiss And Cry (FR) (Nikos 124) [2017 89: **88**
t12.2m^6 p12m^3 t13.9g^2 t13.9g^3 16.5m^3 14.2d p12s 12g p12g^5 Dec 13] fairly useful maiden: placed in maiden at Lingfield and handicaps at Wolverhampton (2) and Doncaster: left Alan King after fifth start: stays 1¾m: acts on polytrack, tapeta and good to firm going: tried in hood. *Laura Mongan*

ARDEN PEARL (IRE) 2 b.f. (Feb 25) Swiss Spirit 117 – Music Pearl (IRE) 77 (Oratorio (IRE) 128) [2017 5m 6d^{3} 6.1g* 6g p6d^{6} t6.1g^{2} p6s f6.1g Dec 21] 30,000F, 23,000Y: rather unfurnished filly: second foal: half-sister to 6f winner Born To Finish (by Dark Angel): dam, 8.5f winner, half-sister to smart winner up to 9f Haami: fair performer: won maiden at Windsor in August: stays 6f: acts on tapeta: wears headgear. *Archie Watson* **77**

ARDHOOMEY (IRE) 5 b.g. Dark Angel (IRE) 113 – Moy Joy (IRE) 90 (Orpen (USA) 116) [2017 116: 5m^{2} 5g^{2} 5f 5f^{3} 5s^{3} 5s^{6} 6s^{3} 5.8v^{6} p5g^{5} Oct 20] smart performer: placed in listed races at Navan (neck behind Washington DC) in April and the Curragh (½ length behind Acapulco) in May, and in Sapphire Stakes at the Curragh (2½ lengths behind Caspian Prince) in July: raced mainly at 5f: acts on polytrack, firm and good to soft going: wears tongue tie: often races towards rear. *G. M. Lyons, Ireland* **116**

AREEN FAISAL (IRE) 2 ch.c. (Mar 29) Bahamian Bounty 116 – Yellow Trumpet 75 (Petong 126) [2017 5m^{3} 5d^{5} 5f 6d* 6d^{3} 6.5g Sep 14] €72,000F, €80,000Y: sparely-made colt: half-brother to several winners, including useful sprinters City of Tribes (by Invincible Spirit) and Viva Verglas (by Verglas), both 2-y-o 5f winners: dam 2-y-o 5f winner: fairly useful performer: won nursery at Pontefract (by 1¼ lengths from The Love Doctor) in July: third in similar event at York in August: left Richard Fahey after fifth start: stays 6f: acts on good to soft going. *David O'Meara* **84**

AREEN HEART (FR) 3 b.g. Exceed And Excel (AUS) 126 – Reine Zao (FR) 107 (Alzao (USA) 117) [2017 82p: 7.5m^{2} 7.6m^{3} p8g^{6} 8m^{2} 8d^{2} 7.9g 7.2s^{5} 8v 8d p8g Nov 17] useful handicapper: placed at Beverley in April, Chester in May, and at Haydock (1¼ lengths behind Calder Prince) and Ripon (½ length behind Shouranour) in July: left Richard Fahey after sixth start: stays 1m: acts on good to firm and good to soft going: wears hood. *David O'Meara* **95**

ARENDELLE 2 b.f. (Feb 8) Camelot 128 – Ape Attack (Nayef (USA) 129) [2017 8.3d 8s^{5} Oct 28] tall, unfurnished filly: first foal: dam unraced half-sister to smart 1¼m winner Mashaahed: fair form when fifth in minor event at Newbury on second of 2 starts: will be suited by 1¼m+: open to further improvement. *Ed Walker* **66 p**

AREYOUTHEWAY (IRE) 3 ch.g. Thewayyouare (USA) 117 – Grenouillere (USA) (Alysheba (USA)) [2017 66: t9.5g p10g 10.4g^{6} 11.9g 10.4g 8.6g a8g a8g^{5} a11.7g^{2} a11.7g^{5} a11.7g^{2} a11.7g* Nov 19] modest handicapper: left Michael Appleby after second outing: won handicap at Bro Park in November: stays 11.7f: acts on dirt and polytrack, best turf form on good going: usually wears headgear. *Annika Sjokvist, Sweden* **55**

ARGAKI (IRE) 7 ch.g. Strategic Prince 114 – Amathusia (Selkirk (USA) 129) [2017 86, a74: t7.1g t9.5g 7.8s 8d^{6} 8g^{4} 8g 8.3s^{2} 8m^{6} Sep 8] fair handicapper nowadays: has form at 11f, raced mainly at shorter: acts on tapeta, firm and soft going: has worn headgear. *Keith Dalgleish* **66**

ARGANTE (FR) 8 b.g. Singspiel (IRE) 133 – Abyaan (IRE) 106 (Ela-Mana-Mou 132) [2017 –: p16s^{3} Dec 15] sturdy gelding: fairly useful handicapper: stays 16.5f: acts on polytrack and tapeta: usually wears blinkers: tried in tongue tie: winning hurdler. *Henry Spiller* **79**

ARGENT BLEU 2 b.c. (Apr 28) Steele Tango (USA) 116 – Silver Marizah (IRE) 74 (Manduro (GER) 135) [2017 p8g Dec 20] 40/1, well held in minor event at Lingfield. *Roger Ingram* **–**

ARGENTERIE 3 ch.f. Archipenko (USA) 127 – Sterling Sound (USA) 95 (Street Cry (IRE) 130) [2017 90p: 11.3m^{6} 9.1g Aug 26] close-coupled filly: fairly useful form at 2 yrs, looked one with problems on both starts in 2017. *Marcus Tregoning* **–**

ARGON 2 b.c. (Apr 8) Kyllachy 129 – Cool Question 99 (Polar Falcon (USA) 126) [2017 t5.1g t5.1d f5g Dec 29] little impact in minor events: tried in cheekpieces. *Sir Mark Prescott Bt* **–**

ARGUS (IRE) 5 b.g. Rip Van Winkle (IRE) 134 – Steel Princess (IRE) 106 (Danehill (USA) 126) [2017 91: 16.8v 12s^{5} p11d p12g Dec 30] good-bodied gelding: fairly useful handicapper: stays 1½m: acts on good to soft going: tried in hood. *Alexandra Dunn* **90**

ARGYLE (IRE) 4 gr.g. Lawman (FR) 121 – All Hallows (IRE) (Dalakhani (IRE) 133) [2017 74: 11.4d Oct 23] tall, good-topped gelding: fair maiden, well beaten sole outing on Flat in 2017: stays 2m: acts on polytrack and soft going: tried in blinkers: modest maiden hurdler. *Gary Moore* **–**

ARIENA (IRE) 3 b.f. Arcano (IRE) 122 – Xena (IRE) (Mull of Kintyre (USA) 114) [2017 85: 6m^{4} 7m^{5} 7m^{3} 7m t8.6g^{5} p7g^{3} Oct 26] close-coupled filly: fairly useful handicapper: third at Newmarket in August: should stay 1m: acts on good to firm going. *Clive Cox* **85**

ARIGATO 2 b.c. (Feb 3) Poet's Voice 126 – Xtrasensory 96 (Royal Applause 124) [2017 **64**
6d 7s p6g p8g^{3} Nov 7] modest form: third in nursery at Kempton in November: best effort at 1m. *William Jarvis*

ARISTOCLES (IRE) 4 b.g. High Chaparral (IRE) 132 – Amathusia (Selkirk (USA) 129) –
[2017 79: p15.8g Dec 28] fair handicapper, well beaten sole start on Flat in 2017: stays 1¾m: in headgear last 4 starts: front runner/races prominently: modest maiden hurdler. *Nikki Evans*

ARISTOCRACY 6 b.g. Royal Applause 124 – Pure Speculation 80 (Salse (USA) 128) **58**
[2017 –: 16d^{6} 14v^{6} 16v^{4} Jul 28] modest handicapper nowadays: stays 2m: acts on polytrack, good to firm and heavy going: tried in blinkers: winning hurdler. *Fergal O'Brien*

ARISTOCRATIC 4 b.f. Exceed And Excel (AUS) 126 – Peeress 124 (Pivotal 124) [2017 **87**
88: 7m^{2} 8m^{6} 8g^{3} Jun 25] good-topped, attractive filly: fairly useful handicapper: second at Salisbury in April: stays 1m: acts on polytrack, best turf form on good going: in headgear last 4 starts: usually races close up. *Sir Michael Stoute*

ARISTODEMUS (IRE) 2 b.g. (Mar 19) Camacho 118 – Sceal Nua (IRE) 92 (Iffraaj 127) **52**
[2017 5m^{3} 5m 6d^{5} 7s 6g^{6} Aug 15] modest maiden: best effort at 5f: acts on good to firm going: tried in blinkers: usually races prominently: sent to Spain. *Tim Easterby*

ARISTO DU PLESSIS (FR) 7 b.g. Voix du Nord (FR) 119 – J'aime (FR) (Royal **67**
Charter (FR)) [2017 12v^{5} Oct 23] useful hurdler: 9/2, fifth in maiden at Pontefract (12¼ lengths behind Darksideoftarnside) on sole outing on Flat. *James Ewart*

ARITHMETIC (IRE) 4 b.g. Invincible Spirit (IRE) 121 – Multiplication 82 (Marju **73 §**
(IRE) 127) [2017 77: 8g 9.9m^{5} 10m^{3} 10m 10s^{2} 10.2m 10g^{2} 10.2m 10.2d 8s 12d^{6} 9.9g Sep 2] close-coupled gelding: fair maiden: stays 1¼m: acts on soft and good to firm going: tried in cheekpieces: not straightforward. *Ruth Carr*

ARIZE (IRE) 4 b.f. Approve (IRE) 112 – Raise (USA) (Seattle Slew (USA)) [2017 74: **74**
t7.1g^{2} p7g^{4} p6g p6g p6g^{6} p6g t7.2g a7g* 7g a6g* a6g^{4} a6g a6g^{2} Nov 22] fair handicapper: left David Brown after second start, Jim Boyle after seventh: won at Bro Park in September and October: stays 7f: acts on dirt and tapeta. *Sandra Brolin, Sweden*

ARIZONA MIST (IRE) 2 br.f. (Jan 25) Exceed And Excel (AUS) 126 – Phoenix City **68**
(USA) 89 (El Prado (IRE) 119) [2017 p6s^{6} 5g^{4} 5d^{2} t5.1g Sep 9] fair form: second in minor event at Ripon in July: best form at 5f: dead. *Simon Crisford*

ARIZONA SNOW 5 b.g. Phoenix Reach (IRE) 124 – Calgary (Pivotal 124) [2017 58: f6g **46**
p6g p6g f6g^{6} 5.7d 5.1s 5.7s 5.7s^{5} Oct 2] modest handicapper, below form in 2017: stays 6f: acts on polytrack, fibresand and soft going: wears headgear: usually races close up. *Ronald Harris*

ARIZONA SUNRISE 4 b.g. Sakhee's Secret 128 – Phoenix Rising (Dr Fong (USA) –
128) [2017 70: 8m 10g 10d t7.1d^{4} t8d t7.1g t7.1s^{6} Nov 30] rather leggy gelding: fair handicapper, no form in 2017. *Tina Jackson*

ARLECCHINO'S ARC (IRE) 2 ch.g. (Feb 24) Arcano (IRE) 122 – Sir Cecil's Girl –
(IRE) 55 (Thunder Gulch (USA) 129) [2017 7m p8g 8d t7.2g Nov 18] no form: in cheekpieces last 3 starts. *Mark Usher*

ARLECCHINO'S LEAP 5 br.g. Kheleyf (USA) 116 – Donna Giovanna 74 (Mozart **75**
(IRE) 131) [2017 91: 7m t8.6g^{6} p7d p7g p7g p6g Nov 29] lengthy gelding: fairly useful handicapper, below form in 2017: stays 7f: acts on polytrack, tapeta and firm going: wears headgear: usually races towards rear. *Mark Usher*

ARMAGNAC (IRE) 3 br.g. Arcano (IRE) 122 – Folle Blanche (USA) (Elusive Quality **73**
(USA)) [2017 76: t8.6g^{3} 8.3g^{5} 8.3d^{4} 8.1m 8.2g^{4} 8s 8.5d^{4} 8g* 8m^{3} Sep 8] angular gelding: fair handicapper: won at Thirsk (apprentice) in September: stays 8.5f: acts on tapeta, good to firm and good to soft going. *Michael Bell*

ARMANDE (IRE) 4 b.f. Sea The Stars (IRE) 140 – Alpine Snow (IRE) 104 (Verglas **118**
(IRE) 118) [2017 10.4g^{2} 9.9g^{2} 10.4g* 11.9g^{3} Jul 2] third foal: half-sister to French 7f winner Alpine Spirit (by Invincible Spirit): dam, French 9.5f (at 2 yrs) and 11.5f winner, out of half-sister to 2000 Guineas winner King's Best and Arc winner Urban Sea (dam of Galileo and Sea The Stars): smart performer: improved last 2 starts, winning Prix Corrida at Saint-Cloud (by 3 lengths from That Which Is Not) in May and third in Grand Prix de Saint-Cloud (2 lengths behind Zarak): stays 1½m: acts on soft going. *A. Fabre, France*

ARMANDIHAN (IRE) 3 b.g. Zoffany (IRE) 121 – Flying Flag (IRE) (Entrepreneur 123) **91**
[2017 83: t8d^{6} 8g^{2} 7m* 7.6d p8g 10g^{2} 10.2d^{4} Oct 27] fairly useful performer: won maiden at Catterick in May: second in handicap at Redcar in October: stays 1¼m: acts on good to firm going: tried in cheekpieces: usually leads (ridden much more patiently last 2 starts). *Kevin Ryan*

ARMED RESPONSE 2 b.c. (Apr 19) Sepoy (AUS) 129 – Respondez (Oasis Dream 129) **89** [2017 5m^4 5m^3 6m* 6s^3 6g^6 t6g* t6g* Dec 6] 44,000F: second foal: dam, French maiden (second at 5.5f), sister to very smart sprinter Prohibit: fairly useful performer: won maiden at Hamilton in June, and nurseries at Newcastle in September and December (by head from Lord of The Glen): will probably stay 7f: acts on tapeta and good to firm going: front runner/races prominently. *Jedd O'Keeffe*

ARMELLE (FR) 6 b.m. Milk It Mick 120 – Park Ave Princess (IRE) 63 (Titus Livius **–** (FR) 115) [2017 58: f6g Jan 2] fair at best, below that level since 2015: stays 1m, usually races at shorter: acts on polytrack, fibresand, good to firm and good to soft going: has worn cheekpieces, including last 3 starts: front runner/races prominently. *Scott Dixon*

ARMUM (IRE) 2 b.f. (Apr 25) Society Rock (IRE) 126 – Good Clodora (IRE) 64 (Red **83** Clubs (IRE) 125) [2017 p6d^4 6.1s* 6m 6d 6s^4 Sep 15] 25,000Y, £70,000 2-y-o: small filly: second foal: half-sister to useful 2-y-o 5f (including Flying Childers Stakes) winner Ardad (by Kodiac): dam lightly-raced half-sister to smart 6f winner Ruby Rocket, herself dam of very smart sprinter Maarek: fairly useful performer: won minor event at Chester (by ½ length from Carouse) in June: left Jamie Osborne after second start: raced only at 6f: acts on soft going: tried in eyeshields: in tongue tie last 2 starts. *Ed Dunlop*

ARNARSON 3 b.c. Exceed And Excel (AUS) 126 – Islandia (USA) (Johar (USA) 130) **79** [2017 77: p7g^3 p8g^4 p8g^3 8.5g^6 t6.1g^3 7.8g^2 7d t6d^2 7d t6.1g^2 p6g^5 p6s^3 Dec 17] fair maiden: stays 7f: acts on polytrack and tapeta: has worn headgear, including last 3 starts: tried in tongue tie: signs of temperament. *Ed Dunlop*

ARNOLD 3 b.g. Equiano (FR) 127 – Azurinta (IRE) 59 (Azamour (IRE) 130) [2017 59: **70** 6g^2 7.2m^4 6m* 6g 6m Jun 21] fair handicapper: won at Ripon in May: stays 6f: acts on good to firm going. *Ann Duffield*

ARNOUL OF METZ 2 b.g. (Mar 18) Kyllachy 129 – Appointee (IRE) 77 (Exceed And **–** Excel (AUS) 126) [2017 p7g Dec 20] 20/1, well held in minor event at Kempton. *Henry Spiller*

AROD (IRE) 6 b.h. Teofilo (IRE) 126 – My Personal Space (USA) 80 (Rahy (USA) 115) **114** [2017 117: 7g 6.5v^2 7.5s 8s 7g 8f^5 Sep 16] tall, useful-looking horse: smart performer: left Peter Chapple-Hyam after penultimate start in 2016: good length second to Rageese in Group 3 L'Oreal Paris Stakes at Flemington final outing that year: length second to McCreery in Group 3 Liverpool City Cup at Randwick in February: left Chris Waller and off 5 months, 3½ lengths fifth to World Approval in Woodbine Mile on final start: effective at 7f and has form up to 1½m: acts on any turf going: tried in cheekpieces. *David Simcock*

ARQUUS (IRE) 4 b.g. Lilbourne Lad (IRE) 111 – Charaig (Rainbow Quest (USA) 134) **–** [2017 –: 8.3g 8v 8s^6 7d p7g f11.1g Dec 4] lengthy gelding: no form: signs of temperament. *Ed de Giles*

ARROGANT (IRE) 2 b.g. (Apr 28) Haatef (USA) 117 – Keep Bacckinhit (IRE) 80 **85** (Raise A Grand (IRE) 114) [2017 5f^4 7d^4 7g 6.5d^5 6.7d* 6.7s^2 7s p7.5g^3 Dec 5] €1,600Y: second foal: dam, 2-y-o 7f winner, half-sister to useful 5f-1m winner Chained Emotion: fairly useful performer: won maiden at Craon in September: placed after in minor event at Cholet and claimer at Deauville: probably stays 7.5f: acts on soft going. *Jose Santos*

ARROGATE (USA) 4 gr.c. Unbridled's Song (USA) 125 – Bubbler (USA) (Distorted **135** Humor (USA) 117) [2017 139: a9f* a9.9g* a8.5f^4 a10f^2 a10f^5 Nov 4]

There is a compulsion about witnessing a top horse gradually falling from grace. Such a decline is more often than not eventually explained by advancing years or recurring injury. Neither applied, however, to Arrogate, described at the height of his powers by his trainer as 'America's dirt version of Frankel' and 'possibly the greatest horse we've seen since Secretariat.' Arrogate's decline, which began when he was a well-beaten fourth of five at 20/1-on in the San Diego Handicap in July and culminated in defeats in the Pacific Classic in August and the Breeders' Cup Classic in early-November, came while he should still have been in his prime, and when he was still said to have been 'training well'. Accounting for Arrogate's dramatic flop is not easy to do and the cause may well remain a mystery. Some pointed to the fact that his three defeats came at Del Mar where the dirt surface was restored in 2015 after California curtailed its short-lived experiment with various artificial surfaces (in place of dirt). Tight and tricky tracks like the one at Del Mar are far from unusual in North American racing and its configuration and surface are unlikely to have been the reason behind Arrogate's disappointing displays (he had won Grade 1s at four different tracks). His trainer seemed to think, in hindsight, that Arrogate's winning effort in the Dubai World Cup at Meydan in March might have 'taken more out of him than any of us thought.'

A number of North American-trained Dubai World Cup winners have never been quite the same afterwards but, if Arrogate did leave his best form behind in Dubai, what is to be made of the subsequent efforts of Gun Runner, second to him at Meydan? Gun Runner ran up a sequence on his return to the States, winning the Stephen Foster Handicap at Churchill Downs (by seven lengths), the Whitney Stakes at Saratoga (by five and a quarter) and the Woodward at the same course (by ten and a quarter) before toppling the pick of America's dirt performers—also including three of Arrogate's Grade 1-winning stablemates—in the Breeders' Cup Classic, the race, according to the organisers, that 'crowns the greatest horse in the world' at the self-proclaimed 'Breeders' Cup World Championships'. Gun Runner and Arrogate's half-length conqueror in the Pacific Classic, his own stable-companion Collected, dominated the Classic from start to finish, belying, incidentally, the seemingly widely-held view that the Del Mar track favours late finishers (the results at the two-day Breeders' Cup meeting also provided some evidence of a bias on the dirt track against the rail runners, but Gun Runner and Collected, going head-to-head from some way out, never looked like being challenged). Arrogate managed to dead heat for fifth in the Classic on his final appearance before being retired to stud, but he was never close enough to get in a blow after jinking left and forfeiting ground at the start from his number-one draw on the inside. Arrogate's performance was lacklustre and it might be that he had simply lost his enthusiasm for racing. It sounded as if his trainer Bob Baffert might have detected signs in his Pacific Classic performance, Baffert saying just before the Breeders' Cup Classic that it had looked to him in the Pacific Classic 'like Arrogate wasn't going to run, then all of a sudden he started running at the end.' Arrogate travelled with no great fluency in the Pacific Classic before making some late ground on all-the-way winner Collected.

Whatever the reasons for Arrogate's failure to show his best form on his final three appearances, he still ended his career as probably the highest-earning horse in history, seemingly surpassing the prize-money earnings of leading Japanese performers T M Opera O, Gentildonna and Orfevre (currency fluctuations make exact comparisons difficult) and, at the same time, certainly taking over from California Chrome (14,752,650 dollars) as the all-time leading earner in North America with total earnings of 17,422,600 dollars. For the North American breeding industry to have produced California Chrome, the Triple Crown-winning American Pharoah and Arrogate in successive crops is remarkable and should, along with the achievements with their European stock of such as Scat Daddy and War Front, help to further restore European interest in North American bloodstock which was once so highly sought after. The boom in American bloodstock values in the 'eighties at venues like the Keeneland July Sale coincided with a succession of top performers in that country in the 'seventies, including three winners of the Triple Crown in six years, while a slightly earlier parallel in Britain saw Nijinsky, Mill Reef and Brigadier Gerard—the first two American-bred—also come along almost at once.

Pegasus World Cup Invitational Stakes, Gulfstream Park—Arrogate and Mike Smith forge clear of Shaman Ghost (noseband) and Neolithic (blinkers) in the inaugural running of what is now the most valuable race in the world; California Chrome (not in picture), a dual winner of America's Horse of the Year award, is well beaten on his final appearance

Dubai World Cup Sponsored By Emirates Airline, Meydan—
Arrogate shows all the hallmarks of a champion to become the highest earner of all time, overcoming a poor start and wide passage to catch Gun Runner (white cap), with Neolithic five lengths further back in third

Unlike the other horses mentioned towards the end of the last paragraph, Arrogate wasn't a classic winner and he missed the American Triple Crown races altogether, first making his mark when bursting on the scene with a thirteen and a half length win in the Travers Stakes at Saratoga (Gun Runner finished third). The Travers was just the fifth start of Arrogate's career—he was unraced at two—and he went on to cement his place among the finest American dirt performers of all time with a narrow victory in the Breeders' Cup Classic over California Chrome, America's Horse of the Year in 2016, as he had been in 2014 when successful in two legs of the Triple Crown, the Kentucky Derby and the Preakness. The newly-instituted 12,000,000-dollar Pegasus World Cup Invitational at Gulfstream Park in January featured a second meeting between Arrogate and California Chrome but, in the end, that particular 'showdown' failed to live up to its billing, with California Chrome beaten some way out and clearly not giving his running. Arrogate's impressive win from Shaman Ghost and Neolithic made his proposed appearance in the Dubai World Cup in March the most eagerly-awaited event of the long Dubai Carnival. At the time of California Chrome's 2016 victory in the World Cup, Arrogate had still not been seen on a racecourse and, when he finally made his debut three weeks later, he was beaten into third, wearing blinkers, in a maiden at lowly Los Alamitos. Arrogate hadn't lost since, though, and the blinkers had been dispensed with straight after Los Alamitos. A victory in the Dubai World Cup, which reverted to a race on dirt in 2015 after five runnings on the synthetic tapeta surface, looked set to stretch Arrogate's winning streak to seven and give him a fourth Grade 1 win in a row.

The Dubai World Cup was Arrogate's first and only appearance outside North America and he and his thirteen rivals faced an unusually wet track after a deluge that caused widespread chaos in the city of Dubai and turned the Meydan track into a sea of standing water at the start of the day, non-stop harrowing making the dirt track raceable just in time for the meeting (the turf course was testing). Arrogate started at 3/1-on for the Emirates Airline-sponsored Dubai World Cup for which there were five challengers in all from North America, also including Arrogate's stablemate Hoppertunity, who had finished third in the race the year before, the Travers third Gun Runner, the Pegasus third Neolithic, and Keen Ice who had finished ten and three quarter lengths third behind Arrogate and California Chrome in the Breeders' Cup Classic. The overseas challenge was completed by Apollo Kentucky, Gold Dream, Lani and Awardee from Japan and Mubtaahij representing South Africa (there were no representatives from Europe). Arrogate made things difficult for himself by fluffing the start and, after also being squeezed by 100/1 outsider Furia Cruzada, found himself in last place and already with plenty to do. Kept wide, Arrogate was being niggled along at times in the back straight where there were ten horses in front of him, but he began to make very good ground from four furlongs out and, moving eye-catchingly into fourth rounding the home turn, soon had the pace-setting Gun Runner in his sights. Keeping on very strongly, Arrogate took the lead over a furlong out and won in astonishing fashion by two and a quarter lengths and five from Gun Runner and Neolithic, giving North America a one, two, three, with Mubtaahij and Awardee next, ahead of Hoppertunity and Keen Ice. The Dubai World Cup might have lost its place to the Pegasus as the world's richest race, but Arrogate put up a towering performance, one that made him look, at the time, worthy of being rated as good as any winner of the race in its illustrious history. Arrogate provided his trainer with his third Dubai World Cup winner, following Silver Charm and Captain Steve in the days when the race was run at Nad Al Sheba. Seventh-placed Keen Ice, incidentally, was the only one of the American challengers in the Dubai World Cup who finished 'out of the money' on what was generally a good night for North American racing. Mind Your Biscuits, placed in the Breeders' Cup Sprint, gave the Americans a second winner on the night in the Dubai Golden Shaheen. The rules in Dubai forbid the administration of drugs on racedays and the likes of Arrogate, Gun Runner and Neolithic all came off their usual pre-race medication of lasix, which is permitted in North America and almost universally used there. The honours on World Cup night were spread among five nations, Vazirabad (Gold Cup) and The Right Man (Al Quoz Sprint) both winning for France, Jack Hobbs (Sheema Classic) for Britain and Vivlos (Turf) for Japan, with Second Summer (Godolphin Mile) and Thunder Snow (UAE Derby) providing the hosts with two of the big winners.

Arrogate (USA) (gr.c. 2013)	Unbridled's Song (USA) (gr 1993)	Unbridled (b 1987)	Fappiano
			Gana Facil
		Trolley Song (gr 1983)	Caro
			Lucky Spell
	Bubbler (USA) (br 2006)	Distorted Humor (ch 1993)	Forty Niner
			Danzigs Beauty
		Grechelle (br 1995)	Deputy Minister
			Meadow Star

Comparisons made between Arrogate and Frankel were partly prompted by the fact that both raced in the colours of Khalid Abdullah, for whom Bobby Frankel trained on the west coast of America until his death from leukaemia in 2009. The Abdullah silks made a return to the Californian tracks after Juddmonte began to buy yearlings to race on the dirt for Bob Baffert. The tall, rather lean Arrogate, who is a long-striding individual, cost 560,000 dollars as a yearling. He is by Unbridled's Song and the first foal of the Distorted Humor minor stakes winner Bubbler who was successful at six to nine furlongs. Unbridled's Song is a son of the influential Unbridled, a Kentucky Derby winner who is also the great grandsire of American Pharoah, whose own grandsire Empire Maker won the Belmont Stakes for Arrogate's owner. Bubbler, who has since had a filly by Medaglia d'Oro go through the sale-ring for 300,000 dollars (as a yearling in September 2016), is a daughter of Grechelle, who was stakes placed, but, much more significantly, a granddaughter of Meadow Star, the champion American two-year-old filly in 1990 when she won the Breeders' Cup Juvenile Fillies in an unbeaten campaign. Meadow Star went on to success as a three-year-old in the Acorn Stakes and the Mother Goose, two legs of the so-called 'triple tiara' at the time. Arrogate, who wore a tongue tie in the Dubai World Cup, raced only on dirt and stayed a mile and a quarter well. He will start his stud career at Juddmonte's Kentucky Farm in 2017 at a fee of 75,000 dollars, nearly twice the initial fee demanded for California Chrome when he was retired, but well short of the 200,000-dollar nomination fee that the same stable's Triple Crown winner American Pharoah commanded in his first season. *Bob Baffert, USA*

ARROWTOWN 5 b.m. Rail Link 132 – Protectress 110 (Hector Protector (USA) 124) **87** [2017 82: 11.9v^2 11.9m^6 12v* 16.3g^2 Oct 14] fairly useful handicapper: won at Pontefract (apprentice) in September: stays 16.5f: acts on polytrack, good to firm and heavy going: wears hood. *Michael Easterby*

ARROWZONE 6 b.g. Iffraaj 127 – Donna Giovanna 74 (Mozart (IRE) 131) [2017 94: **84** p10g t9.5g p10d p8g 8g t9.5g 10m^5 10.2m 10g^6 9.9g p11g p10g^5 t9.5g* t8d^6 t8.6g^4 t9.5g* Nov 25] lengthy gelding: fairly useful handicapper: won at Wolverhampton in October and November: left Ivan Furtado after first start: stays 1¼m: acts on polytrack, tapeta and heavy going: has worn headgear, including last 5 starts: often travels strongly. *Kevin Frost*

ARRUCIAN 4 b.f. Medicean 128 – Arruhan (IRE) 87 (Mujtahid (USA) 118) [2017 10s p8s Sep 30] no form. *Ms N. M. Hugo* –

ARSENIO LUPIN 3 b.c. Delegator 125 – Tenebrae (IRE) (In The Wings 128) [2017 p8g³ p8g⁴ p10g³ 8.3g² 8.1d 8d⁵ Jul 21] 12,000F, 9,000Y: sixth foal: half-brother to 3 winners, including 7f/1m winner Tenbridge (by Avonbridge) and 2-y-o 6f winner Veil of Night (by Val Royal): dam ran once in France: fairly useful maiden: second in handicap at Nottingham in May: stays 8.5f: acts on polytrack: wears tongue tie. *Denis Quinn* **85**

ARTARMON (IRE) 2 b.c. (Feb 10) So You Think (NZ) 133 – Aljumar (IRE) (Marju (IRE) 127) [2017 8.3d 8.3g³ Nov 1] 50,000Y: second foal: dam unraced half-sister to smart winner up to 2m What A Charm: fair form when third at Nottingham on second of 2 starts in maidens: will stay at least 1¼m: open to further improvement. *Michael Bell* **77 p**

ART COLLECTION (FR) 4 b.g. Shakespearean (IRE) 120 – Renascent Rahy (Rahy (USA) 115) [2017 81: t5d* t5s* 5m⁶ 6m⁴ 6s⁶ 6d⁶ 6g⁶ p6.5g 6d² p7.5g Dec 16] neat gelding: useful performer: won handicaps at Newcastle in March and April (by 3¼ lengths from Paddy Power): second in minor event at Fontainebleau (1½ lengths behind Cheikeljack) in November: left Ruth Carr after eighth start: stays 7f: acts on polytrack, tapeta, soft and good to firm going: has worn headgear. *Andrew Hollinshead, France* **97**

ART ECHO 4 b.g. Art Connoisseur (IRE) 121 – Madhaaq (IRE) 87 (Medicean 128) [2017 76: 7m* 8.2g³ 7s* t7.2g⁴ 7d* 7g 7g⁵ 7d 7v⁴ 7.2v² Oct 16] fairly useful handicapper: won at Doncaster in April, Newmarket in May and again at Doncaster (by ½ length from Johnny Cavagin) in July: stays 1m: acts on tapeta, good to firm and heavy going: has worn headgear, including final start: usually wears tongue tie. *John Mackie* **86**

ARTFUL ROGUE (IRE) 6 b.g. Excellent Art 125 – Szabo (IRE) 88 (Anabaa (USA) 130) [2017 81, a90: p12g³ 9.9m² p11g⁶ 9.9d p12s³ p12g⁵ p11g⁴ Oct 4] lengthy gelding: fairly useful handicapper: placed at Lingfield in January, Sandown in June and Kempton in August: stays 13f: acts on polytrack and firm going: has worn headgear: sold to join Keith Dalgleish 11,000 gns in October. *Amanda Perrett* **90**

ARTHENIA (IRE) 2 b.f. (Mar 6) Camelot 128 – Miss Intimate (USA) (War Chant (USA) 126) [2017 7d 8s⁶ 8g³ Oct 7] 50,000Y: closely related to 10.5f winner Honour And Obey (by Hurricane Run) and half-sister to 3 winners, including useful/ungenuine 7f/1m winner Life Partner (by Cape Cross) and useful 2-y-o 7f winner (stays 1¼m) Flirt (by Duke of Marmalade): dam unraced half-sister to Irish 2000 Guineas winner Bachelor Duke: fair form: best effort when third in minor event at Newmarket (6 lengths behind Old Persian) in October: bred to be suited by 1¼m+: remains with potential. *Charles Hills* **74 p**

ARTHENUS 5 b.g. Dutch Art 126 – Lady Hen 68 (Efisio 120) [2017 115: 10d⁶ 12m 10s² 10.5d⁶ 9.9g³ 12s 11.8d⁵ Oct 30] stocky gelding: useful performer: placed in listed races at Newbury (2¾ lengths second to What About Carlo) and Saint-Cloud (1½ lengths third to Uele River): stayed 1¼m: acted on polytrack and soft going: wore headgear: dead. *James Fanshawe* **109**

ART HISTORY (IRE) 9 gr.g. Dalakhani (IRE) 133 – What A Picture (FR) (Peintre Celebre (USA) 137) [2017 –: p12f p16g⁵ 11.9d⁵ 16.5m⁶ Jul 13] lengthy gelding: modest handicapper nowadays: left Zoe Davison after second start: stays 2¼m: acts on polytrack and good to firm going: has worn headgear: tried in tongue tie: not straightforward and can't be relied on. *Philip Kirby* **58 §**

ARTHUR MC BRIDE (IRE) 8 b.g. Royal Anthem (USA) 135 – Lucky Diverse (IRE) (Lucky Guest 109) [2017 88: 16m 16.2f⁴ 14.1s³ 21.6m 20.6v³ 15.9g² 16s* 18d 18m Oct 14] tall gelding: useful handicapper: won at Goodwood (by 2½ lengths from Aurora Gray) in September: placed at Carlisle in June, Goodwood in August and Chester in September: stays 2½m: acts on any turf going: wears tongue tie: front runner/races prominently. *Nigel Twiston-Davies* **95**

ARTHUR'S QUEEN (FR) 6 b.m. Soldier of Fortune (IRE) 131 – Tintagel (Oasis Dream 129) [2017 –: 12m 12g⁵ Jul 20] fair handicapper at best, little impact since 2015: stays 13f: acts on good to soft going. *Carroll Gray* –

ARTHURTHEDELEGATOR 3 b.g. Delegator 125 – Markova's Dance 64 (Mark of Esteem (IRE) 137) [2017 70: p8g 7.5f³ 6.9g² 6.1m⁵ Jun 16] compact gelding: fair handicapper: stayed 1m: acted on fibresand, tapeta and firm going: usually raced prominently: dead. *Oliver Greenall* **72**

ARTIC NEL 3 ch.f. Haafhd 129 – Artic Bliss (Fraam 114) [2017 9.9g 10.2s⁶ t9.5g⁶ 14d⁵ 16s⁵ p13.3d Sep 28] fourth foal: dam, of little account on Flat, 2m hurdle winner: modest maiden: barely stays 2m: acts on soft going. *Ian Williams* **58**

ARTIESHOW (USA) 2 b.c. (Apr 17) Artie Schiller (USA) 124 – Garden Music (USA) **87**
(Pivotal 124) [2017 p7s^{3} p7g^{2} Dec 21] $16,000Y, $50,000 2-y-o: third foal: half-brother to a winner in USA by Heatseeker: dam lightly-raced daughter of Lowther Stakes winner Jemima: fairly useful form: better effort when second in minor event at Chelmsford (head behind Move Swiftly) in December. *Marco Botti*

ARTISTICA (GER) 3 b.f. Areion (GER) 115 – Artica (GER) (Pentire 132) [2017 6s* **111**
6.1g* 6g* 6g^{6} 6g Aug 13] third foal: dam, German 7f and (at 2 yrs) 1m winner, half-sister to Deutches Derby runner-up Acambaro: smart performer: won minor event at Hanover in April, then listed race at Nottingham and Silberne Peitsche at Baden-Baden (by ¾ length from Millowitsch), both in May: sixth to Mystic Dawn in Summer Stakes at York next time: stays 7f: acts on soft going. *D. Moser, Germany*

ART NOUVELLE (IRE) 3 b.f. Art Connoisseur (IRE) 121 – Van de Cappelle (IRE) **90**
(Pivotal 124) [2017 90p: 7d 7m^{3} 6m^{2} 6g 5m 7g 6g p7g p6g* Dec 28] sixth foal: half-sister to German 7f winner Tribal I D (by High Chaparral) and 2-y-o 7f winner Vegas Rebel (by Alfred Nobel): dam unraced half-sister to smart winner up to 12.5f Ruscello: fairly useful handicapper: won at Lingfield (by length from Juan Horsepower) in December: stays 7f: acts on polytrack, good to firm and good to soft going: sometimes in cheekpieces. *Joseph Patrick O'Brien, Ireland*

ART OBSESSION (IRE) 6 b.g. Excellent Art 125 – Ghana (IRE) (Lahib (USA) 129) **89**
[2017 82: t6d^{3} t6d^{2} 6m* 6m^{5} 6d* 6s 6g 6s t6d Oct 24] long-backed gelding: fairly useful handicapper: won at Thirsk in May and Doncaster (by ¾ length from Eccleston) in July: raced mainly at 6f: acts on polytrack, tapeta, good to firm and heavy going: sometimes slowly away, usually races towards rear. *Paul Midgley*

ART OF SWING (IRE) 5 b.g. Excellent Art 125 – Shahmina (IRE) 78 (Danehill (USA) **74**
126) [2017 80p: 14f^{4} 12s^{3} 11.2g 13.3v^{6} 11.2s^{4} p12g^{5} Nov 29] rangy gelding: fair handicapper: probably stays 1½m: acts on polytrack. *Gary Moore*

ARTSCAPE 5 b.g. Iffraaj 127 – Artisti (Cape Cross (IRE) 129) [2017 69: p6g* p6g^{5} 6g 5d^{4} **80**
6d* 6.1s^{6} 7s^{5} 6s^{3} 6.1m^{6} 6s^{6} 5d p6g^{5} Oct 24] sturdy gelding: fairly useful performer: won maiden at Kempton in February and handicap at Goodwood (by head from Curious Fox) in June: stays 6f: acts on polytrack and good to soft going: has worn headgear, including in 2017: front runner/races prominently: sold 2,500 gns in October. *Dean Ivory*

ART SCHOLAR (IRE) 10 b.g. Pyrus (USA) 106 – Marigold (FR) 88 (Marju (IRE) 127) **63**
[2017 73: 10g^{6} 14f^{4} 14d^{4} 10.1d^{5} 11.5m^{6} Aug 17] sturdy gelding: modest handicapper nowadays: stays 1¾m: acts on all-weather, good to firm and heavy going: has worn headgear: usually races towards rear. *Michael Appleby*

ART'S DESIRE (IRE) 3 ch.f. Dutch Art 126 – Zenella 95 (Kyllachy 129) [2017 t7.1g^{3} **71**
6m^{4} 7s^{4} 8.1d p7g^{3} 7m^{3} t8.6g t7.2g^{6} 7.6s^{5} p7d* p8g^{6} Oct 26] 40,000Y: good-topped filly: second foal: half-sister to 2-y-o 7f winner Dark Crescent (by Elnadim): dam 2-y-o 6f-1m winner: fair handicapper: won at Chelmsford in September: stays 7f: acts on polytrack, tapeta and good to firm going. *Ed Walker*

ARTSTEELWORK 3 b.f. Fast Company (IRE) 126 – Etymology (Rail Link 132) [2017 **–**
–: p6g p7g p5d t5.1g p7s Jul 25] no form. *John Butler*

ARTY BUT POOR 2 b.g. (Mar 24) Dutch Art 126 – Libys Dream (IRE) 100 (Invincible **62**
Spirit (IRE) 121) [2017 t6.1g^{4} t5.1g^{6} 6f t6g^{3} t7.2g^{5} t6.1g Nov 29] modest maiden: stays 6f: acts on tapeta: in cheekpieces last 2 starts. *Oliver Greenall*

ARTY CAMPBELL (IRE) 7 b.g. Dylan Thomas (IRE) 132 – Kincob (USA) 63 **89**
(Kingmambo (USA) 125) [2017 89: 16s^{3} 16g^{3} 16s^{5} 15.9v* 14.4v Sep 30] good-bodied gelding: fairly useful handicapper: won at Chester (by neck from Perfect Summer) in September: stays 17f: acts on polytrack, tapeta, good to firm and heavy going: in cheekpieces last 5 starts: sometimes slowly away, often races in rear: consistent. *Bernard Llewellyn*

ARWA (IRE) 3 b.f. Holy Roman Emperor (IRE) 125 – Another Storm (USA) (Gone West **84**
(USA)) [2017 87: 7m 7g May 30] lengthy filly: fairly useful performer: should be suited by at least 1m: acts on good to firm going: has joined David Lanigan. *Charles Hills*

ARYA STARK 3 b.f. Piccolo 121 – Night Affair 83 (Bold Edge 123) [2017 –: t6f t7.1m^{5} **42**
p6d^{3} p7g Feb 24] poor maiden: in cheekpieces last 2 starts. *Tony Carroll*

ARYEH (IRE) 3 ch.f. Exceed And Excel (AUS) 126 – Height of Summer (IRE) 85 **56**
(Alhaarth (IRE) 126) [2017 63p: p7g t8.6g^{4} Jan 26] modest form in maidens: sold 5,500 gns, sent to Greece. *Hugo Palmer*

ARZAAK (IRE) 3 br.g. Casamento (IRE) 118 – Dixieland Kiss (USA) (Dixie Union (USA) 121) [2017 77: p6g^{3} t6d^{3} p6g^{4} t5d^{2} t6g^{5} f5d* p6g^{6} 5.1m^{2} 5m* 5.1m^{4} 5.7f^{2} 5.2s^{2} 5m^{3} 5.2d^{4} p5g^{6} f5g^{2} Nov 16] useful performer: won maiden at Southwell in April and handicap at Catterick (by neck from Merry Banter) in May: placed on 8 other occasions in 2017: stays 6f: acts on all-weather, firm and soft going: wears headgear: front runner/races prominently. *Chris Dwyer* **97**

ASAAS (USA) 3 ch.g. Distorted Humor (USA) 117 – Affectionately (Galileo (IRE) 134) [2017 78: 9m^{2} 8.1m* 8.5m^{4} p10g^{3} Sep 25] medium-sized gelding: fairly useful performer: won maiden at Windsor in July: third in handicap at Kempton in September: probably stays 1¼m: acts on polytrack and good to firm going: tried in blinkers: sent to Saudi Arabia. *Roger Varian* **88**

ASANTA SANA (IRE) 3 b.f. Galileo (IRE) 134 – Milanova (AUS) (Danehill (USA) 126) [2017 p12g^{4} 12g^{4} Apr 11] sister to useful 11f winner Los Barbados and smart winner up to 1½m Pretty Perfect (2-y-o 7f winner) and half-sister to a winner in Australia by Dehere: dam, Australian Group 3 1m winner (stayed 1¼m), sister to high-class 2-y-o 6f/7f winner Holy Roman Emperor: modest form in maidens. *John Gosden* **60**

ASCENDANT 11 ch.g. Medicean 128 – Ascendancy (Sadler's Wells (USA) 132) [2017 t16.5g^{3} p16d* f14g p15.8g^{2} p16g^{6} Jun 28] tall, good-topped gelding: fair handicapper nowadays: won at Kempton in February: stays 16.5f: acts on polytrack, tapeta, soft and good to firm going: has worn headgear/tongue tie: fairly useful hurdler. *Johnny Farrelly* **66**

ASCOT DAY (IRE) 3 b.g. Kheleyf (USA) 116 – My Lucky Liz (IRE) 86 (Exceed And Excel (AUS) 126) [2017 84p: f6g* p5g* 5.1d^{6} 5m^{4} 5g^{6} t6g* Jul 29] lengthy gelding: useful performer: won maiden at Southwell in January, and handicaps at Lingfield later same month and Newcastle (by head from Boundsy) in July: stays 6f: acts on all-weather. *David Simcock* **98**

ASCOT WEEK (USA) 3 br.g. Lonhro (AUS) 128 – Millenia (Unfuwain (USA) 131) [2017 61p: p8g 7.6g^{4} 8m^{3} 8g Aug 20] fairly useful maiden: third in handicap at Doncaster in June: left Owen Burrows after third start: stays 1m: acts on good to firm going. *John Quinn* **85**

ASCRIPTION (IRE) 8 b.g. Dansili 127 – Lady Elgar (IRE) (Sadler's Wells (USA) 132) [2017 –: f7d Mar 21] sturdy gelding: has reportedly had breathing operation: smart at best, lightly raced and well held since 2015: stays 8.5f: acts on soft and good to firm going: has worn hood/tongue tie. *Keith Dalgleish* **–**

ASHADIHAN 4 b.f. Kyllachy 129 – Miss Delila (USA) (Malibu Moon (USA)) [2017 110: p7d* p7g^{3} 7d^{5} May 13] good-topped filly: smart performer: won minor event at Chelmsford (by 1½ lengths from Volunteer Point) in February: stays 1m: acts on polytrack and firm going: has worn headgear, including last 4 starts. *Kevin Ryan* **110**

ASHAZURI 3 b.f. Dick Turpin (IRE) 127 – Shesha Bear 83 (Tobougg (IRE) 125) [2017 69: p8g 9.9f 8.1d^{3} 8g^{3} 8f* 8.5d^{3} 8s^{5} 9s^{3} 8g p8g^{4} Oct 18] compact filly: fair handicapper: won at Salisbury (apprentice) in June: stays 1m: acts on polytrack, firm and good to soft going: wears hood. *Jonathan Portman* **73**

ASHEENA 2 gr.f. (Mar 13) Lethal Force (IRE) 128 – Meddle (Diktat 126) [2017 5m^{6} p5g^{5} 7m Oct 25] workmanlike filly: half-sister to several winners, including useful 6f (including at 2 yrs) winner Munro and winner up to 1m Anastazia (2-y-o 6f winner) (both by Kyllachy): dam of little account: little impact in minor events. *Paul D'Arcy* **–**

ASHFORD ISLAND 4 b.g. Munnings (USA) 118 – Falling Angel 86 (Kylian (USA)) [2017 57: p7s^{6} p8d 7m 6g Jul 4] strong gelding: poor handicapper: stays 7f: acts on polytrack, tapeta and good to firm going: usually wears headgear: sometimes slowly away. *Adam West* **38**

ASHINGTON 2 b.g. (Feb 13) Canford Cliffs (IRE) 133 – Kadoma (Danehill Dancer (IRE) 117) [2017 p8g^{5} p8g^{6} 7d^{3} p8g p10g^{6} Nov 2] fair maiden: should stay 1¼m: acts on polytrack: usually races towards rear. *Luca Cumani* **71**

ASHKOUL (FR) 4 b.g. Tamayuz 126 – Asharna (IRE) (Darshaan 133) [2017 10g 10.3m^{3} 11.9d 10g May 29] useful handicapper: won twice for A. de Royer Dupre in 2016: third at Doncaster (2¾ lengths behind Fidaawy) in April: stays 1½m: acts on good to soft and good to firm going: tried in blinkers: has joined Dan Skelton. *Michael Appleby* **95**

ASHPAN SAM 8 b.g. Firebreak 125 – Sweet Patoopie 72 (Indian Ridge 123) [2017 98: 6s 6m 6m 6f* 6g^{3} 5.1d^{5} 6.1g Aug 7] leggy gelding: fairly useful handicapper: won at Epsom (by ¾ length from Storm Cry) in July: races at 5f/6f: acts on any turf going: wears cheekpieces: front runner/races prominently. *David Drinkwater* **92**

ASHWAQ 3 ch.f. Sepoy (AUS) 129 – Blaugrana (IRE) 76 (Exceed And Excel (AUS) 126) **65**
[2017 82p: p6g* 5.7f^6 6f^6 8s 7.1v^4 p6g Aug 8] fair performer: won maiden at Kempton in March: stays 7f: acts on polytrack and good to firm going: in blinkers last 2 starts. *Richard Hannon*

ASHWASS (USA) 3 b.g. Lonhro (AUS) 128 – Alzerra (UAE) 108 (Pivotal 124) [2017 **98 p**
p8s^6 7.1s* Sep 14] fifth foal: half-brother to 2-y-o 6f-1m winner Majeyda (by Street Cry) and 6f and (at 2 yrs) 7f winner Yattwee (by Hard Spun), both useful: dam 2-y-o 5f/6f winner, including Cornwallis Stakes: useful form: won maiden at Chepstow (impressively, by 8 lengths from Holiday Girl) in September: will go on improving. *Roger Varian*

ASIAN WING (IRE) 8 ch.g. Hawk Wing (USA) 136 – Blue Beacon 68 (Fantastic Light **71**
(USA) 134) [2017 73: p12g^2 p12s t13.9f^3 8m 10s 10g t16.5g p10.7g^4 p10.7g^2 p12g Dec 15] fair handicapper: stays 2m, effective at much shorter: acts on polytrack and soft going: often wears headgear/tongue tie. *J. J. Feane, Ireland*

ASIDIOUS ALEXANDER (IRE) 3 ch.f. Windsor Knot (IRE) 118 – Birthday Present **86**
(Cadeaux Genereux 131) [2017 99: 8d 6.9s Jun 28] compact filly: useful at 2 yrs, below that level in 2017: stays 1m: best form on good going: in headgear last 2 starts. *Simon Crisford*

ASKARI 4 b.g. Sea The Stars (IRE) 140 – Loulwa (IRE) 103 (Montjeu (IRE) 137) [2017 **70**
68: t12.2g^3 p12d 11.6m^4 10d 11.5s* 11.9d Jul 1] sturdy gelding: fair handicapper: won at Yarmouth in June: stays 1½m: acts on tapeta, soft and good to firm going: usually races prominently. *Tom Clover*

ASKING (IRE) 3 b.f. Zoffany (IRE) 121 – Roselita (IRE) (Sadler's Wells (USA) 132) **105**
[2017 88p: p8g* p8g^2 8m^2 9.9d 8d 8m^6 7g* 7g^3 8.1g 6g 7s Aug 4] sturdy filly: third foal: sister to 13f winner Lord Justice: dam unraced half-sister to very smart Japanese 7f/1m performer Fiero out of sister to Rock of Gibraltar: useful performer: won maiden at Dundalk (by length from Sir Danilo) in March and handicap at the Curragh (by ½ length from Honor Oak) in July: stays 1m: acts on polytrack, good to firm and good to soft going: has worn cheekpieces: wears tongue tie: often travels strongly. *Aidan O'Brien, Ireland*

ASK THE GURU 7 b.g. Ishiguru (USA) 114 – Tharwa (IRE) 63 (Last Tycoon 131) [2017 **63**
68: p5g p5m p5f^5 p5g 5.3m^4 5f^2 p5g* 5.3g* 5m p5g p5g* p5g p5g Dec 31] lengthy gelding: modest handicapper nowadays: won at Lingfield in July, Brighton in August and Kempton in October: raced mainly at 5f: acts on polytrack and any turf going: wears headgear. *Michael Attwater*

ASMAHAN 3 b.f. Casamento (IRE) 118 – Finnmark (Halling (USA) 133) [2017 –: t12.2g^{ur} **– §**
May 3] bucked and unseated rider leaving stalls both starts: one to avoid. *Simon Crisford*

ASPASIUS (GER) 5 b.g. Desert Prince (IRE) 130 – Aspasia Lunata (GER) (Tiger Hill **–**
(IRE) 127) [2017 60: p10g Dec 13] angular gelding: fair at best, well held sole outing in 2017: stays 1m: acts on soft going. *Gary Moore*

ASSANILKA (FR) 3 b.f. Diamond Green (FR) 121 – Regal Step 85 (Royal Applause **83**
124) [2017 92: p8g 9.9g 8d p8g^4 8m^4 p8.9g^6 p8g Dec 20] good-topped filly: fairly useful handicapper: probably stays 9f: acts on polytrack and good to firm going: in cheekpieces last 5 starts: usually leads. *Harry Dunlop*

ASSERTAINTY 2 b.g. (Feb 27) Assertive 121 – Layla's Oasis 78 (Oasis Dream 129) **–**
[2017 6d t6g Nov 23] well held in maiden/minor event. *Tim Easterby*

ASSERTIVE AGENT 7 b.m. Assertive 121 – Agent Kensington 65 (Mujahid (USA) **72**
125) [2017 69: p6g^2 p6d* p6g^3 p6g^4 6m^{pu} t6.1g Nov 20] fair handicapper: won at Kempton in February: stays 6f: acts on polytrack and good to soft going: has worn headgear: often races towards rear. *Tony Carroll*

ASSERTOR 3 b.f. Assertive 121 – Blue Goddess (IRE) 94 (Blues Traveller (IRE) 119) **52**
[2017 –: 6g^4 6.1m^6 8s^3 7d^3 8v 8v Oct 19] modest maiden: stays 1m: acts on soft going: tried in hood. *Tony Carroll*

ASSIDUOUS 3 b.g. Sir Percy 129 – Suzi Spends (IRE) 94 (Royal Applause 124) [2017 **74**
11.6m^4 12m^2 p13.3g f12.1g^6 Nov 16] fair form: stays 1½m. *Mark Johnston*

ASTOLAT 2 b.f. (Mar 30) Camelot 128 – Sablonne (USA) 100 (Silver Hawk (USA) 123) **60**
[2017 p8g t8g^5 Dec 6] seventh foal: closely related to 1¼m-1½m winner Classic Villager (by Authorized) and half-sister to 1m winner Royal Hush (by Royal Applause) and winner up to 13f Beat The Tide (2-y-o 7f winner, by Black Sam Bellamy): dam, French 2-y-o 1m winner, half-sister to smart stayer Macorville: modest form in minor event/maiden. *Ed Walker*

ASTONE MAN (FR) 3 gr.c. Rajsaman (FR) 121 – Astonia (FR) (Astarabad (USA) 122) [2017 6.1m4 7.4d3 8s4 Aug 25] modest form when in frame in 3 maidens. *Tony Carroll* **64**

ASTRAEA 2 b.f. (Feb 7) Cityscape 127 – Rapid Revalation (USA) (Bianconi (USA) 123) [2017 6m3 6m3 7d 8v 6g Oct 13] £4,000Y: lengthy filly: fourth foal: half-sister to 2-y-o 6f winner Prophesize (by Captain Rio): dam US 4.5f (including at 2 yrs)/5.5f winner: fair maiden: best effort at 6f: acts on good to firm going. *Michael Easterby* **71**

ASTROBLAZE 2 ch.f. (Feb 22) Havana Gold (IRE) 118 – Astrodonna 83 (Carnival Dancer 123) [2017 7m t7.2g p7g Dec 20] lengthy filly: third foal: dam 1m and (at 2 yrs) 8.6f winner: modest form on second of 3 starts in minor events. *Mark H. Tompkins* **57**

ASTROBREEZE 2 b.f. (Feb 8) Lawman (FR) 121 – Astromagick 84 (Rainbow Quest (USA) 134) [2017 8s6 p7s Dec 8] first foal: dam 2m winner out of useful performer up to 2m Astrocharm: well held in minor events. *Mark H. Tompkins* **–**

ASTROFIRE 2 b.f. (Mar 1) Kheleyf (USA) 116 – Astromancer (USA) 62 (Silver Hawk (USA) 123) [2017 7d p10g p7s6 Dec 15] half-sister to 11.5f winner Cotton Grass (by Medicean): dam 1¾m winner: little impact in minor events/maiden. *Mark H. Tompkins* **–**

ASTROJEWEL 2 b.f. (Mar 21) Havana Gold (IRE) 118 – Astrolibra 67 (Sakhee (USA) 136) [2017 6g Aug 2] second foal: dam, 1¼m/11f winner, also won over hurdles: 50/1, very green when well held in minor event at Leicester. *Mark H. Tompkins* **–**

ASTROLOGIST (IRE) 2 b.c. (Mar 5) Sea The Stars (IRE) 140 – Jumooh (Monsun (GER) 124) [2017 8g 8.3d2 Oct 18] €135,000Y: fourth foal: brother to useful 1¼m winner (stays 1¾m) Shraaoh and smart winner up to 1¾m Raheen House (2-y-o 1m winner): dam lightly-raced half-sister to Queen Mary Stakes winner/1000 Guineas third Maqaasid: fair form: better effort when second in maiden at Nottingham (neck behind Blazing Tunder) in October: will be suited by 1¼m+. *Clive Cox* **75**

ASTRONOMY'S CHOICE 3 b.f. Redoute's Choice (AUS) – Astronomy Domine 61 (Galileo (IRE) 134) [2017 89P: 10m3 12m 9.9d p12g6 Nov 29] big, well-made filly: useful performer: third in listed race at Newmarket (2¼ lengths behind Horseplay) in May: stays 1¼m: acts on good to firm going: tried in blinkers. *John Gosden* **99**

ASTROPHYSICS 5 ch.g. Paco Boy (IRE) 129 – Jodrell Bank (IRE) 63 (Observatory (USA) 131) [2017 83: 5g 5d5 5g 5g 5d2 5s2 5d2 5g6 5s 5g2 t5g6 t5g Nov 24] sturdy, close-coupled gelding: fair handicapper nowadays: stays 6f: acts on tapeta, firm and good to soft going: tried in blinkers/tongue tie. *Lynn Siddall* **75**

ASTROSECRET 4 b.f. Halling (USA) 133 – Optimistic 90 (Reprimand 122) [2017 72: p13.3g 11.5m6 10.2d5 16.3d 11.8g 11.5m Aug 17] leggy filly: maiden: no form in 2017: tried in cheekpieces. *Mark H. Tompkins* **–**

ASTROSHADOW 3 gr.f. Aussie Rules (USA) 123 – Astrodiva 78 (Where Or When (IRE) 124) [2017 p13.3g 11.8d p12s 16.1d2 f16.5g p15.8g Sep 26] second foal: half-sister to German 1¼m winner Heavensfield (by Motivator): dam maiden (stayed 1¾m): standout effort (modest form) when second in handicap at Beverley in July: best effort at 2m on good to soft going. *Mark H. Tompkins* **55**

ASTROSTORM 3 b.g. Medicean 128 – Astrolibra 67 (Sakhee (USA) 136) [2017 p10g p11d6 t12.2g4 14g4 t14g Jul 17] modest maiden: stays 1¾m: acts on tapeta. *Mark H. Tompkins* **52**

ASTUTE BOY (IRE) 3 b.g. Arcano (IRE) 122 – Spa (Sadler's Wells (USA) 132) [2017 65: 11.6d2 11.6s2 11.5m* 14s2 t12.4d5 Sep 29] fairly useful handicapper: won at Yarmouth in August: second at Lingfield in July/August and Haydock in September: stays 1¾m: acts on soft and good to firm going: tried in blinkers: often races prominently, usually responds generously to pressure: sold to join Harry Fry 28,000 gns in October. *Ed Vaughan* **88**

A SURE WELCOME 3 b.g. Pastoral Pursuits 127 – Croeso Bach 73 (Bertolini (USA) 125) [2017 58: t7.1g* p7g* p7g 7d3 t7.2g6 t7.2g t6.1g* t6.1d2 t6.1g3 Dec 18] compact gelding: fair handicapper: won at Wolverhampton and Kempton in April, and again at Wolverhampton in November: effective at 6f/7f: acts on polytrack and tapeta: wears cheekpieces: usually races prominently, often freely. *John Spearing* **79**

ATALANTA BAY (IRE) 7 b.m. Strategic Prince 114 – Wood Sprite 51 (Mister Baileys 123) [2017 74: 16s p13.3g p15.8g p16g6 p12g Dec 6] fair handicapper at best: stayed 2m: acted on polytrack, tapeta and good to soft going: usually wore headgear: dead. *Marcus Tregoning* **62**

ATALANTA QUEEN 2 b.f. (Mar 19) Canford Cliffs (IRE) 133 – Champagne Aerial (IRE) (Night Shift (USA)) [2017 6s^5 5f^6 6m 6f 6d^2 6d* 6d^4 8.1s 6v Sep 25] 24,000F, £15,000Y: second foal: half-sister to 2m winner Navajo Star (by Mastercraftsman): dam twice-raced half-sister to smart performer up to 1m Ishvana: modest performer: won claimer at Lingfield in July: left Brian Meehan after sixth start: stays 6f: acts on good to soft going: in headgear last 5 starts: front runner/races prominently. *Michael Appleby* **60**

ATALANTE 4 b.f. Cape Cross (IRE) 129 – Sabria (USA) (Miswaki (USA) 124) [2017 71: p6g* p6g* Mar 23] angular filly: fairly useful performer: won maiden and handicap (dead-heated with Fredricka) at Chelmsford, both in March: stays 6f: acts on polytrack: often in hood. *Jeremy Noseda* **82**

ATAMAN (IRE) 5 b.g. Sholokhov (IRE) 121 – Diora (IRE) (Dashing Blade 117) [2017 83: 8g p10g^2 9.9g p8s^5 10g 8.3v^3 Aug 8] well-made gelding: fair maiden: stays 1¼m: acts on good to firm going: tried in hood: has worn tongue tie, including last 2 starts: has joined Olly Murphy. *Chris Wall* **78**

ATEEM (FR) 2 b.c. (Mar 19) Dark Angel (IRE) 113 – Jeu de Plume (IRE) (Montjeu (IRE) 137) [2017 7g^4 7d^3 7g^4 7m Sep 23] fair form in minor events/maiden: raced only at 7f *Richard Hannon* **79**

ATHASSEL 8 ch.g. Dalakhani (IRE) 133 – Hope Island (IRE) 69 (Titus Livius (FR) 115) [2017 61: t7.1m* p8d^2 t7.1g* f8g^3 t8.6g^2 t9.5g^4 t6g* p6g* p6g* p6g^3 t7.1g^6 p6g^6 t7.1g^4 t7.1g* 7d^3 7g p7d* 7g 8f 6f^5 6.1m^3 7d^2 7s 7d 7m^5 p7g^4 7.4g p7d p7g^5 t7.2g^4 t7.2g^6 Dec 13] fairly useful handicapper: won 7 times on all-weather between January and May: stays 9.5f, all wins at shorter: acts on polytrack, tapeta, soft and good to firm going: has worn headgear/tongue tie. *David Evans* **88**

ATHENIAN GARDEN (USA) 10 b.m. Royal Academy (USA) 130 – Webee (USA) (Kingmambo (USA) 125) [2017 49: p12g p11d p12g^6 p12g^6 Apr 11] poor handicapper: stays 1½m: acts on polytrack: tried in hood/tongue tie: races towards rear. *Paddy Butler* **48**

ATHLETIC 8 b.g. Doyen (IRE) 132 – Gentle Irony 65 (Mazilier (USA) 107) [2017 75: p8g^3 t7.1g^2 t7.1g t7.1g t7.1m t7.1d^6 p7g* p7m^{pu} Mar 29] sturdy gelding: useful handicapper at best: won at Chelmsford in March: raced mainly at 7f/1m: acted on polytrack, tapeta, good to firm and heavy going: often wore headgear: dead. *David Evans* **72**

ATHOLLBLAIR BOY (IRE) 4 ch.g. Frozen Power (IRE) 108 – Ellxell (IRE) (Exceed And Excel (AUS) 126) [2017 81: t7.1d^4 8.3g 7m^6 8m 6.1m^2 t6g^4 6.1m^2 6v 7g^2 t6d* t6g^3 Oct 20] fairly useful handicapper: won at Newcastle (by ½ length from Major Crispies) in September: stays 7f: acts on tapeta and good to firm going: usually responds generously to pressure. *Nigel Tinkler* **81**

ATKINSON GRIMSHAW (FR) 3 ch.g. Rio de La Plata (USA) 121 – Cosabawn (IRE) 57 (Barathea (IRE) 127) [2017 76: t9.5g* 12.3g* 10m^3 10g^2 p11g^3 Aug 30] sturdy gelding: fairly useful performer: won maiden at Wolverhampton in February and handicap at Chester in May: placed on other 3 starts in 2017: stays 12.5f: acts on polytrack, tapeta, soft and good to firm going: usually leads, often races freely: sold to join Iain Jardine 35,000 gns in November. *Andrew Balding* **93**

ATLANTA BELLE (IRE) 3 ch.f. Zebedee 113 – Tara Too (IRE) 97 (Danetime (IRE) 121) [2017 72: p6m^4 t6m^3 p6g^5 5g t6.1g 5.2s^3 p6d* p6g^2 p5g^6 Oct 17] fair handicapper: won at Kempton in August: best form at 6f: acts on polytrack: front runner/races prominently. *Chris Wall* **73**

ATLETICO (IRE) 5 b.g. Kodiac 112 – Queenofthefairies (Pivotal 124) [2017 6d^3 6m^5 5.1g* 5g^5 6.1s 5g 5d^6 5s t5g* Nov 23] useful-looking gelding: useful handicapper: won at Windsor (by 1¼ lengths from Wiley Post) in July and Newcastle (by 1¼ lengths from Bowson Fred) in November: stays 6f: acts on tapeta and good to firm going. *Roger Varian* **108**

ATOMIC JACK 2 b.g. (Apr 22) Nathaniel (IRE) 129 – Indigo River (IRE) 88 (Kodiac 112) [2017 8g Aug 25] 25/1, well held in maiden at Goodwood. *George Baker* **–**

ATRAFAN (IRE) 3 b.g. Atraf 116 – Up Front (IRE) 61 (Up And At 'Em 109) [2017 62: 5.9s^6 6d^4 6m^5 7m 6m Aug 26] modest maiden: stays 7f: acts on tapeta and good to firm going: tried in cheekpieces. *Alan Brown* **59**

ATTAIN 8 b.g. Dansili 127 – Achieve (Rainbow Quest (USA) 134) [2017 66, a73: t8g p10m^4 p12g* p13g^4 p13g^5 p12f^2 p12g^3 p12m^4 11.7f^3 p12g^3 10.2f* 10.2d^2 10.2f^3 10g^4 10.2f^4 10.2f^6 10m^4 13d 11.5m p10m p12g^3 p10g^3 p10g^6 Dec 30] good-topped gelding: fair handicapper: won at Lingfield (amateur) in January and Bath in May: stays 1½m: acts on polytrack and any turf going: has worn headgear, including in 2017: has worn tongue tie: often races prominently. *Archie Watson* **79**

ATTENTION SEAKER 7 b.m. Bollin Eric 125 – Pay Attention 68 (Revoque (IRE) 122) **82**
[2017 14.5s^{4} 15.9v* 16.1d* 16.3d 15.9s^{2} Oct 31] fairly useful handicapper: won at Catterick and Beverley in August: second at former course in October: stays 17f: acts on any turf going: in tongue tie last 4 starts. *Tim Easterby*

ATTEQ 3 b.c. Invincible Spirit (IRE) 121 – Wallis 104 (King's Best (USA) 132) [2017 78: **90**
t7.1g^{4} t7.1g^{4} t5d^{3} t7.1m^{3} 7.5m* 7.1m^{2} 7m 7.2g^{3} 7d^{6} 7g 6g 6g^{5} 8g Dec 21] compact colt: fairly useful performer: won handicap at Beverley (by 7 lengths from Dapper Man) in April: left Richard Fahey after ninth start: stays 7.5f: acts on fibresand, tapeta and good to firm going: has worn tongue tie. *Zuhair Maki, Qatar*

ATTEST 4 b.g. Cacique (IRE) 124 – Change Course 67 (Sadler's Wells (USA) 132) [2017 **83**
77: 10.2v^{2} Nov 8] well-made gelding: fairly useful form: second in amateur handicap at Nottingham only start on Flat in 2017: should stay 1½m: fairly useful hurdler. *Warren Greatrex*

ATTICUS BOY (IRE) 2 b.c. (Feb 27) Cape Cross (IRE) 129 – Satwa Pearl 91 (Rock of **–**
Gibraltar (IRE) 133) [2017 t8.6d Dec 27] 12/1, well held in minor event at Wolverhampton. *David Lanigan*

ATTY PERSSE (IRE) 3 b.g. Frankel 147 – Dorcas Lane 108 (Norse Dancer (IRE) 127) **109**
[2017 90P: 8.1d* 10.2f^{2} 12m* 13g 11.9d^{6} Aug 23] smallish, strong gelding: useful handicapper: won at Sandown (by short head from Mucho Applause) in April and King George V Stakes at Royal Ascot (by 3 lengths from First Nation) in June: stays 1½m: acts on firm and good to soft going: in cheekpieces last 3 starts. *Roger Charlton*

AT YOUR SERVICE 3 b.c. Frankel 147 – Crystal Gaze (IRE) (Rainbow Quest (USA) **79**
134) [2017 8d^{5} 7g^{2} 6m^{4} p7g 7v 7.2s 8v 10s Nov 5] fair maiden: left W. P. Browne after sixth start: stays 7f: acts on good to firm going: often in headgear: tried in tongue tie: usually races prominently: temperament under suspicion. *Shane Donohoe, Ireland*

AUBERGE DU LAC (IRE) 3 b.c. Lope de Vega (IRE) 125 – Red Kyte 91 (Hawk Wing **99**
(USA) 136) [2017 87p: t8.6m* 8m^{4} 8d^{5} 8m* Jun 30] useful performer: won maiden at Wolverhampton in January and handicap at Yarmouth (by 1½ lengths from To Dibba) in June: stays 8.5f: acts on polytrack, tapeta, good to firm and good to soft going: sometimes slowly away, often travels strongly: sent to Hong Kong, where renamed Multi Facets. *David Simcock*

AUGENBLICK (IRE) 2 b.f. (Mar 23) Epaulette (AUS) 126 – Freezing Love (USA) **79 p**
(Danzig (USA)) [2017 p7g* t7.1g* Nov 3] €25,000F, €20,000Y: seventh foal: half-sister to useful French 1m winner Frozen Ardour (by Dr Fong) and 1m-9.5f winner Zero Game (by High Chaparral): dam French 2-y-o 6f winner: fair form: won minor events at Kempton (by head from Ortiz) in October and Newcastle (by 2 lengths from Riverside Walk) in November: better to come. *Roger Varian*

AUMERLE 5 b.g. Authorized (IRE) 133 – Succinct 104 (Hector Protector (USA) 124) **72**
[2017 74: p15.8f^{6} p15.8g^{4} p14g^{5} 14d^{5} 11.5s^{2} 11.5m^{5} f12.1g^{6} p16g* Dec 20] lengthy gelding: fair handicapper: won at Kempton in December: stays 2m: acts on polytrack, tapeta and soft going: tried in cheekpieces. *Shaun Lycett*

AUMIT HILL 4 b.g. Authorized (IRE) 133 – Eurolinka (IRE) (Tirol 127) [2017 15d^{6} Jun **–**
5] no form: tried in blinkers. *John Quinn*

AUNTIE BARBER (IRE) 4 b.f. Elusive City (USA) 117 – Lady Stardust 95 (Spinning **82**
World (USA) 130) [2017 82: t9.5g^{5} t9.5m* t8.6g^{2} 9.9g^{5} p8g^{4} 8m^{4} 10g 10d p10g p12g^{6} p8g p10s Nov 17] smallish filly: fairly useful handicapper: won at Wolverhampton in March: second there later same month: stays 1¼m: acts on polytrack, tapeta and good to soft going: tried in headgear: wears tongue tie nowadays: sold 5,000 gns in December. *Stuart Williams*

AUNTIE PAM (IRE) 2 b.f. (Mar 31) Sir Prancealot (IRE) 111 – Sans Reserve (IRE) 79 **67**
(Foxhound (USA) 103) [2017 t5.1g^{2} p5g^{4} 5.1m^{2} 5g^{3} t5.1g^{6} 6.1s^{4} 6s^{4} 6s^{4} t6.1g Sep 23] €30,000Y: fifth foal: half-sister to 2-y-o 6f winner En Un Clin d'Oeil (by Chineur), later successful in Hong Kong: dam 1m winner: fair maiden: stays 6f: acts on tapeta, soft and good to firm going: wears cheekpieces. *Tom Dascombe*

AURIC GOLDFINGER (IRE) 3 b.g. Kyllachy 129 – Ghenwah (FR) (Selkirk (USA) **73**
129) [2017 58: t7.1m^{2} p7g* p7g^{4} p8g^{3} p7g t7.1g^{6} 8g^{2} 8.1m^{6} p7s p8g 8d Sep 18] sturdy gelding: fair handicapper: won at Lingfield in January: stays 1m: acts on polytrack and tapeta: wears blinkers: often starts slowly. *Richard Hannon*

AURORA BUTTERFLY (IRE) 3 gr.f. Born To Sea (IRE) 117 – Diamonaka (FR) 105 **102**
(Akarad (FR) 130) [2017 10s^{2} 10g^{5} 9.7m* 6.9s^{3} 12f^{5} 9.5d 9d Aug 27] half-sister to numerous winners, including winner up to 1m (stayed 1¼m) Diamond Green (2-y-o 7f winner, by Green Desert) and 1¼m-12.5f winner Diamilina (by Linamix) (both very

smart), latter grandam of Irish Derby/St Leger winner Capri: dam 10.5f winner: useful performer: won maiden at Clonmel in May: third in listed race at Carlisle next time: barely stays 1½m: acts on firm and soft going: tried in hood. *W. McCreery, Ireland*

AURORA ECLIPSE (IRE) 2 b.f. (Apr 28) Kodiac 112 – Tiltili (IRE) 51 (Spectrum **89**
(IRE) 126) [2017 6g^{2} 5d* 5.8v^{5} 6g^{4} Nov 3] €25,000Y, €70,000 2-y-o: fifth foal: half-sister to 3 winners, including useful winner around 7f (including at 2 yrs) Swift Approval (by Approve): dam staying maiden: fairly useful form: won maiden at Naas in October: will be suited by 7f. *M. D. O'Callaghan, Ireland*

AURORA GRAY 4 gr.f. Rip Van Winkle (IRE) 134 – Summer's Eve 104 (Singspiel (IRE) **96**
133) [2017 70, a76: p15.8m* p16d* 17.1d^{3} 18g^{3} 18g^{2} 20.6v^{2} 16s^{2} 18m Oct 14] good-topped filly: useful handicapper: won at Lingfield and Kempton in January: placed 5 of other 6 starts in 2017: stays 2½m: acts on polytrack and heavy going: tried in cheekpieces: consistent. *Hughie Morrison*

AUSPICION 5 b.g. Dansili 127 – Superstar Leo (IRE) 114 (College Chapel 122) [2017 85, **86**
a73: 8g^{6} t10.2s* t10.2s t10.2s* t10.2g 9.8d^{3} 9.2s t8g* t8d^{4} t8g Oct 10] fairly useful handicapper: won at Newcastle in June, July and September (by 1¼ lengths from Four Wishes): stays 1¼m: acts on tapeta, good to firm and good to soft going: has worn blinkers: usually slowly away: sold £12,000 in November, sent to Saudi Arabia. *Tom Tate*

AUSSIE ANDRE 6 b.g. High Chaparral (IRE) 132 – Hana Dee 72 (Cadeaux Genereux **–**
131) [2017 p12g p12g^{pu} Feb 11] well-made gelding: useful at best, no show in 2017: stayed 1½m: acted on polytrack, tapeta and soft going: dead. *Roger Ingram*

AUSSIE REIGNS (IRE) 7 b.g. Aussie Rules (USA) 123 – Rohain (IRE) (Singspiel **99**
(IRE) 133) [2017 14d^{6} 12s p14g^{5} Nov 2] angular gelding: useful handicapper: left W. P. Mullins after first start: stays 16.5f: acts on polytrack, good to firm and good to soft going: has worn headgear: useful hurdler. *Gary Moore*

AUSSIE WIND 2 b.c. (Mar 11) Aussie Rules (USA) 123 – Ride The Wind 72 (Cozzene **91**
(USA)) [2017 7d^{6} t7.1g* p8g* 8g^{pu} Aug 19] fairly useful form: won minor events at Newcastle in July and Chelmsford (by ½ length from Ibn Al Emarat) in August: in second place when broke down on home turn in listed race won by Francesco Bere at Deauville: stayed 1m: dead. *Hugo Palmer*

AUSTERITY (IRE) 4 br.g. Elnadim (USA) 128 – Royal Reprieve (FR) (Celtic Swing **–**
138) [2017 65: f8.1g^{6} 10g t8s Nov 30] maiden: no form in 2017. *Sally Haynes*

AUSTIN POWERS (IRE) 2 ch.g. (Apr 15) Power 117 – My Lass 91 (Elmaamul (USA) **76**
125) [2017 6g 6s^{2} 6g^{3} 6s^{4} 6m^{3} 6.3s 7s^{4} t7.1d^{4} t8g^{5} Nov 24] good-quartered gelding: fair maiden: stays 7f: acts on soft and good to firm going. *Mark Johnston*

AUSTRIAN SCHOOL (IRE) 2 b.c. (Feb 19) Teofilo (IRE) 126 – Swiss Roll (IRE) 96 **83 p**
(Entrepreneur 123) [2017 8g* p8g^{5} 8v^{3} 10v* Oct 9] 20,000Y: half-brother to very smart winner up to 16.4f (Lonsdale Cup) Ahzeemah (2-y-o 7f winner, by Dubawi) and 9.5f winner Thermal Column (by Vale of York): dam 1½m-1¾m winner who stayed 2m: fairly useful form: won minor events at Ripon in August and Pontefract in October: will be suited by 1½m+: likely to improve further. *Mark Johnston*

AUTHENTIC ART 2 ch.g. (Mar 20) Dutch Art 126 – Tahirah 99 (Green Desert (USA) **– p**
127) [2017 6g^{6} 6.1d^{5} 6g Sep 22] 75,000Y: sturdy gelding: half-brother to several winners, including 5f/6f winner Edward Lewis (by Kyllachy) and 9f/1¼m winner Little Rocky (by Cadeaux Genereux), both useful: dam 7f/1m winner: little impact in minor events/maiden: should do better. *Ralph Beckett*

AUTHORATIVE (IRE) 7 b.g. Refuse To Bend (IRE) 128 – Reasonably Devout (CAN) **44**
(St Jovite (USA) 135) [2017 –: p10.7g p12g t13.9g^{6} Apr 29] poor handicapper: stays 11.5f: acts on polytrack, soft and good to firm going: wears headgear: in tongue tie last 3 starts: modest hurdler. *Anthony McCann, Ireland*

AUTHORIZED TOO 6 b.g. Authorized (IRE) 133 – Audaz (Oasis Dream 129) [2017 **85**
14m p16d* 16d* Jul 25] fairly useful handicapper: won at Kempton (by 2¾ lengths from Fitzwilly) and Ffos Las (by ½ length from Nabhan) in July: stays 2m: acts on polytrack, good to firm and good to soft going: in cheekpieces last 3 starts: fairly useful hurdler/chaser. *Noel Williams*

AUTHOR'S DREAM 4 gr.g. Authorized (IRE) 133 – Spring Dream (IRE) 93 (Kalanisi **74**
(IRE) 132) [2017 –: t16.5g^{2} p15.8g p16s^{4} p16g^{3} t16.5d* Dec 9] fair handicapper: won at Wolverhampton in December: stays 16.5f: acts on polytrack and tapeta: in visor last 2 starts: usually slowly away. *William Knight*

AUTOCRATIC 4 b.c. Dubawi (IRE) 129 – Canda (USA) 100 (Storm Cat (USA)) [2017 **118**
108: 9m^6 9.9m* 10.5d 10m^6 Aug 26] good sort: smart performer: won Brigadier Gerard
Stakes at Sandown (by 1¼ lengths from Algometer) in May: stays 10.5f: acts on polytrack
and firm going. *Sir Michael Stoute*

AUTUMN BELLE 2 b.f. (Mar 17) Canford Cliffs (IRE) 133 – Ballyea (IRE) 70 **–**
(Acclamation 118) [2017 5m^5 5m^6 May 31] £2,000Y: third foal: sister to 2-y-o 6f winner
Canford Belle: dam, 2-y-o 6f winner, half-sister to useful winner up to 1¼m Rakaan: little
impact in minor event/claimer. *Ollie Pears*

AUTUMN GLOW 3 b.f. Sir Percy 129 – Steady Rain 68 (Zafonic (USA) 130) [2017 –: **57**
p10g^4 p10s p13.3s Dec 1] modest form: stays 1¼m. *Miss Joey Ellis*

AUTUMN LEAVES 2 b.f. (Mar 14) Helmet (AUS) 127 – Jadwiga (Pivotal 124) [2017 **79**
6m^2 6g^2 7g* Aug 17] 15,000Y: rather unfurnished filly: third foal: half-sister to winners in
Italy by Royal Applause and Paco Boy: dam unraced half-sister to useful French winner up
to 1¾m Galiteo: fair form: won maiden at Salisbury (by neck from Escape The City) in
August: stays 7f. *Clive Cox*

AUTUMN LODGE 2 b.g. (Feb 10) Stimulation (IRE) 121 – Timeless Elegance (IRE) 83 **68**
(Invincible Spirit (IRE) 121) [2017 5g^5 5m^3 p5g^2 6.1d^3 5f 5f^2 5d^5 5f 6g^2 7g^4 6g^4 5.5g^3
8.9s^6 8d^3 7d^5 8.9s p6.5g p7.5g Dec 26] sturdy gelding: fair maiden: placed 7 times: left
J. S. Moore after twelfth start: stays 1m: acts on firm and good to soft going: tried in
cheekpieces/blinkers. *R. Le Gal, France*

AUTUMN SNOW 2 b.f. (Apr 14) Invincible Spirit (IRE) 121 – Epic Similie (Lomitas **51 p**
129) [2017 t6.1g^5 Nov 18] sixth foal: sister to useful 2-y-o 6f winner Figure of Speech and
half-sister to 2-y-o 6f winner Epithet (by Shamardal): dam, useful French 1½m winner,
half-sister to Prix Jean-Luc Lagardere winner Ultra: 9/4, fifth in minor event at
Wolverhampton: will improve. *Saeed bin Suroor*

AUTUMN TONIC (IRE) 5 b.g. Approve (IRE) 112 – Trempjane 71 (Lujain (USA) 119) **62 §**
[2017 60§: f7g f6g^2 t6g f6m^5 f6g* p5g p6g^5 p7s 6m 6m f6.1g p6g Nov 17] rather leggy
gelding: modest handicapper: won at Southwell in March: left David Barron after fifth
start: stays 7f: acts on polytrack and fibresand: usually wears headgear: temperamental:
sent to Belgium. *Charlie Wallis*

AUXILIARY 4 b.g. Fast Company (IRE) 126 – Lady Xara (IRE) (Xaar 132) [2017 79: **76**
8.3m 9.9m 10s* 11.1g 11.9s^5 11.6g^6 12.1s^5 10.5v^5 12.1s Oct 10] stocky gelding: fair
handicapper: won at Wetherby in June: stays 1¼m: acts on soft and good to firm going:
wears headgear. *Patrick Holmes*

AVAGO JOSH 3 ch.g. Aqlaam 125 – Heart Stopping (USA) 69 (Chester House (USA) **–**
123) [2017 10.3g^{pu} f8g^6 6g^{pu} May 26] little impact in maidens. *Ivan Furtado*

AVANTGARDIST (GER) 3 ch.g. Campanologist (USA) 119 – Avocette (GER) (Kings **70**
Lake (USA) 133) [2017 70: t9.5g^3 14g^6 14g 11.4m^5 14d^5 Sep 16] fair maiden: left Mark
Johnston after first start: stays 11.5f: acts on tapeta, good to firm and good to soft going: in
blinkers last 3 starts: usually races close up. *Pat Phelan*

AV A WORD 3 b.g. Aussie Rules (USA) 123 – Real Me (Mark of Esteem (IRE) 137) [2017 **82**
58: p8g^6 p10g^4 p10g^5 f8g^2 t12.2g^2 p12g^5 9.9g* 9g 11.4m^3 9.9m* 11.6f^6 9.9g* 10.1m*
9.9d^4 t12.4d^3 Sep 29] fairly useful performer: won minor event at Brighton in May,
handicaps there in June/August and handicap at Epsom later in August: stays 12.5f: acts on
all-weather and good to firm going: wears headgear: sold 16,000 gns in November, sent to
USA. *Daniel Kubler*

AVENGING RED (IRE) 2 b.c. (Mar 13) Red Jazz (USA) 125 – Lorena (IRE) (Bishop **56**
of Cashel 122) [2017 5f^3 5.1m 5.7d^4 p6g^4 p6g^3 p5g^6 t7.1g Nov 15] modest maiden: stays
6f: acts on polytrack and firm going: in headgear last 3 starts: often races prominently.
Adam West

AVENTINUS (IRE) 3 b.g. Zoffany (IRE) 121 – Luminous Gold 82 (Fantastic Light **97**
(USA) 134) [2017 86: p7g* 7.6m 7g* 7d^5 p7g^2 6.5g^5 p7g Oct 20] lengthy gelding: useful
handicapper: won at Lingfield in April and Goodwood (by ¾ length from Medburn Dream)
in June: second at Chelmsford (3½ lengths behind Important Mission) in August: stays 7f:
acts on polytrack and good to soft going: tried in cheekpieces: usually races prominently.
Hugo Palmer

AVENTUS (IRE) 3 b.c. Zebedee 113 – Irish Design (IRE) (Alhaarth (IRE) 126) [2017 58: **55**
p10g^3 Jan 19] sturdy colt: modest maiden on Flat: stays 1¼m: acts on all-weather: often
wears headgear: front runner/races prominently: sent to Italy, where won over hurdles in
June. *Jane Chapple-Hyam*

AVENUE DES CHAMPS 5 b.g. Champs Elysees 124 – Penang Cry (Barathea (IRE) 127) [2017 75: 14.1g* 12s 16.3d^3 p16s p13.3g^2 p15.8g^5 Oct 18] strong, compact gelding: fair handicapper: won at Yarmouth in July: stayed 16.5f: acted on polytrack, good to firm and good to soft going: sometimes wore cheekpieces: usually raced prominently: dead. *Jane Chapple-Hyam* **75**

AVENUE OF STARS 4 b.g. Makfi 130 – Clifton Dancer 98 (Fraam 114) [2017 83: t7.1d 6m t6g 6g^4 6v^2 6d t6g^5 t6g t7.1g^4 Nov 24] fair handicapper: stays 6f: acts on tapeta and heavy going: wears headgear. *Karen McLintock* **73**

AVIATOR (GER) 9 br.g. Motivator 131 – Amore (GER) (Lando (GER) 128) [2017 p16s Sep 8] fairly useful handicapper, shaped as if needing run sole outing on Flat in 2017: stays 17f: acts on good to soft going: has worn headgear: fairly useful hurdler. *James Eustace* **–**

AVOCADEAU (IRE) 6 b.g. Lawman (FR) 121 – Christmas Cracker (FR) (Alhaarth (IRE) 126) [2017 –: 11.7f* 11.9m^4 11.6g^3 11.6f^3 10g* 10.2d^4 p11g^6 Oct 4] good-topped gelding: modest handicapper: won at Bath in April and Chepstow in July: stays 1½m: acts on polytrack and firm going: wears headgear: has worn tongue tie, including last 3 starts: usually races close up. *Stuart Kittow* **64**

AVOCET (USA) 4 b.f. Artie Schiller (USA) 124 – Striking Example (USA) (Empire Maker (USA) 129) [2017 10.1s^4 11.8g 12g p10g^3 p10d^6 p10g Oct 12] second foal: dam unraced daughter of high-class US Grade 1 7f-9f winner Sightseek: maiden: fair form for Mme C. Head-Maarek at 3 yrs, below that level in 2017: stays 1¼m: acts on polytrack: has worn headgear, including in 2017. *Julia Feilden* **51**

AVOIDABLE 4 b.g. Iffraaj 127 – Ever Rigg 83 (Dubai Destination (USA) 127) [2017 68: t10.2g^5 Jan 3] maiden: fair form at 3 yrs, below that level sole outing in 2017: best effort at 9.5f: acts on tapeta. *David Simcock* **59**

AVON BREEZE 8 b.m. Avonbridge 123 – African Breeze 79 (Atraf 116) [2017 96: 6g* 6d^4 6.1g^2 5g* 6s^6 6.1s^5 6d* Aug 7] useful handicapper: won at Pontefract (twice) in July and at Ripon (by length from Bossipop) in August: stayed 6f: acted on good to firm and heavy going: sometimes wore headgear: reportedly in foal to Equiano. *Richard Whitaker* **101**

AVON GREEN 2 b.f. (Jan 13) Avonbridge 123 – Greenery (IRE) 81 (Green Desert (USA) 127) [2017 6.1m^6 5.1d 6g t6g^4 p6g^4 p5s^2 p5s^6 p5g^3 t5.1d^5 Dec 26] first foal: dam 2-y-o 5f winner: fair maiden: stays 6f: acts on polytrack and tapeta: usually races prominently. *Joseph Tuite* **68**

AWAKE MY SOUL (IRE) 8 ch.g. Teofilo (IRE) 126 – Field of Hope (IRE) 119 (Selkirk (USA) 129) [2017 103: 10.3d^4 10g 10d 10.3m 10.2s* 10.2d 10s^4 10v* Nov 7] rather leggy gelding: useful handicapper: won at Haydock in September and Redcar (by length from Canberra Cliffs) in November: raced mainly around 1¼m: acts on good to firm and heavy going: tried in hood: front runner/races prominently. *Tom Tate* **98**

AWARE (IRE) 3 b.g. Lawman (FR) 121 – Viz (IRE) 103 (Darshaan 133) [2017 –p: 8f^4 p8s 11.9d^5 10.2f Jul 5] fair maiden: best effort at 1m: acts on firm going: in tongue tie last 2 starts. *Charles Hills* **71**

AWESOME 2 ch.f. (Mar 13) Bahamian Bounty 116 – Ballymore Celebre (IRE) (Peintre Celebre (USA) 137) [2017 5m 5f^2 5f^4 5.1g* 5.4g* Oct 13] close-coupled filly: sister to smart 2-y-o 5f/6f (July Stakes) winner Anjaal and half-sister to several winners, including 1¼m-1½m winner Pintrada (by Tiger Hill) and 2-y-o 7f winner Samharry (by Exceed And Excel): dam French 11.5f-13f winner: fairly useful performer: won minor events at Chepstow (by ½ length from Shaya) in September and York (by length from Midsummer Knight) in October: likely to stay 6f: acts on firm going: front runner/races prominently. *Clive Cox* **84**

AWESOME ALLAN (IRE) 3 b.g. Acclamation 118 – Spring Approach (Tiger Hill (IRE) 127) [2017 85: 5.1g 6.1m 5.1d^2 6d 5.1d 5m 6d^5 5.1s^5 t7.2g 7s^6 7m p7g 5g^2 5.1d^2 6d* 6v* t6.1g^4 t6.1d p5g^4 Dec 23] lengthy gelding: fairly useful handicapper: won at Redcar in October (apprentice) and November: stays 6f: acts on heavy going: often wears tongue tie: usually front runner/races prominently. *David Evans* **85**

AWESOME ROCK (IRE) 8 ch.g. Rock of Gibraltar (IRE) 133 – Dangerous Diva (IRE) 105 (Royal Academy (USA) 130) [2017 51: p12d^2 p10g^5 p10d p12g p10g 11.7f^5 13f^5 11.5m p10s^3 p12g^3 Dec 28] workmanlike gelding: modest handicapper: stays 13.5f: acts on polytrack and good to firm going: has worn headgear. *Roger Ingram* **51**

AWESOMETANK 2 br.f. (Mar 11) Intense Focus (USA) 117 – Janey Muddles (IRE) 98 (Lawman (FR) 121) [2017 5.1m^4 t6d^6 7g^2 7d* 7.9g* 8d^4 Nov 4] 25,000F: second foal: half-sister to 9.5f winner (stays 11.3f) Modern Approach (by New Approach): dam 2-y-o **95**

6f winner who stayed 1m: useful performer: won nurseries at Newmarket in September and York (by neck from Dark Liberty) in October: stays 1m: acts on good to soft going: front runner/races prominently. *William Haggas*

AWFAA (IRE) 3 b.f. Shamardal (USA) 129 – Elraabeya (CAN) 77 (Seeking The Gold (USA)) [2017 55: 8d² 8g⁴ 8m⁵ Aug 31] fairly useful form when second in maiden at Newmarket on return, standout effort: stays 1m: sold 5,000 gns in December. *Sir Michael Stoute* **82**

AWSAAF 2 b.c. (Jan 29) Swiss Spirit 117 – Atheera (IRE) 68 (Shamardal (USA) 129) [2017 t6.1g* 6.1s⁴ 5g⁴ p5d Sep 21] quite attractive colt: fair form: won minor event at Wolverhampton in May: best effort at 6f: tried in hood. *Simon Crisford* **77**

AXE CAP (IRE) 2 b.f. (Mar 22) Zebedee 113 – Clouded Leopard (USA) 81 (Danehill (USA) 126) [2017 5f 5.1d³ t5.1g² t6.1g⁵ Nov 25] 60,000 2-y-o: sixth foal: half-sister to 3 winners, including useful 1m winner Cloudberry (by Pivotal) and 5f winner Dark Leopard (by Dubawi): dam, maiden (raced only at 7f), half-sister to Breeders' Cup Juvenile Turf winner Pounced: fair form: best effort at 5f. *Archie Watson* **72**

AY AY (IRE) 3 b.g. Pour Moi (IRE) 125 – Chatline (IRE) 90 (One Cool Cat (USA) 123) [2017 80p: t8g² p8g⁴ p8g⁶ 10d⁵ 10g⁵ 10d 10.2d* p10g⁶ p11d⁶ Dec 13] lengthy gelding: useful handicapper: won at Nottingham (by head from Fast And Hot) in October: stays 11f: acts on polytrack, tapeta and good to soft going. *David Elsworth* **95**

AYE AYE SKIPPER (IRE) 7 b.g. Captain Marvelous (IRE) 114 – Queenfisher 101 (Scottish Reel 123) [2017 56: t7.1m⁴ p8g p7g⁶ 7m⁶ 7d³ 8f* 8f² 8m⁵ 8g 7.1g p8g p7g Dec 30] tall gelding: modest handicapper: won at Bath in June: stays 8.5f: acts on polytrack, firm and soft going: wears headgear: has worn tongue tie, including in 2017: sometimes slowly away. *Ken Cunningham-Brown* **62**

AYLA'S EMPEROR 8 b.m. Holy Roman Emperor (IRE) 125 – Ayla (IRE) 101 (Daylami (IRE) 138) [2017 –: 14g 16v⁶ 13d Aug 23] modest handicapper: stays 11.5f: acts on soft and good to firm going: wears cheekpieces: fair hurdler. *John Flint* **59**

AYRAD (IRE) 6 ch.g. Dalakhani (IRE) 133 – Sweet Firebird (IRE) 103 (Sadler's Wells (USA) 132) [2017 115: 10m⁵ 9.9m⁵ 10.5d 10.1m⁴ 9.9v* 12s p10g Nov 18] sturdy gelding: smart performer: won handicap at Salisbury (by 4½ lengths from Almoreb) in October: stays 1½m: acts on good to firm and heavy going: has worn headgear, including last 5 starts: front runner/races prominently. *Roger Charlton* **113**

AYRESOME ANGEL 4 ch.f. Captain Gerrard (IRE) 113 – Almunia (IRE) (Mujadil (USA) 119) [2017 71: 5g³ 5v² 5g⁴ 5g f5g 5s Nov 8] fair handicapper: raced only at 5f: acts on good to firm and heavy going: has worn cheekpieces, including in 2017: front runner/races prominently. *John Mackie* **75**

AYR OF ELEGANCE 5 b.m. Motivator 131 – Gaelic Swan (IRE) 80 (Nashwan (USA) 135) [2017 85, a73: p12g⁵ p12g* p15.8g* p16g⁴ 14f² 16m⁵ 14m⁵ 16.3d* p15.8g⁴ 16g⁵ p15.8g⁴ Dec 20] workmanlike mare: fairly useful performer: won maiden in January, and handicaps in March and July (by 2¼ lengths from Fitzwilly), all at Lingfield: stays 16.5f: acts on polytrack, firm and good to soft going: has worn headgear, including in 2017. *Philip Hide* **83**

AYTON (IRE) 2 b.f. (Mar 30) Declaration of War (USA) 128 – Mubashera (USA) (Medaglia d'Oro (USA) 129) [2017 7v t7.1g Nov 15] €65,000 2-y-o: compact filly: first foal: dam, unraced, out of useful half-sister to high-class miler Tamayuz: little impact in minor events. *Ollie Pears* **–**

AY UP MRS 4 b.f. Monsieur Bond (IRE) 120 – Smiddy Hill 85 (Factual (USA) 108) [2017 7m Apr 10] fourth foal: dam 5f winner (including at 2 yrs): no form in bumpers: 100/1, well held in maiden at Redcar. *Rebecca Bastiman* **–**

AYUTTHAYA (IRE) 2 ch.c. (Feb 26) Lope de Vega (IRE) 125 – Pivotal Role 66 (Pivotal 124) [2017 8.3s² 7d² 7v* Sep 30] €100,000F, €50,000Y: tall, good-topped colt: half-brother to 3 winners, including 7f-1½m winner Sheriff of Nawton and 2-y-o 6f winner General Direction (both by Lawman): dam, maiden (stayed 1¼m), closely related to very smart Hong Kong sprinter Dim Sum: fairly useful form: won minor event at Chester (by 2¼ lengths from Zatorius) in September: stays 7f. *Kevin Ryan* **92**

AZALY (IRE) 3 ch.g. Sepoy (AUS) 129 – Azzoom (IRE) 74 (Cadeaux Genereux 131) [2017 61: p8g⁴ 8d⁴ 8m* 8d² p8g* Oct 13] lengthy gelding: fairly useful performer: won maiden at Haydock in July and handicap at Kempton (by short head from Eltezam) in October: stays 1m: acts on polytrack, good to firm and good to soft going: usually races close up. *Owen Burrows* **91**

AZAM 3 b.g. Dansili 127 – Giants Play (USA) 111 (Giant's Causeway (USA) 132) [2017 92p: 10m^6 11s 11.4m^5 12s^3 p11s p11g t12.2g^6 p16d Dec 13] tall, strong gelding: fairly useful handicapper: left John Gosden after third start: stays 1½m: acts on polytrack and tapeta: has worn cheekpieces, including in 2017. *Michael Appleby* **89**

AZAMESSE (IRE) 5 b.m. Azamour (IRE) 130 – Jeunesse Doree (IRE) 68 (Rock of Gibraltar (IRE) 133) [2017 66: t16.5g^4 f14g p13g p13.3d^5 14.1m May 24] fair handicapper, below form in 2017: stays 1¾m: acts on polytrack and good to soft going: often wears headgear: has worn tongue tie, including in 2017. *J. R. Jenkins* **56**

AZARI 5 b.g. Azamour (IRE) 130 – Atasari (IRE) 110 (Whipper (USA) 126) [2017 t12.2g* 11.9m^3 11.9m^2 11.9g^6 11.8d* 11.6g^2 10m 10.3g 11.9s Nov 11] useful performer: won multiple times for various trainers in Italy: also won claimer at Wolverhampton (by 1¾ lengths from Viewpoint) in June and handicap at Haydock (amateur, by nose from Zubayr) in August: left Paul Nicholls after first start: stays 1½m: acts on tapeta, firm and good to soft going: in cheekpieces last 5 starts: has worn tongue tie: sometimes slowly away, often races in rear. *Tom Dascombe* **106**

AZEZATI (IRE) 2 ch.f. (Jan 29) Dream Ahead (USA) 133 – Sweet Nicole 54 (Okawango (USA) 115) [2017 7m^2 p7d^3 Aug 23] 17,000Y: fifth foal: half-sister to 3 winners, including smart 6f (including at 2 yrs) winner Mobsta (by Bushranger) and 6f/7f winner Cincuenta Pasos (by Footstepsinthesand): dam once-raced half-sister to very smart performer up to 1m Tariq: fair form: better effort when second in minor event at Yarmouth (1½ lengths behind Midnight Wilde) in August: remains with potential. *David Simcock* **68 p**

AZPEITIA 2 ch.f. (Mar 3) Showcasing 117 – Leaves You Baby (IRE) 82 (Pivotal 124) [2017 6d^4 p6d Dec 13] first foal: dam 1¼m winner who stayed 1½m out of useful 1¼m-1½m winner Royal Devotion: fair form when fourth in maiden at Doncaster (3¼ lengths behind Raid) on first of 2 starts: will be suited by 7f+. *Ralph Beckett* **70**

AZZIR (IRE) 5 gr.g. Echo of Light 125 – Lady Georgina 88 (Linamix (FR) 127) [2017 84: 11.9s^3 10.2m^3 10.2v^2 11.6g^4 10v 10g Sep 27] fairly useful handicapper: placed 3 times in 2017: stays 1½m: acts on any turf going: tried in visor: sold £9,000 in November. *K. R. Burke* **81**

AZZURI 5 b.g. Azamour (IRE) 130 – Folly Lodge 93 (Grand Lodge (USA) 125) [2017 11.2g Jun 11] fairly useful for G. M. Lyons in 2015, below form sole outing on Flat (wore tongue tie) since: stays 1½m: acts on soft going: fairly useful hurdler/useful chaser. *Dan Skelton* **–**

B

BAASHA 2 b.g. (Feb 9) Havana Gold (IRE) 118 – Tawaasul 83 (Haafhd 129) [2017 8g 8g^6 8s^3 Oct 10] fair form: third in minor event at Brighton (neck behind Enzo) in October. *Ed Dunlop* **69**

BAASHIQ (IRE) 3 b.g. New Approach (IRE) 132 – Fatanah (IRE) 103 (Green Desert (USA) 127) [2017 86p: 10.5m^3 10v^5 8m Aug 16] attractive gelding: fairly useful handicapper: third at Haydock in July: stays 10.5f: acts on good to firm and good to soft going: sold £19,000 in November. *Roger Varian* **89**

BABALUGATS (IRE) 3 br.f. Elzaam (AUS) 115 – Ellanova (Kyllachy 129) [2017 44: 12m 12.1g May 16] poor maiden: often races lazily. *Tim Easterby* **42**

BABAMUNCHKIN 3 b.f. Henrythenavigator (USA) 131 – Babycakes (IRE) 105 (Marju (IRE) 127) [2017 70: 8.1m 10g^4 9.9f Jul 18] lengthy filly: has scope: fair maiden: stays 1¼m: often starts slowly, usually races nearer last than first. *Michael Bell* **68**

BABETTE (IRE) 3 b.f. Cape Cross (IRE) 129 – Crinoline (USA) (Street Cry (IRE) 130) [2017 7m 6.1g 6m 7m t9.5g p12g^4 p13.3s^5 Nov 17] £6,000 3-y-o: second foal: half-sister to useful 2-y-o 7f winner Quality Time (by Exceed And Excel): dam unraced half-sister to Phoenix/Moyglare Stud Stakes winner Saoirse Abu: modest maiden: left Tony Newcombe after fourth start: stays 1½m: in visor last 2 starts. *Alan Bailey* **57**

BABOUSKA 3 b.f. Monsieur Bond (IRE) 120 – Prices Lane 55 (Gentleman's Deal (IRE) 114) [2017 57: t9.5g* p8g^4 Jan 27] modest handicapper: won at Wolverhampton in January: stays 9.5f: acts on polytrack and tapeta: often leads. *Michael Easterby* **62**

BABYFACT 6 b.m. Piccolo 121 – Pennyspider (IRE) 74 (Redback 116) [2017 76: 5m 5.1m3 5.7d* 5.7m5 6m 5.2m3 5f3 5.7g* 5g6 Sep 1] compact mare: fairly useful handicapper: won at Bath in May and July (by 2¾ lengths from Seamster): best at 5f/6f: acts on firm and good to soft going. *Malcolm Saunders* **87**

BABY GAL 3 b.f. Royal Applause 124 – Our Gal 88 (Kyllachy 129) [2017 73: p7g4 p7g 6g3 7m6 6m5 p6g2 6d2 6g5 6m6 p8g4 Dec 30] workmanlike filly: fair handicapper: stays 1m: acts on polytrack and good to soft going. *Jim Boyle* **68**

BABY HELMET 3 ch.g. Helmet (AUS) 127 – Lady Gorgeous 105 (Compton Place 125) [2017 –: t8.6m6 t9.5m3 p8g 8d 8f 7m 7m t7.1s Sep 8] modest maiden: left Mick Channon after third start: stays 9.5f: front runner/races prominently. *Karen Tutty* **59**

BABYLON LANE 2 gr.f. (Mar 18) Lethal Force (IRE) 128 – Crinkle (IRE) (Distant Relative 128) [2017 5d Jul 24] £42,000Y: half-sister to several winners, including useful 6f-1m winner Steed (by Mujahid) and useful 2-y-o 6f winner Wave Aside (by Reset): dam unraced: 14/1, well held in minor event at Beverley. *Michael Dods* **–**

BABY SAY YES 3 b.f. Sayif (IRE) 122 – Baby Princess (BRZ) (Crimson Tide (IRE) 118) [2017 t5.1g4 6m Jun 21] third foal: half-sister to Italian 7.5f/1m winner Black Imagin (by Auction House): dam Brazilian 5.5f winner: no form. *John Norton* **–**

BACACARAT (IRE) 2 b.c. (Apr 14) Raven's Pass (USA) 133 – Mathuna (IRE) (Tagula (IRE) 116) [2017 7d 8d4 Oct 27] 72,000F, €62,000Y, 110,000 2-y-o: sparely-made colt: sixth foal: half-brother to 3 winners, including smart 6f (including at 2 yrs)/7f winner Donjuan Triumphant (by Dream Ahead) and useful 2-y-o 7f/1m winner Caledonian Spring (by Amadeus Wolf), later successful in Hong Kong: dam French 2-y-o 7.5f winner: fair form: better effort when fourth in minor event at Newbury (4¼ lengths behind Military Law) in October: likely to progress further. *Andrew Balding* **73 p**

BACCARAT (IRE) 8 ch.g. Dutch Art 126 – Zut Alors (IRE) 105 (Pivotal 124) [2017 117: 6g* 6g2 6d 6s May 17] sturdy gelding: smart performer: won handicap at Meydan (by neck from Jungle Cat) in January: stays 7f: acts on polytrack, soft and good to firm going. *Charlie Appleby* **116**

BACCHUS 3 ch.g. Kheleyf (USA) 116 – Rumbled 70 (Halling (USA) 133) [2017 92: 7g* 7m3 7m 6g5 6d3 6d* 6d4 Oct 6] lengthy, rather unfurnished gelding: smart handicapper: won at Newbury (by neck from Chessman) in April and Newmarket (by short head from Dakota Gold) in August: stays 7f: acts on good to firm and good to soft going: often wears cheekpieces: consistent. *Brian Meehan* **112**

BACKINANGER 3 b.g. Royal Applause 124 – Giusina Mia (USA) (Diesis 133) [2017 60: t5.1g6 t6g3 t6g3 6g 5m 6m 6d Jun 30] modest maiden: stays 6f: acts on tapeta: in headgear last 4 starts. *Kevin Ryan* **60**

BACK TO LOVE (CAN) 4 b.f. Street Cry (IRE) 130 – Song And Danz (USA) (Unbridled's Song (USA) 125) [2017 34, a44: 8.5g 9.9g 8g 8m p7g p12g Oct 3] maiden: no form in 2017: usually wears headgear: tried in tongue tie. *Mark Gillard* **–**

BAD DOG 2 ch.g. (Feb 4) Pastoral Pursuits 127 – Movie Star (IRE) (Barathea (IRE) 127) [2017 5g 5.5s6 5m6 7.2m p8g p7s3 Dec 14] modest maiden: stays 7f: acts on polytrack and good to firm going: tried in visor: temperamental. *Michael Easterby* **59 §**

BADENSCOTH 3 b.g. Foxwedge (AUS) 128 – Twice Upon A Time 79 (Primo Dominie 121) [2017 p8m5 p7g4 p7g p8g* 8.1d2 8.3d 8m p8d2 p8s* 8.3v3 p8g6 8g2 p8g Oct 5] lengthy gelding: fifth foal: half-brother to winners abroad by Ishiguru and Compton Place: dam, 5f/5.7f winner, half-sister to ungenuine 6f/7f winner Point of Dispute and 6f winner Boomerang Blade (both useful): fairly useful handicapper: won at Kempton in April and Chelmsford in July: second at Sandown in September: stays 8.5f: acts on polytrack and heavy going: has worn hood, including last 2 starts. *Dean Ivory* **90**

BAD GIRL CAOIMHE (IRE) 4 br.f. Big Bad Bob (IRE) 118 – Sumostars (IRE) (Refuse To Bend (IRE) 128) [2017 73: f6g t8d t8.6g 9.9d 7g p8g Nov 24] maiden: below form in 2017: left Marjorie Fife after fifth start: stays 7f: acts on heavy going. *Thomas P. O'Connor, Ireland* **59**

BAGHDAD (FR) 2 b.c. (Apr 9) Frankel 147 – Funny Girl (IRE) 78 (Darshaan 133) [2017 7g5 6g 8.3d4 p10g* Nov 2] €300,000Y: closely related to 3 winners, including useful 1¼m-1½m winner Pippa Greene (by Galileo), and half-brother to several winners, including smart 1m winner Laugh Out Loud (by Clodovil): dam maiden (stayed 7f): fairly useful form: won nursery at Chelmsford (by 2 lengths from Rustang) in November: left Charlie Fellowes after second start: will stay 1½m: will go on improving. *Mark Johnston* **83 p**

BAHAARAH (IRE) 4 b.f. Iffraaj 127 – Love Intrigue (IRE) 107 (Marju (IRE) 127) [2017 **92**
105: p7d^5 p8g^6 Apr 15] small filly: useful performer: below form both starts in 2017: stays 1m: acts on firm going: often starts slowly/races towards rear. *Richard Hannon*

BAHAMADAM 3 b.f. Bahamian Bounty 116 – Pelagia (IRE) 77 (Lycius (USA) 124) **94**
[2017 82: 7g* 6.9s 7.6d^4 8g^5 Aug 25] sturdy filly: fairly useful performer: won handicap at Leicester (by neck from Rely On Me) in May: below form after: stays 7f: acts on good to firm going. *Eve Johnson Houghton*

BAHAMA MOON (IRE) 5 b.g. Lope de Vega (IRE) 125 – Bahama Bay (GER) (Dansili **92**
127) [2017 96: f7g^6 10g^4 8d 10d 9.8d^4 8.5s^3 10d 10.3g^6 10.3v* 10.3v^6 Sep 30] fairly useful handicapper: won at Chester in September: stays 10.5f: acts on heavy going: sold to join Jonjo O'Neill 20,000 gns in October. *David Barron*

BAHAMIAN BIRD 4 b.f. Bahamian Bounty 116 – Ride The Wind 72 (Cozzene (USA)) **83**
[2017 75: 7m* 7m^4 7m* 7g 7.6s 7g^2 7s^3 7g t8d^3 Oct 24] strong filly: fairly useful handicapper: won at Catterick in April and May (by 4 lengths from Courier): stays 7f: acts on tapeta, soft and good to firm going: sold 13,000 gns in October. *Richard Fahey*

BAHAMIAN C 6 b.g. Bahamian Bounty 116 – Amandian (IRE) 84 (Indian Ridge 123) **66 §**
[2017 73§: 10.3g 9.9m^3 10.2f 9.9m 10.2g 9.2g^6 t10.2g Oct 20] fair handicapper: stays 10.5f: acts on good to firm and heavy going: has worn cheekpieces: wears tongue tie: usually races towards rear: ungenuine. *Richard Fahey*

BAHAMIAN DOLLAR 4 b.g. Bahamian Bounty 116 – Penny Ha'penny 84 (Bishop of **89**
Cashel 122) [2017 88: p7d t6g^2 f6g 6m 6.1d^2 6m^2 6.1m* 6d 6.1g* 6.1g^3 6m^5 6.1g^5 6.1d^6 6.1m^3 t6d Oct 24] well-made gelding: fairly useful handicapper: won at Windsor (by ½ length from King of Spin) in June and Chepstow (by head from Farleigh Mac) in July: all wins at 6f: acts on polytrack, tapeta, good to firm and good to soft going: tried in tongue tie. *David Evans*

BAHAMIAN HEIGHTS 6 b.g. Bahamian Bounty 116 – Tahirah 99 (Green Desert **86**
(USA) 127) [2017 83§: 5m 5g^5 6d^5 6.1g^6 5.2m^6 p6g^4 p6g* p6g^2 p5s* p6s^5 p6s^2 Dec 17] strong gelding: fairly useful handicapper: won at Chelmsford in November and December (apprentice, by length from Swendab): stays 7f, raced mainly at shorter: acts on polytrack and good to firm going: has worn headgear: starts slowly, usually races in rear (has refused to race). *Robert Cowell*

BAHAMIAN PARADISE 3 ch.f. Bahamian Bounty 116 – Amanjena 99 (Beat Hollow **68**
126) [2017 62: 5.7m^2 6.1m 6m^5 p6d^2 7d Oct 24] angular filly: fair maiden: stays 7f: acts on polytrack and good to firm going. *Hughie Morrison*

BAHAMIAN SUNRISE 5 ch.g. Bahamian Bounty 116 – Tagula Sunrise (IRE) 101 **90**
(Tagula (IRE) 116) [2017 82: 6m^2 5.3g^6 5.7f 5s* 6d^2 5g^3 6s^5 5g^2 5s Nov 8] good-quartered gelding: fairly useful handicapper: won at Sandown in July: third at same course in September and second at Nottingham in October: stays 6f: acts on soft and good to firm going: wears headgear: front runner/races prominently. *John Gallagher*

BAHAMIAN SUNSHINE 4 ch.g. Bahamian Bounty 116 – Tagula Sunrise (IRE) 101 **44**
(Tagula (IRE) 116) [2017 74, a68: p6g p7g 6m 6g^6 6.8m 6s^5 7.8g Aug 30] close-coupled gelding: poor handicapper nowadays: stays 7f: acts on all-weather and heavy going: wears headgear. *L. Smyth, Ireland*

BAHANGO (IRE) 5 b.g. Bahamian Bounty 116 – Last Tango (IRE) 94 (Lion Cavern **82**
(USA) 117) [2017 51§, a78§: t5g* t5d^4 t5.1g^2 t5.1g* t5.1g t5g Oct 10] fairly useful handicapper: won at Newcastle in January and Wolverhampton (by 2 lengths from Vale of Flight) in April: best form at 5f: acts on tapeta, soft and good to firm going: wears headgear: often races freely. *Patrick Morris*

BAHAR (USA) 3 b.g. First Defence (USA) 119 – La Rignana (USA) (Galileo (IRE) 134) **76**
[2017 66p: p8g^3 8.5g^4 9.9s^2 8d^4 a10.4s^4 8d^6 9m* 9d a10.7g^3 11.9g Nov 29] fair performer: left Richard Hannon after second start: won claimer at Nort-sur-Erdre in October (left J. Phelippon after): stays 10.7f: acts on viscoride and good to firm going: often in cheekpieces. *X-L. Le Stang, France*

BAHKIT (IRE) 3 b.g. Intikhab (USA) 135 – Pink Moon (IRE) 55 (Namid 128) [2017 –: **75**
9.8m* t10.2s* Sep 19] fair handicapper: off 13 months, won at Ripon in August and Newcastle in September: stays 1¼m: acts on tapeta and good to firm going. *Sally Haynes*

BAHUTA ACHA 2 b.g. (May 8) Captain Gerrard (IRE) 113 – Rosein 86 (Komaite (USA)) **78**
[2017 5m 5g 5m^2 5v 5m 5.9v^5 5s* 5.7s^5 5s^2 Oct 31] fair performer: won nursery at Catterick in September: should prove as effective at 6f as 5f: best form on soft/heavy going: sometimes slowly away. *David Loughnane*

BAILEYS APPRENTICE 3 b.f. Mastercraftsman (IRE) 129 – Jalissa 83 (Mister Baileys 123) [2017 71: f8g^5 t12.2g 11.9g^2 8.9v Nov 25] compact filly: fair maiden: left Mark Johnston after second start, J-V. Toux after third: stays 1½m: acts on good to firm going. *P. Adda, France* **71**

BAILEYS EXCEL 2 b.c. (Mar 7) Exceed And Excel (AUS) 126 – Baileys Jubilee 103 (Bahamian Bounty 116) [2017 p5g^6 p6g p6s Nov 17] fair form: best effort when sixth of 7 in minor event at Lingfield (4 lengths behind Three Little Birds) in October: tried in hood. *Chris Dwyer* **65**

BAILEYS EXCELERATE (FR) 2 b.c. (Apr 2) Excelebration (IRE) 133 – Cruel Sea (USA) 94 (Mizzen Mast (USA) 121) [2017 7.2d^3 7.4g* p10g^2 9d^2 Oct 11] third foal: closely related to 1m winner International Law (by Exceed And Excel) and half-brother to 1¼m-1½m winner (stayed 1¾m) Mister Rockandroll (by Rock of Gibraltar): dam, 2-y-o 1m winner who stayed 1½m, sister to useful 1m-1¼m winner Moonday Sun: fairly useful form: won minor event at Beverley in August: second after in minor event at Kempton and nursery at Nottingham: will be suited by at least 1½m. *Mark Johnston* **87**

BAILEYS PURSUIT 5 ch.m. Pastoral Pursuits 127 – Royal Mistress (Fasliyev (USA) 120) [2017 70: f7g t6m t6g Feb 6] good-topped mare: fair handicapper: below form in 2017: stays 6f: acts on tapeta, firm and good to soft going: wears headgear. *Gay Kelleway* **58**

BAILEYS ROCKSTAR 2 b.f. (Mar 20) Rock of Gibraltar (IRE) 133 – Biased 109 (Haafhd 129) [2017 6g p7d t7.1g Oct 20] 22,000Y: fourth foal: half-sister to French 9f winner Azopardo (by Pour Moi): dam, French 9f/1¼m winner, half-sister to smart French winner up to 1¼m Court Canibal: no form. *James Given* **–**

BAILEYS SHOWGIRL (FR) 3 b.f. Sepoy (AUS) 129 – Tanguista (FR) (War Chant (USA) 126) [2017 98: p8g 8m^6 8m Jun 21] tall, unfurnished filly: useful at best, no form in 2017: sometimes slowly away. *Mark Johnston* **–**

BAJAN BEACON 4 gr.g. Hellvelyn 118 – Bajan Rose 89 (Dashing Blade 117) [2017 8.3m t7.1g 7g May 29] no form. *Iain Jardine* **–**

BAJAN GOLD (IRE) 2 ch.c. (May 5) Lope de Vega (IRE) 125 – Charmgoer (USA) (Nureyev (USA) 131) [2017 7g^4 7.4s^4 7s^5 p8g 9m t8g^2 Dec 6] €105,000F, 60,000Y: sturdy colt: half-brother to several winners, including useful French winner up to 13f Beringoer (2-y-o 7f/1m winner, by Bering) and French 6.5f winner Charming Touch (by Elusive Quality): dam, French 13f winner, half-sister to high-class US Grade 1 9f winner Dare And Go: fair maiden: should stay beyond 1m: in tongue tie last 2 starts: usually races nearer last than first: likely to progress further. *Stuart Williams* **71 p**

BAKER STREET 3 ch.g. Bahamian Bounty 116 – Aliante 78 (Sir Percy 129) [2017 59: p7m 10.2m^3 8g 10.3m^6 10.2f t8.6g 9.5g^4 a7.2g^4 a7.5g^6 Oct 24] fair maiden: left Tom Dascombe after sixth start: stays 10.5f: acts on good to firm going: sometimes in cheekpieces: often leads. *M. Schwinn, Germany* **65**

BAKHT KHAN (IRE) 2 ch.g. (Apr 20) Sepoy (AUS) 129 – Naddwah 85 (Pivotal 124) [2017 6g^6 t5.1g^3 p6g Oct 9] fair form: best effort when third in minor event at Wolverhampton (2¼ lengths behind Expecting) in September. *Kevin Ryan* **70**

BALANCING TIME 4 b.g. Pivotal 124 – Time On 114 (Sadler's Wells (USA) 132) [2017 60, a78: p12m* 12g^4 11.2g 13.3g Jul 13] rangy gelding: fairly useful handicapper: won at Lingfield in March: stays 2m: acts on polytrack: wears cheekpieces: races prominently: won on hurdling debut in August: sold 12,000 gns in October. *Amanda Perrett* **85**

BALASHAKH (USA) 3 b.g. Blame (USA) 129 – She Has Aptitude (USA) (Aptitude (USA) 128) [2017 72p: p11d^3 p12g^2 12m^2 10m^5 t12.4g^6 Oct 10] fairly useful maiden: second in maiden at Lingfield in March and handicap at Salisbury in July: stays 1½m: acts on polytrack and good to firm going: in hood last 3 starts: often races towards rear: sold 11,000 gns in October. *David Simcock* **80**

BAL DE RIO (FR) 4 b.g. Vertigineux (FR) 121 – Baldoranic (FR) (Panoramic 120) [2017 9.9d^5 11.2s^3 Aug 7] fairly useful performer: won maiden at Deauville and minor event at Saint-Cloud in 2016: left S. Kobayashi after final (2016) start: stays 15f: acts on polytrack, viscoride and heavy going: fair form over hurdles. *Brian Ellison* **79**

BALDUCCI 10 b.g. Dansili 127 – Miss Meltemi (IRE) 100 (Miswaki Tern (USA) 120) [2017 72: f7g f11d^5 6.7g^2 Sep 3] strong, close-coupled gelding: one-time useful performer: just poor form in 2017, leaving Roger Fell before final outing: stays 8.5f: acts on all- **45**

weather, good to firm and good to soft going: often wears headgear: tried in tongue tie. *C. von der Recke, Germany*

BALESTRA 3 b.c. Bated Breath 125 – Nimble Thimble (USA) 76 (Mizzen Mast (USA) 121) [2017 p7g⁶ 7s 8f* 7.9g p8g⁵ Oct 5] useful-looking colt: first foal: dam, 9.5f winner, half-sister to smart winner up to 8.5f Three Valleys: fairly useful performer: won maiden at Bath (by 7 lengths from Wonderfillo) in July: stays 1m: acts on polytrack and firm going: sold to join Tim Easterby 48,000 gns in November. *Charles Hills* **88**

BALGAIR 3 ch.g. Foxwedge (AUS) 128 – Glencal 74 (Compton Place 125) [2017 76: 8.5g 8.2s⁵ 8d 10g p8g² p7g³ p8g² Nov 1] unfurnished gelding: fairly useful handicapper: second at Kempton in November: left Jonathan Portman after fourth start: stays 8.5f: acts on polytrack and good to soft going: usually races towards rear. *Tom Clover* **83**

BALGOWLAH (IRE) 2 b.g. (Mar 28) Thewayyouare (USA) 117 – Rohain (IRE) (Singspiel (IRE) 133) [2017 p8g p8g t8.6g Nov 11] no form. *David Lanigan* **–**

BALKHASH (IRE) 2 b.g. (Apr 5) Champs Elysees 124 – Balatoma (IRE) 76 (Mr Greeley (USA) 122) [2017 8.3v p8s p8g⁶ Dec 20] modest form in maiden/minor events. *Clive Cox* **50**

BALKINSTOWN (IRE) 7 b.g. Westerner 130 – Graffogue (IRE) 58 (Red Sunset 120) [2017 18d³ Aug 24] modest handicapper, lightly raced on Flat: stays 2¼m: acts on good to soft going: tried in visor/tongue tie: winning hurdler/pointer. *Robert Stephens* **54**

BALLARD DOWN (IRE) 4 b.g. Canford Cliffs (IRE) 133 – Mackenzie's Friend (Selkirk (USA) 129) [2017 90: p8g² t8.6g* p8d⁵ p8s² 8s* Jul 22] smart handicapper: won at Wolverhampton (by 3¾ lengths from Makzeem) in May and Newmarket (by 3½ lengths from Master The World) in July: stays 8.5f: acts on polytrack, tapeta, firm and soft going: in visor last 4 starts: has looked quirky but did nothing wrong last 2 starts. *William Knight* **111**

BALLESTEROS 8 ch.g. Tomba 119 – Flamenco Dancer (Mark of Esteem (IRE) 137) [2017 95: p6g t5g⁶ p6g³ t6d t5.1g⁶ p6g 5.1m p5g⁵ 6.1s⁵ 5.1d⁶ 5f 5.1d 5g³ 5.1g² 5.1v⁴ 5v² 5v³ 6.1d* p6g f5g Dec 11] close-coupled gelding: fairly useful performer: won claimer at Windsor in October, final start for Richard Fahey: stays 6f: acts on polytrack, tapeta, good to firm and heavy going: has worn hood. *Roger Ingram* **84**

BALLET CONCERTO 4 b.g. Dansili 127 – Ballet Ballon (USA) 81 (Rahy (USA) 115) [2017 109: 8g* 9m⁵ 8.5m⁶ 8m⁴ 10.3m* 8g* 8.2s* Sep 9] tall gelding: very smart performer: improved further in 2017, winning handicap at Doncaster in April, John Smith's Cup (Handicap) at York (by ¾ length from Big Country) in July, Sovereign Stakes at Salisbury (by neck from Tabarrak) in August and Superior Mile at Haydock (by 1¼ lengths from Kaspersky) in September: stayed 10.5f: acted on polytrack, good to firm and heavy going: usually raced prominently: collapsed and died on the gallops in late-September. *Sir Michael Stoute* **120**

BALLETOMANE 2 b.c. (Feb 9) Exceed And Excel (AUS) 126 – Alexander Ballet 86 (Mind Games 121) [2017 6m⁴ 8g p6g² p6g³ Oct 24] fair form in minor events. *Richard Hannon* **70**

John Smith's Cup (Heritage Handicap), York—
ill-fated Ballet Concerto beats Big Country (partially hidden by winner) and Mistiroc (right); unusually for York nowadays, they stay far side in the straight rather than coming down the centre

BALLIOL 5 b.g. Exceed And Excel (AUS) 126 – Cinerama (IRE) 68 (Machiavellian (USA) 123) [2017 61: p7g Feb 3] fair at best, disappointing since 3 yrs: stays 6f: acts on good to firm going: in headgear last 3 starts: has worn tongue tie: often starts slowly/races in rear. *Ronald Harris* **–**

BALLYFARSOON (IRE) 6 ch.g. Medicean 128 – Amzara (IRE) (Montjeu (IRE) 137) [2017 66: t12.2g t12.2g p16g p13.3g^5 p16g^2 t16.5g* Oct 21] fair handicapper: won at Wolverhampton in October: stays 16.5f: acts on polytrack, tapeta and good to firm going: usually wears headgear: has worn tongue tie. *Ian Williams* **65**

BALLYLARE 4 b.g. Mullionmileanhour (IRE) 116 – Retainage (USA) (Polish Numbers (USA)) [2017 89: p7g^5 Jan 5] fairly useful handicapper: stays 7f: acts on polytrack, good to firm and good to soft going: often leads: sold 9,000 gns in February. *Lee Carter* **85**

BALLYMORE CASTLE (IRE) 5 br.g. Invincible Spirit (IRE) 121 – Ballymore Lady (USA) (War Chant (USA) 126) [2017 92: 7g^4 7g^5 7s^6 7d^3 7m 7d 6.1m 6s t6d^2 p6g^4 t7.2g^5 t6.1g* Dec 18] strong gelding: fairly useful performer: won seller at Wolverhampton in December: stays 7f: acts on tapeta, firm and soft going: has worn cheekpieces, including last 4 starts: sometimes slowly away: untrustworthy. *Richard Fahey* **87 §**

BALLYNANTY (IRE) 5 gr.g. Yeats (IRE) 128 – Reina Blanca 102 (Darshaan 133) [2017 107: p12g^5 t12.4s p14g^5 14g May 27] good-topped gelding: useful handicapper: largely well below form in 2017: stays 2m: acts on polytrack and tapeta: tried in cheekpieces: has worn tongue tie: often races towards rear: has joined Mrs Denise Foster. *Andrew Balding* **97**

BALLYQUIN (IRE) 2 b.c. (Mar 1) Acclamation 118 – Something Mon (USA) (Maria's Mon (USA) 121) [2017 6.5d^4 Oct 27] half-brother to numerous winners, including useful winner up to 1m Raymi Coya (2-y-o 5f-7f winner, by Van Nistelrooy) and useful 11.7f winner Hikari (by Galileo): dam unraced: 33/1, fourth in maiden at Newbury (4¼ lengths behind Picture No Sound) in October: better to come. *Andrew Balding* **72 p**

BALLYSAMPSON 3 b.c. Equiano (FR) 127 – The Fugative 94 (Nicholas (USA) 111) [2017 –: 5.3g^5 May 15] no form. *Simon Dow* **–**

BALMEC (IRE) 2 bl.g. (Apr 3) Society Rock (IRE) 126 – Crossreadh (USA) 60 (Sahm (USA) 112) [2017 6s 6v t6g^6 t6.1g Dec 22] no form. *Ann Duffield* **–**

BALMONT BELLE (IRE) 7 b.m. Balmont (USA) 117 – Social Set (IRE) (Key of Luck (USA) 126) [2017 49: t9.5g t12.2g^6 10.2d 12m^6 10.2g^{rr} 10d Sep 12] fairly useful at best in Ireland, well below that since 2014: stays 10.5f: acts on polytrack and good to firm going: tried in cheekpieces: sometimes slowly away, often races towards rear: one to treat with caution (refused to race penultimate start). *Barry Leavy* **53 §**

BALMORAL CASTLE 8 b.g. Royal Applause 124 – Mimiteh (USA) 77 (Maria's Mon (USA) 121) [2017 99: 10m 8f 8m^3 9.1d 9.1g 10g Sep 22] lengthy gelding: fairly useful handicapper: third at Ascot (apprentice) in July: stays 1¼m: acts on polytrack, good to firm and good to soft going. *Jonathan Portman* **91**

BALTIC EAGLE (GER) 3 ch.g. Adlerflug (GER) 123 – Baltic Gift (Cadeaux Genereux 131) [2017 t12.2g^2 12.1m^3 12m^5 10.7g* a11.9g Jun 15] fair performer: left Rune Haugen, won minor event at Ovrevoll in June: stays 1½m: acts on tapeta and good to firm going. *Wido Neuroth, Norway* **71**

BALTIC PRINCE (IRE) 7 b.g. Baltic King 120 – Brunswick (Warning 136) [2017 83: p8d p8d^5 t7.1g^6 t7.1m^3 8.2s 7f 7.8s 7.1d^6 7d* 7v 7d t7.2g^2 t7.2g t7.2d^4 Dec 26] fair handicapper: won at Brighton in September: stays 8.5f: acts on all-weather, good to firm and good to soft going: tried in blinkers: front runner. *Tony Carroll* **72 a80**

BALTY BOYS (IRE) 8 b.g. Cape Cross (IRE) 129 – Chatham Islands (USA) 77 (Elusive Quality (USA)) [2017 100: t10.2d Oct 24] useful-looking gelding: smart at best, well held in claimer only start in 2017: stays 1¼m: acts on any turf going: usually wears headgear. *Brian Ellison* **–**

BAMAKO DU CHATELET (FR) 6 gr.g. Voix du Nord (FR) 119 – Royale du Chatelet (FR) (Sleeping Car (FR) 116) [2017 75: t12.4g^2 t12.2m* p12g^4 p15.8g^2 p13g^4 p12g t12.2g^4 p14g^2 p12g 16.3m^4 11.6d^4 16.3d^6 12g^3 16s t16.5g p12g* t14d^2 Dec 27] compact gelding: fair handicapper: won at Wolverhampton in January and Lingfield (apprentice) in December: stays 16.5f: acts on polytrack, tapeta and good to firm going: usually wears headgear. *Ian Williams* **78**

BAMBER BRIDGE (IRE) 3 gr.c. Dark Angel (IRE) 113 – Nashira 78 (Prince Sabo 123) [2017 93: 6d 7d^5 8m^4 8s^4 10v Oct 23] well-made colt: fairly useful handicapper: stays 1m: acts on good to firm going: sometimes slowly away. *Michael Dods* **91**

BAMBINO LOLA 2 b.f. (Feb 19) Helmet (AUS) 127 – Lifetime Romance (IRE) 92 (Mozart (IRE) 131) [2017 7d* 7s^3 6g* 6g Sep 7] 3,500Y: sixth foal: half-sister to 3 winners, including 6f and (including at 2 yrs) 7f winner Amoure Medici (by Medicean) and 6f/7f winner Broughtons Fancy (by Pastoral Pursuits): dam, 2-y-o 7f winner, half-sister to useful winner up to 1½m Hanoverian Baron: fairly useful form: won maiden at Lingfield in June and minor event at Salisbury in August: stays 7f. *Adam West* **85**

BAMO MC 3 gr.g. Hellvelyn 118 – Soft Touch (IRE) 78 (Petorius 117) [2017 8g 8.3v 7g Aug 17] good-topped gelding: down the field in maidens. *Mike Murphy* **50**

BANCNUANAHEIREANN (IRE) 10 b.g. Chevalier (IRE) 115 – Alamanta (IRE) (Ali-Royal (IRE) 127) [2017 102: t8.6g^3 9m p10s 9.1d p8s Dec 14] big, workmanlike gelding: useful handicapper: third in minor event at Wolverhampton (1¾ lengths behind Third Time Lucky) in February: stays 11f: acts on polytrack, tapeta, soft and good to firm going. *Michael Appleby* **100**

BANDITRY (IRE) 5 b.g. Iffraaj 127 – Badalona 90 (Cape Cross (IRE) 129) [2017 95: p10g* 10.1g^2 12m^6 10g^4 p10s^2 10d* 10g^2 Jul 15] angular gelding: useful handicapper: won at Lingfield in February and Newmarket in June: second at Ascot (2 lengths behind Laraaib) in July: stays 10.5f: acts on polytrack, soft and good to firm going: usually in headgear: usually races towards rear: won over hurdles in October. *Ian Williams* **103**

BANFF (IRE) 4 b.g. Papal Bull 128 – Hugs 'N Kisses (IRE) 82 (Noverre (USA) 125) [2017 60: t16.3g* 14.2g^4 Aug 7] modest handicapper: won at Newcastle in July: stays 16.5f: acts on tapeta and heavy going: usually in headgear. *Olly Murphy* **64**

BANISH (USA) 4 b.g. Smart Strike (CAN) 121 – Beyond Our Reach (IRE) 100 (Danehill Dancer (IRE) 117) [2017 90, a102: 10.3m^5 10.3m^5 9.9m^6 p12s^4 p11s t12.4s^4 p12g* p12g^5 t12.4g Oct 19] rangy gelding: fairly useful handicapper: won at Kempton in September: stays 12.5f: acts on polytrack, tapeta and good to firm going: wears headgear/tongue tie: sold 9,000 gns in October: one to treat with caution. *Hugo Palmer* **94 §**

BANJO'S VOICE 2 ch.g. (Apr 8) Poet's Voice 126 – La Jwaab (Alhaarth (IRE) 126) [2017 7m 8g 8.3v Nov 8] well beaten in minor events/maiden. *Jane Chapple-Hyam* **–**

BANK BONUS 8 b.g. Motivator 131 – Small Fortune 81 (Anabaa (USA) 130) [2017 t12.4d t12.4s Jul 1] rather leggy gelding: fairly useful handicapper for Andrew Balding in 2012: lightly raced and little impact on Flat subsequently: stayed 13.5f: acted on polytrack, good to firm and heavy going: wore hood: fair hurdler: dead. *Brian Ellison* **75**

BANKSEA 4 b.g. Lawman (FR) 121 – Stars In Your Eyes 75 (Galileo (IRE) 134) [2017 111: 8m* 8m 8s 10m^5 Sep 23] smart handicapper: won at Newbury (by ½ length from Another Touch) in April: good 2½ lengths fifth of 19 to Brorocco there final start: stays 1¼m: acts on firm going: often races towards rear: sold 130,000 gns in November, sent to UAE. *Luca Cumani* **113**

BAN SHOOF 4 b.g. Shirocco (GER) 129 – Pasithea (IRE) 101 (Celtic Swing 138) [2017 78: t9.5m^5 t13.9m^6 9.9g 11.2g 13.3g 14v^3 11.9g* 10d^4 p10g^2 9.9s p10g* Dec 30] fair handicapper: won at Brighton in August and Lingfield in December: left Ismail Mohammed after second start: stays 1½m: acts on polytrack, tapeta, good to firm and heavy going: wears headgear. *Gary Moore* **75**

BANSURI 2 ch.f. (Apr 5) Piccolo 121 – Trina's Pet 65 (Efisio 120) [2017 t7.2g Jul 3] sister to 5f/6f winner Penny Dreadful and half-sister to 2 winners, including 6f/7f winner Bold Diva (by Bold Edge): dam 2-y-o 5f winner: 80/1, well held in minor event at Wolverhampton. *Jo Hughes* **–**

BANTA BAY 3 b.g. Kheleyf (USA) 116 – Atnab (USA) 64 (Riverman (USA) 131) [2017 58: 7g^6 8s p8g p6d p6g p6g^3 p7g^6 p7g^2 p8s^5 p10g^6 Dec 13] modest maiden: stays 1¼m: acts on polytrack: has worn headgear, including last 3 starts. *John Best* **58**

BAPAK ASMARA (IRE) 5 ro.g. Zebedee 113 – Sheba Five (USA) 73 (Five Star Day (USA) 120) [2017 88: t5s 5m 6s 5d 6d 5g Aug 30] lengthy gelding: fairly useful at best, no form in 2017: has worn headgear, including last 3 starts. *Kevin Ryan* **–**

BAPAK BANGSAWAN 7 b.g. Pastoral Pursuits 127 – Nsx 74 (Roi Danzig (USA)) [2017 53: f5g^5 Jan 10] fairly useful at best, has deteriorated markedly: stays 6f: acts on polytrack, fibresand and any turf going: wears headgear: tried in tongue tie: usually leads. *Ann Stokell* **–**

BARAWEEZ (IRE) 7 b.g. Cape Cross (IRE) 129 – Aquarelle Bleue (Sadler's Wells (USA) 132) [2017 110: p7g t8.6g^5 p7g 7m 7.9m 8.6d^6 7s^2 7.9d^4 p7s^4 7d 7.9g^6 Oct 13] workmanlike gelding: useful handicapper: second at Galway (½ length behind Dream Walker) in August: stays 9f: acts on polytrack, good to firm and heavy going: tried in cheekpieces. *Brian Ellison* **105**

BARBARA VILLIERS 2 b.f. (Apr 12) Champs Elysees 124 – Frances Stuart (IRE) 85 (King's Best (USA) 132) [2017 t8.6d^3 p8s^3 Dec 17] third foal: dam, 1m winner, half-sister to useful 8.5f/1¼m winner Alive Alive Oh: fair form when third in minor events. *Mark Johnston* **67**

BARBARIANATTHEGATE 2 ch.c. (Feb 20) Lethal Force (IRE) 128 – Poetic Dancer 97 (Byron 117) [2017 6.1d p7s^5 p7s^2 7m^2 7v 8.1m^4 7g* Aug 26] sturdy colt: fair performer: won minor event at Chester in August: stays 7f: acts on polytrack and good to firm going: wears blinkers: usually leads. *Brian Meehan* **79**

BARBARY PRINCE 5 ch.g. Dapper – La Vie Est Belle 80 (Makbul 104) [2017 –: f8g t9.5g 11.6d^5 14d t12.2g 12.1d^6 11.6d 11.9d Sep 18] sturdy gelding: poor maiden: tried in blinkers. *Shaun Harris* **44**

BARDD (IRE) 5 b.g. Dylan Thomas (IRE) 132 – Zarawa (IRE) (Kahyasi 130) [2017 p13.3s* Dec 14] won maiden at Chelmsford (by 1¾ lengths from Prerogative) on Flat debut: fair hurdler. *Nicky Henderson* **78**

BAREFOOT BABY (IRE) 2 ch.f. (Mar 25) Choisir (AUS) 126 – Gwen Lady Byron (IRE) 70 (Dandy Man (IRE) 123) [2017 6g^6 5.9s^5 7v^2 8v t8.6g^4 7.9g Oct 13] £17,000Y, €32,000 2-y-o: first foal: dam 2-y-o 5f winner: modest maiden: stays 8.5f: acts on tapeta and heavy going: often races towards rear. *Richard Fahey* **62**

BARFORD (IRE) 2 b.c. (Apr 9) Big Bad Bob (IRE) 118 – Rupa (IRE) 77 (Acclamation 118) [2017 7f^4 7m^2 7d* 7g^5 7s^5 7.9g* Oct 13] €24,000F, €20,000Y, £32,000 2-y-o: lengthy colt: has scope: first foal: dam, maiden (best effort at 1m), half-sister to useful winner up to 9f No Explaining: fairly useful performer: won minor events at Yarmouth in August and York (by 2¾ lengths from Qianlong) in October: stays 1m: acts on soft and good to firm going: usually races close up. *Pam Sly* **91**

BARGAIN BUY 4 ch.f. Tamayuz 126 – Peace Summit (Cape Cross (IRE) 129) [2017 98p: p7g t7.1d^3 Mar 2] fairly useful handicapper: better effort in 2017 when third at Newcastle in March: stays 1m: acts on polytrack and tapeta: usually slowly away/races nearer last than first: temperament under suspicion. *William Haggas* **92**

BARIG AL THUMAMA 2 ch.c. (Mar 1) Kyllachy 129 – Self Centred 88 (Medicean 128) [2017 6.1g^2 6.1g^3 p7d^2 p7g^3 Oct 25] fair form, placed all 4 starts: stays 7f. *Marco Botti* **77**

BARISTA (IRE) 9 b.g. Titus Livius (FR) 115 – Cappuccino (IRE) (Mujadil (USA) 119) [2017 71: 8.1d^3 8.1d^6 p8s 8g* 7.1g^3 7.4v t9.5g f7.1g^3 Dec 4] compact gelding: fair handicapper: won at Salisbury in August: stays 1m: acts on polytrack, fibresand, good to firm and heavy going: tried in visor: often races in rear. *Brian Forsey* **66**

BARITONE (IRE) 2 b.c. (Feb 22) Camelot 128 – Star Ruby (IRE) 109 (Rock of Gibraltar (IRE) 133) [2017 7m^5 Sep 23] fourth foal: half-brother to winner up to 1¼m Stravagante (2-y-o 1m winner, by Rip Van Winkle) and 1¼m winner (stays 1½m) Stargazer (by Canford Cliffs), both smart: dam 1¼m winner: 16/1, caught eye when fifth in minor event at Newbury (11¼ lengths behind Emaraaty) on debut, considerately handled: will be suited by at least 1m: open to significant improvement. *Sir Michael Stoute* **65 P**

BARIZAN (IRE) 11 b.g. Kalanisi (IRE) 132 – Behra (IRE) 101 (Grand Lodge (USA) 125) [2017 77§: 12.1m 16d^3 14v^2 16.5m^4 Jul 13] rather leggy gelding: fair handicapper: stays 2m: acts on good to firm and heavy going: wears headgear: in tongue tie last 5 starts: usually races towards rear: temperamental. *Brendan Powell* **73 §**

BARKSTON ASH 9 b.g. Kyllachy 129 – Ae Kae Ae (USA) (King of Kings (IRE) 125) [2017 88: 6s 5.9d 6d 6g 6v Nov 7] compact gelding: useful at best, no form in 2017: stays 6f: acts on good to firm and heavy going: wears headgear. *Eric Alston* **–**

BARNABY BROOK (CAN) 7 b.g. North Light (IRE) 126 – Mascara (USA) (Milwaukee Brew (USA) 122) [2017 70: 10.9m t9.5g* p10g^6 t9.5m^2 t9.5g Dec 18] fair handicapper: won at Wolverhampton in September: stays 1¼m: acts on polytrack and tapeta: usually wears headgear: often races prominently. *Tom Dascombe* **73**

BARNACLE 8 b.g. Compton Place 125 – Bombalarina (IRE) (Barathea (IRE) 127) [2017 47: p12d^2 p15.8g^5 t13.9g^5 p16d p12g f14g t12.2g Apr 22] big gelding: poor handicapper: stays 2m: acts on polytrack and fibresand: wears headgear/tongue tie: sometimes slowly away, usually races nearer last than first. *Emma Owen* **44**

BARNAY 2 b.g. (Mar 2) Nayef (USA) 129 – Barnezet (GR) 73 (Invincible Spirit (IRE) 121) [2017 p7g p8g p8g[4] Dec 20] lengthy gelding: fourth foal: half-brother to Swedish 6f winner Gobertier (by Avonbridge) and useful 2-y-o 6f winner Rajar (by Archipenko): dam 5f winner: fair form: 5¼ lengths fourth of 9 to Mewtow in minor event at Lingfield final start, having hopeless task from position: will be suited by 1¼m+: tried in hood: remains with potential. *Marcus Tregoning* **70 p**

BARNEY BULLET (IRE) 2 b.g. (Mar 25) Havana Gold (IRE) 118 – Lalinde 50 (Tiger Hill (IRE) 127) [2017 5g 6m 5s[6] Sep 19] down the field in minor events. *Noel Wilson* **53**

BARNEY GEORGE 2 ch.c. (Apr 1) Cityscape 127 – Romantic Retreat 63 (Rainbow Quest (USA) 134) [2017 6m 7.2g 7.2g[5] 8s 8v Oct 23] good-topped colt: modest maiden: should be suited by 1m+. *Iain Jardine* **63**

BARNEY ROY 3 b.c. Excelebration (IRE) 133 – Alina (IRE) (Galileo (IRE) 134) [2017 94P: 7m* 8m[2] 8f* 9.9m[2] 10.3d[3] 10s Oct 21] **126**

One of the changes which followed the summer resignation of Sheikh Mohammed's long-standing adviser John Ferguson was the ending of the Godolphin/Darley boycott of stallions housed at Coolmore, or, more precisely, of their progeny at the yearling sales. That boycott lasted for over a decade and, unfortunately for Godolphin/Darley, proved to be particularly badly timed, coinciding with Galileo's emergence as the dominant stallion in Europe. 'Back door' access to sons of the Coolmore star was gained through the private purchases of top horses Teofilo and New Approach from Jim Bolger (though, following a very good start to his stud career, New Approach's fee has fallen from £80,000 to £30,000 over the last two seasons which tells its own story). The achievements of the offspring of home-bred Dubawi—Galileo's closest rival in the stallion tables nowadays—and of the likes of Shamardal, Exceed And Excel and Teofilo has kept the Darley stallion operation in a prime position, but the insistence on not supporting the phenomenal Galileo has been costly to Sheikh Mohammed's racing division, particularly to its record in the classics.

The dual Guineas triumphs of Galileo's son and daughter Churchill and Winter (and a similar feat by Capri) in the latest season—in the colours of the Coolmore partners—were probably the last straw for Sheikh Mohammed who permitted his team to bid for the choicest yearlings by the Coolmore champion and other Coolmore sires at the major yearling sales in the autumn. They made a relatively low-key start at Keeneland in September when the purchases included a pair of colts by Galileo's son Australia and others by Uncle Mo and Lookin At Lucky, two stallions based at Ashford, Coolmore's Kentucky stud. The purchase of a Galileo filly for €1,200,000 a couple of weeks later at the Orby Sale at Kill was perhaps an even clearer sign that the boycott was over and the addition, at the Newmarket October Sales Book 1, with Coolmore as underbidder, of Galileo's daughter out of Breeders' Cup winner Dank (at 4,000,000 guineas the second most expensive yearling filly to be sold at auction after Al Naamah) evoked memories of some of the bidding battles between the two racing superpowers at the height of the boom in bloodstock values in the 'eighties. John Gosden, who did the bidding for the Dank filly, said 'She's an outstanding physical example with a great pedigree and you must always think that the studs need to be regenerated with new bloodlines, it's very important.' Sheikh Mohammed's team bought four Galileo yearlings from the Book 1 sale, three of which were fillies.

John Ferguson's long tenure at Godolphin/Darley reportedly foundered on internal squabbling over the distribution of the 2017 batch of two-year-olds between the operation's two private stables, a topic touched on in the essay on Thunder Snow. One of the policies that had been abandoned on Ferguson's watch was the automatic transfer to its in-house stables of horses purchased by Godolphin from other trainers. New Approach and his son Dawn Approach (also now a Darley stallion), for example, both remained with Jim Bolger, starting a policy which has certainly paid off for Godolphin. Among the horses who did the operation proud in the latest season were Europe's leading miler Ribchester and the three-year-olds Harry Angel and Barney Roy, who also became Group 1 winners, like Ribchester, after being left with their original trainers when bought by Godolphin. Barney Roy, who is out of a daughter of Galileo, became the latest among a number of good performers in recent years purchased from the Hannon stable, in his case after an impressive victory in a good maiden in the autumn over a mile at Haydock on his only start at two.

A £70,000 yearling by the Coolmore-based stallion Excelebration, Barney Roy held no two-year-old big-race entries and started at 9/1 at Haydock but he looked the part, travelling fluently and quickening well before stretching away under hands and heels to win by three and three quarter lengths from the Varian-trained favourite Fujaira Bridge, with a number of promising types from other powerful stables further back (Barney Roy noticeably took some pulling up afterwards and it was clear he was more likely to be contesting pattern races than handicaps as a three-year-old). Barney Roy didn't take long in his second season to signal his potential as a Group 1 winner, getting the better of another Godolphin-owned colt, the favourite Dream Castle (trained by Saeed bin Suroor), in the seven-furlong JLT Greenham Stakes at Newbury, a race in which the Hannon stable has built up a notable record over the years, though one of its best runners in the race, another out of a daughter of Galileo, Night of Thunder (purchased after his three-year-old season by Godolphin for whom he won the Lockinge), was beaten by the top-notch Kingman in the 2014 edition before turning the tables, starting at 40/1, in a very strong edition of the Two Thousand Guineas, in which he became the only horse to beat Kingman. Barney Roy was again impressive at Newbury, staying on to lead in the final hundred yards for a two-length win and looking sure to benefit from a return to a mile. He started 7/2 second favourite behind Churchill at Newmarket and did extremely well to take second after becoming unbalanced when meeting trouble on the run into the Dip and appearing to stumble. Barney Roy kept on to edge second from French challenger Al Wukair and Churchill's stablemate Lancaster Bomber, with Dream Castle fifth. Just a length separated Churchill and Barney Roy, with some maintaining the latter had been a shade unlucky.

Barney Roy wasn't seen again until Royal Ascot where he met Churchill for the second time. Churchill had gone on in the interim to complete the Anglo-Irish Two Thousand Guineas double and started odds on to emulate Rock of Gibraltar, Henrythenavigator and Gleneagles by completing what is sometimes referred to as the 'triple crown' for three-year-old milers by adding the St James's Palace Stakes. Churchill didn't give his running in fourth, however, while Barney Roy progressed again, staying on to lead well inside the final furlong after being waited with, to win by a length and a head from Lancaster Bomber and Godolphin-owned Thunder Snow, who had finished second to Churchill in the Irish Two Thousand Guineas. Barney Roy was part of a memorable Ascot opening day for his owners, following the success in their royal blue colours of Ribchester in the Queen Anne Stakes (they also had a one, two in the closing Windsor Castle Stakes).

Barney Roy was stepped up in trip after Royal Ascot and he acquitted himself very well in both the Coral-Eclipse and the Juddmonte International. He ran every bit as well at Sandown as he did in the St James's Palace, all but snatching victory in a driving finish with the year-older Ulysses, and was close to his best when third to

St James's Palace Stakes, Royal Ascot—
dual Guineas winner Churchill (striped cap) is well below form as Barney Roy avenges his Newmarket defeat, overhauling Lancaster Bomber (left) and Thunder Snow (white cap)

the same horse at York, where Churchill beat Barney Roy by a neck for second. The official weight-for-age for middle-distance races was changed for the 2017 season and Barney Roy received a pound less from Ulysses in the Eclipse than he would have done twelve months earlier, a pound that surely cost him the race since he went down by the narrowest margin, failing by just a nose to peg back the winner after producing a strong challenge well inside the final furlong (the first two finished clear). Barney Roy's regular jockey in the latest season James Doyle was in trouble with the Sandown stewards for his use of the whip, being referred to the BHA who imposed a fifteen-day ban under the totting-up rules, but he was back in plenty of time to take the ride on Barney Roy in the International in which more use was made of Barney Roy who pressed the front-running Derby runner-up Cliffs of Moher, the pair ensuring a truly-run race, until being sent on fully three furlongs from home. The patiently-ridden Ulysses headed Barney Roy entering the final furlong and Churchill kept on to relegate him to third, beaten two lengths and a neck, with Cliffs of Moher a further four and a half lengths back in fourth.

Barney Roy's final appearance of the season came, after an eight-week break, on British Champions' Day at Ascot, in the Champion Stakes itself (Ribchester and Thunder Snow represented Godolphin in the Queen Elizabeth II Stakes). The going on Champions' Day was much the softest Barney Roy encountered in his career and, although he took the eye with his well-being beforehand, he appeared unable to handle the conditions, eventually beating only one home after raising just a brief effort over two furlongs out following a return to waiting tactics.

Barney Roy (b.c. 2014)	Excelebration (IRE) (b 2008)	Exceed And Excel (b 2000)	Danehill
			Patrona
		Sun Shower (b 2001)	Indian Ridge
			Miss Kemble
	Alina (IRE) (b 2010)	Galileo (b 1998)	Sadler's Wells
			Urban Sea
		Cheyenne Star (b 2003)	Mujahid
			Charita

The tall, good-bodied Barney Roy is an attractive colt with the physique to have developed further if he had been kept in training. He looked in fine shape before nearly all his races in the latest season (he was a shade on edge and had two handlers before the Guineas). Barney Roy is, by some way, the best from the first crop of Excelebration, a top-class miler by Exceed And Excel unfortunate to be foaled in the same year as Frankel. Excelebration's wins included the Prix du Moulin, the Prix Jacques le Marois and the Queen Elizabeth II Stakes, and his record would have looked even better if Frankel hadn't been around (he was placed behind him on five occasions, including when second in three Group 1s). Barney Roy is the first foal out of Alina who was in training in France with Freddie Head but finished down the field on both her outings as a two-year-old before being sent to the December Sales as a three-year-old when she changed hands, carrying Barney Roy, for 65,000 guineas (she had made €200,000 as a foal). As well as being by Galileo, who incidentally is the sire of the dams of two of the last three Two Thousand Guineas winners (Galileo Gold followed Night of Thunder), Alina is out of the smart miler Cheyenne Star who won the Ridgewood Pearl Stakes at the Curragh as a four-year-old and the Brownstown Stakes over seven at Leopardstown at five. Cheyenne Star was as game and consistent as they come, a description that certainly applies to the best representative of this family in recent times before Barney Roy came along. That is the evergreen sprinter-miler Gordon Lord Byron, a Group 1 winner in Britain, France and Australia in his time and still winning in pattern company as a nine-year-old in the latest season; Gordon Lord Byron's unraced dam Boa Estrela is a half-sister to Cheyenne Star, both being daughters of Charita who won a listed race at Naas over a mile as a four-year-old. Alina hit the jackpot with Barney Roy as her first foal and her second Wisdom Mind (a filly by Dark Angel) made the frame in all three of her starts for Criquette Head-Maarek in France, with a yearling filly by Kodiac, who made 400,000 guineas at the December Sales, and a colt foal by Free Eagle following on. Alina was said to be in foal in the latest season to Dubawi (the sire of Night of Thunder among others). The genuine Barney Roy seemed likely to remain in training as a four-year-old but plans were changed and he will stand his

Godolphin's "Barney Roy"

first season at Darley in 2018 at a fee of £10,000. He stayed ten and a half furlongs and wouldn't have been inconvenienced brought back to a mile as a four-year-old. He acted on firm and good to soft going, and was well below form on his only start on soft. *Richard Hannon*

BARNSDALE 4 b.g. Stimulation (IRE) 121 – Seren Teg 80 (Timeless Times (USA) 99) [2017 37: f6g t6g p5d^{3} t5g t6m p5g p5g^{6} p5s^{6} t5.1g^{4} t5.1g^{4} p5g^{4} t5.1g Dec 22] modest maiden: best form at 5f: acts on tapeta: has worn cheekpieces. *John Holt* **52**

BARON BOLT 4 br.g. Kheleyf (USA) 116 – Scarlet Royal 43 (Red Ransom (USA)) [2017 101: 7f 7s^{3} 7s^{5} 7m^{3} p7d^{6} 6.1g* 7d^{5} 6s^{2} 6d^{2} Oct 27] good-topped gelding: useful handicapper: won at Chepstow in August: second at Goodwood and Newbury (½ length behind Alaadel) last 2 starts: stays 7f: acts on polytrack and heavy going: wears cheekpieces. *Paul Cole* **102**

BARONESS (IRE) 2 b.f. (Mar 11) Declaration of War (USA) 128 – Charroux (IRE) 75 (Darshaan 133) [2017 8m^{5} 8d^{5} p7g^{5} 8.1v* 8d^{2} Nov 4] half-sister to several winners, including smart French 1¼m winner Impressionist (by Montjeu), useful 1½m winner Apache (by Galileo) and useful 7f-1¼m winner (stayed 1½m) Beyond Brilliance (by Holy Roman Emperor): dam lightly-raced half-sister to Gold Cup winner Gildoran: useful form: won nursery at Leopardstown in October: second in listed race at Newmarket (1¼ lengths behind Hadith) final start: will stay beyond 1m: acts on heavy going: open to further improvement. *Joseph Patrick O'Brien, Ireland* **101 p**

BARON RUN 7 ch.g. Bertolini (USA) 125 – Bhima (Polar Falcon (USA) 126) [2017 f6g t6d f6d 6g 6d^{4} 7d^{5} 6s^{4} 6d^{6} 7d^{6} 7v Nov 7] well-made gelding: modest handicapper: stays 7f: acts on polytrack, firm and soft going: tried in hood: sometimes slowly away. *K. R. Burke* **57**

BARRACUDA BOY (IRE) 7 b.g. Bahamian Bounty 116 – Madame Boulangere 100 (Royal Applause 124) [2017 105: 7g 7m p6g^{5} t6.1g^{3} p7g t6.1d^{5} Dec 16] robust gelding: useful handicapper: third at Wolverhampton (2½ lengths behind Gulliver) in October: stays 7f: acts on polytrack, tapeta, soft and good to firm going: has worn headgear. *Marjorie Fife* **97**

Qatar Richmond Stakes, Goodwood—Barraquero copes well with the heavy ground as he beats the Superlative Stakes runner-up Nebo and the July Stakes winner Cardsharp

BARRAQUERO (IRE) 2 b.c. (Feb 24) Zebedee 113 – Chica Whopa (IRE) 90 (Oasis Dream 129) [2017 6.5g^3 6.1m* 6v* Aug 3] €40,000F, £30,000Y: compact colt: fourth foal: dam, 7f winner, closely related to useful 2-y-o 5f/6f winner Jezebel: smart form: won minor event at Chepstow (by 6 lengths from Airshow) in July and Richmond Stakes at Goodwood (by 1¼ lengths from Nebo) in August: open to further improvement. *Brian Meehan* **110 p**

BARREN BROOK 10 b.g. Beat Hollow 126 – Carinthia (IRE) 82 (Tirol 127) [2017 76: p10m Jan 21] strong, sturdy gelding: useful at best, behind only start in 2017: stayed 10.5f: acted on polytrack, soft and good to firm going: often in headgear: retired. *Laura Mongan* –

BARRINGTON (IRE) 3 b.c. Casamento (IRE) 118 – Mia Divina (Exceed And Excel (AUS) 126) [2017 100p: 6s^6 7m 5.7f^3 6m^4 6v p6g Sep 25] tall, useful-looking colt: useful handicapper: third at Bath (neck behind Open Wide) in July: stays 5.5f: acts on firm and good to soft going: tried in blinkers: wears tongue tie: sold 37,000 gns in October. *Charles Hills* **102**

BARRSBROOK 3 b.g. Doyen (IRE) 132 – Sayrianna 46 (Sayaarr (USA)) [2017 p10g^4 Dec 30] twice raced in bumpers: fourth in maiden at Lingfield on Flat debut: likely to stay beyond 1¼m. *Gary Moore* **68**

BARSANTI (IRE) 5 b.g. Champs Elysees 124 – Silver Star 105 (Zafonic (USA) 130) [2017 116: 12g^3 12m^2 13.9m^2 Jul 15] well-made gelding: smart performer: second in Hardwicke Stakes at Royal Ascot (½ length behind Idaho) in June: best around 1½m: acts on polytrack and good to firm going. *Roger Varian* **118**

BARTHOLOMEU DIAS 2 b.c. (May 11) Mount Nelson 125 – Lady Francesca 98 (Montjeu (IRE) 137) [2017 6m^3 7m^4 7d^3 Aug 9] 60,000Y: good-topped colt: third foal: dam, 8.6f winner, half-sister to smart performer up to 1¼m Purr Along: useful form: standout effort when fourth in Chesham Stakes at Royal Ascot (5¾ lengths behind September) in June. *Charles Hills* **95**

BARTHOLOMEW J (IRE) 3 ch.g. Fast Company (IRE) 126 – Mana (IRE) (Motivator 131) [2017 –: t7.1m^3 p7g^6 p7g p8g^6 p12g* p12f^5 10.1m* 10.2f^2 12g^6 10.1m^2 10d^6 10g p10s p12g^5 Dec 23] tall, close-coupled gelding: fair handicapper: won at Lingfield in April and Yarmouth in May: best effort when second at latter course in June: stays 1½m: acts on polytrack and firm going: has worn headgear. *Lydia Pearce* **74**

BARTON MILLS 2 b.c. (Feb 4) Iffraaj 127 – Balladonia 103 (Primo Dominie 121) [2017 p7s^2 p7g* 6g Oct 14] 42,000F: brother to smart 2-y-o 6f/7f (Prix Jean-Luc Lagardere) winner Wootton Bassett and useful 2-y-o 6f winner (stays 1¼m) Glenalmond, and half-brother to several winners, including useful 6f and (including at 2 yrs) 7f winner Related (by Kheleyf): dam 9f winner who stayed 1½m: fairly useful form: won minor event at Kempton (by 2½ lengths from Exprompt) in September: stays 7f. *William Haggas* **88**

BARWAH (USA) 6 b.m. Discreet Cat (USA) 127 – Enfiraaj (USA) (Kingmambo (USA) 125) [2017 64, a72: t8d* t7.1g^2 t8g t8g^2 8g t7.1s* 8.8m Jun 17] fair handicapper: won at Newcastle in January and June: stays 1m: acts on polytrack, tapeta and good to firm going: has worn tongue tie. *Peter Niven* **78**

BARWELL (IRE) 3 b.g. Rock of Gibraltar (IRE) 133 – Agata (FR) 114 (Poliglote 121) **99 p** [2017 59p: t7.1g^3 t5s^6 8g^3 9.8d* 10.2m* 10.2g^2 12v* Sep 9] useful handicapper: won at Ripon and Haydock in June, and Thirsk in September: stays 1½m: acts on tapeta, good to firm and heavy going: open to further improvement. *Michael Dods*

BARWICK 9 b.g. Beat Hollow 126 – Tenpence 60 (Bob Back (USA) 124) [2017 96: 12g^3 **95** 12m 12.4d^4 12v 12g* 11.9d^3 a11.4g* p13.4g^5 Oct 23] sturdy gelding: useful performer: won handicap at Les Landes in August and claimer at Mons-Ghlin in September: stays 1½m: acts on polytrack, good to firm and heavy going: sometimes starts slowly. *George Baker*

BARYE 6 b.g. Archipenko (USA) 127 – Oblige 101 (Robellino (USA) 127) [2017 110: **102** t12.4g^5 t12.2g^5 p12g^6 p16g 12m t12.2g^6 p14g p9.4g^3 p12g Dec 30] good-topped gelding: useful handicapper: stays 1¾m: acts on polytrack, tapeta and firm going: in cheekpieces last 2 starts. *Richard Hughes*

BASHEER 3 b.g. Dubawi (IRE) 129 – Reem (AUS) 105 (Galileo (IRE) 134) [2017 t7.1m **66** p7d^4 p6d^6 Feb 23] form in maidens only when fourth at Kempton in February: in hood last 2 starts. *Marco Botti*

BASHIBA (IRE) 6 ch.g. Iffraaj 127 – Nightswimmer (IRE) 75 (Noverre (USA) 125) **93** [2017 96: 5m^5 5m^2 5m^6 5d^3 5m^3 5m^3 5g^3 5g 5g Oct 13] workmanlike gelding: fairly useful handicapper: second at Doncaster in April: best at 5f: acts on good to firm and good to soft going: tried in visor: wears tongue tie: often races towards rear/travels strongly. *Nigel Tinkler*

BASIL BERRY 6 b.g. Tobougg (IRE) 125 – Dolly Coughdrop (IRE) 72 (Titus Livius (FR) **99** 115) [2017 103: p6g^6 p7g^6 7m^4 10.1g^6 8d Aug 12] workmanlike gelding: useful handicapper: stays 9.5f, usually races over shorter: acts on polytrack, tapeta, good to firm and good to soft going: usually in headgear. *Chris Dwyer*

BASINGSTOKE (IRE) 8 b.g. Elusive City (USA) 117 – Ryninch (IRE) 79 (Dr Devious **54** (IRE) 127) [2017 67: f7g^6 t7.1m Jan 13] lengthy gelding: fair handicapper: below form both starts in 2017: stays 8.5f: acts on all-weather and soft going: wears headgear. *Daniel Loughnane*

BASSINO (USA) 4 b.g. Street Cry (IRE) 130 – Show Me The Roses (USA) 91 (Storm Cat **61** (USA)) [2017 57: t9.5m^5 t8.6m^2 t8.6g^6 p8d t8.6g p10g 8g 7m Jun 17] modest maiden handicapper: stays 9.5f: acts on tapeta: wears headgear. *James Bennett*

BASSMAH 3 b.f. Harbour Watch (IRE) 121 – Secret Night 99 (Dansili 127) [2017 72p: 6g^2 **86** 7f^2 7d^2 7d* Aug 12] good-topped filly: fairly useful performer: won maiden at Redcar in August: stays 7f: acts on firm and good to soft going: tried in cheekpieces. *Ismail Mohammed*

BASTIA 3 br.f. Paco Boy (IRE) 129 – Miliana (IRE) 108 (Polar Falcon (USA) 126) [2017 **71** p6d* t6g^5 t6m^2 Mar 14] 10,000F, €40,000Y: half-sister to several winners, including useful 11f/1½m winner (stayed 1¾m) Mildoura (by Sendawar) and French 1½m winner Le Mage (by Dalakhani): dam French 1¼m/10.5f winner: fair form: won maiden at Chelmsford (by ½ length from Zilza) in February: will stay 7f+. *Martyn Meade*

BATAKA 3 ch.f. Mount Nelson 125 – Dominica 115 (Alhaarth (IRE) 126) [2017 63: t7.1g^3 **44** Jan 9] smallish, sparely-made filly: lightly raced, best effort (modest form) on debut in 2016. *Harry Dunlop*

BATEEL (IRE) 5 b.m. Dubawi (IRE) 129 – Attractive Crown (USA) 105 (Chief's **122** Crown (USA)) [2017 112: 14.9g^2 11.8s* 12.4g* 11.9d* 12s^2 Oct 21]

The Saudi Arabian food company Bateel specialises in dates—of the edible variety—and proudly boasts that customers are the 'first people to lay their hands on the dates' as the fruits are hand-picked with special gloves. It was a change of hands that helped the five-year-old mare Bateel secure a first Group 1 success for her owners Al Asayl Bloodstock—and just a second for her trainer Francis-Henri Graffard—when she landed the Prix Vermeille at Chantilly in September. Graffard started at the sales company Arqana in France, before being selected for the Godolphin Flying Start programme, after which he joined Sheikh Mohammed's Darley operation before spending three years as assistant trainer to Alain de Royer-Dupre. After that excellent grounding, Graffard established his own racing stable at Chantilly in October 2011 and to date has sent out more than two hundred winners, with the total prize money earned by the stable exceeding six million euros.

Having left David Simcock after trailing home last of thirteen in the British Champions Fillies' And Mares' Stakes at Ascot on her final start of 2016, Bateel began the latest season in the Prix de Barbeville at Chantilly in late-April, stepped up to fifteen furlongs for the first time. She finished two and a half lengths second to the British-trained Marmelo who went on to gain another good win in France when landing the Prix Kergorlay at Deauville in August. Bateel was dropped back in trip—and returned across the Channel—for the Pinnacle Stakes on soft ground at Haydock on her next start, and she revelled in her optimum conditions, beating the domestic opposition in good style under English rider Richard Kingscote. Dubka, sent off 2/1 favourite, was a length and a half second, with two and three quarters back to Ajman Princess. As it had with the Barbeville, the form again worked out well, with Ajman Princess victorious in the Prix Jean Romanet at Deauville in August. That seaside venue was also the scene for Bateel's next run eight weeks later, when she didn't need to improve to follow up against younger fillies in the Prix de Pomone, beating Traffic Jam by a neck, with a length and a half back to the British challenger Abingdon.

Two of Bateel's vanquished opponents from earlier in the season, Traffic Jam and Ajman Princess, lined up against her in the Prix Vermeille, but both were left in her wake once more. Ajman Princess was one of six British-trained runners in the field and she ensured that the race was a thorough examination of stamina. After she dropped away two furlongs out, it was Bateel and the John Gosden-trained Journey who settled down to fight out the finish. Journey had the rail to help her but she gave best with a furlong to run as Bateel stayed on well for a two and a half length success, with three lengths further back to the previous year's winner Left Hand who edged a tussle with Traffic Jam and Strathspey for third. Although appearing to cause a concertina effect when angling Bateel out on the final bend—leading to a thirty-five-minute stewards' inquiry—jockey Pierre-Charles Boudot received plenty of praise from an emotional Graffard. 'It was in this race in 1955 that my grandfather Henri Champliau won with the filly he owned, Wild Miss,' he explained. 'It has always been in my mind that I would like to win it myself, so I am very happy. This filly was sent to me to try and win a Group 1 race, as there are more opportunities on soft ground in France. She has gone from strength to strength and I knew conditions were right today and she received a perfect ride.'

Bateel, who was not even a pattern winner when the entries for the Prix de l'Arc de Triomphe were first made, wasn't supplemented for that race, with connections deciding to stick with the original plan of running her in the Fillies' And Mares' for the second year in a row, the longer break between the Vermeille and Ascot said to be a key factor in the decision. Bateel faced three of her rivals from Chantilly again at Ascot, including reigning Fillies' And Mares' champion Journey, and she was sent off the 7/4 favourite for what was the weakest of the Group 1 events

Betway Pinnacle Stakes, Haydock—French-trained mare Bateel justifies favouritism with something to spare, recording her first win at pattern level on just her second start for trainer Francis-Henri Graffard; Dubka (right) holds Ajman Princess (hidden by winner) for second, with the first three pulling well clear of the remainder

Qatar Prix Vermeille, Chantilly—daughters of Dubawi dominate as Bateel holds off the challenge of Journey (left), with 2016 winner Left Hand (white sleeves) back in third

on British Champions' Day in the absence, in particular, of three of the leading three-year-old fillies, Enable, Winter and Rhododendron. Travelling strongly, Bateel had every chance but could not match the turn of foot shown by Hydrangea who was stepping up to a mile and a half for the first time and improved on her previous form. Bateel fared easily the best of the older horses, finishing a length and three quarters clear of Coronet, who was in turn five lengths ahead of her nearest pursuer. Despite relinquishing an unbeaten record on soft/heavy ground, Bateel lost nothing in defeat and—if that proves to be her last run—she bowed out with her head held high.

Whenever Bateel is retired to Al Asayl Bloodstock's recently-acquired Haras de Vieux Point in Normandy, she will join over thirty broodmares which include Elle Galante (dam of Al Asayl's first and only Royal Ascot winner Balios, who won the King Edward VII in 2015), French listed winner Khaleesy and the privately purchased Rockery, a three-parts sister to Oaks winner Dancing Rain who visited Frankel in 2017. Sheikha Alyazia Bint Sultan Al Nahyan, along with her father Sheikh Sultan, bought the stud from Sven and Carina Hanson in late-2016, and plans are afoot to breed more horses to offer as yearlings at public auction, as well as to stand their own stallions in future. To this end, a toe has already been dipped into the water with the purchase of shares in the Prix Ganay winner Dariyan and the dual Group 2 winner Battle of Marengo. The stud—which reared Group 1 winners Pride and Reliable Man—is now managed by Johnnie Peter-Hoblyn, who spent seven years at Coolmore before a seventeen-year stint as stud manager at Shadwell. Dubai's Carnival has long been a focal point for the Abu Dhabi-based owners, with their Normandy investment adding to a portfolio which includes a mixed purebred Arabian/thoroughbred training facility in the United Arab Emirates. The South African-born trainer Ernst Oertel sent out forty-six winners from there in the 2013/14 Emirates season and, after two leaner years, bounced back with thirty winners in 2016/17.

Bateel (IRE) (b.m. 2012)	Dubawi (IRE) (b 2002)	Dubai Millennium (b 1996)	Seeking The Gold
			Colorado Dancer
		Zomaradah (b 1995)	Deploy
			Jawaher
	Attractive Crown (USA) (b 1995)	Chief's Crown (b 1982)	Danzig
			Six Crowns
		Attirance (ch 1978)	Crowned Prince
			Arosa

Bateel led home a clean sweep for her sire Dubawi when beating Journey and Left Hand in the Vermeille, and was one of seven new Group/Grade 1 winners for the stallion in 2017. Bateel's dam Attractive Crown was a useful winner at six furlongs (at two) and a mile on soft ground for Kevin Prendergast before finishing second in the Pretty Polly Stakes and then winning over an extended mile in the USA as a four-year-old. She had previously produced the useful Basemah (by Lemon Drop Kid), winner of three races in France at up to a mile and a quarter for Jonathan Pease, including the listed Prix Charles Laffitte at Chantilly, as well as Feathered Crown (by Indian Ridge), a fairly useful handicapper who stayed a mile and a half, and Queen of Skies (by Shamardal), a fair mile winner on fibresand. Bateel's third dam Arosa had a successful racing career, winning the Prix Impudence and Prix

Messidor, and also did well as a broodmare, her notable offspring including the Prix Greffulhe winner Arokar and the dam of Lancashire Oaks winner Spout, in addition to Bateel's grandam Attirance, winner of a listed race at Chantilly over a mile. The useful-looking Bateel, who is said to need time between her races (she had gone completely in her coat at Ascot, though she still ran well), wears a hood and often travels strongly. She acts on heavy going and was last on her only outing on firmer than good in three seasons. *Francis-Henri Graffard, France*

BATH AND TENNIS (IRE) 2 b.f. (Feb 25) Footstepsinthesand 120 – Goldamour (IRE) (Fasliyev (USA) 120) [2017 p6d^3 5.3d^2 5m 5m^5 5.1d^6 p5g^2 p6g* p7g* t7.2g^3 Dec 5] €65,000Y: useful-looking filly: third foal: half-sister to temperamental 6f winner Big Amigo (by Bahamian Bounty): dam French maiden: fairly useful performer: won nursery at Kempton and minor event at Chelmsford (by length from Cwynar) in October: stays 7f: acts on polytrack, tapeta, good to firm and good to soft going: in blinkers last 4 starts. *Sir Mark Prescott Bt* **83**

BATHSHEBA BAY (IRE) 2 b.c. (Apr 3) Footstepsinthesand 120 – Valamareha (IRE) 81 (Val Royal (FR) 127) [2017 7m^5 7s^2 7d^2 7g* Sep 1] €20,000F, €85,000Y: good-topped colt: fourth foal: dam 7.5f/8.5f winner: fairly useful form: won maiden at Sandown in September: raced only at 7f. *Richard Hannon* **92**

BATTAASH (IRE) 3 b.g. Dark Angel (IRE) 113 – Anna Law (IRE) (Lawman (FR) 121) [2017 103: 5m* 5m* 5s* 5g^4 5d* Oct 1] **136**

It must be a long time—if, indeed, it has happened before—since there has been a group of sprinters on the British turf of such superlative merit as those which graced the latest season. Once in every four or five years on average there will be a sprinter in Europe capable of achieving a rating of 130 or higher on the Timeform scale. In the latest season there were no fewer than four, and they were backed up by a supporting cast that was well up to Group 1 standard for sprinters in recent times. The champion sprinter of 2015 Muhaarar (rated 132) was the most recent '130 sprinter' before the latest season and, not counting that force of nature Black Caviar (136) who won the Diamond Jubilee on a flying visit to Britain in 2012, Deacon Blues (130 in 2011) was the last one before Muhaarar, and before that it was the Ballydoyle champions Mozart (131 in 2001) and Stravinsky (133 in 1999). Stravinsky was the best sprinter trained in Britain and Ireland since the brilliant Dayjur who won the King's Stand, the Nunthorpe, the Sprint Cup and the Prix de l'Abbaye on successive outings as a three-year-old in 1990; his Timeform rating of 137 came from his magnificent performance in the Nunthorpe when he also recorded an exceptional timefigure of 1.69 fast (equivalent to a timerating of 142, a mark equalled among sprinters just by the crack filly of the 'eighties Habibti, and bettered only by wide-margin classic winners Troy, Tudor Minstrel and Slip Anchor in Timeform's seventy-year history). Stravinsky's place as the highest-rated sprinter since Dayjur has now been usurped by Battaash, who has also taken over from French-trained middle-distance performer Cirrus des Aigles as the highest-rated gelding in the history of the *Racehorses* series.

Battaash is the latest champion to race in Sheikh Hamdan's royal blue, white epaulets, striped cap, also worn by Dayjur and Muhaarar among many others. The brilliant Battaash was gelded after his first two races as a two-year-old to make him easier to handle, his unruly behaviour—his trainer likened him to 'a bull in a china shop'—manifesting itself when he was very badly behaved in the stalls before the Windsor Castle Stakes at Royal Ascot on his second appearance. The beneficial effect of gelding the evidently temperamental Battaash was not immediately apparent and, after his twelfth in the Windsor Castle, he threw away his next race, a six-furlong conditions event at Doncaster three months later, by hanging badly right after looking all set for an all-the-way victory. His two subsequent performances as a juvenile were a little more straightforward, though he continued to make life look difficult at times for his jockeys by pulling hard and hanging, and he sweated and became worked up before running his best race when third to Mrs Danvers in the Cornwallis Stakes at Newmarket on his final start. That he would be transformed into an outstanding champion couldn't possibly have been predicted from his two-year-old campaign and even his trainer, who trained Muhaarar and has handled

Qatar King George Stakes, Goodwood—Battaash blitzes a high-class field, becoming a rare five-furlong performer to break through the 130 barrier on Timeform ratings; Group 1 winners Profitable (noseband) and Marsha (spots on silks) fill the places, with the 2016 first and second Take Cover (not in picture) and Washington DC (left) chasing up the principals

Battaash with commendable skill, apparently had no real inkling either, stating at the beginning of the latest season that his ambition was to 'try to find a listed race for him.' Battaash achieved that aim in his first race as a three-year-old, in the Randox Health Scurry Stakes at Sandown on the Saturday before Royal Ascot, following up in the Coral Charge over Sandown's same five-furlong course at the beginning of July before announcing his arrival in the top rank of sprinters in the very valuable Qatar King George Stakes at Goodwood's big festival meeting. The second of Battaash's two Sandown victories more than confirmed the impression of the first—that he was a good sprinter in the making. After tracking the pace and quickening (despite hanging right) to win from Koropick and Copper Knight in the Scurry Stakes, Battaash was allowed to stride on from the start in the Coral Charge. A low draw is an advantage on the sprint course at Sandown and the tactics adopted on Battaash from stall two saw him open up a three-length lead from halfway which he never looked like relinquishing on the way to a clear-cut success from Mirza and Goldream, the two others who raced closest to the favoured rail. The form shown by Battaash in the Coral Charge looked well above the standard for a Group 3 race, and the merit of his performance was backed up by a very good timefigure equivalent to a timerating of 123 (the *time value* of his performance was a much more accurate barometer of his merit than the simple fact that his time of 58.57sec lowered the course record set by the tough handicapper Palacegate Touch twenty-one years earlier).

The Qatar King George Stakes has become a richly-endowed event since Qatar signed a long-term deal to sponsor Goodwood's July meeting. It has Group 2 status but is run without penalties and, in the latest season, it was a Group 1 in all but name. The fast-improving Battaash, ridden for the first time by Sheikh Hamdan's number-one in the latest season Jim Crowley, travelled strongly from the start and stormed clear when produced to lead over a furlong out. The Group 1 winners Profitable and Marsha, who had filled the places behind transatlantic visitor Lady Aurelia in the King's Stand at Royal Ascot, couldn't live with Battaash who beat them by two and a quarter lengths and three quarters of a length, with the previous year's first and second Take Cover (attempting a third win in the race) and Washington DC filling fourth and fifth. The form looked as solid as it could be and the *time value* of Battaash's performance was excellent, his timefigure of 1.18 fast (equivalent to a timerating of 130) the fastest recorded by any horse over any distance all year. The going at Goodwood was soft, contrasting sharply with the conditions for Battaash's two Sandown wins and highlighting his versatility in that respect.

The eagerly-awaited clash between Lady Aurelia and Battaash in the Nunthorpe Stakes at York looked like being one of the races—if not *the* race—of the season. Both had produced outstanding performances on their latest appearances (form which put them well clear of the nine other runners) and Britain's premier five-furlong race was the right stage for a showdown. Profitable and Marsha, the previous year's King's Stand and Prix de l'Abbaye winners, again opposed the 'big two', as they had at Royal Ascot and Goodwood respectively, and they were the only other Nunthorpe runners to start at shorter than 20/1. Not for the first time, however, a much anticipated racing head-to-head failed to follow the script. The Nunthorpe produced the expected tight finish but it wasn't between Battaash and Lady Aurelia. Battaash showed at York that there were still issues with his temperament, getting himself too worked up beforehand to be able to do himself justice. He was edgy even when being saddled, seemed het up in the paddock and was then difficult at the start, taking some time to load. He was considerably less tractable in the race too than he had been at Goodwood and, though showing plenty of speed and still being close up until approaching the final furlong, he faltered in the closing stages and finished only fourth, over five lengths behind Marsha and Lady Aurelia, both of whom put up '130 performances' on the day.

The fretful Battaash suffered his only defeat of the campaign in the Nunthorpe but he returned to form in no uncertain fashion in the Prix de l'Abbaye de Longchamp Longines in which he more than confirmed himself the outstanding sprinter he had shown himself to be in the King George Stakes. Marsha started favourite at Longchamp, as she attempted to add a second Prix de l'Abbaye win to her fine record, with the leading French sprinter Signs of Blessing—making his first appearance in the race at the age of six—and the consistent Profitable next in the betting behind second favourite Battaash in the thirteen-strong line-up. Battaash had earned the stable name 'Boltaash' and he was sporting new golden shoes at Chantilly. 'Usain Bolt [who won the 100m and 200m titles at three consecutive Olympics] can have them, so why not him?' joked Battaash's trainer who said that the copper shoes had been the idea of his farrier. Michael Johnson, another of the track and field greats, famously wore gold-coloured spikes at the Atlanta Olympics in 1996 fully aware that 'opting for gold could have been considered downright cocky, but I never doubted my ability to deliver gold medals.' As the American saying goes, if you're gonna talk the talk you've got to walk the walk. Battaash was stabled away from the racecourse and brought in on the morning of racing and, instead of being taken to post early (as he had at York where he had been dismounted), he went down last. Much calmer in the preliminaries and at the start, Battaash dominated his rivals almost throughout, travelling strongly in front nearly all the way and stretching further clear over the final furlong to win by four lengths and a neck from Marsha and Profitable, with Signs of Blessing only twelfth.

Qatar Prix de l'Abbaye de Longchamp, Chantilly—Battaash records the most crushing victory in the race for nearly a quarter of a century, pulling four lengths clear of Marsha (second right) in registering a first Group 1 success and confirming his status as an outstanding sprinter; Profitable (cheekpieces) fills third to complete a clean sweep for the British raiders

Racegoers and television viewers had already witnessed an exemplary performance the same afternoon from Enable in the Prix de l'Arc de Triomphe and Battaash's true merit might not have been fully appreciated at the time by some. Top sprints are rarely won in the manner that Battaash won the Abbaye, a fiercely competitive race that is more often than not won by under a length. Not only was the Abbaye won by the widest margin this century (Benbaun had won by two in 2007), Battaash recorded the most crushing victory in the race for nearly a quarter of a century, since the admirable filly Lochsong won consecutive editions in 1993 and 1994 by six lengths and five lengths. Overdose won the void running of 2008 by three and a half lengths but did not contest the re-run won by Marchand d'Or five hours later. To find the latest male winner by as far as four lengths (geldings were only admitted in 2001) it is necessary to go back to the 'seventies when the three-year-old Deep Diver won by that distance in 1972 and the four-year-old Gentilhombre repeated the feat in 1977 (both ended the year as Europe's leading sprinter).

There could be no doubting that, in routing a good field, Battaash had recorded a tip-top sprinting performance in the Abbaye, one which—the way Timeform interpreted the form at least—was superior even to Enable's splendid Arc-winning effort. The Prix de l'Abbaye gave jockey Jim Crowley his first Group 1 success in the Sheikh Hamdan silks and, having also ridden Ulysses into third in a very good Arc, he described Battaash as 'unbelievable … they just couldn't go fast enough for him and I ended up taking it up, though with him you're just a passenger, it's as simple as that.' While both Marsha and Profitable will be at stud in 2018, Battaash's value to his connections lies only in winning more big races—with The Everest in Australia, the world's richest sprint, said to be his autumn target provided the domestic campaign in the summer goes to plan. The 'golden shoes' will certainly bring a touch of showbiz to any of Battaash's global challenges and it is to be hoped that his performances live up to them (connections were probably wise to spurn another race against Lady Aurelia and Marsha in the Breeders' Cup Turf Sprint—a race dominated in the end by the home team—in anticipation that Battaash's long-term career would benefit more at this stage from being put away to enjoy a quiet winter).

Battaash (IRE) (b.g. 2014)	Dark Angel (IRE) (gr 2005)	Acclamation (b 1999)	Royal Applause
			Princess Athena
		Midnight Angel (gr 1994)	Machiavellian
			Night At Sea
	Anna Law (IRE) (b 2010)	Lawman (b 2004)	Invincible Spirit
			Laramie
		Portelet (b 1992)	Night Shift
			Noirmant

The sturdy Battaash, who is only 15.1 hands, is another fine advert for his sire Dark Angel who was standing at €12,500 (his fee is now €65,000) when Limerick-based Ballyphilip Stud sent two mares, Anna Law and Beatrix Potter, to him in 2013. The story of how the two resulting foals turned out to be Battaash and Harry Angel, who were reared together at the stud before being sold as yearlings, is covered in the

Mr Hamdan Al Maktoum's "Battaash"

essay on the latter. Anna Law was bought by Ballyphilip Stud for just 14,000 guineas at the end of her two-year-old days at the Newmarket Autumn Sales. She had run four times for Charlie Hills and had beaten just two of her forty-five rivals (she was rated a dash in *Racehorses of 2012*). Her first foal fared considerably better at the sales than the dam, fetching 200,000 guineas to a final bid from Shadwell before later being named Battaash. Anna Law may have been of little account herself on the racecourse but there is plenty of speed in her pedigree, although she is by the Prix du Jockey Club winner Lawman. Battaash's grandam Portelet was a fairly useful five-furlong winner who is also the grandam of another of the year's top sprinters the Duke of York Stakes winner and Diamond Jubilee/Sprint Cup/Champion Sprint runner-up Tasleet. Portelet is also the dam of Etlaala who finished third in a July Cup. Further back, Battaash's fourth dam Krakow (who bred a Yorkshire Cup winner Braashee who also dead-heated in the Prix Royal-Oak) is a granddaughter of the five-furlong sprinter Pelting who bred twelve winners (none of them successful over further than a mile) and appears in the further reaches of the pedigrees of such as Priceless, Home of The Brave and Kool Kompany. Pelting, incidentally, is the great grandam of another winner of the Prix de l'Abbaye, Keen Hunter, successful in the 1991 edition and runner-up the following year. Anna Law's second foal Littlelordconford (by Intikhab) was in training in the latest season but showed only poor form. Anna Law has a yearling filly from the first crop of Gutaifan and was said to be in foal again to Dark Angel in the latest season. Battaash is best at five furlongs and acts on soft and good to firm going. He usually races close up. *Charles Hills*

BATTALION (IRE) 7 b.g. Authorized (IRE) 133 – Zigarra (Halling (USA) 133) [2017 108§, a118§: p10g^{3} p10m^{6} p10g p10g^{6} p10g^{6} Dec 23] tall, attractive gelding: smart performer: third in listed race at Lingfield (1¼ lengths behind Decorated Knight) in February: stays 1½m: acts on polytrack, soft and good to firm going: has worn cheekpieces: starts slowly, usually races in rear. *Jamie Osborne* **113**

BATTEN THE HATCHES 3 b.g. Harbour Watch (IRE) 121 – Our Little Secret (IRE) 104 (Rossini (USA) 118) [2017 t6g* 5.1m^{5} 6f^{4} 5m* 5.4d^{2} 5m Aug 26] half-brother to several winners, including smart performer around 5f Pearl Secret (by Compton Place) and 6f-1¼m winner Pearl Bridge (by Avonbridge): dam 5f winner: useful performer: won maiden at Newcastle in February and handicap at Redcar in June: second in handicap at York (¾ length behind Dakota Gold) in July: stays 6f: acts on tapeta, good to firm and good to soft going: in blinkers last 3 starts. *David Barron* **101**

BATTERED 3 b.g. Foxwedge (AUS) 128 – Swan Wings 89 (Bahamian Bounty 116) [2017 87p: 6g^{5} p7g^{4} 7s* 7m^{3} 7g^{5} 7d* 7.9g^{2} 8g^{2} Sep 16] lengthy gelding: useful handicapper: won at York (by 2½ lengths from Lualiwa) in May and Goodwood (by head from Sir Titan) in August: best effort when second at Doncaster (1¾ lengths behind Kryptos) final start: stays 1m: acts on polytrack, soft and good to firm going: in headgear last 5 starts: sold to join Ralph Beckett 200,000 gns in October. *William Haggas* **109**

BATTERSEA 6 b.g. Galileo (IRE) 134 – Gino's Spirits 98 (Perugino (USA) 84) [2017 115: 16f^{6} 13.9m 14.2s^{2} p14g^{6} Nov 2] attractive gelding: useful performer: second in minor event at Salisbury (2½ lengths behind On To Victory) in September: stays 14.5f: acts on firm and soft going: has worn hood. *Roger Varian* **107**

BATTLE COMMENCE (IRE) 2 b.g. (Feb 28) Declaration of War (USA) 128 – Invincible Ash (IRE) 114 (Invincible Spirit (IRE) 121) [2017 6.1g^{5} Aug 18] €35,000Y: tall, quite attractive gelding: has scope: first foal: dam 5f/6f winner: 10/1, fifth in maiden at Nottingham (7¾ lengths behind Eqtidaar) on debut: better to come. *David O'Meara* **64 p**

BATTLE LINES 2 ch.c. (May 7) Sepoy (AUS) 129 – Goslar 92 (In The Wings 128) [2017 7m t8.6g p8g^{3} Dec 20] 15,000F, 40,000Y: seventh foal: half-brother to 1¼m/1¾m winner Gosbeck (by Dubawi) and 1½m winner Hallbeck (by Halling): dam 1½m winner who stayed 1¾m: fair form: best effort when third in minor event at Kempton (4¼ lengths behind Glencadam Master) in December: will be suited by 1¼m+: open to further improvement. *James Tate* **76 p**

BATTLE OF JERICHO (USA) 2 b.c. (Mar 7) War Front (USA) 119 – Together (IRE) 118 (Galileo (IRE) 134) [2017 6g^{3} 6g^{4} 6d* p7g^{2} 5m Oct 13] good-quartered colt: third foal: brother to 7f winner Old Time Waltz and half-brother to useful 8.5f/9.5f winner Earring (by Dansili): dam, winner up to 9f (2-y-o 7f winner) and second in 1000 Guineas, closely related to smart winner up to 1¼m Jan Vermeer: useful performer: won maiden at Leopardstown in July: second in listed race at Dundalk (½ length behind Riyazan) in October: stays 7f: acts on polytrack and good to soft going: tried in blinkers: wears tongue tie. *Aidan O'Brien, Ireland* **102**

BATTLE OF MARATHON (USA) 5 b.g. War Front (USA) 119 – Sayedah (IRE) 105 (Darshaan 133) [2017 116: 8g 8s^{5} p8g 8g^{4} 9d 7d^{5} p8d t9.5g^{3} t9.5g* t9.5d^{6} Dec 26] sturdy gelding: useful handicapper: won at Wolverhampton (by 1¼ lengths from Emenem) in December: stays 9.5f: acts on tapeta, good to firm and heavy going: has worn headgear. *John Ryan* **104**

BATTS ROCK (IRE) 4 b.g. Fastnet Rock (AUS) 127 – Be My Queen (IRE) 104 (Sadler's Wells (USA) 132) [2017 91: 12m^{2} 14g 14g^{5} 12g^{2} t12.2g^{4} p12g^{4} Sep 27] well-made gelding: useful handicapper: second at Newmarket (1¾ lengths behind Quloob) in July: stays 1½m: acts on tapeta and good to firm going: in cheekpieces last 3 starts: often travels strongly: sold 68,000 gns in October. *Michael Bell* **97**

BAYARDS COVE 2 b.f. (Apr 25) Harbour Watch (IRE) 121 – Acicula (IRE) 96 (Night Shift (USA)) [2017 p7d p6g Dec 20] half-sister to several winners, including smart 5f and (including at 2 yrs) 6f winner Elnawin and useful winner up to 1m Elna Bright (2-y-o 6f/7f winner) (both by Elnadim): dam 2-y-o 5f/6f winner: well held in minor events. *Brian Barr* **–**

BAYDAR 4 b.g. Rock of Gibraltar (IRE) 133 – Splashdown 105 (Falbrav (IRE) 133) [2017 115: 9.9m 12m 11.8m 9.9g 10.3m 10m Sep 23] close-coupled gelding: smart handicapper at best, down the field all starts in 2017: left Hugo Palmer after fifth start: stays 1¼m: acts on polytrack, good to firm and good to soft going: in cheekpieces last 2 starts. *Ian Williams* **107**

BAYELSA BOY (IRE) 2 b.g. (Apr 15) Elzaam (AUS) 115 – Extraordinary (IRE) (Swain (IRE) 134) [2017 6m Aug 26] 33/1, well held in minor event at Redcar. *Tim Easterby* **–**

BAY OF POETS (IRE) 3 b.g. Lope de Vega (IRE) 125 – Bristol Bay (IRE) (Montjeu (IRE) 137) [2017 95+: 10.1g^3 10.3d^2 10.4g 10m 8g^2 8.9g* 9.9s^4 Sep 16] good-bodied, attractive gelding: smart performer: won listed race at Clairefontaine (by 1¾ lengths from Born To Be Alive) in August: 2¾ lengths seventh to Brametot in Prix du Jockey Club at Chantilly in June: stays 1¼m: acts on polytrack, good to firm and good to soft going: tried in blinkers. *Charlie Appleby* **114**

BAY STATION 3 b.f. Camacho 118 – Hazelhurst (IRE) 74 (Night Shift (USA)) [2017 74: t5d^5 6m 5m^4 5d^4 5g^5 5m^4 5d^6 6g Sep 27] fair handicapper: left David Nicholls after first start: best form at 5f: acts on good to firm going: in cheekpieces last 4 starts. *Jason Ward* **66**

BAYSTON HILL 3 br.g. Big Bad Bob (IRE) 118 – Jessica Ennis (USA) (English Channel (USA) 126) [2017 73: 8.3m^6 8.5g 10.2f* 12g^5 10.2f^3 10g^6 10.1m^5 p10g^3 9.9s t9.5m^3 p10m^4 p10g* Dec 13] sturdy gelding: fair handicapper: won at Bath in May and Lingfield in December: stays 1¼m: acts on polytrack, tapeta and firm going. *Mark Usher* **77**

BAY WATCH (IRE) 3 b.g. Harbour Watch (IRE) 121 – Karuga 78 (Kyllachy 129) [2017 59: t6g^4 p7g 8f 7d^5 Jul 6] modest maiden: stays 7f: acts on polytrack and good to soft going: in headgear last 3 starts. *Andrew Balding* **61**

BAZOOKA (IRE) 6 b.g. Camacho 118 – Janadam (IRE) 55 (Mukaddamah (USA) 125) [2017 82: t9.5m 11.4d 12v* 12v^3 10d^2 Oct 23] compact gelding: fairly useful handicapper: won at Ffos Las in September: second at Windsor in October: stays 1½m: acts on polytrack, tapeta and heavy going: tried in blinkers: often starts slowly/races towards rear. *David Flood* **80**

BAZWIND (IRE) 3 b.g. Lilbourne Lad (IRE) 111 – Gay Heroine 105 (Caerleon (USA) 132) [2017 71, a60: t9.5g^2 p10g^3 p10g^3 t8.6g* t7.1g^5 t7.1g^5 8.3d Jun 11] fair handicapper: won at Wolverhampton in February: stays 1¼m: acts on polytrack, tapeta and good to soft going: has worn headgear, including last 4 starts: front runner/races prominently. *David Evans* **70**

BAZZAT (IRE) 4 ch.g. Roderic O'Connor (IRE) 119 – Compradore 82 (Mujtahid (USA) 118) [2017 56, a72: t8.6m^6 Jan 10] lengthy, angular gelding: modest handicapper on turf, fair on all-weather: stays 1¼m: acts on polytrack, soft and good to firm going: wears headgear: often races prominently: sold 4,000 gns in February. *John Ryan* **52**

BBOB ALULA 2 ch.g. (Feb 26) Showcasing 117 – Island Rhapsody 78 (Bahamian Bounty 116) [2017 5d^3 6d Sep 6] fair form: better effort when third in maiden at Bath (7½ lengths behind Equilateral) in August: may prove best at 5f: wears tongue tie. *Bill Turner* **65**

BEACH BAR (IRE) 6 b.g. Azamour (IRE) 130 – Toasted Special (USA) 89 (Johannesburg (USA) 127) [2017 105: a8f a9.9f^6 15.9g a9.9f 7.6g^6 9m^5 p8s 7s 7s* 7d p8s p7g* Dec 22] sturdy gelding: fairly useful handicapper: won at Leopardstown in October and Dundalk (by ½ length from Geological) in December: left Brendan Powell after seventh start: stays 1¼m, effective at shorter: acts on polytrack, soft and good to firm going: has often worn hood. *Richard John O'Brien, Ireland* **87 a95**

BEACH BREAK 3 b.g. Cacique (IRE) 124 – Wemyss Bay (Sadler's Wells (USA) 132) [2017 77: 11.6d^2 12.1m* 11.9m^6 13.4g^6 Aug 26] fairly useful performer: won maiden at Catterick (by 5 lengths from Montanna) in June: stays 1½m: acts on tapeta, good to firm and good to soft going: in blinkers last 4 starts: usually leads, often travels strongly: has joined Donald McCain. *Ralph Beckett* **81**

BEACHCOMBER BAY (IRE) 2 b.c. (Jan 29) Invincible Spirit (IRE) 121 – Beach Bunny (IRE) 114 (High Chaparral (IRE) 132) [2017 7v Sep 25] 525,000Y: fourth foal: brother to useful 2-y-o 5f/6f winner Beach Belle and closely related to smart/temperamental 6f and (at 2 yrs) 7f winner Naadirr (by Oasis Dream): dam 1m-1¼m winner who stayed 1½m: 11/2, well held in minor event at Leicester: should do better. *Charlie Appleby* **– p**

BEACH DANCER (IRE) 3 b.g. Footstepsinthesand 120 – All Night Dancer (IRE) 85 (Danehill Dancer (IRE) 117) [2017 –: p5g^6 p6f 5m^3 5g 6.1m p7g^6 p6s 7d^6 Jul 11] leggy gelding: modest maiden: stays 7f: acts on polytrack and good to firm going: has worn headgear: usually leads. *William Knight* **56**

BEACH PARTY 3 b.f. Dutch Art 126 – Musical Sands (Green Desert (USA) 127) [2017 p7g^6 p8s 7.4d^6 f12.1g^{pu} Aug 28] stocky filly: second foal: half-sister to 1m/8.6f winner Pirate's Treasure (by Iffraaj): dam unraced sister to very smart 7f-1¼m winner Alkaadhem: no form. *Hughie Morrison* **–**

BEACHWALK 2 b.g. (May 19) Showcasing 117 – Esplanade 77 (Danehill (USA) 126) [2017 7g p7g^6 t7.2m^4 Oct 31] well-made gelding: fair form: best effort when fourth in minor event at Wolverhampton (¾ length behind Montague) in October. *Sir Michael Stoute* **72**

BEACONSFIELD 3 b.g. Foxwedge (AUS) 128 – Italian Connection (Cadeaux Genereux 131) [2017 70: p8d 8.1g 8.5g p13.3g p12g Oct 9] maiden, standout effort (fair form) on second start in 2016. *Hughie Morrison* **52**

BEADLAM (IRE) 4 ch.f. Frozen Power (IRE) 108 – Pivotal Role 66 (Pivotal 124) [2017 72: 8.5m^5 8.3m 10s 8.5m t7.2g* 8g t8.6g* 8g^3 t7.2g^5 8.5v Sep 26] fair handicapper: won at Wolverhampton in July and August: stays 8.5f: acts on tapeta and firm going: usually in headgear: races prominently. *Roger Fell* **71**

BEAN FEASA 3 b.f. Dubawi (IRE) 129 – Speirbhean (IRE) 111 (Danehill (USA) 126) [2017 84: 7d^5 9.5s^2 8m* 8d^5 8m 12f 8d Sep 9] strong, good-bodied filly: type to carry condition: useful performer: won Derrinstown Stud 1000 Guineas Trial at Leopardstown (by 2¾ lengths from Asking) in May: stays 1m: acts on good to firm and good to soft going: sometimes in tongue tie: often races prominently. *J. S. Bolger, Ireland* **101**

BEARAG 3 b.f. Dutch Art 126 – Cats Eyes 86 (Echo of Light 125) [2017 60p: 7.5f 7m t6.1g^6 t6d p7g t8.6g Oct 21] modest maiden: stays 6f: acts on tapeta and firm going. *David O'Meara* **54**

BEARDWOOD 5 ch.g. Dutch Art 126 – Valentina Guest (IRE) 102 (Be My Guest (USA) 126) [2017 94, a100: 12m 10.3d 10g^5 10g^3 p10s^4 10g^4 9.9m^2 11.9g^5 10.3m p11s Sep 8] big, strong gelding: fairly useful handicapper: second at Sandown in July: stays 1¼m: acts on polytrack, good to firm and heavy going: wears cheekpieces: sold 2,000 gns in October. *Mark Johnston* **94**

BEAR VALLEY (IRE) 3 b.g. Manduro (GER) 135 – Shane (GER) 106 (Kornado 120) [2017 98: 10d^6 9.9m^2 12m^3 10.3m 12g 11.2s 12d^3 12g 9.9g 12s 12m t12.2g Oct 21] strong gelding: useful handicapper: third in King George V Stakes at Royal Ascot (3 lengths behind Atty Persse) in June and back at Ascot (¾ length behind Glenys The Menace) in August: stays 1½m: acts on good to firm and good to soft going: often finds little: sold to join Charlie Mann 17,000 gns in October. *Mark Johnston* **97**

BEAST 3 b.g. Makfi 130 – Wunders Dream (IRE) 107 (Averti (IRE) 117) [2017 76: 6.1m p7g p8g 10d^6 t9.5g Nov 7] angular gelding: modest maiden: left Lee Carter after fourth start: stays 7f: acts on good to soft going: tried in visor/tongue tie: sometimes slowly away. *Johnny Farrelly* **57**

BEATBOX RHYTHM (IRE) 2 ch.c. (Apr 25) Beat Hollow 126 – Birthday Present (Cadeaux Genereux 131) [2017 6d^2 6s* 7d 6d^3 6g* t6d* Oct 24] €62,000Y: good-topped colt: half-brother to several winners, including 2-y-o 5f/6f winner Accepted (by Approve) and 2-y-o 6f/7f winner Asidious Alexander (by Windsor Knot), both useful: dam unraced: useful performer: won minor event at Pontefract in August, and nursery at York (by neck from Kyllachy Dragon) and minor event at Newcastle (by 2¼ lengths from River Boyne) in October: stays 6f: acts on tapeta and soft going: usually leads, often travels strongly. *K. R. Burke* **105**

BEATBYBEATBYBEAT 4 ch.f. Poet's Voice 126 – Beat As One (Medicean 128) [2017 79: 7m 8.3g^5 t8.6g^4 8f^5 7.4m^5 8g t7.1d 7.4v^4 8.3d^2 t8g^5 t8.6g^{ur} t8.6d^4 Dec 9] sturdy filly: fair handicapper: stays 8.5f: acts on polytrack, tapeta, good to firm and heavy going: wears headgear. *Antony Brittain* **71**

BEATISA 3 b.f. Intikhab (USA) 135 – Bea Menace (USA) 93 (Mizzen Mast (USA) 121) [2017 50p: p8g^6 p8g^5 10d 8g^3 9.9d^3 p11g* p13.3s^3 t12.2d^4 Dec 26] fair handicapper: won at Kempton in October, then left Ed Walker: stays 13.5f: acts on polytrack and good to soft going: front runner/races prominently. *Christine Dunnett* **77**

BEAT ROUTE 10 ch.g. Beat Hollow 126 – Steppin Out 63 (First Trump 118) [2017 14.2g Aug 25] tall gelding: fairly useful handicapper at best, well beaten after long absence only start in 2017: stays 2m: acts on polytrack and good to soft going. *Michael Attwater* **–**

BEAT THE BANK 3 b.g. Paco Boy (IRE) 129 – Tiana 99 (Diktat 126) [2017 p7g* 7m* 7m 8g* 8s* 8d* 8s Oct 21] **125**

Vichai Srivaddhanaprabha's King Power operation opened Thailand's first downtown duty free shop in 1989, and seventeen years later the company was granted exclusive rights to all duty free stores at Bangkok's new Suvarnabhumi Airport (the busiest airport in Thailand and the ninth busiest in the world in terms of international traffic). Srivaddhanaprabha is worth an estimated £1.9bn and currently ranked fourth on Thailand's rich list by *Forbes* magazine, though he is perhaps best known in Britain as the owner of Leicester City football club, which he purchased for around £48m in 2010. By the end of 2013, King Power's parent loans to the club had exceeded £100m, the money used to strengthen the team, update

Shadwell Joel Stakes, Newmarket—the improving Beat The Bank puts up a high-class performance; fellow three-year-old Sir John Lavery and Jallota (chevron on silks) trail in his wake

stadium facilities and clear debts, and, by the time the club gained promotion to the Premier League in 2014, it was profitable thanks to new television revenues. 'Our plan is to bring long-term sustainable success to Leicester City,' said Aiyawatt Srivaddhanaprabha (Vichai's son and vice chairman of the club) after King Power had purchased Leicester's ground in 2013 and renamed it the King Power Stadium, but success came much faster than even the Srivaddhanaprabha family could have dreamed at the time, the club defying huge odds (they were 5000/1 in August) to win the Premiership in 2015/16 only two years after promotion from the Championship.

More recently, King Power has turned its attentions to racehorses, and success in racing's 'premiership' may not take long either. Bloodstock agent Alastair Donald of SackvilleDonald was officially acting on behalf of King Power Racing when going to 550,000 guineas for a Frankel colt out of Lady Linda at the Newmarket October Sales Book 1, but the agent mysteriously would not reveal the name of his client when signing for several high-profile fillies at the same sale. Donald went to 2,500,000 guineas for a Frankel filly out of Oaks winner Talent, 725,000 guineas for a Sea The Stars filly out of a half-sister to Arc winner Peintre Celebre, and to 550,000 guineas for another filly by Shamardal. Donald commented after the purchase of the Frankel filly: 'It's a client who wants to keep out of the press, basically. This is the filly he wanted the most and she's a gorgeous filly.' It remains to be seen whether all these purchases were on behalf of King Power Racing (the Frankel filly, to be named King Power, has since been confirmed as a purchase), but all should be excellent broodmare prospects and could potentially be the start of a significant new venture for the King Power operation, whose main representatives in the most recent season were horses bought out of other yards (including the likes of Twin Star, who joined King Power for £260,000 at the Goffs London Sale on the eve of Royal Ascot before running at the meeting).

As a business, King Power had been accused in 2017 of failing to pay the Thai state the agreed 15% of income generated by operations at Bangkok's airport, a sum reportedly amounting to £327m. Pre-race activity before Beat The Bank's run in the Queen Elizabeth II Stakes aroused suspicion too and actually attracted the attention of the Ascot stewards. Beat The Bank's owner—who reportedly flew monks to Britain to bless Leicester City's players before some of their big games—was seen spraying Beat The Bank's legs with a substance in the saddling boxes before the race. The substance, which was sent away for testing, turned out to be harmless and was believed to have been holy water, applied for good luck. The action seemingly did little to help Beat The Bank's chances in the race as he disappointed on what was his first start at Group 1 level, looking ill at ease from an early stage (proving difficult to settle) and eventually finishing tenth. However, the fact that only Ribchester—the winner of the Lockinge, Queen Anne, and Prix du Moulin—was sent off at shorter odds in the fifteen-strong field for the Queen Elizabeth II Stakes reflected the relentless progress Beat The Bank made during his first season, which began when making his debut in a seven-furlong maiden at Dundalk in late-February. Beat The Bank was purchased privately out of the Darren Bunyan yard after winning at the first attempt and he made his debut for Andrew Balding when following up in a minor event at Newmarket's Craven meeting, taking a big step forward in terms of form, for all that he was rather handed victory by the hesitancy of the runner-up Salsabeel, who didn't convince with his attitude when asked to pass Beat The Bank.

Andrew Balding trained the majority of the King Power Racing horses in the most recent season, including the winner of the transferred Ayr Gold Cup in September, Donjuan Triumphant, and he said after Beat The Bank's Newmarket win that 'He's already gelded so we've not got any great plans, but he might make up into a Jersey Stakes horse. The brief from the owner is to try to have runners for Royal Ascot and that is the most likely target'. King Power Racing drew a blank at Royal Ascot in 2017, an unsatisfactory scope providing a possible explanation for Beat The Bank's disappointing effort in the Jersey. Beat The Bank soon regained the thread when stepped up to a mile for the first time in a listed race at Newmarket twenty-two days after the Jersey. Beat The Bank won that race in good style by three lengths, and continued his improvement with a first pattern-level success, by the same margin, in the Thoroughbred Stakes at Goodwood, looking as though he would be well worth a try in a higher grade. That chance came in the Joel Stakes at Newmarket—often a fairly weak Group 2 in recent seasons—and Beat The Bank improved again, putting up a high-class effort, matching the form of Soft Falling Rain's excellent win in the race in 2013 and showing himself to be one of the most progressive horses around, beating a host of smart rivals with authority to win by five lengths. Racing prominently under Oisin Murphy—who was regaining the ride,

King Power Racing's "Beat The Bank"

Jim Crowley and Ryan Moore having partnered Beat The Bank to his two previous victories—Beat The Bank took up the running over a furlong out and responded genuinely to win impressively from Sir John Lavery by his largest margin of victory to date, taking his overall record at the time to five wins from six starts.

Beat The Bank (b.g. 2014)	Paco Boy (IRE) (b 2005)	Desert Style (b 1992)	Green Desert
			Organza
		Tappen Zee (ch 1986)	Sandhurst Prince
			Rossaldene
	Tiana (b 2003)	Diktat (br 1995)	Warning
			Arvola
		Hill Welcome (ch 1998)	Most Welcome
			Tarvie

The sturdy, close coupled Beat The Bank is out of Tiana, a two-year-old six-furlong winner who was placed in the listed Oh So Sharp Stakes for John Gosden and stayed a mile. She was a half-sister to numerous winners including the smart performer up to a mile Above N Beyond, Dubai Hills (one of the best horses on fibresand in Britain at his peak) and Molecomb Stakes second Mary Read (the grandam of 2016 Commonwealth Cup second Kachy). Tiana is by the high-class 6f/7f performer Diktat and Beat The Bank is the first of her progeny to tackle a mile, the pick of her four other winners being the smart sprinter Salt Island (by Exceed And Excel), fourth in the 2015 Commonwealth Cup. SackvilleDonald (again acting on behalf of Srivaddhanaprabha) went to 500,000 guineas for a full-sister to Salt Island at the Newmarket October Sales Book 2. Tiana's filly foal by Showcasing was withdrawn from the December Sales. Beat The Bank is by Paco Boy, whose first classic winner Galileo Gold was retired to stud after reportedly sustaining a soft-tissue injury in the Lockinge on his sole start in 2017, and Beat The Bank may well be his sire's best chance of another Group 1 winner in the immediate future, likely to have even more to offer as a four-year-old given the strides he made at three. Beat The Bank travels strongly in his races and finds plenty under pressure. He stays a mile and acts on polytrack and on soft and good to firm going. *Andrew Balding*

BEAT THE BLUES 5 b.m. Aqlaam 125 – Beat As One (Medicean 128) [2017 50: 11.5m May 2] modest maiden: below form only start in 2017: stays 1¼m. *Miss Joey Ellis* –

BEAU AMADEUS (IRE) 8 b.g. Amadeus Wolf 122 – Degree of Honor (FR) 49 (Highest Honor (FR) 124) [2017 t6g^{6} t6d Feb 4] modest handicapper in 2015, below form after long absence only 2 starts since: stays 1m: acts on polytrack and heavy going: has often worn headgear. *Susan Corbett* 48

BEAUCHAMP OPAL 3 b.f. Pastoral Pursuits 127 – Orange Sunset (IRE) 99 (Roanoke (USA)) [2017 63: p8g^{3} p8g^{3} p8g^{4} p10d^{5} t8g 11.4m Jun 12] modest maiden: stays 1m: acts on polytrack: tried in cheekpieces: often races towards rear. *Charlie Fellowes* 64

BEAUCHAMP ROSE 3 b.f. Pastoral Pursuits 127 – Ashford Castle (USA) (Bates Motel (USA)) [2017 t12.2g^{6} 11.6d Jul 19] half-sister to 3 winners, including 1½m winner Aspasias Tizzy (by Tiznow) and 1m winner Beauchamp Castle (by Motivator): dam US 6f-8.5f (including minor stakes) winner: well beaten in pair of maidens. *Charlie Fellowes* –

BEAUDEN BARRETT 4 b.g. Dick Turpin (IRE) 127 – Riccoche (IRE) 63 (Oasis Dream 129) [2017 84: 6m p6g t7.2g^{3} 8.3s^{5} 10g^{2} 10m 9.2v^{6} t10.2g Oct 20] fair handicapper: left Jeremy Gask after third start: stays 1¼m: acts on polytrack and tapeta: tried in cheekpieces: wears tongue tie. *John Quinn* 79

BEAU MISTRAL (IRE) 8 ch.m. Windsor Knot (IRE) 118 – Carpet Lover (IRE) 46 (Fayruz 116) [2017 66: t6m* p6g* p6d p6d^{2} t7.1g^{6} p6g^{2} 6g* t6g 5s^{6} t6.1g t5.1g t6.1g Dec 13] fair handicapper: won at Wolverhampton and Chelmsford in January, and Brighton in April: stays 6f: acts on all-weather, good to firm and heavy going: has worn headgear: front runner/races prominently. *Tony Carroll* 75

BEAUMONT'S PARTY (IRE) 10 b.g. High Chaparral (IRE) 132 – Miss Champagne (FR) (Bering 136) [2017 –: 11.9g 16.5m Jul 13] well-made, attractive gelding: useful at best, no form on Flat in 2017: stays 1½m: acts on polytrack, good to firm and heavy going: has worn headgear: poor hurdler nowadays. *Laura Morgan* –

BEAUTIFUL ARTIST (USA) 2 b.f. (May 18) Lonhro (AUS) 128 – She's A Beauty (USA) 78 (Storm Cat (USA)) [2017 p7g^{6} 7d p8s p7d^{4} Dec 13] $38,000Y, 110,000 2-y-o: half-sister to 3 winners in USA: dam lightly-raced half-sister to very smart performer up to 1m Lucayan Prince: fair form in minor events/nursery: should stay 1m. *John Gosden* 67

BEAUTIFUL MEMORY (IRE) 2 b.f. (Mar 16) Invincible Spirit (IRE) 121 – Express Way (ARG) (Ahmad (ARG)) [2017 7d^3 p7g^3 Oct 5] half-sister to numerous winners, including very smart winner up to 1¼m Rio de La Plata (2-y-o 7f winner, by Rahy) and 1¼m/1½m winner Arabian Beauty (by Shamardal): dam lightly raced: fair form when third in pair of minor events. *Saeed bin Suroor* **78**

BEAUTIFUL MORNING 4 b.f. Galileo (IRE) 134 – Date With Destiny (IRE) 93 (George Washington (IRE) 133) [2017 105: 9.5s^4 10g^4 9d^5 10s^2 10.1s* Sep 20] rangy filly: smart performer: won listed race at Yarmouth (by 2½ lengths from Vintage Folly) in September: stays 1¼m: acts on soft going: often races prominently: consistent. *Mrs J. Harrington, Ireland* **112**

BEAUTIFUL ROMANCE 5 b.m. New Approach (IRE) 132 – Mazuna (IRE) 110 (Cape Cross (IRE) 129) [2017 114: 14g* 15.9d^2 Mar 25] sturdy mare: smart performer: won Nad Al Sheba Trophy at Meydan (by 1½ lengths from Vazirabad) in February: second in Dubai Gold Cup at same course (neck behind same rival) month later: stays 2m: acts on soft and good to firm going: tried in visor. *Saeed bin Suroor* **118**

BEAUTIFUL STRANGER (IRE) 6 b.g. Iffraaj 127 – Monarchy (IRE) (Common Grounds 118) [2017 78§: t8.6m^3 t9.5m Jan 23] leggy gelding: fair performer: stays 9.5f: acts on fibresand, tapeta, soft and good to firm going: wears headgear: quirky sort, not to be trusted. *Keith Dalgleish* **71 §**

BEAU TIMES (IRE) 2 b.f. (Apr 10) Sepoy (AUS) 129 – Timeless Dream 79 (Oasis Dream 129) [2017 5m 6d Jun 30] fifth foal: half-sister to 6f winner Roman Times (by Holy Roman Emperor) and a winner abroad by Mastercraftsman: dam, 6f winner, half-sister to very smart winner up to 7f Welsh Emperor and smart 5f/6f winner Majestic Times: last in minor events. *Tim Easterby* **–**

BEAUTY FILLY 2 b.f. (May 3) Invincible Spirit (IRE) 121 – Miss Delila (USA) (Malibu Moon (USA)) [2017 6d* Sep 21] 280,000Y: half-sister to several winners, including smart winner up to 7f Ashadihan (2-y-o 6f winner, by Kyllachy) and useful 1m-1¼m winner Mythical Madness (by Dubawi): dam ran twice: 6/4, won minor event at Yarmouth (by length from Flying Sparkle) on debut: will stay 7f: open to improvement. *William Haggas* **84 p**

BEAUTY GENERATION (NZ) 5 b.g. Road To Rock (AUS) 125 – Stylish Bel (AUS) (Bel Esprit (AUS) 125) [2017 8m* 8g^3 8.9m 9.9d^3 10.9m* 11.9m 7d* 8m* 8g^3 8g* Dec 10] very smart performer: successful at Sha Tin in handicaps in January and April, Group 3 Celebration Cup Handicap and Group 2 Sha Tin Trophy Handicap, both in October, and Hong Kong Mile (by length from Western Express, very much having run of race) in December: length third to Seasons Bloom in Group 2 Jockey Club Mile at same course on penultimate start: best form at 1m: acts on good to firm and good to soft going: wears blinkers: in tongue tie nowadays. *J. Moore, Hong Kong* **122**

BE BE KING (IRE) 3 b.g. Bated Breath 125 – Champion Place 109 (Compton Place 125) [2017 p7g f5g Aug 28] fair form: better effort when seventh in maiden at Lingfield in April: likely to prove best at sprint trips. *Eve Johnson Houghton* **68**

BE BOLD 5 ch.g. Assertive 121 – Marysienka 78 (Primo Dominie 121) [2017 81: t6d f6g 6g 6d 6d 5f 6s* 6g^5 6g 5g^4 6v^5 7s^6 8v f6.1g Oct 22] sturdy gelding: fair handicapper: won at Catterick in July: stays 7f: acts on polytrack and heavy going: usually wears headgear: sometimes slowly away, often races prominently: unreliable. *Rebecca Bastiman* **70 §**

BECCA CAMPBELL (IRE) 4 b.f. Roderic O'Connor (IRE) 119 – Scottendale 58 (Zilzal (USA) 137) [2017 77: 9.9g^5 9.9m 10d* 9.9g 10m^6 11.4m^2 13f^3 12d^3 12s* 9.9d^5 Sep 20] neat filly: fairly useful handicapper: won at Lingfield in May and Chepstow (by 2¼ lengths from The Detainee) in August: stays 13f: acts on firm and soft going: wears cheekpieces: often races towards rear. *Eve Johnson Houghton* **81**

BECK AND CALL 3 b.f. Holy Roman Emperor (IRE) 125 – Gosbeck 93 (Dubawi (IRE) 129) [2017 75p: 6m^3 5.1d^2 6m* 6v^6 5.1s^3 6s^2 Sep 16] close-coupled filly: fairly useful handicapper: won at Lingfield (by neck from Pepita) in June: bred to stay 7f: acts on soft and good to firm going: front runner/races prominently: sold 7,000 gns in November. *Henry Candy* **84**

BECKER 2 b.c. (Apr 11) Delegator 125 – Mosa Mine 61 (Exceed And Excel (AUS) 126) [2017 6d^6 t7.2m^5 t6.1g^5 Dec 22] fair form in minor events. *James Given* **70**

BECKFORD 2 b.c. (Feb 22) Bated Breath 125 – Whirly Dancer 93 (Danehill Dancer (IRE) 117) [2017 6g* 6g* 6m² 7s² 6d⁵ 8f⁵ Nov 3] **113**

Saddling three winners at Down Royal on the Friday of the track's big meeting at the beginning of November and then another three on the Saturday, including the Champion Chase with Outlander, may have seemed like business as usual for Grand National and Cheltenham Gold Cup-winning trainer Gordon Elliott. Except that his thoughts that weekend might have been occupied as much by events in southern California as in Northern Ireland with the stable's two-year-old Beckford contesting the Breeders' Cup Juvenile Turf at Del Mar. Ridden by one of America's top jockeys, Joel Rosario, Beckford didn't enjoy the run of the race—in common with a number of the European runners—over the tight turf circuit, racing for much of the way in a detached last after being shuffled back on the very short run to the first turn. After encountering more problems rounding the home turn on the inner, Rosario finally had better luck when persevering with a run up the rail in the straight but Beckford could only keep on into fifth, albeit beaten only around two lengths behind the winner Mendelssohn who had enjoyed a trouble-free run.

A runner at the Breeders' Cup would have seemed an unlikely prospect for a trainer who, at the start of the season, had not even saddled a winner at the Curragh, though that was something which Beckford put right when running out a ready winner of a sixteen-runner maiden auction event on his debut there in May. Like most of Elliott's first batch of two-year-olds, Beckford started out carrying the colours of the Nick Bradley Racing Club for whom Elliott had supplied a Royal Ascot winner in 2016 when Commissioned was successful in the Queen Alexandra Stakes. Commissioned was a former hurdler, but the batch of two-year-olds represented a new challenge for Elliott in the latest season. While remaining very much a side-line among the stable's huge string of jumpers, the two-year-olds, or to be more precise Beckford, quickly took Elliott's involvement on the Flat to the sort of heights he was used to as a jumps trainer. Beckford was returned to the Curragh at the beginning of July for the Railway Stakes, by then in new ownership, having been bought privately by Newtown Anner Stud, best known for campaigning the 2015 Champion Stakes winner Fascinating Rock. Sent off the 11/2 third favourite in a strong renewal of the Group 2 contest sponsored by GAIN, Beckford lowered the colours of representatives from top Flat yards, with the Jim Bolger-trained Verbal Dexterity beaten a length into second and the Aidan O'Brien-trained 6/4 favourite Murillo, a close third in the Coventry Stakes on his previous start, beaten another length and quarter into third. Fourth and fifth were De Bruyne Horse and Folk Tale for Richard Hannon and Charlie Appleby respectively. Beckford showed smart form in following up his course-and-distance debut success (form that had worked out well in the meantime), travelling well behind the pace set by Verbal Dexterity and De Bruyne Horse before leading in the final furlong. Such was Beckford's flying start to his career that he was sent off favourite for Group 1 races on each of his

GAIN Railway Stakes, the Curragh—Beckford takes the step up in class in his stride to give his yard a first pattern race success on the Flat, beating Verbal Dexterity (left) and Murillo (second left)

next three outings. He didn't win any of them, but finished runner-up in the first two, both again at the Curragh. In the Phoenix Stakes he was outpaced in the closing stages by Sioux Nation, going down by half a length, while in the National Stakes, in which the extra furlong was expected to be in his favour, the distance proved to suit Verbal Dexterity even more, and, helped by much softer ground, the Railway Stakes runner-up turned the tables on Beckford to run out the winner by three and a half lengths. Beckford's final start before the Breeders' Cup came back at six furlongs in the Middle Park Stakes at Newmarket. He was a well-backed 7/2 chance in an open-looking Middle Park in which Sioux Nation looked Aidan O'Brien's main hope, but Beckford again shaped as though the trip was on the sharp side in finishing just over three lengths fifth to Sioux Nation's stable-companion U S Navy Flag.

Beckford (b.c. 2015)	Bated Breath (b 2007)	Dansili (b 1996)	Danehill
			Hasili
		Tantina (ch 2000)	Distant View
			Didina
	Whirly Dancer (b 2007)	Danehill Dancer (b 1993)	Danehill
			Mira Adonde
		Whirly Bird (b 2001)	Nashwan
			Inchyre

Beckford was sold for 58,000 guineas as a foal and then for €55,000 at Goffs as a yearling. He comes from the second crop of the high-class sprinter Bated Breath who won the Temple Stakes and had a series of near-misses in Group 1 sprints. Beckford is his sire's best colt to date, though the French-trained Al Johrah, from his first crop, finished second in the Queen Mary and Prix Robert Papin and he also has a promising filly among his latest crop of two-year-olds in Gavota, trained by Roger

Newtown Anner Stud Farm's "Beckford"

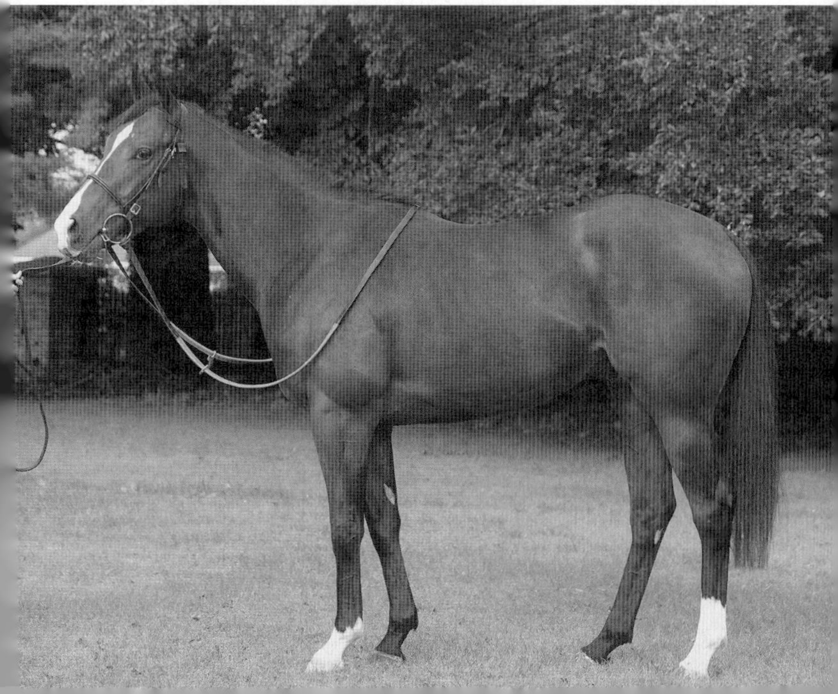

Charlton for Khalid Abdullah, as was Bated Breath himself. Beckford is the second foal out of his fairly useful dam Whirly Dancer, a winner twice over seven furlongs as a three-year-old for Sir Henry Cecil, in a maiden at Folkestone and a handicap at Doncaster. Whirly Dancer's first foal, Lagenda (by Dick Turpin), is also a fairly useful seven-furlong winner, though as a two-year-old. Beckford wasn't the only one to boost his family's fortunes in the latest season as his dam's four-year-old half-brother Poet's Word was much improved for Sir Michael Stoute, progressing from handicaps to win the Glorious Stakes at Goodwood and finish second in the Irish Champion Stakes and the Champion Stakes. Whirly Dancer's other winning siblings include the smart filly Malabar, another winner in pattern company at Goodwood (in the Prestige Stakes and Thoroughbred Stakes) and also fourth in the One Thousand Guineas. Whirly Dancer's dam Whirly Bird was a useful winner of five of her seven starts at up to eleven furlongs and was a half-sister to the St Leger fourth Ursa Major. They are out of Inchyre, a useful daughter (best at a mile and a half) of the smart miler Inchmurrin (runner-up in the Coronation Stakes), whose lack of size made her no less effective as a broodmare for the Oppenheimer family than it had made her as a racehorse. Besides producing the smart colt Inchinor, Inchmurrin's more recent descendants include the 2016 St Leger winner Harbour Law (Inchmurrin is his great grandam).

Whatever else Gordon Elliott goes on to achieve as a trainer on the Flat, Beckford won't be contributing further to his success as he remained in the States after the Breeders' Cup. Effective at six furlongs early on, he had shown by the end of the year that he stays a mile. He ran well enough on both firm and soft ground to suggest that the state of the going makes no real difference to him. *Gordon Elliott, Ireland*

BECKTON 2 b.f. (Mar 17) Finjaan 122 – Stormy Weather (Nashwan (USA) 135) [2017 8s² p8g² Oct 13] 20,000F, 800Y: closely related to German 6.5f-1m winner Hurricane Harry (by Royal Applause) and half-sister to 3 winners, including smart 1m winner Chigun (by Oasis Dream): dam unraced: fairly useful form: better effort when second in maiden at Kempton (½ length behind Preening) in October: sold 50,000 gns in November, sent to Qatar. *Robyn Brisland* **83**

BECKY SHARP 2 b.f. (Feb 27) Foxwedge (AUS) 128 – Perfect Practice 69 (Medicean 128) [2017 7.6s⁶ 7g 7.6d⁵ Sep 16] 2,200F, €20,000Y: tall filly: first foal: dam 1m winner: modest form. *Jim Boyle* **54**

BECKY THE THATCHER 4 b.f. Mastercraftsman (IRE) 129 – Fairmont (IRE) 53 (Kingmambo (USA) 125) [2017 68: 15.9s 14v⁶ Nov 7] fair maiden handicapper: below form both starts on Flat in 2017: stays 1½m: acts on soft and good to firm going: fairly useful hurdler. *Micky Hammond* **54**

BECUNA (USA) 3 b.f. Elusive Quality (USA) – Badalona 90 (Cape Cross (IRE) 129) [2017 p10g⁴ 11.6d⁶ 8.1m⁴ 9.9d 10m⁴ Aug 14] tall, useful-looking filly: fourth foal: half-sister to useful winner up to 1¼m Banditry (2-y-o 1m winner, by Iffraaj): dam, 2-y-o 1m winner, half-sister to useful winner up to 7f Badminton: fair maiden: best effort at 11.5f: acts on good to firm and good to soft going. *Michael Bell* **71**

BEDAZZLING LADY (IRE) 4 gr.f. Zebedee 113 – Malta (USA) (Gone West (USA)) [2017 54: f6g⁶ p6g Jan 27] lengthy filly: modest maiden: below form both starts in 2017: stays 7f: acts on polytrack and good to soft going: tried in visor: often races prominently: sold 1,200 gns in February, sent to Denmark. *Robert Eddery* **–**

BED OF DIAMONDS 3 ch.f. Bated Breath 125 – Bedara 93 (Barathea (IRE) 127) [2017 –: p12g 12d⁶ 14v 11.9m 7d p10g t8.6g⁶ Oct 21] poor maiden: stays 1½m: acts on tapeta and good to soft going. *Adam West* **48**

BEDOUIN (IRE) 3 b.g. High Chaparral (IRE) 132 – Jewel In The Sand (IRE) 107 (Bluebird (USA) 125) [2017 75: 10.2g² 11.9d⁴ 12g⁶ 10.2g* 10v⁴ 9.9g* 9.9g⁶ 10g² 10.3g⁵ Oct 14] sturdy gelding: useful performer: won minor event at Nottingham in July and handicap at Brighton in August: second in handicap at Newbury (short head behind Breden) in September: stays 1½m: acts on heavy going: wears headgear: usually races nearer last than first: sold 30,000 gns in November: not reliable. *Luca Cumani* **95 §**

BEDOUIN'S STORY 2 b.c. (May 4) Farhh 131 – Time Crystal (IRE) 83 (Sadler's Wells (USA) 132) [2017 7m Oct 25] 90,000F: good-topped colt: closely related to useful winner up to 11f Sparkling Portrait (2-y-o 1m winner, by Excellent Art) and half-brother to several winners, including smart 1m-11f winner Start Right (2-y-o 8.6f winner, by Footsteps- **71 p**

inthesand) and 1¼m-1½m winner Loving Your Work (by Royal Applause): dam 1½m winner: 33/1, seventh in minor event at Newmarket (9¼ lengths behind Key Victory) on debut: will be suited by 1m+: will improve. *Saeed bin Suroor*

BEE CASE 3 br.f. Showcasing 117 – Binabee (Galileo (IRE) 134) [2017 84: p8m^3 p6g 7d^6 Jul 1] fairly useful at best, no form in 2017: tried in hood: often races prominently. *Simon Dow* –

BEE INA BONNET 2 ch.f. (Mar 20) Helmet (AUS) 127 – Rosabee (IRE) 96 (No Excuse Needed 123) [2017 5d^5 5g 6s^3 7.4s* 7d 7d Oct 28] fifth foal: dam 2-y-o 5f/6f winner: fair performer: won minor event at Beverley in September: stays 7.5f: acts on soft going: tried in cheekpieces: often races prominently. *Tim Easterby* **73**

BEE MACHINE (IRE) 2 b.g. (Feb 10) Footstepsinthesand 120 – Lady Royale 93 (Monsieur Bond (IRE) 120) [2017 5g 5d 5m t8s 8g^5 8v^6 Oct 23] compact gelding: modest maiden: best effort at 1m. *Declan Carroll* **50**

BEEPEECEE 3 b.g. Henrythenavigator (USA) 131 – Roedean (IRE) 77 (Oratorio (IRE) 128) [2017 62: t7.1m* p7m^5 10m 7m* 7m^3 7d 7g 7s 7.1g 8g p7d^3 p8d* p8g^4 p10m^3 t9.5g p10g Dec 30] fair handicapper: won at Wolverhampton in January, Salisbury in June and Chelmsford in October: stays 1¼m: acts on polytrack, tapeta and good to firm going: wears headgear: quirky and not one to rely on. *Richard Hughes* **75 §**

BEGGING BOWL 2 br.f. (Feb 13) Pastoral Pursuits 127 – Bow Bridge 95 (Bertolini (USA) 125) [2017 t5s^3 Jul 1] seventh foal: half-sister to 3 winning sprinters, including useful 5f (including at 2 yrs) winner Bowson Fred (by Monsieur Bond) and 5f/6f winner Towbee (by Doyen): dam 2-y-o 5f winner: 25/1, third in minor event at Newcastle (4 lengths behind Haddaf) in July: should do better. *Michael Easterby* **63 p**

BEING THERE (FR) 2 b.c. (Feb 27) Dubawi (IRE) 129 – Beauty Parlour 118 (Deep Impact (JPN) 134) [2017 6.5g^2 7m* 7d^6 Jul 29] €1,400,000Y: sturdy colt: first foal: dam 1m winner (including Poule d'Essai des Pouliches, and at 2 yrs) who stayed 10.5f: fairly useful form: won maiden at Newmarket (by head from Doswell) in July: stays 7f. *Charlie Appleby* **88**

BE KOOL (IRE) 4 b.g. Approve (IRE) 112 – Accounting (Sillery (USA) 122) [2017 82, a74: 8m 8.3m^2 8g^5 7m* 7.9m^4 7.2g* 8.4s^6 7s^3 7v Sep 30] fairly useful handicapper: won at York in June and Ayr (by 1¼ lengths from Strong Steps) in July: stays 8.5f: acts on tapeta, soft and good to firm going: wears visor: front runner/races prominently. *Brian Ellison* **92**

BELABOUR 4 b.g. Bernardini (USA) 132 – Criticism 112 (Machiavellian (USA) 123) [2017 62: t8.6m^3 p12g* 13.9m^6 13.4d 12d p12g p12g p11g^6 t12.2g^2 t12.2d Dec 26] fairly useful performer: won maiden at Kempton (by 1½ lengths from Lord Napier) in January: stays 1½m: acts on polytrack and tapeta. *Mark Brisbourne* **85**

BELEAVE 4 gr.f. Avonbridge 123 – Grezie 63 (Mark of Esteem (IRE) 137) [2017 87: p8d^5 p8g Mar 8] fairly useful handicapper: stays 1m: acts on polytrack and good to soft going: in hood last 4 starts: sometimes slowly away/has given trouble at stalls. *Luke Dace* **77**

BELGIAN BILL 9 b.h. Exceed And Excel (AUS) 126 – Gay Romance 71 (Singspiel (IRE) 133) [2017 111: 8g^3 9.9g^3 8g^4 8m 7g a9.9g^5 p8g^2 p8g^5 p8s Dec 7] lengthy, well-made horse: useful handicapper: second at Kempton (head behind Brigliadoro) in October: stays 1¼m: acts on polytrack, firm and soft going: has worn headgear/tongue tie. *George Baker* **105**

BELGRAVIA (IRE) 3 b.c. Galileo (IRE) 134 – Love Me True (USA) 99 (Kingmambo (USA) 125) [2017 70: 10d^3 12m* 13m^4 14m^4 14g^6 12g* Jul 27] well-made colt: brother to high-class 1¼m-1½m (including Derby) winner Ruler of The World and smart 2-y-o 1m winner (stays 1½m) Giovanni Canaletto, and closely related/half-brother to several winners, including top-class winner up to 1½m Duke of Marmalade (2-y-o 7f winner, by Danehill): dam 1m winner: useful performer: won maiden at Leopardstown (by ¾ length from Clongowes) in May and minor event at same course (by neck from Clongowes) in July: stays 1¾m: acts on good to firm and good to soft going: in headgear last 4 starts: wears tongue tie. *Aidan O'Brien, Ireland* **105**

BELGRAVIAN (FR) 3 b.g. Pivotal 124 – Elle Galante (GER) (Galileo (IRE) 134) [2017 8g^5 10.2m^5 12s^{ur} 12d^5 7.1m 7.6d^6 p8g^3 p8d p7g^5 p7g* p8s f8.1g* f8.1g^{pu} Dec 1] fair performer: won minor event at Kempton in October and handicap at Southwell (amateur, by 1¼ lengths from Ingleby Spring) in November: stayed 1m: acted on polytrack and fibresand: wore headgear/tongue tie: sometimes slowly away: dead. *Archie Watson* **72**

BELIEVE IT (IRE) 5 b.h. Rip Van Winkle (IRE) 134 – Have Faith (IRE) 87 (Machiavellian (USA) 123) [2017 59, a80: p10g^{4} p8d p8g* p8g* t9.5g^{4} p7g* p8s* 7m^{2} 9.1m p8g p10g p8s^{2} p8g Dec 31] strong horse: useful handicapper: won 4 times at Kempton in first half of year: stays 9.5f: acts on polytrack, tapeta and good to firm going: usually wears headgear: tried in tongue tie: sometimes slowly away. *Richard Hughes* **95**

BELISA (IRE) 3 ch.f. Lope de Vega (IRE) 125 – Fleche Brisee (USA) (Dynaformer (USA)) [2017 –: 8.3g t8s* 8.3d^{2} 8.2g* Aug 2] fair handicapper: won at Newcastle in June and Leicester in August: stays 8.5f: acts on tapeta and good to soft going: remains capable of better. *Ivan Furtado* **74 p**

BELLA ALISSA 3 b.f. Dutch Art 126 – Crazy Too (IRE) 69 (Invincible Spirit (IRE) 121) [2017 67p: 6g^{4} 5f* 5.7f^{6} 5.3d* 5.3v^{2} Oct 19] fairly useful performer: won maiden at Bath in June and handicap at Brighton in September: second in handicap at latter course in October: stays 5.5f: acts on any turf going: in cheekpieces last 4 starts: sold 3,500 gns later in October. *Robert Cowell* **88**

BELLA DUCHESS (IRE) 3 b.f. Big Bad Bob (IRE) 118 – Spinning Gold 45 (Spinning World (USA) 130) [2017 –: f7g 8.5g 6g^{6} 6g 9.5g Jun 11] little form: left David C. Griffiths after reappearance. *Frau S. Schwinn, Germany* **–**

BELLA FERRARI 2 b.f. (Mar 24) Bated Breath 125 – Massarossa (Mr Prospector (USA)) [2017 t6.1g Nov 18] closely related to French 2-y-o 1¼m winner Desarmante (by Dansili) and half-sister to several winners in France, including useful 7f-9f winner Nid d'Abeilles (by Green Desert): dam ran once in France: 33/1, well held in minor event at Wolverhampton. *George Scott* **–**

BELLAMAY 3 b.f. Foxwedge (AUS) 128 – Steeple (Selkirk (USA) 129) [2017 –: t7.1d Feb 1] no form. *John Weymes* **–**

BELLA'S BOY (IRE) 4 b.g. Lovelace 117 – Cosa Deasa (IRE) 48 (Barathea (IRE) 127) [2017 –: p7d p6g p8g t8.6g^{pu} p6f^{rr} Apr 24] little form: sometimes in headgear: temperamental (virtually refused/refused to race last 2 starts). *John Ryan* **– §**

BELLA'S VENTURE 4 gr.f. Hellvelyn 118 – Fayre Bella 75 (Zafeen (FR) 123) [2017 59: p6g^{5} 7d^{3} 7.1m^{4} 8g^{6} 7d^{2} 7.1g 7d^{3} 7s 6v Oct 19] modest maiden: stays 7f: acts on good to firm and good to soft going: sometimes slowly away. *John Gallagher* **62**

BELLE DE LAWERS 6 b.m. Black Sam Bellamy (IRE) 121 – Scotland The Brave 82 (Zilzal (USA) 137) [2017 t10.2s t10.2g^{5} 8d t8g t16.3g t12.4g^{5} Dec 6] fairly useful handicapper: stays 12.5f: acts on tapeta, best turf form on good going: tried in cheekpieces. *James Bethell* **81**

BELLEDESERT 4 b.f. Pastoral Pursuits 127 – Ocean Blaze 91 (Polar Prince (IRE) 117) [2017 94: 5f^{4} 6.1g 6g^{3} 5.7f^{3} 6m^{3} 6d Jul 21] rather leggy filly: fairly useful handicapper: third at Bath in June: stays 6f: acts on firm and soft going. *Steph Hollinshead* **91**

BELLE DIVA (IRE) 3 b.f. Dark Angel (IRE) 113 – Red Intrigue (IRE) 80 (Selkirk (USA) 129) [2017 86p: p7g Apr 26] tall filly: fairly useful 7f winner at 2 yrs, well held in handicap only start in 2017. *Ralph Beckett* **–**

BELLE MEADE (IRE) 3 ch.f. Roderic O'Connor (IRE) 119 – Hazardous (Night Shift (USA)) [2017 89: 6d^{5} p7g 7s^{6} p8g Nov 2] leggy filly: fairly useful performer: stays 7f: acts on soft and good to firm going. *Andrew Balding* **93**

BELLE PEINTURE (FR) 6 ch.m. Peintre Celebre (USA) 137 – Grosgrain (USA) (Diesis 133) [2017 45: 9.9f 9.9s 12.1d Sep 12] maiden handicapper: well held in 2017: usually in headgear: front runner/races prominently. *Alan Lockwood* **–**

BELLEVARDE (IRE) 3 b.f. Kodiac 112 – Pearl Mountain (IRE) 64 (Pearl of Love (IRE) 112) [2017 75: p5g^{4} 5.1m 6.1d^{5} 6d^{2} 6g^{5} 6.1m^{6} 6v^{2} 6g^{2} 5.1s* 5s^{2} 5s Oct 2] lengthy filly: fair handicapper: won at Chepstow in August: left James Fanshawe after first start: stays 6f: acts on polytrack and heavy going: tried in hood: front runner/races prominently. *Richard Price* **77**

BELL HEATHER (IRE) 4 b.f. Iffraaj 127 – Burren Rose (USA) (Storm Cat (USA)) [2017 83, a76: f6g^{5} t8g t7.1g^{3} t7.2g* 7.6d^{6} t7.2g^{3} t8.6g* 7.6v t8.6g Nov 11] close-coupled filly: fairly useful handicapper: won at Wolverhampton in July and September (apprentice): left Richard Fahey after third start: stays 8.5f: acts on tapeta, good to firm and heavy going. *Patrick Morris* **81**

BELL OF THE BALL (IRE) 7 b.m. Bachelor Duke (USA) 122 – Grangehill Dancer (IRE) 76 (Danehill Dancer (IRE) 117) [2017 59: 13.1g^{6} Jul 17] modest handicapper, very lightly raced on Flat nowadays: stays 13f: best form on good going: modest hurdler. *Liam Lennon, Ireland* **60**

BELL WEIR 9 gr.g. Tobougg (IRE) 125 – Belly Dancer (IRE) 88 (Danehill Dancer (IRE) 117) [2017 77: 13.8m Apr 12] fairly useful at best, well held only start on Flat in 2017: stays 16.5f: acts on good to soft going: often in headgear/tongue tie: modest hurdler. *Kenneth Slack* –

BELOVED KNIGHT 2 ch.c. (Feb 17) Sir Percy 129 – Silent Decision (USA) 91 (Mr Greeley (USA) 122) [2017 p8s p8d p8g Dec 20] down the field in minor events. *Laura Mongan* –

BELTOR 6 b.g. Authorized (IRE) 133 – Carahill (AUS) (Danehill (USA) 126) [2017 90: p16g⁶ Apr 15] lengthy gelding: fairly useful handicapper: stays 2m: acts on polytrack and good to firm going: useful hurdler. *Robert Stephens* **83**

BE MINDFUL (IRE) 2 b.f. (Apr 5) Invincible Spirit (IRE) 121 – Strawberry Roan (IRE) 113 (Sadler's Wells (USA) 132) [2017 6m⁶ p7g 7s Oct 9] rather unfurnished filly: half-sister to several winners, including useful 1m-1½m winner Vivat Rex (by Fastnet Rock): dam, 1m/9f winner (including at 2 yrs) and second in Irish 1000 Guineas, sister to Irish 1000 Guineas/Oaks winner Imagine and half-sister to Derby winner Generous: limited impact in minor events. *Charles Hills* –

BE MY SEA (IRE) 6 b.g. Sea The Stars (IRE) 140 – Bitooh (Diktat 126) [2017 85: t12.2m⁶ p16g⁶ Apr 24] compact gelding: fairly useful handicapper: stays 21f: acts on polytrack, fibresand, good to firm and heavy going: has worn cheekpieces/tongue tie: won over hurdles in June. *Tony Carroll* **81**

BENADALID 2 b.g. (Mar 1) Assertive 121 – Gambatte 58 (One Cool Cat (USA) 123) [2017 5g³ 6m⁴ t6s* t7.1s³ 6m⁶ 7d⁶ Sep 13] first foal: dam maiden (stayed 8.6f): fairly useful performer: won minor event at Newcastle (dead-heated) in June: third in similar event at same course later in month: stays 7f: acts on tapeta: usually races prominently. *Chris Fairhurst* **80**

BENARAS (USA) 2 b.f. (Feb 21) Gio Ponti (USA) 130 – Brocatelle 65 (Green Desert (USA) 127) [2017 5s⁶ May 20] $47,000F, €60,000Y: half-sister to several winners, including useful 2-y-o 7f winner (stayed 1¼m) Ahlaain (by Bernstein) and ungenuine 6f-1¼m winner Penbryn (by Pivotal): dam maiden half-sister to high-class miler Barathea: 6/1, sixth in maiden at Thirsk. *Tim Easterby* –

BENBATL 3 b.c. Dubawi (IRE) 129 – Nahrain 119 (Selkirk (USA) 129) [2017 7g* 8m³ 10.3d² 12m⁵ 10m* 12s⁵ 8.2s⁶ Sep 9] sturdy, attractive colt: first foal: dam, 1m-1¼m winner, including Prix de l'Opera, half-sister to smart 1m-1¼m performers Baharah and Sarrsar: very smart performer: won maiden at Doncaster (by 7 lengths from Made of Honour) in April and Hampton Court Stakes at Royal Ascot (by ½ length from Orderofthegarter) in June: second in Dante Stakes at York and fifth in Derby at Epsom: stays 1½m: acts on good to firm and good to soft going: tried in hood: in tongue tie last 4 starts. *Saeed bin Suroor* **121**

BENBECULA 8 b.g. Motivator 131 – Isle of Flame (Shirley Heights 130) [2017 12m³ 12f⁴ 14.2v⁵ Jul 29] rangy gelding: fair handicapper: stays 1¾m: acts on polytrack and any turf going: has worn headgear, including last 3 starts. *Richard Mitchell* **72**

Hampton Court Stakes, Royal Ascot—Benbatl holds off the late thrust of Orderofthegarter (cheekpieces) to give jockey Oisin Murphy a first Royal Ascot winner

Weatherbys Super Sprint, Newbury—one of five in the race for trainer Richard Fahey, Bengali Boys copes with the heavy going much better than his rivals and finishes clear of the staying-on Declarationoflove (second left, still with plenty to do) and Maggies Angel (striped sleeves)

BENGALI BOYS (IRE) 2 gr.c. (Mar 28) Clodovil (IRE) 116 – Caherassdotcom 79 (Compton Place 125) [2017 5m* 5m² 5g² 5.2v* 5m⁴ Aug 26] €11,000Y: fourth foal: brother to 2-y-o 5f winner Diable d'Or and half-brother to 7f winner Win Lose Draw (by Dark Angel): dam, ungenuine maiden (stayed 7f), half-sister to 1m/9f winner Wannabe Around and winner up to 7f Grantley Adams (both smart): useful performer: won minor event at Beverley (by length from Wahoo) in April and Super Sprint at Newbury (by 6 lengths from Declarationoflove) in July: raced only at 5f: acts on good to firm and heavy going. *Richard Fahey* **106**

BENGAL LANCER 3 gr.g. Hellvelyn 118 – Bens Georgie (IRE) 77 (Opening Verse (USA) 126) [2017 73: 6d⁴ 7d² 7m* 7g* 7d² 7d⁵ Oct 6] good-topped gelding: fairly useful handicapper: won at Salisbury (twice, by 8 lengths from Rebel de Lope second occasion) in August: stays 7f: acts on good to firm and good to soft going: usually races prominently: sold 48,000 gns in October. *Ian Williams* **94**

BENGER'S PURSUIT 2 ch.f. (Feb 18) Pastoral Pursuits 127 – Bengers Lass (USA) (Orientate (USA) 127) [2017 p7g 8s Oct 20] third foal: half-sister to Italian 6f-1m winner Chassis (by Kheleyf): dam of little account: well held in minor event/claimer. *Jo Hughes* **–**

BENISSIMO (IRE) 7 b.g. Beneficial 117 – Fennor Rose (IRE) (Kotashaan (FR) 128) [2017 t12.2g⁴ t12.2g 10.2s 14g 14g t12.2m Oct 28] fair maiden, went wrong way from debut: in cheekpieces last 2 starts: sometimes slowly away: winning hurdler. *Tony Forbes* **66**

BENJAMIN THOMAS (IRE) 3 b.g. Mayson 124 – Strudel (IRE) 94 (Spectrum (IRE) 126) [2017 85p: 7m² 7g³ 6g² 7s³ 6s* 6m 7d² 6d⁵ 7g t6g Oct 20] compact gelding: fairly useful performer: won maiden at Catterick in June: second in handicap at Epsom in August: stays 7f: acts on heavy going: wears visor. *John Quinn* **83**

BEN MY CHREE 2 gr.f. (May 4) Lethal Force (IRE) 128 – Steal The Curtain (Royal Applause 124) [2017 5m⁴ 5f⁵ 5s 6s t6.1g Nov 29] £11,500Y: third foal: half-sister to Italian 7f winner (including at 2 yrs) Il Malandrino (by Kheleyf): dam unraced half-sister to smart 7f/1m winner Mine: modest form: tried in headgear. *Bryan Smart* **62**

BENNELONG 11 b.g. Bahamian Bounty 116 – Bundle Up (USA) (Miner's Mark (USA) 120) [2017 62: p12g Apr 11] rangy gelding: modest handicapper, below form only start in 2017: stays 13f: acts on polytrack, fibresand, firm and soft going: usually wears headgear: tried in tongue tie. *Lee Carter* **–**

BE PERFECT (USA) 8 b.g. Street Cry (IRE) 130 – Binya (GER) 106 (Royal Solo (IRE) 113) [2017 88: t12.4d t12.4g⁴ 12m* 12.1m* 14.6m 11.9g 11.9m 12.1g* 13.1g⁴ 13.9v⁶ 12.1s 12v t12.4s Sep 19] fairly useful handicapper: won at Catterick and Beverley in April, and Hamilton (by ¾ length from Al Destoor) in July: stays 2¼m: acts on all-weather, good to firm and good to soft going: wears headgear: has worn tongue tie: front runner/races prominently: inconsistent. *Ruth Carr* **90**

BEQUIA (IRE) 3 ch.f. Helmet (AUS) 127 – Bunditten (IRE) 92 (Soviet Star (USA) 128) [2017 76: 5.2m³ 7m 7g⁶ t6g⁶ a8.9s⁶ Dec 26] compact filly: fair maiden: left Martyn Meade after third start, David O'Meara after fourth: stays 7f: acts on good to firm going. *C. von der Recke, Germany* **75**

BERENGARIA (IRE) 3 b.f. Teofilo (IRE) 126 – Belle Josephine 80 (Dubawi (IRE) 129) **87** [2017 83: 10.2v^3 9.9d^5 11.4m^4 10g^5 9.9g^3 Aug 11] close-coupled filly: fairly useful handicapper: stays 11.5f: acts on polytrack, good to firm and heavy going: usually leads. *Mark Johnston*

BERGHAIN (IRE) 4 ch.c. Medicean 128 – Basilea Gold (GER) 105 (Monsun (GER) **104** 124) [2017 13.9g 16.2m^5 15.9s 11.4g* Aug 19] sturdy colt: useful performer: won minor event at Mulheim in August by 2¼ lengths from Red Pepper: far from discredited when 14 lengths fifth to Big Orange in Henry II Stakes at Sandown on second outing: seems to stay 2m: acts on soft and good to firm going. *J. Hirschberger, Germany*

BERGHOLT (IRE) 4 b.g. Sir Percy 129 – Sularina (IRE) 74 (Alhaarth (IRE) 126) [2017 **69** 76: p12g 7.1m 9.9g^4 p11g^3 p12g^5 Nov 18] fair maiden: stays 11f: acts on polytrack and firm going: has worn headgear, including last 2 starts. *Tim Vaughan*

BERINGER 2 b.g. (Apr 23) Sea The Stars (IRE) 140 – Edaraat (USA) (Rahy (USA) 115) **76** [2017 7d 7m* p8g^3 7g^6 Aug 25] fair form: won minor event at Salisbury in July: stays 1m. *Alan King*

BERKELEY VALE 6 b.g. Three Valleys (USA) 119 – Intriguing Glimpse 100 (Piccolo **71 §** 121) [2017 81§: t8.6g^6 10.2d* 10g 10.1g^5 8s^4 p10g p11g 8.3g^4 p10m Nov 25] leggy **a64 §** gelding: fair handicapper: won at Bath in May: stays 1¼m: acts on polytrack, good to firm and good to soft going: usually wears headgear: unreliable. *Roger Teal*

BERKSHIRE BOY (IRE) 3 b.g. Elzaam (AUS) 115 – Circuit City (IRE) (Exit To **95 §** Nowhere (USA) 122) [2017 86§: p6g^2 t7.1g^4 7m^4 8g 7.1s* 7d Oct 6] neat gelding: useful handicapper: won at Chepstow (by 1¾ lengths from Mohsen) in September: stays 1m: acts on polytrack, soft and good to firm going: wears blinkers: sometimes slowly away: temperamental. *Andrew Balding*

BERKSHIRE (IRE) 6 b.h. Mount Nelson 125 – Kinnaird (IRE) 113 (Dr Devious (IRE) **104** 127) [2017 112, a97: 10.3m^4 9.9g^5 10g^5 10.2d Aug 5] tall, attractive horse: smart at best, below that in 2017: stays 11.5f: acts on good to firm and good to soft going: often in headgear: usually leads/races freely: tends to get on edge in preliminaries. *Paul Cole*

BERKSHIRE ROYAL 2 b.g. (Feb 27) Sir Percy 129 – Forest Express (AUS) (Kaaptive **66** Edition (NZ)) [2017 7d 7.6d^6 8d^5 8.1g^5 Oct 9] workmanlike gelding: fair form: will stay beyond 1m. *Andrew Balding*

BERKSHIRE SPIRIT 2 gr.c. (Feb 9) Mastercraftsman (IRE) 129 – Rebecca Rolfe 109 **66** (Pivotal 124) [2017 8v^6 8.5m^5 9.9s^6 9d^4 Nov 4] fair form: will stay beyond 1¼m. *Andrew Balding*

BERLIOS (IRE) 4 b.g. Excellent Art 125 – Endless Peace (IRE) 62 (Russian Revival **79** (USA) 125) [2017 82: f5s^5 t6g^2 t6d 5v 6s t5d t7.2g Nov 25] fair handicapper: left David Barron/below form after third start: stays 6.5f: acts on fibresand, tapeta and good to soft going: usually races towards rear. *Rebecca Bastiman*

BERLUSCA (IRE) 8 b.g. Holy Roman Emperor (IRE) 125 – Shemanikha (FR) **83** (Sendawar (IRE) 129) [2017 89: p10g^3 t9.5g t9.5g^6 t8.6g^3 10.2m 10.2m^6 t8.6g 10.3g^2 t12.2g t9.5m p10s^6 t9.5g^2 t9.5g Dec 18] strong gelding: fairly useful handicapper: regressive in 2017: left David O'Meara after sixth start: stays 10.5f: acts on polytrack, tapeta and any turf going: has worn hood, including in 2017: sometimes slowly away, often races towards rear. *David Loughnane*

BERMONDSEY BELLE (IRE) 3 b.f. Sir Percy 129 – Bermondsey Girl 69 (Bertolini **71** (USA) 125) [2017 67: 10g^5 10d^2 11.6d^6 p13.3d p15.8g^6 p12g Nov 1] fair maiden: stays 2m: acts on polytrack and good to soft going: in cheekpieces last 3 starts: in tongue tie last 2: front runner/races prominently. *Lucy Wadham*

BERNARDO O'REILLY 3 b.g. Intikhab (USA) 135 – Baldovina 73 (Tale of The Cat **85** (USA) 113) [2017 7d* 7v^3 7m^5 7d 6.1m^5 Oct 16] £10,000Y: angular gelding: fifth foal: closely related to useful 2-y-o 5f (including Queen Mary Stakes) winner Ceiling Kitty (by Red Clubs) and half-brother to ungenuine 2-y-o 5f winner Van Go Go (by Dutch Art): dam, maiden (stayed 1m), half-sister to Japanese 1000 Guineas winner Jeweler: fairly useful performer: won maiden at Lingfield (by 6 lengths from Joys Delight) in July: best effort at 7f: acts on good to firm and good to soft going: sometimes in hood: sometimes slowly away, usually races nearer last than first. *Richard Spencer*

BERNIE'S BOY 4 b.g. Lilbourne Lad (IRE) 111 – Stoney Cove (IRE) (Needwood Blade **75** 117) [2017 85, a76: 8m 8m^5 6.9g 6g 6m^3 6d^5 7m^3 7s* 7s^4 f6.1g^2 t6.1g^2 p6g Dec 31] rather leggy gelding: fair performer: won claimer at Catterick in July: left Roger Fell after eighth start, Iain Jardine after eleventh: stays 1m: acts on all-weather, firm and soft going: wears headgear: usually races close up. *Phil McEntee*

BE ROYALE 7 b.m. Byron 117 – Sofia Royale 61 (Royal Applause 124) [2017 80: p6g^5 p7g^3 p6g^6 t7.1g 7m^5 8m^2 7m^4 p8s 8.2g Jun 27] fair handicapper: stays 8.5f: acts on all-weather, good to firm and good to soft going: has worn cheekpieces: usually wears tongue tie. *Michael Appleby* **68**

BERRAHRI (IRE) 6 b.g. Bahri (USA) 125 – Band of Colour (IRE) (Spectrum (IRE) 126) [2017 82: p8d a8g^5 a8.9g^4 a8g* p10d^6 p8g^6 8.3m p8g* 8g^3 8s^2 10.1f^2 10.1g* 13.4d* 16d 14.4v^3 14.5d^4 p12g^3 p11d^3 p12g^5 Dec 31] rather leggy gelding: fairly useful performer: won minor event at Saint Moritz in February, and handicaps at Lingfield in May, Epsom in July and Chester (by 2½ lengths from Kajaki) later in July: stays 14.5f: acts on all-weather, snow and any turf going: has worn headgear: front runner/races prominently. *John Best* **92**

BERRYESSA (IRE) 3 b.f. Dandy Man (IRE) 123 – Carrauntoohil (IRE) 49 (Marju (IRE) 127) [2017 p5g^2 p5g* 5m^2 5f^4 5m^5 p5g^6 t5.1g* t5.1g^5 p5s Dec 8] 5,000Y: third foal: half-sister to a winner abroad by Vale of York: dam lightly raced: fairly useful performer: won maiden at Lingfield in February and handicap at Wolverhampton (by ½ length from Kyllukey) in November: raced only at 5f: acts on polytrack, tapeta and good to firm going. *Rae Guest* **80**

BERTHA BURNETT (IRE) 6 gr.m. Verglas (IRE) 118 – Starsazi (Observatory (USA) 131) [2017 55: 9s 7m 10.2d^5 8s^6 Aug 9] sparely-made mare: modest maiden at best, no form in 2017: tried in cheekpieces. *Brian Rothwell* **–**

BERTIE BLU BOY 9 b.g. Central Park (IRE) 123 – Shaymee's Girl 59 (Wizard King 122) [2017 88: p6g p6g^2 p6g p6g p6g Apr 11] workmanlike gelding: fair handicapper: stays 9.5f, usually races over much shorter: acts on polytrack: wears headgear: front runner/races prominently. *Lisa Williamson* **77**

BERTIE MOON 7 b.g. Bertolini (USA) 125 – Fleeting Moon 70 (Fleetwood (IRE) 107) [2017 89: t13.9g 10.1g^6 12s^4 11.9s 14g 14g f16.5g^2 f14.1g^4 f14.1g^4 p12g* Dec 28] fair performer: won seller at Lingfield in December: left Lydia Pearce after fifth start: stays 2m: acts on polytrack, fibresand and any turf going: sometimes in headgear: tried in tongue tie: front runner/races prominently. *Michael Appleby* **77**

BERTIE WALLACE (IRE) 2 b.g. (Feb 1) Fast Company (IRE) 126 – Six Diamonds 84 (Exceed And Excel (AUS) 126) [2017 5m 7g^5 6d^5 8g Sep 27] modest form: best effort at 7f: tried in hood. *Keith Dalgleish* **54**

BERTIEWHITTLE 9 ch.g. Bahamian Bounty 116 – Minette 55 (Bishop of Cashel 122) [2017 100, a93: f7g 7.1g^6 7m 7d^5 7m^5 7s^2 7d 7g* 7g 7s 7d^3 7d^3 t6s^4 t7.1d Dec 16] smallish gelding: useful handicapper: won at Doncaster (by neck from Qeyaadah) in August: stays 1m, usually races over 7f: acts on all-weather, good to firm and heavy going: has worn headgear: often races in rear. *David Barron* **100** **a94**

BERTOG 2 ch.c. (May 23) Sepoy (AUS) 129 – Lucky Token (IRE) 77 (Key of Luck (USA) 126) [2017 7g 8g^5 7g^6 7m^3 Oct 25] 31,000Y: sturdy colt: sixth foal: half-brother to 1m winner (stays 1¼m) Polymnia (by Poet's Voice) and a winner abroad by Exceed And Excel: dam, 8.6f winner, half-sister to 1000 Guineas winner Sky Lantern: fair form: third in nursery at Newmarket final start: stays 1m: open to further improvement. *John Mackie* **79 p**

BE SEEING YOU 6 ch.g. Medicean 128 – Oshiponga 72 (Barathea (IRE) 127) [2017 10g Jul 20] useful-looking gelding: fair maiden at best, well held only start on Flat since 2014: stays 1½m: acts on polytrack, soft and good to firm going: tried in blinkers/tongue tie: modest hurdler. *Trevor Wall* **–**

BESHAAYIR 2 b.f. (Mar 4) Iffraaj 127 – Bahia Breeze 109 (Mister Baileys 123) [2017 6s^2 6g* Sep 22] 19,000F, 120,000Y: sister to 6f-1¼m winner Khalaas and half-sister to 3 winners, including useful Polish 7f-11f winner Brioniya (by Pivotal) and 2-y-o 6f winner Alsaaden (by Acclamation): dam winner up to 1m (2-y-o 6f winner) who stayed 10.5f: fairly useful form: won maiden at Newbury (by 1½ lengths from Foxtrot Lady) in September: open to further improvement. *William Haggas* **87 p**

BESSEMER LADY 3 b.f. Cacique (IRE) 124 – Blast Furnace (IRE) 74 (Sadler's Wells (USA) 132) [2017 –: p8g p10g t12.2g* t12.2g^4 Mar 23] modest performer: won handicap at Wolverhampton in February: stays 1½m: acts on tapeta: in blinkers last 2 starts. *Ralph Beckett* **64**

BESSIE WARFIELD 2 b.f. (Apr 24) Oasis Dream 129 – Wallis 104 (King's Best (USA) 132) [2017 7g 8g 8.3d p7g Nov 17] third foal: closely related to 7.5f winner Atteq (by Invincible Spirit): dam, 6f-1m winner, half-sister to 1¼m-1¾m winner Savarain and 1m-1½m winner Forte dei Marmi (both smart): modest form in maidens/nursery. *Luca Cumani* **57**

BEST BLUE 2 b.c. (Feb 28) Oasis Dream 129 – Filia Regina 76 (Galileo (IRE) 134) [2017 8.3v p8s^2 p8g* Dec 21] 210,000Y: first foal: dam, 1¾m winner, sister to Derby winner Australia out of Oaks winner Ouija Board: fairly useful form: won maiden at Chelmsford (by head from Fleeting Freedom) in December: will stay 1¼m: likely to progress further. *Michael Bell* **84 p**

BEST COMPANY (IRE) 2 b.g. (Apr 16) Fast Company (IRE) 126 – Story (Observatory (USA) 131) [2017 7m 6.1d Sep 4] well held in minor events. *Dean Ivory* **–**

BEST EXAMPLE (USA) 5 ch.g. King's Best (USA) 132 – Born Something (IRE) 105 (Caerleon (USA) 132) [2017 92: p8m 10m 11.5m^4 10g 11.9m^4 11.5m^3 11.5m^2 t12.2g^2 p13.3g^6 p12g^6 t12.2g^5 Dec 2] close-coupled gelding: fair handicapper nowadays: stays 1½m: acts on polytrack, tapeta and good to firm going: has worn headgear. *Julia Feilden* **74**

BEST OF DAYS 3 b.c. Azamour (IRE) 130 – Baisse 83 (High Chaparral (IRE) 132) [2017 108p: 12m 10s^3 10m^4 12d^3 p12g Nov 6] attractive colt: smart performer: third in listed race at Newmarket (1¼ lengths behind Frontiersman) in September: stays 1½m: acts on good to firm and good to soft going: in cheekpieces last 2 starts: wore tongue tie in 2017. *Hugo Palmer* **114**

BEST OF MY LOVE (IRE) 3 b.f. Canford Cliffs (IRE) 133 – Announcing Peace (Danehill (USA) 126) [2017 8f 8s^4 8.3d* 6.9s 8g Jul 22] €16,000F: half-sister to several winners, including smart winner up to 1½m Crosspeace (2-y-o 6f/7f winner) and useful 2-y-o 7f winner (stayed 11.4f) So Sweet (both by Cape Cross): dam of little account: fair performer: standout effort when won maiden at Nottingham in June: stays 8.5f: acts on good to soft going. *Mick Channon* **76**

BEST SOLUTION (IRE) 3 b.c. Kodiac 112 – Al Andalyya (USA) 65 (Kingmambo (USA) 125) [2017 109: a7f^4 a8f 11.6d* 12m 12m 9.9g^2 11.9g^5 12s* Oct 28] compact colt: smart performer: won Derby Trial at Lingfield (by 3¼ lengths from Glencadam Glory) in May and St Simon Stakes at Newbury (by 1¾ lengths from Raheen House) in October: 1½ lengths second to Iquitos in Grosser Dallmayr-Preis at Munich in between: stays 1½m: acts on soft and good to firm going: often races prominently. *Saeed bin Suroor* **119**

BEST TAMAYUZ 6 ch.g. Tamayuz 126 – Pink Ivory 81 (Sakhee (USA) 136) [2017 70: f8.1g^3 f7.1g^2 f8.1g^4 Dec 22] fair handicapper: stays 1¼m: acts on polytrack, fibresand, best turf form on good going: has worn headgear, including last 5 starts: usually races close up. *Scott Dixon* **66**

BEST TRIP (IRE) 10 b.g. Whipper (USA) 126 – Tereed Elhawa 75 (Cadeaux Genereux 131) [2017 95: 6m 7g 6m 7g a4.7g a4.7g Nov 13] useful handicapper at best, no form in 2017: left Marjorie Fife after fourth outing: has worn headgear/tongue tie: usually races close up. *C. von der Recke, Germany* **–**

BETJEMAN 2 b.c. (May 20) Poet's Voice 126 – Respectfilly (Mark of Esteem (IRE) 137) [2017 p8d Dec 13] 33/1, well held in minor event at Kempton. *Hughie Morrison* **–**

BETSALOTTIE 4 gr.g. Aqlaam 125 – Si Belle (IRE) 95 (Dalakhani (IRE) 133) [2017 66: p8g^3 p8g^4 p11g p12g^6 9.9g^2 9.9d 10d^2 9.9g^3 10d^5 10s^5 8g 10g^4 p8g^5 11.4d* p12g^2 p12g^5 p10g^4 Dec 13] compact gelding: fair handicapper: won at Windsor (amateur) in October: stays 1½m: acts on polytrack and good to soft going: tried in blinkers. *John Bridger* **65**

BETTY F 2 ch.f. (Feb 22) Frankel 147 – Instance 106 (Invincible Spirit (IRE) 121) [2017 6m* 6d Sep 30] first foal: dam, 6f (including at 2 yrs) and 7f winner, half-sister to smart performer up to 1¾m Seal of Approval: fairly useful form: won minor event at Newmarket (by ¾ length from Rockies Spirit) in August: eighth in Cheveley Park Stakes at same course (6½ lengths behind Clemmie) month later: will stay at least 7f: will go on improving. *Jeremy Noseda* **92 p**

BETTY GRABLE (IRE) 3 b.f. Delegator 125 – Danella (IRE) (Platini (GER) 126) [2017 7g^6 7d^5 6g^6 7d t7.1d^6 t8d Nov 10] 20,000Y: half-sister to several winners, including useful 9.5f-16.4f winner Gabrial's King (by Hurricane Run) and 9f-1½m winner Master Dan (by Mastercraftsman): dam German 2-y-o 6.5f winner: modest maiden: stays 7f: acts on tapeta: often races in rear. *Wilf Storey* **60**

BEVERLEY BULLET 4 b.g. Makfi 130 – Don't Tell Mary (IRE) 94 (Starcraft (NZ) 128) [2017 68: 7g t8s^4 9s* t8s^2 8m^3 8.3g^3 10s* 9.9g^5 6.9v* 10.5v^4 8v^6 Oct 9] leggy gelding: fair handicapper: won at Carlisle in June, Pontefract in July and Carlisle again in September: stays 1¼m: acts on tapeta, good to firm and heavy going: wears cheekpieces: front runner/races prominently, often travels strongly. *Lawrence Mullaney* **75**

BEYOND BEYOND 3 b.g. Shirocco (GER) 129 – Riverine (Risk Me (FR) 127) [2017 –: 11.4m Jun 12] maiden: hampered and eased in handicap only start in 2017: remains capable of better. *Hughie Morrison* **– p**

BEYOND CONCEIT (IRE) 8 b.g. Galileo (IRE) 134 – Baraka (IRE) 106 (Danehill (USA) 126) [2017 20f Jun 20] tall, attractive gelding: useful at best: in hood, well beaten in Ascot Stakes only start on Flat in 2017: stays 21f: acts on any turf going: smart form over hurdles. *Nicky Henderson* **–**

BEYOND EQUAL 2 b.g. (Feb 28) Kheleyf (USA) 116 – Samasana (IRE) 75 (Redback 116) [2017 6g 7.1s^{2} 7s^{6} Oct 9] fair form: standout effort when second in minor event at Chepstow in September. *Stuart Kittow* **71**

BEYOND RECALL 3 b.f. Cacique (IRE) 124 – Forgotten Dreams (IRE) 44 (Olden Times 121) [2017 58p: 8m^{2} 10.1m^{5} 9.9d 9s p8g^{3} p8g^{3} p8g^{2} t7.2d^{5} f7.1g^{6} Dec 29] fairly useful maiden: second in maiden at Kempton in November: left Luca Cumani after seventh start: stays 1¼m: acts on polytrack and good to firm going: wears headgear. *Archie Watson* **81**

BEZOS (IRE) 2 b.g. (Mar 7) Famous Name 124 – Midnight Oasis 49 (Oasis Dream 129) [2017 6.1m 6.1g^{3} 6s 8.3v 7.4s^{4} p7s^{2} t7.2g^{4} p7g* Dec 28] compact gelding: fair performer: won nursery at Lingfield in December: stays 7f: acts on polytrack: in cheekpieces last 3 starts: usually races prominently. *Richard Hannon* **78**

B FIFTY TWO (IRE) 8 br.g. Dark Angel (IRE) 113 – Petite Maxine 70 (Sharpo 132) [2017 104: 7.1g 6m 5g^{5} 6m 6m 5m^{5} 6g^{3} 5.9s^{6} 5g 6v^{3} 7.6v^{4} t6d 6v^{2} 5v^{4} Oct 16] smallish, leggy gelding: fairly useful handicapper: second at Ripon (apprentice) in September: stays 7f, usually races over shorter: acts on polytrack, good to firm and heavy going: has worn headgear/tongue tie, including often in 2017. *Marjorie Fife* **83**

BHINDI 2 b.f. (Feb 2) Casamento (IRE) 118 – Palkin 76 (Singspiel (IRE) 133) [2017 6g 6.1g^{2} 6.1g^{2} 6g 6.1s^{5} p7.5g Dec 12] sturdy filly: first foal: dam lightly-raced half-sister to useful 2-y-o 6f winner The Paddyman: fair maiden: left Eve Johnson Houghton before final outing: stays 6f. *J. Reynier, France* **70**

BHODI (IRE) 2 b.c. (Feb 1) Dark Angel (IRE) 113 – Modesty's Way (USA) (Giant's Causeway (USA) 132) [2017 6m^{6} Jul 6] first foal: dam, French 9.5f winner, half-sister to useful French 8.5f/9f winner Poupee Flash out of half-sister to high-class North American Grade 1 winners Aldebaran (at 7f/1m) and Good Journey (at 1m): 7/2, considerate introduction when well held in minor event at Newbury: should do better. *Sir Michael Stoute* **– p**

BIANCA MINOLA (FR) 3 ch.f. Shakespearean (IRE) 120 – Transylvania (FR) (Motivator 131) [2017 70: 12d 10.1g 10d^{3} 12v* t12.4g^{4} 15.9s Oct 31] sturdy filly: fair handicapper: won at Ffos Las in August: stays 1½m: acts on heavy going: in cheekpieces last 4 starts. *David Menuisier* **75**

BIBA 3 ch.f. Harbour Watch (IRE) 121 – Acicula (IRE) 96 (Night Shift (USA)) [2017 12g^{5} 9.2s^{4} 9d^{5} 12.5s Oct 9] £14,000Y: half-sister to several winners, including smart 5f and (including at 2 yrs) 6f winner Elnawin and useful winner up to 1m Elna Bright (2-y-o 6f/7f winner) (both by Elnadim): dam 2-y-o 5f/6f winner: little impact in maidens/handicap: in cheekpieces last 3 starts. *Keith Dalgleish* **50**

BIB AND TUCKER 2 br.g. (Apr 21) Dandy Man (IRE) 123 – Dhuyoof (IRE) (Sinndar (IRE) 134) [2017 6.1m 7d 6.1g Jul 20] down the field in minor events/maiden. *David Brown* **–**

BIBBIDIBOBBIDIBOO (IRE) 2 b.f. (Apr 4) Red Jazz (USA) 125 – Provence 83 (Averti (IRE) 117) [2017 6g 5.9m^{4} 7.2d^{4} 8g^{4} 7s t6g^{3} Oct 19] £42,000 2-y-o: sixth foal: half-sister to 1m-1¼m winner Glorious Dancer (by Royal Applause): dam 7f winner: fair maiden: stays 7f: acts on tapeta, good to firm and good to soft going. *Ann Duffield* **65**

BIBLIOTHECA (JPN) 4 b.f. Harbinger 140 – Taygete (USA) (Miswaki (USA) 124) [2017 72: f14g 13.1s^{2} 13.4g^{2} 12s^{3} 14s^{4} 14s p12g Nov 10] third foal: half-sister to useful 1½m winner Plato and 1½m-1¾m winner Chabada (both by Bago), both stayed 2m: dam, US 8.5f/9f winner, closely related to smart French winner up to 1m Byzantium: fair maiden: stays 13.5f: acts on soft going: front runner/races prominently. *W. P. Browne, Ireland* **76**

BICOLOUR (USA) 3 b.f. Tiznow (USA) 133 – Burmilla (USA) 112 (Storm Cat (USA)) [2017 10g t7.2g^{5} 8g^{6} 10.2f^{4} 10.2f Jul 12] sixth foal: half-sister to 3 winners in North America, including US Grade 3 9f winner Snowbell (by Tapit): dam, US Grade 2 6f winner, sister to US 2-y-o Grade 2 6f winner Magicalmysterycat: modest maiden: stays 1¼m: acts on tapeta and firm going: usually races close up. *Mark Johnston* **63**

BIDDING WAR 2 ch.f. (Apr 6) Champs Elysees 124 – Locharia 91 (Wolfhound (USA) 126) [2017 6d^{5} Sep 21] 110,000Y: half-sister to numerous winners, including 7f-8.4f winner Lockantanks (by Compton Place) and 6f-9f winner Credit Swap (by Diktat), both useful: dam 2-y-o 5f winner: 20/1, fifth in minor event at Yarmouth (2¾ lengths behind Beauty Filly) in September: open to improvement. *James Tate* **67 p**

BIDDY BRADY (USA) 2 ch.f. (Feb 22) Street Boss (USA) 124 – October Tempest (USA) (Theatrical) [2017 5s^5 5g^2 5m^3 5s^2 6v* 6d^5 Nov 11] $13,000Y, £18,000 2-y-o: tall, close-coupled filly: second foal: dam third over 8.5f in USA on only start: fair performer: won minor event at Catterick in October: stays 6f: acts on good to firm and heavy going: in hood last 2 starts: usually leads. *Tim Easterby* **73**

BIG AMIGO (IRE) 4 b.g. Bahamian Bounty 116 – Goldamour (IRE) (Fasliyev (USA) 120) [2017 73§: f6g* f6g* f6g^5 t6d t5.1g^3 f6d* f6d^4 f5g^3 t7.1g f6.1g^6 t6g 5d 5d 6g t6.1m^5 f6.1g f7.1g^4 f7.1g^3 Dec 19] fair handicapper: won at Southwell in January (twice) and March: stays 7f: acts on fibresand, tapeta and good to firm going: has worn headgear, including final start: not one to trust. *Daniel Loughnane* **55 § a77 §**

BIGBADBOY (IRE) 4 b.g. Big Bad Bob (IRE) 118 – Elegantly (IRE) (Rock of Gibraltar (IRE) 133) [2017 48: t8s t10.2d* 8.5d* 8.3s^6 10d^3 10.2g^4 t12.4d^6 Dec 16] modest handicapper: won at Newcastle (apprentice) and Beverley (amateur) in August: stays 1¼m: acts on polytrack, tapeta and good to soft going: tried in hood. *Clive Mulhall* **63**

BIG BAD LOL (IRE) 3 b.g. Big Bad Bob (IRE) 118 – Indienne (IRE) 69 (Indian Ridge 123) [2017 8.1m^6 8.3v 8s 8.3g^6 t8.6g* Dec 5] €27,000F, €39,000Y: sixth foal: half-brother to 3 winners, including 7f winner Afkar (by Invincible Spirit) and 1m winner Brave Acclaim (by Acclamation): dam maiden (stayed 1m): fair performer: won handicap at Wolverhampton in December: stays 8.5f: acts on tapeta and soft going: should improve further. *Ed Walker* **67 p**

BIG BAZ (IRE) 7 b.g. Pivotal 124 – Gracefully (IRE) 102 (Orpen (USA) 116) [2017 111: 8g 8m 8.3g^5 8m 7.9d^6 8s^3 8g^5 p8g^6 p8s* Nov 17] strong, quite attractive gelding: useful performer: won claimer at Chelmsford (by 3¾ lengths from Georgian Bay) in November: stays 8.5f: acts on polytrack, soft and good to firm going. *William Muir* **106**

BIG BRAVE BOB 2 br.g. (Feb 15) Big Bad Bob (IRE) 118 – Namaadhej (USA) (Swain (IRE) 134) [2017 5.1d^2 6d^5 Nov 11] fair form: better effort when second in minor event at Windsor (2¼ lengths behind Iconic Knight) in October: should stay 6f. *Richard Hughes* **70**

BIG CHALLENGE (IRE) 3 ch.c. Sea The Stars (IRE) 140 – Something Mon (USA) (Maria's Mon (USA) 121) [2017 90P: p11g^2 Apr 12] useful form: second in handicap at Kempton (length behind Monarchs Glen) sole start in 2017: should improve further. *Saeed bin Suroor* **97 p**

BIG CHILL (IRE) 5 b.g. Acclamation 118 – Royal Consort (IRE) (Green Desert (USA) 127) [2017 81: 7d^5 7d 8.1m^6 7g 7.1d Aug 24] close-coupled gelding: fairly useful handicapper, below form in 2017: stays 8.5f: acts on polytrack, soft and good to firm going: has worn headgear. *Patrick Chamings* **66**

BIG CITY BOY (IRE) 9 b.g. Tamarisk (IRE) 127 – Cuddles (IRE) 89 (Taufan (USA) 119) [2017 –: 6g Jul 27] modest at best, well held only 2 starts since 2015: stays 7f: acts on all-weather and good to firm going: usually wears headgear: wears tongue tie. *Phil McEntee* **–**

BIG COUNTRY (IRE) 4 b.g. High Chaparral (IRE) 132 – Mount Eliza (IRE) 99 (Danehill (USA) 126) [2017 83: t12.2g* p11g* 12m^4 10.3m* 11.8m 10.3m^2 9d 10.3g^5 Oct 14] big, lengthy gelding: smart performer: trained in 2016 by Charles O'Brien, much improved since: won maiden at Wolverhampton in February, and handicaps at Kempton (by 1½ lengths from Wild Hacked) in April and York (by neck from Burguillos) in June: second in John Smith's Cup (Handicap) back at York (¾ length behind Ballet Concerto) in July: effective at 1¼m/1½m: acts on polytrack, tapeta, good to firm and heavy going: often races prominently, usually travels strongly. *Michael Appleby* **113**

BIGDABOG 2 b.g. (May 5) Sayif (IRE) 122 – Alice's Girl (Galileo (IRE) 134) [2017 6m 5.9m Jul 14] well held in minor events. *Eric Alston* **–**

BIG EASY (GER) 10 b.g. Ransom O'War (USA) 117 – Basilea Gold (GER) 105 (Monsun (GER) 124) [2017 16d^6 Oct 6] good-topped gelding: useful handicapper at best, lightly raced on Flat: stays 2½m: acts on good to firm going: in cheekpieces last 3 starts: useful hurdler. *Ian Williams* **88**

BIG KITTEN (USA) 2 ch.c. (Feb 18) Kitten's Joy (USA) 128 – Queen Martha (USA) 85 (Rahy (USA) 115) [2017 7.4v^2 t7.1d^2 p8d^2 Nov 9] €175,000 2-y-o: third foal: closely related to a winner in USA by Medaglia d'Oro: dam, 1m winner, half-sister to US Grade 3 8.5f/9f winner Clearly A Queen: fairly useful form when second all 3 starts in minor events. *Mark Johnston* **81**

BIG LACHIE 3 b.g. Camacho 118 – Ryan's Quest (IRE) 67 (Mukaddamah (USA) 125) [2017 82: f6g^{5} 5.7f 5.1d^{5} 5.7g^{4} 6m^{6} 5m t6.1g p6g p6g^{4} t5g^{2} t5g Nov 24] good-topped gelding: fairly useful handicapper: second at Newcastle in November: left Jamie Osborne after second start: stays 6f: acts on polytrack, tapeta and good to firm going: tried in blinkers: often races towards rear. *Daniel Loughnane* **83**

BIG LES (IRE) 2 b.c. (Jan 17) Big Bad Bob (IRE) 118 – Love Match 88 (Danehill Dancer (IRE) 117) [2017 t5s^{4} t6s^{3} 5.4g^{3} 6v* 7d^{6} t6g^{5} Dec 6] €15,000F, €22,000Y, 25,000 2-y-o: second foal: half-brother to Italian 5f/6f winner (including at 2 yrs) Peppe's Island (by Frozen Power): dam 7f winner: fairly useful performer: won nursery at Pontefract (by length from Camacho Chief) in October: should be suited by 7f: acts on tapeta and heavy going. *Karen McLintock* **81**

BIG ORANGE 6 b.g. Duke of Marmalade (IRE) 132 – Miss Brown To You (IRE) 84 (Fasliyev (USA) 120) [2017 122: 15.9d^{4} 16.2m* 20m* 16g^{2} 16s Oct 21] **122**

It might have had a chequered recent history, but the three-week Tour de France remains like a religious event to many on that side of the Channel, despite the fact there hasn't been a French winner since 1985. Given that drought, it might be expected that the French public would celebrate its past champions, none more than Jacques Anquetil, the most decorated cyclist of the late-'fifties and early-'sixties who became the first five-times winner of the Tour. However, the most popular French cyclist is arguably still Anquetil's arch-rival Raymond Poulidor, even though he never won the Tour, nor even wore the yellow jersey during fourteen attempts at the race. There was more to Poulidor's association with the Tour though, as he made the final podium in Paris no fewer than eight times (including three runner-up finishes), his final appearance being a remarkable third place at the age of forty in 1976. Anquetil was clearly his superior, though, which prompted much discussion and even academic studies as to why Poulidor was the more popular—Anquetil even attracted hissing and whistling from French fans as his domination over Poulidor grew. Poulidor's attacking heart-on-his-sleeve tactics in the mountains, combined with an unpretentious upbringing as a farm worker, certainly appealed more to the French public than Anquetil's more calculated approach to riding, whilst Anquetil's somewhat aloof manner and fondness for fine living didn't really resonate with the common man. Anquetil did himself no favours either when openly admitting to using drugs (or 'stimulants' as they were known then), languidly arguing that it was a cyclist's 'human right' to seek such assistance. By contrast, Poulidor agreed in 1966 to become the first cyclist in Tour de France history to undergo a drugs test, though it was rumoured in some circles that he too may have used something stronger than Perrier water during his lengthy career. The disparity in their popularity clearly irked Anquetil, so much so that he exacted a form of revenge in that same tour of 1966 (Anquetil's final one). Once it became clear that an under-the-weather Anquetil wouldn't be able to win, he and his domestiques rode in support of surprise winner Lucien Aimar in order to ensure that Poulidor (who eventually had to settle for third) wouldn't win.

Cycling certainly isn't the only sport in which a brave and durable trier has been more popular with the public than a rival with more ability and greater achievements. For example, arguably the most popular Flat horse to run in Britain or Ireland during the twentieth century was the remarkable stayer Brown Jack, who recorded seven successive wins (the last six in the Queen Alexandra Stakes) at Royal Ascot after he had won the 1928 Champion Hurdle as a four-year-old. Such longevity is, of course, quite rare in Flat racing and goes some way to explaining Brown Jack's popularity, which led to the publication of a biography, as well as Ascot commissioning a Sir Alfred Munnings bronze statue and even a steam train being named in his honour when he retired after a hugely emotional final win in the 1934 Queen Alexandra Stakes. Brown Jack never contested Royal Ascot's premier race, the Gold Cup, because geldings were ineligible to run in any championship events at that time. It could be argued that this exclusion actually helped to make his legacy. Invershin and Trimdon were dual Gold Cup winners during this period, yet both barely merit a footnote in Flat racing history, whilst the consensus was that

Gold Cup, Royal Ascot—
having made most of the running, Big Orange keeps on gamely to repel the late challenge of odds-on Order of St George, the pair pulling clear of the 2016 St Leger winner Harbour Law

Brown Jack (for all that he managed one notable victory over Trimdon) would have struggled to achieve anything like the same level of success had he been allowed to compete in the Gold Cup.

After Brown Jack's defeat by Singapore (runner-up to Trimdon at Royal Ascot) in the 1931 Doncaster Cup, that year's *Bloodstock Breeders' Review* contained the following verdict: 'When Brown Jack won the Alexandra Stakes at Ascot there were expressions of regret that, because he is a gelding, he had not been able to run for the Gold Cup the previous afternoon. The trouncing he received from Singapore proved that he would have had no chance. Great handicapper though he is, Brown Jack lacks class.' Another popular stayer to capture the public's imagination was Persian Punch, who also had a book published about him and enjoyed a similarly lengthy career with a roll of honour that included wins in the Jockey Club Cup (three times), Goodwood Cup (twice) and Doncaster Cup. Geldings were allowed to contest the Gold Cup by this time and Persian Punch finished runner-up twice from seven attempts in the Ascot showpiece, though it's worth noting that he was never Timeform's champion stayer during that period, his rating regularly between 5 lb and 10 lb below the leading performers in his division.

Big Orange follows firmly in the hoofprints of Brown Jack and Persian Punch, being a gelding with physical presence, deep reserves of stamina and splendid battling qualities, his game front running being another thing he has in common with Persian Punch. These traits have helped Big Orange to build a sizeable following which resulted in his providing the undoubted highlight (at least in terms of crowd reaction) of Royal Ascot in the latest season when bravely holding off defending champion Order of St George in a grandstand finish to the Gold Cup, in doing so becoming the race's seventh winning gelding since the ban on them taking part was lifted in 1986. It was a vintage clash, with the contrasting tactics adopted on the pair adding to the drama. The Ballydoyle-trained Order of St George very much plays the role of Anquetil to Big Orange's Poulidor and has been Timeform's champion stayer in each of the last three seasons. The home-bred Big Orange took longer to reveal his true potential and was actually gelded as a yearling. 'He was a big, ugly, backward box walker without a great pedigree. I didn't think it was the

Mr Bill Gredley's "Big Orange"

plan to even send him into training,' is trainer Michael Bell's recollection of Big Orange as an unraced two-year-old. However, it soon became evident that the gangly youngster could run and there has been steady progression over the seasons as he has grown into his frame, his achievements including a notable Group 2 'double-double' when winning the Princess of Wales's Stakes at Newmarket and the Goodwood Cup in both 2015 and 2016.

After finishing a respectable fourth on his reappearance in the very valuable Dubai Gold Cup at Meydan in late-March (a race in which he had finished second the previous year), Big Orange was warmed up for Royal Ascot when landing the odds in convincing fashion in the Matchbook VIP Henry II Stakes on a scorching evening at Sandown nearly nine weeks later. Frankie Dettori controlled things perfectly from the front at Sandown, and Big Orange was cheered all the way back to the unsaddling enclosure. Dettori was unfortunately forced to miss Royal Ascot through injury, with James Doyle deputising on 5/1-shot Big Orange, who started second favourite behind odds-on Order of St George in a fourteen-runner renewal of the Gold Cup. The tone was set as soon as the stalls opened, with Doyle having Big Orange in his customary position at the head of affairs, and Ryan Moore settling Order of St George down the field with only one behind him. After being briefly headed by Quest For More, Big Orange then dictated it from a circuit out, at just a modest pace for much of the way, Doyle possibly conscious that his mount was tackling two and a half miles for the first time. Order of St George still had plenty to do in Swinley Bottom and was disputing twelfth entering the home turn, where he was forced wide to begin his challenge. Big Orange stole a march when sent for home in earnest entering the straight and, holding a lead of three lengths a furlong out, he had to dig very deep under pressure to withstand Order of St George's strong late surge, just getting home in a head-bobbing finish. It was a fine tactical ride by Doyle, with Big Orange clearly enjoying the run of things compared to the runner-up, though the fact that the pair pulled six lengths clear of 2016 St Leger winner Harbour Law in third showed there was plenty of substance to the form.

Dettori was back on board Big Orange in the Goodwood Cup six weeks later and, although unable to justify short-priced favouritism in his bid for a record-breaking third successive win in the race (another great favourite Double Trigger won the race three times but not successively), Big Orange still ran almost right up to his best in splitting the three-year-olds Stradivarius and Desert Skyline. Big Orange was forced into setting a stronger tempo than he had at Royal Ascot and couldn't hold off Stradivarius inside the final furlong, eventually going down by a length and three quarters—the winner franked the form by finishing a close third in the St Leger on his next start. The Irish St Leger and Prix du Cadran were cited as possible targets for Big Orange, but he was ruled out of both on account of late rain softening the ground, his scratching from the latter coming at the eleventh hour after making the trip to Chantilly—'He is a bit of a worrier on his trips and was put in a particularly noisy stable, so he also had an unsettled night there and worked himself up into a right tizz,' explained Bell.

Given the obvious misgivings about running Big Orange in testing conditions, it was somewhat surprising to see him allowed to take his chance in the Long Distance Cup back at Ascot on British Champions' Day in late-October, when the ground was very soft. Dettori sided with Stradivarius, with Doyle back in the plate on Big Orange. With conditions against him, Big Orange was headed fully five furlongs out and dropped away soon afterwards, eventually finishing a well-beaten eleventh of thirteen behind Order of St George (Stradivarius finished third). To compound matters, Doyle was handed a seven-day careless riding ban for his part in an incident in which rank outsider Stars Over The Sea was nearly brought down at around halfway (Doyle had also picked up a two-day whip ban after his winning Gold Cup ride, which contributed to a fifteen-day ban later in the summer as a result of the totting up procedure).

Big Orange (b.g. 2011)	Duke of Marmalade (IRE) (b 2004)	Danehill (b 1986)	Danzig
			Razyana
		Love Me True (ch 1998)	Kingmambo
			Lassie's Lady
	Miss Brown To You (IRE) (b 2005)	Fasliyev (b 1997)	Nureyev
			Mr P's Princess
		Almaaseh (b 1988)	Dancing Brave
			Al Bahathri

Big by name and big by nature (you can't miss him in the paddock), Big Orange actually has winning form on soft from earlier in his career but, given his giant stride, it's by no means surprising that he has proved ideally suited by less testing conditions (his last six wins have been on good to firm). He isn't a sluggard by any means and has shown his very best form at trips ranging from a mile and a half to two and a half miles. Big Orange's pedigree has been discussed in previous editions of *Racehorses* and, surprisingly for one who stays so well, there is plenty of speed to be found in his family tree, both his grandsires, Danehill and Fasliyev, being sprinters and his dam being a half-sister to the smart five-furlong performer Almaty, as well as Hong Kong champion Military Attack who won good races at a mile and a quarter. Big Orange is one of three winners so far out of the fairly useful miler Miss Brown To You (who also raced for Bell and Big Orange's owner-breeder Bill Gredley), the latest being The Paris Shrug (by Manduro), who won a mile and a half maiden on the all-weather at Dundalk in late-2016 before being retired to the paddocks (she was covered by Pride of Dubai in 2017). Her year-younger half-brother Stormy Blues (by Sepoy) showed fairly useful form when runner-up in a ten-furlong maiden at Nottingham, but was sold cheaply by Godolphin after suffering a breathing problem on his only subsequent outing. Bell and Gredley have Big Orange's latest sibling to reach the racecourse, the Poet's Voice filly India, who hinted at promise when down the field in a couple of two-year-old minor events in the autumn.

The headline name in the bottom line of Big Orange's pedigree is his third dam Al Bahathri, the winner of the 1985 Irish One Thousand Guineas who also did very well for Hamdan Al-Maktoum at stud, her most notable offspring being the Two Thousand Guineas and Champion Stakes winner Haafhd. Miss Brown To You is also a half-sister, incidentally, to the dam of popular globe-trotter Red Cadeaux, who was runner-up three times in the Melbourne Cup. Big Orange has also tried his hand in the 'race that stops a nation', managing fifth on his first trip Down Under in 2015 before finishing a respectable tenth under joint top weight twelve months later. There are several well-held efforts to be found in Big Orange's record, though his loyal followers seem more than willing to forgive these and he always tends to bounce back quickly. He has an excellent attitude to racing (for all that he wears headgear nowadays) and should continue to give his fan club plenty more to cheer about in the seasons to come.

Big Orange ended 2017 with a Timeform rating 6 lb lower than that of divisional leader Order of St George, with whom his head-to-head record stands at one-one. Order of St George will almost certainly be added to Coolmore's stallion roster at some time in the future, but he's due to race on in 2018 and will hopefully face a mouth-watering rematch with Big Orange back at Royal Ascot (they are currently priced at around 7/2 and 7/1 respectively in the ante-post markets). As for those French cycling rivals, they actually became firm friends once both had retired from the saddle, so much so that Poulidor visited the bedside of an ailing Anquetil in his final days. Anquetil, who succumbed to stomach cancer aged just fifty-three, is reported to have indulged in some gallows humour with his former rival: 'Once again my old friend, you will be second to me!' *Michael Bell*

BIG SIGH (IRE) 3 ch.c. Raven's Pass (USA) 133 – Sospira (Cape Cross (IRE) 129) **80** [2017 72: a8f 8.9g^{3} 12s^{2} 11.8v* 11.5d^{5} Oct 24] fairly useful handicapper: won at Haydock in September: stays 1½m: acts on tapeta, best turf form on soft/heavy going: tried in blinkers/tongue tie: often races prominently. *Ismail Mohammed*

BIG STORM COMING 7 b.g. Indesatchel (IRE) 120 – Amber Valley 88 (Foxhound **86** (USA) 103) [2017 84: 7.2m* 6.9g^{2} 8m Aug 26] fairly useful handicapper: won at Musselburgh in June: stays 1m: acts on polytrack, fibresand, good to firm and good to soft going: tried in blinkers: front runner/races prominently. *David Brown*

BIG TIME DANCER (IRE) 4 b.g. Zoffany (IRE) 121 – Final Opinion (IRE) 92 (King's **71** Theatre (IRE) 128) [2017 77p: 7.8s^{6} 8.5f^{5} 7.8s^{6} 8m 10d* 10g 14d^{5} Oct 20] fair handicapper: won at Leicester (apprentice) in September: stays 1¼m: acts on soft and good to firm going: has worn cheekpieces, including last 4 starts. *Brian Ellison*

BIG TIME (IRE) 6 br.g. Kheleyf (USA) 116 – Beguine (USA) 77 (Green Dancer (USA) **105** 132) [2017 108: p6m^{2} 6m 6.3f 7d 6v 6d Oct 27] strong gelding: useful handicapper: second at Lingfield (length behind Kasbah) in January: stays 8.5f, races mainly at shorter: acts on polytrack, fibresand, soft and good to firm going: wears headgear: sold 25,000 gns in October, sent to UAE. *Kevin Ryan*

BIG TIME MAYBE (IRE) 2 b.g. (Apr 30) Dandy Man (IRE) 123 – Divine Design **92** (IRE) 77 (Barathea (IRE) 127) [2017 5f^{2} 5.1m 5s^{4} 5.1d^{3} p5g^{3} 5s^{3} p5g* t5.1m* Oct 28] €31,000F, £44,000Y: fifth foal: half-brother to smart 5f/6f winner (including at 2 yrs) Angelic Lord (by Dark Angel): dam maiden (stayed 1m): fairly useful performer: won nurseries at Kempton and Wolverhampton (by 2¼ lengths from Our Man In Havana) in October: raced only at 5f: acts on polytrack, tapeta and firm going: in headgear last 4 starts: in tongue tie last 2: usually leads, often travels strongly. *Tom Dascombe*

BIG TOUR (IRE) 3 b.c. Dubawi (IRE) 129 – Alsindi (IRE) 106 (Acclamation 118) [2017 **106** 71p: 8m^{2} 8.1m* 10v^{2} t8.6g^{4} p7s* 7d* 7.2v Oct 16] well-made colt: useful performer: won maiden at Windsor (by 3¾ lengths from Hyperloop) in July, and handicaps at Chelmsford (by ½ length from Summer Chorus) and Yarmouth (by 2¼ lengths from Mountain Rescue) in September: best form at 7f: acts on polytrack, good to firm and heavy going: usually races prominently. *Saeed bin Suroor*

BIG WHISKEY (IRE) 7 ch.g. Ad Valorem (USA) 125 – El Opera (IRE) 100 (Sadler's – Wells (USA) 132) [2017 88: p8g Jan 19] sturdy gelding: useful performer at best: tailed off in claimer only start in 2017: stayed 1m: acted on polytrack, firm and soft going: tried in tongue tie: dead. *Clare Ellam*

BILASH 10 gr.g. Choisir (AUS) 126 – Goldeva 104 (Makbul 104) [2017 56: t5.1m t5.1f 5.1m 5g Aug 18] small gelding: fair at best, no form in 2017: tried in cheekpieces/tongue tie. *Sarah Hollinshead* –

BILKO'S BACK (IRE) 5 b.g. Big Bad Bob (IRE) 118 – Chica Roca (USA) 49 (Woodman (USA) 126) [2017 –: t16.3d t10.2g t12.4d t12.4d 8v Nov 7] little form on Flat: wears tongue tie. *Susan Corbett* –

BILL CODY (IRE) 2 b.g. (Apr 3) Declaration of War (USA) 128 – Call This Cat (IRE) 66 (One Cool Cat (USA) 123) [2017 t9.5g t8.6d^5 p8g Dec 20] modest form, best effort on debut. *Jamie Osborne* **59**

BILLESDON BESS 3 br.f. Dick Turpin (IRE) 127 – Coplow 84 (Manduro (GER) 135) [2017 87: 7m^5 9.9d^2 9.9m* 9.9m^2 9.9v* 9.9m* 9.9s^5 Sep 27] lengthy, rather unfurnished filly: useful performer: won handicaps at Salisbury (by ¾ length from Dubara) in June and Goodwood (by length from Titi Makfi) in August, and listed race back at Salisbury (by length from High Hopes) later in August: stays 1¼m: acts on good to firm and heavy going: front runner/races prominently. *Richard Hannon* **106**

BILLESDON BROOK 2 ch.f. (Feb 24) Champs Elysees 124 – Coplow 84 (Manduro (GER) 135) [2017 5m^3 6g^2 6f^2 p7g* 7d^3 7v* 7g* 8g^5 Sep 14] well-made filly: second foal: half-sister to useful winner up to 1¼m Billesdon Bess (2-y-o 7f winner, by Dick Turpin): dam, maiden (stayed 1¼m), half-sister to smart 2-y-o 6f/7f winner Piping Rock: useful performer: won minor event at Kempton in July, and nursery and Prestige Stakes (by ¾ length from Whitefountainfairy) at Goodwood in August: stays 7f: acts on polytrack and any turf going. *Richard Hannon* **99**

BILLIEBROOKEDIT (IRE) 2 ch.c. (Apr 12) Dragon Pulse (IRE) 114 – Klang (IRE) 59 (Night Shift (USA)) [2017 5g^6 5.1d^3 6f 5v^4 5d 5d^6 Oct 11] modest maiden: should stay 6f: acts on heavy going: tried in hood: front runner/races prominently. *Steph Hollinshead* **64**

BILLIE FLYNN 2 b.f. (Mar 16) Lawman (FR) 121 – Lyric Art (USA) 65 (Red Ransom (USA)) [2017 8.3v Nov 8] €13,000Y: fourth foal: half-sister to 1½m winner Knight Music and winner up to 1¼m Mirsaalah (2-y-o 1m winner) (both by Sir Percy): dam, 7f winner, closely related to Park Hill Stakes winner Meeznah: 80/1, well held in maiden at Nottingham. *Harry Dunlop* –

BILLS DELIGHT 3 b.f. Compton Place 125 – Sing Alana Sing 49 (Singspiel (IRE) 133) [2017 –: 5d 5.1d Aug 24] no form: tried in blinkers. *Bill Turner* –

BILLY BOND 5 b.g. Monsieur Bond (IRE) 120 – Princess Cocoa (IRE) 86 (Desert Sun 120) [2017 82: 8.3g^6 t8.6g 8.3m^3 9.2g^5 8m^2 8g^2 7.4s 8g 9v* 8s 8v^6 t8d^3 t8.6g Nov 18] fair handicapper: won at Carlisle in September: stays 9f: acts on all-weather, good to firm and heavy going: usually wears headgear: sometimes slowly away. *Richard Fahey* **67**

BILLY BOOTH (IRE) 2 br.g. (Apr 19) Big Bad Bob (IRE) 118 – Lady Natilda 64 (First Trump 118) [2017 6d 6g^5 5m Jul 8] smallish gelding: modest form at best in maidens/minor event: tried in cheekpieces. *Gay Kelleway* **57**

BILLYCOCK HILL 2 b.c. (Apr 8) Kyllachy 129 – Red Kyte 91 (Hawk Wing (USA) 136) [2017 6g p7d Oct 6] fair form: better effort when seventh in maiden at Newbury (6½ lengths behind Beshaayir) in September: sold 11,000 gns, sent to Spain. *Tom Dascombe* **70**

BILLY DYLAN (IRE) 2 b.g. (Feb 6) Excelebration (IRE) 133 – It's True (IRE) (Kheleyf (USA) 116) [2017 6s^6 5.3d* 5m 5.1d* 6d^3 p5s^2 6g Oct 7] €75,000F, 62,000Y: well-made gelding: second foal: dam once-raced half-sister to very smart winner up to 1m Kahal: fairly useful performer: won minor events at Brighton in June and Chester in July: stays 5.5f: acts on good to firm and good to soft going: often races prominently: sold to join David O'Meara 15,000 gns in October. *Richard Hannon* **87**

BILLYOAKES (IRE) 5 b.g. Kodiac 112 – Reality Check (IRE) 73 (Sri Pekan (USA) 117) [2017 79: p7g^3 p6m^4 t7.1g^5 t6g^6 5.3g^3 p7d p5g^3 p6g 5d^6 p6d^3 p6g^6 t5.1g^5 p6g^3 p6g* p6g^5 Dec 31] stocky gelding: fair handicapper: won at Lingfield in December: stays 7f: acts on polytrack, tapeta, good to firm and heavy going: wears cheekpieces. *Charlie Wallis* **73**

BILLY RAY 2 b.c. (Apr 17) Sixties Icon 125 – Fiumicino 87 (Danehill Dancer (IRE) 117) [2017 9.9s p8g^6 Oct 14] modest form: better effort when sixth in minor event at Kempton. *Mick Channon* **58**

BILLY ROBERTS (IRE) 4 b.g. Multiplex 114 – Mi Amor (IRE) 47 (Alzao (USA) 117) [2017 85: t8g 8g* 8.5f 7.8g 8.3g 9.1g^3 8m Aug 30] compact gelding: fair handicapper: won at Pontefract in April: stays 1m: acts on firm and good to soft going: usually races prominently. *Richard Guest* **79**

BILLY'S BOOTS 3 ch.g. Winker Watson 118 – Solmorin (Fraam 114) [2017 67: t6g^{5} p6g t5.1g p5g^{2} t5d^{4} f5g^{3} 6g^{6} 6g p5g^{3} p6g^{4} t5g 5.1d^{6} p5g^{2} Oct 3] compact gelding: modest handicapper: left Dean Ivory after third start: stays 6f: acts on polytrack, tapeta, good to firm and good to soft going: has worn headgear, including last 2 starts. *J. R. Jenkins* **62**

BILLYS CONNOISSEUR (IRE) 4 b.g. Art Connoisseur (IRE) 121 – Tarziyma (IRE) (Kalanisi (IRE) 132) [2017 t8g^{5} t8d f8d^{6} Mar 21] little impact in maidens. *Tim Easterby* **–**

BILLY STAR 2 b.g. (Apr 10) Sixties Icon 125 – Appreciative (Cockney Rebel (IRE) 127) [2017 p8d p8g Dec 20] well held in minor events. *Jimmy Fox* **–**

BIN BATTUTA 3 ch.c. Dubawi (IRE) 129 – Land of Dreams 115 (Cadeaux Genereux 131) [2017 79: 10.3g* 10m^{3} 10m^{4} 12m 12g* 13.9m^{2} Aug 26] sturdy colt: smart handicapper: won at Doncaster (by neck from First Nation) in April and Ascot (by head from Cape Coast) in July: second in Melrose Stakes at York (neck behind Secret Advisor) in August: stays 1¾m: acts on good to firm going: in headgear last 3 starts: held up. *Saeed bin Suroor* **112**

BIN DAAHIR 2 b.c. (Feb 15) Exceed And Excel (AUS) 126 – Beach Frolic (Nayef (USA) 129) [2017 5.7f 6.1m^{4} Jun 16] modest form on second of 2 starts in minor events. *Charles Hills* **57**

BING BANG BANK (IRE) 3 br.g. Big Bad Bob (IRE) 118 – Causeway Charm (USA) 60 (Giant's Causeway (USA) 132) [2017 –p: 10m^{5} 9.8g^{5} Apr 29] fair form: better effort in 2017 when fifth in maiden at Ripon in April: has joined G. Hayes. *David Barron* **65**

BINGO GEORGE (IRE) 4 b.g. Holy Roman Emperor (IRE) 125 – Kalleidoscope 78 (Pivotal 124) [2017 72, a64: p7m^{6} 7d 6g^{5} 6m^{3} t6.1g 7.1g 6g^{6} 6g^{5} 6m 5.7s 8.1m f6.1g* f6.1g p7g f6.1g f7.1g^{5} Dec 4] good-topped gelding: modest handicapper: won at Southwell in October: left Andrew Balding after fourth start: stays 6f: acts on fibresand and good to firm going: has worn headgear, including final start: often in tongue tie in 2017: races prominently. *Mark Rimell* **60**

BINKY BLUE (IRE) 5 b.m. Approve (IRE) 112 – Sabander Bay (USA) 51 (Lear Fan (USA) 130) [2017 74: t7.1g^{6} t7.1g t6g t7.1g^{bd} t7.1g^{5} p8f^{2} t7.1g p8g^{5} t7.2g 8.3f^{3} 8g^{5} t8.6g 7.1g^{5} p7s^{3} p7g^{3} p7g^{2} p8g p7g^{2} t7.2g p7g Dec 30] modest handicapper on turf, fair on all-weather: stays 1m: acts on polytrack, tapeta, good to firm and heavy going: has worn headgear, including often in 2017. *Daniel Loughnane* **59 a67**

BINT ARCANO (FR) 4 ch.f. Arcano (IRE) 122 – Rosa Mundi (Alhaarth (IRE) 126) [2017 80: t7.1g* t7.1d^{6} t7.1d* t7.1g^{4} 7g 7d^{4} 7m* 7.2m^{3} 7v* 7d^{4} Aug 24] compact filly: useful handicapper: won at Wolverhampton in January, Newcastle in March, Catterick in June and Doncaster (by 2 lengths from Peak Princess) in July: stays 7f: acts on tapeta, good to firm and heavy going: usually races prominently, strong traveller. *Julie Camacho* **98 a90**

BINT DANDY (IRE) 6 b.m. Dandy Man (IRE) 123 – Ceol Loch Aoidh (IRE) 74 (Medecis 119) [2017 90, a101: p7m^{3} p8d^{2} p7g t8.6g^{3} p7g^{6} p8g^{6} 8m* p8s 9.1g^{6} 7s^{4} 7m^{2} 8d^{6} 7.6d^{3} p8g^{5} 8m p8g^{2} p8m Nov 25] smallish, sparely-made mare: fairly useful handicapper: won at Yarmouth in May: second at Kempton in November: best up to 1m: acts on polytrack, tapeta and good to firm going: wears headgear. *Chris Dwyer* **91**

BINT HUWAAR (USA) 2 b.f. (May 9) More Than Ready (USA) 120 – Miss Mary Apples (USA) (Clever Trick (USA)) [2017 6.1m^{5} p7g Oct 5] $390,000Y, $1,000,000 2-y-o: half-sister to several winners in USA: dam US winner up to 6f (4.5f winner at 2 yrs when second in Grade 2 6f event): modest form: blinkered second start: sent to UAE. *George Peckham* **50**

BIOTIC 6 b.g. Aqlaam 125 – Bramaputra (IRE) 88 (Choisir (AUS) 126) [2017 84: 10g^{3} 10m^{2} 10m^{4} 9.9m^{4} 9.1m^{6} p10g p8g p12g^{5} p10d Nov 22] tall, good-topped gelding: fairly useful handicapper: second at Windsor in June, lost form later in year: stays 11f: acts on polytrack and good to firm going: sometimes in headgear in 2017: has worn tongue tie. *Rod Millman* **81 a70**

BIRCH GROVE (IRE) 2 b.f. (Apr 13) Galileo (IRE) 134 – Danehurst 118 (Danehill (USA) 126) [2017 8s^{4} Oct 28] good-bodied filly: half-sister to several winners, including useful 7f winner Time To Reason (by Kyllachy) and 2-y-o 6f winner Ski Slope (by Three Valleys): dam, 5f (including at 2 yrs)/6f winner, half-sister to smart performer up to 1½m Mighty: 5/1, fourth in minor event at Newbury (3¾ lengths behind Red Starlight) in October: will improve. *David Simcock* **70 p**

BIRCHWOOD (IRE) 4 b.c. Dark Angel (IRE) 113 – Layla Jamil (IRE) 85 (Exceed And Excel (AUS) 126) [2017 115: 6g 7m[6] 6m 8s[3] 7s 7s Oct 7] good-topped colt: smart handicapper: third in Betfred Mile at Goodwood (¾ length behind Master The World) in August: stays 1m: acts on firm and soft going: has worn headgear, including once in 2017: front runner/races prominently. *Richard Fahey* **112**

BIRDCAGE 4 b.f. Showcasing 117 – Trinny (Rainbow Quest (USA) 134) [2017 –: 5g May 13] fairly useful at best, last in handicaps all 4 starts since 2015: has worn headgear. *Patrick Morris* **–**

BIRDETTE (IRE) 2 b.f. (Apr 9) Epaulette (AUS) 126 – Madam Ninette (Mark of Esteem (IRE) 137) [2017 5.9s[4] 6g 8d[6] Oct 27] 34,000Y: half-sister to several winners, including 6f (including at 2 yrs) winner Blessington (by Kheleyf) and 5f (including at 2 yrs) winner Excelette (by Exceed And Excel), both smart: dam unraced: modest form in minor events/ maiden. *Mark Johnston* **63**

BIRD FOR LIFE 3 b.f. Delegator 125 – Birdolini 82 (Bertolini (USA) 125) [2017 5.7m[4] 6.1m[6] t7.2g[6] p7g p8d p10g[5] p12g[4] p12g* p12g Nov 21] first foal: dam 2-y-o 7f winner who stayed 1¼m: modest handicapper: won at Kempton in November: stays 1½m: acts on polytrack. *Mark Usher* **58**

BIRDIE MUST FLY 5 ch.m. Major Cadeaux 121 – Musical Day 80 (Singspiel (IRE) 133) [2017 –: t7.1m p7d Jan 17] close-coupled mare: little form: tried in blinkers. *Jimmy Fox* **–**

BIRIKYNO 6 b.g. Piccolo 121 – Alvarinho Lady 72 (Royal Applause 124) [2017 41: 7.4v 8g Oct 16] good-topped gelding: maiden, lightly raced and little form since 2013: tried in cheekpieces. *Matthew Salaman* **45**

BIRTHDAY GIRL (IRE) 2 b.f. (Apr 2) Excelebration (IRE) 133 – Street Style (IRE) 83 (Rock of Gibraltar (IRE) 133) [2017 7s Oct 9] 27,000Y: fifth foal: half-sister to 1¼m winner (stays 13f) Moss Street (by Moss Vale) and smart 1¼m-1½m winner (stays 1¾m) Panama Hat (by Medicean): dam 9.5f winner: 20/1, well held in minor event at Salisbury. *Amanda Perrett* **–**

BIRTHRIGHT 2 b.c. (Mar 29) Mawatheeq (USA) 126 – Pooka's Daughter (IRE) 63 (Eagle Eyed (USA) 111) [2017 8d[6] Sep 20] 800F: half-brother to 3 winners, including useful 6f (including at 2 yrs) winner Avonmore Star (by Avonbridge) and 1m winner Padleyourowncanoe (by Nayef), stays 1¾m: dam 7f-8.5f winner (1m winner at 2 yrs): 50/1, sixth in minor event at Sandown (7¼ lengths behind Kitaabaat) in September: should improve. *Richard Hannon* **72 p**

BISHOP OF BLING (IRE) 4 b.g. Big Bad Bob (IRE) 118 – Convent Girl (IRE) 107 (Bishop of Cashel 122) [2017 77: f11.1g[3] t10.2s 12v[4] 10.2g[6] Aug 10] fair maiden: stays 1½m: best form on soft/heavy going. *Chris Wall* **69**

BISHOPS CANNINGS (IRE) 3 b.f. Cape Blanco (IRE) 130 – Carini 97 (Vettori (IRE) 119) [2017 p10g[3] p10g[2] p12g[3] p12m* Mar 29] 12,000Y: sister to Italian 1¼m winner Zollikon and half-sister to 3 winners abroad, including French 2-y-o 5.5f winner Araneide (by Aragorn): dam, 2-y-o 7f/1m winner, later 1m winner in USA: fair form: won maiden at Lingfield in March: stays 1½m. *David Elsworth* **72**

BISMARCK THE FLYER (IRE) 3 b.g. Requinto (IRE) 109 – Livia's Wake (IRE) 81 (Galileo (IRE) 134) [2017 69: t6m[3] t5d[5] t6f[5] 7g[3] 6g[5] 6m[5] t6.1g Jun 26] modest handicapper: stays 7f: acts on tapeta and good to soft going: tried in cheekpieces: sent to Germany. *Ollie Pears* **62**

BITE MY TONGUE (IRE) 4 b.g. Vale of York (IRE) 117 – Near Relation (Distant Relative 128) [2017 t8.6g t12.2g Apr 22] well beaten in pair of maidens: has joined John O'Neill. *Tony Carroll* **–**

BITHYNIA (IRE) 3 b.f. Kodiac 112 – Alexander Confranc (IRE) 73 (Magical Wonder (USA) 125) [2017 71: t6f[3] p5g[3] p5g[4] 6.1g 5d[2] 5m[6] 5f 5v f5g[3] 5d[5] Sep 12] neat filly: fair maiden: left David Evans after third start: stays 6f: acts on tapeta and good to soft going: sometimes in headgear: has worn tongue tie: usually races prominently. *Christopher Kellett* **74**

BIT OF A QUIRKE 4 ch.g. Monsieur Bond (IRE) 120 – Silk (IRE) (Machiavellian (USA) 123) [2017 63: 10g[2] 9.9m* 10m[5] 9.9m* 10g[4] 10g 8s[4] 9.9m[5] Aug 27] fair handicapper: won at Beverley in April and June: stays 1¼m: acts on soft and good to firm going: front runner/races prominently. *Mark Walford* **74**

BITTERSWEET (IRE) 3 ch.f. Power 117 – Jessie Jane (IRE) 90 (Dylan Thomas (IRE) 132) [2017 8v[5] Oct 9] €10,000Y: first foal: dam, 10.7f winner, half-sister to useful/ ungenuine stayer Icon Dream: well held in maiden. *Jason Ward* **–**

BIZET (IRE) 3 b.g. Helmet (AUS) 127 – Morinda 56 (Selkirk (USA) 129) [2017 68: p10g^{4} 10.2m p10g^{6} 11.4m^{6} 8d^{6} 10d^{3} 16.1d 14s 11.9m^{2} p16g^{5} 9.9d^{5} 11.2m^{2} 9d^{6} 11.6d^{3} 11.5d^{6} 11.5g Oct 16] compact gelding: modest maiden: stays 1½m: acts on polytrack and good to firm going: usually wears headgear: often starts slowly/races in rear: temperamental. *John Ryan* **60 §**

BLACKADDER 5 b.g. Myboycharlie (IRE) 118 – Famcred 89 (Inchinor 119) [2017 –: 7.1g 6s 6.1g^{3} 6s^{6} 7d^{5} 8v p8g p6g^{5} p6g Dec 12] modest maiden handicapper: stays 7f: acts on polytrack and soft going: has worn headgear. *Mark Gillard* **50**

BLACK AGNES (IRE) 4 b.f. Holy Roman Emperor (IRE) 125 – Nice To Know (FR) 89 (Machiavellian (USA) 123) [2017 61, a72: p8g^{2} p8g p12g^{6} 10m 8.3g^{3} 10.3m^{4} p8g Oct 6] fair handicapper: stays 1½m: acts on polytrack, good to firm and heavy going: wears blinkers: often races in rear. *L. Smyth, Ireland* **71**

BLACK BESS 4 br.f. Dick Turpin (IRE) 127 – Spring Clean (FR) 89 (Danehill (USA) 126) [2017 92: p7g 7d* 7g^{2} 6g 7.6d^{3} 7v* 8g^{3} 8s^{6} 7s^{2} Oct 9] angular filly: useful handicapper: won at Lingfield in May and Sandown (by 1½ lengths from Redgrave) in August: second at Brighton (neck behind Staintondale Lass) in May, third at Goodwood (2½ lengths behind Dubara) in August and second in minor event at Salisbury (1¼ lengths behind George William) in October: stays 7f: acts on polytrack and heavy going: usually leads. *Jim Boyle* **98**

BLACK BOLT (IRE) 3 br.c. Cape Cross (IRE) 129 – Safiya Song (IRE) (Intikhab (USA) 135) [2017 86p: 10d 7m Aug 26] fairly useful form when won maiden at 2 yrs: well beaten in handicaps both starts in 2017: best effort at 7f. *Richard Hannon* **–**

BLACK BUBBA (IRE) 3 b.g. Arcano (IRE) 122 – Assumption (IRE) 57 (Beckett (IRE) 116) [2017 69: 7d^{3} 6m^{2} 7g^{2} 6d^{5} 5.7f t6.1g^{5} Jun 26] sturdy gelding: modest maiden: stays 6f: acts on soft and good to firm going: tried in visor. *David Evans* **58**

BLACK CAESAR (IRE) 6 b.g. Bushranger (IRE) 119 – Evictress (IRE) 70 (Sharp Victor (USA) 114) [2017 77: p7g* p7g p7g^{3} 7g^{3} 6g^{2} 6d* 7m^{3} 6.1g^{2} 7s* 7d^{3} 7g^{6} 7d^{5} 7v^{2} p7g^{6} f7.1g Dec 1] good-topped gelding: fairly useful handicapper on turf, fair on all-weather: won at Lingfield in January, and Brighton in June and September (by 6 lengths from Miss Icon): stays 1m: acts on polytrack, good to firm and heavy going: tried in blinkers. *Philip Hide* **86 a79**

BLACK DAVE (IRE) 7 b.g. Excellent Art 125 – Miss Latina (IRE) 74 (Mozart (IRE) 131) [2017 82: t8.6m* t7.1m^{4} p11g p10g^{3} p10g^{4} p10g^{5} p8g t8.6g^{6} 7g^{4} 7.6g* p10g^{5} 7m^{6} 8.1g^{2} 8.1v^{5} t8.6g t9.5g p8s^{pu} p10g* Dec 20] tall gelding: fair performer: won seller at Wolverhampton in January, and claimer in May and seller in December, last 2 at Lingfield: stays 1¼m: acts on all-weather, good to firm and heavy going: has worn visor, including final start: often leads. *David Evans* **69 a77**

BLACK FRIDAY 2 b.c. (Mar 26) Equiano (FR) 127 – The Clan Macdonald 85 (Intikhab (USA) 135) [2017 6g^{4} 5m^{3} 5v^{2} 6g Oct 13] fair form: should be suited by 6f. *Karen McLintock* **79**

BLACK GRASS 4 b.g. Monsieur Bond (IRE) 120 – Alustar 71 (Emarati (USA) 74) [2017 88: 5m* 5g 5m^{4} 5m^{6} 5s^{2} 5m^{6} 5g Jul 14] fairly useful handicapper: won at Ripon (apprentice, dead-heated with Foxtrot Knight) in April: best form at 5f: acted on tapeta, good to firm and heavy going: tried in visor: raced prominently: dead. *Michael Easterby* **88**

BLACK HAMBLETON 4 b.g. Dick Turpin (IRE) 127 – Duena (Grand Lodge (USA) 125) [2017 –: f7g t7.1d* t8d t7.1g Nov 24] fair handicapper: won at Newcastle in January: stays 7f: acts on tapeta and soft going. *Bryan Smart* **72**

BLACKHEATH 2 b.g. (Apr 26) Excelebration (IRE) 133 – Da's Wish (IRE) (Sadler's Wells (USA) 132) [2017 7m 6g^{3} 6g p6d^{2} Nov 9] 15,500F, €50,000Y: fourth foal: closely related to 5f winner (stays 7f) I Will Excel (by Exceed And Excel) and half-brother to useful 2-y-o 6f winner Moral High Ground (by Elnadim): dam unraced half-sister to smart 1½m-1¾m winner Katiykha: fairly useful form: second in nursery at Chelmsford in November: should stay at least 7f: will go on improving. *Ed Walker* **82 p**

BLACK HOLE SUN 5 ch.m. Black Sam Bellamy (IRE) 121 – Black Annie (IRE) (Anshan 119) [2017 53: t9.5g* p12d^{3} Feb 3] modest performer: won handicap at Wolverhampton (apprentice, by 2 lengths from Siouxperhero) in January: stayed 1½m: acted on polytrack and tapeta: front runner/raced prominently: dead. *Ian Williams* **61**

BLACK ICEMAN 9 gr.g. Iceman 117 – Slite 55 (Mind Games 121) [2017 46: t12.2g Aug 10] poor handicapper: stays 16.5f: acts on polytrack and tapeta: has worn headgear. *Lydia Pearce* **–**

BLACK ISLE BOY (IRE) 3 b.g. Elzaam (AUS) 115 – Shadow Mountain (Selkirk (USA) 129) [2017 57p: 6m* 6m* 6m* 6d^{6} 6f^{2} 5.4d 5m Aug 26] fairly useful performer: won maiden at Pontefract in April and handicaps at Hamilton and Ayr (by short head from The McGregornator) in May: stays 6f: acts on good to firm going. *David O'Meara* **90**

BLACK LACE 2 b.f. (Apr 6) Showcasing 117 – Ivory Lace 96 (Atraf 116) [2017 p7g p6g Nov 29] compact filly: third foal: half-sister to 1¼m winner Solveig's Song (by Norse Dancer): dam 5f (including at 2 yrs) to 7f winner: well beaten in minor events: tried in cheekpieces. *Steve Woodman* **–**

BLACKLOOKS (IRE) 2 b.g. (Mar 6) Society Rock (IRE) 126 – Mosaique Beauty (IRE) 77 (Sadler's Wells (USA) 132) [2017 7d^{6} 7g t6s 7v^{5} 7d* 8.3v^{ro} p8s t6g t7.2g* Dec 22] €41,000F, 46,000Y: compact gelding: sixth foal: half-brother to 3 winners, including 2-y-o 5f winner Piranha (by Exceed And Excel) and 2-y-o 7f winner Sekumkum (by Invincible Spirit): dam, 13f winner, half-sister to smart performer up to 1½m Subtle Power: fairly useful performer: won nurseries at Leicester in October and Wolverhampton (by 1¼ lengths from Swissal) in December: stays 8.5f: acts on tapeta and heavy going: tried in cheekpieces: often races freely: has hung badly left (best treated with caution). *Ivan Furtado* **85 §**

BLACK LOTUS 2 b.f. (Feb 1) Declaration of War (USA) 128 – Ravensburg 66 (Raven's Pass (USA) 133) [2017 p7g^{6} 7g^{6} Oct 16] first foal: dam twice-raced half-sister to St Leger runner-up High Accolade: modest form when sixth in minor events: capable of better. *Chris Wall* **64 p**

BLACK MEDUSA (IRE) 2 b.c. (Mar 31) Canford Cliffs (IRE) 133 – Dancer's Leap (Pivotal 124) [2017 t8.6g t7.2g^{4} p8d Dec 13] fair form in minor events: should stay 1m. *Paul Cole* **65**

BLACK NIGHT (IRE) 5 b.h. Excellent Art 125 – Starfish (IRE) (Galileo (IRE) 134) [2017 98: p10g^{4} 8.5g* 10f* 12g^{2} 12.4g 12f* 10d^{2} 11.9d^{6} Oct 28] useful performer: successful at Les Landes in minor event in May and handicaps in July/August: effective at 8.5f to 1½m: acts on polytrack and any turf going. *James Moon, Jersey* **102**

BLACK ORANGE 2 br.c. (Apr 21) Pastoral Pursuits 127 – Mrs Snaffles (IRE) 99 (Indian Danehill (IRE) 124) [2017 5g^{3} p5g^{2} 5m* 5.1m^{2} 6g^{2} 7g^{6} Dec 29] seventh foal: half-brother to 1m/8.6f winner (including at 2 yrs) Karma Chameleon (by Haafhd), later successful abroad: dam 2-y-o 6f winner who stayed 9.5f: fairly useful performer: won minor event at Ripon in April: second after in minor events at Chester and Doha: left Gay Kelleway after fourth start: stays 6f: acts on good to firm going: tried in headgear. *Debbie Mountain, Qatar* **90**

BLACK PRINCE (FR) 3 b.g. Falco (USA) 122 – Thamara (USA) (Street Cry (IRE) 130) [2017 –: p11g^{3} 12d 12f^{3} 16.1d p16g^{3} p16d* p16g^{4} Dec 20] fair handicapper: won at Chelmsford in October: stays 2m: acts on polytrack and firm going: in tongue tie last 5 starts. *Anthony Honeyball* **70**

BLACK REDSTART 3 b.f. Big Bad Bob (IRE) 118 – Red Roxanne (Rock of Gibraltar (IRE) 133) [2017 58: f6g^{4} a10.4g^{2} a8g^{4} a11.7g^{4} a10.4g* 8g^{6} 11.9g^{4} 10.9g^{3} 8.6s^{2} 10.9d 8.6d^{6} 10.4d^{2} a8g a8g^{5} a10.4g a8g^{5} Nov 16] small filly: modest performer: left Alan Bailey after reappearance: won maiden at Bro Park in June: probably stays 1½m: acts on soft going: has worn hood. *Henrik Engblom, Sweden* **58**

BLACK SAILS 2 br.f. (Feb 4) Lope de Vega (IRE) 125 – Missouri Belle 74 (Invincible Spirit (IRE) 121) [2017 6g* 6m 7s^{6} 8d^{6} Aug 27] second foal: dam twice-raced half-sister to useful 1½m winner Dare To Achieve: fairly useful form: won minor event at the Curragh in May: best effort at 6f: sold €25,000 in November, joined Archie Watson. *G. M. Lyons, Ireland* **92**

BLACK SALT 3 b.g. Equiano (FR) 127 – Marine Girl 73 (Shamardal (USA) 129) [2017 53: 6m^{2} 6g* t7.1s 6v^{6} Jul 27] fair performer: won maiden at Redcar in May: stays 6f: acts on good to firm and heavy going. *David Barron* **72**

BLACKTHORN STICK (IRE) 8 b.g. Elusive City (USA) 117 – Hi Lyla (IRE) (Lahib (USA) 129) [2017 65: p6g t7.1g^{4} p7g^{5} p8g^{5} p7m p7g p8g^{6} May 30] modest handicapper: stays 7f: acts on polytrack and soft going: wears headgear: tried in tongue tie. *Paul Burgoyne* **60**

BLACK TRILBY (IRE) 3 ch.c. Helmet (AUS) 127 – Reine de Romance (IRE) (Vettori (IRE) 119) [2017 79: 8.2s^{2} 7m^{3} 7m^{2} 8f^{3} 8m^{6} 8.1g Oct 9] lengthy colt: fairly useful maiden: second in handicaps at Leicester in May and Sandown in June: stays 1m: acts on soft and good to firm going: in hood last 5 starts: usually races close up: sold 11,000 gns in November: held back by attitude. *Clive Cox* **90 §**

BLACK TRUFFLE (FR) 7 b.g. Kyllachy 129 – Some Diva 75 (Dr Fong (USA) 128) [2017 71: t7.1g p7g^{6} t7.2g t7.2g^{2} t7.2g^{4} p7s^{4} 7m p7g^{4} p7g^{3} p7m^{3} p7s^{2} p6g* Dec 21] sturdy gelding: modest handicapper: won at Chelmsford in December: stays 7f: acts on polytrack, tapeta and good to firm going: wears headgear. *Mark Usher* **60**

BLACKWOOD 2 b.g. (Apr 23) Firebreak 125 – Witness 71 (Efisio 120) [2017 7g 7.1s p8g p6g p7d Nov 22] poor maiden: bred to stay at least 7f. *Michael Blanshard* **41**

BLAINE 7 ch.g. Avonbridge 123 – Lauren Louise 55 (Tagula (IRE) 116) [2017 104§: 6s* 6m 6.1g 5d 6v p6g Sep 25] strong, good-topped gelding: useful handicapper: won at Newbury (by 1½ lengths from Ice Age) in May: stays 6f: acts on soft and good to firm going: usually blinkered. *Brian Barr* **106**

BLAIR HOUSE (IRE) 4 ch.g. Pivotal 124 – Patroness (Dubawi (IRE) 129) [2017 105: 8m^{2} 8s 7.9d Aug 24] smart handicapper: second in Royal Hunt Cup at Royal Ascot (½ length behind Zhui Feng) in June: stays 1¼m: acts on firm and soft going: in headgear nowadays. *Charlie Appleby* **110**

BLAKE DEAN 9 b.g. Halling (USA) 133 – Antediluvian 106 (Air Express (IRE) 125) [2017 p13g Feb 9] maiden, well held in handicap only start on Flat since 2011: in headgear last 2 starts: tried in tongue tie: modest hurdler at best, has lost way. *Chris Gordon* **–**

BLAKENEY POINT 4 b.g. Sir Percy 129 – Cartoon 81 (Danehill Dancer (IRE) 117) [2017 98: p16g* 18.6m 14g^{4} 11.8m^{4} 14d^{2} 14m^{4} 12g* 11.8s* Oct 10] angular gelding: smart handicapper: won at Kempton in April, Newbury (by ¾ length from Danehill Kodiac) in September and Leicester (by ½ length from Dance The Dream) in October: stays 2m: acts on polytrack, good to firm and heavy going: usually wears cheekpieces. *Roger Charlton* **112**

BLAME CULTURE (USA) 2 b.c. (Mar 19) Blame (USA) 129 – Pearl In The Sand (IRE) 95 (Footstepsinthesand 120) [2017 7d p8g^{2} p8g^{2} Nov 7] $30,000Y, resold 40,000Y: second foal: half-brother to 2-y-o 6f winner Scudding (by Mizzen Mast): dam, maiden (stayed 7f), half-sister to useful sprinter Reckless Reward: fairly useful form: best effort when second in minor event at Kempton (2 lengths behind Occupy) in November. *George Margarson* **81**

BLAME ME FOREVER (USA) 2 b.f. (Feb 26) Blame (USA) 129 – Empress Josephine (USA) (Empire Maker (USA) 129) [2017 t8.6g Nov 29] third foal: half-sister to winners in North America by Flatter and English Channel: dam unraced half-sister to US Grade 2 9f winner Private Emblem: 40/1, held back by inexperience when ninth in minor event at Wolverhampton (7¼ lengths behind Ghanimah) in November, very slowly away. *Marco Botti* **61**

BLANCHEFLEUR (IRE) 2 b.f. (Apr 20) Camelot 128 – Portrait of A Lady (IRE) 95 (Peintre Celebre (USA) 137) [2017 7.6d^{2} 7m^{3} 7g^{2} 7m p8g Oct 25] €110,000F: rather leggy filly: closely related to 2-y-o 7f winner Vitruvian Man and winner up to 1¼m Miss You Too (2-y-o 7f winner) (both useful and by Montjeu) and half-sister to 6f winner Marshall Art (by Lawman): dam 1½m winner: fairly useful maiden: second in maiden at Salisbury in September: stays 7f: acts on good to firm going. *Richard Hannon* **80**

BLANCO (USA) 4 b.g. Cape Blanco (IRE) 130 – Nimue (USA) 91 (Speightstown (USA) 124) [2017 –: p7d Jan 17] poor maiden: sometimes in tongue tie. *George Baker* **–**

BLANKIEDOODIE 4 b.g. Halling (USA) 133 – Our Day Will Come 75 (Red Ransom (USA)) [2017 –: 10d^{2} 10d^{5} p8g p10.7g Oct 13] modest maiden handicapper: best effort at 1¼m: acts on good to soft going. *John McConnell, Ireland* **58**

BLASTOFMAGIC 3 gr.g. Hellvelyn 118 – Elegant Pursuit (Pastoral Pursuits 127) [2017 53: t6m^{2} t6g 8s p5g Nov 24] modest maiden: left David Dennis after second start: best effort at 6f: acts on tapeta: sometimes in cheekpieces: in tongue tie last 2 starts. *Adrian Brendan Joyce, Ireland* **60**

BLAZED (IRE) 3 gr.g. Dark Angel (IRE) 113 – Sudden Blaze (IRE) (Soviet Star (USA) 128) [2017 t7.2g 7m^{2} 6g^{5} 6d^{6} t5.1g^{2} t5.1g* p5m^{2} t6.1d^{4} Dec 9] 80,000F, 125,000Y: third foal: half-brother to French 6f/6.5f winner Soupcon (by Footstepsinthesand): dam unraced sister to smart US Grade 3 11f winner Rosinka and half-sister to smart US Grade 1 1½m winner King's Drama: fairly useful performer: won handicap at Wolverhampton in November: stays 7f: acts on polytrack, tapeta and good to firm going: sometimes in tongue tie: usually slowly away. *Roger Charlton* **83**

BLAZE OF GLORY (FR) 3 ch.g. Excelebration (IRE) 133 – Roche Ambeau (FR) (Chichicastenango (FR) 119) [2017 p7g^{3} p8g* p7g^{3} t7.1g^{3} p7d May 31] €110,000Y: second foal: half-brother to useful French 10.5f winner Roche Rose (by Rock of Gibraltar): dam, useful French 1¼m/10.5f winner, sister to smart French stayer Blek: fairly useful **89**

performer: won maiden at Lingfield in January: third in handicaps at same course and Wolverhampton after: stays 1m: acts on polytrack: front runner/races prominently: sent to USA. *Jamie Osborne*

BLAZE OF HEARTS (IRE) 4 b.g. Canford Cliffs (IRE) 133 – Shesthebiscuit 76 (Diktat 126) [2017 84: 11.6g^5 10m^6 10g^6 9.1m* 8g 8g* p8s p8g p12g Dec 30] good-topped gelding: fairly useful handicapper: won at Yarmouth in August and October (by 1¼ lengths from Monaadhil): stays 1¼m: acts on good to firm and good to soft going: often leads. *Dean Ivory* **84**

BLAZING BERYL (IRE) 2 b.f. (Jan 24) Most Improved (IRE) 119 – Lady Gray (IRE) (High Chaparral (IRE) 132) [2017 6m^5 6s^4 6.1m p7g 8.1s^6 t7.2g Oct 7] €60,000Y: sturdy filly: third foal: half-sister to French 1m winner La Michodiere (by Power): dam unraced half-sister to useful winner up to 1m Sesmen: modest maiden: best effort at 6f: acts on soft going: in headgear last 2 starts: sent to Sweden. *Brian Meehan* **55**

BLAZING TUNDER (IRE) 2 gr.c. (Mar 25) Casamento (IRE) 118 – La Chita Bonita (IRE) (Verglas (IRE) 118) [2017 8.3d* Oct 18] 11,000F, €16,000Y: second foal: half-brother to Italian 1m winner Apple Scruffs (by Fast Company): dam unraced half-sister to useful performer up to 1½m Sunstone: 9/4, won maiden at Nottingham (by neck from Astrologist) in October: bred to stay beyond 1m: open to improvement. *Henry Candy* **75 p**

BLENDING 3 b.f. Medicean 128 – Panzanella 94 (Dansili 127) [2017 90p: p8g^4 8f^5 8d^5 Sep 23] sturdy filly: fairly useful performer: fourth in minor event at Kempton in April: best effort at 7f: acts on good to firm going: front runner/races prominently: sold 100,000 gns in December. *John Gosden* **85**

BLESSED TO EMPRESS (IRE) 2 b.f. (Feb 1) Holy Roman Emperor (IRE) 125 – Blessing Box 76 (Bahamian Bounty 116) [2017 p5g* 5s p5g^4 6.1g 6s^4 p5g p5s^3 Nov 16] 17,000Y: first foal: dam, 5f winner, sister to smart 6f winner Bounty Box: fair performer: won minor event at Chelmsford in May: stays 6f: acts on polytrack: sometimes slowly away. *Amy Murphy* **66**

BLESS HIM (IRE) 3 b.c. Sea The Stars (IRE) 140 – Happy Land (IRE) (Refuse To Bend (IRE) 128) [2017 p8g^2 p8g* 8m^3 7g^5 8m* 7m^5 Aug 27] 65,000F, 100,000Y, €600,000 2-y-o: strong colt: fourth foal: half-brother to 3 winners, including 7f winner Chewy Round Town (by Roderic O'Connor) and 1¼m winner Thunder In Myheart (by Mastercraftsman): dam unraced half-sister to smart sprinter Dyhim Diamond: useful performer: won maiden at Chelmsford (by ¾ length from Highland Cradle) in April and Britannia Stakes (Handicap) at Royal Ascot (by ½ length from Ronald R) in June: stays 1m: acts on polytrack and good to firm going: in hood last 3 starts: often races in rear/freely. *David Simcock* **108**

Britannia Stakes (Heritage Handicap), Royal Ascot—Bless Him beats Ronald R (striped sleeves) and Tricorn (chevrons on sleeves) in a race dominated by the far-side runners

BLETCHLEY 3 b.f. Makfi 130 – An Ghalanta (IRE) 97 (Holy Roman Emperor (IRE) **103**
125) [2017 103: 7d* 6.9s^2 7s 7s^2 Oct 7] good-topped filly: useful performer: won minor event at Leicester in June: second in listed race at Ascot (1¼ lengths behind One Master) in October: stays 7f: acts on soft going: tried in hood: sold 320,000 gns in December. *Ralph Beckett*

BLEU ET NOIR 6 b.g. Enrique 121 – Gastina (FR) (Pistolet Bleu (IRE) 133) [2017 p8s **57**
8.3g^6 7.1s^6 6.1g p10g^2 t9.5g* f12.1g^5 Dec 4] lengthy, angular gelding: fair performer: won **a78**
maiden at Wolverhampton in November: stays 1¼m: acts on polytrack and tapeta: wears hood. *Tim Vaughan*

BLIND FAITH (IRE) 4 ch.f. Zoffany (IRE) 121 – Guajira (FR) (Mtoto 134) [2017 88: **87**
8m^5 8m^2 10g^5 p10g^3 9.8g Aug 19] angular filly: fairly useful handicapper: second at Doncaster in June: stays 1¼m: acts on polytrack and good to firm going: tried in hood: usually races nearer last than first: sold 11,000 gns in December. *Luca Cumani*

BLING KING 8 b.g. Haafhd 129 – Bling Bling (IRE) 70 (Indian Ridge 123) [2017 68: **72**
t9.5g^2 8.3g^6 9.9m^4 10g^2 10.2m^2 9.2m^2 10g^2 10d^5 Aug 12] sturdy, compact gelding: fair handicapper: stays 1½m: acts on tapeta, viscoride, firm and soft going: wears headgear: usually races prominently. *Geoffrey Harker*

BLISTERING DANCER (IRE) 7 b.g. Moss Vale (IRE) 126 – Datura 74 (Darshaan **43**
133) [2017 58: t5.1g^4 p6g p6g^3 6m^5 5.1s 6.1m 7s 6d^6 5.7s 6v t6.1g Dec 13] poor **a49**
handicapper: stays 7f: acts on polytrack and soft going: often in headgear: front runner/races prominently. *Tony Carroll*

BLITHE SPIRIT 6 b.m. Byron 117 – Damalis (IRE) 106 (Mukaddamah (USA) 125) **91**
[2017 102: 5f 5.1m 6m 5m 5.1d 5.1d^2 5.5g 5.1v Sep 16] rather leggy mare: fairly useful handicapper: second at Chester in July: stays 5.5f: acts on good to firm and heavy going: front runner/races prominently: sold 15,000 gns in December. *Eric Alston*

BLITZ 3 b.f. Exceed And Excel (AUS) 126 – Photo Flash (IRE) 76 (Bahamian Bounty 116) **89**
[2017 84: t5.1m^2 5.1g^4 5g^6 5.1d* 5g^5 5d^4 5.1g^6 Sep 2] well-made filly: half-sister to 3 winners, including 2-y-o 5f/6f (Richmond Stakes) winner Prolific (by Compton Place), later successful in Hong Kong, and winner up to 1m Deal Breaker (2-y-o 5f winner, by Night Shift), both useful: dam 1m winner: fairly useful handicapper: won at Windsor in June: best form at 5f: acts on polytrack, tapeta, good to firm and good to soft going: tried in tongue tie: usually races close up. *Clive Cox*

BLOND ME (IRE) 5 ch.m. Tamayuz 126 – Holda (IRE) 81 (Docksider (USA) 124) **117**
[2017 109: 10.3d* 9.9v^2 11.9d 10s* 9.9g Dec 10] good-bodied mare: smart performer: won Middleton Stakes at York (by 1¼ lengths from The Black Princess) in May and E. P. Taylor Stakes at Woodbine (by length from Kitten's Roar) in October: creditable 1½ lengths second to Winter in Nassau Stakes at Goodwood: last in both Prix Vermeille at Chantilly (squeezed and stumbled badly 5f out) and Hong Kong Cup at Sha Tin on other starts: stays 10.5f: acts on good to firm and heavy going: usually held up. *Andrew Balding*

BLOODSWEATANDTEARS 9 b.g. Barathea (IRE) 127 – Celestial Princess 84 **65**
(Observatory (USA) 131) [2017 71: p8g p8g^3 p8g^3 8v p8g^3 p8g^6 Dec 30] tall gelding: fair handicapper: stays 1¼m: acts on polytrack, good to firm and heavy going: has worn headgear: carries head awkwardly. *William Knight*

BLOOMIN LOVELY (IRE) 3 b.f. Helmet (AUS) 127 – Dorothy Dene (Red Ransom **70**
(USA)) [2017 73: t7.1g^3 t7.1d^2 t6g^3 t7.1m^5 6d Jun 5] fair maiden: stays 7f: acts on tapeta: usually races prominently. *John Quinn*

BLOORIEDOTCOM (IRE) 2 b.g. (May 6) Holy Roman Emperor (IRE) 125 – Peaceful **76**
Kingdom (USA) (King of Kings (IRE) 125) [2017 6m 8d^3 8s^4 9m Oct 25] good-topped gelding: fair form: stays 1m. *Peter Chapple-Hyam*

BLUE BAHIA (IRE) 3 b.f. Big Bad Bob (IRE) 118 – Brazilian Bride (IRE) 103 (Pivotal **73**
124) [2017 79: t6f^2 t6g^4 t7.1g* t6g t7.1g^5 Apr 8] fair performer: won maiden at Wolverhampton in February: stays 7f: acts on tapeta and heavy going: front runner/races prominently. *Mark Johnston*

BLUE BAYOU 4 ch.f. Bahamian Bounty 116 – Oshiponga 72 (Barathea (IRE) 127) [2017 **94**
–: 6g^4 7d May 13] strong filly: useful at best, lightly raced: fourth in listed race (4¼ lengths behind Tupi) at Doncaster in April: stays 7f: acts on firm going: tried in tongue tie. *Brian Meehan*

BLUE CANDY 2 b.c. (Feb 15) Bahamian Bounty 116 – Sally Can Wait (Sakhee (USA) **71**
136) [2017 p7g p8g^5 p7s^2 p7s Dec 1] fair form: best effort at 7f. *Archie Watson*

BLUE DE VEGA (GER) 4 b.c. Lope de Vega (IRE) 125 – Burning Heights (GER) (Montjeu (IRE) 137) [2017 111: 7d³ 6d⁶ p6g² Oct 11] lengthy colt: useful performer: third in Gladness Stakes at Naas (length behind Diamond Fields) in April: left M. D. O'Callaghan after second start: stays 7f: acts on good to soft going: tried in tongue tie. *Robert Cowell* **106**

BLUE HARMONY 2 b.f. (Feb 10) Bahamian Bounty 116 – Fascination Street (IRE) 69 (Mujadil (USA) 119) [2017 6s 6v⁶ t7.1d* t7.1g⁶ t8.6g³ t8.6d³ Dec 26] 9,000F, £13,000Y: lengthy, rather narrow filly: half-sister to a winner in Greece by Pivotal: dam, 7f winner, half-sister to very smart US Grade 1 9f/1¼m winner Golden Apples: fair performer: won minor event at Newcastle in November: third in handicap at Wolverhampton in December: stays 8.5f: acts on tapeta: tried in visor. *K. R. Burke* **70**

BLUE HAVANA (IRE) 2 b.f. (Mar 26) Havana Gold (IRE) 118 – Labyrinthine (IRE) 61 (Pivotal 124) [2017 6d⁵ 5.9g 6d t7.1g⁴ t8s⁴ f8.1g³ f8.1g Dec 29] €28,000F, €23,000Y: sturdy filly: first foal: dam, ran twice, out of useful 1m winner (stayed 1¼m) Madame Cerito: modest maiden: may prove best at 7f: acts on tapeta: in visor last 2 starts. *John Quinn* **55**

BLUE HUSSAR (IRE) 6 b.g. Montjeu (IRE) 137 – Metaphor (USA) (Woodman (USA) 126) [2017 92: 16.3d³ 16.3d* 16.3g Oct 14] good-topped gelding: fairly useful handicapper: won at York (by 3 lengths from Shearling) in September: stays 16.5f: acts on good to firm and heavy going: often wears cheekpieces. *Micky Hammond* **94**

BLUE JACKET (USA) 6 ro.m. Mizzen Mast (USA) 121 – Complex (USA) (Unbridled's Song (USA) 125) [2017 69: t8.6g 6m* 8m 6s⁵ 7.2s⁶ 7m Aug 26] fair handicapper: won at Catterick in April: stays 7f: acts on good to firm and heavy going: front runner/races prominently. *Dianne Sayer* **69**

Mrs Barbara Keller's "Blond Me"

BLUE LAUREATE 2 b.g. (Apr 28) Poet's Voice 126 – Powder Blue 64 (Daylami (IRE) 138) [2017 7s^3 7d^4 8.1g^3 8g* 8g^4 Sep 28] rather unfurnished gelding: half-brother to several winners, including 2-y-o 7f winner (stayed 9.5f) French Blue (by Iffraaj) and winner up to 11.6f Belgrade (2-y-o 8.6f winner, by Rock of Gibraltar): dam ran twice: fairly useful performer: won maiden at Doncaster (by 4½ lengths from Sha La La La Lee) in September: stays 1m: front runner/races prominently: sold 150,000 gns, sent to UAE. *Clive Cox* **88**

BLUE MIST 2 ch.g. (Feb 19) Makfi 130 – Namaskar 84 (Dansili 127) [2017 p8g* 8d^2 p8d^3 Nov 22] well-made gelding: fourth foal: half-brother to smart 1¼m winner Countermeasure (by American Post) and useful French 2-y-o 7f winner Obedient (by Motivator): dam 2-y-o 1m winner who stayed 1¼m: fairly useful form: won minor event at Kempton (by 3 lengths from Communique) in October: placed after in similar events at Newbury and Kempton: raced only at 1m. *Roger Charlton* **88**

BLUE ON BLUE (USA) 3 ch.g. More Than Ready (USA) 120 – Alina (USA) (Came Home (USA) 122) [2017 68: p8g^3 7m* p6g^3 p7d^4 p7d* Oct 6] good-topped gelding: fairly useful handicapper: won at Yarmouth in April and Chelmsford (by ¾ length from Easy Tiger) in October: stays 1m: acts on polytrack and good to firm going: wears hood: sold 47,000 gns, sent to Saudi Arabia. *John Gosden* **92**

BLUE PETAL (IRE) 2 ch.f. (Mar 6) Haatef (USA) 117 – Sapphire Spray (IRE) 79 (Viking Ruler (AUS)) [2017 7.2s 5m^4 7d 7.5s* 7.5s^4 p6g t8d Dec 16] €800Y: fifth foal: sister to French 2-y-o 5f winner My Sapphire and 2-y-o 7f/1m winner Duck Egg Blue: dam 1m winner who stayed 10.7f: fair performer: won maiden claimer at Tipperary in August: left Kevin Prendergast after fifth start: stays 7.5f: acts on soft going: tried in blinkers. *R. K. Watson, Ireland* **65**

BLUE POINT (IRE) 3 b.c. Shamardal (USA) 129 – Scarlett Rose 72 (Royal Applause 124) [2017 118: 6f* 6m^3 6s^4 6s* Oct 7] compact, attractive colt: very smart performer: won Pavilion Stakes at Ascot (by 1½ lengths from Harry Angel) in May and Bengough Stakes at same course (by ½ length from Projection) in October: 1¼ lengths third to Caravaggio in Commonwealth Cup at Royal Ascot: stays 6f: acts on firm and soft going: usually races close up/travels strongly. *Charlie Appleby* **124**

BLUE RAMBLER 7 b.g. Monsun (GER) 124 – La Nuit Rose (FR) 109 (Rainbow Quest (USA) 134) [2017 106: 14g^5 15.9g 14g Jun 10] good-topped gelding: useful handicapper, below best in 2017: stays 2¼m: acts on soft going: tried in cheekpieces. *Ian Williams* **95**

BLUE REFLECTION 2 br.f. (Apr 18) Dansili 127 – Alvee (IRE) 75 (Key of Luck (USA) 126) [2017 p8g^4 Nov 8] fourth foal: sister to winner up to 12.5f Stoney Broke (2-y-o 1m winner): dam maiden half-sister to smart stayer Allegretto: 20/1, fourth in minor event at Kempton (3¼ lengths behind Espadrille) on debut, nearest finish: will stay 1¼m: sure to progress. *James Fanshawe* **69 p**

BLUE REVELATION 4 b.g. Exceed And Excel (AUS) 126 – Epiphany 81 (Zafonic (USA) 130) [2017 78p: p8d 9g^4 Jun 1] lightly-raced 1m winner, below best in handicaps in 2017: tried in tongue tie. *Paul Webber* **51**

BLUE ROCKS 3 b.g. Indesatchel (IRE) 120 – Mabinia (IRE) (Cape Cross (IRE) 129) [2017 60: t5.1g* t6.1g^4 t5.1g 7.6d^6 7.6g^6 6g^5 6d^3 5.1d 5.1g Sep 2] strong gelding: fair handicapper: won at Wolverhampton in April: should stay 7f: acts on tapeta and good to soft going: tried in blinkers. *Lisa Williamson* **65**

BLUE SKIMMER (IRE) 5 b.g. Arcano (IRE) 122 – Cattiva Generosa 109 (Cadeaux Genereux 131) [2017 73: 11.3g^2 12g^3 12s 10s t12.4d^6 Dec 16] fair maiden: stays 12.5f: acts on polytrack, tapeta, good to firm and heavy going: has worn headgear. *Miss Nicole McKenna, Ireland* **70**

BLUE SUEDE (IRE) 3 b.f. Requinto (IRE) 109 – Shoooz (IRE) 63 (Soviet Star (USA) 128) [2017 83: 5.1g 5g 5m^6 6g^6 p5g^5 Aug 18] fair handicapper: left Richard Fahey after third start: best form at 5f: acts on polytrack, tapeta, soft and good to firm going: tried in tongue tie: front runner/races prominently. *R. K. Watson, Ireland* **74**

BLUE SURF 8 ch.g. Excellent Art 125 – Wavy Up (IRE) (Brustolon 117) [2017 100, a106: p12m^5 p12m^2 Feb 25] useful-looking gelding: useful handicapper: second at Lingfield (2 lengths behind Sennockian Star) in February: stays 16.5f: acts on polytrack, tapeta, good to firm and heavy going: has worn cheekpieces. *Amanda Perrett* **96**

BLUE TOP 8 b.g. Millkom 124 – Pompey Blue 71 (Abou Zouz (USA) 109) [2017 65: t13.9m^3 t13.9g^4 Feb 6] plain gelding: fair handicapper: stays 2m: acts on polytrack, tapeta, firm and soft going: has worn headgear, including last 4 starts: tried in tongue tie. *Dai Burchell* **70**

Merriebelle Stable Pavilion Stakes, Ascot—
in receipt of 4 lb from the runner-up Harry Angel (chevrons on sleeves),
Blue Point makes a winning return to stake his claim for the Commonwealth Cup

BLUE VALENTINO 8 b.g. Primo Valentino (IRE) 116 – Blue Water 45 (Shaamit (IRE) 127) [2017 p14g^6 t8.6g^6 Jun 1] maiden, well held in handicaps in 2017: tried in cheekpieces. *Lisa Williamson* –

BLUE WHISPER 2 ch.g. (Mar 25) Bated Breath 125 – Vivid Blue 80 (Haafhd 129) [2017 p7s Sep 8] sturdy gelding: 50/1, well held in minor event at Kempton. *James Eustace* –

BLUFF CRAG 4 b.g. Canford Cliffs (IRE) 133 – Camp Riverside (USA) (Forest Camp (USA) 114) [2017 79: p8g p10g^2 11.6m^4 p12g^2 10s 11.9s p8g* p7g^5 p8g^2 p8g^6 p8g^6 Dec 20] workmanlike gelding: fairly useful handicapper: won at Kempton (by 1½ lengths from Dangerous Ends) in August: left Richard Hughes after tenth start: stays 1½m: acts on polytrack, firm and soft going: has worn headgear: front runner/races prominently. *Philip McBride* 67 a82

BLUSHING RED (FR) 3 ch.g. Le Havre (IRE) 124 – Boliche (Key of Luck (USA) 126) [2017 64: t9.5g^2 t12.4g* 11s^4 11.9d^4 14m^5 12g 10s* 9.9g p10g 10g Oct 17] tall, good-topped gelding: fairly useful performer: won maiden at Newcastle in March and handicap at Chepstow (by 1¼ lengths from Native Prospect) in August: stays 12.5f: acts on tapeta and soft going: sold 38,000 gns in November to join Emma Lavelle. *Ed Dunlop* 84

BLUSHING ROSE 3 ch.f. Dalakhani (IRE) 133 – Russelliana 100 (Medicean 128) [2017 82p: 9m^5 p8s^4 8.1m^3 p10g* p10s* 10g^2 Oct 7] sturdy filly: useful handicapper: won at Chelmsford in August and September: second at Newmarket (1½ lengths behind Neshmeya) in October: stays 1¼m: acts on polytrack and good to firm going. *Sir Michael Stoute* 100

BLYTON LASS 2 ch.f. (Mar 8) Havana Gold (IRE) 118 – Cesseras (IRE) (Cape Cross (IRE) 129) [2017 6d 6v^6 t7.1g t8g Nov 3] 6,000Y: third foal: dam, French 8.5f winner, sister to very smart winner up to 9f Charlie Farnsbarns: no form in minor events. *James Given* –

BOATER (IRE) 3 b.f. Helmet (AUS) 127 – Cercle d'Amour (USA) (Storm Cat (USA)) [2017 84: f6g^5 p7g* Mar 3] fairly useful handicapper: won at Lingfield (by ¾ length from Touch Me) in March: stays 7f: acts on polytrack and firm going: front runner/races prominently: sold 110,000 gns in July. *Mark Johnston* 80

BOBBIE GREEN (IRE) 2 b.f. (Mar 25) Big Bad Bob (IRE) 118 – Sticky Green 75 (Lion Cavern (USA) 117) [2017 7d Oct 20] half-sister to 3 winners, including useful winner up to 1¾m Lethal Glaze (2-y-o 1m-1¼m winner, by Verglas) and useful 2-y-o 6f winner Emerald Hill (by Piccolo), later successful in Hong Kong: dam 1½m winner: 33/1, well held in claimer at Redcar. *Tim Easterby* –

BOBBIO (IRE) 3 ch.c. Choisir (AUS) 126 – Balladiene (IRE) 95 (Noverre (USA) 125) [2017 p7g^6 p7g Apr 1] well held in maidens: sent to Greece. *Marco Botti* –

BOBBY BENTON (IRE) 6 b.g. Invincible Spirit (IRE) 121 – Remarkable Story (Mark of Esteem (IRE) 137) [2017 75: p7g Dec 28] fair handicapper: below form only start in 2017: stays 1¼m: acts on polytrack, fibresand and firm going: sometimes in headgear. *Suzi Best* 60

BOBBY BISCUIT (USA) 2 b.c. (Jan 29) Scat Daddy (USA) 120 – Poupee Flash (USA) (Elusive Quality (USA)) [2017 p7s^4 Sep 8] $8,000Y, 110,000 2-y-o: good-topped colt: first foal: dam useful French 8.5f/9f winner: 20/1, fourth in minor event at Kempton (7 lengths behind Symbolization) in September: likely to stay 1m: will improve. *Simon Dow* **71 p**

BOBBY JOE LEG 3 ch.g. Pastoral Pursuits 127 – China Cherub 94 (Inchinor 119) [2017 t6g* t7.1g f6.1g Dec 19] fair form: won maiden at Newcastle (by ¾ length from Kingofmerrows) in November: best effort at 6f. *Ruth Carr* **79**

BOBBY'S CHARM (USA) 2 b.g. (Apr 2) Shanghai Bobby (USA) 123 – Magic Charm (USA) (Horse Greeley (USA) 114) [2017 6m^4 t5.1g^5 p6g Sep 27] fair form at best in minor events: should stay 6f. *Robert Cowell* **69**

BOBBYS HELMET (IRE) 3 b.g. Helmet (AUS) 127 – Ready When You Are (IRE) 76 (Royal Applause 124) [2017 –: 10m Apr 10] last in maidens. *David C. Griffiths* **–**

BOBBY VEE 3 ch.f. Camacho 118 – Miss Lesley 80 (Needwood Blade 117) [2017 70: t6g p7g 6.1m 5g^4 5d^3 6d p6g^4 Dec 20] workmanlike filly: fair handicapper: stays 6f: acts on polytrack and good to soft going: tried in cheekpieces. *Dean Ivory* **68**

BOBBY WHEELER (IRE) 4 b.g. Pivotal 124 – Regal Rose 110 (Danehill (USA) 126) [2017 98: p7g p7g Dec 13] lengthy gelding: useful handicapper: down the field both starts in 2017: stays 1m: acts on good to firm going: front runner/races prominently, usually finds little. *Clive Cox* **86**

BOB HOPEFUL 4 b.g. Big Bad Bob (IRE) 118 – Trick (IRE) 76 (Shirley Heights 130) [2017 t8.6m^5 t9.5g^4 p8g p7g^4 p6f^5 Apr 24] fair maiden: stays 9.5f: acts on polytrack and tapeta: tried in hood. *Mike Murphy* **66**

BOB MAXWELL (IRE) 3 b.g. Big Bad Bob (IRE) 118 – Catching Stars (IRE) (Halling (USA) 133) [2017 7g^5 t7.1g^2 8d^4 6.9d Jul 8] fair form: best effort at 7f. *David Barron* **79**

BOBOLI GARDENS 7 b.g. Medicean 128 – Park Crystal (IRE) (Danehill (USA) 126) [2017 –: t8.6g t7.1d Feb 4] fair handicapper at best, lightly raced and well held since 2015: has worn hood/tongue tie. *Iain Jardine* **–**

BO BRIDGET (IRE) 4 gr.f. Mastercraftsman (IRE) 129 – Greta d'Argent (IRE) 103 (Great Commotion (USA) 123) [2017 53: 8g^2 7.5d^3 10s 10g^3 8s^3 9v Oct 12] modest maiden handicapper: stays 1¼m: acts on soft going: tried in cheekpieces: front runner/races prominently. *Adrian Murray, Ireland* **64**

BOB'S BOY 4 b.g. Showcasing 117 – Tech Zinne (Zinaad 114) [2017 66: 10.2f^6 12.1m 10.2g^5 9.9v^4 p10g f12.1g 10.2g Nov 1] modest handicapper: trained on reappearance by Warren Greatrex: stays 13f: acts on polytrack, good to firm and heavy going: wears headgear/tongue tie. *Oliver Greenall* **60**

BOB'S GIRL 2 b.f. (Jan 27) Big Bad Bob (IRE) 118 – Linda (FR) (Tamayuz 126) [2017 8d 8d t8g Nov 3] 42,000Y: first foal: dam, French maiden (placed at 1m), half-sister to Prix Saint-Alary winner Ask For The Moon: modest form in minor events. *David Simcock* **58**

BODACIOUS NAME (IRE) 3 b.g. Famous Name 124 – Nice Wee Girl (IRE) 86 (Clodovil (IRE) 116) [2017 57: 14m^4 13.1g^5 16v* 15.9v^2 14.1v^2 15v^4 14d Oct 30] fair handicapper: won at Nottingham in August: stays 2m: acts on tapeta, good to firm and heavy going. *John Quinn* **74**

BODES WELL (IRE) 2 b.g. (Feb 14) Rock of Gibraltar (IRE) 133 – Gypsie Queen (IRE) 83 (Xaar 132) [2017 7s^2 p8d Nov 22] fair form: better effort when second in minor event at Salisbury (length behind N Over J) in October. *Warren Greatrex* **71**

BODIE AND DOYLE 2 ch.g. (Feb 16) Raven's Pass (USA) 133 – Queenofthenorth (IRE) (Halling (USA) 133) [2017 7d 7s 7v p6g t7.2g Nov 18] modest maiden: best effort at 7f: tried in blinkers. *Andrew Balding* **63**

BODYBUILDER 2 b.c. (Feb 1) Power 117 – Looks All Right (IRE) 81 (Danehill Dancer (IRE) 117) [2017 5d 5m^5 5d^3 6f 5s^2 6s 7d^5 t6.1g^4 5.7s^4 p5g Oct 18] modest maiden: best form at 5f: acts on soft and good to firm going: often races prominently. *Richard Hannon* **64**

BOETHIUS 4 b.g. Manduro (GER) 135 – Perfect Note 80 (Shamardal (USA) 129) [2017 –: t14g Nov 25] lightly-raced maiden, little impact in handicap only start on Flat in 2017. *Tim Vaughan* **–**

BOGARDUS (IRE) 6 b.g. Dalakhani (IRE) 133 – Sugar Mint (IRE) 100 (High Chaparral (IRE) 132) [2017 69, a75: t10.2g^5 Mar 9] rather narrow gelding: fair handicapper: below form only start on Flat in 2017: stays 1½m: acts on polytrack, tapeta and good to firm going: has worn headgear. *Patrick Holmes* **55**

BOGART 8 ch.g. Bahamian Bounty 116 – Lauren Louise 55 (Tagula (IRE) 116) [2017 95: 6g 5m^4 6m 5s^3 6g 6d^2 5g^2 5m^6 5d 5g Oct 13] sturdy, good-quartered gelding: fairly useful handicapper nowadays: second at Thirsk (twice) in August: stays 6f: acts on soft and good to firm going: wears cheekpieces/tongue tie: usually races close up: temperamental. *Kevin Ryan* **93 §**

BOGSNOG (IRE) 7 b.g. Moss Vale (IRE) 126 – Lovers Kiss 52 (Night Shift (USA)) [2017 66: t5g t6m t6g* 6m^4 7g^4 6.1g^4 6.1m t7.2g^2 t6.1g* t7.2g t6.1g* t6.1g^4 6g 6s^4 Oct 10] fair handicapper: won at Wolverhampton in March, July and August: effective 6f/7f: acts on polytrack, tapeta and good to firm going: has worn headgear: races prominently. *Ruth Carr* **67**

BOHEMIAN FLAME (IRE) 3 b.g. Zoffany (IRE) 121 – Red Japonica (Daylami (IRE) 138) [2017 91: 6d 7m Aug 26] rangy gelding: fairly useful handicapper: stays 6f: acts on good to soft going: sold 6,000 gns in November, sent to Greece. *Andrew Balding* **81**

BOHEMIAN RHAPSODY (IRE) 8 b.g. Galileo (IRE) 134 – Quiet Mouse (USA) (Quiet American (USA)) [2017 79: 11.6m 10g 12d 14g^5 p15.8g^4 Dec 6] rather leggy gelding: modest handicapper: left Brendan Powell after fourth start: stays 2m: acts on polytrack, soft and good to firm going: usually wears cheekpieces. *Brian Barr* **63**

BOIS D'EBENE (IRE) 3 b.f. Big Bad Bob (IRE) 118 – Mpumalanga 98 (Observatory (USA) 131) [2017 70: 7s 7m p7g 8.1m^6 8s^4 7.1d 8v p8g Oct 14] useful-looking filly: fair maiden: left Roger Charlton after fourth start: stays 1m: acts on polytrack and soft going: has worn headgear, including final start: sometimes slowly away. *John O'Shea* **65**

BOIS DE BOULOGNE (USA) 3 b.c. Street Cry (IRE) 130 – Rosa Parks 103 (Sadler's Wells (USA) 132) [2017 85p: p8g* a7f a8.4f a8.9f^2 Dec 29] fairly useful performer: won maiden at Kempton (by neck from Flight of Fantasy) in February: left John Gosden after: will stay 1¼m: acts on polytrack and tapeta: wears headgear. *S. bin Ghadayer, UAE* **82**

BOITE (IRE) 7 b.g. Authorized (IRE) 133 – Albiatra (USA) (Dixieland Band (USA)) [2017 103: p16d^5 Nov 22] quite good-topped gelding: useful handicapper: fifth at Kempton only start in 2017: stays 17f: acts on polytrack and any turf going: tried in tongue tie: useful hurdler. *Warren Greatrex* **98**

BOKETTO (IRE) 3 b.f. Canford Cliffs (IRE) 133 – Olimpic Girl (IRE) (Darshaan 133) [2017 –: p7g p8g p7g p8s^6 Dec 8] 8,500Y, €13,000 2-y-o: half-sister to several winners abroad, including French 9f winner Prodige (by Aussie Rules) and French 13.5f winner Mandore (by Rock of Gibraltar): dam useful French 1¼m-11.5f winner: modest maiden: left Dermot Murphy after third start: will probably stay 1¼m: acts on polytrack: tried in tongue tie: often races towards rear. *Derek Shaw* **53**

BOKO FITTLEWORTH (IRE) 2 b.g. (Apr 20) Most Improved (IRE) 119 – Sycamores (FR) (Gold Away (IRE) 125) [2017 7.1s 7m 8.3d^6 Oct 18] little impact in minor events/maiden. *Jonjo O'Neill* **–**

BOLD 5 b.g. Oasis Dream 129 – Minority 106 (Generous (IRE) 139) [2017 83: t5g^5 Jan 21] sturdy gelding: fair handicapper: stays 8.5f: acts on polytrack, tapeta, best turf form on soft/heavy going: in visor last 3 starts: wears tongue tie: usually races close up: sent to Macau. *Stuart Williams* **73**

BOLDER BOB (IRE) 3 b.g. Big Bad Bob (IRE) 118 – Semiquaver (IRE) (Mark of Esteem (IRE) 137) [2017 68: 10m^3 9.1g^3 11.8g^4 11.8s* 12.1s* 13.9g Oct 13] workmanlike gelding: fairly useful handicapper: won at Leicester (by 3¼ lengths from Just In Time) in August and Beverley (by 3¼ lengths from Overhaugh Street) in September: stays 1½m: acts on soft and good to firm going. *David Barron* **91**

BOLD GROVE 5 b.g. Proclamation (IRE) 130 – Trysting Grove (IRE) 64 (Cape Cross (IRE) 129) [2017 44§: f7m t8.6g 6.1m 8.2g^{rr} Jul 8] poor maiden handicapper: usually in headgear: temperamental (refused to race final start). *Edward Bevan* **– §**

BOLD MAX 6 b.g. Assertive 121 – Jane's Payoff (IRE) 72 (Danetime (IRE) 121) [2017 55: t7.1m p7g^3 p7g^6 p8g^3 p7d^3 8g 7d Jun 9] lengthy gelding: modest handicapper: stays 1m: acts on all-weather, best turf form on good going: wears headgear: usually races towards rear. *Zoe Davison* **50**

BOLD PREDICTION (IRE) 7 b.g. Kodiac 112 – Alexander Eliott (IRE) 73 (Night Shift (USA)) [2017 98: p8g^3 p8g^4 p8d^3 f7d^4 8m^6 t8.6g^3 8s p8s^5 p8s Jul 7] useful-looking gelding: fairly useful handicapper: third at Chelmsford in March: stays 9f: acts on polytrack, tapeta, firm and good to soft going: has worn headgear: front runner/races prominently. *Ed Walker* **93**

BOLD REASON (GER) 2 b.c. (Apr 24) Invincible Spirit (IRE) 121 – Bufera (IRE) 101 (King's Best (USA) 132) [2017 7s^4 8.2v^2 8.2g^4 9d^5 t8g* Dec 6] 420,000Y: fifth foal: closely related to useful French 1m (including at 2 yrs) winner Chartreuse (by Lawman) and half-brother to a winner abroad by Acclamation: dam, French 1m winner (including at 2 yrs), half-sister to smart winner up to 1m Johnny Barnes: fairly useful performer: won nursery at Newcastle (by 2¼ lengths from Bajan Gold) in December: stays 1m: acts on tapeta and heavy going: tried in blinkers: usually races prominently: likely to progress further. *John Gosden* **89 p**

BOLD SPIRIT 6 b.g. Invincible Spirit (IRE) 121 – Far Shores (USA) (Distant View (USA) 126) [2017 71: 6m 6m^4 8g^5 6d 7m 6m^6 6s^5 8s 7.4g^3 7.4m 6g^2 6d* 7s^3 6s^2 7v f6.1g^2 f7.1g^4 f7.1g* f7.1g^2 Dec 22] compact gelding: fair handicapper on turf, fairly useful on all-weather: won at Catterick in September and Southwell in December: second at latter course later in December: stays 7.5f: acts on fibresand, firm and soft going: has worn headgear: wears tongue tie: usually travels strongly. *Declan Carroll* **69 a84**

BOLLIHOPE 5 ch.g. Medicean 128 – Hazy Dancer 81 (Oasis Dream 129) [2017 80: t10.2g^3 8g^5 t10.2s^5 10f^4 8.1m^5 8.3g^2 8.1g^3 8s 10.5v t10.2g^4 p10s^5 t12.4d Dec 16] fair handicapper: stays 1½m: acts on tapeta, firm and good to soft going. *Richard Guest* **79**

BOLLIN JOAN 2 b.f. (Feb 11) Mount Nelson 125 – Bollin Greta 93 (Mtoto 134) [2017 8g^5 7v Sep 9] second foal: half-sister to 1¼m winner Bollin Ted (by Haafhd): dam, 1½m-1¾m winner, closely related to St Leger winner Bollin Eric and half-sister to smart sprinter Bollin Joanne: little impact in minor events. *Tim Easterby* **54**

BOLLIN TED 3 b.g. Haafhd 129 – Bollin Greta 93 (Mtoto 134) [2017 –: 8m 12.1m^4 9.9m^2 11.2g^5 9.9f* 9.9d* 10s^3 12g^6 9.9m* p10d^5 9.9v^4 10d Oct 20] fair handicapper: won at Beverley in July (twice, awarded race on second occasion) and August: stays 1¼m: acts on any turf going: has flashed tail. *Tim Easterby* **68**

BOLT D'ORO (USA) 2 b.c. (Mar 17) Medaglia d'Oro (USA) 129 – Globe Trot (USA) (A.P. Indy (USA)) [2017 a6.5f* a7f* a8.5f* a8.5f^3 Nov 4] $630,000Y: second foal: half-brother to a winner in USA by Distorted Humor: dam US 1m winner out of US Grade 3 7f-8.5f winner Trip: very smart form: won maiden at Del Mar in August, and Del Mar Futurity then FrontRunner Stakes at Santa Anita (most impressively, by 7¾ lengths from Solomini), both in September: odds on, raced wide when 5¼ lengths third to Good Magic in Breeders' Cup Juvenile at Del Mar final outing: stays 8.5f: wears blinkers: should still progress. *Mick Ruis, USA* **121 p**

BOMAD 2 b.g. (Apr 22) Kheleyf (USA) 116 – Fenella Fudge 77 (Rock Hard Ten (USA) 126) [2017 6m^2 p6s^4 6.1g 7d 6d p5s^3 p6s^5 t5.1g^2 Dec 18] fair maiden handicapper: stays 6f: acts on polytrack and tapeta: often in headgear: usually starts slowly/races nearer last than first: one to treat with caution. *Derek Shaw* **65 §**

BOMBASTIC (IRE) 2 ch.c. (Apr 8) Raven's Pass (USA) 133 – Star of The West (Galileo (IRE) 134) [2017 6g^2 6g^3 6g^2 7g^4 Sep 22] 38,000Y: third foal: half-brother to 2-y-o 7f winner Ava Star (by Amadeus Wolf): dam, unraced, closely related to smart winner up to 1¼m Coordinated Cut: fairly useful form: third in maiden at Goodwood in August: stays 7f. *Ed de Giles* **82**

BOMBAY DREAM 3 ch.f. Sepoy (AUS) 129 – Indiana Blues 90 (Indian Ridge 123) [2017 66: 6d 5.1m Jun 26] compact filly: maiden, fair form at best: stays 6f: in headgear both 2017 starts. *William Haggas* **57**

BOMBAY (IRE) 3 b.g. High Chaparral (IRE) 132 – Cleide da Silva (USA) 84 (Monarchos (USA) 129) [2017 8m^2 8.3v^2 8v^3 Oct 9] fair form: best effort when second in maiden at Ripon in August: should stay 1¼m+: gelded after final start. *David O'Meara* **76**

BOMBAY RASCAL 4 ch.f. Indian Haven 119 – Kohiba (IRE) (Rock of Gibraltar (IRE) 133) [2017 p10g p12g Oct 18] fourth foal: dam, German 2-y-o 7f winner on only start, out of useful half-sister to 1000 Guineas/Oaks winner Kazzia: well beaten in maidens: in cheekpieces second start. *Robert Walford* **–**

BOMBERO (IRE) 3 b.g. Dragon Pulse (IRE) 114 – Mathool (IRE) (Alhaarth (IRE) 126) [2017 8.3d 8v 8.3m 9.9m 10.2v* 10d Aug 18] good-topped gelding: fair performer: won handicap at Nottingham in August: best effort at 1¼m: acts on heavy going: in cheekpieces last 2 starts. *Ed de Giles* **74**

BOMBSHELL BAY 2 b.c. (Mar 10) Foxwedge (AUS) 128 – Cumana Bay 90 (Dansili 127) [2017 6.5m 7g^6 7d^4 p8g^2 8.1d^5 10v p6s^4 p7d Dec 13] good-quartered colt: fair maiden: best effort at 1m: acts on polytrack: tried in cheekpieces: usually races close up. *Richard Hannon* **66**

BOMBYX 2 ch.c. (Feb 7) Sir Percy 129 – Bombazine (IRE) 97 (Generous (IRE) 139) [2017 8g^{3} 8.2g* Oct 17] brother to winners around 1½m Sir Medbury (in France) and Taffeta Lady, closely related to smart French/UAE winner up to 1½m Gravitas (2-y-o 1m winner, by Mark of Esteem) and half-brother to several winners, including smart 11f-15.5f winner Armure (by Dalakhani): dam 1¼m winner who stayed 1½m: fairly useful form: won minor event at Leicester (by 1¾ lengths from Sea Youmzain) in October: will be suited by 1¼m+: will go on improving. *James Fanshawe* **84 p**

BONANZA BOWLS 2 b.g. (Apr 25) Zebedee 113 – Twilight Belle (IRE) 53 (Fasliyev (USA) 120) [2017 5g^{4} 5.9d^{6} 5s t5d Nov 4] modest form. *Bryan Smart* **62**

BOND ANGEL 2 gr.f. (Mar 12) Monsieur Bond (IRE) 120 – Angel Grigio 51 (Dark Angel (IRE) 113) [2017 5.1g^{6} 5f^{5} t6.1g Jun 7] £1,800Y: workmanlike filly: first foal: dam, maiden (stayed 6f), half-sister to 5f-1m winner Ratio and winner up to 1¼m Rochdale (both smart): well held in minor events. *David Evans* **–**

BOND BOMBSHELL 4 ch.f. Monsieur Bond (IRE) 120 – Fashion Icon (USA) 76 (Van Nistelrooy (USA) 108) [2017 82: 5g 5m^{5} 5g 5d 5m^{5} 5d 5d^{3} 5m^{4} 5s 5d^{5} 5g t5g^{5} t5d^{2} 5g t5g^{2} t5.1g^{6} f5g^{4} f5g^{6} Dec 21] fair handicapper on turf, modest on all-weather: best form at 5f: acts on fibresand, tapeta, soft and good to firm going: wears headgear: often races prominently: temperamental. *David O'Meara* **71 § a62 §**

BOND DO TIGRAO 2 b.c. (Feb 24) Monsieur Bond (IRE) 120 – Bahama Bay (Bahamian Bounty 116) [2017 7s 6d p8m t8.6g Dec 18] no form: left Adrian Murray after second start: tried in headgear: in tongue tie last 3 starts. *Sylvester Kirk* **–**

BONDI BEACH BOY 8 b.g. Misu Bond (IRE) 114 – Nice One (Almaty (IRE) 113) [2017 90: 5.1v t5g^{4} t5d t5.1g^{4} t5g^{5} t6.1d^{6} Dec 9] lengthy gelding: fair handicapper: stays 6f: acts on tapeta, firm and soft going: tried in cheekpieces. *Antony Brittain* **76**

BOND STREET BEAU 2 ch.g. (Mar 22) Dandy Man (IRE) 123 – Loveleaves 93 (Polar Falcon (USA) 126) [2017 7m Oct 25] good-topped gelding: 150/1, well held in minor event at Newmarket. *Philip McBride* **–**

BONIFACE (IRE) 2 b.c. (Apr 1) Born To Sea (IRE) 117 – Sassy (FR) (Sinndar (IRE) 134) [2017 7m 8.1m^{4} 8g Sep 28] down the field in maidens/minor event. *Robert Eddery* **60**

BONJOUR STEVE 6 b.g. Bahamian Bounty 116 – Anthea 66 (Tobougg (IRE) 125) [2017 70: f6g* 6.1d 5d^{3} 6.1d^{3} 5s^{5} 5.1m^{5} 6.1g^{4} 6v^{3} 6.1s^{5} 5.1g^{5} 6g Sep 14] tall gelding: fair handicapper: won at Southwell in January: stays 7f: acts on all-weather and any turf going: wears headgear. *Richard Price* **72**

BONNIE ARLENE (IRE) 3 b.f. Excelebration (IRE) 133 – Pioneer Bride (USA) (Gone West (USA)) [2017 65: f8d^{2} p10d^{3} p11g^{2} 10g* p11s^{3} p12g^{3} 10g^{3} 11.1g^{4} 9s* 12g^{3} 12.5m* p11g^{6} 11.5d^{6} 10.2d 10g^{5} Oct 17] angular filly: fairly useful handicapper: won at Pontefract in May, and Sandown and Musselburgh in August: stays 12.5f: acts on polytrack, fibresand, soft and good to firm going: sometimes slowly away: sold 15,000 gns in November. *Mark Johnston* **82**

BONNIE GALS 3 b.f. Delegator 125 – Esteraad (IRE) 90 (Cadeaux Genereux 131) [2017 t7.1g f8g^{2} t7.1g^{2} 7.1m^{5} 7.2d 8.3g^{3} 9.2m 8.3s 9.2v^{3} 7.2s^{4} t7.1d t9.5g^{3} f7.1g t9.5g Dec 2] £7,000Y: half-sister to several winners, including 2-y-o 7f winner Press Baron (by King's Best), later useful winner up to 9f in USA, and 1m-1¾m winner Noora (by Bahhare): dam 2-y-o 6f winner who stayed 1¼m: fair maiden: stays 9.5f: acts on fibresand, tapeta and soft going: has worn headgear, including last 3 starts: usually races towards rear. *Keith Dalgleish* **66**

BON SCOTTE (IRE) 2 b.c. (Apr 15) Kodiac 112 – Bonne 72 (Namid 128) [2017 8g* 8g^{5} Sep 22] €37,000F, £50,000Y: fourth foal: half-brother to 6f winner Made of Honour (by Casamento): dam, 6f winner, half-sister to smart 6f winner Rising Shadow: fairly useful form: won maiden at Goodwood (by ½ length from Kitaabaat) in August. *Richard Hannon* **85**

BOOBOROWIE (IRE) 4 b.g. Big Bad Bob (IRE) 118 – Rejuvenation (IRE) 75 (Singspiel (IRE) 133) [2017 74: 10g Oct 17] fair maiden: stays 1¼m: acts on soft and good to firm going. *Ali Stronge* **70**

BOOGEY WONDERLAND 3 b.f. Paco Boy (IRE) 129 – Western Eyes (IRE) 57 (Rock of Gibraltar (IRE) 133) [2017 6.1m^{6} 7d Aug 21] 13,000F, 15,000Y: third foal: half-sister to 1¼m-1½m winner Hubertas (by Lord of England) and Swiss 6f/1m winner (including at 2 yrs) Ma Petite Folie (by Cockney Rebel), both useful: dam, maiden (stayed 9.5f), half-sister to Australian Group 2 6f winner Newquay: limited impact in maidens. *Scott Dixon* **–**

BOOGIE BABE 3 b.f. Aqlaam 125 – Bahamian Babe 94 (Bahamian Bounty 116) [2017 t6d^6 t6g^6 t6g^6 5d^2 5g^2 t5g 7.2s 6d^5 Oct 30] fourth foal: half-sister to 2-y-o 7f winner Bahamian Boy (by Paco Boy): dam, 5f winner (including at 2 yrs), sister to useful sprinter Reflektor: modest maiden: best form at 5f: acts on good to soft going: tried in hood: usually races nearer last than first. *Richard Fahey* **62**

BOOKMAKER 7 b.g. Byron 117 – Cankara (IRE) 62 (Daggers Drawn (USA) 114) [2017 69§: p10g p7g* p7g^2 p7d p8g^2 p7m^3 p7g^4 p6g^3 p6s^3 7d 7s Jul 22] lengthy gelding: fair handicapper: won at Lingfield (apprentice) in January: stays 1m: acts on polytrack, soft and good to firm going: wears headgear. *John Bridger* **65**

BOOK OF DREAMS (IRE) 2 b.g. (Apr 6) Dream Ahead (USA) 133 – Moonbi Ridge (IRE) 102 (Definite Article 121) [2017 6.1v* 7.4m^2 6.9v^2 7v^4 7.9g^6 Oct 14] €21,000Y: tall gelding: half-brother to several winners, including winner up to 6f Exhibition (by Invincible Spirit) and winner up to 1½m Annaboda (2-y-o 7f winner, by Duke of Marmalade), both useful in Scandinavia: dam 1¼m-1½m winner: fairly useful performer: won minor event at Nottingham in August: second in similar event at Carlisle in September: stays 7.5f: acts on good to firm and heavy going. *Mark Johnston* **82**

BOOK OF DUST 3 ch.f. Pastoral Pursuits 127 – Northern Bows (Bertolini (USA) 125) [2017 8.3g p10g^6 8.5m^4 10.1g Jul 27] fifth foal: half-sister to 6f winner Golden Compass (by Sakhee) and useful 6f-1m winner Subtle Knife (by Needwood Blade): dam unraced: modest form: best effort at 8.5f: in headgear last 2 starts. *Giles Bravery* **58**

BOOMERANG BETTY (IRE) 2 b.f. (Feb 22) Havana Gold (IRE) 118 – Arbeel 83 (Royal Applause 124) [2017 6.1m* 6g 7s^5 6s^5 p7d p7g Dec 28] 10,000Y: rather unfurnished filly: first foal: dam, maiden (stayed 7f), half-sister to useful winner up to 7f Telwaar: fair performer: won maiden at Windsor in June: best effort at 6f: acts on good to firm going: often races towards rear. *Jamie Osborne* **68**

BOOMERANG BOB (IRE) 8 b.h. Aussie Rules (USA) 123 – Cozzene's Pride (USA) (Cozzene (USA)) [2017 96, a103: p6g^4 p6g* a6.5g^{bd} Feb 26] sturdy horse: useful handicapper: won at Chelmsford (by neck from Zac Brown) in February: stayed 7f: acted on all-weather, soft and good to firm going: tried in cheekpieces: dead. *Jamie Osborne* **101**

BOOMSHACKERLACKER (IRE) 7 gr.g. Dark Angel (IRE) 113 – Allegrina (IRE) 70 (Barathea (IRE) 127) [2017 105: 8m 8m 7g 8s 8.9g^2 8.2s 8s^{pu} Oct 16] leggy gelding: useful performer: won 5 times during career: second to Smart Whip in minor event at Clairefontaine in August: stayed 9f: acted on dirt, heavy and good to firm going: often wore headgear: dead. *George Baker* **105**

BOOM THE GROOM (IRE) 6 b.g. Kodiac 112 – Ecco Mi (IRE) (Priolo (USA) 127) [2017 116, a108: p6g^3 t5.1g^6 p5m^4 p6g 5m^6 6m 5g p5g 5m^{ur} 5s Sep 9] lengthy gelding: smart performer: third in listed race at Lingfield (neck behind Lancelot du Lac) in February: stays 6f: acts on polytrack, tapeta, good to firm and good to soft going: has worn tongue tie. *Tony Carroll* **110**

BOOSHBASH (IRE) 3 gr.f. Dark Angel (IRE) 113 – Surrey Storm 76 (Montjeu (IRE) 137) [2017 57, a68: p8d^4 p10g^4 Jan 27] sturdy filly: fair handicapper: stayed 1¼m: acted on polytrack and tapeta: dead. *Ed Dunlop* **66**

BOOST 3 b.f. Pivotal 124 – Hooray 121 (Invincible Spirit (IRE) 121) [2017 72p: t6m* t7.1g* t7.1g^4 t7.2g^5 f6.1g Dec 4] fairly useful performer: won maiden at Wolverhampton in January and handicap at same course in February: stays 7f: acts on polytrack and tapeta: in headgear last 2 starts: usually races prominently. *Sir Mark Prescott Bt* **88**

BOOTS AND SPURS 8 b.g. Oasis Dream 129 – Arctic Char 102 (Polar Falcon (USA) 126) [2017 89: f7g^2 f7g^6 f8g^4 f7g^4 f7m f8m^4 f7g^3 f8g^6 7g^5 8m f8.1g^5 8s^2 8.2d^4 8d* 9m 7.8s 7.9m^3 7.9d^4 9.1d^3 8g^5 10.3d 9d 7.9g 7v* 7s^2 7d Nov 11] lengthy gelding: fairly useful handicapper: won at Ripon in June and Catterick (by length from Lady In Question) in October: second at latter course later in October: stays 9f: acts on all-weather, good to firm and heavy going: wears headgear: has worn tongue tie: races prominently. *Scott Dixon* **91** **a82**

BOP IT 8 b.g. Misu Bond (IRE) 114 – Forever Bond (Danetime (IRE) 121) [2017 77: 6g 6g 5m t5.1g^6 6g^2 6g 5s f6.1g Dec 21] good-topped gelding: just modest handicapper nowadays: stays 6f: acts on polytrack, firm and soft going: has worn headgear: usually tongue tied. *Michael Easterby* **63**

BORAGH STEPS (IRE) 2 br.f. (May 3) Footstepsinthesand 120 – Boragh Jamal (IRE) 76 (Namid 128) [2017 6m^3 6g* 6m^3 5.2s p5g^2 p5g p5g^2 Dec 21] €16,000Y: third foal: sister to a winner in Qatar: dam, 5f winner, half-sister to useful winner up to 7f Whitbarrow: **84**

fairly useful performer: won maiden at Fairyhouse in July: second in nursery at Dundalk final start: stays 6f: acts on polytrack and good to firm going: often races prominently. *Joseph Patrick O'Brien, Ireland*

BORDER BANDIT (USA) 9 b.g. Selkirk (USA) 129 – Coretta (IRE) 118 (Caerleon (USA) 132) [2017 53: f8d^6 Apr 4] fairly useful at best, has deteriorated: best up to 8.5f: acts on tapeta, soft and good to firm going: wears headgear: signs of temperament. *Tracy Waggott* –

BORDERS DREAM 2 b.c. (Jan 7) Dream Ahead (USA) 133 – Songseeker (IRE) (Oasis Dream 129) [2017 5.9s Aug 23] 25/1, well held in maiden at Carlisle. *Donald Whillans* –

BOREAGH LASS (IRE) 2 b.f. (Mar 10) Fast Company (IRE) 126 – Jalasaat (USA) (Lemon Drop Kid (USA) 131) [2017 6d 6.1m* 7g^5 Sep 22] €2,000Y, resold €6,500Y: good-quartered filly: second foal: dam twice-raced half-sister to smart 6f-1¼m winner Alazeyab out of smart 9f-1½m winner Itnab: fair form: won minor event at Windsor (by 1½ lengths from Polly's Gold) in August: will be suited by at least 1m: has joined Ed de Giles: remains open to improvement. *Henry Candy* **76 p**

BORN FOR CHAMPAGNE (IRE) 3 b.f. Born To Sea (IRE) 117 – Roman Locket (IRE) 63 (Holy Roman Emperor (IRE) 125) [2017 f7.1g f11.1g t7.2g Nov 29] 9,000F: first foal: dam, maiden (stayed 1¼m), half-sister to smart winner up to 9f Haami out of smart winner up to 1¼m Oumaldaaya: no form in maidens: wears hood. *Derek Shaw* –

BORN FOR PROSECCO (IRE) 2 ch.f. (Apr 22) Red Jazz (USA) 125 – Kelso Magic (USA) 98 (Distant View (USA) 126) [2017 t5.1g t5.1g Dec 2] half-sister to several winners, including useful 6f (including at 2 yrs) winner Kenny The Captain (by Captain Rio) and 2-y-o 6f winner Jopau (by Dr Fong): dam 2-y-o 5f winner: well held in pair of minor events. *Derek Shaw* –

BORN LEGEND (IRE) 3 b.g. Born To Sea (IRE) 117 – Hallowed Park (IRE) (Barathea (IRE) 127) [2017 –: t9.5m p10g^3 p12g^4 9.9g^4 Jul 4] fair maiden: stays 1¼m: acts on polytrack: in blinkers last 3 starts: often races freely: won over hurdles in November. *Charles Hills* **66**

BORN ON THE CLYDE (IRE) 3 b.g. The Carbon Unit (USA) 106 – There's A Light (IRE) 70 (Fantastic Light (USA) 134) [2017 p7g p6s p7g p8g^5 8s 9.2s Aug 5] modest maiden: best effort at 1m: acts on polytrack: tried in blinkers. *John Patrick Shanahan, Ireland* **57**

BORN TO BE ALIVE (IRE) 3 b.g. Born To Sea (IRE) 117 – Yaria (IRE) 98 (Danehill (USA) 126) [2017 10g^2 8d* 9.1d^2 8.9g^2 9.9s^3 t9.5d^2 Dec 26] 10,000Y: fifth foal: half-brother to 3 winners, including smart 7f/9f winner Father Frost (by Rip Van Winkle) and 1m winner Hurricane Lady (by Hurricane Run): dam, winner up to 7f (2-y-o 6f winner), half-sister to smart winner up to 1m Emirates Gold: smart performer: won maiden at Ayr (by 8 lengths from Lamloom) in June: second in handicap at Wolverhampton (½ length behind Mount Tahan) in December: stays 9.5f: acts on tapeta and good to soft going. *K. R. Burke* **115**

BORN TO BOOGIE 3 b.f. Bahri (USA) 125 – Turtle Dove 65 (Tobougg (IRE) 125) [2017 57: t7.1g f7.1g 8.3s Jul 4] leggy filly: poor maiden: stays 7f: acts on heavy going. *Chris Grant* **45**

BORN TO BOOM (IRE) 3 b.g. Born To Sea (IRE) 117 – La Belle Maison (IRE) 78 (Titus Livius (FR) 115) [2017 8.3g^3 8g^3 9v^5 9.1g 7.8s* 8.9s^6 t8d^6 Oct 24] €80,000Y: first foal: dam, 1m winner, half-sister to very smart winner up to 1½m Housamix: fairly useful performer: won handicap at Carlisle (by head from Heir of Excitement) in August: stays 1m: acts on soft going: front runner/races prominently: sold 4,500 gns in October. *K. R. Burke* **80**

BORN TO FINISH (IRE) 4 b.g. Dark Angel (IRE) 113 – Music Pearl (IRE) 77 (Oratorio (IRE) 128) [2017 66, a75: t6f* p6g* p6d^3 p6g* p6g^6 6g^5 6m 6m^4 6m 7.2g^5 7m 7.1g^6 t6.1g^3 p6g p6g^3 p6g^2 p6g* p6s^2 p6s^3 Dec 15] sturdy gelding: fair handicapper on turf, fairly useful on all-weather: won at Wolverhampton and Kempton in January, Lingfield in February and Kempton again in November: left Jeremy Gask after seventh start: stays 7f: acts on polytrack, tapeta and good to firm going: wears headgear: has worn tongue tie: usually races towards rear. *Jamie Osborne* **75 a90**

BORN TO PLEASE 3 b.f. Stimulation (IRE) 121 – Heart Felt 71 (Beat Hollow 126) [2017 57: 10.2f^4 12g 10.2f 8.3d^3 8s* 9.9m 8v^2 p8g^6 8.1d^3 Oct 23] sturdy filly: modest handicapper: won at Sandown (apprentice) in August: third at Windsor in October: stays 1¼m: acts on any turf going: tried in cheekpieces. *Mark Usher* **61**

BORN TO REASON (IRE) 3 b.g. Born To Sea (IRE) 117 – Laureldean Lady (IRE) (Statue of Liberty (USA) 115) [2017 t9.5m^4 t9.5g^4 t9.5g^4 t9.5m^6 10.2m 10m t8s^3 t8.6g p8d t9.5g* t8.6g* t9.5g t8d^6 t9.5d Dec 26] fair handicapper: won at Wolverhampton (twice) in October: left Jamie Osborne after first start: stays 9.5f: acts on tapeta: wears headgear: tried in tongue tie: often races towards rear. *Kevin Frost* **67**

BORNTOSIN (IRE) 3 b.g. Born To Sea (IRE) 117 – Mrs Beeton (IRE) 80 (Dansili 127) [2017 p8g p10g 8g^2 Jul 6] fair form: standout effort when second in seller at Yarmouth (tongue tied) in July. *Marco Botti* **71**

BORN TO SPEND (IRE) 2 ch.f. (Mar 12) Born To Sea (IRE) 117 – Banco Suivi (IRE) 93 (Nashwan (USA) 135) [2017 8.3v t8g p8g Dec 20] seventh foal: half-sister to useful 1¾m-2m winner Body Language (by Beat Hollow): dam, 1½m winner who stayed 1¾m, half-sister to smart performer up to 14.6f/high-class hurdler Celestial Halo: down the field in maidens/minor event: bred to be suited by 1¼m+. *Ian Williams* **–**

BOROUGH BOY (IRE) 7 b.g. Jeremy (USA) 122 – Ostrusa (AUT) (Rustan (HUN)) [2017 87: f5g f6g f6g^6 p6g f6m^4 f5g^2 p6g^4 f5d^4 f5g* p5g^4 5d^2 5g^4 t5.1g p5s^6 5d 6s^5 5g 5s^6 f5g f6.1g^2 t6g^3 Dec 6] sturdy gelding: fair handicapper: won at Southwell in April: has form at 7f, races at sprint trips nowadays: acts on all-weather and soft going: wears visor. *Derek Shaw* **73**

BORTHWEN (IRE) 3 b.f. Lawman (FR) 121 – Apticanti (USA) 65 (Aptitude (USA) 128) [2017 8m Apr 18] €140,000Y: unfurnished filly: second foal: dam twice-raced half-sister to high-class winner up to 9f Distant Music: 25/1, well held in newcomers race at Newmarket. *Charles Hills* **–**

BOSCASTLE (USA) 2 ch.f. (Jan 24) Sea The Stars (IRE) 140 – Imprecation (USA) (First Defence (USA) 119) [2017 8d 8.3d 8s Oct 28] 60,000Y: first foal: dam, French maiden (stayed 1¼m), half-sister to Prix de Diane winner Nebraska Tornado: mid-division at best in minor events/maiden. *Hughie Morrison* **59**

BO SELECTA (IRE) 3 b.c. Dream Ahead (USA) 133 – Chicane 76 (Motivator 131) [2017 63: p6g^6 f5s^3 f8m 7m^3 7g f7.1g^2 f7.1g^6 f8.1g^2 f7.1g^4 Dec 22] fair maiden: stays 7f: acts on polytrack, fibresand and good to firm going: in cheekpieces last 5 starts. *Richard Spencer* **65**

BOSHAM 7 b.g. Shamardal (USA) 129 – Awwal Malika (USA) 73 (Kingmambo (USA) 125) [2017 83, a105: p5g^4 p6m^6 t6g p5g^6 5m^2 5m* 5m p5s 5m 5g 5g f5g t6s f5g Dec 22] fairly useful handicapper: won at Catterick in May: stays 1m: acts on polytrack, tapeta and firm going: wears headgear: usually tongue tied: front runner/races prominently. *Michael Easterby* **83** **a94**

BOSPHORUS PRINCE (IRE) 5 b.h. Hurricane Run (IRE) 134 – Bosphorus Queen (IRE) 83 (Sri Pekan (USA) 117) [2017 t9.5g^3 p8g^4 t9.5g^2 p12g* May 4] fairly useful performer: won handicap at Lingfield in May: stays 1½m: acts on polytrack and tapeta. *Matthew Salaman* **80**

BOSS FOR A DAY 2 ch.g. (Apr 8) Mastercraftsman (IRE) 129 – Santa Agata (FR) 95 (Anabaa (USA) 130) [2017 p7.5g p8g^6 p10g p7s Dec 14] modest form: best effort at 1m: tried in cheekpieces. *J. S. Moore* **53**

BOSSINEY BAY (IRE) 2 b.f. (Mar 17) Camelot 128 – Ursula Minor (IRE) (Footstepsinthesand 120) [2017 8.3d Oct 4] €60,000Y: fourth foal: half-sister to winners in Hong Kong and South Africa by High Chaparral: dam unraced half-sister to smart 5f-1m winner Alo Pura and to dam of smart performer up to 2m Red Galileo: 28/1, well held in maiden at Nottingham (hooded). *Hughie Morrison* **–**

BOSSIPOP 4 ch.g. Assertive 121 – Opopmil (IRE) 68 (Pips Pride 117) [2017 96: 6g 5.1m^5 6m 6d^2 5g^3 6s* 6d^2 6g 5.5g^2 6v^5 5.6g 6v 5g Oct 13] good-topped gelding: useful handicapper: won at Pontefract (by 2¼ lengths from Gin In The Inn) in July: second at Chester (neck behind Guishan) in August: stays 6f: acts on good to firm and heavy going: wears headgear: races prominently. *Tim Easterby* **97**

BOSS KOKO 2 ch.f. (Feb 5) Cityscape 127 – Speedy Utmost Meg (Medicean 128) [2017 6.5d 6d 7.4m^6 Jun 27] £800Y: first foal: dam little form: well held in minor events. *Tim Easterby* **–**

BOSSY GUEST (IRE) 5 b.g. Medicean 128 – Ros The Boss (IRE) 80 (Danehill (USA) 126) [2017 109§: 8m^5 7m 8m 7g 8s Jul 22] good-topped gelding: smart handicapper: fifth to Banksea at Newbury on reappearance: stays 9f: acts on firm and soft going: often slowly **110 §**

away/races in rear: one to treat with caution (took little interest last 2 starts): sold 5,000 gns in October, sent to Saudi Arabia. *Mick Channon*

BOSTONIAN 7 b.g. Dubawi (IRE) 129 – Bolshaya 74 (Cadeaux Genereux 131) [2017 **88**
p12g p12g^4 t16.5g^5 12g^5 11.5g^2 Jun 13] sturdy gelding: fairly useful maiden handicapper: second at Yarmouth in June: trained by Jo Hughes third outing only, then returned to former trainer: stays 1½m: acts on polytrack and good to firm going: usually races close up. *Shaun Lycett*

BOTTLEOFSMOKE (IRE) 4 b.g. Big Bad Bob (IRE) 118 – Testimonial 63 (Singspiel **75**
(IRE) 133) [2017 53: p12g^2 p12s p10.7g t12.2g* t12.2g^2 12m^6 12g* p12g^6 13m^3 12g 14g^4 **a66**
12s^6 13.8s^3 14d^6 14v Oct 11] fair handicapper: won at Wolverhampton in March and Roscommon in May: stays 1¾m: acts on polytrack, tapeta, soft and good to firm going: has worn hood/tongue tie: sold 4,000 gns, sent to Germany. *Gavin Patrick Cromwell, Ireland*

BOUCLIER (IRE) 7 ch.h. Zamindar (USA) 116 – Bastet (IRE) 110 (Giant's Causeway **83**
(USA) 132) [2017 88: p6g t7.1d^3 p6g* p8f* 8d^3 7.6g 6v 7g 7v f7.1g Dec 11] strong horse: **a90**
fairly useful handicapper: won at Kempton (by ¾ length from Cultured Knight) in March and Lingfield (by ¾ length from Golden Wedding) in April: had various trainers in 2017 (both wins for David Loughnane): stays 1m: acts on polytrack and good to soft going: often races in rear. *Michael Easterby*

BOUDICA BAY (IRE) 2 b.f. (Mar 2) Rip Van Winkle (IRE) 134 – White Shift (IRE) 87 –
(Night Shift (USA)) [2017 6d Sep 12] second foal: dam, winner up to 6f (2-y-o 5f winner), half-sister to useful 7f/1m winner Secret Art: 50/1, well held in minor event at Catterick. *Eric Alston*

BOUNCE 4 b.f. Bahamian Bounty 116 – Black Belt Shopper (IRE) 82 (Desert Prince (IRE) **99**
130) [2017 103p: 6.1g^3 6f^2 5m 5g^4 6g Sep 7] useful performer: second in listed race at Haydock (½ length behind Buying Trouble) in May: stays 6f: acts on polytrack and firm going: often races towards rear. *Henry Candy*

BOUND FOR NOWHERE (USA) 3 b.c. The Factor (USA) 126 – Fancy Deed (USA) **116**
(Alydeed (CAN) 120) [2017 p6f* 5.5f* 6m^4 6.5g Aug 6] $310,000Y: strong colt: fifth foal: half-brother to several winners in USA: dam unraced half-sister to dual Breeders' Cup Sprint winner Midnight Lute: smart form: won maiden at Turfway in January and allowance race at Keeneland in April: fourth in Commonwealth Cup at Royal Ascot (4¼ lengths behind Caravaggio) next time: below form in Prix Maurice de Gheest at Deauville final outing: stays 6f. *Wesley A. Ward, USA*

BOUNDSY (IRE) 3 ch.g. Dandy Man (IRE) 123 – Chiba (UAE) (Timber Country (USA) **99**
124) [2017 80: 5.1m^4 5s 5g^2 5g^2 6.1g* t6g^2 5.1g* 5v* 5d^3 Oct 28] neat gelding: useful handicapper: won at Chester in July and September, and Haydock (by nose from Rasheeq) later in September: stays 6f: acts on tapeta, good to firm and heavy going: consistent. *Richard Fahey*

BOUNTY PURSUIT 5 b.g. Pastoral Pursuits 127 – Poyle Dee Dee 72 (Oasis Dream 129) **76**
[2017 66: t7.1g* f6m* f7g p7g^2 t8.6g^5 7.1m^2 7g^6 7.1g^2 p7g* f7.1g f7.1g^5 Dec 22] fair handicapper: won at Wolverhampton and Southwell in February, and Kempton in October: left Michael Appleby after fifth start: best up to 7f: acts on all-weather and good to firm going: has worn headgear. *Michael Blake*

BOURBONISTO 3 ch.g. Stimulation (IRE) 121 – Psychic's Dream 87 (Oasis Dream 129) **67**
[2017 65: 6d^4 6d^3 5d 7m Aug 26] sturdy gelding: fair maiden: stays 6f: acts on good to firm and good to soft going. *Ben Haslam*

BOURNE 11 gr.g. Linamix (FR) 127 – L'Affaire Monique 101 (Machiavellian (USA) 123) **56**
[2017 14.1s^6 14.1v^5 Sep 13] sturdy gelding: one-time useful handicapper, laboured only 2 starts (blinkered) on Flat since 2011: stays 14.5f: acts on polytrack and good to firm going: fair but temperamental hurdler nowadays. *Donald McCain*

BOWBAN 3 b.c. Makfi 130 – Serafina's Flight 82 (Fantastic Light (USA) 134) [2017 76p: **81**
t10.2g^2 t8g^2 t12.4g Jun 30] fairly useful form: second in maiden at Newcastle in February: best effort at 1m. *Brian Ellison*

BOW BELLES 2 ch.f. (Apr 1) Kyllachy 129 – Rockme Cockney 71 (Cockney Rebel **80**
(IRE) 127) [2017 5m^5 5d* 5d^3 5m 5s^3 5d^2 Oct 11] second foal: half-sister to 1m winner Sheisdiesel (by Harbour Watch): dam 7f winner: fairly useful performer: won minor event at Ripon in July: second in nursery at Nottingham in October: raced only at 5f: acts on soft going: in hood last 2 starts. *Tim Easterby*

BOWDITCH (IRE) 2 b.c. (Mar 27) Nathaniel (IRE) 129 – Kate The Great 79 (Xaar 132) **81** [2017 8g^5 8d^4 8.5v^5 p10g* Oct 18] 75,000Y: half-brother to several winners, including smart winner up to 6f Eastern Impact (2-y-o 5f winner, by Bahamian Bounty) and useful 6f (at 2 yrs) and 6.5f (in Canada) winner Miss Katie Mae (by Dark Angel): dam 2-y-o 5f winner: fairly useful form: won minor event at Lingfield (by 2 lengths from Yabass) in October: stays 1¼m. *John Gosden*

BOWERMAN 3 b.c. Dutch Art 126 – Jamboretta (IRE) 102 (Danehill (USA) 126) [2017 **107 p** 81p: p8g* p8s* Dec 7] useful form: won maiden at Kempton (by 3¾ lengths from Ply) in April and handicap at Chelmsford (by 2¾ lengths from Believe It) in December: raced only at 1m: more to come. *Roger Varian*

BOWGEY MAN 2 bl.g. (Apr 19) Pastoral Pursuits 127 – Black Annis Bower 79 **–** (Proclamation (IRE) 130) [2017 5d Jul 22] 25/1, well held in minor event at Ripon. *Michael Easterby*

BOWLER HAT 2 b.g. (Apr 30) Helmet (AUS) 127 – Fatima's Gift 78 (Dalakhani (IRE) **76** 133) [2017 6.1g^2 p7s p6g t7.1d Nov 4] close-coupled gelding: fair form: best effort at 6f: tried in cheekpieces. *Hugo Palmer*

BOWSERS BOLD 6 gr.g. Firebreak 125 – Cristal Clear (IRE) 92 (Clodovil (IRE) 116) **– §** [2017 –§: p10d Sep 21] sturdy gelding: fair maiden handicapper at best: stayed 1½m: acted on polytrack, tapeta and firm going: tried in headgear: often flattered to deceive: dead. *Roger Ingram*

BOWSON FRED 5 b.g. Monsieur Bond (IRE) 120 – Bow Bridge 95 (Bertolini (USA) **109** 125) [2017 109: t5g^5 f5g^3 t5.1g^2 t6g^5 p5g^2 5.2g^2 5m 5m 5v t5.1g^4 t5g^2 t5.1g^3 Dec 22] good-topped gelding: useful handicapper: second at Lingfield (length behind Kimberella) in March and Newbury (1¼ lengths behind Sir Robert Cheval) in April: best form at 5f: acts on polytrack, tapeta, soft and good to firm going: tried in visor. *Michael Easterby*

BOW STREET 2 ch.c. (Feb 8) New Approach (IRE) 132 – Favourable Terms 120 (Selkirk **93 p** (USA) 129) [2017 p8g^3 8m^2 p8g* Nov 7] compact colt: brother to 7f winner New Terms and half-brother to 3 winners, including useful French 11f winner Semester (by Monsun): dam 7f-1¼m (Nassau Stakes) winner: fairly useful form: won minor event at Kempton (by 2¾ lengths from Podemos) in November: will stay 1¼m: remains with potential. *Charlie Appleby*

BOYCHICK (IRE) 4 b.g. Holy Roman Emperor (IRE) 125 – Al Saqiya (USA) 68 **82** (Woodman (USA) 126) [2017 59: t9.5m* t9.5g* p10d* p11g^2 10.3g^5 p11g^2 t12.2g^2 11.9m^2 11.4g* Jul 31] lengthy gelding: fairly useful handicapper: won at Wolverhampton (twice) in January, Chelmsford in February and Windsor in July: stays 1½m: acts on polytrack, tapeta, soft and good to firm going: has worn blinkers: usually races prominently, often travels strongly. *Ed Walker*

BOYCIE 4 b.g. Paco Boy (IRE) 129 – Eve 81 (Rainbow Quest (USA) 134) [2017 83, a77: **88** p10d^6 10.3g* 9.9g^3 10.4m^4 9.9g* 10.2m^2 10m 10.2d 10s^5 p10g 10.2d t9.5g Dec 5] compact **a77** gelding: fairly useful handicapper: won at Doncaster (apprentice) in April and Sandown (by ½ length from Silver Ghost) in May: stays 10.5f: acts on polytrack, tapeta, soft and good to firm going: has worn headgear. *Richard Hannon*

BOY IN THE BAR 6 ch.g. Dutch Art 126 – Lipsia (IRE) (Dubai Destination (USA) 127) **101** [2017 95: 5f 6s^3 6m* 6g^3 6m^6 p7s^4 t6d* 6d^6 p6g^3 p7s* Nov 17] lengthy, angular gelding: useful handicapper: won at Goodwood in May, Newcastle in October and Chelmsford in November: stays 7f: acts on polytrack, tapeta, soft and good to firm going: wears headgear: usually races prominently. *Ian Williams*

BOYNTON (USA) 3 ch.g. More Than Ready (USA) 120 – Baffled (USA) 89 (Distorted **112** Humor (USA) 117) [2017 112p: p10g^2 10d^3 p10g Nov 18] strong gelding: smart performer: second in minor event at Chelmsford (½ length behind Victory Bond) in October: stays 1¼m: acts on polytrack, good to firm and good to soft going: usually races close up/freely. *Charlie Appleby*

BRACKEN BRAE 5 b.m. Champs Elysees 124 – Azure Mist 79 (Bahamian Bounty 116) **81** [2017 78: p16g^2 p16d* p13.3d^6 p16g^2 t16.5g* t16.5g^4 14.1g^5 p16g^5 p16g p16s Dec 15] big mare: fairly useful handicapper: won at Chelmsford in February and Wolverhampton in April: stays 16.5f: acts on polytrack and tapeta. *Mark H. Tompkins*

BRADFIELD MAGIC (IRE) 3 b.f. Holy Roman Emperor (IRE) 125 – Magic Eye **68** (IRE) 103 (Nayef (USA) 129) [2017 58: t7.2g 7d^3 7.1v 8g^2 8.1d^4 p8g* 9.9d^4 9.9s Oct 10] sturdy filly: fair handicapper: won at Chelmsford in September: may prove best at short of 1¼m: acts on polytrack and good to soft going. *Charles Hills*

BRAEMAR 2 b.c. (Feb 12) Oasis Dream 129 – Spectacle 63 (Dalakhani (IRE) 133) [2017 7m p8g^6 Dec 20] modest form: better effort when eighth in minor event at Yarmouth (6½ lengths behind Il Primo Sole) in August. *Sir Michael Stoute* **61**

BRAES OF LOCHALSH 6 b.g. Tiger Hill (IRE) 127 – Gargoyle Girl 75 (Be My Chief (USA) 122) [2017 81: 16.5m^5 14m^5 15d^2 13.1g^2 14.5s^2 13.1s^5 13.1g^2 15d^5 16.1g^4 13s^5 15v^6 t16.3d Dec 16] fair handicapper: stays 17.5f: acts on good to firm and heavy going: usually wears headgear. *Jim Goldie* **77**

BRAGANZA 2 b.f. (May 3) Nathaniel (IRE) 129 – Amber Queen (IRE) 92 (Cadeaux Genereux 131) [2017 p8s^5 Dec 17] 33,000F, 17,500Y: sixth foal: half-sister to 9f/1¼m winner (stayed 1½m) Diddy Eric (by Oratorio) and useful winner up to 1¼m Mountain Rescue (2-y-o 6f winner, by High Chaparral): dam, 7f winner, half-sister to smart winner up to 1m Spinning Queen: 20/1, well held in minor event at Chelmsford. *Ed Dunlop* **–**

BRAHMA 4 b.g. Mount Nelson 125 – Swan Queen 101 (In The Wings 128) [2017 57p: f12m^5 p12g Apr 5] modest maiden: bred to be suited by 1½m+: tried in blinkers. *Hughie Morrison* **–**

BRAMETOT (IRE) 3 b.c. Rajsaman (FR) 121 – Morning Light (GER) (Law Society (USA) 130) [2017 8g* 8d* 10.4g* 9.9g^5 11.9d^5 10s^6 Oct 21] **124**

August 15th—Assumption Day—is a national holiday in France but the date will be one that Jean-Claude Rouget will want to forget in a hurry. Within the space of an hour at Deauville on that afternoon, the stable's two leading Prix de l'Arc de Triomphe contenders, Almanzor and Brametot, also the last two winners of the Prix du Jockey Club, were each beaten when hot favourite for their respective races. For Almanzor, the best three-year-old in Europe the previous season, it proved both a belated return to action and the final start of his career, as he was retired to stud following his ignominious defeat at 2/1-on in the Prix Gontaut-Biron in which he dead-heated for last in a field of six. As for Brametot's fifth place, following a very slow start, in the Prix Guillaume d'Ornano, that was another disappointment, but, in his case, it was one he put behind him when running a career best to fill the same position in the Arc, while his earlier completion of the double in the French colts' classics when successful in the Jockey Club was the highlight of a difficult season all round in which Rouget, in his own words, endured the worst week of his more than forty years as a trainer.

That had come in April when one of Rouget's barns, housing fifty-seven colts—Almanzor among them, but not Brametot—was struck down in a matter of days by an outbreak of the equine herpes virus or EHV-1. Almanzor was one of those to suffer nothing worse than a fever, but in its neurological form the virus can have a debilitating effect, leading to paralysis. Among those more seriously affected, a couple of three-year-old colts had to be put down. The same virus hit Kevin Ryan's yard in Yorkshire later in the year, while in Louisiana back in January quarantine measures following an EHV outbreak at Fair Grounds racecourse prevented the top-class American colt Gun Runner from contesting the inaugural Pegasus World Cup (he went on to win the 2018 version). Another blow to the Rouget stable came in the spring when the retirement was announced of the stable's unbeaten Poule d'Essai des Pouliches and Prix de Diane winner La Cressonniere as a result of a recurring back problem. Along with the same owners' Almanzor, the filly had been one of the main contributors to Rouget's outstanding season in 2016 when he became champion trainer in France for the second time. Almanzor missed the Arc as a three-year-old in order to contest the Champion Stakes instead, beating the Arc winner Found at Ascot, but he was second favourite for the latest Arc at the time of his belated reappearance at Deauville, after which he had been due to bid for a repeat success in the Irish Champion Stakes before heading to Chantilly. There was no chance of having Almanzor ready in time for Royal Ascot, the long-term plan for the first part of his four-year-old season, and, with other physical problems playing a part, his return was postponed from the York Stakes at the end of July to Deauville the following month. However, Rouget had sounded an ominous warning that Almanzor 'was no longer the same horse as last year' earlier in the summer, having already predicted that the horses from his affected barn would only be sixty or seventy per cent for their return to action.

Abu Dhabi Poule d'Essai des Poulains, Deauville—
Brametot stays on well to deny Le Brevido (spots on cap) on the line, leading home a one, two for the home team with Rivet best of the raiders in third

Whilst the infected barn was quarantined, the remainder of Rouget's string housed elsewhere was unaffected by the outbreak. That much was clear when Brametot lifted the gloom within days of the virus being at its height by making a winning return in the Prix de Fontainebleau at Chantilly. Brametot's two and a half length victory over Stunning Spirit, coming from last place after a slow start, was a smart effort and represented plenty of improvement on his useful two-year-old form. Brametot had won three of his four starts at two, a newcomers race and minor event at Deauville, and the listed Grand Criterium de Bordeaux, a race which Rouget has farmed over the years and which Almanzor had won twelve months earlier. Almanzor had been beaten into third on his return in the Fontainebleau which had prompted connections to step him up in trip straight away, whereas Brametot's win gave him leading claims in the following month's Abu Dhabi Poule d'Essai des Poulains which was once again run over Deauville's straight mile during Longchamp's ongoing redevelopment. The field of thirteen split into two early on, with Brametot at the rear of the smaller stand-side group. Challenging off the good pace approaching the final furlong, Brametot stayed on to snatch the race on the line by a short head from Le Brivido, winner of his two starts for Andre Fabre, who had himself come from well off the pace in the other group. They finished three lengths clear of the Racing Post Trophy winner Rivet in third who fared best of those who raced prominently, himself finishing six lengths or more clear of the remainder. Favourite National Defense, winner of the Prix Jean-Luc Lagardere, raced too freely before finishing a tailed-off last. Brametot, who was Rouget's first winner of the Poule d'Essai des Poulains, carried the Al Shaqab colours for the first time; hitherto, he had raced in the white, purple cap of Gerard Augustin-Normand who had owned Rouget's first Prix du Jockey Club winner Le Havre and was part-owner of Almanzor, La Cressonniere and Avenir Certain. Like La Cressonniere, Avenir Certain was a daughter of Le Havre and had also won both the French fillies' classics.

Augustin-Normand retained an interest in Brametot who was seen next at Chantilly where he was bidding to become his trainer's third winner of the Prix du Jockey Club. Al Shaqab were due to be represented by the Two Thousand Guineas third Al Wukair but, when he went lame days beforehand, Brametot was rerouted from the St James's Palace Stakes. Since the reduction in distance of the Prix du Jockey Club from the traditional Derby trip to ten and a half furlongs, the Poulains/Jockey Club double had been completed by the father and son pair of Shamardal in 2005 and Lope de Vega in 2010. Among the Poulains winners to have been unsuccessful was Silver Frost who had been the last Fontainebleau winner to go on to win the Poulains before Brametot; Silver Frost finished sixth behind Le Havre when favourite at Chantilly in 2009. Le Havre (runner-up to Silver Frost in the Poulains) and Almanzor hadn't been among the favourites in their years whereas Brametot was sent off at 17/10 in a smaller than usual field of twelve in which just three French trainers were represented. Despite Al Wukair's absence, his trainer Andre Fabre was still represented by three colts, including the previous season's Criterium de Saint-Cloud winner Waldgeist. He had been beaten by Recoletos, trained by Carlos Laffon-Parias, in the Prix Greffulhe at Saint-Cloud last time out and that pair figured among the other better-fancied runners, along with Rivet, the shortest-priced of the seven trained outside France. Brametot completed his classic double in what was becoming familiar style. Slowly away again and last early on, he made good headway in the straight after the German outsider Be My Sheriff made the early pace before Taj Mahal, one of three Aidan O'Brien-trained runners, took up the running. However, it was Waldgeist who stayed on to lead in the final fifty yards only for Brametot to arrive on the scene last of all, produced wide to pip Waldgeist on the line by a short head, just as he had that colt's stable-companion at Deauville. Less than three lengths covered the first seven home, with Recoletos a length behind the first two in third, while Taj Mahal finished fourth, just in front of his stable-companions War Decree and Orderofthegarter.

The Prix du Jockey Club was sponsored for the first time by the Al Thani family's investment company Qipco which already sponsors both Guineas at Newmarket, as well as the British Champions' Day programme at Ascot. It had been ten years since France's second most valuable race had the backing of a sponsor. Qatar invests heavily in sponsorship in both Britain and France, but the performances of Qatari-owned horses at the top level didn't provide a commensurate return in the latest season. Apart from Brametot and Al Wukair, who won the Jacques le Marois, the only other Group 1 winner in the Al Shaqab colours was Brametot's four-year-old stable-companion Mekhtaal (beaten favourite in the previous year's Prix du Jockey Club) in the Prix d'Ispahan. Rouget remarked after Brametot's win in the Prix du Jockey Club that it was only by chance that both he and Mekhtaal had been housed in a different barn from the one that had been struck down by EHV. Brametot's Italian-born jockey Cristian Demuro, who rode him in all his races, has now achieved the feat of winning all four traditional French classics—the Prix Royal-Oak (French St Leger) is open to older horses—in the space of just two years as he was La Cressonniere's partner when she won the Poule d'Essai des Pouliches and Prix de Diane the year before.

Almanzor had gone from strength to strength after winning the Prix du Jockey Club as an outsider the previous year, starting with victory in the Prix Guillaume d'Ornano at Deauville. Brametot made his next appearance in the same race, but his habitual slow start was even more pronounced than usual, leaving him trailing the eventual winner Eminent by fifteen lengths at halfway before finishing a never-nearer fifth. Checks on Brametot afterwards revealed a back problem which had perhaps been accounting for his slow starts, making him reluctant to jump away from the stalls. He certainly broke much more alertly in the Prix de l'Arc de Triomphe next time and travelled well just off the pace before making his effort two furlongs out. After initially not getting the best of runs up the rail, he stayed on again in the final furlong to run his best race on what proved his only race over as far as a mile and a half, finishing fifth, six and a half lengths behind impressive winner Enable. With nearly three weeks between the Arc and the Champion Stakes instead of the usual two, Brametot was sent to Ascot for his final start but he couldn't emulate Almanzor, finishing a well-held sixth behind Cracksman, performing as though not over his exertions at Chantilly, though he looked really well beforehand.

Qipco Prix du Jockey Club, Chantilly—
Brametot becomes the first since Lope de Vega in 2010 to complete the Poule d'Essai des Poulains/ Prix du Jockey Club double, staying on strongly again to lead in the final strides; Waldgeist (second right) reverses Prix Greffulhe form with Recoletos who finishes third

The rather leggy, good-topped Brametot was bought for only €26,000 at Arqana's foal sale at Deauville and comes from his sire's first crop. Rajsaman began his career with Alain de Royer Dupre in the ownership of the Aga Khan and unexpectedly registered his first pattern win in the Prix de Fontainebleau when supposedly acting as a pacemaker for his stable-companion Siyouni whom he beat into second, while the aforementioned Lope de Vega finished a close third. Rajsaman's win was no fluke, however, as he went on to prove a very smart miler for Freddie Head as a four-year-old, with Group 2 victories in the Prix du Muguet and Prix Daniel Wildenstein. When Brametot also won the Fontainebleau, he was following not just in the footsteps of his sire, but also those of his grandsire Linamix (who, like Brametot, followed up in the Poulains) and of his great grandsire Mendez who were both also Fontainebleau winners. Rajsaman was given more opportunities than most to make an early impact as a stallion as he covered a total of nearly six hundred mares in his first three years at stud (all at a fee of €4,000), his book of 219 in 2015 thought to be a record for a French-based stallion.

Brametot (IRE) (b.c. 2014)	Rajsaman (FR) (gr 2007)	Linamix (gr 1987)	Mendez
			Lunadix
		Rose Quartz (b 1997)	Lammtarra
			Graphite
	Morning Light (GER) (br 1997)	Law Society (br 1982)	Alleged
			Bold Bikini
		Mosella (b 1985)	Surumu
			Monasia

While Brametot comes from a male line of mainly milers, he is much more stoutly bred on the dam's side which accounts for his staying the Arc trip. His German-bred dam Morning Light is by the Irish Derby winner Law Society and is a half-sister to the Deutsches Derby runner-up Monsun who became Germany's star stallion before his death in 2012. Despite that breeding, Morning Light had been bought for just €12,000 at Deauville in December 2013 carrying Brametot who was subsequently foaled in Ireland. However, his dam's buyer was Chilean, and Morning Light was covered by Monsun's son Manduro to southern hemisphere time later in 2014 before being exported to South America. Morning Light had produced three other winners in Europe from eight foals prior to Brametot. The best of them was Mulan (by Marju), a useful performer in Germany and Scandinavia at up to a mile and a half, while the others are Twilight (by Siyouni), a winner in France over an extended mile, and the Czech winner Miss Kruk (by Soldier of Fortune). Morning Light won twice at around a mile and a half in Germany (in a maiden and handicap) and she and Monsun were among six winners out of their dam Mosella, a listed winner in Germany over ten and a half furlongs. Mosella's other daughters include the grandam of the Prix du Cadran winner Molly Malone and the smart filly Wekeela who won the Prix Chloe for Rouget as a three-year-old and was successful in a Grade 3 contest at Monmouth in the latest season. Both those mares were bought by Qatar Racing when they came up for auction at the end of the year; Wekeela was knocked down for for 1,800,000 guineas at Newmarket, while Molly Malone changed hands for €600,000 at Deauville later in December.

Brametot has been retired by Al Shaqab to their Haras de Bouquetot in Normandy where he'll stand at a fee of €10,000 live foal. As for Almanzor, he begins his stallion career at Haras d'Etreham, where he was raised, and which bought a share in him late in his three-year-old season. His fee is €35,000 live foal. Brametot stayed a mile and a half and was raced only on good or good to soft ground until his final start at Ascot where, as has already been said, there might have been more to his below-form effort than the softer ground. While his best performance came in the Arc, Brametot will be better remembered for his last-gasp victories in the Poule d'Essai des Poulains and the Prix du Jockey Club. Despite what could have been a catastrophic start, and thanks in no small part to those verdicts going Brametot's way, it was pretty much business as usual by the end of the year for his stable, with Rouget once again playing second fiddle to Andre Fabre who was back in his perennial position at the head of the French trainers' championship. *Jean-Claude Rouget, France*

BRANDO 5 ch.g. Pivotal 124 – Argent du Bois (USA) (Silver Hawk (USA) 123) **124**
[2017 125: 6m* 6s 6g[3] 6.5g* 6s 7d 6s[6] Oct 21]

The equine herpes virus is found in horse populations worldwide, with the EHV-1 and EHV-4 supposedly the most common types. The former is said to cause respiratory disease in young horses, abortion in pregnant mares and paralysis in horses of all ages and types. Thankfully, there have been very few instances of the virus causing problems in racing over the years, though the 2017 Flat season saw two high profile outbreaks of the EHV-1 variety, in the stables of Group 1 winning trainers on both sides of the English Channel. Jean-Claude Rouget lost two horses to the disease in April and the barn in Pau in which they were stabled—also home to the top European performer of 2016 Almanzor and the same season's Prix Jean Prat winner Zelzal—was quickly placed under quarantine, with twenty-seven of the fifty-seven inmates having shown signs of the virus. Rouget was fortunate that only one of his three barns was affected and he was allowed to send out runners from the others, including the Poule d'Essai des Poulains and Prix du Jockey Club winner Brametot, whose essay precedes this one. Yorkshire trainer Kevin Ryan, on the other hand, was afforded no such exemption, with the BHA refusing to accept entries 'indefinitely' from his Hambleton stable from June 1st, although the virus had appeared in just one horse (Ryan had notified the authorities immediately and he withdrew the stable's runners that had been declared the next day as a precaution, before a fuller investigation took place). The yards of neighbours Bryan Smart and Michael Herrington were also placed under quarantine as a precaution, because of the proximity to Ryan's yard and the sharing of horse boxes with him, though Smart was having runners just nine days later. Kevin Ryan did not have runners again until much later in the month—Rural Celebration and Futoon finished second and fourth, respectively, in the listed Land o'Burns Fillies' Stakes at Ayr—and the ban denied the stable's top horse Brando the chance to line up in the Diamond Jubilee Stakes at Royal Ascot.

Brando had produced his best effort, and the best handicap performance of the year on Timeform ratings, when winning the Ayr Gold Cup from a BHA mark of 110 the previous September, and didn't have much trouble justifying short odds after six months off in the Abernant Stakes at Newmarket in April, not needing to match his very best form to hold the smart Ornate by a length, having a bit in hand under a confident ride. Brando went into his next race in the Duke of York Stakes with leading claims, sent off the 5/2 favourite in a field of twelve, but he weakened tamely from two out and was afterwards reported to have burst a blood vessel. The restrictions placed on his trainer's yard meant that Brando was not seen on a racecourse again until the July Cup, a race for which he started at 28/1 and finished a length and three quarters third to Harry Angel after starting his effort from some way back in a race run at a false gallop. Even better was to come in

LARC Prix Maurice de Gheest, Deauville—
Brando makes the breakthrough at Group 1 level and leads home a one, two, three, four for the British raiders, with Aclaim (partially hidden by winner), Tupi (checks on cap) and the grey Magical Memory completing the frame; odds-on Caravaggio is only sixth

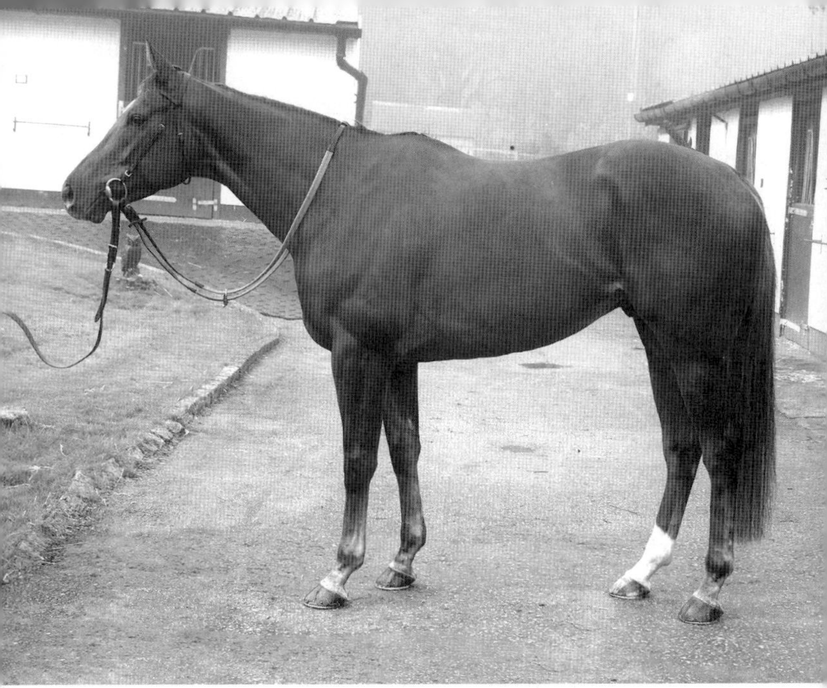

Mrs Angie Bailey's "Brando"

the following month's LARC Prix Maurice de Gheest over an extra half furlong at Deauville. Brando was sent off at 9/1 that day in a race that also featured the home-trained defending champion Signs of Blessing and the Commonwealth Cup winner Caravaggio, who had disappointed when 11/10-on in the July Cup. Caravaggio was sent off at odds on once more to redeem himself in France, but he ran below his best again, leaving British-trained runners to land a one, two, three, four from their four challengers. Brando held off the late thrust of Aclaim to win by half a length, with Tupi a length and three quarters back in third and Magical Memory completing the frame. The most notable aspect of Brando's performance was how strongly he travelled and, after leading inside the final furlong, he was always doing enough to record his first Group 1 victory, and a second for his jockey Tom Eaves, who rode another Yorkshire-trained sprinter Tangerine Trees when he won the Prix de l'Abbaye de Longchamp in 2011. Brando's success was also the undoubted highlight of his trainer's turbulent season, though the stable continued to chalk up the winners. However, for Brando himself, Deauville proved to be as good as it got. He failed to reproduce his form in three subsequent starts, well held in the Sprint Cup at Haydock, the Prix de la Foret at Chantilly and the British Champions Sprint Stakes at Ascot, making little impression when four and a half lengths sixth to Librisa Breeze on the last occasion. That Brando's campaign ended in anti-climax was obviously disappointing, given his July Cup effort and subsequent victory in the Prix Maurice de Gheest, though he is clearly a very smart sprinter when on song. There will be more opportunities for him to add to his tally in 2018, despite the fact that the sprinting division looks likely to be strong once again, with Battaash, Harry Angel, Tasleet and Librisa Breeze among those also set to return, along with the usual crop of up-and-coming three-year-olds.

Brando (ch.g. 2012)	Pivotal (ch 1993)	Polar Falcon (b or br 1987)	Nureyev
			Marie d'Argonne
		Fearless Revival (ch 1987)	Cozzene
			Stufida
	Argent du Bois (USA) (b 1996)	Silver Hawk (b 1979)	Roberto
			Gris Vitesse
		Wiener Wald (ch 1992)	Woodman
			Chapel of Dreams

Brando's pedigree was covered in *Racehorses of 2016* and, in summary, he is by the 1996 Nunthorpe winner Pivotal, who was also represented with distinction, among others, in the latest season, by Remarkable, who emulated Brando's feat in the 2016 Ayr Gold Cup when producing the joint best handicap performance of the year at Ascot in September. Remarkable defied a BHA mark of 107 to score that day and could well make his presence felt in minor pattern company on that evidence if kept in training. Brando is out of the Silver Hawk mare Argent du Bois, a half-sister to the Racing Post Trophy winner Crowded House. Argent du Bois failed to win in three starts at up to a mile for Jonathan Pease in France and Brando is the best of her progeny, though Ticker Tape (by Royal Applause), sold out of Jamie Osborne's stable for 100,000 guineas after winning twice in Britain, went on to win three times for Jim Cassidy in America, including twice in Grade 1 company, winning the American Oaks at Hollywood Park in 2003 and the Queen Elizabeth II Challenge Cup at Keeneland the following year. Saint Elena (by Efisio) also won three races at two to four in Britain and Canada and is the dam of winners, including the Prix Morny and Middle Park winner Reckless Abandon. A Cape Cross yearling half-brother to Brando was sold for 50,000 guineas to Dermot Farrington at the Newmarket October Sales Book 2. A strong gelding, Brando acts on soft and good to firm going. He is best at up to six and a half furlongs and is often held up. *Kevin Ryan*

BRANDON CASTLE 5 b.g. Dylan Thomas (IRE) 132 – Chelsey Jayne (IRE) 57 (Galileo (IRE) 134) [2017 82: 13.8m 11.2v^{6} 10.2m 12.3d t12.2g* 14.2g* 14m^{2} 13.9s* 14.4v* 13s* 15.4g t14d^{4} p12g^{6} Dec 23] sturdy gelding: useful handicapper: had excellent season, winning at Wolverhampton in July, Salisbury in August, Catterick (by 11 lengths from First Quest) and Chester (by 15 lengths from Plymouth Sound) in September, and Ayr (by 6 lengths from Vindicator) in October: left Simon West after fourth start: stays 14.5f: acts on polytrack, tapeta, good to firm and heavy going: wears headgear: usually tongue tied: front runner. *Archie Watson* **106 a99**

BRANDY STATION (IRE) 2 b.c. (Apr 29) Fast Company (IRE) 126 – Kardyls Hope (IRE) 90 (Fath (USA) 116) [2017 5m 5m* 5m^{4} 6d 5m^{2} p5d^{3} 5d^{3} p5g^{5} Oct 18] €5,200F, £8,000Y: sturdy colt: third foal: half-brother to 6f/7f winner Chickenfortea (by Clodovil): dam, 6f-1m winner, half-sister to very smart 1m/1¼m performer Top Notch Tonto: fairly useful performer: won minor event at Pontefract in May: third in nursery at Nottingham in October: left Tony Coyle after fifth start: best form at 5f: acts on polytrack, good to firm and good to soft going: front runner/races prominently. *Lisa Williamson* **82**

BRANSCOMBE 2 b.g. (Apr 16) Invincible Spirit (IRE) 121 – Lacily (USA) 90 (Elusive Quality (USA)) [2017 p5g^{6} t5s^{5} 5m* t5.1g^{2} 5g 6v^{6} Jul 27] second foal: half-brother to smart 2-y-o 5f/6f winner Yalta (by Exceed And Excel): dam, 2-y-o 1m winner who stayed 1¼m, half-sister to smart stayer Ley Hunter out of Irish Oaks winner Lailani: fairly useful performer: won minor event at Sandown (by length from Global Passion) in June: best form at 5f: acts on tapeta and good to firm going: front runner/races prominently. *Mark Johnston* **80**

BRASSBOUND (USA) 9 b.g. Redoute's Choice (AUS) – In A Bound (AUS) (Ashkalani (IRE) 128) [2017 80: f12g^{4} f16d^{4} Apr 6] rather leggy gelding: fairly useful handicapper, below form both starts in 2017: stays 2m: acts on polytrack, fibresand and heavy going: tried in cheekpieces: usually races close up. *Michael Appleby* **–**

BRASTED (IRE) 5 ch.g. Footstepsinthesand 120 – Ellen (IRE) (Machiavellian (USA) 123) [2017 82: p8g^{5} p8s p8g p8d Oct 6] tall gelding: fairly useful handicapper at best, well below that in 2017: stays 1m: acts on polytrack and firm going: usually wears tongue tie: often races prominently. *Lee Carter* **63**

BRAVE ANNA (USA) 3 b.f. War Front (USA) 119 – Liscanna (IRE) 105 (Sadler's Wells (USA) 132) [2017 115: 7m Apr 19] compact, good-bodied filly: smart form at 2 yrs (won Cheveley Park Stakes at Newmarket): well below best in Nell Gwyn Stakes on same course only start in 2017: should have stayed 7f: acted on soft and good to firm going: sometimes slowly away, often raced towards rear: retired, visits Caravaggio. *Aidan O'Brien, Ireland* **–**

Betway Lincoln (Heritage Handicap), Doncaster—
Bravery (far side) makes a winning start for the David O'Meara yard; Ryan Moore had ridden the first three winners on the card and is narrowly denied on the gambled-on Oh This Is Us (stars on sleeves), with Donncha (centre) and the 2015 winner Gabrial (noseband) completing the frame

BRAVERY (IRE) 4 b.g. Galileo (IRE) 134 – Lady Icarus (Rainbow Quest (USA) 134) **109** [2017 103: 8g* 9m 7.9d 8m 10.3m 9.9g 7.9d 10.3m 9d 7.9g^{2} 8.2d^{6} 7d^{5} Nov 11] strong, compact gelding: useful handicapper: won Lincoln at Doncaster (by neck from Oh This Is Us) in April: best up to 1¼m: acts on polytrack and heavy going: has worn hood. *David O'Meara*

BRAVE TART 3 b.f. Pastoral Pursuits 127 – Poyle Kiera 56 (Diktat 126) [2017 8g p8s – 8g Jul 12] tall filly: second foal: dam maiden (stayed 1¼m): no form in maidens. *Martin Smith*

BRAVO ZOLO (IRE) 5 b.g. Rip Van Winkle (IRE) 134 – Set Fire (IRE) 90 (Bertolini **118** (USA) 125) [2017 112: 8g* 7g^{2} 8.9g^{4} 8d* Nov 4] smart performer: won handicap at Meydan (by 1½ lengths from Suyoof) in February and listed race at Newmarket (by neck from Lord Glitters) in November: stays 9.5f: acts on polytrack, tapeta and heavy going: usually races close up. *Charlie Appleby*

BRAZTIME 3 b.f. Canford Cliffs (IRE) 133 – Briery (IRE) 66 (Salse (USA) 128) [2017 **80** 78: p7g^{6} 8.3g* 8m p8g^{4} 8m^{6} 9.9d p8g p8g p8g Oct 3] fairly useful handicapper: won at Nottingham in May: stays 8.5f: acts on polytrack and tapeta. *Richard Hannon*

BREAKABLE 6 ch.m. Firebreak 125 – Magic Myth (IRE) 81 (Revoque (IRE) 122) [2017 **101** 102: p7g 7g 7d^{4} 7.6s* 8d^{5} 7d^{2} 7.6g^{3} 7s 7g Sep 15] lengthy mare: useful handicapper: won at Chester in August: second at York (1¼ lengths behind Lincoln Rocks) later in month: stays 1m: acts on any turf going: has worn cheekpieces: front runner/races prominently. *Tim Easterby*

BREAKHEART (IRE) 10 b.g. Sakhee (USA) 136 – Exorcet (FR) 78 (Selkirk (USA) **58** 129) [2017 71: t9.5m^{6} p10g p8d^{2} p8g p8g 10g 9.9s* 10.2g^{6} 9.1m Aug 27] strong gelding: modest handicapper: won at Sandown (apprentice) in July: stays 10.5f: acts on polytrack, tapeta, firm and soft going: wears headgear: tried in tongue tie: often starts slowly, usually races in rear. *Andrew Balding*

BREAKING BREAD 3 b.c. Nathaniel (IRE) 129 – American Spirit (IRE) (Rock of **72 p** Gibraltar (IRE) 133) [2017 10m^{6} Apr 10] good-topped colt: third foal: half-brother to smart winner up to 7.6f Make It Up (2-y-o 7f winner, by Halling) and 9f winner Girl of The Hour (by Makfi): dam unraced half-sister to Derby winner Authorized: 16/1, badly needed experience when sixth in maiden at Windsor (5¾ lengths behind Comrade Conrad) in April: should improve. *John Gosden*

BREAKING FREE 3 ch.g. Kyllachy 129 – Hill Welcome 52 (Most Welcome 131) [2017 **64** 56: 7g^{6} 7.2m 8.3d p7s^{2} f7.1g^{2} p8d p8g^{6} f7.1g^{5} f8.1g^{4} f8.1g* f8.1g^{6} Dec 21] modest handicapper: won at Southwell in December: stays 1m: acts on polytrack, fibresand and soft going: has worn headgear, including last 5 starts. *John Quinn*

BREAKING RECORDS (IRE) 2 b.c. (Jan 7) Kodiac 112 – Querulous (USA) (Raven's **60 p** Pass (USA) 133) [2017 p7g^{5} Dec 28] 110,000Y: first foal: dam unraced daughter of useful 1m/8.5f winner Contentious: 12/1, fifth in minor event at Lingfield (6½ lengths behind Maverick Officer) in December: should do better. *Hugo Palmer*

BREAK THE SILENCE 3 b.g. Rip Van Winkle (IRE) 134 – In A Silent Way (IRE) 102 **70** (Desert Prince (IRE) 130) [2017 –: 9.9m^{3} 8s^{2} 8g^{3} 8s 8g^{6} 8s^{5} f7.1g^{3} p8g^{3} 8d^{2} p8d^{3} 8v* 8.3g^{2} 7v* f8.1g^{4} Nov 16] fair handicapper: won at Brighton in October and Redcar in November: stays 8.5f: acts on polytrack, fibresand and heavy going: in cheekpieces last 4 starts: usually leads. *Scott Dixon*

BREAKWATER BAY (IRE) 3 b.g. Lilbourne Lad (IRE) 111 – Aqualina (IRE) 104 (King's Theatre (IRE) 128) [2017 63: 8m^5 9g^5 12.1g^2 12.1m^2 14f 12g* 12.1d^4 12d 12.1g^6 Aug 30] fair handicapper: won at Pontefract in July: stays 1½m: acts on good to firm and good to soft going. *Tim Easterby* **74**

BREAN FLYER 3 b.f. Phenomena – Lois Lane 59 (Striking Ambition 122) [2017 –: t6f^6 p5g Jan 18] little impact in seller/maidens. *Bill Turner* **–**

BREANSKI 3 b.g. Delegator 125 – Jubilee 66 (Selkirk (USA) 129) [2017 69: 10.2m^2 8.3m^2 8g* 8.8g^2 8d 9.8m^4 10g t8d^2 t8g* p10s Dec 8] fairly useful handicapper: won at Thirsk in July and Newcastle (by 2¼ lengths from Rey Loopy) in November: stays 1¼m: acts on tapeta and good to firm going: in visor last 4 starts. *David O'Meara* **88**

BREATHABLE 2 b.g. (Apr 19) Bated Breath 125 – Cassique Lady (IRE) 105 (Langfuhr (CAN) 124) [2017 8g 8g^3 8g^3 Sep 1] 10,000Y: third foal: dam, 1¼m/11f winner who stayed 1¾m, half-sister to US Grade 3 9f winner Diamond Tycoon: fair form: best effort when third in minor event at Thirsk (2 lengths behind Trumps Up) in September: likely to progress further. *Tim Easterby* **65 p**

BREATH CAUGHT 2 b.c. (Mar 13) Bated Breath 125 – Double Crossed 102 (Caerleon (USA) 132) [2017 7.1m 7g^2 7d* Oct 27] useful-looking colt: half-brother to high-class winner up to 10.4f Twice Over (2-y-o 1m-1¼m winner, by Observatory) and 2 winners by Oasis Dream, including 1¼m winner Circulation: dam 1¼m-11.5f winner: fairly useful form: won maiden at Doncaster (by 3¾ lengths from Flavius Titus) in October: raced only at 7f: will go on improving. *Ralph Beckett* **90 p**

BREATHLESS 5 b.g. Royal Applause 124 – Ada River 102 (Dansili 127) [2017 69: f8g t9.5g t8g t16.3d^6 t12.2g Feb 20] modest handicapper: stays 9.5f: acts on fibresand and tapeta: in cheekpieces last 4 starts: wears tongue tie: often races towards rear. *Clive Mulhall* **54**

BREATHLESS TIMES 2 b.c. (Mar 17) Bated Breath 125 – Bea Menace (USA) 93 (Mizzen Mast (USA) 121) [2017 p6d^2 Dec 13] €6,000 2-y-o, resold €150,000 2-y-o: fourth foal: half-brother to French winner up to 1¼m Godric (2-y-o 8.5f winner, by Winker Watson) and 11f winner Beatisa (by Intikhab): dam 7f/1m winner: 9/2, second in minor event at Kempton (1½ lengths behind Monadee) on debut: will stay at least 7f: sure to progress. *Roger Charlton* **80 p**

BREATHOFFRESHAIR 3 b.g. Bated Breath 125 – Stormy Weather (Nashwan (USA) 135) [2017 60: t8g p8d^6 f8.1g^4 t7.1d* t6g* t6s* Nov 30] strong gelding: fair handicapper: won last 3 starts, all at Newcastle in November: stays 1m: acts on polytrack and tapeta: sometimes in tongue tie. *Richard Guest* **72**

BREDEN (IRE) 7 b.g. Shamardal (USA) 129 – Perfect Touch (USA) 107 (Miswaki (USA) 124) [2017 8.3g^2 10d^4 10m^6 p11s^6 10g* 8.1g^5 10g^4 Nov 3] lengthy gelding: useful handicapper: won at Newbury in September: stays 11f: acts on polytrack, good to firm and good to soft going: wears hood. *Linda Jewell* **95**

BREEZE (IRE) 3 b.f. Sea The Stars (IRE) 140 – Kitty Matcham (IRE) 102 (Rock of Gibraltar (IRE) 133) [2017 p10.7g^4 8g^4 8m^2 8d^2 9.9d^5 8.1g^5 9g^3 8g^3 t8s* Sep 8] 525,000Y: fourth foal: half-sister to 3 winners, including useful 1m-1½m winner Sam Missile (by Smart Strike) and 6f-1m winner Marciano (by Pivotal): dam, 2-y-o 6f/7f (Rockfel Stakes) winner, closely related to Prix Jean-Luc Lagardere winner Horatio Nelson and winner up to 1¼m Viscount Nelson (both very smart): fairly useful performer: won maiden at Newcastle (by nose from Subhaan) in September: stays 9f: acts on tapeta, good to firm and good to soft going: in blinkers last 3 starts. *J. A. Stack, Ireland* **80**

BREEZE UP 3 b.g. Shirocco (GER) 129 – Lucky Breeze (IRE) 81 (Key of Luck (USA) 126) [2017 10g 9.9s 10s 12s p13.3d p15.8g Oct 18] no form: in headgear last 3 starts. *Ed de Giles* **–**

BREEZOLINI 9 b.m. Bertolini (USA) 125 – African Breeze 79 (Atraf 116) [2017 6d^4 6g^5 7d^2 7d^4 7.5d 6d* 7s 5.8v Oct 8] small mare: fair handicapper: won at Hamilton (amateur) in September: stays 7f: acts on polytrack, good to firm and heavy going: has worn headgear: sometimes slowly away, often races towards rear. *Adrian Brendan Joyce, Ireland* **71**

BRENDAN BRACKAN (IRE) 8 b.g. Big Bad Bob (IRE) 118 – Abeyr 106 (Unfuwain (USA) 131) [2017 108: 8v* 10g^3 8d* 9d^4 8s^6 8.5s* Oct 14] big, rather leggy gelding: smart performer: won handicap at Naas (by 1½ lengths from Aussie Valentine) in March, and listed races at Leopardstown (by 3½ lengths from Elusive Heights) in June and Cork (by 1¾ lengths from Onenightidreamed) in October: stays 8.5f: acts on good to firm and heavy going: tried in blinkers. *G. M. Lyons, Ireland* **117**

Qatar Lennox Stakes, Goodwood—50/1-shot Breton Rock (No.2) swoops late to provide jockey Andrea Atzeni with the second leg of a big-race treble on the day, beating Home of The Brave (left) and the fast-finishing Suedois (second right)

BRENDAN (IRE) 4 b.g. Elnadim (USA) 128 – My 60 (King's Best (USA) 132) [2017 –: 8d 6s 5m³ 5d⁶ 5d 5m⁵ 5m Sep 8] modest maiden: best form at 5f: acts on good to firm going: has worn hood. *Jim Goldie* **51**

BRETON BELLE (IRE) 3 ch.f. Nathaniel (IRE) 129 – Cream Tease 99 (Pursuit of Love 124) [2017 t12.2g 12s 11.6d t14g p16g Sep 6] €55,000Y: half-sister to 3 winners, including useful 2-y-o 1m winner Treat (by Barathea) and 6f and (at 2 yrs) 1m winner Bright Falcon (by Hawk Wing): dam, 7f winner (including at 2 yrs), half-sister to winner up to 1m (stayed 1¼m) Enharmonic and 7f/1m winner Soprano (both smart): modest maiden: often races in rear. *David Simcock* **55**

BRETON BLUES 7 b.g. Street Cry (IRE) 130 – Many Colours 112 (Green Desert (USA) 127) [2017 49: 12g 10g 8g Aug 2] poor maiden: usually wears headgear. *Fred Watson* **–**

BRETON ROCK (IRE) 7 b.g. Bahamian Bounty 116 – Anna's Rock (IRE) 106 (Rock of Gibraltar (IRE) 133) [2017 116: 8s³ 7.2s⁵ 7g³ 7g* 7d⁴ 7g⁵ 8s Oct 21] good-topped gelding: shows plenty of knee action: smart performer: 50/1, won Lennox Stakes at Goodwood (by ½ length from Home of The Brave) in August: effective at 1m, races mostly at 7f: best on good going or softer (acts on heavy): usually races in rear. *David Simcock* **115**

BREX DRAGO (ITY) 5 b.g. Mujahid (USA) 125 – Shibuni's Thea (IRE) (Barathea (IRE) 127) [2017 109: 9.9g³ 8.9g⁶ a8f³ a8f 8m 8s p10s p10g² t9.5g⁶ p8g Dec 31] tall gelding: useful handicapper: twice third at Meydan early in year, beaten 5 lengths by Heavy Metal on latter occasion: stays 10.5f: acts on polytrack, tapeta, good to firm and good to soft going: in blinkers last 3 starts: usually races prominently. *Marco Botti* **103**

BREXIT 3 b.f. Bahamian Bounty 116 – Famcred 89 (Inchinor 119) [2017 52: p8g 7m Jun 1] poor maiden. *Pat Phelan* **–**

BREXITMEANSBREXIT 2 b.f. (Feb 16) Helmet (AUS) 127 – Lady Scarlett (Woodman (USA) 126) [2017 p7g p8g⁶ p8g⁵ Nov 7] half-sister to several winners, including moody 5f/6f winner Sunrise Safari (by Mozart) and winner up to 7f Rosso Corsa (2-y-o 6f winner, by Footstepsinthesand), both smart: dam unraced: fair form: best effort when fifth in minor event at Kempton (6¼ lengths behind Bow Street) in November. *Richard Hannon* **69**

BRIAC (FR) 6 b.g. Kapgarde (FR) – Jarwin Do (FR) (Grand Tresor (FR)) [2017 –: p13g p12g* p16g* p12g p15.8g⁴ p16s p16g 14.2g³ 13d⁶ p16g⁶ p13.3s Nov 17] plain gelding: modest handicapper: won at Kempton (twice) in March: stays 2m: acts on polytrack. *Mark Pattinson* **59**

BRIAN RYAN 2 b.c. (Apr 20) Finjaan 122 – Touching (IRE) 89 (Kheleyf (USA) 116) [2017 p5g⁵ Apr 11] 5/1, fifth in minor event at Lingfield (8 lengths behind Corinthia Knight) in April. *Robyn Brisland* **52**

BRIAN THE SNAIL (IRE) 3 gr.g. Zebedee 113 – Sweet Irish (Shamardal (USA) 129) **105**
[2017 103p: 6g* 5s^5 6f^6 6g 6d 6v Sep 30] strong gelding: useful handicapper: won at Pontefract (by 1¾ lengths from Jule In The Crown) in April: below form after, gelded after final start: raced at 5f/6f: acts on good to firm and heavy going: tried in blinkers. *Richard Fahey*

BRIARDALE (IRE) 5 b.g. Arcano (IRE) 122 – Marine City (JPN) 77 (Carnegie (IRE) **107**
129) [2017 90: f8g^5 10.3g^6 t10.2s* 9g^2 10g* t8s 10.3m 9d Sep 30] strong gelding: useful **a99**
handicapper: won at Newcastle (by 3 lengths from Gaelic Tiger) in April and Redcar (by 6 lengths from Rainbow Rebel) in May: went as if amiss last 3 starts: stays 10.5f: acts on tapeta and good to firm going: tried in headgear: front runner/races prominently. *James Bethell*

BRIDAL MARCH 3 ch.f. Casamento (IRE) 118 – Exultate Jubilate (USA) (With **65**
Approval (CAN)) [2017 62: t7.1g^4 6.9g 8.3d t7.2g t7.2g 10.2v^5 p10d^6 t12.2g^6 t12.2g Dec 22] good-topped filly: fair maiden: probably stays 1½m: acts on polytrack, tapeta, soft and good to firm going: often in cheekpieces in 2017. *John Mackie*

BRIDEY'S LETTUCE (IRE) 5 b.g. Iffraaj 127 – Its On The Air (IRE) (King's Theatre **79**
(IRE) 128) [2017 76: f12g^6 f12g^2 t10.2d^3 f12m^3 p12g^4 p13.3g^2 12s 16.3m^5 13.1g^3 12.1s* **a73**
Aug 1] good-topped gelding: fair handicapper: won at Beverley in August: trained by John Best fifth to eighth starts: stays 16.5f: acts on all-weather, soft and good to firm going: has worn hood. *Ivan Furtado*

BRIDGE BUILDER 7 b.g. Avonbridge 123 – Amazing Dream (IRE) 98 (Thatching 131) **62**
[2017 77: p6g^4 p6m* p7g^5 p6g^6 p6g^5 6g 6s 6g p6g p7g p7g p7g^3 p6g^5 Dec 31] modest **a77**
handicapper on turf, fair on all-weather: won at Lingfield in January: stays 1¼m: acts on polytrack and good to firm going: wears headgear: front runner/races prominently. *Peter Hedger*

BRIDGE OF SIGHS 5 ch.g. Avonbridge 123 – Ashantiana 64 (Ashkalani (IRE) 128) **78**
[2017 82: p12g^3 p12m^3 p10g^6 9.9g^3 11.8m^4 8v^3 p10g 8.5g^5 p12g^4 p11g p10g Dec 21] **a84**
sturdy gelding: fairly useful handicapper: third at Kempton in January: left Martin Smith after fifth start: stays 1½m: acts on polytrack and heavy going: sometimes in cheekpieces in 2017. *Lee Carter*

BRIDGE THAT GAP 9 b.g. Avonbridge 123 – Figura 87 (Rudimentary (USA) 118) **–**
[2017 –: t12.2m p10g p10g Feb 22] good-topped gelding: fair handicapper at best, lightly raced and little form after 2014: stayed 11f: acted on polytrack and tapeta: wore headgear: dead. *Roger Ingram*

BRIEF VISIT 4 b.f. Fastnet Rock (AUS) 127 – Brevity (USA) 108 (Street Cry (IRE) 130) **92**
[2017 88: p11g^4 9.9m 10g^5 10s^2 10g* 10.2s^6 Nov 11] fairly useful handicapper: won at Newmarket (by 7 lengths from Turning Gold) in September: stays 1¼m: acts on soft going: often leads. *Andrew Balding*

BRIGADOON 10 b.g. Compton Place 125 – Briggsmaid 70 (Elegant Air 119) [2017 74: **86**
f12g^2 f14g^2 t12.2g^3 f14g* f14d^2 f11g^3 14.1g^2 14g^3 f11.1g^3 Dec 19] leggy gelding: fairly useful handicapper: won at Southwell (by 10 lengths from Denmead) in March: stays 14.5f: acts on all-weather and any turf going: front runner/races prominently. *Michael Appleby*

BRIGAND 2 b.g. (Feb 3) Dick Turpin (IRE) 127 – Juncea 76 (Elnadim (USA) 128) [2017 **75**
6v^3 p6d* t6.1g Dec 22] well-made gelding: fair form: won minor event at Chelmsford (by ½ length from Maypole) in November: raced only at 6f. *William Haggas*

BRIGHAM YOUNG 2 br.c. (Feb 13) Street Cry (IRE) 130 – Bible Belt (IRE) 116 (Big **77**
Bad Bob (IRE) 118) [2017 p7g^5 p7d p8g^2 Dec 20] workmanlike colt: fair form: best effort when second in minor event at Lingfield (¾ length behind Three Weeks) in December. *Ed Walker*

BRIGLIADORO (IRE) 6 ch.g. Excellent Art 125 – Milady's Pride 82 (Machiavellian **105**
(USA) 123) [2017 105: 8m^5 8s^2 7m^2 7m 8d^4 8m* p8g* 8s Oct 21] angular gelding: useful handicapper: won at Yarmouth (by neck from Mountain Angel) in August and Kempton (by head from Belgian Bill) in October: stays 1¼m: acts on polytrack, soft and good to firm going: has worn visor: sometimes slowly away. *Philip McBride*

BRILLIANT VANGUARD (IRE) 4 b.g. Fast Company (IRE) 126 – Alyska (IRE) 80 **102**
(Owington 123) [2017 92: 7g 8.3m^4 8.3m^5 p8g 8m^2 8d^4 8g* 8m* p8g* p8g^4 p8g^3 8g^6 Nov 3] lengthy gelding: useful handicapper: won at Ripon (twice) in August and Kempton in September: stays 1m: acts on polytrack, good to firm and heavy going: wears cheekpieces. *Kevin Ryan*

BRIMHAM ROCKS 3 b.g. Fastnet Rock (AUS) 127 – Colima (IRE) 101 (Authorized (IRE) 133) [2017 72p: t12.2g* 11.9d6 11.6d* 12g4 12.1d* 12v 12.1s2 13.9g* Oct 13] well-made gelding: useful/progressive handicapper: won at Wolverhampton in May, Haydock (by 7 lengths from Nordic Combined) in June, Hamilton (by 3 lengths from Kajaki) in July and York (by 1¼ lengths from Fools And Kings) in October: stays 1¾m: acts on tapeta and soft going: sold 340,000 gns in November. *Ralph Beckett* **107**

BRINGIT (IRE) 3 b.g. Holy Roman Emperor (IRE) 125 – Challow Hills (USA) 73 (Woodman (USA) 126) [2017 7d 10m6 8f4 Jul 5] fair form: best effort when sixth in maiden at Windsor in June. *Jamie Osborne* **71**

BRING ON A SPINNER 4 b.g. Kheleyf (USA) 116 – Posy Fossil (USA) 70 (Malibu Moon (USA)) [2017 73, a88: f5g5 f6g* f5g6 p7g6 f6g f6d6 p6d5 Jul 12] big, rangy gelding: fairly useful handicapper: won at Southwell (by 1¼ lengths from Sophisticated Heir) in January: stays 6f: acts on fibresand and soft going: wears headgear: sold 16,000 gns in July. *Stuart Williams* **84**

BRISCOLA 2 b.f. (Jan 28) Redoute's Choice (AUS) – La Concorde (FR) 79 (Sadler's Wells (USA) 132) [2017 7m p7g2 p8s5 p7s2 Dec 15] third foal: dam, 1½m winner, out of half-sister to Montjeu: fair form in minor events: should stay 1m. *John Gosden* **73**

BRISE DE MER (FR) 3 b.g. Miesque's Son (USA) 117 – Lisselan Firefly (IRE) (Monashee Mountain (USA) 115) [2017 73: 6g4 8s 8m4 Jun 16] fair maiden: stays 1m: acts on polytrack and good to firm going: tried in cheekpieces. *George Baker* **76**

BRISK TEMPO (FR) 2 b.g. (Feb 5) Dabirsim (FR) 120 – Allegro Vivace (FR) (Muhtathir 126) [2017 p7g t7.1g2 Oct 20] fair form: better effort when second in minor event at Newcastle (2 lengths behind Line House) in October: will stay 1m: open to further improvement. *Richard Fahey* **76 p**

BRISTOL MISSILE (USA) 3 b.c. Kitten's Joy (USA) 128 – Dearest Girl (IRE) 89 (Galileo (IRE) 134) [2017 10m3 11.9m3 10.3m2 10.1m 9.9m* p11d Dec 13] €145,000Y: rather unfurnished colt: first foal: dam 1½m winner who stayed 2m: fairly useful performer: won maiden at Sandown in June: stays 1½m: acts on good to firm going: front runner/races prominently. *Richard Hannon* **88**

BRITISH ART 5 b.g. Iffraaj 127 – Bush Cat (USA) 93 (Kingmambo (USA) 125) [2017 59: 9g 10s t12.4g* p12g2 t12.4g* t16.3d6 Dec 16] strong gelding: fair handicapper: won at Newcastle in September and November: may prove best up to 1¾m: acts on polytrack, tapeta and good to firm going: wears headgear: often races prominently/travels strongly. *R. K. Watson, Ireland* **71**

BRITISH EMBASSY (IRE) 5 b.g. Clodovil (IRE) 116 – Embassy Belle (IRE) 82 (Marju (IRE) 127) [2017 86: 8.3m6 8g6 7m 8m2 7d6 8m5 8g4 8d Aug 23] fair handicapper: stays 10.5f: acts on polytrack, tapeta, soft and good to firm going: wears headgear: front runner/races prominently. *Bill Turner* **77**

BRITTANIC (IRE) 3 ch.c. Excelebration (IRE) 133 – Fountain of Peace (USA) (Kris S (USA)) [2017 83p: t8g* 9.9s p7m5 t7.1d Dec 16] useful performer: won minor event at Newcastle (by 1¾ lengths from Ay Ay) in January: close seventh in handicap at same course in December: stays 1m: acts on tapeta: starts slowly, usually races in rear. *David Simcock* **105**

BRIYOUNI (FR) 4 b.g. Siyouni (FR) 122 – Brianza (USA) 61 (Thunder Gulch (USA) 129) [2017 95: 8m 8m 8s 7.8s5 8.2d4 8d2 10.3d t8d Sep 29] fairly useful handicapper: second at Thirsk in August: stays 8.5f: acts on good to firm and good to soft going: in cheekpieces last 5 starts: sold 20,000 gns in October to join Ralph Beckett. *Kevin Ryan* **86**

BROAD APPEAL 3 ch.g. Medicean 128 – Shy Appeal (IRE) 71 (Barathea (IRE) 127) [2017 p8g* 8.3m 8.3d 10m5 10v5 10m3 10d6 p12g6 p12g Oct 24] close-coupled gelding: fair performer: won maiden at Kempton in February: stays 1½m: acts on polytrack and good to firm going: sometimes in headgear: usually races towards rear. *Jonathan Portman* **75**

BROADHAVEN HONEY (IRE) 3 b.f. Harbour Watch (IRE) 121 – Honeymead (IRE) 95 (Pivotal 124) [2017 81: 5g 5.1m6 5f4 5m 5m 5s4 p5g4 5g t6.1m f5g* t5.1g4 f5g Dec 19] fair handicapper: won at Southwell in November: left Tony Carroll after fourth start: best form at 5f: acts on polytrack, fibresand and firm going: wears headgear. *Ronald Harris* **74**

BROADWAY DREAMS 3 b.g. Oasis Dream 129 – Rosa Eglanteria (Nayef (USA) 129) [2017 10g6 9.2s2 10d4 10m2 Aug 26] 100,000F, £8,000 3-y-o: first foal: dam useful Italian 2-y-o 6f/7.5f winner (stayed 11f): fairly useful form: second in handicap at Redcar (amateur) in August: will stay beyond 1¼m: sold to join Michael Blake £40,000 in September. *Marjorie Fife* **83**

BROCKEY RISE (IRE) 2 ch.g. (Mar 3) Zebedee 113 – Age of Diplomacy (Araafa (IRE) 71
128) [2017 6f 6d^{6} 5.1d^{4} 6s^{2} 7.4v^{5} 6g* 5d 6.3s 6.1s p5g^{5} t5.1g^{6} Dec 18] fair performer: won nursery at Thirsk in August: lost form after: stays 6f: acts on soft going: often in visor: often races towards rear. *David Evans*

BROCKHOLES 4 ch.f. Equiano (FR) 127 – Rivalry (Medicean 128) [2017 83: f5s^{4} Jan 72
26] fairly useful handicapper: stays 7f: acts on soft and good to firm going: front runner/races prominently. *Bryan Smart*

BROCTUNE PAPA GIO 10 b.g. Tobougg (IRE) 125 – Fairlie 70 (Halling (USA) 133) 64
[2017 71: t8g^{2} t8s^{3} t8s 7m^{5} 8g^{4} 7m^{6} t7.1s* t7.1d Sep 29] good-topped gelding: modest handicapper: won at Newcastle in September: stays 1m: acts on tapeta, soft and good to firm going: usually in headgear in 2017: front runner/races prominently. *Gillian Boanas*

BROGAN 3 b.f. Pivotal 124 – Roger Sez (IRE) 103 (Red Clubs (IRE) 125) [2017 79p: 85
7.5m^{6} 7g 7m^{2} 7.2m 7g^{4} 7.2s^{4} p7g Oct 18] smallish filly: fairly useful handicapper: second at Haydock in June: stays 7.5f: acts on soft and good to firm going: in cheekpieces last 3 starts: races prominently. *Tom Dascombe*

BROKEN FORCE (USA) 2 ch.g. (Mar 21) Broken Vow (USA) 117 – New Girlfriend 63
(IRE) 115 (Diesis 133) [2017 7g t8s Sep 19] modest form in maiden/minor event. *K. R. Burke*

BROKEN WINGS (IRE) 2 b.f. (Mar 6) Canford Cliffs (IRE) 133 – Moss Top (IRE) 77 71
(Moss Vale (IRE) 126) [2017 t8g^{2} t8g^{2} t8g^{4} Nov 15] €21,000F, £20,000Y: first foal: dam, maiden (stayed 6f), half-sister to useful 2-y-o 6f winner Crown Dependency: fair form: best effort when second in minor event at Newcastle (2 lengths behind Consolida) in October. *Keith Dalgleish*

BROMANCE 4 b.g. Showcasing 117 – Romantic Destiny 90 (Dubai Destination (USA) 68
127) [2017 70: t8g 9.9m* 9.9m^{2} 9.9m 9.9d 9.9m Aug 27] fair handicapper: won at Beverley in May: second at same course in June: stays 1¼m: acts on tapeta and good to firm going: wears cheekpieces: often races towards rear: quirky sort. *Peter Niven*

BRONZE ANGEL (IRE) 8 b.g. Dark Angel (IRE) 113 – Rihana (IRE) 68 (Priolo (USA) 103
127) [2017 100: 8g 8g^{3} p8g 8.2d^{3} t9.5g p10g^{3} t9.5d Dec 26] quite attractive gelding: useful handicapper: third at Leicester (length behind Fire Brigade) in October: stays 1¼m: acts on polytrack, soft and good to firm going: wears headgear: often races towards rear. *Marcus Tregoning*

BRONZE BEAU 10 ch.g. Compton Place 125 – Bella Cantata (Singspiel (IRE) 133) 82
[2017 74: 5m^{2} 5g* 5g 5g^{5} 5g* 5d^{4} 5d^{2} 5d 5.3m^{2} 5g 5g 5d 5g 5g^{3} Oct 7] lengthy gelding: fairly useful handicapper: won at Hamilton in June and July (by 2 lengths from Vintage Dream): stays 5.5f: acts on firm and soft going: wears cheekpieces/tongue tie: front runner/races prominently. *Kristin Stubbs*

BROOKE'S POINT 4 b.g. Cape Cross (IRE) 129 – Forest Pearl (USA) (Woodman 51
(USA) 126) [2017 59: p11d^{5} p13g^{5} t12.2g^{5} 11.6g 12v Jun 10] modest maiden: best effort at 1m: acts on good to firm going: in cheekpieces last 5 starts: often races prominently. *Neil Mulholland*

BROROCCO 4 b.g. Shirocco (GER) 129 – Lady Brora 83 (Dashing Blade 117) [2017 94: 103
p10g^{5} 10.1g* 10.3m^{2} 10.1m^{5} 11.8m 10.1g^{3} 10g^{2} 10.3m^{4} 10m* 9d^{5} Sep 30] good-bodied gelding: useful handicapper: won at Epsom in April and Newbury (by length from Fidaawy) in September: stays 10.5f: acts on tapeta, good to firm and good to soft going: wears hood: often races towards rear, usually travels strongly: quirky sort. *Andrew Balding*

BROTHER BEAR (IRE) 2 b.c. (Feb 6) Kodiac 112 – Hurricane Emma (USA) (Mr 105
Greeley (USA) 122) [2017 6.4m* 6d* 6f^{4} 6.3f^{3} 7s^{6} 5.8v Oct 8] 125,000Y: strong colt: first foal: dam unraced half-sister to useful performer up to 1m King Hesperus: useful performer: won maiden at Leopardstown (by 2 lengths from Sioux Nation) and listed race at the Curragh (by 3 lengths from Would Be King) in May: fourth in Coventry Stakes at Royal Ascot (½ length behind Rajasinghe) in June: stays 6.5f: acts on firm and good to soft going: tried in cheekpieces: usually races prominently, often travels strongly. *Mrs J. Harrington, Ireland*

BROTHER IN ARMS (IRE) 3 b.g. Kodiac 112 – Cool Cousin (IRE) 102 (Distant 68
Relative 128) [2017 58p: t9.5m^{6} p7g^{5} p5g p6g* p6g^{4} 6.1m^{6} 8f 6d p6g p7g^{5} p7d^{5} p7g Dec 30] workmanlike gelding: fair handicapper: won at Kempton (apprentice) in March: left Jamie Osborne after second start: stays 7f: acts on polytrack. *Tony Carroll*

BROTHERLY COMPANY (IRE) 5 b.g. Fast Company (IRE) 126 – Good Lady (IRE) **76**
(Barathea (IRE) 127) [2017 f11.1g^6 Dec 22] fairly useful handicapper at best: stays 12.5f: acts on fibresand, firm and good to soft going: fairly useful hurdler. *Joanne Foster*

BROTHER MCGONAGALL 3 b.r. Equiano (FR) 127 – Anatase (Danehill (USA) 126) **81**
[2017 66: t5g^5 5f^4 6g 6m^3 8s* 8.3g* 8.5m^3 9g* 8.8g^5 8g^3 7.8s^5 8.9s 10g Sep 27] fairly useful handicapper: won at Wetherby and Hamilton in June, and Carlisle (by ½ length from True Romance) in July: stays 9f: acts on firm and soft going. *Tim Easterby*

BROTHER RALPH (IRE) 2 b.g. (Feb 19) Redoute's Choice (AUS) – Fusion (IRE) 77 **69**
(Cape Cross (IRE) 129) [2017 7m^4 8d Oct 27] fair form: better effort when fourth in minor event at Newbury (10 lengths behind Emaraaty) in September: should stay 1m. *Brian Meehan*

BROTHER TIGER 8 b.g. Singspiel (IRE) 133 – Three Secrets (IRE) 92 (Danehill **85**
(USA) 126) [2017 97: p5g p6g 6g p5g* p5g^5 p5s^5 p5s^6 t6.1g^4 p6s^6 5.1g f5g^2 Dec 29] big, strong gelding: fairly useful handicapper: won at Lingfield (by length from Highly Sprung) in May: stays 6f: acts on all-weather, soft and good to firm going: tried in cheekpieces. *David C. Griffiths*

BROUGH LANE LASS (IRE) 2 b.f. (Jan 24) Big Bad Bob (IRE) 118 – Place de **–**
Moscou (IRE) (Rock of Gibraltar (IRE) 133) [2017 t6s^6 6g t6s Jun 29] fourth foal: half-sister to useful 1¼m-13f winner (including in Australia) Soviet Courage (by Dutch Art) and 2-y-o 6f winner Lady Moscou (by Sir Percy): dam, ran twice in France, closely related to useful French winner up to 15f Pretty Tough: down the field in minor events. *John Weymes*

BROUGHTON EXCELS 2 b.c. (May 2) Kyllachy 129 – Excello 94 (Exceed And Excel **–**
(AUS) 126) [2017 5d t5.1g p6s p7s Dec 14] no form. *Henry Spiller*

BROUGHTONS ADMIRAL 3 b.g. Born To Sea (IRE) 117 – Chanter (Lomitas 129) **72**
[2017 –: p10g 10m^2 10.1g^3 12g^4 11.9d^2 11.5d^2 p16d^3 Oct 6] fair maiden: stays 2m: acts on polytrack, good to firm and good to soft going: in headgear last 4 starts: sometimes slowly away. *Henry Spiller*

BROUGHTONS FANCY 4 b.f. Pastoral Pursuits 127 – Lifetime Romance (IRE) 92 **67**
(Mozart (IRE) 131) [2017 76, a65: t8.6m t8.6m p6g^4 t6m* p8g^4 t7.1g^2 6g^3 p7g 7d p7s 7g f7.1g t7.1s^2 t7.1d^6 t7.2g^4 t7.1d^5 t6g^4 t7.2g^3 t6g^2 Dec 6] lengthy filly: fair handicapper: won at Wolverhampton in March: left Gary Moore after tenth start: stays 1m: acts on polytrack, tapeta and heavy going: tried in cheekpieces. *Karen Tutty*

BROUGHTONS KNIGHT 3 b.g. Foxwedge (AUS) 128 – Disco Ball 75 (Fantastic **79**
Light (USA) 134) [2017 70: 8s^5 8.1d 10g^6 10g^6 12d^5 11.5m^4 10d^3 p10g^5 p8g* p8s^4 p7s* Dec 17] good-topped gelding: fair handicapper: won at Kempton in October and Chelmsford in December: left Henry Spiller after ninth start: best form at 7f/1m: acts on polytrack and soft going: sometimes in cheekpieces: tried in tongue tie. *Jim Boyle*

BROUGHTONS SPORT 3 b.g. Showcasing 117 – Ginger Cookie 47 (Bold Edge 123) **68**
[2017 7v 8.1m^6 Oct 16] fair form: better effort when sixth in maiden at Windsor in October. *Andi Brown*

BROUGHTONS STORY 3 b.g. Royal Applause 124 – News Desk 73 (Cape Cross **67**
(IRE) 129) [2017 64: t9.5g^4 p10g^2 10d 9.8m 8.5s* 9.9s^5 10.1g* t9.5g^4 Dec 22] fair performer: won minor event at Beverley in September and handicap at Yarmouth in October: left Henry Spiller after seventh start: stays 1¼m: acts on polytrack, tapeta and soft going. *Philip McBride*

BRUNDTLAND (IRE) 2 b.c. (Feb 6) Dubawi (IRE) 129 – Future Generation (IRE) 115 **82 p**
(Hurricane Run (IRE) 134) [2017 10m* Oct 25] attractive colt: first foal: dam winner up to 1m (2-y-o 6f winner): 6/1, won maiden at Newmarket (by length from Making Miracles) on debut: will improve. *Charlie Appleby*

BRUNY ISLAND (IRE) 3 ch.g. Bahamian Bounty 116 – Prianca (GER) (Diktat 126) **73**
[2017 55: p7m^4 8s^2 7d^3 t6.1g^3 t7.2g^2 t7.2g Jul 17] strong, lengthy gelding: fair handicapper: stays 1m: acts on polytrack, tapeta and soft going: sometimes in hood. *Charlie Fellowes*

BRYGHT BOY 4 b.g. Paco Boy (IRE) 129 – Bright Moll 88 (Mind Games 121) [2017 76: **69 §**
7d^4 8s 7s^2 7.4v^6 Sep 17] compact gelding: fair maiden handicapper: stayed 7f: acted on polytrack, soft and good to firm going: in cheekpieces last 2 starts: was temperamental: dead. *Ed Walker*

BUBBLE AND SQUEAK 2 b.f. (Feb 24) Mastercraftsman (IRE) 129 – Comeback Queen 91 (Nayef (USA) 129) [2017 p7g^{2} p7g^{2} p8g^{2} p8s^{2} p10s^{3} Nov 23] workmanlike filly: fourth foal: half-sister to useful 8.5f/9.5f winner (stayed 12.5f) Nonchalant (by Oasis Dream) and 2-y-o 6f winner Dheban (by Exceed And Excel): dam, 2-y-o 1m winner, half-sister to smart winner up to 1m Donativum: fairly useful maiden: second in minor events first 4 starts: stays 1m: acts on polytrack. *Sylvester Kirk* **82**

BUBBLES ARCADE 5 b.m. Arkadian Hero (USA) 123 – Alwariah 63 (Xaar 132) [2017 9.9s 8g 8.3g Aug 18] third foal: dam maiden (stayed 7f): bumper winner: little impact in maidens. *Rod Millman* –

BUBBLY BAILEY 7 b.g. Byron 117 – Night Gypsy 74 (Mind Games 121) [2017 –: p5m p5g^{2} p5g p5g p5g p6g Dec 21] smallish gelding: modest handicapper: stays 1m, races mainly at 5f/6f: acts on polytrack, soft and good to firm going: wears headgear. *J. R. Jenkins* **54**

BUCCANEERS COVE (IRE) 3 b.g. Footstepsinthesand 120 – Primissima (GER) (Second Set (IRE) 127) [2017 66: 8m 8.8g 8s Aug 9] maiden, little impact in handicaps in 2017: stays 7f: acts on polytrack and good to firm going. *Richard Fahey* **62**

BUCCANEERS VAULT (IRE) 5 gr.g. Aussie Rules (USA) 123 – Heaven's Vault (IRE) 103 (Hernando (FR) 127) [2017 84, a91: t6g^{5} t6g^{6} p6g^{5} 6g^{6} 6m^{3} 7g^{5} 6g^{4} 6g^{4} 6v^{2} 5.9s 6d^{4} 6g* 6.1m^{2} Oct 16] good-quartered gelding: fairly useful handicapper: won lady riders event at Doncaster in September: second at Windsor final start: stays 7f: acts on polytrack, tapeta and any turf going: has worn headgear, including in 2017: often races prominently. *Paul Midgley* **88** **a81**

BUCKLAND BEAU 6 b.g. Rock of Gibraltar (IRE) 133 – Heavenly Whisper (IRE) 105 (Halling (USA) 133) [2017 87: 8g^{3} 8g^{5} 8.5f 8m^{3} 7m^{6} p8g t9.5m p10d^{5} Nov 22] rather leggy gelding: fair handicapper: stays 11f: acts on polytrack, tapeta, good to firm and good to soft going: has worn visor: tried in tongue tie. *Charlie Fellowes* **79** **a73**

BUCKLE STREET 4 br.g. Cacique (IRE) 124 – Rose Row 86 (Act One 124) [2017 70p: 14.2d^{6} Jun 28] fair maiden: best effort at 2m: acts on polytrack: tried in cheekpieces: in tongue tie last 3 starts: fairly useful hurdler. *Martin Keighley* **60**

BUCKLOW BROOK 2 ch.f. (Apr 25) Sepoy (AUS) 129 – Rivalry (Medicean 128) [2017 t6g p7g Oct 26] fifth foal: half-sister to 3 winners, including 2-y-o 5f winner Back Lane (by Invincible Spirit) and 7f winner Brockholes (by Equiano): dam unraced half-sister to very smart sprinter Pivotal: well held in minor events. *David Brown* –

BUCKS FRIZZ (IRE) 2 b.f. (Apr 8) Havana Gold (IRE) 118 – Frizzante 121 (Efisio 120) [2017 6m 5.1m 6.1v p6g 5s Oct 2] sturdy filly: half-sister to several winners, including useful winner up to 7f Greensward (2-y-o 6f winner, by Green Desert) and 6f winner Pin Cushion (by Pivotal): dam 5f/6f (including July Cup) winner: no form. *David Evans* –

BUCKSTAY (IRE) 7 b.g. Lawman (FR) 121 – Stella Del Mattino (USA) (Golden Gear (USA) 116) [2017 115: 6m 7g 7d Jul 29] lengthy gelding: smart performer at best, out of sorts in 2017: wears headgear: usually races in rear. *Peter Chapple-Hyam* –

BUCKSTOPPER KIT (USA) 2 b.c. (Apr 24) Kitten's Joy (USA) 128 – Prime Silver (USA) (Silver Hawk (USA) 123) [2017 8.3s^{5} 7d^{3} 7.4v* 7.9g^{5} Oct 14] $90,000Y: short-coupled, good-topped colt: brother to 3 winners in North America and half-brother to a winner in USA by Catienus: dam lightly raced: fairly useful form: won minor event at Beverley (by neck from Big Kitten) in September: stays 1m: in blinkers last 3 starts: sold 85,000 gns, sent to USA. *Richard Fahey* **80**

BUDARRI 4 b.g. Supreme Sound 111 – Amtaar 63 (Nayef (USA) 129) [2017 8g Jul 18] well held in bumper/maiden on Flat: third in novice hurdle. *Stuart Coltherd* –

BUDDHA BOY 3 b.g. Bated Breath 125 – Midnight Fantasy 83 (Oasis Dream 129) [2017 66: p7g^{5} p6g^{2} 6g^{2} 6g^{5} 7g 6g 7d 5.8g t6.1g p6g p7g Dec 21] fair handicapper at best, lost way in 2017: left G. M. Lyons after seventh start: stays 7f: acts on polytrack, best turf form on good going: tried in headgear/tongue tie. *Miss Tracy M. Reilly, Ireland* **77**

BUDGIE 2 b.c. (Mar 8) Excelebration (IRE) 133 – Lady Bellatrix 71 (Singspiel (IRE) 133) [2017 p5g^{5} 6g 6m 8g^{3} 8g* 8g* Dec 31] sturdy colt: little form in Britain: left Mark Tompkins 5,000 gns after third start: won minor events at Madrid in November and Dos Hermanas in December: stays 1m. *T. Martins, Spain* **57**

BUFFER ZONE 2 br.c. (Apr 17) Bated Breath 125 – Buffering 101 (Beat Hollow 126) [2017 6m^4 6g^5 p6g* Oct 9] well-made colt: fourth foal: closely related to useful 1m winner Roller (by Rail Link): dam, French 9.5f winner, out of half-sister to dam of Prix de l'Arc de Triomphe winner Rail Link: fairly useful form: won minor event at Kempton (by 1¼ lengths from Perfect Hustler) in October: raced only at 6f: will go on improving. *Roger Charlton* **93 p**

BULAS BELLE 7 b.m. Rob Roy (USA) 122 – Bula Rose (IRE) 57 (Alphabatim (USA) 126) [2017 86: 16.3g^5 13.9v^3 16.1d^6 15.9g^3 17.1v^6 Sep 21] fair handicapper: stays 17f: acts on good to firm and heavy going. *Grant Tuer* **77**

BULDAN 3 b.g. New Approach (IRE) 132 – Meeznah (USA) 115 (Dynaformer (USA)) [2017 8m 10d^5 p12s Jun 14] modest form in maidens: remains with potential. *Sir Michael Stoute* **61 p**

BULLINGDON 2 b.c. (Mar 18) Dansili 127 – Rimth 109 (Oasis Dream 129) [2017 6v^3 7g* Aug 7] stocky colt: third foal: half-brother to 1m winner Garrick (by Galileo): dam 5f (at 2 yrs) and 7f (Fred Darling Stakes) winner: fairly useful form: won minor event at Salisbury (by ½ length from Magnificent) in August: will go on improving. *Richard Hannon* **86 p**

BULLINGTON BANDIT (IRE) 2 br.c. (Mar 6) Canford Cliffs (IRE) 133 – Spiritual Flame 85 (Invincible Spirit (IRE) 121) [2017 6.5g* 7g 6v Aug 3] close-coupled colt: fairly useful form: won minor event at Newbury in June by neck from Being There: seventh of 10 to Gustav Klimt in Superlative Stakes at Newmarket next time: stayed 7f: wore cheekpieces: dead. *Jane Chapple-Hyam* **92**

BULLINGTON BEAR (FR) 4 b.g. Youmzain (IRE) 131 – Maternelle (FR) (Machiavellian (USA) 123) [2017 79: 10g May 15] lengthy gelding: fair form: seventh in maiden at Windsor (in cheekpieces, 7¾ lengths behind Chiefofchiefs) on sole outing in 2017: bred to stay at least 1½m. *Jane Chapple-Hyam* **74**

BULLSEYE BULLET 2 ch.g. (May 14) Kheleyf (USA) 116 – Satin Doll 68 (Diktat 126) [2017 6d t7.2g t6.1g^6 p7d t6.1g 6v^3 Sep 17] strong gelding: modest maiden: stays 6f: acts on tapeta and heavy going: in cheekpieces last 2 starts: usually races towards rear. *Mark Usher* **51**

BUMBLE BAY 7 b.g. Trade Fair 124 – Amica 86 (Averti (IRE) 117) [2017 t12.2g^6 12.1g^2 p13.3g p15.8g t16.5g p16g^4 p15.8g^4 Nov 21] modest maiden: stays 2m: acts on polytrack: has worn headgear, including last 3 starts: wears tongue tie: often races towards rear. *Robert Stephens* **57**

BUMBLE BEEZE (IRE) 2 ch.g. (Mar 24) Zebedee 113 – Choose Me Please (IRE) (Choisir (AUS) 126) [2017 t6.1g 6.1m 7d Jun 30] no form. *Tom Dascombe* **–**

BUMPTIOUS 4 b.f. Acclamation 118 – Cast In Gold (USA) 92 (Elusive Quality (USA)) [2017 8g^6 p8g^4 7m^2 p7g 7.4d* 7m* p7g^2 7g^2 p8g* 7s t7.2g* p7m^4 p8g^4 Dec 23] sturdy filly: fairly useful performer: won maiden at Ffos Las in July, handicaps at Brighton in August and Chelmsford in September, and minor event at Wolverhampton (by neck from Pepita) in November: stays 8.5f: acts on polytrack, tapeta, good to firm and good to soft going: wears cheekpieces: usually races prominently. *Ismail Mohammed* **88 a94**

BUNBURY 5 b.g. Dansili 127 – Ithaca (USA) 100 (Distant View (USA) 126) [2017 96: p10g^2 p8f t9.5g^2 8m 8f^4 p8s^5 Jul 7] rather leggy gelding: useful handicapper: second at Chelmsford (nose behind Monsieur Rieussec) in January: stays 1¼m: acts on polytrack, tapeta, good to firm and good to soft going: tried in cheekpieces: often races freely: sold 45,000 gns, sent to Saudi Arabia. *Richard Hughes* **97**

BUNCE (IRE) 9 b.g. Good Reward (USA) 120 – Bold Desire 58 (Cadeaux Genereux 131) [2017 72: 6m 5g^3 6d^3 5s^4 5s^4 6s^4 5g^5 Jul 14] compact gelding: modest handicapper: winner over 7f, races at shorter nowadays: acts on polytrack, good to firm and heavy going: has worn headgear/tongue tie: usually races towards rear. *Linda Perratt* **61**

BUNCH OF THYME (IRE) 2 b.g. (Jan 15) Elzaam (AUS) 115 – Goodie Goodie 59 (Shirocco (GER) 129) [2017 5g 7.6s 8.1g^6 Aug 28] no form in minor events: tried in cheekpieces. *Bill Turner* **–**

BUNGEE JUMP (IRE) 2 b.f. (Apr 26) Canford Cliffs (IRE) 133 – Starchy 87 (Cadeaux Genereux 131) [2017 t7.1g^4 6g^3 7.4g^6 6.9v* 7s t7.1d Nov 10] 19,000 2-y-o: half-sister to 3 winners, including useful 1m-1¼m winner Tobar Na Gaoise (by Whipper) and 1¼m winner Great Explorer (by Galileo): dam, 2-y-o 6f winner, sister to smart dam of top-class 6f/7f performer Dream Ahead: fair performer: won minor event at Carlisle in September: stays 7f: acts on heavy going. *Kevin Ryan* **76**

BUONARROTI (IRE) 6 b.g. Galileo (IRE) 134 – Beauty Is Truth (IRE) 114 (Pivotal **85**
124) [2017 95: 10.3g 16.3d 11.1g^{4} 10.3s 11.2s 11.9m 11.9s^{4} 10.2g 11.8v^{2} 15v* Oct 12] strong, well-made gelding: fairly useful handicapper: won at Ayr (by 2 lengths from Hurricane Hollow) in October: stays 15f: acts on good to firm and heavy going: has worn headgear: in tongue tie last 4 starts: sometimes slowly away, often races in rear. *Declan Carroll*

BURAUQ 5 b.g. Kyllachy 129 – Riccoche (IRE) 63 (Oasis Dream 129) [2017 63: p6g^{4} **60**
t6m^{4} p6g 5.7f 5.7f^{4} 5.7d^{5} 5.7m^{5} 5.7f 6.1m^{4} 5.7f* 5.7g t6.1g^{2} 5.7d^{3} 5.7m^{3} 5.7s Sep 17] neat gelding: modest handicapper: won at Bath in July: stays 6f: acts on polytrack, tapeta, firm and good to soft going: wears headgear. *Milton Bradley*

BURCAN (FR) 5 ch.g. Astronomer Royal (USA) 121 – Sentimental Union (USA) (Dixie **99**
Union (USA) 121) [2017 101: p10s t10.2d^{2} t12.4g^{3} Nov 23] useful handicapper: third at Newcastle (length behind Sir Chauvelin) in November: stays 12.5f: acts on polytrack and tapeta: often races prominently. *Marco Botti*

BURFORD BROWN 2 br.c. (Mar 20) Swiss Spirit 117 – Sareb (FR) (Indian Ridge 123) **59 p**
[2017 7d Sep 29] 8,000F, €27,000Y: seventh foal: half-brother to 5f (including at 2 yrs) winner Black Moma (by Averti) and ungenuine 2-y-o 5f winner Chartist (by Choisir): dam ran once: 33/1, eighth in maiden at Newmarket (1¾ lengths behind Thrave) on debut: sure to do better. *Hugo Palmer*

BURGUILLOS 4 ch.g. Lope de Vega (IRE) 125 – Hazy Dancer 81 (Oasis Dream 129) **104**
[2017 92: 10g* 11.9d^{2} 10.3m^{2} 10g 11.9d^{5} Oct 28] good-topped gelding: useful handicapper: won at Leicester (by 1½ lengths from Wapping) in May: second at York (neck behind Big Country) in June: stays 1½m: acts on good to firm and good to soft going: has joined Stuart Williams. *Alan King*

BURIDAN (FR) 2 b.c. (Feb 25) Choisir (AUS) 126 – Lady McKell (IRE) (Raven's Pass **80**
(USA) 133) [2017 6.1m* 5.1d^{5} Jul 29] €47,000Y, €360,000 2-y-o: first foal: dam, French 7f winner, out of sister to top-class sprinter Mozart: fairly useful form when won minor event at Windsor (by neck from Mr Top Hat) in June: disappointed in blinkers next time. *Richard Hannon*

BURLINGTON (IRE) 2 b.g. (Jan 18) Zoffany (IRE) 121 – Peig (IRE) (Refuse To Bend **62**
(IRE) 128) [2017 p7g p7g 7m Oct 25] well-made gelding: modest form in minor events: wears tongue tie. *John Gosden*

BURNIEBOOZLE (IRE) 2 b.g. (Mar 25) Frozen Power (IRE) 108 – Tea Chest (IRE) **67**
(In The Wings 128) [2017 7.4m^{4} 6g 7s^{3} 7.2m^{3} 8v Sep 9] fair maiden: should stay 1m: acts on soft and good to firm going. *John Quinn*

BURNING HEAT (IRE) 4 b.g. Rock of Gibraltar (IRE) 133 – Burning Damask (USA) **76**
(Thunder Gulch (USA) 129) [2017 78: p12g^{3} p16d^{6} 14.1g^{3} 12.1s Oct 10] fair maiden: left James Eustace after third start: stays 2m: acts on polytrack and heavy going: in headgear last 2 starts. *Mohamed Moubarak*

BURNING THREAD (IRE) 10 b.g. Captain Rio 122 – Desert Rose (Green Desert **81 d**
(USA) 127) [2017 82§, a89§: t5g^{2} p5g^{3} p6g^{5} p5g^{5} 5.7m 5d^{6} 5d Jul 25] sturdy gelding: fairly useful handicapper: well below form after second start: stays 5.5f: acts on polytrack, tapeta and any turf going: wears headgear: usually races towards rear: temperamental. *David Elsworth*

BURNSIDE (FR) 4 gr.g. Kendargent (FR) 112 – Tishkara (FR) (Xaar 132) [2017 73: **85**
t16.3g^{5} t13.9g^{2} p13g* p13.4g* p15.9g^{3} 15.4g 13.9g 12.9d^{5} 11.9d^{6} Jul 30] fairly useful performer: won handicap at Lingfield (left Ian Williams after) and claimer at Chantilly (only start for Daniel Loughnane), both in February: stays 16.5f: acts on polytrack and tapeta: usually wears headgear: usually races prominently. *Gianluca Bietolini, France*

BURN SOME DUST (IRE) 2 b.g. (Mar 18) Shirocco (GER) 129 – Chilly Filly (IRE) 99 **63**
(Montjeu (IRE) 137) [2017 5s^{5} t6s 5d 8s* 8.3v Nov 8] modest performer: won nursery at Ayr in October: best effort at 1m: acts on soft going: often races towards rear. *Brian Ellison*

BURNS SUPPER (IRE) 2 ch.g. (Feb 7) Poet's Voice 126 – Charming (IRE) 74 **–**
(Invincible Spirit (IRE) 121) [2017 5g May 29] 100/1, well held in minor event at Redcar. *James Ewart*

BURNT CREAM 10 b.m. Exceed And Excel (AUS) 126 – Basbousate Nadia 92 **39**
(Wolfhound (USA) 126) [2017 51: p5g 5.2m t5g Nov 3] good-bodied mare: modest handicapper: below form in 2017: best form at 5f: acts on polytrack and firm going: usually wears hood: wears tongue tie: sometimes slowly away, usually races in rear. *Martin Bosley*

Irish Stallion Farms European Breeders Fund 'Sovereign Path' Handicap, Leopardstown—British raider Burnt Sugar is much the best, beating Silverkode and Withernsea (diamonds)

BURNT SUGAR (IRE) 5 b.g. Lope de Vega (IRE) 125 – Lady Livius (IRE) 102 (Titus Livius (FR) 115) [2017 106: 5m 5m^5 6m 7d* 7m 6d^6 7d 7d^2 7g^2 7d* 7s Oct 7] well-made gelding: smart handicapper: won at Doncaster (by ¾ length from Intense Style) in June and Leopardstown (by 2 lengths from Silverkode) in September: stays 7f: acts on polytrack, firm and good to soft going: has worn blinkers/tongue tie. *Roger Fell* **111**

BURREN VIEW LADY (IRE) 7 br.m. Dansili 127 – Westerly Gale (USA) (Gone West (USA)) [2017 72: p7g p8g p6g^6 p7g^{ur} p7g* 7.5s p7g^3 6m^4 7.2m* 6.7m^6 5d 7s p7g p6g p7g* p7g^5 p7g^3 p6g p7g^6 Dec 21] fair handicapper: won at Lingfield in April, Ayr in May and Dundalk (apprentice) in November: stays 7f: acts on polytrack, tapeta, sand, good to firm and good to soft going: wears headgear/tongue tie: usually races close up. *Denis Hogan, Ireland* **69 a77**

BURRISHOOLE ABBEY (IRE) 3 b.g. Acclamation 118 – Xeralda (IRE) (Xaar 132) [2017 85: t7.1g^6 6m* 6f 7m* 8g^2 7g^4 9.9g Dec 30] lengthy gelding: fairly useful performer: won handicaps at Ayr (by 1½ lengths from El Hombre) in May and Sandown in June: left K. R. Burke, 3 lengths second to Pazeer in Qatar Guineas at Doha in December: stays 1m: acts on good to firm going. *Mohammed Jassim Ghazali, Qatar* **93**

BURRUMBEET (IRE) 3 b.g. Fastnet Rock (AUS) 127 – Bright Bank (IRE) (Sadler's Wells (USA) 132) [2017 p10g^6 Dec 30] 6/1, sixth in maiden at Lingfield (in blinkers, 6¾ lengths behind Colourful Career) on debut: should do better. *Ed Walker* **64 p**

BURTONWOOD 5 b.g. Acclamation 118 – Green Poppy 68 (Green Desert (USA) 127) [2017 74: t6m^4 t6d* t5g^5 t6d t6g^2 t6g^5 5m^6 t6s^2 5g^3 5m^2 6v^6 6d 5g^4 6v Sep 30] strong, close-coupled gelding: fair handicapper: won at Newcastle (apprentice) in February: best at 5f/6f: acts on tapeta, good to firm and good to soft going: wears headgear. *Julie Camacho* **74**

BURY THE EVIDENCE 4 b.f. Phoenix Reach (IRE) 124 – Madam Bijou (Atraf 116) [2017 f11.1g t8.6g Nov 20] fifth foal: dam unraced half-sister to useful 5f winner Treasure Cay: little sign of ability, including in Flat maidens: wears hood. *Derek Shaw* **–**

BUSH BEAUTY (IRE) 6 b.m. Bushranger (IRE) 119 – Scottendale 58 (Zilzal (USA) 137) [2017 78, a67: t7.1g^4 t7.1g 7d^4 7.6s^3 t8.6g^5 6.9s^3 6.9g^5 7.6d^3 8g^3 6.9d^4 t7.1s Sep 19] smallish, close-coupled mare: fair handicapper on turf, modest on all-weather: stays 1m: acts on polytrack, tapeta and soft going: tried in blinkers: sometimes slowly away. *Eric Alston* **71 a60**

BUSHEL (USA) 7 b.g. Street Cry (IRE) 130 – Melhor Ainda (USA) 120 (Pulpit (USA) 117) [2017 71§: p11g f14g^5 f11g* f11.1g Dec 21] modest handicapper: won at Southwell in April: stays 1½m: acts on fibresand and good to firm going: has worn headgear. *Tony Newcombe* **62**

BUSH HOUSE (IRE) 3 b.g. Canford Cliffs (IRE) 133 – Magena (USA) (Kingmambo (USA) 125) [2017 t9.5m^2 t9.5g* 10.3g^4 10s p11d* 13.9m p11s^3 p11g^3 Sep 27] £150,000Y: good-topped gelding: second foal: brother to 2-y-o 7f winner Poplar Close: dam, unraced, out of half-sister to high-class performer up to 1½m Hernando: useful performer: won maiden at Wolverhampton in February and handicap at Kempton in July: third in handicaps at latter course last 2 starts: stays 11f: acts on polytrack and tapeta: wears blinkers: usually races prominently: sold 30,000 gns, sent to Saudi Arabia. *Hugo Palmer* **95**

BUSH WARRIOR (IRE) 6 b.g. Bushranger (IRE) 119 – Lady Corduff (IRE) 78 (Titus Livius (FR) 115) [2017 79: p6m p6g^{3} p6g p6g^{2} t6g^{4} 5.7f^{5} May 26] tall gelding: fair handicapper: stays 6f: acts on polytrack, tapeta and good to firm going: wears headgear: front runner/races prominently. *Anabel K. Murphy* **72**

BUSHWISE (IRE) 4 b.f. Bushranger (IRE) 119 – Validate (Alhaarth (IRE) 126) [2017 60, a50: t6m 6g 5.1s 6.1m 5s^{4} 7.6s^{6} 5.7s^{6} 5.7d 7g^{6} p9.4g Dec 26] modest handicapper: left Milton Bradley after ninth start: stays 6f: acts on polytrack, tapeta, soft and good to firm going: wears headgear: usually races nearer last than first. *Ian Raybould, France* **49**

BUSKIN RIVER (IRE) 3 b.g. Kodiac 112 – Miss Smilla 78 (Red Ransom (USA)) [2017 70: p8g 10.2g 8d* 8s Oct 10] workmanlike gelding: fair handicapper: won at Brighton in September: stays 8.5f: acts on good to soft going. *James Eustace* **70**

BUSTAM (IRE) 2 b.g. (Apr 16) Worthadd (IRE) 124 – Malayan Mist (IRE) 100 (Dansili 127) [2017 6m^{2} t6s^{3} 7m^{6} 7m^{3} 7.2d^{4} 6v^{5} Sep 30] €56,000F, £35,000Y, £130,000 2-y-o: rather leggy gelding: third foal: dam, 9f/9.5f winner, half-sister to useful 6f-9.5f winner Greyfriarschorista: fairly useful maiden: sixth in Chesham Stakes at Royal Ascot in June, standout effort: stays 7f: acts on good to firm going: usually in hood: front runner/races prominently, often freely: temperamental. *John Quinn* **90 §**

BUSY STREET 5 b.g. Champs Elysees 124 – Allegro Viva (USA) (Distant View (USA) 126) [2017 85: f12g^{2} f12d^{2} 12m^{3} 13.1m^{4} 11.9s 11.9m^{4} 11.6g^{3} 12m^{2} Sep 4] good-topped gelding: fairly useful handicapper: second at Ripon in September: should be suited by further than 1½m: acts on fibresand, good to firm and good to soft going. *Sally Haynes* **87**

BUTHELA (FR) 3 b.c. Acclamation 118 – Tribune (FR) (Grand Slam (USA) 120) [2017 p8g* 6g^{5} 8g^{2} 8g* 8d^{2} Sep 30] €240,000Y: first foal: dam useful French 6.5f and (including at 2 yrs) 7.5f winner: smart performer: unraced at 2 yrs: progressed well, winning maiden at Chantilly in June and minor event at Saint-Cloud (by 1½ lengths from Yuman) in August: 1¼ lengths second to Taareef in Prix Daniel Wildenstein at Chantilly final outing, not clear run 2f out and staying on well: stays 1m: acts on polytrack and good to soft going: capable of even better. *A. Fabre, France* **118 p**

BUTHELEZI (USA) 9 b.g. Dynaformer (USA) – Ntombi (USA) (Quiet American (USA)) [2017 –: t12.4g t16.3g t12.4g 11.8g 14.6m 12.1m 13.4d t9.5g^{6} f11.1g Dec 21] big, well-made gelding: useful at best, has deteriorated markedly: stays 2¼m: acts on polytrack, tapeta, soft and good to firm going: has worn headgear: tried in tongue tie: sometimes slowly away, often races in rear. *Brian Ellison* **63**

BUTOOLAT 3 b.f. Oasis Dream 129 – Handassa 110 (Dubawi (IRE) 129) [2017 –: 6d^{5} 7g^{6} 8g^{4} 7g^{6} 7v^{3} 8v p6g^{3} p7g^{2} t7.2g^{6} Dec 13] first foal: dam, winner up to 1m (2-y-o 7f winner), half-sister to smart winner up to 1¼m Euginio: fair maiden: left Kevin Prendergast after eighth start: stays 7f: acts on good to soft going: front runner/races prominently. *Keith Dalgleish* **70**

BUTTERFLY LILY 3 gr.f. Lawman (FR) 121 – Bruxcalina (FR) (Linamix (FR) 127) [2017 7g^{6} Apr 21] third foal: half-sister to high-class sprinter (also winner up to 1¼m) Librisa Breeze (by Mount Nelson) and French 13f winner Belle Dauphine (by Dalakhani): dam French 1¼m winner: 10/3, sixth in maiden at Newbury (2 lengths behind Mulhimatty) on debut: will stay 1m: should improve. *Ralph Beckett* **63 p**

BUTTERFLY SPIRIT 2 gr.f. (Mar 27) Lethal Force (IRE) 128 – Zubova 73 (Dubawi (IRE) 129) [2017 p5g^{5} 5m 5.3d t5.1g 6g p5g^{5} Dec 23] £8,000Y: third foal: half-sister to 5f-7f winner Peachey Carnehan (by Foxwedge): dam, ungenuine 1m winner, half-sister to smart 6f/7f winner Van Ellis: poor maiden: sometimes slowly away: often races freely. *Michael Attwater* **48**

BUTTERSCOTCH (IRE) 2 b.f. (May 2) Galileo (IRE) 134 – Lesson In Humility (IRE) 115 (Mujadil (USA) 119) [2017 6d^{5} 6g^{2} 6d* 6g^{2} 7d^{5} 7m^{4} Oct 13] sturdy filly: fifth foal: sister to 1m winner Puppetshow and half-sister to useful 2-y-o 5f winner Coach House (by Oasis Dream): dam winner up to 6f (Ballyogan Stakes and 2-y-o 5f winner): useful performer: won maiden at Naas in June: fourth in Oh So Sharp Stakes at Newmarket final start: stays 7f: acts on good to firm and good to soft going: wears tongue tie: usually races close up. *Aidan O'Brien, Ireland* **101**

BUTTERWORTH BROW 3 b.f. Acclamation 118 – Rivalry (Medicean 128) [2017 5.9g^{4} Jun 19] 11/2, 12¾ lengths fourth of 5 to Clon Coulis in maiden at Carlisle only start: dead. *Bryan Smart* **–**

BUTTON UP (IRE) 3 b.f. So You Think (NZ) 133 – Star Ruby (IRE) 109 (Rock of Gibraltar (IRE) 133) [2017 61p: 9.9m p12g Jul 5] lengthy filly: modest form: tried in visor. *Sir Michael Stoute* **56**

BUXTED DREAM (USA) 3 gr.g. Dream Ahead (USA) 133 – America Nova (FR) (Verglas (IRE) 118) [2017 62: 8m^4 7d^2 p7g^2 6m^2 7s^2 6d* 6d* p6g^4 6.1m Oct 16] good-topped gelding: fairly useful performer: won maiden at Lingfield and handicap at Brighton (by neck from Bahamian Sunrise) in August: stays 1m, just as effective at shorter: acts on polytrack, good to firm and good to soft going: front runner/races prominently. *Luca Cumani* **89**

BUYER BEWARE (IRE) 5 br.g. Big Bad Bob (IRE) 118 – Adoring (IRE) 86 (One Cool Cat (USA) 123) [2017 –: 12m 14g^6 16m^5 16g^4 17.2s Aug 7] fair handicapper: stays 2m: acts on soft and good to firm going: tried in hood: fair hurdler. *Patrick Holmes* **73**

BUYING TROUBLE (USA) 4 b.f. Hat Trick (JPN) 121 – Lotus Sutra (USA) (Kingmambo (USA) 125) [2017 109: p7d^6 p5m 6g^6 5f 6.1g^5 6f* 6s 6g^4 6g 6g Sep 7] angular filly: useful performer: won listed race at Haydock (by ½ length from Bounce) in May: stays 7f: acts on polytrack, tapeta and firm going. *David Evans* **101**

BUZZ BOY (ITY) 4 ch.g. Buzzword 116 – Echad (IRE) (Kris Kin (USA) 126) [2017 62: 13.1m^2 15d^4 13.1g^6 12.9v Sep 8] modest handicapper: stays 1¾m: acts on good to firm and good to soft going: wears headgear. *A. P. Keatley, Ireland* **62**

BUZZ (FR) 3 gr.g. Motivator 131 – Tiysha (IRE) (Araafa (IRE) 128) [2017 79p: 10g 9.9g^2 Jul 19] tall gelding: fairly useful form: second in handicap at Sandown in July: stays 1¼m: still unexposed. *Hughie Morrison* **92 p**

BUZZ LIGHTYERE 4 b.g. Royal Applause 124 – Lady Gloria 114 (Diktat 126) [2017 65, a57: 8g* 8g^3 p8s^5 9.9g^2 10d^4 9.9m 8m* 8d^2 8g* 8.5g 8s^5 Oct 10] rather sparely-made gelding: fair handicapper: won at Brighton in May, August and September (apprentice): stays 1¼m: acts on good to firm and heavy going: tried in cheekpieces. *Philip Hide* **68**

BYBROOK 4 b.f. Dubawi (IRE) 129 – Diary (IRE) (Green Desert (USA) 127) [2017 82: t12.4g^5 11.8d^3 10v^2 12s* Oct 28] sturdy filly: fairly useful handicapper: won lady riders event at Newbury (by ½ length from Take Two) in October: stays 1½m: acts on heavy going: in cheekpieces last 2 starts. *David Simcock* **82**

BYE BYE BABY (IRE) 2 b.f. (Apr 5) Galileo (IRE) 134 – Remember When (IRE) 111 (Danehill Dancer (IRE) 117) [2017 7m^6 8d^4 7d^2 7d* 8v* 7v^3 Oct 22] fourth foal: sister to 3 winners, including 9f winner Wedding Vow and winner up to 1¼m (stayed 1½m) Beacon Rock (2-y-o 1m winner), both smart: dam, maiden (second in Oaks), closely related to top-class winner up to 1½m Dylan Thomas and 1000 Guineas winner Homecoming Queen: useful performer: won maiden at Newmarket in September and listed race at Navan (by 2¼ lengths from Coeur d'Amour) in October: third in Killavullan Stakes at Leopardstown (1½ lengths behind Kenya) final start: stays 1m: acts on heavy going: front runner/races prominently: remains open to improvement. *Aidan O'Brien, Ireland* **100 p**

BYRES ROAD 4 ch.g. Pivotal 124 – Croeso Cariad 107 (Most Welcome 131) [2017 89: t8.6m^2 t8.6m^4 p8m^5 t8g^2 p8d^5 t8g^4 p8g^6 t12.2g^4 9.9g^6 8s^6 Jul 10] fairly useful handicapper: second at Wolverhampton in January: stays 8.5f: acts on polytrack, tapeta and heavy going: usually races close up: sold 16,000 gns in July. *Mark Johnston* **91**

BYRON BLUE (IRE) 8 br.g. Dylan Thomas (IRE) 132 – High Society (IRE) 97 (Key of Luck (USA) 126) [2017 47: p15.8g p13.3g^5 p16s^6 Jul 25] compact gelding: fair handicapper at best, lightly raced and little form on Flat since 2013: stays 17f: acts on polytrack and soft going: has worn hood: in tongue tie last 3 starts. *Brian Barr* **49**

BYRONEGETONEFREE 6 b.g. Byron 117 – Lefty's Dollbaby (USA) (Brocco (USA) 124) [2017 42: t16.3s 12m^4 16.1g^6 12.5m^5 t16.3g^2 t16.3s Sep 8] modest handicapper: stays 16.5f: acts on polytrack, tapeta, good to firm and good to soft going: tried in hood. *Stuart Coltherd* **57**

BYRON FLYER 6 b.g. Byron 117 – Nursling (IRE) 57 (Kahyasi 130) [2017 86: p15.8g* t16.5g^2 t16.3g^4 13.4g 14g^2 16.3m^2 16d^2 14.5g^2 18m Oct 14] close-coupled gelding: useful handicapper: won at Lingfield in February: second in Mallard Stakes at Doncaster (head behind Time To Study) in September: stays 2m: acts on polytrack and good to soft going: in cheekpieces last 2 starts. *Ian Williams* **104 a96**

BYRON'S CHOICE 2 b.g. (Feb 1) Poet's Voice 126 – Byrony (IRE) 96 (Byron 117) [2017 6g^6 5.9s* t7.1g^6 6s^3 7s^2 Sep 19] 30,000Y: first foal: dam, winner up to 9f (2-y-o 7f/1m winner), closely related to smart sprinter Waffle: fairly useful performer: won minor event at Carlisle in June: second in nursery at Redcar in September: stays 7f: acts on soft going. *Michael Dods* **81**

BY ROYAL APPROVAL (IRE) 2 b.g. (Apr 16) Approve (IRE) 112 – Spring Bouquet (IRE) 60 (King's Best (USA) 132) [2017 6s^6 6m 5m^4 p6g^4 7m t7.2g Dec 22] good-topped gelding: fair maiden: should stay 6f: acts on good to firm going. *Michael Appleby* **74**

BY THE LAW 4 b.g. New Approach (IRE) 132 – Walk On Bye (IRE) 105 (Danehill Dancer (IRE) 117) [2017 62: 7m 8m 5g^6 Jun 23] well-made gelding: maiden, well held in handicaps in 2017: tried in blinkers: sometimes slowly away, often races towards rear: sold 4,000 gns, sent to Greece. *Tim Easterby* –

C

CABAL 10 br.m. Kyllachy 129 – Secret Flame 78 (Machiavellian (USA) 123) [2017 79: f8g t7.1g^6 t8d^4 t8.6g 8.5m^2 7g^2 8m^3 8m^3 7f^5 8g^3 7g 8m Aug 11] lengthy mare: fair handicapper: races around 1m nowadays: acts on polytrack, tapeta, firm and soft going: wears headgear: sometimes slowly away. *Geoffrey Harker* **69**

CABANON BAY 2 b.g. (Feb 14) Dandy Man (IRE) 123 – Eventfull Meet (IRE) (Dalakhani (IRE) 133) [2017 5d 5m^6 6.1m Jul 4] modest form in minor events. *Malcolm Saunders* **56**

CABLE CAR 6 gr.g. Pastoral Pursuits 127 – Nina Fontenail (FR) 66 (Kaldounevees (FR) 118) [2017 12v t9.5g Aug 31] once raced in bumpers: behind in 2 maidens on Flat: in cheekpieces second start. *John Flint* –

CADEAU MAGNIFIQUE 5 b.g. Dutch Art 126 – Cadeau Speciale 54 (Cadeaux Genereux 131) [2017 83: t8g t10.2d^2 Mar 2] rather leggy gelding: fairly useful handicapper: second at Newcastle in March: stays 10.5f: acts on tapeta, soft and good to firm going: in cheekpieces last 3 starts. *Richard Fahey* **85**

CADEAUX BOXER 4 ch.g. Major Cadeaux 121 – Ashantiana 64 (Ashkalani (IRE) 128) [2017 74: 6.1s 7g^2 7g^5 8d^6 p7g^6 p8g^4 p10g f8.1g p10g Dec 13] strong gelding: fairly useful maiden on turf, fair on all-weather: second in handicap at Newbury in July: left Martin Smith after fifth start: stays 1m: acts on soft going: often wears hood: front runner/races prominently. *Lee Carter* **81** **a75**

CADEAUX PEARL 9 b.g. Acclamation 118 – Anneliina 80 (Cadeaux Genereux 131) [2017 54: f6g^4 f6g^2 f7g^5 f6m^4 f6m f6g^2 f6d 6g Apr 22] sturdy gelding: modest handicapper: stays 7f: acts on polytrack, fibresand, soft and good to firm going: usually wears headgear: front runner/races prominently. *Scott Dixon* **54**

CADELA RICA 3 b.f. Compton Place 125 – Millennium Heiress (Singspiel (IRE) 133) [2017 –: 9.9m^4 7d Jul 12] good-topped filly: no form: in tongue tie final start. *Gay Kelleway* –

CADMIUM 6 b.m. Major Cadeaux 121 – Miss Mirasol 92 (Sheikh Albadou 128) [2017 69: 12s 11.1g^5 10g 9.9s^6 8s^4 8.3s a9.7g* 9.9v* 10.4g a9g^3 a8.5g* Dec 26] modest handicapper: left Micky Hammond after sixth start: did well in Germany after, winning minor event at Honzrath in October, and handicaps at Dortmund later same month and in December: stays 1¼m: acts on all-weather, heavy and good to firm going: sometimes wears headgear: sometimes slowly away. *C. von der Recke, Germany* **52**

CADORE (IRE) 9 b.g. Hurricane Run (IRE) 134 – Mansiya 65 (Vettori (IRE) 119) [2017 13.1m^5 15d Jun 5] leggy gelding: fairly useful in 2011: lightly raced and little form on Flat since: stays 10.5f: acts on soft and good to firm going: wears headgear nowadays: poor hurdler nowadays. *Lucy Normile* –

CAESAR'S COMET (IRE) 3 b.g. Acclamation 118 – Star Now 69 (Librettist (USA) 124) [2017 p7g^4 5.8m 6g 5m^3 5d^4 6.1m Oct 16] close-coupled gelding: fair maiden: left M. Halford after third start: stays 7f: acts on polytrack and good to soft going: in hood final start: often races towards rear. *Paul Midgley* **70**

CAESER THE GAESER (IRE) 5 b.g. Captain Rio 122 – Alchimie (IRE) (Sri Pekan (USA) 117) [2017 76: t6s^5 5.9g 6d t6d^5 7m 6v t7.1d Sep 29] fair handicapper: stays 7f: acts on tapeta and good to firm going: wears cheekpieces. *Nigel Tinkler* **60** **a68**

CAGED LIGHTNING (IRE) 7 b.g. Haatef (USA) 117 – Rainbow Melody (IRE) 83 (Rainbows For Life (CAN)) [2017 79: p14d^6 14d^4 p16s* Dec 15] fairly useful handicapper: won at Chelmsford (by head from Fitzwilly) in December: stays 2m: acts on polytrack, fibresand and soft going: usually wears headgear. *Steve Gollings* **80**

CAGLIARI 3 gr.f. Bahamian Bounty 116 – Crocus Rose 89 (Royal Applause 124) [2017 t9.5g^5 11.2m^5 Aug 27] 14,500F, 35,000Y: leggy, unfurnished filly: second foal: half-sister to 1½m winner Mr Marchwood (by Medicean): dam, 1¾m/14.6f winner, half-sister to smart 1¼m-1½m winner Ela Athena: behind in maiden/seller: wears hood: sent to Greece. *Simon Crisford* –

CAHAR FAD (IRE) 5 b.g. Bushranger (IRE) 119 – Tarbiyah 89 (Singspiel (IRE) 133) [2017 65: t9.5g^3 t9.5g p12g^6 p10g^2 p10g^2 t12.2g 8.3g t8.6g^5 p10g Aug 31] angular gelding: modest handicapper: stays 1½m: acts on polytrack, tapeta and good to soft going: wears headgear/tongue tie: front runner/races prominently. *Steph Hollinshead* **56**

CAINHOE STAR 4 ch.g. Pivotal 124 – Celeste (Green Desert (USA) 127) [2017 –: 7m^3 p8s^2 8m* p7s* 8s^6 p7g^2 p7d^3 p7g* p8g f7.1g^4 Dec 11] fairly useful handicapper: won at Yarmouth in June, Chelmsford in July and Kempton (by 3 lengths from Monteverdi) in October: stays 1m: acts on polytrack, fibresand and good to firm going: often races prominently. *Anthony Carson* **78 a89**

CAIUS COLLEGE GIRL (IRE) 5 b.m. Royal Applause 124 – Galeaza (Galileo (IRE) 134) [2017 66: p8d t8.6g^5 p8g^6 9g^4 8.1d 5.7s p7g Oct 17] sturdy mare: modest handicapper: left Natalie Lloyd-Beavis after fourth start: stays 9.5f: acts on soft going: has worn headgear, including last 3 starts. *Adrian Wintle* **54**

CAIYA 2 b.f. (Feb 12) Casamento (IRE) 118 – Louverissa (IRE) (Verglas (IRE) 118) [2017 7s* Oct 9] 15,000F: fifth foal: half-sister to 3 winners, including winner up to 9f Lulani (2-y-o 1m winner, by Royal Applause) and 2-y-o 7f winner (stays 16.5f) Hermarna (by Heliostatic): dam unraced half-sister to 2000 Guineas winner Cockney Rebel: 12/1, won minor event at Salisbury (by neck from Teenage Gal) on debut, despite reportedly bleeding: open to improvement. *Eve Johnson Houghton* **75 p**

CAJMERE 3 b.g. Kyllachy 129 – Percolator 106 (Kheleyf (USA) 116) [2017 79: t5g^2 t5.1m* t5d^4 p6s^2 Jun 14] lengthy gelding: fairly useful handicapper: won at Wolverhampton in January: second at Kempton in June: stays 6f: acts on polytrack, tapeta and good to soft going: has worn cheekpieces: front runner/races prominently: sold 13,000 gns in July, sent to Greece. *Tom Dascombe* **85**

CALARE (IRE) 3 ch.f. Dubawi (IRE) 129 – Calando (USA) 110 (Storm Cat (USA)) [2017 98: a7f^5 a8f a9.4f^5 Feb 23] useful at 2 yrs, below best all 3 starts at Meydan early in 2017: should stay beyond 1m: acts on soft and good to firm going: in cheekpieces last 2 starts. *Charlie Appleby* **93**

CALDER PRINCE (IRE) 4 gr.g. Dark Angel (IRE) 113 – Flame of Ireland (IRE) 85 (Fasliyev (USA) 120) [2017 105: a6f a8f^6 7m^4 7.6d 7d 8m^2 8m* 7.9d^3 7.6s^5 8.2d^2 7.6g^4 7s^3 7v^4 8.2v^6 Sep 30] leggy gelding: useful handicapper: won at Haydock (by 1¼ lengths from Areen Heart) in July: stays 1m: acts on polytrack, dirt, soft and good to firm going: front runner/races prominently. *Tom Dascombe* **99**

CALEDONIA DUCHESS 4 b.f. Dutch Art 126 – Granuaile O'Malley (IRE) 55 (Mark of Esteem (IRE) 137) [2017 74: p8s^5 p8g^2 p8g^5 8.1d^3 Oct 23] sturdy filly: fair maiden: stays 1m: acts on polytrack, tapeta and good to soft going: has worn headgear. *Jo Hughes* **74**

CALEDONIA LAIRD 6 b.g. Firebreak 125 – Granuaile O'Malley (IRE) 55 (Mark of Esteem (IRE) 137) [2017 74: t9.5g^4 t7.1g* 8f^3 t7.2g^2 7f 7g^3 t8.6g t7.2g p8d t7.2g^5 Oct 27] good-topped gelding: fair handicapper: won at Wolverhampton in April: stays 8.5f: acts on polytrack, tapeta, firm and soft going: has worn headgear, including last 5 starts: tried in tongue tie. *Jo Hughes* **69**

CALEDONIAN GOLD 4 b.f. Acclamation 118 – Moonlight Rhapsody (IRE) 73 (Danehill Dancer (IRE) 117) [2017 –: p6d^5 p7g^5 t7.1g^4 f7d^3 p8g p7s^4 7d^4 p7s^5 p7s^3 7d^2 7m^4 p7g^4 p7s^4 p7g^5 f7.1g^4 Nov 16] modest maiden: stays 7f: acts on all-weather: usually wears blinkers nowadays. *Paul D'Arcy* **61**

CALIBRATION (IRE) 3 b.c. Excelebration (IRE) 133 – Dance Troupe 85 (Rainbow Quest (USA) 134) [2017 90: 10g* Jul 20] strong, compact colt: useful performer: won maiden at Leicester (by 7 lengths from Nathan) on sole 2017 start: stays 1¼m: acts on good to firm going: front runner/races prominently: sent to Australia. *Martyn Meade* **97**

CALIFORNIA CHROME (USA) 6 ch.h. Lucky Pulpit (USA) – Love The Chase (USA) (Not For Love (USA)) [2017 138: a9f Jan 28] top-class performer: successful in Kentucky Derby and Preakness Stakes in 2014: ran only twice at 4 yrs: thrived in 2016 (voted US Horse of The Year for a second time), and won 7 of 8 starts, including Dubai World Cup at Meydan, Pacific Classic at Del Mar and Awesome Again Stakes at Santa Anita, and also ½-length second to Arrogate in Breeders' Cup Classic at Santa Anita: well below form in Pegasus World Cup at Gulfstream in January (reportedly returned with a knee injury): stayed 1¼m: acted on polytrack, cushion track, dirt and firm going: wore headgear: tried in tongue tie: usually raced prominently: genuine: retired, and stood at Taylor Made, Kentucky, fee $40,000. *Art Sherman, USA* **–**

CALIFORNIA CLIFFS (IRE) 3 b.f. Canford Cliffs (IRE) 133 – Quiet Waters (USA) (Quiet American (USA)) [2017 t8.6g[6] 8.3g 8m[6] 9.9g[2] 10g[6] 10d[5] 9.8g[4] p10d[2] p10g Oct 12] 10,000Y: angular filly: sixth foal: half-sister to 3 winners by High Chaparral, including useful Scandinavian 1m/10.5f winner Pas de Secrets (stays 1½m) and 1½m winner Rivers Run: dam lightly raced in France: modest maiden: stays 1¼m: acts on polytrack: sent to Germany. *Rae Guest* **60**

CALLAGHAN (GER) 4 b.g. Cacique (IRE) 124 – Cent Cheveux Blanc (GER) (Pentire 132) [2017 –: t12.2g[5] 12d 10.2g p12d 10.2d[5] t12.2g t12.2m Oct 28] modest maiden: stays 1½m: acts on polytrack and tapeta: in headgear last 3 starts: wears tongue tie: sometimes slowly away, usually races nearer last than first. *Tom Gretton* **61**

CALLALOO 3 ch.f. Rip Van Winkle (IRE) 134 – In The Soup (USA) (Alphabet Soup (USA) 126) [2017 8s 8d Aug 5] 8,000Y, 3,000 3-y-o: half-sister to several winners, including useful 9.5f-11f winner General Hazard (by Cacique) and 1¼m-13f winner San Quentin (by Lawman): dam French 1m/9.5f winner: well held in 2 maidens. *Tony Coyle* **–**

CALL DAWN 2 b.f. (Feb 19) Helmet (AUS) 127 – Authoritative (Diktat 126) [2017 5d[4] 5d[4] 5m[5] 6v t7.1g t7.2g[2] Nov 18] 1,500F: fourth foal: dam unraced daughter of useful German winner up to 1¼m Australian Dreams: modest maiden: will stay 1m: acts on tapeta: in hood final start. *Michael Easterby* **62**

CALLING OUT (FR) 6 b.g. Martaline 118 – Exit The Straight (IRE) (Exit To Nowhere (USA) 122) [2017 107: t9.5g* p12g[2] p8s[6] Dec 14] tall gelding: useful performer: won minor event at Wolverhampton (by 1¼ lengths from Mythical Madness) in January: stays 1½m: acts on polytrack, tapeta, good to firm and heavy going. *David Simcock* **105**

CALLING RIO (IRE) 2 b.f. (Mar 30) Canford Cliffs (IRE) 133 – Rio's Pearl 87 (Captain Rio 122) [2017 t6.1g 7.4g[5] 6.9v[3] 7g[3] 8.3d[3] 8.3d[4] t8.6m[4] t8.6g Nov 18] first foal: dam, 2-y-o 7f winner, half-sister to useful 2-y-o 6f winner Medicine Jack: fair maiden: stays 8.5f: acts on tapeta and good to soft going: usually races close up. *David Loughnane* **75**

CALLIOPE 4 b.f. Poet's Voice 126 – Costa Brava (IRE) (Sadler's Wells (USA) 132) [2017 71: 10m t10.2s 14d[3] 12d[5] Aug 21] useful-looking filly: fair handicapper: stays 1¾m: acts on good to soft and good to firm going: tried in hood: often races towards rear. *Kenneth Slack* **68**

CALL ME GRUMPY (IRE) 3 b.g. Holy Roman Emperor (IRE) 125 – Miss Rochester (IRE) 84 (Montjeu (IRE) 137) [2017 69p: 7m* 7g[2] 6.9g[4] 7m[2] 8g[3] Sep 15] fairly useful handicapper: won at Sandown in June: third at same course in September: stays 1m: acts on good to firm going. *Roger Varian* **87**

CALL OUT LOUD 5 b.g. Aqlaam 125 – Winner's Call (Indian Ridge 123) [2017 74: f7g[4] f6g* f6g[6] f7g[3] t7.1g* t7.1m* t7.1g* f7d[2] 7m 7.6g 7v 7d[3] p7d[6] p7s* f6.1g[6] t7.2d Dec 16] fair on turf, fairly useful handicapper on all-weather: won at Southwell in January, completed hat-trick at Wolverhampton in February/March (seller first occasion) and won again at Chelmsford (apprentice, by nose from Human Nature) in December: stays 7.5f: acts on all-weather, good to firm and heavy going: usually wears headgear: often wears tongue tie. *Michael Appleby* **79 a91**

CALL TO MIND 3 b.c. Galileo (IRE) 134 – Memory (IRE) 112 (Danehill Dancer (IRE) 117) [2017 8m* 10d[3] 12m[6] 11.1g[3] 14g* 14.9g[2] Sep 30] useful-looking colt: second foal: brother to smart 2-y-o 7f (including Acomb Stakes) winner Recorder: dam 2-y-o 6f (including Albany and Cherry Hinton Stakes) winner who stayed 1m: smart performer: won maiden at Newbury in April and listed race at Goodwood (by 1¼ lengths from Count Octave) in August: short-neck second to Ice Breeze in Prix Chaudenay at Chantilly final outing: probably stays 15f: acts on good to firm and good to soft going: usually races prominently. *William Haggas* **117**

CALM CHARM (IRE) 3 ch.f. Teofilo (IRE) 126 – Mango Lady 80 (Dalakhani (IRE) 133) [2017 p8g p8g 8.1m[5] Oct 16] well-made filly: fourth foal: half-sister to 3 winners, including smart 7f/7.6f winner (including at 2 yrs) Mix And Mingle (by Exceed And Excel) and 9.5f/1¼m winner May Queen (by Shamardal): dam, 1½m winner, closely related to St Leger runner-up High Accolade: modest form in maidens: will stay beyond 1m: should do better. *Chris Wall* **60 p**

CALVADOS SPIRIT 4 b.g. Invincible Spirit (IRE) 121 – Putois Peace (Pivotal 124) [2017 89: t8.6g* 8s 8.5m 8f[4] 10m[3] 10m[3] 8g p6g Oct 11] sturdy gelding: fairly useful handicapper: won at Wolverhampton in April: barely stays 1¼m: acts on polytrack, tapeta, good to firm and good to soft going: often in hood in 2017: usually races close up: sold to join Richard Fahey 38,000 gns in November. *William Muir* **94**

CALVINIST 4 b.g. Holy Roman Emperor (IRE) 125 – Sharp Relief (IRE) 78 (Galileo (IRE) 134) [2017 98: t16.5g^{5} p16g^{5} t16.3g p10s 14g 12v 14.2g^{5} p16g t12.4g Nov 23] neat gelding: useful handicapper at best: lost his form in 2017: left Archie Watson after third start, Ian Williams after seventh: stays 16.5f: acts on tapeta and good to firm going: often wears cheekpieces: sometimes wears tongue tie. *Ruth Carr* **96 d**

CALVIN'S GAL (IRE) 2 ch.f. (Feb 7) Casamento (IRE) 118 – Spirit of Hope (IRE) (Danehill Dancer (IRE) 117) [2017 5.1m t7.2g t5.1g^{6} Sep 9] 10,000 2-y-o: half-sister to useful Spanish/French 5f-7f (including at 2 yrs) winner Aiboa (by King Charlemagne) and 5.7f/6f winner Fyrecracker (by Kheleyf): dam Greek 5f-9f winner: little impact in maiden/minor events: tried in hood. *Luke McJannet* **–**

CALYPSO BLUE (IRE) 2 b.f. (Mar 6) Dubawi (IRE) 129 – Dark Orchid (USA) 110 (Dansili 127) [2017 t8.6g^{4} p8s^{2} Dec 17] first foal: dam, French 1m-1¼m winner, out of half-sister to high-class 1¼m-1½m winner Hernando: fair form: in cheekpieces, better effort when second in minor event at Chelmsford (½ length behind Ejtyah) in December. *Charlie Appleby* **75**

CALYPSO CHOIR 4 ch.f. Bahamian Bounty 116 – Heavenly Song (IRE) 61 (Oratorio (IRE) 128) [2017 91: p6g Jan 6] angular filly: fairly useful handicapper, well held sole start in 2017: stays 6f: acts on polytrack and firm going: front runner/races prominently. *Sylvester Kirk* **–**

CALYPSO DELEGATOR (IRE) 4 b.g. Lilbourne Lad (IRE) 111 – Amber Nectar (IRE) (Barathea (IRE) 127) [2017 56: 9.8m^{3} 8s 9.8g* Aug 29] modest performer: won seller at Ripon in August: stays 10.5f: acts on good to firm going: wore headgear in 2017: often starts slowly/races in rear. *Micky Hammond* **64**

CALYPSO JO 3 b.g. Bahamian Bounty 116 – Cha Cha Cha 90 (Efisio 120) [2017 p6d^{2} t6g^{4} 6d p8g p6g p6g p6g p6g Dec 21] fair form when second in maiden on debut, standout effort: left Kevin Ryan after third start: sometimes in headgear: tried in tongue tie: tends to find little. *Damian Joseph English, Ireland* **68**

CAMACHO CHIEF (IRE) 2 b.g. (Apr 16) Camacho 118 – Passage To India (IRE) 74 (Indian Ridge 123) [2017 5d^{5} 5g^{2} 5d* 5d* 6d^{3} 6.3s^{5} 6v^{2} Oct 9] €6,000Y: fifth foal: half-brother to 3 winners, including 5f (including at 2 yrs) winner Appleberry (by Approve) and 7f winner Stars N Angels (by Dark Angel): dam, maiden (best at 7f), sister to smart Italian/French 5f-7f winner Rosendhal: fairly useful performer: won minor event at Hamilton in July and nursery at Musselburgh (by 2¾ lengths from Seen The Lyte) in August: stays 6f: acts on heavy going: in cheekpieces final start. *Michael Dods* **90**

CAMAKASI (IRE) 6 b.g. Camacho 118 – Innocence 73 (Unfuwain (USA) 131) [2017 71: p11g* p12d^{5} p11g p11g^{3} 11.5m^{3} 11m 10m^{4} 11.4g^{3} 10.2d* Aug 19] tall gelding: fairly useful handicapper: won at Kempton in January and Bath (by 8 lengths from Silver Dixie) in August: stays 11.5f: acts on polytrack, soft and good to firm going: has worn cheekpieces/tongue tie: often races towards rear. *Ali Stronge* **88 a80**

CAMANCHE GREY (IRE) 6 gr.g. Camacho 118 – Sense of Greeting (IRE) 46 (Key of Luck (USA) 126) [2017 53: 5g 5s* 5g^{3} t5g^{3} 5s^{2} Aug 24] fair handicapper: won at Hamilton in July: best form at 5f: acts on fibresand, soft and good to firm going: tried in headgear. *Ben Haslam* **66**

CAMARADORIE (IRE) 3 ch.f. Camacho 118 – Lady Duxyana 54 (Most Welcome 131) [2017 –: t7.1g^{3} p7g^{6} 6m 8g^{5} t7.2g t9.5g Dec 2] small filly: modest maiden: stays 7f: acts on polytrack and tapeta: often races prominently. *Lydia Pearce* **60**

CAMARGUE 3 b.f. Invincible Spirit (IRE) 121 – Chaquiras (USA) (Seeking The Gold (USA)) [2017 88: f5d^{3} p7g^{5} Apr 12] sturdy filly: fairly useful at 2 yrs, below best in 2017: stays 6f: acts on tapeta and firm going: usually races close up. *Mark Johnston* **76**

CAMBODIA (IRE) 4 ch.g. Fast Company (IRE) 126 – Remarkable Story (Mark of Esteem (IRE) 137) [2017 81: t9.5m p8g^{pu} 8g May 15] fairly useful 1m winner: well below best in 2017 (wore hood). *Chris Wall* **–**

CAMDEN TOWN (IRE) 2 ch.g. (Apr 26) New Approach (IRE) 132 – Antique (IRE) 109 (Dubai Millennium 140) [2017 7v^{6} t6g t8d^{5} Dec 16] well held in minor events. *Roger Fell* **–**

CAMDORA (IRE) 5 b.m. Arcano (IRE) 122 – Crimphill (IRE) 106 (Sadler's Wells (USA) 132) [2017 69: p6g^{3} p6d^{4} Feb 2] fair handicapper: stays 7f: acts on polytrack: wears tongue tie nowadays: often races towards rear. *Jamie Osborne* **65**

CAMEO STAR (IRE) 2 ch.g. (Apr 20) Camacho 118 – Passionforfashion (IRE) 60 (Fasliyev (USA) 120) [2017 5.9g 5f* 5d p6d^{4} 6.1d Oct 4] fair performer: won minor event at Beverley in July: stays 6f: acts on firm going and polytrack. *Richard Fahey* **76**

CAMERONE (IRE) 3 b.f. Galileo (IRE) 134 – Louvain (IRE) 105 (Sinndar (IRE) 134) **95**
[2017 79p: 11.6d^{4} 12.1m* 12g^{6} 11.6d* 11.9d^{4} Sep 14] close-coupled filly: useful handicapper: won at Beverley in June and Bath (by length from Tarte Tropezienne) in August: will stay beyond 1½m: acts on good to firm and good to soft going: sent to France. *Ralph Beckett*

CAMINO 4 b.f. Equiano (FR) 127 – Juncea 76 (Elnadim (USA) 128) [2017 –: p6g p6g **57**
t5.1g^{2} p5g p5g^{3} 5.3m* p5g^{2} 5.3g 5.2m^{2} Aug 17] lengthy filly: modest handicapper: won at Brighton in June: stays 5.5f: acts on polytrack, tapeta and good to firm going: has worn headgear. *Andi Brown*

CAMIYRA (IRE) 3 b.f. Henrythenavigator (USA) 131 – Myrica (Dansili 127) [2017 69p: **75**
6d^{2} 7g^{5} 7m^{5} 5v 7.3s^{2} 7.1d^{3} 7v 7v Oct 24] first foal: dam, useful French 1m winner who stayed 1¼m, closely related to smart 9f/1¼m winner Eddystone Rock: fair maiden: likely to stay 1m: acts on polytrack and soft going: tried in cheekpieces: has worn tongue tie. *John Patrick Murtagh, Ireland*

CAMOMILE LAWN (IRE) 2 b.f. (Mar 21) Camelot 128 – Endure (IRE) (Green Desert **73**
(USA) 127) [2017 p7g^{2} 7m p8s 8v Sep 28] 52,000Y: sturdy filly: closely related to smart 2-y-o 6f/7f winner (stayed 1¼m) Bunker and French 11.5f winner Hallotiere (both by Hurricane Run) and half-sister to 3 winners, including useful 5f/5.7f winner Imtiyaaz (by Starspangledbanner): dam ran twice: fair form when second in minor event at Kempton on debut, standout effort: has joined Eve Johnson Houghton. *Ralph Beckett*

CAMPION 2 b.f. (Apr 10) Exceed And Excel (AUS) 126 – Princess Janie (USA) (Elusive **76**
Quality (USA)) [2017 t5.1g 5m^{4} 5f* 6m^{3} 6g 7d 5.1d^{5} 6d^{5} Sep 5] good-topped filly: closely related to 6f winner Wishsong (by Dansili) and 2-y-o 6f winner Lundy (by Fastnet Rock) and half-sister to 2 winners: dam US 6f winner: fair performer: won minor event at Bath in May: best form at 5f: acts on firm going: tried in hood: has joined Philip Kirby. *Richard Hannon*

CANADIAN DIAMOND (IRE) 10 ch.g. Halling (USA) 133 – Six Nations (USA) **77**
(Danzig (USA)) [2017 73: f16g* p16g* p16g^{6} Apr 1] fair handicapper: won at Southwell (amateur) in January and Kempton in February: stays 2m: acts on polytrack and fibresand: has worn headgear: often travels strongly. *Richard Rowe*

CANADIAN GEORGE (FR) 2 b.c. (Feb 12) George Vancouver (USA) 116 – **75**
Connaissance (IRE) (Choisir (AUS) 126) [2017 7.2m^{5} 7g^{3} 7.2s^{4} t8g^{2} Nov 24] fair form: second in nursery at Newcastle in November: stays 1m. *Keith Dalgleish*

CANADIAN ROYAL 3 b.g. Royal Applause 124 – Emily Carr (IRE) 75 (Teofilo (IRE) **68**
126) [2017 –: 8s 6g^{2} 6d^{6} 6m^{3} p6g t5s^{6} p6g^{3} p6s^{3} f6.1g^{3} Dec 19] good-topped gelding: fair maiden: stays 6f: acts on polytrack, fibresand and good to firm going: in headgear last 3 starts: wears tongue tie: often races prominently. *Stuart Williams*

CANBERRA CLIFFS (IRE) 3 b.f. Canford Cliffs (IRE) 133 – Gloved Hand 105 (Royal **97**
Applause 124) [2017 69: p5g^{6} t7.1g^{5} 10.2m* 10.2g^{3} 9.9g* 10.3g^{3} 10s^{2} 8.1m^{6} 9.9v* 10.2d* 10.2d^{3} 10v^{2} p10g t12.2g^{5} p12g^{4} Dec 31] useful handicapper: won at Nottingham in April, Beverley in May, and Sandown (amateur) and Bath in August: stays 1½m: acts on polytrack, tapeta, good to firm and heavy going. *Don Cantillon*

CAN CAN DREAM 3 b.f. Stimulation (IRE) 121 – Can Can Dancer 55 (Fantastic Light –
(USA) 134) [2017 –: f8.1g Dec 21] leggy filly: little form: tried in cheekpieces. *Olly Williams*

CAN CAN SIXTY TWO 2 b.f. (Apr 23) Sixties Icon 125 – Natalie Jay 88 (Ballacashtal –
(CAN)) [2017 8s Oct 28] sister to 2 winners, including 1½m winner Ingleby Mackenzie, and half-sister to 3 winners, including useful winner up to 1¼m Fork Handles (2-y-o 6f winner, by Doyen): dam 7f/1m winner: 50/1, well held in minor event at Newbury. *Mick Channon*

CANDELARIA 4 b.g. Kyllachy 129 – Gleam of Light (IRE) 81 (Danehill (USA) 126) –
[2017 77: 5f 6.1m 5d 6s 5m^{6} 5.7s Sep 17] fair maiden at best in Ireland, little impact in handicaps in 2017: best form at 5f: has worn headgear, including last 2 starts: usually races close up/finds little. *Jonjo O'Neill*

CANDELISA (IRE) 4 br.g. Dream Ahead (USA) 133 – Vasilia (Dansili 127) [2017 101: **100**
8g^{3} 8s 8d^{4} 8g 9.2s^{5} 7.8v^{5} 8g* 8v Oct 12] well-made gelding: useful performer: won seller at Redcar in September: third in handicap at Doncaster (1¾ lengths behind Ballet Concerto) in April: left Jedd O'Keeffe after seventh start: stays 1m: acts on tapeta, good to firm and heavy going: often wears cheekpieces. *Tony Coyle*

CANDESTA (USA) 7 b.g. First Defence (USA) 119 – Wandesta 121 (Nashwan (USA) 135) [2017 75: p10m p8d^6 8.3g 8m^5 8.1m 9.9f^5 8d^6 p8g p8g 10.2g f8.1g^5 f8.1g* Dec 21] modest handicapper on turf, fair on all-weather: won at Southwell in December: best up to 1m: acts on polytrack, fibresand and firm going: has worn headgear: has worn tongue tie, including last 2 starts. *Julia Feilden* **60 a71**

CANDIDATE (IRE) 2 b.c. (May 1) Camelot 128 – Miss Mariduff (USA) (Hussonet (USA)) [2017 8g 8.1g^4 10m Oct 25] 90,000Y: good-topped colt: half-brother to several winners, including useful Italian/French winner up to 1¼m Porsenna (7f/7.5f winner at 2 yrs, by Dylan Thomas) and smart Italian winner up to 1m Basileus (2-y-o 7.5f winner, by Dream Ahead): dam unraced: fair form: easily best effort when fourth in minor event at Windsor (1¾ lengths behind Delsheer) in October: type to do better in handicaps. *Hughie Morrison* **76 p**

CANDYMAN CAN (IRE) 7 b.g. Holy Roman Emperor (IRE) 125 – Palwina (FR) (Unfuwain (USA) 131) [2017 12g Jun 2] fairly useful at best, below that sole start since 2015: stays 1½m: acts on polytrack and heavy going: in hood last 3 starts. *Henry Spiller* **–**

CANFORD BAY (IRE) 3 b.c. Canford Cliffs (IRE) 133 – Maundays Bay (IRE) 80 (Invincible Spirit (IRE) 121) [2017 65p: 5g^2 5d^5 5g^6 5m t5g^3 t5g t5d* t6g^3 t5d^4 Oct 24] fair handicapper: won at Newcastle (apprentice) in September: stays 6f: acts on tapeta. *Antony Brittain* **72**

CANFORD BELLE 4 b.f. Canford Cliffs (IRE) 133 – Ballyea (IRE) 70 (Acclamation 118) [2017 62: t8g^2 t7.1d^4 t8.6g t8.6g^4 t8.6g f7g^2 f7.1g Aug 28] sturdy filly: modest handicapper: stays 1m: acts on all-weather, good to firm and heavy going: often races prominently. *Grant Tuer* **60**

CANFORD'S JOY (IRE) 2 b.g. (Mar 9) Canford Cliffs (IRE) 133 – Joyful (IRE) 71 (Green Desert (USA) 127) [2017 5s^6 5.9s* 6s* 6g 6d Nov 11] €38,000F, £14,000Y: strong gelding: half-brother to several winners, including useful winner up to 6f Roker Park (2-y-o 5f winner, by Choisir) and useful winner up to 9f Enabling (2-y-o 8.5f winner, by High Chaparral): dam 7f winner: fairly useful performer: won maiden at Carlisle in August and minor event at Catterick (by ½ length from Three Saints Bay) in September: likely to stay 7f: acts on soft going. *Ann Duffield* **81**

CANFORD THOMPSON 4 b.g. Canford Cliffs (IRE) 133 – Sadie Thompson (IRE) 79 (King's Best (USA) 132) [2017 73: p15.8g p12g Dec 6] fair maiden: stays 12.5f: acts on tapeta: usually races towards rear, often freely. *Daniel Steele* **60**

CANFORD TOR (IRE) 3 b.g. Canford Cliffs (IRE) 133 – Igreja (ARG) 101 (Southern Halo (USA)) [2017 7m^6 7s 7m 8m 8.1g^5 Jul 20] sturdy gelding: modest form: tried in blinkers: often races in rear. *Henry Candy* **54**

CANIMAR 2 b.f. (Mar 20) Havana Gold (IRE) 118 – Acquifer 75 (Oasis Dream 129) [2017 7m^6 7m^4 p8d Nov 22] £40,000Y: leggy filly: fourth foal: half-sister to 2-y-o 7f winner Arethusa (by Rip Van Winkle) and 2-y-o 5.7f winner Santafiora (by Poet's Voice): dam, maiden (stayed 7f), half-sister to useful stayer Lady of The Lake: fair form: best effort when fourth in minor event at Newmarket (1½ lengths behind Timpani) in October. *Ed Dunlop* **73**

CANIZAY (IRE) 3 ch.g. Tagula (IRE) 116 – Baltic Dip (IRE) 95 (Benny The Dip (USA) 127) [2017 –: t10.2s 8d^6 7d Jul 28] little impact in maidens/handicap. *Roger Fell* **–**

CANNY KOOL 5 b.g. Kheleyf (USA) 116 – Kool Acclaim 75 (Royal Applause 124) [2017 97: 5.1d^3 5d t6s 7g^{rr} Jul 15] useful at best, has gone wrong way (refused/virtually refused to race last 2 starts): stays 6f: acts on good to firm and good to soft going: sold 4,000 gns in November: one to leave alone. *Brian Ellison* **92 §**

CANNY STYLE 4 b.f. Canford Cliffs (IRE) 133 – Stylish One (IRE) 101 (Invincible Spirit (IRE) 121) [2017 73: 10m^3 t12.2g^3 11.9v^3 13.1s^2 11.9m^5 12.1s* 13d* 14m^3 11.8v^2 Sep 29] fairly useful handicapper: won at Catterick (apprentice) in July and Musselburgh (amateur) in August: stays 13f: acts on tapeta, good to firm and heavy going: tried in blinkers: won over hurdles in November. *Kevin Ryan* **82**

CANTERBURY QUAD (FR) 3 b.f. Motivator 131 – Coiffure (King's Best (USA) 132) [2017 81: 8d^6 10.2d^3 p10s^3 10g 8.1d a10.4g^5 Dec 28] angular filly: fairly useful maiden: third in handicap at Nottingham in May: left Henry Spiller before final outing: stays 1¼m: acts on good to soft going: tried in headgear: often travels strongly. *E. Libaud, France* **80**

CAN'T EXPLAIN 2 ch.f. (Apr 21) Lethal Force (IRE) 128 – Miss Universe (IRE) 99 (Warning 136) [2017 6s^2 Jul 28] 33/1, 1½ lengths second of 12 to Nobleman's Nest in minor event at Newmarket: dead. *Michael Bell* **85**

CANUFEELTHELOVE 2 b.f. (Apr 23) Sayif (IRE) 122 – Lady-Love 70 (Pursuit of Love 124) [2017 t6d t6.1d^6 Dec 27] half-sister to several winners, including 2-y-o 5.3f winner Tongue Twista (by Stimulation) and useful 7f-9f winner Moody Tunes (by Merdon Melody): dam 2-y-o 5f winner who stayed 7f: well held in 2 minor events. *Ben Haslam* –

CANYON CITY 4 b.g. Authorized (IRE) 133 – Colorado Dawn (Fantastic Light (USA) 134) [2017 12d Aug 24] fairly useful maiden for A. Fabre at 3 yrs, well held sole outing on Flat in 2017: stays 13f: acts on heavy going: won over hurdles in October. *Neil King* –

CAPE BANJO (USA) 4 ch.g. Cape Blanco (IRE) 130 – Magic of Love 99 (Magic Ring (IRE) 115) [2017 87: p8g^2 10g^4 p8g^5 9.9m^4 11.4g 10.3g p10g Aug 8] rangy gelding: fairly useful handicapper: second at Kempton in April: stays 1¼m: acts on polytrack and good to firm going: tried in hood: usually races close up. *Ralph Beckett* **79 a85**

CAPE BUNTING (IRE) 2 b.f. (Mar 26) Cape Cross (IRE) 129 – Bergamask (USA) (Kingmambo (USA) 125) [2017 7m* 7.2g* 7d p7s* Sep 2] sixth foal: half-sister to 3 winners, including smart 2-y-o 5f/6f (including Coventry Stakes) winner Buratino and 8.6f winner Tayma (both by Exceed And Excel): dam French 1m winner: fairly useful form: won minor events at Newmarket in June, Musselburgh in July and Chelmsford in September: raced only at 7f: sent to UAE. *Mark Johnston* **92**

CAPE BYRON 3 ch.c. Shamardal (USA) 129 – Reem Three 103 (Mark of Esteem (IRE) 137) [2017 87p: 8s* 8.9s^3 Oct 7] strong colt: useful form: won minor event at Ascot (by neck from Fire Brigade) in September: third in listed race at Chantilly (1¼ lengths behind Glen Shiel) month later: stays 9f. *Roger Varian* **109**

CAPE CASTER (IRE) 6 br.g. Cape Cross (IRE) 129 – Playboy Mansion (IRE) (Grand Lodge (USA) 125) [2017 18m Oct 14] lengthy gelding: useful handicapper at best: probably stays 2¼m: acts on good to firm and heavy going: fairly useful chaser. *Evan Williams* **88**

CAPE COAST 3 b.c. Cape Cross (IRE) 129 – Famusa 104 (Medicean 128) [2017 t10.2s^6 p12s^4 12g* 12m* 12g^2 13.4g^2 Sep 2] 16,000Y: compact colt: second foal: dam, Italian winner up to 11f (2-y-o 7.5f winner), half-sister to very smart 7f-8.5f winner Fanunalter: useful performer: won maiden at Pontefract in June and handicap at Ripon in July: second in handicap at Ascot (head behind Bin Battuta) and listed handicap at Chester (¾ length behind My Reward) last 2 starts: stays 13.5f: acts on polytrack and good to firm going: usually races close up. *Mark Johnston* **100**

CAPE COVA (IRE) 4 b.g. Cape Cross (IRE) 129 – Sina Cova (IRE) 116 (Barathea (IRE) 127) [2017 109: 14s^4 14g^3 12m t16.3d^2 Dec 16] good-topped gelding: smart handicapper: third at Newmarket (1¼ lengths behind Jaameh) in June and second in minor event at Newcastle (2 lengths behind Mountain Bell) in December: left John Gosden after third start: stays 16.5f: acts on polytrack, tapeta, good to firm and good to soft going: has worn headgear. *Michael Appleby* **110**

CAPE CRUISER (USA) 3 ch.g. Cape Blanco (IRE) 130 – Skip A Dare (USA) (Skip Away (USA) 134) [2017 62p: 12d p12g Jun 3] modest form at best: tried in cheekpieces. *Ralph Beckett* –

CAPE DISCOVERY 5 ch.g. Shamardal (USA) 129 – Kotsi (IRE) 103 (Nayef (USA) 129) [2017 92: p12g^6 p12g 11.6m^4 12s 11.9d^4 Jul 11] workmanlike gelding: fairly useful handicapper: stays 1½m: acts on polytrack and good to firm going: sold 18,000 gns in July, sent to Saudi Arabia. *Richard Hughes* **85**

CAPE HIDEAWAY 5 b.g. Mount Nelson 125 – Amiata 89 (Pennekamp (USA) 130) [2017 67: t16.3s^5 Jun 3] fair handicapper: stays 2m: acts on good to firm and heavy going: wears cheekpieces: races prominently: consistent: fair hurdler. *Mark Walford* **58**

CAPE ICON 6 b.g. Mount Nelson 125 – Cape Merino 103 (Clantime 101) [2017 92: 8.3g^3 p7g Aug 22] fairly useful handicapper: stays 8.5f: acts on polytrack, soft and good to firm going: in headgear last 3 starts: usually leads. *Clive Cox* **77**

CAPE LIBERTY (IRE) 2 b.f. (Feb 21) Cape Cross (IRE) 129 – Sharqawiyah 91 (Dubawi (IRE) 129) [2017 p8s Nov 16] first foal: dam 1m winner: 33/1, very green when well held in minor event at Chelmsford: should do better. *Simon Crisford* **– p**

CAPE LOVE (USA) 4 ch.g. Cape Blanco (IRE) 130 – Matroshka (IRE) (Red Ransom (USA)) [2017 68: 12g 8.3m May 19] fairly useful at 2 yrs, lightly raced and disappointing since: stays 1m: acts on good to soft going: sent to Spain. *Mark Johnston* –

CAPE OF GLORY (IRE) 4 br.g. Cape Cross (IRE) 129 – Stairway To Glory (IRE) 86 (Kalanisi (IRE) 132) [2017 93: t12.4g^4 10g^6 12.1g Jul 3] fairly useful handicapper: stays 12.5f: acts on all-weather and good to firm going: often wears headgear. *Keith Dalgleish* **92**

CAPE PENINSULAR 4 b.f. Cape Cross (IRE) 129 – Najam 75 (Singspiel (IRE) 133) **95**
[2017 82: p10g^3 t12.2g* p10g^3 t12.4s^2 t12.4g^4 t12.4s^2 p10g^5 p12g^3 Dec 30] useful performer: won maiden at Wolverhampton in April: second in handicap at Newcastle (short head behind Lopes Dancer) in September: stays 12.5f: acts on polytrack and tapeta: tried in blinkers: usually races prominently, often travels strongly: consistent. *James Tate*

CAPE SPIRIT (IRE) 5 b.m. Cape Cross (IRE) 129 – Fearless Spirit (USA) 74 (Spinning **60**
World (USA) 130) [2017 61: t12.2m^2 p13g^4 t13.9g^2 t13.9m t16.5g^6 t12.2g^5 p14g^5 t12.2g^5 13f May 26] modest maiden: stays 1¾m: acts on tapeta and good to firm going: usually wears headgear: sometimes slowly away. *Andrew Balding*

CAPESTHORNE (IRE) 2 b.f. (Apr 8) Oasis Dream 129 – Eleanora Duse (IRE) 116 **– p**
(Azamour (IRE) 130) [2017 6d Aug 11] third foal: dam, winner up to 1¼m (2-y-o 1m winner) and third in Yorkshire Oaks, half-sister to smart winner up to 1¼m Scottish Stage: 9/1, very green when well held in minor event at Newmarket: likely to prove different proposition in time. *Sir Michael Stoute*

CAPE TO CUBA 3 b.f. Harbour Watch (IRE) 121 – Czarna Roza (Polish Precedent **90**
(USA) 131) [2017 p8g 8d^2 8.3s^2 8v^4 p8g^2 p8g^3 p8g* p8m^3 Nov 25] €130,000Y: half-sister to several winners, including smart winner up to 1m Mabait (2-y-o 6f winner) and 6f/7f winner Jay Bee Blue (both by Kyllachy): dam unraced: fairly useful performer: won maiden at Kempton in November: stays 8.5f: acts on polytrack and soft going: sold 30,000 gns in December. *James Fanshawe*

CAPEZZANO (USA) 3 b.g. Bernardini (USA) 132 – Cableknit (USA) (Unbridled's **100**
Song (USA) 125) [2017 92p: a8f^3 a9.4f^3 8m Jun 22] rather leggy, close-coupled gelding: useful performer: third at Meydan in UAE 2000 Guineas (beaten 9½ lengths by Thunder Snow) and listed race (6 lengths behind Cosmo Charlie): may prove best short of 9.5f: acts on dirt: often races prominently/freely. *Charlie Appleby*

CAPITAL FLIGHT (IRE) 2 ch.g. (Feb 4) Zoffany (IRE) 121 – Mackenzie's Friend **79**
(Selkirk (USA) 129) [2017 7d^3 7g 7m Sep 23] fair form: best effort when third in maiden at Goodwood (6¾ lengths behind Dee Ex Bee) in August. *Paul Cole*

CAPITAL GEARING 4 b.g. Makfi 130 – Dicara (GER) (Royal Applause 124) [2017 62: **60**
f7g^5 f7g^4 a7.5g^5 10.9d^3 a7.5g a11.4g^3 a11.4g^5 8s^6 9g p9.4f^2 10.5g p10.4g^6 Oct 21] sturdy gelding: modest maiden: left Henry Spiller after third start: stays 1m: acts on polytrack, fibresand and good to soft going: wears headgear. *Mme L. Braem, Belgium*

CAPLA DANCER (IRE) 2 ch.f. (Apr 4) Red Jazz (USA) 125 – Greatest Dancer (IRE) **75**
70 (Iffraaj 127) [2017 5m* 5s^6 6m^5 Jul 10] €6,500Y: sturdy filly: second foal: dam, 2-y-o 6f winner, half-sister to useful 7f/1m performer Donncha: fair form when winning minor event at Ripon (66/1, by neck from Faithful Promise) in April: disappointing in hood last 2 starts: sent to Greece. *K. R. Burke*

CAPLA TEMPTRESS (IRE) 2 b.f. (Apr 19) Lope de Vega (IRE) 125 – Mrs Beeton **104**
(IRE) 80 (Dansili 127) [2017 p7s* 7s* 7g^3 8f* 8f Nov 3] €26,000Y: sturdy filly: fourth foal: half-sister to 2-y-o 6f/7f winner Four's Company (by Fast Company): dam, 1m winner, half-sister to very smart 1¼m winner Stotsfold: useful performer: won minor events at Chelmsford in June and Newmarket in July, and Natalma Stakes at Woodbine (by ¾ length from Dixie Moon) in September (left Marco Botti after): 4¼ lengths seventh to Rushing Fall in Breeders' Cup Juvenile Fillies Turf at Del Mar final outing: subsequently returned to former trainer: stays 1m: acts on polytrack, firm and soft going. *William I. Mott, USA*

CAP'N (IRE) 6 b.g. Gamut (IRE) 124 – Dawn Princess (IRE) (Old Vic 136) [2017 16s Oct **–**
21] 150/1, virtually pulled up in Long Distance Cup at Ascot. *Brendan Powell*

CAPOLAVORO (FR) 6 b.g. Sulamani (IRE) 130 – Farnesina (FR) 91 (Anabaa (USA) **81**
130) [2017 85: t7.1d^5 p7d^2 t7.1g^5 7g* May 4] fairly useful performer: in cheekpieces, won claimer at Redcar in May: second in handicap at Chelmsford in March: stays 1m: acts on polytrack, tapeta and soft going: sold 12,000 gns in July. *Robert Cowell*

CAPOMENTO (IRE) 2 b.f. (Feb 10) Casamento (IRE) 118 – Satin Cape (IRE) 62 (Cape **101**
Cross (IRE) 129) [2017 6m* 7d^2 7g^4 7d Sep 29] €13,000Y: half-sister to several winners, including useful winner up to 8.6f Capo Rosso (2-y-o 6f winner, by Red Clubs) and 10.4f winner Caponova (by Bushranger): dam ran twice: useful form: won minor event at Ripon in July: second in listed race at Sandown (nose behind Tajaanus) next time: will be suited by 1m. *Tom Dascombe*

CAPONOVA (IRE) 4 b.g. Bushranger (IRE) 119 – Satin Cape (IRE) 62 (Cape Cross (IRE) 129) [2017 84: 10.4m* 10.3m^6 10.2m 9.9d^6 11.8d^5 11.8d Sep 12] fairly useful handicapper: won at Haydock (by 3 lengths from Zain Arion) in April: stays 10.5f: acts on tapeta, firm and good to soft going: tried in hood: often starts slowly, races well off pace. *Tom Dascombe* **88**

CAPPANANTY CON 3 gr.g. Zebedee 113 – Fairmont (IRE) 53 (Kingmambo (USA) 125) [2017 69: t6m* p6g^2 t6g^2 6.1d^6 6.1m^2 6d^5 p6d^4 t6.1g* 6.1m p6g^5 6.1m p6g^4 p6s* p6g Dec 21] good-topped gelding: fairly useful handicapper: won at Wolverhampton in January and July, and Chelmsford (by ¾ length from Born To Finish) in December: stays 6f: acts on polytrack, tapeta and good to firm going: tried in hood/tongue tie. *Dean Ivory* **90**

CAPPIELOW PARK 8 b.g. Exceed And Excel (AUS) 126 – Barakat 93 (Bustino 136) [2017 –: p11d p16g^4 p11d Feb 15] well-made gelding: poor maiden on Flat nowadays: stays 1½m: acts on polytrack: wears headgear: has worn tongue tie: winning hurdler/chaser. *Ali Stronge* **45**

CAPRICIOUS CANTOR (IRE) 4 b.f. Cape Cross (IRE) 129 – Alleluia 117 (Caerleon (USA) 132) [2017 95: p10s^5 9.9g^2 12s^5 12d 9.9g^6 14.1g^2 Oct 16] good-topped filly: useful performer: second in listed races at Le Lion-d'Angers in June and Yarmouth (1¾ lengths behind Aljezeera) in October: stays 1¾m: acts on polytrack and soft going: often leads. *Ed Dunlop* **100**

CAPRI (IRE) 3 gr.c. Galileo (IRE) 134 – Dialafara (FR) (Anabaa (USA) 130) [2017 113: 10d^4 10m^3 12m^6 12g* 14.5g* 11.9d Oct 1] **124**

'Race meetings like nations are subject to rise and fall … to these causes can be traced the downfall of Doncaster. The St Leger is a dying race. Its days are numbered.' No, not the musings of a contemporary writer, but of an unnamed author in 1839 in an article in the *New Sporting Magazine* which bemoaned the 'rapacity of the overcharging inhabitants, the influence of private interests and changes in high families by death' for introducing 'decay into one of the most popular meetings.' That year's St Leger had seen Charles XII and Euclid produce the first of two dead heats in the history of the oldest classic which was first run in 1776 (Charles XII won the 1839 run-off by a head and went on to win the Doncaster Cup two days later). In the days of the long since defunct *New Sporting Magazine* the St Leger winner was 'usually considered to have been the best three-year-old of the year' and, among those behind Charles XII and Euclid, was the Derby winner Bloomsbury (who started second favourite at Doncaster behind odds-on Charles XII). In 1839, the five classics themselves were still some way off being regarded as a 'series' or a 'set', with the term classics itself only being used at around the same time as the concept of a triple crown began to be recognised around the middle of the nineteenth century to describe the three classics open to colts. The triple crown of Two Thousand Guineas, Derby and St Leger—each run over a different distance—became an aspiration for every owner and breeder in Britain, but the increased specialisation in racing and breeding and the elevation and emergence of major open-aged championships in the period from the middle of the last century, gradually eroded the pre-eminence of the five classics, with the St Leger arguably suffering most.

The concept of the triple crown, however, still remains very much a part of the history of the sport and interest in it was revived in 2012 when the Two Thousand Guineas and Derby winner Camelot arrived at Doncaster for the St Leger. He met defeat for the first time in his career, beaten by 25/1-shot Encke whose reputation was subsequently tarnished when he was named among twenty-two Godolphin horses found to have been injected with anabolic steroids in the biggest doping scandal in the history of British racing. Before Camelot's appearance, no Derby winner had even run in the St Leger since Reference Point in 1987, the race having fallen right out of fashion with commercial breeders, but there was genuine excitement in racing at the prospect of Camelot's becoming the first colt since Nijinsky forty-two years earlier to land the triple crown. A crowd of 30,877 packed into Doncaster and there was prominent coverage of the occasion in the general sports news on the day.

The attention given to the 2012 St Leger has been a boon to the race—it attracted crowds of 30,000 for its next three runnings too—and, after a dip to just above 26,000 in 2016, the figure moved back in the right direction with a crowd of 28,199 for the latest running, the first under the sponsorship of William Hill who took over after the very successful twelve-year tenure of Ladbrokes came to an end when the Arena Racing Company, which runs Doncaster, snubbed that company for refusing to sign up to the sport's controversial 'authorised betting partner' initiative. William Hill had also refused to pay a percentage of its offshore income to racing under the same scheme, which lapsed when a new levy mechanism, ending the offshore loophole, was introduced by the Government in April. That allowed time for Arena to enter and complete negotiations with William Hill over the summer (unlike William Hill, Ladbrokes were among the bookmakers still at loggerheads, over the provision of live pictures to betting shops, with a new media company set up by Arena Racing). The latest St Leger attracted as good and competitive a field as any for the recent runnings of the race and seemed to be anticipated with at least as much excitement as any since 2012.

There may not have been an Epsom Derby winner in the St Leger line-up, but the Irish Derby winner Capri was aimed at the race—and he wasn't even favourite in the ante-post market leading up to St Leger day. Capri's ten opponents included eight who had won pattern races in the current season, among them the winners of nearly all the recognised trials for the St Leger, with the notable exception of the Great Voltigeur at York—a race Capri missed with a minor infection—which had been won by Cracksman, runner-up to Capri at the Curragh where the Epsom Derby winner Wings of Eagles had finished a close third (found to be lame the next day and diagnosed with a career-ending injury). Capri started 3/1 favourite for the St Leger on the day, with the Goodwood Cup winner Stradivarius—a rare three-year-old winner of that particular race—second favourite at 9/2 (Stradivarius had also won the Queen's Vase, a race which recent St Leger winners Leading Light and Harbour Law had used as a stepping stone to Doncaster). The impressive Gordon Stakes winner Crystal Ocean came next in the betting at 5/1, with the progressive Defoe fourth favourite at 6/1 and going for a five-timer after his latest win in the Geoffrey Freer Stakes at Newbury. The only other runner at single-figure odds was the Ribblesdale winner Coronet, an 8/1-shot and the only filly in the line-up, who had been preferred to Stradivarius by Frankie Dettori. The Joseph O'Brien-trained Curragh Cup winner Rekindling, a good second to leading older stayer Order of St George under a penalty in the Irish St Leger Trial at the Curragh on his latest start, was at 10/1, ahead of the second-best of Ballydoyle's four runners, the Chester Vase winner and Great Voltigeur runner-up Venice Beach at 12/1, with Bahrain Trophy winner Raheen House next at 14/1. The Bahrain Trophy runner-up Desert Skyline was barred from the St Leger because he is a gelding and he had contested the previous day's Doncaster Cup instead, which he had won. The St Leger field was completed by Count Octave, who had run Stradivarius to a neck in the Queen's Vase, and the two remaining Ballydoyle runners, the Derrinstown Stud Derby Trial winner Douglas Macarthur, who had finished seventh (a place behind Capri) at Epsom and then fifth in the Irish Derby, and rank outsider The Anvil, who had finished third in the Chester Vase to Venice Beach and Wings of Eagles before being used as a pacemaker in the Derby and Irish Derby.

Dubai Duty Free Irish Derby, the Curragh—the grey Capri proves better than ever, turning around Epsom form with Cracksman (No.2) and Wings of Eagles

William Hill St Leger Stakes, Doncaster—in one of the best recent renewals of the race, Capri holds the challenges of Crystal Ocean (left) and Stradivarius (white face), with subsequent Melbourne Cup winner Rekindling (armlet) back in fourth; this was a fifth St Leger success for Aidan O'Brien and a first for Ryan Moore, completing his collection of British classics

A searching gallop was set in the St Leger by the Ballydoyle quartet, though pacemaker The Anvil, who opened up a big lead, was virtually ignored. Douglas Macarthur and Venice Beach led the main body with Capri close behind them in a planned formation ('We were always going to go forward with them all,' trainer Aidan O'Brien said, adding 'I was very happy the three lads were there together, if any of them wanted to follow The Anvil closer, he was there as a target for them'). The tracking Ballydoyle trio passed The Anvil very early in the home straight as they kept up a relentless gallop, though both Venice Beach and Douglas Macarthur also began to drop away over two furlongs out where Capri was sent for home in earnest. The more patiently-ridden Crystal Ocean drew up to his girths inside the final furlong and, with Stradivarius sticking to his task after being close up from three out, the St Leger produced a thrilling finish, with Capri pulling out more to win by half a length from Crystal Ocean with Stradivarius a short head away in third, and the staying-on Rekindling a length and a half further back in fourth. Coronet and Count Octave both ran creditably to fill fifth and sixth, with a long gap back to the rest (the never-dangerous Defoe beat only The Anvil).

One other point before leaving the St Leger. Except for wartime substitutes and other editions run at different courses (Ayr in 1989 and York in 2006, for example), the distance of the final classic, honoured by time and tradition, has been one mile six furlongs and *132 yards* since 1826. There was a spell in the 'seventies and 'eighties (twentieth century!) when the extra was advertised as *127 yards* but it returned to *132 yards* when the course was remeasured in 1991. There was another general remeasurement of all Flat courses in 2017 (the first since 1991), following a similar review of jumps courses in 2015 which was prompted by research at Timeform which revealed some alarming discrepancies. It seems a shame that one of the unintended consequences of Timeform's vigilance means that we will have to get used to the St Leger being run over its remeasured one mile six furlongs and *115 yards* from now on.

Capri gave his trainer and the Coolmore partners their fifth winner of the St Leger, following Milan (2001), Brian Boru (2003), Scorpion (2005) and Leading Light (2013). Capri's win also meant that his jockey Ryan Moore collected the last British classic that was missing from his record. Victory in the Irish St Leger the previous weekend on Order of St George left Moore requiring only an Irish Derby win to complete a full book of Irish classics. Capri became the first horse to win both the Irish Derby and the St Leger since Nijinsky in 1970 but Moore had been on Wings of Eagles at the Curragh, with Seamus Heffernan taking the ride on Capri who gave him his third winner of the race (he also partnered Soldier of Fortune and Frozen Fire, two of the eleven winners of the race saddled by Aidan O'Brien before Capri in the last twenty years).

Ryan Moore won the Beresford Stakes at the Curragh on Capri, one of three wins for him from five starts as a two-year-old when he showed smart form, but Heffernan rode him on all his three-year-old appearances before the St Leger, except in a very close finish to the Derrinstown Stud Derby Trial over a mile and a quarter at Leopardstown in May when Colm O'Donoghue finished third on him, with Heffernan on runner-up Yucatan behind Douglas Macarthur (Emmet McNamara) in a one, two, three for Ballydoyle. Capri had also followed home Douglas Macarthur and Yucatan when the trio completed the frame behind Rekindling in the Ballysax Stakes over the same course and distance a month earlier. A stiffer test of stamina always looked as if it was going to be needed for Capri who, in the spring, looked more of a St Leger type than a Derby type. With the exception of Yucatan, the principals in the Ballysax and the Derrinstown all ran in the Derby for which, after a spring of inconclusive trials, there was a field of eighteen. Capri was one of six to represent Ballydoyle and he duly improved for the step up to a mile and a half, faring best of the Ballysax/Derrinstown runners in sixth behind two of his stablemates, 40/1-shot Wings of Eagles and Cliffs of Moher (mount of Ryan Moore) and the Gosden-trained favourite Cracksman (Capri's jockey picked up a four-day ban for using his whip above the permitted level).

A major redevelopment at the Curragh, the home of all the Irish classics, meant that restrictions had to be placed on the numbers of spectators at some of the meetings in the latest season, and a crowd of less than 6,000 saw the latest renewal of Ireland's premier classic, the Dubai Duty Free Irish Derby. The winner and the third came on from Epsom, along with Capri, Douglas Macarthur and The Anvil who were also included among five runners from Ballydoyle in the field of nine. There was a rare challenger (nowadays) from France in the Prix du Jockey Club runner-up Waldgeist who was trying to become a third Irish Derby winner for Andre Fabre. Waldgeist had had Capri and Douglas Macarthur back in third and fourth—and Wings of Eagles back in ninth—when winning the Criterium de Saint-Cloud as a two-year-old. Wings of Eagles shaded favouritism at the Curragh from Cracksman and Waldgeist, with 6/1-shot Capri the only other runner at single-figure odds. The Anvil had the field well strung out from an early stage but the race wasn't run at an end-to-end gallop, which probably counted against the more patiently-ridden pair Cracksman (who stalked Wings of Eagles all the way) and Waldgeist the way things turned out, with Cracksman coming wide and Waldgeist being forced to switch two furlongs out and then finding himself short of room after the Ballydoyle runners—who were in the first five places—fanned out turning for home. Capri chased The Anvil from the start and, moving off the rail for the only time, took over in front with over two furlongs to go, keeping on very gamely when tackled by Wings of Eagles and Cracksman entering the final furlong and holding on by a neck and a short head, Cracksman edging ahead of Wings of Eagles late on and only just failing to master the very resolute Capri. Waldgeist completed the frame a further length and a half back.

Capri wasn't seen out between the Irish Derby and the St Leger, a slight setback caused by a minor infection keeping him out of a planned appearance at York in the Great Voltigeur, as already mentioned. His only appearance after the St Leger came fifteen days later in the Prix de l'Arc de Triomphe in which he went off apparently only the fourth choice of a Ballydoyle quintet, according to the betting—he started at 37/1—and also judged on jockey bookings (with Moore switching to Winter, Capri was ridden by Wayne Lordan). No St Leger winner has gone on to win the Arc in the same year and Capri gave the impression in any case that the race came too soon after his exertions at Doncaster. He managed to beat only one home in the field of eighteen and is best forgiven the run.

Capri, a big, strong individual, looks set to remain in training. Running a horse in the St Leger, who has already won a classic over shorter, was swimming against the commercial tide somewhat, and it would be a big surprise to see Capri campaigned at beyond a mile and a half at four. He certainly doesn't *need* further and might not have run in the St Leger at all, except for the fact that Coolmore is already standing two Derby-winning sons of Galileo, and also has two top milers at the stud by him, with another two sons joining them (Churchill and Highland Reel). Capri is the fifth Irish Derby winner to be sired by Galileo, following Soldier of Fortune, Cape Blanco, Treasure Beach and Australia, and the second winner of the St Leger, following Sixties Icon the year it was staged at York.

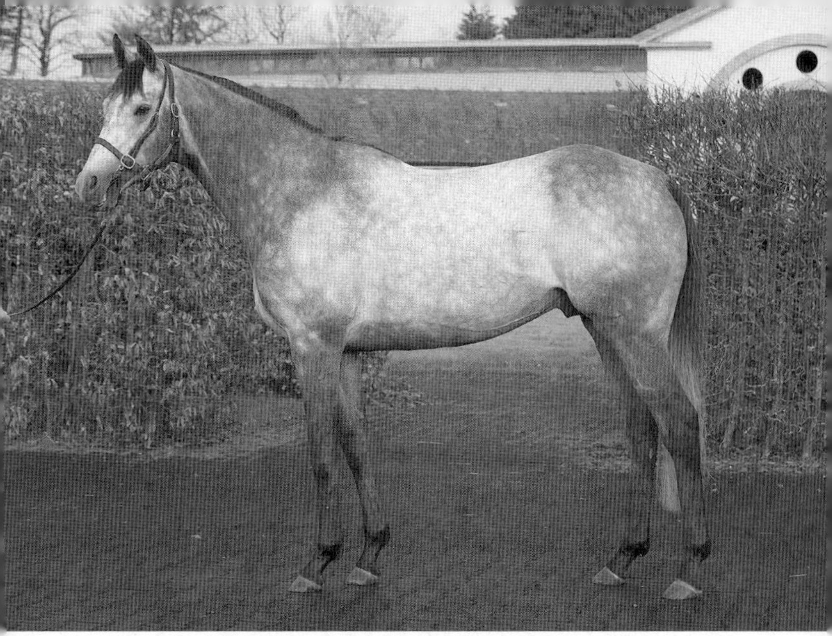

Mr D. Smith, Mrs John Magnier and Mr M. Tabor's "Capri"

Capri (IRE) (gr.c. 2014)	Galileo (IRE) (b 1998)	Sadler's Wells (b 1981)	Northern Dancer
			Fairy Bridge
		Urban Sea (ch 1989)	Miswaki
			Allegretta
	Dialafara (FR) (gr 2007)	Anabaa (b 1992)	Danzig
			Balbonella
		Diamilina (gr 1998)	Linamix
			Diamonaka

Since the success of Frankel (out of the sprinter Kind), much has been made of the increasing number of Galileo's best progeny who have been out of sprinting mares. The second of Galileo's Irish Derby winners Cape Blanco was out of a mare who was all speed, but that hasn't been so with the others. Solder of Fortune's dam stayed a mile and three quarters, Treasure Beach's dam won at a mile and a quarter and Australia was out of Oaks winner Ouija Board. Australia is also one of Galileo's three Epsom Derby winners, the others being New Approach who was out of Irish Champion Stakes winner Park Express and also winner of the Nassau and the Lancashire Oaks and second in the Yorkshire Oaks, while the other Epsom winner Ruler of The World, who won the year before Australia, was out of a mare whose only win in fifteen races came in a maiden over a mile. Galileo's first St Leger winner Sixties Icon was also out of an Oaks winner, Love Divine.

Capri's pedigree on the distaff side contains plenty of middle-distance influences, his dam Dialafara being successful over twelve and a half furlongs in the French Provinces for the Aga Khan who didn't retain her for stud, sending her to the Deauville December Sale at the end of her three-year-old days where she was sold for €175,000. Dialafara's two foals before Capri both turned out to be useful, though their careers were short. They were the seven-furlong two-year-old winner Jamaica and the mile and a quarter maiden winner Sovereign Parade, both also by Galileo, Jamaica trained by Aidan O'Brien and Sovereign Parade by John Gosden. Dialafara has a two-year-old colt (Cypress Creek) who was unplaced in two back-end maidens for O'Brien and a yearling filly, both by Galileo, but she has no foal. Dialafara is out of Diamilina whose career at stud was nowhere near so successful as her racing career, in which her wins included the Prix de Malleret over a mile and a half and a second in the Prix Vermeille in the colours of Jean-Luc Lagardere.

The Lagardere bloodstock empire was absorbed in 2005, after his death, into that of the Aga Khan, a good proportion of the Lagardere mares being the product of American breeding. Diamilina, though, was from a European family, her own dam the useful Diamonaka being a daughter of Diamond Seal, a winning half-sister to the 1977 Irish Two Thousand Guineas winner Pampapaul. Like many of the Lagardere mares, Diamond Seal (who is also the great grandam of Doncaster Cup winner Desert Skyline) became a regular visitor to Linamix, producing the 1995 Prix Greffulhe winner Diamond Mix and the 2003 Prix de Royaumont winner Diasilixa. Diamonaka herself produced a number of winners to Linamix, including the ill-fated 1998 Prix Cleopatre winner Diamonixa, as well as Capri's grandam. Diamonaka's best performer, though, was not by Linamix, as that honour belonged to the Green Desert colt Diamond Green, a pattern winner who was also runner-up in the Poule d'Essai des Poulains, the St James's Palace Stakes and the Prix du Moulin in 2004. Another daughter of Diamonaka (who herself was also eventually offloaded by the Aga Khan's studs), was Dali's Grey who, after being sold by Lagardere, went on to produce the Luca Cumani-trained Melbourne Cup runner-up Bauer. The genuine Capri stays a mile and three quarters but is fully effective at a mile and a half and he acts on soft and good to firm going. He wore a tongue tie in some of his races as a two-year-old, including the Beresford Stakes. *Aidan O'Brien, Ireland*

CAPRIOLETTE (IRE) 2 b.f. (Mar 16) Most Improved (IRE) 119 – Greta d'Argent **61 p**
(IRE) 103 (Great Commotion (USA) 123) [2017 t8.6g^{4} Nov 11] €17,000Y: half-sister to several winners, including smart US 1m winner Beau Recall (2-y-o 7.5f winner in Ireland, by Sir Prancealot) and useful winner up to 7f Coolminx (2-y-o 5f/5.4f winner, by One Cool Cat): dam winner up to 1½m (2-y-o 8.5f winner): 16/1, considerate introduction when fourth in minor event at Wolverhampton (4¾ lengths behind Guvenor's Choice) in November: will improve. *Ed Walker*

CAPTAIN BOB (IRE) 6 b.g. Dark Angel (IRE) 113 – Birthday Present (Cadeaux Genereux **80**
131) [2017 79: t7.1g^{3} t7.1m^{3} f6g^{2} 6m^{3} f6.1g^{2} 6s* 6.1g* a6g p6s^{2} f7.1g f6.1g^{5} Dec 11] good-topped gelding: fairly useful handicapper: won apprentice events at Newmarket in May and Windsor in July: left Robert Cowell after seventh start, Jamie Osborne after ninth: stays 7.5f: acts on all-weather, firm and soft going: often wears headgear. *Philip Kirby*

CAPTAIN BOND 3 b.g. Captain Gerrard (IRE) 113 – Forever's Girl 86 (Monsieur Bond **61**
(IRE) 120) [2017 p6d^{4} 6d^{6} t6g t6.1g^{6} Dec 13] modest form: raced only at 6f. *David O'Meara*

CAPTAIN CAT (IRE) 8 b.g. Dylan Thomas (IRE) 132 – Mother of Pearl (IRE) 113 **99 §**
(Sadler's Wells (USA) 132) [2017 113: p8g^{5} p8g^{5} p8g^{6} p10g^{4} 8s 9d Sep 30] big gelding: useful handicapper nowadays: stays 1¼m: acts on polytrack, soft and good to firm going: has worn headgear: often starts slowly: unreliable (awkward head carriage). *Tony Carroll*

CAPTAIN COCKLE 4 b.g. Indian Haven 119 – Demand 50 (Red Ransom (USA)) [2017 **46**
p8s p8g 8.1m t9.5g Nov 7] sparely-made gelding: poor form. *Roger Teal*

CAPTAIN COLBY (USA) 5 b.g. Bernstein (USA) 115 – Escape To Victory (Salse **100 §**
(USA) 128) [2017 109: 6g^{2} 6m 6s 6m 6m 5.6g 7g^{6} 6d Oct 27] big, lengthy gelding: useful handicapper: second in listed race at Doncaster (4 lengths behind Tupi) in April: stays 6f: acts on firm and good to soft going: usually wears headgear: sometimes slowly away, usually races nearer last than first: sold to Paul Midgley 14,000 gns in November: lazy and isn't one to rely on. *Ed Walker*

CAPTAIN COURAGEOUS (IRE) 4 b.g. Canford Cliffs (IRE) 133 – Annacloy Pearl **100**
(IRE) (Mull of Kintyre (USA) 114) [2017 70p: t9.5m^{2} p8g* p8g^{5} 10m^{5} 10.2f* 8m^{4} 8m* 8g^{3} 9.1g^{4} 9d Sep 29] rangy gelding: useful handicapper: won at Chelmsford in February, and Haydock in May and June: stays 1¼m: acts on polytrack, tapeta and firm going: sold 40,000 gns in November. *Ed Walker*

CAPTAIN DION 4 gr.g. Equiano (FR) 127 – Bandanna 98 (Bandmaster (USA) 97) [2017 **99**
100: t6m^{3} t6g* t7.1g^{3} t6g^{2} t6g^{6} p6g^{4} 6d 6g 6v* 7v^{5} p5g^{3} p6g p7g^{6} Dec 22] lengthy gelding: useful handicapper: won at Newcastle in January and Pontefract in September: left Kevin

Ryan after tenth start: stays 7f: acts on polytrack, tapeta, good to firm and heavy going: wears headgear: in tongue tie last 2 starts: front runner/races prominently. *F. Birrane, Ireland*

CAPTAIN FELIX 5 b.g. Captain Gerrard (IRE) 113 – Sweet Applause (IRE) 84 (Acclamation 118) [2017 78: 10m^3 11.4g^6 Jul 31] good-topped gelding: fair handicapper: stays 1¼m: acts on polytrack, tapeta and good to firm going: tried in hood: front runner/races prominently: won over hurdles in October. *James Eustace* **79**

CAPTAIN GEORGE (IRE) 6 b.g. Bushranger (IRE) 119 – High Society Girl (IRE) (Key of Luck (USA) 126) [2017 70: 11.7f^5 12m^4 14g^3 13d Aug 23] fair handicapper: stays 1¾m: acts on polytrack, tapeta, good to firm and good to soft going: has often worn headgear. *Michael Blake* **70**

CAPTAIN HAWK 3 b.g. Acclamation 118 – Vintage Gardenia (Selkirk (USA) 129) [2017 70: 6.1d 7m^5 6.9d 7v^4 t7.2g t7.2g p8d^4 t7.1g* t7.2g Oct 27] useful-looking gelding: fair handicapper: won at Newcastle in October: stays 1m: acts on polytrack, tapeta and good to firm going: wears headgear. *Ian Williams* **73**

CAPTAIN JAMESON (IRE) 2 b.g. (Mar 27) Camacho 118 – Cross Section (USA) 76 (Cape Cross (IRE) 129) [2017 6.1v^3 5.9s^3 6d* 6g^3 6d* Nov 11] €30,000 2-y-o: fourth foal: half-brother to UAE 7f winner Syncopation (by Dark Angel): dam, maiden (stayed 8.6f), half-sister to smart winner up to 1m Il Warrd: fairly useful performer: won minor event at Catterick in September and nursery at Doncaster (by ½ length from Excellent Times) in November: raced only at 6f: acts on soft going. *John Quinn* **93**

CAPTAIN JOE 6 ch.g. Captain Gerrard (IRE) 113 – Bond Shakira 54 (Daggers Drawn (USA) 114) [2017 p7g Apr 7] lightly-raced maiden, showed nothing only start in 2017 after long absence: tried in hood/tongue tie. *Brian Barr* **–**

CAPTAIN KENDALL (IRE) 8 b.g. Clodovil (IRE) 116 – Queen's Lace (IRE) (King's Best (USA) 132) [2017 49: p7g^4 p7d p7g 7d Oct 30] lengthy gelding: poor handicapper: stays 7f: acts on polytrack, good to firm and heavy going: wears headgear: front runner/races prominently. *Harry Chisman* **49**

CAPTAIN K (IRE) 5 b.g. Captain Rio 122 – Zenana (IRE) 74 (Lucky Guest 109) [2017 56: t7.1m t9.5m^5 t7.1m^5 t9.5g^2 p8d^4 p7g^5 p8g t8.6g^3 7d 8s Apr 30] modest maiden: stays 9.5f: acts on tapeta: wears headgear. *Gordon Elliott, Ireland* **54**

CAPTAIN KISSINGER 2 b.g. (May 29) Captain Gerrard (IRE) 113 – Nigella 92 (Band On The Run 102) [2017 5g t5.1g^5 5.3m^4 6g^5 8m Aug 31] modest form: in blinkers last 2 starts. *Jo Hughes* **52**

CAPTAIN LARS (SAF) 8 b.g. Captain Al (SAF) – Polar Charge 106 (Polar Falcon (USA) 126) [2017 82, a95: f5g^6 f5m^4 f6g^5 p5g* p6g^5 p6s 6g^4 6d^2 5g^5 p6g^6 5.1v 6d 5d f5g p6s* p6s^6 f6.1g* f5g^5 Dec 29] sturdy gelding: fairly useful performer: won handicap in April and claimer in November, both at Chelmsford, and handicap at Southwell (by 1¼ lengths from Tricky Dicky) in December: has form at 9f, races at shorter nowadays: acts on all-weather and heavy going: wears headgear. *Derek Shaw* **90**

CAPTAIN MARMALADE (IRE) 5 gr.g. Duke of Marmalade (IRE) 132 – Elisium (Proclamation (IRE) 130) [2017 63: 7d 7g^5 8g^3 8d^6 8g^5 7.1g^5 8s* 8d Sep 18] good-bodied gelding: fair handicapper: won at Brighton in September: stays 1m: acts on soft and good to firm going: has worn headgear, including last 2 starts: usually slowly away, often races in rear. *Jimmy Fox* **65**

CAPTAIN MORLEY 6 b.g. Hernando (FR) 127 – Oval Office 99 (Pursuit of Love 124) [2017 104: 11.8d Oct 30] big gelding: useful performer, well held sole start on Flat in 2017: stays 12.5f: acts on polytrack, good to firm and heavy going. *David Simcock* **–**

CAPTAIN NAVARRE 5 b.g. Excellent Art 125 – Quantum (IRE) 89 (Alhaarth (IRE) 126) [2017 88: 11.8d 16.3g p16g* t16.5g* p15.8g^4 Dec 28] smallish, close-coupled gelding: useful handicapper: won at Kempton in November and Wolverhampton in December: stays 16.5f: acts on polytrack, tapeta, good to firm and good to soft going: in visor last 3 starts: consistent. *Charlie Fellowes* **97**

CAPTAIN PEACOCK 4 b.g. Champs Elysees 124 – Blast Furnace (IRE) 74 (Sadler's Wells (USA) 132) [2017 85: 11.6m* p11g* 12s p12g^6 11.4g 14s^5 10s 12g^6 p12g^4 Oct 9] strong gelding: fairly useful handicapper: won at Windsor and Kempton in April: stays 2m: acts on polytrack, good to firm and good to soft going: wears headgear: one to treat with caution: has joined Oliver Sherwood. *William Knight* **89 §**

CAPTAIN PEAKY 4 b.g. Captain Gerrard (IRE) 113 – Multi-Sofft 30 (Northern State (USA) 91) [2017 63: 8m p8s^4 8m^3 7.2s 7.2g^6 7.2m p10s^3 Dec 7] modest maiden: stays 1¼m: acts on polytrack, tapeta, soft and good to firm going. *Patrick Holmes* **62**

CAPTAIN PUGWASH (IRE) 3 b.g. Sir Prancealot (IRE) 111 – Liscoa (IRE) 81 (Foxhound (USA) 103) [2017 63: 7g^2 8s^2 8m p8g^6 10.1d p7s* p7g^2 Dec 28] fair handicapper: won at Chelmsford in December: stays 1m: acts on polytrack and soft going. *Henry Spiller* **79**

CAPTAIN REVELATION 5 ch.g. Captain Rio 122 – Agony Aunt 81 (Formidable (USA) 125) [2017 95: f7g^5 f8g^6 f8m^3 t8.6g 8g 8d^4 7f^3 t8.6g 8g 10.2d f7.1g^6 f8.1g^4 f8.1g^4 Dec 19] fair handicapper on turf, fairly useful on all-weather: third at Southwell in March: left Tom Dascombe after ninth start: stays 1m: acts on fibresand, tapeta and firm going: has worn headgear, including last 2 starts: in tongue tie last 3 starts: usually races prominently. *Michael Mullineaux* **77 a85**

CAPTAIN RYAN 6 b.g. Captain Gerrard (IRE) 113 – Ryan's Quest (IRE) 67 (Mukaddamah (USA) 125) [2017 74: 5.7f^5 5.7f^2 6m^3 5.7f^2 5f^3 5s 6.1m^2 5m 5.7s^2 5.1d Oct 23] sturdy gelding: fair handicapper: stays 6f: acts on tapeta, firm and soft going: has worn headgear: usually travels strongly. *Geoffrey Deacon* **70**

CAPTAIN SCOOBY 11 b.g. Captain Rio 122 – Scooby Dooby Do 62 (Atraf 116) [2017 70: f6g 5m 6.1g t6s t6.1g 5.5f 5s^5 5.9g 5d^5 5d^6 5v^3 6.1g 5g 5.7s^6 5.7s^3 5s p5g 5.1d 6d^6 t5g^5 6v t6g^5 p7s t5d p6g t5.1g^5 Dec 22] good-topped gelding: modest handicapper: stays 6f: acts on all-weather, good to firm and heavy going: wears headgear: often starts slowly, usually races towards rear. *Richard Guest* **53**

CAPTAIN SEDGWICK (IRE) 3 b.f. Approve (IRE) 112 – Alinda (IRE) 86 (Revoque (IRE) 122) [2017 –: t6g p6g^4 t6m p7m t7.1g^3 7m^F 7.1m^5 8g* 8g^2 8d^5 p10g p7g t8.6g^6 Dec 13] modest handicapper: won at Ffos Las in July: stays 1m: acts on tapeta and good to firm going. *John Spearing* **58**

CAPTAIN SUE (IRE) 3 ch.f. Tamayuz 126 – Correct 68 (Oasis Dream 129) [2017 65: p6g 6.1g 6.1g Oct 9] lengthy filly: fair maiden at 2 yrs, no form in 2017: tried in tongue tie: sometimes slowly away. *Ian Williams* **–**

CAPTAIN SWIFT (IRE) 6 br.g. Captain Rio 122 – Grannys Reluctance (IRE) 63 (Anita's Prince 126) [2017 71: t13.9m^2 t13.9g^3 p16d^4 t13.9g^3 t12.2g^5 15v t14g 14v^3 t14g* t14d^4 Dec 27] compact gelding: fair handicapper: won at Wolverhampton in November: stays 2m: acts on polytrack, tapeta and soft going: wears headgear: often races prominently. *John Mackie* **72**

CAPTIVE (FR) 3 b.c. Kyllachy 129 – Ukraine (IRE) (Cape Cross (IRE) 129) [2017 7s 7m p6.5g 7g p7.5g p7.5g Dec 16] lengthy colt: well held in maidens/claimer, leaving Richard Hannon £3,500 after second outing: blinkered final start. *Andrew Hollinshead, France* **–**

CAPTON 4 b.g. Cape Cross (IRE) 129 – Flavian 94 (Catrail (USA) 123) [2017 74: 10m^2 8g 8s^2 10d* 9.9g* 10.2d^2 Oct 18] tall gelding: useful handicapper: won at Newbury in August and Sandown in September, and also first past post at Nottingham (demoted after causing interference) in October: stays 1½m: acts on polytrack, soft and good to firm going: usually leads. *Henry Candy* **100**

CAPTOR 3 b.g. Frankel 147 – Hasten (IRE) 72 (Montjeu (IRE) 137) [2017 t10.2s 10g 12s Jul 28] first foal: dam, maiden (should have stayed 1½m), sister to winner up to 1¼m Jan Vermeer and half-sister to 1000 Guineas runner-up/US Grade 1 9f winner Together (both smart): modest form in maidens: open to improvement. *David Simcock* **62 p**

CARACAS 3 b.g. Cacique (IRE) 124 – Bourbonella (Rainbow Quest (USA) 134) [2017 73p: p10m^6 p13.3g p12g p15.8g^4 p16g^2 t16.5d Dec 9] fair maiden: left Roger Charlton after first start: stays 2m: acts on polytrack and tapeta. *Harry Dunlop* **74**

CARADOC (IRE) 2 b.c. (Mar 25) Camelot 128 – Applause (IRE) 102 (Danehill Dancer (IRE) 117) [2017 p8d^4 Dec 13] 270,000Y: fourth foal: half-brother to 3 winners, including useful 2-y-o 7f winner Arcada (by Rip Van Winkle) and 12.5f winner Evening Hush (by Excellent Art): dam, 1m winner, half-sister to winner up to 1½m Snippets and stayer Injam (both useful): 20/1, considerate introduction when fourth in minor event at Kempton (4¾ lengths behind Highbrow) in December: sure to progress. *Ed Walker* **77 p**

CARAMURU (IRE) 3 b.g. Casamento (IRE) 118 – Zaynaba (IRE) (Traditionally (USA) 117) [2017 76: 10g Apr 29] fair form at 2 yrs, well held sole start in 2017. *Richard Hannon* **–**

CARAVAGGIO (USA) 3 gr.c. Scat Daddy (USA) 120 – Mekko Hokte (USA) (Holy Bull (USA) 134) [2017 123p: 6s* 6m* 6g^4 6.5g^6 5s* 6s^3 Oct 21] **126**

Redcar, Sunday July 23rd saw the unexpected and short-lived return of the world's fastest horse …… Stone of Folca. He was back at the age of nine in a six-runner class 4 handicap, in front of a crowd of just 2,881, after two years off the track. Stone of Folca had earned his footnote in the history books by recording an electronically-timed world record of 53.69sec for five furlongs when winning the 'Dash' at Epsom in 2012 at 50/1, one of only two victories in his whole career (he failed to beat a rival at Redcar). Stone of Folca was a useful performer at his best, a better sprinter than Spark Chief, whose time in 1983 he bettered by 0.01sec to take the record, but not so good a racehorse as the more often-quoted world record holder the smart Indigenous whose hand-timed 53.60sec in 1960 bettered by a scarcely-believable one and a fifth seconds the existing record at the time. The main thing that Stone of Folca, Spark Chief and Indigenous had in common was that they all recorded their times at Epsom, where the straight five-furlong course is sharply downhill to the junction with the round course. The contours of the Epsom track, coupled with conditions on the day that were favourable for the setting of fast times, played a major part in the records set by Stone of Folca and Spark Chief, the over-riding importance of prevailing conditions—such as the state of the going and the direction of any wind—being something that applies to most time records in horse racing (the lists of course record holders on Britain's racecourses are filled with the names of ordinary performers). All of which puts the claims made for Ballydoyle's latest sprinting star Caravaggio into some context.

His trainer Aidan O'Brien had described Caravaggio as a two-year-old as 'the fastest we have ever had', quoting him as recording a top speed of forty-five miles per hour on the gallops and saying 'No horse in Ballydoyle has ever been able to do that.' O'Brien repeated the 'fastest we have ever had' quote after Caravaggio made a most impressive winning reappearance, storming nearly five lengths clear of six rivals over the final furlong in the EMS Copiers Lacken Stakes at Naas in May and, in the process, stretching his unbeaten sequence to five (he hadn't been seen since his wide margin victory in the Phoenix Stakes at the Curragh the previous August, having missed his intended autumn targets the Middle Park and the Breeders' Cup Juvenile with an injury to a muscle in his ribcage). Caravaggio's connections had given plenty of thought over the winter to a classic campaign—the Poule d'Essai des Poulains always looking the most likely target, given that the Two Thousand Guineas was earmarked for stablemate Churchill—but, after the Lacken Stakes, it became clear Caravaggio was going to be kept to sprinting. 'He is an unbelievably quick horse,' added Aidan O'Brien. 'We've never seen one quicker than him at home, there's nothing to say he wouldn't get a mile—the petrol gauge never shifted when we worked him over seven furlongs—but he's so quick, sprinting looks the way to go.'

Of course, all the talk of his top speed and how 'quick' Caravaggio was, actually meant little on its own. What had counted as a two-year-old, and what was going to count even more as a three-year-old, was the *form* Caravaggio produced. He was Timeform's highest-rated colt as a juvenile (rated behind the outstanding filly Lady Aurelia), his rating of 123p having been bettered among the two-year-olds handled by his trainer in his career only by his own grandsire Johannesburg, St Nicholas Abbey and Air Force Blue (all of whom, incidentally, failed to win in their three-year-old seasons, though injury-hit St Nicholas Abbey went on to achieve plenty later in his career). The two finest sprinters that have raced for Caravaggio's trainer, named after the composers Stravinsky and Mozart, both followed the well-worn path of so many sprint champions in the era since World War II by spending the early part of their three-year-old season on the classic trail. Stravinsky eventually missed his Two Thousand Guineas because of fears about the firmness of the ground and, rather than taking on older sprinters in the King's Stand or the Cork And Orrery, he ran in the Jersey Stakes over seven at Royal Ascot (where he managed only fourth) before being returned to sprinting and recording successes in the July Cup (track record, if not exactly an outstanding time performance) and in the Nunthorpe. Mozart started out over a mile as a three-year-old, and finished second in the Irish Two Thousand Guineas, before being campaigned in the top sprints, emulating Stravinsky by landing the July Cup-Nunthorpe double (before, like Stravinsky, running well below form on an unfamiliar surface and a turning track in the six-furlong Breeders' Cup Sprint). There was very little incentive, in Stravinsky's and Mozart's day, to race good three-year-olds over sprint distances until the July Cup (which is also open to four-year-olds and above).

Commonwealth Cup, Royal Ascot—one of four winners at Royal Ascot for his much missed sire Scat Daddy, Caravaggio puts up a high-class effort to maintain his unbeaten record, while Harry Angel (second left) and Blue Point (white cap) fill the places for Godolphin

That situation has changed with the advent of the very valuable Commonwealth Cup, over six furlongs for three-year-olds, which was run for the first time in 2015 at Royal Ascot, with a number of listed sprints for three-year-olds promoted to minor pattern level to provide opportunities leading up to the Commonwealth Cup. The first running went to Muhaarar who ended the season as champion sprinter, adding victories over his elders in the July Cup, the Prix Maurice de Gheest and the Champions Sprint, the last-named a much more valuable event that has been developed from the now-defunct Diadem Stakes which had Group 2 status in Stravinsky's and Mozart's day. The Commonwealth Cup provides a worthwhile target for the leading three-year-old sprinters, addressing the previous lack of opportunity for them against their own age group (they can no longer run in the Diamond Jubilee—of which the Cork And Orrery was a forerunner—at the Royal meeting, though they are still able to do so in the five-furlong King's Stand). Caravaggio's connections were, therefore, not under quite the same pressure to pursue a classic campaign with him as they had been with Stravinsky and Mozart (although there is still more prestige attached to the top mile races for three-year-olds than to the top sprints).

The Commonwealth Cup was widely expected to be one of the races of Royal Ascot week with Caravaggio's sky-high reputation being tested by two other potential sprinting champions who, in earlier times, might also have followed the early-season classic route. The transatlantic visitor Lady Aurelia tackled older sprinters in the King's Stand and Caravaggio faced his strongest challenge in the field of twelve for the Commonwealth Cup from two colts carrying the Godolphin colours but racing for different stables. The Mill Reef winner Harry Angel, purchased by Godolphin just before the race but still trained by Clive Cox, had followed what is likely to become a clearly-defined path to the Commonwealth Cup, starting out in the Pavilion Stakes at Ascot in May (the penalised Harry Angel finished second to the Charlie Appleby-trained Blue Point) and then taking in the Sandy Lane Stakes at Haydock later the same month when he demolished his rivals in course-record time (recording an exceptional timefigure too). Caravaggio, Harry Angel and Blue Point (who like Muhaarar had won the Gimcrack at two) monopolised both the betting (6/5-on, 11/4 and 9/2 respectively) and the finish of the Commonwealth Cup which, for the overall strength of the field, was the best edition yet. The principals were separated by three quarters of a length and half a length, with the American challenger Bound For Nowhere (the only other runner to start at shorter than 25/1) three lengths further back in fourth. Harry Angel forced a strong pace into a headwind, pressed much of the way by Caravaggio's stablemate Intelligence Cross, and he looked likely to win the day until Caravaggio, who had plenty to do from two furlongs out, collared him and the always-in-touch Blue Point in the final hundred yards.

Caravaggio looked as if he needed the full six furlongs at Royal Ascot, though the patient tactics adopted on him were apparently planned, with Aidan O'Brien saying 'he is brilliant … he was going to come late and he only raced for two and a half furlongs.' Following Muhaarar's splendid winning sequence after the first Commonwealth Cup, the second winner the filly Quiet Reflection also went on to beat older sprinters, winning the Sprint Cup at Haydock (the runner-up in the first Commonwealth Cup, Limato, went on to win the July Cup as a four-year-old while the fifth Profitable also became a Group 1 winner in the King's Stand at four; the third in Quiet Reflection's Commonwealth Cup, Washington DC, was runner-up in the King George and the Prix de l'Abbaye later in the same season).

The Commonwealth Cup maintained its reputation for revealing new sprinting stars but it was largely through the subsequent exploits of runner-up Harry Angel. Caravaggio himself failed to win another Group 1, with the first thoughts of his connections after Royal Ascot, that he might make a bold bid for the new sprint in Australia, The Everest, the world's richest turf race in 2017, eventually proving a pipedream. Caravaggio's reputation suffered its first blow when he lost his unbeaten record in the July Cup at Newmarket, starting odds on but managing only fourth behind Harry Angel, Limato and Brando after being just about the first in trouble. Another defeat followed behind Brando in the Prix Maurice de Gheest at Deauville, with Caravaggio only sixth after missing the break and reportedly finishing 'sore in front' which his trainer blamed on different racing plates with which he had been fitted.

Back in his 'regular shoes', Caravaggio resumed winning ways in the Derrinstown Stud Flying Five Stakes at the Curragh on Irish Champions' Weekend (a race that will be Group 1 for the first time in 2018). Racing at the minimum trip for the first time since winning the listed Marble Hill Stakes on the second of his four outings as a juvenile, Caravaggio was ridden more prominently and, after looking to be a little outpaced at halfway, he stayed on to reel in his pace-setting stablemate Alphabet well inside the final furlong and win by a length, driven out. There was talk of Caravaggio's being aimed at the Breeders' Cup—which nowadays also stages a Turf Sprint (over five)—but his final appearance came in the Champions Sprint on British Champions' Day at Ascot where, held up again, he ran creditably, with no real excuses, to finish a staying-on third to Librisa Breeze and Tasleet (who had been narrowly beaten in the Diamond Jubilee), with Harry Angel, the Diamond Jubilee winner The Tin Man and Brando the next to finish.

Caravaggio (USA) (gr.c. 2014)	Scat Daddy (USA) (b or br 2004)	Johannesburg (b 1999)	Hennessy
			Myth
		Love Style (ch 1999)	Mr Prospector
			Likeable Style
	Mekko Hokte (USA) (gr 2000)	Holy Bull (gr 1991)	Great Above
			Sharon Brown
		Aerosilver (gr 1992)	Relaunch
			Silver In Flight

The lengthy, good-bodied Caravaggio looked very well and kept his condition throughout his three-year-old campaign, impressing with his demeanour before his races (although he did become restless in the stalls before the Commonwealth Cup). Coolmore supremo John Magnier explained the potential importance to him of Caravaggio after his success in the Commonwealth Cup when he said 'We were unlucky to lose his sire and hopefully this fellow will take his place, it's a cross that we need and it's fortunate for us that he's come along at the right time.' Caravaggio was one of four winners (Lady Aurelia, Sioux Nation and Con Te Partiro were the others) at Royal Ascot for Scat Daddy who stood at Coolmore's Ashford Stud

Mrs John Magnier, Mr M. Tabor and Mr D. Smith's "Caravaggio"

in Kentucky until his premature demise in 2015. Scat Daddy was raced on dirt, winning the Champagne Stakes over a mile at two and the Florida Derby over nine furlongs, and proved something of a surprise package with his turf runners in his short time at stud. The ubiquitous Northern Dancer, the foundation stone on which the success of the Coolmore empire has largely been built, does not appear in the first three generations of Scat Daddy's pedigree and he was one of the stallions with the potential to be used as an outcross for the many Sadler's Wells and Galileo mares owned by Coolmore interests. Australian champion Fastnet Rock and another leading Kentucky-based sire War Front have been among the most successful at fulfilling that task so far and it seems Caravaggio, whose pedigree on the distaff side has no Northern Dancer influences at all, is likely to receive even stronger support.

Given that his sire was proven over the trip, and given that he himself was a tractable racehorse, Caravaggio should, on the face of it, have had good prospects of getting a mile had he been tried. The doubts presumably stemmed from his dam's side, Mekko Hokte having been raced mainly at sprint distances and her four winners at stud before Caravaggio including the Grade 2 Gallant Bloom Handicap winner My Jen (by Fusaichi Pegasus) who was a sprinter. Mekko Hokte's sire Holy Bull won at up to a mile and a quarter as a three-year-old when he was Horse of the Year in North America, but Mekko Hokte's grandsire Great Above (who is the sire of Lady Aurelia's great grandam) was a sprinter out of Ta Wee who was twice champion sprinter in North America. Caravaggio won on going ranging from good to firm (the conditions for both his Group 1 victories) to soft, and he was also successful on polytrack. He was sometimes slowly away. He starts his stallion career at Coolmore at a fee of €35,000, the same as the stud's other major new recruit, dual Guineas winner Churchill. *Aidan O'Brien, Ireland*

CARAVELA (IRE) 3 b.f. Henrythenavigator (USA) 131 – Stella Point (IRE) 93 (Pivotal 124) [2017 8g^3 8g^2 8v* 10.3v Sep 30] second foal: dam, 1¼m winner, out of useful 2-y-o 6f/7f winner Venturi: fair form: won maiden at Thirsk in September: stays 1m. *Mick Channon* **78**

CARBON DATING (IRE) 5 b.g. The Carbon Unit (USA) 106 – Advertising Space (IRE) (Galileo (IRE) 134) [2017 104: 12g^2 14g^2 15.9g^4 12.1g^5 14g 10.9g^3 14g* 13.4d 14m^5 11.4m a9.7f 8g^4 Dec 3] good-topped gelding: useful performer on turf, fairly useful at best on all-weather/dirt: won handicap at Musselburgh (by 1½ lengths from Maleficent Queen) in April: placed earlier in 2 handicaps at Meydan and Group 3 Abu Dhabi Championship (½-length third to Zamaam): trained by John Patrick Shanahan fifth to tenth starts: stays 2m: acts on dirt, soft and good to firm going: has worn blinkers/tongue tie. *S. Seemar, UAE* **109 a–**

CARCHARIAS (IRE) 4 b.g. Kodiac 112 – Princess Atoosa (USA) (Gone West (USA)) [2017 70, a62: p8g 8.3f^5 8g^2 8.1m^2 8.1g 8g 7.1g^2 8g^4 p8g Oct 5] compact gelding: fair handicapper: stays 1m: acts on polytrack, good to firm and good to soft going: tried in cheekpieces: front runner. *Ed de Giles* **70**

CARDAW LILY (IRE) 2 b.f. (Apr 27) Lawman (FR) 121 – Chervil 80 (Dansili 127) [2017 5m^4 6.1m^6 5m p6g 7m p5s^6 Dec 7] €12,000Y, £35,000 2-y-o: good-topped filly: sister to 2 winners, including 1¼m winner Faery Song, and half-sister to several winners, including 1m winner Zeyran (by Galileo): dam 2-y-o 6f winner: fairly useful form when fourth in maiden on debut, disappointing after: in cheekpieces final start. *Richard Hughes* **80**

CARD HIGH (IRE) 7 b.g. Red Clubs (IRE) 125 – Think (FR) 99 (Marchand de Sable (USA) 117) [2017 81: t12.4d t12.4g^6 12m^4 14g 14.1s^2 Jun 9] fairly useful handicapper: second at Carlisle in June: stays 1¾m: acts on tapeta, good to firm and heavy going: wears tongue tie. *Wilf Storey* **82**

CARDSHARP 2 b.c. (Mar 3) Lonhro (AUS) 128 – Pure Illusion (IRE) 95 (Danehill (USA) 126) [2017 5.3m* 5m^4 6m* 5d* 5m^3 6g* 6v^3 6m^3 6d^3 7m^5 Oct 14] tall, rather leggy colt: sixth foal: half-brother to 3 winners, including useful 6f-8.6f winner History Book and French 7f winner Irradiance (both by Raven's Pass): dam winner up to 1m (2-y-o 7f winner): useful performer: won minor events at Brighton in May, and Epsom (awarded race) and Beverley in June, and July Stakes at Newmarket (by 1¾ lengths from U S Navy Flag): third in Norfolk Stakes at Royal Ascot (2 lengths behind Sioux Nation), Richmond Stakes at Goodwood (3½ lengths behind Barraquero), Gimcrack Stakes at York (3¾ lengths behind Sands of Mali) and Middle Park Stakes at Newmarket (2¾ lengths behind U S Navy Flag): should stay 7f: acts on good to firm and good to soft going: usually races prominently. *Mark Johnston* **109**

CARDUCCI 3 b.f. Poet's Voice 126 – Gee Kel (IRE) 91 (Danehill Dancer (IRE) 117) [2017 69: t8.6g 8s^2 8.3g* 8m^6 10d^4 9s^2 8.1s p8g Oct 3] good-topped filly: fairly useful handicapper: won at Nottingham in May: stays 9f: acts on soft and good to firm going: sold 8,000 gns in October. *Richard Hannon* **83**

CAREYANNE 3 ch.f. Mount Nelson 125 – Mayaar (USA) 64 (Grand Slam (USA) 120) [2017 t7.1g 8.2d 7.6d t8.6g Aug 11] third foal: half-sister to 2-y-o 1m/9.5f winner (stayed 1¾m) Keep Calm (by War Chant) and a winner in Italy by Kyllachy: dam, maiden (ran only at 2 yrs, best efforts at 5f), out of sister to Coronation Stakes winner Magic of Life: no form: left David Loughnane after first start: tried in cheekpieces. *Brian Baugh* **–**

Arqana July Stakes, Newmarket—Cardsharp is driven clear to beat U S Navy Flag (blinkers), with Coventry Stakes winner Rajasinghe (second right) back in third under a 3-lb penalty; Invincible Army (striped cap, right) is just run out of a place close home

CARIBBEAN SPRING (IRE) 4 b.g. Dark Angel (IRE) 113 – Bogini (IRE) 95 (Holy Roman Emperor (IRE) 125) [2017 65: p8g⁴ t8.6g* 7m t8.6g⁴ 10.2g 10m 7m p8g⁶ p8g⁶ p8g⁴ t8.6g Dec 5] modest handicapper: won at Wolverhampton (apprentice) in May: stays 8.5f: acts on polytrack, tapeta and good to soft going: has worn visor. *George Margarson* **64**

CARIDADE (USA) 3 b.f. Medaglia d'Oro (USA) 129 – Raffle Ticket (USA) (A P Indy (USA) 131) [2017 7m⁴ 7.9m⁴ 7g* 7d⁵ 7g⁶ 7g Oct 7] 20,000 3-y-o: lengthy filly: first foal: dam unraced sister to top-class US performer up to 1¼m Bernardini: fairly useful performer: won maiden at Redcar (by 6 lengths from Ember's Glow) in August: stays 7f: acts on good to soft going: front runner/races prominently. *Kevin Ryan* **85**

CARIGRAD (IRE) 3 b.g. Excelebration (IRE) 133 – Blissful Beat (Beat Hollow 126) [2017 80p: p7g³ 8g* 8m³ 10m⁴ 10.2m² 10.5m² 8g⁵ 9.9g³ Dec 16] fairly useful performer: won maiden at Redcar in April: second in 2 handicaps at Haydock, then left Hugo Palmer 62,000 gns: stays 10.5f: acts on good to firm going: tried in hood: usually races close up. *Mohammed Jassim Ghazali, Qatar* **91**

CARING TOUCH (USA) 2 b.f. (Feb 9) Elusive Quality (USA) – Blue Petrel (USA) (Distorted Humor (USA) 117) [2017 t8g* Dec 6] second foal: dam, placed at 1¼m-1¾m in France, sister to smart US 2-y-o 6.5f winner (stayed 8.5f) Fortify: 10/3, won maiden at Newcastle (by 2½ lengths from Angelina d'Or) on debut, asserting final 100 yds: should do better. *Saeed bin Suroor* **84 p**

CARLINI (IRE) 2 b.c. (Apr 25) Zoffany (IRE) 121 – Taking Liberties (IRE) 57 (Royal Academy (USA) 130) [2017 7g 7.4g 7v Sep 9] good-topped colt: little impact in minor events. *Brian Meehan* **–**

CARLOVIAN 4 b.g. Acclamation 118 – Mimisel 92 (Selkirk (USA) 129) [2017 58: 6g 6m³ 6m³ 7m* 7d* t7.2g³ 7g⁵ 8.3v² 7s⁵ 8s⁴ 8v Oct 12] strong gelding: modest handicapper: won at Catterick and Leicester (amateur) in July: left Christopher Kellett after second start: stays 8.5f: acts on tapeta, good to firm and heavy going: usually wears cheekpieces nowadays. *Mark Walford* **62**

CARLTON CHOICE (IRE) 3 b.g. Bushranger (IRE) 119 – Choice House (USA) (Chester House (USA) 123) [2017 7.5g⁵ p6.5g* p6.5g² p6.5g⁴ p6.5g* 6g* p6g 6g⁶ 7g⁵ p6.5f⁵ p8g p7.5g³ Dec 6] fairly useful performer: won handicap at Cagnes-sur-Mer in January, and claimer at Deauville and handicap at Maisons-Laffitte in March: well held at Lingfield seventh start: effective at 6f to 1m: acts on polytrack and good to soft going: usually wears headgear (not last 2 starts). *L. Baudron, France* **90**

CARLTON FRANKIE 3 b.f. Equiano (FR) 127 – Valiant Runner 62 (Haafhd 129) [2017 71p: 5g* 5.1m* 6m 5v 5m 5g Oct 13] lengthy filly: useful handicapper: won at Redcar in April and Nottingham (by 1½ lengths from Arzaak) in May: stays 5.5f: acts on good to firm going: front runner. *Michael Easterby* **96**

CARNAGEO (FR) 4 b.g. Pivotal 124 – Sudarynya (IRE) (Sadler's Wells (USA) 132) [2017 91: 10.3g 8.5f 8s⁴ 9.2s³ 7.8s* 8d 9.2s⁴ 10.3d* 10v⁵ 10.3g Oct 14] useful handicapper: won at Carlisle in June and York in September: stays 10.5f: acts on soft and good to firm going: wears headgear. *Richard Fahey* **95**

CARNIVAL KING (IRE) 5 b.g. Arcano (IRE) 122 – Validate (Alhaarth (IRE) 126) [2017 95: 7g 7s 7d⁵ 8.1g³ 10s p8g t7.2m p8s² Nov 16] tall, angular gelding: fairly useful handicapper: stays 1m: acts on polytrack and firm going: usually wears headgear: front runner/races prominently. *Amy Murphy* **87 a81**

CARNTOP 4 b.g. Dansili 127 – Milford Sound (Barathea (IRE) 127) [2017 109: 12m 12m³ 11.8m 14d Aug 5] good-topped gelding: useful handicapper: third at Epsom (3½ lengths behind Soldier In Action) in June: stays 1½m: acts on good to firm and good to soft going: often in headgear: has joined Jamie Snowden. *Ralph Beckett* **109**

CAROLINAE 5 ch.m. Makfi 130 – You Too 74 (Monsun (GER) 124) [2017 84, a93: t8.6g* p8g* p7g 7d⁶ 7m³ 6m² 6g t8.6d³ Dec 27] fairly useful performer: won handicap at Wolverhampton in January and minor event at Lingfield in February: stays 8.5f: acts on polytrack, tapeta and good to firm going: has worn hood, including final start: often races towards rear. *Charlie Fellowes* **94**

CAROL (IRE) 3 b.f. Acclamation 118 – Miss Topsy Turvy (IRE) 85 (Mr Greeley (USA) 122) [2017 80: 10.2g⁴ 10.2d² 9g⁴ 8.1m* 8.1m⁴ p8g⁴ t8g⁶ Sep 22] useful-looking filly: fairly useful performer: won maiden at Chepstow in June: stays 1¼m: acts on good to firm and good to soft going. *Ed Dunlop* **82**

CAROLYN'S VOICE 2 br.f. (Mar 6) Poet's Voice 126 – Two Days In Paris (FR) 78 (Authorized (IRE) 133) [2017 7m p7g Dec 21] good-topped filly: first foal: dam, French 11f-13f winner, half-sister to useful French 1m/9f winner Moonlight In Paris: well held in 2 minor events. *Stuart Williams* **–**

CAROUSE (IRE) 2 b.g. (Jan 31) Excelebration (IRE) 133 – Terre du Vent (FR) 110 (Kutub (IRE) 123) [2017 5m⁶ 6.1s² 6g³ 6s⁵ 7g Sep 2] 30,000Y: neat gelding: first foal: dam French 1¼m-15f winner who stayed 2½m: fairly useful maiden: second in minor event at Chester in June: should be suited by 7f+: acts on soft going. *Andrew Balding* **86**

CARPE DIEM LADY (IRE) 4 b.f. Acclamation 118 – Greenisland (IRE) 100 (Fasliyev (USA) 120) [2017 86: 8.5g³ 7.1m* 6m⁵ 6m 7m Aug 29] lengthy filly: fairly useful handicapper: won at Chepstow (by ½ length from Bounty Pursuit) in June: stays 8.5f: acts on good to firm going: wears headgear: usually races close up: sold 32,000 gns in December. *Ralph Beckett* **81**

CARPET TIME (IRE) 2 b.g. (Mar 23) Intense Focus (USA) 117 – Beal Ban (IRE) (Daggers Drawn (USA) 114) [2017 5g Aug 16] 25/1, well held in minor event at Beverley. *David Barron* **–**

CARP KID (IRE) 2 b.c. (Mar 23) Lope de Vega (IRE) 125 – Homegrown (IRE) 108 (Mujadil (USA) 119) [2017 7m⁶ 8v⁵ p7g p6d p8m* t8g t8.6g* p7g⁴ Dec 31] fair performer: won seller at Lingfield in November and claimer at Wolverhampton in December: left Richard Hannon after fifth start: stays 8.5f: acts on polytrack and tapeta: often travels strongly. *Jamie Osborne* **71**

CARRAGOLD 11 b.g. Diktat 126 – Shadow Roll (IRE) 79 (Mark of Esteem (IRE) 137) [2017 65: f11g Apr 18] workmanlike gelding: fairly useful at best, well held only start in 2017: stays 11f: acts on all-weather, good to firm and heavy going: has worn headgear. *Antony Brittain* **–**

CARRICKLANE 2 b.f. (Apr 23) Zoffany (IRE) 121 – New River (IRE) 78 (Montjeu (IRE) 137) [2017 p6g² Jun 22] second foal: dam, maiden (stayed 11.6f) on Flat, winning hurdler, closely related to useful Scandinavian performer up to 1½m Pas de Secrets: 28/1, promise when second in minor event at Lingfield (head behind Tunes of Glory) on debut: will stay 7f: will improve. *Richard Hughes* **66 p**

CARRIGEEN PRINCE (IRE) 5 ch.g. Strategic Prince 114 – Hi Lyla (IRE) (Lahib (USA) 129) [2017 63, a77: 8s p8g⁶ 10m⁶ 9.5s 8g 8g* 10.5d³ 10s p8g p10.7g p10.7g Dec 1] fair handicapper: won at Naas (apprentice) in July: stays 10.5f: acts on polytrack and heavy going: tried in hood. *Garvan Donnelly, Ireland* **75**

CARRINGTON (FR) 4 b.g. New Approach (IRE) 132 – Winning Family (IRE) (Fasliyev (USA) 120) [2017 96§: 11.8g⁵ Apr 7] useful handicapper: stays 11f: acts on polytrack, good to firm and heavy going: tried in hood: often starts slowly/races in rear: ungenuine. *Charlie Appleby* **91 §**

CARRY ON DERYCK 5 b.g. Halling (USA) 133 – Mullein 110 (Oasis Dream 129) [2017 116: 8g³ 8g⁵ 9d Sep 30] workmanlike gelding: smart performer: third in Sovereign Stakes at Salisbury (neck behind Ballet Concerto) in August: stays 9f: acts on firm and soft going: often races prominently. *Saeed bin Suroor* **116**

CARTAVIO (IRE) 3 b.g. Cacique (IRE) 124 – Star Cluster 106 (Observatory (USA) 131) [2017 –p: t8g⁵ p10g⁵ p12d 9.9m* 9v 10.2m⁵ Jun 24] fair performer: won minor event at Salisbury in May: stays 1¼m: acts on good to firm going: often races prominently. *Andrew Balding* **74**

CARTHAGE (IRE) 6 b.g. Mastercraftsman (IRE) 129 – Pitrizzia (Lando (GER) 128) [2017 79: 11.9s 12g⁴ t12.4s⁵ 16.1g t12.4s⁶ t16.3g Sep 22] attractive gelding: fair handicapper: stays 13.5f: acts on tapeta, soft and good to firm going: has worn headgear: often races towards rear. *Brian Ellison* **73**

CARTOGRAPHER 3 b.f. Henrythenavigator (USA) 131 – Right Answer 95 (Lujain (USA) 119) [2017 86p: 6m* 6m³ 6d* 6g 7d² p6g Nov 29] useful performer: won maiden at Yarmouth in May and handicap at Newmarket (by 3½ lengths from Storm Cry) in June: stays 7f: acts on good to firm and good to soft going: front runner/races prominently. *Martyn Meade* **99**

CARTWRIGHT 4 b.g. High Chaparral (IRE) 132 – One So Marvellous 86 (Nashwan (USA) 135) [2017 98: p14g* 14s⁵ 20f p16g* Sep 5] good-topped gelding: useful handicapper: won at Chelmsford in May and Kempton in September: stays 16.5f: acts on polytrack, tapeta and good to soft going: usually wears headgear. *Sir Mark Prescott Bt* **104**

CARVELAS (IRE) 8 b.g. Cape Cross (IRE) 129 – Caraiyma (IRE) 84 (Shahrastani (USA) 135) [2017 60: p12g^3 p10.7g^4 p12s t12.2m* t13.9m^5 10g^3 12.5g^4 11g^3 12s p10.7g Dec 22] fair handicapper: won at Wolverhampton in February: stays 2m: acts on polytrack, tapeta, good to firm and good to soft going: has worn headgear. *P. J. F. Murphy, Ireland* **68**

CASABLANCA (IRE) 4 b.f. Cape Blanco (IRE) 130 – Wonderful Town (USA) (Bernstein (USA) 115) [2017 82: p12g^4 t12.4g^2 p12g* p13.3d^3 Mar 13] fair performer: won maiden at Lingfield in February: stays 13.5f: acts on polytrack, raced only on good going on turf: front runner/races prominently. *Andrew Balding* **79**

CASACLARE (IRE) 3 b.g. Casamento (IRE) 118 – Sarah Ann (IRE) (Orpen (USA) 116) [2017 53p: 8s^6 12g^2 12s Sep 14] fair maiden: best effort at 1½m: in tongue tie last 2 starts: often races towards rear. *Jonjo O'Neill* **68**

CASA COMIGO (IRE) 2 b.c. (Mar 24) Cape Cross (IRE) 129 – Belanoiva (IRE) (Motivator 131) [2017 7m p8g Nov 7] modest form: better effort when seventh in minor event at Kempton (9¾ lengths behind Bow Street) in November. *John Best* **64**

CASADO (IRE) 3 b.g. Casamento (IRE) 118 – Sense of Greeting (IRE) 46 (Key of Luck (USA) 126) [2017 63p: 10.2g 10.1m^6 p8g^3 p8d^5 p8s 10d Aug 21] workmanlike gelding: fair maiden: stays 1m: acts on polytrack. *John Best* **67**

CASE KEY 4 gr.g. Showcasing 117 – Fluttering Rose 71 (Compton Place 125) [2017 82: 7m^5 5.7f^4 5.7f^2 6g^2 6d* 6g 5.3v^3 7d t7.2g Dec 13] workmanlike gelding: fairly useful handicapper: won at Newmarket (by nose from Zebulon) in August: stays 6f: acts on any turf going: wears cheekpieces: tried in tongue tie. *Michael Appleby* **82**

CASEMATES SQUARE (IRE) 3 b.g. Casamento (IRE) 118 – Marhaba 73 (Nayef (USA) 129) [2017 8m 10.2v^5 t12.2g p12g^3 p16g^3 Nov 8] big gelding: modest maiden: left M. Halford after first start: should stay beyond 1½m: acts on polytrack. *Ian Williams* **62**

CASEMENT (IRE) 3 b.g. Casamento (IRE) 118 – Kirk Wynd 88 (Selkirk (USA) 129) [2017 10m 8g^3 8s* 9.9g 8s^2 Oct 15] €50,000F, 60,000Y: rangy gelding: seventh foal: half-brother to 3 winners, including useful 1½m winner Twin Soul (by Singspiel) and 11.7f winner Uncle Eric (by Alhaarth): dam, 1¼m winner, half-sister to Dubai Duty Free winner Right Approach: fairly useful performer: won maiden at Ffos Las in August: second in handicap at Goodwood in October: stays 1m: acts on soft going. *Roger Charlton* **88**

CASEY BANTER 2 b.f. (Jan 31) Holy Roman Emperor (IRE) 125 – Sinister Ruckus (USA) (Trippi (USA) 121) [2017 6g^3 7m 7d p6g^3 t5g Nov 15] 8,000F, 5,500 2-y-o: third foal: half-sister to 1m-1¼m winner Nouvelle Ere (by Archipenko) and 1¼m-12.5f winner Taopix (by Rip Van Winkle): dam, Canadian 5f/6f winner, sister to Queen Mary Stakes winner Jealous Again: modest maiden: best effort at 6f: acts on polytrack: often races towards rear. *Julia Feilden* **52**

CASHLA BAY 3 b.f. Fastnet Rock (AUS) 127 – Rose Blossom 113 (Pastoral Pursuits 127) [2017 91p: 7g^3 6m t6d^6 f6.1g^4 Dec 4] attractive filly: fairly useful handicapper: third at Leicester in May: stays 7f: acts on fibresand and good to firm going: tried in blinkers: in tongue tie last 2 starts: usually races close up. *John Gosden* **82**

CASIMA 2 b.f. (Feb 5) Dark Angel (IRE) 113 – Caskelena (IRE) 84 (Galileo (IRE) 134) [2017 7d p8g^6 p8g Oct 13] rather unfurnished filly: first foal: dam, 1¼m winner, sister to high-class stayer Age of Aquarius and half-sister to very smart French 1m/9f performer Turtle Bowl: modest form in minor events/maiden: wears hood. *Clive Cox* **55**

CASIMIRO (IRE) 3 ch.g. Casamento (IRE) 118 – Glyndebourne (USA) (Rahy (USA) 115) [2017 p7g* 7.6s^4 p8g^6 8.3d^4 Oct 4] €41,000F, 75,000Y: rangy gelding: third foal: dam lightly-raced half-sister to smart winner up to 1¼m Portrayal: fairly useful form: won maiden at Lingfield in April: will stay 1¼m: sold 42,000 gns in October. *Roger Charlton* **90**

CASINA DI NOTTE (IRE) 3 ch.g. Casamento (IRE) 118 – Nightswimmer (IRE) 75 (Noverre (USA) 125) [2017 72: 8m^6 7s^2 8m t7.2g 8m* p8g Oct 5] fairly useful handicapper: won at Yarmouth in August: stays 1m: acts on soft and good to firm going: usually wears headgear: sometimes slowly away. *Marco Botti* **84**

CASPIAN GOLD (IRE) 3 ch.g. Born To Sea (IRE) 117 – Eminence Gift 60 (Cadeaux Genereux 131) [2017 61p: 8g p12g 9g 8g a10.4g a10.4g a10.4g Nov 13] maiden: no form in 2017: left Richard Hughes after fourth start: tried in blinkers. *Vanessa Bracke, Belgium* **–**

CASPIAN PRINCE (IRE) 8 ch.g. Dylan Thomas (IRE) 132 – Crystal Gaze (IRE) (Rainbow Quest (USA) 134) [2017 116: 5g^3 5g^5 5g^3 6g^3 6g 5.1d^5 5g 5m* 5m^4 5f* 5s^4 5.2m p6g^5 Nov 18] strong, workmanlike gelding: smart performer: won 'Dash' (Handicap) at Epsom (by short head from Dark Shot) in June for third time and Sapphire Stakes at the **117**

*Investec Corporate Banking 'Dash' (Heritage Handicap), Epsom Downs—
the trailblazing Caspian Prince (hood) notches his third win in the race, for the third different trainer; Dark Shot (left) and Duke of Firenze (second left) are second and third in a photo, with Momentofmadness (hidden by winner) and Edward Lewis next*

Curragh (by short head from Marsha) in July: left Roger Fell after fifth start: best at 5f: acts on polytrack, firm and good to soft going: wears headgear/tongue tie: front runner/races prominently. *Tony Coyle*

CASSINI (IRE) 2 b.c. (Jan 12) Galileo (IRE) 134 – Chrysanthemum (IRE) 113 (Danehill Dancer (IRE) 117) [2017 8v³ 8g³ Sep 15] second foal: closely related to useful winner up to 1¼m Cunco (2-y-o 6f winner, by Frankel): dam winner up to 1¼m (2-y-o 7f/1m winner): fair form: better effort when third in minor event at Sandown (3 lengths behind Crossed Baton) in September: will be suited by 1¼m+: wears tongue tie: open to further improvement. *John Gosden* **78 p**

CASTANEA 5 ch.g. Pivotal 124 – Invitee 74 (Medicean 128) [2017 51: t8.6g⁶ p10g⁴ p10d⁵ p12g 10m Jul 4] poor maiden: stays 1½m: acts on polytrack and good to firm going: has worn headgear: tried in tongue tie: often races in rear. *Ronald Harris* **48**

CASTELLATED 3 b.f. Teofilo (IRE) 126 – Portal 108 (Hernando (FR) 127) [2017 77p: 10.3m 11.9d⁶ p11s⁶ 11.4m* 10.9g² 11.9g⁴ 13.9f⁵ Dec 3] neat filly: fairly useful performer: won handicap at Windsor in July: left Richard Hannon 35,000 gns after: should stay 1¾m: acts on polytrack and good to firm going. *J. Maroto, Spain* **92**

CASTERBRIDGE 5 b.g. Pastoral Pursuits 127 – Damalis (IRE) 106 (Mukaddamah (USA) 125) [2017 83: 5gᵘʳ 6g⁴ 5g⁵ 5g* 6g⁵ 5g⁴ 5s 5v⁵ 6g⁵ 5.1v 6.1d⁴ t5d² t5g* t5g* f5g⁵ Dec 22] fairly useful handicapper: won at Leicester in May and Newcastle (twice, by 1½ lengths from Dundunah second occasion) in November: stays 6f: acts on tapeta, soft and good to firm going: wears headgear: usually leads. *Eric Alston* **86**

CASTILO DEL DIABLO (IRE) 8 br.g. Teofilo (IRE) 126 – Hundred Year Flood (USA) (Giant's Causeway (USA) 132) [2017 98: t12.4g t16.5g p15.8f⁵ p12g⁴ t12.2g⁶ 12f⁶ 12d Aug 5] tall, useful-looking gelding: fairly useful handicapper: stays 2m: acts on polytrack, tapeta and firm going: has worn headgear. *David Simcock* **88**

CASTLEACRE 3 ch.f. Exceed And Excel (AUS) 126 – Cloud Castle 119 (In The Wings 128) [2017 90p: 6m⁶ 5.1d⁴ p7g⁶ Aug 31] lengthy filly: fairly useful handicapper: left Hugo Palmer after second start: stays 7f: acts on tapeta and soft going: in hood final start (pulled hard). *James Tate* **90**

CASTLE HARBOUR 4 b.g. Kyllachy 129 – Gypsy Carnival 82 (Trade Fair 124) [2017 106: 8g 7m³ 7m⁵ 8m Jun 21] good-topped gelding: useful handicapper: fifth at Goodwood in May: stays 7f: acts on soft and good to firm going: in headgear last 2 starts: sold 105,000 gns in July, sent to Hong Kong, where renamed Storm Soldier. *John Gosden* **108**

CASTLE HILL CASSIE (IRE) 3 ch.f. Casamento (IRE) 118 – Angel Bright (IRE) 88 (Dark Angel (IRE) 113) [2017 68p: t7.1g² 7g³ 6g* 5.9s² 6.1g⁴ t7.1s* p7g⁴ Oct 18] fairly useful performer: won maiden at Pontefract in May and handicap at Newcastle (by neck from Express Lady) in September: stays 7f: acts on polytrack, tapeta and soft going. *Ben Haslam* **87**

CASTLELYONS (IRE) 5 br.g. Papal Bull 128 – Summercove (IRE) 72 (Cape Cross (IRE) 129) [2017 p11g^4 12v p11s p12g* t12.2g* Dec 2] tall, good-bodied gelding: useful handicapper: won at Kempton in November and Wolverhampton in December: stays 1½m: acts on polytrack and tapeta: has worn hood, including last 2 starts: tried in tongue tie: often races towards rear/freely. *Robert Stephens* **101**

CASTLEREA TESS 4 ch.f. Pastoral Pursuits 127 – Zartwyda (IRE) (Mozart (IRE) 131) [2017 53, a43: t7.1m^2 t6g* t6g^3 t6m^4 t7.1g t6g* t6g 6m* 6d 6.1m* 6.1m t6.1m Oct 28] fair handicapper: won at Wolverhampton (amateur events) in January and April, and Catterick and Chepstow in June: stays 7f: acts on tapeta, soft and good to firm going: wears cheekpieces: sometimes slowly away, often races prominently. *Sarah Hollinshead* **72 a66**

CASTLE TALBOT (IRE) 5 b.g. Rock of Gibraltar (IRE) 133 – Louve Sacree (USA) (Seeking The Gold (USA)) [2017 72§, a61§: 8m^3 10.1m^4 10.2d^2 9.1d^2 10d^6 10.1d^6 Oct 24] leggy gelding: fair handicapper: stays 1¼m: acts on good to firm and good to soft going: often wears headgear: temperamental. *Tom Clover* **74 §**

CATALINAS DIAMOND (IRE) 9 b.m. One Cool Cat (USA) 123 – Diamondiferous (USA) (Danzig (USA)) [2017 61: 6m^6 5.7f^5 5.7d^4 5.7m^6 5.7f^5 5.1m^6 5.7f^5 Jul 12] leggy, angular mare: modest handicapper: races at 5f/6f nowadays: acts on polytrack, firm and soft going: wears hood/tongue tie: often races in rear. *Pat Murphy* **51**

CATALYZE 9 b.g. Tumblebrutus (USA) 102 – Clarita Dear (CHI) (Hussonet (USA)) [2017 p6g p6g p7d p7g p6g p6g^5 p6g Apr 12] sturdy gelding: poor handicapper nowadays: stays 7f: acts on polytrack, soft and good to firm going: has worn headgear, including final start: usually wears tongue tie: sometimes slowly away. *Paddy Butler* **35**

CATAPULT 2 b.g. (Apr 1) Equiano (FR) 127 – Alectrona (FR) (Invincible Spirit (IRE) 121) [2017 5g^4 5.3d^5 6.1m^5 5g p5g 7g^2 7g p7s Nov 16] compact gelding: fair maiden: left Robert Eddery after fifth start: stays 7f: acts on good to soft going: tried in headgear/tongue tie. *Clifford Lines* **67**

CATASTROPHE 4 b.g. Intikhab (USA) 135 – Mrs Snaffles (IRE) 99 (Indian Danehill (IRE) 124) [2017 69: f8g^4 t8g 8g 8.3g^2 8.3g^2 9.2s^2 8.5d 7.8d 8.5s^3 8v^2 8v* a8.4s Dec 12] small gelding: fair performer: first win in seller at Redcar in November: left John Quinn £4,500 after: stays 9f: acts on polytrack, tapeta, good to firm and heavy going: has worn headgear: often travels strongly, tends to find little. *S. Schleppi, Germany* **66**

CAT BALLOU 2 ch.f. (May 9) Equiano (FR) 127 – Flamenco Dancer (Mark of Esteem (IRE) 137) [2017 5d^6 5g t6.1g p6s Dec 1] half-sister to several winners, including smart 5f/6f (including at 2 yrs) winner Ballesteros (by Tomba) and useful 5f (including at 2 yrs) winner Seve (by Exceed And Excel): dam unraced: no form. *David O'Meara* **–**

CATCHER ON THE GO (IRE) 7 b.g. Catcher In The Rye (IRE) 115 – Suspicious Minds (Anabaa (USA) 130) [2017 12v* 14v^5 Aug 15] fairly useful form: won maiden at Ffos Las (by 1¼ lengths from Waterville Dancer) in August: bumper/hurdle winner. *Evan Williams* **89**

CATCH THE PIGEON 2 ch.f. (Feb 23) Paco Boy (IRE) 129 – Jasmick (IRE) 96 (Definite Article 121) [2017 p6d^6 6.1g^6 6.1v^6 p7d^5 7g p7g p6g Oct 14] £3,200Y: sturdy filly: seventh foal: half-sister to 1½m-1¾m winner Jasmeno (by Catcher In The Rye) and smart winner up to 1m Sagramor (2-y-o 7f winner, by Pastoral Pursuits): dam 1½m-14.4f winner: modest maiden: stays 7f: acts on polytrack. *Ed de Giles* **53**

CATCH THE TIDE (FR) 2 ch.f. (Feb 11) Kendargent (FR) 112 – Coiffure (King's Best (USA) 132) [2017 t8g^6 Dec 6] fourth foal: half-sister to French winners around 1¼m Win Coiff (by Raven's Pass) and Combe Hay (by Elusive City): dam unraced daughter of Yorkshire Oaks winner/St Leger runner-up Quiff: in hood, 40/1, sixth in maiden at Newcastle (11¼ lengths behind Caring Touch) in December: should do better. *Henry Spiller* **55 p**

CATCHY LASS (IRE) 8 b.m. Catcher In The Rye (IRE) 115 – Liseraw Lass (IRE) (Grand Lodge (USA) 125) [2017 83§: p10.7g^5 p10.7g* p12g^4 p12g^6 p10.7g^2 p12g^3 t12.4s p12g p12g p12g p12g Dec 21] fairly useful performer: won claimer at Dundalk (by 4¼ lengths from Ineffable) in February: stays 1½m: acts on polytrack and good to firm going: wears tongue tie: quirky. *Anthony Mulholland, Ireland* **80 §**

CATHEADANS FURY 3 ch.f. Firebreak 125 – Dualagi 74 (Royal Applause 124) [2017 p7g Nov 1] second foal: dam 5f/6f winner: in tongue tie, 40/1, pulled very hard when well held in maiden at Kempton. *Martin Bosley* **–**

CATHERINETHEGRACE (IRE) 3 gr.f. Duke of Marmalade (IRE) 132 – Little Miss Gracie 105 (Efisio 120) [2017 p8d p10g Dec 30] fifth foal: closely related to 3 winners, including winner up to 1¼m Graceful James (2-y-o 1m winner, by Rock of Gibraltar) and winner up to 1m Gracious George (2-y-o 7f winner, by Oratorio): dam 1m winner (including at 2 yrs): well held in 2 maidens. *Jimmy Fox* –

CATHIE'S DREAM (USA) 2 b.f. (Apr 14) More Than Ready (USA) 120 – Mantilla (USA) (Gone West (USA)) [2017 5m 6m 5s Oct 31] $25,000Y, £60,000 2-y-o: second foal: dam, maiden (stayed 1m), closely related to smart dam of high-class pair Bated Breath (sprinter) and Cityscape (miler): no form. *Noel Wilson* –

CATIVO RAGAZZO 2 b.c. (Jul 20) Multiplex 114 – Sea Isle 73 (Selkirk (USA) 129) [2017 p7d Nov 22] 250/1, well held in minor event at Kempton. *John E. Long* –

CATOCA (USA) 2 b.f. (Apr 20) Lemon Drop Kid (USA) 131 – Catrageous (USA) (Tale of The Cat (USA) 113) [2017 p7g^4 t7.2g Dec 5] $120,000Y: first foal: dam US 1m/8.5f (minor stakes) winner: fair form: better effort when fourth in minor event at Kempton (3½ lengths behind Lush Life) in November: will stay at least 1m. *Ed Walker* **68**

CAT ROYALE (IRE) 4 b.g. Lilbourne Lad (IRE) 111 – Call This Cat (IRE) 66 (One Cool Cat (USA) 123) [2017 78: t9.5m^2 t9.5g p8d^3 p8g 10d p11d t8.6g* t9.5g^3 p10g t9.5m^4 p12g Nov 29] lengthy gelding: fair handicapper: won at Wolverhampton in July: left Jane Chapple-Hyam after first start: stays 11.5f: acts on polytrack, tapeta and soft going: wears headgear: usually races prominently. *John Butler* **71**

CAT SILVER 4 b.g. Dansili 127 – Catopuma (USA) (Elusive Quality (USA)) [2017 78: 8f^5 p8g p8s 6.1m* 6m^5 6.1m^5 t6.1g p6g Oct 18] good-topped gelding: fair handicapper: won at Windsor (apprentice, by head from Athollblair Boy) in July: left Roger Charlton after fourth start: stayed 1m: acted on polytrack, good to firm and good to soft going: in headgear last 5 starts: dead. *Charlie Wallis* **79** **a67**

CATSKILL 3 b.f. Dutch Art 126 – Catfish (IRE) 96 (One Cool Cat (USA) 123) [2017 t5g t5s 8s 7m Jun 24] first foal: dam 5f and (including at 2 yrs) 6f winner: no form: in tongue tie final start. *Wilf Storey* –

CATWILLDO (IRE) 7 b.m. One Cool Cat (USA) 123 – Hypocrisy 85 (Bertolini (USA) 125) [2017 72: p6g p5g^3 5m p6g 5m^6 5g 5m^3 5g^4 5m^4 5d^4 5g a6g^6 5.8v p5g p5g Nov 24] modest handicapper: stays 6f: acts on polytrack, soft and good to firm going: usually wears headgear: usually races towards rear. *Garvan Donnelly, Ireland* **62**

CAVALIERI (IRE) 7 b.g. Oratorio (IRE) 128 – Always Attractive (IRE) (King's Best (USA) 132) [2017 62, a77: t16.3g^3 t16.3g^3 p14d p16d^6 t16.3g^3 16g* 15.9m^4 16d 15.9s^3 16.1g t16.5g^3 15.9g^5 14s t16.3g Oct 19] fair handicapper: won at Redcar in April: stays 16.5f: acts on polytrack, tapeta, soft and good to firm going: wears headgear/tongue tie. *Philip Kirby* **66** **a74**

CAVALRY REGIMENT 2 gr.g. (May 18) Lethal Force (IRE) 128 – Saddlers Bend (IRE) 90 (Refuse To Bend (IRE) 128) [2017 6.1v^6 6g 7v p6g Nov 2] workmanlike gelding: little impact in minor events. *John Quinn* –

CAVATINA 2 b.f. (Apr 16) Lethal Force (IRE) 128 – Piano 101 (Azamour (IRE) 130) [2017 p7d^4 8s^3 p7g* Oct 13] second foal: dam 1¼m/11f winner: fairly useful form: won minor event at Kempton (by neck from Scandaleuse) in October: stays 1m: will go on improving. *William Haggas* **82 p**

CAVENDISH PLACE 2 b.g. (May 18) Doncaster Rover (USA) 114 – Beauty Pageant (IRE) 90 (Bahamian Bounty 116) [2017 5f 6g Aug 2] well held in 2 minor events. *David Brown* –

CAVIAR ROYALE 2 b.g. (Jan 21) Royal Applause 124 – Precious Secret (IRE) 63 (Fusaichi Pegasus (USA) 130) [2017 6m 7g 6s 7.9g t9.5g Nov 20] big gelding: modest maiden: left Brian Meehan after fourth start: in cheekpieces last 2 starts. *Nikki Evans* **64**

CAYMUS 4 b.f. Compton Place 125 – Midnight Sky 52 (Desert Prince (IRE) 130) [2017 51: 5g 5m 5d Jun 10] small filly: fair at best, no form in 2017: usually wears headgear: wears tongue tie. *Tracy Waggott* –

CECCHINI (IRE) 2 br.f. (Apr 5) Rip Van Winkle (IRE) 134 – Urban Daydream (IRE) 72 (Oasis Dream 129) [2017 p8g* Nov 8] second foal: half-sister to 1m winner Monaadhil (by Dark Angel): dam, maiden (should have stayed beyond 1¼m), half-sister to very smart winner up to 1½m Rainbow Peak out of close relative to Celtic Swing: 9/4, taking debut when won minor event at Kempton (by 1¼ lengths from Bubble And Squeak) in November, making all: useful prospect. *Ralph Beckett* **89 p**

CECILATOR 3 b.f. Delegator 125 – Cecily Parsley 62 (Fantastic Light (USA) 134) [2017 **45**
10g f11.1g^4 9.9d^4 10d 12f 9.9m^6 10g^3 Aug 13] 5,000F, 3,000Y, £1,500 2-y-o: first foal: dam, maiden (stayed 2m) on Flat, winning chaser, out of useful 1¼m-1½m winner Salim Toto: poor maiden: best effort at 1¼m: acts on good to soft going: in headgear last 3 starts. *Noel Williams*

CE DE NULLIS (IRE) 2 ch.f. (Feb 18) Dandy Man (IRE) 123 – Plym 75 (Notnowcato **71**
128) [2017 5d^3 5m^4 5m^5 5g^4 6.1g^2 6.1d 6v Oct 23] €10,000Y, £32,000 2-y-o: good-topped filly: second foal: dam, 2-y-o 1m winner, half-sister to smart 7f winner Frenchmans Bay: fair maiden: stays 6f: acts on good to firm and good to soft going: has worn hood: often races prominently. *Paul Midgley*

CEE JAY 4 ch.g. Kyllachy 129 – Intermission (IRE) (Royal Applause 124) [2017 72: t6m^3 **65**
t5.1g^5 5.7f^4 5.7d 6g* 6.1m^3 5.7s^5 p7g Nov 2] compact gelding: fair handicapper: won at Brighton in July: left Robert Cowell after second start: stays 6f: acts on polytrack, good to firm and good to soft going: has worn headgear. *Patrick Chamings*

CEILIDHS DREAM 2 b.f. (May 8) Oasis Dream 129 – Ceilidh House 107 (Selkirk **71 p**
(USA) 129) [2017 p8g^3 Nov 8] third foal: half-sister to 5f winner Pillar (by Rock of Gibraltar): dam winner up to 1¼m (2-y-o 1m winner): 7/1, shaped well amidst greenness when third in minor event at Kempton (2½ lengths behind Espadrille) in November, not knocked about: sure to progress. *Ralph Beckett*

CE LA VIE 3 ch.f. Dutch Art 126 – Chase The Lady (USA) (Atticus (USA) 121) [2017 **87**
77p: 8v 8m 10.2v^4 8s^5 10.2d Oct 27] angular filly: fairly useful performer: stays 1m: best form on heavy going: sometimes slowly away, usually races nearer last than first. *Keith Dalgleish*

CELEBRATION DAY (IRE) 4 b.g. Raven's Pass (USA) 133 – Bunting 102 (Shaadi **94**
(USA) 126) [2017 82: p10g* 10.1g^2 p10g* p10s 10m* 10m Aug 14] lengthy gelding: fairly useful handicapper: won at Chelmsford in March and June, and Windsor (by 2 lengths from Hollywood Road) in July: stays 1¼m: acts on polytrack, good to firm and good to soft going: tried in visor: usually leads. *Simon Crisford*

CELERITY (IRE) 3 ch.f. Casamento (IRE) 118 – Shinko Dancer (IRE) 90 (Shinko **57**
Forest (IRE)) [2017 –: t6f t6m t6g^3 t5.1g^4 t5.1g^2 t6g^2 p5g^6 p5g^6 p6g^4 p6g^5 5m t5.1g 6.1m^6 t5.1g^6 5.1m 5.1g 5d^2 5d^4 6.1m 5.1d^5 t5g 5s^5 Nov 8] neat filly: modest maiden: left David Evans after twentieth start: stays 6f: acts on polytrack, tapeta and good to soft going: wears headgear: sometimes slowly away. *Lisa Williamson*

CELESTATION 3 b.f. Excelebration (IRE) 133 – Coventina (IRE) 108 (Daylami (IRE) **84**
138) [2017 78: 10m^2 10.2f^3 10.2d 10g^2 9.2g^2 10.1g^3 9.8d^3 10.3g 8.3s 10.3v p10g^4 t10.2g* Oct 20] close-coupled filly: fairly useful handicapper: won at Newcastle in October: stays 1¼m: acts on polytrack, tapeta and good to firm going: usually leads: sold 9,000 gns in October. *Mark Johnston*

CELESTIAL BAY 8 b.m. Septieme Ciel (USA) 123 – Snowy Mantle 54 (Siberian **78**
Express (USA) 125) [2017 78: p12g p12g^4 t12.2g Jan 31] fair handicapper: stays 13.5f: acts on polytrack, tapeta, good to firm and good to soft going: has worn hood. *Sylvester Kirk*

CELESTIAL DANCER (FR) 5 b.m. Dr Fong (USA) 128 – Rabeera 62 (Beat Hollow **–**
126) [2017 55: t16.5g p16g^6 t13.9g^6 t12.2g^6 Mar 27] modest maiden at best, little form in 2017: usually leads. *Nigel Twiston-Davies*

CELESTIAL SPHERES (IRE) 3 b.g. Redoute's Choice (AUS) – Copernica (IRE) **99**
(Galileo (IRE) 134) [2017 85: 10.3g^5 10g* p10g p12g* Dec 31] useful handicapper: won at Newmarket in November and Lingfield (by 1¼ lengths from Al Hamdany) in December: stays 1½m: acts on polytrack and good to firm going: usually wears cheekpieces. *Charlie Appleby*

CELESTIN'S 2 b.f. (Apr 6) Cacique (IRE) 124 – Veenwouden 107 (Desert Prince (IRE) **75**
130) [2017 7.4s^2 8.1g^2 8d^4 Oct 24] rather unfurnished filly: sixth foal: half-sister to French 10.5f winner Jadot (by Motivator): dam, winner up to 1½m (2-y-o 7f winner) who stayed 2m, half-sister to smart performer up to 13.4f Delsarte: fair form: best effort when second in minor event at Windsor (short head behind Delsheer) in October. *William Haggas*

CELSIANA 3 ch.f. Sepoy (AUS) 129 – Generous Lady 98 (Generous (IRE) 139) [2017 **–**
p12g Nov 17] 15,000Y: closely related to a winner in Hong Kong by Raven's Pass and half-sister to several winners, including very smart winner up to 1½m High Accolade (2-y-o 7f winner, by Mark of Esteem), also runner-up in St Leger: dam 1½m-1¾m winner who stayed 2m: behind in 2 bumpers: in blinkers, 25/1, well held in maiden at Lingfield. *Marcus Tregoning*

CELTIC ARTISAN (IRE) 6 ch.g. Dylan Thomas (IRE) 132 – Perfectly Clear (USA) (Woodman (USA) 126) [2017 65: t9.5g^5 t8g t8.6g* p10g* p8d^4 t8.6g* p8d^5 8m^3 9g^5 10.3g 8m^6 8d^4 t8.6g p8d^3 Oct 6] fair handicapper: won at Wolverhampton and Chelmsford (apprentice) in February, and again at Wolverhampton in March: stays 1¼m: acts on polytrack, tapeta, soft and good to firm going: wears headgear/tongue tie: often races close up. *Rebecca Menzies* **76**

CELTIC AVA (IRE) 5 b.m. Peintre Celebre (USA) 137 – Denices Desert 53 (Green Desert (USA) 127) [2017 62, a69: p10g^4 Jan 7] rather sparely-made mare: fair handicapper: stays 1½m: acts on polytrack: often races towards rear. *Pat Phelan* **60**

CELTIC POWER 5 b.g. Rail Link 132 – Biloxi (Caerleon (USA) 132) [2017 72: 11.1m^5 12.5g 12.1m 13.1s^4 16.1g^4 t16.3g^6 15g^5 14s 13.1v Oct 12] modest handicapper: stays 2m: acts on good to firm going: usually wears headgear. *Jim Goldie* **54**

CELTIK SECRET 3 ro.f. Sakhee's Secret 128 – Cill Rialaig 106 (Environment Friend 128) [2017 8.1m^6 9.9g 9.9d 9.9g^5 12g^5 Sep 6] first foal: dam, 1¼m-1½m winner who stayed 1¾m, also won in bumpers: modest form. *Hughie Morrison* **63**

CENOTAPH (USA) 5 b.g. War Front (USA) 119 – Sanserif (IRE) 106 (Fasliyev (USA) 120) [2017 94p: 6d 6d 5g 7f^4 7v p7g^3 Oct 20] useful handicapper: fourth at the Curragh (¾ length behind Severus) in July: stays 1m: acts on polytrack, firm and good to soft going: tried in blinkers: often races towards rear: has joined Jeremy Noseda. *Aidan O'Brien, Ireland* **98**

CENT FLYING 2 b.g. (Apr 14) Sepoy (AUS) 129 – Sea of Leaves (USA) 103 (Stormy Atlantic (USA)) [2017 6d 5d^6 5.1m 5m^4 5.1s Sep 14] modest form: tried in tongue tie. *William Muir* **53**

CENTRAL CITY (IRE) 2 b.g. (Mar 28) Kodiac 112 – She Basic (IRE) 98 (Desert Prince (IRE) 130) [2017 5m^4 5.1m^3 6.1m^4 p6s^4 7v 6g^2 t6.1g* 6d^6 p6d^2 t7.2g^2 Nov 20] €50,000Y: useful-looking gelding: third foal: half-brother to 1m-1¼m winner (including at 2 yrs) Katebird (by Dark Angel): dam, 9f winner, half-sister to useful 7f/1m winner She Breeze: fairly useful performer: won nursery at Wolverhampton (by 2¼ lengths from Gabrial The Devil) in September: stays 7f: acts on polytrack, tapeta and good to firm going: tried in blinkers: front runner/races prominently. *Hugo Palmer* **86**

CENTRAL SQUARE (IRE) 5 b.g. Azamour (IRE) 130 – Lucky Clio (IRE) 59 (Key of Luck (USA) 126) [2017 110: 9m^3 10m 10.3m 10.3g^4 10s^3 9d Sep 30] smart handicapper: third at Newmarket (1¾ lengths behind Playful Sound) in May and fourth in York Stakes (3 lengths behind Success Days) in July: stays 10.5f: acts on good to firm going: has worn headgear: often races towards rear: temperamental. *Roger Varian* **114 §**

CENTRE HAAFHD 6 b.g. Haafhd 129 – Deira Dubai 75 (Green Desert (USA) 127) [2017 56§: t7.1d t7.1g 7.2d Jul 31] fair at best, no form in 2017: often wears headgear: tried in tongue tie: often races prominently. *Kenneth Slack* **–**

CENTURY DREAM (IRE) 3 b.c. Cape Cross (IRE) 129 – Salacia (IRE) 89 (Echo of Light 125) [2017 90p: 10d^3 10s^4 8s* 8g* 8d^6 8.2v* 10s* Oct 28] useful-looking colt: smart/progressive handicapper: won at Doncaster in June, Ayr in July, Haydock (by short head from Original Choice) in September and Newbury (by 1¼ lengths from Abdon) in October: stays 1¼m: acts on good to firm and heavy going: in hood last 5 starts: wears tongue tie: often travels strongly. *Simon Crisford* **116**

CERAMIST 2 b.f. (Jan 22) Mastercraftsman (IRE) 129 – Dalasyla (IRE) (Marju (IRE) 127) [2017 8.3g^3 Aug 15] 165,000Y: sixth foal: half-sister to useful 7f/1m winner Dalkova (by Galileo) and French 1½m winner Diavola (by Duke of Marmalade): dam, French 15f winner, half-sister to very smart winner up to 1¾m Daliapour: 4/1, encouragement when third in minor event at Nottingham (3 lengths behind Perfect Clarity) on debut: will be suited by 1¼m+: open to improvement. *John Gosden* **75 p**

CERTIFICATE 6 ch.g. Pivotal 124 – Graduation 102 (Lomitas 129) [2017 114: 7m^4 6m 7g p7s^3 p8s Dec 14] well-made gelding: smart performer, below best in 2017: left Roger Varian after fourth start: stays 8.5f: acts on polytrack and good to firm going: has worn headgear. *Conor Dore* **106**

CERULEAN SILK 7 b.m. Striking Ambition 122 – Cerulean Rose 78 (Bluegrass Prince (IRE) 110) [2017 51: f6g Jan 19] poor maiden: stayed 6f: acted on all-weather: sometimes wore cheekpieces: dead. *Tony Carroll* **–**

C'EST NO MOUR (GER) 4 b.c. Champs Elysees 124 – C'est L'Amour (GER) (Whipper (USA) 126) [2017 p11g 10m 10g^6 10m* 11.4g* 12d^3 12m* 12g* 12v^6 Oct 1] €110,000Y, 13,000 3-y-o: workmanlike colt: first foal: dam, German 7.5f/1m winner, half-sister to smart performer (best at sprint trips) Calrissian: useful handicapper: won at Lingfield in **96**

June, Windsor in July, and Epsom in August (amateurs) and September (jump jockeys): stays 1½m: acts on good to firm and good to soft going: usually races towards rear. *Peter Hedger*

CEYHAN 5 ch.g. Rock of Gibraltar (IRE) 133 – Alla Prima (IRE) (In The Wings 128) **76** [2017 77: p12m^{2} p12g^{3} t12.2g^{2} f8g^{5} 11.6f^{5} 12m 7m^{5} a7g p10s* p12g^{2} Dec 28] workmanlike gelding: fair performer: won handicap at Chelmsford in December: stays 1½m: acts on polytrack and soft going. *Jamie Osborne*

CHAGATAI (IRE) 2 b.g. (Feb 1) Kodiac 112 – Golden Shine 80 (Royal Applause 124) **85** [2017 5m* 5m^{5} May 25] €110,000Y: useful-looking gelding: third foal: half-brother to 2-y-o 6f winner Arthur Martinleake (by Alfred Nobel) and 5f (including at 2 yrs) winner Moondyne Joe (by Bushranger): dam, 2-y-o 5f winner, half-sister to useful winner up to 6f Falcon Hill: fairly useful form: won minor event at Bath (by head from Last Page) in April: hung badly right next time. *Clive Cox*

CHAI CHAI (IRE) 2 b.g. (Mar 6) Zoffany (IRE) 121 – Flamenco Red 93 (Warning 136) **80** [2017 6.1g^{5} 7m^{3} p7s 7v 7g^{5} 7g^{3} 7v* 7s Oct 10] €120,000F, £45,000Y, £75,000 2-y-o: close-coupled gelding: closely related to French 1½m winner Natural Leader (by Dansili) and half-brother to several winners, including French 8.5f and (at 2 yrs) 1¼m winner Blaze of Fire (by Bering) and 5f/6f winner Scarlet Oak (by Zamindar): dam winner up to 1m (2-y-o 6f winner): fairly useful performer: won nursery at Chester (by 1¾ lengths from Magnus) in September: stays 7f: acts on good to firm and heavy going. *Andrew Balding*

CHAIN OF DAISIES 5 b.m. Rail Link 132 – Puya 88 (Kris 135) [2017 114: 9.9m^{6} **111** t10.2g^{2} 10m^{3} 10m* Oct 13] tall, useful-looking mare: smart performer: won listed race at Newmarket (by 2¼ lengths from Permission) in October: second in similar event at Newcastle (neck behind More Mischief) in June and third in Winter Hill Stakes at Windsor (2½ lengths behind Fabricate) in August: stays 10.5f: acts on polytrack, tapeta and good to firm going: front runner, often travels strongly. *Henry Candy*

CHALKY (IRE) 3 gr.f. Canford Cliffs (IRE) 133 – Beautiful Hill (IRE) 74 (Danehill **74** (USA) 126) [2017 7g^{2} 8g^{3} 8m^{2} 8f^{5} Nov 23] €10,000Y, resold €22,000Y: sixth foal: half-sister to 3 winners, including useful 7f-1¼m winner Chapter And Verse (by One Cool Cat) and 8.5f winner Gris Ladera (by Verglas): dam 9f winner: fair form: left Martyn Meade after third start: will be suited by 9f+. *Philip d'Amato, USA*

CHALLOW (IRE) 3 b.g. Acclamation 118 – Starlight Smile (USA) (Green Dancer **73** (USA) 132) [2017 73: p7g^{5} t7.1g 8f^{3} 10.2g 8.1d^{6} 8m^{3} 10g^{3} 11.8s^{5} 12m^{3} t7.2g^{5} p13.3d^{5} 11.4m Oct 16] lengthy gelding: fair maiden: stays 1½m: acts on polytrack and good to firm going: tried in blinkers: usually races close up. *Sylvester Kirk*

CHAMASAY 3 b.g. Sayif (IRE) 122 – Miss Chamanda (IRE) 86 (Choisir (AUS) 126) **70** [2017 –§: f8g^{6} f8d* p8g f8d* f8g^{3} 7.1d Jun 6] good-topped gelding: fair handicapper: won at Southwell in March (apprentice) and April: stays 1m: acts on fibresand: often races prominently: has looked temperamental. *David Evans*

CHAMPAGNE BOB 5 gr.g. Big Bad Bob (IRE) 118 – Exclusive Approval (USA) (With **75** Approval (CAN)) [2017 67: 6m 6.1v^{3} 6.1g^{3} 6.1m* 6g* 6.1d^{4} 6g 6d 7.1g^{2} 6.9v^{5} 7v 7s^{6} 7d* p7s^{6} Nov 16] workmanlike gelding: fair handicapper: won at Chepstow and Newbury (apprentice) in July, and Leicester (amateur) in October: stays 7f: acts on good to firm and heavy going: has worn headgear, including last 3 starts. *Richard Price*

CHAMPAGNE CHAMP 5 b.g. Champs Elysees 124 – Maramba 97 (Rainbow Quest **97** (USA) 134) [2017 96: 18g^{2} t16.3g^{3} 14d^{3} t16.3s 18g^{3} 14g^{5} 16v^{2} 14.2s^{2} Oct 9] tall gelding: useful handicapper: placed on 6 of 8 starts in 2017: stays 2¼m: acts on polytrack, tapeta, good to firm and heavy going: tried in cheekpieces: front runner/races prominently: has carried head awkwardly but consistent. *Rod Millman*

CHAMPAGNE FREDDIE 4 b.g. Sleeping Indian 122 – Shes Minnie 90 (Bertolini **59** (USA) 125) [2017 56: t7.1m^{4} t7.1m t8.6g 10.2g 7.1g p7g Sep 6] modest maiden: stays 8.5f: acts on tapeta: front runner/races prominently. *John O'Shea*

CHAMPAGNE PINK (FR) 3 b.f. Teofilo (IRE) 126 – Carruba (IRE) (Marju (IRE) 127) **86** [2017 –: t8.6m^{4} 8g^{5} t8.6g^{4} t10.2s^{2} t12.4g^{5} 10d t9.5g* t8.6g* t9.5g* Dec 22] fairly useful handicapper: won at Wolverhampton in November (2) and December: stays 12.5f: acts on tapeta: wears hood. *K. R. Burke*

CHAMPAGNE QUEEN 3 ch.f. Showcasing 117 – Night Haven 99 (Night Shift (USA)) **55** [2017 52: t6m^{6} p6g^{3} t6m^{5} 6g^{2} 6g^{F} 7g May 9] modest maiden: stays 6f: acts on tapeta, best turf form on good going: usually wears tongue tie. *Rae Guest*

CHAMPAGNE REIGN (IRE) 3 b.f. Casamento (IRE) 118 – Reign of Fire (IRE) 69 (Perugino (USA) 84) [2017 –: 8d 9.9g Jun 12] maiden, no form in 2017: in blinkers final start. *J. S. Moore* **–**

CHAMPAGNE RULES 6 gr.g. Aussie Rules (USA) 123 – Garabelle (IRE) (Galileo (IRE) 134) [2017 58: t12.2g 10.2d* 10.2g^{3} 12.1v t10.2s^{5} p10g^{4} t12.4d* p12g* Nov 1] leggy gelding: fair handicapper: won at Nottingham (apprentice) in July, Newcastle (apprentice) in October and Kempton in November: stays 12.5f: acts on polytrack, tapeta, good to firm and heavy going: has worn hood/tongue tie: usually races towards rear. *Sharon Watt* **63 a70**

CHAMPARISI 2 b.f. (Feb 18) Champs Elysees 124 – Parisi (Rahy (USA) 115) [2017 6g^{6} 6g^{3} t7.1g^{3} t8g* t8g^{5} Oct 10] 7,000Y: second foal: half-sister to 1m winner Dreaming of Paris (by Oasis Dream): dam unraced out of half-sister to St Leger winner Mutafaweq: fair performer: won maiden at Newcastle in September: stays 1m: acts on tapeta: front runner/races prominently. *Grant Tuer* **70**

CHAMPION HARBOUR (IRE) 3 b.g. Harbour Watch (IRE) 121 – Drastic Measure 73 (Pivotal 124) [2017 66: 5.1m 8g^{3} t8g* 7.4d^{5} t7.1s^{3} t8g^{4} 6.9g^{3} 7.2d 7.8s^{4} 7.2s^{2} t7.1g Oct 10] fair handicapper: won at Newcastle in May: stays 1m: acts on tapeta, soft and good to firm going: usually races towards rear. *Richard Fahey* **68**

CHAMPS DE REVES 2 b.c. (Apr 15) Champs Elysees 124 – Joyeaux 78 (Mark of Esteem (IRE) 137) [2017 7d 7.1m^{3} 7g^{5} Jul 15] rather unfurnished colt: fair form: best effort when third in minor event at Chepstow (¾ length behind Fortune's Pearl) in July. *Marcus Tregoning* **73**

CHAMPS INBLUE 2 ch.g. (Apr 25) Champs Elysees 124 – Ellablue 63 (Bahamian Bounty 116) [2017 6g^{6} 7g Jul 19] little impact in 2 minor events. *Pat Phelan* **–**

CHANCERY (USA) 9 b.g. Street Cry (IRE) 130 – Follow That Dream 90 (Darshaan 133) [2017 102: 10.3g^{3} 9.8m 11.9s^{5} 11.9g^{2} 11.9s^{4} 11.9m^{6} 11.2s^{3} 11.9m^{2} 11.8d^{4} 14g^{4} 12v t12.4s 10g^{5} t12.4g Oct 19] well-made gelding: fairly useful handicapper: third at Carlisle in June: stays 1½m: acts on polytrack, soft and good to firm going: wears headgear: tried in tongue tie: usually races towards rear. *David O'Meara* **93**

CHANCE TO DREAM (IRE) 3 b.g. Dream Ahead (USA) 133 – Kerry Gal (IRE) (Galileo (IRE) 134) [2017 p8g^{6} p8g^{5} 8.3g^{5} 8.1d* 8g 9.9g^{4} Jul 19] 32,000Y: tall, angular gelding: second foal: half-brother to 1m winner Labyrinth (by Lawman): dam unraced half-sister to dam of very smart miler Al Wukair out of Prix de Diane winner Caerlina: fairly useful performer: won handicap at Windsor in May: stays 8.5f: acts on good to soft going: often races towards rear. *John Best* **81**

CHANDON ELYSEES 4 b.f. Champs Elysees 124 – Upstream 79 (Prince Sabo 123) [2017 71: p12g^{4} p12d Feb 15] close-coupled filly: fair maiden: stays 1¼m: acts on polytrack and good to soft going. *Gary Moore* **62**

CHANDRAYAAN 10 ch.g. Bertolini (USA) 125 – Muffled (USA) 67 (Mizaaya 104) [2017 49: p7g p7d^{5} p7d^{4} p7g p8d^{3} p8d p8g 7m 8s^{5} Jun 6] lengthy gelding: modest handicapper: stays 1m: acts on polytrack, good to firm and good to soft going: wears visor. *John E. Long* **50**

CHANDRESH 4 b.f. Holy Roman Emperor (IRE) 125 – Cloud's End 87 (Dubawi (IRE) 129) [2017 64, a58: p5m^{4} t5.1m^{5} t5.1g^{4} 5.2m^{4} 5m t5.1g^{6} Jun 9] poor maiden: stays 6f: acts on polytrack and tapeta: wears headgear. *Robert Cowell* **48**

CHANGE MAKER 2 ch.c. (Apr 25) Havana Gold (IRE) 118 – Belle Allemande (CAN) (Royal Academy (USA) 130) [2017 8.3g Nov 1] 40,000F, 95,000Y: half-brother to several winners, including smart 1¼m winner Johann Zoffany, later 2m winner in Australia, and useful 1¼m winner Hail (both by Galileo): dam French 11f winner: 16/1, very green when well held in maiden at Nottingham, not knocked about: should do better. *Andrew Balding* **– p**

CHANGING (IRE) 2 b.f. (Jan 17) Intense Focus (USA) 117 – Penny Rose 91 (Danehill Dancer (IRE) 117) [2017 6m 7.1s^{5} 6m p8g Oct 24] £2,400Y: first foal: dam 2-y-o 7f winner who stayed 1¼m out of smart winner up to 1½m Love Everlasting: no form. *Daniel Kubler* **–**

CHANNEL PACKET 3 b.c. Champs Elysees 124 – Etarre (IRE) 69 (Giant's Causeway (USA) 132) [2017 t6g^{5} t7.1m^{4} p10g^{5} 8g 8s 7m^{4} Jul 23] fair maiden: stays 7f: acts on tapeta and good to firm going. *Michael Appleby* **69**

CHANSON DE LA MER (IRE) 2 b.f. (Jan 13) Le Havre (IRE) 124 – Easy To Sing (Johannesburg (USA) 127) [2017 7d Sep 6] 1,500Y: third foal: half-sister to a winner abroad by Kendargent: dam unraced: 12/1, well held in maiden at Lingfield. *David Menuisier* **–**

CHANTECLER 6 b.g. Authorized (IRE) 133 – Snow Goose 111 (Polar Falcon (USA) 126) [2017 79: t12.2m^4 Jan 13] fair handicapper: stays 1½m: acts on polytrack, tapeta, good to firm and good to soft going: has worn hood: in tongue tie last 4 starts: often races freely: fair maiden hurdler. *Neil Mulholland* **72**

CHANT (IRE) 7 b.g. Oratorio (IRE) 128 – Akarita (IRE) 92 (Akarad (FR) 130) [2017 81: 12m^2 t12.4d* Aug 10] strong gelding: fairly useful handicapper: won at Newcastle (by short head from New Society) in August: stays 16.5f: acts on polytrack, tapeta, soft and good to firm going: has worn cheekpieces: front runner/races prominently. *Ann Duffield* **85**

CHANTRESSE (IRE) 2 b.f. (Mar 9) Holy Roman Emperor (IRE) 125 – Woodland Chant (USA) (War Chant (USA) 126) [2017 6s^4 7g 7v^5 Oct 21] €30,000Y: rather narrow filly: fifth foal: half-sister to smart 6f/7f winner Iveagh Gardens (by Mastercraftsman): dam unraced half-sister to Coventry Stakes winner Cd Europe: fair form: best effort when fourth in minor event at Haydock (1¼ lengths behind Pulitzer) on debut: should stay 7f. *K. R. Burke* **67**

CHAPARRACHIK (IRE) 3 b.g. High Chaparral (IRE) 132 – Chocolat Chaud (IRE) 62 (Excellent Art 125) [2017 75p: 10.2g 9.9f^3 11.9d^2 14m^4 p12g^6 p16g^3 12g^6 Aug 26] fair maiden: stays 1½m: acts on polytrack, firm and good to soft going: in hood last 2 starts. *Amanda Perrett* **76**

CHAPARRAL PRINCE (IRE) 2 b.g. (Apr 26) High Chaparral (IRE) 132 – Snow Gretel (IRE) 101 (Green Desert (USA) 127) [2017 7m 8d Oct 27] behind in maiden/minor event. *Charles Hills* **–**

CHAPLIN BAY (IRE) 5 b.g. Fastnet Rock (AUS) 127 – Green Castle (IRE) 101 (Indian Ridge 123) [2017 82: t7.1s* 8m 7.2m^5 7.2g^3 7.2d^2 7m 7m 8s^5 7.4d 7.2g^3 7g 7d 7.4v Sep 26] strong gelding: fairly useful handicapper: won at Newcastle in April: stays 7f: acts on polytrack, tapeta, good to firm and heavy going: has worn headgear, including often in 2017: often races towards rear: temperamental. *Ruth Carr* **83 §**

CHARACTERIZED 3 b.f. Oasis Dream 129 – Hypnology (USA) (Gone West (USA)) [2017 8.1m^5 8g^2 8.1m^3 7.1v^6 7m^4 p7s^3 p8g 8s p8s p10s^4 Dec 7] 130,000Y, 4,000 3-y-o: sturdy filly: fourth foal: half-sister to 1m winner Trust The Wind (by Dansili): dam, unraced, closely related to smart performer up to 1¼m Hathal out of 1000 Guineas winner Sleepytime: fair maiden: stays 1m: acts on good to firm going: often races prominently. *Geoffrey Deacon* **74**

CHARACTER ONESIE (IRE) 5 b.g. Dark Angel (IRE) 113 – Flame Keeper (IRE) (Pivotal 124) [2017 83: 8m^4 8.3m 7.2m^4 8.2d^5 8.5d^2 7.8d^2 8.2g^3 8.5s^6 t8.6g^2 8.5m^6 8d^3 p8g Oct 5] fairly useful handicapper: second at Beverley in June: stays 9f: acts on tapeta, soft and good to firm going: tried in headgear: sometimes slowly away. *Richard Fahey* **81**

CHARACTER WITNESS (IRE) 2 b.g. (Mar 15) Casamento (IRE) 118 – She's A Character 91 (Invincible Spirit (IRE) 121) [2017 6g^6 6s^4 t6d^3 7m^5 8d^6 Oct 27] €28,000F, £38,000Y: rangy gelding: second foal: half-brother to 7f/8.6f winner (including at 2 yrs) Jumping Jack (by Sir Prancealot): dam, winner up to 9f (2-y-o 6f winner), half-sister to useful performer up to 13f Celtic Spirit: fairly useful maiden: third in minor event at Newcastle in August: stays 1m: acts on tapeta and soft going. *Roger Varian* **80**

CHARAVA (IRE) 5 br.g. Captain Marvelous (IRE) 114 – Sweet Compliance 71 (Safawan 118) [2017 69, a56: 7.5f 7.2m 7.2s Jul 10] fair at best, no form in 2017: usually wears headgear: tried in tongue tie. *Patrick Holmes* **–**

CHARISMATIC MAN (IRE) 4 b.g. Dalakhani (IRE) 133 – On Fair Stage (IRE) 103 (Sadler's Wells (USA) 132) [2017 93: t16.5g^4 t13.9m* p16d^2 11.9m^5 Jun 17] useful handicapper: won at Wolverhampton in March: second at Kempton (1¼ lengths behind King Calypso) in May: stays 16.5f: acts on polytrack and tapeta: often races prominently: sold 60,000 gns in July, sent to Saudi Arabia. *Ralph Beckett* **97**

CHARLES FOX 2 b.g. (Mar 28) Power 117 – Jouet 71 (Reprimand 122) [2017 6.1v 6.1g^6 Aug 18] good-topped gelding: half-brother to several winners, including smart 6f (including at 2 yrs) winner Rising Shadow (by Efisio) and useful 1m-1¼m winner Night Cru (by Night Shift): dam maiden (placed at 7f/1m): modest form when sixth in maiden on second of 2 starts at Nottingham: capable of better. *James Fanshawe* **63 p**

CHARLES MOLSON 6 b.g. Monsieur Bond (IRE) 120 – Arculinge 64 (Paris House 123) [2017 108: p7g^3 7f 7m^5 6.1d^5 p7g^5 p8g^6 t7.1d* Dec 16] strong, lengthy gelding: useful handicapper: won at Newcastle (by ½ length from Heaven's Guest) in December: stays 7f: acts on polytrack, tapeta, good to firm and heavy going: has worn headgear: often travels strongly. *Patrick Chamings* **100 a108**

CHARLESTON BELLE 3 b.f. Danehill Dancer (IRE) 117 – Blanche Dubawi (IRE) 108 **70**
(Dubawi (IRE) 129) [2017 6.1m^{2} 6g^{5} 6d^{4} 6s^{5} t6d^{3} Nov 10] first foal: dam 6f winner (including at 2 yrs): fair maiden: will stay 7f: acts on good to firm going: in blinkers final start: often races towards rear. *Giles Bravery*

CHARLIE ALPHA (IRE) 3 b.g. Dandy Man (IRE) 123 – Maroussies Rock (Rock of **–**
Gibraltar (IRE) 133) [2017 p6g 7m^{6} p6g Sep 5] well held in 3 maidens. *Roger Ingram*

CHARLIE CHAPLIN (GER) 3 b.g. Lope de Vega (IRE) 125 – Campina (Oasis Dream **–**
129) [2017 60: 7m p10g p10s Dec 15] maiden, no form in 2017: has worn headgear, including final start: tried in tongue tie: often races towards rear. *Robert Eddery*

CHARLIE LAD 5 b.g. Myboycharlie (IRE) 118 – Night Owl 73 (Night Shift (USA)) **50**
[2017 62: f5g^{4} p5m^{5} f5g Feb 2] modest handicapper: stays 6f: acts on polytrack, fibresand and soft going: has worn blinkers. *Daniel Loughnane*

CHARLIE RASCAL (FR) 3 b.g. Myboycharlie (IRE) 118 – Rascafria (USA) **58**
(Johannesburg (USA) 127) [2017 66: t9.5m^{5} 12m^{6} p12g^{6} Jun 3] modest maiden: should stay beyond 7f: acts on polytrack: has joined Neil Mulholland. *Peter Chapple-Hyam*

CHARLIE'S DREAMER 3 ch.f. Equiano (FR) 127 – Enford Princess 89 (Pivotal 124) **68**
[2017 7m^{6} 6.1m^{2} 7d^{6} 5d^{3} 6s^{3} t6g^{5} f7.1g^{2} f6.1g^{5} f8.1g^{6} Dec 22] sixth foal: half-sister to 3 winners, including 1½m winners Percys Princess and Young Tom (both by Sir Percy): dam 2-y-o 6f winner who stayed 1m: fair maiden: stays 7f: acts on fibresand, tapeta, soft and good to firm going: front runner/races prominently. *Michael Appleby*

CHARLIE VICTOR 3 b.g. Myboycharlie (IRE) 118 – Audrey Brown (Mind Games **52**
121) [2017 –: t5.1g^{4} 6.1m 5v 5.7d Aug 19] modest maiden: left Clive Cox after second start: best effort at 5f. *Malcolm Saunders*

CHARMING GUEST (IRE) 2 b.f. (Mar 16) Kodiac 112 – Na Zdorovie 84 (Cockney **– p**
Rebel (IRE) 127) [2017 5m May 12] €137,000F, 120,000Y: second foal: half-sister to French 2-y-o 6.5f winner Mad Rose (by Royal Applause): dam, 2-y-o 7f winner, closely related to smart US Grade 2 1¼m/1½m winner Slim Shadey: 16/1, badly needed experience when well held in maiden at Ascot: should do better. *Mick Channon*

CHARMING LOZA 3 b.f. Lawman (FR) 121 – Ellbeedee (IRE) 84 (Dalakhani (IRE) **71**
133) [2017 8m t8.6g^{6} 9.9d p12g Jun 22] sturdy filly: second foal: half-sister to 2-y-o 6f winner Bournemouth Belle (by Canford Cliffs): dam, 1¼m winner, half-sister to US Grade 2 1m/9f winner Uncharted Haven: fair form: best effort at 8.5f. *Charlie Fellowes*

CHARMING POWER (IRE) 2 b.g. (Mar 11) Power 117 – Always Attractive (IRE) **–**
(King's Best (USA) 132) [2017 7m 7.4s 10v Oct 9] no form in minor events. *Ann Duffield*

CHARNOCK RICHARD 2 b.c. (Mar 29) Mayson 124 – Velvet Band 73 (Verglas (IRE) **76**
118) [2017 5g 5s^{2} 5d^{3} 5.1d^{2} 5d^{4} 6d 6d^{3} 5d^{4} 5s^{5} p7.5f p6.5g Dec 27] good-quartered colt: fair maiden: left David Brown after ninth start: best form at 5f: acts on soft going: tried in headgear: front runner/races prominently. *P. & F. Monfort, France*

CHARTBREAKER (FR) 6 b.g. Shirocco (GER) 129 – Caucasienne (FR) 79 (Galileo **86**
(IRE) 134) [2017 89: p16d p15.8g^{5} 16m* 16g 15.4d^{2} 15.4d* Oct 10] good-topped gelding: fairly useful performer: won handicap at Goodwood (by ¾ length from Medburn Cutler) in May and claimer at Saint-Cloud in October: left Chris Gordon after fourth start: stays 2m: acts on good to firm and heavy going: often wears headgear. *Frau M. Rotering, Germany*

CHARTBUSTER (IRE) 3 b.g. Mastercraftsman (IRE) 129 – Gift Dancer (Imperial **78**
Dancer 123) [2017 10g^{4} 11.9m^{5} 10.2d^{5} t10.2g^{3} Oct 20] fair form: should stay beyond 1¼m. *Julie Camacho*

CHATBURN (IRE) 2 b.c. (Mar 7) Dream Ahead (USA) 133 – Mistress of Rome 79 **83**
(Holy Roman Emperor (IRE) 125) [2017 5m 6m^{2} 5g* 5d^{4} 5.2g* 5g^{3} 6d p5d^{5} 6g Oct 7] £12,000Y: good-topped colt: first foal: dam, winner up to 1m (2-y-o 6f winner) who stayed 1½m, closely related to smart winner up to 10.4f Arlequin: fairly useful performer: won minor events at Redcar in May and Yarmouth (by neck from Fyre Cay) in July: stays 6f: acts on good to firm and good to soft going. *David O'Meara*

CHATEZ (IRE) 6 b.g. Dandy Man (IRE) 123 – Glory Days (GER) 59 (Tiger Hill (IRE) **109**
127) [2017 8.2d^{2} Oct 30] rather leggy gelding: smart handicapper: second at Leicester (½ length behind Fire Brigade) on sole outing on Flat in 2017: stays 8.5f: acts on heavy going. *Alan King*

CHATOYER (FR) 3 ch.c. Siyouni (FR) 122 – Polyegos (IRE) (Hawk Wing (USA) 136) **80**
[2017 p6g^{4} 5.7m^{4} 6d 6m^{3} t6.1g^{3} 7.1g* p7g 6d 7d^{4} p6.5g Oct 23] €55,000Y: third foal: half-brother to French 10.5f winner Strategic Way (by Strategic Prince): dam 5f-7f winner in

France/Greece: fairly useful performer: won handicap at Chepstow in August: left Richard Hannon after next start: stays 7f: acts on tapeta, good to firm and good to soft going: wears hood: usually races freely: sold 2,500 gns in October. *J. S. Moore*

CHATTING (IRE) 3 b.f. Intikhab (USA) 135 – Kesh Kumay (IRE) 76 (Danehill (USA) 126) [2017 p7g* May 24] €20,000Y, £14,000 2-y-o: smallish filly: half-sister to 3 winners, including useful Italian winner up to 1½m Keshiro (2-y-o 1m/10.5f winner, by Shirocco): dam 2m winner: 7/1, overcame inexperience when won maiden at Kempton (by head from Wigan Warrior) on debut, leading final strides: should improve. *Hugo Palmer* **62 p**

CHAUCER'S TALE 3 b.g. Poet's Voice 126 – Grand Slam Maria (FR) 62 (Anabaa (USA) 130) [2017 66: 10m^6 t7.1d^3 f7.1g^2 t7.1s* p10s^2 Dec 7] fair handicapper: won at Newcastle (apprentice) in November: stays 1¼m: acts on all-weather: often in tongue tie in 2017: front runner/races prominently. *Michael Easterby* **74**

CHAUVELIN 6 b.g. Sir Percy 129 – Enforce (USA) 109 (Kalanisi (IRE) 132) [2017 61: 12.1m^6 14g 14m^6 12.1m^3 11.2g^2 12.1d 9.9m^5 t12.4g^4 11.5g^5 Oct 16] modest handicapper: stays 1¾m: acts on polytrack, tapeta and good to firm going: wears headgear: tried in tongue tie: usually races towards rear. *Nigel Tinkler* **58**

CHEAPO 4 ch.g. Aqlaam 125 – Shy Appeal (IRE) 71 (Barathea (IRE) 127) [2017 p8m Feb 25] 100/1, well held in maiden at Lingfield. *Brett Johnson* **–**

CHE BELLA (IRE) 2 gr.f. (Mar 23) Holy Roman Emperor (IRE) 125 – Satwa Ruby (FR) 96 (Verglas (IRE) 118) [2017 5m^4 5m^5 5s 7.2d^3 8v* 8v^4 7s^2 8d^2 Oct 27] £90,000Y: first foal: dam, French 1¼m-1½m winner, half-sister to Criterium de Saint-Cloud winner/Prix du Jockey Club runner-up Morandi (by Holy Roman Emperor): fairly useful performer: won nursery at Thirsk in September: second in similar event at Doncaster in October: stays 1m: acts on heavy going. *Keith Dalgleish* **89**

CHEBSEY BEAU 7 b.g. Multiplex 114 – Chebsey Belle (IRE) (Karinga Bay 116) [2017 79: 14g 11.9s^6 15g* 14m* 17.1v 16v^3 Oct 16] fair handicapper: won at Ayr in August and Musselburgh in September: stays 15f: acts on soft and good to firm going: tried in cheekpieces: usually races prominently: also won over fences in July. *John Quinn* **79**

CHECK 'EM TUESDAY (IRE) 4 b.f. Kodiac 112 – Wait Watcher (IRE) 96 (Fath (USA) 116) [2017 74: p8g^5 t8d^4 7f p8d p7g p8g Dec 21] sturdy filly: fair handicapper at best, regressed in 2017: left Daniel Loughnane after fourth start: stays 8.5f: acts on polytrack, tapeta and good to soft going. *Christian Delcros, Ireland* **63**

CHEEKY KIKI (IRE) 2 b.f. (Mar 20) Makfi 130 – Manoeuvre (IRE) (Galileo (IRE) 134) [2017 t8g^4 t8g Oct 10] sixth foal: half-sister to 12.4f winner Pereira (by Tiger Hill): dam unraced half-sister to very smart sprinter Astrophysical Jet: modest form: better effort when fourth in maiden at Newcastle (6¾ lengths behind Champarisi) in September. *Giles Bravery* **52**

CHEEKY RASCAL (IRE) 2 b.c. (Mar 15) Most Improved (IRE) 119 – Bessie Lou (IRE) 76 (Montjeu (IRE) 137) [2017 6d 7f^3 7g^5 7v^2 7g^3 9m Oct 25] neat colt: fair maiden: stays 7f: acts on any turf going: often races prominently. *Richard Hannon* **77**

CHEENI 5 ch.m. Orientor 118 – Class Wan 74 (Safawan 118) [2017 49: 5m^2 5m^3 6m^2 5g^2 5s^3 5g^4 6g* 5d^5 6g^3 5s^4 6v^5 5s^6 Sep 16] modest handicapper: won at Ayr in July: stays 6f: acts on soft and good to firm going: usually wears headgear. *Jim Goldie* **55**

CHEERFILLY (IRE) 3 br.f. Excelebration (IRE) 133 – Classic Remark (IRE) 101 (Dr Fong (USA) 128) [2017 59: 7d^3 7.2g^2 8f^3 7g* 7g* 8v^4 t8.6g Oct 7] fairly useful performer: won maiden and handicap (by 2¾ lengths from Bahamian Bird) at Leicester in July: stays 7f: acts on tapeta and good to soft going: in cheekpieces last 4 starts: often races prominently. *Tom Dascombe* **90**

CHEERS BUDDY (IRE) 9 b.g. Acclamation 118 – Victorian Dancer (IRE) 60 (Groom Dancer (USA) 128) [2017 57, a50: 7.2d^5 p8g Aug 18] modest handicapper, below form both starts in 2017: has form at 1¼m, races over shorter nowadays: acts on polytrack, firm and soft going: has worn headgear: often races towards rear. *L. Smyth, Ireland* **43**

CHEERS MONSIEUR 2 ch.g. (Mar 8) Monsieur Bond (IRE) 120 – Cheers For Thea (IRE) 95 (Distant Music (USA) 126) [2017 t6g May 19] 66/1, well held in minor event at Newcastle. *Tim Easterby* **–**

CHEESEANDPICKLE 2 ch.f. (Feb 11) Helmet (AUS) 127 – Branston Gem 59 (So Factual (USA) 120) [2017 t5s* p7g Oct 11] £26,000Y: half-sister to several winners, including 2-y-o 5f winner Plata O Plomo (by Paco Boy) and 7f winner Wear 'Em Out Wilf (by Bahamian Bounty): dam maiden: fair form when won minor event at Newcastle (by 1¼ lengths from Thrifty) in April: well held when next seen 6 months later. *Keith Dalgleish* **70**

CHEF UNITED 2 b.f. (Apr 17) Swiss Spirit 117 – Eurolinka (IRE) (Tirol 127) [2017 6g t7.1g t6s 8s t6g Oct 19] 800F, 3,000Y: half-sister to several winners, including useful 2-y-o 7f/1m winner Art Master (by Peintre Celebre), later successful abroad, and 2m/17f winner Faraway Lady (by Alzao): dam unraced: no form. *Roger Fell* **–**

CHELABELLA 4 b.f. Medicean 128 – Agrippina 99 (Timeless Times (USA) 99) [2017 68: p8d^{5} p10g^{6} t8.6g 7m* May 3] lengthy filly: fair handicapper: won at Yarmouth in May: stays 8.5f: acts on polytrack, tapeta and good to firm going: wears headgear. *Derek Shaw* **65**

CHELSEA CORSAGE (IRE) 3 b.f. Teofilo (IRE) 126 – Galley (Zamindar (USA) 116) [2017 70: p7d t9.5m f12.1g^{6} Nov 28] maiden, fair form at best when trained in Ireland at 2 yrs: stays 7f: acts on polytrack. *Paul D'Arcy* **66**

CHELSEA LAD (IRE) 4 b.g. Clodovil (IRE) 116 – Yali (IRE) 95 (Orpen (USA) 116) [2017 106: 8m^{pu} 7.9d^{2} 8.1g^{3} 7.9d 9d^{4} 10.3g^{6} 11.9s^{2} Nov 11] lengthy gelding: useful handicapper: second in November Handicap at Doncaster (1¼ lengths behind Saunter): stays 1½m: acts on soft going: tried in hood. *Martyn Meade* **109**

CHELSEA'S BOY (IRE) 4 gr.g. Rip Van Winkle (IRE) 134 – St Roch (IRE) (Danehill (USA) 126) [2017 85: p16g^{3} 16d p16g^{5} 11.6d^{6} 17.2s 11.2d 14.1v Sep 13] tall, good-topped gelding: fairly useful handicapper: third at Kempton in April: left Ralph Beckett after fourth start: stays 2m: acts on polytrack and good to firm going: tried in blinkers: one to treat with caution. *Donald McCain* **81 §**

CHELWOOD GATE (IRE) 7 gr.g. Aussie Rules (USA) 123 – Jusoor (USA) (El Prado (IRE) 119) [2017 79: t7.1m^{6} p7g p7g p8g* 7.6g^{2} t7.1s p10s 10m^{2} 10m^{6} t9.5g^{2} 10.2g t8.6g t9.5m^{6} p10m t7.2g^{5} p8g^{3} Dec 30] smallish gelding: fair performer: won seller at Lingfield in May: left Patrick Chamings after fifth start: stays 1¼m: acts on polytrack, tapeta and good to firm going: wears headgear: often races towards rear. *Conor Dore* **76**

CHEMICAL CHARGE (IRE) 5 ch.h. Sea The Stars (IRE) 140 – Jakonda (USA) (Kingmambo (USA) 125) [2017 116: 12g* 12m^{2} 12s^{6} 12m^{3} 12.5g* p12g* 12s^{6} 11.9g^{4} Dec 10] sturdy horse: very smart performer: won minor events at Doncaster in April and Musselburgh in July, and September Stakes at Kempton (by head from Scarlet Dragon): also in frame in John Porter Stakes at Newbury (neck second to Muntahaa), Hardwicke Stakes at Royal Ascot (1¾ lengths third behind Idaho) and Hong Kong Vase at Sha Tin (2¾ lengths fourth to Highland Reel): stays 12.5f: acts on polytrack, good to firm and good to soft going: tried in headgear. *Ralph Beckett* **120**

CHERBOURG (FR) 5 b.g. Dunkerque (FR) 114 – Seduisante (FR) (Anabaa (USA) 130) [2017 p8g^{2} p8d^{6} p8g p8g Dec 31] useful for H-A. Pantall in France prior to 2017: second in handicap at Lingfield in January: went wrong way after: left Ralph Beckett after third start: stays 1m: acts on polytrack, good to firm and good to soft going. *Dr Jon Scargill* **87**

toteplacepot September Stakes, Kempton—Chemical Charge gets up close home to beat Scarlet Dragon (hood), Wild Hacked (striped cap) and Danehill Kodiac (star on cap)

CHERISHED (IRE) 3 b.f. Kodiac 112 – Marasem 86 (Cadeaux Genereux 131) [2017 **68**
6.1m^5 6.1m^3 7.1g^2 7.1s^6 6.1g^6 Oct 9] close-coupled filly: sister to useful winner up to 6f Alutiq (2-y-o 5f winner), closely related to 2-y-o 8.6f winner Maraca (by Danehill Dancer) and half-sister to 3 winners, including very smart 6f (including at 2 yrs) winner Magical Memory (by Zebedee): dam 7f winner: fair maiden: stays 7f: acts on good to firm going. *Geoffrey Deacon*

CHERRY KOOL 4 b.f. Kheleyf (USA) 116 – Pretty Kool 68 (Inchinor 119) [2017 81: **66**
p5m 5.3g^4 5g 5m 5m 5.2d* Jul 6] neat filly: fair handicapper: won at Yarmouth in July: best form at 5f: acts on polytrack and good to soft going: tried in hood/tongue tie: has joined G. O'Leary, Ireland. *Stuart Williams*

CHERRY LEYF 3 b.f. Kheleyf (USA) 116 – Pretty Kool 68 (Inchinor 119) [2017 60p: **54**
p5g p7g p5g^5 5m^4 7d 5.2g^5 p6d 5.3g p5g p7g Oct 17] sturdy filly: modest maiden: in headgear last 2 starts: usually wears tongue tie. *Stuart Williams*

CHERRY OAK (IRE) 2 b.f. (Apr 3) Society Rock (IRE) 126 – Blue Holly (IRE) 83 **61**
(Blues Traveller (IRE) 119) [2017 5g 5m^3 5v^5 t5.1g^5 t5g^4 Nov 15] €25,000 2-y-o: half-sister to several winners, including very smart winner up to 9.5f (best as a sprinter) Monsieur Chevalier (2-y-o 5f winner, by Chevalier) and smart winner up to 7f Outback Traveller (2-y-o 6f winner, by Bushranger): dam winner up to 6f (2-y-o 5f winner): modest maiden: raced only at 5f: acts on tapeta. *Ben Haslam*

CHERUBIC 2 gr.f. (Mar 3) Dark Angel (IRE) 113 – Doula (USA) (Gone West (USA)) **46**
[2017 5m 6s 6.1m p8g^4 t8s Sep 19] €85,000Y: sturdy filly: half-sister to several winners, including smart/moody winner up to 1¼m Humungous (2-y-o 7f winner, by Giant's Causeway), useful 10.7f winner Amazing Beauty (by Galileo) and useful 1¼m-1½m winner Hajaam (by Invincible Spirit): dam US 1m winner: poor maiden: in blinkers last 2 starts: often starts slowly/races towards rear: has joined David Evans. *Charles Hills*

CHESHAM ROSE (IRE) 4 gr.f. Mastercraftsman (IRE) 129 – Rose's Destination (IRE) **–**
(Dubai Destination (USA) 127) [2017 –: f12g Jan 5] little form: in headgear last 2 starts: tried in tongue tie. *Dave Roberts*

CHESSMAN (IRE) 3 b.c. Acclamation 118 – Dulcian (IRE) (Shamardal (USA) 129) **105 p**
[2017 88P: 7g^2 7.2f^2 7m Jun 21] good-topped colt: useful form: neck second in handicaps at Newbury (to Bacchus) and Haydock (behind Silent Echo): seventh to Le Brivido in Jersey Stakes at Royal Ascot only subsequent outing: raced only at 7f: remains open to improvement. *John Gosden*

CHESS MOVE (IRE) 2 b.g. (Apr 14) Kodiac 112 – Azia (IRE) 71 (Desert Story (IRE) **76 +**
115) [2017 p6g^6 6g* 6g Sep 3] compact gelding: fair form: won minor event at Epsom (by 1¾ lengths from Diamond Express) in July, despite missing break: stiff task at Veliefendi next time: raced only at 6f. *George Baker*

CHESTER DEELYTE (IRE) 9 b.m. Desert Style (IRE) 121 – Bakewell Tart (IRE) 92 **–**
(Tagula (IRE) 116) [2017 45: p7g Jan 11] lengthy mare: poor handicapper: stays 7f: acts on polytrack, tapeta, firm and good to soft going: wears headgear. *Lisa Williamson*

CHESTER STREET 4 b.g. Invincible Spirit (IRE) 121 – Expressive 81 (Falbrav (IRE) **95**
133) [2017 99: p8g p8m p8g^4 Oct 14] useful-looking gelding: useful handicapper: stays 8.5f: acts on polytrack and good to firm going: often wears headgear. *Roger Charlton*

CHESTNUT FIRE 5 ch.g. Showcasing 117 – Music In Exile (USA) 58 (Diesis 133) [2017 **94**
87, a100: p8g^4 p8g^4 p8g* p8g^4 7m t8s^3 t8s p7g p8s p8g^2 Dec 20] fairly useful performer: won claimer at Dundalk in February on final start for M. Halford: stays 1m: acts on polytrack, good to firm and good to soft going: often races towards rear. *Daniel Loughnane*

CHESTNUT STORM (IRE) 4 ch.f. Rip Van Winkle (IRE) 134 – Always Attractive **67**
(IRE) (King's Best (USA) 132) [2017 69: f16g^2 t16.5m^6 t13.9g^4 11.4d p15.8g Nov 21] fair handicapper, regressed in 2017: stays 16.5f: acts on fibresand, tapeta, firm and good to soft going: tried in cheekpieces. *Brian Barr*

CHETAN 5 b.g. Alfred Nobel (IRE) 110 – Island Music (IRE) 74 (Mujahid (USA) 125) **70**
[2017 81: p6g^6 p6g^6 p7g^6 6m^4 5.7f^4 6m^4 7g 6m 6.1m^5 6g p8s^3 7m^6 p7g* p8g* p8d* p8g **a81**
p8g p7g^3 t7.2g Nov 25] fairly useful handicapper: completed hat-trick at Kempton (2) and Chelmsford (by 2½ lengths from Prince Jai) in September: stays 1m: acts on polytrack, firm and soft going: has worn headgear: wears tongue tie: front runner/races prominently. *Charlie Wallis*

CHEVAL BLANCHE (USA) 3 gr.f. Stay Thirsty (USA) 123 – Primrose Hill (USA) (Giant's Causeway (USA) 132) [2017 72: p8g* t8d^2 7m* 8m 7g^6 7d 8f^6 Nov 5] useful-looking filly: fairly useful performer: won handicaps at Lingfield (apprentice) in March and Salisbury in April: left Michael Bell before final start (ran well): stays 1m: acts on polytrack and firm going: often leads. *Ben D. A. Cecil, USA* **94**

CHEVALGRIS 7 gr.g. Verglas (IRE) 118 – Danzelline 83 (Danzero (AUS)) [2017 t16.5g 18d^6 Aug 24] fair handicapper, below form only 2 starts on Flat since 2015: stays 17f: acts on good to firm and heavy going: tried in headgear: maiden hurdler. *Dai Burchell* **64**

CHEVALIER DU LAC (IRE) 3 b.g. Sir Prancealot (IRE) 111 – Crimson Sunrise (IRE) 85 (Holy Roman Emperor (IRE) 125) [2017 74: t6.1g 5g^6 7d Jul 28] neat gelding: fair at best, no form in 2017: usually races towards rear. *Conor Dore* **–**

CHEVALLIER 5 b.g. Invincible Spirit (IRE) 121 – Magical Romance (IRE) 110 (Barathea (IRE) 127) [2017 99: t8g^3 p8m^2 p8g* p8m* p8f p8d 8.5m^5 p7m^2 p8s Dec 7] smallish gelding: useful handicapper: won at Lingfield in January and February: stays 1m: acts on polytrack, tapeta, good to firm and good to soft going: in cheekpieces last 2 starts. *Archie Watson* **101**

CHIARA LUNA (USA) 2 br.f. (Mar 16) War Front (USA) 119 – Princess Highway (USA) 119 (Street Cry (IRE) 130) [2017 6g* Aug 17] first foal: dam, 1¼m-1½m (Ribblesdale Stakes) winner, half-sister to smart 1¾m-2m winner Royal Diamond: 4/5, won maiden at Leopardstown on debut by ¾ length from Modern Love, edging ahead 1f out: open to significant improvement. *D. K. Weld, Ireland* **89 P**

CHICA DE LA NOCHE 3 b.f. Teofilo (IRE) 126 – Welsh Cake 76 (Fantastic Light (USA) 134) [2017 76: p8g^5 7f 7m 7d^3 6g* 6m^{ur} Aug 28] leggy filly: fair handicapper: won at Salisbury in August: stays 7f: acts on polytrack: tried in cheekpieces (unseated at start). *Simon Dow* **79**

CHICAGO SCHOOL (IRE) 4 ch.g. Approve (IRE) 112 – Ms Sasha Malia (IRE) (Verglas (IRE) 118) [2017 64: p5g p6g p6g^2 t6g p6g* p6g^6 p5g* Dec 15] fair handicapper: won at Dundalk in October and December: stays 7f: acts on polytrack and tapeta: wears headgear/tongue tie. *Anthony McCann, Ireland* **69**

CHICAGO STAR 3 b.f. Exceed And Excel (AUS) 126 – Librettista (AUS) 81 (Elusive Quality (USA)) [2017 70p: 6g 6g^6 6.9g^4 7m^5 7.1m* 8.1m 6g p7g^5 p8g^5 p7g Oct 5] close-coupled filly: fair handicapper: won at Chepstow in June: stays 7f: acts on polytrack and good to firm going. *Mick Channon* **76**

CHICA LA HABANA (IRE) 2 ch.f. (Apr 4) Havana Gold (IRE) 118 – Esloob (USA) 106 (Diesis 133) [2017 5d* 5m 6d Sep 30] €4,000Y, £64,000 2-y-o: strong, lengthy filly: half-sister to winner up to 9.5f Huroof (2-y-o 7f winner) and useful French 1m winner Halaqa (both by Pivotal): dam, winner up to 1¼m (2-y-o 7f winner), out of Yorkshire Oaks winner Roseate Tern: fairly useful form: won minor event at Beverley (by ¾ length from Maggies Angel) in June: stiff task both starts after: sold 70,000 gns in December. *Robert Cowell* **87**

CHICKENFORTEA (IRE) 3 gr.g. Clodovil (IRE) 116 – Kardyls Hope (IRE) 90 (Fath (USA) 116) [2017 64: 6g 7m^3 5m 6m* 6d^3 6g 5.1g 7s* 6s^6 Oct 31] fair handicapper: won at Catterick in July and September: stays 7f: acts on soft and good to firm going: usually leads. *Eric Alston* **78**

CHICKPEA 2 b.f. (Jan 28) Rip Van Winkle (IRE) 134 – Tahlia Ree (IRE) 77 (Acclamation 118) [2017 6g 7g^6 7m Aug 28] 27,000Y: sturdy filly: second foal: half-sister to useful 2-y-o 6f winner Lost At Sea (by Dutch Art): dam, 6f winner who stayed 1m, half-sister to smart 1m-1½m winner Julienas: no form in minor events/maiden. *Michael Bell* **–**

CHICLET (IRE) 6 b.m. Dandy Man (IRE) 123 – Springfort (IRE) 79 (Captain Rio 122) [2017 103: t5g p5g^5 5m Jul 29] strong mare: useful handicapper, well below best all 3 starts in 2017: best at 5f: acts on polytrack, good to firm and good to soft going: wears hood: usually leads. *Tracey Collins, Ireland* **80**

CHIEF CRAFTSMAN 3 gr.g. Mastercraftsman (IRE) 129 – Eurolink Raindance (IRE) 109 (Alzao (USA) 117) [2017 10.2m^6 10.2g^2 11.9m^2 11.9m^3 12s Jul 28] 37,000F, 125,000Y: seventh foal: half-brother to 3 winners, including useful 7f winner House (by Elusive Quality) and winner up to 14.6f Maastricht (2-y-o 8.5f winner, by Tiger Hill): dam 6f (at 2 yrs) to 9f (in USA) winner: fairly useful maiden: second at Nottingham in May: stays 1½m: acts on good to firm going: usually races prominently, often travels strongly: has joined Paul Nicholls. *Luca Cumani* **82**

CHIEF IRONSIDE 2 b.c. (Feb 23) Lawman (FR) 121 – Moment of Time 97 (Rainbow Quest (USA) 134) [2017 7g Nov 3] 155,000Y: second foal: dam, maiden (stayed 1½m), closely related to Time Ahead and half-sister to Time Away, both placed in Prix de Diane: 10/1, some encouragement when eighth in minor event at Newmarket (6¾ lengths behind Maghaweer) on debut, not knocked about: open to improvement. *William Jarvis* **67 p**

CHIEF JUSTICE 2 b.g. (Apr 14) Acclamation 118 – Freedom Pass (USA) 61 (Gulch (USA)) [2017 6s^2 7d^{ur} t6s^2 7g^2 Oct 14] 62,000Y, 150,000 2-y-o: useful-looking gelding: fourth foal: half-brother to French 7f winners Love Freedom (by Sir Percy) and St Andrew's Day (at 2 yrs, by Showcasing): dam, maiden (stayed 7f), half-sister to smart 2-y-o 5f/6f winner Parliament Square (by Acclamation): fairly useful form: second in minor events all 3 completed starts: stays 7f: temperament under suspicion. *Richard Fahey* **81**

CHIEFOFCHIEFS 4 b.g. Royal Applause 124 – Danvers 63 (Cape Cross (IRE) 129) [2017 84p: 10m 10g* 8m^2 p8g* 7.9m* 8d^3 10m^4 p8g 9d^4 Sep 29] good-topped gelding: useful performer: won maiden at Windsor in May, and handicaps at Kempton in June and York in July: fourth in handicap at Newmarket final start: stays 1¼m: acts on polytrack, good to firm and good to soft going: in cheekpieces last 5 starts: often races towards rear. *Charlie Fellowes* **97**

CHIKOKO TRAIL 2 ch.c. (Apr 28) Sixties Icon 125 – Search Party 78 (Rainbow Quest (USA) 134) [2017 7g 8.3g Nov 1] showed a bit in maidens. *Mick Channon* **63**

CHILDESPLAY 6 ch.m. Byron 117 – Parting Gift (Cadeaux Genereux 131) [2017 87: p7g^3 p7g^6 t7.1g^4 p6g^3 6d^6 7m^4 p7d^3 7v* 7s^2 Aug 8] smallish, plain mare: fairly useful handicapper: won at Newbury (by 5 lengths from Lucky Louie) in July: best up to 7f: acts on polytrack, tapeta, good to firm and heavy going: has worn cheekpieces: front runner/races prominently. *Heather Main* **89**

CHILEAN 2 b.c. (Jan 31) Iffraaj 127 – Childa (IRE) (Duke of Marmalade (IRE) 132) [2017 7d^4 p8g* 8.2s* 8d^6 Oct 28] 130,000Y: first foal: dam, French 9f/1¼m winner (including at 2 yrs), stayed 1½m: smart form: won minor event at Chelmsford (by 1¼ lengths from Kind Act) in August and listed race at Haydock (by 3½ lengths from Learn By Heart) in September: will stay beyond 1m. *Martyn Meade* **111**

CHILLALA (IRE) 2 b.f. (Feb 1) Requinto (IRE) 109 – Positive Step (IRE) 74 (Footstepsinthesand 120) [2017 6m^5 6m 7g^6 6d^3 Oct 30] €38,000F, 125,000Y: well-made filly: third foal: sister to useful 2-y-o 6f winner Broken Stones: dam, maiden (best effort at 11f), half-sister to useful 2-y-o 7f-9f winner Derivative: fair form in minor events: wears hood. *Harry Dunlop* **67**

CHILLI JAM 4 b.g. Mastercraftsman (IRE) 129 – Wosaita 70 (Generous (IRE) 139) [2017 59: 10.2g^4 10.2d^3 p10g* t12.4g^5 p12g^3 p10g^3 Oct 12] fair handicapper: won at Chelmsford in August: stays 1½m: acts on polytrack and good to soft going: often wears cheekpieces. *Ed de Giles* **66**

CHILLILILLI 3 ch.f. Monsieur Bond (IRE) 120 – Stunning Icon (Dr Fong (USA) 128) [2017 –: f7g f8g f8d t5.1g t6g^6 6m t5.1g t5.1m f5g^3 f5g f5g^5 Dec 21] poor maiden: stays 6f: acts on fibresand and tapeta: usually wears headgear: usually races prominently. *Michael Appleby* **50**

CHINA EXCELS 10 b.g. Exceed And Excel (AUS) 126 – China Beauty 64 (Slip Anchor 136) [2017 73: t5.1g^5 5.1m^4 Apr 22] fair handicapper: effective at 5f/6f: acts on fibresand, tapeta, and good to firm going: tried in headgear: front runner/races prominently. *Mandy Rowland* **67**

CHINESE SPIRIT (IRE) 3 gr.g. Clodovil (IRE) 116 – In The Ribbons 88 (In The Wings 128) [2017 –: 9.1g^5 9.2s^4 11.1d^4 7.2d 8d* 11.1d^4 7.2s 9v* t8g Oct 20] fair handicapper: won at Ayr in August and October: stays 11f: acts on heavy going. *R. Mike Smith* **79**

CHINGACHGOOK 2 b.c. (Feb 4) Al Kazeem 128 – Natty Bumppo (IRE) (Kheleyf (USA) 116) [2017 t7.2g^3 p7g^4 Dec 28] first foal: dam unraced half-sister to very smart sprinter Astrophysical Jet: fair form: better effort when fourth in minor event at Lingfield (1½ lengths behind Maverick Officer) in December: remains with potential. *Richard Fahey* **76 p**

CHING CHING LOR (IRE) 3 b.g. Elzaam (AUS) 115 – Art Critic (USA) (Fusaichi Pegasus (USA) 130) [2017 –: 7m 7g 7.2m* t8.6g* 8s^6 8d 9.9m 8m Sep 8] fair handicapper: won at Ayr and Wolverhampton in May: should stay beyond 8.5f: acts on tapeta and good to firm going: in headgear last 2 starts: sold £800, sent to Sweden. *Declan Carroll* **72**

CHINOISERIES 4 b.f. Archipenko (USA) 127 – Robe Chinoise 103 (Robellino (USA) 127) [2017 12f 11.8s Jun 10] leggy filly: fairly useful 1m winner at 2 yrs, very lightly raced since: tried in hood. *David Simcock* **–**

CHIONODOXA 3 ch.f. Haafhd 129 – Bollin Nellie 98 (Rock Hopper 124) [2017 –: 7m 8m 12.1m5 12.1m 16.1d 12.5m 11.2v5 Sep 18] modest maiden: stays 11f: acts on heavy going: tried in cheekpieces: often races prominently. *Tim Easterby* **51**

CHIP OR PELLET 4 b.g. Hellvelyn 118 – Concentration (IRE) (Mind Games 121) [2017 63: 5.1m6 6g t6s6 5m6 5.5f 5m 5g4 t5g* t5.1m p6g4 Dec 12] modest handicapper: won at Newcastle in July: left Nigel Tinkler after sixth start, Paul Midgley after eighth: stays 6f: acts on polytrack, tapeta, good to firm and good to soft going: has worn headgear. *Mark Pattinson* **50 a63**

CHIPPENHAM (IRE) 3 ch.c. Casamento (IRE) 118 – Ohiyesa (IRE) 98 (Noverre (USA) 125) [2017 t8.6g t9.5m3 p11g2 9.9m4 a8.9f Dec 8] fair maiden: left John Gosden after fourth start: stays 11f: acts on polytrack, tapeta and good to firm going: in blinkers last 4 outings. *Ms B. Deutrom, UAE* **69**

CHIPPING (IRE) 3 b.g. Dark Angel (IRE) 113 – Bean Uasal (IRE) 94 (Oasis Dream 129) [2017 78p: 6g 7v 6g2 6m 7m6 7.2g Aug 12] fair handicapper: stays 6f: acts on tapeta and good to soft going: in cheekpieces last 3 starts. *Michael Dods* **78**

CHISWICK BEY (IRE) 9 b.g. Elusive City (USA) 117 – Victoria Lodge (IRE) (Grand Lodge (USA) 125) [2017 78: t8g3 t8d* t8d 8g2 8m5 8g3 7.8v5 7.4m* 8.3g3 8s3 7.4g2 7.4m3 7d 8.5v 8g5 Oct 16] compact gelding: fair performer: won handicap at Newcastle in February and seller at Beverley (dead-heated) in July: stays 8.5f: acts on polytrack, tapeta, soft and good to firm going: has worn headgear/tongue tie: has joined Jacqueline Coward. *Richard Fahey* **78**

CHIVERS (IRE) 6 b.g. Duke of Marmalade (IRE) 132 – Thara (USA) (Hennessy (USA) 122) [2017 f14g4 p14g Apr 27] fairly useful handicapper in 2015, below best only 2 starts on Flat since: stays 1¾m: acts on good to firm and heavy going: usually wears headgear: in tongue tie last 2 starts: maiden hurdler. *Daniel Steele* **65**

CHIZZ DE BIZ (IRE) 2 b.f. (Jan 26) Zebedee 113 – Chizzler (IRE) (Baltic King 120) [2017 6g5 p6g6 t6.1m6 p5s Nov 16] €3,000F, £3,500Y, £20,000 2-y-o: first foal: dam unraced: modest form: in cheekpieces final start. *Daniel Kubler* **57**

CHLOELLIE 2 b.f. (Mar 15) Delegator 125 – Caramelita 79 (Deportivo 116) [2017 6g 6m 6d6 Oct 30] rather leggy filly: first foal: dam 5f-7f winner: no form in minor events. *J. R. Jenkins* **–**

CHLORIS 2 b.f. (Mar 21) Dansili 127 – Primevere (IRE) 113 (Singspiel (IRE) 133) [2017 t8.6g6 Nov 29] second foal: dam winner up to 1¼m (2-y-o 1m winner): 8/1, considerate introduction when sixth in minor event at Wolverhampton (5½ lengths behind Ghanimah) in November, slowly away: capable of better. *John Gosden* **65 p**

CHOCOLATE ACCOUNT (USA) 3 gr.f. Exchange Rate (USA) 111 – Western Vision (USA) (Gone West (USA)) [2017 10.2s t9.5g5 8d p8g5 Sep 7] $70,000F, 52,000Y: sister to minor US winner, closely related to smart 7f-8.3f winner The Rectifier (by Langfuhr) and half-sister to 3 winners: dam unraced half-sister to US Grade 2 1m winner Rahys' Appeal: little impact in maidens/handicap: sold 1,500 gns, sent to Italy. *Ed Dunlop* **–**

CHOCOLATE BOX (IRE) 3 b.c. Zoffany (IRE) 121 – Chocolate Mauk (USA) (Cozzene (USA)) [2017 71: 10.2g 11.9d 12g2 13.3g5 12g2 p14g* t16.3g5 t12.2g3 Oct 27] good-topped colt: fairly useful handicapper: won at Chelmsford in September: stays 16.5f: acts on polytrack, tapeta and good to soft going: wears cheekpieces: sold to join Daniel Loughnane 48,000 gns in November. *Luca Cumani* **89**

CHOCOLAT NOIR (IRE) 4 b.f. Yeats (IRE) 128 – Valrhona (IRE) 93 (Spectrum (IRE) 126) [2017 80p: 10s 13g3 12g2 13g6 13.1s5 12.1s Oct 31] third foal: sister to French 1½m winner Seven Kingdoms and half-sister to a winner abroad by Medicean: dam 1¼m/1½m winner: fairly useful maiden: third in handicap at Navan in April: left John Patrick Murtagh after fifth start: stays 13f: acts on soft going: tried in cheekpieces. *Martin Todhunter* **85**

CHOICE ENCOUNTER 2 ch.g. (Feb 5) Choisir (AUS) 126 – Gimme Some Lovin (IRE) 70 (Desert Style (IRE) 121) [2017 5.1m4 5.2m2 5.1g2 5.1m4 p5g2 p6s2 Dec 7] good-topped gelding: fair maiden: stays 6f: acts on polytrack and good to firm going. *Michael Bell* **79**

CHOOKIE DUNEDIN 2 b.c. (Apr 8) Epaulette (AUS) 126 – Lady of Windsor (IRE) 73 (Woods of Windsor (USA)) [2017 6m* 6f 6m 6.5g Sep 14] close-coupled colt: half-brother to several winners, including smart 6f-9.5f winner Chookie Royale (by Monsieur Bond) and winner up to 1¾m Chookie Hamilton (2-y-o 1m/8.6f winner, by Compton Place): dam ungenuine 7f/1m winner: fairly useful form: won minor event at Ayr in May: should stay 7f. *Keith Dalgleish* **91**

CHOOKIE VALENTINE 4 b.g. Approve (IRE) 112 – Lady of Windsor (IRE) 73 (Woods of Windsor (USA)) [2017 45: 7g 9.2d 11.2v 8s t8.6g Dec 13] little form: wore cheekpieces in 2017. *Keith Dalgleish* –

CHOOSE 3 b.f. Dansili 127 – Insinuate (USA) 99 (Mr Prospector (USA)) [2017 p10g p8g^{5} Nov 6] sister to smart winner up to 1¼m Convey (2-y-o 7f winner), closely related to very smart 7f/1m winner Stronghold (by Danehill) and half-sister to several winners: dam 1m winner: modest form: better effort when fifth in maiden at Kempton in November. *Ralph Beckett* **62**

CHOOSEY (IRE) 2 ch.g. (Apr 1) Choisir (AUS) 126 – Petit Chou (IRE) 73 (Captain Rio 122) [2017 6g 5s^{3} 5d^{4} Aug 19] fair form: best effort when third in minor event at Beverley (2½ lengths behind Arcavallo) in August. *Henry Candy* **72**

CHORAL CLAN (IRE) 6 b.g. Oratorio (IRE) 128 – Campbellite (Desert Prince (IRE) 130) [2017 82: p8g^{2} p12d* p12g^{6} 10m p11d 10g p7g p8g^{5} p8g^{2} p11g^{3} p10g^{3} p10s^{2} t8s* p10g^{2} Dec 21] close-coupled gelding: fairly useful performer: won handicap at Kempton in January and claimer at Newcastle in November: left Philip Mitchell after second start: stays 1½m: acts on polytrack, tapeta and firm going: has worn headgear/tongue tie. *Brendan Powell* **80**

CHORAL MUSIC 2 b.f. (Mar 8) Equiano (FR) 127 – Gospel Music (Beat Hollow 126) [2017 6m 6g 5.1d Oct 23] strong filly: second foal: dam unraced half-sister to smart 6f winner Bounty Box: no form in minor events. *Jonathan Portman* –

CHOSEN CHARACTER (IRE) 9 b.g. Choisir (AUS) 126 – Out of Thanks (IRE) 89 (Sadler's Wells (USA) 132) [2017 86: 8d^{2} 8m^{4} 8.5d^{2} 7.6s^{6} 8g^{2} 7v 8.2v t8.6g t7.2d^{6} Dec 26] workmanlike gelding: fairly useful handicapper: second at Epsom (apprentice) in July: stays 8.5f: acts on any turf going: wears headgear/tongue tie: often races prominently. *Tom Dascombe* **86**

CHOSEN WORLD 3 b.g. Intikhab (USA) 135 – Panoptic 89 (Dubawi (IRE) 129) [2017 7s^{6} 7d^{3} 7d^{5} Aug 21] fair form: third in maiden at Redcar in August. *Julie Camacho* **69**

CHOUGH 3 b.f. Dutch Art 126 – Port Charlotte 77 (Oasis Dream 129) [2017 62: p8g^{5} p8g^{6} p10g^{3} t12.2g^{4} 8d^{2} 8.3d^{6} 8g^{2} 8s^{2} p8d p7g* p8g^{3} t7.2g Nov 7] leggy filly: fair handicapper: won at Kempton in October: stays 8.5f: acts on polytrack and good to soft going: tried in blinkers: usually races prominently. *Hughie Morrison* **71**

CHOUMICHA 3 b.f. Paco Boy (IRE) 129 – Galicuix (Galileo (IRE) 134) [2017 89p: 7m Apr 19] compact filly: fairly useful at 2 yrs, well held in Nell Gwyn Stakes at Newmarket in April: stays 1m: has joined Roger Charlton. *Hugo Palmer* –

CHRISELLAINE (IRE) 2 b.f. (Jan 26) Iffraaj 127 – Janicellaine (IRE) 84 (Beat Hollow 126) [2017 7.2d^{4} t7.1g* Sep 12] first foal: dam, 7f (at 2 yrs) and 1m (in Canada) winner, half-sister to smart winner up to 9f Very Special and Fillies' Mile/Breeders' Cup Juvenile Fillies Turf winner Chriselliam: fair form: won maiden at Newcastle (by 2 lengths from Sharp Reminder) in September: will go on improving. *Charles Hills* **79 p**

CHRISTMAS NIGHT 2 ch.g. (Mar 21) Compton Place 125 – Night Haven 99 (Night Shift (USA)) [2017 5m 6m^{4} 6g^{2} t5.1g^{2} t6.1g 5s^{6} t6g Oct 19] modest maiden: stays 6f: acts on tapeta and good to firm going. *Ollie Pears* **64**

CHRISTOPHER WOOD (IRE) 2 b.c. (Mar 7) Fast Company (IRE) 126 – Surf The Web (IRE) (Ela-Mana-Mou 132) [2017 7d* 7g^{4} 7.4v^{2} Sep 17] 48,000 2-y-o: strong, compact colt: half-brother to several winners, including useful 9f/1¼m winner Legal Waves (by Lawman) and 10.7f winner Kilshannig (by Galileo): dam maiden half-sister to US Grade 3 1m winner Mister Fire Eyes: fairly useful form: won maiden at Salisbury (by ¾ length from Lifeboat) in June: will be suited by 1m. *Ralph Beckett* **85**

CHUNKYFUNKYMONKEY 3 ch.g. Kheleyf (USA) 116 – Give Me High Five 72 (Dubawi (IRE) 129) [2017 7g^{6} 7.1g 8m p10g^{5} 9.9d^{4} 9.9m^{6} 9.9m^{2} 10.1m* 10m^{4} 9.1g* 11.4g 10.1d^{3} 9d Aug 30] angular gelding: fair handicapper: won at Yarmouth in June and July: stays 1¼m: acts on good to firm and good to soft going: has worn headgear: has joined Peter Fahey, Ireland. *John Ryan* **75**

CHUPALLA 3 b.f. Helmet (AUS) 127 – Dubai Sunrise (USA) (Seeking The Gold (USA)) [2017 93: t5.1m^{4} p5g^{5} p6g^{5} 8g 7.4m* 6.1m^{3} p7d 6s Sep 16] well-made filly: fairly useful handicapper: won at Beverley (by ¾ length from Dan Troop) in July: left Mark Johnston before next start: stays 7.5f: acts on polytrack and good to firm going: tried in visor: often leads: not straightforward. *David Evans* **89**

CHURCHILL (IRE) 3 b.c. Galileo (IRE) 134 – Meow (IRE) 108 (Storm Cat (USA)) **126**
[2017 120p: 8m* 8d* 8f[4] 10.3d[2] 10d 8s[3] a10f Nov 4]

The first meeting of the Irish turf season at the end of March took place at Naas after the traditional opening fixture was transferred from the Curragh where a major stands refurbishment was under way. As usual, the occasion itself was arguably of more interest for the opportunity to check on the winter progress of the string at Ballydoyle as Aidan O'Brien—who saddled the winners of both three-year-old maidens on the Naas card—brought eighty horses to be exercised. Among them was the winter favourite for the Two Thousand Guineas and the Derby, Churchill, who had won his last five races as a juvenile, including both the National Stakes at the Curragh and the Dewhurst at Newmarket. After Churchill had been worked over seven furlongs with a group including fellow Guineas hope the unbeaten Caravaggio, Aidan O'Brien announced that Churchill would be sent to Newmarket without a warm-up (none of his seven previous Two Thousand Guineas winners had had a preparatory race), while Caravaggio would be running at Dundalk to 'test his Newmarket credentials'. Caravaggio was sent sprinting in the end but, even when fluid plans for him included the Guineas, Churchill was still a top-priced 6/4 for the Two Thousand Guineas and he was the subject of most of the questions directed at O'Brien at Naas. It is not always easy to get to the substance of O'Brien's public pronouncements about the plans for the good horses in his care—he himself has described the process as 'trying to say something without saying anything'—but he was very clear about Churchill. 'We haven't thought beyond the Guineas,' he said at Naas. 'He was a mature horse last year and you are always worried about whether they will be as good at three.'

Reporting that everything had gone well with Churchill's preparation over the winter, O'Brien was no doubt harking back to the very disappointing performances as a three-year-old of his champion two-year-old of 2015, Air Force Blue, who failed to reach the frame in any of his four races at three, including when starting 5/4-on in the Two Thousand Guineas in which he beat only one home. Like Churchill, Air Force Blue had won both the National Stakes and the Dewhurst, and he completed his campaign with a Timeform rating that was higher than any afforded to O'Brien's previous champion two-year-olds. There has never been any guarantee that one year's champion two-year-old will go on to be the best three-year-old, especially when the honour of being the highest-rated three-year-old is sometimes earned by relatively late developers who were not among the top two-year-olds. A performance, or performances, right at the end of the season can clinch things, as in the latest one when the sprinter Battaash and the middle-distance performer Cracksman tied for that title after tip-top performances on Arc weekend and British Champions' Day respectively. The season for a top three-year-old now extends further into the year than ever, long after the traditional, once dominant classic races have taken place. In that respect, it often seems that the old saying about the Two Thousand Guineas being the last important race of the two-year-old season probably has more than a grain of truth in it. It came as no surprise that the Two Thousand Guineas was regarded by connections as 'D-Day for Churchill' (the naming of the horse provided ample scope for the headline-writers' art).

Racehorses of 2016 described Churchill as strong and compact, though not an imposing sort in appearance. His trainer was at pains to correct any such impression, describing Churchill after his Naas workout as 'a fine, big powerful colt, as physically imposing as any we've had at Ballydoyle.' On paddock inspection at Newmarket before the Two Thousand Guineas, it seemed that our description of Churchill might not really have done him justice. He was more burly than we had remembered him (if lacking that bit of quality), the type to always carry condition and even appear on the gross side. He couldn't have been made fitter than he was on Guineas day—though he spoiled his appearance by starting to sweat before he came into the paddock last—and he took the eye on the way to the start, albeit only being allowed to go to post steadily. A good mover, Churchill showed a fluent action reminiscent of the last Two Thousand Guineas winner sent out from Ballydoyle,

Gleneagles (both are by Galileo who was himself a fine mover). There were other physical similarities between Churchill and Gleneagles, both being heavy-topped, though Churchill was noticeably the taller and heavier of the pair.

The trait of seemingly just doing enough, once put in front in his races as a two-year-old, also evoked memories of Gleneagles, while the two had also been bred on similar lines, being out of Storm Cat mares (the dam of Churchill was a speedy type while the dam of Gleneagles probably stayed a mile and a quarter). In the end, the racing records of Gleneagles and Churchill weren't that dissimilar either. Both were successful in the Tyros Stakes at Leopardstown and the Futurity Stakes at the Curragh, as well as in the National Stakes, as two-year-olds, and both went on to complete the Anglo-Irish Guineas double, as had two of the previous O'Brien-trained Two Thousand Guineas winners, Rock of Gibraltar and Henrythenavigator. Gleneagles went one better than Churchill by emulating Rock of Gibraltar and Henrythenavigator in the St James's Palace Stakes to land what is sometimes called the 'triple crown' for the three-year-old milers. Churchill started odds on at Royal Ascot but managed only fourth and, as with Gleneagles after the St James's Palace, he didn't win again, both eventually following in the footsteps of their sire by ending their career well beaten in the Breeders' Cup Classic on their only start on dirt.

There were only ten runners in the Qipco Two Thousand Guineas, the smallest field for the race in nearly thirty years (Doyoun beat eight rivals in 1988). The creation of the Commonwealth Cup at Royal Ascot, and of a programme of pattern races for three-year-old sprinters leading up to it, has created a lucrative alternative for sprint-bred three-year-olds who might previously have followed the classic trail in the first part of the season, in the absence of much else. Caravaggio, the Dewhurst third Blue Point and the Mill Reef winner Harry Angel were among the previous year's leading two-year-olds who were trained for the Commonwealth Cup, rather than initially for the Two Thousand Guineas. While Churchill went to Newmarket very much the finished article, and was the only runner in the line-up who hadn't had a preparatory race, his better-fancied opponents lacked his race experience and their preparation included a run beforehand in one of the recognised trials.

First up had been Andre Fabre-trained Al Wukair, a winner in listed company on the second of two outings as a juvenile. He put himself in the Guineas picture with a last-to-first victory in the Prix Djebel at Maisons-Laffitte, beating the Prix Jean-Luc Lagardere winner National Defense to maintain an unbeaten record. The two other unbeaten colts in the Two Thousand Guineas line-up had won the two most important British trials, Barney Roy impressive in the Greenham Stakes at Newbury and Eminent similarly so in the Craven at Newmarket where he beat the Champagne Stakes and Racing Post Trophy winner Rivet. For both Barney Roy and Eminent, the Two Thousand Guineas was only their third race, and it came just a fortnight after their exertions in the trials. They started second and third favourite, at 7/2 and 5/1, behind solid 6/4-shot Churchill, with Al Wukair (11/2) and the Greenham second Dream Castle (who hadn't raced at two) the only other runners at single-figure odds.

The race itself for the Guineas wasn't entirely satisfactory because of the relative lack of pace, resulting from Churchill's stablemate Lancaster Bomber (second in the Dewhurst) cutting across to the stands rail and setting just a steady gallop, with Churchill and the third Ballydoyle runner Spirit of Valor close up. With tactics putting the emphasis on speed, and on the importance of being handy, Churchill kept on well against the stands rail, without being able to extend his advantage, after quickening into the lead a furlong out. He won by a length and a neck from Barney Roy and Al Wukair, both challenging towards the centre of the course and seemingly inconvenienced to some degree by the way the race developed, Barney Roy meeting trouble to boot as he made his run and also appearing to stumble in the Dip, while Al Wukair found himself arguably too far back to land a real blow after being dropped out. Lancaster Bomber, who led until Churchill took over, completed the frame, ahead of Dream Castle, Eminent and 100/1-shot Top Score, Eminent being unable to quicken with Churchill and looking ready for a step

Qipco 2000 Guineas Stakes, Newmarket—Churchill gives trainer Aidan O'Brien a record eighth victory in the first British classic of the season; Barney Roy (third left), who had stumbled going into the Dip, and French raider Al Wukair (left) stay on strongly to fill the places

up in trip. A little over three lengths covered the first seven home in what was an up to standard, if not vintage, Two Thousand Guineas in which, because of the pace, a few of the also rans were almost certainly flattered to finish so close.

Churchill's victory in the Two Thousand Guineas marked another milestone in the career of Aidan O'Brien who became the first trainer to win the race eight times (six of his winners won Group 1s as two-year-olds). He also became the most successful trainer in the five British classics since 1900, Churchill's victory taking him to twenty-six, one more than Henry Cecil, and by the end of the season the total had reached twenty-nine with the successes of Winter in the One Thousand Guineas, Wings of Eagles in the Derby and Capri in the St Leger (O'Brien also won four of the five classics in Ireland where his total now stands at thirty-nine). The victory of Wings of Eagles at Epsom enabled O'Brien to match the six victories in the race of Vincent O'Brien, his unrelated namesake who also trained at Ballydoyle. Ballydoyle operated on a much smaller scale in Vincent O'Brien's day and Aidan O'Brien long since overtook his predecessor's outstanding classic totals, although he still has some way to go to wrest the top spot from the nineteenth-century Malton trainer John Scott, the 'Wizard of the North', who trained forty British classic winners between 1827 and 1863, including seven in the Two Thousand Guineas, eight in the Oaks and sixteen in the St Leger. Aidan O'Brien is still only forty-eight and it seems only a matter of time before Scott's record falls to him.

The only Two Thousand Guineas runners to re-oppose Churchill in the Tattersalls Irish Two Thousand Guineas were his stablemates Lancaster Bomber and Spirit of Valor, with the only challenger from overseas being the Saeed bin Suroor-trained Thunder Snow, on a retrieval mission after a puzzling, bucking-bronco display in the Kentucky Derby. The Irish Guineas was run at the Curragh in front of a reported attendance of only 2,500, the decision to keep the Irish classics at the Curragh, while considerable redevelopment work went on, being widely criticised for its lack of regard for the comfort of racegoers, though leading owners and trainers maintained that there was no other suitable venue. Thunder Snow, winner of the Criterium International at two and back on turf after becoming a dual classic winner himself (UAE 2000 Guineas and Derby on the dirt at Meydan) before his Kentucky Derby debacle, started second favourite in the field of six behind Churchill who was sent off at 9/4-on.

In what was no more than an average renewal, Churchill was held up this time (on going softened by incessant rain) and, firmly ridden, he produced a good turn of foot at the end of a soundly-run race, set up again by Lancaster Bomber, to win by two and a half lengths from Thunder Snow with third favourite Irishcorrespondent four and a half lengths further back in third. Churchill was the eleventh Irish Two Thousand Guineas winner saddled by his trainer who has now run four of his Two Thousand Guineas winners in the race, with 2006 winner George Washington, beaten at 7/4-on, the only one not to complete the double. Eight had previously done the double before Churchill, beginning with Right Tack in 1969 and continuing with Don't Forget Me (1987), Tirol (1990) and Rodrigo di Triano (1992) before Cockney Rebel (2007) was successful between Rock of Gibraltar (2002) and Henrythenavigator (2008). The double is not attempted so often as it might be, but those defeated in the attempt—High Top, Nebbiolo, To-Agori-Mou, Lomond, Island Sands, George Washington and Galileo Gold (four of them at odds on)—illustrate that the task does not always prove so straightforward as it might appear at the time.

Only two of Aidan O'Brien's Two Thousand Guineas winners have gone on to contest the Derby, those being King of Kings, who finished last of fifteen and wasn't seen again, and Camelot who went on to success at Epsom before being beaten in the St Leger, that particular defeat—still controversial five years on (as touched on in Capri's essay)—denying Camelot the triple crown and O'Brien the unique feat of saddling all five of Britain's classics in the same season. Gleneagles, supplemented for £8,000 at the second entry stage in April for the Derby before he ran in the Guineas, was briefly in the mix for Epsom before being ruled out, while Henrythenavigator was spoken of as a Derby challenger in his year until there became a prospect of softish going, even though he had shown all the hallmarks of being purely and simply a miler (he went on to get a mile and a quarter well when a good second in the Breeders' Cup Classic in one of the editions run on pro-ride, an artificial surface, rather than the traditional dirt). George Washington was another entered for the Derby at the late-entry stage in early-April before he ran in the Guineas, but there was little talk of the Derby for him after he had won at Newmarket.

Churchill remained generally at around 5/1 in the Derby ante-post market after winning at Newmarket with Aidan O'Brien fending off questions about Epsom by reiterating that the race was a month away and no quick decisions would be made—'The lads [Coolmore partners] make all the decisions about the horses, and he could go any route they want him to.' O'Brien did sound reasonably confident that Churchill would get the Derby trip saying 'He's very relaxed and would probably get as far as you'd want him to get and he has speed as well … horses by Galileo very rarely lack stamina.' For jockey Ryan Moore, Churchill had 'filled me with confidence through the race and is a very straightforward horse, I think he'll keep on performing.' His response to a question about Churchill's Derby prospects was 'I doubt there'd be a better ride in the race.' It wasn't long, though, before Churchill was ruled out of the Derby in favour of his successful crack at the Anglo-Irish Guineas double, which turned out to be the pinnacle of his racing career, with his winning sequence standing at seven after the Irish Guineas (his only defeat in eight starts had come on his debut).

Tattersalls Irish 2000 Guineas, the Curragh—
Churchill overcomes concerns about the testing conditions to complete a Guineas double, beating UAE Derby winner Thunder Snow (left) and Irishcorrespondent (hoops on cap)

Churchill ran five times after the Irish Two Thousand Guineas but didn't add to his victories. He started at 2/1-on for the St James's Palace Stakes at Royal Ascot but didn't give his true running, beaten some way from home when finishing fourth behind Barney Roy, Thunder Snow and his stablemate Lancaster Bomber, all of whom he had already beaten as a three-year-old. Churchill reportedly 'didn't eat up' in the evening after the St James's Palace but his stable could come up with no obvious reason for his poor performance ('He should like fast ground,' said O'Brien, 'it was a baking hot day so maybe it was all the heat, though I don't know'). Goodwood's richly-endowed Sussex Stakes was the next planned port of call but a downpour of biblical proportions turned the track into a morass and Churchill was withdrawn twenty-five minutes before the race, with conditions still deteriorating. O'Brien later felt that the aborted Sussex challenge might have had an effect on the rest of Churchill's campaign ('He's a gross horse that you need to keep working and he missed four days because of Goodwood which he couldn't really afford to do,' said O'Brien).

Churchill was stepped up in trip in the International at York, on his first outing since Royal Ascot, and he started 5/2 favourite in a field of seven which included Barney Roy, who had since gone down very narrowly in a tight finish in the Eclipse to the four-year-old Ulysses (also in the International line-up). The Derby runner-up Cliffs of Moher, a stablemate of Churchill, was also in the field at York. Churchill bounced back to form, maintaining a good challenge over the last two furlongs and being beaten two lengths by Ulysses, with Barney Roy a neck behind Churchill in third, the first three clear of Cliffs of Moher and the rest. Cliffs of Moher and Churchill went on to represent Ballydoyle in the Irish Champion Stakes on the prestigious Irish Champions' Weekend in September. Starting odds on in a field of ten at Leopardstown, Churchill might as well have stayed in his box. He became trapped in a pocket early in the straight, just as the race began to unfold, and Moore couldn't extricate him, eventually having to accept the situation and allow Churchill to come home in his own time in seventh behind Decorated Knight who led home a British one, two, three.

Churchill ran next on British Champions' Day at Ascot, not in the Champion Stakes itself (Highland Reel joined Cliffs of Moher in that) but dropped back to a mile in a very good field for the Queen Elizabeth II Stakes. Churchill came a good third behind Persuasive and Ribchester, doing best of the three-year-olds in a race which didn't, in the end, quite match up to the sum of its parts, with too many of the runners failing to run to their best under the softest conditions some had encountered. Churchill's final appearance came—as it had for so many of his stable's top performers over the years—in the Breeders' Cup Classic over ten furlongs on dirt, the climax of the Breeders' Cup meeting in November. The challenge of taking on America's best dirt performers in their own back yard was again underlined by Churchill's below-form seventh of eleven behind the impressive Gun Runner at Del Mar (Gleneagles had trailed in a long way behind when last of eight to Triple Crown winner American Pharoah two years earlier, while Galileo himself cut no ice in the race in his day). Ballydoyle has yet to win the Breeders' Cup Classic, having gone close in the dirt editions with Giant's Causeway in 2000 and Declaration of War in 2013.

The big, strong Churchill is the third winner of the Two Thousand Guineas for his sire Galileo (following Frankel and Gleneagles) and his fourth in the Irish Two Thousand (following Roderic O'Connor, Magician and Gleneagles). Rather like his own sire, fourteen-times champion Sadler's Wells, who had three Two Thousand Guineas winners and two winners of the Irish Two Thousand, Galileo still tends to be thought of as mainly a sire of middle-distance performers and stayers. In fact, Galileo has sired winners of all six of the Guineas races in Britain, Ireland and France, and, also taking account of the lengthy list of Group 1-winning two-year-olds he has had, he must be regarded as a particularly versatile, as well as the best, stallion of his era. Churchill was one of three dual European classic winners sired by him in the latest season, Churchill's stablemates Winter and Capri completing classic doubles in the One Thousand Guineas and Irish One Thousand,

Mr M. Tabor, Mr D. Smith & Mrs John Magnier's "Churchill"

and in the Irish Derby and the (English) St Leger, respectively. Order of St George gave Galileo his seventh classic victory of the year (four at a mile, one at a mile and a half and two at a mile and three quarters) when romping home in the Irish St Leger.

Churchill (IRE) (b.c. 2014)	Galileo (IRE) (b 1998)	Sadler's Wells (b 1981)	Northern Dancer
			Fairy Bridge
		Urban Sea (ch 1989)	Miswaki
			Allegretta
	Meow (IRE) (b 2008)	Storm Cat (b or br 1983)	Storm Bird
			Terlingua
		Airwave (b 2000)	Air Express
			Kangra Valley

Churchill has something in common with three of Galileo's four other winners in the Two Thousand Guineas and the Irish Two Thousand Guineas, in that they are out of sprinters, or, to be strictly accurate in the case of Roderic O'Connor, out of a listed winner over seven. Magician, who also won the Breeders' Cup Turf over a mile and a half as a three-year-old, is out of the six-furlong winner Absolutelyfabulous, a daughter of the July Cup winner Mozart and a granddaughter of Danehill, who is also the sire of Roderic O'Connor's dam Secret Garden. Another daughter of Danehill, Kind, is the dam of Frankel. Kind won a maiden over seven furlongs before gaining five more wins at five and six including two in listed company. Winter, by the way, is also out of a Danehill-line mare. The dam of Gleneagles, You'resothrilling, a sister to Giant's Causeway, was a useful two-year-old for Aidan O'Brien, winning the Cherry Hinton, but she showed as a three-year-old, when far from disgraced in eighth in the Prix de l'Opera (she also finished a good fourth in the Matron Stakes), that she probably stayed a mile and a quarter.

Because of coughing, Galileo himself ran just once as a two-year-old, winning a maiden in sparkling style in late-October, and Derby winner Ruler of The World wasn't seen at all, but it is much more common to see Ballydoyle's potential classic horses having a full education on the racecourse in their first season. Toughness is built into their make-up, with the expectation that they will already be battle-hardened as three-year-olds, particularly in the early classics in which their experience often stands them in good stead against those from some other yards who regularly have classic runners. Churchill made his racecourse debut when third in a six-furlong maiden at the Curragh's Guineas meeting (a race that had been won the previous year by Air Force Blue). Royal Ascot was the target for Churchill on the second of his six starts as a two-year-old and he began his seven-race winning sequence with a driven-out victory in the seven-furlong Chesham Stakes. Churchill's dam Meow was second in the Queen Mary at Royal Ascot for the Coolmore partners and ran five times as a two-year-old for David Wachman, winning twice (including a listed event) with all her outings coming at five furlongs. She was a speedy and precocious daughter of Storm Cat (whose fee was 500,000 dollars when she was conceived). Storm Cat is the sire of You'resothrilling, also the dam of two sisters to Gleneagles, the Irish One Thousand Guineas winner Marvellous and the Moyglare and Jean-Luc Lagardere winner Happily. Another of Galileo's four Irish One Thousand Guineas winners, Misty For Me, is also out of a Storm Cat mare, as is the latest Irish Champion Stakes winner Decorated Knight who is by Galileo out of a sister to You'resothrilling.

Meow is a daughter of the 2002 Cheveley Park winner Airwave who won the Temple Stakes as a three-year-old when she was also placed in the Golden Jubilee, the July Cup and the Sprint Cup. Airwave was bought by the Coolmore partners out of Henry Candy's yard for 550,000 guineas after her four-year-old days (she won the Ridgewood Pearl Stakes over a mile for Aidan O'Brien at five before being retired to stud). Airwave's dam Kangra Valley was a modest two-year-old five-furlong winner and is also the dam of the ill-fated Nunthorpe Stakes winner Jwala. This is a family that has been noted for producing sprinters over the years, Kangra Valley's dam and grandam, both of whom bred eight winners, also being five-furlong performers, her grandam Spinner being a half-sister to the prolific Clantime who won nine times at the minimum trip. Most of these ancestors of Churchill, by the way, were not in the *General Stud Book*, the family only gaining entry in the 'eighties (when Kangra Valley's dam Thorner Lane was admitted) after years of being included in the *Non-Thoroughbred Register*. As well as producing Meow to Storm Cat, Airwave has herself produced winners to Galileo, including Aloof, a smart winner at up to eleven furlongs, who was sold by Coolmore, carrying a filly by War Front, for a sale-record 3,600,000 dollars at Keeneland in November 2014. Since acquiring Airwave, the Coolmore partners have added further leading sprinting mares—including the likes of Margot Did, Tiggy Wiggy, Mecca's Angel and, in the latest season, Marsha and Quiet Reflection—to their broodmare band, specifically to be mated with Galileo. Churchill's dam Meow has become a perennial visitor to Galileo, the latest offspring to reach the racecourse being Churchill's two-year-old sister Clemmie who also has an essay in this Annual. Clemmie ran five times, completing a hat-trick in the Cheveley Park Stakes at Newmarket on her final outing and looking every inch another classic winner in waiting for Ballydoyle. The next offspring of Meow in the pipeline is a colt by Galileo who will be in training with Aidan O'Brien in the next season.

Galileo is not in the first flush of youth but he seems to have plenty of life left in him yet, having covered 178 mares in 2017, following 158 in 2016 and 181 in 2015. As happened with his own sire Sadler's Wells, he is moving gradually into the role of patriarch among the Coolmore sires, with the retirement of Churchill—who starts at a fee of €35,000—and Highland Reel bringing the number of sons of Galileo on the Flat roster at Coolmore to six (they join Australia, Gleneagles, Ruler of The World and The Gurkha). Churchill stayed ten and a half furlongs, acted on soft and good to firm going, and often raced prominently. He was a good winner of the Two Thousand Guineas, if not an outstanding one, and his two-year-old achievements—including a Royal Ascot win and two Group 1s—will add to his appeal to commercial breeders who look certain to give him strong support in an era when the fashion in the stallion market is for sires likely to produce winning two-year-olds and sprinter-milers. *Aidan O'Brien, Ireland*

CIAOADIOSIMDONE (IRE) 3 ch.f. Arcano (IRE) 122 – Croque Madame (IRE) (Galileo (IRE) 134) [2017 8d 8.1m^{5} 8d^{6} t8.6g* Nov 20] €50,000F, 5,500 3-y-o: close-coupled filly: first foal: dam unraced half-sister to 1000 Guineas/Oaks winner Kazzia: fairly useful form: won maiden at Wolverhampton in November: best effort when seventh in listed event at Newmarket on debut: will stay at least 1¼m. *John Ryan* **90**

CIARAS COOKIE (IRE) 5 b.m. Approve (IRE) 112 – Preach (IRE) (Danehill Dancer (IRE) 117) [2017 56: f5g t7.2g 6.1g Aug 15] lengthy mare: modest at best, has lost her form: usually wears hood: has worn tongue tie, including last 2 starts: sometimes slowly away. *Mandy Rowland* **–**

CIEL ROUGE 3 b.f. Champs Elysees 124 – Artistic Blue (USA) 109 (Diesis 133) [2017 52: p7m p11g 8m Apr 25] medium-sized filly: maiden, no form in 2017: tried in visor: in tongue tie last 2 starts. *Charlie Wallis* **–**

CINCUENTA PASOS (IRE) 6 ch.g. Footstepsinthesand 120 – Sweet Nicole 54 (Okawango (USA) 115) [2017 95: p6g 6.1d 7.1v Jun 10] tall gelding: fairly useful handicapper, below best in 2017: stays 7f: acts on polytrack, good to firm and heavy going: has worn headgear/tongue tie: sometimes slowly away, often races towards rear. *Joseph Tuite* **78**

CINQUE PORT 3 ch.g. Compton Place 125 – Jump Ship 74 (Night Shift (USA)) [2017 76: p6d* p7g^{5} 8m 6.1g Jul 20] fair performer: won maiden at Chelmsford (by 1¾ lengths from Rag Tatter) in March: stayed 7f: acted on polytrack: usually raced close up: dead. *Richard Hughes* **76**

CIRCLING VULTURES 3 ch.g. Monsieur Bond (IRE) 120 – Knavesmire (IRE) 91 (One Cool Cat (USA) 123) [2017 t8g^{5} 10.2g^{6} t10.2s^{5} 10.2v Jul 27] modest form: sprint-bred but seems likely to stay 1½m. *Antony Brittain* **60**

CIRCUIT 3 br.f. Foxwedge (AUS) 128 – Lady Circe (USA) (Spinning World (USA) 130) [2017 –: p7g p8d^{5} 7g t8s 12d Aug 4] poor form: left Mick Quinn after third start: in tongue tie last 2 starts: often starts slowly. *Wilf Storey* **42**

CIRCUIT JUDGE 3 b.c. Lawman (FR) 121 – Gimasha 105 (Cadeaux Genereux 131) [2017 10g^{5} 7g^{6} p8g^{5} Sep 6] sturdy colt: fair form: best effort when fifth in maiden at Kempton in September: has joined Michael Herrington. *William Knight* **71**

CIRCUITOUS 9 b.g. Fasliyev (USA) 120 – Seren Devious (Dr Devious (IRE) 127) [2017 64: 7.2g 7.8m^{6} 6g^{3} 6g^{6} 6.9d^{5} 7.2s 7.2v^{5} Oct 16] modest handicapper: stays 7f: acts on polytrack, soft and good to firm going: wears headgear: tried in tongue tie: front runner/races prominently. *Keith Dalgleish* **62**

CIRCULATE 3 b.f. Dutch Art 126 – Royal Whisper (Royal Applause 124) [2017 70: t7.1g^{2} p7g^{5} p6d^{3} 7g t7.2g p8g a7.5s^{4} Dec 23] fair maiden: left Tom Clover 2,000 gns before final outing: best form at 7f: acts on polytrack and tapeta: tried in blinkers. *Pavel Vovcenko, Germany* **64**

CIRCULATION 3 b.f. Oasis Dream 129 – Double Crossed 102 (Caerleon (USA) 132) [2017 9.9d^{2} 9.8d^{4} 11.2d^{3} 10.2v^{5} p10g* Nov 2] good-topped filly: sister to a winner abroad and half-sister to high-class winner up to 10.4f Twice Over (2-y-o 1m-1¼m winner, by Observatory): dam 1¼m-11.5f winner: fairly useful performer: won handicap at Lingfield in November: stays 1¼m: acts on polytrack and good to soft going: sold 140,000 gns in December. *Ralph Beckett* **82**

CIRENCESTER 3 b.f. Sea The Stars (IRE) 140 – Columella 77 (Kyllachy 129) [2017 77p: 8f May 3] fair 1m winner for Ralph Beckett at 2 yrs, well held sole start in 2017. *Henry Candy* **–**

CIRRUS MINOR (FR) 2 b.f. (Apr 27) George Vancouver (USA) 116 – Porza (FR) (Septieme Ciel (USA) 123) [2017 t6s^{2} t6.1g p7s Dec 15] €80,000Y: half-sister to several winners, including very smart French/Australian winner up to 1¼m Pornichet (2-y-o 1m winner, by Vespone): dam French maiden half-sister to smart French winner up to 6.5f Porlezza: fair form: best effort when second in minor event at Newcastle (1¼ lengths behind Peace Trail) on debut: should be suited by 7f+. *K. R. Burke* **72**

CITY DREAMER (IRE) 3 ch.g. Casamento (IRE) 118 – Cadescia (IRE) (Cadeaux Genereux 131) [2017 66: 10.3m 10.2g^{5} May 12] sturdy gelding: fair maiden on Flat: likely to stay 1½m: races well off pace: fairly useful hurdler, won twice in September. *Alan King* **70**

CITY GENT 2 b.g. (Mar 4) Holy Roman Emperor (IRE) 125 – City Girl (IRE) 103 (Elusive City (USA) 117) [2017 6v 5.7d^{4} 6d^{2} p5g^{3} p6g^{2} p6g* Dec 30] useful-looking gelding: first foal: dam 6f winner (including at 2 yrs): fairly useful performer: won nursery at Lingfield (in blinkers, by 3¾ lengths from Joegogo) in December: stays 6f: acts on polytrack and good to soft going: often travels strongly. *Ralph Beckett* **87**

CITY GROUND (USA) 10 b.g. Orientate (USA) 127 – Magnet (USA) (Seeking The Gold (USA)) [2017 78: 10f* 10g 11.4m 9.1m^{2} Aug 27] angular gelding: fair handicapper: won at Les Landes in April: stays 1¼m: acts on polytrack, firm and good to soft going: tried in visor. *Michael Appleby* **74**

CITY GUEST (IRE) 2 b.g. (Mar 27) Epaulette (AUS) 126 – Union City Blues (IRE) 59 (Encosta de Lago (AUS)) [2017 5.2m^{6} 6g 5.3d^{3} 5f 6m^{5} 5.1g* 6m^{6} Aug 27] good-quartered gelding: fair performer: won maiden at Windsor in July: stays 5.5f: acts on good to soft going. *George Margarson* **73**

CITY LIMITS 3 ch.c. Nathaniel (IRE) 129 – Wait It Out (USA) (Swain (IRE) 134) [2017 74p: 12m 13d^{5} Jun 30] well-made colt: fair maiden: should stay 13f: acts on good to firm going: usually wears tongue tie: often starts slowly/races towards rear. *Luca Cumani* **78**

CITY OF ANGKOR WAT (IRE) 7 b.g. Elusive City (USA) 117 – Kathleen Rafferty (IRE) (Marju (IRE) 127) [2017 79: t6m^{6} p7g^{5} f8g t6g t7.1g t8.6g May 3] good-topped gelding: fairly useful at best, on downgrade nowadays: stays 1¼m: acts on all-weather: wears cheekpieces: has worn tongue tie: often races prominently. *Conor Dore* **57**

CITY OF JOY 3 b.g. Elusive City (USA) 117 – Ammo (IRE) (Sadler's Wells (USA) 132) [2017 84: 8m* p8g* 8m 8g 7.9g^{5} 10d^{4} Sep 23] big, good-topped gelding: useful handicapper: won at Doncaster (by head from Mustarrid) in May and Chelmsford (by ¾ length from Tricorn) in June: stays 1m: acts on polytrack, good to firm and good to soft going: often starts slowly, usually races in rear: sold 200,000 gns, sent to Saudi Arabia. *Sir Michael Stoute* **103**

CLAIM THE ROSES (USA) 6 b.g. Speightstown (USA) 124 – Reboot (USA) (Rubiano (USA)) [2017 99: t8s^{5} 7m p7g a8f^{2} Dec 29] rather leggy gelding: fairly useful performer: left Ed Vaughan, second in minor event at Jebel Ali in December: stays 1m: acts on all-weather: has worn headgear/tongue tie. *S. bin Ghadayer, UAE* **94**

CLAIRE'S SECRET 3 ch.f. Sakhee's Secret 128 – Akathea (Barathea (IRE) 127) [2017 70: 8.3m t8.6g^{6} 8s^{4} 8m 7d t8.6g t9.5g Dec 2] angular filly: fair handicapper, largely out of sorts in 2017: stays 8.5f: acts on polytrack and tapeta. *Philip McBride* **69**

CLAIRETTE (IRE) 2 b.f. (Mar 7) Al Kazeem 128 – Petit Calva (FR) 108 (Desert King (IRE) 129) [2017 7g^{4} 7g* p7g^{3} Oct 13] 115,000Y: useful-looking filly: seventh foal: half-sister to 3 winners, including useful French 2-y-o 1m winner Rosay (by Raven's Pass) and French 2-y-o 5.5f winner Anyaar (by Green Desert): dam, French winner up to 1m (2-y-o 5f/6f winner), half-sister to smart French/US winner up to 11f Mauralakana: fairly useful form: won maiden at Salisbury (cosily by 1½ lengths from Goodnight Girl) in September: will stay 1m. *Roger Charlton* **82**

CLANDON 4 b.g. Sakhee's Secret 128 – Whassup (FR) (Midyan (USA) 124) [2017 –: 7m 8g p7g p7m Nov 25] no form: tried in visor. *Brett Johnson* **–**

CLAN MCGREGOR (IRE) 2 b.c. (Apr 12) Dragon Pulse (IRE) 114 – Riymaisa (IRE) (Traditionally (USA) 117) [2017 9.9s 8s p8g Nov 7] little impact in maiden/minor events. *Seamus Durack* **–**

CLANVELLYN 3 b.f. Hellvelyn 118 – Clancassie (Clantime 101) [2017 t6m Jan 14] closely related to 2 winners by Ishiguru, including 5f winner Mecca's Team, and half-sister to 2 winners, including useful 5f/6f winner Mecca's Mate (by Paris House): dam of little account: 12/1, well held in maiden at Wolverhampton. *K. R. Burke* **–**

CLARABEL 4 b.f. Major Cadeaux 121 – Neardown Beauty (IRE) 95 (Bahhare (USA) 122) [2017 61: 9.2s^{4} 10d^{6} Aug 14] modest form: stays 9f. *John Weymes* **62**

CLARAMARA (IRE) 2 b.f. (Apr 29) Epaulette (AUS) 126 – Yaqootah (USA) 72 (Gone West (USA)) [2017 6.1v^{5} 6d 7g^{2} 7.2m 6.9v^{2} t7.1g^{pu} Oct 10] €19,000Y: seventh foal: half-sister to useful 2-y-o 6f winner Sweet Cecily (by Kodiac): dam 5f winner who stayed 7f: fair maiden: reportedly bled final start: stays 7f: acts on heavy going. *Mark Johnston* **66**

CLASSICAL TIMES 3 b.f. Lawman (FR) 121 – Sunday Times 109 (Holy Roman Emperor (IRE) 125) [2017 90: 6g* 7.9d^{4} 8m^{5} 6g^{3} 7g 6m Oct 14] compact filly: useful performer: won maiden at Redcar in May: third in listed race at Pontefract (½ length behind Queen Kindly) in August: likely to prove best up to 7f: acts on good to firm going: often races towards rear. *Peter Chapple-Hyam* **101**

CLASSIC CHARM 2 b.f. (Feb 22) Rip Van Winkle (IRE) 134 – Classic Lass 68 (Dr Fong (USA) 128) [2017 7d^3 p7d p8g^6 Dec 20] fifth foal: half-sister to 7f/1m winner Echo of Lightning (by Echo of Light) and 6f winner Sexy Legs (by Dutch Art): dam, lightly raced, out of half-sister to Derby second Walk In The Park: fair form: best effort when third in minor event at Newmarket (3 lengths behind Perfect Thought) on debut. *Dean Ivory* **66**

CLASSIC FLYER 5 b.g. Stimulation (IRE) 121 – Tranquil Flight (Oasis Dream 129) [2017 75: p5g^6 5g 5g^6 t6.1g^6 6m 6s p6g^5 f5g p6g Sep 7] fair handicapper at best, below form in 2017: stays 6f: acts on tapeta, good to firm and good to soft going: wears headgear: inconsistent. *Christine Dunnett* **50**

CLASSIC MISSION 6 ch.g. Bahamian Bounty 116 – Triple Cee (IRE) 73 (Cape Cross (IRE) 129) [2017 76§: p11d 10g 11m Jun 29] good-topped gelding: maiden, no form in 2017: wears headgear: often starts slowly: temperamental. *Jonathan Portman* **– §**

CLASSIC PURSUIT 6 b.g. Pastoral Pursuits 127 – Snake's Head 81 (Golden Snake (USA) 127) [2017 77: p6g^6 p7g^6 6g p5g* 5g^2 p5s 5g^3 5d 5s^6 5d^3 5g* 5g 5g^3 5d* 5s Nov 8] good-topped gelding: fairly useful handicapper: won at Chelmsford in May, and Nottingham in August and October (by 6 lengths from Jacob's Pillow): stays 6f: acts on polytrack, firm and good to soft going: wears headgear: sometimes slowly away. *Michael Appleby* **90 a71**

CLASSIC SENIORITY 5 b.g. Kyllachy 129 – Dramatic Solo 76 (Nayef (USA) 129) [2017 98: 6m^5 6s^6 7m^3 7m* 6g* 7s^5 6d 6g 6g^2 6v 7.9g Oct 13] angular gelding: useful performer: won minor event at Doncaster and handicap at Hamilton (by 1¼ lengths from Dark Defender) in July: stays 7.5f: acts on polytrack, tapeta, soft and good to firm going: often wears cheekpieces. *Marjorie Fife* **102**

CLASSIC VILLAGER 5 b.g. Authorized (IRE) 133 – Sablonne (USA) 100 (Silver Hawk (USA) 123) [2017 –: p10s^2 10m^6 p10g Sep 7] lengthy gelding: fairly useful handicapper: second at Chelmsford in June: stays 1½m: acts on polytrack, tapeta, good to firm and good to soft going: tried in hood. *Dean Ivory* **81**

CLAUDE GREENWOOD 7 b.g. Lucky Story (USA) 128 – Greenmeadow 70 (Sure Blade (USA) 130) [2017 58: p7g^6 t9.5g Jan 20] smallish, rather sparely-made gelding: poor handicapper nowadays: stays 1½m: acts on polytrack, fibresand, soft and good to firm going: wears headgear: front runner/races prominently. *Tony Carroll* **46**

CLAUDINE (IRE) 2 b.f. (Mar 4) Zoffany (IRE) 121 – Hamalka (IRE) 83 (Alhaarth (IRE) 126) [2017 6g^6 7d* p7g^6 Oct 3] €15,000F, £7,000Y: second foal: dam, 1¼m winner, also won over hurdles: fair form: won maiden at Lingfield (by ½ length from Vera Drake) in September: will stay further than 7f. *Henry Candy* **70**

CLAYTON HALL (IRE) 4 b.g. Lilbourne Lad (IRE) 111 – Hawk Dance (IRE) 73 (Hawk Wing (USA) 136) [2017 79, a71: 10.3g 10g 9.9m 9.8m^5 11.1g 10v^6 f8.1g f11.1g Dec 22] fair handicapper, below best in 2017: stays 10.5f: acts on tapeta and good to firm going: often wore headgear in 2017: tried in tongue tie. *John Wainwright* **58**

CLEAN CUT 3 b.f. Kheleyf (USA) 116 – Regal Asset (USA) (Regal Classic (CAN)) [2017 p6g t6d p5g f8d 7.5f^4 7m^4 9.9m^6 Jun 27] 2,500F: sixth foal: half-sister to 3 winners, including 2-y-o 7f/1m winner Regal Gold (by Exceed And Excel) and 7f-1¼m winner Shearian (by Royal Applause): dam, US maiden, half-sister to high-class Hong Kong 1m/1¼m performer Olympic Express: modest maiden: best effort at 7.5f: acts on firm going: in cheekpieces last 3 starts: often leads. *Ivan Furtado* **52**

CLEARANCE 3 b.g. Authorized (IRE) 133 – Four Miracles 96 (Vettori (IRE) 119) [2017 9m 10.2s 11.9m 16v 11.5d 11.9s Oct 10] poor maiden: should be suited by further than 1¼m: often races in rear. *Mark H. Tompkins* **51**

CLEAR AS A BELL (IRE) 3 ch.f. Choisir (AUS) 126 – Brilliant Crystal (Compton Place 125) [2017 65: 6g 6m 7.2m* 8.2g^2 t8s 7.4m* 7m* t7.2g^4 7d 6d Sep 12] fair handicapper: won at Musselburgh in June, and Beverley and Redcar in July: stays 1m: acts on good to firm and good to soft going: tried in blinkers: front runner/races prominently. *Tim Easterby* **71**

CLEARLY 3 b.f. Invincible Spirit (IRE) 121 – Concordia (Pivotal 124) [2017 10g p8g* 8d^3 8g^5 8m Oct 25] tall, lengthy filly: fourth foal: half-sister to 3 winners, including smart winner up to 2m Polarisation (2-y-o 6f winner, by Echo of Light) and 1¼m winner First Voyage (by Dubawi): dam, French 11f winner, half-sister to Derby/Prix de l'Arc de Triomphe winner Lammtarra: fairly useful performer: won maiden at Kempton in September: third in handicap at Sandown next start: stays 1m: acts on polytrack and good to soft going: tried in blinkers: usually slowly away: sold 125,000 gns in December, sent to Germany. *John Gosden* **91**

CLEAR SPRING (IRE) 9 b.g. Chineur (FR) 123 – Holly Springs 81 (Efisio 120) [2017 107: 6m 6s^4 6m 6m 6d^4 6g^2 6d^5 p6g^3 6.1s^2 6v* 6s^6 6d^5 Oct 27] leggy gelding: useful handicapper: won at Salisbury (by 2¾ lengths from Satchville Flyer) in October: best up to 6f: acts on polytrack, fibresand and any turf going: tried in cheekpieces: sometimes slowly away. *John Spearing* **98**

CLEAR WATER (IRE) 4 b.f. Hard Spun (USA) 124 – Storm Lily (USA) 55 (Storm Cat (USA)) [2017 99: 7m 6.1g^6 6g 6g^2 7d 6g^4 6g p7g^6 Dec 6] workmanlike filly: fairly useful handicapper: second at Haydock in August: stays 7f: best form on good going: usually races nearer last than first. *Michael Wigham* **92**

CLEF 3 b.f. Dutch Art 126 – Humouresque 110 (Pivotal 124) [2017 85: 10.3g 7.8v 8s^2 8.1m^2 7d^4 p7s Nov 23] fairly useful handicapper: second at Ayr and Windsor in October: stays 1m: acts on soft and good to firm going: sold 55,000 gns in December. *Richard Fahey* **85**

CLEMENCY 6 b.m. Halling (USA) 133 – China Tea (USA) (High Chaparral (IRE) 132) [2017 12.3g^2 10.3v^5 12.1v^3 Sep 26] £12,000 6-y-o: tall mare: first foal: dam unraced sister to smart French 1¼m-1½m winner Magadan: fair form: best effort when second in maiden at Chester in August: will stay beyond 1½m: fair hurdler. *Donald McCain* **71**

CLEMENT (IRE) 7 b.g. Clodovil (IRE) 116 – Winnifred (Green Desert (USA) 127) [2017 91: t7.1g^4 p7g t7.2d Dec 26] fair handicapper: stays 7f: acts on polytrack, tapeta and good to firm going: has worn headgear: tried in tongue tie: sometimes slowly away. *John O'Shea* **76**

CLEMENTO (IRE) 3 b.g. Canford Cliffs (IRE) 133 – Street Style (IRE) 83 (Rock of Gibraltar (IRE) 133) [2017 –p: 10m^5 9.9d^4 9.9s^4 11.8v^3 p12g^3 Oct 18] good-topped gelding: fairly useful maiden: stays 1½m: acts on polytrack, good to firm and heavy going: often races towards rear: sold to join John Quinn 35,000 gns in October. *Roger Charlton* **82**

CLEM FANDANGO (FR) 3 b.f. Elzaam (AUS) 115 – Question (USA) 56 (Coronado's Quest (USA) 130) [2017 102: 5.5g^4 5g^4 5.5d^6 5s^2 5s^2 p6g Nov 18] compact filly: useful performer: second in listed race at Musselburgh (¾ length behind Mabs Cross) in October and handicap at Nottingham (1¼ lengths behind Perfect Pasture) in November: stays 5.5f: acts on soft and good to firm going: sold 100,000 gns in December. *Keith Dalgleish* **108**

CLEMMIE (IRE) 2 b.f. (Feb 14) Galileo (IRE) 134 – Meow (IRE) 108 (Storm Cat (USA)) [2017 6d^3 6m 6g* 6m* 6d* Sep 30] **118 p**

Ballydoyle has had some excellent fillies in recent seasons. Hot on the heels of the likes of Found and Minding came the latest three-year-old crop that included Winter, Roly Poly, Hydrangea and Rhododendron who between them accounted for almost half of the stable's record haul of Group 1 races. The indications from the latest group of two-year-olds in Aidan O'Brien's care are that another strong batch of fillies is coming through. In due course, all of these are destined to join the Coolmore broodmare band which produced them in the first place. Coolmore has long been synonymous with its stallions, exclusively so, perhaps, but some of its broodmares are making a name for themselves too, and their influence was particularly hard to ignore in the latest season. Roly Poly and U S Navy Flag are both out of Misty For Me, whose wins included the Irish One Thousand Guineas, and another Irish Guineas winner to be represented by both a leading three-year-old and two-year-old was Halfway To Heaven, the dam of Rhododendron and Magical. Giant's Causeway's sister You'resothrilling could already boast two classic winners among her offspring—Gleneagles and Marvellous—before two-year-old Happily became her third Group 1 winner in the latest season (her three-year-old Taj Mahal won a Group 2 in Australia late in the year). And then there was the Queen Mary Stakes runner-up Meow, whose three-year-old son Churchill became a dual Guineas winner and whose two-year-old daughter Clemmie looked a potential classic winner herself when winning the Cheveley Park Stakes.

On the same card that Churchill completed his Guineas double at the Curragh, Clemmie made an eye-catching debut in the opening fillies maiden, showing her inexperience early on before staying on to be beaten just two heads into third. Churchill had also finished third on his debut in the corresponding race for colts the same weekend twelve months earlier before going on to win the Chesham Stakes, but Royal Ascot came a bit too soon in Clemmie's development. She was sent off second favourite for the Albany Stakes but could only stay on into seventh behind the French-trained winner Different League, shaping as though a step up

Juddmonte Cheveley Park Stakes, Newmarket—Clemmie rubber stamps her credentials for the 2018 One Thousand Guineas with a commanding victory, asserting late on to beat Albany Stakes winner Different League (striped sleeves) and Lowther Stakes runner-up Madeline (spots)

to seven furlongs would see her in a better light. Churchill had raced exclusively over seven furlongs at two after his debut whereas Clemmie ended up doing all her racing at six, but that didn't stop her winning her three remaining starts. The first of those was back at the Curragh just nine days after the Albany Stakes in the Group 3 Grangecon Stud Stakes which she won well by two and three quarter lengths from her stable-companion Butterscotch who had made her own debut in the same race as Clemmie, finishing just behind her in fifth. Roly Poly had won the same race in 2016 before following up in the Duchess of Cambridge Stakes at the July meeting, and Clemmie was sent off the 11/8 favourite to complete the same double at Newmarket. Clemmie's rivals included Mamba Noire, who had finished third behind her last time out, and Mistress of Venice, three places ahead of her in the Albany, but her main opponent looked to be Nyaleti who had finished second to Clemmie's stable-companion September in the Chesham Stakes. Nyaleti gave her all at Newmarket, but the thriving Clemmie stayed on too strongly for her. Clemmie took over entering the final furlong and won by a length and three quarters with Mamba Noire half a length behind Nyaleti in third. The combination of quite a strong pace, firmish ground and a tailwind resulted in Clemmie breaking the two-year-old course record.

As at Royal Ascot, Clemmie's two subsequent wins had strongly suggested that a step up in trip would suit, making the Moyglare Stud Stakes at the Curragh the obvious next race for her, as it was for her stable-companions Magical and Happily, after they had fought out a close finish to the Debutante Stakes over the same course and distance (September, sent off favourite, finished only fourth). Ryan Moore had ridden all four of these Ballydoyle fillies to victory at one time or another over the summer so it was significant that Clemmie was his original pick of them in the Moyglare. However, when the official going in the straight was changed to 'soft to heavy' after the second race on the card, Clemmie was withdrawn, leaving her stable-companions to complete a one, two, three without her, with Happily beating Magical and September (Moore switched to the runner-up who was beaten a short head).

Clemmie didn't have long to wait to be given her chance of Group 1 success as she was back at Newmarket later in September, on good to soft ground, for the Juddmonte Cheveley Park Stakes, a race which her trainer had won for the first time twelve months earlier when Brave Anna had got the better of stable-companion Roly Poly (ridden by Moore) by a short head. Clemmie was her stable's sole representative in the Cheveley Park (one of the few Group 1 races O'Brien won in his record-breaking year in which he ran just one), so there was no danger of the stable's number-one jockey being on the wrong filly this time. It was more a question of whether Clemmie would be quick enough against more speedily-bred fillies. For all his many achievements, Clemmie's sire Galileo had never had a Group 1 winner over six furlongs, even at two. Notwithstanding that Churchill had proved suited by seven furlongs at two, and later by a mile, the bottom half of Clemmie's pedigree is extremely speedy and provided plenty of encouragement. Like her daughter, Meow also won the Grangecon Stud Stakes, though it was then a listed contest over five furlongs and run later in the year. Meow was all speed and might not even have stayed in the Cheveley Park had she been tried, though she never got the chance to prove herself beyond the minimum trip in a truncated career, trailing home after losing her action in the Flying Childers on her final start. There was some family history a bit further back as Clemmie's grandam Airwave won the Cheveley Park for Henry Candy in 2002. In doing so, she beat the odds-on Russian Rhythm, winner of the Lowther Stakes and future winner of the One Thousand Guineas. Clemmie faced a bigger field than her grandam had done, and she too had the Lowther winner as her chief rival, sent off the 15/8 favourite ahead of the York winner Threading at 5/2 in an eleven-runner field. Different League (4/1), who had finished third against colts in the Prix Morny on her only start since beating Clemmie at Royal Ascot, and the Lowther runner-up Madeline (8/1), who also finished in front of Clemmie when fifth in the Albany, were the only others at shorter than 14/1. Showing no sign of rustiness despite the two and a half month absence since her last start, Clemmie was soon handy behind the pace set by Different League and one of the outsiders Treasuring. Different League was travelling more smoothly than Clemmie, who was being pushed along by Moore to join issue with the leaders from two furlongs out, but, though the pair were still upsides each other entering the final furlong, Clemmie's stamina began to tell on hitting the rising ground and she drew a length and three quarters clear by the line, with Different League finishing a length and a half ahead of Madeline in third. The 50/1 maiden Now Your Talking, fourth in the Queen Mary, completed the frame close behind, while Threading was the only one of the main contenders to disappoint, finishing seventh after becoming unbalanced in the Dip.

Clemmie (IRE) (b.f. 2015)	Galileo (IRE) (b 1998)	Sadler's Wells (b 1981)	Northern Dancer
			Fairy Bridge
		Urban Sea (ch 1989)	Miswaki
			Allegretta
	Meow (IRE) (b 2008)	Storm Cat (b or br 1983)	Storm Bird
			Terlingua
		Airwave (b 2000)	Air Express
			Kangra Valley

The only Cheveley Park winners this century to win the One Thousand Guineas the following spring were the French-trained pair Natagora in 2007 and Special Duty two years later, the latter awarded the race in the stewards' room. The record of the five Cheveley Park winners who have attempted the double since Special Duty isn't good, with only Tiggy Wiggy (third in 2015) managing to reach a place. Clemmie is very much a Guineas prospect, though, and is a very worthy favourite at this stage. As well as being almost guaranteed to be better suited by a mile—her elder brother actually showed himself fully effective over an extended ten furlongs when second in the Juddmonte International—Clemmie's form in the Cheveley Park looks better than the form of the Fillies' Mile in which September was narrowly beaten, looking unlucky. Clemmie's Guineas prospects certainly contrast with those of her grandam immediately after she had won the Cheveley Park: Airwave looked a sprinter purely and simply, at least at that stage of her career, and the Guineas never came into the reckoning for her. Airwave made a winning reappearance at three in the Temple Stakes and spent the next couple of seasons in top sprinting company. She was placed later at three in the Golden Jubilee, July Cup and Sprint Cup, though, after being bought for 550,000 guineas by Coolmore at the end of her four-year-old season, she did have three races over longer trips for Aidan O'Brien, winning an albeit uncompetitive Group 2 contest over a mile at the Curragh, the Ridgewood Pearl Stakes. Like Meow, Airwave has been regularly mated with Galileo in recent seasons, and her latest winner by him is the fairly useful three-year-old Auckland, a versatile colt who was successful twice over a mile at

Leopardstown in the latest season (he was also placed twice at a mile and a quarter and wasn't beaten far when fourth in a handicap at Navan at just short of six furlongs on his final start). Further details of Clemmie's pedigree can be found in the essays on Churchill, the one which appeared in *Racehorses of 2016* also giving an account of Sir Winston Churchill's close ties with racing. Churchill married Clementine Hozier in 1908 and was on record as saying that persuading 'Clemmie' to marry him was his 'most brilliant achievement'. Exemplifying the phrase 'behind every great man …', Churchill's wife may have had her own close connection with the sport. Her paternity was a matter of some dispute, but it was her mother Lady Blanche's claim that Clemmie's father was Captain George 'Bay' Middleton, one of the leading steeplechase jockeys of his day (Bay Middleton was a Derby winner earlier in the nineteenth century).

The well-made Clemmie wore a tongue tie for all her starts, except in the Albany Stakes. She acts on good to firm and good to soft going, and, despite her withdrawal from the Moyglare, softer conditions won't inconvenience her if she takes after Churchill who showed his form on a variety of surfaces. Airwave's success in the Cheveley Park Stakes helped her dam Kangra Valley earn the Thoroughbred Breeders' Association's broodmare of the year award that year as she was among four of her dam's foals to be successful in 2002. Thanks to Churchill and Clemmie, Meow would be a strong contender for similar honours in 2017, though she wouldn't be the only candidate among the Coolmore broodmare band. *Aidan O'Brien, Ireland*

CLENYMISTRA (IRE) 3 ch.f. Poet's Voice 126 – Expedience (USA) 74 (With Approval **76**
(CAN)) [2017 59: 10m* 9.2m^{3} 8m^{5} 9.9f^{2} 12d^{3} 12g* 14m^{2} t12.4d 12.1s^{5} Oct 10] fair handicapper: won at Redcar in May and Thirsk in August: stays 1¾m: acts on polytrack, firm and good to soft going: tried in cheekpieces: often races towards rear. *David O'Meara*

CLEONTE (IRE) 4 ch.g. Sir Percy 129 – Key Figure (Beat Hollow 126) [2017 12m^{5} 20f **98**
14d 14s^{4} 14v^{6} Sep 30] sturdy gelding: useful 15f winner for A. Fabre at 3 yrs, below best in 2017: acts on soft going: in headgear last 3 starts. *Andrew Balding*

CLERGYMAN 5 b.g. Pastoral Pursuits 127 – Doctor's Note (Pursuit of Love 124) [2017 **60**
70: f6g^{4} 6m^{2} f6.1g^{2} Dec 29] modest handicapper: stays 6f: acts on polytrack, tapeta, good to firm and heavy going. *Rebecca Bastiman*

CLEVERCONVERSATION (IRE) 4 ro.f. Thewayyouare (USA) 117 – Monet's Lady **62 §**
(IRE) 51 (Daylami (IRE) 138) [2017 75§: p8g^{4} p8g^{5} p8f Apr 24] lengthy filly: modest maiden: stays 8.5f: acts on polytrack, best turf form on good going: wears headgear: sometimes slowly away: has flashed tail and can't be trusted. *Jane Chapple-Hyam*

CLEVER COOKIE 9 b.g. Primo Valentino (IRE) 116 – Mystic Memory 74 (Ela-Mana- **113**
Mou 132) [2017 116: 13.9d^{6} 13.9g t16.3s 13.9m^{3} 13.9m^{6} 17.9g^{4} 16s^{6} Oct 21] big, strong gelding: smart performer: fourth in Doncaster Cup (2 lengths behind Desert Skyline) in September: stays 2¼m: acts on tapeta, good to firm and heavy going: wears cheekpieces: held up. *Peter Niven*

CLEVER DIVYA 4 b.f. Archipenko (USA) 127 – Clever Omneya (USA) 73 (Toccet **–**
(USA) 118) [2017 59: f7g p6d^{4} 8m Jun 30] good-topped filly: modest 6f winner at 3 yrs, no form in 2017: often races nearer last than first. *J. R. Jenkins*

CLEVER LADY (IRE) 3 b.f. Big Bad Bob (IRE) 118 – Muneera (USA) 67 (Green **51**
Dancer (USA) 132) [2017 5.7m^{6} p7g p7g^{6} 5.1s^{6} 6.1m^{6} 8.2g^{3} 8g Jul 17] 45,000 2-y-o: half-sister to several winners, including winner up to 9f Bolton Hall (2-y-o 5f winner, by Imperial Ballet) and 2-y-o 7f winner Cleodora (by One Cool Cat): dam ran twice: modest maiden: stays 1m: acts on good to firm going. *David Evans*

CLEVERLEY (IRE) 2 gr.f. (Apr 4) Mastercraftsman (IRE) 129 – Turning Point **57**
(Dalakhani (IRE) 133) [2017 p10g p8g^{5} Dec 20] first foal: dam unraced half-sister to French 9f/1¼m winner Rainbow Dancing and winner up to 1¾m Handsome Man (both useful): modest form: better effort when fifth in minor event at Lingfield (6½ lengths behind Mewtow) in December. *Henry Candy*

CLIFF BAY (IRE) 3 b.g. Elzaam (AUS) 115 – Lost Highway (IRE) 66 (Danehill Dancer **78**
(IRE) 117) [2017 57: f8g^{2} 9g^{2} 9.2g^{5} 8.3m* 9g^{5} 9.2g^{5} 7.2d^{5} 8m^{5} 8.3s^{4} 8.3v^{3} 8s* 9v^{3} Oct 12] fair handicapper: won at Hamilton in June and Ayr (apprentice) in October: stays 9f: acts on fibresand, tapeta, good to firm and heavy going: has worn headgear: often starts slowly. *Keith Dalgleish*

CLIFF FACE (IRE) 4 b.f. Canford Cliffs (IRE) 133 – Kotdiji (Mtoto 134) [2017 98: p14s6 12g5 12g2 12d 13.4g 14.1d t12.2g p12d2 p11d4 Dec 13] good-topped filly: useful handicapper: second at Ascot (3 lengths behind Dawn Horizons) in July: stays 1½m: acts on polytrack, good to firm and good to soft going: often in headgear: often starts slowly/ races in rear. *Sir Mark Prescott Bt* **98 a92**

CLIFFHANGER 4 b.f. Canford Cliffs (IRE) 133 – Copy-Cat 60 (Lion Cavern (USA) 117) [2017 78: p7d Aug 23] fair handicapper, below form only start in 2017: stays 7f: acts on polytrack and good to soft going. *Paul Cole* **59**

CLIFF (IRE) 7 b.g. Bachelor Duke (USA) 122 – Silesian (IRE) (Singspiel (IRE) 133) [2017 74: t7.1m2 t7.1g* t7.1g6 7g 7g 6d 6m* 5.9d2 6g4 5.9s* 6g6 5.9d2 7d6 6v3 6v5 Sep 30] fair handicapper: won apprentice races at Wolverhampton in January and Ripon in June, and lady riders event at Carlisle in August: stays 1m, usually races over shorter: acts on tapeta, good to firm and heavy going: has worn headgear: often races towards rear. *Nigel Tinkler* **77**

CLIFFS OF CAPRI 3 b.g. Canford Cliffs (IRE) 133 – Shannon Spree 77 (Royal Applause 124) [2017 85p: p7g* p7s2 p8g5 Dec 31] useful handicapper: won at Kempton (by 3 lengths from Human Nature) in October: left Simon Crisford after first start: should stay 1m: acts on polytrack and tapeta: responds generously to pressure. *Jamie Osborne* **108**

CLIFFS OF MOHER (IRE) 3 b.c. Galileo (IRE) 134 – Wave (IRE) 81 (Dansili 127) [2017 110P: 10.3d* 12m2 9.9m4 10.3d4 10d6 10s 12f Nov 4] sturdy, attractive colt: very smart performer: won listed Dee Stakes at Chester (by 1½ lengths from Bay of Poets) in May: second in Derby at Epsom (¾ length behind Wings of Eagles) 3 weeks later: didn't repeat that effort, including when fourth in Eclipse Stakes at Sandown and International Stakes at York and when eighth in Breeders' Cup Turf at Del Mar final outing: stays 1½m: acts on good to firm and good to soft going: wears tongue tie. *Aidan O'Brien, Ireland* **123**

CLINE 4 ch.f. Pivotal 124 – Graduation 102 (Lomitas 129) [2017 t7.1m6 8.3m t8s 8.3d* 8.3g 8g Aug 15] fair handicapper: won at Hamilton in July: stays 8.5f: acts on polytrack and good to soft going: in cheekpieces last 3 starts. *Kevin Ryan* **69**

Mrs John Magnier, Mr M. Tabor and Mr D. Smith's "Cliffs of Moher"

CLIP ART 3 b.f. Acclamation 118 – Semaphore (Zamindar (USA) 116) [2017 –p: 6m t6.1g p7g Jun 28] sturdy filly: no form. *Jamie Osborne* –

CLOAK AND DEGAS (IRE) 5 b.g. Sakhee's Secret 128 – Coup de Torchon (FR) 61 (Namid 128) [2017 52: p7s Sep 30] fair at best, below that since 2015: stays 6f: acts on polytrack, tapeta and soft going: wears headgear: front runner/races prominently. *Tim McCarthy* –

CLOCK CHIMES 3 b.g. Foxwedge (AUS) 128 – Passing Hour (USA) 80 (Red Ransom (USA)) [2017 f8g² f7g* t7.1g³ p8g t8g f7.1g⁴ Dec 22] 47,000F, £36,000 2-y-o: half-brother to several winners, including 6f-1m winner Passing Star (by Royal Applause) and 5f/6f winner Sixty Minutes (by Compton Place), both useful: dam 1m winner who stayed 1¼m: fairly useful performer: won maiden at Southwell in March: stays 7f: acts on fibresand and tapeta: tried in visor: often races prominently. *David Brown* **81**

CLON COULIS (IRE) 3 b.f. Vale of York (IRE) 117 – Cloneden (IRE) 79 (Definite Article 121) [2017 5.9g* 6d² 6s* Aug 25] fifth foal: half-sister to smart winner around 1¼m Clon Brulee (by Modigliani) and a winner in USA by Antonius Pius: dam 1½m winner: smart form: won maiden at Carlisle (by 4 lengths from World Power) in June and handicap at Hamilton (by 2½ lengths from Rutherford) in August: will stay further than 6f: unexposed. *David Barron* **111 p**

CLONDAW BANKER (IRE) 8 b.g. Court Cave (IRE) – Freya Alex 58 (Makbul 104) [2017 t12.4g⁵ Feb 17] 9/2, found little when fifth in maiden at Newcastle on belated Flat debut: fairly useful hurdler/chaser at best, has lost way. *Nicky Henderson* **62**

CLON ROCKET (IRE) 4 b.g. Lilbourne Lad (IRE) 111 – Ryalahna (IRE) (High Chaparral (IRE) 132) [2017 69: t6g⁵ t6g 5.1m 6.1g May 12] fair handicapper at best, has deteriorated markedly: stays 7f: acts on soft going: has worn headgear: sometimes slowly away. *John Holt* **39**

CLOTH OF STARS (IRE) 4 b.c. Sea The Stars (IRE) 140 – Strawberry Fledge (USA) (Kingmambo (USA) 125) [2017 116: 9.9d* 9.9m* 10.4g* 11.9d² 11.9d² Oct 1] **132**

Those who believe that the Derby comes too soon in the career of many three-year-olds would have found some good examples to support their case in the latest season. It certainly came too early for the season's top three-year-old colt Cracksman who was a stone better horse in the autumn than he had been in June when having just the third start of his life at Epsom. There was also the result of the Prix de l'Arc de Triomphe in which the placed horses, four-year-olds Cloth of Stars and Ulysses, put up top-class efforts in defeat behind the outstanding three-year-old filly Enable. The pair had been well fancied—both 8/1 shots—for the previous season's Derby in which they had finished only eighth and twelfth respectively. However, as more mature individuals a year on, they proved themselves among the best older middle-distance performers in Europe.

It might have taken a couple of years for Cloth of Stars to reach his full potential, but he had already shown plenty of ability at two, enough to make a winning debut at Deauville before following up in the Prix des Chenes at Longchamp and ending his first season with second place in the Criterium de Saint-Cloud. The main issue holding Cloth of Stars back in his early days was his headstrong nature and that was still in evidence when he was sent to Epsom after winning the Prix La Force and Prix Greffulhe (beating Criterium de Saint-Cloud winner Robin of Navan in the latter). His intractability certainly cost him dearly on his first try at a mile and a half, and, after leading the Derby field briefly over two furlongs out, he weakened to finish more than fifteen lengths behind the winner Harzand. Cloth of Stars was seen out only once more at three, taking a strong hold again early on but seeing out the Derby trip much better this time to finish third to Mont Ormel in the Grand Prix de Paris at Saint-Cloud.

It was clear from very early on in the latest season that Cloth of Stars was an improved four-year-old, and a more tractable one, and by the beginning of May he had run up a hat-trick in the Prix Exbury at Saint-Cloud, the Prix d'Harcourt at Chantilly and the Prix Ganay, Europe's first Group 1 for older horses, back at Saint-Cloud. Cloth of Stars progressed with each race, beginning with a stylish win conceding weight all round to just smart rivals at best in the Exbury. Under firmer conditions at Chantilly which resulted in the track record being broken, he had to

Prix Ganay, Saint-Cloud—Cloth of Stars repels the late thrust of Zarak (whose jockey has lost his whip) to land the first Group 1 of the European season, his third consecutive victory in pattern company, with Silverwave (hood), Erupt (head only just in shot extreme left) and Hawkbill (cheekpieces) just behind

work a bit harder to land the odds by a neck from the very smart Mekhtaal in the Prix d'Harcourt, with old rival Robin of Navan back in fourth. It was those two rivals who disputed much of the running, and Cloth of Stars, coming from much further back, did well to get up near the line. Mekhtaal and Robin of Navan went on to fight out the finish of the Prix d'Ispahan at Chantilly in May by which time Cloth of Stars had gained his own Group 1 win in the Ganay. It was still early in the season and fitness played its part, with 13/10 favourite Cloth of Stars and Zarak, next in the betting at 5/2, taking the first two places in a field of seven in which the others were all making their seasonal returns. Zarak had twice finished second to Europe's top three-year-old Almanzor the previous season, including in the Prix du Jockey Club, and had made his return even earlier than Cloth of Stars, winning a Group 3 contest at Meydan in February. The rest of the field comprised the first two from the previous season's Grand Prix de Saint-Cloud, Silverwave and Erupt, the Eclipse winner Hawkbill and the German pair Guignol and Potemkin, the latter having had Zarak back in third when winning the Prix Dollar at the Arc meeting. Early in the straight, Cloth of Stars looked in danger of being hemmed in behind the leading pair Guignol and Hawkbill but, when a gap appeared between them over a furlong out, Cloth of Stars quickened into the lead, getting first run on Zarak who had been shuffled back to last. Zarak finished strongly from out of the pack to reduce Cloth of Stars' advantage to just a short neck at the line, though Christophe Soumillon dropped his whip and had to resort to slapping Zarak down the neck with the flat of his hand in the closing stages. Silverwave and Erupt, the trip on the short side for both of them, kept on to complete the frame, beaten another three quarters of a length and a head, ahead of Hawkbill, Guignol and Potemkin. Cloth of Stars was Andre Fabre's fifth winner of the Ganay, equalling the record of Alain de Royer Dupre in the race.

Although Cloth of Stars had been given entries in the Coronation Cup and at Royal Ascot, nothing more was seen of him for more than four months until he turned out for the Prix Foy at Chantilly. Back at a mile and a half in the Arc trial, he ran creditably to go down by a length and a half to the German colt Dschingis Secret in a race where much of the attention beforehand was focussed on the latest Japanese challenger for the Arc, the well-touted Satono Diamond, who finished only fourth. While the winner of the Foy, who had a good record in the mud, attracted some support for the Arc when conditions were forecast to be softer still the following month, the Foy form was otherwise disregarded and Cloth of Stars, one of three runners for his stable in the Arc, started at over 20/1 on the pari-mutuel. Cloth of Stars, though, had clearly been laid out for the Arc since the spring and, in typical fashion for one from his stable, improved a good deal for his run in the trial three weeks earlier. Making smooth headway in the straight as he picked his way through the field, Cloth of Stars stayed on the better in a private battle for second with

Ulysses in the closing stages but without making any impression on the impressive winner Enable. While Fabre's seven Arc winners constitutes a record, it is now more than ten years since the last of them, Rail Link, and Cloth of Stars was his third runner-up in the last four runnings after Flintshire's second places in 2014 and 2015. Masterstroke, Intello and New Bay have all finished third for Fabre since 2012. The only four-year-old among Fabre's Arc winners (the rest were three) remains Subotica who got the better of User Friendly (who completed the same Oaks treble as Enable in the latest season, before adding the St Leger) in 1992. Like Cloth of Stars, Subotica had won the Ganay earlier in the year and also finished second in the Foy after a summer break. Subotica ran below form subsequently in the Breeders' Cup Turf, though that wasn't the next destination for Cloth of Stars; Fabre and owners Godolphin went on to win the Turf with Talismanic instead who had finished a place behind Cloth of Stars in the Foy.

Cloth of Stars (IRE) (b.c. 2013)	Sea The Stars (IRE) (b 2006)	Cape Cross (b 1994)	Green Desert
			Park Appeal
		Urban Sea (ch 1989)	Miswaki
			Allegretta
	Strawberry Fledge (USA) (b 2005)	Kingmambo (b 1990)	Mr Prospector
			Miesque
		Lingerie (b 1988)	Shirley Heights
			Northern Trick

Cloth of Stars and Ulysses have much more in common than a similar career profile. Both are from a top Niarchos family and are bred on very similar lines, with their dams being full sisters and their sires being the half-brothers Sea The Stars and Galileo. That pair were sons of the 1993 Arc winner Urban Sea, with Sea The Stars emulating his dam at Longchamp in 2009. There's Arc history in their distaff family too, as their grandam Lingerie, a maiden in France (runner-up four times at up to a mile and a half), was a daughter of the top-class 1984 Arc runner-up Northern Trick, winner beforehand of the Prix de Diane and Prix Vermeille. While Ulysses has the Oaks winner Light Shift as his dam, Cloth of Stars' dam Strawberry Fledge ran just once, finishing third in a mile maiden at Nantes as a two-year-old for Dominique Sepulchre. Based in the Provinces, Sepulchre, who retired at the end of 2016, trained some of the lesser lights in the Niarchos colours, though one of the best horses he trained was Limnos, a half-brother to Strawberry Fledge and Light Shift (and a full brother to the high-class mile and a quarter filly Shiva). Limnos won the Prix Foy as a much improved four-year-old but met with a setback which prevented him contesting that year's Arc. Sepulchre also trained another of Lingerie's daughters, Burning Sunset, in the latter part of her career, as well as Burning Sunset's daughter Ikat, another useful filly, who in turn produced another of this family's best performers, Main Sequence, the Derby runner-up who as a five-year-old beat Flintshire in the Breeders' Cup Turf.

The third foal of Strawberry Fledge, Cloth of Stars was bought by John Ferguson for 400,000 guineas at the Newmarket October Sales as a yearling and became his dam's second winner after Warrior of Light (by High Chaparral), a useful performer at his best who won over a mile at two and a mile and a half at three. High Chaparral is also the sire of the latest pair of Strawberry Fledge's foals to reach the racecourse. Gelded three-year-old Apollonian finished second in a mile and a half newcomers race at Clairefontaine for Andre Fabre, while two-year-old filly Niku showed promise when mid-division in a maiden at the Curragh for Jessica Harrington. That pair were retained to race in the 'Niarchos' (nowadays Flaxman Stables) colours, whereas their yearling half-sister by War Command was sold for €300,000 at Goffs in September. Cloth of Stars, an attractive colt, has belatedly proven himself fully effective at a mile and a half, a trip he's very much bred for after all. He acts on soft and good to firm ground and is usually held up in his races so that a well-run race suits him ideally. His winning debut came in cheekpieces but he has never worn headgear of any sort since. *A. Fabre, France*

CLOUD DRAGON (IRE) 3 br.g. Dark Angel (IRE) 113 – Karliysha (IRE) (Kalanisi **77**
(IRE) 132) [2017 65p: p8g^{3} p8g* 8m 10d Jun 5] fair performer: won maiden at Lingfield in February: stays 1m: acts on polytrack: sent to Singapore. *Hugo Palmer*

CLOUDED GOLD 5 ch.g. Resplendent Glory (IRE) 115 – Segretezza (IRE) 48 (Perugino (USA) 84) [2017 39: 6d f6.1g^6 t5g^5 f5g Nov 13] little form: in cheekpieces last 3 starts: front runner/races prominently. *Michael Appleby* –

CLOUD EIGHT (IRE) 2 b.c. (Mar 14) Dream Ahead (USA) 133 – Night Cam (IRE) 65 (Night Shift (USA)) [2017 p6g t5.1d^4 Dec 26] €65,000F, 42,000Y: fourth foal: half-brother to 3 winners, including 1m winners Camrock Star (including at 2 yrs, by Rock of Gibraltar) and No Approval (by Approve): dam lightly-raced half-sister to smart winner up to 7f Ugo Fire: fair form: better effort when fourth in minor event at Wolverhampton (3¾ lengths behind Reiffa) in December: should be suited by 6f: wears tongue tie: capable of better again. *Marco Botti* **66 p**

CLOUD MONKEY (IRE) 7 b.g. Marju (IRE) 127 – Sweet Clover 67 (Rainbow Quest (USA) 134) [2017 74: 13.8m 12.1s Jul 26] rather leggy gelding: fairly useful at best, no form on Flat in 2017: stays 12.5f: acts on polytrack, soft and good to firm going: has worn headgear: fair maiden hurdler. *Martin Todhunter* –

CLOUD NINE (FR) 4 b.f. Sakhee (USA) 136 – Heaven 84 (Reel Buddy (USA) 118) [2017 50: p6g^5 7m^5 7d^5 8s 8f^5 8g^4 p8g p11g t8.6g^6 t8.6g Dec 13] lengthy filly: modest maiden: stays 1m: acts on polytrack and good to firm going: usually races towards rear. *Tony Carroll* **57**

CLOVELLY BAY (IRE) 6 b.g. Bushranger (IRE) 119 – Crystalline Stream (FR) (Polish Precedent (USA) 131) [2017 83: t12.2m t12.2m^2 p13.3d^6 p12g^2 11.4g^6 13.3s p12g^4 Sep 6] angular gelding: fairly useful handicapper: second at Kempton in April: stays 1½m: acts on polytrack, tapeta and soft going. *Marcus Tregoning* **82**

CLOWANCE ONE 5 b.g. Oasis Dream 129 – Clowance 117 (Montjeu (IRE) 137) [2017 p12g^3 p11g^3 p16g* 14s^4 p16s* p16g^4 Sep 5] sturdy gelding: useful handicapper: won at Kempton in July and August (by 3½ lengths from Dominating): stays 2m: acts on polytrack and soft going: usually wears headgear: front runner/races prominently: sold to join Kristin Stubbs 5,000 gns in October. *Roger Charlton* **97**

CLUBBABLE 2 b.f. (Mar 9) Mayson 124 – Invitee 74 (Medicean 128) [2017 6g^3 6g^2 6d^3 6d^2 6.5g^2 7d^2 7m^6 6d* Oct 30] rather leggy filly: fourth foal: half-sister to 7f-1¼m winner Visitant (by Pivotal): dam, maiden, closely related to smart French sprinter Titus Livius: fairly useful performer: won minor event at Leicester in October: stays 7f: acts on good to soft going. *Richard Fahey* **86**

CLUB HOUSE (IRE) 7 b.g. Marju (IRE) 127 – Idesia (IRE) 78 (Green Desert (USA) 127) [2017 –: t7.1m Jan 4] workmanlike gelding: fairly useful at best, lightly raced and no form since 2015: sometimes wears headgear. *Kevin Frost* –

CLUBLAND (IRE) 8 b.g. Red Clubs (IRE) 125 – Racjilanemm 77 (Kyllachy 129) [2017 86: f5g 7d 6g Aug 2] compact gelding: fair handicapper: left Garry Moss after first start and rejoined former yard: stays 6f: acts on all-weather, firm and soft going: tried in cheekpieces/tongue tie. *Roy Bowring* **66**

CLUB TROPICANA 2 ch.f. (Feb 16) Helmet (AUS) 127 – Twenty Seven (IRE) 75 (Efisio 120) [2017 6m^6 p7s^3 7d p7g Oct 13] £25,000Y: tall filly: half-sister to 2-y-o 5f winners Beat Seven (useful, by Beat Hollow) and Kirtling Belle (by Pastoral Pursuits): dam 2-y-o 6f winner: fair form: stays 7f. *Richard Spencer* **78**

C NOTE (IRE) 4 b.g. Iffraaj 127 – Alexander Queen (IRE) 96 (King's Best (USA) 132) [2017 105: p7m^6 p8s^4 Dec 7] strong gelding: useful performer: stays 1m: acts on polytrack and heavy going: has worn blinkers: in tongue tie last 2 starts. *Heather Main* **100**

COACH BOMBAY (IRE) 9 b.g. Ad Valorem (USA) 125 – Molly-O (IRE) 101 (Dolphin Street (FR) 125) [2017 66: p8g^4 p10.7g t8.6g p8g p8g Nov 17] modest handicapper: stays 1½m: acts on polytrack, tapeta, good to firm and good to soft going: usually wears headgear: wears tongue tie. *Adrian Brendan Joyce, Ireland* **61**

COACHELLA (IRE) 3 gr.g. Kyllachy 129 – Indian Belle (IRE) 83 (Indian Ridge 123) [2017 –: t8g 7m^4 p7g 7.4g 7m^6 6.1g^6 8.1d p10d Sep 21] sturdy gelding: poor maiden: stays 7f: acts on good to firm going: tried in cheekpieces. *Ed de Giles* **47**

COAL STOCK (IRE) 2 ch.g. (Mar 26) Red Jazz (USA) 125 – Scar Tissue 63 (Medicean 128) [2017 6.1m 7.1m 7.4g^2 7.4d^4 7.4v^3 p7d Dec 13] fair maiden: left David Evans after fifth start: stays 7.5f: acts on good to soft going. *Christian Williams* **71**

COASTAL CYCLONE 3 b.g. Canford Cliffs (IRE) 133 – Seasonal Cross 80 (Cape Cross (IRE) 129) [2017 82p: 6d^4 p7d 7m^3 6m^4 6d^6 6.1d^3 5m^4 5d 6.1m Oct 16] sturdy gelding: fairly useful handicapper: third at Newbury in June: stays 7f: acts on polytrack and good to firm going: sometimes in headgear: temperament under suspicion. *Harry Dunlop* **81**

COASTAL DRIVE 2 gr.c. (Apr 19) Harbour Watch (IRE) 121 – Added Attraction (FR) (Kendor (FR) 122) [2017 7m^3 7d^5 7m^2 p7g^6 Aug 8] fair form: raced only at 7f: acts on good to firm going: has joined Paul Midgley. *Richard Hannon* **73**

COAST GUARD 2 b.f. (Mar 16) Harbour Watch (IRE) 121 – Epernay 86 (Tiger Hill (IRE) 127) [2017 7g^3 8s p7g^3 p7g Oct 18] 5,000Y: second foal: dam, 1m/8.6f winner, half-sister to smart winner up to 9.5f Nimr: modest form: best effort at 7f: in cheekpieces last 2 starts: sold 5,000 gns, sent to Italy. *Tom Dascombe* **61**

COAT OF ARMS (IRE) 2 b.c. (May 21) Galileo (IRE) 134 – La Traviata (USA) 112 (Johannesburg (USA) 127) [2017 7m 8g^3 8g^2 7s^2 7s^4 7d^3 8d Oct 28] brother to high-class 1m-1½m (including Irish Oaks) winner Seventh Heaven and half-brother to 3 winners, including smart 2-y-o 6f (including Middle Park Stakes) winner Crusade (by Mr Greeley): dam US Grade 3 6f winner: useful maiden: second in Futurity Stakes at the Curragh (short head behind Rostropovich) in August: stays 1m: acts on soft going: sent to Denmark. *Aidan O'Brien, Ireland* **100**

COBALTY ISLE (IRE) 3 b.g. Kodiac 112 – Shamarlane 75 (Shamardal (USA) 129) [2017 6m^2 6.1m^2 t7.1g^4 Jun 30] €48,000Y: first foal: dam 7f-9f winner: fairly useful form: best effort when second in maiden at Windsor (neck behind Think Fashion) in June: bred to stay 7f: sold to join Keith Dalgleish 7,500 gns in July. *Henry Candy* **81**

COBBLER QUINN (IRE) 2 b.g. (Apr 18) Tagula (IRE) 116 – Skyscape 89 (Zafonic (USA) 130) [2017 5m Jun 2] 22/1, well held in minor event at Catterick. *Keith Dalgleish* **–**

COCKNEY BOY 4 ch.g. Cockney Rebel (IRE) 127 – Menha 70 (Dubawi (IRE) 129) [2017 –: p12g 11.7f^2 11.9m 10d 12.1s t9.5g f12.1g t9.5g^2 t8.6g^4 f8.1g^3 f8.1g^4 Dec 4] modest maiden: left John Gallagher after fourth start: stays 11.5f: acts on tapeta and firm going: usually wears headgear: tried in tongue tie: usually races close up. *Michael Appleby* **62**

COCKTAIL (IRE) 2 ch.c. (Mar 9) Dream Ahead (USA) 133 – Pina Colada 77 (Sabrehill (USA) 120) [2017 6.1d 6d t6g^2 Nov 23] fair form: best effort when second in minor event at Newcastle (1¾ lengths behind Gowanbuster) in November. *Jedd O'Keeffe* **71**

COCONUT CREME 3 b.f. Cape Cross (IRE) 129 – Soft Centre 109 (Zafonic (USA) 130) [2017 64p: 9.9f* 9.9m^2 12m 9.9m^4 10m^4 Oct 13] tall, rather leggy filly: useful performer: won maiden at Beverley in May: fourth in listed race at Salisbury (2½ lengths behind Billesdon Bess) in August: stays 1¼m: acts on firm going. *William Haggas* **99**

CODESHARE 5 b.g. Dansili 127 – Clepsydra 78 (Sadler's Wells (USA) 132) [2017 66p: t12.4g^3 t12.4g* t12.4d* t12.4g^3 t10.2s^4 14.6m^2 14.1s 16.3g^3 14m^4 14m Aug 26] fairly useful performer: won maiden in February and handicap in March, both at Newcastle: stays 14.5f: acts on tapeta and good to firm going. *Sally Haynes* **91**

CODICIL 2 b.f. (Feb 19) Lawman (FR) 121 – Macleya (GER) 115 (Winged Love (IRE) 121) [2017 p7g* 7.4s* 8.1m* t8s* Sep 8] rangy filly: has plenty of scope: sixth foal: half-sister to 1¼m winner Mediation (by Azamour) and 2-y-o 7f winner Saltonstall (by Pivotal): dam German/French 1¼m-15f winner: fairly useful form: unbeaten in 4 starts, winning minor events at Kempton in June and Beverley in August, and nurseries at Windsor in August and Newcastle (by short head from Weellan) in September: stays 1m: will go on improving. *Sir Mark Prescott Bt* **85 p**

COEUR DE LION 4 b.g. Pour Moi (IRE) 125 – Hora 79 (Hernando (FR) 127) [2017 81p: 16d* 18d^2 16.3g^3 Oct 14] rangy gelding: fairly useful handicapper: won at Nottingham in May: second at Newmarket in September and third at York in October: stays 2¼m: acts on good to soft going: often races prominently: useful hurdler. *Alan King* **93**

COHESION 4 b.g. Champs Elysees 124 – Winter Bloom (USA) 89 (Aptitude (USA) 128) [2017 p12m^4 p12g^3 t12.2g* p15.8g^4 14.9g 11.9s t12.2g^4 t14d^2 t16.3d Dec 16] smart handicapper: won at Wolverhampton (by 1¼ lengths from Winterlude) in March: second at same course (short head behind Velvet Revolution) in December: stays 1¾m: acts on polytrack, tapeta and heavy going: tried in cheekpieces: usually races prominently. *David Bridgwater* **113**

COILLTE CAILIN (IRE) 7 b.m. Oratorio (IRE) 128 – Forest Walk (IRE) (Shinko Forest (IRE)) [2017 81, a98: p10g* p10g^5 t9.5g^3 p10g^4 t9.5g 9.8m^5 8d^6 9.8d^6 p10s^6 t12.2g p10g t9.5d^6 Dec 16] fairly useful handicapper on turf, useful on all-weather: won at Lingfield in January: third at Wolverhampton (½ length behind Pactolus) in February: stays 11f: acts on polytrack, tapeta and good to firm going: tried in blinkers: often races towards rear: has joined Daniel Loughnane. *David O'Meara* **87 a102**

COISTE BODHAR (IRE) 6 b.g. Camacho 118 – Nortolixa (FR) (Linamix (FR) 127) **62**
[2017 80, a74: f6d f6g f5g 5d 5d 5d^5 5g f6.1g 5s^3 5s^3 f5g^6 f6.1g^4 f5g^5 f5g* Dec 21] sturdy gelding: modest handicapper: won at Southwell in December: stays 6f: acts on polytrack, fibresand, good to firm and heavy going: usually wears headgear. *Scott Dixon*

COLD FIRE (IRE) 4 ch.g. Frozen Power (IRE) 108 – Eleanor Eloise (USA) 61 (Minardi **65**
(USA) 119) [2017 p6g^4 p6f Mar 4] fair form: better effort when fourth in maiden at Kempton in February: went as if amiss next time: has joined Hughie Morrison. *Jeremy Gask*

COLD FUSION (IRE) 4 b.f. Frozen Power (IRE) 108 – Tuscania (USA) (Woodman **60**
(USA) 126) [2017 77: t8.6m p12g^5 t8.6m^5 f8g^6 t8.6g p13.3g^2 p12g t16.5g^4 p16g^5 t12.2g^4 11.7f^6 t12.2g 16.2m^2 16d^2 11.6g^5 Jun 1] angular filly: modest handicapper: stays 2m: acts on polytrack, tapeta, good to firm and good to soft going: wears headgear: in tongue tie last 3 starts. *David Flood*

COLD SHOULDER 3 b.g. Passing Glance 119 – Averami 68 (Averti (IRE) 117) [2017 **74**
12d^4 11.2d Jul 8] fair form: better effort when fourth in maiden at Chepstow in June. *Andrew Balding*

COLD SNAP (IRE) 4 b.g. Medicean 128 – Shivering 80 (Royal Applause 124) [2017 **87**
82p: 6m 6m^2 6d^4 Aug 18] lengthy gelding: fairly useful handicapper: second at Newmarket in June: raced only at 6f: acts on good to firm and good to soft going. *William Jarvis*

COLD STARE (IRE) 2 b.g. (Mar 29) Intense Focus (USA) 117 – Ziria (IRE) 109 **96**
(Danehill Dancer (IRE) 117) [2017 7g* 7g* 7g 7s Oct 4] €10,000F, €46,000Y: strong, workmanlike gelding: half-brother to several winners, including smart 7f (including at 2 yrs) winner Fadhayyil (by Tamayuz) and useful French winner up to 1¼m Zipzip (2-y-o 1m/9f winner, by Whipper): dam French 5f winner (including at 2 yrs): useful form: won newcomers race at Maisons-Laffitte in June and listed event at Saint-Cloud (by head from Ghost Serge) in July: well below best in better company after: raced only at 7f: sold to join David O'Meara 68,000 gns in October. *E. J. O'Neill, France*

COLIBRI (IRE) 3 b.g. Redoute's Choice (AUS) – High Days (IRE) 77 (Hennessy (USA) **100**
122) [2017 96: 8.1d^4 8m 10m 8g^4 8.2v^3 Sep 29] sturdy gelding: useful handicapper: fourth at Sandown in April: stays 1m: acts on heavy and good to firm going: tried in cheekpieces: has joined F. Rohaut in France. *Hugo Palmer*

COLLATERAL BEAUTY 2 b.f. (Apr 7) Pastoral Pursuits 127 – Nicola's Dream 76 **68**
(Alhaarth (IRE) 126) [2017 6g^4 6m^5 6g^3 7d 6.9v^6 Sep 18] rather unfurnished filly: third foal: half-sister to 7f winner Back To Bond (by Monsieur Bond): dam maiden (should have stayed 1¼m): fair maiden: stays 6f: acts on good to firm going. *Richard Fahey*

COLLATERAL (IRE) 2 b.g. (Mar 1) Reckless Abandon 119 – May Day Queen (IRE) **75**
79 (Danetime (IRE) 121) [2017 6g^4 6m^6 7m^2 7.2d^5 6.1m^6 p7g^2 p8g Oct 5] compact gelding: fair maiden: stays 7f: acts on polytrack and good to firm going: tried in blinkers: sent to Macau. *James Tate*

COLLECTED (USA) 4 ch.c. City Zip (USA) 112 – Helena Bay (Johannesburg (USA) **129**
127) [2017 a8f* a9f* a8.5f* a10f* a10f^2 a8.5f^3 Dec 26] developed into top-class performer at 4 yrs after missing second half of 2016: won listed race and Grade 2 Californian Stakes in April, and Grade 3 Precisionist Stakes (by 14 lengths) in June, all at Santa Anita, and Pacific Classic at Del Mar (by ½ length from Arrogate, making all) in August: placed after in Breeders' Cup Classic at Del Mar (beaten 2¼ lengths by Gun Runner) and Grade 2 San Antonio Stakes at Santa Anita (odds on when 3½ lengths third to Giant Expectations): stays 1¼m: acts on dirt and firm going: used to wear blinkers (didn't in 2017): usually races up with the pace. *Bob Baffert, USA*

COLLEGE KING 2 b.g. (Mar 30) Baltic King 120 – Flaming Telepath (Storming Home **–**
128) [2017 p7d 8.3d Oct 18] well held in minor event/maiden. *Christine Dunnett*

COLLEGIATE (IRE) 2 b.f. (Mar 4) Declaration of War (USA) 128 – Cochabamba **–**
(IRE) 102 (Hurricane Run (IRE) 134) [2017 p7g Oct 26] €350,000Y: second foal: half-sister to 7f winner Multicultural (by Fastnet Rock): dam winner up to 1m (2-y-o 6f winner): 33/1, very green when well held in minor event at Chelmsford. *Sir Michael Stoute*

COLLINGHAM PARK (IRE) 2 b.g. (Feb 24) Dragon Pulse (IRE) 114 – Curraline **80**
(IRE) 59 (Bachelor Duke (USA) 122) [2017 5m^5 5m^3 6d* 6m^2 6d^6 6.1v^3 6g Oct 13] €16,000F: second foal: dam maiden: fairly useful performer: won minor event at Ripon (by 4 lengths from Go Now Go Now) in June: will stay 7f+: acts on good to firm and good to soft going. *Jedd O'Keeffe*

COLLODI (GER) 8 b.g. Konigstiger (GER) 112 – Codera (GER) (Zilzal (USA) 137) **82**
[2017 85: 12.1s* Jun 10] fairly useful performer: won claimer at Catterick (by 8 lengths from Never Say) on sole start on Flat in 2017: stays 1½m: acts on polytrack and heavy going: has worn cheekpieces: sometimes slowly away, often travels strongly: fair hurdler. *Neil Mulholland*

COLOMANO 3 b.c. Cacique (IRE) 124 – Codera (GER) (Zilzal (USA) 137) [2017 104p: **119**
8.4g^4 10.9g* 11.9s 11.9g^4 11.9g^3 11.9s^3 10.2s^5 Nov 5] €43,000Y: half-brother to several winners, including useful German 10.5f/11f winner Codoor (by Sabiango) and 1m-1½m winner Collodi (by Konigstiger): dam, German 1¼m winner, half-sister to smart German performer up to 1½m Concepcion: smart performer: won Union-Rennen at Cologne (by ½ length from Windstoss) in June: best effort when third in Grosser Preis von Baden (2½ lengths behind Guignol) on fifth start: stays 1½m: acts on soft going: usually races towards rear. *Markus Klug, Germany*

COLONEL FRANK 3 b.g. Dutch Art 126 – Loquacity (Diktat 126) [2017 86: 7d^6 7g^5 6v^4 **90**
8d* Oct 27] fairly useful handicapper: won at Newbury (by ¾ length from Redgrave) in October: stays 1m: acts on tapeta, good to soft and good to firm going: sold to join Mick Quinn 28,000 gns in November. *Ed Walker*

COLONIAL CLASSIC (FR) 4 br.f. Dansili 127 – Flame of Hestia (IRE) 79 (Giant's **98**
Causeway (USA) 132) [2017 97: 12f^4 12g 12d^4 14.1g^5 Oct 16] good-topped, attractive filly: useful performer: stays 1½m: acts on tapeta and firm going: often races prominently. *James Fanshawe*

COLORADO DREAM 2 b.g. (Feb 7) Oasis Dream 129 – Colorado Dawn (Fantastic **71**
Light (USA) 134) [2017 5g 7d^5 7g 8.5m 8.3d^2 Oct 18] lengthy, rather unfurnished gelding: fair maiden: best effort at 8.5f: acts on good to soft going: often wears headgear. *George Baker*

COLOR FORCE (IRE) 4 gr.f. Dark Angel (IRE) 113 – Amistad (GER) (Winged Love **48**
(IRE) 121) [2017 61: p7m p11d^5 p13.3g^6 10.1d^4 10.2d 10.1m^4 t12.4d^4 p15.8g Nov 21] big, **a60**
rangy filly: modest maiden: left Gay Kelleway after sixth start: stays 12.5f: acts on tapeta and good to firm going: has worn headgear: often wears tongue tie: front runner/races prominently. *Daniel Kubler*

COLOURBEARER (IRE) 10 ch.g. Pivotal 124 – Centifolia (FR) 112 (Kendor (FR) **73**
122) [2017 75: t6m^5 p6g* f6g p6g^6 t6g^6 p6g^5 p6g^3 Mar 24] fair handicapper: won at Chelmsford in January: stays 6f: acts on all-weather and soft going: has worn headgear: wears tongue tie: front runner/races prominently. *Charlie Wallis*

COLOUR CONTRAST (IRE) 4 b.g. Rock of Gibraltar (IRE) 133 – Colour Coordinated **65**
(IRE) 70 (Spectrum (IRE) 126) [2017 –: 9.1m^5 9s^2 9.2m^6 10g^3 10d^4 11.1g^5 9.2s 8.3s^3 9.2d^4 11.2v 9.9v Sep 26] fair maiden: stays 1¼m: acts on soft and good to firm going: usually wears headgear. *Iain Jardine*

COLOURFIELD (IRE) 2 b.f. (Mar 15) Makfi 130 – Rainbow Desert (USA) 86 **71**
(Dynaformer (USA)) [2017 7m 7m^3 Oct 25] 21,000Y: good-topped filly: fourth foal: dam, 1m winner, closely related to smart US Grade 1 9f winner Dublino: fair form: better effort when third in minor event at Newmarket (4¼ lengths behind Wild Impala) in October: bred to be suited by 1m+. *Ed Vaughan*

COLOURFUL CAREER (USA) 3 b.g. More Than Ready (USA) 120 – Rainbow Luck **79**
(USA) (Honour And Glory (USA) 122) [2017 t8.6g^4 p8s^3 8.1m^3 t7.2g^5 p8s^4 p10g* Dec 30] good-topped gelding: fair performer: won maiden at Lingfield in December: stays 1¼m: acts on polytrack and good to firm going: tried in cheekpieces: front runner/races prominently. *Ed Dunlop*

COLUMBIA KID (IRE) 2 b.f. (Mar 19) Big Bad Bob (IRE) 118 – Tinaheely (IRE) 75 **75**
(Intikhab (USA) 135) [2017 6m 6m^3 May 24] €5,500F, €4,500Y: second foal: sister to 2-y-o 1m-1¼m winner Count Calabash: dam maiden (stayed 1m): fair form: better effort when third in minor event at Ayr (1½ lengths behind Chookie Dunedin) in May. *L. Smyth, Ireland*

COLUMBIAN CARTEL 4 b.g. Indesatchel (IRE) 120 – Find The Answer (Vital Equine –
(IRE) 121) [2017 p7g t12.2g^6 10m Jun 17] lengthy, rather dipped-backed gelding: no form. *J. S. Moore*

COMBE HAY (FR) 4 b.f. Elusive City (USA) 117 – Coiffure (King's Best (USA) 132) **69**
[2017 73: p12g 8d^3 7.5g^3 8.4g^5 9.7g* Aug 8] tall filly: fair performer: left Henry Spiller after first outing: won minor event at Les Sables-d'Olonne in August: stays 1¼m: acts on polytrack and good to soft going: has worn hood: front runner/races prominently. *E. Libaud, France*

COME BACK KING (IRE) 4 ch.g. Pivotal 124 – Queen Consort (USA) (Kingmambo (USA) 125) [2017 86: f12g^{2} t13.9g^{3} Feb 6] fairly useful handicapper: second at Southwell in January: stays 1¾m: acts on fibresand and good to firm going: sometimes in blinkers: front runner/races prominently. *Michael Appleby* **86**

COMEDY HOUSE 9 b.g. Auction House (USA) 120 – Kyle Akin (Vettori (IRE) 119) [2017 61: p15.8g Jan 4] fair at best, down the field sole start in 2017: stays 2m: acts on polytrack and good to firm going: often wears headgear. *Michael Madgwick* **–**

COMEDY SCHOOL (USA) 3 b.f. Distorted Humor (USA) 117 – Cheeky Charm (USA) (A P Indy (USA) 131) [2017 96: p7g 12m 9m 7.9m^{5} 8.3g^{4} 6g 8.2s^{4} 8d^{3} p9.4f^{6} Nov 29] useful-looking filly: fairly useful performer: left Mark Johnston after fifth start: close third in minor event at Maisons-Laffitte in October: left Gianluca Bietolini before final outing: probably stays 1m: acts on soft and good to firm going: has worn blinkers. *A. Marcialis, Italy* **85**

COME ON COME ON (IRE) 3 br.c. Lord Shanakill (USA) 121 – Maridiyna (IRE) (Sinndar (IRE) 134) [2017 83p: 8m^{pu} May 12] fairly useful form when winning 7f maiden at 2 yrs, broke down sole start in 2017. *Clive Cox* **–**

COME ON DAVE (IRE) 8 b.g. Red Clubs (IRE) 125 – Desert Sprite (IRE) 62 (Tagula (IRE) 116) [2017 86: p5g p5g^{4} p5g^{4} t5.1g^{3} p5g^{6} 5.3g* 5d* 5.3g^{2} 5.1g 5.1v^{3} p5g^{3} p5m* Nov 25] tall gelding: fairly useful handicapper: won at Brighton in June, and Lingfield in July and November (by ½ length from Blazed): stays 5.5f: acts on all-weather, good to firm and heavy going: wears headgear: front runner/races prominently, often travels strongly. *John Butler* **88**

COME ON PERCY 3 b.c. Sir Percy 129 – Collette's Choice 72 (Royal Applause 124) [2017 67: f7g^{2} f8g Jan 24] modest maiden: stays 7f: acts on fibresand: sent to the Netherlands. *Richard Fahey* **58**

COME ON SAL 2 b.f. (Mar 11) Sayif (IRE) 122 – Immortelle (Arazi (USA) 135) [2017 t9.5g Nov 18] half-sister to several winners, including 1½m winner Corker (by Grand Lodge) and 2-y-o 5f winner Lothian Countess (by Auction House): dam unraced half-sister to Poule d'Essai des Pouliches winner Danseuse du Soir: 200/1, well held in minor event at Wolverhampton. *Daniel Loughnane* **–**

COME ON TIER (FR) 2 b.c. (Mar 6) Kendargent (FR) 112 – Milwaukee (FR) (Desert King (IRE) 129) [2017 8.1g^{3} 8.3g* Nov 1] €10,000Y, €65,000 2-y-o: useful-looking colt: half-brother to several winners, including 7f-8.6f winner Two No Bids (by Footstepsinthesand) and 1¼m winner Kachou (by Excellent Art): dam useful French 10.5f-12.5f winner: fairly useful form: won maiden at Nottingham (by 3¾ lengths from Rich Identity) in November: will go on improving. *David Simcock* **91 p**

COME WITH ME 2 b.f. (Apr 16) Dansili 127 – Fantasia 116 (Sadler's Wells (USA) 132) [2017 8m^{5} 8.3d 8d^{2} t8.6g p8s^{4} Dec 17] third foal: half-sister to useful 7f-1¼m winner Jupiter Light (by Lonhro) and a winner in USA by Tapit: dam winner up to 9.5f (2-y-o 6f/7f winner): fair maiden: best effort at 1m: acts on good to soft going: in tongue tie last 3 starts. *John Gosden* **74**

COMICAS (USA) 4 ch.g. Distorted Humor (USA) 117 – Abby's Angel (USA) (Touch Gold (USA) 127) [2017 102: a6f* a6f^{4} a6g^{2} 6s^{3} 6m a6f^{2} Dec 21] good-bodied gelding: smart performer: won handicap at Meydan (by length from Dundonnell) in February: second in Dubai Golden Shaheen at same course (3 lengths behind Mind Your Biscuits) in March: below best after: stays 7f: acts on dirt and good to firm going: wears headgear. *Charlie Appleby* **115**

COMMANCHE 8 ch.g. Sleeping Indian 122 – Happy Memories (IRE) (Thatching 131) [2017 72§: p6g^{4} t6d^{2} t6g* p6g^{6} t6g^{6} 7g^{4} 7d^{5} 7m^{5} 6m^{3} t6.1g^{6} p6d 6s 6d^{5} 6s^{6} Oct 31] compact gelding: modest handicapper on turf, fair on all-weather: won at Wolverhampton in February: stays 7f: acts on polytrack, tapeta and any turf going: wears headgear. *Chris Dwyer* **64 a74**

COMMANDER 3 b.c. Frankel 147 – Model Queen (USA) 76 (Kingmambo (USA) 125) [2017 66p: 8m^{2} 8d* Jun 2] strong, compact colt: fairly useful form: won maiden at Doncaster (by head from Cape To Cuba) in June, showing good attitude: raced only at 1m: remains with potential. *Roger Varian* **90 p**

COMMANDER HAN (FR) 2 ch.c. (Mar 6) Siyouni (FR) 122 – Acentela (IRE) (Shirocco (GER) 129) [2017 7g 7g^{4} Oct 7] €62,000Y, 400,000 2-y-o: strong, useful-looking colt: second foal: half-brother to French 7f-9.5f winner (including at 2 yrs) Blue **75 p**

Hills (by Myboycharlie): dam, French maiden, out of half-sister to Poule d'Essai des Poulains winner Tin Horse: fair form: better effort when fourth in minor event at Redcar (1¾ lengths behind Three Saints Bay) in October: open to further improvement. *Kevin Ryan*

COMMISSAR 8 b.g. Soviet Star (USA) 128 – Sari 83 (Faustus (USA) 118) [2017 68: f12g^4 t9.5g^5 f12g^5 p12g f11g^5 t8.6g 10.1m May 17] tall gelding: modest handicapper: stays 1½m: acts on all-weather, firm and soft going: wears headgear/tongue tie. *Mandy Rowland* **59**

COMMODITY (IRE) 4 ch.g. Dutch Art 126 – Royale Danehill (IRE) (Danehill (USA) 126) [2017 79: 8.3m* 8m* p8g* 8.2s^4 t8.6g^3 p8g^6 Sep 9] good-topped gelding: fairly useful handicapper: won at Windsor in April, and Yarmouth and Kempton in May: stays 8.5f: acts on polytrack, tapeta and good to firm going: front runner: sold 30,000 gns in October, sent to Saudi Arabia. *Sir Michael Stoute* **91**

COMMUNIQUE (IRE) 2 ch.c. (Feb 10) Casamento (IRE) 118 – Midnight Line (USA) 114 (Kris S (USA)) [2017 p8g^2 p8g^2 Oct 26] half-brother to several winners, including useful 1½m winner Timekeeping (by New Approach) and useful 1¼m winner Moon Quest (by Rainbow Quest): dam winner up to 1½m (US Grade 2 event, also 2-y-o 7f/1m winner): fairly useful form: better effort when second in minor event at Chelmsford (length behind Dukhan) in October, clear of rest: will go on improving. *Mark Johnston* **83 p**

COMPANY ASSET (IRE) 4 ch.f. Fast Company (IRE) 126 – Changari (USA) 90 (Gulch (USA)) [2017 85: 7m^3 7d^3 8.3s* 9.2g* 10.3g^6 9.2s^3 10.5s* 9.9s^2 10.4g Oct 22] useful handicapper: won at Hamilton in June and July, and Haydock (by 6 lengths from Empress Ali) in September: second in listed race at Saint-Cloud (2½ lengths behind Rosental) in October: stays 10.5f: acts on soft and good to firm going: usually held up. *Kevin Ryan* **107**

COMPANY TRADER (IRE) 3 b.g. Fast Company (IRE) 126 – Akariyda (IRE) (Salse (USA) 128) [2017 12g^6 10m^5 12s 11.6d 16v Aug 3] no form: tried in blinkers. *Sharon Watt* **–**

COMPAS SCOOBIE 4 br.g. Kheleyf (USA) 116 – Fantastic Santanyi (Fantastic Light (USA) 134) [2017 89: t6g* 6m^5 6g^2 5d^2 5g 5d* 5d* 5m^5 5.6g t5.1g^5 Dec 22] useful handicapper: won at Wolverhampton (apprentice) in April, Newmarket in July and Bath (by 4½ lengths from Seamster) in August: left Roger Varian after ninth start: best at 5f/6f: acts on polytrack, tapeta and soft going: wears headgear: tried in tongue tie: races towards rear. *Stuart Williams* **103**

COMPASS POINT 2 b.c. (Feb 28) Helmet (AUS) 127 – Takarna (IRE) 70 (Mark of Esteem (IRE) 137) [2017 7d 8g Sep 15] sturdy colt: well held in 2 minor events. *Laura Mongan* **–**

COMPASS ROSE (IRE) 3 b.f. Henrythenavigator (USA) 131 – Raydaniya (IRE) 78 (In The Wings 128) [2017 7m 8g t7.1g^4 p7g f8.1g Oct 22] £20,000Y: neat filly: half-sister to several winners, including smart winner around 1¼m Roseburg (by Tamayuz) and useful 7.5f-1½m winner Raydiya (by Marju): dam maiden (stayed 12.5f): little form: in tongue tie last 2 starts. *Scott Dixon* **–**

COMPETENT 5 b.g. Compton Place 125 – Pantita 74 (Polish Precedent (USA) 131) [2017 72: f11g t12.2g May 3] fair maiden at best, failed to beat a rival last 3 starts: stays 1½m: acts on polytrack and tapeta: usually races close up. *Tim Fitzgerald* **–**

COMPETITION 5 b.g. Multiplex 114 – Compolina (Compton Place 125) [2017 t12.2g^6 8g^5 t7.1g 10.2d^4 9g^6 10.2m^6 12.1s^5 Jul 26] placed in bumper: fair maiden: stays 1¼m: acts on good to soft going: wears tongue tie. *Brian Rothwell* **66**

COMPLIANCE (IRE) 2 b.c. (Mar 26) Exceed And Excel (AUS) 126 – Saadiah (IRE) (Dubai Destination (USA) 127) [2017 7m p8s^2 t8s^5 t8.6g^6 Nov 18] fair form: stays 8.5f. *James Tate* **69**

COMPLICIT (IRE) 6 b.g. Captain Rio 122 – Molomo 104 (Barathea (IRE) 127) [2017 85, a102: p5g^5 p7s^4 p8g^6 p8g^5 7g^5 8g 7v 5d 7s p8g^2 p8g^2 p8g^2 p7g* Dec 21] good-topped gelding: fair handicapper: won at Chelmsford (amateur) in December: stays 1¼m, usually races over 7f/1m nowadays: acts on all-weather, good to firm and heavy going: often wears headgear: has worn tongue tie. *J. F. Levins, Ireland* **73**

COMPORTA 2 b.c. (Jan 26) Iffraaj 127 – Hot Wired (Rock of Gibraltar (IRE) 133) [2017 7s 7g Oct 7] fair form: better effort when seventh in maiden at Yarmouth (5 lengths behind Regal Reality) in September. *Ismail Mohammed* **67**

COMPRISE 3 b.g. Pivotal 124 – Constitute (USA) 85 (Gone West (USA)) [2017 77p: f6g* 6m^2 5s 6.1m^3 p6g* 6.1g t6g^4 6d^5 Sep 20] well-made gelding: fairly useful performer: won maiden at Southwell in March and handicap at Kempton (by 3¼ lengths from Father McKenzie) in July: stays 6f: acts on polytrack, fibresand and good to firm going: often leads: sold to join Keith Dalgleish 20,000 gns in October. *Michael Bell* **91**

COMPTON ABBEY 3 b.f. Compton Place 125 – Bolsena (USA) (Red Ransom (USA)) [2017 p8d^4 Dec 13] 2,500F, £12,000Y: half-sister to several winners, including useful 1m winners Cactus Rose (by Zamindar) and Peru (including at 2 yrs, by Motivator): dam unraced: 50/1, well held in maiden at Kempton. *Brett Johnson* **–**

COMPTON BRAVE 3 b.g. Compton Place 125 – Willmar (IRE) 53 (Zafonic (USA) 130) [2017 –: 6m 6g p8g p7g^4 t8.6g^3 f7.1g Dec 22] modest maiden: stays 8.5f: acts on polytrack and tapeta. *J. R. Jenkins* **52**

COMPTON GRACE 2 ch.f. (Apr 15) Compton Place 125 – Janet Girl (Polar Falcon (USA) 126) [2017 6.1g 6.1g 5s^5 p7g Sep 6] 4,500Y: unfurnished filly: seventh foal: half-sister to Italian 7.5f winner Invincible Girl (by Orpen): dam ran twice in Italy: no form. *Mick Channon* **–**

COMPTON LANE 3 b.g. Compton Place 125 – Dubai Affair 73 (Dubawi (IRE) 129) [2017 75: t6g^6 5.1m^6 7d^6 5m Jun 13] sturdy gelding: fair handicapper, below form in first half of 2017: stays 6f: acts on soft going: usually races prominently: sent to Italy, where won handicap at Pisa in November. *Rod Millman* **61**

COMPTON MILL 5 b.g. Compton Place 125 – Classic Millennium 72 (Midyan (USA) 124) [2017 86: 10g^3 10s^3 10.1f^6 11.8d* 14s^6 12v^4 10.2d* 10.2d 10v^6 Nov 7] rather leggy gelding: fairly useful handicapper: won at Leicester in July and Nottingham (by short head from Indian Chief) in October: stays 1½m: acts on polytrack and any turf going: has worn tongue tie. *Hughie Morrison* **93**

COMPTON PARK 10 ch.h. Compton Place 125 – Corps de Ballet (IRE) 92 (Fasliyev (USA) 120) [2017 82: t6g^3 t6g 6g^3 5m 6d 7g^5 7d t6d t6g Oct 19] tall horse: fair handicapper: stays 7f: acts on polytrack, tapeta, good to firm and heavy going: has worn headgear: usually wears tongue tie: sometimes slowly away. *Les Eyre* **72**

COMPTON POPPY 3 b.f. Compton Place 125 – Miss Poppy 68 (Averti (IRE) 117) [2017 80: 5m^6 6d^3 5f 5.1m^2 5.1v^4 Jul 28] fairly useful handicapper: second at Chepstow in July: best form at 5f: acts on good to firm going. *Tony Carroll* **82**

COMPTON PRINCE 8 ch.g. Compton Place 125 – Malelane (IRE) 48 (Prince Sabo 123) [2017 46, a71: p6g* p6m p6g^5 p6g^3 p6g^4 p6g^6 p6g^2 5.7f^3 5.7f* p6g 5.7m* 5.7f 6.1m^6 5.7f t6.1g p6g p6g* Dec 12] lengthy gelding: modest handicapper on turf, fair on all-weather: won at Kempton in January, Bath in May and June, and Lingfield in December: raced up to 6f nowadays: acts on polytrack, tapeta and firm going: wears headgear. *Milton Bradley* **62** **a70**

COMPTON RIVER 5 b.g. Compton Place 125 – Inagh River 71 (Fasliyev (USA) 120) [2017 83: t5.1g^6 t5g^6 t5.1g^6 5m^4 5g^5 5d^3 5s 5s^3 5d^2 5g 5s 5v^3 5s^5 Oct 31] stocky, close-coupled gelding: fair handicapper: best form at 5f: acts on tapeta, good to firm and heavy going: has worn headgear: sometimes slowly away. *Bryan Smart* **75**

COMPULSIVE (IRE) 2 ch.c. (Apr 26) Lope de Vega (IRE) 125 – Fand (USA) (Kingmambo (USA) 125) [2017 p7s 7g p7g Nov 6] fair form in minor event/maidens. *Roger Varian* **71**

COMPUTABLE 3 ch.g. Compton Place 125 – Kummel Excess (IRE) 81 (Exceed And Excel (AUS) 126) [2017 84: 5g^2 5s 5m^6 5g Aug 19] strong, workmanlike gelding: fairly useful handicapper: below form after second at Thirsk in April: best form at 5f: acts on good to soft going: tried in tongue tie: often races towards rear. *Tim Easterby* **88**

COMRADE CONRAD (IRE) 3 br.c. Canford Cliffs (IRE) 133 – View (IRE) 56 (Galileo (IRE) 134) [2017 10m* 10g^5 10d^5 13.3s^2 12g^6 14v Sep 29] €78,000Y: attractive colt: second foal: dam, ran twice, out of half-sister to dam of Prix de l'Arc de Triomphe winner Rail Link: fairly useful performer: won maiden at Windsor in April: second in handicap at Newbury in August: stays 13.5f: acts on soft and good to firm going: tried in cheekpieces: usually races prominently: sold to join Dan Skelton 25,000 gns in October. *Roger Charlton* **92**

COMRADE IN ARMS (USA) 2 b.g. (Feb 15) War Front (USA) 119 – Maryinsky (IRE) 107 (Sadler's Wells (USA) 132) [2017 7d^5 p7g t7.2m^2 Oct 31] $650,000F: well-made gelding: half-brother to 3 winners, including high-class 1m-1½m (Irish Oaks) winner **73 p**

Peeping Fawn (by Danehill) and smart 2-y-o 7.5f/1m winner (stayed 10.5f) Thewayyouare (by Kingmambo): dam 2-y-o 7f winner: fair form: best effort when second in minor event at Wolverhampton (½ length behind Montague) in October: will stay at least 1m: gelded after final start, and open to further improvement. *Sir Michael Stoute*

COMSELLE 2 b.f. (Feb 16) Compton Place 125 – M'selle (IRE) 75 (Elnadim (USA) 128) **58** [2017 5m 5d^4 5d^6 5g 6.1s 5.1m Oct 16] workmanlike filly: first foal: dam 2-y-o 5f winner: modest maiden: best effort at 5f: acts on good to soft going: tried in hood/tongue tie. *Stuart Kittow*

CONCUR (IRE) 4 ch.g. Approve (IRE) 112 – Tradmagic (IRE) (Traditionally (USA) 117) **61** [2017 55: 6m 7m^5 6m* 6g* 6g^4 6s 5.7s 6.1g Oct 9] stocky gelding: modest handicapper: won amateur events at Redcar in May and Hamilton in June: stays 1m, usually races over shorter: acts on soft and good to firm going: wears headgear/tongue tie. *Rod Millman*

CONDAMINE (IRE) 4 b.g. Duke of Marmalade (IRE) 132 – Miracolia (IRE) (Montjeu **78** (IRE) 137) [2017 81p: p12g^2 Jan 6] fair form: stays 1½m: sent to Australia, where won 7f maiden at Ballarat in June. *Jeremy Gask*

CONFESSIONAL 10 b.g. Dubawi (IRE) 129 – Golden Nun 108 (Bishop of Cashel 122) **99** [2017 100: 5.1m^3 5g 5d^3 5m t5g 5s 5.1d* 5g 5s^3 5.5g^3 5.5g 5s^3 5v^4 5v^3 5d^4 Oct 28] lengthy, good-topped gelding: useful handicapper: won at Chester in July: third at same course (length behind El Astronaute) in May: stays 6f: acts on all-weather, good to firm and heavy going: wears headgear. *Tim Easterby*

CONFLAGRATION 2 b.c. (Apr 8) Exceed And Excel (AUS) 126 – Please Sing 103 **59** (Royal Applause 124) [2017 6.1m^6 p6g p6g^6 p6s p7g Dec 28] sturdy colt: modest form. *Ed Dunlop*

CONISTONE 3 ch.f. Poet's Voice 126 – Protectress 110 (Hector Protector (USA) 124) **62** [2017 68: 8m 9.9g^4 12.1m^3 9.9m^4 12g 9d* Aug 30] modest performer: won claimer at Lingfield in August: stays 1¼m: acts on good to soft going: in cheekpieces last 2 starts: usually races close up: has joined Dan Skelton. *James Bethell*

CONJUROR'S BLUFF 9 b.g. Tiger Hill (IRE) 127 – Portmeirion 96 (Polish Precedent **–** (USA) 131) [2017 t8d 7.1m^6 7m Jun 24] leggy gelding: lightly-raced maiden, no worthwhile form for a long time: usually wears headgear. *Fred Watson*

CONKERING HERO (IRE) 3 ch.g. Arakan (USA) 123 – Brioney (IRE) 70 (Barathea **77** (IRE) 127) [2017 67: p8d p10d^4 p12g* t12.4g^4 11.6d^6 p16g^4 p14d p16s Dec 15] fair handicapper: won at Lingfield in June: stays 1½m: acts on polytrack: front runner/races prominently. *Joseph Tuite*

CONNACHT GIRL (IRE) 3 b.f. Dark Angel (IRE) 113 – Fairy Flight (USA) 80 **–** (Fusaichi Pegasus (USA) 130) [2017 80: 7d 7s 6m^4 May 31] fair maiden at best: failed to beat a rival in 3 starts in 2017: stayed 6f: acted on soft going: tried in blinkers: dead. *A. P. Keatley, Ireland*

CONNAUGHT RANGER (IRE) 2 ch.g. (Jan 24) Finsceal Fior (IRE) – Mona Brown **74** (IRE) 92 (Dylan Thomas (IRE) 132) [2017 7g^5 p7s^5 p8g* p8g^3 Oct 14] sturdy gelding: fair form: won maiden at Lingfield in September: stays 1m. *Denis Coakley*

CONNECT 2 b.c. (Mar 23) Roderic O'Connor (IRE) 119 – Robema 89 (Cadeaux **102** Genereux 131) [2017 7m^4 7s* 7g^6 8v* Oct 23] 38,000F, €67,000Y: leggy colt: sixth foal: brother to useful winner up to 8.5f Atlantic Sun (2-y-o 1m winner) and half-brother to useful 2-y-o 6f winner Leontes (by Paco Boy): dam, 7.4f/1m winner, half-sister to smart US performer up to 1¼m Lucky Chappy: useful form: won minor event at Sandown in August and listed race at Pontefract (by 2¾ lengths from Lisheen Castle) in October: will stay 1¼m. *Clive Cox*

CONNECTICUT 6 b.g. New Approach (IRE) 132 – Craigmill 85 (Slip Anchor 136) **104** [2017 12d^5 p12g^6 Nov 6] attractive gelding: smart at best, below that both starts in 2017 after 2-year absence: stays 1¾m: acts on good to firm going. *Roger Varian*

CONNEMERA QUEEN 4 ch.f. Major Cadeaux 121 – Cashleen (USA) 73 (Lemon Drop **74** Kid (USA) 131) [2017 68: 8g^2 8g^6 7s^6 p7g^5 p8g^2 p8g^4 t7.1g Nov 24] fair handicapper: left Chris Grant after second start: stays 1m: acts on polytrack and good to firm going. *John Butler*

CONNERY (IRE) 2 gr.g. (May 4) Clodovil (IRE) 116 – Ringarooma 61 (Erhaab (USA) **74** 127) [2017 5g^2 6f 5f* 5m^5 5.2v p6g 6g Oct 7] sturdy gelding: fair performer: won minor event at Bath in July: best form at 5f: acts on firm going: sent to Qatar. *Sylvester Kirk*

CONNOISSEUR 2 gr.f. (Apr 29) Mastercraftsman (IRE) 129 – Critical Acclaim 87 (Peintre Celebre (USA) 137) [2017 6d p7g t8.6g Nov 25] fourth foal: half-sister to useful 1¾m winner (stays 21f) William of Orange (by Duke of Marmalade) and 1¼m winner Wave Reviews (by Fastnet Rock): dam, 1½m winner, half-sister to smart 1¼m-1½m winner Eagles Peak: little impact in minor events: type to do better in handicaps. *Sir Mark Prescott Bt* **– p**

CONQUERESS (IRE) 3 ch.f. Dandy Man (IRE) 123 – Sesmen 106 (Inchinor 119) [2017 75: 8s 7m 8f^{5} 8g^{4} 8.1m^{2} t7.1s t6.1m Oct 28] fair handicapper: stays 1m: acts on firm and soft going: in cheekpieces last 5 starts: front runner/races prominently. *Tom Dascombe* **72**

CONSELICE 4 gr.f. Showcasing 117 – Dictatrix 91 (Diktat 126) [2017 105: 7.2m 8.2d^{4} 8d Sep 5] fourth foal: dam 2-y-o 6f winner: useful performer: won 3 times in Italy at 3 yrs, including Premio Regina Elena at Rome for A. & S. Botti: below best in 2017: stays 1m: acts on good to firm and good to soft going. *K. R. Burke* **93**

CONSEQUENCES (IRE) 2 b.c. (Jan 9) Dandy Man (IRE) 123 – Originate (Oasis Dream 129) [2017 5s^{2} 5m* 5m 5s 6g* Nov 3] €16,000F, £31,000Y: first foal: dam, unraced, out of useful close relative to Falmouth Stakes winner Timepiece: useful performer: won minor events at Catterick in June and Newmarket (by 3½ lengths from Rajar) in November: stays 6f: acts on good to firm going: often races prominently, usually travels strongly. *David O'Meara* **97**

CONSIDERED OPINION 3 b.f. Redoute's Choice (AUS) – Forest Crown 105 (Royal Applause 124) [2017 81p: p8g^{2} t7.2g* p8g Nov 6] good-topped filly: fairly useful form: won maiden at Wolverhampton in October: stays 1m. *Ralph Beckett* **80**

CONSOLIDA 2 b.f. (Mar 19) Sir Percy 129 – Red Larkspur (IRE) 86 (Red Clubs (IRE) 125) [2017 8d^{5} t8g* Oct 10] 25,000Y: first foal: dam, 6f winner (including at 2 yrs), half-sister to smart 1m-1¼m winner Blond Me: fairly useful form: won minor event at Newcastle (by 2 lengths from Broken Wings) in October, asserting under hands-and-heels ride: will stay 1¼m: sent to USA: likely to progress further. *Luca Cumani* **80 p**

CONSORTIUM (IRE) 5 b.g. Teofilo (IRE) 126 – Wish List (IRE) 98 (Mujadil (USA) 119) [2017 75: t13.9g^{4} t12.2g Mar 23] stocky gelding: fair handicapper: stays 16.5f: acts on polytrack and tapeta: wears headgear: tried in tongue tie. *Miss Imogen Pickard* **73**

CONSTANTINO (IRE) 4 b.g. Danehill Dancer (IRE) 117 – Messias da Silva (USA) 89 (Tale of The Cat (USA) 113) [2017 97: t8g^{2} p8m^{2} t8s* 7.9m p7s^{5} 8.2v Sep 30] good-topped gelding: useful handicapper: won at Newcastle in June: stays 1m: acts on polytrack, tapeta, soft and good to firm going: wears headgear. *Richard Fahey* **100**

CONSTRUCT 2 b.c. (Mar 22) Maxios 123 – Airfield (Dansili 127) [2017 8s Sep 15] first foal: dam unraced sister to smart performers Early March (stayed 1m) and Aviate (stayed 10.5f): 6/1, badly needed experience when well held in minor event at Salisbury: should do better. *Ralph Beckett* **– p**

CONSULTANT 2 b.g. (Mar 11) Kodiac 112 – Mary Goodnight 86 (King's Best (USA) 132) [2017 7v^{4} 7d^{4} f7.1g^{5} Nov 28] big gelding: fair form: best effort when fourth in minor event at Salisbury (5¼ lengths behind Jamil) on debut. *Andrew Balding* **68**

CONSULTING 4 ch.g. Kyllachy 129 – Doctor's Note (Pursuit of Love 124) [2017 92: p6g^{6} 5s 6g 7m 6m 6s^{3} 6d^{6} Aug 12] strong gelding: fair handicapper: left Martyn Meade after first start: stays 7f: acts on polytrack, tapeta, soft and good to firm going: often wears headgear: wears tongue tie: sold 2,500 gns in November, sent to Italy. *Stuart Williams* **75**

CONTANGO (IRE) 3 ch.g. Casamento (IRE) 118 – Call Later (USA) (Gone West (USA)) [2017 8.2d* 10.3d* 10s* 12d^{2} Aug 12] 50,000Y: good-topped gelding: half-brother to several winners, including smart 2-y-o 7f winner Be Ready (by New Approach) and 5f-13f winner Trending (by Dark Angel): dam, unraced, closely related to very smart North American Grade 1 7f/1m winner Ventura: useful form: won first 3 starts, maiden at Leicester in June, and handicaps at Chester and Newmarket in June/July: stays 1½m. *Andrew Balding* **103**

CONTENTMENT 3 b.f. Cacique (IRE) 124 – Cartimandua 115 (Medicean 128) [2017 76: 7g* 6.9g^{2} p8s^{6} 8s^{6} p6g Nov 17] useful-looking filly: fairly useful performer: won maiden at Goodwood in May: second in handicap at Carlisle in June: stays 7f: acts on polytrack, best turf form on good going: tried in cheekpieces: often in tongue tie: sold 10,000 gns in December. *William Haggas* **83**

CON TE PARTIRO (USA) 3 b.f. Scat Daddy (USA) 120 – Temple Street (USA) (Street Cry (IRE) 130) [2017 7f^{4} 8m* 9f^{4} 9f Oct 14] $130,000Y: compact filly: third foal: half-sister to smart US 7f/8.5f winner Donworth (by Tiznow): dam US 6f/6.5f winner (including **112**

Sandringham Handicap, Royal Ascot—American trainer Wesley Ward comes to the bookmakers' rescue as 20/1-shot Con Te Partiro finishes best of all to deny the gambled-on Rain Goddess (third left), with Paco's Angel and Queen of Time completing the frame

at 2 yrs), runner-up in Grade 1 7f event: smart performer: won listed Sandringham Handicap at Royal Ascot (by 1¼ lengths from Rain Goddess) in June: 1¾ lengths fourth to Dream Dancing in Del Mar Oaks next time: stays 9f: acts on dirt and firm going: has worn blinkers/tongue tie. *Wesley A. Ward, USA*

CONTINGENT 2 b.f. (Feb 7) Frankel 147 – Proportional 115 (Beat Hollow 126) [2017 8.1v* Oct 22] fourth foal: half-sister to smart 1½m winner Variable (by Sea The Stars) and a winner abroad by Dansili: dam 2-y-o 7f/1m (Prix Marcel Boussac) winner: 9/4, looked excellent prospect when won maiden at Leopardstown on debut by 1¾ lengths from Alghabrah, quickening to lead over 1f out: sort to improve markedly. *D. K. Weld, Ireland* **93 P**

CONTINUUM 8 b.g. Dansili 127 – Clepsydra 78 (Sadler's Wells (USA) 132) [2017 99: 14.5d^{6} p16d^{6} p16d^{4} p15.8g^{5} Dec 28] tall, good-topped gelding: fairly useful handicapper: stays 2m: acts on polytrack, good to firm and good to soft going: wears headgear: usually slowly away, often races towards rear: not straightforward. *Peter Hedger* **91**

CONTRAPPOSTO (IRE) 3 b.c. Cacique (IRE) 124 – Interim Payment (USA) 88 (Red Ransom (USA)) [2017 90: 8m^{4} 10.3d May 18] strong, compact colt: useful performer: best effort when fourth in Craven Stakes at Newmarket (4 lengths behind Eminent) in April, though always last in his group: stays 8.5f: acts on good to firm going: often races towards rear. *David Menuisier* **104**

CONTRAST (IRE) 3 ch.g. Dutch Art 126 – Israar (Machiavellian (USA) 123) [2017 96: 8.1d^{6} 10s May 20] good-topped gelding: useful handicapper: should stay 1¼m: acts on firm and soft going: slowly away both starts in 2017, markedly so second time. *Richard Hannon* **98**

CONTREBASSE 2 b.g. (Mar 13) Champs Elysees 124 – Viola da Braccio (IRE) 58 (Vettori (IRE) 119) [2017 7.8v 7.9g^{6} t7.1g^{5} Nov 3] 16,000Y: tall, lengthy gelding: closely related to 7f-8.6f winner (stayed 1¼m) Skytrain (by Exceed And Excel) and half-brother to several winners, including useful French 9f/1¼m winner Sarinda (by Dubawi) and smart Hong Kong 1m/9f winner Pleasure Gains (by Cape Cross): dam maiden (stayed 12.5f): modest form: best effort when sixth in minor event at York (9½ lengths behind Barford) in October: will stay beyond 1m: remains capable of better. *Tim Easterby* **59 p**

CONTRIBUTE 2 ch.g. (Feb 26) Bahamian Bounty 116 – Myth And Magic (IRE) (Namid 128) [2017 5m 5.2m^{5} 7m^{4} 6m^{6} 6.1g^{3} t7.1g^{3} 7m Oct 25] angular gelding: fair maiden: stays 7f: acts on good to firm going: tried in blinkers: front runner/races prominently: sent to Spain. *Martyn Meade* **66**

CONTROL CENTRE (IRE) 3 b.g. Dragon Pulse (IRE) 114 – Margaux Magique (IRE) (Xaar 132) [2017 72: 6g* 6d^{6} 6s^{3} 7.2d 5.9s^{4} t6g t5g t6.1g Nov 20] sturdy gelding: fairly useful handicapper: won at Hamilton in June: stays 7f: acts on tapeta and soft going: usually in headgear in 2017. *Marjorie Fife* **80**

CONTROVERSIAL LADY (IRE) 2 b.f. (Feb 26) Holy Roman Emperor (IRE) 125 – Eleanor Roosevelt (IRE) (Dalakhani (IRE) 133) [2017 5m t5s^{5} 5.3m^{4} 6d^{4} 6m^{2} 7m^{4} 7g^{5} 7d* 8g* p6.5g^{4} 6.3s 8g^{5} p7.5f Oct 18] €7,000Y: small filly: first foal: dam lightly-raced half-sister to smart winner up to 7f Captain Marvelous: fairly useful performer: won claimers at Clairefontaine (apprentice) and Deauville, both in August: stays 1m: acts on good to firm and good to soft going. *J. S. Moore* **81**

CONVERSANT (IRE) 2 gr.g. (Apr 6) Zebedee 113 – Tea Cup 83 (Danehill Dancer (IRE) 117) [2017 7v p7g 7g t6d^{6} Nov 4] modest form: tried in blinkers: has joined David O'Meara. *Hugo Palmer* **64**

CONVEY 5 b.g. Dansili 127 – Insinuate (USA) 99 (Mr Prospector (USA)) [2017 116: p10m* p10g* 8m^{6} May 7] well-made, attractive gelding: smart performer: won Winter Derby at Lingfield (by neck from Pinzolo) in February and Easter Classic AW Middle Distance Championships Stakes at same course (by 1¾ lengths from Absolute Blast) in April: below form in Champions Mile at Sha Tin only subsequent outing: stays 1¼m: acts on polytrack, soft and good to firm going: has worn cheekpieces: often races freely. *Sir Michael Stoute* **113**

CONVINCED (IRE) 2 b.g. (Feb 11) Invincible Spirit (IRE) 121 – Personified (GER) 77 (Doyen (IRE) 132) [2017 p8g Nov 7] 25/1, very green when well held in minor event at Kempton. *Richard Hannon* –

COOKIE RING (IRE) 6 b.g. Moss Vale (IRE) 126 – Talah 87 (Danehill (USA) 126) [2017 64: 7m 6g p7s t7.1s 9.9m p7s p10g t8.6g p8g t8d^{4} p8g* t8.6g^{5} p8s* Dec 17] modest handicapper: won at Kempton (apprentice) in November and Chelmsford in December: left Patrick Holmes after seventh start: stays 9.5f: acts on polytrack, tapeta, firm and soft going: has worn headgear: wears tongue tie: sometimes slowly away, usually races nearer last than first/often travels strongly. *Kristin Stubbs* **63**

COOKIE'S STAR 3 b.f. Kyllachy 129 – Bling Bling (IRE) 70 (Indian Ridge 123) [2017 p10g^{5} p12g^{6} t12.2g^{4} 7g^{4} 8g Jun 13] 2,500Y: workmanlike filly: half-sister to several winners, including 1¼m winner Go Sakhee (by Sakhee's Secret) and winner up to 1¼m Bling King (2-y-o 6f winner, by Haafhd): dam, maiden (stayed 9.7f), sister to smart sprinter Watching: no worthwhile form. *Philip McBride* –

COOL BABY 2 b.f. (Mar 12) Intense Focus (USA) 117 – Dead Cool 73 (Kyllachy 129) [2017 5m 5g^{4} 5.1d^{6} p5s^{5} p5s^{5} Nov 23] third foal: half-sister to 5f/6f winner Cool Breeze (by Dream Ahead): dam, 6f winner, out of Cheveley Park Stakes winner Dead Certain: modest maiden: raced only at 5f: tried in cheekpieces. *Robert Cowell* **54**

COOL BAHAMIAN (IRE) 6 b.g. Bahamian Bounty 116 – Keritana (FR) (One Cool Cat (USA) 123) [2017 91: 6m^{4} 7d^{4} 6.1d^{5} 6.1m^{3} 6d^{5} 6s^{2} 6m^{6} 6s^{4} Sep 8] sparely-made gelding: fairly useful handicapper: fourth at Lingfield in May: usually races around 6f nowadays: acts on polytrack, tapeta, soft and good to firm going: wears headgear: usually races prominently. *Eve Johnson Houghton* **86**

COOL BREEZE (IRE) 3 b.f. Dream Ahead (USA) 133 – Dead Cool 73 (Kyllachy 129) [2017 –: p7g^{5} 6d 5m^{2} 5.2g* t5g^{4} 5.2s^{5} t5.1m^{4} t5.1g^{4} p6g* Dec 20] fair handicapper: won at Yarmouth in July and Kempton in December: stays 6f: acts on polytrack, tapeta and good to firm going: often races towards rear. *David Simcock* **72**

COOL ECHO 3 b.f. Mount Nelson 125 – Ellcon (IRE) 71 (Royal Applause 124) [2017 75: f5g^{4} f6s^{5} p6g^{6} 6.1g^{5} 6d 7d^{2} f8.1g^{5} Nov 28] tall filly: modest maiden: stays 7f: acts on good to soft going: often in headgear: often starts slowly. *J. R. Jenkins* **59**

Betway Easter Classic All-Weather Middle Distance Championships Conditions Stakes, Lingfield—Convey follows up his Winter Derby victory under Ryan Moore, beating Absolute Blast (second left) and French raider Allez Henri (left)

COOLFITCH (IRE) 3 b.f. Roderic O'Connor (IRE) 119 – Farbenspiel (IRE) (Desert Prince (IRE) 130) [2017 89: 5.1g^6 5m^6 5s* 5d^5 5m^2 5g* 5.1g^5 5g^2 5d 5m 5v 5s 5d t5.1g^6 Nov 7] useful handicapper: won at York in May and Ayr in June: largely below form after: best form at 5f: acts on tapeta, good to firm and heavy going: in visor last 3 starts: often races towards rear/travels strongly. *David O'Meara* **99**

COOL MACAVITY (IRE) 9 b.g. One Cool Cat (USA) 123 – Cause Celebre (IRE) 80 (Peintre Celebre (USA) 137) [2017 93: 13.3s^6 Aug 18] good-topped gelding: fairly useful handicapper: stays 1¾m: acts on polytrack, good to firm and heavy going: has worn hood: fairly useful hurdler. *Nicky Henderson* **93**

COOL MUSIC (IRE) 7 b.m. One Cool Cat (USA) 123 – Musicology (USA) (Singspiel (IRE) 133) [2017 65: t12.2g t12.2g^6 t12.2g^3 10.2m^3 12.1m^6 12.1m* 12.1m^2 12.1s^2 t12.4d 12.1d^3 t12.2g^6 Dec 22] modest handicapper: won at Beverley in July: stays 1½m: acts on tapeta, soft and good to firm going: wears cheekpieces: often races prominently. *Antony Brittain* **62**

COOLONGOLOOK 2 b.c. (Apr 6) Invincible Spirit (IRE) 121 – Cascata (IRE) 86 (Montjeu (IRE) 137) [2017 8g^3 p8g^2 Oct 25] fourth foal: closely related to 1¼m-1½m winner (stayed 1¾m) Richard of Yorke and 1¼m-1½m winner Pacharana (both useful and by Oasis Dream): dam, 2-y-o 1m winner who stayed 1½m, sister to high-class winner up to 13.4f St Nicholas Abbey: fairly useful form when placed in minor events at Newmarket and Kempton: will be suited by further than 1m: remains open to improvement. *Luca Cumani* **80 p**

COOL RUN GIRL (IRE) 3 br.f. Lord Shanakill (USA) 121 – Fantastic Anna (IRE) (Fantastic Light (USA) 134) [2017 –: t5g^6 5s^3 6g 6g 6g 8.3s^5 11.2v Sep 18] poor maiden: in tongue tie last 2 starts. *Iain Jardine* **47**

COOL SKY 8 b.g. Millkom 124 – Intersky High (USA) (Royal Anthem (USA) 135) [2017 16.2f^6 14m^6 20.6v* Aug 2] good-topped gelding: fairly useful handicapper: won at Goodwood (by 1¼ lengths from Aurora Gray) in August: stays 21f: acts on polytrack and any turf going: tried in cheekpieces: fairly useful hurdler. *Ian Williams* **92**

COOL SPIRIT 2 b.g. (Feb 25) Swiss Spirit 117 – Marmot Bay (IRE) 65 (Kodiac 112) [2017 5d^3 6g^3 5g* Aug 30] £34,000Y, £78,000 2-y-o: first foal: dam 2-y-o 6f winner: fairly useful form: won minor event at Catterick (by ½ length from Paco Escostar) in August. *James Given* **85**

COOL STRUTTER (IRE) 5 b.g. Kodiac 112 – Cassava (IRE) (Vettori (IRE) 119) [2017 72: t8g^6 t7.1d^5 t7.1d^6 t7.1d^5 7g^3 6g^3 t6s^6 6.9v^2 6m^2 t8s^4 7m^4 8g 7g^4 t7.1s^6 6d^3 6s^2 6v^4 Nov 7] modest handicapper nowadays: stays 1m: acts on fibresand, tapeta, good to firm and heavy going: has worn headgear, including last 3 starts. *Karen Tutty* **64**

COOL TEAM (IRE) 3 b.g. Tamayuz 126 – Coolminx (IRE) 99 (One Cool Cat (USA) 123) [2017 75p: 8.3g^2 p8s^2 8m^3 8g* t8.6g^5 p8s^3 t8d* p8g* Oct 13] fairly useful performer: won maiden at Yarmouth in July, and handicaps at Newcastle in September and Kempton (by ½ length from Traveller) in October: stays 8.5f: acts on polytrack, tapeta, best turf form on good going: wears cheekpieces/tongue tie: sent to Hong Kong. *Hugo Palmer* **91**

COOPERESS 4 b.f. Sixties Icon 125 – Vilnius 67 (Imperial Dancer 123) [2017 65: t7.1g t6m 6m^6 7m 6d^4 7.1v^3 7m 8v^6 Sep 17] workmanlike filly: modest handicapper: left John O'Shea after seventh start: stays 1m: acts on good to firm and heavy going: usually wears headgear: has worn tongue tie. *Dai Burchell* **55**

COPA BEECH 3 ch.g. Paco Boy (IRE) 129 – My Girl Jode 70 (Haafhd 129) [2017 –: f7g Jan 5] no form: in blinkers last 2 starts. *Olly Williams* **–**

COPING STONE 3 b.f. Bahamian Bounty 116 – Brick Tops 82 (Danehill Dancer (IRE) 117) [2017 66: p5g^4 p6g^6 t5.1g^5 6g 8.2g^6 8.9g 7g 5.5d 5g p7g^6 8d Sep 24] stocky filly: modest maiden: left David Brown after third start: stays 1m: acts on polytrack, tapeta and good to firm going: often wears headgear. *P. & F. Monfort, France* **60**

COPPER BAKED (FR) 3 b.f. Never On Sunday (FR) 125 – Shakila (Cadeaux Genereux 131) [2017 78: f7d* 8m^3 9.9g^4 9.9s^4 8.9d^2 9.9g* 9.9g^2 p9.4g Sep 30] fairly useful performer: won maiden at Southwell in April and handicap at Vichy in July: left K. R. Burke after fifth start: stays 1¼m: acts on fibresand, good to firm and good to soft going: has rejoined former yard. *Mme G. Rarick, France* **86**

COPPER KNIGHT (IRE) 3 b.g. Sir Prancealot (IRE) 111 – Mystic Dream 85 (Oasis Dream 129) [2017 90: 5m^2 5.1d* 5g* 5m^3 5m 5d^4 5m^6 5s Sep 9] compact gelding: useful handicapper: won at Chester (by 2¼ lengths from Evergate) and York (by 1¼ lengths from Rasheeq) in May: raced only at 5f: acts on good to firm and good to soft going: tried in blinkers: in tongue tie last 2 starts: front runner/races prominently. *Tim Easterby* **108**

COQUINE 4 b.f. Monsieur Bond (IRE) 120 – Stolen Glance 84 (Mujahid (USA) 125) [2017 74: t6m^{3} t7.1m^{6} t7.1m^{2} 6m^{5} Apr 12] fair handicapper: stays 7f: acts on tapeta: wears headgear. *David O'Meara* **70**

CORAL CAYE 3 b.f. Pastoral Pursuits 127 – Vermilion Creek 68 (Makbul 104) [2017 –: 7s^{5} 7d 6.1g 5.7s^{4} 6v^{4} Oct 19] close-coupled filly: modest maiden: best effort at 5.5f: acts on soft going: tried in hood: often races in rear. *Steph Hollinshead* **53**

CORAL PRINCESS (IRE) 3 b.f. Elzaam (AUS) 115 – Ohwhatalady (IRE) (Invincible Spirit (IRE) 121) [2017 t8g^{5} t8d t7.1g^{4} 8m^{5} 9v 7.2m t8s 7.2s 8.3d^{5} 8.9m^{3} 8.9d^{6} 7.2g^{6} 7.2s 8v^{5} t7.1d f8.1g Dec 22] €5,000Y, 6,000 2-y-o: second foal: half-sister to 5f winner Pink Martini (by Tagula): dam of little account: modest maiden: stays 1m: acts on tapeta, good to firm and heavy going: tried in blinkers: usually races towards rear. *Keith Dalgleish* **53**

CORAL SEA 3 gr.f. Excelebration (IRE) 133 – Tropical Paradise (IRE) 116 (Verglas (IRE) 118) [2017 75: p6g 6d* 6d^{6} 6v^{5} 7d* 7m 7s^{4} Sep 16] fairly useful handicapper: won at Goodwood in June and Epsom (by 1½ lengths from Nightingale Valley) in August: stays 7f: acts on heavy going: often wears hood: often races towards rear. *Charles Hills* **89**

CORAZON ESPINADO (IRE) 2 b.c. (Jan 29) Iffraaj 127 – Three Decades (IRE) 83 (Invincible Spirit (IRE) 121) [2017 6.5g 5d^{6} p7d p7g^{2} p7g^{2} Dec 28] 120,000Y: rather unfurnished colt: fourth foal: half-brother to useful 2-y-o 5f/6f winner (stayed 1m) Melbourne Memories (by Sleeping Indian) and 1m/9f winner Big McIntosh (by Bushranger): dam 2-y-o 6f winner: fair maiden: stays 7f: acts on polytrack. *Simon Dow* **72**

CORDITE (IRE) 6 ch.g. Footstepsinthesand 120 – Marion Haste (IRE) 69 (Ali-Royal (IRE) 127) [2017 90: 10m^{3} 10g^{6} 9.9g^{5} 11.2g^{3} 11.4g^{5} 11.4g^{4} 12m* 12g 12v^{5} 11.5d Oct 24] sturdy gelding: fair handicapper: won at Epsom in August: stays 1½m: acts on polytrack, fibresand, good to firm and heavy going: usually wears headgear: often races freely. *Jim Boyle* **79**

CORECZKA (IRE) 6 b.m. Intense Focus (USA) 117 – Szewinska 87 (Green Desert (USA) 127) [2017 77: p8s p8g 8s p8g* 8m^{6} 10.3m 8m^{4} 8d a6g* p7g* p7g p8g Nov 17] fair handicapper: won at Dundalk in May, Laytown in September and again at Dundalk (by ¾ length from Silk Cravat) in October: best up to 1m: acts on polytrack, sand, soft and good to firm going: has worn hood: usually races towards rear. *Miss Clare Louise Cannon, Ireland* **73** **a80**

CORELLI (USA) 2 b.c. (May 20) Point of Entry (USA) 128 – Vignette (USA) 93 (Diesis 133) [2017 8.3v^{6} t9.5g* Nov 18] closely related to 3 winners by Dynaformer, including 1m-14.6f (St Leger) winner Lucarno and winner up to 2m Flying Officer (2-y-o 1m winner), both very smart, and half-brother to several winners: dam 2-y-o 6f winner (later winning sprinter in USA): fairly useful form: won minor event at Wolverhampton (by neck from Craving) in November: will be suited by 1¼m+: will go on improving. *John Gosden* **88 p**

CORGI 2 b.c. (Mar 7) So You Think (NZ) 133 – Ermyn Express 68 (Selkirk (USA) 129) [2017 8v^{4} 8.3d^{2} Oct 18] 30,000F, 85,000Y: third foal: dam, 1¼m winner, half-sister to smart US Grade 1 9f winner Byrama: fair form: better effort when second in maiden at Nottingham (length behind Msayyan) in October: will be suited by 1¼m+: capable of better again. *Hughie Morrison* **79 p**

CORINTHIA KNIGHT (IRE) 2 ch.c. (Jan 26) Society Rock (IRE) 126 – Victoria Lodge (IRE) (Grand Lodge (USA) 125) [2017 p5g* p5g* 5f^{2} 5f 5.2v^{4} t5.1g* p6g^{2} 5f^{4} t6.1d^{3} Dec 9] €15,000Y: good-quartered colt: half-brother to several winners, including useful winner up to 1m Chiswick Bey (2-y-o 5f/6f winner, by Elusive City) and 5f winner Kodimoor (by Kodiac): dam unraced: useful performer: won minor events at Lingfield and Kempton in April, and Wolverhampton (by 6 lengths from Mokaatil) in August: second in Sirenia Stakes at Kempton (1½ lengths behind Invincible Army) in September: stays 6f: acts on polytrack, tapeta and firm going: front runner/races prominently. *Archie Watson* **106**

CORKED (IRE) 4 b.f. Mastercraftsman (IRE) 129 – Dama'a (IRE) 85 (Green Desert (USA) 127) [2017 76: p10d^{2} t8g^{2} p10s* p8s^{2} p8g^{3} Dec 21] fairly useful performer: won maiden at Chelmsford in November: left Hugo Palmer after fourth start: stays 1¼m: acts on polytrack, tapeta, best turf form on good going: front runner. *Ed Walker* **85**

CORNBOROUGH 6 ch.g. Sir Percy 129 – Emirates First (IRE) 77 (In The Wings 128) [2017 79: 8g 10.2g 10g* 10.3g^{4} 10.2g* 9.8d^{4} 12.1m^{3} Aug 27] leggy gelding: fairly useful handicapper: won at Redcar in May and Haydock in July: stays 1½m: acts on good to firm and heavy going: usually wears cheekpieces. *Mark Walford* **86**

CORNELIOUS (IRE) 5 b.g. Cape Cross (IRE) 129 – Fantastic Spring (USA) (Fantastic Light (USA) 134) [2017 74: f12g^{5} p10d 8.3d Oct 11] rather leggy gelding: fair handicapper, out of form in 2017: sometimes wears headgear: tried in tongue tie. *Clifford Lines* **–**

CORNELIUS (FR) 5 b.g. Country Reel (USA) 113 – Dinaha (FR) (Octagonal (NZ) 126) [2017 p12d p12g p13.3g 11.4g Aug 7] fair maiden at best, no form in 2017: tried in visor/ tongue tie: has looked awkward. *Jonathan Geake* –

CORNERSTONE LAD 3 b.g. Delegator 125 – Chapel Corner (IRE) (Alhaarth (IRE) 126) [2017 –: 8g 9.8d² 12g³ 12s 13.9d⁵ 12v* 14d³ Oct 30] has reportedly had soft palate operation: fair handicapper: won at Pontefract in October: stays 1¾m: acts on heavy going. *Micky Hammond* 75

CORNISH POINT (IRE) 2 b.g. (Mar 19) Thewayyouare (USA) 117 – Griffin Point (IRE) 74 (Tagula (IRE) 116) [2017 p8m p8g Dec 23] last in seller/minor event. *J. S. Moore* –

CORNWALLVILLE (IRE) 5 ch.h. Makfi 130 – Morinqua (IRE) 99 (Cadeaux Genereux 131) [2017 107: 8g 8g a8f Feb 16] small horse: useful handicapper, below best at Meydan early in 2017: best at 6f/7f: acts on polytrack, tapeta, soft and good to firm going: has worn headgear: tried in tongue tie: usually races towards rear. *Roger Fell* 94

COROBEREE (IRE) 4 b.g. Dansili 127 – Cabaret (IRE) 105 (Galileo (IRE) 134) [2017 95p: 10.3g 10v⁵ f12.1g⁴ f14.1g⁶ Dec 11] useful 1¼m winner on debut at 3 yrs, little impact in handicaps/claimer in 2017: in cheekpieces last 3 starts: often races prominently: maiden hurdler. *Tony Coyle* 81

CORONATION COTTAGE 3 b.f. Pastoral Pursuits 127 – Avrilo 78 (Piccolo 121) [2017 58: t6g⁵ 5m³ 5f³ 5.7f* 5d⁶ 5.1s⁶ 5m* 5.7s⁵ p6g Oct 18] sturdy filly: fairly useful handicapper: won at Bath in July and August (by 1¾ lengths from Dandilion): stays 5.5f: acts on firm going. *Malcolm Saunders* 82

CORONATION DAY 4 b.f. Bahamian Bounty 116 – Queensgate 60 (Compton Place 125) [2017 88: 7m² 7m⁴ p7s 6g* 6m⁴ p6g³ t6.1d Dec 16] useful-looking filly: useful handicapper: won at Brighton in August: stays 7f: acts on polytrack, tapeta and good to firm going: front runner/races prominently. *James Tate* 96

CORONET 3 gr.f. Dubawi (IRE) 129 – Approach 105 (Darshaan 133) [2017 102P: 9.9d³ 12m⁵ 12m* 12f⁴ 11.9d² 14.5g⁵ 12s³ Oct 21] sturdy filly: smart performer: won Ribblesdale Stakes at Royal Ascot (by neck from Mori) in June: second in Yorkshire Oaks at York (5 lengths behind Enable) in August, fifth in St Leger at Doncaster (3¼ lengths behind Capri) in September and third in Fillies' And Mares' Stakes at Ascot (3¾ lengths behind Hydrangea) in October: stays 14.5f: acts on firm and soft going. *John Gosden* 116

CORPORAL MADDOX 10 b.g. Royal Applause 124 – Noble View (USA) 68 (Distant View (USA) 126) [2017 86: t7.1m p7g⁵ t7.1g 7g³ 7.6g³ p7g 7.1m 7m 7s⁵ 7m² 7.1d 7.1g* p7g f6.1g t7.2g p7g⁴ Dec 13] good-topped gelding: fair handicapper: won at Chepstow in August: stays 7f: acts on polytrack, tapeta and any turf going: wears headgear: tried in tongue tie. *Ronald Harris* 73

CORPUS CHORISTER (FR) 4 b.f. Soldier of Fortune (IRE) 131 – Bridge of Peace (Anabaa (USA) 130) [2017 88: p15.8g⁴ 14g² 15.9d² 16.1f* p16d⁶ 18d Sep 23] rather leggy filly: fairly useful handicapper: won at Beverley (by 3 lengths from Angel Gabrial) in July: stays 2m: acts on polytrack, firm and good to soft going: usually leads: sent to France. *David Menuisier* 94

Ribblesdale Stakes, Royal Ascot—Olivier Peslier delivers Coronet, one of four runners in the race for trainer John Gosden, with a perfectly-timed challenge to get the better of Mori (centre) and stablemate Hertford Dancer (left)

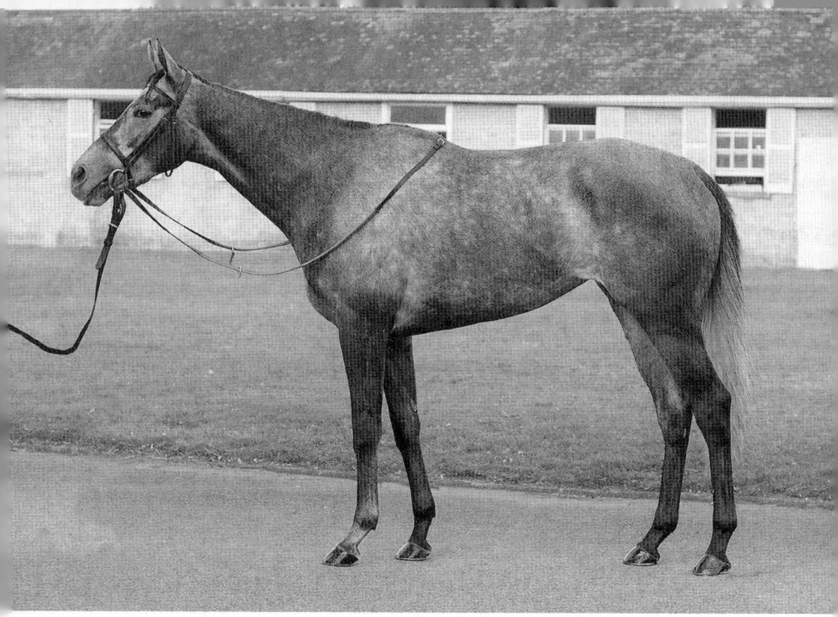

Denford Stud's "Coronet"

CORREDORDEL VIENTO (USA) 3 b.g. Lonhro (AUS) 128 – Asheville (USA) (Clever Trick (USA)) [2017 8.5g^5 10s 9.9m p11g p12g Oct 24] good-topped gelding: modest maiden: sometimes in headgear: usually races towards rear. *Simon Dow* **55**

CORREGGIO 7 ch.g. Bertolini (USA) 125 – Arian Da 81 (Superlative 118) [2017 78: 9.9m 12g 12.1m^6 12g^2 10s^2 12d^4 12.1s Oct 10] rangy gelding: fair handicapper: stays 1½m: acts on soft and good to firm going: has worn cheekpieces: often races towards rear. *Micky Hammond* **68**

CORRIDOR KID (IRE) 4 b.g. Kodiac 112 – All In Clover (IRE) 74 (Bahri (USA) 125) [2017 77: f5g^6 p5g^3 5d^5 p5s 5d^5 5g^6 p6d Sep 21] stocky gelding: fair maiden: best form at 5f: acts on polytrack and good to soft going: wears visor: sometimes slowly away, usually races nearer last than first. *Derek Shaw* **69**

CORROSIVE (USA) 2 b.c. (Mar 30) Uncle Mo (USA) 127 – Lovely Syn (USA) (Freud (USA) 113) [2017 7g^5 p7g* Sep 27] $40,000Y, 150,000 2-y-o: attractive colt: first foal: dam won all 4 starts in USA at 6f-7f: fairly useful form: won minor event at Kempton (readily by 1¾ lengths from Manthoor) in September: will go on improving. *Hugo Palmer* **88 p**

CORTON LAD 7 b.g. Refuse To Bend (IRE) 128 – Kelucia (IRE) 101 (Grand Lodge (USA) 125) [2017 93: 12.5m* 13.1m* 12.1m^5 11.9m t16.3s 12d 10d^5 12.1s^5 13s^3 t12.4g^5 t10.2g Nov 23] useful handicapper: won at Musselburgh and Hamilton (by head from Kensington Star) in May: stays 13f: acts on polytrack, tapeta, good to firm and heavy going: wears headgear/tongue tie: front runner/races prominently. *Keith Dalgleish* **96**

CORTON LASS 2 gr.f. (Feb 3) Showcasing 117 – Elbow Beach 76 (Choisir (AUS) 126) [2017 5m^4 5g^3 5d 6s^5 6d 6d f6.1g Nov 16] 12,000Y: second foal: half-sister to 7f winner African Grey (by Kheleyf): dam, 1¼m winner, half-sister to smart 6f-1m winner Santefisio: modest maiden: in cheekpieces last 2 starts: usually races prominently/freely. *Keith Dalgleish* **62**

COSA NOSTRA (IRE) 2 ch.c. (Apr 1) Society Rock (IRE) 126 – Gilded Truffle (IRE) 69 (Peintre Celebre (USA) 137) [2017 6.1m^5 6s^2 7.2d^2 8g^2 7g^3 6.5g 7.9g^3 8f Nov 24] 28,000Y: fifth foal: half-brother to winner up to 1¼m Kalon Brama (2-y-o 7f winner, by Kodiac) and 6f/7.5f winner Diatomic (by Bushranger): dam, maiden (stayed 1¼m), half- **84**

sister to smart winner up to 1m Birdman: fairly useful maiden: placed 5 times: left Richard Fahey after seventh start: stays 7f: acts on soft going: often races prominently. *Jack Carava, USA*

COSMEAPOLITAN 4 b.g. Mawatheeq (USA) 126 – Cosmea 87 (Compton Place 125) **95** [2017 105: 12m 10.3d 11.8m 10.2s^3 p10g^5 Dec 12] strong gelding: useful handicapper: stays 1¾m: acts on tapeta, soft and good to firm going: often races in rear. *Alan King*

COSMELLI (ITY) 4 b.g. Mr Vegas (IRE) 110 – Victorian Girl (GER) (Lomitas 129) **105** [2017 106: 14g 14g t16.3s 16d 16d 13.4d t14d^3 t16.3d^6 Dec 16] rather leggy gelding: useful handicapper: won 5 times in Italy in 2016, including listed event at Rome: best effort in 2017 when eighth in Northumberland Plate at Newcastle (2½ lengths behind Higher Power) in July: stays 16.5f: acts on tapeta and heavy going: wears headgear: tried in tongue tie: often races towards rear. *Gay Kelleway*

COSMIC CHATTER 7 b.g. Paris House 123 – Paradise Eve 81 (Bahamian Bounty 116) **82** [2017 93: t6g 6g 6g 6s 6m 6d 6m^2 6.1d^2 6s* 6d^6 6s 6s 6s 5v^4 t6g^5 t6d^3 p6g^5 Nov 17] **a75** workmanlike gelding: fairly useful handicapper on turf, fair on all-weather: won at Pontefract (by 4½ lengths from Harwoods Volante) in August: stays 6f: acts on tapeta, good to firm and heavy going: wears headgear. *Ruth Carr*

COSMIC DUST 4 b.f. Equiano (FR) 127 – Cosmic Song 58 (Cosmonaut) [2017 50: **55** 10.2m 9m 8g^4 8.5s^2 8v 8v^4 t8d Nov 10] modest maiden: stays 8.5f: acts on tapeta and soft going: has worn headgear: usually leads. *Richard Whitaker*

COSMIC LOVE 2 ch.f. (Apr 3) Sea The Stars (IRE) 140 – Soodad (King's Best (USA) **80 p** 132) [2017 p7g^2 Dec 20] 90,000Y: fourth foal: half-sister to 3 winners, including useful 6f (including at 2 yrs) winner Symposium (by Exceed And Excel): dam, ran 3 times in France, out of half-sister to 1000 Guineas winner Virginia Waters: 12/1, promising second in minor event at Lingfield (length behind Dancing Brave Bear) on debut, conceding first run: sure to progress. *William Haggas*

COSMIC RAY 5 b.g. Phoenix Reach (IRE) 124 – Beat Seven 102 (Beat Hollow 126) **85** [2017 –: f8s p8g^6 p8g^6 t9.5g 8.3g^2 8.3g* 8m^4 9m* 8g* 9.2s^4 8m* 7d^5 Jun 30] sturdy **a61** gelding: fairly useful handicapper on turf, modest on all-weather: won at Nottingham in April, Musselburgh (twice) in May and Ripon (by 3¾ lengths from Billy Bond) in June: stays 9.5f: acts on polytrack, tapeta, good to firm and heavy going: wears headgear: tried in tongue tie: often travels strongly. *Les Eyre*

COSMIC SKY 3 b.f. Harbour Watch (IRE) 121 – Foolish Lady (IRE) 75 (Exceed And **62** Excel (AUS) 126) [2017 50: 6g^6 8g^5 t7.1g^6 t6.1g 9.9m^6 7d* 7.2m^5 7.2s^5 Sep 16] modest handicapper: won at Thirsk in July: stays 1m: acts on good to soft going: wears headgear: front runner/races prominently, often freely. *Tim Easterby*

COSMIC TIGRESS 6 b.m. Tiger Hill (IRE) 127 – Cosmic Case 66 (Casteddu 111) [2017 **65** 65: t16.3d t13.9g* f14g 14m^3 14g^2 16m^6 13.1s^6 12.5m^4 13d^6 Aug 4] fair handicapper: won at Wolverhampton in March: stays 16.5f: acts on tapeta, soft and good to firm going: won over hurdles in August. *John Quinn*

COSMOPOLITAN GIRL (IRE) 4 b.f. Dream Ahead (USA) 133 – Absolute Music **94** (USA) 98 (Consolidator (USA) 121) [2017 89: 5.3g* 5g^5 5d^5 5s^5 Oct 9] lengthy filly: fairly useful performer: won handicap at Brighton (by 2¼ lengths from Sandfrankskipsgo) in May: best form at 5f: acts on polytrack and firm going: tried in cheekpieces: sometimes slowly away. *Robert Cowell*

COSMOPOLITAN QUEEN 2 ch.f. (Feb 10) Dubawi (IRE) 129 – Barshiba (IRE) 116 **80** (Barathea (IRE) 127) [2017 6g p6g^2 6m 7v^5 8.3g^2 p8g^4 7d Sep 30] sturdy filly: third foal: sister to smart winner up to 10.4f (Juddmonte International) Arabian Queen (2-y-o 5f/6f winner) and half-sister to 1m/14.5f winner Australian Queen (by Fastnet Rock): dam 1m-1½m (including dual Lancashire Oaks) winner: fairly useful maiden: runner-up in 2 minor events: stays 8.5f: acts on polytrack and heavy going: tried in cheekpieces: front runner/races prominently. *David Elsworth*

COSTA FILEY 6 b.g. Pastoral Pursuits 127 – Cosmic Destiny (IRE) 79 (Soviet Star **54** (USA) 128) [2017 72: p5m^6 Jan 20] leggy gelding: fair handicapper, not seen to best effect only start in 2017: stays 6f: acts on polytrack, soft and good to firm going: has worn headgear. *Ed Vaughan*

COSTA PERCY 3 b.g. Sir Percy 129 – Costa Brava (IRE) (Sadler's Wells (USA) 132) **73** [2017 –: t9.5m t8d^5 10.2g 14g^6 12.5m* 12v^3 t14g^5 Oct 27] fair handicapper: won at Musselburgh in September: left K. R. Burke after fourth start: stays 1¾m: acts on tapeta, good to firm and heavy going: tried in cheekpieces: won twice over hurdles in June. *Jennie Candlish*

COSY CLUB (IRE) 3 br.g. So You Think (NZ) 133 – Bali Breeze (IRE) 85 (Common Grounds 118) [2017 65: 8.5v4 11.3m 8m 6g 7.5mpu 7.2g* 8.4v 7.5d 11.1d p10.7g Nov 8] modest handicapper: won at Ayr in July: stays 7f: best form on good going: tried in blinkers: usually races close up: has joined Dan Skelton. *A. P. Keatley, Ireland* **64**

COTAI GLORY 5 ch.h. Exceed And Excel (AUS) 126 – Continua (USA) (Elusive Quality (USA)) [2017 117: 5m 5f 5f 5m3 6.1s4 5g3 5s5 5.2m2 6s2 5f Nov 4] tall horse: smart performer: winner of 4 races, including Molecomb Stakes at Goodwood at 2 yrs and World Trophy at Newbury in 2016: placed in 2017 in listed race (¾ length behind Take Cover) and Nunthorpe Stakes (3¾ lengths third to Marsha and Lady Aurelia), both at York, and World Trophy at Newbury (¾-length second to Take Cover): best at 5f: acted on firm and good to soft going: to stand at Tally-Ho Stud, Mullingar, Co. Westmeath, fee €6,000. *Charles Hills* **117**

COTE D'AZUR 4 ch.g. Champs Elysees 124 – Florentia 75 (Medicean 128) [2017 105: t9.5g 10g5 8m* 7.9d6 8m 8m6 8g 9d3 7.9g Oct 13] strong, compact gelding: useful handicapper: won at Thirsk in May: third in Cambridgeshire Handicap at Newmarket (1¾ lengths behind Dolphin Vista) in September: stays 10.5f: acts on polytrack, good to firm and good to soft going: usually races close up. *Les Eyre* **104**

COTINGA 3 ch.f. Paco Boy (IRE) 129 – Hobby 100 (Robellino (USA) 127) [2017 75: 9.9d4 10d2 12.3d6 10g3 10s4 10v3 9.9s Oct 9] rather unfurnished filly: fairly useful handicapper: second at Leicester in June: stays 1¼m: acts on soft going: tried in cheekpieces: often races towards rear: sold 4,000 gns in November, sent to Spain. *Ralph Beckett* **82**

COTO (IRE) 5 b.m. Fast Company (IRE) 126 – Let Me Shine (USA) 79 (Dixie Union (USA) 121) [2017 84: p5g t5g p5g Dec 15] small, close-coupled mare: fairly useful handicapper, below best in 2017: best form at 5f: acts on all-weather, soft and good to firm going: tried in hood: has worn tongue tie: often races towards rear. *M. J. Tynan, Ireland* **71**

COTTESLOE (IRE) 8 b.g. Teofilo (IRE) 126 – Vignelaure (IRE) 74 (Royal Academy (USA) 130) [2017 82: t12.2m6 11.6d Jul 1] tall gelding: fairly useful handicapper: last both starts in 2017, including in seller: stays easy 2m: acts on polytrack, tapeta, good to firm and heavy going: often wears headgear: has worn tongue tie: often starts slowly, usually races in rear. *Neil Mulholland* **–**

COTTON CLUB (IRE) 6 b.g. Amadeus Wolf 122 – Slow Jazz (USA) 106 (Chief's Crown (USA)) [2017 85, a92: p16g t16.5g* p16d4 14.1m5 16m 12m* 14.2d3 12m3 11.9m3 12m6 Aug 28] quite good-topped gelding: fairly useful handicapper: won at Wolverhampton in January and Salisbury in June: stays 17f: acts on polytrack, tapeta, good to firm and good to soft going. *Rod Millman* **81 a93**

COUGAR KID (IRE) 6 b.g. Yeats (IRE) 128 – Western Skylark (IRE) (Westerner 130) [2017 56: 12g Jul 17] lengthy gelding: maiden, well held sole start on Flat in 2017: likely to stay 2m: acts on polytrack: in headgear last 3 starts: often races towards rear: fair hurdler. *John O'Shea* **–**

COUGAR MOUNTAIN (IRE) 6 b.h. Fastnet Rock (AUS) 127 – Descant (USA) (Nureyev (USA) 131) [2017 120: 8g2 8.9d 8.1d6 8m3 8f 7m5 6m2 6s5 6s4 5.8v 7m5 Oct 13] strong, attractive horse: smart performer: placed in Irish Thoroughbred Marketing Cup at Doha (½ length behind Sovereign Debt) in February, Amethyst Stakes at Leopardstown (½ length behind Custom Cut) in May and Phoenix Sprint Stakes at the Curragh (½ length behind Washington DC) in August: stays 1m: acts on firm and good to soft going: wears headgear/tongue tie. *Aidan O'Brien, Ireland* **115**

COULDN'T COULD SHE 2 b.f. (Apr 10) Sixties Icon 125 – Emperatriz 81 (Holy Roman Emperor (IRE) 125) [2017 6.1s 7f5 7m 6d5 p7g4 6v 8.2g3 p10g6 f8.1g* Dec 29] rather lightly-built filly: first foal: dam winner up to 1m (2-y-o 7f winner): fair performer: won nursery at Southwell in December: stays 1m: acts on fibresand, polytrack, firm and good to soft going: tried in eyeshields: front runner/races prominently. *Adam West* **71**

COUNT CALABASH (IRE) 3 b.g. Big Bad Bob (IRE) 118 – Tinaheely (IRE) 75 (Intikhab (USA) 135) [2017 93p: 10m5 10s6 10g3 11.2s5 10.1m3 Aug 28] useful-looking gelding: fairly useful handicapper: third at Windsor in July: left Paul Cole after second start: stays 1¼m: acts on good to soft and good to firm going: tried in hood: front runner/races prominently. *Eve Johnson Houghton* **94**

COUNTERFEIT 2 b.f. (Feb 15) Iffraaj 127 – Money Note 68 (Librettist (USA) 124) [2017 6m 5d 7g4 t6.1g5 p8m6 Nov 25] 62,000Y: third foal: half-sister to 6f winner Kyllukey (by Kyllachy) and winner up to 1m Stringybark Creek (2-y-o 5f winner, by Bushranger): dam maiden half-sister to very smart 6f-1m winner Lend A Hand: modest maiden: best effort at 7f: in headgear last 3 starts: tried in tongue tie. *Richard Hughes* **53**

COUNTER SPIRIT (IRE) 3 b.f. Invincible Spirit (IRE) 121 – Counterclaim 98 (Pivotal 124) [2017 6g^4 p7d^3 Aug 16] 80,000Y: fifth foal: half-sister to 3 winners, including useful 7f/1m winner (including at 2 yrs) Good Trip (by Dansili) and useful 1m-1¼m winner Power Game (by Shamardal): dam, French 10.5f winner, half-sister to useful winner up to 1½m Teofonic: fair form: better effort when third in maiden at Kempton in August. *Ismail Mohammed* **67**

COUNT MONTECRISTO (FR) 5 b.g. Siyouni (FR) 122 – Blackberry Pie (USA) 74 (Gulch (USA)) [2017 90: t9.5g* t9.5g^2 9.8m^3 t8.6g^4 8s t8.6g p10g 10g f7.1g^3 Dec 22] fairly useful handicapper: won at Wolverhampton (by 2¼ lengths from Hairdryer) in February: stays 1¼m: acts on tapeta, good to firm and good to soft going: tried in cheekpieces: usually races close up. *Kevin Ryan* **90**

COUNT OCTAVE 3 b.c. Frankel 147 – Honorine (IRE) 89 (Mark of Esteem (IRE) 137) [2017 77p: t12.2g* 12.3m^5 14m^2 14g^2 14.5g^6 Sep 16] rangy colt: smart performer: won maiden at Wolverhampton (by 3 lengths from Utopian Dream) in March: second in Queen's Vase at Royal Ascot (neck behind Stradivarius) in June and listed race at Goodwood (1¼ lengths behind Call To Mind) in August, and sixth in St Leger at Doncaster (5½ lengths behind Capri) in September: stays 14.5f: acts on tapeta and good to firm going. *Andrew Balding* **115**

COUNT OTTO (IRE) 2 b.g. (Apr 29) Sir Prancealot (IRE) 111 – Dessert Flower (IRE) (Intikhab (USA) 135) [2017 6.1s p6g* p6g^3 Dec 20] €12,000Y, £33,000 2-y-o: fourth foal: brother to 1m winner Sir Plato and half-brother to 2 winners in Italy by Zebedee: dam French maiden (third at 7f): fairly useful form: won minor event at Kempton (by 2¾ lengths from City Gent) in November: will stay 7f: in hood last 2 starts. *Amanda Perrett* **83**

COUNTRY'N'WESTERN (FR) 5 b.g. Samum (GER) 126 – Cracking Melody (Shamardal (USA) 129) [2017 p12g Oct 3] 66/1, seventh in maiden at Kempton (11½ lengths behind Isaac Bell) in October: bumper winner. *David Elsworth* **62**

COUNT SIMON (IRE) 3 b.g. Rip Van Winkle (IRE) 134 – Wedding Cake (IRE) 71 (Groom Dancer (USA) 128) [2017 10m^4 12g^2 12g^2 11.8s^4 12d^3 12s^3 11.8v* 13.9g Oct 13] €26,000Y: leggy, close-coupled gelding: sixth foal: half-brother to moody 11f winner (stayed 1¾m) Mehendi (by Indian Danehill) and useful winner up to 1½m Croquembouche (2-y-o 7.5f winner, by Acclamation): dam, 1½m winner, half-sister to very smart 1½m/1¾m performer Gamut: fairly useful performer: won handicap at Haydock in September: stays 1¾m: acts on heavy going. *Andrew Balding* **89**

COUP DE VENT 6 b.m. Tobougg (IRE) 125 – Pigment (Zamindar (USA) 116) [2017 58: p8m p8g 10.2m^6 11.6d 10s 10.2s^4 Aug 9] poor handicapper: stays 1¼m: acts on polytrack and soft going: has worn headgear: often starts slowly/races prominently/freely. *John O'Shea* **47**

COURIER 5 b.m. Equiano (FR) 127 – Pivotal Drive (IRE) (Pivotal 124) [2017 92: t7.1s 7m^2 7.8g 7d* 7m 6d^6 7v^4 6g^5 6s^3 6v^5 6v p6s^4 p7g^3 Dec 20] rather leggy mare: fairly useful handicapper on turf, fair on all-weather: won at Haydock (by ½ length from Rebel Surge) in June: left Marjorie Fife after eleventh start: stays 9f: acts on polytrack, good to firm and heavy going: has worn cheekpieces: front runner/races prominently. *Michael Appleby* **91** **a79**

COURTEOUS CROWN 2 ch.f. (Apr 4) Helmet (AUS) 127 – Speak Softly To Me (USA) (Ogygian (USA)) [2017 5.7d 7g 7d p7g^6 t8.6g Oct 7] €10,500Y: smallish, plain filly: half-sister to several winners, including 7f winner Charlotte Bronte (by Danehill Dancer) and 11f/1½m winner Contra Mondum (by Giant's Causeway): dam unraced: modest maiden: best effort at 7f: acts on good to soft going: has joined David Evans. *Richard Hannon* **60**

COURT HOUSE (IRE) 2 b.c. (Feb 15) Dawn Approach (IRE) 132 – Crossanza (IRE) (Cape Cross (IRE) 129) [2017 p7g^6 p7s^2 Dec 8] €200,000Y: fourth foal: half-brother to 3 winners, including useful 2-y-o 6f/7f winner Cape Factor (by Oratorio) and useful 1m/8.5f winner Benzanno (by Refuse To Bend): dam unraced out of useful 5f winner Alegranza: fairly useful form: better effort when second in minor event at Chelmsford (2¾ lengths behind Nice Shot) in December: remains with potential. *John Gosden* **81 p**

COURT OF JUSTICE (FR) 2 b.c. (Feb 19) Dabirsim (FR) 120 – Great News (FR) (Bering 136) [2017 7s^2 Sep 9] €50,000Y, €70,000 2-y-o: half-brother to several winners in France, including useful 2-y-o 1m winner Galveston (by Green Tune) and useful 9f-1½m winner Great Event (by Anabaa): dam useful French 7f and (at 2 yrs) 1m winner: 2/1, shaped well when second in minor event at Ascot (½ length behind Fajjaj) on debut: open to improvement. *David Simcock* **80 p**

COURTSIDE (FR) 2 ch.g. (Mar 12) Siyouni (FR) 122 – Memoire (FR) (Sadler's Wells (USA) 132) [2017 8g^5 10m^6 Oct 25] €35,000Y, €155,000 2-y-o: good-topped gelding: half-brother to 3 winners in France, including very smart 11f/1½m winner Ming Dynasty (by King's Best) and 13f winner Moscow Nights (by Peintre Celebre), latter dam of very smart performer up to 2m Heartbreak City: dam French 1¼m winner: fair form: better effort when fifth in minor event at Newmarket (7½ lengths behind Old Persian) in October: remains with potential. *David Simcock* **74 p**

COUSIN KHEE 10 b.g. Sakhee (USA) 136 – Cugina 99 (Distant Relative 128) [2017 –: 11.9m 18g^5 14g^5 16.3d^6 14.2v^6 f12.1g^4 f14.1g^2 Dec 11] well-made gelding: fair handicapper nowadays: stays 16.5f: acts on all-weather and soft going: tried in blinkers: usually races nearer last than first. *Hughie Morrison* **75**

COVE BEACH 2 ch.f. (Jan 20) Harbour Watch (IRE) 121 – Dubai Affair 73 (Dubawi (IRE) 129) [2017 5g 5f^5 6m 5f 5.1s^3 5s p5g^3 p6g Nov 1] 23,000Y: second foal: half-sister to 2-y-o 6f winner Compton Lane (by Compton Place): dam, 2-y-o 5f winner, out of smart winner up to 7f Palace Affair, herself half-sister to high-class sprinter Sakhee's Secret: modest maiden: should prove best at 5f: acts on polytrack and soft going: sometimes in blinkers: tried in tongue tie. *Paul Cole* **62**

COVERHAM (IRE) 3 b.g. Bated Breath 125 – Mark Too (IRE) (Mark of Esteem (IRE) 137) [2017 59: p6g^3 p7g^2 7g^2 7d^2 8m^3 p8g^6 7v^5 8g^3 Oct 16] compact gelding: fair maiden: stays 1m: acts on polytrack, good to firm and good to soft going: has worn headgear. *James Eustace* **72**

COVIGLIA (IRE) 3 ro.c. Invincible Spirit (IRE) 121 – Bright Snow (USA) (Gulch (USA)) [2017 71p: 7d 6g 7.4g^4 t6d Sep 29] fair form in maiden at 2 yrs, standout effort: left D. K. Weld after first start: stays 7f: acts on heavy going: tried in blinkers: has joined Jacqueline Coward. *David O'Meara* **50**

COWBOY SOLDIER (IRE) 2 b.c. (Mar 26) Kodiac 112 – Urgele (FR) 102 (Zafonic (USA) 130) [2017 5d^2 Oct 4] 105,000Y: closely related to useful 2-y-o 6f winner Al Aasifh and 2-y-o 6f/7f winner Invincible Gold (both by Invincible Spirit) and half-brother to 3 winners, including useful 1m (including at 2 yrs) winner Cordell (by Fasliyev): dam French 1m winner (including at 2 yrs): 3/1, second in maiden at Nottingham (head behind Kodiac Express) in October: likely to improve. *Robert Cowell* **80 p**

COYA 3 b.f. Paco Boy (IRE) 129 – Toffee Vodka (IRE) 86 (Danehill Dancer (IRE) 117) [2017 p7g p8g^6 7m 8.1m Aug 26] rather leggy filly: half-sister to several winners, including 1¼m-1½m winner Carry Me Home (by Dark Angel) and 2-y-o 6f winner Toffee Tart (by Dutch Art): dam winner up to 1m (2-y-o 6f winner): modest form: best effort at 1m: wears hood: sent to the Netherlands. *Charles Hills* **58**

CRACKER FACTORY 2 b.g. (Apr 15) Poet's Voice 126 – Pure Song 75 (Singspiel (IRE) 133) [2017 7m^4 p8g^5 t8g^4 Nov 3] fair form in minor events: will stay beyond 1m. *William Haggas* **66**

CRACK ON CRACK ON 2 ch.c. (Mar 15) Havana Gold (IRE) 118 – Almunia (IRE) (Mujadil (USA) 119) [2017 6.1m^5 7m^5 p7d^2 Nov 22] 24,000F, €70,000 2-y-o: tall colt: seventh foal: half-brother to 3 winners, including ungenuine 5f/6f winner Lewisham (by Sleeping Indian) and 11f winner Second Page (by Harbour Watch): dam unraced: fairly useful form: best effort when fifth in minor event at Newmarket (4 lengths behind Key Victory) in October: remains with potential. *Clive Cox* **88 p**

CRACKSMAN 3 b.c. Frankel 147 – Rhadegunda 103 (Pivotal 124) [2017 105P: 10.1g* 12m^3 12g^2 11.9d* 11.9d* 10s* Oct 21] **136**

Racing should be glad that the sparkling Frankie Dettori, its most recognisable face and a 'Pol Roger' in the world of sport, isn't planning to hang up his saddle for another three or four years. There is no other figure in Flat racing with anything like the level of general public recognition or appeal, and the game owes him a huge debt of gratitude, not just for his virtuoso performances in the saddle over the years but for his role in broadening racing's appeal. He isn't going to be around forever, more's the pity, and the sport will lose its most valuable marketing asset when he goes. Ask the organisers of the latest British Champions' Day, the nation's richest raceday. The richly-endowed meeting at Ascot in October attracted a crowd of 31,187 on a day when winds sometimes close to gale force and the prevailing soft ground (for the fifth time in seven years) threatened to detract from the significance of some of the main events. Successive winning appearances by Frankel at the first two editions of British Champions' Day in 2011 and 2012 got the occasion off to a dream start and it was on the three-year-old Cracksman, the first of Frankel's offspring to appear on a Champions' Day programme (which has no race for two-year-olds), that Dettori orchestrated British Champions' Day's defining moment.

On any other card, trainer Aidan O'Brien's equalling the world record for Group/Grade 1 wins with Hydrangea in the Fillies' And Mares' Stakes, would have been a certainty to draw the biggest headline. But, on a day when even celebrating Silvestre de Sousa's runaway jockeys' championship was reduced almost to a footnote, it was Cracksman's brilliance, accentuated by Dettori's showmanship (including the trademark flying dismount!), that will be remembered for longest. Ridden right out by Dettori, after leading over two furlongs out, Cracksman forged ahead of his nine rivals in most impressive fashion to win by seven lengths and a neck from Poet's Word, a good second in the Irish Champion Stakes on his previous start, and the high-class 'globe-trotter' Highland Reel. The likes of Prix du Jockey Club winner Brametot, Derby runner-up Cliffs of Moher and St James's Palace Stakes winner Barney Roy were among Cracksman's rivals who were a long way below form on ground softer than they had encountered previously, but that tempered enthusiasm for Cracksman's performance only slightly, as did the eleventh-hour withdrawal—because of the going—of the Eclipse and International winner Ulysses. Soft ground undoubtedly helped to stretch the margin of Cracksman's victory, but Dettori's firmness and his desire 'to provide a thrill for everyone' enabled Cracksman to show exactly what he is capable of. It was one of the best—if not *the* best—performances of the year and Cracksman certainly gave British Champions' Day a real champion it could celebrate. There are two statues fifty yards apart at Ascot, one of Frankel and another of Frankie Dettori, and they should serve as a reminder in years to come of the occasion the pair combined (Frankel won the Champion Stakes himself on his final appearance) to provide as fitting a finale as anyone could wish to an event rather optimistically promoted as 'the day that champions are crowned'.

Cracksman's performance on British Champions' Day, on which Dettori also won the Queen Elizabeth II Stakes on the same stable's Persuasive, was a measurable improvement on anything he had achieved before. It wasn't altogether the biggest surprise, though, given that he had been progressing all season and had already shown, when winning both the Great Voltigeur Stakes at York and the Prix Niel at Chantilly in clear-cut fashion, that he was a very strong and relentless galloper once fully opened out, those performances in particular looking a portent of even better things to come from him as a four-year-old, with another year on his back. Whether Cracksman can actually show further improvement on his Champion

Betway Great Voltigeur Stakes, York—Cracksman records his first pattern win with a devastating performance, forging six lengths clear of the Chester Vase winner Venice Beach (partially hidden by winner), with Mirage Dancer (white sleeves) another six lengths back in third

Stakes performance looks open to doubt now—but, even if he can just reproduce that effort, he must have the world at his feet. His stablemate Enable, assuming she trains on fully from three to four, will certainly have her work cut out to repeat her historic King George/Arc double if Cracksman turns up in the sort of form he displayed at Ascot.

Frankie Dettori also partnered Enable for her magnificent performances in the latest season and it is clear that he would always have chosen to ride the five-times Group 1-winning filly if she and Cracksman had met in the latest season. Indeed, in his pronouncements leading up to Europe's richest race, the Prix de l'Arc de Triomphe, which took place three weeks before British Champions' Day, Dettori seemed almost to gloss over Cracksman when discussing Enable's chances. 'If she wants to be the best in Europe, Enable has got to show her stuff in the Arc,' he said. 'It's the biggest prize of the season, the race everybody wants to win, and everybody's turned up.' But *everybody* didn't turn up. Cracksman's connections may now say they are 'relishing' a clash with Enable as a four-year-old, but they seemed hell bent on ducking one in the latest season, knowing that Dettori was committed to Enable. 'He is not far off being as good as Golden Horn [who won the 2015 Arc in the Oppenheimer colours],' said Cracksman's owner after the colt had won the Prix Niel, a recognised trial over the Arc course and distance, 'but, as far as the Arc goes, Dettori will be riding another horse and I don't think that Cracksman would like to be ridden by anyone else. There are a lot of good jockeys but there's only one Frankie.'

The aim was said to be to 'preserve' Cracksman for his four-year-old season and it was thought that a hard race in the Arc could compromise those plans. 'To not run in the Arc this year [with the horse at the top of his form] is a risk, but one I am willing to take,' was how Anthony Oppenheimer put it. It was very hard to argue, after Cracksman's scintillating victory in the Qipco Champion Stakes, that Oppenheimer and trainer John Gosden made the wrong decision in not running Cracksman in the Arc. For one thing, the stable won two of the richest races in Europe by saving Cracksman for Ascot. The unforeseen can put paid to long-term plans, as with 2016 Horse of the Year Almanzor, whose connections opted to wait another year for an Arc challenge, taking in the Champion Stakes as a three-year-old instead. Almanzor ran only once as a four-year-old when disappointing in the Prix Gontaut-Biron at Deauville in August. That doesn't mean, of course, that a similar thing might happen with Cracksman, but no-one knows what the future holds. However, even if Cracksman doesn't go on to meet the highest expectations as a four-year-old, he has already shown himself to be one of the best middle-distance colts trained in Britain and Ireland in years. His owner's assessment that Cracksman is 'not far off being as good as Golden Horn' might even be doing a disservice to Cracksman, so far as pure merit is concerned (Golden Horn achieved a Timeform rating of 134).

Anthony Oppenheimer, the owner-breeder of both Golden Horn and Cracksman, is one of a diminishing band of English owner-breeders who still operate a stud of any size. He maintains his broodmare strength at Hascombe and Valiant studs in Newmarket at around thirty but, unlike his father Sir Philip Oppenheimer who raced most of his home breds, Anthony Oppenheimer sells more yearlings to help to defray costs (the annual running costs of the stud are said to be around £1.5m). Golden Horn was led out unsold at 190,000 guineas in 2013 at Newmarket's principal yearling sale, the October Sales Book 1, and was put into training with John Gosden. On the back of Golden Horn's success as a three-year-old, Oppenheimer decided to retain more of his 2015 yearlings to race himself. One of them was Cracksman. Like Golden Horn, he appeared on a racecourse just once as a two-year-old, winning a back-end maiden (at Newmarket) in fine style, looking a good prospect and rated 105P in *Racehorses of 2016*. Neither Golden Horn (eventually supplemented at a cost of £75,000 five days before the race) nor Cracksman began their three-year-old season holding a Derby entry. Cracksman was put in the race in April at a cost of £9,000 which jokingly led to his owner asking for his money back when Cracksman won the Investec Derby Trial at Epsom on his reappearance later in April, a victory that brought with it a free entry to the Derby.

Qipco Champion Stakes, Ascot—Cracksman puts his rivals to the sword again to provide a fitting climax to British Champions' Day, drawing seven lengths clear of Poet's Word (spots on cap) and Highland Reel (striped sleeves) to give jockey Frankie Dettori a first victory in the race; it is also a first Group 1 winner in Europe for Cracksman's sire Frankel, in a race he himself won

Cracksman had to pull out all the stops to catch a race-fit Permian almost on the line, winning by a short head, with Bay of Poets a length and three quarters back in third. Cracksman was caught out by the steady gallop, coupled with the fact that Permian got first run on him, but he responded really well under pressure and remained an exciting prospect.

Cracksman seemed set to follow in the footsteps of Golden Horn by tackling the Dante Stakes at York next (which was won by Permian) but, in the end, he arrived at Epsom—via another workout on the course at the Breakfast With The Stars event—with just two runs under his belt. Cracksman was pulled out of the Dante on the morning of the race because of the soft ground ('I don't want him involved in a battle just sixteen days out from the Derby, but he's in great form,' said his trainer). Golden Horn won the Derby on his fourth start, and Cracksman put up a fine performance in the race on only his third, despite, according to Dettori who picked up a four-day ban for excessive use of the whip, giving a 'raw and immature' display. Cracksman was sent off 7/2 favourite in a field of eighteen and was beaten only by the O'Brien-trained pair, 40/1 outsider Wings of Eagles and joint second favourite Cliffs of Moher, the distances three quarters of a length and a neck. Cracksman was prominent in the main group most of the way, going slightly in snatches after suffering some interference in the early stages and not handling the downhill run towards Tattenham Corner as smoothly as he might have done. He took on the Derby winner again in the Irish Derby (Golden Horn had been dropped back in trip after Epsom, winning the Eclipse and then the Irish Champion—after a surprise defeat in the International at York—before reverting to a mile and a half to gain his fourth championship win of the year in the Arc). Cracksman turned the tables on Wings of Eagles, who was afterwards found to have fractured a sesamoid bone, but the Derby sixth Capri held off Cracksman by a neck at the Curragh as he stayed on well after being ridden entering the straight and delivering his challenge wide.

Still to win a pattern event—let alone a Group 1—Cracksman corrected that first omission on his next two outings, beating his five rivals hollow in the Betway Great Voltigeur Stakes at York where he turned the race into a procession and won by six lengths from the Chester Vase winner and Grand Prix de Paris third Venice Beach, storming clear from three furlongs out and having the race well won by the time Dettori allowed him to take things easily towards the finish. The Voltigeur, won in recent seasons by Storm The Stars and Idaho who had also been in the frame in the Derby and the Irish Derby, often serves as a trial for the St Leger, but Doncaster had never been on Cracksman's agenda (he wasn't even entered). His performance in the five-runner Prix Niel was almost a carbon copy of the Voltigeur, though the race was slowly run which didn't enable Cracksman to turn it on quite so strikingly as he had at York. Cracksman still had the Niel won some way out and looked full of running at the line where he had three and a half lengths in hand of runner-up Avilius. The decision by Cracksman's connections to bypass the Arc was naturally the subject of comment, with plenty keen to offer an opinion as they felt it robbed Europe's most prestigious race of a most important contender (three-year-olds have a fine record in the race). Chantilly's loss was Ascot's gain, however, though Frankie Dettori struck a discordant note beforehand when saying he was praying for more rain—'it will help him and disadvantage some of the others'—when almost everyone else, including the British Champions' Day organisers, were hoping just as fervently for the rain to hold off in the hope of more 'normal' conditions for the big day.

British Champions' Day, however, is not the be-all and end-all. It is simply one of a number of key meetings over the season with the potential to provide the sport with an Enable or a Battaash or a Cracksman. The two first-named both missed British Champions' Day but that didn't affect their status, which was established by a tip-top performance—*more* than one in both cases—at a previous festival meeting in another race (or races) with the potential to confer championship status on its winners. Becoming a champion racehorse can never be dependent on producing a performance on just one specific day. Enable had her best day(s) at Ascot and Chantilly, when she won the King George and the Arc, while Battaash trounced the opposition at both Goodwood (in the King George Stakes, a Group 1 in all but name) and at the Arc meeting at Chantilly (in the Prix de l'Abbaye). Frankie Dettori's admission after Cracksman's victory in the Champion Stakes that 'The horse I rode today is not the horse I rode at Epsom' illustrates the point that horses change and develop (and sometimes go backwards). The Derby gave Cracksman an early opportunity to stake his claim to be one of the best horses in training, but he wasn't ready; British Champions' Day gave him another shot when he *was* well and truly ready. What could be fairer than a racing programme with that sort of scope?

Cracksman (b.c. 2014)	Frankel (b 2008)	Galileo (b 1998)	Sadler's Wells
			Urban Sea
		Kind (b 2001)	Danehill
			Rainbow Lake
	Rhadegunda (b 2005)	Pivotal (ch 1993)	Polar Falcon
			Fearless Revival
		St Radegund (b 1994)	Green Desert
			On The House

The well-made, long-striding Cracksman is the first offspring of Frankel to win a Group 1 in Europe (he had already sired the Japanese Oaks winner Soul Stirring). Some of the Frankels have acquired a reputation for being a little over-

Mr Anthony Oppenheimer's "Cracksman"

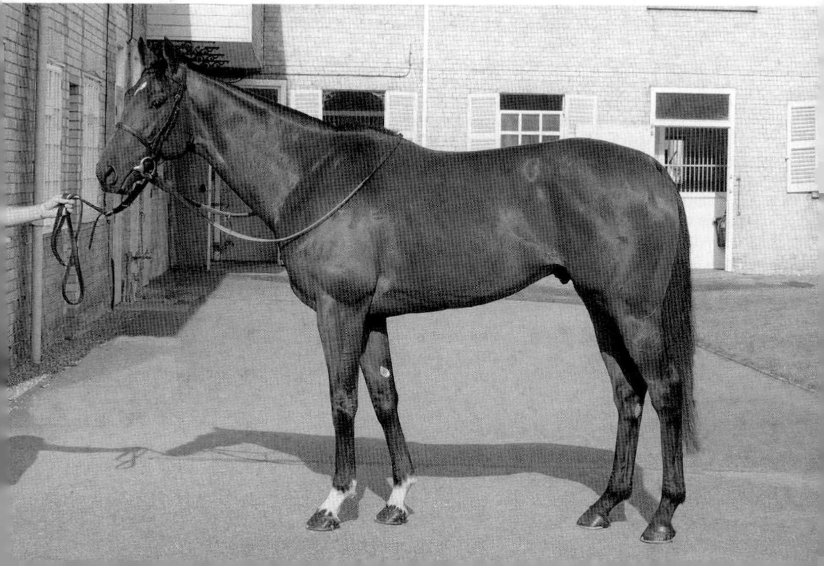

exuberant but Cracksman was reportedly always green and lazy at home and, apart from becoming briefly upset in the saddling boxes before the Champion Stakes (perhaps because of the close attention of a film crew), he was nearly always calm and relaxed in the racecourse preliminaries (he was sweating when he arrived in the paddock before the Derby but cooled off and took the preliminaries well). With the notable exception of Montjeu, who had an Arc winner (Hurricane Run), a Derby winner (Motivator) and a St Leger winner (Scorpion) in his first crop, Frankel has made as good a start to his stud career as almost any stallion in recent times. His first two crops have contained fourteen individual European pattern winners so far, just four fewer than record-holding Dubawi achieved in the same two years of his stallion career (Frankel's sire Galileo started his own stud career relatively slowly). Frankel's offspring won fourteen pattern races in Europe in the latest season (only the offspring of Galileo and Dubawi won more), with Eminent's win in the Prix Guillaume d'Ornano at Deauville and Monarchs Glen's in the Darley Stakes at Newmarket probably the most important of them after Cracksman's Champion Stakes (the Somerville Tattersall winner Elarqam and the Aidan O'Brien-trained pair Nelson and Rostropovich were among Frankel's two-year-old pattern winners). Frankel covered 195 mares in the latest season, the year after his first two-year-old runners, a significant increase on the book sizes of 2015 and 2016 when he had 114 and 130 mares respectively. His fee for 2018 has been raised from £125,000 to £175,000.

Cracksman's dam the Pivotal mare Rhadegunda was a useful performer on the track for Cracksman's owner and trainer and stayed a mile and a quarter. She was successful three times as a three-year-old, winning a listed event at Fontainebleau over nine furlongs on her final start. Cracksman is her fifth foal and her third winner. Her first was the useful Fantastic Moon (by Dalakhani) who won the Solario Stakes as a two-year-old and finished sixth in the King Edward VII Stakes at Royal Ascot (barely getting the mile and a half) as a three-year-old, before ending up being sent to Qatar as a four-year-old. Rhadegunda's other winner is Strong Force (by Sea The Stars) who showed fairly useful form for Saeed bin Suroor when winning a maiden at Chelmsford over a mile and a quarter. Cracksman's grandam St Radegund was a seven-furlong winner and, apart from Rhadegunda, her other winners include the one-time useful staying handicapper Halla San who was beaten a head in the Northumberland Plate and was twice third in the Chester Cup.

St Radegund was a daughter of one of the best performers produced by the Oppenheimer family studs, the One Thousand Guineas and Sussex Stakes winner On The House, a home bred who raced for Anthony Oppenheimer's father and was trained by Harry Wragg. Geoff Wragg, who died at the age of eighty-seven in September, took over the Abington Place stables from his father in 1983 after being his assistant for nearly thirty years and continued to train there until 2008 when he retired. Most of Geoff Wragg's owners, like the Oppenheimers, were owner-breeders and he was rarely seen at the sales until after the deaths of the Moller brothers who set up a trust fund, managed by John Ferguson, to enable horses to continue racing in their colours. Geoff Wragg also kept enjoying success for the Oppenheimers until late in his career, one of his Group 1 winners being the 1997 Coronation Stakes winner Rebecca Sharp, a half-sister to the dam of Golden Horn.

Cracksman is effective at a mile and a quarter to a mile and a half and he acts on soft and good to firm going. He is a straightforward, genuine and reliable racehorse, his only defeats so far coming in the Derby and the Irish Derby, and he should continue to carry the famous Oppenheimer black and white (halved), sleeves reversed, red cap, with distinction in Europe's major races as a four-year-old. He is a credit to those who have handled him at Clarehaven. *John Gosden*

CRAFTINESS 2 b.f. (Jan 19) Al Kazeem 128 – Artful (IRE) (Green Desert (USA) 127) – [2017 p7g Dec 20] fifth foal: half-sister to 2-y-o 6f winner (stayed 1m) Duplicity (by Cadeaux Genereux): dam, French 7.5f winner, half-sister to smart 2-y-o 7f winner Chintz, herself dam of high-class miler The Gurkha: in hood, 16/1, very green when well held in minor event at Kempton. *Roger Charlton*

CRAFTSMANSHIP (FR) 6 ch.g. Mastercraftsman (IRE) 129 – Jennie Jerome (IRE) 87 **82**
(Pivotal 124) [2017 91: t9.5g p10d^5 9.9g^5 10g^3 p10s 10m^5 10m^6 12d^4 9.1g^5 Jul 27] workmanlike gelding: fairly useful handicapper: stays 1¼m: acts on polytrack, firm and soft going: has worn cheekpieces. *Robert Eddery*

CRAFTY MADAM (IRE) 3 gr.f. Mastercraftsman (IRE) 129 – Dani Ridge (IRE) 92 **88**
(Indian Ridge 123) [2017 72p: 6m^2 6m* 7g 7g* 7d p7g^3 Oct 18] fairly useful performer: won maiden at Salisbury in May and handicap at Sandown in September: stays 7f: acts on polytrack and good to firm going. *Clive Cox*

CRAGGAKNOCK 6 b.g. Authorized (IRE) 133 – Goodie Twosues 91 (Fraam 114) **74**
[2017 90: t12.4d^5 12v Sep 9] lengthy, rather leggy gelding: fairly useful handicapper, below best both starts in 2017: stays 14.5f: acts on heavy going. *Mark Walford*

CRAKEHALL LAD (IRE) 6 ch.g. Manduro (GER) 135 – My Uptown Girl (Dubai **52**
Destination (USA) 127) [2017 50: f12s^4 f12g^6 f14g 15.9m^2 14m^2 14m 16g t16.3d f11.1g Dec 29] smallish, leggy gelding: modest handicapper: stays 2m: acts on fibresand, tapeta, firm and good to soft going: wears headgear. *Andrew Crook*

CRANWELL 5 b.m. Nayef (USA) 129 – First Bloom (USA) 71 (Fusaichi Pegasus (USA) **–**
130) [2017 61: p12g 9.9g 11.6d Jun 24] lengthy mare: maiden, no form in 2017: in hood last 2 starts: often races towards rear. *George Baker*

CRANWORTH PHOENIX 2 b.f. (Apr 6) Lilbourne Lad (IRE) 111 – Kahalah (IRE) 77 **50**
(Darshaan 133) [2017 5f^4 5d 5g^6 6d^2 6d 5.1s p8g Oct 24] half-sister to several winners, including useful winner up to 1¼m Emenem (2-y-o 7f/8.6f winner, by Sir Percy) and winner up to 1¼m Masaraat (2-y-o 1m winner, by Alhaarth): dam 1½m winner: poor maiden. *Brian Barr*

CRAVING (IRE) 2 b.c. (Mar 19) Equiano (FR) 127 – Pretty Bonnie 94 (Kyllachy 129) **81**
[2017 p8g^4 t8.6g^2 t9.5g^2 t9.5g^3 Dec 18] £40,000Y: second foal: dam 5f/6f winner: fairly useful form: placed in 3 minor events at Wolverhampton: stays 9.5f. *Simon Crisford*

CRAY (IRE) 3 b.g. Rip Van Winkle (IRE) 134 – Amaya (USA) (Kingmambo (USA) 125) **80**
[2017 61: t8d^3 t10.2g^4 12g^3 14g* 14m^6 p14s^2 14m^6 14.4s^6 16.1d^5 Aug 17] fairly useful handicapper: won at Wetherby (by ½ length from Padrinho) in May: stays 1¾m: acts on polytrack, tapeta and good to firm going: often in cheekpieces. *James Bethell*

CRAZIE MAISIE 2 ch.f. (Mar 13) Intikhab (USA) 135 – Maisie's Moon (USA) 60 **–**
(Curlin (USA) 134) [2017 t6.1g p7g Dec 20] first foal: dam maiden (best form at 7f): well held in 2 minor events. *Brian Barr*

CRAZY HORSE 4 b.g. Sleeping Indian 122 – Mainstay 86 (Elmaamul (USA) 125) [2017 **–**
118: 8g Apr 1] lengthy gelding: smart at 3 yrs, well below form and looked ungainly on sole start in 2017: stays 1m: acts on heavy going. *John Gosden*

CRAZY TORNADO (IRE) 4 b.g. Big Bad Bob (IRE) 118 – All Day (CHI) (Jaded **77**
Dancer (USA)) [2017 78: 7m^6 8m^6 8m^2 8.3m^5 8m 6.9v^4 7.2m 8d^5 8g* 8d^2 8d^4 8m^5 7.8v 9s^6 8v^3 Oct 12] fair handicapper: won at Ayr in July: stays 1m: acts on polytrack, soft and good to firm going: wears hood. *Keith Dalgleish*

CRAZY WORLD 2 b.g. (May 9) Sleeping Indian 122 – Mis Chicaf (IRE) 101 (Prince **57**
Sabo 123) [2017 5m 7m 6.1v 6g* Sep 27] sturdy gelding: modest form: won 20-runner nursery at Redcar on final start by ½ length from Excellent Times: best effort at 6f: dead. *Declan Carroll*

CREEK WALK (USA) 3 b.g. Street Cry (IRE) 130 – Badminton 106 (Zieten (USA) 118) **78**
[2017 83p: 9m^4 p6g^5 Sep 5] fair form: better effort in 2017 when fourth in maiden at Lingfield in June: may prove best at shorter than 9f. *Saeed bin Suroor*

CREEL 2 b.c. (Feb 11) Aussie Rules (USA) 123 – Spate Rise (Speightstown (USA) 124) **78**
[2017 8g 8.2v^3 8d 8.3v^3 t8g^3 Nov 24] fair maiden: stays 8.5f: acts on tapeta, best turf form on heavy going: usually races prominently. *David Brown*

CREGGS PIPES (IRE) 5 ch.m. Rip Van Winkle (IRE) 134 – Sophie Germain (IRE) **114**
(Indian Ridge 123) [2017 109: 9.5s^5 10g^3 8d* 10g Jul 2] first foal: dam unraced out of Oaks d'Italia winner Nydrion: smart performer: won Lanwades Stud Stakes at the Curragh (by 3¾ lengths from Opal Tiara) in May: stays 1¼m, all wins at shorter: acts on polytrack and heavy going: front runner. *A. Slattery, Ireland*

CRESENDO (IRE) 4 b.g. Vocalised (USA) 114 – Rachida (IRE) (Hurricane Run (IRE) **68**
134) [2017 72: p7g 9.5g p8g^2 p10.7g^5 f11.1g^6 Dec 21] fair handicapper: left J. S. Bolger after fourth start: stays 1m: acts on polytrack, best turf form on good going: has worn cheekpieces: has worn tongue tie, including last 3 starts. *Gavin Patrick Cromwell, Ireland*

CRIBBS CAUSEWAY (IRE) 3 b.f. Rip Van Winkle (IRE) 134 – Bristol Fashion (Dansili 127) [2017 –: 8.3g^5 8.3g 10.2f^5 p11s* p12g* 11.5m* 14m 12g* 12d^2 12g* p13g^3 Nov 2] sturdy filly: useful handicapper: won at Kempton, Lingfield and Yarmouth, all in June, Salisbury (by 1½ lengths from Notice) in August and Newmarket (by length from Teofonic) in October: stays 13f: acts on polytrack, good to firm and good to soft going: in cheekpieces last 2 starts: often races prominently. *Roger Charlton* **105**

CRICKLEWOOD GREEN (USA) 6 ch.g. Bob And John (USA) 117 – B Berry Brandy (USA) (Event of The Year (USA) 125) [2017 91: p8g 8m 8.5m 8g^6 10m 7g* 8m^4 8d^2 7d p8g Dec 13] workmanlike gelding: fairly useful handicapper: won at Ascot in July: stays 1m: acts on polytrack, good to firm and good to soft going: usually races in rear. *Sylvester Kirk* **88**

CRIKEYITSWHYKIE 2 b.g. (Mar 25) Piccolo 121 – Kitty Kitty Cancan 73 (Warrshan (USA) 117) [2017 5s^3 t5.1g p6s^6 Nov 17] modest form: best effort when third in minor event at Catterick (6 lengths behind Machree) in October. *Derek Shaw* **51**

CRIMEAN TATAR (TUR) 4 b.c. Sea The Stars (IRE) 140 – Unity (IRE) 103 (Sadler's Wells (USA) 132) [2017 117p: 12m^4 13.9d 13.3d^4 11.9g^4 Sep 3] good-topped colt: smart performer: fourth in John Porter Stakes (2 lengths behind Muntahaa) and Geoffrey Freer Stakes (beaten 6¾ lengths by Defoe), both at Newbury, and Bosphorus Cup at Veliefendi (2¾ lengths behind Secret Number): stays 1½m: acts on polytrack and good to firm going: blinkered last 2 starts. *Hugo Palmer* **114**

CRIMSON ROCK (USA) 3 b.f. Fastnet Rock (AUS) 127 – Maryinsky (IRE) 107 (Sadler's Wells (USA) 132) [2017 86P: 10m p12g Nov 6] sturdy filly: useful form: won sole start at 2 yrs: possibly flattered when seventh in listed race at Kempton (5¾ lengths behind Titi Makfi) in November: should be suited by 1¼m+. *Ralph Beckett* **98 ?**

CRIMSON ROSETTE (IRE) 3 b.f. Teofilo (IRE) 126 – Crimson Ribbon (USA) 92 (Lemon Drop Kid (USA) 131) [2017 66: 8m^3 10.3g^5 8.1m* p10g* Nov 17] useful-looking filly: fairly useful performer: won maiden at Windsor in October and handicap at Lingfield (awarded race after beaten head by Stellar Surprise) in November: stays 1¼m: acts on polytrack and good to firm going: in hood last 2 starts: sometimes slowly away. *Charlie Fellowes* **89**

CRIMSON SKIES (IRE) 2 ch.f. (Mar 23) Declaration of War (USA) 128 – Emily Blake (IRE) 115 (Lend A Hand 124) [2017 p8g t8.6g Nov 25] fifth foal: half-sister to winner up to 6f Gallena (2-y-o 5.7f winner, by Invincible Spirit): dam 6f-1m winner: modest form: better effort when seventh in minor event at Wolverhampton (7½ lengths behind Thunderbolt Rocks) in November. *Tom Dascombe* **52**

CRINDLE CARR (IRE) 3 ch.g. Compton Place 125 – Arley Hall 79 (Excellent Art 125) [2017 t8g t8g^2 t8d^4 t12.2m^3 9.8m^2 May 12] fair maiden: stays 1¼m: acts on tapeta and good to firm going: often races lazily: has joined John Flint. *David Barron* **71**

CRISTAL FIZZ (IRE) 3 ch.f. Power 117 – Effervesce (IRE) 84 (Galileo (IRE) 134) [2017 104p: 8d 8g^5 7d Aug 24] good-topped filly: useful performer: eighth in Poule d'Essai des Pouliches at Deauville on reappearance: stays 1m: acts on soft going: tried in cheekpieces: often races in rear. *William Haggas* **100**

CRISTAL PALLAS CAT (IRE) 2 b.g. (Apr 24) Kodiac 112 – Flower of Kent (USA) 78 (Diesis 133) [2017 p7d^4 6d^6 p6g p7d* p7g^2 Dec 31] fair performer: won nursery at Kempton in December: stays 7f: acts on polytrack: in hood last 2 starts: usually leads. *Roger Ingram* **72**

CRISTAL SPIRIT 2 b.g. (Mar 31) Nathaniel (IRE) 129 – Celestial Girl 84 (Dubai Destination (USA) 127) [2017 7d 7g p7g Nov 6] 55,000Y: third foal: half-brother to useful 7f/1m winner Mystique Moon (by Shamardal): dam 1¼m winner who stayed 1½m: little impact in maidens/minor event: will be suited by 1¼m: should do better. *William Haggas* **– p**

CRITICAL THINKING (IRE) 3 b.g. Art Connoisseur (IRE) 121 – Cookie Cutter (IRE) 71 (Fasliyev (USA) 120) [2017 56: p8g^6 p7g^2 p10g^4 p10g* t9.5m^3 8m^3 10.2f^5 11.6d 8.1m^3 10.3d^4 10.3d^6 t9.5g^4 t9.5g t9.5g t9.5g^6 p7g^3 Dec 30] fair performer: won claimer at Lingfield in February for Julia Feilden: left Kevin Frost after thirteenth start: stays 1¼m: acts on polytrack, tapeta and firm going. *David Loughnane* **70**

CROMER (IRE) 2 b.c. (Apr 1) Footstepsinthesand 120 – Boga (IRE) 63 (Invincible Spirit (IRE) 121) [2017 p6d May 29] in hood, 10/1, very green when well held in minor event at Chelmsford: sold 4,500 gns in November, sent to Sweden. *Martyn Meade* **–**

CROPLEY (IRE) 8 gr.g. Galileo (IRE) 134 – Niyla (IRE) (Darshaan 133) [2017 16s Sep 19] maiden, well held sole start on Flat in 2017: stays 2m: acts on heavy going: usually wears headgear: modest hurdler. *Dai Burchell* **–**

CROQUEMBOUCHE (IRE) 8 b.g. Acclamation 118 – Wedding Cake (IRE) 71 (Groom Dancer (USA) 128) [2017 96: 11.6g^2 12.3d 11.4d^4 11.4m^4 12g* 12g^5 12m Sep 23] good-topped gelding: fairly useful handicapper: won at Pontefract (by nose from Melting Dew) in August: stays 1½m: acts on polytrack, firm and soft going: in cheekpieces last 3 starts: front runner. *Ed de Giles* **91**

CROSS COUNTER 2 b.c. (Apr 5) Teofilo (IRE) 126 – Waitress (USA) (Kingmambo (USA) 125) [2017 t8.6d* Dec 9] second foal: dam, French winner around 7f, out of very smart French 5f-7f winner Do The Honours: 7/2, looked useful prospect when won minor event at Wolverhampton (by 2¼ lengths from Kaser) on debut with bit in hand: sure to progress. *Charlie Appleby* **89 p**

CROSSED BATON 2 b.c. (Feb 28) Dansili 127 – Sacred Shield 87 (Beat Hollow 126) [2017 8d^6 8g* Sep 15] third foal: half-brother to 1¼m winner The Begum (by Zamindar): dam, 9.5f/1¼m winner, half-sister to useful dam of high-class 1¼m performer Twice Over: fairly useful form: won minor event at Sandown (by length from Stephensons Rocket) in September: will be suited by 1¼m: likely to progress further. *John Gosden* **85 p**

CROSSE FIRE 5 b.g. Monsieur Bond (IRE) 120 – Watersilk (IRE) (Fasliyev (USA) 120) [2017 59, a95: f5g^6 f5g^4 f6g^6 f6g^3 f5s f6g^4 f5m^2 f5m^3 f6g* f6d^5 f6d* f6g^6 5m* 5d^4 6g 5s^4 5d 5s* 5s 5g 5g^4 5d 5v t5g f5g^6 6s^3 f5g^3 f6.1g f6.1g f5g^4 f5g^4 Dec 29] fair handicapper on turf, fairly useful on all-weather: won at Southwell in March and April (by 1¼ lengths from Meshardal), Beverley in May and Pontefract in July: stays 6f: acts on fibresand, soft and good to firm going: has worn headgear, including usually in 2017: front runner/races prominently. *Scott Dixon* **74 a84**

CROSSING THE LINE 2 br.f. (Apr 1) Cape Cross (IRE) 129 – Terentia 108 (Diktat 126) [2017 6g* 6g^6 6d Sep 30] 75,000Y: third foal: half-sister to 6f winner Shades of Silk (by Bahamian Bounty) and 2-y-o 6f winner Publilia (by Makfi): dam, 5f winner (including at 2 yrs), half-sister to smart 6f winner Cartimandua: fairly useful form: won minor event at Newmarket (by neck from Gabr) in August: best effort when sixth in Dick Poole Fillies' Stakes at Salisbury (3 lengths behind Anna Nerium) in September: raced only at 6f. *Andrew Balding* **87**

CROSSLEY 8 ch.g. Monsieur Bond (IRE) 120 – Dispol Diamond 72 (Sharpo 132) [2017 t8s t8.6g Jun 1] maiden, well held in handicaps in 2017: wears headgear. *Neville Bycroft* **–**

CROSS MY MIND (IRE) 2 b.f. (Mar 26) Cape Cross (IRE) 129 – Zaaqya 94 (Nayef (USA) 129) [2017 p8g^6 Nov 18] €58,000Y: fourth foal: sister to 2-y-o 1m winner Laafiraaq: dam, winner up to 1½m (2-y-o 7f/1m winner), half-sister to useful/unreliable winner up to 1m Brave Hero: 8/1, sixth in minor event at Lingfield (8½ lengths behind Masaarr) in November: should do better. *Ralph Beckett* **60 p**

CROSS STEP (USA) 3 b.g. Kitten's Joy (USA) 128 – Maid Service (USA) (Arch (USA) 127) [2017 63p: 10m^2 11.6g* 12m^5 11.2s 10.9g a8.9f^5 a8.9f a8f Dec 21] rangy gelding: fairly useful performer: won maiden at Lingfield (by short head from Humble Hero) in May: left Charlie Appleby after fourth start: stays 11.5f: acts on good to firm going: wears headgear. *A. Al Rayhi, UAE* **89**

CROTCHET 2 gr.f. (Apr 18) Lethal Force (IRE) 128 – Humouresque 110 (Pivotal 124) [2017 5v* 7v t6.1g^3 Nov 18] rather lightly-made filly: half-sister to several winners, including useful 1¼m/11f winner Piano (by Azamour) and 2-y-o 5f-7f winner Clef (by Dutch Art): dam 1m-11f winner: fairly useful form: won minor event at Nottingham (by ½ length from Dandy's Beano) in August: should be suited by 6f+. *Richard Fahey* **81**

CROWNED EAGLE 3 b.g. Oasis Dream 129 – Gull Wing (IRE) 108 (In The Wings 128) [2017 92p: 10g* 12m 13g 10d^3 12m^4 t12.2g^3 Dec 2] strong, attractive gelding: useful handicapper: won at Windsor in May: left John Gosden after fifth start: stays 1½m: acts on tapeta, good to firm and good to soft going: sometimes in cheekpieces: front runner/races prominently. *Marco Botti* **104**

CROWNING GLORY (FR) 4 b.f. Speightstown (USA) 124 – Forest Crown 105 (Royal Applause 124) [2017 96: p8g 8f^4 8.5m^5 8g* 8g p8g^6 Oct 27] leggy filly: useful performer: won handicap at Pontefract (by 1¼ lengths from Red Tea) in July: stays 8.5f: acts on polytrack, tapeta and firm going. *Ralph Beckett* **103**

CROWN OF CORTEZ 2 ch.g. (Feb 24) Pivotal 124 – Bahia Emerald (IRE) 80 (Bahamian Bounty 116) [2017 5m^6 6s^6 7.2m t7.1g* t6g* Oct 19] 48,000F: third foal: closely related to 2-y-o 5f winner Emerald Bay (by Kyllachy): dam, 6f winner, half-sister to useful 2-y-o 6f winner Vital Statistics out of useful 5f performer Emerald Peace: fair performer: won nurseries at Newcastle in September and October: stays 7f: acts on tapeta: in blinkers last 2 starts: often races towards rear: will go on improving. *Richard Fahey* **78 p**

CROWNTHORPE 2 b.g. (Mar 24) Monsieur Bond (IRE) 120 – Normandy Maid 75 **89**
(American Post 121) [2017 p5g^3 5f t6.1g^3 7s^2 7.4d^2 7g* 7d^2 6g Oct 7] sturdy gelding: second foal: dam, 2-y-o 5f winner, half-sister to useful winner up to 7f Charles Molson: fairly useful performer: won nursery at Sandown in September: second in similar event at Doncaster next time: stays 7.5f: acts on tapeta and soft going: often races towards rear. *Richard Fahey*

CROWN VALLARY (FR) 2 b.f. (Mar 8) Manduro (GER) 135 – Troiecat (FR) (One **87**
Cool Cat (USA) 123) [2017 7d^2 7g* 7.5d^2 8d Sep 30] €30,000Y: fifth foal: sister to useful French/Scandinavian 1m-1½m winner High As A Kite and half-sister to 2 winners, including useful winner up to 1m London Protocol (2-y-o 6.5f winner, by Muhtathir): dam French maiden: fairly useful form: won maiden at Clairefontaine in August: second in minor event at Maisons-Laffitte (1½ lengths behind Red Line) in September: bred to stay at least 1m. *K. R. Burke*

CROWN WALK 2 ch.f. (Mar 25) Dubawi (IRE) 129 – Dunnes River (USA) 84 (Danzig **83 p**
(USA)) [2017 p7s* Dec 15] sister to French 7f winner Pirate's Cove and half-sister to several winners, including very smart winner up to 10.5f Cutlass Bay (2-y-o 1¼m winner) and smart winner up to 1½m Boscobel (2-y-o 7f winner) (both by Halling): dam 1m winner: in hood, 7/2, won minor event at Chelmsford (by 4½ lengths from Briscola) on debut: will stay 1m+: will improve. *Charlie Appleby*

CRUCIAL MOMENT 3 b.g. Pivotal 124 – Moonglow 65 (Nayef (USA) 129) [2017 63: **61**
p8g^5 f8g* 8d^6 10.2f^6 14d^6 Aug 19] good-topped gelding: modest handicapper: won at Southwell in April: probably stays 1¾m: acts on polytrack, fibresand and soft going: took well to hurdling, winning twice before end of year. *Bill Turner*

CRUEL CLEVER CAT 2 b.f. (Mar 12) Bated Breath 125 – Satin Braid 78 (Diktat 126) **51**
[2017 5g^5 5m 6m^5 6.1m^6 5v^4 p6g Sep 5] rather unfurnished filly: fourth foal: half-sister to 5f/6f winner Ada Lovelace (by Byron): dam 1m winner: modest maiden: best effort at 5f: usually races close up. *John Gallagher*

CRUISE TOTHELIMIT (IRE) 9 b.g. Le Vie dei Colori 126 – Kiva (Indian Ridge 123) **72**
[2017 71: t5g t6g^6 t5.1f^2 t6g t5.1g* 5m t5.1g^2 t5.1g^2 5f 5d^3 6.1g^2 t5.1g t5.1d Dec 27] lengthy gelding: fair handicapper: won at Wolverhampton in March: stays 6f: acts on tapeta, good to firm and heavy going: usually wears headgear/tongue tie nowadays: front runner/races prominently. *Patrick Morris*

CRUMBLECREEK (IRE) 3 b.f. Sir Prancealot (IRE) 111 – Larkfield Empress (IRE) **63 p**
55 (Holy Roman Emperor (IRE) 125) [2017 t8.6g^3 Dec 18] €7,500Y, resold £10,000Y: first foal: dam once-raced daughter of useful Italian sprinter Shifting Place: 10/1, some encouragement when third in maiden at Wolverhampton (5 lengths behind Pure Shores) in December: entitled to progress. *Clive Cox*

CRUSHED (IRE) 3 b.g. Beat Hollow 126 – Sel 58 (Salse (USA) 128) [2017 70p: 10.2m^2 **86**
12m^4 11.8s^3 10d* 10g 12.1s^3 Oct 10] good-topped gelding: fairly useful handicapper: won at Windsor in September: stays 1¼m: acts on tapeta, good to firm and good to soft going: usually races close up/freely: sold to join Alan King 40,000 gns in October. *William Haggas*

CRY FURY 9 b.g. Beat Hollow 126 – Cantanta 74 (Top Ville 129) [2017 69: 10g Sep 6] –
useful at best, well held sole start on Flat in 2017: stays 1½m: acts on polytrack, tapeta and good to firm going: tried in cheekpieces/tongue tie: sometimes slowly away: poor maiden hurdler/chaser. *Matt Sheppard*

CRYPTONITE (IRE) 3 br.g. Dark Angel (IRE) 113 – Bowness 84 (Efisio 120) [2017 54: **65**
8.3g t7.1g* f7.1g^6 6m^3 5d t7.2g^6 t7.2g 6s^4 6g 5.7d* 6m^6 6g Sep 27] fair handicapper: won at Wolverhampton in May and Bath in August: stays 7f: acts on tapeta and good to soft going: has worn headgear. *Michael Appleby*

CRYSTAL CASQUE 2 ch.f. (May 5) Helmet (AUS) 127 – Crystal Moments 96 (Haafhd **66**
129) [2017 6d p7g^4 p6g^5 p7d^2 Nov 22] angular filly: fifth foal: half-sister to 1¼m winner Al Nasser Alwashik (by Intikhab): dam winner up to 7f (2-y-o 5f/6f winner): fair form: best effort at 7f. *Rod Millman*

CRYSTAL DEAUVILLE (FR) 2 b.g. (May 3) Equiano (FR) 127 – Crystal Plum (IRE) **63**
67 (Rock of Gibraltar (IRE) 133) [2017 p6.5f^5 p6.5g^6 6d p5m^5 t5.1d^6 p5g* f5g^3 Dec 29] modest performer: won seller at Lingfield in December: stays 6.5f: acts on polytrack and viscoride: sometimes in headgear: in tongue tie last 2 starts: front runner/races prominently. *Gay Kelleway*

CRYSTAL HOPE 2 ch.f. (Mar 1) Nathaniel (IRE) 129 – Crystal Etoile 76 (Dansili 127) [2017 8.3d⁶ Oct 18] second foal: half-sister to 1m (including at 2 yrs)/8.6f winner Stellar Surprise (by Notnowcato): dam, maiden (stayed 1¼m), half-sister to very smart winners up to 1½m Crystal Capella, Hillstar and Crystal Ocean: 20/1, sixth in maiden at Nottingham (9½ lengths behind Hadith) in October: will improve. *Sir Michael Stoute* **71 p**

CRYSTAL MOONLIGHT 2 ch.f. (Mar 29) New Approach (IRE) 132 – Crystal Capella 122 (Cape Cross (IRE) 129) [2017 p8g⁵ Nov 8] third foal: dam, 1¼m-1½m (including Princess of Wales's Stakes) winner, closely related to St Leger runner-up Crystal Ocean: 14/1, fifth in minor event at Kempton (8¾ lengths behind Cecchini) in November, not knocked about: will stay at least 1¼m: sure to progress. *Sir Michael Stoute* **60 p**

CRYSTAL OCEAN 3 b.c. Sea The Stars (IRE) 140 – Crystal Star 100 (Mark of Esteem (IRE) 137) [2017 82P: 10.2m* 10.3d³ 12m³ 12d* 14.5g² Sep 16] **123 p**

The Gordon Stakes is unlikely to rank too highly among the big races won by Sir Michael Stoute during his glittering career, but the Group 3 mile and a half contest for three-year-olds at Glorious Goodwood—now the Qatar Goodwood Festival—has proved a good race for the trainer down the years. Freemason Lodge has saddled a record ten winners of this long-established St Leger trial and, although the 2008 winner Conduit is the only one of those who went on to win at Doncaster too, it is significant that some of the yard's best recent performers feature on the Gordon Stakes roll of honour. Conduit also went on to have a memorable four-year-old career, winning both the King George VI and Queen Elizabeth Stakes and the Breeders' Cup Turf. The 2009 Gordon Stakes winner Harbinger also landed the Ascot showpiece the following summer, putting up one of the best performances in that race's exalted history during an unbeaten, if truncated, four-year-old campaign. In the latest season, Ulysses developed into one of the leading older horses in Europe twelve months on from his Goodwood win, his achievements including a memorable Group 1 double in the Eclipse at Sandown and International Stakes at York. All of which bodes well for Stoute's latest Gordon Stakes winner Crystal Ocean, who still looked a top-class colt in the making at the end of his three-year-old campaign and is just the sort that his trainer does well with as a four-year-old. Watch out for Crystal Ocean being turned into a Group 1 winner in 2018.

In truth, the latest renewal of the Qatar-sponsored Gordon Stakes didn't look a vintage one, attracting the smallest field since just four lined up in 2002 (and the joint-smallest since the quintet in 2005), with the market focussing on 6/4 favourite Crystal Ocean and 9/4-shot Khalidi, the pair having finished third and

Qatar Gordon Stakes, Goodwood—a fine shot of Crystal Ocean as he confirms earlier promise to give trainer Sir Michael Stoute a tenth victory in the race

second respectively in the King Edward VII Stakes at Royal Ascot on their previous start. The market leaders dominated the race itself too, with Crystal Ocean reversing those Royal Ascot placings in smooth fashion under Ryan Moore, who was riding the colt for the first time since Crystal Ocean made a promising debut when second in a Newbury maiden on his only two-year-old outing. Produced to lead over a furlong out, Crystal Ocean wasn't fully extended by any means to pull three and a half lengths clear of his market rival, with the pace-setting Mount Moriah a further length back in third. It was Crystal Ocean's first win since romping home on his reappearance in a ten-furlong maiden at Nottingham in April, but he had hardly been standing still since then. His never-nearer third to the ill-fated Permian in the Dante Stakes at York next time was a performance full of promise, whilst his third behind the same rival when a well-backed favourite for the King Edward VII (a race his half-brother Hillstar had won four years earlier) didn't tell the whole story either, as he wasn't seen to best effect, being rushed up out wide at a vital stage by Andrea Atzeni (who had also been on board at York).

With Moore and Atzeni claimed by their respective retainers, 2016 champion jockey Jim Crowley (who struck up a good relationship with Ulysses over the summer) came in for the ride on Crystal Ocean in the St Leger, in which he was sent off a 5/1-shot in a field of eleven, with only Irish Derby winner Capri (the mount of Moore) and Goodwood Cup winner Stradivarius at shorter odds. It looked one of the best St Legers—both in terms of depth and competitiveness—for many years, and it says plenty for Crystal Ocean that he shaped like the best horse in the race for most of the way. With Ballydoyle pacemaker The Anvil ensuring a furious gallop, Crystal Ocean travelled noticeably strongly under a patient ride before being produced with what looked a winning challenge just over a furlong out. Capri, however, found plenty under pressure for Moore and held him off by half a length, with a short head back to Stradivarius in third, and subsequent Melbourne Cup winner Rekindling a further length and a half away in fourth. 'Thrilled' and 'outstayed' were the contrasting post-race verdicts from Stoute, who added: 'We won't run him beyond a mile and a half again.'

Whilst Stoute has just the one St Leger win to his name, the wait for another success in Britain's oldest classic dates much further back for the famous dark blue, yellow cap carried by Crystal Ocean. The de Rothschild banking dynasty has had strong links with British racing for some one hundred and seventy-five years and was responsible for several key individuals in the Flat racing establishment during the nineteenth and twentieth centuries, notably Baron Mayer de Rothschild, who registered the colours in 1843 and saw them carried to a famous victory in the St Leger twenty-eight years later, his horse Hannah completing the fillies' triple crown in the process, having won the One Thousand Guineas and Oaks. The baron's nephew, Leopold, also saw the colours carried to a surprise 40/1 success with Doricles in the 1901 St Leger, but there have been no further family victories in the Doncaster showpiece. The 1901 St Leger, by the way, featured in a story told by Timeform's founder Phil Bull who credits the race with converting his father who was a member of the Salvation Army and used to paint religious slogans on walls with whitewash. On the eve of the 1901 St Leger he painted 'What shall we do to be saved?' on the wall of the Doncaster grandstand, only to return the following day to find some wag had chalked underneath it 'Back Doricles for the St Leger.' Bull's father backed the horse—was it divine intervention?—which started his life-long interest from then on in racing.

Crystal Ocean (b.c. 2014)	Sea The Stars (IRE) (b 2006)	Cape Cross (b 1994)	Green Desert
			Park Appeal
		Urban Sea (ch 1989)	Miswaki
			Allegretta
	Crystal Star (ch 2000)	Mark of Esteem (b 1993)	Darshaan
			Homage
		Crystal Cavern (ch 1992)	Be My Guest
			Krisalya

The current de Rothschild racing and breeding empire operates on a smaller scale than those overseen by the family's illustrious ancestors, but Crystal Ocean's octogenarian owner Sir Evelyn de Rothschild (Leopold's grandson) has still enjoyed plenty of success with Crystal Ocean's family in recent years. A son of Sea The Stars, Crystal Ocean is the seventh foal out of the useful seven-furlong performer Crystal Star, who finished runner-up in the 2003 Fred Darling Stakes before disappointing when prominent in the betting for the Poule d'Essai des Pouliches on her next start. Her most notable representatives before Crystal Ocean include Crystal Ocean's close relative Crystal Capella (by Cape Cross), who was a very smart mile and a half performer with three wins at Group 2 level, the Pride Stakes (twice) and the Princess of Wales's Stakes at Newmarket, before she was retired to the paddocks. The biggest money-spinner among Crystal Ocean's four winning siblings, however, is the aforementioned Hillstar (by Danehill Dancer), who landed the Canadian International at Woodbine in 2014 at the end of a very consistent four-year-old campaign. The signs are that Crystal Ocean takes far more after the durable pair Crystal Capella and Hillstar than another half-sister Crystal Zvezda (by Dubawi), who was a listed winner at ten furlongs but was increasingly held back by her attitude towards the end of her career and ended up with a Timeform squiggle. Hillstar, meanwhile, isn't the only member of this family to have tasted success in Canada, as Crystal Ocean's grandam Crystal Cavern won over a mile there after being exported to North America after showing fairly useful form (seven-furlong winner at two) for Roger Charlton. Both Crystal Cavern and Crystal Ocean's great grandam Krisalya proved a prolific source of winners at stud, the most notable performers associated with them being useful middle-distance stayer Waila, the final foal out of Crystal Cavern, and the 2001 Poule d'Essai des Pouliches winner Rose Gypsy, who was the highest-rated of Krisalya's seven winners from ten runners to reach the track.

A useful-looking colt, Crystal Ocean has yet to race on extremes of ground but has seemed equally as effective on good to firm and good to soft so far. Although it would be stretching things to say he didn't stay the extended mile and three quarters at Doncaster, given he posted a career-best effort there, it seems reasonable to assume shorter trips will play to his strengths more. Indeed, he travels so strongly that a return to ten furlongs might not be out of the question, with the Eclipse at Sandown appealing as a possible early-summer target. Stoute is also the most successful trainer in the Eclipse too (albeit tied with Alec Taylor) and has won it for the de Rothschild family before, his 2007 winner Notnowcato being owned by Sir Evelyn's sons Anthony and David. *Sir Michael Stoute*

CRYSTAL RIVER 3 b.f. Dubawi (IRE) 129 – Inner Secret (USA) 85 (Singspiel (IRE) 133) [2017 69p: 8.3v* 8.9d* Oct 15] useful form: won maiden at Hamilton (by 13 lengths from Bombay) in September and listed race at Chantilly (by 1½ lengths from Garance) in October: stays 9f: likely to progress further. *William Haggas* **108 p**

CRYSTAL SECRET 3 b.f. Sayif (IRE) 122 – Laser Crystal (IRE) 67 (King's Theatre (IRE) 128) [2017 52: 8.5g 7f 9.9m 11.4m^4 11.6d^5 11.6d 9.9m^3 8.5d^6 10g^5 10m p12d^6 11.2m^6 p15.8g p12g Oct 3] leggy, narrow filly: modest maiden: stays 11.5f: acts on good to firm going: sometimes wears headgear: usually races close up. *John Bridger* **54**

CRYSTAL STANZA (IRE) 3 b.g. Poet's Voice 126 – Clear Impression (IRE) 103 (Danehill (USA) 126) [2017 –: t7.1g^2 Jan 9] modest form: in visor, better effort when second in maiden at Wolverhampton on sole outing in 2017: sent to Greece. *Charlie Fellowes* **55**

CRYSTAL SUNSTONE 3 b.g. Henrythenavigator (USA) 131 – Crystal Power (USA) (Pleasant Colony (USA)) [2017 p8s t9.5g 9.9s^5 9.9s 8v^2 Oct 19] fair maiden: best effort at 1m: raced only on soft/heavy going on turf: sometimes slowly away: has joined Alex Hales. *Eve Johnson Houghton* **72**

CRY WOLF 4 ch.g. Street Cry (IRE) 130 – Love Charm (Singspiel (IRE) 133) [2017 73: p12g Sep 27] fair maiden, down the field sole start in 2017: stays 1½m: tried in cheekpieces. *James Evans* **–**

CTHULHU (USA) 3 b.f. Henrythenavigator (USA) 131 – So Stylish (USA) 87 (Johannesburg (USA) 127) [2017 11.6g^5 t12.2g^4 p11g Oct 11] 20,000Y: second foal: half-sister to French 1½m winner Natty (by Fastnet Rock): dam, 2-y-o 5f winner, half-sister to very smart winner up to 7f One Cool Cat: modest form: best effort when fifth in maiden at Lingfield in June. *William Muir* **61**

CUBAN HEEL 2 gr.g. (Apr 16) Havana Gold (IRE) 118 – Tipping Over (IRE) 88 (Aussie **81**
Rules (USA) 123) [2017 6.5g 7g^2 7d^3 7m^4 7s^2 Oct 10] 20,000F, €55,000Y: rather unfurnished gelding: first foal: dam 2-y-o 6f winner: fairly useful maiden: second in minor event at Leicester in October: best effort at 7f: acts on soft going: tried in cheekpieces. *Clive Cox*

CUBAN QUEEN (USA) 4 ro.f. Elusive Quality (USA) – One Smokin' Lady (USA) **55**
(Smoke Glacken (USA) 120) [2017 56: p7g^3 p7g p7d p8d^6 f7d^4 t6g^6 7m May 3] angular filly: modest handicapper: stays 7f: acts on polytrack and tapeta: has worn headgear: sent to Sweden. *Julia Feilden*

CUBSWIN (IRE) 3 b.f. Zamindar (USA) 116 – Moonlight Rhapsody (IRE) 73 (Danehill **80**
Dancer (IRE) 117) [2017 –p: 10g^4 10m^4 12g^3 t12.2g^5 11.6f* Jul 18] fairly useful handicapper: won at Bath (by 2 lengths from Plato's Kode) in July: stays 1½m: acts on firm going: tried in hood: sold to join Neil King £20,000 in August and won over hurdles in November. *Roger Charlton*

CUCKOO'S CALLING 3 b.f. So You Think (NZ) 133 – Sinndarina (FR) (Sinndar (IRE) **71**
134) [2017 t12.4d^5 Dec 16] first foal: dam, useful French winner up to 1½m (2-y-o 9f winner), out of smart French performer up to 1½m Ana Marie: 5/1, fifth in maiden at Newcastle (4¼ lengths behind Warm Oasis) in December. *James Bethell*

CUDDINGTON (IRE) 2 gr.c. (Jan 23) Dark Angel (IRE) 113 – Pindrop 56 (Exceed And **63**
Excel (AUS) 126) [2017 7g^4 Aug 11] 12/1, fourth in minor event at Haydock (4 lengths behind Exhort) in August, very slowly away and hanging badly left from 3f out. *Tom Dascombe*

CUE'S FOLLY 2 b.f. (Apr 20) Nathaniel (IRE) 129 – Island Odyssey 93 (Dansili 127) **–**
[2017 t8.6g Nov 29] fifth foal: half-sister to useful 2-y-o 9f winner (stays 1¾m) Island Remede (by Medicean): dam, 1¼m-1½m winner, half-sister to useful 1¼m-1½m winner Scrutinise: 40/1, very green when well held in minor event at Wolverhampton. *Ed Dunlop*

CUILLIN HILLS 2 ch.g. (Mar 27) Pastoral Pursuits 127 – Justbetweenfriends (USA) 85 **62**
(Diesis 133) [2017 t6s 6s^4 7.2d^3 7.2m 8s Oct 3] modest maiden: best effort at 7f: tried in cheekpieces: sometimes slowly away, often races in rear. *Keith Dalgleish*

CULLINGWORTH (IRE) 3 b.g. Kodiac 112 – Think (FR) 99 (Marchand de Sable **100**
(USA) 117) [2017 81: 8g* 8.1d 8.2f 10.3m^5 10m^6 8d 8g* Aug 14] good-topped gelding: useful handicapper: won at Musselburgh in April and Ripon (by 7 lengths from Fujaira Bridge) in August: stays 10.5f: acts on good to firm and heavy going: sent to Australia. *Richard Fahey*

CULLODEN 5 b.g. Kyllachy 129 – Mamounia (IRE) 101 (Green Desert (USA) 127) **72**
[2017 67: f6g f6m p5g* p6g^5 5m^2 f5g^4 5g 5g^3 5d^2 5.5f^3 5s 5g* 5d* 5d* 5g^5 5g 5s 5s p5g Dec 23] lengthy gelding: fair handicapper: won at Chelmsford in March (awarded race), Musselburgh and Thirsk (apprentice) in July, and again at Musselburgh in August: best at 5f: acts on all-weather, good to firm and good to soft going: sometimes wears headgear: front runner/races prominently. *Shaun Harris*

CULMINATION 5 b.g. Beat Hollow 126 – Apogee 113 (Shirley Heights 130) [2017 **–**
14.1g^5 13.4d May 12] fair form when winning 1½m maiden at Argentan at 3 yrs: out of depth both starts on Flat in 2017: fair hurdler. *Donald McCain*

CULPABILITY (USA) 2 b.c. (Apr 1) Blame (USA) 129 – Princess Consort (USA) **58 p**
(Dixieland Band (USA)) [2017 p8g^5 Dec 20] $350,000Y: closely related to 2 winners by Arch, including useful 2-y-o 6f/7f (Oh So Sharp Stakes) winner Waterway Run (later Grade 3 8.5f winner in USA), and half-brother to several winners in USA: dam ran twice in USA: 9/2, fifth in minor event at Lingfield (9 lengths behind Three Weeks) in December: will be suited by 1¼m: capable of better. *John Gosden*

CULTURATI 4 b.g. Dubawi (IRE) 129 – Whazzis 109 (Desert Prince (IRE) 130) [2017 **111**
6g* Jun 10] lengthy, good sort: lightly-raced smart handicapper: won at Newmarket (by 1½ lengths from Scorching Heat) in June: best form at 6f: acts on soft going. *Charlie Appleby*

CULTURED KNIGHT 4 ch.g. Compton Place 125 – Cultured Pride (IRE) 81 (King's **88**
Best (USA) 132) [2017 85: p6g^2 5m^5 t6g^2 p5g^2 p5g^{pu} May 30] lengthy gelding: fairly useful handicapper: runner-up 3 times in 2017: stayed 6f: acted on all-weather and good to soft going: tried in blinkers: usually raced prominently, often freely: dead. *Richard Hughes*

CULTURE SHOCK 2 b.f. (Mar 14) Zoffany (IRE) 121 – No Song (Zamindar (USA) **–**
116) [2017 t7.2g Dec 22] 20,000F, £16,000Y, €20,000 2-y-o: second foal: dam unraced half-sister to Derby third/St Leger runner-up Romsdal: 11/2, well held in minor event at Wolverhampton. *Richard Hannon*

CUM SPIRO SPERO (IRE) 2 ch.f. (Apr 26) Casamento (IRE) 118 – Bon Ton Roulet **57**
63 (Hawk Wing (USA) 136) [2017 7d 7.4s^5 7.4g Aug 16] sixth foal: half-sister to 3
winners, including 7f winner Glanely (by Exceed And Excel) and 6f/7f winner Acadian
Angel (by Dark Angel): dam maiden (stayed 1¼m): modest form: best effort when fifth in
minor event at Beverley (5½ lengths behind Codicil) in August. *Tony Coyle*

CUNCO (IRE) 3 b.c. Frankel 147 – Chrysanthemum (IRE) 113 (Danehill Dancer (IRE) **106**
117) [2017 105: 10d* 12.3m^6 May 11] smallish, sturdy colt: useful performer: won Classic
Trial at Sandown (by head from Intern) in April: stays 1¼m: acts on soft and good to firm
going: tried in hood: has joined Chad Brown in USA. *John Gosden*

CUPID'S ARROW (IRE) 3 b.g. Majestic Missile (IRE) 118 – Kiss And Don'tell (USA) **70**
(Rahy (USA) 115) [2017 71: 6m 6m 6g^4 7m^4 6g^4 t7.1s^4 7m^2 6s* 7v^3 7d 6d^3 6s^5 Oct 10]
fair handicapper: won at Catterick in July: stays 7f: acts on soft and good to firm going.
Ruth Carr

CUPPACOCO 2 b.f. (Mar 26) Stimulation (IRE) 121 – Glen Molly (IRE) 97 (Danetime **74**
(IRE) 121) [2017 7s 7v 5s^5 t6g* t5d* Nov 4] 14,000Y: fifth foal: half-sister to French 5.5f
and (including at 2 yrs) 6.5f winner If I Say So (by Sayif): dam winner up to 7f (2-y-o 6f
winner): fair performer: won nurseries at Newcastle in October and November: stays 6f:
acts on tapeta: often leads. *Ann Duffield*

CURBYOURENTHUSIASM (IRE) 6 gr.g. Mastercraftsman (IRE) 129 – Mohican **103**
Princess (Shirley Heights 130) [2017 115: 14g 15.9g 13.9g^6 May 27] big gelding: smart
performer at 4 yrs, below that level in 2017: stays 14.5f: acts on polytrack, good to firm and
heavy going: dropped out (often starts slowly). *David Simcock*

CURIOSITY (IRE) 2 b.g. (Mar 20) High Chaparral (IRE) 132 – Precautionary 73 (Green **86**
Desert (USA) 127) [2017 6.5g^3 t6s* 7g* 7g^6 t8s Sep 8] €46,000F, €65,000Y: rather
unfurnished gelding: seventh foal: half-brother to 5f (including at 2 yrs) winner Best Be
Careful (by Exceed And Excel) and 2-y-o 7f winner Summer Stroll (by Hurricane Run):
dam, maiden (stayed 7f), closely related to very smart sprinter Prohibit: fairly useful
performer: won minor events at Newcastle in June and Ascot in July: will prove best at
short of 1m: acts on tapeta, raced only on good going on turf. *Hugo Palmer*

CURIOUS FOX 4 b.f. Bertolini (USA) 125 – Doric Lady 91 (Kyllachy 129) [2017 75: **89**
6m^6 p6g* 6d^2 6s* 6.1v^5 6m 6s^3 6.1d p6s Dec 7] sturdy filly: fairly useful handicapper: won
at Lingfield in May and Newmarket (by 1¾ lengths from Cool Bahamian) in July: stays 6f:
acts on polytrack, tapeta and soft going: often starts slowly/races in rear. *Anthony Carson*

CURLEW RIVER 3 b.f. Casamento (IRE) 118 – Dubai Opera (USA) (Dubai Millennium **103**
140) [2017 75: p10g* p10g 10g* 11.9m* 11.9d 13.4g^5 10.5s^5 10m 12g^5 Oct 7] tall filly:
useful performer: won maiden at Chelmsford in April, and handicaps at Leicester and
Brighton in August: probably stays 13.5f: acts on polytrack and good to firm going: usually
leads: sold 16,000 gns in December. *Mark Johnston*

CURTSY (IRE) 3 ch.f. Galileo (IRE) 134 – Acts of Grace (USA) 109 (Bahri (USA) 125) **63**
[2017 52p: p12f^4 p12g 14m^3 t14g 16v^5 14d^4 Aug 19] useful-looking filly: modest maiden:
stays 2m: acts on polytrack, good to firm and heavy going. *Hughie Morrison*

CURZON (IRE) 2 b.c. (May 5) Roderic O'Connor (IRE) 119 – Anna Karenina (USA) **69**
(Atticus (USA) 121) [2017 6g 5m^4 5f^3 5d^3 Aug 4] fair form: dead. *David O'Meara*

CURZON LINE 8 b.g. Dubawi (IRE) 129 – Polska (USA) 103 (Danzig (USA)) [2017 88: **76**
t7.1g^3 t7.1d^2 p7d 7m^5 t6g 8m^5 7.8g^5 7.8m^2 7.2d^5 Aug 4] strong gelding: fair handicapper **a82**
on turf, fairly useful on all-weather: second at Newcastle in February: stays 1m: acts on
polytrack, tapeta, sand and good to firm going: has worn eyeshields/tongue tie. *Michael
Easterby*

CUSTARD THE DRAGON 4 b.g. Kyllachy 129 – Autumn Pearl 102 (Orpen (USA) **93**
116) [2017 61+, a79: f7g* t7.1d^3 f7g* f7m^4 t7.1g^2 f7d* f7g* t7.1s^2 7d^6 7g f7.1g^6 t7.2g
f7.1g^2 Dec 11] lengthy gelding: fairly useful handicapper: won 4 times at Southwell in
early-2017: stays 7f: acts on all-weather: wears cheekpieces: usually races towards rear.
John Mackie

CUSTOM CUT (IRE) 8 b.g. Notnowcato 128 – Polished Gem (IRE) 89 (Danehill (USA) **112**
126) [2017 118: 8g^6 7g^2 8m* 8.5m 7.9m 8s^2 8g^3 8d 8d^5 7g Oct 17] smallish, workmanlike
gelding: smart performer: won Amethyst Stakes at Leopardstown (by ½ length from
Raymonda) in May: second in listed race at Pontefract (neck behind Another Touch) in July
and third in Desmond Stakes at Leopardstown (1½ lengths behind Alexios Komnenos) in
August: stays 9f: acts on polytrack, good to firm and heavy going: has worn headgear: front
runner/races prominently. *David O'Meara*

CWYNAR 2 b.f. (Feb 27) Kodiac 112 – Modern Art (New Approach (IRE) 132) [2017 6m **73**
p6g^{4} p7g^{2} p7g Nov 17] 35,000F, 110,000Y: first foal: dam, of little account, out of close relative to smart 6f performers Camacho and Showcasing: fair form: best effort at 7f. *Charles Hills*

CYFLYMDER (IRE) 11 b.g. Mujadil (USA) 119 – Nashwan Star (IRE) 68 (Nashwan **57**
(USA) 135) [2017 57: p8d p8f^{4} 7.1m 8g^{6} 7.2m^{3} 7d* 7.2s^{5} 7.2g^{4} 7s^{3} 7s^{3} 7.6d^{3} 8m Aug 30] smallish gelding: modest handicapper: won at Lingfield in July: stays 8.5f: acts on polytrack, fibresand and any turf going: has worn headgear: tried in tongue tie. *David C. Griffiths*

CYMRIC (USA) 4 b.c. Kitten's Joy (USA) 128 – Fastbridled (USA) (Unbridled's Song **114**
(USA) 125) [2017 106: 8g* 8g^{3} 8g Apr 1] tall, attractive colt: smart performer: won handicap at Meydan (by ½ length from Elite Excalibur) in February: third in Zabeel Mile at same course (2¾ lengths behind Championship) next time: stays 1m: acts on soft and good to firm going: has worn cheekpieces: usually races prominently. *Charlie Appleby*

CYMRO (IRE) 5 gr.g. Dark Angel (IRE) 113 – Dictatrice (FR) (Anabaa (USA) 130) **105**
[2017 110: 10g^{6} 11.9d^{5} 14.1v^{4} Aug 4] lengthy gelding: useful handicapper: left Tom Dascombe after second start: stays 1½m: acts on any turf going: often races prominently. *Joseph Patrick O'Brien, Ireland*

CYMRU LADY 3 ch.f. Equiano (FR) 127 – Racina 103 (Bluebird (USA) 125) [2017 7.1g **–**
p6g Nov 18] last both starts in maidens: dead. *Nikki Evans*

CYPRIA CHARIS (IRE) 2 b.f. (Mar 8) Henrythenavigator (USA) 131 – Amathusia **–**
(Selkirk (USA) 129) [2017 7g Aug 30] half-sister to several winners, including useful 1¼m winner (stayed easy 13f) Troas (by Dalakhani) and 1¼m/11f winner Kinyras (by Peintre Celebre): dam unraced: 7/1, well held in minor event at Lingfield. *Sir Michael Stoute*

CYRUS DALLIN 3 b.g. Roderic O'Connor (IRE) 119 – Munaawashat (IRE) 87 (Marju **87**
(IRE) 127) [2017 p8g* t8.6m^{4} 8f 7g* 7d^{4} p8s 7d^{4} Aug 19] 16,000F, €40,000Y: rather leggy gelding: fifth foal: half-brother to German 6f-1m winner Haarib (by Bushranger): dam, winner up to 1m (2-y-o 6f winner), half-sister to useful winner up to 1¼m Windsor Palace: fairly useful performer: won maiden at Lingfield in January and handicap at Goodwood (by 2 lengths from Alemaratalyoum) in June: left John Gosden after first start: stays 1m: acts on polytrack: sometimes in hood. *William Muir*

CYTRINGAN 4 b.f. Equiano (FR) 127 – Scisciabubu (IRE) (Danehill (USA) 126) [2017 **44**
51: t7.1m t6m^{6} p5g^{6} Mar 16] poor maiden: tried in cheekpieces. *Lydia Pearce*

CZABO 4 b.f. Sixties Icon 125 – Fiumicino 87 (Danehill Dancer (IRE) 117) [2017 107: 8s^{6} **106**
8v* 8.5m Jun 3] rather sparely-made filly: useful performer: won Park Express Stakes at Naas (by ½ length from Somehow) in March: stays 1m: best on ground softer than good (acts on heavy). *Mick Channon*

D

DAAWY (IRE) 3 ch.g. Teofilo (IRE) 126 – Juno Marlowe (IRE) 100 (Danehill (USA) **96**
126) [2017 10m^{6} 9.8g* 10.2s^{2} 10m 10.1m^{6} Aug 27] 110,000Y: compact gelding: half-brother to several winners, 3 smart, including 1½m-1¾m winner Stellar Mass (by Sea The Stars) and 1m-11f winner Marzelline (by Barathea): dam 7f winner (including at 2 yrs): useful performer: won maiden at Ripon in April: second in minor event at Doncaster in June: raced only at 1¼m: acts on soft going: tried in cheekpieces: usually races close up: sold to join David O'Meara 28,000 gns in October. *William Haggas*

DABAN (IRE) 3 b.f. Acclamation 118 – Malaspina (IRE) (Whipper (USA) 126) [2017 **114**
82p: 7m* 8m^{3} 7m^{6} 7g^{pu} Aug 25] well-made filly: smart performer: won Nell Gwyn Stakes at Newmarket (by ¾ length from Unforgetable Filly) in April: third in 1000 Guineas at same course (2¼ lengths behind Winter) in May: went amiss final outing: stays 1m: acts on polytrack and good to firm going. *John Gosden*

DABYAH (IRE) 3 b.f. Sepoy (AUS) 129 – Samdaniya 79 (Machiavellian (USA) 123) **114**
[2017 110p: 7m* 8m^{4} 7m Oct 13] strong, attractive filly: smart performer: won Fred Darling Stakes at Newbury (by 1¼ lengths from Urban Fox) in April: 3½ lengths fourth to Winter in Coronation Stakes at Royal Ascot next time: stays 1m: acts on soft and good to firm going. *John Gosden*

DADDIES GIRL (IRE) 2 b.f. (Mar 18) Elzaam (AUS) 115 – La Cuvee 48 (Mark of Esteem (IRE) 137) [2017 5m^3 5m^4 5m* 5s^5 6g 5.1m^3 7g 8g^4 6s* 6.1d* 6g^6 7s^4 Oct 28] €7,500F, £5,500Y: rather leggy filly: third foal: half-sister to 1¼m/11f winner Whiz Replay (by Alhaarth): dam, maiden (stayed 1¼m), half-sister to useful winner up to 1m She Bat: useful performer: won minor event at Salisbury in April, and nurseries at same course in September and Nottingham (by 2 lengths from Roman Spinner) in October: stays 1m: acts on soft and good to firm going: tried in cheekpieces. *Rod Millman* **95**

DADDYS POPPIT (USA) 2 ch.f. (Apr 23) Scat Daddy (USA) 120 – Valiant Girl 93 (Lemon Drop Kid (USA) 131) [2017 6s t7.1g^6 6d Oct 30] rather unfurnished filly: first foal: dam, 1m-11f winner, sister to very smart winner up to 1½m Bronze Cannon: modest form in minor events/maiden: should be suited by 7f. *William Haggas* **59**

DADDY TYRRELL (USA) 2 b.c. (Feb 9) Scat Daddy (USA) 120 – My Hopeful Heart (USA) (Strong Hope (USA) 120) [2017 p8g Nov 18] 33/1, well held in minor event at Lingfield. *J. S. Moore* –

DAFFRAH 2 b.f. (Mar 28) Dawn Approach (IRE) 132 – Island Babe (USA) (Kingmambo (USA) 125) [2017 6.5d 7m 7d^6 p8g p7g 8.2g^2 p10g^4 Oct 26] 50,000 2-y-o: seventh foal: half-sister to 2 winners, including useful 1m (including at 2 yrs) winner (stays 10.5f) Billingsgate (by Exceed And Excel): dam once-raced half-sister to smart Japanese 9f-11.5f winner Er Nova: modest maiden: stays 1¼m: acts on polytrack: sold 6,000 gns, sent to Hungary. *James Tate* **59**

DAFFY GREY (IRE) 2 ro.g. (Feb 25) Zebedee 113 – Pahokee (IRE) (Almutawakel 126) [2017 7v^6 7g t8g Nov 3] little impact in minor events/maiden. *Michael Easterby* –

DAFFY JANE 2 b.f. (Apr 16) Excelebration (IRE) 133 – Final Dynasty 104 (Komaite (USA)) [2017 5m 5m 5.4g^4 5d^6 5m^3 5d* Sep 16] £40,000Y: fourth foal: closely related to useful 5f/5.4f winner Thesme (by Exceed And Excel) and half-sister to 6f winner Crazee Diamond (by Rock of Gibraltar): dam, 5f winner (including at 2 yrs), sister to useful 2-y-o 5f winner Castelletto: fair performer: won nursery at Musselburgh in September: likely to stay 6f: acts on good to firm and good to soft going. *Nigel Tinkler* **73**

DAGHASH 8 b.g. Tiger Hill (IRE) 127 – Zibet 90 (Kris 135) [2017 81: 14g^6 16.3m 14g 17.1d Aug 4] sturdy gelding: fairly useful handicapper, below form in 2017: stays 17f: acts on polytrack, tapeta, firm and good to soft going: has worn headgear, including in 2017: often races towards rear. *Stuart Kittow* **73**

DAGIAN (IRE) 2 ch.g. (Feb 24) Dawn Approach (IRE) 132 – Hen Night (IRE) 110 (Danehill Dancer (IRE) 117) [2017 7d p7g^5 Oct 11] modest form in maiden/minor event. *Amanda Perrett* **63**

DAGONET (IRE) 3 b.g. Sir Prancealot (IRE) 111 – Dubai Diamond (Octagonal (NZ) 126) [2017 85p: 6f 5.1m Jun 12] fairly useful form at 2 yrs, little impact either start in 2017: stays 6f: acts on polytrack: tried in hood: sometimes in tongue tie: sold 10,000 gns, sent to Qatar. *Roger Charlton* –

DAGUENEAU (IRE) 2 b.g. (Mar 8) Champs Elysees 124 – Bright Enough 78 (Fantastic Light (USA) 134) [2017 8g p8g^6 p8g Nov 7] good-topped gelding: little impact in maiden/minor events. *Ed Dunlop* –

DAHIK (IRE) 2 ch.c. (Mar 6) Society Rock (IRE) 126 – Bishop's Lake 87 (Lake Coniston (IRE) 131) [2017 5m^2 5.1m^4 5m* 5f p5d^6 Sep 21] £62,000Y: compact colt: half-brother to several winners, including smart 9f/1¼m winner (stayed 12.5f) Euphrasia (by Windsor Knot) and useful 2-y-o 5f winner Langavat (by Bushranger): dam 2-y-o 6f winner: fairly useful performer: won minor event at Bath (by 5 lengths from Haveoneyerself) in June: raced only at 5f: acts on good to firm going: sold to join Michael Easterby 18,000 gns in October. *Roger Varian* **84**

DAILY TRADER 3 ch.g. Medicean 128 – Danehill Destiny 104 (Danehill Dancer (IRE) 117) [2017 62: f8g* t10.2d* 10.2g^6 12d 8.1d^4 10.2g^4 10.2g^3 9s^2 p12g^5 9.9s^3 p10g^5 f12.1g^4 t12.2d* Dec 16] rather leggy gelding: fair handicapper: won at Southwell in January, Newcastle in March and Wolverhampton in December: stays 1½m: acts on fibresand, tapeta and soft going. *David Evans* **76**

DAIMOCHI (IRE) 3 b.c. Excelebration (IRE) 133 – Quiritis (Galileo (IRE) 134) [2017 71p: p8g 8.1m^3 9.1m 10.2f^4 9.7d 7g^6 Sep 27] fair maiden: left Clive Cox after fourth start: stays 1m: acts on polytrack and good to firm going: front runner/races prominently. *P. & F. Monfort, France* **79**

DAINTY DANDY (IRE) 3 b.f. Dandy Man (IRE) 123 – Pinewoods Lily (IRE) 66 (Indian Ridge 123) [2017 91: 6g^5 5.1m 5m^3 6m Jul 6] compact filly: fairly useful handicapper: third at Haydock in June: stays 6.5f: acts on good to firm going: often in headgear: tried in tongue tie: usually races close up. *Paul Cole* **80**

DAIRA BRIDGE (IRE) 3 b.g. Dream Ahead (USA) 133 – Lady Livius (IRE) 102 (Titus Livius (FR) 115) [2017 7g^3 May 4] 110,000Y, 8,000 2-y-o: half-brother to several winners, including smart winner up to 7f Burnt Sugar (2-y-o 5f/6f winner, by Lope de Vega) and useful 2-y-o 5f/6f winner Brown Sugar (by Tamayuz): dam, winner up to 6f (2-y-o 5f winner), half-sister to smart winner up to 7f Galeota: 14/1, third in maiden at Redcar (length behind Grinty) in May: sold 11,000 gns, sent to Qatar. *David O'Meara* **65**

DAIRA PRINCE (IRE) 3 b.g. Dubawi (IRE) 129 – Chiang Mai (IRE) 113 (Sadler's Wells (USA) 132) [2017 78p: 8.1m^2 10.1m* 9.1s^4 8.2g* 9d Sep 29] rather leggy gelding: fairly useful handicapper: won at Yarmouth in June and Leicester in July: stays 1¼m: acts on good to firm going: remains with potential. *Roger Varian* **92 p**

DAISY BERE (FR) 4 b.f. Peer Gynt (JPN) – Jackette (USA) (Mr Greeley (USA) 122) [2017 88: t9.5g^6 8g t10.2g^6 t8.6d^5 Dec 27] fairly useful handicapper: stays 10.5f: acts on all-weather, good to firm and good to soft going: has worn cheekpieces, including last 5 starts. *K. R. Burke* **86**

DAISY BOY (IRE) 6 b.g. Cape Cross (IRE) 129 – Muluk (IRE) 83 (Rainbow Quest (USA) 134) [2017 83, a90: p12g^5 p11g^6 16m 10m^4 11.8m^2 13m^4 14.1g^4 Jul 12] big gelding: fairly useful handicapper: second at Leicester in June: stays 2m: acts on polytrack, soft and good to firm going: tried in visor: wears tongue tie: front runner/races prominently: sold 14,000 gns in July. *Stuart Williams* **81**

DAKOTA CITY 6 b.g. Three Valleys (USA) 119 – West Dakota (USA) (Gone West (USA)) [2017 76, a82: t9.5m^4 p11g^5 p15.8g^4 11.6m^6 p14g^3 t12.2g^4 11.4d^3 14v t16.5g Nov 20] good-topped gelding: fair handicapper nowadays: left Julia Feilden after sixth start: stays 1½m: acts on polytrack, tapeta, firm and soft going: wears headgear: often starts slowly/races in rear: best treated with caution. *Olly Murphy* **75 §**

DAKOTA GOLD 3 b.g. Equiano (FR) 127 – Joyeaux 78 (Mark of Esteem (IRE) 137) [2017 83: 5g* 5m^2 5.4d* 6d^2 6d^2 5.2d^3 Sep 20] rather leggy gelding: useful handicapper: won at Thirsk (by 2 lengths from Computable) in April and York (by ¾ length from Batten The Hatches) in July: placed other 4 starts in 2017: stays 6f: acts on good to firm and good to soft going: sometimes slowly away, often races towards rear/travels strongly. *Michael Dods* **109**

DALALAH 4 b.f. Exceed And Excel (AUS) 126 – Bashasha (USA) 69 (Kingmambo (USA) 125) [2017 53: 6m 6g^5 t6g^4 6g 6m p5g^5 p5g^4 p7g t6.1m Oct 31] modest maiden: stays 6f: acts on polytrack, tapeta and good to firm going: wears headgear. *Richard Guest* **53**

DALASIRI (IRE) 8 gr.g. Dylan Thomas (IRE) 132 – Dalataya (IRE) (Sadler's Wells (USA) 132) [2017 t16.5g t16.5d^6 Dec 9] fair handicapper for Sabrina J. Harty in 2015, below that level in 2017 after long absence: stays 13f: acts on good to firm and good to soft going: has worn headgear: in tongue tie last 2 starts. *Johnny Farrelly* **64**

DALAVAND (IRE) 4 ch.g. Tamayuz 126 – Kirunavaara (IRE) (Galileo (IRE) 134) [2017 61: t9.5m p12g^4 p13g^4 p13.3g p15.8g 9.9g 11.6g Jun 1] modest maiden: stays 13f: acts on polytrack, tapeta and good to firm going: tried in cheekpieces: has worn tongue tie, including in 2017: usually races nearer last than first. *Laura Mongan* **56**

DALAVIDA (FR) 3 gr.f. Kendargent (FR) 112 – Dalawysa (FR) (Dalakhani (IRE) 133) [2017 t8d^3 p10g^3 t8.6g^5 12g Aug 4] 68,000Y: second foal: sister to 2-y-o 6f winner Kendala: dam, runner-up at 12.5f (also over hurdles), half-sister to useful winner up to 7.5f Valima: modest form: stays 1¼m: in hood first 3 starts. *David Simcock* **58**

DALAWYNA (FR) 2 gr.f. (Feb 5) Kendargent (FR) 112 – Dalawysa (FR) (Dalakhani (IRE) 133) [2017 7f^6 6s^4 Sep 23] third foal: sister to 2-y-o 6f winner Kendala: dam, runner-up at 12.5f, half-sister to useful dam of Prix de Diane winner Valyra: modest form in 2 minor events. *Kevin Ryan* **58**

DALEELAK (IRE) 4 b.g. Arcano (IRE) 122 – Alshamatry (USA) (Seeking The Gold (USA)) [2017 69: p10g t7.1d 8v t9.5g Oct 21] fair at best, no form in 2017: tried in blinkers. *Mark Johnston* **–**

DALGIG 7 b.g. New Approach (IRE) 132 – Bright Halo (IRE) (Bigstone (IRE) 126) [2017 10m^6 t12.2g Jul 17] compact gelding: fairly useful at best, lightly raced and little form since 2014: stays 1½m: acts on polytrack, good to firm and good to soft going: has worn hood: temperamental (has refused to race). *Jennie Candlish* **– §**

DAL HARRAILD 4 ch.g. Champs Elysees 124 – Dalvina 113 (Grand Lodge (USA) 125) [2017 120p: 12m^6 13.9g* 12m^6 16.3g^6 Aug 25] close-coupled gelding: very smart performer: won listed race at York (by 3½ lengths from Nakeeta) in May: should stay 2m: acts on any turf going. *William Haggas* **120**

DALILEO (IRE) 2 b.c. (Mar 7) Galileo (IRE) 134 – Snow Queen (IRE) 109§ (Danehill Dancer (IRE) 117) [2017 8s^4 p10g^2 Oct 5] €150,000Y: first foal: dam, ungenuine 2-y-o 6f/7f winner, sister to smart 7f/1m winner Carribean Sunset: fair form when runner-up at Chelmsford (2¼ lengths behind Deyaarna) on second of 2 starts in maidens: open to further improvement. *Mark Johnston* **78 p**

DALNESS EXPRESS 4 b.g. Firebreak 125 – Under My Spell 80 (Wizard King 122) [2017 51: p7g p7d t6.1g^6 Dec 13] modest maiden: stays 7f: acts on polytrack and tapeta: tried in tongue tie. *John O'Shea* **51**

DALSHAND (FR) 4 ch.g. New Approach (IRE) 132 – Daltaiyma (IRE) (Doyoun 124) [2017 9.9s 11.4f^5 16.3g 12.1s Oct 31] half-brother to several winners, including smart French 1m winner (including at 2 yrs) Daltaya (by Anabaa), herself dam of Prix de l'Opera winner Dalkala: dam, French 1¼m winner, sister to Daylami and half-sister to Dalakhani: useful form at 3 yrs, won newcomers race at Saint-Cloud: well below that level in 2017: left A. de Royer Dupre after second start: stays 15f: acts on good to soft going. *David O'Meara* **76**

DALTON 3 b.c. Mayson 124 – Pious 74 (Bishop of Cashel 122) [2017 72: 6m* 6f 6d^6 7d Nov 4] fairly useful performer: won maiden at Ayr (by 3¾ lengths from Hee Haw) in May: best effort at 6f: acts on good to firm going. *David O'Meara* **83**

DALTREY 2 b.c. (Mar 30) Iffraaj 127 – Roger Sez (IRE) 103 (Red Clubs (IRE) 125) [2017 7g p7d^6 Nov 22] €65,000Y: second foal: half-brother to 2-y-o 7f winner Brogan (by Pivotal): dam 2-y-o 5f/6f winner: fair form when sixth at Kempton on second of 2 starts in minor events: remains with potential. *John Gosden* **72 p**

DAME NELLIE 2 b.f. (Feb 2) Aussie Rules (USA) 123 – Eminencia (Sadler's Wells (USA) 132) [2017 p8d Dec 13] half-sister to 1¼m winner (stayed 1½m) Archduchess (by Archipenko) and useful 1¼m winner Edya (by Makfi): dam unraced half-sister to smart winner up to 11f Red Rocks Point: in hood, 50/1, very green when well held in minor event at Kempton. *Rae Guest* **–**

DAMO 3 ch.g. New Approach (IRE) 132 – Umlilo 64 (Mtoto 134) [2017 p8g t9.5m^4 p7d t8.6g Aug 11] modest form on debut, standout effort. *Simon Dow* **62 ?**

DAMOCLES (GER) 3 b.c. Siyouni (FR) 122 – Duty And Destiny (IRE) 82 (Montjeu (IRE) 137) [2017 8m^4 8.3g^4 p7g* Nov 1] 130,000Y: first foal: dam 9f-1½m winner: fairly useful form: won maiden at Kempton (by length from Domitilla) in November: stays 8.5f: wears tongue tie: sold £8,500 later same month: open to further improvement. *John Gosden* **83 p**

DAMSELFLY (IRE) 2 b.f. (Feb 17) Power 117 – Flavia Tatiana (IRE) 90 (Holy Roman Emperor (IRE) 125) [2017 5d^6 5g^5 5m^2 5g^3 5m^2 5m^3 5g^4 5v* 6v^5 p7g^6 6s^3 7s* 8d Nov 4] second foal: dam 10.7f winner: fairly useful performer: won maiden at Down Royal in September and nursery at Leopardstown (by 2 lengths from Its My Turn) in October: stays 7f: acts on good to firm and heavy going. *Joseph Patrick O'Brien, Ireland* **91**

DANA'S PRESENT 8 ch.g. Osorio (GER) 114 – Euro Empire (USA) 111 (Bartok (IRE) 94) [2017 77: t8.6m^5 t7.1m^5 t8.6g^5 t8.6g^3 p8g^3 8.1d t8.6g Nov 11] lengthy, useful-looking gelding: fair performer: left Tom Dascombe after fifth start: stays 9.5f: acts on polytrack, tapeta, firm and good to soft going: has worn headgear, including in 2017: tricky ride (races freely). *Tony Newcombe* **74**

DANCE DAN DAN (IRE) 3 b.c. Danehill Dancer (IRE) 117 – Justly Royal (USA) (Royal Academy (USA) 130) [2017 t8g^4 p10m^5 p10g Jan 27] fair form on second of 3 starts in maidens: will stay 1½m: tried in blinkers: sold 6,000 gns, won over hurdles in Italy in November. *Mark Johnston* **65**

DANCE DIVA 2 b.f. (Mar 13) Mayson 124 – Dance East 101 (Shamardal (USA) 129) [2017 6m* 6m* 6g* 6d^2 7g 6g Oct 14] strong, lengthy filly: fourth foal: sister to winner abroad and half-sister to 1m winner The Groove (by Azamour): dam 7.4f-9f winner: useful performer: won minor events at Redcar in May and Haydock in June, and listed race at Newmarket (by 1¼ lengths from Maggies Angel) in July: stays 6f: acts on good to firm going. *Richard Fahey* **97**

DANCE EMPEROR (IRE) 2 b.c. (Mar 19) Holy Roman Emperor (IRE) 125 – Dance Avenue (IRE) (Sadler's Wells (USA) 132) [2017 6m 6d^5 7v^2 8.3v^4 p7s^2 p7d^5 Dec 13] sturdy colt: fair maiden: stays 7f: acts on polytrack and heavy going. *Ed Walker* **79**

DANCE KING 7 ch.g. Danehill Dancer (IRE) 117 – One So Wonderful 121 (Nashwan (USA) 135) [2017 95: 9.8m 9.8m^2 11.9g^4 10.3m^3 10g^4 11.2s* 11.8d 11.9g^6 10.3d^4 10v* 10.3g^4 Oct 14] rather leggy gelding: useful handicapper: won at Carlisle in June and Pontefract (by ½ length from Empress Ali) in September: stays 12.5f, usually races at shorter: acts on good to firm and heavy going: wears cheekpieces/tongue tie. *Tim Easterby* **98**

DANCE ME (USA) 2 b.f. (Apr 28) Bernardini (USA) 132 – Stormy Saturday (USA) (Stormy Atlantic (USA)) [2017 7m^3 p7g^4 t8.6g^2 p7s^3 Dec 15] $165,000Y, resold 70,000Y: first foal: dam lightly-raced sister to US Grade 2 1m winner Icy Atlantic and US Grade 3 9f winner Wild Promises (both smart): fair form when in frame in minor events: stays 7f. *Sylvester Kirk* **73**

DANCE OF FIRE 5 b.g. Norse Dancer (IRE) 127 – Strictly Dancing (IRE) 95 (Danehill Dancer (IRE) 117) [2017 95: t10.2d Oct 24] good-topped gelding: useful at best, well held sole outing on Flat in 2017: stays 10.5f: acts on polytrack, good to firm and heavy going: has worn headgear. *N. W. Alexander* **–**

DANCE ON THE DAY (IRE) 2 b.f. (Mar 3) Epaulette (AUS) 126 – Skeleton (IRE) 65 (Tobougg (IRE) 125) [2017 7m Oct 25] 16,000F, 55,000Y: lengthy filly: fourth foal: half-sister to winner abroad by Dark Angel and 2-y-o 7f winner November Tale (by Casamento): dam, 2-y-o 1m-9.5f winner, half-sister to very smart winner up to 11f Mulaqat: 8/1, hinted at ability when well held in minor event at Newmarket: capable of better. *Tom Dascombe* **– p**

DANCE REBEL 4 b.g. Cockney Rebel (IRE) 127 – Slave To The Rythm (IRE) 63 (Hamas (IRE) 125) [2017 70: p6g^3 p6g p7g^6 Apr 13] fair maiden: stays 7f: acts on polytrack and tapeta: sold 4,000 gns, sent to Italy. *Dr Jon Scargill* **70**

DANCE ROCK 4 b.g. Oasis Dream 129 – Zee Zee Top 116 (Zafonic (USA) 130) [2017 11.6d 9.9d^6 7.1s^3 p12g Oct 3] fair form: best effort at 11.5f: in visor last 2 starts. *Neil Mulholland* **73**

DANCE TEACHER (IRE) 3 ch.f. Lope de Vega (IRE) 125 – Fairnilee 67 (Selkirk (USA) 129) [2017 74: 8s^3 8d 8m^6 7g^2 7d* p8g* Dec 20] fairly useful performer: won maiden at Thirsk in August and handicap at Kempton (by length from Chestnut Fire) in December: left Ralph Beckett after fifth start: stays 1m: acts on polytrack and soft going: usually travels strongly. *David Elsworth* **90**

DANCETERIA (FR) 2 b.c. (May 7) Redoute's Choice (AUS) – Bal de La Rose (IRE) 110 (Cadeaux Genereux 131) [2017 8g^6 7s^3 8.3d^4 Oct 11] fair form: best effort when fourth in maiden at Nottingham (4 lengths behind Merlin Magic) in October. *David Menuisier* **79**

DANCE THE DREAM 4 b.f. Sir Percy 129 – Shadow Dancing 110 (Unfuwain (USA) 131) [2017 101: 12f^3 12g^6 11.8s^2 11.8d* 11.9s^6 Nov 11] sturdy filly: useful handicapper: won at Leicester (by 1½ lengths from Top Tug) in October: likely to stay beyond 1½m: acts on soft and good to firm going: often races prominently. *Marcus Tregoning* **109**

DANCE TO PARIS 2 b.f. (Mar 13) Champs Elysees 124 – Riabouchinska (Fantastic Light (USA) 134) [2017 6d^2 7g 8d^4 p8d^2 Oct 6] 7,000F, 20,000Y: fifth foal: half-sister to 1¼m winner Rakmanova (by Kheleyf) and 5.5f winner Rambert (by Acclamation): dam, 1¼m winner, half-sister to 10.3f-1½m winner Yawmi and 9f winner Earl's Court (both useful): fair form: likely to stay 1¼m. *Lucy Wadham* **68**

DANCE WITH KATE 6 b.m. Hamairi (IRE) 112 – Vercheny (Petoski 135) [2017 –: 7d p10g 14v Nov 7] no form: left Bill Turner after first start: in headgear last 2 starts. *Olly Murphy* **–**

DANCIN ALPHA 6 ch.g. Bahamian Bounty 116 – Phoebe Woodstock (IRE) 76 (Grand Lodge (USA) 125) [2017 61: t8g^3 f8g^5 t10.2g^4 Mar 9] modest maiden: stays 9.5f: acts on fibresand, tapeta and good to firm going: tried in blinkers. *Alan Swinbank* **59**

DANCING BRAVE BEAR (USA) 2 b.f. (Apr 12) Street Cry (IRE) 130 – Baghdaria (USA) (Royal Academy (USA) 130) [2017 p7g* Dec 20] $230,000Y: seventh foal: half-sister to 3 winners, including useful Japanese 1¼m/11f winner Dilga (by Curlin) and minor US winner by Giant's Causeway: dam multiple US Grade 3 8.5f winner: 20/1, won minor event at Lingfield (by length from Cosmic Love) in December: open to improvement. *Ed Vaughan* **78 p**

DANCING BREEZE (IRE) 3 ch.f. New Approach (IRE) 132 – Posterity (IRE) (Indian Ridge 123) [2017 8m* 7.9d^6 8g^5 8m 8m^3 8.2d^3 8g^6 8g^3 8.5g^2 Nov 23] strong filly: fifth foal: sister to useful 2-y-o 7f winner Rasmeyaa and half-sister to smart winner up to 1m Future Generation (2-y-o 6f winner, by Hurricane Run): dam unraced half-sister to very smart winner up to 7f Do The Honours: useful performer: won maiden at Newmarket in April: **103**

best effort when 5½ lengths sixth to Aljazzi in Atalanta Stakes at Sandown in September: left John Gosden after: raced only around 1m: acts on good to firm and good to soft going. *H. Graham Motion, USA*

DANCING DRAGON (IRE) 3 b.f. Dragon Pulse (IRE) 114 – Abbeyleix Lady (IRE) **63**
(Montjeu (IRE) 137) [2017 51p: 8.3g 8g 9d^{5} 11.4g 9.9s^{4} Sep 4] rather unfurnished filly: modest maiden: stays 9f: acts on good to soft going: tried in cheekpieces. *George Baker*

DANCING RAINBOW (GR) 4 b.f. Tiantai (USA) – Rainbow Way (High Chaparral **–**
(IRE) 132) [2017 51: p12d Jan 17] neat filly: maiden, modest at best: in blinkers last 5 starts: sent to Greece. *Amanda Perrett*

DANCING STAR 4 b.f. Aqlaam 125 – Strictly Dancing (IRE) 95 (Danehill Dancer (IRE) **109**
117) [2017 117: 5m 6.1m^{2} 6m Jun 24] sturdy filly: smart performer at 3 yrs, not quite as good in 2017: second in listed race at Windsor (neck behind Perfect Pasture) in May: stays 6f: acts on good to firm and good to soft going: usually races prominently. *Andrew Balding*

DANDIESQUE (IRE) 2 b.f. (Apr 24) Dandy Man (IRE) 123 – Marigold (FR) 88 (Marju **68**
(IRE) 127) [2017 6g^{6} t6.1g^{6} 6.1g^{3} 7g^{2} 7s^{4} p7g Oct 18] €46,000Y: big filly: has scope: seventh foal: half-sister to useful winner up to 1½m Art Scholar (2-y-o 5.7f winner, by Pyrus) and 6f winner Jaeger Train (by Captain Rio): dam, 1½m/13f winner who stayed 15f, half-sister to 10.4f-1¾m winner (stayed 2m) Mount Athos and winner up to 1½m Imperial Monarch (both very smart): fair maiden: stays 7f: best form on good going: tried in cheekpieces. *Richard Hannon*

DANDILION (IRE) 4 b.f. Dandy Man (IRE) 123 – Free Angel (USA) 73 (Mystery Storm **73**
(USA)) [2017 61: t5.1m^{2} t5.1g^{3} t5.1f* t5g 5m t6g^{5} p5g^{2} t5.1g^{3} t5.1g* 5m^{3} 5m* 5m^{2} 5.7s **a67**
Sep 17] fair handicapper: won at Wolverhampton in February/June and Beverley in July: best form at 5f: acts on tapeta and good to firm going: wears tongue tie. *Alex Hales*

DANDY BIRD (IRE) 3 b.f. Dandy Man (IRE) 123 – Labba (Tiger Hill (IRE) 127) [2017 **65**
67: 6d t6d^{4} t6g t7.1s^{4} Nov 30] fair maiden: likely to stay 1m: acts on tapeta. *Julie Camacho*

DANDY DUDE (IRE) 4 b.g. Dandy Man (IRE) 123 – Queen of Fibres (IRE) 65 (Scenic **74**
128) [2017 71: p8g^{2} p8g 8g 8g 8m^{4} 6s^{4} 7.9g 10s Aug 20] fair maiden: stays 1m: acts on polytrack and good to firm going: often wears tongue tie. *Keith Henry Clarke, Ireland*

DANDY FLAME (IRE) 3 ch.g. Dandy Man (IRE) 123 – Nouveau Riche (IRE) 84 **86**
(Entrepreneur 123) [2017 82: t7.1f* p7g* t6g* t5.1g 5.7f^{5} 6d^{3} 6.1d^{5} p6g 6m* 6.1g* 5m^{5} 6v Oct 4] leggy, plain gelding: fairly useful performer: won handicap at Wolverhampton and claimers at Lingfield/Wolverhampton in January, and handicaps at Salisbury and Windsor (lady riders) in July: left William Haggas after third start: stays 7f: acts on polytrack, tapeta, good to firm and good to soft going: has worn headgear, including final start: sold 9,000 gns, sent to France. *Richard Hughes*

DANDY HIGHWAYMAN (IRE) 3 ch.g. Dandy Man (IRE) 123 – Paradise Blue (IRE) **94**
63 (Bluebird (USA) 125) [2017 80: 6m* 6m^{3} 6d^{2} 6g* 6g^{6} Jun 24] close-coupled gelding: fairly useful handicapper: won at Ripon in April and Hamilton (by 1½ lengths from Hee Haw) in June: stays 6f: acts on soft and good to firm going. *Ollie Pears*

DANDYLEEKIE (IRE) 5 b.g. Dandy Man (IRE) 123 – Cockaleekie (USA) (Alphabet **83 §**
Soup (USA) 126) [2017 89: 6v^{3} 6s^{3} 6d 6s^{6} 6m 6g 6v 8s^{2} 8g 8v 8g^{3} 8v f8.1g Oct 22] tall gelding: fairly useful handicapper: best efforts in 2017 when third at Doncaster in May and second at Pontefract in August: stays 1m: acts on polytrack and heavy going: has worn headgear, including last 4 starts: sold 3,500 gns in October: untrustworthy. *David O'Meara*

DANDYMAN PORT (IRE) 3 b.f. Dandy Man (IRE) 123 – Fillthegobletagain (IRE) **88**
(Byron 117) [2017 6v^{4} 5.8g 5.1d 7.1d^{6} 5d 7.4v^{5} 7v^{6} 7d Oct 28] €17,000Y: second foal: half-sister to winner abroad by Footstepsinthesand: dam unraced half-sister to useful winner up to 1m Romancero: fairly useful performer: won maiden at Dieppe in 2016 for E. J. O'Neill: stays 7.5f: acts on heavy going: in headgear last 3 starts: often races towards rear. *Des Donovan, Ireland*

DANDY'S BEANO (IRE) 2 ch.f. (Apr 15) Dandy Man (IRE) 123 – Hear My Cry (USA) **83**
(Giant's Causeway (USA) 132) [2017 5f^{6} 5v^{2} 5g 5s* Sep 19] €1,000Y, €20,000 2-y-o: fourth foal: half-sister to 7f-8.5f (including at 2 yrs) winner Magia Nera (by Bellamy Road): dam once-raced half-sister to smart 8.6f-1¼m winner Gulf Express: fairly useful form: won minor event at Redcar (by 2 lengths from Biddy Brady) in September: will stay at least 6f. *Kevin Ryan*

DANDYS DENOUEMENT 3 b.g. Pastoral Pursuits 127 – Engaging 62 (Oasis Dream **70**
129) [2017 6s 7g^{2} 7m^{2} 6d^{5} t7.1g Nov 3] fair maiden: best effort at 7f: acts on good to firm going: tried in hood. *Brian Ellison*

DANECASE 4 ch.g. Showcasing 117 – Yding (IRE) (Danehill (USA) 126) [2017 84: 6g^6 7d^2 6m* 6m 7m^5 p6g* p6g p6s p6g^6 Dec 28] neat, good-quartered gelding: fairly useful handicapper: won at Goodwood (apprentice) in May and Lingfield (by neck from Alkashaaf) in October: stays 7f: acts on polytrack and good to firm going: tried in cheekpieces. *David Dennis* **83**

DANEHILL DESERT (IRE) 2 b.g. (Mar 30) Clodovil (IRE) 116 – Misplace (IRE) (Green Desert (USA) 127) [2017 5m^4 5s^5 5g* 5.2v t6.1g 5s^3 6v^4 Oct 9] stocky gelding: fair performer: won minor event at Hamilton in June: best form at 5f: acts on good to firm going. *Richard Fahey* **75**

DANEHILL KODIAC (IRE) 4 b.c. Kodiac 112 – Meadow 72 (Green Desert (USA) 127) [2017 107: 12d* p12g^4 12g^2 12s* 12s^3 11.9g Dec 10] workmanlike colt: smart performer: won handicap at Newmarket (by 3½ lengths from Sofia's Rock) in August and Cumberland Lodge Stakes at Ascot (by neck from Waldgeist) in October: third in St Simon Stakes at Newbury (3¼ lengths behind Best Solution) later in October: below form in Hong Kong Vase at Sha Tin final outing: will stay 1¾m: acts on polytrack, soft and good to firm going: usually races close up. *Richard Hannon* **116**

DAN EMMETT (USA) 7 ch.g. Flower Alley (USA) 127 – Singing Dixie (USA) (Dixieland Band (USA)) [2017 21.6m 16d^4 18v Oct 9] strong gelding: fair handicapper: stays 2m: acts on soft going: has worn cheekpieces: fairly useful hurdler. *Michael Scudamore* **69**

DANGEROUS ENDS 3 b.g. Monsieur Bond (IRE) 120 – Stolen Glance 84 (Mujahid (USA) 125) [2017 –: p8g* p8g* p10g^3 8.1d^6 p8d* p8d^3 p8g^2 p12g^5 p10s* p10s^2 Dec 1] rather leggy gelding: fairly useful handicapper: won at Kempton in January, February and July, and at Chelmsford (by ½ length from Choral Clan) in November: best up to 1¼m: acts on polytrack: usually wears headgear: often travels strongly. *Brett Johnson* **83**

DANGEROUS LADY 2 b.f. (Jan 5) Bahamian Bounty 116 – Purple Silk (Holy Roman Emperor (IRE) 125) [2017 5d^5 6g^2 5g 5v^6 Sep 21] £13,000Y: first foal: dam unraced: fair form: best effort at 6f. *Tim Easterby* **67**

DANGLYDONTASK 6 b.g. Lucky Story (USA) 128 – Strat's Quest 65 (Nicholas (USA) 111) [2017 65: 17.2f* 16.3m^3 16m 18d p15.8g p16g Nov 1] rather leggy gelding: fair handicapper: won at Bath in April: stays 2¼m: acts on polytrack, firm and good to soft going: has worn headgear, including last 5 starts: sometimes slowly away. *David Arbuthnot* **71**

DANICA ASHTON 3 b.f. Fast Company (IRE) 126 – Spirit of Success 68 (Invincible Spirit (IRE) 121) [2017 6m 7d^4 p8d p7g f6.1g Dec 4] first foal: dam maiden (stayed 7f): no form: tried in visor/tongue tie. *Miss Joey Ellis* **–**

DANIELSFLYER (IRE) 3 b.g. Dandy Man (IRE) 123 – Warm Welcome (Motivator 131) [2017 93: 6m* 6m 6g 6d 6d^5 Aug 19] good-quartered gelding: useful handicapper: won at Newmarket (by ½ length from Eqtiraan) in May: stays 6f: acts on soft and good to firm going. *David Barron* **104**

DANISH DANCER (IRE) 2 ch.g. (Feb 28) Sir Prancealot (IRE) 111 – Daneville (IRE) (Danetime (IRE) 121) [2017 8s p7g Oct 5] in blinkers, well held in minor events. *Ed Walker* **–**

DANISH DUKE (IRE) 6 ch.g. Duke of Marmalade (IRE) 132 – Bridge Note (USA) 49 (Stravinsky (USA) 133) [2017 78, a67: t6s^3 6d^6 5.9g 6d 6g^6 6d* 6g^3 f6.1g^4 6s^4 6v 7.2v 6d^2 t6.1g Nov 20] strong gelding: fair handicapper: won at Thirsk (apprentice) in August: stays 7f: acts on fibresand, tapeta, soft and good to firm going: wears headgear. *Ruth Carr* **76**

DANNY MC D 4 b.g. Kheleyf (USA) 116 – Thorntoun Piccolo 64 (Groom Dancer (USA) 128) [2017 6s^5 8g^6 8s^6 8g 10d 8m t12.4s Sep 8] no form: in cheekpieces last 4 starts: often races towards rear. *Iain Jardine* **–**

DANOT (IRE) 5 ch.g. Zebedee 113 – Hapipi (Bertolini (USA) 125) [2017 73§: t8d f7g^5 7.4m^6 7f 7m^4 7d^2 t7.2g^2 7g^2 7m^5 7s^5 7.2s^2 t7.2g Oct 27] fair handicapper: stays 7f: acts on tapeta, soft and good to firm going: wears cheekpieces: front runner/races prominently: sold £3,000, sent to Poland. *Jedd O'Keeffe* **67**

DAN'S DREAM 2 br.f. (Jan 22) Cityscape 127 – Royal Ffanci (Royal Applause 124) [2017 6.1g^4 Jul 20] first foal: dam unraced: 5/1, fourth in minor event at Chepstow (4½ lengths behind Demons Rock) in July: should improve. *Mick Channon* **63 p**

DAN'S HOPEFORGLORY 5 b.m. Bahri (USA) 125 – Silvan Stream 67 (Observatory (USA) 131) [2017 t10.2d^4 t10.2g 8g 10g t10.2s 12.1m Jun 21] modest maiden: stays 1¼m: acts on tapeta: sometimes slowly away. *Peter Niven* **53**

DAN TROOP 3 b.g. Lawman (FR) 121 – Full Mandate (IRE) 98 (Acclamation 118) [2017 75: 7.1m* 7s* 7.4m² 7.6d* 7.6v* Sep 16] useful performer: won maiden at Musselburgh in May, and handicaps at Wetherby in June and Chester in July/September (latter by ½ length from King's Pavilion): stays 7.5f: acts on tapeta, good to firm and heavy going: often races prominently: sold 75,000 gns, sent to Qatar. *Richard Fahey* **105**

DANZAN (IRE) 2 b.c. (Apr 1) Lawman (FR) 121 – Charanga (Cadeaux Genereux 131) [2017 p7s⁶ t7.2g³ 6g* 7d⁵ 6.5g² 6d Sep 30] 6,500F, £12,000Y: good-topped colt: first foal: dam unraced: useful performer: won minor event at Pontefract in July: second in valuable event at Doncaster (1¼ lengths behind Laugh A Minute) in September: best effort at 6f: acts on tapeta and good to soft going: front runner/races prominently. *Andrew Balding* **103**

DANZAY (IRE) 2 b.c. (Feb 6) Raven's Pass (USA) 133 – La Chapelle (IRE) (Holy Roman Emperor (IRE) 125) [2017 t8.6d² Dec 27] €62,000F: third foal: half-brother to winner abroad by Harbour Watch: dam, ran once, closely related to very smart winner up to 1½ Zhukova: 11/4, second in minor event at Wolverhampton (2½ lengths behind Antonian) in December: better to come. *Mark Johnston* **73 p**

DANZELLA 5 b.m. Desideratum 118 – Danzatrice 76 (Tamure (IRE) 125) [2017 49: 12g⁵ 11.6m Jun 15] poor maiden: stays 16.5f: acts on tapeta and good to firm going: tried in visor. *Chris Fairhurst* **42**

DANZENO 6 b.g. Denounce 89 – Danzanora (Groom Dancer (USA) 128) [2017 116: 7g⁶ 6m⁵ 5g* 6d 6s⁴ 6s 6d³ Nov 11] strong gelding: smart handicapper: won at Ascot (by ¾ length from Polybius) in July: stays 6.5f: acts on soft and good to firm going: often starts slowly. *Michael Appleby* **115**

DAPHNE 4 b.f. Duke of Marmalade (IRE) 132 – Daring Aim 89 (Daylami (IRE) 138) [2017 93: 12m* 14.1g⁴ p13g* p12g³ Nov 29] useful-looking filly: useful performer: won handicap at Newbury (by ¾ length from Weekender) in September and listed race at Lingfield (by 1½ lengths from Melodic Motion) in November: stays 1¾m: acts on polytrack and good to firm going: tried in cheekpieces. *William Haggas* **108**

DAPPER MAN (IRE) 3 b.g. Dandy Man (IRE) 123 – Gist (IRE) 104 (Namid 128) [2017 74: t8d⁶ 7.5m² 7.1m 6.9g⁶ 6g 5.5f* 5m³ 5m² 5d⁶ 5d⁴ 6g 5g 5m⁶ 5g² Sep 1] fair handicapper: won at Wetherby in June: stays 7.5f, raced mainly at shorter: acts on firm going: usually wears headgear: usually races prominently. *Roger Fell* **72**

DARCEY LOU 3 b.f. Mullionmileanhour (IRE) 116 – Balletlou (IRE) 85 (Peintre Celebre (USA) 137) [2017 –: p8g 10.1m⁵ 11.4m Jun 12] no form. *John Best* **–**

DAREBIN (GER) 5 ch.g. It's Gino (GER) 128 – Delightful Sofie (GER) (Grand Lodge (USA) 125) [2017 –: p12g³ p12g* p12d² Feb 22] workmanlike gelding: fairly useful performer: won maiden at Lingfield (by neck from Remember The Man) in February: stays 1½m: acts on polytrack: in blinkers last 3 starts: fairly useful hurdler/chaser. *Gary Moore* **87**

DARING GUEST (IRE) 3 b.g. Fast Company (IRE) 126 – Balm 72 (Oasis Dream 129) [2017 63: p6f* 6.1m⁵ p7g⁶ 8.2g⁵ 7g* 7g⁶ p7g* p7g² t7.2m⁴ p7s Nov 16] sturdy gelding: fairly useful performer: won maiden at Lingfield in March, and handicaps at Yarmouth in July and Kempton (by ½ length from Medicean El Diablo) in September: stays 7f: acts on polytrack and good to firm going. *George Margarson* **82**

DARING KNIGHT 4 b.g. Dick Turpin (IRE) 127 – Fairy Slipper (Singspiel (IRE) 133) [2017 66: 7m 11.5m Jun 14] sturdy gelding: fair maiden, well beaten both starts on Flat in 2017: stays 1m: acts on polytrack and good to firm going: has worn blinkers, including last 2 starts: sometimes slowly away, often races in rear/lazily: has joined Dan Skelton. *Clare Ellam* **–**

DARK ACCLAIM (IRE) 2 gr.c. (Feb 11) Dark Angel (IRE) 113 – Sistine 71 (Dubai Destination (USA) 127) [2017 7m⁴ 7s* 8.2s⁴ 8v³ Oct 23] £45,000 2-y-o: second foal: dam, 1¾m winner, closely related to useful dam of 2000 Guineas/Derby winner Camelot: useful form: won minor event at Doncaster (by 3¾ lengths from Qaroun) in July: third in listed race at Pontefract (2¾ lengths behind Connect) in October: likely to stay 1¼m. *Marco Botti* **96**

DARK ALLIANCE (IRE) 6 b.g. Dark Angel (IRE) 113 – Alinda (IRE) 86 (Revoque (IRE) 122) [2017 79, a87: p7g p8g³ 7s 6m⁶ 7s 8d p6g t7.2d⁵ Dec 26] fair handicapper on turf, fairly useful on all-weather: third at Dundalk in February: left A. P. Keatley after sixth start: stays 7f: acts on polytrack and good to soft going: has worn headgear, including in 2017: has worn tongue tie: sometimes slowly away. *Daniel Loughnane* **73 a85**

DARK AMBER 7 b.m. Sakhee (USA) 136 – Donna Vita 85 (Vettori (IRE) 119) [2017 67: **64**
p10g^{2} t12.2g p10.7g^{6} p10.7g 8s^{pu} p7g^{6} 8s 10d 12g^{2} p12g 12d 15g 11.8g^{5} p12g p10.7g p8g Dec 21] rather leggy mare: fair handicapper: left Brendan Powell after second start: stays 1½m: acts on polytrack, firm and soft going: has worn cheekpieces, including final start: has worn tongue tie: sometimes slowly away. *Damian Joseph English, Ireland*

DARKANNA (IRE) 2 br.f. (Jan 16) Dark Angel (IRE) 113 – Jadanna (IRE) 97 (Mujadil **102**
(USA) 119) [2017 5m 5.1m^{6} 5s* 5m 6m 6g^{2} 6d^{5} 6d^{5} 6g* Oct 7] £205,000Y: small filly: first foal: dam 2-y-o 5f winner: useful performer: won minor event at Haydock in June and listed Two-Year-Old Trophy at Redcar (by ½ length from Flying Sparkle) in October: stays 6f: acts on soft and good to firm going: usually races prominently: sold 320,000 gns in December. *Richard Fahey*

DARK BLUE (IRE) 2 b.f. (Feb 18) Dark Angel (IRE) 113 – Lapis Blue (IRE) 78 **65**
(Invincible Spirit (IRE) 121) [2017 7m 7d 7s^{4} 7s 8m^{2} 8.1s^{2} p7g* 7d p8g Nov 7] €75,000Y: rather leggy filly: first foal: dam, 6f winner, half-sister to useful winner up to 1m Go For Goal: fair performer: won nursery at Kempton in October: stays 1m: acts on polytrack, soft and good to firm going. *Mick Channon*

DARK CONFIDANT (IRE) 4 b.g. Royal Applause 124 – Sleek Gold 81 (Dansili 127) **69**
[2017 58, a74: t7.1g t7.1m 7g^{5} 6g^{5} t7.2g^{5} 7.2s t7.2g^{4} t7.2g^{3} 7.8m* 7d 8g 7g* 5.9s Aug 23] fair handicapper: won amateur events at Carlisle in July and Thirsk in August: left Richard Fahey after eighth start: stays 1m: acts on polytrack, tapeta and good to firm going: has worn headgear, including in 2017. *Donald McCain*

DARK CRYSTAL 6 b.m. Multiplex 114 – Glitz (IRE) 54 (Hawk Wing (USA) 136) [2017 **80**
73: 8m^{3} 9.1m 8.3g^{4} 8.3s* 7.2s* 8.3m^{3} 8.3s^{3} 7.2d^{5} 8d 8.3s^{2} 7.2g Aug 12] fairly useful handicapper: won at Hamilton and Ayr in June: stays 9f: acts on polytrack, good to firm and heavy going. *Linda Perratt*

DARK DEFENDER 4 b.g. Pastoral Pursuits 127 – Oh So Saucy 90 (Imperial Ballet **95**
(IRE) 110) [2017 96: 6v 6m 7m 5s^{2} 6g^{3} 6d^{4} 6s* 6g^{2} 5s^{5} 5v^{5} 6v 6d Nov 11] rather slightly-built gelding: useful handicapper: won at Ayr (by 1¼ lengths from Kenny The Captain) in July: second at Hamilton later same month: stays 6f: acts on good to firm and heavy going: wears headgear. *Keith Dalgleish*

DARK DESTROYER (IRE) 3 b.g. Helmet (AUS) 127 – Oeuvre d'Art (IRE) 100 (Marju **85**
(IRE) 127) [2017 79: p6g^{2} p7d* t7.1g* 7g 7g 7d 7m p7g Oct 11] rangy gelding: fairly useful performer: won maiden at Kempton in February and handicap at Wolverhampton (by ¾ length from Sidewinder) in March: stays 7f: acts on polytrack, tapeta and good to firm going: in visor last 2 starts: sold 16,000 gns in November. *Joseph Tuite*

DARK DEVIL (IRE) 4 gr.g. Dark Angel (IRE) 113 – Ride For Roses (IRE) (Barathea **94**
(IRE) 127) [2017 95: p8d^{6} 9.1s 7.8s 8.2d^{6} 7.6g^{3} 7.6v* 7v^{2} 8v 8.1d^{2} Oct 23] lightly-made gelding: fairly useful handicapper: won at Chester (amateur) in September: second there later same month and at Windsor in October: stays 1m: acts on heavy going: sold £23,000 in November. *Richard Fahey*

DARK EMERALD (IRE) 7 gr.g. Dark Angel (IRE) 113 – Xema (Danehill (USA) 126) **94**
[2017 114: 7g^{5} 8g 7g 8g 6f 8.1g Jul 2] lengthy gelding: smart at best, little impact in various events in 2017: stays 8.5f: acts on polytrack, soft and good to firm going: usually wears visor: wears tongue tie. *Brendan Powell*

DARKEST LIGHT 2 b.c. (Feb 20) Lethal Force (IRE) 128 – Deora De (Night Shift **–**
(USA)) [2017 p6g Nov 29] in tongue tie, 12/1, well held in minor event at Kempton. *Jamie Osborne*

DARK FOREST 4 b.g. Iffraaj 127 – Through The Forest (USA) 62 (Forestry (USA) 121) **78**
[2017 70, a62: t8g f7g* f7g^{3} t7.1m f7g^{3} f6d* f6g^{3} 7m^{2} 7g 7.8s 6g^{2} 6s 7s Sep 19] fair handicapper: won at Southwell in January and April: stays 7f: acts on fibresand and good to firm going: wears cheekpieces: usually races prominently. *Marjorie Fife*

DARK FREEDOM (IRE) 2 b.g. (Jan 29) Canford Cliffs (IRE) 133 – Arctic Freedom **56**
(USA) 75 (War Chant (USA) 126) [2017 6m 6s 6.1v 6v^{6} p7g Dec 28] good-quartered gelding: modest maiden: sometimes slowly away. *Charles Hills*

DARK HEDGES 2 b.f. (Feb 17) Zebedee 113 – Bella Chica (IRE) 95 (Bigstone (IRE) **–**
126) [2017 5m 5g 5m^{3} 6d 5m 5m p6g 5s 5s t5g Nov 15] £6,500Y: half-sister to 3 winners, including useful winner up to 5.7f Sleepy Sioux and 5f/6f winner Mother Jones (both by Sleeping Indian): dam 2-y-o 5f/6f winner: no form. *Olly Williams*

DARK ILLUSTRATOR 4 b.f. Dutch Art 126 – Xtrasensory 96 (Royal Applause 124) **–**
[2017 56: t8.6g 8.3s 9.2d 11.2v 8g 10d 14v Nov 7] maiden: no form in 2017: often starts slowly/races in rear. *Lynn Siddall*

DARK INTENTION (IRE) 4 b.f. High Chaparral (IRE) 132 – Ajiaal 72 (Cape Cross (IRE) 129) [2017 84: 7d5 10.3g4 8.8m3 11.1d6 10s4 7d* 7v 7g5 8d4 Nov 4] lengthy filly: fairly useful handicapper: won at York (apprentice, by 2¼ lengths from Roll On Rory) in September: effective from 7f to 11f: acts on tapeta, soft and good to firm going: has worn hood: often races towards rear. *Lawrence Mullaney* **88**

DARK LIBERTY (IRE) 2 gr.f. (Feb 24) Dark Angel (IRE) 113 – Extricate (IRE) (Exceed And Excel (AUS) 126) [2017 p7s3 7d6 8.3g4 7s* 7d3 7.9g2 7s* Oct 29] 88,000Y: first foal: dam, 5f/6f winner, half-sister to smart 7f-1½m winner Entangle: useful performer: won nursery at Redcar in September and listed race at Hanover (by ½ length from Wonderful Gorl) in October: stays 8.5f: acts on soft going. *Simon Crisford* **95**

DARK MAGIC 3 b.g. Invincible Spirit (IRE) 121 – Dark Promise 114 (Shamardal (USA) 129) [2017 6.1m5 7s* 6d p7s p8g2 Dec 31] 575,000Y, £14,000 2-y-o: first foal: dam, 1m-1¼m winner, half-sister to Oaks winner Love Divine, herself dam of St Leger winner Sixties Icon: fairly useful performer: won maiden at Newmarket in July: second in handicap at Lingfield in December: stays 1m: acts on polytrack and soft going: hooded on debut. *Dean Ivory* **84**

DARKOLVA (IRE) 2 gr.c. (Jan 26) Dark Angel (IRE) 113 – Penolva (IRE) 65 (Galileo (IRE) 134) [2017 7g4 7d2 7s4 p6g3 p7g4 p7g3 t7.1g3 p7s5 Dec 8] €38,000Y: fourth foal: brother to 6f winner Alfie's Angel: dam, 1¾m winner who would have stayed 2m, half-sister to useful 1¼m-1½m winner Far From Old: fairly useful maiden: in frame first 7 starts: stays 7f: acts on polytrack and soft going: tried in blinkers: usually races prominently. *Joseph Patrick O'Brien, Ireland* **80**

DARK PEARL (IRE) 3 b.g. Born To Sea (IRE) 117 – Luanas Pearl (IRE) (Bahri (USA) 125) [2017 10s3 12d2 12m* 12v3 13.9m Aug 26] 70,000Y: lengthy gelding: fourth foal: half-brother to 11.6f-2m winner Cosette (by Champs Elysees): dam unraced half-sister to 8.6f-12.3f winner Hattan and winner up to 2m (stayed 2¼m) Tastahil (both smart): fairly useful performer: won maiden at Chepstow in June: third in handicap at Ascot (3 lengths behind Royal Associate) in July: gelded after final start: stays 1¾m: acts on good to firm and heavy going: remains open to improvement. *Ed Walker* **94 p**

DARK PHANTOM (IRE) 6 b.g. Dark Angel (IRE) 113 – Stoneware (Bigstone (IRE) 126) [2017 46: 8m5 p11g3 11.6g 10m Jul 17] good-topped gelding: poor maiden: stays 11f: acts on polytrack, tapeta and good to firm going: has worn headgear/tongue tie: usually races close up. *Eve Johnson Houghton* **44**

DARK POWER (IRE) 3 gr.g. Dark Angel (IRE) 113 – Sixfields Flyer (IRE) 66 (Desert Style (IRE) 121) [2017 84p: 6.1g5 6.1d* 6d* 6d 6d Oct 6] compact gelding: useful handicapper: won at Nottingham in July and Leicester (by length from Stanhope) in August: raced only at 6f: acts on good to soft going: in tongue tie last 4 starts: often races prominently. *Clive Cox* **96**

DARK PROFIT (IRE) 5 gr.g. Dark Angel (IRE) 113 – Goldthroat (IRE) 79 (Zafonic (USA) 130) [2017 f7g2 f6d4 7.2m3 7.2g* 7.2d 6.9g* 7.4g6 7.2m* 7.2s Oct 9] good-topped gelding: useful handicapper: won at Ayr in June, Carlisle in July and Musselburgh (by 2 lengths from Roaring Forties) in September: stays 7.5f: acts on polytrack, fibresand and good to firm going: wears cheekpieces. *Keith Dalgleish* **96**

DARK RED (IRE) 5 gr.g. Dark Angel (IRE) 113 – Essexford (IRE) 92 (Spinning World (USA) 130) [2017 105: 8s4 p10s4 10.3m 10d3 9.9g2 10.3m3 10.2d4 p10s6 10.3g* 8s3 10d4 Nov 4] good-topped gelding: smart handicapper: first past post at Goodwood (demoted after causing interference) in August and York (by 2¼ lengths from Syphax) in October: third in Balmoral Handicap at Ascot (1½ lengths behind Lord Glitters) later in October: stays 10.5f: acts on polytrack, soft and good to firm going: in blinkers last 3 starts. *Ed Dunlop* **112**

DARKROOM ANGEL 3 gr.f. Dark Angel (IRE) 113 – Framed (Elnadim (USA) 128) [2017 69: 8g* 9.9f* 12m6 10.1g4 8g 9.9m6 8d p10g Oct 5] angular filly: fairly useful handicapper: won at Brighton in April and Goodwood in May: stays 1¼m: acts on firm going: front runner/races prominently. *Philip Hide* **83**

DARK ROSE ANGEL (IRE) 2 b.f. (Jan 24) Dark Angel (IRE) 113 – Roseraie (IRE) 99 (Lawman (FR) 121) [2017 7d5 8g* 8g2 7m Oct 13] 60,000Y: compact filly: first foal: dam, 2-y-o 6f winner, half-sister to smart 5f-7f winner Rose Bonheur: useful form: won maiden at Doncaster in August: second in May Hill Stakes at same course (head behind Laurens) in September: stays 1m. *Simon Crisford* **102**

DARK SHOT 4 b.g. Acclamation 118 – Dark Missile 114 (Night Shift (USA)) [2017 92: 5m^4 5f^3 5m^2 6f^5 6.1g^5 5.1m^4 5g Aug 1] sturdy gelding: useful handicapper: third at Goodwood (1½ lengths behind Vibrant Chords) in May and second in 'Dash' at Epsom (short head behind Caspian Prince) in June: stays 6f: acts on firm and soft going: tried in tongue tie: sold 40,000 gns in November. *Andrew Balding* **99**

DARK SIDE DREAM 5 b.g. Equiano (FR) 127 – Dream Day 98 (Oasis Dream 129) [2017 81: t5g^3 t6g^2 t6g^3 t5d^5 t6g* p6g^2 p7d* p6s^3 p7s^3 p6g^2 p7s^3 p7d^5 p6g* p6s^5 Oct 24] tall gelding: fairly useful handicapper: won at Wolverhampton in April, Chelmsford in May and Kempton (by head from Summerghand) in October: stays 7f: acts on polytrack and tapeta: has worn cheekpieces, including last 2 starts: front runner/races prominently: consistent. *Chris Dwyer* **87**

DARK SIDE JAZZ (IRE) 2 ch.g. (May 28) Red Jazz (USA) 125 – Marianne's Dancer (IRE) 67 (Bold Fact (USA) 116) [2017 7g 7m Oct 25] lengthy gelding: fair form on first of 2 starts in minor events. *John Ryan* **69**

DARKSIDEOFTARNSIDE (IRE) 3 b.g. Intense Focus (USA) 117 – Beautiful Dancer (IRE) 50 (Danehill Dancer (IRE) 117) [2017 t12.4g^2 12v* Oct 23] €7,000F, €9,000Y: fifth foal: half-brother to 3 winners, including 2-y-o 6f winner Our Cool Cat (by One Cool Cat) and 9.5f winner (stays 2m) The Way You Dance (by Thewayyouare): dam twice-raced half-sister to useful winner up to 1m Beautiful Fire: fairly useful form: won maiden at Pontefract (by head from Tranquil Star) in October: will be suited by further than 1½m. *Sally Haynes* **88**

DARK SPEC 2 b.c. (May 16) Dark Angel (IRE) 113 – Speciosa (IRE) 115 (Danehill Dancer (IRE) 117) [2017 7g 7d^2 7g^6 7d^4 Sep 29] good-topped colt: seventh foal: half-brother to 3 winners, including 1¼m winner Vernatti (by Teofilo) and 1½m winner Asteroidea (by Sea The Stars): dam, winner up to 1m (1000 Guineas, also 2-y-o 7f/7.4f winner) who stayed 1¼m: fairly useful form: raced only at 7f. *Pam Sly* **83**

DARK TITAN (IRE) 3 b.g. Sepoy (AUS) 129 – Kournikova (SAF) (Sportsworld (USA) 121) [2017 t7.1m p8m^3 t8.6g* t9.5m^2 p10g Sep 25] €120,000Y: half-brother to several winners, including very smart winner up to 1¼m Spark Plug (2-y-o 1m winner, by Dylan Thomas) and smart 1m winner Pearl of Africa (by Jeremy): dam 7f-1¼m winner: fairly useful performer: won maiden at Wolverhampton in February: second in handicap there in March: stays 9.5f: acts on tapeta: sold 8,500 gns in November. *Ed Walker* **80**

DARMA (IRE) 5 b.m. Acclamation 118 – Dark Dancer (FR) (Danehill (USA) 126) [2017 88: p6d Feb 3] fairly useful handicapper, below form sole outing in 2017: stays 6f: acts on polytrack, tapeta and good to firm going: usually races close up. *Martyn Meade* **–**

DARTMOOR GIRL (IRE) 3 b.f. So You Think (NZ) 133 – Preveza (FR) (Dalakhani (IRE) 133) [2017 12m^6 9.9d p12s^4 p12g^5 16s Sep 19] first foal: dam 1¾m winner out of smart 11f winner Mystic Lips: no form: in blinkers last 3 starts: signs of temperament. *Mark Gillard* **–**

DARTMOUTH 5 b.h. Dubawi (IRE) 129 – Galatee (FR) 115 (Galileo (IRE) 134) [2017 123: 13.9d* 12m^4 16.3g^2 14s 16s Oct 21] strong horse: very smart performer: won Yorkshire Cup at York (by neck from Simple Verse) in May: second in Lonsdale Cup at same course (nose behind Montaly) in August: stayed 2m: acted on polytrack, firm and good to soft going: to stand at Shade Oak Stud, Shropshire, fee £3,000. *Sir Michael Stoute* **120**

DARVIE 3 b.g. Stimulation (IRE) 121 – Timeless Elegance (IRE) 83 (Invincible Spirit (IRE) 121) [2017 –: f5g^3 t5g^3 6g^6 5m 6d^5 7m^2 7.2d 7g^4 t7.1s^3 Sep 8] fair maiden: stays 7f: acts on tapeta, good to firm and good to soft going: often starts slowly, usually races towards rear. *David Barron* **65**

Betway Yorkshire Cup, York—
separated by the width of the track, there is just a neck between Dartmouth (left) and 2015 St Leger winner Simple Verse at the line, the Royal runner finding plenty under Ryan Moore; High Jinx (star on cap) and Endless Time (third left) are not beaten far in a thrilling renewal

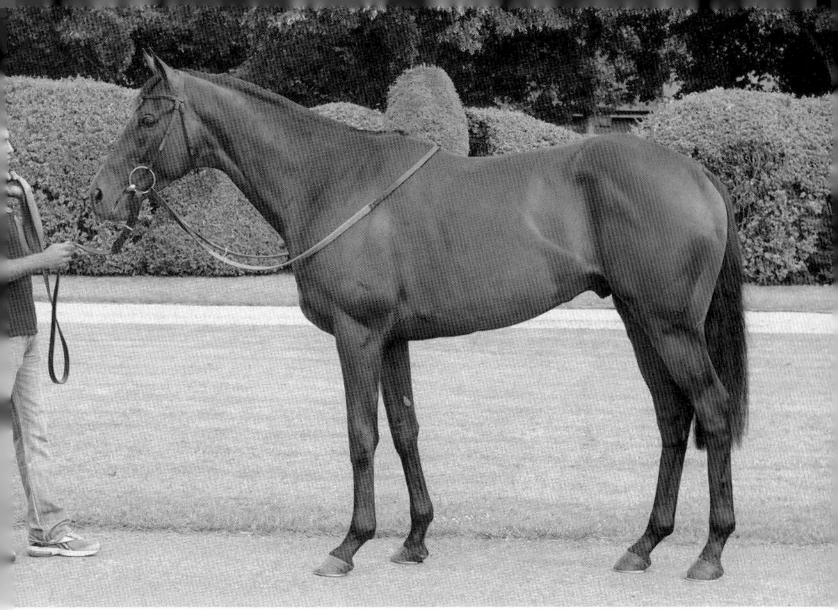

The Queen's "Dartmouth"

DARWASL 3 b.f. Sepoy (AUS) 129 – Hakeeka (Cape Cross (IRE) 129) [2017 64: 10m 10.2m Jun 15] maiden, little impact in 2017: tried in blinkers. *Brian Meehan* **–**

DASCHAS 3 b.g. Oasis Dream 129 – Canada Water (Dansili 127) [2017 85p: p8g p8g 7d 7d Oct 6] good-bodied gelding: fairly useful handicapper, little impact in 2017: left Amanda Perrett after second start: stays 7f: acts on polytrack: wears tongue tie. *Stuart Williams* **80**

DASHANTI 3 gr.f. Medicean 128 – Daheeya 76 (Daylami (IRE) 138) [2017 p10g^{6} p12g t12.2g^{5} Apr 25] third foal: dam, 2-y-o 7f winner, half-sister to 1m-11f winner Moonlight Dash and 2-y-o 5f/6f winner King Electric (both useful) out of smart winner up to 1½m (2-y-o 7.5f winner) Kind Regards: failed to beat a rival in 3 maidens. *Jonathan Portman* **–**

DASHING DUSTY (IRE) 2 b.g. (Apr 28) Elzaam (AUS) 115 – Zuppa Inglese (IRE) (Orpen (USA) 116) [2017 7s^{6} 6d^{4} p7d^{4} p7d^{4} p7g p7s Dec 14] neat gelding: modest maiden: stays 7f: acts on polytrack: tried in cheekpieces. *Jamie Osborne* **60**

DASHING POET 3 b.f. Poet's Voice 126 – Millisecond 85 (Royal Applause 124) [2017 58p: t6f^{6} p5m p6g^{2} p6g p5g* t5.1g* 5m^{5} 5.1m^{3} 5d^{6} t5.1g^{3} 5m 5m p7g^{2} p8g* p8g p8s^{3} p7g^{4} Dec 6] lengthy, angular filly: fair handicapper: won at Chelmsford/Wolverhampton in March and Lingfield in October: left Jeremy Gask after eleventh start: stays 1m: acts on polytrack and tapeta: has worn hood. *Heather Main* **74**

DASHING STAR 7 b.g. Teofilo (IRE) 126 – Dashiba 102 (Dashing Blade 117) [2017 103: p12g^{5} p12g Mar 24] lengthy gelding: smart handicapper at best: stayed 1¾m: acted on good to firm and heavy going: often wore hood: dead. *David Elsworth* **102**

DASH OF SPICE 3 br.c. Teofilo (IRE) 126 – Dashiba 102 (Dashing Blade 117) [2017 8m^{4} 10.1v^{2} p10g* Dec 13] brother to smart winner up to 12.4f Dashing Star (2-y-o 8.3f winner) and half-brother to several winners, including smart 1m-1½m winner Barshiba (by Barathea) and useful 2-y-o 1m winner Doctor Dash (by Dr Fong): dam 9f-1¼m winner: fairly useful form: won maiden at Lingfield (by 3¾ lengths from Past Master) in December: stays 1¼m: likely to progress further. *David Elsworth* **88 p**

DATA PROTECTION 2 b.g. (Apr 6) Foxwedge (AUS) 128 – Midnight Sky 52 (Desert Prince (IRE) 130) [2017 t5.1g^{4} 5.1d^{4} 5m^{5} 5d^{6} 6d^{6} 7.4s* p7g^{2} t8.6g Oct 7] sturdy gelding: fair performer: won nursery at Ffos Las in August: stays 7.5f: acts on polytrack and soft going: tried in blinkers: sometimes slowly away. *William Muir* **68**

DATHANNA (IRE) 2 b.f. (Mar 18) Dubawi (IRE) 129 – Colour (AUS) (More Than Ready (USA) 120) [2017 6.1m 6m^4 7d* 7d* 8v^2 Sep 28] well-made filly: fourth foal: half-sister to a winner in Australia by Exceed And Excel: dam Australian 5f/6f (Group 3) winner: fairly useful performer: won minor event and nursery (by short head from Amourice) in August, both at Newmarket: stays 1m: acts on heavy going: in hood last 4 starts: often travels strongly: capable of better still. *Charlie Appleby* **89 p**

DAVID FALLOW 2 b.g. (Mar 21) Assertive 121 – Dimashq 65 (Mtoto 134) [2017 6m 7m Jul 23] well beaten in 2 minor events. *Paul Midgley* –

DAVID'S BEAUTY (IRE) 4 b.f. Kodiac 112 – Thaisy (USA) (Tabasco Cat (USA) 126) [2017 68, a57: t5.1g^3 t5.1g^5 t5.1f^4 t5g^6 t6g^5 5m^4 5s^5 5.1m^5 5.1g^3 5s 5s^3 5d^2 5.1g* 5.7s^4 t5.1g^6 Sep 23] modest handicapper: won at Chepstow in September: raced mainly at 5f: acts on polytrack, tapeta, firm and soft going: usually wears headgear: front runner/races prominently. *Brian Baugh* **63**

DAVINA 2 b.f. (Apr 25) Delegator 125 – Devon Diva 60 (Systematic 121) [2017 p8g Oct 14] first foal: dam 1m winner who stayed 1¼m: 50/1, well held in minor event at Kempton. *Jeremy Scott* –

DAVINCI DAWN 3 b.f. Poet's Voice 126 – Bonnie Brae 111 (Mujahid (USA) 125) [2017 –: t8d^6 f8g 6m May 24] no form: tried in cheekpieces. *Ann Duffield* –

DAVY'S DILEMMA 3 b.g. Sixties Icon 125 – Wansdyke Lass 59 (Josr Algarhoud (IRE) 118) [2017 81: 9m^4 14f* 13.1s* Jul 4] useful handicapper: won at Wetherby in June and Hamilton (by 1¼ lengths from Addicted To You) in July: stays 1¾m: acts on tapeta, firm and soft going. *Michael Dods* **96**

DAWAALEEB (USA) 3 b.c. Invincible Spirit (IRE) 121 – Plaza (USA) (Chester House (USA) 123) [2017 8m^5 10g 8g^2 8.3g^3 p8g* Oct 5] $325,000Y: fourth foal: half-brother to 3 winners, including 1½m winner Important Message (by New Approach) and 1½m-1¾m winner (stays 16.5f) High Command (by High Chaparral), both useful: dam, 1¼m winner, half-sister to useful 1m-1¼m winner Eaton Square: fairly useful performer: won maiden at Lingfield (by neck from Mr Tyrrell) in October: should stay 1¼m: acts on polytrack, best turf form on good going: tried in blinkers: front runner/races prominently: sold to join Les Eyre 65,000 gns in November. *Charles Hills* **86**

DAWN BREAKING 2 b.g. (Mar 20) Firebreak 125 – Jubilee Dawn 52 (Mark of Esteem (IRE) 137) [2017 7v^5 6v* 7g^6 6v* 6d Nov 11] tall gelding: fair performer: won minor events at Pontefract in September and October: should be suited by 7f: best form on heavy going. *Richard Whitaker* **75**

DAWN DANCER 2 b.c. (Mar 1) Dawn Approach (IRE) 132 – Ballet Ballon (USA) 81 (Rahy (USA) 115) [2017 8.3g f7.1g^2 Nov 28] half-brother to several winners, including very smart 1m-10.2f winner Ballet Concerto (by Dansili) and smart winner up to 7.5f Havane Smoker (by Dubawi): dam 1¼m winner who stayed 1½m: fair form when second in minor event at Southwell (2¾ lengths behind On The Warpath) on second of 2 starts: likely to do better still. *Andrew Balding* **73 p**

DAWN DASH 2 ch.f. (May 14) Dawn Approach (IRE) 132 – Dashiba 102 (Dashing Blade 117) [2017 8.2g p8g p8g Dec 20] half-sister to several winners, including smart 1m-1½m winner Barshiba (by Barathea), smart winner up to 12.4f Dashing Star (2-y-o 8.3f winner, by Teofilo) and useful 2-y-o 1m winner Doctor Dash (by Dr Fong): dam 9f-1¼m winner: modest form on second of 3 starts in minor events. *Ralph Beckett* **53**

DAWN GODDESS 3 b.f. Dick Turpin (IRE) 127 – Aurora Sky (IRE) 81 (Hawk Wing (USA) 136) [2017 –: p8g 6m^4 5.7f 7s 9.9m^5 9.9d^6 8d^2 p10g p7g^4 p10s p10s^2 Dec 15] modest maiden: stays 1¼m: acts on good to soft going: often starts slowly/races towards rear. *Gary Moore* **52**

DAWN HORIZONS 4 ch.f. New Approach (IRE) 132 – Hidden Hope 111 (Daylami (IRE) 138) [2017 95: 12g* 14v Aug 3] useful-looking filly: useful performer: won handicap at Ascot (by 3 lengths from Cliff Face) in July: stays 1½m: acts on firm and soft going: front runner/races prominently. *William Haggas* **96**

DAWN OF HOPE (IRE) 4 ch.f. Mastercraftsman (IRE) 129 – Sweet Firebird (IRE) 103 (Sadler's Wells (USA) 132) [2017 105: 8g^3 8.1d 8m 8d^2 9d^3 8.9d^5 8g^5 Oct 7] compact filly: smart performer: third in listed race at Doncaster (½ length behind Kool Kompany) in April and Dance Design Stakes at the Curragh (length behind Rain Goddess) in August: stays 10.5f: acts on polytrack, good to firm and good to soft going. *Roger Varian* **113**

DAWN OF RECKONING 2 b.f. (Mar 7) Dawn Approach (IRE) 132 – Reckoning (IRE) 103 (Danehill Dancer (IRE) 117) [2017 8s^6 p8g Nov 8] first foal: dam, 2-y-o 1m winner who stayed 1½m, half-sister to useful 1m winner Hope Cross: modest form on first of 2 starts in minor events. *Jonathan Portman* **60**

DAWOODI 3 ch.g. Exceed And Excel (AUS) 126 – Anna Amalia (IRE) (In The Wings 128) [2017 82: 6m^6 6d 7.2g 6s 5d^4 5g^4 6d 5d^6 6d^3 5m^5 5s* t5d 5s^3 5s^4 Oct 9] fair handicapper: won at Musselburgh in September: stays 6f: acts on soft and good to firm going: wears headgear. *Linda Perratt* **69**

DAYBREAK 2 b.f. (Apr 8) Dawn Approach (IRE) 132 – Walk On Bye (IRE) 105 (Danehill Dancer (IRE) 117) [2017 6g^4 6d^2 6s^2 p6s^6 p7g Dec 20] 65,000Y: compact filly: fourth foal: dam, 2-y-o 6f/6.3f winner, half-sister to smart 12.4f/13f winner Motherland out of very smart sprinter Pipalong: fair maiden: stays 6f: acts on good to soft going. *Hughie Morrison* **74**

DAYDREAM (IRE) 4 b.f. Dream Ahead (USA) 133 – Intricate Dance (USA) (Aptitude (USA) 128) [2017 62: t5.1g^6 p6d p7s May 25] modest maiden, below form in 2017: stays 1m: acts on polytrack and tapeta: has worn tongue tie, including final start. *Tony Newcombe* **45**

DAYKING 3 b.c. Dubawi (IRE) 129 – Birjand 99 (Green Desert (USA) 127) [2017 t8.6g^2 Apr 29] brother to very smart winner up to 1m Lucky Nine (2-y-o 6f winner) and half-brother to 3 winners, including smart Japanese Grade 3 6f winner Teehaff (by Storming Home): dam 6f-7f winner: 9/4, plenty of promise when second in maiden at Wolverhampton (head behind Manchego) in April: should improve. *Saeed bin Suroor* **90 p**

DAY OF REST (FR) 2 gr.g. (Apr 28) Sunday Break (JPN) 121 – Nakiya (FR) (Kendor (FR) 122) [2017 6d^3 7d^4 7.5g^4 7g^2 7.5s^5 7d^3 7g^5 8.2s p9.4g^5 a8.9g^3 p9.4g^2 Dec 26] fair maiden: left George Baker after sixth start: stays 9.5f: acts on polytrack and good to soft going: tried in cheekpieces. *M. Boutin, France* **76**

DAZACAM 3 b.f. Camacho 118 – Dazakhee 74 (Sakhee (USA) 136) [2017 84p: t5.1m^3 t5.1m* p6g^3 t5g^2 t5.1m^3 t6g^4 5.1g^6 6m^6 Apr 28] fairly useful handicapper: won at Wolverhampton in January: stays 6f: acts on polytrack, tapeta and good to firm going: usually races nearer last than first. *Michael Herrington* **88**

DAZEEKHA 4 b.f. Captain Gerrard (IRE) 113 – Dazakhee 74 (Sakhee (USA) 136) [2017 –: t7.1g t7.1g t6g^6 f5g^4 Dec 21] modest maiden: stays 7f. *Michael Herrington* **52**

DAZZLE GOLD (USA) 2 b.c. (Feb 22) Lemon Drop Kid (USA) 131 – Tustarta (USA) 105 (Trempolino (USA) 135) [2017 6.5m^5 p7g^3 p8g Oct 25] fair form: best effort when third in minor event at Kempton (3¼ lengths behind Barton Mills) in September. *Robert Cowell* **75**

D'BAI (IRE) 3 b.g. Dubawi (IRE) 129 – Savannah Belle 84 (Green Desert (USA) 127) [2017 100: 8g^2 10.4g 8g^3 8d* 8s^3 8d^6 8.9s^5 Oct 7] close-coupled, attractive gelding: smart performer: won handicap at Ascot (by neck from Pealer) in July: stays 10.5f: acts on good to firm and heavy going: wears headgear: often races towards rear. *Charlie Appleby* **119**

DEADLY ACCURATE 2 br.g. (Mar 25) Lethal Force (IRE) 128 – Riccoche (IRE) 63 (Oasis Dream 129) [2017 7g 7d^5 7m* 7g^3 7s Oct 15] 28,000Y: fourth foal: half-brother to 5f/6f winner Burauq (by Kyllachy) and 6f winner (stays 1¼m) Beauden Barrett (by Dick Turpin): dam lightly-raced half-sister to useful winner up to 1m City of Joy: fairly useful performer: won minor event at Epsom in August: third in nursery at Newbury in September: raced only at 7f: acts on good to firm going. *Hughie Morrison* **80**

DEADLY REEL (IRE) 2 b.f. (Feb 23) Pour Moi (IRE) 125 – Lady Ederle (USA) (English Channel (USA) 126) [2017 6.5d^6 7f^3 7.1m^4 6.9g^5 8g^3 8v^5 p10g^3 Nov 2] €60,000F, €60,000Y: first foal: dam lightly-raced half-sister to smart 1m/9f winner (stayed 1¾m) Fathayer out of smart winner up to 1½m Bright Generation: fair maiden: will stay at least 1½m: acts on polytrack and firm going: tried in cheekpieces: front runner/races prominently. *Archie Watson* **72**

DEALER'S CHOICE (IRE) 3 gr.f. Exchange Rate (USA) 111 – Micaela's Moon (USA) (Malibu Moon (USA)) [2017 79: 6d^2 5.7m^2 6d* 5.9g^5 6.1v^4 p6g^6 p7g* p8m Nov 25] lengthy, rather unfurnished filly: fairly useful performer: won maiden at Lingfield in June and handicap there (by ¾ length from Dashing Poet) in October: stays 7f: acts on polytrack, tapeta and good to soft going: has worn headgear. *Roger Varian* **81**

DEANSGATE (IRE) 4 b.g. Dandy Man (IRE) 123 – Romarca (IRE) 61 (Raise A Grand (IRE) 114) [2017 85: t7.1s^4 7g t7.1g^4 7.4m 7f^4 7g* t7.1d^5 t7.1g^4 t7.1g^2 Dec 6] fairly useful handicapper: won at Doncaster in August: second at Newcastle in December: raced mainly around 7f: acts on fibresand, tapeta and good to firm going: has worn headgear, including in 2017: quirky sort and not one to rely on. *Julie Camacho* **83 §**

DEAUVILLE DIVA (IRE) 3 b.f. Lawman (FR) 121 – Sheila Toss (IRE) 81 (Galileo (IRE) 134) [2017 8.1m^{6} t8.6g^{5} Nov 20] €46,000Y, resold €95,000Y: unfurnished filly: second foal: dam, 7f winner, half-sister to smart 1m winner Diamond Tycoon out of useful 1m/9f winner Palacoona: modest form in 2 maidens. *Marcus Tregoning* **62**

DEAUVILLE (IRE) 4 b.c. Galileo (IRE) 134 – Walklikeanegyptian (IRE) 77 (Danehill (USA) 126) [2017 119: 8.9d 10d^{2} 10.3m* 10.5d^{3} 8f^{3} 9d^{2} 10f^{3} 8f 9.9g Dec 10] lengthy colt: very smart performer: won Huxley Stakes at Chester (by neck from Poet's Word) in May: placed in Gordon Richards Stakes at Sandown (length second to Ulysses), Tattersalls Gold Cup at the Curragh (3½ lengths third to Decorated Knight), Queen Anne Stakes at Royal Ascot (1½ lengths third behind Ribchester), Meld Stakes at Leopardstown (head second to Moonlight Magic) and Arlington Million (¾-length third behind Beach Patrol): below form in Woodbine Mile and Hong Kong Cup at Sha Tin last 2 starts: stays 10.5f: acts on any turf going: often wears headgear: has worn tongue tie: front runner/races prominently. *Aidan O'Brien, Ireland* **123**

DEAUVILLE SOCIETY (IRE) 2 b.f. (Mar 5) Society Rock (IRE) 126 – Dorothy Dene (Red Ransom (USA)) [2017 6m p6s 6.1f^{5} 6.1g^{5} 7g p7g Oct 13] €34,000F, 20,000Y: rather unfurnished filly: fourth foal: half-sister to useful 6f (including at 2 yrs) winner Navigate (by Iffraaj): dam, unraced, closely related to useful 2-y-o 6f winner Dora Carrington and half-sister to smart 6f winner Primo Valentino: poor maiden: stays 6f: acts on good to firm going: tried in cheekpieces. *Sir Mark Prescott Bt* **49**

DEBAWTRY (IRE) 2 b.f. (Apr 28) Camacho 118 – Muluk (IRE) 83 (Rainbow Quest (USA) 134) [2017 5d^{2} 5m* Aug 31] €10,000Y: sixth foal: half-sister to 3 winners, including winner up to 1m (stays 1¼m) Intiwin (2-y-o 7f winner, by Intikhab) and 8.3f-13.3f winner (stays 2m) Daisy Boy (by Cape Cross): dam 1m winner: fair form: won minor event at Musselburgh (by neck from Brandy Station) in August: will be suited by 6f: remains open to improvement. *David O'Meara* **70 p**

DEBEN 4 b.g. Lilbourne Lad (IRE) 111 – Mocca (IRE) 99 (Sri Pekan (USA) 117) [2017 66: 6m^{6} 6m^{4} 7.2m 6m^{2} 6s^{2} 6v^{2} 7g 6g^{6} t6.1d Dec 27] leggy gelding: modest handicapper: stays 7f: acts on fibresand, good to firm and heavy going: has worn headgear. *John Weymes* **58**

DEBONAIRE DAVID 3 b.c. Sir Prancealot (IRE) 111 – Peyto Princess 85 (Bold Arrangement 127) [2017 70: p6g* t6.1g* 5.7g 6g^{4} p6g^{3} t7.2m^{4} p6g^{5} Nov 2] fairly useful handicapper: won at Lingfield in June and Wolverhampton in July: stays 7f: acts on polytrack and tapeta: tried in cheekpieces: wears tongue tie: sometimes slowly away. *Richard Hughes* **81**

DE BRUYNE HORSE 2 b.c. (Feb 26) Showcasing 117 – Right Rave (IRE) 84 (Soviet Star (USA) 128) [2017 5m^{5} 6m* 6m*^{d} 6f 6g^{4} 5.5g^{6} 7d* 6d 7g 7g 6g 7.5g Oct 22] 10,000F, £50,000Y: compact colt: third foal: half-brother to 1m winner Right Rebel (by Cockney Rebel): dam, winner up to 9f (2-y-o 5f winner): useful performer: first past post in minor events at Ripon in May and Epsom (disqualified after failing drugs test) in June, and listed race at Vichy (by neck from Red Line) in August: stays 7f: acts on good to firm and good to soft going: in headgear last 6 starts: often races prominently: sold 40,000 gns, has joined Brendan Powell. *Richard Hannon* **102**

DEBUTANTE'S BALL (IRE) 2 ch.f. (Apr 28) Society Rock (IRE) 126 – Query (USA) (Distant View (USA) 126) [2017 5.1d* 5m 5d^{5} 5.2v 6g^{4} 7d^{6} 7g p5g 6d^{5} Nov 1] €5,500Y, resold £6,000Y: close-coupled filly: sixth foal: half-sister to several winners, including winner up to 1m Sensei (2-y-o 7f winner, by Dr Fong) and ungenuine 9.5f/1¼m winner Saturation Point (by Beat Hollow): dam unraced: fair performer: won minor event at Chepstow in May: flattered in pattern races in France third/fifth starts: little impact after: stays 6f: acts on good to soft going: in cheekpieces last 5 starts: often races towards rear. *J. S. Moore* **73**

DECADENT TIMES (IRE) 3 b.g. Art Connoisseur (IRE) 121 – Be Special (IRE) (Sri Pekan (USA) 117) [2017 67: 6m 7m 6g 5m Jun 24] fair form at 2 yrs, below that level in Britain first 4 starts in 2017: sent to Germany, where won (for first time) over 5.5f at Neuss in November. *Marjorie Fife* **58**

DECIDING VOTE 3 b.f. Pivotal 124 – Clincher Club 77 (Polish Patriot (USA) 128) [2017 6m^{5} 7g 6d^{6} 6d^{2} 6d* 6s Sep 15] sister to smart 6f/7f winner Intense Pink and half-sister to numerous winners, including smart 2-y-o 6f winner Henrik (by Primo Dominie) and useful 1¼m-1½m winner Fractal (by High Chaparral): dam winner up to 7f (2-y-o 5f winner): fair performer: won handicap at Yarmouth in August: stays 6f: acts on good to soft going. *Chris Wall* **70**

DECIMA (IRE) 3 b.f. Dream Ahead (USA) 133 – Snowtime (IRE) (Galileo (IRE) 134) **77** [2017 6g 7g^4 7m 9.9s^3 12d^5 9.9v* 10.2d 10d^3 Oct 20] 12,500Y: fifth foal:half-sister to 1m-9.5f winner Heavens Eyes (by Oasis Dream): dam unraced half-sister to high-class winner up to 9f Ali-Royal and 1000 Guineas winner Sleepytime: fair handicapper: won at Beverley (amateur) in September: stays 1¼m: acts on heavy going: tried in tongue tie. *Michael Easterby*

DECISION MAKER (IRE) 3 b.g. Iffraaj 127 – Consensus (IRE) 91 (Common Grounds **72** 118) [2017 8.3m 8.3s^3 6m^2 6v t6d^2 t6g^4 f5g^2 Dec 21] fair maiden: best form at sprint trips: acts on fibresand, tapeta, soft and good to firm going: tried in tongue tie. *Roy Bowring*

DECLAMATION (IRE) 7 ch.g. Shamardal (USA) 129 – Dignify (IRE) 105 (Rainbow **69** Quest (USA) 134) [2017 66: t7.1g 7.2g 7.2g f6.1g^2 f6.1g* Dec 29] fair performer: won minor event at Southwell in December: left Alistair Whillans after third start: raced mainly at 6f/7f nowadays: acts on all-weather, firm and good to soft going: front runner/races prominently. *John Butler*

DECLARATIONOFLOVE (IRE) 2 b.c. (Mar 23) Declaration of War (USA) 128 – **82** Mary's Daughter 94 (Royal Applause 124) [2017 5m^4 5.3m^3 5.1m* 5f 5.2v^2 5m p6g p6d Sep 28] €28,000Y: smallish colt: first foal: dam 2-y-o 5f/6f winner: fairly useful performer: won minor event at Windsor (by 1¼ lengths from Spoof) in May: second in Super Sprint at Newbury (6 lengths behind Bengali Boys) in July: should stay 6f: acts on good to firm and heavy going: sold 15,000 gns in October. *Tom Clover*

DECLARATIONOFPEACE (USA) 2 b.c. (Apr 16) War Front (USA) 119 – Serena's **108** Cat (USA) (Storm Cat (USA)) [2017 5.8m^3 p5g* 5f 6m 6d p5g* p5g^3 5f* Nov 4] $2,600,000F: lengthy, well-made colt: sixth foal: half-brother to several winners, including high-class US Grade 1 1m/9f winner Honor Code (by A P Indy) and US Grade 2 8.5f winner Noble Tune (by Unbridled's Song), runner-up in Breeders' Cup Juvenile Turf: dam 5.5f (minor US stakes) winner: useful performer: won maiden at Dundalk in May, minor event on same course in October and listed race at Del Mar (beat Sound And Silence by head, showing impressive burst of speed) in November: needs strongly-run race at 5f and stays 6f: acts on polytrack, firm and good to soft going: wears tongue tie. *Aidan O'Brien, Ireland*

DECORATED KNIGHT 5 ch.h. Galileo (IRE) 134 – Pearling (USA) (Storm Cat **125** (USA)) [2017 120: p10g* 8.9g* 8.9d^6 10.5d* 10m^2 9.9m^6 10.3d^5 10d* 12f Nov 4]

Ireland's most important all-aged middle-distance event began life as the Joe McGrath Memorial at Leopardstown in 1976, though its prestige (and value) received a significant boost when the race was both moved and rebranded as the Phoenix Champion Stakes in 1984. Back at Leopardstown since 1991 (following the closure of Phoenix Park) and now known as the Irish Champion Stakes, the Group 1 ten-furlong contest has experienced very few shock winners during its long history. The only winner at double-figure odds before 2017 had come in the period during the race's original guise, when a lesser light from the all-powerful Robert Sangster and Vincent O'Brien camp, Fordham, sprang a 14/1 surprise under an enterprising ride from Tommy Carberry (who died aged seventy-five in July). Carberry, of course, was much better known for his exploits over jumps—four-times Irish National Hunt champion—but it is often forgotten that he also liked to keep his hand in on the Flat, having started off as a talented apprentice in that sphere. By contrast, Roger Charlton's brief riding career centred firmly on the winter game, the undoubted highlight being his win on Pride of Kentucky in the Kim Muir at the 1969 Cheltenham Festival, but he has become a stalwart of the British Flat racing scene since taking over the reins at Beckhampton in 1990 from Jeremy Tree (after a lengthy spell as his assistant trainer), saddling over seventy pattern winners during that period. Charlton's biggest money-spinner in recent years has been Decorated Knight, who became by far the longest-priced winner in Irish Champion Stakes history when landing the latest renewal in September as an unconsidered 25/1-shot.

In truth, Decorated Knight hardly fitted the usual profile of a rank outsider. The Irish Champion Stakes was his third Group 1 prize of the season, following lucrative wins in the Jebel Hatta at Meydan in March and the Tattersalls Gold Cup at the Curragh in May. He'd also put up a fine performance when runner-up, splitting Highland Reel and Ulysses, in the Prince of Wales's Stakes at Royal Ascot, though two subsequent finishes down the field in the Eclipse at Sandown and the International Stakes at York (both won by Ulysses) were enough to persuade most punters that

Decorated Knight found Group 1 races during the main core of the season too hot for him. At 25/1, he was sent off sixth choice in a field of ten at Leopardstown, with the market dominated by three-year-olds, the 11/8-on favourite being dual Guineas winner Churchill (who'd finished runner-up in the International). Waited with as usual, Decorated Knight was still last turning for home and was forced to challenge widest of all in the home straight, though this might have turned out to be a blessing in disguise given what happened in the latter stages. In fact, both Decorated Knight and runner-up Poet's Word swooped down the outer to take over in the final furlong as others met trouble in running, Decorated Knight's strong late surge taking him to a half length victory over Poet's Word. There was a further length and three quarters back to the front-running Eminent, who fared best of the three-year-old contingent in third—Churchill, who became trapped in a pocket along the inside rail, eventually finished seventh after being eased late on. It was a one, two, three for British stables, the first such clean sweep since Cezanne won in 1994, when British raiders made up seven of the eight runners (the sole Irish representative Perfect Imposter finished last).

On a more pertinent note, Decorated Knight recorded the lowest Timeform rating by a winner in the race since 2008, not needing to improve much, if at all, on the pick of his form from earlier in the campaign. That said, as a whole, Decorated Knight did take his form to a new level from four to five, his first season with Charlton in 2016 (trained by Roger Varian before then) seeing him competing only at listed and Group 3 level, signing off that campaign with a win in the Group 3 Meld Stakes at Leopardstown under George Baker—who was forced into retirement in autumn 2017 as a result of head injuries sustained in a fall racing on the ice at St Moritz in February. Andrea Atzeni, however, has been Decorated Knight's regular rider for the bulk of his career and was thankful to have such a willing partner under him when hardly enjoying the breaks on each of his first two starts in 2017. A short head was the winning margin when an easy-to-back Decorated Knight edged out Arab Spring in the Winter Derby Trial at Lingfield in February, holding on gamely after Atzeni had been forced to wait for a gap on the home turn. Decorated Knight did even better to overcome unfavourable circumstances when winning the Jebel Hatta, getting up

Tattersalls Gold Cup, the Curragh—Decorated Knight emulates dual winner Al Kazeem to give trainer Roger Charlton a third victory in the race, forging on to beat the Aidan O'Brien-trained pair Somehow (blinkers) and Deauville (not in picture)

Qipco Irish Champion Stakes, Leopardstown—Decorated Knight swoops wide and late to register a third win at Group 1 level, beating Poet's Word (spots on cap) and the three-year-old Eminent (right); dual Guineas winner Churchill (second right) suffers interference and is eased in the closing stages

in the final strides to deprive Folkswood by a neck in a bunched finish, showing a fine turn of foot (particularly after being short of room over two furlongs out) in a muddling race which essentially developed into a sprint. After finishing a below-par sixth in the Dubai Turf back at Meydan later the same month, Decorated Knight got back on track in the Tattersalls Gold Cup some nine weeks later, quickening smartly to beat the Aidan O'Brien-trained pair Somehow and Deauville after being ridden closer to the pace than usual. It was also Charlton's third Tattersalls Gold Cup win in the last five renewals, following on from Al Kazeem in both 2013 and 2015—five of the trainer's last nine Group 1 wins have now been on Irish soil.

Decorated Knight (ch.h. 2012)	Galileo (IRE) (b 1998)	Sadler's Wells (b 1981)	Northern Dancer
			Fairy Bridge
		Urban Sea (ch 1989)	Miswaki
			Allegretta
	Pearling (USA) (br 2006)	Storm Cat (b or br 1983)	Storm Bird
			Terlingua
		Mariah's Storm (b 1991)	Rahy
			Immense

It is somewhat ironic that Decorated Knight's surprise Irish Champion Stakes win came at the expense of a Coolmore-owned hotpot, as he hails from one of the most fruitful bloodlines developed by that breeding empire in recent years. He is actually a three-parts brother to the equine Coolmore—O'Brien's smart ten-furlong performer Coolmore (fifth in the 2016 Prix de Diane) is also by Galileo and out of the yard's 2007 Cherry Hinton Stakes winner You'resothrilling, who is a sister of Decorated Knight's dam Pearling (whose only other winner to date is the Frankel filly Ambrosia, who landed a lowly all-weather mile maiden on her debut for Charlton in November having also made the switch from Varian's yard). You'resothrilling is better known for her first two foals (both also by Galileo), the Irish One Thousand Guineas winner Marvellous and the top-class miler Gleneagles, who completed a Group 1 hat-trick in the St James's Palace Stakes at Royal Ascot after completing the Anglo-Irish Two Thousand Guineas double. Their two-year-old sister Happily, winner of the Moyglare Stud Stakes and Prix Jean-Luc Lagardere, also has an essay in this Annual. Pearling is also a half-sister to the dam of Storm The Stars, who was placed in the Derby at both Epsom and the Curragh in 2015. However, all that came after Pearling (carrying Decorated Knight at the time) fetched 1,300,000 guineas at the 2011 December Sales, a sum which certainly wasn't triggered by the dam's own modest racing career (she finished runner-up—over five furlongs—on the first of just two starts as a three-year-old in Canada). Interest in Pearling stemmed from her being a sister to Giant's Causeway, the top-class miler/ten-furlong performer who notched up six Group 1 wins, the last of them in the Irish Champion Stakes, during a wonderfully consistent career. The famed durability of Giant's Causeway—which

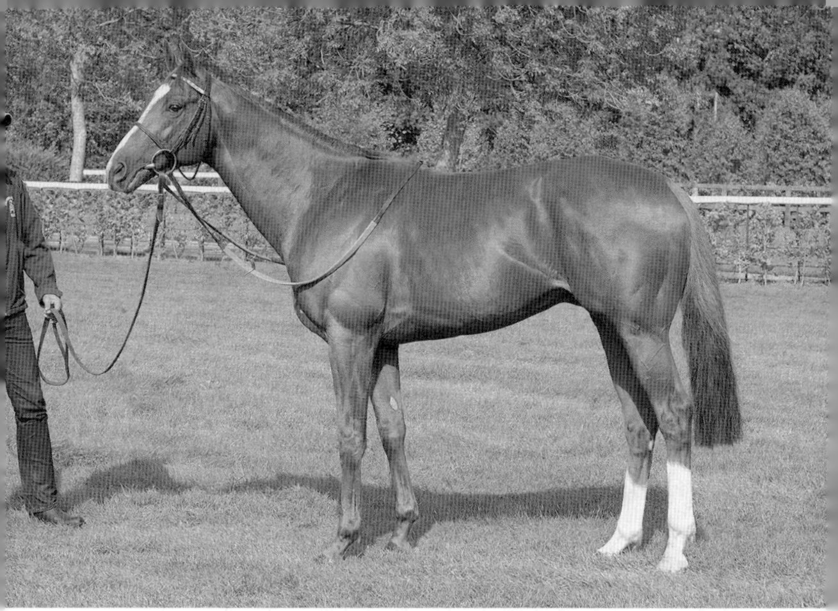

Mr S. Al Homaizi and Mr I. Al Sagar's "Decorated Knight"

earned him the tag of the 'The Iron Horse'—has since been passed on to many of his offspring as he has gone on to become a leading sire. Pearling's dam Mariah's Storm showed similar toughness during her racing career in the States where she won ten of her sixteen starts (showing high-class form), including the Arlington-Washington Lassie Stakes as a two-year-old. Her record is all the more remarkable as she fractured her near-fore cannon bone on her final start at two, only to make a full recovery from that serious injury and race on, winning three times back at Arlington the following year—the track has since named a race in her honour. The mare's legacy doesn't end there, however, as Mariah's Storm became the inspiration for the 2005 film *Dreamer*, in which the fictional filly Sonador is nursed back from a broken leg to win the Breeders' Cup Classic!

There was no such Hollywood happy ending for Giant's Causeway, who suffered an agonisingly narrow defeat on his final start, going down by a neck to Tiznow in the 2000 Breeders' Cup Classic after a rare slip by jockey Mick Kinane saw him lose his reins late on. Alas, Decorated Knight didn't come nearly so close when making his own American swansong, managing just tenth of thirteen in the Breeders' Cup Turf at Del Mar in November, though there must be a chance that this first try at a mile and a half stretched his stamina. A useful-looking horse, Decorated Knight was effective at a mile up to ten and a half furlongs, and he proved versatile with regards to the going, acting on polytrack and on soft and good to firm on turf (the Breeders' Cup Turf was on firm). His racing career and his fashionable pedigree should make him attractive to commercial breeders. He will be standing at the Irish National Stud for a fee of €15,000 in 2018. *Roger Charlton*

DEDUCE (FR) 4 b.f. Iffraaj 127 – Count The Cost (USA) (Cozzene (USA)) [2017 p10g Oct 5] fairly useful handicapper, won twice for Francois Rohaut at 3 yrs: below that level sole outing on Flat in 2017: stays 13.5f: acts on soft going. *James Eustace* **70**

DEEBAJ (IRE) 5 br.g. Authorized (IRE) 133 – Athreyaa (Singspiel (IRE) 133) [2017 –: p12g Dec 20] lengthy gelding: fair maiden, below form only 2 starts on Flat since 2015: stays 1½m: acts on soft going: fair hurdler. *Gary Moore* **–**

DEECIDER 2 b.c. (Feb 21) Captain Gerrard (IRE) 113 – Plead (FR) (Bering 136) [2017 6g^4 6.1v 6v^6 Sep 29] modest form when fourth in minor event at Haydock on first of 3 starts: tried in visor: sold 3,500 gns, sent to Norway. *Tom Dascombe* **59**

DEEDS NOT WORDS (IRE) 6 b.g. Royal Applause 124 – Wars (IRE) 60 (Green Desert (USA) 127) [2017 76: 7m^4 6.1g^2 p6g* t6.1g* 6g* 6m^5 5d^2 p6g^6 p6g^6 p6g^4 p6s Dec 15] smallish gelding: fair handicapper: won at Kempton in May, and at Wolverhampton and Brighton in June: stays 7f: acts on polytrack, tapeta, good to firm and good to soft going: usually wears headgear: has worn tongue tie. *Michael Wigham* **79**

DEE EX BEE 2 b.c. (May 3) Farhh 131 – Dubai Sunrise (USA) (Seeking The Gold (USA)) [2017 7d* 7d^6 8.2s^3 8.5v* 10m^2 Oct 14] lengthy, attractive colt: sixth foal: closely related to 1m winner Solar Moon (by Pivotal) and half-brother to 1m-1¼m winner Bewilder (by Invincible Spirit) and winner up to 7.4f Chupalla (2-y-o 5f winner, by Helmet): dam unraced sister to top-class winner up to 1¼m Dubai Millennium: useful performer: won maiden at Goodwood in August and minor event at Epsom (by ¾ length from Move Over) in October: placed in listed races at Haydock (4 lengths behind Chilean) in September and Newmarket (3½ lengths behind Kew Gardens) in October: stays 1¼m: acts on heavy and good to firm going: front runner/races prominently. *Mark Johnston* **100**

DEELEY'S DOUBLE (FR) 4 ch.g. Makfi 130 – Habilea (FR) (Grand Lodge (USA) 125) [2017 69: t6m^3 t7.1g p8g^4 10.3g^2 10.2d^4 t12.2g^4 Dec 2] fair maiden: left Tony Carroll after fourth start: stays 1½m: acts on polytrack, tapeta and good to soft going. *Daniel Loughnane* **75**

DEEP CHALLENGER (IRE) 5 b.g. Galileo (IRE) 134 – Healing Music (FR) (Bering 136) [2017 71p: f7g^4 p8g^4 t9.5g* t9.5g^2 9.9g^2 12g^3 11.8m^5 t12.2g t12.2g* 14d f12.1g Nov 16] workmanlike gelding: fairly useful handicapper: won at Wolverhampton in April and October: stays 1½m: seems most effective on tapeta: tried in tongue tie: often races prominently. *Jamie Osborne* **84**

DEEP DREAM 4 b.f. Dream Ahead (USA) 133 – Jessica's Dream (IRE) 114 (Desert Style (IRE) 121) [2017 52p: t6d^4 p6g Feb 18] modest form: better effort in 2017 when fourth in maiden at Newcastle in February. *Andrew Balding* **58**

DEEP RESOLVE (IRE) 6 b.g. Intense Focus (USA) 117 – I'll Be Waiting (Vettori (IRE) 119) [2017 74: f12m* 12g^3 f12.1g^3 11.2s 11.1v^6 f16.5g^3 Dec 29] fair handicapper: won at Southwell in March: stays 1½m: acts on fibresand and heavy going: has worn headgear, including in 2017. *Sally Haynes* **68** **a76**

DEER SONG 4 b.g. Piccolo 121 – Turkish Delight 67 (Prince Sabo 123) [2017 54, a62: p5g^3 p5f p6g p6g 6m^3 6m^2 5.3m^6 5.2m 6.1m 5.1m^5 6g 5m p7g p5g* p6g p6g Dec 12] compact gelding: modest handicapper: won at Kempton in October: stays 6f: acts on polytrack and good to firm going: has worn headgear. *John Bridger* **56** **a62**

DEFINING MOMENT 3 b.f. Camacho 118 – Elfine (IRE) 78 (Invincible Spirit (IRE) 121) [2017 57: f5g^5 6m^5 5m^2 6g* 5.3g^4 5.2m* Aug 22] compact filly: fair handicapper: won at Yarmouth in July and August: stays 6f: acts on good to firm going: usually races towards rear, often travels strongly. *Rae Guest* **79**

DEFINITELY MAYBE (IRE) 3 b.g. Elusive Quality (USA) – Ebony Street (USA) (Street Cry (IRE) 130) [2017 t5s Apr 14] 25/1, well held in maiden at Newcastle. *Keith Dalgleish* **–**

DEFOE (IRE) 3 gr.c. Dalakhani (IRE) 133 – Dulkashe (IRE) 90 (Pivotal 124) [2017 95: 10s* 10.3m* 11.1g* 13.3d* 14.5g Sep 16] good-topped colt: smart performer: won handicaps at Newbury in May and York in July, listed race at Hamilton (by 1½ lengths from **119**

Betfred Geoffrey Freer Stakes, Newbury—Defoe continues his rise through the ranks with a victory over older horses, taking his record for the season to four wins from four starts; Wall of Fire (quartered cap) keeps on well having been forced to switch around the winner—the placings were left unaltered after a stewards' inquiry—with Frontiersman back in third

Frankuus) later in July and Geoffrey Freer Stakes at Newbury (by ¾ length from Wall of Fire) in August: shaped as if amiss in St Leger at Doncaster final start: stays 13.5f: acts on soft and good to firm going. *Roger Varian*

DEFTERA FANTUTTE (IRE) 6 b.m. Amadeus Wolf 122 – Carranza (IRE) (Lead On Time (USA) 123) [2017 p7d p8d p7s May 25] maiden: no form in 2017: tried in cheekpieces. *Natalie Lloyd-Beavis* **–**

DEFTERA LAD (IRE) 5 b.g. Fast Company (IRE) 126 – Speedbird (USA) 76 (Sky Classic (CAN)) [2017 52, a68: t9.5m^{2} Jan 7] sparely-made gelding: fair handicapper: stays 9.5f: acts on polytrack and tapeta: tried in headgear: usually races nearer last than first. *Natalie Lloyd-Beavis* **64**

DEINONYCHUS 6 b.g. Authorized (IRE) 133 – Sharp Dresser (USA) 80 (Diesis 133) [2017 t16.5g^{5} 13.8m 10g 10.2s^{2} 11.8d^{2} 10.2v* 14g^{6} Aug 15] fair handicapper nowadays: won at Nottingham in August: stays 13f: acts on polytrack and heavy going: often wears hood: often races freely. *Michael Appleby* **76**

DEJA (FR) 2 b.c. (Mar 24) Youmzain (IRE) 131 – Atarfe (IRE) (Anabaa (USA) 130) [2017 7m^{5} t8.6g* Aug 18] €62,000F, 350,000 2-y-o: first foal: dam unraced half-sister to winner up to 9f Arasin and 2-y-o 9f winner (stayed 1¾m) Obligation (both useful): fairly useful form: won maiden at Wolverhampton (by 2¾ lengths from Miss Mumtaz) in August: remains with potential. *Jeremy Noseda* **83 p**

DELAGATE THIS LORD 3 b.g. Delegator 125 – Lady Filly 92 (Atraf 116) [2017 –: p8g t7.1g 7g^{3} 6m^{3} 6m* 5d* 5s* 5s Oct 7] good-topped gelding: fairly useful handicapper: won at Newbury in June, and at Bath in August and September (by 1¼ lengths from Bellevarde): left Bill Turner after fourth start: best at 5f/6f: acts on polytrack, tapeta, soft and good to firm going: tried in cheekpieces. *Michael Attwater* **88**

DELAGOA BAY (IRE) 9 b.m. Encosta de Lago (AUS) – Amory (GER) (Goofalik (USA) 118) [2017 67: p15.8g^{3} t16.5m^{3} t16.5g^{2} p16d^{6} Feb 22] compact mare: fair handicapper: stays 17f: acts on polytrack, tapeta and good to firm going: tried in blinkers. *Sylvester Kirk* **65**

DELAHAY 3 b.f. Delegator 125 – Harryana To 57 (Compton Place 125) [2017 –: 5.7m^{5} 7f^{5} 6s^{6} 5.7s p6g Dec 12] no form. *Michael Blanshard* **–**

DELANNOY 3 ch.g. Le Havre (IRE) 124 – Raving Monsun 76 (Monsun (GER) 124) [2017 68: p8g^{6} 12m 9.9f^{4} 10.2g 10.2g^{4} 14s 11.2m* 14.1d Sep 21] leggy gelding: fair performer: won seller at Goodwood in August, subsequently left Eve Johnson Houghton: stays 11f: acts on firm going: wears headgear. *Neil Mulholland* **68**

DELANO ROOSEVELT (IRE) 2 b.c. (Feb 4) Galileo (IRE) 134 – Again (IRE) 115 (Danehill Dancer (IRE) 117) [2017 8g* 8d^{3} 8s^{2} Sep 24] fourth foal: brother to useful 2-y-o 7.4f/1m winner Indian Maharaja: dam, 7f/1m winner (including Moyglare Stud Stakes at 2 yrs and Irish 1000 Guineas), closely related to dam of very smart performer up to 1m Aclaim: useful form: won maiden at Leopardstown (by head from Coat of Arms) in July: best effort when second in Beresford Stakes at Naas (2½ lengths behind Saxon Warrior) in September: will stay at least 1¼m: remains with potential. *Aidan O'Brien, Ireland* **108 p**

DELECTATION 3 b.f. Delegator 125 – Chushka 81 (Pivotal 124) [2017 104p: 8g* 8d 8g^{4} 8m^{5} 8s* 8f Oct 7] smart performer: trained by Bryan Smart at 2 yrs: won Schwarzgold-Rennen at Cologne in April and Europa Meile at Dusseldorf (by 3½ lengths from Millowitsch) in September: 4½ lengths fifth to Roly Poly in Falmouth Stakes at Newmarket: stays 1m: acts on soft and good to firm going: often races towards rear. *Andreas Wohler, Germany* **115**

DELEGATION 3 b.g. Delegator 125 – Rosabee (IRE) 96 (No Excuse Needed 123) [2017 9g 8m^{6} 7m 8v Oct 12] no form. *Tim Easterby* **–**

DE LESSEPS (USA) 9 ch.g. Selkirk (USA) 129 – Suez 109 (Green Desert (USA) 127) [2017 66: f7g Jan 2] lengthy gelding: fair handicapper, well held sole outing in 2017: stays 1m: acts on polytrack and fibresand: usually slowly away/races nearer last than first. *John Murray* **–**

DELEYLA 3 b.f. Acclamation 118 – Alwarga (USA) (Street Sense (USA) 128) [2017 7g^{3} 8g^{6} p7g^{2} t8g^{5} Sep 22] attractive filly: first foal: dam unraced half-sister to smart winner up to 1¼m Kabool: fair form: stays 1m. *Roger Varian* **76**

DELEYLL 3 ch.g. Sepoy (AUS) 129 – Strings (Unfuwain (USA) 131) [2017 58: p8g p7g 10.1m p10g* 11.4m^{2} Jun 12] modest handicapper: won at Lingfield in June: stays 11.5f: acts on polytrack: sometimes wears headgear. *John Butler* **61**

DELFIE LANE 3 b.g. Harbour Watch (IRE) 121 – Anneliina 80 (Cadeaux Genereux 131) **82** [2017 66: p7d^2 p8g^2 p8g* p8g^3 8.3m^2 6.1m^2 6.1m^2 7m^2 6d* Jul 11] good-topped gelding: fairly useful handicapper: won at Chelmsford in March and Brighton (by ½ length from Maazel) in July: placed all other starts in 2017: stays 8.5f: acts on polytrack, good to firm and good to soft going: wears cheekpieces: sold 25,000 gns later in July. *Richard Hughes*

DELIBERATOR 3 b.g. Delegator 125 – Purest (Shamardal (USA) 129) [2017 53p: p8g^3 **76** p8d^5 p11g^6 t9.5g^4 p8g^3 p8g^3 Dec 28] fair maiden: stays 1m: acts on polytrack: tried in hood. *William Knight*

DELICATE KISS 3 b.f. Delegator 125 – Desert Kiss 100 (Cape Cross (IRE) 129) [2017 **71** p8g p12g p10g^4 Dec 13] second foal: half-sister to 7f/1m winner Whispered Kiss (by Medicean): dam 1m-10.3f winner: fair form when fourth at Lingfield on last of 3 starts in maidens: in blinkers last 2 starts. *John Bridger*

DELILAH PARK 3 b.f. Delegator 125 – Sarah Park (IRE) 100 (Redback 116) [2017 **84 p** t7.2g^6 8g^4 t7.2g* Nov 29] second foal: dam, 7f-8.5f winner, sister to useful winner up to 7f Gouray Girl: fairly useful form: won maiden at Wolverhampton (by 2½ lengths from Gustavo Fring) in November: left Philip McBride after second start: stays 1m: likely to do better still. *Clive Cox*

DELIRIUM (IRE) 3 b.f. Tamayuz 126 – Coeur de La Mer (IRE) 87 (Caerleon (USA) **61** 132) [2017 –: 8.2d 8.2g^6 8.1m^2 8g 8.1d^6 p8g 9.9d* p12g Oct 9] modest handicapper: won at Sandown in September: should stay 1½m: acts on polytrack, good to firm and good to soft going: wears cheekpieces. *Ed de Giles*

DE LITTLE ENGINE (IRE) 3 ch.g. Power 117 – Reveuse de Jour (IRE) 79 (Sadler's **–** Wells (USA) 132) [2017 72: t7.2g^6 Nov 29] fair form at 2 yrs, well held sole outing in 2017. *Jamie Osborne*

DELLAGUISTA (IRE) 3 gr.f. Sea The Stars (IRE) 140 – Lady Springbank (IRE) 109 **89** (Choisir (AUS) 126) [2017 74: 8m^3 8m 6g^4 8g^5 6.9v 10.3v^6 9v^2 8.3g^3 t8.6d* p8g* Dec 21] fairly useful handicapper: won at Wolverhampton and Chelmsford in December: left William Haggas after third start: stays 9f: acts on polytrack, tapeta and heavy going: tried in cheekpieces. *Tim Easterby*

DELLA VALLE (GER) 4 b.f. Lando (GER) 128 – Denial (Sadler's Wells (USA) 132) **70** [2017 82: 10m 10s^5 10.2d^2 10d 11.4g 9.9d^6 Sep 20] lengthy filly: fair handicapper: stays 1¼m: acts on soft and good to firm going. *Mike Murphy*

DEL PARCO 3 b.g. Delegator 125 – Sparkle Park 52 (Kyllachy 129) [2017 p7g^2 7m^2 7s^3 **82** 5.7f^4 6d^2 6.1s Aug 17] rangy gelding: second foal: dam, maiden, closely related to useful 7f-9f winner Violet Park: fairly useful maiden: stays 7f: acts on soft and good to firm going: tried in headgear: in tongue tie last 2 starts: usually leads. *Clive Cox*

DELPH CRESCENT (IRE) 2 gr.g. (Apr 20) Dark Angel (IRE) 113 – Zut Alors (IRE) **66** 105 (Pivotal 124) [2017 7m^3 7d^6 7v^4 Sep 9] fair form: best effort when third in minor event at Haydock (4 lengths behind Mildenberger) in July. *Richard Fahey*

DELPHYNE 5 ch.m. Mount Nelson 125 – Darmiana (USA) (Lemon Drop Kid (USA) **67** 131) [2017 f7g t9.5g^4 t10.2g^3 10m Apr 10] fair form: will stay at least 1½m. *Shaun Harris*

DELSHEER (FR) 2 b.c. (Feb 8) Iffraaj 127 – Rose Et Noire (IRE) (Dansili 127) [2017 7g **80** 8d^3 8.1g* Oct 9] €260,000Y: good-topped colt: second foal: half-brother to useful 1m-1¼m winner Alfarris (by Shamardal): dam, 11f winner, half-sister to smart winner up to 11f Free Port Lux out of smart 9.5f-1½m winner Royal Highness: fairly useful form: won minor event at Windsor (by short head from Celestin's) in October: will stay beyond 1m. *Hugo Palmer*

DEMAND RESPECT 4 ch.g. Paco Boy (IRE) 129 – Brilliance 74 (Cadeaux Genereux **–** 131) [2017 –: p12g f8d^5 f7g Apr 18] no form: tried in blinkers. *Henry Spiller*

DEMBABA (IRE) 5 b.g. Moss Vale (IRE) 126 – Wildsplash (USA) (Deputy Minister **–** (CAN)) [2017 t12.2g Apr 5] modest form at best, never on terms sole outing in 2017: in headgear last 4 starts: tried in tongue tie: usually races towards rear. *Gordon Elliott, Ireland*

DEMI'S QUEST 3 b.f. Roderic O'Connor (IRE) 119 – Demi Voix (Halling (USA) 133) **–** [2017 –: t7.1m p8g Mar 2] no form: tried in cheekpieces. *Tony Carroll*

DEMOGRAPHIC (USA) 8 b.g. Aptitude (USA) 128 – Private Line (USA) 105 (Private **–** Account (USA)) [2017 68: p12m Jan 21] twice-raced maiden on Flat: will stay beyond 1½m: tried in visor: fair hurdler. *Emma Lavelle*

DEMONS AND WIZARDS (IRE) 2 b.g. (Mar 5) Elnadim (USA) 128 – Crystal **71** Theatre (IRE) 72 (King's Theatre (IRE) 128) [2017 p8g 7s^4 p6d^4 p7s^2 p8g^2 Dec 23] fair maiden: stays 1m: acts on polytrack. *Sylvester Kirk*

DEMONS ROCK (IRE) 2 b.c. (Apr 30) Requinto (IRE) 109 – Afnoon (USA) 76 (Street **103**
Cry (IRE) 130) [2017 5m 5d^3 5g^2 5.1m^5 5.1d^2 6.1g* 6.1s* 6g* 6d* 6d^4 Sep 13] €27,000F, €45,000Y: strong colt: second foal: dam, 2-y-o 7f winner, half-sister to useful winner up to 1m Shebebi out of Falmouth Stakes winner Tashawak: useful performer: won minor event at Chepstow in July and nurseries at Chester, Catterick and York (by head from Queen's Sargent) in August: stays 6f: acts on soft going: front runner/races prominently: sold 50,000 gns in November, sent to Hong Kong. *Tom Dascombe*

DEMURRER (USA) 2 br.g. (Apr 28) First Defence (USA) 119 – Seeking Ema (USA) **53**
(Seeking The Gold (USA)) [2017 p8g p8g t7.2g p7g Dec 21] modest form in maiden/minor events. *Michael Bell*

DENAAR (IRE) 2 b.c. (Mar 10) Acclamation 118 – Clever Millie (USA) 81 (Cape **94**
Canaveral (USA) 115) [2017 p5g* 6s* 6f 6g 5v 5g^4 p6.5g* p7.5g^2 p6.5g p8g^5 Dec 19] €34,000F, €80,000Y, 300,000 2-y-o: close-coupled colt: half-brother to several winners, including smart 9.5f-11f winner Majeed (by Mount Nelson) and 7f winner (stays 1¼m) Clever Bob (by Big Bad Bob): dam, 7f winner, half-sister to smart Canadian Grade 2 9f winner Points of Grace: fairly useful performer: successful in minor events at Chelmsford and Newbury, both in May, and claimer at Deauville in August: left Richard Hannon after sixth start, Julien Phelippon after seventh: stays 7.5f: acts on polytrack and soft going. *A. Marcialis, Italy*

DENHAM 2 b.f. (Apr 22) Denounce 89 – Fareham (Komaite (USA)) [2017 p6g Oct 12] –
fifth foal: half-sister to useful 5f-6f winner Guishan (by Ishiguru): dam of little account: 50/1, very green when well held in minor event at Chelmsford. *Michael Appleby*

DENMEAD 4 b.g. Champs Elysees 124 – Glorious Dreams (USA) 76 (Honour And Glory **87**
(USA) 122) [2017 77: f14g^2 f14d^4 t16.5g* 14f^3 p16g* 20.6v^5 p16d^2 18d Sep 23] workmanlike gelding: fairly useful handicapper: won at Wolverhampton (dead-heated) in May and Kempton in June: stays 2m: acts on polytrack, tapeta and any turf going: front runner/races prominently, usually travels strongly. *John Butler*

DENVER SPIRIT (IRE) 3 b.f. Invincible Spirit (IRE) 121 – Leavingonajetplane (IRE) –
76 (Danehill (USA) 126) [2017 –: 7s 7g Jun 3] no form. *Luca Cumani*

DEPENDABLE (GER) 2 ch.f. (May 3) Reliable Man 128 – Dessau (GER) 100 (Soldier –
Hollow 121) [2017 p8g Aug 30] €49,000Y: second foal: dam, winner up to 1m (2-y-o 7f winner), half-sister to useful winner up to 1¼m Damour: 33/1, well held in minor event at Kempton. *Charles Hills*

DEREK DUVAL (USA) 3 b.g. Lope de Vega (IRE) 125 – Lady Raj (USA) (El Prado **86**
(IRE) 119) [2017 –: t6g* t6g^3 7m 7m* 7g^2 7d^5 8d 8g t8d p8g^5 Oct 25] fairly useful performer: won maiden at Wolverhampton in March and handicap at Newmarket (by 1½ lengths from Merlin) in June: stays 1m: acts on polytrack, tapeta and good to firm going: wears tongue tie. *Stuart Williams*

DERVISH 3 b.g. Cacique (IRE) 124 – Doggerbank (IRE) 106 (Oasis Dream 129) [2017 –: –
p7g Jan 28] no form: bred to be suited by 1½m+. *John Berry*

DESERT ACE (IRE) 6 ch.g. Kheleyf (USA) 116 – Champion Place 109 (Compton Place **88**
125) [2017 89: 5m^4 5m^4 5m 5m 5g 5s* 5m 5g^6 5g^2 5g^2 5s^2 5.1v^2 5v^2 Oct 21] good-topped gelding: fairly useful handicapper: won at Hamilton (by 1¼ lengths from Black Grass) in June: runner-up last 5 starts: left Iain Jardine after twelfth start: raced mainly at 5f: acts on any turf going: usually wears headgear: has worn tongue tie: front runner. *Paul Midgley*

DESERT CHIEF 5 b.g. Kheleyf (USA) 116 – African Breeze 79 (Atraf 116) [2017 50: – §
f8g f6g p8d^{rr} Feb 8] maiden: no form in 2017: usually wears headgear: starts slowly, often races in rear: one to treat with caution (refused to race final start). *Michael Appleby*

DESERT CROSS 4 b.g. Arcano (IRE) 122 – Secret Happiness (Cape Cross (IRE) 129) **78**
[2017 66: p12g^2 11.6m* 12s 11.8m^3 14g^3 14g* 14.1d 12.1s^2 11.5d^3 Oct 24] compact gelding: fair handicapper: won at Windsor in April and Bath in July: stays 1¾m: acts on polytrack, firm and good to soft going: often races towards rear, usually travels strongly. *Jonjo O'Neill*

DESERT DIAMOND 2 b.f. (Apr 21) Dubawi (IRE) 129 – Arizona Jewel 91 (Dansili **70 p**
127) [2017 p7g p8s^5 Nov 16] third foal: sister to 7f winner Jewel House: dam, 1¼m winner, half-sister to high-class winner up to 1½m Powerscourt and closely related to dam of Frankel: fair form when fifth at Chelmsford on second of 2 starts in minor events: will stay 1¼m: will go on improving. *Sir Michael Stoute*

DESERT DOCTOR (IRE) 2 ch.g. (Jan 29) Society Rock (IRE) 126 – Dorn Hill 55 **85**
(Lujain (USA) 119) [2017 6g^{3} p6g* p6g^{2} Dec 20] 115,000Y: fifth foal: half-brother to 3 winners, including smart 5f/6f (including at 2 yrs) winner Gracious John and 1½m winner Helmsley Flyer (both by Baltic King): dam 6f winner: fairly useful form: won minor event at Kempton (by neck from Lashabeeh) in November: best effort when second in similar event there (½ length behind Worship) in December: raced only at 6f. *Ed Walker*

DESERT DREAM 3 b.c. Oasis Dream 129 – Rosika 112 (Sakhee (USA) 136) [2017 65p: **85**
8.3g^{5} 8.3g* 8m^{5} 10.3d 10m^{6} Aug 25] fairly useful performer: won maiden at Windsor (by ½ length from Cool Team) in May: should be suited by 1¼m+: best form on good going: tried in cheekpieces: sold 10,000 gns in November, joined Michael Easterby. *Sir Michael Stoute*

DESERT ENCOUNTER (IRE) 5 b.g. Halling (USA) 133 – La Chicana (IRE) **121**
(Invincible Spirit (IRE) 121) [2017 109p: 12m* 12g^{2} 9.9m^{3} 12s^{6} 11m* 10s^{5} Oct 21] strong, lengthy gelding: very smart performer: won listed race at Ascot (by 2¾ lengths from Star Storm) in May and Legacy Cup at Newbury (by neck from Second Step) in September: third in Eclipse Stakes at Sandown (3½ lengths behind Ulysses) in July: stays 1¾m: acts on good to firm and heavy going: wears hood: races well off pace. *David Simcock*

DESERT EXPLORER (IRE) 3 b.g. Henrythenavigator (USA) 131 – Bee Eater (IRE) **77**
105 (Green Desert (USA) 127) [2017 p8g^{3} 8f^{3} 8.3g^{4} 11.6g^{pu} Jun 1] fair form in maidens: should stay 1¼m. *Eve Johnson Houghton*

DESERT FOX 3 b.g. Foxwedge (AUS) 128 – Snow Moccasin (IRE) (Oasis Dream 129) **76**
[2017 61p: t6.1g^{2} p7d Dec 13] fair maiden: stays 6f: acts on polytrack and tapeta. *Mike Murphy*

DESERT FROST (IRE) 3 b.c. Dark Angel (IRE) 113 – Layla Jamil (IRE) 85 (Exceed **89 p**
And Excel (AUS) 126) [2017 6m* 7d^{6} May 20] £270,000Y: second foal: brother to smart 5f-7f winner (including at 2 yrs) Birchwood: dam 7f winner: fairly useful form: won maiden at Doncaster (by 1¼ lengths from Crafty Madam) in May: remains with potential. *Saeed bin Suroor*

DESERT GOD (IND) 5 ch.h. Burden of Proof (IRE) 118 – Running Flame (IND) **100**
(Steinbeck (USA) 119) [2017 12g 12g 11.4g^{4} 16d^{4} 14g 16v^{3} 11.4g^{5} p12g^{6} p16d^{6} Dec 13] brother/half-brother to several winners abroad: dam won Indian 1000 Guineas/Oaks: good-topped horse: won 12 of 17 races in India, including Calcutta Derby at Kolkata, Indian Derby at Mumbai, Indian Turf Invitational Cup at Chennai and Indian St Leger at Pune in 2016: useful form at best in handicaps in UAE/Britain in 2017, leaving S. Padmanabhan after second start: stays 2m: acts on good to soft going: in cheekpieces last 2 starts: front runner/races prominently. *Richard Hughes*

DESERT GREY (IRE) 3 b.g. Mastercraftsman (IRE) 129 – Endure (IRE) (Green Desert **77**
(USA) 127) [2017 74: p7s p8g p6g^{2} p6g p10.7g Nov 24] good-topped gelding: fair maiden: left Roger Charlton after fourth start: stays 7f: acts on polytrack: tried in blinkers: often in tongue tie: inconsistent. *Denis Hogan, Ireland*

DESERT HAZE 4 br.f. New Approach (IRE) 132 – Ensemble (FR) (Iron Mask (USA) **99**
117) [2017 102: p8g 8f^{3} p9.4g^{6} 8d Sep 29] sturdy filly: useful performer: third in listed race at Goodwood (5 lengths behind Laugh Aloud) in May: stays 9.5f: acts on polytrack and any turf going: tried in cheekpieces. *Ralph Beckett*

DESERT LAW (IRE) 9 b.g. Oasis Dream 129 – Speed Cop 104 (Cadeaux Genereux 131) **107**
[2017 101: 5g* 5m 5m 5g 5g 5d^{5} 5g* 5.4d* 5g^{6} 5d^{6} Sep 13] strong gelding: useful performer: won minor event at Musselburgh (by 3¼ lengths from Lexington Abbey) in April, and handicaps at Doncaster (by length from Vibrant Chords) and York (by 1¼ lengths from Edward Lewis) in August: raced mainly at 5f: acts on firm and good to soft going: has worn hood: tried in tongue tie: usually races prominently, often travels strongly. *Paul Midgley*

DESERT MOUNTAIN (IRE) 2 b.g. (Apr 29) Epaulette (AUS) 126 – Al Andalyya **63**
(USA) 65 (Kingmambo (USA) 125) [2017 6s a7g^{6} a6f^{6} Nov 23] modest form in minor event/maidens at Newmarket and Meydan (2). *Saeed bin Suroor*

DESERT PATH 2 ch.g. (Jan 29) Champs Elysees 124 – Desert Image 99 (Beat Hollow **71 p**
126) [2017 p8g p8g^{4} Oct 25] first foal: dam, 2-y-o 7f winner, half-sister to useful 1m winner Full Steam: fair form: fourth in minor event at Kempton (3½ lengths behind King And Empire) in October: should do better. *Amanda Perrett*

DESERT RAIN (IRE) 3 b.f. Invincible Spirit (IRE) 121 – Ballantrae (IRE) 96 (Diktat **85**
126) [2017 p6g^{2} 6m^{2} 7d^{5} t6.1g* Jul 17] third foal: closely related to winner up to 9f Tautira (2-y-o 6f winner, by Kheleyf) and winner up to 1¼m Berland (2-y-o 7f winner, by Cape

Cross): dam, 2-y-o 7f winner, half-sister to useful winner up to 7f Badminton: fairly useful form: won handicap at Wolverhampton (by short head from Samarmadi) in July: stays 6f: tried in visor: sold £28,000 in August. *Saeed bin Suroor*

DESERT RIVER (IRE) 4 b.g. Showcasing 117 – Kathy's Rocket (USA) (Gold Legend **69**
(USA)) [2017 73: 6m^3 May 3] fair handicapper: stays 7f: acts on polytrack and good to firm going: has worn tongue tie. *Mark H. Tompkins*

DESERT RULER 4 b.g. Kheleyf (USA) 116 – Desert Royalty (IRE) 96 (Alhaarth (IRE) **86**
126) [2017 79: 8g^2 8m^3 8g^2 9.2g^2 10g^2 p11g^2 p11g Nov 6] workmanlike gelding: fairly useful handicapper: placed on 6 of 7 starts in 2017: stays 11f: acts on polytrack, best turf form on good going: consistent. *Jedd O'Keeffe*

DESERT SKYLINE (IRE) 3 ch.g. Tamayuz 126 – Diamond Tango (FR) 115 **118**
(Acatenango (GER) 127) [2017 95p: 10d^2 10.1m^3 14m^6 13g^2 16g^3 14.9g^2 17.9g* 16s Oct 21]

Not many three-year-olds contest the Cup races these days, which made the achievements of such as Stradivarius, Desert Skyline and Irish-trained Rekindling particularly worthy of note in the latest season. Before he made a big name for himself by winning the Melbourne Cup, Rekindling, who contested both the Derby and St Leger, won the Curragh Cup at the Irish Derby meeting in July (the third successive three-year-old winner of the race), while Stradivarius won the first running of the Goodwood Cup since its upgrade to Group 1 before reverting to three-year-old company to finish a good third in an above-average St Leger (a place ahead of Rekindling). One good, staying three-year-old who couldn't contest any of the major classics was Desert Skyline, who was barred because he is a gelding, a considerable source of irritation to his veteran trainer David Elsworth who joked that he would consider making a personal sacrifice if the vets could perform a transplant!

Desert Skyline had been gelded before he even ran, after proving difficult to handle as a two-year-old, but he went on to win his last two races that season, a maiden over a mile at Yarmouth and a nursery over nine furlongs at Newmarket, looking open to further improvement. Staying was probably going to be Desert Skyline's game eventually and he was stepped up considerably in trip after a couple of placed efforts on his first two starts at three, in listed and handicap company. He didn't shine particularly on his third start, in the Queen's Vase at Royal Ascot, managing only sixth behind Stradivarius, after being dropped right out, but he was then a good second, ridden more prominently, to Raheen House in the Bahrain Trophy at Newmarket, having every chance approaching the final furlong and sticking to his task. Desert Skyline well and truly rose to the occasion in the Goodwood Cup, improving again (in cheekpieces for the first time) to finish third (justifying the £25,000 spent to supplement him) behind Stradivarius and the six-year-old Big Orange who was seeking a hat-trick in the race. Another fine placed effort followed when the staying-on Desert Skyline found only Marmelo too good for him in the Prix Kergorlay at Deauville in August (no three-year-old had contested that race since 2009). That Desert Skyline got to September, though, without a victory as a three-year-old must have been a disappointment to his stable after a run of consistent performances.

'I'm not going to be able to change the rules, am I? But this horse should be lining up for the St Leger,' said Desert Skyline's trainer in the run up to Doncaster. 'I don't know why geldings can't run in the classics, we want to know what the best three-year-old is and if it happens to be a gelding, then he's the best.' David Elsworth was right on both counts. *Racehorses* has been advocating for half a century now that geldings should be allowed to run in all the top weight-for-age events—including the classics—but the traditionalists are no more likely to give way now than they have been for all that time. To them the gelding operation is 'performance-enhancing'—Desert Skyline wouldn't have been the same horse if he hadn't been 'cut'—and, for that reason, geldings cannot run in races which, it is claimed, exist for the purpose of selecting the best colts for breeding (they actually exist for the purpose of providing entertainment!). The fact that high-class colts regularly come up against geldings in the North American triple crown races, and in Australia's classics, for example, has not damaged those races. Far from it. Admitting the best geldings can only provide a stiffer test for the colts which, for breeders, as well as for the entertainment of the general racing public, should be welcome. In any case, what is the justification for still barring geldings from the classics, which test a single generation, when for years they have been allowed to run in races like the King George VI and Queen Elizabeth Stakes, which is potentially a more significant event than any of the classics as it is designed to bring together different generations? It is staggering that the subject still has to be raised at all.

The answer for Desert Skyline's connections was to run him the day before the St Leger in the Doncaster Cup, a race that has traditionally formed part of the so-called 'stayers' triple crown'—last landed by Double Trigger in 1995—along with the Gold Cup at Royal Ascot and the Goodwood Cup. While the two last-named races have gone from strength to strength, with first prizes of £226,840 and £296,593 respectively in the latest season, the Doncaster Cup has been allowed to stagnate and in the latest season its value (first prize £56,710) was half that of York's equivalent staying event the Lonsdale Cup (£113,420)—which is to be linked to the Gold Cup and the Goodwood Cup by a million-pound bonus in 2018—and a long way adrift of that for the Long Distance Cup (£263,418) on British Champions' Day, a race being groomed for elevation to Group 1 status. The fact that the Doncaster St Leger meeting follows fairly closely on the heels of York's richly-endowed Ebor meeting serves only to accentuate the prize money differences between the two meetings nowadays, one that is by no means confined to their Cup races (every race at York had a minimum prize money fund of £70,000, with even the five-furlong apprentice handicap which closes the York meeting having a larger prize than Doncaster's historic sprint handicap the Portland which nowadays opens the St Leger day programme).

More worrying, perhaps, for the St Leger itself are plans reportedly floated to make York's signature handicap the Ebor (run over roughly the same distance as the final classic) into a £1m race, turning it into a northern hemisphere version of the Melbourne Cup. Although three-year-olds rarely get into the Ebor these days (Fields of Athenry finished fifth in the 2015 Ebor before coming third in the St Leger), a £1m Ebor would be a big draw for the top three-year-old stayers. To return to Desert Skyline, he was the only three-year-old in the twelve-strong Doncaster Cup line-up which also included the last two winners, Sheikhzayedroad and Pallasator, as well as the Lonsdale Cup winner Montaly, the Ascot Stakes winner Thomas Hobson, the Gold Cup fourth and Goodwood Cup fifth She Is No Lady (the only mare), Maisons-Laffitte listed winner Fun Mac and those Cup veterans Clever Cookie and High Jinx. Desert Skyline, ridden for the first-time by champion-jockey-elect Silvestre de Sousa, started favourite and proved well suited by the two and a quarter miles, beginning his effort early in the home straight and making good progress to lead inside the final furlong, staying on strongly to win by a length and a half and a head from Thomas Hobson and Sheikhzayedroad, with Clever Cookie, High Jinx and Montaly completing the first six. Desert Skyline was the first three-

Doncaster Cup, Doncaster—following excellent placed efforts in the Bahrain Trophy and Goodwood Cup, Desert Skyline notches a deserved first success in pattern company, beating Ascot Stakes winner Thomas Hobson (third left) and 2016 winner Sheikhzayedroad (hood)

year-old to win the Doncaster Cup since 2011, when Saddler's Rock slammed the Goodwood Cup winner and Gold Cup runner-up Opinion Poll and recorded the best single performance by an out-and-out stayer that year (only the St Leger winner Masked Marvel bettered the effort of Saddler's Rock in a race beyond a mile and a half). The only three-year-old winners in the thirty years before Saddler's Rock were Protection Racket (who went on to success in the Irish St Leger), the ill-fated Kneller, Weld (who beat only two opponents in 1989, though he went on to beat the St Leger runner-up in the Jockey Club Cup) and the filly Alleluia who broke down on her only subsequent outing.

Desert Skyline's only appearance after the Doncaster Cup came in the Long Distance Cup at Ascot where the ground he encountered was much the softest in any of his races so far. He chased the leaders but was being ridden with over half a mile to go and managed only ninth of thirteen behind Order of St George, Torcedor and Stradivarius. Desert Skyline was the only ride on the British Champions' Day card for Silvestre de Sousa whose crowning as the season's champion jockey (the curtain comes down on the 'official' championship nowadays on Champions' Day) was overshadowed by other events on the card, not least a Queen Elizabeth II/ Champion Stakes double for Frankie Dettori, and Aidan O'Brien's achievement of matching the world record by a trainer for Group 1s in a calendar year when winning the Fillies' And Mares' with Hydrangea. Ironically, de Sousa would have had a full book of rides at the afternoon's other Flat fixture, everyday Catterick, had he not been required to attend at Ascot, and it was equally ironic that the ceremony to crown the season's champion apprentice took place at the North Yorkshire track where David Egan and his nearest challenger Kieran Shoemark both had a number of last-day rides (neither rode a winner, with Egan winning the championship by one). Of course, all championships should run from January 1st to December 31st. If a ceremony can take place at Catterick, it can surely take place at Lingfield on December 31st (it is not so long ago that the championships ended three weeks later than they do now, at Doncaster on November Handicap day, at the end of the turf season, which, at least, has a little more logic to it than the present abridged version).

Desert Skyline (IRE) (ch.g. 2014)	Tamayuz (ch 2005)	Nayef (b 1998)	Gulch
			Height of Fashion
		Al Ishq (ch 1997)	Nureyev
			Allez Les Trois
	Diamond Tango (FR) (b 2001)	Acatenango (ch 1982)	Surumu
			Aggravate
		Diamond Dance (b 1991)	Dancehall
			Diamond Seal

The wiry, rather unfurnished Desert Skyline, who is often on his toes and sometimes sweating in the preliminaries, is by the miler Tamayuz who enjoyed a good year, siring the Poule d'Essai des Pouliches winner Precieuse and the E. P. Taylor Stakes winner Blond Me, among others. Desert Skyline's dam Diamond Tango, who won the Prix de Pomone over an extended mile and a half, had six foals before Desert Skyline, the best of them the smart Aga Khan stayer Doumaran (by Authorized) and the useful eleven-furlong winner Dounyapour (by Lope de Vega) who carried the Aga Khan's colours to success in the French Provinces. The family is one of those developed by Jean-Luc Lagardere, whose bloodstock interests were acquired in 2005, after his death, by the Aga Khan. Desert Skyline's great grandam Diamond Seal, who bred nine winners for Jean-Luc Lagardere, is the fourth dam of Irish Derby and St Leger winner Capri in whose essay more can be found about the family. Khalidi, runner-up in the King Edward VII Stakes and the Gordon Stakes, is another smart staying type from the family, his dam Dali's Grey (the dam of Melbourne Cup runner-up Bauer) being a half-sister to the grandam of Capri, Diamilina. Desert Skyline stays two and a quarter miles and acts on good to firm and good to soft going. He has worn cheekpieces in all his races since the Goodwood Cup and is usually held up. *David Elsworth*

DESERT SONG 3 b.g. Makfi 130 – Lyra's Daemon 82 (Singspiel (IRE) 133) [2017 10g 10g^{6} 9.9d 8s p11g^{2} p12g^{6} Nov 21] tall, good-topped gelding: fair maiden: stays 11f: acts on polytrack. *Pat Phelan* **67**

DESERT SPORT (USA) 3 b.g. Hat Trick (JPN) 121 – Desert Sky (IRE) 97 (Green Desert (USA) 127) [2017 80: 5.1m^{4} 5f* 5m^{6} p5d Sep 28] fairly useful handicapper: won at Bath (by 2½ lengths from Fabric) in May: stays 6f: acts on tapeta and firm going. *Robert Cowell* **82**

DESERT STRIKE 11 b.g. Bertolini (USA) 125 – Mary Jane 77 (Tina's Pet 121) [2017 82: f6g p6g p5g Feb 28] rangy gelding: fairly useful handicapper, below best early in 2017: stays 6f: acts on all-weather, firm and good to soft going: wears headgear: tried in tongue tie: front runner/races prominently. *Conor Dore* **58**

DESERT TRIP (FR) 2 b.g. (May 6) Fuisse (FR) 124 – Sea Life (FR) (Anabaa (USA) 130) [2017 6.1m 6.5d Oct 27] tall gelding: little impact in minor event/maiden. *David Menuisier* **–**

DESERT WATER (IRE) 3 b.f. Sepoy (AUS) 129 – Desert Sunrise 75 (Green Desert (USA) 127) [2017 83: 10.3g May 27] fairly useful form on debut at 2 yrs, has gone wrong way: best effort at 1m. *Richard Hannon* **–**

DESERT WAY (IRE) 4 ch.f. Giant's Causeway (USA) 132 – Desert Sage 91 (Selkirk (USA) 129) [2017 88p: 10m^{4} 12g^{3} 9.9m^{6} 10.2d* 10d Aug 14] fairly useful handicapper: won at Doncaster (by 3½ lengths from Parish Boy) in July: stays 1½m: acts on good to firm and good to soft going: sold 17,000 gns in December: has refused to enter stalls. *Rebecca Menzies* **90**

DESERT WIND (IRE) 2 b.c. (Apr 17) Worthadd (IRE) 124 – Matula (IRE) 86 (Halling (USA) 133) [2017 8.3v f7.1g^{3} Nov 28] €10,000Y, £62,000 2-y-o: third foal: half-brother to winner abroad by Invincible Spirit: dam 2-y-o 1m winner who stayed 1¼m: fair form when third in minor event at Southwell on second of 2 starts: should stay beyond 7f: likely to progress further. *Ed Vaughan* **69 p**

DESHAN (GER) 6 b.g. Soldier Hollow 121 – Desimona (GER) (Monsun (GER) 124) [2017 t12.4d^{5} Nov 4] modest form in bumpers/over hurdles: in tongue tie, 12/1, well held in maiden at Newcastle only outing on Flat. *Tim Vaughan* **–**

DESI DARU (IRE) 5 b.g. Indian Haven 119 – Daiquiri (IRE) (Houmayoun (FR) 114) [2017 10.2s 11.6v 8.3g p7s Sep 30] no form, including in bumper/over hurdles. *Conrad Allen* **–**

DESIDERO (SPA) 3 b.f. Sixties Icon 125 – Atasari (IRE) 110 (Whipper (USA) 126) [2017 –: 10d Aug 21] workmanlike filly: no form: tried in cheekpieces. *Pat Phelan* **–**

DESIGNAMENTO (IRE) 3 b.g. Casamento (IRE) 118 – Designed (Zamindar (USA) 116) [2017 –: 10.2g 8d p8g 8.3g Nov 1] poor maiden. *Ed de Giles* **46**

DESIRABLE 4 b.f. Stimulation (IRE) 121 – Hot Pursuits 89 (Pastoral Pursuits 127) [2017 51: f5g^{6} Jan 24] workmanlike filly: modest at best: in tongue tie, well held sole outing in 2017: best effort at 6f: acts on polytrack. *Brian Barr* **–**

DESKTOP 5 b.g. Desideratum 118 – First Harmony (First Trump 118) [2017 66: 14m p16s^{2} 15.9v^{3} f16.5g t16.3s t12.4g t16.3g t16.5d Dec 9] modest handicapper: stays 16.5f: acts on polytrack, tapeta, good to firm and good to soft going. *Antony Brittain* **59**

DESPACITO 2 b.f. (Jan 14) Equiano (FR) 127 – Dongola (IRE) 52 (Xaar 132) [2017 6.1d^{3} 7.4v^{3} Sep 17] compact filly: third foal: dam maiden (probably stayed 1½m): modest form when third in minor events. *Brendan Powell* **62**

DESPERADOS DESTINY 3 b.g. Delegator 125 – Muara 73 (Wolfhound (USA) 126) [2017 82: 6m 6d 6g t5d^{4} 5v^{2} Sep 18] fair handicapper: stays 6f: acts on tapeta and heavy going: in cheekpieces last 3 starts. *Michael Dods* **77**

DESTINATA 2 b.f. (Feb 10) Canford Cliffs (IRE) 133 – Hurricane Lady (IRE) 87 (Hurricane Run (IRE) 134) [2017 p7g^{5} t7.1d^{5} Nov 10] 11,000Y: first foal: dam, 1m/8.3f winner, half-sister to smart performer up to 9.5f Born To Be Alive: modest form when fifth at Kempton on first of 2 starts in minor events: in tongue tie second one. *James Fanshawe* **58**

DESTINATION AIM 10 b.g. Dubai Destination (USA) 127 – Tessa Reef (IRE) (Mark of Esteem (IRE) 137) [2017 59: 7g^{2} t7.1s 7.2d^{4} 7.2m* t7.1d Aug 10] fair handicapper: won at Musselburgh in July: raced mainly at 7f: acts on good to firm and good to soft going: front runner/races prominently. *Fred Watson* **69**

DESTINYS ROCK 2 b.f. (Apr 13) Zoffany (IRE) 121 – Special Destiny (Tobougg (IRE) 125) [2017 t8.6g^{5} t8.6g^{6} Nov 29] €4,000F, €2,500Y, €5,000 2-y-o: fourth foal: dam unraced: modest form in minor events. *Daniel Loughnane* **60**

DESTROYER 4 b.g. Royal Applause 124 – Good Girl (IRE) 100 (College Chapel 122) [2017 87: 7g^{2} 8.8m^{4} 8g* 8g^{4} 8d 7d Sep 10] strong gelding: fairly useful handicapper: won at Pontefract (by short head from Full of Promise) in July: stays 1m: acts on polytrack, tapeta and good to firm going: has worn cheekpieces: front runner/races prominently. *Tom Tate* **86**

DETACHMENT 4 b.g. Motivator 131 – Argumentative 101 (Observatory (USA) 131) **84**
[2017 p8g^{2} t10.2s^{5} 8.5f^{6} 8.5g 8d^{4} 8v Oct 9] fairly useful maiden: raced twice for Mme C. Head-Maarek in 2016: should stay 1¼m: acts on polytrack and good to soft going. *Les Eyre*

DETAILED (IRE) 3 b.f. Motivator 131 – Seraya (FR) (Danehill (USA) 126) [2017 75: **108**
p10.7g^{5} 9.7m^{2} 9.5d^{6} 11.1d^{2} 9.9g* 11.8v^{2} 12s* 10.3v* 14.5d^{4} 12.5v* 12s^{4} Oct 15] useful performer: won handicaps at Ballinrobe in July, the Curragh in August and Roscommon (by 1¾ lengths from Secret Existence) in September, and listed race at Limerick (by ½ length from Cannonball) in October: stays 14.5f: acts on good to firm and heavy going: often races towards rear. *Joseph Patrick O'Brien, Ireland*

DE VEGAS KID (IRE) 3 ch.c. Lope de Vega (IRE) 125 – Fravolina (USA) (Lemon **64**
Drop Kid (USA) 131) [2017 73: f5g^{5} t8.6g t7.1g^{3} p8g^{5} p8g^{4} 10.1m^{4} 8.3d 7d 7.4g^{3} 7m^{2} 9d^{5} 8s^{2} Sep 4] modest maiden: stays 1m: acts on polytrack, tapeta, soft and good to firm going: sometimes wears cheekpieces. *Tony Carroll*

DEVIATE (IRE) 2 b.f. (Apr 18) Acclamation 118 – Divert (IRE) 91 (Averti (IRE) 117) **80**
[2017 6g t5.1g* 5g^{2} 6.1g^{6} 5s^{2} p5g^{3} p5g^{4} t5.1g^{5} Dec 18] sister to winner up to 7f The Art of Racing (2-y-o 5.4f winner) and useful 2-y-o 5f winner Reroute, and half-sister to 3 winners, including 5f-7f winner Available (by Moss Vale): dam 5f winner: fairly useful performer: won minor event at Wolverhampton in July: second in similar event at Ripon in August and in nursery at Bath in September: best form at 5f: acts on tapeta and soft going: front runner/races prominently. *Tom Dascombe*

DEVIL OR ANGEL 2 ch.f. (Mar 13) Assertive 121 – Level Pegging (IRE) 48 (Common **58**
Grounds 118) [2017 5d 5m^{5} 5m p5g Oct 18] £11,000Y: sister to winner up to 1m Go For Broke (2-y-o 6f winner) and 2-y-o 5f/6f winner Goldcrest, and closely related to 2 winners by Bold Edge, including 5f/6f winner Even Bolder: dam ran twice: modest form: raced only at 5f. *Bill Turner*

DEVIL'S BRIDGE (IRE) 3 b.c. Casamento (IRE) 118 – Cantaloupe (Priolo (USA) 127) **92**
[2017 88: 10.3g 8m^{2} 8m^{5} 7.6s^{3} p8g 8f^{4} 8g t8.6g^{3} p8g Oct 26] good-topped colt: fairly useful handicapper: second at Ripon in April and third at Chester in June: stays 9f: acts on tapeta and any turf going: in cheekpieces last 3 starts: front runner/races prominently: sold 10,000 gns in November, sent to Greece. *Richard Hannon*

DEVIL'S COWBOY (IRE) 2 b.c. (Apr 5) Helmet (AUS) 127 – Naseem Sea (IRE) 91 **70**
(Bahri (USA) 125) [2017 5m 6g 6m^{6} 7v 6m Aug 27] angular colt: fair maiden: best effort at 6f: front runner/races prominently. *Charles Hills*

DEVIL'S GUARD (IRE) 3 br.g. Dark Angel (IRE) 113 – Visual Element (USA) 47 **59**
(Distant View (USA) 126) [2017 –: 9v^{6} 7.2m^{4} 8.3s^{2} 9.2s 8.9m t8.6g Oct 21] modest maiden: stays 8.5f: acts on soft and good to firm going: often wears headgear. *Keith Dalgleish*

DEVIOUS SPIRIT (IRE) 5 br.g. Intikhab (USA) 135 – Unintentional 60 (Dr Devious **56 §**
(IRE) 127) [2017 66: t12.4g t8.6m^{rr} t8g^{5} t7.1d 7g Apr 30] workmanlike gelding: modest handicapper: stays 1¼m, effective at shorter: acts on tapeta, good to firm and good to soft going: has worn hood: often slowly away: one to treat with caution (has refused to race). *Iain Jardine*

DEYAARNA (USA) 2 b.c. (Feb 22) Kitten's Joy (USA) 128 – Tanaami (USA) 89 (Elusive **83 p**
Quality (USA)) [2017 7m^{5} 8s^{2} p10g* t9.5g* Oct 27] second foal: dam, 1m winner, half-sister to US Grade 1 9f winner Alwajeeha: fairly useful form: won maiden at Chelmsford (by 2¼ lengths from Dalileo) and minor event at Wolverhampton (by length from Sassie) in October: stays 1¼m: open to further improvement. *Saeed bin Suroor*

DHAHMAAN (IRE) 4 b.c. Kodiac 112 – Heroine Chic (IRE) 69 (Big Bad Bob (IRE) **99**
118) [2017 97, a105: p6m^{4} Jan 20] good-quartered colt: useful performer: stays 6f: acts on polytrack and soft going: has worn headgear, including sole outing in 2017: sent to Bahrain. *David O'Meara*

DHALAM (USA) 3 b.c. Lonhro (AUS) 128 – War Tigress (USA) (War Chant (USA) 126) **89**
[2017 p8g^{2} 8m^{3} t7.2g* p8g^{4} Oct 26] $72,000Y, €160,000 2-y-o: attractive colt: second foal: dam 2-y-o 1m (minor US stakes) winner: fairly useful form: won maiden at Wolverhampton (by nose from Narjes) in May: stays 1m: in tongue tie last 2 starts: sold 18,000 gns in October. *John Gosden*

DHAROOS (IRE) 4 ch.g. New Approach (IRE) 132 – Cailiocht (USA) (Elusive Quality **56**
(USA)) [2017 88: p14g^{5} Sep 7] fairly useful form at 3 yrs, below that level sole outing on Flat in 2017: best effort at 1¼m. *Nigel Hawke*

DIABLE D'OR (IRE) 3 gr.g. Clodovil (IRE) 116 – Caherassdotcom 79 (Compton Place 125) [2017 84: 5.1g 5.7f 7g^4 7m^4 7g^5 t7.2g^5 p7s^6 8d^6 p6s^3 5.3v^6 Oct 19] good-quartered gelding: fairly useful handicapper: stays 7f: acts on polytrack, good to firm and good to soft going: in headgear last 5 starts: sold 8,000 gns in November. *Eve Johnson Houghton* **80**

DIABLERY 2 b.f. (Mar 12) Dalakhani (IRE) 133 – Magical Romance (IRE) 110 (Barathea (IRE) 127) [2017 p8s p8g^4 Dec 20] half-sister to several winners, including 6f-8.3f winner Modern Tutor (by Selkirk) and 1m-13f winner Tall Ship (by Sea The Stars), both useful: dam 2-y-o 6f (including Cheveley Park Stakes) winner, closely related to Oaks/Irish Oaks winner Alexandrova: modest form when fourth at Lingfield on second of 2 starts in maidens. *John Gosden* **51**

DIAGNOSTIC 3 gr.f. Dutch Art 126 – Holistic (Pivotal 124) [2017 7.1s^2 p7d* p7g* p6g* Nov 2] first foal: dam unraced half-sister to smart winner up to 1¼m Cupid's Glory: useful form: won maiden and handicap in October, and another handicap (by 4 lengths from Impart) in November, all at Chelmsford: stays 7f: open to further improvement. *William Haggas* **103 p**

DI ALTA (IRE) 3 b.f. High Chaparral (IRE) 132 – Dibiya (IRE) 102 (Caerleon (USA) 132) [2017 78p: 10.2d^5 t12.4s^6 11.9m^2 11.4g* 12g^5 16.3d^5 Sep 10] small filly: fairly useful handicapper: won at Windsor in July: stays 1½m: acts on soft and good to firm going: has worn hood, including in 2017. *Ed Walker* **89**

DIAMANTE (IRE) 3 b.f. Big Bad Bob (IRE) 118 – Miracle Steps (CAN) 77 (Theatrical) [2017 –p: p8g t8.6g^5 12.1g 9.9g Jun 12] lengthy filly: modest maiden. *Daniel Kubler* **55**

DIAMOND AVALANCHE (IRE) 4 b.g. Alfred Nobel (IRE) 110 – Queens Flight 56 (King's Best (USA) 132) [2017 66: 8.3m 7.2d 7.2m 7m^6 6s t8g^4 t7.1g t8.6g* Dec 5] fair performer: won maiden at Wolverhampton in December: left Patrick Holmes after fifth start: stays 8.5f: acts on tapeta, best turf form on good going: often in headgear: usually races prominently. *Kristin Stubbs* **69**

DIAMOND BEAR (USA) 3 b.f. First Dude (USA) 120 – Lady Mariah (USA) (Giant's Causeway (USA) 132) [2017 74p: 8g^5 10.1m 8.5g^4 p10g^4 p10g p11g^4 Oct 24] fairly useful handicapper: stays 11f: acts on polytrack and good to firm going: tried in visor: sold 7,000 gns in October. *Sir Mark Prescott Bt* **80**

DIAMOND CHARLIE (IRE) 9 br.g. Diamond Green (FR) 121 – Rosy Lydgate 53 (Last Tycoon 131) [2017 61, a79: p6g^4 Jan 11] compact gelding: fair handicapper nowadays: stays 6f: acts on polytrack, soft and good to firm going: has worn cheekpieces. *Simon Dow* **65**

DIAMOND DOUGAL (IRE) 2 b.g. (Apr 7) Zebedee 113 – Blue Saphire (Acclamation 118) [2017 5f^3 5s^3 6.1v^5 7g 6s* 5.9v^2 6.1s^4 5v* 6.1d^4 6s^5 Oct 28] £22,000Y: rather unfurnished gelding: first foal: dam unraced half-sister to smart 6f winner Minalisa: fairly useful performer: won nurseries at Brighton and Haydock (by 2½ lengths from Up Sticks And Go) in September: stays 6f: best form on soft/heavy going. *Mick Channon* **80**

DIAMOND EAGLE (IRE) 5 b.g. Moss Vale (IRE) 126 – Purify (Sinndar (IRE) 134) [2017 –: t8d Feb 4] no form. *Shaun Harris* **–**

DIAMOND EXPRESS (IRE) 2 b.f. (Jan 31) Fast Company (IRE) 126 – South Ring (IRE) 79 (Titus Livius (FR) 115) [2017 5f^6 6g^2 6v^4 5.7d^6 p5g 6s^4 t7.2g Nov 7] €5,000Y, £9,000 2-y-o: compact filly: first foal: dam, 5f winner, sister to useful 5f-7f winner Crimson Fern: fair maiden: stays 6f. *Roger Teal* **65**

DIAMOND INDULGENCE 4 b.f. Cockney Rebel (IRE) 127 – Shaws Diamond (USA) 81 (Ecton Park (USA) 124) [2017 53: t6g^4 p6g^4 p7d 6g^6 6g Aug 15] modest maiden: should stay 7f: acts on fibresand and tapeta: wears hood. *Derek Shaw* **54**

DIAMOND JOEL 5 b.g. Youmzain (IRE) 131 – Miss Lacroix 32 (Picea 99) [2017 85: p16s Sep 8] plain gelding: fairly useful handicapper, well beaten sole outing on Flat in 2017: stays 2m: acts on polytrack, tapeta, good to firm and good to soft going: tried in cheekpieces: front runner/races prominently. *David Dennis* **–**

DIAMOND KUT 4 gr.g. Rock of Gibraltar (IRE) 133 – Diamond Line (FR) (Linamix (FR) 127) [2017 74: t10.2g* Jan 3] fair form: won maiden at Newcastle (by neck from Fastnet Blast) on sole outing in 2017: will stay 1¾m+. *Andrew Balding* **77**

DIAMOND LADY 6 b.m. Multiplex 114 – Ellen Mooney 83 (Efisio 120) [2017 87: p6g* 6g^4 6g^5 6g* 6m 6g^5 5d^2 6d 5m^2 p5d 5g p6g^3 p6g^4 p6g^4 Dec 21] rather leggy mare: fairly useful handicapper: won at Lingfield in April and June (by ¾ length from Compas Scoobie): second at Newmarket in July and August: stays 6f: acts on polytrack, firm and good to soft going: tried in cheekpieces: usually races prominently. *William Stone* **91**

DIAMOND PRINCESS 3 b.f. Bahri (USA) 125 – Rainbow's Destiny (Dubai Destination (USA) 127) [2017 –: f8m Feb 21] no form: wears hood. *Michael Appleby* –

DIAMOND PURSUIT 2 b.f. (Apr 11) Pastoral Pursuits 127 – Broughtons Jewel (IRE) (Bahri (USA) 125) [2017 t5.1g^5 5.3m* 5.7f^4 6m^4 6g 5f^4 6g 7m 5.7s^2 7s^4 p7g^5 t7.2g* p7g^6 p7g^4 Dec 20] 6,500Y: close-coupled filly: first foal: dam unraced half-sister to useful 2-y-o 6f winner Sweet Cecily: fair performer: won maiden at Brighton in April and nursery at Wolverhampton in November: stays 7f: acts on tapeta, firm and soft going: tried in blinkers. *Jo Hughes* 73

DIAMOND REFLECTION (IRE) 5 b.g. Oasis Dream 129 – Briolette (IRE) 112 (Sadler's Wells (USA) 132) [2017 p10g p10g Dec 30] maiden: no form in 2017 (including over hurdles): raced only at 1¼m: in tongue tie last 2 starts. *Alexandra Dunn* –

DIAMOND RUNNER (IRE) 5 b.g. Amadeus Wolf 122 – Hawk Eyed Lady (IRE) 75 (Hawk Wing (USA) 136) [2017 62: 10g t10.2s^2 10.2m* 9.9m^5 12.1m^5 12s^3 10d* 10.2g^3 8d 9.9v t10.2g Oct 20] fair handicapper: won at Nottingham in June and Redcar in August: stays 1¼m: acts on tapeta, good to firm and good to soft going: wears headgear. *Lawrence Mullaney* 65

DIAMONDS A DANCING 7 ch.g. Delta Dancer – Zing (Zilzal (USA) 137) [2017 70: 7.2m^6 10g^5 10.2g* 9.9f^3 11.2s* 10.2g^2 11.6g Sep 7] sturdy gelding: fairly useful handicapper: won at Nottingham (amateur) in July and Carlisle (lady riders) in August: stays 11f: acts on polytrack, tapeta, firm and soft going: wears headgear: front runner/races prominently. *Donald McCain* 81

DIAMONDSARETRUMPS (IRE) 4 b.f. Dick Turpin (IRE) 127 – Serial Sinner (IRE) 65 (High Chaparral (IRE) 132) [2017 –: 6m 8g p7s Jul 7] sturdy filly: little form: left Chris Dwyer after first start: tried in headgear: in tongue tie last 2 starts. *Phil McEntee* –

DIAMOND SET 2 b.c. (Apr 29) Dutch Art 126 – Asaawir 97 (Royal Applause 124) [2017 6f^2 6g^5 Aug 10] fair form: better effort when second in minor event at Haydock (2¼ lengths behind Prestbury Park) in July. *Tom Dascombe* 73

DIAMONDS POUR MOI 4 b.f. Pour Moi (IRE) 125 – Diamond Light (USA) 70 (Fantastic Light (USA) 134) [2017 107: 13.4d 14v^6 Aug 3] tall filly: useful performer, below best in 2017: stays 12.5f: acts on polytrack and heavy going: front runner/races prominently. *Ralph Beckett* 92

DIAMOND VINE (IRE) 9 b.g. Diamond Green (FR) 121 – Glasnas Giant 60 (Giant's Causeway (USA) 132) [2017 59§: p6g t6m^5 p6g t6g p6g 5.7d^2 5.1s^4 6.1m 6.1m 5.7f^6 6s 5.7g Jul 26] good-topped gelding: modest handicapper: stays 6f: acts on polytrack, tapeta, soft and good to firm going: wears headgear: often races in rear. *Ronald Harris* 52

DIANA LADY (CHI) 5 gr.m. Dunkirk (USA) 121 – Lady Kitty Karson (USA) (Carson City (USA)) [2017 p11g p10g p8g p10s 8.3g p10s^5 t12.2g Dec 22] third foal: half-sister to several winners abroad: dam 6f winner in US on only start: won minor event and placed in graded events in Chile in 2015: modest handicapper in Britain: left Rune Haugen after third start: stays 1¼m: acts on polytrack: in headgear last 5 starts: sometimes in tongue tie: sometimes slowly away, often races towards rear. *Luke McJannet* 58

DIBLOAM (USA) 4 ch.g. Hard Spun (USA) 124 – Nuqoosh 103 (Machiavellian (USA) 123) [2017 t7.1g^6 t8d^6 f8m^5 t9.5m t8.6g t12.2g^5 p10g p10g^4 p13.3s^2 p15.8g^5 t12.2g Dec 13] modest maiden: stays 2m: acts on polytrack: in hood last 4 starts. *David Evans* 56

DICHATO (USA) 2 b.g. (Feb 11) Scat Daddy (USA) 120 – Dolce Lemone (CAN) (Lemon Drop Kid (USA) 131) [2017 6f 6g^3 6d^2 7d^3 Jul 20] second foal: brother to minor US winner: dam Canadian 8.5f winner: fairly useful form: placed in minor events at Newmarket (2) in June and maiden in Epsom in July: should stay 7f: sold to join Stuart Williams 20,000 gns in October. *John Gosden* 82

DICKTATION 2 b.g. (Mar 7) Dick Turpin (IRE) 127 – Curly Come Home 87 (Notnowcato 128) [2017 7v 8v^5 Oct 12] no form. *Richard Whitaker* –

DI FEDE (IRE) 2 b.f. (Apr 20) Shamardal (USA) 129 – Dibiya (IRE) 102 (Caerleon (USA) 132) [2017 5m^5 p6g* 7m 7s^2 p8g^3 8v^3 p7g* Oct 25] lengthy filly: sister to very smart winner up to 11f Dibayani (2-y-o 7f winner) and half-sister to several winners, including smart winner up to 1¾m (stayed 2¼m) Dirar (2-y-o 1m winner, by King's Best) and winner up to 1m (stays 1¼m) Dilinata (2-y-o 7f winner, by Spinning World): dam 1½m-1¾m winner: fairly useful performer: won minor event at Kempton in May and nursery there (by nose from Motown Mick) in October: stays 1m: acts on polytrack, best turf form on soft/heavy going: often travels strongly. *Ralph Beckett* 94

DIFFERENT JOURNEY 4 b.g. Poet's Voice 126 – Vintage Gardenia (Selkirk (USA) 129) [2017 78p: 8g^4 6.9g 8d 8g t10.2s 10.2g^5 t8.6g Nov 18] fair maiden: probably stays 1¼m: acts on good to soft going: in blinkers last 2 starts. *Michael Easterby* **69**

DIFFERENT LEAGUE (FR) 2 b.f. (Apr 24) Dabirsim (FR) 120 – Danseuse Corse (IRE) (Danehill Dancer (IRE) 117) [2017 5g* 6s* 6m* 6g^3 6d^2 Sep 30] €8,000F: strong filly: fourth foal: half-sister to French winner up to 1¼m Whipcorse (2-y-o 9f winner, by Whipper) and German 7.5f winner Dream On Me (by Kendargent): dam French 9f-10.5f winner: smart performer: won maiden at Lyon Parilly and minor event at Angers, both in May, and Albany Stakes at Royal Ascot (by neck from Alpha Centauri) in June: placed in Prix Morny at Deauville (1¼ lengths third behind Unfortunately) and Cheveley Park Stakes at Newmarket (1¾ lengths second to Clemmie): bred to stay 7f: acts on soft and good to firm going: sold 1,500,000 gns in December, has joined Aidan O'Brien. *M. Palussiere, France* **110**

DIFFERENT VIEWS (USA) 3 b.g. Proud Citizen (USA) 122 – Elite 71 (Invincible Spirit (IRE) 121) [2017 –: p8g p8g^4 7.5d p9.4g^5 8g^5 9.9g 8d p8g 9.9g^5 7g* 7g^3 8m^4 p9.4f^5 8g* p7.5g p8g p6.5g p9.4g Dec 14] fair handicapper: won at Dieppe in July and Saint-Cloud in September: left Gay Kelleway after third start: stays 1¼m: acts on polytrack and good to firm going: tried in blinkers. *F-X. Belvisi, France* **75**

DIGEANTA (IRE) 10 b.g. Helissio (FR) 136 – Scolboa Gold (IRE) (Accordion) [2017 16m^6 16.8v^4 14.1v^6 14d 18m Oct 14] rather leggy gelding: useful handicapper: stays 2¼m: acts on good to firm and heavy going: tried in cheekpieces: wears tongue tie: often races towards rear. *W. P. Mullins, Ireland* **102**

DIGITAL REVOLUTION 3 ch.f. Monsieur Bond (IRE) 120 – Lujiana 67 (Lujain (USA) 119) [2017 –: 5g^6 t5.1g^3 t6.1g t5g^4 5s^6 5m^5 t5.1g^4 Sep 23] modest maiden: best form at 5f: acts on tapeta. *Antony Brittain* **52**

DILINGER 3 b.g. Equiano (FR) 127 – Dilys 84 (Efisio 120) [2017 7.1s 6.1g p6g Nov 18] lengthy gelding: closely related to useful 5f (including at 2 yrs) winner Macdillon (by Acclamation) and half-brother to 3 winners, including 5.7f-7f winner Dilgura (by Ishiguru) and winner up to 6f Our Piccadilly (by Piccolo): dam 2-y-o 6f winner: little impact in maidens: type to do better in handicaps. *Stuart Kittow* **– p**

DILLIE DALLIE (IRE) 2 b.f. (Mar 28) Zoffany (IRE) 121 – Dalliefour (IRE) 62 (Cape Cross (IRE) 129) [2017 t7.2g^4 Dec 22] 16,000F, 5,000 2-y-o: first foal: dam maiden (stayed 11.5f): 16/1, green when fourth in minor event at Wolverhampton (2½ lengths behind Unveiling) in December: likely to stay 1m: will improve. *Henry Spiller* **63 p**

DIMINUTIVE (IRE) 5 ch.m. Fast Company (IRE) 126 – Take It Easee (IRE) 89 (Noverre (USA) 125) [2017 56, a46: 6.1g 6d 5.1s^5 6.1m 5d^6 5v 6v^4 6.1g 5.7s Sep 17] neat mare: modest handicapper, below form in 2017: stays 6f: acts on polytrack, tapeta, soft and good to firm going: wears headgear. *Grace Harris* **46**

DIMITRE 3 gr.g. Showcasing 117 – Devoted (IRE) 81 (Dalakhani (IRE) 133) [2017 78p: p6s^3 Jun 14] compact gelding: fairly useful form: third in handicap at Kempton sole outing in 2017: raced only at 6f: remains with potential. *Henry Candy* **80 p**

DING DING 6 ch.m. Winker Watson 118 – Five Bells (IRE) (Rock of Gibraltar (IRE) 133) [2017 47: p15.8g^2 p16g Dec 20] small, angular mare: modest handicapper: stays 2m: acts on polytrack, soft and good to firm going: fair hurdler. *Sheena West* **62**

DINNERATMIDNIGHT 6 b.g. Kyllachy 129 – The Terrier 76 (Foxhound (USA) 103) [2017 89: t5.1g^4 t6g^5 5s 6g 5g Jul 3] fair handicapper: stays 6f: acts on polytrack and good to soft going: usually wears headgear: tried in tongue tie. *Richard Guest* **76**

DINSDALE 4 b.g. Cape Cross (IRE) 129 – Emmy Award (IRE) (Sadler's Wells (USA) 132) [2017 71: p12g Oct 3] lightly-raced maiden: well held sole outing on Flat in 2017: fair hurdler. *Michael Scudamore* **–**

DIOCLES OF ROME (IRE) 2 b.c. (Mar 19) Holy Roman Emperor (IRE) 125 – Serisia (FR) 107 (Exit To Nowhere (USA) 122) [2017 7m^6 Sep 23] €38,000Y: half-brother to several winners, including very smart winner up to 1¼m Contributer (2-y-o 8.6f winner, by High Chaparral) and useful 7f-1¼m winner Saimaa (by Zoffany): dam 1¼m/10.5f winner: 50/1, sixth in minor event at Newbury in September: will improve. *Ralph Beckett* **64 p**

DIOCLETIAN (IRE) 2 b.c. (Jan 31) Camelot 128 – Saturday Girl (Peintre Celebre (USA) 137) [2017 8g 8g^6 10m^5 Oct 25] fair form in minor events/maiden. *Andrew Balding* **76**

DIODORUS (IRE) 3 b.c. Galileo (IRE) 134 – Divine Proportions (USA) 125 (Kingmambo (USA) 125) [2017 92: 10d^{4} 12m^{3} p10.7g* t12.4g^{4} Nov 23] useful performer: won maiden at Dundalk in July: left Aidan O'Brien after third start: will be suited by 1¾m+: acts on polytrack, tapeta and good to soft going: in blinkers last 5 starts: sometimes in tongue tie. *Karen McLintock* **99**

DIORE LIA (IRE) 3 b.f. Yeats (IRE) 128 – Cyclonic Storm 78 (Catrail (USA) 123) [2017 8.5g 11.6d^{5} May 12] fifth foal: dam, 1m-9.3f winner, half-sister to smart winner up to 12.5f (stayed 16.4f) Anna Pavlova: modest form when fifth at Lingfield on second of 2 starts in maidens. *Jane Chapple-Hyam* **54**

DIPLOMACY (IRE) 2 b.g. (Mar 30) Champs Elysees 124 – Winter Bloom (USA) 89 (Aptitude (USA) 128) [2017 7v^{4} Nov 7] sixth foal: brother to 7f-1¼m winner Marmot and useful 1¼m-1½m winner Cohesion: dam, 2-y-o 7f winner who stayed 11.6f, half-sister to high-class winner up to 9f Phoenix Tower: 17/2, fourth in minor event at Redcar (8 lengths behind Up Sticks And Go) in November: open to improvement. *David O'Meara* **50 p**

DIPTYCH (USA) 3 b.f. Hat Trick (JPN) 121 – Fork Lightning (USA) 99 (Storm Cat (USA)) [2017 60p: p10d^{5} p10g Nov 2] good-topped filly: modest maiden: should stay 1m+: acts on polytrack: in cheekpieces last 2 starts. *Sir Mark Prescott Bt* **58**

DIRAYAH (IRE) 3 b.f. Dark Angel (IRE) 113 – Folga 104 (Atraf 116) [2017 p6s^{4} Dec 8] 825,000Y: third foal: sister to high-class 5f (including at 2 yrs) winner Mecca's Angel and very smart winner up to 7f Markaz (2-y-o 6f winner): dam winner up to 6f (2-y-o 5f winner): in blinkers, 7/2, green when well held in maiden at Chelmsford. *George Peckham* **–**

DIRCHILL (IRE) 3 b.g. Power 117 – Bawaakeer (USA) (Kingmambo (USA) 125) [2017 6m^{3} 6v^{3} 6.1m^{2} 6d^{2} 6.1d^{3} 6s* 6s^{3} 5s^{6} Sep 20] 9,000F, €48,000Y: lengthy gelding: second foal: dam unraced half-sister to useful 7.5f-9.5f winner Ipswich out of Prix de l'Abbaye de Longchamp winner Imperial Beauty: fairly useful performer: won maiden at Hamilton (by 4 lengths from Hamidans Girl) in August: raced mainly at 6f: acts on good to firm and heavy going: tried in blinkers. *David Barron* **83**

DIRECTORSHIP 11 br.g. Diktat 126 – Away To Me (Exit To Nowhere (USA) 122) [2017 98?: 8f^{2} 8.2d^{2} 8g 8m^{5} 8d 8g^{6} 8g^{5} Sep 15] well-made gelding: fairly useful handicapper nowadays: second at Ascot (apprentice) and Leicester in May: raced mainly at 1m: acts on firm and good to soft going: often races towards rear. *Patrick Chamings* **85**

DIRECT TIMES (IRE) 6 b.g. Acclamation 118 – Elegant Times (IRE) 68 (Dansili 127) [2017 5m Jul 7] strong gelding: useful handicapper at best, below that level sole outing since 2015: stays 6f: acts on good to firm and heavy going. *Peter Chapple-Hyam* **89**

DIRE STRAITS (IRE) 6 b.g. Teofilo (IRE) 126 – Kalagold (IRE) 81 (Magical Strike (USA) 114) [2017 p16d 16d Jul 25] rather leggy gelding: fairly useful at best, little impact in 2017 after long absence: stays 1¾m: acts on polytrack and tapeta: wears cheekpieces: in tongue tie last 2 starts. *Stuart Kittow* **–**

DIRTY RANDY (IRE) 3 b.g. Notnowcato 128 – Regal Fairy (IRE) (Desert King (IRE) 129) [2017 –: f12g^{2} 14m^{6} 12.5s^{6} Oct 9] fair maiden: should stay 1¾m: acts on fibresand: in cheekpieces last 3 starts. *Keith Dalgleish* **66**

DISAPPROVAL (IRE) 2 b.f. (Jan 9) Approve (IRE) 112 – Disko (IRE) 87 (Kodiac 112) [2017 6g 5m p6g^{5} p6g p7g Oct 13] €15,000Y: first foal: dam 2-y-o 5f winner: modest maiden: best effort at 6f: in hood last 3 starts. *Daniel Kubler* **56**

DISCLOSURE 6 b.g. Indesatchel (IRE) 120 – Gemini Gold (IRE) 97 (King's Best (USA) 132) [2017 65: t6f^{2} t7.1m t7.1d^{3} p6g^{5} t6g t6g^{5} 6m 7g p7s 6m^{6} Jun 2] fair handicapper: stayed 8.5f, usually raced at shorter: acted on polytrack, tapeta and good to firm going: often wore headgear: often raced in rear: unreliable: dead. *Declan Carroll* **63 §**

DISCOVERED (IRE) 3 ch.g. Bated Breath 125 – Sandglass 101 (Zafonic (USA) 130) [2017 –: 8m 8g^{6} 7g^{6} p8g Sep 25] good-topped gelding: fair maiden: best effort at 1m: acts on good to firm going: tried in tongue tie: usually races towards rear. *Roger Charlton* **72**

DISCREET HERO (IRE) 4 ch.g. Siyouni (FR) 122 – Alfaguara (USA) (Red Ransom (USA)) [2017 90: 5f^{3} 5.2s* 5m^{4} Aug 28] fairly useful handicapper: won at Yarmouth (by ½ length from Arzaak) in August: stays 6f: acts on polytrack, tapeta and good to firm going: wears tongue tie: races towards rear: sold £7,500 in November. *Simon Crisford* **92**

DISPLAYING AMBER 2 ch.f. (Apr 15) Showcasing 117 – Amber Lane (Compton Place 125) [2017 t6.1g t6s t6.1d^{5} Dec 27] 10,000F, 20,000Y: first foal: dam unraced: little impact in minor events. *Ben Haslam* **–**

DI'S PRIDE 4 b.f. Paco Boy (IRE) 129 – Bramalea 102 (Whitmore's Conn (USA) 117) [2017 f7.1g^{3} Dec 29] first foal: dam 1m-1½m winner: 33/1, well held in maiden at Southwell. *David Bridgwater* **–**

DISTANT HIGH 6 b.m. High Chaparral (IRE) 132 – Distant Dreamer (USA) (Rahy (USA) 115) [2017 68: 10.2m^4 10d 10m 10m^3 12m Jul 14] stocky mare: modest handicapper nowadays: stays 1½m: acts on good to firm and heavy going: wears headgear: usually slowly away, often races towards rear. *Richard Price* **59**

DISTANT PAST 6 b.g. Pastoral Pursuits 127 – Faraway Lass 94 (Distant Relative 128) [2017 102: p5g^5 f5g^5 f5g^2 6m 5d^3 t5g 6s^2 5s Sep 9] compact gelding: useful handicapper: second at Southwell (¾ length behind Sir Billy Wright) in February and Hamilton (nose behind Manshood) in August: raced at 5f/6f: acts on all-weather, good to firm and heavy going: usually wears headgear: usually races prominently: sold to join Ruth Carr 5,000 gns in October. *Kevin Ryan* **97**

DISTANT (USA) 3 br.f. First Defence (USA) 119 – Ventoux (Galileo (IRE) 134) [2017 p12d^5 p10s* p11d^4 p12s p8g Oct 3] first foal: dam, French 1½m winner, half-sister to 1000 Guineas winner Special Duty and to dam of Vintage Stakes winner Expert Eye: fairly useful performer: won maiden at Chelmsford in June: stays 11f: acts on polytrack: in cheekpieces last 2 starts: usually races close up: sold 28,000 gns in December. *Roger Charlton* **84**

DISTURB 5 ch.g. Halling (USA) 133 – Ataraxy (Zamindar (USA) 116) [2017 t12.4g Oct 10] modest form in bumpers: 100/1, well held in maiden at Newcastle sole start on Flat. *Andrew Crook* **–**

DIVA STAR 2 ch.f. (Mar 12) Siyouni (FR) 122 – Kissin Sign (Turtle Bowl (IRE) 121) [2017 6.5g^5 7m^4 7.1s^6 t7.2g Dec 5] €185,000Y: rather leggy filly: second foal: dam unraced half-sister to very smart 9f-12.5f winner Irish Wells: fair form in minor events: stays 7f: tried in tongue tie. *Marcus Tregoning* **65**

DIVINE CALL 10 b.g. Pivotal 124 – Pious 74 (Bishop of Cashel 122) [2017 72: t6m p6g^6 t6g 6m 6.1d^5 6m 6.1m 6m 5.7g t7.2g 6g^4 Aug 30] well-made gelding: fair handicapper, below form in 2017: stays 7f: acts on all-weather and heavy going: wears headgear: tried in tongue tie: usually races nearer last than first. *Milton Bradley* **48** **a56**

DIVINE INTUITION (IRE) 2 b.g. (May 12) Showcasing 117 – Sea Fret (Nayef (USA) 129) [2017 6m^6 6d^3 6.9v^4 7g Oct 16] fair form: left Richard Hannon after second start: best form at 6f: sold £5,800, sent to Italy. *Kevin Ryan* **70**

DIVINE MESSENGER 3 b.c. Firebreak 125 – Resentful Angel 95 (Danehill Dancer (IRE) 117) [2017 7s^4 p6g p6g^4 Nov 18] first foal: dam, 9.5f-11f winner, half-sister to useful winners up to 2m Ascalon and Captain John Nixon: modest form when fourth at Lingfield on last of 3 starts in maidens: bred to be suited by 1m+: capable of better again. *Emma Owen* **58 p**

DIVINE PRINCE (GR) 4 ch.g. Apotheosis (USA) – Pringipessa's Way 72 (Machiavellian (USA) 123) [2017 –: p15.8g p12d p12g Jan 28] modest maiden: stays 1½m: acts on polytrack: blinkered in 2017: sent to Greece. *Amanda Perrett* **51**

DIXIELAND DIVA (USA) 2 b.f. (Apr 4) Cape Blanco (IRE) 130 – Winnie Dixie (USA) 78 (Dixie Union (USA) 121) [2017 7d^2 Jul 21] second foal: sister to a winner in USA: dam 6f winner (in Britain at 2 yrs, later in USA): 20/1, second in minor event at Newmarket (¾ length behind Quivery) on debut: will improve. *Andrew Balding* **79 p**

DIXIE'S DOUBLE 3 b.f. Multiplex 114 – Dress Design (IRE) 84 (Brief Truce (USA) 126) [2017 70: f5g^6 p5g^5 p7g p6g 5m Apr 12] modest handicapper: stays 6f: acts on polytrack and soft going: tried in blinkers: often races prominently. *Daniel Kubler* **62**

DIXON 3 b.c. Lawman (FR) 121 – Pure Song 75 (Singspiel (IRE) 133) [2017 11.5m^6 8s 11.9m p10d^4 t9.5g^2 10.1g^5 p12g p12g Nov 1] fair maiden: stays 1¼m: acts on polytrack and tapeta. *Mark H. Tompkins* **65**

DIZOARD 7 b.m. Desideratum 118 – Riviere (Meadowbrook 83) [2017 16g 11.1g t16.3g Jul 29] maiden: no form in 2017: wears hood. *Iain Jardine* **–**

DIZZEY HEIGHTS (IRE) 5 b.m. Halling (USA) 133 – Extreme Pleasure (IRE) 72 (High Chaparral (IRE) 132) [2017 75: p10m f12g^4 10d^5 12d^3 Jun 6] fair maiden: stays 1½m: acts on heavy going. *Stuart Kittow* **71**

DIZZY G (IRE) 2 b.f. (Apr 28) Red Jazz (USA) 125 – Altogether (IRE) (King's Best (USA) 132) [2017 6v 5.7d^6 Aug 23] €26,000Y, €115,000 2-y-o: fourth foal: half-sister to useful US 1m winner Jeremy's Legacy (including at 2 yrs, by Jeremy) and 7f winner Mollie The Moo (by Requinto): dam, of little account, half-sister to smart 7f/1m winner Tamweel: modest form when sixth in minor event at Bath on second of 2 starts: open to further improvement. *K. R. Burke* **58 p**

D K TRAVEL (IRE) 3 b.g. Jeremy (USA) 122 – Guth Na Gaoithe (IRE) 36 (Invincible Spirit (IRE) 121) [2017 p6g^6 p6s p7g p8g^5 10d p6g^5 6m^3 7d^5 6g 6.3s 7.5s^6 7.2s^3 5s^3 5.8v p7g p7s Dec 8] modest maiden: stays 1m: acts on polytrack, good to firm and good to soft going: often wears headgear/tongue tie. *J. J. Feane, Ireland* **53**

DLTRIPLESEVEN (IRE) 4 gr.g. Dark Angel (IRE) 113 – Namu 76 (Mujahid (USA) 125) [2017 66, a73: p15.8m^3 Jan 9] fair handicapper: stays 17f: acts on polytrack and soft going: tried in blinkers: sometimes slowly away. *Richard Hughes* **75**

DOCK OF THE BAY 3 b.g. Sixties Icon 125 – Kaylianni 101 (Kalanisi (IRE) 132) [2017 12d Aug 19] 25/1, well held in maiden at Newbury. *Mick Channon* **–**

DOC SPORTELLO (IRE) 5 b.g. Majestic Missile (IRE) 118 – Queen of Silk (IRE) 93 (Brief Truce (USA) 126) [2017 88: t6g^2 t5g* t5.1g p6g t5g 5d^6 6v 6v t5.1g p6g Dec 30] fairly useful on turf, useful on all-weather: won minor event at Newcastle (by short head from Justice Good) in January: left Michael Herrington after fifth start: stays 6f: acts on tapeta and heavy going: usually wears cheekpieces: tried in tongue tie: often races in rear. *Tony Carroll* **93 a109**

DOCTOR BARTOLO (IRE) 3 gr.g. Sir Prancealot (IRE) 111 – Operissimo (Singspiel (IRE) 133) [2017 78§: t10.2g* 11.7m^6 8s^3 10.5d 10m* 10d^2 t12.4g^3 Sep 12] fairly useful performer: won maiden at Newcastle in January and handicap at Newbury (by ¾ length from Pilgrim's Treasure) in June: third in handicap at Newcastle in September: barely stays 1½m: acts on tapeta, soft and good to firm going. *Charles Hills* **92**

DOCTOR BONG 5 b.g. Sleeping Indian 122 – Vax Rapide 80 (Sharpo 132) [2017 80: 7d 7.1m^6 8.1m^6 7.4g^5 7m 8.1d* 7.1g^5 7.4v p8g^2 p8g Oct 24] tall, angular gelding: modest handicapper nowadays: won at Chepstow in August: stays 1m: acts on polytrack, good to firm and good to soft going: wears headgear: tried in tongue tie: front runner/races prominently. *Grace Harris* **64**

DOCTOR CROSS (IRE) 3 b.g. Cape Cross (IRE) 129 – Doctrine 97 (Barathea (IRE) 127) [2017 72: 7.4m^3 8.5v^2 10g^5 Nov 3] fairly useful maiden: second in handicap at Beverley in September: stays 8.5f: acts on tapeta, good to firm and heavy going: often races towards rear: remains with potential. *Richard Fahey* **84 p**

DOCTOR DYNAMITE (IRE) 3 b.g. Alfred Nobel (IRE) 110 – Alhaadh (USA) 57 (Diesis 133) [2017 68: 9.9m Jun 27] fair form at 2 yrs, never a threat sole outing in 2017: should stay at least 1m. *Tim Easterby* **–**

DOCTOR JAZZ (IRE) 2 b.c. (Feb 27) Most Improved (IRE) 119 – Daliyana (IRE) 80 (Cadeaux Genereux 131) [2017 p8g Oct 14] €32,000F, £90,000Y: half-brother to 2-y-o 1m winner (stayed 1¼m) Daliyra (by Refuse To Bend) and 1m-12.5f winner Daliyan (by Red Ransom): dam, placed all 3 starts (stayed 1½m), half-sister to smart performer up to 1¾m Daliapour and smart 1½m and 2m winner Dalampour: 14/1, seventh in minor event at Kempton (6¼ lengths behind Indiscretion) in October: entitled to do better. *Richard Hannon* **62 p**

DOCTOR KEHOE 5 b.g. Cockney Rebel (IRE) 127 – Ogre (USA) 84 (Tale of The Cat (USA) 113) [2017 64: t12.2m a14.2g^5 a10.4g^5 a14.2g* 15.9g^6 a11.4g^4 a10.4g a11.4g^4 a11.4g Dec 24] modest performer: left Tim Vaughan after first start: won handicap at Mons in May: stays 1¾m: acts on tapeta, fibresand and firm going: usually wears headgear/tongue tie. *A. M. Verschueren, Belgium* **57**

DOCTOR KNOX (IRE) 2 b.c. (Feb 19) Dawn Approach (IRE) 132 – Queen of Carthage (USA) (Cape Cross (IRE) 129) [2017 8.3v p7d^5 Nov 22] fair form: in tongue tie, better effort when fifth in minor event at Kempton in November. *Paul Cole* **67**

DOCTOR PARKES 11 b.g. Diktat 126 – Lucky Parkes 108 (Full Extent (USA) 113) [2017 84: p6g^5 f5g^5 p5d^4 t6g t5.1g^6 t5.1g 6g^2 5.1m p5s^2 t6.1g^5 6.1m^3 6.1m 6s^6 p6g^6 Sep 26] strong gelding: fair handicapper nowadays: left Stuart Williams after ninth start: stays 6f: acts on polytrack, tapeta and good to firm going: tried in eyeshields. *Natalie Lloyd-Beavis* **63 a76**

DOCTOR SARDONICUS 6 ch.g. Medicean 128 – Never A Doubt 107 (Night Shift (USA)) [2017 102: p5g^2 p6g p5g* 5g p5g* t5.1g^4 Dec 22] strong gelding: smart handicapper: won at Chelmsford in March (by 1½ lengths from Stepper Point) and August (by 1¾ lengths from El Astronaute): raced mainly at sprint trips: acts on polytrack, tapeta, best turf form on good going: front runner/races prominently. *David Simcock* **113**

DODGY BOB 4 b.g. Royal Applause 124 – Rustam (Dansili 127) [2017 82: f6g^4 t6d^6 t7.1g^4 5f^4 6m^4 7.4m 5g^2 5d^4 6.1m^5 7s 6g^6 5.1s^2 5.9s* 6v* 6v 6s^6 f6.1g t6.1g Dec 13] fair handicapper: won at Carlisle (amateur) in August and Hamilton in September: left Kevin Ryan after third start: stays 7f: acts on tapeta, good to firm and heavy going: wears headgear. *Michael Mullineaux* **74**

DOEADEER (IRE) 4 b.f. Dandy Man (IRE) 123 – Bloomsday Babe (USA) (Cherokee **63**
Run (USA) 122) [2017 69: f7g t6m^2 t7.1g t6g f6m 6m Apr 12] modest handicapper: stays 6f: acts on polytrack, tapeta and good to firm going: often wears headgear: often races towards rear/freely. *Keith Dalgleish*

DOHA DREAM (FR) 4 b.c. Shamardal (USA) 129 – Crystal Reef (King's Best (USA) **118**
132) [2017 118: 11.9g^5 11.9g^{ur} 12.4g^2 12.4g^2 11.9d Oct 1] smart performer: twice runner-up to Tiberian at Deauville, in Prix de Reux (beaten short head) and Grand Prix de Deauville (went down by short neck): far from discredited when 8½ lengths twelfth behind Enable in Prix de l'Arc de Triomphe at Chantilly final outing: stays 15f: acts on soft going: usually races prominently. *A. Fabre, France*

DOLLAR AND A DREAM (IRE) 8 b.g. Fruits of Love (USA) 127 – Gorgeous **–**
Georgina (IRE) 68 (Tirol 127) [2017 12v^6 Sep 30] fair hurdler at best: 40/1, well held in maiden at Ripon only start on Flat. *Michael Mullineaux*

DOLLAR REWARD 4 b.g. Shamardal (USA) 129 – Cape Dollar (IRE) 107 (Cape Cross **93**
(IRE) 129) [2017 90: p8g^3 Jan 7] compact gelding: fairly useful performer: third in minor event at Lingfield only start in 2017: stays 1m: acts on polytrack, tapeta and good to soft going: sent to Hong Kong. *Stuart Williams*

DOLLAR VALUE (USA) 2 gr.g. (Apr 17) Exchange Rate (USA) 111 – Makoma (USA) **62**
(Malibu Moon (USA)) [2017 p6g^5 p7g^4 Dec 21] modest form in minor events. *Robert Cowell*

DOLLY DAGGER 2 ch.f. (Apr 8) Pastoral Pursuits 127 – Dance Away 94 (Pivotal 124) **–**
[2017 5m 5s 5g^4 Jun 11] half-sister to several winners, including winner up to 5.5f Foghorn Leghorn (by Medicean) and 6f winner Barron's Lad (by Compton Place): dam 2-y-o 5f winner: no form. *Mark Usher*

DOLLY DIMPLES 3 gr.f. Sir Percy 129 – Brave Mave 83 (Daylami (IRE) 138) [2017 57:
p7m 10.9g 9d 9f^6 a9.5g^6 10.9g^3 10.9g^2 10.9s* 10.9f* 10.4f^5 10.9g^4 Nov 19] modest form **?**
at 2 yrs: left William Jarvis after first outing in 2017: won at San Sebastian in September and Madrid in October: stays 11f: acts on firm and soft going: has worn hood. *J. Lopez, Spain*

DOLLYWAGGON PIKE 3 b.f. Hellvelyn 118 – Once Removed 65 (Distant Relative **40**
128) [2017 6.1m 6m^6 f5g 5.1d f5g^6 Nov 13] £800Y: half-sister to several winners, including 6f winner (including at 2 yrs) Ray of Joy (by Tobougg) and 1¼m winner Tybalt (by Polar Falcon): dam maiden (stayed easy 7f): poor maiden. *J. R. Jenkins*

DOLPHIN VILLAGE (IRE) 7 b.g. Cape Cross (IRE) 129 – Reform Act (USA) 112 **83**
(Lemon Drop Kid (USA) 131) [2017 93: p12g^2 t13.9m^4 p11g^5 12g^3 11.9g t12.4s 12d **a92**
p10g p11g 11.5d 12.1s^6 t12.2g t12.2d^3 t12.2d^5 Dec 26] smallish gelding: fairly useful handicapper: second at Lingfield in January: left Jane Chapple-Hyam after first start: stays 12.5f: acts on polytrack, tapeta, good to firm and heavy going: usually wears hood: has worn tongue tie, including in 2017. *Shaun Harris*

DOLPHIN VISTA (IRE) 4 b.g. Zoffany (IRE) 121 – Fiordiligi (Mozart (IRE) 131) [2017 **111**
105: 8g^5 9m 10g^6 9d* p10g^5 Dec 23] sturdy gelding: smart handicapper: won Cambridgeshire Handicap at Newmarket (by 1½ lengths from Sands Chorus) in September: left Richard Fahey after second start: stays 1¼m: acts on good to firm and heavy going: often races prominently. *Martyn Meade*

DOLYDAYDREAM 2 b.f. (Feb 7) Equiano (FR) 127 – Ellie In The Pink (IRE) 85 **–**
(Johannesburg (USA) 127) [2017 6.1g p7g p8g Nov 1] angular filly: first foal: dam 6f-7.6f winner who stayed 1¼m: little impact in minor events. *Pat Phelan*

Betfred Cambridgeshire (Heritage Handicap), Newmarket—Dolphin Vista (right) resumes winning ways on just his second start for the Martyn Meade yard, springing a 50/1 surprise under 3-lb claimer George Wood; Sands Chorus (pale colours and dark cap), Cote d'Azur (white face) and Dolphin Vista's stablemate Chelsea Lad (near rail) complete the frame; Brorocco, chasing the winner, finishes fifth

totepool Live Info Download The App Phil Bull Trophy Conditions Stakes, Pontefract—Dominating stays on strongly to provide trainer Mark Johnston with a 4000th winner on the Flat in Britain; the win is also a 100th of the season for jockey PJ McDonald

DOMINANNIE (IRE) 4 b.f. Paco Boy (IRE) 129 – English Rose (USA) (Kafwain (USA) 118) [2017 70: t8g 8d^4 8g^4 8.3v^4 8g^3 8g^6 Aug 29] fair maiden: stays 8.5f: acts on good to firm and heavy going: sometimes slowly away. *Sally Haynes* **65**

DOMINATING (GER) 3 ch.g. Jukebox Jury (IRE) 123 – Dominante (GER) 107 (Monsun (GER) 124) [2017 73: 9.9f^6 11.9d 14g* 14m* 14m^2 16g* p16s^2 13.9m 14s^2 t16.3g^3 16d* 13.9g 18v* Oct 23] strong gelding: useful handicapper: won at Nottingham in May, Sandown in June, Musselburgh in July, and at Ascot (by neck from Altaayil) and Pontefract (Phil Bull Trophy) in October: stays 2¼m: acts on polytrack, tapeta, good to firm and heavy going: usually races prominently, often travels strongly. *Mark Johnston* **101**

DOMINIUM (USA) 10 b.g. E Dubai (USA) 124 – Sudenlylastsummer (USA) (Rinka Das (USA) 107) [2017 77, a83: t7.1m^4 t6m^6 t7.1g p7d^5 p6g p7g Mar 29] leggy gelding: shows traces of stringhalt: fair handicapper nowadays: stays 7f: acts on polytrack, tapeta and good to firm going: wears headgear: often races towards rear. *Jeremy Gask* **73**

DOMITILLA 3 b.f. Cape Cross (IRE) 129 – Dan Loose Daughter (Sakhee (USA) 136) [2017 7g^4 p7g^2 p7d^2 p7g* Dec 6] €45,000Y, 72,000 2-y-o: first foal: dam, Italian 1¼m winner (including at 2 yrs), half-sister to smart winner up to 11f Storming Loose: fairly useful form: won handicap at Lingfield (by 2¼ lengths from Temeraire) in December: bred to be suited by 1m+: tried in hood: open to further improvement. *Marco Botti* **87 p**

DONERAILE (IRE) 3 b.g. Requinto (IRE) 109 – Yaky Romani (IRE) (Victory Note (USA) 120) [2017 –: f6g^6 Jan 10] no form: in cheekpieces sole outing in 2017. *Robert Eddery* **–**

DONJUAN TRIUMPHANT (IRE) 4 b.c. Dream Ahead (USA) 133 – Mathuna (IRE) (Tagula (IRE) 116) [2017 117, a109: p8g 7g^3 6d 7g* 6v* 6s Oct 21] strong, lengthy colt: smart performer: won minor event (by 1¼ lengths from Yattwee) and Gold Cup Handicap (by short head from Stake Acclaim), both at Haydock in September: stays 7f: acts on polytrack, good to firm and heavy going: wears hood: tried in tongue tie. *Andrew Balding* **119**

DONNACHIES GIRL (IRE) 4 b.f. Manduro (GER) 135 – Russian Society 103 (Darshaan 133) [2017 12m 6.9g 8d^4 12.1m* 13.1s* 13.1g^2 t12.4g* 11.6g^2 12.1s^3 13s^6 12.5v^2 12g* Nov 3] £7,000 3-y-o: half-sister to 3 winners, including useful winner up to 1½m Petrovsky (2-y-o 1m winner, by Daylami) and 1¼m-1½m winner Scarab (by Machiavellian): dam, 1¼m winner, half-sister to winner up to 11f Tahaamah and 10.5f winner Buckwheat (by Manduro) (both smart): modest form in bumpers: fairly useful handicapper: won at Hamilton (twice) in June, Newcastle in July and Newmarket in November: stays 13f: acts on tapeta, good to firm and heavy going: tried in cheekpieces. *Alistair Whillans* **82**

DONNA FINCHELLA (IRE) 3 b.f. Casamento (IRE) 118 – Air Maze 80 (Dansili 127) **56**
[2017 8.3g 8.1m 9.9d May 18] €24,000F, £34,000Y: useful-looking filly: third foal: half-sister to winner up to 8.3f Harlequin Striker (2-y-o 7f winner, by Bahamian Bounty): dam, 9.5f/1¼m winner, half-sister to useful 1¼m/11f winner (stayed 13f) Pivotal Answer: modest form when seventh at Windsor on second of 3 starts in maidens. *Brian Meehan*

DONNCHA (IRE) 6 br.g. Captain Marvelous (IRE) 114 – Seasonal Style (IRE) 93 **108**
(Generous (IRE) 139) [2017 111: 8g^3 8m 7.9d 8.1g 7g Jul 15] tall gelding: useful handicapper: third in Lincoln at Doncaster (½ length behind Bravery) in April: stays 8.5f: acts on polytrack, good to firm and heavy going: usually races nearer last than first. *Robert Eddery*

DONNELLY'S RAINBOW (IRE) 4 b.g. Lilbourne Lad (IRE) 111 – Donnelly's **73**
Hollow (IRE) 71 (Docksider (USA) 124) [2017 77: 7.1m 7d^4 7g 7s^2 7s^3 7.2v^3 Oct 16] fair handicapper: raced only at 7f: acts on heavy going: tried in hood/tongue tie: sometimes slowly away. *Rebecca Bastiman*

DONNY BELLE 2 b.f. (Feb 20) Doncaster Rover (USA) 114 – Speedy Senorita (IRE) 79 **71**
(Fayruz 116) [2017 5s^3 5g^2 5m^5 6d^6 5m Sep 4] second foal: dam 5f winner including at 2 yrs: fair maiden: best form at 5f: acts on soft going. *David Brown*

DON PADEJA 7 br.g. Dansili 127 – La Leuze (IRE) (Caerleon (USA) 132) [2017 –: 12m **–**
Jul 4] fairly useful at best, lightly raced and little form on Flat since 2013: stays 1¾m: acts on polytrack, good to firm and good to soft going: tried in cheekpieces/tongue tie: fairly useful hurdler. *Fergal O'Brien*

DON PEPE (IRE) 2 b.c. (Mar 25) Havana Gold (IRE) 118 – Woodmaven (USA) (Woodman **61 p**
(USA) 126) [2017 6m^6 Jun 17] 57,000F, €100,000 2-y-o: half-brother to several winners, including 7f winner Sylvestris (by Arch) and 2-y-o 5f winner (stayed 7f) Roof Fiddle (by Cat Thief), both useful: dam, ran twice in USA, half-sister to 1000 Guineas runner-up Arch Swing: 6/1, sixth in maiden at York (6 lengths behind International Man) in June: entitled to do better. *Richard Hannon*

DON'T BLAME ME 4 b.g. Captain Gerrard (IRE) 113 – Dragon Flyer (IRE) 105 **81**
(Tagula (IRE) 116) [2017 80: p6g^2 6.1g t6.1g p6g p6g^6 t6.1g^3 p5g Dec 12] sturdy gelding: fairly useful handicapper: placed at Lingfield in March and Wolverhampton in November: stays 6f: acts on polytrack, tapeta and soft going. *Clive Cox*

DON'T CRY ABOUT IT (IRE) 2 ch.g. (Mar 1) Casamento (IRE) 118 – Back At de **–**
Front (IRE) 70 (Cape Cross (IRE) 129) [2017 p6g p6g^6 p7g Oct 18] little impact in minor events. *Ali Stronge*

DONTFORGETTOCALL 3 ch.g. Foxwedge (AUS) 128 – Shaken And Stirred **64**
(Cadeaux Genereux 131) [2017 69: t5d^6 6g 6s p5g^2 t5.1m^3 p6g^3 Nov 17] modest maiden: best form at 5f: acts on polytrack, best turf form on heavy going: tried in headgear. *Joseph Tuite*

DON'T GIVE UP 3 b.c. Dubawi (IRE) 129 – Avongrove 108 (Tiger Hill (IRE) 127) [2017 **104**
p7g* 8d^2 10m* 10.2s p8g^5 Oct 4] sturdy colt: second foal: brother to 2-y-o 7f winner (stays 1½m) Welford: dam, 11f winner, half-sister to smart 1½m-2¼m winner Veracity: useful performer: won maiden at Kempton in June and handicap at Windsor (by head from New Agenda) in August: second in handicap at Newmarket (½ length behind Pillar of Society) in July: stays 1¼m: acts on polytrack, good to firm and good to soft going: tried in cheekpieces. *Saeed bin Suroor*

DONTGIVEUPONBOB 2 b.g. (Apr 26) Pastoral Pursuits 127 – Parsonagehotelyork **72**
(IRE) 62 (Danehill (USA) 126) [2017 5m^5 6s^4 5.5s^3 6m^2 7.2m^5 7m 8v^3 7s 10v^3 Oct 9] sturdy gelding: fair maiden: stays 1¼m: acts on good to firm and heavy going. *Richard Fahey*

DON'T TELL NIK (IRE) 4 b.f. Lawman (FR) 121 – Karliysha (IRE) (Kalanisi (IRE) **–**
132) [2017 –: t10.2g Jan 11] no form: tried in hood: usually races towards rear. *Roger Fell*

DON'T TOUCH 5 b.g. Dutch Art 126 – Expressive 81 (Falbrav (IRE) 133) [2017 117: 7g^2 **106**
t6s 7g 6d^6 7g^6 Oct 7] strong gelding: useful performer nowadays: second in Ballycorus Stakes at Leopardstown (2½ lengths behind Flight Risk) in June: stays 7f: acts on tapeta, good to firm and good to soft going: has worn headgear, including in 2017. *Richard Fahey*

DONTTOUCHTHECHIPS (IRE) 4 b.g. Lilbourne Lad (IRE) 111 – Trim (IRE) (Ela- **–**
Mana-Mou 132) [2017 72: 6.1d 10m Jul 4] fair maiden, well beaten both starts in 2017: stays 1m: acts on soft and good to firm going: tried in hood: front runner/races prominently. *Nikki Evans*

DON VALENTINO (IRE) 3 b.g. Dandy Man (IRE) 123 – My Funny Valentine (IRE) 105 (Mukaddamah (USA) 125) [2017 7.1m^4 6g^3 6s^2 6m* 6g* Jul 3] €18,000F, €40,000Y: half-brother to several winners, including smart 2-y-o 6f winner Murbeh (by Elusive City) and 1m-1¼m winner Pink Ribbon (by Dark Angel): dam winner up to 1m (2-y-o 5f/6f winner): fairly useful performer: won maiden at Ripon in June and minor event at Pontefract (by 2¼ lengths from Acadian Angel) in July: stays 6f: acts on soft and good to firm going: usually races close up/travels strongly: sold 100,000 gns later in July, sent to Qatar. *David O'Meara* **91**

DOODLE DANDY (IRE) 4 b.f. Starspangledbanner (AUS) 128 – Grid Lock (IRE) (Van Nistelrooy (USA) 108) [2017 p8g^6 f8g 8.3g p7g^5 7d 8.1m^4 9.9d Sep 20] €7,000F, £4,000 3-y-o: compact filly: first foal: dam unraced: fair maiden: should stay 1¼m: acts on polytrack: tried in cheekpieces: front runner/races prominently. *David Bridgwater* **61 a67**

DORA'S FIELD (IRE) 4 b.f. Rip Van Winkle (IRE) 134 – Rydal Mount (IRE) 96 (Cape Cross (IRE) 129) [2017 77: 10d^2 10g^6 10d 10g Oct 17] angular filly: fair maiden: stays 1¼m: acts on good to soft going: tried in cheekpieces: sometimes slowly away. *Stuart Kittow* **76**

DORCAS 2 b.f. (Feb 27) Havana Gold (IRE) 118 – Mortitia 97 (Dansili 127) [2017 p5g^4 6g^4 6g* 7m 7v^6 Sep 30] £8,500Y: second foal: half-sister to 1¼m winner (stays 1½m) Huddersfilly Town (by Major Cadeaux): dam 2-y-o 6f winner: fair performer: won minor event at Ripon in August: best form at 6f on good going. *James Given* **67**

DOREEN 3 b.f. Dansili 127 – Hi Calypso (IRE) 114 (In The Wings 128) [2017 –p: t12.2g^3 11.8d p12g Jun 22] fair form: best effort at 1½m. *Sir Michael Stoute* **66**

DORELLA (GER) 2 b.f. (Feb 27) Reliable Man 128 – Diacada (GER) 108 (Cadeaux Genereux 131) [2017 t8.6g^4 p8d^6 Dec 13] 48,000F: half-sister to numerous winners, including useful winner up to 7f Diatribe (2-y-o 6f winner, by Tertullian) and useful winner up to 9f Daktani (2-y-o 7f/1m winner, by Kallisto): dam winner up to 1m (2-y-o 6f winner): fair form: better effort when fourth in minor event at Wolverhampton (3½ lengths behind Ghanimah) in November. *Eve Johnson Houghton* **70**

DORIAN GRAY (IRE) 2 b.g. (Feb 21) So You Think (NZ) 133 – Flawless Beauty 91 (Excellent Art 125) [2017 p7s p8g f7.1g^3 f8.1g^6 Dec 11] €25,000F, 40,000Y: big gelding: first foal: dam, 2-y-o 6f winner who stayed 1m, half-sister to Breeders' Cup Juvenile Turf winner Wrote: modest form: should stay 1m+: should do better. *Hughie Morrison* **63 p**

DORIA ROAD (USA) 3 b.f. Quality Road (USA) 131 – Celestic (USA) (Sky Classic (CAN)) [2017 65p: 6g^3 p7g^6 8g^3 8d p8g^3 t8g* t8.6g^5 Nov 11] compact filly: fair handicapper: won at Newcastle in October: stays 8.5f: acts on polytrack and tapeta. *Kevin Ryan* **73**

DOR'S LAW 4 b.f. Lawman (FR) 121 – Law of Chance (Pennekamp (USA) 130) [2017 65: t9.5g t9.5g p10g 10.1g^4 8m^5 p10g^6 p10d 8g^3 p8g^2 t9.5g^5 p8s^2 p8s^4 Dec 8] modest maiden: stays 11.5f, effective at shorter: acts on polytrack and heavy going: in cheekpieces last 5 starts. *Dean Ivory* **63**

DOSE 4 b.f. Teofilo (IRE) 126 – Prescription 103 (Pivotal 124) [2017 64: t9.5m^3 f8g* t8.6g^2 t7.1g^3 f8g^5 8.5m^3 10g^4 f8.1g Dec 22] fair handicapper: won at Southwell in January: stays 1¼m: acts on fibresand, tapeta, good to firm and good to soft going. *Richard Fahey* **71**

DOSWELL (USA) 2 br.g. (May 26) Giant's Causeway (USA) 132 – Ballet Pacifica (USA) 104 (Minardi (USA) 119) [2017 7m^2 Jul 14] sixth foal: brother to US 6.5f-8.5f winner Entrechat and half-brother to 8.5f (minor US stakes) winner Secretary At War (by War Front), both useful: dam, 7f-1¼m winner, half-sister to smart 8.4f winner Ariege: 20/1, shaped well when second in maiden at Newmarket (head behind Being There) on debut: useful prospect. *John Gosden* **87 p**

DOT GREEN (IRE) 4 b.f. Lawman (FR) 121 – Katajan (Halling (USA) 133) [2017 88: 8m^5 8.3g^6 7.4f 7m Aug 17] rather leggy filly: fairly useful handicapper, below form in 2017: stays 1¼m: acts on polytrack and firm going: sometimes slowly away, often races towards rear. *Mark H. Tompkins* **70**

DOTTED SWISS (IRE) 2 b.f. (Mar 3) Swiss Spirit 117 – Luxuria (IRE) 59 (Kheleyf (USA) 116) [2017 p6g* p7g p7g p5g^2 Nov 21] 35,000F, £80,000Y: fifth foal: half-sister to 3 winners, including temperamental 5f/6f winner Crisis Averted (by Compton Place) and 2-y-o 5f winner Moving Melody (by Equiano): dam, 2-y-o 6f winner, half-sister to useful winner up to 1m Sweepstake: fairly useful form: won minor event at Lingfield in May: second in nursery there in November: stays 6f. *Richard Hannon* **80**

DOUBLE DUTCH 3 ch.g. Dutch Art 126 – Duchess Dora (IRE) 108 (Tagula (IRE) 116) [2017 –p: p6g f8g 7s Jul 22] no form. *John Butler* –

DOUBLE REFLECTION 2 b.f. (Mar 21) Showcasing 117 – Green And Bleue (Green **77**
Tune (USA) 125) [2017 5g^4 6.1v* 7.2d 8.1g^3 8v^6 Sep 28] £7,000Y: fourth foal: half-sister to winner up to 1¼m Mister Anthony (2-y-o 1m winner, by Sakhee's Secret): dam unraced: fair performer: won minor event at Chepstow in July: stays 1m: acts on heavy going. *K. R. Burke*

DOUBLE SPIN 3 b.f. Hard Spun (USA) 124 – Dear Lavinia (USA) (Grand Slam (USA) **67**
120) [2017 74p: p7g^6 p6g^5 t5s^2 5d^4 5f 6.1m^5 p6d Aug 23] good-topped filly: fair maiden: left John Gosden after first start: stays 7f: acts on polytrack and tapeta: tried in cheekpieces. *Robert Cowell*

DOUBLET (IRE) 2 b.c. (Mar 21) Epaulette (AUS) 126 – Biaraafa (IRE) 82 (Araafa (IRE) **96**
128) [2017 7f^6 7d* 7d* a7f^6 Dec 7] €130,000F: second foal: dam, winner up to 7f (2-y-o 6f winner), half-sister to dam of top-class performer up to 1½m Postponed: useful form: successful at Epsom in maiden in July and minor event (by 2¾ lengths from Guvenor's Choice) in August: left Mark Johnston after: will stay 1m. *S. bin Ghadayer, UAE*

DOUBLE UP 6 b.g. Exceed And Excel (AUS) 126 – My Love Thomas (IRE) 84 (Cadeaux **115**
Genereux 131) [2017 111: 5.2g^5 5.1d^2 p6g* t6.1d^4 Dec 26] workmanlike gelding: smart performer: won handicap at Kempton (by ¾ length from Intisaab) in November: stays 6f: acts on polytrack, tapeta and firm going: wears tongue tie. *Roger Varian*

DOUGAN 5 b.g. Dutch Art 126 – Vive Les Rouges 91 (Acclamation 118) [2017 108: t5g^3 **106**
p6g p7g 6.1d^6 6m^2 6.1g 5g^6 6g^5 6.1s 6.5g^3 p6g 6d Oct 27] good-topped gelding: useful performer: placed in minor event at Newcastle (1¼ lengths behind Doc Sportello) in January and handicaps at Doncaster in June (head behind Pipers Note) and September: stays 7f: acts on polytrack, tapeta and good to firm going. *David Evans*

DOUGLAS MACARTHUR (IRE) 3 b.c. Galileo (IRE) 134 – Alluring Park (IRE) 97 **116**
(Green Desert (USA) 127) [2017 108: 10d^2 10m* 12m 12g^5 11.9d^4 14.5g Sep 16] rather leggy colt: smart performer: won Derrinstown Stud Derby Trial at Leopardstown (by head from Yucatan) in May: stays 1½m: acts on good to firm and good to soft going: tried in hood: usually races close up: has joined Liam Howley in Australia. *Aidan O'Brien, Ireland*

DOURADO (IRE) 3 b.c. Dark Angel (IRE) 113 – Skehana (IRE) 69 (Mukaddamah **89**
(USA) 125) [2017 78: 7g^5 7d* 7m* 7m p7g^3 p7g* Nov 6] good-topped colt: fairly useful handicapper: won at Epsom (twice) in August and Kempton (by head from Glenn Coco) in November: stays 7.5f: acts on polytrack, good to firm and good to soft going: often travels strongly. *Patrick Chamings*

DOVE MOUNTAIN (IRE) 6 b.g. Danehill Dancer (IRE) 117 – Virginia Waters (USA) **68**
116 (Kingmambo (USA) 125) [2017 69: t9.5m^4 t8.6m^2 t9.5g^6 t9.5m t12.2g 11.5m^3 9.9g* 11.8g Jul 20] fair handicapper: won at Brighton in July: left Anabel K. Murphy after sixth start: stays 1½m: acts on polytrack, tapeta, soft and good to firm going: wears headgear/tongue tie: sometimes slowly away, often races towards rear. *Olly Murphy*

DOVILS DATE 8 gr.g. Clodovil (IRE) 116 – Lucky Date (IRE) 91 (Halling (USA) 133) **79**
[2017 78: t12.2g t13.9g t12.2g p12g^6 14g* 16m* p15.8g* Oct 18] sturdy gelding: fair handicapper: won at Lingfield in May, Chepstow in June and Lingfield again in October: stays 16.5f: acts on polytrack, tapeta, soft and good to firm going. *Tim Vaughan*

DOVIL'S DUEL (IRE) 6 b.g. Clodovil (IRE) 116 – Duelling 80 (Diesis 133) [2017 70: **67 §**
t8.6m^6 t9.5g^4 10m^2 10g p8g^5 7.5d 8.2s 7.8g a7g 7v 7v p7g p8g Nov 8] leggy, dipped-backed gelding: fair handicapper: left Tony Newcombe after second start, Gavin Patrick Cromwell after ninth: stays 1¼m: acts on polytrack, firm and soft going: has worn headgear, including in 2017: has worn tongue tie: front runner/races prominently, tends to find little: one to treat with caution. *Richard John O'Brien, Ireland*

DOWAYLA (IRE) 3 b.f. Sepoy (AUS) 129 – Baheeja 100 (Dubawi (IRE) 129) [2017 83: **97**
t8.6g^6 9.8m^2 8f* 8d^2 p10s^3 8g^3 a8f Nov 9] neat filly: useful handicapper: won at Bath in July: second at Newmarket (2¼ lengths behind Zymyran) in August and third at Chelmsford (3 lengths behind Blushing Rose) in September: stays 1¼m: acts on tapeta and firm going: tried in cheekpieces: front runner/races prominently. *Saeed bin Suroor*

DOWITCHER (USA) 2 b.f. (Apr 18) Lonhro (AUS) 128 – Danelagh (AUS) (Danehill **– p**
(USA) 126) [2017 6s^6 Aug 9] half-sister to several winners, including high-class Hong Kong performer up to 1½m Vengeance of Rain and Australian 6.5f-1½m (Group 1) winner Dizelle (both by Zabeel): dam Australian Group 1 6f winner: 8/1, well held in minor event at Pontefract: should do better. *Mark Johnston*

DOWNFORCE (IRE) 5 b.g. Fast Company (IRE) 126 – Spinning Ruby 94 (Pivotal 124) **115**
[2017 106: 6v* 5m 6d^{4} 6d^{2} 6s^{5} 7.5v^{2} 6d Nov 1] tall gelding: smart performer: won listed race at Cork (by 12 lengths from Penny Pepper) in April: second after in similar event at York (nose behind Tommy Taylor) and Concorde Stakes at Tipperary (½ length behind Psychedelic Funk): stays 7.5f: acts on good to firm and heavy going: usually travels strongly. *W. McCreery, Ireland*

DOWN TIME (USA) 7 b.g. Harlan's Holiday (USA) 124 – Frappay (USA) (Deputy **50**
Minister (CAN)) [2017 77: 16v^{6} 10.2d 10.2g Nov 1] fair handicapper at best, below that level in 2017: stays 2m: acts on fibresand and good to firm going: usually wears headgear: tried in tongue tie: modest hurdler/chaser. *Paul Midgley*

DOWNTON KITTEN (USA) 3 b.f. Kitten's Joy (USA) 128 – Manda Bay (USA) **91**
(Empire Maker (USA) 129) [2017 8m* 10.5g* a13g^{6} 9.5f Dec 30] first foal: dam, 7f winner, sister to useful 1m winner Bahama Bound out of US Grade 2 1¼m winner Summer Wind Dancer: fairly useful form: won maiden at Haydock in April (left David Lanigan after) and allowance race at Kentucky Downs in September: stays 10.5f. *Eduardo Caramori, USA*

DOWNTOWN MOMBASA (IRE) 2 b.f. (Mar 31) Lord Shanakill (USA) 121 – **66**
Mattinata (Tiger Hill (IRE) 127) [2017 6.1m^{3} p6d^{4} Jul 12] lengthy, useful-looking filly: sister to 7f winner Moreno and half-sister to 3 winners, including 1m/8.3f winner Reaver (by Sabiango) and 1m winner Magica Von Tryll (by Lomitas): dam, 9f winner who stayed 1½m, half-sister to 1¼m-15f winner Macleya and 1½m winner Montclair (both smart): fair form: better effort when third in maiden at Windsor (¾ length behind Boomerang Betty) in June: will stay 7f. *Eve Johnson Houghton*

DOWNTOWN REBEL (USA) 3 b.g. Arch (USA) 127 – Downtown Drifter (USA) **–**
(Devil His Due (USA) 126) [2017 –: p10.7g^{pu} 10d 10m 10m 13f^{6} Jun 23] no form on Flat: tried in blinkers: fair hurdler. *A. Slattery, Ireland*

DO YOU KNOW (IRE) 3 b.f. So You Think (NZ) 133 – Queen of Lyons (USA) 61 **70**
(Dubai Destination (USA) 127) [2017 64: t8.6m^{3} p8g^{4} 8.3g t7.2g^{3} p7s p8d 7g^{3} 7d^{4} Aug 10] fair maiden in Britain: stays 8.5f: acts on polytrack and tapeta: often in headgear: in tongue tie last 5 starts: sent to Italy, where won 2 handicaps at Rome in December. *Marco Botti*

DRACARYS 2 b.c. (Apr 16) Sepoy (AUS) 129 – Fen Guest 73 (Woodborough (USA) 112) **–**
[2017 6d 6g p7g Oct 11] little impact in maidens/minor event. *Jose Santos*

DRAGO (IRE) 5 b.g. Cape Cross (IRE) 129 – Eden (USA) (Holy Bull (USA) 134) [2017 **72**
84: t9.5g^{4} t9.5g 10.3g 8g^{5} Jun 23] fair handicapper: stays 9.5f: acts on tapeta: wears hood: usually races prominently: sent to Germany. *David O'Meara*

DRAGON DREAM (IRE) 3 b.f. Dragon Pulse (IRE) 114 – Night Scent (IRE) 85 **70**
(Scenic 128) [2017 62: p8g p7g p7g p8g^{6} p7g* 7g^{3} 8s^{2} p7d^{6} 7m^{6} 7s p7d Dec 13] compact filly: fair handicapper: won at Kempton (apprentice) in June: stays 1m: acts on polytrack and soft going: tried in hood. *Roger Ingram*

DRAGONFLY DREAM 2 b.f. (Mar 25) Sepoy (AUS) 129 – Tartaria 70 (Oasis Dream **–**
129) [2017 p7g Oct 5] first foal: dam maiden (stayed 1¼m): 66/1, well held in minor event at Chelmsford. *John Best*

DRAGONITE (IRE) 3 ch.g. Dragon Pulse (IRE) 114 – Glamorous (GER) 96 (Red **51**
Ransom (USA)) [2017 –: t9.5g 9.9m^{5} 9.9m^{3} 11.5d^{4} 9.9v f11.1g^{6} f8.1g Dec 4] modest maiden: barely stays 11.5f: acts on good to firm and good to soft going. *Daniel Loughnane*

DRAGON KHAN (IRE) 8 b.g. Dr Fong (USA) 128 – Desert Magic (IRE) 110 (Green **51**
Desert (USA) 127) [2017 65: 8.3g 7m May 3] modest handicapper: stays 1¼m, raced mainly at shorter: acts on heavy going: usually wears headgear: has worn tongue tie: one-time fair hurdler. *John O'Shea*

DRAGON KING (IRE) 5 ch.g. Dylan Thomas (IRE) 132 – Alexander Queen (IRE) 96 **91**
(King's Best (USA) 132) [2017 94: 6m 7.2m 6.1s* 6d 6s Jul 10] strong gelding: fairly useful handicapper: won at Chester (by short head from Russian Realm) in June: stays 6f: acts on tapeta and soft going: usually wears headgear nowadays. *Iain Jardine*

DRAGON MALL (USA) 4 b.g. Blame (USA) 129 – Petition The Lady (USA) **110**
(Petionville (USA)) [2017 112: 7g^{6} 8g^{5} 9.9g 8.3g^{3} 10m 10.3m Jul 15] good-topped gelding: smart handicapper: fifth to Bravo Zolo at Meydan in February, best effort in 2017: stays 1¼m: acts on polytrack and good to firm going: usually wears headgear: sometimes slowly away, usually races in rear. *David Simcock*

DRAGON MOUNTAIN 2 b.c. (Feb 1) Sir Percy 129 – Rouge Dancer (Elusive City **75**
(USA) 117) [2017 p8s^{3} p8g p8g^{5} Oct 14] fair form in minor events. *Hugo Palmer*

DRAGONS TAIL (IRE) 2 b.c. (Apr 29) Dragon Pulse (IRE) 114 – Mastoora (IRE) 85 (Acclamation 118) [2017 5g³ 5.1m* 5f 6m² 6.1d⁴ 7g² 6.3s³ 7g⁶ Sep 22] €30,000Y: well-made colt: fourth foal: half-brother to sprint winner Knoxville Bullet (by Clodovil) and ungenuine 5f winner (stays 7f) Mr Michael (by Big Bad Bob): dam 7f winner: fairly useful performer: won maiden at Chester (by 4½ lengths from Auntie Pam) in May: second in nursery at Ascot in July: best at sprint trips: acts on good to firm and good to soft going: usually races prominently. *Tom Dascombe* **94**

DRAGON'S TEETH (IRE) 2 b.g. (Apr 15) Dragon Pulse (IRE) 114 – Lamassu (IRE) (Entrepreneur 123) [2017 5g p5g² 5s⁵ 6m⁵ 5.5g² 6g⁴ 5.5g² 7v* 8s³ 7g* 8d⁴ p7.5g² p6.5g² p9.4g Dec 26] €5,000Y: rather leggy gelding: half-brother to 11.5f winner Dalby Spook (by Jeremy) and a winner abroad by Dark Angel: dam twice-raced half-sister to smart 7f/1m winner Montecastillo: fairly useful performer: left Jo Hughes after seventh start: won claimers at Compiegne (apprentice) in September and Saint-Cloud in October: stays 1m: acts on polytrack and heavy going: wears headgear. *R. Le Gal, France* **81**

DRAGONS THUNDER (IRE) 3 ch.g. Dragon Pulse (IRE) 114 – Boschendal (IRE) (Zamindar (USA) 116) [2017 7.4d Jun 10] well held in maiden: dead. *Brian Ellison* **–**

DRAGONS VOICE 3 b.g. Poet's Voice 126 – China 74 (Royal Academy (USA) 130) [2017 70: p8m⁶ p8g³ 8.3d* 8.3d³ 8.1g* 8d 8g 8.1g* Oct 9] sturdy gelding: fairly useful performer: won minor event at Nottingham in May and handicaps at Windsor in July and October (by 1¼ lengths from Ghalib): stays 8.5f: acts on polytrack and good to soft going: races prominently. *Philip Hide* **89**

DRAGON TATTOO (IRE) 2 b.f. (Mar 1) Zoffany (IRE) 121 – Geisha Lily (FR) (Gone West (USA)) [2017 7.4s⁶ p7g t7.1g⁴ t7.2g f8.1g Dec 11] €12,000F, €15,000Y: first foal: dam ran once: modest maiden: best effort at 7f: acts on tapeta: tried in cheekpieces. *Hugo Palmer* **51**

DRAKEFELL (IRE) 2 b.c. (Feb 10) Canford Cliffs (IRE) 133 – Cake (IRE) 100 (Acclamation 118) [2017 p5g³ 6.5d⁵ p5g* p5m² Nov 25] fourth foal: brother to useful winner up to 6f Tomily (2-y-o 5f/5.3f winner) and half-brother to useful 2-y-o 5f/6f winner Fig Roll (by Bahamian Bounty): dam 5f winner (including at 2 yrs): fairly useful form: won minor event at Lingfield (by 1¼ lengths from Choice Encounter) in November: best form at 5f. *Richard Hannon* **81**

DRAMATIC QUEEN (USA) 2 ch.f. (Mar 27) Kitten's Joy (USA) 128 – Midnight Music (IRE) 106 (Dubawi (IRE) 129) [2017 8.2v³ 8d* Oct 24] $150,000Y: second foal: half-sister to 1m winner Archer's Arrow (by Lonhro): dam winner up to 2m (2-y-o 1m winner): fairly useful form: won minor event at Yarmouth (by 1¼ lengths from Heather Lark) in October: will go on improving. *William Haggas* **80 p**

DRAMATIC VOICE 4 ch.f. Poet's Voice 126 – Darwinia (GER) (Acatenango (GER) 127) [2017 –: f7m p6g 5s⁶ t6.1g p6g f5g Dec 21] no form: tried in hood/tongue tie. *Ken Cunningham-Brown* **–**

DRAVID 3 b.g. Famous Name 124 – Sweet Power (Pivotal 124) [2017 55: p8g 7g 7d 6g⁴ 7g p12g p8g p7g Dec 21] maiden: no form in 2017: left Rod Millman after fourth start: has worn headgear: in tongue tie last 2 starts: often starts slowly/races in rear. *E. D. Delany, Ireland* **–**

DRAW SWORDS 3 br.c. Dansili 127 – Sacred Shield 87 (Beat Hollow 126) [2017 83: p10g² t9.5m⁵ Jan 16] lengthy, rather unfurnished colt: fairly useful maiden: second at Chelmsford in January: stays 1¼m: acts on polytrack and tapeta: in headgear last 2 starts: tried in tongue tie: usually races freely: sold 52,000 gns in February, sent to Qatar. *John Gosden* **80**

DR DORO (IRE) 4 b.f. Holy Roman Emperor (IRE) 125 – Stellarina (IRE) 71 (Night Shift (USA)) [2017 p5g t7.1g t7.1g 6m Jul 8] fairly useful form at 2 yrs, little impact in handicaps in 2017 after long absence: best effort at 5f: acts on tapeta: wears headgear: tried in tongue tie. *Ian Williams* **–**

DREAM ALLY (IRE) 7 b.g. Oasis Dream 129 – Alexander Alliance (IRE) 106 (Danetime (IRE) 121) [2017 60: t5.1g³ t5.1f⁵ p6g* t6m⁶ t6s* t5.1g* t6g t5.1d Dec 27] fair handicapper: won at Chelmsford in March, and at Newcastle and Wolverhampton in June: stays 6f: acts on polytrack, tapeta and good to firm going: has worn headgear, including in 2017: tried in tongue tie. *John Weymes* **71**

DREAM BALLAD (IRE) 3 b.c. Dream Ahead (USA) 133 – Royal Alchemist 109 (Kingsinger (IRE) 94) [2017 t7.1g 8m⁴ Jul 7] fair form when fourth at Haydock on second of 2 starts in maidens: wears tongue tie: sold 1,200 gns, sent to Spain. *Hugo Palmer* **67**

DREAMBOAT ANNIE 2 b.f. (Mar 30) Piccolo 121 – Bold Rose 69 (Bold Edge 123) **70**
[2017 6.1d^5 5m 5f* 5f^2 t5.1g^5 5g^4 5s^4 Sep 17] lengthy filly: third foal: dam, 5f-7f winner, half-sister to smart winner up to 9f Wise Dennis out of useful sprinter (including at 2 yrs) Bowden Rose: fair performer: won maiden at Bath in June: best form at 5f: acts on firm going. *Mark Usher*

DREAM BOUNTY 5 b.m. Bahamian Bounty 116 – Dream In Waiting 88 (Oasis Dream **–**
129) [2017 67p: 6g 6d Sep 19] fair at best, well held both starts in 2017: trained by Steph Hollinshead only on reappearance: raced only at 6f: acts on soft going. *Michael Appleby*

DREAM CASTLE 3 b.c. Frankel 147 – Sand Vixen 107 (Dubawi (IRE) 129) [2017 7g* **117**
7m^2 8m^5 7m^5 7g 8g^2 Sep 3] sturdy colt: second foal: dam, 2-y-o 5f/6f winner, half-sister to smart 6f winner So Will I: smart performer: won maiden at Doncaster (by 3½ lengths from To Dibba) in April: second in Greenham Stakes at Newbury (2 lengths behind Barney Roy) later in month and Topkapi Trophy at Veliefendi (length behind Wonnemond) in September: fifth in 2000 Guineas at Newmarket (3 lengths behind Churchill) on third outing: stays 1m: acts on good to firm going: tried in hood. *Saeed bin Suroor*

DREAMDANCER (IRE) 2 b.f. (Mar 21) Rip Van Winkle (IRE) 134 – Silver Samba 88 **–**
(Dalakhani (IRE) 133) [2017 p7g Oct 11] first foal: dam, 1½m-2m winner, half-sister to useful 1¼m-1½m winner Fort Moville: 100/1, well held in minor event at Kempton. *Joseph Tuite*

DREAM DESTROYER (IRE) 3 gr.f. Vale of York (IRE) 117 – Lady Georgina 88 **–**
(Linamix (FR) 127) [2017 t6d t6g t8s f8.1g Dec 21] €4,500F, £12,000Y: half-sister to several winners, including 1¼m winner (stays 1½m) Azzir (by Echo of Light) and 2-y-o 5f winner (stayed 7f) King's Approach (by Fasliyev): dam 7f winner who stayed 9f: no form. *Geoffrey Harker*

DREAM FACTORY (IRE) 4 ch.g. Manduro (GER) 135 – Istishaara (USA) 90 **82**
(Kingmambo (USA) 125) [2017 76: p12g* t12.2m^3 Jan 23] fairly useful handicapper: won at Kempton (by ½ length from Santiburi Spring) in January: stayed 1¾m: acted on polytrack, tapeta and good to firm going: in headgear last 4 starts: often raced prominently: dead. *Marco Botti*

DREAM FARR (IRE) 4 b.g. Dream Ahead (USA) 133 – French Lady (NZ) (Entrepreneur **74**
123) [2017 84p: t6m* p5d^3 p6g* p6g^5 6v^5 p7g p6g^3 7v^3 6d^3 6.1g^2 p6g Sep 13] workmanlike **a84**
gelding: fair handicapper on turf, fairly useful on all-weather: won at Wolverhampton in January and Kempton in February: stays 6f: acts on polytrack, tapeta and good to firm going: tried in blinkers: wears tongue tie: front runner/races prominently. *Ed Walker*

DREAM FREE 4 b.g. Oasis Dream 129 – Freedonia 117 (Selkirk (USA) 129) [2017 73p: **68**
9.9m^3 9.9d 11.9d^3 10.2g 12d^3 12.1v t10.2s 10d^4 t9.5m^4 t8.6g^3 Nov 7] lengthy gelding: fair maiden: stays 1½m: acts on polytrack: wears headgear: tried in tongue tie: inconsistent. *Mark Walford*

DREAMING OF PARIS 3 b.f. Oasis Dream 129 – Parisi (Rahy (USA) 115) [2017 70p: **80**
p7g^3 p8d* Jan 18] fairly useful form: won maiden at Kempton (by 1¾ lengths from Driver's Girl) in January: likely to stay further than 1m: sold 25,000 gns in February, sent to Greece. *William Haggas*

DREAMING TIME 3 b.f. Oasis Dream 129 – Maskunah (IRE) (Sadler's Wells (USA) **86**
132) [2017 t7.1g^5 p8g* p8g^5 t9.5g^6 8g^3 p8g* t7.2m* p8s Nov 16] sister to 2-y-o 1m winner Natural Beauty, closely related to very smart 1¼m-1½m winner Laaheb and smart 6f-7f winner Ruwaiyan (both by Cape Cross) and half-sister to 3 winners: dam unraced: fairly useful performer: won maiden at Lingfield in February, and handicaps there and at Wolverhampton (by short head from Tavener) in October: left Hugo Palmer after third start: stays 1m: acts on polytrack and tapeta: often races prominently. *James Tate*

DREAM LOVE 4 b.f. Rail Link 132 – Love Always 81 (Piccolo 121) [2017 72p: p12g^3 **82**
p12g^4 11.6m Apr 24] fairly useful form: dead. *Simon Dow*

DREAM MACHINE (IRE) 3 ch.g. Dream Ahead (USA) 133 – Last Cry (FR) (Peintre **89**
Celebre (USA) 137) [2017 –p: 10.2f* 9.9m^3 10.1g^2 9.9v^2 9.8m^3 10.1g* 10g^3 Oct 7] lengthy gelding: fairly useful handicapper: won at Haydock in May and Epsom (by length from Music Lesson) in September: stays 1¼m: acts on any turf going: often travels strongly: sold to join Neil Mulholland 48,000 gns in October. *Michael Bell*

DREAM MAGIC (IRE) 3 b.g. Lord Shanakill (USA) 121 – Pursuit of Passion 67 **78**
(Pastoral Pursuits 127) [2017 –: t9.5m^3 p10g^2 9.9f p10g^2 t8.6g^4 t8.6g p8g f8.1g t12.2g* f11.1g^5 Dec 29] fair handicapper: won at Wolverhampton in December: stays 1½m: acts on polytrack and tapeta. *Daniel Loughnane*

DREAM MALFUNCTION (IRE) 2 ch.f. (Jan 22) Mastercraftsman (IRE) 129 – Limetree Lady 109 (Selkirk (USA) 129) [2017 7d^4 7m^4 6m p7g Nov 17] first foal: dam, 2-y-o 5f winner, half-sister to useful winner up to 1m Volunteer Point: fair form: left Joseph Patrick O'Brien after third start: stays 7f. *Joseph Tuite* **76**

DREAM MOUNT (IRE) 2 b.c. (Feb 12) Dream Ahead (USA) 133 – Mistify (IRE) (Elusive Quality (USA)) [2017 7g p8s p8g* t8.6m^5 Oct 31] €31,000 2-y-o: first foal: dam unraced out of smart winner up to 7.5f (including at 2 yrs) Modeeroch: fairly useful form: won maiden at Lingfield in September: stays 1m: remains with potential. *Marco Botti* **80 p**

DREAM OF CAMELOT (IRE) 2 b.f. (Apr 21) Camelot 128 – Definite Opinion (IRE) 75 (Kheleyf (USA) 116) [2017 7s^3 8s^4 Oct 28] €16,000Y, €31,000 2-y-o: third foal: half-sister to 2-y-o 5.4f winner Kruger Park (by Requinto): dam unreliable 2-y-o 6f winner: fair form when in frame in 2 minor events. *Gary Moore* **76**

DREAM OF DELPHI (IRE) 2 b.f. (Feb 16) Camacho 118 – Kitty Softpaws (IRE) (Royal Applause 124) [2017 6d 6g 6g 7g* p8g^2 8g 8.2g Oct 17] £33,000Y: smallish filly: second foal: dam unraced half-sister to smart winner up to 1¼m Miblish: fair performer: won nursery at Lingfield in August: stays 1m: acts on polytrack: in headgear last 4 starts: sold 8,000 gns, sent to Spain. *William Haggas* **65**

DREAMOFDISCOVERY (IRE) 3 b.g. Henrythenavigator (USA) 131 – Dreamwriter (USA) 92 (Tale of The Cat (USA) 113) [2017 61: t8g t8d^3 10m^3 8.2d* 8.5d^5 7.8v^5 Sep 13] fair performer: won seller at Leicester in July: stays 1m: acts on tapeta and good to soft going: in cheekpieces last 3 starts: sometimes slowly away. *Julie Camacho* **67**

DREAM OF DREAMS (IRE) 3 ch.c. Dream Ahead (USA) 133 – Vasilia (Dansili 127) [2017 105: 5m^2 6m 7s* 7g^5 6d* Nov 11] smart performer: won minor event at Lingfield (by 5 lengths from Mutawathea) in September and listed race at Doncaster (by length from Perfect Pasture) in November: left Kevin Ryan after first start: stays 7f: acts on soft and good to firm going. *Sir Michael Stoute* **117**

DREAM OF JOY (IRE) 3 b.f. Dream Ahead (USA) 133 – Love And Laughter (IRE) 74 (Theatrical) [2017 75: 6g^2 Jul 27] workmanlike filly: fair form: second in maiden at Yarmouth (3½ lengths behind Thafeera) on sole outing in 2017: likely to stay 1m: remains open to improvement. *Roger Varian* **76 p**

DREAM OF SUMMER (IRE) 4 b.g. Canford Cliffs (IRE) 133 – Danehill's Dream (IRE) (Danehill (USA) 126) [2017 91: p8f^3 7.6d^5 p8s p8s p8g Oct 5] strong gelding: fairly useful handicapper: third at Lingfield in April: left Andrew Balding after third start: stays 1m: acts on polytrack and good to firm going: tried in blinkers: usually leads: sold 3,500 gns in October. *Jeremy Noseda* **84**

DREAM ON DREAMER (IRE) 3 b.f. Dream Ahead (USA) 133 – Marula (IRE) (Sadler's Wells (USA) 132) [2017 66: 8g^6 Jul 18] fair maiden, well beaten sole start in 2017: stays 1m: acts on soft going: tried in headgear: usually leads. *Antony Brittain* **–**

DREAM PROSPECT 2 b.g. (Mar 2) Invincible Spirit (IRE) 121 – Turama (Pivotal 124) [2017 5m^6 6.1m^4 5.1g^3 5m^6 Aug 31] modest form: best form at 5f. *Roger Charlton* **63**

DREAM REVERSION 3 b.c. Oasis Dream 129 – Last Second (IRE) 121 (Alzao (USA) 117) [2017 68: p5m p7g^2 Jan 28] modest maiden: stays 7f: acts on polytrack and good to soft going: sometimes slowly away. *Tom Dascombe* **60**

DREAM REVIVAL 4 br.f. Captain Gerrard (IRE) 113 – Passkey 83 (Medicean 128) [2017 64: t7.1s 8.5s^6 p6g^2 p7g^6 t6d^2 t7.1g^3 t6g^3 t5g* t5d Dec 16] modest performer: won maiden at Newcastle in December: stays 7f: acts on tapeta: wears cheekpieces: often starts slowly/races towards rear. *Paul Collins* **61**

DREAM SERENADE 4 b.f. Dream Eater (IRE) 119 – Lady Santana (IRE) 61 (Doyoun 124) [2017 58: t16.5g^3 t13.9m^4 t16.5g* t13.9f^5 p16g 18g^4 15.9m^3 14.1m^2 14v p13.3g t14g t16.5g f11.1g^3 t12.2g^3 f11.1g^3 Dec 22] leggy, close-coupled filly: modest handicapper: won at Wolverhampton in February: stays 2¼m: acts on fibresand, tapeta, soft and good to firm going: wears headgear: front runner/races prominently. *Michael Appleby* **63**

DREAMS OF GLORY 9 ch.g. Resplendent Glory (IRE) 115 – Pip's Dream 52 (Glint of Gold 128) [2017 76: t5.1g* p6g^5 t5.1g p5g p6g Dec 31] rather leggy gelding: fair handicapper: won at Wolverhampton in January: stays 6f: acts on polytrack, tapeta and any turf going: has worn blinkers. *Ron Hodges* **75**

Irish Stallion Farms European Breeders Fund 'Ahonoora' Handicap, Galway— the grey Dream Walker repeats his 2016 victory and leads home a one, two, three for the latest Galway raiding party sent over by Brian Ellison, with 2014 and 2015 winner Baraweez (centre) and Be Kool (rail) filling the places

DREAM START 3 b.f. Exceed And Excel (AUS) 126 – Calipatria 110 (Shamardal (USA) 129) [2017 8m 8m 7d⁴ 7s⁵ p8s⁴ p6g³ 6s² p7g 6d² p7g⁶ p6s⁶ t6s Nov 30] £22,000 2-y-o: rather leggy filly: first foal: dam 1m-11f winner: fair maiden: stays 1m: acts on polytrack and soft going: wears tongue tie: sometimes slowly away: sent to the Netherlands. *John Ryan* **67**

DREAM TEAM 3 b.g. Captain Gerrard (IRE) 113 – Mimi Mouse 98 (Diktat 126) [2017 59, a80: f8s⁵ t8g⁴ 9v⁵ 7.8g⁵ 7.4g⁶ 8s t8d Nov 4] fair performer at 2 yrs, below that level in 2017: stays 1m: acts on fibresand, tapeta and soft going: wears headgear: sold £3,000, sent to Germany. *Michael Dods* **61**

DREAMTIDE 3 b.f. Champs Elysees 124 – Moraine 71 (Rainbow Quest (USA) 134) [2017 11.6d⁶ 11.8d⁶ 11.6f³ Jun 28] fifth foal: half-sister to 1½m winner (stayed 21.5f) Brass Ring (by Rail Link) and 1¾m-2m winner Wicklow Brave (by Beat Hollow), both smart: dam 1½m winner: fair form when third at Bath on last of 3 starts in maidens: tried in visor. *Amanda Perrett* **66**

DREAM TODAY (IRE) 2 b.c. (Mar 9) Dream Ahead (USA) 133 – Macheera (IRE) (Machiavellian (USA) 123) [2017 7g* 7g⁵ 8m² 7s⁶ Oct 28] 42,000Y: tall, lengthy colt: has scope: sixth foal: brother to very smart 7f/1m (including at 2 yrs) winner Al Wukair, and half-brother to winner up to 7f Ballyorban (by Cape Cross) and 7f winner Witches Brew (by Duke of Marmalade), both useful: dam 2-y-o 1m winner: useful form: won maiden at York (by 1½ lengths from Gabr) in August: second in Autumn Stakes at Newmarket (1¾ lengths behind Ghaiyyath) in October: stays 1m. *Mark Johnston* **106**

DREAM WALKER (FR) 8 gr.g. Gold Away (IRE) 125 – Minnie's Mystery (FR) (Highest Honor (FR) 124) [2017 105: t8.6g 8g 8m 7.2s 7.6d⁴ 8s 8.6d³ 7s* 8d 9v⁵ 8.2v Sep 30] strong gelding: useful handicapper: won at Galway (by ½ length from Baraweez) in August: stays 9f: acts on tapeta, good to firm and heavy going: has worn headgear: wears tongue tie: often races towards rear. *Brian Ellison* **101**

DREAM WARRIOR 2 b.c. (Jan 29) Dubawi (IRE) 129 – I'm A Dreamer (IRE) 119 (Noverre (USA) 125) [2017 7v³ 7s³ 7s* Oct 7] 575,000Y: first foal: dam 1m-9.5f winner, including US Grade 1 8.5f event: fairly useful form: won maiden at Chantilly (by nose from Corsen) in October: raced only at 7f: should continue to progress. *Charlie Appleby* **91 p**

DR GOODHEAD (FR) 3 b.f. Zoffany (IRE) 121 – Whoosh (FR) (Muhtathir 126) [2017 7g 7s³ 7g⁶ p7g 10m Jul 17] €20,000F, £50,000Y: fifth foal: dam unraced sister to smart French/US winner up to 11f Mauralakana: modest maiden: stays 7f: sold £800, sent to Greece. *Charles Hills* **54**

DRILL 2 b.c. (Apr 15) Dansili 127 – Pongee 110 (Barathea (IRE) 127) [2017 7m Jul 14] **– p** closely related to 9.5f winner (stayed 12.5f) Petrol (by Danehill Dancer) and half-brother to several winners, including smart winner up to 1¾m Pinzolo (2-y-o 1m winner, by Monsun) and useful 2-y-o 1m winner Poplin (by Medicean): dam 1¼m-1½m winner who stayed 1¾m: 25/1, well held in maiden at Newmarket: should do better. *Luca Cumani*

DRIVER'S GIRL (USA) 3 b.f. Candy Ride (ARG) 133 – Sharbat (USA) (Dynaformer **78** (USA)) [2017 –: p8d^{2} p8d* 8.5f 8.5f t8.3f^{3} 8.5d^{5} Oct 16] fairly useful performer: won maiden at Chelmsford in February: left Marco Botti after: stays 8.3f: has worn headgear. *H. Graham Motion, USA*

DR JULIUS NO 3 b.g. Dick Turpin (IRE) 127 – Royal Assent 56 (Royal Applause 124) **96** [2017 94: t7.1g^{2} p7f 8g^{3} 8.1d 7m^{4} 9m^{3} 8m^{2} 10g^{4} 9.1g^{3} 8s^{6} 8.5v^{4} Oct 1] sturdy gelding: useful handicapper: placed 5 times in 2017: left Ralph Beckett after fourth start: stays 9f: acts on tapeta and good to firm going: in cheekpieces last 2 starts: sold 42,000 gns in October. *Richard Hughes*

DROCHAID 3 ch.c. Mastercraftsman (IRE) 129 – Avon Lady 96 (Avonbridge 123) [2017 **101** 81: p8g^{2} p10g* 10.1m* 12m^{4} Jun 22] tall, rather leggy colt: useful handicapper: won at Chelmsford in May and Epsom (by neck from Emenem) in June: stays 1½m: acts on polytrack, tapeta and firm going: front runner/races prominently: sent to Australia. *Andrew Balding*

DROP KICK MURPHI (IRE) 3 b.g. Sir Prancealot (IRE) 111 – Rindiseyda (IRE) **59** (Arakan (USA) 123) [2017 83: p7g p6g^{6} 6s 6d 6s 7d 5s^{4} Nov 8] fairly useful performer at 2 yrs, well below that level in 2017: left George Baker after first start: stays 7f: acts on good to firm and good to soft going: tried in cheekpieces. *Christine Dunnett*

DROVER 2 ch.g. (Mar 17) Foxwedge (AUS) 128 – Brooksby 77 (Diktat 126) [2017 6m^{6} **–** 7m^{6} 6g^{6} Jul 24] little impact in maiden/minor events. *Keith Dalgleish*

DR RED EYE 9 ch.g. Dr Fong (USA) 128 – Camp Fire (IRE) 81 (Lahib (USA) 129) [2017 **57** 71, a53: f7g t7.1m* t7.1g^{5} t7.1g f7g 7m^{3} May 3] strong gelding: modest handicapper nowadays: won at Wolverhampton in January: raced mainly at 6f/7f: acts on all-weather, good to firm and heavy going: wears headgear: tried in tongue tie: front runner/races prominently. *Scott Dixon*

DR RICHARD KIMBLE (IRE) 2 b.g. (Mar 19) Lawman (FR) 121 – Aoife Alainn **75** (IRE) 117 (Dr Fong (USA) 128) [2017 7.2g 8.3s 7.8v^{3} t8.6m* Oct 31] fair form: won nursery at Wolverhampton in October: stays 8.5f. *Mark Johnston*

DRUIDS CROSS (IRE) 3 b.c. Cape Cross (IRE) 129 – Shell Garland (USA) 80 (Sadler's **99** Wells (USA) 132) [2017 85p: 12.3m 13g^{5} 11.3m^{2} 12.7m^{6} 8.1g^{su} Jul 18] strong, lengthy colt: useful performer: won maiden at Dundalk in 2016: second in minor event at Limerick (½ length behind Steel Prince) in June: stayed 13f: acted on polytrack and good to firm going: in tongue tie last 4 starts: dead. *Joseph Patrick O'Brien, Ireland*

DRUID'S DIAMOND 4 b.g. Piccolo 121 – Faithful Beauty (IRE) (Last Tycoon 131) **62** [2017 –: 10m 10g^{5} 9.1m t10.2s 12.1m^{4} 11.2g^{4} 9.9d^{2} 10.2g^{2} 10.2g^{6} 13.1v Oct 12] modest maiden: demoted after first past post in handicap at Beverley in July: stays 1½m: acts on good to firm and good to soft going: in headgear last 5 starts. *Mark Walford*

DRUMFAD BAY (IRE) 3 b.f. Acclamation 118 – Manieree (IRE) 120 (Medicean 128) **102** [2017 92: 7d 7g^{2} 7s^{2} 8m 8.1g* 7s^{2} 7.5s^{2} 7g Sep 15] good-bodied filly: useful performer: won listed race at Killarney (by 1½ lengths from Music Box) in July: second in similar events at Naas (2) in May and Galway in August, and also in Fairy Bridge Stakes at Tipperary (1¾ lengths behind Realtra) later in August: stays 1m: acts on soft and good to firm going. *Mrs J. Harrington, Ireland*

DRUMOCHTER 3 br.f. Bated Breath 125 – Dixey 98 (Diktat 126) [2017 p8g 8d^{3} 7.9m^{5} **80** 8s^{3} 10.2s* 10m 10.3v^{4} 10d^{6} p10g^{4} Dec 20] 20,000F, £70,000Y: leggy filly: third foal: half-sister to 2-y-o 1¼m winner Dullingham (by Dubawi): dam, 7f winner (including at 2 yrs), half-sister to useful winner up to 6f Harry Patch: fairly useful handicapper: won at Bath (by 2¾ lengths from Saint Helena) in August: left Charles Hills after eighth start: stays 1¼m: acts on soft going. *Jamie Osborne*

DSCHINGIS SECRET (GER) 4 b.c. Soldier Hollow 121 – Divya (GER) (Platini (GER) **125** 126) [2017 115: 11.9g* 10.9g^{5} 11.9s* 11.9g* 11.9d* 11.9d^{6} 11.9s^{3} Nov 1] €200,000Y: first foal: dam, German 1¼m-1½m winner, sister to useful German/Italian Group 3 1¼m/11f winner Deva and half-sister to smart German stayer Duke d'Alba: high-class performer: won Gerling-Preis at Cologne in May, Grosser Hansa-Preis at Hamburg (beat Iquitos 3¾ lengths) in July, Grosser Preis von Berlin at Hoppegarten (by length from Hawkbill) in August and Prix Foy at Chantilly (by 1½ lengths from Cloth of Stars) in September:

Qatar Prix Foy, Chantilly—German raider Dschingis Secret beats Prix Ganay winner Cloth of Stars and his stablemate Talismanic (white face); Japanese Arc hope Satono Diamond, odds-on favourite, is only fourth

creditable efforts last 2 starts, in Prix de l'Arc de Triomphe at Chantilly (7 lengths sixth to Enable) and Grosser Preis von Bayern at Munich (close third to Guignol): stays 1¾m: acts on heavy going. *Markus Klug, Germany*

DUBAI ACCLAIM (IRE) 2 b.c. (Feb 27) Acclamation 118 – Bahati (IRE) 99 (Intikhab (USA) 135) [2017 p6d^4 Dec 13] 50,000Y: third foal: brother to smart winner up to 1m Tabarrak (2-y-o 7f winner) and useful winner up to 6f The Wagon Wheel (2-y-o 5f/6f winner): dam 2-y-o 6f winner who stayed 1m: 10/1, fourth in minor event at Kempton (4¼ lengths behind Monadee) in December: sure to progress. *Richard Fahey* **70 p**

DUBAI ART 3 b.c. Dutch Art 126 – Enact 104 (Kyllachy 129) [2017 70p: p7g* p7d 6g t7.2g^4 Jul 11] fair performer: won maiden at Lingfield in January: stays 7f: acts on polytrack and tapeta. *Richard Fahey* **78**

DUBAI CELEBRITY 5 b.g. Sakhee (USA) 136 – Aljana (IRE) (Exceed And Excel (AUS) 126) [2017 t16.3g^{pu} Jul 29] fair maiden, went wrong sole outing on Flat in 2017: stays 1½m: acts on good to firm going: tried in visor. *Chris Grant* **–**

DUBAI CLASSIC (IRE) 2 b.f. (Apr 11) Fast Company (IRE) 126 – Dubai Pearl (IRE) (Refuse To Bend (IRE) 128) [2017 5s^5 6.5d Jun 3] €8,000Y: third foal: dam unraced half-sister to useful 1¼m winner (stayed 1½m) Saab Almanal: fair form when fifth in maiden at Thirsk on first of 2 starts. *K. R. Burke* **66**

DUBAI DYNAMO 12 b.g. Kyllachy 129 – Miss Mercy (IRE) 62 (Law Society (USA) 130) [2017 93: 7g 8g^4 8.5f May 1] stocky gelding: fairly useful handicapper: stays 8.5f: acts on polytrack, fibresand and any turf going: has worn headgear. *Ruth Carr* **81**

DUBAI ELEGANCE 3 ch.f. Sepoy (AUS) 129 – Some Sunny Day 89 (Where Or When (IRE) 124) [2017 80: t8.6g^4 p7d^4 t8d^6 Sep 29] fairly useful handicapper: stays 8.5f: acts on polytrack and tapeta: in cheekpieces last 2 starts: races prominently. *Saeed bin Suroor* **86**

DUBAI EMPIRE (FR) 2 ch.c. (Apr 14) Motivator 131 – Cable Beach (USA) (Langfuhr (CAN) 124) [2017 7d^5 7g^4 8s* 10m^6 Oct 14] €11,000Y, €40,000 2-y-o: strong colt: seventh foal: closely related to 1½m winner Rennsenas (by Montmartre) and half-brother to 1m-10.5f winner Calcutta (by Panis) and 7f/1m winner Huang Ho (by Kentucky Dynamite): dam 9f/1¼m winner: fairly useful form: won maiden at Musselburgh in September: should stay 1¼m. *John Quinn* **80**

DUBAI FRAME 2 b.c. (Mar 2) Sixties Icon 125 – Strictly Lambada 77 (Red Ransom (USA)) [2017 7m 8.3g^5 p8g^5 Nov 18] 140,000Y: sturdy colt: fourth foal: closely related to 1½m-1¾m winner (stays 2m) Sleep Easy (by Rip Van Winkle) and half-brother to useful 2-y-o 1m winner (stays 1½m) Last Tango Inparis (by Aqlaam) and 1½m winner Hawridge Flyer (by Sir Percy): dam maiden (stayed 1½m): fair form: best effort when fifth in maiden at Nottingham in November: will be suited by 1¼m+: remains with potential. *Ed Dunlop* **65 p**

DUBAI HORIZON (IRE) 3 b.g. Poet's Voice 126 – Chibola (ARG) (Roy (USA)) [2017 91: p10g* 10m^2 May 7] good-topped gelding: useful form: won maiden at Lingfield (by 3 lengths from Impact Point) in April: second in handicap at Newmarket (neck behind Leshlaa) in May: stays 1¼m: tried in cheekpieces. *Saeed bin Suroor* **106**

DUBAI LANDMARK (IRE) 2 b.c. (May 9) Helmet (AUS) 127 – Cairncross (IRE) 76 (Cape Cross (IRE) 129) [2017 p7g p7g Dec 28] little impact in minor events. *Hugo Palmer* **–**

DUBAI ONE (IRE) 3 ch.f. Exceed And Excel (AUS) 126 – Dresden Doll (USA) 78 (Elusive Quality (USA)) [2017 92: t6g* p6g p6g* Dec 30] useful handicapper: won at Wolverhampton (by neck from King Robert) in March and Lingfield (by ½ length from Kasbah) in December: stays 6f: acts on polytrack and tapeta: tried in hood: often races prominently, usually travels strongly. *Saeed bin Suroor* **106**

DUBAI SILK 2 ch.f. (Mar 22) Helmet (AUS) 127 – Silken Express (IRE) 105 (Speightstown (USA) 124) [2017 p5g⁴ Nov 17] first foal: dam 5f winner: 9/1, fourth in minor event at Lingfield (3¾ lengths behind Drakefell) in November. *Robert Cowell* **59**

DUBAI'S SECRET 4 ch.g. Paco Boy (IRE) 129 – Lilli Marlane 82 (Sri Pekan (USA) 117) [2017 95: 8g⁶ p8g 8g 7.6d³ 8s⁶ 7m⁴ 8.5m⁴ 10g p8g Oct 26] angular gelding: fairly useful handicapper: stays 8.5f: acts on good to firm and good to soft going: tried in headgear: sold 5,000 gns, sent to Spain. *David Brown* **87**

DUBAI THUNDER 3 b.c. Dubawi (IRE) 129 – Gonbarda (GER) 117 (Lando (GER) 128) [2017 10s* 12m Jun 3] sturdy colt: half-brother to several winners, including top-class winner up to 1¼m Farhh (2-y-o 7f winner), very smart 1m-10.3f winner Racing History and smart 1m winner (stays 10.5f) Basem (all by Pivotal): dam winner up to 1½m (2-y-o 6f winner): smart form: won maiden at Newbury (by 10 lengths from Hawridge Flyer) in May: eleventh in Derby at Epsom (8 lengths behind Wings of Eagles) only other start: remains with potential. *Saeed bin Suroor* **110 p**

DUBAITWENTYTWENTY 3 br.f. Poet's Voice 126 – Cairncross (IRE) 76 (Cape Cross (IRE) 129) [2017 67p: t8g* 9.9d⁶ 10.2d t8d f8.1g⁵ f8.1g² Dec 22] fair performer: won maiden at Newcastle in January: stays 1m: acts on fibresand and tapeta: in cheekpieces last 2 starts: in tongue tie last 5 starts: front runner/races prominently. *Hugo Palmer* **77**

DUBAI WAVES 3 b.f. Poet's Voice 126 – Pencarrow 80 (Green Desert (USA) 127) [2017 p8d² p10g⁵ p8g³ 8m⁶ 8.1d t8.6g f8.1g Dec 11] first foal: dam maiden half-sister to smart 11f-1¾m winner (stayed 2m) Tenenbaum: fair maiden: left Hugo Palmer after fifth start: stays 1m: acts on polytrack: often races prominently. *Tony Newcombe* **74**

DUBARA 3 b.f. Dubawi (IRE) 129 – Kibara 88 (Sadler's Wells (USA) 132) [2017 83p: 8m³ 9.9m² 9.1g⁴ 8g* 8d³ 7s Oct 7] compact filly: useful handicapper: won at Goodwood (by neck from Panova) in August: third at Newmarket in September: stays 1¼m: acts on polytrack, firm and good to soft going: tried in hood: often races towards rear/travels strongly: sold 180,000 gns in December. *Luca Cumani* **98**

DUBAWI FIFTY 4 b.g. Dubawi (IRE) 129 – Plethora (Sadler's Wells (USA) 132) [2017 88: 15d* 14g* 18m⁴ Oct 14] sturdy gelding: useful handicapper: won at Ayr in July and Nottingham in August: probably stays 2¼m: acts on tapeta and good to soft going: often races towards rear, usually responds generously to pressure. *Karen McLintock* **103**

DUBAWI PRINCE 3 b.c. Dubawi (IRE) 129 – Flawly 106 (Old Vic 136) [2017 71p: 10.3g* 10g⁶ Apr 21] rather leggy, unfurnished colt: fairly useful form: won maiden at Doncaster (by ½ length from Never Surrender) in April: will be suited by 1½m. *Roger Varian* **90**

DUBHE 2 b.c. (Mar 11) Dubawi (IRE) 129 – Great Heavens 120 (Galileo (IRE) 134) [2017 7g⁴ 8v* 8.2s⁵ 8d⁵ Oct 27] well-made colt: second foal: dam, 1¼m-1½m (including Irish Oaks) winner, sister to high-class 1¼m-1½m winner Nathaniel: fairly useful form: won maiden at Sandown in August: stays 1m. *Charlie Appleby* **92**

DUBKA 4 b.f. Dubawi (IRE) 129 – Rosika 112 (Sakhee (USA) 136) [2017 104p: 12f⁶ 11.8s² 11.8m 14v² 13.9m 14.5d⁶ 14.1g⁶ Oct 16] stocky filly: useful performer: second in Pinnacle Stakes at Haydock (1½ lengths behind Bateel) in June and Lillie Langtry Stakes at Goodwood (neck behind Endless Time) in August: stays 1¾m: acts on good to firm and heavy going: usually races close up. *Sir Michael Stoute* **109**

DUC DE SEVILLE (IRE) 5 b.g. Duke of Marmalade (IRE) 132 – Splendid (IRE) (Mujtahid (USA) 118) [2017 60: f14g 21.6m Apr 24] modest at best, no form in 2017: stays 1½m: acts on tapeta, good to firm and heavy going: often wears headgear: often races prominently. *Michael Chapman* **–**

DUCHESS OF FIFE 3 ch.f. Dutch Art 126 – La Adelita (IRE) 94 (Anabaa (USA) 130) [2017 65p: 9.9f t8.6g⁵ 8.2g² 8.3g 8.1g⁵ 8.2d* 10d⁴ 8.2v⁴ 8.1d Oct 23] fair handicapper: won at Leicester in August: stays 1m: acts on good to soft going: wears headgear. *William Knight* **73**

DUCHESS OF FRANCE (IRE) 4 b.f. Dylan Thomas (IRE) 132 – Miss Champagne (FR) (Bering 136) [2017 77: 8m 6d² 7s* 7g³ 7s³ 8.2s³ 7.5s 7d 5.8v Oct 8] useful handicapper: won at the Curragh (by 2¾ lengths from Tobacco Bay) in June: third in **97**

listed races at Galway (2¾ lengths behind Music Box) and Killarney (length behind Canary Row) in August: stays 1m: acts on soft going: wears tongue tie: front runner/races prominently. *A. P. Keatley, Ireland*

DUCHY 4 b.f. Kyllachy 129 – Albavilla 82 (Spectrum (IRE) 126) [2017 –: 10d^5 9s^6 10d^2 Aug 18] rangy filly: fairly useful maiden: second in handicap at Newmarket in August: stays 1¼m: acts on good to soft going. *Michael Bell* **80**

DUCISSA 4 b.f. Exceed And Excel (AUS) 126 – Baize 95 (Efisio 120) [2017 66: t7.1m p6d Mar 13] modest maiden: stays 7f: acts on polytrack: tried in hood: often races prominently. *Daniel Kubler* **62**

DUCK A L'ORANGE (IRE) 4 ch.g. Duke of Marmalade (IRE) 132 – Incheni (IRE) 100 (Nashwan (USA) 135) [2017 82: p12g^4 p13.3d^5 p12g^2 Mar 25] sturdy gelding: fairly useful handicapper: stays 1½m: often wore headgear: front runner/raced prominently: dead. *Michael Bell* **79**

DUCK EGG BLUE (IRE) 3 b.f. Haatef (USA) 117 – Sapphire Spray (IRE) 79 (Viking Ruler (AUS)) [2017 75: 7m 8.3s^2 8.3d^5 10.2v^3 9.8g^2 9s^3 11.1d^3 10.2d Oct 4] fair handicapper: stays 11f: acts on heavy going: often wears headgear. *Patrick Holmes* **79**

DUFFY 2 b.c. (Apr 14) Redoute's Choice (AUS) – Kunegunda 88 (Pivotal 124) [2017 8g 7g^6 Sep 27] little impact in minor event/maiden: bred to be suited by 1¼m+. *Richard Fahey* **–**

DUGGARY 2 b.g. (Feb 10) Champs Elysees 124 – Waitingonacloud (In The Wings 128) [2017 t7.2g 7d 8g^6 t7.1g p10g 10v^5 Oct 9] modest maiden: stays 1¼m: acts on heavy going: tried in blinkers. *Kevin Frost* **60**

DUHR (IRE) 3 b.g. Mawatheeq (USA) 126 – Dijlah (Linamix (FR) 127) [2017 10.4d^5 8g p10g p8g^6 Dec 28] fair form in maidens: left F. Head after second start: best effort at 1m: tried in blinkers. *Ralph Smith* **69**

DUKE COSIMO 7 ch.g. Pivotal 124 – Nannina 121 (Medicean 128) [2017 91: 6g 6m 6d^5 6s 6g^3 6s 6d^4 6s^5 6s^6 t6d^3 t5g^2 t5d^4 t6.1d Dec 9] lengthy gelding: fairly useful handicapper: placed at Redcar in July and Newcastle in September/October: stays 6f: acts on polytrack, tapeta, soft and good to firm going: has worn headgear, including last 3 starts: often races towards rear. *Michael Herrington* **80**

DUKE OF ALBA (IRE) 2 b.c. (Mar 21) Lope de Vega (IRE) 125 – Royal Alchemist 109 (Kingsinger (IRE) 94) [2017 p7d Nov 22] 50/1, well held in minor event at Kempton. *Jamie Osborne* **–**

DUKE OF BRONTE 3 b.g. Mount Nelson 125 – Reaf (In The Wings 128) [2017 p8g p8g 8m* 10s^5 12m^4 12m* 14d^4 12s* 12m^3 13.3d^2 Oct 27] lengthy gelding: seventh foal: half-brother to 3 winners, including 1¼m-16.4f winner Deauville Flyer (by Dubai Destination) and 1¾m-17f winner (stays 21.5f) Taws (by Hernando), both useful: dam unraced sister to smart stayer Boreas: useful performer: won maiden at Newbury in April, and handicaps at same course in July and Ascot (by neck from Melting Dew) in September: stays 13.5f: acts on soft and good to firm going. *Rod Millman* **103**

DUKE OF CLARENCE (IRE) 8 gr.g. Verglas (IRE) 118 – Special Lady (FR) (Kaldoun (FR) 122) [2017 –: 18.6m May 10] well-made gelding: useful handicapper, lightly raced in recent years: stays 2¼m: acts on polytrack, good to firm and heavy going: has worn headgear. *Ian Williams* **94**

DUKE OF DIAMONDS 5 gr.g. Duke of Marmalade (IRE) 132 – Diamond Line (FR) (Linamix (FR) 127) [2017 81: 11.8g^4 12s May 18] fairly useful handicapper: stays 2¼m: acts on soft and good to firm going. *Julia Feilden* **78**

DUKE OF DORSET 2 b.c. (Apr 7) Sepoy (AUS) 129 – Zuleika Dobson 106 (Cadeaux Genereux 131) [2017 p7g p8g Nov 1] little impact in minor events. *Harry Fry* **–**

DUKE OF FIRENZE 8 ch.g. Pivotal 124 – Nannina 121 (Medicean 128) [2017 113: 5.2g^6 5.1d^4 5s* 5m^3 5m 6m 5d^5 6d 5s 5.6g 5d^4 Oct 1] good-topped gelding: smart performer: won handicap at York (by neck from Rasheeq) in May: very close third to Caspian Prince in 'Dash' at Epsom next time: 5¼ lengths fourth to Battaash in Prix de l'Abbaye at Chantilly final outing: best at 5f: acts on polytrack, good to firm and heavy going: has worn cheekpieces: waited with. *David C. Griffiths* **116**

DUKE OF FREEDOM 2 b.g. (Feb 8) Equiano (FR) 127 – Duchess of Seville 88 (Duke of Marmalade (IRE) 132) [2017 7.4m^3 7.4m^6 6s^5 t6g 6s t6g t6.1g^6 Oct 27] modest maiden: in headgear last 3 starts. *Ann Duffield* **58**

DUKE OF NORTH (IRE) 5 b.g. Danehill Dancer (IRE) 117 – Althea Rose (IRE) (Green Desert (USA) 127) [2017 75: p8g^4 8.3m^4 7g^2 7d* 6g^6 7d^6 p8g 8.5g^4 7.6s^4 7v^6 8s 8.1d Oct 23] tall gelding: fair handicapper: won at Lingfield (amateur) in May: stays 8.5f: **76**

acts on polytrack, good to firm and good to soft going: has worn headgear, including last 2 starts: tried in tongue tie: sometimes slowly away. *Jim Boyle*

DUKE OF SONNING 5 ch.g. Duke of Marmalade (IRE) 132 – Moonshadow 75 (Diesis 133) [2017 –: f14g^{5} 15.9s^{5} 11.5s^{3} 12.1d t16.5g Sep 23] big, strong gelding: modest handicapper nowadays: probably stays 1¾m: acts on fibresand, soft and good to firm going: in blinkers last 4 starts: winning hurdler. *Shaun Harris* **61**

DUKEOFWALLINGFORD 2 b.g. (Mar 18) Equiano (FR) 127 – Hazelberry (Bertolini (USA) 125) [2017 7g^{5} 8s^{2} t8.6g^{6} Nov 25] fair form: best effort when second in minor event at Brighton (head behind Enzo) in October: should stay beyond 1m. *Eve Johnson Houghton* **71**

DUKE OF YORKSHIRE 7 b.g. Duke of Marmalade (IRE) 132 – Dame Edith (FR) (Top Ville 129) [2017 76: 12g p10g^{2} 10g^{3} 13.1s^{5} 12g^{5} t10.2g 12.1g^{6} 10d Oct 20] tall gelding: fair handicapper: stays 1¾m, usually raced at shorter: acts on polytrack, tapeta, good to firm and heavy going: wears headgear: has worn tongue tie: usually races close up. *Tim Easterby* **77**

DUKE'S GIRL 3 b.f. Poet's Voice 126 – Juniper Girl (IRE) 108 (Revoque (IRE) 122) [2017 65: p8d^{5} 9.9d^{5} 12s^{2} 14m^{2} 14s^{5} 14.2g^{4} 13.9d^{3} 12v^{2} Oct 9] rather unfurnished filly: fair maiden: stays 1¾m: acts on good to firm and heavy going: has worn hood: front runner/races prominently. *Michael Bell* **76**

DUKES MEADOW 6 b.g. Pastoral Pursuits 127 – Figura 87 (Rudimentary (USA) 118) [2017 57, a73: t9.5m^{3} t8.6m^{6} p8d^{2} p8g p8g p8g^{5} t8.6g^{3} p8d 8g^{5} 9.9m p10g^{4} p8d^{3} t8.6g^{6} p8s^{2} p8s^{6} Dec 17] rather leggy gelding: modest handicapper nowadays: stays 1¼m: acts on polytrack and tapeta: has worn headgear. *Roger Ingram* **60**

DUKE STREET (IRE) 5 b.g. Duke of Marmalade (IRE) 132 – Act of The Pace (IRE) 86 (King's Theatre (IRE) 128) [2017 89: p16d* 18m Oct 14] workmanlike gelding: useful handicapper: won at Chelmsford (by head from Aldreth) in February: stays 2m: acts on polytrack, tapeta, soft and good to firm going: tried in cheekpieces: useful hurdler/chaser. *Dr Richard Newland* **96**

DUKHAN 2 br.c. (Apr 5) Teofilo (IRE) 126 – Vedela (FR) (Selkirk (USA) 129) [2017 7g^{2} 7m^{4} p8g* Oct 26] €260,000Y: good-topped colt: fourth foal: half-brother to 1¼m winner Sea of Knowledge (by Sea The Stars): dam unraced half-sister to winner up to 1¾m (stayed 2½m) Vadamar and 2-y-o 7.5f winner Vedevani (both smart): fairly useful form: won minor event at Chelmsford (by length from Communique) in October: likely to stay 1¼m: open to further improvement. *Hugo Palmer* **86 p**

DUKINTA (IRE) 3 b.f. Dubawi (IRE) 129 – Misskinta (IRE) 81 (Desert Sun 120) [2017 9.9g 10.2s^{6} 11.6d 14s* p16g^{6} 14.1d Sep 21] half-sister to several winners, including very smart winner up to 1½m Grandeur (2-y-o 7f winner, by Verglas) and useful 2-y-o 1m winner (stays 11f) Magnolia Beach (by Footstepsinthesand): dam 1½m winner: fairly useful performer: won handicap at Bath (by 8 lengths from Percy Thrower) in August: stays 1¾m: acts on soft going: in headgear last 5 starts: front runner/races prominently. *Hugo Palmer* **85**

DULCINA 3 b.f. Compton Place 125 – Alushta 60 (Royal Applause 124) [2017 –: p6g^{2} Mar 29] modest form: best effort at 6f. *R. P. McNamara, Ireland* **53**

DUNCAN OF SCOTLAND (IRE) 4 ch.g. Roderic O'Connor (IRE) 119 – Cantando (IRE) (Hamas (IRE) 125) [2017 55: 6m* p6g* 6m 6.8m^{3} 6g^{2} 6g^{2} 5d^{5} 6d^{3} 5.8g Sep 2] fair handicapper: won at Ayr and Dundalk in May: seems best at 6f: acts on polytrack and good to firm going: wears blinkers: usually races prominently. *L. Smyth, Ireland* **71**

DUNDUNAH (USA) 3 ch.f. Sidney's Candy (USA) 124 – Sealedwithapproval (USA) (With Approval (CAN)) [2017 72: 5g^{3} 6g t5s^{3} 5m^{2} 5g^{5} 5m* 5.2g^{2} t5d 5g t5g t5g^{2} p5s Dec 8] fairly useful handicapper: won at Haydock in July: second at Yarmouth later same month and Newcastle in November: best form at 5f: acts on tapeta and good to firm going: wears tongue tie. *David O'Meara* **82**

DUNGANNON 10 b.g. Monsieur Bond (IRE) 120 – May Light 62 (Midyan (USA) 124) [2017 91, a99: f5g^{2} f5g* f5g^{4} f5m^{6} f5g* 5m p5g^{4} 5g^{5} f5g Nov 16] good-topped gelding: useful performer: won seller at Southwell in January and handicap there (by 2¼ lengths from New Road Side) in March: races at 5f nowadays: acts on polytrack, fibresand, good to firm and heavy going: wears headgear. *Andrew Balding* **96**

DUNQUIN (IRE) 5 b.g. Cape Cross (IRE) 129 – Last Resort 116 (Lahib (USA) 129) [2017 76: t9.5m t9.5g* t12.2g* t12.2g 10s 11.9m^{5} Jul 7] good-bodied gelding: fairly useful handicapper: won at Wolverhampton in February and March (by 1¼ lengths from Surround Sound): stays 1½m: acts on tapeta and good to soft going: often leads: sold £8,000 in August. *John Mackie* **80**

DURETTO 5 ch.g. Manduro (GER) 135 – Landinium (ITY) 109 (Lando (GER) 128) [2017 112: 13.4d^3 12.3v* 16s^5 Oct 21] tall gelding: smart performer: won listed race at Chester (by ½ length from Across The Stars) in September: third in Ormonde Stakes at same course (¾ length behind Western Hymn) in May: stays 2m: acts on polytrack, good to firm and heavy going: has worn hood: patiently ridden. *Andrew Balding* **114**

DUSKY DAWN 5 b.m. Kheleyf (USA) 116 – Piddies Pride (IRE) 75 (Indian Lodge (IRE) 127) [2017 84: t8g^5 t8d^3 f7m^5 t7.1d^4 t8g* f7d^5 f6d^3 Apr 6] fairly useful handicapper: won at Newcastle (by 3½ lengths from Barwah) in March: stays 1m: acts on fibresand and tapeta. *Alan Swinbank* **85**

DUSKY MAID (IRE) 3 b.f. Dark Angel (IRE) 113 – Dream Scape 74 (Oasis Dream 129) [2017 t7.1g^4 t7.1g^2 t8.6g t8d^4 7m* t7.2g* p7g^2 7m^6 t6.1g* t7.2g^2 p7g^5 p6g^6 Dec 12] €47,000F, £62,000Y: compact filly: first foal: dam 9.4f winner: fairly useful performer: won maiden at Catterick in May, and handicaps at Wolverhampton in June and August (by 5 lengths from Tooty Fruitti): stays 7f: acts on polytrack, tapeta and good to firm going: front runner/races prominently. *James Given* **87**

DUSTY 2 ch.f. (Apr 25) Paco Boy (IRE) 129 – Hairspray 92 (Bahamian Bounty 116) [2017 5m 5.1m^3 6v Sep 29] third foal: half-sister to useful winner up to 8.5f Epsom Icon (2-y-o 7f winner, by Sixties Icon): dam 6f winner (including at 2 yrs): fair form when third in minor event at Windsor (3½ lengths behind Flying Sparkle) on second of 3 starts: should stay 6f. *Mick Channon* **68**

DUSTY BERRY 3 ch.f. Sixties Icon 125 – Hazelberry (Bertolini (USA) 125) [2017 59: p12g Feb 8] lengthy filly: modest form on debut at 2 yrs, standout effort: tried in cheekpieces. *Eve Johnson Houghton* **–**

DUSTY BIN 3 b.g. Sepoy (AUS) 129 – Short Affair 99 (Singspiel (IRE) 133) [2017 71: t7.1g^6 p7d 7d^6 5d^5 t7.2g f6.1g Dec 29] fair form at 2 yrs, below that level in 2017: left Garry Moss after first start, Scott Dixon after second: stays 7f: acts on polytrack, tapeta and good to soft going: tried in headgear: usually races nearer last than first. *Roy Bowring* **58**

DUSTY BLUE 5 ch.m. Medicean 128 – Jazz Jam 100 (Pivotal 124) [2017 75: f5g f5m* f5d^3 p5f* 5m 5g 6d Jul 28] fair handicapper: won at Southwell (for Michael Appleby) in March and Lingfield (for David Loughnane) in April: had left Tony Carroll after first start: raced mainly at 5f/6f: acts on polytrack, fibresand, good to firm and good to soft going: has worn tongue tie. *Michael Easterby* **75**

DUTCH ACADEMY 2 b.c. (Feb 26) Dutch Art 126 – Katimont (IRE) 90 (Montjeu (IRE) 137) [2017 6s^5 6s^5 t7.1g Oct 20] modest form: best effort when fifth in minor event at Goodwood (5½ lengths behind Lady Dancealot) in October: should be suited by 7f: sold 5,500 gns, sent to Germany. *K. R. Burke* **60**

DUTCH ART DEALER 6 b.g. Dutch Art 126 – Lawyers Choice 86 (Namid 128) [2017 89: t7.1g* p7d t7.1d^4 7g 8m^6 7d 8s^4 Aug 9] smallish, lengthy gelding: fair handicapper on turf, fairly useful on all-weather: won at Newcastle (by 2¼ lengths from Roller) in January: stays 1m: acts on polytrack, tapeta, firm and good to soft going: wears headgear: often starts slowly, usually races nearer last than first: one to treat with caution. *Ivan Furtado* **79 §** **a90 §**

DUTCH ARTIST (IRE) 5 ch.g. Dutch Art 126 – Baltic Princess (FR) 81 (Peintre Celebre (USA) 137) [2017 87: 7m^3 7g 8s^2 7.2s 7.4m 10m^3 8.3v^5 12m 10.3v 8v^3 7d Oct 20] fairly useful handicapper: left David O'Meara after seventh start: stays 1m: acts on soft and good to firm going: often wears headgear: temperament under suspicion. *Alan Brown* **82**

DUTCH BARNEY 7 b.g. Dutch Art 126 – Celeb Style (IRE) 54 (Tagula (IRE) 116) [2017 –: 8m 12g Jun 5] no form: tried in cheekpieces. *Barry Leavy* **–**

DUTCH CONNECTION 5 ch.h. Dutch Art 126 – Endless Love (IRE) (Dubai Destination (USA) 127) [2017 122: 8f^6 7m^6 7m* 8f^6 7m^{pu} Oct 13] rangy, good sort: very smart performer: won Supreme Stakes at Goodwood (by 2 lengths from Salateen) in August: barely stays 1m: acts on firm and good to soft going. *Charles Hills* **117**

DUTCH DESIRE 2 b.f. (Mar 2) Dutch Art 126 – Danehill Destiny 104 (Danehill Dancer (IRE) 117) [2017 5d Jul 27] fifth foal: sister to useful winner up to 7f Dutch Destiny, closely related to 1m-1¼m winner Daily Trader (by Medicean) and half-sister to useful 6f winner Danehill Revival (by Pivotal): dam winner up to 6f (2-y-o 5f winner): 11/4, given considerate introduction when seventh in maiden at Sandown in July: will improve. *William Haggas* **51 p**

DUTCH DREAM 4 ch.f. Dutch Art 126 – Starry Sky 81 (Oasis Dream 129) [2017 51: 6m 5m^6 6m 5g* 5s^2 5d* 5d 5s 6v Sep 5] modest handicapper: won at Hamilton in June and July: best at 5f/6f: acts on soft and good to firm going: sometimes slowly away, often races in rear. *Linda Perratt* **60**

DUTCH GOLDEN AGE (IRE) 5 b.g. Kodiac 112 – Magic Melody 62 (Petong 126) [2017 86: p6g* p7g p6d* p6g⁶ p6g t5.1g² Jun 1] sturdy gelding: useful handicapper: won at Kempton in January and February (by 2½ lengths from Fairway To Heaven): stays 7f: acts on polytrack: tried in visor: has worn tongue tie: front runner/races prominently: sold 9,000 gns in July. *Gary Moore* **96**

DUTCH MELODY 3 b.f. Dutch Art 126 – Mystic Melody (IRE) (Montjeu (IRE) 137) [2017 8.3d 10.2s Jun 30] good-topped filly: first foal: dam once-raced sister to smart stayer Steve Rogers and half-sister to smart winner up to 7f The Right Man: well held in maidens. *Chris Wall* **–**

DUTCH MIST 4 ch.f. Dutch Art 126 – Solstice 84 (Dubawi (IRE) 129) [2017 92: p7m⁵ p7g Jan 28] neat filly: fairly useful handicapper, below form in 2017: stays 6f: acts on good to firm and good to soft going: usually wears headgear nowadays: often races in rear. *Kevin Ryan* **74**

DUTCH QUALITY 3 b.g. Dutch Art 126 – Miss Quality (USA) (Elusive Quality (USA)) [2017 71: 8m 10.2f May 26] fair form: stays 1m: tried in tongue tie. *Marco Botti* **68**

DUTCH STRANGER 2 b.f. (May 13) Dutch Art 126 – Passing Stranger (IRE) 74 (Dixie Union (USA) 121) [2017 5.1m⁴ May 8] unfurnished filly: third foal: dam, 6f winner, half-sister to useful 1m winner Beat of The Drum: 28/1, fourth in minor event at Windsor (3¾ lengths behind Declarationoflove) in May: should improve. *Harry Dunlop* **60 p**

DUTCH UNCLE 5 b.g. Dutch Art 126 – Evasive Quality (FR) (Highest Honor (FR) 124) [2017 92: p10g² t8.6m⁶ t9.5g* p10g² t9.5g⁵ 10.1g⁶ 8f 7m 7s⁶ p8d 7s 8.1g⁴ 8.1d t9.5d Dec 16] compact gelding: useful handicapper: won at Wolverhampton (by 1½ lengths from Final) in February: second at Lingfield in January and later in February: left Ed Dunlop after sixth start, Robert Cowell after thirteenth: stays 11f, usually races at shorter: acts on polytrack, tapeta, good to firm and good to soft going: has worn headgear, including in 2017. *Archie Watson* **95**

DUTIFUL SON (IRE) 7 b.g. Invincible Spirit (IRE) 121 – Grecian Dancer 114 (Dansili 127) [2017 93: p8m³ p8g p7g p7g³ p6g* 5g p8g t7.2g⁶ p6d p6s⁵ p7d p6g⁵ p6g p7g⁵ p7g³ p7g* p7g* t7.2d Dec 26] sturdy gelding: fairly useful performer: won handicap at Kempton (by length from Steelriver) in March, and handicap and seller at Lingfield in December: stays 1m: raced almost exclusively on all-weather: tried in cheekpieces: usually races prominently. *Simon Dow* **87**

DUXBURY 3 b.c. Dutch Art 126 – Triskel 101 (Hawk Wing (USA) 136) [2017 –: f8g Jan 30] well held in 2 maidens. *Richard Fahey* **–**

D'WATERSIDE 3 b.g. Sir Percy 129 – Santorini Sunset (Haafhd 129) [2017 6.1g 7s 7.4d⁴ 7.6d⁵ p8g⁵ p11g⁵ p12g t9.5g⁵ t9.5g⁶ t8.6g⁴ p7g⁵ Dec 30] modest maiden: stays 9f: acts on polytrack and tapeta: in blinkers last 2 starts: front runner/races prominently. *David Loughnane* **63**

DWIGHT D 4 b.g. Duke of Marmalade (IRE) 132 – Almatinka (IRE) (Indian Ridge 123) [2017 94: 10.2s 8.2v 9v⁶ 10v Oct 23] well-made gelding: fairly useful at best, little impact in handicaps in 2017: tried in cheekpieces: usually races nearer last than first. *Stuart Coltherd* **–**

DYLAN MOUTH (IRE) 6 b.h. Dylan Thomas (IRE) 132 – Cottonmouth (IRE) 109 (Noverre (USA) 125) [2017 117: 9.9g² 12.1g³ 12g⁵ 12m p14g³ 13.9g 11.8m* 11m p12g³ Nov 6] strong, compact horse: smart performer: won Old Newton Cup (Handicap) at Haydock (by 2¼ lengths from Soldier In Action) in July: placed in handicaps at Meydan **115**

bet365 Old Newton Cup (Heritage Handicap), Haydock—
Dylan Mouth defies top weight to run out a clear-cut winner from Soldier In Action (stripes on cap), with 9/2 favourite Shraaoh (third right) and Blakeney Point (left) coming home just behind

(2) in February, minor event at Chelmsford in May and listed race at Kempton (length behind Titi Makfi) in November: should stay 1¾m: acts on firm and good to soft going: tried in cheekpieces. *Marco Botti*

DYLAN'S CENTENARY 6 b.g. Kyllachy 129 – Sheka 68 (Ishiguru (USA) 114) [2017 7m 7d p8d^{rr} 7s Oct 10] sturdy gelding: maiden: no form in 2017: has worn headgear, including final start: most temperamental (twice refused to race). *Phil McEntee* **§§**

DYLAN'S STORM (IRE) 5 b.g. Zebedee 113 – Storm Lady (IRE) (Alhaarth (IRE) 126) [2017 –: 8m 7f 8.5m 9m 8g Aug 2] fair handicapper at best, well below that level since 2015: stays 7f: acts on polytrack, good to firm and good to soft going: in cheekpieces last 5 starts: tried in tongue tie. *Peter Niven* **43**

DYLLAN (IRE) 4 b.g. Zebedee 113 – Luvmedo (IRE) 57 (One Cool Cat (USA) 123) [2017 83: 5f 5.7f 7s^2 7v 6g^5 Aug 20] compact gelding: fair handicapper: stays 7f: acts on soft and good to firm going: in cheekpieces last 2 starts: temperament under suspicion: sold £1,800, sent to Germany. *Ruth Carr* **73**

DYNAMIC 3 b.f. Teofilo (IRE) 126 – White Cay (Dalakhani (IRE) 133) [2017 77P: 8m* 8d^5 8m* Oct 25] big filly: has plenty of scope: fairly useful form: won maiden at Newmarket in August and handicap at same course (by neck from Al Nafoorah) in October: will stay 1¼m: will go on improving. *William Haggas* **93 p**

DYNAMIC GIRL (IRE) 4 b.f. Holy Roman Emperor (IRE) 125 – Boca Dancer (IRE) 96 (Indian Ridge 123) [2017 78: p6g^4 6g 7f 8.1m 7d 7.6s 7v^3 7s 8.3g p7g^5 p7m^6 p8s p8s Dec 17] sturdy filly: fair handicapper at 3 yrs, below that level in 2017: stays 7f: acts on polytrack, good to firm and heavy going: has worn headgear, including in 2017: in tongue tie last 5 starts: usually slowly away: best treated with caution. *Brendan Powell* **64 §**

DYNA MIGHT 3 b.f. Foxwedge (AUS) 128 – Dyna Bowl (USA) (Dynaformer (USA)) [2017 49: t9.5g 12.1g* 12.1m^2 12s* 12g^4 t14g^4 12d 12.5s t12.4d Oct 24] modest handicapper: won at Beverley in May and Thirsk in June: stays 1¾m: acts on tapeta, soft and good to firm going: wears cheekpieces: has high head carriage. *Ollie Pears* **64**

DYNAMO (IRE) 6 b.g. Galileo (IRE) 134 – Trading Places (Dansili 127) [2017 a56: t13.9m^6 p12g p13g Feb 28] fair handicapper, below best in 2017: stays 2m: acts on polytrack and good to firm going: wears tongue tie. *Richard Hughes* **54**

DYNAMO WALT (IRE) 6 b.g. Acclamation 118 – Cambara 97 (Dancing Brave (USA) 140) [2017 99: t5g^4 p5d^2 p5g p5f^5 p5g^5 p5g^4 p5g* p5g^4 p5s^6 p5g t5.1g^4 Dec 5] fairly useful handicapper: won at Chelmsford (by ½ length from Cultured Knight) in May: raced mainly at 5f: acts on polytrack, tapeta and good to firm going: wears visor. *Derek Shaw* **91**

DYSON'S GIRL 2 ch.f. (Feb 12) Equiano (FR) 127 – Choisette 75 (Choisir (AUS) 126) [2017 5m 6m^4 6m^4 6m^2 6d^4 5d^4 5d^5 p6g^6 t6g^6 t5d Nov 4] £22,000Y: fifth foal: half-sister to 6f (including at 2 yrs) winner Straightothepoint (by Kyllachy) and smart 6f (including at 2 yrs) winner Flying Pursuit (by Pastoral Pursuits): dam 5f winner (including at 2 yrs): fair maiden: stays 6f: acts on good to firm going: in cheekpieces last 4 starts: often races prominently. *Bryan Smart* **65**

E

EADAOINS PET (IRE) 4 b.f. Tagula (IRE) 116 – Ice Rock (IRE) (Rock of Gibraltar (IRE) 133) [2017 72: 7m^5 8.7m^3 7.5g^6 p8g^3 7d 7.8g^5 p8g p7g^4 Oct 6] fifth foal: half-sister to useful 7.5f/1m winner Ice Slice (by Dark Angel) and 2-y-o 9f winner Shadow Rock (by Verglas): dam, French maiden (stayed 1¼m), half-sister to 1m winner Khateeb and winner up to 1½m Chock A Block (both smart): fair maiden: stays 8.5f: acts on polytrack and good to firm going: tried in cheekpieces. *J. J. Feane, Ireland* **71**

EAGLE CREEK (IRE) 3 b.g. Raven's Pass (USA) 133 – Blue Angel (IRE) 107 (Oratorio (IRE) 128) [2017 69P: p8g* 8m 8g^2 8s p8g^3 p8g Nov 18] useful-looking gelding: useful performer: won maiden at Lingfield (by 6 lengths from Mathix) in April: third in handicap at Kempton (neck behind Brigliadoro) in October: raced only at 1m: acts on polytrack: front runner/races prominently, sometimes finds little. *Simon Crisford* **105**

EARLY DAWN 2 ch.f. (Apr 22) Dawn Approach (IRE) 132 – Born Something (IRE) 105 (Caerleon (USA) 132) [2017 6g^4 6m^4 Jul 6] 60,000Y: half-sister to several winners, including useful winner up to 9.5f Red Label (2-y-o 1m winner, by Dubawi) and useful UAE 1¼m winner Tarbawi (by Anabaa): dam, French/US 7f-8.5f winner, half-sister to top-class miler Goldikova: fair form when fourth in maiden/minor event: should do better. *Marco Botti* **67 p**

Darley EBF Stallions Boadicea Stakes, Newmarket—a daughter of the yard's Queen Mary Stakes winner Ceiling Kitty, the Tom Dascombe-trained Eartha Kitt gains a valuable 'black-type' success from Marie of Lyon (No.6, partially hidden by winner) and Pixeleen (spots on cap)

EARLY MORNING (IRE) 6 gr.g. New Approach (IRE) 132 – Summer's Eve 104 (Singspiel (IRE) 133) [2017 110: 8m² 8m 8d 7s p8g p7m* p7.5g³ Dec 16] workmanlike gelding: useful performer: won minor event at Lingfield (by 5 lengths from Chevallier) in November: stays 10.5f, usually races over shorter: acts on polytrack, good to firm and good to soft going: usually races close up. *Harry Dunlop* **103 a109**

EARTHA KITT 3 br.f. Pivotal 124 – Ceiling Kitty 107 (Red Clubs (IRE) 125) [2017 92p: 7d 6m* 6g³ 6g² 7g 6g³ 6m* Oct 14] lengthy, useful-looking filly: useful performer: won handicap at York (by ½ length from Southern Belle) in June and listed race at Newmarket (by ¾ length from Marie of Lyon) in October: third in handicap at Newmarket (head behind Pixeleen) in October: should stay 7f: acts on good to firm going: wears cheekpieces. *Tom Dascombe* **105**

EARTHLY (USA) 3 b.c. Spring At Last (USA) 122 – Geographic (USA) (Empire Maker (USA) 129) [2017 74p: p10g* t9.5g⁵ 9.9m⁶ p12g* 10.2d⁵ 12s 14.4v⁶ p12g⁶ Nov 1] fairly useful performer: won maiden at Lingfield in February and handicap at same course (by ¾ length from Starshell) in May: left Ralph Beckett after fourth start: stays 1½m: acts on polytrack and good to firm going: tried in cheekpieces. *Bernard Llewellyn* **81**

EARTHWINDORFIRE 6 br.g. High Chaparral (IRE) 132 – Elemental 82 (Rudimentary (USA) 118) [2017 72: t13.9m Jan 13] fair maiden handicapper: well below form only start in 2017: stays 1½m: acts on polytrack and soft going: in cheekpieces last 4 starts: front runner/races prominently. *Geoffrey Deacon* **–**

EAST COAST LADY (IRE) 5 b.m. Kodiac 112 – Alexander Anapolis (IRE) 94 (Spectrum (IRE) 126) [2017 78§: t7.1m⁶ p7g⁶ t8.6g³ t7.1g² p7g² p7g 6s³ p7d* 6d⁵ 6d 6s⁵ 7d⁶ 7v* 8.1d* Oct 23] useful-looking mare: fairly useful handicapper: won at Chelmsford in May, Leicester (apprentice) in September and Windsor (dead-heated with International Law) in October: has form at 1¼m, races mainly over shorter: acts on polytrack, tapeta, good to firm and heavy going: tried in headgear. *William Stone* **80**

EASTERN DRAGON (IRE) 7 b.g. Elnadim (USA) 128 – Shulammite Woman (IRE) (Desert Sun 120) [2017 84: t8g* t8d⁵ t8g⁵ t8g⁶ 8g 10g 12d Aug 5] sturdy gelding: fairly useful handicapper: won at Newcastle (by ¾ length from Rock Warbler) in January: stays 8.5f: acts on polytrack, tapeta, good to firm and heavy going: wears headgear: usually slowly away, often races in rear. *Iain Jardine* **81**

EASTERN IMPACT (IRE) 6 b.g. Bahamian Bounty 116 – Kate The Great 79 (Xaar 132) [2017 113: 6g 6g 6g t6g³ 6m² 6m 6d 6g 5.6g 6g⁴ Oct 14] good-topped gelding: useful handicapper: second at Newmarket (1¼ lengths behind Mr Lupton) in May: stays 6f: acts on tapeta, firm and good to soft going: in cheekpieces last 4 starts: races prominently. *Richard Fahey* **107**

EASTERN (IRE) 3 b.f. Shamardal (USA) 129 – Thought Is Free 88 (Cadeaux Genereux 131) [2017 8m⁴ 9.9s⁶ Sep 15] fifth foal: half-sister to 3 winners, including 1m winners Merry Me (useful, by Invincible Spirit) and Westward Ho (by Fastnet Rock): dam maiden (best up to 1m): fair form: better effort when fourth in maiden at Bath in August. *Andrew Balding* **69**

EASTERN LADY (IND) 4 ch.f. Dancing Forever (USA) 119 – Oriental Lady (IRE) (King's Best (USA) 132) [2017 76: 10.2s^4 8.1g^6 12g^6 12s^6 Aug 17] rangy filly: fair maiden: below form in 2017: stays 1½m: acts on soft going: in tongue tie last 4 starts. *Richard Price* **58**

EASTERN RACER (IRE) 5 b.g. Bushranger (IRE) 119 – Queen Cobra (IRE) 80 (Indian Rocket 115) [2017 91: 7g 6m^6 Apr 20] good-topped gelding: fairly useful handicapper, below form in 2017: stays 7f: acts on good to firm and heavy going: usually wears cheekpieces. *Brian Ellison* **77**

EASTERN SUNRISE 2 b.f. (Mar 20) Dawn Approach (IRE) 132 – Desert Sunrise 75 (Green Desert (USA) 127) [2017 7d 7d 5.1g Sep 6] rather unfurnished filly: second foal: half-sister to 2-y-o 1m winner Desert Water (by Sepoy): dam, maiden (stayed 7f), half-sister to Middle Park Stakes winner Primo Valentino and Cherry Hinton Stakes winner Dora Carrington: modest form: standout effort when seventh in minor event at Newmarket (6 lengths behind Quivery) on debut. *Richard Hannon* **60**

EAST INDIA 5 ch.g. Galileo (IRE) 134 – Field of Hope (IRE) 119 (Selkirk (USA) 129) [2017 85: 10.2f^3 12g^6 10.1g^3 10.9g* 11.9g^5 9.7d^3 9.9d p9.4g 10.4d^6 p11.9g Dec 17] workmanlike gelding: fairly useful performer: won claimer at Clairefontaine in August, then left George Baker: stays 1½m: acts on firm going: sometimes wears headgear. *P. Nicot, France* **81**

EAST INDIES 4 b.g. Authorized (IRE) 133 – Elan (Dansili 127) [2017 –: 10.1m^6 p12g Dec 30] good-topped gelding: fairly useful at 2 yrs, lightly raced on Flat since: best effort at 1¼m: acts on polytrack: tried in hood: fairly useful hurdler. *Gary Moore* **–**

EAST STREET REVUE 4 ch.g. Pastoral Pursuits 127 – Revue Princess (IRE) 80 (Mull of Kintyre (USA) 114) [2017 101: 5m^2 6m^4 5g 5m 5g^6 5.5g^4 5g* 5d Oct 28] useful handicapper: won at York (by 1¼ lengths from Memories Galore) in October: best at 5f: acts on good to firm and good to soft going: wears blinkers: usually races prominently. *Tim Easterby* **104**

EAST WIND 2 b.f. (Apr 19) Dick Turpin (IRE) 127 – Angel Rays 68 (Unfuwain (USA) 131) [2017 10v Oct 9] third foal: dam, maiden (stayed 7f), half-sister to smart 5.4f-7f winner Barney McGrew: 50/1, well held in minor event at Pontefract. *Tony Coyle* **–**

EASY CODE 4 b.g. Bahamian Bounty 116 – Skirrid (Halling (USA) 133) [2017 71: 6m p8s^3 8d^4 7s^4 t7.2g* 7g^3 p7g^3 p8g* p8g^5 Oct 5] sturdy gelding: fair handicapper: won at Wolverhampton in July and Lingfield in September: stays 1m: acts on polytrack, tapeta and good to soft going: often races towards rear. *William Haggas* **72** **a79**

EASY TIGER 5 b.g. Refuse To Bend (IRE) 128 – Extremely Rare (IRE) 82 (Mark of Esteem (IRE) 137) [2017 93: 8.1g^2 7g* 7v^4 7g 7d^2 7d^4 p7d^2 p7g^6 t7.2g^3 p8g^2 Dec 13] rangy gelding: useful handicapper: won at Leicester (by 1¼ lengths from Twin Appeal) in July: second at Chelmsford (¾ length behind Blue On Blue) in October: stays 1m: acts on polytrack, tapeta, good to firm and good to soft going: has worn cheekpieces, including once in 2017: front runner/races prominently. *Malcolm Saunders* **96**

EASY VICTORY 3 b.f. Dubawi (IRE) 129 – Independence 116 (Selkirk (USA) 129) [2017 89: 7d Nov 11] close-coupled filly: fairly useful form: well held only start in 2017: best effort at 6f: acts on good to firm going: tried in cheekpieces. *Saeed bin Suroor* **–**

EASY WIND 3 b.f. Shirocco (GER) 129 – Attainable 72 (Kalanisi (IRE) 132) [2017 t7.1g t7.2g 7m^5 13.1g^3 16v^2 t14g^2 Aug 10] second foal: dam maiden (stayed 1½m): fair maiden: stays 2m: acts on tapeta and heavy going: tried in cheekpieces. *Sir Mark Prescott Bt* **67**

EATON SQUARE 3 b.g. Invincible Spirit (IRE) 121 – Loch Jipp (USA) 95 (Belong To Me (USA)) [2017 91p: 7m Jun 2] good-quartered gelding: fairly useful form: well held only start in 2017: stays 7f: in cheekpieces last 3 starts: sent to Hong Kong. *John Gosden* **–**

EBBESBOURNE (IRE) 3 b.f. Teofilo (IRE) 126 – Ebble 77 (Oasis Dream 129) [2017 78p: p8g^5 10.3g* 10g^2 12d 12g Oct 7] rather unfurnished filly: useful handicapper: won at York in May: second in listed race at Newbury (3¾ lengths behind Elas Ruby) in June: should stay beyond 1¼m: acts on polytrack, best turf form on good going: in hood last 4 starts. *Sir Michael Stoute* **101**

EBBISHAM (IRE) 4 b.g. Holy Roman Emperor (IRE) 125 – Balting Lass (IRE) (Orpen (USA) 116) [2017 76: p8g p8g* 10m^6 p8s p8g t7.2m* p7s t7.2d^3 Dec 26] workmanlike gelding: fair handicapper: won at Kempton in April and Wolverhampton in October: left Jim Boyle after fifth start: stays 1m: acts on polytrack and tapeta: often in cheekpieces in 2017: usually races prominently. *John Mackie* **79**

EBEN DUBAI (IRE) 5 b.g. New Approach (IRE) 132 – Eldalil 106 (Singspiel (IRE) 133) [2017 8f^6 11.7f^6 10.2d^3 12d 12v^5 11.6f^2 11.6f^2 10.2f^5 10.2d^3 14.1d^3 10.5v^3 11.9s^6 Oct 10] modest maiden handicapper: left Tracey Barfoot-Saunt after ninth start: stays 1¾m: acts on firm and good to soft going: has worn headgear, including last 3 starts. *John Flint* **61**

EBITDA 3 b.f. Compton Place 125 – Tipsy Girl 79 (Haafhd 129) [2017 f5s^5 t6g t5.1f^6 5m* 6g^6 5.5f^4 5m 5d* 5.2m* 5g^6 5d* 5s* 5s* Nov 8] 12,500Y: second foal: half-sister to winner up to 6f Socialites Red (2-y-o 5f winner, by Sakhee's Secret): dam 2-y-o 5.7f winner who stayed 1m: fairly useful/most progressive handicapper: won at Redcar in May, Ripon and Yarmouth in August, Catterick in September and October, and Nottingham (by 1¼ lengths from Angel Palanas) in November: best form at 5f: acts on soft and good to firm going. *Scott Dixon* **93**

EBONY N IVORY 4 b.g. Equiano (FR) 127 – Ile Deserte (Green Desert (USA) 127) [2017 80: t6m^3 p5d t6g^4 t5.1g p6g^5 f6d Mar 21] fair handicapper: third at Wolverhampton in January: stayed 6f: acted on polytrack, tapeta, best turf form on good going: wore headgear: front runner/raced prominently: dead. *Archie Watson* **76**

EBONY PRINCESS (IRE) 7 b.m. Camacho 118 – Maripova (IRE) (Marju (IRE) 127) [2017 p8g 7d 9.1m 7d^5 p8g Sep 22] first foal: dam once-raced half-sister to very smart 1m/9f winner Autumn Glory: maiden, only poor form in 2017: tried in tongue tie: races towards rear. *Kieran Patrick Cotter, Ireland* **49**

EBQAA (IRE) 3 b.f. Cape Cross (IRE) 129 – Estedaama (IRE) 97 (Marju (IRE) 127) [2017 60p: 10.3v^4 7.6v^2 t10.2g^2 t12.2d^4 Dec 9] fair maiden: should stay 1½m: raced only on heavy going on turf. *James Unett* **79**

EBTKAAR (IRE) 3 b.g. Cape Cross (IRE) 129 – Clare Glen (IRE) 101 (Sakhee (USA) 136) [2017 73p: 8.2d^3 8.1m^3 p7s^2 Dec 17] sturdy gelding: fairly useful form: second in handicap at Chelmsford in December: left Roger Varian after second start: stays 1m. *Michael Appleby* **83**

EBURACI (IRE) 3 b.c. Vale of York (IRE) 117 – Dubai Pearl (IRE) (Refuse To Bend (IRE) 128) [2017 64p: 7g f8g^4 8s May 19] leggy, rather unfurnished colt: modest form: best effort at 1m: in visor last 2 starts. *Charlie Fellowes* **64**

ECCLESTON 6 b.g. Acclamation 118 – Miss Meggy 97 (Pivotal 124) [2017 98: 6g 6s^4 6d^4 6d 6d^2 6g^6 6v 5v^3 t6s^3 t7.2d^6 Dec 16] sparely-made gelding: fairly useful handicapper: second at Doncaster in July: left David O'Meara after sixth start: stays 6f: acts on tapeta and heavy going: wears headgear: often races towards rear. *Julie Camacho* **93**

ECHO COVE (IRE) 2 ch.c. (Mar 22) Roderic O'Connor (IRE) 119 – Russian Rave 97 (Danehill Dancer (IRE) 117) [2017 7g 7g 8g^4 Oct 7] workmanlike colt: fair form: best effort when fourth in minor event at Newmarket (7 lengths behind Old Persian) final start. *Jane Chapple-Hyam* **76**

ECHO (IRE) 2 b.g. (Apr 15) Zoffany (IRE) 121 – Aweebounce (IRE) (Dubawi (IRE) 129) [2017 7m 7.4s 7.4m^5 t8s 8g* Sep 27] modest performer: won nursery at Redcar in September: will probably stay further than 1m: acts on tapeta. *Jedd O'Keeffe* **64**

ECHOISM (IRE) 3 ch.f. Casamento (IRE) 118 – Epic Similie (Lomitas 129) [2017 60: 7g^5 t7.1g Nov 15] poor maiden on balance of form: best effort at 7f: acts on heavy going: tried in hood: front runner/races prominently. *Peter Hiatt* **–**

ECHO OF LIGHTNING 7 b.g. Echo of Light 125 – Classic Lass 68 (Dr Fong (USA) 128) [2017 84: 6.1s 7d 7.2g* 7.2d^3 8s* 7.6g 7.6v 8v^3 7g^2 7v f7.1g t8d Nov 10] quite good-topped gelding: fairly useful handicapper: won at Musselburgh in July and Pontefract (by 5 lengths from Stanley) in August: left Brian Ellison after seventh start: stays 1m: acts on good to firm and heavy going: wears headgear: usually leads. *Roger Fell* **91**

ECONOMIC CRISIS (IRE) 8 ch.m. Excellent Art 125 – Try The Air (IRE) (Foxhound (USA) 103) [2017 85: 5m^2 5g 5s^5 5g^3 5m^6 5d^6 5g^4 5s^5 5m 5m^5 5s* 5s^2 5v* 6s^2 t6d^3 Nov 10] leggy mare: fairly useful handicapper: won at Musselburgh (twice) in October: left Colin Teague after tenth start: stays 6f: acts on all-weather, good to firm and heavy going: tried in cheekpieces. *Alan Berry* **82**

EDDIEBET 3 ch.g. Monsieur Bond (IRE) 120 – Champagne Katie (Medicean 128) [2017 t6g^6 p6d^5 f7d^2 f8g^3 8m^3 t8g^5 t7.1d p7g^3 p7g Dec 28] fair maiden: stays 7f: acts on polytrack and fibresand. *David O'Meara* **72**

EDDIEMAURICE (IRE) 6 ch.g. Captain Rio 122 – Annals 74 (Lujain (USA) 119) [2017 13.1m^2 Apr 14] fairly useful handicapper: second at Bath sole run on Flat in 2017: stays 13f: acts on good to firm and tapeta: often wears headgear: fairly useful hurdler. *John Flint* **83**

EDDIETHEBUNG (IRE) 2 ch.g. (Mar 22) Casamento (IRE) 118 – Ma Paloma (FR) (Highest Honor (FR) 124) [2017 6v 7.9g Oct 13] strong gelding: well held in minor events. *Nigel Tinkler* **–**

EDDY MERCS 5 bl.g. Striking Ambition 122 – Bella Tutrice (IRE) 78 (Woodborough (USA) 112) [2017 –: t7.1m Jan 13] no form: tried in hood/tongue tie. *Michael Appleby* **–**

EDDYSTONE ROCK (IRE) 5 ch.g. Rock of Gibraltar (IRE) 133 – Bayberry (UAE) 109 (Bering 136) [2017 100: p10g^3 a9g^4 a8.9g 8g^6 10.1g 12m^2 12m 10.3m^6 9.9g 10g^4 10.3m* 10m 9d 8s 11.9s^3 Nov 11] close-coupled gelding: smart handicapper on turf, useful on all-weather: won at York (by short head from Titi Makfi) in August: third in November Handicap at Doncaster (2½ lengths behind Saunter) final start: stays 1½m: acts on polytrack, soft and good to firm going: has worn hood: often races towards rear: consistent. *John Best* **110** **a100**

EDEN ROSE 2 b.f. (May 3) Dansili 127 – Gallic Star (IRE) 105 (Galileo (IRE) 134) [2017 8.3d Oct 18] third foal: half-sister to 1m winner Star Blaze (by Shamardal): dam 2-y-o 6f-1m winner who stayed 1½m: 50/1, well held in maiden at Nottingham. *Mick Channon* –

EDE'S A WINNER 2 ch.f. (Mar 10) Archipenko (USA) 127 – Run For Ede's 89 (Peintre Celebre (USA) 137) [2017 6.1g p8g p6g^5 p7d Dec 13] narrow filly: third foal: dam 1m-1½m winner: little form. *Pat Phelan* –

EDE'S E RIDER 3 b.g. Equiano (FR) 127 – Run For Ede's 89 (Peintre Celebre (USA) 137) [2017 –: p8g 8.1d p7g Oct 11] modest maiden: best effort at 1m: acts on polytrack. *Pat Phelan* **50**

EDE'S THE MOVER 4 b.f. Bahamian Bounty 116 – Run For Ede's 89 (Peintre Celebre (USA) 137) [2017 59: 9.9g p8g^3 p8g^5 8.5d^6 8d Sep 11] modest maiden: stays 1¼m: acts on polytrack and soft going: often races prominently. *Pat Phelan* **59**

EDGAR ALLAN POE (IRE) 3 b.g. Zoffany (IRE) 121 – Swingsky (IRE) (Indian Ridge 123) [2017 66: 6g 8f^6 8.3s* 8s* 8m^4 9s^4 8.3d^6 8.1d^2 7v^2 Nov 7] fairly useful handicapper: won at Hamilton and Pontefract in July: second at Redcar in November: stays 8.5f: acts on polytrack, good to firm and heavy going: tried in blinkers. *Rebecca Bastiman* **83**

EDGAR BALTHAZAR 5 b.g. Pastoral Pursuits 127 – Assistacat (IRE) (Lend A Hand 124) [2017 91§: t8d^4 Nov 10] fairly useful handicapper: stays 1m: acts on tapeta, good to firm and good to soft going: wears headgear: sometimes slowly away, often races towards rear: temperamental. *Keith Dalgleish* **84 §**

EDGAR (GER) 7 b.g. Big Shuffle (USA) 122 – Estella (GER) (Acatenango (GER) 127) [2017 72: f12g Jan 1] fair form: well held in claimer only start on Flat in 2017: stays 1¾m: acts on fibresand and tapeta: wears headgear: tried in tongue tie: front runner/races prominently: modest hurdler/chaser. *David Bridgwater* –

EDGED IN BLUE 3 b.f. Acclamation 118 – Dutch Diamond 83 (Dutch Art 126) [2017 60: p6g^2 p7d^6 6m* 6m^6 7d^4 7m^2 Aug 16] fair handicapper: won at Yarmouth in April: left K. R. Burke before final outing: stays 7f: acts on polytrack, good to firm and good to soft going. *S. Brogi, France* **70**

EDGED OUT 7 b.m. Piccolo 121 – Edge of Light 94 (Xaar 132) [2017 80: 5.1m 5m^3 5f* Jun 18] plain mare: fairly useful handicapper: won at Salisbury (by ¾ length from Mr Pocket) in June: stays 6f: acts on firm and soft going: front runner/races prominently. *Christopher Mason* **82**

EDGE (IRE) 6 b.g. Acclamation 118 – Chanter (Lomitas 129) [2017 64: 7d^5 8.1d 8f 8g^6 8s^5 8g^3 10.2d^2 9.9s* 9.9d^2 7s* 7d t9.5g t8.6g^3 t8.6d^5 Dec 9] fair handicapper: won at Brighton (amateur) in September and Salisbury in October: third at Wolverhampton in November: effective at testing 7f, stays 1¼m: acts on tapeta, firm and soft going: wears headgear: sometimes slowly away. *Bernard Llewellyn* **69**

EDGE OF HEAVEN 5 b.m. Pastoral Pursuits 127 – Halfwaytoparadise 69 (Observatory (USA) 131) [2017 75: t9.5g^5 Jan 6] compact mare: fairly useful handicapper at best: stays 8.5f: acts on polytrack, tapeta, good to firm and good to soft going: tried in cheekpieces. *Jonathan Portman* **70**

EDGE OF SANITY (IRE) 8 b.g. Invincible Spirit (IRE) 121 – Saor Sinn (IRE) 60 (Galileo (IRE) 134) [2017 16.3m^3 16.3d Aug 23] leggy gelding: useful handicapper: third at York (1½ lengths behind Theydon Grey) on return from long absence: stays 16.5f: acts on polytrack, soft and good to firm going: has worn tongue tie, including last 2 starts. *Iain Jardine* **98**

EDGE OF THE WORLD (IRE) 2 b.f. (Apr 4) Fastnet Rock (AUS) 127 – Lady Links 100 (Bahamian Bounty 116) [2017 7.1s p7g t7.2g Dec 2] 62,000F, €110,000Y: angular filly: half-sister to several winners, including smart/moody winner up to 1m (stayed 1¼m) Selinka (2-y-o 6f/7f winner, by Selkirk) and 2-y-o 7f winner Tidal Wave (by Canford Cliffs): dam 6f winner (including at 2 yrs): little impact in minor events. *Ralph Beckett* –

EDITH WESTON 4 b.f. Showcasing 117 – Twitch Hill 67 (Piccolo 121) [2017 55: t5.1m t5.1g 5.2m Apr 25] maiden, well held in 2017: usually wears headgear: often starts slowly, usually races in rear: one to treat with plenty of caution. *Robert Cowell* – §

EDWARD LEWIS 4 b.g. Kyllachy 129 – Tahirah 99 (Green Desert (USA) 127) [2017 100: 5m* 5m² 5d* 5s⁴ 5m⁵ 6m⁶ 5g 6d 5.4d² 5v⁵ 6g Oct 14] good-quartered, dipped-backed gelding: useful handicapper: won at Beverley (by head from East Street Revue) in April and Lingfield (by 1¼ lengths from Orvar) in May: best at 5f/6f: acts on good to firm and good to soft going. *David O'Meara* **109**

EEH BAH GUM (IRE) 2 b.g. (May 16) Dandy Man (IRE) 123 – Moonline Dancer (FR) 79 (Royal Academy (USA) 130) [2017 6g 5v 7g Oct 7] €24,000F, €30,000 2-y-o: third foal: dam 2-y-o 6f winner: little impact in maiden/minor events: type to do better in handicaps. *David O'Meara* **– p**

EENY MAC (IRE) 10 ch.g. Redback 116 – Sally Green (IRE) 79 (Common Grounds 118) [2017 54, a42: 9m 9s 7.4m Jul 7] modest handicapper: below form in 2017: stayed 1¼m: acted on any turf going: wore headgear: usually raced close up: dead. *John Wainwright* **–**

EESHA BEAUTY (IRE) 2 b.f. (Apr 3) Born To Sea (IRE) 117 – Eastern Glow (Cape Cross (IRE) 129) [2017 6.1f 6.1g³ t7.2g* Aug 31] €28,000Y: good-topped filly: third foal: dam ran once in France: fair form: won minor event at Wolverhampton (by 1¼ lengths from Merkava) in August: stays 7f: likely to do better still. *Marco Botti* **67 p**

EESHA SAYS (IRE) 2 b.f. (Mar 22) Fast Company (IRE) 126 – Admire The View (IRE) 94 (Dubawi (IRE) 129) [2017 t6.1g p5m⁴ p6d Dec 13] €15,000F, £20,000Y, 800 2-y-o: fourth foal: half-sister to useful 2-y-o 5f winner Silver Line (by Dark Angel): dam winner up to 1m (2-y-o 7f winner) out of useful 1m-1¼m winner Miss Honorine: no form in seller/minor events. *Tony Carroll* **–**

EEZ EH (IRE) 4 b.g. Jeremy (USA) 122 – Step With Style (USA) 81 (Gulch (USA)) [2017 80: 10m 10m⁵ 10m⁶ 10s 9g³ 9d⁵ 10g Aug 2] lengthy gelding: fair handicapper: stays 1½m, usually races over shorter: acts on soft and good to firm going: wears headgear: well held in novice hurdle. *Keith Dalgleish* **72**

EFAADAH (IRE) 2 b.f. (Mar 20) Dansili 127 – Albaraah (IRE) 114 (Oasis Dream 129) [2017 7.5g* 8d² 8m Oct 13] third foal: half-sister to useful French 2-y-o 5.5f/6f (Prix de Cabourg) winner Alrahma (by Shamardal): dam French 1m/9f winner: useful form: won newcomers race at Deauville (by 3 lengths from Soustraction) in August: second in Prix d'Aumale at Chantilly (length behind Soustraction) in September: only eighth behind Laurens in Fillies' Mile at Newmarket final outing: stays 1m. *F. Head, France* **101**

EGGESFORD 3 b.g. Foxwedge (AUS) 128 – Elegant Pride (Beat Hollow 126) [2017 p11d⁴ Feb 22] half-brother to several winners, including 1¼m-1½m winner Age of Elegance (by Makfi) and 2-y-o 1m winner Edification (by Dream Ahead): dam unraced: 10/1, fourth in maiden at Kempton: no form over hurdles. *Martyn Meade* **57**

EHTIRAAS 4 b.g. Oasis Dream 129 – Kareemah (IRE) (Peintre Celebre (USA) 137) [2017 92: 8.3g² 8.1g⁵ Sep 6] well-made gelding: fairly useful handicapper: second at Nottingham in July: stays 8.5f: acts on polytrack and soft going: often races prominently. *Owen Burrows* **90**

EINSTEIN 4 b.c. Aqlaam 125 – Park Crystal (IRE) (Danehill (USA) 126) [2017 62: f8g⁶ f8g⁴ f7g t9.5g⁵ t12.2m p10g³ 10.2d t8.6g* Jun 26] fair handicapper: won at Wolverhampton in June: stays 1¼m: acts on all-weather: tried in visor: wears tongue tie: front runner/races prominently. *Mrs Ilka Gansera-Leveque* **74**

EIRENE 2 b.f. (Mar 28) Declaration of War (USA) 128 – Za Za Zoom (IRE) 99 (Le Vie dei Colori 126) [2017 6g³ 6d* 6.1v² 5.2s* 6g² 6d⁶ Sep 30] 85,000F: third foal: half-sister to 2-y-o 7f winner Colour Me Happy (by Poet's Voice), later successful in USA, and French 8.5f-10.5f winner Be My Lady (by Duke of Marmalade): dam, 2-y-o 6f winner, sister to very smart winner up to 1m Highland Colori: useful performer: won minor event at Doncaster in June and listed race at Newbury (by 1¾ lengths from Sankari Royale) in August: stays 6f: acts on heavy going: often races towards rear. *Dean Ivory* **96**

EIUM MAC 8 b.g. Presidium 124 – Efipetite 54 (Efisio 120) [2017 64: f7g f8.1g t8s⁶ t8.6g² t8.6g Oct 21] modest handicapper: best around 1m: acts on fibresand, tapeta and good to firm going: usually wears headgear: front runner. *Neville Bycroft* **56**

EJAABY 3 ch.g. Helmet (AUS) 127 – Vivid Blue 80 (Haafhd 129) [2017 80p: t7.1g* 7g² 6d³ 7g a7f⁶ Dec 15] fairly useful performer: won maiden at Wolverhampton in April: second in handicap at Leicester in May: left Roger Varian after fourth start: stays 7f: acts on polytrack and tapeta: often races prominently. *D. Watson, UAE* **92**

EJABAH (IRE) 3 b.f. Iffraaj 127 – Relinquished 80 (Royal Applause 124) [2017 64: f7g⁶ f6g⁴ 6g 6m f5g⁴ 10.3v⁶ f8.1g f7.1g³ f6.1g⁴ f7.1g Dec 22] angular filly: modest maiden: best effort at 6f: acts on firm going: in visor last 3 starts. *Charles Smith* **53**

bet365 Handicap, Newmarket—strong form as Ekhtiyaar beats Tommy Taylor (quartered cap), Ultimate Avenue (second left) and Golden Apollo (spots on cap)

EJAYTEEKAY 4 b.f. Big Bad Bob (IRE) 118 – Lovely Dream (IRE) 69 (Elnadim (USA) 128) [2017 85: p8d* p8g 8m 9g 8.1g^pu p7d^6 10d^3 8v* 11.6d* 11.6d^2 11.9s Oct 3] rather leggy filly: fairly useful performer: won handicaps at Chelmsford (by neck from Skidby Mill) in March and Ffos Las in August, and claimer at Lingfield in September: stays 11.5f: acts on polytrack, tapeta, good to firm and heavy going: tried in hood: has joined Gavin Patrick Cromwell. *Hughie Morrison* **81**

EJTYAH 2 b.f. (Feb 5) Frankel 147 – Darysina (USA) (Smart Strike (CAN) 121) [2017 p8s* Dec 17] first foal: dam, placed at around 1¼m in France, half-sister to Hong Kong Vase winner Daryakana out of Prix de Diane/Vermeille winner Daryaba: 7/2, won minor event at Chelmsford (by ½ length from Calypso Blue) in December: will stay 1¼m: should make considerable progress. *David Simcock* **79 P**

EKHTIYAAR 3 b.c. Bated Breath 125 – Bayja (IRE) (Giant's Causeway (USA) 132) [2017 89p: 6m^2 6d* 6m^5 6g* 6d^5 Oct 6] useful handicapper: won at Newmarket in May (by head from Poet's Princess) and July (by head from Tommy Taylor): raced only at 6f: acts on good to firm and good to soft going: often travels strongly. *Roger Varian* **109**

ELAND ALLY 9 b.g. Striking Ambition 122 – Dream Rose (IRE) 80 (Anabaa (USA) 130) [2017 49, a66: p5m^2 t5.1m p5g May 5] big gelding: modest handicapper: stays 7f, usually races over shorter: acts on polytrack, tapeta, soft and good to firm going: wears headgear: sometimes slowly away: sold £600, sent to Belgium. *Anabel K. Murphy* **57**

ELAPIDAE 2 b.g. (Mar 17) Helmet (AUS) 127 – Al Cobra (IRE) 70 (Sadler's Wells (USA) 132) [2017 t8.6d^6 t8.6d Dec 27] modest form in minor events. *David Lanigan* **62**

ELARQAM 2 b.c. (Feb 23) Frankel 147 – Attraction 125 (Efisio 120) [2017 7d* 7g* Sep 28] **112 p**

Topping the list at one of the major yearling sales is no guarantee of success on the racecourse. The world's most expensive yearling of 2012, 2,500,000-guinea purchase Hydrogen, a close relative of Derby winner Authorized, saw the racecourse once as a three-year-old and once as a four-year-old and failed to make the frame either time, though faithfulness to first impressions still resulted in his being given a chance at stud in Ireland by his owners Qatar Racing. By contrast, the 1,600,000 guineas paid by Shadwell for Elarqam at Newmarket's principal yearling sale in 2016, the October Sales Book 1, looks likely to prove money well spent. The price made Elarqam the most expensive Frankel yearling to be sold at public auction and he hasn't put a foot wrong on the racecourse so far, winning both his starts as a two-year-old in the style of a colt who might well develop into something out of the ordinary, the Two Thousand Guineas—a race he is bred for—said to be his first big target. Mark Johnston trained Elarqam's dam Attraction to win the One Thousand Guineas, among other races, and he trained her twice-raced first foal Elation (by Cape Cross), who won a maiden at Lingfield as a two-year-old, as well as that filly's close relative the useful miler Huntlaw (by another Green Desert stallion, Oasis Dream). Johnston reckons that Elarqam looks more like Attraction than any of her earlier foals and he must be hoping he turns out to be as good as her. Kingsley Park suffered the misfortune of losing its stable star in the latest season, the Dante and King Edward VII Stakes winner Permian, when he had to be put down after fracturing his near-fore in the Secretariat Stakes at Arlington in August. That was the lowest point in another landmark season for the Middleham yard which reached a double century in a calendar year on the Flat in Britain for the seventh time in the last nine years (a century has been chalked up in each of the last twenty-four). The stable's final total of two hundred and fifteen winners in Britain was short of the calendar year record held jointly by Richard Fahey and Richard Hannon senior on two hundred and thirty-five, but it is only a matter of time before Mark Johnston overtakes Richard Hannon senior's overall domestic total of 4,193 winners (4,145 on the Flat) to become the most successful trainer in British racing history by number of winners (he is currently third behind Hannon and fifteen-times champion jumps trainer Martin Pipe). Johnston's 4,000th winner on the Flat in Britain came at Pontefract in October when Dominating won the Phil Bull Trophy.

Johnston was asked, after Dominating's victory, for his career highlights (he first took out a licence in 1987 with just a handful of horses) and, after nominating Shamardal (whom he had as a two-year-old) as the best horse he has trained, he said that Attraction was 'the one I'm most proud of because I think many people would have given up on her, she didn't have the best of conformation and she also fractured a pedal bone as a two-year-old and strained a suspensory at four, but we managed to keep her racing.' Johnston also mentioned the 1994 Two Thousand Guineas victory of Mister Baileys ('It moved us up another level, we went from a sixty-five-horse stable to more than a hundred'), and he also paid tribute to the part played by his wife Deirdre who worked as a teacher in Grimsby in the early days when the couple were so short of money. 'I used to ride out, go to work and then come back and do evening stables, Mark used to do a bit of vetting as well,' said Deirdre Johnston at

Mr Hamdan Al Maktoum's "Elarqam"

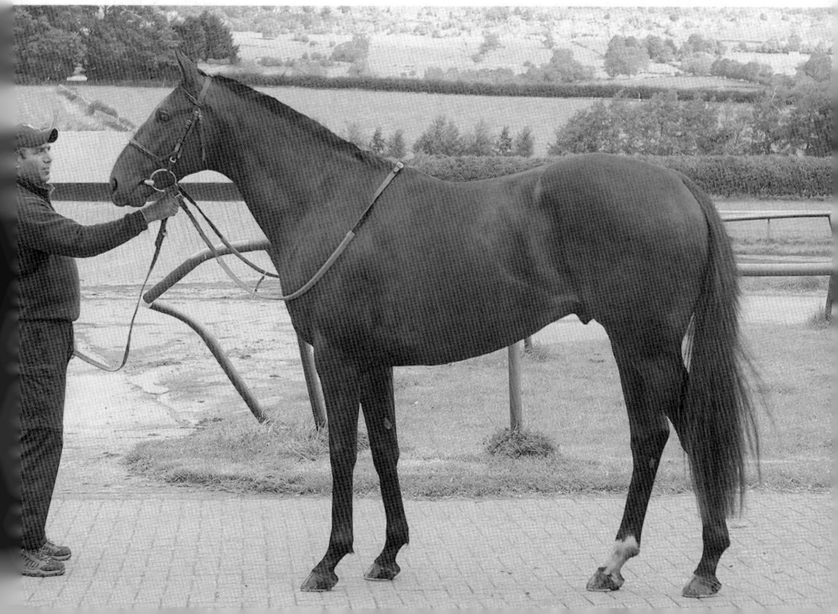

Pontefract as she reflected on the early years spent at a small yard near Louth in Lincolnshire, before the couple moved to Middleham where they started with fifteen horses ('which meant I was able to give up teaching'). The Kingsley Park two-year-olds make a much bigger contribution to the success of the stable now that Darley sends a much larger draft of juveniles to the yard each year. Cardsharp won the July Stakes at Newmarket in the latest season (and was placed in the Middle Park) and, of the fillies, Threading won the Lowther Stakes at York and Nyaleti the Princess Margaret at Ascot. There is no doubting, though, that Elarqam is regarded by the stable as its main classic hope. He was all the rage in the betting when he made his debut in a minor event at York in September and landed the odds with plenty in hand from the fairly useful Ayutthaya (the runner-up, third and fourth all won next time). The Group 3 Somerville Tattersall Stakes at Newmarket was chosen for Elarqam's other outing as a two-year-old, eighteen days after York, and he again justified strong market support (sent off 11/8 favourite in the field of nine) to win by two and a quarter lengths from close finishers Tip Two Win and Tangled. Elarqam was well on top at the finish after taking time, as at York, to assert fully before showing himself a powerful galloper once fully opened out and looking very much the type to train on well.

Elarqam (b.c. 2015)	Frankel (b 2008)	Galileo (b 1998)	Sadler's Wells
			Urban Sea
		Kind (b 2001)	Danehill
			Rainbow Lake
	Attraction (b 2001)	Efisio (b 1982)	Formidable
			Eldoret
		Flirtation (b 1994)	Pursuit of Love
			Eastern Shore

The good-topped Elarqam is already the pick of several winners out of Attraction, a list previously headed by her fifth foal, the smart sprinter Fountain of Youth (a brother to Huntlaw) who won the Sapphire Stakes at the Curragh for Aidan O'Brien. Probably the pick of the others was a close relative to Elarqam, the useful middle-distance filly Cushion (by Frankel's sire Galileo) who was placed in listed company as a three-year-old for John Gosden and went on to be pattern-placed at nine furlongs in the States before being returned to join Attraction in the broodmare band at the Duke of Roxburghe's Floors Stud. Attraction's yearling half-brother by Dubawi, named Maydanny, was bought by Shadwell at Newmarket in October for 1,350,000 guineas. Elarqam will be suited by at least a mile and should go on improving for a while yet. *Mark Johnston*

ELAS RUBY 3 b.f. Raven's Pass (USA) 133 – Elas Diamond 98 (Danehill Dancer (IRE) 117) [2017 85: 9.9m^2 9.9m^4 10g* 11.9g^3 12.4d^4 12d Sep 29] well-made filly: useful performer: won listed race at Newbury (by 3¾ lengths from Ebbesbourne) in June: third in Prix de Malleret at Saint-Cloud (1¼ lengths behind Strathspey) in July: stays 1½m: acts on polytrack, soft and good to firm going. *John Gosden* **109**

EL ASTRONAUTE (IRE) 4 ch.g. Approve (IRE) 112 – Drumcliffe Dancer (IRE) 66 (Footstepsinthesand 120) [2017 97: 5m* 5.1m* 5m 5m 5g 5g* p5g^2 5.5g^2 p5s^5 Sep 30] good-bodied gelding: useful handicapper: won at Newmarket in April, Chester in May and Goodwood (by short head from A Momentofmadness) in August: stays 5.5f: acts on polytrack, good to firm and good to soft going: front runner, often travels strongly. *John Quinn* **103**

ELATION (IRE) 2 b.f. (Apr 1) Invincible Spirit (IRE) 121 – Hallowed Park (IRE) (Barathea (IRE) 127) [2017 6g^5 6d* 6v^3 Sep 30] 75,000Y, 130,000 2-y-o: sturdy filly: sixth foal: half-sister to 3 winners, including useful 9f/1¼m winner Stetchworth (by New Approach) and 2-y-o 1m winner Taqwaa (by Iffraaj): dam, unraced, closely related to Derby runner-up Walk In The Park: fair form: won minor event at Ripon (by ½ length from Perfect Thought) in August: raced only at 6f. *Roger Varian* **79**

ELBERETH 6 b.m. Mount Nelson 125 – Masandra (IRE) (Desert Prince (IRE) 130) [2017 108: p10.7g* p10g^4 9m^2 12m^4 10m 10.3g^6 11.9g^2 12d Sep 29] sturdy mare: smart performer: won minor event at Dundalk (by ½ length from Fire Fighting) in March: second in Dahlia Stakes at Newmarket (3¼ lengths behind Somehow) and Bosphorus Cup at Veliefendi (beaten 2 lengths by Secret Number): stays 1½m: acts on polytrack, tapeta, good to firm and good to soft going: usually races prominently. *Andrew Balding* **110**

EL BERTIE (IRE) 2 b.g. (Apr 22) Elzaam (AUS) 115 – Emily Jane (IRE) 76 (Acclamation **54**
118) [2017 5v t7.1g t6d t6g^5 6s^6 8v Oct 23] compact gelding: modest maiden: best effort at 6f: acts on tapeta. *Tim Easterby*

EL BORRACHO (IRE) 2 br.g. (Feb 26) Society Rock (IRE) 126 – Flame of Hibernia **70**
(IRE) (One Cool Cat (USA) 123) [2017 6.5g p6g 7d^5 8g* p8g^4 t8.6g Nov 18] strong gelding: fair performer: won nursery at Salisbury in August: stays 1m: acts on polytrack and good to soft going. *Simon Dow*

EL CAMPEON 5 b.g. Multiplex 114 – Villabella (FR) (Hernando (FR) 127) [2017 86: **85**
p16d^2 p14d^5 t13.9g^5 p13g^2 Mar 31] good-topped gelding: fairly useful handicapper: second at Kempton in January: stays 2m: acts on polytrack, tapeta and heavy going: often races in rear/freely. *Simon Dow*

EL CAP (USA) 3 b.g. Speightstown (USA) 124 – Divine Presence (USA) (A P Indy **108 p**
(USA) 131) [2017 80p: t7.1g^3 t8.6g^5 8d* 8.5s^2 8.2d* Aug 12] useful performer: won maiden at Thirsk (by 4 lengths from Mathix) in July and handicap at Haydock (by 3½ lengths from Calder Prince) in August: likely to stay 1¼m: acts on polytrack, tapeta and soft going: gelded, and sent to Hong Kong, where renamed Dark Knight: open to further improvement. *Sir Michael Stoute*

EL CHAPO 2 b.g. (May 2) Lethal Force (IRE) 128 – Never Lose 95 (Diktat 126) [2017 **82**
7d^4 7.2g^3 t7.1g^5 7m^5 8v^2 7s* 7s* Oct 10] 19,000F, 40,000Y: fifth foal: half-brother to winner up to 1¼m Miss Lillie (2-y-o 7f winner, by Exceed And Excel): dam, 6f/7f winner, half-sister to smart 6f/7f winner Morache Music: fairly useful performer: won nurseries at Catterick in September and October (by ½ length from Che Bella): stays 1m: acts on good to firm and heavy going: sold 58,000 gns, sent to UAE. *Richard Fahey*

ELDRITCH (IRE) 3 b.g. Dark Angel (IRE) 113 – Henties Bay (IRE) (Cape Cross (IRE) **100**
129) [2017 77p: 10.3m* 9.1m^5 p11g^4 t12.4g^2 t12.2g^2 8f Nov 25] useful handicapper: won at Doncaster in April: second at Newcastle and Wolverhampton in October: left John Gosden 200,000 gns after: stays 12.5f: acts on polytrack, tapeta and good to firm going: tried in cheekpieces: sometimes slowly away, often races towards rear. *Mark Glatt, USA*

ELECTION DAY 3 b.g. Invincible Spirit (IRE) 121 – Missisipi Star (IRE) 98 (Mujahid **87**
(USA) 125) [2017 83: 9.9m^2 9m^3 p8g^4 p8g^3 8.5m^2 8v^5 p11g p8g^6 Oct 26] useful-looking gelding: fairly useful handicapper: second at Beverley in August: stays 1¼m: acts on polytrack, tapeta, good to firm and heavy going: sold 25,000 gns, sent to Saudi Arabia. *Mark Johnston*

ELECTOR 2 b.c. (Feb 4) Dansili 127 – Enticement 102 (Montjeu (IRE) 137) [2017 7v* **80 P**
Sep 9] fourth foal: half-brother to useful 7f/1m winner Pick Your Choice (by Elusive Quality) and smart winner up to 10.4f Diploma (2-y-o 7f winner, by Dubawi): dam, winner up to 1¼m (2-y-o 1m winner), half-sister to smart winner up to 7f Surfrider: 7/1, won minor event at Ascot (by ½ length from Agar's Plough) on debut: will stay 1m: open to significant improvement. *Sir Michael Stoute*

ELECTRIC LANDLADY (IRE) 2 b.f. (Mar 8) Red Jazz (USA) 125 – Margie (IRE) **83**
(Marju (IRE) 127) [2017 p6d* 6m 6g* 7d^4 Aug 19] 7,000Y: angular filly: first foal: dam unraced: fairly useful form: won minor events at Kempton in May and Newbury (by nose from Autumn Leaves) in July: stays 7f. *Denis Coakley*

ELEGANCE (IRE) 2 ch.f. (Mar 25) Famous Name 124 – Royal Crescent (IRE) 43 **–**
(Spectrum (IRE) 126) [2017 7g p7g Oct 3] €9,000F, €5,500Y, €15,000 2-y-o: fourth foal: dam twice-raced daughter of very smart miler Marling: well held in minor events. *Martin Smith*

ELEGANT JOAN 2 ch.f. (Mar 11) Assertive 121 – Fangfoss Girls 68 (Monsieur Bond **–**
(IRE) 120) [2017 6m 6.1m Jul 4] well-grown filly: third foal: half-sister to 5f and (including at 2 yrs) 6f winner Pancake Day and useful winner up to 1m Roll On Rory (2-y-o 5f winner) (both by Mullionmileanhour): dam 2-y-o 5f winner: well held in minor events. *Kevin Frost*

ELEGANTLY BOUND (IRE) 3 b.g. Choisir (AUS) 126 – Boundless Joy (AUS) 55 **84**
(Montjeu (IRE) 137) [2017 72: f8g^2 f7g^2 f8m^2 Feb 21] fairly useful maiden: second at Southwell all 3 starts in 2017: may prove best at short of 1m: acts on fibresand and tapeta: often in blinkers: usually races close up/travels strongly: sent to Greece. *James Given*

ELEGIAC 2 b.c. (Feb 28) Farhh 131 – Lamentation (Singspiel (IRE) 133) [2017 p10g^3 **90 p**
t8g* Nov 3] 22,000Y: fourth foal: half-brother to Italian 7.5f winner Bravo (by Indian Charlie) and useful 1¼m winner Lawless Secret (by Lawman): dam useful Italian/US 1m/1½m winner: fairly useful form: won minor event at Newcastle (by 6 lengths from Broken Wings) in November: will go on improving. *Mark Johnston*

ELEMENTARY 3 b.g. Exceed And Excel (AUS) 126 – Humdrum 101 (Dr Fong (USA) 128) [2017 71: p8g* p8m^2 Jan 21] rather unfurnished gelding: fair handicapper: won at Lingfield in January: stays 1m: acts on polytrack, good to firm and good to soft going: tried in hood: sold 23,000 gns in February, sent to Greece. *Michael Bell* **76**

ELEMENTO 3 ch.g. Assertive 121 – Black Baccara 78 (Superior Premium 122) [2017 –: t6g f5g^5 6m Aug 22] no form. *Phil McEntee* **–**

ELEMENTS LEGACY 3 b.g. Kheleyf (USA) 116 – New Romantic 57 (Singspiel (IRE) 133) [2017 57: f7g t6g^6 t8d 7g May 4] maiden: well held at 3 yrs: left K. R. Burke after second start: usually in headgear. *Tracy Waggott* **–**

ELEMENTS QUEST (IRE) 2 b.f. (Mar 29) Elzaam (AUS) 115 – Sweet Chilli (IRE) 87 (Intikhab (USA) 135) [2017 5s 5d^4 5g^4 6g Sep 27] £23,000Y: second foal: dam 2-y-o 5f winner: little form. *K. R. Burke* **–**

ELHAAME (IRE) 7 b.g. Acclamation 118 – Gold Hush (USA) 96 (Seeking The Gold (USA)) [2017 110: 9.9g* Jan 12] strong, sturdy gelding: smart handicapper: raced only twice since 2015: won at Meydan (by ¾ length from Good Trip) in January: stays 1½m: acts on firm and good to soft going. *Saeed bin Suroor* **115**

ELHAFEI (USA) 2 br.c. (Mar 16) Speightstown (USA) 124 – Albamara 104 (Galileo (IRE) 134) [2017 p8g^4 Nov 21] 525,000Y: first foal: dam, 2-y-o 8.5f winner who stayed 1½m, half-sister to smart winner up to 11f Algometer out of smart winner up to 1½m Albanova: 6/1, shaped well from wide draw when fourth in minor event at Lingfield (4 lengths behind Rajaam) in November: sort to improve markedly. *John Gosden* **69 P**

EL HAYEM (IRE) 4 b.g. Invincible Spirit (IRE) 121 – Winning Sequence (FR) (Zafonic (USA) 130) [2017 96: 8m^6 7.6d^2 8s 8m* 7.9d^5 9d Sep 30] strong, lengthy gelding: useful handicapper: won at Sandown (by neck from GM Hopkins) in July: stays 1m: acts on good to firm and good to soft going: often starts slowly. *Sir Michael Stoute* **103**

EL HOMBRE 3 ch.c. Camacho 118 – Nigella 92 (Band On The Run 102) [2017 84p: t5d^4 t7.1g^3 6m^2 6m* 6f* 6d^3 5g^2 5g* 6g* Sep 1] useful handicapper: won at Hamilton and Haydock in May, Carlisle in July and Thirsk (by ¾ length from Classic Seniority) in September: stays 6f: acts on tapeta and firm going. *Keith Dalgleish* **101**

ELIDOR 7 br.g. Cape Cross (IRE) 129 – Honorine (IRE) 89 (Mark of Esteem (IRE) 137) [2017 115: 14.1g* 16.2m^6 14g^3 13.9m 14.5g^5 Sep 15] strong, rangy gelding: smart performer: won listed race at Nottingham (by nose from Wall of Fire) in April: third in Curragh Cup (1½ lengths behind Rekindling) in July: stays 1¾m: acts on any turf going: tried in visor: often races towards rear. *Mick Channon* **113**

ELITE ICON 3 b.g. Sixties Icon 125 – Sailing Days 67 (Kris 135) [2017 t8g^6 t8g^6 t12.2g^3 9v^4 11.2g^4 t12.2g^5 12.1s^4 12.5m^4 14.1v* Sep 13] modest handicapper: won at Carlisle in September: best effort at 1¾m: acts on heavy going. *Iain Jardine* **62**

ELITE SHADOW 2 gr.g. (Mar 3) Finjaan 122 – Silver Elite 67 (Forzando 122) [2017 6g^2 5.1d Oct 23] fair form: better effort when second in minor event at Yarmouth (2¼ lengths behind Foreseeable Future) in October. *Gay Kelleway* **73**

ELITE TREATY 3 b.g. Mawatheeq (USA) 126 – Silver Elite 67 (Forzando 122) [2017 p8g^4 Dec 28] sixth foal: dam 5f/6f winner: 10/1, fourth in maiden at Lingfield (5½ lengths behind Swiss Vinnare) in December: capable of better. *Gay Kelleway* **69 p**

ELIXSOFT (IRE) 2 b.f. (Mar 10) Elzaam (AUS) 115 – Grandegrandegrande (IRE) (High Chaparral (IRE) 132) [2017 5g 6m 5.5s 7d f6.1g Dec 19] €4,250F, €11,000Y: first foal: dam Italian 7.5f winner: modest maiden: best effort at 7f: acts on good to soft going: sometimes slowly away. *Roger Fell* **54**

ELIZABETH BENNET (IRE) 2 b.f. (Mar 14) Acclamation 118 – Littlepromisedland (IRE) 40 (Titus Livius (FR) 115) [2017 6g^3 p6s* 6g^5 7d p6d* 7d^6 7m Oct 13] €85,000F, €140,000Y: lengthy filly: third foal: dam, maiden (stayed 1m), half-sister to high-class 6f/7f winner Lethal Force: fairly useful performer: won minor event at Lingfield (by 5 lengths from Sardenya) in June and nursery at Kempton (by length from George) in August: stays 7f: acts on polytrack and good to soft going. *Charles Hills* **89**

ELIZABETH DARCY (IRE) 2 b.f. (Mar 15) Camacho 118 – Regency Girl (IRE) 76 (Pivotal 124) [2017 5f* 5f^6 5d^2 5m 5f^6 Nov 4] €88,000Y: strong filly: second foal: dam, maiden (stayed 1½m), half-sister to useful winner around 1¼m This Is The Day: useful performer: won maiden at Indiana Grand (by 7¾ lengths) in May: second in Prix du Bois at Deauville (¾ length behind Zonza) in July: below form at Royal Ascot and York second/fourth starts: raced only at 5f: acts on firm and good to soft going: wears blinkers. *Wesley A. Ward, USA* **98**

ELJADDAAF (IRE) 6 b.g. Shamardal (USA) 129 – Almansoora (USA) 78 (Bahri (USA) 125) [2017 85: p6g* p6g³ t6g p6g 6s⁵ 6.1d p7g Dec 13] compact gelding: useful handicapper: won at Kempton in January: third at Chelmsford (½ length behind Boomerang Bob) in February: stays 7f: acts on polytrack and tapeta: usually hooded: often races towards rear. *Dean Ivory* **98**

ELLAAL 8 b.g. Oasis Dream 129 – Capistrano Day (USA) 110 (Diesis 133) [2017 84, a68: f8g 8g 8.3m 8m 8g⁴ 7.2m⁴ 7.8g 8.5m⁵ 8g 8g* 8.5d 8m² 8m p8d⁵ 7d Oct 20] big, strong, close-coupled gelding: fair handicapper: won at Redcar (amateur) in August: stays 1¼m: acts on polytrack, tapeta, soft and good to firm going: wears cheekpieces: front runner/races prominently. *Ruth Carr* **71**

ELLEN GATES 2 b.f. (Feb 6) Mayson 124 – Mrs Greeley 91 (Mr Greeley (USA) 122) [2017 p6g⁶ p7g⁶ Dec 21] 30,000F, 30,000Y: second foal: dam, 6f/7f winner, half-sister to high-class winner up to 1½m Jack Hobbs: well held in minor events. *Richard Hughes* **–**

ELLER BROOK 2 ch.f. (Mar 28) Sepoy (AUS) 129 – Haigh Hall 84 (Kyllachy 129) [2017 5m⁶ 5d 5d⁵ 5d³ 5s³ Oct 1] fourth foal: half-sister to 6f winner Robin Park (by Invincible Spirit) and 2-y-o 5f winner Astley Hall (by Dutch Art), later successful in Qatar: dam, 2-y-o 5f winner, half-sister to useful 7f/1m winner Balducci: modest maiden: raced only at 5f: acts on soft going. *Michael Dods* **64**

ELLEVAL (IRE) 7 b.g. Kodiac 112 – Penny Rouge (IRE) 59 (Pennekamp (USA) 130) [2017 111: 9.9g⁵ 12g 8.9g² 9.9g 8.9g p10.7g³ 10d⁶ 8m⁶ 8m 10m 8g p8s³ p7g³ Dec 22] strong gelding: useful performer: placed in 2017 at Meydan and Dundalk (3 times, ½-length third to Beach Bar in handicap on last occasion): stays 10.5f: acts on polytrack, tapeta, good to firm and good to soft going: usually in headgear: tried in tongue tie: often races towards rear. *David Marnane, Ireland* **107**

ELLTHEA (IRE) 2 b.f. (Apr 15) Kodiac 112 – Tropical Lady (IRE) 117 (Sri Pekan (USA) 117) [2017 5.1m⁴ 5v* 7d⁶ 7g 6.5g* 7s* 8m⁵ Oct 13] €88,000Y: good-topped filly: half-sister to 3 winners, including useful 1m (including at 2 yrs) winner Von Blucher (by Zoffany) and 7f winner Tropical Mist (by Marju): dam 7f-1¼m winner: useful performer: won minor event at Carlisle (by 2 lengths from Mable Lee) in June, and nursery at Doncaster (by 3¾ lengths from Clubbable) and C. L. & M. F. Weld Park Stakes at Naas (by 2¾ lengths from Sizzling) in September: stays 7f: acts on heavy going: tried in blinkers: often races prominently. *K. R. Burke* **107**

ELM GROVE (IRE) 5 b.m. Arcano (IRE) 122 – Ladytown (IRE) 77 (Bertolini (USA) 125) [2017 79: 8.5v* 10s⁴ 9.7m* 10m⁵ 10g 8.4s 10.2s³ 10.3v 8.5s⁶ 10v⁵ Oct 25] fairly useful handicapper: won at Cork (apprentice) in April and Clonmel in May: third at Roscommon in August: stays 12.5f: acts on good to firm and heavy going: has worn hood: often races in rear. *W. McCreery, Ireland* **94**

ELMLEY QUEEN 3 b.f. Piccolo 121 – All Business 92 (Entrepreneur 123) [2017 –: t6m t5.1g Feb 27] no form. *Roy Brotherton* **–**

ELNADIM STAR (IRE) 2 ch.f. (Mar 27) Elnadim (USA) 128 – Fancy Feathers (IRE) 79 (Redback 116) [2017 5m 5d* 5s* Sep 20] €8,000F, 20,000Y: fifth foal: half-sister to 2-y-o 5f winner Just Past Andover (by Amadeus Wolf) and useful 6f winner Red Pike (by Kheleyf): dam, 6f/7f winner, half-sister to smart winner up to 1½m Come On Jonny: fairly useful form: won minor events at Beverley in August (by 1¼ lengths from Zip Along) and September (by ½ length from Palmer): likely to stay 6f: remains open to improvement. *Kevin Ryan* **84 p**

EL NEFOUS (IRE) 3 gr.f. Choisir (AUS) 126 – Light And Airy (Linamix (FR) 127) [2017 t6.1g⁴ Jun 1] €120,000Y: seventh foal: sister to useful winner up to 7f Gossamer Seed (2-y-o 5f winner) and a winner in Italy: dam unraced: 16/1, fourth in maiden at Wolverhampton (6¾ lengths behind Always Amazing) in June: sent to UAE. *George Peckham* **55**

EL NINO SEA (IRE) 3 b.g. Sea The Stars (IRE) 140 – Mayano Sophia (IRE) (Rock of Gibraltar (IRE) 133) [2017 8m⁴ 8.3m⁴ 9g May 21] fair form: best effort when fourth in maiden at Hamilton in May: sold 2,500 gns in October. *Richard Fahey* **65**

EL PRINCIPE 4 b.g. Strategic Prince 114 – Shamrock Lady (IRE) 88 (Orpen (USA) 116) [2017 75: p6g² p6g² 6g³ 5m⁶ t6s⁴ 6g² 7.4d* 7.4s³ 7.8s* 8.3d⁵ t7.1g² 7d Nov 11] fairly useful handicapper: won at Beverley in July and Carlisle (lady riders) in August: stays 8.5f: acts on polytrack, tapeta, soft and good to firm going: usually wears headgear/tongue tie: front runner/races prominently. *Les Eyre* **86**

ELSAAKB (USA) 2 ch.g. (Apr 25) Exchange Rate (USA) 111 – Bella Jolie (USA) (Broken Vow (USA) 117) [2017 7g 7d p7d6 7m4 p7g* p7s6 Dec 1] useful-looking gelding: has scope: fair performer: won nursery at Kempton in November: raced only at 7f: acts on polytrack and good to firm going: in headgear last 4 starts. *John Gosden* **76**

ELTANIN (IRE) 3 ch.g. Dragon Pulse (IRE) 114 – Maigh Nuad (IRE) (Alhaarth (IRE) 126) [2017 67: t5s3 6m6 6g3 t7.1s5 6g6 6v3 t5g3 Sep 22] fair maiden: stays 6f: acts on tapeta and heavy going: in headgear last 5 starts. *John Quinn* **72**

EL TEL 5 ch.g. Sixties Icon 125 – Chelsea (USA) (Miswaki (USA) 124) [2017 –: t7.1g t7.1d t9.5m6 t8.6g Mar 27] rather leggy gelding: modest maiden: best effort at 8.5f: acts on tapeta: tried in hood: often races freely. *Shaun Harris* **53**

ELTEZAM (IRE) 4 b.g. Kodiac 112 – Tymora (USA) 63 (Giant's Causeway (USA) 132) [2017 t7.1g p6g5 7f 7s5 6d 7m5 p8d 8.1g3 8s4 8g p8g2 10g p10s2 p8g5 Dec 20] lengthy gelding: useful handicapper on turf, fairly useful on all-weather: second at Chelmsford in December: left Richard Hannon after sixth start: stays 1¼m: acts on polytrack and firm going: often in headgear. *Amanda Perrett* **97** **a90**

EL TORITO (IRE) 3 ch.g. Tagula (IRE) 116 – April Green (FR) (Green Tune (USA) 125) [2017 78: p7g4 p8d4 p7g6 7m* 8.1d 7m t7.2g 7d4 7d 7g 7v 7v 6.1d5 p7s p6g p7g4 Dec 28] useful-looking gelding: fairly useful handicapper: won at Brighton (by ½ length from Spirit of Sarwan) in May: stays 7f: acts on polytrack, soft and good to firm going: often in headgear. *Jim Boyle* **80**

ELUCIDATION (IRE) 3 b.g. Oasis Dream 129 – Mimalia (USA) (Silver Hawk (USA) 123) [2017 95p: 10m p10g5 8g4 Sep 1] compact gelding: fairly useful handicapper: should stay 1¼m: acts on good to firm going: sold 26,000 gns, sent to USA. *Sir Michael Stoute* **91**

ELUSIF (IRE) 2 b.c. (Apr 13) Elusive Quality (USA) – Appealing (IRE) 98 (Bertolini (USA) 125) [2017 7s4 7d5 t8.6g Nov 25] fair form: best effort when fourth in minor event at Ascot (4¾ lengths behind Fajjaj) in September. *Marco Botti* **66**

ELUSIVE BEAUTY (IRE) 3 b.f. Elusive Pimpernel (USA) 117 – Lost Icon (IRE) (Intikhab (USA) 135) [2017 92: 7v6 8.5v2 8m3 7s* 9.5d4 8d4 6s5 6.9s* 7g 7s 8d 7.5s 7d p7g6 8.5s Oct 14] sister to Italian winner up to 11f La Grande Bellezza (2-y-o 9f winner) and half-sister to several winners, including 10.7f/1½m winner Atmospheric High (by Hurricane Run): dam French 9f winner: useful performer: won handicap at Gowran in April and listed race at Carlisle (by ½ length from Bletchley) in June: fourth in handicap at the Curragh in May: stays 8.5f: acts on good to firm and heavy going: has worn headgear, including last 4 starts: sometimes slowly away, often races in rear. *K. J. Condon, Ireland* **99**

ELUSIVE BIRD 2 ch.f. (Apr 10) Choisir (AUS) 126 – Ermena (Dalakhani (IRE) 133) [2017 5g 6g5 6m t6g p6g p7g p8g Oct 24] 27,000Y: fourth foal: half-sister to 9.5f/1¼m winner Nearly Famous (by Rip Van Winkle) and a winner in Czech Republic by So You Think: dam unraced out of smart winner up to 12.5f Fairy Queen: modest maiden: best effort at 6f. *Giles Bravery* **51**

ELUSIVE COWBOY (USA) 4 ch.g. Elusive Quality (USA) – Sarmad (USA) 56 (Dynaformer (USA)) [2017 81: t13.9f6 p11g 12g 11m5 13.3v 10d5 p12g p12g p15.8g Dec 6] fair handicapper: left Stuart Edmunds after third start: stays 12.5f: acts on tapeta: often in headgear. *Chris Gordon* **69**

ELUSIVE OLIVIA (USA) 3 b.f. Elusive Quality (USA) – Kenza (USA) (Menifee (USA) 124) [2017 52p: t7.1d* t8d4 t8.6g4 8.3g 8.2g Jun 27] fair performer: won maiden at Newcastle in February: fourth in handicap at Wolverhampton in May: stays 8.5f: acts on tapeta: wears tongue tie: often races in rear. *Joseph Tuite* **71**

ELUSIVITY (IRE) 9 b.g. Elusive City (USA) 117 – Tough Chic (IRE) 82 (Indian Ridge 123) [2017 88: t5g t5.1g f6g* f5g3 t6m4 f7g t6g f6.1g 5d6 t5.1g p5g3 t6.1g2 6g6 t6.1g f7.1g t5.1g Sep 23] well-made gelding: fair handicapper: won at Southwell in January: stays 1m: acts on all-weather, good to firm and heavy going: wears headgear: front runner/races prominently. *Conor Dore* **77**

EL VIP (IRE) 4 b.g. Pivotal 124 – Elle Danzig (GER) 118 (Roi Danzig (USA)) [2017 106p: 8m3 8m t8s* 8m 7.9d Aug 24] useful handicapper: won at Newcastle (by 2¼ lengths from Torrid) in June: stays 10.5f: acts on tapeta and good to firm going. *Luca Cumani* **105**

ELWAZIR 2 ch.c. (Apr 3) Frankel 147 – Dash To The Front 105 (Diktat 126) [2017 7d2 7m4 Oct 25] 500,000Y: big, long-backed colt: closely related to useful 13f/1¾m winner Joshua Reynolds (by Nathaniel) and half-brother to several winners, including smart 1¼m/10.5f winner Speedy Boarding (by Shamardal) and useful 1m (including at 2 yrs) **93 p**

winner Next Stage (by Dubawi): dam 8.6f-11f winner: fairly useful form: fourth in minor event at Newmarket (2¼ lengths behind Key Victory) in October: will be suited by 1m+: should do better. *Owen Burrows*

ELYAASAAT (USA) 3 b.c. Frankel 147 – Lahudood 119 (Singspiel (IRE) 133) [2017 8m^6 Apr 18] well-made colt: fifth foal: half-brother to French 1¼m winner Aghareed (by Kingmambo) and a winner in USA by Bernardini: dam 9f (in France) to 11f (Breeders' Cup Filly & Mare Turf) winner: 7/4, sixth in newcomers race at Newmarket (tongue tied, 9 lengths behind Night Circus) in April, first home in group: should improve. *William Haggas* **71 p**

ELYSEE STAR 2 b.f. (Mar 14) Champs Elysees 124 – Alushta 60 (Royal Applause 124) [2017 6g^2 6d^3 7m^3 6.9v^4 t7.1g Oct 10] third foal: dam once-raced sister to smart 2-y-o 6f winner Auditorium and smart winner up to 9f Mister Cosmi: modest maiden: best effort at 7f: acts on good to firm and heavy going: tried in cheekpieces. *Ben Haslam* **64**

ELYSIAN FIELDS (GR) 6 ch.m. Champs Elysees 124 – Second of May 72 (Lion Cavern (USA) 117) [2017 102: 12f^2 p14s^5 12g 12d^4 12g p13g p12g p12g^4 p12g^5 Dec 30] sturdy mare: useful handicapper: second in listed race at Goodwood (5 lengths behind Ajman Princess) in May: stays 1¾m: acts on polytrack, firm and good to soft going: in cheekpieces last 2 starts. *Amanda Perrett* **96**

ELYSIAN FLYER (IRE) 5 b.g. Majestic Missile (IRE) 118 – Starisa (IRE) (College Chapel 122) [2017 –: t6d^4 t6g 5s* 5d^4 5g 5d 5s^3 5g 5s^5 5v^4 5v Sep 28] good-quartered gelding: fairly useful handicapper: won at Thirsk (by 1¼ lengths from Lucky Beggar) in May: stays 6f: acts on tapeta, soft and good to firm going: tried in cheekpieces. *Paul Midgley* **92**

ELYSIAN PRINCE 6 b.g. Champs Elysees 124 – Trinkila (USA) 74 (Cat Thief (USA) 126) [2017 79, a86: p10g* p12g p12g^3 p12g Sep 27] rangy, useful-looking gelding: fairly useful handicapper: won at Lingfield in January: third at Kempton in March: stays 1½m: acts on polytrack, tapeta and good to firm going: has worn tongue tie: modest hurdler. *Neil King* **89**

ELYSIUM DREAM 2 b.f. (Feb 25) Champs Elysees 124 – Dream of Wunders (Cape Cross (IRE) 129) [2017 5d^4 6.1m* 7m^5 7m 6d^4 7d^3 6.5g^6 6g* 7s 8d Nov 4] 5,000F: lengthy filly: second foal: dam, of little account, half-sister to useful winner up to 6.5f Inyordreams out of Flying Childers Stakes winner Wunders Dream: fairly useful performer: won minor event at Windsor in May and quite valuable sales race at Newmarket in October: stays 7f: acts on soft and good to firm going. *Richard Hannon* **87**

EMARAATY 2 b.c. (Apr 2) Dubawi (IRE) 129 – Zee Zee Top 116 (Zafonic (USA) 130) [2017 7g^4 7m* 7m Oct 14] 2,600,000Y: well-made, attractive colt: half-brother to 3 winners, including 9f-10.5f winner Izzi Top (by Pivotal) and 1m-1¼m winner Jazzi Top (by Danehill Dancer), both very smart: dam, 1m-10.4f winner, including Prix de l'Opera, half-sister to Opera House and Kayf Tara: useful form: won minor event at Newbury (by 2¼ lengths from Magnificent) in September: bred to be suited by 1m+: remains open to improvement. *John Gosden* **100 p**

EMBANKMENT 8 b.g. Zamindar (USA) 116 – Esplanade 77 (Danehill (USA) 126) [2017 65§: p8g^4 t10.2g^3 p10g* 10d p11d p8d 9.9s Jul 26] sturdy, attractive gelding: fair handicapper: won at Lingfield in April: stays 1¼m: acts on polytrack, tapeta and soft going: has worn cheekpieces: untrustworthy. *Michael Attwater* **65 §**

EMBER'S GLOW 3 ch.g. Sepoy (AUS) 129 – Fading Light 103 (King's Best (USA) 132) [2017 8d^5 8.3g^5 7g^2 7d^6 7.4g^3 7s^4 Sep 23] compact gelding: fair maiden: stays 7.5f: best form on good going. *Jason Ward* **69**

EMBLETON 3 b.f. Cacique (IRE) 124 – Morzine 84 (Miswaki (USA) 124) [2017 57: 6m t8.6g 10.2f p6g Jul 19] maiden, no form in 2017: tried in visor. *Charlie Wallis* **–**

EMBOUR (IRE) 2 b.c. (Apr 28) Acclamation 118 – Carpet Lady (IRE) 70 (Night Shift (USA)) [2017 5.2g^3 Apr 21] €98,000F, £145,000Y: brother to several winners, including useful 5f (including at 2 yrs) winner Cake and winner up to 7f Young John (2-y-o 5f winner) and half-brother to several winners, including useful 7f/1m winner Suited And Booted (by Tagula): dam maiden: 5/1, third in maiden at Newbury (neck behind Gold Town) on debut. *Richard Hannon* **81**

EMELL 7 ch.g. Medicean 128 – Londonnetdotcom (IRE) 101 (Night Shift (USA)) [2017 107: t8.6g 8g 6.1m 8s p8g Oct 14] strong gelding: useful handicapper, below form in 2017: left Richard Hannon after second start: stays 8.5f: acts on tapeta, soft and good to firm going: wears headgear. *Tim Vaughan* **94**

EMENEM 3 b.g. Sir Percy 129 – Kahalah (IRE) 77 (Darshaan 133) [2017 78: p10g* 11.7m5 8.5g* 10.1m2 10.3m3 9.9v 9.9m3 p11g 10.1v3 p10g3 t9.5g2 p10g* t9.5d4 Dec 26] compact gelding: useful handicapper: won at Lingfield in January, Epsom in April and again at Lingfield (by short head from Kyllachy Gala) in December: stays 11.5f: acts on polytrack, tapeta, good to firm and heavy going. *Simon Dow* **101**

EMERALD BAY 4 b.f. Kyllachy 129 – Bahia Emerald (IRE) 80 (Bahamian Bounty 116) [2017 63: f5g p6g Mar 2] neat filly: modest handicapper: best form at 5f: acted on tapeta, good to firm and good to soft going: tried in headgear: dead. *Ronald Thompson* **38**

EMERALD CROSS (IRE) 4 b.g. Cape Cross (IRE) 129 – Yaqootah (USA) 72 (Gone West (USA)) [2017 p12g5 t12.4d2 Dec 16] fifth foal: half-brother to useful 2-y-o 6f winner Sweet Cecily (by Kodiac): dam 5f winner who stayed 7f: fairly useful form: better effort when second in maiden at Newcastle (neck behind Warm Oasis) in December. *Adam West* **82**

EMERALD ROCKET (IRE) 2 b.g. (Mar 11) Society Rock (IRE) 126 – Lady From Limerick (IRE) 61 (Rainbows For Life (CAN)) [2017 6m 6g3 6m4 7s4 8g t7.1g* t8g* t7.1d6 Nov 4] fair performer: won nurseries at Newcastle (twice) in October: stays 1m: acts on tapeta and good to firm going: tried in visor. *K. R. Burke* **77**

EMERALD SECRET (IRE) 3 b.f. Arcano (IRE) 122 – Limit (IRE) 69 (Barathea (IRE) 127) [2017 60: t5d3 5g 6g 5m 5g5 6s 5d Aug 4] fair maiden: stays 5.5f: acts on tapeta: wears headgear. *Paul Midgley* **66**

EMIGRATED (IRE) 4 b.g. Fastnet Rock (AUS) 127 – Ecoutila (USA) (Rahy (USA) 115) [2017 –: 14g f8.1g6 p8s5 p10s Dec 15] poor maiden handicapper: trained on reappearance only by Gavin Patrick Cromwell: usually wears headgear: modest maiden hurdler. *Derek Shaw* **49**

EMILENE 3 b.f. Clodovil (IRE) 116 – Spark Up 81 (Lahib (USA) 129) [2017 t7.2g t7.2g t7.2g 5s t6.1g Oct 27] fourth foal: half-sister to 5f/6f winner Monumental Man (by Vital Equine): dam winner up to 8.6f (2-y-o 5f winner): modest maiden: best effort at 7f: acts on tapeta: sometimes in hood: often leads. *Mark Brisbourne* **55**

EMILIA JAMES 2 ch.f. (Feb 2) Poet's Voice 126 – Dozy (IRE) 90 (Exceed And Excel (AUS) 126) [2017 5m2 5m* 5.1m4 p5g* 5m 6g p5d2 p6d6 Oct 6] 24,000F, €19,000Y: workmanlike filly: second foal: dam, 2-y-o 5f winner, closely related to useful 2-y-o 5f winner Patience Alexander: fairly useful performer: won minor events at Beverley in April and Chelmsford (by 3¼ lengths from Queen of Kalahari) in June: best form at 5f: acts on polytrack and good to firm going: front runner/races prominently. *Mark Johnston* **89**

EMILY GOLDFINCH 4 ch.f. Prime Defender 118 – Lakelands Lady (IRE) 85 (Woodborough (USA) 112) [2017 64: t6f6 p6d p6d6 p8d2 7m* p7s4 7d2 7g 6s Sep 20] fair handicapper: won at Lingfield in June: second at Newmarket in July: stays 1m: acts on polytrack, good to firm and good to soft going: usually leads. *Phil McEntee* **67 a57**

EMILYSBUTTERSCOTCH 3 ch.f. Kyllachy 129 – Solfilia 91 (Teofilo (IRE) 126) [2017 p6s 5.1m4 p6g p5g6 t5.1m p6s Dec 7] 10,000Y: plain filly: first foal: dam 2-y-o 6f winner who stayed 1½m: modest maiden: best effort at 5f: acts on good to firm going. *Rae Guest* **53**

EMINENT (IRE) 3 b.c. Frankel 147 – You'll Be Mine (USA) 107 (Kingmambo (USA) 125) [2017 83p: 8m* 8m6 12m4 9.9m5 9.9g* 10d3 Sep 9] big, strong colt: very smart performer: won Craven Stakes at Newmarket (by 1¾ lengths from Rivet) in April and Prix Guillaume d'Ornano at Deauville (by 3 lengths from Salouen) in August: also in frame in Derby at Epsom (1¾ lengths fourth to Wings of Eagles) and Irish Champion Stakes at Leopardstown (2¼ lengths third to Decorated Knight): effective at 1¼m to 1½m: acts on good to firm and good to soft going: usually races close up. *Martyn Meade* **122**

EMIRATES FLIGHT 3 ch.f. New Approach (IRE) 132 – Flying Cloud (IRE) 115 (Storming Home 128) [2017 72p: 11.6d May 12] fair form on first of 2 starts, in maiden at 2 yrs: tried in tongue tie. *Saeed bin Suroor* **–**

EMJAYEM 7 ch.g. Needwood Blade 117 – Distant Stars (IRE) 69 (Distant Music (USA) 126) [2017 81, a71: t5.1g5 t5.1g4 5.3g4 5g 5m5 5f 5f5 6g Aug 2] strong gelding: fair handicapper: best form at 5f: acts on tapeta and firm going: has worn cheekpieces. *John Holt* **69**

EMMAUS (IRE) 3 b.c. Invincible Spirit (IRE) 121 – Prima Luce (IRE) 111 (Galileo (IRE) 134) [2017 94: 7g* Oct 17] smart form: won handicap at Leicester (by nose from Sir Dancealot) on sole outing in 2017: stays 1m: capable of better still. *Roger Varian* **113 p**

EMOTIONLESS (IRE) 4 b.g. Shamardal (USA) 129 – Unbridled Elaine (USA) 124 (Unbridled's Song (USA) 125) [2017 101: a8f^{6} a9.9f^{2} 12g^{3} Mar 4] good sort: smart performer: placed at Meydan in handicap and Dubai City of Gold (length third to Prize Money) early in year: stays 1½m: acts on dirt, good to firm and good to soft going: tried in cheekpieces. *Charlie Appleby* **119**

EMPEROR NAPOLEON 4 b.g. Champs Elysees 124 – Amarullah (FR) (Daylami (IRE) 138) [2017 100p: 13.4g^{4} May 27] useful handicapper: fourth at Chester, only outing in 2017: likely to prove best up to 13f: acts on good to firm and heavy going: often travels strongly. *Andrew Balding* **95**

EMPHATIC (IRE) 2 b.c. (Jan 24) Epaulette (AUS) 126 – Wild Ocean (Pivotal 124) [2017 5m 6s^{3} 6v^{2} Oct 21] neat, attractive colt: fair form: best effort when second in minor event at Catterick (1¼ lengths behind Biddy Brady) in October. *Robert Cowell* **73**

EMPLOYER (IRE) 2 b.c. (Jan 23) Camelot 128 – Close Regards (IRE) (Danehill (USA) 126) [2017 p7d^{3} Nov 22] €180,000F: closely related to 2 winners by Hurricane Run, including very smart 7f-1½m winner (including in Australia) Magic Hurricane, and half-brother to 3 winners, including useful 7f-1¼m winner Maybe Grace (by Hawk Wing): dam unraced: 7/1, third in minor event at Kempton (2¾ lengths behind Qaysar) on debut: will stay at least 1m: sure to progress. *Hugo Palmer* **73 p**

EMPRESS ALI (IRE) 6 b.m. Holy Roman Emperor (IRE) 125 – Almansa (IRE) (Dr Devious (IRE) 127) [2017 99: 9g^{5} 10.3d^{3} 10.3g^{4} 10.2g* 10.5s^{2} 10v^{2} 10.2d^{5} 10.2s^{4} Nov 11] smallish, sturdy mare: useful handicapper: won at Nottingham (by 1¼ lengths from Indulged) in August: second at Pontefract (½ length behind Dance King) in September: stays 10.5f: acts on good to firm and heavy going: has worn cheekpieces. *Tom Tate* **100**

EMPRESS ROSE 2 ch.f. (Feb 19) Makfi 130 – Ittasal 86 (Any Given Saturday (USA) 128) [2017 7g Sep 7] €20,000Y: second foal: dam, 2-y-o 7f winner, half-sister to 7f/1m winner Paper Talk and 2-y-o 6f winner La Presse (both useful): 50/1, well held in maiden at Salisbury: sold 4,000 gns, sent to Spain. *Richard Hughes* **–**

Sir Peter Vela's "Eminent"

ENABLE 3 b.f. Nathaniel (IRE) 129 – Concentric 107 (Sadler's Wells (USA) 132) **134**
[2017 83p: 10g^3 11.3m* 12m* 12f* 12s* 11.9d* 11.9d* Oct 1]

Perhaps the highest compliment that can be paid to Enable is that there hasn't been a better filly trained in Britain since Pebbles. Pebbles made an indelible impression as a four-year-old in that vintage year for British racing of 1985 which also featured, among others, the last winner of the fillies' triple crown Oh So Sharp, those paragons Never So Bold and Shadeed, a sprinter and miler of the highest class, and a seven-length Derby winner in Slip Anchor. Kept in training after winning the One Thousand Guineas, Pebbles enjoyed a scintillating year in 1985, winning four of her five races and earning Horse of the Year honours, her last three victories coming in the Eclipse (she was the first filly to win that race since its inception in 1886), the Champion Stakes (by three lengths, easing down, from Slip Anchor) and the Breeders' Cup Turf (supplemented for 240,000 dollars, she won by showing a superb turn of foot after looking to be trapped on the sharp final turn). Pebbles had been given the target of either the King George VI and Queen Elizabeth Stakes or the Arlington Million after her success in the Eclipse but she went off her food and was on the easy list over the summer, more than three months elapsing before she raced again. With the exception of the flying machine Habibti, Pebbles (rated 135) was the best of her sex aged three and above trained in Britain in the second half of the twentieth century, just ahead of Petite Etoile (134) and a group (on 133) comprising Dunfermline, Indian Skimmer, Marwell and Rose Bowl.

Pebbles may just have the edge on Enable on Timeform ratings, but it would be hard for any filly to better the overall achievements in a single season of Enable who, after being beaten on her reappearance, won her six remaining races, culminating in Europe's richest race the Prix de l'Arc de Triomphe, which was run at Chantilly for the second time and for which she was only the fourth horse this century to be sent off at odds on (following Treve when finishing fourth trying for a third victory in the race in 2015; Sea The Stars when successful in 2009; and the 1999 winner Montjeu when he was also beaten into fourth in 2000). Like those other notable European champions of recent times, Frankel and Treve, Enable developed something of an air of invincibility as a three-year-old by demolishing the opposition in race after race. Treve won all four of her starts at three, her victories including the Prix de Diane by four lengths and the Arc, before which she did not meet any of the top colts, by five (though it looked more like four), while Frankel won his five starts as a three-year-old (four of them Group 1s) by an aggregate of nearly twenty lengths, winning the Two Thousand Guineas by the widest margin for sixty-five years and the Sussex Stakes by the widest winning margin for thirty-three.

Before Enable crowned her magnificent year by becoming the first three-year-old filly to win the Arc since Treve (winning impressively by two and a half lengths in a style reminiscent of Treve herself), she had already won four Group 1s—the Oaks by five lengths, the Irish Oaks by five and a half, 'Britain's Arc' and traditionally Europe's mid-season middle-distance championship the King George VI and Queen Elizabeth Stakes by four and a half, and the Yorkshire Oaks by five. Three of Enable's Group 1 victories came in races against her own sex—four of Minding's five Group 1 wins the previous season had also been against fillies and mares—but Enable's quintet was achieved in successive races and equalled the feat by Giant's Causeway and Rock of Gibraltar of winning five straight Group 1s as a three-year-old, matching Nijinsky's five championship races in a row in 1970, the year before the official pattern system was introduced. Sea The Stars holds the European record for winning six successive Group 1s as a three-year-old, which, like Nijinsky's wins, were achieved over a variety of distances. Enable's achievement of winning the Oaks, the Irish Oaks and Yorkshire Oaks in the same season placed her in some illustrious company, including that of User Friendly (trained like Pebbles by Clive Brittain) who also won the St Leger before being narrowly beaten in the Arc.

However, it is the achievement of landing the King George/Prix de l'Arc double in the same season that makes Enable unique among fillies (Danedream won both races but in different seasons). Only six colts have also won the King George and the Arc in the same campaign—Ribot (rated 142), Ballymoss (136), Mill Reef (141), Dancing Brave (140), Lammtarra (134) and Dylan Thomas (132). Enable became the fifth winner of the Arc for Frankel's owner-breeder Khalid Abdullah (putting him one ahead of the Aga Khan and Daniel Wildenstein), following Rainbow Quest in 1985 (when he was runner-up to Pebbles in the Eclipse), Dancing Brave in 1986 (when he also won the King George) and the home breds Rail Link in 2006 and Workforce in 2010. Frankie Dettori had the mount on Enable for all her wins as a three-year-old and she gave him a record fifth winning ride in the Arc (following Lammtarra who completed the King George/Arc double in 1995, Sakhee in 2001, Marienbard in 2002 and Golden Horn in 2015). Dettori had previously been joint holder of the record with six other jockeys who have four Arc wins to their name, Jacko Doyasbere, Freddie Head, Yves Saint-Martin, Pat Eddery, Olivier Peslier and Thierry Jarnet (who partnered Treve to her two victories).

Frankie Dettori may well have a good opportunity to enhance his record in the Prix de l'Arc de Triomphe even further in the next season, as Enable remains in training, along with her stablemate Cracksman whom Dettori partnered to a most impressive victory in the Champion Stakes. Keeping a classic or Group 1-winning three-year-old in training at four does not always meet with the success it deserves, for the very obvious reason that not many tip-top three-year-olds are capable of making more than the normal improvement from three to four as measured by the weight-for age scale (of which more later in the essay). Frankel and Treve were notable exceptions and Enable's connections will be hoping for a similar outcome after their decision to race on, with the principal aim of winning a second Arc (when the race will be back at its traditional home Longchamp).

History is against Enable, though, as Treve is the only Arc-winning filly to have followed up her victory as a three-year-old with a further success in the race the following year, overcoming setbacks to do so. Since the prize-money for the Prix de l'Arc de Triomphe was raised five-fold in 1949 to make it a race of truly international importance, nine three-year-old fillies won the race before Enable. The Aga Khan-owned Akiyda and Zarkava were both retired but the seven others stayed in training. Danedream raced on at four, when she won the King George, but she was prevented from defending her Arc crown by a swamp-fever ban imposed in her native Germany. Coronation V, La Sorellina, San San and Detroit didn't make the first ten in the Arc as four-year-olds. The 1979 winner Three Troikas, trained like Treve by Criquette Head, came close to achieving successive wins when beaten less than a length into fourth behind Detroit in the 1980 renewal, recovering from a broken bone in her foot earlier in the season to take part. Apart from Treve, Corrida is the only other filly or mare to have won the Arc twice, her successes coming at the ages of four and five in the 'thirties when the race was less important (Corrida was owned by Marcel Boussac whose six Arc wins remain the record for a breeder as well as for an owner, although most of his wins were in the era before the massive increase in the Arc's prize money and when the Grand Prix de Paris was still France's most valuable race).

Investec Oaks, Epsom—
Enable stamps herself as the clear leader of her age and sex over middle distances, quickly putting daylight between herself and Rhododendron, with Alluringly leading home the others

Darley Irish Oaks, the Curragh—
Enable becomes the fourteenth filly, and the first since Snow Fairy in 2010, to complete the Anglo-Irish Oaks double; she wins in authoritative fashion, beating Rain Goddess and Eziyra

Enable made only one appearance as a two-year-old, winning a fillies maiden right at the end of November on the all-weather at Newcastle (which replaced its Flat turf course with tapeta in 2016). Although it still comes as something of a surprise to see a classic winner emerge from among those who have started off in the all-weather ranks, Enable is not the first and won't be the last to do so. Ghanaati, Jack Hobbs and Covert Love are other recent classic winners who made their debuts in races on an artificial surface, at Kempton, Wolverhampton and Lingfield respectively (Covert Love's first win was achieved at Chelmsford). Enable started her three-year-old season a little way down the pecking order among the potential classic fillies at Clarehaven and she was still available at 25/1 for the Oaks in early-May, after she had finished a staying-on third behind well-regarded stablemate Shutter Speed (short-priced favourite and ridden by Dettori) in a conditions event at Newbury on her reappearance (turf debut). Shutter Speed was installed as joint favourite for the Oaks after her Newbury victory and another stablemate, Coronet, was a 10/1-chance for the race at the time. John Gosden, who made a flying start to the season, particularly in the classic trials, described Enable in a *Racing Post* feature on his Oaks prospects (in which he mentioned six of his fillies being considered for the race) as 'a nice middle-distance prospect, but we'll know more after she runs in the Cheshire Oaks.'

The Arkle Finance Cheshire Oaks has only listed status and it had been ten years since the winner had gone on to score at Epsom (Light Shift for Henry Cecil). John Gosden wasn't the only Oaks-winning trainer with a runner in the latest edition, with Aidan O'Brien represented by Alluringly, Ralph Beckett by Rich Legacy and Andrew Balding by Hidden Steps, the seven-runner line-up making for a better renewal than some in recent years. Alluringly (evens favourite) and Enable (2/1) dominated both the betting and the race itself, in which they showed themselves clearly a cut above their rivals. Enable benefited from being stepped up in trip again and, with Dettori taking the mount on her for the first time, she travelled with plenty of zest and quickened into the lead three furlongs out before staying on to beat Alluringly by a length and three quarters, eased down in the final strides (third-placed Tansholpan finished nine lengths further back). With more improvement in her, and seemingly certain to relish the full mile and a half of the Oaks, Enable looked a genuine contender for Epsom, although some regarded her Chester performance at the time as more of a boost for the form of her Newbury conqueror Shutter Speed who was due to contest the following week's Musidora Stakes at York before a final decision was made about her own participation in the Oaks. Shutter Speed won the Musidora but, in the same ownership as Enable, she didn't go on to Epsom, being sent instead to Chantilly for the Prix de Diane (in which she finished only fourth). While Shutter Speed's career faltered after a very bright start, Enable's went from strength to strength, starting at Epsom where she was sent off 6/1 joint second favourite in a representative field for the Investec Oaks.

The One Thousand Guineas runner-up Rhododendron, whose conqueror Winter (from the same stable) had followed up in the Irish Guineas, was sent off at odds on for the Oaks in which most of the other principals had made an impact in good races or in the traditional Oaks trials. Sobetsu, joint second favourite with Enable, had won the Prix Saint-Alary at Deauville, a Group 1 that often has more bearing on the Prix de Diane than the Oaks. Enable's stablemate Coronet had shaped well in third in the Saint-Alary and started at 12/1 for the Oaks, the same odds as Natavia (carrying the Abdullah colours) who had won the listed Fillies' Trial at Newbury. Horseplay was a 14/1-shot after her success in Newmarket's Pretty Polly Stakes which had been won by three previous Oaks winners this century, Ouija Board, Talent and Taghrooda. Alluringly was also in the Oaks line-up, a 16/1-shot and the Ballydoyle second string behind Rhododendron. The Ballydoyle runners on the day were late arriving at Epsom after a problem with the aircraft bringing them over from Ireland and they finally got to the course around two o'clock, just over an hour before Highland Reel's appearance in the Coronation Cup, which he won, and around two and a half hours before the Oaks.

By the time the Oaks was run, torrential rain was falling at Epsom, with accompanying thunder and lightning, which probably contributed to the unfortunate incident in which Daddys Lil Darling, who would have been the first North American-trained runner in the Oaks, bolted on the way to the start and eventually parted company with her jockey Olivier Peslier before having to be withdrawn (thankfully both horse and rider seemed to emerge from the experience unscathed). When the race got under way, the third Ballydoyle runner Pocketfullofdreams, who had come second in the Lingfield Oaks Trial, forced the pace, going clear before halfway as she set a searching gallop which contributed to the Oaks being run in 2m 34.13sec, a record for the race since official times were kept (the 1993 winner Intrepidity had held the record). Enable got the better of a gripping duel with Rhododendron in the home straight, leading three furlongs out and again staying on strongly, forging clear inside the final furlong and well on top at the finish.

Wide-margin winners of the Oaks are not so rare as might be imagined. Sun Princess, a twelve-length winner in 1983 (when she also won the St Leger), holds the record, ahead of the ten-length winners Formosa (1868), Noblesse (1963) and 50/1-shot Jet Ski Lady (1991), with Lady Carla (1996) having won by nine lengths, Saucy Sue (1925) by eight, and Blue Wind (1981) and Ouija Board (2004) by seven. A wide-margin victory isn't always evidence of a high-class performance, as it can also sometimes serve to expose a lack of strength in depth among the other runners, particularly in a searching race like the Oaks. In most renewals nowadays, only a handful in the line-up prove capable of showing much more than useful form over Epsom's stiff mile and a half in a race which comes at the halfway stage in their three-year-old campaign. Enable's five-length Oaks win, with Alluringly a further six lengths back in third and another three and three quarters to fourth-placed Horseplay (Coronet came fifth and went on to turn the tables on Alluringly in the Ribblesdale at Royal Ascot), did clearly represent high-class form, however. Enable's performance was on a par with that in the race of Ouija Board, which had been the best since those outstanding winners in the early-'nineties, Salsabil and User Friendly (Oh So Sharp's very fine performance in the race in 1985, when she won by six lengths, represents the high-water mark for Oaks performances in the last thirty years or so).

For most fillies, winning the Oaks is the pinnacle of their achievements. Indeed, it is fairly unusual for an Oaks winner to go on to enhance her reputation much—if at all—after Epsom. Minding had done so twelve months earlier when beating the very best of the milers among the colts in the Queen Elizabeth II Stakes on British Champions' Day, and the 2014 winner Taghrooda had been another outstanding example. Taghrooda, trained like Enable by John Gosden, went on to success in the King George VI and Queen Elizabeth Stakes, becoming only the third three-year-old filly to win the Ascot showpiece, after the French-trained pair Dahlia and Pawneese back in the 'seventies. Taghrooda didn't run between the Oaks and the King George but Enable took in another classic on the way, as had Dahlia (who won the Irish Oaks when there was only a week between that race and the King George) and Pawneese (who added the Prix de Diane nine days after Epsom).

Enable started at 5/2-on for the Darley Irish Oaks at the Curragh where Frankie Dettori, who injured a shoulder in a parade-ring incident at Yarmouth in mid-June which forced him to miss Royal Ascot, made an earlier than expected return to the saddle to partner Enable to another wide-margin victory. Enable made mincemeat of the opposition, which included Alluringly and Coronet from those defeated at Epsom. Coronet, who started second favourite, and Alluringly managed only fourth and sixth, leaving another of the Ballydoyle fillies, the runner-up in the Pretty Polly at the Curragh, Rain Goddess, to chase home easy winner Enable, ahead of 20/1-shot Eziyra in third. Enable could have produced more, and won by further than five and a half lengths, had the situation required it, and she didn't need to match her Epsom form, having the Irish Oaks in the bag soon after quickening to lead two furlongs out ('When I asked her to go she flew, and it was hands and heels from there,' said Dettori). The widest margin of victory achieved in the Irish Oaks since the *Racehorses* series began is the eight lengths by which Snow Fairy crushed her rivals in 2010 when she became the thirteenth to complete the Oaks/Irish Oaks double. Enable became the fourteenth to do the double and, like Snow Fairy, who added further big victories as a three-year-old in the Queen Elizabeth II Commemorative Cup at Kyoto and the Hong Kong Cup at Sha Tin, Enable wasn't finished for the year by a long way.

The year of Snow Fairy's Oaks/Irish Oaks double was also the year of Harbinger's record-breaking eleven-length victory in the King George VI and Queen Elizabeth Stakes. The King George was inaugurated in 1951 as a championship event that would bring the pick of the different generations of middle-distance horses together, on weight-for-age terms, at the end of July, after Europe's major classic races had been decided. The King George hasn't always succeeded in fulfilling that particular aim in recent times, but the 2010 edition featured not just one, but two, Derby winners, Harbinger's stablemate Workforce who had won at Epsom and was odds on for the King George, and Cape Blanco who had won the Irish Derby and went on to add the Irish Champion. Workforce's disappointing performance (which he more than made up for by winning the Arc on his next start) was as big a letdown as Harbinger's wide-margin victory was a revelation. Workforce and Kris Kin (third behind Irish Derby winner Alamshar in the 2003 King George) are the only Epsom Derby winners to have contested the Ascot showpiece since Galileo who was the last to complete the Derby/King George double, back in 2001. Alamshar, Enable's sire Nathaniel, who missed the classics, and Taghrooda had been the only winning three-year-olds in the King George since Galileo (five of the last fourteen runnings have taken place without a single three-year-old in the line-up as the King George has increasingly seemed to be shaping up as more of a race for older horses). There were two three-year-olds in the ten-runner line-up for the latest King George VI and Queen Elizabeth Stakes (sponsored by Qipco), Enable and the Derby fifth Benbatl who had since won the Hampton Court Stakes at Royal Ascot.

Enable's participation was confirmed when she came out of the Irish Oaks 'full of herself', in the words of her trainer. There was a fortnight between the two races, during which time Frankie Dettori existed on a diet of 'white fish, vegetables and water' to ensure that he lost 7 lb to get down to his minimum riding weight of 8-7, a mark at which he has ridden only rarely in recent years. The prevailing soft ground (further significant rain in the hour before the race made conditions unusually testing) resulted in Enable replacing ante-post favourite Highland Reel, the previous year's winner, at the head of the market in the week leading up to the race. She was sent off at 5/4 on the day, with Highland Reel, who had won the Coronation Cup and the Prince of Wales's Stakes on his last two starts, starting at 9/2, ahead of Enable's senior stablemate the 2015 Irish Derby winner Jack Hobbs who was an 11/2-shot. The presence of the Hardwicke Stakes winner Idaho (Highland Reel's brother) and the Eclipse winner Ulysses, the only others sent off at single-figure odds, contributed to a representative field which included a quixotic challenger from South America, the four-year-old Sixties Song who had won the most recent runnings of two of that continent's biggest races, the Gran Premio Carlos Pellegrini in Argentina and the Gran Premio Latinoamericano in Chile.

Conditions were not ideal for some in the King George field, most notably for Highland Reel who clearly wasn't at his best and managed only fourth after racing wide for a long way, with his rider seemingly in search of better ground. There was no reason, however, to think that the placed horses, Ulysses and Idaho, did not run to form. Enable beat them comprehensively, taking the lead early in the home straight and staying on strongly when ridden over two furlongs out to draw clear for an impressive win by four and a half lengths and three quarters of a length. Highland Reel was four lengths behind Idaho, with Benbatl below form in fifth and the Eclipse third Desert Encounter in sixth; Jack Hobbs beat only Sixties Song, who was always behind. Trainers are sometimes reluctant to place their best horses in a pecking order but John Gosden had no hesitation after the King George in hailing Enable as 'the best filly I've trained.' Gosden has handled plenty of good fillies. In addition to King George winners Enable and Taghrooda, the list is headed by the likes of the Lloyd-Webber-owned pair The Fugue and Dar Re Mi, both fillies out of the top drawer, Nathaniel's Irish Oaks-winning sister Great Heavens, multiple Group 1 winner Elusive Kate, dual Group 1 winner Izzi Top and, further back, the Breeders' Cup Mile winner Royal Heroine. John Gosden, incidentally, has now trained three of the last seven King George winners, all of them three-year-olds, and his 2015 Derby winner Golden Horn (who would have been odds on) would also have contested the race had significant rain not arrived the day before the race, leading to his late withdrawal after connections had walked the course on raceday. Enable's performances in the latest season weren't enough for her trainer to regain the British trainers' championship from Irish-based Aidan O'Brien, but Clarehaven's domestic earnings of £6,188,845 were a record for a British-based operation. Gosden also headed the table for earnings on foreign soil by a British trainer by a very wide margin (thanks largely to Enable's win in the Arc and the success of Jack Hobbs in the Dubai Sheema Classic); according to figures compiled by the International Racing Bureau, Clarehaven horses won £6,125,688 on their travels in the latest season, contributing to a total haul of £22,166,769 won by British-trained horses overseas, the best since the bumper year of 2009 (£24.6m), though, as in that year (at the height of the global banking crisis), the 2017 total owed much to a particularly weak pound, attributed to the Brexit vote.

One unexpected consequence of Enable's victory in the King George VI and Queen Elizabeth Stakes was the debate which took place, in the columns of some commentators and in the letters pages of the *Racing Post*, over the weight-for-age scale in horseracing. The idea that younger horses should receive a weight allowance from their elders, to compensate for their lack of maturity, has been recognised for

King George VI and Queen Elizabeth Stakes, Ascot—significant rain in the hour before the all-aged summer championship makes the conditions unusually testing, but it matters little to Enable as she beats Eclipse winner Ulysses (noseband) in good style, with the brothers Idaho (striped cap) and Highland Reel (right) completing the frame

Darley Yorkshire Oaks, York—Enable records a fourth Group 1 success of the summer under a change of tactics, making all to beat stablemate Coronet (noseband) and Queen's Trust (white face)

more than a hundred and fifty years—the original weight-for-age scale of Admiral Rous, modified from time to time since, was introduced in 1851—but the fact that Enable received 14 lb in weight-for-age and fillies' allowances from the seven northern hemisphere older horses in the King George line-up ('a *full* stone' as one commentator emphasised) was claimed by some to have given her an 'unfair advantage'. The fact that Enable carried less weight than all her rivals, something which also applied later to her and four-times Group 1-winning Winter in the Prix de l'Arc, seemed to be used to devalue her victory ('Small wonder Enable was such a good thing, but can we call this a true championship race in any meaningful sense?'). There was talk of the older horses 'having a mountain to climb to beat the best of the classic generation,' though King George runner-up Ulysses had thwarted St James's Palace winner Barney Roy in the Eclipse and went on to do so again—more comprehensively—in the International at York where the dual Two Thousand Guineas winner Churchill split the pair. Furthermore, in the King George itself, the four-year-olds and upwards, as a group, lead the three-year-olds by thirty-seven victories to thirty, a gap that has widened in recent times, after rough parity between the groups over the period when the race was in its prime. With powerful stables such as Ballydoyle now viewing the King George as a race for its top older horses rather than for its classic three-year-olds, the gap between the two age groups seems likely to widen further, rather than to close, over the next decade or so. The latest 'tweaking' of the official weight-for-age scale took place in the latest season, incidentally, and is discussed in a little more detail in the essay on Ulysses. Enable would have carried 1 lb less in the King George, and later in the Arc, in previous seasons.

The average thoroughbred reaches full maturity at the age of four and, having a weight-for-age allowance allows three-year-olds to compete on relatively fair terms in open-aged championship races like the King George and the Arc, the races that count most in the racing year. Some three-year-olds, however, inevitably and naturally mature faster than others, with the result, as inferred earlier, that many tip-top three-year-olds might be said to have owed their success not only to their intrinsic merit but also to the fact that they were already a good deal closer to full maturity than many of their three-year-old contemporaries. By the same token, they were probably favoured by the weight-for-age scale in their encounters with older rivals. The fact that all racehorses are given a common birthday of January 1st, and treated for weight-for-age purposes, within their own age group, as if they were the same age, is another reason why the weight-for-age scale cannot be a perfect model. But, for all its inevitable shortcomings, it brings clear benefits to the sport by helping to capture the public imagination through intensifying competition in open-aged events like the King George and the Arc. The top three-year-olds wouldn't run without the allowance, although there is an argument that the weight-for-age scale results in many of the sport's most prestigious events being won by horses which are short of full maturity and, as a result of enhancing their reputations through successes in open-aged championship events, in particular, end up leaving racing prematurely and being retired to stud at the end of their three-year-old days. It has nearly always been like that, though the creation of richly-endowed races like the King George provided more of an incentive to keep top horses in training than in the days when the classic races were well and truly dominant and there were fewer top races for older horses. That said, among the highest-rated horses that have appeared in this Annual over the years, Sea-Bird, Dancing Brave, Shergar, Vaguely Noble, Sea The Stars and Nijinsky were all retired after their three-year-old season, during which they received a statutory weight-for-age allowance when recording major victories over older horses. Were they not among the greatest horses to have graced the game in the *Racehorses* era?

Enable became a short-priced favourite for the Qatar Prix de l'Arc de Triomphe the moment she passed the post in the King George and had a final warm-up for Chantilly with an all-the-way win in the Darley Yorkshire Oaks in August, winning with plenty in hand from Coronet and the four-year-olds Queen's Trust and Nezwaah. Enable's five-length winning margin was the widest in the race since the same owner's Quiff won the 2004 edition by eleven lengths. No three-year-old filly trained in Britain or Ireland had ever won the Arc, and no British-trained filly or mare of any age had done so, Leggera joining User Friendly in coming closest when beaten a neck by Sagamix in 1998 (she was also fourth the next year). The five-year-old Park Top was a fast-finishing runner-up to Levmoss in 1969 after winning the King George, while Sun Princess (third in the King George) was also second in the Arc in 1983. Of the trio of three-year-old fillies before Enable who had won the King George, the 1973 winner Dahlia finished sixteenth behind Rheingold at Longchamp after an interrupted preparation, the 1976 winner Pawneese finished eleventh behind Ivanjica, and the 2014 winner Taghrooda came third to Treve and Flintshire.

The latest Arc was hosted by Chantilly for the second year running while the redevelopment was completed at Longchamp. Chantilly is France's major training centre, as well as being home to the Prix du Jockey Club and Prix de Diane among other races. Chantilly's track is tighter than that at Longchamp and Enable's trainer felt that 'things could well go wrong in an eighteen-runner field and I'd feel a lot

Qatar Prix de l'Arc de Triomphe, Chantilly—
Enable puts herself in the history books as the first three-year-old filly from Britain or Ireland to win Europe's richest race, producing a top-class performance to provide jockey Frankie Dettori with a record fifth victory in the race; Enable is also a fifth winner for her owner Khalid Abdullah, whose second winner, Dancing Brave, also completed the King George/Arc double; four-year-olds Cloth of Stars (second right) and Ulysses (noseband) do best of the rest, with Order of St George (striped cap) in the frame for the second successive year

more confident if the race was at Longchamp.' He need not have worried. Everything went like clockwork for Enable (who looked very well beforehand and still had her summer coat), with Dettori keen not to end up trapped on the rail, from a potentially awkward draw in stall two, and quickly securing an ideal spot. Enable was settled behind a couple of the Ballydoyle runners, Idaho and Order of St George, as they set the pace ('I had toyed with the idea of making the running if I needed to, but was soon where I wanted to be, with plenty of room and free air on my left,' said Dettori afterwards). Enable travelled with her usual enthusiasm and was sent to the front two furlongs out, soon bursting clear and then sustaining her run to win smoothly by two and a half lengths, well on top in the closing stages. 'She was running away rounding the home turn,' said Dettori, 'I was going so well, striking Order of St George's heels, and I couldn't wait to get to the four-hundred-metre mark. When I asked her, it was just a question of counting the furlong sticks, it was so effortless for her, too perfect.'

The Prix Ganay winner Cloth of Stars produced a career best to finish second to Enable, becoming the third runner-up in the race for his trainer Andre Fabre in the last four runnings, but he never looked like making any impression on the winner. Ulysses came a creditable third, a further length and a quarter behind Cloth of Stars and a little closer to Enable than he had been at Ascot, while Order of St George completed the frame, doing best of the five runners saddled by Aidan O'Brien who had trained the first three the previous year when Order of St George had finished third behind Found and Highland Reel (who didn't contest the latest running). The Prix du Jockey Club winner Brametot was the first of the three-year-old colts to finish, running on for fifth, ahead of German-trained Dschingis Secret, who had won the Prix Foy from Cloth of Stars after landing the Group 1 Grosser Preis von Berlin in August. Of the first ten home, only eighth-placed Idaho hadn't won a Group 1 in the current season (though the Group 2 Hardwicke is run without penalties and is being groomed for promotion). Enable was the seventh filly or mare to win the Arc in the last ten runnings and Ryan Moore, who had won on Found, chose another Ballydoyle filly in the latest edition, the dual One Thousand Guineas winner Winter who had been imperious in races against her own sex until narrowly beaten in the Matron Stakes at Leopardstown, before which she was reported to have missed some home work because of a stone bruise. Winter, stepping up to a mile and a half for the first time, raced too freely early on and shaped as if the trip stretched her stamina. The Arc form had a solid look to it with Enable's top-class performance matching that of Treve in the race at the same age. French racegoers, incidentally, had little to cheer about on Arc day as all six Group 1 events on the card were won by British- or Irish-trained runners. It was the first time that French stables had drawn a blank since the Arc card has been in its present format (the last 'Group 1 whitewash' had come back in 1985, when Arc day featured just three Group 1s, the Marcel Boussac, the Abbaye and the Arc, with Midway Lady and Committed supplementing Rainbow Quest's triumph—promoted after a stewards' inquiry—in the Arc).

Enable (b.f. 2014)	Nathaniel (IRE) (b 2008)	Galileo (b 1998)	Sadler's Wells
			Urban Sea
		Magnificient Style (b 1993)	Silver Hawk
			Mia Karina
	Concentric (b 2004)	Sadler's Wells (b 1981)	Northern Dancer
			Fairy Bridge
		Apogee (b 1990)	Shirley Heights
			Bourbon Girl

After a busy summer, it came as no surprise to see Enable retired for the season after winning the Arc. There was never any talk of her being considered for the Breeders' Cup and she wouldn't have been the ideal type for the tight, turning North American tracks in any case. A rangy filly, strong and attractive, she stood out physically in the Oaks field and strengthened further through the season, something confirmed by the scales ('she is weighing heavier than she did before the Oaks,' John Gosden said in the run-up to the Arc). Enable took the eye in the preliminaries before all her races, being particularly calm and relaxed except before the Yorkshire Oaks when, after being saddled in the racecourse stables prior to being walked across the course, she was sweating in the paddock and became a little on edge, though it had no effect on her performance. Enable is from the first crop of Frankel's contemporary Nathaniel, a strapping individual who improved markedly himself from two to three (as did his Irish Oaks-winning sister Great Heavens). It was, therefore, not the greatest surprise when Nathaniel's first crop did not particularly shine as two-year-olds. Enable has put him on the map, though, and his fee for 2018 has been raised from £17,500 to £20,000. Nathaniel, like Frankel, is a son of Galileo, and therefore a grandson of Sadler's Wells who is also the sire of Enable's dam Concentric who won three times at a mile and a quarter for Andre Fabre, including in listed company, and is a sister to the Prix de Diane runner-up Dance Routine and closely related to the smart miler Apsis.

When Enable won the Oaks, she recorded the two-hundredth Group 1 win by a horse bred by Khalid Abdullah's Juddmonte operation which is built on the foundation of a varied set of broodmares, all either proven at stud or with good racing records, acquired during the 'eighties through a series of private purchases and shrewd dealing at the sales (mostly in North America). Enable's family has been at Juddmonte since Ferrans Stud in Ireland, and its mares, were acquired in 1982 (Ferrans still plays an important role as the base where the Juddmonte yearlings are put through their pre-training). Not all the Ferrans Stud broodmares were deemed good enough for Juddmonte at the time but Fleet Girl, Enable's fourth dam, went on to have a considerable influence. Fleet Girl bred the Oaks and Irish Oaks runner-up Bourbon Girl for Khalid Abdullah and, although Bourbon Girl herself died at the age of thirteen, she produced three daughters who all eventually joined the Juddmonte broodmare band. The first of them Shining Bright finished fifth in the Oaks and went on to breed the Ribblesdale winner Spanish Sun and her brother Spanish Moon who won the Grand Prix de Saint-Cloud; the third daughter Daring Miss, a Grand Prix de Chantilly winner and Grand Prix de Saint-Cloud runner-up, was the least successful of the trio at stud. Bourbon Girl's middle daughter, Enable's grandam Apogee, won the Prix de Royaumont, and the racecourse performances of her offspring Dance

Mr K. Abdullah's "Enable"

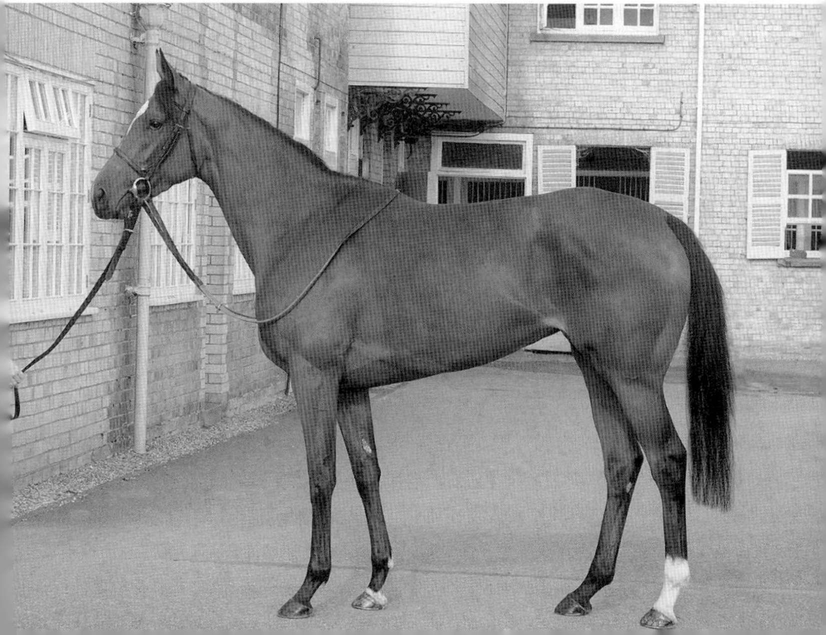

Routine and Apsis, in particular, made her the most successful of Bourbon Girl's daughters at stud. Enable is the fifth foal out of Apogee's daughter Concentric and the best of three winners bred by her for Khalid Abdullah, the two others being the miler Tournament (by Oasis Dream) and the middle-distance stayer Contribution (by Champs Elysees). Both were useful performers for Andre Fabre, Contribution finishing third in the Prix de Pomone. Concentric has a two-year-old, Centroid, and a yearling, both by Dansili, the sire of Flintshire (a son of Concentric's sister Dance Routine) whose string of Group/Grade 1 wins and two Arc seconds make him Juddmonte's leading home-bred money earner (its record-earning American champion Arrogate was bought as a yearling). Following on after unraced Centroid and his yearling sister is a filly foal by Frankel, while Concentric was in foal to Sea The Stars in the latest season.

The thoroughly genuine Enable stays a mile and a half well and acts on tapeta, firm and soft going. She travels strongly in her races and usually tracks the pace (though she made the running in the Yorkshire Oaks). The selecting of a 'horse of the year' in *Racehorses* began in the 'sixties and Enable is only the sixth filly to have won the title, following Allez France in 1974, Habibti in 1983, Pebbles in 1985, Zarkava in 2008 and Treve in 2013. Allez France and unbeaten Zarkava were French-trained winners of the Prix de l'Arc de Triomphe, like Treve, and victory in Europe's pre-eminent weight-for-age race was a dominant factor in earning the award, as it was for Enable. Allez France was Timeform Horse of the Year as a four-year-old, as was Pebbles, while the others picked up the award as three-year-olds. Habibti won, successively, the July Cup, the William Hill Sprint Championship (Nunthorpe), the Sprint Cup (by seven lengths) and the Prix de l'Abbaye, all races also open to colts and, had she stuck to sprinting instead of first being aimed at the One Thousand Guineas and its Irish equivalent, she might well have gone through her three-year-old season unbeaten. Enable was tested in a full series of top races for a three-year-old middle-distance filly, and her overall achievements stand comparison with those of Habibti or any of her female predecessors in the season they were Timeform Horse of the year. We wish her well as a four-year-old. *John Gosden*

ENCAPSULATED 7 b.g. Zamindar (USA) 116 – Star Cluster 106 (Observatory (USA) 131) [2017 67: p7g p6d* p6g p6g² p6g p6g⁶ t7.2g p6g p7g p7g p6g p7s Dec 14] good-topped gelding: fair handicapper: won at Chelmsford in February: stays 7f: acts on polytrack, tapeta, good to firm and good to soft going: has worn cheekpieces: usually races towards rear: inconsistent. *Roger Ingram* **65**

ENCHANTED MOMENT 5 b.m. Lawman (FR) 121 – Gentle Thoughts 73 (Darshaan 133) [2017 64: 10.2g 10d⁵ t9.5g Aug 11] lengthy mare: modest maiden handicapper: stays 1¾m: acts on tapeta and heavy going: usually wears headgear: sometimes slowly away: ungenuine. *Olly Murphy* **58 §**

ENCHANTING ENYA (IRE) 2 ch.f. (May 15) Champs Elysees 124 – Miss Honorine (IRE) 109 (Highest Honor (FR) 124) [2017 p8d Nov 22] 5,000Y: closely related to 6f winner Sirajiah (by Exceed And Excel) and half-sister to 3 winners, including 11.5f-1¾m winner Onorina (by Arcano): dam 1m-1¼m winner: 100/1, well held in minor event at Kempton. *Steph Hollinshead* **–**

ENCODED (IRE) 4 ch.f. Sakhee's Secret 128 – Confidentiality (IRE) 93 (Desert Style (IRE) 121) [2017 7d t5g⁴ t5g t6d⁴ Nov 10] poor maiden: best effort at 6f: acts on tapeta. *Lynn Siddall* **46**

ENCORE D'OR 5 b.g. Oasis Dream 129 – Entente Cordiale (IRE) 72 (Ela-Mana-Mou 132) [2017 113: f5g t5.1g⁵ p5f* p6g³ 5f p5s* 5m 5g³ p5g 5d* 5.2m Sep 23] strong gelding: smart performer: won handicaps at Lingfield (by head from Zac Brown) in March and Chelmsford (by neck from Royal Birth) in June, and listed race at Doncaster (by length from Razzmatazz) in September: stays 6f: acts on polytrack, tapeta, good to firm and good to soft going: tried in cheekpieces. *Robert Cowell* **112**

ENCRYPTED 2 b.c. (Feb 16) Showcasing 117 – Disclose 100 (Dansili 127) [2017 6g p6g* 6m³ 5v 5m p5d* t6d Oct 24] compact colt: fourth foal: closely related to winner up to 6f Impart (2-y-o 5f winner, by Oasis Dream) and half-brother to a winner abroad by Beat Hollow: dam 1m winner: fairly useful performer: won minor event at Kempton in June and nursery at Chelmsford (by ½ length from Emilia James) in September: stays 6f: acts on polytrack and good to firm going. *Hugo Palmer* **92**

ENCRYPTION (IRE) 2 b.g. (Feb 25) High Chaparral (IRE) 132 – Challow Hills (USA) 73 (Woodman (USA) 126) [2017 t8s 8d 7g Nov 3] fifth foal: dam, 1m winner who probably stayed 1¼m, out of half-sister to Oaks winner Diminuendo: modest form: best effort when ninth in minor event at Newcastle (4½ lengths behind Tansheet) in September: remains open to improvement. *George Scott* **60 p**

ENDEAVOUR (IRE) 3 b.g. Acclamation 118 – Miss Hawai (FR) (Peintre Celebre (USA) 137) [2017 70: p5g³ p5g⁵ t6g⁶ 6g* 5.3g* 6m⁴ 7g 6d t6.1g Aug 18] fair performer: won seller at Leicester and handicap at Brighton in April: left Richard Hannon after fifth start: stays 6f: acts on polytrack and good to firm going: front runner/races prominently. *Marjorie Fife* **69**

ENDLESS ACRES (IRE) 4 b.g. Champs Elysees 124 – Eternity Ring (Alzao (USA) 117) [2017 88: p16g* p16g³ t16.3g² 20f² 18mᵖᵘ Oct 14] lengthy gelding: useful handicapper: won at Kempton (by 4½ lengths from Glan Y Gors) in April: second in Ascot Stakes at Royal Ascot (6 lengths behind Thomas Hobson) in June: suffered career-ending injury in Cesarewitch: stayed 2½m: acted on polytrack, tapeta, firm and soft going: wore visor. *Charlie Fellowes* **108**

ENDLESS CHARM 3 ch.f. Dubawi (IRE) 129 – Whazzis 109 (Desert Prince (IRE) 130) [2017 76P: p7g May 4] won maiden on debut at 2 yrs, last in handicap only start in 2017: should stay 7f. *Charlie Appleby* **–**

ENDLESS GOLD 3 b.g. Dubawi (IRE) 129 – Love Charm (Singspiel (IRE) 133) [2017 67: 8.3g² 8m 7m² 8d² 8.3g² Jul 8] well-made, attractive gelding: fairly useful maiden: second in handicaps at Newmarket in June: will stay 1¼m: acts on good to firm and good to soft going: in headgear last 3 starts: front runner/races prominently. *Charlie Appleby* **91**

ENDLESSLY (IRE) 2 b.c. (Jan 31) Nathaniel (IRE) 129 – What's Up Pussycat (IRE) 100 (Danehill Dancer (IRE) 117) [2017 7g Nov 3] 10/3, well held in minor event at Newmarket. *Martyn Meade* **–**

ENDLESS TANGENT (IRE) 2 b.f. (Mar 21) Lawman (FR) 121 – Passion Planet (IRE) 75 (Medicean 128) [2017 7.2d 8.2v² 8s⁵ Oct 28] 7,500F, €26,000Y: first foal: dam, 14.4f winner, half-sister to smart stayers Pale Mimosa and Nearly Caught: fair form: best effort when second in minor event at Haydock (1¾ lengths behind Pioneer Spirit) in September: bred to stay 1¼m+. *Tom Dascombe* **71**

ENDLESS TIME (IRE) 5 b.m. Sea The Stars (IRE) 140 – Mamonta 65 (Fantastic Light (USA) 134) [2017 117: 13.9d⁴ 20m 14v* 11.9d Sep 10] big, leggy mare: smart performer: won Lillie Langtry Stakes at Goodwood (by neck from Dubka) in August: fourth earlier in Yorkshire Cup at York (½ length behind Dartmourth): tailed off in Prix Vermeille at Chantilly final outing: stays 15.5f: acts on polytrack, good to firm and heavy going: in cheekpieces last 2 starts. *Charlie Appleby* **110**

Markel Insurance Fillies' Stakes, Goodwood—
Endless Time overcomes trouble in running to win a good renewal of this Group 3, registered as the Lillie Langtry and set for promotion to Group 2 in 2018, with Dubka (second left), Melodic Motion and Natural Scenery completing the frame

ENDURING POWER (IRE) 4 b.g. Approve (IRE) 112 – Our Dear Ruth (USA) **75** (Baldski (USA)) [2017 75: 8g p7.5f Aug 22] good-bodied gelding: fair performer: ran only in claimers in France in 2017: stays 1m: acts on polytrack: tried in blinkers. *Jo Hughes*

ENERGIA FLAVIO (BRZ) 7 gr.g. Agnes Gold (JPN) 115 – Lira da Guanabara (BRZ) **85** (Pitu da Guanabara (BRZ)) [2017 81: 8m t7.2g^{2} t7.2g^{2} t8.6g t7.2d Dec 16] angular gelding: fairly useful handicapper: second at Wolverhampton in July: stays 9.5f: acts on tapeta, soft and good to firm going: has worn headgear: often races towards rear. *Patrick Morris*

ENERGIA FOX (BRZ) 7 ch.m. Agnes Gold (JPN) 115 – Super Eletric (BRZ) (Choctaw **89** Ridge (USA)) [2017 89: t12.2m^{5} t10.2d* 10.3m^{3} 10.3g* 10.3s^{4} 9.8m^{4} 10.2d^{6} 10.3s^{4} 10.2s 10.3v Sep 16] lengthy mare: fairly useful handicapper: won at Newcastle in February and Chester (by head from Kapstadt) in May: stays 12.5f: acts on polytrack, tapeta, good to firm and heavy going: usually races prominently. *Richard Fahey*

ENFOLDING (IRE) 3 b.g. Fastnet Rock (AUS) 127 – Althea Rose (IRE) (Green Desert **96 p** (USA) 127) [2017 77p: t8.6g^{2} t9.5g* t9.5g* p11d^{2} Dec 13] useful performer: won maiden at Wolverhampton and handicap at same course (by 3¼ lengths from Peace And Plenty) in March: second in handicap at Kempton (nose behind General Hazard) in December: stays 11f: acts on polytrack and tapeta: responds generously to pressure: will go on improving. *James Fanshawe*

ENFORCEMENT (IRE) 2 b.g. (Mar 26) Lawman (FR) 121 – Elodie (Dansili 127) **–** [2017 7d^{6} 8.1g p6g Oct 24] strong, compact gelding: down the field in minor events: tried in hood. *Martin Keighley*

ENGLAND EXPECTS 3 b.f. Mount Nelson 125 – Fanny's Fancy 99 (Groom Dancer **71** (USA) 128) [2017 t8d^{5} 6g^{6} 6m^{4} 8s 8f^{2} 8.3s^{5} 9.9v^{3} 10.2d^{2} 10.2g^{2} 10.2v Nov 8] €28,000Y: seventh foal: half-sister to 2-y-o 6f winner Jolah (by Oasis Dream), later successful abroad, and 6f winner Lead Role (by Exceed And Excel): dam 6f winner: fair maiden: stays 1¼m: acts on any turf going: wears hood: often races towards rear. *K. R. Burke*

ENGLISH HERO 4 b.g. Royal Applause 124 – Merton Matriarch 64 (Cadeaux Genereux **70** 131) [2017 78: f6g^{4} Apr 16] fair handicapper: stays 7f: acts on fibresand, tapeta, soft and good to firm going. *John Mackie*

ENGLISHMAN 7 b.g. Royal Applause 124 – Tesary 98 (Danehill (USA) 126) [2017 94: **91** 5m 6m 6.1g* 6g^{4} 6.1d 6.1m^{4} 6.1g^{2} 6d 6.1g^{6} 6.1s^{4} 6s^{4} 6v 6s Oct 15] big, good-topped gelding: fairly useful handicapper: won at Windsor in May: second at same course in July: stays 7f, usually races over shorter: acts on good to firm and heavy going: tried in cheekpieces: often races prominently. *Milton Bradley*

ENGLISH SUMMER 10 b.g. Montjeu (IRE) 137 – Hunt The Sun (Rainbow Quest **66** (USA) 134) [2017 95: t13.9f p13m^{2} t13.9g^{6} t12.2g t12.2g^{6} Mar 23] sturdy, close-coupled gelding: fair handicapper: stays 16.5f: acts on polytrack, tapeta and any turf going: has worn headgear, including last 3 starts: usually wears tongue tie: often races prominently. *Ian Williams*

ENGLISHWOMAN 4 b.f. Acclamation 118 – Tesary 98 (Danehill (USA) 126) [2017 81: **81** f5g^{3} f6g* f6g^{4} f5s^{2} t6d^{3} Feb 4] fairly useful handicapper: won at Southwell in January: stays 6f: acts on fibresand, tapeta and good to firm going. *David Evans*

ENIGMATIC (IRE) 3 b.g. Elnadim (USA) 128 – Meanwhile (IRE) 63 (Haafhd 129) **82** [2017 49p: p8d* p8g* t8g^{2} p10s^{4} p8g Dec 31] fairly useful performer: won maiden at Chelmsford in September and claimer at Lingfield in November: second in handicap at Newcastle in December: stays 1m: acts on polytrack and tapeta: front runner/races prominently, often freely. *Jamie Osborne*

ENJAZAAT 2 b.c. (Feb 18) Acclamation 118 – Miliika 92 (Green Desert (USA) 127) **105** [2017 6s 6s* 6g^{6} 6m* 6m Sep 23] 115,000F: attractive colt: first foal: dam 6f winner out of useful 5f/6f winner Miss Anabaa: useful performer: won minor event at Yarmouth (by 6 lengths from Zaaki) in June and listed race at Ripon (by 2 lengths from Tip Two Win) in August: raced only at 6f: acts on soft and good to firm going. *Owen Burrows*

ENJOY LIFE (IRE) 4 b.f. Acclamation 118 – Jeu de Plume (IRE) (Montjeu (IRE) 137) **86** [2017 87: t7.1g^{4} t6g^{4} 6g^{5} 7g^{6} 6.9s^{5} 6.1g^{2} 5.8g^{5} 8v^{4} 6v^{2} Oct 24] fairly useful handicapper: second at Nottingham in July: left Kevin Ryan after sixth start: stays 7f: acts on tapeta and heavy going: has worn cheekpieces, including often in 2017: races prominently. *W. McCreery, Ireland*

ENMESHING 4 ch.g. Mastercraftsman (IRE) 129 – Yacht Club (USA) (Sea Hero (USA) **76** 124) [2017 84: p12m* Jan 21] fair performer: won maiden at Lingfield in January: stays 1½m: acts on polytrack and tapeta: tried in cheekpieces: has joined Alexandra Dunn: poor form over hurdles. *James Fanshawe*

ENNAADD 4 b.c. King's Best (USA) 132 – Zayn Zen 107 (Singspiel (IRE) 133) [2017 120p: p8g^{4} 8f^{2} 8f Jun 20] well-made colt: smart performer: second in listed race at Ascot (neck behind Tabarrak) in May: stays 1m: acts on polytrack and firm going: often races prominently/travels strongly: has joined G. Selvaratnam in UAE. *Roger Varian* **119**

ENNJAAZ (IRE) 3 b.c. Poet's Voice 126 – Hall Hee (IRE) 103 (Invincible Spirit (IRE) 121) [2017 10s^{2} p10g^{2} p10d* p11g^{2} a9.9f Nov 23] fourth foal: closely related to 2-y-o 1m winner Here Now (by Dubawi) and half-brother to 2-y-o 7f winner Sherinn (by Refuse To Bend) and 1m winner (stays 1¼m) Saafarr (by Teofilo): dam 1m winner out of close relative to Derby winner Sir Percy: useful performer: won maiden at Chelmsford in September: second in handicap at Kempton (nose behind Seniority) in October: stays 11f: acts on polytrack: in cheekpieces last 3 starts. *Saeed bin Suroor* **97**

ENOLA (IRE) 3 b.f. Lawman (FR) 121 – Kelowna (IRE) 93 (Pivotal 124) [2017 11.6g* 11.6d^{6} 10.1g p12g p13.3s^{6} p16g^{6} Dec 20] 8,500Y: third foal: half-sister to winner up to 11f Nebulla (2-y-o 1m winner, by Iffraaj) and 7f-8.6f winner Dommersen (by Dutch Art), both useful: dam 1m winner: fair performer: won maiden at Lingfield in June: left Ed Dunlop after third start: stays 2m: acts on polytrack: tried in cheekpieces. *Amy Murphy* **67**

ENRICHING (USA) 9 ch.g. Lemon Drop Kid (USA) 131 – Popozinha (USA) (Rahy (USA) 115) [2017 74: t12.2g^{4} Oct 7] close-coupled gelding: fair handicapper: stays 1½m: acts on polytrack, tapeta, firm and good to soft going: tried in blinkers: has worn tongue tie: usually races prominently. *Robyn Brisland* **70**

ENROLMENT 2 b.f. (Feb 2) Equiano (FR) 127 – Enrol 102 (Pivotal 124) [2017 5g^{5} 5s 6d^{3} t7.1d* p7g^{4} Nov 17] first foal: dam, 6f/7f winner, closely related to useful 6f winner Enact: fair performer: won nursery at Newcastle in November: stays 7f: acts on polytrack, tapeta and good to soft going. *Richard Fahey* **75**

ENTANGLING (IRE) 3 b.g. Fastnet Rock (AUS) 127 – Question Times 97 (Shamardal (USA) 129) [2017 p8g^{6} p8g^{3} p8g 10.2v^{2} 10.1d* 10g^{2} p12d* Nov 22] €380,000Y: second foal: brother to useful winner up to 7f (2-y-o 6f winner) Diamond Fields: dam, 6f winner, half-sister to useful 5f/6f winner Udontdodou (by Fastnet Rock): useful handicapper: won at Yarmouth in August and Kempton in November: demoted after dead-heating with Villette at Leicester in between: stays 1½m: acts on polytrack and heavy going: races towards rear, usually responds generously to pressure. *Chris Wall* **99**

ENTERTAINING BEN 4 b.g. Equiano (FR) 127 – Fatal Attraction 65 (Oasis Dream 129) [2017 80: t5g t5.1g t5g^{3} t5g^{5} 5g^{2} t5.1g^{2} 5m^{2} 5.3g^{5} 5m^{4} 5d^{4} p6g^{4} t6.1g^{5} 5.7m^{5} p5g p5g* p5s* p5g^{4} p5g^{6} Dec 23] fair handicapper: won at Lingfield in October and Chelmsford in November: left Iain Jardine after sixth start: best form at 5f: acts on polytrack, tapeta and good to firm going: often wears headgear: tried in tongue tie: usually races close up. *Amy Murphy* **77**

ENTIHAA 9 b.g. Tiger Hill (IRE) 127 – Magic Tree (UAE) 52 (Timber Country (USA) 124) [2017 f12g^{4} p12g^{6} t16.5g^{6} t13.9g t16.5g^{3} p16g 14v^{5} t12.2g^{3} 16d^{5} 12d Aug 24] sturdy gelding: fair handicapper on turf, fairly useful on all-weather: third at Wolverhampton in March: stays 16.5f: acts on fibresand, tapeta, good to firm and heavy going: sometimes in headgear in 2017: usually races close up. *Dai Burchell* **63** **a84**

ENTSAR (IRE) 4 b.f. Fastnet Rock (AUS) 127 – Starfish (IRE) (Galileo (IRE) 134) [2017 109: 10.2g^{3} t10.2g^{4} 10.3d* Jul 28] well-made filly: useful performer: won listed race at York (in cheekpieces, by 1¼ lengths from Ajman Princess) in July: stays 10.5f: acts on polytrack and good to soft going: often races prominently/travels strongly: sent to Australia. *William Haggas* **108**

ENVISAGING (IRE) 3 b.g. Zoffany (IRE) 121 – Star of Stars (IRE) (Soviet Star (USA) 128) [2017 76p: p8g^{2} p8g^{4} 8m^{2} 8d^{4} p7d^{3} t7.2g^{4} p7d t6d* p6g^{2} Dec 21] fairly useful performer: won maiden at Newcastle in November: second in handicap at Chelmsford in December: stays 1m: acts on polytrack, tapeta and good to firm going: in tongue tie last 5 starts. *James Fanshawe* **90**

ENVOY 3 gr.g. Delegator 125 – La Gessa 69 (Largesse 112) [2017 68: 8.3d* 8g Jun 8] big, strong gelding: fairly useful form: won maiden at Nottingham (by 2¾ lengths from Maratha) in May: badly hampered next time: stays 8.5f: remains open to improvement. *James Eustace* **87 p**

ENZEMBLE (IRE) 2 b.c. (Mar 17) Zoffany (IRE) 121 – Fifer (IRE) (Soviet Star (USA) 128) [2017 7d 7g^{2} Sep 1] 110,000Y: useful-looking colt: third foal: half-brother to smart 7f/1m winner Udododontu (by Lope de Vega): dam of little account: fairly useful form: better effort when second in maiden at Sandown (1¼ lengths behind Rum Runner) in September. *David Elsworth* **81**

ENZO (IRE) 2 b.g. (Apr 11) Exceed And Excel (AUS) 126 – Zamhrear 73 (Singspiel (IRE) 133) [2017 6g 8d* 8d⁶ 8s* 9d⁶ Nov 4] fair performer: won minor events at Brighton in August and October: stays 1m: acts on soft going: in tongue tie last 4 starts: usually races towards rear. *Ed Walker* **77**

ENZO'S LAD (IRE) 2 b.g. (May 10) Society Rock (IRE) 126 – Geht Fasteur (IRE) (Chineur (FR) 123) [2017 p6g⁶ t6g³ t6d⁴ Nov 4] fair form: best effort when third in minor event at Newcastle (1½ lengths behind Mountain Breath) in October. *K. R. Burke* **75**

EOLIAN 3 b.g. Poet's Voice 126 – Charlecote (IRE) (Caerleon (USA) 132) [2017 64§: 12d³ 11.8s⁵ 12f⁶ 10v* 9.9g 12v³ Sep 17] rather leggy gelding: fair handicapper: won at Ffos Las in August: stays 1½m: acts on any turf going: has worn headgear, including last 4 starts: one to treat with caution. *Andrew Balding* **79 §**

EPAULEMENT (IRE) 2 b.g. (Mar 10) Epaulette (AUS) 126 – Little Whisper (IRE) 95 (Be My Guest (USA) 126) [2017 7m⁵ Sep 23] 13,000F, 12,000Y: sixth foal: half-brother to several winners, including useful 1¼m-1½m winner Ex Oriente and 2-y-o 7f winner (stayed 1½m) If You Whisper (by Iffraaj): dam, 2-y-o 6f/7f winner, half-sister to smart 6f/7f winner Confuchias: 40/1, fifth in minor event at Newbury (4¾ lengths behind Fennaan) in September: sure to progress. *Tom Dascombe* **73 p**

EPEIUS (IRE) 4 b.g. Arakan (USA) 123 – Gilda Lilly (USA) 80 (War Chant (USA) 126) [2017 71: t6g* 6g⁵ t6s t6g³ t6d³ 5.9s t7.1d⁶ Nov 10] fair handicapper: won at Newcastle in March: stays 7.5f: acts on tapeta and good to soft going: tried in cheekpieces/tongue tie: sometimes slowly away. *Ben Haslam* **71**

EPIC FANTASY 2 b.c. (Apr 24) Invincible Spirit (IRE) 121 – Impressionism (IRE) (Elusive Quality (USA)) [2017 7m³ 7d² t7.2g² t6.1g² Dec 22] fourth foal: half-brother to 7f/9f winner Pointillism (by Manduro) and a winner in Greece by Exceed And Excel: dam French 6f/7f winner: fairly useful form: second in minor event at Wolverhampton in December: stays 7f. *Charles Hills* **80**

EPICURIOUS (IRE) 3 ch.g. Makfi 130 – Indolente (IRE) (Diesis 133) [2017 –: 10m 11.6d May 12] angular gelding: modest form in maidens: should do better. *Brian Meehan* **59 p**

EPISCIA (IRE) 2 b.f. (Apr 1) Arcano (IRE) 122 – Violet Flame (IRE) 60 (Kalanisi (IRE) 132) [2017 6.1g⁴ 5.3g² p6g* 7m Oct 25] 14,000 2-y-o: good-topped filly: fourth foal: closely related to 1m winner Kubali (by Approve) and half-sister to a winner in Italy by Intense Focus: dam twice-raced half-sister to Breeders' Cup Juvenile winner Vale of York: fair form: won minor event at Chelmsford in September: stays 6f. *Stuart Williams* **71**

EPITAPH (IRE) 3 b.g. Henrythenavigator (USA) 131 – Chartres (IRE) 105 (Danehill (USA) 126) [2017 66: p8g⁵ 10d 11.3g² 11.3m² 12m⁵ 10g³ 10.3d³ 10.1d² 12g⁶ t12.2g 10.2d² t9.5m³ t8.6g⁶ f11.1g² f12.1g² f12.1g³ Dec 21] fair maiden: left Joseph Patrick O'Brien after fifth start: stays 1½m: acts on all-weather, good to firm and good to soft going: wears headgear: usually races prominently. *Michael Appleby* **79**

EPONINA (IRE) 3 b.f. Zoffany (IRE) 121 – Dame Rochelle (IRE) 49 (Danehill Dancer (IRE) 117) [2017 61: t7.1g⁵ f7.1g² 7d⁴ 6d⁶ 7g³ f7.1g³ Oct 22] fair maiden: stays 7f: acts on fibresand and tapeta. *Ben Haslam* **67**

EPSOM BOUNTY 2 ch.g. (Apr 8) Bahamian Bounty 116 – My Amalie (IRE) 92 (Galileo (IRE) 134) [2017 6g p8g Nov 1] well held in minor events: in tongue tie second start. *Pat Phelan* **–**

EPSOM DAY (IRE) 4 b.g. Teofilo (IRE) 126 – Dubai Flower (Manduro (GER) 135) [2017 80: p13g⁶ p13g Feb 3] good-topped gelding: fairly useful at best, little impact in handicaps in 2017: stays 1½m: acts on polytrack and tapeta: has worn headgear: sometimes starts slowly. *Laura Mongan* **–**

EPSOM ICON 4 b.f. Sixties Icon 125 – Hairspray 92 (Bahamian Bounty 116) [2017 105: 9.9g 8g 8.9g 8f⁵ 8m⁴ 8.5m 7.9m t10.2g Jun 30] compact filly: useful performer: fourth in handicap at Ascot (4¾ lengths behind Tisbutadream) in May: stays 1¼m: acts on soft and good to firm going: often races towards rear: sold 130,000 gns in December. *Mick Channon* **101**

EPSOM SECRET 3 ch.f. Sakhee's Secret 128 – My Amalie (IRE) 92 (Galileo (IRE) 134) [2017 46: p8g³ p8g² 9g⁶ p8g² 10m* p12g 10.1m p12g⁴ p12g² Nov 1] sturdy filly: fair handicapper: won at Windsor (apprentice) in July: stays 1½m: acts on polytrack and good to firm going: has worn hood. *Pat Phelan* **65**

EQLEEM 4 b.g. Acclamation 118 – Blessing (Dubai Millennium 140) [2017 90: 7g 7m t7.2g² 7d⁴ Jun 30] good-topped gelding: fairly useful handicapper: second at Wolverhampton in June: stays 7f: acts on tapeta and good to soft going: sold 3,000 gns in November, sent to UAE. *David Evans* **87**

EQTIDAAR (IRE) 2 b.c. (May 4) Invincible Spirit (IRE) 121 – Madany (IRE) 94 (Acclamation 118) [2017 6.1g* p6g^4 Sep 9] well-made, attractive colt: third foal: half-brother to very smart 7f winner (including at 2 yrs) Massaat (by Teofilo), runner-up in 2000 Guineas, and 2-y-o 6f winner Hathiq (by Exceed And Excel): dam 2-y-o 6f winner: fairly useful form: won maiden at Nottingham (by 2½ lengths from Mountain Guard) in August: will stay 7f: remains with potential. *Sir Michael Stoute* **91 p**

EQTIRAAN (IRE) 3 b.g. Helmet (AUS) 127 – Miranda Frost (IRE) (Cape Cross (IRE) 129) [2017 99p: p8g^3 6m^2 6d 6f* 6d^5 6d 6g^6 Oct 14] well-made gelding: smart performer: won listed race at Salisbury (by neck from Mythmaker) in June: sixth in handicap at York (2½ lengths behind Teruntum Star) final start: best form at 6f: acts on polytrack, firm and soft going: often races towards rear: has joined A. Al Rayhi in UAE. *Richard Hannon* **111**

EQUALLY FAST 5 b.g. Equiano (FR) 127 – Fabulously Fast (USA) 120 (Deputy Minister (CAN)) [2017 88: p6g^6 t7.1g t7.1d 6m 6.1d 6.1g Jul 8] good-quartered gelding: fairly useful handicapper at best, below that in 2017: best form at 5f: acts on polytrack, tapeta and good to firm going: usually wears headgear: front runner/races prominently. *Peter Hiatt* **72**

EQUAL RIGHTS 3 b.g. Equiano (FR) 127 – Australia Fair (Pivotal 124) [2017 53: 8g^4 p8g^4 7g 9g^3 7.6s t9.5g^4 Oct 7] modest maiden: stays 9.5f: acts on polytrack, tapeta, best turf form on good going: in cheekpieces last 4 starts: often races prominently. *Eve Johnson Houghton* **60**

EQUIANO SPRINGS 3 b.g. Equiano (FR) 127 – Spring Clean (FR) 89 (Danehill (USA) 126) [2017 –: 6g^4 6m^2 5m^4 6s^4 6g^3 7.4g* 7.4v t7.1g* t7.1g* Dec 6] useful performer: won maiden at Beverley in September, and handicaps at Newcastle in November and December (by ½ length from Deansgate): stays 7.5f: acts on tapeta and good to firm going: usually leads. *Tom Tate* **93**

EQUIDAE 2 ch.c. (Feb 7) Equiano (FR) 127 – Dularame (IRE) (Pivotal 124) [2017 7.4m^2 p10g Nov 29] fair form: better effort when second in minor event at Beverley (4½ lengths behind Ventura Knight) in June. *James Tate* **68**

EQUIJADE 4 b.f. Equiano (FR) 127 – Royal Jade 82 (Last Tycoon 131) [2017 74: p5m Mar 29] fair form, well held only start in 2017: raced only at 5f: acts on polytrack. *Robert Stephens* **–**

EQUILATERAL 2 b.c. (May 2) Equiano (FR) 127 – Tarentaise (Oasis Dream 129) [2017 5d* 5.4d^6 Sep 10] first foal: dam unraced half-sister to winner up to 9f Cityscape and 5f/6f winner Bated Breath (both high-class) out of smart 7f winner Tantina: useful form: won maiden at Bath (by 3½ lengths from Swing Out Sister) in August. *Charles Hills* **95**

EQUILIBRIUM 2 b.f. (Mar 27) Equiano (FR) 127 – Piste 74 (Falbrav (IRE) 133) [2017 p6g 5.3g 6d^3 t7.2g Dec 22] 1,500F, £7,000Y: first foal: dam, 5f winner, half-sister to useful performers up to 1¼m Black Cherry and Alfathaa: fair form: left Robert Eddery after third start: best effort at 6f: tried in blinkers. *Ivan Furtado* **65**

EQUIMOU 3 ch.f. Equiano (FR) 127 – Culture Queen 91 (King's Best (USA) 132) [2017 101: 5.7m^4 5m* 5m 5m^5 6g p5g 5m 5.2d* 5s^4 5v^4 t5g Nov 23] sparely-made filly: useful performer: won minor event at Hamilton in May and handicap at Yarmouth (by ½ length from Jumira Bridge) in September: best form at 5f: acts on polytrack, good to firm and heavy going: tried in cheekpieces. *Robert Eddery* **103**

EQUINETTE (IRE) 4 b.f. Equiano (FR) 127 – Rougette 86 (Red Ransom (USA)) [2017 58: p5m Jan 20] rather leggy filly: maiden, last in handicap only start in 2017: best effort at 5f: acts on polytrack: in headgear last 3 starts. *Amanda Perrett* **–**

EQUIPE 3 b.f. Equiano (FR) 127 – Charlevoix (IRE) 78 (King Charlemagne (USA) 120) [2017 –: 6m 5m t5g Sep 12] no form: tried in hood. *Richard Whitaker* **–**

EQUITANT 2 ch.c. (Mar 8) Equiano (FR) 127 – Intrusion 74 (Indesatchel (IRE) 120) [2017 5g* 6d^3 p6g^3 5.4g^6 Oct 13] strong colt: fourth foal: half-brother to 5f winner Kings Academy (by Mayson) and a winner abroad by Major Cadeaux: dam, 2-y-o 6f winner, half-sister to useful 1¼m winner Maid of Camelot: fairly useful form: won minor event at Beverley (by 2¾ lengths from Kyllachy Dragon) in August: should stay 6f. *Richard Fahey* **80**

EQUITATION 3 b.g. Equiano (FR) 127 – Sakhee's Song (IRE) 102 (Sakhee (USA) 136) [2017 6s^3 6g* 6d* Sep 20] 47,000Y: fourth foal: half-brother to 3 winners, including useful 6f (including at 2 yrs) winner Taayel (by Tamayuz) and useful 2-y-o 7f winner Alfajer (by Mount Nelson): dam Italian 5f/6f winner: fairly useful form: won maiden at Doncaster (by length from Mohsen) in August and handicap at Yarmouth (by ¾ length from Stanhope) in September: raced only at 6f: likely to progress further. *Roger Varian* **91 p**

EQUITY 3 ch.g. Equiano (FR) 127 – Trinny (Rainbow Quest (USA) 134) [2017 63: 6g 5m 7.2m t6.1g^{3} t5.1g^{4} Jul 3] modest maiden: stays 7f: acts on good to firm going: in headgear last 4 starts: usually leads. *David Brown* **52**

EQUO 2 b.g. (Apr 7) Equiano (FR) 127 – Catfish (IRE) 96 (One Cool Cat (USA) 123) [2017 7s 6g^{5} Oct 16] well held in maiden/minor event. *Chris Wall* **–**

ERAAD (IRE) 2 b.c. (Feb 3) Dark Angel (IRE) 113 – Tickled Pink (IRE) 117 (Invincible Spirit (IRE) 121) [2017 p6g^{5} Oct 24] 500,000Y: first foal: dam, 5f/6f winner, half-sister to Irish 1000 Guineas/Nassau Stakes winner Halfway To Heaven, herself dam of 1000 Guineas/Oaks runner-up Rhododendron: 8/1, fifth in minor event at Kempton (8¾ lengths behind Perfect Hustler) in October: will improve. *Charles Hills* **52 p**

ERASMUS (GER) 2 b.c. (Apr 24) Reliable Man 128 – Enora (GER) 111 (Noverre (USA) 125) [2017 8s^{3} 8s* 8s* Oct 15] fourth foal: half-brother to German 9f winner Kizingo (by Oasis Dream) and French 11f winner Eskandar (by Teofilo): dam, German 11f winner (including Preis der Diana), half-sister to very smart German winner up to 1½m Egerton: smart form: successful at Cologne in maiden in September and Preis der Winterfavoriten (beat Salve del Rio by 8 lengths) in October: will stay 1¼m+: likely to go on to better things. *Markus Klug, Germany* **112 p**

ERASTUS 2 b.g. (Apr 29) Swiss Spirit 117 – Blakeshall Rose 38 (Tobougg (IRE) 125) [2017 5d^{6} 5.7f^{6} 7d 5.3m^{4} 6d t5.1g 7g Aug 30] modest maiden: best effort at 5.5f: acts on good to firm going: often starts slowly/races towards rear. *Mick Channon* **54**

ERDOGAN 3 b.c. Frankel 147 – Dar Re Mi 124 (Singspiel (IRE) 133) [2017 12d^{3} Aug 19] 750,000Y: third foal: half-brother to smart French winner up to 1¼m De Treville (2-y-o 7f winner, by Oasis Dream) and very smart winner up to 10.4f So Mi Dar (2-y-o 1m winner, by Dubawi): dam, 1¼m-12.5f winner (including Yorkshire Oaks), half-sister to top-class winner up to 1½m Rewilding: 7/2, third in maiden at Newbury (4¼ lengths behind Gold Star) on debut: should do better. *John Gosden* **87 p**

ERHAAF (USA) 5 b.g. Street Sense (USA) 128 – Saraama (USA) (Bahri (USA) 125) [2017 95: p12m Jan 21] useful performer, well held in handicap only start in 2017: stays 1¼m: acts on polytrack. *Charlie Fellowes* **–**

ERICA BING 3 b.f. Captain Gerrard (IRE) 113 – Monica Geller 86 (Komaite (USA)) [2017 90: 11.3m 8g 7d^{5} Jul 1] short-coupled filly: fairly useful performer: fifth in handicap at Chester in July: stays 7f: acts on soft going: usually leads. *Jo Hughes* **82**

ERIK THE RED (FR) 5 b.g. Kendargent (FR) 112 – Norwegian Princess (IRE) (Fairy King (USA)) [2017 106: t12.4s^{6} 10.3d 10.3m 10.2d* 11.9g^{3} 10m Sep 23] good-topped gelding: smart handicapper: won at Doncaster (by 1½ lengths from Another Eclipse) in August: third at York (3¼ lengths behind Fidaawy) later in month: stays 1½m: acts on soft and good to firm going: has worn headgear, including last 4 starts. *Kevin Ryan* **110**

ERINYES (IRE) 3 gr.f. Dalakhani (IRE) 133 – Endearing 78 (Selkirk (USA) 129) [2017 62p: p12g* 12d 12.5m^{4} p12g^{6} Dec 13] rather leggy filly: fairly useful performer: won maiden at Kempton in July: sixth in handicap at Lingfield in December: stays 1½m: acts on polytrack: in cheekpieces last 2 starts. *Archie Watson* **84**

ERISSIMUS MAXIMUS (FR) 3 b.c. Holy Roman Emperor (IRE) 125 – Tegan (IRE) 77 (Cape Cross (IRE) 129) [2017 77: t5g* t5g^{2} t6g f5d* 5.1g^{3} 5g^{4} 6d 5g^{2} 5.2g* 5.2s^{2} 5v* 5s* 5d Oct 28] lengthy colt: useful/progressive handicapper: won at Newcastle in January, Southwell in March, Yarmouth in July, Thirsk (dead-heated) in September and Ascot (by ½ length from Evergate) in October: stays 6f: acts on all-weather, good to firm and heavy going: wears headgear: front runner/races prominently. *Chris Dwyer* **99**

ERNSTSTAVROBLOFELD (USA) 3 ch.c. Elusive Quality (USA) – Minute Limit (IRE) 78 (Pivotal 124) [2017 88p: 8m^{5} 8m^{2} 8m p7g^{5} p8s^{5} Sep 8] sturdy colt: fairly useful handicapper: second at Yarmouth in May: stays 1m: acts on polytrack and good to firm going: sold 32,000 gns in November, sent to Saudi Arabia. *Martyn Meade* **92**

ERSHAAD (IRE) 5 b.g. Acclamation 118 – Emerald Peace (IRE) 103 (Green Desert (USA) 127) [2017 52, a59: f7g t7.1m^{5} p7g t8.6g 8m^{6} 6s 7m^{4} Aug 1] lengthy gelding: modest handicapper: stays 7f: acts on polytrack, tapeta and good to firm going: usually wears headgear: tried in tongue tie. *Shaun Harris* **50**

ERTIDAAD (IRE) 5 b.g. Kodiac 112 – Little Scotland 92 (Acclamation 118) [2017 60: p8d p7d p8d p10d^{2} p10g^{6} p10g f8d^{3} f8g p8s* p10s^{5} Dec 15] close-coupled gelding: modest handicapper: won at Chelmsford in December: left Emma Owen after eighth start: stays 1¼m: acts on polytrack and fibresand: wears headgear: has worn tongue tie. *Suzi Best* **56**

ERTIJAAL (IRE) 6 b.g. Oasis Dream 129 – Shabiba (USA) 103 (Seeking The Gold (USA)) [2017 124: 5g* 5g* 6d^3 Mar 25] strong, attractive gelding: high-class performer: successful at Meydan in handicap (by 1¾ lengths from The Happy Prince) in January and Meydan Sprint (by 2¾ lengths from Jungle Cat) in February: 1¼ lengths third to The Right Man in Al Quoz Sprint on same course in March: has won at 6f/7f, best at 5f: acts on polytrack and soft going: has worn headgear: front runner/races prominently, strong traveller. *A. Al Rayhi, UAE* **129**

ERTIYAD 2 b.f. (Mar 8) Dark Angel (IRE) 113 – Lily Again 95 (American Post 121) [2017 5m^2 6s* 6m 7g^4 7g^6 Aug 26] £90,000Y: useful-looking filly: second foal: dam 2-y-o 6f/7f winner: fairly useful performer: won maiden at Haydock in June: fourth in Sweet Solera Stakes at Newmarket (2 lengths behind Tajaanus) in August: stays 7f: acts on soft and good to firm going. *William Haggas* **94**

ERUPT (IRE) 5 b.h. Dubawi (IRE) 129 – Mare Nostrum 117 (Caerleon (USA) 132) [2017 124: 10.4g^4 11.9g 12f^5 12s^5 Oct 15] sturdy horse: very smart performer: best effort in 2017 when length fourth to Cloth of Stars in Prix Ganay at Saint-Cloud: left Francis-Henri Graffard before final outing: stays 1½m: acts on firm and good to soft going: tried in cheekpieces. *H. Graham Motion, USA* **121**

ESCALATING 5 ch.g. Three Valleys (USA) 119 – Pure Joy (Zamindar (USA) 116) [2017 88: f5m* f6g^2 p6g^3 5g^3 5d* t5g 5s 5g 5v Oct 23] strong, attractive gelding: useful handicapper: won at Southwell in February and Nottingham (by neck from Stake Acclaim) in June: stays 6f: acts on polytrack, fibresand and soft going: has worn headgear, including sometimes in 2017: wears tongue tie: often races towards rear: sold 10,000 gns in October. *Michael Appleby* **95**

ESCALATOR 2 b.c. (Apr 5) Cape Cross (IRE) 129 – Sayyedati Symphony (USA) 90 (Gone West (USA)) [2017 8.2g^5 t8.6m^2 Oct 31] fifth foal: half-brother to UAE 6f winner Daar Rashid (by Exceed And Excel): dam, maiden (stayed 1¼m), out of 1000 Guineas winner Sayyedati: fair form: better effort when second in minor event at Wolverhampton (2¼ lengths behind Laieth) in October: remains with potential. *Charlie Fellowes* **74 p**

ESCAPE CLAUSE (IRE) 3 b.g. Lawman (FR) 121 – Discophilia (Teofilo (IRE) 126) [2017 79: 8m^6 8s^2 10g 8s^6 8.1v t8d f7.1g^5 Dec 1] fairly useful handicapper: standout effort when second at Naas in May: left Mrs J. Harrington after fifth start: stays 1m: best form on soft/heavy going: often races in rear: temperament under suspicion. *Grant Tuer* **94**

ESCAPE THE CITY 2 b.f. (Apr 5) Cityscape 127 – Jasmeno 78 (Catcher In The Rye (IRE) 115) [2017 6g^4 6.1g^4 7g^2 7m* 6g^4 7s t7.2g^3 p8s^4 Dec 15] 9,000Y: neat filly: third foal: half-sister to 11f/1½m winner (stays 2m) Pastoral Music (by Pastoral Pursuits): dam, 1½m-1¾m winner, half-sister to smart performer up to 1½m Sagramor: fairly useful performer: won minor event at Redcar in August: third in nursery at Wolverhampton (neck behind Our Man In Havana) in November: stays 7f: acts on tapeta, soft and good to firm going. *Hughie Morrison* **82**

ESCOBAR (IRE) 3 b.g. Famous Name 124 – Saying Grace (IRE) 108 (Brief Truce (USA) 126) [2017 106: 8m^2 7m 8s^5 7g 8d p8g Oct 14] useful-looking gelding: useful performer: second in listed race at Sandown (neck behind Khafoo Shememi) in May: stays 1m: acts on good to firm going: in headgear last 4 starts: in tongue tie last 2: often races in rear/freely: sold 100,000 gns in October to join David O'Meara: temperament under suspicion. *Hugo Palmer* **106**

ESKENDASH (USA) 4 ch.g. Eskendereya (USA) 126 – Daffaash (USA) (Mr Greeley (USA) 122) [2017 p11g* 10m^2 10s^6 10s^3 p11g^5 p11g^6 Oct 11] $105,000Y: big gelding: fifth foal: half-brother to 3 winners, including useful 7f (including at 2 yrs) winner Ebn Arab (by Dixie Union): dam unraced half-sister to smart US Grade 1 11f winner Request For Parole: fairly useful performer: won maiden at Kempton in March: second in handicap at Windsor in May: stays 11f: acts on polytrack and good to firm going: often races towards rear: fairly useful hurdler. *Pam Sly* **86**

ESKIMO BAY (IRE) 3 b.g. Kodiac 112 – Magilini (IRE) 54 (Bertolini (USA) 125) [2017 68: 5.1d^5 p6g Jul 5] angular gelding: fair form: stays 6f. *Clive Cox* **66**

ESME KATE (IRE) 2 b.f. (Apr 16) Arch (USA) 127 – Francisca (USA) (Mizzen Mast (USA) 121) [2017 7m 8d Oct 24] 72,000Y: second foal: dam, US 8.5f-9.5f winner, half-sister to smart US Grade 2 9.5f winner Willcox Inn: well held in maiden/minor event. *Michael Bell* **–**

ESPADRILLE 2 b.f. (Mar 25) Dubawi (IRE) 129 – High Heeled (IRE) 122 (High Chaparral (IRE) 132) [2017 8.3d^5 p8g* Nov 8] 800,000F: fourth foal: sister to useful French 1m winner Pabouche and half-sister to useful 1¼m winner Neshmeya (by **78 p**

Lawman): dam winner up to 1½m (2-y-o 1m winner): fair form: won minor event at Kempton (by 1½ lengths from Ruffina) in November: open to further improvement. *Charlie Appleby*

ESPRESSO FREDDO (IRE) 3 b.g. Fast Company (IRE) 126 – Spring Bouquet (IRE) **86**
60 (King's Best (USA) 132) [2017 76: f6g^{3} t7.1m* t7.1d* t7.1g^{5} t7.1d^{2} 7g t8d t9.5g^{5} t9.5d p8g^{4} Dec 31] fairly useful performer: won maiden at Wolverhampton in January and handicap at Newcastle in February: fifth in handicap at former course in December: left Sir Mark Prescott Bt after third start: stays 9.5f: acts on polytrack and tapeta: usually wears headgear: tried in tongue tie: often races freely. *Robert Stephens*

ESPRESSO MARTINI 3 b.g. Royal Applause 124 – Sceilin (IRE) 69 (Lil's Boy (USA) **–**
109) [2017 8m p7g 10s May 19] lengthy gelding: well held in maidens. *Brian Meehan*

ESPRIT DE CORPS 3 b.g. Sepoy (AUS) 129 – Corps de Ballet (IRE) 92 (Fasliyev **92**
(USA) 120) [2017 72: 5.7m* 6d 6d^{4} 7g^{2} 7d^{4} p8g^{5} 7m^{2} 7d Oct 6] tall gelding: fairly useful performer: won maiden at Bath in April: stays 7f: acts on polytrack, good to firm and good to soft going: in cheekpieces last 2 starts: sometimes slowly away, often races towards rear: sold 28,000 gns in October to join David Barron. *Roger Charlton*

ESSAKA (IRE) 5 b.g. Equiano (FR) 127 – Dream Vision (USA) (Distant View (USA) **62**
126) [2017 67, a51: 6g^{4} 6g^{5} 6g t5.1g t6.1g^{6} 5.7g^{5} 5.7s^{5} 5.3g^{3} 5.7d^{5} 5.7m 5.7s^{4} p5g^{3} p5g^{5} **a55**
Oct 13] modest handicapper: stays 6f: acts on tapeta, soft and good to firm going: often races towards rear. *Tony Carroll*

ESSENAITCH (IRE) 4 b.g. Zoffany (IRE) 121 – Karlisse (IRE) 90 (Celtic Swing 138) **82**
[2017 80: f7g* f7g* f8s^{6} f7m t7.1g^{6} 8.3m 10s^{2} 10m^{2} 11.4d^{3} 11.2g^{6} 10m 8s 8.6d 10s* **a76**
11.4d^{3} 10.2d* 10g^{3} 10d^{6} Oct 23] sturdy gelding: fairly useful handicapper: won at Southwell (twice) in January, Windsor in August and Nottingham (apprentice, by ½ length from Epitaph) in October: stays 11.5f: acts on fibresand, soft and good to firm going: often races prominently. *David Evans*

ESSENDON (FR) 2 b.g. (Apr 14) Aussie Rules (USA) 123 – Inhibition 96 (Nayef (USA) **–**
129) [2017 p8g p7s t8.6d Dec 9] well beaten in minor events. *Andrew Balding*

ESSENTIAL 3 b.g. Pivotal 124 – Something Blue (Petong 126) [2017 p6d^{5} p6g^{3} 6s^{2} 7d **65**
t6.1g p8s^{6} Dec 15] fair maiden: stays 6f: acts on polytrack and tapeta: in headgear last 3 starts: often races prominently. *George Scott*

ESSPEEGEE 4 b.g. Paco Boy (IRE) 129 – Goldrenched (IRE) 78 (Montjeu (IRE) 137) **66**
[2017 56: 11.5m 14.1m^{5} 15d^{5} 16.3d^{3} 14v^{2} 15g f16.5g^{3} 11.9d* 11.9s* t12.4d* Dec 16] compact gelding: fair handicapper: won at Brighton in September and October (apprentice), and Newcastle in December: stays 16.5f: acts on fibresand, tapeta, good to firm and heavy going: wears cheekpieces: races prominently. *Alan Bailey*

ESTEAMING 7 b.g. Sir Percy 129 – Night Over Day 57 (Most Welcome 131) [2017 –: **87**
t16.5g^{5} f12g^{3} t16.3g f11g^{4} Apr 18] compact gelding: fairly useful handicapper: third at Southwell in February: stays 1¾m: acts on fibresand, good to firm and heavy going: in cheekpieces in 2017. *Keith Dalgleish*

ESTHER (IRE) 2 b.f. (May 11) Kodiac 112 – Good For Her 72 (Rock of Gibraltar (IRE) **49**
133) [2017 5m 5f May 26] £20,000 2-y-o: fourth foal: half-sister to 3 winners, including 5f (including at 2 yrs)/6f winner Sandra's Secret (by Zebedee) and 2-y-o 6f/7f winner Pranceleya (by Sir Prancealot): dam, maiden (stayed 1m), closely related to very smart performer up to 1m Zoffany: down the field in minor events: tried in hood. *Amy Murphy*

ESTIBDAAD (IRE) 7 b.g. Haatef (USA) 117 – Star of Siligo (USA) (Saratoga Six **66**
(USA)) [2017 76: p10m^{4} p11g^{3} p10g^{4} p10g^{4} p8s^{6} t12.2g^{6} p10d* p10g p10g^{5} Dec 30] lengthy gelding: fair handicapper: won at Chelmsford in September: stays 1½m: acts on polytrack and tapeta: tried in cheekpieces: wears tongue tie: front runner/races prominently. *Paddy Butler*

ESTRELLADA 3 b.f. Oasis Dream 129 – Gallic Star (IRE) 105 (Galileo (IRE) 134) [2017 **60**
9.9m 8g^{5} 10.2f^{5} 9.9m Jul 15] second foal: half-sister to 1m winner Star Blaze (by Shamardal): dam 2-y-o 6f/1m winner who stayed 1½m: modest form, standout effort on third start (possibly flattered). *Mick Channon*

ESTRELLA ERIA (FR) 4 gr.f. Mastercraftsman (IRE) 129 – Madrid Beauty (FR) **77**
(Sendawar (IRE) 129) [2017 71: p10g* 10.2f^{4} p10g^{4} 10d p10g p11g a8.9g^{6} p9.9g^{4} p9.4g Dec 26] fair handicapper: won at Chelmsford in April: left George Peckham after sixth start: stays 1¼m: acts on polytrack: used to wear hood, *M. Palussiere, France*

ETAAD (USA) 6 b.g. Intidab (USA) 115 – Red's Lucky Lady (USA) (Lucky Lionel (USA) 112) [2017 79: p8g p10m* p10m^2 10m 9.9g 10d 9.9v t10.2g t12.4g f11.1g^5 f14.1g^5 t16.3d Dec 16] fair handicapper: won at Lingfield in January: left Gary Moore after sixth start: stays 1¼m: acts on polytrack, tapeta and soft going: usually wears headgear: tried in tongue tie: often starts slowly, usually races towards rear. *Lucinda Egerton* **76**

ETEFAAQ (IRE) 2 b.c. (Mar 29) Kodiac 112 – Sheila Blige 83 (Zamindar (USA) 116) [2017 6.1m 6d* 7g 6v^4 6d 7m Oct 14] €75,000F, 110,000 2-y-o: good-quartered colt: brother to a winner in Sweden, closely related to 8.7f winner Apt (by Danetime) and half-brother to 2 winners, including useful 5f/6f winner Lady Lily (including at 2 yrs, by Desert Sun): dam 2-y-o 5f winner: fairly useful performer: won minor event at Newmarket in June: fourth in Richmond Stakes at Goodwood (5¾ lengths behind Barraquero) in August: stays 7f: acts on heavy going. *Richard Hannon* **88**

ETERNAL 5 ch.g. New Approach (IRE) 132 – Sharp Mode (USA) (Diesis 133) [2017 –: 7.1g^4 8.5f^3 8.5g* 10d^6 8m Jun 15] workmanlike gelding: fairly useful handicapper: won at Beverley (by nose from Mohab) in May: stays 1¼m: acts on firm and soft going: front runner/races prominently. *Declan Carroll* **93**

ETERNAL DREAM 3 ch.g. Dream Ahead (USA) 133 – Get Happy (IRE) (Zamindar (USA) 116) [2017 –p: 8.2d^4 10d 7g p8d p8g 6s Sep 15] smallish gelding: fair maiden: best effort at 1m: acts on good to soft going: tried in cheekpieces: front runner/races prominently, usually finds little. *William Knight* **67**

ETERNALIST 4 ch.f. Equiano (FR) 127 – Eternal Instinct 77 (Exceed And Excel (AUS) 126) [2017 63: 5g^5 5g* 5f^4 5g t5.1g^3 t5.1g^2 t5.1d^5 Dec 27] good-quartered filly: fair handicapper: won at Thirsk in June: second at Wolverhampton (½ length behind Hamish McGonagain) in November: best form at 5f: acts on tapeta: has worn hood. *Jim Goldie* **72**

ETERNALLY 4 b.f. Dutch Art 126 – Ardent 92 (Pivotal 124) [2017 112p: 7s^2 7g^2 7s^3 Oct 7] tall filly: useful performer: second in Oak Tree Stakes at Goodwood (1¼ lengths behind Al Jazi) in August and Sceptre Stakes at Doncaster (length behind Music Box) in September: stays 8.5f, usually races over shorter: acts on tapeta, firm and probably soft going: usually leads. *John Gosden* **106**

ETIENNE GERARD 5 b.g. Captain Gerrard (IRE) 113 – Alucica 64 (Celtic Swing 138) [2017 82: 6g 6v 6g 7g^6 6d 6.1m^6 6g^2 t6d^5 6g p7d Sep 28] fair handicapper: stays 6f: acts on good to firm and good to soft going: wears cheekpieces. *Nigel Tinkler* **68**

ETIKAAL 3 ch.g. Sepoy (AUS) 129 – Hezmah 106 (Oasis Dream 129) [2017 81: 6m^6 p7s* p7s p7s Sep 2] useful handicapper: won at Chelmsford in May: stays 7f: acts on polytrack and good to firm going: in cheekpieces last 3 starts: front runner/races prominently: sold £14,000 in November to join Grant Tuer. *Simon Crisford* **96**

ETISALAT 2 gr.c. (Feb 26) Lethal Force (IRE) 128 – Chalet Girl (Oasis Dream 129) [2017 p6g^3 p6g* Nov 2] 20,000F, £42,000Y, 110,000 2-y-o: second foal: dam unraced half-sister to useful performer up to 1½m Senate: fairly useful form: won minor event at Chelmsford (by length from Jack Taylor) in November: will be suited by 7f: will go on improving. *Owen Burrows* **85 p**

ETTIE HART (IRE) 4 b.f. Bushranger (IRE) 119 – Miss Megs (IRE) 81 (Croco Rouge (IRE) 126) [2017 61: 8m^2 8g^6 8g^3 t7.2g 7d^5 7g Jun 12] modest handicapper: stays 1m: acts on good to firm and good to soft going: inconsistent. *Mick Channon* **55**

ETTIHADI (IRE) 3 b.g. Rip Van Winkle (IRE) 134 – Bright And Clear 106 (Danehill (USA) 126) [2017 77p: 11.9d 14g^6 Jul 17] rather lightly-built gelding: fair maiden: stayed 1¾m: acted on good to firm going: tried in cheekpieces: dead. *Tim Vaughan* **71**

ETTU 3 b.f. Excelebration (IRE) 133 – Tragic Moment (USA) (Pivotal 124) [2017 77: p8g^6 t6d* p6.5g p7g^4 6g p8g 8d* 8d^2 7d^6 p6.5g Dec 5] fair performer: won maiden at Newcastle in January (left Jeremy Noseda after) and claimer at Compiegne in July: stays 1m: acts on polytrack, tapeta, good to firm and good to soft going: blinkered last 4 starts. *S. Wattel, France* **78**

EUCHEN GLEN 4 b.g. Authorized (IRE) 133 – Jabbara (IRE) 65 (Kingmambo (USA) 125) [2017 94: t12.4g t12.4g 10m* 10g^3 10.3m 13.1g* 11.8m 16d* 16.3d^3 18m 11.9s Nov 11] good-topped gelding: useful handicapper: won at Ayr in May and June, and Ascot (by neck from Byron Flyer) in August: stays 16.5f: acts on good to firm and good to soft going: tried in hood: often races in rear. *Jim Goldie* **101**

EUGENIC 6 br.g. Piccolo 121 – Craic Sa Ceili (IRE) 83 (Danehill Dancer (IRE) 117) [2017 61: 11.6m 10.2f^5 12v^4 10.2f^2 11.9m^3 10.2d f12.1g^2 Oct 22] modest handicapper: left Rod Millman after sixth start: stays 1½m: acts on polytrack, fibresand and any turf going: tried in visor. *Tracey Barfoot-Saunt* **61**

EUGINIO (IRE) 3 b.c. Fastnet Rock (AUS) 127 – Starstone (Diktat 126) [2017 93: 10m^2 **116** 9.9m* 10.5d^4 9.9g^5 10.2d* Sep 14] good-bodied colt: smart handicapper: won at Sandown (by head from Beardwood) in July and Doncaster (by neck from Another Eclipse) in September: stays 1¼m: acts on tapeta, good to firm and good to soft going. *Richard Hannon*

EULA VARNER 3 b.f. Showcasing 117 – Tremelo Pointe (IRE) 73 (Trempolino (USA) **72** 135) [2017 59p: 7m^3 8.3g^3 May 31] fair form: stays 8.5f. *Henry Candy*

EUQRANIAN (USA) 3 b.f. Galileo (IRE) 134 – Anne of Kiev (IRE) 110 (Oasis Dream **80** 129) [2017 8.1m^2 7g^5 8.1g^2 8g^4 p7g* Aug 30] $320,000Y: second foal: sister to French 1¼m winner Anneli: dam, 5f/6f winner, half-sister to useful/ungenuine winner up to 1¼m Big Robert: fairly useful performer: won maiden at Kempton (by 1¼ lengths from Deleyla) in August: stays 1m: acts on polytrack and good to firm going: often in hood: front runner/races prominently, often freely. *Jeremy Noseda*

EURATO (FR) 7 ch.g. Medicean 128 – Double Green (IRE) 104 (Green Tune (USA) 125) **81** [2017 74: t13.9m^2 t13.9m^2 p13.3d^2 f14m^3 f14d* f14d^3 14g Nov 1] good-topped gelding: fairly useful handicapper: won at Southwell (by neck from Brigadoon) in March: third at same course in April: stays 2m: acts on all-weather and heavy going: usually wears cheekpieces. *Steve Gollings*

EUREKA SPRINGS 4 b.f. Mullionmileanhour (IRE) 116 – Shaymee's Girl 59 (Wizard **–** King 122) [2017 6g t5s Sep 8] sixth foal: half-sister to 5f-9.5f winner Bertie Blu Boy (by Central Park): dam 5f winner: well beaten in pair of maidens. *Lisa Williamson*

EURO MAC 5 ch.m. Sir Percy 129 – Oomph 83 (Shareef Dancer (USA) 135) [2017 56: **60** 9.9f 9.9d^5 8g* 7.8d 8.5s^{pu} Sep 20] modest handicapper: won at Ripon (apprentice) in August: stays 1¼m: acts on good to firm and good to soft going: tried in hood. *Neville Bycroft*

EURO NIGHTMARE (IRE) 3 b.f. Kodiac 112 – Kilakey (IRE) (Key of Luck (USA) **103** 126) [2017 81: 9m* 14m^3 9.8m* 9.2g^3 12g^5 11.1g^4 10d* 11.9d^6 9.9g^6 10g Oct 7] close-coupled filly: useful handicapper: won at Musselburgh in May, Ripon in June and Ayr (by ½ length from Weekend Offender) in July: stays 1¾m, effective at shorter: acts on soft and good to firm going. *Keith Dalgleish*

EURYSTHEUS (IRE) 8 b.g. Acclamation 118 – Dust Flicker 63 (Suave Dancer (USA) **67** 136) [2017 87: t8g Jan 21] well-made gelding: fairly useful handicapper, below form only start in 2017: stays 10.5f: acts on polytrack, tapeta, firm and soft going: wears cheekpieces/ tongue tie: often races prominently. *Michael Appleby*

EVA DOCC (IRE) 2 ch.f. (Apr 23) Dandy Man (IRE) 123 – La Rochelle (IRE) 80 (Salse **62** (USA) 128) [2017 5g^2 6s 5v^3 6d f6.1g^6 Nov 16] €6,500Y: half-sister to several winners, including 2-y-o 6f winner Doctor Kananga (by Dr Fong) and 2-y-o 7f winner (stayed 11f) Citelle (by City On A Hill): dam, 1m winner who stayed 1¼m, half-sister to useful 1¼m-1½m winner Rudagi: modest maiden: best effort at 5f. *Keith Dalgleish*

EVANESCENT (IRE) 8 b.g. Elusive City (USA) 117 – Itsanothergirl 77 (Reprimand **76** 122) [2017 85: t7.1m f5m p7m^2 p7g 7.1v^3 5.7s^6 t7.2g p8g Dec 30] good-topped gelding: fair handicapper: stays 7f: acts on good to firm and heavy going: front runner/races prominently: inconsistent. *Tony Carroll*

EVENING ATTIRE 6 b.g. Pastoral Pursuits 127 – Markova's Dance 64 (Mark of Esteem **91** (IRE) 137) [2017 80, a90: p7g^4 p7d^5 7g^2 7d May 13] good-topped gelding: fairly useful handicapper: second at Leicester (short head behind Gallipoli) in April: stays 7f: acts on polytrack, tapeta, best turf form on good going: usually leads. *William Stone*

EVENING HILL 3 b.c. Harbour Watch (IRE) 121 – Al Hawa (USA) (Gulch (USA)) **88** [2017 69p: 8.1d* 10d 8m^6 10g^2 10g^4 10d p8g* p8g* Oct 5] close-coupled colt: fairly useful performer: won maiden at Chepstow in May, and handicaps at Kempton in September and Lingfield (by ¾ length from Sandy Shores) in October: stays 1¼m: acts on polytrack and good to soft going: in cheekpieces last 3 starts: usually races prominently: sold 62,000 gns, sent to Saudi Arabia. *Richard Hughes*

EVENING STARLIGHT 4 gr.f. Kyllachy 129 – Night Haven 99 (Night Shift (USA)) **67** [2017 75: t6m 5.1m^4 5.7f^5 6g 5.7s 5d^4 5.7s* p5g^3 Sep 26] fair handicapper: won at Bath in September: third at Lingfield (head behind Prominna) final start: stays 6f: acts on polytrack and soft going: front runner/races prominently. *Ron Hodges*

EVERDINA 3 b.f. Pour Moi (IRE) 125 – Silent Music (IRE) (Peintre Celebre (USA) 137) **53** [2017 –: p8g p8g^5 t12.2g 8v^5 p8g Oct 18] modest maiden: best effort at 1m: acts on polytrack: sold 800 gns, sent to Spain. *Ed Walker*

EVERGATE 3 b.g. Exceed And Excel (AUS) 126 – Lion Forest (USA) (Forestry (USA) 121) [2017 89: t5.1g^2 5.7f^2 5.1d^2 5.1d* 6m^5 5m^3 5.6g 5s^2 Oct 7] rangy gelding: useful handicapper: won at Windsor in May: second at Ascot (½ length behind Erissimus Maximus) final start: stays 6f: acts on polytrack, tapeta, firm and soft going. *Robert Cowell* **104**

EVERKYLLACHY (IRE) 3 br.f. Kyllachy 129 – Superfonic (FR) (Zafonic (USA) 130) [2017 59: t7.1m^6 6.1m^3 6m* 6g^6 6d^5 7.1g 6.1m 5.1s* 5.3g^3 5.3d^3 5s* 5.3s 5g p6g^6 t5.1d^3 Dec 27] angular filly: fair handicapper: won at Yarmouth in May, Chepstow in August and Bath in October: stays 7f: acts on tapeta, soft and good to firm going: wears headgear: usually races nearer last than first: temperamental. *J. S. Moore* **74 §**

EVERLASTING SEA 3 b.f. Harbour Watch (IRE) 121 – Doliouchka (Saumarez 132) [2017 –: 9m^5 12m^3 12v 12g 9.9d p15.8g^3 Oct 18] tall, unfurnished filly: fair maiden: stays 2m: acts on polytrack and good to firm going: signs of temperament. *Stuart Kittow* **65**

EVERY CHANCE (IRE) 4 b.g. Frozen Power (IRE) 108 – Runway Dancer (Dansili 127) [2017 t9.5g^5 p11g^2 p12g^3 t13.9g* t12.2g^4 t10.2d p16d t9.5g^3 f11.1g^2 p12g^4 Dec 30] useful handicapper: won at Wolverhampton (by head from Midtech Star) in April: stays 1¾m: acts on polytrack and tapeta: in tongue tie last 4 starts: sometimes slowly away. *Jamie Osborne* **98**

EVERY NICE GIRL (USA) 3 gr.f. Mizzen Mast (USA) 121 – Joop (USA) (Zilzal (USA) 137) [2017 53: 8.3m t12.2g Jun 1] rather sparely-made filly: modest maiden: best effort at 1m. *Marco Botti* **–**

EVERYTHING FOR YOU (IRE) 3 b.g. Pivotal 124 – Miss Delila (USA) (Malibu Moon (USA)) [2017 66P: t8.6g^2 8g* 10.3m 8.5m^3 8.9s^4 Sep 16] fairly useful performer: won maiden at Redcar in April: third in handicap at Beverley (2½ lengths behind Rinaria) in August: stays 8.5f: acts on tapeta and good to firm going: in cheekpieces last 2 starts. *Kevin Ryan* **86**

EVIDENT (IRE) 7 b.g. Excellent Art 125 – Vestavia (IRE) (Alhaarth (IRE) 126) [2017 59: t7.1m p7g Jan 19] strong, lengthy gelding: modest handicapper: well below form both starts in 2017: stays 7f: acts on polytrack, fibresand and good to soft going: has worn headgear. *Tony Carroll* **–**

EVIES WISH (IRE) 3 b.f. Holy Roman Emperor (IRE) 125 – Sharapova (IRE) 87 (Elusive Quality (USA)) [2017 77: 5.9g^3 5g^5 6v^6 7.8g p7g^2 t6d* p6g Dec 6] fifth foal: sister to useful 2-y-o 6f winner Rockaway Valley, and half-sister to French 1m winner Floriade and 6f winner Lottie Dod (both by Invincible Spirit): dam, 7f winner, half-sister to smart performer up to 9f Tamweel: fairly useful performer: won maiden at Newcastle (by 7 lengths from Dream Revival) in November: stays 7f: acts on polytrack, tapeta, good to firm and good to soft going: tried in cheekpieces/tongue tie. *John McConnell, Ireland* **84**

EVIL SPELL 5 b.m. Dutch Art 126 – Yajala (Fasliyev (USA) 120) [2017 5f^5 6.1g 6s 5d 5.5d Oct 2] first foal: dam, Italian 6f-7.5f winner, half-sister to useful Italian sprinter Dasami: useful performer at best: won listed race at Rome in 2016 (trained by E. Botti): not in same form in listed/pattern races in 2017: stays 6f: acts on viscoride, good to firm and good to soft going: tried in blinkers: has worn tongue tie. *Robert Cowell* **86**

EXACTING 3 b.f. Excelebration (IRE) 133 – Blue Azure (USA) 67 (American Chance (USA) 117) [2017 8.3g May 12] fifth foal: half-sister to 2-y-o 6f winner (stayed 1m) Distinctive (by Tobougg) and 5f (including at 2 yrs) winner Blue Aegean (by Invincible Spirit), both useful: dam lightly raced: 66/1, well held in maiden at Nottingham. *Daniel Kubler* **–**

EXAMINER (IRE) 6 ch.g. Excellent Art 125 – Therry Girl (IRE) (Lahib (USA) 129) [2017 102: t8.6g^4 8g 10.1m^4 8d* 8s 8.6d 8d^6 9d^6 Sep 30] sturdy gelding: useful handicapper: won at Salisbury (by 1¾ lengths from Morning Suit) in June: stays 10.5f: acts on polytrack, tapeta, soft and good to firm going: wears tongue tie: often races towards rear. *Stuart Williams* **104**

EXCEEDINGLY DIVA 2 b.f. (Feb 17) Exceed And Excel (AUS) 126 – Anqooda (USA) 56 (Oasis Dream 129) [2017 6.1m^2 6m* Aug 16] €46,000Y: good-topped filly: second foal: dam twice-raced half-sister to smart winner up to 1m Algaith out of half-sister to 1000 Guineas winner Ghanaati: fairly useful form: won minor event at Salisbury (by length from Kick On Kick On) in August: likely to progress further. *Marcus Tregoning* **86 p**

EXCEEDING POWER 6 b.g. Exceed And Excel (AUS) 126 – Extreme Beauty (USA) 89 (Rahy (USA) 115) [2017 82: p10g^3 p10g^4 p10g* 8g^4 8m* 8m 8d^4 8g^2 p10g^2 Sep 25] sturdy gelding: fairly useful handicapper: won at Lingfield in February and Salisbury in **88**

July: second at Sandown (¾ length behind Al Nafoorah) in September: stays 1¼m: acts on polytrack, fibresand, good to firm and heavy going: tried in cheekpieces/tongue tie. *Martin Bosley*

EXCEED THE LIMIT 4 b.g. Exceed And Excel (AUS) 126 – Clinet (IRE) 110 **83**
(Docksider (USA) 124) [2017 96: p5g^{2} 6s 5m p5s 5d 5.2s^{4} p6g* Sep 5] strong gelding: **a98**
useful handicapper: won at Kempton (by neck from Secondo) in September: second at Chelmsford (head behind Zac Brown) in May: stays 6f: acts on polytrack, soft and good to firm going: has worn headgear, including last 3 starts: often races prominently: sold 23,000 gns in October. *Robert Cowell*

EXCEL AGAIN 3 b.c. Exceed And Excel (AUS) 126 – Adonesque (IRE) 106 (Sadler's **91**
Wells (USA) 132) [2017 p8g^{3} t8g* 8f^{3} 8g^{4} t8g* t8.6g^{5} t8d^{3} Sep 29] 110,000Y: half-brother to several winners, including smart/unreliable UAE 7f-1¼m winner Busker (by Street Cry) and useful 2-y-o 6f winner Alderney (by Elusive Quality): dam 9f/1¼m winner: fairly useful performer: won maiden at Newcastle in February and handicap at same course (by ½ length from Amood) in June: stays 8.5f: acts on tapeta and firm going: sold 28,000 gns in October. *James Tate*

EXCELLENT ADDITION (IRE) 7 ch.g. Excellent Art 125 – Race The Wild Wind **–**
(USA) 121 (Sunny's Halo (CAN)) [2017 –: 8g 5d Sep 12] fair maiden handicapper at best: lightly raced and no form since 2013: stays 1m: acts on polytrack and good to soft going: tried in visor: in tongue tie last 3 starts. *Lee James*

EXCELLENT AIM 10 b.g. Exceed And Excel (AUS) 126 – Snugfit Annie 49 (Midyan **63**
(USA) 124) [2017 69: p5g p5g t6g^{4} p5d^{2} f6m^{6} f5g^{5} f5g Dec 4] tall, lengthy gelding: modest handicapper: effective 5f/6f: acts on all-weather and good to firm going: has worn tongue tie. *George Margarson*

EXCELLENT GEORGE 5 b.g. Exceed And Excel (AUS) 126 – Princess Georgina 78 **73**
(Royal Applause 124) [2017 89: p6d^{6} t5.1g^{2} 5m p5g^{2} p5s^{4} 5d^{5} 5m p6s* Dec 17] good- **a89**
quartered gelding: fairly useful handicapper: won at Chelmsford (by 1¼ lengths from Bahamian Heights) in December: stays 6f: acts on polytrack, tapeta and good to firm going: wears tongue tie. *Stuart Williams*

EXCELLENTLY POISED 2 b.g. (Jan 28) Sepoy (AUS) 129 – Excelette (IRE) 111 **81**
(Exceed And Excel (AUS) 126) [2017 5g* 5d^{6} 5f 5g^{4} Jul 14] rather unfurnished gelding: first foal: dam, 5f winner (including at 2 yrs), half-sister to smart 6f winner Blessington: fairly useful form: won minor event at Musselburgh (by ¾ length from Requinto Dawn) in April: raced only at 5f: tried in cheekpieces. *Bryan Smart*

EXCELLENT PUCK (IRE) 7 b.g. Excellent Art 125 – Puck's Castle 92 (Shirley **79**
Heights 130) [2017 83: p16g^{6} t16.5g^{6} 14.1g^{5} 12s^{5} 13m^{3} 14.1d^{2} t12.2d^{4} t12.2d^{3} Dec 26] sturdy gelding: fair handicapper: stays 2m: acts on all-weather, soft and good to firm going: tried in blinkers: usually races prominently: has hung left under pressure. *Shaun Lycett*

EXCELLENT RESULT (IRE) 7 b.g. Shamardal (USA) 129 – Line Ahead (IRE) **94**
(Sadler's Wells (USA) 132) [2017 –: t16.3g^{4} 21.6m Jun 24] lengthy gelding: fairly useful performer: fourth in handicap at Newcastle in May: stays 16.5f: acts on tapeta, firm and good to soft going: often in headgear: fairly useful hurdler. *Richard Spencer*

EXCELLENT SOUNDS 4 b.f. Exceed And Excel (AUS) 126 – Siren Sound 80 **92**
(Singspiel (IRE) 133) [2017 88: 7.2m 7f* 7.2m* 7d^{6} 6g^{6} Aug 20] fairly useful handicapper: won at Salisbury in June and Haydock (by neck from Aljuljalah) in July: stays 7f: acts on polytrack and firm going. *Hughie Morrison*

EXCELLENT STORY 3 b.g. Excelebration (IRE) 133 – Storyland (USA) 103 (Menifee **64**
(USA) 124) [2017 7.8g^{4} 8s 8d^{6} t7.1s Sep 8] modest form: best effort at 1m. *John Davies*

EXCELLENT SUNSET (IRE) 3 b.f. Exceed And Excel (AUS) 126 – Sunset Avenue **75**
(USA) 82 (Street Cry (IRE) 130) [2017 –p: t7.1g^{2} 6g^{2} 6m^{2} 6m^{6} Jun 29] sturdy filly: fair maiden: stays 7f: acts on tapeta and good to firm going. *David Lanigan*

EXCELLENT TIMES 2 b.f. (Mar 9) Excelebration (IRE) 133 – Al Janadeirya 79 (Oasis **87**
Dream 129) [2017 6s 6g 5d^{4} 6g^{2} 5.9v^{4} 6g^{2} 6.1d^{3} 6d* 6d^{2} Nov 11] second foal: half-sister to Spanish 5.5f (including at 2 yrs)/6f winner Antonella (by Dream Ahead): dam, 5.5f winner, half-sister to useful 6f winner Direct Times: fairly useful performer: won nursery at Redcar (by 2¾ lengths from Istanbul Pasha) in October: second in nursery at Doncaster (½ length behind Captain Jameson) final start: stays 6f: acts on good to soft going. *Tim Easterby*

EXCELLENT WORLD (IRE) 4 b.f. Excellent Art 125 – Granny Kelly (USA) 60 (Irish River (FR) 131) [2017 63: 7g⁶ f5g⁴ 6g⁶ 6v⁴ 5d f6.1g⁴ t5.1m⁴ 6s f5g² t5g⁵ f5g⁴ f5g⁴ Dec 21] modest maiden: stays 7f, usually races over shorter: acts on fibresand, good to firm and heavy going: has worn cheekpieces: often in tongue tie: usually races prominently. *Tony Coyle* **55**

EXCESSABLE 4 ch.g. Sakhee's Secret 128 – Kummel Excess (IRE) 81 (Exceed And Excel (AUS) 126) [2017 89: t5s³ 5m* 5m* 5m 5m 5m 5g* 5m⁶ Sep 4] workmanlike gelding: useful handicapper: won at Thirsk and Redcar in May, and York (by ½ length from Coolfitch) in July: best form at 5f: acts on firm going: tried in eyeshields: has worn tongue tie, including usually in 2017. *Tim Easterby* **99**

EXCHEQUER (IRE) 6 ch.g. Exceed And Excel (AUS) 126 – Tara's Force (IRE) 56 (Acclamation 118) [2017 92, a99: t7.2g t7.2d³ Dec 16] lengthy gelding: useful handicapper: third at Wolverhampton (1¼ lengths behind Twin Appeal) in December: stays 1m: acts on polytrack, tapeta, good to firm and good to soft going. *David O'Meara* **96**

EXCLUSIVE WATERS (IRE) 7 b.g. Elusive City (USA) 117 – Pelican Waters (IRE) 97 (Key of Luck (USA) 126) [2017 55: t10.2d* 10g* 10s⁶ t10.2g t12.4g² Nov 23] good-topped gelding: fair handicapper: won at Newcastle (apprentice) in February and Pontefract (amateur) in July: left Garry Moss after first start: stays 12.5f: acts on all-weather, good to firm and good to soft going: has worn headgear: often races towards rear. *Tina Jackson* **73**

EXEC CHEF (IRE) 2 ch.g. (Mar 13) Excelebration (IRE) 133 – Donnelly's Hollow (IRE) 71 (Docksider (USA) 124) [2017 p8g³ p8g² Nov 1] €35,000Y: sixth foal: half-brother to 3 winners, including useful 1¼m-1½m winner Headline News (by Peintre Celebre) and 7f winner Donnelly's Rainbow (by Lilbourne Lad): dam, maiden (stayed 1½m), half-sister to high-class 1½m performer White Muzzle: fair form when placed in maiden/minor event: should improve. *David Simcock* **70 p**

EXECUTIVE FORCE 3 b.g. Sepoy (AUS) 129 – Mazuna (IRE) 110 (Cape Cross (IRE) 129) [2017 103: p8g² 8.9g⁴ 8m 8g 7s⁴ 8d 8g⁵ 7.4g⁵ 8d⁴ Oct 27] strong gelding: useful handicapper: second in minor event at Kempton (3½ lengths behind Khafoo Shememi) in April: stays 9f: acts on polytrack and soft going: tried in cheekpieces: often races towards rear: sold 32,000 gns in October to join Michael Wigham. *William Haggas* **97**

EXEMPLAR (IRE) 3 ro.c. Galileo (IRE) 134 – Miarixa (FR) (Linamix (FR) 127) [2017 107p: 10.3d 11.6d⁶ 12d² Sep 9] well-made colt: smart performer: second in Enterprise Stakes at Leopardstown (blinkered, ¾ length behind Eziyra) in September: stays 1½m: acts on soft going: wears tongue tie: has joined Liam Howley in Australia. *Aidan O'Brien, Ireland* **111**

EXHORT 2 ch.f. (Apr 16) Dutch Art 126 – Entreat 87 (Pivotal 124) [2017 7d² 7g* 8g* 7d⁶ Sep 30] fourth foal: sister to 1¼m winners Suitor and Plead (latter at 2 yrs): dam, 9.7f winner, half-sister to smart winner up to 1m Producer (by Dutch Art): fairly useful form: won minor events at Haydock in August and Thirsk (by neck from Gamesters Icon) in September: stays 1m. *Richard Fahey* **86**

EXIT EUROPE 5 ch.g. Bahamian Bounty 116 – Depressed 80 (Most Welcome 131) [2017 p7g⁵ p7g² p7s Nov 23] sturdy gelding: fair handicapper: stays 7f: acts on polytrack, tapeta and soft going. *Sir Mark Prescott Bt* **73**

EXMOUTH 3 b.f. Elusive Quality (USA) – Havant 111 (Halling (USA) 133) [2017 85p: 6m May 6] tall filly: fairly useful form: last of 9 in handicap at Newmarket (5½ lengths behind Danielsflyer) on sole outing in 2017: stays 7f: sold 90,000 gns in December. *Sir Michael Stoute* **84**

EXOTIC GUEST 7 ch.g. Bahamian Bounty 116 – Mamoura (IRE) 97 (Lomond (USA) 128) [2017 73: 6s 6m² 5s* 5.9g³ 6g* Jul 3] fair handicapper: won at Carlisle in June and Hamilton (amateur) in July: best at 5f/6f nowadays: acts on soft and good to firm going: wears headgear. *Ruth Carr* **77**

EXPECTING 2 b.c. (Feb 16) Bated Breath 125 – Oasis Jade 65 (Oasis Dream 129) [2017 6.1m⁵ 5.1m⁴ 5.1m³ 5.7d² t5.1g* p6d* Oct 6] 90,000Y: fourth foal: half-brother to Italian 5f and (at 2 yrs) 6f winner Hot Sun (by Equiano): dam, maiden (stayed 6f), half-sister to useful 6f winner Secondo: fairly useful performer: won minor event at Wolverhampton in September and nursery at Chelmsford (by 2¼ lengths from Central City) in October: stays 6f: acts on polytrack, tapeta and good to firm going: front runner/races prominently. *Charles Hills* **90**

EXPEDIATE 2 ch.g. (Apr 10) Bahamian Bounty 116 – Welanga (Dansili 127) [2017 6g⁵ 6g⁶ 6d⁵ Aug 10] modest form: best effort when fifth in minor event at Goodwood (7 lengths behind Royal Household) in June. *Robert Cowell* **55**

EXPELLED 2 b.c. (Apr 16) Exceed And Excel (AUS) 126 – Pellinore (USA) (Giant's Causeway (USA) 132) [2017 6.1m t6.1g^4 6d^4 p5g^5 p6d t7.2g^3 Nov 29] fair maiden: fourth in minor event at Wolverhampton in August: stayed 7f: acted on tapeta: dead. *James Fanshawe* **69**

EXPENSIVE LIAISON (IRE) 2 b.f. (Apr 11) Camelot 128 – Indigo Lady 101 (Sir Percy 129) [2017 8.3d^5 8s^2 Oct 28] 155,000Y: first foal: dam winner up to 1¼m (2-y-o 7f winner): fair form: better effort when second in minor event at Newbury (length behind Red Starlight) in October: will be suited by at least 1¼m: open to further improvement. *Hugo Palmer* **76 p**

EXPERT EYE 2 b.c. (Jan 31) Acclamation 118 – Exemplify (Dansili 127) [2017 6.5g* 7g* 7m Oct 14] **117 p**

The excellent record of odds-on favourites in the Dewhurst Stakes came to an abrupt halt in the latest edition with the hugely disappointing performance of Expert Eye, sent off at 7/4-on, who came home last of the nine runners. The race is usually the season's top two-year-old contest and three of the four previous editions had gone to odds-on shots—War Command, Air Force Blue and Churchill—all trained by Aidan O'Brien, and it was he who was responsible for the latest winner, U S Navy Flag, along with the next three home as well. Nine of the last ten Dewhurst favourites to start at odds on had been successful, a sequence that had begun with Khalid Abdullah's Zafonic in 1992 and included two other colts also belonging to Expert Eye's owner, Distant Music and, of course, Frankel. The only odds-on favourite beaten in this period was another O'Brien hotpot, Horatio Nelson, who somewhat unluckily lost his unbeaten record when going down by a neck in 2005 to the future Derby winner Sir Percy.

The most famous, or infamous, defeat of an odds-on favourite in the Dewhurst, as well as perhaps the most baffling, has to be that of the Dick Hern-trained Gorytus in 1982. Like Expert Eye, Gorytus was ante-post favourite for the Two Thousand Guineas after winning both his previous starts, and was sent off at 2/1-on in a four-runner Dewhurst, but the scale of his loss was far greater than Expert Eye's as he trailed home thirty lengths behind the third horse, the maiden Tough Commander who started at 200/1. The winner was Diesis, coincidentally the last Middle Park Stakes winner to follow up in the Dewhurst before U S Navy Flag. However, it was the eclipse of Gorytus which made most of the headlines afterwards and the inquest into his sensational defeat took up the majority of his essay in *Racehorses*, certainly more space was devoted to it than to his seven-length win in course-record time in the Acomb Stakes and his even better display when winning the Champagne Stakes by five lengths, performances which accounted for his scaring off all bar three rivals at Newmarket. Gorytus was 'beaten in a matter of strides three furlongs from home' before 'falling further and further behind until being virtually pulled up before the final furlong. When brought back to the unsaddling enclosure Gorytus was shaking badly and appeared both distressed and exhausted.' Plenty of theories were put forward to account for Gorytus' abject display but there was little or no evidence to substantiate any of them. His jockey Willie Carson reportedly thought Gorytus had choked, saying he'd 'run like a horse that had been got at.' There was certainly nothing in the colt's appearance or demeanour beforehand to suggest anything was amiss—a particularly impressive-looking individual, he was described as looking 'absolutely magnificent' in the paddock. Rumours that Gorytus had been coughing were dismissed by his stable who reported him to be 'perfectly normal' just a day after the race. In the apparent absence of any natural physical ailment to account for the colt's distress, something more sinister was the obvious alternative explanation and, inevitably, a more fascinating one for sections of the media. One theory was that Gorytus might have been given a purgative, and another that he'd been exposed to something like a pepper spray, though a dope test proved negative and a statement by Racecourse Security Services said that no evidence of foul play had been found.

Compared to that of Gorytus, Expert Eye's flop in the latest Dewhurst doesn't seem so bad—he finished only a length behind the horse in front of him and a total of just over ten lengths behind the winner and, unlike Gorytus, there was less of a mystery about what went wrong. Although he looked in good shape (just starting to grow his winter coat) and was relaxed in the preliminaries, he became noticeably warm on his neck and was sweating between his hind legs at the start where he became restless in the short time he was in the stalls, after being put in last by a stable representative rather than one of the stalls team. Once under way, Expert Eye pulled too hard, close up behind the eventual winner, and was labouring over two furlongs out, dropping back through the field with his tongue out and just nursed home in the end. Routine testing of Expert Eye afterwards found him to be slightly lame on his off-hind though he was reported to be fine the next day.

The Dewhurst was Expert Eye's first start for ten weeks—he had missed an engagement in the meantime when an unsatisfactory scope had ruled him out of the previous month's National Stakes at the Curragh. However, by all accounts, he was back in top form before the Dewhurst, pleasing his trainer and once again the subject of glowing reports from the gallops as he had been before his two wins in the summer. Sir Michael Stoute's last Group 1-winning two-year-old had been Red Bloom in the 2003 Fillies' Mile and he described Expert Eye, who was bidding to become his second Dewhurst winner, Ajdal having landed odds of 9/4-on back in 1986, as 'the best two-year-old I've had for a while.' 'We don't seem to get so many naturally precocious juveniles now,' remarked Stoute, who, for example, has won the Flying Childers Stakes five times (the last of those wins in 2001), including with Marwell, one of his three Cheveley Park winners.

Expert Eye was only the second two-year-old runner of the year for his stable when making his debut the week before Royal Ascot in a minor event at Newbury. He looked a good prospect in beating the only runner with previous experience, odds-on Mutakatif, by a length and a half with something to spare. The form worked out well, with the third, Barraquero, winning both his subsequent starts, including the Richmond Stakes. By then, though, Expert Eye had registered his own win at Goodwood two days earlier, winning the Vintage Stakes in a manner which far exceeded what could have been gleaned from his debut promise and was arguably the most striking performance by a two-year-old in a pattern race all year, certainly the best by that stage of the season, and one which shot Expert Eye to the head of the Guineas betting. Although less highly tried than some of his rivals, there was no shortage of confidence in Expert Eye who started at 7/4 at Goodwood. Dual winner Zaman had only been beaten just over a length into fourth in the Superlative Stakes last time out, but Expert Eye's main market rivals, like him, were unbeaten and stepping up in grade: Mildenberger had won both his starts in minor events for Mark Johnston, defying a penalty by five lengths at Newbury on the second occasion, while Aidan O'Brien's representative was Seahenge, one of the few Ballydoyle two-year-olds at that stage of the season to have made a winning debut, when successful in a maiden at Naas. Expert Eye appeared more relaxed beforehand on this occasion, though he did suddenly spook away from the rails when walking to the start, unseating his jockey Andrea Atzeni, who led him on foot the rest of the way to the stalls. Atzeni, who ended up riding four winners on the card, including the two other pattern races with 50/1-shot Breton Rock in the Lennox Stakes and Stradivarius in the Goodwood Cup, had few anxious moments on Expert Eye once the stalls opened. With Zaman taking a strong hold in front, Expert Eye travelled strongly in mid-division before cruising into the lead on the outside of the field around two furlongs

Qatar Vintage Stakes, Goodwood—
Expert Eye produces at least as good a performance as has been put up by any recent winner of the race; he's well ahead of Zaman (blinkers) at the line, with Mildenberger (light colours, right) back in third

out. Atzeni got an immediate response when shaking him up and Expert Eye quickly shot clear before just being kept up to his work in the closing stages to pass the post four and a half lengths clear of Zaman.

The runner-up wasn't seen out again but otherwise the Vintage Stakes form could hardly have worked out better during Expert Eye's own absence over the next couple of months. Mildenberger, who kept on well into third just over five lengths behind the winner, won a listed race at Salisbury next time out before finishing two lengths third to Roaring Lion in the Royal Lodge Stakes. James Garfield, who was fourth, was beaten a nose in the Acomb Stakes next time before dropping back in trip to win a good edition of the Mill Reef Stakes. Seahenge, who still looked inexperienced in fifth at Goodwood, was another to go on to pattern-race success, winning the Champagne Stakes before finishing third in the Dewhurst. It was little wonder, therefore, that Expert Eye's next appearance was so keenly awaited. However, his defeat at Newmarket threw the ante-post market on the Two Thousand Guineas into disarray, with Expert Eye out to 10/1 in places by the end of the turf season behind the Racing Post Trophy winner Saxon Warrior, U S Navy Flag and a third Ballydoyle colt Gustav Klimt who wasn't seen out again after winning the Superlative Stakes.

Expert Eye (b.c. 2015)	Acclamation (b 1999)	Royal Applause (b 1993)	Waajib
			Flying Melody
		Princess Athena (b 1985)	Ahonoora
			Shopping Wise
	Exemplify (b 2008)	Dansili (b 1996)	Danehill
			Hasili
		Quest To Peak (b 2002)	Distant View
			Viviana

Expert Eye's sire Acclamation is best known for his sprinters, who are headed by Marsha, and for his stallion son Dark Angel, an even more potent source of speed to which the performances of the likes of Battaash and Harry Angel attested in the latest season. But there are smart performers at up to a mile among Acclamation's offspring too, and the dam's side of Expert Eye's pedigree lends encouragement to those who have backed him for the Guineas. His dam's half-sister Special Duty was a speedy two-year-old, winning the Prix Robert Papin and Cheveley Park Stakes, and, while she didn't get her head in front at three, she was involved closely enough in the finishes of both the One Thousand Guineas and Poule d'Essai des Pouliches to be awarded both of them in the stewards' room, after going down by a nose to Jacqueline Quest at Newmarket and by a head to Liliside at Longchamp. Special Duty's trainer Criquette Head-Maarek, who announced her retirement at the end of the year and has a tribute in 'Top Horses Abroad', also trained Expert Eye's dam Exemplify, though she failed to reach the frame in three subsequent starts after winning a newcomers race over a mile at Deauville at two. Expert Eye is Exemplify's second foal after the fairly useful maiden Divisionist (by Oasis Dream) whose best efforts for Sir Michael Stoute came when placed in a maiden and a handicap over an extended mile at Wolverhampton. Exemplify's other winning siblings include Icespire, a Frankel filly who won her only start at two in good style but didn't quite fulfil that promise in the latest season, and the Spanish-trained Presidency who was third in a listed race over six furlongs at Maisons-Laffitte in the spring. Expert Eye's grandam Quest To Peak ran once in the States and was sister and half-sister respectively to the prolific graded stakes winners Sightseek and Tates Creek. Although half-sisters, Tates Creek was a turf filly whereas Sightseek, the better of the pair, was a high-class dirt performer. With six Grade 1 wins between them in 2003, they were major contributors that year to their trainer Bobby Frankel's world record total of top-level successes which Aidan O'Brien surpassed in the latest season.

Expert Eye looked such a promising colt at Goodwood, and the Vintage form worked out so well, that he must be given another chance to prove himself as good as he looked that day. A good-topped colt—'very athletic' and 'well balanced' is how his trainer describes him—he certainly possesses the physical scope to train on. Perhaps a return in the Craven Stakes might give him a chance to restore his reputation before the Guineas, while there are always options at seven furlongs, or maybe even six, if things don't work out for him at a mile. Hopefully, Expert Eye will bounce back from his Dewhurst defeat better than Gorytus did. There was still sufficient confidence in Gorytus for him to be sent off 7/2 second favourite for the Two Thousand Guineas, but he managed only fifth behind Lomond, and was subsequently fourth and then fifth in the Benson & Hedges Gold Cup and the Waterford Crystal Mile before two more defeats in Florida as a four-year-old. *Sir Michael Stoute*

EXPLAIN 5 ch.g. Kyllachy 129 – Descriptive (IRE) 83 (Desert King (IRE) 129) [2017 89: t6g^{5} 7g^{6} 6m* 7g 6g^{2} 7d* 7d 7d 7.6g 7s^{2} 7v* 6v 7.2s Oct 9] good-topped gelding: useful handicapper: won at Ripon in May, and Chester in June and September (by 1½ lengths from Luis Vaz de Torres): best at 6f/7f: acts on tapeta, good to firm and heavy going: wears headgear. *Ruth Carr* **98**

EXPRESSIY (FR) 2 b.f. (Apr 28) Siyouni (FR) 122 – Express American (FR) (American Post 121) [2017 7d^{3} 7m* 8d^{5} p7g* 7m^{6} 7s^{3} Oct 28] €260,000 2-y-o: compact filly: second foal: dam, French 11.5f winner, half-sister to useful French performer around 1¼m Saint Elier: useful performer: won minor events at Newmarket in August and Chelmsford in October: third in listed race at Newbury (1¼ lengths behind Hikmaa) later in October: should be suited by 1m: acts on polytrack, soft and good to firm going: usually in hood: front runner/races prominently. *Charlie Appleby* **96**

EXPRESS LADY (IRE) 3 b.f. Helmet (AUS) 127 – Star Express 80 (Sadler's Wells (USA) 132) [2017 7d* 7d^{5} t7.1s^{2} p8g* Nov 6] 40,000Y: half-sister to several winners, including 1m/8.5f winner Dubai Sunshine (by Dubawi) and 7f winner Desert Shine (by Green Desert): dam French 1½m winner: fairly useful form: won maiden at Lingfield in May and handicap at Kempton (by neck from Bint Dandy) in November: stays 1m: in hood/tongue tie last 2 starts. *Hugo Palmer* **88**

EXPROMPT (FR) 2 b.c. (Apr 1) Choisir (AUS) 126 – Councilofconstance (IRE) 78 (Footstepsinthesand 120) [2017 6s p7s^{3} p7g^{2} p7g^{6} Oct 11] fair form in minor events: stays 7f. *Hugo Palmer* **77**

EXQUISITE RUBY 3 b.f. Exceed And Excel (AUS) 126 – Ruby Rocket (IRE) 113 (Indian Rocket 115) [2017 t6f^{5} t6g^{3} 6m^{6} 5g^{5} 5f^{3} 5.1d^{2} p5g^{4} p6g^{5} p6g^{6} Nov 17] seventh foal: sister to useful 6f-1m winner Mississippi and half-sister to 2 winners, including very smart 5f/6f winner Maarek (by Pivotal): dam 6f winner (including at 2 yrs): fair maiden: stays 6f: acts on polytrack, tapeta, firm and good to soft going: front runner/races prominently. *Charles Hills* **69**

EXSPECTATION (IRE) 3 b.g. Excelebration (IRE) 133 – Emeralds Spirit (IRE) 76 (Rock of Gibraltar (IRE) 133) [2017 67p: 8.3m 9.9f p8g p11g^{ur} p10g p8g^{5} Dec 30] compact gelding: modest maiden: stays 1m: acts on polytrack and good to soft going. *Michael Blanshard* **62**

EXTORTION 4 b.g. Kheleyf (USA) 116 – Virtuality (USA) 60 (Elusive Quality (USA)) [2017 78: t7.1g Jan 3] fair handicapper: well held only start in 2017: stays 6f: acts on good to firm and good to soft going: signs of temperament. *Bryan Smart* **–**

EXTRACTION (USA) 2 b.c. (Mar 6) More Than Ready (USA) 120 – Coppermine (USA) (Unbridled's Song (USA) 125) [2017 7m^{6} p10g^{4} Oct 18] fair form: better effort when fourth in minor event at Lingfield (5¾ lengths behind Bowditch) in October. *Martyn Meade* **68**

EXTRA ELUSIVE 2 ch.c. (Apr 10) Mastercraftsman (IRE) 129 – Nessina (USA) (Hennessy (USA) 122) [2017 8d* Oct 27] tall, leggy, unfurnished colt: third foal: half-brother to smart 2-y-o 5.4f/6f (Gimcrack Stakes) winner Ajaya (by Invincible Spirit): dam unraced: 7/1, won minor event at Newbury (by 2¾ lengths from First Eleven) on debut: open to significant improvement. *Roger Charlton* **90 P**

EXTRA MILE 3 b.f. Frankel 147 – Marie de Medici (USA) 104 (Medicean 128) [2017 p8g^{4} 9.9f^{2} 9.9f^{4} Jun 18] third foal: half-sister to useful winner up to 9.5f Local Time (2-y-o 7f/1m winner, by Invincible Spirit): dam, winner up to 1¼m (2-y-o 7f winner), half-sister to high-class 1½m performer Erupt: fairly useful form: best effort when second in maiden at Beverley (½ length behind Coconut Creme) in May: in visor last 2 starts. *Saeed bin Suroor* **83**

EXTRASOLAR 7 b.g. Exceed And Excel (AUS) 126 – Amicable Terms 88 (Royal Applause 124) [2017 87: t6g f5g t5d 6g 6m^{3} 6m^{2} 5m^{5} 6m t6.1g 5.9d 6d^{6} Sep 12] sturdy gelding: fair handicapper: stays 7f: acts on polytrack, tapeta, firm and good to soft going: has worn headgear, including in 2017: has worn tongue tie, including last 2 starts. *Geoffrey Harker* **78**

EYE BURNER 3 ch.g. Equiano (FR) 127 – Tilly's Dream 87 (Arkadian Hero (USA) 123) –
[2017 6d 6.1g t5.1g p6s f5g Dec 21] workmanlike gelding: no form in maidens. *J. R. Jenkins*

EYECATCHER (IRE) 2 b.g. (Mar 14) Camelot 128 – For Joy (Singspiel (IRE) 133) **67 p**
[2017 t8.6g^3 p8s^6 10v^4 Oct 9] 78,000F, 150,000Y: fourth foal: half-brother to useful French 1m and (at 2 yrs) 9f winner Victoria Regina (by Mastercraftsman): dam, French 9.5f-1½m winner, sister to smart French stayer Gloomy Sunday: fair form: still unexposed. *Simon Crisford*

EYE OF THE STORM (IRE) 7 ch.g. Galileo (IRE) 134 – Mohican Princess (Shirley **103**
Heights 130) [2017 106: 9.9g 12d^4 13.4g^6 12g 16d^4 t12.2g Oct 21] angular gelding: reportedly has only one eye: useful handicapper: stays 16.5f: acts on good to firm and heavy going: tried in hood: front runner/races prominently, often finds little: sold 9,000 gns in October to join Keith Dalgleish. *Amanda Perrett*

EYE ON YOU (IRE) 4 b.f. Tagula (IRE) 116 – Hollow Haze (USA) 90 (Woodman –
(USA) 126) [2017 t8g Jan 12] €7,500Y: half-sister to numerous winners, including useful 7f-9.5f winner Ella Woodcock (by Daggers Drawn) and 5f winner (including at 2 yrs) Phoenix Clubs (by Red Clubs): dam 8.5f winner: 33/1, well held in maiden at Newcastle. *John Murray*

EYESIGHT 3 ch.g. Medicean 128 – Look So 92 (Efisio 120) [2017 p12g Apr 20] 20/1, –
well held in maiden at Lingfield (visored). *Charlie Fellowes*

EYES OF FIRE 2 gr.g. (Feb 4) Helmet (AUS) 127 – Lady Xara (IRE) (Xaar 132) [2017 –
5m 6g^5 6m 6g Sep 27] little form. *Ollie Pears*

EYES ON ASHA (IRE) 3 b.f. Redoute's Choice (AUS) – Sunday Nectar (IRE) 101 **79**
(Footstepsinthesand 120) [2017 t8g* p11g^5 Aug 30] €75,000Y, €775,000 2-y-o: first foal: dam French 7.5f/1m winner: fair form: won maiden at Newcastle (by 2½ lengths from Sulafah) in March. *Kevin Ryan*

EYNHALLOW 3 b.g. Nathaniel (IRE) 129 – Ronaldsay 108 (Kirkwall 118) [2017 73p: **105**
9.1m* 9.9m^3 9.9g* 9.9d^2 9.9m^4 11.5d^3 12m^2 Oct 13] well-made gelding: useful handicapper: won at Goodwood (by ½ length from Secret Advisor) in May and Sandown (by 2¾ lengths from Buzz) in July: second at Newmarket (¾ length behind First Nation) final start: stays 1½m: acts on good to firm and good to soft going: often races towards rear: sold 300,000 gns, has joined Charlie Appleby. *Roger Charlton*

EYREBORN (IRE) 3 b.f. Born To Sea (IRE) 117 – Eyrecourt (IRE) 64 (Efisio 120) [2017 **74**
61: 11.1s^4 12g^2 14m^5 11.1d^2 14.1v^5 11.8v^5 13.1v^2 14d^4 14v^5 f12.1g Nov 16] fair maiden handicapper: stays 1¾m: acts on heavy going: has worn hood: often races towards rear. *Keith Dalgleish*

EZIYRA (IRE) 3 ch.f. Teofilo (IRE) 126 – Eytarna (IRE) 104 (Dubai Destination (USA) **112**
127) [2017 105p: 12d^2 12f^3 12s* 12d* Sep 9] smart performer: won Give Thanks Stakes at Cork (by 2½ lengths from Bloomfield) in August and Enterprise Stakes at Leopardstown (by ¾ length from Exemplar) in September: stays 1½m: acts on firm and soft going: often in hood. *D. K. Weld, Ireland*

EZZ (IRE) 2 b.c. (Apr 14) Intello (GER) 129 – Looby Loo 71 (Kyllachy 129) [2017 p7g –
Oct 18] 100/1, well held in minor event at Kempton. *Mrs Ilka Gansera-Leveque*

F

FAADHEL (GER) 2 b.c. (Apr 22) Maxios 123 – Firedance (GER) (Lomitas 129) [2017 **67**
7g^6 8.2g Oct 17] fair form: better effort when seventh in minor event at Leicester (6¾ lengths behind Bombyx) in October. *Roger Varian*

FAAY (IRE) 2 gr.f. (Apr 19) Dark Angel (IRE) 113 – Folga 104 (Atraf 116) [2017 7m t6s **64**
7d^4 Sep 30] 400,000Y: fourth foal: sister to high-class 5f (including at 2 yrs) winner Mecca's Angel and very smart winner up to 7f Markaz (2-y-o 6f winner): dam winner up to 6f (2-y-o 5f winner): modest form when fourth in maiden at Newmarket (11 lengths behind Bye Bye Baby) on last of 3 starts: tail flasher. *Ed Dunlop*

FABELLA BERE (FR) 2 b.f. (Mar 31) Peer Gynt (JPN) – L'Ete (CHI) (Hussonet (USA)) **52**
[2017 5.9v^3 7f 7d t7.1g f8.1g^4 Dec 11] €22,000Y: half-sister to several winners, including useful French winner up to 1¼m The Turning Point (2-y-o 6f winner, by Hurricane Cat): dam winner up to 7.5f in Chile (2-y-o 6f winner): modest maiden: will stay beyond 1m. *K. R. Burke*

Bet & Watch At sunbets.co.uk Winter Hill Stakes, Windsor—
Royal runner Fabricate gets off the mark in pattern company at the first attempt, beating Spark Plug (right) and the previous year's winner Chain of Daisies

FAB (IRE) 2 br.f. (Mar 2) Society Rock (IRE) 126 – Dubai Princess (IRE) 105 (Dubai Destination (USA) 127) [2017 5f² t5.1g 5.1m⁵ f5g⁵ 5s⁴ 5.1m⁴ Oct 16] £42,000 2-y-o: rather leggy filly: half-sister to several winners, including 5f/6f winner Taquka (by Kodiac) and winner up to 7f Zebs Lad (2-y-o 5f winner, by Zebedee): dam, 5f/6f winner (including at 2 yrs), half-sister to 5f winner Swiss Lake and 5f-7f winner Hajoum (both smart): fair maiden: raced only at 5f: acts on firm going: front runner/races prominently. *Jamie Osborne* **70**

FABRIC 3 b.f. Acclamation 118 – Decorative (IRE) 100 (Danehill Dancer (IRE) 117) [2017 79: 5.1m⁶ 5f² 6g 6g³ 5v p7g Nov 8] rather unfurnished filly: fair handicapper: left Richard Hannon after fourth start: stays 6f: acts on firm going: in hood last 2 starts. *J. F. Levins, Ireland* **75**

FABRICATE 5 b.g. Makfi 130 – Flight of Fancy 114 (Sadler's Wells (USA) 132) [2017 108: t12.2g³ t12.4s⁴ p14g⁴ 11.8m⁶ 9.9g* 10m* 11m⁵ Sep 23] well-made gelding: smart performer: won handicap at Goodwood (awarded race) and Winter Hill Stakes at Windsor (by 1¼ lengths from Spark Plug) in August: stays 1¾m: acts on polytrack, tapeta, good to firm and good to soft going: wears cheekpieces. *Michael Bell* **117 a107**

FABULOUS FLYER 4 b.f. Equiano (FR) 127 – Lucky Flyer 79 (Lucky Story (USA) 128) [2017 51: p5m* p5g² t5.1g² p5f² p5g³ p6g³ 5g p5g² 5d⁶ Jul 1] modest handicapper: won at Lingfield in January: stays 6f: acts on polytrack, best turf form on good going. *Jeremy Gask* **58**

FABULOUS RED 2 b.f. (Feb 17) Red Jazz (USA) 125 – Red Fantasy (IRE) 98 (High Chaparral (IRE) 132) [2017 6d² 6g⁴ t6d⁴ p7g* Sep 9] third foal: half-sister to 1½m winner Rock 'N Red (by Fastnet Rock): dam, 1¼m winner, half-sister to smart 6f/7f winner Desert Fantasy out of smart 5f/6f winner Petite Fantasy: fairly useful form: won nursery at Kempton (by ¾ length from Collateral) in September: will stay 1m. *Ed Dunlop* **80**

FACE LIKE THUNDER 2 b.g. (Feb 25) Passing Glance 119 – Violet's Walk (Dr Fong (USA) 128) [2017 7m 7s³ Oct 10] fourth foal: brother to 1m winner Reedcutter and half-brother to 7f winner Tunnager Grove (by Piccolo): dam unraced: fair form: better effort when third in minor event at Leicester (1¼ lengths behind Indomeneo) in October: open to further improvement. *Andrew Balding* **74 p**

FACE THE FACTS (IRE) 3 ch.g. Nathaniel (IRE) 129 – Aricia (IRE) 88 (Nashwan (USA) 135) [2017 75p: 11.8g² 11m* 11.9f⁴ 14m 13g⁶ 14s² 16g* 13.9g Oct 13] angular gelding: shows traces of stringhalt: smart performer: won maiden at Newbury (by ¾ length from Karawaan) in April and listed race at Newmarket (by length from Nearly Caught) in September: stays 2m: acts on soft and good to firm going: tried in hood: often races towards rear: sold 100,000 gns in October. *John Gosden* **115**

FAHEEM 6 b.g. Halling (USA) 133 – White Star (IRE) 108 (Darshaan 133) [2017 p10g Dec 30] fair form in bumpers: 20/1, well held in maiden at Lingfield on sole Flat outing: maiden hurdler. *Lydia Richards* **–**

FAIENCE 3 b.f. Holy Roman Emperor (IRE) 125 – Delft 93 (Dutch Art 126) [2017 p7g p8d* t8g^5 Mar 4] first foal: dam 6f/7f winner (including at 2 yrs): fair form: won maiden at Chelmsford (by neck from Dubai Waves) in February: best effort at 1m. *William Haggas* **74**

FAINTLY (USA) 6 b.g. Kitten's Joy (USA) 128 – Tinge (USA) (Kingmambo (USA) 125) [2017 75: t7.1g^4 7m t7.1g^6 7.5f t8s^2 t7.1s^5 7.4m^4 t7.1d 7m Aug 26] fair handicapper: stays 1m: acts on polytrack, tapeta and firm going: usually wears headgear: usually races towards rear, often travels strongly: has looked hesitant under pressure: sent to Germany. *Ruth Carr* **58 § a69 §**

FAIR COMMENT 7 b.m. Tamayuz 126 – Cliche (IRE) 108 (Diktat 126) [2017 70: p12g^{pu} Apr 11] rather leggy mare: fair handicapper: stayed 1¾m: acted on polytrack and any turf going: often raced freely: dead. *Michael Blanshard* **–**

FAIR COP 3 b.f. Exceed And Excel (AUS) 126 – Speed Cop 104 (Cadeaux Genereux 131) [2017 p6g^2 5.7f^2 5.1d* 6.1m^5 5g^3 5v^2 Aug 3] tall, angular filly: fifth foal: half-sister to 3 winners, including smart winner up to 6f Desert Law (by Oasis Dream) and useful winner up to 6f Top Cop (2-y-o 5.7f winner, by Acclamation): dam 5f winner (including at 2 yrs): fairly useful performer: won maiden at Windsor (by 1¾ lengths from Beck And Call) in May: best effort at 5f: acts on good to soft going: front runner/races prominently, usually travels strongly. *Andrew Balding* **88**

FAIR EVA 3 ch.f. Frankel 147 – African Rose 119 (Observatory (USA) 131) [2017 112: 8m^5 May 7] well-made filly: smart performer: fifth of 14 to Winter in 1000 Guineas at Newmarket on sole outing in 2017: stays 1m: acts on good to firm going: often travels strongly. *Roger Charlton* **104**

FAIR ISLAND 2 b.f. (Mar 30) Trans Island 119 – La Vie Est Belle 80 (Makbul 104) [2017 8d Oct 27] £3,500Y: fourth foal: dam, 5f winner (including at 2 yrs), sister to useful winner up to 6f Phantom Whisper: 150/1, well held in maiden at Doncaster. *Sarah Hollinshead* **–**

FAIR LOCH 9 gr.g. Fair Mix (IRE) 123 – Ardentinny (Ardross 134) [2017 t16.3g^2 t16.3g^4 Mar 24] fair maiden: stays 16.5f: acts on polytrack, tapeta and heavy going: tried in cheekpieces/tongue tie: fairly useful hurdler/chaser. *Brian Ellison* **73**

FAIR POWER (IRE) 3 b.g. Power 117 – Pitrizzia (Lando (GER) 128) [2017 77: 8.5g^4 8.1d^5 9.9g* 10.1g* 12v 9.9g^3 p12g Oct 9] leggy gelding: fairly useful handicapper: won at Brighton and Epsom (by ½ length from Dream Machine) in July: third at Sandown in September: stays 1¼m: acts on polytrack and good to soft going: often races towards rear. *Sylvester Kirk* **89**

FAIR SELENE 3 b.f. Equiano (FR) 127 – Jane Jubilee (IRE) 91 (Mister Baileys 123) [2017 63: t7.1g^6 7g^2 7g^3 7d^2 8.1m^3 8.1v* 8g Aug 17] compact filly: fair handicapper: won at Chepstow in July: stays 1m: acts on polytrack, tapeta and heavy going: often wears headgear: sometimes slowly away. *Heather Main* **75**

FAIRWAY TO HEAVEN (IRE) 8 b.g. Jeremy (USA) 122 – Luggala (IRE) 90 (Kahyasi 130) [2017 87: t6m^4 p6d^2 t6g p6g^2 6g 6m p7g 7m p6d 7d^5 6d^4 p6d^5 p6g^3 t6.1m^2 t6.1g Nov 11] rather leggy gelding: fairly useful handicapper, on decline in 2017: left Michael Wigham after fourth start: stays 7f: acts on polytrack, tapeta, soft and good to firm going: has worn headgear, including final start. *Lee Carter* **82 d**

FAIRYLAND (USA) 2 ch.f. (Feb 4) Scat Daddy (USA) 120 – Dame Ursula (Elusive Quality (USA)) [2017 a4.5f* 6m 5.5f^2 5f p5.5f* Dec 6] $375,000Y: powerful filly: third foal: half-sister to minor US winner by City Zip: dam, ran once in US, half-sister to top-class Japanese 1m-1¼m performer Agnes Digital: useful performer: won maiden at Keeneland in April and optional claimer at Turfway in December: well held in Albany Stakes at Royal Ascot on second start: stays 5.5f: acts on polytrack, dirt and firm going: often in blinkers. *Wesley A. Ward, USA* **95**

FAIRY LIGHTS 3 b.f. Shamardal (USA) 129 – Suba (USA) 85 (Seeking The Gold (USA)) [2017 74p: p8g^6 8.3g 7g^4 Aug 30] fair form on sole start at 2 yrs, little impact in maidens in 2017. *Roger Varian* **–**

FAIRY LOCK (IRE) 3 b.f. Sir Prancealot (IRE) 111 – Too Close (IRE) (Danehill Dancer (IRE) 117) [2017 58: f7g^5 t7.1m^4 8g^2 t8g^4 8.3d^6 8f^5 Jun 19] modest maiden: stays 1m: acts on tapeta and firm going: sometimes slowly away. *David Barron* **59**

FAIRY MIST (IRE) 10 b.g. Oratorio (IRE) 128 – Prealpina (IRE) (Indian Ridge 123) [2017 61: p8m^6 p8g 8g^2 8g^6 9.1g^6 8g p10g^6 7m p10s p7g Dec 30] modest handicapper: stays 1¼m, raced mainly at shorter: acts on polytrack and any turf going: usually wears headgear: has worn tongue tie. *John Bridger* **55**

FAITHFUL CREEK (IRE) 5 b.g. Bushranger (IRE) 119 – Open Verse (USA) 69 (Black Minnaloushe (USA) 123) [2017 94: t8g^4 t12.2m^5 f12g* t12.4d^3 11.8g^2 10.1g 10.1s^3 p12g 10v^4 Oct 23] compact gelding: fairly useful handicapper: won at Southwell (by head from Serenity Now) in February: placed at Newcastle in March, Leicester in April and Yarmouth in September: stays 12.5f: acts on fibresand, tapeta and any turf going: wears headgear: has worn tongue tie: front runner/races prominently: consistent: sold 11,000 gns, sent to Saudi Arabia. *Michael Appleby* **91**

FAITHFUL PROMISE 2 b.f. (Feb 18) Acclamation 118 – Devotion (IRE) 102 (Dylan Thomas (IRE) 132) [2017 t5.1g^6 5m^2 5m* 5s 5v^4 6m* 6d^2 6d 6d^6 Sep 5] 48,000Y: sturdy filly: second foal: half-sister to 1m winner Nick Vedder (by Rip Van Winkle): dam, 2-y-o 7f winner who stayed 1½m, closely related to useful 1½m winner Thomas Edison, also smart hurdler: fairly useful performer: won maiden at Musselburgh in May and nursery at Catterick in July: second in nursery at Newmarket in August: stays 6f: acts on good to firm and good to soft going: usually races close up. *Mark Johnston* **81**

FAJJAJ (IRE) 2 ch.c. (Mar 1) Dawn Approach (IRE) 132 – Pleasantry (Johannesburg (USA) 127) [2017 7s* 7g^4 Sep 28] 140,000Y: third foal: half-brother to 2-y-o 7f winner Parlance (by Invincible Spirit): dam unraced half-sister to top-class miler Kingman out of Poule d'Essai des Pouliches winner Zenda: useful form: won minor event at Ascot (by ½ length from Court of Justice) in September: fourth in Somerville Tattersall Stakes at Newmarket (4 lengths behind Elarqam) later same month: likely to stay 1m: open to further improvement. *Hugo Palmer* **99 p**

FAKE NEWS 2 b.g. (Apr 8) Paco Boy (IRE) 129 – Day Creek (Daylami (IRE) 138) [2017 6d 5.9d* 6g Oct 7] 9,000Y: third foal: half-brother to winner up to 6f Lackaday (by Kyllachy) and 1m winner River Echo (by Equiano): dam unraced half-sister to smart winner up to 1¼m With Interest: fairly useful form: won minor event at Carlisle (by 1¾ lengths from Lucky Lucky Man) in August: raced only at 6f. *David Barron* **84**

FAKHOOR (IRE) 2 b.c. (Mar 28) Oasis Dream 129 – Darajaat (USA) 101 (Elusive Quality (USA)) [2017 p6g^2 p6s^2 Nov 17] third foal: dam, 2-y-o 6f winner, half-sister to useful winner up to 1m Shabiba: fairly useful form when second in minor events at Kempton and Chelmsford: remains with potential. *Owen Burrows* **85 p**

FALABELLE (IRE) 2 ch.f. (Feb 21) Choisir (AUS) 126 – Mooching Along (IRE) (Mujahid (USA) 125) [2017 5s^3 5.2v 5m* 5m Aug 26] 23,000Y: half-sister to several winners, including smart 5f (including at 2 yrs) winner Primo Uomo (by Strategic Prince) and useful winner up to 7f Safari Sunseeker (by Tagula): dam unraced: fair form: won minor event at Musselburgh in August: raced only at 5f. *Kevin Ryan* **78**

FALAK (IRE) 4 b.g. Teofilo (IRE) 126 – Family (USA) (Danzig (USA)) [2017 –p: t8.6g^3 p8s^6 11.5g^3 14g* Jul 8] fairly useful performer: won handicap at Nottingham (by ½ length from Graceful Lady) in July: stays 1¾m: best form on good going: remains capable of better. *Roger Varian* **88 p**

FALBON 3 b.g. Mayson 124 – Eleodora (Dubawi (IRE) 129) [2017 70: p8g^2 p7s^2 7m p7d p8g^3 Sep 5] fairly useful maiden: placed in handicaps at Chelmsford in May and Kempton in September: stays 1m: acts on polytrack: tried in cheekpieces: races prominently. *Marco Botti* **85**

FALCAO (IRE) 5 br.g. Majestic Missile (IRE) 118 – Cafe Lassere (USA) (Giant's Causeway (USA) 132) [2017 83: p7g f7g^6 p7d Feb 15] fairly useful at best, no form in 2017: has worn headgear/tongue tie. *John Butler* **–**

FALCON CLIFFS (IRE) 3 b.f. Canford Cliffs (IRE) 133 – Circle (IRE) 88 (Galileo (IRE) 134) [2017 p10g* 9.9m^6 p11g 11.6d^2 12m^5 Aug 27] €25,000Y: rather unfurnished filly: first foal: dam 7f winner who stayed 9f: fairly useful performer: won maiden at Lingfield in February: second in handicap there in August: left Joseph Tuite after third start: stays 11.5f: acts on polytrack and good to soft going. *William Muir* **84**

FALCON EYE (IRE) 2 gr.g. (Mar 7) Dubawi (IRE) 129 – Asi Siempre (USA) 123 (El Prado (IRE) 119) [2017 7m^6 8d^5 p10g^4 p10g Nov 2] fair form: best effort at 1m. *Charlie Appleby* **74**

FALCON'S FIRE (IRE) 4 ch.g. Thewayyouare (USA) 117 – Matadora (IRE) 69 (Kris 135) [2017 80: f11g^5 f12d 13.8m^2 t12.2g^5 12.5m^3 14g^3 11.1g 16m t12.4s 11.1d 11.1g^3 13d^5 12.5m^5 12.1d t10.2s^5 14s t12.4g^3 p10m^6 t12.4d t12.2g^4 Dec 22] fairly useful handicapper: placed 5 times in 2017: stays 1¾m: acts on polytrack, tapeta, good to firm and heavy going: wears headgear: tried in tongue tie: has carried head awkwardly: untrustworthy. *Keith Dalgleish* **81 §**

FALCON'S REIGN (FR) 8 ch.g. Haafhd 129 – Al Badeya (IRE) 68 (Pivotal 124) [2017 60: f8g Jan 24] rather leggy gelding: modest handicapper nowadays, well held sole outing on Flat in 2017: stays 9f: acts on fibresand and heavy going: wears headgear: lightly-raced maiden hurdler. *Michael Appleby* –

FALCON'S VISION 2 b.f. (Feb 10) Iffraaj 127 – New Falcon (IRE) 81 (New Approach (IRE) 132) [2017 6.5d⁴ 7f³ p7s 7d Sep 30] 52,000Y: first foal: dam, 2-y-o 7f winner, half-sister to useful winner up to 1m Sharnberry out of useful 2-y-o 5f/6f winner (stayed 1m) Wimple: fair form: stays 7f. *David Simcock* **72**

FALLING WOOD (IRE) 2 gr.c. (May 4) Zebedee 113 – Wood Nymph (IRE) 50 (Acclamation 118) [2017 p7g Dec 21] 20/1, well held in minor event at Chelmsford. *Marco Botti* –

FALMOUTH LIGHT (FR) 2 b.g. (Feb 1) Cape Cross (IRE) 129 – Wonderous Light (IRE) (Montjeu (IRE) 137) [2017 7m* 7g⁴ 7m⁴ 6d 7v Sep 15] strong gelding: fair performer: won maiden at Sandown in June: stays 7f: acts on good to firm going: often races prominently. *Mark Johnston* **79**

FALSE ID 4 b.g. Aqlaam 125 – Miss Dutee 68 (Dubawi (IRE) 129) [2017 75: p6m⁶ p7g p8g 10m⁶ p10g⁴ 10.2f⁶ 10s³ 8s 7.4d t8.6g⁵ 8.3s 9.8g³ p7s⁶ 8d⁵ p10g Oct 12] sturdy gelding: fair handicapper, lost form in 2017: left Robert Eddery after fifth start, Marjorie Fife after thirteenth: stays 1¼m, effective at shorter: acts on polytrack and tapeta: has worn headgear/tongue tie, including in 2017. *Daniel Steele* **71 d**

FAMILY FORTUNES 3 ch.g. Paco Boy (IRE) 129 – Barawin (IRE) 87 (Hawk Wing (USA) 136) [2017 p5m* p6g* p7g³ 7g⁴ 7s⁵ p8g³ p7g p8s Dec 1] 25,000F, 18,000Y: third foal: half-brother to useful winner up to 1½m Sir Jack Layden (2-y-o 7f winner, by Sir Percy) and 9f-13f winner Kelvin Hall (by Halling): dam 2-y-o 1m winner who stayed 1¾m: fairly useful performer: won maiden at Lingfield in February and handicap at Kempton (by head from Berkshire Boy) in April: stays 1m: acts on polytrack: often races towards rear. *Sylvester Kirk* **94**

FAMILY TREE 2 ch.c. (Apr 30) Galileo (IRE) 134 – Sant Elena 88 (Efisio 120) [2017 7s* Sep 6] 420,000Y: closely related to 8.6f winner Jumbo Prado (by El Prado) and a winner in Japan by New Approach, and half-brother to 2 winners, including smart 2-y-o 5f/6f (including Prix Morny/Middle Park Stakes) winner Reckless Abandon (by Exchange Rate): dam, 6f (including at 2 yrs)/1m winner, half-sister to high-class sprinter Brando: in tongue strap, 5/1, won maiden at Gowran on debut cosily by ¾ length from Meagher's Flag: will stay 1m: open to improvement. *Aidan O'Brien, Ireland* **88 p**

FAMOUS DYNASTY (IRE) 3 b.g. Famous Name 124 – Daffodil Walk (IRE) 93 (Captain Rio 122) [2017 65: p8g 10.2f³ 8.1d 12f⁴ 11.6d⁴ 9.9m² 10.2g⁶ 9.9g⁶ 8g³ 8d⁶ p8g p10g Nov 2] close-coupled gelding: fair maiden: stays 1½m: acts on firm and good to soft going: often races towards rear. *Michael Blanshard* **68**

FAMOUS KID (USA) 6 ch.g. Street Cry (IRE) 130 – Moyesii (USA) (Diesis 133) [2017 118: t16.5m² 12g 15.9d Mar 25] well-made gelding: smart performer: second in minor event at Wolverhampton (1¾ lengths behind Antiquarium) in January: below form at Meydan after: stays 1¾m: acts on polytrack, dirt and any turf going. *Saeed bin Suroor* **113**

FANAN 2 ch.g. (May 7) Iffraaj 127 – Paradise Isle 112 (Bahamian Bounty 116) [2017 7.6v⁵ p7g Oct 5] finely-made gelding: well held in minor events. *Simon Crisford* –

FANCIFUL ANGEL (IRE) 5 gr.g. Dark Angel (IRE) 113 – Fanciful Dancer (Groom Dancer (USA) 128) [2017 113: 8g* 8g⁶ 8g⁶ 8m p10s* 9.9m⁶ 10f² 12f² 12f Nov 4] good-topped gelding: smart performer: won handicaps at Meydan (by length from Hors de Combat) in January and Chelmsford (by head from Noble Gift) in May: twice second to Beach Patrol, in Arlington Million (beaten ½ length, left Marco Botti after) and Joe Hirsch Turf Classic (went down by 5 lengths): behind in Breeders' Cup Turf at Del Mar final start: stays 1½m: acts on polytrack, firm and good to soft going: tried in hood: often starts slowly/races in rear. *Chad C. Brown, USA* **116**

FANCIFUL MISS 2 b.f. (Mar 8) New Approach (IRE) 132 – Fann (USA) 96 (Diesis 133) [2017 6g Jul 21] 32,000Y: rather unfurnished filly: sixth foal: sister to useful 2-y-o 7f winner (stayed 2m) Future Empire, and closely related to smart winner up to 11f Black Arrow (2-y-o 1m winner) and winner up to 1½m Muhtaris (2-y-o 8.3f winner) (both by Teofilo): dam 9f winner: 25/1, well held in minor event at Newbury. *Tom Dascombe* –

FANFAIR 3 b.f. Royal Applause 124 – Fugnina 89 (Hurricane Run (IRE) 134) [2017 53: 7g³ 7g⁴ 10.2f* 10d* 10.2s³ 10m² 9.9s⁶ Oct 10] smallish filly: fair handicapper: won at Bath and Lingfield in July: stays 1¼m: acts on firm and good to soft going. *Richard Hannon* **74**

FANFARE LADY (IRE) 2 br.f. (Feb 14) Society Rock (IRE) 126 – Silk Fan (IRE) 100 **56**
(Unfuwain (USA) 131) [2017 5.7s^{4} t6.1m Oct 28] €19,000Y: half-sister to several winners, including useful 2-y-o 5f/6f winner Haikbidiac (by Kodiac) and useful 2-y-o 5f winner (stays 1m) Risk Adjusted (by Bushranger): dam 7f winner (including at 2 yrs) who stayed 1¼m: modest form when fourth at Bath on first of 2 starts in minor events. *William Knight*

FANG 4 b.g. Lawman (FR) 121 – Desert Tigress (USA) 83 (Storm Cat (USA)) [2017 90: **63**
6m p5s 6m 6d^{6} Sep 18] sturdy gelding: fairly useful handicapper, below form in 2017: stays 6f: acts on polytrack and firm going: tried in blinkers: has worn tongue tie. *William Jarvis*

FANOULPIFER 6 b.g. High Chaparral (IRE) 132 – Furbeseta 84 (Danehill Dancer (IRE) **99 d**
117) [2017 108: 9.9f^{2} 9.9m^{5} 8.9m 10.1m^{5} p10g p12g^{6} Dec 31] €100,000Y: third foal: dam, 1m winner, half-sister to very smart winner up to 7f Pretend: useful performer at best: won 6 races in Italy prior to 2017, including listed race at Milan at 2 yrs: second in minor event on same course (head behind Freedom Beel) in March: left A. & S. Botti, looked tricky ride when well held last 3 outings: stays 1¼m: acts on firm and good to soft going: has worn headgear, including last 3 starts: tried in tongue tie. *Michael Attwater*

FANTASY GLADIATOR 11 b.g. Ishiguru (USA) 114 – Fancier Bit (Lion Cavern **70**
(USA) 117) [2017 82: t9.5m^{5} p10d^{pu} p8g t10.2d^{5} p11g^{4} 8.3g^{3} 10.1m^{6} 10.2g^{2} 10.2d^{6} 8.3g^{5} 9.1d^{6} p8g* p10d^{2} p8d^{4} Oct 6] fair handicapper nowadays: won at Chelmsford in September: stays 10.5f: acts on all-weather, soft and good to firm going: wears headgear: quirky sort. *Michael Appleby*

FANTASY JUSTIFIER (IRE) 6 b.g. Arakan (USA) 123 – Grandel (Owington 123) **64**
[2017 77: 6.1d 6.1v 6.1m 6s^{3} 6.1g^{2} 5d^{5} 5.7s^{5} 5.7s^{5} t6.1m^{2} f6.1g Nov 13] lengthy gelding: fair handicapper: stays 6f: acts on tapeta, good to firm and heavy going: often in headgear in 2017: usually slowly away, often races towards rear. *Ronald Harris*

FANTASY KEEPER 3 b.g. Mayson 124 – Expressive 81 (Falbrav (IRE) 133) [2017 70: **83**
p5g^{3} 6.1d* 6d^{3} 6.1g^{2} p7s 6d 6.1d^{2} 5s^{2} Nov 8] strong, lengthy gelding: fairly useful handicapper: won at Nottingham in May: second there in October and November: stays 6f: acts on polytrack and soft going. *Michael Appleby*

FANTASY KING 11 b.g. Acclamation 118 – Fantasy Ridge 92 (Indian Ridge 123) [2017 **–**
67: 14m^{6} May 13] fairly useful at best, little impact sole outing on Flat in 2017: stays 2m: acts on polytrack, good to firm and good to soft going: has worn tongue tie: fair hurdler/fairly useful chaser. *James Moffatt*

FANTASY QUEEN 4 b.f. Aqlaam 125 – Regal Curtsy 67 (Royal Applause 124) [2017 **75**
67: p7g^{3} 7m^{5} 8.1m* 8.1m^{3} 8.1g* 8.1d^{5} 8g^{4} p8g Oct 5] workmanlike filly: fair handicapper: won at Chepstow in June and July: stays 1m: acts on polytrack, good to firm and good to soft going: tried in cheekpieces. *Eve Johnson Houghton*

FARAASAH (IRE) 2 br.g. (Mar 28) Arcano (IRE) 122 – Falsafa (Dansili 127) [2017 6g^{2} **82**
6m^{6} 6.5g p6d Sep 28] first foal: dam unraced half-sister to smart 2-y-o 7f winner (stays 1¼m) Mustadeem (by Arcano): fairly useful form when second in minor event at Newmarket on debut, standout effort. *Brian Meehan*

FARADAYS SPARK (IRE) 2 br.c. (Apr 23) Dragon Pulse (IRE) 114 – High Reserve 95 **60**
(Dr Fong (USA) 128) [2017 5m 5m^{4} 5g^{6} 6m 7g* 7d^{3} 7s^{3} p7g^{4} 7g* 8v^{6} 8g p10g Oct 26] modest performer: won sellers at Redcar in June and Catterick in August: stays 1¼m: acts on polytrack, soft and good to firm going: often races prominently: sold 5,000 gns, sent to Italy. *Richard Fahey*

FARAGE (IRE) 3 b.f. High Chaparral (IRE) 132 – Advertising Space (IRE) (Galileo **–**
(IRE) 134) [2017 12d 8.3v^{4} Sep 5] fifth foal: half-sister to smart 1¼m-1¾m winner Ralston Road (by Dylan Thomas) and useful 11f-1¾m winner Carbon Dating (by The Carbon Unit), both stay 2m: dam unraced: well held in maidens. *John Patrick Shanahan, Ireland*

FARAWAY FIELDS (USA) 2 b.c. (Feb 22) First Defence (USA) 119 – Faraway Flower **64**
(USA) 98 (Distant View (USA) 126) [2017 8d^{6} Oct 27] lengthy, unfurnished colt: 40/1, sixth in minor event at Newbury (7½ lengths behind Military Law) in October: will be suited by 1¼m+. *Charles Hills*

FAR DAWN 2 ch.g. (Mar 20) Helmet (AUS) 127 – Windlass (IRE) 67 (Teofilo (IRE) 126) **70**
[2017 t6g 7.4m^{5} 7s^{3} 8.3v 8m^{3} t8s^{2} t8.6g^{3} p10g^{4} t8.6g^{5} t8g^{4} Dec 6] angular gelding: fair maiden: stays 8.5f: acts on tapeta, soft and good to firm going: in headgear last 4 starts. *Simon Crisford*

FAREEQ 3 gr.g. Dark Angel (IRE) 113 – Spate (IRE) (Danehill Dancer (IRE) 117) [2017 81: 7.2s^5 7d 6g^5 6d p6s^6 p7g t6.1g p7s p6g^6 Dec 31] smallish gelding: fair handicapper: left William Haggas after second start: stays 7f: acts on tapeta, best turf form on good going: in headgear last 4 starts: wears tongue tie. *Charlie Wallis* **73**

FARHH AWAY 2 ch.g. (Apr 18) Farhh 131 – Bukhoor (IRE) (Danehill (USA) 126) [2017 t6s^6 7g^5 Sep 27] 40,000Y: closely related to winner up to 1m Hawfinch (2-y-o 6f winner, by Kyllachy) and half-brother to unreliable 2-y-o 7f winner Rescent (by Reset) and 7f winner Flynn's Boy (by Tobougg): dam unraced: modest form in maiden/minor event: remains open to improvement. *Michael Dods* **63 p**

FARLEIGH MAC 3 ch.g. Equiano (FR) 127 – Le Badie (IRE) (Spectrum (IRE) 126) [2017 84: 7m p7s^6 6.1m* 6f^3 6.1g^2 5.7g^3 6d 5g 6d Sep 23] workmanlike gelding: fairly useful performer: won minor event at Windsor (by 1¼ lengths from Cappananty Con) in June: second in handicap at Chepstow in July: stays 6f: acts on good to firm going: has worn headgear, including last 2 starts: front runner/races prominently: sold 24,000 gns in November, sent to Macau. *Andrew Balding* **88**

FARLOW (IRE) 9 ch.g. Exceed And Excel (AUS) 126 – Emly Express (IRE) (High Estate 127) [2017 105: 7m t6s 7d 7s Jul 29] good-topped gelding: useful handicapper, well below best in 2017: raced mainly at 7f: acts on any turf going: has worn headgear: lazy. *Richard Fahey* **65**

FAROOK (IRE) 3 ro.g. Raven's Pass (USA) 133 – Wrong Answer 102 (Verglas (IRE) 118) [2017 74: p7g^2 t6g^2 6m* 7m^6 a6f* Dec 29] rangy gelding: useful performer: won maiden at Yarmouth in May and handicap at Jebel Ali (by 4¼ lengths from Call To War) in December: left Charles Hills after fourth start: stays 7f: acts on polytrack, tapeta, sand and good to firm going: front runner/races prominently. *E. Charpy, UAE* **95**

FARQUHAR (IRE) 6 ch.g. Archipenko (USA) 127 – Pointed Arch (IRE) 68 (Rock of Gibraltar (IRE) 133) [2017 10.3m^6 14s^3 p10s 11.8m 10g^6 12d^5 Aug 19] sturdy gelding: fairly useful handicapper nowadays: third at Newmarket in May: stays 1½m: acts on soft and good to firm going: often in hood in 2017: often races freely: sold 1,000 gns, sent to Italy. *Michael Appleby* **93**

FARRAH'S CHOICE 5 b.m. Equiano (FR) 127 – Esplanade 77 (Danehill (USA) 126) [2017 –: t9.5g Jan 20] modest maiden at 3 yrs, little form since: stays 6f: acts on good to firm going: has worn headgear: tried in tongue tie. *James Grassick* **–**

FASCINATOR 2 ch.f. (Mar 23) Helmet (AUS) 127 – Mary Read 100 (Bahamian Bounty 116) [2017 t7.1g^2 Nov 24] £28,000Y: fifth foal: half-sister to winner up to 12.3f Dubai Bounty (2-y-o 8.6f winner, by Dubai Destination) and unreliable winner up to 7f Jacquotte Delahaye (2-y-o 6f winner, by Kyllachy): dam, 2-y-o 5f winner, half-sister to smart winner up to 1m Above N Beyond: 20/1, green when second in minor event at Newcastle (1½ lengths behind Windsor Cross) on debut: will stay 1m: sure to progress. *Ann Duffield* **68 p**

FASHAAK (IRE) 4 b.g. Starspangledbanner (AUS) 128 – Szabo (IRE) 88 (Anabaa (USA) 130) [2017 90: 8m^2 8m^6 8m^6 8d^4 8s^2 Sep 19] strong, compact gelding: fairly useful handicapper: second at Yarmouth in May and Redcar in September: stays 1m: acts on soft and good to firm going: often leads: sold 6,000 gns in October. *John Butler* **85**

FASHAAR 4 b.g. Showcasing 117 – Avessia 65 (Averti (IRE) 117) [2017 8d 8.6s 8g^6 10v p8g* Dec 21] fair performer: won handicap at Dundalk in December: stays 1m: acts on polytrack: tried in hood. *Anthony McCann, Ireland* **79**

FASHION BUSINESS 3 b.g. Frankel 147 – Icon Project (USA) 121 (Empire Maker (USA) 129) [2017 p8g^2 p10g* 8f 9f^3 9f 9f^2 8.5f^2 9f^5 Sep 3] third foal: dam, 8.5f-1½m (including US Grade 1 1¼m) winner, half-sister to US Grade 2 9f winner Lasting Approval: useful performer: won maiden at Lingfield in January: left Roger Charlton after: placed in optional claimers at Santa Anita and Del Mar, and Grade 3 La Jolla Handicap (head second to Sharp Samurai) on latter course: stays 1¼m: raced only on firm going on turf, winner on polytrack: blinkered in USA. *Philip d'Amato, USA* **108**

FASHION PARADE 4 b.f. Fastnet Rock (AUS) 127 – Festivale (IRE) 107 (Invincible Spirit (IRE) 121) [2017 92: 12g Jul 14] workmanlike filly: fairly useful handicapper, seemed amiss sole outing in 2017: stays 1½m: acts on polytrack and good to firm going. *Charles Hills* **–**

FASHION QUEEN 3 b.f. Aqlaam 125 – Pizzarra 62 (Shamardal (USA) 129) [2017 89p: 5s* 5m^6 5d^3 5d Oct 1] good-topped filly: smart performer: won listed race at York (by head from Kyllang Rock) in May: neck third to Lady Macapa in Prix du Petit Couvert at **111**

Chantilly in September: below form in Prix de l'Abbaye on latter course final outing: likely to prove best at 5f: acts on soft and good to firm going: usually races close up/travels strongly. *David O'Meara*

FASHION SENSE (IRE) 2 b.f. (Apr 26) Clodovil (IRE) 116 – Speckled Hen (IRE) 60 (Titus Livius (FR) 115) [2017 6s^3 5.7s^6 Oct 2] €23,000F, £22,000Y: sixth foal: sister to smart 7f-9f winner Third Time Lucky, and half-sister to useful winner up to 8.2f Baba O'Riley (2-y-o 6f winner, by Whipper) and winner up to 1½m Rockfield Last (2-y-o 5f/6f winner, by Frozen Power): dam maiden (stayed 7f): fair form when third at Ascot (6½ lengths behind Odyssa) on first of 2 starts in minor events. *Clive Cox* **66**

FASHION THEORY 3 b.f. Dubawi (IRE) 129 – Lady's Purse 107 (Doyen (IRE) 132) [2017 73p: 10d^5 11.6d^4 9.9d^2 10.9g* 10.9s* 9.9g^2 11.4d^5 10.4s^2 Nov 15] good-topped filly: fairly useful performer: left Charlie Appleby after second start: won maiden at Niort and minor event at La-Roche-Posay, both in September: stays 11.5f: acts on soft going: tried in cheekpieces: sold €45,000 in December, has joined Tim Easterby. *H-A. Pantall, France* **85**

FAS (IRE) 3 b.c. Fastnet Rock (AUS) 127 – Sotka (Dutch Art 126) [2017 6d* 6m* 6.5g 6g Aug 27] first foal: dam, 2-y-o 5f winner, half-sister to high-class 5f winner Sole Power: smart performer: successful at Chantilly in listed race in March and Prix Sigy (beat subsequent Poule d'Essai des Pouliches winner Precieuse 3½ lengths) in April, making all both times: off 4 months, last at Deauville in Prix Maurice de Gheest and Prix de Meautry (blinkered): stays 6.5f: acts on good to firm and good to soft going. *Mme Pia Brandt, France* **117**

FAS LE FIOS (IRE) 2 b.f. (Feb 19) Epaulette (AUS) 126 – Saffa Garden (IRE) 49 (King's Best (USA) 132) [2017 4.5g t5s^4 5g* Apr 25] half-sister to 3 winners, including useful winner up to 1½m Paddys Motorbike (2-y-o 1m winner, by Fast Company) and winner up to 7f Blue Lotus (2-y-o 5f winner, by Elnadim): dam maiden half-sister to very smart 6f winner Danetime: fair form: won claimer at Maisons-Laffitte (by short neck from So Sora) in April: best effort at 5f. *J. S. Moore* **72**

FAST ACT (IRE) 5 ch.g. Fast Company (IRE) 126 – Nullarbor (Green Desert (USA) 127) [2017 93: 5m 5g^6 5g^6 5g 5d p5d 5v^5 t5.1g^2 t5.1g p5g^5 Dec 15] fairly useful handicapper: second at Wolverhampton in November: best at 5f: acts on polytrack, tapeta and good to firm going: has worn headgear, including last 3 starts: front runner/races prominently. *Kevin Ryan* **81**

FASTALONG (IRE) 2 b.f. (Apr 13) Fastnet Rock (AUS) 127 – Nidina (IRE) (Hurricane Run (IRE) 134) [2017 6d^6 7d^4 7d 8g^6 5.9v 6.9v^5 Sep 18] 21,000Y: first foal: dam, 1¼m winner, half-sister to winner up to 1m Joanna and winner up to 11f Cazals (both smart): modest maiden: should be suited by 1m. *Tim Easterby* **60**

FAST AND FURIOUS (IRE) 4 b.g. Rock of Gibraltar (IRE) 133 – Ocean Talent (USA) (Aptitude (USA) 128) [2017 t7.1g Feb 14] fairly useful at 2 yrs, well beaten sole start since: stays 6f: best form on good going. *James Bethell* **–**

FAST AND HOT (IRE) 4 gr.g. Fastnet Rock (AUS) 127 – Hotelgenie Dot Com 107 (Selkirk (USA) 129) [2017 77: p12d p10m p10g^2 p10g^5 10g^5 10s* 10m* 11.2g^4 10m^2 10g* 10g^3 10d^3 9.9g p10g^6 10.2d^2 10d Oct 23] leggy gelding: fairly useful handicapper: won at Newbury (apprentice) and Windsor in May, and at Windsor again (by 2¼ lengths from Squiggley) in July: stays 1¼m: acts on polytrack, soft and good to firm going: wears headgear: usually races prominently. *Richard Hannon* **89** **a78**

FASTAR (IRE) 3 ch.g. Fast Company (IRE) 126 – Asterism 83 (Motivator 131) [2017 72p: p7g^3 p8g^5 8.1g* 8.2d^2 8m^6 8g* 8.2v* Sep 29] lengthy gelding: useful handicapper: won at Windsor in July, and at Sandown and Haydock (by 1¾ lengths from Silvery Moon) in September: stays 1m: acts on polytrack and heavy going. *Brian Meehan* **97**

FAST DANCER (IRE) 5 b.g. Fast Company (IRE) 126 – Tereed Elhawa 75 (Cadeaux Genereux 131) [2017 92: 7m^4 7m^6 10.3g^5 7m^2 8.1m^3 8g* 9.1d 10d^2 9.9g^4 10.1v^4 Oct 1] lengthy gelding: fairly useful handicapper: won at Bath (by 2¼ lengths from Zlatan) in July: second at Newbury in August: stays 1¼m: acts on polytrack, tapeta, good to firm and heavy going: has worn headgear, including in 2017: often races towards rear. *Joseph Tuite* **92**

FAST KAR (IRE) 3 b.f. Fast Company (IRE) 126 – Karlinha (IRE) (Desert Style (IRE) 121) [2017 p6g^5 p6g p5g^5 t6g^4 t7.1g^6 t7.1g p8g 5g 5m 5g 6g 6d 7d 5d 5d t7.1s Nov 30] second foal: dam, 1m-9.5f winner, half-sister to useful winner up to 1½m Filios: modest handicapper: won maiden at Lyon Parilly for M. Palussiere in 2016: stays 6f: acts on polytrack and soft going: tried in headgear. *Barry John Murphy, Ireland* **58**

Totescoop6 Victoria Cup (Heritage Handicap), Ascot—
Fastnet Tempest is produced to land this valuable handicap, with George William (left), Zhui Feng (cheekpieces) and Shady McCoy (star on cap) completing the frame

FAST LANDING 3 b.g. Raven's Pass (USA) 133 – Miss Lucifer (FR) 119 (Noverre (USA) 125) [2017 –p: t7.1g^{2} t7.1g* Jan 31] fairly useful form: in cheekpieces, won maiden at Wolverhampton (by 2¾ lengths from Naab) in January: raced only at 7f. *Saeed bin Suroor* **85**

FASTNET BLAST (IRE) 4 b.g. Fastnet Rock (AUS) 127 – Bright Bank (IRE) (Sadler's Wells (USA) 132) [2017 76: t10.2g^{2} t9.5m^{4} Jan 23] strong gelding: fair maiden: stays 1½m: acts on polytrack, tapeta and good to firm going: wears blinkers: often races towards rear: sent to Singapore. *Ed Walker* **77**

FASTNET SPIN (IRE) 3 b.f. Fastnet Rock (AUS) 127 – Lucky Spin 116 (Pivotal 124) [2017 79§: 8.1m^{5} 10g 8.2d^{3} 7g^{6} 8.1m^{3} 8m^{2} 8.1m^{5} 7.1v^{2} 6v^{2} 8.1s^{3} 8v* 8.2v* 8.1m^{6} 8d^{6} Oct 27] rather leggy filly: fairly useful handicapper: won at Ffos Las and Leicester (dead-heated with Zaria) in September: stays 8.5f: acts on good to firm and heavy going: wears headgear/tongue tie: usually races nearer last than first: sold 35,000 gns in October, sent to Saudi Arabia. *David Evans* **86**

FASTNET TEMPEST (IRE) 4 b.g. Fastnet Rock (AUS) 127 – Dame Blanche (IRE) 67 (Be My Guest (USA) 126) [2017 97: 8m^{3} 7m* 7.6g* 8m 7d p7s 7g 8s^{2} 8g* Nov 11] lengthy gelding: useful handicapper: won at Ascot (Victoria Cup, by ¾ length from George William) and Chester (by neck from Penwortham), both in May, and Flemington (by head from Raw Impulse) in November: stays 10.5f: acts on soft and good to firm going: wears headgear: often races towards rear. *William Haggas* **106**

FAST ON (IRE) 8 gr.g. Verglas (IRE) 118 – Dream State (IRE) (Machiavellian (USA) 123) [2017 58: p10g^{5} 10d Apr 15] modest handicapper, below form both outings in 2017: stays 11.5f: acts on polytrack, fibresand, good to firm and heavy going: wears headgear: sometimes slowly away, often races towards rear. *Seamus Fahey, Ireland* **44**

FAST PLAY (IRE) 5 b.m. Fast Company (IRE) 126 – Akariyda (IRE) (Salse (USA) 128) [2017 75: p12g* t12.2g^{3} t12.2g* t13.9g t12.2g^{5} p13.3d t9.5g p11g t12.2g^{6} 14v t12.2g f12.1g Aug 28] sturdy mare: fair performer: won seller at Lingfield in January and handicap at Wolverhampton in February: left Richard Hughes after second start: stays 1½m: acts on polytrack, tapeta, best turf form on good going: wears headgear. *Conor Dore* **78**

FAST TACK (IRE) 3 b.g. Fast Company (IRE) 126 – Green Vision (IRE) (Green Desert (USA) 127) [2017 –: t6m^{5} t5g Mar 3] little impact in maidens. *John Quinn* **–**

FAST TRACK 6 b.g. Rail Link 132 – Silca Boo 99 (Efisio 120) [2017 98: t6m* p6g^{4} t6g^{3} t6g^{3} p6g^{3} p5g^{3} 5m p6g t5g t5.1g^{2} t6.1d^{4} Dec 16] strong gelding: useful handicapper: won at Wolverhampton (by neck from Oriental Relation) in January: placed 5 times after: stays 6f: acts on polytrack, tapeta, good to firm and good to soft going: has worn hood: often races prominently. *David Barron* **96**

FATA MORGANA 2 b.f. (Apr 3) Society Rock (IRE) 126 – Life's A Whirl 77 **–**
(Machiavellian (USA) 123) [2017 8d Oct 24] third foal: dam, 1m winner, half-sister to
smart 6f winner Musical Comedy out of useful 1¼m winner Spinning Top: 250/1, well held
in minor event at Yarmouth. *Christine Dunnett*

FATHER AILBE (IRE) 2 b.g. (Mar 30) Excelebration (IRE) 133 – Ms Sophie Eleanor **71 p**
(USA) 70 (Grand Slam (USA) 120) [2017 p7s p7s^{4} t8.6d^{3} Dec 27] fifth foal: half-brother
to 6f winner Trillian Astra (by Bahamian Bounty): dam, 7f winner, half-sister to smart
winner up to 10.4f Saratoga Springs: fair form: best effort when third in minor event at
Wolverhampton (3½ lengths behind Antonian) in December: open to further improvement.
John Butler

FATHER BERTIE 5 b.g. Firebreak 125 – Magical Music 96 (Fraam 114) [2017 101: 8g **84**
8g 8g^{6} 8m 7.8v^{6} 8s^{6} 8g Oct 7] useful handicapper, below form in 2017: stays 1m: acts on
soft and good to firm going: wears cheekpieces/tongue tie: usually races prominently.
Tim Easterby

FATHER MCKENZIE 3 b.g. Sixties Icon 125 – Queen of Narnia 67 (Hunting Lion **80**
(IRE) 115) [2017 82: 5.1g^{5} 6m 6d^{2} 6.1d^{3} p6g^{2} 6d^{4} 5d p6g^{5} Oct 18] stocky gelding: fairly
useful handicapper: placed at Lingfield/Nottingham in May and Kempton in July: stays 6f:
acts on polytrack, good to firm and good to soft going: races prominently: consistent.
James Eustace

FATTSOTA 9 b.g. Oasis Dream 129 – Gift of The Night (USA) (Slewpy (USA)) [2017 98: **95**
t12.4g^{5} p12m^{6} f11g^{5} Apr 18] lengthy gelding: smart handicapper at best: stayed 12.5f:
acted on tapeta, firm and soft going: tried in visor: front runner/raced prominently: dead.
David O'Meara

FAULKWOOD 3 gr.g. Hellvelyn 118 – Sleep Dance 62 (Sleeping Indian 122) [2017 75: **–**
f5g 6s 6d Oct 20] fair form at 2 yrs, little impact in 2017: in visor last 2 starts. *K. R. Burke*

FAVORITE GIRL (GER) 9 b.m. Shirocco (GER) 129 – Favorite (GER) (Montjeu (IRE) **76**
137) [2017 74: t9.5g^{4} t12.2g* t12.2g* 10.1g^{2} 10.2d^{4} t12.2g Dec 2] compact mare: fair
handicapper: won at Wolverhampton in January and February: stays 14.5f, usually raced at
shorter: acts on all-weather, soft and good to firm going: front runner/races prominently:
fairly useful hurdler. *Michael Appleby*

FAVOURITE ROYAL (IRE) 3 b.f. Acclamation 118 – Affirmative (Pivotal 124) [2017 **89 §**
71: t7.1g^{2} 7g^{4} t8.6g* 6.9s p8s 7m* 7g 8g p8g p8m* p7g^{5} Dec 6] tall filly: fairly useful
handicapper: won at Wolverhampton in May, Epsom in August and Lingfield (by ¾ length
from Ifubelieveindreams) in November: stays 8.5f: acts on polytrack, tapeta and good to
firm going: often in headgear in 2017: far from straightforward (has flashed tail). *Eve
Johnson Houghton*

FAVOURITE TREAT (USA) 7 b.g. Hard Spun (USA) 124 – Truart (USA) (Yes It's **79**
True (USA) 116) [2017 84: 7m 8g 7m^{3} 7.2g^{3} 7.6d^{6} t6.1g* t6.1g^{5} 7d^{3} 7.4m^{5} 7g^{4} 6v Sep 28]
strong gelding: fair performer nowadays: won claimer at Wolverhampton in July: stays 1m:
acts on polytrack, tapeta, good to firm and heavy going: wears eyeshields. *Ruth Carr*

FAWAAREQ (IRE) 4 b.g. Invincible Spirit (IRE) 121 – Ghandoorah (USA) (Forestry **99**
(USA) 121) [2017 99: 7m^{3} 7m^{3} 7d 7.2v Oct 16] useful-looking gelding: useful handicapper:
third at Haydock (2½ lengths behind Afjaan) in April and Newmarket (3¾ lengths behind
Parfait) in July: stays 1m: acts on firm and soft going: often travels strongly. *Owen Burrows*

FAYEZ (IRE) 3 b.g. Zoffany (IRE) 121 – Gems 73 (Haafhd 129) [2017 84: 7.5m^{5} 7.2m^{3} **102**
8m^{5} 6.9d^{5} 7d^{2} 7d^{6} t8.6g* p8g^{4} 8.9s^{5} t8d* t10.2d^{3} p10g* t9.5g Dec 2] rather leggy gelding:
useful handicapper: won at Wolverhampton (lady riders) in August, Newcastle in
September and Lingfield (by neck from Brex Drago) in November: stays 1¼m: acts on
polytrack, tapeta, firm and good to soft going: often races towards rear. *David O'Meara*

FAYROUZ 2 ch.f. (Jan 17) Sepoy (AUS) 129 – Mango Mischief (IRE) 110 (Desert King **–**
(IRE) 129) [2017 7d Sep 12] 48,000Y: fourth foal: half-sister to smart 1m-1¼m winner
Mango Diva (by Holy Roman Emperor): dam winner up to 10.3f (2-y-o 7f winner): 40/1,
very green when well held in minor event at Leicester: sent to UAE. *Ismail Mohammed*

FAYROUZ ROSE (IRE) 2 b.f. (Apr 28) Epaulette (AUS) 126 – Very Nice (Daylami **81 p**
(IRE) 138) [2017 8.3d* Oct 4] 26,000Y: half-sister to 3 winners, including useful 6f/7f
winner Seek N' Destroy (by Exceed And Excel) and winner up to 1m Very Elusive (2-y-o
6f winner, by Elusive City): dam unraced: 25/1, won maiden at Nottingham (by ½ length
from La Diva) on debut: should progress. *Mick Channon*

FEARLESS LAD (IRE) 7 b.g. Excellent Art 125 – Souffle 105 (Zafonic (USA) 130) **59**
[2017 75: 11.6d^{5} p15.8g^{6} Sep 26] good-topped gelding: fair handicapper, below form both
starts in 2017: should stay 2m: acts on polytrack: has worn tongue tie. *John Best*

FEARSOME 3 b.c. Makfi 130 – Lixian (Linamix (FR) 127) [2017 p10m^3 10s^3 9.9d^3 p12g^3 Oct 18] 38,000F, €70,000Y: seventh foal: half-brother to 3 winners, including useful 9.5f-1½m winner Bit By Bit (by Rail Link): dam, placed up to 1¾m, half-sister to useful 9f-1½m winner Weald: fairly useful form when placed in maidens: will stay beyond 1½m: sold 24,000 gns in October. *Ralph Beckett* **84**

FEAR THE FURY (USA) 3 ch.g. Elusive Quality (USA) – O Beautiful (USA) (Unbridled's Song (USA) 125) [2017 60p: t7.1m* t7.1g^5 8m^3 8f 7d a7f a7f* a8f a8.4f Dec 23] fairly useful performer: won maiden at Wolverhampton in January and handicap at Jebel Ali in November: left K. R. Burke after fifth start: stays 8.5f: acts on tapeta, sand and good to firm going: in tongue tie last 4 starts. *A. bin Harmash, UAE* **83**

FEEBS 2 ch.g. (Apr 28) Assertive 121 – Fujakka (IRE) (Vettori (IRE) 119) [2017 5g 5g^3 6v* 6v^6 6d^6 Nov 11] fair performer: won maiden at Haydock in September: best effort at 6f: acts on heavy going. *Michael Easterby* **77**

FEELTHERHYTHM (IRE) 6 b.m. Yeats (IRE) 128 – Queen Althea (IRE) 89 (Bach (IRE) 121) [2017 58: t16.3g^6 Mar 15] modest maiden: stayed 15f: acted on polytrack, raced only on good going on turf: wore headgear last 5 starts: dead. *Chris Grant* **47**

FEEL THE VIBES 3 b.g. Medicean 128 – Apple Dumpling 50 (Haafhd 129) [2017 68: 7g 7g^6 p8d^4 t8.6g^5 p12d Aug 16] smallish gelding: fair maiden: stays 1m: acts on polytrack, good to firm and good to soft going: in headgear last 3 starts. *Michael Blanshard* **65**

FEEL THE WRATH (IRE) 2 br.g. (Mar 8) Arcano (IRE) 122 – Takaliya (IRE) (Darshaan 133) [2017 p7d 7m 7g Nov 3] well held in minor events. *Denis Quinn* **–**

FEINT 3 ch.f. Teofilo (IRE) 126 – Ruse 66 (Diktat 126) [2017 8m^3 8.3g^5 10.2f^2 p10g* Oct 5] half-sister to several winners, including useful 7f/1m winner Flying Hammer (by Acclamation) and useful winner up to 6f Alkhor (2-y-o 5f winner, by Exceed And Excel): dam maiden (stayed 1½m), half-sister to smart winner up to 7f Ardkinglass: fairly useful form: won handicap at Chelmsford (by ½ length from Rayaa) in October: stays 1¼m: tried in tongue tie: open to further improvement. *William Haggas* **84 p**

FEISTY GIRL 7 ch.m. Erhaab (USA) 127 – Dolly Duff (Alflora (IRE) 120) [2017 –: p12g Jan 28] well held both starts in Flat maidens: in blinkers second time. *Michael Mullineaux* **–**

FEISTY ONE U R 3 b.f. Monsieur Bond (IRE) 120 – Formidable Girl (USA) 57 (Roman Ruler (USA) 122) [2017 p8d p8g Feb 1] second foal: dam, maiden (stayed 8.6f), half-sister to useful US 2-y-o 8.5f (minor stakes) winner House of Grace: modest form on second of 2 starts in maidens. *George Baker* **55**

FELISA 2 b.f. (Mar 28) Multiplex 114 – Limegrove 79 (Captain Gerrard (IRE) 113) [2017 t5.1g^4 5.3m^3 5.1m^5 6.1g^6 6m^5 7s^6 t6.1g^4 7g^2 6m^2 7d* 6v^4 7g^4 7d^4 p7g^3 f8.1g^2 Dec 29] small filly: first foal: dam 2-y-o 5f/6f winner: fair performer: won seller at Leicester in September: stays 1m: acts on all-weather, good to firm and heavy going: has worn visor, including last 2 starts: often races prominently: consistent. *David Evans* **68**

FELIX MENDELSSOHN (IRE) 6 b.g. Galileo (IRE) 134 – Ice Queen (IRE) 118 (Danehill Dancer (IRE) 117) [2017 104: 12d^3 14d p12g 16v Oct 8] rangy gelding: useful handicapper: third at the Curragh (2¼ lengths behind Glamorous Approach) in May: should stay 1¾m: acts on firm and good to soft going: in tongue tie last 4 starts: often races towards rear: sold £6,500 in November. *Joseph Patrick O'Brien, Ireland* **99**

FELSTEAD KNIGHT (IRE) 2 b.g. (Mar 27) Tough As Nails (IRE) 108 – Fine Day (Fantastic Light (USA) 134) [2017 p6g Oct 24] 66/1, well held in minor event at Kempton. *Joseph Tuite* **–**

FELSTEAD QUEEN 3 ch.f. Bated Breath 125 – Today's The Day 72 (Alhaarth (IRE) 126) [2017 –: 7.1d Jun 6] workmanlike filly: no form. *Joseph Tuite* **–**

FENAGH (IRE) 2 b.f. (Feb 7) Dabirsim (FR) 120 – Book of Manners (King's Best (USA) 132) [2017 6s 6.1g^4 p7d 7g Sep 7] first foal: dam 12.5f winner: fair form when fourth in minor event at Chepstow in July, standout effort: tried in cheekpieces. *David Loughnane* **66**

FEN CAROLINE 2 gr.f. (Apr 9) Sir Percy 129 – Half Moon Hotel (With Approval (CAN)) [2017 8.3d Oct 18] 5,500Y: third foal: dam unraced half-sister to useful/temperamental winner up to 2m Bowdler's Magic: 100/1, well held in maiden at Nottingham. *Robert Cowell* **–**

FENDALE 5 b.g. Exceed And Excel (AUS) 126 – Adorn 105 (Kyllachy 129) [2017 99: 6g Aug 19] strong, good-topped gelding: useful handicapper, well beaten sole start in 2017: stays 6f: acts on soft and good to firm going: tried in cheekpieces: often travels strongly. *Antony Brittain* **–**

FENGATE 4 ch.f. Champs Elysees 124 – Allegro Viva (USA) (Distant View (USA) 126) [2017 9.9m4 10.3g2 10.2g4 11.5d Sep 21] sister to 1½m winner Busy Street, closely related to smart French 1½m/15f (Group 2) winner Canticum (by Cacique) and half-sister to 2 winners, including useful 1m-1½m winner Uphold (by Oasis Dream): dam unraced sister to Dewhurst Stakes winner Distant Music: fairly useful performer: won minor event at Marseilles Vivaux for D. Smaga in 2016: second in handicap at York in July: stays 10.5f: acts on polytrack and good to firm going: tried in tongue tie: sold 9,000 gns in October, sent to Saudi Arabia. *Roger Charlton* **86**

FENISA'S HOOK 2 ch.g. (Mar 10) Lope de Vega (IRE) 125 – Islandia (USA) (Johar (USA) 130) [2017 8d p10g4 Nov 29] fair form: better effort when fourth in maiden at Kempton (3½ lengths behind Ispolini) in November. *Warren Greatrex* **76**

FENNAAN (IRE) 2 br.c. (Feb 16) Footstepsinthesand 120 – Sanadaat (Green Desert (USA) 127) [2017 p7s5 7m* Sep 23] €50,000Y: second foal: dam, unraced, out of half-sister to Phoenix Stakes winner Alfred Nobel: fairly useful form: won minor event at Newbury (by head from Sam Gold) in September: will stay 1m+: wears hood/tongue tie: open to further improvement. *John Gosden* **89 p**

FENNANN 6 b.g. Dutch Art 126 – Embraced 103 (Pursuit of Love 124) [2017 p15.8m t16.5g Feb 13] rangy gelding: fair at best, no form in 2017 (including over hurdles) after long absence: wears headgear: temperamental. *Natalie Lloyd-Beavis* **– §**

FENNER HILL NEASA (IRE) 4 b.f. Alfred Nobel (IRE) 110 – A Woman In Love 87 (Muhtarram (USA) 125) [2017 52: 11.9m 9.9g 9.9m Jun 27] maiden: no form in 2017: usually wears hood: usually slowly away. *Pat Phelan* **–**

FERAGUST 2 b.g. (Mar 4) Poet's Voice 126 – Faciascura (Oratorio (IRE) 128) [2017 p8s 8.3d t8.6m5 Oct 31] best effort (fair form) in minor events/maiden on final start. *Marco Botti* **66**

FERGALL (IRE) 10 br.g. Norwich 118 – Gaybrook Girl (IRE) (Alderbrook 120) [2017 90: p11g p12g4 Jun 7] fairly useful handicapper: stays 13f: raced exclusively on polytrack: useful hurdler. *Seamus Mullins* **87**

FERIK (IRE) 2 b.g. (May 10) Arcano (IRE) 122 – Love And Laughter (IRE) 74 (Theatrical) [2017 6f6 7m6 7.1m2 7g2 8.1m2 Aug 14] €44,000Y: rather unfurnished gelding: half-brother to 3 winners, including very smart winner up to 1½m Wigmore Hall (2-y-o 1m winner, by High Chaparral) and useful 1¼m winner Lady Liberty (by Shirocco): dam 2-y-o 7f winner: fairly useful maiden: second in nurseries at Leicester in July and Windsor in August: stays 1m: acts on good to firm going: usually races close up. *David Evans* **84**

FERNGROVE (USA) 6 gr.g. Rockport Harbor (USA) 114 – Lucky Pipit 102 (Key of Luck (USA) 126) [2017 t10.2d 12.1g3 t16.3s 12.5s 10d Oct 20] tall gelding: modest maiden: stays 1½m: acts on heavy going: wears hood/tongue tie. *Susan Corbett* **53**

FERN OWL 5 ch.g. Nayef (USA) 129 – Snow Goose 111 (Polar Falcon (USA) 126) [2017 89: f16g* f16d3 Apr 6] rangy gelding: fairly useful handicapper: won at Southwell (by ¾ length from Start Seven) in February: stays 2m: acts on all-weather and firm going: wears headgear: sold to join Eoin Doyle 20,000 gns in July. *Hughie Morrison* **93**

FEROCITY (IRE) 3 b.g. Poet's Voice 126 – Foreign Language (USA) 80 (Distant View (USA) 126) [2017 81p: p6g5 t5.1m6 t7.1d p6g t7.2m6 Oct 28] fair handicapper: stays 7f: acts on tapeta: in cheekpieces last 2 starts. *Robyn Brisland* **75**

FERRIER 2 b.f. (Mar 25) Iffraaj 127 – Ratukidul (FR) 79 (Danehill (USA) 126) [2017 6.1v5 6m 7d Sep 12] half-sister to several winners, including useful winner up to 1½m Kithonia (2-y-o 7f winner, by Sadler's Wells) and useful 1m winner Rifle Range (by Shamardal): dam, 2-y-o 7f winner, half-sister to high-class 1¼m-1½m winner Hernando: little impact in minor events: hooded first 2 starts. *Sir Mark Prescott Bt* **–**

FERRYVIEW PLACE 8 b.g. Compton Place 125 – Songsheet 74 (Dominion 123) [2017 61: t9.5m t9.5m4 t8.6m t9.5g4 t9.5g5 p11d6 Feb 15] tall gelding: modest handicapper: stays 11.5f, raced mainly at shorter: acts on polytrack, tapeta, best turf form on good going: wears headgear: often wears tongue tie: often starts slowly, usually races towards rear. *Ian Williams* **56**

FESTIVAL OF AGES (USA) 3 b.g. Medaglia d'Oro (USA) 129 – November (USA) (A P Indy (USA) 131) [2017 11.6m2 12s* Jul 28] first foal: dam, ran once, half-sister to US Grade 1 9f winner The Cliff's Edge: fairly useful form: won maiden at Newmarket (by ½ length from Kohinur) in July: will go on improving. *Charlie Appleby* **92 p**

FETHIYE BOY 3 br.g. Pastoral Pursuits 127 – Ocean Blaze 91 (Polar Prince (IRE) 117) **85** [2017 74: t6m p5g* 5g* 5d^{3} 5.1d^{4} 5f* 5m* 5f^{4} 5m Aug 16] big, strong gelding: fairly useful performer: won maiden at Chelmsford in February, and handicaps at Windsor in May, Bath in June and Sandown (by head from Kasbah) in July: raced mainly at 5f: acts on polytrack, firm and good to soft going: front runner. *Ronald Harris*

FEVER FEW 8 b.m. Pastoral Pursuits 127 – Prairie Oyster 68 (Emperor Jones (USA) 119) **63** [2017 78: 6m 7g 6m p7g^{2} p6g Sep 26] tall, lengthy mare: modest handicapper nowadays: raced at 6f/7f: acts on polytrack and good to firm going: tried in cheekpieces: often races prominently: inconsistent. *Chris Wall*

FIBONACCI 3 ch.c. Galileo (IRE) 134 – Tereschenko (USA) (Giant's Causeway (USA) **85** 132) [2017 76p: p10g^{3} 11.5m^{2} 11.9m^{5} 11.6g* 11.8s^{4} Oct 10] big colt: fairly useful performer: won maiden at Haydock (by 3¼ lengths from Line of Beauty) in September: barely stays 1½m: acts on polytrack and good to firm going: often travels strongly: sent to France. *Hugo Palmer*

FICANAS 2 b.f. (Mar 5) Sepoy (AUS) 129 – Windermere Island 81 (Cadeaux Genereux **85 p** 131) [2017 8d^{2} Oct 27] 48,000Y: half-sister to several winners, including 2-y-o 5f winner Lady Ro (by Showcasing) and 6f-7f winner Flexible Flyer (by Exceed And Excel): dam 7f winner: 50/1, second in maiden at Doncaster (1¼ lengths behind Mrs Sippy) in October: should improve. *Marco Botti*

FIDAAWY 4 ch.g. New Approach (IRE) 132 – Haymana (IRE) (Pivotal 124) [2017 101: **116** 10.3m* 10.1m 12d 11.9g* 10m^{2} 9m Oct 14] workmanlike gelding: smart handicapper: won at Doncaster (by ½ length from Sam Missile) in April and York (by ½ length from Red Galileo) in August: second at Newbury (length behind Brorocco) in September: stays 1½m: acts on good to firm and good to soft going: tried in hood: often races prominently. *Sir Michael Stoute*

FIDELMA MOON (IRE) 5 b.m. Dylan Thomas (IRE) 132 – Ridiforza (FR) **59** (Starborough 126) [2017 82: 8.5m 7m 7g^{3} 6.9v^{5} t7.2g^{5} 7.4s^{6} 8.3s 7m 9v 8g^{6} 8v Nov 7] leggy mare: fairly useful handicapper, well below form in 2017: left K. R. Burke after fifth start: stays 8.5f: acts on tapeta and heavy going: has worn headgear, including last 2 starts: tried in tongue tie: usually races close up. *Tracy Waggott*

FIDRA BAY (IRE) 4 b.f. Roderic O'Connor (IRE) 119 – Halicardia 104 (Halling (USA) **58** 133) [2017 78: 7.1m^{6} 8g May 15] maiden, below best both starts in 2017: stays 1m: acts on heavy going. *Alan Swinbank*

FIELD OF VISION (IRE) 4 b.g. Pastoral Pursuits 127 – Grand Design 64 (Danzero **84** (AUS)) [2017 102: 6.1d^{6} 7m 6m^{3} 6g^{2} 6g^{6} 6g* 5.7d^{2} 6.1m^{3} 7d^{5} p6g p6s^{4} t6.1g^{5} Dec 18] lengthy, dipped-backed gelding: fairly useful handicapper nowadays: won at Salisbury (by ¾ length from Whitecrest) in August: placed on 4 other occasions in 2017: left Joseph Tuite after eleventh start: stays 6f: acts on polytrack, tapeta, firm and soft going: has worn cheekpieces, including final start: tried in tongue tie. *John Flint*

FIELDSMAN (USA) 5 b.g. Hard Spun (USA) 124 – R Charlie's Angel (USA) (Indian **87** Charlie (USA) 126) [2017 96: 7g^{6} 8s 7.2m^{4} 7.2d^{5} 7g 6g 7d^{2} 7m^{2} 7g^{3} p7d^{6} p7d^{5} 7v Oct 21] rather leggy gelding: fairly useful handicapper: second at Redcar and Yarmouth in August: stays 7f: acts on polytrack, soft and good to firm going: has worn headgear, including final start: sold 20,000 gns in October. *David O'Meara*

FIELDS OF FORTUNE 3 b.g. Champs Elysees 124 – Widescreen (USA) (Distant View **78** (USA) 126) [2017 71: 8.3m^{5} 9.9f^{5} 9.9m^{3} 9.9d 12m^{6} p12g^{5} p16g^{4} 14.2v^{2} Oct 4] good-topped gelding: fair maiden: left Richard Hannon after fifth start: stays 1¾m: acts on good to firm and heavy going: tried in hood. *Alan King*

FIENDISH (USA) 3 ch.f. Street Cry (IRE) 130 – Evil (USA) (Hennessy (USA) 122) **75** [2017 t8g^{3} p8g^{2} p10g^{3} 8f^{5} 10m^{2} 8.2s 8m 8g^{4} p8d^{6} Jul 12] closely related to a winner in USA by Street Sense and half-sister to 3 winners there, including Grade 2 2-y-o 8.5f winner Tiz Wonderful (by Tiznow): dam US 6f winner: fair maiden: stays 1¼m: acts on polytrack and good to firm going: temperament under suspicion. *Mark Johnston*

FIERCE IMPACT (JPN) 3 b.c. Deep Impact (JPN) 134 – Keiai Gerbera (JPN) (Smarty **100** Jones (USA) 134) [2017 77p: 10d^{5} 11.2m^{2} 14m 11.1g^{6} 10.1m^{3} t12.2g^{4} Oct 21] good sort: useful performer: placed in listed race at Goodwood (5 lengths behind Khalidi) in May and minor event at Epsom (7½ lengths behind Midterm) in August: stays 1½m: acts on tapeta and good to firm going: in headgear last 3 starts: often races towards rear: sold 120,000 gns in November. *David Simcock*

FIERY BREATH 2 br.c. (Mar 10) Bated Breath 125 – Sunset Kitty (USA) 95 (Gone West (USA)) [2017 6.1m^{4} 6g^{5} 7m Aug 25] modest form in minor events: tried in tongue tie. *Robert Eddery* **55**

FIERY SPICE (IRE) 3 ch.g. Dream Ahead (USA) 133 – High Spice (USA) 92 (Songandaprayer (USA) 118) [2017 –: p6m^{3} f5s* t5d* f5g* f5d^{2} Mar 21] fair performer: won maiden at Southwell in January, and handicaps at Newcastle and again at Southwell (by 2 lengths from Scotch Myst) in March: best at 5f: acted on tapeta and fibresand: dead. *Robert Cowell* **79**

FIFTYSHADESOFGREY (IRE) 6 gr.g. Dark Angel (IRE) 113 – Wohaida (IRE) 71 (Kheleyf (USA) 116) [2017 93: p7d^{3} p7g^{4} 7f 7m^{5} Jun 16] good-topped gelding: useful handicapper: third at Kempton (½ length behind Intransigent) in January: stays 1m: acts on polytrack, good to firm and good to soft going: has worn headgear, including final start: has worn tongue tie. *George Baker* **96**

FIGHTING IRISH (IRE) 2 b.c. (Mar 19) Camelot 128 – Quixotic (Pivotal 124) [2017 6g^{4} 6m^{5} 6s* 7d^{4} 6d* 6d* Oct 13] €50,000F, £70,000Y: strong, sturdy colt: fourth foal: half-brother to 2-y-o 5f winner Well Done (by Lawman): dam unraced sister to very smart 7f-9f winner Virtual: useful performer: won maiden at Salisbury in July, nursery at Yarmouth in September and Criterium de Maisons-Laffitte (3 ran, by head from Nebo) in October: stays 6f: acts on soft going: usually races close up. *Harry Dunlop* **102**

FIGHTING TEMERAIRE (IRE) 4 b.g. Invincible Spirit (IRE) 121 – Hot Ticket (IRE) (Selkirk (USA) 129) [2017 104: 7d 7m^{4} 7d p8s p8g Dec 20] well-made gelding: useful handicapper at best: below form in 2017: stays 1m: acts on polytrack, good to firm and good to soft going. *Dean Ivory* **83**

FIKHAAR 3 b.f. Oasis Dream 129 – Fawaayed (IRE) (Singspiel (IRE) 133) [2017 t7.1g 8d 8.3g t7.1s^{4} p6g* p6g t6s^{4} t5.1g^{6} Dec 13] 4,000 3-y-o: first foal: dam unraced half-sister to Queen Mary Stakes winner Maqaasid out of close relative to 1000 Guineas winner Ghanaati: fair handicapper: won at Chelmsford in September: stays 7f: acts on polytrack and tapeta: front runner/races prominently. *Kevin Ryan* **67**

FILAMENT OF GOLD (USA) 6 b.g. Street Cry (IRE) 130 – Raw Silk (USA) (Malibu Moon (USA)) [2017 68: t9.5g^{3} t9.5g t12.2g* 11.6f^{2} 12g t12.2g t9.5g^{3} t9.5g Nov 7] good-topped gelding: modest handicapper nowadays: won at Wolverhampton (amateur) in May: stays 1½m: acts on polytrack, tapeta and firm going: wears headgear: inconsistent. *Roy Brotherton* **64**

FILATORE (IRE) 8 ch.g. Teofilo (IRE) 126 – Dragnet (IRE) 72 (Rainbow Quest (USA) 134) [2017 –: 16.2m May 5] rather leggy gelding: fairly useful at best, very lightly raced and no form on Flat since 2013: wears headgear: tried in tongue tie: modest hurdler nowadays. *Bernard Llewellyn* **–**

FILBERT STREET 2 ch.c. (Mar 14) Poet's Voice 126 – Tinnarinka 84 (Observatory (USA) 131) [2017 p6s^{4} p6s^{6} Dec 7] modest form when fourth at Chelmsford on first of 2 starts in minor events. *Robert Cowell* **62**

FILLE DE REVE 2 b.f. (Apr 7) Iffraaj 127 – Danehill Dreamer (USA) (Danehill (USA) 126) [2017 p7s^{2} 7g^{3} p7g* Oct 18] 85,000Y: seventh foal: half-sister to 3 winners, including useful 2-y-o 1m winner (stayed 10.5f) Madeed (by Nayef) and useful winner up to 7f Sulaalaat (2-y-o 6f winner, by New Approach): dam unraced half-sister to Eclipse Stakes winner Compton Admiral and Queen Elizabeth II Stakes winner Summoner: fairly useful form: won minor event at Kempton (by 1¼ lengths from Light Relief) in October: bred to stay 1m: remains open to improvement. *Ed Walker* **80 p**

FILLE THE FORCE 3 b.f. Sakhee's Secret 128 – Coup de Torchon (FR) 61 (Namid 128) [2017 6v^{6} 6d 5m^{5} Jul 8] fourth foal: sister to 6f winner Cloak And Degas: dam maiden half-sister to 2 useful winners, including 1¼m-12.5f winner Tashtikar: modest form in maidens: stays 6f. *Scott Dixon* **50**

FILLYDELPHIA (IRE) 6 b.m. Strategic Prince 114 – Lady Fonic 77 (Zafonic (USA) 130) [2017 69: 12g^{2} 10g^{4} 12.5g 12s 12m 13.1s^{3} 12.1m^{6} 12.1s 12.5s 13.9v t12.4d Dec 16] modest handicapper nowadays: stays 13f: acts on tapeta, soft and good to firm going: has worn hood, including final start: usually slowly away, often races in rear: moody. *Patrick Holmes* **62 §**

FILLY MIGNON 2 b.f. (Feb 6) Piccolo 121 – One Pixel (Primo Valentino (IRE) 116) [2017 7m 7d p8g Aug 30] neat filly: first foal: dam unraced half-sister to smart 7f-8.3f winner Fire Ship: little impact in minor events. *Brendan Powell* **–**

FINAL 5 b.g. Arabian Gleam 122 – Caysue (Cayman Kai (IRE) 114) [2017 90: t9.5g^2 p10g* p10d^2 t12.4g* p11g 10g^2 t12.4s^{ur} 9.8m^2 12m^5 10.3d 10.1m Jun 2] sturdy gelding: useful handicapper: won at Lingfield in February and Newcastle (by 1½ lengths from On Fire) in March: also runner-up 4 times in 2017: stays 12.5f: acts on polytrack, tapeta and good to firm going: tried in blinkers. *Mark Johnston* **101**

FINALE 3 b.f. Holy Roman Emperor (IRE) 125 – Sell Out 107 (Act One 124) [2017 p7g^6 f8g^2 f8m^3 8.3s* 8d* 7m^4 8d^2 8.1m^5 Oct 16] fifth foal: closely related to useful 1¼m/11f winner Landwade Lad (by Dansili) and half-sister to 7.5f/1m winner Living Desert (by Oasis Dream) and 7f-11f winner Ariolo (by Teofilo): dam winner up to 1½m (2-y-o 7f winner): fairly useful handicapper: won at Nottingham in June and Sandown (by short head from Kyllachys Tale) in July: stays 8.5f: acts on fibresand and soft going: sometimes idles. *Hughie Morrison* **88**

FINAL FRONTIER (IRE) 4 b.g. Dream Ahead (USA) 133 – Polly Perkins (IRE) 100 (Pivotal 124) [2017 –: 7d 7g Jul 8] angular gelding: useful at 2 yrs, not in same form since: stays 7f: acts on good to firm going: tried in cheekpieces: often races towards rear. *Clive Cox* **79**

FINAL GO 2 b.g. (Apr 16) Equiano (FR) 127 – Ipsa Loquitur 69 (Unfuwain (USA) 131) [2017 5.9s^6 Aug 23] 11/1, green when well held in maiden at Carlisle. *Sally Haynes* **–**

FINAL ROCK 2 b.g. (Feb 26) Rock of Gibraltar (IRE) 133 – Up At Last 67 (Cape Cross (IRE) 129) [2017 6.1m p6g 7f 6m Jul 13] good-bodied gelding: no form in minor events/maiden: tried in cheekpieces. *Sir Mark Prescott Bt* **–**

FINAL SET (IRE) 2 b.f. (Mar 11) Dark Angel (IRE) 113 – Two Sets To Love (IRE) (Cadeaux Genereux 131) [2017 p7s^5 7g^6 Sep 7] €145,000F, 700,000Y: sister to 7f-1¼m winner Emman Bee and useful winner up to 1m Midnite Angel (2-y-o 5f winner) and half-sister to 3 winners, including smart 1¼m winner (stays 12.5f) Cannonball (by Lope de Vega): dam unraced: fair form: better effort when fifth in minor event at Kempton (4½ lengths behind Verandah) in August. *Sir Michael Stoute* **68**

FINAL TREAT (IRE) 2 b.f. (Apr 24) Acclamation 118 – Musical Treat (IRE) 98 (Royal Academy (USA) 130) [2017 6g^4 7m^3 p8s Nov 16] half-sister to several winners, including 1000 Guineas winner (stayed 10.5f) Finsceal Beo (2-y-o 6f-1m winner, by Mr Greeley) and useful winner up to 1m Frozen Power (2-y-o 6f/7f winner, by Oasis Dream): dam 7f/1m winner: fairly useful form when third in maiden at Newmarket (5½ lengths behind Veracious) on second of 3 starts: remains with potential. *William Haggas* **82 p**

FINAL VENTURE 5 b.g. Equiano (FR) 127 – Sharplaw Venture 95 (Polar Falcon (USA) 126) [2017 112: 6g* 6g^3 6g* 6g^5 6d 5f^4 5d* 5f t6s^5 5m^2 5s 5g 5g^2 5d^4 Sep 13] big gelding: smart performer: won handicaps at Meydan in January/February and listed race at Haydock (by neck from Kyllang Rock) in June: second in listed races at York in July and Beverley in September: best at 5f/6f: acts on good to firm and heavy going: often in hood in 2017: usually races prominently. *Paul Midgley* **117**

FINANCIAL CRIME (IRE) 2 b.g. (Mar 1) Red Jazz (USA) 125 – Clodilla (IRE) (Clodovil (IRE) 116) [2017 6.5d p7s^6 p8m^5 Nov 25] no form: in visor last 2 starts. *Mick Channon* **–**

FINE EXAMPLE 4 b.g. Showcasing 117 – Belle Reine (King of Kings (IRE) 125) [2017 75: 8g 7g^2 7.5f* 6.9g^4 7.4m 7.2g^2 7.2m^2 7m^2 7s p7g 7.2v t7.2m Oct 28] strong, compact gelding: fair handicapper: won at Beverley in May: stays 7.5f: acts on polytrack, tapeta, firm and soft going: wears headgear: front runner/races prominently. *Kevin Ryan* **77**

FINELCITY (GER) 4 b.g. Elusive City (USA) 117 – Finity (USA) 94 (Diesis 133) [2017 95: p7g p7g^4 p8g 6d Oct 27] rather leggy gelding: fairly useful handicapper: stays 8.5f: acts on polytrack, best turf form on soft/heavy going: wears headgear: front runner/races prominently: sold 20,000 gns in October. *Harry Dunlop* **92**

FINGAL'S CAVE (IRE) 5 ch.g. Fast Company (IRE) 126 – Indiannie Moon (Fraam 114) [2017 90: t7.1g t7.1g* 7m* 7g^3 8m^3 7.8g 7s* 7m 7.9m 7g^2 8.2d 7.6g 7.6v^5 6v 7s 7d Nov 11] leggy, angular gelding: useful performer: won handicap at Newcastle (apprentice) in March, claimer at Catterick in April and handicap at latter course (by 1¾ lengths from Shouranour) in June: left Iain Jardine after third start: stays 1m: acts on tapeta, firm and soft going. *Philip Kirby* **98**

FINISHER (USA) 2 br.g. (Apr 12) Street Cry (IRE) 130 – Morena (PER) (Privately Held (USA)) [2017 t8s Sep 19] $385,000Y: fourth foal: half-brother to US Grade 1 9f-1½m (Belmont Stakes) winner Creator (by Tapit): dam Grade 2 11f/1½m winner in Peru: 15/2, eighth in minor event at Newcastle (3½ lengths behind Tansheet) in September: should progress. *Kevin Ryan* **63 p**

FINISHING TOUCH 3 b.f. Invincible Spirit (IRE) 121 – Dubai Smile (USA) (Pivotal **83**
124) [2017 7.9m* 8m^3 8v^3 a8.9f Nov 17] second foal: half-sister to 7f-8.5f winner Second Life (by Dubawi): dam 1m winner out of smart 1¼m winner (stayed 1½m) Hi Dubai: fairly useful form: won maiden at York (by ¾ length from Spinnaka) in July: third in handicap at Newmarket next time: stays 1m: in tongue tie last 2 starts. *Saeed bin Suroor*

FINK HILL (USA) 2 b.g. (Feb 9) The Factor (USA) 126 – Matroshka (IRE) (Red **73**
Ransom (USA)) [2017 t6g^6 6d^4 6m^3 t6g^4 p6d^3 7g Oct 16] fair maiden: stays 6f: acts on polytrack, tapeta and good to firm going: in blinkers last 2 starts. *Richard Guest*

FINN CLASS (IRE) 6 b.g. Exceed And Excel (AUS) 126 – Finnmark (Halling (USA) **92 §**
133) [2017 95§: 7g 8m 8s* 9.1s^3 8g^6 8d^2 8d 8s 8.2v 8s^6 Oct 3] useful-looking gelding: fairly useful handicapper: won at Thirsk (by short head from Boots And Spurs) in May: placed at Ayr in June and July: stays 1m: acts on polytrack, soft and good to firm going: has worn headgear, including last 3 starts: tried in tongue tie: carries head awkwardly: hard to catch right: sold 4,000 gns in October, sent to Belgium. *Michael Dods*

FINNION FOX 2 b.g. (Apr 20) Foxwedge (AUS) 128 – Chushka 81 (Pivotal 124) [2017 **66**
7g^5 5.9s^4 6.1v 6v^5 Oct 9] fair form when fourth in maiden at Carlisle in August, standout effort: should stay 7f. *Tim Easterby*

FINNISTON FARM 2 b.c. (Mar 18) Helmet (AUS) 127 – Logic 94 (Slip Anchor 136) **94**
[2017 6f* 7g^6 Jul 15] 65,000Y: half-brother to numerous winners, including useful winner up to 1m Crowley's Law (2-y-o 7.4f winner, by Dubawi) and useful 8.3f-9.7f winner Everybody Knows (by King's Best): dam lightly raced: fairly useful form: won minor event at Haydock (by 1½ lengths from Mutakatif) in May: sixth in Superlative Stakes at Newmarket (2½ lengths behind Gustav Klimt) in July. *Tom Dascombe*

FINN MCCOOL (IRE) 3 b.c. Galileo (IRE) 134 – Mystical Lady (IRE) 106 (Halling **101**
(USA) 133) [2017 96: 12.3m 13m^3 10d^3 12d^5 12.7m 10v Oct 22] strong, well-made colt: useful performer: third in listed race at Navan (2½ lengths behind Naughty Or Nice) and Gallinule Stakes at the Curragh (2 lengths behind Homesman) in May: stays 13f: acts on soft and good to firm going: wears headgear: usually races close up. *Aidan O'Brien, Ireland*

FINSBURY PARK 2 b.g. (Mar 13) Finjaan 122 – Fonnie (IRE) 58 (Barathea (IRE) 127) **83**
[2017 t7.2g^5 7g* 7g 7d^3 7m^3 p8g p7g^5 Oct 25] 2,200Y: tall gelding: third foal: half-brother to 7f winner Reinforced (by Equiano): dam lightly-raced half-sister to useful 2-y-o 6f winner Crown Dependency: fairly useful performer: won minor event at Sandown in July: third in similar event and nursery in August, both at Newmarket: stays 7f: acts on good to soft going: sold to join Ruth Carr 12,000 gns in October. *Robyn Brisland*

FINSBURY SQUARE (IRE) 5 b.g. Siyouni (FR) 122 – Diamond Square (FR) (Dyhim **115**
Diamond (IRE) 117) [2017 115: p6.5g* 6d 5d^3 5g^2 6m^5 6g^2 5d Oct 1] rangy gelding: smart performer: won minor event at Chantilly (by head from Saon Secret) in March: placed after in Prix de Saint-Georges at Deauville, Prix du Gros-Chene at Chantilly (length second to Muthmir) and Prix de Meautry back at Deauville (2 lengths second to Signs of Blessing): 3 lengths fifth to The Tin Man in Diamond Jubilee Stakes at Royal Ascot on fifth outing: stays 6.5f: acts on polytrack, soft and good to firm going: wears headgear: often races towards rear: not straightforward (has flashed tail/wandered under pressure). *F. Chappet, France*

FINTECH (IRE) 3 b.g. Dark Angel (IRE) 113 – Final Legacy (USA) (Boston Harbor **70**
(USA) 122) [2017 t9.5g^5 p8g 6d^4 6s t9.5m p10s^2 p10s^5 Dec 14] fair maiden: left Mrs Ilka Gansera-Leveque after fifth start: stays 1¼m: acts on polytrack and tapeta: wears tongue tie. *Philip Hide*

FINTRY FLYER 3 ch.f. Compton Place 125 – Primo Heights 87 (Primo Valentino (IRE) **59 p**
116) [2017 5g 5d 6g 5m 5s t6s^3 t5d^3 Dec 16] fifth foal: half-sister to 5f/6f winner New Lease of Life (by Orientor) and 7f winner Tommy G (by Makfi): dam 2-y-o 5f winner: modest maiden: stays 6f: acts on tapeta: often in headgear: often races in rear: capable of better again. *Jim Goldie*

FIRBY (IRE) 2 b.g. (Mar 31) Rock of Gibraltar (IRE) 133 – Huffoof (IRE) 83 (Dalakhani **62**
(IRE) 133) [2017 7.2g^4 7g^5 7.4s^5 t7.1g^4 Oct 10] modest form in minor events/nursery: stays 7f. *James Bethell*

FIRE BRIGADE 3 b.g. Firebreak 125 – Island Rhapsody 78 (Bahamian Bounty 116) **108**
[2017 79p: 7m^3 8s* 8.2f^4 8m* 8m^5 8d^3 8.2d* 8s^2 9d^3 8.2d* Oct 30] sturdy gelding: useful handicapper: won at Newmarket (by ½ length from Trading Punches) in May, Haydock in June (by head from Original Choice) and August (by 1¾ lengths from Glorious Forever), and Leicester (by ½ length from Chatez) in October: stays 9f: acts on polytrack, soft and good to firm going: often races towards rear, usually travels strongly. *Michael Bell*

FIRE DIAMOND 4 b.g. Firebreak 125 – Diapason (IRE) 80 (Mull of Kintyre (USA) 114) [2017 75: t7.1g* p7g^4 p8d^4 p7g p7g^5 p8g^6 7.2m 8g p8g t8g p7g t7.2g* t8.6g* p8s^6 t7.2d^2 Dec 26] fairly useful handicapper: won at Wolverhampton in January, October and November (by 1½ lengths from Luang Prabang): second there in December: stays 8.5f: acts on polytrack, tapeta and firm going: wears headgear: has worn tongue tie, including in 2017. *Tom Dascombe* **80**

FIRE EMPRESS 4 b.f. Firebreak 125 – Tedsmore Dame 81 (Indesatchel (IRE) 120) [2017 51: t8.6g p8d^6 t9.5g^6 10.2d^6 Aug 23] leggy filly: maiden: no form in 2017: wears hood: often starts slowly. *James Unett* **–**

FIRE FIGHTING (IRE) 6 b.g. Soldier of Fortune (IRE) 131 – Savoie (FR) (Anabaa (USA) 130) [2017 116: p10.7g^2 p10g^5 p10g 12g^3 12m May 13] medium-sized gelding: smart performer: second in minor event at Dundalk (½ length behind Elbereth) in March: stays 1½m: acts on polytrack, firm and soft going: wears headgear. *Mark Johnston* **111**

FIREFRIGHT (IRE) 3 b.g. Dragon Pulse (IRE) 114 – Emsiyah (USA) 53 (Bernardini (USA) 132) [2017 91: 7m^3 7m* 7m 7m^3 7d* 6g^5 7m^2 Aug 27] compact gelding: useful performer: won maiden at Doncaster in April and handicap there (by 2¼ lengths from Athassel) in July: placed in handicaps at Sandown in between and Yarmouth (1¼ lengths behind Hyde Park) in August: stays 7f: acts on good to firm and good to soft going: gelded, and sent to Singapore. *Jeremy Noseda* **97**

FIREGUARD 4 b.g. Firebreak 125 – Leaping Flame (USA) (Trempolino (USA) 135) [2017 p6s^6 f6.1g f7.1g^5 Dec 29] well held in maidens. *Emma Owen* **–**

FIRE IN BABYLON (IRE) 9 b.g. Montjeu (IRE) 137 – Three Owls (IRE) 79 (Warning 136) [2017 t13.9g p13.3g f12g^5 f11g^6 Apr 18] fair at best, no form in 2017 after long absence: wears headgear: has worn tongue tie. *Giles Bravery* **–**

FIRE JET (IRE) 4 ch.f. Ask 126 – Lightning Jet (Dutch Art 126) [2017 86: t16.5g^4 16.5m^2 14g* 14m^3 14.5s^4 13.3g 14m* 14s^6 14d* p13g Nov 2] small filly: useful handicapper: won at Nottingham in May, Newmarket in August and Nottingham again (by neck from St Mary's) in October: stays 16.5f: acts on good to firm and good to soft going. *John Mackie* **97**

FIRE LEOPARD 3 b.f. Lawman (FR) 121 – Catopuma (USA) (Elusive Quality (USA)) [2017 11.6d^5 10g^3 10d^5 12d^3 12g* 12g 12.1g^2 t12.4g 10g* 12.1s^4 Oct 10] third foal: half-sister to 1½m winner Kip (by Rip Van Winkle) and 6f winner Cat Silver (by Dansili): dam unraced half-sister to smart 7f/1m winner Pounced out of useful 1m winner (stayed 1¼m) Golden Cat: fairly useful handicapper: won at Ripon in August and Redcar (by head from Desert Ruler) in September: stays 1½m: acts on good to soft going: wears hood: sometimes slowly away, usually races in rear. *David O'Meara* **87**

FIRENZE ROSA (IRE) 2 b.f. (Apr 7) Zebedee 113 – Our Nana Rose (IRE) 81 (Viking Ruler (AUS)) [2017 5m 5.3g^4 5m^3 5m^3 5d* 5v 6.1m^4 5g Sep 1] £4,000Y: neat filly: third foal: sister to 1m winner Zebosprint and half-sister to 7f/1m winner Lady Rosebud (by Sir Prancealot): dam, 1m-1¾m winner, also won over hurdles: fair performer: won nursery at Lingfield in July: best form at 5f: acts on good to firm and good to soft going: front runner/races prominently. *John Bridger* **79**

FIRE ORCHID 2 gr.f. (Mar 24) Lethal Force (IRE) 128 – Ring of Love 77 (Magic Ring (IRE) 115) [2017 p7g^5 7d p8g^4 t7.2g^2 p7g* Dec 6] 17,000F, 70,000Y: half-sister to several winners, including useful winner up to 1m (stayed 10.5f) Bahia Breeze (2-y-o 6f winner, by Mister Baileys) and 5f winner Ring For Baileys (by Kyllachy): dam 5f winner (including at 2 yrs): fair performer: won nursery at Lingfield in December: stays 1m: acts on polytrack and tapeta: usually races prominently. *Richard Hannon* **72**

FIRE PALACE 3 b.f. Royal Applause 124 – Inflammable 76 (Montjeu (IRE) 137) [2017 86: 8m 7m 8.1m^4 10.3g^5 10m^5 8d^2 8.2v^5 7d p7g t8g^5 p8s Dec 15] sturdy filly: fair handicapper: stays 1m: acts on polytrack and good to soft going: tried in cheekpieces: usually slowly away, often markedly so, and is not one to rely on. *Robert Eddery* **72 §**

FIRESNAKE (IRE) 4 b.g. Dandy Man (IRE) 123 – La Bataille (USA) (Out of Place (USA)) [2017 71: p6g p6g^5 t7.2g 6d 6s^4 p6g* 6g p6g^5 p6g^3 6s p5s^3 t6.1d Dec 16] good-topped gelding: modest handicapper nowadays: won at Chelmsford in August: stays 7f: acts on polytrack, tapeta, soft and good to firm going: wears headgear: often races prominently: temperamental. *Lisa Williamson* **53 §** **a62 §**

FIRESTORM (GER) 6 b.g. Dylan Thomas (IRE) 132 – Fitness (IRE) (Monsun (GER) **62**
124) [2017 74, a68: p12g^{3} p10d p12g^{6} t13.9m p10g^{4} p10g 13.1s^{6} 10g^{6} 10.2g^{6} 13.3v* 11.2s Aug 7] sturdy gelding: modest handicapper nowadays: won at Newbury (amateur) in July: left Michael Attwater after sixth start: stays 13.5f: acts on heavy going: has worn eyecover, including in 2017: sometimes slowly away, often races in rear. *Richard Ford*

FIRE TREE (IRE) 4 b.g. Cacique (IRE) 124 – Monicalew 77 (Refuse To Bend (IRE) **90**
128) [2017 84: p10m^{3} 8.3g^{5} 8g* 8m* 9.1d 8g 9d Sep 29] sturdy gelding: fairly useful handicapper: won at Wetherby in May and Ascot (apprentice, by ½ length from Brilliant Vanguard) in July: stays 1¼m: acts on polytrack, good to firm and good to soft going: has worn tongue tie, including in 2017. *Charlie Fellowes*

FIRE WHIRL 3 b.g. Sixties Icon 125 – Cyclone Connie 98 (Dr Devious (IRE) 127) [2017 **–**
p10g p8g p8g p11g Oct 25] little form, including in handicap: sold 800 gns, sent to Germany. *William Knight*

FIRGROVE BRIDGE (IRE) 5 ch.g. Dandy Man (IRE) 123 – Over Rating 74 (Desert **–**
King (IRE) 129) [2017 60: t7.1m t6m Jan 13] stocky, close-coupled gelding: fairly useful at best, no form in 2017: stays 1m: acts on polytrack, good to firm and good to soft going: often wears headgear: sometimes slowly away, usually races nearer last than first. *Kevin Frost*

FIRMAMENT 5 b.g. Cape Cross (IRE) 129 – Heaven Sent 116 (Pivotal 124) [2017 121: **117**
8f^{3} 7g^{2} 7g^{5} 8g^{6} 7d^{5} 8g^{5} 7.9d^{3} 7s^{5} 7s 8s Oct 21] close-coupled, good-topped gelding: smart performer: placed in listed race at Ascot (2 lengths behind Tabarrak) in May and handicaps at York later in May and in August: stays 1m: acts on polytrack, tapeta, good to firm and heavy going. *David O'Meara*

FIRMDECISIONS (IRE) 7 b.g. Captain Rio 122 – Luna Crescente (IRE) (Danehill **97**
(USA) 126) [2017 96: p7g^{2} p7d^{6} p7g^{3} p7g^{5} 7m^{3} 7m p8g p7g^{3} 7d 7d p7d p7s^{5} t7.2d Dec 16] big, workmanlike gelding: useful handicapper: placed at Chelmsford/Kempton in January and Yarmouth (neck behind Taurean Star) in May: stays 7f: acts on polytrack and firm going: has worn headgear, including final start. *Dean Ivory*

FIRNAS 4 b.g. Dubawi (IRE) 129 – Crystal Music (USA) 114 (Nureyev (USA) 131) [2017 **103**
93p: 10g 10d^{4} 7.9m Jul 15] rangy gelding: useful handicapper: stays 1¼m: acts on good to soft going: tried in cheekpieces. *Charlie Appleby*

FIRST BOMBARDMENT 4 br.g. Pastoral Pursuits 127 – Magic Myth (IRE) 81 **85**
(Revoque (IRE) 122) [2017 85, a93: t5s^{5} 5m 5m^{6} 5g 5m 5m^{4} 5m^{6} 5d^{5} 5d 5d t5g t5g^{3} p5s t5.1g Nov 29] fairly useful handicapper: best form at 5f: acts on tapeta, good to firm and good to soft going: has worn headgear/tongue tie, including in 2017: often races prominently/freely. *David O'Meara*

FIRST DANCE (IRE) 3 b.f. Cape Cross (IRE) 129 – Happy Wedding (IRE) (Green Tune **81**
(USA) 125) [2017 88: 8m p7d* 7g^{6} p7g Oct 18] useful-looking filly: fairly useful performer: won maiden at Kempton (by 3 lengths from Natheer) in August: stays 7f: acts on polytrack and good to firm going: sold 36,000 gns in October. *James Tate*

FIRST DRIVE 2 b.f. (Jan 30) Street Cry (IRE) 130 – Dawn Glory 76 (Oasis Dream 129) **74**
[2017 6g^{2} p7g 6.1g* 6d 6m^{5} p6d Nov 9] lengthy, rather unfurnished filly: second foal: dam, maiden (stayed 1m), half-sister to 1m-1¼m winner (stayed 1½m) Kingdom of Fife and winner up to 1m Four Winds (both smart) out of smart 1¼m winner Fairy Godmother: fair performer: won maiden at Nottingham in July: should be suited by at least 7f: best form on good going: tried in visor. *Michael Bell*

FIRST ELEVEN 2 b.c. (Feb 9) Frankel 147 – Zenda 115 (Zamindar (USA) 116) [2017 8d **79 p**
8.3d^{6} 8d^{2} Oct 27] strong, good-bodied colt: half-brother to several winners, including top-class winner up to 1m Kingman (2-y-o 7f winner, by Invincible Spirit) and smart 1m-1¼m winner Remote (by Dansili): dam 1m winner, including Poule d'Essai des Pouliches: fair form when second in minor event at Newbury (2¾ lengths behind Extra Elusive) on last of 3 starts: will stay beyond 1m: open to further improvement. *John Gosden*

FIRST EXCEL 5 ch.g. First Trump 118 – Exceedingly Good (IRE) 71 (Exceed And Excel **57**
(AUS) 126) [2017 62: t6g* t8d 7m 5m^{4} 6.1m t6.1m^{6} f6.1g* f6.1g* f7.1g^{6} Dec 22] modest **a78**
handicapper on turf, fair on all-weather: won at Newcastle in January and Southwell in November/December: stays 7f: acts on fibresand, tapeta and good to firm going: wears headgear: front runner/races prominently. *Roy Bowring*

bet365 Old Rowley Cup (Heritage Handicap), Newmarket— First Nation deservedly gets his head in front after several good efforts in defeat, beating Eynhallow, Duke of Bronte (noseband) and Crowned Eagle

FIRST EXPERIENCE 6 b.m. Tamayuz 126 – Lolla's Spirit (IRE) 68 (Montjeu (IRE) 137) [2017 82: p8g^3 p8g^2 p8g^2 p8g^2 t7.1g^6 p10f^4 p8g^4 p8g^3 8.1m^5 7g p8g^4 p7g p10d p7g^5 p7g Dec 20] well-made mare: fairly useful handicapper: placed 5 times in 2017: barely stays 1¼m: acts on polytrack, tapeta, good to firm and good to soft going: often wears headgear: usually races prominently. *Lee Carter* **79**

FIRST FLIGHT (IRE) 6 b.g. Invincible Spirit (IRE) 121 – First of Many 83 (Darshaan 133) [2017 10g^2 10.1g 10.3m^6 10s 10m 11.9d^4 p12g^4 t9.5g^4 p11d Dec 13] attractive gelding: useful handicapper: second at Newmarket (length behind Kapstadt) in June: stays 1½m: acts on polytrack, tapeta, good to firm and heavy going: has worn headgear, including in 2017: often races towards rear. *Heather Main* **103 a96**

FIRST MOHICAN 9 ch.g. Tobougg (IRE) 125 – Mohican Girl 112 (Dancing Brave (USA) 140) [2017 109: p16d^3 p15.8g* p15.8g 18.6m 21.6m 18m Oct 14] smallish, well-made gelding: useful performer: won minor event at Lingfield (by 1¾ lengths from Isharah) in March: stays 2¼m: acts on polytrack, tapeta, good to firm and heavy going: wears headgear: sometimes slowly away. *Alan King* **102**

FIRST MOON 3 b.f. Oasis Dream 129 – Flood Plain 94 (Orpen (USA) 116) [2017 p8g^2 t8.6g^4 p8g^4 8m^6 May 22] second foal: dam, 2-y-o 7f winner, half-sister to smart 1m winner The Nile: fair form: stays 1m: wears tongue tie. *Hugo Palmer* **71**

FIRST NATION 3 b.g. Dubawi (IRE) 129 – Moyesii (USA) (Diesis 133) [2017 83p: 10.3g^2 10m 10d^2 12m^2 12v^4 12s^5 10d^2 12m* Oct 13] strong, compact gelding: smart handicapper: won at Newmarket (by ¾ length from Eynhallow) in October: runner-up 4 times earlier in year: stays 1½m: acts on tapeta, good to firm and heavy going: often travels strongly. *Charlie Appleby* **110**

FIRST OF NEVER (IRE) 11 b.g. Systematic 121 – Never Promise (FR) 72 (Cadeaux Genereux 131) [2017 –: t10.2g Jan 11] no form. *Lynn Siddall* **–**

FIRST QUEST (USA) 3 b.g. First Defence (USA) 119 – Dixie Quest (USA) (Coronado's Quest (USA) 130) [2017 80: 10.1m p12g^5 11.6d^4 13.9s^2 12.1s^4 11.5d^2 Oct 24] lengthy gelding: fairly useful handicapper: second at Catterick in September and Yarmouth in October: stays 1¾m: acts on soft going: often wears blinkers/tongue tie: sold 32,000 gns in November. *Ed Dunlop* **81**

FIRST RATE 4 b.g. Kyllachy 129 – Hooray 121 (Invincible Spirit (IRE) 121) [2017 55: 5g^6 5d 8.7g* 4.7g^5 7.5g Sep 27] fair form at 2 yrs, little impact in Britain since: left Marjorie Fife after second start: won maiden at Quakenbruck in September: stays 8.7f: tried in hood. *Frau D. Floryn, Germany* **51**

FIRST SELECTION (SPA) 4 b.g. Diktat 126 – Villa Sonata 77 (Mozart (IRE) 131) [2017 112: a8f^5 7g^5 9.9g 6m 7.9m^5 8s Aug 4] close-coupled gelding: useful handicapper: stays 1m: acts on fibresand and firm going: has worn headgear, including last 2 starts: front runner/races prominently. *Simon Crisford* **104**

FIRST SITTING 6 b.g. Dansili 127 – Aspiring Diva (USA) (Distant View (USA) 126) [2017 111: 10d 9.9g* 9.9m^3 9.9g* 9.9d 9m Oct 14] tall gelding: smart performer: won listed race at Goodwood (by nose from Spark Plug) in May and Prix Gontaut-Biron at Deauville (by ¾ length from Garlingari) in August: third in La Coupe at Chantilly (2½ lengths behind Robin of Navan) in between: stays 11.5f: acts on good to firm and heavy going. *Chris Wall* **117**

FIRST SUMMER 5 b.g. Cockney Rebel (IRE) 127 – Silken Dalliance 91 (Rambo Dancer (CAN) 107) [2017 69: t9.5m t9.5g[6] 10g 10.2g[5] p10g Aug 31] leggy gelding: fair handicapper, below form in 2017: stays 11f: acts on polytrack, tapeta and good to firm going: has worn cheekpieces, including often in 2017. *Shaun Harris* **61**

FIRST UP (IRE) 3 b.g. Rip Van Winkle (IRE) 134 – Doregan (IRE) (Bahhare (USA) 122) [2017 90: 8.1d 8m 8.2f[6] 10.1d[2] t8.6g[6] t9.5d[3] Dec 27] sturdy gelding: fairly useful handicapper: placed at Epsom in July and Wolverhampton in December: left Jeremy Noseda after fifth start: stays 1¼m: acts on polytrack, tapeta and good to soft going: tried in blinkers/tongue tie. *Oliver Greenall* **89**

FIRST VOYAGE (IRE) 4 ch.g. Dubawi (IRE) 129 – Concordia (Pivotal 124) [2017 87: 11.6m[3] 9.1g[ur] 10.2d[4] Jul 20] fairly useful handicapper: third at Haydock in June: stays 11.5f: acts on good to firm going: sometimes in cheekpieces: front runner/races prominently. *Charlie Appleby* **89**

FIRST WHEAT 4 b.g. Monsieur Bond (IRE) 120 – Ballet Fame (USA) 79 (Quest For Fame 127) [2017 79: 10.3g 8g 7.5f[6] May 1] fair handicapper: stayed 9f: acted on soft going: tried in headgear/tongue tie: dead. *Michael Easterby* **68**

FISHERGATE 4 b.g. Pastoral Pursuits 127 – Miss Meggy 97 (Pivotal 124) [2017 70: p12d 9.9s p8m t8.6g 9.9g 11.6d Jul 12] lengthy gelding: fair handicapper, well below form in 2017: stays 1½m: acts on heavy going: has worn blinkers, including in 2017: usually slowly away. *Richard Rowe* **42**

FISHERMAN'S BLUES (IRE) 4 b.g. Zebedee 113 – Southern Barfly (USA) (Southern Halo (USA)) [2017 76: p10.7g p12g[5] p10.7g 10.3g 12.5m[5] 12m[4] 12.1m 9.2s[2] a11.4g[6] a10.4g* a9.5s Dec 9] fair performer: left G. M. Lyons after third start and Peter Niven after seventh: won (for first time) handicap at Mons in November: barely stays 1½m: best form on good going: has worn blinkers: signs of temperament. *C. von der Recke, Germany* **68**

FIT FOR THE JOB (IRE) 5 b.g. Lawman (FR) 121 – Spesialta 80 (Indian Ridge 123) [2017 78: 8.1d 8.1m[3] 8.1m* 8.5d[3] 8.1s p8g Oct 13] fairly useful handicapper: won at Windsor (by 1¼ lengths from Jumping Jack) in July: stays 1m: acts on good to firm and good to soft going: has worn cheekpieces, including last 4 starts: sent to Germany. *Jonjo O'Neill* **82**

FITZROVIA 2 br.c. (Mar 6) Poet's Voice 126 – Pompey Girl (Rainbow Quest (USA) 134) [2017 6g p6g p6g[5] Oct 24] 45,000Y: sixth foal: closely related to 8.3f winner Sharqawiyah (by Dubawi) and half-brother to useful winner up to 1m Ptolemaic (2-y-o 7f winner, by Excellent Art): dam unraced half-sister to smart 1¼m winner (stayed 1½m) Inchila: poor form in minor events: type to do better in handicaps. *Ed de Giles* **49 p**

Prix Gontaut-Biron Hong Kong Jockey Club, Deauville—First Sitting continues his progression and reverses La Coupe form with Garlingari (cheekpieces); Almanzor (spots), the top European performer in 2016, who disappoints on his return after ten months off, is subsequently retired

FITZWILLIAM 5 ch.g. Sixties Icon 125 – Canadian Capers 70 (Ballacashtal (CAN)) **41**
[2017 56: 9.9g^{5} t8.6g 7g 8f Jun 17] sparely-made gelding: modest maiden, below form in 2017: stays 1½m: acts on polytrack, tapeta and soft going. *Mick Channon*

FITZWILLY 7 b.g. Sixties Icon 125 – Canadian Capers 70 (Ballacashtal (CAN)) [2017 **77**
82: 14f^{5} 14g^{4} 16g^{6} 16m^{3} p16d^{2} 16.3d^{2} 17.1d^{6} 16.3d^{2} 16g* p16s p15.8g^{5} 16s 16d^{3} p16s^{2} Dec 15] workmanlike gelding: fair handicapper: won at Ripon in August: stays 2¼m: acts on polytrack and any turf going: tried in visor. *Mick Channon*

FIVEHUNDREDMILES (IRE) 4 b.g. The Carbon Unit (USA) 106 – There's A Light **88**
(IRE) 70 (Fantastic Light (USA) 134) [2017 75: a8.9f 8.3m^{4} 8.3m* 9.2s^{2} 9.2g^{4} 8.3s^{6} 9s* **a65**
a9.9f^{5} a9.7f^{3} Dec 15] fairly useful handicapper on turf, fair on all-weather: won at Hamilton in May and Newbury (apprentice, by ½ length from Daily Trader) in August: left S. Seemar after first start, John Patrick Shanahan after seventh: stays 9f: acts on dirt, soft and good to firm going: often blinkered: has worn tongue tie, including last 2 starts. *S. Seemar, UAE*

FIVE STAR FRANK 3 b.g. Exceed And Excel (AUS) 126 – Anadolu (IRE) 93 (Statue **76**
of Liberty (USA) 115) [2017 78: p6g^{3} 5.1d^{6} t6.1g^{4} Jun 26] sturdy gelding: fair maiden: stays 6f: acts on polytrack. *Eve Johnson Houghton*

FIVETWOEIGHT 3 b.c. Kyllachy 129 – Super Midge 50 (Royal Applause 124) [2017 **90**
79p: 6m^{3} 6s^{5} 6.1m^{4} p6g Oct 3] neat colt: fairly useful handicapper: raced only at 6f: acts on polytrack and good to firm going. *Peter Chapple-Hyam*

FIVOS 3 ch.g. Piccolo 121 – Bold Diva 65 (Bold Edge 123) [2017 7f^{6} p7g 6.1m^{3} 6g 5s^{5} **50**
6.1g^{6} 5.1d^{6} t6.1g f7.1g^{6} f8.1g^{ur} p8d p8s Dec 17] rather unfurnished gelding: modest maiden: stays 6f: acts on good to firm going: often wears headgear. *David Bridgwater*

FLAG FESTIVAL 2 gr.g. (Mar 9) New Approach (IRE) 132 – Blue Bunting (USA) 122 **56 p**
(Dynaformer (USA)) [2017 p8d Nov 9] third foal: half-brother to useful 1m winner Blue Creek (by Street Cry) and 11f winner Blue Illusion (by Dubawi): dam winner up to 1½m (2-y-o 1m winner), including 1000 Guineas and Irish Oaks: 14/1, seventh in minor event at Chelmsford (13½ lengths behind Gronkowski) in November: entitled to progress. *Charlie Appleby*

FLAG OF HONOUR (IRE) 2 b.c. (Feb 7) Galileo (IRE) 134 – Hawala (IRE) 97 **100**
(Warning 136) [2017 7s 7d* 8m^{5} 9s* Oct 28] close-coupled colt: brother to 2-y-o 8.4f winner Galilean and half-brother to numerous winners, including smart 7f (including at 2 yrs) winner Air Chief Marshal and smart winner up to 1m Foxtrot Romeo (2-y-o 6f winner) (both by Danehill Dancer): dam 8.3f winner: useful form: won maiden at Naas and Eyrefield Stakes at Leopardstown (by 1½ lengths from Giuseppe Garibaldi) in October: will stay 1½m. *Aidan O'Brien, Ireland*

FLAMIN AUDI (GER) 2 b.f. (Apr 13) Medicean 128 – Flames To Dust (GER) (Oasis **65**
Dream 129) [2017 7.2d 7.5s^{6} 5.8v 6s 7s^{2} Nov 5] €13,000Y: fifth foal: dam unraced half-sister to winner up to 1½m Bahamian Dancer and 8.6f-1½m winner Flag War (both useful): fair maiden: stays 7f: acts on soft going: tried in cheekpieces. *L. Smyth, Ireland*

FLAMING FYNN 4 ch.g. Paco Boy (IRE) 129 – La Polka 69 (Carnival Dancer 123) **–**
[2017 p8g Oct 18] no form: tried in tongue tie. *Paul Burgoyne*

FLAMING MARVEL (IRE) 3 b.g. Redoute's Choice (AUS) – Flame of Hestia (IRE) **78**
79 (Giant's Causeway (USA) 132) [2017 82p: 10.2g^{3} May 12] fair form when placed in 3 maidens. *James Fanshawe*

FLAMING SPEAR (IRE) 5 ch.g. Lope de Vega (IRE) 125 – Elshamms 107 (Zafonic **114**
(USA) 130) [2017 106: t7.1g* 7d 7.9d* 8.2s 7s Oct 7] strong gelding: smart handicapper: won at Newcastle (by neck from Fort Bastion) in January and York (by 1¾ lengths from Qassem) in August: best up to 1m: acts on polytrack, tapeta, good to firm and heavy going: tried in cheekpieces: often travels strongly. *Kevin Ryan*

FLANNERY (IRE) 6 b.g. Excellent Art 125 – Magic Sister 63 (Cadeaux Genereux 131) **46**
[2017 63: 16.8m 11.3g 12v^{5} 11.9m^{6} 12g 16s Sep 19] fair handicapper for Andrew Oliver in 2015, below that level since: left David Harry Kelly after second start: stays 1½m: acts on heavy going: tried in hood: has worn tongue tie, including last 4 starts. *Tim Vaughan*

FLASH CITY (ITY) 9 b.g. Elusive City (USA) 117 – Furnish 87 (Green Desert (USA) **75**
127) [2017 79: f5g^{4} 5m^{6} t5s 5g^{2} 5s^{2} 5d^{6} 5s^{3} 5g 5s^{2} 5g Sep 27] robust gelding: fair handicapper: raced mainly at 5f: acts on polytrack, fibresand, firm and soft going: has worn headgear, including in 2017: has worn tongue tie: often races in rear. *Ruth Carr*

FLASH FIRE (IRE) 5 b.g. Shamardal (USA) 129 – Flamelet (USA) 94 (Theatrical) **116**
[2017 115: 7g* 7g^2 7g^2 8g Feb 16] useful-looking gelding: smart performer: won handicap at Meydan (by 2½ lengths from Rene Mathis) in January: second there in Al Fahidi Fort (3½ lengths behind Championship) and handicap (beaten nose by Salateen): stays 1m: acts on good to firm going: usually races nearer last than first. *Charlie Appleby*

FLASHING LIGHT 3 b.f. Compton Place 125 – Heliograph (Ishiguru (USA) 114) **58**
[2017 59: 5m^3 5m^5 5d Jun 11] modest maiden: best form at 5f: acts on good to firm going: usually races close up. *Tim Easterby*

FLASH OF WHITE 3 b.g. Excelebration (IRE) 133 – Aberdovey 82 (Mister Baileys **–**
123) [2017 78: 6m 7g Jun 23] fair form at 2 yrs, little impact either start in 2017: best effort at 6f: tried in hood: sometimes slowly away. *Bryan Smart*

FLASHY SNAPPER 3 ch.g. Raven's Pass (USA) 133 – Super Sleuth (IRE) 113 (Selkirk **96**
(USA) 129) [2017 –: f8g* 8m 7s p8g p8g^5 a8f^2 a8.9f a8f^2 Dec 21] lengthy, good-quartered gelding: useful performer: won maiden at Southwell in April: second in handicaps at Jebel Ali and Meydan, both in December: left Simon Crisford after fifth start: stays 1m: acts on fibresand, sand and good to firm going: often races freely. *S. bin Ghadayer, UAE*

FLAVIUS TITUS 2 ch.c. (Feb 22) Lethal Force (IRE) 128 – Furbelow 83 (Pivotal 124) **93 p**
[2017 6.1m 7d^2 p7d* Nov 22] 37,000F, 100,000Y: second foal: dam, 6f winner, closely related to useful 2-y-o 6f winner Adorn: fairly useful form: won minor event at Kempton (by length from Salute The Soldier) in November: stays 7f: will go on improving. *Roger Varian*

FLAWED DIAMOND (FR) 3 b.f. Tin Horse (IRE) 120 – Anaphora (IRE) 53 (Goofalik **–**
(USA) 118) [2017 52: f8d^6 p11g 9.9s p7.5g 8.2d^4 Jul 26] modest form at 2 yrs, little impact in various events in 2017: in headgear last 3 starts. *K. R. Burke*

FLAWLESSLY (FR) 3 b.f. Exceed And Excel (AUS) 126 – Privalova (IRE) (Alhaarth **76**
(IRE) 126) [2017 72p: t5s 5g^2 5m^2 5g^3 5g* 5m^2 5d p5g^6 5s^4 p5g^2 p5g^3 Dec 15] fair handicapper: won at Redcar in June: left James Bethell after fifth start: raced only at 5f: acts on polytrack and good to firm going: often starts slowly. *Ms Sheila Lavery, Ireland*

FLECKERL (IRE) 7 b.g. Danehill Dancer (IRE) 117 – Spinola (FR) 103 (Spinning **77**
World (USA) 130) [2017 95: p6g p8d t7.1g t6g^3 t6g^2 p6g t6g p6g^5 6d^3 p6g t6.1g^6 6g^5 t6.1g^5 Aug 18] lengthy gelding: fair handicapper nowadays: stays 8.5f, raced mainly at shorter: acts on polytrack, tapeta, good to firm and good to soft going: usually wears headgear: often starts slowly. *Conor Dore*

FLEDERMAUS (IRE) 7 br.g. Jeremy (USA) 122 – Khayrat (IRE) (Polar Falcon (USA) **46**
126) [2017 45: 12m 12.1m 8g 8.5d^5 10.9m^6 9.9v Sep 26] poor maiden: stays 1¼m: wears tongue tie. *Tina Jackson*

FLEETFOOT JACK (IRE) 3 b.g. Kyllachy 129 – Move 79 (Observatory (USA) 131) **78**
[2017 66p: 7.5m^6 10.2m^6 10.2v 8d^5 8.3s* 8.3v* Sep 5] fair handicapper: won at Hamilton in August and September: stays 8.5f: acts on heavy going: in cheekpieces last 4 starts. *David O'Meara*

FLEETING FRANCESCA 3 ch.f. Paco Boy (IRE) 129 – Fleeting Echo 99 (Beat **65**
Hollow 126) [2017 52: p8g* p8g^2 8m May 26] fair handicapper: won at Kempton in April: stays 1m: acts on polytrack. *Chris Gordon*

FLEETING FREEDOM 2 b.f. (Mar 24) Equiano (FR) 127 – Fleeting Image 99 (Sir **80**
Percy 129) [2017 6s^6 7g^5 7d^3 7g^3 8s^4 p8g^2 p8s^3 p8g^2 Dec 21] second foal: half-sister to 2-y-o 1m winner Fleeting Motion (by Sepoy): dam, 1½m winner, half-sister to very smart winner up to 10.5f Rebelline: fairly useful maiden: placed on 5 occasions in 2017: stays 1m: acts on polytrack: front runner/races prominently. *Alan Bailey*

FLEETING GLIMPSE 4 b.f. Passing Glance 119 – Perfect Act 96 (Act One 124) [2017 **64 §**
70: p6g^6 p7g p6g* 7m^4 6g^6 p6g 6g t6.1g^5 p6s^5 5.7s^2 p5g 5s t8.6g Dec 5] fair handicapper: won at Kempton in April: left Andrew Balding after fifth start, Patrick Chamings after twelfth: stays 7f: acts on polytrack and soft going: has worn hood, including in 2017: tried in tongue tie: often races towards rear/freely: temperamental. *Dai Burchell*

FLEETING MOTION 3 ch.f. Sepoy (AUS) 129 – Fleeting Image 99 (Sir Percy 129) **86**
[2017 83p: 8f^4 8s 8m^3 8m^5 7m^5 Aug 9] compact filly: fairly useful handicapper: third at Newmarket in June: stays 1m: acts on firm going: sold 3,000 gns in October, sent to Saudi Arabia. *Richard Hannon*

FLEETING STEPS (IRE) 2 b.g. (Apr 13) Footstepsinthesand 120 – Breedj (IRE) 94 **53**
(Acclamation 118) [2017 p6g p6g^6 p6g Nov 2] modest form on first of 3 starts in minor events: in hood last 2 starts. *Sir Mark Prescott Bt*

British EBF & Sir Henry Cecil Galtres Stakes, York—
Ribblesdale runner-up Mori (third right) disappoints as Fleur Forsyte shows improved form to win this listed prize from More Mischief (armlets)

FLEETING VISIT 4 b.g. Manduro (GER) 135 – Short Affair 99 (Singspiel (IRE) 133) [2017 94: 10m^5 12m^6 p12g^2 11.2s^2 12d^2 16d^4 p16d^3 16s^4 t16.5g^6 p12g^3 Oct 9] fairly useful handicapper: placed 5 times in 2017: stays 2m: acts on polytrack, soft and good to firm going: wears cheekpieces: sold 31,000 gns in November. *Eve Johnson Houghton* **92**

FLEET REVIEW (USA) 2 b.c. (Jan 21) War Front (USA) 119 – A Star Is Born (IRE) 49 (Galileo (IRE) 134) [2017 6.4m^6 6g^3 6m* 6m* 7d 6d^2 Sep 30] well-made colt: first foal: dam, 8.4f winner, sister to top-class winner up to 10.4f Rip Van Winkle: smart performer: won maiden at the Curragh (by neck from Goodthingstaketime) in July and minor event there (by length from I Am Power) in August: second in Middle Park Stakes at Newmarket (½ length behind U S Navy Flag) in September: should stay 7f: acts on good to firm and good to soft going: wears tongue tie: front runner/races prominently. *Aidan O'Brien, Ireland* **116**

FLEETWOOD POPPY 5 br.m. Kheleyf (USA) 116 – Steppin Out 63 (First Trump 118) [2017 53: p12g p13g p12g^5 11.9g^4 13d Aug 23] smallish mare: modest at best, little form in 2017. *Michael Attwater* **–**

FLERE IMSAHO (IRE) 2 b.c. (Apr 25) Kodiac 112 – Florida City (IRE) (Pennekamp (USA) 130) [2017 5d 6.1v^3 6.1d Oct 11] modest form when third at Chester (7½ lengths behind Shaya) on second of 3 starts in minor events. *Tom Dascombe* **62**

FLEUR FORSYTE 3 b.f. Teofilo (IRE) 126 – Fleurissimo 79 (Dr Fong (USA) 128) [2017 60p: 9.9d* 10g 12d^3 11.9d* 12d^4 Sep 29] well-made filly: useful performer: won maiden at Salisbury (by neck from Lightening Dance) in May and listed race at York (by 2¼ lengths from More Mischief) in August: stays 1½m: acts on good to soft going: in hood last 3 starts. *James Fanshawe* **106**

FLEURTILLE 8 b.m. Tillerman 123 – Miss Fleurie 50 (Alzao (USA) 117) [2017 65: 8m May 22] fair handicapper, well held sole outing in 2017: stays 7f: acts on good to firm and heavy going: tried in cheekpieces. *Ray Craggs* **–**

FLEXIBLE FLYER 8 b.g. Exceed And Excel (AUS) 126 – Windermere Island 81 (Cadeaux Genereux 131) [2017 74: p6g^3 p7g^2 7g 7d^4 6d^3 Jun 9] lengthy gelding: fairly useful handicapper: placed at Lingfield (claimer) in February and Brighton in June: stays 7f: acts on polytrack, soft and good to firm going: wears headgear: has worn tongue tie. *Chris Dwyer* **83**

FLICKA'S BOY 5 b.g. Paco Boy (IRE) 129 – Selkirk Sky 65 (Selkirk (USA) 129) [2017 77: 5.1m^5 5m^5 5m^3 7g^5 6d 5.5g 7d Jul 20] strong gelding: fair performer: left Tony Coyle/below form after third start: stays 6f: acts on good to firm going: has worn headgear, including last 5 starts: has worn tongue tie. *P. & F. Monfort, France* **67**

FLIGHT OF FANTASY 3 b.f. Nathaniel (IRE) 129 – Luminda (IRE) (Danehill (USA) 126) [2017 73p: p8g^{2} p8g^{3} 11.8g* 11.6d^{6} 13.3g^{2} 13.3g^{4} 14s^{4} 10g p12g^{2} Nov 1] well-made filly: fairly useful performer: won maiden at Leicester in April: second in handicaps at Newbury in July and Kempton in November: stays 13.5f: acts on polytrack, best turf form on good going: tried in hood: front runner/races prominently. *Harry Dunlop* **85**

FLIGHT OFFICER 6 b.g. New Approach (IRE) 132 – Danuta (USA) 108 (Sunday Silence (USA)) [2017 100: t16.3s Jul 1] attractive gelding: useful at best, gone wrong way since 2016 return: stays 1¼m: best form on heavy going: usually races freely close up. *Michael Easterby* –

FLIGHT RISK (IRE) 6 ch.g. Teofilo (IRE) 126 – Raghida (IRE) 102 (Nordico (USA)) [2017 113: 7g* 8g^{4} 7m 8g 6s 7.5v^{4} 7s^{5} Oct 28] stocky gelding: smart performer: won Ballycorus Stakes at Leopardstown (by 2½ lengths from Don't Touch) in June: stays 8.5f: acts on heavy going: has worn tongue tie: often races in rear. *J. S. Bolger, Ireland* **112**

FLINTY FELL (IRE) 4 b.f. Rock of Gibraltar (IRE) 133 – Manoeuvre (IRE) (Galileo (IRE) 134) [2017 79: 7.1m^{4} 8.3g^{5} 7.2m^{4} 7.2m^{5} 7.2g 8m Aug 30] fair maiden: stays 1m: acts on tapeta and good to soft going: sometimes wears hood. *Keith Dalgleish* **70**

FLIRTARE (IRE) 2 b.f. (Jan 30) Oasis Dream 129 – Federation 94 (Motivator 131) [2017 p6g^{5} May 24] 105,000Y: sturdy filly: first foal: dam, 1m winner, half-sister to 1000 Guineas winner Attraction: 10/1, fifth in minor event at Kempton (1½ lengths behind Di Fede) in May: should do better. *Amanda Perrett* **65 p**

FLOOD DEFENCE (IRE) 3 b.f. Harbour Watch (IRE) 121 – Krynica (USA) 80 (Danzig (USA)) [2017 66: 8s 8.3d^{2} 8s* 8.1v^{3} 10d^{4} 9.9d* 9.9s Oct 9] lengthy, angular filly: fair handicapper: won at Doncaster in June and Sandown in September: stays 1¼m: acts on polytrack, tapeta and heavy going: often races towards rear. *Chris Wall* **79**

FLOODED 3 ch.g. Archipenko (USA) 127 – Spate Rise (Speightstown (USA) 124) [2017 p12s 10d Jul 1] in hood, little show in 2 maidens. *Daniel Kubler* –

FLOOD WARNING 3 ch.f. Pivotal 124 – Sabreon 85 (Caerleon (USA) 132) [2017 61p: t8.6g* t9.5m* 10.3g^{6} 10d* 10s^{2} 10.1s^{5} 9.9d^{2} Nov 7] sturdy filly: useful performer: won maiden at Wolverhampton in February, and handicaps there in March and Sandown (by 1¼ lengths from First Nation) in April: second in listed races after at Newbury (beaten 3¾ lengths by Natavia) and Saint-Cloud (1¼ lengths behind Gaining): stays 1¼m: acts on tapeta and soft going: often races towards rear. *Clive Cox* **99**

FLORA SANDES (USA) 2 b.f. (Feb 8) War Front (USA) 119 – Aloof (IRE) 110 (Galileo (IRE) 134) [2017 p7g^{6} p8s* Nov 16] $900,000Y: first foal: dam, winner up to 10.7f (2-y-o 1m winner), sister to useful 1¼m winner Orator and half-sister to useful dam of Churchill and Clemmie: fairly useful form: won minor event at Chelmsford (by ½ length from Bubble And Squeak) in November: wears hood: open to further improvement. *Charlie Appleby* **84 p**

FLORA TRISTAN 2 ch.f. (Mar 4) Zoffany (IRE) 121 – Red Roxanne (Rock of Gibraltar (IRE) 133) [2017 p7s^{5} Dec 15] second foal: half-sister to 1¼m winner Black Redstart (by Big Bad Bob): dam unraced: 12/1, well held in minor event at Chelmsford. *Marco Botti* –

FLOR DE SEDA (FR) 2 b.f. (Jan 30) George Vancouver (USA) 116 – Toile de Soie (FR) (Peintre Celebre (USA) 137) [2017 p7g Sep 25] €7,000Y, £27,000 2-y-o: first foal: dam unraced half-sister to useful 9f/1¼m winner Grand Opening: 100/1, well held in minor event at Kempton. *Jo Hughes* –

FLOREAT FLOREAT (IRE) 2 b.c. (Mar 26) Epaulette (AUS) 126 – Flying Flag (IRE) (Entrepreneur 123) [2017 7g^{6} Jul 22] attractive colt: 7/1, well held in minor event at Haydock: dead. *Tom Dascombe* –

FLORENCIO 4 b.g. Equiano (FR) 127 – Mary Pekan (IRE) 97 (Sri Pekan (USA) 117) **78**
[2017 92: p6g^{5} p6d* p6g t7.1s 6m 6s^{5} 6m t7.1s^{2} 7.4m^{6} t7.1g^{5} 7d t7.2g^{3} f7.1g* t6d^{4} t7.2g **a92**
t6s^{6} Nov 30] tall gelding: fair handicapper on turf, fairly useful on all-weather: won at Kempton in February and Southwell (by neck from Pearl Spectre) in October: left Marco Botti after fourth start: stays 7.5f: acts on all-weather, firm and soft going: wears headgear: has worn tongue tie, including in 2017. *Roger Fell*

FLORENZA 4 b.f. Haafhd 129 – Danzatrice 76 (Tamure (IRE) 125) [2017 86: 7g^{6} 7m^{2} 7d^{2} 7d* 7m^{6} 8m^{3} 8d* 8d^{3} 8m 10.1s 8.2v Sep 30] useful handicapper: won at Doncaster in June and Thirsk (dead-heated with Moonlightnavigator) in August: stays 1m: acts on good to firm and good to soft going: usually leads. *Chris Fairhurst* **96**

FLORIDA TIMES (IRE) 3 b.f. Elzaam (AUS) 115 – Brooklands Time (IRE) 63 (Danetime (IRE) 121) [2017 5v^2 5d* 6s^3 6s^4 6g Jul 14] sturdy filly: fifth foal: half-sister to 3 winners, including 5f winner Majestic Timeline (by Majestic Missile) and ungenuine 2-y-o 8.6f winner (stayed 1½m) Brooklands Bay (by Pyrus): dam maiden half-sister to useful winner up to 1m Cat Belling: useful performer: won maiden at Cork in April: third in listed race at Newbury (1½ lengths behind Visionary) in May: left Adrian Brendan Joyce after second start: raced at 5f/6f: acts on soft going. *David O'Meara* **95**

FLO'S MELODY 2 br.f. (Feb 17) Swiss Spirit 117 – Ginger Cookie 47 (Bold Edge 123) [2017 5m^3 5v 6d^4 6m^5 t5.1g t6.1g* 6m* t6.1g 5s^2 Sep 20] £28,000Y: fifth foal: half-sister to 3 winners, including 5f (including at 2 yrs) winners Threes Grand (by Milk It Mick) and Biscuiteer (by Byron): dam maiden half-sister to useful winner up to 8.2f Peculiarity: fair performer: won sellers at Wolverhampton and Ripon in August: best at 6f: acts on tapeta, good to firm and good to soft going. *Richard Fahey* **66**

FLOSS THE HOSS (IRE) 2 b.f. (Apr 13) Havana Gold (IRE) 118 – Paradise Way (Elusive Quality (USA)) [2017 5m^4 5.3g^3 6.1g 6m 5.1d^3 5d t6.1g Oct 27] 8,000F, €27,000Y: third foal: half-sister to useful winner up to 6f Lostinparadise (by Exceed And Excel): dam unraced half-sister to useful 1¼m winner Haalan: modest maiden: best form at 5f: acts on good to firm and good to soft going. *David Evans* **64**

FLOURISHING 3 b.f. Exceed And Excel (AUS) 126 – Mi Anna (GER) (Lake Coniston (IRE) 131) [2017 7g 7.4m^2 7.6d* 8g^3 t7.2g* Aug 14] 155,000 2-y-o: closely related to useful 7f winner Mi Rubina (by Rock of Gibraltar) and half-sister to numerous winners, including 7f/1m winner Mi Emma (by Silvano) and 1m winner Anna's Pearl (by Pivotal), both smart: dam 2-y-o 7f winner: fairly useful performer: won maiden at Chester in July and handicap at Wolverhampton (by ½ length from Dusky Maid) in August: stays 7.5f: acts on tapeta, good to firm and good to soft going: tried in hood: front runner/races prominently. *Sir Michael Stoute* **88**

FLOWER CUP 4 b.f. Acclamation 118 – Amber Queen (IRE) 92 (Cadeaux Genereux 131) [2017 t6g p7g 6g 6m^2 p7s^2 6g^3 6d^2 t7.2g Aug 31] good-topped filly: fair maiden: stays 7f: acts on polytrack and good to soft going: often wears headgear: tried in tongue tie. *Chris Dwyer* **71**

FLOWERS ON VENUS (IRE) 5 ch.g. Raven's Pass (USA) 133 – Chelsea Rose (IRE) 121 (Desert King (IRE) 129) [2017 96: p7g* p6g* p6g* May 4] lengthy gelding: fairly useful performer: won claimers at Lingfield in February, March and May (by 3 lengths from Major Crispies): stays 7f: acts on all-weather and firm going: tried in visor. *Tom Dascombe* **89**

FLOWERS WILL BLOOM (IRE) 3 b.f. Fastnet Rock (AUS) 127 – Natural Bloom (IRE) 79 (Galileo (IRE) 134) [2017 12.1m^4 11.6m^6 11.2d t12.2g^6 Aug 10] first foal: dam, 9.7f winner, half-sister to Falmouth Stakes winner Tashawak and Ribblesdale Stakes winner Fairy Queen: modest form: stays 1½m. *David O'Meara* **53**

FLOWING CLARETS 4 ch.f. Pastoral Pursuits 127 – Flying Clarets (IRE) 115 (Titus Livius (FR) 115) [2017 81, a60: p6g p6g p6d^6 6g 6g 5g* 5.3g^4 6m 5d^3 6d^3 5.1g^2 5m^6 6d^3 6g^4 5s^2 5.3s^2 5.1d* p6g Nov 17] narrow filly: fair handicapper on turf, modest on all-weather: won at Lingfield in June and Windsor in October: stays 6f: acts on soft going: front runner/races prominently. *John Bridger* **72** **a61**

FLY AT DAWN (USA) 3 ch.g. Discreet Cat (USA) 127 – Emirates Girl (USA) (Unbridled's Song (USA) 125) [2017 98: a7f* 7g^2 a9.4g^5 a9.9f^6 Dec 21] well-made gelding: smart performer: won minor event at Meydan (by length from Cosmo Charlie) in January: best effort when 4 lengths fifth to Thunder Snow in UAE Derby on same course in March: stays 9.5f: acts on polytrack, dirt and good to firm going: has worn hood: tongue tied in 2017: usually travels strongly. *Charlie Appleby* **110**

FLYBOY (IRE) 4 b.g. Zoffany (IRE) 121 – In Dubai (USA) 91 (Giant's Causeway (USA) 132) [2017 92: 8m 8m 6.9g^3 7d^2 7m^6 7d^2 7m 6.9v^2 7v Oct 21] rather leggy gelding: fairly useful handicapper: second at Leicester in June/July and Carlisle in September: left David O'Meara after second start: stays 8.5f: acts on good to firm and heavy going: wears headgear: sold 10,000 gns in October. *Richard Fahey* **87**

FLYING AUTHOR (IRE) 6 b.g. Authorized (IRE) 133 – Fly Free 97 (Halling (USA) 133) [2017 p10g^3 p10d p13.3g p10g^3 p12g 10.1s^2 10f^2 11.4m^5 Jun 19] tall gelding: modest maiden: stays 1¼m: acts on polytrack, firm and soft going: wears headgear: often wears tongue tie: front runner/races prominently. *Phil McEntee* **53**

FLYING BEAR (IRE) 6 b.g. Kodiac 112 – Marinebird (IRE) 66 (Bad As I Wanna Be (IRE) 115) [2017 76, a85: p5g^6 May 5] rather leggy gelding: fairly useful handicapper: stays 6f, raced mainly at 5f: acts on polytrack and firm going: has worn headgear. *Jeremy Gask* **79**

FLYING EXPECTATION (ITY) 3 gr.g. Zebedee 113 – Folcara (IRE) (Brief Truce (USA) 126) [2017 51: p7g t6.1g^6 6g 5d Jul 25] poor maiden: stays 6f: in headgear last 2 starts: tried in tongue tie: often races prominently. *Des Donovan, Ireland* **44**

FLYING FANTASY 5 b.g. Oasis Dream 129 – Disco Volante 105 (Sadler's Wells (USA) 132) [2017 83: p7g p7d p7g p7g^3 8m^4 8m^2 7d^3 10g^5 t7.2g p7s^5 7d* 7m t8.6g 7s^{pu} Sep 19] lengthy gelding: fair handicapper nowadays: won at Yarmouth (apprentice) in August: left Stuart Williams after sixth start: stays 1m: acts on polytrack, tapeta, good to firm and heavy going: has worn headgear, including last 4 starts: has worn tongue tie: sometimes slowly away. *Michael Appleby* **76**

FLYING FOXY 3 b.f. Foxwedge (AUS) 128 – Fauran (IRE) (Shamardal (USA) 129) [2017 56p: 5m* 5.2g t5.1g^4 Aug 18] fair form: won maiden at Beverley in July: best form at 5f. *Michael Wigham* **72**

FLYING FYNN (IRE) 3 ch.g. Byron 117 – Can She Dance (IRE) 56 (Danehill Dancer (IRE) 117) [2017 –: p7g^3 p8d^3 p7d p10g^6 Mar 8] modest maiden: best effort at 7f: in cheekpieces last 4 starts: dead. *Jose Santos* **58**

FLYING HOPE (IRE) 3 ch.f. Tagula (IRE) 116 – Unknowndestination (IRE) (Authorized (IRE) 133) [2017 47: t5g t5d^2 t5.1g t5.1g^5 t5d 5m^6 5g Apr 22] modest maiden: raced only at 5f: acts on tapeta and firm going: sometimes wears headgear/tongue tie: front runner/races prominently. *Nigel Tinkler* **54**

FLYING NORTH 3 b.f. Raven's Pass (USA) 133 – Round The Cape 94 (Cape Cross (IRE) 129) [2017 85p: p8g^6 8m 10m* 10g^3 10v 8d^5 8g^4 8d Sep 20] good-topped filly: fairly useful handicapper: won at Windsor (by 1¾ lengths from Lightening Dance) in June: third at Leicester in July: stays 1¼m: acts on good to firm going: front runner/races prominently. *Richard Hannon* **89**

FLYING ONSITE (FR) 3 ro.g. Rajsaman (FR) 121 – Infinitely (Fantastic Light (USA) 134) [2017 56: 7g 8g t7.1g 6d 6d^4 7d^5 Jul 28] maiden: no form in 2017: in headgear last 2 starts. *Nigel Tinkler* **–**

FLYING POWER 9 b.g. Dubai Destination (USA) 127 – Rah Wa (USA) (Rahy (USA) 115) [2017 56: 12g^4 11.6d^4 14g^5 11.8g t12.2g^3 t12.4g t12.2m^5 f11.1g Dec 4] stocky gelding: modest handicapper nowadays: stays 1¾m: acts on polytrack, tapeta, good to firm and good to soft going: has worn headgear, including last 4 starts: front runner/races prominently. *John Norton* **55**

FLYING PURSUIT 4 ch.g. Pastoral Pursuits 127 – Choisette 75 (Choisir (AUS) 126) [2017 100: 6g p6g^5 6s^5 6d^6 6g* 6g 6g* 6g^5 6v* 6g^3 6d^2 6d Nov 11] good-quartered gelding: smart handicapper: won at Ayr (by 1¼ lengths from Explain) in June, York (by 2 lengths from Al Qahwa) in July and Ripon (by ½ length from Nameitwhatyoulike) in September: placed at York (Coral Sprint Trophy) and Doncaster in October: stays 6f: acts on good to firm and heavy going: wears headgear: usually leads. *Tim Easterby* **113**

FLYING RACONTEUR 3 b.g. Bated Breath 125 – Abunai 100 (Pivotal 124) [2017 7d^5 t8g^2 f8.1g^2 Dec 1] fair form: best effort when second in maiden at Southwell in December: will stay beyond 1m: in tongue tie last 2 starts. *Nigel Tinkler* **78**

FLYING SAKHEE 4 b.f. Sakhee's Secret 128 – Sister Moonshine 65 (Averti (IRE) 117) [2017 57§: 6m 7d 6g^2 6d 7m^5 5s^6 6s^5 6g^6 6g^3 6g 6.1g^5 p6g p8g^2 p8g Dec 13] compact filly: modest maiden: stays 1m: acts on polytrack: has worn headgear, including in 2017: races towards rear: one to treat with caution (has virtually refused to race). *John Bridger* **57 §**

FLYING SPARKLE (IRE) 2 b.f. (Apr 17) Fast Company (IRE) 126 – Titian Saga (IRE) 74 (Titus Livius (FR) 115) [2017 5.1m* 6d^2 6g^2 Oct 7] 70,000Y: fifth foal: sister to 2-y-o 5f winner Pres Rapide, and half-sister to 5f winner Imperial Legend (by Mujadil) and 5f (including at 2 yrs) winner Hay Chewed (by Camacho), both useful: dam 2-y-o 6f winner: fairly useful form: won minor event at Windsor (by 2¼ lengths from Hunni) in July: best effort when second in listed Two-Year-Old Trophy at Redcar (½ length behind Darkanna) in October: stays 6f: open to further improvement. *Michael Bell* **92 p**

FLYING TIGER (IRE) 4 bl.g. Soldier of Fortune (IRE) 131 – Ma Preference (FR) 109 (American Post 121) [2017 12s^5 Oct 7] €38,000Y: strong gelding: second foal: dam French 9.5f-1½m winner: useful hurdler: 33/1, fifth in Cumberland Lodge Stakes at Ascot (4½ lengths behind Danehill Kodiac) only start on Flat. *Nick Williams* **108**

MPR LII, Mrs Jones and Osborne House's "Flymetothestars"

FLYMETOTHESTARS 4 b.g. Sea The Stars (IRE) 140 – Precious Gem (IRE) 109 (Sadler's Wells (USA) 132) [2017 95p: t16.3g* t16.3s3 13.9m2 14.9d4 Sep 10] smart performer: won handicap at Newcastle (by 2 lengths from Endless Acres) in May: placed in Northumberland Plate at Newcastle (third to Higher Power) and Ebor at York (head second to Nakeeta): below form in Prix Gladiateur at Chantilly final start: stays 2m: acts on all-weather and good to firm going: sold only 5,000 gns in October, has joined Michael Easterby. *Sir Mark Prescott Bt* **114**

FLY TRUE 4 b.f. Raven's Pass (USA) 133 – Have Faith (IRE) 87 (Machiavellian (USA) 123) [2017 79: t5.1g2 p5g 5g 5m p6g6 f5g Dec 19] fair handicapper: left Jeremy Gask after fifth start: stays 7f: acts on polytrack, tapeta and good to firm going: usually wears headgear: usually slowly away, sometimes markedly so, and can't be relied on. *Suzzanne France* **74 §**

FOIE GRAS 7 b.g. Kyllachy 129 – Bint Zamayem (IRE) 95 (Rainbow Quest (USA) 134) [2017 72: p8g6 t8d2 t8.6g p8d* t8.6g5 p7g5 p8s3 p10s3 p10g6 p10s p8g6 p8d Oct 6] good-topped gelding: fair handicapper: won at Chelmsford in March: stays 8.5f: acts on all-weather, good to firm and good to soft going: usually wears headgear. *Chris Dwyer* **73**

FOLIES BERGERES 2 ch.f. (Mar 26) Champs Elysees 124 – May Fox (Zilzal (USA) 137) [2017 p8g 8s Oct 19] 22,000Y: seventh foal: closely related to 8.3f winner Down To Earth (by Aussie Rules) and half-sister to winner up to 8.6f Meglio Ancora (2-y-o 6f winner, by Best of The Bests) and smart winner up to 1m Annecdote (2-y-o 7f winner, by Lucky Story): dam unraced: little impact in maiden/minor event. *Jonathan Portman* **–**

FOLKLORE (GER) 2 b.f. (Mar 15) Lethal Force (IRE) 128 – Focal 76 (Pivotal 124) [2017 6g Aug 27] 26,000Y, 50,000 2-y-o: third foal: dam twice-raced maiden: 109/10, well held in minor event at Baden-Baden. *Mrs Ilka Gansera-Leveque* **–**

FOLKSWOOD 4 b.g. Exceed And Excel (AUS) 126 – Magic Nymph (IRE) (Galileo (IRE) 134) [2017 109: 9.9g2 8.9g* 8.9g2 9m2 10.3m3 8.5m5 10.1g* 10.1g3 9.9g5 Nov 11] rangy gelding: very smart performer: won handicaps at Meydan (by 2 lengths from Elleval) in February and Cranbourne (listed event, by 2¾ lengths from Berisha) in October: runner- **120**

up in between in Jebel Hatta on former course (neck behind Decorated Knight) and Earl of Sefton Stakes at Newmarket (beaten ½ length by Steel of Madrid): good efforts last 2 starts, in Cox Plate at Moonee Valley (4¾ lengths third to Winx) and Emirates Stakes at Flemington (1¾ lengths fifth to Tosen Stardom): stays 1¼m: acts on good to firm going: wears cheekpieces: races prominently. *Charlie Appleby*

FOLK TALE (IRE) 2 ch.g. (May 2) Dubawi (IRE) 129 – Causeway Lass (AUS) (Giant's Causeway (USA) 132) [2017 6m⁴ 6g* 6g⁵ Jul 1] seventh foal: half-brother to 3 winners, including useful 2-y-o 7f/1m winner Good Place and winner up to 1¼m Press Room (2-y-o 9.5f winner) (both by Street Cry): dam, 5f/5.5f winner (including at 2 yrs), out of Australian Group 1 winner up to 1m Canny Lass: useful form: won minor event at Newmarket (by neck from Faraasah) in June: fifth in Railway Stakes at the Curragh (4½ lengths behind Beckford) in July: raced only at 6f: tried in hood: open to further improvement. *Charlie Appleby* **95 p**

FOLLOWING BREEZE (IRE) 2 b.f. (Apr 26) Kodiac 112 – Xaloc (IRE) 57 (Shirocco (GER) 129) [2017 5.1g 6.1m 6g⁶ 5m² 5.1m Oct 16] €42,000F, £38,000 2-y-o: close-coupled filly: second foal: dam once-raced half-sister to smart 2-y-o 1m winner Foundation: poor maiden: best effort at 5f: acts on good to firm going. *Jim Boyle* **43**

FOLLOW ME (IRE) 3 b.f. Zoffany (IRE) 121 – Flower of Kent (USA) 78 (Diesis 133) [2017 –: p8g p8g p8g 9.9d⁶ t9.5g⁶ p12g Nov 8] modest maiden: stays 1¼m: acts on tapeta and good to soft going: tried in headgear: often races prominently. *Lee Carter* **55**

FOLLOW THE FEELING (USA) 2 br.f. (Mar 12) More Than Ready (USA) 120 – Crystal Lake Drive (USA) (Giant's Causeway (USA) 132) [2017 7s⁴ 7m⁵ p6g a7f a7f Dec 29] $15,000 2-y-o: first foal: dam unraced: modest maiden: left Henry Spiller after third start: stays 7f: acts on soft and good to firm going: tried in hood. *A. bin Harmash, UAE* **58**

FOLLOWTHESTEPS (IRE) 2 b.g. (Feb 12) Footstepsinthesand 120 – Excellent Mariner (IRE) 69 (Henrythenavigator (USA) 131) [2017 6d⁶ t5.1g* Jun 26] €68,000F, 25,000Y: sturdy gelding: second foal: dam, maiden (stayed 7.5f), half-sister to smart winner up to 9f Steinbeck: fair form: won minor event at Wolverhampton (by ¾ length from Branscombe) in June: will go on improving. *Ivan Furtado* **77 p**

FONDEST 2 b.f. (Mar 8) Mayson 124 – Fondled 101 (Selkirk (USA) 129) [2017 p7g p7g⁵ Nov 8] half-sister to several winners, including smart 7f-8.6f winner Keystroke, useful 1m-10.3f winner Cosseted (both by Pivotal) and useful 1¼m winner Indulged (by Teofilo): dam 1m winner: fair form: better effort when fifth in minor event at Kempton (4½ lengths behind Lush Life) in November. *James Fanshawe* **65**

FONT VERT (FR) 2 b.g. (Mar 6) Sinndar (IRE) 134 – Fontaine Margot (FR) (Ballingarry (IRE) 123) [2017 7m 7f 7d⁶ 8.3v⁵ 8m⁴ Aug 31] close-coupled gelding: modest maiden: stays 1m: acts on good to firm going. *Ralph Beckett* **61**

FOOLAAD 6 ch.g. Exceed And Excel (AUS) 126 – Zayn Zen 107 (Singspiel (IRE) 133) [2017 72: t8g⁴ t6d* t7.1d* 6g* 6m³ 6s³ f5g* Dec 29] useful handicapper: won at Newcastle (twice) in March, Thirsk in April and Southwell (by 1¾ lengths from Brother Tiger) in December: stays 7f: acts on fibresand, tapeta, soft and good to firm going: wears tongue tie. *Roy Bowring* **95**

FOOL FOR YOU (IRE) 2 b.f. (Apr 2) Lawman (FR) 121 – Bosphorus Queen (IRE) 83 (Sri Pekan (USA) 117) [2017 5.4d⁴ 5s* Oct 10] €16,000F, €13,000Y, €47,000 2-y-o: fourth foal: half-sister to 1½m winner Bosphorus Prince (by Hurricane Run): dam lightly raced (should have stayed 1m): fair form: won minor event at Catterick (by 1½ lengths from Paco Escostar) in October: will stay 6f+: will go on improving. *Richard Fahey* **74 p**

FOOLS AND KINGS 3 b.g. Sakhee (USA) 136 – Mookhlesa 94 (Marju (IRE) 127) [2017 10d⁵ t9.5g* 10s³ 12s* 13.9g² Oct 13] 2,500F: tall gelding: fifth foal: half-brother to 3 winners, including 6f winner Najd (by Dick Turpin) and 5f winner Traditionelle (by Indesatchel): dam 2-y-o 5f winner: useful performer: won maiden at Wolverhampton in July and handicap at Chepstow (by 1¾ lengths from Knight Destroyer) in September: second in handicap at York in October: stays 1¾m: acts on tapeta and soft going: often races towards rear/travels strongly: sold 46,000 gns later in October. *Robyn Brisland* **95**

FOOTLIGHT 4 br.f. Showcasing 117 – Wood Fairy 74 (Haafhd 129) [2017 82: p10g² f11g* t10.2g³ p10d³ 9.8m⁴ 12.1m 9.9d³ 10.3g⁴ 10d⁵ 10.2g⁴ Aug 19] fair handicapper on turf, fairly useful on all-weather: won at Southwell (by length from Storm King) in February: should stay 1½m: acts on all-weather and soft going: front runner/races prominently. *Richard Fahey* **79 a86**

FOOTMAN (GER) 3 b.g. Cacique (IRE) 124 – Flames To Dust (GER) (Oasis Dream 129) [2017 74p: 8.1m p11g^2 11.4m^5 p12g^2 12d^6 p10d^2 p10g^2 Oct 12] strong gelding: fairly useful maiden: second in maidens at Chelmsford in September and October: stays 1½m: acts on polytrack and good to firm going: tried in cheekpieces: often races prominently/travels strongly: sold 30,000 gns later in October. *Richard Hughes* **86**

FOOTSTEPS FOREVER (IRE) 2 ch.f. (Mar 20) Footstepsinthesand 120 – Ceoil An Aith (IRE) 81 (Accordion) [2017 6.1s^6 6g* 7.2m^2 t8s^3 Sep 8] tall filly: fourth foal: half-sister to 9.3f-1½m winner Novancia (by Fastnet Rock): dam, 1½m winner, sister to very smart 7f-15.5f winner Yavana's Pace and smart winner up to 1¼m Littlepacepaddocks: fair form: won minor event at Pontefract in June: will be suited by further than 1m: remains open to improvement. *Mark Johnston* **78 p**

FOOTSTEPSINTHERAIN (IRE) 7 b.g. Footstepsinthesand 120 – Champagne Toni (IRE) (Second Empire (IRE) 124) [2017 90: p7g^5 Dec 13] sturdy gelding: fairly useful at best, well held in seller sole outing in 2017: stays 1m: acts on polytrack, tapeta and good to firm going: has worn tongue tie. *Daniel Steele* **54**

FOR AYMAN 6 b.g. Bertolini (USA) 125 – Saharan Song (IRE) 64 (Singspiel (IRE) 133) [2017 79: t7.1m p6g p6g^6 p6g Feb 18] rather sparely-made gelding: fair handicapper: stayed 7f: acted on polytrack, tapeta, good to firm and good to soft going: wore tongue tie: often raced in rear: dead. *Joseph Tuite* **65**

FORCED FAMILY FUN 7 b.g. Refuse To Bend (IRE) 128 – Juniper Girl (IRE) 108 (Revoque (IRE) 122) [2017 80: p15.8m Jan 9] lengthy gelding: fairly useful handicapper, well held sole outing in 2017: stays 13f: acts on soft going: has worn hood, including last 2 starts. *George Baker* **64**

FORCEFUL APPEAL (USA) 9 b.g. Successful Appeal (USA) 118 – Kinetic Force (USA) (Holy Bull (USA) 134) [2017 102: t9.5g^3 p10g p10g^5 t8.6g^2 p10d^6 p7g* 8f* 8m 8.5m^4 p8g t9.5g p7g Dec 13] workmanlike gelding: fairly useful handicapper on turf, useful on all-weather: won apprentice events at Lingfield (by nose from War Glory) in April and Ascot (by neck from Directorship) in May: stays 1¼m: acts on all-weather and firm going: often races towards rear. *Simon Dow* **91 a101**

FORECAST 5 ch.g. Observatory (USA) 131 – New Orchid (USA) 106 (Quest For Fame 127) [2017 62: t12.2m^2 p16g Mar 22] modest maiden: stays 1½m: acts on tapeta: in hood/tongue tie in 2017: fairly useful hurdler. *Martin Keighley* **63**

FORESEEABLE FUTURE (FR) 2 b.c. (Mar 16) Harbour Watch (IRE) 121 – Russian Spirit 105 (Falbrav (IRE) 133) [2017 6g^6 6g* Oct 16] 32,000Y: second foal: dam 5f/6f winner: fair form: won minor event at Yarmouth (by 2¼ lengths from Elite Shadow) in October: remains open to improvement. *James Tate* **79 p**

FORESEE (GER) 4 b.g. Sea The Stars (IRE) 140 – Four Roses (IRE) (Darshaan 133) [2017 88: 10.3g p16d 12.3d 12d^5 14s p12g Oct 13] fairly useful at 3 yrs, well below that level in 2017: stays 15f: acts on heavy going: has worn headgear. *Tony Carroll* **62**

FORESIGHT (FR) 4 b.g. Dream Ahead (USA) 133 – Madhya (USA) 103 (Gone West (USA)) [2017 84: t6d t7.1g 6g 6m^6 7f 8m 7.8v Sep 13] good-topped gelding: fairly useful handicapper, below form in 2017: stays 6f: acts on soft going: tried in cheekpieces: in tongue tie last 2 starts. *Kevin Ryan* **72**

FOREST ANGEL (IRE) 3 gr.f. Dark Angel (IRE) 113 – Fruit O'The Forest (IRE) (Shinko Forest (IRE)) [2017 63: t8.6g^4 t7.1g f8g^6 Apr 16] leggy, rather unfurnished filly: modest maiden: stays 8.5f: acts on tapeta and good to firm going: tried in cheekpieces. *James Tate* **63**

FOREST DRAGON 2 b.f. (Mar 25) Teofilo (IRE) 126 – Lion Forest (USA) (Forestry (USA) 121) [2017 7d 7d 7m^6 6s^4 t6g Oct 19] 55,000Y: fifth foal: half-sister to 2-y-o 7f winner Gaspirali (by Oasis Dream) and useful winner up to 6f Evergate (by Exceed And Excel): dam unraced sister to US 2-y-o Grade 1 8.5f winner Diplomat Lady: modest form: standout effort when fourth in nursery at Catterick in October: best effort at 6f: acts on soft going: in cheekpieces last 2 starts: sold 7,000 gns, sent to Russia. *Hugo Palmer* **61**

FOREST LAKES (IRE) 4 b.f. Iffraaj 127 – Cala (FR) 98 (Desert Prince (IRE) 130) [2017 66: t7.1m^6 Jan 13] fair maiden: stayed 1m: acted on polytrack and heavy going: sometimes wore headgear: dead. *Paul D'Arcy* **56**

FOREST RANGER (IRE) 3 b.c. Lawman (FR) 121 – Alava (IRE) (Anabaa (USA) 130) [2017 96p: t8s* 10.3d^6 8f^5 8g^2 8s^3 8.8m^2 9m Oct 14] strong, rangy colt: smart performer: won minor event at Newcastle (by 2¾ lengths from Syphax) in April: second in listed race **115**

at Newmarket (3 lengths behind Beat The Bank) in July and Strensall Stakes at York (¾ length behind Mustashry) in August: stays 9f: acts on tapeta, good to firm and heavy going. *Richard Fahey*

FORESTRY 3 b.g. Firebreak 125 – Oak Leaves 61 (Mark of Esteem (IRE) 137) [2017 –
t8.6g^{6} p10g Apr 26] little impact in maidens. *Jonathan Portman*

FOREST STEPS (IRE) 3 b.f. Footstepsinthesand 120 – Zeena 61 (Unfuwain (USA) **44**
131) [2017 –: t9.5g p10g p10g Feb 9] poor maiden: tried in hood. *J. S. Moore*

FOREVER A LADY (IRE) 4 b.f. Dark Angel (IRE) 113 – Unicamp 84 (Royal Academy **80**
(USA) 130) [2017 81: t8g^{3} 8.5m^{4} 8m^{2} 6.9g* 8.3g^{2} 7.6s^{2} 8m 8.3s^{5} 8.3d^{4} 7.8s 7.2m^{5} 6s^{4} 7.2m^{4} 8s^{4} 8s^{3} 7.2v Oct 16] smallish, good-topped filly: fairly useful handicapper: won at Carlisle in May: second at Hamilton and Chester in June: stays 8.5f: acts on soft and good to firm going. *Keith Dalgleish*

FOREVER EXCEL (IRE) 3 b.f. Excelebration (IRE) 133 – Never A Doubt 107 (Night –
Shift (USA)) [2017 –: 7g^{5} May 27] sparely-made filly: well held in maidens. *Charles Hills*

FOREVER IN LOVE 2 ch.f. (May 9) Dutch Art 126 – Ardent 92 (Pivotal 124) [2017 **71**
p6g^{5} t6.1g^{2} 6s^{2} 6d^{4} p6g^{4} Oct 17] fourth foal: sister to smart winner up to 8.3f Eternally (2-y-o 7f winner): dam 6f winner: fair maiden: raced only at 6f: acts on tapeta and soft going: tried in headgear. *Sir Michael Stoute*

FOREVER SONG 3 b.g. Dubawi (IRE) 129 – Echoes In Eternity (IRE) 111 (Spinning **72**
World (USA) 130) [2017 10.2m p12s^{5} a7g a9.9f^{pu} Nov 24] fair form: left Charlie Appleby after second start: best effort at 1½m: in headgear last 2 starts. *A. bin Harmash, UAE*

FOREVER YOURS (IRE) 4 b.g. Canford Cliffs (IRE) 133 – Gilded (IRE) 101 **68**
(Redback 116) [2017 66: p7d p6g^{5} t6.1g^{2} p7s 6.1m^{4} 7g^{4} p7s p6g^{3} Dec 31] fair maiden: stays 6f: acts on polytrack, tapeta and good to firm going. *Dean Ivory*

FORGOTTEN HERO (IRE) 8 b.g. High Chaparral (IRE) 132 – Sundown 71 (Polish –
Precedent (USA) 131) [2017 102: t12.2g Oct 21] strong, sturdy gelding: useful handicapper, below form sole outing on Flat in 2017: stays 1½m: acts on polytrack, good to firm and good to soft going: has worn hood: wears tongue tie: sometimes slowly away. *Kim Bailey*

FORMATIVE 4 ch.g. Champs Elysees 124 – Chasing Stars 103 (Observatory (USA) 131) –
[2017 9.8d Jun 7] in tongue tie, 66/1, well held in maiden at Ripon. *Noel Wilson*

FORMIDABLE KITT 2 b.f. (Feb 16) Invincible Spirit (IRE) 121 – Ceiling Kitty 107 **84**
(Red Clubs (IRE) 125) [2017 5m* 5m 5m^{4} 5d Sep 3] compact, sprint type: second foal: half-sister to useful 6f (including at 2 yrs) winner Eartha Kitt (by Pivotal): dam 2-y-o 5f winner, including Queen Mary Stakes: fairly useful form: won maiden at Newmarket in April: quite highly tried after: raced only at 5f. *Tom Dascombe*

FORMIGA (IRE) 2 b.f. (Apr 12) Worthadd (IRE) 124 – Hymn of Love (IRE) 100 **65**
(Barathea (IRE) 127) [2017 5g^{6} t6.1g^{3} p7.5g^{2} t7.1g^{5} p6.5g^{6} Oct 30] seventh foal: half-sister to 10.4f winner Stroke of Love (by Smart Strike) and 2-y-o 7f winner What About Bob (by Big Bad Bob): dam 7f-8.5f winner: fair maiden: will stay 1m: acts on polytrack and tapeta. *Jose Santos*

FORRICHERFORPOORER (IRE) 2 gr.g. (Feb 7) Casamento (IRE) 118 – Ghedi –
(IRE) (Aussie Rules (USA) 123) [2017 8d p8g Dec 20] well held in 2 minor events. *William Knight*

FORT BASTION (IRE) 8 b.g. Lawman (FR) 121 – French Fern (IRE) 81 (Royal **95**
Applause 124) [2017 104, a96: p10g^{4} t7.1g^{2} 7g 8m^{4} 8g^{2} a7.5g Nov 19] well-made gelding: useful handicapper: second at Newcastle (neck behind Flaming Spear) in January: left Brian Ellison before final outing: best form up to 1m: acts on polytrack, tapeta, firm and soft going: has worn headgear: usually slowly away. *Claes Bjorling, Sweden*

FOR THE ROSES 3 b.f. Nathaniel (IRE) 129 – Ivory Rose (Green Desert (USA) 127) **67**
[2017 68: 9.5d^{6} 11d 9v^{3} Sep 18] fair maiden: stays 9.5f: acts on good to firm and heavy going: in tongue tie last 3 starts. *John Patrick Murtagh, Ireland*

FORTIA 3 b.f. Nathaniel (IRE) 129 – Veenwouden 107 (Desert Prince (IRE) 130) [2017 –: **65**
p13.3g^{5} 11.5d^{3} p16d Oct 6] fair maiden: stays 11.5f: acts on polytrack and good to soft going. *Dean Ivory*

FORTINBRASS (IRE) 7 b.g. Baltic King 120 – Greta d'Argent (IRE) 103 (Great **69**
Commotion (USA) 123) [2017 68: f6g^{6} f6g* f7g^{5} f6m^{3} f6g^{3} f6g^{6} f6d^{6} f7g* f6.1g 6.1m^{5} f5g f6.1g^{6} f6.1g^{5} f7.1g^{6} Dec 19] smallish gelding: fair handicapper: won at Southwell in January and April: stays 7f: acts on all-weather, good to firm and heavy going: tried in cheekpieces: has worn tongue tie: usually races prominently. *John Balding*

FORTITUDE (IRE) 3 b.f. Oasis Dream 129 – Sweepstake (IRE) 98 (Acclamation 118) **88** [2017 6d^4 5d* 5g p6d^6 6.1g^3 6.1g^3 6s* Sep 20] 240,000Y: neat filly: fourth foal: half-sister to useful 1½m winner Horseshoe Bay (by Arch) and minor US winner by Empire Maker: dam winner up to 1m (2-y-o 5f winner): fairly useful performer: won maiden at Doncaster in June and handicap at Yarmouth (by 2 lengths from Dream Start) in September: stays 6f: acts on polytrack and soft going: sold 90,000 gns in December. *Hugo Palmer*

FORT JEFFERSON 4 br.g. Passing Glance 119 – Florida Heart 78 (First Trump 118) **77** [2017 90: f8g 10.1f 10.3s 8g 9.9s* Oct 10] lengthy gelding: fair handicapper: won at Brighton in October: stays 1¼m: acts on good to firm and heavy going. *Andrew Balding*

FORTUITIES (IRE) 3 b.f. Soldier of Fortune (IRE) 131 – Inez (Dai Jin 123) [2017 61p: **71** t8d^3 t10.2s^6 8d^4 8.3g^6 7.2d 6.9d p7s t9.5g Dec 22] fair maiden: left Jedd O'Keeffe after sixth start: stays 8.5f: acts on tapeta and soft going: tried in hood: often races prominently. *J. J. Feane, Ireland*

FORTUNATE VISION 2 b.g. (Mar 25) Libranno 119 – How Fortunate 69 (Haafhd 129) **73** [2017 5.2g^4 5s^4 6d^3 6s* 6v^2 t7.1d^3 Nov 4] lengthy gelding: fair performer: won nursery at Catterick in October: stays 6f: best form on soft/heavy going: in visor last 3 starts. *David Brown*

FORTUNE AND GLORY (USA) 4 b.g. War Front (USA) 119 – Spain (USA) 123 **71** (Thunder Gulch (USA) 129) [2017 6d^5 5.1m f5g^2 Aug 28] strong gelding: half-brother to several winners, including smart winner up to 9f Plan (2-y-o 7f winner, by Storm Cat) and useful 2-y-o 1m winner Dreamtheimpossible (by Giant's Causeway): dam won Breeders' Cup Distaff: fair form when second at Southwell on last of 3 starts in maidens: should be suited by 6f+. *Joseph Tuite*

FORTUNE'S PEARL (IRE) 2 ch.c. (Mar 7) Harbour Watch (IRE) 121 – Princess Mood **97** (GER) (Muhtarram (USA) 125) [2017 7.1m* 7d^4 7m* 7g^5 Sep 28] 30,000F: half-brother to several winners, including very smart Hong Kong 6f-1m winner Sunny King (by Desert Sun), formerly Kingsgate Prince in Britain, and smart 6f/7f winner (including at 2 yrs) Captain Ramius (by Kheleyf): dam German maiden: useful form: won minor events at Chepstow in July and Newmarket (by head from Thrave) in August: likely to stay 1m. *Andrew Balding*

FORWARD CONTRACT (USA) 3 ch.g. Exchange Rate (USA) 111 – Persistent Penny **–** (USA) (A P Indy (USA) 131) [2017 p12g^6 10.2g May 12] well held in maidens: dead. *Hughie Morrison*

FORWARD THINKER 2 ch.f. (Feb 5) Dream Ahead (USA) 133 – Avodale (IRE) **73 p** (Lawman (FR) 121) [2017 7m^5 Oct 25] lengthy filly: has scope: second foal: sister to useful winner up to 7f Visionary (2-y-o 5.3f winner): dam lightly-raced maiden in France: 20/1, fifth in minor event at Newmarket (2 lengths behind Timpani) in October: sure to improve. *David Simcock*

FOSSA 7 b.g. Dubai Destination (USA) 127 – Gayanula (USA) 67 (Yonaguska (USA) 112) **54** [2017 41, a57: t7.1m^3 t7.1m^3 p6g^5 t6g^5 t7.1g^3 p8d f7m* t7.1g^5 t7.2g t7.2g t7.2g t7.2g f7.1g^3 Aug 28] good-topped gelding: modest handicapper: won at Southwell in March: stays 7f: acts on all-weather: has worn headgear, including in 2017. *Mark Brisbourne*

FOUR CHAMPS 2 gr.c. (Apr 15) Champs Elysees 124 – Lana Jolie (GER) (Whipper **–** (USA) 126) [2017 t9.5g Oct 27] 20/1, well held in minor event at Wolverhampton. *Tom Dascombe*

FOUR DRAGONS 3 ch.f. Dragon Pulse (IRE) 114 – Mysterious Girl (IRE) (Teofilo **78** (IRE) 126) [2017 78: 5.1g 5s t6.1g t6.1g^2 a6g^2 Dec 6] close-coupled filly: fair handicapper: left Tom Dascombe after fourth start: stays 6f: acts on tapeta, good to firm and good to soft going: tried in cheekpieces: races prominently. *Charlotte Sjogren, Sweden*

FOUR FIFTY THREE 2 b.g. (Mar 31) Kheleyf (USA) 116 – Velvet Waters 80 **65** (Unfuwain (USA) 131) [2017 6d p7s t7.2g^4 7m^4 p8g* p8g^3 Sep 7] compact gelding: fair performer: won nursery at Chelmsford in August: will stay 1¼m: acts on polytrack and good to firm going. *Mark H. Tompkins*

FOUR KINGDOMS (IRE) 3 b.g. Lord Shanakill (USA) 121 – Four Poorer (IRE) **72** (Oasis Dream 129) [2017 –: 7g 9.2g^6 t8.6g^6 10s^2 11.5g* p12g* 14v t12.4g Nov 23] fair handicapper: won at Yarmouth and Kempton in October: stays 1½m: acts on polytrack and soft going. *K. R. Burke*

FOUR MILE BEACH 4 gr.g. Dalakhani (IRE) 133 – Rappel (Royal Applause 124) **–** [2017 77: 10.2d Oct 27] fair maiden, well held sole outing on Flat in 2017: stays 1¼m: acts on tapeta and heavy going: modest maiden hurdler. *Malcolm Jefferson*

FOURTH WAY (IRE) 4 b.f. Iffraaj 127 – Spiritual Air 93 (Royal Applause 124) [2017 **84**
93: 7d^4 7m Jul 1] lengthy, unfurnished filly: fairly useful handicapper: stays 7f: acts on good to firm and heavy going. *Ralph Beckett*

FOUR WISHES 3 b.g. Sepoy (AUS) 129 – Postage Stampe 95 (Singspiel (IRE) 133) **72**
[2017 57: 7g* 6.9g^4 8d^6 8.3m^3 10.2v 8.5d^6 t8g^2 Sep 12] fair handicapper: won at Catterick in April: stays 8.5f: acts on tapeta and good to firm going: tried in blinkers. *Tim Easterby*

FOXANGEL 2 ch.f. (May 7) Foxwedge (AUS) 128 – Tech Zinne (Zinaad 114) [2017 7d –
6s 7m Sep 23] fourth foal: half-sister to 1¼m winner Bob's Boy (by Showcasing): dam, placed in bumper, half-sister to useful 1m-1¼m winner Tech Exceed: in hood, well held in maidens/minor event. *Jose Santos*

FOXCATCHER 3 ch.f. Foxwedge (AUS) 128 – Copy-Cat 60 (Lion Cavern (USA) 117) **72**
[2017 77: 6d 5m 5f^6 Jul 6] well-made filly: fair handicapper: stays 6f: acts on good to firm and good to soft going: in headgear last 5 starts: often races prominently. *Clive Cox*

FOXFORD 6 b.m. Clodovil (IRE) 116 – Pulau Pinang (IRE) 101 (Dolphin Street (FR) **64 §**
125) [2017 60§: p6g p5g 6g^5 5.1s* 5s Oct 2] lengthy mare: modest handicapper: won at Chepstow in June: stays 7f: acts on polytrack and soft going: has high head carriage and isn't one to trust. *Patrick Chamings*

FOXINTHEHENHOUSE 4 ch.f. Bahamian Bounty 116 – Pants 78 (Pivotal 124) [2017 –
–: t7.1g Apr 17] neat filly: fair form at 2 yrs, little impact since: stays 7f: acts on polytrack: usually races close up. *John Holt*

FOX KING 3 b.g. Foxwedge (AUS) 128 – King's Siren (IRE) 77 (King's Best (USA) 132) –
[2017 –: p7g Apr 26] little show in 3 maidens. *Ralph Beckett*

FOX MINT 3 ch.f. Foxwedge (AUS) 128 – Unasuming (IRE) 59 (Orpen (USA) 116) –
[2017 –p: 7.1d Aug 24] no form: in cheekpieces last 2 starts. *Karen George*

FOXRUSH TAKE TIME (FR) 2 b.g. (Apr 9) Showcasing 117 – Stranded (Montjeu **65**
(IRE) 137) [2017 6m^4 6m 6g 7.4v^2 7g^3 7.4s^3 7d t7.2g t7.2g^3 t8s^5 Nov 30] fair maiden: stays 7.5f: acts on tapeta and heavy going: often races towards rear. *Richard Guest*

FOXTRIX 3 b.f. Foxwedge (AUS) 128 – Royal Pardon 61 (Royal Applause 124) [2017 6g –
May 29] fifth foal: half-sister to 3 winners, including useful 5f (including at 2 yrs) winner March (by Dutch Art) and unreliable winner up to 6f Lord Buffhead (2-y-o 5f winner, by Iceman): dam maiden (stayed 9f): 16/1, very green when well held in maiden at Redcar. *Michael Dods*

FOXTROT KNIGHT 5 b.g. Kyllachy 129 – Rustam (Dansili 127) [2017 89: t5.1g 5m* **87**
5m^5 5.5g 5m^3 5m^4 5s 5s^2 5f^6 5v^4 5g^4 5g^4 5d^4 5v 5g Oct 7] smallish, robust gelding: fairly useful handicapper: won at Ripon (apprentice, dead-heated with Black Grass) in April: placed at Redcar in May and Ayr in July: stays 6f: acts on polytrack, tapeta, soft and good to firm going: tried in blinkers. *Ruth Carr*

FOXTROT LADY 2 ch.f. (Feb 6) Foxwedge (AUS) 128 – Strictly Dancing (IRE) 95 **86**
(Danehill Dancer (IRE) 117) [2017 6v 6m^3 6m^2 6g^2 6g^3 Oct 7] third foal: half-sister to useful winner up to 1¼m Dance of Fire (2-y-o 1m/8.5f winner, by Norse Dancer) and smart 6f (including at 2 yrs) winner Dancing Star (by Aqlaam): dam 6f winner out of smart winner up to 6f (including at 2 yrs) Lochangel: fairly useful maiden: third in listed Two-Year-Old Trophy at Redcar (2¼ lengths behind Darkanna) in October: raced only at 6f: acts on good to firm going. *Andrew Balding*

FOX TROTTER (IRE) 5 br.g. Bushranger (IRE) 119 – Miss Brief (IRE) 72 (Brief Truce **93**
(USA) 126) [2017 98: 7f 7.6d^3 7m 7.1v^2 7f^6 7m^6 7s* 7g^6 8s^3 8g 7d Oct 6] rangy gelding: fairly useful handicapper: won at Sandown (by head from Sultan Baybars) in July: second at Chepstow in June: stays 7f: acts on good to firm and heavy going: tried in hood. *Brian Meehan*

FOXXY BROWN 2 b.f. (Apr 28) Paco Boy (IRE) 129 – Odense (USA) (Medaglia d'Oro –
(USA) 129) [2017 5s 5.9v^5 6m 7g^4 Jun 23] 24,000Y: third foal: half-sister to useful winner up to 1m Enjoy Yourself (2-y-o 7f winner, by Sir Percy): dam unraced: no form. *Richard Fahey*

FOXY BOY 3 ch.g. Foxwedge (AUS) 128 – Suzy Wong 80 (Auction House (USA) 120) **85**
[2017 64: 5m 6g^5 5m* 5m* 5f* 5m^5 5s^3 5g^6 5v^6 5s^4 5d 5g Oct 7] fairly useful handicapper: won at Redcar in June, and apprentice events at Beverley later in June and Haydock in July: stays 6f: acts on firm and good to soft going: sold to join Rebecca Bastiman 6,000 gns in October. *Michael Dods*

FOXY FOREVER (IRE) 7 b.g. Kodiac 112 – Northern Tara (IRE) 84 (Fayruz 116) **100**
[2017 91: t5.1f t5g^3 t5d^2 p5g t5.1g* p5g 5m 5s 5m^3 5g^5 5f* 5m* p5s^2 p5g^4 p5g* 5d Oct 28] lengthy gelding: useful handicapper: won at Wolverhampton in March, Haydock in July,

Newmarket in August and Kempton (by ¾ length from Alsvinder) in October: stays 5.5f: acts on polytrack, tapeta and firm going: has worn headgear, including in 2017: wears tongue tie. *Michael Wigham*

FOXY LADY 2 b.f. (Apr 21) Foxwedge (AUS) 128 – Catherine Palace 60 (Grand Lodge **66** (USA) 125) [2017 6d^6 5f^4 6d 7.2m^4 t7.1g^2 t7.1g^6 7d^4 Oct 20] 15,000Y: sixth foal: half-sister to useful 2-y-o 5f winner (stayed 1¼m) Sleeper King (by Holy Roman Emperor): dam lightly-raced half-sister to useful winner up to 1½m Alessandria, herself dam of smart performer up to 1½m Saint Baudolino: fair maiden: stays 7f: acts on tapeta and firm going. *Kevin Ryan*

FOXY LASS 3 b.f. Foxwedge (AUS) 128 – Domitia (Pivotal 124) [2017 p7g^6 t8.6g 7.5g **62** 11g 12.4v 11.3v Oct 7] 32,000Y: first foal: dam unraced half-sister to useful 2-y-o 6f winner Elronaq out of smart 6f winner Cartimandua: modest maiden: left William Haggas after second start: tried in blinkers. *Denis Hogan, Ireland*

FOXY REBEL 3 ch.g. Cockney Rebel (IRE) 127 – Foxholes Lodge (Nasheyt) [2017 8g **–** 8g 10g 8.3m 8s^4 8.3d Jul 25] rangy, rather unfurnished gelding: no form. *Ruth Carr*

FOXY'S SPIRIT 2 b.f. (Feb 6) Foxwedge (AUS) 128 – Jessie's Spirit (IRE) 85 (Clodovil **51** (IRE) 116) [2017 5m 7m 7d 8g^4 8v Sep 9] £5,000Y: first foal: dam, winner up to 7f (2-y-o 6f winner), closely related to useful 6f-1m winner Film Maker: modest form when fourth in minor event at Ripon in August, standout effort: often leads. *Tim Easterby*

FOYLESIDEVIEW (IRE) 5 b.g. Dark Angel (IRE) 113 – Showerproof (Peintre Celebre **48** (USA) 137) [2017 59: t9.5m^6 t8.6g t8.6g^6 p10g Apr 8] sturdy gelding: poor handicapper nowadays: stays 1¼m: acts on polytrack and tapeta: has worn headgear, including last 2 starts. *Harry Chisman*

FRAMLEY GARTH (IRE) 5 b.g. Clodovil (IRE) 116 – Two Marks (USA) 73 **72** (Woodman (USA) 126) [2017 79: t10.2d 10g^6 10.4m 8g^6 8.3s^2 7.8d^3 8.3g^5 8.3s Aug 5] rather leggy gelding: fair handicapper: stays 10.5f: acts on polytrack, soft and good to firm going: has worn headgear, including final start: tried in tongue tie: often races in rear. *Patrick Holmes*

FRANCA FLORIO (IRE) 3 b.f. Acclamation 118 – Lyca Ballerina 76 (Marju (IRE) **54** 127) [2017 76: 5g 5.2m^5 Jun 30] fair at 2 yrs, below that level in Britain in 2017: stays 6f: acts on soft going: often travels strongly: sold 8,000 gns, sent to Spain. *Kevin Ryan*

FRANCISCO 5 b.g. Paco Boy (IRE) 129 – Blue Goddess (IRE) 94 (Blues Traveller (IRE) **84** 119) [2017 90: 5s^2 7d 6s^3 6v^5 6d Oct 27] sturdy gelding: fairly useful handicapper: placed at Sandown in July and Goodwood in September: stays 7f: acts on polytrack, soft and good to firm going. *Tony Carroll*

FRANCIS OF ASSISI (IRE) 7 b.g. Danehill Dancer (IRE) 117 – Queen Cleopatra **–** (IRE) 112 (Kingmambo (USA) 125) [2017 120: 10.5d Aug 12] very smart performer, below form sole outing in 2017: stays 1¾m: acts on good to firm and heavy going: has worn cheekpieces: reported in October to have fractured pelvis. *Charlie Appleby*

FRANCIS XAVIER (IRE) 3 b.g. High Chaparral (IRE) 132 – Missionary Hymn (USA) **83** (Giant's Causeway (USA) 132) [2017 p8g^3 t8g^2 t8g* Nov 15] 125,000Y: third foal: brother to 1¼m winner (stayed 1½m) High And Flighty: dam unraced: fairly useful form: won maiden at Newcastle (by 3 lengths from Flying Raconteur) in November: raced only at 1m. *Hugo Palmer*

FRANCO'S SECRET 6 b.g. Sakhee's Secret 128 – Veronica Franco 90 (Darshaan 133) **95** [2017 90: p8m* p8d* p8d^2 p8m p8f^2 Mar 4] sturdy gelding: useful handicapper: won at Lingfield in January and Kempton (by head from Ice Royal) in February: second at former course (½ length behind My Target) in March: stays 1¼m, usually raced at shorter: acts on polytrack and good to firm going: wears headgear: sometimes slowly away, usually races nearer last than first. *Peter Hedger*

FRANGARRY (IRE) 5 b.g. Lawman (FR) 121 – Divert (IRE) 91 (Averti (IRE) 117) **65** [2017 67: p6g t6g p5g* t5.1g^5 6d 6.1m 6s 5.2m p7g^5 p7s^2 p6g p8g f7.1g^6 f8.1g^6 Nov 28] fair handicapper: won at Lingfield in May: stays 7.5f: acts on polytrack, tapeta and good to firm going: has worn headgear, including in 2017: in tongue tie last 5 starts. *Alan Bailey*

FRANK BRIDGE 4 b.g. Avonbridge 123 – First Among Equals 59 (Primo Valentino **99** (IRE) 116) [2017 77: p8g^5 8.2d* 7.8s 8.5f^2 7d* 8s* 7v^3 7g 8g^6 Sep 15] smallish gelding: useful handicapper: won at Leicester in May, Epsom in July and Sandown (by 4½ lengths from See The Master) in August: stays 8.5f: acts on polytrack, firm and soft going: tried in cheekpieces. *Eve Johnson Houghton*

FRANK COOL 4 b.g. Royal Applause 124 – Queen of Heaven (USA) 54 (Mr Greeley (USA) 122) [2017 –: p7m^4 p6g^3 t7.1g^3 p6f* 6g^2 6.1m 5.7d^2 5.7s^3 p6g^4 Oct 11] compact gelding: modest performer: won maiden at Lingfield in April: stays 7f: acts on polytrack, tapeta and good to soft going. *Tony Carroll* **64**

FRANKIE 6 gr.g. Firebreak 125 – Winterbourne 49 (Cadeaux Genereux 131) [2017 –: p10g^3 p12g^5 10d May 13] sturdy gelding: poor maiden: stays 1½m: acts on polytrack: often races towards rear. *Jimmy Fox* **49**

FRANKO FOLIE (FR) 4 b.f. Kendargent (FR) 112 – Atlantic Festival (USA) (Theatrical) [2017 a8.4g^5 p9.7g^4 p8g 10.7g^6 p9.4f 11.9g^4 12.4s^5 10.4g^6 11.9s 12.4s p9.4f Nov 29] €32,000Y: second foal: dam ran once: modest performer, lost form later in year: has had several trainers, including Gay Kelleway: stays 10.7f: acts on polytrack: tried in cheekpieces. *Mlle M. Henry, France* **63 d**

FRANK'S LEGACY 3 ch.g. Aqlaam 125 – Quite A Thing 93 (Dutch Art 126) [2017 f5g p5g t5g^6 t6.1g* p7g^2 p7d^4 Sep 28] fair performer: won handicap at Wolverhampton in June: stays 7f: acts on polytrack and tapeta: in cheekpieces last 3 starts. *Ivan Furtado* **66**

FRANKSTER (FR) 4 b.g. Equiano (FR) 127 – Milwaukee (FR) (Desert King (IRE) 129) [2017 75: 8m 10s 9.9m^5 10v^2 8v* Oct 9] fair performer: won maiden at Pontefract in October: stays 1¼m: acts on heavy going: has worn headgear, including last 2 starts: wears tongue tie: usually races towards rear: temperamental. *Micky Hammond* **77 §**

FRANK THE BARBER (IRE) 5 gr.g. Zebedee 113 – Red Rosanna 82 (Bertolini (USA) 125) [2017 64: p5g^6 t5.1g^2 t5.1g^5 p5f* p5g^3 p5g^3 5.1m^3 5f^3 p5s^4 p5s^3 5g t5.1m^3 p5s t6.1d^2 t5.1g^4 Dec 22] modest handicapper on turf, fair on all-weather: won at Lingfield in March: stays 6f: acts on polytrack, tapeta and firm going: has worn headgear, including in 2017: wears tongue tie: none too resolute. *Steph Hollinshead* **60 a69**

FRANKUUS (IRE) 3 gr.c. Frankel 147 – Dookus (IRE) (Linamix (FR) 127) [2017 105: 10d^3 11.6d^4 12m 9.9m^4 11.1g^2 10.5d* 10m^5 9.9s^6 Sep 27] good-topped colt: smart performer: won Rose of Lancaster Stakes at Haydock (by ¾ length from Mount Logan) in August: second in listed race at Hamilton (1½ lengths behind Defoe) in July: stays 1½m: acts on firm and soft going: in blinkers last 4 starts: front runner/races prominently. *Mark Johnston* **117**

FRANNY NISBET 3 b.f. Mount Nelson 125 – Don't Stop Me Now (FR) (Zamindar (USA) 116) [2017 –: 11.8d 12m 14s^3 16g^5 p16g* 16s^3 Sep 19] fair handicapper: won at Kempton in September: stays 2m: acts on polytrack and soft going: often races towards rear. *William Muir* **72**

FRANTICAL 5 b.g. Observatory (USA) 131 – Quest For Freedom (Falbrav (IRE) 133) [2017 63: 7d^3 10.2g^3 10m^5 10g^4 10d* 14s^6 p10g Sep 26] fair handicapper: won at Ffos Las in July: stays 1¼m: acts on polytrack, good to firm and good to soft going: sometimes wears headgear: usually races nearer last than first. *Tony Carroll* **67**

FRAP 4 b.g. Makfi 130 – Frizzante 121 (Efisio 120) [2017 64: t8.6g t9.5g^4 t9.5g t12.2g^5 t12.2g t12.2g p8s 8m^3 9s^3 9.9s 9.2d^6 9.2d^3 8.7g^4 9.9g Sep 17] modest handicapper: left Ian Williams after eighth start: stays 9.5f: acts on polytrack, tapeta, firm and soft going: often in headgear in 2017. *Frau L. Steudle, Germany* **61**

Betfred Rose of Lancaster Stakes, Haydock—a strong Group 3 on paper is dominated by Frankuus, who holds the late thrust of Mount Logan (spots on cap) with the pair well clear

FREDDY WITH A Y (IRE) 7 b.g. Amadeus Wolf 122 – Mataji (IRE) (Desert Prince (IRE) 130) [2017 76: f6g f6g p8g^2 p8g^5 p7g^3 p8g^4 p8g^4 7d p8s^5 f7.1g p7g p7g* p8g^5 Oct 24] tall gelding: fair handicapper: won at Kempton in October: stays 1¼m, effective over much shorter: acts on polytrack, good to firm and heavy going: sometimes wears headgear: tried in tongue tie. *J. R. Jenkins* **70**

FREDERIC 6 b.g. Zamindar (USA) 116 – Frangy 77 (Sadler's Wells (USA) 132) [2017 82: 17.2g* 17.1d* 18g^4 20.6v^6 18m t16.5g^5 Dec 5] well-made gelding: fairly useful handicapper: won at Carlisle in May and Pontefract (by 1½ lengths from All For The Best) in June: stays 17f: acts on polytrack, good to firm and good to soft going: often travels strongly. *Keith Dalgleish* **94**

FREDRICKA 6 ch.m. Assertive 121 – Vintage Steps (IRE) 76 (Bahamian Bounty 116) [2017 90: t5g^5 t5g t5g^2 t5d^3 t6g^2 p6g^2 p6g* 5f p6g^3 t6s^2 5g p5s^3 6v^4 6v^6 5d t5d^5 p6g^4 p7s* p7s^5 p6s^5 Dec 17] workmanlike mare: fairly useful handicapper: won at Chelmsford in March (dead-heated) and November (by head from Kreb's Cycle): placed on several other occasions in 2017: left David Barron after fourth start, Jose Santos after ninth, Chris Dwyer after twelfth: stays 7f: acts on polytrack, tapeta, firm and good to soft going: wears headgear: often races prominently. *Ivan Furtado* **86**

FRED'S FILLY 4 ch.f. Avonbridge 123 – Regal Quest (IRE) 91 (Marju (IRE) 127) [2017 –: t6.1g Dec 13] maiden: no form since 2015: wears headgear. *Nick Mitchell* **–**

FREEBE ROCKS (IRE) 2 ch.g. (Mar 15) Camacho 118 – Shamardyh (IRE) 69 (Shamardal (USA) 129) [2017 7g 6s 6d^4 7g^5 Aug 30] strong gelding: modest form: will stay 1m+. *Michael Bell* **50**

FREE BOUNTY 4 b.g. Dick Turpin (IRE) 127 – Native Ring (FR) (Bering 136) [2017 52+, a74: p16g^4 f14g* f14g^4 p15.8g^4 t13.9g^4 Mar 28] angular gelding: fair handicapper: won at Southwell (amateur) in January: stays 2m: acts on all-weather: wears tongue tie: front runner/races prominently. *Philip McBride* **74**

FREE CODE (IRE) 6 b.g. Kodiac 112 – Gerobies Girl (USA) 86 (Deposit Ticket (USA)) [2017 94: t7.1d* t7.1g^6 t7.1d^6 t7.1g^3 7g 6.7m 7.1d 7d 9d 11.2s p10.7g p12g Dec 21] strong gelding: fairly useful handicapper: won at Newcastle in February: third there in March: left David Barron after fifth start: unproven beyond 7f: acts on polytrack, tapeta, good to firm and good to soft going: has worn headgear, including final start: in tongue tie last 3 starts. *Eugene M. O'Sullivan, Ireland* **90**

FREEDIVER 3 ch.f. Bated Breath 125 – Grand Coral (Grand Lodge (USA) 125) [2017 –: t8.6g t9.5g Dec 22] modest form. *John Berry* **54**

FREEDOM FIGHTER (IRE) 7 b.g. Danehill Dancer (IRE) 117 – Rose of Petra (IRE) 91 (Golan (IRE) 129) [2017 12v^5 p8g^6 p8s^6 Sep 30] very lightly-raced maiden: best effort in 2017 after 5-year absence when sixth in maiden at Kempton: wears tongue tie nowadays. *Tim Pinfield* **67**

FREE FORUM (IRE) 3 b.g. Holy Roman Emperor (IRE) 125 – Kentucky Warbler (IRE) 77 (Spinning World (USA) 130) [2017 p8g p8g 8m 10.1m* 9.9g^3 p12g^3 p12g^6 Oct 3] fair handicapper: won at Yarmouth in August: stays 1½m: acts on polytrack and good to firm going. *David Simcock* **77**

FREE SPIRITED 2 ch.g. (Apr 7) Equiano (FR) 127 – Tagula Sunrise (IRE) 101 (Tagula (IRE) 116) [2017 6g 5m 5m^5 5s Sep 20] useful-looking gelding: has scope: modest form: best form at 5f: tried in cheekpieces. *Richard Fahey* **55**

FREE TALKIN 2 b.f. (Apr 26) Equiano (FR) 127 – Where's Broughton 77 (Cadeaux Genereux 131) [2017 7.6s 8m^6 p7g^5 p7g^6 Dec 28] 14,000Y: sturdy filly: half-sister to several winners, including 1¼m winner Near Kettering (by Medicean) and 7f winner Colourfilly (by Compton Place): dam, 9.5f winner, sister to very smart 1m-1¼m winner Desert Deer: poor form. *Michael Attwater* **46**

FREE TO ROAM (IRE) 4 gr.f. Bushranger (IRE) 119 – Operissimo (Singspiel (IRE) 133) [2017 62: p7d p8g^2 p8g t7.1g^5 p8d^3 p8s 7g 7d^4 7d 7.5d^3 7.2d^5 7.8g^5 a6g^3 6.3v^2 5s^2 5.8v 7v p5g^3 p7s^2 p6g* Dec 21] good-topped filly: modest handicapper: won at Dundalk in December: left Luke McJannet after sixth start: stays 8.5f, effective over shorter: acts on polytrack, tapeta, sand and heavy going: wears cheekpieces. *Adrian McGuinness, Ireland* **59**

FREE ZONE 8 b.g. Kyllachy 129 – Aldora 109 (Magic Ring (IRE) 115) [2017 93: p6g^3 p6g^2 p7g^4 a5g* a6g 6g^6 6g^5 6g* a6g* a6g^4 a6g^2 a6g a6g^2 Nov 6] smallish, good-topped gelding: useful performer: won handicaps at Bro Park in April and August (2): left Lee Carter after third start: best at 5f/6f: acts on polytrack, dirt, good to firm and heavy going: wears headgear: front runner/races prominently. *Claes Bjorling, Sweden* **100**

FREIGHT TRAIN (IRE) 5 b.g. Manduro (GER) 135 – Sigonella (IRE) (Priolo (USA) 127) [2017 85: t9.5m p8d p8g p8g p8g Oct 24] fairly useful at best, no form in 2017: often wears cheekpieces. *Adrian Wintle* –

FRENCH 4 ch.f. Monsieur Bond (IRE) 120 – Guadaloup 70 (Loup Sauvage (USA) 125) [2017 63: 6m⁶ 6m² 6s* 6.1g² t7.2g² 6d⁵ t6g t6.1g t6d t6.1g³ Dec 13] workmanlike filly: fair handicapper: won at Thirsk in May: stays 6f: acts on tapeta, soft and good to firm going: wears cheekpieces: often races prominently. *Antony Brittain* 77 a71

FRENCH CRICKET (FR) 2 b.g. (May 10) Sunday Break (JPN) 121 – Hambye 97 (Distant Relative 128) [2017 p8d p7g Dec 31] little impact in minor events. *George Baker* –

FRENCH FLYER (IRE) 2 b.g. (Mar 31) Pour Moi (IRE) 125 – Leavingonajetplane (IRE) 76 (Danehill (USA) 126) [2017 6g* 7.2g³ 7.2g⁴ 8g² Sep 1] fair form: won minor event at Ayr in June: bred to stay beyond 1m. *Michael Dods* 75

FRENCH HEROINE 2 b.f. (May 12) Redoute's Choice (AUS) – Hasaiyda (IRE) 84 (Hector Protector (USA) 124) [2017 7d Sep 30] 78,000Y: seventh foal: half-sister to 3 winners, including smart 1¼m-1½m winner Glorious Protector and 11.6f/1½m winner Full Moon Fever (both by Azamour): dam 9f-1¼m winner: 16/1, seventh in maiden at Newmarket (14¼ lengths behind Bye Bye Baby) in September: capable of better. *William Haggas* 54 p

FRENCH KISS (IRE) 2 b.g. (Feb 17) French Fifteen (FR) 122 – Ms Cordelia (USA) (Anabaa (USA) 130) [2017 8s 9.9s 8.3d Oct 18] little impact in minor event/maidens. *Hughie Morrison* –

FRENCH MIX (USA) 3 b.f. Dalakhani (IRE) 133 – Alharmina (Linamix (FR) 127) [2017 11.3g 12g⁵ 9.9d 11g⁶ p12g* p12g⁶ p12g⁴ p10.7g⁴ p10.7g Dec 21] seventh foal: half-sister to 10.5f/11f winner Amok (by Shirocco) and useful 10.5f winner Rio Amable (by Dylan Thomas): dam, 11.5f winner, half-sister to smart 1¼m/11f winner Albahri: fair handicapper: won at Dundalk in October: stays 1½m: acts on polytrack: often races prominently. *Joseph Patrick O'Brien, Ireland* 78

FRENCH RESISTANCE (IRE) 2 b.g. (Mar 16) Elusive Pimpernel (USA) 117 – Ivy Batty (IRE) (King's Best (USA) 132) [2017 8.3s⁶ 8g⁶ 8.9s³ 8.3d 8v Oct 23] tall gelding: fair maiden: stays 9f: acts on soft going. *Roger Fell* 66

FRENCH SILK 2 b.f. (Apr 10) Pour Moi (IRE) 125 – Green Silk (IRE) (Namid 128) [2017 5s 6d 6g 5g⁶ t6g⁴ Sep 22] 9,000Y: fifth foal: half-sister to 6f winner (stayed 1m) The Fulwell End (by Amadeus Wolf): dam unraced half-sister to winner up to 9f Singhalese and ungenuine winner up to 1m Docofthebay (both smart): modest maiden: best effort at 6f: acts on tapeta. *Chris Fairhurst* 55

FRENCH SILVER (FR) 3 gr.f. Rajsaman (FR) 121 – Senanque (IRE) (Pivotal 124) [2017 –: 10.2s 9d 11.6s Jul 29] angular filly: no form: sent to France. *Tony Carroll* –

FRENCH SPARKLE 2 b.f. (Mar 18) Swiss Spirit 117 – Chantilly Jewel (USA) 66 (Century City (IRE) 124) [2017 6d p6s t6.1d Dec 27] second foal: dam, 5f/6f winner, half-sister to US minor sprint stakes winner Cherokee Jewel: modest form when eighth at Chelmsford (4¾ lengths behind Lady Willpower) on second of 3 starts in minor events. *Robert Cowell* 53

FRESH FOX 3 ch.f. Sakhee's Secret 128 – May Fox (Zilzal (USA) 137) [2017 –: 10g Apr 21] well held in maidens. *Jonathan Portman* –

FRESH TERMS 2 b.f. (Feb 25) New Approach (IRE) 132 – Best Terms 116 (Exceed And Excel (AUS) 126) [2017 t7.2g⁶ Dec 5] second foal: half-sister to 5.3f winner Her Terms (by Pivotal): dam 2-y-o 5f/6f winner: 6/1, sixth in minor event at Wolverhampton (3¼ lengths behind Point Hope) in December: open to improvement. *Ralph Beckett* 60 p

FREUD (FR) 7 b.g. Dalakhani (IRE) 133 – Ailette (Second Set (IRE) 127) [2017 84: t9.5g t12.2g t8.6g t12.2d Dec 26] fairly useful at best, no form in 2017: tried in visor: in tongue tie in 2017. *Ian Williams* –

FRIDAY NIGHT LIGHT (FR) 4 b.g. Air Chief Marshal (IRE) 115 – Peninsula (FR) (Dansili 127) [2017 18m Oct 14] fairly useful performer for E. Lellouche in 2016, successful in maiden at Compiegne: well held in Cesarewitch at Newmarket only outing on Flat in 2017: stays 1½m: acts on heavy going: tried in tongue tie. *David Pipe* –

FRIGHTENED RABBIT (USA) 5 b.g. Hard Spun (USA) 124 – Champagne Ending (USA) (Precise End (USA)) [2017 63: t10.2g 11.2s Aug 7] modest handicapper, below form both Flat outings in 2017: stays 9f: acts on soft going: sometimes wears headgear: in tongue tie last 2 starts. *Susan Corbett* –

FRIVOLOUS PRINCE (IRE) 4 b.g. Baltic King 120 – Sweet Reflection (IRE) (Victory Note (USA) 120) [2017 56: t9.5m² t12.2m* p11d² p12g² t12.2g* 12f⁴ 12g⁵ 10f⁶ Jul 7] modest handicapper: won at Wolverhampton in January (apprentice) and February (amateur): left David Evans after fifth start: stays 1½m: acts on polytrack, tapeta, soft and good to firm going: wears headgear/tongue tie. *K. Kukk, Jersey* **62**

FROLIC 2 b.f. (Feb 22) Dutch Art 126 – Jamboretta (IRE) 102 (Danehill (USA) 126) [2017 7d³ 7.2d 7.4g² 7.1s² p7g⁶ Oct 5] well-made filly: fifth foal: sister to useful 1m winner Bowerman, and half-sister to 7f/1m winner Messila Star (by Pivotal) and 2-y-o 7f winner Music And Dance (by Galileo): dam, 1m/9f winner, half-sister to smart/ungenuine 5f-7f winner Excusez Moi: fair maiden: stays 7f: acts on soft going: tried in blinkers: front runner/races prominently. *Sir Mark Prescott Bt* **74**

FROM A DISTANCE (IRE) 3 b.f. Power 117 – Meek Appeal (USA) (Woodman (USA) 126) [2017 p6g⁵ p7g⁵ t7.1g p8g Apr 24] half-sister to several winners, including 2-y-o 1m winner (stayed 2m) Triumphant (by Danehill Dancer) and 1¼m winner Ferdinand Magellan (by Montjeu), both useful: dam Japanese 6f-9f winner: no form: tried in hood. *David Simcock* **–**

FRONTIERSMAN 4 br.c. Dubawi (IRE) 129 – Ouija Board 125 (Cape Cross (IRE) 129) [2017 106: 12g⁴ 12m* 12m² 12g² 13.3d³ 12.4g⁶ 12d* 12s⁶ Oct 28] sturdy colt: very smart performer: won handicap at Newmarket (by 2½ lengths from Top Tug) in May and listed race there (by ½ length from Red Galileo) in September: second in Coronation Cup at Epsom (1¾ lengths behind Highland Reel) in June and Princess of Wales's Stakes at Newmarket (¾ length behind Hawkbill) in July: stays 1½m: acts on good to firm and good to soft going: in headgear last 5 starts: quirky and can't be trusted. *Charlie Appleby* **120 §**

FRONTISPIECE 3 b.c. Shamardal (USA) 129 – Free Verse 102 (Danehill Dancer (IRE) 117) [2017 90p: 9.9g* 9.9m³ 9.9v² 9.9m Aug 27] useful-looking colt: useful handicapper: won at Sandown (by neck from On To Victory) in June: second at Goodwood (1¼ lengths behind Good Omen) in August: stays 1¼m: acts on good to firm and heavy going. *Sir Michael Stoute* **96**

Godolphin's "Frontiersman"

FRONTLINE PHANTOM (IRE) 10 b.g. Noverre (USA) 125 – Daisy Hill (Indian Ridge 123) [2017 t8g p11d p10g^{3} 10.2m^{4} 10g 8.9m Jul 25] strong, close-coupled gelding: modest handicapper nowadays: stays 10.5f: acts on polytrack, firm and good to soft going: has worn headgear: tried in tongue tie: held up. *K. R. Burke* **53**

FROSTBITE 2 gr.g. (Feb 1) Lethal Force (IRE) 128 – Red Sovereign 81 (Danzig Connection (USA)) [2017 6g 5.1s^{2} p6g^{6} Oct 24] fair form: second in minor event at Chepstow in June. *Eve Johnson Houghton* **65**

FROSTING 3 ch.f. Kyllachy 129 – Ice Palace 100 (Polar Falcon (USA) 126) [2017 8m^{4} 9.9g^{2} 10.2g* 9.9m^{3} 10s^{5} Aug 25] half-sister to 3 winners, including winner up to 1½m Queen of Ice (2-y-o 7f winner, by Selkirk) and 1m-11f winner Gone Dutch (by Dutch Art), both useful: dam, 1m-1¼m winner, closely related to smart 2-y-o 7f winner White Lake: fairly useful performer: won maiden at Nottingham (by neck from Sea Tide) in July: third in handicap at Brighton in August: stays 1¼m: best form on good going: front runner/races prominently. *William Haggas* **84**

FROWN 3 b.f. Nathaniel (IRE) 129 – Scorn (USA) 84 (Seeking The Gold (USA)) [2017 t9.5g^{3} Nov 7] third foal: half-sister to 1m winner Skimp (by Exceed And Excel): dam, maiden (stayed 1¼m), sister to smart 7f winner (stayed 9f) Ibn Battuta out of smart 2-y-o 7f-1m winner (stayed 15.5f) Sulk: 11/2, third in maiden at Wolverhampton (1½ lengths behind Al Kout) in November: open to improvement. *Ralph Beckett* **71 p**

FROZEN ANGEL (IRE) 2 gr.c. (Jan 27) Dark Angel (IRE) 113 – Cut No Ice (IRE) 80 (Verglas (IRE) 118) [2017 5m 5f* 5m^{2} 5m^{4} 5.5g^{2} 6m^{5} 6m 6d Sep 30] £165,000Y: strong, well-made colt: first foal: dam, 2-y-o 5f winner, half-sister to very smart 5f/6f winner Pipalong: useful performer: won minor event at Ascot (by 3¼ lengths from Corinthia Knight) in May: second in Prix Robert Papin at Maisons-Laffitte (½ length behind Unfortunately) on fifth start: stays 6f: acts on firm going: sold 335,000 gns, sent to Hong Kong, where renamed Patriotism. *Tom Dascombe* **106**

FROZEN LAKE (USA) 5 b.g. Elusive Quality (USA) – Creative Design (USA) (Stravinsky (USA) 133) [2017 77: p8g^{4} 8m^{6} t7.2g t7.2g Dec 13] fair handicapper: left Mary Hambro after second start: stays 1m: acts on polytrack and good to firm going: has worn headgear, including final start: tried in tongue tie. *John O'Shea* **73**

FROZON 4 b.g. Kheleyf (USA) 116 – Crozon 68 (Peintre Celebre (USA) 137) [2017 66: 9.2m^{5} 10g^{5} t12.2g^{2} t12.2g* t12.2g t12.2g* t12.4g Oct 10] fair handicapper: won at Wolverhampton in August and September: stays 1½m: acts on tapeta and good to firm going: wears headgear. *Brian Ellison* **65**

FRUIT SALAD 4 ch.f. Monsieur Bond (IRE) 120 – Miss Apricot 48 (Indian Ridge 123) [2017 83: 5m^{3} 6m^{6} t5g^{2} 5g^{5} 5g t5g^{6} t5d* t6d Nov 10] fairly useful handicapper: won at Newcastle (by neck from Impart) in October: stays 6f: acts on polytrack, tapeta, soft and good to firm going: wears headgear: usually races in rear. *James Bethell* **85**

FUEL INJECTION 6 gr.g. Pastoral Pursuits 127 – Smart Hostess 101 (Most Welcome 131) [2017 62: t5.1m^{4} t5d^{6} p5g^{6} 5g Apr 26] rather leggy gelding: modest handicapper: best at 5f: acts on fibresand, tapeta, soft and good to firm going: wears headgear: usually races close up. *Paul Midgley* **57**

FUJAIRA BRIDGE (IRE) 3 b.g. Sea The Stars (IRE) 140 – Garanciere (FR) (Anabaa (USA) 130) [2017 77p: 8m* 10.3d 8g^{3} 8f^{6} 8g^{2} 8.5m* 8.5v^{2} Oct 1] fairly useful performer: won maiden at Ripon in April and handicap at Epsom (by 1½ lengths from Lord Clenaghcastle) in August: stays 8.5f: acts on good to firm going: sold 82,000 gns in November. *Roger Varian* **91**

FUJAIRA PRINCE (IRE) 3 gr.g. Pivotal 124 – Zam Zoom (IRE) (Dalakhani (IRE) 133) [2017 10g^{2} Jul 24] 90,000Y: tall gelding: fourth foal: half-brother to 3 winners, including smart winner up to 15.5f Nichols Canyon (2-y-o 9f winner, by Authorized) and useful 1¼m winner Bright Approach (by New Approach): dam unraced: 12/1, promise when second in maiden at Windsor (½ length behind Al Mayda) in July: should improve. *Roger Varian* **88 p**

FUJIN 6 b.g. Oasis Dream 129 – Phantom Wind (USA) 111 (Storm Cat (USA)) [2017 70, a76: f5g p6g* p6g* f6g^{2} f7g^{6} t6g^{5} p6g* p6g* f6g p6g^{3} p6g^{4} 5g^{2} 5.1g^{4} 6g* 5s^{5} 6s^{ur} Oct 10] strong, good-bodied gelding: fairly useful handicapper on turf, useful on all-weather: won at Chelmsford and Lingfield in January, Chelmsford again in March and April (by 1¾ lengths from Lightning Charlie), and Brighton (by neck from Iseemist) in September: stays 6f: acts on polytrack, fibresand and good to firm going: usually wears headgear: usually races close up. *Shaun Harris* **83 a95**

FULHAM (IRE) 3 b.g. Sir Prancealot (IRE) 111 – Bond Deal (IRE) 104 (Pivotal 124) [2017 p10g^{2} t12.2m* 14s^{6} 13.9s^{3} p15.8g^{2} Oct 5] 20,000F, 13,000Y: fifth foal: half-brother to smart winner up to 1m Arcanada (2-y-o 7f winner, by Arcano): dam Italian/US winner up to 9.5f (2-y-o 7.5f winner): fairly useful performer: won maiden at Wolverhampton (by 1¾ lengths from Specialist) in February: second in handicap at Lingfield in October: stays 2m: acts on polytrack, tapeta and soft going: sold 4,500 gns later in October. *Robyn Brisland* **90**

FULL COURT PRESS (IRE) 4 b.g. Frozen Power (IRE) 108 – Share The Feeling (IRE) 80 (Desert King (IRE) 129) [2017 89: 8d 9.5s 12d 13.4g* 10.2s^{6} 12d^{4} 9v^{5} 14v Oct 11] fairly useful handicapper: won at Ballinrobe in July: stays 13.5f: acts on polytrack and heavy going: has worn headgear: sold 4,000 gns, sent to France. *John Patrick Murtagh, Ireland* **87**

FULL DRAGO (ITY) 4 b.c. Pounced (USA) 112 – Almata (IRE) (Almutawakel 126) [2017 119: 11.9g* 11.9m* 13.9g^{5} 10.9d* 11.9g* Oct 22] very smart performer: won Premio Carlo d'Alessio at Rome in May, Gran Premio di Milano in June, Premio Federico Tesio at Milan (for second year running) in September and Gran Premio del Jockey Club on same course (by 3 lengths from Savoir Vivre) in October: only defeat of year when fifth to Talismanic in Prix Maurice de Nieuil at Saint-Cloud: stayed 1¾m: acted on good to firm and good to soft going: front runner: to stand at Allevamento Si. Fra, Italy. *A. & S. Botti, Italy* **120**

FULL INTENTION 3 b.g. Showcasing 117 – My Delirium 83 (Haafhd 129) [2017 88: t5.1g* t5.1g^{5} 6.1m^{5} 6f^{2} 6d^{4} 6m 5d^{3} 6g Sep 1] compact gelding: fairly useful performer: won maiden at Wolverhampton (by 2½ lengths from Secret Strategy) in March: placed in handicaps at Haydock in May and Ripon in August: stays 6f: acts on tapeta, firm and good to soft going: in headgear last 3 starts: front runner/races prominently. *Tom Dascombe* **89**

FULL OF PROMISE 4 b.f. Kyllachy 129 – Arculinge 64 (Paris House 123) [2017 68: 6s^{6} 7.2m^{2} 7.8g* 8g^{2} 7.4f 8g^{4} 7.8d t8g Sep 22] fair handicapper: won at Carlisle in June: stays 1m: acts on tapeta, good to firm and heavy going. *Richard Fahey* **74**

FULLON CLARETS 5 ch.g. Equiano (FR) 127 – Palinisa (FR) 106 (Night Shift (USA)) [2017 84: p8g 6.1d p7g p7g p6g Dec 20] good-topped gelding: fair handicapper: stays 7f: acts on polytrack, good to firm and heavy going: often wears cheekpieces: front runner/races prominently: temperament under suspicion (has hung left/carried head awkwardly). *Laura Mongan* **66**

FULL TILT LAD (IRE) 3 b.g. Lilbourne Lad (IRE) 111 – Tiltili (IRE) 51 (Spectrum (IRE) 126) [2017 12g^{5} 7m 7g 14m May 30] no form. *Tim Easterby* **–**

FULLY FOCUSSED (IRE) 3 br.f. Intense Focus (USA) 117 – Folcungi (IRE) (Mukaddamah (USA) 125) [2017 –: t6f Jan 5] no form. *Ann Duffield* **–**

FUMBO JUMBO (IRE) 4 b.f. Zebedee 113 – Baraloti (IRE) 71 (Barathea (IRE) 127) [2017 94: 5m^{2} 5s^{3} 5d^{3} 5.5g^{4} 5m^{4} 5d^{5} 5g Oct 13] strong, close-coupled filly: fairly useful handicapper: placed first 3 starts in 2017: best at 5f: acts on fibresand, soft and good to firm going. *Michael Dods* **92**

FUNDING DEFICIT (IRE) 7 ch.g. Rakti 130 – Bukat Timah (Inchinor 119) [2017 85, a77: 6s 7m 6g^{5} 6d 8m 6g Sep 27] fairly useful at best, no form in 2017: wears hood. *Jim Goldie* **–**

FUNKADELIC 2 ch.c. (Apr 4) Dandy Man (IRE) 123 – Cape Elizabeth (IRE) (Invincible Spirit (IRE) 121) [2017 5m^{6} 5g^{6} 5.5s^{6} 5f^{3} 5g t5.1g* 5s^{4} t5d^{6} Nov 4] fair performer: won claimer at Wolverhampton in August: best form at 5f: acts on tapeta and firm going: tried in cheekpieces. *Ben Haslam* **66**

FUNKY FOOTSTEPS (IRE) 3 ch.f. Footstepsinthesand 120 – Felin Gruvy (IRE) 69 (Tagula (IRE) 116) [2017 74: 8s^{6} 8.1g^{3} 8d^{3} 10g^{2} 9.9m^{3} 9.9s Oct 9] angular filly: fair handicapper: stays 1¼m: acts on good to firm and good to soft going: in cheekpieces last 4 starts: sold 3,000 gns, sent to Switzerland. *Eve Johnson Houghton* **79**

FUN MAC (GER) 6 ch.g. Shirocco (GER) 129 – Favorite (GER) (Montjeu (IRE) 137) [2017 109: 18.6m^{3} 21.6m^{5} 16.2m^{4} 15.4g* 17.9g 18m 11.9s Nov 11] good-topped gelding: smart performer: won listed race at Maisons-Laffitte (by nose from Vent de Force) in July: third in Chester Cup (length behind Montaly) in May: stays 2½m: acts on polytrack and any turf going: has worn blinkers, including in 2017: usually wears tongue tie: often races towards rear. *Hughie Morrison* **111**

FUNNY OYSTER (IRE) 4 gr.f. Dark Angel (IRE) 113 – Carpet Lover (IRE) 46 (Fayruz 116) [2017 65: f8d 9.9g^{6} 9.9d^{6} 8v^{3} Oct 1] sturdy filly: maiden, just poor form in 2017: left Chris Gordon after third start: stays 1¼m: acts on heavy going: has worn headgear. *D. Henderson, France* **45**

FUN RAISER (IRE) 3 ch.f. Dream Ahead (USA) 133 – Party Appeal (USA) (Mr Greeley **57**
(USA) 122) [2017 p7g^{6} p7g^{4} p8g p6g^{5} Mar 29] 7,000Y: second foal: dam maiden half-sister to useful 1¼m winner Cozy Maria: modest form: stays 7f: tried in visor: sent to France. *Harry Dunlop*

FURIA CRUZADA (CHI) 6 b.m. Newfoundland (USA) 122 – Nuestra Machi (CHI) **115**
(Hussonet (USA)) [2017 112: a9.4f* a9.9f^{3} a9.9g 8m 8g 9.9g 9.9s^{4} 11.9d^{6} 10.4g Oct 22] smart performer: won Maktoum Challenge Round 2 at Meydan (by nose from Second Summer) in February: third in Round 3 on same course (2½ lengths behind Long River) in March: left E. Charpy after third start: stays 1½m: acts on dirt and soft going: tried in hood. *S. Kobayashi, France*

FURNI FACTORS 2 b.g. (Mar 9) Captain Gerrard (IRE) 113 – Calgary (Pivotal 124) **40**
[2017 5g 5m 5d^{6} 5g 6g t5g Nov 15] poor maiden: raced mainly at 5f. *Ronald Thompson*

FURZE BOY 2 b.g. (May 26) Mazameer (IRE) 107 – Alustar 71 (Emarati (USA) 74) **–**
[2017 5f 5s May 17] workmanlike gelding: well held in minor events. *Michael Easterby*

FURZIG 2 b.g. (Mar 26) Monsieur Bond (IRE) 120 – Princess Cocoa (IRE) 86 (Desert Sun **76**
120) [2017 t6d^{3} t6g^{5} p7g* Dec 31] fair form: won minor event at Lingfield (by 1¼ lengths from Kath's Lustre) in December: stays 7f. *Richard Fahey*

FUSION CENTRAL (IRE) 2 ch.f. (Feb 6) Bahamian Bounty 116 – Whatever You Do **62**
(IRE) 67 (Barathea (IRE) 127) [2017 6g p6d^{4} 6.1g 6d^{5} 8.1g^{2} 7.1s p7g^{2} Oct 12] €13,000Y: angular filly: first foal: dam, maiden (stayed 6f), half-sister to useful winner up to 1¼m Rakaan: modest maiden: stays 1m: acts on polytrack and good to soft going: sold 6,000 gns, sent to Spain. *Richard Hannon*

FUTOON (IRE) 4 b.f. Kodiac 112 – Vermilliann (IRE) 98 (Mujadil (USA) 119) [2017 93: **98**
5f^{2} 6.1g^{2} 6f^{3} 5g^{4} 6g 6g^{6} 6g 5.5d Oct 2] sturdy filly: useful performer: placed in listed races at Bath, Nottingham (½-length second to Artistica) and Haydock (length third to Buying Trouble): stays 6f: acts on tapeta, firm and soft going: front runner/races prominently: sold 100,000 gns in December. *Kevin Ryan*

FUTURE SCORE (IRE) 2 br.g. (Apr 28) Cape Cross (IRE) 129 – Theola (IRE) 93 **70**
(Kalanisi (IRE) 132) [2017 p8g p10s^{4} Nov 23] fair form in 2 minor events. *Saeed bin Suroor*

FUWAIRT (IRE) 5 b.g. Arcano (IRE) 122 – Safiya Song (IRE) (Intikhab (USA) 135) **96**
[2017 101: 8g 7.6d^{4} 7.6g^{3} 8m^{4} 8.6d 6d 7v p7g^{2} p7g Dec 22] stocky, close-coupled gelding: useful handicapper: placed at Chester (2 lengths behind Fastnet Tempest) in May and Dundalk (neck behind Katiymann) in October: left Roger Fell after fourth start: stays 1m: acts on polytrack, tapeta, soft and good to firm going: tried in hood/tongue tie: sometimes slowly away, often races towards rear. *Gavin Patrick Cromwell, Ireland*

FYRE CAY (IRE) 2 b.c. (Apr 7) Red Jazz (USA) 125 – Anklesocks (IRE) (Night Shift **81**
(USA)) [2017 5.2g^{2} 6g* 6m* Aug 26] €13,000F, £12,000 2-y-o: third foal: half-brother to 5f winner Run Rio Run (by Captain Rio): dam, ran once, out of useful 6f/7f winner Cool Cousin: fairly useful form: won minor events at Yarmouth (by neck from Take Shelter) in July and Redcar (by head from Mistress of Venice) in August: stays 6f: sold 34,000 gns in October. *Kevin Ryan*

FYRECRACKER (IRE) 6 ch.g. Kheleyf (USA) 116 – Spirit of Hope (IRE) (Danehill **–**
Dancer (IRE) 117) [2017 76: 6g Apr 22] angular gelding: fair handicapper, well held sole outing in 2017: stays 7f: acts on good to firm going: has worn headgear. *Grant Tuer*

FYXENNA 2 ch.f. (Feb 5) Foxwedge (AUS) 128 – Good Enough (FR) 109 (Mukaddamah **57**
(USA) 125) [2017 6d^{5} t7.2g^{pu} Dec 5] lengthy filly: half-sister to several winners, including smart 1m/9f winner Smart Enough (by Cadeaux Genereux) and smart winner up to 1m Oasis Dancer (2-y-o 7f winner, by Oasis Dream): dam 9f winner: modest form when fifth in minor event at Leicester: in cheekpieces, went wrong soon after start next time. *Clive Cox*

G

GABR 2 ch.c. (Mar 11) Intello (GER) 129 – Spacious 119 (Nayef (USA) 129) [2017 6g^{2} 7g^{2} **108 p**
8d* 8d^{5} Oct 28] 300,000Y: fourth foal: closely related to useful 2-y-o 7f winner Spatial (by New Approach): dam 7f/1m winner (including at 2 yrs) and second in 1000 Guineas: useful

form: won minor event at Yarmouth (by 1¾ lengths from Istanbul Sultan) in September: fifth in Racing Post Trophy at Doncaster (5¼ lengths behind Saxon Warrior) final start: stays 1m: open to further improvement. *Sir Michael Stoute*

GABRIAL (IRE) 8 b.g. Dark Angel (IRE) 113 – Guajira (FR) (Mtoto 134) [2017 116: 8.9g 8.9g^5 11.9g 8g^4 8.1d^2 10.3m^4 8.5m^2 7.9m^4 8g^4 8s^3 10.5d^5 8.8m^5 7.6g 8s^5 p8g^3 Nov 18] big, strong gelding: smart performer: fourth in Lincoln Handicap at Doncaster (length behind Bravery) and second in Mile at Sandown (½ length behind Sovereign Debt) in April: stays 10.5f: acts on polytrack and any turf going: tried in headgear: often starts slowly, usually races in rear. *Richard Fahey* **114**

GABRIALS CENTURION (IRE) 2 b.g. (Apr 30) Society Rock (IRE) 126 – Flamanda 67 (Niniski (USA) 125) [2017 6s^5 7g^5 6.1v^4 7d^6 Oct 30] fair form: stays 7f. *David O'Meara* **73**

GABRIAL'S KAKA (IRE) 7 b.g. Jeremy (USA) 122 – Love In May (IRE) 80 (City On A Hill (USA) 114) [2017 102: 8g 7.6d 7.6g 8.2s 7.6d^5 7.9d 7.6s^3 t8.6g^5 7.6g 10.3v^4 10.3v^5 Sep 30] lengthy gelding: fairly useful handicapper: third at Chester (1¼ lengths behind Breakable) in August: stays 1¼m: acts on polytrack, soft and good to firm going: has worn headgear, including in 2017: often starts slowly. *Richard Fahey* **88**

GABRIAL'S KING (IRE) 8 b.g. Hurricane Run (IRE) 134 – Danella (IRE) (Platini (GER) 126) [2017 97: 12g* 16g 10.3m^6 13.4g^3 14g t16.3s^5 16.3m^4 11.8d 15.9g 14.4v^6 11.8v Sep 30] sturdy gelding: fairly useful handicapper: won at Thirsk (by ¾ length from Airton) in April: third at Chester in May: stays 2¼m: acts on polytrack, tapeta and any turf going: has worn headgear. *Richard Fahey* **94**

GABRIAL'S STAR 8 b.g. Hernando (FR) 127 – Grain Only (Machiavellian (USA) 123) [2017 97: 12.3d t16.5g* 12.3s^4 15.9d^4 16.3m 15d^4 14g 15.9g^6 14.4v^5 14.4v^4 15v^3 16d^4 f16.5g* t16.5g^4 t16.5g f14.1g* Dec 22] tall gelding: fairly useful performer: won handicaps at Wolverhampton (by 2 lengths from Little Stampy) in May and Southwell in November, and claimer at latter course in December: stays 2¼m: acts on all-weather and any turf going: wears headgear. *Richard Fahey* **90**

GABRIAL THE DEVIL (IRE) 2 b.g. (Apr 7) Epaulette (AUS) 126 – Grasshoppergreen (IRE) (Barathea (IRE) 127) [2017 6.1s 6m^5 7.2g^5 7s^6 t6.1g^2 7v^4 t6g^2 Oct 19] strong gelding: fair maiden: stays 7f: acts on tapeta: tried in hood. *David O'Meara* **76**

GABRIAL THE DUKE (IRE) 7 ch.g. Duke of Marmalade (IRE) 132 – Literacy (USA) 74 (Diesis 133) [2017 87§: 12.1s^3 15.9d^6 12.1m 13.4d t12.2g^4 t16.5g Oct 21] fairly useful handicapper at best: below form in 2017: stayed 2m: acted on all-weather, firm and soft going: wore headgear: often started slowly, usually raced nearer last than first: was one to treat with caution: dead. *Patrick Morris* **62 §**

GABRIAL THE HERO (USA) 8 b.g. War Front (USA) 119 – Ball Gown (USA) (Silver Hawk (USA) 123) [2017 101: 14g Apr 15] strong gelding: useful handicapper: stays 2¼m: acts on all-weather, firm and good to soft going: has worn cheekpieces. *Richard Fahey* **91**

GABRIAL THE SAINT (IRE) 2 ch.g. (Feb 23) Society Rock (IRE) 126 – Green Briar (Compton Place 125) [2017 6.1v^2 7v^3 Sep 30] €26,000Y, €35,000 2-y-o: first foal: dam unraced: fairly useful form when placed in minor events at Chester in September: should do better. *Richard Fahey* **84 p**

GABRIAL THE TERROR (IRE) 7 b.g. Kheleyf (USA) 116 – Simla Bibi 69 (Indian Ridge 123) [2017 68, a77: f8g t13.9m^3 t13.9g^2 t10.2g 12.1m^5 t12.2g^3 t14g t12.2d^5 Dec 16] fair handicapper: left Ian Williams after fourth start: stays 16.5f: acts on polytrack, tapeta, good to firm and good to soft going: has worn headgear: usually slowly away, often races towards rear: not one to trust. *Patrick Morris* **75 §**

GABRIAL THE THUG (FR) 7 b.g. Azamour (IRE) 130 – Baliyna (USA) (Woodman (USA) 126) [2017 61: f8g t8.6m* t8.6g* t8.6m^2 t9.5g^3 t8.6g t8.6g* 9.1g^3 10d^4 Jun 24] fair handicapper: won at Wolverhampton in January, February (amateur) and May: stays 10.5f: acts on polytrack, tapeta, good to firm and good to soft going: tried in cheekpieces: usually wears tongue tie: quirky: has joined Patrick Morris. *Ian Williams* **71**

GABRIAL THE TIGER (IRE) 5 b.g. Kodiac 112 – Invincible 76 (Slip Anchor 136) [2017 94: 7g 6m 7m 7s 7d^3 7.6s^2 6d 7.4g 7v^5 7v* 7.2v^3 Oct 16] fairly useful handicapper: won at Chester (by ½ length from Dark Devil) in September: stays 7f: acts on good to firm and heavy going: has worn hood: front runner/races prominently. *Richard Fahey* **85**

GABRIELLE 4 b.f. Paco Boy (IRE) 129 – Bounty Box 115 (Bahamian Bounty 116) [2017 78: p6g t7.1g 7s 7d^5 7.6s 8g 7d^2 Oct 24] angular filly: fair handicapper: best up to 7f: acts on good to soft going: has worn hood, including in 2017. *Dr Jon Scargill* **65**

GABRIEL'S OBOE (IRE) 2 b.g. (Feb 11) Rip Van Winkle (IRE) 134 – Tinaar (USA) **55**
99 (Giant's Causeway (USA) 132) [2017 8g Sep 1] 66/1, seventh in minor event at Thirsk. *Mark Walford*

GAELIC SILVER (FR) 11 b.g. Lando (GER) 128 – Galatza (FR) (Johann Quatz (FR) **73**
120) [2017 77, a89: p10g^5 p10g^2 p10g^5 p8g^6 9.1g 10g Jun 15] sturdy gelding: fair performer: stays 11.5f: acts on polytrack, good to firm and good to soft going: wears headgear: often starts slowly. *Gary Moore*

GAELIC SPIRIT (IRE) 2 b.f. (Jan 25) Fast Company (IRE) 126 – Mystic Dream 85 **66**
(Oasis Dream 129) [2017 5d^4 5g^5 5g p5s^3 5m^6 p5g^5 Sep 26] fair maiden: raced only at 5f: acted on polytrack, best turf form on good going: usually raced close up: dead. *Joseph Tuite*

GAELIC TIGER 4 b.g. Teofilo (IRE) 126 – Green Swallow (FR) 107 (Green Tune (USA) **97**
125) [2017 95p: t10.2s^2 12.1m^2 16.3d 11.1g* 11.4m^3 12.1g 12v^5 14g^{pu} Aug 14] tall gelding: useful handicapper: won at Hamilton in June: second at Newcastle (3 lengths behind Briardale) in April: stays 1½m: acts on tapeta, good to firm and good to soft going: in headgear last 5 starts: usually races close up. *David O'Meara*

GAELIC WIZARD (IRE) 9 b.g. Fasliyev (USA) 120 – Fife (IRE) 95 (Lomond (USA) **63**
128) [2017 71: f6d^4 5m 6g t6s 6g 6m^5 6d^6 5.9g^4 6g* 6g^4 6g 6m 7.2s 6d^5 t7.1d^6 Nov 4] modest handicapper: won at Redcar in August: stays 7.5f: acts on polytrack, fibresand, soft and good to firm going: wears headgear: often starts slowly. *Karen Tutty*

GAIA PRINCESS (IRE) 3 gr.f. Dark Angel (IRE) 113 – Mount Eliza (IRE) 99 (Danehill **56**
(USA) 126) [2017 65: 8.1d 7m 6g^3 p5g^5 p6g 6v Oct 19] rather leggy filly: modest maiden: stays 6f: acts on polytrack and good to soft going: in cheekpieces last 2 starts: often races prominently. *Gary Moore*

GAINSAY 2 b.f. (Feb 24) Sayif (IRE) 122 – Pesse (IRE) (Eagle Eyed (USA) 111) [2017 6g **–**
6.1g 7d Sep 6] 15,000Y: smallish filly: seventh foal: sister to 2-y-o 5f/6f winner Sayesse and half-sister to a winner in Italy by Refuse To Bend: dam, Italian winner up to 9.5f (2-y-o 7.5f winner), half-sister to Racing Post Trophy winner Kingsbarns: down the field in minor event/maidens. *Jonathan Portman*

GAKKU 3 ch.f. Pivotal 124 – Gakalina (IRE) 86 (Galileo (IRE) 134) [2017 8m^2 9.9m^5 **84 +**
9.8m^2 10.3v^2 p13g^4 f12.1g^3 Nov 28] leggy filly: second foal: dam, 1½m winner, sister to smart performer up to 1m Prima Luce: fairly useful maiden: probably flattered when fourth in listed event at Lingfield in November: stays 13f: acts on polytrack and heavy going: in blinkers last 4 starts. *Roger Varian*

GALA CELEBRATION (IRE) 3 b.g. Excelebration (IRE) 133 – Elusive Galaxy (IRE) **73 §**
98 (Elusive City (USA) 117) [2017 66: p7m* p7g^3 p7s 7g^3 7.6d 7.1d 7s^4 6s t7.2g 8s^3 8.1d^4 Oct 23] robust gelding: fair handicapper: won at Lingfield in March: stays 1m: acts on polytrack, soft and good to firm going: usually wears headgear: sometimes slowly away, often races freely: untrustworthy. *John Gallagher*

GALACTIC (IRE) 2 b.c. (Mar 23) Roderic O'Connor (IRE) 119 – Star Cluster 106 **67**
(Observatory (USA) 131) [2017 7m^5 7g^6 7s^5 8g^6 p7g^5 p8g 8.3d 7m 9d^2 Nov 4] good-topped colt: fair maiden: probably stays 9f: acts on polytrack: in blinkers last 2 starts. *Richard Hannon*

GALACTIC PRINCE 3 ch.g. Dubawi (IRE) 129 – Opera Gal (IRE) 108 (Galileo (IRE) **89**
134) [2017 78: 9.9m p10s^3 9.9d^3 12m* 12g^3 12v 13.4g^2 12m Sep 23] stocky gelding: fairly useful handicapper: won at Goodwood (by neck from Road To Dubai) in June: third at Ascot in July: stays 13.5f: acts on polytrack, soft and good to firm going: sold 65,000 gns, sent to Qatar. *Andrew Balding*

GALACTIC SPIRIT 2 ch.c. (Mar 31) Dutch Art 126 – Gino's Spirits 98 (Perugino **77 p**
(USA) 84) [2017 t8.6d^2 Dec 9] half-brother to several winners, including smart 1½m-1¾m winner Battersea (by Galileo), very smart 8.6f-10.7f winner Gitano Hernando (2-y-o 9.5f winner) and useful 11f-1¾m winner (stayed 2½m) Sizzler (both by Hernando): dam winner up to 1¼m (2-y-o 7f winner): 7/1, second in minor event at Wolverhampton (1½ lengths behind Mr Reckless) in December: will be suited by 1¼m+: will improve. *Marco Botti*

GALAHAD 3 ch.g. Sir Prancealot (IRE) 111 – Miss Mediator (USA) 77 (Consolidator **66**
(USA) 121) [2017 65, a71: t7.1g^5 Jan 25] fair handicapper: stays 1m: acts on tapeta and good to firm going: often starts slowly: hurdling in Italy. *Richard Fahey*

GALAPIAT 4 b.c. Galileo (IRE) 134 – Lady Jane Digby 118 (Oasis Dream 129) [2017 11.8g* 12g* 12m^{4} 12g^{4} 11.9g^{6} 12d 11.6g Sep 7] stocky, good-quartered colt: smart handicapper: won at Leicester (by 5 lengths from Faithful Creek) and Epsom (by 4½ lengths from Whinging Willie) in April: stays 12.5f: acts on polytrack, good to firm and good to soft going. *Mark Johnston* **114**

GALILEE CHAPEL (IRE) 8 b.g. Baltic King 120 – Triple Zero (IRE) 70 (Raise A Grand (IRE) 114) [2017 78: 11.1g 9.2g 11.2s t10.2s 12.5s t12.4g^{3} t12.4d Dec 16] compact gelding: fair handicapper: stays 12.5f: acts on polytrack, tapeta, good to firm and heavy going: wears headgear. *Alistair Whillans* **67**

GALILEO GOLD 4 ch.c. Paco Boy (IRE) 129 – Galicuix (Galileo (IRE) 134) [2017 126: 8s^{5} May 20] useful-looking colt: high-class performer: won 2000 Guineas at Newmarket and St James's Palace Stakes at Royal Ascot in 2016: well below best in Lockinge Stakes only start in 2017 (sustained soft-tissue injury): stayed 1m: acted on soft and good to firm going: keen sort, raced prominently: to stand at Tally-Ho Stud, Mullingar, Co. Westmeath, fee €15,000. *Hugo Palmer* **101**

GALINTHIAS 5 b.g. Sixties Icon 125 – Tidie France (USA) (Cape Town (USA) 125) [2017 74p: p8m 9.9g^{6} 8d* 8.5f^{5} 8m 10.1m 8d p8g Nov 7] fair handicapper: won at Brighton in June: stays 1m: acts on polytrack and good to soft going. *Simon Dow* **70**

GALIZZI (USA) 6 b.g. Dansili 127 – Dancing Abbie (USA) 105 (Theatrical) [2017 101: 20f 14.9m^{4} a11.9g* Dec 8] useful-looking gelding: useful performer at best: left Tim Vaughan after reappearance: won claimer at Lyon La Soie in December: stays 2m: acts on polytrack, viscoride and any turf going: has worn visor/tongue tie. *J. Reynier, France* **75**

GALLIFREY 3 b.f. Sir Percy 129 – Crystal Gal (IRE) 106 (Galileo (IRE) 134) [2017 79p: 9g^{2} 12g^{2} 12s 12g^{4} 14s^{4} p13g t12.4g* Dec 6] angular filly: fairly useful handicapper: won at Newcastle (by ½ length from Zabeel Star) in December: stays 12.5f: acts on polytrack and tapeta, acts on soft going: in headgear last 4 starts: often races prominently. *Lucy Wadham* **94**

GALLIPOLI (IRE) 4 b.g. Compton Place 125 – Altadena Lady (IRE) (Imperial Ballet (IRE) 110) [2017 96: 7g* 7m^{2} 7d 7m Jun 17] rangy gelding: useful handicapper: won at Leicester in April: second at Doncaster (½ length behind Aardwolf) in May: stays 7f: acts on polytrack and good to firm going. *Richard Fahey* **96**

GALLOPING HOGAN (IRE) 2 b.g. (Feb 15) Most Improved (IRE) 119 – Rapparee (USA) 78 (Red Ransom (USA)) [2017 p7s 7f 7d 8.1s 8.2g* Oct 17] fair performer: won nursery at Leicester in October: stays 1m. *Sylvester Kirk* **65**

GALLOWAY HILLS 2 b.c. (Feb 16) Kyllachy 129 – Bonnie Brae 111 (Mujahid (USA) 125) [2017 p5m^{3} Nov 25] 95,000Y: second foal: dam 6f/7f winner: 7/1, needed experience when third in minor event at Lingfield (6½ lengths behind Hit The Beat) on debut: sort to improve markedly. *David Elsworth* **63 P**

GALUPPI 6 b.g. Galileo (IRE) 134 – La Leuze (IRE) (Caerleon (USA) 132) [2017 64§: p12d^{5} p12g^{5} p13g^{5} p12g p12g 11.6s^{3} 11.5m^{5} p13.3s Nov 17] tall gelding: modest maiden: stays 1¾m: acts on polytrack and heavy going: wears headgear: temperamental. *J. R. Jenkins* **53 §**

GAMBINO (IRE) 7 b.g. Red Clubs (IRE) 125 – Temptation Island (IRE) 67 (Spectrum (IRE) 126) [2017 –: t8.6g t8.6g t6.1g^{pu} Aug 31] modest handicapper: stayed 8.5f: acted on tapeta, good to firm and good to soft going: often in cheekpieces in 2014: often started slowly: dead. *John David Riches* **64**

GAMBIT 4 b.g. New Approach (IRE) 132 – Sospel (Kendor (FR) 122) [2017 82, a95: 7g 8.3m^{5} 8m^{6} 10m p8g p8g p8g Oct 13] good-topped gelding: fairly useful handicapper: below best in 2017: left Tom Dascombe after sixth start: sole win at 1½m, raced over shorter otherwise: acts on polytrack, tapeta and good to firm going: tried in headgear/tongue tie: usually races prominently, often finds little: sold 15,000 gns in October. *Robert Cowell* **80**

GAMBOL (FR) 7 ch.g. New Approach (IRE) 132 – Guardia (GER) 109 (Monsun (GER) 124) [2017 –: t13.9m t12.2g^{6} t12.2m^{5} 13f* 14.5m^{3} 13.3g Jul 13] workmanlike gelding: fair handicapper: won at Bath in May: probably stays 2m: acts on tapeta and firm going: wears headgear: has worn tongue tie, including final start: sometimes slowly away, often races in rear: fair hurdler. *Ian Williams* **67**

GAME PLAYER (IRE) 2 gr.c. (Feb 4) Dark Angel (IRE) 113 – Lucky Clio (IRE) 59 (Key of Luck (USA) 126) [2017 6f 7d^{4} Jul 29] 185,000F, 300,000Y: half-brother to several winners, including temperamental 1¼m winner Central Square (by Azamour) and 5f (including at 2 yrs)/6f winner Lucky Beggar (by Verglas), both smart, and useful winner up **78 p**

to 1¼m Kingsdesire (2-y-o 1m winner, by King's Best): dam maiden (stayed 7f): fair form: better effort when fourth in minor event at Newmarket (2¼ lengths behind Anna Nerium) in July: should improve further. *Roger Varian*

GAMESOME (FR) 6 b.g. Rock of Gibraltar (IRE) 133 – Hot Coal (USA) (Red Ransom (USA)) [2017 104: 5m³ 5f⁴ 5g⁶ 5m 5g³ 5.1d 5g 5m⁵ 5v⁴ t5g⁵ 5v Oct 23] compact gelding: useful handicapper: third at Beverley (1½ lengths behind Edward Lewis) in April: stays 6f: acts on any turf going: has worn headgear: usually races towards rear: temperamental. *Paul Midgley* **100 §**

GAME STARTER (IRE) 3 b.c. Dubawi (IRE) 129 – Opera Cloak (IRE) (Cape Cross (IRE) 129) [2017 76p: 8m* 10g* 11.9g* Sep 16] smart form: won maiden at Newmarket (by ½ length from Mafaaheem) in June, and handicaps at same course (by 4½ lengths from Brorocco) in August and Doncaster (by 3½ lengths from Amazing Red) in September: stays 1½m: in cheekpieces last 2 starts: capable of better still. *Saeed bin Suroor* **114 p**

GAMESTERS ICON 2 b.f. (Apr 22) Sixties Icon 125 – Gamesters Lady 84 (Almushtarak (IRE) 122) [2017 7f⁵ 7d 8g² 8s² 8v⁴ Oct 23] lightly-made filly: third foal: dam, winner up to 1½m (2-y-o 6f/7f winner), also won over hurdles: fair maiden: stays 1m: acts on soft going. *Bryan Smart* **68**

GAMESTERS LAD 5 b.g. Firebreak 125 – Gamesters Lady 84 (Almushtarak (IRE) 122) [2017 p11d f12m⁶ p10g t8.6g⁶ t8.6g 9.9g May 15] modest maiden handicapper: below form in 2017 after long absence: stays 1¼m: acts on firm going: wears headgear: sometimes slowly away, often races towards rear. *Oliver Greenall* **39**

GAMRAH (IRE) 4 ch.f. Exceed And Excel (AUS) 126 – Fashionable 102 (Nashwan (USA) 135) [2017 69: t8.6m⁴ p7g⁶ Jan 25] fair maiden: below form both starts in 2017: best effort at 8.5f. *James Tate* **–**

GANAYEM (IRE) 2 gr.f. (Feb 20) Frankel 147 – Rose of Summer (USA) (El Prado (IRE) 119) [2017 6m⁴ Aug 27] $900,000Y: half-sister to several winners, including US Grade 2 8.5f winner Summer Front (by War Front) and US 2-y-o Grade 1 8.5f winner Laragh (by Tapit), both smart: dam unraced: 3/1, fourth in minor event at Yarmouth (4 lengths behind Zain Hana) in August: likely to improve. *Owen Burrows* **69 p**

GANGLAND 2 gr.g. (Mar 29) Lethal Force (IRE) 128 – Miss Dutee 68 (Dubawi (IRE) 129) [2017 t6g 5d² 6m² 6.1g⁵ 5m⁴ 6.3s t6g² 6d* 6d³ Nov 11] €38,000Y, resold €42,000Y: second foal: half-brother to 6f/7f winner (stays 1¼m) False ID (by Aqlaam): dam, winner up to 7f (2-y-o 6f winner), half-sister to useful 2-y-o 6f winner Yajbill: fairly useful performer: won nursery at Yarmouth in October: third in nursery at Doncaster (1¼ lengths behind Captain Jameson) in November: stays 6f: acts on tapeta, good to firm and good to soft going: usually wears hood: often races towards rear. *Richard Fahey* **80**

GANG WARFARE 6 b.g. Medicean 128 – Light Impact (IRE) (Fantastic Light (USA) 134) [2017 100, a109: t16.5m⁵ t16.5g Feb 15] sturdy gelding: useful performer: below form both 2017 starts: stays 16.5f: acts on all-weather, good to firm and good to soft going: wears headgear: fair hurdler. *Jamie Osborne* **94**

GANNICUS 6 b.g. Phoenix Reach (IRE) 124 – Rasmani 40 (Medicean 128) [2017 77: 8f⁵ 9.9g 10.1d⁵ 11.4m 8d Sep 18] strong, close-coupled gelding: fair handicapper: below form in 2017: stays 1½m: acts on polytrack, good to firm and heavy going: usually wears headgear: wears tongue tie: modest hurdler. *Brendan Powell* **63**

GANTON PAR 2 b.g. (Mar 11) Frozen Power (IRE) 108 – Sheer Indulgence (FR) (Pivotal 124) [2017 5.4g⁵ 7g Aug 25] well held in minor event/maiden. *Michael Easterby* **–**

GARAM (IRE) 3 b.f. Pivotal 124 – Coy (IRE) 112 (Danehill (USA) 126) [2017 t6f* p6g Jan 28] 23,000F, €30,000Y, £95,000 2-y-o: sister to 3 winners, including 2-y-o 7f winner Resolute (later successful abroad) and 6f winner Redden, and closely related to 6f (including at 2 yrs) winner Modest (by Kyllachy): dam, winner up to 1m (2-y-o 6f winner), half-sister to smart winner up to 1m Il Warrd (by Pivotal): fairly useful form: won maiden at Wolverhampton (by length from Blue Bahia) in January. *Hugo Palmer* **80**

GARBOESQUE (IRE) 3 b.f. Elzaam (AUS) 115 – Princess Nicole (IRE) 61 (Alhaarth (IRE) 126) [2017 –: f5g Jan 1] well held in maidens. *Shaun Harris* **–**

GARCIA 4 b.g. Paco Boy (IRE) 129 – Birdie 99 (Alhaarth (IRE) 126) [2017 107p: 10.3m⁵ 9.9g Aug 1] useful handicapper: fifth in John Smith's Cup at York (length behind Ballet Concerto) in July: stays 10.5f: acts on soft and good to firm going: sent to Germany. *Richard Fahey* **107**

Qatar Prix Dollar, Chantilly—representing the same stable as former triple winner Cirrus des Aigles, Garlingari battles on well to record a fourth win in pattern company, beating rank outsider Subway Dancer (rail) and British raider Salouen (right)

GARCON DE SOLEIL 4 b.g. Danehill Dancer (IRE) 117 – Darinza (FR) (Dalakhani (IRE) 133) [2017 12m 12g^5 14.2g p12g^4 p12g^6 p12g t16.5d Dec 9] modest maiden: stays 1½m: acts on polytrack and good to soft going: often races towards rear. *Michael Blanshard* **51**

GARDEN OASIS 2 b.c. (Feb 21) Excelebration (IRE) 133 – Queen Arabella (Medicean 128) [2017 6.1g^6 7.6s^4 Aug 5] €75,000F, 100,000Y: first foal: dam unraced half-sister to very smart 1m-10.4f winner Poet: modest form in minor events: should do better. *Sir Michael Stoute* **60 p**

GARDINIA 2 b.f. (Feb 4) Pivotal 124 – Garden Row (IRE) (Invincible Spirit (IRE) 121) [2017 7m 7g Aug 5] 26,000Y: first foal: dam unraced sister to useful 2-y-o 5f winner Madame Trop Vite: well held in minor events: sent to Norway. *Tim Easterby* **–**

GARLINGARI (FR) 6 b.g. Linngari (IRE) 124 – Garlinote (FR) 106 (Poliglote 121) [2017 120: 9.9m^2 9.9g^2 9.9g^2 12.4g^5 9.9s* 9.9d* 9.9g Dec 10] smart performer: won La Coupe de Maisons-Laffitte (by ¾ length from One Foot In Heaven) and Prix Dollar at Chantilly (by short neck from Subway Dancer) in September: below form in Hong Kong Cup at Sha Tin final outing: stays 12.5f: acts on polytrack, good to firm and heavy going: wears headgear. *Mme C. Barande-Barbe, France* **118**

GARNETTA 3 b.f. Poet's Voice 126 – Petit A Petit (IRE) (Holy Roman Emperor (IRE) 125) [2017 p7g p7g 8.3g May 1] 20,000Y: first foal: dam, French 12.5f winner, closely related to smart performer up to 1½m Inchila: well held in maidens: tried in cheekpieces: sent to Spain. *Amanda Perrett* **–**

GARRICK 3 b.c. Galileo (IRE) 134 – Rimth 109 (Oasis Dream 129) [2017 t8d* 10m 10g^2 Nov 3] sturdy colt: second foal: dam 5f (at 2 yrs) and 7f (Fred Darling Stakes) winner: useful form: won maiden at Newcastle (by 1¼ lengths from War At Sea) in February: second in handicap at Newmarket (head behind Celestial Spheres) in November: stays 1¼m: will go on improving. *John Gosden* **95 p**

GARSINGTON 2 b.c. (Apr 10) Intello (GER) 129 – Ruse 66 (Diktat 126) [2017 t8.6g p7s p7g Dec 28] well held in minor events. *Ed Dunlop* **–**

GARTER (IRE) 4 b.f. Fastnet Rock (AUS) 127 – Princess Iris (IRE) 99 (Desert Prince (IRE) 130) [2017 79: p7g^3 p7g^3 7d t7.1d^6 7.2v^6 Oct 16] fair handicapper: left Charles Hills after second start: stays 7f: acts on polytrack and good to soft going. *Richard Fahey* **76**

GARTH ROCKETT 3 b.g. Delegator 125 – Leelu 73 (Largesse 112) [2017 –: 10.2f 7.1m 7g^4 7m* 8d p8g p7g* p7g^4 Dec 6] strong gelding: fair handicapper: won at Yarmouth in August and Lingfield (apprentice) in November: stays 1m: acts on polytrack and good to firm going: in cheekpieces last 5 starts: in tongue tie last 2: races prominently. *Brendan Powell* **68**

GAS MONKEY 2 b.g. (Feb 16) Cityscape 127 – Bavarica 82 (Dansili 127) [2017 7d 7m 7s^4 Oct 10] modest form: best effort when fourth in minor event at Brighton (4½ lengths behind Move To The Front) final start. *Julia Feilden* **54**

GATHER 2 b.f. (Apr 16) Showcasing 117 – Acquisition 94 (Dansili 127) [2017 7g p7g2 p8g3 Oct 13] fifth foal: half-sister to 3 winners, including useful French 1¼m/10.5f winner Gaining (by American Post): dam, 1½m-1¾m winner, out of sister to Racing Post Trophy winner/St Leger runner-up Armiger: fairly useful form: best effort when third in maiden at Kempton (¾ length behind Preening) final start: will be suited by 1¼m+. *Amanda Perrett* **82**

GATILLO 4 gr.g. Showcasing 117 – Crystal Gale (IRE) 71 (Verglas (IRE) 118) [2017 79: f8g6 p8g 10.3g 7d 8m6 7v 8g4 7d4 f7.1g3 f8.1g f8.1g Dec 4] modest maiden handicapper: left Philip McBride after first start: stays 8.5f: acts on fibresand and soft going: tried in cheekpieces/tongue tie: sometimes slowly away. *Julia Feilden* **61**

GATTAIA (USA) 2 ch.f. (May 6) Kitten's Joy (USA) 128 – Shaaraat (USA) (Distorted Humor (USA) 117) [2017 p8g p8g5 Dec 20] $35,000Y, €95,000 2-y-o: third foal: dam, US 6f winner, half-sister to very smart 7f/1m winner Snaafy: fair form: better effort when fifth in minor event at Kempton (4¼ lengths behind Native Appeal) in December. *Ralph Beckett* **68**

GAUDI (IRE) 2 b.c. (Mar 28) Invincible Spirit (IRE) 121 – Alava (IRE) (Anabaa (USA) 130) [2017 p8g5 p8g2 Nov 18] 260,000Y: fifth foal: closely related to smart winner up to 1m Forest Ranger (2-y-o 7f winner, by Lawman) and half-brother to useful winner up to 8.6f Home Cummins (2-y-o 6.5f/7f winner, by Rip Van Winkle): dam useful French winner up to 9.5f (2-y-o 1m winner): fair form: better effort when second in minor event at Lingfield (short head behind Rusper) in November: likely to progress further. *John Gosden* **77 p**

GAVAL 3 b.g. Major Cadeaux 121 – Bold Bidder 92 (Indesatchel (IRE) 120) [2017 69: t5s3 6g6 6d* 6g* 6d5 Aug 13] strong, lengthy gelding: fairly useful handicapper: won at Leicester in July and August (by 4 lengths from Jacksonfire): stays 6f: acts on tapeta and good to soft going: front runner/races prominently: sold 2,000 gns, sent to Italy. *David Barron* **84**

GAVARNIE ENCORE 5 b.h. Intikhab (USA) 135 – Greeley Bright (USA) 64 (Mr Greeley (USA) 122) [2017 61: p8d5 p8g3 p8g p8g6 8f Jun 17] good-topped horse: modest handicapper: stays 1m: acts on polytrack and tapeta: has worn cheekpieces. *Michael Blanshard* **53**

GAVLAR 6 b.g. Gentlewave (IRE) 120 – Shawhill 93 (Dr Fong (USA) 128) [2017 98: t16.5g4 t16.3g* p15.8g 16g4 t16.3g 14d6 t16.3s 16d6 16d6 p16g5 t16.5g3 16d5 Oct 6] sturdy gelding: useful handicapper: won at Newcastle (by ¾ length from Good Run) in March: stays 2¼m: acts on polytrack, tapeta, soft and good to firm going: has worn headgear, including usually in 2017: often races towards rear. *William Knight* **99**

GAVOTA 2 b.f. (Feb 13) Bated Breath 125 – Ombre (Galileo (IRE) 134) [2017 6d* 7g* 7d3 7m2 Oct 13] tall filly: second foal: dam unraced half-sister to smart/temperamental performer up to 1m Grand Vista: useful form: won minor events at Newmarket (by short head from Daybreak) and Lingfield (by 6 lengths from Unchaining Melody) in August: second in Oh So Sharp Stakes at Newmarket (neck behind Altyn Orda) in October: stays 7f: should do better still. *Roger Charlton* **105 p**

GAWDAWPALIN (IRE) 4 b.g. Holy Roman Emperor (IRE) 125 – Dirtybirdie 63 (Diktat 126) [2017 95: p12g2 p11g4 10.1g3 12m 12d* 12d2 12s4 12g4 14.2s6 11.8d4 11.9s5 Nov 11] useful-looking gelding: useful handicapper: won at Ascot (by 1¼ lengths from Red Galileo) in July: stays 1½m: acts on polytrack and heavy going: often races freely. *Sylvester Kirk* **102**

GEALACH GHORM (IRE) 3 b.g. Finsceal Fior (IRE) – Saintly Wish (USA) (St Jovite (USA) 135) [2017 71: 10g 10.3m6 t9.5m t12.2d Dec 9] fair maiden: left John Patrick Murtagh after second start. *Sarah Hollinshead* **72**

GEESALA BRAVE (IRE) 2 b.c. (Apr 8) Arcano (IRE) 122 – Wong Again 62 (Araafa (IRE) 128) [2017 5f 6g4 5.9s2 t6g5 6v5 p9.4g Dec 26] neat colt: fair maiden: left John Quinn after fifth start: stays 6f: acts on tapeta and soft going: usually races prominently. *P. & F. Monfort, France* **70**

GEE SIXTY SIX 3 b.g. Mount Nelson 125 – Azure Mist 79 (Bahamian Bounty 116) [2017 p10g6 p10g5 p10g2 p14g5 p10s5 14g3 p16g6 p16g p16g Oct 12] fair maiden: stays 1¾m: acts on polytrack: often starts slowly, usually races in rear/freely. *Mark H. Tompkins* **71**

GEETANJALI (IRE) 2 b.f. (Apr 2) Roderic O'Connor (IRE) 119 – Scylla Cadeaux (IRE) 61 (Cadeaux Genereux 131) [2017 p7g Oct 5] third foal: half-sister to 8.5f-1½m winner Aussie Guest (by Aussie Rules) and 2-y-o 6f winner Hoku (by Holy Roman Emperor), later useful winner up to 9f in Scandinavia: dam maiden (stayed 1m): 100/1, well held in minor event at Chelmsford. *Michael Bell* **–**

GEMBARI 2 b.g. (Feb 1) Denounce 89 – Zagarock 56 (Rock of Gibraltar (IRE) 133) [2017 7m^6 7g t6s 7g p10g t8.6g^2 p10s* Dec 15] fair performer: won nursery at Chelmsford in December: stays 1¼m: acts on polytrack and tapeta: in headgear last 4 starts: often races prominently. *Ivan Furtado* **68**

GEMINI 2 b.f. (Apr 13) Makfi 130 – Gaze 74 (Galileo (IRE) 134) [2017 7m Oct 25] leggy, unfurnished filly: looks weak at present: half-sister to several winners, including smart performer up to 1½m Greatwood (2-y-o 1m winner, by Manduro), later successful in Australia, and 1½m/12.4f winner Musaanada (by Sea The Stars): dam, German 1¼m/10.5f winner, closely related to Irish Derby/Gold Cup winner Fame And Glory: 8/1, hinted at ability when well held in minor event at Newmarket: should improve. *Charles Hills* **– p**

GEMOLOGIST (IRE) 2 b.f. (Mar 20) Sir Percy 129 – Tiffany Diamond (IRE) 101 (Sadler's Wells (USA) 132) [2017 p7s 7d^3 7s 8.3v^6 8.3v Nov 8] leggy filly: fourth foal: half-sister to German 1¼m winner Mr Copperfield (by Shamardal): dam 1¼m winner: fair maiden: best effort at 7f: acts on good to soft going. *Mark Johnston* **68**

GENDARME (IRE) 2 b.c. (Mar 4) Lawman (FR) 121 – Gravitation 112 (Galileo (IRE) 134) [2017 8s 8.3d^3 Oct 18] half-brother to several winners, including smart winner up to 1¼m Gibeon (2-y-o 7f winner, by Cape Cross) and 2-y-o 7f winner Gemina (by Holy Roman Emperor): dam, 1½m-1¾m winner who stayed 2m, out of half-sister to Irish Derby/Gold Cup winner Fame And Glory: fair form: better effort when third in maiden at Nottingham (1¼ lengths behind Blazing Tunder) in October: will be suited by 1¼m+: likely to progress further. *Richard Hannon* **73 p**

GENERAL ALEXANDER (IRE) 4 gr.g. Zebedee 113 – Alexander Express (IRE) 102 (Sri Pekan (USA) 117) [2017 87: 5m^3 6g 5.9s 6m^2 7.4g 6s^2 Oct 10] fairly useful handicapper: second at Leicester (neck behind Rapid Ranger) in October: stays 7f: acts on good to firm and heavy going: usually wears cheekpieces: sold £10,000 in November. *Brian Ellison* **85**

GENERAL ALLENBY 3 b.g. Medicean 128 – Cat Hunter 77 (One Cool Cat (USA) 123) [2017 –: t9.5g p12g^6 14m^5 11.9d^6 15.9m^4 16.1d^5 16v^2 16g^4 p16g^2 16s^3 15.9s* p15.8g Dec 6] stocky gelding: modest handicapper: won at Catterick in October: stays 2m: acts on polytrack, good to firm and heavy going: wears headgear: often races prominently. *Henry Tett* **62**

GENERAL BROOK (IRE) 7 b.g. Westerner 130 – Danse Grecque (IRE) (Sadler's Wells (USA) 132) [2017 58: t9.5g^6 7m^6 p12g Dec 6] lengthy gelding: modest handicapper: stays 1¼m: acts on polytrack, good to firm and heavy going: has worn headgear, including in 2017: usually races close up. *John O'Shea* **50**

GENERAL GERRARD 3 b.g. Captain Gerrard (IRE) 113 – Dockside Strike (Docksider (USA) 124) [2017 –: 7m 5.3g^4 5.1d 6g 5.3g^6 5.3g^6 6v^5 Oct 19] neat gelding: modest maiden handicapper: best effort at 5.5f: best form on good going: in visor last 3 starts: usually wears tongue tie. *Michael Madgwick* **45**

GENERAL HAZARD (IRE) 4 gr.g. Cacique (IRE) 124 – In The Soup (USA) (Alphabet Soup (USA) 126) [2017 84: p12g^2 t10.2d* p10g* p11g 11.2s 11.9d^5 t9.5g* p11d* Dec 13] useful performer: won handicaps at Newcastle and Chelmsford in March, claimer at Wolverhampton in November and handicap at Kempton (by nose from Enfolding) in December: left Michael Bell after first start: stays 1½m: acts on polytrack, tapeta and firm going: tried in cheekpieces. *Archie Watson* **96**

GENERAL JACK (IRE) 2 br.c. (Mar 19) Society Rock (IRE) 126 – City Dazzler (IRE) 65 (Elusive City (USA) 117) [2017 p7g^4 Dec 31] first foal: dam maiden (stayed 1m): 2/1, fourth in minor event at Lingfield (2½ lengths behind Furzig) in December: capable of better. *Eve Johnson Houghton* **68 p**

GENERAL MACARTHUR (USA) 4 b.c. War Front (USA) 119 – Imagine (IRE) 119 (Sadler's Wells (USA) 132) [2017 103: 8g 8g t8.6g^5 8m^4 8.1g^4 7.9m 8f^4 5.5s^6 Oct 25] useful handicapper: fourth at Sandown and Windsor: left David Simcock after sixth start: stays 1¼m: acts on polytrack and good to firm going: tried in blinkers: often wears tongue tie. *Wesley A. Ward, USA* **99**

GENERAL MARIUS (IRE) 2 gr.c. (Mar 23) Holy Roman Emperor (IRE) 125 – Megaspiel (Singspiel (IRE) 133) [2017 7s^6 7m^6 6.1g^5 6s^3 7s 7g^5 Oct 16] modest maiden: best effort at 6f: in headgear last 3 starts: sold 12,000 gns, sent to Italy. *Roger Varian* **64**

GENERAL TUFTO 12 b.g. Fantastic Light (USA) 134 – Miss Pinkerton 104 (Danehill (USA) 126) [2017 60§: f8g^3 f8g^3 f8g^5 f8g^2 p10g f7m^2 f7g^2 f8d^3 f7g^4 f7g^6 p8d f8.1g^5 Dec 21] sturdy gelding: modest handicapper: winner at 1½m, races mostly over shorter nowadays: acts on polytrack, fibresand, firm and soft going: wears headgear: usually races nearer last than first: not one to rely on (tends to get well behind). *Charles Smith* **59 §**

GENERALYSE 8 b.g. Cadeaux Genereux 131 – Dance To The Blues (IRE) 73 (Danehill Dancer (IRE) 117) [2017 67§: t6f 5.7f² p6g⁴ t6.1g⁶ 5g⁶ 6g Jul 20] lengthy gelding: fair handicapper: stays 6f: acts on polytrack, tapeta, firm and good to soft going: wears headgear: tried in tongue tie: inconsistent. *Anabel K. Murphy* **67 a58**

GENERAL ZOFF 2 b.g. (Feb 18) Zoffany (IRE) 121 – Aunt Julia 106 (In The Wings 128) [2017 6g 6.1m⁶ 7m³ 7s 8g Aug 25] good-topped gelding: fair maiden: best effort at 7f: acts on good to firm going. *William Muir* **69**

GENEROUS TIMES 3 b.f. Bahri (USA) 125 – Gerardina (Generous (IRE) 139) [2017 –: f12g Apr 16] little form. *Chris Grant* **–**

GENETICS (FR) 3 b.c. Manduro (GER) 135 – Garmerita (FR) (Poliglote 121) [2017 89: 10m 10s p8g⁵ Dec 13] sturdy colt: fairly useful handicapper: stays 1¼m: acts on good to firm going: tried in hood. *Andrew Balding* **92**

GENRES 5 b.g. Champs Elysees 124 – Musical Horizon (USA) (Distant View (USA) 126) [2017 72: t12.4g* t12.4d³ t10.2gᵖᵘ 11.1m* t10.2s May 23] big gelding: fair handicapper: won at Newcastle (amateur) in January and Hamilton in May: stays 12.5f: acts on tapeta, firm and good to soft going: front runner/races prominently: has joined Rebecca Menzies. *Sally Haynes* **77**

GENTLEMAN GILES (IRE) 3 b.c. Dutch Art 126 – Sularina (IRE) 74 (Alhaarth (IRE) 126) [2017 51: t6m* t6m⁶ p6g⁵ Jan 28] good-topped colt: modest handicapper: won at Wolverhampton in January: best effort at 6f: acts on tapeta: sold 8,000 gns, sent to Italy. *Jamie Osborne* **62**

GENTLEMEN 6 ch.g. Ad Valorem (USA) 125 – Stoney Cove (IRE) (Needwood Blade 117) [2017 104§: t6g p6g² p6m p6g⁴ p6g⁴ t6g t6g t6g⁴ p7g p6g⁴ t6.1g p5g p5g t7.2g p7sᵘʳ p8g⁶ Dec 13] useful handicapper: second in minor event at Kempton (1½ lengths behind Pretend) in January: stays 7f: acts on polytrack and tapeta: wears headgear: tried in tongue tie: has looked reluctant and refused to race. *Phil McEntee* **101 §**

GENUINE APPROVAL (IRE) 4 ch.f. Approve (IRE) 112 – Genuinely (IRE) 43 (Entrepreneur 123) [2017 86, a74: p10g p10g p12f p12g 10m t8.6g t8.6g p10g Dec 13] fairly useful handicapper: below form in 2017: stays 1½m: acts on polytrack, good to firm and good to soft going. *John Butler* **67**

GEOFF POTTS (IRE) 4 ch.g. Zebedee 113 – Our Sheila 82 (Bahamian Bounty 116) [2017 81: p6m³ p6g² 6m 5.7m⁶ 5m 6s* 5s⁵ 6s³ 6s⁴ p6g³ p6g Nov 29] fairly useful handicapper: won at Leicester (by 1¼ lengths from Operative) in August: left Jeremy Gask after fifth start: stays 6f: acts on polytrack and soft going: has worn hood. *Richard Fahey* **80**

GEOFFREY'S GIRL (FR) 4 b.f. Croco Rouge (IRE) 126 – Camas (FR) (Hamas (IRE) 125) [2017 12.4g 11.9d² 11.4g⁶ Jul 24] lengthy filly: second foal: dam French 1m-10.6f winner: fairly useful performer: won twice in 2016, including handicap at Saint-Cloud: second in claimer at Compiegne in May: left J-F. Doucet after: stays 15f: acts on heavy going: tried in hood. *Richard Rowe* **81**

GEOPHONY (IRE) 3 b.g. Canford Cliffs (IRE) 133 – Dawn Chorus (IRE) (Mukaddamah (USA) 125) [2017 76: 8m⁴ 7.5m 9.9g 9.2g 7.2v Oct 16] rangy gelding: fair handicapper: stays 7f: acts on polytrack: tried in blinkers: sold 1,000 gns, sent to Spain. *Mark Johnston* **72**

GEORDIE GEORGE (IRE) 5 b.g. Kodiac 112 – Trika (First Trump 118) [2017 f7g³ t8s⁶ 7.8v* 9d 7.4s f7.1g⁶ Aug 28] quite attractive gelding: fair handicapper: won at Carlisle in June: stays 1½m: acts on fibresand, good to firm and heavy going: has worn cheekpieces: in tongue tie last 5 starts. *Rebecca Menzies* **67**

GEORDIELAD 3 ch.g. Geordieland (FR) 122 – Adees Dancer 65 (Danehill Dancer (IRE) 117) [2017 p10g 10.2g p7g p12g p10d Sep 21] tall gelding: little form. *Jamie Osborne* **–**

GEORGE BAILEY (IRE) 5 b.g. Zebedee 113 – Zuzu (IRE) 94 (Acclamation 118) [2017 50: t7.1d⁶ t6g 5g 5m⁵ 5f 6g f6.1g t7.1d Nov 4] poor handicapper: stays 7f: acts on fibresand, tapeta and good to firm going: has worn headgear, including in 2017. *Suzzanne France* **48**

GEORGE BAKER (IRE) 10 b.g. Camacho 118 – Petite Maxine 70 (Sharpo 132) [2017 72: t7.1g⁵ t7.1g⁶ p8g p7g 8d⁴ 8.5g³ Aug 13] modest handicapper nowadays: stays 9.5f, usually races at shorter: acts on polytrack, tapeta and firm going: tried in cheekpieces/ tongue tie. *George Baker* **64**

GEORGE BOWEN (IRE) 5 gr.g. Dark Angel (IRE) 113 – Midnight Oasis 49 (Oasis Dream 129) [2017 101: 6g 6m 6s⁶ 6m³ 6.1m* 6.3f 6g 6d⁶ 6g⁶ 6s 6v³ 6d Oct 27] sturdy gelding: useful handicapper: won at Nottingham (by 4½ lengths from Love Island) in June: stays 7f: acts on tapeta, good to firm and heavy going: has worn headgear, including last 5 starts. *Richard Fahey* **100**

GEORGE CINQ 7 b.g. Pastoral Pursuits 127 – Fairnilee 67 (Selkirk (USA) 129) [2017 102§: t7.1g6 f7g* 8g Apr 1] good-bodied gelding: useful handicapper: won at Southwell (by 1½ lengths from Outer Space) in March: stays 1m: acts on all-weather, firm and soft going: has worn headgear: usually travels strongly: temperamental. *George Scott* **99 §**

GEORGE DRYDEN (IRE) 5 gr.g. Zebedee 113 – Key To Fortune (GER) 86 (Big Shuffle (USA) 122) [2017 109: 6m5 6m 7d 6g t6.1g Oct 7] lengthy gelding: useful handicapper: below best in 2017: stays 6f: acts on soft and good to firm going: tried in cheekpieces: sold 40,000 gns in November to join Charlie Wallis: has hung left. *Ann Duffield* **97**

GEORGE (IRE) 2 b.g. (Apr 7) Dragon Pulse (IRE) 114 – Before The Storm 78 (Sadler's Wells (USA) 132) [2017 6s3 6g5 6g p6d2 7v2 8s2 Oct 19] 45,000Y: lengthy gelding: half-brother to 3 winners, including useful 2-y-o 7f winner Storm Rising (by Canford Cliffs) and 9.5f/1¼m winner Landau (by Aussie Rules): dam, maiden (stayed 1m), half-sister to useful performer up to 14.6f Valentine Girl: fairly useful maiden: second in nursery at Epsom in October: stays 7f: acts on polytrack, best turf form on soft/heavy going. *Sylvester Kirk* **83**

GEORGE OF HEARTS (FR) 2 gr.c. (Mar 7) Kendargent (FR) 112 – Bugie d'Amore 107 (Rail Link 132) [2017 6g4 6.5d2 Oct 27] €155,000Y, €470,000 2-y-o: second foal: half-brother to 2-y-o 7f winner Dubai Hero (by Dark Angel): dam Italian 2-y-o 7f/1m winner who stayed 1¼m: fairly useful form: fourth in maiden at Newbury (2¾ lengths behind Beshaayir) in September: remains capable of better. *Richard Hughes* **83 p**

GEORGE REME (IRE) 3 ch.g. Power 117 – My Sweet Georgia (IRE) 79 (Royal Applause 124) [2017 84: 7.5m4 9m5 8d 8.5m3 8.5m5 7.4f6 8d p8d t8s6 Nov 30] fairly useful handicapper: fourth at Beverley in April: stays 1m: acts on tapeta, good to firm and good to soft going: wears headgear. *John Quinn* **83**

GEORGE VILLIERS (IRE) 2 b.c. (Feb 17) Dubawi (IRE) 129 – Comic (IRE) 87 (Be My Chief (USA) 122) [2017 7m3 7g4 p7g* Nov 6] 750,000Y: brother to 2-y-o 8.5f winner Nice Future and half-brother to several winners, including smart US Grade 1 9f/1¼m winner Laughing (by Dansili) and high-class Hong Kong performer up to 1½m Viva Pataca (by Marju, 2-y-o 6f-8.5f winner in Britain as Comic Strip): dam 1¼m-11.5f winner: fair form: won maiden at Kempton (by ½ length from Medal of Honour) in November: raced only at 7f: open to further improvement. *John Gosden* **79 p**

GEORGE WILLIAM 4 b.g. Paco Boy (IRE) 129 – Basque Beauty 96 (Nayef (USA) 129) [2017 101: 8.3g* 8m4 7m2 8m 8m 7g3 7s* 8s Oct 21] good-topped gelding: useful performer: won handicap at Nottingham (by neck from G K Chesterton) in April and minor event at Salisbury (by 1¼ lengths from Black Bess) in October: third in listed race at Newbury (1¼ lengths behind Tabarrak) in September: stays 8.5f: acts on polytrack, tapeta, soft and good to firm going. *Richard Hannon* **108**

GEORGIAN BAY (IRE) 7 b.g. Oratorio (IRE) 128 – Jazzie (FR) (Zilzal (USA) 137) [2017 93, a101: p7g 7m6 8m4 7.8g3 7.8s3 8.1g 7s* p8d6 p8g 7g p8s2 Nov 17] lengthy gelding: useful handicapper: won at Ascot (amateur, by neck from Bertiewhittle) in July: stays 1m: acts on polytrack, tapeta, firm and soft going: wears headgear: has worn tongue tie: often travels strongly. *K. R. Burke* **96 a90**

GEORGIAN MANOR (IRE) 2 br.g. (Mar 4) Iffraaj 127 – Southern House (IRE) 100 (Paris House 123) [2017 6g6 p7g3 Sep 27] 115,000Y: half-brother to several winners abroad, including Japanese Group 3 1¼m winner Cosmo Phantom (by Stephen Got Even): dam Italian/US 6.5f-1m winner (7.5f winner at 2 yrs): fair form: better effort when third in minor event at Kempton (4 lengths behind Corrosive) in September: likely to progress further. *Sir Michael Stoute* **73 p**

GEORGIEZAR 4 ch.f. Winker Watson 118 – Quaker Parrot 83 (Compton Place 125) [2017 t7.2g f6.1g6 Dec 19] second foal: sister to French 6f/6.5f winner Duquesa Penguin: dam 2-y-o 5f/5.5f winner: well held in maidens. *Brian Forsey* **–**

GEORGIO (GER) 3 b.g. Approve (IRE) 112 – Gillenia (GER) (Greinton 119) [2017 60p: f8g p8g f8g 6g 8g May 27] modest form at 2 yrs: well held in 2017, leaving Andrew Balding after third start: tried in hood: often races prominently. *Frau R. Weissmeier, Germany* **–**

GERALDINE (GER) 3 b.f. Royal Applause 124 – Golden Whip (GER) 105 (Seattle Dancer (USA) 119) [2017 70: t7.1m3 p7m2 a6.5g4 8m2 7m3 8m2 8m2 7m* 7m* 8m3 6m2 Dec 8] fair handicapper: left Stuart Williams after second start: successful at Syracuse in minor event in July and handicap in September: stays 1m: acts on polytrack, tapeta and good to firm going: often travels strongly. *S. Postiglione, Italy* **69**

GERMAN BIGHT (IRE) 2 br.f. (Mar 1) Makfi 130 – Saint Lucia (IRE) 50 (Whipper (USA) 126) [2017 f7.1g* Nov 16] £13,000Y: second foal: half-sister to 1m-1¼m winner Hawridge Glory (by Royal Applause): dam once-raced half-sister to useful 5.7f-7f winner Redvers and useful stayer Mamlook: 7/1, won minor event at Southwell (by ¾ length from The Jungle Vip) in November: will improve. *Keith Dalgleish* **70 p**

GERMAN WHIP 4 b.g. Zoffany (IRE) 121 – Tan Tan (King's Best (USA) 132) [2017 67, a79: 7.6d5 7s p8g p7g p7g Dec 28] dipped-backed gelding: fair handicapper: stays 1m: acts on polytrack and good to soft going. *Gary Moore* **68**

GERRY 4 ch.f. Captain Gerrard (IRE) 113 – Bhima (Polar Falcon (USA) 126) [2017 t6g t6g Mar 6] fourth foal: half-sister to 6f winner Baron Run (by Bertolini): dam Italian 7f/7.5f winner: well beaten in maidens. *Matthew Salaman* **–**

GERRY THE GLOVER (IRE) 5 b.g. Approve (IRE) 112 – Umlani (IRE) (Great Commotion (USA) 123) [2017 88: 8m4 8f6 8.5g3 t10.2s2 10g4 t8g3 t8d3 t10.2d4 Oct 24] workmanlike gelding: fairly useful handicapper: third at Beverley (short head behind Eternal) in May: stays 1¼m: acts on tapeta, soft and good to firm going: wears cheekpieces: often starts slowly/races towards rear: sold £13,000 in November to join Lee Carter: quirky sort (hard to win with). *Brian Ellison* **86 §**

GETBACK IN PARIS (IRE) 4 ch.g. Galileo (IRE) 134 – Elusive Wave (IRE) 120 (Elusive City (USA) 117) [2017 p10g2 p11g5 10g2 p11g4 10d2 14d* 14g2 14d3 14v 18m5 Oct 14] compact gelding: useful handicapper: won at Goodwood (by ½ length from Rydan) in June: second at Windsor (short head behind Toulson) in May: stays 2¼m: acts on polytrack, soft and good to firm going. *Richard Hughes* **102 a95**

GET EVEN 2 b.f. (May 16) Multiplex 114 – Retaliator 80 (Rudimentary (USA) 118) [2017 4.5d2 t5.1g* 5s6 5g p6g3 7g5 7d 7d Sep 30] sister to 2-y-o 5f winner Queens Revenge and half-sister to several winners, including useful winner up to 13f Kings Bayonet (2-y-o 7f winner, by Needwood Blade): dam 6f (including at 2 yrs)/7f winner: fairly useful performer: won minor event at Wolverhampton in April: fifth in listed race at Deauville in July: stays 7f: acts on polytrack, tapeta, best turf form on good going: usually races prominently. *Jo Hughes* **83**

GETGO 3 b.g. Excelebration (IRE) 133 – Hip 88 (Pivotal 124) [2017 75: 7m5 8.3g 8.5m 8.3g6 10.1m2 9.9m t10.2s4 9.9s4 p10.7g5 Dec 21] fair handicapper: left David Lanigan after eighth start: stays 10.5f: acts on polytrack, tapeta, soft and good to firm going: usually wears blinkers: often races in rear: temperament under suspicion. *Keith Henry Clarke, Ireland* **71**

GET KNOTTED (IRE) 5 ch.g. Windsor Knot (IRE) 118 – Genuinely (IRE) 43 (Entrepreneur 123) [2017 109: 7m6 7.9d5 7g3 7m t6s4 6g5 7g* 7g4 6v3 6v5 7.2v6 7d Nov 11] tall, quite good-topped gelding: useful handicapper: won at York (by 1¾ lengths from Fingal's Cave) in July: stays 1m, usually races over shorter: acts on tapeta, good to firm and heavy going: wears cheekpieces: often races towards rear. *Michael Dods* **103**

GETNA (USA) 3 b.f. Lonhro (AUS) 128 – Aquarius Star (IRE) 85 (Danehill Dancer (IRE) 117) [2017 77: p7g3 10m5 t7.2g2 8.1m2 7s3 8.1d Aug 24] fair maiden: stays 1m: acts on polytrack, tapeta and good to firm going: tried in blinkers: often races prominently. *Richard Hannon* **76**

GETTIN' LUCKY 4 ch.g. Bertolini (USA) 125 – Loose Caboose (IRE) 82 (Tagula (IRE) 116) [2017 52: t5.1m4 t5d f6m2 t6g6 p6g f6.1g3 f5g3 f6.1g6 Dec 29] modest maiden: stays 6f: acts on fibresand and tapeta: has worn headgear, including usually in 2017: front runner/races prominently. *John Balding* **61**

G EYE JOE 2 ch.c. (Feb 18) Lethal Force (IRE) 128 – Winifred Jo 52 (Bahamian Bounty 116) [2017 6d f7.1g4 f7.1g Dec 11] sturdy colt: fair form: best effort when fourth in minor event at Southwell (4¼ lengths behind On The Warpath) in November. *James Given* **69**

G FORCE (IRE) 6 b.g. Tamayuz 126 – Flanders (IRE) 110 (Common Grounds 118) [2017 108: 6d 6m 6.3f 7d 5.8v4 7s 6d p6g Dec 15] good-topped gelding: useful performer nowadays: fourth in listed race at Navan (¾ length behind Texas Rock) in October: stays 6.5f: acts on good to firm and heavy going: has worn headgear, including usually in 2017: has worn tongue tie: usually races nearer last than first: temperament under suspicion. *A. P. Keatley, Ireland* **106**

GHADAAYER (IRE) 3 b.f. Shamardal (USA) 129 – Eldalil 106 (Singspiel (IRE) 133) [2017 72: 7g* t8.6g2 8m* 8g4 7d p8g Sep 26] good-topped filly: fairly useful performer: won maiden at Catterick in April and handicap at Newmarket (by neck from Angel's Quest) in June: stays 8.5f: acts on polytrack, tapeta and good to firm going: usually races prominently: sold 80,000 gns in December. *Sir Michael Stoute* **91**

GHAIYYATH (IRE) 2 b.c. (Apr 19) Dubawi (IRE) 129 – Nightime (IRE) 113 (Galileo (IRE) 134) [2017 8g³ 8g* 8m* Oct 14] €1,100,000F: lengthy colt: half-brother to several winners, including very smart 1¼m-1½m winner Zhukova (by Fastnet Rock) and useful 8.6f-1½m winner New Year's Night (by Raven's Pass): dam 1m (Irish 1000 Guineas)/8.7f winner: smart form: won maiden at Newmarket (by 5 lengths from Proschema) in September and Autumn Stakes at same course (by 1¾ lengths from Dream Today) in October: will stay at least 1¼m: in hood last 2 starts: open to further improvement. *Charlie Appleby* **111 p**

GHALIB (IRE) 5 ch.g. Lope de Vega (IRE) 125 – Gorband (USA) 59 (Woodman (USA) 126) [2017 102: p7g⁵ 7.6d² 7d 7s⁶ p7g 8.1g² 8.1d* Oct 23] quite attractive gelding: useful handicapper: won at Windsor (by 1¼ lengths from Dark Devil) in October: stays 1m: acts on polytrack and heavy going: has worn headgear/tongue tie, including often in 2017: usually races close up: sold 12,000 gns in November to join David Simcock. *Amy Murphy* **95**

GHANIMAH 2 b.f. (Apr 13) Invincible Spirit (IRE) 121 – Gile Na Greine (IRE) 117 (Galileo (IRE) 134) [2017 p7g⁴ p7g⁴ t8.6g* Nov 29] neat filly: third foal: half-sister to 9f winner Mawjood and 1m winner Alwahsh (both by Dubawi), both useful: dam, 2-y-o 7f winner, placed in 1000 Guineas/Coronation Stakes: fairly useful form: won minor event at Wolverhampton (by 1¼ lengths from Spring Waterfall) in November: stays 8.5f. *William Haggas* **80**

GHASEEDAH 3 b.f. Kyllachy 129 – Represent (IRE) 80 (Exceed And Excel (AUS) 126) [2017 60p: 7g 7m³ 7d p7d³ f6.1g* Dec 4] fair performer: won maiden at Southwell (by 5 lengths from Ladies First) in December: stays 7f: acts on fibresand and good to firm going: in headgear in 2017: usually races prominently. *Simon Crisford* **77**

GHAYADH 2 b.g. (Mar 25) Kyllachy 129 – Safe House (IRE) 79 (Exceed And Excel (AUS) 126) [2017 5m* 6v⁴ 6g⁴ 6d p6d⁴ p7g⁴ Oct 25] 28,000Y, 190,000 2-y-o: good-topped gelding: second foal: half-brother to French 7.5f winner Raaghib (by Dutch Art): dam, 7f winner, closely related to smart US Grade 2 7f winner Rebellion: fairly useful performer: won maiden at Beverley (by ¾ length from Regulator) in July: should stay 7f: acts on good to firm going. *Hugo Palmer* **81**

GHAYYAR (IRE) 3 b.g. Power 117 – Al Ihtithar (IRE) 106 (Barathea (IRE) 127) [2017 89: 8g p10g⁴ 9.9g⁶ 12d Aug 24] sturdy gelding: fairly useful handicapper: stays 1¼m: acts on polytrack and good to firm going: sold 14,000 gns in November to join Tim Easterby. *Richard Hannon* **86**

GHAZAN (IRE) 2 ch.c. (Feb 4) Iffraaj 127 – Sweet Firebird (IRE) 103 (Sadler's Wells (USA) 132) [2017 7g 8.2d⁵ 8.3d³ Oct 18] fair form: best effort when third in maiden at Nottingham (1½ lengths behind Msayyan) final start. *Clive Cox* **77**

GHEEDAA (USA) 3 b.f. Tamayuz 126 – Soohaad (USA) 75 (Hard Spun (USA) 124) [2017 91p: 5m⁴ 6g⁵ 7d⁶ Aug 24] good-topped filly: useful performer: fourth in listed race at Sandown (3¾ lengths behind Battaash) in June: may prove best at 6f: acts on polytrack, tapeta and good to firm going. *William Haggas* **96**

GHEPARDO 2 b.f. (Apr 30) Havana Gold (IRE) 118 – Clincher (Royal Applause 124) [2017 5f³ 5g t5.1g² 7g 5.3g* p6g² t5.1g³ p6s² p5g² t6.1d³ Dec 27] €20,000Y: third foal: dam, of little account, half-sister to smart 6f/7f winner Intense Pink: fair performer: won maiden at Brighton in September: stays 6f: acts on polytrack and tapeta. *Richard Hannon* **78**

GHINIA (IRE) 6 b.m. Mastercraftsman (IRE) 129 – Jorghinia (FR) (Seattle Slew (USA)) [2017 87: 8.3m⁶ 10.2m³ 9.9g³ 10m² 10g 10d² 9.9d⁵ 10g Oct 17] lengthy mare: fairly useful handicapper: stays 1¼m: acts on good to firm and good to soft going. *Pam Sly* **79**

GHOST 2 gr.f. (Jan 31) Footstepsinthesand 120 – Actionplatinum (IRE) (Act One 124) [2017 5d⁴ 5g⁵ 5g Aug 30] 4,000F, €19,000 2-y-o: third foal: dam unraced: modest form: best effort when fourth in minor event at Thirsk (4¾ lengths behind Abel Handy) in August. *John Quinn* **60**

GHOSTLY ARC (IRE) 5 b.g. Arcano (IRE) 122 – Cheyenne's Spirit (IRE) 56 (Sadler's Wells (USA) 132) [2017 71: 11.2d⁵ 14s t12.4d Oct 24] fair handicapper: stays 1¾m: acts on good to firm and good to soft going: front runner/races prominently. *Noel Wilson* **67**

GHOST SERGE (IRE) 2 gr.c. (Mar 20) Zebedee 113 – Cornakill (USA) 97 (Stormin Fever (USA) 116) [2017 6m* 5.9g* 7g² 7d⁵ 8g⁶ Aug 25] €28,000Y: second foal: half-brother to winner up to 7f The Stalking Moon (2-y-o 6f winner, by Arcano): dam, 2-y-o 7f/7.5f winner who stayed 1¼m, half-sister to useful US Grade 3 9f winner Fast And Accurate: useful performer: won minor events at Lingfield and Carlisle (by 1¼ lengths from Arcavallo) in June: second in listed race at Saint-Cloud (head behind Cold Stare) in July: stays 7f: acts on good to firm going. *Archie Watson* **95**

GHOST TRAIN (IRE) 8 b.g. Holy Roman Emperor (IRE) 125 – Adrastea (IRE) (Monsun (GER) 124) [2017 68§: p6g^{rr} p6g^{rr} Apr 1] fair handicapper at best: refused to race both starts in 2017: stays 7.5f: acts on polytrack and firm going: wears headgear: one to avoid. *Tim McCarthy* **– §**

GHOSTWATCH (IRE) 2 b.c. (Mar 4) Dubawi (IRE) 129 – Nature Spirits (FR) (Beat Hollow 126) [2017 8d^{3} 8g^{3} Sep 7] 2,100,000Y: second foal: half-brother to French 1½m winner Nature's Order (by Dansili): dam, useful French 1¼m (including at 2 yrs) to 1½m winner, closely related to winner up to 1¼m Curtain Call and French 1½m/12.5f winner Launched (both smart): fairly useful form: better effort when third in minor event at Haydock (3 lengths behind The Revenant) in September: will be suited by 1¼m+: should do better. *Charlie Appleby* **82 p**

GIANT REDWOOD (IRE) 5 b.g. Galileo (IRE) 134 – Gwynn (IRE) (Darshaan 133) [2017 80: f16.5g^{pu} Nov 13] fairly useful handicapper: pulled up only start in 2017: stays 2¼m: acts on good to soft going: usually in cheekpieces: has worn tongue tie: front runner/races prominently. *Ben Haslam* **–**

GIANT SEQUOIA (USA) 13 ch.g. Giant's Causeway (USA) 132 – Beware of The Cat (USA) (Caveat (USA)) [2017 –: p13g^{6} t12.2g^{4} Feb 20] poor handicapper nowadays: stays 1¾m: acts on all-weather: tried in cheekpieces: usually wears tongue tie. *Des Donovan, Ireland* **49**

GIANT SPARK 5 b.g. Orientor 118 – Annie Gee (Primo Valentino (IRE) 116) [2017 100: t6g 6v 6s 6g^{4} 6d 6.1g^{5} 6s Jul 30] strong gelding: useful handicapper, below form in 2017: stays 6f: acts on good to firm and heavy going: has worn headgear, including final start. *Paul Midgley* **86**

GIANTSTEPSAHEAD (IRE) 8 br.g. Footstepsinthesand 120 – Salty Air (IRE) (Singspiel (IRE) 133) [2017 93: t12.2m p11g p12g^{5} Mar 20] fairly useful handicapper: stays 1½m: acts on polytrack and soft going: has worn hood: tried in tongue tie: front runner. *Alan Bailey* **85**

GIANT'S TREASURE (IRE) 3 b.c. Shamardal (USA) 129 – Ballybacka Lady (IRE) 115 (Hurricane Run (IRE) 134) [2017 t7.1m* Mar 17] 105,000F, 525,000Y: second foal: dam winner up to 1m (2-y-o 6f winner): 7/4, won maiden at Wolverhampton (by 4½ lengths from Trenchard) on debut: should do better. *Richard Hannon* **89 p**

GIBBS HILL (GER) 4 gr.g. Mastercraftsman (IRE) 129 – Gold Charm (GER) 100 (Key of Luck (USA) 126) [2017 94p: t12.2g* 11.9d^{3} p12g* Jul 5] well-made gelding: smart handicapper: won at Wolverhampton (by 2½ lengths from Marmajuke Bay) in April and Kempton (by 7 lengths from Zubayr) in July: stays 1½m: acts on polytrack, tapeta and soft going: tried in blinkers: strong traveller: open to further improvement. *Roger Varian* **119 p**

GIENNAH (IRE) 3 b.f. Tamayuz 126 – Jamaayel 99 (Shamardal (USA) 129) [2017 83: p6g^{5} 7g^{6} 6m^{5} p8g Nov 17] fair handicapper: left Daniel Loughnane after third start: best effort at 6f: acts on tapeta: has worn hood. *J. L. Hassett, Ireland* **74**

GIFTED HEIR (IRE) 13 b.g. Princely Heir (IRE) 111 – Inzar Lady (IRE) (Inzar (USA) 112) [2017 t9.5g 7.1d Aug 24] small gelding: fair handicapper at best, well beaten both starts in 2017: stays 9.5f: acts on polytrack, best turf form on good to firm going: has worn headgear. *Ray Peacock* **–**

GIFTED MASTER (IRE) 4 b.g. Kodiac 112 – Shobobb (Shamardal (USA) 129) [2017 112: 8g^{4} a8g 6s 6g* 6m* 7m p6g* Nov 18] rather leggy gelding: smart performer: won minor event at Doncaster (by 3½ lengths from Mr Lupton) and listed race at Newmarket (by short head from Steady Pace) in August, and listed race at Lingfield (by 1½ lengths from Mythmaker) in November: best up to 7f: acts on polytrack, good to firm and good to soft going: wears blinkers: front runner. *Hugo Palmer* **117**

GIFT FROM GOD 4 b.g. Teofilo (IRE) 126 – Piffling (Pivotal 124) [2017 58: p7s^{5} Dec 14] compact gelding: modest maiden: below form only start on Flat in 2017: should stay 1m: acts on polytrack and soft going: in tongue tie last 3 starts: usually races nearer last than first. *Hugo Froud* **–**

GIFT IN TIME (IRE) 2 b.g. (Apr 29) Society Rock (IRE) 126 – Gift of Time (Cadeaux Genereux 131) [2017 5s^{2} 5m 5.1g* 6s^{3} 6d p5d 5s^{4} Oct 10] €15,000Y, £75,000 2-y-o: fourth foal: dam unraced: fairly useful performer: won minor event at Chester (by neck from Ginbar) in July: stays 6f: acts on soft going: tried in blinkers: sometimes slowly away. *James Given* **81**

GIFT OF HERA 2 ch.f. (Apr 4) Nathaniel (IRE) 129 – Premier Prize 106 (Selkirk (USA) 129) [2017 8d 8d^{5} 7s^{5} 9m^{5} Oct 25] useful-looking filly: half-sister to several winners, including smart winner up to 12.5f Cocktail Queen (2-y-o 1m winner, by Motivator) and **71**

useful 1m (including at 2 yrs) winner (stayed 2m) Gold Prince (by Nayef): dam, winner up to 1¼m (2-y-o 7f winner), half-sister to smart stayer Gold Medallist: fair form: best effort at 1m. *Sylvester Kirk*

GIFT OF LOULINS 2 b.f. (Apr 22) Aussie Rules (USA) 123 – Gift of Love (IRE) 72 (Azamour (IRE) 130) [2017 t7.1s 7d 8g Aug 14] £5,800Y: second foal: dam, maiden (should have stayed 1¼m), half-sister to smart stayer Gold Medallist: well held in minor events. *Tony Coyle* **–**

GIGI (IRE) 2 b.f. (Apr 3) Iffraaj 127 – Dubai Flower (Manduro (GER) 135) [2017 p6g^{5} 6m 8.3g^{6} Aug 15] £50,000Y: good-topped filly: third foal: half-sister to 1½m winner Epsom Day (by Teofilo): dam unraced half-sister to very smart winner up to 1¼m Best of The Bests: fair form: best effort when sixth in minor event at Nottingham (6¼ lengths behind Perfect Clarity) final start: likely to stay 1¼m: sold 3,500 gns, sent to Spain. *Charles Hills* **66**

GILDED HEAVEN 2 ch.f. (Jan 26) Medicean 128 – Heavenly (Pivotal 124) [2017 7g^{6} Aug 12] strong filly: first foal: dam, ran twice, out of half-sister to US Grade 1 9f/1¼m winner Megahertz: 33/1, well held in maiden at Newmarket. *Roger Varian* **–**

GILDED HOUR (IRE) 2 b.f. (Feb 27) Bated Breath 125 – Mimisel 92 (Selkirk (USA) 129) [2017 p6g^{2} 6d^{3} Nov 11] £40,000 2-y-o: sixth foal: half-sister to 3 winners, including French winner up to 10.5f Keep The Dream (2-y-o 5f winner, by Oasis Dream) and 7f winner Carlovian (by Acclamation): dam 2-y-o 7f winner: fair form: third in maiden at Doncaster (2¾ lengths behind Tallow) in November: remains open to improvement. *Ralph Beckett* **73 p**

GILDED REFLECTION 4 b.f. Zoffany (IRE) 121 – Vanity (IRE) 75 (Thatching 131) [2017 83: 7m^{6} 8m^{5} 8.1m^{4} 9s^{4} p10.7g* p8g Dec 22] well-made filly: half-sister to several winners, including smart winner up to 6f Lesson In Humility (2-y-o 5f winner, by Mujadil) and useful 5f-1m winner Boastful (by Clodovil): dam sprint maiden: fairly useful handicapper: won at Dundalk (by ¾ length from Miss Snossyboots) in October: left Ralph Beckett after fourth start: stays 10.5f: acts on polytrack and good to soft going: tried in blinkers. *N. Madden, Ireland* **86**

GILGAMESH 3 b.g. Foxwedge (AUS) 128 – Flaming Cliffs (USA) (Kingmambo (USA) 125) [2017 84p: t7.1f* t7.1g* 7g* p7s^{4} Nov 17] useful handicapper: won at Wolverhampton in February and March, and Redcar in May: will stay 1m+: acts on polytrack, tapeta, best turf form on good going: tried in tongue tie: usually responds generously to pressure: remains open to improvement. *George Scott* **104 p**

GILMER (IRE) 6 b.g. Exceed And Excel (AUS) 126 – Cherokee Rose (IRE) 122 (Dancing Brave (USA) 140) [2017 80: 7s^{2} 6g* 6g^{3} t7.1g 6d^{6} 6.9v^{6} 6s 6.1d^{4} Oct 23] fairly useful handicapper: won at Ayr (by 1¼ lengths from Chipping) in June: has form at 9.5f, races mainly over shorter: acts on polytrack, tapeta, good to firm and heavy going: has worn headgear, including in 2017: has worn tongue tie: often races towards rear. *James Ewart* **83**

GINBAR (IRE) 2 b.c. (May 14) Kodiac 112 – Double Fantasy (GER) (Indian Ridge 123) [2017 5.1g^{2} 5d^{2} 5g^{3} 6g* 6.1v* 6g Oct 13] €30,000Y, resold 20,000Y: close-coupled, good-quartered colt: closely related to 2 winners by Rock of Gibraltar, including 6f/7f winner (including at 2 yrs) George Rooke, and half-brother to 2 winners, including 6f winner (including at 2 yrs) Magical Dreamer (by Acclamation): dam, German 1m winner, half-sister to smart UAE 1m winner Zafeen Speed: fairly useful performer: won minor event at Haydock (by 4 lengths from Knighted) and nursery at Chester (by ¾ length from It Dont Come Easy) in September: stays 6f: acts on heavy going: front runner/races prominently. *Tom Dascombe* **86**

GINGER CHARLIE 4 ch.g. Haafhd 129 – Mandarin Lady 60 (Timeless Times (USA) 99) [2017 56: f8d t8s 9.2g Jun 1] modest maiden handicapper: no form in 2017: often races in rear. *Ruth Carr* **–**

GINGER JACK 10 ch.g. Refuse To Bend (IRE) 128 – Coretta (IRE) 118 (Caerleon (USA) 132) [2017 94: 8g^{2} 8g^{4} 8d Aug 5] workmanlike gelding: useful handicapper: second at Redcar (½ length behind Mutahaady) in June: best at 1m: acts on polytrack, firm and soft going: tried in cheekpieces: usually leads. *Jo Hughes* **96**

GINGER LADY (IRE) 3 ch.f. Helmet (AUS) 127 – Theola (IRE) 93 (Kalanisi (IRE) 132) [2017 8s^{6} p8g^{4} p8d Dec 13] third foal: half-sister to French 10.5f-1½m winner Theomour (by Azamour): dam, 2m-2¼m winner, half-sister to useful 1¼m winner Ajman King: modest form in maidens: will be suited by 1¼m+. *Mark H. Tompkins* **58**

GINGER LOVE 3 ch.g. Kheleyf (USA) 116 – La Peinture (GER) (Peintre Celebre (USA) 137) [2017 55: 7m 6m 6g^{4} Aug 30] modest form: will prove suited by 7f+. *Bryan Smart* **58**

GINGER TRUFFLE 3 ch.f. Sixties Icon 125 – Whassup (FR) (Midyan (USA) 124) [2017 47: p5g p6g5 5.3m5 6m4 6g 5.1g Jul 20] modest maiden: stays 6f: acts on polytrack and good to firm going. *Brett Johnson* **55**

GIN IN THE INN (IRE) 4 b.g. Alfred Nobel (IRE) 110 – Nose One's Way (IRE) 57 (Revoque (IRE) 122) [2017 85: 6g* 6m* 7m2 6g 6.3f 6s2 6d 6s6 6d f6.1g Dec 4] useful handicapper: won at Redcar in April and Pontefract (by 6 lengths from Johnny Cavagin) in May: stays 6f: acts on soft and good to firm going. *Richard Fahey* **99**

GINZAN 9 b.m. Desert Style (IRE) 121 – Zyzania 96 (Zafonic (USA) 130) [2017 89: 6.1d6 6.1m4 5.3m* 5f5 Jul 12] good-topped mare: fairly useful handicapper: won at Brighton (by neck from Mr Pocket) in June: stays 6f: acts on polytrack, firm and soft going: tried in cheekpieces. *Malcolm Saunders* **88**

GIOVANNI MEDICI 2 b.c. (Apr 22) Medicean 128 – Hadeeya (Oratorio (IRE) 128) [2017 7m 7.1m5 7d3 8m p7g 7m Oct 25] good-topped colt: modest maiden: bred to stay 1m: acts on good to firm and good to soft going. *Seamus Durack* **64**

GIRLOFINKANDSTARS (IRE) 3 b.f. Power 117 – Gaselee (USA) 83 (Toccet (USA) 118) [2017 54: p10g Feb 9] maiden, well held only start in 2017: best effort at 1m: tried in blinkers. *Rae Guest* **–**

GIRL SQUAD 3 b.f. Intikhab (USA) 135 – Foxtrot Alpha (IRE) 82 (Desert Prince (IRE) 130) [2017 –: p7g4 8g p8g Aug 22] modest form: best effort at 7f: tried in hood. *William Jarvis* **63**

GIRLS TALK (IRE) 2 b.f. (Apr 6) Shamardal (USA) 129 – Tasha's Dream (USA) 74 (Woodman (USA) 126) [2017 7m5 8.3d 8d Oct 24] 125,000Y: half-sister to several winners, including smart winner up to 1¼m Basateen (2-y-o 7f winner, by Teofilo): dam maiden (stayed 8.5f): modest form in minor events/maiden: should do better. *Michael Bell* **64 p**

GISELE'S ANGEL 2 br.f. (Feb 17) Dark Angel (IRE) 113 – Lovely Thought 92 (Dubai Destination (USA) 127) [2017 5m* Apr 24] £60,000Y: fourth foal: half-sister to smart 5f/6f winner High On Life (by Invincible Spirit) and useful 5f and (at 2 yrs) 6f winner Vibrant Chords (by Poet's Voice): dam 6f and (at 2 yrs) 7f winner: 4/1, won minor event at Pontefract (by length from Lord Riddiford) on debut: should improve. *Richard Guest* **80 p**

GIUSEPPE GARIBALDI (IRE) 2 b.c. (Feb 12) Galileo (IRE) 134 – Queenscliff (IRE) 78 (Danehill Dancer (IRE) 117) [2017 8v 9s2 Oct 28] second foal: dam, 1m winner, sister to smart 7f/1m winner Carribean Sunset: useful form: still green when 1½ lengths second to Flag of Honour in Eyrefield Stakes at Leopardstown, nearest finish: wears tongue tie: open to further improvement. *Aidan O'Brien, Ireland* **98 p**

GIVE AND TAKE 2 b.f. (Feb 4) Cityscape 127 – Grace And Glory (IRE) (Montjeu (IRE) 137) [2017 7d2 8m2 7.6d* Sep 16] rather unfurnished filly: first foal: dam unraced sister to Irish Derby/Gold Cup winner Fame And Glory: fairly useful form: won minor event at Lingfield (by 4½ lengths from Lady of Aran) in September: stays 1m: remains open to improvement. *William Haggas* **86 p**

GIVEAWAY GLANCE 4 br.f. Passing Glance 119 – Giving 98 (Generous (IRE) 139) [2017 83: 11.4m5 10s* 11.4g6 Oct 9] lengthy filly: fairly useful handicapper: won at Leicester (by ¾ length from Mikmak) in May: stays 1¼m: acts on heavy going: tried in hood: fairly useful hurdler. *Alan King* **88**

GIVE EM A CLUMP (IRE) 2 br.c. (Apr 28) Camacho 118 – Pixie's Blue (IRE) 89 (Hawk Wing (USA) 136) [2017 5m 5f5 6.1m3 7g2 7d* 7.4s2 8m5 p7g6 6v* 6d6 f6.1g2 p7d f6.1g Dec 21] lengthy colt: fair performer: won seller at Thirsk in July and nursery at Ffos Las in September: stays 7.5f: acts on fibresand, good to firm and heavy going: often wears visor. *David Evans* **69**

GIVEITSOMEGINGER 3 ch.f. Stimulation (IRE) 121 – Glaze 56 (Kyllachy 129) [2017 –: 7s 7.1s 8g 10g6 Oct 9] little form: in blinkers last 2 starts. *Jo Hughes* **–**

GIVE IT SOME TEDDY 3 b.g. Bahamian Bounty 116 – Croeso Cariad 107 (Most Welcome 131) [2017 7g5 8g4 6d* 7d2 Nov 4] 1,000Y, €19,000 2-y-o: half-brother to several winners, including useful 1m winner (including at 2 yrs) Saboteur (by Shamardal): dam 2-y-o 5f-7.5f winner who stayed 1½m: fairly useful form: won maiden at Redcar in October: second in handicap at Newmarket (¾ length behind Yellowhammer) in November: left Alan Swinbank after second start: stays 1m: likely to improve further. *Tim Easterby* **86 p**

GIVE US A BELLE (IRE) 8 b.g. Kheleyf (USA) 116 – Bajan Belle (IRE) 72 (Efisio 120) [2017 63: p5g t5.1g2 t5.1f f5g 5.2m5 5g 5g t5.1g Jun 9] modest handicapper: best form at 5f: acts on polytrack, tapeta, good to firm and heavy going: wears headgear: usually wears tongue tie. *Christine Dunnett* **48 a54**

GIVING GLANCES 2 b.f. (Apr 18) Passing Glance 119 – Giving 98 (Generous (IRE) 139) [2017 8.3g^5 7s^3 8d Oct 24] sixth foal: sister to winner up to 1¼m Giveaway Glance (2-y-o 7f winner): dam, 2-y-o 7f winner who stayed 1¼m, half-sister to smart performer up to 12.5f Burn The Breeze: fair form: best effort when fifth in minor event at Nottingham (4¾ lengths behind Perfect Clarity) in August. *Alan King* **69**

G K CHESTERTON (IRE) 4 ch.g. Poet's Voice 126 – Neptune's Bride (USA) 110 (Bering 136) [2017 88: 8.3g^2 8s* 8.5m* 8m 8s 7.9d Aug 24] well-made gelding: useful handicapper: won at Newmarket (by 2 lengths from Moonlightnavigator) in May and Epsom (by length from Mythical Madness) in June: stays 8.5f: acts on soft and good to firm going: in headgear last 4 starts: usually races close up. *Charlie Appleby* **106**

GLACEON (IRE) 2 b.f. (Apr 14) Zoffany (IRE) 121 – Ihtiraam (IRE) 80 (Teofilo (IRE) 126) [2017 5g^3 5m^3 p7g^5 5.2v 6s^5 Sep 15] €22,000F, €70,000Y: rather unfurnished filly: second foal: half-sister to 1½m winner Warnaq (by Arcano): dam 2-y-o 6f winner: fair maiden: should stay beyond 5f: acts on good to firm going. *Richard Hannon* **73**

GLACIER FOX 2 ch.g. (Mar 16) Foxwedge (AUS) 128 – Beat Seven 102 (Beat Hollow 126) [2017 7m^2 7s^4 t7.1g Nov 3] fair form: best effort when fourth in minor event at Leicester (1¾ lengths behind Indomeneo) in October. *Tom Tate* **76**

GLACIER (IRE) 2 b.c. (Apr 18) Canford Cliffs (IRE) 133 – Ice Pie 85 (Mount Nelson 125) [2017 6.5g 7g 8d Aug 18] lengthy colt: well held in minor events. *Richard Hannon* **–**

GLACIER POINT 3 ch.f. Foxwedge (AUS) 128 – Ahwahnee (Compton Place 125) [2017 76: 5.7m^3 6.1d 5d^2 5.1m* 5d^2 5.1s^4 5.3v^4 5g^5 Nov 1] workmanlike filly: fairly useful handicapper: won at Chepstow (by neck from Compton Poppy) in July: stays 6f: acts on good to firm and good to soft going: in headgear last 5 starts: races prominently. *Clive Cox* **84**

GLADYS COOPER (IRE) 4 b.f. Arcano (IRE) 122 – Anthyllis (GER) (Lycius (USA) 124) [2017 65: t8d p10d Feb 23] angular filly: modest maiden: below form both starts in 2017: will stay 1½m: acts on polytrack and tapeta: sent to France. *Richard Fahey* **–**

GLAMOROUS APPROACH (IRE) 4 ch.f. New Approach (IRE) 132 – Maria Lee (IRE) (Rock of Gibraltar (IRE) 133) [2017 102: 12d^3 12d* 10s* 12m^3 11.6d^2 12s^4 9.5d^4 9d^6 12d^3 9.5s^6 12.5v^6 10v^4 Oct 22] tall filly: useful performer: won handicap (by 2 lengths from Spruce Meadows) in May and listed race (by 1¼ lengths from Laganore) in June, both at the Curragh: second in listed race at Roscommon (1¼ lengths behind Flying Fairies) in July and third in Enterprise Stakes at Leopardstown (¾ length behind Eziyra) in September: effective at 9.5f to 2m: acts on good to firm and heavy going: often in cheekpieces in 2017. *J. S. Bolger, Ireland* **109**

GLAMOROUS DREAM (IRE) 2 b.f. (Apr 15) Dark Angel (IRE) 113 – Glamorous Air (IRE) (Air Express (IRE) 125) [2017 7.1s p6g^6 t6.1g Nov 18] 50,000Y: sister to 2 winners, including 7.5f winner Tobacco Bay, and half-sister to 3 winners, including very smart 5f/5.4f winner Just Glamorous (by Arcano): dam Italian 6f-1m winner (including at 2 yrs): modest form: best effort when sixth in maiden at Kempton (6¼ lengths behind Tivoli) in October. *Ronald Harris* **63**

GLAMOROUS ROCKET (IRE) 2 gr.f. (Mar 17) Dark Angel (IRE) 113 – Glamorous Spirit (IRE) 109 (Invincible Spirit (IRE) 121) [2017 5f^6 t5.1g 5.1m^5 5s^4 Aug 5] 62,000Y: third foal: dam, 5f winner (including at 2 yrs), half-sister to very smart 5f/5.4f winner Just Glamorous: modest form: raced only at 5f: should do better. *Ronald Harris* **52 p**

GLAM'SELLE 3 b.f. Elnadim (USA) 128 – Town And Gown 72 (Oasis Dream 129) [2017 48: p5g^5 t5.1g^2 t5.1g^6 p5g^4 5m 6.1m p5d^4 5f 5d Jul 25] lengthy filly: modest maiden handicapper: best effort at 5f: acts on tapeta: wears headgear: sometimes slowly away. *Ronald Harris* **51**

GLANCE MY WAY (IRE) 4 ch.g. Rock of Gibraltar (IRE) 133 – Glympse (IRE) 59 (Spectrum (IRE) 126) [2017 81: 9.9f 11.9s 10.3g 10f^6 9s 13.1v^5 Oct 12] rather leggy gelding: fairly useful handicapper: well below form in 2017: stays 10.5f: acts on good to firm and soft going: in blinkers last 5 starts: often races lazily. *Tim Easterby* **60**

GLAN Y GORS (IRE) 5 b.g. High Chaparral (IRE) 132 – Trading Places (Dansili 127) [2017 97: p16d p16g^3 p16g^2 Apr 1] leggy gelding: fairly useful handicapper: third at Chelmsford in March and second at Kempton in April: stays 16.5f: acts on polytrack, tapeta and good to firm going: usually wears headgear: sometimes slowly away, usually races in rear: fair form over hurdles for Alan Fleming. *David Simcock* **87**

GLARING 6 b.h. Champs Elysees 124 – Brightest (Rainbow Quest (USA) 134) [2017 103: 14.1m^6 14g 14d 14.2d Jun 28] strong horse: useful handicapper, below form in 2017: stays 15.5f: acts on good to firm going: in cheekpieces last 3 starts: tried in tongue tie: sold 10,000 gns in July. *Amanda Perrett* **93**

GLASGON 7 gr.g. Verglas (IRE) 118 – Miss St Tropez (Danehill Dancer (IRE) 117) [2017 **60**
59: t12.4g^{4} Jan 11] modest handicapper: stays 12.5f: acts on tapeta and good to soft going:
tried in cheekpieces. *Ray Craggs*

GLASSALT 3 b.f. Medaglia d'Oro (USA) 129 – Abergeldie (USA) 81 (Street Cry (IRE) **73**
130) [2017 63: p8s 11.5m^{3} p13.3d^{2} p12g Oct 9] fair maiden: stays 13.5f: acts on polytrack
and good to firm going. *Michael Bell*

GLASS OFFICE 7 gr.h. Verglas (IRE) 118 – Oval Office 99 (Pursuit of Love 124) [2017 **104**
6f^{4} 5s 6m^{6} Aug 26] tall, good-topped horse: smart performer: below best in 2017 after long
absence: best up to 6f: acts on polytrack and firm going. *David Simcock*

GLASSY WATERS (USA) 3 ch.c. Distorted Humor (USA) 117 – Captivating Lass **88 p**
(USA) (A P Indy (USA) 131) [2017 11.8g^{3} 11.6g^{3} 8g* Aug 20] first foal: dam, useful US
1m winner (including at 2 yrs), out of UAE 1000 Guineas/Oaks winner Folk: fairly useful
form: won maiden at Pontefract (by 1½ lengths from Caravela) in August: stays 1½m:
remains open to improvement. *Saeed bin Suroor*

GLASTONBURY SONG (IRE) 3 ch.g. Casamento (IRE) 118 – Nesmeh (USA) (More **113**
Than Ready (USA) 120) [2017 88: 8d^{5} p8g* 8d^{4} 7m 7d^{6} p8d p8s^{2} Dec 8] rather leggy
gelding: third foal: half-brother to 1m-9.5f winner Roman de Brut (by Rock of Gibraltar)
and 1¼m winner Spirit of The Vale (by Royal Applause): dam unraced: smart performer:
won minor event at Dundalk (by 2½ lengths from Asking) in April: second in handicap at
same course (1¾ lengths behind Katiymann) in December: stays 1m: acts on polytrack and
good to soft going: tried in blinkers: sometimes slowly away, often races towards rear. *G.
M. Lyons, Ireland*

GLEAMING GIRL 5 b.m. Arabian Gleam 122 – Desert Liaison 68 (Dansili 127) [2017 **82**
76, a86: t8.6g* p8d^{6} t8.6g^{4} Jan 31] fairly useful handicapper: won at Wolverhampton (by
neck from Stosur) in January: stays 8.5f: acts on polytrack, tapeta, good to firm and good
to soft going: tried in hood: often starts slowly, usually races in rear: sold 12,000 gns in
February. *David Simcock*

GLEAMING SUN 2 b.g. (Mar 12) Arabian Gleam 122 – Cara's Delight (AUS) (Fusaichi **58**
Pegasus (USA) 130) [2017 5s^{4} 6v^{4} 7g Oct 7] modest form: best effort when fourth in minor
event at Redcar (5¼ lengths behind Dandy's Beano) in September. *Michael Easterby*

GLENALMOND (IRE) 5 b.g. Iffraaj 127 – Balladonia 103 (Primo Dominie 121) [2017 **76**
83: t9.5m^{4} p10d^{2} t8.6m^{3} f11d^{4} 9.9g 9.9g^{4} May 2] attractive gelding: fair handicapper: stays
1¼m: acts on polytrack, tapeta and good to firm going: has worn headgear, including in
2017: often races towards rear. *Daniel Steele*

GLENAMOY LAD 3 b.g. Royal Applause 124 – Suzy Alexander 72 (Red Ransom **107**
(USA)) [2017 83: 7d^{3} 6g* 6d^{4} 6d* t6s* Nov 30] rather leggy gelding: first foal: dam, 5.7f
winner, half-sister to smart US Grade 2 9f winner Medici Code: useful handicapper: won
at Newmarket in August (by ½ length from Bellevarde) and September (by ¾ length from
Mont Kiara), and Newcastle (by 2¾ lengths from Tropics) in November: stays 6f: acts on
tapeta and soft going: usually wears tongue tie: sometimes slowly away, often races in rear.
Michael Wigham

GLENBANK KING (IRE) 9 b.g. Desert King (IRE) 129 – Miss Glenbank (IRE) (Over **76**
The River (FR)) [2017 –: p12g p12g^{4} p12g 16.8m 12g 13.1s* 12.5d^{3} 11.8g 18v Sep 8] fair **a69**
handicapper: won at Ayr in July: stays 13f: acts on polytrack and soft going: wears
headgear: tried in tongue tie. *L. Smyth, Ireland*

GLENCADAM GLORY 3 b.g. Nathaniel (IRE) 129 – Lady Grace (IRE) 110 (Orpen **112**
(USA) 116) [2017 88p: 10d^{5} 11.6d^{2} 12m 12m^{5} Jun 23] well-made gelding: smart performer:
fifth in King Edward VII Stakes at Royal Ascot (3 lengths behind Permian) in June: will
stay beyond 1½m: acts on good to firm and good to soft going: in hood last 4 starts:
sometimes slowly away. *John Gosden*

GLENCADAM MASTER 2 gr.c. (Feb 11) Mastercraftsman (IRE) 129 – Coquet 109 **88 p**
(Sir Percy 129) [2017 8.3v^{3} p10g^{2} p8g* Dec 20] 150,000Y: first foal: dam, winner up to
1¼m (2-y-o 1m/8.6f winner) who stayed 1½m, half-sister to 1m-9.5f winner Genius Boy
and 1¼m-2m winner Cartwright (both useful): fairly useful form: won minor event at
Kempton (by 1¾ lengths from Tum Tum) in December: stays 1¼m: likely to progress
further. *John Gosden*

GLENDEVON (USA) 2 ch.c. (Mar 3) Scat Daddy (USA) 120 – Flip Flop (FR) 114 **95 p**
(Zieten (USA) 118) [2017 p7s^{2} p7g* Oct 11] €140,000 2-y-o: well-made colt: fourth foal:
half-brother to 1m/8.6f winner Birdy Boy (by Elusive Quality) and smart French winner up

to 1m Qurbaan (2-y-o 6.5f winner, by Speightstown): dam French/US 1m/1¼m winner: useful form: won minor event at Kempton (by 5 lengths from Moqarrar) in October: will go on improving. *Richard Hughes*

GLENDUN (USA) 3 b.g. First Defence (USA) 119 – La Mina (USA) (Mineshaft (USA) 132) [2017 73: 7m^2 p7s^3 8g^2 10.2g^2 p8g* p8s^6 p10s^3 Dec 14] fairly useful handicapper: won at Kempton (by neck from Archie) in October: stays 1¼m: acts on polytrack, tapeta and good to firm going: in cheekpieces last 3 starts: front runner/races prominently. *James Eustace* **87**

GLENGARRY 4 b.g. Monsieur Bond (IRE) 120 – Lady McBeth (IRE) (Avonbridge 123) [2017 97: 7.2m^2 7.2g^2 6g^5 6s Jul 10] useful handicapper: second at Musselburgh (¾ length behind Luis Vaz de Torres) in May: stays 1m: acts on soft and good to firm going. *Keith Dalgleish* **95**

GLENN COCO 3 gr.g. Aussie Rules (USA) 123 – Las Hilanderas (USA) (El Prado (IRE) 119) [2017 7d^3 8.3v^3 7d^4 t7.2g* p7g^2 p8s* p8s^3 Dec 17] second foal: half-brother to winner up to 1m Fable of Arachne (2-y-o 6f/7f winner, by Dick Turpin): dam, lightly raced, out of smart winner up to 1½m Lilium: fairly useful handicapper: won at Wolverhampton in September and Chelmsford (by 2¾ lengths from Samphire Coast) in December: stays 8.5f: acts on polytrack, tapeta and heavy going: usually races close up. *Stuart Williams* **88**

GLENROWAN ROSE (IRE) 4 b.f. Bushranger (IRE) 119 – Choice House (USA) (Chester House (USA) 123) [2017 105: 5g 5f 5d 5g 6g 6g* 5s* 5s* 6g^{pu} 6v 5s^3 Oct 9] useful performer: won handicaps at Hamilton (by 4 lengths from Harwoods Volante) and Catterick (by 2¼ lengths from Landing Night) in July, and minor event at Hamilton (by ¾ length from Alpha Delphini) in August: stays 6f: acts on firm and soft going: tried in hood: front runner/races prominently. *Keith Dalgleish* **105**

GLENS WOBBLY 9 ch.g. Kier Park (IRE) 114 – Wobbly (Atraf 116) [2017 82: 12.1m^4 10.2f^2 12v^3 10.2f* 10v^4 9s^5 12s Oct 28] fairly useful handicapper: won at Bath (by 1¼ lengths from Sharjah) in June: second at same course in May: stays 13f: acts on polytrack and any turf going: tried in cheekpieces: usually leads. *Jonathan Geake* **82**

GLEN VALLEY (IRE) 2 ch.f. (Jan 26) Society Rock (IRE) 126 – Glen Ginnie (IRE) 72 (Red Clubs (IRE) 125) [2017 f5d^4 5m 5g May 4] £10,000Y: first foal: dam, 1m winner, half-sister to very smart winner up to 1m Killybegs: no form: tried in cheekpieces. *Keith Dalgleish* **–**

GLENYS THE MENACE (FR) 3 b.f. American Post 121 – Elle S'voyait Deja (USA) (Carson City (USA)) [2017 67: 8.3m^4 9.9f^3 p12g^4 p12g^2 10d* 10.3d* 9.9v^2 12d* 13.9m 12s 10.2d^6 p10g^3 p11d Dec 13] close-coupled filly: fairly useful handicapper: won at Newmarket and Chester in July, and Ascot (by ½ length from Contango) in August: stays 1½m: acts on polytrack and any turf going: has worn hood. *John Best* **94**

GLIMPSE OF DIRHAMS 2 b.f. (May 13) Passing Glance 119 – Jemiliah 64 (Dubai Destination (USA) 127) [2017 5m Apr 10] small, angular filly: third foal: dam 1m winner: 100/1, well held in minor event at Windsor. *Chris Gordon* **–**

GLITTERDUST 2 b.f. (May 8) Intello (GER) 129 – Glitterball (IRE) (Smart Strike (CAN) 121) [2017 7d 8d^3 Oct 24] second foal: half-sister to useful 2-y-o 6.5f/7f winner Glitter Girl (by Invincible Spirit): dam unraced half-sister to smart performer up to 11.5f High End out of Fillies' Mile winner Crystal Music: fair form: better effort when third in minor event at Yarmouth (4½ lengths behind Lady of Shalott) in October: open to further improvement. *Sir Michael Stoute* **69 p**

GLITTER GIRL 3 b.f. Invincible Spirit (IRE) 121 – Glitterball (IRE) (Smart Strike (CAN) 121) [2017 100: 7m 6.1g 7.2m^3 Jun 3] quite attractive filly: useful performer: third in listed race at Musselburgh (1¾ lengths behind Unforgetable Filly) final start: likely to stay 1m: acts on soft and good to firm going. *William Haggas* **98**

GLITTERING 4 ch.f. Firebreak 125 – Razzle (IRE) 68 (Green Desert (USA) 127) [2017 57: 8m^4 Jun 30] modest maiden: stays 8.5f: acts on soft and good to firm going: tried in cheekpieces. *James Eustace* **55**

GLITTERING JEWEL (USA) 3 b.f. Bernardini (USA) 132 – Bedazzle (USA) (Dixieland Band (USA)) [2017 8m^4 10m^2 11.9g^6 t9.5g* p10g^5 8.5f^3 Dec 1] attractive filly: half-sister to 3 winners abroad, notably Breeders' Cup Juvenile and Kentucky Derby winner Street Sense (by Street Cry): dam US 6f-7.5f winner: fairly useful performer: won maiden at Wolverhampton in July: left Charlie Appleby after fifth start: stays 1¼m: acts on polytrack, tapeta and good to firm going: front runner/races prominently. *Michael Stidham, USA* **92**

GLOBAL ACADEMY (IRE) 2 b.g. (Apr 20) Zebedee 113 – Lady Meagan (IRE) 80 (Val Royal (FR) 127) [2017 5g^4 6v^6 5.1g^2 5m^6 t5.1g^4 p5s* Dec 7] £28,000 2-y-o: good-topped gelding: fourth foal: half-brother to German 1¼m winner Lady Mac Ben (by Mastercraftsman) and a winner abroad by Bushranger: dam, 2-y-o 5.8f winner, half-sister to smart winner up to 1m Canwinn: fairly useful performer: won nursery at Chelmsford (by 4 lengths from Angel of The South) in December: best form at 5f: acts on polytrack and tapeta, best turf form on good going: often in headgear: front runner/races prominently. *Gay Kelleway* **85**

GLOBAL ALEXANDER (IRE) 3 br.f. Dark Angel (IRE) 113 – Taraeff (IRE) (Cape Cross (IRE) 129) [2017 p7g^2 p7g^4 5.7m^2 6g 6d^6 Jun 9] €160,000Y: first foal: dam unraced half-sister to useful 1m/9f winner Tazffin out of smart winner up to 1¼m Tarfshi, herself half-sister to Cheveley Park Stakes winner Embassy: fair maiden: stays 7f: acts on polytrack and good to firm going: front runner/races prominently. *Clive Cox* **73**

GLOBAL ANGEL 2 br.c. (Feb 15) Dark Angel (IRE) 113 – Authoritarian 84 (Authorized (IRE) 133) [2017 8.2d 8d p10g p10g^5 t9.5g Nov 20] fair maiden: stays 1¼m: acts on polytrack and tapeta: in blinkers last 2 starts. *Ed Dunlop* **66**

GLOBAL APPLAUSE 3 b.c. Mayson 124 – Crown (IRE) 91 (Royal Applause 124) [2017 104: 6g^3 7s^5 5d^5 Oct 28] good-topped, attractive colt: useful performer: fifth in handicap at Doncaster (1¾ lengths behind Tomily) final start: stays 6f: acts on good to firm and good to soft going: often travels strongly. *Ed Dunlop* **109**

GLOBAL ART 2 b.c. (Apr 9) Dutch Art 126 – Constant Dream 68 (Kheleyf (USA) 116) [2017 6d^5 Jul 28] 110,000Y: well-made colt: first foal: dam, 2-y-o 5f winner, half-sister to smart winner up to 1m Grecian Dancer: 10/1, fifth in newcomers race at Ascot (5¼ lengths behind Mythical Magic) in July: likely to improve. *Ed Dunlop* **79 p**

GLOBAL CONQUEROR 2 b.c. (Feb 9) Dubawi (IRE) 129 – Nargys (IRE) 109 (Lawman (FR) 121) [2017 7m^6 7.4g^3 8g^2 8g^2 Sep 28] first foal: dam winner up to 7f (2-y-o 6f winner): fairly useful form: second in nursery at Newmarket (¾ length behind Rastrelli) final start: best effort at 1m: remains capable of better. *Simon Crisford* **91 p**

GLOBAL EMPIRE (IRE) 3 b.g. New Approach (IRE) 132 – Lady Zonda 95 (Lion Cavern (USA) 117) [2017 t12.2g Apr 29] half-brother to several winners, including very smart winner up to 1½m Hibaayeb (Fillies' Mile winner at 2 yrs, by Singspiel), herself dam of Breeders' Cup Filly & Mare Turf winner Wuheida, and useful 1½m/12.4f winner (stayed 2m) Halifax (by Halling): dam 7f/1m winner: 20/1, well held in maiden at Wolverhampton: should do better. *Simon Crisford* **– p**

GLOBAL EXCEED 2 b.c. (Jan 21) Exceed And Excel (AUS) 126 – Blue Maiden 113 (Medicean 128) [2017 5.3m^5 6.1d^3 t6.1g^5 6.1g^4 6d^2 p7d^6 6d* 5.1s^2 5.1m* t5.1g^6 Nov 11] compact colt: fair performer: won nurseries at Lingfield in September and Windsor in October: stays 6f: acts on soft and good to firm going: wears blinkers: temperamental. *Ed Dunlop* **76 §**

GLOBAL EXCEL 2 b.c. (Apr 24) Exceed And Excel (AUS) 126 – Seta 113 (Pivotal 124) [2017 7.4s^6 p8g 8.3g^6 Nov 1] fair form in minor events/maiden. *Ed Walker* **67**

GLOBAL GIANT 2 b.c. (Apr 11) Shamardal (USA) 129 – Aniseed (IRE) 103 (Dalakhani (IRE) 133) [2017 7m^3 7m* Jul 14] 120,000F, 185,000Y: first foal: dam, 1½m winner, half-sister to useful winner up to 1¼m Soviet Rock: fairly useful form: won maiden at Newmarket (by short head from Tribal Quest) in July: will go on improving. *Ed Dunlop* **90 p**

GLOBAL HUMOR (USA) 2 b.c. (Mar 8) Distorted Humor (USA) 117 – In Bloom (USA) (Discreet Cat (USA) 127) [2017 t5s^3 t7.2g* Jul 3] $120,000Y, 300,000 2-y-o: first foal: dam US 5f winner: fairly useful form: won minor event at Wolverhampton (by length from Indomeneo) in July: open to further improvement. *Ed Dunlop* **83 p**

GLOBAL PASS 2 b.g. (May 1) Exceed And Excel (AUS) 126 – Mary Boleyn (IRE) 108 (King's Best (USA) 132) [2017 p6g^4 Nov 29] 160,000Y: fourth foal: half-brother to useful 1m winner Clotilde (by Dubawi) and 2-y-o 7f winner Marylebone (by Shamardal): dam, French 9f/1¼m winner, sister to smart 6f winner Kaldoun Kingdom: 7/1, hooded when fourth in minor event at Kempton (4¼ lengths behind Count Otto) on debut: will stay 7f+: sure to progress. *Ed Walker* **67 p**

GLOBAL PASSION (FR) 2 b.g. (Jan 19) Penny's Picnic (IRE) 111 – Lili St Cyr (IRE) (Rock of Gibraltar (IRE) 133) [2017 5m^2 5.5d^2 6.1g p5s* p5d Sep 21] fair performer: won minor event at Chelmsford in September: stays 5.5f: acts on polytrack and good to soft going. *Charles Hills* **79**

GLOBAL REVIVAL (IRE) 3 b.g. Kyllachy 129 – Soliza (IRE) 93 (Intikhab (USA) 135) [2017 76: t9.5g^3 p10g^2 p10g* 12.1m* 12.3m May 10] sturdy gelding: fairly useful handicapper: won at Lingfield in February and Beverley (by ¾ length from The Blues Master) in April: stays 1½m: acts on polytrack, tapeta and good to firm going: sold 1,000 gns in November, sent to Spain. *Ed Dunlop* **81**

GLOBAL ROAR 4 b.g. Arabian Gleam 122 – Kungfu Kerry (Celtic Swing 138) [2017 8v^6 8m^3 t8s Sep 8] modest form: best effort when third in maiden at Ripon in August, having run of race. *John Weymes* **71 ?**

GLOBAL ROSE (IRE) 2 b.f. (Mar 5) Dark Angel (IRE) 113 – Classic Falcon (IRE) 73 (Dubawi (IRE) 129) [2017 5.1m^2 5d^3 5.1g^4 t6.1d Dec 27] €40,000Y, €135,000 2-y-o: second foal: dam, 7.6f/1m winner, half-sister to useful winner up to 1m Dingle View: fair form: best effort at 5f: tried in hood. *Gay Kelleway* **74**

GLOBAL SPIRIT 2 b.c. (Feb 23) Invincible Spirit (IRE) 121 – Centime 75 (Royal Applause 124) [2017 6m 7d p6g^3 t7.2g^2 p7g Nov 17] fair maiden: stays 7f: acts on tapeta: tried in hood. *Ed Dunlop* **71**

GLOBAL STYLE (IRE) 2 b.c. (Apr 6) Nathaniel (IRE) 129 – Danaskaya (IRE) 106 (Danehill (USA) 126) [2017 8d 8.5m^3 8g Sep 15] fair form: best effort when third in maiden at Epsom (5½ lengths behind Lynwood Gold) in August: will be suited by 1¼m+. *Ed Dunlop* **72**

GLOBAL TANGO (IRE) 2 gr.g. (Mar 22) Zebedee 113 – Beautiful Dancer (IRE) 50 (Danehill Dancer (IRE) 117) [2017 5f^4 6s^6 6.1m^2 t6d* Nov 4] €29,000F, €42,000Y: useful-looking gelding: sixth foal: half-brother to several winners, including 2-y-o 6f winner Our Cool Cat (by One Cool Cat) and 1½m winner Darksideoftarnside (by Intense Focus): dam ran twice: fairly useful form: won minor event at Newcastle (by ½ length from I'm Yer Man) in November: stays 6f. *Charles Hills* **83**

GLOBAL WEALTH 2 b.g. (Mar 13) Havana Gold (IRE) 118 – Inner Sea (USA) (Henrythenavigator (USA) 131) [2017 6g^5 7.4m^3 p7s 7s^5 Jul 28] fair form: best effort at 6f. *Ed Dunlop* **72**

GLOBAL WONDER (IRE) 2 b.c. (Apr 22) Kodiac 112 – Traveller's Tales 84 (Cape Cross (IRE) 129) [2017 7g^6 7.6d^5 p6g t8.6g p10s^4 Dec 15] modest maiden: stays 8.5f: acts on tapeta and good to soft going: sometimes slowly away, often races towards rear. *Ed Dunlop* **61**

GLOBETROTTER (IRE) 3 ch.g. Helmet (AUS) 127 – Shimna 62 (Mr Prospector (USA)) [2017 t8g^2 10m 12m* 12d^5 t12.4g Oct 19] 24,000Y: strong gelding: half-brother to several winners, including 1¼m winner Black Eagle (by Cape Cross) and winner up to 1¼m (stayed 1½m) Hazeymm (2-y-o 1m winner, by Marju), both smart: dam once-raced half-sister to St Leger winner Shantou: fairly useful performer: won maiden at Thirsk (by head from Key Bid) in May: stays 12.5f: acts on tapeta, good to firm and good to soft going: sold 21,000 gns in October to join Julia Brooke. *James Tate* **81**

GLORIOSUS (USA) 3 b.c. Lonhro (AUS) 128 – Sky Song (IRE) (Sadler's Wells (USA) 132) [2017 7.1m^6 7.4g^5 7.4m* 8m 8g^6 8f^6 Jul 12] seventh foal: closely related to very smart French winner up to 1½m Laverock (2-y-o 1m winner, by Octagonal) and half-brother to French winner up to 1½m Right Note (2-y-o 1m winner, by Daylami) and French 1¼m winner Spinning Cloud (by Street Cry): dam, French maiden, (stayed 12.5f), half-sister to Ribblesdale Stakes winner Flying Cloud: fairly useful performer: won maiden at Beverley (by nose from Time's Arrow) in May: bred to stay at least 1m: acts on good to firm going: front runner/races prominently: temperament under suspicion: sold 15,000 gns in July, sent to Spain. *Mark Johnston* **84**

GLORIOUS ARMY 2 ch.c. (Apr 21) Declaration of War (USA) 128 – Shibina (IRE) 95 (Kalanisi (IRE) 132) [2017 p7g^5 Nov 6] 60,000Y: half-brother to several winners, including smart French/Australian 1m-11f winner Shikarpour (by Dr Fong) and useful 7f winner (stayed 1¼m) Shebella (by Dubai Destination): dam 1¼m-1½m winner: 66/1, fifth in maiden at Kempton (1½ lengths behind George Villiers) on debut: will improve. *Ed Walker* **81 p**

GLORIOUS ARTIST (IRE) 3 b.g. Zoffany (IRE) 121 – Queenie Keen (IRE) 92 (Refuse To Bend (IRE) 128) [2017 80: t7.1g^3 t7.1g* p7g^3 8m^5 t8.6g* Jul 31] strong gelding: useful handicapper: won at Wolverhampton in April and July (by 2½ lengths from Pushaq): stays 8.5f: acts on polytrack, tapeta and good to firm going: sent to Hong Kong. *Charles Hills* **95**

GLORIOUS ASSET 5 b.g. Aqlaam 125 – Regal Asset (USA) (Regal Classic (CAN)) [2017 65: f12g^3 t9.5g t9.5g^3 t9.5g^2 f8g* 10.3g Apr 1] fair handicapper: won at Southwell in March: stays 1¼m: acts on all-weather. *Ivan Furtado* **67**

GLORIOUS FOREVER 3 ch.g. Archipenko (USA) 127 – Here To Eternity (USA) 74 (Stormy Atlantic (USA)) [2017 83p: 10.3m^2 10s 8g^3 10g^4 8.2d^2 9.9g* Sep 2] rangy gelding: useful handicapper: won at Sandown (by head from Swilly Sunset) in September: stays 10.5f: acts on good to firm and good to soft going: in visor last 2 starts: sent to Hong Kong. *Ed Walker* **98**

GLORIOUS JOURNEY 2 b.c. (Feb 9) Dubawi (IRE) 129 – Fallen For You 121 (Dansili 127) [2017 6g* 7g* Sep 8] 2,600,000Y: second foal: dam, winner up to 1m (Coronation Stakes and 2-y-o 7f winner), out of half-sister to very smart 1m performer Fly To The Stars: useful form: won minor event at Newmarket (by neck from Grand Koonta) in June and Prix La Rochette at Saint-Cloud (4 ran, by 1¼ lengths from Feralia) in September: will improve further. *Charlie Appleby* **105 p**

GLORIOUS PLAYER (IRE) 2 b.g. (Feb 21) Kyllachy 129 – Playwithmyheart (Diktat 126) [2017 t7.2g^5 Dec 2] €64,000F, 90,000Y: third foal: half-brother to 2-y-o 1¼m winner Silas R (by Pour Moi): dam, French 2-y-o 1m winner, half-sister to Prix de la Foret winner Toylsome: 25/1, fifth in minor event at Wolverhampton (7½ lengths behind Moqarrab) on debut: better to come. *Tom Dascombe* **63 p**

GLORIOUS POET 4 ch.g. Poet's Voice 126 – Sky Wonder (Observatory (USA) 131) [2017 82: t7.1g 7g p8g^3 7d p8g^2 8.1g^6 10s^6 10g^5 7.6s* 7.4v 8.1d^3 Oct 23] workmanlike gelding: fairly useful handicapper: won at Lingfield (by 5 lengths from Lucky Louie) in September: left Tony Carroll after third start: best up to 1m: acts on polytrack and soft going: often races freely. *John Spearing* **84**

GLORIOUS POLITICS 3 b.g. Delegator 125 – Pelican Key (IRE) 80 (Mujadil (USA) 119) [2017 90p: t6g* t6g^6 7g p7g Nov 6] fair performer: won maiden at Newcastle in January: stays 6f: acts on tapeta. *David Barron* **73**

GLORIOUS POWER (IRE) 3 ch.g. Power 117 – Arpege (IRE) (Sadler's Wells (USA) 132) [2017 –: p8g* 8.5g 10.2g p10s^6 May 25] good-topped gelding: fair performer: won maiden at Lingfield in March: best effort at 1m: acts on polytrack: sold 4,000 gns in July, sent to Spain. *Charles Hills* **76**

GLORIOUS ROCKET 3 b.g. Bated Breath 125 – Up And About 77 (Barathea (IRE) 127) [2017 82p: p7g 6d 6m^5 6f^4 t7.1g f6.1g Dec 11] good-topped gelding: fair handicapper: left Luca Cumani after first start: stays 7f: acts on polytrack and good to firm going: often in headgear: sometimes slowly away, often races towards rear/freely. *David Barron* **75**

GLORIUX 3 b.g. Exceed And Excel (AUS) 126 – Najraan (Cadeaux Genereux 131) [2017 79: 5.7f^3 6m 6d 6g^4 Jul 21] fair maiden: stays 6f: acts on firm going: sometimes in headgear. *Charles Hills* **78**

GLORVINA (IRE) 3 b.f. Dragon Pulse (IRE) 114 – Hawk Dance (IRE) 73 (Hawk Wing (USA) 136) [2017 67p: 8g^5 8.5m^2 10.2g p10g^3 10s^3 8g* Jul 6] fair performer: won seller at Yarmouth in July: stays 8.5f: acts on tapeta and good to firm going: front runner/races prominently: modest form over hurdles for Charlie Mann. *David O'Meara* **69**

GLORY AWAITS (IRE) 7 ch.g. Choisir (AUS) 126 – Sandbox Two (IRE) (Foxhound (USA) 103) [2017 105§: 7m 7.9d 8m^3 8m 7.6d^2 8m^3 7s Sep 9] close-coupled gelding: useful handicapper: third at Yarmouth (neck behind Brigliadoro) in August: stays 9f: acts on soft and good to firm going: wears headgear: front runner/races prominently: unreliable. *David Simcock* **98 §**

GLORY OF PARIS (IRE) 3 b.g. Sir Prancealot (IRE) 111 – Paris Glory (USA) (Honour And Glory (USA) 122) [2017 72: p7g* 7g 6d^2 8g^6 p8g^5 7g 8m^5 6.1s^5 Sep 14] good-topped gelding: fairly useful handicapper: won at Kempton (by 4 lengths from Sea Shack) in April: stays 1m: acts on polytrack and good to soft going. *Rod Millman* **90**

GLYDER 3 b.f. Camacho 118 – Blades Princess 92 (Needwood Blade 117) [2017 61: 6g 5m^2 5m* 5m^6 5m^6 5g 5s^4 5.1d^4 5d Sep 12] fair handicapper: won at Catterick in June: stays 5.5f: acts on tapeta and good to firm going: inconsistent. *John Holt* **66**

GM HOPKINS 6 b.g. Dubawi (IRE) 129 – Varsity 109 (Lomitas 129) [2017 117: 7m 8m 8m^2 8s 9d 8s^2 Oct 21] attractive, good-quartered gelding: smart handicapper: second in Balmoral Handicap at Ascot (neck behind Lord Glitters) final start: stays 9f: acts on firm and soft going: tried in hood: usually races nearer last than first: sold 95,000 gns later in October, sent to UAE. *John Gosden* **117**

GNAAD (IRE) 3 b.g. Invincible Spirit (IRE) 121 – Areyaam (USA) 75 (Elusive Quality (USA)) [2017 62: p5g^2 t5.1g^3 f5g* p5g^3 f5g* t5.1g^3 5g^{ur} 5s* 5g* 6d f5g^6 f6.1g^5 f5g^3 Dec 19] workmanlike gelding: fairly useful handicapper: won at Southwell in March (maiden) **84**

and April, Ffos Las in August and Sandown (by length from John Joiner) in September: left Robert Cowell after sixth start: stays 6f: acts on all-weather and soft going: has worn cheekpieces: sometimes slowly away. *Alan Bailey*

GOADBY 6 gr.m. Kodiac 112 – Gone Sailing (Mizzen Mast (USA) 121) [2017 66: f6d **50**
6.1g t6.1g^3 6m^4 6g 6s^2 6v p6g^6 t6.1m t6.1d^5 Dec 27] modest handicapper: stays 6f: acts on polytrack, tapeta and any turf going: wears headgear. *John Holt*

GO AMBER GO 5 ch.m. Compton Place 125 – Lady Chef 75 (Double Trigger (IRE) 123) **73**
[2017 63: p6g* 6m* 5.7f^6 5.7m 6.1m^2 5f^4 6.1g^6 Aug 28] fair handicapper: won at Kempton and Windsor in April: stays 6f: acts on polytrack, good to firm and good to soft going: has worn headgear, including in 2017: tried in tongue tie: front runner/races prominently. *Rod Millman*

GO BANANAS 2 b.f. (Mar 20) Bahamian Bounty 116 – Ribbon Royale (Royal Applause **54**
124) [2017 5m^4 p6s 5m 7g 6g^4 5m Aug 31] £20,000Y: close-coupled filly: first foal: dam unraced half-sister to smart winner up to 1½m Broche: modest maiden: may prove best at 5f: acts on good to firm going: tried in cheekpieces. *Brian Meehan*

GOBI DESERT 2 b.c. (Feb 24) Oasis Dream 129 – Household Name (Zamindar (USA) **102 p**
116) [2017 7s* 6v^2 5.8v* Oct 8] 95,000F: first foal: dam, French maiden (second at 1½m), half-sister to smart/very smart French stayers Coastal Path and Reefscape: useful form: won maiden at the Curragh in August and listed race at Navan (by ½ length from Golden Spell) in October: stays 7f: open to further improvement. *G. M. Lyons, Ireland*

GO CHARLIE 6 b.g. Myboycharlie (IRE) 118 – Branston Gem 59 (So Factual (USA) **42**
120) [2017 50: t6g t6.1d^5 p5g Dec 31] poor handicapper: stays 6f: acts on polytrack, tapeta and firm going: wears hood: often starts slowly/races in rear. *Lisa Williamson*

GOD GIVEN 3 b.f. Nathaniel (IRE) 129 – Ever Rigg 83 (Dubai Destination (USA) 127) **110**
[2017 75p: 12s^2 11.6d* 12s* 12.4d* 11.9d^6 Sep 10] smart performer: won maiden at Haydock in June, listed race at Newmarket (by length from Isabel de Urbina) in July and Prix Minerve at Deauville (by 1¾ lengths from Calayana) in August: far from discredited when 7¾ lengths sixth to Bateel in Prix Vermeille at Chantilly final outing: stays 12.4f: acts on soft going: races prominently. *Luca Cumani*

GODODDIN 2 b.c. (Jan 28) Camelot 128 – Spritza (IRE) 71 (Spectrum (IRE) 126) [2017 **69 p**
p8s^4 8g Sep 28] 300,000Y: fifth foal: closely related to smart winner up to 10.5f (2-y-o 7f/1¼m winner) Rougemont and French 11f winner Surrealist (both by Montjeu) and half-brother to a winner in Sweden by Pivotal: dam, 11f/1½m winner, half-sister to dam of Irish Oaks winner Covert Love: fair form: 16/1, shaped better than distance beaten suggests when 12 lengths eighth of 16 to Ghaiyyath in maiden at Newmarket: should still improve. *Hugo Palmer*

GOD WILLING 6 b.g. Arch (USA) 127 – Bourbon Ball (USA) (Peintre Celebre (USA) **92**
137) [2017 100: t6g^5 8g 7.1g^5 8m^6 6s 7m 6d 6g^5 7d 7g^2 7d^5 6.9v^4 7v^3 Oct 21] lengthy, quite attractive gelding: fairly useful handicapper: stays 9f: acts on polytrack and heavy going: often wears blinkers: has worn tongue tie. *Declan Carroll*

GO FAR 7 b.g. Dutch Art 126 – Carranita (IRE) 111 (Anita's Prince 126) [2017 99: t6g^4 **105**
t6g* p6g p6g 6m^3 6m^3 6g^6 5g 6d 6s^2 t6.1g 6d Oct 27] good-topped gelding: useful handicapper: won at Wolverhampton (by ¾ length from Upavon) in March: races at 5f/6f: acts on all-weather and good to firm going: wears headgear. *Alan Bailey*

GO FOX 2 ch.g. (Feb 19) Foxwedge (AUS) 128 – Bling Bling (IRE) 70 (Indian Ridge 123) **67**
[2017 7s 7g p8g^3 Nov 1] fair form: best effort when third in minor event at Kempton (3¾ lengths behind Pompey Chimes) final start. *Tom Clover*

GOG ELLES (IRE) 3 b.f. Helmet (AUS) 127 – Hear My Cry (USA) (Giant's Causeway **57**
(USA) 132) [2017 47: p12g^5 t9.5g^4 p12g^5 p10g^4 8d 14.9g p12.4f t8.6g^6 p8g t8.6g^5 p7g Nov 2] modest maiden: stays 15f: acts on polytrack, tapeta and good to soft going: often wears headgear: usually races prominently. *J. S. Moore*

GO GEORGE GO (IRE) 4 gr.g. Zebedee 113 – La Bella Grande (IRE) 86 (Giant's **84**
Causeway (USA) 132) [2017 79p: t12.4g* t12.4d^3 f11g^4 t12.2g^2 13.8m^3 12.5m^2 t12.4s Jul 1] fairly useful handicapper: won at Newcastle (by ½ length from Bamako du Chatelet) in January: second at Musselburgh in May: stays 12.5f: acts on tapeta and good to firm going. *Sally Haynes*

GOING NATIVE 2 ch.f. (Mar 16) Speightstown (USA) 124 – Latin Love (IRE) 112 **65**
(Danehill Dancer (IRE) 117) [2017 7m^4 t8s^3 p10g^5 p7g^4 Oct 18] 110,000Y: fourth foal: half-sister to a winner in Japan by Galileo: dam winner up to 9f (2-y-o 1m winner): fair form: stays 1¼m. *Ed Walker*

GOING UP (IRE) 4 ch.g. Duke of Marmalade (IRE) 132 – Guilia 106 (Galileo (IRE) 134) [2017 87: 12m 14.2m^3 p16s p14g^{pu} Sep 7] sturdy gelding: fairly useful handicapper: third at Salisbury in May: stays 1¾m: acts on polytrack, tapeta and good to soft going: tried in hood: sold 5,000 gns in October, sent to Saudi Arabia. *Rae Guest* **86**

GOLCONDA PRINCE (IRE) 3 b.g. Arcano (IRE) 122 – Mujarah (IRE) 59 (Marju (IRE) 127) [2017 67: 8m^3 9.8g^4 9v^2 8.3s^3 8s^2 8.9d^2 8.5d^3 10m Aug 26] fair maiden: stays 1¼m: acts on good to firm and heavy going. *Richard Fahey* **74**

GOLDAKOYA 2 ch.f. (Mar 2) Captain Gerrard (IRE) 113 – Just Lille (IRE) 98 (Mull of Kintyre (USA) 114) [2017 t5.1g Jul 31] first foal: dam 7f-15f winner: 100/1, well held in minor event at Wolverhampton. *Daniel Loughnane* **–**

GOLD AWARD (IRE) 3 gr.g. Bushranger (IRE) 119 – Sandtail (IRE) 58 (Verglas (IRE) 118) [2017 71: 8.1m 8.2s May 22] lengthy gelding: fair 6f winner at 2 yrs, well held both starts in 2017: tried in visor. *Mick Channon* **–**

GOLD CHAIN (IRE) 7 b.m. Authorized (IRE) 133 – Mountain Chain (USA) (Royal Academy (USA) 130) [2017 65§: 13.8m^5 17.2s^5 12.5m^3 Aug 31] medium-sized mare: modest handicapper: stays 17f: acts on soft and good to firm going: usually wears headgear: tried in tongue tie: usually races nearer last than first: temperamental: fair hurdler. *Dianne Sayer* **63 §**

GOLD CLASS 6 ch.g. Firebreak 125 – Silken Dalliance 91 (Rambo Dancer (CAN) 107) [2017 49: t12.2g^4 11.9g^2 p16g Oct 12] poor handicapper nowadays: stays 1¾m: acts on fibresand and soft going: wears headgear/tongue tie: often races towards rear: fair hurdler. *Olly Murphy* **47**

GOLD CLUB 6 b.g. Multiplex 114 – Oceana Blue 89 (Reel Buddy (USA) 118) [2017 85: p6g p6g^3 t6g^2 6m^4 6g^6 6m^6 t6.1g t6.1g^3 p7g p6g^2 p6g* Dec 31] big gelding: fair handicapper: won at Lingfield in December: left Ed McMahon after first start, Tom Clover after ninth: stays 7f: acts on polytrack, tapeta and good to firm going: has worn cheekpieces: sometimes in tongue tie. *Lee Carter* **78**

GOLD DUST 3 b.f. Choisir (AUS) 126 – Afrodita (IRE) (Montjeu (IRE) 137) [2017 7g^4 8.1g^5 8g^5 8.3d Oct 11] 15,000F: second foal: half-sister to UAE 6f winner Ajwad (by Rock of Gibraltar): dam, ran once in Germany, half-sister to smart 7f-9f winner Polar Bear: modest form: may prove best at short of 1m. *Clive Cox* **62**

GOLD EAGLE 2 b.f. (Apr 21) Paco Boy (IRE) 129 – Fin (Groom Dancer (USA) 128) [2017 6g 6g 6g^4 p6g p7g^3 t8.6g^2 9m Oct 25] lengthy filly: half-sister to several winners, including 1¼m winner Haalan (by Sir Percy) and winner up to 1½m Je Suis Charlie (2-y-o 7.5f winner, by High Chaparral), both useful: dam French/US 7f-9f winner: fair maiden: stays 8.5f: acts on polytrack and tapeta. *Philip McBride* **69**

GOLDEN AMBER (IRE) 6 b.m. Holy Roman Emperor (IRE) 125 – Time of Gold (USA) (Banker's Gold (USA) 116) [2017 101: p6g^4 p7d^4 p7g 6g^5 p6g^4 p7g 6s 7d Nov 11] workmanlike mare: useful handicapper: fifth at Doncaster (1½ lengths behind Wentworth Falls) in April: stays 7f: acts on polytrack and soft going: has worn hood: sometimes slowly away, usually races in rear: sold 30,000 gns in December. *Dean Ivory* **96**

GOLDEN APOLLO 3 ch.g. Pivotal 124 – Elan (Dansili 127) [2017 86: 7s^4 7s^3 6d* 6m* 6g^4 6d 6d* 6v^3 6g Oct 14] lengthy gelding: useful handicapper: won at Pontefract (by 5 lengths from Parnassian) and York (by neck from The Wagon Wheel) in June, and Ascot (by length from Lualiwa) in August: stays 7f: acts on soft and good to firm going: tried in headgear. *Tim Easterby* **107**

GOLDEN BIRTHDAY (FR) 6 b.g. Poliglote 121 – Gold Or Silver (FR) (Glint of Gold 128) [2017 11.8v* p12g* 14.5d* Oct 27] half-brother to French 15f winner Or Ou Argent and smart French 1½m-15.5f winner Diamond Boy (both by Mansonnien): dam French 1¼m/10.5f winner: useful form: won maiden at Leicester (by 1¼ lengths from Lester Kris) in September, and handicaps at Kempton (by ¾ length from St Malo) and Doncaster (by 2½ lengths from Zaidiyn) in October: stays 14.5f: wears tongue tie: open to further improvement: useful hurdler. *Harry Fry* **98 p**

GOLDEN BOWL (FR) 7 b.g. Turtle Bowl (IRE) 121 – Maid of Dawkins (IRE) 105 (Kendor (FR) 122) [2017 14.4v 12.1v^{pu} Oct 21] useful performer in 2013 when trained in France, lightly raced and very little impact since: stays 15f: acts on good to firm and heavy going. *John Quinn* **–**

GOLDEN CANNON 6 b.m. Winker Watson 118 – Kalmina (USA) (Rahy (USA) 115) [2017 7g 7d^5 7g 7d 6v p8g p8g Dec 13] second foal: dam unraced: modest maiden: best effort at 7f: acts on good to soft going: usually races nearer last than first. *Sheena West* **51**

GOLDEN CAPE 4 ch.f. Native Ruler 119 – Lake Sabina 77 (Diktat 126) [2017 54: t7.1g –
11.8d 12v Jun 10] maiden, well held in handicaps in 2017: tried in cheekpieces. *Michael Mullineaux*

GOLDEN DEAL (IRE) 2 b.f. (May 3) Havana Gold (IRE) 118 – Lady Rockfield (IRE) **57**
71 (Rock of Gibraltar (IRE) 133) [2017 6.1g^{6} 7d p6g p7d Nov 22] 21,000 2-y-o: compact filly: fifth foal: half-sister to 6f winner Belle Dormant (by Rip Van Winkle) and 9.5f/1¼m winner Cape Crystal (by Cape Cross): dam, maiden (stayed 1m), half-sister to smart performer up to 1m Ugo Fire: modest form: wears hood. *Richard Phillips*

GOLDEN DOYEN (GER) 6 b.g. Doyen (IRE) 132 – Goldsamt (GER) (Rienzi (EG)) **68**
[2017 87: 20.6v Aug 2] fairly useful handicapper: below form only start on Flat in 2017: stays 16.5f: acts on good to firm and heavy going: tried in cheekpieces: useful hurdler. *Philip Hobbs*

GOLDEN EASTER (USA) 3 ch.f. Distorted Humor (USA) 117 – Easterette (USA) **57**
(Hard Spun (USA) 124) [2017 79p: 5.3g^{3} 5.1m f5g Aug 28] medium-sized filly: fair maiden at 2 yrs, well below form in 2017: stays 6f: acts on tapeta, best turf form on good going: sometimes in headgear. *Robert Cowell*

GOLDEN EYE 3 ch.g. Kheleyf (USA) 116 – Gennie Bond 73 (Pivotal 124) [2017 66: **61**
8.3m p8g 7g^{6} p7g 7s Jul 29] sturdy gelding: modest maiden: stays 7f: acts on tapeta and good to firm going. *Sylvester Kirk*

GOLDEN FOOTSTEPS (IRE) 2 b.f. (Mar 17) Footstepsinthesand 120 – Contemplate **68**
55 (Compton Place 125) [2017 p6s^{4} 6m^{3} p7d 7g Sep 7] €22,000F: third foal: dam, maiden (stayed 7f), closely related to smart winner up to 7f Tumbleweed Ridge: fair form: best effort at 6f: tried in hood. *Ed Walker*

GOLDEN GLIMMER (IRE) 4 b.f. Danehill Dancer (IRE) 117 – Gilded Vanity (IRE) –
83 (Indian Ridge 123) [2017 91: 7d^{5} Jun 9] fairly useful performer: well held only start in 2017: stays 1m: acts on good to firm going. *Tom Dascombe*

GOLDEN GOAL (IRE) 3 gr.c. Dark Angel (IRE) 113 – Golden Rosie (IRE) 74 (Exceed **98**
And Excel (AUS) 126) [2017 p7s* p7s* p7g^{6} p8g* 8d p7s^{6} Nov 17] £240,000Y: second foal: half-brother to useful winner up to 6f Rosie's Premiere (2-y-o 5f winner, by Showcasing): dam, 2-y-o 6f winner, half-sister to very smart winner up to 8.5f Sovereign Debt (by Dark Angel): useful performer: won 3 times at Chelmsford, maiden in July and handicaps later in July and in August (dead-heated with Almoreb): stays 1m: acts on polytrack: tried in hood: usually races freely. *Saeed bin Suroor*

GOLDENGROUND (IRE) 2 b.c. (Apr 1) Zebedee 113 – Bryana Gold (IRE) (Namid **72**
128) [2017 6m^{6} p6s^{2} p6s^{5} a6f^{5} a6f^{4} a5f Dec 16] fair maiden: left Henry Spiller after third start: raced only at 5f/6f: acts on dirt: in blinkers/tongue tie last 3 starts. *A. bin Harmash, UAE*

GOLDEN GUEST 3 ch.g. Bated Breath 125 – Si Belle (IRE) 95 (Dalakhani (IRE) 133) **82**
[2017 70: 8.3m^{2} 7.5f^{2} 8s 7s^{3} 7g 7g* 7g* 7d^{5} 7m^{2} 8g p8g* t7.2m Oct 28] neat gelding: fairly useful handicapper: won at Brighton and Yarmouth in July, and Kempton (by head from Choral Clan) in October: stays 8.5f: acts on polytrack and firm going: has worn visor: often races towards rear: sold 19,000 gns later in October to join Les Eyre. *George Margarson*

GOLDEN GUIDE 2 b.f. (Feb 1) Havana Gold (IRE) 118 – Blonde (IRE) 58 (Pivotal 124) **57**
[2017 8g^{4} 8d t8g^{5} Nov 15] 15,000F, 13,000Y, £12,000 2-y-o: second foal: dam once-raced half-sister to useful performer up to 1¼m Alexis: modest form in minor events/maiden. *K. R. Burke*

GOLDEN HARBOUR (FR) 3 b.g. Harbour Watch (IRE) 121 – Make Up 67 (Kyllachy –
129) [2017 –: p7d 7m p7s p8g Sep 7] no form: left Brian Barr after third start: tried in blinkers: wears tongue tie. *Alex Hales*

GOLDEN IMAGE 2 b.f. (Mar 12) Havana Gold (IRE) 118 – Photographic (USA) **72**
(Trempolino (USA) 135) [2017 7g^{3} 7d t7.2g^{2} Dec 22] angular filly: half-sister to several winners, including useful 1½m-1¾m winner Duty Free (by Rock of Gibraltar) and winner up to 1½m Little Dutch Girl (2-y-o 1m winner, by Dutch Art): dam lightly raced: fair form: best effort when third in maiden at Salisbury (2 lengths behind Autumn Leaves) in August: will stay 1m. *Jonathan Portman*

GOLDEN ISLES (IRE) 4 ch.f. Mastercraftsman (IRE) 129 – Aphorism 84 (Halling **63**
(USA) 133) [2017 66: 8g^{6} 10m^{6} 10d* 10m^{6} Jul 6] modest handicapper: won at Lingfield in June: stays 1¼m: acts on firm and good to soft going. *Heather Main*

GOLDEN JEFFREY (SWI) 4 b.g. Soldier Hollow 121 – Ange Doree (FR) (Sinyar (IRE)) [2017 11.2d 12.1m^4 8g^4 16m* 15g^4 15v Oct 12] fair performer: won handicap at Musselburgh in August: stays 2m: acts on good to firm going: front runner/races prominently: fairly useful hurdler. *Iain Jardine* **78**

GOLDEN JUBILEE (USA) 8 b.g. Zavata (USA) 111 – Love Play (USA) (Friendly Lover (USA) 117) [2017 84: p12g^5 p16g^5 12.1m p16d May 31] good-topped gelding: fairly useful handicapper: stays 13f: acts on all-weather, soft and good to firm going: wears headgear: often races prominently. *Nigel Twiston-Davies* **80**

GOLDEN MUSCADE (USA) 4 b.f. Medaglia d'Oro (USA) 129 – Kinda Spicy (USA) (A P Indy (USA) 131) [2017 64: p12d t9.5g^6 p11g 11.7f^2 13f^4 11.6f^5 12g a8f^6 10f^5 9.5g^5 a8.5f^5 Dec 29] strong filly: fair maiden: left Brian Barr after seventh start: stays 11.5f: acts on polytrack and firm going: front runner/races prominently. *Kiaran P. McLaughlin, USA* **75**

GOLDEN NECTAR 3 ch.f. Sakhee's Secret 128 – Mildoura (FR) 96 (Sendawar (IRE) 129) [2017 81p: 8m^5 10m^5 Jul 10] lengthy, rather unfurnished filly: fairly useful handicapper: stays 1¼m: acts on polytrack and good to firm going: often races prominently. *Laura Mongan* **80**

GOLDEN OPPORTUNITY 3 ch.c. Kheleyf (USA) 116 – Golden Waters 80 (Dubai Destination (USA) 127) [2017 70: t6g* t6g^3 p6g^3 Jan 28] fairly useful handicapper: won at Newcastle (by length from Marquee Club) in January: stays 7f: acts on all-weather: tried in cheekpieces: sold 21,000 gns in February, sent to Italy. *James Tate* **81**

GOLDEN RAVEN (IRE) 5 b.g. Raven's Pass (USA) 133 – Superfonic (FR) (Zafonic (USA) 130) [2017 –: p8g p8g t7.2g 7m Jun 24] lengthy gelding: fairly useful handicapper: stays 1m: acts on polytrack and soft going: sometimes slowly away. *Jamie Osborne* **82**

GOLDEN SALUTE (IRE) 2 b.f. (Apr 5) Acclamation 118 – Golden Shadow (IRE) 77 (Selkirk (USA) 129) [2017 6.1g 5.1m* 5g* 6d^2 Sep 5] €88,000F: sister to useful 6f (including at 2 yrs) winner Victory Angel and half-sister to several winners, including 1m winner Reckless Gold (by Pivotal) and 2-y-o 5f-1m winner Lord Ofthe Shadows (by Kyllachy), both useful: dam maiden (raced at 1m): fairly useful form: won maiden at Windsor and minor event at Bath (by head from Little Boy Blue) in July: stays 6f. *Andrew Balding* **85**

GOLDEN SET 3 b.f. Bated Breath 125 – Match Point (Unfuwain (USA) 131) [2017 10.2d^6 12d 11.6d^3 11.8v t12.4g^3 f14.1g Dec 11] 10,000F, 25,000Y: half-sister to several winners, including useful 11f-1¾m winner Deuce Again (by Dubawi) and useful 1½m winner (stays 15.5f) Return Ace (by Zamindar): dam unraced: fair maiden: left James Fanshawe after fifth start: stays 1½m: acts on good to soft going. *Eve Johnson Houghton* **73**

GOLDEN SPEAR 6 ch.g. Kyllachy 129 – Penmayne 95 (Inchinor 119) [2017 100: 18.6m May 10] useful handicapper: stays 2¼m: acts on good to firm and heavy going: has worn headgear: in tongue tie last 3 starts: useful hurdler. *A. J. Martin, Ireland* **91**

GOLDEN STATE (USA) 3 b.f. Elusive Quality (USA) – Bronze Route (USA) (Mud Route (USA) 116) [2017 78: t8.6g 7m* 8g Jun 22] sister to a winner in USA and closely related/half-sister to 3 other winners there: dam, US 2-y-o 5f winner, half-sister to US Grade 1 1m/8.5f winner Golden Ballet, herself dam of Belmont Stakes/Breeders' Cup Classic winner Drosselmeyer: fair form: won maiden at Redcar in May: may prove best at short of 1m: sold 42,000 gns in July, sent to USA. *Archie Watson* **73**

GOLDEN STEPS (FR) 6 b.g. Footstepsinthesand 120 – Kocooning (IRE) (King's Best (USA) 132) [2017 109: p6s^5 Nov 23] lengthy gelding: smart handicapper (for Marco Botti): well held in claimer only start in 2017: stays 7.5f: acts on polytrack, soft and good to firm going: has worn hood: has joined Jim Goldie. *Jamie Osborne* **–**

GOLDEN STUNNER (IRE) 4 ch.f. Dream Ahead (USA) 133 – Pina Colada 77 (Sabrehill (USA) 120) [2017 101: 7g* 7.9m^2 7g^2 8d 7g Sep 22] tall filly: useful performer: won handicap at York (by 2 lengths from Firmament) in May: second in listed race at same course (head behind Arabian Hope) in June: stays 9f: acts on polytrack, soft and good to firm going: often leads. *Ralph Beckett* **109**

GOLDEN WEDDING (IRE) 5 b.g. Archipenko (USA) 127 – Peace Lily 69 (Dansili 127) [2017 87: p8f^2 7d^2 p8g^2 p7d^6 8g^2 8m p8d^2 8g^4 p8g^3 p8g 8.1d p8g Dec 20] good-topped gelding: fairly useful handicapper: second at Newbury in June and third at Kempton in September: best up to 1m: acts on polytrack, fibresand, soft and good to firm going: has worn cheekpieces, including last 2 starts: races prominently. *Eve Johnson Houghton* **91**

GOLDEN WOLF (IRE) 3 b.g. Big Bad Bob (IRE) 118 – Jeunesse Doree (IRE) 68 (Rock of Gibraltar (IRE) 133) [2017 72p: t8.6g^2 p10g^4 t9.5g^2 10.3s^2 10d* 9.9g^3 12v^2 Oct 1] fairly useful performer: won maiden at Lingfield (by ¾ length from Rainbow Rising) in August: second in handicap at Epsom (apprentice) final start: stays 1½m: acts on polytrack, tapeta and heavy going: often travels strongly. *Richard Hughes* **93**

GOLD FILIGREE (IRE) 2 gr.f. (Mar 10) Dark Angel (IRE) 113 – Gold Lace (IRE) 83 (Invincible Spirit (IRE) 121) [2017 5m^5 6d^3 5f^4 5v^2 p5g^2 p6g^2 p5g^2 t6.1g* Nov 18] €40,000Y: workmanlike filly: second foal: dam, 2-y-o 5f winner, half-sister to smart winner up to 9f Emerald Commander: fair performer: won minor event at Wolverhampton in November: raced at 5f/6f: acts on polytrack, tapeta and good to soft going: races prominently. *Richard Hughes* **77**

GOLD FLASH 5 b.g. Kheleyf (USA) 116 – My Golly (Mozart (IRE) 131) [2017 81: t7.1m* t7.1m* p7d^6 t8.6g^2 p7g^4 p6g 6m 10s p6s p6s Dec 17] lengthy gelding: fairly useful performer: won handicap and claimer, both at Wolverhampton in January: second in claimer at same course in March: left Keith Dalgleish after fifth start, Hugo Froud after eighth: stays 8.5f: acts on polytrack, tapeta, soft and good to firm going: has worn headgear: often races in rear. *Richenda Ford* **85**

GOLDFOX GIRL 2 b.f. (Mar 25) Phenomena – Baileys Honour 61 (Mark of Esteem (IRE) 137) [2017 7m^6 f7.1g^4 Nov 16] £1,000Y: sturdy filly: fifth foal: dam, 9.5f winner, closely related to dam of high-class 1¼m-1½m performer Al Kazeem: poor form in minor events. *Michael Appleby* **46**

GOLD HUNTER (IRE) 7 b.g. Invincible Spirit (IRE) 121 – Goldthroat (IRE) 79 (Zafonic (USA) 130) [2017 84: 6g 6m* 6m^6 6.1m^2 7m^3 5.7d^4 7g^3 p7d* p7d p7g p7s Dec 1] sturdy gelding: fairly useful handicapper: won at Salisbury (apprentice) in June and Chelmsford (by neck from Rouge Nuage) in September: left Steve Flook after tenth start: stays 7f: acts on polytrack, firm and good to soft going: wears cheekpieces: often travels strongly. *Adrian Wintle* **86**

GOLDMADCHEN (GER) 9 b.m. Ivan Denisovich (IRE) 115 – Goldkatze (GER) (Czaravich (USA)) [2017 48: p10g t12.2g Feb 20] fair handicapper at best, lightly raced and little form since 2015: stays 1¾m: acts on all-weather, best turf form on heavy going: tried in cheekpieces. *James Given* **39**

GOLDMEMBER 4 ch.g. New Approach (IRE) 132 – Sister Act 85 (Marju (IRE) 127) [2017 106: 13.9g 16.2m^6 14m t12.2g^2 Oct 21] useful performer: second in handicap at Wolverhampton (length behind Master Singer) in October: stays 2m: acts on tapeta, soft and good to firm going: tried in tongue tie. *David Simcock* **96**

GOLD MERLION (IRE) 4 b.f. Alhaarth (IRE) 126 – Sea of Time (USA) (Gilded Time (USA)) [2017 59: p10g 12d^5 10.2g p10g* 10.1d^2 11.6g 12m 12.1d t12.2g p10g^2 f12.1g Oct 22] fair handicapper: won at Lingfield in July: stays 1¼m: acts on polytrack and good to soft going: tried in blinkers: front runner/races prominently. *Mark Johnston* **73**

GOLDREAM 8 br.g. Oasis Dream 129 – Clizia (IRE) (Machiavellian (USA) 123) [2017 116: 5m^3 5f^2 5f 5m^3 5m^6 5d^3 5g 5.2m 5g^4 Oct 17] compact gelding: smart performer: second in Temple Stakes at Haydock (½ length behind Priceless) in May: stays 1m: acts on polytrack, firm and soft going: wears headgear: sometimes slowly away, usually races towards rear. *Robert Cowell* **118**

GOLD RETURN (IRE) 4 b.f. Gold Away (IRE) 125 – Ourika (IRE) (Danehill Dancer (IRE) 117) [2017 70: p7g p8g^6 t9.5g^4 p8g^4 p13.3d^5 Mar 13] fair handicapper: stays 13.5f: acts on polytrack and tapeta: tried in tongue tie: usually races in rear: sent to Italy, where won 3 times. *John Ryan* **67**

GOLDSLINGER (FR) 5 b.g. Gold Away (IRE) 125 – Singaporette (FR) (Sagacity (FR) 125) [2017 77: p14g^6 12m^4 11.9m^6 12v^2 14g^4 18d^4 16s^4 p15.8g Oct 5] sturdy gelding: fair handicapper: stays 1¾m: acts on fibresand, good to firm and heavy going: tried in hood: sold 1,000 gns in November. *Dean Ivory* **70**

GOLDSPUN 2 b.f. (Apr 2) Nathaniel (IRE) 129 – Dream Day 98 (Oasis Dream 129) [2017 8d Oct 24] sixth foal: half-sister to 3 winners, including useful French 2-y-o 9.5f winner Delhi (by High Chaparral) and 5f-7f winner Dark Side Dream (by Equiano): dam, 2-y-o 6f winner who stayed 1m, half-sister to smart winner up to 1m Sabbeeh: 28/1, seventh in minor event at Yarmouth (7¼ lengths behind Lady of Shalott) in October. *Ed Dunlop* **61**

GOLD STAR 3 b.c. Nathaniel (IRE) 129 – Tanzania (USA) (Darshaan 133) [2017 12s^3 12d* t12.2g* 13.9g Oct 13] strong, good sort: closely related to smart 1¼m-2m winner Winning Story (by New Approach) and half-brother to useful winner up to 1¼m Serengeti **111**

(2-y-o 8.6f winner, by Singspiel) and very smart winner up to 9f True Story (2-y-o 7f winner, by Manduro): dam unraced: smart form: won maiden at Newbury (by 3 lengths from Reverend Jacobs) in August and handicap at Wolverhampton (by 3¾ lengths from Abjar) in September: stays 1½m. *Saeed bin Suroor*

GOLD STONE 2 b.f. (Mar 31) Havana Gold (IRE) 118 – Slatey Hen (IRE) 66 (Acclamation 118) [2017 5d² 5d* Aug 17] £45,000Y: first foal: dam, 5f and (including at 2 yrs) 6f winner, half-sister to smart sprinter Masta Plasta: fair form: won minor event at Beverley (by 1¼ lengths from Debawtry) in August: will go on improving. *Kevin Ryan* **70 p**

GOLD TOWN 2 b.g. (Mar 28) Street Cry (IRE) 130 – Pimpernel (IRE) 110 (Invincible Spirit (IRE) 121) [2017 5.2g* t6g⁵ 6d⁵ 7m 7m³ 7g* Aug 12] close-coupled gelding: second foal: dam 2-y-o 5f-7f winner: useful performer: won maiden at Newbury in April and nursery at Newmarket (by 3¾ lengths from Dragons Tail) in August: stays 7f: acts on good to firm and good to soft going: in cheekpieces last 4 starts. *Charlie Appleby* **99**

GOLLY MISS MOLLY 6 b.m. Exceed And Excel (AUS) 126 – Amicable Terms 88 (Royal Applause 124) [2017 54, a71: p8g⁶ p8g p10g p15.8g³ p16s* p16g* p16sᵘʳ p15.8g p16g⁵ Nov 1] sturdy mare: fair handicapper: won at Kempton (twice) in June: left Jeremy Gask after fourth start: stays 2m: acts on polytrack and tapeta: wears headgear. *Martin Bosley* **73**

GONE TO SEA (IRE) 2 b.f. (Apr 18) Born To Sea (IRE) 117 – Chaguaramas (IRE) 93 (Mujadil (USA) 119) [2017 6.1d 7g⁶ 6g⁵ Jul 8] €7,500Y: half-sister to several winners, including winner up to 1½m Jersey Bull (2-y-o 6f winner, by Clodovil): dam 2-y-o 5f winner who stayed 1m: well held in minor event/sellers. *David Evans* **–**

GONE VIRAL (IRE) 6 ch.g. Virtual 122 – Dorinda Gray (IRE) (Docksider (USA) 124) [2017 p12g t9.5m Jan 23] workmanlike gelding: fairly useful handicapper: below form both starts in 2017 after lengthy absence: stays 10.5f: acts on soft going: has worn headgear: often in tongue tie. *George Baker* **–**

GONE WITH THE WIND (GER) 6 b.g. Dutch Art 126 – Gallivant 93 (Danehill (USA) 126) [2017 72: 8m⁶ f8.1g Dec 11] useful-looking gelding: fair handicapper: below form both starts in 2017: stays 9f: acts on polytrack, tapeta, good to firm and heavy going: has worn cheekpieces/tongue tie: often races towards rear. *Rebecca Bastiman* **–**

GONINODAETHAT 9 b.g. Proclamation (IRE) 130 – Big Mystery (IRE) 53 (Grand Lodge (USA) 125) [2017 64: 5g⁴ 6m 6m* 6d⁶ 5s³ 6g 6s⁶ 6g⁴ 6g² 5d⁶ 6g 6d⁴ 5.9s⁶ 5m⁶ 5v 5s⁴ 7.2s Oct 9] fair handicapper: won at Ayr in May: second at same course in July: stays 1m: acts on good to firm and heavy going: has worn hood: unreliable. *Jim Goldie* **67 §**

GO NOW GO NOW (IRE) 2 b.g. (Apr 16) Kodiac 112 – Ms Mary C (IRE) 68 (Dolphin Street (FR) 125) [2017 5m⁴ 5g 6d² 6m⁴ 7s* 7.4d* 8.1d² 7s⁶ 8.1g⁴ Oct 9] angular gelding: fair performer: won nurseries at Catterick in July and Beverley in August: stays 1m: acts on soft going: front runner/races prominently. *Mark Johnston* **76**

GOOD BOND 5 b.g. Monsieur Bond (IRE) 120 – Seminole Sun (IRE) (Invincible Spirit (IRE) 121) [2017 p7g 6m³ p7s p10gᵖᵘ Jul 26] plain gelding: no form: in hood last 2 starts: dead. *Linda Jewell* **–**

GOOD BOY JASPER 3 ch.g. Doncaster Rover (USA) 114 – Mitchelland 72 (Namaqualand (USA)) [2017 59: 7.2m 6v 7g Aug 18] maiden, no form in 2017: left Linda Perratt after first start. *James Moffatt* **–**

GOOD BUSINESS (IRE) 3 ch.f. Dutch Art 126 – Parakopi (IRE) 53 (Green Desert (USA) 127) [2017 8s 8.1g⁴ 8g 8s⁴ p7g⁴ Sep 26] €50,000Y: fourth foal: half-sister to 7f/1m winner Tanawar (by Elusive City) and German 9f/1¼m winner Mesaria (by Montjeu): dam German 9.5f winner out of useful 1m winner Siringas: modest maiden: stays 1m: acts on polytrack and soft going: tried in visor: often races prominently. *Jeremy Noseda* **59**

GOODBYE LULU (IRE) 2 b.f. (Feb 12) Exceed And Excel (AUS) 126 – Guarantia 92 (Selkirk (USA) 129) [2017 6.1m 6g p6g Oct 4] 80,000Y: half-sister to several winners, including winner up to 7f Certified (2-y-o 6f winner, by Raven's Pass) and 6f winner Surety (by Cape Cross): dam, 7f winner, half-sister to very smart 1¼m-1½m winner Laaheb: modest form in minor event/maidens: in hood last 2 starts. *George Baker* **61**

GOODBY INHERITENCE 5 b.g. Medicean 128 – Chili Dip (Alhaarth (IRE) 126) [2017 74: p12d p12g⁵ p11g 11.6m⁵ Apr 24] close-coupled gelding: fair maiden handicapper, below form in 2017: stays 1½m: acts on polytrack, tapeta and good to firm going: has worn headgear, including last 2 starts: wears tongue tie. *Seamus Durack* **59**

GOOD IMPRESSION 2 b.g. (Mar 17) Showcasing 117 – Daintily Done (Cacique (IRE) 124) [2017 6g 6m 6d f6.1g² Dec 19] compact gelding: modest form: left Amanda Perrett after second start: likely to stay 7f: tried in blinkers. *Ali Stronge* **65**

GOOD LUCK CHARM 8 b.g. Doyen (IRE) 132 – Lucky Dice (Perugino (USA) 84) [2017 81: 8.3m 7m p7g 7m^4 7m^2 7d 7g* 7g^5 7d* 7v 7v Oct 19] rather leggy gelding: fairly useful handicapper: won at Brighton in August and September (by length from King of Swing): stays 8.5f: acts on polytrack and any turf going: wears headgear: has worn tongue tie. *Gary Moore* **83**

GOODLUCK JOEY 3 b.g. Sayif (IRE) 122 – Cozette (IRE) 49 (Danehill Dancer (IRE) 117) [2017 –: p7g^{rr} Feb 9] no form: refused to race only start in 2017. *Emmet Michael Butterly, Ireland* **– §**

GOOD MAGIC (USA) 2 ch.c. (Mar 1) Curlin (USA) 134 – Glinda The Good (USA) (Hard Spun (USA) 124) [2017 a6.5f^2 a8f^2 a8.5f* Nov 4] $1,000,000Y: second foal: half-brother to US 6f winner Goodzapper (by Ghostzapper): dam, useful US 1m (including at 2 yrs) winner, out of half-sister to US Grade 1 1m/8.5f (including at 2 yrs) winner Magical Maiden: very smart form: second in maiden at Saratoga and Champagne Stakes at Belmont (beaten ½ length by Firenze Fire) prior to winning Breeders' Cup Juvenile at Del Mar (beat Solomini impressively by 4¼ lengths) in November: will stay 1¼m: should progress further. *Chad C. Brown, USA* **120 p**

GOOD MAN (IRE) 4 ch.g. New Approach (IRE) 132 – Garden City (FR) (Majorien 118) [2017 t7.1g 8s^5 10v^6 12.5s^3 13.9v t12.4d^6 Nov 4] poor maiden: in cheekpieces last 5 starts. *Karen McLintock* **45**

GOOD MOVE (IRE) 5 b.m. Aussie Rules (USA) 123 – Lady Lafitte (USA) 73 (Stravinsky (USA) 133) [2017 –: 5g May 13] of little account: wears headgear: tried in tongue tie. *Brian Rothwell* **–**

GOODNIGHT GIRL (IRE) 2 ro.f. (Apr 11) Clodovil (IRE) 116 – Leenavesta (USA) 72 (Arch (USA) 127) [2017 6d^3 7g^2 7.1s^5 7d^5 Sep 30] €97,000 2-y-o: third foal: closely related to a winner in Canada by Kodiac: dam maiden (stayed 7f): fair form: stays 7f. *Jonathan Portman* **78**

GOOD NIGHT OUT (IRE) 2 b.f. (Apr 25) Fast Company (IRE) 126 – Titus Tina (IRE) (Titus Livius (FR) 115) [2017 t5.1g May 2] 8/1, well held in minor event at Wolverhampton: dead. *David Evans* **–**

GOOD OMEN 3 b.g. Holy Roman Emperor (IRE) 125 – Magic Nymph (IRE) (Galileo (IRE) 134) [2017 98p: a7f 7g 10.2s* 12m 10.1g* 9.9v* Aug 3] lengthy gelding: smart performer: won minor event at Doncaster (by 1¾ lengths from Daawy) in June, and handicaps at Yarmouth (by ¾ length from Petite Jack) in July and Goodwood (by 1¼ lengths from Frontispiece) in August: stays 1¼m: acts on polytrack and heavy going: waited with: sent to Hong Kong. *David Simcock* **110**

GOOD RUN (FR) 4 ch.g. Iffraaj 127 – Tadawul (USA) 73 (Diesis 133) [2017 108p: t16.3g^2 t12.4s 16g^6 t16.3s Jul 1] well-made gelding: useful handicapper: second at Newcastle (¾ length behind Gavlar) in March: stays 2m: acts on tapeta and soft going: tried in headgear. *Saeed bin Suroor* **105**

GOOD TIME AHEAD (IRE) 3 b.g. Iffraaj 127 – Good Time Sue (IRE) 96 (Commander Collins (IRE) 120) [2017 75: t9.5g^3 t9.5m* p10g^2 t10.2d^2 t9.5m^5 9.8g 11.6d^6 12m^4 12g^5 t10.2d^3 12d^2 t12.4s^3 t12.4d t12.4g* 14d f12.1g^3 f12.1g* f14.1g* f12.1g^2 Dec 21] angular gelding: fairly useful performer: won maiden at Wolverhampton in January, and handicaps at Newcastle in October and Southwell in November and December (by 3¾ lengths from Cousin Khee): stays 1¾m: acts on fibresand, tapeta and good to soft going. *Philip Kirby* **90**

GOOD TRADITION (IRE) 6 b.g. Pivotal 124 – Token Gesture (IRE) 113 (Alzao (USA) 117) [2017 68: 18.6m May 10] useful at best, lightly raced on Flat nowadays: down the field in Chester Cup only start in 2017: stays 1¾m: acts on soft going: often in headgear: fair hurdler. *Donald McCain* **–**

GOOD WAY OFF (USA) 4 b.f. Northern Afleet (USA) 117 – Out of Reach 109 (Warning 136) [2017 8m* 8d 10m^4 Oct 16] lengthy filly: half-sister to several winners, including useful US Grade 3 1¾m winner Inordinate (French 2-y-o 7f/7.5f winner, by Harlan's Holiday): dam 6f (at 2 yrs) to 8.5f (US Grade 3 winner): fairly useful performer: won maiden at Bath in August: fourth in handicap at Windsor (1¼ lengths behind Jus Pires) final start: stays 1¼m: acts on polytrack and good to firm going: sold 20,000 gns in December. *Luca Cumani* **90**

GOODWOOD CRUSADER (IRE) 3 b.g. Sir Prancealot (IRE) 111 – Pale Orchid (IRE) 97 (Invincible Spirit (IRE) 121) [2017 63: p5m^6 p6g^2 p5g^2 t5.1g^6 5.7m* 5.7f* 6d* 6m* 6m* 6g 6d 6d p6g 6s Oct 15] sturdy gelding: useful handicapper: won at Bath twice in April (maiden first occasion, dead-heated second time) and Brighton, Leicester and **100**

Newmarket (by 2 lengths from Cold Snap), all in June: stays 6f: acts on polytrack, tapeta, firm and good to soft going: usually races towards rear: sold 30,000 gns in October to join Luke McJannet. *Richard Hughes*

GOODWOOD SHOWMAN 2 b.g. (Apr 20) Showcasing 117 – Polly Floyer 66 (Halling (USA) 133) [2017 7g p8g^{5} Nov 18] fair form: better effort when fifth in minor event at Lingfield (8 lengths behind Masaarr) in November. *William Knight* **67**

GO ON GAL (IRE) 4 b.f. Approve (IRE) 112 – Jeritza (Rainbow Quest (USA) 134) [2017 63: p10g^{6} f12s^{2} f12m^{3} f12g^{2} f14d^{5} 11.9m^{3} 11.6g 11.5s^{4} 11.5s^{5} 11.9m^{5} f12.1g* f11.1g^{4} Dec 29] workmanlike filly: fair handicapper: won at Southwell in August: stays 1½m: acts on polytrack, fibresand, good to firm and good to soft going: has worn cheekpieces, including final start: often travels strongly. *Julia Feilden* **65**

GO ON GO ON GO ON 4 b.f. Medicean 128 – Piranha (IRE) 82 (Exceed And Excel (AUS) 126) [2017 106: 6f 5g 5d^{3} 5.2m Sep 23] useful performer: third in listed race at Doncaster (2 lengths behind Encore d'Or) in September: stays 6f: acts on polytrack, tapeta and good to firm going: tried in tongue tie. *Clive Cox* **96**

GO ON MAYSON 3 br.g. Mayson 124 – Red Tiara (USA) 60 (Mr Prospector (USA)) [2017 72: 8.3g 8f 10d 8.1m^{5} 10d 8.1d Aug 24] maiden, no form in 2017: left David Evans after fourth start: tried in blinkers. *Christian Williams* **–**

GORDON LORD BYRON (IRE) 9 b.g. Byron 117 – Boa Estrela (IRE) (Intikhab (USA) 135) [2017 115: 6g 6g p6g^{2} 7d^{5} 8m^{4} 6d* 7g^{4} 6g^{2} 7m^{4} 6m^{3} 7g 6s^{6} 7.5v^{6} 7m^{3} 6d^{6} p8s^{5} Dec 8] tall, good-topped gelding: smart performer: won Greenlands Stakes at the Curragh (by 1½ lengths from Only Mine) in May: fifth in handicap at Dundalk (2¼ lengths behind Katiymann) final start: stays 8.5f: acts on polytrack and any turf going: genuine. *T. Hogan, Ireland* **116**

GORGEOUS (FR) 4 b.f. Assertive 121 – Agent Kensington 65 (Mujahid (USA) 125) [2017 57: t5.1g^{2} t5.1g^{4} Dec 13] lengthy filly: modest handicapper: should be suited by 6f: acts on fibresand and tapeta: sometimes slowly away. *Tony Carroll* **64**

GORGEOUS NOORA (IRE) 3 b.f. Raven's Pass (USA) 133 – Aneedah (IRE) 101 (Invincible Spirit (IRE) 121) [2017 89p: 6d p5g^{4} p5g^{2} p6g* Nov 21] useful handicapper: won at Lingfield (by ½ length from Rose Berry) in November: stays 6f: acts on polytrack and tapeta. *Luca Cumani* **101**

GORHAM'S CAVE 3 b.g. Rock of Gibraltar (IRE) 133 – Moiava (FR) 112 (Bering 136) [2017 7s^{5} 7s^{5} p6g^{3} Oct 25] fair form: best effort when fifth in maiden at Doncaster in July. *Roger Varian* **75**

Weatherbys Ireland Greenlands Stakes, the Curragh—the veteran Gordon Lord Byron adds to his considerable haul of pattern-race wins; Only Mine (left) and Suedois (star on cap) fill the places

GORING (GER) 5 b.g. Areion (GER) 115 – Globuli (GER) (Surako (GER) 114) [2017 91: 6g^{2} 6.1g^{5} 6g^{4} 7.1v* 7.8s 7v^{5} 6d 6.1s 6.1s* 6v^{5} p6s^{6} p8g* p8g* Dec 31] compact gelding: fairly useful handicapper on turf, useful on all-weather: won at Chepstow in June and September, and Lingfield (twice, by 2 lengths from Alfred Hutchinson second occasion) in December: stays 8.5f: acts on polytrack, good to firm and heavy going: in headgear last 5 starts. *Eve Johnson Houghton* **93 a106**

GOROKAI (IRE) 4 b.g. Kodiac 112 – Damask (IRE) 66 (Red Clubs (IRE) 125) [2017 83: t5g Jan 12] fairly useful handicapper: well below form only start in 2017: stays 6f: acts on polytrack, tapeta and soft going: tried in cheekpieces: often races towards rear. *David Simcock* –

GO ROO 2 br.c. (Mar 29) Kyllachy 129 – Cross My Heart 72 (Sakhee's Secret 128) [2017 5.7d^{3} 6g p6g^{2} Oct 9] fair form: best effort when second in minor event at Kempton (neck behind Sergio Leone) final start. *Clive Cox* **75**

GORSE (IRE) 2 b.g. (Mar 22) Zebedee 113 – Golden Flower 83 (Royal Applause 124) [2017 t6d 6m^{5} 5m^{4} 6s^{3} 6d t6g^{6} Dec 6] modest maiden: stays 6f: acts on soft and good to firm going: in cheekpieces last 2 starts. *Ann Duffield* **63**

GO SANDY 2 ch.f. (Mar 29) Captain Gerrard (IRE) 113 – Lily Jicaro (IRE) 59 (Choisir (AUS) 126) [2017 5.1g^{6} 5.1d t6.1g 5m Aug 31] first foal: dam sprint maiden: no form. *Lisa Williamson* –

GOSSIP COLUMN (IRE) 2 b.c. (Apr 8) Arcano (IRE) 122 – Monicalew 77 (Refuse To Bend (IRE) 128) [2017 6.1m^{4} 6g^{4} 6d 7v^{5} p8g^{4} 7m Oct 25] compact, good-quartered colt: fair maiden: stays 7f: acts on good to firm going: often races prominently. *Charles Hills* **71**

GOSSIPING 5 b.g. Dubawi (IRE) 129 – Gossamer 118 (Sadler's Wells (USA) 132) [2017 75: t8.6m* t9.5m^{5} p8g* p8g* p8g^{3} 7f* 7m* 7g 7d 8s p8g p8g Oct 4] sturdy gelding: useful handicapper on turf, fairly useful on all-weather: won at Wolverhampton and Kempton in January, Kempton again in March and Goodwood (twice, by 1¾ lengths from The Warrior second occasion) in May: stays 8.5f: acts on polytrack, tapeta and firm going: has worn headgear, including last 3 starts. *Gary Moore* **103 a94**

GOTHIC EMPIRE (IRE) 5 b.g. Dark Angel (IRE) 113 – Box of Frogs (IRE) 50 (One Cool Cat (USA) 123) [2017 99: p7g 7m^{5} 7m t7.1g 7m^{5} 7d p7g^{4} p10g p11d^{5} Dec 13] lengthy gelding: fairly useful handicapper: left James Fanshawe after seventh start: stays 11f: acts on polytrack, tapeta, good to firm and good to soft going: has worn hood: often starts slowly/races towards rear. *Richard Rowe* **92**

GOT MY MOJO 7 b.g. Motivator 131 – Habla Me (IRE) (Fairy King (USA)) [2017 f7.1g 7d Oct 30] well beaten in pair of maidens. *Gary Sanderson* –

GOTTI (USA) 2 b.c. (Feb 15) More Than Ready (USA) 120 – Soot Z (USA) (Empire Maker (USA) 129) [2017 5.3d^{4} 5.1m* 6g^{4} Jul 6] fair form: won minor event at Windsor (by head from Indian Warrior) in June: stays 5.5f: tried in blinkers: has joined A. Al Rayhi, UAE. *Jeremy Noseda* **77**

GOWANBUSTER 2 b.g. (Apr 26) Bahri (USA) 125 – Aahgowangowan (IRE) 88 (Tagula (IRE) 116) [2017 t7.1d^{5} t6g* Nov 23] fair form: won minor event at Newcastle (by 1¾ lengths from Cocktail) in November: wears tongue tie: open to further improvement. *Susan Corbett* **77 p**

GOWANLESS 4 b.g. Monsieur Bond (IRE) 120 – Aahgowangowan (IRE) 88 (Tagula (IRE) 116) [2017 63: t5g t6g Mar 15] fair handicapper at best: well below form both starts in 2017: stays 6f: acts on good to firm and good to soft going: wears headgear. *Michael Dods* –

GOWER GOLD 2 b.f. (Mar 11) Mayson 124 – Mistressofthelake (IRE) (Mastercraftsman (IRE) 129) [2017 p6g May 30] €5,000Y, resold £3,500Y: first foal: dam unraced: 33/1, well held in minor event at Lingfield. *John Gallagher* –

GOWING GOWING GONE (IRE) 2 ch.f. (Jan 30) Society Rock (IRE) 126 – Face The Storm (IRE) 72 (Barathea (IRE) 127) [2017 6d p6g p6g Oct 14] £36,000Y: half-sister to several winners, including smart winner up to 7f Roi de Vitesse (2-y-o 5f/6f winner, by Chineur) and useful winner up to 7f Rebel Surge (2-y-o 6f winner, by Kodiac): dam 2-y-o 1m winner: well held in maidens/minor event. *Richard Spencer* –

GOZO GIRL 2 b.f. (Feb 27) Nayef (USA) 129 – Trust The Wind 66 (Dansili 127) [2017 8v Oct 4] first foal: dam 1m winner: 33/1, well held in minor event at Salisbury. *Joseph Tuite* –

GRACEFUL ACT 9 b.m. Royal Applause 124 – Minnina (IRE) (In The Wings 128) [2017 53: 10m 8m 12m 10.2g 9.9f* 9m^{2} 9.9s^{5} 10d 8.5d^{2} 10m^{5} 9.9v^{6} 10d Oct 20] modest handicapper: won at Beverley (amateur) in July: stays 1½m: acts on polytrack, firm and soft going: wears headgear: usually races prominently. *Ron Barr* **56**

GRACEFUL JAMES (IRE) 4 ch.g. Rock of Gibraltar (IRE) 133 – Little Miss Gracie 105 (Efisio 120) [2017 83: 9.9g p11d^{3} p10g* p10g^{4} 10g p11g p11d Dec 13] tall, strong gelding: fairly useful handicapper: won at Chelmsford (by 3 lengths from Zorba The Greek) in August: stays 11f: acts on polytrack. *Jimmy Fox* **90**

GRACEFUL LADY 4 b.f. Sixties Icon 125 – Leitzu (IRE) 74 (Barathea (IRE) 127) [2017 65: p12d^{6} p13g^{3} p12g^{2} p12g^{4} 11.5m^{2} 14.1m* 14.5m* p16s* 14g^{2} 16.3g* 16.3d^{4} 18d^{5} 16d^{5} 16g Nov 3] compact filly: fairly useful handicapper: won at Yarmouth in May, Doncaster (apprentice) and Chelmsford in June, and York (by 2¾ lengths from Angel Gabrial) in July: stays 16.5f: acts on polytrack, tapeta, good to firm and good to soft going: often races in rear/travels strongly. *Robert Eddery* **90** **a72**

GRACELAND (FR) 5 gr.m. Mastercraftsman (IRE) 129 – Jeunesse Lulu (IRE) (Montjeu (IRE) 137) [2017 93: 16m* 16.3d^{2} p14s^{4} t16.3s^{2} 16d^{3} 13.4g 14s^{2} 14s Sep 27] workmanlike mare: useful handicapper: won at Ascot (apprentice) in May: second at Haydock (3 lengths behind Sepal) in September: stays 16.5f: acts on polytrack, tapeta, soft and good to firm going: often starts slowly/races freely. *Michael Bell* **100**

GRACESOME (IRE) 6 b.m. Shirocco (GER) 129 – Simonda 95 (Singspiel (IRE) 133) [2017 72: p12g p12g Nov 29] lengthy mare: fair handicapper: well below form both starts in 2017: stays 1½m: acts on polytrack, tapeta, good to firm and good to soft going. *Michael Blanshard* **–**

GRACE'S SECRET 2 ro.f. (Feb 5) Mastercraftsman (IRE) 129 – Silent Music (IRE) (Peintre Celebre (USA) 137) [2017 7d p7g p7g^{6} p7g^{3} t8g Dec 6] second foal: dam, French 7.5f winner, half-sister to useful 8.5f-11.4f winner Hammiya: fair maiden: should be suited by 1m: acts on polytrack: often travels strongly. *Ed Walker* **74**

GRACIOUS DIANA 3 ch.f. Foxwedge (AUS) 128 – Generous Diana 90 (Generous (IRE) 139) [2017 –p: 10g* 10s^{4} 12m 10.2s p9.4g Nov 28] strong, well-made filly: useful performer: won maiden at Newbury (by 3½ lengths from Star Rock) in April: best effort at 1¼m: acts on good to firm going: tried in tongue tie: sometimes slowly away. *John Gosden* **97**

GRACIOUS GEORGE (IRE) 7 b.g. Oratorio (IRE) 128 – Little Miss Gracie 105 (Efisio 120) [2017 76: p8g p8g^{5} p8g^{5} p8s p11g p8s^{3} p8g^{6} Dec 30] sturdy gelding: modest handicapper: stays 1m: acts on polytrack, good to firm and good to soft going: has worn headgear. *Jimmy Fox* **64**

GRACIOUS JOHN (IRE) 4 b.g. Baltic King 120 – Dorn Hill 55 (Lujain (USA) 119) [2017 119: t5g^{4} p6g^{4} 6g^{4} p6g^{2} 5m 5f 5m 5g^{6} 5.4d 5.5g^{6} 5d^{3} 5.2d^{5} 5g* 5s^{5} p5g* t5.1g* Dec 22] useful-looking gelding: useful on turf, smart on all-weather: won handicaps at Leicester (by ½ length from Just Glamorous) in October, and Lingfield (by length from Royal Birth) and Wolverhampton (by short head from Tomily) in December: stays 6f: acts on polytrack, tapeta, soft and good to firm going: front runner/races prominently. *David Evans* **106** **a118**

GRACIOUS TOM (IRE) 3 b.c. Roderic O'Connor (IRE) 119 – Bigalo's Laura B (IRE) 50 (Needwood Blade 117) [2017 76: t5.1m^{5} f5g* t5.1m^{2} p5g^{3} p6g^{6} Jan 28] fairly useful handicapper: won at Southwell (by 1½ lengths from Major Jumbo) in January: stays 6f: acts on all-weather: sold 12,000 gns in February. *David Evans* **84**

GRAFFITI MASTER 2 b.c. (Apr 1) Dubawi (IRE) 129 – Independence 116 (Selkirk (USA) 129) [2017 7g^{4} p10g* 10m^{3} Oct 14] 575,000Y: strong colt: brother to 2-y-o 6f winner Easy Victory and half-brother to several winners, including high-class winner up to 1¼m (Eclipse Stakes) Mount Nelson (2-y-o 7f/1m winner, by Rock of Gibraltar) and very smart winner up to 1½m (Great Voltigeur Stakes) Monitor Closely (2-y-o 1m winner, by Oasis Dream): dam 7f/1m (including Sun Chariot Stakes) winner: useful form: won minor event at Kempton (by 1¾ lengths from Baileys Excelerate) in September: third in listed race at Newmarket (4 lengths behind Kew Gardens) in October: stays 1¼m: open to further improvement. *John Gosden* **101 p**

GRAFFITISTA (IRE) 2 b.f. (Feb 12) Kodiac 112 – Noble Galileo (IRE) 99 (Galileo (IRE) 134) [2017 6d^{5} p6g^{6} 6.1s^{5} p7g Sep 13] €56,000F, £42,000Y: third foal: dam 1½m winner: modest form: stays 7f. *George Scott* **61**

GRAMERCY (IRE) 10 b.g. Whipper (USA) 126 – Topiary (IRE) (Selkirk (USA) 129) [2017 73: p8g^{4} p7g t6g t7.1g^{3} 6m^{4} 6.1s 7.6d^{4} 7g Jul 13] well-made gelding: fair handicapper: trained third to fifth starts by Patrick Morris: stays 7.5f: acts on polytrack, tapeta and any turf going: usually wears headgear: usually races towards rear: not one to trust. *Ian Williams* **67 §** **a79 §**

GRAMS AND OUNCES 10 b.g. Royal Applause 124 – Ashdown Princess (IRE) (King's Theatre (IRE) 128) [2017 66: t12.2m 12v* 11.6f* 11.6f4 10g 12v* 11.4m5 12g6 14.1d Sep 21] strong gelding: fair handicapper: won at Chepstow and Bath in June, and Chepstow again in July: stays 17f: acts on polytrack and any turf going: wears cheekpieces/ tongue tie: often races towards rear. *Grace Harris* **67**

GRAND ACCLAIM (IRE) 2 ch.g. (Mar 28) Monsieur Bond (IRE) 120 – Endless Applause 62 (Royal Applause 124) [2017 6m t6.1g5 5s4 p6g Sep 5] modest form: best effort at 6f. *Harry Dunlop* **54**

GRANDAD CHUNK (IRE) 6 gr.g. Acclamation 118 – Silverdreammachine (IRE) 51 (Marju (IRE) 127) [2017 48: 7.1m 6m May 30] maiden, well held both starts in 2017: stays 6f: acts on good to firm and good to soft going. *Colin Teague* **–**

GRANDAD'S WORLD (IRE) 5 b.g. Kodiac 112 – Nose One's Way (IRE) 57 (Revoque (IRE) 122) [2017 93: 6g3 6g5 5g 5s 5g6 5g4 6g2 6v Sep 28] lengthy gelding: fairly useful handicapper: third at Redcar (¾ length behind Wentworth Falls) in April: stays 6f: acts on soft going: tried in headgear: unreliable. *Richard Fahey* **87 §**

GRANDEE (IRE) 3 b.g. Lope de Vega (IRE) 125 – Caravan of Dreams (IRE) 74 (Anabaa (USA) 130) [2017 96p: 10d6 13m2 12d* 12g 14d3 12g6 10v Oct 22] useful performer: won listed race at Leopardstown (by 2¼ lengths from Eziyra) in June: placed in similar events at Navan (head behind Naughty Or Nice) in May and Down Royal (1½ lengths behind The Tartan Spartan) in July: stays 1¾m: acts on soft and good to firm going: front runner/races prominently: sold to join David O'Meara 22,000 gns in October. *Mrs J. Harrington, Ireland* **106**

GRAND FACILE 5 b.g. Henrythenavigator (USA) 131 – Santolina (USA) 101 (Boundary (USA) 117) [2017 56: p15.8g2 p15.8g p13g* p12g 11.6d4 16.3d Jul 12] strong gelding: modest handicapper: won at Lingfield in February: stays 2m: acts on polytrack: wears headgear. *Gary Moore* **62**

GRANDFATHER TOM 2 b.c. (Mar 24) Kheleyf (USA) 116 – Kassuta 72 (Kyllachy 129) [2017 p6s5 Dec 7] second foal: dam 1m winner: 50/1, fifth in minor event at Chelmsford (5½ lengths behind Mushtaq) in December: entitled to do better. *Robert Cowell* **62 p**

GRAND INQUISITOR 5 b.g. Dansili 127 – Dusty Answer 97 (Zafonic (USA) 130) [2017 102: p7g p7g 8s6 7d 8d3 8g3 8g4 10.2d4 10.3g* t9.5d Dec 26] good-topped gelding: useful handicapper: won at York (by 5 lengths from Swift Emperor) in October: stays 10.5f: acts on good to firm and good to soft going: wears headgear: often races towards rear. *Ian Williams* **100**

GRAND KOONTA (IRE) 2 gr.c. (May 4) Dark Angel (IRE) 113 – Wrong Key (IRE) 108 (Key of Luck (USA) 126) [2017 6s4 6g2 6.1g* 6g 6m5 Sep 23] €140,000Y: good-topped colt: closely related to winner up to 1¼m Epic Battle (2-y-o 7f winner, by Acclamation) and half-brother to 3 winners, including very smart 1m winner Albaasil (by Dansili) and useful 2-y-o 5f winner Wrong Answer (by Verglas): dam winner up to 1m (2-y-o 6.5f/7f winner) who stayed 1¼m: fairly useful performer: won minor event at Windsor (by 3¾ lengths from Popsicle) in July: fifth in Mill Reef Stakes at Newbury (5½ lengths behind James Garfield) final start: will be suited by 7f+: acts on good to firm going. *Clive Cox* **91**

GRANDMA TILLY 2 b.f. (Mar 31) Hellvelyn 118 – Sleep Dance 62 (Sleeping Indian 122) [2017 5g May 9] 20,000Y: third foal: dam, 5f winner, out of useful 5f performer Crofters Ceilidh: 33/1, eighth in maiden at Leicester (7½ lengths behind Marchingontogether) in May. *Steph Hollinshead* **55**

GRAND MEISTER 6 gr.g. Mastercraftsman (IRE) 129 – Wait It Out (USA) (Swain (IRE) 134) [2017 85: t16.3g t12.2g6 t12.2g5 13.8m Apr 12] big gelding: fair handicapper: stays 2m: acts on polytrack, tapeta and good to soft going: has worn headgear, including last 3 starts. *John Quinn* **75**

GRAND MYLA (IRE) 3 gr.f. Dark Angel (IRE) 113 – Selfara 87 (Oasis Dream 129) [2017 66: 5.7f4 6g p6g p5g2 p5g p5g3 Dec 31] strong, compact filly: fair maiden handicapper: stays 6f: acts on polytrack and firm going: wears headgear: often leads. *Gary Moore* **71**

GRANDSCAPE 2 b.c. (Feb 2) Lemon Drop Kid (USA) 131 – Unnatural (USA) (Proud Citizen (USA) 122) [2017 7s4 7d4 Oct 27] 72,000Y: first foal: dam, lightly raced in Japan, half-sister to smart winner up to 6f Land of Dreams, herself dam of top-class 6f/7f performer Dream Ahead: fair form: better effort when fourth in maiden at Doncaster (4¼ lengths behind Breath Caught) in October: should improve further. *Ed Dunlop* **77 p**

GRANITE CITY DOC 4 b.g. Arabian Gleam 122 – Hansomis (IRE) 73 (Titus Livius (FR) 115) [2017 –: 10d 9.2d^2 8s Oct 3] modest maiden: stays 9f: acts on good to soft going. *Lucy Normile* **55**

GRAN MAESTRO (USA) 8 ch.g. Medicean 128 – Red Slippers (USA) 111 (Nureyev (USA) 131) [2017 18v Oct 9] fairly useful handicapper at best: tailed off only start on Flat in 2017: stays 2m: acts on polytrack and any turf going: usually wears headgear: sometimes in tongue tie: fair hurdler. *Peter Winks* **–**

GRANNY ANNE (IRE) 9 ch.m. Redback 116 – Krayyalei (IRE) 94 (Krayyan 117) [2017 8.5f^2 12v Jun 10] modest handicapper at best, off 5 years before return: stays 8.5f: acts on polytrack, fibresand and good to firm going: often wears headgear. *Natalie Lloyd-Beavis* **43**

GRANNY ROZ 3 b.f. Bahamian Bounty 116 – Hulcote Rose (IRE) 100 (Rock of Gibraltar (IRE) 133) [2017 6g^5 7m 6s^2 6m^2 6d* 5g^2 5g^2 5g Sep 27] 22,000Y: second foal: half-sister to 7f winner Bear Faced (by Intikhab): dam winner up to 8.6f (2-y-o 6f winner): fair performer: won handicap at Ripon in July: stays 7f: acts on good to firm and good to soft going: tried in blinkers: front runner/races prominently. *David Barron* **76**

GRAN PARADISO (IRE) 5 ch.g. Galileo (IRE) 134 – Looking Lovely (IRE) 77 (Storm Cat (USA)) [2017 –: 18g^6 21.6m^5 Apr 24] modest maiden: stays 21.5f: acts on good to firm and good to soft going: in headgear last 5 starts: sometimes in tongue tie: sold £4,800 in August to join Dan Skelton. *Micky Hammond* **63**

GRANTCHESTER (IRE) 3 ch.g. Exceed And Excel (AUS) 126 – Emily Blake (IRE) 115 (Lend A Hand 124) [2017 p10g^4 p10g^6 Sep 7] modest form: better effort when fourth in maiden at Chelmsford in August. *James Eustace* **63**

GRAPEVINE (IRE) 4 b.g. Lilbourne Lad (IRE) 111 – High Vintage (IRE) 97 (High Chaparral (IRE) 132) [2017 96: 10m^2 9m 10.1m 9.9m^4 10g^5 10.1m^5 10g 10m^6 Oct 16] lengthy gelding: useful handicapper: second at Newbury (nose behind Signe) in April: stays 10.5f: acts on soft and good to firm going: sometimes slowly away, often races towards rear: has joined Nicky Henderson. *Charles Hills* **96**

GRAPHITE GIRL (IRE) 2 gr.f. (Feb 3) Kodiac 112 – My Girl Lisa (USA) (With Approval (CAN)) [2017 5.1g 5d 5.9s 7s^5 6g t5d Nov 4] £42,000Y: closely related to 1¼m winner Darling Lexi (by Dylan Thomas) and half-sister to several winners, including winner up to 7f Explosive Power (2-y-o 6f winner, by Alfred Nobel): dam US 5f/5.5f winner, including at 2 yrs: modest maiden: stays 6f: acts on soft going. *Tim Easterby* **50**

GRAPHITE (IRE) 3 ro.g. Galileo (IRE) 134 – Simply Perfect 116 (Danehill (USA) 126) [2017 8.1g^3 10g^4 10.2d 8v^2 t7.2m^6 Oct 28] fair maiden: best effort at 1m: acts on heavy going: tried in cheekpieces. *David Simcock* **79**

GRAPHITE STORM 3 gr.g. Delegator 125 – Ice Haven (IRE) (Verglas (IRE) 118) [2017 87p: 7g^6 8m^2 8.2f 7.6d^5 7d^2 7d* 7d^6 Oct 6] useful handicapper: won at Leicester (by 1¼ lengths from Easy Tiger) in September: stays 1m: acts on good to firm and good to soft going: sometimes slowly away, often races in rear. *Clive Cox* **102**

GRASMERE (IRE) 2 b.f. (Apr 15) Society Rock (IRE) 126 – Silk Point (IRE) (Barathea (IRE) 127) [2017 8m 7d^5 6.1v p6s^6 p7s Dec 14] €21,000Y: half-sister to several winners, including 7f (including at 2 yrs) winner All of Me (by Xaar) and 7f/1m winner (stays 1¼m) Ixelles Diamond (by Diamond Green): dam unraced: modest maiden: best effort at 7f: acts on polytrack. *Alan Bailey* **54**

GRAVINA 2 b.f. (Feb 16) Havana Gold (IRE) 118 – Dolcetto (IRE) 83 (Danehill Dancer (IRE) 117) [2017 6s May 19] sturdy filly: third foal: half-sister to smart winner up to 1½m Primitivo (2-y-o 1m winner, by Excellent Art) and 1m/1¼m winner Shadow Warrior (by Born To Sea): dam 1¼m-1½m winner: 25/1, well held in maiden at Newbury. *Alan King* **–**

GRAVITY FLOW (IRE) 4 ch.f. Exceed And Excel (AUS) 126 – Landela 64 (Alhaarth (IRE) 126) [2017 108: 6f 6g p5g 6g Oct 7] rather leggy filly: useful performer at 3 yrs: no form in 2017: stays 6f: acts on polytrack and good to firm going. *William Haggas* **–**

GRAVITY WAVE (IRE) 3 br.g. Rip Van Winkle (IRE) 134 – Phrase 72 (Royal Anthem (USA) 135) [2017 75: 10.2g 10d p11g 10m^6 11.8g^6 Jul 8] lengthy gelding: fair handicapper: stays 1¼m: acts on good to firm going: often races towards rear. *Sylvester Kirk* **73**

GREAT AND SMALL 4 b.f. Galileo (IRE) 134 – Gryada 93 (Shirley Heights 130) [2017 95p: 14.1m Apr 30] fairly useful at 3 yrs, went as if amiss only start in 2017: stays 1¾m: acts on good to firm going. *Andrew Balding* **–**

GREAT BEYOND 2 b.c. (Mar 29) Dansili 127 – Solar Pursuit (Galileo (IRE) 134) [2017 8.3v Nov 8] 14/1, eighth in maiden at Nottingham (4½ lengths behind Kinaesthesia). *Roger Charlton* **70**

GREAT COLACI 4 b.g. Sulamani (IRE) 130 – Fairlie 70 (Halling (USA) 133) [2017 64: 7.2m* 7m 7m t7.1s 7.2s⁶ Sep 16] modest handicapper: won at Musselburgh in June: stays 7f: acts on tapeta and good to firm going: tried in cheekpieces. *Gillian Boanas* **63**

GREAT COURT (IRE) 3 gr.f. Mastercraftsman (IRE) 129 – Neat Shilling (IRE) (Bob Back (USA) 124) [2017 77: 9.9f⁵ 9s³ t9.5g* 9.9g² 10g⁵ t12.2g* p12g Nov 29] sturdy filly: useful performer: won maiden at Wolverhampton in August and handicap at same course (by 1¾ lengths from Eldritch) in October: left Luca Cumani after first start: stays 1½m: acts on polytrack, tapeta, best turf form on good going. *Roger Varian* **100**

GREAT EXPECTATIONS 9 b.g. Storming Home 128 – Fresh Fruit Daily 92 (Reprimand 122) [2017 71: p6g³ p6g⁴ t5g p6g⁶ 6m 7m 6s 8m Jun 30] compact gelding: modest handicapper nowadays: stays 7f: acts on all-weather, good to firm and heavy going: has worn headgear, including in 2017: wears tongue tie: often races towards rear. *J. R. Jenkins* **45 a56**

GREAT FIGHTER 7 b.g. Street Cry (IRE) 130 – Evil Empire (GER) 108 (Acatenango (GER) 127) [2017 83: t12.4d⁶ 14g* 16m* 16.3m⁵ 14m² 14s⁵ 18d Sep 23] fairly useful handicapper: won at Musselburgh in May and June (by 1½ lengths from Kensington Star): second at same course in August: stays 17.5f: acts on polytrack, soft and good to firm going: wears headgear: often starts slowly/races in rear: fairly useful hurdler. *Jim Goldie* **94**

GREAT HALL 7 b.g. Halling (USA) 133 – L'Affaire Monique 101 (Machiavellian (USA) 123) [2017 108: p12g⁴ 10g 10.1g⁴ 9m⁶ 10.1m⁶ 10g 11.4g³ 10.1g⁵ 10d⁶ 12d* 12s* 14.1d* 12s⁶ Oct 7] good-topped gelding: smart handicapper: won at Ascot in August (by 1¼ lengths from Gawdawpalin) and September (by ½ length from Alqamar), and Yarmouth (by 1½ lengths from Zenon) later in September: stays 1¾m: acts on polytrack, soft and good to firm going: has worn headgear. *Mick Quinn* **110**

GREAT PROSPECTOR (IRE) 2 b.c. (Apr 19) Elzaam (AUS) 115 – Guana (IRE) (Dark Angel (IRE) 113) [2017 6.1m* 7g³ 6d² 6.5g⁴ 7m⁶ Oct 14] €48,000F, £95,000Y: lengthy, useful-looking colt: second foal: half-brother to 2-y-o 7f winner Red Guana (by Famous Name): dam unraced: useful performer: won minor event at Nottingham in June: third in Superlative Stakes at Newmarket (½ length behind Gustav Klimt) in July: stays 7f: acts on good to firm and good to soft going: often races prominently. *Richard Fahey* **100**

GREAT RETURN 4 b.g. New Approach (IRE) 132 – Under The Rainbow 107 (Fantastic Light (USA) 134) [2017 71p: 6.9g⁶ 7.6g 9.9m 10d⁵ p15.8g³ p16g² Dec 20] fair maiden: left Lisa Williamson after fourth start: stays 2m: acts on polytrack and good to firm going. *Warren Greatrex* **69**

GREAT ROAR (USA) 9 b.g. Thunder Gulch (USA) 129 – Boasting (USA) (Kris S (USA)) [2017 t10.2g⁶ t12.2g⁶ Feb 11] placed in bumpers in 2012: tailed off in Flat maidens: wears tongue tie. *Ronald Thompson* **–**

GREAT SHOT SAM (USA) 2 ch.f. (Mar 23) Shackleford (USA) 124 – Universal Peace (JPN) (Sunday Silence (USA)) [2017 p8g² 8v⁶ t7.1g* Nov 23] $13,000F, $15,000Y: fifth foal: half-sister to a winner in Japan by Bluegrass Cat: dam, Japanese 6f winner, out of US Grade 2 8.5f/9f winner Sixieme Sens: fair form: won minor event at Newcastle (by 1½ lengths from Ideal Candy) in November: stays 1m: remains with potential. *Andrew Balding* **67 p**

GREAT SOUND (IRE) 3 b.g. Galileo (IRE) 134 – Wanna (IRE) 95 (Danehill Dancer (IRE) 117) [2017 12d* 12d³ 13.3s* 14s⁶ 14.5d⁵ Oct 27] 320,000Y: fourth foal: closely related to 2 winners, including smart winner up to 1¼m Tannaaf (2-y-o 7f winner, by High Chaparral), and half-brother to 1m winner Just Joan (by Pour Moi): dam, 1½m winner, closely related to Cheveley Park Stakes winner/1000 Guineas runner-up Wannabe Grand: useful performer: won maiden at Chepstow in June and handicap at Newbury (by ½ length from Comrade Conrad) in August: stays 13.5f: acts on soft going: tried in cheekpieces: sometimes slowly away, often races lazily. *John Gosden* **102**

GREAT VIZIER 2 b.g. (Mar 30) Sir Percy 129 – Special Green (FR) (Sadler's Wells (USA) 132) [2017 7g⁶ 7.1s² 8d Sep 5] fair form: second in minor event at Chepstow (4½ lengths behind Shepherd Market) in August: should stay 1m+. *Eve Johnson Houghton* **73**

GREAT WHITE SHARK (FR) 3 gr.f. Le Havre (IRE) 124 – Trip To Fame (FR) (Lordmare (FR) 105) [2017 9.9g⁵ 10.2s* 11.9d* 11.9g Sep 8] €60,000Y: seventh foal: half-sister to useful French 7.5f/1m winner (including at 2 yrs) Trip To Glory (by Where Or **97**

When) and French 1m/8.5f winner Grey Caviar (by Air Chief Marshal): dam unraced: useful form: won maiden at Doncaster in June and handicap at same course (by ½ length from Mister Belvedere) in August: stays 1½m. *James Fanshawe*

GRECIAN DIVINE (IRE) 3 b.f. Kodiac 112 – Grecian Glory (IRE) 88 (Zafonic (USA) 130) [2017 82, a75: p5g⁴ f5d⁵ p5g 5.1g 5m⁶ 6s Sep 15] closely related to useful 5f/6f winner Marmalady (by Duke of Marmalade) and half-sister to 2 winners, including 1¼m-1½m winner Amber Grey (by Galileo): dam 1m winner: fairly useful at 2 yrs for Denis Hogan in Ireland: below form in 2017: stays 6.5f: acts on polytrack and heavy going: tried in cheekpieces. *Joseph Tuite* **70**

GRECIAN KING 4 b.g. Kheleyf (USA) 116 – Grecian Air (FR) (King's Best (USA) 132) [2017 67: t6g 7g 5m⁵ May 8] maiden, no form in 2017: wears headgear. *David Barron* **–**

GRECIAN LIGHT (IRE) 3 b.f. Shamardal (USA) 129 – Akrivi (IRE) (Tobougg (IRE) 125) [2017 100: 8d³ 8m Jun 21] compact filly: useful performer: third in listed race at Saint-Cloud (2½ lengths behind Melesina) in March: stays 1m: acts on soft and good to firm going: often races freely. *Charlie Appleby* **96**

GRECIAN SPIRIT 2 b.c. (Mar 25) Teofilo (IRE) 126 – Ghar Shoop (IRE) 60 (Dubai Destination (USA) 127) [2017 t8.6m³ p10g³ Nov 29] third foal: half-brother to useful French 1½m winner Cap Verite (by Cape Cross): dam once-raced half-sister to very smart winner up to 11f Blue Monday: fair form: better effort when third in maiden at Kempton (3 lengths behind Ispolini) in November: bred to be suited by 1½m+: open to further improvement. *James Tate* **76 p**

GREEN DOOR (IRE) 6 b.g. Camacho 118 – Inourhearts (IRE) 111 (Pips Pride 117) [2017 110: 5g 5g³ 5d 5g³ 5s⁴ 5s 5v 5g³ 5v⁶ 5s³ t5g Nov 23] attractive gelding: useful handicapper: third at Goodwood (length behind El Astronaute) in August: races at 5f nowadays: acts on polytrack, firm and soft going: wears headgear: has refused to enter stalls. *Robert Cowell* **105**

GREENEYEDAFGHAN 2 b.g. (Apr 2) Sepoy (AUS) 129 – Extremely Rare (IRE) 82 (Mark of Esteem (IRE) 137) [2017 6v* 6.1d⁶ 7.4v⁵ Sep 17] neat gelding: fair form: won minor event at Ffos Las (by 1¾ lengths from Lope de Loop) in August: best effort at 6f. *William Muir* **71**

GREEN FORTUNE 2 b.c. (Feb 14) Sayif (IRE) 122 – Shyrl 98 (Acclamation 118) [2017 6m* 6f³ p6s* 6d p6g⁵ 6g Oct 7] good-topped colt: fifth foal: half-brother to smart 5f/6f winner (including at 2 yrs) Raucous (by Dream Ahead): dam 2-y-o 5f winner: fairly useful performer: won minor events at Lingfield in June and Chelmsford (by length from Amazing Alice) in July: raced only at 6f: acts on polytrack and good to firm going: in headgear last 4 starts. *William Haggas* **89**

GREENGAIRS 3 b.g. Delegator 125 – Shore Light (USA) (Gulch (USA)) [2017 57: f8g⁶ 6g⁶ 7.2s³ 7.2g⁴ 7.2d⁵ Jul 31] modest maiden handicapper: stays 1m: acts on soft going: in cheekpieces last 5 starts: in tongue tie last 3. *Keith Dalgleish* **59**

GREEN HOWARD 9 ch.g. Bahamian Bounty 116 – Dash of Lime 67 (Bold Edge 123) [2017 87: t9.5m⁶ t7.1g t8d⁶ t8.6g⁶ 8.3g⁵ 7.5f 8g² 8.5d³ 9.2m 8g 9.2s³ 8g² 8.3v⁵ 8s² 8v² 8.1d⁶ 8.3g Nov 1] fair handicapper: stays 1¼m: acts on good to firm and heavy going: wears headgear: has worn tongue tie: usually races nearer last than first. *Rebecca Bastiman* **70**

GREEN LIGHT 6 b.g. Authorized (IRE) 133 – May Light 62 (Midyan (USA) 124) [2017 98: 12g⁴ 12.5m⁴ 12m t16.3s t10.2g Jul 29] lengthy gelding: useful handicapper, on downgrade in 2017: stays 1½m: acts on any turf going: has worn headgear, including often in 2017: often races towards rear: suspect temperament. *Brian Ellison* **87**

GREEN OR BLACK (IRE) 5 gr.m. Zebedee 113 – Boucheron 89 (Galileo (IRE) 134) [2017 84: p12m⁵ t10.2d⁶ 11.6d³ Aug 23] first foal: dam 1½m winner: fairly useful maiden, below best in 2017: stays 1¼m: acts on soft going: front runner/races prominently. *Neil Mulholland* **75**

GREEN POWER 2 b.c. (Mar 18) Kheleyf (USA) 116 – Hakuraa (IRE) (Elnadim (USA) 128) [2017 5.1m 6.1d* 6f² 6v⁵ 6m⁶ Aug 28] £7,000Y: strong colt: second foal: half-brother to 5f winner Zavikon (by Compton Place): dam unraced: fairly useful performer: won minor event at Nottingham (by neck from Raydiance) in May: stays 6f: acts on any turf going: front runner/races prominently. *John Gallagher* **89**

GREENSIDE 6 b.g. Dubawi (IRE) 129 – Katrina (IRE) (Ela-Mana-Mou 132) [2017 99: 8m² 8m* 8m⁶ 8s 9d 8s Oct 21] good-topped gelding: useful handicapper: won at Sandown (by 1¼ lengths from Laidback Romeo) in June: stays 1m: acts on polytrack, good to firm and good to soft going. *Henry Candy* **108**

GREENVIEW PARADISE (IRE) 3 gr.f. Exchange Rate (USA) 111 – Senza Rete (IRE) (Barathea (IRE) 127) [2017 58: 6m 7.5f 7m^2 7.4d^2 6.9g^3 7.6d^2 9.9m^2 9.9d^4 9.2v^2 9.9s p7d^4 t9.5g Nov 25] fair maiden: left Richard Fahey after ninth start: stays 1¼m: acts on good to firm and good to soft going: often leads. *Brian Barr* **72**

GRENDISAR (IRE) 7 b.h. Invincible Spirit (IRE) 121 – Remarkable Story (Mark of Esteem (IRE) 137) [2017 118: p10g^4 p10m^5 p10g Apr 14] strong horse: smart performer: fourth in listed race at Lingfield in February: stays 1½m: acts on polytrack and heavy going: wears headgear: sold £45,000 in May. *Marco Botti* **111**

GRETA G (ARG) 4 gr.f. Exchange Rate (USA) 111 – Gringa Nativa (ARG) (Orpen (USA) 116) [2017 8m 8m^6 8g Sep 2] sturdy filly: first foal: dam unraced half-sister to smart US Grade 1 9f winner Global Hunter: smart performer in Argentina, successful twice in 2016, including in Gran Premio Mil Guineas at San Isidro: below best in Britain: stays 1m: acts on heavy going: tried in tongue tie: sent to USA. *John Gosden* **100**

GREY BRITAIN 3 gr.g. Arcano (IRE) 122 – Reaching Ahead (USA) (Mizzen Mast (USA) 121) [2017 96: 7g^5 7g^6 p7f^4 8g^2 8m^4 10d* 10m 8g^5 9.9v^4 Aug 3] leggy, unfurnished gelding: useful performer: won listed race at Newmarket (by nose from Desert Skyline) in May: fourth in handicap at Goodwood (2¾ lengths behind Good Omen) final start: stays 1¼m: acts on any turf going: has worn headgear: usually leads. *John Ryan* **107**

GREY DANUBE (IRE) 8 gr.g. Verglas (IRE) 118 – Redrightreturning 81 (Diktat 126) [2017 95: p7g* p6g p7g p7g^4 p6g p8s Dec 8] leggy gelding: useful handicapper: won at Dundalk (by ½ length from Cocoa Beach) in January: stays 1m: acts on polytrack: has worn blinkers, including last 3 starts: wears tongue tie: often leads. *Darren Bunyan, Ireland* **99**

GREY DESTINY 7 gr.g. Desideratum 118 – Mother Corrigan (IRE) 64 (Paris House 123) [2017 66§: t7.1g* f7g^6 t7.1g t8s^2 t8.6g^3 7f^6 t8.6g^4 7m^2 7.4s 8s f7.1g^6 t7.1s^5 t8s t7.1d^3 t7.1g t7.2g^2 t7.2g* t7.2g* Dec 13] fair handicapper: won at Wolverhampton in March, November and December: stays 8.5f: acts on fibresand, tapeta and good to firm going: has worn cheekpieces: usually slowly away, races well off pace, often travels strongly: temperamental. *Antony Brittain* **67 §** **a74 §**

GREY DIAMOND 3 gr.g. Shamardal (USA) 129 – Tiffany Diamond (IRE) 101 (Sadler's Wells (USA) 132) [2017 9.2s 8m^5 10g^3 t8.6g 10s^5 10d p16g Dec 20] good-topped gelding: fair maiden: left Mark Johnston after sixth start: should stay at least 1¼m: acts on good to firm going: tried in blinkers: sometimes slowly away. *Denis Quinn* **65**

GREYFRIARSCHORISTA 10 ch.g. King's Best (USA) 132 – Misty Heights 105 (Fasliyev (USA) 120) [2017 84: f8g p7g p8g f7g p8g^4 f7g^4 f8g^3 p8d p8g^2 7d^4 8g 7.4g 8.1d Aug 24] tall, angular gelding: modest handicapper on turf, fair on all-weather: stays 9.5f: acts on polytrack, fibresand, firm and good to soft going: wears headgear/tongue tie: front runner/races prominently. *David Evans* **53** **a67**

GREYJOY (IRE) 3 gr.g. Mastercraftsman (IRE) 129 – American Jewel (USA) (Quiet American (USA)) [2017 63: p8g p8g f8d^4 t7.1g 8g^6 p12f 8d t8.6g 9.9g^4 9.9m t8.6g 7.6d 7m 11.6d 9.9d Sep 18] smallish gelding: modest maiden handicapper: stays 1¼m: acts on polytrack. *Sylvester Kirk* **54**

GREY MIRAGE 8 b.g. Oasis Dream 129 – Grey Way (USA) 109 (Cozzene (USA)) [2017 102: t7.1g p6.5g p8g^5 p6.5g^3 p6.5g^3 p7.5g^2 p7.5g 8g 7d p6.5f a8.5g p6.5f 9m a7.5g Dec 21] lengthy, good-topped gelding: useful handicapper: left Gay Kelleway after second start, J. M. G. Lefebvre after fourth: short-head second at Marseilles Vivaux in March: disappointing after: stays 8.5f: acts on polytrack, fibresand, good to firm and heavy going: often in headgear. *Cedric Boutin, France* **95 d**

GREY MIST 3 gr.g. Mastercraftsman (IRE) 129 – Kekova (Montjeu (IRE) 137) [2017 11.9m 12g^3 10.2d 14m 14.1v 14s 12v Oct 23] fair maiden: best effort at 1¾m: acts on good to firm going: in headgear last 4 starts. *Tim Easterby* **66**

GREY SPIRIT (IRE) 2 gr.g. (Mar 3) Dark Angel (IRE) 113 – Buttonhole 64 (Montjeu (IRE) 137) [2017 7.1s^6 p7g p7g Oct 18] modest form in minor events. *Sir Mark Prescott Bt* **59**

GREY WATERS (IRE) 3 gr.f. Mastercraftsman (IRE) 129 – Pelican Waters (IRE) 97 (Key of Luck (USA) 126) [2017 64: 11.3g 10.3g^6 12m^2 9.5s^3 12g^5 11g^3 p12g^4 p16g* Nov 7] fifth foal: sister to 7f winner Crafted Mastery and half-sister to 2 winners, including 1m-1¼m winner (stays 12.5f) Exclusive Waters (by Elusive City): dam 9.5f winner: fair handicapper: won at Kempton in November: stays 2m: acts on polytrack, soft and good to firm going: has worn headgear. *Joseph Patrick O'Brien, Ireland* **74**

GRIEG HALL 3 b.g. Halling (USA) 133 – Woven Lace (Hard Spun (USA) 124) [2017 10m5 p10g2 9.9d3 Jun 9] well-made gelding: first foal: dam, useful French 1m winner, out of very smart French 5f-7f winner Do The Honours: fairly useful form: best effort when fifth in maiden at Newmarket (5¾ lengths behind Tamleek) in April: sold 35,000 gns in July. *John Gosden* **88**

GRIMEFORD LANE (IRE) 2 b.g. (Apr 16) Zoffany (IRE) 121 – Bean Uasal (IRE) 94 (Oasis Dream 129) [2017 5.9g 7.4m 7.2g2 8.3v 7d3 t7.2g* 7d2 Oct 20] good-topped gelding: fair performer: won seller at Wolverhampton in October: second in claimer at Redcar final start: stays 7f: acts on tapeta and good to soft going: in cheekpieces last 3 starts: often races prominently: sent to Sweden. *Michael Dods* **73**

GRINTY (IRE) 3 b.c. Elnadim (USA) 128 – Fire Line (Firebreak 125) [2017 76: 7g* 7s6 6g3 6g 5.9s6 7d6 7s2 7d2 7v3 Nov 7] fair performer: won maiden at Redcar in May: placed in handicaps at Redcar last 2 starts: stays 7f: acts on heavy going. *Michael Dods* **76**

GRIPPER 2 b.g. (Mar 30) Thewayyouare (USA) 117 – Hold On Tight (IRE) 90 (Hernando (FR) 127) [2017 t7.2g4 p8g5 Sep 26] fair form: better effort when fourth in minor event at Wolverhampton (2 lengths behind Eesha Beauty) in August: should stay 1m+. *Ralph Beckett* **66**

GRISE LIGHTNING (FR) 2 gr.f. (Mar 16) Wootton Bassett 119 – Tcncpia (FR) (Keltos (FR) 132) [2017 6s2 t7.1g4 Sep 12] €6,500F, €45,000Y, €77,000 2-y-o: seventh foal: half-sister to 3 winners in France, including 9f/1¼m winner Tianjin City (by Holy Roman Emperor) and 2-y-o 1m winner La Cumparsita (by American Post): dam French 8.5f winner: fair form: better effort when second in maiden at Hamilton (3½ lengths behind Queen Penn) in August: should still improve. *Richard Fahey* **69 p**

GRONKOWSKI (USA) 2 b.c. (Feb 1) Lonhro (AUS) 128 – Four Sugars (USA) (Lookin At Lucky (USA) 127) [2017 7m 8g2 p8d* Nov 9] $75,000F, 50,000Y, 300,000 2-y-o: first foal: dam unraced half-sister to smart US Grade 1 9f winner Flashy Bull: fairly useful form: won minor event at Chelmsford (by 4½ lengths from Big Kitten) in November: stays 1m: tried in blinkers: will go on improving. *Jeremy Noseda* **93 p**

GROOR 5 b.h. Archipenko (USA) 127 – Alta Moda (Sadler's Wells (USA) 132) [2017 8g 8.9g a9.4f4 8.9gpu 8g a8f 8m4 8m6 11.9s 8.5m5 8.5gur p8g6 Sep 26] fairly useful handicapper: left Ali Jan after sixth start: best at around 1m: acts on dirt and good to firm going: has worn headgear: sold 14,000 gns in November. *Mohamed Moubarak* **89**

GROOVEJET 6 b.m. Cockney Rebel (IRE) 127 – Vino Veritas (USA) 72 (Chief's Crown (USA)) [2017 104: 12d5 14m3 14.5d 12g Oct 7] sturdy mare: useful performer: third in handicap at Newmarket (¾ length behind Fire Jet) in August: stays 14.5f: acts on polytrack, fibresand, good to firm and heavy going: tried in cheekpieces: often races in rear. *Richard Spencer* **99**

GROUNDFROST (IRE) 3 gr.f. Excelebration (IRE) 133 – Evening Time (IRE) 117 (Keltos (FR) 132) [2017 p6.5g p6.5g4 8d2 7d5 7g4 8m6 7s6 8.2s5 8.1d2 8v5 7v3 p8g p7g2 p8g Dec 31] half-sister to several winners, including 6f/7f winner Penny Pepper (by Fast Company) and 7f-1¼m winner Shaan (by Iffraaj), both useful: dam 6f winner (including at 2 yrs): fairly useful performer: fourth in handicap at the Curragh in July: left C. Ferland after second start: stays 1m: acts on polytrack and soft going: has worn hood. *J. J. Feane, Ireland* **91**

GROUNDNUT 2 b.g. (Mar 1) Rip Van Winkle (IRE) 134 – Hard Walnut (IRE) 82 (Cape Cross (IRE) 129) [2017 6.1d4 6m2 7g 7d* 7s3 Oct 10] workmanlike gelding: fair performer: won maiden at Brighton in September: stays 7f: acts on good to firm and good to soft going: in cheekpieces last 2 starts: often races prominently. *Jonathan Portman* **75**

GROUNDSKEEPERWILLY 3 ch.g. Camacho 118 – Hello Deauville (FR) (Alhaarth (IRE) 126) [2017 t6g t7.1g4 t6g 6f 6d 8d a7.5g 5.5s Nov 6] little form: left David Evans after third start. *Frank Sheridan, Italy* **–**

GROUNDWORKER (IRE) 6 b.g. Tagula (IRE) 116 – Notepad 63 (King's Best (USA) 132) [2017 74§: t5g6 t5.1g4 5m 5g 5g6 5m5 5d5 5m4 t5g* t5g 5s t5g Nov 3] compact gelding: fair handicapper: won at Newcastle in September: stays 6f: acts on tapeta, soft and good to firm going: tried in cheekpieces: wears tongue tie: usually races prominently: temperamental. *Paul Midgley* **66 §**

GROUPIE 3 b.f. Requinto (IRE) 109 – Amour Fou (IRE) 81 (Piccolo 121) [2017 88: 6m 6d 6g6 7f* 7d 7.2m p7d Oct 6] compact filly: fairly useful handicapper: won at Haydock (by ¾ length from Manners Please) in July: stays 7f: acts on firm and soft going. *Tom Tate* **84**

GROVEMAN 2 b.g. (Mar 24) Holy Roman Emperor (IRE) 125 – Raving Monsun 76 (Monsun (GER) 124) [2017 7m^4 7d^6 7m^5 Aug 9] fair form: best effort when sixth in minor event at Newmarket (4 lengths behind Anna Nerium) in July: will be suited by 1m+. *Charles Hills* **74**

GROWL 5 b.g. Oasis Dream 129 – Desert Tigress (USA) 83 (Storm Cat (USA)) [2017 119: 6s 7.2s 6m^{ur} 6g^6 6d^4 6g 6s 6v 6g Oct 14] attractive gelding: smart performer: fourth in Stewards' Cup Handicap at Goodwood (length behind Lancelot du Lac) in August: stays 7f: acts on firm and soft going: usually wears headgear: has worn tongue tie. *Richard Fahey* **116**

GRUMETI 9 b.g. Sakhee (USA) 136 – Tetravella (IRE) (Groom Dancer (USA) 128) [2017 94: t16.5g* 16.3d^6 p16g^4 16.1f^3 16g^4 Aug 12] tall, good-topped gelding: fairly useful handicapper: won at Wolverhampton (by ½ length from All For The Best) in March: third at Beverley in July: stays 2¼m: acts on polytrack, tapeta, firm and soft going: in cheekpieces last 2 starts: often races towards rear. *Alan King* **87**

GUARD OF HONOUR (IRE) 6 b.g. Galileo (IRE) 134 – Queen of France (USA) 95 (Danehill (USA) 126) [2017 93: p16g^5 18g^4 21.6m^6 20.6v Aug 2] angular gelding: fairly useful handicapper: fourth at Newbury in April: stays 2¾m: acts on polytrack, tapeta, firm and soft going: wears headgear: races towards rear. *George Baker* **93**

GUIDING PASSION (FR) 3 b.f. Iffraaj 127 – Right Ted (IRE) 78 (Mujadil (USA) 119) [2017 7g^4 7s^5 8v 8.9v Nov 25] €12,000Y: sixth foal: half-sister to 10.7f winner Miss Forde (by Clodovil) and a winner in Italy by Fast Company: dam, winner up to 1m (2-y-o 7f winner), half-sister to useful 1¼m/1½m winner Torcello: modest form: best effort at 7f: in cheekpieces last 2 starts. *K. R. Burke* **61**

GUIDING STAR 3 b.f. Iffraaj 127 – Still I'm A Star (IRE) 70 (Lawman (FR) 121) [2017 67: p6g^4 p5g p7g 5m 7.2m 6m^3 5.9s^3 6g* 6.8m 6g 5m 6m 7.8g p7g p7g t6g^5 p6g Dec 21] sturdy filly: modest handicapper: won at Fairyhouse in June: left John Patrick Murtagh after first start: stays 6f: acts on polytrack, soft and good to firm going: usually wears headgear. *P. J. McKenna, Ireland* **62**

GUIGNOL (GER) 5 b.h. Cape Cross (IRE) 129 – Guadalupe (GER) 113 (Monsun (GER) 124) [2017 119: 10.4g^6 10.9g* 11.9s^4 11.9g* 11.9s* 11.9f Nov 26] very smart performer: won Grosser Preis der Badischen Wirtschaft at Baden-Baden in May, Grosser Preis von Baden (by 2½ lengths from Iquitos) in September and Grosser Preis von Bayern at Munich (beat same rival by neck) in October: ninth to Cheval Grand in Japan Cup at Tokyo final outing: stays 1½m: acts on heavy going: usually makes running. *J-P. Carvalho, Germany* **124**

GUISHAN 7 b.m. Ishiguru (USA) 114 – Fareham (Komaite (USA)) [2017 99: f5g^4 p6g^6 6d 6.1v* 6g^4 5.5g* 6v* Sep 5] angular mare: useful handicapper: won at Nottingham (by 6 lengths from Magical Dreamer) and Chester (by neck from Bossipop) in August, and at Hamilton (by neck from Southern Belle) in September: best up to 6f: acted on polytrack, fibresand, good to firm and heavy going: tried in cheekpieces: usually raced close up: reportedly in foal to Cable Bay. *Michael Appleby* **105**

GUITAR PETE (IRE) 7 gr.g. Dark Angel (IRE) 113 – Innishmore (IRE) (Lear Fan (USA) 130) [2017 13.1s^2 Jul 10] fair maiden: stays 1¾m: acts on soft going: tried in visor: useful chaser. *Nicky Richards* **69**

GULF OF POETS 5 b.g. Oasis Dream 129 – Sandglass 101 (Zafonic (USA) 130) [2017 81: 10g* t9.5g* 9.2s* 10.2m* 8.3s^4 7.9d 10.3m 10.3v 10.3g 10v^3 Nov 7] fairly useful handicapper: won at Pontefract (apprentice) and Wolverhampton in April, and Hamilton and Haydock (by 1¼ lengths from Boycie) in June: stays 1¼m: acts on tapeta, good to firm and heavy going: has worn headgear. *Michael Easterby* **94**

GULLAND ROCK 6 b.g. Exceed And Excel (AUS) 126 – Sacre Coeur 90 (Compton Place 125) [2017 75: p7g* p7g^3 7m^3 8m^5 p7g^4 7d 7g^6 Jul 12] attractive gelding: fair handicapper: won at Kempton in March: fourth at same course in June: stays 1m: acts on all-weather, soft and good to firm going: has worn headgear: usually leads: inconsistent. *Anthony Carson* **72** **a78**

GULLANE ONE (IRE) 2 ch.g. (Feb 25) Dream Ahead (USA) 133 – Shamsalmaidan (IRE) 67 (Fantastic Light (USA) 134) [2017 7v 6v^3 5.4g Oct 13] good-topped gelding: modest form: best effort when seventh in minor event at York (5 lengths behind Awesome) final start. *Tim Easterby* **62**

GULLIVER 3 b.g. Sayif (IRE) 122 – Sweet Coincidence 69 (Mujahid (USA) 125) [2017 94p: 8m 6.1g^4 6m 6m^2 7g 6.1s^6 6v^2 t6.1g* p7g* p6g* p7m t6.1d^2 Dec 26] well-made gelding: smart handicapper: won at Wolverhampton (by neck from Sign of The Kodiac) in **113**

October, and Lingfield (by neck from Sacred Act) and Kempton (by ¾ length from Intransigent) in November: second in minor event at Wolverhampton (length behind Intisaab) final start: stays 1m: acts on polytrack, tapeta, good to firm and heavy going: usually wears headgear: wears tongue tie. *Hugo Palmer*

GUMRIYAH 2 b.f. (Mar 11) Shamardal (USA) 129 – Yummy Mummy 86 (Montjeu (IRE) 137) [2017 7m 8d³ Oct 27] 870,000Y: well-made filly: fifth foal: half-sister to 3 winners, including very smart winner (including 1000 Guineas) up to 1¼m Legatissimo (2-y-o 7f winner, by Danehill Dancer) and useful 1½m winner (stayed 2½m) Another Cocktail (by Dalakhani): dam, 1¼m winner who probably stayed 1½m, sister to Irish Derby/Gold Cup winner Fame And Glory: fairly useful form: better effort when third in maiden at Doncaster (2½ lengths behind Mrs Sippy) in October: likely to progress further. *John Gosden* **81 p**

GUN CASE 5 b.g. Showcasing 117 – Bassinet (USA) 84 (Stravinsky (USA) 133) [2017 80: t6s 5.9g 7.2d 8g³ 8d⁵ 7m⁴ t8g t7.1d² t7.1g⁴ t7.1d* t7.1d² t8g³ t7.1g Dec 6] good-bodied gelding: fair handicapper: won at Newcastle in November: stays 1m: acts on tapeta, good to firm and good to soft going: usually wears headgear: races towards rear. *Alistair Whillans* **67 a76**

GUNG HO JACK 8 b.g. Moss Vale (IRE) 126 – Bijan (IRE) 75 (Mukaddamah (USA) 125) [2017 85: a6.5g⁶ a6.5g⁵ a6.5g⁴ 6m 6m 6.1m⁴ Jun 15] good-topped gelding: fair on turf, fairly useful on all-weather: stays 7f: acts on polytrack, snow and good to firm going. *John Best* **65 a82**

GUNMAKER (IRE) 3 b.g. Canford Cliffs (IRE) 133 – Can Dance (Manduro (GER) 135) [2017 p8g⁴ p7g⁵ t7.1g⁴ 9.9m 7g 7d² 7v⁵ 6d⁴ 6s⁴ Sep 19] fair maiden: stays 7f: acts on polytrack, tapeta and good to soft going: tried in hood: sometimes slowly away, often races towards rear: temperamental. *David Simcock* **73 §**

GUNMETAL (IRE) 4 gr.g. Clodovil (IRE) 116 – March Star (IRE) 109 (Mac's Imp (USA) 116) [2017 95: 6g 6m* 6m 6s⁶ 6g 7m 6d Oct 27] rangy gelding: useful handicapper: won at Newmarket (by 2¾ lengths from Normandy Barriere) in April: stays 7f: acts on good to firm and good to soft going: has joined David Barron. *Charles Hills* **99**

GUNNAR JULIUS (USA) 2 b.c. (Feb 28) Lonhro (AUS) 128 – Peinture Ancienne (USA) (Seeking The Gold (USA)) [2017 7.1s p5m⁶ t5.1d Dec 26] well held in minor events. *Ed Walker* **–**

GUNNER LINDLEY (IRE) 10 ch.g. Medicean 128 – Lasso 58 (Indian Ridge 123) [2017 64: 13.1s⁵ Jun 12] modest handicapper: well held only start on Flat in 2017: stays 13f: acts on soft and good to firm going: has worn headgear: front runner/races prominently: poor hurdler. *Stuart Coltherd* **–**

GUNNER MOYNE 5 b.g. Excellent Art 125 – Maramkova (IRE) (Danehill Dancer (IRE) 117) [2017 69: p10g p7g⁶ f8d* p10g 10d p10g³ f12.1g p11g p7g p8s f8.1g³ Dec 21] lengthy gelding: fair handicapper: won at Southwell in April: left Gary Moore after ninth start: stays 1¼m: acts on all-weather: wears headgear: has worn tongue tie. *Emma Owen* **66**

GUN RUNNER (USA) 4 ch.c. Candy Ride (ARG) 133 – Quiet Giant (USA) 120 (Giant's Causeway (USA) 132) [2017 127: a8.5f* a9.9g² a9f* a9f* a9f* a10f* Nov 4] first foal: dam, US Grade 2 8.5f winner, half-sister to Breeders' Cup Classic winner Saint Liam: top-class performer: won 5 of his 6 starts in 2017, Grade 3 Razorback Handicap at Oaklawn in February, Stephen Foster Handicap at Churchill Downs (beat Honorable Duty by 7 lengths) in June, Whitney Stakes at Saratoga (by 5¼ lengths from Keen Ice) in August, Woodward Stakes on last-named course (beat Rally Cry 10¼ lengths) in September and Breeders' Cup Classic at Del Mar (by 2¼ lengths from Collected) in November: 2¼ lengths second to Arrogate, pair 5 lengths clear, in Dubai World Cup at Meydan on other start: stays 1¼m: raced only on dirt: has worn tongue tie: front runner/races prominently. *Steven M. Asmussen, USA* **133**

GUNS DRAWN (IRE) 2 b.f. (Mar 8) Dandy Man (IRE) 123 – Just Like Ivy (CAN) 68 (Street Cry (IRE) 130) [2017 p7g⁴ p6g⁴ p6g* Oct 17] €8,500F, €22,000Y: fourth foal: half-sister to 1½m winner Creeping Ivy (by Mustameet): dam 1¾m winner: fair form: won minor event at Kempton (by ½ length from Gilded Hour) in October: stays 6f. *Richard Hannon* **74**

GURKHA FRIEND 5 b.g. Showcasing 117 – Parabola 72 (Galileo (IRE) 134) [2017 95: 7.1g³ 8g* 9g* 8d³ 7m 8m⁶ 7.2s 8.2d 7d t12.4g Nov 23] good-bodied gelding: useful handicapper: won at Ripon in April and May (by neck from Briardale): third at same course (½ length behind Boots And Spurs) in June: stays 9f: acts on firm and soft going: usually races prominently. *Karen McLintock* **101**

GUSTAV KLIMT (IRE) 2 b.c. (Mar 28) Galileo (IRE) 134 – Massarra 99 (Danehill (USA) 126) [2017 6d⁵ 7g* 7g* Jul 15] **112 p**

The Newmarket July meeting is usually the time of the year when things start to get serious for the two-year-olds, but for Gustav Klimt it marked the premature end of his season. Despite missing the chance to further his classic claims in the autumn, he still went into the winter vying for favouritism for the Two Thousand Guineas with stable-companions U S Navy Flag and Saxon Warrior, winners of the Middle Park/Dewhurst Stakes and the Racing Post Trophy. The Dewhurst would almost certainly have come into the reckoning for Gustav Klimt had things gone to plan for him beforehand in the National Stakes at the Curragh in September, for which he was forecast to start odds on until he was taken out on the morning of the race due to a stone bruise.

Aidan O'Brien had won the three previous editions of the National Stakes with Gleneagles, Air Force Blue and Churchill. While Gustav Klimt's bare form might not rank him alongside those top Ballydoyle two-year-olds of recent seasons, the campaign being planned for him gave every indication that he was considered to be at or near the top of the pecking order in the latest crop. As it is, Gustav Klimt can only be judged on a couple of starts in maidens and a narrow success in the Superlative Stakes, which he did really well to win at all. Like many of his stable's debutants, Gustav Klimt wasn't ready to do himself full justice first time up, finishing a never-nearer fifth in a maiden at the Curragh (won by Air Force Blue two years earlier) at the end of May but, with that run behind him, and over another furlong, he was a different proposition in a similar event there at the beginning of July, justifying favouritism in a race Gleneagles had won in 2014. Newmarket was chosen for Gustav Klimt's first big test and, less than a fortnight later, he took on nine rivals in the bet365 Superlative Stakes, a race O'Brien had won twice before, most recently with Horatio Nelson, the top-rated two-year-old of 2005. The Godolphin colt Aqabah, who had fared best of the three in the line-up who had contested the Coventry Stakes last time (beaten just over a length in fifth at Ascot), was the one to beat on form but Gustav Klimt started a strongly-backed favourite at 6/5-on and didn't let his backers down, though they must have been close to tearing up their tickets at one stage. After being up with the pace for much of the way, Gustav Klimt lost his place when a gap closed on him around two furlongs out, costing him valuable momentum. With the lead being fought over by three of his rivals, Gustav Klimt renewed his effort when switched by Ryan Moore to find a clear run up the far rail approaching the final furlong and kept on really well to take a narrow advantage and maintain it in the last fifty yards. Only a head, half a length and three quarters of a length separated the first four home, with Gustav Klimt landing the odds from Nebo, Great Prospector and Zaman. Had he not suffered interference, Gustav Klimt would have run out a clear-cut winner and he has been rated accordingly. The colts Gustav Klimt beat in the Superlative weren't among the season's top two-year-olds, but those who finished in the frame behind him all proved useful, with Nebo ending

bet365 Superlative Stakes, Newmarket—Gustav Klimt does well to catch Nebo (dark sleeves) after a troubled passage, with Great Prospector (hooped cap) in third

the year winning the Horris Hill Stakes at Newbury and Zaman faring best of the rest behind the most impressive Expert Eye in the Vintage Stakes at Goodwood on his only subsequent outing.

Gustav Klimt (IRE) (b.c. 2015)	Galileo (IRE) (b 1998)	Sadler's Wells (b 1981)	Northern Dancer
			Fairy Bridge
		Urban Sea (ch 1989)	Miswaki
			Allegretta
	Massarra (b 1999)	Danehill (b 1986)	Danzig
			Razyana
		Rafha (b 1987)	Kris
			Eljazzi

Gustav Klimt isn't the first foal out of his dam Massarra to have classic aspirations entertained for him. His brother Mars shot to the head of both the Guineas and Derby betting after winning a maiden at Dundalk on his debut, but he too wasn't seen out after July in his two-year-old season. Given his lack of experience, his sixth place in both classics were good efforts (particularly at Epsom where he finished less than four lengths behind stable-companion Ruler of The World) and Mars went on to reach the frame in the St James's Palace Stakes and Eclipse before suffering a fatal injury in the following year's Dubai Sheema Classic, by which time he had joined Mike de Kock, without having added to his debut success. Massarra had been carrying Mars when she was bought by the Coolmore partners for 600,000 guineas at the 2009 December Sales and she has produced three useful winners to Galileo between Mars and Gustav Klimt, all doing their winning as two-year-olds in what were rather anti-climactic careers. Wonderfully won twice, including the Group 3 Silver Flash Stakes over seven furlongs though, apart from finishing fourth in the Fillies' Mile, she failed to cut much ice subsequently. Toscanelli won a seven-furlong maiden at Limerick and ended his two-year-old season pacemaking for Gleneagles in the National Stakes, while Cuff won twice over six furlongs at Naas, including in a listed race, before fracturing a knee when sent off favourite for the 2016 Albany Stakes in which she finished fifth. Massarra's earlier foals, before she joined the Coolmore fold, included Nayarra (by Cape Cross) who gained her only career success in Italy's top two-year-old race, the Gran Criterium, when it still had Group 1 status.

Although Gustav Klimt's grandam Rafha won the Prix de Diane and some of her winners have stayed well, including St Leger fourth Sadian and Queen's Vase third Aquarius, Rafha is best known as the dam of the highly successful stallions Invincible Spirit and Kodiac, both sprinters. Sprint Cup winner Invincible Spirit was the better of the pair, though Kodiac (who sired a world-record sixty-one individual two-year-old winners in 2017) was a smart performer and Massarra, a useful filly and a full sister to Kodiac, was likewise best at sprint trips. All three of her wins came at six furlongs, including a listed contest at Newmarket at two, when she was also beaten a neck in the Prix Robert Papin, though she did also finish second in the Nell Gwyn Stakes over seven furlongs. This is also the family of the dual Australian Group 1 winner Pride of Dubai, a son of Street Cry, who joins Coolmore's Irish stallion roster in 2018; he is out of a half-sister to Rafha. If Gustav Klimt is to make his mark in a classic, it looks more likely to be a Guineas than a Derby, given that his full brothers and sisters have tended to take more after their dam, despite Galileo's stamina input. His withdrawal from the National Stakes, when the ground was soft, means he has only encountered good or good to soft ground to date. He was tongue tied on his last two starts. *Aidan O'Brien, Ireland*

GUSTAVO FRING (IRE) 3 b.g. Kodiac 112 – Maleha (IRE) (Cape Cross (IRE) 129) **78**
[2017 p7g^4 t7.2g^2 f5g* Dec 21] fair form: won maiden at Southwell (by ½ length from Decision Maker) in December: stays 7f. *Richard Spencer*

GUVENOR'S CHOICE (IRE) 2 ro.g. (Feb 25) Intikhab (USA) 135 – Exempt 75 **83**
(Exceed And Excel (AUS) 126) [2017 7g^4 7d^2 t8.6g* t8.6g^5 t8.6d* Dec 26] €7,000F, £20,000Y: first foal: dam lightly-raced half-sister to smart 6f/7f winner Mehronissa and US Grade 2 8.5f winner Three Degrees: fairly useful performer: won minor event at Wolverhampton in November and nursery at same course (by neck from Jellmood) in December: stays 8.5f: acts on tapeta and good to soft going: wears tongue tie. *K. R. Burke*

GUZMAN (IRE) 2 b.g. (Mar 31) Camacho 118 – Casablanca Jewel (IRE) 76 (Kalanisi **77**
(IRE) 132) [2017 5m* t6s* 7m^{5} 6d 7d^{4} p6d 6g^{5} 7m^{5} Oct 25] lengthy, useful-looking gelding: fair performer: won minor events at Thirsk in May and Newcastle (dead-heated) in June: fifth in nursery at Newmarket final start: stays 7f: acts on tapeta and good to firm going: in hood last 5 starts. *Richard Fahey*

GWENDOLYN (GER) 4 b.f. Invincible Spirit (IRE) 121 – Golden Whip (GER) 105 **75**
(Seattle Dancer (USA) 119) [2017 89: p5g p6g 5m^{6} Apr 20] sturdy filly: fairly useful handicapper: below form in 2017: stays 6f: acts on polytrack, tapeta, firm and soft going: tried in cheekpieces: sometimes slowly away. *Amy Murphy*

GWORN 7 b.g. Aussie Rules (USA) 123 – Crochet (IRE) (Mark of Esteem (IRE) 137) **90**
[2017 86: 8m^{4} 10m* 10m* 9.1s^{2} 10g* 10d^{6} 10g^{2} 10d^{3} 10d^{4} 12.1s 13s Oct 3] good-topped gelding: fairly useful handicapper: won at Ayr in May (twice) and again in June (by head from Kasperenko): stays 1½m: acts on polytrack, soft and good to firm going: has worn headgear: usually races towards rear. *R. Mike Smith*

GYMNASTE (IRE) 3 b.f. Shamardal (USA) 129 – Galipette 79 (Green Desert (USA) **101**
127) [2017 86p: 7d* p7d^{2} 8m 7g^{2} 7d 6m^{6} Oct 14] compact filly: useful performer: won maiden at Chester in May: second in handicap at Newmarket (neck behind Inshiraah) in July: stays 7f: acts on polytrack and good to soft going. *John Gosden*

GYPSY MAJOR 5 ch.g. Major Cadeaux 121 – Romany Gypsy (Indesatchel (IRE) 120) **59**
[2017 72: 6d^{4} 6s Sep 19] fair handicapper: below form both starts in 2017: stays 1m: acts on tapeta and firm going: wears headgear. *John Weymes*

GYPSY RIDER 8 b.g. Ishiguru (USA) 114 – Spaniola (IRE) (Desert King (IRE) 129) **55**
[2017 –: p7g t6g^{6} 7m^{5} 7m* 7m^{4} p7g^{6} Sep 6] close-coupled gelding: modest handicapper: won at Brighton in May: stays 7f: acts on polytrack, tapeta, soft and good to firm going: tried in headgear. *Henry Tett*

H

HAABIS (USA) 4 b.g. Super Saver (USA) 121 – Raise Fee (USA) (Menifee (USA) 124) **–**
[2017 65: p8g p10g t12.2g p10g^{3} 10.1m May 17] fair form on first 2 starts in 2016, little show since: usually in headgear: often wears tongue tie: has joined Patrick Chamings. *George Peckham*

HAADER (FR) 2 ch.c. (Jan 11) Sepoy (AUS) 129 – Idle Tears 59 (Selkirk (USA) 129) **71 p**
[2017 p7g^{5} Oct 18] €32,000Y, €120,000 2-y-o: fourth foal: half-brother to 12.5f winner Invernata (by Holy Roman Emperor) and French 2-y-o 1¼m winner Padoga (by Iffraaj): dam maiden half-sister to top-class 6f/7f winner Dream Ahead: 25/1, fifth in minor event at Kempton (4½ lengths behind Archie McKellar) in October, left poorly placed: open to improvement. *Owen Burrows*

HAAF A SIXPENCE 8 b.g. Haafhd 129 – Melody Maker 62 (Diktat 126) [2017 98: p8m^{4} **95**
Feb 25] rather leggy gelding: useful handicapper: stays 1m: acts on polytrack, fibresand and soft going: front runner/races prominently. *Ralph Beckett*

HAAFDASEE 2 b.g. (May 4) Haafhd 129 – See Clearly 83 (Bertolini (USA) 125) [2017 **–**
5g May 16] 50/1, well held in minor event at Beverley. *Tim Easterby*

HAAFFA SOVEREIGN 6 ch.g. Haafhd 129 – Royal Nashkova (Mujahid (USA) 125) **–**
[2017 54: p11d t12.2g Apr 8] modest maiden, below best both starts in 2017: stays 1½m: acts on tapeta: has worn headgear, including last 2 starts. *Laura Morgan*

HABBAD (FR) 3 ch.c. Choisir (AUS) 126 – Arikaria (IRE) (Sri Pekan (USA) 117) [2017 **79**
83p: 8.1m 8m 8g^{6} 7d^{3} 7g* p8g^{4} 8.1s Sep 14] fair handicapper: won at Doncaster in August: stays 1m: acts on polytrack: often wears cheekpieces. *Richard Hannon*

HAB REEH 9 gr.g. Diktat 126 – Asian Love (Petong 126) [2017 62: f6g t7.1g 6g 6g t6s **–**
Jun 1] big, good-topped gelding: fair at best, no form in 2017: wears headgear: has worn tongue tie. *Ruth Carr*

HACKBRIDGE 2 br.g. (Mar 14) Archipenko (USA) 127 – Famcred 89 (Inchinor 119) **62**
[2017 p8g p8d^{6} Dec 13] modest form: better effort when sixth in minor event at Kempton (10¼ lengths behind Highbrow) in December: in cheekpieces first start. *Pat Phelan*

HACKNEY ROAD 4 b.f. Aqlaam 125 – West Lorne (USA) 60 (Gone West (USA)) [2017 **88**
84p: p6g^{2} 6m^{3} p6g* p6d^{2} p6g^{3} p6g^{6} p6g Nov 7] fairly useful handicapper: won at Kempton (apprentice, by ½ length from Nightingale Valley) in July: left Henry Spiller after first start: raced only at 6f: acts on polytrack, tapeta and good to firm going. *John Butler*

HADDAF (IRE) 2 b.g. (Feb 1) Dawn Approach (IRE) 132 – Deveron (USA) 105 (Cozzene (USA)) [2017 5g^{2} 5m^{3} 5m^{3} 6f t5s* 5d^{3} 6.1d^{5} 5m Aug 26] 85,000Y: well-grown gelding: closely related to ungenuine 2-y-o 1m winner Open Letter (by New Approach) and half-brother to 3 winners, including smart winner up to 9.5f Lamar (2-y-o 6f winner, by Cape Cross): dam 2-y-o 7f winner: fairly useful performer: won minor event at Newcastle in July: third in listed races at Sandown (1¼ lengths behind Havana Grey) in May and Vichy (½ length behind Rioticism) in July: best form at 5f: acts on tapeta, good to soft and good to firm going. *James Tate* **93**

HADDEYA 3 b.f. Poet's Voice 126 – Sakhya (IRE) (Barathea (IRE) 127) [2017 t8.6g 8g 9g^{6} 10.9g 9d 10.9g^{5} 10.9g^{6} 8g 8f 8g 7.5g^{6} 8g^{6} 7v^{2} 7g 7.5m 7s^{5} Dec 14] half-sister to several winners, including useful 7f (including at 2 yrs) winner Dagher (by New Approach) and winner up to 1¼m Al Mukhdam (2-y-o 7f winner, by Exceed And Excel): dam ran once: well held in maiden at Wolverhampton: left Ed Walker, modest form in Spain/France after: stays 7f. *R. Avial-Lopez, Spain* **53**

HADEEQA (IRE) 3 b.f. Cape Cross (IRE) 129 – Khulood (USA) 103 (Storm Cat (USA)) [2017 65p: 8m 9.9m* 9.9m 8g^{3} 10s^{3} 10.2d Oct 11] good-topped filly: fairly useful performer: won maiden at Goodwood (dead-heated) in May: third in handicap there in August: stays 1¼m: acts on good to firm going: in hood last 3 starts. *Simon Crisford* **89**

HADFIELD (IRE) 5 b.g. Sea The Stars (IRE) 140 – Rezyana (AUS) (Redoute's Choice (AUS)) [2017 p12g Oct 18] fairly useful form for A. Fabre in 2015, down the field on sole start on Flat since: will be suited by 1¾m+: tried in cheekpieces/tongue tie: fairly useful hurdler. *Neil Mulholland* **–**

HADITH (IRE) 2 b.f. (Mar 6) New Approach (IRE) 132 – Discourse (USA) 116 (Street Cry (IRE) 130) [2017 8d^{3} 8.3d* 8d* Nov 4] second foal: half-sister to French 1m winner Discursus (by Dubawi): dam, 2-y-o 6f/7f winner, including Sweet Solera Stakes, half-sister to very smart US Grade 1 9f winner Bandini: useful form: won maiden at Nottingham (by 2½ lengths from Sheikha Reika) in October and listed race at Newmarket (by 1¼ lengths from Baroness) in November: likely to stay 1¼m: will go on improving. *Charlie Appleby* **102 p**

HADLEY 4 b.g. Royal Applause 124 – Brush Strokes (Cadeaux Genereux 131) [2017 52: f6g^{2} f6g f6g^{3} t6d^{3} t5g^{3} 6g^{4} 6g^{2} t6s^{3} 5g^{2} 5g^{3} t5g^{2} 5s^{3} 6g* 5m^{2} t5g Sep 22] fair handicapper on turf, modest on all-weather: won at Thirsk in August: best at 5f/6f: acts on fibresand, tapeta and good to firm going: wears cheekpieces: usually leads. *Tracy Waggott* **70 a59**

HAIL CLODIUS (IRE) 5 gr.g. Clodovil (IRE) 116 – Dhairkana (IRE) (Soviet Star (USA) 128) [2017 93: f8g^{4} t8g t7.1g^{5} 10.3g^{2} 9.8m May 12] tall gelding: fairly useful handicapper: second at Doncaster in April: left Richard Hannon after first start: stays 10.5f: acts on polytrack, soft and good to firm going: tried in hood: front runner/races prominently: has carried head awkwardly. *Roger Fell* **90**

HAIL CLOUD (IRE) 3 b.c. Hail (IRE) 100 – Wasmi (IRE) 81 (Exceed And Excel (AUS) 126) [2017 p8d p10g Dec 30] modest form: better effort when seventh in maiden at Lingfield in December. *Marco Botti* **63**

HAINES 6 ch.g. Shirocco (GER) 129 – Spring Dream (IRE) 93 (Kalanisi (IRE) 132) [2017 99: t16.5g* t12.2g^{6} p15.8g t14d^{5} Dec 9] lengthy gelding: useful handicapper: won at Wolverhampton in February: stays 16.5f: acts on all-weather, good to firm and good to soft going: usually races towards rear. *Andrew Balding* **99**

HAIRDRYER 4 b.g. Motivator 131 – Londonnetdotcom (IRE) 101 (Night Shift (USA)) [2017 84: t9.5g^{2} p11g^{3} p10g^{3} p10g^{2} p10d^{2} Nov 22] well-made gelding: fairly useful handicapper: second at Kempton in November: stays 11f: acts on polytrack, tapeta and good to firm going: usually races prominently, often freely. *Andrew Balding* **90**

HAJAAM (IRE) 3 b.g. Invincible Spirit (IRE) 121 – Doula (USA) (Gone West (USA)) [2017 p8m^{6} p8g 10s^{5} p12g^{4} 10.5v* p12g* 10g* 11.5d* p12g^{5} p12g* Dec 23] 170,000F, 250,000Y: brother to 2-y-o 7f winner Better Announce, later successful in Hong Kong, and half-brother to several winners, including smart/moody winner up to 1¼m Humungous (2-y-o 7f winner, by Giant's Causeway) and useful 10.7f winner Amazing Beauty (by Galileo): dam US 1m winner: useful handicapper: completed 4-timer at Haydock (apprentice), Kempton, Leicester and Yarmouth in September/October, and also won at Lingfield (by ¾ length from Primero) in December: stays 1½m: acts on polytrack and heavy going: tried in tongue tie: front runner/races prominently. *Charlie Fellowes* **100**

HAJAJ (IRE) 3 b.g. Dark Angel (IRE) 113 – And Again (USA) 83 (In The Wings 128) [2017 77: p8g^{3} 8m* 10.1m 9m^{2} 10g^{5} 8g^{5} 9.1m* Aug 17] smallish gelding: fairly useful handicapper: won at Ascot in May and Yarmouth in August: stays 1¼m: acts on polytrack and good to firm going. *Charlie Fellowes* **90**

HAJJAM 3 b.g. Paco Boy (IRE) 129 – Amanda Carter 92 (Tobougg (IRE) 125) [2017 74: p7m* p7g 7s^4 7g* 8.5m^4 7d^3 7d* 7s^3 7d^2 7d^3 7d^2 Nov 11] fairly useful performer: won maiden at Lingfield in March, and handicaps at Redcar in June and August: second in handicaps at Ascot in October and Doncaster (apprentice) in November: left William Knight after second start: stays 8.5f: acts on polytrack, soft and good to firm going: wears hood: often races towards rear. *David O'Meara* **91**

HAKAM (USA) 5 b.g. War Front (USA) 119 – Lauren Byrd (USA) (Arch (USA) 127) [2017 96: p7g* p6g* p7g 6m a6g^4 6m^2 5.6g t6.1g^6 p7m^3 t7.1d^6 Dec 16] strong gelding: useful handicapper: won at Chelmsford in January and Kempton in April: second at Ascot (short head behind Lightning Charlie) in July: best at 6f/7f: acts on polytrack, tapeta, dirt and good to firm going: often wears cheekpieces: usually races towards rear. *Michael Appleby* **104**

HAKEEM 3 b.g. Exceed And Excel (AUS) 126 – Khazeena 84 (Oasis Dream 129) [2017 8m* 8g Jun 13] first foal: dam, 1m winner who stayed 1¼m, half-sister to smart performer up to 1½m Shamali: fair form: won maiden at Yarmouth (by short head from Alwahsh) in April: will be suited by at least 1¼m: should still do better. *William Haggas* **79 p**

HALAWAIN (USA) 3 b.g. Congrats (USA) 118 – Screen Giant (USA) (Giant's Causeway (USA) 132) [2017 80: 6m^3 7m^3 6g^4 7m^5 Jul 12] fair handicapper: stays 7f: acts on good to firm going: sold 20,000 gns, sent to Qatar. *John Quinn* **78**

HALDAW 3 b.f. Halling (USA) 133 – Dawnus (IRE) 103 (Night Shift (USA)) [2017 –: t12.2g^2 p13.3g^6 11.8s^6 14v^4 14s t14g^6 11.9d^4 p10g^2 t9.5g t9.5m^5 p10s^6 t12.2g p10s^5 Dec 17] good-topped filly: modest maiden: stays 1½m: acts on tapeta and polytrack. *Mick Channon* **63**

HALIMA HATUN (USA) 2 ch.f. (Feb 26) Algorithms (USA) 120 – Extravaganza (USA) (Elusive Quality (USA)) [2017 7g a6f* Nov 23] $62,000Y, $110,000 2-y-o: first foal: dam US 5.5f/6f winner: useful form: won maiden at Meydan (impressively, by 9½ lengths from Hucklebuck) in November: should progress further, *Ismail Mohammed* **102 p**

HALINKA (IRE) 3 gr.f. Dark Angel (IRE) 113 – Mahaazen (IRE) 86 (Cape Cross (IRE) 129) [2017 73: 7m^6 8f^2 8.1m^4 7g^4 7s^3 8g^2 t7.1s p8g Oct 18] fair maiden: stays 1m: acts on tapeta and firm going: has worn headgear. *Roger Varian* **76**

HALLINGHAM 7 b.g. Halling (USA) 133 – In Luck 72 (In The Wings 128) [2017 64: p12g^2 11.7f^3 11.6f* 11.6f^3 11.9d^5 p10g Dec 30] workmanlike gelding: fair handicapper: won at Bath in June: stays 1½m: acts on polytrack and any turf going: has worn headgear. *Ken Cunningham-Brown* **67**

HALLINGS COMET 8 ch.g. Halling (USA) 133 – Landinium (ITY) 109 (Lando (GER) 128) [2017 67: p11g^4 Feb 18] fair handicapper: stays 11f: acts on polytrack, good to firm and heavy going: inconsistent: fairly useful hurdler, won 4 times in 2017. *Shaun Lycett* **66**

HALLING'S WISH 7 br.g. Halling (USA) 133 – Fair View (GER) (Dashing Blade 117) [2017 74: p13g^3 p11g^2 p12g^3 p11d^3 11.9g^3 13f^4 14g^4 11.9m 11.6d^3 Aug 30] modest handicapper on turf, fair on all-weather: stays 2m: acts on polytrack, good to firm and good to soft going: wears headgear: has worn tongue tie. *Gary Moore* **63 a71**

HALLSTATT (IRE) 11 ch.g. Halling (USA) 133 – Last Resort 116 (Lahib (USA) 129) [2017 72: t16.3g^4 t13.9g* 14.1g^3 14d^3 14f^2 14g^6 17.1g^5 t16.3s* t16.3g^3 t16.5g^2 t16.5d^4 Dec 9] fair performer: won claimer at Wolverhampton in January and handicap at Newcastle in September: stays 2¼m: acts on polytrack, tapeta, firm and good to soft going: has worn cheekpieces: wears tongue tie. *John Mackie* **74**

HAMBA KASHE (IRE) 3 gr.g. Clodovil (IRE) 116 – Final Favour (IRE) (Unblest 117) [2017 63: 6m 5.9s^2 Jun 9] fair maiden: raced only at 6f: acts on soft going: sold 7,000 gns, sent to Sweden. *Tim Easterby* **65**

HAMBA MOYO (IRE) 2 gr.f. (Feb 17) Mastercraftsman (IRE) 129 – Back In The Frame 68 (Dutch Art 126) [2017 6g 7.4m 7m^3 7.2m 8v 7d^5 Oct 20] 13,000F, £24,000Y: first foal: dam, maiden (stayed 7f), out of half-sister to St Leger winner Kingston Hill (by Mastercraftsman): modest maiden: best effort at 7f: usually wears headgear. *Tim Easterby* **52**

HAMEEM 2 br.f. (Feb 10) Teofilo (IRE) 126 – Tres Ravi (GER) 108 (Monsun (GER) 124) [2017 8d^5 Oct 24] €500,000Y: closely related to French 12.5f winner Tres Rush (by Rip Van Winkle) and half-sister to numerous winners, including smart French winner up to 12.5f Tres Blue (2-y-o 9f winner, by Anabaa Blue) and smart German 10.5f-2m winner Tres Rock Danon (by Rock of Gibraltar): dam German 8.5f winner who stayed 11f: 6/4, fifth in minor event at Yarmouth (5½ lengths behind Lady of Shalott) in October: sure to improve. *John Gosden* **66 p**

HAMELIN (IRE) 7 b.g. Cape Cross (IRE) 129 – Love Divine 120 (Diesis 133) [2017 105: t12.4g* t16.3g^5 t12.4s^5 p10s May 25] rangy gelding: useful handicapper: won at Newcastle (by ¾ length from Petite Jack) in February: stays 2m: acts on polytrack, tapeta, good to firm and good to soft going: has worn headgear: tried in tongue tie. *George Scott* **103**

HAMELIN POOL 3 b.g. High Chaparral (IRE) 132 – Presbyterian Nun (IRE) 100 (Daylami (IRE) 138) [2017 12m^5 10.2g May 12] well held in 2 maidens: tried in blinkers: has joined Michael Chapman. *Henry Candy* **–**

HAMIDANS GIRL (IRE) 3 ch.f. Bahamian Bounty 116 – Moynsha Lady (IRE) (Namid 128) [2017 71: 5m^4 5m^3 t5s 5m^5 5m^5 5g^3 5.9g^4 6d^3 6s^2 6g^4 5s^4 5m* 5m* 5d^4 p6g^6 Oct 18] leggy filly: fairly useful handicapper: won at Beverley in August and Musselburgh (by 2 lengths from The Night Before) in September: stays 6f: acts on tapeta and good to firm going: tried in cheekpieces: often travels strongly: sold 10,000 gns in October. *Keith Dalgleish* **83**

HAMISH MCGONAGAIN 4 b.g. Kyllachy 129 – Inya Lake 101 (Whittingham (IRE) 104) [2017 69: t6m* p5m* p6g^4 t7.1g^5 t6g t6g^3 6m p6g^4 6d^5 p6g^4 5d^3 5g* 5.2m^5 t6g t5g^4 t6.1g^3 t5.1g* t6.1g^2 p6g^3 Dec 28] fair handicapper: won at Wolverhampton and Lingfield in January, Nottingham in August and again at Wolverhampton in November: left Jeremy Gask after tenth start: stays 6f: acts on polytrack, tapeta, soft and good to firm going: usually wears cheekpieces: often races towards rear, usually responds generously to pressure. *David O'Meara* **79**

HAMMER GUN (USA) 4 b.g. Smart Strike (CAN) 121 – Caraboss 98 (Cape Cross (IRE) 129) [2017 73: f7g* f7g* p8g* f8g* p8g^4 p7g 8.2s p8s^4 t8s p8s f7.1g^4 7s p7d^4 p7s p8s f7.1g* f6.1g^4 Dec 19] fairly useful handicapper: completed 4-timer at Southwell (3) and Chelmsford in March, and also won at former course (by length from Custard The Dragon) in December: best up to 1m: acts on polytrack, fibresand and good to soft going: wears headgear. *Derek Shaw* **92**

HAMRIYAH 3 ch.g. Harbour Watch (IRE) 121 – Golden Dirham (Kheleyf (USA) 116) [2017 6.9g 5m^6 7m^4 6g 7g 8.3s 6s Sep 19] modest maiden: stays 7f: acts on good to firm going: wears headgear. *Tim Easterby* **53**

HAMSTER JAM (IRE) 3 ch.f. Dutch Art 126 – Hecuba 93 (Hector Protector (USA) 124) [2017 7g^6 8.3m^2 8f^5 8g^5 8.5m^2 8.5g^3 Jul 13] €52,000Y: sturdy, lengthy filly: half-sister to several winners, including smart 6f (including at 2 yrs) winner Shanghai Glory (by Exceed And Excel) and useful winner up to 1¼m Choose Me (2-y-o 6f/7f winner, by Choisir): dam 1¼m winner: fair maiden: stays 8.5f: acts on firm going: usually leads. *Mark Johnston* **78**

HANDAZAN (IRE) 8 b.g. Nayef (USA) 129 – Handaza (IRE) 93 (Be My Guest (USA) 126) [2017 p16g Jul 5] workmanlike gelding: useful at best, lightly raced since 2012: last in handicap on sole start in 2017: stays 2m: acts on good to firm and heavy going: sometimes in cheekpieces: tried in tongue tie. *Ivan Furtado* **–**

HANDIWORK 7 ch.g. Motivator 131 – Spinning Top 105 (Alzao (USA) 117) [2017 82: 16.5m* 16m May 12] workmanlike gelding: fairly useful handicapper: won at Doncaster (by 2¾ lengths from Fire Jet) in April: stays 16.5f: acts on polytrack, fibresand, soft and good to firm going: wears headgear. *Steve Gollings* **90**

HANDSOME BOB (IRE) 2 b.c. (May 9) Most Improved (IRE) 119 – Beautiful Dreamer (Red Ransom (USA)) [2017 5.9s^6 8.9s^4 t7.2m^3 t8.6g^3 t8g^4 Nov 24] fair maiden: will stay 1¼m: acts on tapeta: in headgear last 3 starts: sometimes slowly away. *Keith Dalgleish* **72**

HANDSOME DAN (IRE) 11 b.g. Busy Flight 122 – Beautiful City (IRE) (Jurado (USA)) [2017 75: t12.2m^3 t16.5g t12.2g t12.2g t12.2g Jul 31] fair maiden: stays 1½m: acts on polytrack and tapeta: tried in cheekpieces: fairly useful hurdler. *Sarah Hollinshead* **71**

HANDSOME DUDE 5 b.g. Showcasing 117 – Dee Dee Girl (IRE) 60 (Primo Dominie 121) [2017 94§: t6g* 6g 6g^5 6m 6s^2 6d* 6v t6s f6.1g^3 Dec 19] useful handicapper: won at Newcastle (by 2 lengths from Bahamian Dollar) in February and Haydock in June: stays 6f: acts on fibresand, tapeta and soft going: wears blinkers: front runner/races prominently, often travels strongly: temperamental. *David Barron* **96 §**

HANDYTALK (IRE) 4 b.g. Lilbourne Lad (IRE) 111 – Dancing With Stars (IRE) (Where Or When (IRE) 124) [2017 80: 7g^6 p8g^2 7m^3 6.1m^6 5.7f* 7d^2 6.1g^5 6m^2 p5s^4 Sep 30] rather leggy gelding: fairly useful handicapper: won at Bath (by 1¼ lengths from Case Key) in July: stays 8.5f: acts on polytrack, firm and soft going: usually leads. *Rod Millman* **92**

HANG MAN (IRE) 3 ch.g. Windsor Knot (IRE) 118 – Halliard 72 (Halling (USA) 133) [2017 12s^2 Sep 8] €15,000Y: fifth foal: dam, maiden (best effort at 1¼m), closely related to smart winner up to 10.4f Lateen Sails: 33/1, second in maiden at Ascot (short head behind Reverend Jacobs) in September: entitled to progress. *Ed Vaughan* **85 p**

HANGMAN JURY 4 gr.g. Indian Haven 119 – Non Disclosure (IRE) (Clodovil (IRE) 116) [2017 50: f8g Jan 5] modest maiden, well held sole start in 2017: best effort at 1½m: often races freely. *Richard Hughes* –

HANNAH JUST HANNAH 8 gr.m. Proclamation (IRE) 130 – Evaporate 51 (Insan (USA) 119) [2017 66: p12g^5 p13g Feb 28] fair form on Flat debut in 2016, standout effort: best effort at 1½m: wears headgear/tongue tie: fair hurdler. *Matthew Salaman* –

HANNINGFIELD 3 ch.g. Mayson 124 – Arch of Colours 73 (Monsun (GER) 124) [2017 p7g 7m 8g 7m Aug 1] no form. *Michael Bell* –

HANNINGTON 6 ch.g. Firebreak 125 – Manderina (Mind Games 121) [2017 71: t8.6m t9.5g^6 t9.5g t12.2m^6 p10g* t8.6g p8g^2 p10g^2 10g^2 12g 10d* 10m^2 10.2g 10.1m* 9.9g p10g 10d^6 10.1d^2 Oct 24] lengthy gelding: fair performer: won handicap at Chelmsford in March, seller at Lingfield in July and handicap at Yarmouth (apprentice) in August: left Barry Brennan after first start: stays 1½m: acts on polytrack, tapeta, firm and good to soft going: has worn headgear: wears tongue tie. *Michael Appleby* **68**

HANSEATIC 8 b.g. Galileo (IRE) 134 – Insinuate (USA) 99 (Mr Prospector (USA)) [2017 84: 10.3g 8m^4 8g^2 8.8m^6 7.8s 7d^5 9s^4 8.3d Oct 11] rangy gelding: fairly useful handicapper: second at Pontefract in May: stays 10.5f: acts on polytrack, soft and good to firm going: has worn headgear: usually wears tongue tie: often races prominently. *Michael Easterby* **83**

HAN SOLO BERGER (IRE) 2 b.g. (Feb 24) Lord Shanakill (USA) 121 – Dreamaway (IRE) (Oasis Dream 129) [2017 5.9g^3 6g* 5.9d^4 7.2s* Oct 9] €5,000F, €14,000Y: fourth foal: half-brother to useful 2-y-o 6f winner Bing Bang Bong (by Big Bad Bob), later successful in Hong Kong: dam, unraced, closely related to Solario Stakes winner Foss Way: fairly useful form: won minor events at Hamilton (by nose from Clubbable) in July and Musselburgh in October: stays 7f: sold to join Chris Wall 28,000 gns in October. *Keith Dalgleish* **80**

HAPPILY (IRE) 2 b.f. (Feb 27) Galileo (IRE) 134 – You'resothrilling (USA) 117 (Storm Cat (USA)) [2017 7d 7d* 7g* 7s^2 7s* 8d* 8f Nov 3] **116**

In the autumn of 1984 owner Alan Clore had two of the best two-year-old fillies over a mile in Europe. In Ireland, Alydar's Best had made a winning debut for David O'Brien in the Silken Glider Stakes at Leopardstown, while in France the David Smaga-trained Triptych was beaten a nose in the Prix d'Aumale at Chantilly after her own successful debut at Deauville. The Prix Marcel Boussac on Arc day was the logical next step for both fillies (the Fillies' Mile at Ascot was still only a Group 3 contest at the time), but rather than run both in the same race or leave one of them at home, and just a week after Triptych had put up the best performance by a French-trained two-year-old of either sex when running away with the Marcel Boussac by four lengths, Alydar's Best took her chance instead at Longchamp against the colts in the Grand Criterium. The decision to aim the two fillies at different races paid off in the best possible way, with Alydar's Best landing the odds in the even more valuable Grand Criterium by a short neck. Alydar's Best was actually the second filly in a sequence of four to land France's top two-year-old contest in successive years during the 'eighties; Treizieme had won it the year before, and Femme Elite and Danishkada took the next two editions. However, it was not until Happily in the latest season—thirty-one years after Danishkada—that another filly beat the colts in the Grand Criterium, or what is now the Prix Jean-Luc Lagardere. The Coolmore partners aren't averse to running their best horses against each other in the top races—far from it—but the Jean-Luc Lagardere is open to fillies as well as colts and nowadays part of the Arc card alongside the Marcel Boussac (the two races are run over the same trip again after the Jean-Luc Lagardere was shortened to seven furlongs for a time). The Coolmore partners saw a good opportunity for the smart fillies Happily and Magical, both of whom carry Derrick Smith's colours, each to bring back a big prize rather than go for the same one though, in the end, unlike the Clore-owned pair in 1984, they couldn't pull off the double, with Magical managing only fourth when sent off favourite for the Marcel Boussac.

The Criterium des Pouliches (which became the Prix Marcel Boussac in 1980), a fillies' equivalent of the Grand Criterium, albeit a less valuable alternative, was not created until 1969. Before then, if a filly was good enough to beat colts in the Grand Criterium it was usually a sign that she was destined for a top-notch career at three. Marcel Boussac's 1955 winner Apollonia won both French fillies' classics the following year, while the 1957 winner Bella Paola and 1962 winner Hula Dancer both went on to win the One Thousand Guineas and Champion Stakes, Bella Paola also winning the Oaks. All three were top-class fillies. Inevitably, the creation of the race that was to become the Marcel Boussac led to a drop in the number of fillies contesting the Grand Criterium and, when Treizieme was successful in 1983, she was the first of her sex to be successful for seventeen years. Treizieme's trainer Maurice Zilber wasn't afraid to run his top fillies against colts as he'd proven in 1975 when saddling Nobiliary (herself sixth in the Grand Criterium the year before) to finish second in the Derby. Zilber was also the trainer of the 1985 winner Femme Elite who had won the same newcomers race as Treizieme beforehand, just a week before the Marcel Boussac, so contesting the Grand Criterium instead gave both fillies an extra week between races. Danishkada's participation in the Grand Criterium in 1986 was more due to the fact that it looked an easier option than the Marcel Boussac that year, and the first two in the fillies' race, Miesque and Milligram, duly proved themselves top class at three.

Ryan Moore, for one, must have been pleased with the arrangement to keep Happily and Magical apart on Arc day as choosing between them, if they'd met for a third time, wouldn't have been easy. There was precious little between the pair on the evidence of their two meetings at the Curragh, with the score one apiece. On both occasions, Moore chose the wrong filly, riding Happily when she was unable to peg back all-the-way winner Magical in the Debutante Stakes in August, going down by a length and a quarter. Moore had ridden Happily to a five-length victory in the Jockey Club of Turkey Silver Flash Stakes at Leopardstown the previous month when she had looked an exciting prospect in storming clear in a race run at a steady pace. That followed an odds-on success in a maiden at the Curragh in June after Happily had finished seventh on her debut at Leopardstown earlier the same month in a maiden won by another of her stable's leading fillies September. The Moyglare Stud Stakes at the Curragh on Irish Champions' Weekend should have brought all the top Ballydoyle fillies together but, when the first string Clemmie was a late withdrawal due to the softening ground, Moore switched to Magical who, at 9/4, started the shortest-priced of the stable's remaining runners, ahead of September on 4/1 and Happily (ridden by Donnacha O'Brien, who'd won the Debutante on Magical) on 13/2. A fourth Ballydoyle filly Ballet Shoes was sent off at 14/1 but the 2/1 favourite was Alpha Centauri who had won a listed race on soft ground and had been beaten a neck by the French-trained filly Different League in the Albany Stakes at Royal Ascot on her last start. Moore attempted to repeat the tactics on Magical which had worked against him on Happily in the Debutante, but this time Happily

Moyglare Stud Stakes, the Curragh—the late withdrawal of Clemmie fails to detract from a good-quality renewal of the race, Happily leading home Magical (left) and September (dark colours) in a one, two, three for Aidan O'Brien

Qatar Prix Jean-Luc Lagardere, Chantilly—Happily becomes the first of her sex to win this Group 1 since Danishkada in 1986, collaring Olmedo (rail) and Masar (centre) close home; the win is also a first in the race for Aidan O'Brien since Holy Roman Emperor in 2006, though Happily's brother Gleneagles was demoted from first in 2014

proved just the stronger in the closing stages, challenging in the last half furlong and staying on in the final strides to win by a short head. The first two pulled three and three quarter lengths clear of September in third, with the favourite only fifth. Happily was an eighth winner of the Moyglare for Aidan O'Brien who repeated the feat of saddling the first three home which he had achieved two years earlier with Minding, Ballydoyle and Alice Springs who filled the same places in the One Thousand Guineas the following spring. Happily was Donnacha O'Brien's second Moyglare winner as he had partnered outsider Intricately, trained by elder brother Joseph, twelve months earlier, when Intricately beat their father's pair Hydrangea and Rhododendron (Moore finished fifth on another Ballydoyle filly, Promise To Be True, the even-money favourite).

Aidan O'Brien has won the Prix Marcel Boussac four times, with two of his Moyglare winners, Rumplestiltskin (2005) and Misty For Me (2010), as well as with Found in 2014, third in the Moyglare beforehand, and the 2015 Moyglare runner-up Ballydoyle. Just over half an hour after Magical failed in her bid to add to those successes at Chantilly, it was the turn of Happily in the Qatar Prix Jean-Luc Lagardere, a race O'Brien had won with seven colts at its usual home of Longchamp. Happily had something of a family score to settle, as her brother Gleneagles would have been an eighth winner for the stable had he not been demoted from first to third for causing interference three years earlier. Sent off favourite, Happily faced just five colts, with Olmedo, beaten a nose in the Prix des Chenes over course and distance, after a winning debut at Deauville, next in the betting. Rather than relying on Stage Magic who had beaten Olmedo in the Chenes, Charlie Appleby and Godolphin were represented by the ready Solario Stakes winner Masar and by Mythical Magic who had been a close third in the Champagne Stakes. It was Mythical Magic who set the pace but, for much of the last couple of furlongs, it became a duel between Olmedo, who had loomed up on the bridle two out, and Masar, the race appearing to be between the two of them. Waited with on her first try at a mile, Happily only began to overhaul the leaders inside the final furlong and, having edged ahead with little more than fifty yards to run, she went on to win by a length and a quarter with Olmedo getting the better of Masar by a short neck for second. Outsider Woodmax took a never-dangerous fourth, while Mythical Magic faded to finish fifth with Francesco Bere bringing up the rear. Happily's last place when favourite in the Breeders' Cup Juvenile Fillies Turf at Del Mar on her final start, in which September finished third, can safely be ignored as little went right for her. Early interference left Happily poorly placed and she met further trouble in trying to come from the rear, Ryan Moore not persevering with her in the end. Happily had been due to contest

Mr D. Smith, Mrs John Magnier and Mr M. Tabor's "Happily"

the Fillies' Mile at Newmarket three weeks before the Breeders' Cup but she was withdrawn with a temperature on the day of the race, in which stable-companions September and Magical finished second and fourth behind Laurens.

Happily (IRE) (b.f. 2015)	Galileo (IRE) (b 1998)	Sadler's Wells (b 1981)	Northern Dancer
			Fairy Bridge
		Urban Sea (ch 1989)	Miswaki
			Allegretta
	You'resothrilling (USA) (b or br 2005)	Storm Cat (b or br 1983)	Storm Bird
			Terlingua
		Mariah's Storm (b 1991)	Rahy
			Immense

Happily is the fifth foal resulting from the repeat unions of Galileo and the Cherry Hinton Stakes winner You'resothrilling. All five of those foals have either won, or been placed, at Group/Grade 1 level. Gleneagles, whose own Breeders' Cup experience is best forgotten (he failed to handle the dirt in the Classic on his final start) added to his National Stakes success at two with further Group 1 wins in the Two Thousand Guineas at both Newmarket and the Curragh and the St James's Palace Stakes. He was You'resothrilling's second classic winner after the Irish One Thousand Guineas winner Marvellous. The next foal after Gleneagles was Coolmore, who didn't quite live up to the name she was given, but still won the C. L. Weld Stakes at the Curragh at two and finished third in the Belmont Oaks. You'resothrilling's three-year-old Taj Mahal became his dam's latest pattern winner when successful in the Group 2 Zipping Classic in Australia on his first start for Robert Hickmott. Taj Mahal had had a busy campaign for O'Brien which had included finishing a close fourth in the Prix du Jockey Club and second in the Secretariat Stakes. Taj Mahal also ran well when fifth in the Irish Champion Stakes which was won by his relative Decorated Knight (also by Galileo) who is out of a sister to You'resothrilling. After showing useful form at two, Giant's Causeway's sister You'resothrilling made a belated reappearance at three but ran her best race, showing smart form, on her return to finish fourth in the Matron Stakes (Magical's dam Halfway To Heaven was third in the same race). Like Meow, the dam of the Galileo pair Churchill and Clemmie, You'resothrilling is a daughter of Storm Cat which has put something of a limit on the stamina of most of her offspring despite all of them being sired by Galileo. Marvellous ran below form in the Oaks and Irish Oaks, though Taj Mahal's win in Australia came at a mile and a half—he's You'resothrilling's only other foal to have been tried at the trip. Happily was staying on well at the end of the Jean-Luc Lagardere, but she is likely to prove best at not much more than a mile and a quarter at three, no doubt after bidding to become a third Guineas winner of some sort for her dam. Happily had raced only on good ground or softer (acts on soft) until the Breeders' Cup and wears a tongue tie. *Aidan O'Brien, Ireland*

HAPPY ENDING (IRE) 2 b.f. (May 8) Big Bad Bob (IRE) 118 – Heroic Performer (IRE) (Royal Applause 124) [2017 7g 6s p7g Oct 18] sixth foal: half-sister to 1½m winner MacNicholson (by Definite Article) and 9f winner Camile (by Captain Rio): dam unraced half-sister to winner up to 13f Banksters Bonus and winner up to 11f Backbench Blues (both smart, by Big Bad Bob): little impact in minor events/maiden. *Seamus Mullins* –

HAPPY ESCAPE 3 ch.f. Delegator 125 – Saharan Song (IRE) 64 (Singspiel (IRE) 133) [2017 p7m^4 p7g p8g p7g^2 p7d^3 Dec 13] compact filly: seventh foal: half-sister to 6f winner For Ayman (by Bertolini): dam maiden (stayed 9.5f): fair maiden: left Joseph Tuite after fourth start: stays 7f: acts on polytrack: wears tongue tie. *Neil Mulholland* **73**

HAPPY JACK (IRE) 6 b.g. Elusive City (USA) 117 – Miss Pelling (IRE) 75 (Danehill Dancer (IRE) 117) [2017 61: t12.2g p10g Feb 22] modest handicapper, below form both starts in 2017: stays 1½m: acts on polytrack and tapeta: wears headgear: usually races prominently. *Dai Burchell* –

HAPPY LIKE A FOOL (USA) 2 ch.f. (Apr 12) Distorted Humor (USA) 117 – Lastofthsummerwine (USA) (Sky Mesa (USA) 116) [2017 a4.5f* 5m^2 6d^6 a6f* Oct 15] strong filly: fourth foal: half-sister to 2 winners in North America by Kitten's Joy, including smart Canadian Grade 2 7f winner Conquest Panthera: dam ran once (second at 6f at 2 yrs) in USA: useful form: won maiden at Keeneland in April and Grade 3 Matron Stakes at Belmont (by 2¼ lengths from Take Charge Paula) in October: ran in Britain in between, second in Queen Mary Stakes at Royal Ascot (2½ lengths behind Heartache) and sixth in Lowther Stakes at York (3¾ lengths behind Threading): stays 6f: blinkered first 3 starts: has worn tongue tie. *Wesley A. Ward, USA* **108**

HARAKA (IRE) 3 b.f. Fastnet Rock (AUS) 127 – Luna Wells (IRE) 119 (Sadler's Wells (USA) 132) [2017 74: f8s^2 t9.5g^4 Feb 13] sturdy filly: fair handicapper: likely to stay 1¼m: acts on fibresand: in blinkers last 3 starts: often starts slowly/races towards rear. *Ralph Beckett* **72**

HARAZ (IRE) 4 b.g. Acclamation 118 – Hanakiyya (IRE) 84 (Danehill Dancer (IRE) 117) [2017 88: t7.1g^4 8.3g^4 8.5m^2 8.3m^4 7.6d^5 7g^4 6g 7g^3 a7g^2 8d^5 t8.6g^2 p7g f7.1g^4 p7g^2 t6.1g^3 p7g^3 p6g^2 Dec 31] sturdy gelding: fairly useful maiden: second in handicap at Beverley in May: left David O'Meara after eighth start: stays 9f, effective at shorter: acts on polytrack, tapeta, sand, good to firm and good to soft going: wears headgear: irresolute. *Jamie Osborne* **83 §**

HARBA (IRE) 3 ch.f. Frankel 147 – Kirinda (IRE) 106 (Tiger Hill (IRE) 127) [2017 64: 8m^3 7.4m* 7g* 7g* 7.6d^2 p8g p7g Oct 18] lengthy, rather unfurnished filly: fairly useful performer: won maiden at Beverley in June, and handicaps at Sandown (by 7 lengths from Captain Pugwash) and Yarmouth in July: second in handicap at Lingfield in August: stays 1m: acts on good to firm going. *William Haggas* **88**

HARBOUR BELLE 3 b.f. Harbour Watch (IRE) 121 – Sans Reward (IRE) 99 (Barathea (IRE) 127) [2017 55p: 7m 8s^5 10d Jul 9] modest form on sole start at 2 yrs, standout effort. *Michael Dods* –

HARBOUR BREEZE (IRE) 2 b.c. (Apr 3) Le Havre (IRE) 124 – Retiens La Nuit (USA) (Grand Slam (USA) 120) [2017 p10g^5 Nov 29] 66/1, fifth in maiden at Kempton (7½ lengths behind Ispolini) in November. *Lucy Wadham* **68**

HARBOUR FORCE (FR) 3 b.g. Harbour Watch (IRE) 121 – Dam Beautiful 98 (Sleeping Indian 122) [2017 8.1m6 8.3d6 7m 7.6d Aug 12] compact gelding: fair form: best effort at 1m: tried in blinkers: has joined Neil Mulholland. *William Muir* **66**

HARBOUR GREY (IRE) 3 b.f. Zoffany (IRE) 121 – Caterina di Cesi (Cape Town (IRE) 119) [2017 76p: 6m* 7s 6mpu 7g6 6v Jul 27] lengthy filly: fairly useful performer: won maiden at Doncaster in April: stays 7f: acts on polytrack and good to firm going. *Richard Hannon* **81**

HARBOURING 3 ch.f. Harbour Watch (IRE) 121 – Juncea 76 (Elnadim (USA) 128) [2017 p8g 9.9d May 18] £5,500Y: fifth foal: closely related to 5f winner Camino (by Equiano) and half-sister to 2-y-o 5f/6f winner Juncart (by Dutch Art): dam 2-y-o 6f winner: little impact in 2 maidens. *Jonathan Portman* **–**

HARBOUR LAW 4 b.c. Lawman (FR) 121 – Abunai 100 (Pivotal 124) [2017 119: 16f 20m3 Jun 22] strong, attractive colt: smart performer: third in Gold Cup at Royal Ascot (6 lengths behind Big Orange) in June: subsequently found to have tendon injury: stays 2½m: acts on good to firm and good to soft going. *Laura Mongan* **117**

HARBOUR LIGHTNING 3 ch.f. Harbour Watch (IRE) 121 – Divine Power 84 (Kyllachy 129) [2017 69: 5g 7.2g 6d5 5.5f6 5f Jul 18] modest maiden: left Ann Duffield after first start: stays 6f: acts on tapeta, good to firm and good to soft going: tried in cheekpieces: sometimes slowly away. *Noel Wilson* **61**

HARBOUR NIGHTS 2 b.g. (Mar 5) Harbour Watch (IRE) 121 – Irtahal (USA) 94 (Swain (IRE) 134) [2017 p10g5 p10g p10g Nov 29] modest form: in headgear last 2 starts. *Hugo Palmer* **56**

HARBOUR PATROL (IRE) 5 b.g. Acclamation 118 – Traou Mad (IRE) 107 (Barathea (IRE) 127) [2017 47: t7.1g6 t7.1g f7d6 7.1m3 7.2m3 8m 6s2 7.1g* 7.2d3 7.2d4 6m 7.2s4 7.2s5 Oct 9] workmanlike gelding: modest handicapper on turf, poor on all-weather: won at Chepstow in July: stays 7f: acts on soft and good to firm going: wears blinkers: often races towards rear. *Rebecca Bastiman* **60 a44**

Merriebelle Stable, Mr M. Tabor, Mr D. Smith and Mrs John Magnier's "Happy Like A Fool"

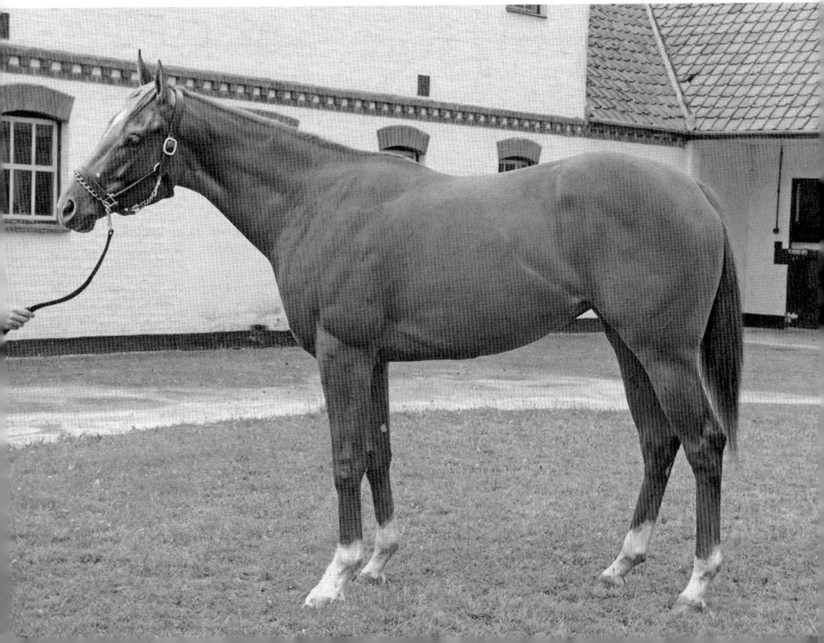

HARBOUR PILOT 2 b.c. (Apr 9) Harbour Watch (IRE) 121 – Bountiful Girl 82 – (Bahamian Bounty 116) [2017 t6.1g Dec 22] 50/1, well held in minor event at Wolverhampton. *David Loughnane*

HARBOUR QUAY 3 b.c. Foxwedge (AUS) 128 – Whatcameoverme (USA) (Aldebaran – (USA) 126) [2017 p8g Mar 8] seventh foal: half-brother to 3 winners, including 1m winner (stayed 11.6f) Dream Ruler (by Holy Roman Emperor): dam unraced: 50/1, very green when well held in maiden at Kempton. *Jeremy Gask*

HARBOUR ROCK 3 b.c. Harbour Watch (IRE) 121 – Rock Lily 81 (Rock of Gibraltar **91** (IRE) 133) [2017 83: 8m* 8m^{2} 9.9g^{2} 10d^{2} 10d^{6} p8g Oct 26] fairly useful performer: won maiden at Goodwood in June: second in handicap at Salisbury in July: stays 1¼m: acts on good to firm and good to soft going: races towards rear: sold 30,000 gns in October. *David Simcock*

HARBOUR ROSE 2 b.f. (Feb 14) Harbour Watch (IRE) 121 – Serrenia (IRE) (High – Chaparral (IRE) 132) [2017 6s 6.1f 7d 8.3v t7.1g Sep 12] 15,000F, £27,000Y, £16,000 2-y-o: leggy filly: fifth foal: half-sister to 3 winners, including useful 1¼m-1½m winner/smart hurdler Penhill (by Mount Nelson) and 8.6f winner Duchess of Seville (by Duke of Marmalade): dam unraced half-sister to smart French/US winner up to 1½m Fast And Furious: no form: tried in hood. *Philip Kirby*

HARBOUR SEAL 2 b.f. (May 13) Archipenko (USA) 127 – River Naiad (Nayef (USA) – 129) [2017 6g 6s 6.1v^{6} p7g Oct 13] fourth foal: half-sister to 2-y-o 7.4f winner Peak Hill (by Bahamian Bounty): dam twice-raced half-sister to useful performer up to 1½m Dorcas Lane: no form: in headgear last 3 starts. *Henry Spiller*

HARBOUR SIREN 3 b.f. Harbour Watch (IRE) 121 – Dee Dee Girl (IRE) 60 (Primo **59** Dominie 121) [2017 t7.1g^{3} Mar 9] £34,000Y: fifth foal: half-sister to 3 useful winners, including 2-y-o 6f/7f winner Magic Casement (by Proclamation), later successful in Hong Kong, and winner up to 6f Handsome Dude (2-y-o 5.4f winner, by Showcasing): dam 2-y-o 7f winner: 5/2, green when third in maiden at Newcastle (4½ lengths behind Rutherford) in March. *David Brown*

HARBOUR STORM 2 b.c. (Apr 21) Sayif (IRE) 122 – Minette 55 (Bishop of Cashel – 122) [2017 6d^{5} p6g Sep 26] workmanlike colt: little impact in minor events. *Laura Mongan*

HARBOUR SUNRISE 2 b.f. (Apr 25) Harbour Watch (IRE) 121 – Nairobi (FR) (Anabaa – (USA) 130) [2017 8d Oct 27] half-sister to 2 winners, including 1¼m/11f winner Kenyan Cat (by One Cool Cat): dam, French maiden, half-sister to useful 7f/1m performer Chief Commander: 150/1, well held in maiden at Doncaster. *Shaun Harris*

HARBOUR TOWN 3 ch.g. Harbour Watch (IRE) 121 – Dress Code (IRE) 83 (Barathea **58** (IRE) 127) [2017 66: p6g^{6} p7g 7m 8g p7g p6g^{6} Oct 25] sturdy gelding: modest maiden: best effort at 1m: in cheekpieces last 3 starts. *Harry Dunlop*

HARBOUR VISION 2 gr.c. (Apr 27) Harbour Watch (IRE) 121 – Holy Nola (USA) **75** (Silver Deputy (CAN)) [2017 7m^{3} 7g^{6} p7d* t7.1d^{3} p7s^{4} Dec 1] fair performer: won minor event at Chelmsford in September: raced only at 7f: acts on polytrack, tapeta and good to firm going: usually races close up. *David Brown*

HARD GRAFT 2 gr.g. (Apr 16) Lethal Force (IRE) 128 – Molly Brown 95 (Rudimentary **78** (USA) 118) [2017 6f^{4} 5m t5s^{5} 6.1g^{4} 6d^{5} 6.1d 7m f6.1g* Dec 21] workmanlike gelding: fair performer: won nursery at Southwell in December: stays 6f: acts on fibresand: tried in hood. *David Brown*

HARD TOFFEE (IRE) 6 b.g. Teofilo (IRE) 126 – Speciale (USA) (War Chant (USA) **78** 126) [2017 78: p12g 11.5m^{4} 11.6d^{5} 10d^{5} 10d^{4} 10.1m^{2} 11.2s^{5} p10s^{4} 10.2d^{5} p10s^{4} p10s^{4} Dec 1] well-made gelding: fair handicapper: left Conrad Allen after ninth start: stays 1½m: acts on polytrack, good to firm and good to soft going: front runner/races prominently. *Louise Allan*

HARD TO HANDEL 5 b.g. Stimulation (IRE) 121 – Melody Maker 62 (Diktat 126) **73** [2017 92: t9.5m^{3} p11g t9.5g t8.6m^{6} t8.6g^{6} t8.6g^{3} 10.3g 10f^{3} t8.6g^{6} 8.5g^{2} 8.5f^{2} 9f^{2} 8.5g^{4} 10g 8.5f^{3} 10d^{4} Sep 10] rather leggy gelding: fair handicapper: left Clare Ellam after tenth start: effective at 8.5f to 1½m: acts on tapeta, firm and soft going: usually wears headgear. *Mrs A. Malzard, Jersey*

HAREBELL (IRE) 3 ch.f. Halling (USA) 133 – Prairie Flower (IRE) (Zieten (USA) 118) **90** [2017 70: 10g 10.2d* 9.9m^{3} 11.9m^{3} 11.4m* 12g^{6} 11.8d^{3} Sep 12] rangy, rather unfurnished filly: fairly useful handicapper: won at Nottingham in May and Windsor in July: will stay further than 1½m: acts on good to firm and good to soft going: sometimes in hood: usually races nearer last than first: sold 18,000 gns in December. *Ralph Beckett*

HARIPOUR (IRE) 3 b.c. Shamardal (USA) 129 – Hazariya (IRE) 109 (Xaar 132) [2017 **97**
77: 10s^5 12g^3 13m^5 13g* 14m Jun 23] well-made colt: half-brother to several winners, notably high-class 1¼m-1½m (including Derby) winner Harzand (by Sea The Stars) and smart 1¼m-1½m winner Hazarafa (by Daylami): dam 7f-9.5f winner: useful performer: won maiden at Navan in June: should be suited by 1¾m+: acts on good to firm going: in blinkers last 2 starts: sent to Australia. *D. K. Weld, Ireland*

HARLEQUEEN 4 b.f. Canford Cliffs (IRE) 133 – Aurelia 80 (Rainbow Quest (USA) **104 §**
134) [2017 112: 14v 13.3d^5 11.4m^5 13.4g^3 14.5d 16g Sep 28] useful performer: third in listed handicap at Chester (2 lengths behind My Reward) in September: stays 13.5f: acts on soft going: often wears visor: races freely: sold 400,000 gns in December: no easy ride and can't be relied on. *Mick Channon*

HARLEQUIN ROCK 4 bl.g. Rock of Gibraltar (IRE) 133 – Berry Baby (IRE) 74 **68**
(Rainbow Quest (USA) 134) [2017 67: 8.3g^4 8m^2 8m^3 10.1m 8s^3 8m 9.1d^4 8m 8s 8g* 8.3g^5 Nov 1] leggy gelding: fair handicapper: won at Yarmouth in October: stays 9f: acts on polytrack, fibresand, good to firm and heavy going: has worn headgear, including last 2 starts. *Mick Quinn*

HARLEQUIN ROSE (IRE) 3 ch.f. Dutch Art 126 – Miss Chaussini (IRE) 76 (Rossini **62**
(USA) 118) [2017 56: 6.1m 5.7f^2 6g^2 5.7d p6g p7m Nov 25] modest handicapper: stays 6f: acts on polytrack and firm going: usually wears visor. *Patrick Chamings*

HARLEQUIN STORM (IRE) 3 gr.g. Clodovil (IRE) 116 – Convidada (IRE) (Trans **78**
Island 119) [2017 t6g^3 t6g^4 p6d^4 5.1m^3 p6d* p6g Oct 24] lengthy gelding: fair performer: won handicap at Chelmsford in September: stays 6f: acts on polytrack, tapeta and good to firm going: front runner/races prominently. *Dean Ivory*

HARLEQUIN STRIKER (IRE) 5 b.g. Bahamian Bounty 116 – Air Maze 80 (Dansili **86**
127) [2017 91: p8g p8g^4 10m^3 8.5g^4 8s^4 8d 8.5g 8.3d* 8.1d^6 p8s f7.1g^5 t9.5d Dec 27] angular gelding: fairly useful handicapper: won at Nottingham in October: third at Windsor in June: stays 1¼m: acts on polytrack, good to firm and heavy going: has worn headgear, including last 5 starts: front runner/races prominently. *Dean Ivory*

HARLOW 3 b.g. Harlan's Holiday (USA) 124 – Glowing (IRE) 108 (Dansili 127) [2017 **94**
t8d* p8g^3 10m 12v t8g^4 Oct 10] tall gelding: third foal: dam, 7f and (including at 2 yrs) 1m winner, closely related to smart performer up to 15.5f Glaring: fairly useful performer: won maiden at Newcastle in March: third in handicap at Chelmsford in April: should stay beyond 1m: acts on polytrack and tapeta: often in hood: sometimes slowly away, usually races towards rear: has joined A. J. Martin. *Hugo Palmer*

HARMONICA 2 b.f. (Mar 28) Pivotal 124 – Affinity 76 (Sadler's Wells (USA) 132) [2017 **71**
5v^4 7.6d^3 p8g^2 Aug 30] fourth foal: half-sister to useful 1m (including at 2 yrs)/1¼m winner Zest (by Duke of Marmalade): dam, 1½m winner, closely related to grandam of top-class 5f performer Marsha and half-sister to high-class miler Soviet Song: fair form: best effort when second in minor event at Kempton (4 lengths behind Mahaarat) in August: bred to stay further than 1m. *Sir Mark Prescott Bt*

HARMONIC WAVE (IRE) 4 b.f. Zebedee 113 – Pure Folly (IRE) 58 (Machiavellian **69**
(USA) 123) [2017 73: t6f^4 t6m^2 t6g p6g^3 Jan 28] fair handicapper: stays 6f: acts on tapeta and good to firm going: wears headgear: sometimes slowly away. *Rebecca Menzies*

HARMONISE 3 b.f. Sakhee's Secret 128 – Composing (IRE) 71 (Noverre (USA) 125) **81**
[2017 75: 8.3g^6 8s* 7g 8m^6 8.1m^6 p8g 8.2v^3 10.2d^4 10d Oct 27] useful-looking filly: fairly useful handicapper: won at Newmarket in May: stays 1¼m: acts on tapeta, soft and good to firm going: in hood last 2 starts: inconsistent: sold to join Sheena West 7,000 gns in November. *Mick Channon*

HAROME (IRE) 3 ch.g. Bahamian Bounty 116 – Clytha 57 (Mark of Esteem (IRE) 137) **88**
[2017 86: 5d 5m* 5f^5 5m^4 t6g^6 5d^2 6m^3 5v^4 Sep 9] fairly useful handicapper: won at Ripon in June: placed at same course twice in August: stays 6f: acts on tapeta, good to firm and heavy going: front runner/races prominently. *Roger Fell*

HAROON (IRE) 3 ch.c. Lope de Vega (IRE) 125 – Hazarista (IRE) 113 (Barathea (IRE) **78**
127) [2017 8.5d 10m^6 8m^3 9.2s^2 9d^2 9v Sep 18] fair maiden: left M. Halford after third start: stays 9f: acts on soft and good to firm going: often wears tongue tie. *Tony Coyle*

HARPERS RUBY 7 b.m. Byron 117 – La Belle Katherine (USA) (Lyphard (USA) 132) **46**
[2017 65: f5g t5.1g^2 t5.1g^4 5g^4 5s 5g Jul 14] poor handicapper on turf, modest on all- **a60**
weather: best form at 5f: acts on tapeta: tried in hood: front runner/races prominently. *Lynn Siddall*

HARRISON 4 b.g. Sixties Icon 125 – Excellent Day (IRE) 78 (Invincible Spirit (IRE) 121) **110** [2017 109: p14g* 13.9g[4] 20m Jun 22] good-topped gelding: smart performer: won minor event at Chelmsford (by 2¼ lengths from St Michel) in May: fourth in listed race at York (5 lengths behind Dal Harraild) later in month: stays 1¾m: acts on polytrack, good to firm and good to soft going: often races prominently: sent to Australia. *Mick Channon*

HARRISON STICKLE 5 gr.g. Hellvelyn 118 – Hollybell 87 (Beveled (USA)) [2017 –: **68** 5.7f[2] 5.7m 6m 6s 5m 5s[6] Oct 2] workmanlike gelding: fair handicapper: stays 6f: acts on firm going: tried in cheekpieces: usually races close up. *John Gallagher*

HARROGATE (IRE) 2 br.g. (Apr 18) Society Rock (IRE) 126 – Invincible Me (IRE) **83** (Invincible Spirit (IRE) 121) [2017 6g 6g[2] 5m[2] 5v[3] 5.4g Oct 13] 50,000F, 60,000Y: workmanlike gelding: second foal: half-brother to 2-y-o 5f winner Monte Cinq (by Bushranger): dam, lightly raced in France, half-sister to smart 5f winner Kyllang Rock: fairly useful maiden: second in maiden at Ripon in September: best form at 5f: acts on good to firm and heavy going: front runner/races prominently. *James Bethell*

HARRY ANGEL (IRE) 3 b.c. Dark Angel (IRE) 113 – Beatrix Potter (IRE) 75 **132** (Cadeaux Genereux 131) [2017 111p: 6f[2] 6f* 6m[2] 6g* 6s* 6s[4] Oct 21]

The sprinting scene in Britain has been transformed in recent times by the elevation or restoration to Group 1 status of existing five- and six-furlong races such as the King's Stand (originally the only Group 1 sprint for three-year-olds and upwards in Britain which had its top status restored in 2008 after a spell as a Group 2), the Diamond Jubilee at Royal Ascot (elevated in 2002), and what is now the British Champions Sprint (formerly the Diadem) at Ascot in October which became a Group 1 in 2015, the same year that the Commonwealth Cup for three-year-olds was added to the Royal Ascot programme to give that meeting a third Group 1 sprint. There are now seven Group 1 sprints in Britain for three-year-olds and upwards. Three-year-olds can no longer contest the Diamond Jubilee but, as a group, the top sprinters are catered for much better than they used to be. At the turn of the century, for example, there wasn't a single Group 1 in Europe over five or six furlongs until the July Cup which, like all sprints of that status, was also open to four-year-olds and upwards. The financial reward for sprinters in those days did not compare to those for the milers and middle-distance horses either, but that is not a charge that can be made nowadays. The first prize money for the three British Group 1 sprints in 1999 amounted to just under £260,000 in total. The seven such Group 1s in the latest season with their first prize money were: King's Stand (£226,840), Commonwealth Cup (£226,840), Diamond Jubilee (£340,260), July Cup (£283,550), Nunthorpe (£198,485), Sprint Cup (£147,446) and Champions Sprint (£340,260). The King George Stakes at Goodwood (£176,992) is also a Group 1 in everything but name, and its eventual promotion will give the five-furlong specialists a third official Group 1, along with the King's Stand and Nunthorpe.

The creation of the Commonwealth Cup means that potential sprint champions among the leading three-year-olds now have a good prize to aim at against horses of their own age in the first part of the season. Before the advent of the Commonwealth Cup, connections of three-year-olds like Caravaggio, the Mill Reef Stakes winner Harry Angel and Blue Point—the first three in the latest running—had little incentive to race them over sprint distances from the outset of their second season and were often tempted to try to make them into milers. Like so many before them, Harry Angel's connections considered running him in a Two Thousand Guineas trial (in his case, the Greenham) before deciding whether to take up the Two Thousand Guineas entry that had been made for him. In the end, though, with the Commonwealth Cup to aim at, and a new 'pattern pathway' leading to the Royal Ascot showpiece, Harry Angel was sent sprinting straight away. 'As soon as we got busy with him in the spring, it was clear that he's a sprinter through and through,' said his trainer Clive Cox. 'We would have been spreading him too thinly trying to go further.' Various setbacks restricted Harry Angel's two-year-old career to just two races—a minor event at Ascot in May, in which he was beaten a nose, and the Mill Reef at Newbury in September which he won in good style—but he made up for lost time in the latest season when he trained on into one of the top sprinters around (he was the only one to win two of Britain's Group 1 sprints, landing both the July Cup and the Sprint Cup).

The Group 3 Pavilion Stakes at Ascot at the beginning of May and the Group 2 Sandy Lane Stakes at Haydock at the end of the same month, both over six furlongs, and restricted to three-year-olds, were the stepping stones to Harry Angel's appearance at Royal Ascot. By a quirk of the race conditions, Harry Angel had to shoulder a 4-lb penalty against the Gimcrack winner Blue Point in the Pavilion Stakes (only four weeks separated the Group 2 wins of Blue Point and Harry Angel but the cut-off point for penalties in the Pavilion is August 31st, which snares the Mill Reef but not the earlier Gimcrack). Nine of the ten runners in the Pavilion Stakes held an entry in the Commonwealth Cup and the first two, Blue Point and Harry Angel, who were separated by a length and a half at the end, both shaped like serious Commonwealth Cup contenders in a race run in course record time. Harry Angel fought his jockey for a long way at Ascot and any idea of adopting patient tactics with him was abandoned when he lined up next in the Armstrong Aggregates Sandy Lane Stakes. He demolished his six rivals with a straightforward front-running performance, beating Second Thought by four and a half lengths, with the Pavilion Stakes third Mubtasim (who had finished only a length and a half behind Harry Angel at Ascot) a further length and three quarters back in third. Like the Pavilion, the Sandy Lane Stakes was run in course record time (the runner-up also broke the old record) and Harry Angel returned an excellent timefigure, 1.08 fast (equivalent to a timerating of 127), which was bettered over the season in sprint races only by the 1.18 fast (130) recorded by Battaash in the King George Stakes at Goodwood.

By the time Harry Angel took his place in the Commonwealth Cup field, he had been acquired privately from his owner Peter Ridgers by Godolphin, the owners of Blue Point. The Godolphin royal blue enjoyed a fine Royal Ascot but neither Harry Angel nor Blue Point could quite handle Irish-trained Caravaggio on the day, though both ran well to be beaten three quarters of a length and half a length by the odds-on favourite. Harry Angel forced the pace, as he had at Haydock, though the attentions of Caravaggio's stablemate Intelligence Cross, who pressed him much of the way, coupled with the fact that the runners had to race into a stiff headwind, probably weren't ideal for Harry Angel, though he still confirmed himself a high-class sprinter. He couldn't hold the late burst of Caravaggio and was headed in the final hundred yards. Caravaggio (again odds on) and Harry Angel met again in the Darley July Cup in which they came up against some of the seasoned older sprinters, among them the first three in the Diamond Jubilee, The Tin Man, Tasleet and Limato (trying for a second July Cup win). The field of ten may have been the smallest for the July Cup since Agnes World beat nine rivals in 2000, but it lacked nothing in quality. Harry Angel sat behind Caravaggio's 100/1-stablemate Intelligence Cross this time and, in a race that developed into a falsely-run, muddling affair, he was always in the best place. Harry Angel was never in much danger after taking over in the lead approaching the final furlong and he kept on well to win by a length and a quarter and half a length from Limato and the Abernant Stakes winner Brando (who

Darley July Cup, Newmarket—Harry Angel is always well positioned in a falsely-run race and keeps on well; 2016 winner Limato (light cap, second left) and Brando (halved sleeves) are his closest pursuers at the line; favourite Caravaggio (left) is only fourth

32Red Sprint Cup Stakes, Haydock—Harry Angel proves without question that he is the best around at six furlongs with a top-class effort, overcoming concerns about the soft going to beat Tasleet (striped cap, left) and The Tin Man, with Blue Point (white cap) completing the frame

won the Prix Maurice de Gheest on his next start), with Caravaggio, pushed along soon after halfway, finishing fourth but never threatening to land a blow. Intelligence Cross was flattered in fifth, beaten around two lengths by the winner, his proximity cautioning strongly against taking the bare form literally.

Harry Angel was almost certainly better suited by Newmarket's sharper six-furlong course (than he had been by Ascot's stiffer one), and the sprint course at Haydock, which rises only slightly, is also less testing than Ascot which provides a particularly stiff test, more so when the going is soft (it was good to firm at the Royal meeting). Harry Angel's participation in the 32Red Sprint Cup at Haydock in early-September was in doubt until fairly close to the race after heavy rain turned the going soft (causing the course executive to reschedule the Sprint Cup from the sixth race to the third), but the decision to let Harry Angel take his chance was rewarded with another fine victory. Prominent all the way, travelling strongly, Harry Angel drew clear over the final furlong to win in clear-cut fashion by four lengths and a length and a half from Tasleet and The Tin Man, with Blue Point, having his first race since the Commonwealth Cup, completing the frame. Harry Angel's Sprint Cup performance confirmed without much doubt that he was the best six-furlong sprinter around and he can be forgiven his below-form fourth behind Librisa Breeze, Tasleet and Caravaggio on soft going at Ascot in October when attempting to become the first to complete the July Cup/Sprint Cup/Champions Sprint treble. Harry Angel reared leaving the stalls in the Champions Sprint and didn't settle fully, while his jockey also arguably pressed on too early, sending him for home in earnest two furlongs out. He edged left and also caught a bump as he faded inside the final furlong.

Harry Angel (IRE) (b.c. 2014)	Dark Angel (IRE) (gr 2005)	Acclamation (b 1999)	Royal Applause
			Princess Athena
		Midnight Angel (gr 1994)	Machiavellian
			Night At Sea
	Beatrix Potter (IRE) (ch 2005)	Cadeaux Genereux (ch 1985)	Young Generation
			Smarten Up
		Great Joy (b 1996)	Grand Lodge
			Cheese Soup

The good-topped Harry Angel, who sometimes spoils his appearance by sweating and getting on edge, isn't the first July Cup winner sired by Dark Angel. Lethal Force, like Harry Angel, was very well bought at the yearling sales by trainer Clive Cox and is now a Cheveley Park stallion; he won the Diamond Jubilee as well as the July Cup for Cox as a four-year-old in 2013. Lethal Force is from the first crop of the speedy Dark Angel who took up stud duties after the end of his juvenile campaign, when he won the Mill Reef Stakes and the Middle Park. Dark Angel has become a stallion sensation—challenging for the speed-sire mantle held for so long by the likes of Invincible Spirit and Oasis Dream—and he covered 223 mares in the latest season when he was the busiest designated Flat sire in Britain and Ireland (his fee goes up from €65,000 to €85,000 in 2018). Dark Angel's three Group 1 winners in the latest season included the Queen Elizabeth II Stakes winner Persuasive but, apart from her, Dark Angel's best offspring—conceived in the six years when his fee ranged from €7,000 to €12,500—have made their names as sprinters, most notable among them, apart from Harry Angel and Lethal Force, being the dual Nunthorpe winner Mecca's Angel, her very smart brother Markaz (now a stallion) and the very fast Battaash who won the King George Stakes and France's Prix de l'Abbaye in the latest season (the continued smart form shown by veteran milers Sovereign Debt and Gabrial—both members of his first crop—serves as a reminder that Dark Angel is not a wholly one-dimensional sire).

In a strange twist to the story of Britain's two top sprinters, Harry Angel and Battaash were reared together at the same stud, where they shared a paddock. Family-run Ballyphilip Stud in County Limerick houses around a dozen broodmares, including the dams of both Battaash and Harry Angel. Harry Angel's dam Beatrix Potter, a daughter of another July Cup winner in Cadeaux Genereux, was sold by the stud as a yearling but then bought back—after fifteen runs without a win—when her half-brother Xtension met with Group 1 success in Hong Kong after originally being sold for €15,000 by Ballyphilip Stud to Harry Angel's trainer for whom he finished fourth in the Two Thousand Guineas. Beatrix Potter bred one winner before Harry Angel, the fairly useful handicapper Golden Journey (by Nayef) who won for the Cox stable over a mile and a quarter. Harry Angel's grandam Great Joy was a fairly useful seven-furlong winner in Germany and a half-sister to the useful mile winner A La Carte. Two other daughters of Great Joy, Our Joy (a fairly useful seven-furlong winner for Cox by Kodiac) and an unraced filly by Rip Van Winkle, are also members of the broodmare band at Ballyphilip and both were reported in foal in the latest season to sprinting sons of Dark Angel, Markaz and the smart Heeraat respectively. The Darley/Godolphin operation bought into Dark Angel back in 2015

Godolphin's "Harry Angel"

and he has been visited by around two dozen Darley mares in each of the last two years. Harry Angel will become an important Darley/Godolphin stallion once his racing days are over, but he will be in training again as a four-year-old. He has been kept to six furlongs since his debut but will prove at least as effective at five and it will come as no surprise to see the King's Stand as his Royal Ascot target, given his previous performances over Ascot's stiff six furlongs. A clash with Battaash at the Royal meeting, or anywhere else for that matter, would be something to savour. Harry Angel is versatile with regards to the going, unraced on heavy but effective on any other. An exuberant type, he is usually taken early and quietly to post. *Clive Cox*

HARRY BEAU 3 ch.g. Kheleyf (USA) 116 – Lovellian (Machiavellian (USA) 123) [2017 65p: $7f^3$ $9.9m^5$ 9.9d $10.2f^5$ 7g $8g^2$ $7d^5$ 7d t8.6d Dec 9] fair maiden: left Richard Hannon after fifth start: stays 1m: acts on firm going: tried in tongue tie: front runner/races prominently. *David Evans* **71**

HARRY CALLAHAN (IRE) 2 b.g. (Feb 22) Dutch Art 126 – Sovana (IRE) 103 (Desert King (IRE) 129) [2017 7m 7d 8.3v Nov 8] modest form in minor event/maidens. *Tom Dascombe* **54**

HARRY HOLLAND 5 b.g. Dutch Art 126 – Common Consent (IRE) 68 (Common Grounds 118) [2017 85: p7g* t7.1d p7d 7.6d t7.2g 10.2d Jul 25] good-bodied gelding: fair handicapper: won at Lingfield (apprentice) in January: little form after: left Tom Dascombe after third start: stays 1m: acts on polytrack: often wears headgear. *Oliver Greenall* **68**

HARRY HUNT 10 b.g. Bertolini (USA) 125 – Qasirah (IRE) 97 (Machiavellian (USA) 123) [2017 87: $14.2m^5$ $16s^4$ Oct 15] workmanlike gelding: fairly useful handicapper: stays 16.5f: acts on polytrack and heavy going: has worn headgear: fair hurdler/chaser. *Graeme McPherson* **83**

HARRY HURRICANE 5 b.g. Kodiac 112 – Eolith 99 (Pastoral Pursuits 127) [2017 108: $5g^2$ 5g 5g $5g^4$ $5m^2$ 6m 5g 5g 6d 5.6g Sep 16] sturdy gelding: useful handicapper: second at Musselburgh (neck behind Line of Reason) in June: best at 5f: acts on polytrack, tapeta, good to firm and good to soft going: usually wears headgear. *George Baker* **109**

HARRY SPEED (IRE) 4 b.g. Dark Angel (IRE) 113 – Starfly (IRE) 79 (Invincible Spirit (IRE) 121) [2017 68: 6d $7d^4$ $7d^3$ $7d^2$ 7.5d 7.2d* $7v^2$ 7v $7v^5$ $7v^2$ $5s^5$ Nov 5] fair handicapper: won at Ayr in August: stays 7f: acts on heavy going: wears tongue tie: front runner/races prominently. *Garvan Donnelly, Ireland* **72**

HARTSIDE (GER) 8 b.g. Montjeu (IRE) 137 – Helvellyn (USA) 83 (Gone West (USA)) [2017 65: 18g Apr 11] fairly useful at best, well held sole start on Flat in 2017: stays 2m: acts on heavy going: has worn headgear: modest hurdler. *Peter Winks* **–**

HART STOPPER 3 b.g. Compton Place 125 – Angel Song 68 (Dansili 127) [2017 60p: $t7.1m^3$ $f5d^4$ $t7.1g^3$ 6.1m* $6d^2$ 6m* 6g* 6d $6d^5$ $6g^4$ 6d Sep 23] angular gelding: fairly useful handicapper: won at Windsor in May, and Haydock and Yarmouth (amateur, by ½ length from Case Key) in July: stays 7f: acts on tapeta and good to firm going: usually races towards rear: sold to join Stuart Williams 37,000 gns in October. *Michael Bell* **92**

HARVEST DAY 2 b.f. (Apr 10) Harbour Watch (IRE) 121 – Miss Wells (IRE) (Sadler's Wells (USA) 132) [2017 $6g^6$ 6g $6d^6$ $t5g^5$ $p5s^4$ f6.1g Dec 19] 1,600F, £5,000Y: fifth foal: half-sister to 3 winners, including 1m-1¼m winner Bocking End (by Paco Boy) and 5f/6f winner (including at 2 yrs) Archie Stevens (by Pastoral Pursuits): dam unraced: modest maiden: best effort at 5f: acts on tapeta: tried in eyeshields: wears tongue tie: often starts slowly. *Michael Easterby* **55**

HARVEST MOON 3 b.f. Mayson 124 – Hamsat Elqamar 78 (Nayef (USA) 129) [2017 65: 6g $7g^5$ $7.4m^6$ Jul 8] modest maiden: best effort at 6f: acts on good to soft going. *Richard Fahey* **60**

HARVEST RANGER 3 b.g. Bushranger (IRE) 119 – Time of Gold (USA) (Banker's Gold (USA) 116) [2017 –: $f6g^4$ $f8.1g^5$ $p7s^6$ f7.1g Dec 22] poor maiden: best effort at 6f. *Michael Appleby* **46**

HARVEST WIND (IRE) 3 b.c. Elzaam (AUS) 115 – Harvest Joy (IRE) 89 (Daggers Drawn (USA) 114) [2017 79: $7.4d^2$ $p8s^3$ 8g Sep 1] sturdy colt: fairly useful maiden: placed at Ffos Las in July and Kempton in August: stays 1m: acts on polytrack and good to soft going: often races prominently: sold 16,000 gns in November. *Clive Cox* **84**

HARVEY'S HOPE 11 b.g. Sinndar (IRE) 134 – Ancara 109 (Dancing Brave (USA) 140) [2017 14s Sep 19] fairly useful at best, showed nothing on sole start in 2017 after long absence: stays 2m: acts on good to firm and heavy going: tried in blinkers: has worn tongue tie. *Paul Collins* **–**

HARWOOD 3 b.g. Dutch Art 126 – Amicable Terms 88 (Royal Applause 124) [2017 –: 6m^6 6g^5 5d^5 Jun 3] modest form: best effort at 6f. *David O'Meara* **64**

HARWOODS STAR (IRE) 7 br.g. Danehill Dancer (IRE) 117 – Showbiz (IRE) 89 (Sadler's Wells (USA) 132) [2017 65, a80: f7g^3 f7g^5 f5g^4 f7m f7g^5 f6g Mar 29] fair handicapper: third at Southwell (¾ length behind Custard The Dragon) in January: stayed 1¼m: acted on polytrack, fibresand, soft and good to firm going: wore headgear: tried in tongue tie: often started slowly, usually raced nearer last than first: dead. *John Butler* **77**

HARWOODS VOLANTE (IRE) 6 ch.g. Kheleyf (USA) 116 – Semiquaver (IRE) (Mark of Esteem (IRE) 137) [2017 98: 6s 6m^3 7s^3 6g 6s^2 6g^2 t7.1g 6s^2 6g 6s^5 6s Sep 8] sturdy gelding: fairly useful handicapper: third at Catterick in June: stays 7f: acts on polytrack, good to firm and good to soft going: has worn headgear. *David O'Meara* **92**

HASANOANDA 2 b.c. (Apr 9) Champs Elysees 124 – Indian Mystery (IRE) 69 (Indian Ridge 123) [2017 p8s^4 t9.5g^6 Dec 18] 31,000 2-y-o: sixth foal: closely related to smart winner up to 1m Medicine Path (2-y-o 7f winner, by Danehill Dancer) and a winner in Sweden by Exceed And Excel: dam 5f winner: fair form in 2 minor events. *John Gosden* **79**

HASTENPLACE 2 b.f. (Mar 23) Compton Place 125 – Hasten (USA) (Lear Fan (USA) 130) [2017 5m 5d 6m^6 5d^4 5f 5s^5 p7g p6g^6 Oct 14] compact filly: sister to 2-y-o 7f winner Great Run, later successful in Hong Kong, and half-sister to several winners, including 2-y-o 1m winner Clutchingatstraws (by Showcasing) and 2-y-o 6f winner Hellofahaste (by Hellvelyn): dam lightly raced: modest maiden: best effort at 6f: often in headgear. *Rod Millman* **60**

HATEEL (IRE) 2 b.f. (Feb 16) Kodiac 112 – Vee Gita (IRE) (Vettori (IRE) 119) [2017 7d^3 Nov 4] €140,000F, 260,000Y: fifth foal: closely related to 2 winners, including smart Italian/US winner up to 11f Responsibleforlove (2-y-o 9f winner, by Duke of Marmalade): dam unraced half-sister to Breeders' Cup Juvenile winner Vale of York: 8/1, third in minor event at Newmarket (6½ lengths behind Nawassi) in November: will improve. *William Haggas* **61 p**

HATEYA (IRE) 2 b.f. (Apr 5) Footstepsinthesand 120 – Selfsame (USA) 82 (Dansili 127) [2017 6g^2 6g^6 7m^2 7g^3 7v^6 Oct 1] €20,000F, £8,500Y: second foal: half-sister to Spanish 5.5f winner Azkarra (by Royal Applause): dam, 1m winner who stayed 1¼m, half-sister to smart 1¼m winner Mirror Lake: fair maiden: best effort at 7f: acts on good to firm going. *Jim Boyle* **72**

HATHAL (USA) 5 ch.h. Speightstown (USA) 124 – Sleepytime (IRE) 121 (Royal Academy (USA) 130) [2017 118: 8g^3 10.3g^3 8g^3 8d^4 Sep 30] attractive horse: smart performer: third in Summer Mile Stakes at Ascot (4¼ lengths behind Mutakayyef), York Stakes (beaten 1¼ lengths by Success Days) and Celebration Mile at Goodwood (¾ length behind Lightning Spear): 2 lengths fourth to Taareef in Prix Daniel Wildenstein at Chantilly final outing: stays 10.3f: acts on firm and soft going: often wears cheekpieces. *William Haggas* **117**

HATHFA (FR) 3 gr.f. Dark Angel (IRE) 113 – Nepali Princess (IRE) (Mr Greeley (USA) 122) [2017 68: t6f^2 p5g* p5g^5 Feb 8] rather leggy filly: fair performer: won maiden at Lingfield in January: stayed 6f: acted on polytrack, tapeta and good to firm going: often wore headgear: usually raced close up: covered by Toronado. *Richard Hughes* **75**

HATSAWAY (IRE) 6 b.g. Dubawi (IRE) 129 – Scotch Bonnet (IRE) 95 (Montjeu (IRE) 137) [2017 86: 16m^6 p16d^5 14.2d 12v p16g p15.8g^5 Nov 21] fair handicapper: stays 2m: acts on soft and good to firm going: has worn headgear. *Pat Phelan* **78 a67**

HATS OFF TO LARRY 3 b.g. Sixties Icon 125 – Highland Jig (Norse Dancer (IRE) 127) [2017 10g^3 10d^3 12.3g^3 9.9d^2 10v^4 p8g^4 Oct 5] lengthy, angular gelding: first foal: dam unraced: fairly useful maiden: second at Goodwood in September: stays 1½m: acts on good to soft going: front runner/races prominently. *Mick Channon* **82**

HAULANI (USA) 3 ch.g. Algorithms (USA) 120 – License To Speed (USA) (Thunder Gulch (USA) 129) [2017 87: 9.9m p10s 8m p8g^5 10g^3 9.9d^3 9.9s^2 10d^3 Oct 23] workmanlike gelding: fairly useful handicapper: second at Salisbury and third at Windsor in October: stays 1¼m: acts on polytrack, tapeta and soft going: usually wears headgear: wears tongue tie: sold to join Brian Ellison 43,000 gns in October. *Philip Hide* **84**

HAVANA BEAT (IRE) 7 b.g. Teofilo (IRE) 126 – Sweet Home Alabama (IRE) 56 (Desert Prince (IRE) 130) [2017 101: t16.3g 18g 11.9g 18d Sep 23] leggy gelding: smart performer at best, not same force nowadays: stays 2½m: acts on firm and soft going: has worn visor/tongue tie. *Tony Carroll* **91**

HAVANA GREY 2 gr.c. (Feb 12) Havana Gold (IRE) 118 – Blanc de Chine (IRE) 96 (Dark Angel (IRE) 113) [2017 5.1m^2 5m* 5m* 5m 5m* 5v* 6g^2 5g^2 Sep 15] 42,000F, €70,000Y: stocky colt: first foal: dam 5f winner (including at 2 yrs): smart performer: won **112**

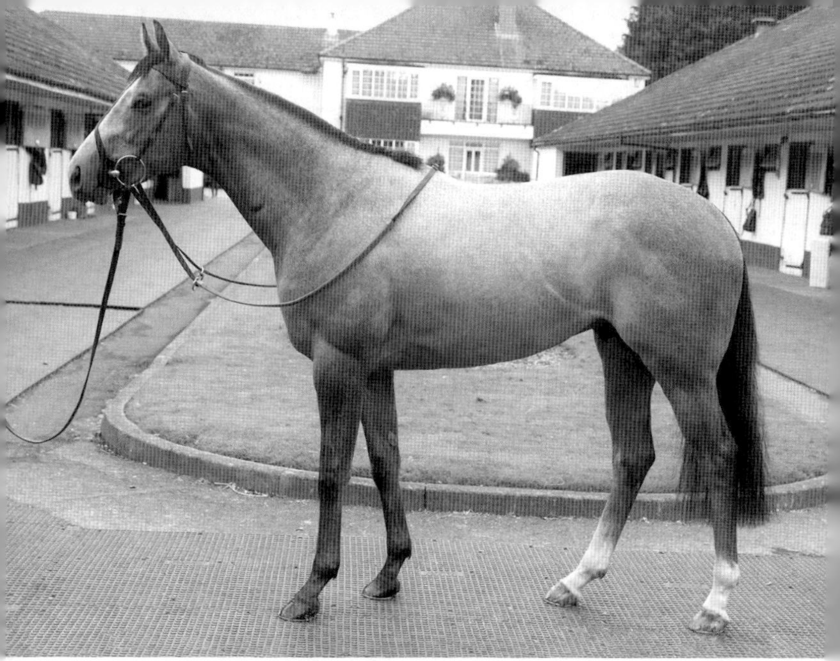

Global Racing Club and Mrs E. Burke's "Havana Grey"

minor event at Ayr in May, listed races at Sandown later same month and in July, and Molecomb Stakes at Goodwood (by 1¾ lengths from Invincible Army) in August: second after in Prix Morny at Deauville (1¼ lengths behind Unfortunately) and Flying Childers Stakes at Doncaster (½ length behind Heartache): stays 6f: acts on good to firm and heavy going: usually leads. *K. R. Burke*

HAVANA HEART 2 ch.f. (Jan 30) Havana Gold (IRE) 118 – Glee Club 64 (Kyllachy 129) [2017 6d 6d² 6s⁵ p6g⁵ 6d⁵ Oct 30] 16,000Y: smallish filly: first foal: dam, maiden (stayed 8.7f), sister to useful performer up to 1m Kylayne: fair maiden: raced only at 6f: acts on soft going: front runner/races prominently: sold £3,000, sent to Germany. *Ismail Mohammed* **65**

HAVANA MARIPOSA 2 b.f. (Apr 29) Havana Gold (IRE) 118 – Critical Path (IRE) 87 (Noverre (USA) 125) [2017 5d 5.9d³ t8g 6d³ t7.2g⁴ Nov 20] 5,000F, €5,500Y, €32,000 2-y-o: third foal: half-sister to 6f (including at 2 yrs) winner Krazy Paving (by Kyllachy) and a winner in Sweden by Royal Applause: dam 1¼m winner who stayed 1½m: fair maiden: best effort at 6f: acts on good to soft going. *K. R. Burke* **70**

HAVANASTAR (IRE) 2 b.g. (Jan 21) Havana Gold (IRE) 118 – Nagham (IRE) 96 (Camacho 118) [2017 5f* 6g³ 6g³ 6s² 5.9v 6g Oct 13] sturdy gelding: fair performer: won minor event at Beverley in May: stays 6f: acts on firm and soft going: tried in cheekpieces. *Kevin Ryan* **77**

HAVELOCK (IRE) 3 ch.g. Helmet (AUS) 127 – Pearl Grey 98 (Gone West (USA)) [2017 80: t7.1g⁴ f7g³ p7g² p7g² p6d 5g 5g 8.4v f11.1g⁴ Dec 21] fair maiden: left Mark Johnston after seventh start: seems to stay 11f: acts on polytrack, fibresand and good to soft going. *Peter Fahey, Ireland* **76**

HAVEN'S VIEW 2 b.g. (Feb 12) Reckless Abandon 119 – Haven's Wave (IRE) (Whipper (USA) 126) [2017 5.1m⁶ 5m 6.1g t6.1g p7s⁶ Dec 14] good-topped gelding: poor maiden: often starts slowly. *Richard Hughes* **47**

HAVEONEYERSELF (IRE) 2 b.c. (Apr 25) Requinto (IRE) 109 – Charismas Birthday (IRE) 65 (Choisir (AUS) 126) [2017 5.1m⁵ 5m² 5m² 5.2g³ 5.3m* p5g⁶ p6g t5.1g Nov 11] fair performer: won nursery at Brighton in August: stays 5.5f: acts on good to firm going. *John Butler* **71**

HAVERLAND (IRE) 2 b.g. (Feb 15) Big Bad Bob (IRE) 118 – Pivotal's Princess (IRE) 107 (Pivotal 124) [2017 6.1m p7s⁵ p7g⁵ Dec 21] smallish gelding: fair form: best effort when fifth in minor event at Chelmsford (3 lengths behind I'm Yer Man) in December. *Charlie Fellowes* **65**

HAVRE DE PAIX (FR) 5 b.m. Le Havre (IRE) 124 – Bridge of Peace (Anabaa (USA) 130) [2017 99: 8m 7.9d 8g² 7d 8s² 7s 8d* Nov 7] tall mare: useful performer: won listed race at Saint-Cloud (by neck from Dallas Affair) in November: second earlier in 2 handicaps at Ascot (beaten 3¼ lengths by Mittens, then 3½ lengths by Amabilis): stays 1¼m, usually races over shorter: acts on polytrack and soft going: usually races close up. *David Menuisier* **100**

HAWAIIAN FREEZE 8 b.m. Avonbridge 123 – Autumn Affair 100 (Lugana Beach 116) [2017 p12g⁴ 12f³ 12g³ 9f⁶ 7f⁴ 14g² 8.5g² 10f² 14d⁴ Sep 10] modest handicapper: effective at 8.5f to 1¾m: acts on polytrack and firm going: has worn headgear. *James Moon, Jersey* **55**

HAWATIF (IRE) 4 b.f. Royal Applause 124 – Excellerator (IRE) 101 (Exceed And Excel (AUS) 126) [2017 89: p8g⁶ t8.6g⁵ p7g 9.9g⁶ 8s³ p8g³ p8m⁶ p8g Dec 21] lengthy, angular filly: fairly useful handicapper: stays 8.5f: acts on polytrack, tapeta and good to firm going. *Anthony Carson* **85**

HAWKBILL (USA) 4 ch.c. Kitten's Joy (USA) 128 – Trensa (USA) (Giant's Causeway (USA) 132) [2017 125: 10.4g⁵ 12s* 12m³ 11.9g⁶ 12g* 11.9g² 12f² Sep 16] good-topped colt: very smart performer: won Aston Park Stakes at Newbury (by 2 lengths from My Dream Boat) in May and Princess of Wales's Stakes at Newmarket (by ¾ length from Frontiersman) in July: second after in Grosser Preis von Berlin at Hoppegarten (length behind Dschingis Secret) and Northern Dancer Turf Stakes at Woodbine (below best when beaten head by Johnny Bear): stays 1½m: acts on polytrack and soft going: wears headgear: front runner/races prominently. *Charlie Appleby* **123**

HAWKER HURRICANE (IRE) 3 gr.g. Dalakhani (IRE) 133 – Kitty Hawk 88 (Danehill Dancer (IRE) 117) [2017 p8s Aug 9] 66/1, well held in maiden at Kempton. *Luke McJannet* **–**

HAWKERLAND (IRE) 4 b.g. Sea The Stars (IRE) 140 – Zarara (USA) (Manila (USA)) [2017 p11g⁶ 10m⁴ 11.5g* 16m* 20.6v 18d Sep 23] tall gelding: fairly useful handicapper: won at Yarmouth in June and Chepstow in July: will stay beyond 2m: acts on good to firm going. *Marcus Tregoning* **90**

HAWORTH 3 b.g. Showcasing 117 – Some Diva 75 (Dr Fong (USA) 128) [2017 75: 7v 7d⁵ 6d⁵ 6m³ 7m⁵ 6g* 5.9s 5g t6d⁶ Sep 29] fair handicapper: won at Haydock in August: stays 6f: acts on tapeta, soft and good to firm going: often wears blinkers. *James Bethell* **75**

HAWRIDGE FLYER 3 b.g. Sir Percy 129 – Strictly Lambada 77 (Red Ransom (USA)) [2017 78p: 10s² 12d³ 12v* 14s Sep 8] compact gelding: fairly useful performer: won maiden at Ffos Las in August: stays 1½m: best form on soft/heavy going. *Stuart Kittow* **83**

HAWRIDGE GLORY (IRE) 3 b.g. Royal Applause 124 – Saint Lucia (IRE) 50 (Whipper (USA) 126) [2017 61: 8.1d⁵ 10m³ 10g* 8s² 10s² 8g* 10.1g⁴ p10d⁴ 11.4m³ 10.2d⁶ Oct 27] lengthy gelding: fairly useful handicapper: won amateur events at Newbury in July and Salisbury in August: stays 11.5f: acts on polytrack, soft and good to firm going: tried in blinkers. *Rod Millman* **82**

HAXBY JUNIORS 2 ch.f. (Apr 8) Monsieur Bond (IRE) 120 – Mozayada (USA) 85 (Street Cry (IRE) 130) [2017 5m⁶ t6d t5.1g Dec 2] second foal: dam 7f/1m winner: no form: tried in hood. *Antony Brittain* **–**

Princess of Wales's Arqana Racing Club Stakes, Newmarket—Hawkbill (white face) outbattles stablemate Frontiersman to gain his fourth pattern success, the pair clear of the grey Algometer; also pictured are Western Hymn (right) and Wings of Desire

Queen Mary Stakes, Royal Ascot—Heartache shows smart form on just her second start to record a comfortable success, beating US raider Happy Like A Fool (blinkers, right) and Out of The Flames (to the winner's immediate right)

HAYLAH (IRE) 2 b.f. (Apr 12) Epaulette (AUS) 126 – Pearls of Wisdom (Kyllachy 129) [2017 6g^{5} 5.7s^{2} p6s^{5} Nov 17] €32,000Y, 220,000 2-y-o: fifth foal: half-sister to 2-y-o 5.4f winner Alphabet Rap (by Amadeus Wolf), later successful in Hong Kong, and French 5f/5.5f winner Range of Knowledge (by Bushranger): dam once-raced half-sister to useful winner up to 7f Presto Vento: fair form: best effort when second in minor event at Bath (head behind Lady Marigold) in October. *Richard Hannon* **77**

HAYMARKET 8 b.g. Singspiel (IRE) 133 – Quickstyx 72 (Night Shift (USA)) [2017 70: t8g 9.2g^{3} 10s^{3} 10g* 10d^{5} 8.3g* 8.9m* 8g^{3} 10d 10m^{3} 10d t8d Nov 4] fair handicapper: won at Ayr (amateur) in June, and Hamilton and Musselburgh in July: stays 12.5f: acts on polytrack, soft and good to firm going: front runner/races prominently. *R. Mike Smith* **71**

HAYWARD FIELD (IRE) 4 b.g. Cape Blanco (IRE) 130 – Keepers Hill (IRE) 99 (Danehill (USA) 126) [2017 77p: 13.1m^{6} 12d^{6} 12g* t12.4d 12.1m^{6} t12.2g p12g^{3} t12.4g Nov 23] sturdy gelding: fair handicapper: won at Thirsk in July: stays 1½m: acts on polytrack, best turf form on good going. *Noel Wilson* **75**

HAZAMAR (IRE) 4 gr.g. Manduro (GER) 135 – Hazarafa (IRE) 110 (Daylami (IRE) 138) [2017 –: t9.5m^{5} t12.2g^{4} Aug 11] fair maiden: should be suited by 1¼m+: acts on good to soft going: often wears tongue tie: fair hurdler. *Sophie Leech* **65**

HAZARFAN 2 b.c. (Feb 3) Frankel 147 – Debonnaire 82 (Anabaa (USA) 130) [2017 8g^{6} 8d^{2} Oct 20] 250,000Y: fourth foal: closely related to useful 2-y-o 7f winner Roz (by Teofilo) and half-brother to high-class winner up to 2m Hartnell (2-y-o 1m-1¼m winner, by Authorized) and winner up to 1½m Phyllis Maud (2-y-o 1¼m winner, by Halling): dam winner up to 1m (2-y-o 7f winner): fair form: better effort when second in minor event at Redcar (3½ lengths behind Stephensons Rocket) in October: capable of better again. *Ed Dunlop* **73 p**

HAZARFIYA 2 b.f. (Apr 8) Fastnet Rock (AUS) 127 – Hazariya (IRE) 109 (Xaar 132) [2017 8s^{3} Oct 28] strong, rangy filly: has scope: half-sister to several winners, notably high-class 1¼m-1½m (including Derby) winner Harzand (by Sea The Stars) and smart 1¼m-1½m winner Hazarafa (by Daylami): dam 7f-9.5f winner: 11/1, plenty of promise when third in minor event at Newbury (3¼ lengths behind Red Starlight) in October, not knocked about: will be suited by 1¼m+: has scope for plenty of improvement. *Sir Michael Stoute* **70 P**

HAZARIBAN (IRE) 8 b.g. Kahyasi 130 – Hazarista (IRE) 113 (Barathea (IRE) 127) [2017 69: p16d^{5} p16g 14g Sep 2] fair handicapper: stays 17f: acts on fibresand, good to firm and heavy going: has worn headgear: wears tongue tie: fair hurdler. *Seamus Fahey, Ireland* **63**

HAZELL BERRY (IRE) 3 b.f. Big Bad Bob (IRE) 118 – Mudalalah (IRE) 70 (Singspiel (IRE) 133) [2017 47: t7.1m^{2} p7g^{6} f8m^{6} p8g^{3} t7.2g t8.6g Oct 21] leggy filly: poor maiden: left David Evans after fourth start: stays 8.5f: acts on polytrack and tapeta: wears headgear. *Karen George* **48**

HAZY MANOR (IRE) 3 b.f. Tagula (IRE) 116 – Hazarama (IRE) 91 (Kahyasi 130) [2017 48: 10m 8.3g^{6} 8.9m^{6} 11.2v Sep 18] poor maiden: tried in cheekpieces/tongue tie. *Julia Brooke* **–**

HEADLINE ACT 2 ch.f. (Apr 2) Helmet (AUS) 127 – Accede 88 (Acclamation 118) [2017 p6d^{6} 6.1f 7d p8g^{5} Aug 15] £23,000Y: fifth foal: half-sister to winner up to 1m Miss Van Gogh (2-y-o 7f winner, by Dutch Art) and 2-y-o 6f winner Poster Girl (by Excellent Art), later 6.5f winner in USA: dam 2-y-o 6f winner who stayed 1¼m: little impact in minor events/nursery: tried in cheekpieces. *Archie Watson* **–**

HEAD SPACE (IRE) 9 b.g. Invincible Spirit (IRE) 121 – Danzelline 83 (Danzero (AUS)) [2017 76: t6m p6m^2 p6g^2 p6g^6 p6g^5 t6g p6g^4 f5g^3 p6g^4 t6g p6g^6 t6.1g 6g^3 5.7s 7s 6.1d p6g^6 Dec 21] rangy gelding: fair handicapper: left David Evans after tenth start: stays 6f: acts on polytrack, tapeta and any turf going: often wears headgear: has worn tongue tie, including last 2 starts: often races in rear. *Brian Barr* **77**

HEADS YOU WIN 4 ch.f. Compton Place 125 – Miss Rimex (IRE) 84 (Ezzoud (IRE) 126) [2017 69: p10g* p10d Feb 2] fair handicapper: won at Lingfield in January: stays 1¼m: acts on polytrack and tapeta. *Jamie Osborne* **76**

HEADWAY 2 b.c. (Mar 14) Havana Gold (IRE) 118 – On Her Way 92 (Medicean 128) [2017 5.2g^2 6.1g* 6f^2 6v^6 6m^3 Aug 26] 38,000F, 60,000Y: sturdy colt: third foal: dam, temperamental 1¼m/11f winner, half-sister to smart Hong Kong miler Chater Way: useful performer: won maiden at Chester in May: second in Coventry Stakes at Royal Ascot (beaten head by Rajasinghe) and third in Gimcrack Stakes at York: will be suited by 7f: acts on firm going. *William Haggas* **107**

HEADWEAR (IRE) 2 ch.f. (Apr 28) Helmet (AUS) 127 – Indian Dumaani 51 (Indian Ridge 123) [2017 7m 7d 6g Aug 2] 30,000Y: third foal: half-sister to winner up to 16.5f Masterson (2-y-o 1¼m winner, by Lawman): dam Italian winner up to 7.5f (2-y-o 6f winner): well held in minor events/maiden. *David Brown* **–**

HEARTACHE 2 b.f. (Feb 8) Kyllachy 129 – Place In My Heart 105 (Compton Place 125) [2017 5f* 5m* 5.5g^3 5g* Sep 15] strong filly: first foal: dam, 5f winner (including at 2 yrs), half-sister to smart winner up to 1m Leitrim House: smart form: won minor event at Bath (by 6 lengths from Fab) in May, Queen Mary Stakes at Royal Ascot (by 2½ lengths from Happy Like A Fool) in June and Flying Childers Stakes at Doncaster (by ½ length from Havana Grey) in September: third in Prix Robert Papin at Maisons-Laffitte (½ length behind Unfortunately) in July: best form at 5f. *Clive Cox* **111**

The Hot To Trot Syndicate's "Heartache"

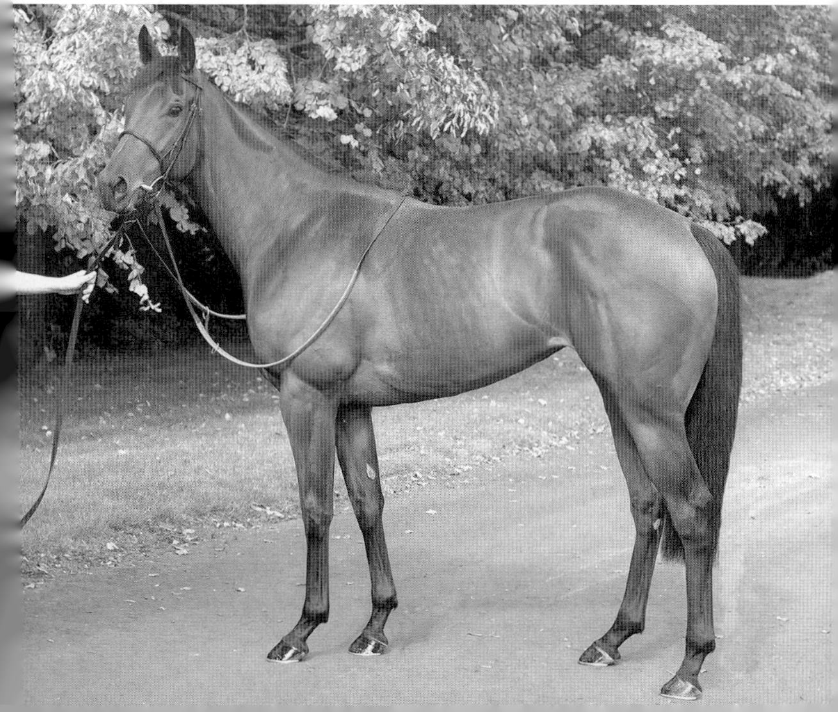

HEARTBREAK CITY (FR) 7 b.g. Lando (GER) 128 – Moscow Nights (FR) (Peintre Celebre (USA) 137) [2017 123: 15.9d Mar 25] good-topped gelding: very smart in 2016, winning Ebor Handicap at York and head second in Melbourne Cup at Flemington: well held in Dubai Gold Cup at Meydan, only outing on Flat in 2017: stayed 16.5f: acted on viscoride, good to firm and heavy going: wore tongue tie: fairly useful form over hurdles: put down after breaking leg in gallop in May. *A. J. Martin, Ireland* **–**

HEART LOCKET 5 b.m. Champs Elysees 124 – Zante 108 (Zafonic (USA) 130) [2017 80: p12g^5 t12.2g^4 t12.2g^2 p13.3d Mar 13] fair handicapper: stays 1¾m: acts on polytrack, tapeta, firm and good to soft going: has worn blinkers. *Michael Easterby* **76**

HEART OF AN ANGEL 4 ro.f. Dark Angel (IRE) 113 – How High The Sky (IRE) (Danehill Dancer (IRE) 117) [2017 60: p12g t8.6g p8d^5 Feb 16] smallish filly: modest maiden at best, no form in 2017: often wears headgear: often starts slowly, usually races in rear. *Henry Spiller* **–**

HEART OF GOLD 3 b.f. Kyllachy 129 – Secret Era 69 (Cape Cross (IRE) 129) [2017 58: 7g^4 8m^4 8.3g^2 8s^3 Aug 9] workmanlike filly: fair maiden: stays 8.5f: acts on good to firm going: usually races close up. *William Muir* **78**

HEARTSTONE (IRE) 4 b.f. Fastnet Rock (AUS) 127 – Eva's Request (IRE) 115 (Soviet Star (USA) 128) [2017 76: t9.5g^2 p12g^2 t12.2g^4 t10.2d t12.2g^2 t8.6g^2 t9.5m^5 10g 8.1m* 8d^3 p10g Aug 8] fairly useful handicapper: won at Chepstow in July: stays 1½m, effective at shorter: acts on polytrack, tapeta, good to firm and good to soft going: tends to find little. *David Evans* **80**

HEARTY (IRE) 4 b.g. Big Bad Bob (IRE) 118 – Ulanova (IRE) (Noverre (USA) 125) [2017 71: 10m^3 11.6d Jul 12] lengthy gelding: fair handicapper: stays 1½m: acts on polytrack, good to firm and heavy going: sometimes in cheekpieces: sometimes slowly away, usually races nearer last than first. *Richard Rowe* **69**

HEATHER LARK (IRE) 2 b.f. (Apr 24) Shamardal (USA) 129 – Heather Rose (GER) (Montjeu (IRE) 137) [2017 8d^3 p10g^6 8d^2 p8g^3 Nov 8] fourth foal: dam, German 11f winner, sister to top-class winner up to 1½m Hurricane Run: fair form: will prove suited by 1¼m: remains with potential. *John Gosden* **78 p**

HEATONGRAD (IRE) 3 b.g. Kodiac 112 – Best Mother (IRE) (King's Theatre (IRE) 128) [2017 72: 8g 8.3g^5 8d* 8.3m^5 8.3s 8.9s* 8.5v* 8v^4 Oct 9] compact gelding: fairly useful handicapper: won at Ripon in June, Musselburgh in September and Epsom (by 9 lengths from Fujaira Bridge) in October: stays 9f: acts on good to firm and heavy going: usually races close up: sold 25,000 gns, sent to Macau. *Richard Fahey* **89**

HEAT STORM (IRE) 6 b.g. Lawman (FR) 121 – Coconut Show (Linamix (FR) 127) [2017 50: 10.2g^6 May 31] modest maiden, well held sole start on Flat in 2017: stays 9f: acts on tapeta and good to firm going: wears visor: has worn tongue tie: often starts slowly, usually races towards rear. *James Unett* **–**

HEATSTROKE (IRE) 5 b.g. Galileo (IRE) 134 – Walklikeanegyptian (IRE) 77 (Danehill (USA) 126) [2017 95: 8.3g Apr 12] lengthy gelding: fairly useful handicapper: stays 1m: acts on polytrack. *Charles Hills* **87**

HEAVENLY ANGEL 3 gr.f. Dark Angel (IRE) 113 – Ballyalla 90 (Mind Games 121) [2017 79: 6m 7f 7d t7.1d Aug 10] sturdy filly: fair maiden at best, no form in 2017: left Richard Hannon after second start. *Ruth Carr* **–**

HEAVENLY CRY 3 b.g. Dick Turpin (IRE) 127 – Acclamatory 61 (Royal Applause 124) [2017 61: f5g^2 p5g^6 p5g^4 p5g Feb 18] modest maiden: stays 6f: acts on polytrack and fibresand: wears headgear: often races prominently: has joined Martin Smith. *Phil McEntee* **61**

HEAVENLY GAIT 5 b.m. Revoque (IRE) 122 – Still Runs Deep (Karinga Bay 116) [2017 t10.2d t10.2g Mar 22] third foal: half-sister to useful 16.5f-2¼m winner Lieutenant Miller (by Beat All): dam third in bumper: little impact in 2 maidens: tried in hood. *Jason Ward* **–**

HEAVENLY GUEST 2 ch.g. (Jan 14) Havana Gold (IRE) 118 – Maid In Heaven (IRE) 99 (Clodovil (IRE) 116) [2017 6.1m^4 7d Oct 27] stocky gelding: modest form in minor event/maiden. *George Margarson* **50**

HEAVENLY PULSE (IRE) 2 ch.g. (Mar 23) Dragon Pulse (IRE) 114 – Bogini (IRE) 95 (Holy Roman Emperor (IRE) 125) [2017 p5g^6 5g 6g 6m^6 6.9g 6d 7s^5 6d^5 p8g^6 p7d a7g* a8g^3 a6g* Nov 22] lengthy gelding: modest performer: left Ann Duffield after tenth start: won maiden (dead-heat) at Bro Park in October and minor event at same course in November: stays 7f: acts on dirt and soft going: tried in blinkers: sometimes slowly away. *Sandra Brolin, Sweden* **63**

HEAVEN SCENT 4 ch.f. Phoenix Reach (IRE) 124 – Hel's Angel (IRE) 86 (Pyrus (USA) 106) [2017 59: 12.1s⁶ 11.2v Sep 18] modest handicapper, no form in 2017: stays 1¼m: acts on good to soft going: usually in headgear: tried in tongue tie: often races prominently: winning hurdler: has joined Ken Wingrove. *Donald McCain* –

HEAVENSFIELD 4 b.f. Motivator 131 – Astrodiva 78 (Where Or When (IRE) 124) [2017 74: p12g 9.9g* 10.9g 10.2g³ 9s² 9.2g 8s³ 9.9g³ 9.2s 9.2d² 8d² Oct 20] modest performer: left Mark Tompkins after first start: won maiden at Mulheim in April: effective at 1m to 1¾m: acts on soft going: often wore headgear in Britain. *C. J. M. Wolters, the Netherlands* **61**

HEAVEN'S GUEST (IRE) 7 b.g. Dark Angel (IRE) 113 – Bakewell Tart (IRE) 92 (Tagula (IRE) 116) [2017 112: 8g 8m 7m 7m 7d 7s³ 8d⁴ 7.2v 7d t7.1d² Dec 16] good-topped gelding: useful handicapper: third at Ascot (1¾ lengths behind Remarkable) in September: stays 7f: acts on tapeta and any turf going: often races prominently. *Richard Fahey* **96**

HEAVEN'S ROCK (IRE) 3 b.g. Requinto (IRE) 109 – Rockfleet Castle 69 (Rock of Gibraltar (IRE) 133) [2017 71: 7d³ 8g* 8.3d⁶ 8d Oct 27] sturdy gelding: fair handicapper: won at Haydock in September: stays 1m: acts on polytrack, tapeta and good to soft going: has worn headgear/tongue tie: front runner/races prominently. *Tom Dascombe* **78**

HEDGING (IRE) 3 gr.g. Mastercraftsman (IRE) 129 – Privet (IRE) 79 (Cape Cross (IRE) 129) [2017 74: 7g⁴ 6g⁶ 7.1d* 7.1g⁴ 7.6s* 8.3d⁵ 8.1d⁶ Oct 23] good-topped gelding: fairly useful handicapper: won at Chepstow in August and Lingfield (by 1½ lengths from Spun Gold) in September: stays 8.5f: acts on soft going: wears cheekpieces. *Eve Johnson Houghton* **80**

HEDIDDODINTHE (IRE) 3 gr.g. Kendargent (FR) 112 – Damoiselle (USA) 100 (Sky Classic (CAN)) [2017 58: t10.2g p10s² p10s Dec 7] fair maiden: stays 1¼m: acts on polytrack: usually slowly away/races nearer last than first. *Richard Guest* **69**

HEDONISM (IRE) 2 b.f. (Apr 21) Excelebration (IRE) 133 – Knapton Hill 88 (Zamindar (USA) 116) [2017 5s⁵ Sep 19] €20,000Y: half-sister to several winners, including 2-y-o 6f winner Vallado (by Clodovil) and 2-y-o 1m winner Anythingknappen (by Arcano): dam 7f winner: 7/1, badly needed experience when fifth in minor event at Redcar (6¼ lengths behind Dandy's Beano) in September: open to improvement. *Hugo Palmer* **52 p**

HEE HAW (IRE) 3 b.g. Sleeping Indian 122 – My American Beauty 93 (Wolfhound (USA) 126) [2017 71: 6m² 6g² 5.9g* 6s* 6g⁵ 6s⁶ 6g 6m* 6d⁵ 6v³ Sep 28] fairly useful handicapper: won at Carlisle and Hamilton in June, and Ripon (by length from Sfumato) in August: left Keith Dalgleish after fourth start: stays 6f: acts on good to firm and heavy going. *Paul Midgley* **91**

HEEYAAM 2 b.f. (Mar 3) Invincible Spirit (IRE) 121 – Shalwa 88 (Galileo (IRE) 134) [2017 t8.6g² Nov 29] first foal: dam, maiden (stayed 1½m), sister to very smart winner up to 15.5f Kite Wood: 18/1, shaped best when second in minor event at Wolverhampton (head behind West Palm Beach) in November: open to improvement. *Marco Botti* **77 p**

HEEZARARITY 9 b.g. Librettist (USA) 124 – Extremely Rare (IRE) 82 (Mark of Esteem (IRE) 137) [2017 75: 11.4g 10.2d⁶ Aug 19] tall gelding: fair at best, down the field in 2 starts in 2017: stays 1¼m: acts on polytrack and any turf going: has worn tongue tie. *Jonathan Geake* –

HEIDI 2 b.f. (Feb 18) Swiss Spirit 117 – Mysterious Girl (IRE) (Teofilo (IRE) 126) [2017 6.1s⁶ Aug 21] 3,000F: second foal: half-sister to 2-y-o 5f winner Four Dragons (by Dragon Pulse): dam unraced: 17/2, sixth in minor event at Windsor (8¾ lengths behind Snazzy Jazzy) in August: should improve. *Richard Hannon* **51 p**

HEIR OF EXCITEMENT (IRE) 3 b.g. Tagula (IRE) 116 – Gimli's Treasure (IRE) 63 (King's Best (USA) 132) [2017 74: t7.1g⁶ 8m² 8m² 6.9g* 7.6d³ 7m² 8g⁴ 7.8s² 7d² 7.2sᵖᵘ Oct 1] fairly useful handicapper: won at Carlisle in May: went as if amiss final start: stays 1m: acts on tapeta, soft and good to firm going: in cheekpieces last 3 starts. *Kevin Ryan* **85**

HEIR TO A THRONE (FR) 4 ch.g. Siyouni (FR) 122 – Boaka (FR) (Kahyasi 130) [2017 92: 8m² 8m 7.8g 7d² 7.2g⁴ 8d 7.6g 7.6v 7g p7.5g⁴ Dec 19] fairly useful handicapper: second at Redcar in April and Chester in June: left Kevin Ryan after ninth start: stays 1m: acts on good to firm and good to soft going: sometimes in cheekpieces. *Mme L. Braem, Belgium* **91**

HELEN SHERBET 2 br.f. (Apr 1) Makfi 130 – Clifton Dancer 98 (Fraam 114) [2017 6g 6s⁶ 7.4s⁶ t7.2g f6.1g* f6.1g⁵ Dec 21] €37,000Y: fifth foal: sister to 6f winner Avenue of Stars: dam 7f winner (including at 2 yrs): fair performer: won nursery at Southwell in November: stays 6f: acts on fibresand. *K. R. Burke* **69**

HELFIRE 4 b.f. Archipenko (USA) 127 – Relkida 76 (Bertolini (USA) 125) [2017 75: p7g^5 p7g* p7g^2 p8g* 8g^3 8m^3 7g^2 Sep 1] rather leggy filly: fairly useful handicapper: won at Kempton in May and Lingfield in June: second at Sandown in September: stays 1m: acts on polytrack and good to firm going: usually races nearer last than first/responds generously to pressure: consistent. *Hughie Morrison* **85**

HELF (IRE) 3 b.c. Helmet (AUS) 127 – Causeway Song (USA) (Giant's Causeway (USA) 132) [2017 11.9m^3 11.9m^6 11.6v^4 11.6s^4 9.9m^6 12g p12g Oct 9] useful-looking colt: fair maiden: best effort at 1½m: acts on good to firm going: tried in tongue tie: usually races close up: has joined Oliver Greenall. *Richard Hannon* **74**

HELIS (FR) 4 b.g. Footstepsinthesand 120 – Xaara (SWE) (Xaar 132) [2017 p6g Dec 28] fairly useful performer in France, successful 3 times prior to 2017: well held in handicap on British debut in December: stays 1¼m: acts on polytrack and good to soft going: tried in cheekpieces. *Michael Scudamore* **–**

HELIUM (FR) 12 b.g. Dream Well (FR) 127 – Sure Harbour (SWI) (Surumu (GER)) [2017 57: p13g^6 Feb 9] modest maiden: stays 17f: acts on fibresand and heavy going: tried in blinkers: winning hurdler/fair chaser. *Alexandra Dunn* **52**

HELLARIOUS 4 gr.g. Hellvelyn 118 – Yarrita 77 (Tragic Role (USA)) [2017 –: t6g p6g 10d 8m Aug 10] poor maiden: often wears tongue tie. *Geoffrey Deacon* **43**

HELLAVASHOCK 4 gr.g. Hellvelyn 118 – Surprise Statement (Proclamation (IRE) 130) [2017 71: t8s 8.3s^3 10g 9.2s^6 12.1s 12.1v^3 8s^4 8v^5 t8s^4 t8.6g^5 Dec 13] modest maiden: stays 8.5f: acts on tapeta and soft going: usually wears headgear. *Alistair Whillans* **57**

HELLO BRIGETTE (IRE) 2 b.f. (Apr 30) Kodiac 112 – Fern Tycoon (IRE) (College Chapel 122) [2017 7s^4 p7g^5 t6.1d* Dec 27] €33,000F, €80,000 2-y-o: fourth foal: half-sister to German 6f/7f winner Fashion Tycoon (by Chineur): dam unraced half-sister to very smart winner up to 7f Balthazaar's Gift: fair form: won minor event at Wolverhampton (by 4 lengths from Sugar Coating) in December, having run of race: stays 7f. *M. D. O'Callaghan, Ireland* **78**

HELL OF A BAND 2 b.c. (Mar 16) Kyllachy 129 – Chilli Green 94 (Desert Sun 120) [2017 6g^{pu} Aug 1] 80/1, broke down over 1f out in maiden at Goodwood: dead. *Richard Hughes* **–**

HELL OF A LADY 3 gr.f. Hellvelyn 118 – Lady Killer (IRE) 76 (Daggers Drawn (USA) 114) [2017 p7g 7d^4 5.7m^3 f6.1g t6.1d Dec 16] sixth foal: dam 2-y-o 5f winner: no form. *Michael Attwater* **–**

HELLO GIRL 2 ch.f. (Apr 3) Bated Breath 125 – Elysee (IRE) (Fantastic Light (USA) 134) [2017 p6g^6 p6d^2 6.1f^2 5.2v t5.1g* 6d^6 t5.1g^4 Sep 9] sturdy filly: third foal: half-sister to 5f (including at 2 yrs)/5.7f winner Juan Horsepower (by Foxwedge) and a winner in Italy by Modigliani: dam unraced half-sister to smart winner up to 9.5f Nimr: fairly useful performer: won minor event at Wolverhampton in August: stays 6f: acts on polytrack, tapeta and firm going: usually leads. *Dean Ivory* **80**

HELLOMOTO 3 b.g. Firebreak 125 – Dayville (USA) 86 (Dayjur (USA) 137) [2017 –: 7g^2 8.3s^4 8s^5 8m^4 8.9m^5 8.5s^4 p10g 11.5g^6 Oct 16] modest maiden: stays 8.5f: acts on soft going: wears cheekpieces: sold £2,500, sent to Germany. *Kevin Ryan* **61**

HELLO MY SUNSHINE 2 ch.c. (Feb 15) Captain Gerrard (IRE) 113 – Dalmunzie (IRE) (Choisir (AUS) 126) [2017 t6s t7.1s^4 7.2m^3 t7.1d t6g Dec 6] fair maiden: stays 7f: acts on tapeta and good to firm going. *Karen McLintock* **66**

HELLOVAQUEEN 2 gr.f. (Apr 6) Hellvelyn 118 – Regal Quest (IRE) 91 (Marju (IRE) 127) [2017 5g^4 t5.1g Apr 8] fourth foal: dam 2-y-o 7f winner: modest form: better effort when fourth in minor event at Doncaster (5 lengths behind Requinto Dawn) in April. *Bill Turner* **55**

HELLS BABE 4 gr.f. Hellvelyn 118 – Blues In Cee (IRE) 91 (Sinndar (IRE) 134) [2017 76: t7.1g^3 t8.6g^5 7m* 7d* 7.2m^4 7g^6 7s 7d^6 Nov 11] good-topped filly: useful handicapper: won at Doncaster in April and York in May: stays 7f: acts on tapeta, soft and good to firm going: front runner/races prominently. *Michael Appleby* **101**

HELOVAPLAN (IRE) 3 b.g. Helmet (AUS) 127 – Watsdaplan (IRE) (Verglas (IRE) 118) [2017 74: 7.1g^5 8g* 8m* 8s^4 8g^4 10.2g^6 Sep 15] rangy gelding: fairly useful handicapper: won at Thirsk in April and Doncaster (by 1¾ lengths from Komodo) in June: stays 1m: acts on good to firm going. *Bryan Smart* **90**

HELVETIAN 2 b.c. (Apr 14) Swiss Spirit 117 – Lucky Dip 68 (Tirol 127) [2017 6v 5.7d* 6m 6m^4 6.3s 6.5g 6v^4 Oct 4] €33,000Y: good-topped colt: half-brother to numerous winners, including 2-y-o 5f winner Fortunately (by Forzando) and 5f-1m winner Halsion Chancer (by Atraf), both useful: dam 5f winner: fairly useful performer: won maiden at Bath in August: stays 6f: acts on good to soft going: often races prominently. *Mick Channon* **87**

HEMINGFORD (IRE) 2 ch.c. (Feb 11) Famous Name 124 – Fantastic Anna (IRE) (Fantastic Light (USA) 134) [2017 6.1d t7.1s^{6} 7m 8.3v* 8d^{4} 10v 8v Oct 23] useful-looking colt: fair performer: won nursery at Nottingham in August: best effort at 8.5f: acts on heavy going. *Charlie Fellowes* **70**

HEMINGWAY (IRE) 3 ch.g. Dragon Pulse (IRE) 114 – Degree of Honor (FR) 49 (Highest Honor (FR) 124) [2017 79: t6g^{2} t6g 6g^{3} 5g 5m^{5} t7.1g Oct 10] strong gelding: fairly useful handicapper: third at Pontefract in April: should stay 7f: acts on tapeta and good to firm going: often wears cheekpieces: sometimes slowly away: sold 4,000 gns in October. *Kevin Ryan* **84**

HENLEY 5 b.g. Royal Applause 124 – Making Waves (IRE) 70 (Danehill (USA) 126) [2017 75: f5d^{2} 5m^{2} 5g* 5s^{5} t5s* 5g* 5m 5s^{6} 5v^{5} t5g 5v^{2} Oct 23] angular gelding: fairly useful handicapper: won at Beverley in May, and Newcastle (by ½ length from Manshood) and Hamilton in June: stays 5.5f: acts on fibresand, tapeta, good to firm and heavy going: tried in tongue tie: usually races close up. *Tracy Waggott* **93**

HENPECKED 7 b.m. Footstepsinthesand 120 – Poule de Luxe (IRE) 75 (Cadeaux Genereux 131) [2017 79: t12.4g^{3} t10.2g^{4} t10.2s^{2} t10.2s^{2} 11.1s^{5} 9.8g^{4} 11.1v^{2} t12.4g^{2} 12.1s t10.2g t12.4g Dec 6] fair handicapper on turf, fairly useful on all-weather: second at Newcastle in June: stays 13f: acts on tapeta and heavy going: wears cheekpieces. *Alistair Whillans* **73 a80**

HENRIETTA'S DREAM 3 b.f. Henrythenavigator (USA) 131 – Timeless Dream 79 (Oasis Dream 129) [2017 –: t7.1m 5m 5g^{5} t6.1g 5d^{6} 6m^{5} 6d^{3} t5g^{5} 5g 5m 6d^{4} 6d^{2} 6v Nov 7] modest maiden: stays 6f: acts on good to soft going: wears headgear. *John Wainwright* **55**

HENRIQUA 3 b.f. Henrythenavigator (USA) 131 – Child Bride (USA) (Coronado's Quest (USA) 130) [2017 p7g 7m 7s Jul 29] 12,000Y: angular filly: closely related to smart US Grade 2 1½m/1¾m winner Juniper Pass (by Lemon Drop Kid) and half-sister to several winners, including 2-y-o 1¼m winner Jassur (by Canford Cliffs): dam unraced: no form in maidens. *Denis Coakley* **–**

HENRY CROFT 4 b.g. Dubawi (IRE) 129 – Karen's Caper (USA) 115 (War Chant (USA) 126) [2017 85: t12.4g^{4} p12d^{3} 12d p16d Jul 12] strong, sturdy gelding: fair maiden: stays 1½m: acts on tapeta and good to firm going. *Tony Carroll* **71**

HENRY DID IT (IRE) 3 b.g. Henrythenavigator (USA) 131 – The Fairies Did It (USA) (Elusive Quality (USA)) [2017 59: 8d 9.9g^{3} 9d^{6} 9.9m^{4} 11.6m^{6} t8.6g^{3} Oct 21] strong gelding: modest maiden: stays 9f: acts on polytrack, tapeta and good to soft going: usually races towards rear. *Tony Carroll* **57**

HENRY GRACE (IRE) 6 b.g. Oratorio (IRE) 128 – Little Miss Gracie 105 (Efisio 120) [2017 58: p8d^{3} p8d* p10g p11g^{6} p10g p8s Dec 8] modest handicapper: won at Kempton in February: stays 1m: acts on polytrack: wears blinkers: often races towards rear. *Jimmy Fox* **60**

HENRYHUDSONBRIDGE (USA) 5 b.g. Henrythenavigator (USA) 131 – Harlan Ash (USA) (Harlan (USA) 118) [2017 68: t12.2g 10.2d^{5} 10.2f^{5} 10m^{4} 10.2f* Jul 12] modest handicapper: won at Bath in July: stays 1¼m: acts on firm going: wears headgear: often wears tongue tie. *John Flint* **63**

HENRY SMITH 5 b.g. Firebreak 125 – So Discreet (Tragic Role (USA)) [2017 93: 12d^{4} 12v^{4} 12v^{4} 12.1v^{3} 12.1s^{2} Oct 31] lightly-built gelding: fairly useful handicapper: in frame all starts in 2017: stays 12.5f: acts on all-weather and heavy going: wears headgear: races prominently: sold £22,000 in November. *John Weymes* **85**

HEPPLEWHITE 4 b.g. Rail Link 132 – Millistar 88 (Galileo (IRE) 134) [2017 89: 11.4m^{3} 14g^{3} p16g 11.6d^{2} 11.9d^{3} 12d^{2} 12m^{4} 11.6m^{4} p12g* Oct 3] good-topped gelding: fair handicapper: won at Kempton in October: stays 1¾m: acts on polytrack, tapeta, good to firm and good to soft going: wears cheekpieces: tried in tongue tie. *William Muir* **78**

HEPTATHLETE (IRE) 2 gr.f. (Feb 17) Mount Nelson 125 – Jessica Ennis (USA) (English Channel (USA) 126) [2017 p7g^{4} Sep 25] third foal: half-sister to 2-y-o 7f/1m winner Indigo (by Medicean) and winner up to 1¼m Bayston Hill (2-y-o 7f winner, by Big Bad Bob): dam unraced: 50/1, fourth in minor event at Kempton (1¼ lengths behind Homeopathic) in September. *George Baker* **75**

HERCULEAN 2 ch.c. (Apr 21) Frankel 147 – African Rose 119 (Observatory (USA) 131) [2017 7s* Sep 8] fifth foal: brother to smart 2-y-o 6f winner Fair Eva, and half-brother to useful 1m/8.6f winner Hakka and French 8.5f winner Cosmos Pink (both by Dansili): dam 6f (Sprint Cup)/7f winner (including at 2 yrs): 11/10, overcame inexperience when won maiden at Ascot (by 1¾ lengths from Wadilsafa) on debut, responding well: exciting prospect. *Roger Charlton* **95 P**

HERCULLIAN PRINCE 5 b.g. Royal Applause 124 – Thara'a (IRE) 69 (Desert Prince (IRE) 130) [2017 67: t7.1g p8g t9.5g p8g t8.6g p8s⁶ 9.9m⁵ Jun 27] modest handicapper: stays 8.5f: acts on polytrack and tapeta: usually wears headgear: sometimes slowly away: has hinted at temperament. *Conor Dore* **52**

HERDWICK 2 b.c. (Apr 28) Makfi 130 – Bellwether (Three Valleys (USA) 119) [2017 7s⁴ 7g⁵ Oct 16] first foal: dam twice-raced half-sister to very smart performer up to 1¼m Mirage Dancer out of very smart US Grade 1 1m/9.5f winner Heat Haze: fair form in maiden/minor event: bred to be suited by 1m+: remains open to improvement. *Sir Michael Stoute* **78 p**

HERE AND NOW 3 b.g. Dansili 127 – Look Here 123 (Hernando (FR) 127) [2017 p11d² p12g* p11g³ 12.3m* 14.4g⁴ 14.4s² 13.9m³ 12m Oct 13] strong gelding: third foal: half-brother to 1¼m-14.4f winner Hereawi (by Dubawi) and a winner abroad by Sea The Stars: dam winner up to 1½m (2-y-o 1m winner), including Oaks: useful performer: won maiden at Lingfield in March and handicap at Chester in May: third in Melrose Stakes (Handicap) at York (½ length behind Secret Advisor) in August: stays 14.5f: acts on polytrack, soft and good to firm going. *Ralph Beckett* **100**

HERECOMESTHESUN (IRE) 2 b.f. (Feb 18) Invincible Spirit (IRE) 121 – Intimacy (IRE) (Teofilo (IRE) 126) [2017 7g* 7m 8d³ Nov 4] €150,000F: good-topped filly: second foal: half-sister to winner up to 1m Intimate Art (2-y-o 7f winner, by Dutch Art): dam unraced half-sister to smart 1¼m-1½m winner Folk Opera: useful form: won maiden at Salisbury (by 1½ lengths from Blanchefleur) in September: third in listed race at Newmarket (2 lengths behind Hadith) in November: stays 1m: open to further improvement. *Archie Watson* **96 p**

HERE COMES WHEN (IRE) 7 br.g. Danehill Dancer (IRE) 117 – Quad's Melody (IRE) 107 (Spinning World (USA) 130) [2017 111: 7.9d* 8.1g³ 8v* 8s Oct 21] **121**

Some illustrious names have adorned the winning roll of the Sussex Stakes over the years, but the latest edition is much more likely to be remembered for the conditions of extreme meteorological misery under which it took place, rather than for its winner. Rain lashed the Goodwood track, as forty millimetres fell in seven hours turning the course into a morass, with clerk of the course Seamus Buckley, officiating at his twenty-third and final Glorious Goodwood meeting, describing the weather as 'probably the worst I've encountered in my time here.' The day's programme was depleted by non-runners and late absentees, the most disappointing withdrawal being that of dual Two Thousand Guineas winner Churchill whose clash with the Lockinge and Queen Anne winner Ribchester in the Qatar Sussex Stakes promised to be one of the races of the week. Once at the track, Ballydoyle rarely withdraws its runners because of a late going change but the decision not to risk Churchill was perhaps understandable in the extreme circumstances. The withdrawal of Zonderland further reduced the Sussex field to seven, with Ribchester sent off at 13/8-on and the very smart French miler Zelzal at 4/1 second favourite (Churchill's stablemate Lancaster Bomber and the smart six-year-old Lightning Spear were the only others at single-figure odds). One for whom the significant rainfall came at the right time was the oldest runner in the line-up, 20/1-shot Here Comes When, a seven-year-old gelding who is a proven mudlark. A pattern winner as a four-year-old (when he won a Group 2 in Germany and was also successful in the Challenge Stakes at Newmarket), Here Comes When has had his chances over the years to make a mark in Group 1 company but, before the latest Sussex Stakes, he had simply seemed just not good enough, including when fourth at 33/1 to odds-on Solow in the 2015 Sussex. Here Comes When's most recent victory had come in the well-contested Hambleton Handicap at York in May when his performance showed that he was still a smart performer, though he had subsequently managed just third of five behind Morando in listed company at Windsor on his only other outing before Goodwood.

How the veteran Here Comes When came to win the richly-endowed Sussex, in which he trebled his career prize-money earnings at a stroke, is perhaps less pertinent than asking how Ribchester came to lose it. Less than five lengths covered the seven runners at the line after a muddling race in which Ribchester made the running (his intended pacemaker Toscanini was never dangerous). Zelzal's jockey Frankie Dettori stole up on the inside of William Buick on Ribchester at around the

Qatar Sussex Stakes, Goodwood—Here Comes When handles the morass-like conditions best to spring a 20/1-shock, with odds-on Ribchester (noseband) and Lightning Spear (left) filling the places; dual Guineas winner Churchill is a late non-runner on account of the ground

two-furlong pole, which seemed to unsettle Ribchester who didn't find as much at first as he usually does when asked for his finishing effort. Headed by Here Comes When approaching the final furlong, Ribchester briefly looked like dropping away, especially after his jockey seemed to stop riding at one point and Ribchester found himself short of room. In the end, Here Comes When was all out to hold on by a neck from Ribchester, who rallied strongly in the closing stages and would have got back up had there been another fifty yards to go. Lightning Spear finished three quarters of a length behind Ribchester in third, not quite seeing it out after challenging strongly, and Zelzal completed the frame, finding less than had seemed likely when looming up alongside Ribchester.

The somewhat puzzling performance of Ribchester's jockey prompted the stewards to hold an inquiry 'to consider why William Buick, the rider of Ribchester, had appeared to ease for a few strides approaching the final furlong.' The stewards noted the rider's explanation that 'the gelding (*sic*) had lugged right handed, and being mindful that he may run onto the heels of the winner Here Comes When he eased for a few strides before continuing to ride when the colt became re-balanced and ran straight again'. Buick himself cited the ground as the main reason for Ribchester's defeat, while Ribchester's trainer Richard Fahey described it as 'a strange race' and thought the jockey 'should have taken a lead for a bit … perhaps the horse pulled up in front, it's not the ground for a Flat horse but he showed good heart and nearly got up again.' The connections of Here Comes When conceded that 'everything dropped right in terms of the ground being almost unraceable and Ribchester getting a little bit unlucky, but that's racing isn't it?' Here Comes When had been declared under top weight for the Betfred Mile forty-eight hours after the Sussex but he didn't take up the engagement, the official reason given as 'the going'! Winning the Sussex Stakes entitled Here Comes When to a slot, with all entry fees paid and a generous travel allowance, in the Breeders' Cup Mile at Del Mar. However, he made just one more appearance after Goodwood, finishing ninth of fifteen on soft going (starting at 20/1) behind Persuasive, Ribchester and Churchill in the Queen Elizabeth II Stakes on British Champions' Day at Ascot (Lightning Spear was sixth).

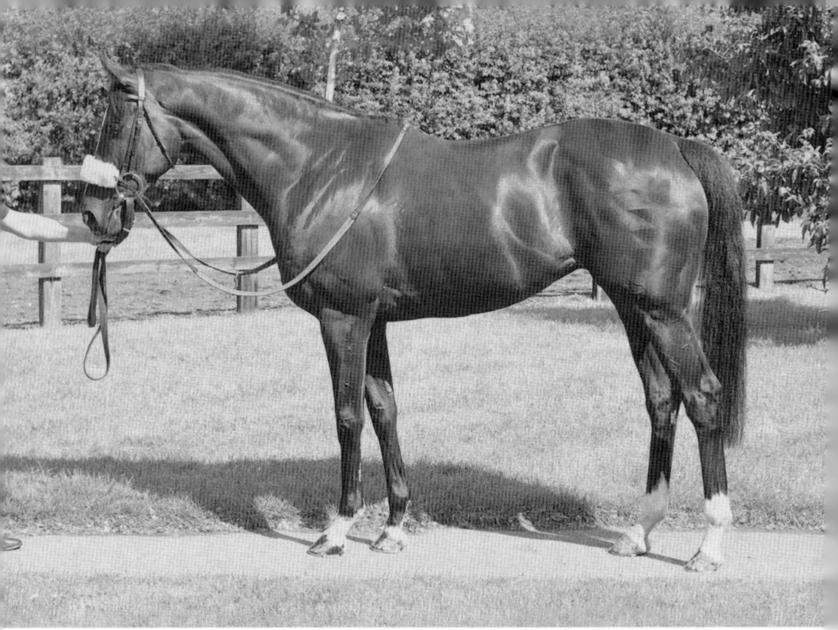

Mrs Fitri Hay's "Here Comes When"

Here Comes When (IRE) (br.g. 2010)	Danehill Dancer (IRE) (b 1993)	Danehill (b 1986)	Danzig
			Razyana
		Mira Adonde (b or br 1986)	Sharpen Up
			Lettre d'Amour
	Quad's Melody (IRE) (b 1999)	Spinning World (ch 1993)	Nureyev
			Imperfect Circle
		Fab's Melody (b or br 1989)	Devil's Bag
			Distinctive Moon

The tall, lengthy Here Comes When and the smart four-year-old French filly Qemah, who won the Duke of Cambridge Stakes at Royal Ascot, kept Danehill Dancer's name in lights for another season (he was retired from stud duties in 2014 and Qemah is from his final crop of any size). Champion sire in 2009, Danehill Dancer had to be put down at Coolmore in March due to the infirmities of old age. Quad's Melody, the dam of Here Comes When, did her racing in France, winning the Prix d'Aumale over a mile as a two-year-old. A half-sister to the smart Bonapartiste, who won in France and North America (the Grade 2 Del Mar Handicap), Quad's Melody has bred several other winners, including the fairly useful filly Morant Bay (by Montjeu) who won at a mile and a quarter for Sir Henry Cecil, and the Ralph Beckett-trained three-year-old Melodic Motion (by Nathaniel) who won at a mile and a quarter and twice at a mile and a half before finishing second in the Park Hill Stakes over a mile and three quarters. Here Comes When stays a mile and acts on good to firm and heavy going. He has a tendency to sweat and races in a hood. *Andrew Balding*

HERE I GO AGAIN (IRE) 3 b.g. Fast Company (IRE) 126 – Jaldini (IRE) (Darshaan 133) [2017 –: 8.1g 10g 7d Aug 13] rather sparely-made gelding: of no account: in hood last 3 starts. *Christine Dunnett* –

HERE IN THE DARK 2 b.g. (Feb 12) Harbour Watch (IRE) 121 – Behest 47 (Rainbow Quest (USA) 134) [2017 6s[3] 6s[4] 7.2m[4] 7.4d 7.2m[3] 8g[4] 8s[2] Oct 3] fair maiden: stays 1m: acts on soft and good to firm going: in cheekpieces last 3 starts. *Keith Dalgleish* **72**

HERE'S THE DEAL 3 b.f. Sakhee's Secret 128 – Quite Something 69 (Footstepsinthesand 120) [2017 6.1m 6g^6 Jul 27] no show in 2 maidens: dead. *Lisa Williamson* –

HERE'S TWO 4 b.f. Hellvelyn 118 – There's Two (IRE) 85 (Ashkalani (IRE) 128) [2017 81: 8.3m^5 p8g^5 7m 10d^4 p8g^3 8.1m^2 t7.2g 7.1v* 8.1d^2 7g* 7v Sep 30] good-topped filly: fairly useful handicapper on turf, fair on all-weather: won at Chepstow in July and Sandown (by ¾ length from Helfire) in September: stays 1¼m: acts on polytrack, tapeta, good to firm and heavy going: usually races prominently. *Ron Hodges* **82 a70**

HERMANA SANTA (IRE) 2 b.f. (Mar 1) Arabian Gleam 122 – La Zamora 93 (Lujain (USA) 119) [2017 6g 5m^3 5d^4 6.1g^5 5d^2 Aug 29] second foal: sister to 6f winner Semana Santa: dam, 5f-7f winner, half-sister to useful winner up to 1½m Latenightrequest: fair maiden: will probably stay 7f: acts on good to soft going. *David Barron* **70**

HERMANN 4 b.c. Authorized (IRE) 133 – Alamanni (USA) 109 (Elusive Quality (USA)) [2017 88p: t12.2m^2 11.4m^4 12s* 11.9s^2 10m^4 Jun 12] fairly useful handicapper: won at Newmarket in May: stays 1½m: acts on tapeta, soft and good to firm going: in cheekpieces last 2 starts: front runner/races prominently. *Richard Hannon* **91**

HERMARNA (IRE) 4 br.f. Heliostatic (IRE) 115 – Louverissa (IRE) (Verglas (IRE) 118) [2017 66: 11.6g^5 16.3d^2 18d t16.5g^2 Oct 21] good-topped filly: fair handicapper: stays 16.5f: acts on tapeta and soft going: often races lazily. *Neil King* **67**

HERMENEUTICS (USA) 3 b.g. Scat Daddy (USA) 120 – Rosangela (USA) (El Prado (IRE) 119) [2017 –p: p7g t9.5m Jan 16] little impact in maidens. *Ed Walker* –

HERMINIO (FR) 5 b.g. New Approach (IRE) 132 – Histoire Sainte (FR) 109 (Kendor (FR) 122) [2017 p11g Oct 11] fairly useful in France in 2015, eased off sole start on Flat since: stays 1½m: acts on polytrack, best turf form on good going: tried in hood: fair form over hurdles for W. P. Mullins. *Gary Moore* –

HERM (IRE) 3 b.g. Bushranger (IRE) 119 – School Holidays (USA) 90 (Harlan's Holiday (USA) 124) [2017 69: 6.1m 7g 8m 6.1m 7.1g 6.1g t7.2g* Dec 2] good-topped gelding: fair handicapper: won at Wolverhampton in December: stays 7f: acts on tapeta and good to firm going: sometimes in tongue tie. *David Evans* **67**

HERMOSA VAQUERA (IRE) 7 b.m. High Chaparral (IRE) 132 – Sundown 71 (Polish Precedent (USA) 131) [2017 56: 11.6s* 11.6d* 11.6d* 9.9v^3 p12g Dec 6] good-topped mare: fair handicapper: completed hat-trick at Lingfield in July, August and September: stays 1½m: acts on polytrack, good to firm and heavy going: usually wears cheekpieces: has worn tongue tie. *Gary Moore* **68**

HERMOSITA 2 b.f. (Mar 28) Exceed And Excel (AUS) 126 – Honorlina (FR) (Linamix (FR) 127) [2017 6g* Jun 13] fifth foal: half-sister to 9.5f winner Al Kout (by Oasis Dream) and 1½m winner Horseguardsparade (by Montjeu): dam, French 2-y-o 1m winner, sister to very smart French miler Vahorimix: 9/4, won maiden at Yarmouth (by neck from First Drive) in June: should progress. *Roger Varian* **80 p**

HERNANDES (FR) 3 gr.g. Clodovil (IRE) 116 – Gontcharova (IRE) (Zafonic (USA) 130) [2017 70: 7v^4 8.1d^2 10.3d^5 10g^5 10.4d^3 Aug 20] rather leggy gelding: fair maiden: left Ed Walker after fourth start: best form up to 1m: acts on heavy going. *Ian Williams* **78**

HERNANDOSHIDEAWAY 5 b.g. Hernando (FR) 127 – Alba Stella 92 (Nashwan (USA) 135) [2017 90§: 12g 9.9d^3 t10.2s^6 10s^3 10g^6 10g* Aug 2] compact gelding: fair performer nowadays: won seller at Redcar in August: stays 12.5f: acts on soft going: usually wears headgear/tongue tie: sometimes slowly away, usually races freely: one to treat with caution: has joined Miss Amanda Mooney, Ireland. *Michael Dods* **79 §**

HERNANDO TORRES 9 b.g. Iffraaj 127 – Espana 69 (Hernando (FR) 127) [2017 76: p8d* t7.1g t7.1m^4 10.3g 8.3m 8m t7.1s^6 t8.6g^3 8m^2 8.3g* 8.1v^2 10d 8g^2 t7.1d t8g f8.1g f7.1g f7.1g Dec 19] workmanlike gelding: fair handicapper: won at Chelmsford (amateur) in February and Hamilton (apprentice) in July: stays 1½m, effective at much shorter: acts on polytrack, tapeta and any turf going: has worn cheekpieces: usually wears tongue tie: often races towards rear/lazily. *Michael Easterby* **79**

HERON (USA) 3 b.c. Quality Road (USA) 131 – Dreamt 107 (Oasis Dream 129) [2017 10g^2 11.9m 10v^3 p12g Dec 20] fair form: left Hugo Palmer after third start: best effort at 1¼m. *Brett Johnson* **77**

HERSIGH 3 ch.f. Poet's Voice 126 – Zayn Zen 107 (Singspiel (IRE) 133) [2017 84: 8.2s^3 8g^5 p8g^3 Jul 5] lengthy filly: fairly useful handicapper: stays 9f: acts on polytrack: tried in cheekpieces: usually leads: sold £52,000 in August. *Saeed bin Suroor* **85**

HER TERMS 3 ch.f. Pivotal 124 – Best Terms 116 (Exceed And Excel (AUS) 126) [2017 75: 5m^3 5.3g* 5s^5 Oct 2] smallish filly: fair handicapper: won at Brighton in September: stays 6f: acts on soft and good to firm going: often in cheekpieces: front runner/races prominently. *Clive Cox* **76**

HERTFORD DANCER 3 ch.f. Foxwedge (AUS) 128 – Tebee 89 (Selkirk (USA) 129) [2017 75p: t9.5g^3 10.2g^2 11.6d* 12m^3 11.8m^4 Jul 8] strong, lengthy filly: useful performer: won listed Oaks Trial at Lingfield (by 1½ lengths from Pocketfullofdreams) in May: third in Ribblesdale Stakes at Royal Ascot (1¼ lengths behind Coronet) in June: stays 1½m: acts on tapeta, good to firm and good to soft going. *John Gosden* **105**

HE'S A LAD (IRE) 3 b.g. Lilbourne Lad (IRE) 111 – Make Amends (IRE) 79 (Indian Ridge 123) [2017 66p: p8g^2 f7g^5 f8g* Mar 9] rather unfurnished gelding: fairly useful form: won maiden at Southwell (by 5 lengths from Clock Chimes) in March: stays 1m: sold 3,500 gns in November. *Andrew Balding* **83**

HE'S AMAZING (IRE) 2 b.g. (Mar 19) Fastnet Rock (AUS) 127 – Kahyasi Moll (IRE) 35 (Brief Truce (USA) 126) [2017 7g^3 7d^2 Aug 18] sturdy gelding: fair form: better effort when second in maiden at Newbury (length behind Qaroun) in August: will be suited by 1m. *Clive Cox* **78**

HE'S A TOFF (IRE) 3 br.g. Dandy Man (IRE) 123 – Prevarication (IRE) (In The Wings 128) [2017 61: 7.5m^3 9.9g 8s 8f^3 Jun 19] modest maiden: stays 1m: acts on firm going: has worn blinkers: usually races towards rear: temperament under suspicion. *Tim Easterby* **58**

HESHEM (IRE) 4 b.c. Footstepsinthesand 120 – Doohulla (USA) 100 (Stravinsky (USA) 133) [2017 121: p9.4g^2 8.9d^2 Mar 25] very smart performer: second in minor event at Chantilly (beaten 1¼ lengths by Best Fouad) and Dubai Turf at Meydan (went down by ½ length to Vivlos): stays 1¼m: acts on polytrack, good to firm and good to soft going. *C. Ferland, France* **123**

HE'S MAGIC 6 b.g. Court Masterpiece 127 – Lady Magician (Lord Bud 121) [2017 –: t16.5g^6 t16.3d t16.3d^5 Mar 2] poor maiden: in cheekpieces last 2 starts. *Tim Fitzgerald* **38**

HE'S MY BOY (IRE) 6 gr.g. Dark Angel (IRE) 113 – Rose of Battle 80 (Averti (IRE) 117) [2017 79: 6g 7d 6d Aug 19] lengthy, rather leggy gelding: fair handicapper: stays 8.5f: acts on polytrack and good to firm going: often wears headgear: sometimes slowly away, often races towards rear. *James Fanshawe* **70**

HE'S MY CRACKER 4 ch.g. Captain Gerrard (IRE) 113 – Dalmunzie (IRE) (Choisir (AUS) 126) [2017 88: p6d 7g 6v May 20] sturdy gelding: fairly useful at 3 yrs, below that level in 2017: stays 7f: acts on soft and good to firm going. *Clive Cox* **68**

HE'S OUR STAR (IRE) 2 b.g. (Apr 13) Lord Shanakill (USA) 121 – Afilla (Dansili 127) [2017 6g^3 5.7d^5 7d^6 7d Oct 30] smallish gelding: fair form: should be suited by 7f+: tried in cheekpieces. *Ali Stronge* **69**

HESTINA (FR) 4 b.f. Soldier of Fortune (IRE) 131 – Diagora (FR) (Highest Honor (FR) 124) [2017 93: 12d Aug 5] lengthy filly: fairly useful performer, well held sole start on Flat in 2017: stays 1½m: acts on good to firm going: tried in hood/tongue tie: often races towards rear: fairly useful hurdler. *Dan Skelton* **–**

HEWOULDWOULDNTHE 3 b.f. Sixties Icon 125 – Gib (IRE) 81 (Rock of Gibraltar (IRE) 133) [2017 p10g f11.1g^4 t12.2d^3 Dec 9] fourth foal: half-sister to 7f/1m winner Waspy (by King's Best): dam 1¼m winner: fair form: best effort when third in maiden at Wolverhampton in December. *Jonathan Portman* **73**

HEY GAMAN 2 b.c. (Mar 5) New Approach (IRE) 132 – Arsaadi (IRE) 107 (Dubawi (IRE) 129) [2017 6g^2 7m 6g* 6g 6d* 7d* 7g^2 Sep 16] well-made colt: first foal: dam 2-y-o 7f winner (stayed 1¼m): useful performer: won minor events at Yarmouth (by 4 lengths from Arbalet) and Newmarket (by 5 lengths from Roussel) in July, and listed race at Newbury (by short head from Red Mist) in August: second in Champagne Stakes at Doncaster (neck behind Seahenge) in September: stays 7f: acts on good to soft going: front runner. *James Tate* **108**

HEY JONESY (IRE) 2 b.c. (Mar 23) Excelebration (IRE) 133 – Fikrah 92 (Medicean 128) [2017 5.9m^2 6g* 6d^3 6d^4 Sep 30] £35,000Y: good-quartered colt: third foal: half-brother to useful 7f/1m winner Loaded (by Kodiac): dam 2-y-o 1m winner: useful form: won minor event at York (by 2¾ lengths from Staxton) in July: fourth in Middle Park Stakes at Newmarket (2¾ lengths behind U S Navy Flag) in September: will probably stay 7f: remains with potential. *Kevin Ryan* **107 p**

HIBOU 4 ch.g. Street Cry (IRE) 130 – Arlette (IRE) (King of Kings (IRE) 125) [2017 100: 8m^6 10g^6 10g 10g^3 8.3s* 8.6d^2 8d 8.2v 10.3g Oct 14] useful handicapper: won at Hamilton (by 1¼ lengths from Masham Star) in July: second at Galway (1½ lengths behind Riven **105**

Light) in August: stays 10.5f: acts on polytrack, firm and soft going: wears headgear: often races towards rear: quirky sort (carries head awkwardly): sold 60,000 gns, sent to Saudi Arabia. *Iain Jardine*

HIC BIBI 2 b.f. (Mar 9) Cityscape 127 – Real Me (Mark of Esteem (IRE) 137) [2017 6f 7g^{5} 5.9s p6g* p6s^{2} Nov 16] leggy, light-framed filly: second foal: half-sister to 1¼m winner Av A Word (by Aussie Rules): dam unraced: modest performer: won nursery at Kempton in November: stays 6f: acts on polytrack: usually races close up. *David Brown* **64**

HIDDEN AFFAIR 2 b.g. (Apr 22) Equiano (FR) 127 – Love Action (IRE) 80 (Motivator 131) [2017 6s^{5} 6d^{3} Nov 11] fair form: better effort when third in maiden at Doncaster (3 lengths behind Raid) in November. *Henry Candy* **76**

HIDDEN CHARMS (IRE) 3 b.f. Canford Cliffs (IRE) 133 – Gilded Vanity (IRE) 83 (Indian Ridge 123) [2017 t8.6g* 9.9m 8v^{6} p8g t8g Sep 22] 200,000Y: half-sister to several winners, including smart winner up to 1m Birdman (2-y-o 6f winner) and useful 7f winner Predominance (both by Danehill Dancer): dam 5f winner: fair performer: won maiden at Wolverhampton in March: best effort at 8.5f: acts on tapeta: tried in cheekpieces: often starts slowly/races towards rear. *David Simcock* **77**

HIDDEN DEPTHS (IRE) 2 b.c. (Mar 21) Dark Angel (IRE) 113 – Liber Nauticus (IRE) 105 (Azamour (IRE) 130) [2017 7d Aug 11] 12/1, very green when well held in maiden at Newmarket. *Sir Michael Stoute* **–**

HIDDEN DREAM (IRE) 2 b.f. (Feb 22) Casamento (IRE) 118 – Anything (IRE) (Rock of Gibraltar (IRE) 133) [2017 p8g^{5} p8d^{6} 8.3d Oct 18] €22,000F: second foal: dam, unraced, closely related to useful 2-y-o 6f winner Rockaway Valley: modest form. *Christine Dunnett* **56**

HIDDEN GEM 4 b.f. Shamardal (USA) 129 – Hidden Brief 100 (Barathea (IRE) 127) [2017 68: p7d^{2} t7.1g p7g^{2} 7m^{6} Apr 25] fair maiden: stays 1m: acts on polytrack and tapeta: wears headgear/tongue tie: often races lazily: sent to France. *Stuart Williams* **65**

HIDDEN OASIS (IRE) 6 b.g. Lawman (FR) 121 – Spesialta 80 (Indian Ridge 123) [2017 83: 10s 8d 6m 7.4d^{3} 8.3v^{6} Aug 3] sturdy gelding: fair handicapper nowadays: stays 1m: acts on heavy going: usually wears headgear: often starts slowly, usually races in rear. *Jonjo O'Neill* **74**

HIDDEN REBEL 5 b.m. Cockney Rebel (IRE) 127 – Medicea Sidera 101 (Medicean 128) [2017 93: t8.6g^{4} 8g^{3} 8m 7.8g^{4} 8m^{3} 9.2g^{4} 9.2g^{6} 8s^{5} Sep 16] lengthy mare: fairly useful handicapper: third at Redcar in April: stays 1¼m, usually races at shorter: acts on good to firm going: has worn headgear: sometimes slowly away: tail flasher. *Alistair Whillans* **90**

HIDDEN STASH 3 b.g. Sakhee's Secret 128 – Marajuana 82 (Robellino (USA) 127) [2017 72: t6m^{3} t7.1g^{6} p6g^{6} 6g^{4} 7g 7m^{5} 7g^{5} p8g^{4} p10d 10s^{5} p7g^{ur} p7m* p7s* Dec 14] sturdy gelding: fair handicapper: won at Lingfield in November and Chelmsford in December: left Andrew Balding after seventh start: stays 7f: acts on polytrack and good to soft going: has worn headgear, including last 3 starts: usually races close up. *William Stone* **69**

HIDDEN STEPS 3 b.f. Footstepsinthesand 120 – Hidden Valley 82 (Haafhd 129) [2017 74p: p8g^{6} 11.3m^{5} 10.5m^{5} 8.1m* 8m^{5} p10g^{5} Nov 17] leggy, sparely-made filly: fairly useful handicapper: won at Windsor (by 1½ lengths from Clef) in October: stays 1m: acts on good to firm going: wears hood: often races freely. *Andrew Balding* **93**

HIER ENCORE (FR) 5 ch.g. Kentucky Dynamite (USA) 118 – Hierarchie (FR) (Sillery (USA) 122) [2017 64: t13.9m^{6} 18g Apr 11] rather sparely-made gelding: modest maiden: stays 16.5f: acts on polytrack, tapeta and soft going: front runner/races prominently. *David Menuisier* **62**

HIGGY'S HEARTBEAT 3 b.g. Acclamation 118 – Adorn 105 (Kyllachy 129) [2017 p8g 8.3g 6m^{3} p6g 7.1g^{4} 7.6s p7d Sep 28] modest maiden: stays 7f: acts on good to firm going: sometimes slowly away. *Dean Ivory* **63**

HIGH ACCLAIM (USA) 3 b.g. Elusive Quality (USA) – La Reine Lionne (USA) (Leroidesanimaux (BRZ) 127) [2017 89: p7f^{5} t7.1g^{5} 8m^{3} 8v^{3} 7m^{3} 6.1g^{4} 8g^{3} 7d^{6} 7d p7g Oct 25] compact gelding: fairly useful handicapper: third at Newmarket in May and Sandown in September: stays 1m: acts on polytrack, good to firm and good to soft going: wears headgear: races prominently. *Roger Teal* **94**

HIGH ANXIETY 3 ch.f. Bated Breath 125 – Odense (USA) (Medaglia d'Oro (USA) 129) [2017 8d^{6} t5s^{5} t5g^{5} Sep 22] €10,000Y: second foal: half-sister to useful 7f (at 2 yrs)/1m (in USA) winner Enjoy Yourself (by Sir Percy): dam unraced: poor form. *John Weymes* **48**

HIGH BAROQUE (USA) 5 b.g. Lookin At Lucky (USA) 127 – Yesterday (IRE) 119 (Sadler's Wells (USA) 132) [2017 94: p12g t9.5g^{6} 10.2f^{6} t10.2s Jul 1] fairly useful handicapper: stays 1¼m: acts on polytrack and good to soft going: often races prominently: sold 2,000 gns, sent to Spain. *Richard Fahey* **86**

HIGHBROW 2 b.c. (Feb 24) Intello (GER) 129 – Wild Gardenia 58 (Alhaarth (IRE) 126) [2017 p8g³ p8d* Dec 13] 120,000Y: fifth foal: half-brother to 8.6f/9f winner Raheeba (by Invincible Spirit): dam, maiden (stayed 1½m), half-sister to Irish 2000 Guineas winner Power and closely related/half-sister to Ribblesdale Stakes winners Thakafaat and Curvy: fairly useful form: won minor event at Kempton (by 4½ lengths from Returning Glory) in December: will stay 1¼m: will go on improving. *David Simcock* **90 p**

HIGHCASTLE (IRE) 2 b.g. (Apr 23) High Chaparral (IRE) 132 – Green Castle (IRE) 101 (Indian Ridge 123) [2017 8g 10m p8g Nov 18] down the field in maidens/minor event. *Ed Dunlop* **–**

HIGH COMMAND (IRE) 4 b.g. High Chaparral (IRE) 132 – Plaza (USA) (Chester House (USA) 123) [2017 98: 14.2m⁶ t16.3s³ p16s³ p16d Aug 23] fairly useful handicapper: third at Kempton in August: stays 16.5f: acts on all-weather and firm going: sold 6,000 gns in November to join Gary Moore. *Roger Varian* **92**

HIGH DRAW (FR) 4 ch.g. Falco (USA) 122 – Augusta Lucilla (USA) (Mr Greeley (USA) 122) [2017 88: 8g 10s 8.9g* 9.9d³ 8v² 8g 9s² 9.9s² p8g Nov 8] well-made gelding: fairly useful performer: won claimer at Fontainebleau in June: second after in handicaps at Sandown and Ayr, and claimer at Compiegne (left K. R. Burke after): stays 1¼m: acts on polytrack and heavy going: front runner/races prominently. *Julien Phelippon, France* **82**

HIGH END 3 b.g. Dubawi (IRE) 129 – Crystal Music (USA) 114 (Nureyev (USA) 131) [2017 p8s* t8.6g* 10.1m* 11.5d² 12m Oct 13] good-topped gelding: brother to useful 1¼m winner Firnas and half-brother to 3 winners, including useful 2-y-o 7f winner Treasury Devil (by Bernardini): dam, 2-y-o 7f/1m (Fillies' Mile) winner and second in 1000 Guineas, closely related to smart performer up to 1¾m Dubai Success: smart performer: won maiden at Chelmsford (by head from Hyperloop) in July, and handicaps at Wolverhampton (by 2¼ lengths from Almoreb) and Epsom (by 2¼ lengths from Lorelina) in August: stays 11.5f: acts on polytrack, tapeta, good to firm and good to soft going: tried in cheekpieces. *Saeed bin Suroor* **111**

HIGHER COURT (USA) 9 b.g. Shamardal (USA) 129 – Nawaiet (USA) (Zilzal (USA) 137) [2017 79: p6g⁵ p6g³ p6g p6g⁴ p7d³ p7g² t6.1g p6g* p6g* Nov 29] fairly useful handicapper: won at Kempton in October and November (by ½ length from Bahamian Heights): stays 7f: acts on polytrack and dirt: tried in tongue tie: front runner/races prominently. *Emma Owen* **85**

HIGHER POWER 5 b.g. Rip Van Winkle (IRE) 134 – Lady Stardust 95 (Spinning World (USA) 130) [2017 110: p16g² 16.2m² t16.3s* 16g 16.3g 16g Sep 28] well-made gelding: smart performer: won Northumberland Plate (Handicap) at Newcastle (by ½ length from Natural Scenery) in July: second in handicap at Kempton (1¼ lengths behind Blakeney Point) in April and Henry II Stakes at Sandown (5 lengths behind Big Orange) in May: well below form last 3 starts: stays 16.5f: acts on polytrack, tapeta and good to firm going: tried in tongue tie: often races prominently. *James Fanshawe* **114**

Stobart Rail Northumberland Plate (Heritage Handicap), Newcastle—
Higher Power produces a smart performance on the tapeta under his big weight to beat Natural Scenery (white cap with darker silks); the well-backed favourite Flymetothestars (right) and the winner's stablemate Lord George (white blaze) are also close up

HIGHEST RANK (IRE) 2 b.c. (Apr 14) Epaulette (AUS) 126 – La Noe (Nayef (USA) 129) [2017 5.9s* 7v 7g Oct 14] fair form: won maiden at Carlisle (by neck from Geesala Brave) in August: best effort at 6f: tried in visor. *K. R. Burke* **71**

HIGH EXPECTATIONS (FR) 6 b.g. High Rock (IRE) 114 – Tashifiya (FR) (Sendawar (IRE) 129) [2017 54: 13.1m* 13.1s^3 12s* 11.8g* 14g^2 12s^3 Sep 19] fair handicapper: won at Ayr (amateur) in May, and Tramore and Bellewstown in August: stays 1¾m: acts on good to firm and heavy going: races prominently, usually travels strongly: fairly useful hurdler, won handicap in November. *Gordon Elliott, Ireland* **77**

HIGHFIELD LASS 6 b.m. Cayman Kai (IRE) 114 – Jendorcet 57 (Grey Ghost 98) [2017 54: 9s 10d t8g Nov 3] maiden, no form in 2017: left Michael Dods after first start: tried in cheekpieces: tends to find little. *Tracy Waggott* **–**

HIGHGARDEN 2 b.f. (Apr 24) Nathaniel (IRE) 129 – Regalline (IRE) 79 (Green Desert (USA) 127) [2017 8s* Oct 28] fifth foal: half-sister to useful 2-y-o 7f winner Reglisse (by Verglas) and a winner in Qatar by Lord Shanakill: dam, 1m winner, closely related to smart performer up to 10.5f Recharge: 13/8, won minor event at Newbury (comfortably by 2¼ lengths from Spirit of Appin) on debut: will stay at least 1¼m: useful prospect. *John Gosden* **86 p**

HIGH HOPES 4 b.f. Zamindar (USA) 116 – Dixielake (IRE) 84 (Lake Coniston (IRE) 131) [2017 95p: 10.2v^2 9.9d* 12s 9.9m^2 10.1s^3 10m Oct 13] tall, attractive filly: useful performer: won handicap at Beverley (by 1¾ lengths from Prying Pandora) in June: second in listed race at Salisbury (length behind Billesdon Bess) in August: stays 1¼m: acts on good to firm and heavy going: often starts slowly, usually races towards rear. *David Simcock* **105**

HIGH JINX (IRE) 9 b.g. High Chaparral (IRE) 132 – Leonara (GER) (Surumu (GER)) [2017 13.9d^3 13.9m^5 16g 16.3g^5 17.9g^5 20.4d^4 15.4d Nov 10] good-topped gelding: smart performer: best efforts in 2017 when third in Yorkshire Cup at York (½ length behind Dartmouth) and fifth in Lonsdale Cup at same course (beaten 3½ lengths by Montaly) on first/fourth outings: stays 2½m: acts on good to firm and heavy going: in cheekpieces last 2 starts: tried in tongue tie: front runner/races prominently. *Tim Easterby* **113**

HIGHLAND ACCLAIM (IRE) 6 b.g. Acclamation 118 – Emma's Star (ITY) (Darshaan 133) [2017 98§: f5g p6g^6 p6d 6g^2 6f 6g* 6m^5 5g 6m* t6.1g 6d p7g p7s p6g p6s Dec 15] good-topped gelding: useful handicapper on turf, fairly useful on all-weather: won at Epsom in July and August (by ¾ length from Handytalk): all wins at 6f: acts on polytrack, firm and good to soft going: wears hood: often leads: not straightforward and is one to treat with caution. *David O'Meara* **97 §** **a89 §**

HIGHLAND BOBBY 2 b.g. (Mar 6) Big Bad Bob (IRE) 118 – Eolith 99 (Pastoral Pursuits 127) [2017 5f^5 5m^5 5g 7.4m^6 6g t6.1g^4 t7.1g^3 Sep 12] modest maiden: stays 6f: acts on tapeta and firm going: sometimes slowly away. *David O'Meara* **64**

HIGHLAND CASTLE 9 b.g. Halling (USA) 133 – Reciprocal (IRE) 88 (Night Shift (USA)) [2017 93: t16.3g 16.1f^6 14g^6 12v Sep 9] strong gelding: one-time smart performer: well held in 2017: usually in tongue tie: often races in rear. *Lucinda Egerton* **–**

HIGHLAND CLEARANCE (FR) 3 b.f. Kyllachy 129 – Let My People Go (FR) (Country Reel (USA) 113) [2017 –: p6d f8.1g Oct 22] no form. *Giles Bravery* **–**

HIGHLAND COLORI (IRE) 9 b.g. Le Vie dei Colori 126 – Emma's Star (ITY) (Darshaan 133) [2017 108: 8g 8m^4 8.3g^4 8.3s^6 8s 8.1m^5 7.8v^4 7d^4 7.9g 7d^4 Nov 4] good-bodied gelding: useful handicapper: stays 8.5f: acts on fibresand, good to firm and heavy going: wears headgear: front runner/races prominently. *Andrew Balding* **99**

HIGHLAND CRADLE 3 b.g. Bated Breath 125 – Orford Ness 107 (Selkirk (USA) 129) [2017 –p: p8g^2 10g 8d^5 Jun 8] tall gelding: fairly useful form: second in maiden at Chelmsford in April: best effort at 1m: tried in cheekpieces: sold to join Michael Appleby 9,000 gns in July. *Sir Michael Stoute* **86**

HIGHLAND MARY 2 b.f. (Mar 22) Dark Angel (IRE) 113 – Albertine Rose 89 (Namid 128) [2017 5m^6 6g^5 5d^2 5v^5 5d^5 5.1g t6.1g 5.7s Oct 2] £36,000Y: rather unfurnished filly: fifth foal: half-sister to 3 winners, including 8.6f winner Mandria (by Duke of Marmalade) and 2-y-o 5f winner Paytheprice (by Lawman): dam 2-y-o 6f winner: fair maiden: stays 6f: acts on good to soft going: tried in visor: usually races close up. *Richard Hannon* **72**

HIGHLAND PASS 3 b.f. Passing Glance 119 – Lady Brora 83 (Dashing Blade 117) [2017 83: 7d^2 7.6g* 8m^6 7.2m^5 8d^5 p8s Nov 16] rather unfurnished filly: fairly useful performer: won maiden at Chester in May: stays 1m: acts on good to firm and good to soft going: sometimes in hood: temperament under suspicion. *Andrew Balding* **82**

HIGHLAND REEL (IRE) 5 b.h. Galileo (IRE) 134 – Hveger (AUS) (Danehill (USA) 126) [2017 129: 12d 12m* 10m* 12s⁴ 10s³ 12f³ 11.9g* Dec 10] **128**

The blue chip might of Coolmore Stud and its racing arm Ballydoyle has made it the dominant force in European racing in the twenty-first century. That domination was taken to fresh heights in 2017 when Aidan O'Brien, who has had two decades in charge at Ballydoyle, set a new world record for Group/Grade 1 wins on the Flat when Saxon Warrior landed the Racing Post Trophy at Doncaster to overtake the twenty-five Group/Grade 1 wins by the North American trainer Bobby Frankel in 2003 (Frankel took the record from O'Brien who had set a mark of twenty-three in 2001, a number he had since matched in 2008). O'Brien ended the latest season with twenty-eight top-level successes—including five fillies' races promoted to Group 1s since 2003 and the Commonwealth Cup which is a new race—when that renowned Ballydoyle 'globe-trotter' Highland Reel won the Hong Kong Vase at Sha Tin in December for the second time in three years to complete another splendid campaign in which he also won two other Group 1s, the Coronation Cup at Epsom and the Prince of Wales' Stakes at Royal Ascot. Those two races were among sixteen (of the thirty-six) British Group 1s which were won by Ballydoyle in 2017 when O'Brien was champion trainer in Britain for the sixth time. He won the Irish trainers' title for the twentieth time (winning seven of the twelve Group 1s) and set a record by winning eight of the ten British and Irish classics in one year (if Enable had not contested the Oaks and Irish Oaks, all ten would have fallen to an O'Brien-trained horse). The victory of Wings of Eagles in the Derby was Aidan O'Brien's sixth in the race, bringing him level with the number achieved by his famed Ballydoyle predecessor and namesake Vincent, while Capri's Irish Derby win was O'Brien's twelfth in that classic (he has had the first three on five occasions).

Highland Reel may not be the best horse Aidan O'Brien has trained—he himself gives that palm to tip-top hurdler Istabraq while Hawk Wing (Timeform 136) is the highest-rated Flat horse he has had—but not many of O'Brien's top performers over the years (with the notable exception of Galileo) have contributed more towards their trainer's burgeoning legend. Highland Reel himself hasn't often enjoyed top billing among the blue bloods in his time at Ballydoyle but his victory in the Hong Kong Vase was his seventh Group 1, taking him level with the miler Rock of Gibraltar, the stayer Yeats and the filly Minding at the head of the list of O'Brien's multiple top-level scorers on the Flat (Istabraq achieved fourteen top-level victories over jumps including three Champion Hurdles). Highland Reel's victory in the 2016 King George VI and Queen Elizabeth Stakes was O'Brien's two hundred and eightieth Group/Grade 1 win (Flat and jumps combined) which took him past the generally acknowledged world record for 'top-level victories' held by Australian trainer Tommy 'TJ' Smith whose tally could be challenged as he achieved many of his wins before there was such a thing as official pattern status. When Highland Reel won the Prince of Wales's Stakes, O'Brien became the first trainer to win three hundred Group/Grade 1 races across both codes and, when Highland Reel's prize-

Investec Coronation Cup, Epsom—the Aidan O'Brien-trained runners are delayed getting to the track, arriving just over an hour before the race, but it clearly has no ill effects on Highland Reel as he battles on well to beat the Godolphin pair Frontiersman and Hawkbill

Prince of Wales's Stakes, Royal Ascot—dropped down in trip, Highland Reel responds generously to regain the lead having been headed briefly by Decorated Knight (third left) and Ulysses (noseband)

money earnings passed the £6,089,233 earned by Cirrus des Aigles (which they did when he won the Prince of Wales's Stakes), O'Brien also became the trainer of the horse who has won more prize money than any other based in Europe.

Victory in the Hong Kong Vase took Highland Reel's total earnings to £7,920,350, calculating them at the exchange rate prevailing at the time of his races. The accuracy of prize-money figures, in these days of so much international racing, is always open to question but we should perhaps point out that overseas prize money earnings quoted in most other publications, including the *Racing Post*, are calculated using a fixed conversion rate for the whole year—the 'official' rate as used by Weatherbys—and therefore do not take into account currency fluctuations that occur. The prize money for the last three races which Highland Reel contested in 2016 differs by as much as £510,000, depending on the exchange rates used (at the start of the year, for example, the dollar stood at 1.47 to the pound but at the time Highland Reel won the Breeder's Cup Turf in early-November it was 1.22). Whatever figures are used, it seems likely to be some time before Highland Reel is toppled from his pedestal. No wonder Aidan O'Brien, who once compared Highland Reel's constitution and racing character to 'concrete', described him as 'irreplaceable' after he had run his final race in the Hong Kong Vase. 'Where do you get a horse who did what he did? He has toured the world and passed every test, but he has to go to stud at some time.' In the past two and a half seasons, after finishing a traditional campaign for a classic three-year-old in Europe (including runner-up in the Prix du Jockey Club), Highland Reel has become a truly international performer. Since finishing a below-form fifth in the Irish Derby, he has run just twice in his native Ireland (when failing to reach a place in two runnings of the Irish Champion Stakes). Over that time, Highland Reel has raced on four continents, running in North America (three times), Australia, Hong Kong (four times) and Dubai (twice), as well as also contesting top races in Europe in both Britain and France (he was second in the 2016 Arc in which his trainer set another record when saddling the first three in Europe's richest and most prestigious race).

Highland Reel showed as a racehorse that he could handle most things—he maintained his form remarkably well, frequently turning up next time as fresh as paint after a hard race—but he wasn't at his best when the going was soft. He was only narrowly beaten in softish conditions in the Hardwicke as a four-year-old but ideally needed good going or firmer and relished what this Annual used to call 'top-of-the-ground conditions.' His two Grade 1 wins in North America, in the Secretariat Stakes at Arlington as a three-year-old and the Breeders' Cup Turf at Santa Anita as a four-year-old, both came on firm and the going was good to firm when he won the King George VI and Queen Elizabeth Stakes at Royal Ascot as four-year-old. Highland Reel's campaign as a five-year-old coincided with a sometimes wet summer but he still made the most of the opportunities when they came his way, finding conditions ideal when winning the Coronation Cup and the Prince of Wales's Stakes (which was run on one of the hottest June days on record). The rain leading up to World Cup night at Meydan in March didn't do Highland Reel any favours and he finished last of seven behind Jack Hobbs in the Dubai Sheema Classic (a race

Longines Hong Kong Vase, Sha Tin—Highland Reel produces a trademark game effort on his final start, fending off his Breeders' Cup conqueror Talismanic (broad white face); the win is Highland Reel's second in the race (first in 2015) and establishes him as the clear leader among the leading European money-earners of all time

in which he had finished a respectable fourth the previous year). Back on a sound surface in the Coronation Cup, Highland Reel had to overcome other difficulties when a problem fuelling the aircraft flying the Ballydoyle horses to Epsom resulted in them arriving at the course at around the time of the first race at two o'clock, just over an hour before the time of Highland Reel's scheduled appearance (he had left Ballydoyle at four in the morning). Highland Reel was dripping with sweat in the paddock—by no means unusual for him—and generally failed to take the eye. But neither the travel difficulties nor his appearance and pre-race demeanour had the slightest effect on his performance.

Sent off the 9/4 favourite at Epsom in a field of ten, and the first favourite for the Coronation Cup to start at longer than evens since Youmzain, who was beaten narrowly in 2009, Highland Reel dictated the pace all the way, travelling well, and was in control even when pressed strongly by Hawkbill early in the home straight. Highland Reel was sent for home in earnest two furlongs from home and won by a length and three quarters and three and a half lengths from the Godolphin pair Frontiersman and Hawkbill. Highland Reel's stablemates, his brother Idaho and the previous year's Derby runner-up US Army Ranger, managed only sixth and tenth (neither looking at their best beforehand). Highland Reel was Aidan O'Brien's eighth winner of the Coronation Cup, three of the earlier victories achieved by the ill-fated St Nicholas Abbey, another international performer who became the first horse trained in Britain or Ireland to win over £5m in prize money. Like Highland Reel, St Nicholas Abbey did most of his racing at a mile and a half but when tried in a couple of the top mile and a quarter events he showed himself every bit as effective at that trip as over further. Highland Reel did exactly the same, confirming his versatility dropped back in trip in the Prince of Wales's Stakes (he had been runner-up in the Juddmonte International the previous year), in the process becoming the first winner of the Coronation Cup to complete that particular double since Royal Palace won the Prince of Wales's in 1968, the year the race was restored to give the Royal meeting a top mile and a quarter race. Sweating freely in the paddock again at Royal Ascot, Highland Reel came up against three others who had won Group 1s on their most recent appearances, including French challenger Mekhtaal who had won the Prix d'Ispahan and Decorated Knight who had won the Tattersalls Gold Cup at the Curragh. The favourite was Jack Hobbs who hadn't been seen out since winning the Sheema Classic. Decorated Knight and the Gordon Richards Stakes winner Ulysses both looked like getting the better of Highland Reel when they edged past him a furlong out, but Highland Reel pulled out all the stops to regain the lead and win by a length and a quarter and a short head from Decorated Knight and Ulysses in what turned out to be a superb horse race in which the only disappointment was Jack Hobbs who finished last.

Soft ground for the King George VI and Queen Elizabeth Stakes and for the Champion Stakes, both at Ascot (and won respectively by Enable and Cracksman), counted against Highland Reel, though he made the frame, taken wide both times presumably in the hope of encountering better ground. The late withdrawal of King

George runner-up Ulysses from the Breeders' Cup Turf seemed to leave the way clear for Highland Reel to follow up his victory the previous year but he was beaten by Talismanic and Beach Patrol, keeping on gamely but seeming tapped for finishing speed in the very short home straight on the tight Del Mar turf track. Highland Reel bounced back at Sha Tin in the Longines Hong Kong Vase in which he showed all his trademark tenacity to turn the tables on Talismanic who looked poised to pounce for much of the home straight before Highland Reel found plenty under pressure to win going away again by a length and three quarters, with Japanese-trained Tosen Basil and the September Stakes winner Chemical Charge completing the frame.

Highland Reel (IRE) (b.h. 2012)	Galileo (IRE) (b 1998)	Sadler's Wells (b 1981)	Northern Dancer
			Fairy Bridge
		Urban Sea (ch 1989)	Miswaki
			Allegretta
	Hveger (AUS) (b 2001)	Danehill (b 1986)	Danzig
			Razyana
		Circles of Gold (ch 1991)	Marscay
			Olympic Aim

The pedigree of the good-topped Highland Reel emphasises—just as much as his racing record—the cosmopolitan aspects to Flat racing at the highest level nowadays. His sire and dam made their names in different hemispheres, his dam Hveger being placed in the Australasian Oaks and a sister to globe-trotting Australian champion Elvstroem and a half-sister to Haradasun, who also made a name for himself in Europe after being a top performer in Australia. Hveger has been a habitual visitor to Galileo since she was imported into Europe in 2009 and, as mentioned, is also the dam of the high-class brother to Highland Reel, the 2016 Derby third and Irish Derby runner-up Idaho, who won the Hardwicke Stakes at Royal Ascot in the latest season and also has an essay in this edition of *Racehorses*. There is also more background to the family in the extended entries on Highland Reel in the last two Annuals. Highland Reel and Idaho share a propensity to sweat freely before their races—though, unusually, Highland Reel did not do so before the Champion Stakes—and, while Idaho has shown that he acts on any turf going, Highland Reel put up his very best performances on good going or firmer. A front runner who was thoroughly genuine and reliable, Highland Reel was effective at a mile and a quarter to a mile and a half. He starts his stud career alongside five other sons of Galileo on Coolmore's specialist Flat roster, Australia, Gleneagles, Ruler of The World, The Gurkha and newly-retired Churchill. Highland Reel's fee in 2018 has been set at a relatively modest €17,500, below that for the other Galileos with the exception of Derby winner Ruler of The World (€8,000). Of that select group, only Australia can justifiably be held to have been a better racehorse than Highland Reel, whose splendid, all-round qualities—not least his toughness and tenacity—should ensure him strong support from breeders. *Aidan O'Brien, Ireland*

HIGHLAND SKY (IRE) 2 b.c. (Apr 22) Camelot 128 – Healing Music (FR) (Bering 136) [2017 8d t9.5g^{6} Nov 18] €360,000Y: closely related to useful 11f/1½m winner Kuda Huraa (by Montjeu) and half-brother to 3 winners by Galileo, including Derby runner-up At First Sight (2-y-o 1m winner): dam French 2-y-o 7f winner: fair form: better effort when sixth in minor event at Wolverhampton (7¾ lengths behind Corelli) in November: capable of better. *David Simcock* **65 p**

HIGHLIGHT REEL (IRE) 2 b.g. (Mar 13) Big Bad Bob (IRE) 118 – Dance Hall Girl (IRE) 81 (Dansili 127) [2017 6m^{2} 7m t7.1g^{3} 7d* Aug 18] €40,000Y: good-topped gelding: fourth foal: brother to useful 2-y-o 7f winner Tashweeq and half-brother to useful 5f (including at 2 yrs)/6f winner Kasbah (by Acclamation): dam, 6.7f winner, closely related to smart winner up to 9.5f Solar Deity: fairly useful form: won minor event at Newmarket (by ½ length from Alternative Fact) in August: stays 7f: tried in hood: remains open to improvement. *Michael Bell* **83 p**

HIGHLY FOCUSSED (IRE) 3 b.g. Intense Focus (USA) 117 – Mood Indigo (IRE) 91 (Indian Ridge 123) [2017 62p: t5g^{4} f5s t5.1g f5g^{5} t7.1g^{2} 7.2d^{6} Jun 5] modest maiden: stays 7f: acts on tapeta. *Ann Duffield* **60**

HIGHLY SPRUNG (IRE) 4 b.g. Zebedee 113 – Miss Donovan 100 (Royal Applause 124) [2017 94: p7g^5 6g 6g^3 p5g^2 p5g^3 5g 6g^5 5m 5.7f^5 6d^6 6g* 6g 6g 6d^4 p6g t7.2m^3 Oct 28] rather leggy gelding: fairly useful handicapper: won at Redcar in July: third at Leicester in April and Chelmsford in May: stays 7f: acts on polytrack, tapeta and good to firm going: sometimes slowly away, usually races in rear: sold to join Les Eyre 13,000 gns in October. *Mark Johnston* **88**

HIGH ON LIGHT 4 b.f. Makfi 130 – Estephe (IRE) 91 (Sadler's Wells (USA) 132) [2017 80: t12.2g^2 t12.4d^2 t10.2g^5 12.1m^2 t12.4g^3 14g* 14s Sep 8] fairly useful handicapper: won at Haydock (by 2¾ lengths from Takbeer) in August: stays 1¾m: acts on tapeta, soft and good to firm going: has worn hood: front runner/races prominently. *David Barron* **87**

HIGH ON LOVE (IRE) 3 br.f. Requinto (IRE) 109 – Cant Hurry Love (Desert Prince (IRE) 130) [2017 85: 8m 8.1m^2 p8g p7g^5 p7g Oct 26] strong, compact filly: fairly useful handicapper: stays 1m: acts on polytrack and good to firm going: tried in cheekpieces: front runner/races prominently: sold 8,000 gns, sent to Saudi Arabia. *Charlie Fellowes* **83**

HIGHSALVIA COSMOS 6 b.g. High Chaparral (IRE) 132 – Salvia (Pivotal 124) [2017 p15.8g 14g May 24] fair at best, well below that level in 2017: stays 1½m: acts on polytrack: usually wore blinkers prior to 2017: wears tongue tie. *Mark Hoad* **–**

HIGH SEAS (IRE) 2 b.f. (Mar 15) Henrythenavigator (USA) 131 – High Days (IRE) 77 (Hennessy (USA) 122) [2017 t6s^6 7s^4 7m^2 p7g Nov 17] rather unfurnished filly: fourth foal: half-sister to 3 winners, including useful 2-y-o 7f winner Colibri (by Redoute's Choice): dam, 2-y-o 6f winner, out of smart sister to top-class 1¼m/1½m performer Fantastic Light: fair form: will be suited by 1m+. *Hugo Palmer* **74**

HIGH SECRET (IRE) 6 b.g. High Chaparral (IRE) 132 – Secret Question (USA) (Rahy (USA) 115) [2017 14g^2 20f p14g^3 Nov 2] rangy gelding: useful handicapper: second at Goodwood (1¾ lengths behind Top Tug) in May: stays 17f: acts on polytrack, tapeta and any turf going: useful hurdler. *Paul Nicholls* **103**

HIGH SHAW 3 b.g. Paco Boy (IRE) 129 – Mondovi 97 (Kyllachy 129) [2017 8.5m^6 8g 7g May 29] no form: dead. *Ann Duffield* **–**

HIGHTIME GIRL 4 ch.f. Pivotal 124 – Hightime Heroine (IRE) 89 (Danetime (IRE) 121) [2017 68: t8g Jan 4] modest maiden: stays 1¼m: acts on tapeta: often wears cheekpieces: wears tongue tie: sometimes slowly away. *Roger Fell* **59**

HIGH WAVES (IRE) 3 br.c. Dream Ahead (USA) 133 – Lake Moon (Tiger Hill (IRE) 127) [2017 82p: 10.5d 12m^6 Jul 10] fairly useful form: won sole start at 2 yrs, down the field in handicaps in 2017: should stay at least 1m: tried in visor. *Saeed bin Suroor* **81**

HIGHWAYMAN 4 b.g. Dick Turpin (IRE) 127 – Right Rave (IRE) 84 (Soviet Star (USA) 128) [2017 65: t12.4d^5 t12.4g^5 t12.4d 10d f11.1g Dec 4] sturdy gelding: modest maiden: stays 1¼m: acts on polytrack, fibresand and good to soft going: has worn headgear: often races freely. *David Thompson* **60**

HIGHWAY ONE (USA) 3 b.f. Quality Road (USA) 131 – Kinda Wonderful (USA) (Silver Train (USA) 120) [2017 7g^4 7s^2 8g 7.4d 7g 7.6s^3 8.1d Oct 23] $120,000Y: lengthy, rather unfurnished filly: second foal: dam twice-raced daughter of US Grade 3 6f winner Voodoo Lily: fair maiden: stays 7.5f: acts on soft going: tried in blinkers. *George Baker* **77**

HIGHWAY ROBBER 4 b.g. Dick Turpin (IRE) 127 – Lawyers Choice 86 (Namid 128) [2017 55: t10.2g^2 t10.2d^2 t10.2s^4 11.1g* t16.3g^3 t12.4d^3 12.1s^5 12.1v^4 8v^6 t12.4d^3 Oct 24] modest handicapper: won at Hamilton in June: stays 16.5f: acts on tapeta and good to soft going: front runner/races prominently. *Wilf Storey* **59**

HIGH WELLS 3 b.g. High Chaparral (IRE) 132 – Valencha 103 (Domedriver (IRE) 128) [2017 10.2m 9.9g 9.9m 10.2f^2 9.9m^4 14s 11.6m* 12.5m^2 Sep 8] fair handicapper: won at Bath in August: stays 12.5f: acts on firm going: usually wears blinkers: sometimes slowly away, often races in rear. *Seamus Durack* **78**

HI HO SILVER 3 gr.g. Camacho 118 – Silver Spell 54 (Aragon 118) [2017 7s^3 p7g^5 t7.2g^4 Nov 29] half-brother to 3 winners, including useful winner up to 7f Brassini (2-y-o 5f winner) and 1m-1¼m winner Don Pietro (both by Bertolini): dam 2-y-o 5f winner: modest form: will stay beyond 7f: better to come. *Chris Wall* **63 p**

HIJRAN (IRE) 4 ch.f. Mastercraftsman (IRE) 129 – Sunny Slope 77 (Mujtahid (USA) 118) [2017 73: t7.1m 8.3g 8.3g^3 7.4m 7d 8.3v^2 Aug 8] tall filly: fair handicapper: stays 8.5f: acts on polytrack, good to firm and heavy going: wears headgear: has joined Henry Oliver. *Michael Appleby* **70**

HIKMAA (IRE) 2 b.f. (Apr 15) Roderic O'Connor (IRE) 119 – Alice Liddel (IRE) (Dark Angel (IRE) 113) [2017 t6d* p6g* 7d4 7m5 7s* Oct 28] 10,000 2-y-o: sturdy filly: first foal: dam unraced: useful performer: won minor events at Newcastle in August and Chelmsford in September, and listed race at Newbury (by ¾ length from Shepherd Market) in October: will stay 1m: acts on polytrack, tapeta and soft going: tried in tongue tie. *Ed Vaughan* **98**

HILARIO 3 b.g. Sepoy (AUS) 129 – Persario 96 (Bishop of Cashel 122) [2017 93p: 6m Apr 20] useful-looking gelding: fairly useful form at 2 yrs, well held in handicap sole start in 2017: stays 6f. *Charles Hills* **–**

HILARY J 4 b.f. Mount Nelson 125 – The Terrier 76 (Foxhound (USA) 103) [2017 94: 5m5 6m4 5m 6s 5g5 t5d* t5g3 Nov 23] fairly useful handicapper: won at Newcastle (by 1¾ lengths from Casterbridge) in October: stays 6f: acts on tapeta, good to firm and good to soft going: has worn hood: usually races prominently. *Ann Duffield* **91**

HILBOROUGH 2 b.c. (Mar 17) Makfi 130 – Ambrix (IRE) 64 (Xaar 132) [2017 8.3d5 7g6 p7s5 t8.6g4 Dec 18] fair form: best effort at 7f: has joined Les Eyre. *Mick Channon* **72**

HILLBILLY BOY (IRE) 7 b.g. Haafhd 129 – Erreur (IRE) 84 (Desert King (IRE) 129) [2017 112: 7.6d 7g Jul 15] useful performer: down the field both starts in 2017: stayed 1m: acted on polytrack, tapeta and heavy going: tried in cheekpieces: usually raced close up: dead. *Tom Dascombe* **–**

HIMALAYAN QUEEN 4 b.f. Poet's Voice 126 – Annapurna (IRE) 101 (Brief Truce (USA) 126) [2017 74: p6g4 p6g6 6m 6g 7g* t7.2g2 7d 8.1m3 p8g5 p7g Oct 26] fair handicapper: won at Yarmouth in June: stays 1m: acts on polytrack, tapeta and good to firm going. *William Jarvis* **73**

HI MILADY (IRE) 3 b.f. Sir Prancealot (IRE) 111 – Hi Katriona (IRE) 63 (Second Empire (IRE) 124) [2017 66: 7m 10m 10d 8g6 7d5 Aug 13] leggy filly: modest handicapper: stays 7f: acts on tapeta and good to soft going: often wears headgear. *Dominic Ffrench Davis* **53**

HIMSELF 3 b.g. High Chaparral (IRE) 132 – Self Centred 88 (Medicean 128) [2017 78: 7g 7g 6.1m2 p6g6 Oct 9] compact gelding: fairly useful handicapper: second at Windsor in August: stays 7f: acts on polytrack and good to firm going. *Richard Hannon* **81**

HINDSIGHT 3 b.f. Sayif (IRE) 122 – Classic Vision 59 (Classic Cliche (IRE) 128) [2017 6g3 7g2 8.3d3 7.9m6 7d* 6s4 6s Oct 10] 2,000Y: seventh foal: half-sister to 2-y-o 7f winner Farsighted (by Where Or When) and 8.6f winner Excellent Vision (by Exceed And Excel): dam 6f-1m winner: fair performer: won maiden at Lingfield in September: stays 8.5f: acts on soft going: tried in hood: front runner/races prominently. *Michael Appleby* **75**

HINT OF GREY (IRE) 4 gr.f. Mastercraftsman (IRE) 129 – Anamarka 57 (Mark of Esteem (IRE) 137) [2017 68: p12g 11.5m3 12v6 11.5g4 p7g6 Dec 21] workmanlike filly: modest handicapper: stays 1½m: acts on good to firm and heavy going: tried in headgear: fair hurdler. *Don Cantillon* **62**

HIORNE TOWER (FR) 6 b.g. Poliglote 121 – Hierarchie (FR) (Sillery (USA) 122) [2017 65: 16.3d* 16.3s* Jul 29] rather leggy gelding: fair handicapper: won at Lingfield (twice) in July: stays 16.5f: acts on polytrack and soft going: tried in visor: often leads. *John Best* **73**

HIPPEIA (IRE) 2 b.f. (Jan 27) Lilbourne Lad (IRE) 111 – Majestic Oasis 90 (Oasis Dream 129) [2017 6d4 6d4 7.2m5 6v3 Sep 25] €2,500F: first foal: dam, French 7f/7.5f winner, half-sister to useful French 1½m-2m winner Minotaur: fair form: should be suited by at least 7f. *Jedd O'Keeffe* **73**

HIPPOCAMPUS (IRE) 3 b.c. Born To Sea (IRE) 117 – Tolzey (USA) 94 (Rahy (USA) 115) [2017 p8g5 p8g 8m 9.9f 10.2f p8g Jun 22] compact colt: modest maiden: should be suited by further than 1m: acts on polytrack: sold 1,500 gns, sent to Greece. *Richard Hannon* **57**

HIPSTER BOY 2 b.c. (Apr 12) Dubawi (IRE) 129 – Mandellicht (IRE) (Be My Guest (USA) 126) [2017 8.3v3 t8.6g* Nov 25] brother to French 9f winner Mightily and half-brother to several winners, notably top-class winner up to 1½m Manduro (2-y-o 7f/1m winner, by Monsun): dam German 7.5f winner: fairly useful form: won minor event at Wolverhampton (by head from Profound) in November: will be suited by 1¼m: will go on improving. *John Gosden* **82 p**

HIPZ (IRE) 6 br.m. Intense Focus (USA) 117 – Radha (Bishop of Cashel 122) [2017 68: p7d p7g2 p7g6 p7g* f7g p7g4 p7d5 May 29] angular mare: fair handicapper: won at Chelmsford in April: left Laura Mongan after third start: stays 7f: acts on polytrack, soft and good to firm going: wears headgear: has joined George Margarson. *Ivan Furtado* **72**

HISAR (IRE) 3 ch.g. Dragon Pulse (IRE) 114 – Delphie Queen (IRE) 104 (Desert Sun 120) [2017 –: p6g^2 t5.1g^6 p7g^4 8.1m^6 7s^6 7g^6 8.1m^5 7.4d 6d^5 6.1g^4 7v t6.1g^6 t6.1m^4 p7m^3 t7.1s^4 t6.1d* Dec 16] workmanlike gelding: fair performer: won handicap at Wolverhampton in December: left Ronald Harris after eleventh start: stays 1m: acts on polytrack, tapeta and soft going: often wears headgear: often races prominently. *Michael Appleby* **73**

HIS DREAM (IRE) 4 b.g. Yeats (IRE) 128 – Rosa Muscosa (USA) 79 (Dixie Union (USA) 121) [2017 21.6m Jun 24] 66/1, well held in Queen Alexandra Stakes at Royal Ascot: bumper winner. *Jonjo O'Neill* –

HISTORIC EVENT (IRE) 3 gr.f. Invincible Spirit (IRE) 121 – Scenica (ARG) (Interprete (ARG)) [2017 t6g^2 p6g* 6g^2 May 13] 120,000F: second foal: dam, Argentinian Group 1 2-y-o 7.5f winner, later 7f winner in Australia: fairly useful form: won maiden at Chelmsford (by ½ length from Fair Cop) in April: raced only at 6f: tried in cheekpieces: sold 16,000 gns in July, sent to Greece. *Saeed bin Suroor* **85**

HISTORY WRITER (IRE) 2 b.c. (Feb 12) Canford Cliffs (IRE) 133 – Abhasana (IRE) (Hawk Wing (USA) 136) [2017 7g^3 Sep 1] tall, rather unfurnished colt: first foal: dam, lightly raced in Italy, half-sister to French 11f/1½m winner Sub Rose and 1½m winner Astonishing (both smart): 20/1, promise when third in maiden at Sandown (3 lengths behind Rum Runner) in September: will stay 1m: sure to progress. *David Menuisier* **80 p**

HITCHCOCK 3 b.g. Equiano (FR) 127 – George's Gift (Haafhd 129) [2017 t6g^2 6m^5 6m t7.1s 7.4m 7m 6g 7.2s* 8.3g^2 7v^5 Nov 7] fair handicapper: won at Musselburgh in September: stays 8.5f: acts on soft going: usually wears headgear. *Kevin Ryan* **77**

HI THERE SILVER (IRE) 3 gr.g. Clodovil (IRE) 116 – Elaborate 88 (Sadler's Wells (USA) 132) [2017 –: p8g p12g^4 p11g^6 9.9g p12g^5 p12g^3 Dec 23] modest maiden: stays 1½m: acts on polytrack: has worn headgear, including last 3 starts: often races prominently. *Michael Madgwick* **54**

HITMAN 4 b.g. Canford Cliffs (IRE) 133 – Ballymore Celebre (IRE) (Peintre Celebre (USA) 137) [2017 82: 8s^3 8.8m 8g^5 8d^6 7v^3 7g 8d 7.4v^6 7.2s^6 7d* Oct 20] tall gelding: fair handicapper: won at Redcar in October: stays 1m: acts on good to firm and heavy going: tried in blinkers. *Rebecca Bastiman* **79**

HIT THE BEAT 2 br.f. (Mar 14) Fast Company (IRE) 126 – Dance Express (IRE) 82 (Rail Link 132) [2017 p6g^4 p5m* Nov 25] first foal: dam 7f winner: fair form: won minor event at Lingfield (by 2 lengths from Drakefell) in November, making all: will go on improving. *Clive Cox* **78 p**

HIT THE BID 3 b.c. Exceed And Excel (AUS) 126 – Selinka 110 (Selkirk (USA) 129) [2017 96: p7g^6 5g 5m* 5g^2 5f^4 5.2m p5g^2 Oct 20] very smart performer: won listed race at Cork (by ¾ length from Go Kart) in June: second in handicap at the Curragh (neck behind Tithonus) in July and in listed race at Dundalk (neck behind Take Cover) in October: best form at 5f (raced too freely over 7f): acts on polytrack and good to firm going: in tongue tie last 2 starts. *Darren Bunyan, Ireland* **120**

HIT THE LIGHTS (IRE) 7 b.g. Lawman (FR) 121 – Dawn Chorus (IRE) (Mukaddamah (USA) 125) [2017 76: 5m^5 6m 6s Jul 10] fair handicapper, well below best in 2017: stays 6f: acts on fibresand, good to firm and heavy going: often wears headgear. *Marjorie Fife* **48**

HOCHFELD (IRE) 3 b.g. Cape Cross (IRE) 129 – What A Charm (IRE) 115 (Key of Luck (USA) 126) [2017 86: p10g^4 t8.6g^2 12.3d* 14.4g* 13.1g^2 12v^6 14m* 14s 14.2d^3 12m^5 Oct 13] well-made gelding: smart handicapper: won at Chester (twice, by 8 lengths from Look My Way second occasion) in July and Newmarket (by 6 lengths from Kajaki) in August: third in listed race at Ascot (¾ length behind Weekender) in October: stays 14.5f: acts on polytrack, tapeta, good to firm and good to soft going: front runner/races prominently. *Mark Johnston* **113**

HOCUS FOCUS (IRE) 2 b.c. (Apr 6) Intense Focus (USA) 117 – Hedera (USA) 90 (Woodman (USA) 126) [2017 t7.1s^5 t6.1g^6 Dec 22] well held in 2 minor events. *Richard Guest* –

HOGAR SEGURO (IRE) 2 b.f. (Apr 13) Casamento (IRE) 118 – Gemma's Pearl (IRE) (Marju (IRE) 127) [2017 6g^5 7.4m^5 Jul 8] €2,500F, €1,600Y: good-topped filly: third foal: half-sister to a winner abroad by Clodovil: dam, placed at 1½m in Italy, half-sister to smart winner up to 2m Yes Mr President: modest form in 2 minor events. *David Loughnane* **62**

HOLDENHURST 2 gr.g. (Mar 16) Hellvelyn 118 – Michelle Shift (Night Shift (USA)) [2017 5.1d^5 6g* 6m^6 6m^2 6m 5.2v Jul 22] lengthy gelding: fair performer: won maiden at Brighton in May: stays 6f: acts on good to firm going: usually races close up. *Sylvester Kirk* **73**

HOLD FIRM 5 b.h. Refuse To Bend (IRE) 128 – Four Miracles 96 (Vettori (IRE) 119) [2017 63: t8.6m^4 p10g^2 p8g* p8g* p8g^6 t8.6g^5 p8g^6 9.9g^3 p8g* p8s^5 8m^3 Jun 14] fair handicapper: won at Lingfield (apprentice) in February, and at Chelmsford in March (apprentice) and May: stays 1¼m: acts on polytrack, tapeta, best turf form on good going: often races prominently. *Mark H. Tompkins* **69**

HOLD HANDS 6 b.m. Lawman (FR) 121 – Tiponi (IRE) (Traditionally (USA) 117) [2017 71: t9.5d Dec 26] fair maiden, down the field on sole start in 2017: stays 1½m: acts on polytrack, tapeta and soft going: tried in tongue tie: often starts slowly. *Brendan Powell* **–**

HOLD ME TIGHT (IRE) 3 b.g. Zoffany (IRE) 121 – All Embracing (IRE) 82 (Night Shift (USA)) [2017 55: p7g p7g^3 f8g^5 p7m^3 8d 8.1d 10m^3 p12.4f 8d^6 8.9m Aug 16] sturdy gelding: modest maiden: stays 1¼m: acts on polytrack, tapeta and good to firm going: has worn blinkers: has joined Polly Gundry. *J. S. Moore* **59**

HOLD ON MAGNOLIA 4 ch.g. Monsieur Bond (IRE) 120 – Mawjoodah 80 (Cadeaux Genereux 131) [2017 73: f6g^3 f6g^3 8s 7g^6 8g 8g^4 9.7g 7.5g a7.5g a7.5g^3 a7.5g* a7.5g^5 a7.5g* Dec 10] fair handicapper: left Richard Fahey after second start: won handicaps at Mons in November and December: stays 7.5f: acts on fibresand and tapeta: has worn headgear. *M. Keller, Germany* **71**

HOLD SWAY (IRE) 3 b.g. Dubawi (IRE) 129 – Annabelle's Charm (IRE) 107 (Indian Ridge 123) [2017 p8g^2 10.3g^3 10m^2 10d* 9.9g^3 9.9v^5 12d Aug 12] well-made gelding: third foal: half-brother to smart 2-y-o 6f (including Middle Park Stakes) winner Charming Thought (by Oasis Dream) and 5f/6f winner Spanish City (by Exceed And Excel): dam 1m-1¼m winner: useful performer: won maiden at Newmarket (by length from Zenon) in May: stays 10.5f: acts on good to firm and good to soft going: often wears headgear. *Charlie Appleby* **95**

HOLDTHASIGREEN (FR) 5 ch.g. Hold That Tiger (USA) 117 – Greentathir (FR) (Muhtathir 126) [2017 116: 15.4g* 14.9g 11.9g* 11.9g^2 14.9g^3 14.9d^2 15.4g^3 11.9s* Dec 10] smart performer: won listed races at Maisons-Laffitte in March, Lyon Parilly in June and Toulouse (beat Ison 6½ lengths) in December: also placed 4 times, including in Prix Kergorlay at Deauville, Prix Gladiateur at Chantilly (¾-length second to Vazirabad) and Prix Royal-Oak at Saint-Cloud (3¼ lengths third to Ice Breeze): stays 15.4f: acts on polytrack and soft going: wears cheekpieces. *C. Le Lay, France* **118**

HOLD YOUR BREATH 2 b.f. (Jan 25) Bated Breath 125 – Chittenden (USA) 74 (Raven's Pass (USA) 133) [2017 6g 6g 5m Sep 15] first foal: dam lightly-raced half-sister to US Grade 3 8.5f winner Kilgowan: no form. *Tony Carroll* **–**

HOLIDAY GIRL (IRE) 3 b.f. Acclamation 118 – Bikini Babe (IRE) 104 (Montjeu (IRE) 137) [2017 84p: p8g^6 p5g^6 8m^3 7.1s^2 6.1g^2 7d^3 Oct 30] sturdy filly: second foal: half-sister to French 2-y-o 5f/6f winner Rkaya (by Exceed And Excel): dam, 2-y-o 7f winner who stayed 12.5f, half-sister to very smart performers Scottish (stays 1½m) and Royal Empire (winner up to 13f) and to dam of Poule d'Essai des Pouliches winner Precieuse: fair maiden: left W. McCreery after second start: stays 7f: best form on good going: tried in visor: usually races prominently. *Eve Johnson Houghton* **77**

HOLIDAY MAGIC (IRE) 6 gr.g. Dark Angel (IRE) 113 – Win Cash (IRE) (Alhaarth (IRE) 126) [2017 102: f7g* t7.1g^4 t7.1g^2 t8.6g^3 8g p7g 7m^6 6m^6 6d^5 7g f7.1g p7s p8s Dec 7] strong gelding: useful handicapper: won at Southwell in January: second at Newcastle (head behind Suzi's Connoisseur) in February and third at Wolverhampton (1¾ lengths behind Nimr) in March: stays 8.5f: acts on all-weather and good to firm going: tried in blinkers: usually races towards rear. *Michael Easterby* **102**

HOLLANDER 3 ch.g. Dutch Art 126 – Thrill 97 (Pivotal 124) [2017 6.1g^2 6m^6 5.1g^5 5g^5 5.1g* Aug 7] sturdy gelding: fair performer: won handicap at Windsor in August: stays 6f: best form on good going: front runner/races prominently. *William Muir* **78**

HOLLIE'S DREAM 2 ch.f. (Apr 16) Rip Van Winkle (IRE) 134 – In A Silent Way (IRE) 102 (Desert Prince (IRE) 130) [2017 5.1m^5 6.1s 7g^6 5.1s p6g Oct 5] sister to 7f/1m winner Break The Silence, closely related to 1¼m winner Al Destoor (by Teofilo) and half-sister to several winners, including useful French 2-y-o 1m winner Crecy (by Refuse To Bend): dam winner up to 1¼m (2-y-o 6f winner): no form: tried in tongue tie. *David Evans* **–**

HOLLY BUSH HENRY (IRE) 6 b.g. Yeats (IRE) 128 – Maslam (IRE) (Robellino (USA) 127) [2017 p12m^6 Jan 21] in tongue tie, 10/1, well held in maiden at Lingfield: has joined Phil Middleton: useful hurdler/chaser. *Graeme McPherson* **–**

HOLLYDAZE (IRE) 2 b.f. (May 5) Big Bad Bob (IRE) 118 – Fashionable 102 (Nashwan (USA) 135) [2017 7g^3 7g* 8.2v^5 Sep 30] €72,000Y: half-sister to several winners, including smart winner up to 9.4f Jack Naylor (2-y-o 7f/1m winner, by Champs Elysees) and 1¼m winner Seamless (by Beat Hollow), both stayed 1½m: dam 1m-1¼m winner: fair form: won minor event at Epsom (by 2 lengths from King of The Sand) in September: should be suited by 1m. *Richard Hughes* **76**

HOLLYWOOD ALL STAR (IRE) 8 b.g. Kheleyf (USA) 116 – Camassina (IRE) 62 (Taufan (USA) 119) [2017 43: f12s Jan 26] maiden, well held sole start on Flat in 2017: stays 1½m: acts on polytrack and soft going: winning hurdler. *Graeme McPherson* **–**

HOLLYWOOD DREAM 2 b.f. (Apr 28) Delegator 125 – Royal Obsession (IRE) (Val Royal (FR) 127) [2017 6m 6v^4 6m^5 6v^5 p7g p7d^6 p7g Dec 28] third foal: half-sister to 2-y-o 5f winners Harleys Rocket (by Proclamation) and Just Emma (by Bertolini): dam ran twice: fair maiden: left William Muir after fifth start: stays 6f: acts on good to firm going. *Neil Mulholland* **68**

HOLLYWOOD HARRY (IRE) 3 ch.g. Dandy Man (IRE) 123 – Alifandango (IRE) 78 (Alzao (USA) 117) [2017 55: t7.1g t7.1g^2 t7.1g^6 6g 7.2m^2 7.2g^5 7.2d^3 8f t7.1s 7m Jul 12] stocky gelding: fair maiden: stays 7f: acts on tapeta and good to firm going: wears headgear. *Keith Dalgleish* **65**

HOLLYWOOD ROAD (IRE) 4 b.g. Kodiac 112 – Rinneen (IRE) 67 (Bien Bien (USA) 125) [2017 91: 10m* 10m^3 10m^2 9.9g^2 12m^3 12g^4 Sep 14] stocky gelding: useful handicapper: won at Windsor in June: second at Beverley (head behind Save The Bees) in August: stays 1½m: acts on good to firm and heavy going: wears headgear: sometimes slowly away. *Don Cantillon* **95**

HOLLYWOOD STYLE 3 b.f. Royal Applause 124 – Brazilian Style 67 (Exit To Nowhere (USA) 122) [2017 45: p8g 7m^{rr} Aug 1] unfurnished filly: little form: left William Knight after first start: temperamental. *Brendan Powell* **– §**

HOLMESWOOD 3 b.g. Mayson 124 – Anglezarke (IRE) 109 (Acclamation 118) [2017 92p: 6m^3 6d^4 6d^5 6s^4 5g* 5d* 5m* 5s^4 Sep 9] useful handicapper: won at Ayr (by length from Desert Ace) in July, and Ripon (by ½ length from Harome) and York (apprentice, dead-heated with Intense Romance) in August: stays 6f: acts on tapeta, soft and good to firm going: has worn headgear: often races prominently. *Michael Dods* **105**

HOLMFIRST 2 b.g. (Feb 21) Finjaan 122 – Forrest Star 57 (Fraam 114) [2017 5m^5 5m^5 6m 5d Aug 4] modest form: best effort at 5f. *Paul Midgley* **51**

HOLTE END 2 b.f. (Mar 19) Stimulation (IRE) 121 – Ellway Queen (USA) 71 (Bahri (USA) 125) [2017 t7.1g Nov 3] 3,000Y: half-sister to several winners, including useful US winner up to 1¼m Ghetto (2-y-o 7f winner in Britain, by Auction House) and 6f winner Artistic Queen (by Dutch Art): dam 1m winner: 150/1, well held in minor event at Newcastle. *Kevin Frost* **–**

HOLY HEART (IRE) 2 b.c. (Apr 30) Holy Roman Emperor (IRE) 125 – Heart of Ice (IRE) (Montjeu (IRE) 137) [2017 t8.6d^3 Dec 9] closely related to 2 winners in Germany, including 1¼m-12.5f winner Heart Storm (by Dansili), and half-brother to 2 winners by Lope de Vega, including 7f/1m winner Alemaratalyoum: dam, French 2-y-o 9f winner, half-sister to smart French/US winner up to 1½m Fast And Furious: 13/2, third in minor event at Wolverhampton (3¾ lengths behind Mr Reckless) in December, not knocked about: sure to improve. *John Gosden* **76 p**

HOLYROMAN PRINCESS 3 b.f. Holy Roman Emperor (IRE) 125 – Princess Ellen 114 (Tirol 127) [2017 51: 10.2m 8d^5 12m 9.9g 11.6f f8.1g^5 Dec 4] little form: left Rod Millman after fifth start: usually wears headgear: often races towards rear. *Daniel Kubler* **–**

HOLY SHAMBLES (IRE) 2 b.c. (Apr 25) Holy Roman Emperor (IRE) 125 – Shim Sham (IRE) 91 (Danehill Dancer (IRE) 117) [2017 p8d^5 Dec 13] third foal: dam, 2-y-o 7f winner, sister to smart winner up to 9f Decado: 25/1, considerate introduction when fifth in minor event at Kempton (3¼ lengths behind Rusper) in December: better to come. *Marco Botti* **71 p**

HOLY TIBER (IRE) 2 b.f. (Apr 27) Holy Roman Emperor (IRE) 125 – Quiet Waters (USA) (Quiet American (USA)) [2017 5v* 6.1d^6 6.1s* 6s^4 6m^4 6g Oct 7] 20,000Y: seventh foal: half-sister to 3 winners by High Chaparral, including useful Scandinavian 1m/10.5f winner Pas de Secrets (stays 1½m) and 1½m winner Rivers Run: dam lightly raced in France: fair performer: won minor events at Doncaster in May and Nottingham in June: will stay at least 7f: acts on good to firm and heavy going. *George Scott* **79**

HOMBRE CASADO (FR) 2 b.c. (Jan 31) Siyouni (FR) 122 – Storma (FR) (Starborough 126) [2017 8.3v Nov 8] 33/1, well held in maiden at Nottingham. *Ed Walker* **–**

HOME AGAIN 4 b.g. Bahamian Bounty 116 – Celestial Welcome 96 (Most Welcome **60 §**
131) [2017 53§: p7d^{2} p6g^{3} p7d^{2} p8g^{3} p7s May 25] smallish gelding: modest maiden: stays 1m: acts on polytrack: tried in visor: usually races close up: temperamental. *Lee Carter*

HOME CUMMINS (IRE) 5 b.m. Rip Van Winkle (IRE) 134 – Alava (IRE) (Anabaa **102**
(USA) 130) [2017 102: 8m 7.9d 8.5m^{3} 8m^{6} 7.9m 8d^{4} 7.9d^{2} 8m^{2} 7.9g^{3} 8.2d^{5} Oct 30] lengthy mare: useful handicapper: second at Ripon (2 lengths behind Brilliant Vanguard) in August and third at York (3½ lengths behind Zabeel Prince) in October: stays 8.5f: acts on tapeta, good to firm and good to soft going: wears cheekpieces. *Richard Fahey*

HOME OF THE BRAVE (IRE) 5 ch.g. Starspangledbanner (AUS) 128 – Blissful Beat **119**
(Beat Hollow 126) [2017 119: 7g* 7g* 7g^{2} 7g^{3} 8f Nov 4] lengthy gelding: smart performer: won listed race at Leicester in April and Criterion Stakes at Newmarket (by ¾ length from Jungle Cat) in July: placed in Lennox Stakes at Goodwood (½-length second to Breton Rock) and Park Stakes at Doncaster (1¾ lengths third to Aclaim): last of 14 in Breeders' Cup Mile at Del Mar final outing, then gelded: stays 7f: acts on good to firm and good to soft going: wears tongue tie: usually leads. *Hugo Palmer*

HOMEOPATHIC 2 b.f. (Mar 20) Dark Angel (IRE) 113 – Holistic (Pivotal 124) [2017 **78 p**
p7g* Sep 25] second foal: half-sister to useful 6f/7f winner Diagnostic (by Dutch Art): dam unraced half-sister to smart winner up to 1¼m Cupid's Glory: 7/1, won minor event at Kempton (by neck from Odyssa with bit in hand) in September: open to improvement. *Sir Michael Stoute*

HOMERTON 2 b.c. (Mar 23) Finjaan 122 – Canis Star (Wolfhound (USA) 126) [2017 **68**
7m^{4} 8d^{4} 8d 7s^{5} t8g^{3} Oct 20] sturdy colt: fair maiden: stays 1m: acts on tapeta, soft and good to firm going: often races prominently. *Robyn Brisland*

HOMESMAN (USA) 3 b.c. War Front (USA) 119 – My Annette (USA) 78 (Red Ransom **112**
(USA)) [2017 83P: 10m^{4} 11.3m* 8g^{2} 10d* 12m^{5} 10f^{3} Jul 8] big, heavy-topped colt: smart performer: progressed to win maiden at Limerick in April and Gallinule Stakes at the Curragh (by head from Born To Play) in May: third in Belmont Derby (2¾ lengths behind Oscar Performance) final start: stays 1½m: acts on firm and good to soft going: wears headgear. *Aidan O'Brien, Ireland*

HOMING STAR 2 b.f. (Apr 1) Harbour Watch (IRE) 121 – Nightunderthestars **62**
(Observatory (USA) 131) [2017 8s p8g Nov 8] third foal: dam unraced half-sister to smart sprinter Definightly: modest form on second start in minor events. *Jonathan Portman*

HONEY BADGER 6 b.g. Pastoral Pursuits 127 – Taminoula (IRE) 82 (Tagula (IRE) 116) **75**
[2017 66§: 8m^{2} t8s^{2} p7s* p8g t7.1d* t7.1g^{3} Nov 24] fair handicapper: won at Chelmsford in September and Newcastle in November: stays 11f, races over much shorter nowadays: acts on polytrack, tapeta and firm going: wears headgear: often races prominently. *Michael Herrington*

HONEY BLOSSOM 2 b.f. (Apr 12) Makfi 130 – Seasonal Blossom (IRE) (Fairy King **–**
(USA)) [2017 6g 7d 7d^{6} Aug 11] half-sister to several winners, including useful 6f-1½m winner Brushing (by Medicean) and 1¼m-1¾m winner Wee Charlie Castle (by Sinndar): dam of little account: no form: left Mark H. Tompkins after second start: sent to Belgium. *Denis Quinn*

HONEY GG 2 b.f. (Mar 3) Mayson 124 – Local Fancy 85 (Bahamian Bounty 116) [2017 **42**
5d 6s 5s^{5} 6d^{5} Oct 30] £800Y: half-sister to several winners, including useful 5f (including at 2 yrs) winner Kyleakin Lass (by Kyllachy) and winner up to 1m Local Flier (2-y-o 5f winner, by Byron): dam 2-y-o 5f winner who stayed 7f: poor form. *Declan Carroll*

HONEYSUCKLE LIL (IRE) 5 b.m. Alfred Nobel (IRE) 110 – Twinberry (IRE) **80**
(Tagula (IRE) 116) [2017 86: 6m^{4} 6m^{4} 6m^{5} 6s^{2} 5g^{2} 5s^{4} 5.9g 6g 6s^{5} 6s^{3} 6v Sep 30] fairly useful handicapper: second at Hamilton in June: stays 7f: acts on good to firm and heavy going: wears headgear: usually races close up: sold 2,000 gns in November. *Tim Easterby*

HONG KONG JOE 7 b.g. Oasis Dream 129 – Singed (Zamindar (USA) 116) [2017 **55**
p12g^{4} p12g 12v 11m 9.9s p12g^{3} p12g p10s^{4} Dec 15] modest maiden: stays 1½m: acts on polytrack and soft going: usually wears headgear. *Lydia Richards*

HONIARA 4 b.g. Rock of Gibraltar (IRE) 133 – Indian Maiden (IRE) 115 (Indian Ridge **95**
123) [2017 84: p7g^{3} p8d^{5} p7g^{2} 7m* 8m^{2} 7m* p8g 8s^{5} p7g p7.5g^{3} Dec 19] good-topped gelding: useful handicapper: won at Brighton in June and lady riders event on same course in August: left Paul Cole before final outing: stays 1m: acts on polytrack and good to firm going: usually wears headgear: has worn tongue tie. *J-M. Capitte, France*

HONOURABLE KNIGHT (IRE) 9 b.g. Celtic Swing 138 – Deemeh (IRE) 35 (Brief Truce (USA) 126) [2017 –: p15.8g 14g 14m⁴ 16.3d 14d⁶ p12g³ Oct 17] tall gelding: modest handicapper nowadays: stays 2m: acts on polytrack and good to firm: has worn headgear: usually races prominently. *Mark Usher* **51**

HOOFALONG 7 b.g. Pastoral Pursuits 127 – Baymist 68 (Mind Games 121) [2017 107: 6g 6g 5.4d 6g 5v Sep 30] useful-looking gelding: useful handicapper, below best in 2017: stays 6.5f: acts on all-weather, soft and good to firm going: wears headgear: sometimes slowly away. *Michael Easterby* **95**

HOOF IT 10 b.g. Monsieur Bond (IRE) 120 – Forever Bond (Danetime (IRE) 121) [2017 107: 6g 6d⁶ 5.4d⁶ 6g 6d⁴ 5s⁴ Nov 8] big, strong gelding: useful handicapper: sixth in Stewards' Cup at Goodwood (1¾ lengths behind Lancelot du Lac) in August: stays 6.5f: acts on polytrack, soft and good to firm going: has worn headgear. *Michael Easterby* **104**

HOOVER FEVER 3 b.f. Compton Place 125 – Aswaaq (IRE) 74 (Peintre Celebre (USA) 137) [2017 –: 8g 14d Aug 19] no form: tried in cheekpieces: often races towards rear. *Carroll Gray* **–**

HOPE AGAINST HOPE (IRE) 3 b.f. Dark Angel (IRE) 113 – Hope of An Angel (IRE) 79 (Intikhab (USA) 135) [2017 65: 8.2g* Jun 27] well-made filly: fair handicapper: won at Leicester in June: stays 1m: best form on good going: tried in blinkers: often races prominently. *Mark Johnston* **75**

HOPE AND GLORY (IRE) 2 ch.f. (Apr 5) Dandy Man (IRE) 123 – Tashyra (IRE) 59 (Tagula (IRE) 116) [2017 5g 5m 5g⁵ 6s³ 6d t6.1g³ 5.1s p6g² t6.1g³ Oct 27] 10,000Y: half-sister to several winners, including 2-y-o 6f winner I'malwaysright (by Namid), later successful abroad, and 5f winner Simply Black (by Kheleyf): dam sprint maiden: modest maiden: stays 6f: acts on polytrack, tapeta and soft going: tried in cheekpieces: front runner/races prominently: sold 5,000 gns, sent to Norway. *Tom Dascombe* **57**

HOPE IS HIGH 4 b.f. Sir Percy 129 – Altitude 88 (Green Desert (USA) 127) [2017 62: 11.5m⁴ 11.6g⁴ 11.5m* 11.4m² 13f³ 11.5m² 11.5m* 13d* 14.1d* Sep 21] fairly useful handicapper: won at Yarmouth in June, and at same course (twice) and Bath in August/September: stays 1¾m: acts on tapeta, firm and good to soft going: tried in cheekpieces: usually responds generously to pressure. *John Berry* **88**

HOPE SOLO (IRE) 3 ch.f. Dutch Art 126 – In Safe Hands (IRE) 92 (Intikhab (USA) 135) [2017 84: 6m 6g⁴ 6.1g 6g 6m* 6d⁴ 6v³ Sep 21] rather leggy filly: fairly useful handicapper: won at Ripon (by 2¾ lengths from Pepita) in September: stays 6f: acts on good to firm and heavy going: in cheekpieces last 3 starts: sold 22,000 gns, sent to Qatar. *Tim Easterby* **91**

HORNBY 2 b.g. (Apr 2) Equiano (FR) 127 – Kindia (IRE) 78 (Cape Cross (IRE) 129) [2017 6m p6g p5g⁵ p5g⁶ Dec 12] modest form. *Michael Attwater* **53**

HORROOB 3 b.c. Showcasing 117 – Funny Enough 64 (Dansili 127) [2017 78p: p7g* p7g* 7g⁴ 8m t7.1g² 7.9g Aug 25] well-made colt: useful performer: won maiden at Lingfield in April and handicap there in May: stays 7f: acts on polytrack and tapeta: often travels strongly: sent to UAE. *Roger Varian* **98**

HORS DE COMBAT 6 ch.g. Mount Nelson 125 – Maid For Winning (USA) (Gone West (USA)) [2017 108: 8g² 8.9g³ 8m² 7m 8m 8m⁴ 8d² 8s Oct 21] strong gelding: smart performer: placed in handicaps at Meydan (2) and Bath (neck second to Oh This Is Us), and listed race at Sandown: stays 9f: acts on polytrack, firm and good to soft going: tried in blinkers: hard to win with. *Denis Coakley* **110**

HORSEGUARDSPARADE 6 b.g. Montjeu (IRE) 137 – Honorlina (FR) (Linamix (FR) 127) [2017 73: f12m⁶ Feb 21] fair handicapper, missed break sole start on Flat in 2017: stays 2m: acts on fibresand, tapeta and heavy going: usually wears cheekpieces: usually races nearer last than first: maiden hurdler/chaser. *Nigel Twiston-Davies* **58**

HORSEPLAY 3 b.f. Cape Cross (IRE) 129 – Mischief Making (USA) 101 (Lemon Drop Kid (USA) 131) [2017 97p: 10m* 12m⁴ 11.9g⁴ 12s Oct 21] sturdy filly: useful performer: won listed race at Newmarket (by ¾ length from Isabel de Urbina) in May: fourth after in Oaks at Epsom (14¾ lengths behind Enable) and Prix de Malleret at Saint-Cloud (beaten 2¼ lengths by Strathspey): stays 1½m: acts on good to firm and good to soft going. *Andrew Balding* **107**

HORSFORTH 5 b.m. Kyllachy 129 – Lady McBeth (IRE) (Avonbridge 123) [2017 79: t5g² t5g³ 5m⁴ t5s⁴ t5s* 5g 5d⁵ Jul 9] fair handicapper: won at Newcastle in June: stays 5.5f: acts on polytrack, tapeta, good to firm and good to soft going: wears headgear. *Richard Guest* **76**

HORSTED KEYNES (FR) 7 ch.g. Giant's Causeway (USA) 132 – Viking's Cove (USA) (Miswaki (USA) 124) [2017 88: t7.1g p8g^3 t7.1g^3 p7g^3 p8d 7m^2 7m^3 7m^2 7m* t7.1g^3 7d^4 7m^3 t7.2g^3 Sep 9] sturdy gelding: useful handicapper: won at Yarmouth (by neck from Brigliadoro) in June: also placed on 9 occasions: stays 1m: acts on polytrack, tapeta and good to firm going: has worn headgear: usually races towards rear. *David Simcock* **101**

HOT BEAT (IRE) 5 b.g. Dylan Thomas (IRE) 132 – Hungry Heart (IRE) (Hawk Wing (USA) 136) [2017 97: t12.2m* t16.3g^3 14g t16.3s 12s^4 Aug 9] useful handicapper: won at Wolverhampton in January: stays 16.5f: acts on tapeta: tried in hood: usually races in rear: has joined W. P. Mullins. *David Simcock* **102**

HOTFILL 3 b.g. Showcasing 117 – Reel Cool (Reel Buddy (USA) 118) [2017 65, a73: t7.1m^5 t7.1g^2 t6d^6 8g 6.9g^5 May 22] fair maiden: stays 7f: acts on tapeta: tried in hood. *David Barron* **69**

HOT GOSSIP (IRE) 3 b.f. Fast Company (IRE) 126 – On The Make (IRE) (Entrepreneur 123) [2017 –: t10.2g 7g 12g 11.2v^6 Sep 18] poor maiden. *Dianne Sayer* **43**

HOT HANNAH 3 gr.f. Hellvelyn 118 – Toy Top (USA) 86 (Tactical Cat (USA) 116) [2017 74: 5g^6 6g t5s^5 5d 5d* 5s^2 5d 5g Sep 27] fair handicapper: won at Ayr (apprentice) in July: best form at 5f: acts on soft going: has worn headgear: usually races close up. *Michael Dods* **75**

HOT LICK 3 b.g. Phoenix Reach (IRE) 124 – Sweet Mandolin (Soviet Star (USA) 128) [2017 –: p12g^3 t12.2g 12d May 16] modest maiden: left Andrew Balding after second start: best effort at 1½m: acts on polytrack: often in hood: tried in tongue tie: sometimes slowly away, often races towards rear. *Dan Skelton* **57**

HOT MUSTARD 7 b.g. Pastoral Pursuits 127 – Lihou Island 89 (Beveled (USA)) [2017 78: 8f^2 10.2f^4 8m^5 8f^6 8m 8d^5 p8g^4 p7s t8.6g* t8.6g Nov 18] angular gelding: fair handicapper: won at Wolverhampton in October: stays 9f: acts on polytrack, tapeta, firm and soft going: usually wears headgear. *William Muir* **68**

HOT NATURED (IRE) 3 b.f. Canford Cliffs (IRE) 133 – Teddy Bears Picnic (Oasis Dream 129) [2017 t8d^2 t8g^5 f8g Apr 16] £65,000Y: fifth foal: half-sister to 3 winners, including 6f/7f winner (including at 2 yrs) Nezar (by Mastercraftsman) and 1m winner Ottilie (by High Chaparral): dam unraced: fair form: best effort when second in maiden at Newcastle in February. *K. R. Burke* **70**

HOT OFF THE PRESS (IRE) 2 b.f. (Mar 24) Camelot 128 – Jewel In The Sand (IRE) 107 (Bluebird (USA) 125) [2017 8.3d p8g Nov 8] 38,000Y: closely related to useful 9.5f-10.5f winner Falkirk (by Montjeu) and half-sister to several winners, including useful 1¼m winner Bedouin (by High Chaparral): dam 5f/6f winner (including at 2 yrs): modest form. *Michael Bell* **59**

HOT ROCK (IRE) 2 ch.g. (Feb 26) Society Rock (IRE) 126 – Red Roar (IRE) 77 (Chineur (FR) 123) [2017 5m^4 5f^6 6m May 22] modest form: best effort when fourth in minor event at Beverley (4¾ lengths behind Bengali Boys) in April: should stay 6f. *Bryan Smart* **63**

HOT STUFF 4 b.g. Assertive 121 – Even Hotter 63 (Desert Style (IRE) 121) [2017 64: p5g* p5g^3 p5g^6 p5f^5 p5s^3 5.1g 5.2m^6 p8g p5g Dec 15] useful-looking gelding: fair performer: won maiden at Lingfield in February: lost form later in year: left Tony Carroll after seventh start, Damian Joseph English after eighth: best form at 5f: acts on polytrack, tapeta and good to soft going: sometimes in headgear: tried in tongue tie. *James McAuley, Ireland* **65 d**

HOULTON 2 ch.c. (Mar 4) Declaration of War (USA) 128 – Greek Goddess (IRE) 87 (Galileo (IRE) 134) [2017 t9.5g p8g Dec 20] well held in 2 minor events: wears tongue tie. *Marco Botti* –

HOURGLASS (IRE) 2 b.f. (May 13) Galileo (IRE) 134 – Helsinki (Machiavellian (USA) 123) [2017 8d^6 Oct 24] closely related to French 1½m winner Shamarbelle and smart 2-y-o 1m (Beresford Stakes) winner Geoffrey Chaucer (both by Montjeu) and half-sister to several winners, notably high-class winner up to 10.5f (Prix du Jockey Club) Shamardal (2-y-o 6f/7f winner, by Giant's Causeway): dam, French 1¼m winner, sister to Dubai World Cup winner Street Cry: 7/1, sixth in minor event at Yarmouth (6½ lengths behind Lady of Shalott) in October: will stay at least 1¼m: will do better. *Marco Botti* **63 p**

HOUSE EDGE 2 gr.c. (Mar 12) Nathaniel (IRE) 129 – Bezique 97 (Cape Cross (IRE) 129) [2017 8g^5 8.9s* Oct 1] 85,000Y: second foal: half-brother to smart winner up to 11f Khalidi (2-y-o 1m winner, by High Chaparral): dam Italian winner up to 1m (2-y-o 7.5f winner): useful form: won minor event at Musselburgh (by 5 lengths from Lynwood Gold) in October: will be suited by 1¼m+: will go on improving. *Michael Bell* **98 p**

HOUSE OF COMMONS (IRE) 4 b.g. Sea The Stars (IRE) 140 – Reality (FR) (Slickly (FR) 128) [2017 82: f8g* p10g5 t9.5g5 f8g5 8g3 8.3m 8.3g 10s4 8d 11.4d6 8.1s2 10g4 f8.1g3 Oct 22] tallish, lean gelding: fair handicapper on turf, fairly useful on all-weather: won at Southwell (by 2½ lengths from Anton Chigurh) in January: stays 8.5f: acts on fibresand, tapeta, soft and good to firm going: tried in headgear: front runner/races prominently: sold 14,000 gns in October. *Michael Appleby* **79 a85**

HOUSE OF FRAUDS (IRE) 9 b.g. Storming Home 128 – Bogus Penny (IRE) 80 (Pennekamp (USA) 130) [2017 –: t7.1g f7g 12d 11.9d Sep 18] no form. *Tony Newcombe* **–**

HOWARDIAN HILLS (IRE) 4 b.g. Vale of York (IRE) 117 – Handsome Anna (IRE) 67 (Bigstone (IRE) 126) [2017 65: 11.8g t12.2g* p12d p12g2 12s p12g t14g5 p16g Dec 20] fair performer: won claimer at Wolverhampton in July: stays 1¾m: acts on polytrack and tapeta: often wears headgear. *Victor Dartnall* **67**

HOWBAAR (USA) 2 b.g. (Mar 23) Lonhro (AUS) 128 – Going Day (USA) (Daylami (IRE) 138) [2017 t7.1d Oct 24] 33/1, well held in minor event at Newcastle. *James Bethell* **–**

HOW BIZARRE 2 ch.g. (May 5) Society Rock (IRE) 126 – Amanda Carter 92 (Tobougg (IRE) 125) [2017 7.2m4 7.4s4 7g4 Oct 7] 15,000Y: fourth foal: half-brother to 7f winners Salateen (smart, and including at 2 yrs, by Dutch Art) and Hajjam (by Paco Boy): dam, 9f-13f winner, also won over hurdles: modest form: best effort when fourth in minor event at Musselburgh (3¾ lengths behind Arabian Jazz) in September: may prove best up to 7f: remains open to improvement. *Kevin Ryan* **64 p**

HOW'S LUCY 3 b.f. Approve (IRE) 112 – Murielle 68 (Diktat 126) [2017 56: p8g 7m2 p8g5 p7g6 p8s3 p8s3 Dec 17] modest maiden: stays 1m: acts on polytrack and good to firm going: usually races prominently. *Jane Chapple-Hyam* **63**

HUDDERSFILLY TOWN 3 b.f. Major Cadeaux 121 – Mortitia 97 (Dansili 127) [2017 50: p6g4 f7g p7g t8g5 t9.5g6 p12g6 p10s* p10s4 p10s* Dec 17] fair handicapper: won at Chelmsford in November and December: stays 1½m: acts on polytrack and tapeta: in cheekpieces last 3 starts: often races towards rear. *Ivan Furtado* **66**

HUGGING THE RAILS (IRE) 3 b.g. Royal Applause 124 – Aqraan 100 (In The Wings 128) [2017 62: 8g4 9.9g5 10.2f May 26] modest maiden: stays 1m: acts on heavy going: tried in blinkers: often races towards rear. *Tim Easterby* **59**

HUGIE BOY (IRE) 5 ch.g. Art Connoisseur (IRE) 121 – Piece Unique (Barathea (IRE) 127) [2017 –: f7.1g f7.1g f6.1g3 f6.1g6 f6.1g Dec 29] modest handicapper: stays 6f: acts on fibresand and good to firm going: wears headgear: usually wears tongue tie. *Scott Dixon* **56**

HUGIN (IRE) 3 b.g. Henrythenavigator (USA) 131 – Silver Star 105 (Zafonic (USA) 130) [2017 76: t7.1g* 8m3 10.5m4 8g* 8g2 8d2 Sep 21] half-brother to numerous winners, including smart 1¼m-1½m winner Barsanti (by Champs Elysees) and dam of very smart US Grade 1 8.5f/9f winner Close Hatches: dam, French 2-y-o 1m winner, sister to Dewhurst Stakes winner Xaar: useful performer: won maiden at Newcastle in May and handicap at Redcar in August: stays 1m: acts on tapeta, good to firm and good to soft going: usually travels strongly: sold 130,000 gns in October. *David Simcock* **99**

HUGOIGO 3 b.g. Sulamani (IRE) 130 – Gargoyle Girl 75 (Be My Chief (USA) 122) [2017 10m5 12s5 10d5 Jul 9] modest form. *Jim Goldie* **51**

HUGS AND PATS 2 b.g. (Apr 8) Big Bad Bob (IRE) 118 – Zambujeiro (Dutch Art 126) [2017 5f5 Jun 23] 11/4, shaped as if amiss when well held in maiden at Bath. *Dean Ivory* **–**

HULA GIRL 2 gr.f. (Mar 15) Oasis Dream 129 – Tropical Paradise (IRE) 116 (Verglas (IRE) 118) [2017 6s4 7d5 6g Nov 3] 120,000Y: third foal: half-sister to 6f/7f winner Coral Sea (by Excelebration): dam winner up to 7f (2-y-o 6f winner): fairly useful form: best effort when seventh in listed race at Newmarket (3¾ lengths behind Alwasmiya) in November. *Charles Hills* **88**

HUMAN NATURE (IRE) 4 b.g. Kodiac 112 – Sundown 71 (Polish Precedent (USA) 131) [2017 84: 6g6 6m5 p7d* 7d4 p7g p7g2 p7s2 p6s* Dec 15] compact gelding: fairly useful handicapper on turf, useful on all-weather: won at Kempton (apprentice) in July and Chelmsford (by 1¼ lengths from Nautical Haven) in December: stays 7f: acts on polytrack, firm and soft going: tried in cheekpieces: wears tongue tie: front runner/races prominently. *Stuart Williams* **81 a101**

HUMBERT (IRE) 3 b.g. Kodiac 112 – Fee Eria (FR) (Always Fair (USA) 121) [2017 82p: p8d* Dec 13] fairly useful form: won maiden at Kempton (by 4½ lengths from Maximinus Thrax) in December: stays 1m: tried in cheekpieces: open to further improvement. *Hugo Palmer* **89 p**

HUMBLE GRATITUDE 2 ch.g. (May 3) Foxwedge (AUS) 128 – Gilt Linked 85 (Compton Place 125) [2017 6f^4 6g^2 6d* 6.5g Sep 14] 58,000Y: seventh foal: half-brother to smart 5f-7f winner (including at 2 yrs) Lincoln (by Clodovil) and 5f/6f winner Operative (by Pastoral Pursuits): dam, 2-y-o 5f winner, half-sister to smart performer up to 1¼m Chil The Kite: fairly useful form: won minor event at Hamilton (by 1¾ lengths from Up Sticks And Go) in September: raced around 6f: tried in cheekpieces. *K. R. Burke* **89**

HUMBLE HERO (IRE) 3 b.g. High Chaparral (IRE) 132 – Alamouna (IRE) 85 (Indian Ridge 123) [2017 11.9m^2 11.6g^2 11.9m* 14m^4 t12.4g* 12m Oct 13] 300,000Y: strong gelding: sixth foal: closely related to useful French/US 1m/9f winner Almoradi (by Barathea) and half-brother to French 11f winner Almadan (by Azamour): dam, 1¼m winner, half-sister to smart performer up to 1¼m Alasha: useful performer: won maiden at Doncaster in June and handicap at Newcastle in September: stays 1¾m: acts on tapeta and good to firm going: usually races towards rear. *William Haggas* **100**

HUMBOLT CURRENT 2 b.c. (Feb 23) Fastnet Rock (AUS) 127 – Humdrum 101 (Dr Fong (USA) 128) [2017 7g^2 Oct 16] third foal: closely related to 1m winner Elementary (by Exceed And Excel) and half-brother to 2-y-o 6f winner Husbandry (by Paco Boy): dam, 7f/1m winner (including at 2 yrs), half-sister to smart 6f winner Musical Comedy: 12/1, promise when second in minor event at Yarmouth (2½ lengths behind Willie John) in October: will be suited by 1m: sure to do better. *William Haggas* **83 p**

HUMOUR (IRE) 6 b.g. Invincible Spirit (IRE) 121 – Hucking Hot 102 (Desert Prince (IRE) 130) [2017 63: p6g^6 p6d t7.1g 5.2m 7m^6 p7s^3 6m 7g p7s Jul 25] modest on all-weather, poor on turf nowadays: stays 7f: acts on polytrack, tapeta and good to soft going: wears headgear: tried in tongue tie: temperament under suspicion. *Christine Dunnett* **44 a56**

HUNGARIAN RHAPSODY 3 b.g. Exceed And Excel (AUS) 126 – Sharp Terms (Kris 135) [2017 p6g^5 f5g^2 f6g^2 7.4g^4 t6.1g^5 Aug 11] 80,000Y: brother to smart 2-y-o 5f/6f (including Queen Mary/Lowther Stakes) winner Best Terms and 5f/6f winner Miracle Garden, and half-brother to 3 winners, including 1¼m/11f winner Sunsemperchi (by Montjeu): dam unraced: fair maiden: stays 7.5f: acts on fibresand: remains capable of better. *Jamie Osborne* **65 p**

HUNNI 2 b.f. (Mar 25) Captain Gerrard (IRE) 113 – Lady O Malley (IRE) 89 (Oratorio (IRE) 128) [2017 p6g 5m^5 5.1m^2 6d* 6g Oct 7] compact filly: first foal: dam, 9f winner, half-sister to useful 1m-10.7f winner Nice Style: fair performer: won nursery at Newmarket in August: stays 6f: acts on good to firm and good to soft going: usually races prominently. *Tom Clover* **78**

HUNTSMANS CLOSE 7 b.g. Elusive Quality (USA) – Badminton 106 (Zieten (USA) 118) [2017 102: 5d^6 p5s 6g^2 6m^3 6m^5 6d Oct 27] lengthy gelding: useful handicapper: second at Epsom (short head behind Highland Acclaim) in July: races at 5f/6f: acts on polytrack and any turf going: has worn hood, including last 4 starts: sold 18,000 gns in October. *Robert Cowell* **96**

HURRICANE ALERT 5 b.g. Showcasing 117 – Raggle Taggle (IRE) 95 (Tagula (IRE) 116) [2017 52: p5g p5d^6 p5g^2 p5g^4 p6g^4 p5g^2 5.2m* 5.7f^6 5.3g^2 5d^4 5.2m 5.3g 6s Sep 4] modest handicapper: won at Yarmouth in April: best at 5f: acts on polytrack, good to firm and good to soft going: has worn visor: tried in tongue tie: often races towards rear. *Mark Hoad* **63 a55**

HURRICANE HOLLOW 7 b.g. Beat Hollow 126 – Veenwouden 107 (Desert Prince (IRE) 130) [2017 t10.2g^5 t12.2g 12s^3 12d^2 15.9m^5 12d^5 11.6g^3 11.8v^4 15v^2 15.9s^3 f16.5g^5 Nov 13] fair maiden: stays 15f: acts on heavy going: sometimes slowly away, often races towards rear: useful hurdler at best, and has rejoined Dan Skelton. *David Barron* **79**

HURRICANE LIL (IRE) 2 b.f. (Apr 20) Big Bad Bob (IRE) 118 – Ladylishandra (IRE) 82 (Mujadil (USA) 119) [2017 6s 6g^6 7.1s 7s^5 p8g^6 p8m^3 p7g Dec 6] 20,000Y: half-sister to several winners, including smart winner up to 7f Tropical Paradise (2-y-o 6f winner, by Verglas), smart Italian 5f/6f winner Harlem Shake (by Moss Vale) and useful winner up to 1m Shenanigans (2-y-o 7f winner, by Arcano): dam 2-y-o 6f winner: modest maiden: best effort at 1m: tried in blinkers. *George Baker* **58**

HURRICANE ROCK 4 ch.g. Rock of Gibraltar (IRE) 133 – Seasonal Cross 80 (Cape Cross (IRE) 129) [2017 60: p6g p7m 6d^4 7d 7s t7.2g t6.1g* p6g^2 t6.1g^5 Oct 27] modest handicapper: won at Wolverhampton in August: stays 6f: acts on polytrack and tapeta. *Simon Dow* **60**

HURRICANE VOLTA (IRE) 6 ch.g. Hurricane Run (IRE) 134 – Haute Volta (FR) –
(Grape Tree Road 122) [2017 74: 11.6d^3 Jun 24] fair handicapper, well held sole start in 2017: stays 2m: acts on polytrack, tapeta and good to firm going: wears headgear. *Peter Hedger*

HUSHOOD (IRE) 3 b.c. Champs Elysees 124 – Cochin (USA) (Swain (IRE) 134) [2017 **101**
89: 11.7m* Apr 14] good-topped colt: useful form: won handicap at Bath (by head from Mister Manduro) in April: stayed 11.5f: dead. *Richard Hannon*

HUSSAR BALLAD (USA) 8 b.g. Hard Spun (USA) 124 – Country Melody (USA) **67**
(Gone West (USA)) [2017 76: t12.2g^4 t12.2g^3 t10.2s^3 t12.2g^3 12.3d 9.9s^4 10d t12.2g* **a76**
t12.2g^4 t12.4g^4 t10.2g^6 t14g* t12.2g Dec 2] strong gelding: fair handicapper: won at Wolverhampton in September and October: stays 1¾m: acts on fibresand, tapeta, best turf form on good going. *Antony Brittain*

HUSTLE (IRE) 12 ch.g. Choisir (AUS) 126 – Granny Kelly (USA) 60 (Irish River (FR) –
131) [2017 p8g 8m Jun 30] fairly useful at best, well held only 2 starts on Flat since 2010: has worn headgear/tongue tie. *Clare Hobson*

HYANNA 2 b.f. (Apr 7) Champs Elysees 124 – Highly Spiced (Cadeaux Genereux 131) **61**
[2017 7.4s^3 8v^4 7.9g 8v^5 Oct 23] 15,000Y: rather lightly-made filly: third foal: half-sister to French 5f-9f winner (including at 2 yrs) Rainbow Black (by Kheleyf): dam unraced: modest form: bred to stay beyond 1m. *Tim Easterby*

HYDEANDSEEK (FR) 3 b.f. Mullionmileanhour (IRE) 116 – Retainage (USA) (Polish –
Numbers (USA)) [2017 6d^3 7d^5 7s^5 Jul 29] sturdy filly: little form in maidens: dead. *John Best*

HYDE PARK 3 b.g. Oasis Dream 129 – Deliberate (King's Best (USA) 132) [2017 95: 7g^3 **106**
8m 6g 7m* 7d^5 7d 7g^3 Oct 17] compact gelding: useful handicapper: won at Yarmouth (by 1¼ lengths from Firefright) in August: stays 7f: acts on good to firm and good to soft going: tried in cheekpieces: tongue tied last 4 starts: sold 210,000 gns, sent to UAE. *John Gosden*

HYDRANGEA (IRE) 3 b.f. Galileo (IRE) 134 – Beauty Is Truth (IRE) 114 (Pivotal **123**
124) [2017 112: 7d* 8m 8d^3 8m^3 9.9v^4 8d* 9.9d^2 12s* Oct 21]

Ballydoyle housed another outstanding collection of three-year-old fillies in the latest season and, with them meeting (and beating) each other regularly in the big races, the exact pecking order took some time to establish itself. The three major autumn championship meetings in Europe, Irish Champions' Weekend, Arc Weekend and British Champions' Day, provided the stage for late-blooming Hydrangea to move herself up a few places, in the process tackling Group 1s over three different distances at those headline meetings. Starting the season at Ballydoyle as 'number 4' behind Rhododendron (to whom Hydrangea had come second in the Moyglare and the Fillies' Mile) and also behind the Cheveley Park first and second Brave Anna and Roly Poly, Hydrangea narrowly beat new recruit Winter (with other stablemates Promise To Be True and Rain Goddess behind) in the One Thousand Guineas Trial at Leopardstown in early-April to book her place in the field for the One Thousand Guineas at Newmarket. She seemed to have claims for making the frame at least but managed only tenth as Winter pulled off something of a surprise to win from hot favourite Rhododendron. Hydrangea finished behind all-conquering Winter on her next three outings too, making the frame in the Irish One Thousand Guineas at the Curragh, the Coronation Stakes at Royal Ascot (in both of which Roly Poly also beat her, finishing a place ahead) and the Nassau Stakes at Goodwood.

Hydrangea went into the Coolmore Fastnet Rock Matron Stakes at Leopardstown on Irish Champions' Weekend as still the only filly to have beaten Winter during the season (though their true relationship seemed to have been firmly established since). As in all the major races at Ireland's big autumn championship meeting, Ballydoyle was strongly represented in the Matron over a mile with hot favourite Winter, Roly Poly and the returning Rhododendron (not seen since bursting a blood vessel when beaten in the Prix de Diane after coming second in the Oaks) all starting considerably shorter than Hydrangea who was a 20/1-shot. Prominently-ridden Hydrangea foiled Winter's bid for a fifth successive Group 1 victory, achieving her own Group 1 breakthrough by battling back gamely after looking held by Winter entering the final furlong. The winning margin was a head, with British challenger Persuasive (second the previous year) and Wuheida, both of whom went on to frank the form, close up in third and fourth. Roly Poly (winner of Group 1s

Coolmore Fastnet Rock Matron Stakes, Leopardstown—having finished behind stablemate Winter (rail) on each of her last four starts, Hydrangea (No.6) produces a career best to make the breakthrough at Group 1 level, battling back well to get the better of her old rival and the grey Persuasive; also pictured are Wuheida and Roly Poly (striped cap)

on her two previous starts) and the considerately-handled Rhododendron finished sixth and seventh in an excellent, international field which must have delighted the organisers of Irish Champions' Weekend which was in its fourth year.

Trainer Aidan O'Brien's reaction to the unexpected win in the Matron of the seemingly exposed Hydrangea was a throwaway 'Nothing surprises me any more.' He made excuses for Winter, saying that she had been held up in her work at home, and the stable's top filly went on to contest the Prix de l'Arc de Triomphe in which Ryan Moore chose to ride her from Ballydoyle's multiple entry. Moore also elected to partner Hydrangea, rather than Rhododendron, in the Prix de l'Opera at the same meeting but Hydrangea found her stablemate—gaining her first win of the year—just too strong, keeping on gamely but unable to get back up after being headed by Rhododendron over a furlong out, and going down by a head. The improved Lady Frankel and Wuheida completed the frame in a race in which there wasn't much between the principals at the line. The Prix de l'Opera is over a mile and a quarter, a trip Hydrangea had shown to be within her compass in the Nassau, and she was stepped up again, to a mile and a half for the first time, in the Qipco British Champions Fillies' And Mares' Stakes, the weakest of the Group 1s on British Champions' Day at Ascot in the absence, in particular, of Enable, Winter and Roly Poly who, between them, had won the six designated races in the fillies and mares category in the British Champions' Series leading up to Champions' Day (Winter had won the One Thousand Guineas, the Coronation and the Nassau, Enable the Oaks and Yorkshire Oaks, and Roly Poly the Falmouth). The first and second in the Prix Vermeille, Bateel and Journey (winner of the Fillies' and Mares' the previous year), started at shorter odds than Hydrangea whose stable, unusually, wasn't 'mob-handed', 66/1-shot Wild Irish Rose being its only other runner (Winter wasn't seen out after finishing ninth to Enable in the Arc and Roly Poly and Rhododendron were both in reserve for the Breeders' Cup—where Rhododendron came second to Wuheida in the Filly & Mare Turf). Hydrangea showed herself better than ever at Ascot, seeming to relish the extra distance and finding extra after being waited with and leading two furlongs out. She won by two lengths and a length and three quarters from Bateel and the Ribblesdale winner and Yorkshire Oaks runner-up Coronet (Journey managed only sixth on the softest ground she had encountered). The Fillies' And Mares' Stakes was Hydrangea's eighth outing of the year and she had been on the go since the very start of the turf season. Her victory gave her trainer his twenty-fifth Group/Grade 1 of the year which took him level with the record set

Qipco British Champions Fillies' And Mares' Stakes, Ascot—
Hydrangea stays on strongly to beat Prix Vermeille winner Bateel and Ribblesdale winner Coronet; the win is a 25th at Group 1 level for Aidan O'Brien in 2017, equalling the world record for a calendar year set by American trainer Bobby Frankel in 2003

by American Bobby Frankel in 2003 (O'Brien went on to set a new mark of twenty-eight and there is more about his training achievements in the latest season in the essay on Highland Reel).

Hydrangea (IRE) (b.f. 2014)	Galileo (IRE) (b 1998)	Sadler's Wells (b 1981)	Northern Dancer
			Fairy Bridge
		Urban Sea (ch 1989)	Miswaki
			Allegretta
	Beauty Is Truth (IRE) (b 2004)	Pivotal (ch 1993)	Polar Falcon
			Fearless Revival
		Zelding (b 1995)	Warning
			Zelda

Hydrangea wasn't carrying a lot of condition by the time she ran in the Fillies' And Mares' Stakes, perhaps understandable after her long season, but she is an attractive filly who will be a valuable addition to the ranks of the Coolmore broodmares when the time comes to retire her. Her dam Beauty Is Truth, a smart five-furlong sprinter who won the Prix du Gros-Chene at three for Robert Collet, was acquired by one of the Coolmore syndicates after her racing days and has been a regular visitor to Galileo over the years. Her first mating, though, was with Dansili, to whom she produced the smart five- to-six-furlong winner Fire Lily. Her clutch of Galileo foals include two others who won at a mile and a half or further, the very smart The United States who won the Group 1 Ranvet Stakes over a mile and a quarter and the mile and a half Moonee Valley Gold Cup after being exported to Australia, and the useful Buonarroti, who has been successful at up to one mile seven furlongs. Hydrangea's family descends from the prolific Kilfrush Stud foundation mare Mill Princess, a half-sister to Irish Derby winner Irish Ball and to Irish Bird who bred two Prix du Jockey Club winners Bikala and Assert (who also won the Irish Derby) and an Irish St Leger winner Eurobird. Mill Princess herself was the dam of the versatile Last Tycoon, a champion sprinter who ended his career winning the Breeders' Cup Mile for Collet. Among the daughters of Mill Princess were the winning sprinter Save Me The Waltz, who became the dam of Poule d'Essai des Pouliches winner Valentine Waltz, and the listed winner at a mile Side of Paradise, the dam of Prix Jacques le Marois and Coronation Stakes winner Immortal Verse who held the European record for a filly or mare in training sold at auction (4.7m guineas) until Marsha went through the ring at the latest December Sales. Kilfrush Stud retained Zelda, a minor sprint winner out of Mill Princess, and she bred them the consistent French sprinter Zipping, a Prix Robert Papin winner, and the Prix du Bois winner Zelding (who was third in the Robert Papin), among others. Zelding is the grandam of Hydrangea, as well as being the dam of Poule d'Essai des Pouliches runner-up and Prix de Diane third Glorious Sight, in addition to Beauty Is Truth. Beauty Is Truth is not the only Coolmore mare by Pivotal (the sire of Immortal Verse) to have had great success crossed with Galileo. Halfway To Heaven is the dam of the sisters Rhododendron and the smart two-year-old Magical. The tough and resolute Hydrangea stays a mile and a half and acts on good to firm and heavy going. She wears cheekpieces and usually races prominently. She remains in training. *Aidan O'Brien, Ireland*

HYDRANT 11 b.g. Haafhd 129 – Spring 112 (Sadler's Wells (USA) 132) [2017 69: p10g p12g6 t10.2d p10g5 t10.2g p10gpu Mar 11] strong, good-bodied gelding: modest handicapper nowadays: stays 16.5f, effective at much shorter: acts on all-weather, good to firm and heavy going: tried in eyeshields: usually races close up. *Richard Guest* **61**

HYDROXIDE 3 b.g. Lope de Vega (IRE) 125 – Craighall 66 (Dubawi (IRE) 129) [2017 87: t6g3 7s5 7g3 9.9g* 8g7 Dec 21] fairly useful performer: left Hugo Palmer 45,000 gns in July: won maiden at Doha in November: stays 1¼m: acts on soft and good to firm going: tried in blinkers: often wears tongue tie: often races prominently. *Jassim Mohammed G. Jahromi, Qatar* **83**

HYLAND HEATHER (IRE) 4 b.f. Lilbourne Lad (IRE) 111 – Maidservant (USA) (Seeking The Gold (USA)) [2017 83: t7.1g5 p7g Mar 3] fairly useful performer, below that level in 2017: left Richard Fahey after first start: should stay 7f: acts on soft and good to firm going: sometimes in cheekpieces. *J. J. Feane, Ireland* **59**

HYMN FOR THE DUDES 4 br.g. Sakhee's Secret 128 – Hermione's Dream (Oasis Dream 129) [2017 61: t8.6m t8.6g3 p10g 8m2 Jun 30] compact gelding: modest maiden: left John Berry after third start: stays 8.5f: acts on tapeta and good to firm going: tried in cheekpieces: often in tongue tie: usually travels strongly. *L. Smyth, Ireland* **60**

HYPERFOCUS (IRE) 3 b.g. Intense Focus (USA) 117 – Jouel (FR) (Machiavellian (USA) 123) [2017 88: p6g6 5g3 6m4 6d6 6s* 6v* 6d Oct 27] useful-looking gelding: useful handicapper: won at Haydock (twice, by 2¼ lengths from Letmestopyouthere second occasion) in September: stays 6f: acts on tapeta and heavy going: often races prominently. *Hugo Palmer* **106**

HYPERLINK (IRE) 8 b.g. Cape Cross (IRE) 129 – Surf The Web (IRE) (Ela-Mana-Mou 132) [2017 68: t13.9g Feb 15] big, strong gelding: fair handicapper at best, down the field on sole start in 2017: stayed 16.5f: acted on polytrack, tapeta, good to firm and heavy going: tried in headgear/tongue tie: dead. *Clare Ellam* **–**

HYPERLOOP 3 br.c. So You Think (NZ) 133 – Fabulous Speed (USA) (Silver Hawk (USA) 123) [2017 p7g3 8.1m2 p8s2 p8s* Sep 30] 70,000F, 100,000Y: strong, rangy colt: half-brother to several winners abroad, including useful Italian/US winner up to 8.5f Facoltoso (2-y-o 6f winner, by Refuse To Bend): dam, French 9f-1½m winner, half-sister to dam of high-class miler Solow: fairly useful form: won maiden at Chelmsford (by 3¼ lengths from Ifubelieveindreams) in September: stays 1m: sold 45,000 gns in October, sent to Saudi Arabia: should improve further. *William Haggas* **88 p**

HYPNOTIC DANCER (IRE) 2 b.f. (Apr 8) Sir Prancealot (IRE) 111 – Red Trance (IRE) 79 (Soviet Star (USA) 128) [2017 t5.1g 5m5 5m4 t5.1g2 5d6 t6g Oct 19] £15,000Y: half-sister to several winners, including 2-y-o 5f winner Kodi da Capo (by Kodiac) and 1½m winner Hypnotic Gaze (by Chevalier): dam 2-y-o 5f winner: modest maiden: best effort at 5f: acts on tapeta: tried in tongue tie: sold 800 gns, sent to Italy. *Keith Dalgleish* **53**

I

I AM DANDY (IRE) 2 b.c. (Mar 23) Dandy Man (IRE) 123 – Acushladear (IRE) 99 (Tagula (IRE) 116) [2017 5g5 t6g 5m5 6f t5.1g 7.2m5 Aug 31] modest maiden. *James Ewart* **53**

I AM NOT HERE (IRE) 6 b.g. Amadeus Wolf 122 – Newgate Lodge (IRE) 101 (Namid 128) [2017 94: 8.2s6 11.2s t16.3s Jul 1] workmanlike gelding: fairly useful handicapper: stays 13f: acts on polytrack, tapeta and any turf going: hurdling in USA. *Brian Ellison* **89**

IBALLISTICVIN 4 b.g. Rail Link 132 – Guntakal (IRE) (Night Shift (USA)) [2017 75: p11d6 10m3 11.6d3 11.6s* p13.3g4 p12g2 p11g* Oct 24] sturdy gelding: fairly useful handicapper: won at Lingfield in August and Kempton (by 1¾ lengths from Abel Tasman) in October: stays 13.5f: acts on polytrack, good to firm and heavy going: often travels strongly. *Gary Moore* **81**

IBAZZ 4 br.f. Kyllachy 129 – Quite Elusive (USA) (Elusive Quality (USA)) [2017 p7g t7.1d^{5} p10d 11.4d 8m 10m t8.6g^{2} p8g^{5} t8g* p7g^{5} Oct 26] tall filly: sixth foal: half-sister to 1m winner Quadrant (by Shamardal) and a winner in Germany by Teofilo: dam unraced: fairly useful handicapper: won twice in France for A. & G. Botti in 2016: also won at Newcastle (by ½ length from Table Manners) in September: left Archie Watson after third start: best up to 1m: acts on polytrack, tapeta, best turf form on good going: in headgear last 2 starts: sometimes slowly away: sold 15,000 gns in October. *Ian Williams* **84**

IBERICA ROAD (USA) 4 b.g. Quality Road (USA) 131 – Field of Clover (CAN) (Bluegrass Cat (USA) 120) [2017 86: p10g 10m^{6} 7m^{4} 7.4m* 10.2d t7.1d^{5} Aug 10] workmanlike gelding: fairly useful at 3 yrs, below that level in 2017: won seller at Beverley (dead-heated) in July: left Andrew Balding after first start: stays 1¼m: acts on polytrack, tapeta and good to firm going: tried in blinkers: has worn tongue tie: front runner/races prominently. *Grant Tuer* **71**

IBN AL EMARAT (IRE) 2 b.g. (Feb 2) Excelebration (IRE) 133 – Grace of Dubai (FR) (Dubai Destination (USA) 127) [2017 p7s^{5} t7.1g^{2} p8g^{2} 8m* Aug 27] €35,000Y: neat gelding: second foal: dam useful French 2-y-o 9.5f winner who stayed 1½m: fairly useful form: won minor event at Goodwood (by ½ length from Macaque) in August: stays 1m. *David Simcock* **87**

IBN MALIK (IRE) 4 ch.g. Raven's Pass (USA) 133 – Moon's Whisper (USA) (Storm Cat (USA)) [2017 113: 7g^{4} 7g^{2} 7d^{6} p7s 7s^{5} Sep 16] strong gelding: smart performer at 3 yrs: below best in 2017: second in minor event at Haydock (5 lengths behind Jungle Cat) in July: stays 7f: acts on good to firm and good to soft going: usually leads: sent to UAE. *Charles Hills* **100**

IBRAZ 2 b.c. (Mar 8) Farhh 131 – Wadaa (USA) 97 (Dynaformer (USA)) [2017 7m^{5} Jul 14] 100,000Y: first foal: dam, 11.5f winner who stayed 2m, half-sister to smart dam of Breeders' Cup Filly & Mare Turf winner Queen's Trust: 8/1, fifth in maiden at Newmarket (5¾ lengths behind Global Giant) in July: better to come. *Roger Varian* **72 p**

IBREEQ (IRE) 4 b.g. Intikhab (USA) 135 – Cerulean Sky (IRE) 114 (Darshaan 133) [2017 t12.4g t12.4g^{6} 10m^{6} 14m 13.9m^{3} 10g Jul 3] well held in bumpers: modest maiden: in headgear last 2 starts: front runner/races prominently. *Roger Fell* **56**

I CAN FLY 2 b.f. (Mar 3) Fastnet Rock (AUS) 127 – Madonna Dell'orto 83 (Montjeu (IRE) 137) [2017 p7g* 7m^{3} Oct 13] 240,000Y: good-topped filly: third foal: half-sister to useful 7f/7.6f winner Viscount Barfield (by Raven's Pass) and 1½m winner All of Me (by Teofilo): dam, maiden (stayed 1m), half-sister to high-class miler Landseer and very smart 1m-1¼m winner Ikhtyar: useful form: won maiden at Dundalk (by 4 lengths from Raynama) in September: third in Oh So Sharp Stakes at Newmarket (1¼ lengths behind Altyn Orda) in October: bred to stay at least 1m: better to come again. *Aidan O'Brien, Ireland* **104 p**

I CAN (IRE) 2 b.g. (Feb 23) So You Think (NZ) 133 – Walk On Water 99 (Exceed And Excel (AUS) 126) [2017 p7d^{3} Nov 22] €35,000Y: third foal: half-brother to 7f winner Showing Off (by Notnowcato): dam 2-y-o 6f winner: 33/1, third in minor event at Kempton (4½ lengths behind Flavius Titus) in November: likely to stay 1m: will improve. *Henry Candy* **86 p**

I CAN'T STOP 4 gr.f. Kyllachy 129 – Vellena (Lucky Story (USA) 128) [2017 66: t8.6m t7.1g p7g^{4} p8d p8d p7g t8.6g 7m May 17] modest maiden: stays 1m: acts on polytrack: often wears blinkers: usually races nearer last than first. *Milton Bradley* **50**

ICART POINT 2 br.g. (Mar 10) Poet's Voice 126 – Maziona 89 (Dansili 127) [2017 7m p8g^{3} p8d^{6} Nov 22] 14,000Y: fourth foal: dam, 2-y-o 7f winner who stayed 10.4f, half-sister to St Leger runner-up The Geezer: fair form: best effort when third in minor event at Kempton (neck behind Losingmyreligion) in November: will stay 9f+: remains capable of better. *Clive Cox* **68 p**

ICE AGE (IRE) 4 b.g. Frozen Power (IRE) 108 – Incendio (Siberian Express (USA) 125) [2017 92: 7m* 7f^{4} 6s^{2} 6.1d^{3} 6.1g^{4} 5g 6.1g* 6.1s* 6s* 6v^{3} Sep 30] workmanlike gelding: useful handicapper: won at Brighton (by 2¼ lengths from Coronation Day) in April, Windsor (twice, by length from Upstaging second occasion) in August and the Curragh (by 1¼ lengths from Al Qahwa) in September: third in Gold Cup at Haydock in September: stays 7f, usually raced at shorter: acts on polytrack, soft and good to firm going: tried in cheekpieces: usually leads, often travels strongly. *Eve Johnson Houghton* **109**

ICE ALERT (IRE) 4 b.g. Frozen Power (IRE) 108 – Karenka (IRE) (Arakan (USA) 123) [2017 77: 8d 8g^{2} Jul 12] lengthy gelding: fair handicapper: stays 9.5f: acts on polytrack and tapeta: sometimes wears tongue tie. *John Ryan* **68**

ICEAXE 4 b.f. Stimulation (IRE) 121 – Laser Crystal (IRE) 67 (King's Theatre (IRE) 128) [2017 76: p7g5 7.5f t7.2g6 7g 7s 7s6 p7g Nov 8] fair handicapper, below form in 2017: stays 7f: acts on tapeta and soft going: front runner/races prominently. *John Holt* **57**

ICE BREEZE 3 b.c. Nayef (USA) 129 – Winter Silence 103 (Dansili 127) [2017 9.9g2 11.9g* 11.9g2 11.9m* 11.9g4 11.9d4 14.9g* 15.4g* Oct 22] **124**

The Arc meeting will return in 2018 to a redeveloped Longchamp, where racing is due to resume in April, after a two-year spell at Chantilly. Considering the dominance of British- and Irish-trained horses on Arc Sunday in particular over the last two seasons, the French presumably can't wait for the meeting's return to its traditional home. The aptly-named National Defense prevented the hosts from suffering a whitewash in 2016 when taking the Prix Jean-Luc Lagardere, but the British and Irish took all six of the Sunday Group 1s in the most recent season. The Karl Burke-trained London Protocol won an all-weather handicap on the Saturday of Arc weekend, but the day was made up of French-trained winners apart from that, with Vazirabad providing the home team with its only Group 1 of the weekend when taking a six-runner renewal of the Prix du Cadran. Vazirabad made hard work in the end of justifying very short odds, jockey Christophe Soumillon eventually having to get serious with him to go past 2015 winner Mille Et Mille after looming up in the straight.

Vazirabad has been the top French stayer in recent seasons and was recording his thirteenth win from his last sixteen starts in the Cadran, though signs of temperament had been creeping in (he had made hard work of winning the Group 3 Prix Gladiateur earlier in September). It wasn't a complete surprise, therefore, when Vazirabad was beaten at odds on by Ice Breeze in the Prix Royal-Oak at Saint-Cloud on his final start of 2017. He was notably easy to back on the pari mutuel in a race which he was bidding to win for the third successive year. Like Vazirabad, Ice Breeze had also won on Arc weekend, keeping on well to take the Qatar Prix Chaudenay for three-year-olds over fifteen furlongs by a short neck from the British challenger Call To Mind. Ice Breeze was unraced at two but he made up for lost time in the latest season, racing eight times, starting out over a mile and a quarter in a Saint-Cloud newcomers event. He won a minor event on his second start, over a mile and a half at the same track, before improving to finish second in the Group 3 Prix du Lys, a trial for the Grand Prix de Paris over the same course and distance in July. The Prix du Lys was won by Called To The Bar, who was ineligible to run in the Grand Prix de Paris because he is a gelding, but the form was franked in the Group 2

Prix Royal-Oak, Saint-Cloud—Ice Breeze (rail) puts up a very smart performance to deny Vazirabad a third victory in the race, with Holdthasigreen third

Prix Hocquart at Chantilly the following month, the former Prix du Jockey Club trial moving to a later date and run over a mile and a half to serve as the main preparatory race for the Grand Prix de Paris instead. In a race also confined to entires, the three that had chased home Called To The Bar at Saint-Cloud filled the places in the same order, Ice Breeze getting up late to win by a head and three quarters of a length from Shakeel and Falcon Wings. The second in the Prix Hocquart Shakeel went on to win the Grand Prix de Paris, with Ice Breeze fourth and Falcon Wings fifth. Ice Breeze seemed to have reached his ceiling at a mile and a half, and he was unable to land a glove on Cracksman in the Prix Niel on his next start over that trip. Stepped up in trip, however, his form regained its progressive curve as he first took the Prix Chaudenay at Chantilly before improving further to beat Vazirabad by a length and a quarter in the Royal-Oak, finding plenty under pressure on both occasions and relishing the extra distance.

Ice Breeze (b.c. 2014)	Nayef (USA) (b 1998)	Gulch (b 1984)	Mr Prospector
			Jameela
		Height of Fashion (b 1979)	Bustino
			Highclere
	Winter Silence (b 2002)	Dansili (b 1996)	Danehill
			Hasili
		Hunt The Sun (b 1992)	Rainbow Quest
			Suntrap

Ice Breeze is a brother to Snow Sky who was third in the 2014 St Leger and won the Yorkshire Cup and Hardwicke Stakes the following season. Snow Sky and Ice Breeze are out of the useful Winter Silence who won at up to an extended thirteen furlongs for Andre Fabre and is also dam of a couple of winners by Zamindar, including the useful French eleven-furlong winner Clariden. There is plenty of stamina on his dam's side as Ice Breeze's grandam Hunt The Sun is a sister to Sunshack and Raintrap, both winners of the Prix Royal-Oak. Hunt The Sun, who failed to win in four attempts, made up for it at stud, becoming the dam of a number of winners, including Host Nation who won the Group 3 Prix de Barbeville over nearly two miles. Hunt The Sun is also the dam of Meteor Storm, winner of the Grade 1 Manhattan Handicap in the States as well as the Grade 2 San Juan Capistrano Handicap over a mile and three quarters, and the Dubai Sheema Classic winner Polish Summer and she is also the great grandam of the Nassau Stakes winner Winsili, a daughter of Dansili like Winter Silence. Ice Breeze's sire Nayef also won the Sheema Classic but not all his best progeny have been stayers, the likes of Tamayuz (himself now a successful stallion), Mustajeeb and Spacious being speedier types. Ice Breeze has primarily been campaigned on ground described as good or firmer (he was below his best on his only start on good to soft in the Prix Niel) and he will stay further than two miles. He may well have even more to offer as a four-year-old and would be an interesting challenger for the Gold Cup. *P. Bary, France*

ICEBUSTER 9 ch.g. Iceman 117 – Radiate (Sadler's Wells (USA) 132) [2017 89, a81: p10g^{6} t8.6m p12g^{3} p13.3d^{3} p15.8g^{2} t16.5g^{6} 13.1m^{4} t16.5g^{2} 12.1m May 5] compact gelding: fairly useful handicapper: stays 16.5f: acts on polytrack, tapeta, good to firm and heavy going: sometimes slowly away, often races in rear/freely. *Rod Millman* **83**

ICE CANYON 3 b.g. Raven's Pass (USA) 133 – Picture Hat (USA) (El Prado (IRE) 119) [2017 91: p5g^{3} 5v 5m^{4} 6m t12.2g^{3} Dec 2] fairly useful maiden: third in handicap at Wolverhampton in December: left M. Halford after fourth start: stays 1½m: acts on tapeta and good to soft going: often in headgear: often races prominently. *Mark Brisbourne* **80**

ICE DANCING (IRE) 3 ch.f. Raven's Pass (USA) 133 – Dancing Abbie (USA) 105 (Theatrical) [2017 t8.6g* 10.3g 8m^{5} 10.2g^{4} t9.5g* p10g^{2} 10g^{3} 10.2d Oct 27] fifth foal: half-sister to useful 1½m-2m winner Galizzi (by Dansili): dam, 9.5f-1½m winner, out of US Grade 1 9f winner Sicy d'Alsace: fairly useful performer: won maiden at Wolverhampton in March and handicap there (by 1¼ lengths from My Brother Mike) in August: stays 1¼m: acts on polytrack and tapeta: in hood last 5 starts: sold 35,000 gns, sent to Saudi Arabia. *Michael Bell* **88**

ICEFALL (IRE) 4 b.g. Frozen Power (IRE) 108 – Silvertine (IRE) 84 (Alzao (USA) 117) [2017 92: 9.8m^{5} 12s^{5} 12v t12.4s 16.3g 14.5d Oct 27] tall gelding: fairly useful handicapper: stays 1½m: acts on any turf going: tried in cheekpieces/tongue tie. *Tim Easterby* **80**

ICE GALLEY (IRE) 4 br.g. Galileo (IRE) 134 – Ice Queen (IRE) 118 (Danehill Dancer (IRE) 117) [2017 74: 10.3g 13.1m^2 16.3d 14.5s 11.9m^6 11.9s 17.1g Aug 20] fair maiden: stays 13f: acts on tapeta, good to firm and good to soft going: tried in cheekpieces. *Philip Kirby* **73**

ICE LORD (IRE) 5 gr.g. Verglas (IRE) 118 – Special Lady (FR) (Kaldoun (FR) 122) [2017 97: p7g 7s^2 7d^4 7d 6g^3 6v* 7d^2 Sep 30] lengthy gelding: useful handicapper: won at Ascot (by 1¼ lengths from Gulliver) in September: stays 7f: acts on heavy going: tried in blinkers: sometimes slowly away, often races in rear. *Chris Wall* **102**

ICE ROYAL (IRE) 4 b.g. Frozen Power (IRE) 108 – Salford Princess (IRE) (Titus Livius (FR) 115) [2017 94: p8g^4 t8.6m^3 p8d^2 p8m^3 p8d^4 p10d^4 p10g p8g p7d p8g^5 p8s* p10s^5 p8g^3 Dec 20] good-topped gelding: useful handicapper: won at Chelmsford (by 1½ lengths from Corked) in December: placed on 4 other occasions in 2017: stays 1¼m: acts on all-weather and good to firm going: has worn cheekpieces. *Jamie Osborne* **97**

ICE SLICE (IRE) 6 b.g. Dark Angel (IRE) 113 – Ice Rock (IRE) (Rock of Gibraltar (IRE) 133) [2017 102: 8.3g 7.6d^3 7.6g 8m^5 7.6d^6 7.6v^6 8s^4 Oct 15] angular gelding: useful handicapper: third at Chester (3½ lengths behind Sound Advice) in May: stays 8.5f: acts on polytrack, good to firm and heavy going: front runner/races prominently. *James Eustace* **96**

ICESPIRE 3 b.f. Frankel 147 – Quest To Peak (USA) (Distant View (USA) 126) [2017 80P: 8f^2 9.9m 8g^2 Sep 1] well-made filly: useful form: second in minor event at Ascot (short head behind Prosper) in May and handicap at Sandown (2½ lengths behind Archetype) in September: should stay 1¼m: wears hood: sent to USA. *John Gosden* **95**

ICKYMASHO 5 b.m. Multiplex 114 – Icky Woo (Mark of Esteem (IRE) 137) [2017 90: p12g^4 p12g^5 p10d* p10d* p10g^2 10d p10s* p9.4g^3 p10s^2 p10s^5 p10g^4 p10d^5 Nov 9] tall mare: useful handicapper: won at Chelmsford in March (2) and June (by neck from Banditry): placed at Deauville (listed race, 1½ lengths behind Syrita) in July and Chelmsford (2½ lengths behind Blushing Rose) in September: stays 1½m: acts on polytrack, tapeta and good to firm going: front runner/races prominently. *Jonathan Portman* **104**

ICONIC BELLE 3 ch.f. Sixties Icon 125 – Five Bells (IRE) (Rock of Gibraltar (IRE) 133) [2017 74: 9.9d^4 10.2f^3 11.2m^4 Aug 27] smallish filly: fair maiden: stays 1¼m: acts on good to firm and good to soft going. *Mick Channon* **76**

ICONIC BOY 2 b.c. (Mar 20) Cape Cross (IRE) 129 – Snoqualmie Girl (IRE) 103 (Montjeu (IRE) 137) [2017 7d p8g Nov 18] little impact in maiden/minor event: in hood second start. *David Elsworth* **–**

ICONIC CODE 2 ch.f. (Apr 14) Sixties Icon 125 – Silca Key 94 (Inchinor 119) [2017 t8.6g^4 8.5m^4 7.8v^6 8v* Oct 23] rather slightly-built filly: sixth foal: half-sister to 7f/1m winners Fiducia (by Lawman) and Bajan Rebel (by Bahamian Bounty): dam 9f/1¼m winner: fair form: won nursery at Pontefract in October: will stay 1¼m. *Mick Channon* **75**

ICONIC KNIGHT (IRE) 2 b.g. (May 2) Sir Prancealot (IRE) 111 – Teutonic (IRE) 55 (Revoque (IRE) 122) [2017 5.1m 6m^3 6.1m^3 6s p6g^2 p5g^2 5.1d* Oct 23] £18,000 2-y-o: good-topped gelding: half-brother to several winners, including 2-y-o 5f winner Kotonic (by Kodiac) and winner up to 1½m Red Tyke (2-y-o 7f winner, by Red Clubs): dam, maiden (stayed 2m) on Flat, winning hurdler: fairly useful performer: won minor event at Windsor (by 2¼ lengths from Big Brave Bob) in October: stays 6f: acts on polytrack, good to firm and good to soft going: often races freely, and has looked hard ride. *Ed Walker* **81**

ICONIC SUNSET 2 ch.c. (Mar 19) Farhh 131 – Manila Bay (IRE) (Halling (USA) 133) [2017 6d^5 7m^2 7.4m^2 7s p7d* t8.6m^3 Oct 31] fair performer: won minor event at Kempton in August: stays 8.5f: acts on polytrack, tapeta and good to firm going. *James Tate* **79**

ICONS IMAGE 4 ch.g. Sixties Icon 125 – Marrimeclaire (IRE) 72 (Spartacus (IRE) 107) [2017 –: 10.1m May 17] no form. *Alan Bailey* **–**

IDAHO (IRE) 4 b.c. Galileo (IRE) 134 – Hveger (AUS) (Danehill (USA) 126) [2017 122: 12m^6 12m* 12s^3 12f^6 11.9d 12s^4 11.9f^5 Nov 26] **126**

A career haul of six Grand Prix wins is something most Formula One drivers would happily boast about—it is the same total as John Surtees and Jochen Rindt, world champions in 1964 and 1970 respectively, whilst it's more than that achieved by title-holders such as Giuseppe Farina, Keke Rosberg, Mike Hawthorn and Phil Hill. Ralf Schumacher, however, was always having his achievements behind the wheel measured against those of his older brother Michael who won more world championship titles (seven) than the number of individual Grand Prix wins recorded by six-years-younger Ralf. Michael Schumacher's record-breaking achievements (which included a staggering ninety-one race wins) led many to

Hardwicke Stakes, Royal Ascot—Highland Reel's younger brother Idaho lands a well-contested renewal, beating the fast-finishing Barsanti (right) and Chemical Charge

regard him as the greatest Formula One driver of all time. Patrick McEnroe reached a very high standard in the world of tennis, contesting the semi-final of the 1991 Australian Open and quarter-final of the 1995 US Open (losing to Boris Becker in four sets both times), but was always destined to be a mere footnote in that sport's history on account of his older brother John being one of the greatest players of the same era. Similarly, Anton Ferdinand represented England twenty-three times at youth levels and played for three Premier League clubs, but his footballing exploits have inevitably been overshadowed by those of older brother Rio, who played for teams who won six Premier League titles and also collected a Champions League winner's medal during a career that also saw him capped eighty-one times at senior international level.

The chances are that most racegoers will view the Aidan O'Brien-trained Idaho as another example of a performer who has been in the shadow of a more talented older sibling. Idaho's year-older brother Highland Reel developed into one of the most popular horses in training thanks to his globe-trotting exploits, which yielded no fewer than seven Group 1 wins (ten career wins in total) and saw him accrue a European record of more than £7.9m in total prize money. By contrast, Idaho has managed just three wins (none at Group 1 level) from sixteen starts to date, and he has now been beaten six times as a short-priced favourite, including on all three of his sorties to North America. That doesn't tell the whole story, however, as Idaho is a high-class performer in his own right and ended 2017 rated just 2 lb inferior to his older brother. Idaho actually had a head-to-head record of one-all with Highland Reel in the latest season and could yet step up on to the biggest stage.

Idaho's only win of 2017, in the Group 2 Hardwicke Stakes, came immediately before and after those two meetings with Highland Reel and capped a fine week at Royal Ascot for the brothers, coming seventy-two hours after Highland Reel had won the Prince of Wales's Stakes. With Ryan Moore opting to ride the favourite, the Queen's Dartmouth who had been a narrow winner (from Highland Reel) of the 2016 renewal, Seamus Heffernan took the ride on Idaho in the Hardwicke. Heffernan had partnered Idaho to a smooth victory in the Great Voltigeur Stakes the previous summer, in a three-year-old campaign that seems arguably destined to be remembered more for his unfortunate unseating of Heffernan when looking likely to justify favouritism in the St Leger. There were no such scares for Heffernan in the Hardwicke as Idaho (fitter for his reappearance when sixth to Highland Reel in the Coronation Cup) was always going best after being ridden a bit closer to the pace than usual, tactics which proved advantageous in a race run at just a fair gallop. Sent off 9/2 second favourite in what looked a good renewal, Idaho stayed on well to lead inside the final furlong and was always holding his main challengers thereafter, winning from the outsiders Barsanti and Chemical Charge by half a length and a length and a quarter, with a further length and a half back to Dartmouth in fourth. Idaho seemed set for a very good summer at this stage, a view which was strengthened by an even better performance (in form terms at least) when third in the King George VI and Queen Elizabeth Stakes back at Ascot the following month. Heavy rain rendered conditions vastly different to those in the Hardwicke—the ground was soft as opposed to good to firm—but Idaho coped well and, although no match for the clear-cut winner Enable, arguably should have finished a bit closer having been shuffled back at a vital stage. Ironically, Highland Reel (preferred by Moore) was the cause of Idaho's momentary loss of position as he dropped to sixth on the home turn, with Heffernan forced to sit and suffer with Idaho briefly trapped behind his brother. Rallying strongly once in the clear, Idaho finished three quarters of a length behind runner-up Ulysses (the impressive Enable was a further four and a half lengths ahead), with four lengths back to a below-form Highland Reel in fourth.

True to form, Highland Reel bounced back later in the season, rounding off his glittering career with that seventh Group 1 win in the Hong Kong Vase in December. However, those two Ascot performances proved to be as good as it got for Idaho, as he fared nothing like so well afterwards. Admittedly, Idaho's eighth in the Prix de l'Arc de Triomphe wasn't too bad a run in form terms, particularly as he was effectively pressed into service as pacemaker from Ballydoyle's other runners. However, there were two very disappointing runs in North America either side of Chantilly, with Idaho flopping when well fancied for both the Sword Dancer Stakes at Saratoga in August and the Canadian International at Woodbine in October. A tardy break compromised his chances in the latter contest and it was a similar story in the Japan Cup at Tokyo on his final outing when he did quite well in the circumstances to finish a never-nearer fifth of seventeen (beaten five and a half lengths) to Cheval Grand. Idaho fared best of the three European raiders in his bid to become the first Irish-trained winner of the Japan Cup since Stanerra in 1983.

Idaho (IRE) (b.c. 2013)	Galileo (IRE) (b 1998)	Sadler's Wells (b 1981)	Northern Dancer
			Fairy Bridge
		Urban Sea (ch 1989)	Miswaki
			Allegretta
	Hveger (AUS) (b 2001)	Danehill (b 1986)	Danzig
			Razyana
		Circles of Gold (ch 1991)	Marscay
			Olympic Aim

Idaho's pedigree has, of course, been covered in the essays on Highland Reel and also in his own extended entry in *Racehorses of 2016*. To recap, both are out of the winning Australian miler Hveger, who is a sister to versatile Australasian champion Elvstroem and a half-sister to Haradasun, who won the 2008 Queen Anne Stakes for Ballydoyle having also been a champion Down Under earlier in his career. Idaho's year-younger sister Cercle de La Vie hasn't looked anything out of the ordinary in five starts to date for Andre Fabre, her only placing being when runner-up in a ten-furlong handicap in the French Provinces, though she'll clearly have broodmare potential given her pedigree—a comment which also applies to Via Condotti, Hveger's as-yet-unraced 2015 filly by Galileo. Hveger has produced two colts to the same stallion since then, with the 2016 foal (as yet unnamed) snapped up by Coolmore for 240,000 guineas as a yearling.

The tall, good-topped Idaho takes after Highland Reel in more ways than just racing ability, with his tendency to sweat and/or get on edge during the preliminaries also very much a trait of his older brother. Idaho is more versatile with regards to underfoot conditions, though, having shown his form on all types of turf going, and it is also not out of the question that, usually being more patiently ridden than his habitually front-running brother, he might stay a bit further too. The manner in which he saw things out in both the King George VI and Queen Elizabeth Stakes and the Japan Cup suggests he is well worth another try over further than a mile and a half, his only previous venture being that luckless tilt at the St Leger. Unlike its Doncaster counterpart, the Irish St Leger has been open to older horses since the early-'eighties and appeals as a possible target for Idaho to finally break his Group 1 duck, if he hasn't done so already by then. *Aidan O'Brien, Ireland*

I DARE TO DREAM 3 b.f. Mullionmileanhour (IRE) 116 – Shaymee's Girl 59 (Wizard King 122) [2017 –: 6g 8g 7d⁶ 7.2m Aug 31] lengthy filly: no form: in cheekpieces last 3 starts. *Lisa Williamson* –

IDEAL CANDY (IRE) 2 b.f. (Mar 19) Canford Cliffs (IRE) 133 – Forever More (IRE) (Galileo (IRE) 134) [2017 7f⁶ t7.1g³ t7.1g² t8g⁵ t7.2g³ Dec 22] €18,000F, £4,000Y: third foal: dam unraced half-sister to smart 1m-1¼m winner Pinpoint: modest maiden: left Andrew Crook after first start: stays 1m: acts on tapeta. *Karen Tutty* **63**

IDEAL SPIRIT 2 b.f. (Jan 28) Swiss Spirit 117 – Silver Sail 49 (Daylami (IRE) 138) [2017 5m 5m⁵ t6g t5.1d³ f5g⁴ Dec 29] £5,000Y: fifth foal: half-sister to 6f winner Friendship Is Love (by Byron): dam, maiden (probably stayed 1¼m), half-sister to smart performer up to 1½m Medici Code: modest maiden: left Andrew Crook after second start: should stay 6f: acts on tapeta: often races prominently. *Karen Tutty* **52**

IDIDITFORYOOOO (IRE) 3 b.g. Fast Company (IRE) 126 – Ann's Annie (IRE) 78 (Alzao (USA) 117) [2017 8.2d⁶ 9.9m⁵ 8.3v² 11.6g³ 11.8v⁵ 10g⁵ Oct 9] compact gelding: fair maiden: stays 11.5f: acts on heavy going. *Brian Meehan* **78**

IDLE TALKER (IRE) 5 b.g. Dandy Man (IRE) 123 – Special Pearl (IRE) 75 (Alhaarth (IRE) 126) [2017 –: f14g⁵ 16d May 16] fair at best, lightly raced and no form since 2015: stays 1½m: acts on polytrack, tapeta and soft going: often wears cheekpieces: tried in tongue tie. *Nick Gifford* –

IDOL DEPUTY (FR) 11 gr.g. Silver Deputy (CAN) – Runaway Venus (USA) (Runaway Groom (CAN)) [2017 83: t9.5m t9.5m³ t9.5m t8.6m* t9.5g t8.6g t8.6g t8.6g t9.5g t8.6g p10m t8.6d Dec 9] fair handicapper nowadays: won at Wolverhampton in February: stays 1¼m: acts on polytrack and tapeta: wears headgear: tried in tongue tie. *James Bennett* **79**

I DON'T BELIEVE IT 3 ch.g. Choisir (AUS) 126 – Special Destiny (Tobougg (IRE) 125) [2017 –: t7.1g Mar 10] lightly-made gelding: no form: tried in cheekpieces. *Micky Hammond* –

IFAN (IRE) 9 b.g. Ivan Denisovich (IRE) 115 – Montana Miss (IRE) 80 (Earl of Barking (IRE) 119) [2017 68: t9.5g t9.5g Feb 11] fairly useful at best, well held both starts in 2017: stays 1½m: acts on polytrack, fibresand and good to firm going: wears headgear: front runner/races prominently. *Tim Vaughan* –

IFTITAH (IRE) 3 b.g. Harbour Watch (IRE) 121 – Solstice 84 (Dubawi (IRE) 129) [2017 71: p7s 8.3d 7d⁵ p8d⁶ t7.2g* p7g p7g a5f³ Dec 16] sturdy gelding: fair handicapper: won at Wolverhampton in August: left George Peckham after seventh start: stays 7f: acts on polytrack and tapeta: in blinkers last 5 starts: usually in tongue tie: often races towards rear. *Fawzi Abdulla Nass, Bahrain* **77**

IFUBELIEVEINDREAMS (IRE) 3 b.f. Iffraaj 127 – Oratrix (IRE) 47 (Oratorio (IRE) 128) [2017 67p: 8.3g³ p8s² t8g⁴ p7d* p8m² Nov 25] fairly useful performer: won maiden at Chelmsford (by 3 lengths from Domitilla) in November: stays 8.5f: acts on polytrack and tapeta: tried in hood: often races towards rear. *Ismail Mohammed* **90**

IFWECAN 6 b.g. Exceed And Excel (AUS) 126 – Kirk 79 (Selkirk (USA) 129) [2017 101: 7s* 7g⁶ 7v 7d Sep 30] big gelding: useful handicapper: won at Newmarket (by nose from Ice Lord) in May: stays 1m: acts on firm and soft going: tried in blinkers: front runner/races prominently. *Martin Smith* **101**

IF WE CAN CAN 2 ch.g. (Apr 2) Sepoy (AUS) 129 – Kirk 79 (Selkirk (USA) 129) [2017 6d 6s³ 7.4m⁵ Jun 27] modest form: best effort when third in minor event at Hamilton (5½ lengths behind Miss Bar Beach) in June: should stay 7f. *Mark Johnston* **55**

IGNACIO ZULOAGA (IRE) 3 ch.g. Lope de Vega (IRE) 125 – Indian Express 61 (Indian Ridge 123) [2017 –: f8.1g³ p8d⁵ Dec 13] modest form: better effort in 2017 when third in maiden at Southwell in November. *Jo Hughes* **58**

I KNOW HOW (IRE) 2 b.g. (Apr 12) Epaulette (AUS) 126 – Blue Crystal (IRE) 77 (Lure (USA) 131) [2017 6.1d 6d⁶ Oct 30] modest form: better effort when sixth in minor event at Redcar (3½ lengths behind Aljady) in October. *Julie Camacho* **62**

ILEY BOY 3 b.g. Delegator 125 – Menha 70 (Dubawi (IRE) 129) [2017 11.6g p12s 10g⁴ 12g⁴ 12s⁵ 11.9s p12g² p13.3s⁶ t12.2g* p12g⁶ Dec 23] modest handicapper: won at Wolverhampton in December: stays 1½m: acts on polytrack and tapeta: in cheekpieces last 4 starts. *John Gallagher* **61**

ILLAUNMORE (USA) 3 b.f. Shamardal (USA) 129 – Illaunglass (IRE) 96 (Red Clubs (IRE) 125) [2017 85: p8g³ p8g³ p8g² p7s 8g a8.4g³ p8g* p9.4g⁵ Nov 28] useful performer: placed in 3 handicaps at Chelmsford before leaving John Gosden after fourth start: won minor event at Chantilly in October: 3 lengths fifth to Indian Blessing in listed race at Deauville final start: stays 9.5f: acts on polytrack. *Mme Pia Brandt, France* **99**

I'LL BE GOOD 8 b.g. Red Clubs (IRE) 125 – Willisa 67 (Polar Falcon (USA) 126) [2017 89: f5g³ 5v⁵ Oct 16] fairly useful performer: third in handicap at Southwell in January: left Brian Ellison after first start: raced mainly at 5f: acts on polytrack, fibresand, good to firm and heavy going: has worn cheekpieces/tongue tie. *Alan Berry* **86**

ILLEGALLY BLONDE (IRE) 4 b.f. Lawman (FR) 121 – Kayak (Singspiel (IRE) 133) [2017 82: p6g p6g⁶ Jan 13] fairly useful performer, little impact either start in 2017: stays 6f: acts on polytrack, tapeta, good to firm and good to soft going: tried in cheekpieces. *Jamie Osborne* **–**

ILLUSIONAL 2 b.g. (Mar 29) Bernardini (USA) 132 – Illustrious Miss (USA) 115 (Kingmambo (USA) 125) [2017 7d² t7.1g³ t6g⁶ Nov 23] fair form in minor events. *Mark Johnston* **66**

ILLUSTRISSIME (USA) 4 b.g. Mizzen Mast (USA) 121 – Ghost Friendly (USA) (Ghostzapper (USA) 137) [2017 95: t8s Jun 1] useful performer, well beaten sole outing in 2017: stays 9.5f: acts on polytrack and good to soft going. *Tony Coyle* **–**

IL PRIMO SOLE 2 b.c. (Mar 17) Raven's Pass (USA) 133 – Sweet Alabama 56 (Johannesburg (USA) 127) [2017 7m* 7d² p7g³ Nov 2] 20,000F, €40,000Y, £55,000 2-y-o: rangy colt: first foal: dam maiden (stayed 1½m): useful form: won minor event at Yarmouth (by 4½ lengths from Tanseeq) in August: third in similar event at Lingfield (neck behind Statehood) in November: raced only at 7f: remains open to improvement. *John Gosden* **100 p**

IL SICARIO (IRE) 3 b.g. Zebedee 113 – Starring (FR) 74 (Ashkalani (IRE) 128) [2017 68: 8g³ 7.5f* 7g³ 6.9g⁵ 7.4d⁴ 10m* p10g⁶ Dec 21] small, angular gelding: fair performer: won apprentice handicap at Beverley in May and claimer at Leicester in June: left Mark Johnston after sixth start: stays 1¼m: acts on firm going: tried in visor: usually races prominently. *Bill Turner* **78**

I'M A BELIEVER 3 b.f. Sixties Icon 125 – Fascinatin Rhythm 83 (Fantastic Light (USA) 134) [2017 7d⁵ Aug 22] fourth foal: sister to 11.5f winner Da Do Run Run: dam maiden (barely stayed 1¾m): 4/1, well held in maiden at Brighton. *Mick Channon* **–**

IMAGE 2 b.f. (Mar 6) Sepoy (AUS) 129 – The Terrier 76 (Foxhound (USA) 103) [2017 6m 6d⁶ p6g³ 7m p6d³ Nov 9] useful-looking filly: half-sister to several winners, including 5f/6f winners Dutch Masterpiece (smart, by Dutch Art) and Hilary J (by Mount Nelson): dam 2-y-o 5f winner who stayed 7f: fair maiden: stays 6f: acts on polytrack. *Philip McBride* **71**

IMAGINATIVE (IRE) 2 b.c. (Jan 29) Camelot 128 – Just Wondering (IRE) 51 (Danehill Dancer (IRE) 117) [2017 8.3d⁴ Oct 18] €70,000F, 100,000Y: second foal: dam, lightly raced (bred to have been suited by 1m+), out of half-sister to Kentucky Derby runners-up Desert Wine and Menifee: 7/2, shaped as if in need of experience when fourth in maiden at Nottingham (4¼ lengths behind Blazing Tunder) in October: entitled to progress. *Roger Varian* **65 p**

IMAGING 2 b.c. (Mar 5) Oasis Dream 129 – Mirror Lake 112 (Dubai Destination (USA) 127) [2017 8s² 7v* Oct 7] third foal: brother to 7f winner Catchment and half-brother to useful 2-y-o 1m winner Titus (by Dansili): dam winner around 1¼m: useful form: improved from debut when won 7-runner maiden at Limerick by 9½ lengths from Spanish Point, making all and quickening clear over 1f out: better to come. *D. K. Weld, Ireland* **96 p**

I'M A STAR (IRE) 2 b.g. (Feb 26) High Chaparral (IRE) 132 – Etoile de Lune (Zamindar (USA) 116) [2017 7d⁵ 8.5m² t9.5g Nov 18] fair form in minor events/maiden: stays 8.5f. *Stuart Williams* **74**

IMBUCATO 3 b.g. Paco Boy (IRE) 129 – L'Invitata (Dr Fong (USA) 128) [2017 6v p6g 8.5d 7d³ 7.3s⁵ 8.1d² t5.1g Dec 22] modest maiden: left John Patrick Murtagh after sixth start: stays 1m: acts on good to soft going: tried in visor. *Tony Carroll* **60**

IMDANCINWITHURWIFE (IRE) 3 b.f. Sir Prancealot (IRE) 111 – Bishop's Lake 87 (Lake Coniston (IRE) 131) [2017 73p: t5.1m³ t5g⁶ Jan 25] fair form: best form at 5f. *Tom Dascombe* **70**

IM DAPPER TOO 6 b.g. Dapper – Lonely One (Perryston View 114) [2017 69: 8m 9s* 9d* 8s* 9s² 7.8v³ 10g Sep 27] fair handicapper: won at Carlisle in June/July and Pontefract in August: stays 9f: acts on fibresand and heavy going: usually races prominently. *John Davies* **79**

I'M IMPROVING (IRE) 2 b.c. (Apr 16) Most Improved (IRE) 119 – Shebelia (GER) (Black Sam Bellamy (IRE) 121) [2017 7.2g³ 8.3s³ 9d* Oct 30] €30,000 2-y-o: fifth foal: half-brother to smart 1m-9.5f winner String Theory (by Medicean): dam unraced half-sister to very smart/high-class German performers up to 1½m Sabiango and Silvano: fairly useful form: won minor event at Redcar (by 6 lengths from Sea Youmzain) in October: will stay at least 1¼m: will go on improving. *Keith Dalgleish* **90 p**

IMJIN RIVER (IRE) 10 b.g. Namid 128 – Lady Nasrana (FR) (Al Nasr (FR) 126) [2017 57: t5.1m f5g^3 f5g f5g^4 Mar 14] good-topped gelding: modest handicapper: best at 5f/6f: acted on all-weather and good to firm going: wore headgear/tongue tie: dead. *William Stone* **54**

IMMINENT APPROACH 2 b.f. (Jan 21) New Approach (IRE) 132 – Nashmiah (IRE) 114 (Elusive City (USA) 117) [2017 p8g^5 p10g^5 Oct 18] 35,000Y: third foal: half-sister to 7f winner A Legacy of Love (by Sea The Stars) and French 6.5f-1m winner Fond Words (by Shamardal): dam winner up to 1¼m (2-y-o 7.6f winner): modest form in 2 minor events. *James Tate* **63**

IMMORTALISED 3 ch.c. Frankel 147 – Noahs Ark (IRE) 102 (Charnwood Forest (IRE) 125) [2017 10.3g 10.2m^4 9g^6 11.2s^2 13d^6 7g 11.9g Dec 17] 100,000 2-y-o: half-brother to several winners, including smart performer up to 1m After (2-y-o 6f winner, by Danehill Dancer) and useful French 2-y-o 7f winner Temps Au Temps (by Invincible Spirit): dam winner up to 1¼m (2-y-o 7f/1m winner): fairly useful maiden: second in handicap at Carlisle in June: left K. R. Burke after fifth start: stays 11f: acts on soft and good to firm going: in blinkers last 2 starts: usually leads. *S. Seemar, UAE* **86**

IMMORTAL ROMANCE (IRE) 2 br.g. (May 1) Society Rock (IRE) 126 – Sundown 71 (Polish Precedent (USA) 131) [2017 6s^3 6.1m 6s^5 6v^3 Oct 21] rather unfurnished gelding: fair form in minor events: raced only at 6f: tried in visor. *Michael Bell* **72**

IMPACT POINT (JPN) 3 b.c. Deep Impact (JPN) 134 – Rumba Boogie (Rainbow Quest (USA) 134) [2017 p10g^2 t12.2g^2 Aug 11] ¥35,000,000F: half-brother to winners in Japan by Afleet (2) and Wild Rush: dam, lightly raced in Japan (second at 7.5f), half-sister to dam of very smart Japanese winner up to 2m Suzuka Mambo: fairly useful form when second in maidens at Lingfield and Wolverhampton: sold 7,000 gns in November, sent to Saudi Arabia. *Andrew Balding* **86**

IMPART 3 b.g. Oasis Dream 129 – Disclose 100 (Dansili 127) [2017 79: 6.1m^6 6d* 5.1s^5 6m^6 5.1d 5.4d^6 5d^6 5m 5.1g^5 5.1v 5v t5d^2 p6g^2 Nov 2] compact gelding: fairly useful handicapper: won maiden at Navan in 2016 for D. K. Weld: also won at Ripon (by neck from Dandy Highwayman) in June: second at Newcastle in October: stays 6f: acts on tapeta, soft and good to firm going: tried in headgear: usually races close up. *David O'Meara* **91**

IMPERIAL CITY (USA) 3 ch.f. City Zip (USA) 112 – Imperial Pippin (USA) 108 (Empire Maker (USA) 129) [2017 72: p7m^6 Jan 20] fair maiden: stays 7f: tried in hood: sold 6,000 gns, sent to Greece. *Charles Hills* **65**

IMPERIAL FOCUS (IRE) 4 b.g. Intense Focus (USA) 117 – Mrs Cee (IRE) 71 (Orpen (USA) 116) [2017 82: 8g 8.3m^2 Jun 21] fairly useful maiden: second in handicap at Hamilton in June: stays 1¼m: acts on good to firm going: front runner/races prominently. *Simon Waugh* **82**

IMPERIAL LEGEND (IRE) 8 b.g. Mujadil (USA) 119 – Titian Saga (IRE) 74 (Titus Livius (FR) 115) [2017 83, a74: t5g 5g 5d 5d^4 5s^5 t5g^4 t5d 5g 5s^3 5s^4 t5g^6 f5g Nov 13] modest handicapper nowadays: left David Nicholls after first start: best at 5f: acts on firm and soft going: often wears headgear. *Alan Brown* **61**

IMPERIAL LINK 5 b.m. Rail Link 132 – Imperia (GER) (Tertullian (USA) 115) [2017 66, a53: t9.5m p10g 7m 8.2d 8.1d 8.2g^3 10d^6 8g 8.1d^3 8v 8.2v^5 Sep 25] modest handicapper: stays 8.5f: acts on heavy going: wears headgear: front runner: unreliable. *John O'Shea* **58 §**

IMPERIAL PAST 2 b.c. (Mar 17) Dubawi (IRE) 129 – Divorces (AUS) 116 (Domesday (AUS)) [2017 7s* Sep 20] second foal: dam Australian 7f/9f winner: in tongue tie, 5/2, won maiden at Yarmouth (by ¾ length from Prime Minister) on debut: will improve. *Charlie Appleby* **75 p**

IMPERIAL RED (IRE) 2 ch.g. (Mar 15) Zoffany (IRE) 121 – Scoville (GER) (Sholokhov (IRE) 121) [2017 8d t7.2g p7s Dec 8] fair form when seventh in minor event at Newbury on debut, standout effort. *William Haggas* **70**

IMPERIAL STATE 4 b.g. Holy Roman Emperor (IRE) 125 – Seldemosa 67 (Selkirk (USA) 129) [2017 92: p8g^6 8.3g 7m^3 p7s^3 8m* 7s^4 Jul 29] close-coupled gelding: fairly useful handicapper: won at Sandown (amateur, by ¾ length from Honiara) in July: stays 1m: acts on polytrack, tapeta, soft and good to firm going: in headgear last 4 starts: wears tongue tie: sold to join Michael Easterby 15,000 gns in October. *George Scott* **90**

IMPHAL 3 b.g. Nathaniel (IRE) 129 – Navajo Rainbow (Rainbow Quest (USA) 134) [2017 –: 13m^2 13f* 13f* 16g* p15.8g* Oct 5] rather unfurnished gelding: useful handicapper: won at Bath in June/July, Goodwood (by short head from Kozier) in August and Lingfield (by short head from Fulham) in October: stays 2m: acts on polytrack and firm going: in cheekpieces last 4 starts: open to further improvement. *Marcus Tregoning* **95 p**

IMPLAUSIBLE 3 b.f. Royal Applause 124 – Tease (IRE) 81 (Green Desert (USA) 127) [2017 –: t7.1g^5 p7g* Jan 25] fair form: won maiden at Lingfield (by 4½ lengths from Allegheny Bay) in January: raced only at 7f: sent to USA: open to further improvement. *Jonathan Portman* **71 p**

IMPORTANT MISSION (USA) 3 b.g. More Than Ready (USA) 120 – Laura's Pleasure (USA) (Cactus Ridge (USA) 109) [2017 7m t7.1g* p8s^4 p7g* 7d^4 Sep 13] $175,000Y: first foal: dam, US winner up to 5.5f (2-y-o 5f winner), half-sister to useful US Grade 2 1m winner Withgreatpleasure: useful performer: won maiden at Newcastle in June and handicap at Chelmsford (by 3½ lengths from Aventinus) in August: stays 1m: acts on polytrack and tapeta: usually races towards rear. *William Haggas* **101**

IMPRESSIVE DAY (IRE) 4 b.f. Cape Cross (IRE) 129 – Shieldmaiden (USA) 85 (Smart Strike (CAN) 121) [2017 p8g 8.3m p10f^6 9.9g* 11.9g^2 11.6d^6 9.9m* 9.9g* Sep 3] well-made filly: fairly useful handicapper: won at Brighton in May, August and September (by neck from Great Court): stays 1½m: acts on polytrack and good to firm going: in cheekpieces last 5 starts: sold 25,000 gns in November. *Gary Moore* **88**

I'M RIGHT ON TIME 3 ch.g. Dutch Art 126 – Euroceleb (IRE) 76 (Peintre Celebre (USA) 137) [2017 t12.2g^5 p12d^{pu} p8g^6 p10g^5 Dec 30] modest form: stays 1¼m. *Dean Ivory* **64**

I'M RUNNING LATE 3 ch.g. Sepoy (AUS) 129 – Clinet (IRE) 110 (Docksider (USA) 124) [2017 p11g t12.2g^6 p10g* p11s 14.2v p12g^5 p12g^3 p13.3s Dec 1] fair performer: won maiden at Lingfield in May: stays 1½m: acts on polytrack: tried in cheekpieces. *Dean Ivory* **79**

IMSHIVALLA (IRE) 6 b.m. Acclamation 118 – Subtle Affair (IRE) 96 (Barathea (IRE) 127) [2017 99: 10g 8m 9.8m^5 10.2v^5 10.1m 11.9m Jun 17] good-topped mare: fair handicapper: stays 10.5f: acts on good to firm and heavy going: usually in hood: usually races freely. *Richard Fahey* **79**

I'M SUPER TOO (IRE) 10 b.g. Fasliyev (USA) 120 – Congress (IRE) 86 (Dancing Brave (USA) 140) [2017 64: f8d^2 7.5f^4 10g^6 t8s 7.4m^3 8.3g 9.9m 7.4m^3 9.9f^4 7.4d 8.5d^6 9.9m 9.9g^6 9.9v Sep 26] workmanlike gelding: modest handicapper nowadays: stays 1¼m: acts on fibresand, firm and soft going: usually wears headgear: sometimes slowly away. *Karen Tutty* **63**

IMTIYAAZ (IRE) 5 b.m. Starspangledbanner (AUS) 128 – Endure (IRE) (Green Desert (USA) 127) [2017 97: 5f^3 6.1g May 13] useful performer at best: third in listed race at Bath (6½ lengths behind Priceless) in April: best at sprint trips: acts on good to firm going. *Roger Varian* **84**

I'MWAITINGFORYOU 8 ch.m. Needwood Blade 117 – Elegant Lady 89 (Selkirk (USA) 129) [2017 12v 8s p8g Oct 18] no form, including in bumpers: tried in tongue tie. *Peter Bowen* **–**

IM WAITING (IRE) 4 b.f. Excellent Art 125 – Margot (Sadler's Wells (USA) 132) [2017 69: t12.4g^5 p12s p12g t16.3g^4 Oct 19] half-sister to 3 winners, including 2m winner Strolling Home (by Medicean): dam twice-raced half-sister to 2000 Guineas winner Footstepsinthesand: fair maiden: stays 16.5f: acts on polytrack, tapeta and good to soft going: wears headgear: in tongue tie last 3 starts. *Anthony McCann, Ireland* **65**

I'M YER MAN 2 b.g. (Mar 13) Foxwedge (AUS) 128 – Coffee Cup (IRE) 70 (Royal Academy (USA) 130) [2017 5.4g t6d^2 t7.1g^4 t6g^3 p7s* Dec 14] 2,000F: workmanlike gelding: second foal: dam, 2-y-o 7f winner, half-sister to smart sprinter Lexi's Hero: fairly useful performer: won minor event at Chelmsford in December: third in nursery at Newcastle earlier in month: stays 7f: acts on polytrack and tapeta. *Ann Duffield* **82**

INAAM (IRE) 4 b.g. Camacho 118 – Duckmore Bay (IRE) (Titus Livius (FR) 115) [2017 86: t7.1g^5 t8g* t7.1g* t7.1s^2 8m^4 t7.1s^4 t8g^5 t7.1g t7.2g^2 Dec 13] lengthy gelding: fairly useful handicapper: won at Newcastle in February and March: second there in April and at Wolverhampton in December: stays 1m: acts on all-weather, soft and good to firm going: has worn headgear, including in 2017: carries head high. *Richard Fahey* **90**

INCENTIVE 3 b.f. Stimulation (IRE) 121 – Folly Drove 71 (Bahri (USA) 125) [2017 65: 6g^5 5.7d^2 6d 5s^5 6v* 6s Sep 15] fair handicapper: won at Ffos Las in August: stays 6f: acts on good to firm and heavy going: in cheekpieces last 3 starts: front runner/races prominently. *Stuart Kittow* **74**

INCH PINCHER 2 b.f. (Apr 23) Captain Gerrard (IRE) 113 – Elfine (IRE) 78 (Invincible Spirit (IRE) 121) [2017 p7s t7.2g Dec 5] third foal: half-sister to 5f/6f winner Defining Moment (by Camacho): dam, maiden (stayed 11f), half-sister to useful 1¼m-1½m winner Headline News: little impact in minor events. *Rae Guest* **–**

INCH WING (IRE) 9 b.m. Winged Love (IRE) 121 – Incharder (IRE) 86 (Slip Anchor 136) [2017 10m May 8] workmanlike mare: no form in bumpers/over hurdles: 250/1, well held in maiden at Windsor sole outing on Flat. *Mark Hoad* **–**

INCLUDED 5 b.m. Champs Elysees 124 – Cordoba 77 (Oasis Dream 129) [2017 p12g t12.2g^5 p12d^5 Feb 22] fair handicapper: stays 1½m: acts on polytrack, tapeta and good to firm going: tried in cheekpieces/tongue tie. *David Dennis* **77**

INCONCEIVABLE (IRE) 3 b.f. Galileo (IRE) 134 – Mohican Princess (Shirley Heights 130) [2017 71p: 10g^3 p13.3g^2 12m^3 13.3g^3 14.2v^3 11.9g^2 12v^2 Sep 17] fairly useful maiden: placed all 7 starts in 2017: stays 13.5f: acts on polytrack and heavy going: sent to USA. *Ralph Beckett* **87**

INCREDIBLE DREAM (IRE) 4 b.g. Vale of York (IRE) 117 – Finnmark (Halling (USA) 133) [2017 p8g t9.5g p10g^5 10.2d* 10.1m 11.4g^2 12g^3 12s* 14.2v^5 11.5d Oct 24] fair handicapper: won at Nottingham in June and Chepstow in September: stays 1½m: acts on soft going: wears cheekpieces: sometimes slowly away, often races in rear. *Dean Ivory* **79**

INCREDIBLE RED 3 b.f. Invincible Spirit (IRE) 121 – Sweet Stream (ITY) 117 (Shantou (USA) 125) [2017 10.2s Jun 30] 97,000Y: sixth foal: closely related to 2-y-o 1m winner Sweet Dream (by Oasis Dream) and half-sister to useful French 12.5f-14.5f winner Tidespring (by Monsun): dam winner up to 14.6f (2-y-o 1m/8.5f winner), including Prix Vermeille and Park Hill Stakes: 33/1, well held in maiden at Doncaster. *Ed Dunlop* **–**

INCUS 4 b.g. Bertolini (USA) 125 – Cloudchaser (IRE) (Red Ransom (USA)) [2017 52: 14g^5 14.5s* 14d* 14.5s 14d^2 14.2g 14s* 14s^5 16d* Oct 27] fair handicapper: won at Doncaster and Nottingham in June, Ffos Las in August and Newbury (apprentice) in October: stays 2m: acts on polytrack and soft going: tried in cheekpieces: usually races close up. *Ed de Giles* **76**

INDEPENDENCE DAY (IRE) 4 b.c. Dansili 127 – Damson (IRE) 113 (Entrepreneur 123) [2017 –: 5m p5g 5s 5m^6 5g 6g 5m^4 6d 5.8g^3 p5g 5v 5v 5s Nov 5] fairly useful handicapper: left Robert Cowell after third start: stays 6f: acts on good to firm going: sometimes wears headgear: tried in tongue tie. *Shane Donohoe, Ireland* **90**

INDIA 2 b.f. (May 2) Poet's Voice 126 – Miss Brown To You (IRE) 84 (Fasliyev (USA) 120) [2017 8d^6 p8g^6 Oct 14] sixth foal: half-sister to 3 winners, including very smart 1¼m-2½m (Gold Cup) winner Big Orange (by Duke of Marmalade) and 1½m winner The Paris Shrug (by Manduro): dam, 1m winner, half-sister to high-class Hong Kong 1m-1¼m winner Military Attack: modest form: better effort when sixth in minor event at Kempton (4 lengths behind Indiscretion) in October: will go on improving. *Michael Bell* **63 p**

INDIA JANE (FR) 3 b.f. Zoffany (IRE) 121 – Irisijana (GER) (Diktat 126) [2017 t7.1g Jan 6] €20,000Y: second foal: half-sister to German 11f winner Identity (by Manduro): dam, German 7f winner, half-sister to very smart German/Hong Kong 1m-1¼m performer Irian: 15/2, well held in maiden at Wolverhampton. *Henry Spiller* **–**

INDIANA DAWN 4 b.f. Sleeping Indian 122 – Street Diva (USA) 69 (Street Cry (IRE) 130) [2017 63: 7.4g^6 7.1v^5 8m^3 9.9d^4 8v^3 t9.5g^3 t8.6g Nov 20] modest maiden: stays 1¼m: acts on polytrack, tapeta, good to firm and heavy going: has worn headgear, including last 5 starts. *Robert Stephens* **60**

INDIAN ADMIRAL 2 ch.c. (Feb 16) Sepoy (AUS) 129 – Love And Cherish (IRE) 98 (Excellent Art 125) [2017 6g^5 7v^5 t8.6d Dec 9] modest form in minor events. *Mark Johnston* **55**

INDIAN AFFAIR 7 b.h. Sleeping Indian 122 – Rare Fling (USA) (Kris S (USA)) [2017 76: t6m^2 p6g^5 p7d^6 t6g t6g^4 p6g t6g^2 6.1d* 6m^6 6.1v^6 6.1m^3 6m^4 6.1m^4 6.1g^5 5.7s^2 t6.1g^2 t6.1g t6.1m^2 t6.1g^4 p6g* Dec 12] stocky horse: fair handicapper: won at Chepstow in May and Lingfield in December: stays 7f: acts on polytrack, tapeta, good to firm and heavy going: wears headgear/tongue tie. *Milton Bradley* **78**

INDIAN BLESSING 3 ch.f. Sepoy (AUS) 129 – Alpen Glen 96 (Halling (USA) 133) [2017 77p: p8g^3 9.9m^3 10g^4 9.9d^4 9.9m 8g p9.4g* Nov 28] good-topped filly: useful performer: won listed race at Deauville (by 2 lengths from Vintage Folly) in November: stays 1¼m: acts on polytrack, tapeta, good to firm and good to soft going. *Ed Walker* **105**

INDIAN CHIEF (IRE) 7 b.g. Montjeu (IRE) 137 – Buck Aspen (USA) (Seeking The Gold (USA)) [2017 86: f11d 9.9f^6 12g^6 9d^4 9.2g^3 9.9s* 11.1s^2 10.2g^2 11.1v* 10.3d^3 10v^6 10.2d^2 10.2d^5 10.2d Oct 18] tall, lengthy, attractive gelding: useful handicapper: won at Beverley (amateur) in August and Hamilton (by 7 lengths from Henpecked) in September: second at Nottingham in October: stays 1½m: acts on heavy going: tried in headgear/tongue tie: often starts slowly, races towards rear/travels strongly. *Rebecca Bastiman* **95**

INDIAN DANDY (IRE) 3 b.g. Dandy Man (IRE) 123 – Danealla (IRE) (Indian Danehill (IRE) 124) [2017 p8g* t8d^{2} p8d* 8m*^{d} 8.2f^{2} 8m^{4} Jun 22] workmanlike gelding: first foal: dam, well held both starts in bumpers, closely related to useful sprinter Kohala: useful form: won maiden at Lingfield in January and handicap at Chelmsford (by ½ length from Ourmullion) in March: also first past post in handicap at Yarmouth in May (subsequently disqualified due to prohibited substance): fourth in Britannia Stakes (Handicap) at Royal Ascot in June, first home in group: raced only at 1m: acts on polytrack, tapeta and firm going: in hood last 5 starts: often travels strongly: gelded, and sent to Hong Kong, where renamed Enshrining: remains open to improvement. *Marco Botti* **108 p**

INDIAN GIVER 9 b.m. Indesatchel (IRE) 120 – Bint Baddi (FR) (Shareef Dancer (USA) 135) [2017 64: 8.3m^{6} 9.2g 12.1m 8.3g 8.9m^{5} 9s 9.2d Sep 2] small, leggy mare: modest handicapper: stays 11f: acts on tapeta and any turf going: often wears headgear. *John David Riches* **52**

INDIAN PURSUIT (IRE) 4 b.g. Compton Place 125 – Church Melody (Oasis Dream 129) [2017 69: t6g^{2} t5g* t5g^{2} t5d 6m^{3} t6g 5g 5s^{5} t6d 6g* 6d* t5d Oct 24] fair handicapper: won at Newcastle in February and Catterick in August/September: stays 7f: acts on tapeta, good to firm and heavy going: tried in cheekpieces: usually races prominently. *John Quinn* **75**

INDIAN RAJ 3 b.g. Iffraaj 127 – Princess Georgina 78 (Royal Applause 124) [2017 5.1g^{2} 5d* t5d* Aug 10] half-brother to several winning sprinters, including smart 5f (including at 2 yrs) winner Royal Birth and 5f/6f winner Excellent George (both by Exceed And Excel): dam 2-y-o 5f winner: fairly useful form: won maiden at Leicester (by 2¾ lengths from Tea El Tee) in July and handicap at Newcastle (by ¾ length from Suwaan) in August: raced only at 5f: likely to progress further. *Stuart Williams* **90 p**

INDIAN RED 3 ch.g. Sir Percy 129 – Missouri 86 (Charnwood Forest (IRE) 125) [2017 p8d p12g^{4} t12.2g^{4} 11.9d p14d p16d p16g^{5} Nov 7] tall, close-coupled gelding: modest maiden: stays 2m: acts on polytrack and tapeta: often races freely. *Mark H. Tompkins* **64**

INDIAN TINKER 8 b.g. Sleeping Indian 122 – Breakfast Creek 63 (Hallgate 127) [2017 74: f5g^{2} Apr 16] fair handicapper: stays 5.5f: acts on good to firm and heavy going: sometimes in headgear: usually races prominently. *Robert Cowell* **66**

INDIAN VISION (IRE) 3 ch.g. Iffraaj 127 – Sweet Fairnando 66 (Hernando (FR) 127) [2017 –: 8m^{6} 10.2v 8g 10d^{5} Oct 20] modest maiden: likely to stay beyond 1¼m: acts on good to soft going: often starts slowly. *Micky Hammond* **53**

INDIAN WARRIOR 2 b.g. (Feb 18) Sepoy (AUS) 129 – Night Gypsy 74 (Mind Games 121) [2017 5.2m^{4} 5.1g^{3} 5.1m^{2} 5d^{3} 6g^{3} t6.1g t6g^{3} p6d^{5} Nov 9] rather leggy gelding: fair maiden: stays 6f: acts on tapeta and good to firm going. *Ed Dunlop* **79**

INDICIA 2 b.f. (Mar 19) Bated Breath 125 – Indication 76 (Sadler's Wells (USA) 132) [2017 6g^{2} 7d^{4} t6.1g^{4} 6s^{6} Sep 15] good-topped filly: seventh foal: closely related to smart/untrustworthy winner up to 9f Stipulate (2-y-o 7f winner) and 2-y-o 7f winner Syndicate (both by Dansili) and half-sister to a winner in Belgium by Oasis Dream: dam, 9.5f winner, half-sister to very smart 7f/1m winner Stronghold and smart winner up to 1¼m Convey: fair form: should stay at least 7f. *Charles Hills* **76**

INDIGO PRINCESS 4 b.f. Native Ruler 119 – Red To Violet 85 (Spectrum (IRE) 126) [2017 74: p8g t8d^{6} t9.5g^{5} 7m^{2} 8.3g* 7d^{2} 8.3f 10.2d^{6} p8g^{6} Dec 21] sturdy filly: fair handicapper: won at Nottingham (apprentice) in May: best at around 1m: acts on polytrack, tapeta, good to firm and good to soft going. *Michael Appleby* **71**

INDIRA 6 ch.m. Sleeping Indian 122 – Forever Loved 86 (Deploy 131) [2017 96: 10d^{3} May 29] smallish, close-coupled mare: useful handicapper: third at Windsor (3¾ lengths behind Toulson) on sole outing in 2017: stays 13.5f: acts on polytrack, tapeta, soft and good to firm going: usually races prominently. *John Berry* **96**

INDISCRETION (IRE) 2 b.f. (Apr 4) Big Bad Bob (IRE) 118 – Fleeting Affair (USA) (Gone West (USA)) [2017 7.6d p8g* p8d^{ur} Nov 22] sixth foal: half-sister to 1m-9.5f winner Marital (by Montjeu) and useful winner around 7f (including at 2 yrs) Sevenleft (by Manduro): dam once-raced sister to very smart US Grade 2 8.5f winner/Kentucky Derby runner-up Proud Citizen: fair form: won minor event at Kempton (by ¾ length from Jazeel) in October: unseated soon after start next time: stays 1m. *Jonathan Portman* **74**

INDOMENEO 2 b.c. (Feb 7) Piccolo 121 – Cherrycombe-Row 77 (Classic Cliche (IRE) 128) [2017 t6g^{2} 7f* t7.2g^{2} 7s* 7.4v^{2} t8s^{6} 8v* 7s* Oct 10] 25,000F, £62,000Y: brother to smart 7f-9.5f winner (including in USA) St Trinians and 7f-8.6f winner Beat Goes On: dam 2-y-o 7f winner who stayed 1¼m: fairly useful performer: won minor events at **89**

Wetherby in June, Lingfield in July and Leicester (by length from Cuban Heel) in October, and nursery at Ripon (by neck from Poet's Dawn) in September: stays 1m: acts on tapeta and any turf going: often races prominently. *Richard Fahey*

INDOMITABLE SPIRIT 5 b.g. Zebedee 113 – Gayala (IRE) (Iron Mask (USA) 117) [2017 –: p7s Jul 7] fair at best, no form since 2015: stays 1m: acts on polytrack and fibresand. *Martin Smith* **–**

IN DREAMS 3 b.c. Sixties Icon 125 – Tidal Run 80 (Hurricane Run (IRE) 134) [2017 12v5 t9.5g Aug 31] in cheekpieces, fair form when seventh at Wolverhampton on second of 2 starts in maidens. *Brian Meehan* **68**

IN DUE TIME (IRE) 5 br.g. Big Bad Bob (IRE) 118 – Bravada (GER) (Dai Jin 123) [2017 8g Apr 17] little impact in maidens/handicap: dead. *Alan Swinbank* **–**

INDULGED 4 b.f. Teofilo (IRE) 126 – Fondled 101 (Selkirk (USA) 129) [2017 95: 10.2v* 9.9v3 10.2g2 10.1s4 10.2s5 p12g Nov 29] tall, rather unfurnished filly: useful performer: won handicap at Doncaster (by 1¼ lengths from High Hopes) in May: placed in similar events at Goodwood (1¾ lengths behind Billesdon Bess) and Nottingham (1¼ lengths behind Empress Ali) in August: stays 11f: acts on polytrack, good to firm and heavy going. *James Fanshawe* **101**

INDULGENT 4 b.g. Makfi 130 – Santa Agata (FR) 95 (Anabaa (USA) 130) [2017 57: f12m Feb 21] compact gelding: modest maiden, well held only outing on Flat in 2017: stays 1½m: acts on good to firm and good to soft going: tried in cheekpieces. *Mike Sowersby* **–**

INDUS VALLEY (IRE) 10 ch.g. Indian Ridge 123 – Gloriously Bright (USA) 69 (Nureyev (USA) 131) [2017 62, a51: p6d p8g5 p7m6 p6g 7m 8g May 2] well-made gelding: modest handicapper, below form in 2017: stays 9f, effective at shorter: acts on polytrack, firm and soft going: usually wears headgear: tried in tongue tie: often races in rear. *Lee Carter* **48**

INDY (IRE) 6 b.g. Indian Haven 119 – Maddie's Pearl (IRE) 62 (Clodovil (IRE) 116) [2017 89: 10s5 9.8d4 12d* 11.6g* 12.1s6 12v2 Sep 30] sturdy gelding: fairly useful handicapper: won at Ripon in July and Haydock (by neck from Starplex) in August: second at Ripon in September: stays 1½m: acts on heavy going: often races prominently. *John Quinn* **93**

INEXES 5 gr.g. Exceed And Excel (AUS) 126 – Likeable (Dalakhani (IRE) 133) [2017 84: 8m2 8m2 6s* 7.2s4 6d2 7.8s 6s4 7g 6v* t6d5 p7g4 t7.2g6 p6s Dec 7] fairly useful handicapper: won at Hamilton (by ¾ length from Honeysuckle Lil) in June and Pontefract (by neck from Mujassam) in September: stays 1m: acts on polytrack, tapeta, good to firm and heavy going: wears cheekpieces: often starts slowly, usually races towards rear/travels strongly. *Marjorie Fife* **87**

INFAMOUS LAWMAN (IRE) 3 b.g. Lawman (FR) 121 – Infamous Angel 101 (Exceed And Excel (AUS) 126) [2017 6.9g5 7.6d3 8g3 10g6 8.5v5 9v4 t10.2g4 Oct 20] fair maiden: left Brian Ellison after fourth start: stays 1¼m: acts on tapeta and heavy going: races prominently: sold 12,000 gns, sent to the Netherlands. *David O'Meara* **75**

INFANTA ISABELLA 3 b.f. Lope de Vega (IRE) 125 – Shemissa (IRE) (Fairy King (USA)) [2017 12m5 Jun 16] 50,000Y: half-sister to several winners, including smart French/US 5.5f-1m winner Shediak (2-y-o 7.5f winner, by Selkirk): dam unraced out of Prix de Diane winner Shemaka: 16/1, looked unlucky not to finish closer when fifth in maiden at Chepstow (6½ lengths behind Sure To Explore) in June: should progress. *George Baker* **68 p**

INFINITI (IRE) 4 b.f. Arcano (IRE) 122 – Seraphina (IRE) 99 (Pips Pride 117) [2017 67: 8.3g t12.2g4 t12.2g* 11.8g t12.2g6 12d t12.2g6 t14g Oct 27] good-topped filly: modest handicapper: won at Wolverhampton in May: stays 1½m: acts on tapeta and good to firm going: has worn cheekpieces, including in 2017: sometimes slowly away. *Barry Leavy* **63**

IN FIRST PLACE 3 b.g. Bated Breath 125 – Carved Emerald 88 (Pivotal 124) [2017 82: 8m3 8m4 8f6 8m4 10.3g3 8.8g* 10.2d4 10.2s5 10.2d3 Oct 18] good-topped gelding: fairly useful handicapper: won at York (apprentice, by 2 lengths from Breanski) in July: stays 10.5f: acts on soft and good to firm going: tried in blinkers: sold 20,000 gns in October. *Richard Fahey* **89**

INFLEXIBALL 5 b.m. Refuse To Bend (IRE) 128 – Sphere (IRE) 77 (Daylami (IRE) 138) [2017 66: t12.2g2 f11g4 t12.2g 10g6 10.2m5 10.2d* 10d* 9.9g3 10d3 10.5v6 t12.2d Dec 16] lightly-built mare: fair handicapper: won at Doncaster and Leicester in July: stays 1½m: acts on tapeta, good to firm and good to soft going: often races prominently. *John Mackie* **70**

INFLUENT (IRE) 3 b.f. Shamardal (USA) 129 – Kaabari (USA) 89 (Seeking The Gold (USA)) [2017 57p: p8g* p8g p8g^4 t9.5d^3 Dec 16] fairly useful performer: won maiden at Kempton in August: third in handicap at Wolverhampton in December: will be suited by 1¼m: acts on polytrack and tapeta: often races prominently. *James Tate* **88**

IN FOCUS (IRE) 6 ch.g. Intense Focus (USA) 117 – Reine de Neige 96 (Kris 135) [2017 –: t10.2g 7g^4 8m^5 8g 7.8g 13d^2 12d 14.1v^2 15.9s^2 15.9s Oct 31] modest handicapper: left Philip Kirby after fifth start: stays 2m: acts on good to firm and heavy going: in hood last 5 starts: tried in tongue tie: front runner/races prominently: inconsistent. *Dianne Sayer* **63**

INGENUITY 2 b.c. (Mar 24) Slickly (FR) 128 – Onlyyouknowme (IRE) (Martino Alonso (IRE) 113) [2017 5.9s^3 5.9m* t6d^2 Aug 10] 11,000F: first foal: dam useful Italian 5f-1m winner: fairly useful form: won minor event at Carlisle (by nose from Hey Jonesy) in July: raced only at 6f. *Jedd O'Keeffe* **88**

INGLEBY ANGEL (IRE) 8 br.g. Dark Angel (IRE) 113 – Mistress Twister 83 (Pivotal 124) [2017 86: 8d 8.8m 7.8s 8.5m^2 8g^3 8.3g^4 8.3v 9.9g t7.1d^4 8s^3 8v 8.3g^3 t8.6g^2 t9.5g^5 t8s^3 t9.5d^5 Dec 26] leggy gelding: fair handicapper nowadays: left Colin Teague after eighth start: stays 9.5f: acts on fibresand, tapeta, good to firm and heavy going: tried in headgear: usually races towards rear. *David O'Meara* **69**

INGLEBY ERIN 4 b.f. Medicean 128 – Mistress Twister 83 (Pivotal 124) [2017 –: 8s t10.2d Aug 10] little form: tried in cheekpieces. *Colin Teague* **–**

INGLEBY HOLLOW 5 ch.g. Beat Hollow 126 – Mistress Twister 83 (Pivotal 124) [2017 87: 12g 16d^5 14f^6 14g^3 13.9v^2 17.1g 15.9g^4 11.8v 14d* 15.9s^6 14v^4 t12.2g Dec 2] fair handicapper nowadays: won at Redcar in October: stays 2m: acts on tapeta, good to firm and heavy going: often wears cheekpieces: in tongue tie last 4 starts. *David O'Meara* **76**

INGLEBY MACKENZIE 3 b.g. Sixties Icon 125 – Natalie Jay 88 (Ballacashtal (CAN)) [2017 70: 8.1d^5 10.2m 11.4m t12.2g^3 12.1m^2 11.9d* 12d^2 14s p12g 10d^2 Sep 4] sturdy gelding: fair handicapper: won at Doncaster in July: stays 1½m: acts on tapeta, good to firm and good to soft going: front runner/races prominently. *Mick Channon* **73**

INGLEBY MOLLY (IRE) 2 ch.f. (May 17) Choisir (AUS) 126 – Mistress Twister 83 (Pivotal 124) [2017 t5.1g^4 t6.1d^4 Dec 27] half-sister to several winners, including useful 6f-9f winner Ingleby Angel (by Dark Angel) and 1½m-2m winner Ingleby Hollow (by Beat Hollow): dam 1m-1¼m winner: little impact in minor events. *David O'Meara* **–**

INGLEBY SPRING (IRE) 5 br.m. Zebedee 113 – Jouel (FR) (Machiavellian (USA) 123) [2017 68: 10s 7.4d^4 8g^5 8.5d 9.2d 7.8v 8s 10d* 10.2g^6 f8.1g^2 p10g^4 f11.1g* Dec 29] fair handicapper: won at Redcar (amateur) in October and Southwell in December: stays 11f: acts on polytrack, fibresand, soft and good to firm going. *Richard Fahey* **71**

INGLORIOUS 3 gr.g. Kheleyf (USA) 116 – Impulsive Decision (IRE) 71 (Nomination 125) [2017 61: 7.2d^2 7.2g^3 7.2g t8.6g 8.9d^3 7.2g* 7d^5 7.8s 7.2m^3 8m^2 8s 7.2v* t7.2g^4 Nov 25] fair handicapper: won at Ayr in August and Musselburgh in October: stays 9f: acts on tapeta, good to firm and heavy going: wears headgear. *Keith Dalgleish* **77**

INICIAR (GER) 7 b.g. Galileo (IRE) 134 – Iota (GER) 115 (Tiger Hill (IRE) 127) [2017 20f Jun 20] smart performer at best for J-P. Carvalho, well beaten sole outing on Flat in 2017: stays 1½m: acts on good to soft going: tried in blinkers: fairly useful hurdler. *David Pipe* **–**

INIESTA (IRE) 6 b.g. Galileo (IRE) 134 – Red Evie (IRE) 117 (Intikhab (USA) 135) [2017 10m^5 12v^2 p16d^4 f14.1g^3 Dec 22] fair handicapper: stays 2m: acts on polytrack, fibresand, good to firm and heavy going: has worn headgear, including final start: fair hurdler. *Fergal O'Brien* **74**

INITIATIVE (IRE) 2 b.c. (Feb 1) Excelebration (IRE) 133 – Viking Fair (Zamindar (USA) 116) [2017 6d^2 6m* Jun 13] sixth foal: half-brother to 7f winner Beauty's Forte (by Kyllachy): dam unraced close relative to very smart 7f winner Trade Fair: fairly useful form: won minor event at Salisbury (by length from Autumn Leaves) in June: will stay 7f: remains with potential. *Henry Spiller* **81 p**

INJAM (IRE) 4 b.g. Pour Moi (IRE) 125 – Sniffle (IRE) 60 (Shernazar 131) [2017 91: t16.3g 16.3d* 14.1s^5 14.5s* Jun 30] lengthy gelding: useful handicapper: won at York (by length from Graceland) in May and Doncaster (by 2 lengths from Braes of Lochalsh) in June: stays 16.5f: acts on heavy going: often races prominently. *Jedd O'Keeffe* **99**

INJUN SANDS 6 b.g. Halling (USA) 133 – Serriera (FR) 51 (Highest Honor (FR) 124) [2017 87: p12g^{pu} Feb 11] attractive gelding: fairly useful handicapper, amiss sole outing in 2017: stays 2m: acts on polytrack and good to firm going: tried in hood. *Jane Chapple-Hyam* **–**

INKE (IRE) 5 br.m. Intikhab (USA) 135 – Chifney Rush (IRE) (Grand Lodge (USA) 125) [2017 87: p10g^6 p10f^2 10d^2 9.9d^4 t12.2g 9.9g 12v p12g Oct 18] lengthy mare: fairly useful handicapper: second at Lingfield in April and May: stays 1¼m: acts on polytrack and heavy going: often in headgear. *Jim Boyle* **83**

IN KEN'S MEMORY 4 b.f. Sakhee (USA) 136 – Suzi Spends (IRE) 94 (Royal Applause 124) [2017 72: 7g* 8m^4 7g^2 7g^3 6s^5 Aug 9] fairly useful handicapper: won at Brighton in May: placed at Yarmouth (twice) in July: stays 1m: acts on polytrack and good to soft going: front runner/races prominently. *Michael Appleby* **82**

INLAWED 3 b.g. Bahamian Bounty 116 – Regent's Park 83 (Green Desert (USA) 127) [2017 66: 6.1m^3 6f 8.1m 7g^6 6d^6 p6g* p7g^3 p6g* t6.1g^6 Nov 20] good-topped gelding: fair handicapper: won at Kempton in August and October: stays 7f: acts on polytrack and good to firm going. *Ed Walker* **78**

INNER CIRCLE (IRE) 3 b.c. Choisir (AUS) 126 – Eternity Ring (Alzao (USA) 117) [2017 80: p8g^3 8m 8f^2 8m^4 7g 7d^2 7m Sep 23] good-topped colt: fairly useful handicapper: second at Haydock in May and Newmarket (1¼ lengths behind Kynren) in August: stays 1m: acts on polytrack, firm and good to soft going: front runner/races prominently: sold to join Roger Fell 13,500 gns in October. *Richard Hannon* **88**

INNISCASTLE LAD 5 b.g. Kyllachy 129 – Glencal 74 (Compton Place 125) [2017 89: p10d p10g^6 9.9g^2 10.3g Aug 26] strong gelding: fairly useful handicapper: second at Brighton in April: left Stuart Williams after third start: stays 10.5f: acts on polytrack, firm and good to soft going: wears headgear: usually leads. *Donald McCain* **86**

INNISH MAN (IRE) 5 b.g. Fastnet Rock (AUS) 127 – Super Gift (IRE) 96 (Darshaan 133) [2017 74: t12.2g t12.2g t14g Oct 27] modest handicapper: stays 1¾m: acts on tapeta: has worn headgear, including final start. *John Mackie* **59**

INNOCENT TOUCH (IRE) 6 bl.g. Intense Focus (USA) 117 – Guajira (FR) (Mtoto 134) [2017 101: 10g^3 10.1g 10.3d^6 10.1m^2 10.3m^4 7.9d^5 10.1m^4 10.3d^5 Sep 10] rather leggy gelding: useful handicapper: placed at Pontefract (3½ lengths behind Snoano) in April and Epsom (neck behind Not So Sleepy) in June: has form at 14.5f, usually raced over shorter: acts on good to firm and heavy going: tried in visor: races prominently. *Richard Fahey* **99**

INNOKO (FR) 7 gr.g. Carlotamix (FR) 113 – Chalana (Ashkalani (IRE) 128) [2017 68: p11g^6 t10.2g t12.2g^4 11.9m^2 11.6g^2 12d^6 13f* 14g^2 17.1d^3 14.1d^2 p16g^2 t16.3g^5 Nov 15] sturdy gelding: fair handicapper: won at Bath in July: left Tony Carroll after sixth start: stays 16.5f: acts on polytrack, tapeta, firm and soft going: wears headgear: has worn tongue tie. *Robert Stephens* **75**

INNS OF COURT (IRE) 3 b.c. Invincible Spirit (IRE) 121 – Learned Friend (GER) (Seeking The Gold (USA)) [2017 7g* 8d^6 7s* 7d* 8d^2 8d^5 Sep 10] second foal: half-brother to French 1½m winner (stays 2m) Age of Wisdom (by Pivotal): dam lightly-raced daughter of smart French 1¼m-12.5f winner Lune d'Or: very smart performer: won minor event at Saint-Cloud in April, Prix du Palais-Royal at Maisons-Laffitte in June and Prix de la Porte Maillot at Deauville (beat African Ride ¾ length) in July: short-head second to Al Wukair in Prix Jacques le Marois at Deauville (caught on line) next time: stays 1m: acts on soft going. *A. Fabre, France* **123**

INNSTIGATOR 3 b.g. Delegator 125 – Page (Elmaamul (USA) 125) [2017 60: 7m 6d 6g p6d^4 p7g Oct 17] modest maiden: stays 6f: acts on polytrack: temperament under suspicion. *Ralph Smith* **53**

INN THE BULL (GER) 4 ch.g. Lope de Vega (IRE) 125 – Ile Rousse (Danehill (USA) 126) [2017 76: 10m 11m^2 13.3g Jul 13] angular gelding: fair handicapper: stays 11f: acts on soft and good to firm going: in tongue tie last 2 starts. *Alan King* **77**

INSCRIBE (USA) 3 b.g. Harlan's Holiday (USA) 124 – Reflections (Sadler's Wells (USA) 132) [2017 –: p10g^5 8g^5 8v* 10s* Nov 5] fairly useful performer: won handicaps at Gowran in October and Naas (by neck from Lucky Mistake) in November: left Sir Michael Stoute after first start: stays 1¼m: acts on heavy going: will go on improving. *G. M. Lyons, Ireland* **92 p**

INSHAA 5 b.g. Dansili 127 – Hidden Brief 100 (Barathea (IRE) 127) [2017 72: t6g^5 t6g^3 p7g t6g^3 t6g^3 t6s t7.1d^5 t7.1g^6 f8.1g Dec 1] lengthy gelding: fair maiden: left Michael Herrington after sixth start: stays 1m: acts on fibresand and tapeta: wears cheekpieces: tried in tongue tie. *Simon West* **71**

INSHIRAAH (FR) 3 b.f. Holy Roman Emperor (IRE) 125 – Blessed Catch (USA) (Storm Cat (USA)) [2017 7.4g^3 t7.2g^3 t7.2g* 7d^3 7g* 7d* Jul 29] €75,000Y: third foal: sister to French winner around 1¼m Dream of Life: dam unraced sister to smart winner up **104 p**

to 1m Brave Tin Soldier out of sister to Kentucky Derby winner Fusaichi Pegasus: useful performer: won maiden at Wolverhampton in June and handicaps at Newmarket (twice, by 4½ lengths from Cartographer second occasion) in July: will stay 1m: acts on tapeta and good to soft going: usually responds generously to pressure: open to further improvement. *George Peckham*

INSOLENCEOFOFFICE (IRE) 9 b.g. Kodiac 112 – Sharp Diversion (USA) 42 (Diesis 133) [2017 62: t5d t6d t5.1g p6g t7.1g t6g² t6.1g 5s³ 6d Sep 2] modest handicapper: stays 6f: acts on all-weather, soft and good to firm going: wears headgear. *Richard Ford* **55**

INSPECTOR (IRE) 3 b.c. Lawman (FR) 121 – Helter Helter (USA) (Seeking The Gold (USA)) [2017 –: 12s⁴ 11.6m 11.8g 16.1d p16g⁴ Aug 15] fair maiden: fourth at Thirsk in May: standout effort at 1½m: acts on soft going: in headgear last 3 starts: wears tongue tie: sold £4,000, sent to Sweden. *Hugo Palmer* **65**

INSPECTOR NORSE 6 b.g. Norse Dancer (IRE) 127 – Indiana Blues 90 (Indian Ridge 123) [2017 –: 11.6m⁶ 10g⁴ 10g⁶ 10.2g 9.9f 11.2v⁴ 9.9v² 12.5s² 13.9v³ Oct 21] lengthy gelding: modest handicapper: stays 12.5f: acts on polytrack, good to firm and heavy going: sometimes wears headgear: usually races prominently. *Tim Easterby* **64**

INSPIRE 5 gr.m. Hellvelyn 118 – Time Clash 67 (Timeless Times (USA) 99) [2017 t6g Feb 6] well held in maidens. *Matthew Salaman* **–**

INSTANT ATTRACTION (IRE) 6 b.g. Tagula (IRE) 116 – Coup de Coeur (IRE) (Kahyasi 130) [2017 106: 8g 7.9d t8s 7.9m 7.9d 7.8v² 7.6v³ 8.2v⁵ 7g 8.3g Nov 1] small, close-coupled gelding: useful handicapper: stays 8.5f: acts on polytrack, tapeta, good to firm and heavy going: in visor last 3 starts. *Jedd O'Keeffe* **100**

INSTANT KARMA (IRE) 6 b.g. Peintre Celebre (USA) 137 – Kotdiji (Mtoto 134) [2017 81: p12g* 12m p11g Jun 28] leggy gelding: fairly useful handicapper: won at Kempton (by ¾ length from Safira Menina) in March: stays 13f: acts on polytrack and heavy going: has worn visor: sold to join Jamie Snowden £11,000 in July: fairly useful hurdler. *Michael Bell* **90**

INSTILL 5 ch.g. Pivotal 124 – Insijaam (USA) 112 (Secretariat (USA)) [2017 t9.5m t12.2g⁵ t9.5g⁵ 11.5m May 17] fair handicapper at 3 yrs, below that level in 2017 after long absence: stays 11.5f: acts on good to soft going: tried in visor. *Mandy Rowland* **64**

INSTITUTION (IRE) 2 ch.c. (Apr 20) Zoffany (IRE) 121 – Became (USA) (Giant's Causeway (USA) 132) [2017 8g 8g Oct 7] fair form: better effort when seventh in minor event at Newmarket (6¾ lengths behind Just Brilliant) in October. *Charles Hills* **67**

INSURGENCE 2 ch.g. (Mar 14) Sepoy (AUS) 129 – Isis (USA) 71 (Royal Academy (USA) 130) [2017 7m 6m⁶ 6d p7g* Nov 17] good-topped gelding: seventh foal: half-brother to 6f winner (stayed 1m) Mawjoodah (by Cadeaux Genereux) and 2-y-o 7f winner Iberis (by Nayef): dam twice-raced half-sister to smart 6f winner Sir Gerry: fairly useful form: won nursery at Lingfield in November: best effort at 7f: will go on improving. *James Fanshawe* **89 p**

INSURPLUS (IRE) 4 b.g. Bushranger (IRE) 119 – Emly Express (IRE) (High Estate 127) [2017 70: 5m⁴ 6m⁶ 6d⁵ 6g 6g³ 7.2d 6g² 7g³ 7m* 7s⁵ t6g³ t7.1d³ t7.1g* Nov 24] fair handicapper: won at Redcar in August and Newcastle in November: stays 7f: acts on tapeta and good to firm going: has worn headgear, including in 2017: usually races nearer last than first/responds generously to pressure. *Jim Goldie* **76**

INTELLECT (IRE) 3 b.c. Nathaniel (IRE) 129 – Shesasmartlady (IRE) (Dolphin Street (FR) 125) [2017 p10g⁶ 10.2s* 12v* 13.9m 11.5d⁴ Sep 19] 115,000F, 145,000Y: useful-looking colt: half-brother to several winners, including smart winner up to 7f Captain Marvelous (2-y-o 5f/6f winner, by Invincible Spirit) and useful 1¼m-1½m winner Hero Worship (by Kalanisi): dam of little account: useful performer: won maiden at Nottingham in June and handicap at Newbury (by 9 lengths from Amelia Dream) in July: stays 1½m: best form on soft/heavy going: usually races close up: sold 23,000 gns, sent to Saudi Arabia. *Sir Michael Stoute* **101**

INTELLIGENCE CROSS (USA) 3 b.c. War Front (USA) 119 – Good Vibes (USA) (Unbridled's Song (USA) 125) [2017 109: p7g⁴ 5.8g³ 6m 6g⁵ 6.5g 6m⁶ 5.8g* 6s Oct 21] compact colt: smart performer: won minor event at Navan (by 2¾ lengths from Mr Scarlet) in September: stays 6f: acts on good to firm and good to soft going: wears blinkers: usually wears tongue tie. *Aidan O'Brien, Ireland* **113**

INTENSE ROMANCE (IRE) 3 b.f. Intense Focus (USA) 117 – Hedera (USA) 90 (Woodman (USA) 126) [2017 t5d* t6g* t6g⁴ 6m³ 6m⁶ t5s* 6g⁴ t5g* 5m² 5d* 5v⁴ 5m* 5s Oct 9] €21,000Y: sturdy filly: half-sister to numerous winners, including French winner up to 11.5f Ivy League (2-y-o 9.5f winner, by Doyoun) and winner up to 1¼m Deia Sunrise **105**

(2-y-o 1m winner, by Clodovil), both useful: dam 2-y-o 7f winner: useful performer: won maiden at Newcastle in February, handicaps there in March, May and June, and other handicaps at Ascot (by 1¾ lengths from Savannah Beau) in July and York (apprentice, dead-heated with Holmeswood) in August: stays 6f: acts on tapeta, good to firm and good to soft going. *Michael Dods*

INTENSE STARLET (IRE) 6 ch.m. Intense Focus (USA) 117 – Glady Starlet (GER) (Big Shuffle (USA) 122) [2017 58, a69: f6g^{6} t6g t6g^{6} 7g 5d^{6} 6m 6.3v^{4} 5s 7v p5g p6g^{6} p5g Nov 24] rather lightly-made mare: modest handicapper: left Marjorie Fife after third start: stays 6.5f: acts on polytrack, tapeta and heavy going: often wears headgear: wears tongue tie: often races prominently. *Thomas P. O'Connor, Ireland* **52**

INTENSE STYLE (IRE) 5 ch.g. Intense Focus (USA) 117 – Style Queen (IRE) 82 (Galileo (IRE) 134) [2017 98: t6g^{4} 6g 6s 7d^{2} 7s 7d 6s 8d^{6} 8g 7s^{2} 7.4v* 7v p8g^{4} Nov 17] leggy, quite good-topped gelding: fairly useful handicapper nowadays: won at Beverley (by neck from Kirkham) in September: stays 1m: acts on polytrack and heavy going: has worn headgear. *Les Eyre* **92**

INTENSE TANGO 6 b.m. Mastercraftsman (IRE) 129 – Cover Look (SAF) (Fort Wood (USA) 117) [2017 101: t16.5m^{6} p16d^{4} t12.4s 16g 14g 11.8d 14m^{5} 14s 14v Sep 30] rangy mare: useful handicapper, generally well below form in 2017: stays 1¾m: acts on polytrack, tapeta, soft and good to firm going: tried in cheekpieces: often wears tongue tie: front runner/races prominently. *K. R. Burke* **93**

INTENSICAL (IRE) 6 b.g. Intense Focus (USA) 117 – Christinas Letter (IRE) (Galileo (IRE) 134) [2017 81: p7g^{2} p8g^{3} p10g^{4} f7g^{6} 7g^{3} p7d^{6} 8m*^{d} 7.8s 8.1g^{3} 8m^{6} 8s^{3} a7.5s a7.5g 8s^{5} Dec 14] fairly useful handicapper: first past post at Doncaster in June, but later disqualified due to prohibited substance: left Ivan Furtado after eleventh start and C. Rossi after thirteenth: stays 1m: acts on polytrack, soft and good to firm going: wears headgear: has worn tongue tie: usually races prominently. *C. Escuder, France* **84**

INTERCHOICE STAR 12 b.g. Josr Algarhoud (IRE) 118 – Blakeshall Girl 64 (Piccolo 121) [2017 39: f6.1g^{5} f6.1g Nov 13] fair at best, little form since 2015: stays 7f: acts on polytrack, fibresand, good to firm and good to soft going: wears headgear. *Ray Peacock* **–**

INTERCONNECTION 6 ch.g. Mount Nelson 125 – Lacework 91 (Pivotal 124) [2017 97: 8.3g 10s^{2} 9.1g^{2} 9.1d^{4} 10.9g a9.9f a9.7f^{6} Dec 29] sturdy gelding: useful handicapper: second at Newmarket (2 lengths behind Zzoro) in May and Yarmouth (¾ length behind Rotherwick) in July: left Ed Vaughan after fourth start: stays 12.5f: acts on polytrack, firm and soft going: wears headgear: front runner/races prominently. *S. bin Ghadayer, UAE* **97**

INTERLINK (USA) 4 b.g. Kitten's Joy (USA) 128 – Seattle Tac (USA) (Seattle Slew (USA)) [2017 82: 8g t6g^{2} p5s^{5} 6g 6d^{3} 5g f6.1g^{2} 6s^{2} t7.1g Nov 3] fair handicapper: left Michael Appleby after eighth start: best form at 6f: acts on all-weather and soft going. *Marjorie Fife* **78**

INTERMODAL 3 b.g. Rail Link 132 – Rule of Nature 88 (Oasis Dream 129) [2017 82p: p10g^{5} 10m p10s^{6} t8s^{5} p8s^{3} Dec 8] strong gelding: fair handicapper: left Amanda Perrett after second start: best effort at 1m: acts on polytrack: front runner/races prominently, often races freely. *Jamie Osborne* **76**

INTERNATIONAL LAW 3 gr.g. Exceed And Excel (AUS) 126 – Cruel Sea (USA) 94 (Mizzen Mast (USA) 121) [2017 82: 8f* 8m 8m 8f^{5} 9.9g 10.3d 8.1d* Oct 23] fairly useful performer: won maiden at Bath in April and handicap at Windsor (dead-heated with East Coast Lady) in October: stays 1m: acts on firm and good to soft going: wears headgear: sold to join Antony Brittain 30,000 gns later in October. *Brian Meehan* **80**

INTERNATIONAL MAN 2 b.g. (Apr 27) Epaulette (AUS) 126 – Right Answer 95 (Lujain (USA) 119) [2017 6m* 7.4s^{4} 7.4g^{2} 6.5g 6g 8d Oct 27] 72,000Y: good-topped gelding: half-brother to several winners, including smart 2-y-o 5f/6f winner Galtymore Lad (by Indesatchel), later successful in Hong Kong, and useful 6f winner Cartographer (by Henrythenavigator): dam 2-y-o 5f winner: fairly useful performer: won maiden at York (by 1½ lengths from Arbalet) in June: second in minor event at Beverley in August: stays 7.5f: acts on good to firm going. *Richard Fahey* **81**

INTERN (IRE) 3 b.g. Rip Van Winkle (IRE) 134 – Uliana (USA) 95 (Darshaan 133) [2017 94p: 10d^{2} 12m p10g^{3} p10g^{4} Dec 23] compact gelding: closely related to 1m (including at 2 yrs) winner So Amazing (by Galileo) and half-brother to several winners, including useful 1m winner (stayed 1¼m) Festival Princess (by Barathea): dam 1¼m winner: useful performer: won maiden at Leopardstown in 2016 for David Wachman: second in Classic Trial at Sandown (head behind Cunco) in April and third in minor event **108**

at Lingfield (1¾ lengths behind Toast of New York) in December: left Ralph Beckett after second start: stays 1¼m: acts on polytrack, good to firm and good to soft going: usually races towards rear. *David Simcock*

INTERWEAVE 3 ch.f. Dutch Art 126 – Interlace 78 (Pivotal 124) [2017 79: p8g* 10d Jun 5] workmanlike filly: fair performer: won maiden at Chelmsford in April: stays 1m: acts on polytrack and good to firm going: tried in visor: often races prominently. *Sir Michael Stoute* **75**

IN THE HOUSE (IRE) 5 b.m. Montjeu (IRE) 137 – O' Bella Ballerina (USA) 80 (Fusaichi Pegasus (USA) 130) [2017 67: p16s 10m Jul 23] compact mare: fair maiden, well beaten both starts in 2017: stays 2m: acts on polytrack, good to firm and good to soft going: tried in blinkers/tongue tie: usually races nearer last than first. *Lucinda Egerton* –

IN THE LOPE (IRE) 3 b.g. Lope de Vega (IRE) 125 – Biswa (USA) 48 (Kafwain (USA) 118) [2017 8.9g* 8g* 8s^{5} p9.4g* p10g^{4} Nov 18] fourth foal: brother to smart French 6f (including at 2 yrs)/7f winner Ride Like The Wind and useful 6.5f-1m winner Qassem, and half-brother to French 6f winner Royale du Buisson (by Invincible Spirit): dam twice-raced half-sister to smart US Grade 1 8.5f winner Ariege: useful performer: won claimer at Saint-Malo in August, and handicaps at Deauville later same month and Chantilly in October: best effort when 2½ lengths fourth to Master The World in listed race at Lingfield on final outing: stays 1¼m: acts on polytrack and soft going. *Mme Pia Brandt, France* **104**

IN THE RED (IRE) 4 b.g. Elusive Pimpernel (USA) 117 – Roses From Ridey (IRE) 78 (Petorius 117) [2017 91: p8d* 8m 7.6d^{6} 6m 7m* 7f 8m^{6} 9.1d 10g 6.1m 7d p8g Nov 17] good-topped gelding: useful handicapper: won at Kempton (by 2¾ lengths from Pendo) in January and Goodwood (apprentice) in June: left Richard Hannon after first start: stays 1m: acts on polytrack, soft and good to firm going: has worn headgear, including in 2017. *Martin Smith* **95**

IN THE SPOTLIGHT (IRE) 3 b.f. Exceed And Excel (AUS) 126 – Naruko (USA) (Street Cry (IRE) 130) [2017 60: t6f^{2} p6g* p7d^{3} 6g^{5} 6m* 5.7f^{5} 6.1m^{5} 6m* 6m^{6} Aug 25] fairly useful handicapper: won at Kempton in January, and Yarmouth in June and August (by 2¾ lengths from Mulzim): stays 6f: acts on polytrack, tapeta, good to firm and good to soft going: in cheekpieces last 2 starts: sometimes slowly away, often races towards rear: sold 130,000 gns in December. *Henry Spiller* **89**

INTIBAAH 7 b.g. Elnadim (USA) 128 – Mawaared 61 (Machiavellian (USA) 123) [2017 100, a86: t5g 5g^{4} 5d^{2} 5.5d^{6} Jul 22] good-quartered gelding: fairly useful handicapper: second at Salisbury in June: best up to 6f nowadays: acts on polytrack, good to firm and heavy going: wears headgear. *George Baker* **87**

INTIMATE ART (IRE) 3 ch.g. Dutch Art 126 – Intimacy (IRE) (Teofilo (IRE) 126) [2017 85: 7g p8g^{3} 8m p8s* 7.6d^{6} p8g Dec 20] compact gelding: fairly useful handicapper: won at Chelmsford (by short head from Makaarim) in July: third there in June: stays 1m: acts on polytrack: sometimes slowly away. *Andrew Balding* **91**

INTIMATELY 4 b.g. Intense Focus (USA) 117 – Midnight Fling 66 (Groom Dancer (USA) 128) [2017 65: p7m 7m^{6} 7d* 7d^{5} 8m^{5} 8g^{3} 7d 7d^{4} 7m 8d* 7v 7s Oct 9] compact gelding: fair handicapper: won apprentice events at Salisbury in May and Brighton in September: stays 1m: acts on polytrack, good to firm and good to soft going: tried in blinkers: usually slowly away, often races towards rear. *Jonathan Portman* **67**

INTIMATION 5 b.m. Dubawi (IRE) 129 – Infallible 114 (Pivotal 124) [2017 107: 8f^{2} 9d^{2} 8g^{5} 9m^{6} 10.4g* Oct 22] tall mare: smart performer: won Prix de Flore at Saint-Cloud (by ½ length from Son Macia) in October: second earlier in listed race at Goodwood and Dance Design Stakes at the Curragh (½ length behind Rain Goddess): stays 10.5f: acts on any turf going. *Sir Michael Stoute* **110**

INTIMIDATOR (IRE) 6 b.g. Intikhab (USA) 135 – Zither 93 (Zafonic (USA) 130) [2017 63: p16s^{2} p16g^{5} p16g p16g Oct 4] sturdy gelding: fair maiden: stays 2m: acts on polytrack. *Miss Joey Ellis* **65**

INTISAAB 6 b.g. Elnadim (USA) 128 – Katoom (IRE) 75 (Soviet Star (USA) 128) [2017 114: 6m* 6m^{5} 6.1m^{5} 6m t6s^{2} 6g 6s^{6} 6d 6m^{3} p7s^{4} 6s^{6} 7d^{4} p6g^{4} p6g^{2} t6.1d* Dec 26] sturdy gelding: smart performer: won handicap at Ripon (by neck from Muntadab) in April and minor event at Wolverhampton (by length from Gulliver) in December: placed in Chipchase Stakes at Newcastle in July, listed race at Newmarket in August and handicap at Kempton (¾ length behind Double Up) in November: best at 6f/7f: acts on polytrack, tapeta, good to firm and good to soft going: wears headgear: often races towards rear. *David O'Meara* **117**

INTISHA (IRE) 3 b.f. Intikhab (USA) 135 – Shawaaty (IRE) (Monsun (GER) 124) [2017 67: t12.2g 8.3m Apr 10] smallish filly: fair form at 2 yrs, well held both outings in 2017: tried in tongue tie. *Jonathan Portman* –

INTIWIN (IRE) 5 b.g. Intikhab (USA) 135 – Muluk (IRE) 83 (Rainbow Quest (USA) 134) [2017 85: 10m 10m 10g5 8d 8.3s t8s5 t7.1d* t7.1g3 t7.1d Nov 4] neat gelding: fair handicapper: won at Newcastle in September: stays 1¼m: acts on tapeta, firm and soft going. *Linda Perratt* **68**

INTOXIKATING 3 b.g. Phoenix Reach (IRE) 124 – Chocolada (Namid 128) [2017 6.1m t7.1g5 t6d6 Sep 29] little impact in maidens: wears tongue tie. *Gay Kelleway* **56 ?**

INTRANSIGENT 8 b.g. Trans Island 119 – Mara River 86 (Efisio 120) [2017 104: t6g4 p7d* p7g2 p8g2 p7g5 p7g 7.6d p7g2 7.6g p6g2 Nov 6] tall gelding: useful handicapper: won at Kempton (by ½ length from Joey's Destiny) in January: second at same course on 3 other occasions in 2017: stays 1m: acts on polytrack, firm and soft going: has worn hood, including in 2017. *Andrew Balding* **100**

INTREPIDLY (USA) 3 b.g. Medaglia d'Oro (USA) 129 – Trepidation (USA) (Seeking The Gold (USA)) [2017 93p: 9m4 10m* p11g 12m p10g4 Dec 12] useful handicapper: won at Windsor (by neck from Anythingtoday) in July: stays 1¼m: acts on polytrack and good to firm going: sometimes slowly away. *Jeremy Noseda* **100**

INTRICATELY (IRE) 3 b.f. Fastnet Rock (AUS) 127 – Inner Realm (IRE) 62 (Galileo (IRE) 134) [2017 110: 7d4 8m 8d4 10g6 12f 8g5 8d Sep 9] strong, well-made filly: smart performer: fourth in Irish 1000 Guineas at the Curragh (5 lengths behind Winter) on third start: stays 1m: acts on soft and good to firm going: tried in blinkers: sold 1,700,000 gns in December. *Joseph Patrick O'Brien, Ireland* **112**

INTRUDE 5 b.g. Intikhab (USA) 135 – Don't Tell Mum (IRE) 99 (Dansili 127) [2017 85, a102: p7g p8m6 t9.5g4 p10g2 p10g5 8m2 8s* 8m 8g Sep 28] good-topped gelding: useful handicapper: won at Yarmouth (by 16 lengths from Berrahri) in June: stays 1¼m: acts on polytrack, tapeta, firm and soft going: tried in cheekpieces: has worn tongue tie, including last 3 starts. *Stuart Williams* **98**

INUK (IRE) 2 b.f. (Feb 23) Kodiac 112 – Elkmait 80 (Trade Fair 124) [2017 p6g4 6.1d 5d5 7g6 p7d4 6v4 p6g* p5g3 p6g* Dec 12] 55,000Y: second foal: dam, 2-y-o 6f winner, half-sister to 2000 Guineas third Stubbs Art: modest performer: won nursery at Kempton in October and seller at Lingfield in December: stays 6f: acts on polytrack: in cheekpieces last 4 starts. *Richard Hughes* **64**

INVERMERE 4 b.f. Kyllachy 129 – Kootenay (IRE) 109 (Selkirk (USA) 129) [2017 87: 7g2 8m 7m5 7m5 7m 8.3d3 7.8s5 8.3d4 8s2 8s 8d Nov 4] good-topped filly: fairly useful handicapper: second at Doncaster in April and Musselburgh in September: stays 8.5f: acts on firm and soft going: usually races prominently. *Richard Fahey* **85**

INVESTIGATION 3 gr.g. Rip Van Winkle (IRE) 134 – Syann (IRE) 97 (Daylami (IRE) 138) [2017 t12.2g3 11.5g* 11.9d p11g 12d 14.2v p12g Dec 23] good-topped gelding: fair performer: won maiden at Yarmouth in April: left Andrew Balding after sixth start: best effort at 11.5f: in hood last 3 starts: often starts slowly, races freely. *Shaun Harris* **78**

INVICTUS (GER) 5 b.g. Exceed And Excel (AUS) 126 – Ivowen (USA) 104 (Theatrical) [2017 88: p10g 8.3g6 9.9g 12d 10g* 9d 11.6g4 11.1v3 10v Sep 21] fair handicapper nowadays: won at Leicester in June: stays 11f: best form on good going: often wears headgear: front runner/races prominently. *David Loughnane* **72**

INVINCIBLE ARMY (IRE) 2 b.c. (Jan 28) Invincible Spirit (IRE) 121 – Rajeem 116 (Diktat 126) [2017 6m2 6m* 6g4 5v2 6m2 p6g* 6m2 Sep 23] 95,000Y: sturdy colt: seventh foal: dam 1m winner (including at 2 yrs and Falmouth Stakes): smart performer: won minor event at Newmarket (by 5 lengths from Tribal Quest) in June and Sirenia Stakes at Kempton (by 1½ lengths from Corinthia Knight) in September: second in Gimcrack Stakes at York in August and Mill Reef Stakes at Newbury in September: likely to prove best at 5f/6f: acts on polytrack, good to firm and heavy going: strong traveller. *James Tate* **112**

INVINCIBLE MAN (IRE) 3 b.c. Invincible Spirit (IRE) 121 – Elshabakiya (IRE) 102 (Diktat 126) [2017 t7.1m5 p8g3 t7.1g2 f7g2 Mar 15] fair form in maidens: stays 1m. *James Tate* **73**

INVINCIBLE RIDGE (IRE) 9 b.g. Invincible Spirit (IRE) 121 – Dani Ridge (IRE) 92 (Indian Ridge 123) [2017 89: t5.1f6 t5.1g2 t6m2 t5.1g t5.1g* 5m3 5m5 5.1d4 5s6 5g5 5.1g 5s 5g t5.1g3 t6.1g* t6.1d Dec 9] quite good-topped gelding: fairly useful handicapper: won at Wolverhampton in April and November (by head from Arnarson): raced at sprint trips: acts on polytrack, tapeta, soft and good to firm going: tried in blinkers: has worn tongue tie. *Eric Alston* **85**

INVIOLABLE SPIRIT (IRE) 2 b.g. (Mar 28) Zebedee 113 – Mediska 59 (Medicean 128) [2017 5m* 5f^{3} 6g^{2} 5.2v 6.1s^{5} 6d 7d 6g Oct 7] compact, good-quartered gelding: fair performer: won minor event at Redcar in April: stays 6f: acts on firm and soft going. *Richard Fahey* **77**

IONA ISLAND 4 b.f. Dutch Art 126 – Still Small Voice (Polish Precedent (USA) 131) [2017 71: p12d^{3} t13.9f* p16g^{3} 13d^{4} p16g 14.2g Aug 25] leggy filly: fair handicapper: won at Wolverhampton in February: stays 2m: acts on polytrack, tapeta, and good to firm going. *Peter Hiatt* **70**

IONIZATION (IRE) 4 ch.f. The Carbon Unit (USA) 106 – The Mighty Atom (USA) 78 (Sky Mesa (USA) 116) [2017 90: 7.1g 7.2m^{3} 8.3m^{2} 8.2s^{2} 8.3s^{3} 7d^{4} 7.5s 9.5s Sep 16] useful handicapper: second at Haydock (head behind Zwayyan) in June stays 8.5f: acts on polytrack, soft and good to firm going. *John Patrick Shanahan, Ireland* **102**

IPCRESS FILE 2 ch.g. (Apr 27) Sixties Icon 125 – Solmorin (Fraam 114) [2017 7d^{3} p8g^{6} f7.1g^{5} Nov 16] modest form: best effort when third in maiden at Brighton (4½ lengths behind Groundnut) in September. *Scott Dixon* **61**

IPSILANTE 2 b.f. (Mar 18) Nayef (USA) 129 – Rosacara 71 (Green Desert (USA) 127) [2017 7.6d 6g p8g Nov 1] 8,000Y: half-sister to several winners, including useful 2-y-o 6f winner Russelliana (by Medicean) and winner up to 1¾m Kingarrick (2-y-o 7f winner, by Selkirk): dam, maiden (stayed 1m), half-sister to high-class 1m-10.5f winner Notnowcato: no form. *Jonathan Portman* **–**

IQUITOS (GER) 5 b.h. Adlerflug (GER) 123 – Irika (GER) (Areion (GER) 115) [2017 121: 10.9g^{2} 11.9s^{2} 9.9g* 11.9g^{2} 11.9d 11.9s^{2} 11.9f Nov 26] very smart performer: won Grosser Dallmayr-Preis Bayerisches Zuchtrennen at Munich (by 1½ lengths from Best Solution) in July: second in Grosser Preis der Badischen Wirtschaft at Baden-Baden (neck behind Guignol), Grosser Hansa-Preis at Hamburg (3¾ lengths behind Dschingis Secret), Grosser Preis von Baden (beaten 2½ lengths by Guignol) and Grosser Preis von Bayern at Munich (neck behind Guignol): creditable seventh to Enable in Prix de l'Arc de Triomphe at Chantilly but behind in Japan Cup at Tokyo on other starts: stays 1½m: acts on any turf going: usually races towards rear. *H-J. Groschel, Germany* **123**

IRISHCORRESPONDENT (IRE) 3 b.g. Teofilo (IRE) 126 – Contrary (IRE) 79 (Mark of Esteem (IRE) 137) [2017 8d* 8g* 8d^{3} 10m^{5} 7m^{5} 8g^{2} 9.9g* Dec 23] close-coupled gelding: fourth foal: half-brother to 3 winners, including useful 10.4f-1½m winner Chilli Spice (by Manduro) and 7f-1m winner Nonno Giulio (2-y-o 7.5f winner, by Halling): dam, French 2-y-o 7f winner, half-sister to smart/very smart sprinters Caspian Prince and Spirit Quartz: smart performer: won maiden at Leopardstown in April and minor event at the Curragh (by 4½ lengths from Homesman) in May: third in Irish 2000 Guineas at the Curragh (7 lengths behind Churchill) in May: gelded and left M. Halford after fourth start: renamed Exultant, won handicap at Sha Tin in December: stays 1¼m. *A. S. Cruz, Hong Kong* **111**

IRISH HAWKE (IRE) 5 b.g. Montjeu (IRE) 137 – Ahdaab (USA) 73 (Rahy (USA) 115) [2017 t12.2g Jun 7] good-topped gelding: fair at 3 yrs, well held sole outing on Flat since: stays 11.5f: tried in blinkers/tongue tie: modest hurdler. *Donald McCain* **–**

IRISH SKY (IRE) 3 b.f. Elnadim (USA) 128 – Royal Aly (USA) (Royal Academy (USA) 130) [2017 p7g 6g^{3} p6g t5g^{3} p6g Dec 21] €8,000F, €25,000Y: third foal: half-sister to winner up to 1¾m Nice Story (2-y-o 1m winner, by Suave): dam, US 5f winner, out of sister to Kentucky Derby winner Strike The Gold: modest form when third in seller at Leicester in April, standout effort: tried in cheekpieces/tongue tie. *Henry Spiller* **53**

IRISH TIMES 2 b.c. (Apr 17) Swiss Spirit 117 – Amouage Royale (IRE) (Mr Greeley (USA) 122) [2017 p7g Dec 21] 33/1, well held in minor event at Chelmsford. *Henry Spiller* **–**

IRON ISLANDS 3 b.g. Dutch Art 126 – Night Premiere (IRE) 63 (Night Shift (USA)) [2017 72: 8m 8g 8.3s^{6} Jun 29] fair maiden: stays 1m: acts on soft going: in headgear last 2 starts: often races prominently. *K. R. Burke* **71**

IRON LADY (IRE) 3 b.f. Exceed And Excel (AUS) 126 – Kahlua Kiss 103 (Mister Baileys 123) [2017 –: 7g t6.1g* 5.7f^{2} 6g^{6} 5.3g Sep 3] sturdy filly: modest handicapper: won at Wolverhampton in June: stays 6f: acts on tapeta and firm going: tried in tongue tie: front runner/races prominently. *William Muir* **62**

IRON SKY 2 b.g. (Mar 19) Showcasing 117 – Addiena 72 (Golan (IRE) 129) [2017 f7.1g Nov 28] 22,000F, €44,000 2-y-o: second foal: dam 1m winner: 14/1, well held in minor event at Southwell: entitled to do better. *Keith Dalgleish* **– p**

IRVINE LADY (IRE) 4 ch.f. Footstepsinthesand 120 – Ascot Lady (IRE) 85 (Spinning **54**
World (USA) 130) [2017 –: p7g^{6} t5.1g p6g^{6} 7.2s^{2} 7.2g 7.2d^{6} 9.2d 8.3v^{3} 7.2s 8v Oct 12]
modest maiden: left Gay Kelleway after third start: best effort at 7f: acts on soft going:
often wears headgear. *R. Mike Smith*

ISAAC BELL (IRE) 9 b.g. Fruits of Love (USA) 127 – Oso Well (IRE) (Oscar (IRE) **92**
122) [2017 p12g* p12g^{2} p12d^{6} p16d^{5} Dec 13] fairly useful form: won maiden at Kempton
(by neck from Stanley) in October: second in handicap there in November: stays 1½m:
wears tongue tie: bumper/hurdle winner. *Alex Hales*

ISABEL DE URBINA (IRE) 3 b.f. Lope de Vega (IRE) 125 – Roscoff (IRE) (Daylami **105**
(IRE) 138) [2017 73P: 10m^{2} 12m^{6} 12s^{2} 12d^{4} 12d Sep 29] rather unfurnished filly: useful
performer: second in listed races at Newmarket in May (¾ length behind Horseplay) and
July (length behind God Given): stays 1½m: acts on soft and good to firm going.
Ralph Beckett

ISABELLA (IRE) 3 ch.f. Galileo (IRE) 134 – Song of My Heart (IRE) 107 (Footstepsin- **100**
thesand 120) [2017 56p: 8d* 8g* 8.3d^{2} Sep 2] useful form: won maiden at Thirsk and
handicap at Pontefract (by 1½ lengths from Eagle Creek) in August: second in handicap at
Hamilton (neck behind Whatsthemessage) in September: stays 8.5f. *David O'Meara*

ISABELLA MAYSON 2 b.f. (Apr 28) Mayson 124 – Sydney Star 91 (Machiavellian **62**
(USA) 123) [2017 6m^{6} 6g^{2} 7d^{6} 6v^{6} Sep 25] seventh foal: half-sister to 7f winner Hold The
Star (by Red Ransom) and a winner abroad by Compton Place: dam 7f winner: modest
form: stays 7f. *Stuart Kittow*

ISABELLA RUBY 2 b.f. (Apr 18) Power 117 – Scarlet Rocks (IRE) 83 (Chineur (FR) **56**
123) [2017 6.9v 6.1v^{5} 6v^{5} t6g Oct 19] second foal: dam winner up to 6f (2-y-o 5f winner)
out of useful 2-y-o 7f winner Alexander Duchess: modest form when fifth in minor event
at Chepstow in September, standout effort: wears hood. *Lisa Williamson*

ISABEL'S ON IT 3 ch.f. Dubawi (IRE) 129 – Check The Label (USA) 112 (Stormin **94**
Fever (USA) 116) [2017 77p: 7m^{3} p7g^{2} 7g* 6.9s^{4} 6g 8f Sep 20] rather unfurnished filly:
fairly useful performer: won maiden at Lingfield in June: left William Haggas after fifth
start: stays 7f: acts on polytrack, tapeta, soft and good to firm going. *Arnaud Delacour, USA*

ISEEMIST (IRE) 6 gr.m. Verglas (IRE) 118 – Krasivaya (IRE) (Soviet Star (USA) 128) **100**
[2017 101: p5g^{3} 5f^{6} 6.1g^{6} 6g^{2} 6m 6.1g 6g^{6} 6g^{2} 5v^{3} 6s^{3} Oct 15] workmanlike mare:
useful handicapper: placed 5 times in 2017: stays 7f: acts on polytrack, good to firm and
heavy going: has worn headgear, including last 2 starts: front runner/races prominently.
John Gallagher

ISHARAH (USA) 4 b.g. Kitten's Joy (USA) 128 – Menekineko (USA) (Kingmambo **99**
(USA) 125) [2017 90: t16.3g* f12g* t16.5g^{3} p15.8g^{2} 14g 16g^{5} t16.3g 16d 16.3d 15.9v^{4}
t12.2g Oct 21] sturdy gelding: useful handicapper: won at Newcastle and Southwell (by
short head from L'Inganno Felice) in January: placed at Wolverhampton in February and
Lingfield (minor event) in March: stays 16.5f: acts on all-weather and good to soft going.
Mark Johnston

I SHOULD COCO 4 b.f. With The Flow (USA) 114 – Follow The Dream 69 (Double **–**
Trigger (IRE) 123) [2017 p12g p10s^{4} p8d Dec 13] first foal: dam 1¾m-2¼m winner: well
held in maidens: tried in cheekpieces. *Karen George*

ISIS BLUE 7 b.g. Cockney Rebel (IRE) 127 – Bramaputra (IRE) 88 (Choisir (AUS) 126) **71**
[2017 78: 10m^{5} p8g^{2} May 5] lengthy, angular gelding: fair performer: stays 11f: acts on
polytrack, soft and good to firm going: has worn cheekpieces. *Rod Millman*

IS IT OFF (IRE) 2 b.c. (Mar 7) Clodovil (IRE) 116 – French Doll (IRE) 66 (Titus Livius **70**
(FR) 115) [2017 6s^{2} 6.5d p8d p7d p7g^{5} Dec 31] fair maiden: should stay 7f: acts on soft
going: sometimes slowly away, often races in rear. *Gary Moore*

ISLAND AFFAIR (IRE) 2 b.f. (Mar 22) Tagula (IRE) 116 – Subtle Affair (IRE) 96 **64**
(Barathea (IRE) 127) [2017 7g^{5} 6g^{4} 7g* 7v^{4} 7.2d^{6} 6v^{5} 5d Oct 4] €5,500Y: sister to 2-y-o 7f
winner Cascading Stars and half-sister to several winners, including useful winner up to
1¼m Imshivalla (2-y-o 7f winner, by Acclamation): dam 11f/11.5f winner: modest
performer: won claimer at Leopardstown in July: stays 7f: acts on good to soft going:
wears hood: often races towards rear. *Adrian McGuinness, Ireland*

ISLAND AUTHORITY 5 b.m. Authorized (IRE) 133 – Island Odyssey 93 (Dansili 127) **60**
[2017 p12g^{5} p16g Oct 4] modest maiden: should stay 2m: acts on polytrack: has worn hood.
Eugene Stanford

ISLAND BRAVE (IRE) 3 b.c. Zebedee 113 – Tip The Scale (USA) (Valiant Nature **92**
(USA) 118) [2017 p7g^{3} p8g* p7g 8g p9.4f^{6} p6.5g 10m t9.5m* t12.2g* p15.8g^{3} Dec 28]
18,000Y, £32,000 2-y-o: good-topped colt: sixth foal: half-brother to useful 2-y-o 6f/7f

winner Wildcat Wizard (by Forest Wildcat) and a winner in USA by Hussonet: dam, US 1m/9f winner, half-sister to smart French winner up to 12.5f Eleusis: fairly useful performer: won maiden at Lingfield in March, and handicaps at Wolverhampton in October and November (by length from Star Story): left J. S. Moore after sixth start: stays 2m: acts on polytrack and tapeta: tried in blinkers. *Heather Main*

ISLAND CLOUD 3 b.f. Harbour Watch (IRE) 121 – Cloud Illusions (USA) 85 (Smarty Jones (USA) 134) [2017 70: 6g³ 6d⁵ 5.1m³ 5.7f² 6g² 6g* 6s Sep 27] rather leggy filly: fairly useful handicapper: won at Goodwood (apprentice, by 1½ lengths from Jashma) in August: stays 7f: acts on polytrack and firm going: tried in cheekpieces. *Heather Main* **80**

ISLAND COURT (IRE) 2 b.c. (Feb 10) Camelot 128 – First Breeze (USA) 87 (Woodman (USA) 126) [2017 6g⁶ p8g t8.6g³ p8g⁵ t8.6d⁶ Dec 26] fair maiden: stays 8.5f: acts on tapeta. *J. S. Moore* **70**

ISLAND DRIVE (IRE) 2 b.f. (Mar 1) Kodiac 112 – Redstone Dancer (IRE) 115 (Namid 128) [2017 p6d* 6.1v⁴ 6g Oct 14] 44,000F, 88,000Y: fifth foal: half-sister to a winner abroad by Teofilo: dam 7f/1m winner: fairly useful form: won minor event at Kempton (by ¾ length from Angel Islington) in July: raced only at 6f. *William Haggas* **80**

ISLAND FLAME (IRE) 4 b.f. Kodiac 112 – Noble Flame (IRE) 58 (Doyoun 124) [2017 84: 11.9s t12.4s⁵ 10g³ 11.9m t10.2g⁴ 11.6g⁶ 12.1m⁵ t12.4g⁶ t9.5m Oct 28] fair handicapper: stays 12.5f: acts on polytrack, tapeta, soft and good to firm going: has worn headgear, including final start. *Richard Fahey* **72**

ISLAND OF LIFE (USA) 3 b.f. Dubawi (IRE) 129 – Pimpernel (IRE) 110 (Invincible Spirit (IRE) 121) [2017 7m³ 8d³ Aug 5] first foal: dam 2-y-o 5f-7f winner: fair form: better effort when third in maiden at Salisbury in July. *Saeed bin Suroor* **72**

ISLAND REMEDE 6 b.m. Medicean 128 – Island Odyssey 93 (Dansili 127) [2017 91: 12d² 11.8s Jun 10] good-topped mare: useful performer: second in listed race at Cork (2 lengths behind Zhukova) in April: stays 1¾m: acts on polytrack, good to firm and heavy going: has worn headgear, including last 2 starts: usually leads. *Henry de Bromhead, Ireland* **99**

ISLAND SOUND 2 gr.c. (Apr 8) Havana Gold (IRE) 118 – Cloud Illusions (USA) 85 (Smarty Jones (USA) 134) [2017 7d 8.1g⁴ 7g⁶ Sep 16] fair form. *Heather Main* **67**

ISLAND VISION (IRE) 3 ch.f. Arcano (IRE) 122 – Boo Boo Bear (IRE) 81 (Almutawakel 126) [2017 92: a7f 7g 7g 7m 7g Jul 15] angular filly: fairly useful at 2 yrs, below that level in 2017: stays 1m: acts on polytrack, tapeta and good to firm going: usually races nearer last than first. *David Simcock* **71**

ISLE OF AVALON (IRE) 2 b.f. (Feb 10) Camelot 128 – Adeste 76 (Dansili 127) [2017 6.9v⁵ p7g 8.3d Oct 4] first foal: dam, 1½m winner, out of sister to Fillies' Mile winner Listen and Moyglare Stud Stakes winner Sequoyah, latter dam of 2000 Guineas winner Henrythenavigator: modest form: best effort when eighth in maiden at Nottingham (4¼ lengths behind Fayrouz Rose) in October: capable of better again. *Sir Mark Prescott Bt* **63 p**

ISLE OF MAN 2 b.c. (Apr 29) Exceed And Excel (AUS) 126 – One So Marvellous 86 (Nashwan (USA) 135) [2017 7g t8.6g Oct 21] well-made colt: little impact in maiden/minor event. *Clive Cox* **–**

ISNTSHESOMETHING 5 br.m. Assertive 121 – Princess Almora 88 (Pivotal 124) [2017 57: p7d* p7g² t7.1g² 7.1m* p7d p7g t7.1s⁶ p7s² p7g* t7.2g² t7.2g Nov 7] fair handicapper: won at Chelmsford in March, Musselburgh in May and Kempton in October: stays 7f: acts on polytrack, tapeta and good to firm going: wears headgear: often travels strongly. *Richard Guest* **68**

ISOLETTA 2 b.f. (Feb 25) Oasis Dream 129 – Miss Cap Estel 104 (Hernando (FR) 127) [2017 5.1m 6.1d p6g⁴ 7s³ p7g p7g³ Dec 28] first foal: dam 1m-1½m winner: fair maiden: stays 7f: acts on polytrack and soft going. *Ed Walker* **65**

ISOMER (USA) 3 ch.g. Cape Blanco (IRE) 130 – Nimue (USA) 91 (Speightstown (USA) 124) [2017 98: 9.9m 8g⁶ 8.2v Sep 30] lengthy, attractive gelding: useful performer at best: little impact in various events in 2017: stays 1m: acts on good to firm going. *Andrew Balding* **–**

ISPOLINI 2 b.c. (Feb 7) Dubawi (IRE) 129 – Giants Play (USA) 111 (Giant's Causeway (USA) 132) [2017 8.3g⁴ p10g* Nov 29] 1,200,000Y: third foal: half-brother to useful 9f-10.4f winner Playful Sound (by Street Cry) and 2-y-o 1¼m winner Azam (by Dansili): dam 1¼m (US Grade 2)/1½m winner: fairly useful form: won maiden at Kempton (by 2 lengths from Glencadam Master) in November: wears tongue tie: will go on improving. *Charlie Appleby* **90 p**

ISSTOORA (IRE) 3 b.f. Fastnet Rock (AUS) 127 – Shegotloose (USA) (Dynaformer **76**
(USA)) [2017 p8g^{4} t8s p8g^{5} p8g^{6} p7g^{2} f8.1g* t9.5g^{6} Dec 18] first foal: dam unraced half-sister to smart/ungenuine 5f-7f winner Excusez Moi out of half-sister to outstanding broodmare Hasili: fair performer: won maiden at Southwell in December: left Marco Botti after fifth start: stays 1m: acts on polytrack and fibresand: tried in hood. *Archie Watson*

ISTANBUL PASHA (IRE) 2 b.g. (Feb 19) Fast Company (IRE) 126 – Red Red Rose **57**
(Piccolo 121) [2017 7d 5.1m^{5} 5.1g^{4} p7d 8.1s^{5} 6g^{3} 6d^{2} t7.1g^{6} t6.1g Nov 29] modest maiden: stays 6f: acts on soft going: in visor last 4 starts. *David Evans*

ISTANBUL SULTAN (IRE) 2 gr.g. (Feb 8) Zoffany (IRE) 121 – Far Away Eyes (IRE) **80 p**
(High Chaparral (IRE) 132) [2017 7d^{5} 8d^{2} 9.1s* Oct 15] €150,000F, 100,000Y: first foal: dam, ran once in Sweden, half-sister to dam of Australian Group 1 1½m winner Magic Hurricane: fairly useful form: won minor event at Goodwood (dead-heated with Loxley) in October: will stay 1¼m: still unexposed. *William Haggas*

ISTIMRAAR (IRE) 6 b.g. Dansili 127 – Manayer (IRE) (Sadler's Wells (USA) 132) **–**
[2017 69: f16g Jan 2] angular gelding: fairly useful at best, well held sole outing on Flat in 2017: stays 1¾m: acts on polytrack, soft and good to firm going: wears cheekpieces: in tongue tie last 2 starts: poor hurdler nowadays. *Alexandra Dunn*

ITALIAN BEAUTY (IRE) 5 b.m. Thewayyouare (USA) 117 – Edelfa (IRE) (Fasliyev **53**
(USA) 120) [2017 76: p8g^{5} p8g 7.4m 10.3v 8v^{5} f8.1g Dec 1] fair handicapper, below form in 2017: stays 8.5f: acts on polytrack, tapeta, good to firm and heavy going: usually wears headgear. *John Wainwright*

ITALIAN HEIRESS 3 ch.f. Medicean 128 – Regal Heiress 76 (Pivotal 124) [2017 67p: **89**
8.1m^{3} 9.9g^{3} 10g^{5} 10g^{2} 12d 9.9s* 10.2d^{6} Oct 11] workmanlike filly: fairly useful performer: won maiden at Salisbury (by ¾ length from Ajman King) in September: stays 1¼m: acts on soft and good to firm going. *Clive Cox*

ITALIAN RIVIERA 8 b.g. Galileo (IRE) 134 – Miss Corniche 104 (Hernando (FR) 127) **71**
[2017 73: 16.1g^{2} 15.9v^{4} 15.9g^{2} Aug 30] fair handicapper: stays 16.5f: acts on polytrack, fibresand and heavy going: wears headgear. *Kenneth Slack*

IT DONT COME EASY (IRE) 2 b.g. (Feb 19) Kyllachy 129 – Eleganza (IRE) **102**
(Balmont (USA) 117) [2017 5s^{4} 5m* 5m^{5} 6g 5v^{6} 6.1v^{2} 6g^{2} t6d^{3} Oct 24] strong, compact gelding: useful performer: won minor event at Musselburgh (by head from Rebel Assault) in June: second in listed race at York (1¼ lengths behind Rebel Assault) in October: raced at 5f/6f: acted on good to firm and heavy going: usually raced prominently: dead. *Richard Fahey*

ITLAAQ 11 b.g. Alhaarth (IRE) 126 – Hathrah (IRE) 113 (Linamix (FR) 127) [2017 88: **82**
12m 14g 12g^{2} 11.9m^{4} 14.5s^{6} 13.1g^{5} 13.9v^{5} 12m 10.2d^{3} t16.5g^{5} Nov 20] attractive gelding: fairly useful handicapper: second at Pontefract in May: stays 16.5f: acts on polytrack, firm and soft going: has worn cheekpieces, including in 2017: wears tongue tie: often races towards rear. *Michael Easterby*

IT MUST BE FAITH 7 b.g. Mount Nelson 125 – Purple Rain (IRE) 46 (Celtic Swing **76**
138) [2017 77: t8.6m^{5} f6g t6g^{2} t5.1f t5d 5.5g^{4} May 14] fair handicapper: stays 7f: acts on polytrack, tapeta, good to firm and good to soft going: has worn headgear: front runner/races prominently. *Michael Appleby*

ITSAKINDAMAGIC 3 b.g. Mount Nelson 125 – Carsulae (IRE) (Marju (IRE) 127) **93 §**
[2017 79p: p8d* p8g^{4} 7.6s^{5} 8d^{2} 8s^{3} 9.1g^{6} 10.3v^{4} Sep 30] quite attractive gelding: fairly useful performer: won maiden at Chelmsford in March: placed in handicaps at Thirsk and Sandown in July: stays 9f: acts on polytrack and soft going: wears hood: in tongue tie last 5 starts: temperamental, usually pulls hard/carries head high. *Andrew Balding*

ITSALONGLONGROAD 3 b.c. Lawman (FR) 121 – Alabelle 89 (Galileo (IRE) 134) **79**
[2017 79: 10d^{2} 12.1g^{5} 9.5s^{5} Sep 16] fair maiden: stays 1¼m: acts on soft going: in tongue tie last 3 starts: usually leads. *John McConnell, Ireland*

ITS A SHEILA THING 4 ch.f. Sir Percy 129 – Sefemm (Alhaarth (IRE) 126) [2017 57: **51**
9.9g 10.2m 10d^{2} p10g Jul 26] rather sparely-made filly: modest maiden: stays 1¼m: acts on tapeta and good to soft going: usually wears hood. *Tony Carroll*

IT'S A WISH 2 b.f. (Feb 26) Invincible Spirit (IRE) 121 – Sun Bittern (USA) (Seeking **57**
The Gold (USA)) [2017 t6.1g^{3} t5.1g Dec 2] €300,000Y: sixth foal: sister to very smart 5f-6.5f winner Signs of Blessing, closely related to winner up to 12.5f Admire Fuji (2-y-o

1m winner, by Oasis Dream) and half-sister to 7f/7.5f winner Lucrece (by Pivotal), all in France: dam unraced: modest form when third on first of 2 starts in minor events at Wolverhampton: will stay 7f. *Clive Cox*

IT'S HOW WE ROLL (IRE) 3 b.g. Fastnet Rock (AUS) 127 – Clodora (FR) 113 **72**
(Linamix (FR) 127) [2017 70: p7d^{4} f7g^{3} 8.1d^{4} 10m^{4} 8.1m 10v^{2} p12g^{6} 9.9s 8.1d^{5} Oct 23] angular gelding: fair maiden: left Charles Hills after second start: stays 1¼m: acts on polytrack, fibresand, good to firm and heavy going: wears blinkers. *John Spearing*

IT'S NOT UNUSUAL 2 b.f. (Mar 4) Exceed And Excel (AUS) 126 – Welsh Anthem 77 **64**
(Singspiel (IRE) 133) [2017 p7g^{4} 6m^{5} p6g^{5} Sep 27] 175,000Y: good-quartered filly: third foal: half-sister to useful 6f winner Dream Dubai (by Kyllachy): dam, 1¼m winner, half-sister to smart winners up to 8.5f Trans Island and Mujaazef: modest form in minor events. *Roger Charlton*

IVAN GROZNY (FR) 7 b.g. Turtle Bowl (IRE) 121 – Behnesa (IRE) (Suave Dancer **–**
(USA) 136) [2017 106: 13.9m Aug 26] tall gelding: useful at best, well held sole outing on Flat in 2017: stays 1¾m: acts on heavy going: in hood last 3 starts: smart hurdler: sold to race in Australia. *W. P. Mullins, Ireland*

IVANHOE 7 b.g. Haafhd 129 – Marysienka 78 (Primo Dominie 121) [2017 75: 14f 12s^{5} **68**
14.5s^{5} 14g^{4} 14.2v 13d 16s^{2} p16g p15.8g Oct 18] workmanlike gelding: fair handicapper: stays 17f: acts on polytrack, good to firm and heavy going: often wears headgear. *Michael Blanshard*

I'VEGOTTHEPOWER (IRE) 3 b.g. Power 117 – Waterways (IRE) 99 (Alhaarth **97**
(IRE) 126) [2017 65: 10.2g^{4} 8f* 10.2f^{2} 10s 8m* 8f* Jul 5] tall gelding: useful performer: won minor event at Bath in May, and handicaps at Goodwood in June and Bath (by nose from Pillar of Society) in July: stays 1¼m: acts on firm and good to soft going: usually wears headgear: front runner/races prominently. *Brian Meehan*

IVOR'S FANTASY (IRE) 3 ch.f. Zebedee 113 – Fantasy Princess (USA) 85 **53**
(Johannesburg (USA) 127) [2017 p5m^{4} 6g^{6} 7d 7f^{2} 9.2m a7.2g^{2} a5.5g a6s a8.5s* a9s* Dec 26] €8,000Y: third foal: dam 2-y-o 7f winner who stayed 1¼m: modest performer: left David Elsworth after second start: won 2 handicaps at Dortmund in December: stays 9f: acts on dirt. *Frau R. Weissmeier, Germany*

IVORS INVOLVEMENT (IRE) 5 b.g. Amadeus Wolf 122 – Summer Spice (IRE) 88 **56**
(Key of Luck (USA) 126) [2017 48: t8s 8.5d 6m^{6} 7m 9.9s^{3} 8g 8.5d 12d^{3} 12.5m^{4} 9.9g* 9.9v 8s^{6} Oct 3] modest handicapper: won at Beverley (apprentice) in September: stays 1½m: acts on polytrack, soft and good to firm going: has worn headgear, including last 3 starts: usually leads/travels strongly. *Tina Jackson*

IVOR'S MAGIC (IRE) 3 ch.f. Zebedee 113 – Rinneen (IRE) 67 (Bien Bien (USA) 125) **59**
[2017 63: p7g p7g^{4} p8g 7.6g May 24] sturdy filly: modest handicapper: stays 7f: acts on polytrack and good to firm going: sold £600 in June. *David Elsworth*

IVY LEAGUER 2 b.c. (Mar 25) Compton Place 125 – Brick Tops 82 (Danehill Dancer **70**
(IRE) 117) [2017 6.1m 6f 5m 5f^{3} p5g 5g^{3} 5.1d Oct 23] sturdy colt: fair maiden: should stay 6f: acts on firm going: tried in cheekpieces: sold 8,000 gns, sent to Spain. *Brian Meehan*

IVY MATILDA 4 b.f. Monsieur Bond (IRE) 120 – Ingleby Princess 78 (Bold Edge 123) **–**
[2017 t7.1d^{6} t8d 6g^{6} 6s^{6} Jun 10] no form: tried in cheekpieces/tongue tie. *Colin Teague*

I WAS ONLY JOKING (IRE) 2 ch.f. (Apr 15) Helmet (AUS) 127 – Lady Angele (FR) **71**
98 (Ski Chief (USA) 115) [2017 6v^{4} t6.1d^{2} Dec 27] €55,000Y: big filly: seventh foal: half-sister to French 2-y-o 5f-6.5f winner Lady Jak (by American Post): dam French 2-y-o 5f winner: fair form: better effort when second in minor event at Wolverhampton (2¼ lengths behind Angel of The South) in December. *Richard Fahey*

I WOULDN'T BOTHER 3 b.g. Captain Gerrard (IRE) 113 – Dalmunzie (IRE) (Choisir **–**
(AUS) 126) [2017 69: 5.9s 5m Jun 17] good-quartered gelding: fair form at 2 yrs, well held both starts in 2017: best effort at 6f: acts on polytrack: tried in blinkers: in tongue tie last 2 starts. *Daniel Kubler*

IXELLES DIAMOND (IRE) 6 br.m. Diamond Green (FR) 121 – Silk Point (IRE) **63**
(Barathea (IRE) 127) [2017 60, a72: p8d^{3} p8g* p8d^{4} p7g^{4} p10g^{2} 9g p8g 7d p8g^{3} t8.6g^{3} p8s^{5} Dec 17] leggy mare: modest handicapper nowadays: won at Lingfield in March: stays 1¼m: acts on polytrack, tapeta and any turf going: often wears hood. *Lee Carter*

IZZY BIZU (IRE) 2 br.f. (May 5) Kodiac 112 – Dame Hester (IRE) 92 (Diktat 126) [2017 5m* 5s 5.9v* 6m* 6g^3 7g* 7g 6g 6g^2 t6.1d^6 Dec 9] €30,000Y: small filly: seventh foal: half-sister to 3 winners, including smart German 6f/7f winner Donnerschlag (by Bahamian Bounty) and useful 2-y-o 6f winner De Boss Man (by Dandy Man): dam 1m-9.7f winner: fairly useful performer: won minor events at Catterick in May, and Carlisle and Leicester in June, and listed race at Deauville (by short neck from Model) in July: second in listed race at Newmarket (3 lengths behind Alwasmiya) in November: stays 7f: acts on good to firm and heavy going: front runner. *Mark Johnston* **93**

J

JAALBOOT 2 b.g. (Feb 3) Invincible Spirit (IRE) 121 – Selinka 110 (Selkirk (USA) 129) [2017 t6.1g 7d^4 Jul 11] modest form: better effort when fourth in minor event at Brighton (3¾ lengths behind Wildnightinvegas) in July. *Owen Burrows* **62**

JAAMEH (IRE) 4 b.g. Iffraaj 127 – Miss Gibraltar (Rock of Gibraltar (IRE) 133) [2017 92: 14m^2 13.4g* 14g* t16.3s 12d^5 14d^5 14m^3 14s^3 12g^3 Sep 28] useful-looking gelding: useful handicapper: won at Chester in May and Newmarket (by head from Byron Flyer) in June: stays 1¾m: acts on good to firm and heavy going: tried in blinkers. *Mark Johnston* **104**

JAARIH (IRE) 5 ch.g. Starspangledbanner (AUS) 128 – Bridge Note (USA) 49 (Stravinsky (USA) 133) [2017 81: p5g Apr 1] fairly useful performer, well held sole start in 2017: best form at 5f: acts on fibresand, tapeta, soft and good to firm going: wears headgear: has worn tongue tie. *George Scott* **–**

JABBAAR 4 ch.g. Medicean 128 – Echelon 120 (Danehill (USA) 126) [2017 83, a69: 8g 8m^5 10g^2 10.3s^3 8.3m^6 7.2m 10.3v^3 10g 10.3v^3 12.1v* 12.1s^5 Oct 31] fairly useful handicapper: won at Catterick (by neck from Only Orsenfoolsies) in October: left David Barron after fifth start: stays 1½m: acts on heavy going: tried in blinkers: often races towards rear. *Iain Jardine* **83**

JABBAROCKIE 4 b.g. Showcasing 117 – Canina 70 (Foxhound (USA) 103) [2017 65: 5d^2 5s 5d^3 f5g* 5g^6 5g* 5s^3 Nov 8] strong, compact gelding: fairly useful performer: won maiden at Southwell in August and handicap at Nottingham in October: best form at 5f: acts on fibresand, soft and good to firm going: front runner/races prominently. *Eric Alston* **83**

JACBEQUICK 6 b.g. Calcutta 112 – Toking N' Joken (IRE) (Mukaddamah (USA) 125) [2017 95: t8g 8.5f^4 8.5g 8.5m^6 9.8d^3 10.2m^4 9m^3 11.9m* 10.3g 9.8d^2 11.8d 9.2s 9.8g^3 10.3d 12v^3 10.3g Oct 14] strong gelding: fairly useful handicapper: won at York (amateur, by neck from Azari) in July: stays 1½m: acts on polytrack and any turf going: wears headgear: inconsistent. *David O'Meara* **93**

JACK BEAR 6 b.g. Joe Bear (IRE) 109 – Colins Lady (FR) (Colonel Collins (USA) 122) [2017 85: p16s^6 16s^5 Oct 15] sturdy gelding: fairly useful handicapper: stays 1¾m: acts on polytrack and soft going: has joined Roger Teal. *Harry Whittington* **78**

JACKBLACK 5 b.g. Crosspeace (IRE) 118 – Saharan Royal 70 (Val Royal (FR) 127) [2017 63?: p12d^5 p16s Jun 14] modest maiden: stays 1½m: acts on polytrack: in hood last 2 starts: usually races towards rear: fairly useful hurdler. *Brett Johnson* **63**

JACK BLANE 3 br.g. Kheleyf (USA) 116 – Blane Water (USA) 93 (Lomond (USA) 128) [2017 52: t5.1f^4 t7.1g* t7.1g^5 p7g^5 8f^4 8d^5 7.2d^2 7v^4 7.2d^2 7.2m^3 t7.1s^2 t8s t7.1d 7.2s^4 t7.2g p7m^2 t7.2g^5 t6.1g* Dec 13] fair handicapper: won at Wolverhampton in March and December: left Daniel Kubler after sixth start: stays 1m: acts on polytrack, tapeta, firm and good to soft going: wears headgear. *Keith Dalgleish* **67**

JACK CROW 2 b.c. (Mar 11) Bahamian Bounty 116 – Here To Eternity (USA) 74 (Stormy Atlantic (USA)) [2017 p7d^2 6g^2 Sep 22] 20,000Y: third foal: half-brother to very smart Hong Kong winner up to 1¼m (Hong Kong Cup) Time Warp (2-y-o 7f/1m winner) and useful winner up to 1¼m Glorious Forever (2-y-o 1m winner) (both by Archipenko): dam 7f winner: fairly useful form: better effort when second in maiden at Newbury (neck behind Orange Suit) in September. *Eve Johnson Houghton* **90**

JACK DEXTER 8 b.g. Orientor 118 – Glenhurich (IRE) 59 (Sri Pekan (USA) 117) [2017 109: 6m 5s^6 5m t5g^4 5s^5 6g^4 5d* 7d 6g^{pu} Aug 19] lengthy gelding: very smart at best: won handicap at Ascot (by 1½ lengths from Pettochside) in July: stayed 7f, raced mainly at shorter: acted on any turf going: dead. *Jim Goldie* **101**

JACKFINBAR (FR) 2 b.c. (Mar 1) Whipper (USA) 126 – Anna Simona (GER) (Slip Anchor 136) [2017 8s5 8d t9.5g* Dec 18] €41,000Y: brother to 2-y-o 6f/1m winner Willie The Whipper, later smart 10.5f winner in Qatar, and half-brother to several winners abroad, including French 2-y-o 1m winner Santanna (by Country Reel): dam German/French 9.5f-1¾m winner: fairly useful form: won minor event at Wolverhampton (by neck from Voyager Blue) in December: likely to stay 1½m: open to further improvement. *Harry Dunlop* **82 p**

JACK FLASH (FR) 3 gr.g. Dark Angel (IRE) 113 – Lexi The Princess (IRE) 62 (Holy Roman Emperor (IRE) 125) [2017 80: p6g* t6d2 p6g* 5.1g 5g3 5m* 5s 5m2 5f3 p7.5g5 p6.5g3 Dec 19] fairly useful performer: won maiden at Lingfield in January, and handicaps there in February and at Ripon in April: left Les Eyre after ninth start: stays 6.5f: acts on polytrack, tapeta and good to firm going: often wears headgear: has worn tongue tie: usually leads. *Mme G. Rarick, France* **90**

JACKHAMMER (IRE) 3 b.g. Thewayyouare (USA) 117 – Ask Annie (IRE) (Danehill (USA) 126) [2017 92: p11g4 9.9m6 8m 10v 7g5 10.2d Oct 27] fairly useful handicapper: left William Knight after fifth start: probably stays 11f: acts on polytrack and soft going: sometimes in hood. *Dianne Sayer* **89**

JACK HOBBS 5 br.h. Halling (USA) 133 – Swain's Gold (USA) (Swain (IRE) 134) [2017 124: 12d* 10m 12s Jul 29] strong, good sort: high-class performer: runner-up in Derby before winning Irish Derby at the Curragh in 2015: better effort in 2016 when third in Champion Stakes at Ascot for second year running: back to winning ways in Dubai Sheema Classic at Meydan (by 2¼ lengths from Seventh Heaven) in March, but disappointing afterwards in Prince of Wales's Stakes and King George VI and Queen Elizabeth Stakes, both at Ascot: stayed 1½m: acted on polytrack, tapeta, good to firm and good to soft going: wore blinkers in 2017: to stand at Overbury Stud, near Tewkesbury, Gloucestershire, fee £4,000 Oct 1st. *John Gosden* **126**

JACKIE ELLIS (IRE) 6 b.m. Excellent Art 125 – Dancing With Stars (IRE) (Where Or When (IRE) 124) [2017 66: 7.5s2 8m5 7.2s6 9g4 8.3d* 8g 9d5 10v Aug 28] fair handicapper: won at Hamilton in July: stays 10.5f: acts on polytrack, good to firm and heavy going: has worn headgear/tongue tie: often races towards rear. *Paul W. Flynn, Ireland* **69**

JACK LUEY 10 b.g. Danbird (AUS) – Icenaslice (IRE) 78 (Fayruz 116) [2017 82, a72: 5m3 5g 5g2 5s4 5d4 5s 5s 5g 5g Oct 7] rather leggy gelding: fairly useful handicapper: second at Hamilton in June: stays 6f: acts on fibresand, good to firm and heavy going: usually wears headgear: often races prominently. *Lawrence Mullaney* **80**

JACKMAN 3 gr.g. Aussie Rules (USA) 123 – Fit To Burst (Pastoral Pursuits 127) [2017 45: 7d5 8.5s Sep 20] no form: left Tony Carroll after first start: sometimes in cheekpieces. *Lee James* **–**

JACK NEVISON 4 b.g. Dick Turpin (IRE) 127 – Creative Mind (IRE) 95 (Danehill Dancer (IRE) 117) [2017 83: 6m 6d2 8s 8g3 p8g 7s p7g* p8g5 Oct 26] tall gelding: modest handicapper on turf, fair on all-weather: won at Chelmsford (apprentice) in September: left John O'Shea after second start: stays 7f: acts on polytrack and good to firm going: has worn headgear, including last 2 starts. *Michael Appleby* **61 a70**

Longines Dubai Sheema Classic, Meydan—Jack Hobbs produces a high-class performance in first-time headgear as he beats Seventh Heaven (striped sleeves), with 2016 winner Postponed (spots on cap) back in third and the hooded Prize Money fourth

JACK OF DIAMONDS (IRE) 8 b.g. Red Clubs (IRE) 125 – Sakkara Star (IRE) 94 (Mozart (IRE) 131) [2017 89, a96: t8.6m p8g p8g t8.6g^4 11.6m^2 11.4m^6 9.9g^6 10m^4 11m^4 t12.2g 9.9s 8g^2 t8.6g* 10.2d t8.6g^2 p10s^2 t9.5g^3 p10g* Dec 21] compact gelding: fair handicapper: won at Wolverhampton (apprentice) in September and Chelmsford in December: stays 11.5f: acts on all-weather and good to firm going: has worn headgear: usually races towards rear. *Roger Teal* **79**

JACKONTHEROCKS 2 b.g. (Apr 4) Bated Breath 125 – Desert Kiss 100 (Cape Cross (IRE) 129) [2017 6m 6s* 5.9m^6 7.4d 8v 7s Sep 19] fair performer: won minor event at Ayr in June: best effort at 6f: acts on soft going: often races towards rear. *Michael Dods* **69**

JACKPOT ROYALE 2 b.g. (Mar 23) Sixties Icon 125 – Sofia Royale 61 (Royal Applause 124) [2017 p6g^5 7s^6 f7.1g^6 Nov 28] fair form. *Michael Appleby* **65**

JACK REGAN 2 b.g. (Mar 28) Rock of Gibraltar (IRE) 133 – Chelsey Jayne (IRE) 57 (Galileo (IRE) 134) [2017 7g^3 7g^6 7d^6 6s 8v Sep 30] useful-looking gelding: fair maiden: should stay 1m: tried in blinkers/tongue tie: has joined Ian Williams. *Charles Hills* **77**

JACKSONFIRE 5 ch.g. Firebreak 125 – Fitolini 72 (Bertolini (USA) 125) [2017 53: 6m 6g 6.1m^5 7d^3 6g^2 6.1s^2 7.1d 6v^4 5v^4 7.6v^4 7s t6.1m t6.1g t6.1d f6.1g Dec 21] modest maiden on turf, poor on all-weather: stays 6f: acts on soft and good to firm going: wears headgear: usually races towards rear. *Michael Mullineaux* **59 a43**

JACK'S REVENGE (IRE) 9 br.g. Footstepsinthesand 120 – Spirit of Age (IRE) 83 (Indian Ridge 123) [2017 96: p8g^5 t8.6m^6 Jan 14] leggy gelding: fairly useful handicapper: stays 10.5f, usually races at shorter: acts on polytrack, fibresand, soft and good to firm going: wears headgear: usually wears tongue tie. *George Baker* **86**

JACK TAYLOR (IRE) 2 b.g. (Apr 17) Invincible Spirit (IRE) 121 – Glory Power (IRE) (Medicean 128) [2017 6s^6 p6g^2 p6.5g* Dec 5] €42,000Y: second foal: dam useful French 7.5f-9f winner: fairly useful form: won maiden at Deauville (by nose from Rozanne) in December: gelded after: will stay 7f. *Richard Hughes* **81**

JACK THE LAIRD (IRE) 4 b.g. Acclamation 118 – Pretty Demanding (IRE) 84 (Night Shift (USA)) [2017 69, a77: p6g p6g^4 t6g^3 t5.1g t5.1f^3 p7g^3 p7g^4 p7g^3 6m 7m^5 7.6g^4 6g^4 6m^5 Jun 27] modest handicapper on turf, fair on all-weather: stays 7f: acts on polytrack, tapeta and good to firm going: usually wears headgear: tried in tongue tie. *Dean Ivory* **61 a68**

JACK THE TRUTH (IRE) 3 ch.g. Dandy Man (IRE) 123 – Friendly Heart (CAN) (Lion Heart (USA) 124) [2017 p5g^4 t5.1f^2 f6.1g* Dec 19] fair form: won maiden at Southwell (by 3 lengths from Ladies First) in December: stays 6f. *George Scott* **79**

JACOB BLACK 6 b.g. Amadeus Wolf 122 – First Eclipse (IRE) 66 (Fayruz 116) [2017 –: t8s 8m 7m 7.8d^5 10g t6d 7.2s^6 t7.1d Sep 29] lengthy gelding: useful at best, little form since 2015: stays 8.5f: acts on good to firm and good to soft going: sometimes in headgear: usually wears tongue tie: has rejoined Keith Dalgleish. *Kenny Johnson* **63**

JACOB CATS 8 b.g. Dutch Art 126 – Ballet 61 (Sharrood (USA) 124) [2017 93: p11g* p12g* p11g^3 11.4m^2 11.4g 12d 12d^3 16s^3 12s^6 Oct 15] angular gelding: useful handicapper: won at Kempton (twice) in April: stays 2m: acts on polytrack, good to firm and good to soft going: wears headgear: tried in tongue tie: often starts slowly, usually races nearer last than first. *William Knight* **100**

JACOB'S PILLOW 6 b.g. Oasis Dream 129 – Enticing (IRE) 116 (Pivotal 124) [2017 76: f6g f5g^4 t5g f5g* f5d^6 f5g^2 f6.1g^5 5m* 5d^2 5g^6 5s 6s* 6d^2 7d 5s^3 5d^2 5v^2 6s^5 Oct 31] fairly useful handicapper on turf, fair on all-weather: won at Southwell in March, Beverley in May and Hamilton in August: stays 6f: acts on fibresand and any turf going: usually wears headgear: front runner/races prominently. *Rebecca Bastiman* **85 a75**

JACQUARD (IRE) 3 b.c. Pivotal 124 – Camlet 94 (Green Desert (USA) 127) [2017 90: 7g 8v^5 t8d t8d^4 Oct 24] fairly useful at 2 yrs, well below that level in 2017: stays 6f: acts on tapeta and good to firm going: front runner/races prominently. *Mark Johnston* **57**

JACQUES 4 b.g. Sixties Icon 125 – Laminka (Intikhab (USA) 135) [2017 10m Apr 10] 100/1, well held in maiden at Redcar. *John Balding* **–**

JACQUOTTE DELAHAYE 6 ch.m. Kyllachy 129 – Mary Read 100 (Bahamian Bounty 116) [2017 80§: p8g^6 p7g* p7g* Feb 18] fairly useful handicapper: won at Kempton (twice, by ½ length from Threebagsue second occasion) in February: stays 7f: acts on polytrack, tapeta and good to firm going: has worn headgear, including last 2 starts: tried in tongue tie: unreliable. *David Brown* **88 §**

JAFETICA 3 ch.f. New Approach (IRE) 132 – Fann (USA) 96 (Diesis 133) [2017 t9.5g^3 10g p8g^3 p10g^4 t8g^3 Oct 19] 100,000Y: rather leggy filly: fifth foal: sister to useful performer up to 2m Future Empire (2-y-o 7f winner) and closely related to smart German winner up to 11f Black Arrow (2-y-o 1m winner) and winner up to 1½m Muhtaris (2-y-o 1m winner) (both by Teofilo): dam 9f winner: fair maiden: best effort at 1m: acts on polytrack and tapeta: in hood last 4 starts: has joined Mark Johnston. *James Fanshawe* **78**

JAFFAR 2 b.g. (Jan 13) Mawatheeq (USA) 126 – Velvet Jaguar (Hurricane Run (IRE) 134) [2017 6g 7m^5 7.4m^4 7.4g f7.1g f6.1g f8.1g Dec 29] modest maiden: best effort at 7f: acts on good to firm going: usually wears headgear. *Scott Dixon* **50**

JAGANORY (IRE) 5 b.g. Dylan Thomas (IRE) 132 – Jacquelin Jag (IRE) (Fayruz 116) [2017 64: 6.1d^4 5.7m^3 5.1s 5.7f* 6m 5f^4 5.7g 5s* 5d* 5.7m^4 5.7s 5.7s^5 Oct 2] fair handicapper: won at Bath in June and August (twice): stays 6f: acts on polytrack, firm and soft going: wears headgear: front runner/races prominently. *Christopher Mason* **70**

JAHAAFEL (FR) 2 gr.c. (May 12) Style Vendome (FR) 116 – Irisijana (GER) (Diktat 126) [2017 p7s^4 Nov 16] €45,000Y, €400,000 2-y-o: third foal: half-brother to German 11f winner Identity (by Manduro): dam, German 7f winner, half-sister to very smart German/ Hong Kong 1m-1¼m performer Irian: 5/2, fourth in minor event at Chelmsford (8¾ lengths behind Music Society) in November: sure to progress. *William Haggas* **54 p**

JAI HANUMAN (IRE) 3 b.g. Requinto (IRE) 109 – Almost Blue (USA) (Mr Greeley (USA) 122) [2017 –: t7.1m^6 f5s Jan 26] modest form: wears tongue tie: has joined Michael Wigham. *Seamus Durack* **55**

JAIMIE'S JOY 2 b.g. (Apr 8) Sleeping Indian 122 – Mad Jazz 78 (Sir Percy 129) [2017 6d^6 5f 6d^5 6m Aug 28] poor form: tried in cheekpieces. *Tony Coyle* **49**

JAKEBOY 3 ch.g. Equiano (FR) 127 – Teyateyaneng (IRE) (Hawk Wing (USA) 136) [2017 p6g^6 t7.2d^6 Dec 16] well held in 2 maidens. *Sylvester Kirk* **–**

JAKE'S HILL 3 b.c. Mount Nelson 125 – Flower Market 68 (Cadeaux Genereux 131) [2017 79: 10g^2 9.9g* 9.9m^3 12d^4 Aug 5] tall, rather unfurnished colt: useful performer: won maiden at Sandown (by ¾ length from Mafaaheem) in June: third in listed race there (1¾ lengths behind Spark Plug) in July: stays 1½m: acts on good to firm and good to soft going: front runner/races prominently. *Eve Johnson Houghton* **109**

JALELA 3 b.f. Canford Cliffs (IRE) 133 – Divine Grace (IRE) (Definite Article 121) [2017 8m^2 t8.6g^2 7s* p7g p8s* 8d^4 8g Oct 7] 60,000F, 180,000Y: lengthy filly: has a quick action: half-sister to several winners, including smart German 6f (including at 2 yrs)/7f winner Electric Beat (by Shinko Forest) and useful 2-y-o 6f winner Gray Pearl (by Excellent Art): dam ran twice: useful performer: won maiden at Newmarket in May and handicap at Kempton (apprentice) in September: stays 1m: acts on polytrack and soft going: sent to France. *Richard Hannon* **97**

JALINGO (IRE) 6 b.g. Cape Cross (IRE) 129 – Just Special 109 (Cadeaux Genereux 131) [2017 p15.8g^6 Dec 20] useful at best, little show sole start in 2017 after long absence: stays 1½m: acts on polytrack, fibresand and firm going. *Ali Stronge* **–**

JALLOTA 6 b.g. Rock of Gibraltar (IRE) 133 – Lady Lahar 106 (Fraam 114) [2017 116: 8.1d^3 7.2s^2 8f 7g^3 7g 7g^4 7d^5 8d^3 7g* 7d^2 8d^4 Nov 4] tall, good-topped gelding: smart performer: won listed race at Redcar (by 4½ lengths from Von Blucher) in October: placed on 5 occasions, including in Mile at Sandown (2 lengths behind Sovereign Debt), John of Gaunt Stakes at Haydock (½ length behind Absolutely So) and Joel Stakes at Newmarket (7¼ lengths behind Beat The Bank): stays 1m: acts on firm and soft going. *Charles Hills* **116**

JAL MAHAL 2 b.f. (Jan 23) Sepoy (AUS) 129 – Eminently 75 (Exceed And Excel (AUS) 126) [2017 p7d Nov 22] £84,000Y: first foal: dam, 2-y-o 6f winner, half-sister to high-class sprinter Reverence: 12/1, green when well held in minor event at Kempton. *John Gosden* **–**

JAMACHO 3 ch.g. Camacho 118 – Obsessive Secret (IRE) (Grand Lodge (USA) 125) [2017 70: 7g^3 9m^2 9.9g^2 9v^3 10g^6 Jul 24] fairly useful maiden: second in handicaps at Beverley in May: stays 1¼m: acts on tapeta, soft and good to firm going: usually leads. *Brian Ellison* **81**

JAMAICAN JILL 2 b.f. (Apr 4) Teofilo (IRE) 126 – Kahlua Kiss 103 (Mister Baileys 123) [2017 p7g^3 p8s^6 Nov 16] half-sister to several winners, including very smart winner up to 1¼m Windhoek (2-y-o 6f winner, by Cape Cross) and 1½m winner Eager Beaver (by Duke of Marmalade): dam winner up to 10.4f (2-y-o 7f winner): fair form: better effort when third in minor event at Chelmsford (1¼ lengths behind Bath And Tennis) in October: should stay at least 1m. *William Muir* **73**

Dubai Duty Free Mill Reef Stakes, Newbury—
having married owner Bill Gredley's daughter Polly just seven days earlier, trainer George Scott receives a belated wedding present when James Garfield beats Invincible Army (striped cap) and Nebo (dark sleeves) to give his handler a first pattern-race success

JAMEERAH 4 b.f. Dansili 127 – Jira 95 (Medicean 128) [2017 96: 6s 6g p6g⁵ t5g p6s Dec 7] good-topped filly: useful handicapper, generally well below form in 2017: stays 6f: acts on polytrack and tapeta. *Bryan Smart* **83**

JAMES COOK (IRE) 2 b.c. (Apr 7) Galileo (IRE) 134 – Red Evie (IRE) 117 (Intikhab (USA) 135) [2017 7s² 8.1v* Oct 22] brother to several winners, including high-class winner up to 1½m (including Prix de l'Arc de Triomphe) Found and smart winner up to 1½m Best In The World (both 2-y-o 1m winners): dam 7f/1m (including Lockinge Stakes) winner: fairly useful form: won maiden at Leopardstown in October by ½ length from Latrobe, making most: will be suited by further than 1m: wears tongue tie: open to further improvement. *Aidan O'Brien, Ireland* **93 p**

JAMES GARFIELD (IRE) 2 b.c. (Mar 24) Exceed And Excel (AUS) 126 – Whazzat 105 (Daylami (IRE) 138) [2017 6g³ 5f³ 6m* 7g⁴ 7d² 6m* 8f Nov 3] compact colt: seventh foal: closely related to useful winner up to 1m The Shrew (2-y-o 7.5f winner, by Dansili) and half-brother to winner up to 7f Theladyinquestion (2-y-o 6f winner, by Dubawi) and 1¼m winner Trainnah (by Pivotal): dam, 2-y-o 6f/7f winner, stayed 1¼m: smart performer: won maiden at Doncaster in July and Mill Reef Stakes at Newbury (by ¾ length from Invincible Army) in September: second in Acomb Stakes at York (nose behind Wells Farhh Go) in August: tenth in Breeders' Cup Juvenile Turf at Del Mar final outing: stays 7f: acts on firm and good to soft going. *George Scott* **111**

JAMIH 2 ch.c. (Apr 16) Intello (GER) 129 – Hannda (IRE) 74 (Dr Devious (IRE) 127) [2017 p8d⁶ p10g Nov 29] 300,000Y: half-brother to several winners, including smart 11f/1½m winner (stayed 1¾m) Seal of Approval (by Authorized) and useful winner around 2m Gale Force (by Shirocco): dam 1¼m winner: modest form in minor event/maiden: remains with potential. *John Gosden* **60 p**

JAMIL (IRE) 2 b.c. (Mar 26) Dansili 127 – Havant 111 (Halling (USA) 133) [2017 7v* Oct 4] 240,000F, 95,000 2-y-o: second foal: half-brother to 2-y-o 6f winner Exmouth (by Elusive Quality): dam, 2-y-o 7f winner, half-sister to very smart winner up to 1½m Leadership: 4/1, overcame inexperience when won minor event at Salisbury (by 2¼ lengths from Dance Emperor) on debut, asserting final 100 yds: should do better. *Roger Varian* **82 p**

JAMPOWER 2 b.g. (Mar 11) Equiano (FR) 127 – Wiki Tiki 70 (Dixie Union (USA) 121) [2017 p6g p7g Dec 20] well held in minor events. *Stuart Williams* **–**

JANABIYA 2 b.f. (Jan 28) Nathaniel (IRE) 129 – Date With Destiny (IRE) 93 (George Washington (IRE) 133) [2017 7g Jul 15] 130,000Y: second foal: closely related to smart winner up to 1¼m Beautiful Morning (2-y-o 7f winner, by Galileo): dam 2-y-o 7f winner who stayed 11.5f: 66/1, tenth in maiden at Newmarket (6¾ lengths behind Poetic Charm) in July: should do better. *George Peckham* **67 p**

JAN DE HEEM 7 ch.g. Dutch Art 126 – Shasta 81 (Shareef Dancer (USA) 135) [2017 71: 14g⁵ 9.9d⁴ 11.9m⁴ 14g² 12s⁴ 14d 10m⁶ 14s* 13.9v² 14v² Nov 7] sturdy gelding: fair handicapper: won at Redcar in September: stays 1¾m: acts on tapeta and any turf going: has worn headgear, including last 3 starts: often travels strongly. *Tina Jackson* **68**

JANE ROSE (IRE) 2 b.f. (Mar 9) Acclamation 118 – Miss Champagne (FR) (Bering 136) [2017 6d⁴ p6d 6g⁶ Jul 21] €65,000F, 100,000Y: well-made filly: half-sister to several winners, including 2-y-o 7f winner Minor Vamp (by Hawk Wing) and 1m-1¼m winner **68**

Beaumont's Party (by High Chaparral), both useful, and to dam of smart performer up to 1¾m Quest For Peace: dam unraced: fair form: best effort when fourth in minor event at Doncaster (3¾ lengths behind Eirene) in June. *Richard Hannon*

JANNIA 3 b.f. Iffraaj 127 – Fairy Moss (IRE) 43 (Amadeus Wolf 122) [2017 –: p7g Jan 4] poor form in maidens in Britain: sent to Spain, where won minor event over 1m at San Sebastian in July. *Eve Johnson Houghton* **48**

JAN'S JOY 2 br.f. (May 3) Kheleyf (USA) 116 – Overwing (IRE) 84 (Fasliyev (USA) 120) [2017 6s^4 5.1m p6g^4 p6g^5 Aug 22] fourth foal: dam 5f (including at 2 yrs)/6f winner: modest form: stays 6f: in tongue tie last 2 starts. *Stuart Williams* **61**

JAN SMUTS (IRE) 9 b.g. Johannesburg (USA) 127 – Choice House (USA) (Chester House (USA) 123) [2017 77, a69: t16.3g* t12.4g t16.3g^5 t16.3d^2 t16.3d^4 t16.3g^5 13.8m^6 16.5m^4 16m^3 17.2g^5 t16.3s^4 14.1g^3 16.1g 16m^5 15.9v 16g^2 t16.3s^4 15.9s^6 t16.3g 15.9s^5 Oct 31] lengthy, useful-looking gelding: fair handicapper: won at Newcastle in January: stays 17f: acts on tapeta, good to firm and heavy going: wears headgear/tongue tie. *Wilf Storey* **67**

JANSZOON 3 gr.g. Dubawi (IRE) 129 – Adventure (USA) (Unbridled's Song (USA) 125) [2017 10m^2 11.6d* 11.9f^6 12m 14d^5 a9.9f^4 Nov 23] lengthy gelding: sixth foal: half-brother to 3 winners, including smart 2-y-o 7f winner (stayed 1½m) Laughing Lashes (by Mr Greeley) and smart winner up to 1½m (stayed 1¾m) Adventure Seeker (2-y-o 1m winner, by Dalakhani): dam, US 8.5f/9f winner, half-sister to Racing Post Trophy winner Palace Episode: useful performer: won maiden at Lingfield in May: left Charlie Appleby after fifth start: stays 1½m: acts on good to firm and good to soft going: often in blinkers. *A. Al Rayhi, UAE* **95**

JASHMA (IRE) 3 b.g. Power 117 – Daganya (IRE) 104 (Danehill Dancer (IRE) 117) [2017 –p: p5g^3 t6g^5 5g^4 5d* 5m^3 5m^4 5f^2 5d^2 6g^2 6s^2 5m* 5s* Sep 27] fairly useful handicapper: won at Bath in May, and Sandown and Goodwood (apprentice, by ¾ length from Flowing Clarets) in September: stays 6f: acts on tapeta, firm and soft going: in cheekpieces last 3 starts: usually travels strongly. *Richard Hughes* **87**

JASI (IRE) 2 b.g. (Apr 15) Kodiac 112 – Late Night Movie (IRE) (Holy Roman Emperor (IRE) 125) [2017 f5d* 5m^2 5.1g^4 t5.1m Oct 28] fair form: won minor event at Southwell in April: left Richard Fahey after third start: raced only at 5f: has joined Ivan Furtado. *David O'Meara* **74**

JASMINCITA (IRE) 3 b.f. Dark Angel (IRE) 113 – Jasmine Flower (Kyllachy 129) [2017 69: p7g 8.3m p8g p7g^6 p6g p7g^4 Oct 17] leggy filly: modest maiden: stays 7f: acts on polytrack: in cheekpieces last 3 starts. *George Baker* **54**

JAVELIN 2 ch.f. (Mar 2) Lethal Force (IRE) 128 – Amitola (IRE) 100 (Choisir (AUS) 126) [2017 6g^5 Jun 20] 12,000F, £40,000Y: third foal: dam, winner up to 1m (2-y-o 6f winner), half-sister to useful 5f-7f winner Farlow: 11/4, fifth in minor event at Thirsk (2½ lengths behind Silca Mistress) in June: has joined William Muir: capable of better. *Richard Fahey* **60 p**

JAWAN 2 b.c. (Mar 28) Sepoy (AUS) 129 – Luluti (IRE) 55 (Kheleyf (USA) 116) [2017 7g Oct 16] fourth foal: half-brother to 2-y-o 6f winner Dutch Gallery (by Dutch Art) and a winner in Greece by Poet's Voice: dam once-raced half-sister to useful sprinter Excellerator: 100/1, well held in minor event at Yarmouth: should do better. *Michael Bell* **– p**

JAWWAAL 2 ch.c. (Jan 26) Bahamian Bounty 116 – Avenbury (Mount Nelson 125) [2017 7d^3 7d^3 Aug 18] 45,000F, £140,000Y: first foal: dam unraced half-sister to very smart 7f/1m performer Ouqba: fairly useful form: third in minor event at Newmarket in July and maiden at Newbury in August: will prove effective at 6f. *John Gosden* **80**

JAYCOLS STAR 2 ch.g. (Feb 21) Medicean 128 – A Lulu Ofa Menifee (USA) (Menifee (USA) 124) [2017 7d 7m^6 7v 8g 8.2g^6 Oct 17] modest maiden: best effort at 7f: acts on good to soft going. *Philip Kirby* **57**

JAY EM GEE (IRE) 4 gr.g. Mastercraftsman (IRE) 129 – Pallas Athena (IRE) (Sadler's Wells (USA) 132) [2017 7g Aug 2] no form in 2 maidens 22 months apart. *Bryan Smart* **–**

JAY KAY 8 b.g. Librettist (USA) 124 – Turn Back 73 (Pivotal 124) [2017 81: f7g 7.2m^2 7.2d^3 7.2s^6 7.2d 7d^4 8d^2 7.8d^3 7.8v^2 8s* 8v* f8.1g Oct 22] fairly useful handicapper: won at Ayr (twice, by 3 lengths from Le Chat d'Or second occasion) in October: stays 8.5f: acts on fibresand, good to firm and heavy going: wears hood: front runner/races prominently, usually travels strongly. *K. R. Burke* **87**

JAYWALKER (IRE) 6 b.g. Footstepsinthesand 120 – Nipping (IRE) 113 (Night Shift (USA)) [2017 87, a94: t6g* t6g 6g⁴ 6m² 6g 6d³ p6g* Sep 25] good-quartered gelding: useful handicapper: won at Newcastle in March and Kempton (by head from Seeking Magic) in September: stays 6f: acts on polytrack, tapeta, good to firm and good to soft going: front runner/races prominently. *Rebecca Bastiman* **99**

JAZAALAH (USA) 3 ch.f. Hard Spun (USA) 124 – Teeba (USA) 100 (Seeking The Gold (USA)) [2017 –p: 8g p8g³ t7.2g³ Oct 7] fair form: stays 1m: in hood last 2 starts. *Owen Burrows* **71**

JAZEEL (IRE) 2 b.c. (Apr 25) Roderic O'Connor (IRE) 119 – Simla Bibi 69 (Indian Ridge 123) [2017 7g³ 7.6s* 7d p8g² p8g² Oct 14] €42,000F, 40,000Y: close-coupled colt: half-brother to several winners, including 1m-11f winner Emerald Wilderness (by Green Desert), winner up to 1½m Swift Alhaarth (2-y-o 8.6f winner, by Alhaarth) and 7f/1m winner Simla Sunset (by One Cool Cat), all useful: dam maiden (stayed 1¼m): fairly useful performer: won minor event at Lingfield in August: second in nursery at Kempton in September: stays 1m: acts on polytrack and soft going. *Mick Channon* **88**

JAZIRAT (IRE) 2 b.g. (Feb 6) Dark Angel (IRE) 113 – Layla Jamil (IRE) 85 (Exceed And Excel (AUS) 126) [2017 7g³ 7d² Jul 11] 220,000Y: third foal: brother to smart 5f-7f winner (including at 2 yrs) Birchwood and 6f winner Desert Frost: dam 7f winner: fair form when placed in minor events: wears hood: should do better. *Charlie Appleby* **72 p**

JAZRI 6 b.g. Myboycharlie (IRE) 118 – Read Federica 90 (Fusaichi Pegasus (USA) 130) [2017 66§: t9.5m p10g² p10d⁴ p10g³ p10g 10.2f 10.2d 9.9s³ p10d p10g Oct 5] big, robust gelding: modest handicapper: stays 11f: acts on polytrack, tapeta, good to firm and heavy going: wears headgear: tried in tongue tie: starts slowly, usually races in rear: temperamental. *Milton Bradley* **56 §**

JAZZ AFFAIR (IRE) 2 b.g. (Apr 28) Red Jazz (USA) 125 – Kiss And Don'tell (USA) (Rahy (USA) 115) [2017 6.1g 6g 7g p6g⁶ t7.2g t6.1g p6g³ Dec 12] modest maiden: best effort at 6f: acts on polytrack: tried in visor. *Jamie Osborne* **55**

JAZZ LEGEND (USA) 4 b.g. Scat Daddy (USA) 120 – Champion Ride (USA) (Candy Ride (ARG) 133) [2017 70: f5g 6.1g 6m⁵ 6m⁶ t7.2g⁵ 6g* 6v⁵ t6.1g⁶ p7g 5v p6g Sep 26] modest handicapper: won at Leicester (apprentice) on final start for Olly Murphy in July: left Anabel K. Murphy after fourth start: stays 6f: acts on polytrack, tapeta, good to firm and good to soft going: wears headgear: tends to find little. *Mandy Rowland* **58**

JAZZ MAGIC (IRE) 2 ch.g. (Mar 25) Red Jazz (USA) 125 – Caerella (IRE) (Alzao (USA) 117) [2017 6g May 27] 20/1, well held in minor event at York. *Sally Haynes* **–**

JAZZY GIRL (IRE) 2 br.f. (Apr 21) Red Jazz (USA) 125 – Intimate Secret (IRE) 75 (Invincible Spirit (IRE) 121) [2017 6g p6g 5.1d p6s p7d⁵ Nov 22] €5,000Y, £16,000 2-y-o: fourth foal: half-sister to 2-y-o 5f winner Secret Tale (by Zoffany), later successful in Qatar, and a winner in Italy by Alhaarth: dam maiden (stayed 7f): poor maiden. *Brendan Powell* **49**

JAZZY (IRE) 4 b.g. Roderic O'Connor (IRE) 119 – Lucayan Beauty (IRE) 80 (Marju (IRE) 127) [2017 80: 11.4d⁶ p16s⁵ 11.6d* Jul 12] compact gelding: fairly useful handicapper: won at Lingfield (by ¾ length from Maroc) in July: stays 1½m: acts on polytrack and good to soft going: often wears headgear/tongue tie: sold 17,000 gns in July. *Martin Keighley* **82**

JEANIE'S PLACE 4 ch.f. Compton Place 125 – Good Again 104 (Dubai Destination (USA) 127) [2017 48: p6g p6d p6g⁶ 5.7f 6g t6.1g Jun 7] lengthy filly: modest handicapper: stays 6f: acts on good to firm going: tried in headgear: usually wears tongue tie. *Charlie Wallis* **55**

JEAN PAGET (IRE) 2 b.f. (Feb 24) Choisir (AUS) 126 – Betty Fontaine (IRE) 88 (Mujadil (USA) 119) [2017 6g 5s⁴ 6d t6.1g⁶ p6g 6m Aug 28] close-coupled filly: second foal: dam 2-y-o 5f/5.7f winner: modest maiden: best effort at 5f: acts on soft going: tried in visor: sold €1,000, sent to Germany. *Mick Channon* **54**

JEANY (IRE) 3 b.f. Kodiac 112 – Flower Bowl (IRE) (Noverre (USA) 125) [2017 69: 5m² t5.1g⁶ 5m² Aug 30] fair maiden: raced only at 5f: acts on good to firm and good to soft going. *Bryan Smart* **72**

JEBEL TARA 12 b.g. Diktat 126 – Chantilly (FR) (Sanglamore (USA) 126) [2017 67, a61: 6g 6d³ 7.2s⁵ t5d Sep 29] lengthy, good-topped gelding: modest handicapper: stays 8.5f, usually races at shorter nowadays: acts on fibresand, tapeta and any turf going: wears headgear/tongue tie. *Alistair Whillans* **52**

JEBULANI 7 b.g. Jelani (IRE) 115 – Susan's Dowry 74 (Efisio 120) [2017 t12.2g 14m⁶ 12.5g 13.1s⁴ 10d 15.9v⁶ Aug 8] poor performer: has worn headgear, including last 4 starts: tried in tongue tie. *Barry Murtagh* **–**

JEDI MASTER (IRE) 2 ch.c. (Feb 22) Red Jazz (USA) 125 – Misrepresent (USA) 72 (Distorted Humor (USA) 117) [2017 5g^6 5g^4 5v^2 6g* 5.5s* 6m^5 7v^4 7g^6 6.5g 6g Oct 7] €15,000F, €27,000Y: lengthy colt: second foal: half-brother to Italian 7.5f-11f winner Titanic Blond (by Frozen Power): dam 7f winner out of US Grade 2 1m/9f winner Halory Leigh: fairly useful performer: won minor events at Thirsk and Wetherby in June: stays 7f: acts on good to firm and heavy going: sold 17,000 gns, sent to Italy. *Richard Fahey* **85**

JEDLITZKA (IRE) 2 b.f. (May 14) Kodiac 112 – Jeritza (Rainbow Quest (USA) 134) [2017 6g 7s Jul 22] €20,000F, 20,000Y: seventh foal: closely related to German 10.5f winner Joker Hill (by Tiger Hill) and half-sister to 1½m winner Go On Gal (by Approve): dam, French 11f/1½m winner, sister to useful 9f-13f winner Jade Quest: well held in 2 minor events. *Mick Channon* **–**

JELLMOOD 2 b.g. (Mar 3) Acclamation 118 – Emotif (ARG) (Giant's Causeway (USA) 132) [2017 5m^3 5m^2 6m^2 6g t7.2g* t8.6d^2 Dec 26] sturdy gelding: first foal: dam South African 7f winner out of half-sister to South African Horse of the Year Empress Club: fairly useful performer: won minor event at Wolverhampton in December: second in nursery there later in month: stays 8.5f: acts on tapeta and good to firm going: in hood last 2 starts: has hinted at temperament (once refused to enter stall). *Marco Botti* **92**

JELLY MONGER (IRE) 5 b.m. Strategic Prince 114 – Royal Jelly 82 (King's Best (USA) 132) [2017 86: 12m^4 12m^2 p14s^2 14g^6 13.3g^5 12g^3 12g^5 10.1s 12g^3 10m 11.9d Oct 28] tall mare: useful handicapper: third at Salisbury (¾ length behind So Sleek) in August: stays 1¾m: acts on polytrack, soft and good to firm going: has worn headgear: has looked ungainly. *Dominic Ffrench Davis* **95**

JENJI (IRE) 3 b.f. Pour Moi (IRE) 125 – Distant Symphony (FR) (Dalakhani (IRE) 133) [2017 –: 7d^4 May 18] no form: dead. *David Evans* **–**

JENNIES GEM 4 b.g. Mount Nelson 125 – Kaspirit (IRE) 88 (Invincible Spirit (IRE) 121) [2017 6.9g 6s^3 6m^4 7m 9.9d f7.1g^4 t7.1g^4 f8.1g^5 f11.1g Dec 22] poor maiden: stays 7f: acts on fibresand and tapeta. *Ollie Pears* **49**

JEOPARDY JOHN 2 b.g. (Apr 19) Delegator 125 – Daysiwaay (IRE) (Daylami (IRE) 138) [2017 p7g^6 p6g^4 p7g p7d^3 p7g^3 Dec 31] tall gelding: fair maiden: stays 7f: acts on polytrack: front runner/races prominently. *Michael Attwater* **68**

JEREMIAH 2 ch.c. (Feb 5) Kheleyf (USA) 116 – Tessie (Tiger Hill (IRE) 127) [2017 p10g^3 10m^3 Oct 25] big, strong colt: third foal: dam unraced close relative to smart 1m winner Dolores, herself dam of Irish St Leger winner Duncan and smart stayer Samuel: fairly useful form: third in maidens at Chelmsford and Newmarket (1¼ lengths behind Brundtland) in October: open to further improvement. *Charlie Fellowes* **80 p**

JEREMY'S JET (IRE) 6 b.g. Jeremy (USA) 122 – Double Vie (IRE) (Tagula (IRE) 116) [2017 70: 8.3g t8.6g 12v 11.5s^6 f16.5g^{pu} 11.9d^6 Sep 18] fair form for A. J. Martin in 2016, well below that level in 2017: has worn tongue tie, including last 2 starts. *Tony Carroll* **–**

JERSEY BREEZE (IRE) 4 gr.f. Dark Angel (IRE) 113 – Sixfields Flyer (IRE) 66 (Desert Style (IRE) 121) [2017 7m^4 7d^6 6g^3 6g^6 6m* 5.7f* 6m 5d^6 5d^3 6g 6d 6d^5 p7g Oct 18] angular filly: fairly useful handicapper: won at Brighton and Bath (by 2¼ lengths from Powerful Dream) in June: stays 6f: acts on firm going: has worn visor. *Mick Channon* **86**

JERSEY BULL (IRE) 5 b.g. Clodovil (IRE) 116 – Chaguaramas (IRE) 93 (Mujadil (USA) 119) [2017 71: p11g p12d^4 p11g^5 p12g^3 p11g^6 10m 11.6d p12g^3 p12g^6 p12g Oct 17] good-quartered gelding: fair handicapper: stays 1½m: acts on polytrack, good to firm and good to soft going: wears headgear: often races towards rear. *Michael Madgwick* **67**

JERSEY JEWEL (FR) 5 b.m. Naaqoos 117 – Nikolenka (IRE) (Indian Ridge 123) [2017 78: p10g^4 13.3v 11.4m t9.5g Dec 18] workmanlike mare: fair handicapper: left Tom Dascombe after third start: stays 1½m: acts on polytrack, tapeta, good to firm and good to soft going: has worn cheekpieces: in tongue tie last 2 starts: usually races prominently. *Peter Bowen* **75**

JESS 4 b.f. Equiano (FR) 127 – Poyle Meg 91 (Dansili 127) [2017 53, a69: t7.1g t5g t6g^6 t5g 6s^3 6g 6g Aug 15] modest handicapper: stays 6f: acts on all-weather, soft and good to firm going: wears headgear. *Kevin Ryan* **55**

JESSE TREE (IRE) 4 ch.f. Approve (IRE) 112 – Dane Blue (IRE) 97 (Danehill Dancer (IRE) 117) [2017 47: 8g 5.7m p6g^3 5.7f Jul 12] poor maiden: stays 7f: in tongue tie last 3 starts: front runner/races prominently. *John Flint* **37**

JESSICA JO (IRE) 4 ch.f. Mastercraftsman (IRE) 129 – Naomh Geileis (USA) 95 (Grand Slam (USA) 120) [2017 65: p8d f12g Feb 2] fair maiden on Flat, well held both starts in 2017: stays 9f: acts on good to firm going: wears blinkers: sent to Italy, where won over hurdles in October. *Mark Johnston* **–**

JESSIE ALLAN (IRE) 6 b.m. Bushranger (IRE) 119 – Ishimagic 52 (Ishiguru (USA) 114) [2017 52?: t7.1d t7.1d t7.1d^4 t8g t6g^6 7.1m^4 6m^6 6m^4 7.2m^5 t8s^3 7.2s^2 7.2g^3 7.2d^4 8g 7.2d^2 8v^4 t7.1d t6g^2 t7.1s^2 t6.1d^4 t6.1d^3 Dec 27] modest maiden: stays 1m: acts on tapeta, soft and good to firm going: has worn headgear: often races towards rear. *Jim Goldie* **59**

JESSINAMILLION 3 b.g. Mine (IRE) 117 – Miss Apricot 48 (Indian Ridge 123) [2017 6m 6g^3 t7.1g^5 6v^3 6d^6 6d* 6d^6 Sep 20] fair performer: won maiden at Hamilton in September: stays 7f: acts on tapeta and heavy going: often races towards rear. *James Bethell* **79**

JE SUIS CHARLIE 3 b.g. High Chaparral (IRE) 132 – Fin (Groom Dancer (USA) 128) [2017 76: 10m 11.9d^2 11.9d^3 10.3d^2 10.2m 10.2d^5 12.1g* 12.1s^2 13.9g^5 Oct 13] rather unfurnished gelding: useful handicapper: won at Catterick in August: stays 1¾m: acts on firm and soft going: often travels strongly: sold to join John Quinn 80,000 gns in October. *Michael Bell* **96**

JETHRO (IRE) 6 b.g. Craigsteel 122 – Wee Mo (IRE) (Zaffaran (USA) 117) [2017 –: f8.1g^4 May 8] modest form in maidens: tried in hood: maiden jumper. *Brian Ellison* **53**

JETPAC 2 b.g. (Feb 21) Paco Boy (IRE) 129 – Emperor's Hope (IRE) 79 (Holy Roman Emperor (IRE) 125) [2017 p7g p8g Dec 20] last in 2 minor events. *Laura Mongan* **–**

JET SETTER (IRE) 3 ch.g. Fast Company (IRE) 126 – Raven One (IRE) 45 (Titus Livius (FR) 115) [2017 75: f6g^4 f6g^3 p6g^4 t6f^2 t6g 6g^4 7g* 7g^5 7.6d 7d 7g^5 8g^5 7v^6 10s^4 t7.2g Oct 27] angular gelding: fair performer: won claimer at Leicester in May: left Brian Meehan after second start: stays 1m: acts on polytrack, tapeta and soft going: has worn headgear: sold £3,000, sent to Germany. *Tony Carroll* **66**

JET STREAMING (IRE) 3 ch.f. Born To Sea (IRE) 117 – Sateen 87 (Barathea (IRE) 127) [2017 6v^3 7.5s^4 7s^3 8g* 8m 8.6s* 10s 12d^5 12s Oct 15] €72,000F: sixth foal: closely related to useful 1¼m winner Vita Venturi and 9.5f/1¼m winner Do The Bosanova (both by Galileo) and half-sister to French 1m winner Sendora (by Kendor): dam, 6f-11f winner, half-sister to very smart stayer Golden Quest and to dams of Oaks winner Alexandrova and Melbourne Cup winner Rekindling: useful performer: won handicaps at Leopardstown (apprentice) in June and Galway (by ½ length from So You Thought) in August: seemingly best effort when fifth in Princess Royal Stakes at Newmarket (3 lengths behind Apphia) in September: stays 1½m: acts on soft going: in hood/tongue tie last 2 starts. *A. P. Keatley, Ireland* **103 ?**

JETSTREAM (IRE) 2 b.c. (Jan 11) Galileo (IRE) 134 – Bewitched (IRE) 120 (Dansili 127) [2017 7m Jul 14] in tongue tie, 33/1, well held in maiden at Newmarket. *Charles Hills* **–**

JEWEL HOUSE 3 b.c. Dubawi (IRE) 129 – Arizona Jewel 91 (Dansili 127) [2017 82: 7g^3 7m* 7m May 12] compact colt: fairly useful performer: won maiden at Newmarket (by 1¾ lengths from Top Mission) in April: stays 8.5f: acts on good to firm going: usually races close up: sold 215,000 gns in July, sent to Qatar. *John Gosden* **88**

JIMENEZ (IRE) 4 b.c. Acclamation 118 – Fritta Mista (IRE) (Linamix (FR) 127) [2017 85: p8g* Jan 5] tall colt: fairly useful handicapper: won at Chelmsford (by 1¼ lengths from Squire) in January: stays 1¼m: acts on polytrack and good to firm going: wears cheekpieces: front runner/races prominently: sold 26,000 gns in February. *Brian Meehan* **90**

JIMMY TWO TIMES (FR) 4 gr.c. Kendargent (FR) 112 – Steel Woman (IRE) (Anabaa (USA) 130) [2017 117: 8g* 8g* May 1] very smart performer: won Prix Edmond Blanc at Saint-Cloud (by 3½ lengths from Dicton) in April and Prix du Muguet at same course (by ½ length from Kourkan) in May: stays 1m: acts on soft going. *A. Fabre, France* **120**

JIM ROCKFORD 2 ch.g. (Mar 23) Showcasing 117 – Positivity 79 (Monsieur Bond (IRE) 120) [2017 5.2g^6 5m^4 5d^5 6f^2 6m f5g^2 5s* 5.7s* Oct 2] £47,000Y: third foal: half-brother to 2-y-o 6f winner Cumbrianna (by Hellvelyn): dam, 7.5f/1m winner, half-sister to useful 1m winner Peculiarity: fairly useful performer: won nurseries at Bath in September and October (by ¾ length from Diamond Pursuit): stays 6f: acts on firm and soft going: sold 24,000 gns in November. *Ralph Beckett* **82**

JINKIE PINK (IRE) 3 b.f. Teofilo (IRE) 126 – Hurricane Havoc (IRE) 106 (Hurricane Run (IRE) 134) [2017 7g^5 7.1s^3 8.1m^4 Jun 26] 17,000Y: second foal: dam winner up to 1¼m (2-y-o 7f winner): fair form: best effort when fifth in maiden at Newbury in April: should stay 1m. *Ed Walker* **65**

JIRO BOY 2 b.c. (Apr 21) Compton Place 125 – Foolish Lady (IRE) 75 (Exceed And Excel (AUS) 126) [2017 7g 7d Oct 27] well held in minor event/maiden. *Rebecca Bastiman* **–**

JIVE FACTOR (USA) 3 b.g. The Factor (USA) 126 – Jive Talk (USA) (Kingmambo (USA) 125) [2017 –: p10d^6 f8g^4 Apr 16] tall gelding: modest maiden. *Ed Dunlop* **59**

JIVE LADY (IRE) 2 b.f. (May 3) Exceed And Excel (AUS) 126 – Fair Sailing (IRE) 62 (Docksider (USA) 124) [2017 5m 5g 5m^2 5g^3 5g* 5g^5 p5g^4 5m^6 Aug 27] 82,000Y: rather unfurnished filly: sixth foal: sister to smart 6f (including at 2 yrs)/7f winner Windfast, and half-sister to useful 2-y-o 1m winner (stayed 1¼m) Montalcino (by Big Bad Bob) and 11.5f-1¾m winner West Drive (by Sea The Stars): dam, maiden (stayed 1¼m), half-sister to high-class 1½m performer White Muzzle: fairly useful performer: won minor event at Hamilton in July: raced only at 5f: acts on polytrack and good to firm going: front runner/races prominently: sold 32,000 gns in October. *Mark Johnston* **80**

JIVE TALKING (IRE) 3 ch.f. Zoffany (IRE) 121 – Inis Boffin 81 (Danehill Dancer (IRE) 117) [2017 73: 10.2m^2 9.9m* 11.4g^2 12g^4 9.9g 11.5d^4 12g^6 p10d^3 Nov 22] lengthy filly: fairly useful handicapper: won at Beverley in July: stays 11.5f: acts on polytrack, tapeta, soft and good to firm going: in hood last 2 starts: sold 21,000 gns in December. *Michael Bell* **87**

JOALDO 5 b.g. Monsieur Bond (IRE) 120 – Labba (Tiger Hill (IRE) 127) [2017 46: f8d^5 t6.1g^4 t7.2g^4 t8.6g Jul 3] poor maiden: best effort at 7f: acts on tapeta: in cheekpieces last 3 starts: sometimes slowly away, often races towards rear. *Antony Brittain* **49**

JOCK TALK (IRE) 3 b.g. Famous Name 124 – Katdogawn 114 (Bahhare (USA) 122) [2017 –: 9.7s^3 10g 7.5d 8.1d^4 11.3v^3 p10.7g^2 p8g f8.1g Dec 4] fair maiden: left Seamus Fahey after fourth start: stays 11.5f: acts on polytrack, best turf form on soft/heavy going: usually wears tongue tie. *Gordon Elliott, Ireland* **69**

JOE CABLE (IRE) 2 b.g. (Mar 13) Camacho 118 – Happy Talk (IRE) 74 (Hamas (IRE) 125) [2017 5v^6 7g 7.9g 6d Oct 30] sturdy gelding: no form: tried in visor. *Nigel Tinkler* **–**

JOEGOGO (IRE) 2 b.g. (Mar 4) Approve (IRE) 112 – Joyfullness (USA) (Dixieland Band (USA)) [2017 5d^2 5m^3 6m^4 6s^6 p6g^3 5.1v 5.7s^3 t5.1g* p5g* t6.1g* t6.1d^5 p6g^2 Dec 30] €22,000Y: half-brother to several winners, including useful winner up to 1m Chesturo (2-y-o 7f winner, by Manduro) and 2-y-o 6f winner Academy House (by Kodiac): dam unraced: fairly useful performer: won nurseries at Wolverhampton (twice) and Lingfield in November: stays 6f: acts on polytrack, tapeta, soft and good to firm going: front runner, often travels strongly. *David Evans* **87**

JOE PACKET 10 ch.g. Joe Bear (IRE) 109 – Costa Packet (IRE) (Hussonet (USA)) [2017 81§: 6g* 7m^4 6s^4 Sep 5] quite good-topped gelding: fairly useful handicapper: won at Goodwood (by nose from Morache Music) in May: stays 7f: acts on firm and soft going: has worn headgear. *Jonathan Portman* **84**

JOE'S SPIRIT (IRE) 2 b.g. (Apr 1) Swiss Spirit 117 – Dimensional (Dansili 127) [2017 5f^2 p6d* 5d 6m^3 7s^4 p7g* p6d Sep 28] 17,000F, £42,000Y: third foal: dam unraced close relative to very smart US Grade 1 1¼m winner Light Jig: fairly useful performer: won minor event at Chelmsford in May and nursery there (by 2 lengths from Kit Marlowe) in August: stays 7f: acts on polytrack and firm going. *Michael Bell* **86**

JOEY'S DESTINY (IRE) 7 ch.g. Kheleyf (USA) 116 – Maid of Ailsa (USA) 65 (Pivotal 124) [2017 95: p7d^2 t7.1g^4 p7g 7m^3 t7.2g t7.2g* p7s t7.2g^6 t6.1g 6s t5g t6.1g Nov 20] leggy gelding: fairly useful performer: won claimer at Wolverhampton in July for Antony Brittain: left George Baker after fourth start: stays 7f: acts on polytrack, tapeta, soft and good to firm going: has worn cheekpieces: sometimes slowly away, often races in rear. *Kevin Frost* **93**

JOHANNES VERMEER (IRE) 4 b.c. Galileo (IRE) 134 – Inca Princess (IRE) 82 (Holy Roman Emperor (IRE) 125) [2017 111: 10g^4 10.5d^5 10m 10g* 12g^2 9.9g^2 11.9g^3 15.9g^2 Nov 7] good-topped colt: very smart performer: won International Stakes at the Curragh (by ½ length from Success Days) in July: placed after in Ballyroan Stakes at Leopardstown (probably should have won when beaten ½ length by Spanish Steps), Ladbrokes Stakes at Caulfield (went down by head to Gailo Chop), Caulfield Cup (Handicap) (1½ lengths third to Boom Time) and Melbourne Cup (Handicap) at Flemington (½-length second to Rekindling): stays 2m: acts on soft and good to firm going: usually wears tongue tie. *Aidan O'Brien, Ireland* **122**

JOHN CAESAR (IRE) 6 b.g. Bushranger (IRE) 119 – Polish Belle (Polish Precedent (USA) 131) [2017 70: t8.6m^4 t9.5g t8g^5 t9.5g^5 8m 10d^6 9.9d^3 9.9s^2 10d 8.5s* 9.9v* 8s^5 10.2d^3 11.4d Oct 23] modest performer: won minor event and amateur handicap at Beverley in September: stays 1¼m: acts on polytrack, tapeta, good to firm and heavy going: wears cheekpieces/tongue tie: usually races prominently. *Rebecca Bastiman* **64**

JOHN CONSTABLE (IRE) 6 b.g. Montjeu (IRE) 137 – Dance Parade (USA) 107 (Gone West (USA)) [2017 18m Oct 14] useful at best, well held in Cesarewitch Handicap on sole Flat start in 2017: stays 2m: acts on good to firm and heavy going: usually wears headgear: tried in tongue tie: smart hurdler. *Evan Williams* **–**

Grosvenor Sport Handicap, Goodwood—Johnny Barnes runs out a decisive winner from Burnt Sugar and Straight Right (noseband on rail)

JOHNI BOXIT 2 ch.g. (Feb 21) Sakhee's Secret 128 – Pink Supreme 70 (Night Shift (USA)) [2017 6g³ 5f² 5.1d⁴ 6d Oct 24] fair form: best effort at 5f. *Gay Kelleway* **66**

JOHN JOINER 5 b.g. Captain Gerrard (IRE) 113 – Nigella 92 (Band On The Run 102) [2017 79: 5g 5g⁶ 5d 5s³ 5.1g³ 5g² 5.1g⁴ 5s³ 5.1d Oct 23] good-topped gelding: fair handicapper: stays 5.5f: acts on tapeta, firm and soft going: has worn headgear. *Peter Hedger* **65**

JOHN KIRKUP 2 ch.g. (Feb 22) Assertive 121 – Bikini 80 (Trans Island 119) [2017 6m 5s* 5s* 6m² 5d* 6d⁴ 6d² 6g Oct 7] 6,000F, £16,000Y: well-made gelding: fourth foal: brother to useful 7f winner Tight Fit and 5f/6f winner Kommander Kirkup: dam maiden (stayed 1m): fairly useful performer: won minor events at Carlisle (twice) in June and nursery at Thirsk (by 1½ lengths from Angel Force) in August: stays 6f: acts on soft and good to firm going. *Michael Dods* **94**

JOHNNY BARNES (IRE) 5 b.h. Acclamation 118 – Mahalia (IRE) 107 (Danehill (USA) 126) [2017 108: 6.1m 7d⁴ 7s³ 7d⁴ 7g* 6v⁶ 7s⁵ Oct 7] good-topped horse: smart handicapper: won at Goodwood (by length from Burnt Sugar) in August: stayed 1m: acted on heavy going: often raced towards rear/travelled strongly: to stand at Haras des Granges, France, fee €2,500. *John Gosden* **117**

JOHNNY CAVAGIN 8 b.g. Superior Premium 122 – Beyond The Rainbow (Mind Games 121) [2017 93: 7g 6m² 6m³ 6v² 6d 6.1m⁵ 7d² 6d⁵ 6s³ 7g⁶ 7g⁵ 6v² t6d⁶ t8d p6s Dec 15] strong gelding: fairly useful handicapper on turf, fair on all-weather: second at Doncaster in May and July: stays 7f: acts on polytrack, good to firm and heavy going: tried in hood: wears tongue tie: sometimes slowly away. *Ronald Thompson* **88** **a79**

JOHN REEL (FR) 8 b.g. Country Reel (USA) 113 – John Quatz (FR) (Johann Quatz (FR) 120) [2017 105: p12m⁶ t9.5g t12.4g t12.2g p15.8g⁴ t13.9g⁵ p15.8g Apr 14] big gelding: useful handicapper: stays 2¼m: acts on polytrack, tapeta and good to soft going: tried in visor/tongue tie: front runner/races prominently: won on chasing debut in May. *David Evans* **99**

JOLLY ROGER (IRE) 10 b.g. Oratorio (IRE) 128 – Chalice Wells (Sadler's Wells (USA) 132) [2017 p15.8g⁶ Feb 22] smallish gelding: fairly useful at best, well held on sole Flat start in 2017: stays 2m: acts on soft and good to firm going: fairly useful hurdler at best, on downgrade nowadays. *Dai Burchell* **–**

JONATHANS GIRL 2 b.f. (Apr 29) Equiano (FR) 127 – Jewelled 85 (Fantastic Light (USA) 134) [2017 p7g Oct 9] 800Y: first foal: dam 1m-1½m winner: 100/1, well held in minor event at Kempton. *Christine Dunnett* **–**

JONBOY 2 b.c. (Apr 12) Delegator 125 – Cavallo da Corsa (Galileo (IRE) 134) [2017 6s⁶ 5v* Sep 21] 9,000F: fifth foal: half-brother to useful 2-y-o 5f winner Muhadathat (by Showcasing): dam unraced half-sister to useful 6f/7f winner Cansili Star: fairly useful form: won maiden at Pontefract (by ½ length from Black Friday) in September. *David Barron* **81**

JON H THE LAWMAN (IRE) 4 b.g. Lawman (FR) 121 – Lan Pham Ti (IRE) (Librettist (USA) 124) [2017 47: t8.6g 7m Jun 24] poor maiden: stays 1¼m: acts on good to firm going: has worn headgear, including last 3 starts. *Ronald Thompson* **–**

JONNIE SKULL (IRE) 11 b.g. Pyrus (USA) 106 – Sovereign Touch (IRE) (Pennine Walk 120) [2017 51: 8m² 8g 8m⁵ Jun 14] compact gelding: fairly useful performer at best, winner of 19 of 196 starts on Flat: stayed 1½m, usually raced over shorter: acted on all-weather, firm and good to soft going: usually wore headgear/tongue tie: front runner: retired. *Phil McEntee* **47**

JONNY DELTA 10 ch.g. Sulamani (IRE) 130 – Send Me An Angel (IRE) 75 (Lycius (USA) 124) [2017 –: 14m^{2} 13.1m* 13.1m^{3} 14m^{3} 13.1s 12.5g^{6} 12.5m* 16m^{3} 12.5m^{2} 14m^{6} 14s* 16v^{4} Oct 16] fair handicapper: won at Ayr in May, and Musselburgh in July and October: stayed 2¼m: acted on good to firm and heavy going: tried in hood: front runner/raced prominently: dead. *Jim Goldie* **68**

JONNYSIMPSON (IRE) 2 gr.f. (Feb 25) Zebedee 113 – Applauding (IRE) (Royal Applause 124) [2017 5m^{4} p6d^{3} 5m 5m^{3} 5s^{2} p5g* Oct 18] seventh foal: half-sister to 3 winners, including temperamental 6f/7f winner Loud (by Dutch Art) and 1m-1¼m winner Stoneboat Bill (by Virtual): dam unraced half-sister to useful winner up to 1¼m Tomintoul Flyer: fair performer: won nursery at Kempton in October: best form at 5f: acts on polytrack, soft and good to firm going: usually races close up. *Brendan Powell* **73**

JORDAN JAMES (IRE) 4 b.g. Equiano (FR) 127 – Deira (USA) 79 (Green Desert (USA) 127) [2017 80: 8.3m 8m 7.8v^{3} t8g 7.8v Sep 13] fair handicapper: stays 1m: acts on soft going: in cheekpieces last 3 starts: often races prominently. *Brian Ellison* **72**

JORDAN SPORT 4 b.g. Dubawi (IRE) 129 – Wonder Why (GER) (Tiger Hill (IRE) 127) [2017 95: p6g* t5.1g^{4} 6.1d^{4} p5s^{4} 6m^{3} 6d* 6v^{4} 7g^{4} Oct 7] well-made gelding: useful handicapper: won at Lingfield (by 2 lengths from Kasbah) in January and Newmarket (by 2¾ lengths from Major Pusey) in August: best form at 6f: acts on polytrack, tapeta, soft and good to firm going: wears hood: usually leads: sold to join Fawzi Abdulla Nass 90,000 gns in October. *David Simcock* **106**

JORDAURA 11 br.g. Primo Valentino (IRE) 116 – Christina's Dream 74 (Spectrum (IRE) 126) [2017 –: t9.5m 10d Oct 20] sturdy gelding: fairly useful at best, retains little ability: tried in eyeshields/tongue tie. *Alan Berry* **41**

JORVIK PRINCE 3 br.g. Kheleyf (USA) 116 – Wotatomboy 65 (Captain Rio 122) [2017 67: 5m^{4} 5m^{4} 5m^{3} 5d 5m 5m t5d t6.1g^{2} 6s^{4} t6g t6.1d^{2} t5.1g* t6.1d* Dec 27] fairly useful handicapper: won at Wolverhampton (twice, by 1½ lengths from Tasaaboq second occasion) in December: stays 6f: acts on polytrack, tapeta, good to firm and good to soft going: has worn headgear: front runner/races prominently. *Karen Tutty* **81**

JO'S GIRL (IRE) 2 b.f. (Jan 21) Zebedee 113 – Diamond Finesse (IRE) 78 (Red Clubs (IRE) 125) [2017 5f^{4} 5.5s^{4} 6m 7d^{3} 7s 7s^{2} t8.6g t8g^{6} Dec 6] £42,000 2-y-o: compact filly: second foal: dam lightly-raced half-sister to useful 2-y-o 6f winner Beatbox Rhythm: fair maiden: left Jamie Osborne after seventh start: stays 7f: acts on soft going: tried in tongue tie: sometimes slowly away, often races in rear. *Micky Hammond* **72**

JOSHLEE (IRE) 3 b.f. Dark Angel (IRE) 113 – Kay Es Jay (FR) 99 (Xaar 132) [2017 56: p8g^{6} 7s 7m p5g^{4} p5g p6s f5g^{6} Dec 21] modest maiden: left Richard Hughes after third start: probably stays 1m: acts on polytrack: tried in headgear. *Emma Owen* **56**

JOSH THE PLOD (IRE) 3 b.g. Arcano (IRE) 122 – Dune Breeze (IRE) (Azamour (IRE) 130) [2017 10g^{3} 10d^{6} t9.5g^{3} 10g^{3} 9.9m Aug 16] sturdy gelding: fair maiden: best effort at 9.5f: acts on tapeta: sometimes slowly away. *Andrew Balding* **75**

JOSHUA REYNOLDS 3 b.g. Nathaniel (IRE) 129 – Dash To The Front 105 (Diktat 126) [2017 62p: 10.3g^{5} 11.6m^{3} 13d* 14d* 14s 13.9g p14g* Nov 2] useful-looking gelding: useful handicapper: won at Newmarket (by 4½ lengths from Maori Bob) in June, Sandown (by ¾ length from Nadaitak) in July and Chelmsford (by 2½ lengths from Watersmeet) in November: will stay 2m: acts on polytrack, good to firm and good to soft going: wears headgear: sold £160,000 in November. *John Gosden* **106**

JOURNEY 5 b.m. Dubawi (IRE) 129 – Montare (IRE) 116 (Montjeu (IRE) 137) [2017 124: 12m^{5} 10g 11.9d^{2} 12s^{6} Oct 21] sturdy mare: smart performer: second in Prix Vermeille at Chantilly (2½ lengths behind Bateel) in September, below best other starts in 2017: stays 1½m: acts on good to firm and good to soft going: wears hood: keen sort, races prominently. *John Gosden* **118**

JOUSI 2 ch.f. (Jan 27) Dubawi (IRE) 129 – Soon (IRE) 106 (Galileo (IRE) 134) [2017 7g^{4} 7d* 7g p7s^{2} 7m Oct 13] close-coupled filly: second foal: dam, winner up to 8.5f (2-y-o 7f winner), closely related to Derby runner-up Walk In The Park out of Irish 1000 Guineas winner Classic Park: fairly useful performer: won minor event at Ascot (by length from Give And Take) in July: raced only at 7f: acts on polytrack and good to soft going. *Hugo Palmer* **82**

JOY 3 b.f. Equiano (FR) 127 – On Wings of Love (IRE) 69 (Hawk Wing (USA) 136) [2017 p6g^{6} p7g p7g 7g 10m Jun 17] first foal: dam, maiden (best at 6f), half-sister to useful 1m/1¼m winner Prince Kalamoun: no form. *Laura Mongan* **–**

JOYFUL DREAM (IRE) 3 ch.f. Dream Ahead (USA) 133 – Tearsforjoy (USA) 51 (Street Cry (IRE) 130) [2017 66: t7.1g^{6} p7g^{4} t7.1g^{4} p7g^{5} 6g p6g^{5} t9.5m^{3} t8.6g Dec 13] modest maiden: left J. S. Moore after sixth start: stays 9.5f: acts on polytrack, tapeta and good to firm going: has worn cheekpieces: often races prominently. *John Butler* **57**

JOYFUL STAR 7 b.g. Teofilo (IRE) 126 – Extreme Beauty (USA) 89 (Rahy (USA) 115) [2017 60: 8m^{3} 8m^{4} 9s^{4} 10d^{6} 8m Aug 11] modest handicapper: probably stays 1¼m: acts on soft and good to firm going: has worn headgear: races towards rear. *Fred Watson* **56**

JOYROO (IRE) 3 b.g. Tagula (IRE) 116 – Memphis Belle 61 (Linamix (FR) 127) [2017 –: f6g^{5} f5s^{6} Jan 26] modest form: dead. *Michael Easterby* **55**

JOYS DELIGHT 3 b.f. Stimulation (IRE) 121 – Lambadora 55 (Suave Dancer (USA) 136) [2017 54: t7.1m t7.2g^{3} 7d^{2} t8.6g t7.2g^{4} t7.2g^{4} t7.1g^{2} 7s t7.2g^{6} t9.5g^{3} t8.6g^{2} t9.5d^{6} Dec 26] compact filly: fair maiden: stays 9.5f: acts on tapeta and good to soft going: sometimes slowly away. *Daniel Loughnane* **68**

JOYSUNNY 3 b.f. Camacho 118 – Alustar 71 (Emarati (USA) 74) [2017 35: f5g^{6} f5d^{5} 5m^{2} p5d^{6} 5m^{3} 5m 5s^{4} 5g 5f^{2} 5d 5m Aug 27] modest maiden: left Michael Easterby after seventh start: raced only at 5f: acts on firm going: front runner/races prominently. *Jacqueline Coward* **54**

JUAN HORSEPOWER 3 b.g. Foxwedge (AUS) 128 – Elysee (IRE) (Fantastic Light (USA) 134) [2017 77, a83: f5g^{4} p5g^{2} p6g^{3} p5g* p6g^{3} 5.7f* 5m^{5} 6d 6f 6.1g 6.1g^{6} p6g^{4} p7s p5s p6g^{2} Dec 28] fairly useful handicapper: won at Lingfield in March and Bath (by ½ length from Evergate) in May: stays 7f: acts on polytrack, tapeta and firm going: wears headgear: usually races prominently. *Richard Hannon* **89**

JUANITO CHICO (IRE) 3 br.g. Pour Moi (IRE) 125 – Miss Kittyhawk (IRE) 66 (Hawk Wing (USA) 136) [2017 83: 8.1d^{5} 8m^{3} 7m* 7g^{4} 8g^{2} 8d^{4} Jul 29] lengthy gelding: useful handicapper: won at Epsom (by length from Wahash) in June: second at Ascot (neck behind Addeybb) in July: stays 1m: acts on polytrack, good to firm and good to soft going: wears hood: often races towards rear. *William Jarvis* **105**

JUBILEE BRIG 7 b.g. Kheleyf (USA) 116 – Voile (IRE) 102 (Barathea (IRE) 127) [2017 74: t7.1g^{3} t7.1g^{6} t7.1d^{3} t8d^{3} f8g^{4} 7m^{5} Apr 12] useful-looking gelding: fair handicapper: stays 1m: acts on all-weather, good to firm and good to soft going: has worn headgear. *Alan Swinbank* **74**

JUDICIAL (IRE) 5 b.g. Iffraaj 127 – Marlinka 95 (Marju (IRE) 127) [2017 110: t5.1g t6g^{6} p6g^{5} 5m* 5.1d* 5m* 5m^{4} 6.1s^{2} 5.2m^{6} Sep 23] smart on turf, useful on all-weather: won handicap at Pontefract (by 1½ lengths from Edward Lewis) in April, and minor events at Chester (by 4 lengths from Double Up) in May and Beverley (by 3¼ lengths from Soie d'Leau) in June: stays 5.5f: acts on polytrack, tapeta, good to firm and good to soft going: wears headgear. *Julie Camacho* **116** **a98**

JUDICIOUS 10 ch.g. Pivotal 124 – Virtuous 92 (Exit To Nowhere (USA) 122) [2017 65: 12g 9.9m^{6} 9.9d t10.2d 9.9g Sep 2] sturdy, attractive gelding: modest handicapper: stays 1½m, usually races over shorter: acts on firm and good to soft going: often wears cheekpieces. *Geoffrey Harker* **60**

JUDY WOODS (IRE) 3 b.f. Excelebration (IRE) 133 – Snowpalm (Halling (USA) 133) [2017 68p: 6g^{2} 6g^{6} 6m May 30] fair maiden: stays 6f: acts on tapeta: usually races towards rear/freely. *Bryan Smart* **68**

JUFN 4 b.g. Nayef (USA) 129 – Deyaar (USA) (Storm Cat (USA)) [2017 76p: p8g^{6} 10g 10s^{4} 10m* 10.1f^{5} 9.1d p10g^{3} p11g t12.2g^{6} Oct 27] sturdy gelding: fairly useful handicapper: won at Chepstow in June: stays 1¼m: acts on polytrack, firm and soft going: wears hood: usually races close up: sold 20,000 gns, sent to Bahrain. *John Butler* **87**

JUKEBOX JIVE (FR) 3 b.g. Jukebox Jury (IRE) 123 – Sweetheart 84 (Sinndar (IRE) 134) [2017 70: t12.2g* 12.3m^{3} 14g* 14m 18g* 16g^{4} Sep 28] useful performer: won maiden at Wolverhampton (by 1½ lengths from Pealer) in April, and handicaps at Sandown (by neck from Veiled Secret) in June and Newbury (by short head from Aurora Gray) in July: stays 2¼m: acts on tapeta and good to firm going: in tongue tie last 3 starts: front runner/races prominently. *Anthony Honeyball* **107**

JULE IN THE CROWN 3 b.f. Harbour Watch (IRE) 121 – Jules (IRE) 76 (Danehill (USA) 126) [2017 81: 6g^{2} 7g 7g 6m^{5} 6v* 6.1v^{3} 6m^{3} Aug 26] useful handicapper: won at Newbury (by neck from Bellevarde) in July: left Mick Channon after fourth start: stayed 6f: acted on good to firm and heavy going: dead. *Richard Hannon* **95**

JULIET CAPULET (IRE) 2 b.f. (Mar 13) Dark Angel (IRE) 113 – Capulet Monteque (IRE) 84 (Camacho 118) [2017 6.5d 7m^{4} 7g^{3} 7d* 7g^{2} 7d* 8f Nov 3] €235,000Y: compact filly: third foal: sister to 2-y-o 6f winner Juliette Fair: dam, 6f winner in Qatar, half-sister **105**

to smart 5f winner Flanders (dam of Sprint Cup winner G Force) and to dam of high-class 6f/7f winner Lethal Force (by Dark Angel): useful performer: won minor event at Thirsk in July and Rockfel Stakes at Newmarket (by head from Nyaleti) in September: did too much too soon when eleventh in Breeders' Cup Juvenile Fillies Turf at Del Mar final outing: stays 7f: acts on good to firm and good to soft going: often in cheekpieces: usually leads. *John Gosden*

JULIET FOXTROT 2 b.f. (Mar 21) Dansili 127 – Kilo Alpha 104 (King's Best (USA) 132) [2017 7g^5 7d* 7s^5 Sep 24] rather unfurnished filly: fourth foal: sister to useful 2-y-o 1m winner Cartago (stayed 1¼m) and half-sister to useful French 2-y-o 1m winner Alpha Bravo (by Oasis Dream): dam, French 7.5f (at 2 yrs)/1m winner, sister to smart performer up to 1½m Runaway: fairly useful form: won minor event at Goodwood (by 7 lengths from Richenza) in September: raced only at 7f: remains open to improvement. *Charles Hills* **89 p**

JUMBO PRADO (USA) 8 gr.g. El Prado (IRE) 119 – Sant Elena 88 (Efisio 120) [2017 76: t8.6m p8g^4 t8.6m t8.6g Mar 6] rather leggy gelding: fair performer: stays 1¼m: acts on polytrack, tapeta and soft going: wears headgear: tried in tongue tie. *Daniel Loughnane* **70**

JUMBO'S BOY 3 b.g. Multiplex 114 – Silver Gyre (IRE) 65 (Silver Hawk (USA) 123) [2017 8s 7.1g^5 7.1s Sep 14] well held in maidens. *Peter Bowen* **–**

JUMIRA BRIDGE 3 b.g. Invincible Spirit (IRE) 121 – Zykina (Pivotal 124) [2017 88p: 5.3g* 5g* 5s^3 5m^2 5g 5.2d^2 5g Oct 17] strong gelding: sprint type: useful performer: won maiden at Brighton (by 2½ lengths from Secret Strategy) and handicap at Sandown (by ½ length from Queen In Waiting) in April: second in handicaps at Newmarket (neck behind Queen In Waiting) in June and Yarmouth (½ length behind Equimou) in September: best form at 5f: acts on good to firm and good to soft going: usually travels strongly: sold to join Robert Cowell 100,000 gns in November. *Roger Varian* **108**

JUMIRA PRINCE (IRE) 3 ch.g. Exceed And Excel (AUS) 126 – Aoife Alainn (IRE) 117 (Dr Fong (USA) 128) [2017 –p: 7m^6 7m^4 8.3d* 8m^5 8g^2 8d^5 Aug 18] angular gelding: fairly useful handicapper: won at Nottingham in June: stays 8.5f: acts on good to soft going: in headgear last 2 starts. *Roger Varian* **86**

JUMP AROUND 3 b.f. Medicean 128 – Mountain Leap (IRE) (Sadler's Wells (USA) 132) [2017 10.3g 9.8g 12m 8g 8m^6 p10g 9.9d p16d Oct 6] of little account: tried in hood: usually wore tongue tie: dead. *Ali Stronge* **–**

JUMPING AROUND (IRE) 3 b.f. Dark Angel (IRE) 113 – Box of Frogs (IRE) 50 (One Cool Cat (USA) 123) [2017 84: t5.1g 5m^5 7.2s 8m 7m t7.2g^3 p7s^2 t7.2g p6g t5.1d^6 Dec 27] fair handicapper: stays 7f: acts on polytrack, tapeta and good to firm going: often wears headgear. *Ian Williams* **70**

JUMPING JACK (IRE) 3 b.g. Sir Prancealot (IRE) 111 – She's A Character 91 (Invincible Spirit (IRE) 121) [2017 75: p7g^2 t8.6g^4 p8g^6 7m^5 8.3g 7m 7m* 8.1m^2 8.1m^6 p8g Dec 20] stocky gelding: fairly useful handicapper: won at Brighton in June: left Richard Hughes after ninth start: stays 8.5f: acts on polytrack, tapeta and good to firm going: tried in hood. *Chris Gordon* **83**

JUNDERSTAND 2 ch.f. (Mar 19) Champs Elysees 124 – Sienna Sunset (IRE) 68 (Spectrum (IRE) 126) [2017 p7g^3 Oct 18] seventh foal: half-sister to 1m winner Wrekin Sunset (by Doyen) and winner up to 10.4f Now My Sun (2-y-o 7f winner, by Notnowcato): dam 1¼m winner: 25/1, third in minor event at Kempton (4¾ lengths behind Fille de Reve) in October: should improve. *Alan King* **61 p**

JUNE DOG 2 b.c. (Apr 5) Helmet (AUS) 127 – Broadway Dancer 74 (Fantastic Light (USA) 134) [2017 5m 6g* 5f 6f^4 5f 6.1v Sep 30] 5,500F, £62,000 2-y-o: sturdy colt: fourth foal: dam 9f winner who stayed 11.6f: fairly useful performer: won maiden at Leicester (by head from Prince Ahwahnee) in May: stays 6f: acts on firm going: usually races close up: sold 13,000 gns in October. *Richard Hannon* **80**

JUNGLE CAT (IRE) 5 b.h. Iffraaj 127 – Mike's Wildcat (USA) (Forest Wildcat (USA) 120) [2017 116: 6g^2 5g^2 6g* 6d^4 6s 7g^2 7g^2 7g* 7g 7g^6 Aug 25] good-topped horse: smart performer: won minor events at Meydan (by 2 lengths from Baccarat) in March and Haydock (by 5 lengths from Ibn Malik) in July: second in handicap at Meydan (neck behind Baccarat) in January, Meydan Sprint (2¾ lengths behind Ertijaal) in February and Criterion Stakes at Newmarket (¾ length behind Home of The Brave) in July: stays 7f: acts on firm going: wears headgear. *Charlie Appleby* **117**

JUNGLE GEORGE 3 b.g. Kheleyf (USA) 116 – Amouage Royale (IRE) (Mr Greeley (USA) 122) [2017 –: p5g f5s 7.4g f7.1g p10g 9.9v f11.1g Nov 13] poor maiden: has worn headgear. *Scott Dixon* **45**

JUNGLE QUEEN (IRE) 2 ch.f. (Jan 23) Leroidesanimaux (BRZ) 127 – Elusive Gold (IRE) 76 (Elusive City (USA) 117) [2017 5m^6 5g^6 6m^3 Jun 13] €16,000Y: smallish, angular filly: first foal: dam, 6f winner, half-sister to smart 1m winner Duntle: fair form: best effort when third in minor event at Salisbury (3¼ lengths behind Initiative) in June. *Eve Johnson Houghton* **65**

JUNGLE ROOM (USA) 2 b.g. (Apr 30) Violence (USA) 125 – Raised Right (USA) (Giant's Causeway (USA) 132) [2017 6.5m 6g^4 Jul 24] $7,000Y, 210,000 2-y-o: third foal: half-brother to winners in USA by Mineshaft and Kitten's Joy: dam unraced half-sister to smart 2-y-o 5f/6f winner Rossini: modest form: better effort when fourth in minor event at Ayr (6½ lengths behind Regulator) in July: open to further improvement. *Kevin Ryan* **63 p**

JUNOESQUE 3 b.f. Virtual 122 – Snake Skin 68 (Golden Snake (USA) 127) [2017 66: 8.3d^6 9g^6 7g 8s^3 p8g^4 9.9s p8g^3 p8g^2 p8s^2 Dec 8] rather leggy filly: fair maiden: stays 1m: acts on polytrack, soft and good to firm going: wears cheekpieces. *John Gallagher* **66**

JUPITER 2 b.g. (Feb 21) Finjaan 122 – Medicea Sidera 101 (Medicean 128) [2017 6.1g^4 7s^2 6.1m^2 6d^3 p6d Sep 28] 16,500F, 35,000Y: good-topped gelding: fourth foal: half-brother to 3 winners, including 1m winner Hidden Rebel (by Cockney Rebel) and 7f winner Brick Lane (by Bahamian Bounty): dam 7f winner: fairly useful maiden: second in minor event at Windsor in August and third in maiden at Lingfield in September: stays 7f: acts on soft and good to firm going: usually leads. *Henry Candy* **83**

JUPITER ASCENDING 3 b.g. Excelebration (IRE) 133 – Habita (IRE) (Montjeu (IRE) 137) [2017 –: 12.1m 8.3d 8.3s Jun 29] no form: tried in blinkers: in tongue tie last 3 starts. *Michael Appleby* **–**

JUPITER LIGHT 3 b.g. Lonhro (AUS) 128 – Fantasia 116 (Sadler's Wells (USA) 132) [2017 53p: t7.1g* 8.1d 8m t8.6g 9.9m* 9.9m^5 9.9d^2 10.2d* Oct 18] well-made gelding: useful performer: won maiden at Wolverhampton (by short head from Tafaakhor) in March, and handicaps at Sandown (by short head from Archetype) in June and Nottingham (awarded race) in October: stays 1¼m: acts on tapeta, good to firm and good to soft going: tried in headgear: sold 220,000 gns, sent to UAE. *John Gosden* **105**

JURISPRUDANCE (FR) 2 b.f. (Jan 10) Panis (USA) 112 – L'Aventura (FR) (Librettist (USA) 124) [2017 4.5d^3 5g^6 5g^2 5d^3 6g^3 6d^3 5.5g^4 5.5g^6 7d^5 7s 7d^6 6.5d 8d 7d^3 5.5d^4 5.5s^3 7s^5 Dec 10] €30,000Y: first foal: dam French 2-y-o 9f winner: fair maiden: in frame 9 times: left George Baker after third start: stays 7f: often in cheekpieces. *M. Boutin, France* **68**

JURZ (IRE) 2 ch.c. (Apr 30) Exceed And Excel (AUS) 126 – Bahja (USA) 76 (Seeking The Gold (USA)) [2017 7m^3 Aug 17] 22,000F, 55,000Y: half-brother to 6f winners Ghazwah (by Shamardal) and Ferjaan (at 2 yrs, by Oasis Dream), both later successful abroad: dam twice-raced daughter of Poule d'Essai des Pouliches winner Valentine Waltz: 20/1, third in minor event at Yarmouth (4½ lengths behind Il Primo Sole) in August: will improve. *Roger Varian* **67 p**

JUS PIRES (USA) 3 b.g. Scat Daddy (USA) 120 – Liza Lu (USA) (Menifee (USA) 124) [2017 8s 8.1m^2 p8s* 10m* Oct 16] $120,000F, $280,000Y: useful-looking gelding: fourth foal: brother to 2-y-o 7f winner Good Intent: dam US 5.5f-7f winner out of US Grade 2 9f winner Chamrousse: fairly useful form: won maiden at Kempton in August and handicap at Windsor in October: best effort at 1¼m: in tongue tie last 3 starts: likely to progress further. *Jeremy Noseda* **94 p**

JUST AN IDEA (IRE) 3 b.g. Lilbourne Lad (IRE) 111 – Emreliya (IRE) (Danehill Dancer (IRE) 117) [2017 79: p6m* p5g^4 5g 6s^4 5.1g^3 7s p6s p6g Nov 21] workmanlike gelding: fair performer: won maiden at Lingfield in January: stays 6f: acts on polytrack and soft going: has worn visor. *Harry Dunlop* **79**

JUSTANOTHERBOTTLE (IRE) 3 ch.g. Intense Focus (USA) 117 – Duchess K (IRE) (Bachelor Duke (USA) 122) [2017 77: 5.1g* 5s 5.1d^3 6m^3 5.6d* 6g 5.1d 5m^4 5.6g^3 5g^3 Oct 13] workmanlike gelding: useful handicapper: won at Nottingham in April and Doncaster in July: probably best at 5f: acts on good to firm and good to soft going: usually races close up. *Declan Carroll* **104**

JUST BE LUCKY (IRE) 5 ch.g. Intense Focus (USA) 117 – Anda (Selkirk (USA) 129) [2017 85: 7m Apr 28] fairly useful at best, has lost his form: stays 9f: acts on good to firm and good to soft going: wears headgear. *Conor Dore* **–**

JUST BRILLIANT (IRE) 2 b.c. (Feb 27) Lope de Vega (IRE) 125 – Mauresmo (IRE) (Marju (IRE) 127) [2017 8g* Oct 7] 150,000Y: third foal: half-brother to smart 2-y-o 7f/1m (Racing Post Trophy) winner Marcel (by Lawman): dam unraced sister to smart **84 p**

sprinter Munjiz: 10/3, won minor event at Newmarket (by length from Silver Quartz) on debut: will improve. *Peter Chapple-Hyam*

JUSTE POUR NOUS 4 b.g. Pour Moi (IRE) 125 – Steam Cuisine 104 (Mark of Esteem (IRE) 137) [2017 91: p12f^{6} Mar 4] well-made gelding: fairly useful handicapper, below form sole start on Flat in 2017: stays 12.5f: acts on polytrack and any turf going: often in headgear: tried in tongue tie: front runner/races prominently: modest maiden hurdler. *David Pipe* **67**

JUST FAB (IRE) 4 b.f. Canford Cliffs (IRE) 133 – Unlock (IRE) 78 (Key of Luck (USA) 126) [2017 63: p6d p8d p8g p7g p8d* p8s 8g^{3} p10g^{2} p8d^{5} p8g^{4} p10s p8g Nov 29] modest handicapper: won at Chelmsford in May: stays 1¼m: acts on polytrack and heavy going: wears headgear: has worn tongue tie: often races towards rear. *Lee Carter* **59**

JUST FOR FUN 2 b.f. (Mar 5) Showcasing 117 – Lady Le Quesne (IRE) 78 (Alhaarth (IRE) 126) [2017 6.1f^{4} 6d^{5} 5d^{4} 6g^{5} t6.1g* t6.1g 6g t6g^{2} 8d^{5} p7.5g p6.5g^{4} Dec 27] 9,000Y: compact filly: half-sister to 3 winners, including winner up to 1m Excuse To Linger (2-y-o 6f winner, by Compton Place) and 2-y-o 1m winner Little Pippin (by Sir Percy): dam 2-y-o 5f/6f winner: fair performer: won nursery at Wolverhampton in August: left Richard Fahey after eighth start: stays 6f: acts on tapeta and good to soft going: often wears headgear: sometimes slowly away. *P. & F. Monfort, France* **71**

JUST FOR SHOW (IRE) 4 b.f. Poet's Voice 126 – Starchy 87 (Cadeaux Genereux 131) [2017 –: t9.5g Jan 26] angular filly: little form: sent to Germany. *Shaun Lycett* **–**

JUST FOR THE CRAIC (IRE) 2 b.g. (Mar 25) Most Improved (IRE) 119 – Beziers (IRE) (Fasliyev (USA) 120) [2017 5m 5m^{3} 5m^{5} 5m^{4} 5s 5m* 5m 5.1s^{5} 5s* p5s Nov 16] fair performer: won claimer at Catterick in July and nursery at Bath in October: left Ruth Carr after sixth start: raced only at 5f: acts on soft and good to firm going: often races prominently. *Neil Mulholland* **72**

JUST FRED (IRE) 4 br.g. Excellent Art 125 – Consignia (IRE) 67 (Definite Article 121) [2017 58: t12.2m t9.5g^{6} p10g t12.2g^{5} 9.9g t12.2g^{5} 11.6f 10.2f^{4} 10.2d^{4} p10g p12g f11.1g^{4} f11.1g^{5} Dec 22] modest maiden: stays 1½m: acts on polytrack, tapeta, firm and good to soft going: wears headgear/tongue tie. *Neil Mulholland* **53**

JUST GLAMOROUS (IRE) 4 ch.g. Arcano (IRE) 122 – Glamorous Air (IRE) (Air Express (IRE) 125) [2017 120: 5m 5g 5f 5d 5.2m 5s* 5g^{2} 5d Oct 28] tall gelding: smart performer: won listed race at Ascot (by ¾ length from Sir Robert Cheval) in October: second in handicap at Leicester (½ length behind Gracious John) later in month: best at 5f: acts on polytrack, tapeta, soft and good to firm going: usually leads. *Ronald Harris* **114**

JUST HEATHER (IRE) 3 gr.f. Zebedee 113 – Miss Sundance (IRE) 74 (Desert Sun 120) [2017 –: p8g^{6} t12.2g 8.3d 10.2d 12.3g 10.3v 7.6v^{6} 10v f8.1g^{6} Dec 1] no form: often in headgear. *John Wainwright* **–**

JUST HISS 4 b.g. Lawman (FR) 121 – Feather Boa (IRE) 81 (Sri Pekan (USA) 117) [2017 98: 10.3m 8d^{6} 10.3m 7.9m* 7.9m^{4} 10.2d^{6} 8.2d^{5} 8g^{bd} 8g^{6} 8.2v^{3} 7.9g^{5} 8.2d Oct 30] tall gelding: useful handicapper: won at York (by length from Truth Or Dare) in July: stays 10.5f: acts on good to firm and heavy going: usually wears cheekpieces: often races towards rear. *Tim Easterby* **99**

JUSTICE FREDERICK (IRE) 3 br.g. Lawman (FR) 121 – Sheer Spirit (IRE) 86 (Caerleon (USA) 132) [2017 83: t7.1g 8.3m 8g t6.1g 10.2g^{5} 10.1g p16g Aug 15] neat gelding: fairly useful at 2 yrs, well below that level in 2017: stays 7f: acts on good to soft going: often wears headgear: wears tongue tie: often races in rear: sent to the Netherlands. *Paul D'Arcy* **58**

JUSTICE GOOD (IRE) 5 b.g. Acclamation 118 – Qui Moi (CAN) 88 (Swain (IRE) 134) [2017 103, a110: t5g^{2} p6g^{6} p6g 5s May 18] sturdy gelding: useful performer: second in minor event at Newcastle (short head behind Doc Sportello) in January: stayed 6f: acted on polytrack, tapeta, soft and good to firm going: tried in tongue tie: dead. *David Elsworth* **109**

JUSTICE (IRE) 4 b.f. Lawman (FR) 121 – Sheboygan (IRE) 95 (Grand Lodge (USA) 125) [2017 46: p7g Jan 25] good-topped filly: little form: sometimes in cheekpieces: front runner/races prominently. *Jose Santos* **–**

JUSTICE LADY (IRE) 4 br.f. Dream Ahead (USA) 133 – Celestial Dream (IRE) 69 (Oasis Dream 129) [2017 86: 5s^{3} 5f^{5} 5d^{3} 5m* 5d^{4} 5m^{4} 5g* 5s Oct 7] sturdy filly: fairly useful handicapper: won at Doncaster in July and Sandown (by 1¼ lengths from Super Julius) in September: best form at 5f: acts on polytrack, good to firm and good to soft going: often races in rear. *David Elsworth* **94**

JUSTICE PLEASING 4 b.g. Kodiac 112 – Spangle (Galileo (IRE) 134) [2017 65: f7g^6 t8g t7.1d^2 t7.1d^2 t7.1d^2 t7.1g* t7.1d t7.1s Nov 30] fair handicapper: won at Newcastle in March: stays 1m: acts on tapeta: wears headgear: tried in tongue tie: front runner/races prominently. *Roger Fell* **67**

JUSTICE ROCK 4 b.g. Acclamation 118 – Fashion Rocks (IRE) 97 (Rock of Gibraltar (IRE) 133) [2017 53, a61: p5g^6 p5m^6 p6g^2 t6g^4 p5g^3 p6g^2 t6m^5 p6g^2 t5.1g^4 p6g p6g t6.1g^5 6m* 7f^3 6d^2 5.2m^3 5.2m^3 7d^6 p7g^3 p7s^6 p6g* p5g^6 6d^4 t6.1m p6g t6.1d^6 Dec 27] close-coupled gelding: modest handicapper: won at Yarmouth in June and Chelmsford in October: stays 7f: acts on polytrack, tapeta, good to firm and good to soft going: has worn headgear: wears tongue tie. *Phil McEntee* **58**

JUST IN TIME 3 b.g. Excelebration (IRE) 133 – Flying Finish (FR) (Priolo (USA) 127) [2017 52: 11.8s^2 12g* p12g* 11.8s* p11g Nov 6] fairly useful handicapper: won at Goodwood in August, Kempton in September and Leicester in October: likely to stay 1¾m: acts on polytrack and soft going: usually responds generously to pressure. *Alan King* **88**

JUST MARION (IRE) 5 b.m. Bushranger (IRE) 119 – Dolphin Stamp (IRE) (Dolphin Street (FR) 125) [2017 49: f7g p8d 7g^{ur} Jun 12] small, leggy mare: fair performer in 2015, little subsequent form: tried in headgear: dead. *Clare Ellam* **–**

JUST OVER 4 b.f. Bahamian Bounty 116 – Kassuta 72 (Kyllachy 129) [2017 –: t6f p6g t5.1g p6g Mar 22] no form: in headgear last 2 starts. *Robert Cowell* **–**

JUST RIGHT 2 ch.f. (Mar 13) Medicean 128 – Rightside 78 (High Chaparral (IRE) 132) [2017 t7.2g Dec 5] 12,500F, 18,000Y: third foal: half-sister to 7f/1m winner Love And Be Loved (by Lawman): dam 2-y-o 8.5f winner out of useful winner up to 1¾m Right Key: 100/1, well held in minor event at Wolverhampton. *John Flint* **–**

JUST SURPRISE ME (IRE) 4 b.g. Makfi 130 – Bayalika (IRE) (Selkirk (USA) 129) [2017 8s 7s^3 8g f6.1g p8s^4 Nov 17] fair maiden: best effort at 7f: acts on soft going: tried in hood: wears tongue tie: front runner/races prominently. *Mohamed Moubarak* **75**

JUST THAT LORD 4 ch.g. Avonbridge 123 – Lady Filly 92 (Atraf 116) [2017 95: p5g^3 5g^2 5f May 6] well-made gelding: fairly useful handicapper: third at Kempton and second at Epsom in April: raced only at 5f: acts on polytrack, tapeta and good to firm going: usually races close up: has joined Michael Attwater. *Bill Turner* **90**

JUST US TWO (IRE) 5 b.g. Royal Applause 124 – Sarah's First 68 (Cadeaux Genereux 131) [2017 91: p5g^5 t5d* p5g^3 p5g^3 p5g^6 5f 5m^6 5m 5m* 5.2s^5 5m^6 5m^6 Sep 8] strong, lengthy gelding: fairly useful handicapper: won at Newcastle (by length from Aprovado) in March and Doncaster in July: raced only at 5f: acts on tapeta and good to firm going: wears headgear: sold to join Mark Pattinson 6,500 gns in October. *Robert Cowell* **91**

K

KAABA STONE (IRE) 2 b.f. (Feb 20) Society Rock (IRE) 126 – Wattrey 62 (Royal Academy (USA) 130) [2017 5g^6 5.1g^3 Sep 6] €92,000 2-y-o: half-sister to 2m winner Quitit (by Kalanisi) and a winner in Italy by Spectrum: dam ran once: fair form: better effort when third in minor event at Chepstow (1¾ lengths behind Awesome) in September: will stay 6f: likely to progress further. *David Simcock* **76 p**

KAABER (USA) 6 b.g. Daaher (CAN) 120 – Taseel (USA) (Danzig (USA)) [2017 61: t7.1m^4 t7.1g 6.1d^3 6.1m 6.1m 6.1g* 5.7s 7s f6.1g* f6.1g Nov 28] lengthy gelding: modest handicapper on turf, fair on all-weather: won at Nottingham in August and Southwell in October: left Roy Brotherton after fifth start: stays 6f: acts on fibresand, tapeta, good to firm and good to soft going: often wears headgear: in tongue tie last 2 starts. *Michael Blake* **57 a70**

KAATSKILL NAP (FR) 4 ch.g. Rip Van Winkle (IRE) 134 – Last Cast (FR) (Marju (IRE) 127) [2017 98: 12d Aug 12] fairly useful handicapper: stays 1½m: acts on good to firm going. *Venetia Williams* **90**

KABRIT (IRE) 2 ch.c. (Feb 7) Mastercraftsman (IRE) 129 – Twinkling Ice (USA) 49 (Elusive Quality (USA)) [2017 8g Sep 15] 50/1, well held in minor event at Sandown. *Andrew Balding* **–**

KACHESS 3 b.f. Kyllachy 129 – Fibou (USA) (Seeking The Gold (USA)) [2017 77: 5g^3 6g t5s^5 5m^5 t7.2g 5g t6.1g t6.1g t7.1g p7d p8g Dec 30] sturdy filly: fair handicapper: left Tom Dascombe after sixth start: best form at 5f: acts on good to firm going: has worn headgear, including in 2017: usually races prominently. *David Loughnane* **75**

KACHUMBA 2 b.f. (May 7) Mayson 124 – Native Nickel (IRE) (Be My Native (USA) 122) [2017 p6s p6d³ p7g⁶ Dec 31] half-sister to several winners, including smart winner up to 9f Five Cents (2-y-o 7f winner, by Exceed And Excel): dam unraced: fair form when third at Kempton (3¾ lengths behind Monadee) on second of 3 starts in minor events: should stay 7f. *Rae Guest* **66**

KACHY 4 b.c. Kyllachy 129 – Dubai Bounty 89 (Dubai Destination (USA) 127) [2017 116: 5m⁴ 5f⁵ 6m 6m² 5s 5d² Sep 12] useful-looking colt: smart performer: second in minor event at Haydock (short head behind Magical Memory) in July: stays 6f: acts on good to firm going: tried in hood: in tongue tie last 4 starts: front runner/races prominently. *Tom Dascombe* **114**

KADRIZZI (FR) 4 ch.g. Hurricane Cat (USA) 111 – Kadiania (FR) (Indian Rocket 115) [2017 112: p6g⁶ p7g p7g⁵ p6g² 7m 6m⁶ 6.1g 7g p6s⁴ t6s p7g Dec 13] useful handicapper: second in minor event at Chelmsford (1¾ lengths behind Raucous) in April: stays 7f: acts on polytrack, tapeta, good to firm and heavy going: often in headgear in 2017: tried in tongue tie. *Dean Ivory* **96** **a102**

KAESO 3 b.g. Excelebration (IRE) 133 – Bahia Breeze 109 (Mister Baileys 123) [2017 –: 7g 6g* 6m* 6d* 6v* 6m⁴ Aug 28] fairly useful handicapper: won at Thirsk in April, Redcar in May, Ripon in June and Doncaster (by ½ length from Marseille) in July: stays 6f: acts on good to firm and heavy going: often travels strongly. *Nigel Tinkler* **82**

KAFEEL (USA) 6 b.g. First Samurai (USA) 119 – Ishraak (USA) (Sahm (USA) 112) [2017 66: f7g t7.1g⁴ 8g⁴ t8.6g⁶ p7g² p8g* p8g* Dec 30] sturdy gelding: fair handicapper: won at Kempton in October and Lingfield in December: left Linda Jewell after second start: stays 1m: acts on polytrack and good to firm going: wears headgear: has worn tongue tie, including in 2017. *Gary Moore* **70**

KAFOO 4 b.g. Dansili 127 – Nidhaal (IRE) 107 (Observatory (USA) 131) [2017 71: t9.5g⁶ 8.3f 8g 7.2d t8.6g 8v⁶ t7.2g⁴ t7.2g² t7.1s⁵ p7g⁵ Dec 28] fair handicapper: left Ed Dunlop after third start: stays 1m: acts on polytrack, tapeta and good to firm going: has worn headgear, including last 4 starts when also in tongue tie. *Michael Appleby* **71**

KAHLO (IRE) 2 b.f. (Mar 22) Mastercraftsman (IRE) 129 – Sky Boat (IRE) (Dansili 127) [2017 7g p7g Sep 25] second foal: half-sister to French 1¼m/1½m winner Helmsdale (by Nathaniel): dam unraced daughter of smart US Grade 1 9f/9.5f winner Angara: little impact in maiden/minor event. *Jonathan Portman* **–**

KAISAN 4 b.g. Rip Van Winkle (IRE) 134 – Orinoco (IRE) 53 (Darshaan 133) [2017 75: 12v⁶ 14g⁵ 16v⁴ 12s⁵ 11.6d⁵ t12.2g p12g t12.2m² p13.3s* p15.8g² t12.2g⁴ Dec 13] fair handicapper: won at Chelmsford in November: stays 2m: acts on polytrack, tapeta, firm and soft going: has worn headgear, including in 2017: wears tongue tie. *Bernard Llewellyn* **68**

KAI TAK AND BACK 3 b.g. Exceed And Excel (AUS) 126 – Beldarian (IRE) 101 (Last Tycoon 131) [2017 9d⁴ p10g⁴ 11.8v⁶ Sep 25] fair form when fourth at Chelmsford on second on 3 starts in maidens. *William Muir* **65**

KAJAKI (IRE) 4 gr.g. Mastercraftsman (IRE) 129 – No Quest (IRE) (Rainbow Quest (USA) 134) [2017 78: 13.8m* 16.3d 12.3d² 12.1d² 13.4d² 14m² 14.4v* 14.4v⁵ Sep 30] good-topped gelding: fairly useful handicapper: won at Catterick in April and Chester (by 4½ lengths from St Mary's) in September: stays 2m: acts on tapeta and any turf going: wears cheekpieces. *Kevin Ryan* **94**

KALAGIA (IRE) 2 b.f. (Mar 16) Kodiac 112 – Esuvia (IRE) 95 (Whipper (USA) 126) [2017 5m³ 5g* 5s² 6d Aug 23] €105,000Y: compact filly: third foal: sister to useful 2-y-o 5f (including Norfolk Stakes) winner Prince of Lir: dam, 5f and (including at 2 yrs) 6f winner, half-sister to smart 5f/6f winner Resplendent Glory: fair form: won minor event at Hamilton in July: best effort at 5f. *Mark Johnston* **74**

KALAKCHEE 2 b.c. (Apr 8) Kyllachy 129 – Maysarah (IRE) 77 (Green Desert (USA) 127) [2017 t7.2g⁵ p8g⁶ 7d⁶ p7g⁵ p8g⁵ Oct 24] modest maiden: stays 1m: acts on polytrack: wears headgear. *Amy Murphy* **54**

KALAMKAN (USA) 4 b.g. Kitten's Joy (USA) 128 – Kaloura (IRE) 113 (Sinndar (IRE) 134) [2017 55: p10.7g t16.5g p12g Dec 6] modest maiden: left P. D. Deegan after first start: bred to stay 1½m: acts on polytrack and soft going: in headgear last 5 starts. *T. G. McCourt, Ireland* **55**

KALANI ROSE 3 b.f. Sixties Icon 125 – Dance To The Blues (IRE) 73 (Danehill Dancer (IRE) 117) [2017 8.1m 8g⁴ 8.1m 7d Aug 22] sixth foal: half-sister to 6f winners Generalyse (by Cadeaux Genereux) and Byron's Gold (by Byron): dam 5f/6f winner: modest form: best effort at 1m: tried in cheekpieces. *Ben De Haan* **56**

KALANN (IRE) 10 b.g. Barathea (IRE) 127 – Karkiyla (IRE) (Darshaan 133) [2017 97, a82: p12g^5 10s 12s 13g 16.8m p12g 12.8g 15g^3 11.3g^4 13m^2 12m p15.8g Oct 5] fair handicapper: stays 2¼m: acts on polytrack, good to firm and good to soft going: wears headgear/tongue tie. *Denis Hogan, Ireland* **71**

KALIMANTAN (IRE) 7 b.g. Azamour (IRE) 130 – Kalamba (IRE) (Green Dancer (USA) 132) [2017 14.1m 16.3d 16s^6 Sep 19] good-topped gelding: fair maiden, below form in 2017 after long absence: stays 15f: acts on tapeta: has worn headgear, including final start. *Tim Vaughan* **52**

KALK BAY (IRE) 10 b.g. Hawk Wing (USA) 136 – Politesse (USA) (Barathea (IRE) 127) [2017 91: 7g t7.1s^3 6g^2 Apr 30] big, strong gelding: fairly useful handicapper: placed at Newcastle and Thirsk in April: has won over 1¼m, raced mainly at shorter: acts on fibresand, tapeta and any turf going: tried in headgear: wears tongue tie: held up: temperamental. *Michael Easterby* **89 §**

KAMRA (USA) 3 b.g. Stay Thirsty (USA) 123 – Milliondollarbill (USA) (Speightstown (USA) 124) [2017 80: p6g^2 t6g^6 6m 5g^4 5m^3 p6g^6 6.1g^4 t6.1g^2 6g 5.1g^3 Sep 2] compact gelding: fairly useful handicapper: placed 4 times in 2017: left Jeremy Noseda after second start: stays 6f: acts on polytrack, tapeta and good to firm going: wears headgear: in tongue tie last 4 starts: usually races prominently. *Michael Herrington* **86**

KANADE (IRE) 4 b.f. Poet's Voice 126 – Ra Hydee (USA) (Rahy (USA) 115) [2017 –: p7g f6g^5 8s Apr 30] half-sister to several winners, including smart 1m-9.5f winner Jack Junior and 2-y-o 5f winner Perfect Paula (both by Songandaprayer): dam US 8.5f winner: no form. *Emmet Mullins, Ireland* **–**

KANDY KOVE (IRE) 2 b.f. (Apr 16) Kodiac 112 – Kondakova (IRE) 87 (Soviet Star (USA) 128) [2017 5g^6 5v Aug 3] €16,000Y, £32,000 2-y-o: sixth foal: half-sister to 3 winners, including 2-y-o 5f winner Hopefilly (by Compton Place) and 5f and (at 2 yrs) 6f winner Buy Art (by Acclamation): dam 6f winner (including at 2 yrs): modest form when sixth at Nottingham (4¼ lengths behind Mrs Gallagher) on first of 2 starts in minor events: in hood second start: remains open to improvement. *Robert Cowell* **58 p**

KANNAPOLIS (IRE) 2 b.g. (Mar 28) Makfi 130 – Alta Definizione (IRE) (Hawk Wing (USA) 136) [2017 6g^2 7g 10v^6 Oct 9] 5,000Y: second foal: dam Italian 5.5f-8.5f winner (including at 2 yrs): modest form in minor events/maiden: remains open to improvement. *Michael Easterby* **58 p**

KAPSTADT (FR) 7 b.g. Country Reel (USA) 113 – King's Parody (IRE) (King's Best (USA) 132) [2017 94: p10.4g^2 10.3m^2 10.3g^2 10g* 11.8m 12d^6 Aug 12] useful handicapper: won at Newmarket (by length from First Flight) in June: second at Chester (twice) in May: stays 1½m: acts on polytrack and any turf going: has worn headgear: often races prominently. *Ian Williams* **99**

KARAM ALBAARI (IRE) 9 b.h. King's Best (USA) 132 – Lilakiya (IRE) 60 (Dr Fong (USA) 128) [2017 76: p12g* f12g p13.3d p12f^5 p12g p12g^4 11.5m^5 t12.2g p16g 10.2d p12d p12g^6 p12g^4 Dec 6] sturdy horse: fair handicapper: won at Lingfield in January: stays 2m: acts on polytrack, fibresand, good to firm and good to soft going: wears headgear: sometimes slowly away, usually races nearer last than first. *J. R. Jenkins* **73**

KARAPIRO BOY 3 b.g. Arabian Gleam 122 – Littlemiss (Cosmonaut) [2017 12.1m^6 Jun 2] 100/1, well held in maiden at Catterick. *Roger Fell* **–**

KARAR 5 b.g. Invincible Spirit (IRE) 121 – In The Light 99 (Inchinor 119) [2017 119: 8g 7s^3 7g^2 7d* 7d^3 8f 8g Dec 10] very smart performer: won Prix du Pin at Chantilly (by 1½ lengths from Empire of The Star) in September: placed in race for second year running when ¾-length third to Aclaim in Prix de la Foret at Chantilly next time: stays 1m: acts on firm and soft going: tried in cheekpieces. *Francis-Henri Graffard, France* **120**

KARAWAAN (IRE) 3 b.g. Sea The Stars (IRE) 140 – Magic Sister 63 (Cadeaux Genereux 131) [2017 76p: 11m^2 11.6d^3 p10g* 9.9m^6 Aug 27] well-made gelding: fairly useful performer: won maiden at Chelmsford in August: stays 11f: acts on polytrack and good to firm going: in tongue tie last 2 starts: usually races close up. *Sir Michael Stoute* **87**

KAREVA 2 b.f. (Mar 17) Oasis Dream 129 – Kilasiki (IRE) (Pivotal 124) [2017 6d^2 6g^3 6.1v^3 6g^4 p6g Oct 4] 36,000Y: first foal: dam unraced half-sister to Lowther Stakes winner Threading: fairly useful maiden: third in minor event at Newbury in July: raced only at 6f. *Charles Hills* **80**

KARIJINI (GER) 3 b.f. Siyouni (FR) 122 – Kalahari Dancer (Dalakhani (IRE) 133) **81 p** [2017 p7g^3 t7.2g^6 p6s* Dec 8] 65,000Y: fourth foal: dam unraced half-sister to dam of very smart 1m-1¼m winner Ballet Concerto: fairly useful form: won maiden at Chelmsford (by 2 lengths from Kingofmerrows) in December: left Simon Crisford after second start: best effort at 6f: will go on improving. *Archie Watson*

KARISMA (IRE) 4 gr.f. Lawman (FR) 121 – Lucky Clio (IRE) 59 (Key of Luck (USA) **83** 126) [2017 78p: p8g^2 7m^4 p8g^2 Jun 7] good-topped filly: fairly useful handicapper: second at Lingfield in April and Kempton in June: stays 1m: acts on polytrack and good to firm going: often travels strongly. *Roger Varian*

KASBAAN 2 br.c. (Feb 17) Dansili 127 – Aghareed (USA) (Kingmambo (USA) 125) **76 p** [2017 8d^4 Oct 27] quite attractive colt: second foal: dam, useful French 1¼m winner, out of Breeders' Cup Filly & Mare Turf winner Lahudood: 6/1, fourth in minor event at Newbury (4 lengths behind Extra Elusive) in October: better to come. *Owen Burrows*

KASBAH (IRE) 5 b.g. Acclamation 118 – Dance Hall Girl (IRE) 81 (Dansili 127) [2017 **97** 102: p6g^2 p6m* p6g^2 p5f^4 p6g^4 5f^5 6m 5m^2 5g 5g^5 p6g p6g p5g^6 p6g^2 Dec 30] lengthy **a104** gelding: useful handicapper: won at Lingfield in January: second at same course in February (nose behind Zac Brown) and December (½ length behind Dubai One): stays 6f: acts on polytrack, tapeta and good to firm going: has worn headgear. *Amanda Perrett*

KASER (IRE) 2 b.c. (Mar 11) Invincible Spirit (IRE) 121 – Lethal Quality (USA) (Elusive **80 p** Quality (USA)) [2017 t8.6d^2 Dec 9] €500,000Y: fourth foal: dam US 5.5f/6f winner: evens, second in minor event at Wolverhampton (2¼ lengths behind Cross Counter) in December: sure to improve. *Saeed bin Suroor*

KASHGAR 8 b.g. Hernando (FR) 127 – Miss Katmandu (IRE) (Rainbow Quest (USA) **74** 134) [2017 75: 16.2m* 16m^4 Jun 16] sturdy gelding: fair handicapper: won at Chepstow in May: stays 2m: acts on polytrack, soft and good to firm going: tried in headgear: has worn tongue tie. *Bernard Llewellyn*

KASHMIRI SUNSET 6 b.g. Tiger Hill (IRE) 127 – Sagamartha (Rainbow Quest (USA) **84** 134) [2017 –: 13.1g* 14g^4 14.1s^2 16.3d Sep 10] strong gelding: fairly useful handicapper: won at Ayr (apprentice) in July: second at Carlisle in August: stays 2¼m: acts on good to firm and heavy going: in cheekpieces/tongue tie last 5 starts. *Iain Jardine*

KASHTAN 4 ch.f. Sakhee's Secret 128 – Gitane (FR) (Grand Lodge (USA) 125) [2017 83: **70** p6g p6d^4 p7.5g Mar 7] sturdy filly: fairly useful at best: below form in 2017: stays 6f: acts on tapeta and good to firm going: tried in cheekpieces. *J. S. Moore*

KASPERENKO 3 b.g. Archipenko (USA) 127 – Jardin (Sinndar (IRE) 134) [2017 77: **102** p10g^2 p10g* 10g^2 11.9m* 12d^6 p11s t12.2g^3 Oct 21] useful performer: won maiden at Chelmsford in May and handicap at Doncaster (by 2¾ lengths from Chancery) in July: third in handicap at Wolverhampton (2½ lengths behind Master Singer) in October: stays 1½m: acts on polytrack, tapeta and good to firm going: in blinkers last 4 starts: usually races nearer last than first: sold to join Brendan Powell 95,000 gns in November. *David Lanigan*

KASPERSKY (IRE) 6 b.h. Footstepsinthesand 120 – Croanda (IRE) (Grand Lodge **116** (USA) 125) [2017 118: 8f^5 8.3g^2 8f^5 8g^2 7d 8.2s^2 8g Oct 14] good-bodied horse: smart performer: second in handicap at Nottingham (2½ lengths behind Another Touch), Summer Mile Stakes at Ascot (3 lengths behind Mutakayyef) and Superior Mile at Haydock (1¼ lengths behind Ballet Concerto): stays 8.5f: acts on firm and soft going: has worn tongue tie: front runner/races prominently: withdrawn from Cox Plate at Moonee Valley Oct 28 on morning of race due to a swelling on near-fore. *Jane Chapple-Hyam*

KASSANDRA (IRE) 3 b.f. Dandy Man (IRE) 123 – Gala Style (IRE) (Elnadim (USA) **69** 128) [2017 –p: p6d^3 t8.6g^4 8.3m 8g Aug 17] neat filly: fair maiden: left Richard Hannon after third start: best effort at 8.5f: acts on tapeta: tried in cheekpieces. *Amy Murphy*

KASSAR (IRE) 2 b.g. (Mar 2) Exceed And Excel (AUS) 126 – Inchiri 108 (Sadler's Wells **85** (USA) 132) [2017 p8g* p8g^6 Nov 21] 100,000Y: closely related to 3 winners, including smart 1¼m winner Inchila (by Dylan Thomas), and half-brother to 3 winners, including useful 11.6f-13f winner Inchwood (by Dubai Destination): dam 1¼m-1½m winner: fairly useful form: won minor event at Kempton (by neck from Msayyan) in October: will stay beyond 1m. *Roger Charlton*

KASSIA (IRE) 4 b.f. Acclamation 118 – Speedy Sonata (USA) (Stravinsky (USA) 133) **104** [2017 108: 6m^4 6m 6m^5 6g^2 6g^5 Oct 7] rather unfurnished filly: useful performer: second in handicap at Salisbury (3 lengths behind Thafeera) in September: stays 6f: acts on soft and good to firm going. *Mick Channon*

KATABATIKA 3 b.f. Shirocco (GER) 129 – Landinium (ITY) 109 (Lando (GER) 128) [2017 –: p8s^{6} 10d^{5} 12v^{3} 12g^{4} p12g* p12g^{5} p12g^{3} p12g Dec 23] fair handicapper: won at Kempton in October: stays 1½m: acts on polytrack and good to soft going: sometimes slowly away, often races towards rear. *Hughie Morrison* **73**

KATALAN (GER) 4 b.g. Adlerflug (GER) 123 – Kalla 110 (Monsun (GER) 124) [2017 –: p12d^{rr} p11d^{4} p12g^{4} t16.5d Dec 9] no form: in hood last 3 starts: one to treat with caution (has refused to race). *John Butler* **– §**

KATEBIRD (IRE) 3 gr.f. Dark Angel (IRE) 113 – She Basic (IRE) 98 (Desert Prince (IRE) 130) [2017 72: 9g^{6} 9.9g^{6} p12g 9.8m^{3} 9.9m* 10.1g 9.9d^{3} 10.2v^{4} 9.8g* 10.3g^{4} 11.1d^{5} 10.3v^{2} 10g 10g^{6} Oct 17] close-coupled filly: fairly useful handicapper: won at Beverley in June and Ripon (by 3 lengths from Duck Egg Blue) in August: second at Chester in September: stays 10.5f: acts on polytrack, tapeta, good to firm and heavy going: usually leads: sold to join Oliver Greenall 15,000 gns in November. *Mark Johnston* **84**

KATHEEFA (USA) 3 gr.g. Street Cry (IRE) 130 – Wid (USA) 100 (Elusive Quality (USA)) [2017 t7.1g 6m^{4} 6g^{4} 7.1g* 7m Sep 23] sixth foal: closely related to 7f winner Tawteen (by Street Sense): dam, 2-y-o 6f winner, half-sister to very smart 7f-9f winner Haatheq: fairly useful performer: won maiden at Chepstow (by 1¾ lengths from Cherished) in September: stays 7f: sold to join Ruth Carr 8,000 gns in October. *Charles Hills* **80**

KATHERINE PLACE 2 b.f. (Apr 28) Showcasing 117 – Folly Drove 71 (Bahri (USA) 125) [2017 5g May 9] 5,000Y: third foal: half-sister to 6f winners Mr Conundrum (by Paco Boy) and Incentive (by Stimulation): dam 2-y-o 7f winner: 14/1, well held in maiden at Leicester. *Sylvester Kirk* **–**

KATH'S BOY (IRE) 3 b.g. Bushranger (IRE) 119 – Elayoon (USA) 76 (Danzig (USA)) [2017 54: t6.1g 5d p7g^{4} 7.4g^{5} 6.1m^{4} 8.1d 5.7s Oct 2] sturdy gelding: poor maiden: stays 7f: acts on polytrack, soft and good to firm going: tried in tongue tie. *Tony Carroll* **49**

KATH'S LEGACY 4 ch.f. Cockney Rebel (IRE) 127 – It's Dubai Dolly 82 (Dubai Destination (USA) 127) [2017 80: p10f^{3} 11.4g^{4} 9s^{5} 9.9g^{3} p10g 10d^{pu} p12d p12g^{5} Dec 20] leggy filly: fairly useful handicapper: third at Lingfield in April and Brighton in September: left Ben De Haan after sixth start: stays 11.5f: acts on polytrack, soft and good to firm going. *Richard Hughes* **80**

KATH'S LEGEND 3 b.f. Dick Turpin (IRE) 127 – It's Dubai Dolly 82 (Dubai Destination (USA) 127) [2017 –: 7d p10g 8.1d Oct 23] poor form: tried in hood. *Ben De Haan* **48**

KATH'S LUSTRE 2 b.f. (Mar 30) Dick Turpin (IRE) 127 – It's Dubai Dolly 82 (Dubai Destination (USA) 127) [2017 6.1s p7g^{2} Dec 31] third foal: half-sister to 9f winner (stays 11.5f) Kath's Legacy (by Cockney Rebel): dam 1¼m-1½m winner: fair form when runner-up at Lingfield (1¼ lengths behind Furzig) on second of 2 starts in minor events: left Ben De Haan after first start: will be suited by 1m+: open to further improvement. *Richard Hughes* **67 p**

KATHY 2 b.f. (Feb 25) Bated Breath 125 – Lolita Lebron (IRE) 85 (Royal Applause 124) [2017 6.1g 5.1d 6d^{5} Jul 22] second foal: dam, winner around 7f (including at 2 yrs), half-sister to useful performer up to 9.5f Assume: no form. *Scott Dixon* **–**

KATIE CANFORD 4 b.f. Canford Cliffs (IRE) 133 – Serafina's Flight 82 (Fantastic Light (USA) 134) [2017 57: 8m^{pu} p7g Sep 26] lengthy filly: modest maiden at best, no form in 2017: tried in blinkers. *Mark Hoad* **–**

KATIE GALE 7 b.m. Shirocco (GER) 129 – Karla June (Unfuwain (USA) 131) [2017 80: f16g^{3} f14m^{2} p16g^{5} f12.1g^{5} p16s f16.5g^{6} Dec 29] angular mare: fairly useful handicapper: placed at Southwell in February and March: stays 2m: acts on polytrack and fibresand: has worn headgear, including in 2017: usually races close up. *Michael Appleby* **81**

KATIE LEE (IRE) 2 b.f. (Feb 6) Camacho 118 – Katherine Lee (IRE) 91 (Azamour (IRE) 130) [2017 5s^{3} 6d^{6} 6d^{4} p7g^{6} Dec 20] €26,000F, £5,000 2-y-o: neat filly: second foal: dam 1m winner: modest form in maidens/minor events: stays 7f. *Henry Candy* **64**

KATMANDOO (USA) 3 b.c. Kitten's Joy (USA) 128 – Granny Franny (USA) (Grand Slam (USA) 120) [2017 58p: 10.2m^{5} 10.3m 14m May 30] fair form: best effort at 1¼m. *Tom Dascombe* **67**

KATRINE (IRE) 3 b.f. Kodiac 112 – Falcolnry (IRE) 86 (Hawk Wing (USA) 136) [2017 75: 5.3g^{6} 5g 6g Jun 27] compact filly: fair performer at 2 yrs, below that level in 2017: left William Knight after first start: stays 6f: acts on polytrack, good to firm and good to soft going: has worn hood, including last 2 starts. *David O'Meara* **53**

KAVORA 2 b.f. (Feb 13) Havana Gold (IRE) 118 – Anadiya (FR) (Bahri (USA) 125) [2017 p7g5 Sep 25] 10,000F: second foal: dam once-raced half-sister to smart French 1m winner Alnadana out of useful French 1¼m-1½m winner Alnamara: 66/1, fifth in minor event at Kempton (9 lengths behind Teppal) in September: should improve. *George Baker* **55 p**

KAWASIR (USA) 2 ch.c. (Feb 7) Speightstown (USA) 124 – Bashful Bertie (USA) (Quiet American (USA)) [2017 p7g3 Oct 11] $400,000F: third foal: half-brother to 2 winners abroad, notably very smart US Grade 1 1¼m (including Arlington Million)/1½m winner Beach Patrol (by Lemon Drop Kid): dam, US maiden, sister to US Grade 2 9f winner Allamerican Bertie: 10/1, third in minor event at Kempton (6½ lengths behind Glendevon) in October: likely to stay 1m: sure to progress. *Roger Varian* **71 p**

KAYLEN'S MISCHIEF 4 ch.g. Doyen (IRE) 132 – Pusey Street Girl 87 (Gildoran 123) [2017 8m4 t5s t5g 8v Oct 12] modest form when fourth in maiden at Ripon on debut, standout effort: tried in hood. *Philip Kirby* **63**

KAY SERA 9 b.g. Kayf Tara 130 – Inflation 68 (Primo Dominie 121) [2017 58, a68: t12.2g5 p13.3d* t13.9g6 10.2d6 13f f12.1g f11.1g Dec 21] modest handicapper: won at Chelmsford in February: stays 13.5f: acts on all-weather and firm going: held up. *Tony Newcombe* **63**

KAZANAN (IRE) 3 b.f. Tamayuz 126 – Bosphorus Queen (IRE) 83 (Sri Pekan (USA) 117) [2017 –: t7.1g2 t7.1g 8g 10m May 22] modest maiden: best effort at 7f: acts on tapeta. *Michael Dods* **51**

KAZAWI 3 ch.g. Dubawi (IRE) 129 – Kazeem 73 (Darshaan 133) [2017 11m 11.6g4 12d2 11.6v3 Jul 22] well-made gelding: brother to high-class winner up to 1½m Al Kazeem (2-y-o 1m winner), closely related to smart 7f-1¼m winner Makzeem (by Makfi) and half-brother to 2 winners, including 1m winner Park Lane (by Royal Applause): dam lightly raced: fairly useful form: second in maiden at Chepstow in June: stays 1½m: temperament under suspicion. *Roger Charlton* **86**

KAZEERA 2 ch.f. (Apr 29) Dubawi (IRE) 129 – Kazeem 73 (Darshaan 133) [2017 7m Aug 25] sister to high-class winner up to 1½m Al Kazeem (2-y-o 1m winner), closely related to smart 7f-1¼m winner Makzeem (by Makfi) and half-sister to 2 winners, including 1m winner Park Lane (by Royal Applause): dam lightly raced: 33/1, well held in minor event at Newmarket. *Roger Charlton* **–**

KAZIMIERA 3 b.f. Dubawi (IRE) 129 – Kailani 105 (Monsun (GER) 124) [2017 94: 7m 10m6 May 7] compact filly: fairly useful performer: should stay at least 1¼m: acts on good to firm and good to soft going. *Charlie Appleby* **88**

KAZOEY 4 b.f. Stimulation (IRE) 121 – Dubawi's Spirit (IRE) (Dubawi (IRE) 129) [2017 56: t13.9g t16.3s f11.1g Dec 22] modest at best, no form in 2017. *Chris Fairhurst* **–**

KEEM BAY 3 b.f. Multiplex 114 – Copsehill Girl (IRE) (Carroll House 132) [2017 11.6g5 Sep 7] first foal: dam winning hurdler/pointer: 150/1, well held in maiden at Haydock. *Michael Mullineaux* **–**

KEENE'S POINTE 7 br.g. Avonbridge 123 – Belle's Edge (Danehill Dancer (IRE) 117) [2017 67: t7.1m4 t7.1g3 t7.1g6 p7g4 p7g 6.1g p7g 7d t7.2g 5.9d 5.7s4 7s Oct 10] sturdy gelding: fair handicapper: lost form in 2017: stays 1m, usually races at shorter: acts on polytrack, tapeta, soft and good to firm going: has worn headgear, including last 5 starts: sometimes slowly away. *Steph Hollinshead* **65 d**

KEEPER'S CHOICE (IRE) 3 ch.f. Intikhab (USA) 135 – Crossing 102 (Cape Cross (IRE) 129) [2017 8.1m5 8f2 8g* 9.9g6 10g Oct 7] €6,000F, 14,000Y: workmanlike filly: fourth foal: half-sister to 8.6f winner Saltwater Creek (by Marju): dam, 1m-1¼m winner, also won in bumpers: fair performer: won maiden at Salisbury in August: stays 1m: acts on firm going. *Denis Coakley* **75**

KEEP IT DARK 8 b.g. Invincible Spirit (IRE) 121 – Tarneem (USA) 87 (Zilzal (USA) 137) [2017 70§: 6m p6g Jun 22] strong gelding: fairly useful at best, well held both starts in 2017: best up to 6f: acts on polytrack, fibresand, good to firm and heavy going: has worn headgear: tried in tongue tie: carries head high, one to treat with caution. *William Knight* **– §**

KEEPUP KEVIN 3 b.g. Haafhd 129 – Black Salix (USA) 54 (More Than Ready (USA) 120) [2017 76: 8s* 8.1d6 8m5 7.4f3 8.2d3 8v5 Oct 9] neat gelding: fair handicapper: won at Newmarket in May: stays 1m: acts on polytrack, firm and soft going: races prominently. *Pam Sly* **78**

KEIBA (IRE) 4 gr.g. Dark Angel (IRE) 113 – True Magic 80 (Magic Ring (IRE) 115) [2017 65: f7g Jan 30] fair maiden at best: stayed 6f: acted on polytrack: tried in headgear: dead. *Murty McGrath* –

KELPIE SPIRIT (IRE) 3 b.g. Born To Sea (IRE) 117 – Lady of Kildare (IRE) 100 (Mujadil (USA) 119) [2017 –: 10m^5 9.8g 7.2m^6 7.2m^2 8f 8.3g^6 7d t7.1s Sep 8] modest maiden: stays 1¼m: acts on good to firm going: usually races towards rear. *John Weymes* **59**

KENCUMIN (FR) 3 ch.c. Kendargent (FR) 112 – Cumin (USA) 100 (Fusaichi Pegasus (USA) 130) [2017 t7.1m^3 f7g* 8f^4 9f^2 8f* 8f^3 Nov 23] €47,000Y, €65,000 2-y-o: sixth foal: half-brother to 3 winners, including French 2-y-o 5f winner Cucuma (by Invincible Spirit) and 1¾m winner Divea (by Dylan Thomas): dam 2-y-o 7f winner: useful performer: won maiden at Southwell in February and optional claimer at Santa Anita in October: left Ralph Beckett after second start: stays 9f: acts on fibresand, raced only on firm going on turf. *Peter Eurton, USA* **98**

KENDERGARTEN KOP (IRE) 2 ch.g. (Mar 25) Kendargent (FR) 112 – Elsa T (IRE) (Duke of Marmalade (IRE) 132) [2017 7.6v^6 6v^5 t7.2g^2 Oct 7] leggy gelding: fair form when second in seller at Wolverhampton (½ length behind Grimeford Lane) on last of 3 starts: has joined David Flood. *Tom Dascombe* **67**

KENMARE RIVER 2 gr.g. (Apr 22) Kendargent (FR) 112 – Isabella Glyn (IRE) 75 (Sadler's Wells (USA) 132) [2017 6.9v 7g Oct 7] well held in minor events. *Jedd O'Keeffe* –

KENNY GEORGE 2 b.g. (Feb 23) Mawatheeq (USA) 126 – One For Philip (Blushing Flame (USA) 109) [2017 8d Oct 27] 50/1, well held in minor event at Newbury. *Mick Channon* –

KENNY THE CAPTAIN (IRE) 6 ch.g. Captain Rio 122 – Kelso Magic (USA) 98 (Distant View (USA) 126) [2017 97: 6g 6g 6m 6s 6d 6m^6 6s^4 6s^2 6d^3 5.9s^4 6d 6v* 6g^2 6v^4 7g t6d^2 t6s^5 Nov 30] useful-looking, athletic gelding: fairly useful handicapper: won at Thirsk in September: second at same course (lady riders) in September and Newcastle in October: stays 6f: acts on tapeta, good to firm and heavy going: has worn headgear, including in 2017. *Tim Easterby* **91**

KENSINGTON PALACE (IRE) 4 b.g. Kodiac 112 – Anthyllis (IRE) (Night Shift (USA)) [2017 f8g^4 7m 6v^5 6m^2 6g^4 7f^4 8.3d 7.2d t8s t8.6g f6.1g f8.1g Dec 4] modest maiden: stays 7f: acts on firm going: has worn cheekpieces, including last 4 starts: tried in tongue tie. *Marjorie Fife* **63** **a52**

KENSINGTON STAR 4 b.g. Pivotal 124 – Wild Silk 71 (Dansili 127) [2017 77p: 10m* 13.1m^2 12.1m^2 14.1s* 16m^2 t16.3s^4 12d^6 14m^5 12.1s 14.5d^3 Oct 27] useful performer: won maiden at Redcar in April and handicap at Carlisle (by short head from Card High) in June: placed in handicaps at Musselburgh later in June and Doncaster in October: stays 14.5f: acts on soft and good to firm going: wears headgear. *Keith Dalgleish* **96**

KEN'S SAM'S (IRE) 4 b.f. Intense Focus (USA) 117 – Hannah's Smile (IRE) 69 (Cape Cross (IRE) 129) [2017 69: p6g^3 p5g^4 t5g p6g* 6d 5.8g* 6d 7g 7v 7.3v p7g p7g p6g Dec 6] fair handicapper: won at Dundalk in March and Navan (apprentice) in April: left Adrian Brendan Joyce after eighth start: stays 7f: acts on polytrack and good to firm going: often wears cheekpieces: has worn tongue tie, including in 2017: often races in rear. *E. Sheehy, Ireland* **74**

KENSTONE (FR) 4 gr.g. Kendargent (FR) 112 – Little Stone (FR) (One Cool Cat (USA) 123) [2017 74: t7.1g^2 p8g^2 p8g* p8g^3 p8g^3 8g* p8s^3 7.8s^2 7.6g* 7.6v p8g p7d Nov 9] angular gelding: fairly useful handicapper: won at Chelmsford in March, Thirsk in June and Chester (by 3½ lengths from Sun Lover) in August: stays 1m: acts on polytrack, tapeta and soft going: wears headgear: often races prominently. *Adrian Wintle* **93**

KENTISH WALTZ (IRE) 2 ch.f. (Mar 4) Dandy Man (IRE) 123 – Imelda Mayhem 84 (Byron 117) [2017 5g* 5s 6g* 5d^6 6g 5s Oct 7] €18,000Y: second foal: dam 2-y-o 6f winner out of useful 2-y-o 5f/6f winner Halland Park Girl: fairly useful performer: won newcomers race at Chantilly in April and minor event at Maisons-Laffitte (by nose from Sagres) in June: below form in listed races otherwise, including at York on second outing: stays 6f: best form on good going. *E. J. O'Neill, France* **89**

KENTUCKY BLUEBLOOD (USA) 2 ch.f. (Feb 13) Awesome Again (CAN) 133 – All Due Respect (USA) (Value Plus (USA) 117) [2017 p6d 7m^6 Aug 1] £800 2-y-o: second foal: half-sister to a winner in USA by Speightstown: dam, smart US 1m/8.5f winner, also placed in Grade 1 7f/8.5f events: little show in 2 minor events: sent to USA. *Richard Guest* –

KENTUCKYCONNECTION (USA) 4 b.g. Include (USA) 121 – Youcanringmybell (USA) (Street Cry (IRE) 130) [2017 110: 7g^5 10.3d 8g^5 t8s^2 10.3m p8g p8s Dec 7] lengthy gelding: useful handicapper: second at Newcastle (1½ lengths behind Constantino) in June: stays 1¼m: acts on tapeta and good to firm going: has worn headgear, including in 2017. *Bryan Smart* **96**

KENYA (IRE) 2 b.c. (Jan 26) Galileo (IRE) 134 – Tender Morn (USA) (Dayjur (USA) 137) [2017 7d^3 7s* 7v* Oct 22] half-brother to several winners, including French 2-y-o 7.5f/1m winner Zantenda (by Zamindar) and French 1m winner (including at 2 yrs) Single (by Singspiel), both useful: dam French 2-y-o 5f winner: useful form: won maiden at Cork (by 8 lengths from Stellar Eclipse) and Killavullan Stakes at Leopardstown (by length from Mcmunigal) in October: will stay 1m: wears tongue tie: will go on improving. *Aidan O'Brien, Ireland* **107 p**

KENYAN (FR) 3 b.g. Kendargent (FR) 112 – Landora (FR) (Lando (GER) 128) [2017 –p: p12g^5 Jun 3] poor form: best effort at 1½m: tried in hood: in tongue tie last 2 starts: fair hurdler. *Seamus Durack* **49**

KERRE (IRE) 3 b.f. Pour Moi (IRE) 125 – Double Green (IRE) 104 (Green Tune (USA) 125) [2017 p10g^6 Oct 12] €75,000Y: seventh foal: closely related to Spanish 11f/11.5f winner Lady Dari (by Montjeu) and half-sister to 11f-1¾m winner Eurato (by Medicean): dam French 1½m-15f winner: 50/1, well held in maiden at Chelmsford. *William Jarvis* **–**

KERRERA 4 ch.f. Champs Elysees 124 – Questa Nova (Rainbow Quest (USA) 134) [2017 57: 10d^5 12g* p12g^3 p14d Sep 21] workmanlike filly: fair handicapper: won at Newmarket in August: stays 1½m: acts on polytrack and good to soft going: usually races nearer last than first. *Paul Webber* **77**

KERRY ICON 4 b.f. Sixties Icon 125 – La Gifted 79 (Fraam 114) [2017 54: t8.6g^5 t10.2d^2 t10.2g^2 10m* 9m^3 10g^5 t10.2s^5 8.3d 8.9m^2 t10.2d^4 10.9m^3 t12.4g t9.5g^5 Oct 21] modest handicapper: won at Redcar in April: stays 1½m: acts on tapeta, soft and good to firm going: wears hood: usually races close up: sold £3,000, sent to Italy. *Iain Jardine* **57**

KERRYMERRY (IRE) 5 b.g. Vale of York (IRE) 117 – Reasonably Devout (CAN) (St Jovite (USA) 135) [2017 p14g^3 14g^2 May 24] fair handicapper: stays 1¾m: acts on polytrack and good to soft going. *Dr Richard Newland* **73**

KESTREL CALL (IRE) 4 b.g. Acclamation 118 – Winged Harriet (IRE) 85 (Hawk Wing (USA) 136) [2017 84§: f6g 6g 5m^5 5d 5.3g^4 Jul 4] fairly useful handicapper, well below form in 2017: stays 6f: acts on polytrack, fibresand and good to soft going: tried in cheekpieces: wears tongue tie: unreliable. *Michael Appleby* **57 §**

KESTREL DOT COM 5 br.g. Oasis Dream 129 – Tanfidh 93 (Marju (IRE) 127) [2017 88: p8g^4 p8g^6 8m^4 8m* p8d 8g* Jun 15] fairly useful handicapper: won at Yarmouth in May and Newbury (by ½ length from Golden Wedding) in June: stays 1m: acts on good to firm going: wears headgear: sometimes slowly away: sold 52,000 gns in July, sent to Bahrain. *Chris Dwyer* **93 a84**

KESWICK 3 b.c. Dansili 127 – Marywell 87 (Selkirk (USA) 129) [2017 p10g^3 p10m* Jan 20] third foal: brother to smart 1¼m-1½m winner Martlet and half-brother to 1m/8.5f winner Palmerston (by Oasis Dream): dam 11f winner out of Irish Oaks winner Margarula: fairly useful form: won maiden at Lingfield (by 1¼ lengths from Tomorrow Mystery) in January: wears tongue tie: sold to join Heather Main £4,000 in September. *John Gosden* **85**

KEVLAR 2 b.g. (Apr 27) Helmet (AUS) 127 – Madhaaq (IRE) 87 (Medicean 128) [2017 p8d Dec 13] 100/1, well held in minor event at Kempton. *Jonathan Portman* **–**

KEW GARDENS (IRE) 2 b.c. (Jan 20) Galileo (IRE) 134 – Chelsea Rose (IRE) 121 (Desert King (IRE) 129) [2017 7m 8.2s* 8d^2 8s^4 10m* Oct 14] good-topped colt: seventh foal: half-brother to 3 winners, including smart French 6f-1m winner Thawaany (by Tamayuz) and useful 5f/6f winner Pale Orchid (by Invincible Spirit): dam winner up to 1½m (2-y-o 7f winner, including Moyglare Stud Stakes): useful performer: won maiden at Killarney (by 4½ lengths from Tonkin) in August and listed race at Newmarket (by 3½ lengths from Dee Ex Bee) in October: second in Willis Champions Juvenile Stakes at Leopardstown (3 lengths behind Nelson) in September: will stay 1½m: acts on soft and good to firm going: open to further improvement. *Aidan O'Brien, Ireland* **108 p**

KEY BID 3 ch.g. Dubawi (IRE) 129 – Silca Chiave 106 (Pivotal 124) [2017 10m 12m^2 12s* 11.9d^3 14.2g^5 13.4g* 15.9v^3 14.5d Oct 27] 375,000F: compact gelding: fifth foal: half-brother to 6f/1m winner Strictly Silca (by Danehill Dancer): dam, 2-y-o 6f winner, half-sister to Prix Morny winner Silca's Sister and smart performers Green Manalishi (sprinter) **97**

and Golden Silca (best at 1m-1¼m): useful performer: won maiden at Thirsk in May and handicap at Chester (by 3½ lengths from Galactic Prince) in August: stays 1¾m: acts on soft and good to firm going: wears headgear. *Charlie Appleby*

KEYNOTE (IRE) 2 b.g. (Mar 30) Dragon Pulse (IRE) 114 – Taalluf (USA) 82 (Hansel (USA)) [2017 6.1m t6.1g Dec 22] stocky gelding: well held in maiden/minor event: left Roger Varian after first start. *David C. Griffiths* **–**

KEY PLAYER 2 ch.g. (Feb 15) Kheleyf (USA) 116 – My Pretty Girl (Arakan (USA) 123) [2017 p7g² 8s⁵ p8g² t7.2g⁶ Dec 2] fair form in minor events: stays 1m. *Eve Johnson Houghton* **76**

KEYSER SOZE (IRE) 3 ch.g. Arcano (IRE) 122 – Causeway Queen (IRE) (Giant's Causeway (USA) 132) [2017 83: 7g* p7d* 8m Jun 22] good-quartered gelding: useful performer: won maiden at Thirsk in April and handicap at Kempton (by 2¼ lengths from Gymnaste) in May: stays 7f: acts on polytrack, best turf form on good going. *Richard Spencer* **96**

KEYSTROKE 5 b.h. Pivotal 124 – Fondled 101 (Selkirk (USA) 129) [2017 109: p7g* t7.1g² p8g⁶ p8d² Nov 22] smart performer: won handicap at Kempton (by 2½ lengths from Intransigent) in January: second in listed races at Wolverhampton (nose behind Salateen) in March and Kempton (½ length behind Second Thought) in November: stays 8.5f: acts on polytrack, tapeta and good to soft going: often races towards rear, strong traveller. *Jeremy Noseda* **114**

KEY VICTORY (IRE) 2 b.c. (Feb 9) Teofilo (IRE) 126 – Patroness (Dubawi (IRE) 129) [2017 7m* Oct 25] compact colt: second foal: half-brother to smart 1m winner Blair House (by Pivotal): dam, French maiden (second at 9f), sister to high-class winner up to 1m Poet's Voice: 10/3, won minor event at Newmarket (by length from Qaysar) on debut: will stay at least 1m: will improve. *Charlie Appleby* **103 p**

K'GARI SPIRIT 4 b.f. Major Cadeaux 121 – Ivory Silk 94 (Diktat 126) [2017 60: p5g* p5d⁵ t6g* p6g p6g t5.1g⁴ p6g² p6g⁶ 5m⁶ Jul 13] fair handicapper: won at Chelmsford in January and Wolverhampton in March: raced at 5f/6f: acts on polytrack and tapeta: tried in hood: wears tongue tie. *Jeremy Gask* **74**

KHAFOO SHEMEMI (IRE) 3 b.c. Dark Angel (IRE) 113 – Appleblossom Pearl (IRE) 79 (Peintre Celebre (USA) 137) [2017 95: p8g* 7m⁵ 8m* 7.9m 8d* p8d⁴ Nov 22] useful-looking colt: smart performer: won minor event at Kempton (by 3½ lengths from Executive Force) in April, and listed races at Sandown in May (by neck from Escobar) and September (by ¾ length from Hors de Combat): stays 1m: acts on polytrack, good to firm and good to soft going: front runner/races prominently. *Richard Hannon* **116**

KHAIRAAT (IRE) 4 b.g. Shamardal (USA) 129 – Mumayeza 80 (Indian Ridge 123) [2017 98p: 10.3m* 10m 9.9g³ 10.3m Aug 26] smart handicapper: won at Chester (by 4½ lengths from Brorocco) in May: third at Goodwood (¾ length behind Dark Red) in August: stays 10.5f: acts on good to firm going: usually travels strongly. *Sir Michael Stoute* **116**

KHALEEFA BAY 3 br.f. Kheleyf (USA) 116 – Langland Bay 61 (Diktat 126) [2017 p8g Feb 11] 50/1, well held in maiden at Lingfield: dead. *Martin Smith* **–**

KHALIDI 3 br.c. High Chaparral (IRE) 132 – Bezique 97 (Cape Cross (IRE) 129) [2017 97p: 10.3g³ 9m* 10m³ 11.2m* 12m 12m² 12d² Aug 5] sturdy colt: smart performer: won listed races at Newmarket (by neck from Salouen) in April and Goodwood (by 5 lengths from Fierce Impact) in May: second in King Edward VII Stakes at Royal Ascot (½ length behind Permian) in June and Gordon Stakes at Goodwood (3½ lengths behind Crystal Ocean) in August: will stay 1¾m: acts on good to firm and good to soft going. *John Gosden* **116**

KHAMAARY (IRE) 3 br.f. Tamayuz 126 – Nufoos 110 (Zafonic (USA) 130) [2017 76p: 8m* 8m² 7d⁵ 7.6d* 7g⁶ 7.6g⁴ 8g* p8g Nov 2] sturdy filly: useful performer: won handicap at Redcar (by 7 lengths from Mama Africa) in May, minor event at Lingfield (by 3¾ lengths from Glory Awaits) in July and another handicap at Redcar (by ¾ length from Zeshov) in October: stays 1m: acts on good to firm and good to soft going: usually leads, often travels strongly. *Mark Johnston* **107**

KHAMRY 4 b.g. Poet's Voice 126 – Poppets Sweetlove 73 (Foxhound (USA) 103) [2017 t8g³ Nov 3] 525,000Y: fourth foal: half-brother to 3 winners, including smart winner up to 9f Patentar (2-y-o 7f winner, by Teofilo) and 9f/1¼m winner Exclusive Diamond (by Iffraaj): dam, 7f/1m winner, half-sister to high-class sprinter Overdose: 5/1, third in maiden at Newcastle (4¾ lengths behind Al Galayel) in November: should do better. *Owen Burrows* **76 p**

KHARBETATION (IRE) 4 b.g. Dream Ahead (USA) 133 – Anna's Rock (IRE) 106 (Rock of Gibraltar (IRE) 133) [2017 100P: 7.9d⁶ p8g 8m 10v³ 10.1v⁵ 10.3g Oct 14] useful 1m winner on debut at 3 yrs, went wrong way in handicaps in 2017: front runner/races prominently. *David O'Meara* **94**

Mr Nizar Anwar's "Khalidi"

KHATAAF (IRE) 3 b.g. Shamardal (USA) 129 – Sana Abel (IRE) 78 (Alhaarth (IRE) 126) [2017 8s 8.3m 6g* a9.9g* 9.9g* 9.9g Dec 30] fourth foal: half-brother to useful 1¼m winner (stayed 1½m) Reesha (by Teofilo) and 2-y-o 8.6f winner Mutawaaly (by Cape Cross): dam, 1¾m winner, closely related to Oaks winner Eswarah: fairly useful performer: left Roger Varian after second start: successful at Doha in maiden and handicap in November, and another handicap in December: stays 1¼m: acts on dirt: in headgear last 4 starts, tongue tied last 5. *I. Al Malki, Qatar* **86**

KHAZAF 2 b.c. (Feb 9) Dawn Approach (IRE) 132 – Winds of Time (IRE) 91 (Danehill (USA) 126) [2017 8g[6] Sep 22] 44,000F, 175,000Y: sixth foal: half-brother to useful 2-y-o 6f winner The Paddyman (by Giant's Causeway) and 1¼m winner Julia Dream (by Montjeu): dam 6f (at 2 yrs) to 9f (in Canada) winner: 9/1, well held in minor event at Newbury: should do better. *Marcus Tregoning* **– p**

KHELEYF'S GIRL 2 br.f. (Feb 9) Kheleyf (USA) 116 – Handsome Molly 59 (Halling (USA) 133) [2017 f5d[2] t5s t6.1g[4] 6.9g[5] 7d[4] 6v[2] t7.2g f7.1g[2] t8.6g[6] Dec 18] £1,000Y: first foal: dam maiden (stayed 13f): modest maiden: stays 7f: acts on fibresand and heavy going: in visor last 2 starts: often races prominently. *David Evans* **61**

KHELMAN (IRE) 7 b.g. Kheleyf (USA) 116 – Mandolin (IRE) 69 (Sabrehill (USA) 120) [2017 92: 7g 6m 6v* 6.1s 7d 6g[4] 6d* 6g 6v 7g 6s 7d Nov 11] sturdy gelding: fairly useful handicapper: won at Doncaster in May and Ayr (by 1¼ lengths from Tatlisu) in July: stays 7f: acts on good to firm and heavy going: has worn cheekpieces, including last 2 starts: unreliable. *Richard Fahey* **90 §**

KHESKIANTO (IRE) 11 b.m. Kheleyf (USA) 116 – Gently (IRE) (Darshaan 133) [2017 –§: 9.9v Sep 26] leggy mare: fair at best, no form since 2014: has worn headgear/tongue tie: often races towards rear: one to treat with caution. *Michael Chapman* **– §**

KHITAAMY (IRE) 3 b.g. Approve (IRE) 112 – Halliwell House 59 (Selkirk (USA) 129) [2017 8.3g[3] p7g[4] p6s[5] 7m* Jul 19] good-topped gelding: fair form: won maiden at Catterick in July: stays 8.5f. *Ed Dunlop* **75**

KIBAAR 5 b.g. Pastoral Pursuits 127 – Ashes (IRE) 77 (General Monash (USA) 107) [2017 96: 5m 5m 5.1d 5g^5 6g 5g 5g 5g Oct 7] well-made gelding: useful handicapper, well below form in 2017: left Kevin Ryan after sixth start: stays 6f: acts on soft and good to firm going: has worn headgear, including last 5 starts: often races prominently. *Ruth Carr* **62**

KICKBOXER (IRE) 6 gr.g. Clodovil (IRE) 116 – Ajig Dancer 86 (Niniski (USA) 125) [2017 96: 5s* 6v 6g 5v 6d p7s p8s f5g^2 Dec 22] close-coupled gelding: useful handicapper: won at Thirsk (by 2 lengths from Ladweb) in May: best at 5f/6f: acts on fibresand, good to firm and heavy going: has worn headgear: usually races nearer last than first. *Michael Appleby* **106 a98**

KICKING THE CAN (IRE) 6 gr.g. Aussie Rules (USA) 123 – Silk Meadow (IRE) (Barathea (IRE) 127) [2017 72: t10.2g^5 t8d^2 t9.5g^3 t10.2g 8g* 8m p10d t10.2g Oct 20] fair handicapper: won at Redcar in June: left David Thompson after fifth start: stays 12.5f, effective over much shorter: acts on polytrack and tapeta: has worn headgear/tongue tie. *Noel Wilson* **71**

KICK ON KICK ON 2 b.c. (Mar 14) Swiss Spirit 117 – Catmint 85 (Piccolo 121) [2017 5g* 6m^6 6m^2 5d* Oct 11] 16,500F, £52,000Y: sturdy colt: fourth foal: half-brother to 2-y-o 7f/1m winner Firecruise (by Firebreak): dam 2-y-o 5f winner: fairly useful form: won minor event at Leicester in April and nursery at Nottingham (by head from Bow Belles) in October: stays 6f. *Clive Cox* **94**

KIDMENEVER (IRE) 4 b.c. Baltic King 120 – Pepys Tillergirl (IRE) (Tillerman 123) [2017 12.1g^4 9.9g^2 10m^3 9.9m^2 12g 9g^2 Nov 18] well-made colt: smart performer: placed in handicap at Meydan, Wolferton Handicap at Royal Ascot (1¼ lengths third to Snoano), listed race at Sandown (1¾ lengths second to Spark Plug) and Group 3 Eclipse Stakes Handicap at Sandown (Australia) (short-head second to Payroll): stays 1½m: acts on polytrack, soft and good to firm going: has worn cheekpieces, including last 2 starts: often races prominently: reportedly had thumps and bled fifth outing. *Charlie Appleby* **113**

KI KI 5 ch.m. Kheleyf (USA) 116 – Peryllys 67 (Warning 136) [2017 69: t6d^4 t6g* t6g^5 5.9d^6 6d* 5.9d 6v Sep 21] fair handicapper: won at Newcastle in March and Thirsk in July: raced only at 6f: acts on tapeta and soft going: sometimes slowly away. *Bryan Smart* **72**

KIKINI BAMALAAM (IRE) 2 b.f. (Mar 15) Society Rock (IRE) 126 – Crimson Sunrise (IRE) 85 (Holy Roman Emperor (IRE) 125) [2017 5m 5m^5 5m 5m^2 5d^6 7.2m* 7.2m* 8v^4 t8.6g f7.1g^5 Nov 28] €16,500F, £20,000Y: second foal: half-sister to 2-y-o 5.5f/7f winner Chevalier du Lac (by Sir Prancealot): dam 2-y-o 6f/8.5f winner: fair performer: won nurseries at Musselburgh (twice) in August: stays 7f: acts on good to firm going: sometimes slowly away. *Keith Dalgleish* **69**

KILBAHA LADY (IRE) 3 b.f. Elnadim (USA) 128 – Sidney Girl (Azamour (IRE) 130) [2017 66: 7.5f 7.4d^6 7g^3 8s^3 9.9f 8d^4 8g^4 t8s* p8d 8g* Oct 16] close-coupled filly: fair handicapper: won at Newcastle in September and Yarmouth in October: stays 1m: acts on tapeta, firm and soft going: wears tongue tie: often starts slowly, usually races nearer last than first. *Nigel Tinkler* **73**

KILIM 4 b.f. Dansili 127 – Kibara 88 (Sadler's Wells (USA) 132) [2017 64: p12g^6 p13g t12.2m^4 t13.9g^5 11.6f^6 10m^6 12v 11.9d* 11.9d^2 11.9s^2 Oct 10] fair handicapper: won at Brighton in August: stays 1½m: acts on polytrack, tapeta, soft and good to firm going: tried in cheekpieces: wears tongue tie: often races towards rear. *John Berry* **66**

KILLAY 3 b.f. Aqlaam 125 – Avessia 65 (Averti (IRE) 117) [2017 7m^2 6s^2 7g* 7m^3 8.1m^3 Oct 16] compact filly: closely related to 5f-7.5f winner Avertor (by Oasis Dream) and 1m winner Fashaar (by Showcasing) and half-sister to useful 2-y-o 6f/7f winner Trading Profit (by Kheleyf), later successful in Qatar: dam twice-raced sister/half-sister to Prix de l'Abbaye winners Avonbridge and Patavellian: fairly useful performer: won maiden at Salisbury in August: third in handicaps at Newbury in September and Windsor in October: stays 1m: acts on soft and good to firm going: sold 60,000 gns, sent to USA. *Eve Johnson Houghton* **90**

KILLERMONT STREET (IRE) 3 b.f. Dream Ahead (USA) 133 – Leopard Creek 60 (Weldnaas (USA) 112) [2017 75: t6g^4 p8g^3 t8d* t7.1g^2 t8.6g^3 t7.1m^4 f8g^5 Mar 29] fair handicapper: won at Newcastle (apprentice) in February: stays 8.5f: acts on polytrack and tapeta: sometimes slowly away. *Mark Johnston* **73**

KILMAH 3 b.f. Sepoy (AUS) 129 – Perfect Star 107 (Act One 124) [2017 99: 7m^6 8m 8.5m 8m Jun 21] strong, compact filly: useful performer at 2 yrs, below form in 2017: should stay 1m: acts on firm going: front runner/races prominently. *Mark Johnston* **93**

KILOWATT 3 ch.g. Power 117 – Bogside Theatre (IRE) 102 (Fruits of Love (USA) 127) [2017 10.3g 9.8g^2 12s^2 9.8d^2 12m* 12m^2 Jul 10] second foal: half-brother to smart 1½m winner Lord Yeats (by Yeats): dam, 1¼m-13f winner who stayed 2¼m, also won over **89**

hurdles: fairly useful performer: won handicap at Ripon (by head from Londinium) in June: second in similar event there in July: stays 1½m: acts on soft and good to firm going: usually races prominently. *Tim Easterby*

KIMBERELLA 7 b.g. Kyllachy 129 – Gleam of Light (IRE) 81 (Danehill (USA) 126) [2017 113: p5g* p6g* 5m 5m 5m^3 t6s^3 a6g 6.1s* 6m 5g^4 6s t6.1d Dec 26] close-coupled, attractive gelding: smart performer: won handicap at Lingfield (by length from Bowson Fred) in March, valuable event at same course (by ½ length from Gracious John) in April and listed race at Chester (by 1¾ lengths from Judicial) in August: third in handicap at Musselburgh in June and in Chipchase Stakes at Newcastle (neck behind Koropick) in July: best at 5f/6f: acts on polytrack, tapeta and any turf going: tried in cheekpieces. *Richard Fahey* **117**

KIMENE 3 b.f. Aqlaam 125 – Aditi (Dansili 127) [2017 p8g 12s p10s^4 t9.5g Jul 17] 21,000F: first foal: dam, French/Italian 1¼m winner, closely related to useful Italian/French performer up to 1¼m Bugie d'Amore: modest form when fourth in maiden at Chelmsford in June, standout effort. *William Stone* **61**

KIMIFIVE (IRE) 2 ch.c. (Apr 23) Born To Sea (IRE) 117 – Appletreemagic (IRE) 72 (Indian Danehill (IRE) 124) [2017 6m^4 6d^4 6.1g^2 6.1s^2 7v^4 6s^3 6d^4 Nov 11] fair maiden: stays 6f: acts on soft and good to firm going. *Joseph Tuite* **79**

KINAESTHESIA 2 b.f. (Feb 14) Sea The Stars (IRE) 140 – Kinetica 100 (Stormy Atlantic (USA)) [2017 8.3v* Nov 8] 90,000F: second foal: dam 2-y-o 7f winner out of useful winner up to 1¾m Kiswahili: 4/1, won maiden at Nottingham (by short head from Qawamees) on debut: will improve. *Ralph Beckett* **84 p**

KIND ACT (USA) 2 b.g. (Feb 26) Distorted Humor (USA) 117 – Kind Words (USA) (A P Indy (USA) 131) [2017 8d^5 p8g^2 t8.6g* 9d^3 Nov 4] fourth foal: half-brother to a winner abroad by Shamardal: dam twice-raced sister to top-class US 9f/1¼m performer Bernardini out of US Grade 1 2-y-o 8.5f winner Cara Rafaela: fairly useful form: won minor event at Wolverhampton in September: stays 8.5f. *Charlie Appleby* **84**

KIND OF BEAUTY (IRE) 3 ch.f. Helmet (AUS) 127 – Extreme Beauty (USA) 89 (Rahy (USA) 115) [2017 78p: 9.9m^5 11.4g^5 12d Aug 5] rather unfurnished filly: fair handicapper: stays 11.5f: acts on good to firm and good to soft going: tried in cheekpieces: sold £15,000, sent to Greece. *Hugo Palmer* **79**

KING AND EMPIRE (IRE) 2 b.c. (Apr 24) Intello (GER) 129 – Fraloga (IRE) 111 (Grand Lodge (USA) 125) [2017 p8g* Oct 25] 125,000Y: seventh foal: half-brother to 3 winners in France, including useful 1½m winner Feyzabad (by Pivotal): dam, French winner up to 1½m (2-y-o 1m winner) who stayed 15f, half-sister to very smart French 10.5f-1½m winner Fragrant Mix: 12/1, won minor event at Kempton (by length from Coolongolook) in October: bred to stay at least 1¼m: sure to progress. *Andrew Balding* **81 p**

KING ATHELSTAN (IRE) 2 b.g. (Apr 16) Mayson 124 – Ashtaroute (USA) 60 (Holy Bull (USA) 134) [2017 7m^6 7g p7g Oct 3] limited impact in minor events. *John Best* **–**

KING BOLETE (IRE) 5 b.g. Cape Cross (IRE) 129 – Chanterelle (FR) (Trempolino (USA) 135) [2017 113: 12g 10g 11.4g* 12d^3 11.4m^3 11.9g^4 Sep 16] good-topped gelding: smart handicapper: won at Windsor (by neck from What About Carlo) in July: third at Ascot (1½ lengths behind Gawdawpalin) later in month and Windsor (listed race, 3¾ lengths behind Second Step) in August: stays 1½m: acts on any turf going: has worn headgear, including last 4 starts: sold 130,000 gns in November. *Roger Varian* **110**

KING CALYPSO 6 ch.g. Sir Percy 129 – Rosa de Mi Corazon (USA) 86 (Cozzene (USA)) [2017 87: p16g^2 p16d* p16g^2 p16s^5 p16g^3 t16.5g^5 p16g^6 Nov 1] lengthy gelding: fairly useful handicapper: won at Kempton (by 1¼ lengths from Charismatic Man) in May: placed there on 3 other occasions in 2017: stays 16.5f: acts on polytrack, tapeta and firm going: has worn headgear: often races towards rear. *Denis Coakley* **88**

KING CRIMSON 5 ch.g. Captain Gerrard (IRE) 113 – Elegant Lady 89 (Selkirk (USA) 129) [2017 90: f5s t5.1g f5m f5g Apr 16] smallish gelding: fairly useful at best, no form in 2017: sometimes slowly away, often races towards rear. *John Butler* **–**

KINGDOMFORAKITTEN (USA) 3 b.c. Kitten's Joy (USA) 128 – Mayakoba (USA) (War Chant (USA) 126) [2017 p10g Aug 8] 10/1, well held in maiden at Chelmsford. *David Lanigan* **–**

KINGFAST (IRE) 2 b.g. (Mar 7) Fast Company (IRE) 126 – Monarchy (IRE) (Common Grounds 118) [2017 7f^5 8.1m^5 6.1m Oct 16] workmanlike gelding: modest form in minor events. *David Dennis* **57**

KINGFISHER GIRL 4 gr.f. Hellvelyn 118 – Caribbean Star 81 (Soviet Star (USA) 128) **52**
[2017 52: p7g^{6} 6g 7g^{5} 8m^{3} 7d p7s 6v Oct 19] modest maiden: stays 1m: acts on soft and good to firm going: wears cheekpieces: in tongue tie last 5 starts: often starts slowly/races towards rear. *Michael Appleby*

KING JULIEN (IRE) 4 b.g. Canford Cliffs (IRE) 133 – Western Sky 56 (Barathea (IRE) **48**
127) [2017 58: t8.6g t12.2g^{3} t12.2g^{4} p14g^{4} 16g t13.9g^{4} Apr 29] tall gelding: poor maiden: stays 1¾m: acts on polytrack, tapeta and good to firm going: usually wears headgear: has worn tongue tie, including in 2017: usually races prominently. *John Ryan*

KING KEVIN 3 b.g. Holy Roman Emperor (IRE) 125 – Annalina (USA) (Cozzene **74**
(USA)) [2017 10.2m 10g p8s 9.9g^{6} 10m^{5} 8.5s p10g^{3} 10.1g^{3} p10s* t9.5g* t12.4d^{2} t9.5d* Dec 26] compact, good-bodied gelding: fair handicapper: won at Chelmsford in November and Wolverhampton (twice) in December: stays 12.5f: acts on polytrack and tapeta: wears headgear: sometimes slowly away, usually races nearer last than first, often travels strongly. *Ed Dunlop*

KINGLAMI 8 b.g. Kingsalsa (USA) 118 – Red Japonica (Daylami (IRE) 138) [2017 81: **87**
6g 5s* 6.1v* 6g^{3} 6.1m^{6} 5.1v* 6v* 6s^{4} 5.1s^{2} 6s^{6} 5v p6g p6s Dec 7] sturdy gelding: fairly useful handicapper: won at Hamilton (apprentice) and Chepstow in June, Chepstow again in July and Ffos Las (by nose from Alaadel) in August: raced mainly at sprint trips nowadays: acts on polytrack, good to firm and heavy going: wears headgear: tried in tongue tie: often races towards rear. *John O'Shea*

KING OF CASTILLA 3 br.g. Sayif (IRE) 122 – Thicket 87 (Wolfhound (USA) 126) **–**
[2017 62: 5m 5s 5g 7d Jul 28] modest at 2 yrs, no form in 2017: sometimes wears headgear: has worn tongue tie. *Colin Teague*

KING OF DREAMS 4 ch.g. Dream Ahead (USA) 133 – Complexion 92 (Hurricane Run **81**
(IRE) 134) [2017 85: t8d^{4} p8d^{2} p8g^{3} p8g^{5} 9.9g 7g 10s^{4} 10.1m^{3} Aug 27] fairly useful handicapper: stays 1¼m: acts on polytrack, tapeta, soft and good to firm going: sometimes wears headgear: often races towards rear. *David Simcock*

KINGOFMERROWS (IRE) 3 br.g. Kodiac 112 – Tamara Gervasoni (IRE) 73 (Namid **78**
128) [2017 76: t6g^{2} p6s^{2} t7.2d^{3} Dec 16] fair maiden: stays 7f: acts on polytrack, tapeta and good to firm going. *Jamie Osborne*

KING OF NAPLES 4 b.g. Excellent Art 125 – Avon Lady 96 (Avonbridge 123) [2017 93: **91**
7g 7s 7d^{3} Jul 1] rather finely-made gelding: fairly useful handicapper: third at Doncaster in July: stays 7f: acts on soft and good to firm going: sold 23,000 gns, sent to Greece. *James Fanshawe*

KING OF NEPAL 3 b.g. Sepoy (AUS) 129 – Empress Anna (IRE) (Imperial Ballet (IRE) **85**
110) [2017 82p: 7g t7.1g t7.2d* Dec 26] fairly useful handicapper: won at Wolverhampton (by 1¼ lengths from Fire Diamond) in December: stays 7f: acts on polytrack and tapeta: often races prominently. *Henry Candy*

KING OF PARADISE (IRE) 8 b.g. Hurricane Run (IRE) 134 – Silly Game (IRE) **–**
(Bigstone (IRE) 126) [2017 69: 12g 10g 9.2g 11.6m^{4} 10.2m Jul 7] fair handicapper, little impact in 2017: has worn headgear, including in 2017: front runner/races prominently. *Eric Alston*

KING OF PARIS 3 b.g. Exceed And Excel (AUS) 126 – Dubai Queen (USA) 103 **82**
(Kingmambo (USA) 125) [2017 74p: 7g^{2} 10d 7m^{4} 6m^{6} Jul 13] fairly useful maiden: should stay beyond 7f: tried in cheekpieces: front runner/races prominently: temperament under suspicion. *Roger Varian*

KING OF ROOKS 4 b.g. Acclamation 118 – Slap Shot (IRE) 115 (Lycius (USA) 124) **95**
[2017 101: 5g Jul 13] good-topped gelding: useful handicapper: stays 6f: acts on good to firm and good to soft going: tried in hood. *Henry Spiller*

KING OF SCOTLAND (FR) 3 b.g. Rip Van Winkle (IRE) 134 – Water Fountain (Mark **70**
of Esteem (IRE) 137) [2017 67: t8.6m 11.8s* 11.6d 11.8v^{5} 13.1v Oct 12] lengthy gelding: fair handicapper: won at Leicester in May: stays 1½m: best form on soft/heavy going: tried in cheekpieces: often leads. *Hughie Morrison*

KING OF SPIN 4 b.g. Pivotal 124 – Regina 97 (Green Desert (USA) 127) [2017 83: 6g* **91**
6.1d^{4} 6.1m^{2} 6.1d^{5} 6.1g Aug 7] strong gelding: fairly useful handicapper: won at Windsor (by 1½ lengths from Goring) in May: second there in June: best at 6f: acts on tapeta, good to firm and good to soft going: tried in cheekpieces: sometimes wears tongue tie: usually races close up: sold 6,000 gns in October *Richard Hughes*

KING OF SWING 4 b.g. Dutch Art 126 – Mystic Spirit (IRE) (Invincible Spirit (IRE) 121) [2017 87: t5.1f t6m p6d p6g p6g 5m 6.1d^{6} p6g^{2} 7d^{5} 7.6s^{3} p7s* 7d^{2} 7v^{2} Oct 1] good-topped gelding: fairly useful handicapper: won at Chelmsford (apprentice, by 5 lengths from Jumping Around) in September: stays 7.5f: acts on polytrack, good to firm and heavy going: usually wears headgear: sometimes slowly away: sold 18,000 gns in October. *Richard Hughes* **80**

KING OF THE CELTS (IRE) 9 b.g. Celtic Swing 138 – Flamands (IRE) 92 (Sadler's Wells (USA) 132) [2017 73: 9.9f^{5} 9.9m^{6} 9.9d^{5} 9.9m 12.1m^{2} 12.1s^{6} 9.9s^{2} 11.2s 11.6g Sep 7] lengthy gelding: fair handicapper: stays 1½m: acts on firm and soft going: wears cheekpieces: front runner/races prominently. *Tim Easterby* **72**

KING OF THE SAND (IRE) 2 ch.c. (Feb 16) Footstepsinthesand 120 – Lough Mewin (IRE) (Woodman (USA) 126) [2017 8d^{3} 7g^{2} 8s* Oct 19] £60,000Y: fifth foal: brother to winner up to 1¼m (US Grade 3 event) Queen of The Sand (2-y-o 7f winner) and closely related to 1¼m-1½m winner (stays 2m) Rydan (by Intense Focus), both smart: dam unraced: fairly useful form: won minor event at Brighton (by 4½ lengths from George) in October: will stay 1¼m. *Gary Moore* **84**

KINGOFTHESINGERS 2 b.c. (Apr 11) Leroidesanimaux (BRZ) 127 – Songerie 115 (Hernando (FR) 127) [2017 p7d p8g p8g Oct 26] €38,000Y: seventh foal: half-brother to 3 winners, including useful 1½m/13f winner Hardstone (by Birdstone) and 2-y-o 1m winner Valitop (by Pivotal): dam 2-y-o 7f/1m (Prix des Reservoirs) winner who stayed 14.6f: little impact in minor events: type to do better in handicaps. *Sir Mark Prescott Bt* **– p**

KING OLAV (UAE) 12 ch.g. Halling (USA) 133 – Karamzin (USA) (Nureyev (USA) 131) [2017 69: p15.8g* p13g^{3} 11.6d^{3} p16s^{4} Jul 25] tall, angular gelding: fair performer: won handicap at Lingfield in January: stays 16.5f: acts on polytrack, tapeta, good to firm and good to soft going. *Tony Carroll* **72**

KING OSWALD (USA) 4 b.g. Street Cry (IRE) 130 – Northern Melody (IRE) (Singspiel (IRE) 133) [2017 60, a74: t9.5m^{5} t9.5g^{2} t9.5g^{5} t9.5g^{5} t10.2g^{6} t12.2g^{6} 8m^{3} 8m* 8m^{3} 8m^{5} 8g^{5} 8m^{5} t8.6d^{2} Dec 9] fair handicapper: won at Yarmouth in May: stays 9.5f: acts on tapeta and good to firm going: wears cheekpieces: has worn tongue tie, including in 2017: usually races nearer last than first. *James Unett* **72**

KING OTTO 3 b.g. Holy Roman Emperor (IRE) 125 – Que Puntual (ARG) (Contested Bid (USA) 120) [2017 –: p7g^{6} p8g t7.1g 7g 8g Jun 27] little form: in headgear/tongue tie last 2 starts. *Phil McEntee* **–**

KING ROBERT 4 b.g. Royal Applause 124 – Generously Gifted (Sakhee (USA) 136) [2017 105: p6g t6g* t6g^{2} 6m 6s 6d^{3} 6g 6g^{6} t6.1g Oct 7] rather leggy gelding: fairly useful handicapper on turf, useful on all-weather: won at Wolverhampton (by neck from Upavon) in February: second there (neck behind Dubai One) in March: stays 6f: acts on tapeta and heavy going: usually in headgear in 2017. *Bryan Smart* **94 a102**

KINGS ACADEMY 3 ch.g. Mayson 124 – Intrusion 74 (Indesatchel (IRE) 120) [2017 74: 7g 6d 6m^{4} 7g^{6} 5m^{6} 5.1g^{3} 5d* 6.1d^{4} p6g^{3} 7v^{2} Sep 25] sturdy gelding: fair performer: won handicap at Leicester in August: stays 6f: acts on polytrack, tapeta, good to firm and good to soft going: has worn cheekpieces, including last 2 starts: often in tongue tie: often races towards rear. *Paul Cole* **76**

KINGS CITY (IRE) 3 b.g. Rock of Gibraltar (IRE) 133 – Muluk (IRE) 83 (Rainbow Quest (USA) 134) [2017 10m p12d 9.9m 9.9g^{2} 9.9d^{4} p12g^{5} p12g Oct 24] useful-looking gelding: fair maiden: stays 1½m: acts on polytrack: in headgear last 4 starts: usually races prominently: temperamental. *Luca Cumani* **68 §**

KING'S COINAGE (IRE) 3 b.g. Holy Roman Emperor (IRE) 125 – Seducing (IRE) 71 (Galileo (IRE) 134) [2017 67: 10.2m^{2} 12g* 12d^{6} 12g^{4} 12m^{6} t12.4s t12.2g t10.2g Oct 20] close-coupled gelding: fairly useful handicapper: won at Newbury (by ¾ length from Chocolate Box) in June: left Ed Walker after second start: stays 1½m: acts on polytrack and good to firm going: usually wears hood. *Ruth Carr* **82**

KINGS FULL (IRE) 2 b.g. (Mar 27) Galileo (IRE) 134 – Half Queen (USA) (Deputy Minister (CAN)) [2017 8g^{4} Sep 7] $500,000Y: half-brother to several winners in USA, notably Breeders' Cup Juvenile Fillies winner Halfbridled (by Unbridled): dam US 6.5f winner: 10/1, fourth in minor event at Haydock (5¼ lengths behind The Revenant) on debut, not knocked about: open to significant improvement. *Kevin Ryan* **77 P**

KINGS GIFT (IRE) 3 ch.g. Casamento (IRE) 118 – Jawaaneb (USA) 87 (Kingmambo (USA) 125) [2017 99: 7m^{4} 8d 10m 7.9m^{3} 9.9v 7.9g^{3} 9d Sep 30] rangy gelding: useful handicapper: third at York in July (½ length behind Chiefofchiefs) and August (3¼ lengths behind Mojito): stays 1¼m: acts on soft and good to firm going. *Michael Dods* **106**

KINGS HEART (IRE) 3 b.c. Zoffany (IRE) 121 – Queens Flight 56 (King's Best (USA) 132) [2017 70: 5.7f 6d^{4} 6.1d t6.1g^{2} t6.1g^{2} p7s^{5} p6g^{4} p6g^{6} 7s^{4} Jul 29] smallish colt: fair handicapper: stays 6f: acts on tapeta and good to soft going: wears headgear: often races freely. *Mark Usher* **69**

KINGSLEY KLARION (IRE) 4 b.g. Arcano (IRE) 122 – May Day Queen (IRE) 79 (Danetime (IRE) 121) [2017 81, a93: p7g p6g t7.1s^{6} t7.1g 7.2m p7d^{2} t7.2g^{3} 7s p6s p7d^{2} t7.2g p8g p6g t6.1g Dec 18] fairly useful handicapper: placed at Chelmsford in May, Wolverhampton in June and Kempton in July: left Mark Johnston after tenth start: stays 7f: acts on polytrack, tapeta and good to firm going. *John Butler* **86**

KINGS OF LUXOR 4 b.g. Royal Applause 124 – Tut (IRE) 84 (Intikhab (USA) 135) [2017 54: p6g 6m 7.2d 7g 6.3v Sep 11] little form: tried in blinkers: often races towards rear. *R. P. Burns, Ireland* **–**

KING'S PAVILION (IRE) 4 b.g. King's Best (USA) 132 – Embassy 114 (Cadeaux Genereux 131) [2017 99: 8.3g^{5} 8m^{5} 7.8s^{2} 8g^{4} 8d 7.8v* 7.6v^{2} 8.2v^{4} 8.2d Oct 30] tall, angular gelding: useful handicapper: won at Carlisle (by 3½ lengths from Instant Attraction) in September: second at Chester (½ length behind Dan Troop) later same month: stays 8.5f: acts on good to firm and heavy going: has worn cheekpieces: often races towards rear: sold to join Jason Ward £35,000 in November. *David Barron* **103**

KING'S PROCTOR (IRE) 2 b.c. (Apr 12) Cape Cross (IRE) 129 – Alimony (IRE) 77 (Groom Dancer (USA) 128) [2017 7m^{5} 8.3g* Nov 1] €85,000F: half-brother to several winners, including 5f winner Jane's Payoff (by Danetime): dam, 7f winner, sister to smart winner up to 8.5f Thrilling Day: fairly useful form: won maiden at Nottingham (by 1¼ lengths from Tamkeen) in November: will go on improving. *Mark Johnston* **91 p**

KINGS SHIELD (USA) 2 b.c. (Jan 22) Scat Daddy (USA) 120 – Gender Dance (USA) (Miesque's Son (USA) 117) [2017 t7.1g* Nov 15] 675,000 2-y-o: half-brother to several winners, including smart 2-y-o 6f winner Great White Eagle (by Elusive Quality) and useful 2-y-o 6f winner Quarrel (by Maria's Mon): dam US 7f/1m winner: 8/11, won minor event at Newcastle (by 1¼ lengths from Ostilio) on debut: sure to progress. *John Gosden* **86 p**

KINGSTON KURRAJONG 4 b.g. Authorized (IRE) 133 – Kingston Acacia 87 (King of Roses (AUS)) [2017 95: p8g^{4} p8g^{6} p8m f7g^{5} p8g^{4} 8m 8.3g^{5} p8d 8g 8d^{3} 8g^{3} 8s^{2} 8d 8g^{5} Sep 2] sturdy gelding: fairly useful handicapper: placed at Salisbury, Newbury and Sandown in June/July: left Andrew Balding after second start: stays 8.5f: acts on polytrack, soft and good to firm going: in cheekpieces last 4 starts. *Michael Attwater* **93**

KINGSTON MIMOSA 5 b.g. Kheleyf (USA) 116 – Derartu (AUS) (Last Tycoon 131) [2017 11m Jun 29] angular gelding: maiden, well held sole outing on Flat in 2017: stays 1¼m: acts on good to firm and heavy going: in headgear last 5 starts: modest hurdler. *Mark Gillard* **–**

KINGSTON TASMANIA 3 b.g. Kheleyf (USA) 116 – Derartu (AUS) (Last Tycoon 131) [2017 –: p8g Jan 6] no form: has worn blinkers, including on sole outing in 2017. *Andrew Balding* **–**

KINGSTREET LADY 4 b.f. Royal Applause 124 – Intellibet One 74 (Compton Place 125) [2017 54: t6g^{5} t7.1g^{6} p6d t7.1g^{3} 5.7f* 5.7d^{4} 5.7m 6.1m^{4} 5.7f^{4} 7.4g 6v^{3} 5s^{3} 5.1g^{3} Sep 6] modest handicapper: won at Bath in May: stays 7f: acts on tapeta, firm and good to soft going: tried in headgear. *Richard Price* **59**

KINGS WILL DREAM (IRE) 3 ch.g. Casamento (IRE) 118 – Road Harbour (USA) (Rodrigo de Triano (USA) 130) [2017 8d^{3} 8m^{3} 8s* Jul 30] €50,000Y, 7,500 2-y-o: half-brother to several winners, including 11.6f-2½m winner Leg Spinner (by Intikhab) and 5f-1m winner Togoville (by Verglas), both useful: dam unraced: fairly useful form: won maiden at Pontefract (by head from Sharja Bridge) in July: will be suited by further than 1m: has joined Darren Weir in Australia: open to further improvement. *Micky Hammond* **90 p**

KINGTHISTLE 4 ch.g. Monsieur Bond (IRE) 120 – Chez Cherie 108 (Wolfhound (USA) 126) [2017 74: t9.5m* p10d^{3} p11g* 10g^{3} 10.4m^{6} 9.9f^{2} 11.1g^{5} 10g^{3} 11.1d^{3} 9s Aug 7] fairly useful handicapper: won at Wolverhampton in January and Kempton (by nose from Every Chance) in February: stayed 11f: acted on polytrack, tapeta, firm and good to soft going: in cheekpieces/tongue tie last 3 starts: dead. *Rebecca Menzies* **82**

KING TUT (USA) 2 b.c. (Jan 30) Animal Kingdom (USA) 129 – St Malo's Gate (USA) (Dynaformer (USA)) [2017 p8g t9.5g^{5} Nov 18] fair form: better effort when fifth in minor event at Wolverhampton (6¾ lengths behind Corelli) in November. *Roger Charlton* **67**

KINGWILLIAMSTOWN 3 gr.g. Hellvelyn 118 – Honesty Pays (Dr Fong (USA) 128) [2017 –: 7v^{6} 8g 5g 6g 10d 11.9d p12g Oct 9] no form: left Susan A. Finn after fourth start: tried in headgear. *Jose Santos* **–**

KINLOCH PRIDE 5 ch.m. Kyllachy 129 – Pride of Kinloch 80 (Dr Devious (IRE) 127) **79**
[2017 60: t5g* 5m* 5g^{2} 5g* 5g* 6m t5g^{3} 5g^{4} 5m* Aug 30] fair handicapper: won at Newcastle in March, Catterick (twice) in April, Thirsk in May and Musselburgh in August: best at 5f: acts on tapeta, soft and good to firm going: wears cheekpieces: often races prominently. *Noel Wilson*

KIRBEC (IRE) 2 b.f. (Feb 7) Lord Shanakill (USA) 121 – Monsusu (IRE) 86 (Montjeu **75**
(IRE) 137) [2017 5m 6s^{3} 6s^{2} 7.2d^{2} 6s^{3} 7v^{6} 7d^{3} 8.3v Nov 8] €6,000Y: close-coupled filly: seventh foal: half-sister to 3 winners, including 2-y-o 6f winner Tro Nesa (by Chineur) and 2-y-o 5.5f winner Kidmenot (by Ad Valorem): dam, 7f winner, half-sister to useful 9f-10.4f winner Military Power: fair maiden: stays 7f: acts on soft going: in cheekpieces last 2 starts: often races prominently. *Keith Dalgleish*

KIRIBATI 3 b.g. Poet's Voice 126 – Oasis Jade 65 (Oasis Dream 129) [2017 74: 6g 7.2g^{6} **70**
8.3m^{4} 8.1m 7m^{6} p7s^{6} Jul 25] fair maiden: stays 1m: acts on good to firm going: in blinkers last 2 starts: often leads: sold £6,000, sent to Greece. *Mark Johnston*

KIRINGA 4 ch.f. Kyllachy 129 – Good Health 78 (Magic Ring (IRE) 115) [2017 70: t5.1g^{5} **61**
5g 5f^{4} 5d^{6} Jul 20] fair handicapper, below form in 2017: best form at 5f: acts on tapeta and good to firm going: tried in headgear: often races prominently. *Robert Cowell*

KIRKBY'S PHANTOM 3 gr.f. Sayif (IRE) 122 – Demolition Jo 89 (Petong 126) [2017 **–**
–: 7g 7d 7s^{6} t5g 6v t5g^{4} Dec 6] no form: left Colin Teague after second start: in cheekpieces last 3 starts. *Alan Berry*

KIRKHAM 4 b.g. Pastoral Pursuits 127 – Royal Grace 66 (Royal Applause 124) [2017 76: **82**
7m^{6} 7g t7.1s^{2} 7g^{2} 7d^{2} 7d^{4} 7d^{6} 7g* 7.4v^{2} Sep 26] fairly useful handicapper: won at Thirsk in September: stays 7.5f: acts on tapeta, good to firm and heavy going: wears cheekpieces: usually races prominently, often travels strongly. *Julie Camacho*

KIRKLAND FOREVER 3 ch.f. Sakhee (USA) 136 – Maystock 87 (Magic Ring (IRE) **67**
115) [2017 11.6d 12d 11.4d^{6} p11g^{4} 11.4m Oct 16] sturdy filly: third foal: dam 1½m-17f winner: fair maiden: stays 11f: acts on polytrack. *Brendan Powell*

KIRKMAN (IRE) 6 ch.g. Virtual 122 – Validate (Alhaarth (IRE) 126) [2017 –: 16m Jun **–**
16] fair at best, has lost his way: tried in hood: front runner/races prominently. *Peter Hiatt*

KIRUNA PEAK (IRE) 3 ch.f. Arcano (IRE) 122 – Kirunavaara (IRE) (Galileo (IRE) **71**
134) [2017 72: 10.2g 10.2g^{5} 14g^{3} 13m^{6} 14f^{5} 11.6f^{5} 10m* 11.4g^{3} 10.2g^{2} Jul 26] smallish, leggy filly: fair performer: won claimer at Windsor in July: stays 1¾m: acts on good to firm going: in visor 4 of last 5 starts. *Mick Channon*

KISMAT 2 b.f. (Apr 2) Sepoy (AUS) 129 – Magic Destiny 96 (Dubai Destination (USA) **59**
127) [2017 p7g Oct 18] first foal: dam, 7f/1m winner, half-sister to useful winner up to 1m Magic Cat: 50/1, very green when ninth in minor event at Kempton (6¾ lengths behind Revalue) in October. *Alan King*

KISS ME DAILY (FR) 2 b.f. (Mar 16) Reliable Man 128 – Via Saleria (IRE) 77 (Arazi **56**
(USA) 135) [2017 7.6s 8s p8s Nov 23] half-sister to numerous winners, including very smart French/Australian 7f-1½m winner I'm Your Man (raced as He's Your Man in Australia, by Cape Cross) and smart winner up to 11f Perfect Hedge (2-y-o 9f winner, by Unfuwain): dam 9f winner: modest form when seventh at Newbury on second of 3 starts in minor events: will be suited by 1¼m+. *Ralph Beckett*

KISSY SUZUKI 5 b.m. Sakhee's Secret 128 – Yonder 71 (And Beyond (IRE) 113) [2017 **–**
65: p12g^{6} Jan 14] fair handicapper, well held in seller sole outing in 2017: stays 1½m: acts on tapeta. *Hughie Morrison*

KISUMU 5 b.g. High Chaparral (IRE) 132 – Arum Lily (USA) (Woodman (USA) 126) **– §**
[2017 69§: 15.9m^{6} 15.9s t16.3s t16.3g Oct 19] fair maiden at best, little impact in 2017: has worn headgear, including last 2 starts: temperamental (carries head awkwardly). *Micky Hammond*

KITAABAAT 2 b.c. (Feb 11) Dansili 127 – Ausus (USA) (Invasor (ARG) 133) [2017 7g^{4} **89 p**
8g^{2} 8d* Sep 20] first foal: dam smart US 6f-9.5f (Grade 3) winner: fairly useful form: won minor event at Sandown (by ¾ length from Sevenna Star) in September: remains with potential. *Owen Burrows*

KITASAN BLACK (JPN) 5 b.h. Black Tide (JPN) 115 – Sugar Heart (JPN) (Sakura **128**
Bakushin O (JPN)) [2017 126: 9.9f* 15.9g* 10.9g 9.9s* 11.9f^{3} 12.4f* Dec 24] high-class performer: won Osaka Hai at Hanshin and Tenno Sho (Spring) at Kyoto (beat Cheval Grand 1¼ lengths), both in April, Tenno Sho (Autumn) at Tokyo (by neck from Satono Crown) in October and Arima Kinen at Nakayama (by 1½ lengths from Queens Ring) in

December: reportedly lost near-fore shoe when 1½ lengths third to Cheval Grand in Japan Cup at Tokyo on penultimate start (had won race in 2016): stayed 2m: acted on firm and soft going: raced prominently: to stand at Shadai Stallion Station, fee ¥5,000,000. *Hisashi Shimizu, Japan*

KIT MARLOWE 2 b.g. (Feb 25) Poet's Voice 126 – La Nuit Rose (FR) 109 (Rainbow Quest (USA) 134) [2017 5m^2 6s^5 6.1m^3 t7.1s* p7g^2 p8s^3 t8s^4 t8g^2 Oct 20] well-grown gelding: closely related to French 7f winner Lunar Halo (by Dubawi) and half-brother to numerous winners, including very smart/ungenuine 1m-11f winner Tam Lin (by Selkirk) and useful 10.5f-1½m winner (stays 2¼m) Blue Rambler (by Monsun): dam, 2-y-o 7f winner, third in Poule d'Essai des Pouliches/Irish 1000 Guineas: fairly useful performer: won minor event at Newcastle in June: second in nurseries at Chelmsford in August and Newcastle in October: stays 1m: acts on polytrack, tapeta and good to firm going: front runner/races prominently. *Mark Johnston* **85**

KITSEY (IRE) 3 b.f. High Chaparral (IRE) 132 – Thistlestar (USA) 64 (Lion Heart (USA) 124) [2017 67: 10.2m 10.2f 10m^6 14v^6 9.9d 10g Oct 7] tall filly: modest maiden in Britain: sold 2,000 gns, sent to Italy, where won 10.7f claimer at Varese in December. *Richard Hannon* **53**

KITTEN'S JOHNSTOWN (USA) 3 ch.c. Kitten's Joy (USA) 128 – Cellars Shiraz (USA) (Kissin Kris (USA) 122) [2017 88p: 8m^5 10g^6 8d p8g^5 t8.6g Oct 27] leggy colt: fairly useful 7f winner on sole start at 2 yrs, disappointing in 2017. *Kevin Ryan* **73**

KITTY BOO 3 b.f. Invincible Spirit (IRE) 121 – Kitty Wells 90 (Sadler's Wells (USA) 132) [2017 76: 8.3d^2 10.2s^4 8d^2 9.9g p8g* 8.1m p8g^3 Nov 6] fairly useful performer: won maiden at Chelmsford (by 2 lengths from Considered Opinion) in September: third in handicap at Kempton (neck behind Express Lady) in November: stays 1¼m: acts on polytrack and good to soft going: wears hood: sold 55,000 gns in December. *Luca Cumani* **90**

KIWI BAY 12 b.g. Mujahid (USA) 125 – Bay of Plenty (FR) (Octagonal (NZ) 126) [2017 83: t8g t8d t8d* t8g^4 t8d^3 8g^4 8m 9.1m* 8g^4 10g^2 7.8m^4 10m* 9s^6 8v 7v t7.1g Nov 24] tall gelding: fair handicapper nowadays: won at Newcastle in March, Ayr (apprentice) in May and Redcar (claimer) in July: stays 10.5f, effective at shorter: acts on polytrack, tapeta, good to firm and heavy going: has worn cheekpieces. *Michael Dods* **75**

KLOSTERS (IRE) 2 b.f. (Feb 19) Kodiac 112 – Seminova (Cape Cross (IRE) 129) [2017 p6g^3 6.1m* 8f^4 8f 8f^4 t6f^6 t8f^3 Dec 10] €57,000F, 45,000Y: neat filly: fourth foal: dam once-raced daughter of US Grade 1 9.5f winner Snow Polina: fair performer: won minor event at Chepstow in June: left Roger Charlton after second start: stays 1m: acts on dirt and firm going. *Jonathan Wong, USA* **77**

KNIGHT COMMANDER 4 br.g. Sir Percy 129 – Jardin (Sinndar (IRE) 134) [2017 80: p16g^3 Oct 12] compact gelding: fair maiden: probably stays 2m: acts on soft going: often races in rear: fair hurdler. *Olly Murphy* **74**

KNIGHT DESTROYER (IRE) 3 b.g. Dark Angel (IRE) 113 – Do The Deal (IRE) 67 (Halling (USA) 133) [2017 56p: 12d^2 12d* 12v^6 12s^2 Sep 19] tall gelding: fairly useful handicapper: won at Chepstow (by 4½ lengths from Rahmah) in June: second there in September: stays 1½m: acts on soft going: won over hurdles in October. *Jonjo O'Neill* **86**

KNIGHTED (IRE) 2 b.g. (Mar 9) Sir Prancealot (IRE) 111 – Olympia Theatre (Galileo (IRE) 134) [2017 6g^2 6.1d^5 7v^2 Nov 7] €45,000Y: sixth foal: half-brother to 2-y-o 7f winner Mandeville (by Kodiac) and a winner in Italy by Bushranger: dam unraced: fair form: second in minor event at Redcar (length behind Up Sticks And Go) in November: will stay 1m: remains capable of better. *Kevin Ryan* **75 p**

KNIGHT ERRANT (IRE) 2 b.c. (May 5) So You Think (NZ) 133 – Lamanka Lass (USA) 79 (Woodman (USA) 126) [2017 p8s^5 Dec 15] 25/1, very green when well held in minor event at Chelmsford. *William Jarvis* –

KNIGHT IN ARMOUR (IRE) 2 b.g. (Apr 6) Camelot 128 – Madeira Mist (IRE) 80 (Grand Lodge (USA) 125) [2017 7m^4 7d^2 7g^4 8v^3 9d^6 Oct 11] close-coupled gelding: fair maiden: should stay at least 1m: acts on good to firm and good to soft going: front runner/races prominently. *Mark Johnston* **71**

KNIGHTLY SPIRIT 2 br.c. (Mar 4) Dalakhani (IRE) 133 – Elysian 79 (Galileo (IRE) 134) [2017 8d 8d^3 9.9s^3 Sep 27] 90,000Y: second foal: half-brother to 7f winner Noble Masterpiece (by Dutch Art): dam, 1½m winner, half-sister to very smart 1m winner Integral (by Dalakhani): fair form: best effort when third in maiden at Goodwood (4¼ lengths behind Setting Sail) in September: remains with potential. *Roger Varian* **74 p**

KNIGHT MUSIC 5 b.g. Sir Percy 129 – Lyric Art (USA) 65 (Red Ransom (USA)) [2017 90: 12d4 p12g 11.5d4 Oct 24] sturdy gelding: fairly useful handicapper: stays 1½m: acts on polytrack, good to firm and heavy going: sold 9,000 gns in October. *Michael Attwater* **82**

KNIGHT OF THE AIR 5 b.g. Bushranger (IRE) 119 – Picolette 56 (Piccolo 121) [2017 74: p6g4 7m 9.1g4 6g6 p7s 9.1m4 9.9s6 p7g Oct 11] angular gelding: fair handicapper: stays 9f: acts on polytrack, soft and good to firm going: in tongue tie last 3 starts. *Joseph Tuite* **68**

KNIGHT OWL 7 b.g. Rock of Gibraltar (IRE) 133 – Miss Ivanhoe (IRE) 107 (Selkirk (USA) 129) [2017 101: 9g3 8s 8d 8g2 Sep 28] rather leggy gelding: useful handicapper: placed at Ripon (1¼ lengths behind Gurkha Friend) in May and Newmarket (5 lengths behind Repercussion) in September: stays 9f: acts on polytrack, firm and good to soft going: tried in hood. *James Fanshawe* **99**

KNIGHTSBRIDGE LIAM (IRE) 3 b.g. Lilbourne Lad (IRE) 111 – Carmona 65 (Rainbow Quest (USA) 134) [2017 –: t8g6 f8g6 t9.5g2 t12.2g 11.2g3 12g5 9.9f4 12.1d2 12.5m5 t10.2s4 t10.2g Oct 20] modest maiden: stays 1½m: acts on tapeta, firm and good to soft going: often races towards rear: temperament under suspicion: sold 5,000 gns, sent to the Netherlands. *Michael Easterby* **64**

KNIGHTS TABLE 4 b.c. Sir Percy 129 – Whole Grain 72 (Polish Precedent (USA) 131) [2017 101: 12g* 12m4 May 13] smart performer: won handicap at Ripon (by 5 lengths from Tawdeea) in April: should stay beyond 1½m: acts on tapeta and good to firm going: often races prominently: sold to join Tim Easterby 10,000 gns in October. *James Tate* **111**

KNIGHT TO BEHOLD (IRE) 2 b.c. (Mar 16) Sea The Stars (IRE) 140 – Angel of The Gwaun (IRE) (Sadler's Wells (USA) 132) [2017 8g2 8m* Oct 25] neat colt: half-brother to several winners, including smart Japanese 11f-17f winner Cosmo Meadow (by King's Best) and useful winner up to 1¼m Beauty O' Gwaun (2-y-o 7f winner, by Rainbow Quest): dam unraced: useful form: won minor event at Newmarket (by neck from Bow Street) in October: will be suited by 1¼m: remains open to improvement. *Harry Dunlop* **95 p**

KNOCKAMANY BENDS (IRE) 7 b.g. Majestic Missile (IRE) 118 – Sweet Compliance 71 (Safawan 118) [2017 54§: 5m 5g 5s5 6g 5s2 5s* 6d2 5s 5v 5s* 5g Oct 18] modest handicapper: won at Hamilton in August and Musselburgh in October: stays 6f: acts on polytrack, fibresand, soft and good to firm going: wears headgear: has worn tongue tie, including in 2017: front runner/races prominently: unreliable. *John Wainwright* **60 §**

KNOCKOUT BLOW 2 b.g. (Apr 14) Lethal Force (IRE) 128 – Elidore 95 (Danetime (IRE) 121) [2017 5s 6.1g2 6m4 5.1d6 p5g* p6g6 Oct 9] good-quartered gelding: fair performer: won minor event at Kempton in September: seems best at 5f: acts on polytrack and good to firm going: front runner/races prominently. *Mark Johnston* **79**

KNOTTY JACK (IRE) 5 b.g. Zebedee 113 – Half-Hitch (USA) 88 (Diesis 133) [2017 –: 7.4g5 7.2s Sep 16] lightly-raced maiden. *Chris Grant* **–**

KNOWING GLANCE (IRE) 2 b.g. (Apr 5) Kodiac 112 – Shauna's Princess (IRE) 79 (Soviet Star (USA) 128) [2017 6m5 t5s4 7m3 7v3 Sep 15] €52,000F, 65,000Y: fifth foal: closely related/half-brother to winners abroad by Oratorio and Mastercraftsman: dam 5f winner: fair form: best effort at 7f: remains with potential. *Richard Fahey* **72 p**

KNOW THE TRUTH 3 br.f. Lawman (FR) 121 – Snow Key (USA) 103 (Cozzene (USA)) [2017 p7g6 8.1m 8g p7g4 8m p7s p7g 7v6 6.1g4 f7.1g4 f5g* Nov 13] neat filly: fifth foal: half-sister to 3 winners, including 1½m-14.6f winner Paris Snow (by Montjeu): dam French 1m-11f winner: fair performer: won maiden at Southwell in November: stays 1m, effective over much shorter: acts on polytrack and fibresand. *Andrew Balding* **72**

KNOW YOUR LIMIT (IRE) 3 ch.g. Tamayuz 126 – Rapid Ransom (USA) 88 (Red Ransom (USA)) [2017 71p: 8.3m3 8m2 8.1g2 9.9m2 9.9g2 12v3 Oct 23] well-made gelding: fairly useful maiden: placed on all 6 starts in 2017: stays 1¼m: acts on polytrack, good to firm and heavy going: temperament under suspicion. *Ed Walker* **87**

KNOW YOUR NAME 6 ch.g. Halling (USA) 133 – Lady Agnes 53 (Singspiel (IRE) 133) [2017 79: t8.6g4 7.8g t8.6g* 7.8m5 8g6 t8.6g5 t7.2g t8.6g3 7.6v t9.5m t8.6g5 t8.6g6 Nov 18] close-coupled gelding: fair handicapper: won at Wolverhampton (amateur) in July: stays 8.5f: acts on polytrack, tapeta, good to firm and good to soft going: has worn headgear, including in 2017: front runner/races prominently. *Donald McCain* **71**

KODIAC EXPRESS (IRE) 2 b.f. (Apr 12) Kodiac 112 – Excel Yourself (IRE) 85 (Exceed And Excel (AUS) 126) [2017 p5g4 p5g3 5.1m3 5.3d6 5.7f2 6g p5g4 5g2 6d2 5d* Oct 4] €64,000Y, resold 50,000Y: rather leggy filly: second foal: dam, 2-y-o 5f/6f winner, sister to smart sprinter Taajub: fair performer: won maiden at Nottingham in October: stays 6f: acts on polytrack, firm and good to soft going. *Mike Murphy* **75**

KODIAC KHAN (IRE) 3 b.c. Kodiac 112 – Mirwara (IRE) (Darshaan 133) [2017 83: **80**
7.5m^4 8g t8g^6 10d Jul 9] fairly useful handicapper: stays 1m: acts on polytrack and good to
firm going: tried in blinkers: sold 15,000 gns in July, sent to Sweden. *Mark Johnston*

KODIAC LADY (IRE) 5 b.m. Kodiac 112 – Weeping Willow (IRE) 57 (Kheleyf (USA) **47**
116) [2017 64: t7.1m^5 t8.6g^4 Jan 26] poor handicapper nowadays: stays 9.5f: acts on
polytrack and tapeta: wears headgear: has worn tongue tie. *Simon West*

KODIAC PEARL (IRE) 3 b.f. Kodiac 112 – Valmirez (USA) (Smart Strike (CAN) 121) **40**
[2017 5m^5 t5s 5g^6 5.1d t5.1g 6v^6 Oct 19] £42,000Y: first foal: dam, unraced, closely related
to useful US 1m/8.5f winner Maybellene: poor maiden: stays 6f: in hood last 3 starts.
Robert Cowell

KODI BEACH 2 b.g. (Mar 18) Kodiac 112 – Annie Beach (IRE) 95 (Redback 116) [2017 **64**
5d 5d^6 Oct 4] modest form when sixth in maiden at Nottingham (3½ lengths behind Kodiac
Express) on second of 2 starts. *David Barron*

KODICAT (IRE) 3 b.f. Kodiac 112 – Mimiteh (USA) 77 (Maria's Mon (USA) 121) [2017 **79**
67: t5g^3 5g* 6g 5.6d^4 6m^4 6d^3 6.1d^2 t6.1g^3 t5g Nov 3] leggy filly: fair handicapper: won at
Catterick in April: stays 6f: acts on tapeta, good to firm and good to soft going: tried in
cheekpieces. *Kevin Ryan*

KODILINE (IRE) 3 b.c. Kodiac 112 – Kris Spring (Kris S (USA)) [2017 94: 7m^6 6m **98**
6m^5 p5g^5 p6g^4 Nov 21] sturdy colt: useful handicapper: stays 6f: acts on polytrack and
good to firm going: in headgear last 4 starts. *Clive Cox*

KODIMOOR (IRE) 4 b.g. Kodiac 112 – Victoria Lodge (IRE) (Grand Lodge (USA) **67**
125) [2017 62: f5g^3 t5.1g^6 f5g^2 5m* 5d^6 5g* 5d^4 5g f5g^5 6d 5s^2 5s Nov 8] fair handicapper **a58**
on turf, modest on all-weather: won at Catterick (apprentice) in May and Hamilton in July:
stays 6f: acts on tapeta, good to firm and heavy going: usually wears headgear/tongue tie.
Christopher Kellett

KODINA 2 b.f. (Jan 16) Kodiac 112 – Quan Am (FR) (Invincible Spirit (IRE) 121) [2017 **64**
6s 5.1g^5 Sep 6] £65,000Y: first foal: dam ran once in France: modest form: better effort
when fifth in minor event at Chepstow (4¼ lengths behind Awesome) in September.
Charles Hills

KODITIME (IRE) 2 b.c. (Feb 1) Kodiac 112 – Eponastone (IRE) 72 (Footstepsinthesand **94**
120) [2017 5m* 6s^3 5m 5v Aug 2] £65,000Y: compact colt: first foal: dam, maiden (stayed
1¼m), half-sister to St Leger runner-up Unsung Heroine: fairly useful form: won maiden at
Doncaster (by ½ length from Dahik) in April: stays 6f: tried in blinkers. *Clive Cox*

KODY RIDGE (IRE) 3 b.g. Kodiac 112 – Top of The Ridge (IRE) (Celtic Swing 138) **80**
[2017 74: 7g 5d 6d* 6m* 6m^3 6g 5s^5 5.9s^2 f5g^6 Dec 19] fairly useful performer: won seller
at Leicester in June and handicap at Ripon in July: left David Dennis after third start: stays
6f: acts on soft and good to firm going: usually wears hood: front runner/races prominently.
Roger Fell

KOEMAN 3 b.c. Dutch Art 126 – Angelic Note (IRE) 68 (Excellent Art 125) [2017 79: **93**
p8g^4 9.9m^3 12.3g^2 11.9d^4 12m^3 12d^5 12m* p12g* 12g^3 p11g^3 p11g* 12m p11g Nov 6]
workmanlike colt: fairly useful handicapper: won at Salisbury/Lingfield in July and
Kempton (by ½ length from Al Hamdany) in September: stays 12.5f: acts on polytrack,
good to firm and good to soft going. *Mick Channon*

KOHINOOR DIAMOND (IRE) 3 b.f. Excelebration (IRE) 133 – Gems of Araby 80 **75 §**
(Zafonic (USA) 130) [2017 50p: p10g* p10g^6 p12g^2 p12g f16.5g Dec 29] fair handicapper:
won at Chelmsford in October: stays 1½m: acts on polytrack: in headgear last 3 starts:
ungenuine. *Sir Mark Prescott Bt*

KOHINUR 3 b.f. Dubawi (IRE) 129 – Vita Nova (IRE) 121 (Galileo (IRE) 134) [2017 **86**
12s^2 p12s^3 12.1v^2 Sep 26] first foal: dam 1¼m-1½m winner: fairly useful form: placed all
3 starts in maidens. *Hugo Palmer*

KOIN 2 b.f. (Feb 9) Kheleyf (USA) 116 – Tenpence 60 (Bob Back (USA) 124) [2017 6s 6m **–**
7d p7g Oct 12] half-sister to several winners, including useful 1m-1½m winner Barwick
(by Beat Hollow) and 1¼m winner Zenarinda (by Zamindar): dam ran twice: no form: tried
in blinkers. *Mark H. Tompkins*

KOLO TAMAM 2 b.c. (Jan 27) Al Kazeem 128 – Sensiz (IRE) 82 (Marju (IRE) 127) **– p**
[2017 t8.6d Dec 9] first foal: dam, 1m winner, half-sister to smart winner up to 1¼m High
Twelve out of Prix Robert Papin winner Much Faster: 8/1, very green when well held in
minor event at Wolverhampton: capable of better. *Roger Charlton*

KOMMANDER KIRKUP 6 ch.g. Assertive 121 – Bikini 80 (Trans Island 119) [2017 87§: 6.1s 6g^3 6v 6g 5g 7s t6g^2 t6g f6.1g* f6.1g* Dec 21] fair handicapper nowadays: won at Southwell in November and December: stays 6f: acts on fibresand, tapeta, soft and good to firm going: sometimes wears headgear: signs of temperament. *Michael Herrington* **77**

KOMODO (IRE) 3 ch.g. Dragon Pulse (IRE) 114 – Salydora (FR) (Peintre Celebre (USA) 137) [2017 7m^4 7g^2 7g* 8m^2 10d* 9.8d* Aug 7] €30,000F: half-brother to several winners abroad, including French 1¼m winner Effervescent (by Green Tune): dam French 9f-10.5f winner: useful performer: won maiden at Wetherby in May, and handicaps at Ayr in July and Ripon (by 1¼ lengths from Save The Bees) in August: stays 1¼m: acts on good to firm and good to soft going: usually races prominently: sent to Hong Kong, where renamed Amazing Wonder: will go on improving. *Jedd O'Keeffe* **98 p**

KONIG DAX (GER) 7 b.g. Saddex 124 – Konigin Shuttle (GER) (Big Shuffle (USA) 122) [2017 7g^6 11.1g^3 10d^4 10g^5 9v Sep 18] fairly useful handicapper, lightly raced: won maiden in France for L. Viel in 2013: third at Hamilton in June: stays 11f: acts on good to soft going: in tongue tie last 4 starts: usually races close up: winner over hurdles in France. *Alistair Whillans* **83**

KONIG HALL 9 b.g. Halling (USA) 133 – Konigin Shuffle (GER) (Big Shuffle (USA) 122) [2017 64: 11.3g* t12.2g^4 p10.7g^2 p12g^4 Oct 3] fair handicapper: won at Limerick in June: stays 1½m: acts on polytrack, tapeta, best turf form on good going: wears headgear: often in tongue tie: fair hurdler. *Anthony McCann, Ireland* **69**

KOOL KOMPANY (IRE) 5 br.h. Jeremy (USA) 122 – Absolutely Cool (IRE) 74 (Indian Ridge 123) [2017 112: 8g* 8.1d 8.5m^4 8f 7g^6 8v 8g 8d Sep 20] good-topped horse: smart performer: won 5 times at 2 yrs, including Railway Stakes at the Curragh and Prix Robert Papin at Maisons-Laffitte, and successful in Craven Stakes at Newmarket in 2015: also won listed race at Doncaster (by short head from Stormy Antarctic) in April: stayed 1m: acted on good to firm and good to soft going: sold 110,000 gns in November: to stand at Dehesa de Milagro, Spain, fee €3,000. *Richard Hannon* **112**

KOPASSUS (IRE) 5 b.g. Holy Roman Emperor (IRE) 125 – Couverture (USA) 82 (Lear Fan (USA) 130) [2017 60, a44: f6g^5 f7g Jan 30] modest maiden, below form both starts in 2017: stays 9f: acts on good to firm going: often wears headgear. *Lawrence Mullaney* **42**

KORAK BOY (IRE) 2 b.g. (Mar 3) Zebedee 113 – Facce Tarzan (IRE) (Exceed And Excel (AUS) 126) [2017 p6s 5f^5 5.1m^6 Jul 14] little impact in minor events: tried in blinkers. *Joseph Tuite* **–**

KORBOUS (IRE) 8 ch.g. Choisir (AUS) 126 – Puppet Play (IRE) 82 (Broken Hearted 124) [2017 82: 7s^5 7m^2 8d^5 7g^3 8m^2 7.1d^2 8g^2 a7g 7.6v Sep 15] stocky gelding: fairly useful handicapper: second at Leopardstown (twice) in July: stays 8.5f: acts on sand, good to firm and good to soft going: has worn headgear, including in 2017. *Richard Brabazon, Ireland* **86**

KOROPICK (IRE) 3 b.c. Kodiac 112 – Kathoe (IRE) (Fayruz 116) [2017 100: 6s 7m^5 5m^2 t6s* 6s 6m 7g Sep 22] compact colt: smart performer: won Chipchase Stakes at Newcastle (by head from Intisaab) in July: second in listed race at Sandown (1¼ lengths behind Battaash) in June: stayed 6f: acted on polytrack, tapeta and good to firm going: sold 50,000 gns in October: to stand at Annshoon Stud, Co. Kilkenny, fee €3,000. *Hugo Palmer* **115**

Betfred TV Chipchase Stakes, Newcastle—Koropick provides jockey Josephine Gordon with a first pattern-race victory, beating Intisaab (cheekpieces) and Kimberella (left); Gordon later becomes just the second female jockey after Hayley Turner to ride 100 winners in a calendar year in Britain

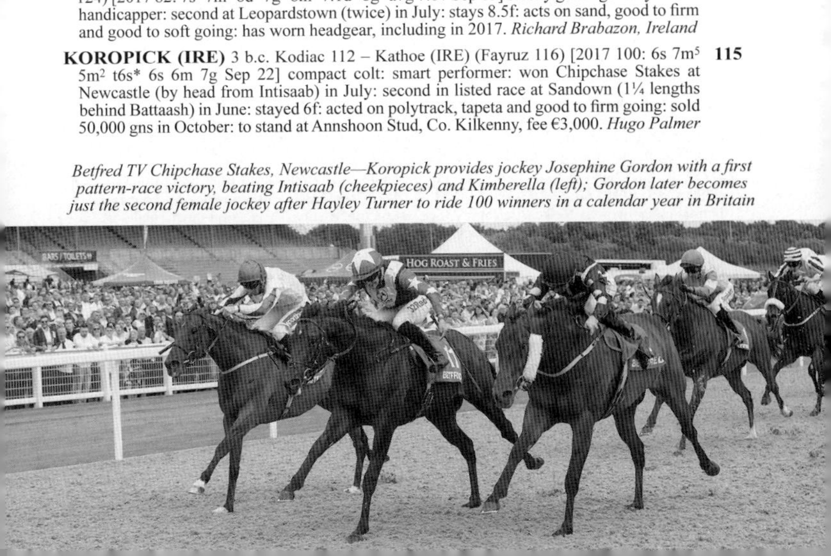

KOUBBA (IRE) 4 b.f. Peintre Celebre (USA) 137 – Elyaadi 106 (Singspiel (IRE) 133) [2017 11.6d 9.9s 8g 10.2d p13.3s^4 Nov 17] first foal: dam, 1½m-2m winner who stayed 21.7f, also won over hurdles: modest maiden: stays 13.5f: acts on polytrack: wears tongue tie: usually races nearer last than first. *Neil Mulholland* **51**

KOWAIYESS (IRE) 3 b.g. Exceed And Excel (AUS) 126 – Nidhaal (IRE) 107 (Observatory (USA) 131) [2017 82p: p5g^2 5.7m^5 6g* p6g Oct 9] fairly useful performer: won handicap at Epsom (by neck from Grandad's World) in September: left Owen Burrows after second start: stays 6f: acts on polytrack: often races freely: sent to UAE. *Mohamed Moubarak* **81**

KOZIER (GER) 3 ch.g. Muhtathir 126 – Kasumi (GER) 106 (Poliglote 121) [2017 58: t14g^5 16g^2 16s* Sep 19] well-made gelding: fair handicapper: won at Chepstow in September: stays 2m: acts on soft going: usually races in rear: open to further improvement. *Alan King* **77 p**

KRAFTY ONE 5 ch.m. Mastercraftsman (IRE) 129 – Wonderful Desert 57 (Green Desert (USA) 127) [2017 57: t12.2m 10.2s^{pu} 10.2d 11.9d Sep 18] maiden: no form in 2017: tried in cheekpieces: sometimes slowly away. *Michael Scudamore* **–**

KRAKA (IRE) 2 b.g. (Feb 2) Dark Angel (IRE) 113 – Manuelita Rose (ITY) (Desert Style (IRE) 121) [2017 7m t7.2g^3 7g^2 6.3s Sep 10] fair form: stays 7f. *Tom Dascombe* **77**

KRAZY PAVING 5 b.g. Kyllachy 129 – Critical Path (IRE) 87 (Noverre (USA) 125) [2017 60: p6g^2 p6g* p6g^2 p6g* p6g^6 p6g^6 p6g p6g p6g^3 p6g Dec 31] modest handicapper: won at Lingfield in January and Chelmsford in March: stays 6f: acts on polytrack, tapeta and heavy going: wears headgear: usually races prominently. *Anabel K. Murphy* **63**

KREB'S CYCLE (IRE) 3 ch.g. Helmet (AUS) 127 – La Noe (Nayef (USA) 129) [2017 86: 6.1m 6d^6 7m 7g^4 8d^4 8m t7.1g^2 t8g p7s^2 t7.2d Dec 16] stocky gelding: fairly useful handicapper: second at Newcastle in October and Chelmsford in November: stays 1m: acts on polytrack, tapeta, good to firm and heavy going: wears cheekpieces: tried in tongue tie. *Ian Williams* **88**

KRIPKE (IRE) 2 b.g. (Apr 18) Fast Company (IRE) 126 – Tranquil Sky 91 (Intikhab (USA) 135) [2017 7d^3 Oct 27] €20,000F, £28,000Y: half-brother to several winners, including useful 5f (including at 2 yrs) winner Wolowitz (by Intense Focus) and useful 5f/6f winner Discussiontofollow (by Elusive City): dam 2-y-o 6f/7f winner who stayed 1¼m: 8/1, third in maiden at Doncaster (3¾ lengths behind Breath Caught) on debut: capable of better. *David Barron* **78 p**

KRISTAL HART 8 b.m. Lucky Story (USA) 128 – Moly (FR) (Anabaa (USA) 130) [2017 63: p10g Jan 14] modest handicapper: stays 1¼m: acts on polytrack, tapeta, firm and soft going: wears cheekpieces: front runner/races prominently. *Neil Mulholland* **61**

KRISTJANO (GER) 5 b.g. Nayef (USA) 129 – Kalahari Dancer (Dalakhani (IRE) 133) [2017 78: 14v^4 Jun 8] well-made gelding: fair maiden, well held sole outing on Flat in 2017: stays 2m: acts on polytrack, tapeta and good to soft going: in cheekpieces last 5 starts: races prominently. *Jimmy Frost* **–**

KRISTOFF (IRE) 4 b.g. Frozen Power (IRE) 108 – Easter Girl (Efisio 120) [2017 54: p8d^3 p8d p8g p8m^5 p6f^2 8m^6 6g^4 p7g 7s^5 7.6s Aug 5] compact gelding: poor maiden on turf, modest on all-weather: stays 1m: acts on polytrack and tapeta: has worn cheekpieces, including in 2017: usually races prominently. *Jim Boyle* **42 a52**

KROY 3 b.g. Sleeping Indian 122 – Valley of The Moon (IRE) 84 (Monashee Mountain (USA) 115) [2017 60: 6g^5 6m 6g^3 6s t6g* t7.1d^2 f7.1g t6s^5 Nov 30] compact gelding: fair handicapper: won at Newcastle (apprentice) in October: stays 7f: acts on tapeta and soft going: wears cheekpieces. *Ollie Pears* **70**

KRYPTOS 3 b.g. Cacique (IRE) 124 – Posteritas (USA) 91 (Lear Fan (USA) 130) [2017 58: 8m^3 7.6g* 8m^2 8v* 8g* Sep 16] smart handicapper: won at Chester (apprentice) in July, and at Thirsk (by 5 lengths from Mountain Angel) and Doncaster (by 1¾ lengths from Battered) in September: will stay 9f: acts on good to firm and heavy going: tried in blinkers: open to further improvement. *John Berry* **111 p**

KRYSTALLITE 4 ch.f. Kheleyf (USA) 116 – Chrystal Venture (IRE) 71 (Barathea (IRE) 127) [2017 86: f5g t5.1g* 5g t5g t6.1g t6.1g^5 f6.1g^6 p5g t5.1g^6 t5.1g^4 f5g^6 t5.1d Dec 27] fair handicapper: won at Wolverhampton in June: best form at 5f: acts on polytrack and tapeta: has worn cheekpieces, including last 2 starts: sometimes slowly away. *Scott Dixon* **76**

KUIPER BELT (USA) 3 b.g. Elusive Quality (USA) – Youre So Sweet (USA) (Storm Cat (USA)) [2017 –: 7d^6 t8s t7.2g^6 Jul 11] modest maiden: should stay 1m: acts on tapeta. *David Lanigan* **51**

KULGRI 3 ch.f. Monsieur Bond (IRE) 120 – Jord (IRE) 80 (Trans Island 119) [2017 –: 6m 5m 7m^3 7v^5 8.3s^3 8.5s^2 10.1g Oct 16] modest maiden: stays 8.5f: best form on soft/heavy going: tried in cheekpieces: usually races close up: sold £2,000, sent to Germany. *Kevin Ryan* **62**

KULLU (IRE) 4 b.f. Oasis Dream 129 – Mussoorie (FR) 108 (Linamix (FR) 127) [2017 80: 10d* t12.4s^2 Jun 3] fairly useful handicapper: won at Lingfield (by 5 lengths from Inke) in May: stayed 12.5f: acted on tapeta and good to soft going: wore hood: front runner/raced prominently, usually responded generously to pressure: dead. *Charlie Fellowes* **94**

KUNANI (USA) 3 b.g. Arch (USA) 127 – Sweet Sonnet (USA) 95 (Seeking The Gold (USA)) [2017 8g^5 Aug 4] third foal: half-brother to a winner in USA by Bernardini: dam, 2-y-o 6f winner (stayed 1m), sister to smart US Grade 1 9f winner Bob And John: in blinkers, 11/1, fifth in maiden at Newmarket (12¼ lengths behind Mountain Hunter) in August: sent to UAE: should progress. *John Gosden* **55 p**

KURAKA 3 b.g. Cacique (IRE) 124 – Puzzling (Peintre Celebre (USA) 137) [2017 72: 9m^6 12.1m^4 11.6d 10.2m^2 Jul 7] fair maiden: barely stays 1½m: acts on soft and good to firm going: usually races prominently. *K. R. Burke* **74**

KWIKSTEP 3 b.f. Nathaniel (IRE) 129 – Enchufla (Danehill Dancer (IRE) 117) [2017 p12g^6 11.8v t12.2d Dec 9] first foal: dam, French 1m winner, half-sister to smart 1¼m-12.5f winner Gatewood: well held in maidens. *Andi Brown* **–**

KYLEQUE (IRE) 2 br.g. (Feb 21) Equiano (FR) 127 – Dispol Kylie (IRE) 82 (Kheleyf (USA) 116) [2017 5m 5v 5d^5 Jun 10] little impact in minor events. *Paul Midgley* **–**

KYLIE RULES 2 bl.f. (Apr 21) Aussie Rules (USA) 123 – Africa's Star (IRE) 63 (Johannesburg (USA) 127) [2017 6d^4 5.9m 7d^4 t7.1d^3 t8s^6 Sep 19] fourth foal: half-sister to 1m winner Thanks Harry (by Lucky Story): dam maiden (stayed 7f): fair maiden: stays 1m: acts on tapeta and good to soft going. *Ann Duffield* **68**

KYLIE STYLE 2 b.f. (Jan 30) Aussie Rules (USA) 123 – Stilettoesinthemud (IRE) 68 (Footstepsinthesand 120) [2017 t5.1g 5v 6.1d p5s t6.1g^5 f6.1g p7g Dec 28] first foal: dam 6f winner: modest maiden: stays 6f: acts on tapeta: tried in cheekpieces. *Steph Hollinshead* **52**

KYLLA 4 b.f. Kyllachy 129 – Mamounia (IRE) 101 (Green Desert (USA) 127) [2017 –: 6m 5s 5g^6 5d 6s^6 Sep 19] no form: left Shaun Harris after fourth start: wears headgear nowadays. *Alan Brown* **–**

KYLLACH ME (IRE) 5 b.g. Kyllachy 129 – Good For Her 72 (Rock of Gibraltar (IRE) 133) [2017 59, a66: t6f t6m^3 t6g^2 f6m 6m 6g* 6g^2 6m 6d t6g t6g^6 t6.1g^5 Dec 13] fair handicapper: won at Thirsk in April: stays 6f: acts on fibresand, tapeta and good to firm going: wears headgear: signs of temperament. *Bryan Smart* **67**

KYLLACHY DRAGON (IRE) 2 b.g. (Feb 19) Dragon Pulse (IRE) 114 – Lafayette (GER) (Artan (IRE) 119) [2017 5d^6 5g^2 5s^3 6g^2 Oct 13] €4,000Y, €14,000 2-y-o: second foal: dam, 1m winner in France, half-sister to smart German performer up to 1½m Lecroix: fairly useful form: second in nursery at York (neck behind Beatbox Rhythm) in October: will stay 7f. *Iain Jardine* **87**

KYLLACHY GALA 4 b.g. Kyllachy 129 – Tenuta di Gala (IRE) (Nashwan (USA) 135) [2017 p10g^2 8.9g 9.9g 8m^3 p10s^6 p8g t9.5g^4 p10g^2 t9.5d^3 Dec 26] useful handicapper: won 3 times in Italy for A. & S. Botti in 2016: placed at Lingfield in January, Haydock in April, and Lingfield (short head behind Emenem) and Wolverhampton (length behind Mount Tahan) in December: stays 1¼m: acts on polytrack, tapeta, good to firm and good to soft going. *Marco Botti* **107**

KYLLACHYS TALE (IRE) 3 b.f. Kyllachy 129 – Betray 103 (King's Best (USA) 132) [2017 60: p8g p8g^6 f8m* 9.9m^6 8m* 8d^2 8.1s* 8d 8.1d Oct 23] fairly useful handicapper: won at Southwell in February, Newbury in June and Windsor (by 5 lengths from Uae Queen) in August: stays 1m: acts on polytrack, fibresand, soft and good to firm going: tried in hood: usually leads. *Roger Teal* **88**

KYLLANG ROCK (IRE) 3 b.g. Kyllachy 129 – Megec Blis (IRE) 92 (Soviet Star (USA) 128) [2017 96: 5.1g* 5s^2 5d^2 5m 5s^6 5g^2 5d^4 5s^6 Oct 7] compact gelding: smart performer: won minor event at Nottingham (by neck from Major Jumbo) in April: second in listed races at York (head behind Fashion Queen) and Haydock (neck behind Final Venture) in June: raced only at 5f: acts on soft and good to firm going: tried in headgear. *James Tate* **112**

KYLLUKEY 4 b.g. Kyllachy 129 – Money Note 68 (Librettist (USA) 124) [2017 87: 6m 6g^{6} p5g^{6} 5.7f^{3} 5m^{6} 5f^{5} p6g t6.1g^{3} t6.1g 5.7d p6d p5g^{3} p6g^{2} p5g^{2} t6.1g^{4} t5.1g^{2} t5.1g^{5} p6g Dec 12] strong gelding: fairly useful handicapper: third at Bath in May: stays 6f: acts on all-weather and good to firm going: wears headgear: tried in tongue tie: front runner/races prominently. *Milton Bradley* **81**

KYNETON (IRE) 3 b.c. Fastnet Rock (AUS) 127 – Kahyasi Moll (IRE) 35 (Brief Truce (USA) 126) [2017 p12d Feb 15] in blinkers, 10/1, well held in maiden at Kempton. *John Gosden* **–**

KYNREN (IRE) 3 b.g. Clodovil (IRE) 116 – Art of Gold 46 (Excellent Art 125) [2017 t7.1g^{3} 7.8g* 7d* 8s* Sep 19] 25,000Y: lengthy gelding: first foal: dam, maiden (best effort at 1¾m), out of half-sister to smart sprinter Balmont Mast: useful form: won maiden at Carlisle in July, and handicaps at Newmarket (by 1¼ lengths from Inner Circle) in August and Redcar (by 3 lengths from Fashaak) in September: stays 1m: will go on improving. *David Barron* **104 p**

KYSHONI (IRE) 3 ch.f. Casamento (IRE) 118 – Curious Lashes (IRE) (Footstepsinthesand 120) [2017 8.1d 8s^{5} 8.1m^{ro} 8.1m 10.1d^{5} p10g Aug 31] €12,500F, £20,000 2-y-o: workmanlike filly: third foal: half-sister to useful winner up to 1m Shaakis (2-y-o 7f winner, by Dark Angel) and 1m winner Rupert Boy (by Frozen Power): dam unraced half-sister to smart winner up to 1m Close To You: fair form when fifth in maiden at Yarmouth in June, standout effort: usually slowly away/races nearer last than first. *Mike Murphy* **65**

L

LA BACOUETTEUSE (FR) 12 b.g. Miesque's Son (USA) 117 – Toryka (Vettori (IRE) 119) [2017 74: 17.2g 17.1d 16g^{5} t16.3g 17.2s^{4} 16m^{3} 15s^{3} 15.9s 16v^{2} 15.9s 14v t16.3d Dec 16] modest handicapper: stays 17f: acts on soft and good to firm going: wears headgear: sometimes slowly away, usually races nearer last than first: lazy. *Iain Jardine* **64**

LA BELLE MAYSON 2 ch.f. (Apr 11) Mayson 124 – Excellent Show 89 (Exceed And Excel (AUS) 126) [2017 5m^{5} 5d^{3} 6v^{4} 5.1m^{5} Oct 16] 3,500F: workmanlike filly: first foal: dam, winner up to 6f (2-y-o 5f winner), half-sister to useful winner up to 1m Better Built: fair form: best effort at 6f: sold 6,000 gns, sent to France. *Richard Fahey* **65**

LABHAY (IRE) 3 b.f. New Approach (IRE) 132 – Sooraah 111 (Dubawi (IRE) 129) [2017 8f^{6} p8s* p8m Nov 25] first foal: dam 1m winner: fair form: won maiden at Chelmsford (by neck from Verity) in July: raced only at 1m. *William Haggas* **77**

LABREGA 2 b.f. (Mar 23) Cacique (IRE) 124 – Postale (Zamindar (USA) 116) [2017 p7g^{6} Nov 6] 47,000F, 180,000Y: second foal: closely related to 2-y-o 1m winner Star Archer (by Champs Elysees): dam once-raced half-sister to very smart 1m-1½m winner Mutual Trust (by Cacique): 12/1, sixth in maiden at Kempton (1½ lengths behind George Villiers) in November: will improve. *Hugo Palmer* **69 p**

LA CABANA 2 b.f. (Jan 31) Havana Gold (IRE) 118 – Mania (IRE) (Danehill (USA) 126) [2017 t6s t6g 6d^{6} t6.1g^{6} f8.1g Dec 11] small, sparely-made filly: half-sister to numerous winners, including smart 6f winner Domineer (by Shamardal) and 2-y-o 6f winner Nautical Haven (by Harbour Watch): dam unraced: modest maiden: stays 6f: acts on tapeta and good to soft going: sometimes slowly away, often races towards rear. *Richard Fahey* **53**

LACAN (IRE) 6 b.g. New Approach (IRE) 132 – Invincible Isle (IRE) 89 (Invincible Spirit (IRE) 121) [2017 90: t8.6m p8d^{6} t8.6g* p8g p8g 8f 7m 10m 10.1d^{6} p7d p8g p8g^{5} p8g* p8g^{4} Dec 20] well-made gelding: fairly useful performer: won claimer at Wolverhampton in March and handicap at Kempton (by 1¾ lengths from Balgair) in November: left Ralph Beckett after third start: stays 8.5f: acts on polytrack, tapeta and good to firm going: has worn headgear: sometimes slowly away, often races towards rear. *Brett Johnson* **75** **a88**

LA CASA TARIFA (IRE) 3 b.f. Casamento (IRE) 118 – Cool Tarifa (IRE) 80 (One Cool Cat (USA) 123) [2017 80: p7g* 8m* 8.3g^{5} 9.9v 8g^{5} p10s^{rr} 10v t10.2d* Oct 24] stocky filly: fairly useful performer: won handicaps at Chelmsford and Ripon (by length from Devil's Bridge) in April, and claimer at Newcastle (by ½ length from Burcan) in October: stays 1¼m: acts on polytrack, tapeta and good to firm going: temperamental: sold 16,000 gns, sent to Saudi Arabia. *Mark Johnston* **88 §**

LACAZAR (GER) 3 ch.f. Adlerflug (GER) 123 – Laey Diamond (GER) (Dai Jin 123) **112**
[2017 8.4s^3 10.9g* 10.4g* 10.9s* 10.9s* 9.9d Oct 1] second foal: sister to useful German 2-y-o 1m winner Liberry Gold: dam unraced sister to smart German 1m-11f winner Liang Kay: smart performer: progressed well, winning maiden at Krefeld in May, minor event at Cologne in June, Hamburger Stuten-Preis at Hamburg in July and Preis der Diana at Dusseldorf (by ¾ length from Megera) in August: 4 lengths ninth to Rhododendron in Prix de l'Opera at Chantilly final outing: stays 11f: acts on soft going. *P. Schiergen, Germany*

LA CELEBS VILLE (IRE) 4 b.f. Sea The Stars (IRE) 140 – Bryanstown (IRE) 69 **83**
(Galileo (IRE) 134) [2017 78: 8m* 8d* 8f^4 10.2g^5 8.1s^5 7g^5 8.1m Oct 16] close-coupled filly: fairly useful handicapper: won at Haydock in April (by ½ length from Whitkirk) and June (by head from Chosen Character): best at around 1m: acts on firm and soft going: wears cheekpieces: often races prominently: sold 10,000 gns in November. *Tom Dascombe*

LACKADAY 5 gr.g. Kyllachy 129 – Day Creek (Daylami (IRE) 138) [2017 73, a79: t5g^3 **66**
6g 6m^3 5d* 6s^5 6s 6s 5m 5d 5s 6s f5g Dec 4] rather leggy, close-coupled gelding: fair handicapper: won at Catterick in June: stays 6f: acts on all-weather, good to firm and heavy going: wears headgear: often leads. *Noel Wilson*

LAC LEMAN (GER) 6 b.g. Doyen (IRE) 132 – Learned Lady (JPN) (Fuji Kiseki (JPN)) **86**
[2017 –: t16.3g^2 t12.4d* t12.4d^2 t10.2s^3 11.9s^6 11.2v^4 t12.4s^4 t10.2g^6 Jul 29] fairly useful handicapper: won at Newcastle (by short head from High On Light) in February: second at same course in March: stays 16.5f, effective at shorter: acts on tapeta, best turf form on good going: wears hood. *Pauline Robson*

LA CORONEL (USA) 3 b.f. Colonel John (USA) 121 – Listen (USA) (Chester House **115**
(USA) 123) [2017 8.5f^2 8f* 8.5d* 8m^5 9g^4 9f^2 9f* Oct 14] useful-looking filly: half-sister to 3 winners, including 1m-1½m winner General Bunching (by Vindication): dam, US 6f/6.5f winner, closely related to US Grade 2 6f winner Listen Here: smart performer: won Grade 3 Appalachian Stakes at Keeneland in April, Grade 3 Edgewood Stakes at Churchill Downs in May and Queen Elizabeth II Challenge Cup at Keeneland (beat Daddys Lil Darling ½ length) in October: 5¼ lengths fifth to Winter in Coronation Stakes at Royal Ascot: neck second to Uni in Grade 2 Sands Point Stakes at Belmont on penultimate start: stays 9f: acts on firm and good to soft going. *Mark E. Casse, North America*

LADAKHI 3 b.f. Compton Place 125 – Charpoy Cobra 65 (Mark of Esteem (IRE) 137) **64**
[2017 p8g 6.1g^5 p7g Nov 1] smallish filly: first foal: dam maiden (stayed 1m): modest form: best effort when fifth in maiden at Windsor in October. *Rod Millman*

LADIES FIRST 3 b.f. Monsieur Bond (IRE) 120 – Forever Bond (Danetime (IRE) 121) **65**
[2017 t8.6g^3 f6.1g^2 f6.1g^2 p8g Dec 31] sister to 3 winners, including high-class winner up to 6.5f Hoof It (2-y-o 6f winner) and smart 5f/6f (including at 2 yrs) winner Ladies Are Forever, and closely related to 2 winners, including 6f-9.5f winner Chosen Forever (by Choisir): dam unraced: fair form: stays 8.5f. *Michael Easterby*

LA DIVA 2 b.f. (Feb 15) Helmet (AUS) 127 – Craigmill 85 (Slip Anchor 136) [2017 7s^2 7d^4 **80**
8.3d^2 7m^3 Oct 25] 30,000Y: workmanlike filly: closely related to 6f/7f winner Represent (by Exceed And Excel) and half-sister to numerous winners, including smart 1¼m-1½m winner (stays 1¾m) Connecticut (by New Approach) and smart 1m winner Castleton (by Cape Cross): dam 2-y-o 7f winner: fairly useful form: second in minor event at Newmarket in July: stays 7f: sold 32,000 gns, sent to USA. *Roger Varian*

LADOFASH 3 b.g. Canford Cliffs (IRE) 133 – Curras Spirit (Invincible Spirit (IRE) 121) **66**
[2017 70: t7.1g^5 t8d^4 t10.2d^6 t12.2g* f12d^4 t12.2g^6 14g^6 11.6d Sep 6] fair handicapper: won at Wolverhampton in March: left K. R. Burke after seventh start: stays 1½m: acts on tapeta and soft going: wears headgear. *Chris Gordon*

LADURELLI (IRE) 5 b.g. Mastercraftsman (IRE) 129 – Chanter (Lomitas 129) [2017 **83**
90: 10m^5 10.1f 8g^6 Jul 26] sturdy gelding: fairly useful handicapper: stays 11f: acts on polytrack and good to firm going: tried in blinkers/tongue tie. *Paul Cole*

LADWEB 7 ch.g. Bertolini (USA) 125 – Adweb 88 (Muhtarram (USA) 125) [2017 89: 5s^2 **87**
5g 5.2s^5 5v 6d^3 Sep 18] leggy gelding: fairly useful handicapper: second at Thirsk (2 lengths behind Kickboxer) in May: best at 5f: acts on good to firm and heavy going: tried in visor: front runner/races prominently. *John Gallagher*

LADY ALAVESA 2 b.f. (Feb 17) Westlake 100 – Matilda Peace (Namaqualand (USA)) **68**
[2017 5m 5s^2 p6d^5 t6.1g^4 7.4v* t8s^4 7d Sep 30] 2,500Y: angular filly: half-sister to 3 winners, including winner up to 9.5f Poppy Bond (2-y-o 5f winner, by Misu Bond) and 9f winner Swiss Lait (by Milk It Mick): dam unraced half-sister to winner up to 6f Blue Iris and 6f winner Abbajabba (both useful): fair performer: won nursery at Ffos Las in August: fourth in similar event at Newcastle in September: stays 1m: acts on tapeta and heavy going: often races in rear. *Gay Kelleway*

LADY AL THUMAMA 2 gr.f. (Mar 12) Leroidesanimaux (BRZ) 127 – Mrs Micawber 78 (Nayef (USA) 129) [2017 p7g^3 7m^4 p6g^4 Dec 20] 20,000Y: useful-looking filly: first foal: dam, 9.5f winner, half-sister to smart 1¼m-2m winner Watersmeet: fair form: best effort when third in minor event at Kempton (2 lengths behind Augenblick) in October: will stay 1m+: tried in tongue tie. *Charlie Fellowes* **69**

LADY ANJORICA (IRE) 2 ch.f. (Apr 10) Camacho 118 – Adaria 84 (Sleeping Indian 122) [2017 5m^5 5m^2 5g^5 5m 6m^2 5.2v 6d^6 6.1v^4 6g 7.9g 7v* 7d^3 Oct 28] €13,000F, £18,000Y: sturdy filly: third foal: half-sister to 11.5f winner Star The First (by Born To Sea): dam, 1m winner, half-sister to smart 9f/1¼m winner Thattinger: fairly useful performer: won minor event at Catterick (by ¾ length from Lady Willpower) in October: stays 7f: acts on good to firm and heavy going: has worn headgear, including last 2 starts: sometimes slowly away, usually races nearer last than first: sold 25,000 gns, sent to Qatar. *Keith Dalgleish* **82**

LADY AURELIA (USA) 3 b.f. Scat Daddy (USA) 120 – D' Wildcat Speed (USA) (Forest Wildcat (USA) 120) [2017 127: 5.5f* 5f* 5g^2 5f Nov 4] **133**

Another Royal Ascot, another demolition job by the American speedball Lady Aurelia. Her all-the-way seven-length triumph in the 2016 Queen Mary Stakes—the widest margin of victory in the race since the legendary Mumtaz Mahal won by ten lengths in 1923—earned Lady Aurelia the highest Timeform rating achieved by a two-year-old filly for over forty years, putting her at the top of the Timeform juvenile ratings for 2016, ahead of the Ballydoyle colts Caravaggio and Churchill. None of Lady Aurelia's other form came within a stone of her outstanding effort in the Queen Mary—she bled when beaten into third behind Brave Anna and Roly Poly in the Cheveley Park on her other run in Britain—but there was no reason to doubt that she put up a tip-top effort for a juvenile that day at Royal Ascot (her timefigure of 1.08 fast—in line with her form rating of 127—was the fastest recorded by a two-year-old filly since Timeform timefigures were reintroduced in 1975).

If Lady Aurelia's Queen Mary performance was exhilarating, what could be said of her even more memorable Royal Ascot victory in the latest King's Stand Stakes? The firmer terrain (the going had been good to soft for the Queen Mary) played perfectly to her strengths and, ridden a little more circumspectly than in the scorching Queen Mary, Lady Aurelia returned one of the best five-furlong performances by a filly in the history of the *Racehorses* series. Her rating in this Annual puts her on the same mark as two exceptional fillies from over thirty-five years ago, French-trained sprinter-miler Lianga, who was never beaten in a sprint race at three and four, and the brilliant Marwell who won the King's Stand, July Cup and Abbaye as a three-year-old. It is very rare for a filly to make it to the top of the sprinting tree and sprinting has had only two fillies rated more highly than Lianga, Marwell and Lady Aurelia. They are Habibti, who dominated the European sprinting scene as a three-year-old in 1983 and 'The Wonder From Down Under' Black Caviar. Sprinting will be fortunate if another filly as fast as Lady Aurelia comes along in the near future, and it is good news that she remains in training as a four-year-old.

Lady Aurelia made her three-year-old debut at Keeneland in mid-April, setting herself up for another Royal Ascot appearance with a smooth victory in a double-figure field in the Giant's Causeway Stakes, a listed event for fillies and mares in which she was the only three-year-old. She shaped well, ridden with noticeably more restraint than as a two-year-old, her stable apparently having concentrated in her home work on harnessing her raw speed a little more. Breaking in mid-division, Lady Aurelia was produced wide into the home straight and drew clear after leading over a furlong out to win by two and a half lengths from the four-year-old Nobody's Fault. Lady Aurelia's trainer Wesley Ward, a regular visitor to Royal Ascot in recent times (five North American trainers saddled runners at the latest renewal), said that connections were 'excited to get back over to Britain to Ascot, but the ultimate goal is the Breeders' Cup. Five-eighths on the turf at Del Mar should suit her perfect.' Lady Aurelia's victory at Keeneland was her fourth in five career starts but she didn't start favourite for a strong renewal of the King's Stand, that distinction going to another fine filly, the previous year's Prix de l'Abbaye winner Marsha who had put up an even better effort than that when winning the

King's Stand Stakes, Royal Ascot—Lady Aurelia produces one of the best performances seen in the long history of this race as she beats the 2016 winner Profitable (noseband) and Marsha (spots); Lady Aurelia's display is also one of the best from a sprinting filly in the history of the **Racehorses** *series, while the time is only just outside Miss Andretti's course record set in this race in 2007*

Palace House Stakes at Newmarket on her reappearance, conceding weight all round under her Group 1 penalty. Marsha met all those who renewed rivalry with her from the Palace House on better terms in the King's Stand, headed by the second and third at Newmarket, Washington DC (who had also been runner-up to Marsha in the Abbaye) and Goldream (winner of the 2015 King's Stand). Goldream had gone on to finish second in the Temple Stakes at Haydock to another smart sprinting filly in the King's Stand line-up, Priceless, a stablemate of the previous year's King's Stand winner Profitable, who gave trainer Clive Cox a second string to his bow in a seventeen-strong line-up in which there was no shortage of established domestic sprinters with strong form in pattern races. If it lacked anything, the King's Stand field wasn't so cosmopolitan as it has sometimes been in recent times, with only two of the runners trained outside Britain and Ireland, Lady Aurelia and French-trained Signs of Blessing (whose connections had had a row with racecourse officials over rehydration, after his journey to Ascot). The King's Stand has regularly fallen to overseas challengers since Choisir won it (and followed up in the Golden Jubilee) for Australia in 2003, his victory paving the way for what has become a regular flow of Australian sprinters to the Royal meeting (Takeover Target, Miss Andretti and Scenic Blast have followed in Choisir's footsteps by winning the King's Stand which also had a Hong Kong-trained winner Little Bridge in 2012, the last time the race had been won by a sprinter trained outside Britain and Ireland). South African-trained Shea Shea came second in 2013 but the international challenge has gradually become less of a feature of the race. The familiar Australian tilt at Royal Ascot, particularly in the sprint races, was always a point of interest but, for the first time since 2004, the Australians were absent from the Royal meeting altogether.

Lady Aurelia was among a group of Wesley Ward-trained Royal Ascot runners who worked on the course the week before the meeting (the workout was switched from Newmarket where the ground was deemed too firm). The move didn't go down well with some of the home trainers and other individuals who claimed that allowing Ward to use the course gave his runners an unfair advantage. Ascot defended its action, saying that the same courtesy had been extended in previous years to the likes of California Chrome and Animal Kingdom when their connections had requested it, although it was 'not practical to do it for British trainers as there would be too much demand and it would risk the track.' One important change for the Ward team after the Ascot workout was forced by a shoulder injury suffered in a paddock incident at Yarmouth by Frankie Dettori, who had ridden Lady Aurelia in all three of her races in Europe as a two-year-old (she also won the Prix Morny at Deauville). Dettori had been pencilled in to ride nearly all the Ward raiding party at the Royal meeting, but, after the full effects of the injury had become clearer, he had to withdraw from Royal Ascot at the eleventh hour and was in hospital in Cambridge having scans on his injured shoulder on the day Lady Aurelia won the King's Stand Stakes. American jockey John Velasquez, specially booked to ride the Ward-trained Arawak in the Coventry Stakes, the race before the King's Stand, only found out he was riding Lady Aurelia (whom he had partnered at Keeneland) after his plane landed at Heathrow just a few hours before the race.

Velasquez had Lady Aurelia handy from the start in the King's Stand, after she broke well from her high draw, and, edging slightly right from halfway towards the centre of the track, she soon quickened clear when Velasquez let out a little rein. Doing everything under just a hands-and-heels ride, Lady Aurelia kept on strongly inside the final furlong to win, almost certainly with something in hand, by three lengths from Profitable who ran right up to his best but was no match for a spectacular winner. Marsha would have grabbed second in another few strides, finishing a head behind Profitable, while the veterans Muthmir, Take Cover and Alpha Delphini all ran well to complete the first six in a red-hot renewal in which the previous year's runner-up Cotai Glory also ran creditably to finish seventh, ahead of below-form Signs of Blessing who had been sent off third favourite. The winner's time was only just outside Miss Andretti's course record for the decade or so since the Ascot course was redeveloped. The time performance was a good one too, though Lady Aurelia, the first three-year-old to win the King's Stand since 2008, went on to better it in the Nunthorpe at York.

Lady Aurelia wasn't seen out between the King's Stand and the Nunthorpe Stakes at York in August when nine of her ten opponents renewed rivalry from Royal Ascot, headed by the second and third Profitable and Marsha. The tenth opponent was another three-year-old, Battaash, who had won his last three races, impressively accounting for Profitable and Marsha in the King George Stakes at Goodwood in the most recent of them. Reunited with Frankie Dettori, who partnered her in an

Stonestreet Stables LLC and Mr Peter Leidel's "Lady Aurelia"

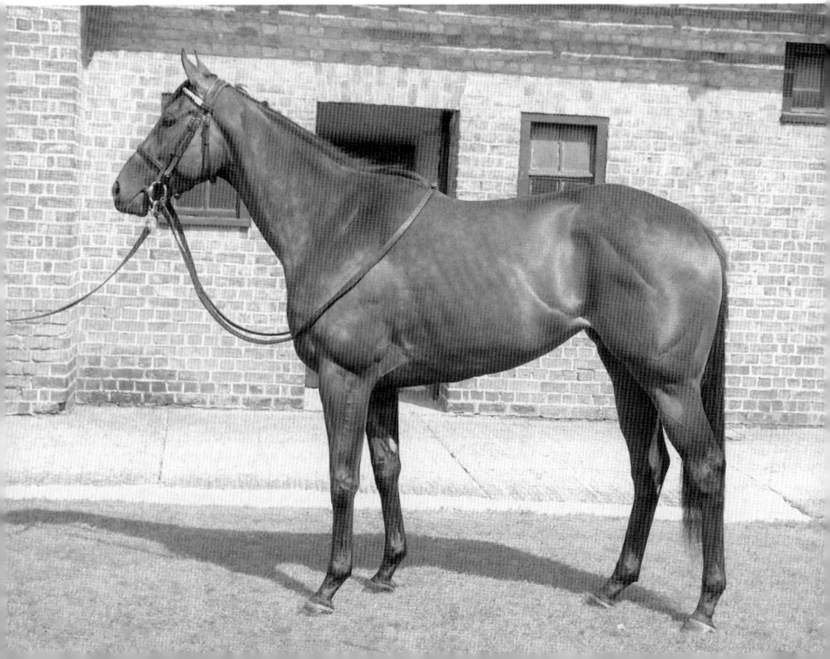

apparently sparkling piece of work at York the week before the race, Lady Aurelia was sent off at a shade of odds on in the Nunthorpe, with Battaash at 11/4 and Profitable and Marsha at 8/1, and 20/1 and upwards the rest. The race was run on good going, though there was still some cut in it after heavy rain earlier in the week, and it produced a memorable head-to-head encounter, though not the expected one between Lady Aurelia and Battaash. The latter got too worked up beforehand to be able to give his true running and faltered inside the final furlong of a race that was run flat out from start to finish. Lady Aurelia made most of the running and was out on her own for much of the race, ending up a little isolated towards the far side of the track as Marsha moved into second and steadily whittled away at the two-length advantage that Lady Aurelia held entering the final furlong. Marsha edged left towards Lady Aurelia as she challenged and the pair passed the post locked together, with Frankie Dettori's obvious jubilation soon proving misplaced. The ITV commentator Richard Hoiles delivered a description that caught the mood—'Lady Aurelia needs the line,' he said as Marsha drew alongside. 'Marsha dives, the Nunthorpe's a head-bob…Frankie punches the air. He's sure! I'm not!' Hoiles was right. The photo-finish showed that Marsha had won by the shortest possible margin, a nose, with third-placed Cotai Glory three and three quarter lengths further back in third, and Battaash only fourth, just ahead of stablemates Priceless and Profitable. Both Marsha and Lady Aurelia produced top-class performances on the day and, although Lady Aurelia didn't quite repeat her King's Stand form, she shaped like clearly the best horse in the race—on the bridle much of the way—until showing unexpected vulnerability to be worn down very late indeed. Judged on time, Lady Aurelia's performance was fractionally ahead of the one in the King's Stand, her timefigure at York of 1.03 fast equivalent to a timerating of 126, which was bettered, among sprinters in the latest season, only by Battaash (1.18 fast) in the King George Stakes and Harry Angel (1.08 fast) in the Sandy Lane Stakes at Haydock in May.

Lady Aurelia and Marsha met for a third time in the Breeders' Cup Turf Sprint at Del Mar in November but both turned in efforts that are best forgotten. There must have been something not quite right with Lady Aurelia in particular for her to fall so short in a race that had always been her principal target. She tracked the very strong pace but couldn't respond when asked for her effort in the home straight, eventually trailing in tenth of twelve behind surprise winner Stormy Liberal. The three European challengers, Marsha (who fared best in sixth), Washington DC and Cotai Glory, all finished ahead of Lady Aurelia.

Lady Aurelia (USA) (b.f. 2014)	Scat Daddy (USA) (b or br 2004)	Johannesburg (b 1999)	Hennessy Myth
		Love Style (ch 1999)	Mr Prospector Likeable Style
	D' Wildcat Speed (USA) (ch 2000)	Forest Wildcat (b or br 1991)	Storm Cat Victoria Beauty
		Velvet Panther (gr 1991)	Pentaquod Blue Eyed Cat

The good-quartered Lady Aurelia, who is on the small side, did not grow much from two to three but she clearly lost none of her speed and there is every reason to hope she will reproduce her best if she is returned to Royal Ascot as a four-year-old (presumably to try for a repeat in the King's Stand which is also likely to be the target for Battaash—and possibly for Harry Angel too). If Royal Ascot has proved the perfect stage for Lady Aurelia so far, the same can be said for her American sire Scat Daddy whose sudden death at the age of eleven in December 2015 was a blow (his demise came not long after an announcement that his fee had been raised from 35,000 dollars to 100,000 dollars). Scat Daddy, who himself was raced on dirt, had no fewer than four winners at the Royal meeting in the latest season, headed by Lady Aurelia and the Commonwealth Cup winner Caravaggio, the same pair who had pulled off the Coventry/Queen Mary double the previous year. Lady Aurelia's dam and grandam, D'Wildcat Speed and Velvet Panther, both raced with distinction on the Caribbean island of Puerto Rico, D'Wildcat Speed, who won sixteen races there, including fourteen in a row, being Horse of the Year in 2003 before going on to win the Rampart Handicap over nine furlongs at Gulfstream Park as a five-year-old after being transferred to the United States. Seeing that Scat

Daddy also stayed nine furlongs, winning the Florida Derby over that trip, if could be said that Lady Aurelia was bred to stay at least a mile. Of D'Wildcat Speed's first two winners before Lady Aurelia, Distorsionada (by Distorted Humor) was a sprinter and Titletown Five (by Tiznow) won at seven furlongs as a two-year-old. D'Wildcat Speed is now also dam of a fourth winner, the four-year-old filly Sudden Fame (by Congrats), who is also a sprinter. Lady Aurelia has won at six furlongs but she is all speed and five is clearly her trip. She acts on firm going and good to soft on turf, as well as on polytrack. She was blinkered as a two-year-old but didn't wear headgear at three. A strong traveller, she usually races prominently or makes the running. *Wesley A. Ward, USA*

LADY BACCHUS 4 b.f. Compton Place 125 – Beauty (IRE) 74 (Alzao (USA) 117) [2017 63: t5.1m* t5d t5.1g^4 t5g^6 p5g^3 t6g Mar 25] modest handicapper: won at Wolverhampton in January: stays 6f: acts on polytrack and tapeta: wears headgear: often races towards rear. *Richard Guest* **64**

LADY BAYSIDE 9 ch.m. Ishiguru (USA) 114 – Seldemosa 67 (Selkirk (USA) 129) [2017 75: 8.1d Jun 6] fair handicapper: well held only start in 2017: stays 1¼m: acts on polytrack, tapeta, soft and good to firm going: has worn headgear. *Malcolm Saunders* **–**

LADY BERGAMOT (FR) 3 gr.f. Mastercraftsman (IRE) 129 – Mahima (FR) (Linamix (FR) 127) [2017 68p: 10g t10.2s* 10g* 10.3g^3 12m* 12d^3 Sep 23] lengthy filly: fairly useful performer: won maiden at Newcastle in June, and handicaps at Leicester in July and Goodwood (by head from White Chocolate) in August: should stay 1¾m: acts on tapeta, good to firm and good to soft going: front runner/races prominently. *James Fanshawe* **86**

LADY BUTTONS 7 b.m. Beneficial 117 – Lady Chapp (IRE) (High Chaparral (IRE) 132) [2017 14.2s^6 Sep 15] useful hurdler/chaser: 33/1, well held in minor event at Salisbury. *Philip Kirby* **–**

LADYCAMMYOFCLARE (IRE) 2 b.f. (Apr 13) Camacho 118 – County Clare 77 (Barathea (IRE) 127) [2017 5.7f^5 6m 6s 7.2m 7.2m^4 t7.1g^6 8g^6 p8g^4 p8g Nov 7] second foal: half-sister to 2-y-o 1m winner Step Dancer (by Footstepsinthesand): dam maiden: modest maiden: stays 1m: acts on polytrack and good to firm going: usually races prominently: sold £2,000, sent to Italy. *Mark Johnston* **50**

LADY CARDUROS (IRE) 3 b.f. Byron 117 – Saranjo (IRE) 68 (Carrowkeel (IRE) 106) [2017 p7g f7.1g f8.1g Nov 28] first foal: dam 11f/1½m winner: no form in maidens. *Neil Mulholland* **–**

LADY CASHMERE (IRE) 2 b.f. (May 10) Lord Shanakill (USA) 121 – Erreur (IRE) 84 (Desert King (IRE) 129) [2017 6g t6d 8.3s t7.1g Sep 12] fifth foal: half-sister to smart winner up to 1m Hillbilly Boy (2-y-o 6f winner, by Haafhd): dam 6f winner: no form: tried in visor. *Alistair Whillans* **–**

LADY CLITICO (IRE) 6 b.m. Bushranger (IRE) 119 – Villa Nova (IRE) 55 (Petardia 113) [2017 74: t10.2g^5 t12.2g 12g^5 15.9m* 14m^4 t16.3g t16.3d Dec 16] fair handicapper: won at Catterick in May: stays 16.5f: acts on tapeta, good to firm and heavy going: has worn cheekpieces, including in 2017. *Rebecca Menzies* **72**

LADY CRISTAL (IRE) 3 b.f. Footstepsinthesand 120 – Scarborough Lily 70 (Dansili 127) [2017 74: t5g^4 t6d* t5d^3 t6g^6 p6g^2 5.7f^4 5m* 5g t5g^4 5d t5g t5d t6.1g^2 p6g^4 Dec 20] fair performer: won maiden at Newcastle in February and handicap at Musselburgh in May: stays 6f: acts on polytrack, tapeta and firm going: wears cheekpieces: front runner/races prominently. *K. R. Burke* **77**

LADY DANCEALOT (IRE) 2 b.f. (Apr 25) Sir Prancealot (IRE) 111 – Mayorstone (IRE) (Exceed And Excel (AUS) 126) [2017 6g^3 6v 6s^2 p5g^4 6s* Oct 15] €11,000F, €30,000Y: good-topped filly: first foal: dam twice-raced half-sister to smart 2-y-o 5f winner Light The Rocket: fair performer: won minor event at Goodwood in October: stays 6f: acts on soft going: usually travels strongly. *David Elsworth* **76**

LADY EMMA 4 b.f. Mount Nelson 125 – Songbook (Singspiel (IRE) 133) [2017 –: p14g t16.5g Aug 11] little form: sometimes in headgear. *Steph Hollinshead* **–**

LADY ENSIGN 2 ch.f. (Mar 25) Captain Gerrard (IRE) 113 – Ensign's Trick 72 (Cayman Kai (IRE) 114) [2017 6m 5.1d t6.1g Aug 11] third foal: dam unreliable 6f winner (including at 2 yrs): well held in sellers/minor event. *Mark Brisbourne* **–**

LADY FREYJA 3 b.f. Mayson 124 – Third Party 63 (Terimon 124) [2017 58: 8m^3 7g* 8m 8m 7d Nov 4] fairly useful performer: won maiden at Newmarket (by 7 lengths from Alouja) in June: stays 1m: acts on good to firm going: usually races close up. *John Ryan* **84**

LADY GODIVA (IRE) 2 b.f. (Feb 8) Camelot 128 – For Evva Silca 60 (Piccolo 121) [2017 7d 6d^6 6s^4 7s 6d^4 Oct 24] €80,000Y: useful-looking filly: half-sister to several winners, including smart winner up to 7f Warsaw (2-y-o 5f/6f winner, by Danehill Dancer): dam maiden (stayed 6f): fair maiden: stays 6f: acts on soft going. *Richard Hannon* **71**

LADY GRAND 2 ch.f. (May 12) Poet's Voice 126 – Lady Gorgeous 105 (Compton Place 125) [2017 6g 5d 5d Aug 5] 40,000Y: second foal: dam, 2-y-o 6f winner, half-sister to useful 2-y-o 1m winner Kartica: well held in minor events: tried in hood. *Richard Fahey* **–**

LADY GRIGIO (IRE) 2 ro.f. (Apr 27) Casamento (IRE) 118 – Park Approach (IRE) 77 (Indian Ridge 123) [2017 t8g Dec 6] half-sister to ungenuine winner up to 7f Tasmeem (2-y-o 6f winner, by Acclamation) and winner up to 6f Musical Molly (2-y-o 5f winner, by Mastercraftsman): dam maiden half-sister to useful 1m winner Poetical: 50/1, well held in maiden at Newcastle. *Iain Jardine* **–**

LADY GWHINNYVERE (IRE) 3 b.f. Sir Prancealot (IRE) 111 – Johar Jamal (IRE) 84 (Chevalier (IRE) 115) [2017 –: 7.4g^3 8s 7d Sep 18] modest maiden: best effort at 7.5f. *John Spearing* **50**

LADY HESTER (USA) 3 b.f. Bernardini (USA) 132 – Questing 127 (Hard Spun (USA) 124) [2017 54: t7.1g^3 t8g^4 p10d^2 Mar 30] fair maiden: stays 1¼m: acts on polytrack and tapeta: sold 22,000 gns in July, sent to USA. *John Gosden* **74**

LADY IN QUESTION (IRE) 3 b.f. Elzaam (AUS) 115 – Black Meyeden (FR) 45 (Black Minnaloushe (USA) 123) [2017 87: 7v^5 7.2s^4 6d^3 7m^4 7.6d^5 7.2g^2 7d^2 6.9d* t7.1s^3 p7g^3 7v^2 7d^4 Nov 11] rather leggy filly: fairly useful handicapper: won at Carlisle (by neck from Reinforced) in August: second at Catterick in October: stays 7f: acts on polytrack, tapeta, good to firm and heavy going: tried in cheekpieces. *Richard Fahey* **85**

LADY ISLE 2 b.f. (Mar 22) Monsieur Bond (IRE) 120 – Ailsa Craig (IRE) 85 (Chevalier (IRE) 115) [2017 7s 7.4g Aug 16] first foal: dam 1m-1½m winner: well held in minor events. *Grant Tuer* **–**

LADY JAYNE (IRE) 2 b.f. (Apr 26) Henrythenavigator (USA) 131 – Stellavera (FR) (Anabaa (USA) 130) [2017 6m 7g 7d t7.1g^3 p7g^5 Dec 6] unfurnished filly: second foal: half-sister to 2m winner St Andrews (by Rip Van Winkle): dam unraced half-sister to useful winner up to 1½m Peligroso: poor maiden: best effort at 7f: acts on tapeta. *Ian Williams* **46**

LADY JOANNA VASSA (IRE) 4 ch.f. Equiano (FR) 127 – Lady Natilda 64 (First Trump 118) [2017 65: 5m t5s 5d^3 5g^5 5.5f 5m^6 5.9g t5g^6 5v^2 5s^2 5d^3 5g^3 5s^4 5m t5.1g 5s* 5s^3 5s^2 p5g* t5.1m t5g^4 Nov 3] modest handicapper: won at Musselburgh (apprentice) and Kempton in October: stays 6f: acts on polytrack, tapeta, good to firm and heavy going: wears headgear: tried in tongue tie: front runner/races prominently. *Richard Guest* **58**

LADY KAVIAR (IRE) 3 b.f. Lope de Vega (IRE) 125 – Maoin Dor (IRE) (Manduro (GER) 135) [2017 62: 8s 10.1m 9.9g p8g* p7g Oct 25] fair performer: won minor event at Kempton in October: stays 1m: acts on polytrack: often races prominently. *George Margarson* **67**

LADY LINTERA (IRE) 2 b.f. (Mar 14) Lilbourne Lad (IRE) 111 – Lintera (GER) (Night Shift (USA)) [2017 5m 5m 5d^4 6g 6m^5 5.1s 5s^4 5s^6 t6.1g^2 t5g^3 t6.1g^4 f6.1g^3 Dec 19] €5,500Y: third foal: half-sister to 1¼m winner Lintisham (by Shamdinan): dam 5f/6f winner: modest maiden: stays 6f: acts on fibresand, tapeta, soft and good to firm going: wears headgear. *Ann Duffield* **54**

LADY LUNCHALOT (USA) 7 b.m. More Than Ready (USA) 120 – Betty Johanne (USA) (Johannesburg (USA) 127) [2017 74d: p11d 12v^2 Jun 10] angular mare: fair handicapper: stayed 1½m: acted on polytrack, good to firm and heavy going: usually wore cheekpieces: sometimes slowly away, often raced towards rear: dead. *Polly Gundry* **65**

LADY LYDIA (IRE) 6 b.m. Kheleyf (USA) 116 – Piece Unique (Barathea (IRE) 127) [2017 86: f7g p8d^5 t8.6g^6 p6d^5 t7.1g* t7.1g p7g 7m 8g^4 t8.6g 8g^6 p7g p8g p7s p7g Dec 20] fair handicapper on turf, fairly useful on all-weather: won at Wolverhampton (by length from East Coast Lady) in March: trained mostly in 2017 by Gay Kelleway: stays 1m: acts on polytrack, tapeta, soft and good to firm going: often wears headgear/tongue tie: sometimes finds little. *Hugo Froud* **72** **a84**

LADY MACAPA 4 b.f. Equiano (FR) 127 – Brazilian Style 67 (Exit To Nowhere (USA) 122) [2017 107: 5.2g^3 6.1g 6s^3 5d* Sep 10] useful-looking filly: smart performer: won Prix du Petit Couvert at Chantilly (by neck from Gold Vibe) in September: third earlier at Newbury in handicap and Hackwood Stakes (3 lengths behind Magical Memory): stays 6f: acts on soft and good to firm going: has worn hood: usually leads: sold 170,000 gns in December. *Clive Cox* **110**

LADY MACHA 3 b.f. Mount Nelson 125 – Lady Francesca 98 (Montjeu (IRE) 137) [2017 p10s p12g^5 p12s^2 p12d^5 Aug 23] good-topped filly: second foal: dam, 8.6f winner, half-sister to smart winner up to 1m (stayed 1¼m) Purr Along: fair form: stays 1½m. *Marco Botti* **76**

LADY MAKFI (IRE) 5 b.m. Makfi 130 – Dulcet Tones (IRE) (Singspiel (IRE) 133) [2017 86: t16.5g t16.5g^4 16d^6 t16.5g^2 p13g Nov 2] sturdy mare: fair handicapper: stays 16.5f: acts on polytrack and tapeta: usually races nearer last than first. *Johnny Farrelly* **79**

LADY MALDIVA (IRE) 2 b.f. (Mar 14) Thewayyouare (USA) 117 – Rapid Review (IRE) (Observatory (USA) 131) [2017 7d 7d^5 7g Aug 17] €1,800F, €2,200Y: compact filly: first foal: dam unraced: well beaten in maidens/minor event: tried in cheekpieces/tongue tie. *Jose Santos* **–**

LADY MARIGOLD (IRE) 2 b.f. (Mar 23) Intense Focus (USA) 117 – Peace Lily 69 (Dansili 127) [2017 5m^6 6.1g^6 7g^4 5.7s* Oct 2] sixth foal: half-sister to 7f-1m winner Golden Wedding (by Archipenko): dam, 7f winner, half-sister to useful winner up to 6f Bannister: fair form: won minor event at Bath in October: stays 7f. *Eve Johnson Houghton* **77**

LADY MARITIME (IRE) 3 b.f. Delegator 125 – No Song (Zamindar (USA) 116) [2017 p8g p10g^3 p12g Apr 20] 9,000F, £9,000Y: first foal: dam unraced half-sister to Derby third/St Leger runner-up Romsdal: modest form: best effort when third in maiden at Lingfield in March. *Brett Johnson* **55**

LADY MOLLY (IRE) 3 b.f. Kodiac 112 – Beth 79 (Deportivo 116) [2017 65: f5g^6 5g^6 6m^6 7.2g 5.5f^6 5s 7.2d^6 8.9m 5s^2 t5d 5s^6 5s Oct 9] modest maiden: best form at 5f: acts on firm and soft going: has worn headgear, including last 4 starts: front runner/races prominently. *Keith Dalgleish* **55**

LADY MOMOKA (IRE) 2 b.f. (May 4) Shamardal (USA) 129 – Juno Marlowe (IRE) 100 (Danehill (USA) 126) [2017 7d^6 Jul 28] €470,000Y: compact, attractive filly: half-sister to numerous winners, 3 smart, including 1½m-1¾m winner Stellar Mass (by Sea The Stars) and 1m-11f winner Marzelline (by Barathea): dam 7f winner (including at 2 yrs): 8/1, sixth in minor event at Ascot (4½ lengths behind Jousi) in July: should improve. *Roger Varian* **69 p**

LADY MOREL (IRE) 3 b.f. Arcano (IRE) 122 – Heart's Desire (IRE) 79 (Royal Applause 124) [2017 65: p8g^4 t7.1g p7s^5 8g 7m^2 7d^4 6s* 7d^5 p8s Nov 23] modest handicapper: won at Brighton in September: stays 1m, effective over shorter: acts on polytrack, soft and good to firm going: tried in blinkers. *Joseph Tuite* **64**

LADY NAHEMA (IRE) 4 b.f. Zoffany (IRE) 121 – Jamary (IRE) (Grand Reward (USA) 112) [2017 68: 10s p8g 10.1g p10g^6 Aug 31] modest maiden handicapper: stays 1¼m: acts on polytrack and good to firm going. *Martin Bosley* **52**

LADY NATASHA (IRE) 4 b.f. Alfred Nobel (IRE) 110 – Hot To Rock (IRE) (Kalanisi (IRE) 132) [2017 68: 14.5s^2 13.1s^3 13.1s^5 14d^5 11.6g^5 14.1v Sep 13] plain, sparely-made filly: fair maiden handicapper: stays 14.5f: acts on soft going. *K. R. Burke* **66**

LADY NAYEF 4 b.f. Nayef (USA) 129 – Luck Will Come (IRE) 82 (Desert Style (IRE) 121) [2017 74, a82: f5g* p5g* f5g^4 f5g^3 f5m^3 f5g^5 Mar 9] rather leggy filly: fairly useful handicapper: won at Southwell (by 1¼ lengths from Piazon) and Lingfield (apprentice, by ¾ length from Temple Road) in January: has won at 6f, races mainly at 5f: acts on all-weather, good to firm and heavy going: tried in visor: wears tongue tie: front runner/races prominently. *John Butler* **87**

LADY NOORAH 2 ch.f. (Feb 10) Nathaniel (IRE) 129 – Vital Statistics 102 (Indian Ridge 123) [2017 p8g^6 t7.2g^2 Dec 5] fifth foal: half-sister to useful winner up to 7f Ashaadd (2-y-o 6f winner, by Dansili): dam 2-y-o 6f winner: fair form: better effort when second in minor event at Wolverhampton (neck behind American Endeavour) in December: open to further improvement. *Richard Fahey* **71 p**

LADY OF ARAN (IRE) 2 b.f. (Mar 13) Sir Prancealot (IRE) 111 – Tipperary Boutique (IRE) 86 (Danehill Dancer (IRE) 117) [2017 7d^4 7.6d^2 p7g* p7g^2 Nov 8] €24,000Y: fourth foal: half-sister to winner abroad by Footstepsinthesand: dam, 2-y-o 7f winner, half-sister to useful winner up to 1¼m (stayed 12.5f) Leitmotiv: fairly useful form: won minor event at Kempton in October: second in nursery at same course final start: stays 7.5f. *Charlie Fellowes* **83**

LADY OF AUTHORITY 2 b.f. (Mar 6) Kheleyf (USA) 116 – Miss Authority (Authorized (IRE) 133) [2017 6.1m p6d p6g t7.2g^3 p7g^4 Dec 28] 1,300F: compact filly: first foal: dam unraced: modest maiden: stays 7f: acts on polytrack and tapeta. *Murty McGrath* **63**

LADY OF PETRA 2 b.f. (May 13) Compton Place 125 – Aqaba 65 (Lake Coniston (IRE) 131) [2017 6v^3 p7s 7g^5 p6g Oct 5] half-sister to 5.3f/6f winner Amazing Win (by Marju) and useful 7f winner Secret Talent (by Sakhee's Secret): dam maiden half-sister to stayer Alcazar and French miler Lady of Chad (both smart): modest form: stays 7f. *Eve Johnson Houghton* **60**

LADY OF SHALOTT 2 b.f. (Feb 1) Camelot 128 – Silent Act (USA) 86 (Theatrical) [2017 8d* Oct 24] 80,000Y: third foal: half-sister to 1¼m winner Harold Lloyd (by Cape Cross): dam, 11.5f/1½m winner, sister to US Grade 3 9f winner Roman Dynasty: 12/1, won minor event at Yarmouth (by 2¾ lengths from Come With Me) on debut: bred to be suited by 1¼m+: sure to go on to better things. *David Simcock* **81 p**

LADY OF STEEL 3 b.f. Sir Percy 129 – Steel Free (IRE) 81 (Danehill Dancer (IRE) 117) [2017 p8g p8d p12g p12g p12g Dec 6] second foal: half-sister to 1¼m-11f winner Tommys Geal (by Halling): dam, 7f winner who stayed 9f, half-sister to useful 1¼m winner System Overload: modest maiden: stays 1½m: acts on polytrack. *John Butler* **58**

LADY OF THE COURT (IRE) 2 b.f. (Jan 11) Camelot 128 – Caserta (Dansili 127) [2017 6g 7g 8g^6 Aug 9] neat filly: first foal: dam, useful French 1m-9.5f winner, out of smart French 1½m winner Daring Miss: fair form: seemingly best effort when ninth in listed race at Deauville (6 lengths behind Izzy Bizu) on second start: should stay 1m: tried in cheekpieces. *J. S. Moore* **74 ?**

LADY OF THE LAMP (IRE) 3 b.f. Invincible Spirit (IRE) 121 – Lady Angola (USA) 83 (Lord At War (ARG)) [2017 6g t5s^2 t5g* t6g* t6d* Nov 10] half-sister to several winners, including smart 1m winner Duntle (by Danehill Dancer) and useful 9f-1½m winner Edmaaj (by Intikhab): dam 1½m winner: fair performer: won last 3 starts, all at Newcastle, maiden in September and handicaps in November: stays 6f: acts on tapeta. *Rae Guest* **80**

LADY OF YORK 3 b.f. Sir Percy 129 – Parsonagehotelyork (IRE) 62 (Danehill (USA) 126) [2017 –: 9.9g^5 p12g^3 11.6d* 9.9d^4 p12d^5 Aug 16] sturdy filly: modest handicapper: won at Lingfield in June: stays 1½m: acts on polytrack and good to soft going: tried in hood. *Alan Bailey* **58**

LADY OF YUE 7 b.m. Manduro (GER) 135 – Desert Royalty (IRE) 96 (Alhaarth (IRE) 126) [2017 72: p15.8m^6 11.8d^5 18v Oct 9] sturdy mare: fair handicapper: below best in 2017: stays 2m: acts on polytrack and any turf going: in cheekpieces last 4 starts: often races prominently. *Eugene Stanford* **63**

LADY PARKER (IRE) 3 gr.f. Zebedee 113 – Westering Home (IRE) 71 (Mull of Kintyre (USA) 114) [2017 –: t7.1g p10g p12m^4 Mar 29] poor maiden: stays 1½m: acts on polytrack and tapeta: tried in cheekpieces. *J. S. Moore* **46**

LADY PERIGNON 4 b.f. Poet's Voice 126 – Amallna (Green Desert (USA) 127) [2017 87: 8.1g 9.9v 8g 8.5g* 8g^4 f7.1g^3 p8m^4 Nov 25] big, workmanlike filly: fairly useful handicapper: won at Epsom (by ½ length from Masarzain) in September: stays 8.5f: acts on polytrack, fibresand and good to firm going: usually leads. *Andrew Balding* **84**

LADY PRIMA 3 b.f. Sir Percy 129 – Alla Prima (IRE) (In The Wings 128) [2017 p7g 7s^6 8.3v 10m p16g p13.3d Sep 28] half-sister to several winners, including winner up to 10.4f All Annalena (2-y-o 1m winner, by Dubai Destination) and winner up to 1¾m Winner's Wish (2-y-o 1¼m winner, by Clodovil): dam maiden: modest form: often races prominently/ freely. *Mike Murphy* **52**

LADY ROCKA 4 ch.f. Rock of Gibraltar (IRE) 133 – Tap Dance Way (IRE) 77 (Azamour (IRE) 130) [2017 65: t12.2g^{pu} 11.7f Apr 21] leggy filly: modest handicapper at best: stays 1¼m: acts on good to firm and good to soft going: in headgear last 5 starts. *Anabel K. Murphy* **–**

LADY ROWENA 3 ch.f. Sepoy (AUS) 129 – Miss Ivanhoe (IRE) 107 (Selkirk (USA) 129) [2017 –: p10g Jan 19] no form. *Mark Johnston* **–**

LADY SANDY (IRE) 2 ch.f. (Apr 27) Dandy Man (IRE) 123 – Surf's Up (IRE) 58 (Encosta de Lago (AUS)) [2017 6d 5d^5 5g 5.9v 6g^6 t7.1g f6.1g^4 Dec 19] €12,000F, £17,000Y, £40,000 2-y-o: first foal: dam, maiden (stayed 1¾m), half-sister to high-class Hong Kong sprinter Peniaphobia (by Dandy Man): modest maiden: stays 6f: acts on fibresand and good to soft going. *David Barron* **55**

LADY SOPHIEBELLA 2 b.f. (Mar 30) Monsieur Bond (IRE) 120 – Lady Paris (IRE) 96 (Invincible Spirit (IRE) 121) [2017 6v 6d t6.1g^6 f6.1g^3 Dec 21] third foal: dam, 6f winner (including at 2 yrs), half-sister to useful 7f winner Lukrecia: modest form: raced only at 6f. *Bryan Smart* **59**

LADY SUNDEW (IRE) 4 b.f. Roderic O'Connor (IRE) 119 – Dawaama (IRE) (Dansili 127) [2017 t8g t8g Nov 15] €10,000F, €3,500Y: first foal: dam unraced half-sister to smart 5.5f-1m winner Baqah: well beaten in maidens. *Iain Jardine* **–**

LADY TURPIN (IRE) 4 gr.f. Arakan (USA) 123 – Proficiency 68 (El Prado (IRE) 119) [2017 61: t12.4g^{3} f12g* t12.2g^{4} 12s^{4} Jun 5] fair handicapper: won at Southwell (apprentice) in March: stays 1½m: acts on fibresand, soft and good to firm going. *Richard Fahey* **65**

LADY VALDEAN 3 ch.f. Helmet (AUS) 127 – Symphonic Dancer (USA) 73 (Smart Strike (CAN) 121) [2017 73: 10.4d^{2} 10.4d^{3} 11.6d^{6} 11.9g* 9.9s 10d 11.9d^{2} p12.4g^{6} Nov 27] fairly useful performer: won maiden at Clairefontaine in August: stays 1½m: acts on good to firm and good to soft going: in hood last 3 starts: usually leads. *Jose Santos* **82**

LADY VOLANTE (IRE) 3 b.f. Teofilo (IRE) 126 – Empress of Rome (IRE) 53 (Holy Roman Emperor (IRE) 125) [2017 70: t8.6m^{5} f6s^{6} f7g t7.1g^{2} t7.1g t7.1g^{5} t7.1g 6g^{5} p7g^{3} 7.1m^{3} 8g t7.1d 10g^{6} 11.5g Oct 16] modest maiden: left David Evans after ninth start, Lucinda Egerton after tenth: stays 1m: acts on tapeta, soft and good to firm going: has worn headgear. *Rebecca Menzies* **61**

LADY WILLPOWER 2 b.f. (Mar 8) Multiplex 114 – Gagajulu 75 (Al Hareb (USA) 123) [2017 6d 6.1g^{4} 7d^{5} 7v^{2} 6d^{2} 6d^{2} p6s* Dec 1] compact filly: sister to useful winner up to 7f Radio Gaga (2-y-o 6f winner) and half-sister to several winners, including useful winner up to 1m Ardbrae Lady (2-y-o 7f winner, by Overbury) and smart winner up to 1m Obe Gold (2-y-o 5f/6f winner, by Namaqualand): dam 2-y-o 5f winner: fair performer: won minor event at Chelmsford in December: stays 7f: acts on polytrack and heavy going: front runner/races prominently. *John Quinn* **74**

LA ESTRELLA (USA) 14 b.g. Theatrical – Princess Ellen 114 (Tirol 127) [2017 f16g^{5} f14g^{6} Mar 15] lengthy, useful-looking gelding: fairly useful performer: won 27 times on all-weather, 16 of them at Southwell: below form both starts in 2017 after long absence: stays 2½m: acts on all-weather and good to firm going: has worn headgear. *Don Cantillon* **70**

LA FIGLIA (IRE) 3 ch.f. Frankel 147 – Finsceal Beo (IRE) 123 (Mr Greeley (USA) 122) [2017 p6g^{2} 8d^{4} Sep 29] €1,800,000F: fifth foal: closely related to useful 1¼m winner (stayed 1½m) An Cailin Orga (by Galileo) and half-sister to 1¼m winner Too The Stars (by Sea The Stars) and smart 2-y-o 1m winner (stays 1½m) Ol' Man River (by Montjeu): dam, 6f-1m winner (including at 2 yrs, and 1000 Guineas), stayed 10.5f: useful form: better effort when fourth in listed race at Newmarket (1¼ lengths behind Muffri'ha) in September: open to further improvement. *Jeremy Noseda* **101 p**

LA FORTUNA 4 b.f. Zamindar (USA) 116 – Hyperspace 69 (Dansili 127) [2017 56: p6d t6.1g t6.1g p6s^{6} p6g^{5} Dec 21] modest maiden: stays 6f: acts on polytrack and fibresand: tried in tongue tie. *Charlie Wallis* **54**

LA FRITILLAIRE 5 b.m. Champs Elysees 124 – Generous Diana 90 (Generous (IRE) 139) [2017 68: 21.6m^{6} 16m* 17.2g^{3} 18g^{2} 16.1f^{4} 17.1g^{6} 16g^{3} 17.1v* 18v^{3} 18v^{3} Oct 23] fairly useful handicapper: won at Ripon in May and Pontefract in September: third in minor event at latter course final start: stays 2¼m: acts on polytrack, good to firm and heavy going: in cheekpieces last 3 starts: front runner/races prominently. *James Given* **86**

LAGANORE (IRE) 5 b.m. Fastnet Rock (AUS) 127 – Lady Bones (IRE) (Royal Applause 124) [2017 113: 9.5s^{3} 10g^{2} 10s^{2} 10g^{5} 9m^{3} 9.5s* 9.9m* Oct 29] strong mare: smart performer: won Denny Cordell Lavarack & Lanwades Stud Fillies Stakes at Gowran (by 2 lengths from I'm So Fancy) in September and Premio Lydia Tesio at Rome (by same margin from A Raving Beauty) in October: stays 1¼m: acts on good to firm and heavy going: sometimes slowly away, often travels strongly. *A. J. Martin, Ireland* **114**

L'AGE D'OR 2 b.f. (Apr 18) Iffraaj 127 – Goleta (IRE) (Royal Applause 124) [2017 t6.1g Nov 18] sixth foal: sister to smart winner up to 6.5f Dibajj and half-sister to 2 winners, including useful winner up to 10.5f Black Sea (2-y-o 1m winner, by Dubai Destination): dam twice-raced half-sister to very smart 5f/6f winner Chineur: 33/1, 7¾ lengths eighth of 11 in minor event at Wolverhampton. *Robert Cowell* **53**

LAGENDA 4 b.g. Dick Turpin (IRE) 127 – Whirly Dancer 93 (Danehill Dancer (IRE) 117) [2017 94: 6g 7g^{4} 7m^{3} 8m^{6} 7.8s 7g^{6} 7g^{2} 7d^{4} 7g p8s^{3} t7.2g^{3} p8s^{2} Dec 17] smallish gelding: fairly useful handicapper: third at Chester in May: left Kevin Ryan after ninth start: stays 1m: acts on polytrack, tapeta, soft and good to firm going: wears headgear. *Kristin Stubbs* **89**

LAGERTHA (IRE) 3 b.f. Oasis Dream 129 – Tafiya 83 (Bahri (USA) 125) [2017 –: 12s^{6} 9.9f 8d Jul 11] little form: tried in cheekpieces. *Hugo Palmer* **–**

LAGOPUS 4 b.f. Shirocco (GER) 129 – Pelagia (IRE) 77 (Lycius (USA) 124) [2017 p12g^5 11.6d p10s 11.5s Jul 6] 45,000Y: sixth foal: half-sister to 3 winners, including useful/temperamental winner up to 8.3f Upper Hand (2-y-o 6f winner, by Mark of Esteem) and winner up to 8.3f Dutiful (2-y-o 7f winner, by Dubawi): dam maiden half-sister to smart stayer Alcazar and Prix Marcel Boussac winner Lady of Chad: well held in maidens/handicap. *David Simcock* **–**

LAGOSTOVEGAS (IRE) 5 b.m. Footstepsinthesand 120 – Reine de Coeur (IRE) 68 (Montjeu (IRE) 137) [2017 81: 17d* 16.8v^3 18m^3 12s^2 Nov 5] useful performer: won handicap at Killarney (by 4¼ lengths from Shinghari) in July: second in listed race at Naas (3 lengths behind Tocco d'Amore) in November: stays 2¼m: acts on good to firm and heavy going: smart hurdler. *W. P. Mullins, Ireland* **101**

LA GOULUE 3 ch.f. Kheleyf (USA) 116 – Quotation 100 (Medicean 128) [2017 p8g^5 8.3g 8g t7.2g p10s t9.5g^6 t8.6g^4 t12.2d p12g^4 Dec 28] fourth foal: dam 1m winner: modest maiden: stays 1½m: acts on polytrack and tapeta: wears headgear: sometimes slowly away. *John Gallagher* **51**

LA GUAPITA 3 ch.f. Bahamian Bounty 116 – Somersault 69 (Pivotal 124) [2017 74p: p7g^2 p7g t6m^4 7.1s^4 Jun 10] fair maiden: left Hugo Palmer after third start: best effort at 7f: acts on tapeta: tried in hood: sold 3,500 gns in July, sent to Italy. *Andrew Balding* **69**

LAHARNA (IRE) 2 b.f. (Feb 24) Epaulette (AUS) 126 – Maughami 63 (Manduro (GER) 135) [2017 6g 6d t7.1d Nov 10] €12,000Y, €16,000 2-y-o: first foal: dam, maiden (stayed 1¼m), half-sister to winner up to 10.5f Distant Way and 1¼m winner Way To Paris (both smart): well beaten in minor events. *Noel Wilson* **–**

LA HAULE LADY 3 ch.f. Helmet (AUS) 127 – Sea of Leaves (USA) 103 (Stormy Atlantic (USA)) [2017 61: t7.1g 6g^4 5m^5 5m 5s 5f^5 5m^3 t5g 5s Oct 10] lengthy filly: modest maiden handicapper: stays 6f: acts on soft going: sometimes in headgear in 2017. *Paul Midgley* **55**

LA HAVRESE (FR) 6 ch.m. Le Havre (IRE) 124 – La Buena (IRE) (Big Shuffle (USA) 122) [2017 72: 10g 8.5d^6 10.2m^5 10d^6 10.2g 9.9g^3 Sep 2] fair handicapper: stays 10.5f: acts on tapeta, good to firm and good to soft going: has worn headgear. *Lynn Siddall* **66**

LAHAYEB 5 b.m. High Chaparral (IRE) 132 – Tea Break (Daylami (IRE) 138) [2017 10.2v 9.9d^5 10.2f^5 10g Jul 8] useful handicapper at best: no form in 2017: stayed 1¼m: acted on polytrack and heavy going: tried in hood: dead. *Michael Appleby* **–**

LAHORE (USA) 3 b.c. Elusive Quality (USA) – Nayarra (IRE) 105 (Cape Cross (IRE) 129) [2017 5m* 6.1g* 6g^5 7d* 7g^3 Oct 7] first foal: dam, 2-y-o 1m (Gran Criterium) winner, half-sister to very smart performer up to 1¼m Mars and Superlative Stakes winner Gustav Klimt: useful performer: won maiden at Doncaster in April, and handicaps at Windsor in July and Doncaster (by 4 lengths from Bengal Lancer) in September: 4½ lengths third to Jallota in listed race at Redcar final start: stays 7f: acts on good to firm and good to soft going: usually races nearer last than first, often travels strongly. *Roger Varian* **109**

LAIDBACK ROMEO (IRE) 5 b.g. Kodiac 112 – Belmora (USA) (Scrimshaw (USA)) [2017 100: 8m* 8m^2 8m^3 8d^5 Sep 20] tall gelding: useful performer: won handicap at Sandown (by length from Greenside) in May: fifth to Khafoo Shememi in listed race at same course final outing: stays 8.5f: acts on good to firm and good to soft going: sent to Bahrain. *Clive Cox* **107**

LAIETH 2 b.c. (Mar 26) Dubawi (IRE) 129 – First City 116 (Diktat 126) [2017 p7g^4 t8.6m* Oct 31] 550,000Y: second foal: dam winner up to 1m (2-y-o 6f winner), including Group 2 event in UAE: fairly useful form: won minor event at Wolverhampton (by 2¼ lengths from Escalator) in October: will go on improving. *Saeed bin Suroor* **84 p**

LA ISLA BONITA 3 b.f. Foxwedge (AUS) 128 – Excello 94 (Exceed And Excel (AUS) 126) [2017 –: p7m^6 p7g t7.2g* t7.2g^3 p8g^2 p7d^2 p7g Nov 2] fair handicapper: won at Wolverhampton in August: second at Chelmsford in September: stays 1m: acts on polytrack and tapeta: front runner/races prominently. *Richard Spencer* **72**

LAITH ALAREEN 2 b.g. (Apr 3) Invincible Spirit (IRE) 121 – Bewitchment 70 (Pivotal 124) [2017 5g 5m^5 5d t5.1g Jul 31] modest form: raced only at 5f: in tongue tie last 3 starts. *David O'Meara* **64**

LAKE SHORE DRIVE (IRE) 5 b.g. Thewayyouare (USA) 117 – Labrusca 58 (Grand Lodge (USA) 125) [2017 –: 17.1d 16s p15.8g* t14g^2 Nov 25] fair handicapper: won at Lingfield in November: second at Wolverhampton final start: stays 2m: acts on polytrack, tapeta and good to soft going. *Johnny Farrelly* **73**

LAKESKI 3 b.f. Sir Percy 129 – Floating (Oasis Dream 129) [2017 f8d^4 f7d^6 9.9f^6 8f 8s 7.4g Jul 17] 4,000Y, resold 5,000Y: fourth foal: half-sister to 1m winner (stays 10.5f) Like A Prayer (by Compton Place) and 2-y-o 6f winner Star Jeanie (by Kyllachy): dam French maiden: modest maiden: stays 1m: acts on fibresand and firm going: tried in cheekpieces. *Scott Dixon* **52**

LAKE VOLTA (IRE) 2 b.g. (Mar 11) Raven's Pass (USA) 133 – Ghanaian (FR) 101 (Shamardal (USA) 129) [2017 6g 6g* 6g* 6m^3 p6g^3 p7g^3 t6d^6 Oct 24] useful-looking gelding: first foal: dam, 7f winner (including at 2 yrs), half-sister to useful 5f/6f winner Free Roses: useful performer: won minor events at Brighton and Ripon (by 5 lengths from Simmy's Copshop) in August: stays 7f: acts on polytrack, best turf form on good going: front runner/races prominently. *Mark Johnston* **100**

LA LA LAND (IRE) 2 br.c. (Feb 20) Dark Angel (IRE) 113 – Taraeff (IRE) (Cape Cross (IRE) 129) [2017 7s^3 p8s^5 9.9s^5 t8.6m^2 t8.6g* Nov 18] €165,000Y: good-bodied colt: second foal: dam unraced half-sister to useful 8.3f/9f winner Tazffin out of smart winner up to 1¼m Tarfshi: fairly useful performer: won nursery at Wolverhampton (by 1½ lengths from Gembari) in November: stays 1¼m: acts on tapeta and soft going: in cheekpieces last 2 starts: sometimes slowly away: open to further improvement. *Jamie Osborne* **84 p**

LALANIA 2 br.f. (Mar 9) Kheleyf (USA) 116 – George's Gift (Haafhd 129) [2017 6d^3 Aug 10] third foal: half-sister to 7f winner Hitchcock (by Equiano): dam unraced out of useful 5f-1m winner Miss George: 40/1, third in minor event at Yarmouth (2¼ lengths behind Luis Fernandez) in August: will improve. *Stuart Williams* **62 p**

LA MAQUINA 2 b.c. (Apr 6) Dutch Art 126 – Miss Meltemi (IRE) 100 (Miswaki Tern (USA) 120) [2017 p7d^4 p7g^2 Dec 20] 52,000Y: half-brother to several winners, including 7f-8.3f winner Balducci, 1m winner (stayed 1¼m) Ada River and winner up to 1m (stayed 1½m) Dont Dili Dali (all useful by Dansili): dam 2-y-o 7.5f/1m winner who stayed 11f: fairly useful form: better effort when second in minor event at Kempton (length behind Mr Ritz) in December: likely to progress further. *George Baker* **92 p**

LAMB CHOP 2 b.f. (Apr 7) Havana Gold (IRE) 118 – Mutoon (IRE) 64 (Erhaab (USA) 127) [2017 6g 6.1g 7.1s^3 7s^3 8s p7s Dec 1] neat filly: half-sister to several winners, including winner up to 7f Rattling Jewel (by Royal Applause) and 7f winner Mutoondresdashorse (by Harbour Watch): dam, maiden (stayed 1¼m), half-sister to smart 1¼m-14.6f winner Ranin: fair maiden: best effort at 7f: acts on soft going: in cheekpieces last 4 starts: often races prominently. *Rod Millman* **68**

LAMBRINI LEGACY 3 b.f. Captain Gerrard (IRE) 113 – Lambrini Lace (IRE) 65 (Namid 128) [2017 5.3g^4 5.2m^2 5.3g^2 5m^4 5m 5m 6.1g 6g^6 5.3g Sep 3] good-bodied filly: second foal: dam 5f winner: modest maiden: stays 5.5f: acts on good to firm going: wears hood: usually races freely. *Lisa Williamson* **60**

LA MERNANCIA (IRE) 2 b.f. (Mar 25) Kodiac 112 – Nashatara (USA) (Nashwan (USA) 135) [2017 t7.2g^5 t8.6d^5 Dec 27] €13,000F: closely related to 12.2f winner Whisky Marmalade (by Duke of Marmalade) and half-sister to 2 winners, including useful Italian 2-y-o 1m winner Nantha (by King's Best): dam useful Italian 1¼m winner: modest form in minor events. *Jamie Osborne* **61**

L'AMI DE ROUGE 4 b.f. Excellent Art 125 – Coup de Torchon (FR) 61 (Namid 128) [2017 p8d p8g p12g^4 t12.2g 11.6g^4 p16s^6 16.3d^{pu} p11g p12g Nov 18] sturdy filly: third foal: half-sister to 6f winner Cloak And Degas (by Sakhee's Secret): dam maiden: modest maiden handicapper: best effort at 1½m: acts on polytrack: has worn hood. *Ralph Smith* **59**

Qatar Stewards' Cup (Heritage Handicap), Goodwood—
the far side dominates as Lancelot du Lac claims a deserved big-race success,
beating Aeolus (cheekpieces), Upstaging (quartered cap) and Growl (star on cap)

LAMLOOM (IRE) 3 b.g. Cape Cross (IRE) 129 – Lulua (USA) (Bahri (USA) 125) [2017 64p: 7g3 8m2 9g4 8d2 9.1g* 8s2 8.3d2 8d6 8.5m5 8v Sep 21] lengthy gelding: fairly useful performer: won maiden at Ayr (by 3¼ lengths from Liquid Gold) in June: stays 9f: acts on soft and good to firm going: front runner/races prominently. *David O'Meara* **88**

LAMYA (GER) 2 b.f. (Jan 27) Choisir (AUS) 126 – Livia's Wake (IRE) 81 (Galileo (IRE) 134) [2017 6g6 6.1m* 7g4 Sep 22] €30,000Y, €260,000 2-y-o: second foal: half-sister to 2-y-o 6f/7f winner Bismarck The Flyer (by Requinto): dam, maiden (stayed 11f), out of useful 9f winner Liska: fair form: won minor event at Windsor (by 2¼ lengths from Angel's Whisper) in August: should stay 7f. *Richard Hannon* **77**

LANCASTER BOMBER (USA) 3 b.c. War Front (USA) 119 – Sun Shower (IRE) (Indian Ridge 123) [2017 113: a9.4g4 8m4 8d5 8f2 8v6 8f2 8s 8f2 8g5 Dec 10] well-made colt: very smart performer: in frame 5 times, in UAE Derby at Meydan, 2000 Guineas at Newmarket (1¼ lengths fourth to Churchill), St James's Palace Stakes at Royal Ascot (length second to Barney Roy), Woodbine Mile (2½ lengths second to World Approval) and Breeders' Cup Mile at Del Mar (1¼ lengths second to World Approval): 3¼ lengths fifth to Beauty Generation in Hong Kong Mile at Sha Tin final start: stays 9.5f: best form on firm/good to firm going, probably acts on dirt: front runner/races prominently. *Aidan O'Brien, Ireland* **122**

LANCELOT DU LAC (ITY) 7 b.g. Shamardal (USA) 129 – Dodie Mae (USA) (Capote (USA)) [2017 112: p5g* p6g* p5m2 p6g4 6m 6d* 6d5 5.6g Sep 16] good-topped gelding: smart performer: won handicap at Chelmsford (by ¾ length from Doctor Sardonicus) in January, listed race at Lingfield (by nose from Mythmaker) in February and Stewards' Cup (Handicap) at Goodwood (by ¾ length from Aeolus) in August: best at 5f/6f nowadays: acts on polytrack, good to firm and heavy going: has worn hood, including last 3 starts: usually races prominently. *Dean Ivory* **115**

LANCEUR (FR) 8 b.g. Rail Link 132 – Lanciana (IRE) (Acatenango (GER) 127) [2017 t8.6g5 p10d p12g5 12s p16g2 p16g5 16g Aug 12] good-topped gelding: fairly useful handicapper: second at Kempton (1¾ lengths behind Denmead) in June: stayed 2m: acted on all-weather, best turf form on good going: dead. *William Stone* **86**

LANDING NIGHT (IRE) 5 b.g. Kodiac 112 – Night Delight (IRE) 86 (Night Shift (USA)) [2017 89: f5g t6m6 5.5g3 5m4 5g6 5m4 5f3 5s2 5g 5g2 5m* 5.1v6 t5g* t5.1g2 t5g5 t5.1g5 Dec 5] fairly useful handicapper: won at Musselburgh in September and Newcastle (by ¾ length from Duke Cosimo) in October: best form at 5f: acts on fibresand, tapeta, firm and good to soft going: wears cheekpieces/tongue tie: often travels strongly. *Rebecca Menzies* **89**

LANDSHARK 2 b.c. (Apr 5) Bated Breath 125 – Tremelo Pointe (IRE) 73 (Trempolino (USA) 135) [2017 6g* 6d2 Aug 27] 5,000Y, €210,000 2-y-o: fifth foal: half-brother to 2 winners by Pastoral Pursuits, including 8.3f winner Aldair: dam, 1m winner, half-sister to winner up to 7f Dream Eater and winner up to 13f Dreamspeed (both smart): fairly useful form: won maiden at Leopardstown in August by ½ length from Sappho: second in Round Tower Stakes at the Curragh (6 lengths behind U S Navy Flag) later in month: will be suited by 7f+: remains open to improvement. *Mrs J. Harrington, Ireland* **94 p**

LANDSMAN (IRE) 4 b.g. Canford Cliffs (IRE) 133 – Mowaadah (IRE) 93 (Alzao (USA) 117) [2017 91: 12g5 12d6 12g* 11.9g 12.8d 12.1s 14s Nov 5] useful handicapper: won at Fairyhouse (apprentice, by short head from Political Policy) in July: stays 13f: acts on polytrack, good to firm and heavy going: wears tongue tie: races towards rear. *A. J. Martin, Ireland* **95**

LANDUE 2 b.c. (Apr 13) Champs Elysees 124 – Time of Gold (USA) (Banker's Gold (USA) 116) [2017 7d 7.1m p6g Sep 6] 10,000F, €25,000Y: seventh foal: closely related to useful 6f (including at 2 yrs) winner Golden Amber (by Holy Roman Emperor) and half-brother to 2 winners in Italy, including useful winner up to 9f Tauman (by Blu Air Force): dam winner up to 1m (2-y-o 6f/7f winner): modest form: remains with potential. *Marcus Tregoning* **54 p**

LANGHAM 4 b.f. Royal Applause 124 – Three Ducks 89 (Diktat 126) [2017 71: t7.1g4 t7.1g5 7m 6m t7.2g6 t7.2g 8m Aug 22] compact filly: fair maiden: stays 7f: acts on polytrack and tapeta: has worn headgear, including last 5 starts. *Michael Appleby* **71**

LANGLAUF (USA) 4 gr.f. Raven's Pass (USA) 133 – Emirates Girl (USA) (Unbridled's Song (USA) 125) [2017 t9.5g p11g3 p12d* 12m5 p12g* p14s* 12g5 12d 14d p12d p12g Dec 30] fairly useful handicapper: won at Kempton in February and June, and Chelmsford (by neck from Jelly Monger) later in June: stays 1¾m: acts on polytrack and soft going: wears cheekpieces. *Rod Millman* **83 a91**

LANGLEY VALE 8 b.g. Piccolo 121 – Running Glimpse (IRE) 84 (Runnett 125) [2017 73: t6g^4 6m^2 6d 6.1m^3 5.7s 5.7s* p6g Oct 18] good-topped gelding: fair handicapper: won at Bath in September: stays 6f: acts on polytrack, tapeta, firm and soft going: has worn headgear: often races towards rear. *Roger Teal* **70**

LANGTREE LANE 2 b.f. (Feb 21) Equiano (FR) 127 – Saunta 62 (Invincible Spirit (IRE) 121) [2017 5.9m Jul 14] second foal: dam, maiden (stayed 6f), half-sister to winner up to 9f Singhalese and ungenuine winner up to 1m Docofthebay (both smart): 18/1, well held in minor event at Carlisle. *Bryan Smart* **–**

LANJANO 3 ch.r. Foxwedge (AUS) 128 – Hot Property (USA) (Thunder Gulch (USA) 129) [2017 82: 6m 6.1v^4 6m 7d^5 t7.2g^5 Nov 25] fair handicapper: stays 7f: acts on good to firm and good to soft going: front runner/races prominently. *Kevin Ryan* **73**

LANSKY (IRE) 2 b.c. (Feb 27) Dark Angel (IRE) 113 – Goldthroat (IRE) 79 (Zafonic (USA) 130) [2017 6.1m* 7d^3 6m^4 p6g* Oct 14] 175,000F, 125,000Y, 300,000 2-y-o: good-quartered colt: brother to useful 5f-7f winner Dark Profit and half-brother to several winners, including very smart winner up to 1¼m Zafisio (2-y-o 7f/1m winner, by Efisio) and smart winner up to 1½m Gold Trail (2-y-o 1m winner, by Teofilo): dam ungenuine 2-y-o 7f winner: useful form: won minor events at Windsor in August and Kempton (blinkered) in October: third in Acomb Stakes at York (3¾ lengths behind Wells Farhh Go) in August: best effort at 7f: remains open to improvement. *Jeremy Noseda* **98 p**

LAPILLI 4 b.g. Bahamian Bounty 116 – Blue Lyric 81 (Refuse To Bend (IRE) 128) [2017 95p: 5g p5g^4 p5g Dec 1] fairly useful handicapper: left William Haggas after first start, Damian Joseph English after second: raced only at 5f: acts on tapeta and good to firm going. *James McAuley, Ireland* **88**

LA PLUSBELLE 2 b.f. (Feb 13) Champs Elysees 124 – Cat O' Nine Tails 84 (Motivator 131) [2017 6m t7.1g 7m^{pu} Aug 26] no form: dead. *Richard Fahey* **–**

L'APOGEE 4 ch.g. Rip Van Winkle (IRE) 134 – Pappas Ruby (USA) 63 (Red Ransom (USA)) [2017 67: t9.5g^2 f8g Jan 30] fair handicapper: stays 1¼m: acts on tapeta, good to firm and good to soft going: often in headgear: sold 6,500 gns, sent to Italy. *Richard Fahey* **65**

LAQAB (IRE) 4 b.g. Teofilo (IRE) 126 – Ghaidaa (IRE) 105 (Cape Cross (IRE) 129) [2017 89p: 10.1m^5 t12.2g Sep 9] fairly useful form: best effort at 1¼m: sold £20,000 in November to join Derek Shaw. *Roger Varian* **80**

LARAAIB (IRE) 3 b.c. Pivotal 124 – Sahool 109 (Unfuwain (USA) 131) [2017 10.2m* 10.2f* 10g* 10.5d^3 Aug 12] rangy colt: seventh foal: half-brother to useful 1¼m winner (stayed 1½m) Arwaah (by Dalakhani) and 1¼m-17f winner Tawseef (by Monsun): dam winner up to 1½m (2-y-o 8.2f winner): smart form: won maiden at Chepstow and handicap at Haydock (by 1¾ lengths from Atty Persse) in May, and handicap at Ascot (by 2 lengths from Banditry) in July: stays 1¼m. *Owen Burrows* **110**

LA RAV (IRE) 3 b.g. Footstepsinthesand 120 – Swift Acclaim (IRE) 56 (Acclamation 118) [2017 8s^5 7m* 8g* p8g^3 7.9g Aug 25] 10,000Y, 120,000 2-y-o: first foal: dam, maiden (stayed 6f), half-sister to smart 6f winner Presto Shinko: useful performer: won maiden at Salisbury in June and handicap at Newbury (by 3¼ lengths from Mr Minerals) in July: stays 1m: acts on polytrack and good to firm going. *Luca Cumani* **102**

LARCHMONT LAD (IRE) 3 b.c. Footstepsinthesand 120 – Fotini (IRE) (King's Best (USA) 132) [2017 109: 8m^5 8m 7d^2 8g^4 10.5d 8d^3 7s^2 Oct 28] good-topped colt: smart performer: first past post in listed race at Leopardstown in October, beating Making Light a nose, but demoted after idling/hanging right late on: left Richard Hannon after fifth start: stays 1m: acts on soft and good to firm going: front runner/races prominently. *David O'Meara* **110**

LASHABEEH (IRE) 2 gr.c. (Apr 24) Acclamation 118 – Do The Honours (IRE) 121 (Highest Honor (FR) 124) [2017 p6g^2 Nov 29] 65,000Y: half-brother to several winners, including 1m winner Woven Lace (by Hard Spun) and 6f/7f winner Waitress (by Kingmambo), both useful: dam French 5f-7f winner: 4/1, second in minor event at Kempton (neck behind Desert Doctor) on debut: will improve. *Roger Varian* **78 p**

LA SIOUX (IRE) 3 ch.f. Casamento (IRE) 118 – Dakota Sioux (IRE) 90 (College Chapel 122) [2017 7g* p8g Dec 31] fifth foal: half-sister to 3 winners, including useful 2-y-o 6f winner Max One Two Three (by Princely Heir) and winner up to 9.5f Dakota Canyon (2-y-o 6f winner, by Rock of Gibraltar): dam 7f-8.3f winner: fair form: won maiden at Catterick (by nose from Nuns Walk) in August. *Richard Fahey* **70**

LASSANA ANGEL 3 b.f. High Chaparral (IRE) 132 – Diara Angel (IRE) (Hawk Wing **71**
(USA) 136) [2017 59p: 8.3g^{6} 9.9d^{5} 10d^{4} Jun 6] fair form: stays 1¼m: sometimes in hood.
Roger Charlton

LAST CHANCE PADDY (USA) 3 gr.g. Paddy O'Prado (USA) 121 – Mizzcan'tbewrong **65**
(USA) (Mizzen Mast (USA) 121) [2017 f8g^{4} 8.3m^{5} 8g May 13] fair form: best effort when
fifth in maiden at Hamilton in May. *Alan Swinbank*

LAST ENCHANTMENT (IRE) 2 b.f. (Jan 21) Camelot 128 – Illandrane (IRE) 73 **77**
(Cape Cross (IRE) 129) [2017 p7g^{2} 6v 6s^{2} 7d Sep 30] 32,000Y: sturdy filly: second foal:
dam, lightly raced (bred to have been suited by 1¼m), half-sister to smart winner up to 9f
Adagio: fair form: stays 7f. *Eve Johnson Houghton*

LASTMANLASTROUND (IRE) 4 b.g. Azamour (IRE) 130 – Lastroseofsummer **88**
(IRE) 82 (Haafhd 129) [2017 80: 7g* p8d^{2} p8s^{6} p8g Sep 9] medium-sized gelding: fairly
useful handicapper: won at Brighton in May: second at Kempton later that month: stays
1m: acts on polytrack, raced only on good going on turf. *Rae Guest*

LASTONEFORTHECRAIC (IRE) 2 b.f. (May 1) Red Jazz (USA) 125 – Charming **47**
Vista (Josr Algarhoud (IRE) 118) [2017 6.1d 5.1m 5.1m p6s Nov 16] €5,000Y: rather
unfurnished filly: sixth foal: half-sister to 2 winners, including 6f (including at 2 yrs)
winner Silver Springs (by Zebedee): dam unraced half-sister to useful winner up to 1m
Distant Valley: poor form. *David Evans*

LAST PAGE 2 b.g. (Apr 17) Pastoral Pursuits 127 – No Page (IRE) 81 (Statue of Liberty **88**
(USA) 115) [2017 5g^{2} 5m^{2} 5.1g^{ur} 5.7f^{2} 5f^{5} 5m^{6} Jul 7] rather unfurnished gelding: third
foal: half-brother to 7f-1m winner Rocco's Delight (by Multiplex): dam 2-y-o 6f winner:
fairly useful maiden: stays 5.5f: acts on firm going: in cheekpieces last 2 starts: needs
treating with some caution (threw rider just after start third outing). *David Evans*

LAST STAR FALLING (IRE) 4 b.f. Acclamation 118 – Star Port (Observatory (USA) **67**
131) [2017 59, a76: p6g^{5} p6g^{6} p6g f7g Apr 16] fair handicapper: stays 7.5f: acts on all-
weather and soft going: usually wears headgear: sent to Belgium. *Henry Spiller*

LAST SUMMER 6 ch.g. New Approach (IRE) 132 – Evil Empire (GER) 108 (Acatenango **–**
(GER) 127) [2017 51: f12s p16d Feb 22] bumper winner: modest maiden on Flat, well
beaten in 2017: stays 1½m: acts on tapeta: tried in cheekpieces: often starts slowly/races
towards rear. *Grace Harris*

LAST VOYAGE (USA) 2 br.c. (Feb 6) Eskendereya (USA) 126 – Shipboard Romance **92**
(USA) (Pulpit (USA) 117) [2017 5.1g* 7d^{3} p7g^{4} Oct 18] $52,000F, $90,000Y, $335,000
2-y-o: well-made colt: first foal: dam unraced out of smart 7f winner Captain's Lover:
fairly useful form: won minor event at Windsor (by short head from Choice Encounter) in
May: best effort when third in similar event at Sandown (2¼ lengths behind Wafy) in
September: stays 7f: tried in hood. *Charlie Appleby*

LAST WORD 3 b.f. Bated Breath 125 – Intermission (IRE) (Royal Applause 124) [2017 **60**
–p: p7m Nov 25] modest form: best effort at 7f. *Joseph Tuite*

LATE CHANGE 2 b.f. (May 1) Exceed And Excel (AUS) 126 – Khione 108 (Dalakhani **– p**
(IRE) 133) [2017 7g 8d^{6} 7d Sep 30] 72,000 2-y-o: good-topped filly: first foal: dam
8.3f-1½m winner: signs of ability in maidens/minor event: remains capable of better.
David Simcock

LATEST QUEST (IRE) 3 b.g. Zebedee 113 – Fancy Theory (USA) (Quest For Fame **53**
127) [2017 71: 8.3m 8m^{3} 8d 7d^{4} p7g^{3} p7d p7g p7g t7.2g t6.1d Dec 16] angular gelding:
modest handicapper: stays 7f: acts on polytrack and good to soft going: tried in blinkers.
Sylvester Kirk

LAT HAWILL (IRE) 6 b.g. Invincible Spirit (IRE) 121 – Arbella 106 (Primo Dominie **99**
121) [2017 105: 8g 7.1g^{2} 8m 7.6d 7.6g^{5} 8g 8.3s 7.2v t10.2d Oct 24] sturdy, attractive
gelding: useful handicapper: second at Musselburgh (1¾ lengths behind Twin Appeal) in
April: stays 9.5f: acts on firm and good to soft going: wears headgear: often races in rear:
sold only 3,000 gns, sent to Belgium. *Keith Dalgleish*

LATHOM 4 b.g. Compton Place 125 – Wigan Lane 66 (Kheleyf (USA) 116) [2017 98: 5g **89**
p5g^{5} 6m^{6} 5m 5s^{3} 5f^{4} 5d^{4} 6d 5v^{4} 5g^{5} 5s^{4} t5g Nov 24] good-topped gelding: fairly useful
handicapper: fourth at Musselburgh (½ length behind Rural Celebration) in August: left
David O'Meara after eighth start: best form at 5f: acts on soft and good to firm going: has
worn headgear: on long losing run. *Julie Camacho*

Weatherbys Racing Bank £300,000 2-Y-O Stakes, Doncaster—Laugh A Minute lands a very big prize, with Danzan (noseband), Alba Power (stars on sleeves) and favourite Great Prospector (hooped cap) leading the chasing pack

LAUBALI 2 ch.c. (Feb 22) Kyllachy 129 – Different 75 (Bahamian Bounty 116) [2017 6m 6d³ 5s³ 6d t6g⁴ t7.2g³ Dec 22] useful-looking colt: fair maiden: left Owen Burrows after fourth start: stays 7f: acts on tapeta and soft going: often races prominently. *David O'Meara* **72**

LAUGH ALOUD 4 ch.f. Dubawi (IRE) 129 – Opera Comique (FR) 100 (Singspiel (IRE) 133) [2017 110: p8g⁵ 8f* 8.5m* Jun 3] well-made filly: very smart performer: won listed race at Goodwood (by 3¼ lengths from Intimation) in May and Princess Elizabeth Stakes at Epsom (by 5 lengths from Absolute Blast) in June: stays 8.5f: acts on firm and good to soft going: wears tongue tie: strong traveller: usually leads, stalked pace at Epsom. *John Gosden* **121**

LAUGH A MINUTE 2 b.c. (Apr 12) Mayson 124 – Funny Enough 64 (Dansili 127) [2017 7g³ 7d² 7g³ 6.5g* Sep 14] 45,000Y: tall, rather unfurnished colt: third foal: half-brother to 2-y-o 7f winner Puzzled Look (by Sakhee's Secret) and useful 7f winner Horroob (by Showcasing): dam lightly-raced half-sister to 1m/9f winner Smart Enough and winner up to 1m Oasis Dancer (both smart): useful form: won valuable event at Doncaster (by 1¼ lengths from Danzan) in September: should prove as effective at bare 6f: should improve further. *Roger Varian* **104 p**

LAUGHTON 4 b.g. Acclamation 118 – Peach Pearl (Invincible Spirit (IRE) 121) [2017 92: 6g 5m⁴ 6s 6d⁵ 6g 6s 5v 6s Oct 31] fairly useful handicapper: fourth at Doncaster (length behind Acclaim The Nation) in April: stays 6f: acts on good to firm and good to soft going: tried in tongue tie: sometimes slowly away. *Kevin Ryan* **86**

LAUNCESTON PLACE (FR) 2 br.c. (Feb 1) Le Havre (IRE) 124 – Last Song (Singspiel (IRE) 133) [2017 7s 7g³ p7g³ Nov 6] fair form: best effort when third in minor event at Redcar (1¼ lengths behind Three Saints Bay) in October. *Henry Spiller* **77**

LAURA KNIGHT (IRE) 2 gr.f. (Mar 3) Dark Angel (IRE) 113 – Mauri Moon 104 (Green Desert (USA) 127) [2017 6g p6s⁵ p7g 5f⁶ p6g² t6.1g² p7g p5g⁴ Sep 26] €48,000F, £54,000Y: rather leggy filly: half-sister to several winners, including useful winner up to 9f Karaka Jack (2-y-o 7f winner) and 2-y-o 7f winner Shamayel (both by Pivotal): dam winner up to 8.2f (2-y-o 6f winner): fair maiden: best effort at 6f: acts on polytrack and tapeta: in cheekpieces last 3 starts. *Gary Moore* **68**

LAUREATE 3 b.f. Poet's Voice 126 – Step This Way (USA) 93 (Giant's Causeway (USA) 132) [2017 72: t9.5m⁴ t12.2g³ 11.8s 14f² 16.1d⁴ Jul 24] fair maiden: stays 2m: acts on tapeta and firm going. *Mark Johnston* **75**

LAURENS (FR) 2 b.f. (Apr 12) Siyouni (FR) 122 – Recambe (IRE) (Cape Cross (IRE) 129) [2017 7d* 7g² 8g* 8m* Oct 13] **112**

Karl Burke's stable star Quiet Reflection, winner of the Commonwealth Cup and Sprint Cup in 2016, was restricted by a niggling injury to just three starts in the latest season, with her only win coming in the Group 3 Renaissance Stakes at Naas. But it was another excellent season for the Middleham trainer who again passed the million-pound mark in domestic earnings and set another new seasonal high of seventy-four wins. The key to the stable's success this time was a batch of two-year-olds which included two Group 1 winners: Unfortunately won the Prix Morny in France, while the May Hill Stakes winner Laurens went on to win the Fillies' Mile. Another smart youngster was the Molecomb winner Havana Grey who completed a one, two for the stable in the Morny and also finished runner-up in the Flying Childers. Quiet Reflection had been a smart two-year-old herself, winning the Cornwallis Stakes under Graham Lee, while at three she became the regular ride of Dougie Costello. It was yet another former jump jockey, P. J. McDonald, winner of the 2007 Scottish Grand National on Hot Weld, who rode Havana Grey and Laurens in all their races, the filly giving McDonald, who is retained by owner John Dance, his first Group 1 success.

First, though, for Laurens came two wins at Doncaster either side of finishing second to one of the top French two-year-old fillies, Polydream, in the Prix du Calvados at Deauville on the same weekend as the Morny. Laurens stepped up a good deal on the form of her debut success in a fillies maiden in July but still looked green at Deauville when going down by a length and three quarters to the future Marcel Boussac runner-up. Back at Doncaster for the St Leger meeting, Laurens was a well-backed 11/4 favourite for the William Hill May Hill Stakes and she came off best in a tight four-way finish at the end of a steadily-run race. The step up to a mile suited her, but she did well to stay on from mid-division to lead in the final fifty yards and get the better of Dark Rose Angel, Nyaleti and Sizzling, with the margins between them just a head, a head and a neck. Nyaleti set the standard beforehand judged on her five-length win in the Princess Margaret Stakes at Ascot, though she'd since run below that form when sixth behind Laurens' stable-companions in the Morny. Laurens came out best in another thrilling finish to the bet365 Fillies' Mile at Newmarket the following month, a race that attracted a grand-looking bunch of fillies and took a good deal more winning, despite the late absence with a temperature of the Moyglare Stud Stakes and Prix Jean-Luc Lagardere winner Happily who was forecast to start favourite. Aidan O'Brien, successful in the last three editions of the race, still fielded the first two in the betting, however, with the placed fillies from the Moyglare, Magical (15/8 favourite, and fourth since in the Marcel Boussac) and September (9/2). Polydream's trainer Freddie Head sent over the Prix d'Aumale runner-up Efaadah (the third from that race, Wild Illusion, had won the Marcel Boussac) and was next in the betting on 11/2, ahead of 8/1-shots Nyaleti, a close second in the Rockfel Stakes since the May Hill, and Godolphin's Magic Lily, a daughter of Oaks winner Dancing Rain and winner of her only start over the same course and distance by eight lengths. Laurens was 10/1 with the five other fillies in the line-up at long odds, including Laurens' stable-companion Ellthea

bet365 Fillies' Mile, Newmarket—
September (almost hidden on rail) stays on strongly after encountering trouble in running, but just fails to peg back the front-running Laurens; the success is a first Group 1 for jockey PJ McDonald in a race weakened by the defection of morning favourite Happily due to a high temperature; Magic Lily (blaze) finishes a close third while Ellthea (left), a stablemate of the winner, comes fifth

who had finished a long way behind her at Deauville but had won both her starts since, including a Group 3 at Naas from the May Hill fourth Sizzling. Making the running up the stand rail, Laurens ran out the gamest of winners as she repelled several different challengers in the last couple of furlongs. At one stage, her trainer had prospects of having the first two in a Group 1 for the second time in the season as Ellthea was close up until the final furlong, while Magical briefly looked a danger wider out, as did Magic Lily who burst through from behind the leaders to challenge in the final furlong before edging right in the closing stages. However, it was September who went closest to pegging back Laurens in the end after failing to get a clear run until the final furlong, staying on strongly once doing so between Laurens and Magic Lily and unlucky to be beaten just a nose. Magic Lily was only three quarters of a length behind the first two and clear of the rest, with Magical seeing things out a bit better than Ellthea to ensure that it was O'Brien, not Burke, who had two fillies in the frame. September shaped like much the best filly in the race, but, equally, Laurens would have been an undeserving loser given how generously she responded in fending off her challengers.

The imposing Laurens, a strong, rangy individual, became the first Fillies' Mile winner to be trained in the North and her defeat of a pair of blue-blooded fillies representing two of racing's superpowers was an act of giant-killing of sorts. However, by any standards, Laurens cost plenty as a yearling. At £220,000 she was the top-priced filly at Doncaster's Premier Sale in 2016—and she cost a lot more than the €24,000 paid for Unfortunately as a yearling, or, for that matter, the £44,000 Quiet Reflection had cost at a breeze-up sale. Laurens has already proven a good investment for John Dance, owner of a Newcastle asset management firm, who has a growing string—'We never really meant to have thirty or forty horses a year but you get a bit addicted to it'. The Dance horses are spread among several yards, mostly in the North. It was Dance's background in finance which got him interested in racing in the first place—'The finance industry is very analytical, so the skills lend themselves well to form study'—and it was as a result of his firm sponsoring races at his local track and presenting trophies that he decided he wanted to experience the thrill of being on the receiving end as an owner. His ambitions don't end there, either, as in time Laurens will be a foundation mare for what Dance intends to be a commercial breeding operation, following the purchase of Fair Winter Farm, the Buckinghamshire stud formerly owned by the Barnett family who bred and raced the likes of Master Willie and Time Charter.

Laurens (FR) (b.f. 2015)	Siyouni (FR) (b 2007)	Pivotal (ch 1993)	Polar Falcon
			Fearless Revival
		Sichilla (b 2002)	Danehill
			Slipstream Queen
	Recambe (IRE) (b 2005)	Cape Cross (b 1994)	Green Desert
			Park Appeal
		Razana (b 1992)	Kahyasi
			Raysiya

The Aga Khan's Prix Jean-Luc Lagardere winner Siyouni was still covering at his original fee of €7,000 when Laurens, from his fourth crop, was conceived in 2014. However, his first-crop daughter Ervedya won the Poule d'Essai des Pouliches, Coronation Stakes and Prix du Moulin the following year and Siyouni's fee has rocketed ever since to make him one of Europe's most sought-after young sires. In 2018 he'll be standing at his owner's Haras de Bonneval for €75,000 (up from €45,000) after a year in which his three-year-old son Le Brivido was narrowly beaten in the Poule d'Essai des Poulains before winning the Jersey Stakes and when his latest crop of two-year-olds also included the smart French colt Sacred Life who is unbeaten in three starts, including the Prix Thomas Bryon. Laurens, her fourth foal, has certainly boosted the stud record of her dam Recambe whose only other winner to date is Autignac (by Solon), a fairly useful winner over hurdles at Auteuil. Recambe's other foal to have raced, Murviel, was a sister to Laurens, but she made the frame only once from seven starts on the Flat in France and was pulled up on her only start over hurdles. Recambe won two races for Robert Collet, a mile and a quarter maiden at Compiegne and a minor event at Clairefontaine over an extended mile and three quarters. Among Recambe's winning siblings are Ovambo, who was

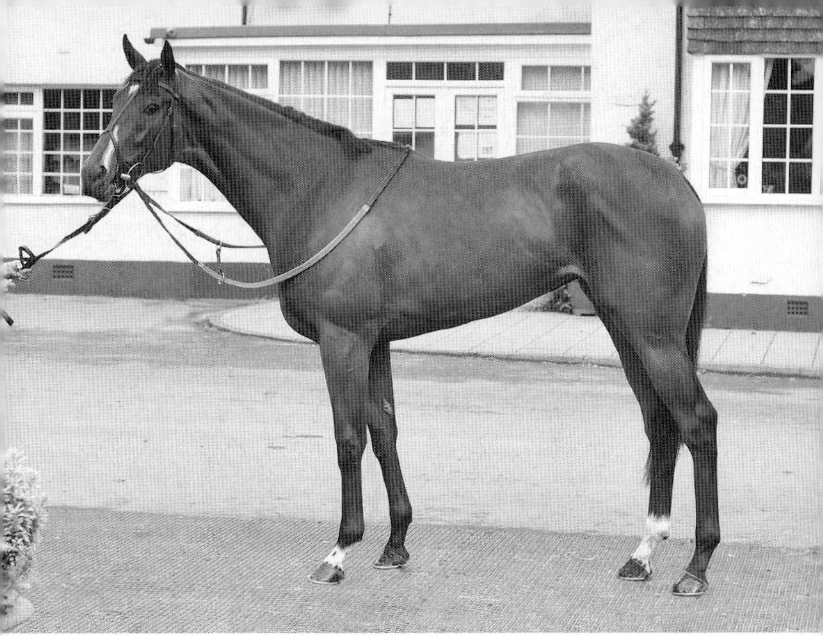

Mr John Dance's "Laurens"

smart at up to a mile and three quarters, and Salford Mill, another smart colt, who ran sixth in Authorized's Derby, and became a Derby winner in Hong Kong the following year when renamed Helene Mascot. Grandam Razana won a maiden at Chepstow at three and went on to win three more races in France as a four-year-old, showing useful form at around a mile and a half. The stoutly-bred Razana was owned by Sheikh Mohammed but she is very much an Aga Khan product, being by Derby winner Kahyasi out of a half-sister to his Irish St Leger runner-up Rayseka. Great grandam Raysiya won at a mile and a quarter and a mile and a half in Ireland and Laurens is just the latest among several pattern winners descending from her. Another Middleham-trained Group 1 winner to do so was the Prix de l'Opera winner Kinnaird (another May Hill winner, too), a career highlight for her trainer Pat Haslam who died in October. Kinnaird, a granddaughter of Raysiya and a half-sister to the Chester Vase winner Mickdaam, is herself the dam of the Royal Lodge Stakes winner Berkshire and grandam of the smart two-year-old sprinter Ivawood.

In short, there's plenty of stamina in Laurens' family, enough to think she'll stay further than her sire who never raced beyond a mile. As a French-bred filly, she's eligible for bonuses on top of any prize money she picks up across the Channel, which must make a return to France at some stage, perhaps for the most valuable race for fillies in Europe the Prix de Diane—'the ideal race' for her according to her trainer—a strong likelihood in 2018. She has won on good to firm and good to soft ground. Laurens will need to improve further to win more races at the top level but, if the attitude she showed at Newmarket is anything to go by, she won't fail for the want of trying. *K. R. Burke*

LAVETTA 5 b.m. Peintre Celebre (USA) 137 – Card Games 89 (First Trump 118) [2017 92: 8m t8s 8d^5 7d^2 7d 7d^6 Oct 28] lengthy mare: fairly useful handicapper: second in minor event at Thirsk (2½ lengths behind Mitchum Swagger) in August: stays 1m: acts on heavy going: races prominently. *Sally Haynes* **91**

LA VIE EN ROSE 3 b.f. Henrythenavigator (USA) 131 – Lady Jane Digby 118 (Oasis Dream 129) [2017 64: t9.5g p10g^2 p10g^4 p12f* 12.1m* t12.2g^2 12.1m^3 t12.2g^2 15.9g^4 t12.4d^2 Sep 29] fairly useful handicapper: won at Lingfield in April and Catterick (by 2¼ lengths from Breakwater Bay) in May: second at Newcastle final start: stays 12.5f: acts on polytrack, tapeta and good to firm going. *Mark Johnston* **82**

LAW AND ORDER (IRE) 3 b.c. Lawman (FR) 121 – Catbells (IRE) 80 (Rakti 130) [2017 99: p8g* 9m^3 8m 8m^4 7g 8m^4 10.1g^4 11.4m^2 p12g^5 10m 12s 10.3g Oct 14] strong, lengthy colt: smart performer: won listed race at Lingfield (by neck from Mr Scaramanga) in April: second in similar event at Windsor (2½ lengths behind Second Step) in August: stays 1½m: acts on polytrack, soft and good to firm going: tried in visor: sometimes slowly away: sold 120,000 gns, sent to Saudi Arabia. *James Tate* **113**

LAWFILLY 3 b.f. Lawman (FR) 121 – Red Boots (IRE) 66 (Verglas (IRE) 118) [2017 60§: 6.1m^5 7m^3 7g^3 7g^5 8g^2 8d^3 7.1g^2 7m^6 8s^3 Sep 4] modest maiden handicapper: stays 1m: acts on polytrack, soft and good to firm going: sometimes wears headgear: usually races towards rear, often travels strongly: temperamental (flashes tail). *Richard Hughes* **59 §**

LAWLESS LOUIS 3 ch.g. Equiano (FR) 127 – Peace And Love (IRE) 75 (Fantastic Light (USA) 134) [2017 84: 5m^3 5f^3 6m^5 t5s 5m^2 t5.1g^2 5d^2 6g^3 6g^5 6g 6g Dec 20] fairly useful handicapper: second at Ripon, Wolverhampton and Pontefract: left David O'Meara after seventh start: stays 6f: acts on tapeta, firm and good to soft going: usually in headgear nowadays. *Ahmed Al Jehani, Qatar* **80**

LAWLESS SECRET 3 b.f. Lawman (FR) 121 – Lamentation (Singspiel (IRE) 133) [2017 10g* 10.2g^2 11.4g^3 11.9d^2 12.4s Nov 17] 48,000Y: unfurnished filly: third foal: half-sister to 7f winner Bravo (by Indian Charlie): dam 1m-1½m winner: useful performer: won maiden at Windsor in August: second in handicap at Doncaster (3¾ lengths behind Reshoun) in October: stays 1½m: acts on good to soft going: wears hood. *Simon Crisford* **96**

LAWMAKING 4 b.g. Zamindar (USA) 116 – Canada Water (Dansili 127) [2017 95: 6.1g 6.1m 7.4m 8s* 8d^5 9.1g^2 9d 10m 8d^6 Nov 4] strong gelding: fairly useful handicapper: won at Newmarket (by head from Capton) in July: stays 9f: acts on soft and good to firm going: in hood last 4 starts. *Henry Spiller* **88**

LAWMAN'S JUSTICE (IRE) 4 b.g. Lawman (FR) 121 – Brazilian Bride (IRE) 103 (Pivotal 124) [2017 –: p10g 8.3s^6 Jun 7] lightly-raced maiden, little form. *John Quinn* **–**

LAWN RANGER 2 b.g. (Mar 23) Cityscape 127 – Baylini 102 (Bertolini (USA) 125) [2017 p8g* Dec 23] 20/1, won minor event at Lingfield (by ½ length from Demons And Wizards) on debut. *Michael Attwater* **75**

LAWS OF SPIN (IRE) 4 b.g. Lawman (FR) 121 – Spinning Well (IRE) 83 (Pivotal 124) [2017 105: 16g^4 14d^5 14d^6 12.8d* 18m 12s^5 Nov 5] good-topped gelding: useful handicapper: won at Leopardstown (by head from Machine Learner) in September: fourth at the Curragh in July: stays 2m: acts on soft going: usually tongue tied: often races nearer last than first. *W. P. Mullins, Ireland* **106**

LAWYER (IRE) 6 b.g. Acclamation 118 – Charaig (Rainbow Quest (USA) 134) [2017 87: t7.1g^4 Mar 15] good-topped gelding: fairly useful handicapper: fourth at Newcastle (¾ length behind Inaam) only start in 2017: stays 8.5f: acts on polytrack, tapeta, soft and good to firm going: tried in blinkers: sold £11,000 in May. *David Barron* **89**

LAYDEE VICTORIA (IRE) 2 b.f. (Feb 3) Sir Prancealot (IRE) 111 – Damask (IRE) 66 (Red Clubs (IRE) 125) [2017 6m 6m 7d^4 6d^3 t5g f6.1g^5 Dec 19] £10,000Y: third foal: half-sister to 5f winner Gorokai (by Kodiac): dam, maiden (should have stayed 7f), half-sister to very smart winner up to 1¼m Zafisio and smart winner up to 1½m Gold Trail: modest maiden: stays 6f: acts on fibresand and good to soft going: tried in cheekpieces. *Ollie Pears* **54**

LAYLA'S HERO (IRE) 10 b.g. One Cool Cat (USA) 123 – Capua (USA) (Private Terms (USA)) [2017 82: t7.1m p7d Feb 15] good-topped gelding: fairly useful handicapper: well below form in 2017: stays 1m: acts on polytrack, fibresand, good to firm and heavy going: usually wears headgear: tried in tongue tie: often races in rear. *Roger Teal* **–**

LAYTOWN (IRE) 2 ch.f. (Feb 16) Footstepsinthesand 120 – Miss Mocca 70 (Bahamian Bounty 116) [2017 t7.2g p7d^3 p7g^4 Oct 9] 8,000Y: first foal: dam, maiden (stayed 7f), half-sister to smart winner up to 7f Kiyoshi: modest form: best effort when third in minor event at Chelmsford (2 lengths behind Harbour Vision) in September. *Jamie Osborne* **63**

LAZARUS (IRE) 3 b.g. Zoffany (IRE) 121 – Knysna (IRE) 69 (Rock of Gibraltar (IRE) 133) [2017 10.2v^6 11.4d^2 12v^5 11.5d 10.2v p10g^2 Dec 20] €33,000F, €160,000Y: tall gelding: fourth foal: half-brother to 2 winners abroad, including French/Spanish winner **80**

up to 11.5f Irish Sand (2-y-o 7f winner, by Footstepsinthesand): dam maiden (stayed 1¼m): fair maiden: stays 11.5f: acts on good to soft going: tried in cheekpieces: wears tongue tie. *Amy Murphy*

LAZIO (IRE) 4 b.g. Intikhab (USA) 135 – La Spezia (IRE) 94 (Danehill Dancer (IRE) 117) [2017 76: p16d 16.3s^5 Jul 29] fair maiden, below best in 2017: best effort at 13f. *Jamie Osborne* –

LAZIZAH 4 b.f. Medicean 128 – Atyaab 78 (Green Desert (USA) 127) [2017 61: 9.9g p8g 9.9v Oct 19] compact filly: modest maiden at best: no form in 2017: sometimes in hood: tried in tongue tie: often races towards rear. *Marcus Tregoning* –

LBRETHA (FR) 4 b.f. Exceed And Excel (AUS) 126 – Actrice Francaise (USA) (Dynaformer (USA)) [2017 p7.5g^2 7g^3 8d* 8g^6 8s* 8g 8d^6 Oct 15] sturdy filly: fifth foal: closely related to French 2-y-o 1m winner Absolutely True (by Westerner) and half-sister to 2 winners in France, including 9f-1½m winner Accent Francais (by Halling): dam French 10.5f winner: useful performer: won handicap at Compiegne in May and listed race at Vichy (by neck from Maximum Aurelius) in July: below form last 2 starts, in Atalanta Stakes at Sandown first occasion: stays 1m: acts on polytrack and soft going. *Francis-Henri Graffard, France* **106**

L C SALOON 4 ch.g. Equiano (FR) 127 – Aberdovey 82 (Mister Baileys 123) [2017 80: f6d^5 5g Aug 21] fairly useful handicapper: below form in 2017: best effort at 5f: acts on good to firm going: sometimes finds little: sold £1,200, sent to Germany. *David C. Griffiths* **72**

LEAD A DANCE (IRE) 3 b.f. Henrythenavigator (USA) 131 – Dancing Diva (FR) (Sadler's Wells (USA) 132) [2017 7.1s p10d^5 Sep 28] sixth foal: half-sister to 3 winners, including 7f winner (stayed 1¼m) Cnocandancer and 1m winner Cnocan Diva (both by Danehill Dancer): dam unraced: little show in 2 maidens. *John Butler* –

LEADEROFTHEPACK 2 gr.g. (Feb 16) Lethal Force (IRE) 128 – Spontaneity (IRE) 59 (Holy Roman Emperor (IRE) 125) [2017 5m 5f^5 t5.1g^3 t6.1g^6 t6g^5 Oct 19] fair maiden: stays 6f: acts on tapeta: tried in cheekpieces. *Bryan Smart* **72**

LEADER'S LEGACY (USA) 3 b.c. War Front (USA) 119 – Bauble Queen (USA) (Arch (USA) 127) [2017 66p: 8.5g* 8m* 8m Jun 22] well-made colt: useful form: won maiden at Epsom in April and handicap at Haydock (by 1½ lengths from The Grape Escape) in May: stays 8.5f: in tongue tie last 3 starts. *Saeed bin Suroor* **102**

LEADER WRITER (FR) 5 b.h. Pivotal 124 – Miss Emma May (IRE) 84 (Hawk Wing (USA) 136) [2017 p8g^6 8d^3 p6s 8d^3 8s* 9d Sep 30] useful handicapper: won at Ascot (by 2¼ lengths from Storm Ahead) in September: left H-A. Pantall after second start: stays 1m: acts on viscoride, soft and good to firm going: in cheekpieces last 3 starts. *Henry Spiller* **107**

LEAHCAR 2 b.f. (May 4) Delegator 125 – Certral 86 (Iffraaj 127) [2017 t7.1d t7.1g t8g^4 Dec 6] first foal: dam, 1m-1¼m winner who stayed 1½m, half-sister to smart 1¼m-1½m winner (stays 1¾m) Connecticut: modest form: best effort when fourth in maiden at Newcastle (8¾ lengths behind Caring Touch) final start: will be suited by 1¼m: open to further improvement. *James Ewart* **62 p**

LEANDA J 2 ch.f. (Apr 15) Equiano (FR) 127 – Wedding Dream 81 (Oasis Dream 129) [2017 5s t6.1g Oct 27] third foal: half-sister to 2-y-o 6f winner (stayed 8.5f) As A Dream (by Azamour): dam winner up to 9.3f (2-y-o 1m winner): well held in minor event/seller: sold £800, sent to Denmark. *Ann Duffield* –

LEAN ON PETE (IRE) 8 b.g. Oasis Dream 129 – Superfonic (FR) (Zafonic (USA) 130) [2017 68, a74: f11g^3 10g 9.9m^5 9.9m^4 12.1m* 9.9f t12.2g 12.1d^4 f12.1g^2 9.9v f11.1g^2 f11.1g* Dec 21] good-topped gelding: fair handicapper: won at Beverley in June and Southwell in December: stays 1½m: acts on all-weather, good to firm and heavy going: has worn headgear: usually races close up. *Ollie Pears* **65** **a72**

LEAPT 3 b.g. Nathaniel (IRE) 129 – Liel 58 (Pivotal 124) [2017 71: 10d 14g^5 14s^2 14s^4 16s^4 11.8v^4 p12g Oct 9] lengthy gelding: fair maiden handicapper: stays 1¾m: acts on soft going: usually in hood: irresolute. *Richard Hughes* **76 §**

LEARN BY HEART 2 b.c. (Feb 12) Frankel 147 – Memory (IRE) 112 (Danehill Dancer (IRE) 117) [2017 6f^3 7d* 7d^4 8.2s^2 8v^4 Oct 23] smallish, lightly-made colt: third foal: closely related to 2-y-o 7f winner Recorder and 1m/1¾m winner Call To Mind (both by Galileo), both smart: dam 2-y-o 6f winner (including Albany and Cherry Hinton Stakes) who stayed 1m: useful performer: won minor event at Doncaster in June: second in listed race at Haydock (3½ lengths behind Chilean) in September: stays 1m: acts on soft going: sold 160,000 gns, sent to Denmark. *William Haggas* **101**

LE BRIVIDO (FR) 3 b.c. Siyouni (FR) 122 – La Bugatty (IRE) (Dr Fong (USA) 128) [2017 p6g* 8d² 7m* Jun 21] rather leggy colt: second foal: dam once-raced half-sister to smart winner up to 14.6f Dansant: very smart form: won newcomers race at Chantilly at 2 yrs: also won minor event at Chantilly in April and Jersey Stakes at Royal Ascot (by neck from Spirit of Valor) in June: only defeat when second in Poule d'Essai des Poulains at Deauville (short head behind Brametot) in between: stays 1m: acts on good to firm and good to soft going. *A. Fabre, France* **123**

LE CHAT D'OR 9 b.g. One Cool Cat (USA) 123 – Oh So Well (IRE) (Sadler's Wells (USA) 132) [2017 95: 8g 9.1s⁶ 8s* 8.2v 8v² Oct 12] fairly useful handicapper: won at Ayr (by neck from Lamloom) in July: stays 9f: acts on heavy going: usually wears headgear: wears tongue tie: races towards rear. *Michael Dods* **94**

LEDBURY (IRE) 5 b.g. Lawman (FR) 121 – Truly Magnificent (USA) 62 (Elusive Quality (USA)) [2017 –: p10g p10g⁵ t12.2g p12g⁶ p15.8g May 4] poor maiden nowadays: stays 1½m: acts on polytrack and fibresand: has worn headgear. *Lee Carter* **49**

LE DELUGE (FR) 7 b.g. Oratorio (IRE) 128 – Princess Sofia (UAE) (Pennekamp (USA) 130) [2017 74: 10g³ t12.4s t10.2s Sep 19] strong gelding: fair handicapper: well below form in 2017: wears tongue tie. *Micky Hammond* **–**

LEDHAM (IRE) 2 b.c. (Mar 27) Shamardal (USA) 129 – Pioneer Bride (USA) (Gone West (USA)) [2017 7s⁴ Aug 2] 115,000F, 200,000Y: big, rangy colt: brother to useful 1¼m winner Global Force and half-brother to 3 winners, including smart 6f-1m winner Yamal and unreliable winner up to 1m (stayed 1¼m) Trailblazing (2-y-o 6f winner) (both by Green Desert): dam ran once: 7/1, plenty of promise when fourth in minor event at Sandown (8½ lengths behind Connect) on debut: will stay 1m: open to significant improvement. *Sir Michael Stoute* **72 P**

LEESHAAN (IRE) 2 b.c. (Jan 26) Bated Breath 125 – La Grande Elisa (IRE) (Ad Valorem (USA) 125) [2017 5f³ 6g⁴ 7m* 7.1m⁶ 7g t6g⁶ Sep 22] good-topped colt: fair performer: won minor event at Haydock in June: stays 7f: acts on good to firm going. *James Tate* **76**

LEFORTOVO (FR) 4 b.g. Arcano (IRE) 122 – Lorientaise (IRE) (Xaar 132) [2017 96: p8g³ 7d⁵ 7m³ 7m Jul 14] useful performer: third in minor events at Chantilly (beaten 2 lengths by Lord Glitters) and Doncaster (1½ lengths behind Classic Seniority): stays 8.5f: acts on polytrack, tapeta, good to firm and good to soft going: in cheekpieces last 2 starts. *Jo Hughes* **95**

LEFT ALONE 2 b.f. (Jan 28) Reckless Abandon 119 – Akhmatova 100 (Cape Cross (IRE) 129) [2017 6d³ p6g² 7m² Oct 25] 47,000F, €120,000Y: attractive filly: second foal: half-sister to 2-y-o 6f winner Walaaa (by Exceed And Excel): dam, 8.3f-1¼m winner who stayed 1½m, closely related to useful winner up to 1m Rudolf Valentino: fairly useful form: best effort when second in maiden at Kempton (1¼ lengths behind Tivoli) in October: should prove as effective at 7f as 6f. *Hugo Palmer* **86**

LEFT HAND 4 ch.f. Dubawi (IRE) 129 – Balladeuse (FR) 113 (Singspiel (IRE) 133) [2017 117: 10.4g⁶ 11.9g⁴ 11.9g⁵ 9.9g³ 11.9d³ 9.9d⁵ 12s Oct 21] close-coupled filly: smart performer: third in Prix Jean Romanet at Deauville (1¼ lengths behind Ajman Princess) and Prix Vermeille at Chantilly (5½ lengths behind Bateel, had won race in 2016): stays 1½m: acts on good to firm and good to soft going: usually wears headgear. *C. Laffon-Parias, France* **114**

LEGAL HISTORY (IRE) 2 b.c. (Apr 13) Lawman (FR) 121 – Nina Celebre (IRE) (Peintre Celebre (USA) 137) [2017 p8g Dec 20] fourth foal: half-brother to useful 2-y-o 6f winner Ninas Terz (by Tertullian) and very smart but temperamental Hong Kong 6f/7f winner Pakistan Star (by Shamardal): dam winner up to 1¼m (2-y-o 7f winner): 25/1, eighth in minor event at Kempton (5¾ lengths behind Native Appeal) in December: capable of better. *Ed Walker* **69 p**

LEGALIZED 3 br.f. Authorized (IRE) 133 – Laurena (GER) (Acatenango (GER) 127) [2017 –: 16.1d⁶ f16.5g 14s⁶ p16d⁴ t16.3g Oct 19] modest maiden handicapper: stays 2m: acts on polytrack and good to soft going. *James Given* **53**

LEGATO (IRE) 3 ch.g. Power 117 – Lisa Gherardini (IRE) 53 (Barathea (IRE) 127) [2017 –: 8.3g⁶ 8.5m⁴ 10.3m 11.6d³ 11.8g 11.8s Aug 8] fair maiden: stays 11.5f: acts on good to firm and good to soft going: tried in cheekpieces: sometimes slowly away. *Tom Dascombe* **70**

LEGENDARY LUNCH (IRE) 3 ch.c. Dragon Pulse (IRE) 114 – Taalluf (USA) 82 (Hansel (USA)) [2017 104: 6f 6m Jun 23] well-made colt: useful performer at 2 yrs: well held both starts in 2017: stays 6f: acts on soft going: sold 35,000 gns in July, sent to Bahrain. *Richard Hannon* **–**

Jersey Stakes, Royal Ascot—Le Brivido (spots on cap) overhauls Spirit of Valor (blinkers), with Mubtasim (far right) and Parfait (cheekpieces) completing the frame

LEGENDOIRE (IRE) 3 b.g. Fast Company (IRE) 126 – Last Shaambles (IRE) (Shaamit (IRE) 127) [2017 62: p8g 7g^{3} 6.1m May 5] modest maiden: stays 7f: acts on polytrack. *John Gallagher* **62**

LEGEND STATUS (IRE) 3 b.c. Sir Prancealot (IRE) 111 – Baby Bunting 63 (Wolfhound (USA) 126) [2017 –: 5.8g 7.2d^{4} Jun 5] modest maiden: stays 7f: acts on polytrack and good to soft going: sometimes in tongue tie. *A. P. Keatley, Ireland* **55**

LE GROS SERPANT (IRE) 2 b.c. (May 3) Zoffany (IRE) 121 – Fatwa (IRE) 95 (Lahib (USA) 129) [2017 5g^{5} 6s 5d p8g^{4} Aug 15] poor form: stays 1m. *Keith Dalgleish* **46**

LEIGH'S LAW (IRE) 2 b.f. (Mar 8) Lawman (FR) 121 – Delira (IRE) 75 (Namid 128) [2017 p8g Nov 8] 50,000Y: third foal: half-sister to useful 2-y-o 1m winner (stays 1¼m) Wahash (by Dark Angel): dam, 5.5f winner, half-sister to smart winner up to 1½m Barrier Reef: 33/1, well held in minor event at Kempton. *Hugo Palmer* –

LEITH BRIDGE 5 b.g. Avonbridge 123 – Ishibee (IRE) 64 (Ishiguru (USA) 114) [2017 52: p5g 7.4g 7s 6.1m 5.7d^{6} f7.1g Aug 28] poor maiden handicapper: stays 6f: acts on polytrack and good to soft going: has worn headgear, including last 4 starts. *Mark Usher* **48**

LE LAITIER (FR) 6 b.g. Milk It Mick 120 – La Brigitte 92 (Tobougg (IRE) 125) [2017 64: 6d 7g 6g 6g^{4} f6.1g^{5} 6s f5g f7.1g Dec 4] modest handicapper on turf, poor on all-weather: stays 7f: acts on firm going: in headgear last 5 starts. *Scott Dixon* **52** **a46**

LE MANEGE ENCHANTE (IRE) 4 gr.g. Zebedee 113 – Beth 79 (Deportivo 116) [2017 67§: t6f 6d^{3} 6v^{4} 6d 6g* 6d^{6} 6d 6d^{3} Oct 24] good-topped gelding: modest handicapper: won at Thirsk in August: stays 6f: acts on tapeta and good to soft going: usually wears headgear: often races towards rear: one to treat with caution. *Derek Shaw* **64 §**

LEMON DROP 3 b.f. Paco Boy (IRE) 129 – Zia (GER) (Grand Lodge (USA) 125) [2017 55: 8.3m 8m^{6} 9.9g^{3} 11.6s^{4} 11.6s^{5} p12g 11.9s^{5} Oct 10] sparely-made filly: modest maiden: in headgear last 5 starts: sometimes slowly away. *Jim Boyle* **50**

LEMON THYME 4 b.f. Sakhee's Secret 128 – Limonia (GER) 64 (Perugino (USA) 84) [2017 53: p8g^{5} t9.5g t9.5g t9.5g Mar 27] modest maiden: stays 1m: acts on polytrack: often in headgear: sold £600, sent to Germany. *Mike Murphy* **53**

LENIN (IRE) 2 gr.c. (May 25) Arakan (USA) 123 – Virginia Woolf 105 (Daylami (IRE) 138) [2017 p7s p8g^{6} Dec 23] modest form: better effort when sixth in minor event at Lingfield (6¾ lengths behind Lawn Ranger) in December. *J. S. Moore* **54**

LENOIRE 3 b.f. Galileo (IRE) 134 – Latice (IRE) 121 (Inchinor 119) [2017 58: 10.2v^{6} 8d 10d^{3} Aug 14] modest maiden: stays 1¼m: tried in cheekpieces. *Michael Appleby* **60**

LEODIS (IRE) 5 ch.g. Shirocco (GER) 129 – Leonica 92 (Lion Cavern (USA) 117) [2017 11.9m f12.1g^{5} Nov 28] fair form in bumpers: well held in maidens on Flat. *Tom Tate* –

LEO MINOR (USA) 3 b.c. War Front (USA) 119 – Kissed (IRE) 110 (Galileo (IRE) 134) [2017 94: p6g p6g^6 Dec 30] fairly useful handicapper: stays 7.5f: acts on polytrack and soft going: front runner/races prominently. *Robert Cowell* **92**

LEONARDO (GER) 5 ch.g. Areion (GER) 115 – Lolli Pop (GER) (Cagliostro (GER)) [2017 –: 11.6m^2 t12.2g 10m 12g p5g p8g Dec 30] angular gelding: modest maiden: form in 2017 only on return: left Mark Pitman after fifth start: stays 11.5f: acts on good to firm going: tried in tongue tie: front runner/races prominently. *Shaun Lycett* **59 d**

LEONARD THOMAS 7 b.g. Singspiel (IRE) 133 – Monawara (IRE) 73 (Namaqualand (USA)) [2017 63, a72: t8d^3 t9.5g p12f^3 t10.2g 7g^6 10g 9s^4 t10.2s 7m^5 8g^6 9.9m^6 t12.4d Dec 16] modest handicapper on turf, fair on all-weather: left Tony Carroll after fourth start, Philip Kirby after eleventh: stays 1½m: acts on polytrack, tapeta, soft and good to firm going: usually wears headgear: tried in tongue tie: sometimes slowly away, usually races nearer last than first. *Rebecca Menzies* **54 a67**

LEONIDAS (IRE) 3 b.g. Dalakhani (IRE) 133 – Marque Royale 107 (Royal Academy (USA) 130) [2017 70: 9.9d^6 11.4m^4 Oct 16] rather leggy gelding: fair maiden: will stay beyond 1½m: acts on good to firm going: sometimes slowly away, often races in rear. *Marcus Tregoning* **76**

LEONTES 3 ch.g. Paco Boy (IRE) 129 – Robema 89 (Cadeaux Genereux 131) [2017 96: t6g^5 5.1s 6s p7g^2 Sep 9] rather leggy gelding: fairly useful handicapper: second at Kempton final start: stays 7f: acts on polytrack and soft going: sometimes slowly away. *Andrew Balding* **92**

LEOPARD (IRE) 3 b.g. Iffraaj 127 – Appletreemagic (IRE) 72 (Indian Danehill (IRE) 124) [2017 –: p8g 7.4m^4 t8.6g^6 8m 7.8d 11.2v^3 10g 14v^3 Nov 7] modest maiden: left Paul Cole after first start: stays 1¾m: acts on polytrack, tapeta, good to firm and heavy going: sometimes in headgear. *Tony Coyle* **63**

LE PINCHY (GER) 3 ch.g. Adlerflug (GER) 123 – Lady Manners (USA) (Montbrook (USA)) [2017 –: 12v Sep 30] well held in maidens. *Tom Dascombe* **–**

LE ROI DU TEMPS (USA) 4 ch.g. Leroidesanimaux (BRZ) 127 – Minute Limit (IRE) 78 (Pivotal 124) [2017 83: 7g 7g t8g Dec 6] fairly useful handicapper: well below form in 2017: sometimes in cheekpieces. *Tom Tate* **–**

LESANTI 3 b.g. Royal Applause 124 – Kammaan 85 (Diktat 126) [2017 –: 7g t7.1g^4 7m^2 8.5d^5 8s^6 7m^3 p6d^5 8s p7g t8.6g p10s Nov 16] sturdy gelding: modest maiden handicapper: stays 7f: acts on good to firm going: tried in cheekpieces: often races prominently. *Ed de Giles* **58**

LES ARCEAUX (IRE) 3 b.g. Arcano (IRE) 122 – Amoureux (USA) (Deputy Minister (CAN)) [2017 –: p8g^5 10m^4 9.5s* 9.7s^6 11.2v* 12v* Oct 24] fair handicapper: won at Gowran in June, Carlisle in September and Fairyhouse in October: stays 1½m: acts on polytrack, good to firm and heavy going: often races prominently. *John Patrick Murtagh, Ireland* **79**

LES DARCY 6 b.g. Haatef (USA) 117 – Overcome (Belmez (USA) 131) [2017 –: p8d f7m Mar 7] fair handicapper at best, no form since 2014: in hood last 2 starts: tried in tongue tie: usually races nearer last than first. *Ken Cunningham-Brown* **–**

L'ES FREMANTLE (FR) 6 b.g. Orpen (USA) 116 – Grand Design 64 (Danzero (AUS)) [2017 46: 9.9v Sep 26] poor maiden handicapper: best effort at 1¼m: acts on good to firm and heavy going: has worn headgear: sometimes slowly away, often races prominently. *Michael Chapman* **43**

LES GAR GAN (IRE) 6 b.m. Iffraaj 127 – Story (Observatory (USA) 131) [2017 66: t9.5m p8d t8.6g t9.5g^5 Feb 23] angular mare: one-time fairly useful handicapper: no form in 2017: usually wears headgear: sometimes slowly away, usually races towards rear. *Daniel Loughnane* **–**

LESHLAA (USA) 3 ch.c. Street Cry (IRE) 130 – Vine Street (IRE) 88 (Singspiel (IRE) 133) [2017 91p: t8s 10m* 10d^4 8m^5 10m^4 p8g a9.9g* 10m^6 Sep 23] strong, good-bodied colt: smart performer: won handicap at Newmarket (by neck from Dubai Horizon) in May and Anatolia Trophy at Veliefendi (by 1½ lengths from Cerastes) in September: fifth in Britannia Stakes (Handicap) at Royal Ascot in June: stays 1¼m: acts on polytrack and good to firm going: has worn hood: often travels strongly. *Saeed bin Suroor* **117**

LES PECHEURS (IRE) 3 b.f. Lilbourne Lad (IRE) 111 – Sweet Kristeen (USA) 69 (Candy Stripes (USA) 115) [2017 6g^5 8s^3 8g^3 10d 9.9s^4 9.2s f12.1g Aug 28] €25,000F: half-sister to several winners, including 8.3f winner Cliche (by Diktat) and winner up to 7f Al Shahaniya (by Zoffany), both useful/stayed 1¼m: dam 7f winner: modest maiden: stays 1¼m: acts on soft going: in hood last 3 starts. *James Ewart* **59**

LESTER KRIS (IRE) 3 b.g. Fame And Glory 133 – Wood Sprite 51 (Mister Baileys 123) **83**
[2017 76: 12.1m^4 11.9d^2 12.1m^3 11.4d^2 p12g 11.8v^2 14.2v^3 11.9g^4 Oct 29] workmanlike gelding: fairly useful maiden: in frame 7 times in 2017: gelded after final outing: stays 1¾m: acts on good to firm and heavy going: tried in cheekpieces: front runner/races prominently. *Richard Hannon*

LETBYGONESBEICONS 4 b.g. Sixties Icon 125 – Composing (IRE) 71 (Noverre **64**
(USA) 125) [2017 65: f6g^4 t6g Jan 21] fair handicapper: stays 7.5f: acts on fibresand, tapeta, good to firm and heavy going: sent to Poland. *John Balding*

LETHAL ANGEL 2 gr.f. (Mar 19) Lethal Force (IRE) 128 – Heliograph (Ishiguru (USA) **69 p**
114) [2017 7m^6 t6.1g p6s^3 Dec 7] 3,500 2-y-o: good-topped filly: third foal: half-sister to winner abroad by Compton Place: dam once-raced half-sister to useful winner up to 6f Prolific: fair form: best effort when third in minor event at Chelmsford (3 lengths behind Mushtaq) final start: remains with potential. *Stuart Williams*

LETHAL IMPACT (JPN) 3 b.c. Deep Impact (JPN) 134 – Musical Way (FR) 112 (Gold **84**
Away (IRE) 125) [2017 79p: 11m^6 11.6g 14m^5 p16g^3 p16g^6 Sep 13] compact colt: fairly useful maiden: third in handicap at Kempton in August: stays 2m: acts on polytrack and tapeta: in headgear last 2 starts: sold 13,000 gns in October. *David Simcock*

LETHAL LADY 2 ch.f. (Feb 10) Lethal Force (IRE) 128 – Lady In The Bath (Forzando **–**
122) [2017 6m 7m^6 Jul 23] fourth foal: half-sister to 6f winner Especial (by Misu Bond): dam very lightly raced: well held in pair of minor events. *Michael Dods*

LETHAL LUNCH 2 gr.c. (Apr 14) Lethal Force (IRE) 128 – Pin Cushion 85 (Pivotal **88**
124) [2017 5m 5.1m^3 6m* 7g^4 7g Sep 22] 30,000F, £62,000Y: workmanlike colt: third foal: half-brother to 2-y-o 7f winner Pinch A Kiss (by Sakhee's Secret) and 2-y-o 5f winner Tadkhirah (by Acclamation): dam, 6f winner, half-sister to useful winner up to 7f Greensward out of July Cup winner Frizzante: fairly useful performer: won minor event at Ascot (by 1¾ lengths from Rebel Streak) in July: fourth in nursery at Sandown in September: left Richard Hannon after third start: stays 7f: acts on good to firm going: sometimes slowly away. *Clive Cox*

LE TISSIER 4 ch.g. Sir Percy 129 – Incarnation (IRE) 72 (Samum (GER) 126) [2017 68: **61**
p15.8g^2 p13g^2 p16d p16g^4 11.6m p15.8g 14m 16.3d^6 11.9m Aug 9] angular gelding: modest maiden handicapper: stays 2m: acts on polytrack and good to firm going: wears headgear. *Michael Attwater*

LET IT GO 5 b.m. Halling (USA) 133 – Kisses (Sakhee (USA) 136) [2017 –: p7d t6m **–**
Mar 17] of no account: has worn hood. *Tony Carroll*

LETMESTOPYOUTHERE (IRE) 3 b.g. Sir Prancealot (IRE) 111 – Romanylei (IRE) **91**
106 (Blues Traveller (IRE) 119) [2017 90: t7.1g* p6d^4 p8g^5 t7.1f^6 t7.1g t6g^2 p6g 7.6m^6 7.2s 6.1m^3 6f^3 6d 6.1g^3 6.1s^3 6v^3 6v^2 6s 7d^6 p7g^6 f6.1g^5 Dec 19] leggy gelding: fairly useful handicapper: won at Newcastle (by ½ length from Dr Julius No) in January: third at Chepstow in August and September: stays 1m: acts on polytrack, tapeta, good to firm and heavy going: usually races towards rear: consistent. *David Evans*

LET RIGHT BE DONE 5 gr.g. Lawman (FR) 121 – Cheerfully 67 (Sadler's Wells **56**
(USA) 132) [2017 65: t8g 9m^5 9.1m 8g^3 8m 7.2m^6 7.2g^5 10d 7.2s* 7.2g^6 8.9m^4 7.2d 8m^3 8g^4 7.2d 8.3s 6d 8s 7.2s* 8v 7.2v t7.1d^5 Nov 4] modest handicapper: won at Ayr (apprentice) in July and Musselburgh in October: stays 1¼m: acts on tapeta, soft and good to firm going: wears headgear. *Linda Perratt*

LETSBE AVENUE (IRE) 2 b.c. (May 4) Lawman (FR) 121 – Aguilas Perla (IRE) **79**
(Indian Ridge 123) [2017 7g^6 7g 7d^6 p7g* 7m Oct 25] well-made colt: fair performer: won nursery at Kempton in September: raced only at 7f: acts on polytrack. *Richard Hannon*

LET'S BE HAPPY (IRE) 3 gr.f. Mastercraftsman (IRE) 129 – Corrozal (GER) (Cape **72**
Cross (IRE) 129) [2017 69: p8g^6 p12g^2 9.9m* 9.9g^2 11.4g^3 12m^5 p12g^3 p12g^4 Oct 24] fair handicapper: won at Brighton in June: third at Kempton in October: stays 1½m: acts on polytrack, tapeta and good to firm going: wears cheekpieces: usually races close up. *Richard Hughes*

LET'S SWAY 3 b.f. Authorized (IRE) 133 – Let's Dance (IRE) 70 (Danehill Dancer (IRE) **–**
117) [2017 –: 8m 9.9g^4 p10g^4 11.4m 11.6d^6 Jun 24] modest maiden: in hood last 5 starts: often races freely. *Amy Murphy*

LET'S TWIST 5 ch.g. Piccolo 121 – Takes Two To Tango 69 (Groom Dancer (USA) 128) **67**
[2017 82: p7d^6 7g^3 7g^6 6.9d 8g Sep 27] fairly useful handicapper: below form in 2017: stays 1m: acts on polytrack, tapeta and good to soft going: usually wears blinkers. *Kristin Stubbs*

LEVANTE PLAYER (IRE) 2 b.g. (Mar 15) Kodiac 112 – Isolde's Return (Avonbridge 123) [2017 5m 6.1g^{3} 5.1d^{5} 6d p8g^{4} p10g^{6} Oct 18] tall gelding: fair maiden: stays 1m: acts on polytrack: in cheekpieces last 3 starts. *Tom Dascombe* **70**

LEVEN (IRE) 3 b.g. The Carbon Unit (USA) 106 – The Real Thing (IRE) 84 (Traditionally (USA) 117) [2017 8m 10m^{4} 12s 13.1s^{6} 8.3g^{5} 11.1s Aug 5] modest maiden: best effort at 1¼m: acts on good to firm going: tried in blinkers. *John Patrick Shanahan, Ireland* **56**

LEVER DU SOLEIL (FR) 2 b.g. (Feb 16) Le Havre (IRE) 124 – Morning Dust (IRE) (Invincible Spirit (IRE) 121) [2017 6m 7m 7g Sep 27] little form in minor events/maiden. *Tim Easterby* **–**

LEWINSKY (IRE) 3 b.f. Famous Name 124 – Happy Flight (IRE) (Titus Livius (FR) 115) [2017 p10s^{2} t9.5g^{4} 10s^{4} p8d^{4} t8g^{2} t10.2g^{3} t9.5g Dec 22] €6,500Y, resold £38,000Y: half-sister to 2-y-o 1m winner (stays 1¼m) Dodgybingo (by Roderic O'Connor) and a winner in Italy by Denon: dam Italian 5f/6f winner (including at 2 yrs): fair maiden: left Hugo Palmer after fifth start: best effort at 1¼m: acts on polytrack: often races prominently. *Antony Brittain* **73**

LEXINGTON ABBEY 6 b.g. Sleeping Indian 122 – Silvereine (FR) (Bering 136) [2017 105: 5g^{2} t5g^{2} 5g^{4} 5d^{3} 5.6g^{4} Sep 16] sturdy gelding: useful handicapper: second at Newcastle (½ length behind Line of Reason) in June: stays 6f: acts on tapeta, good to firm and heavy going: wears headgear: usually races prominently. *Kevin Ryan* **105**

LEXINGTON EMPIRE 2 ch.g. (Jan 28) Intello (GER) 129 – Emperice (USA) (Empire Maker (USA) 129) [2017 p8g t8.6g Nov 25] well held in minor events. *David Lanigan* **–**

LEXINGTON GRACE (IRE) 2 b.f. (May 1) Sir Prancealot (IRE) 111 – Bronze Baby (USA) (Silver Charm (USA) 132) [2017 5.1m^{6} 5g^{2} 5m^{3} 6.1f* 6m^{5} 6m^{4} 5.2v 7d* 7m* 7s^{3} 7m* 8f^{4} Nov 25] €36,000Y: leggy filly: fifth foal: half-sister to 3 winners, including 2-y-o 7f winner Scutum and 7f winner Sunbaked (both by Kodiac): dam lightly-raced half-sister to 1000 Guineas runner-up Arch Swing: useful performer: won minor event at Nottingham in June, seller at Newmarket in August, and nurseries at Epsom in August and Newmarket in October: left Richard Hannon before 3 lengths fourth to Daddy Is A Legend in Grade 3 Jimmy Durante Stakes at Del Mar final start: stays 1m: acts on firm and soft going: usually wears headgear. *Ian Kruljac, USA* **97**

LEXINGTON LAW (IRE) 4 b.g. Lawman (FR) 121 – Tus Nua (IRE) (Galileo (IRE) 134) [2017 83: t12.2g^{2} 14m^{4} 12d^{3} 10.2d^{3} 10.2v^{3} 10s p12g* Dec 30] sturdy gelding: fairly useful handicapper: won at Lingfield (by ½ length from Zubayr) in December: stays 1½m: acts on polytrack and tapeta: in headgear last 2 starts. *Alan King* **93**

LEXINGTON PLACE 7 ch.g. Compton Place 125 – Elidore 95 (Danetime (IRE) 121) [2017 93: 5m^{6} 5m^{4} 5m^{6} 5d 5g 5m^{4} 5d^{4} 5s* 5s^{6} 5m 5v Sep 28] good-quartered gelding: fairly useful handicapper: won at Pontefract (by ½ length from Muatadel) in August: stays 6f: acts on fibresand, tapeta, firm and soft going: has worn headgear: often races towards rear. *Ruth Carr* **82**

LEXINGTON SKY (IRE) 3 b.f. Iffraaj 127 – Hurricane Lily (IRE) 61 (Ali-Royal (IRE) 127) [2017 78: 6m 6d^{5} 6g 6.1v* 6g^{3} 6.1g^{5} 6s^{6} f6.1g 6s 7.2v^{6} 7d^{5} Oct 30] compact filly: fairly useful handicapper: won at Nottingham (by 2½ lengths from Stringybark Creek) in August: stays 7f: acts on polytrack and heavy going: tried in cheekpieces: sold 6,000 gns in October. *Roger Fell* **81**

LEXINGTON TIMES (IRE) 5 b.g. Paco Boy (IRE) 129 – Fuaigh Mor (IRE) 68 (Dubai Destination (USA) 127) [2017 97: f7g p7g^{5} t7.1d^{2} p7g^{2} p7g 7s^{2} 7d 7m 6.1s^{2} 6s^{5} 6.1g^{2} 6g* 6d^{3} 6g 6g^{5} 6v^{6} 7g Oct 13] fairly useful handicapper: won at York (by ¾ length from Pomme de Terre) in July: stays 7f: acts on polytrack, tapeta, soft and good to firm going: wears cheekpieces: sometimes slowly away, usually races towards rear. *Ruth Carr* **92**

LEXI'S HERO (IRE) 9 b.g. Invincible Spirit (IRE) 121 – Christel Flame (Darshaan 133) [2017 90: 5s 5.1d^{5} Jul 1] big, strong gelding: fairly useful handicapper: below form both starts in 2017: stays 6f: acts on polytrack, fibresand, soft and good to firm going: wears headgear: often races prominently. *Patrick Morris* **74**

L'EXPLORA (USA) 2 b.f. (Apr 28) War Front (USA) 119 – Damson (IRE) 113 (Entrepreneur 123) [2017 p6g Oct 4] $320,000Y: half-sister to several winners, including 2-y-o 5f winners Requinto (smart) and Independence Day (useful) (both by Dansili): dam 2-y-o 5f/6f winner: 10/1, very considerately handled when well held in maiden at Kempton: will prove different proposition in time. *Roger Charlton* **– P**

L FRANK BAUM (IRE) 10 b.g. Sinndar (IRE) 134 – Rainbow City (IRE) 85 (Rainbow Quest (USA) 134) [2017 16.2m May 5] fairly useful handicapper in 2013: well held only start on Flat since: stays 21.5f: acts on soft going: has worn headgear: poor hurdler nowadays. *Bernard Llewellyn* –

LIAMBA 2 b.f. (Feb 5) Equiano (FR) 127 – Hisaronu (IRE) 75 (Stravinsky (USA) 133) [2017 5s^5 Oct 31] fourth foal: half-sister to useful 7f/1m winner Philba (by Cockney Rebel): dam, ran twice, closely related to useful 1¼m winner (stayed 1½m) Dream To Dress: 33/1, hinted at ability when well held in minor event at Catterick: should do better. *David O'Meara* – **p**

LIBERATUM 3 b.g. Paco Boy (IRE) 129 – Fine Lady 70 (Selkirk (USA) 129) [2017 63: 5g^3 5m^2 5d^3 5.7s 5.1s* 5.1g^2 5m^4 t6.1g^3 6s^2 t5d^5 Oct 24] fairly useful handicapper: won at Windsor (by 1¼ lengths from Lydia's Place) in August: second at Chester (neck behind Boundsy) in September: stays 6f: acts on tapeta and soft going: tried in tongue tie. *Ruth Carr* **83**

LIBERTY LYNX 2 b.f. (Mar 20) High Chaparral (IRE) 132 – Stella Point (IRE) 93 (Pivotal 124) [2017 p7g Dec 28] third foal: half-sister to 1m winner Caravela (by Henrythenavigator): dam, 10.3f winner, half-sister to useful 1m-11f winner Cilium out of useful 2-y-o 6f/7f winner Venturi: 12/1, well held in minor event at Lingfield. *William Haggas* –

LIBRISA BREEZE 5 gr.g. Mount Nelson 125 – Bruxcalina (FR) (Linamix (FR) 127) [2017 123: 6m^4 7g 7d^2 6s* Oct 21] **125**

'I have no idea whether a "gamble" was landed but I did notice he was well backed,' said Roger Charlton after his 5/1 favourite Withhold—who had been as long as 12/1 in the morning—had run away with the Cesarewitch by three and three quarter lengths in track-record time. 'Everyone did their due diligence and I was asked just before the race if everything was okay, and I said yes'. The man asking Charlton the question was Withhold's owner Tony Bloom who had bought the horse for 170,000 guineas at the 2016 Newmarket Autumn Horses In Training Sales from Juddmonte Farms. Withhold had been in training with Charlie Hills and won two of his eight starts, including a two-mile handicap at Haydock just twelve days before he was sold. The new connections kept Withhold off the course until late-September, three weeks before the Cesarewitch, Charlton adding 'I insisted on the horse being gelded, the offspring of Champs Elysees improve and we knew he stayed two miles, so I thought if we didn't run him, he wouldn't go up the handicap.' Withhold ran for Charlton at Newbury over an inadequate mile and a half, finishing third behind Daphne and Weekender when making a comeback full of promise. With an entire year dedicated to the race, Withhold justified the considerable faith placed in him by putting up an impressive display in the Cesarewitch, leading a mile from home and gradually being brought across from his wide draw to the stands side by Silvestre de Sousa and having the race to himself in the final furlong.

Withhold's win began an excellent seven-day period for Tony Bloom, with his football club Brighton & Hove Albion trouncing West Ham 3-0 the following Friday, and Librisa Breeze winning the Champions Sprint on British Champions'

Qipco British Champions Sprint Stakes, Ascot—Librisa Breeze proves better than ever and provides trainer Dean Ivory with a first Group 1 success, following near misses with the likes of Tropics in the 2015 July Cup; Tasleet (striped cap, cheekpieces) and Caravaggio (No.9) fill the places, with July Cup/Sprint Cup winner Harry Angel below form in fourth

Mr Tony Bloom's "Librisa Breeze"

Day on the Saturday. Bloom had bought Librisa Breeze from the equivalent Horses In Training Sales in 2015 out of Jeremy Noseda's yard for 60,000 guineas. Sent to Dean Ivory, Librisa Breeze quickly went about repaying his new connections, going from a handicap win at Wolverhampton to finishing an unfortunate but still lucrative second in the Royal Hunt Cup on his second start. Librisa Breeze had won for Noseda over a mile and a quarter, but his strong-travelling style and sharp turn of foot prompted his new trainer to drop him down to seven furlongs on his third start for the yard, a move that led to further improvement as Librisa Breeze landed a pair of very valuable handicaps over that trip at Ascot, the International in July and the Challenge Cup in October. Librisa Breeze overcame plenty of trouble in running to win the Challenge Cup from a BHA mark of 108, marking himself down as a pattern winner in waiting. Things didn't fall right for Librisa Breeze either on his first try at pattern level in the 2016 Champions Sprint Stakes; ridden to come from a long way back, as had become usual, he also found himself short of room a furlong out and could manage only sixth behind The Tin Man. Given the way he is ridden, Librisa Breeze can be something of a hostage to fortune in his races, borne out further during his first three starts of 2017, when he met trouble when fourth again behind The Tin Man in the Diamond Jubilee Stakes at Royal Ascot, before enduring an even more torrid passage in a muddling Lennox Stakes at Goodwood. He met minor interference on his third start in the Hungerford Stakes at Newbury but, even with a clearer run, wouldn't have beaten the revitalised Massaat, who had been second in the previous season's Two Thousand Guineas.

Librisa Breeze had been all the rage for the Hungerford but was sent off at double-figure odds for his second crack at the Champions Sprint in October. That was due in no small part to the presence of three-year-old Harry Angel, who had put up one of the performances of the season when winning the Sprint Cup at Haydock on his previous start. Harry Angel and Librisa Breeze had very different records at Ascot, with the former having been beaten on all three of his starts at the track (his only defeats) while Librisa Breeze had enjoyed his best days on Ascot's straight seven-furlong course in the previous season. Harry Angel was below his best once again at Ascot, finishing only fourth, while Librisa Breeze belatedly stepped up on his best form from the previous season to land a first pattern success. The patient tactics that had proven Librisa Breeze's downfall on more than one occasion worked out ideally in the Champions Sprint, which was run on testing ground and into a headwind, placing more emphasis on stamina. Smuggled into the race by regular jockey Robert Winston (who reportedly postponed his retirement from the saddle when Librisa Breeze came along), Librisa Breeze challenged last of all and led inside the final hundred yards, beating a field of sprinters that contained a number who had already scored at Group 1 level earlier in the season. The win—by a length and a quarter from Tasleet—was a first Group 1 for trainer Dean Ivory and capped a memorable season for his stable which also landed the Stewards' Cup with Lancelot du Lac.

Librisa Breeze (gr.g. 2012)	Mount Nelson (b 2004)	Rock of Gibraltar (b 1999)	Danehill
			Offshore Boom
		Independence (b 1998)	Selkirk
			Yukon Hope
	Bruxcalina (FR) (gr 2004)	Linamix (gr 1987)	Mendez
			Lunadix
		Brusca (b or br 1998)	Grindstone
			Chic Corine

As has been said, Librisa Breeze won at a mile and a quarter when trained by Jeremy Noseda and has plenty of stamina in his pedigree, for all that he has proved best as a sprinter. A sturdy gelding, he is a first Group 1 winner for former Newsells Park stallion Mount Nelson who now stands as a jumps stallion at Boardsmill Stud in Ireland and is also the sire of Spa Hurdle winner Penhill who is also owned by Tony Bloom. Librisa Breeze is out of the Linamix mare Bruxcalina, a mile and a quarter winner who was listed placed in France for Andre Fabre and is a half-sister to several other winners, notably the Prix La Force winner Baraan, who finished third in the Prix du Jockey Club, and Brampour, a useful stayer in France who became a very smart hurdler for Paul Nicholls. Bruxcalina's second and third foals have both made the racecourse, Belle Dauphine (by Dalakhani) winning over thirteen furlongs in the French Provinces, and three-year-old Butterfly Lily (by Lawman) finishing sixth over seven furlongs at Newbury for Ralph Beckett on her only start to date. Bruxcalina's fourth foal is a sister to Librisa Breeze and made 120,000 guineas at the Newmarket October Yearling Sales in 2016, while a brother to Butterfly Lily was sold for only 25,000 guineas at the equivalent sales in 2017. Librisa Breeze will continue to be a force in the best six- and seven-furlong races in the next season, though the exaggerated waiting tactics used on him mean he will need things to drop right. He travels strongly and acts on good to firm and soft going, as well as on polytrack and tapeta. *Dean Ivory*

LICENSE TO THRILL (USA) 3 b.g. Mizzen Mast (USA) 121 – Mystic Miracle (Dalakhani (IRE) 133) [2017 66: p8g^3 p8g^5 p8d^5 Jan 18] fair maiden handicapper: stays 1m: acts on polytrack. *Simon Dow* **64**

LICINIUS 2 b.g. (Mar 28) Rock of Gibraltar (IRE) 133 – Vespasia (Medicean 128) [2017 p7g Dec 28] 33/1, well held in minor event at Lingfield. *Charles Hills* **–**

LIFEBOAT (IRE) 2 b.g. (Mar 28) Born To Sea (IRE) 117 – Mrs Seek (Unfuwain (USA) 131) [2017 6.5g^5 7d^2 7g^6 7g Oct 7] €26,000F, 55,000Y: rather unfurnished gelding: half-brother to several winners, including smart winner up to 1½m Change The World (2-y-o 9f winner, by Sakhee) and 7.4f/1m winner (stayed 10.5f) Mamma Rosa (by Footstepsinthesand): dam 1m-1¼m winner: fairly useful form: second in maiden at Salisbury in June: stays 7f. *Charles Hills* **80**

LIFEBOAT LAD (USA) 3 br.g. Exchange Rate (USA) 111 – Bema (USA) (Pulpit (USA) 117) [2017 8.1m 7s 8.1m Jun 26] rangy gelding: no form in maidens: wears hood. *Dean Ivory* **–**

LIFE FOR RENT 2 b.g. (Feb 12) Sleeping Indian 122 – Sea Flower (IRE) 70 (Acclamation 118) [2017 5g^4 6g^3 t6d 5d^5 5m* 6.1d^5 Oct 4] fair performer: won nursery at Ripon in September: best at 5f: acts on good to firm and good to soft going. *Tim Easterby* **69**

LIFE HAPPENS 3 b.f. Pastoral Pursuits 127 – Halfwaytoparadise 69 (Observatory (USA) 131) [2017 –: p10g^6 p10s Dec 7] little impact in maidens/handicap: tried in cheekpieces. *Jonathan Portman* **–**

LIFE KNOWLEDGE (IRE) 5 ch.g. Thewayyouare (USA) 117 – Rosa Bellini (IRE) (Rossini (USA) 118) [2017 62: t12.4g* 12g^4 11.1m^2 9.9v t12.4g^6 t12.4d^3 Dec 16] modest handicapper: won at Newcastle (apprentice) in February: stays 12.5f: acts on tapeta and good to firm going: tried in cheekpieces: often starts slowly, usually races nearer last than first. *Patrick Holmes* **64**

LIFE OF FAME 4 b.f. Equiano (FR) 127 – Fame Is The Spur 81 (Motivator 131) [2017 66: t8g t6m^4 f6g 6m t7.1g Apr 25] modest handicapper: left Mark Walford after third start: has worn headgear/tongue tie: usually races close up; sent to Germany, where won 6.5f handicap at Leipzig in September. *Rebecca Menzies* **58**

LIFE OF LUXURY 4 b.g. Shamardal (USA) 129 – Champagnelifestyle 97 (Montjeu (IRE) 137) [2017 66: t7.1m t8.6g^6 t8.6g^4 t7.2g^5 t8.6g^2 t8.6g^3 9.1m^5 t12.2g t12.2g^6 p12g p12g^6 t8.6g Dec 5] modest maiden handicapper: stays 1½m: acts on tapeta. *Mark Brisbourne* **63**

LIFE WON'T WAIT 3 b.g. Showcasing 117 – Manbaa (USA) 58 (Jazil (USA) 122) [2017 59p: t6g^2 t8g^3 p10g^6 Feb 16] modest form: temperament under suspicion. *John Quinn* **61**

LIGETI (IRE) 4 b.g. Rip Van Winkle (IRE) 134 – Dollar Chick (IRE) 99 (Dansili 127) [2017 –: p8g p8g* p10.7g* p10.7g^2 p12g^2 p12g^2 9.7m^5 13m^2 12g^6 12.1d^5 p12g* p12g^5 Oct 6] fairly useful handicapper: won at Dundalk in February (twice) and again in September (apprentice): stays 13f: acts on polytrack and good to firm going: wears headgear/tongue tie: sold 20,000 gns in October. *Joseph Patrick O'Brien, Ireland* **86**

LIGHTENING DANCE 3 b.f. Nathaniel (IRE) 129 – Dance Lively (USA) (Kingmambo (USA) 125) [2017 9.9d^2 9.9g* 10m^2 12g 10d Oct 27] useful-looking filly: closely related to 6f winner Emirati Spirit (by New Approach) and half-sister to several winners, including 1m winner Live Concert (by Singspiel) and winner up to 13f Charleston Lady (2-y-o 1m winner, by Hurricane Run), both useful: dam unraced: fairly useful performer: won maiden at Goodwood (by neck from Sileel) in June: second in handicap at Windsor (1¾ lengths behind Flying North) later that month: stays 1¼m: acts on good to firm and good to soft going. *Amanda Perrett* **86**

LIGHTENING FAST 3 b.g. Frankel 147 – Lightening Pearl (IRE) 113 (Marju (IRE) 127) [2017 83: 10d^5 8m* 8m 8m* 8.6s^6 p7g Oct 20] smallish, quite attractive gelding: useful handicapper: won at Navan in April and Leopardstown (by neck from I'm So Fancy) in July: stayed 1¼m: acted on good to firm and good to soft going: tried in blinkers: inconsistent: dead. *G. M. Lyons, Ireland* **100**

LIGHTENING QUICK 2 b.f. (Mar 10) Frankel 147 – Lightening Pearl (IRE) 113 (Marju (IRE) 127) [2017 7d* 7d Sep 29] second foal: sister to useful 1m winner Lightening Fast: dam, 2-y-o 6f/7f winner (including Cheveley Park Stakes), sister to high-class Japanese winner up to 1½m Satono Crown: fairly useful form: won maiden at Leopardstown (by neck from Bye Bye Baby) in September: remains with potential. *G. M. Lyons, Ireland* **93 p**

LIGHT FROM MARS 12 gr.g. Fantastic Light (USA) 134 – Hylandra (USA) (Bering 136) [2017 79: t7.1g^3 p8g p7g^2 p7g 6m t7.2g^5 Dec 5] good-topped gelding: fair handicapper: stays 8.5f: acts on polytrack, good to firm and good to soft going: usually wears cheekpieces: has worn tongue tie. *Ronald Harris* **74**

Grosvenor Sport Celebration Mile Stakes, Goodwood—Lightning Spear records a second victory in this Group 2, again beating Zonderland (second left) who was making his first start since this race in 2016; also pictured are Hathal (rail) and Oh This Is Us

LIGHT GUNNER (IRE) 3 b.g. Lawman (FR) 121 – Neve Lieve (IRE) 89 (Dubai 57
Destination (USA) 127) [2017 –: p10g p12f 12m^{3} 11.4m 14s^{6} 11.6d^{4} Sep 6] modest maiden: stays 1½m: acts on polytrack, good to firm and good to soft going: tried in hood. *Henry Tett*

LIGHT HUMOR (USA) 3 b.f. Distorted Humor (USA) 117 – Aldebaran Light (USA) –
(Seattle Slew (USA)) [2017 8.1m Jul 3] half-sister to several winners, including high-class US Grade 1 9f winner Eskendereya (by Giant's Causeway) and smart 2-y-o 6f winner (including Gimcrack and Middle Park Stakes) Balmont (by Stravinsky): dam, won at around 1m in USA, half-sister to US Grade 2 7f winner Blazonry: 10/1, well held in maiden at Windsor: sent to USA. *Jeremy Noseda*

LIGHTLY SQUEEZE 3 b.g. Poet's Voice 126 – Zuleika Dobson 106 (Cadeaux Genereux 84
131) [2017 –: t9.5g* 10g^{6} 10d^{6} 10.2g^{6} 10.2v* 10d 9.9d^{4} 11.8s^{6} Oct 10] useful-looking gelding: fairly useful performer: won maiden at Wolverhampton in April and handicap at Doncaster (by 2¼ lengths from Entangling) in July: stays 1¼m: acts on tapeta and heavy going: usually wears headgear: often races freely: inconsistent. *Philip Hide*

LIGHTNING CHARLIE 5 b.g. Myboycharlie (IRE) 118 – Lighted Way 66 (Kris 135) 97
[2017 95: p6g^{2} 6m^{2} 7f^{5} 6m* 6d 6.1s p6g Sep 25] close-coupled gelding: useful handicapper: won at Ascot (by short head from Hakam) in July: stays 7f: acts on polytrack, soft and good to firm going. *Amanda Perrett*

LIGHTNING MARK (IRE) 3 b.f. Invincible Spirit (IRE) 121 – Maakrah (Dubai – p
Destination (USA) 127) [2017 7s^{5} May 18] 130,000F: third foal: closely related to 7f/1m winner (stays 1¼m) Matravers (by Oasis Dream): dam unraced sister to high-class winner up to 10.4f Farraaj and half-sister to high-class winner up to 7f Iffraaj: 9/4, well held in maiden at Newmarket: should do better. *John Gosden*

LIGHTNING SPEAR 6 ch.h. Pivotal 124 – Atlantic Destiny (IRE) 99 (Royal Academy 119
(USA) 130) [2017 125: 8s^{2} 8f 9.9m 8v^{3} 8g* 8d^{6} 8s^{6} 8g Dec 10] rangy horse: smart performer: won Celebration Mile at Goodwood (for second year running, by nose from Zonderland) in August: placed earlier in Lockinge Stakes at Newbury (3¾ lengths second to Ribchester) and Sussex Stakes at Goodwood (length third to Here Comes When): below form in Queen Elizabeth II Stakes at Ascot and Hong Kong Mile at Sha Tin last 2 starts: stays 8.5f: acts on polytrack, firm and good to soft going. *David Simcock*

LIGHT OF AIR (FR) 4 b.g. Youmzain (IRE) 131 – Height of Vanity (IRE) 56 (Erhaab 84
(USA) 127) [2017 81: p12d^{2} p13g^{3} p12g^{4} 10m^{4} 9.9m^{3} 11.9g* 12g^{2} 12f^{3} 11.6d^{2} Aug 21] good-topped gelding: fairly useful handicapper: won at Brighton (by 5 lengths from Melabi) in May: second at Goodwood (1½ lengths behind Thames Knight) in June: stays 13f: acts on polytrack, soft and good to firm going: has worn blinkers: front runner/races prominently, often travels strongly. *Gary Moore*

LIGHT OF JOY (USA) 3 ch.f. Kitten's Joy (USA) 128 – Light Blow (USA) 83 86
(Kingmambo (USA) 125) [2017 t8.6g t10.2s^{3} 10.2f* 10g^{2} 9.9m^{4} 11.6d^{4} p10g p10g^{3} Oct 5] second foal: dam, 15f winner, sister to Oaks winner Light Shift (dam of Ulysses) and to dam of Arc runner-up Cloth of Stars: fairly useful performer: won maiden at Bath (by 1¼ lengths from Feint) in June: third at Chelmsford (½ length behind Feint) final start: stays 1¼m: acts on polytrack, tapeta and firm going: often races towards rear. *David Lanigan*

LIGHTOLLER (IRE) 3 ch.g. Harbour Watch (IRE) 121 – April (IRE) 84 (Rock of 90
Gibraltar (IRE) 133) [2017 67: t7.1g t7.1g 5.1m 5g^{5} 6.1m^{2} 6.1m 5d^{ur} 5m^{2} 5d^{4} 5m^{5} 5.7f* 5.1m^{2} 5.2m^{5} 5d^{3} 5d^{3} 6d^{2} 7m^{4} 6d^{2} 6s^{6} 6.7s^{3} p8g p6.5g Dec 5] light-framed gelding: fairly useful handicapper: won at Bath in June: in frame 10 other times, leaving Mick Channon following seventeenth start: stays 7f: acts on firm and good to soft going: wears headgear. *P. & F. Monfort, France*

LIGHT RELIEF 2 b.f. (Jan 26) Medicean 128 – Tickle Me (GER) (Halling (USA) 133) 72
[2017 7m^{6} p7g^{2} p7g Nov 8] 45,000Y: first foal: dam unraced half-sister to useful winner up to 9f Tickle Me Blue: fair form: best effort when second in minor event at Kempton (1¼ lengths behind Fille de Reve) in October: likely to stay 1m. *James Tate*

LIGHTS 3 b.f. Delegator 125 – Sirenuse (IRE) 91 (Exceed And Excel (AUS) 126) [2017 –
39: 5m Apr 12] poor maiden: raced only at 5f. *Declan Carroll*

LIGHTSCAMERACTION (IRE) 5 ch.g. Pastoral Pursuits 127 – Silca Boo 99 (Efisio 81
120) [2017 108: t5g f5g 5.1d 5d^{6} 5.1d p5s Sep 30] one-time smart performer on all-weather, a93
fairly useful nowadays: stays 6f: acts on polytrack, tapeta, soft and good to firm going: wears headgear: tried in tongue tie: sometimes slowly away. *Gay Kelleway*

LIGHTSOME 4 b.f. Makfi 130 – Aunty Mary 82 (Common Grounds 118) [2017 55, a63: 59
p6g^{4} t6g^{3} Jan 31] modest maiden handicapper: stays 7f: acts on polytrack and soft going: has worn headgear. *Harry Dunlop*

LIGHT UP DUBAI 2 b.c. (Jan 22) Kodiac 112 – Tuscan Light 88 (Medicean 128) [2017 p8d⁴ Nov 9] 90,000F: first foal: dam, 11.7f winner, half-sister to very smart winner Exosphere: 7/1, fourth in minor event at Chelmsford (10¾ lengths behind Gronkowski): sure to progress. *Charlie Appleby* **64 p**

LIKE A DIAMOND (IRE) 7 b.g. Antonius Pius (USA) 123 – Silk Law (IRE) 80 (Barathea (IRE) 127) [2017 87: t8g Jan 21] big, lengthy gelding: fairly useful handicapper: well beaten only start in 2017: stays 1½m: acts on polytrack: tried in headgear. *Brian Ellison* **–**

LIKE LIGHTNING (IRE) 2 b.c. (Feb 27) Fast Company (IRE) 126 – Sara Mana Mou 41 (Medicean 128) [2017 6s 6d* 7g* 7g Jul 14] compact colt: sixth foal: half-brother to winner abroad by Shirocco: dam maiden half-sister to useful winner up to 10.4f Saratov: fairly useful form: won claimers at Saint-Cloud (twice, by ¾ length from All This Time second occasion, claimed from J. S. Moore €30,200) in June: stays 7f. *Julien Phelippon, France* **87**

LIKE MINDS 3 b.f. Royal Applause 124 – Creative Mind (IRE) 95 (Danehill Dancer (IRE) 117) [2017 44: t5.1g⁶ t6.1g p7d Nov 9] poor maiden: stays 6f: acts on polytrack: often races prominently. *David Brown* **38**

LIKE NO OTHER 4 b.g. Approve (IRE) 112 – Blue Beacon 68 (Fantastic Light (USA) 134) [2017 80, a90: t7.1g t7.1d t7.1s 7g² 8s 7.4m 7v 7.6s 7.4v Sep 26] fairly useful handicapper: second at Wetherby (1¼ lengths behind Theodorico) in May: stays 8.5f: acts on polytrack, tapeta and good to soft going: wears headgear: has worn tongue tie, including final start: often races prominently. *Les Eyre* **80 a71**

LIL GEM (IRE) 2 b.f. (Apr 21) Sepoy (AUS) 129 – Cynthia Calhoun 70 (Exceed And Excel (AUS) 126) [2017 5s 5v⁵ 5m 7.2m 6.9v 8s Oct 3] €9,000F: first foal: dam maiden (stayed 7f): little form. *Keith Dalgleish* **–**

LILLY BALLERINA (IRE) 3 b.f. Lilbourne Lad (IRE) 111 – Entrechat 59 (Green Desert (USA) 127) [2017 –: 6.1m 8g Aug 15] no form: left Tony Carroll after first start: tried in tongue tie. *Lee James* **–**

LIL SOPHELLA (IRE) 8 ch.m. Indian Haven 119 – Discotheque (USA) 73 (Not For Love (USA)) [2017 94, a88: 7d 7s 8m 8g 8g⁴ 8m⁴ 8m⁵ 8.5v t10.2g t9.5m Oct 28] fair handicapper: stays 1¼m: acts on tapeta, soft and good to firm going: has worn hood: sometimes slowly away, often races in rear. *Patrick Holmes* **71**

LILY ASH (IRE) 4 b.f. Lilbourne Lad (IRE) 111 – Ashdali (IRE) (Grand Lodge (USA) 125) [2017 p6d⁵ p6g² p7g⁶ 6d p7s⁴ Sep 30] modest maiden: stays 7f: acts on polytrack and tapeta. *Mike Murphy* **58**

LILY CLIFF 3 b.f. Canford Cliffs (IRE) 133 – Night Lily (IRE) 102 (Night Shift (USA)) [2017 –: f6g p7g Jan 28] no form: tried in tongue tie. *Paul D'Arcy* **–**

LILY EDGE 8 b.m. Byron 117 – Flaming Spirt 78 (Blushing Flame (USA) 109) [2017 58: p15.8g⁴ p12d⁶ Jan 17] plain mare: modest handicapper: stays 2m: acts on polytrack and good to firm going: wears headgear. *John Bridger* **49**

LILY FONTANA (IRE) 3 b.f. Dandy Man (IRE) 123 – Lily's Dream (IRE) (Celtic Swing 138) [2017 –: p7m t7.1g Mar 25] poor maiden: often starts slowly/usually races in rear. *Richard Fahey* **33**

LIMATO (IRE) 5 b.g. Tagula (IRE) 116 – Come April 77 (Singspiel (IRE) 133) [2017 129: 6d 6m³ 6g² 7g⁴ 7m* Oct 13] **127**

The Everest, a weight-for-age event held for the first time in 2017 at Randwick in Sydney, Australia, is not your average horse race. With an eye-watering entry fee of 600,000 Australian dollars to guarantee one of twelve berths, the six-furlong contest—worth a total of ten million Australian dollars (rising to $13m in 2018, and $15m by 2020)—follows the same 'buy-to-let' format as the nine-furlong Pegasus World Cup, another new 'super race' designed to attract the very best horses in the world and raise the profile of the sport. The inaugural running of the Pegasus, which took place at Gulfstream Park in late-January, was billed as a match between California Chrome, twice American Horse of the Year, and Arrogate, the highest-rated horse of 2016. The Pegasus didn't live up to the hype, but at least the star names were of a much higher calibre than The Everest managed to attract. The Everest winner Redzel, trained by the father and son team of Peter and Paul Snowden, earned a rating of 125 when beating eleven opponents. Not only was that rating 8 lb inferior to the one recorded by Arrogate in the Pegasus, it was 2 lb lower than the rating given to the British sprinter Limato for his clear-cut success in the

Godolphin Stud And Stable Staff Awards Challenge Stakes, Newmarket—
Limato returns to his best with a clear-cut victory over Massaat (striped cap, rail), the pair finishing ahead of the veteran Gordon Lord Byron (left)

Challenge Stakes at Newmarket the previous afternoon. Food for thought there for the connections of some of Europe's top sprinters (Caravaggio had been pencilled in for the first running of The Everest after winning the Commonwealth Cup at Royal Ascot but he didn't make the trip in the end).

Following a pair of top-level wins the previous season—in the July Cup at Newmarket and Prix de la Foret at Chantilly—hopes were high ahead of Limato's seasonal reappearance in the Al Quoz Sprint at Meydan in late-March. However, an unseasonal spell of wet weather led to the race, which was run over six furlongs for the first time since 2010, taking place on ground that was good to soft. The weather itself was a major bone of contention with Limato's owner Paul Jacobs, who suggested that cloud seeding—using scientific technology to create rain—during Dubai World Cup week had led to the rainfall, some of it of biblical proportions: 'If we had not put a lot of time, effort and money into getting him here he wouldn't have run. They were still watering until the Thursday, as I could see from my hotel, and I believe that human intervention pushed conditions over the edge,' said Jacobs. Bustled along soon after halfway, Limato was never involved and eventually beaten over nine lengths behind the French-trained winner The Right Man. The experience evidently took its toll on Limato, who needed time to recover from the exertions of both the race and the travelling to and from Dubai. Ryan Moore took over from Harry Bentley for Limato's next start, the Diamond Jubilee. Sent off the well-supported 2/1 favourite at Royal Ascot, Limato was the form pick on his win in the July Cup the previous summer in a field that, unusually, contained not a single runner from Ireland, Australia or Hong Kong. Limato ran creditably, beaten a neck and three quarters of a length into third behind The Tin Man and Tasleet, after holding every chance when hitting the front a furlong out.

The defence of his July Cup crown was next for Limato, who was up against just nine rivals at Newmarket, the lowest turnout since 2000 and eight fewer than he had triumphed over the previous season. Despite the small field, the July Cup looked a good renewal, with six of the ten having shown high-class form, the principals including the first three from the Diamond Jubilee and the first two from the Commonwealth Cup. With Harry Bentley back in the saddle, Limato turned the tables on The Tin Man and Tasleet, who managed to beat just one home between them. The anticipated defining championship clash failed to materialise, largely because the muddling pace set by outsider Intelligence Cross resulted in a falsely-run race, the timefigure being notably poor. Intelligence Cross was tracked by both Limato and eventual winner Harry Angel, who made his challenge towards the centre of the track and produced the best turn of foot with a furlong to run to seal a win by a length and a quarter over Limato, with Brando running on for a never-nearer third. Despite initial concerns over the reliability of the form, both the first and third won on their next outing, Brando taking the Prix Maurice de Gheest at Deauville the following month, and Harry Angel winning the Sprint Cup at Haydock in September, a race missed by Limato on account of soft ground.

Limato was stepped back up in trip for the Lennox Stakes at Goodwood next, his participation confirmed on the morning of the race despite the track getting plenty of rain on the day. Although a Group 2 (Goodwood has a Group 1 over only a furlong further in the Sussex Stakes), the valuable seven-furlong Lennox is worth over £170,000 to the winner and is one of the races that Goodwood is keen to upgrade to Group 1. 'We are in a position to guarantee half a million pounds in prize money the day it is upgraded,' said Alex Eade, the track's general manager. 'It is a bit frustrating but there is a process and it has to be followed.' Goodwood's frustration may be temporary as it seems that money talks nowadays when it comes to upgrading pattern races (look at Ascot's record with races at the Royal meeting over the years, and the creation of another big day at Ascot, British Champions' Day, which has seen lesser pattern races promoted to Group 1s through the largesse heaped upon them). Unfortunately for Goodwood, the 2017 renewal of the Lennox was more noteworthy for the quantity of its runners than for the quality of them: Breton Rock's winning performance was rated lower than any since Fath's victory in 2001. Breton Rock's winning margin over Home of The Brave was half a length, with the next five home covered by less than a length, that group including Limato who finished fourth, travelling as well as anything before leading under pressure a furlong out, but ultimately shaping as though he'd perhaps have benefited from having his effort delayed for a bit longer.

Unsuitable going was thought by connections to have been the reason behind Limato's below-par performance at Goodwood. 'We talked ourselves into running him when we shouldn't have,' said his trainer. A proposed bid to win a second Foret was scuppered by yet more inclement weather, and it wasn't until Newmarket's Cesarewitch meeting that Limato was seen on the racecourse again, when he was sent off the 6/4 favourite for the Challenge Stakes. With the ground good to firm, and the race run at the end-to-end gallop which suits him, Limato signed off his campaign in style, somewhat belatedly showing that he retained all his ability as he made short work of his rivals. The field split into two groups, with Limato travelling strongly behind Massaat in a group of six on the stands rail. That party soon became five as Dutch Connection was pulled up before halfway but, as the leaders encountered The Dip, there were five left with a chance overall, before the front-running Gifted Master weakened quickly and it soon became evident that Limato had the measure of his field. He surged clear inside the final furlong, winning in fine style by three and a half lengths from Massaat, with the veteran Gordon Lord Byron, who fared best of those who raced down the centre of the course throughout, a further length and a half back in third.

Limato (IRE) (b.g. 2012)	Tagula (IRE) (b 1993)	Taufan (b 1977)	Stop The Music
			Stolen Date
		Twin Island (ch 1989)	Standaan
			Jolly Widow
	Come April (b 2004)	Singspiel (b 1992)	In The Wings
			Glorious Song
		So Admirable (b 1998)	Suave Dancer
			Sumoto

Referring to the success of the David O'Meara-trained Suedois, who finished a short head in front of Limato in the Lennox before winning the Shadwell Turf Mile at Keeneland and finishing fourth in the Breeders' Cup Mile at Del Mar, Limato's owner has suggested that there could be a change of tack for Limato as a six-year-old, with a step back up to a mile being considered. Though Limato has made little impression on either of his two starts outside Europe, the more favourable weather and the tighter turns of the American tracks might prompt a different campaign, especially as Limato has limited opportunities over seven furlongs at the top level in Europe and has more chance of getting a mile on the less demanding courses in North America. Limato's owner, a former solicitor, has now been an owner for a quarter of a century and his dark green silks—a similar hue to Plymouth Argyle, the football club he supports—are carried under both codes, his jumpers with trainers near Lambourn, notably Emma Lavelle and Harry Whittington.

Limato, whose name is made up from the first two letters of Jacobs' wife Linda, mother Marjorie and father Tom, has had his pedigree covered in the last three editions of *Racehorses*. The most recent season saw two more of Limato's siblings make it to the racecourse. Two-year-old half-brother Tullyallen (by Arcano) progressed on each of his three starts in maiden company for Richard Hannon, though it seems likely he will be with a new trainer having been sold for 16,000 guineas at the Newmarket Autumn Horses In Training Sales. Tullyallen's three-year-old sister Limoncino benefited from the step up to a mile when winning on her handicap debut at Newcastle for Michael Dods very early in 2018. The compact Limato acts on polytrack, firm and good to soft going, his sparkling Park Stakes win as a three-year-old having been achieved on softish ground. *Henry Candy*

LIME AND LEMON (IRE) 4 b.f. Makfi 130 – Nimboo (USA) (Lemon Drop Kid **85** (USA) 131) [2017 84: 10.3g^5 11.6g^3 11.4d^2 10m^2 10d Oct 27] lengthy, rather sparely-made filly: fairly useful handicapper: second at Windsor (nose behind Jus Pires) in October: stays 1½m: acts on good to firm and heavy going: sold 15,000 gns in December. *Clive Cox*

LI MEI (IRE) 3 b.f. Iffraaj 127 – Rose of Battle 80 (Averti (IRE) 117) [2017 t8g^5 Nov 3] **– p** 40,000Y: half-sister to several winners, including winner up to 7f Winter Rose and 6f-8.3f winner He's My Boy (both by Dark Angel): dam, 2-y-o 5f winner, half-sister to smart 5f/6f winner Orpen Grey: 8/1, well held in maiden at Newcastle: should do better. *William Haggas*

LIMELITE (IRE) 3 b.f. Dark Angel (IRE) 113 – Light It Up (IRE) 79 (Elusive City **80** (USA) 117) [2017 72: 6g 7m^2 7g* 7g^3 7g^3 7g Sep 14] close-coupled filly: fairly useful handicapper: won at Newbury (by ¾ length from Pyjamarama) in June: stays 7f: acts on good to firm going: in headgear last 2 starts. *Richard Hannon*

LIME PICKLE 2 b.g. (Apr 29) Major Cadeaux 121 – Ocean Grove (IRE) 84 (Fairy King **–** (USA)) [2017 t6d Nov 4] 66/1, well held in minor event at Newcastle. *John Davies*

LIMERICK LORD (IRE) 5 b.g. Lord Shanakill (USA) 121 – Hollow Green (IRE) 90 **57** (Beat Hollow 126) [2017 66: f8g^5 f8g^3 f7g p8d^5 p7d^4 f7m^5 f7g^4 p7g 6s^4 7m^3 8s^5 7d^2 f7.1g^6 f8.1g^2 Dec 21] neat gelding: modest handicapper: stays 1m: acts on polytrack, fibresand, good to firm and good to soft going: wears headgear: front runner/races prominently. *Julia Feilden*

LIMONATA (IRE) 4 b.f. Bushranger (IRE) 119 – Come April 77 (Singspiel (IRE) 133) **–** [2017 69: t9.5g Jan 9] neat filly: fair maiden: below form only start in 2017: stays 1½m: acts on tapeta and good to firm going: in cheekpieces last 2 starts: front runner/races prominently. *Harry Whittington*

LIMONCINO (IRE) 3 b.f. Arcano (IRE) 122 – Come April 77 (Singspiel (IRE) 133) **68** [2017 6d t6d^3 t6g^3 f6.1g^4 Dec 19] fourth foal: half-sister to high-class winner up to 7f Limato (2-y-o 6f winner, by Tagula): dam 1¼m winner: fair form: should stay 7f+: wears hood. *Michael Dods*

LINA'S STAR (IRE) 2 b.f. (Feb 22) Lawman (FR) 121 – Readyandaway (USA) (More **69** Than Ready (USA) 120) [2017 6s^4 5d^3 5s^2 5d^3 t6g* t6.1g f6.1g^6 Dec 21] 9,000 2-y-o: second foal: dam lightly-raced half-sister to smart 2-y-o 6f winner (should have stayed 1m) Sander Camillo: fair performer: won nursery at Newcastle in September: left Richard Fahey after fourth start: stays 6f: acts on tapeta and soft going. *David O'Meara*

LINCOLN (IRE) 6 b.g. Clodovil (IRE) 116 – Gilt Linked 85 (Compton Place 125) [2017 **100** 102: 6g 6s^3 6.1g 5s^3 Oct 7] tall gelding: useful handicapper: third at York (1½ lengths behind Al Qahwa) in May: stays 7.5f, at least as effective over 5f/6f: acts on polytrack, soft and good to firm going: usually races nearer last than first. *Mick Channon*

LINCOLN ROCKS 4 b.f. Rock of Gibraltar (IRE) 133 – Redskin Dancer (IRE) 90 **111** (Namid 128) [2017 94: 8.3g^2 9.8m^4 t8g^3 8m* 8m^4 8d* 8v^2 8g^2 8.2d^2 7d* 8g 8d^5 Sep 29] angular filly: smart performer: won handicap at Musselburgh (by ½ length from Khamaary) in June, listed race at Pontefract (by neck from Dawn of Hope) in July and handicap at York (by 1¼ lengths from Breakable) in August: stays 8.5f: acts on good to firm and heavy going: usually leads. *David O'Meara*

LINDA DORIS (IRE) 3 b.f. Art Connoisseur (IRE) 121 – Kai Mook 73 (Littletown Boy **52** (USA)) [2017 7g 6.1g p6g^4 t7.1g p8g^5 p10s Dec 15] compact filly: first foal: dam winner up to 1½m (2-y-o 7f winner): modest maiden: stays 1m: acts on polytrack: often in tongue tie. *Gay Kelleway*

LINE HOUSE 2 ch.f. (Mar 11) Kheleyf (USA) 116 – Wood Fairy 74 (Haafhd 129) [2017 **79** p7g^3 p7g^4 t7.1g* f7.1g^2 Dec 11] 2,200Y: second foal: half-sister to 7f-11f winner Footlight (by Showcasing): dam, 7f-9f winner, half-sister to winner up to 1m Polar Ben and winner up to 1¾m Franklins Gardens (both smart): fair form: won minor event at Newcastle (by 2 lengths from Brisk Tempo) in October: second in similar event at Southwell (3½ lengths behind On The Warpath) final start: left Robyn Brisland after third start: raced only at 7f. *K. R. Burke*

LINEMAN 7 b.g. Rail Link 132 – Shamana (USA) (Woodman (USA) 126) [2017 66: t16.5g^2 t16.5g^5 t13.9f t16.5g t12.2g 14m Jun 15] modest handicapper: stays 16.5f: acts on polytrack, tapeta and good to firm going: wears headgear: tried in tongue tie. *Sarah Hollinshead* **62**

LINE OF BEAUTY 3 b.f. Helmet (AUS) 127 – Bisou (Tiger Hill (IRE) 127) [2017 9.9f 10.2g^5 p10g^2 11.6g^2 9.9d f11.1g^3 p8s^2 p10g^3 Dec 30] first foal: dam, twice second at 9f in France, closely related to smart 7f-9f winner Musaddas out of useful 9f winner Zuleika Dobson: fair maiden: stays 1¼m: acts on polytrack: front runner/races prominently. *Simon Crisford* **74**

LINEOFINTELLIGENCE 2 b.g. (Feb 23) Intello (GER) 129 – Linea (King's Best (USA) 132) [2017 7d^5 7g Sep 27] modest form: better effort when fifth in minor event at Chester (8 lengths behind Zoffalee) in August. *Richard Fahey* **57**

LINE OF REASON (IRE) 7 br.g. Kheleyf (USA) 116 – Miss Party Line (USA) (Phone Trick (USA)) [2017 110: 5g^5 5g^4 5g^6 6g^5 5g 5g^3 5m^4 5g 5m 5m* t5g* 5m 5g 5g 5.6g 5.2m 5v^2 t6.1d Dec 26] strong, compact gelding: smart handicapper: won at Musselburgh (by neck from Harry Hurricane) and Newcastle (by ½ length from Lexington Abbey) in June: second in minor event at Beverley (neck behind Alpha Delphini) in September: mainly races at 5f: acts on polytrack, tapeta and any turf going: has worn cheekpieces: often races towards rear. *Paul Midgley* **113**

L'INGANNO FELICE (FR) 7 br.g. Librettist (USA) 124 – Final Overture (FR) 57 (Rossini (USA) 118) [2017 77: t10.2g* f12g* f12g^2 t12.4d t12.4g^5 Mar 22] big gelding: fairly useful performer: won minor event at Newcastle (by ½ length from Siren's Cove) and handicap at Southwell (by 7 lengths from Come Back King) in January: second in handicap at latter course (short head behind Isharah) later that month: stays 1½m: acts on fibresand, tapeta, good to firm and heavy going: wears headgear: often races prominently. *Iain Jardine* **93**

LINGUINE (FR) 7 ch.g. Linngari (IRE) 124 – Amerissage (USA) (Rahy (USA) 115) [2017 66: 16.3d^6 16.3d^4 p16s Sep 8] good-topped gelding: fair handicapper: stays 16.5f: acts on any turf going: in headgear last 5 starts: tried in tongue tie. *Seamus Durack* **79**

LINGUISTIC (IRE) 4 b.g. Lope de Vega (IRE) 125 – Dazzle Dancer (IRE) 84 (Montjeu (IRE) 137) [2017 111: p10g^2 9d 10.3g^3 8s a9.9f Dec 21] sturdy gelding: smart performer: placed in listed race at Kempton (neck second to Absolute Blast) in April and handicap at York (3 lengths third to Dark Red) in October: left John Gosden after next start: stays 1½m: acts on polytrack, good to firm and good to soft going: often in headgear. *S. bin Ghadayer, UAE* **111**

LINKS BAR MARBELLA (IRE) 4 ch.g. Intense Focus (USA) 117 – Silesian (IRE) (Singspiel (IRE) 133) [2017 –: 7d 10.1s^6 Jun 6] tall gelding: of little account: often in headgear. *Eric Wheeler* **–**

LIONS CHARGE (USA) 10 ch.g. Lion Heart (USA) 124 – Fellwaati (USA) (Alydar (USA)) [2017 69: p12d Jan 17] fair handicapper: well held only start in 2017: stays 1½m: acts on polytrack, tapeta and good to firm going: usually wears headgear/tongue tie: often races prominently. *Seamus Mullins* **–**

LIQUID AMBER (USA) 2 ch.f. (Feb 11) Kitten's Joy (USA) 128 – Pachattack (USA) 115 (Pulpit (USA) 117) [2017 8d^2 8d* Aug 27] second foal: half-sister to useful 1m winner Dilmun (by War Front): dam winner up to 1½m (2-y-o 7f winner and US Grade 3 8.5f/9f winner): useful form: won Flame of Tara Stakes at the Curragh (by 5 lengths from Ballet Shoes) in August: open to further improvement. *W. McCreery, Ireland* **106 p**

LIQUID GOLD (IRE) 3 b.f. Nathaniel (IRE) 129 – Northern Mischief (USA) (Yankee Victor (USA) 121) [2017 7.4g^2 8d^2 9.1g^2 12s^6 9.9g* 10.3v^4 10d Oct 23] €95,000F: seventh foal: half-sister to 3 winners, notably very smart 1m winner (stays 1¼m) North America (by Dubawi): dam, 1m winner (2-y-o 7f winner), half-sister to US Grade 1 8.5f/9f winner Gourmet Girl: fairly useful handicapper: won at Beverley (by neck from Yensir) in August: fourth at Chester (1¾ lengths behind Marsh Pride) in September: stays 10.5f: acts on heavy going. *Richard Fahey* **80**

LIQUID (IRE) 3 ch.g. Zoffany (IRE) 121 – Playful Promises (IRE) 55 (Elnadim (USA) 128) [2017 70: 5m^2 5m^2 5g* 5d 5m^4 5m t5g^2 t5d^3 Oct 24] fairly useful performer: won maiden at Thirsk in July: placed in handicaps at Newcastle last 2 starts: raced only at 5f: acts on tapeta and good to firm going: tried in blinkers: temperament under suspicion. *David Barron* **85**

LISBON LEGEND 2 b.c. (Feb 24) Kyllachy 129 – Expect 87 (Invincible Spirit (IRE) 121) [2017 5.3d 6g^6 5s^6 Jul 29] well held in minor events/seller: sold £800, sent to Sweden. *Tony Carroll* **–**

William Hill Scottish Sprint Cup Handicap, Musselburgh—Line of Reason wins the richest sprint handicap run in Scotland in the latest season, with the abandonment of Ayr's Gold Cup meeting due to waterlogging; Harry Hurricane (partially hidden by winner) and Kimberella (No.2) are best of the remainder

LISHEEN CASTLE (IRE) 2 b.c. (Apr 3) Most Improved (IRE) 119 – Mafaaza (USA) (Jazil (USA) 122) [2017 8.3s* 8.5v^4 8v^2 Oct 23] €39,000F, €30,000Y, £50,000 2-y-o: compact colt: second foal: dam unraced half-sister to smart winner up to 1m Tazahum: useful form: won minor event at Hamilton (by 1¼ lengths from Ayutthaya) in August: best effort when second in listed race at Pontefract (2¾ lengths behind Connect) final start: will stay 1¼m: sold 185,000 gns in November. *John Quinn* **96**

LISNAMOYLE LADY (IRE) 2 ch.f. (Feb 9) Roderic O'Connor (IRE) 119 – Allegheny Dawn (IRE) (Teofilo (IRE) 126) [2017 t8.6g Oct 21] 12,000F: first foal: dam unraced half-sister to very smart 6f winner Danetime: 100/1, well held in minor event at Wolverhampton. *Martin Smith* **–**

LISP (IRE) 3 ch.g. Poet's Voice 126 – Hora 79 (Hernando (FR) 127) [2017 69p: 10m May 8] good-topped gelding: lightly-raced maiden on Flat: should be suited by at least 1¼m: fairly useful form over hurdles, won in December. *Charles Hills* **–**

LISTEN ALEXANDER (IRE) 2 br.f. (Jan 15) Kodiac 112 – Private Alexander (IRE) 98 (Footstepsinthesand 120) [2017 5m^4 5.1m^2 5g^6 5.1m* 6g^6 5.2s 6g Sep 7] compact filly: first foal: dam, 2-y-o 7f winner, half-sister to useful winner up to 11f Menhoubah: fair performer: won minor event at Chepstow in July: best form at 5f: acts on good to firm going: front runner/races prominently. *David Evans* **76**

LITTLE AUB 2 b.g. (Mar 16) Milk It Mick 120 – Makindi 63 (Makbul 104) [2017 p6g p7s^6 Dec 14] modest form on second start in minor events. *Mark Usher* **51**

LITTLE BELTER (IRE) 5 gr.g. Dandy Man (IRE) 123 – On Thin Ice (IRE) (Verglas (IRE) 118) [2017 61: t5g t5g t6g^3 7.1m 6m 6g Jul 24] neat gelding: modest maiden handicapper: stays 6f: acts on tapeta and good to firm going: wears headgear: temperamental. *Keith Dalgleish* **53 §**

LITTLE BOY BLUE 2 gr.g. (Mar 16) Hellvelyn 118 – Dusty Dazzler (IRE) 102 (Titus Livius (FR) 115) [2017 5g^2 5d^2 p5g* t5.1d^3 Dec 26] sixth foal: half-brother to 2-y-o 5f winner Dusty Spirit (by Invincible Spirit) and winner up to 1½m A Little Bit Dusty (2-y-o 1m winner, by Needwood Blade): dam winner up to 6f (2-y-o 5f winner): fairly useful form: won minor event at Lingfield (by head from Ghepardo) in December: third in similar event at Wolverhampton (length behind Reiffa) final start: raced only at 5f. *Bill Turner* **84**

LITTLE CHOOSEY 7 ch.m. Cadeaux Genereux 131 – Little Nymph 89 (Emperor Fountain 112) [2017 69: f8g^{6} f8g^{2} f8g p8g^{3} p8d^{4} t8.6g^{2} 8.3g^{2} 10.2d 9.9g p8d t7.2g^{5} t7.1d^{4} t9.5g f8.1g Dec 21] smallish mare: fair handicapper: stays 1½m, usually races over shorter: acts on all-weather, firm and soft going: wears headgear: usually wears tongue tie. *Roy Bowring* **68**

LITTLE CUPCAKE 6 b.m. Myboycharlie (IRE) 118 – Imco Cracking (IRE) (Piccolo 121) [2017 56: p5g^{2} p6g^{3} p5g^{6} p6g^{5} 6m p6s^{4} p5g^{4} 6g^{6} 5f Jul 18] poor handicapper: left Paul W. Flynn after fifth start: stays 7f: acts on polytrack, best turf form on good going: usually in headgear in 2017: tried in tongue tie. *Denis Quinn* **39 a48**

LITTLE INDIAN 7 b.g. Sleeping Indian 122 – Once Removed 65 (Distant Relative 128) [2017 65: p7g* p8d^{5} p6g p6g^{4} 7m t7.2g 7m p7g Sep 6] compact gelding: modest handicapper: won at Kempton in January: stays 1m: acts on all-weather, firm and good to soft going: tried in headgear: often races towards rear. *J. R. Jenkins* **57**

LITTLE JO 3 b.g. Major Cadeaux 121 – Discoed 38 (Distinctly North (USA) 115) [2017 8s^{4} 8g 9d^{3} 14.1v^{6} 12v t8d* Nov 10] modest performer: won handicap at Newcastle in November: left Chris Grant after fifth start: best effort at 1m: acts on tapeta and heavy going: sometimes slowly away. *Brian Ellison* **63**

LITTLE KINGDOM (IRE) 3 b.f. Royal Applause 124 – Hadba (IRE) 95 (Cape Cross (IRE) 129) [2017 –: t5g^{4} t5d* 6g 6m^{2} t5s 5m 6m 7v^{6} 6m 7.2s^{4} t7.1d t6g t6s t5d^{6} Dec 16] modest handicapper: won at Newcastle in February: stays 6f: acts on tapeta and good to firm going: often races towards rear. *Tracy Waggott* **63**

LITTLE KIPLING 4 b.f. Royal Applause 124 – Victoria Sponge (IRE) 96 (Marju (IRE) 127) [2017 72: t8.6g^{4} p8g^{2} p7g^{3} 9.9g^{4} Apr 15] lengthy filly: fair handicapper: stays 1m: acts on polytrack and good to soft going: usually races prominently. *Stuart Williams* **74**

LITTLE LADY KATIE (IRE) 5 b.m. Lord Shanakill (USA) 121 – Akarita (IRE) 92 (Akarad (FR) 130) [2017 92: 8.2s 8g^{4} 8d^{4} 7v^{5} 8.2d 8.3d^{5} Sep 2] compact mare: fairly useful handicapper: stays 8.5f: acts on good to firm and heavy going: tried in visor: sold 6,000 gns in December. *K. R. Burke* **85**

LITTLE LIZZIE 4 ch.f. Sleeping Indian 122 – Quality Street 86 (Fraam 114) [2017 –: 5.3g^{6} Apr 15] no form. *Paddy Butler* **–**

LITTLELORDCONFORD (IRE) 2 b.g. (Feb 15) Intikhab (USA) 135 – Anna Law (IRE) (Lawman (FR) 121) [2017 5s^{5} 5d p6g Oct 14] limited impact in minor events/ maiden. *Richard Spencer* **50**

LITTLE LOTTE (IRE) 4 b.f. Kodiac 112 – Dancing Steps (Zafonic (USA) 130) [2017 –: t9.5g 14d^{5} Sep 10] small, leggy filly: maiden, well held both starts on Flat in 2017: left Tom Gretton after first start: stays 9f: acts on polytrack and soft going: has worn headgear: modest hurdler. *Mrs A. Corson, Jersey* **–**

LITTLE MISS DAISY 3 b.f. Arabian Gleam 122 – Desert Liaison 68 (Dansili 127) [2017 69: p5m^{2} p5g* t5d^{2} 5.3g 5g 5.7f^{3} t5d^{3} 5s^{2} 5d 5.3s t5.1g Nov 25] fair handicapper: won at Kempton in February: stays 5.5f: acts on polytrack, tapeta and firm going: sometimes slowly away, usually races nearer last than first. *William Muir* **77**

LITTLE MISS KODI (IRE) 4 b.f. Kodiac 112 – Sensasse (IRE) 83 (Imperial Ballet (IRE) 110) [2017 82: t7.1g 6.9g^{2} 7m^{6} 7g t7.2g p7g^{5} Dec 20] fair handicapper: stays 7f: acts on polytrack, tapeta and good to firm going: tried in blinkers: sometimes finds little. *Daniel Loughnane* **80 a72**

LITTLE MISS LILLY 2 b.f. (Feb 25) Lethal Force (IRE) 128 – Malilla (IRE) 89 (Red Clubs (IRE) 125) [2017 6.1m 6m^{3} 6m p6g p7g^{4} Dec 6] lengthy filly: first foal: dam 2-y-o 6f winner: fair maiden: stays 7f: acts on polytrack and good to firm going. *Clive Cox* **70**

LITTLE MISS LOLA 3 ch.f. Dandy Man (IRE) 123 – Purepleasureseeker (IRE) (Grand Lodge (USA) 125) [2017 60: 6g^{5} 6g 6g^{5} 6d t5d^{6} t5g* t6s^{6} t5d^{2} Dec 16] fair handicapper: won at Newcastle in November: second at same course final start: left Sally Haynes after fourth start: stays 6f: acts on tapeta and good to firm going: often races prominently. *Lynn Siddall* **67**

LITTLE MISS TANGO 3 ch.f. Steele Tango (USA) 116 – Many Welcomes 70 (Young Ern 120) [2017 8f^{5} t8.6g Nov 20] second foal: dam 6f-7.6f winner: well held in maidens (slowly away). *Roger Teal* **–**

LITTLE MONKEY 2 b.f. (Apr 17) Monsieur Bond (IRE) 120 – Lujiana 67 (Lujain (USA) 119) [2017 5m 5m 6d^{2} 6g t6g Oct 19] second foal: dam 5f winner: poor maiden: best effort at 6f: acts on good to soft going: tried in cheekpieces. *Antony Brittain* **45**

LITTLE NOSEGAY (IRE) 3 gr.f. Clodovil (IRE) 116 – Bank On Black (IRE) 90 (Big Bad Bob (IRE) 118) [2017 61: t6f^4 p6g t5.1g t5.1g* f5g^4 p5g Mar 16] small, dipped-backed filly: modest handicapper: won at Wolverhampton in February: stays 6f: acts on polytrack, tapeta, and probably on soft going. *David Evans* **61**

LITTLE ORCHID 4 b.f. Observatory (USA) 131 – Bushy Dell (IRE) 81 (King Charlemagne (USA) 120) [2017 57: 11.5m 14.1m^4 14m 11.9g^6 Jun 27] modest maiden handicapper: stays 1¾m: acts on polytrack, tapeta and good to firm going: often races towards rear. *Julia Feilden* **53**

LITTLE PALAVER 5 b.g. Showcasing 117 – Little Nymph 89 (Emperor Fountain 112) [2017 98: 6m* 6m^3 6.1d 6m 6.1g^6 Aug 7] close-coupled gelding: useful handicapper: won at Windsor (by 2 lengths from Lightning Charlie) in April: stays 7f: acts on polytrack, soft and good to firm going: front runner/races prominently. *Clive Cox* **99**

LITTLE PIPPIN 4 b.f. Sir Percy 129 – Lady Le Quesne (IRE) 78 (Alhaarth (IRE) 126) [2017 56: t8s 9.9d 9.2s^4 8.3s^5 8.5s^5 8v^3 10d^3 10v^4 f8.1g Dec 21] small filly: modest handicapper: stays 8.5f: best form on soft/heavy going: in cheekpieces last 4 starts. *Tony Coyle* **56**

LITTLE POEM 2 b.f. (Apr 8) Holy Roman Emperor (IRE) 125 – Gerika (FR) (Galileo (IRE) 134) [2017 7d^3 7d^6 p7g^5 Oct 12] unfurnished filly: second foal: half-sister to 2-y-o 7f winner (stays 1¼m) Pirate Look (by Canford Cliffs): dam, 9f-1½m winner, closely related to useful 1¼m winner Right Connection: modest form: will stay 1m: wears hood. *Marco Botti* **50**

LITTLE RED BERRY (IRE) 2 b.f. (Mar 20) Red Jazz (USA) 125 – Passi di Danza (IRE) (Bertolini (USA) 125) [2017 6m t6s 5v^5 Sep 26] 4,500F: second foal: dam 7f/1m winner: no form in minor events. *James Given* **–**

LITTLE STAMPY (IRE) 6 ch.m. Artan (IRE) 119 – Gold Stamp (Golden Act (USA)) [2017 74: p16g^4 t16.5g^2 13.1s^4 16s^6 Aug 19] fair handicapper: stays 16.5f: acts on polytrack, tapeta and soft going: usually wears headgear: fair hurdler. *D. Broad, Ireland* **74**

LIVA (IRE) 2 ch.g. (Apr 10) Champs Elysees 124 – Resistance Heroine 75 (Dr Fong (USA) 128) [2017 6s^5 6.1m^3 7.4g* 7.4v^2 Aug 15] good-bodied gelding: fair form: won minor event at Ffos Las in July: bred to stay 1m. *David Evans* **70**

LIVE DANGEROUSLY 7 b.g. Zamindar (USA) 116 – Desert Lynx (IRE) 79 (Green Desert (USA) 127) [2017 70: 10m 8m 11.9g^4 9.9g^4 7d* 8m^5 8.5f^6 10d^3 7s^2 8m^3 7g 7d 7.6s^3 p11g 7s^5 p7g Oct 17] smallish gelding: fair handicapper: won at Brighton in June: second at Lingfield (short head behind Arctic Flower) in July: stays 1¼m: acts on good to firm and heavy going: tried in headgear: has worn tongue tie. *John Bridger* **67**

LIVELLA FELLA (IRE) 4 b.f. Strategic Prince 114 – Ardent Lady 79 (Alhaarth (IRE) 126) [2017 82: t8g^4 10m^6 8.5m^6 10g^2 10.2d* 10.2d^2 10.3d^4 9.8g^5 12.5m^5 10g^6 t10.2g f8.1g p10s^3 p10s Dec 1] rather lightly-made filly: fairly useful handicapper: won at Doncaster (by ¾ length from Miss Ranger) in June: stays 1¼m: acts on polytrack, tapeta, soft and good to firm going: front runner/races prominently: sold 6,000 gns in December. *Keith Dalgleish* **80**

LIVING IN THE NOW 2 b.f. (Mar 15) Elzaam (AUS) 115 – Jardin (Sinndar (IRE) 134) [2017 6s Sep 4] half-sister to 2 winners, including useful 1¼m-1½m winner Kasperenko (by Archipenko): dam unraced half-sister to very smart 7f-8.3f winner Sleeping Indian: 20/1, well held in maiden at Brighton. *Charles Hills* **–**

LIVING LEADER 8 b.g. Oasis Dream 129 – Royal Jade 82 (Last Tycoon 131) [2017 56: t9.5m p8d* p8m* 7m^2 p8s 8f^5 8g p8g t8.6g^6 t8.6g^3 p8g^2 Dec 30] leggy gelding: modest handicapper: won at Kempton (apprentice) in February and Lingfield in March: stays 1½m, usually races over shorter: acts on polytrack, tapeta, good to firm and good to soft going: has worn headgear/tongue tie. *Grace Harris* **53 a61**

LIVINGSTONES QUEST (IRE) 2 b.g. (May 3) Showcasing 117 – Maramba 97 (Rainbow Quest (USA) 134) [2017 7d 6s^2 7.4v* 7g 8.1g Oct 9] compact gelding: fair performer: won minor event at Ffos Las in August: stays 7.5f: best form on soft/heavy going: often leads. *Rod Millman* **73**

LIVVYS DREAM (IRE) 2 b.f. (Apr 10) Declaration of War (USA) 128 – Briolette (IRE) 112 (Sadler's Wells (USA) 132) [2017 7.6d 7d^5 Sep 30] half-sister to several winners, including useful 2-y-o 1m winner (stayed 13f) Thomasgainsborough (by Dansili) and useful 5f-8.3f winner Point North (by Danehill Dancer): dam, 1¼m-1½m winner, half-sister to top-class 1¼m-1½m winner Pilsudski: modest form: better effort when fifth in maiden at Newmarket (13¼ lengths behind Bye Bye Baby) in September. *Charles Hills* **56**

LIZZY'S DREAM 9 ch.g. Choisir (AUS) 126 – Flyingit (USA) 90 (Lear Fan (USA) 130) **56** [2017 61: f5g p5g[5] t5.1g[5] t6f[5] t6m[3] t5.1g[3] 5g 5m[2] 6m[4] 5.5f[4] 5d 5d[3] 5.2m 5m[4] Sep 8] modest handicapper: stays 6f: acts on polytrack, tapeta and good to firm going: tried in blinkers. *Rebecca Bastiman*

LLAMREI 2 b.f. (Jan 30) Multiplex 114 – Nalear (FR) (Lear Fan (USA) 130) [2017 5.3g[5] **58** 5f[5] 5.7f[4] 5f[5] 5.3m[2] t5.1g[4] t6.1g 6s[5] 5.1m[3] p6g p5g[4] Dec 12] £1,000Y: close-coupled filly: sixth foal: half-sister to useful French 9.5f-14.5f winner Norashman (by Sinndar) and winner abroad by Siyouni: dam 1¼m/10.5f winner: modest maiden: stays 5.5f: acts on polytrack, tapeta and firm going: usually races prominently. *Jo Hughes*

LLEWELLYN 9 b.g. Shamardal (USA) 129 – Ffestiniog (IRE) 96 (Efisio 120) [2017 74: **66** f7g f6m 7m[4] 7g f5g* 6s t5.1g[4] f5g f6.1g[3] Nov 28] rather leggy gelding: fair handicapper: won at Southwell in May: best up to 7f nowadays: acts on fibresand, good to firm and heavy going: usually wears headgear: front runner/races prominently. *Declan Carroll*

LMNTRIX 5 b.g. Mount Nelson 125 – Big Mystery (IRE) 53 (Grand Lodge (USA) 125) **51** [2017 66: f7g Jan 2] fair maiden handicapper: below form only start in 2017: stays 1m: acts on polytrack and fibresand: tried in hood: often races prominently. *George Margarson*

LOBSTER COCKTAIL (IRE) 4 b.c. Footstepsinthesand 120 – Sanpala (Sanglamore **69** (USA) 126) [2017 65: p12d* Jan 17] fair handicapper: won at Kempton in January: stays 1½m: acts on polytrack, tapeta and good to soft going: tried in cheekpieces: in tongue tie last 4 starts: sold 10,000 gns in February, sent to Italy. *Ed Walker*

LOCAL ARTIST (IRE) 3 b.f. Requinto (IRE) 109 – A L'Aube (IRE) (Selkirk (USA) **59** 129) [2017 64: t5g[3] t5g[6] t5d t6m[6] Mar 17] modest maiden: stays 6f: acts on tapeta and good to firm going: tried in blinkers: often races prominently. *John Quinn*

LOCKHEED 3 gr.c. Exceed And Excel (AUS) 126 – Clinical 109 (Motivator 131) [2017 **110** 104: 8g[2] 6g[5] Dec 10] sturdy colt: smart performer: second in Mehl-Mulhens-Rennen (German 2000 Guineas) at Cologne (neck behind Poetic Dream): left William Haggas £900,000 after: stays 1m: acts on good to firm and good to soft going. *C. S. Shum, Hong Kong*

LOCOMMOTION 5 gr.g. Proclamation (IRE) 130 – Miss Madame (IRE) 74 (Cape **61** Cross (IRE) 129) [2017 57: p8g p7m* p7d t7.1g 7d[4] 7.6g[5] 7d p7g[3] 7.6s p7g p7m[5] p7g* Dec 30] good-topped gelding: modest handicapper: won at Lingfield in March and December: stays 1m: acts on polytrack and good to soft going: has worn headgear/tongue tie: sometimes slowly away. *Matthew Salaman*

LOGI (IRE) 3 b.g. Kodiac 112 – Feet of Flame (USA) 59 (Theatrical) [2017 79: t5.1f* 6m **82** 5m[3] 6m[3] 6m[2] 6g[6] t6.1g[2] p6g[3] Nov 2] neat gelding: fairly useful performer: won maiden at Wolverhampton (by 3½ lengths from Jack The Truth) in February: second in handicap at same course (short head behind Qatari Riyals) in September: left David Barron after sixth start: stays 6f: acts on tapeta and good to firm going: often blinkered: has joined Rebecca Bastiman. *Richard Guest*

LOG OFF (IRE) 3 b.f. Sir Prancealot (IRE) 111 – Dolphin Stamp (IRE) (Dolphin Street **65** (FR) 125) [2017 –: f7g[3] f8g* p8g[5] f8m[5] t12.2g[6] p10d f12g[6] t9.5g* 12.1m 10d[4] 10m[4] 9.9m[3] 9.9g[3] 10m[5] t8.6g p10s[6] Dec 7] sturdy filly: fair performer: won maiden at Southwell in January and handicap at Wolverhampton (dead-heated) in April: left David Evans after fourteenth start: stays 1¼m: acts on all-weather and good to firm going. *Karen George*

LOLITA 5 ch.m. Sir Percy 129 – Miss Ippolita 84 (Diktat 126) [2017 77: t6m[5] Jan 10] tall **64** mare: fair handicapper: below form only start in 2017: stays 6f: acts on polytrack, good to firm and good to soft going: tried in cheekpieces: sometimes slowly away, often races prominently: sent to Malaysia. *J. R. Jenkins*

LOMU (IRE) 3 ch.g. Dandy Man (IRE) 123 – Miss Me 107 (Marju (IRE) 127) [2017 85p: **94** 7.2g* 8g[4] 7.2s Oct 1] fairly useful handicapper: won at Ayr (by ½ length from Navarone) in June: stays 7f: acts on tapeta, soft and good to firm going: usually races freely. *Keith Dalgleish*

LONDINIUM 3 b.g. New Approach (IRE) 132 – Historian (IRE) (Pennekamp (USA) 130) **105** [2017 84p: 12m[2] 10.3d[3] 12v* 11.2s[2] 11.9g[5] 12s[4] Sep 9] useful handicapper: won at Goodwood (by 1½ lengths from On To Victory) in August: fourth at Ascot (2½ lengths behind Duke of Bronte) final start: stays 1½m: acts on any turf going. *Mark Johnston*

LONDON (FR) 4 b.g. Galileo (IRE) 134 – Altana (USA) (Mountain Cat (USA)) [2017 89: **97** t8.6m p8d[6] f8m[6] p8g[2] p7d* p8g 8s[2] 7v* 7g 7d[3] 7d p8s[5] p8s[2] p8g Dec 31] useful handicapper: won at Chelmsford in March and Epsom (by 3¼ lengths from King of Swing) in October: stays 8.5f: acts on polytrack and heavy going: wears hood: has worn tongue tie: front runner/races prominently. *Phil McEntee*

LONDON GLORY 4 b.g. Archipenko (USA) 127 – Reflected Image (IRE) 71 (Refuse To Bend (IRE) 128) [2017 80p: t7.1g 8.3g 10.4m^{3} 12g^{3} t10.2s^{5} 15.9s^{4} 14m^{3} t12.4s^{6} 14g^{6} t16.3g 12.1v* 14s^{2} 15v f12.1g t12.4g^{4} Nov 23] lengthy gelding: fair handicapper: won at Hamilton in September: stays 1¾m: acts on polytrack, tapeta, good to firm and heavy going: wears blinkers. *David Thompson* **71**

LONDON GRAMMAR (IRE) 3 b.f. Sir Prancealot (IRE) 111 – Emmas Princess (IRE) 96 (Bahhare (USA) 122) [2017 63: p8g p8g p8g* p8g 9g 10s 10s^{3} t9.5g^{5} p12g p8g Dec 13] modest handicapper: won at Kempton in April: stays 1¼m: acts on polytrack, tapeta and soft going: tried in headgear: often races in rear: temperamental. *Ralph Smith* **59 §**

LONDONIA 5 gr.g. Paco Boy (IRE) 129 – Snowdrops (Gulch (USA)) [2017 72: 13f^{2} 13f^{2} Jul 18] fair maiden handicapper: stays 1¾m: acts on polytrack and firm going: in hood/tongue tie last 4 starts. *Graeme McPherson* **71**

LONDON MASTER 3 ch.c. Mastercraftsman (IRE) 129 – Reflected Image (IRE) 71 (Refuse To Bend (IRE) 128) [2017 –p: t9.5g* 12d^{5} 11.9d^{5} 10d t10.2s^{6} Sep 19] fair handicapper: won at Wolverhampton (dead-heated) in April: stays 9.5f: acts on tapeta: sometimes slowly away. *Chris Wall* **70**

LONDON PRIZE 6 b.g. Teofilo (IRE) 126 – Zibet 90 (Kris 135) [2017 92: t16.3g^{2} 16g* t16.3s* 18m^{2} Oct 14] sturdy gelding: useful handicapper: won at Goodwood (by 8 lengths from Medburn Cutler) in June and Newcastle (by neck from Graceland) in July: second in Cesarewitch Handicap at Newmarket (3¾ lengths behind Withhold) final start: stayed 2¼m: acted on tapeta, soft and good to firm going: useful hurdler: dead. *Ian Williams* **108**

LONDON PROTOCOL (FR) 4 ch.g. Muhtathir 126 – Troiecat (FR) (One Cool Cat (USA) 123) [2017 102: 8g 8m 7s^{4} 8m 8d^{5} 8d* 8f 8g^{4} p8g* 8.2d p8d Nov 22] strong gelding: useful performer: won minor event at Compiegne (by ¾ length from Prince Apache) in July and handicap at Chantilly (by 1¾ lengths from Sky Ship) in September: stays 8.5f: acts on polytrack, tapeta, firm and soft going: has worn cheekpieces: front runner/races prominently. *K. R. Burke* **106**

LONDON REBEL (IRE) 4 ch.f. Arcano (IRE) 122 – Piccadilly Filly (IRE) 111 (Exceed And Excel (AUS) 126) [2017 –: p7g f5s p7d Feb 16] little form: tried in cheekpieces. *Richard Spencer* **–**

LONDON'S BURNING 2 ch.g. (Mar 2) Cityscape 127 – Even Hotter 63 (Desert Style (IRE) 121) [2017 6f Jun 18] 33/1, well held in minor event at Salisbury. *Ralph Beckett* **–**

LONELY THE BRAVE (IRE) 3 b.g. Lawman (FR) 121 – Luckbealadytonight (IRE) 53 (Mr Greeley (USA) 122) [2017 82: 7.6s 7.6d 7.8d^{4} 7s^{6} p7s Aug 9] rangy gelding: fairly useful handicapper: below form in 2017: best form at 5f: acts on polytrack and good to soft going: often races prominently. *Mark Johnston* **73**

LONG EMBRACE 2 b.f. (Mar 5) Poet's Voice 126 – Loveable (Oasis Dream 129) [2017 t6.1g^{5} 6s 6d p6g^{5} t7.2g Nov 18] second foal: dam unraced half-sister to high-class winner up to 1m Delegator: modest maiden: should stay 7f: acts on tapeta. *Simon Crisford* **62**

LONG JOHN SILVER (IRE) 3 b.g. Rip Van Winkle (IRE) 134 – Tropical Lady (IRE) 117 (Sri Pekan (USA) 117) [2017 p8g^{2} t9.5m* Mar 14] 50,000F, €160,000Y: seventh foal: half-brother to 7f winner (stayed 9f) Tropical Mist (by Marju) and useful 1m (including at 2 yrs) winner Von Blucher (by Zoffany): dam 7f-1¼m winner: fairly useful form: won maiden at Wolverhampton (by 2¾ lengths from Oxford Don) in March: should improve further. *Jamie Osborne* **84 p**

LONG ON VALUE (USA) 6 b.h. Value Plus (USA) 117 – Long Message (USA) (Orientate (USA) 127) [2017 5f^{3} 6d^{2} 6m 5.5f^{3} 8f^{3} Sep 16] tall horse: smart performer: best effort when second in Al Quoz Sprint at Meydan (nose behind The Right Man) in March: 3 lengths third to World Approval in Woodbine Mile final outing: effective at 5.5f to 9f: acts on firm and soft going: has worn tongue tie: hung right when well held in Diamond Jubilee Stakes at Royal Ascot on third outing. *William I. Mott, USA* **119**

LONGROOM 5 b.g. Oasis Dream 129 – Phantom Wind (USA) 111 (Storm Cat (USA)) [2017 67: 5m* 5m* 5m* 5g^{2} 5.5g 5v Oct 21] stocky gelding: fairly useful handicapper: won at Musselburgh (apprentice) and Ayr in May, and Musselburgh again (by 2½ lengths from Midnight Malibu) in June: best form at 5f: acts on firm and good to soft going: usually races close up, strong traveller. *Noel Wilson* **89**

LONGSIDE 5 b.g. Oasis Dream 129 – Hypoteneuse (IRE) 86 (Sadler's Wells (USA) 132) [2017 76: 12g 10.1m^{2} 11.5m^{5} 11.9m^{4} p10g Sep 26] fair handicapper: stays 1½m: acts on polytrack and good to firm going: tried in blinkers/tongue tie. *James Eustace* **69**

LONG SOCKS 3 ch.g. Notnowcato 128 – Sienna Sunset (IRE) 68 (Spectrum (IRE) 126) **69 p** [2017 8.3d^5 8m^6 8.3v^4 Aug 3] tall, angular gelding: sixth foal: brother to winner up to 10.4f Now My Sun (2-y-o 7f winner) and half-brother to 1m winner Wrekin Sunset (by Doyen): dam 1¼m winner: fair form: best effort when fourth in maiden at Nottingham final start: should improve further. *Alan King*

LOOKING GOOD 5 b.m. Makfi 130 – Primo Heights 87 (Primo Valentino (IRE) 116) **72** [2017 7d 8g^2 10v Aug 28] fair maiden handicapper: stays 1m: acts on soft going: in cheekpieces last 2 starts: in tongue tie last 3. *S. Curling, Ireland*

LOOKINTOMYEYES 3 b.f. Cockney Rebel (IRE) 127 – Wizby 59 (Wizard King 122) **–** [2017 8m 7m p8s Sep 30] fourth foal: sister to 2-y-o 6.5f-1m winner Cockney Bob: dam winner up to 1m (2-y-o 5f-6f winner) who stayed 1¼m: well held in maidens: tried in hood: wears tongue tie. *Mrs Ilka Gansera-Leveque*

LOOK MY WAY 3 b.g. Pour Moi (IRE) 125 – Casual Glance 102 (Sinndar (IRE) 134) **106** [2017 57p: p12g^3 f12g* p14g^2 14m^5 14m^2 14m^3 14.4g^2 16g^3 13.9m 16v* Sep 17] useful handicapper: won at Southwell (by 4 lengths from Dirty Randy) in April and Ffos Las (by 22 lengths from Champagne Champ) in September: will stay 2¼m: acts on polytrack, fibresand, good to firm and heavy going: sold 70,000 gns in November to join John Quinn. *Andrew Balding*

LOOKS A MILLION 2 b.f. (Feb 26) Kyllachy 129 – Look Busy (IRE) 113 (Danetime (IRE) 121) **89** [2017 5g^2 5g* 6g 5.2s^5 5m 5s^3 6g^6 Nov 3] neat filly: second foal: dam, winner up to 6f (2-y-o 5f winner), half-sister to Prix Morny winner Unfortunately: fairly useful performer: won minor event at Sandown (by ¾ length from Validator) in June: third in listed race at Chantilly (1¼ lengths behind Beau Ideal) in October: stays 6f: acts on soft and good to firm going: usually races close up. *Joseph Tuite*

LOOK SURPRISED 4 ch.f. Kier Park (IRE) 114 – Cloridja (Indian Ridge 123) [2017 **73** 6.1m 5.1m* 5m^4 5d^6 t6.1g^5 t5.1g^3 p6g Dec 20] smallish filly: sixth foal: sister to 6f winner One Big Surprise: dam unraced half-sister to smart 1¼m/10.5f winner Colombian: fair performer: won maiden at Windsor in August: third at Wolverhampton in November: stays 6f: acts on tapeta and good to firm going: often races prominently. *Roger Teal*

LOPE DE LOOP (IRE) 2 b.f. (Apr 28) Lope de Vega (IRE) 125 – Patroller (USA) 59 **66** (Grand Slam (USA) 120) [2017 6.1v^4 6v^2 Aug 3] €9,000 2-y-o: fifth foal: half-sister to 3 winners, including 2-y-o 5f winner Lady Story (by Lucky Story) and 2-y-o 6f winner Yorkshire Relish (by Amadeus Wolf): dam maiden: fair form on first of 2 runs in minor events when fourth at Chepstow (2¾ lengths behind Double Reflection) in July. *David Evans*

LOPES DANCER (IRE) 5 b.g. Lope de Vega (IRE) 125 – Ballet Dancer (IRE) 77 **88** (Refuse To Bend (IRE) 128) [2017 83: t10.2g* t10.2s^6 10.2m^6 t10.2s^4 10s 12v^2 t12.4s* t12.4g Oct 19] fairly useful performer: won maiden at Newcastle (by 2¼ lengths from Wefait) in March and handicap at same course (by short head from Cape Peninsular) in September: stays 12.5f: acts on tapeta, good to firm and heavy going. *Sally Haynes*

LOPITO 2 b.c. (Mar 2) Lope de Vega (IRE) 125 – Stellar Brilliant (USA) 85 (Kris S **60 p** (USA)) [2017 8.3v Nov 8] £32,000Y: half-brother to several winners, including useful winner up to 1m He's No Saint (2-y-o 6f winner, by Dutch Art) and winner up to 11f Keepax (2-y-o 7f winner, by Dubai Destination): dam 1¼m winner: 14/1, eighth in maiden at Nottingham (12¾ lengths behind My Lord And Master): should do better. *Andrew Balding*

LOPITO DE VEGA (IRE) 5 ch.g. Lope de Vega (IRE) 125 – Athenian Way (IRE) 104 **72** (Barathea (IRE) 127) [2017 73: 9.9m 11.9v^4 10s^6 11.6m 10d^4 10.1g^4 10.2g 9.9m 12.1d p11g Oct 4] rather leggy gelding: fair handicapper: stays 1½m: acts on good to firm and heavy going: tried in cheekpieces: often races towards rear: sold £2,000, sent to Italy. *David C. Griffiths*

LORD CAPRIO (IRE) 2 b.g. (Feb 19) Lord Shanakill (USA) 121 – Azzurra du Caprio **71 p** (IRE) 96 (Captain Rio 122) [2017 7s^6 5.9s t6s t7.1g* t8g* Nov 24] first foal: dam, 5f/6f winner (including at 2 yrs), half-sister to useful 9.5f/1¼m winner Kilmore Quay: fair performer: won 2 nurseries at Newcastle in November: stays 1m: acts on tapeta: in tongue tie last 2 starts: sometimes slowly away, often races towards rear: open to further improvement. *Ben Haslam*

LORD CLENAGHCASTLE (IRE) 3 b.g. Big Bad Bob (IRE) 118 – Clenaghcastle **89** Lady (IRE) (Acclamation 118) [2017 74: p7g^6 7g^2 8.5d* 8m* 8.5m^2 7g 8.5v^5 Oct 1] fairly useful handicapper: won at Epsom (by 2 lengths from Sandy Shores) in July and Brighton (by 2 lengths from Pendo) in August: should stay 1¼m: acts on polytrack, good to firm and good to soft going: usually races prominently. *Gary Moore*

LORD COMMANDER 3 b.g. Nayef (USA) 129 – Kashoof 83 (Green Desert (USA) **77**
127) [2017 76: 10m^{4} 8.3g^{2} 11.9d 8m^{6} t8.6g 8.5g^{6} 8.3d^{4} t8g* Oct 19] fair performer: won maiden at Newcastle in October: stays 8.5f: acts on tapeta, good to firm and good to soft going. *Richard Fahey*

LORD COOPER 3 b.g. Sir Percy 129 – Zooming (IRE) (Indian Ridge 123) [2017 49, **83**
a72: p7m^{5} p6g* t6f* t6g* 7m 6d^{5} 6s^{5} 6d^{4} t6g p6.5g t6.1g^{2} p6g p6g^{6} 5.5v Nov 25] sturdy gelding: fairly useful handicapper: won at Kempton and Wolverhampton in February, and again at latter course (by head from Cappananty Con) in March: stays 6f: acts on polytrack, tapeta and soft going: wears cheekpieces: often wears tongue tie. *Jose Santos*

LORD DEL BOY 2 b.g. (Mar 27) Delegator 125 – Lady Prodee 74 (Proclamation (IRE) –
130) [2017 5m May 27] 33/1, well held in minor event at Salisbury. *Bill Turner*

LORD E (IRE) 3 b.g. Lord Shanakill (USA) 121 – Elouges (IRE) (Dalakhani (IRE) 133) **59**
[2017 p8g^{5} p7m 7m 9.9g^{6} 11.6g^{3} 11.6d^{3} Jun 24] modest maiden: stays 11.5f: acts on polytrack and good to soft going: tried in visor: winning hurdler: sold 1,500 gns in November, sent to Italy. *Gary Moore*

LORD FRANKLIN 8 ch.g. Iceman 117 – Zell (IRE) 65 (Lend A Hand 124) [2017 88: 8m **80**
10.3m 10.2g 10g^{2} 10.3s^{6} 12.3d^{4} 10.3g^{6} 10s^{5} 11.8d 10.5v 10.2d f12.1g Oct 22] tall, leggy gelding: fairly useful handicapper: second at Leicester in May: stays 10.5f: acts on polytrack and any turf going: has worn cheekpieces: front runner/races prominently: sold £4,500 in November to join Andrew Crook. *Eric Alston*

LORD GEORGE (IRE) 4 gr.g. Sir Percy 129 – Mahima (FR) (Linamix (FR) 127) [2017 **108**
98: t12.4s^{3} 12m^{3} t16.3s^{4} 15.4g 14.5g p14g^{4} p16d^{2} t16.3d^{4} Dec 16] good-topped gelding: useful handicapper: third at Ascot (5¼ lengths behind Appeared) in May: stays 16.5f: acts on polytrack, tapeta and good to firm going: tried in tongue tie: often races prominently. *James Fanshawe*

LORD GLITTERS (FR) 4 gr.g. Whipper (USA) 126 – Lady Glitters (FR) (Homme de **120 p**
Loi (IRE) 120) [2017 p8g* 8d* 7s^{2} 8s* 8d^{2} Nov 4] good-topped gelding: half-brother to several winners in France, including 1m-1¼m winner Glittering Star (by Lomitas) and 1½m-17f winner Blue Saphire (by Anabaa Blue): dam French maiden (stayed 1m): very smart performer: won minor events at Chantilly in April and Saint-Cloud (by 2½ lengths from Instant de Reve) in May, and Balmoral Handicap at Ascot (by neck from GM Hopkins) in October: sold from C. Lotoux €270,000 after second start: has won over 1¼m, best form at 7f/1m: acts on polytrack and soft going: often races in rear: capable of better still. *David O'Meara*

LORD HUNTINGDON 4 b.g. Lord of England (GER) 119 – Marajuana 82 (Robellino –
(USA) 127) [2017 88: 14.2v^{6} Jul 29] fairly useful handicapper: well below form only start on Flat in 2017: stays 1¼m: acts on polytrack, fibresand and good to soft going: front runner/races prominently: fairly useful hurdler. *Alan King*

LORD KITTEN (USA) 3 b.g. Kitten's Joy (USA) 128 – Iteration (USA) (Wild Again **73**
(USA)) [2017 10g 9.9d^{5} 8m^{3} 7.4m^{3} t8.6g 9.9m^{3} t10.2s^{3} p8d Oct 6] fair maiden: stays 1¼m: acts on tapeta and good to firm going: usually wears headgear: in tongue tie last 3 starts. *David Lanigan*

Balmoral Handicap (Sponsored by Qipco), Ascot—the grey Lord Glitters gets up on the line to land a gamble, winning from GM Hopkins, the other grey Dark Red (blinkers) and Accidental Agent (left)

LORD MURPHY (IRE) 4 b.g. Holy Roman Emperor (IRE) 125 – Tralanza (IRE) 77 **71**
(Traditionally (USA) 117) [2017 –: p8d t8.6g* t8.6g^{2} p8g^{2} t8.6g* t8.6g^{5} t8.6g t8.6g^{4} 11.4m t9.5g^{3} t9.5g t9.5d Dec 26] fair handicapper: won at Wolverhampton in March and April: stays 11.5f: acts on polytrack, tapeta and good to firm going. *Daniel Loughnane*

LORD NAPIER (IRE) 4 b.g. Galileo (IRE) 134 – Jacqueline (IND) (King Charlemagne **88**
(USA) 120) [2017 82: p12g^{2} p12m^{4} p16g^{3} 12m May 7] good-bodied gelding: fairly useful maiden: third in handicap at Kempton in April: stays 2m: acts on polytrack and soft going: usually wears headgear: sold £24,000 in June to join Peter Bowen. *John Ryan*

LORD OF THE GLEN 2 b.g. (Apr 6) Orientor 118 – Glenlini 68 (Bertolini (USA) 125) **69**
[2017 5m 5m^{6} 5m^{5} 6s 5d^{5} 6s 5d^{4} 6g t6g^{6} t5d^{2} t5g* t6g^{2} Dec 6] fair performer: won nursery at Newcastle in November: second in similar event at same course final start: stays 6f: acts on tapeta and good to soft going: wears headgear. *Jim Goldie*

LORD OF THE ROCK (IRE) 5 b.g. Rock of Gibraltar (IRE) 133 – La Sylphide 94 **101**
(Rudimentary (USA) 118) [2017 102: 8g 7.9d* 8.2v 7d Nov 11] useful handicapper: won at York (by ½ length from Home Cummins) in July: stays 1m: acts on good to firm and heavy going: usually races close up, sometimes finds little: inconsistent. *Michael Dods*

LORD OF THE STORM 9 b.g. Avonbridge 123 – Just Run (IRE) 45 (Runnett 125) **67**
[2017 73: t9.5m^{4} p8g p8g^{5} p8g 9.9g p8g^{4} p10g 9.9v p10s Dec 7] lengthy gelding: fair handicapper: stays 1½m: acts on polytrack, tapeta, good to firm and heavy going: has worn cheekpieces/tongue tie. *Michael Attwater*

LORD REASON 5 b.g. Sixties Icon 125 – Luck Will Come (IRE) 82 (Desert Style (IRE) **84**
121) [2017 82: 8.5f* 8.5f 9.1m^{5} Aug 17] fairly useful handicapper: won at Epsom (by short head from Frank Bridge) in July: stays 1¼m: acts on polytrack, firm and soft going: usually races close up. *John Butler*

LORD RIDDIFORD (IRE) 2 gr.g. (Mar 23) Zebedee 113 – Beacon of Hope (IRE) **81**
(Barathea (IRE) 127) [2017 5m^{2} 5g* 5.1d^{4} Oct 23] €27,000Y: half-brother to several winners, including 6f winner Mister Freeze (by Frozen Power) and 5f/6f winner Fly By Wire (by Excellent Art): dam once-raced half-sister to useful 7f/1m winner Kehaar: fairly useful form: won minor event at Beverley (by 1¾ lengths from Porchy Party) in May: raced only at 5f. *John Quinn*

LORD ROB 6 b.g. Rob Roy (USA) 122 – First Grey (Environment Friend 128) [2017 51: **54**
t10.2g^{3} t10.2d^{4} t10.2g^{3} t12.4d^{6} t8s^{4} t10.2s Jun 3] modest maiden handicapper: stays 1¼m: acts on tapeta and good to soft going: has worn headgear, including last 4 starts: usually races prominently. *David Thompson*

LORD VETINARI 2 br.g. (Mar 10) Lethal Force (IRE) 128 – Princess Luna (GER) **77 p**
(Grand Lodge (USA) 125) [2017 6d^{6} 6m^{5} Aug 16] 27,000F, 42,000Y: sturdy gelding: half-brother to 3 winners, including useful 6f-8.6f winner Space War (by Elusive City) and 7f winner Lunette (by Teofilo): dam 1m winner: fair form: better effort when sixth in newcomers race at Ascot (5¾ lengths behind Mythical Magic) in July: remains open to improvement. *Andrew Balding*

LORD YEATS 4 b.g. Yeats (IRE) 128 – Bogside Theatre (IRE) 102 (Fruits of Love (USA) **116**
127) [2017 95: 11.9d* 12g* 12s^{5} 13.9m 14s^{5} Sep 10] rangy gelding: smart performer: won handicap at York (by 6 lengths from Burguillos) in May and listed race at Newmarket (by neck from Second Step) in July: stays 13f: acts on heavy going: front runner. *Jedd O'Keeffe*

LORELEI 5 b.m. Excellent Art 125 – Light Dreams 70 (Fantastic Light (USA) 134) [2017 **–**
66: p15.8g Jan 27] fair handicapper: well below form only start in 2017: stays 16.5f: acts on polytrack and tapeta: tried in cheekpieces: often races towards rear. *William Muir*

LORELINA 4 b.f. Passing Glance 119 – Diktalina 61 (Diktat 126) [2017 88: 9.9g^{3} 11.4m^{3} **92**
10.3s^{2} 10.1m^{2} 10v* 10g 10d^{2} Oct 27] fairly useful handicapper: won at Ffos Las (by ¾ length from Bybrook) in September: second at Newbury (head behind Precious Ramotswe) in October: stays 1¼m: acts on good to firm and heavy going: often races prominently. *Andrew Balding*

LORIKEET (USA) 3 ch.g. Street Cry (IRE) 130 – Ishitaki (ARG) (Interprete (ARG)) **59**
[2017 70: t9.5g Jan 6] fair maiden: below form only start in 2017: stays 8.5f: acts on tapeta. *Mark Johnston*

LOS CAMACHOS (IRE) 2 b.c. (Mar 21) Camacho 118 – Illuminise (IRE) 109 (Grand **65**
Lodge (USA) 125) [2017 t5.1d^{2} t5.1d^{6} Dec 26] fair form: better effort in minor events at Wolverhampton when second to Ty Rock Brandy. *David Evans*

LOS CERRITOS (SWI) 5 ch.g. Dr Fong (USA) 128 – La Coruna (SWI) (Arazi (USA) 135) [2017 60: p8d^4 a9g^3 a8.9s^2 a9.7g^4 Mar 14] modest performer nowadays: stays 9.7f: acts on polytrack, dirt, snow and good to soft going: has worn headgear, including in 2017: tried in tongue tie: usually races prominently. *Oliver Greenall* **62**

LOSINGMYRELIGION (FR) 2 b.g. (Mar 1) Planteur (IRE) 124 – Marie Dar (FR) (Sinndar (IRE) 134) [2017 7d^5 t8g^5 p8g* Nov 1] fair form: won minor event at Kempton (by short head from Exec Chef) in November: stays 1m. *Marco Botti* **70**

LOST AT SEA 3 b.g. Dutch Art 126 – Tahlia Ree (IRE) 77 (Acclamation 118) [2017 94: 8g 7v 7d Nov 11] fairly useful performer: below form in 2017: stays 6f: best form on good going: tried in cheekpieces. *K. R. Burke* **–**

LOSTOCK 3 b.c. Kodiac 112 – Green Silk (IRE) (Namid 128) [2017 67p: t5.1f^3 t6g^4 Mar 6] lightly-raced maiden, form only on debut at 2 yrs. *Michael Dods* **–**

LOST THE MOON 4 b.f. Authorized (IRE) 133 – Missouri 86 (Charnwood Forest (IRE) 125) [2017 77p: p13.3d* p15.8f^2 p14g^{pu} p16d^4 p14g^6 16.3g 16g^6 t16.5g^2 p15.8g^2 Dec 20] workmanlike filly: fairly useful handicapper: won at Chelmsford (by 2¼ lengths from Eurato) in February: second at Lingfield (apprentice) in March: stays 16.5f: acts on polytrack and tapeta: sometimes races in rear. *Mark H. Tompkins* **85**

LOTARA 5 b.m. Monsieur Bond (IRE) 120 – Cheviot Heights 72 (Intikhab (USA) 135) [2017 68: t5g 6d^4 5m 6g 6g^5 7.2g^5 5.9d t5g^5 t6.1m t7.1s* t6g Dec 6] modest handicapper: won at Newcastle (apprentice) in November: stays 7f: acts on tapeta and good to soft going: tried in headgear: usually races nearer last than first. *Jim Goldie* **62**

LOUD AND CLEAR 6 b.g. Dalakhani (IRE) 133 – Whispering Blues (IRE) (Sadler's Wells (USA) 132) [2017 t12.4g^5 Oct 10] dual bumper winner: 8/1, fifth in maiden at Newcastle (2 lengths behind Magellan): will be suited by 1¾m+: open to improvement. *Iain Jardine* **81 p**

LOUGH SALT (IRE) 6 b.g. Brian Boru 124 – Castlehill Lady (IRE) (Supreme Leader 123) [2017 12v^3 Sep 30] 9/1, third in maiden at Ripon (9½ lengths behind Mixboy): fair hurdler. *Richard Guest* **65**

LOUIS VEE (IRE) 9 b.g. Captain Rio 122 – Mrs Evans (IRE) 97 (College Chapel 122) [2017 41, a66: p7g t6g p6g^5 t6m 6m p6g^3 5.7f^3 7m 5.1s 6.1m p6g p7s 5.7s 6.1g^2 f6.1g p6s Dec 7] modest handicapper: stays 6f: acts on polytrack, tapeta, firm and soft going: wears headgear: has worn tongue tie: front runner/races prominently. *John O'Shea* **53**

LOUJAIN (IRE) 3 ch.g. Dubawi (IRE) 129 – Eshaadeh (USA) (Storm Cat (USA)) [2017 74p: 7g^4 7s^2 May 22] sturdy gelding: fairly useful form: second in maiden at Leicester (2½ lengths behind To Dibba) in May: tried in blinkers: open to further improvement. *John Gosden* **86 p**

LOULIN 2 ch.g. (Apr 24) Exceed And Excel (AUS) 126 – Wimple (USA) 101 (Kingmambo (USA) 125) [2017 5g^5 5s^6 5s^6 Oct 31] modest form: best effort when fifth in minor event at Pontefract (5¾ lengths behind Viscount Loftus) in August. *David O'Meara* **57**

LOUMARIN (IRE) 5 b.m. Bushranger (IRE) 119 – Masela (IRE) 71 (Medicean 128) [2017 58, a69: t7.1g f6g t6g^3 t6g^3 t5.1g^3 t5.1g^3 p5g 6.1g^3 5m^3 6d^6 Jun 5] rather leggy mare: modest handicapper on turf, fair on all-weather: stays 6f: acts on polytrack, tapeta and good to firm going: wears cheekpieces: tried in tongue tie: often races prominently. *Michael Appleby* **59 a65**

LOVE AND BE LOVED 3 b.f. Lawman (FR) 121 – Rightside 78 (High Chaparral (IRE) 132) [2017 60: p7g t6m t7.1g^3 t9.5g^4 t8.6g^4 7.1d* 8f^3 7.1m^6 8g* 8.2v* 8.1d* Oct 23] fair handicapper: won at Chepstow in June, Salisbury in August, Leicester in September and Windsor in October: left Peter Chapple-Hyam after first start: stays 8.5f: acts on tapeta and heavy going: tried in hood: front runner. *John Flint* **79**

LOVEATFIRSTSIGHT 4 b.f. Bertolini (USA) 125 – Starbeck (IRE) 94 (Spectrum (IRE) 126) [2017 70: p7d^6 6.1m t7.2g^3 t7.2g^2 t7.2g^3 t7.2g p8g p8g p7g* p7m* p7s^5 p7g^6 Dec 20] fair handicapper: won at Kempton and Lingfield in November: left Michael Attwater after sixth start: stays 7f: acts on polytrack and tapeta: usually in cheekpieces in 2017. *Jane Chapple-Hyam* **67**

LOVE CANDY (IRE) 3 b.f. Canford Cliffs (IRE) 133 – Love Thirty 93 (Mister Baileys 123) [2017 8s 12g^3 12d^6 Aug 7] €28,000Y: half-sister to several winners, including 1¼m winner Chefchaouen (by Dylan Thomas) and useful 7f/1m winner Royal Temptress (by Strategic Prince): dam 2-y-o 6f winner: modest form: best effort when third in maiden at Pontefract in June. *Sally Haynes* **54**

LOVE CONQUERS (JPN) 3 b.f. Deep Impact (JPN) 134 – Love And Bubbles (USA) 112 (Loup Sauvage (USA) 125) [2017 10d 10m^2 10g^2 11.4m^2 p10g^6 t12.4d* Nov 4] rather leggy filly: sister to several winners in Japan, including smart winner up to 1½m (Japanese Derby) Deep Brillante (2-y-o 9f winner), and half-sister to Japanese 6f winner Love In The Dark (by Dance In The Dark): dam French 7f (at 2 yrs) to 9f (Prix Chloe) winner, out of unraced half-sister to Japanese St Leger winner That's The Plenty: fairly useful performer: won maiden at Newcastle in November: stays 12.5f: acts on tapeta and good to firm going. *Ralph Beckett* **84**

LOVE DREAMS (IRE) 3 b.c. Dream Ahead (USA) 133 – Kimola (IRE) (King's Theatre (IRE) 128) [2017 92p: 7m^5 6g^6 7s* 7d^3 7g 7.6g^6 Sep 2] angular colt: smart handicapper: won at Newmarket (by 5 lengths from Mountain Rescue) in July: stays 7f: acts on soft and good to firm going: front runner/races prominently. *Mark Johnston* **110**

LOVE IN THE DARK 4 b.f. Sleeping Indian 122 – Love In The Park 78 (Pivotal 124) [2017 –: p7g p7g t7.1g Mar 27] little form: in hood last 5 starts: temperamental. *Nikki Evans* **– §**

LOVE IS ENOUGH (JPN) 2 b.f. (Mar 23) Deep Impact (JPN) 134 – Soinlovewithyou (USA) 79 (Sadler's Wells (USA) 132) [2017 t8.6g Nov 29] fourth foal: dam, 2-y-o 7f winner, closely related to Derby winner Ruler of The World and half-sister to top-class winner up to 1½m Duke of Marmalade: 12/1, well held in minor event at Wolverhampton. *John Gosden* **–**

LOVE ISLAND 8 b.m. Acclamation 118 – Sally Traffic 57 (River Falls 113) [2017 91: 6m 6.1g^4 t6s* 6.1m^2 Jun 15] angular mare: fairly useful handicapper: won at Newcastle (by head from Fredricka) in June: stays 6f: acts on polytrack, tapeta, good to firm and heavy going: wears headgear: has worn tongue tie. *Richard Whitaker* **89**

LOVELL 4 b.g. Dubawi (IRE) 129 – Cosmodrome (USA) 108 (Bahri (USA) 125) [2017 103p: 10.3d May 17] good-topped gelding: useful handicapper: returned lame only start in 2017: stays 1¼m: acts on soft going. *Charlie Appleby* **–**

LOVELY ACCLAMATION (IRE) 3 b.f. Acclamation 118 – Titova (Halling (USA) 133) [2017 68p: 7m^6 p6s^6 7g 8.2g^4 t7.2g p7d^6 8s 6d Oct 24] fair maiden: stays 1m: acts on good to firm going: tried in cheekpieces: front runner/races prominently. *Ismail Mohammed* **67**

LOVELY STORY (IRE) 6 b.m. Cape Cross (IRE) 129 – Hush Money (CHI) (Hussonet (USA)) [2017 81: 11.6m^6 13.3g Jul 13] lengthy mare: useful maiden at best: well held both starts in 2017: stays 1½m: acts on good to firm going: tried in cheekpieces/tongue tie. *Seamus Durack* **–**

LOVE ME AGAIN 3 b.f. Kheleyf (USA) 116 – Midnight Allure 85 (Aragon 118) [2017 –: 8g^6 8.3v^5 8.1m 7d p8g^6 p10s Dec 7] modest maiden: stays 1m: acts on polytrack, best turf form on good ground. *Charlie Fellowes* **64**

LOVE NOT WAR 3 b.f. Sepoy (AUS) 129 – Jumeirah Palm (USA) 64 (Distorted Humor (USA) 117) [2017 7m Apr 30] 12/1, well held in maiden at Salisbury: dead. *George Scott* **–**

LOVE OASIS 3 b.f. Oasis Dream 129 – Pickle 84 (Piccolo 121) [2017 68: 6m^3 6g^2 6d* 6m^5 6g* 6g 6.1g^2 6m^2 5.7g^2 6g^6 6m 6s^5 6v 6s^6 t6.1g* p6g p6g Nov 17] sturdy filly: fairly useful handicapper: won at Ayr and Leicester (by 3½ lengths from Screaming Gemini) in June, and Wolverhampton (by ½ length from Four Dragons) in October: stays 6f: acts on tapeta, soft and good to firm going: front runner/races prominently: sold 50,000 gns in December. *Mark Johnston* **86**

LOVE ON THE ROCKS (IRE) 4 ch.f. Exceed And Excel (AUS) 126 – My Love Thomas (IRE) 84 (Cadeaux Genereux 131) [2017 93: 5m* 5g 5m 5.1m* 5g 5m^2 p5g^6 Oct 20] good-quartered filly: useful handicapper: won at Bath (by head from Seamster) in April and Windsor (by length from Spring Loaded) in July: best at 5f: acts on firm going: wears hood: races freely. *Charles Hills* **99**

LOVE RAT 2 b.g. (Mar 16) Mawatheeq (USA) 126 – Watersilk (IRE) (Fasliyev (USA) 120) [2017 f7.1g^5 Dec 11] 100/1, fifth in minor event at Southwell (6½ lengths behind On The Warpath). *Scott Dixon* **72**

LOVE TO BREEZE 2 b.f. (Jan 20) Azamour (IRE) 130 – Burn The Breeze (IRE) 115 (Beat Hollow 126) [2017 7d Nov 4] fourth foal: half-sister to 6f/7f winner Roman Holiday (by Holy Roman Emperor): dam, 1¼m/10.5f winner who stayed 12.5f, half-sister to smart 1m winner Lethals Lady: 20/1, well held in minor event at Newmarket. *Ed Vaughan* **–**

LOVE TO ROCK (IRE) 4 b.f. Fastnet Rock (AUS) 127 – I'm In Love (USA) 88 (Zafonic (USA) 130) [2017 –: 15g 13.1s t8.6g^5 8.9m Jul 25] modest maiden: stays 15f: acts on tapeta: in blinkers last 2 starts. *A. P. Keatley, Ireland* **56**

LOVING 3 gr.f. Mayson 124 – Courting 108 (Pursuit of Love 124) [2017 79: 5.6d^{6} 5.2g^{4} t6.1g^{4} 6m^{5} Aug 28] close-coupled filly: fair handicapper: stays 6f: acts on good to firm and good to soft going: tried in cheekpieces: front runner/races prominently, often freely: temperament under suspicion. *William Haggas* **70**

LOVING YOUR WORK 6 b.g. Royal Applause 124 – Time Crystal (IRE) 83 (Sadler's Wells (USA) 132) [2017 74§: p13g 10m^{4} 12m^{5} 11m^{3} 10s^{4} p12g Dec 6] strong gelding: modest handicapper: stays 1½m: acts on polytrack, soft and good to firm going: has worn headgear: often races towards rear: quirky sort, carries head awkwardly. *Ken Cunningham-Brown* **62 §**

LOW PROFILE 2 ch.g. (Mar 16) Galileo (IRE) 134 – Dynaforce (USA) 118 (Dynaformer (USA)) [2017 8.1g^{6} Oct 9] €100,000Y: lengthy gelding: fourth foal: closely related to useful winner up to 1¾m Aljezeera (2-y-o 1m winner, by Frankel) and half-brother to a winner in USA by Tapit: dam French/US 1m-1½m winner: 9/1, sixth in minor event at Windsor (4½ lengths behind Delsheer): will stay at least 1¼m: should improve. *Roger Charlton* **69 p**

LOWRIE 4 b.f. Assertive 121 – Miacarla 67 (Forzando 122) [2017 57: 5m May 8] modest maiden: well beaten only start in 2017: best effort at 5f: acts on firm going: usually wears headgear: front runner. *John David Riches* **–**

LOXLEY (IRE) 2 b.c. (Feb 11) New Approach (IRE) 132 – Lady Marian (GER) 125 (Nayef (USA) 129) [2017 9.1s* 8d Oct 28] fourth foal: half-brother to useful winner up to 1m Forest Maiden (2-y-o 7f winner, by Invincible Spirit) and French 9.5f winner Edwinstowe (by Shamardal): dam 1¼m/11f winner: useful form: won minor event at Goodwood (dead-heated with Istanbul Sultan) in October: seventh in Racing Post Trophy at Doncaster (8¼ lengths behind Saxon Warrior) 2 weeks later: will be suited by 1¼m: remains with potential. *Charlie Appleby* **100 p**

LOYALTY 10 b.g. Medicean 128 – Ecoutila (USA) (Rahy (USA) 115) [2017 95: p8g^{6} p8m^{4} p7d^{2} p8d* p8f^{4} p8d^{5} p7g p7g^{5} t7.1s p7s^{5} p8s^{6} t7.2d^{5} Dec 16] compact gelding: useful handicapper: won at Chelmsford (by 7 lengths from King of Dreams) in February: stays 1¼m: acts on polytrack: wears visor. *Derek Shaw* **96**

LOZAH 4 b.f. Lawman (FR) 121 – Princess Luna (GER) (Grand Lodge (USA) 125) [2017 75: t8g^{6} t8d^{4} t10.2d^{5} t8s^{5} 8m^{4} 8f 9m^{3} t10.2d 8g 9.9m^{2} 7.8d^{6} t8s t12.4d^{6} t8d^{3} t8.6g Dec 5] fair handicapper: stays 1¼m: acts on tapeta, good to firm and good to soft going: has worn headgear/tongue tie: sometimes slowly away. *Roger Fell* **68**

LUALIWA 3 b.g. Foxwedge (AUS) 128 – Sunpearl (Compton Place 125) [2017 79: p7g* 7.5m^{3} 7s^{2} 7d* 7g* 6d^{2} 7s^{6} 7.2v Oct 16] compact gelding: useful performer: won maiden at Chelmsford in March, and handicaps at Chester and York (apprentice, by 1½ lengths from Derek Duval) in July: second in handicap at Ascot (length behind Golden Apollo) in August: stays 7.5f: acts on polytrack, soft and good to firm going: front runner/races prominently. *Kevin Ryan* **100**

LUANG PRABANG (IRE) 4 b.f. Invincible Spirit (IRE) 121 – Sauvage (FR) (Sri Pekan (USA) 117) [2017 80p: 7m 7s^{4} p7g^{4} 7.6s p8g^{3} t8.6g* t8.6g^{2} p8m Nov 25] modest handicapper on turf, fairly useful on all-weather: won at Wolverhampton in October: second at same course in November: stays 8.5f: acts on polytrack, tapeta and good to firm going. *Chris Wall* **58 a81**

LUATH 4 ch.g. Archipenko (USA) 127 – Delaware Dancer (IRE) 68 (Danehill Dancer (IRE) 117) [2017 58: t8g f7g* 7g^{6} t8s^{3} 8s t7.1d^{6} f7.1g^{4} t8s^{6} t7.1g f8.1g^{3} f8.1g^{2} Dec 1] fair handicapper: won at Southwell in April: stays 1m: acts on fibresand and tapeta: tried in headgear. *Suzzanne France* **67**

LUBINKA (IRE) 2 ro.f. (Feb 19) Mastercraftsman (IRE) 129 – Petite Nymphe (Golan (IRE) 129) [2017 8g^{2} 8s^{3} 8m^{6} Oct 13] workmanlike filly: fourth foal: half-sister to 2-y-o 7f winner Paulownia (by Nathaniel): dam, 15f winner, half-sister to very smart winner up to 1m Danseuse du Soir: fairly useful form: best effort when sixth in Fillies' Mile at Newmarket (6¼ lengths behind Laurens) final start: will be suited by 1¼m+. *Peter Chapple-Hyam* **94**

LUCATA (IRE) 3 b.g. Sir Prancealot (IRE) 111 – Toy Show (IRE) 86 (Danehill (USA) 126) [2017 78: 6d Oct 20] fair maiden: well held only start in 2017: best effort at 5f: acts on heavy going: tried in visor. *Alan Berry* **–**

LUCENT DREAM (IRE) 6 b.g. Teofilo (IRE) 126 – Cheyenne Star (IRE) 115 (Mujahid (USA) 125) [2017 69: p10.7g p10.7g t9.5m* t8.6g^{2} 9.1m^{6} 9g* 10d^{2} 10g* 11.8g^{5} Aug 30] fairly useful handicapper on turf, fair on all-weather: won at Wolverhampton in March, **87 a67**

Carlisle in June and Ayr (by 1½ lengths from Zealous) in July: stays 1½m: acts on polytrack, tapeta and good to soft going: tried in hood: wears tongue tie: often races towards rear. *John McConnell, Ireland*

LUCIFUGOUS (IRE) 2 gr.f. (Apr 28) Footstepsinthesand 120 – Krasotka (IRE) (Soviet Star (USA) 128) [2017 6g^6 7d^3 7s^5 8m^3 8d^6 Sep 19] €8,500Y, 10,000 2-y-o: sixth foal: half-sister to 5f/6f winner The Grey Rebel (by Tagula) and temperamental winner up to 1m Pumaflor (2-y-o 6f winner, by Aussie Rules): dam of little account: modest maiden: stays 7f: acts on good to firm and good to soft going. *Stuart Williams* **64**

LUCKY BEGGAR (IRE) 7 gr.g. Verglas (IRE) 118 – Lucky Clio (IRE) 59 (Key of Luck (USA) 126) [2017 89: t5d^6 6g^2 5m^4 5m^3 5.5g* 5s^2 6m* 6m 6.1s^4 5.1d^2 5g 5g^5 6d 6d 5.5g 5.5g 5g f5g 6s^4 Oct 31] strong gelding: useful handicapper: won at Wetherby in May and Catterick (by 1¼ lengths from Stanghow) in June: second at Chester (short head behind Reflektor) in July: stays 6f: acts on tapeta and any turf going: has worn headgear: sold £6,000 in November. *David C. Griffiths* **95**

LUCKY CLOVER 6 ch.m. Lucky Story (USA) 128 – Willisa 67 (Polar Falcon (USA) 126) [2017 69: 5.7f t5.1g 5.7f^5 5.2m 5f* 5.1g^2 5s^4 p6g p5g* Oct 17] fair handicapper: won at Bath in July and Kempton in October: best form at 5f: acts on polytrack, tapeta, firm and good to soft going: usually wears headgear: front runner/races prominently. *Malcolm Saunders* **71**

LUCKY DEAL 2 ch.c. (May 7) Mastercraftsman (IRE) 129 – Barter 62 (Daylami (IRE) 138) [2017 9d^3 p10s* Nov 23] 85,000Y: fifth foal: half-brother to 3 winners, including smart winner up to 10.5f Haggle (2-y-o 1m winner, by Pivotal) and useful 1m-1¼m winner Bermondsey (by Galileo): dam lightly-raced half-sister to very smart stayer Golden Quest and to dams of Oaks winner Alexandrova and Melbourne Cup winner Rekindling: fairly useful form: won minor event at Chelmsford (by 2 lengths from Wissahickon) in November: will stay at least 1½m: open to further improvement. *Mark Johnston* **88 p**

LUCKY DI 7 br.m. Araafa (IRE) 128 – Lucky Date (IRE) 91 (Halling (USA) 133) [2017 78d: p6s^2 t7.2g 6g 6s 6.1g^5 p7g^3 p7m^6 p7g^6 Dec 13] sturdy mare: modest handicapper nowadays: stays 7f: acts on polytrack, tapeta and good to firm going: tried in cheekpieces: races towards rear. *Peter Hedger* **54**

LUCKY ELLEN (IRE) 3 b.f. Elusive Pimpernel (USA) 117 – Dona Alba (IRE) 99 (Peintre Celebre (USA) 137) [2017 52: p7g^5 8.5d 8.5s^3 t9.5m^6 t12.4d^5 t12.2g Dec 22] modest maiden: left David Kenneth Budds after second start: stays 12.5f: acts on tapeta and soft going: sometimes slowly away. *Jennie Candlish* **55**

LUCKY ESTEEM 3 b.f. Yorgunnabelucky (USA) 102 – Dream Esteem 65 (Mark of Esteem (IRE) 137) [2017 67: 8g^6 10d 9.9s 8.3g Nov 1] sturdy filly: modest maiden: should stay beyond 1m: best form on good going: tried in tongue tie. *Neil Mulholland* **61**

LUCKY GAL 7 b.m. Overbury (IRE) 116 – Lucky Arrow 60 (Indian Ridge 123) [2017 t12.2g^4 Feb 11] maiden hurdler: 50/1 and hooded, fourth in maiden at Wolverhampton (8 lengths behind Big Country) on Flat debut. *Martin Hill* **65**

LUCKY LODGE 7 b.g. Lucky Story (USA) 128 – Melandre 74 (Lujain (USA) 119) [2017 73: t6g^3 t7.1g^2 7m^4 t7.1s^4 6.1m^3 6d^4 7m^6 6v^5 6v t6d* 6g t6d Nov 10] leggy gelding: fair handicapper: won at Newcastle in August: stays 7f: acts on tapeta, good to firm and heavy going: wears headgear. *Antony Brittain* **71**

LUCKY LOUIE 4 ch.g. Dutch Art 126 – Ardessie (Bahamian Bounty 116) [2017 69: f6g **78**
p8g^2 f8g p7g* p8g^2 7m^3 7d^2 7v^2 8v^2 7.6s^2 Sep 16] lengthy, angular gelding: fair handicapper: **a72**
won at Lingfield in February: second at Ffos Las in August: stays 1m: acts on polytrack, good to firm and heavy going: wears headgear: usually races towards rear. *Roger Teal*

LUCKY LUCKY MAN (IRE) 2 gr.g. (Apr 25) Clodovil (IRE) 116 – Regrette Rien (IRE) 70 (Chevalier (IRE) 115) [2017 6m t5.1g^4 t5.1g^2 5.9d^2 5.9v* Sep 13] €10,000F, £13,000Y: second foal: dam maiden (stayed 1½m): fairly useful performer: won nursery at Carlisle (by 4½ lengths from Diamond Dougal) in September: stays 6f: acts on heavy going. *Richard Fahey* **88**

LUCKY LUCRECIA (IRE) 3 b.f. Dansili 127 – Politesse (USA) (Barathea (IRE) 127) [2017 7m* Jul 7] half-sister to several winners, including very smart 6f/7f winner King's Apostle (by King's Best) and smart 6f/6.5f winner Cape Classic (by Cape Cross): dam unraced: 5/2, won maiden at Doncaster (by ½ length from Pretty Passe) on debut: should progress. *William Haggas* **73 p**

LUCKY RESET 2 ch.f. (Mar 11) Yorgunnabelucky (USA) 102 – Reset City 87 (Reset (AUS) 124) [2017 7d p7d p8g Aug 30] second foal: dam, 1¼m-1½m winner, half-sister to useful winner up to 11f I'm So Lucky: well held in maiden/minor events. *David Evans* **–**

LUCKY'S DREAM 2 ch.g. (Mar 21) Yorgunnabelucky (USA) 102 – Dream Esteem 65 (Mark of Esteem (IRE) 137) [2017 6.5g 7g 7.4v^{4} 8g Sep 27] lengthy gelding: modest form: best effort when seventh in minor event at Newbury on second start. *David Evans* **56**

LUCKY VIOLET (IRE) 5 b.m. Dandy Man (IRE) 123 – Rashida 73 (King's Best (USA) 132) [2017 79p: 8s 7.2v^{5} t8d^{5} Oct 24] fair handicapper: stays 9f: acts on good to firm going: usually wears hood. *Iain Jardine* **73**

LUCREZIA 3 b.f. Nathaniel (IRE) 129 – Nannina 121 (Medicean 128) [2017 71p: p10m Jan 9] fair form at best: stays 8.5f: in visor last 2 starts. *Sir Michael Stoute* **57**

LUCYMAI 4 b.f. Multiplex 114 – Miss Lesley 80 (Needwood Blade 117) [2017 78: p8g p7g^{2} p8g^{3} p7g* p7d^{2} p8g p7s^{3} p7s* Nov 23] fairly useful handicapper: won at Chelmsford in May and November (by 4½ lengths from Samphire Coast): stays 1m: acts on polytrack. *Dean Ivory* **90**

LUCY'S LAW (IRE) 3 b.f. Lawman (FR) 121 – Lucy Limelites 81 (Medicean 128) [2017 72: 8m^{6} 8g^{2} 9.8g^{2} 10g^{4} 10d^{3} 9.8g^{3} Aug 19] fair handicapper: stays 1¼m: acts on tapeta, soft and good to firm going. *Tom Tate* **77**

LUCY THE PAINTER (IRE) 5 b.m. Excellent Art 125 – Royal Bounty (IRE) 80 (Generous (IRE) 139) [2017 101: 8g p8g 8f^{6} 10.2g^{5} 11.8s^{4} 12g^{2} 11.8m^{6} 14v 12g^{6} 10.5s^{4} 12d^{6} 10d^{5} p8g^{6} Nov 6] angular mare: useful performer: probably flattered when sixth in Lancashire Oaks at Haydock (3¾ lengths behind The Black Princess) in July: stays 1½m: acts on polytrack, tapeta and any turf going: in headgear last 4 starts. *Ed de Giles* **96**

LUDORUM (IRE) 3 ch.g. Lope de Vega (IRE) 125 – Savignano (Polish Precedent (USA) 131) [2017 8d^{5} 8g^{4} 9.8m* 10v^{6} Sep 21] fair form: won maiden at Ripon in September: stays 1¼m: acts on good to firm going. *Richard Fahey* **76**

LUDUAMF (IRE) 3 ch.c. Tamayuz 126 – Aphorism 84 (Halling (USA) 133) [2017 62: t7.1g^{3} t7.1g^{4} p8g^{6} t7.1g 7d 7.6g 7s 7s^{6} 7d^{3} 8.1d^{5} 9d^{2} p7d p7m p7s^{4} Dec 14] compact colt: modest handicapper: stays 9f: acts on polytrack, tapeta, soft and good to firm going: tried in blinkers. *Richard Hannon* **63**

LUGANO 4 b.g. Galileo (IRE) 134 – Swiss Lake (USA) 115 (Indian Ridge 123) [2017 81p: t12.2g* 11.6m* 14f* 13.1g^{3} 12d^{5} Aug 5] big gelding: fairly useful handicapper: won at Wolverhampton, Haydock (apprentice) and Nottingham (by 4½ lengths from Hallstatt), all in June: stays 1¾m: acts on tapeta, firm and soft going: front runner/races prominently: sold 8,000 gns in October. *Sir Mark Prescott Bt* **93**

LUIS FERNANDEZ (USA) 2 b.c. (Mar 27) Gio Ponti (USA) 130 – Escape To Victory (Salse (USA) 128) [2017 5f^{3} 6m* 6g* 6d* Aug 10] $35,000F, £5,000 2-y-o: brother to 1m winner Time Constraints and half-brother to several winners, including high-class winner up to 6f Benbaun (2-y-o 5f winner, by Stravinsky) and useful winner up to 6f Captain Colby (2-y-o 5f/5.5f winner, by Bernstein): dam 2-y-o 7f winner: fairly useful form: won minor events at Redcar in May, Newbury in July and Yarmouth (by head from Manthoor) in August: stays 6f: sent to Hong Kong, where renamed Gameplayer Emperor. *Kevin Ryan* **85**

LUIS VAZ DE TORRES (IRE) 5 b.g. Tagula (IRE) 116 – Tekhania (IRE) (Dalakhani (IRE) 133) [2017 89: t6g^{6} t6g t6g p7g^{5} 7g* 7.2g* 7s^{6} 7.2g^{3} 7v^{6} 7.4g^{4} 7v^{2} 7v 7g^{6} 7d Nov 11] fairly useful handicapper: won at Catterick in April and Musselburgh (by ¾ length from Glengarry) in May: stays 7.5f: acts on polytrack, tapeta, good to firm and heavy going: wears headgear. *Richard Fahey* **92**

LUKOUTOLDMAKEZEBAK 4 b.g. Arabian Gleam 122 – Angelofthenorth 76 (Tomba 119) [2017 46: 7g t7.1g^{5} 6.9v 7f 7m^{6} 10g^{4} 9s 6g 7s f6.1g t7.1d^{3} t7.1s^{3} Nov 30] modest maiden handicapper: stays 7f: acts on tapeta and soft going: tried in headgear: often races towards rear. *David Thompson* **54**

LULU STAR (IRE) 2 b.f. (Feb 16) Oasis Dream 129 – Jeanie Johnston (IRE) 91 (One Cool Cat (USA) 123) [2017 t6s Sep 19] £100,000Y: first foal: dam, winner up to 13f (2-y-o 6f winner), half-sister to useful 2-y-o 6f winner Switcher: 40/1, well held in minor event at Newcastle. *Richard Fahey* **–**

LULU THE ROCKET 3 b.f. Authorized (IRE) 133 – Sagina (Shernazar 131) [2017 61: p10g t14g p10g p16d p12g Nov 8] modest maiden handicapper: left Peter Chapple-Hyam after first start: stays 1m: acts on tapeta: in hood last 3 starts. *John Butler* **51**

LUMINATE (IRE) 2 b.f. (Mar 2) Lawman (FR) 121 – Kalandara (IRE) 72 (Rainbow Quest (USA) 134) [2017 8g* 8.9s* Oct 7] €85,000Y: fifth foal: half-sister to useful 11.3f winner Kalabaya (by Sinndar): dam lightly-raced half-sister to top-class winner up to 1½m winner Kalanisi: useful form: won newcomers race at Deauville in August and Prix de Conde at Chantilly (by 3 lengths from Kingstar, leading over 1f out) in October: will stay 1½m: should improve further. *F. Head, France* **108 p**

LUMINOUS 3 b.f. Champs Elysees 124 – Tamzin (Hernando (FR) 127) [2017 –: t8.6g^{3} 8.5m^{2} 10g t8s^{6} 9.9d^{2} p10g t9.5g^{2} Nov 18] fair maiden: stays 1¼m: acts on tapeta, good to firm and good to soft going: has worn hood: races prominently: suspect temperament. *Simon Crisford* **78**

LUNA BEAR 3 b.f. Dick Turpin (IRE) 127 – Royal Tavira Girl (IRE) 62 (Orpen (USA) 116) [2017 p7g p10g 7d^{2} 8m* 8g Jul 15] rather leggy filly: fourth foal: half-sister to winner up to 9f El Duque (2-y-o 6f winner, by Byron): dam maiden (stayed 8.5f): fairly useful performer: won handicap at Newmarket (by ½ length from Turning Gold) in June: best effort at 1m: acts on good to firm going: usually races close up. *Gary Moore* **81**

LUNA ECLIPSE (IRE) 2 b.c. (Feb 10) Bahamian Bounty 116 – Luna Forest (IRE) 86 (Holy Roman Emperor (IRE) 125) [2017 5d^{3} 6f Jun 18] fair form in minor events. *Andrew Balding* **65**

LUNA LADY 2 ch.f. (Feb 17) Paco Boy (IRE) 129 – Tamara Moon (IRE) 75 (Acclamation 118) [2017 t7.1g Nov 3] £6,000Y: sixth foal: half-sister to useful 5f/6f (including at 2 yrs) winner Chilworth Icon (by Sixties Icon): dam 2-y-o 7f-1m winner: 33/1, well held in minor event at Newcastle. *Ann Duffield* **–**

LUNA MAGIC 3 b.f. Mayson 124 – Dayia (IRE) 98 (Act One 124) [2017 p10g^{4} 10g^{4} 10.2d^{4} p12d^{4} 9.9d 8g^{5} f8.1g p8g* Dec 30] second foal: dam, 1¾m-2m winner who stayed 21.7f, also won in bumpers: fair performer: won handicap at Lingfield in December: stays 1¼m: acts on polytrack, best turf form on good going: usually in hood: sometimes slowly away. *Lydia Pearce* **73**

LUNA MARE (IRE) 4 b.f. Galileo (IRE) 134 – Pale Moon Rising (IRE) (Kingmambo (USA) 125) [2017 84: 10m^{5} 11.4m^{5} May 22] angular filly: fairly useful handicapper: stays 1¼m: acts on polytrack, soft and good to firm going: tried in cheekpieces: often races lazily. *Richard Fahey* **81**

LUNAR CORONA 2 br.f. (Jan 28) Dansili 127 – Starscope 112 (Selkirk (USA) 129) [2017 8d Oct 27] first foal: dam, temperamental 2-y-o 7f winner who stayed 10.5f, half-sister to useful 1m winner Solar Magic: 7/1, eighth in maiden at Doncaster (9¾ lengths behind Mrs Sippy): should do better. *Sir Michael Stoute* **63 p**

LUNAR DEITY 8 b.g. Medicean 128 – Luminda (IRE) (Danehill (USA) 126) [2017 67, a102: p8g^{2} p8g^{5} p8g^{5} 7m^{3} 8m* 8m* 8g^{4} 8g^{4} p7d p7g p8g Dec 13] strong, good-topped gelding: fairly useful handicapper: won at Yarmouth (apprentice) and Brighton in June: stays 8.5f: acts on polytrack, good to firm and heavy going: has worn headgear: has worn tongue tie, including often in 2017: often starts slowly/races towards rear. *Stuart Williams* **87**

LUNAR JET 3 ch.g. Ask 126 – Lightning Jet (Dutch Art 126) [2017 64: 10.3g 8m^{4} 10.2g^{2} 9.9m 10.2m^{6} 10m^{2} 9.9s* 10d^{4} Oct 23] fairly useful handicapper: won at Goodwood (by 3¼ lengths from Zamperini) in September: stays 10.5f: acts on tapeta, soft and good to firm going: often travels strongly. *John Mackie* **89**

LUNAR MARIA 2 b.f. (Mar 1) Dubawi (IRE) 129 – Ama (USA) (Storm Cat (USA)) [2017 7.6d^{3} Sep 16] fourth foal: half-sister to 3 winners, including 2-y-o 1m winner Mirror City (by Street Cry) and 9f winner Nightster (by Raven's Pass): dam lightly-raced half-sister to high-class winner up to 1m Kingmambo and very smart winner up to 1¼m East of The Moon: 7/2, third in minor event at Lingfield (6¾ lengths behind Give And Take): will improve. *Charlie Appleby* **64 p**

LUNAR MIST 3 b.f. Bated Breath 125 – Time Will Show (FR) (Exit To Nowhere (USA) 122) [2017 t9.5g^{6} t10.2g^{4} p8s^{5} Dec 17] closely related to a winner and half-sister to several winners, including useful winner up to 1m Choose Your Moment (2-y-o 6f-7f winner, by Choisir) and useful 8.6f-1½m winner Dragonera (by Doyen): dam maiden: modest form in maidens. *Ed Dunlop* **61**

LUNCH (IRE) 3 br.c. Big Bad Bob (IRE) 118 – All Day (CHI) (Jaded Dancer (USA)) [2017 p10g* 10.9g^{3} 10.9d^{4} 11.9m 11.9g* 10.9g^{2} 10.9g^{6} 10.4f^{6} 9f^{6} Oct 15] €15,000Y: brother to 6f-1m winner Crazy Tornado and half-brother to several winners, including winner up to 7f Bachelor Son (2-y-o 5f/6f winner, by Bachelor Duke) and 2-y-o 7f winner (stays 9.5f) Could Should Would (by Jeremy): dam 6f-1¼m winner: fairly useful form: won maiden at Lingfield (by neck from Fulham) in February (left Jamie Osborne after) and 4-runner minor event at Madrid in July: stays 1½m. *A. Carrasco, Spain* **83**

LUNGARNO PALACE (USA) 6 b.g. Henrythenavigator (USA) 131 – Good Time Sally (USA) (Forestry (USA) 121) [2017 85: t12.2g p12g Dec 13] workmanlike gelding: fairly useful handicapper: well below form both starts in 2017 after long absence: stays 14.5f: acts on polytrack, good to firm and good to soft going: often in headgear: tried in tongue tie: quirky sort. *John Gallagher* **65**

LUPIN (USA) 3 b.f. Medaglia d'Oro (USA) 129 – Promising Lead 121 (Danehill (USA) 126) [2017 9.9d 8.3d^{6} Jun 11] half-sister to several winners, including useful 1¼m winner Vital Evidence and 2-y-o 8.3f winner Surcingle (both by Empire Maker): dam, 7f-10.4f winner, half-sister to smart performer up to 1¼m Visit: modest form in maidens: in visor second start. *Sir Michael Stoute* **56**

LUQYAA 3 b.f. Smart Strike (CAN) 121 – Maqaasid 112 (Green Desert (USA) 127) [2017 74p: 7g^{5} Jun 10] fair form: better effort on debut at 2 yrs: sent to USA. *John Gosden* **55**

LUSH LIFE (IRE) 2 b.f. (Feb 8) Mastercraftsman (IRE) 129 – Break of Day (USA) (Favorite Trick (USA) 121) [2017 p7g* Nov 8] 110,000Y: sister to German 2-y-o 7f winner Rakete, closely related/half-sister to several winners, including smart 6f/7f winner Laddies Poker Two (dam of 1000 Guineas winner Winter) and useful 6f (including at 2 yrs) winner Chooseday (both by Choisir): dam unraced: 16/1, won minor event at Kempton (by 1¾ lengths from Briscola) on debut: will improve. *Jamie Osborne* **79 p**

LUSTROUS LIGHT (IRE) 4 ch.c. Galileo (IRE) 134 – Glinting Desert (IRE) 73 (Desert Prince (IRE) 130) [2017 111: 10d^{5} 14g^{4} 10.3d 12m 11.9g^{3} 14.2s^{3} 11.9d^{6} Oct 28] well-made colt: useful handicapper: seventh (4¼ lengths behind Rare Rhythm) in Duke of Edinburgh Stakes (Handicap) at Royal Ascot in June: left G. M. Lyons after second start: stays 1½m: acts on good to firm and good to soft going: tried in cheekpieces: sold 40,000 gns in November. *Ralph Beckett* **106**

LUTINE CHARLIE (IRE) 10 br.g. Kheleyf (USA) 116 – Silvery Halo (USA) 68 (Silver Ghost (USA)) [2017 58: t8.6g^{2} p7d^{6} t9.5g p8d^{4} p10g^{6} t8.6g^{3} f7d 8m^{3} 8g 8g 8g t8.6g 7m* 8s^{4} 7d^{2} p7g 6v^{3} p8g^{4} p8s p7s Dec 14] compact gelding: modest handicapper: won at Brighton in August: stays 1¼m: acts on polytrack, tapeta and any turf going: has worn headgear, including last 3 starts: inconsistent. *Emma Owen* **53**

LUV U ALWAYS 3 b.f. Captain Gerrard (IRE) 113 – Lady Suesanne (IRE) 66 (Cape Cross (IRE) 129) [2017 53: f5s^{2} f6g^{3} t5g 5d^{5} 5m^{6} t5g 5s^{3} 5s^{5} Oct 9] modest maiden: best form at 5f: acts on fibresand, tapeta and soft going: usually in cheekpieces. *Iain Jardine* **63**

LUV U WHATEVER 7 b.g. Needwood Blade 117 – Lady Suesanne (IRE) 66 (Cape Cross (IRE) 129) [2017 100: f12g^{3} t12.2m f12g^{3} p14d^{4} p16d f12g* p13g* t13.9g^{4} f11g^{2} 12.3s t12.2g^{2} 11.9m^{2} 13.3v^{5} 11.2s^{6} 12d t12.4s p10g p11g^{6} t10.2d p11g^{6} f12.1g^{2} f12.1g^{2} p12g t9.5g^{3} Dec 18] fair on turf, fairly useful on all-weather: won seller at Southwell and claimer at Lingfield in March: left Michael Attwater after eleventh start: stays 2m: acts on all-weather and good to firm going: wears headgear/tongue tie. *Marjorie Fife* **74** **a91**

LUXFORD 3 b.f. Mullionmileanhour (IRE) 116 – Dolly Parton (IRE) 79 (Tagula (IRE) 116) [2017 49: p7m^{4} p8g^{4} 7g^{4} 8g* p7g^{3} 8d* 8s 8d^{6} p10g* p10g^{4} p10s p10g^{5} Dec 13] smallish, close-coupled filly: fair handicapper: won at Brighton in June and July, and Chelmsford in October: stays 1¼m: acts on polytrack and good to soft going: tried in blinkers: often races prominently. *John Best* **68**

LYDIA'S PLACE 4 ch.f. Equiano (FR) 127 – Peace And Love (IRE) 75 (Fantastic Light (USA) 134) [2017 83: t5d^{3} 5g^{5} 5m* 5m 5m* 5f^{5} 5m 5.2s^{3} 5m^{3} 5.1s^{2} 5m 5g^{6} 5m 5s 5d Oct 4] sturdy filly: fairly useful handicapper: won at Beverley in April and Redcar (by ½ length from Economic Crisis) in May: best form at 5f: acts on tapeta, firm and soft going: usually leads. *Richard Guest* **87**

LYDIATE LADY 5 b.m. Piccolo 121 – Hiraeth 76 (Petong 126) [2017 63, a50: 5g^{4} 5d^{5} 5g^{3} f5g* 5d* 5g* 5g^{2} t5.1g^{4} t5.1g* Nov 25] fair handicapper: won at Southwell in August, Catterick in September, Redcar in October and Wolverhampton in November: races at 5f: acts on fibresand, tapeta, soft and good to firm going: has worn cheekpieces: front runner/races prominently. *Eric Alston* **79**

LYFKA 5 ch.m. Kheleyf (USA) 116 – Tarkamara (IRE) 80 (Medicean 128) [2017 90: 7m^{6} 7g^{3} p7g p7g p7g p7g Dec 21] compact mare: fair handicapper: left Paul Cole after second start: stays 7f: acts on polytrack, tapeta, good to firm and good to soft going: usually wears headgear/tongue tie: usually races towards rear. *J. J. Feane, Ireland* **79**

LYFORD (IRE) 2 ch.g. (Feb 19) Intense Focus (USA) 117 – Nurture (IRE) 104 (Bachelor Duke (USA) 122) [2017 6m^{5} 7d^{5} 7.1m p7d Aug 16] modest form: best effort at 7f. *Sylvester Kirk* **53**

LYIN EYES 3 b.f. Equiano (FR) 127 – Christmas Tart (IRE) 74 (Danetime (IRE) 121) [2017 70: 5v p5g f5g^{4} Nov 13] fair maiden at 2 yrs, well below form in 2017: stays 6f: acts on good to soft going: sometimes in headgear: tried in tongue tie. *K. J. Condon, Ireland* **50**

LYNIQUE (IRE) 3 ch.f. Dylan Thomas (IRE) 132 – Danse Grecque (IRE) (Sadler's Wells (USA) 132) [2017 10g Jul 13] €100,000Y: sister to smart 8.5f-11.3f (including Canadian 1¼m Grade 1 event) winner Tannery and closely related to winner up to 1¼m General Brook (by Westerner): dam unraced half-sister to very smart 1½m/1¾m performer Gamut: 12/1, well held in maiden at Newbury. *William Haggas* –

LYNN'S MEMORY 2 b.f. (Feb 15) Acclamation 118 – Roxelana (IRE) 86 (Oasis Dream 129) [2017 6m 5g^5 5f^3 5f* 5m^6 5.2v Jul 22] 38,000F, 40,000Y: first foal: dam, 1m winner, closely related to useful 1m/8.3f winner Spirit Raiser out of smart winner up to 1¼m (2-y-o 1m winner) Macadamia: fair performer: won minor event at Bath in June: best form at 5f on firm going. *Joseph Patrick O'Brien, Ireland* **76**

LYNWOOD GOLD (IRE) 2 ro.c. (Mar 31) Mastercraftsman (IRE) 129 – Witch of Fife (USA) 91 (Lear Fan (USA) 130) [2017 8.5m* 8.2d^6 8.9s^2 8v^2 9m* Oct 25] €60,000Y: lengthy, rather unfurnished colt: closely related to smart winner up to 1¼m (stayed 1¾m) Drumfire (2-y-o 7f/7.4f winner, by Danehill Dancer) and half-brother to several winners, including smart winner up to 1m Ho Choi (2-y-o 6f winner, by Pivotal) and useful 2-y-o 7f winner Cabaret (by Galileo): dam 2-y-o 6f/7f winner: useful performer: won maiden at Epsom in August and nursery at Newmarket (by 2½ lengths from Simpson) in October: will be suited by 1¼m+: acts on good to firm and heavy going: front runner/races prominently: will go on improving. *Mark Johnston* **97 p**

LYRICAL PURSUIT 2 ch.f. (Jan 15) Poet's Voice 126 – Crinklelini (Bertolini (USA) 125) [2017 6g t5s^2 6m Jul 15] £3,500Y: second foal: dam, unraced, closely related to useful 6f-1m winner Steed: modest form: best effort when second in minor event at Newcastle (4 lengths behind Haddaf) in July. *Michael Easterby* **63**

LYRICA'S LION (IRE) 3 b.g. Dragon Pulse (IRE) 114 – Shishangaan (IRE) (Mujadil (USA) 119) [2017 –: p8g p12g^5 8.1m 9.9m* 8v^6 11.9g^3 p11g^5 p12g* Oct 17] fair handicapper: won at Salisbury in July and Kempton in October: left Mark Hoad after first start, Paddy Butler after second: stays 1½m: acts on polytrack and good to firm going. *Michael Attwater* **66**

LYRIC HARMONY (IRE) 3 b.f. Teofilo (IRE) 126 – Musical Bar (IRE) 93 (Barathea (IRE) 127) [2017 7m 7m^5 8s* 8m 8.1g^3 8g^2 10s Aug 25] sturdy filly: fourth foal: half-sister to 2-y-o 6f winner Chord Chart (by Acclamation): dam, 7f winner, half-sister to very smart winner up to 1m (stayed 10.5f) Finsceal Beo: fairly useful performer: won maiden at Thirsk (by ¾ length from White Rosa) in June: stays 1m: acts on soft and good to firm going. *Giles Bravery* **82**

M

MAAKAASIB 3 b.g. Equiano (FR) 127 – Majoune (FR) 105 (Take Risks (FR) 116) [2017 89p: p7g 6d^6 p6d* 5v^3 p6g* Aug 22] workmanlike gelding: useful handicapper: won at Kempton in July and August (by neck from Dark Side Dream): should stay 7f: acts on polytrack: in eyeshields last 4 starts: usually races close up. *Simon Crisford* **95**

MAAREK 10 b.g. Pivotal 124 – Ruby Rocket (IRE) 113 (Indian Rocket 115) [2017 110: 6v^3 5m^5 5m^5 6d^5 5g 6.3f 6g 5s^4 6s 5s^4 5.8v^3 5.8v* 6d Nov 11] smallish, strongly-made gelding: useful handicapper nowadays: won at Navan (by ½ length from Kupa River) in October: raced at sprint trips: acts on good to firm and heavy going: waited with. *Miss Evanna McCutcheon, Ireland* **107**

MAARIT (IRE) 3 b.f. Harbour Watch (IRE) 121 – Atamana (IRE) 82 (Lahib (USA) 129) [2017 –: p7d Feb 3] well held in 2 maidens, tongue tied on second occasion. *Denis Coakley* –

MAAWARD (IRE) 2 b.c. (Feb 11) Kodiac 112 – Caterina di Cesi (Cape Town (IRE) 119) [2017 p8g^2 Oct 25] £78,000Y: third foal: brother to 5f (including at 2 yrs)/6f winner Mignolino and half-brother to 6f winner Harbour Grey (by Zoffany): dam, Italian 6f winner, half-sister to useful 2-y-o 5f winner Risky: 9/2, second in minor event at Kempton (2 lengths behind Tenedos) in October, faring best of those ridden prominently: sure to progress. *Richard Hannon* **83 p**

MAAZEL (IRE) 3 b.g. Elzaam (AUS) 115 – Laylati (IRE) 64 (Green Desert (USA) 127) [2017 80: 5m^4 6d^2 t5d^6 5.1s^6 p6g^2 Oct 9] compact gelding: fairly useful handicapper: second at Brighton in July and Kempton in October: stays 6f: acts on polytrack, good to firm and good to soft going: tried in blinkers: sometimes slowly away, usually races nearer last than first: sold to join Julia Fielden 3,000 gns in November. *Roger Varian* **84**

MABLE LEE (IRE) 2 ch.f. (May 3) Zoffany (IRE) 121 – Mexican Milly (IRE) 60 (Noverre (USA) 125) [2017 5m⁵ 5v² 6s⁶ 5d* 5.1v² 5v⁴ 6d Nov 11] third foal: half-sister to 6f winner Yes You (by Choisir): dam maiden (best efforts at 6f): fair performer: won nursery at Thirsk in August: best form at 5f: acts on heavy going: often races prominently. *Iain Jardine* **73**

MABO 2 gr.c. (Feb 26) Aussie Rules (USA) 123 – Crochet (IRE) (Mark of Esteem (IRE) 137) [2017 5v⁵ 6g 5.4g 6d 6.1s 6s 5.9v³ t6g Oct 19] modest maiden: will stay 7f: best form on heavy going: sometimes slowly away, usually races in rear. *Richard Fahey* **64**

MABROOK 3 b.c. Dubawi (IRE) 129 – Mahbooba (AUS) 116 (Galileo (IRE) 134) [2017 p8g⁴ 10s⁵ 8s² Jun 6] well-made colt: fair form in maidens: in hood last 2 starts: has joined S. Seemar in UAE. *Marco Botti* **79**

MABS CROSS 3 b.f. Dutch Art 126 – Miss Meggy 97 (Pivotal 124) [2017 6g 6g³ t5s* 5.1m* 5m* 5s* Oct 9] £3,000Y: sixth foal: half-sister to 3 winners, including winner up to 1½m in USA Charlie Em (2-y-o 7f/1m winner in Britain, by Kheleyf) and 5f (including at 2 yrs)/6f winner Eccleston (by Acclamation), both useful: dam winner up to 7f (2-y-o 5f winner): smart performer: won maiden at Newcastle in May, handicaps at Windsor (by ¾ length from Open Wide) and Haydock (by 2¼ lengths from Midnight Malibu) in June, and listed race at Musselburgh (by ¾ length from Clem Fandango) in October: stays 6f: acts on tapeta, soft and good to firm going. *Michael Dods* **112**

MACAQUE 2 b.g. (Feb 6) Rock of Gibraltar (IRE) 133 – Spiliada (FR) (Falco (USA) 122) [2017 7d 7g² 8m* 8m² 8g⁴ Sep 22] €33,000Y: rather unfurnished gelding: first foal: dam, French winner up to 1m (2-y-o 7f winner), half-sister to smart winner up to 1¼m Riven Light: fairly useful performer: won maiden at Brighton (by 24 lengths from sole rival, Secratario) in August: second in minor event at Goodwood (½ length behind Ibn Al Emarat) later same month: stays 1m: acts on good to firm going: usually races prominently. *Andrew Balding* **88**

MACHIAVELIAN STORM (IRE) 5 gr.m. Dark Angel (IRE) 113 – Terri's Charmer (USA) (Silver Charm (USA) 132) [2017 50: 8g 7m⁵ 8g⁴ 9.9d 11.6f⁵ 8g f8.1g t8.6g Dec 13] rather leggy mare: poor maiden: has worn cheekpieces/tongue tie, including last 2 starts. *Richard Mitchell* **42**

MACHINE LEARNER 4 b.g. Sir Percy 129 – My First Romance 61 (Danehill (USA) 126) [2017 90: 14m* 14m² 13.3s⁴ 12.8d² 12s 11.9s Nov 11] sturdy gelding: useful handicapper: won at Sandown (by nose from Taper Tantrum) in June: second at same course (¾ length behind Uae King) in July and Leopardstown (head behind Laws of Spin) in September: stays 1¾m: acts on polytrack, tapeta, good to firm and heavy going: usually wears headgear. *Joseph Tuite* **100**

MACHO GUEST (IRE) 2 b.g. (Apr 10) Camacho 118 – Alabama Grace (IRE) (Teofilo (IRE) 126) [2017 6.1d 6s Jun 6] useful-looking gelding: well held in minor events. *George Margarson* **–**

MACHO MAC 4 ch.g. Pastoral Pursuits 127 – Clarice Orsini (Common Grounds 118) [2017 86: f7g f6g⁵ f8s f7g⁶ p7g⁶ Mar 17] fair handicapper: stays 7f: acts on fibresand, good to firm and good to soft going: tried in hood: often races towards rear/freely: temperamental. *Hughie Morrison* **74 §**

MACHO MOVER (IRE) 2 b.g. (Apr 25) Camacho 118 – Fanciful Dancer (Groom Dancer (USA) 128) [2017 7m p7d 8d Oct 27] modest form: best effort when seventh in minor event at Chelmsford (6½ lengths behind Society Power) in October. *Mick Channon* **59**

MACH ONE 3 b.g. Makfi 130 – Perfect Spirit (IRE) (Invincible Spirit (IRE) 121) [2017 68: 8.3d p8d⁵ p10g³ p8g² p8g* f8.1g² f8.1g* f8.1g³ p8g⁵ Dec 31] good-topped gelding: fairly useful handicapper: won at Chelmsford in November and Southwell in December: left Clive Cox after first start: stays 1¼m: acts on polytrack and fibresand: wears headgear: often starts slowly. *Archie Watson* **88**

MACHREE (IRE) 2 b.f. (Apr 28) Lord Shanakill (USA) 121 – Faleena (IRE) 95 (Verglas (IRE) 118) [2017 5g³ 5.4g⁴ 5s* Oct 31] rather sparely-made filly: first foal: dam 5f/6f winner: fair form: won minor event at Catterick (by 1½ lengths from Bahuta Acha) in October: stays 5.5f: remains with potential. *Declan Carroll* **78 p**

MACKIRI (IRE) 4 b.g. Makfi 130 – Inchiri 108 (Sadler's Wells (USA) 132) [2017 51: f12g Jan 5] neat gelding: maiden, well held sole outing in 2017: best effort at 2m: acts on polytrack: tried in visor. *Michael Appleby* **–**

MACKSVILLE (IRE) 4 gr.g. Mastercraftsman (IRE) 129 – Fairest of All (IRE) (Sadler's **69**
Wells (USA) 132) [2017 72: p12g^2 t13.9m^5 11.9m^3 14d^3 18d^5 p16g^6 p14d* p15.8g^5 11.5d Oct 24] fair handicapper: won at Chelmsford in September: left Jeremy Gask after second start: stays 2m: acts on polytrack, tapeta, good to firm and good to soft going: wears headgear. *James Eustace*

MAC MAHON (ITY) 3 b.c. Ramonti (FR) 126 – Miss Sultin (IRE) (Celtic Swing 138) **115**
[2017 10.4m* 9.9m* 10.9g* 11.9g 10.9d^3 9.9d^2 9.9g* Dec 30] half-brother to Italian winner up to 11f Mickai (2-y-o 9f winner, by Mujahid): dam useful Italian winner up to 1¼m (2-y-o 1m winner): smart performer: won minor event at Rome in March, listed race at Milan in April, Derby Italiano at Rome (by 5 lengths from Back On Board) in May and Qatar Derby at Doha (by 2¼ lengths from Pazeer) in December: second in Premio Roma (½ length behind Anda Muchacho) in November: stays 11f: acts on good to firm and good to soft going. *A. & S. Botti, Italy*

MAC O'POLO (IRE) 3 b.g. Henrythenavigator (USA) 131 – Topka (FR) 100 (Kahyasi **77 p**
130) [2017 7.6g^6 7s^5 t7.2g^5 8g^3 t8.6d^3 t9.5g^2 Dec 22] 15,000F: fifth foal: closely related to very smart French 9.5f-11f winner (stayed 2½m) Top Trip (by Dubai Destination): dam French 2-y-o 9f winner (stayed 1½m): fair maiden: will be suited by 1½m+: acts on tapeta: often races prominently: remains with potential. *Tom Dascombe*

MAC'S KYLLACHY 3 ch.g. Kyllachy 129 – Folly Lodge 93 (Grand Lodge (USA) 125) **66**
[2017 58p: p8g p8g^2 Feb 1] fair maiden: best effort at 1m: acts on polytrack: tried in visor. *James Fanshawe*

MADAKHEEL (USA) 6 b.m. Mr Greeley (USA) 122 – Manaal (USA) 93 (Bahri (USA) **–**
125) [2017 44: f7.1g f8.1g Dec 21] maiden, well held both starts in 2017: tried in cheekpieces: has worn tongue tie. *Simon West*

MADAME BOUNTY (IRE) 3 b.f. Bahamian Bounty 116 – Madame Boulangere 100 **88**
(Royal Applause 124) [2017 77: 6.1m* 5.2m* p6d 5.2s^6 6g^4 p6g Nov 2] compact filly: fairly useful performer: won maiden at Windsor in June and handicap at Newbury (apprentice, by length from Our Lord) in July: stays 6f: acts on good to firm going: sometimes slowly away, often travels strongly. *Ed Walker*

MADAME CLAUD 4 ch.f. Champs Elysees 124 – Change Partners (IRE) 79 (Hernando **–**
(FR) 127) [2017 68: 11.4d Oct 23] fair at best, well held sole outing on Flat in 2017: stays 2m: acts on polytrack and soft going. *Mark Gillard*

MADAME JO JO 2 ch.f. (Mar 14) Havana Gold (IRE) 118 – Paradise Place 69 (Compton **63**
Place 125) [2017 6g 7d 5.7d^5 5.1s^4 5.7s^6 Oct 2] 6,500 2-y-o: second foal: dam, 6f winner, half-sister to useful performers Zomerlust (at 6f/7f) and Pirouette (at 7f/1m): modest maiden: stays 5.5f: acts on soft going. *Sarah Hollinshead*

MADAME MIME ARTIST 6 b.m. Dutch Art 126 – Silent Waters (Polish Precedent **–**
(USA) 131) [2017 f8.1g Dec 4] lightly-raced maiden: tried in tongue tie. *Natalie Lloyd-Beavis*

MADAME RITZ (IRE) 2 b.f. (Feb 17) Canford Cliffs (IRE) 133 – Sky Red 75 (Night **50**
Shift (USA)) [2017 t5.1g^3 Dec 2] €15,000Y, 15,000 2-y-o: half-sister to several winners, including smart 2-y-o 5f/6f winner Orpen Grey (by Orpen) and useful 6f winner Dawn's Early Light (by Starspangledbanner): dam 5f winner: in hood, 80/1, third in minor event at Wolverhampton (8¼ lengths behind Al Asef) in December. *Richard Phillips*

MADAM LILIBET (IRE) 8 b.m. Authorized (IRE) 133 – Foxilla (IRE) 68 (Foxhound **67 §**
(USA) 103) [2017 68§: 18g^5 21.6m^2 16d t16.3s 17.1g^4 17.1v^5 18v* Oct 9] good-bodied mare: fair handicapper: won at Pontefract in October: stays 21.5f: acts on good to firm and heavy going: temperamental. *Sharon Watt*

MADAM MAI TAI 5 ch.m. Compton Place 125 – Dash of Lime 67 (Bold Edge 123) **–**
[2017 54: f7m Mar 7] modest handicapper, well held sole outing in 2017: stays 7f: acts on heavy going: sometimes slowly away, often races towards rear. *Rebecca Bastiman*

MADAM POMFREY 2 b.f. (Feb 11) Sayif (IRE) 122 – Miss Poppy 68 (Averti (IRE) **–**
117) [2017 5m 6d Oct 30] 5,000Y: stocky filly: fifth foal: half-sister to 3 winners, including 2-y-o 5f winner Compton Poppy (by Compton Place) and 6f winner Reflation (by Stimulation): dam, maiden (stayed 6f), half-sister to high-class 5f performer Kyllachy: well held in minor events. *Jonathan Portman*

MADAM PRANCEALOT (IRE) 3 b.f. Sir Prancealot (IRE) 111 – Delia (IRE) **49**
(Darshaan 133) [2017 60: p8g p7g^6 t7.1g^5 p7g^4 7d^2 p10g 8.2g^5 Aug 2] modest performer at 2 yrs, below that level in 2017: left David Evans after sixth start: stays 1m: acts on good to firm and good to soft going: tried in visor. *Karen George*

MADDI 2 b.f. (Mar 29) Foxwedge (AUS) 128 – Sulis Minerva (IRE) 96 (Arakan (USA) **–**
123) [2017 5d Aug 19] first foal: dam 5f/6f winner out of useful winner up to 11f Lacinia: 25/1, well held in maiden at Bath. *Luke Dace*

MADDYS DREAM 4 b.g. Arabian Gleam 122 – Group Force (IRE) 64 (Montjeu (IRE) **59**
137) [2017 56: 7g^5 7m^6 7g Oct 17] leggy, close-coupled gelding: modest maiden: stays 7f: acts on good to soft going. *Lydia Pearce*

MADELEINE BOND 3 ch.f. Monsieur Bond (IRE) 120 – Spin A Wish 58 (Captain Rio **90**
122) [2017 58: p7g^5 7.1s* 7g* 8d* 8g^{ur} 8d Sep 20] unfurnished filly: fairly useful performer: won maiden at Chepstow in June, and handicaps at Newbury in July and Bath (by 1¾ lengths from Stosur) in August: stays 1m: acts on polytrack and soft going. *Henry Candy*

MADELINE (IRE) 2 b.f. (Mar 15) Kodiac 112 – Madhulika (FR) (Marchand de Sable **105**
(USA) 117) [2017 5m^5 6g* 6m^5 6g* 6d^2 6d^3 8f Nov 3] 140,000Y: smallish filly: first foal: dam, Swiss 9f-1½m winner, sister to smart French 6f/7f performer Dolma: useful performer: won minor event at Goodwood in May and listed race at Newbury (by 2¼ lengths from Natural) in July: placed in Lowther Stakes at York (1¾ lengths second to Threading) and Cheveley Park Stakes at Newmarket (3¼ lengths third to Clemmie): well held in Breeders' Cup Juvenile Fillies Turf at Del Mar final outing: stays 6f: acts on good to firm and good to soft going: often races prominently. *Roger Varian*

MAD ENDEAVOUR 6 b.g. Muhtathir 126 – Capefly 71 (Cape Cross (IRE) 129) [2017 **72**
73: p6g* 6d 5.1m^6 6g^4 t6.1g 5d^4 6s^4 Oct 10] compact gelding: fair handicapper: won at Lingfield in May: raced mainly at 6f: acts on polytrack, tapeta, soft and good to firm going: wears headgear: tried in tongue tie: often leads. *Stuart Kittow*

MADE OF HONOUR (IRE) 3 ch.f. Casamento (IRE) 118 – Bonne 72 (Namid 128) **83**
[2017 7g^2 7m^3 6m* 6v 8v p6.5g* Oct 23] €14,000Y, resold £26,000Y: third foal: dam, 6f winner, half-sister to smart 6f winner Rising Shadow: fairly useful performer: won maiden at Ayr (by 3¼ lengths from Excellent Sunset) in May and claimer at Chantilly (blinkered) in October: stays 7f: acts on polytrack and good to firm going (well below form on heavy). *K. R. Burke*

MADRASA (IRE) 9 b.g. High Chaparral (IRE) 132 – Shir Dar (FR) (Lead On Time **–**
(USA) 123) [2017 –: t12.2g^5 t12.2m Oct 28] smallish, leggy gelding: fairly useful at best, little form since 2014: usually wears headgear: has worn tongue tie, including last 2 starts. *Ken Wingrove*

MADRINHO (IRE) 4 ch.g. Frozen Power (IRE) 108 – Perfectly Clear (USA) (Woodman **81**
(USA) 126) [2017 94: 8s^6 8.8m 7.4m^4 7g^6 6s^6 t7.1g t7.2g^6 p7s Dec 17] useful-looking gelding: fairly useful handicapper, below best in 2017: left Tony Coyle after fourth start, Neville Bycroft after fifth: stays 9f: acts on firm and soft going: tried in headgear/tongue tie. *John Butler*

MADROOS 4 ch.g. Teofilo (IRE) 126 – Hedaaya (IRE) 92 (Indian Ridge 123) [2017 84: **86**
7g^2 7g^3 10.3m 7.8s^3 8.3g^3 t8.6g^4 t8g 7v Oct 21] strong gelding: fairly useful handicapper: second at Catterick in April: stays 8.5f: acts on tapeta and good to soft going: tried in tongue tie. *Michael Easterby*

MAD ROSE (IRE) 3 b.f. Royal Applause 124 – Na Zdorovie 84 (Cockney Rebel (IRE) **67**
127) [2017 p7g 6.1m 6d^3 p7g 6g 6d f6.1g p7g Dec 30] leggy filly: first foal: dam, 2-y-o 7f winner, closely related to smart US performer up to 1½m Slim Shadey: fair handicapper: won claimer in France for J. Reynier at 2 yrs: left Jonathan Portman after fifth start: stays 7.5f: acts on polytrack and good to soft going: tried in headgear/tongue tie: often races prominently. *Denis Quinn*

MAESTRO MAC (IRE) 4 b.g. Roderic O'Connor (IRE) 119 – Union City Blues (IRE) **82**
59 (Encosta de Lago (AUS)) [2017 85: p12g 14f 10m^3 11m^6 10.1d* 11.2s^2 p10s* 11.5d Oct 24] useful-looking gelding: fairly useful handicapper: won at Yarmouth in August and Chelmsford (by 2¾ lengths from Archimento) in September: left Hughie Morrison after fourth start: stays 11f: acts on polytrack, tapeta, soft and good to firm going: tried in tongue tie. *Tom Clover*

MAFAAHEEM (IRE) 3 b.g. Shamardal (USA) 129 – Hammiya (IRE) 103 (Darshaan **98**
133) [2017 76p: 10m^2 9.9g^2 8m^2 10.2v* 10.1m^2 Aug 27] sturdy gelding: useful performer: won maiden at Nottingham (by 11 lengths from Raining Stars) in August: second in handicap at Yarmouth (2½ lengths behind Teodoro) later in month: stays 1¼m: acts on polytrack, good to firm and heavy going: usually races close up, often travels strongly. *Owen Burrows*

MAFDET 2 b.f. (Feb 20) Rip Van Winkle (IRE) 134 – Fabulous Speed (USA) (Silver Hawk (USA) 123) [2017 7d^{5} 8d^{5} t7.1g^{6} Nov 15] half-sister to 1m winner Hyperloop (by So You Think) and several winners abroad, including useful Italian/US winner up to 8.5f Facoltoso (2-y-o 6f winner, by Refuse To Bend): dam, French 9f-1½m winner, half-sister to dam of high-class miler Solow: modest form: best effort when fifth in minor event at Thirsk in July: should be suited by 1m+. *Bryan Smart* **57**

MAFEKING 2 b.g. (Mar 17) Makfi 130 – Save Me The Waltz (FR) (Halling (USA) 133) [2017 6s 7g 7.4d^{6} 8s^{6} 8d Sep 30] modest maiden: best effort at 7.5f: acts on good to soft going: tried in cheekpieces: sold £6,500 in November. *Harry Dunlop* **61**

MAGDALENE FOX 3 ch.c. Foxwedge (AUS) 128 – Malelane (IRE) 48 (Prince Sabo 123) [2017 56: t6f* t6m^{2} t5g^{3} 6d^{5} 5g^{6} 6m 6m 6m Sep 7] fair performer: won handicap at Wolverhampton in January: left Ed Dunlop after third start: best efforts at 6f: acts on polytrack and tapeta: wears blinkers: front runner/races prominently. *Devis Grilli, Italy* **70**

MAGELLAN 3 b.g. Sea The Stars (IRE) 140 – Hector's Girl 99 (Hector Protector (USA) 124) [2017 8m^{6} 10s 9.9g^{6} t12.4g* Oct 10] 62,000F: tall gelding: half-brother to several winners, including very smart 1m-10.4f winner Class Is Class (by Montjeu) and useful 1¼m winner Ascot Lime (by Pivotal): dam 2-y-o 6f winner: fairly useful form: won maiden at Newcastle (by neck from Darksideoftarnside) in October: stays 12.5f: open to further improvement. *Roger Charlton* **85 p**

MAGGIE JONKS 2 ch.f. (Apr 27) Sixties Icon 125 – Lighted Way 66 (Kris 135) [2017 7s 7m Oct 25] sturdy filly: half-sister to several winners, including 2-y-o 6f winner Rosie Briar (by Mayson) and 6f (including at 2 yrs) winner Lightning Charlie (by Myboycharlie), both useful: dam sprint maiden: little impact in minor events. *Andrew Balding* **–**

MAGGIE PINK 8 b.m. Beat All (USA) 120 – Top Notch (Alderbrook 120) [2017 76, a86: t8.6g^{4} p8d p7g 7m 7.6d 7.6v p7g^{6} p7s^{4} p7s f7.1g Dec 4] fairly useful handicapper: stays 8.5f: acts on all-weather, good to firm and heavy going: tried in cheekpieces: usually races close up. *Michael Appleby* **81**

MAGGIES ANGEL (IRE) 2 b.f. (Jan 26) Dark Angel (IRE) 113 – Last Bid 99 (Vital Equine (IRE) 121) [2017 5m* 5s^{4} 5d^{2} 6g^{2} 5.2v^{3} Jul 22] €36,000Y: smallish, angular filly: first foal: dam 2-y-o 5f winner: fairly useful performer: won minor event at Ripon (by 2¼ lengths from Mount Victoria) in April: second in listed race at Newmarket (1¼ lengths behind Dance Diva) in July: stays 6f: acts on soft and good to firm going. *Richard Fahey* **93**

MAGGIE THE THIRD M 3 b.f. Haafhd 129 – Markila (FR) (Mark of Esteem (IRE) 137) [2017 t12.4g Oct 10] second foal: dam, French maiden (second at 9f)/winning hurdler, half-sister to useful stayer Ile de Re: 100/1, well held in maiden at Newcastle. *John Davies* **–**

MAGGI MAY (IRE) 3 b.f. Kodiac 112 – Virevolle (FR) (Kahyasi 130) [2017 –: f6g^{3} f5g^{2} t5.1g^{2} t5.1g^{2} 5m^{3} 5s 5f^{4} t5g 5.2m^{6} Aug 22] slightly-built filly: modest maiden: stays 6f: acts on fibresand, tapeta and good to firm going: tried in cheekpieces: often races prominently: sold £1,800, sent to Italy. *David Brown* **58**

MAGHAWEER (IRE) 2 ch.c. (Apr 27) Dubawi (IRE) 129 – Indian Ink (IRE) 122 (Indian Ridge 123) [2017 p6g^{4} 7g^{3} 7g* Nov 3] fifth foal: half-brother to 3 winners, including 6f (including at 2 yrs)/7f winner Wahaab (by Tamayuz): dam winner up to 1m (2-y-o 6f/6.5f winner), including Cheveley Park Stakes and Coronation Stakes: fairly useful form: won minor event at Newmarket (by length from dead-heaters Porth Swtan and Plunger) in November: stays 7f: open to further improvement. *Richard Hannon* **89 p**

MAGHFOOR 3 b.g. Cape Cross (IRE) 129 – Thaahira (USA) 89 (Dynaformer (USA)) [2017 86p: p10g^{2} 11.9m* 9.1m 16.1d^{4} p14g t12.4g Oct 19] fairly useful performer: won maiden at Haydock in April: stays 1½m: acts on good to firm and good to soft going: in headgear last 2 starts: often travels strongly, tends to find little: sold to join Eric Alston £48,000 in November. *Saeed bin Suroor* **94**

MAGICAL DREAMER (IRE) 3 b.f. Acclamation 118 – Double Fantasy (GER) (Indian Ridge 123) [2017 74p: 6m 6g* 6d^{4} 6.1v^{2} 5s^{2} 5.2d^{2} 6g^{2} Oct 7] sturdy filly: fairly useful handicapper: won at Leicester (by 1¼ lengths from Bassmah) in May: second 4 times subsequently: stays 6f: acts on polytrack and soft going: tried in hood: front runner/races prominently, often travels strongly: has suspect attitude (flashes tail). *James Fanshawe* **93**

MAGICAL EFFECT (IRE) 5 ch.g. New Approach (IRE) 132 – Purple Glow (IRE) 96 (Orientate (USA) 127) [2017 88: 6m* 6m^{2} 6.1m^{6} 6d^{3} 6s^{5} 6d* 6g^{3} 7g^{3} 7.2m^{5} 6v^{5} Sep 30] useful handicapper: won at Ripon in April and Redcar (by 2 lengths from Tricky Dicky) in August: stays 7f: acts on good to firm and heavy going. *Ruth Carr* **95**

Breast Cancer Research Debutante Stakes, the Curragh—
Magical upstages better fancied stablemate Happily (dark cap) to emulate her sister Rhododendron, who won this race in 2016; Mary Tudor is back in third

MAGICAL FOREST (IRE) 3 b.f. Casamento (IRE) 118 – Hurry Home Hydee (USA) (Came Home (USA) 122) [2017 76: a8f5 a9.4f f8d2 8d4 8.9d3 10.4g* 10g 10.4v 10.4d6 a8.9g* Nov 23] fairly useful performer: won claimers at Maisons-Laffitte in July and Lyon La Soie in November: left Marco Botti after third start: stays 10.5f: acts on polytrack, dirt, good to firm and good to soft going: has worn headgear. *A. & G. Botti, France* **83**

MAGICAL (IRE) 2 b.f. (May 18) Galileo (IRE) 134 – Halfway To Heaven (IRE) 118 (Pivotal 124) [2017 6m2 8s* 7s* 7s2 8d4 8m4 Oct 13] strong, attractive filly: fifth foal: sister to 3 winners, including smart winner up to 1¼m (Prix de l'Opera) Rhododendron (2-y-o 7f/1m winner) and smart winner up to 1¼m Flying The Flag (2-y-o 7f winner): dam winner up to 1¼m (2-y-o 7f winner), including Irish 1000 Guineas and Nassau Stakes: smart performer: won maiden at Cork (by head from Mary Tudor) and Debutante Stakes at the Curragh (by 1¼ lengths from Happily) in August: second in Moyglare Stud Stakes at latter course (short head behind Happily) in September: stays 1m: acts on soft going: front runner/races prominently. *Aidan O'Brien, Ireland* **115**

MAGICAL MEMORY (IRE) 5 gr.g. Zebedee 113 – Marasem 86 (Cadeaux Genereux 131) [2017 123: 6s2 6m 6m* 6s* 6.5g4 6s 6s3 Oct 7] strong gelding: smart performer: won minor event at Haydock (by short head from Kachy) and Hackwood Stakes at Newbury (by 1¼ lengths from Perfect Angel) in July: placed in Duke of York Stakes at York (2½ lengths behind Tasleet) in May and Bengough Stakes at Ascot (3¾ lengths behind Blue Point) in October: stays 6f: acts on soft and good to firm going. *Charles Hills* **115**

MAGICAL MOLLY JOE 3 b.f. Arabian Gleam 122 – Magical Music 96 (Fraam 114) [2017 –: t6d5 t6d2 t7.1g 6d 7g 6v 8v3 Oct 12] modest maiden: stays 1m: acts on tapeta and heavy going: often races towards rear. *David Barron* **61**

MAGICAL PEAK 5 gr.m. Hellvelyn 118 – Enjoy The Magic 59 (Namaqualand (USA)) [2017 –: p8d p8g 6g5 Apr 15] no form: in blinkers last 2 starts. *John O'Shea* **–**

MAGIC APPLAUSE (IRE) 2 b.f. (Feb 8) Zebedee 113 – Last Hooray 68 (Royal Applause 124) [2017 5g4 5m2 5g* 6m f5g Dec 29] £6,000Y, £19,000 2-y-o: first foal: dam, maiden (stayed 7f), half-sister to smart performers Nota Bene (5f/6f winner), Tarjman and Raphinae (both up to 7f): fair performer: won maiden at Lingfield in June: should stay 6f: best form on good going: tried in hood. *George Scott* **68**

MAGIC APPROACH 3 b.f. Piccolo 121 – Diane's Choice 95 (Komaite (USA)) [2017 t8g6 t6m* 6m6 6d5 t6.1g3 Aug 10] 2,000Y: third foal: half-sister to 6f winner Minister of Fun (by Pastoral Pursuits): dam 5f/6f winner: modest performer: won maiden at Wolverhampton in March: best effort at 6f: acts on tapeta: tried in blinkers: sometimes slowly away. *David Simcock* **63**

MAGIC BEANS 3 br.g. Pastoral Pursuits 127 – Jasmeno 78 (Catcher In The Rye (IRE) 115) [2017 67p: 10.2m5 12m4 14g4 t14g 14m4 11.5d p12g Oct 3] modest maiden: stays 1¾m: acts on polytrack and good to firm going: tried in cheekpieces: front runner/races prominently. *Hughie Morrison* **64**

MAGIC BUDDY 2 ch.f. (Apr 29) Captain Gerrard (IRE) 113 – Magic By Bell (Reel Buddy (USA) 118) [2017 f5g 6d Oct 30] first foal: dam unraced half-sister to useful sprinter Beat The Bell: well held in minor events. *J. R. Jenkins* **–**

MAGIC CIRCLE (IRE) 5 b.g. Makfi 130 – Minkova (IRE) (Sadler's Wells (USA) 132) [2017 108: p16g^{5} 18.6m^{5} 20f 16.3d* 13.9m^{5} 18m Oct 14] big gelding: useful handicapper: won at York (by length from My Reward) in August: stays 16.5f: acts on good to firm and good to soft going: sold to join Patrick Morris 70,000 gns in November. *Ralph Beckett* **107**

MAGIC CITY (IRE) 8 b.g. Elusive City (USA) 117 – Annmarie's Magic (IRE) 28 (Flying Spur (AUS)) [2017 83: t8.6m^{4} p8d^{3} t7.1g^{2} p7g t8g* p10g^{5} 8m^{6} 8.3g^{3} 8s* 9m* 9.8m^{6} 9.1d^{5} 8.2v^{6} 10.2d 10.3g 8.3g^{3} 10v Nov 7] tall gelding: fairly useful handicapper: won at Newcastle in March, and at Wetherby and Ripon (by ¾ length from Mulligatawny) in June: stays 9f: acts on polytrack, tapeta, soft and good to firm going: tried in headgear: sometimes slowly away. *Michael Easterby* **92**

MAGICINTHEMAKING (USA) 3 br.f. Wildcat Heir (USA) 118 – Love In Bloom (USA) (More Than Ready (USA) 120) [2017 –: p6s Jun 21] neat filly: no form: tried in hood. *Mike Murphy* **–**

MAGIC JAZZ (IRE) 2 b.g. (Mar 19) Red Jazz (USA) 125 – Ishimagic 52 (Ishiguru (USA) 114) [2017 5m 5g^{5} 5d^{2} 6s* 6d* 6.5g Sep 14] €15,000Y: fifth foal: half-brother to 1m-10.7f winner Honor Oak (by Zebedee): dam, maiden (stayed 1m), closely related to smart US Grade 2 8.5f/1¼m winner Foxysox: fairly useful performer: won nurseries at Hamilton in August and September (by 1¼ lengths from Clubbable): stays 6f: acts on soft going: sold 12,000 gns, sent to Italy. *Kevin Ryan* **86**

MAGIC JOURNEY (IRE) 3 gr.g. Zebedee 113 – Journey's End (IRE) (In The Wings 128) [2017 57: f7g t7.1m^{3} t7.1g^{5} t7.1g 7.2d^{2} 7.2m 7.2s* 7.1g^{3} 7.2g^{2} 7.2d^{2} 7.2d^{4} Aug 14] fair handicapper: won at Ayr (apprentice) in July: stays 7f: acts on tapeta and soft going: sometimes wears headgear. *John Quinn* **67**

MAGIC LILY 2 ch.f. (Feb 11) New Approach (IRE) 132 – Dancing Rain (IRE) 120 (Danehill Dancer (IRE) 117) [2017 8d* 8m^{3} Oct 13] good-topped filly: second foal: dam, 1¼m-1½m winner (including Oaks), half-sister to dam of Moyglare Stud Stakes winner Maybe, herself dam of Racing Post Trophy winner Saxon Warrior: smart form: won minor event at Newmarket (by 8 lengths from Mystic Meg) in September: third in Fillies' Mile at same course (¾ length behind Laurens) in October: will be suited by 1¼m+: wears tongue tie: open to further improvement. *Charlie Appleby* **110 p**

MAGIC MARK 2 b.g. (Mar 15) Helmet (AUS) 127 – Silken Aunt 60 (Barathea (IRE) 127) [2017 5g^{3} 5m^{3} 6m^{6} 5d^{6} t5.1g^{3} Dec 18] fair maiden: stays 6f: acts on tapeta and good to firm going. *K. R. Burke* **71**

MAGIC MIRROR 4 b.f. Dutch Art 126 – Balatoma (IRE) 76 (Mr Greeley (USA) 122) **58**
[2017 –: p8d* p7g* p8g 8m^{6} 8g^{4} 7d^{3} 8.3f^{4} p7g p7g^{2} 8.2v^{6} p7g^{2} p7g* p8g* p7g^{3} Dec 20] **a74**
modest handicapper on turf, fair on all-weather: won at Kempton in January, March, October and November: stays 1m: acts on polytrack: wears headgear: often races towards rear. *Mark Rimell*

MAGIC MOMENTS 4 b.f. Kheleyf (USA) 116 – Magic Rhythm 65 (Librettist (USA) 124) [2017 62: t7.1m t7.1g^{2} 8m^{5} 7m* 7d^{5} 7f^{5} t6.1g* t6.1g^{4} t6.1g^{6} Oct 21] fair handicapper: won at Yarmouth in May and Wolverhampton in August: stays 1m: acts on polytrack, tapeta and good to firm going: front runner/races prominently, often travels strongly. *Alan King* **74**

MAGIC PASS 3 ch.g. Raven's Pass (USA) 133 – Magic America (USA) 112 (High Yield (USA) 121) [2017 t8.6g^{6} t8.6g^{4} f8g^{3} 9.9f May 6] modest form: best effort at 8.5f: often in hood. *Andrew Balding* **63**

MAGIC PULSE (IRE) 2 b.f. (Feb 1) Dragon Pulse (IRE) 114 – Invincible Magic (IRE) 66 (Invincible Spirit (IRE) 121) [2017 5s 5m 5s^{4} p5g^{2} p5s* p5s^{5} f5g^{2} Dec 29] €5,000F, €11,000Y: first foal: dam, lightly raced, out of half-sister to Japan Cup winner Alkaased: fair performer: won nursery at Chelmsford in November: left Ann Duffield after fourth start: raced only at 5f: acts on polytrack and fibresand: has worn tongue tie: often races towards rear. *David C. Griffiths* **65**

MAGIC SHIP (IRE) 2 b.c. (May 4) Kodiac 112 – Baltic Belle (IRE) 86 (Redback 116) [2017 5f 5d 5g^{6} 6g t7.1g t6g Oct 19] little impact in minor events/nurseries: tried in hood. *Ollie Pears* **–**

MAGISTRAL 7 b.g. Manduro (GER) 135 – Tamalain (USA) 80 (Royal Academy (USA) 130) [2017 t12.4d^2 t10.2d t12.2g^4 13.8m 13.1m^3 7.2s^2 7.2g^2 8d 8d 9s^5 12.5v^6 t8d^4 t7.1g t12.4d^2 Dec 16] well-made gelding: fair handicapper nowadays: left Iain Jardine after fifth start, R. Mike Smith after eleventh: stays 12.5f: acts on tapeta, soft and good to firm going: wears headgear: sometimes slowly away. *Linda Perratt* **77**

MAGNETIC BOUNDARY (USA) 2 ch.c. (Feb 17) Union Rags (USA) 124 – Enthused (USA) 109 (Seeking The Gold (USA)) [2017 f7.1g^2 f7.1g^3 Dec 11] half-brother to several winners, including smart 1m winner Ea (by Dynaformer), later winner up to 2m in USA, and useful winner up to 1¼m Flow (2-y-o 1m winner, by Medaglia d'Oro): dam 2-y-o 6f winner (including Lowther Stakes) who stayed 1m: fairly useful form when placed in minor events at Southwell: will stay at least 1m: wears tongue tie. *George Scott* **80**

MAGNIFICENT 2 b.c. (Apr 6) Zebedee 113 – Barathea Dancer (IRE) 83 (Barathea (IRE) 127) [2017 6.5g^6 7m^4 7g^2 7m^2 Sep 23] 12,000F: rangy colt: has scope: first foal: dam 1¼m winner: fairly useful form: second in minor event at Newbury (2¼ lengths behind Emaraaty) in September: will probably stay 1m. *Richard Hannon* **93**

MAGNIFICENT MADIBA 4 b.g. Mount Nelson 125 – Mrs Penny (AUS) 98 (Planchet (AUS)) [2017 71: 9.9g May 2] angular gelding: fair at 3 yrs, well held sole outing on Flat in 2017: stays 1¼m: tried in cheekpieces. *George Baker* **–**

MAGNOLIA RIDGE (IRE) 7 b.g. Galileo (IRE) 134 – Treasure The Lady (IRE) 95 (Indian Ridge 123) [2017 54: 12.1m Jul 19] smallish gelding: modest handicapper, below form sole outing on Flat in 2017: stays 12.5f: acts on polytrack, tapeta, good to firm and good to soft going: wears headgear: winning hurdler. *Mark Walford* **44**

MAGNOLIA SPRINGS (IRE) 2 b.f. (Mar 3) Shamardal (USA) 129 – Rainbow City (IRE) 85 (Rainbow Quest (USA) 134) [2017 7g* 7s^6 Oct 28] €105,000Y: half-sister to several winners, including useful 9f-17f winner L Frank Baum (by Sinndar) and winner around 1¼m Mythical City (by Rock of Gibraltar): dam, 1¼m winner, closely related to very smart 11f-13f winner Gamut: fairly useful form: won minor event at Newbury (by 3½ lengths from Melodies) in September: still in need of experience when sixth to Hikmaa in listed race there next time: will be suited by 1m: remains with potential. *Eve Johnson Houghton* **91 p**

MAGNUS (IRE) 2 b.c. (Apr 7) Makfi 130 – Royale Danehill (IRE) (Danehill (USA) 126) [2017 5m 6m^6 5.5s* 5f 6f^3 7g^4 6.1s^6 7g^5 7v^2 Sep 15] smallish colt: fair performer: won minor event at Wetherby (by neck from Tough Remedy) in June: stayed 7f: acted on any turf going: dead. *Tom Dascombe* **77**

MAGNUS MAXIMUS 6 b.g. Holy Roman Emperor (IRE) 125 – Chanrossa (IRE) 72 (Galileo (IRE) 134) [2017 114: 5g 6g 6g p6g^6 6v p7s^6 Sep 30] dipped-backed gelding: smart performer, below form in 2017: stays 7f: acts on polytrack, good to firm and good to soft going: tried in blinkers: front runner/races prominently: sold 14,000 gns in October. *Robyn Brisland* **99**

MAGNUS ROMEO 6 b.g. Manduro (GER) 135 – Chili Dip (Alhaarth (IRE) 126) [2017 –: 13f p15.8g Sep 26] maiden: no form in 2017, including over hurdles: best effort at 1¼m: acts on polytrack: wears tongue tie. *Johnny Farrelly* **–**

MAGOJIRO (USA) 2 b.g. (May 14) Hat Trick (JPN) 121 – Rebuke (USA) (Carson City (USA)) [2017 p8g^6 Oct 25] in blinkers, 12/1, sixth in minor event at Kempton (13½ lengths behind Tenedos) in October. *Jeremy Noseda* **51**

MAGS WELL (IRE) 3 gr.f. Thewayyouare (USA) 117 – Sliabh Aniaran (IRE) (Oratorio (IRE) 128) [2017 57: 7m 8.2d t7.2g^4 6.7g t6.1g^4 5.7s p6g t5.1g Dec 13] first foal: dam unraced half-sister to useful 1¼m winner Leningrad: fair maiden: left E. D. Linehan after fifth start: stays 7f: acts on tapeta: usually races close up. *Geoffrey Deacon* **65**

MAHAARAT 2 ch.f. (Jan 28) Dubawi (IRE) 129 – Ashaaqah (IRE) (Dansili 127) [2017 7m 7d^5 p8g* 8v Sep 28] good-quartered filly: first foal: dam, ran twice in France, out of useful half-sister to Breeders' Cup Filly & Mare Turf winner Lahudood: fairly useful form: won minor event at Kempton (by 4 lengths from Harmonica) in August: will be suited by further than 1m. *Sir Michael Stoute* **82**

MAHABBA (IRE) 3 gr.f. Galileo (IRE) 134 – Bewitched (IRE) 120 (Dansili 127) [2017 9.9f^3 10.2g^3 t12.4g^4 p13.3g^6 Oct 26] 360,000Y: second foal: dam, winner up to 7f (2-y-o 5f winner), out of Prix de Diane runner-up Abbatiale: fairly useful form in maidens: stays 12.5f. *Luca Cumani* **81**

MAHICAN (IRE) 7 b.g. Cape Cross (IRE) 129 – Dark Indian (IRE) (Indian Ridge 123) [2017 t13.9m p15.8g^{4} Jan 25] lengthy gelding: useful performer in 2013, lightly raced and well below that level since: stays 1½m: acts on polytrack, soft and good to firm going: has worn cheekpieces, including final start. *Jennie Candlish* –

MAHNA MAHNA (IRE) 3 b.g. Kodiac 112 – Namu 76 (Mujahid (USA) 125) [2017 t7.1m^{6} p7m^{5} t8.6g 7g t6.1g^{5} 5.7f^{6} p6d Aug 23] modest maiden: stays 6f: acts on polytrack and tapeta: front runner/races prominently, usually freely. *David Drinkwater* **52**

MAID IN BRITTAIN 3 ch.f. Monsieur Bond (IRE) 120 – Guadaloup 70 (Loup Sauvage (USA) 125) [2017 7g 8.3g t7.1g 7g t8.6g Oct 21] fourth foal: sister to winner up to 6f French (2-y-o 5f winner): dam 6f/7f winner: no form: tried in tongue tie. *Antony Brittain* –

MAID IN INDIA (IRE) 3 br.f. Bated Breath 125 – Indian Maiden (IRE) 115 (Indian Ridge 123) [2017 6m* 6g* 6.1g^{2} 6.1d^{5} Oct 4] half-sister to several winners, including smart French 5.5f-1m winner Love Spirit (by Elusive City) and useful 7f/1m winner Honiara (by Rock of Gibraltar): dam 5f/6f winner: fairly useful form: won maiden at Doncaster in July and handicap there (by ¾ length from Seyasah) in August: second in handicap at Nottingham later in August: raced only at 6f: remains with potential. *Eric Alston* **89 p**

MAID OF ROCK (IRE) 3 b.f. Rock of Gibraltar (IRE) 133 – Embark (Soviet Star (USA) 128) [2017 p8g p8g p8g Nov 6] €10,000Y, 16,500 2-y-o: sixth foal: closely related to smart North American 1m-11f (Canadian Grade 2) winner Can'thelpbelieving (by Duke of Marmalade) and half-sister to a winner in Sweden by Medicean: dam once-raced sister to dual Lockinge Stakes winner Soviet Line: well held in 3 maidens at Kempton. *Mike Murphy* –

MAID OF TUSCANY (IRE) 6 b.m. Manduro (GER) 135 – Tuscania (USA) (Woodman (USA) 126) [2017 58: p16g Dec 20] angular mare: modest handicapper, well held sole outing on Flat in 2017: stays 1¾m: acts on polytrack, tapeta, soft and good to firm going: wears headgear: often races towards rear: winning hurdler. *Neil Mulholland* –

MAID TO REMEMBER 3 b.f. Redoute's Choice (AUS) – Maid To Believe 106 (Galileo (IRE) 134) [2017 8.3g* 10m^{5} Jun 26] €200,000Y: rather unfurnished filly: fifth foal: dam winner up to 1½m (2-y-o 1m winner): fairly useful form: won maiden at Nottingham (by neck from Sasini) in May: should still improve. *Ralph Beckett* **84 p**

MAID UP 2 gr.f. (Mar 2) Mastercraftsman (IRE) 129 – Complexion 92 (Hurricane Run (IRE) 134) [2017 p8g 8s Oct 28] third foal: half-sister to 1¼m winner King of Dreams (by Dream Ahead) and 1m winner (stays 11f) Rumpole (by Lawman): dam, 1m winner who stayed 1¼m, half-sister to high-class winner up to 1m Zacinto: little impact in maiden/minor event. *Andrew Balding* –

MAIFALKI (FR) 4 b.g. Falco (USA) 122 – Makila (IRE) (Entrepreneur 123) [2017 91p: 8m 9.8m 8g 10g 8d t12.2g^{4} t9.5d Dec 16] fairly useful handicapper: left Mark Walford after fourth start: barely stays 1½m: acts on tapeta: tried in hood. *Jason Ward* **89**

MAIL ORDER 2 b.f. (Feb 19) Nathaniel (IRE) 129 – Mail The Desert (IRE) 110 (Desert Prince (IRE) 130) [2017 7.4d^{5} p8g^{4} 7.4g^{3} 8s^{3} 7s^{6} Oct 29] half-sister to several winners, including very smart winner up to 7f Desert Force (2-y-o 6f winner, by Equiano) and useful 7f/1m winner Zwayyan (by Pivotal): dam 2-y-o 6f/7f (Moyglare Stud Stakes) winner: fair maiden: stays 1m: acts on soft going. *Mark Johnston* **66**

MAILSHOT (USA) 3 ch.c. Hard Spun (USA) 124 – Newsreel (IRE) (A P Indy (USA) 131) [2017 95: t8g^{3} p8m* p7g^{2} p8g* 8g 7.6m 8.2f May 27] rather unfurnished colt: useful handicapper: won at Lingfield in January and Chelmsford (by 2¼ lengths from Mutawatheb) in March: stays 8.5f: acts on polytrack, tapeta, good to firm and good to soft going: sent to UAE. *Mark Johnston* **100**

MAIN DESIRE (IRE) 2 b.f. (Mar 18) High Chaparral (IRE) 132 – Purple Glow (IRE) 96 (Orientate (USA) 127) [2017 5.1m* 5s* May 19] €40,000Y: second foal: half-sister to useful 5f/6f winner Magical Effect (by New Approach): dam, 2-y-o 6f winner, out of sister to US Grade 1 1m winner Easy Now, herself half-sister to Belmont Stakes winner Easy Goer: useful form: won minor event at Nottingham (by 1¼ lengths from She Believes) and listed race at York (by ½ length from Neola) in May: will stay 6f: open to further improvement. *Michael Bell* **98 p**

MAIN FACT (USA) 4 b.g. Blame (USA) 129 – Reflections (Sadler's Wells (USA) 132) [2017 t8g t12.4g 13.8m 13.1v^{3} Oct 12] fairly useful in France for D. Smaga at 3 yrs, below that level in 2017: stays 13f: acts on heavy going: in hood last 3 starts: winning hurdler. *Dianne Sayer* **67**

MAINSTREAM 4 b.g. Dansili 127 – Golden Stream (IRE) 110 (Sadler's Wells (USA) 132) [2017 108: 12m^{3} 12m^{6} 11.9g^{2} 14d Aug 5] rather leggy gelding: useful handicapper: placed at Newmarket (2¾ lengths third to Frontiersman) in May and York (1¾ lengths second behind Mukhayyam) in July: stays 1½m: acts on soft and good to firm going: usually wears hood: sometimes slowly away, usually races nearer last than first: best treated with caution (carries head awkwardly): sent to Australia. *Sir Michael Stoute* **109 §**

MAIN STREET 2 b.c. (Feb 6) Street Cry (IRE) 130 – My Special J's (USA) 109 (Harlan's Holiday (USA) 124) [2017 7m^{5} p8g* Oct 12] first foal: dam, 2-y-o 7f (Debutante Stakes) winner, later 1m winner in USA: fairly useful form: won minor event at Chelmsford (impressively, by 1¾ lengths from Rua Augusta) in October: will go on improving. *John Gosden* **89 p**

MAISON BRILLET (IRE) 10 b.g. Pyrus (USA) 106 – Stormchaser (IRE) (Titus Livius (FR) 115) [2017 62: 14.1m May 24] good-topped gelding: poor handicapper: stays 2m: acts on polytrack and good to firm going: wears headgear: often races towards rear. *Clive Drew* **49**

MAIS SI 4 b.f. Montjeu (IRE) 137 – Magic America (USA) 112 (High Yield (USA) 121) [2017 12g^{3} 13.1s^{6} 13.4g^{4} 16g^{4} 11.6g^{5} Sep 7] fourth foal: half-sister to 2 winners abroad, including useful French 5f (including at 2 yrs) winner Sara Lucille (by Dansili): dam French 5f/7f winner, including at 2 yrs: fair maiden: runner-up in handicap at Maisons-Laffitte for F. Head in 2016: in frame 3 times in 2017: stays 15f: acts on soft going: often wears headgear. *Gordon Elliott, Ireland* **77**

MAITRESSE (IRE) 3 ch.f. Mastercraftsman (IRE) 129 – L'Amour Toujours (IRE) 69 (Montjeu (IRE) 137) [2017 10.2m 12m Jun 16] €11,000Y, £32,000 2-y-o: third foal: half-sister to Italian 6f winner Amour Amour (by Bushranger): dam maiden (stayed 11f): well held in maidens. *Seamus Durack* **–**

MAJBOOR (IRE) 3 ch.g. Dragon Pulse (IRE) 114 – City Vaults Girl (IRE) 78 (Oratorio (IRE) 128) [2017 6s^{3} 7g^{2} 7.1g^{3} 10g^{5} 8.1m^{2} t9.5g^{2} Nov 7] 34,000F, 72,000Y, £9,000 3-y-o: good-topped gelding: third foal: half-brother to 2-y-o 7f winner City of Stars (by Lilbourne Lad), later 7f/1m winner in Italy: dam, 1¼m winner, closely related to smart Hong Kong performer up to 1½m King Dancer: fairly useful maiden: placed on 5 of 6 starts: stays 1¼m: acts on good to firm going: front runner/races prominently. *Dominic Ffrench Davis* **86**

MAJDOOL (IRE) 4 b.g. Acclamation 118 – Maany (USA) 62 (Mr Greeley (USA) 122) [2017 92: t7.1s 7.2d 6g 6v t8g^{4} t7.1g^{ur} t8g^{6} t7.1g Dec 6] fair handicapper nowadays: stays 1m: acts on polytrack, tapeta and good to firm going: tried in headgear: often starts slowly: temperamental. *Noel Wilson* **77 §**

MAJEED 7 b.g. Mount Nelson 125 – Clever Millie (USA) 81 (Cape Canaveral (USA) 115) [2017 112: 9.9g 12g^{4} 12.1g 10g 10m^{2} 10.3m 12s^{6} p12g Dec 23] strong, useful-looking gelding: useful handicapper: second in Wolferton Handicap at Royal Ascot (neck behind Snoano) in June: stays 12.5f: acts on polytrack and good to firm going: often starts slowly, races well off pace. *David Simcock* **108**

MAJESTE 3 b.g. Acclamation 118 – Winged Valkyrie (IRE) 73 (Hawk Wing (USA) 136) [2017 95: 7m^{6} 10.3d 7s^{6} 7d^{6} p7g 8g 6d Sep 23] well-made gelding: useful form at 2 yrs, disappointing in 2017: stays 7f: acts on good to firm going: tried in blinkers: sold 17,000 gns in October. *Richard Hannon* **–**

MAJESTIC GIRL (IRE) 4 b.f. Royal Applause 124 – Pretty Majestic (IRE) 92 (Invincible Spirit (IRE) 121) [2017 60: 5.7d^{3} p7s^{5} p8d 5.1s t7.2g^{6} 7m 7m 7d Oct 30] sturdy filly: modest maiden: stays 1m: acts on polytrack and good to soft going: has worn headgear, including in 2017: usually slowly away/races towards rear. *Steve Flook* **50**

MAJESTIC HERO (IRE) 5 b.g. Majestic Missile (IRE) 118 – Xena (IRE) (Mull of Kintyre (USA) 114) [2017 96: 5m^{2} 5g* 5.1m 5m 5g 5.1m^{3} 5.1g 5d^{5} 5m^{3} 5g p5d^{5} p5g Oct 13] strong gelding: useful handicapper: won at Epsom (by ¾ length from Just That Lord) in April: best form at 5f: acts on good to firm and heavy going. *Ronald Harris* **98**

MAJESTIC MAN (IRE) 4 b.g. Majestic Missile (IRE) 118 – Windomen (IRE) (Forest Wind (USA) 111) [2017 t8g^{4} Nov 15] well held in bumper/Flat maiden. *Ronald Thompson* **–**

MAJESTIC MOON (IRE) 7 b.g. Majestic Missile (IRE) 118 – Gala Style (IRE) (Elnadim (USA) 128) [2017 105: p7g 7m 7s 7m^{5} 7m^{2} 7.6d^{2} 7d 7m 6g^{3} 7s 6g 6d^{5} f8.1g^{4} f7.1g^{3} Dec 1] good-topped gelding: fairly useful handicapper nowadays: placed at Goodwood (apprentice) in June and Yarmouth (amateur) in July: stays 7f: acts on polytrack, fibresand, soft and good to firm going: has worn headgear, including in 2017. *Julia Feilden* **91**

MAJESTIC MYLES (IRE) 9 b.g. Majestic Missile (IRE) 118 – Gala Style (IRE) **58**
(Elnadim (USA) 128) [2017 86: p7g p7g p8g p6g^{5} Apr 20] tall gelding: smart handicapper at best, well below that level in 2017: stayed 7f: acted on polytrack, good to firm and heavy going: tried in headgear/tongue tie: dead. *Lee Carter*

MAJESTIC STONE (IRE) 3 b.g. Casamento (IRE) 118 – Pretty Majestic (IRE) 92 **61**
(Invincible Spirit (IRE) 121) [2017 –: t7.1m t5d 6g^{2} 6d^{2} 6d^{5} 5.9s 6m Aug 26] modest maiden: stays 6f: acts on good to soft going: in headgear last 5 starts: held up. *Julie Camacho*

MAJOR ASSAULT 4 b.c. Kyllachy 129 – Night Premiere (IRE) 63 (Night Shift (USA)) –
[2017 72: p7d 8m 6.1d t7.2g Nov 7] fair form at 3 yrs, little impact in 2017. *Matthew Salaman*

MAJOR BEN 4 ch.g. Major Cadeaux 121 – La Jwaab (Alhaarth (IRE) 126) [2017 72: **72**
p13g^{2} t14d Dec 27] lengthy gelding: fair handicapper: left David Evans after first start: stays 13f: acts on polytrack, tapeta and good to firm going: often races prominently. *Michael Blake*

MAJOR CORNWALLIS (IRE) 3 ch.g. Dandy Man (IRE) 123 – Macnas (USA) 80 **68**
(Orientate (USA) 127) [2017 71: t8d^{3} t8g t8.6g^{4} t9.5g^{4} 7.5f^{5} 7m 7g^{4} 7g* 7d^{4} Aug 13] sturdy gelding: fair performer: won seller at Leicester in July: stays 1m: acts on tapeta, firm and good to soft going. *Richard Fahey*

MAJOR CRISPIES 6 b.g. Pastoral Pursuits 127 – Nellie Melba 82 (Hurricane Sky **81 §**
(AUS)) [2017 91§: p8d p6d p7g^{6} 7g p6g* p6g^{2} t6s p6d^{3} 7d^{3} 7.4f^{2} 7.2m^{4} 6g^{3} p7g p6g 6v^{6} t6d^{2} t6g* t6d^{4} t6.1d^{5} t7.2d^{4} Dec 26] good-quartered gelding: fairly useful performer: won claimer at Lingfield in April and handicap at Newcastle (by neck from Samarmadi) in October: left Jeremy Gask after sixth start: stays 1m: acts on polytrack, tapeta, firm and good to soft going: wears headgear: has worn tongue tie, including in 2017: often starts slowly, usually races nearer last than first: temperamental. *David O'Meara*

MAJORETTE 3 ch.f. Major Cadeaux 121 – So Discreet (Tragic Role (USA)) [2017 7g^{6} **62**
p6g^{4} 6d^{3} Sep 19] 2,200Y: half-sister to several winners, including 7f (including at 2 yrs)/1m winner Reel Buddy Star (by Reel Buddy) and 6f/7f winner Fireback (by Firebreak), both useful: dam unraced: modest form in maidens. *Martin Smith*

MAJOR FRANKO 5 ch.g. Major Cadeaux 121 – Royal Future (IRE) (Royal Academy –
(USA) 130) [2017 –: t16.5g Jan 6] workmanlike gelding: little form: has worn headgear, including in 2017. *Sarah-Jayne Davies*

MAJORIS (IRE) 3 b.g. Frankel 147 – Drops (IRE) 62 (Kingmambo (USA) 125) [2017 **93**
94: p8g^{5} 10m^{4} 12m Jun 22] small, workmanlike gelding: fairly useful performer: should stay 1m: acts on good to firm going: tried in blinkers: wears tongue tie: sometimes slowly away: sold 82,000 gns in July, then gelded and sent to Hong Kong, where renamed Enjoyable Success. *Hugo Palmer*

MAJOR JUMBO 3 gr.g. Zebedee 113 – Gone Sailing (Mizzen Mast (USA) 121) [2017 **103**
72: f5g^{2} t5g* t5d^{2} t5.1m* 5.1g^{2} 5s^{3} 5.1g^{2} 5m 6d* Sep 10] tall, good-quartered gelding: useful handicapper: won at Newcastle in January, Wolverhampton in February and York (by neck from Dakota Gold) in September: stays 6f: acts on fibresand, tapeta and good to soft going: front runner/races prominently. *Kevin Ryan*

MAJOR MINUS 3 b.g. Sir Percy 129 – Eminencia (Sadler's Wells (USA) 132) [2017 7d –
8m^{6} t8s Sep 8] well held in maidens. *Tim Easterby*

MAJOR MUSCARI (IRE) 9 ch.g. Exceed And Excel (AUS) 126 – Muscari 68 (Indian **64**
Ridge 123) [2017 68: t6f^{3} p7g^{2} p7g^{3} t7.1d^{5} p7g f6m p6g^{3} t7.1g^{6} 5m t7.2g^{5} 6g Aug 21] lengthy gelding: fair handicapper: stays 7f: acts on all-weather, firm and soft going: wears headgear: sometimes slowly away. *Shaun Harris*

MAJOR PEIRSON (IRE) 2 b.g. (Mar 31) Society Rock (IRE) 126 – Snowtime (IRE) **85**
(Galileo (IRE) 134) [2017 5.1d^{6} 6d^{4} 6m* 6g^{5} 7g^{6} Sep 15] rather sparely-made gelding: sixth foal: half-brother to 1m-9.5f winner Heavens Eyes (by Oasis Dream) and 1¼m winner Decima (by Dream Ahead): dam unraced half-sister to high-class winner up to 9f Ali-Royal and 1000 Guineas winner Sleepytime: fairly useful performer: won minor event at Newbury (by 5 lengths from Warsaan) in July: stays 6f: acts on good to firm going: usually races close up. *Jo Hughes*

MAJOR PUSEY 5 ch.g. Major Cadeaux 121 – Pusey Street Lady 103 (Averti (IRE) 117) **97**
[2017 91: p6g 5g 5s 6.1d* 6d^{2} 6m 5d^{3} 6.1g^{2} 6d^{2} 6.1s 5s* 5.6g 6v Sep 30] close-coupled gelding: useful handicapper: won at Windsor in May and Haydock (by 1¼ lengths from Magical Dreamer) in September: best at 5f/6f: acts on any turf going: tried in tongue tie: usually races close up. *John Gallagher*

MAJOR ROWAN 6 b.g. Captain Gerrard (IRE) 113 – Julie's Gift (Presidium 124) [2017 76: t12.4d^4 t12.4d f12d^3 16g^4 14g^4 14v^4 14m t12.4d^5 t12.4s^4 t12.4g Oct 10] fair handicapper: stays 2m: acts on fibresand, tapeta, best turf form on good going: has worn blinkers. *John Davies* **65 a75**

MAJOR TOM 3 b.g. Native Ruler 119 – Top Level (IRE) 55 (Fasliyev (USA) 120) [2017 –: t9.5m f7g^6 f8g Mar 9] modest form when sixth in maiden at Southwell in February, standout effort. *Michael Appleby* **50**

MAJOR VALENTINE 5 b.g. Major Cadeaux 121 – Under My Spell 80 (Wizard King 122) [2017 58, a79: p6g t6g^4 p6g* 6m* 5.1m* 5g^3 5m* 5.2m^4 5g* 5v^3 5.1m^2 5.1s^3 6.1g^2 6d^3 t6.1g Sep 23] fairly useful handicapper: won at Kempton in March, Catterick/Nottingham (apprentice) in April, Bath in June and Ffos Las (by 1¼ lengths from The Daley Express) in July: stays 6f: acts on polytrack, tapeta, good to firm and good to soft going: tried in cheekpieces: usually races close up. *John O'Shea* **83**

MAKAARIM 3 b.g. Tamayuz 126 – Dubawi Cheetah (IRE) 74 (Dubawi (IRE) 129) [2017 84p: p8g^2 p8g^6 10m p8s^2 8d t7.2g* p7g^5 Dec 13] useful handicapper: won at Wolverhampton (by neck from Twin Appeal) in November: left Marco Botti after fourth start: stays 8.5f: acts on polytrack and tapeta. *Hughie Morrison* **106**

MAKAMBE (IRE) 2 gr.g. (Mar 3) Dark Angel (IRE) 113 – Pink Diva (IRE) 80 (Giant's Causeway (USA) 132) [2017 6g 6m 6.1m^4 Aug 26] useful-looking gelding: second foal: dam, 2-y-o 1m winner, out of Irish 1000 Guineas winner Saoire: fair form when seventh in minor event at Salisbury (4 lengths behind Rogue) on second of 3 starts: will be suited by 7f: remains with potential. *Charles Hills* **66 p**

MAKANAH 2 b.g. (Mar 8) Mayson 124 – Diane's Choice 95 (Komaite (USA)) [2017 6s^3 t6.1g^2 p6g^5 5.4g^5 Oct 13] strong gelding: fair form in maidens/minor event: left Simon Crisford after third start: stays 6f. *Julie Camacho* **76**

MAKE GOOD (IRE) 2 b.g. (Mar 12) Fast Company (IRE) 126 – Rectify (IRE) (Mujadil (USA) 119) [2017 6.5m 6d* 7g^2 7m^5 7v Oct 1] €7,500F, €31,000Y: seventh foal: brother to a winner in Greece, and half-brother to 5f-7f winner (including at 2 yrs) Transfixed (by Trans Island) and 6f winner Red Tide (by Tamayuz): dam unraced: fairly useful performer: won minor event at Doncaster (by 2½ lengths from Beatbox Rhythm) in July: stays 7f: acts on good to soft going. *David Brown* **80**

MAKE MUSIC 4 b.f. Acclamation 118 – Come What May 67 (Selkirk (USA) 129) [2017 89: p7m p7g* p7d p7g^5 p6g* p7g^4 7f^2 p7g^4 Dec 13] rangy filly: useful handicapper: won at Lingfield in January and March (by neck form Rosealee): second at Goodwood (½ length behind Gossiping) in May: stays 7.5f: acts on polytrack, tapeta and any turf going: usually races close up. *Andrew Balding* **100**

MAKE ON MADAM (IRE) 5 b.m. Captain Rio 122 – Rye (IRE) 75 (Charnwood Forest (IRE) 125) [2017 71, a62: t7.1g^3 8.5m* 7.5f^3 8g 7.4m^2 8.5m^5 7.4m^2 8f^6 8.5f^6 8.5s^4 7g 8.5v^6 t8g Oct 19] short-coupled mare: fair handicapper: won at Beverley in April: stays 8.5f: acts on fibresand, tapeta, firm and soft going: often wears headgear: tried in tongue tie: front runner/races prominently, often freely. *Les Eyre* **76**

MAKE SAIL 3 b.f. Assertive 121 – Mabel's Song 62 (Sakhee (USA) 136) [2017 6.1m 5.1g^6 7d^6 Sep 6] first foal: dam maiden (stayed 11f): well held in maidens. *Tony Carroll* **–**

MAKE TIME (IRE) 3 ch.c. Makfi 130 – Poppet's Lovein 89 (Lomitas 129) [2017 92p: 7m 8g* 8s^2 8.8m Aug 26] sturdy colt: smart performer: won handicap at Sandown (by 6 lengths from Selection) in July: second in Thoroughbred Stakes at Goodwood (3 lengths behind Beat The Bank) in August: stayed 1m: acted on soft and good to firm going: dead. *David Menuisier* **110**

MAKHFAR (IRE) 6 b.g. Bushranger (IRE) 119 – Let Me Shine (USA) 79 (Dixie Union (USA) 121) [2017 70: p8g^4 p8g^4 t8.6g^2 t8.6g* t8.6g^2 p8d^2 p8g t9.5m t8.6d Dec 9] fair handicapper: won at Wolverhampton in June: stays 8.5f: acts on polytrack, tapeta and good to firm going: wears headgear. *Mark Usher* **72**

MAKING LIGHT (IRE) 3 b.f. Tamayuz 126 – Instant Sparkle (IRE) 88 (Danehill (USA) 126) [2017 101p: 8d^3 9.5d^2 9d 8s^2 7s* Oct 28] third foal: half-sister to a winner in Qatar by Pivotal: dam, 1½m winner, sister to Ribblesdale Stakes winner Irresistible Jewel, herself dam of Irish St Leger winner Royal Diamond: useful performer: won listed event at Leopardstown (awarded race after beaten nose by Larchmont Lad) in October: second in similar events at Gowran (neck behind Alluringly) in August and Naas (short head behind Elegant Pose) in October: stays 9.5f: acts on heavy going: usually races prominently. *D. K. Weld, Ireland* **106**

MAKING MIRACLES 2 b.g. (Mar 6) Pivotal 124 – Field of Miracles (IRE) 114 (Galileo (IRE) 134) [2017 t8s 8.9s^{6} 10v^{2} 10m^{2} p10d^{5} Nov 9] 47,000Y: good-topped gelding: second foal: dam, ungenuine 1½m winner, sister to smart 9f-11.6f winner Cameron Highland: fairly useful maiden: stays 1¼m: acts on polytrack and good to firm going: sometimes slowly away, often races towards rear. *Mark Johnston* **80**

MAKING TROUBLE (GER) 5 b.g. Paco Boy (IRE) 129 – Making Hay (Dr Fong (USA) 128) [2017 6.5g^{2} 6g^{5} 6.5s^{5} 6.5s^{2} p6g Nov 18] useful performer: won 3 times in Germany, including listed race at Dusseldorf in 2015: second in minor events at Bad Doberan (2 lengths behind Shining Emerald) in August and Hanover (length behind Mc Queen) in October: below form in listed race at Lingfield final start: stays 7.5f: acts on soft going. *D. Moser, Germany* **104**

MAKIN IT 2 b.f. (Feb 16) North Light (IRE) 126 – Saltpetre (IRE) (Selkirk (USA) 129) [2017 p8g Nov 8] second foal: dam unraced half-sister to useful winner up to 1½m Seafarer: 66/1, ninth in minor event at Kempton (6 lengths behind Espadrille) in November. *William Knight* **62**

MAKKAAR (IRE) 3 b.g. Raven's Pass (USA) 133 – Beneventa 110 (Most Welcome 131) [2017 84p: 7.2m 8m Jun 14] fairly useful handicapper: stays 7f: acts on good to firm going: sold £15,000 in September, sent to Greece. *Mark Johnston* **82**

MAKKADANGDANG 3 ro.g. Mastercraftsman (IRE) 129 – Penny Cross 99 (Efisio 120) [2017 75p: 9.9m^{2} 9.9d p15.8g 11.4m p11g^{5} Oct 24] rather leggy gelding: fair maiden: should be suited by 1½m+: acts on polytrack and good to firm going: sent to USA. *Andrew Balding* **72**

MAKOFITWHATYOUWILL 2 b.g. (Feb 3) Makfi 130 – Frequent (Three Valleys (USA) 119) [2017 6g^{6} 6d 6m 8g Sep 27] no form, including in nursery: tried in tongue tie. *Nigel Tinkler* **–**

MAKSAB (IRE) 2 b.c. (Mar 9) Makfi 130 – Azeema (IRE) 82 (Averti (IRE) 117) [2017 6g^{5} 7g* 7g 7m* 8g^{4} 8g^{5} 7m^{4} Oct 14] 48,000Y: compact colt: sixth foal: half-brother to 3 winners, including 6f winner Major Jack (by Kheleyf) and winner up to 1¼m Trader Jack (2-y-o 1m winner, by Trade Fair), both useful: dam, 7f winner, half-sister to high-class winner up to 1½m Al Kazeem: fairly useful performer: won minor event at Leicester in June and nursery at Newmarket (by nose from Tadleel) in August: stays 7f: acts on good to firm going. *Mick Channon* **86**

MAKZEEM 4 b.g. Makfi 130 – Kazeem 73 (Darshaan 133) [2017 97: t8.6g^{2} 8m 7d* 7m^{2} 7d^{6} 7d* 7s^{4} Oct 7] sturdy gelding: smart handicapper: won at Newmarket in June (by length from Supersta) and September (by 3¼ lengths from Ice Lord): best form at 7f: acts on soft and good to firm going: tried in cheekpieces: often travels strongly. *Roger Charlton* **115**

MALASPINA (ITY) 5 b.m. Pounced (USA) 112 – Modern Goddess (USA) 68 (Gulch (USA)) [2017 7.5m^{3} 8g* 8f* 9.9g* 8.9d^{5} 8s^{5} 8g* p7.5f^{3} 8s* t8g* f7.1g* Dec 1] seventh foal: half-sister to 3 winners in Italy, including 5.5f-7.5f winner Morgante (by Orpen): dam maiden (best effort at 7f): useful performer: won 5 times in France/Italy between February and September, and also successful in handicaps at Newcastle in November and Southwell (by head from Mr Christopher) in December: left A. Marcialis after ninth start: stays 1¼m: acts on fibresand, tapeta, firm and soft going: in headgear last 5 starts. *Ivan Furtado* **97**

MALAYSIAN BOLEH 7 ch.g. Compton Place 125 – Orlena (USA) (Gone West (USA)) [2017 69, a77: p7g^{2} t7.1g^{2} t6g^{4} t5.1g* p5g* p5g^{5} 7m 6g^{6} 5m^{6} 6g^{6} 5s 6d p6g p5s^{6} p6g^{5} p7g Dec 28] modest on turf, fair on all-weather: won claimer at Wolverhampton and handicap at Chelmsford in March: left Brian Ellison after fourth start: has form at 1m, raced over shorter nowadays: acts on polytrack, tapeta and soft going: wears headgear: tried in tongue tie. *Phil McEntee* **51 a78**

MALCOLM THE PUG (IRE) 3 b.c. Acclamation 118 – La Zona (IRE) 110 (Singspiel (IRE) 133) [2017 74p: p7g^{5} 6.1m^{5} 6d^{2} p6g 6.1m^{4} 5.7g^{6} 5g^{5} 6g* 7d 6.1m t6.1m Oct 28] sturdy colt: fair performer: won seller at Lingfield in August: left Richard Hannon after eighth start: stays 6f: acts on good to firm going: front runner/races prominently: sold 1,000 gns, sent to Spain. *David Brown* **75**

MALDONADO (FR) 3 ch.g. Rio de La Plata (USA) 121 – Spanish Winner (IRE) (Choisir (AUS) 126) [2017 83: 7.2s 8g^{5} 8.3g^{5} 8g^{6} 7d 6v 8.3d^{6} t7.1d t6s Nov 30] fair handicapper: stays 7f: acts on good to firm going: tried in cheekpieces. *Michael Easterby* **75**

MALEFICENT QUEEN 5 b.m. Mount Nelson 125 – Manila Selection (USA) (Manila (USA)) [2017 112: 12g^{5} 14g^{2} 16f^{4} 10m^{3} 11.8s^{6} t16.3s^{pu} 12.5g^{4} 13.9m Aug 26] workmanlike mare: useful performer: second in handicap at Musselburgh (1½ lengths behind Carbon Dating) in April: stays 1¾m: acts on soft and good to firm going: has worn headgear, including final start. *Keith Dalgleish* **108**

MALLORY HEIGHTS (IRE) 7 gr.g. Dalakhani (IRE) 133 – My Dark Rosaleen 84 (Sadler's Wells (USA) 132) [2017 10s 11.3g 13.1m 12g 12.5g^{5} 13.4g^{bd} 12s 10g^{4} p10.7g p12g Oct 3] good-topped gelding: modest handicapper: stays 1½m: acts on polytrack and good to soft going: usually in headgear: wears tongue tie: often starts slowly/races towards rear. *Garvan Donnelly, Ireland* **54**

MALLYMKUN 5 b.m. Kheleyf (USA) 116 – Harriet's Girl 88 (Choisir (AUS) 126) [2017 67, a76: 6.1m^{4} 7.2g 6s 7.1d Aug 24] fair handicapper, below form in 2017: stays 7f: acts on tapeta: tried in cheekpieces. *David Loughnane* **60**

MALT TEASER (FR) 3 ch.g. Muhtathir 126 – Abondante (USA) (Thunder Gulch (USA) 129) [2017 50: p6g^{4} p7g^{5} p8g 9.9f p10g^{2} p11s^{5} 10.1g^{5} 8v^{4} 12g^{6} p10g^{6} p12g^{2} p12g p12g^{2} p12g^{4} Dec 23] well-made gelding: fair maiden: stays 1½m: acts on polytrack. *John Best* **75**

MAMA AFRICA (IRE) 3 br.f. Big Bad Bob (IRE) 118 – Colourpoint (USA) 81 (Forest Wildcat (USA) 120) [2017 66: t6g^{4} t7.1d^{4} t7.1g^{4} 8m^{5} 7.1m^{5} 8m^{2} 8d^{2} 8.3d^{5} 8.3s^{2} 7.8g^{4} 8.2g 8d^{2} 8g 8.2v^{2} 8v f7.1g* f8.1g* Dec 19] fairly useful performer: won maiden at Southwell in October and handicap there (by 2¼ lengths from Muqarred) in December: stays 8.5f: acts on fibresand, tapeta, good to firm and heavy going: sometimes wears headgear: front runner/races prominently, often freely. *David Barron* **87**

MAMBA NOIRE (FR) 2 b.f. (Feb 21) Wootton Bassett 119 – Baileys Applause 59 (Royal Applause 124) [2017 5m* 5s^{5} 5m 6g^{3} 6m^{3} 7g 6d^{3} Aug 24] €60,000Y: sturdy filly: half-sister to several winners, including 2-y-o 5f winner Royal Raider (by Piccolo) and French 2-y-o 6f winner Pepite Noire (by Redback): dam 5f winner: useful performer: won maiden at Cork in May: third in Duchess of Cambridge Stakes at Newmarket (2¼ lengths behind Clemmie) in July and Lowther Stakes at York (2½ lengths behind Threading) in August: stays 6f: acts on good to soft and good to firm going: tried in visor. *K. J. Condon, Ireland* **101**

MAMBO DANCER 3 b.g. So You Think (NZ) 133 – Mambo Halo (USA) (Southern Halo (USA)) [2017 –: p10g^{5} 12.5m^{2} 11.5m^{2} 12.1g^{3} 13.9d 12v^{5} t12.2g^{3} 13.1v p12g Oct 24] fair maiden: stays 12.5f: acts on tapeta and good to firm going. *Mark Johnston* **77**

MAMBO SPIRIT (IRE) 13 b.g. Invincible Spirit (IRE) 121 – Mambodorga (USA) (Kingmambo (USA) 125) [2017 73: t5.1g t5.1g^{6} p6d^{2} p6g^{6} 7m^{3} p5s^{5} 5f^{5} Jul 12] tall, good-topped gelding: fair handicapper: raced mainly over sprint trips: acted on polytrack, tapeta, firm and soft going: tried in blinkers/tongue tie: usually raced towards rear: dead. *Tony Newcombe* **71**

MAMDOOD (IRE) 3 gr.g. Clodovil (IRE) 116 – Fact (American Post 121) [2017 81: 8m^{4} 7d^{4} t8d 7.2s^{6} 8.3g Nov 1] fairly useful handicapper: left Richard Hannon after first start: stays 1m: acts on polytrack, soft and good to firm going: in tongue tie last 4 starts. *Susan Corbett* **80**

MAMETZ WOOD (IRE) 2 b.g. (Apr 27) Elzaam (AUS) 115 – Shaanbar (IRE) 53 (Darshaan 133) [2017 7g^{2} t7.1g^{3} 7v^{3} Nov 7] €10,000F, €20,000Y: seventh foal: half-brother to useful winner up to 1m Shaiyem (2-y-o 7.4f winner, by Starspangledbanner) and a winner abroad by Ad Valorem: dam maiden (stayed 1½m): fair form when placed in maiden/minor events: will be suited by 1m+: remains with potential. *K. R. Burke* **74 p**

MAMILLIUS 4 b.g. Exceed And Excel (AUS) 126 – Laika Lane (USA) (Street Cry (IRE) 130) [2017 87: 7g^{4} 7m* 8m 6.1g Aug 28] good-topped gelding: fairly useful handicapper: won at Leicester (by neck from Peak Princess) in June: stays 7f: acts on good to firm going: tried in cheekpieces: tends to find little. *George Baker* **92**

MAMNOON (IRE) 4 b.g. Cape Cross (IRE) 129 – Masaafat (Act One 124) [2017 –: p12g^{4} p11d^{5} t12.2g^{5} p12g 10.2f* 8f^{3} 10.2f^{3} 10.2g 10.2g t9.5g t9.5g f11.1g^{4} Dec 22] fair handicapper: won at Bath in May: stays 11f: acts on polytrack, fibresand, best turf form on firm going: wears blinkers: often races prominently. *Roy Brotherton* **66**

MAMOO 4 ch.g. Sir Percy 129 – Meredith (Medicean 128) [2017 67: t13.9m^{6} p13g^{5} p10d^{6} Feb 23] modest maiden: stays 1½m: acts on polytrack, good to firm and good to soft going: usually wears headgear nowadays. *Mike Murphy* **58**

MAM'SELLE (IRE) 3 b.f. Teofilo (IRE) 126 – Coquette Rouge (IRE) 93 (Croco Rouge (IRE) 126) [2017 9.9d* 9.9d^{5} 11.6d* 12d* 12s^{3} 12.4s Nov 17] 80,000Y: half-sister to several winners, including smart/ungenuine 2-y-o 7f winner Jacqueline Quest (by Rock of Gibraltar), first past post in 1000 Guineas, and 7f winner Coquette Noire (by Holy Roman Emperor): dam, 1½m-17f winner, half-sister to smart performer up to 1½m Regime: useful performer: won maiden at Salisbury in May, and handicaps at Lingfield in July and Newbury (lady amateur) in August: third in handicap at Ascot (1½ lengths behind Duke of Bronte) in September: stays 1½m: acts on soft going: often races prominently. *William Haggas* **104**

MANAAHIL 3 b.f. Dubawi (IRE) 129 – Mudaaraah 106 (Cape Cross (IRE) 129) [2017 **72**
p7g^2 7m^5 p8s^5 p7d^3 Nov 9] smallish filly: third foal: sister to French winner up to 1½m Mushawweq (2-y-o 1¼m winner): dam, 2-y-o 6f/7f winner who stayed 10.4f, closely related to smart 7f/1m performer Muwaary: fair form in maidens: stays 1m. *Charles Hills*

MAN ABOUT TOWN (IRE) 3 ch.g. Dandy Man (IRE) 123 – Zanida (IRE) 91 (Mujadil **74**
(USA) 119) [2017 67: t7.1d^6 p6g t6g* t7.1g* 6g 6m t6g Jun 30] good-quartered gelding: fair handicapper: won at Newcastle (twice) in March: stays 7f: acts on tapeta: tried in tongue tie: front runner/races prominently. *K. R. Burke*

MANANGATANG (IRE) 3 b.g. Fastnet Rock (AUS) 127 – Mona Lisa 114 (Giant's **80**
Causeway (USA) 132) [2017 76P: 9.9m^3 10g 10d p8g p8g^4 Oct 13] well-made gelding: fairly useful handicapper: third at Beverley in April: stays 1¼m: acts on polytrack and good to firm going: often races towards rear: sent to Australia. *Luca Cumani*

MANATEE BAY 7 b.g. Royal Applause 124 – Dash of Lime 67 (Bold Edge 123) [2017 **77**
88: 7g^6 7g 6m^4 6s^4 6m^3 5.9d* 6s t6g t6d Nov 10] fair handicapper nowadays: won at Carlisle in August: stays 7f: acts on tapeta, soft and good to firm going: wears headgear. *Noel Wilson*

MANCHEGO 3 b.g. Lope de Vega (IRE) 125 – Gooseberry Pie 63 (Green Desert (USA) **90**
127) [2017 79p: t8.6g* 11s 8s 8.1g t12.2g Oct 27] good-topped gelding: fairly useful performer: won maiden at Wolverhampton in April, standout effort in 2017: best effort at 8.5f: acts on tapeta: tried in cheekpieces: in tongue tie last 2 starts: sold to join Jamie Osborne 10,000 gns in October. *Hugo Palmer*

MANCINI 3 ch.g. Nathaniel (IRE) 129 – Muscovado (USA) 71 (Mr Greeley (USA) 122) **83**
[2017 11.6g^6 10g^2 9.9d^4 12g* 12g Aug 26] 67,000F, 27,000Y: fourth foal: half-brother to 1m-1¼m winner (stayed 1½m) Monsieur Rieussec (by Halling) and useful 1¼m winner Maybelater (by Mount Nelson): dam twice-raced daughter of dual Yorkshire Oaks winner Only Royale: fairly useful performer: won maiden at Pontefract in July: stays 1½m: best form on good going. *Jonathan Portman*

MANCO INCA (IRE) 2 b.g. (Apr 10) Sir Prancealot (IRE) 111 – Night Delight (IRE) 86 **–**
(Night Shift (USA)) [2017 5g 5m 6v^5 6d Aug 12] close-coupled gelding: no form, including in nursery: tried in blinkers. *Joseph Tuite*

MANDALAYAN (IRE) 2 b.g. (Jan 30) Arakan (USA) 123 – Danza Nera (IRE) 64 **78 p**
(Dansili 127) [2017 8v^2 Oct 4] €10,000Y: third foal: half-brother to useful Italian winner up to 11.5f Jalapeno (2-y-o 7.5f winner, by Windsor Knot): dam, maiden (stayed 7f), half-sister to useful sprinter Cheveton: 40/1, second in minor event at Salisbury (head behind Ace Ventura) in October: should improve. *Jonathan Portman*

MANDARIN (GER) 3 ch.c. Lope de Vega (IRE) 125 – Margarita (GER) (Lomitas 129) **98**
[2017 88p: 8v^5 p8g^5 p7g^5 Oct 25] useful handicapper: stays 1m: acts on polytrack and tapeta: tried in tongue tie: usually races close up: sold to join Archie Watson 50,000 gns in November. *Marco Botti*

MANDARIN PRINCESS 2 b.f. (Feb 16) Vale of York (IRE) 117 – Little China 77 **62**
(Kyllachy 129) [2017 7d p7s 6d^5 7g Oct 16] 2,000Y: first foal: dam 5f winner (including at 2 yrs): modest form when fifth in minor event at Yarmouth in September, standout effort. *Philip McBride*

MANDRELL (USA) 4 b.f. Dubawi (IRE) 129 – Country Star (USA) 116 (Empire Maker **–**
(USA) 129) [2017 t8g^5 Mar 9] fairly useful form on debut at 2 yrs, shaped as if amiss only subsequent start: covered by Golden Horn. *Charlie Appleby*

MANGATA (FR) 3 b.g. Cape Cross (IRE) 129 – Kong Moon (FR) (Hernando (FR) 127) **66**
[2017 p9.4g p8g 8.9v^5 9.7g 9.9d 11.7g^4 f11.1g Dec 29] fair maiden: left H-A. Pantall after sixth start: stays 11.5f: tried in cheekpieces. *Philip Kirby*

MANGO CHUTNEY 4 b.g. Sleeping Indian 122 – Crimson Topaz 75 (Hernando (FR) **79**
127) [2017 72: 7m 8g^3 7f* 7d* 7v^2 7g Sep 1] fair handicapper: won at Wetherby in June and Thirsk in July: stays 1m: acts on fibresand, firm and soft going: wears cheekpieces. *John Davies*

MANIACO 4 b.c. Galileo (IRE) 134 – Plumania 117 (Anabaa (USA) 130) [2017 114: **117**
9.9m^3 Apr 9] second foal: brother to useful French 1½m winner Solilea: dam 1m (at 2 yrs) to 1½m (Grand Prix de Saint-Cloud) winner: smart performer: won twice at 3 yrs, including listed race at Deauville: third in Prix d'Harcourt at Chantilly (1¾ lengths behind Cloth of Stars) only outing in 2017: stays 12.5f: acts on soft and good to firm going. *A. Fabre, France*

MANIPURA 4 gr.f. Sleeping Indian 122 – Ming Meng (IRE) 85 (Intikhab (USA) 135) **58 §**
[2017 70: 6m 6.1g t5s^{6} 6m^{3} 5m^{6} 6g^{4} 6g^{4} 6g^{3} 6.1g p6g Sep 26] modest handicapper nowadays: stays 6f: acts on polytrack, soft and good to firm going: wears cheekpieces: temperamental. *Derek Shaw*

MANJAAM (IRE) 4 ch.g. Tamayuz 126 – Priory Rock (IRE) 79 (Rock of Gibraltar (IRE) **100**
133) [2017 99: p13g^{2} 14g 12m 12d p11s Sep 8] workmanlike gelding: useful handicapper: second at Lingfield (½ length behind Royal Marskell) in March: stays 13f: acts on polytrack, tapeta and good to firm going: tried in headgear: often races towards rear. *Ed Dunlop*

MANKIND (FR) 2 b.g. (Feb 7) Dabirsim (FR) 120 – Pastiches 78 (Street Cry (IRE) 130) **76**
[2017 6m^{4} 6s Jul 28] fair form when fourth at Ascot (2¼ lengths behind Lethal Lunch) on first of 2 starts in minor events: will be suited by 7f+. *George Scott*

MANNERS MAKETH MAN (IRE) 3 b.c. Lope de Vega (IRE) 125 – Dabawiyah **54**
(IRE) 61 (Intikhab (USA) 135) [2017 8s^{6} p8g 10.1v^{6} Oct 1] modest form in maidens. *Ralph Beckett*

MANNERS PLEASE 3 b.g. Sixties Icon 125 – Humility 66 (Polar Falcon (USA) 126) **78**
[2017 77p: 7f^{2} 7.4d^{6} Jul 25] compact gelding: fair handicapper: stays 7f: acts on polytrack, firm and soft going: sold 2,000 gns, sent to Greece. *Ralph Beckett*

MANNY OWENS (IRE) 5 b.g. Manduro (GER) 135 – Arabian Coral (IRE) (Intikhab **74**
(USA) 135) [2017 75: 13.3v^{4} 11.6g^{3} Sep 7] sturdy gelding: fair handicapper: stays 13.5f: acts on polytrack, good to firm and heavy going: has worn headgear: usually wears tongue tie: winning hurdler. *Jonjo O'Neill*

MAN OF LA MANCHA (IRE) 4 b.g. Zoffany (IRE) 121 – Sarella Loren (USA) 69 **–**
(Theatrical) [2017 50: p7d Feb 3] modest maiden, well held sole outing in 2017: stays 7f: acts on good to firm going: in cheekpieces last 2 starts: tried in tongue tie: often races towards rear. *Ben Haslam*

MAN OF VERVE (IRE) 3 b.g. Dandy Man (IRE) 123 – She's Our Rock (IRE) (Rock **–**
of Gibraltar (IRE) 133) [2017 77: 6g 7s Jun 6] fair form at 2 yrs, little impact in handicaps in 2017: best effort at 6f: acts on heavy going: usually races close up. *John Quinn*

MANOLITO 5 b.g. High Chaparral (IRE) 132 – Break Time (Dansili 127) [2017 79: f8g^{5} **–**
Jan 2] good-bodied gelding: fairly useful at best, shaped as if amiss sole outing in 2017: stays 8.5f: acts on polytrack and tapeta: usually wears tongue tie. *Hughie Morrison*

MANOMINE 8 b.g. Manduro (GER) 135 – Fascinating Hill (FR) (Danehill (USA) 126) **67**
[2017 53: 9.7m^{2} p12g^{2} 10.2m 12.8g^{4} 10.3m^{5} 12.5g* p10.7g t12.4d^{3} Dec 16] lengthy gelding: fair handicapper: won at Musselburgh in July: stays 2m: acts on polytrack, tapeta, good to firm and good to soft going: has worn headgear: front runner/races prominently. *R. K. Watson, Ireland*

MANOR PARK 2 b.g. (Feb 13) Medicean 128 – Jadeel (Green Desert (USA) 127) [2017 **73**
7s^{6} 7g^{6} 7.6v^{2} Sep 15] smallish, close-coupled gelding: fair form: best effort when sixth in minor event at Chester (5¾ lengths behind Mutakatif) in September. *Alan King*

MANSFIELD 4 b.g. Exceed And Excel (AUS) 126 – Jane Austen (IRE) 104 (Galileo **80**
(IRE) 134) [2017 p8f p6g^{6} 8g 8s 8.2s 9m 10d p7g^{2} t7.2g^{2} Dec 13] fairly useful handicapper: second at Lingfield and Wolverhampton in December: stays 1m: acts on polytrack and good to soft going: in hood last 2 starts: sometimes slowly away, usually races freely. *Michael Wigham*

MANSHOOD (IRE) 4 b.g. Iffraaj 127 – Thawrah (IRE) (Green Desert (USA) 127) [2017 **94**
71: 7.1g^{4} 6v^{6} t5s^{2} 5s^{2} 6s^{2} 6d* 6d 6s* 6s^{6} Sep 8] fairly useful handicapper: won at Hamilton in July and August (by nose from Distant Past): best at 6f: acts on tapeta and soft going: wears blinkers. *Paul Midgley*

MANSON 4 ch.g. Equiano (FR) 127 – Swain's Gold (USA) (Swain (IRE) 134) [2017 104: **101**
9.9g p10g^{3} 8m^{5} p8g^{3} 8g p8g Oct 4] rather leggy gelding: useful handicapper: third at Kempton (4½ lengths behind Abareeq) in March and Chelmsford (2¼ lengths behind Mustashry) in August: stays 1¼m: acts on polytrack and good to firm going: in cheekpieces last 3 starts. *Dominic Ffrench Davis*

MANTHOOR (IRE) 2 gr.c. (Feb 6) Swiss Spirit 117 – Enchanting Way (Linamix (FR) **85**
127) [2017 6.1m^{6} 6d^{2} 6d^{2} p7g^{2} t6d^{5} Nov 4] €72,000F, £110,000Y: sixth foal: half-brother to 3 winners, including smart 5f to (at 2 yrs) 7f winner Silver Rainbow (by Starspangledbanner): dam unraced half-sister to very smart winner up to 1¼m Ashkal Way: fairly useful maiden: stays 7f: acts on polytrack and good to soft going: front runner/races prominently. *Owen Burrows*

MANTON GRANGE 4 b.g. Siyouni (FR) 122 – Emulate 81 (Alhaarth (IRE) 126) [2017 **96**
80: 8f^{2} 8.3g^{3} 7d* 8.1m^{2} p7g* Aug 22] lengthy gelding: useful handicapper: won at Leicester in June and Kempton (by 3 lengths from Intransigent) in August: stays 8.5f: acts on polytrack, firm and good to soft going: tried in cheekpieces: often races towards rear. *George Baker*

MANY A TALE 3 br.f. Poet's Voice 126 – Rustam (Dansili 127) [2017 82: 7m^{5} 7.4d^{4} **76**
t7.2g^{6} p8g p7g Oct 5] fair handicapper: stays 7.5f: acts on tapeta and good to soft going: tried in cheekpieces. *Ismail Mohammed*

MANY DREAMS (IRE) 4 b.f. Kodiac 112 – Deeday Bay (IRE) 78 (Brave Act 119) [2017 **75**
72: 7d* 8d^{2} 8.1g^{6} 8v^{5} 8g^{6} 7.6s^{6} 7g^{2} Oct 17] lengthy filly: fair handicapper: won at Salisbury (apprentice) in May: stays 1m: acts on polytrack and good to soft going. *Gary Moore*

MANY WATERS (USA) 3 b.f. Street Cry (IRE) 130 – Satulagi (USA) 98 (Officer (USA) **84**
120) [2017 p8m^{4} p10g^{2} 10g^{6} 10d^{2} t12.2g^{4} 9.9d^{2} 10.5g 9.5f^{5} a7f^{2} a5.5g^{2} a8.3f^{2} Nov 29] fifth foal: half-sister to 6f/7f winner (including at 2 yrs) One More Roman (by Holy Roman Emperor), later successful in Qatar, and winner up to 11f Teolagi (2-y-o 1m winner, by Teofilo): dam 2-y-o 5f-7f winner: fairly useful maiden: runner-up 6 times: left Andrew Balding after sixth start, Wesley Ward after ninth: stays 1½m: acts on polytrack, tapeta and good to soft going: tried in headgear. *Brett T. Santangelo, USA*

MAOI CHINN TIRE (IRE) 10 b.g. Mull of Kintyre (USA) 114 – Primrose And Rose **74**
72 (Primo Dominie 121) [2017 79: 14g^{5} 14f^{5} Jun 19] sturdy gelding: fair handicapper: stays 2m: acts on polytrack, fibresand, firm and soft going: has worn headgear, including last 4 starts: has worn tongue tie. *Jennie Candlish*

MAORI BOB (IRE) 3 b.g. Big Bad Bob (IRE) 118 – Tekhania (IRE) (Dalakhani (IRE) **92**
133) [2017 59: p10g* t10.2d^{5} 12g^{2} 13d^{2} 16v^{4} 12.1g* 12.1m* 11.8d* Sep 12] fairly useful handicapper: won at Lingfield (apprentice) in February, Beverley (twice) in August and Leicester (by ¾ length from Medalla de Oro) in September: stays 13f: acts on polytrack, good to firm and good to soft going: often races prominently/travels strongly. *Michael Bell*

MA PEEK (USA) 4 b.c. Arch (USA) 127 – Downtown Drifter (USA) (Devil His Due **–**
(USA) 126) [2017 68: 12.1m May 5] tall colt: lightly-raced maiden: in tongue tie last 2 starts: dead. *Brian Meehan*

MAPLE STIRRUP (IRE) 5 b.m. Duke of Marmalade (IRE) 132 – Street Shaana (FR) **57**
111 (Darshaan 133) [2017 66: t16.3g t16.3g 14g 16m^{4} 16g^{4} 17.1v Sep 21] modest maiden: stays 16.5f: acts on polytrack, tapeta and good to soft going: has worn headgear, including in 2017. *Patrick Holmes*

MAPPED (USA) 2 b.c. (Apr 14) Mizzen Mast (USA) 121 – Geographic (USA) (Empire **79 p**
Maker (USA) 129) [2017 8d^{3} Oct 27] useful-looking colt: has scope: brother to 2 winners, including 7f winner Market Town (later smart performer up to 1½m in Hong Kong as Harbour Master), and half-brother to 3 winners, including 1¼m-1½m winner Earthly (by Spring At Last): dam unraced half-sister to Kentucky Derby and Belmont Stakes runner-up Aptitude: 33/1, third in minor event at Newbury (3 lengths behind Extra Elusive) on debut: will be suited by 1¼m: sure to do better. *Charles Hills*

MAPPIN TIME (IRE) 9 b.g. Orientate (USA) 127 – Different Story (USA) (Stravinsky **90**
(USA) 133) [2017 85, a93: f5g^{3} Jan 1] sturdy gelding: fairly useful handicapper: third at Southwell on sole outing in 2017: stays 6f: acts on all-weather, firm and good to soft going: wears headgear: often races towards rear. *Tim Easterby*

MARAAKIB (IRE) 5 b.g. Dark Angel (IRE) 113 – Mrs Cee (IRE) 71 (Orpen (USA) 116) **78**
[2017 99: 9.8m 10.3m 11.9s 9.8d^{5} 9.1s 10s^{6} 9.9g^{5} 10.1m^{2} t9.5g^{6} 9v 10g 10g^{2} t10.2g^{2} 10.2d 10.2v^{3} p10s^{4} t8s^{2} t8.6d^{6} f11.1g^{5} Dec 21] tall gelding: fair handicapper nowadays: stays 1¼m: acts on all-weather, good to firm and heavy going: has worn cheekpieces. *David O'Meara*

MARATHA (IRE) 3 gr.g. Cape Cross (IRE) 129 – Middle Persia 76 (Dalakhani (IRE) **90**
133) [2017 f8.1g^{2} 8.3d^{2} 9.8d^{5} 8.3g* 10m 8d^{4} 8.3d^{3} 8.3g p8s^{4} p8g^{3} t9.5d* Dec 27] 90,000Y: sturdy gelding: fourth foal: half-brother to 10.7f/11.5f winner Kilimanjaro (by High Chaparral) and 1¼m/10.7f winner Mawaany (by Teofilo), both useful: dam, 1m winner, half-sister to very smart performer up to 1¼m Mars and smart 2-y-o 7f winner Gustav Klimt: fairly useful handicapper: won at Nottingham in July and Wolverhampton (by 2 lengths from Perfect Soldier) in December: left Simon Crisford after fourth start: should stay 1¼m: acts on all-weather and good to soft going: tried in visor: in tongue tie last 5 starts: often races prominently. *Stuart Williams*

MARAUDER 5 b.g. Thewayyouare (USA) 117 – Louise d'Arzens 73 (Anabaa (USA) **–**
130) [2017 p8g^{5} p12g^{4} p12g^{6} p10g Apr 26] little form. *Henry Candy*

MARBLE BAR 2 b.g. (Apr 3) Makfi 130 – Presbyterian Nun (IRE) 100 (Daylami (IRE) 138) [2017 7m^{6} 7g^{5} 7m 8.3v^{2} Nov 8] sturdy gelding: fair form: will stay beyond 1m. *Henry Candy* **69**

MARBLE STATUE 2 b.f. (Feb 15) Makfi 130 – Czarna Roza (Polish Precedent (USA) 131) [2017 7g^{5} Sep 7] 35,000Y: half-sister to several winners, including smart winner up to 1m Mabait (2-y-o 6f winner, by Kyllachy) and 1m winner Cape To Cuba (by Harbour Watch): dam unraced: 10/1, fifth in maiden at Salisbury (4¾ lengths behind Clairette) in September: entitled to progress. *Ralph Beckett* **69 p**

MARBOOH (IRE) 4 b.g. Dark Angel (IRE) 113 – Muluk (IRE) 83 (Rainbow Quest (USA) 134) [2017 88: 8m p7d^{3} 8.5m^{6} t7.2g^{6} 7g 7.6d^{6} p8d^{6} t9.5m p7s Dec 8] lengthy gelding: fair handicapper: lost form in 2017 (had several trainers): stays 1m: acts on polytrack, tapeta and good to firm going: tried in visor: often wears tongue tie. *Miss Joey Ellis* **78 d**

MARCANO (IRE) 5 b.g. Arcano (IRE) 122 – Aquatint (Dansili 127) [2017 88: 8.3m^{2} 8m p10g^{pu} Jun 3] fairly useful handicapper: second at Windsor (neck behind Commodity) in April: stayed 1m: acted on soft and good to firm going: wore headgear/tongue tie: dead. *Rod Millman* **85**

MARCELLA 2 b.f. (Mar 30) Showcasing 117 – Cool In The Shade 80 (Pastoral Pursuits 127) [2017 6v 7g Oct 14] £2,000Y: second foal: dam 5f winner: well beaten in maiden/minor event. *David C. Griffiths* **–**

MARCHINGONTOGETHER 2 ch.f. (Apr 29) Havana Gold (IRE) 118 – Transvaal Sky 90 (Avonbridge 123) [2017 5g* 5f p6g^{6} 7.2s^{5} Oct 9] 1,000F, £800Y: rather leggy filly: third foal: dam 2-y-o 6f winner: fair form: won maiden at Leicester in May: should stay 7f. *Ivan Furtado* **79**

MARCONI 2 ch.g. (Apr 28) Monsieur Bond (IRE) 120 – Tamara Bay 69 (Selkirk (USA) 129) [2017 5d 6s^{5} 6g 6g Sep 27] little impact in minor events/nursery. *John Davies* **–**

MARETTIMO (IRE) 3 b.g. Harbour Watch (IRE) 121 – Renowned (IRE) (Darshaan 133) [2017 67p: p10m 10m p12g 10.2g 6g^{6} Jul 17] tall gelding: modest maiden: stays 1¼m. *Charles Hills* **59**

MARGHERITA 3 b.f. Mayson 124 – Phillipina 105 (Medicean 128) [2017 71p: t8.6g^{3} p7g^{3} 7m^{3} Jun 17] close-coupled filly: fair form in maidens: stays 8.5f: sold 25,000 gns in July, sent to Qatar. *Roger Varian* **72**

MARGUB 2 ch.c. (Apr 24) Bated Breath 125 – Bahamian Babe 94 (Bahamian Bounty 116) [2017 6g^{5} Jun 2] £30,000Y: fifth foal: half-brother to 2-y-o 7f winner Bahamian Boy (by Paco Boy): dam, 5f winner (including at 2 yrs), sister to useful sprinter Reflektor: 12/1, fifth in minor event at Goodwood (2¾ lengths behind Snazzy Jazzy) in June: better to come. *Marcus Tregoning* **66 p**

MARIAH'S MELODY (IRE) 2 gr.f. (May 22) Graydar (USA) 122 – In Seconds (USA) (Giant's Causeway (USA) 132) [2017 5.1d 7g^{4} 6.1g^{5} 7v^{6} Sep 15] €12,000Y: neat filly: sixth foal: half-sister to 3 winners in USA: dam, US 1m/8.5f winner, half-sister to very smart 1m-1½m winner Lear Spear: little impact in minor events/nursery: tried in hood. *Lisa Williamson* **–**

MARICRUZ (IRE) 2 gr.f. (Feb 27) Most Improved (IRE) 119 – Miss Fancy Pants 92 (Act One 124) [2017 p7g^{6} t7.1d^{4} Nov 10] €15,000Y: third foal: dam, 1¼m-1½m winner (also won over hurdles), half-sister to very smart 1m-1½m winner Sweet Lightning: modest form when sixth in maiden at Dundalk on first of 2 starts: should stay 1m+. *John McConnell, Ireland* **62**

MARIEE 4 b.f. Archipenko (USA) 127 – Maria di Scozia 90 (Selkirk (USA) 129) [2017 87: p8g^{3} t8d^{2} t10.2g^{2} p8g^{5} 9.9f^{3} 10g^{5} May 9] lengthy filly: fairly useful handicapper: placed 4 times in 2017: stays 1¼m: acts on polytrack, tapeta, firm and good to soft going: has hinted at temperament. *Mark Johnston* **87**

MARIE JOSEPHE 3 b.f. Cape Cross (IRE) 129 – Maria Letizia 78 (Galileo (IRE) 134) [2017 10m^{4} 12s^{4} 10m* 10m^{2} 9.9m^{2} 9.9g Sep 3] rather unfurnished filly: first foal: dam, maiden (stayed 1¾m), half-sister to useful performer up to 1½m Queen of Naples out of useful half-sister to Derby winner Oath: fairly useful performer: won maiden at Windsor in June: second in handicaps at same course in July and Brighton in August: stays 1¼m: acts on good to firm going: front runner/races prominently, often travels strongly: sold 26,000 gns in December. *Richard Hughes* **88**

MARIE OF LYON 3 b.f. Royal Applause 124 – Virginia Hall 107 (Medicean 128) [2017 85: 8m 7g^{4} 7d^{3} 6s 6d* 6v* 6g 6m^{2} Oct 14] sturdy filly: useful handicapper: won at Brighton and Pontefract (by 2¼ lengths from Tirania) in September: second in listed race at **100**

Newmarket (¾ length behind Eartha Kitt) in October: stays 7f: acts on good to firm and heavy going. *Richard Fahey*

MARIE TOULOUSE (IRE) 2 b.f. (Apr 2) Oasis Dream 129 – Virginia Waters (USA) 116 (Kingmambo (USA) 125) [2017 t8.6g Nov 29] €180,000Y: half-sister to useful winner up to 1m Emperor Claudius (2-y-o 6f winner, by Giant's Causeway), later successful in Hong Kong, and 7f-1¼m winner Dove Mountain (by Danehill Dancer): dam 7f (including at 2 yrs)/1m (1000 Guineas) winner: 28/1, needed experience when well held in minor event at Wolverhampton: should do better. *K. R. Burke* **– p**

MARILYN 3 ch.f. Sixties Icon 125 – Donatia (Shamardal (USA) 129) [2017 75p: 8m 10.2d⁶ 10.1g p8d p8g⁶ 8g⁶ Oct 16] well-made filly: fair handicapper: probably stays 1m: best form on good going: tried in cheekpieces. *Chris Wall* **66**

MARILYN M (IRE) 2 b.f. (Apr 25) Red Jazz (USA) 125 – Jilly Choo 69 (Bahamian Bounty 116) [2017 5g p7g Dec 20] €5,000F, 52,000 2-y-o: third foal: dam, maiden (stayed 7f), half-sister to useful winner up to 9f Kinsya: little impact in maiden/minor event. *George Scott* **–**

MARINE ONE 3 b.g. Frankel 147 – Marine Bleue (IRE) 109 (Desert Prince (IRE) 130) [2017 8m⁵ 10d⁴ p12s³ t12.4g² p13.3g² Oct 26] half-brother to several winners, including useful French 9f-1½m winner Marina Piccola (by Halling) and useful performer up to 1m Wednaan (2-y-o 6f winner, by Dubawi): dam French 7f/1m winner: fairly useful maiden: stays 12.5f: acts on polytrack and tapeta: usually races nearer last than first, often freely. *David Simcock* **84**

MARJU'S QUEST (IRE) 7 b.g. Marju (IRE) 127 – Queen's Quest (Rainbow Quest (USA) 134) [2017 p12g⁶ p16g Nov 7] fairly useful at best, very lightly raced and little form since 2013: stays 1½m: acts on firm going: free-going sort. *Adrian Wintle* **–**

MARKET CHOICE (IRE) 4 b.g. Majestic Missile (IRE) 118 – Ron's Secret 92 (Efisio 120) [2017 81: 6g⁶ 7s⁶ 5g 5.9d⁵ 6s³ 5.9d 6v⁵ 6s 6g 5s⁶ 6v⁵ t6g Dec 6] fair handicapper: stays 6f: acts on heavy going: sometimes in headgear in 2017: often races towards rear: temperament under suspicion. *Tracy Waggott* **71**

MARKHAN (USA) 4 b.g. Birdstone (USA) 129 – Royal Flush (USA) (Smart Strike (CAN) 121) [2017 101: 8g 7s 9g³ 8.1g⁵ p8g p8g Oct 26] useful performer at 3 yrs, below that level in 2017: stays 1m: acts on polytrack and good to soft going: has worn headgear, including final start: wears tongue tie: sometimes slowly away: sold 14,000 gns in November. *David Marnane, Ireland* **85**

MARK HOPKINS 5 b.g. Mount Nelson 125 – Halska (Unfuwain (USA) 131) [2017 –: 14.1m 12m⁴ 14.2m* 13.9m⁵ 14g 16d³ 16g Aug 12] strong gelding: useful handicapper: won at Salisbury (by 3½ lengths from Volpone Jelois) in May: third at Ascot (8 lengths behind Uae King) in July: stays 2m: acts on soft and good to firm going: usually leads. *David Elsworth* **95**

MARK OF APPROVAL (USA) 3 ch.g. Lemon Drop Kid (USA) 131 – Agreeable Miss (USA) (Speightstown (USA) 124) [2017 8m³ f8.1g* May 8] $400,000Y: good-topped gelding: fourth foal: half-brother to useful 2-y-o 6f winner Faydhan (by War Front) and a winner in USA by Arch: dam unraced out of US Grade 2 8.5f winner Sweet And Ready: useful form: won maiden at Southwell (by 5 lengths from Maratha) in May: remains with potential. *John Gosden* **99 p**

MARK OF EXCELLENCE (IRE) 3 ch.g. Sepoy (AUS) 129 – Cheyenne Star (IRE) 115 (Mujahid (USA) 125) [2017 7s⁶ 8.1g⁶ 8m⁴ 8.2g p7.5g Dec 16] maiden: left Saeed bin Suroor after fourth start: seemingly best effort at 7.5f: tried in headgear. *N. Clement, France* **73 ?**

MARMAJUKE BAY 4 b.g. Duke of Marmalade (IRE) 132 – Shimoni 90 (Mark of Esteem (IRE) 137) [2017 91: p12g² t12.2g² 11.9s 11.6m* 14g⁴ 14g 11.6g* 12g⁵ 11.8d Oct 30] good-topped gelding: useful handicapper: won at Haydock in June and September (by 2 lengths from Azari): stays 1¾m: acts on polytrack, tapeta, soft and good to firm going: wears cheekpieces: often races prominently. *Mark Usher* **99**

MARMALAD (IRE) 5 b.g. Duke of Marmalade (IRE) 132 – Primissima (GER) (Second Set (IRE) 127) [2017 69§: t9.5g p8g Mar 24] close-coupled gelding: fair handicapper, well held both starts in 2017: stays 1¼m: acts on polytrack, tapeta and good to firm going: has worn headgear: temperamental. *Shaun Lycett* **–**

MARMELO 4 b.c. Duke of Marmalade (IRE) 132 – Capriolla 55 (In The Wings 128) [2017 106: 14.9g* 13.9d⁵ 13.9g² 14.9g* 11.9g⁶ 15.9g Nov 7] very smart performer: won Prix de Barbeville at Chantilly (by 2½ lengths from Bateel) in April and Prix Kergorlay at Deauville (by 1¼ lengths from Desert Skyline) in August: also creditable efforts in **120**

Yorkshire Cup at York (1¼ lengths fifth to Dartmouth), Prix Maurice de Nieuil at Saint-Cloud (1¼ lengths second to Talismanic) and Caulfield Cup (Handicap) (2¾ lengths equal sixth to Boom Time): ninth behind Rekindling in Melbourne Cup (Handicap) at Flemington final outing: should stay 2m: acts on polytrack and soft going: often races close up. *Hughie Morrison*

MARMION 5 b.g. Cape Cross (IRE) 129 – Margarula (IRE) 120 (Doyoun 124) [2017 t13.9m^{6} 10.3g p10g 12d* 12m^{5} 13.1s 9.8d 11.6g^{6} 12.1s^{3} t12.4g 10.2d p12g Nov 18] tall gelding: fair handicapper: won at Ripon in June: stays 1½m: acts on good to firm and good to soft going: usually wears hood: usually races freely. *Les Eyre* **76 a56**

MARNIE JAMES 2 b.g. (Mar 30) Camacho 118 – Privy Garden (IRE) (Oasis Dream 129) [2017 5m^{5} 5m^{2} 5m^{6} 5m 5g* 6d 5v* Oct 16] 34,000F, £35,000Y: stocky gelding: second foal: dam, French 9f winner (including at 2 yrs), half-sister to smart performer up to 2m Century and useful 1¼m/1½m winner Apphia: fairly useful performer: won nursery at York in July and minor event at Musselburgh (by 3½ lengths from Ace of Spades) in October: best form at 5f: acts on good to firm and heavy going: in tongue tie last 3 starts. *Iain Jardine* **83**

MAROC 4 b.g. Rock of Gibraltar (IRE) 133 – Zietory 107 (Zieten (USA) 118) [2017 80, a66: t12.2m^{5} 11.6m^{3} 10s^{4} 10.2d^{3} 11.6d^{2} 11.4g^{2} 11.4m^{4} Aug 13] tall gelding: fairly useful maiden: second in handicaps at Lingfield and Windsor in July: stays 11.5f: acts on soft and good to firm going: wears cheekpieces: has worn tongue tie: front runner/races prominently: has looked tricky ride. *Nikki Evans* **80**

MARQOOM 3 ch.c. New Approach (IRE) 132 – Night Frolic 68 (Night Shift (USA)) [2017 t8g^{6} 12g^{2} 9.8g^{3} 12g 12g Jul 3] fair maiden: stays 1½m: raced only on tapeta/good going: front runner/races prominently: temperament under suspicion: sold 22,000 gns, sent to Germany. *Mark Johnston* **73**

MARQUEE CLUB 3 b.c. Sixties Icon 125 – Rose Cheval (USA) 74 (Johannesburg (USA) 127) [2017 81: t6g^{2} t6g* p6g* p6g^{2} t5g^{4} p7f^{6} p6g Apr 14] fairly useful handicapper: won at Newcastle and Kempton (by 2 lengths from Kamra) in January: second at Lingfield in February: stays 6f: acts on polytrack, tapeta, good to firm and good to soft going: tried in blinkers: usually races close up. *Jamie Osborne* **94**

MARSEILLE (IRE) 3 b.f. Excelebration (IRE) 133 – Marlinka 95 (Marju (IRE) 127) [2017 71p: t5s* t5s^{2} 5.6d^{2} 6v^{2} 6.1g Aug 18] sturdy filly: fairly useful performer: won maiden at Newcastle in April: runner-up 3 times in handicaps: stays 6f: acts on tapeta and heavy going: often travels strongly. *Julie Camacho* **81**

MARSHA (IRE) 4 b.f. Acclamation 118 – Marlinka 95 (Marju (IRE) 127) [2017 121: 5m* 5f^{3} 5f^{2} 5s^{3} 5g* 5d^{2} 5f^{6} Nov 4] **130**

It's often said that such-and-such a top filly 'will be worth her weight in gold' as a broodmare. Although not literally true, Marsha came closer to it than any filly or mare previously sold at auction in Europe when she made 6,000,000 guineas at the December Sales. Her sale price—a record for any thoroughbred sold at auction in Europe—smashed the previous record for a filly of racing age or a broodmare sold in Europe which had been set by Irish Oaks winner Chicquita who fetched €6,000,000 at the Goffs November Sale in 2013, the same year that Immortal Verse set the previous mark for the Newmarket December Sales when changing hands for 4,700,000 guineas. The fighting policy adopted with Marsha by her owners the long-standing Elite Racing Club, which draws its members from a wide base, and trainer Sir Mark Prescott saw her establish herself as one of the top sprinting fillies trained in Britain in the past forty years. Her victories in the Prix de l'Abbaye de Longchamp (as a three-year-old) and the Nunthorpe Stakes, in which she snatched victory from American speedball Lady Aurelia in most dramatic fashion, gave her a record that few sprinting fillies can match.

In those forty years under review, no filly has a record in European sprints that compares with Habibti's successive victories as a three-year-old in the July Cup, the Nunthorpe (then the William Hill Sprint Championship), the Sprint Cup at Haydock (by seven lengths) and the Prix de l'Abbaye in 1983 (she added the King's Stand as a four-year-old before a winning run of six came to an end). Habibti shares top spot among the female sprinters of Timeform's experience with Black Caviar, 'The Wonder From Down Under'. Apart from that pair, and Black Caviar's illustrious Australian compatriot Miss Andretti, who won the King's Stand Stakes on a visit to Royal Ascot in 2007, there have been very few fillies who have recorded

Lot 1848
6,000,000 gns
EUR 7,134,120
JPY 955,628,730
AUD 11,136,510
USD 8,469,090
Lot 1847 8,000 gns
£25,000
Tattersalls October
Book 1 Bonus
£25,000
Tattersalls October
Book 1 Bonus
Tattersalls
Tattersalls

two or more Group 1 sprint victories (not counting two-year-olds) among those who have had essays in *Racehorses*. There are no all-aged Group 1 sprints in Europe restricted to fillies and mares, who, by contrast, have a programme of races against their own sex at a mile and over middle distances, and soon will have over long distances too. The top sprinting fillies have to do it the hard way, by taking on the top colts in receipt of the standard weight-for-sex allowance. Marsha's victory at York maintained the good run by fillies in the Nunthorpe in recent years—they have now won six of the last seven renewals, two of those achieved by another of the top sprinting fillies of recent times Mecca's Angel—but fillies have generally struggled in the top races (their best long-term record is in the Abbaye, not the Nunthorpe). The estimable Lochsong won all three of the principal European events over five furlongs open to three-year-olds and upwards, winning the Prix de l'Abbaye twice, in 1993 and 1994, the Nunthorpe in 1993 and the King's Stand (which was a Group 2 at the time) in 1994. Irish-trained Committed is another with three Group 1 five-furlong sprints to her name, having won the Nunthorpe (as the William Hill Sprint Championship) and the Prix de l'Abbaye—with Habibti behind her in both races—as a four-year-old in 1984, and the Abbaye for a second time as a five-year-old. The brilliant Marwell included the King's Stand and the Abbaye in her run of sprint victories as a three-year-old in 1981, but she completes the scanty list of European fillies who have won two or more open-aged Group 1 races over the minimum trip in the last forty years. Marwell, Habibti, Committed, Lochsong and Mecca's Angel provide illustrious company for Marsha.

Marsha began her campaign as a four-year-old in the Longholes Palace House Stakes on Two Thousand Guineas day. The Palace House is a Group 3 with a scale of penalties for pattern winners which meant that Marsha carried an extra 7 lb for her win in the Prix de l'Abbaye the previous autumn and had to concede weight all round at Newmarket in a field of fifteen which also included the unpenalised runner-up in the Abbaye, Washington DC, who started 100/30 favourite, with Priceless and Muthmir also preferred to 8/1-shot Marsha in the betting. Just as Lochsong had done twenty-three years earlier (the season after her first win in the Abbaye), Marsha was able to defy the Group 1 penalty and record an effort that was even more meritorious—judged on form—than the one she had recorded at Chantilly seven months earlier. Always handily placed and travelling well on the stands rail, in a race run at a strong gallop, Marsha led approaching the final furlong and was driven out to hold off Washington DC by a neck with the 2015 King's Stand and Abbaye winner Goldream a length away third. It seemed unlikely that Marsha's very smart performance would be bettered in too many of the top sprints over the course of the season and she was sent off favourite to beat transatlantic challenger Lady Aurelia, a stunning winner of the Queen Mary at Royal Ascot the previous year, in the King's Stand Stakes. Lady Aurelia turned in a brilliant display—one of the very best from a sprinting filly in the history of the *Racehorses* series—and Marsha was far from disgraced in finishing third, reproducing her Palace House form. Finishing strongly, she would have snatched second in another few strides from the previous year's King's Stand winner Profitable who also ran right up to his very best. Marsha was beaten in her next two races, at odds on (beaten a short head by Caspian Prince) dropped in grade in the Sapphire Stakes at the Curragh and then by Battaash and Profitable in the very valuable King George Stakes at Goodwood (a Group 1 in all but name nowadays).

The Coolmore Nunthorpe Stakes at York in August looked like being one of the races of the season—over any distance—and was widely billed as a match-up between the spectacular Lady Aurelia (reunited with Frankie Dettori who had missed the ride at Royal Ascot through injury) and another three-year-old, the potential new 'king of the sprinters' Battaash whose top-class performance in the King George Stakes had followed two equally impressive victories in lesser company at Sandown earlier in the summer. That pair dominated the betting at 11/10-on and

December Sales—a battle between representatives of Coolmore and Godolphin has the Newmarket sale-ring spellbound before the filly Marsha finally falls to Coolmore for 6,000,000 guineas, a record for any horse at a European auction

11/4 respectively, while Marsha shared third favouritism at 8/1 with Profitable, with the seven other runners starting at odds ranging from 20/1 to 66/1. York's flat five-furlong course suits performers with all-out speed, which both Lady Aurelia and Battaash had spectacularly displayed, and, as the ground dried out to good (though with some ease still in it) after heavy rain earlier in the week, everything seemed set fair for a much heralded showdown. Not for the first time, however, a so-called two-horse race failed to live up to its billing and produced a story different from the one widely anticipated. Battaash got himself too worked up in the preliminaries to do himself justice on the day and, with Lady Aurelia out in front entering the final furlong, it looked as if the Nunthorpe's first prize was going to follow that for the King's Stand across the Atlantic. Without detracting too much from Marsha's splendid victory, it could be that going flat out from the moment the stalls opened, and ending up a little isolated towards the far side, contributed to Lady Aurelia's defeat by her strong-finishing and very game rival. Lady Aurelia was on the bridle until Dettori asked her to quicken approaching the final furlong where she extended her lead to at least two lengths. Marsha was making headway, though, after being covered up for a long way, and was soon into second with Lady Aurelia to aim at. Edging left towards her rival over the final furlong as she came under very strong pressure, Marsha kept on strongly to join Lady Aurelia right on the post, the pair three and three quarter lengths clear of third-placed Cotai Glory and clearly having recorded top-class form (Battaash came fourth).

In the immediate moments after Lady Aurelia and Marsha had crossed the line, Frankie Dettori seemed certain Lady Aurelia had won, standing up in his irons, punching the air and putting a finger to his lips. 'I'm speechless, I thought I had won a neck,' Dettori said after the photo-finish decided the race in Marsha's favour by a nose, the minimum margin of victory. Marsha's jockey Luke Morris initially also seemed to think he had been beaten, dropping his head in evident disappointment after crossing the line. Dettori couldn't be blamed for Lady Aurelia's defeat—his wasn't a case of being caught unawares—and he suffered only the embarrassment of having started celebrating prematurely, much as Kevin Shea had done on South African challenger Lizard's Desire in the Dubai World Cup in 2010 when another of the riders in a three-way photo had extended his whip to him in a congratulatory gesture just after crossing the line. The uncertainty over which horse had won that day—the verdict went to the third horse in the finish Gloria de Campeao by a nose—lasted longer than it did at York, with the judge taking several minutes to decipher the photo (Channel 4's live coverage of the race ran out of air time before the result was announced). Gloria de Campeao couldn't hold off Lizard's Desire and Kevin Shea for a second time when they met two months later, going down by half a length when the pair filled the first two places in the International Cup at Kranji in Singapore.

Marsha and Lady Aurelia met for a third time in the Breeders' Cup Turf Sprint at Del Mar in November, a race that has yet to be won by a European challenger and which Lady Aurelia was expected to dominate. The Del Mar turf track is tight, even by American standards, with the sprint races run round two bends

Longholes Palace House Stakes, Newmarket—Marsha successfully concedes weight all round, beating Washington DC and Goldream (cheekpieces)

Coolmore Nunthorpe Stakes, York—
Marsha produces a career best to catch Lady Aurelia (No.12), the first two pulling clear and both showing top-class form; Battaash (epaulets) is below form in fourth

before a short finishing straight of just over a furlong. The track hardly seemed ideal for Marsha but connections decided to take on Lady Aurelia after Marsha followed up her Nunthorpe win with second place in the Prix de l'Abbaye in October. Marsha started favourite at Chantilly but Battaash returned to form in some style to beat her by four lengths, with third-placed Profitable replicating his earlier placed efforts in the King's Stand and the King George Stakes. Marsha clearly didn't reproduce her Nunthorpe form, unable to make any impression on Battaash, and she was below form at Del Mar too where she still managed sixth, beaten a length and a quarter, behind 40/1 winner Stormy Liberal, beating the other European challengers Washington DC and Cotai Glory, as well as the very disappointing Lady Aurelia.

The lengthy, well-made Marsha is by the sprint stallion Acclamation whose own achievements on the track, which included a win in the Diadem and placed efforts in the King's Stand and the Nunthorpe, hardly foretold the influence he was to have at stud. Another of his Group 1 winners, Dark Angel (who was retired to stud after his two-year-old days), is now the busiest specialist Flat sire in Britain and Ireland (he covered 223 mares in 2017) and is the sire of Battaash and another of the season's top sprinters, the July Cup and Sprint Cup winner Harry Angel, as well as of Mecca's Angel. Acclamation's own fee at Rathbarry Stud in Ireland has been increased from €30,000 to €40,000 for 2018 after he was also represented in the latest season by another Group 1 performer, the Prix de la Foret winner Aclaim. Acclamation's ability to sire fast-maturing stock, and sprinters renowned for their toughness as well as their ability, accounts only partly for his popularity. The fact that the ubiquitous Northern Dancer is so far back in his pedigree (he is descended from him through his great grandsire, El Gran Senor's full brother Try My Best, the sire of Waajib) makes Acclamation—not to mention his son Dark Angel—an interesting outcross.

Diversity has been anything but a notable feature in the bloodstock industry over the last forty years or so as breeders have become fixated on Northern Dancer and his sons and grandsons. The Coolmore empire was built largely on the success of Northern Dancer's son Sadler's Wells which has been consolidated by the remarkable achievements of Sadler's Wells's own son Galileo, both stallions proving versatile while being renowned principally as influences for stamina. Northern Dancer, however, became virtually all things to all breeders, some of his other sons, such as Danzig and Nureyev, and his important grandson Storm Cat, becoming noted influences for speed. But where does thoroughbred breeding go from here? Coolmore is addressing a more particular problem—where does it go after Galileo?—by looking to top sires in places like North America (including to Danzig's son War Front), Japan (to Deep Impact who has no Northern Dancer within three generations) and Australia (to the shuttling grandson of Danzig, Fastnet Rock). Coolmore and its various syndicates have a large broodmare band which is top heavy with Sadler's Wells and Galileo mares for which it needs an outcross.

Elite Racing Club's "Marsha"

Galileo's own fee has been listed as 'private' for a number of years now but demand for his services hasn't prevented Coolmore from snapping up prospective broodmares for him when they become available. One notable thread has been the continuing acquisition of good sprinting mares, a group that has done well with Galileo in recent times, the most recent purchases to supplement its collection including such as Mecca's Angel (bought privately after her racing days), Easton Angel (another daughter of Dark Angel) and Tiggy Wiggy (a daughter of the prolific Kodiac, a grandson of Danzig). It was Coolmore (after a battle with Godolphin's representatives) who finally lodged the winning bid for Marsha in a frenzied Tuesday evening session at the December Sales in which it also paid 2,100,000 guineas for another dual Group 1-winning sprinter, the six-furlong performer (Commonwealth Cup and Sprint Cup in 2016) Quiet Reflection, a daughter of Showcasing who is a great grandson of Danzig. Quiet Reflection has been the flagship horse of the Ontoawinner syndicate and a number of its members were at Newmarket to watch her go through the ring, just as nearly fifty members of the Elite Racing Club were present to see home-bred Marsha sold.

Marsha (IRE) (b.f. 2013)	Acclamation (b 1999)	Royal Applause (b 1993)	Waajib
			Flying Melody
		Princess Athena (b 1985)	Ahonoora
			Shopping Wise
	Marlinka (b 2008)	Marju (br 1988)	Last Tycoon
			Flame of Tara
		Baralinka (b 1999)	Barathea
			Kalinka

The Elite Racing Club runs a breeding programme and it also bred and owned Marsha's dam Marlinka, a useful sprinter who won in listed company at Vichy, and her grandam Baralinka. Marsha's great grandam Kalinka was purchased at auction as an unraced two-year-old for the Elite Racing Club in the first years after its formation in 1992. She won a two-year-old maiden but lost her way on the racetrack, eventually being tried over hurdles. Retained for breeding, she proved a splendid foundation mare for her owners, her second foal being none other than that grand racemare Soviet Song (sired incidentally by a grandson of Try My Best in Marju) whose five Group 1 wins included the Sussex Stakes as a four-year-old (she was raced until she was six). Kalinka also produced the 2005 Triumph Hurdle winner Penzance for the club, as well as the fairly useful miler Sister Act (a sister to Soviet Song) who became the dam of Ribbons, the second Group 1 winner on the Flat to carry the Elite Racing Club's white, large black spots, black cap before Marsha did her bit to keep the club's name in lights (one of the club members Marsha Holliman won a competition to name her).

Marsha is Marlinka's second foal and her first and third foals are also sprinters who were both in training in the latest season: the smart Judicial (by Iffraaj) won three times, at Pontefract, Chester and Beverley, and the fairly useful Marseille (by Excelebration) won a maiden at Newcastle, both of them in the Elite Racing Club silks. Marlinka had no foal in 2017 but her reward for her fine start at stud is a visit in 2018 to Frankel, paid for out of the proceeds of Marsha's sale. Frankel's own dam, Kind, was best at sprint trips and Frankel himself is the finest advertisement for sending sprinting mares to Galileo, a 'formula' also responsible for dual classic winners Churchill and Winter, among others, in the latest season. Five furlongs was the optimum trip for the tough and genuine Marsha who showed her best form on turf on good or firmer going (also won on polytrack). Her career reflected great credit on her trainer Sir Mark Prescott and all who worked with her at Heath House. Sir Mark thinks that, because she is a filly, Marsha 'will be remembered for her best performances, unlike colts who are remembered for their worst.' In the immediate years ahead, however, she will probably be remembered as 'the six-million guinea filly', as much as for her performances. It goes almost without saying that she starts life as a broodmare with a visit to Galileo, the racing career of the resulting offspring no doubt attended by the highest expectations. *Sir Mark Prescott Bt*

MARSHAL DAN (IRE) 2 b.c. (Apr 22) Lawman (FR) 121 – Aunt Nicola 85 (Reel **59**
Buddy (USA) 118) [2017 t7.2g p7g^{6} Dec 28] modest form: better effort when sixth in minor event at Lingfield (6½ lengths behind Maverick Officer) in December. *Heather Main*

MARSHAL DAN TROOP (IRE) 4 b.c. Lawman (FR) 121 – Corrozal (GER) (Cape **64**
Cross (IRE) 129) [2017 73: p11g^{6} p12g^{2} t13.9g^{4} Jan 26] sturdy colt: modest performer: stays 1½m: acts on polytrack and heavy going: has worn headgear, including last 3 starts: sold 6,000 gns, sent to Norway. *Robyn Brisland*

MARSHALL AID (IRE) 4 b.g. Lawman (FR) 121 – Dievotchkina (IRE) (Bluebird **62**
(USA) 125) [2017 75: t13.9m p13g^{2} t13.9g^{2} p15.8g^{3} p15.8g^{3} p13.3g^{3} 14g 14d^{4} 11.4m^{4} **a73**
p15.8g p15.8g t12.2g Dec 22] sturdy gelding: modest maiden on turf, fair on all-weather: stays 2m: acts on polytrack and tapeta: sometimes wears headgear: has worn tongue tie, including last 2 starts. *Mark Usher*

MARSHGATE LANE (USA) 8 b.g. Medaglia d'Oro (USA) 129 – Louvain (IRE) 105 **99**
(Sinndar (IRE) 134) [2017 98: f8g^{2} p10g^{5} p8g^{5} t9.5g^{6} t9.5g^{2} a8g* a8g* 8.9g 8g 8g^{2} 10.5g^{5} a10.4g* 8d^{2} 10.4g a10.4g^{5} Nov 6] sturdy gelding: useful performer: left Neil Mulholland after fifth start: successful at Bro Park in handicap in April, minor event in May and handicap in August: effective at 1m to 11f: acts on dirt, all-weather and soft going: wears cheekpieces. *Claes Bjorling, Sweden*

MARSH PRIDE 5 b.m. Stimulation (IRE) 121 – Peneia (USA) (Nureyev (USA) 131) **90**
[2017 96: 8.3g 10.3m^{4} 11.4m^{4} 12.3s^{3} 12g^{6} t12.4g^{6} 10.3v^{2} 10.3v* Sep 30] workmanlike mare: fairly useful handicapper: won at Chester (by length from Katebird) in September: stays 12.5f: acts on heavy going: often races towards rear. *K. R. Burke*

MARSH STORM (IRE) 2 b.f. (Mar 13) Choisir (AUS) 126 – Margaret's Dream (IRE) **61**
61 (Muhtarram (USA) 125) [2017 t5s^{3} 5m^{5} 7d t6.1g t7.1g^{4} t8s t7.1g Oct 10] €38,000F: fifth foal: sister to 2-y-o 1m winner (stays 13f) Olympic Legend, and half-sister to winner up to 7f Whats For Pudding (2-y-o 6f winner, by Kheleyf) and 1m winner Balmont Blast (by Balmont): dam maiden half-sister to top-class winner up to 1m Olympic Glory (by Choisir): modest maiden: unproven beyond 5f: acts on tapeta: often races prominently. *K. R. Burke*

MARTINENGO (IRE) 2 b.c. (Jun 2) Elusive Pimpernel (USA) 117 – Albiatra (USA) –
(Dixieland Band (USA)) [2017 8d Oct 27] 66/1, well held in minor event at Newbury. *Peter Chapple-Hyam*

MARWA 3 b.f. Exceed And Excel (AUS) 126 – La Cucina (IRE) (Last Tycoon 131) [2017 **59**
59: p7g^{5} p8g Jan 27] modest form: sold 80,000 gns in February, sent to USA. *Ed Dunlop*

MARY ANNE EVANS 3 b.f. Oasis Dream 129 – Gertrude Bell 112 (Sinndar (IRE) 134) [2017 72p: t9.5g⁶ 10.2g⁵ 11.6d⁵ May 13] well-made filly: fair performer: stays 1¼m: acts on good to firm going: tried in cheekpieces. *John Gosden* **69**

MARY ELISE (IRE) 2 b.f. (Jan 26) Mastercraftsman (IRE) 129 – Je T'adore (IRE) (Montjeu (IRE) 137) [2017 p8g Nov 8] 21,000F: first foal: dam, ran twice in France, closely related to useful performer up to 1¾m Snowmane: 66/1, seventh in minor event at Kempton (4¾ lengths behind Espadrille) in November: will improve. *Ed Walker* **66 p**

MARYLEBONE 4 b.g. Shamardal (USA) 129 – Mary Boleyn (IRE) 108 (King's Best (USA) 132) [2017 –: 8m p7g³ p7g Oct 11] rangy gelding: fairly useful handicapper: third at Kempton in September: stays 7f: acts on polytrack: in tongue tie last 2 starts: sold 10,000 gns in November. *Ed Walker* **87**

MARY LE BOW 6 b.m. Sir Percy 129 – Bermondsey Girl 69 (Bertolini (USA) 125) [2017 72: t9.5m⁶ p10m⁵ Jan 21] fair handicapper: stays 1½m: acts on polytrack, tapeta and firm going: has worn headgear: wears tongue tie: often races in rear. *Victor Dartnall* **67**

MARZOUQ (USA) 3 b.c. Spring At Last (USA) 122 – Smart 'N Special (USA) (Smart Strike (CAN) 121) [2017 78p: p7g³ t8g² 8m² 8d⁴ 8m² 10m* Jul 14] good-topped colt: useful handicapper: won at Newmarket (by ¾ length from Oasis Charm) in July: second at Goodwood (head behind I'vegotthepower) in June: stays 1¼m: acts on polytrack, tapeta, good to firm and good to soft going: sent to Hong Kong. *Jeremy Noseda* **103**

MASAARR (USA) 2 ch.c. (Mar 28) Distorted Humor (USA) 117 – Aryaamm (IRE) 94 (Galileo (IRE) 134) [2017 7m³ p8g* Nov 18] compact colt: half-brother to several winners, including very smart 2-y-o 7f (including Champagne Stakes) winner Saamidd (by Street Cry) and smart 1¼m/1½m winner Talmada (by Cape Cross): dam 1¼m winner: useful form: won minor event at Lingfield (impressively by 4½ lengths from Poetic Imagination) in November: exciting prospect. *Roger Varian* **101 p**

MASAMAH (IRE) 11 gr.g. Exceed And Excel (AUS) 126 – Bethesda 91 (Distant Relative 128) [2017 84: p6g p6m⁵ t7.1g* t7.1g t6m⁶ t7.1m⁵ Mar 14] good-topped gelding: fair handicapper: won at Wolverhampton in January: stays 7f: acts on polytrack, tapeta, firm and soft going: wears headgear: has worn tongue tie, including final start. *Ian Williams* **74**

MASAR (IRE) 2 ch.c. (Apr 16) New Approach (IRE) 132 – Khawlah (IRE) 114 (Cape Cross (IRE) 129) [2017 6m* 7m³ 7g* 8d³ 8f⁶ Nov 3] good-topped colt: second foal: dam, winner up to 9.5f (2-y-o 1m winner), half-sister to smart French 1¼m winner Vancouverite: smart performer: won minor event at Goodwood in May and Solario Stakes at Sandown (by 2 lengths from Romanised) in September: third in Prix Jean-Luc Lagardere at Chantilly (1½ lengths behind Happily) in October: met trouble when 2½ lengths sixth to Mendelssohn in Breeders' Cup Juvenile Turf at Del Mar final outing: stays 1m: acts on firm and good to soft going. *Charlie Appleby* **115**

MASARZAIN (IRE) 4 br.g. Kodiac 112 – Cache Creek (IRE) 104 (Marju (IRE) 127) [2017 83: f7g p6g t6m t6g⁴ 6m⁶ 7g³ 7.6s⁵ 8g* 8g² 8m* 8m* 8.5g² p8g⁵ Sep 25] good-topped gelding: fairly useful handicapper: won at Salisbury/Musselburgh in August and Musselburgh again (by 5 lengths from Inglorious) in September: second at Epsom later in September: left James Given after sixth start: stays 8.5f: acts on polytrack, good to firm and good to soft going: tried in blinkers: sold 18,000 gns in October. *Archie Watson* **93 a87**

MASHAHEER 2 b.g. (Jan 27) Dutch Art 126 – Faustinatheyounger (IRE) 64 (Antonius Pius (USA) 123) [2017 6g 6m⁶ 6d⁶ Sep 19] 110,000Y: first foal: dam, maiden (stayed 1½m), half-sister to US Grade 2 1m winner Uncharted Haven, herself dam of very smart performer up to 1½m High Heeled: fair form: best effort when sixth in minor event at Yarmouth (4¾ lengths behind Mutaaqeb) in September: should still improve. *William Haggas* **67 p**

MASHAM STAR (IRE) 3 b.g. Lawman (FR) 121 – Croisiere (USA) 109 (Capote (USA)) [2017 101: a7f 7g⁶ 7g⁴ t8s 7.6m² 7d⁵ 8.2f³ 10.1m⁵ 8m 8.3s² 8g² 8s⁵ 8d⁵ 8s⁶ p8g² 7g 7g⁵ p7s* 7s 7.2v⁵ Oct 16] sturdy gelding: smart handicapper: won at Chelmsford (by head from Sutter County) in September: second at Hamilton/Newmarket in July and Chelmsford (½ length behind Mustashry) in August: stays 8.5f: acts on polytrack, tapeta, firm and soft going: front runner/races prominently. *Mark Johnston* **112**

MASKED BANDIT 4 b.g. Dick Turpin (IRE) 127 – Plaisterer 100 (Best of The Bests (IRE) 122) [2017 –: p10g Apr 26] no form, including over hurdles: tried in hood. *Suzy Smith* **–**

MASKED DEFENDER (USA) 2 b.c. (Feb 16) First Defence (USA) 119 – Costume 111 (Danehill (USA) 126) [2017 6m 7g⁵ p7g⁴ p6g² Oct 24] big colt: fifth foal: half-brother to temperamental 6f winner (stayed 1m) Epic Voyage (by Empire Maker): dam 1m/9f winner: fairly useful form: second in minor event at Kempton in October: best effort at 6f: sold 62,000 gns, sent to Qatar. *Amanda Perrett* **82**

MASK OF TIME (IRE) 3 b.c. Holy Roman Emperor (IRE) 125 – Mission Secrete (IRE) (Galileo (IRE) 134) [2017 p8g^{3} 8d* 8g^{3} 9.4g* 11.9m^{4} 8g^{5} 9.9g^{6} 8g^{4} Oct 14] third foal: closely related to French winner up to 1½m Mahari (2-y-o 9.7f winner, by Duke of Marmalade): dam, French 14.5f winner, half-sister to 1000 Guineas winner Miss France: useful performer: won maiden at Fontainebleau in March and listed race at Bordeaux (by neck from Troarn) in May: fourth after in Prix Hocquart at Chantilly (1½ lengths behind Ice Breeze) and Toorak Handicap at Caulfield (first race after leaving A. Fabre, beaten 2 lengths by Tosen Stardom): effective at 1m to 1½m: acts on polytrack, good to firm and good to soft going: often races in rear. *Hugo Palmer* **108**

MASKOON 6 ch.g. Aqlaam 125 – Tamazug 101 (Machiavellian (USA) 123) [2017 74: 12g 10m^{6} May 9] fairly useful handicapper at best, on downgrade: stays 10.5f: acts on polytrack, soft and good to firm going: has worn blinkers/tongue tie. *Philip Kirby* **55**

MASONIC (IRE) 3 b.g. Intense Focus (USA) 117 – Green Tambourine 84 (Green Desert (USA) 127) [2017 73: p10g^{6} p8g^{5} 7m 8.3d t9.5g t8.6g^{4} p8g Oct 26] close-coupled gelding: fair maiden: stays 1m: acts on polytrack: tried in headgear: sometimes slowly away. *Robyn Brisland* **71**

MASONS BELLE 2 b.g. (Mar 23) Piccolo 121 – Edge of Gold 81 (Choisir (AUS) 126) [2017 7.4s 8v t9.5g Oct 27] no form in minor events. *Ronald Harris* **–**

MASQUERADE BLING (IRE) 3 b.f. Approve (IRE) 112 – Mataji (IRE) (Desert Prince (IRE) 130) [2017 62: p8g f6s^{4} p7g^{2} p7g^{5} p8g^{4} p8g^{2} p8g^{3} 7m^{2} 8g^{5} t7.1s* t7.1d^{5} f8.1g p7d^{4} p7g^{2} Dec 28] compact filly: fair handicapper: won at Newcastle in September: left Simon Hodgson after seventh start, Daniel Loughnane after eleventh: stays 1m: acts on polytrack, tapeta and good to firm going: tried in cheekpieces. *Neil Mulholland* **70**

MASSAAT (IRE) 4 b.c. Teofilo (IRE) 126 – Madany (IRE) 94 (Acclamation 118) [2017 122: 7d* 8d^{3} 7m^{2} Oct 13] tall, good sort: very smart performer: won Hungerford Stakes at Newbury (by 1¾ lengths from Librisa Breeze) in August after 12-month absence: placed after in Prix du Moulin de Longchamp at Chantilly (4¼ lengths third behind Ribchester) and Challenge Stakes at Newmarket (3½ lengths second to Limato): stays 1m: acts on good to firm and good to soft going: front runner/races prominently. *Owen Burrows* **121**

Mr Hamdan Al Maktoum's "Massaat"

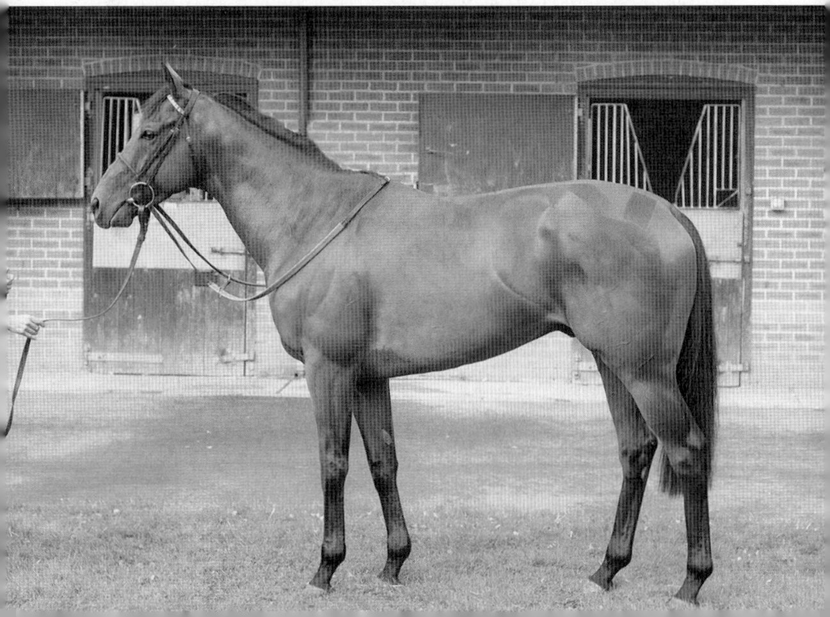

MASTER ARCHER (IRE) 3 gr.g. Mastercraftsman (IRE) 129 – Kinigi (IRE) 83 **88**
(Verglas (IRE) 118) [2017 66p: 10m^{4} 10.3m^{4} p12s 13.3g^{4} 14s^{2} 14g^{2} p16g^{2} 14g^{2} Nov 1] strong gelding: fairly useful maiden: second 4 times between August and November: barely stays 1¾m: acts on polytrack, soft and good to firm going: in cheekpieces last 4 starts. *James Fanshawe*

MASTER BILLIE (IRE) 3 ro.g. Mastercraftsman (IRE) 129 – Billie Jean 65 (Bertolini **–**
(USA) 125) [2017 –: p10g^{6} p12g t12.2g f8g Mar 9] no form, including over hurdles: left William Muir after third start: in headgear last 2 starts. *Roger Teal*

MASTER CARPENTER (IRE) 6 ch.h. Mastercraftsman (IRE) 129 – Fringe 93 (In **108**
The Wings 128) [2017 112: 8g 8m 10.3d* 12m 10.3m 9.9g 8g 9.9v^{4} 10.3g^{4} 10s Oct 28] smallish, good-topped horse: useful handicapper: won at York (by 5 lengths from Al Neksh) in May: stays 10.5f: acts on good to firm and heavy going. *Rod Millman*

MASTER DANCER 6 gr.g. Mastercraftsman (IRE) 129 – Isabella Glyn (IRE) 75 **80**
(Sadler's Wells (USA) 132) [2017 71: 16.2m^{3} p16s^{6} 16s* Sep 19] workmanlike gelding: fairly useful handicapper: won at Chepstow (by 10 lengths from Ivanhoe) in September: stays 2m: acts on soft and good to firm going: often wears headgear: fairly useful hurdler. *Tim Vaughan*

MASTERFILLY (IRE) 3 gr.f. Mastercraftsman (IRE) 129 – Waldena (USA) (Storm Cat **59**
(USA)) [2017 54: t9.5g^{5} p12g 12g^{3} 10.2v 11.6m t9.5g Oct 7] sturdy filly: modest maiden: should be suited by 1½m: acts on tapeta and good to firm going: tried in visor: usually races prominently. *Ed Walker*

MASTERFUL ACT (USA) 10 ch.g. Pleasantly Perfect (USA) 130 – Catnip (USA) **–**
(Flying Paster (USA)) [2017 75: t9.5g t16.3g^{6} t10.2s t10.2g f12.1g^{6} f11.1g Dec 29] tall, workmanlike gelding: useful at best, no form in 2017: tried in visor/tongue tie. *John Balding*

MASTER GREY (IRE) 2 gr.g. (Apr 30) Mastercraftsman (IRE) 129 – Market Day 105 **61**
(Tobougg (IRE) 125) [2017 6.1d^{5} 7d^{6} 7.4d Jul 25] compact gelding: modest form. *Rod Millman*

MASTER ME (IRE) 3 b.f. Masterofthehorse (IRE) 122 – Miss Starlight 111 (Trade Fair **69**
124) [2017 8f 10s^{2} t12.2g Jul 3] first foal: dam winner up to 11f (2-y-o 8.6f winner): fair form: best effort when second in maiden at Ayr in June: sold 2,000 gns in November, sent to Spain. *K. R. Burke*

MASTEROFDISCOVERY 3 b.c. Henrythenavigator (USA) 131 – Wonderful Desert **78**
57 (Green Desert (USA) 127) [2017 74: 8.3m* 8.5g 8m^{5} 8d^{3} p8g^{5} p10g Sep 25] sturdy colt: fair handicapper: won at Windsor in April: stays 8.5f: acts on good to firm and good to soft going: wears blinkers. *Clive Cox*

MASTER OF FINANCE (IRE) 6 ch.g. Mastercraftsman (IRE) 129 – Cheal Rose **– §**
(IRE) 83 (Dr Devious (IRE) 127) [2017 105§: 11.9g Aug 25] strong gelding: useful handicapper, well held sole outing on Flat in 2017: stays 12.5f: acts on good to firm and heavy going: has worn blinkers: usually races prominently: temperamental: fairly useful hurdler. *Malcolm Jefferson*

MASTER OF HEAVEN 4 b.g. Makfi 130 – Maid In Heaven (IRE) 99 (Clodovil (IRE) **59**
116) [2017 71: p11d p10g^{6} p10d p10g* 9.9g* 10g 9.9g^{6} 10d 9.9m p10g^{3} 9.9s^{5} p10d^{3} p10g^{3} p10s p8g p10s^{3} Dec 17] sturdy gelding: modest handicapper: won at Chelmsford in March and Brighton in May: stays 1½m: acts on polytrack: wears headgear: has worn tongue tie, including in 2017: usually leads. *Jim Boyle*

MASTER OF IRONY (IRE) 5 b.g. Makfi 130 – Mother of Pearl (IRE) 113 (Sadler's **88**
Wells (USA) 132) [2017 103: 12m 12.1m 14v^{5} Sep 30] useful handicapper, below form in 2017: stays 1½m: acts on polytrack and soft going: wears headgear: often starts slowly/ races in rear: useful hurdler. *John Quinn*

MASTER OF SONG 10 ch.g. Ballet Master (USA) 92 – Ocean Song 61 (Savahra Sound **51**
111) [2017 63: p10g p10d f6.1g^{3} f11.1g^{3} Dec 29] modest handicapper: stays 1½m: acts on polytrack, fibresand, good to firm and good to soft going: wears headgear: has worn tongue tie. *Roy Bowring*

MASTER OF WINE (GER) 2 b.g. (Apr 13) Maxios 123 – Magma (GER) (Dubai **78**
Destination (USA) 127) [2017 7m^{2} 7m^{6} Jul 7] good-topped gelding: fair form when second in maiden at Sandown (head behind Falmouth Light) on first of 2 starts. *Andrew Balding*

MASTERPAVER 6 gr.g. Mastercraftsman (IRE) 129 – Most-Saucy 86 (Most Welcome **96**
131) [2017 96: t12.4g^{2} t16.3g^{4} p12m^{5} p12g^{2} 11.9m^{4} 12g* Jun 20] useful handicapper: won at Thirsk (by 2 lengths from New World Power) in June: stays 16.5f, effective over shorter: acts on all-weather and good to firm going: has worn headgear: sold 27,000 gns in July, sent to Bahrain. *Richard Fahey*

MASTER PEKAN 4 b.g. Piccolo 121 – Lady Pekan 87 (Sri Pekan (USA) 117) [2017 45: t5.1m f5s t5.1g t5.1g Mar 30] modest maiden: best effort at 5f: acts on fibresand: in headgear last 4 starts: front runner/races prominently. *Roy Brotherton* **51**

MASTER POET 2 b.g. (Feb 5) Poet's Voice 126 – Lilli Marlane 82 (Sri Pekan (USA) 117) [2017 p6g Oct 9] 25/1, well held in minor event at Kempton. *Robert Cowell* **–**

MASTERS APPRENTICE (IRE) 2 ch.g. (Mar 11) Mastercraftsman (IRE) 129 – Maghzaa (IRE) (Aqlaam 125) [2017 7g 8m5 p10g4 p10g2 p10g5 Nov 2] compact gelding: fair maiden: stays 1¼m: acts on polytrack. *Sylvester Kirk* **68**

MASTER SINGER (USA) 3 br.c. Giant's Causeway (USA) 132 – Ring of Music (Sadler's Wells (USA) 132) [2017 76p: 11m3 t10.2s* 12m 13.9m 16d t12.2g* t12.4g5 t16.3d5 Dec 16] good-bodied colt: useful performer: won maiden at Newcastle (by 16 lengths) in May and handicap at Wolverhampton (by length from Goldmember) in October: stays easy 16.5f: acts on tapeta and good to firm going: usually in headgear. *John Gosden* **101**

MASTERSON (IRE) 4 gr.g. Lawman (FR) 121 – Indian Dumaani 51 (Indian Ridge 123) [2017 74: p16g* p14g* t16.5g* 14g5 t16.5g3 16.5s Aug 2] fairly useful handicapper: won at Chelmsford (twice) in April and Wolverhampton (dead-heated with Denmead) in May: left Mick Channon after fifth start: stays 16.5f: acts on polytrack, tapeta, firm and soft going: tried in visor/tongue tie: fairly useful hurdler. *Gordon Elliott, Ireland* **85**

MASTER THE WORLD (IRE) 6 gr.g. Mastercraftsman (IRE) 129 – Zadalla 68 (Zaha (CAN) 106) [2017 115: 9.9g 9.9g4 9.9g5 8m 8s2 8s* 8g4 8.8m4 9d 8s 11.8d6 11.9s p10g* p12g2 p10g Dec 23] good-topped gelding: smart performer: won Betfred Mile (Handicap) at Goodwood (by ¾ length from Tony Curtis) in August and listed race at Lingfield (by 1¾ lengths from Victory Bond) in November: second in handicap at Newmarket (3½ lengths behind Ballard Down) in July and listed race at Kempton (½ length behind Red Verdon) in November: stays 1½m: acts on polytrack, good to firm and heavy going: wears headgear. *David Elsworth* **115**

MATCH MAKER (IRE) 2 b.c. (Jan 12) Declaration of War (USA) 128 – I'm In Love (USA) 88 (Zafonic (USA) 130) [2017 6g3 7m Jun 24] 180,000 2-y-o: well-made colt: fifth foal: half-brother to 2-y-o 6f winner Masai (by Oasis Dream) and US Grade 3 2-y-o 1m winner More Than Love (by More Than Ready), both useful: dam, 7f and (at 2 yrs) 1m winner, later 8.5f winner in USA: fairly useful form when third in maiden at Leicester (1¾ lengths behind Westerland) on first of 2 starts: in tongue tie second one. *Simon Crisford* **85**

MATCHMAKING (GER) 2 ch.g. (Mar 20) Mastercraftsman (IRE) 129 – Monami (GER) 107 (Sholokhov (IRE) 121) [2017 6d p7g p7g Oct 11] little impact in minor events. *Sir Mark Prescott Bt* **–**

Betfred Mile Handicap, Goodwood—2016 runner-up Master The World goes one better, beating Tony Curtis (right) and the Richard Fahey-trained pair Birchwood (No.8) and Withernsea (No.18)

William Hill Great St Wilfrid Handicap, Ripon—
clearly all the better for his reappearance after an aborted spell at stud, Mattmu keeps going well to beat Pipers Note (noseband) and Shanghai Glory (not in picture)

MATCH MY FIRE (IRE) 4 ch.g. Makfi 130 – High Lite 54 (Observatory (USA) 131) **72**
[2017 75: 10.3g 13.1m 8.3g^2 10.2d Oct 27] sturdy gelding: fair maiden: stays 1¼m: acts on heavy going: has worn cheekpieces, including last 3 starts. *Michael Dods*

MATERIALIST 3 b.c. Dansili 127 – Mundana (IRE) 103 (King's Best (USA) 132) [2017 **86**
79p: 8g^2 9g* 10.5d^6 8s^3 Jun 30] fairly useful performer: won maiden at Ripon (by neck from Another Eclipse) in May: stays 9f: acts on good to firm going: has worn hood: usually races freely: sent to Sardinia, where won minor event at Villacidro in November. *Roger Varian*

MATERIALISTIC 4 b.f. Oasis Dream 129 – Pongee 110 (Barathea (IRE) 127) [2017 **101**
101: p8g^2 8f t10.2g^6 8d 8.2d^5 Aug 12] close-coupled filly: useful performer: second in listed race at Kempton (1½ lengths behind Aljazzi) in April: stays 1¼m: acts on good to firm and good to soft going: in cheekpieces last 2 starts. *Luca Cumani*

MATEWAN (IRE) 2 b.g. (Apr 24) Epaulette (AUS) 126 – Cochin (USA) (Swain (IRE) –
134) [2017 7m 7g 7m Sep 23] little impact in minor events. *Ian Williams*

MATHIX (FR) 3 b.g. Kendargent (FR) 112 – Matwan (FR) 90 (Indian Rocket 115) [2017 **86**
78p: p8g^2 9g^3 8d^2 a8.4s* 8d^5 a8.4g^6 p8g 9.9g^5 Nov 29] fairly useful performer: left William Haggas, won maiden at Pornichet in August: stays 1¼m: acts on polytrack, viscoride and good to soft going: tried in cheekpieces. *S. Kobayashi, France*

MATHS PRIZE 3 b.g. Royal Applause 124 – Hypoteneuse (IRE) 86 (Sadler's Wells **93**
(USA) 132) [2017 98p: 10g^5 8m 8g^3 8s^4 8s^4 7d Oct 6] well-made gelding: fairly useful handicapper: third at Newmarket in July: should stay 1¼m: acts on good to firm and good to soft going: has worn cheekpieces, including last 3 starts: sold 15,000 gns in October. *Roger Charlton*

MATILDA GRACE (IRE) 2 gr.f. (Apr 21) Lilbourne Lad (IRE) 111 – New Deal 76 –
(Rainbow Quest (USA) 134) [2017 t6g t7.2g p7g Dec 31] €800Y: closely related to several winners by Acclamation, including useful winner up to 1½m Alrasm (2-y-o 6f winner) and 2-y-o 6f winner War Queen: dam French 1m winner: well held in minor events. *Lisa Williamson*

MATORICO (IRE) 6 gr.g. Mastercraftsman (IRE) 129 – Hashbrown (GER) 95 (Big –
Shuffle (USA) 122) [2017 95: 10m Jul 3] useful at best, well held sole outing on Flat in 2017: stays 16.5f: acts on soft and good to firm going: tried in cheekpieces/tongue tie: useful hurdler/maiden chaser. *Jonjo O'Neill*

MATRAVERS 6 b.g. Oasis Dream 129 – Maakrah (Dubai Destination (USA) 127) [2017 **77**
p8d p10d^4 8f 10m^3 8.5f^3 10g^5 Jul 20] sturdy gelding: fairly useful handicapper at 3 yrs, mostly respectable efforts after long absence in 2017: stays 1¼m: acts on polytrack and good to firm going. *Mary Hambro*

MATTMU 5 b.h. Indesatchel (IRE) 120 – Katie Boo (IRE) 92 (Namid 128) [2017 111: 6g4 6g* Aug 19] tall horse: smart performer: had aborted spell at stud prior to return in August: won Great St Wilfrid Stakes (Handicap) at Ripon (by ¾ length from Pipers Note) later in month: stayed 6f: acted on good to firm and heavy going: wore cheekpieces: front runner/raced prominently: to stand at Bearstone Stud, Market Drayton, Shropshire, fee £3,000. *Tim Easterby* **111**

MAULESDEN MAY (IRE) 4 b.f. Dark Angel (IRE) 113 – Jemima's Art 61 (Fantastic Light (USA) 134) [2017 76: 10m3 9g2 10g* 10.2d6 10g* 10g* t12.4g6 10g Oct 7] small filly: fairly useful handicapper: won at Redcar in June, and at Ayr in July and August (by 1½ lengths from Beauden Barrett): stays 12.5f: acts on tapeta, soft and good to firm going: tried in cheekpieces. *Keith Dalgleish* **83**

MAUREB (IRE) 5 br.m. Excellent Art 125 – Almost Blue (USA) (Mr Greeley (USA) 122) [2017 81: 7m5 6m4 6.9g 6.1g 7m2 5.9s4 8g6 5.9g* 5d 7.2m3 7g t6.1m* Oct 28] quite good-topped mare: fair handicapper: won at Carlisle in July and Wolverhampton (apprentice) in October: stays 7f: acts on polytrack, tapeta and firm going: wears headgear. *Tony Coyle* **75**

MAVERICK OFFICER 2 b.g. (May 3) Exceed And Excel (AUS) 126 – Gradara 108 (Montjeu (IRE) 137) [2017 7m 7.4s5 p7g* Dec 28] €85,000Y: third foal: half-brother to smart winner up to 1¼m Gershwin (2-y-o 1m winner, by Shamardal): dam, French 9.5f-12.5f winner, half-sister to French 1m-1¼m winner Giofra and 1m/8.6f winner Big Baz (both smart): fairly useful form: won minor event at Lingfield (by ¾ length from Ode To Autumn) in December: will be suited by 1m+: will go on improving. *David Simcock* **86 p**

MAVERICK WAVE (USA) 6 ch.h. Elusive Quality (USA) – Misty Ocean (USA) (Stormy Atlantic (USA)) [2017 116: 10m4 12s 10s Oct 21] sturdy horse: useful performer nowadays: stays 10.5f: acts on polytrack, tapeta, soft and good to firm going: front runner/races prominently. *John Gosden* **106**

MAVERIK 9 ch.g. Iceman 117 – Nouvelle Lune (Fantastic Light (USA) 134) [2017 70: p10g* p10d Feb 2] lengthy gelding: fair handicapper: won at Lingfield (by ½ length from Dark Amber) in January: stayed 1¼m: acted on polytrack, tapeta, snow, good to firm and good to soft going: wore headgear/tongue tie: front runner/raced prominently: dead. *Neil Mulholland* **70**

MAVEWAY (IRE) 2 b.f. (May 1) Sir Prancealot (IRE) 111 – Stef's Girl (IRE) 73 (Petardia 113) [2017 6.1d t7.2g 6.1m 7g Aug 30] €16,000Y: neat filly: fourth foal: half-sister to 7f winner (including at 2 yrs) Princess Way (by Zebedee) and a winner in Sweden by Kodiac: dam, 6f-1m winner, half-sister to useful 7f winner Cakestown Lady: no form, including in nursery. *David Evans* **–**

MAWAQEET (USA) 8 b.g. Dynaformer (USA) – Lady Ilsley (USA) (Trempolino (USA) 135) [2017 16.3m 14g5 Aug 11] well-made gelding: fairly useful handicapper: stays 2m: acts on good to firm and heavy going: has worn headgear. *Michael Appleby* **83**

MAX BEDDOW (IRE) 4 b.g. Tagula (IRE) 116 – Copper Harbour (IRE) (Foxhound (USA) 103) [2017 –: 8g 8f Jun 17] little form: tried in tongue tie. *Geoffrey Deacon* **–**

MAX DYNAMITE (FR) 7 b.g. Great Journey (JPN) – Mascara (GER) (Monsun (GER) 124) [2017 107: 17d* 15.9g3 11.9g6 Dec 10] quite attractive gelding: smart performer: won minor event at Killarney (by 3 lengths from Sandymount Duke) in August: placed for second time in race when third in Melbourne Cup (Handicap) at Flemington (3 lengths behind Rekindling) in November: 3¾ lengths sixth to Highland Reel in Hong Kong Vase at Sha Tin final start: stays 17f: acts on good to firm and good to soft going. *W. P. Mullins, Ireland* **118**

MAXIMINUS THRAX (FR) 3 b.c. Holy Roman Emperor (IRE) 125 – Ziride (FR) (Valanour (IRE) 125) [2017 p8d2 Dec 13] €37,000Y, €70,000 2-y-o: fourth foal: half-brother to French 2-y-o 6f winner Sissi Pompon (by Whipper) and French 6f-7.5f winner Pulgar (by Excellent Art): dam French winner up to 1¼m (2-y-o 5.5f/7f winner): 3/1, promise when second in maiden at Kempton (4½ lengths behind Humbert) in December: sure to progress. *David Simcock* **82 p**

MAX ZORIN (IRE) 3 b.g. Cape Cross (IRE) 129 – My 60 (King's Best (USA) 132) [2017 92: 9m4 10.3d3 May 12] useful performer: third in listed Dee Stakes at Chester (2¼ lengths behind Cliffs of Moher) in May: stays 10.5f: acts on good to firm and good to soft going: front runner/races prominently. *Andrew Balding* **106**

MAYALEE 2 b.f. (Feb 28) Iffraaj 127 – Moma Lee 79 (Duke of Marmalade (IRE) 132) – [2017 6d Oct 30] 17,000Y: first foal: dam, 7f winner, closely related to useful performer up to 7f Danehill Destiny: 22/1, very green when well held in minor event at Redcar. *Richard Fahey*

MAYASA (IRE) 4 ch.f. Iffraaj 127 – Lanzana (IRE) (Kalanisi (IRE) 132) [2017 83: 14v **70** 11.6m^6 t12.2g p15.8g p16g Nov 7] sturdy filly: fairly useful handicapper, below form in 2017: stays 1½m: acts on all-weather: wears headgear: tried in tongue tie. *John Flint*

MAYASEEN (FR) 2 gr.f. (Mar 23) Style Vendome (FR) 116 – Wing Stealth (IRE) 76 **59** (Hawk Wing (USA) 136) [2017 p8g Nov 8] €200,000Y: fifth foal: half-sister to 7f (including at 2 yrs) winner Stealth Missile (by Invincible Spirit) and very smart 1¼m-1½m (Irish Oaks) winner Covert Love (by Azamour): dam maiden (stayed 1½m): 12/1, eleventh in minor event at Kempton (7 lengths behind Espadrille) in November. *Hugo Palmer*

MAYBRIDE 2 b.f. (Apr 7) Mayson 124 – Wedding Party 91 (Groom Dancer (USA) 128) **88** [2017 6s^2 5m 6g^5 6v^2 6g^5 6d* Oct 30] good-topped filly: sister to 2-y-o 5f/6f winner Rosebride and half-sister to several winners, including useful 8.6f winner Party Doctor (by Dr Fong), later successful abroad, and 5f-7f winner Firstknight (by Kyllachy): dam 2-y-o 6f/7f winner: fairly useful performer: won minor event at Leicester in October: stays 6f: acts on heavy going. *Richard Fahey*

MAYER 2 b.c. (Feb 21) Nathaniel (IRE) 129 – Paisley 80 (Pivotal 124) [2017 p8d t8.6d – Dec 27] well held in minor events. *Luca Cumani*

MAYFAIR LADY 4 b.f. Holy Roman Emperor (IRE) 125 – Lady Luachmhar (IRE) 94 **81** (Galileo (IRE) 134) [2017 109: 6m^5 6f 5g Jun 24] useful performer, below form in 2017: stays 6f: acts on good to firm and good to soft going: front runner/races prominently. *Richard Fahey*

MAYFIELD BOY 6 b.g. Authorized (IRE) 133 – Big Pink (IRE) (Bigstone (IRE) 126) **57** [2017 64: t9.5g t8s 7.4d^5 7.4s Aug 1] modest handicapper: stays 1m: acts on soft and good to firm going: tried in cheekpieces. *Antony Brittain*

MAYFLAIR 3 b.f. Zamindar (USA) 116 – Madhaaq (IRE) 87 (Medicean 128) [2017 –: **67** p10m^6 p8d^3 t9.5g^3 11.4m^4 Jul 3] fair maiden: stays 9.5f: acts on polytrack and tapeta: tried in blinkers. *Jonathan Portman*

MAY GIRL 2 b.f. (Mar 25) Mayson 124 – Instructress 66 (Diktat 126) [2017 5.2m^4 5m^2 **87** 5d* 5.4d* 5g^3 5s Oct 7] sturdy filly: third foal: dam unreliable 5f winner (including at 2 yrs): fairly useful performer: won maiden at Sandown in July and minor event at York (by ½ length from Pretty Baby) in September: third in Flying Childers Stakes at Doncaster (5 lengths behind Heartache) 5 days later: stays 5.5f: acts on good to soft going: usually races close up: sold 140,000 gns in December. *Robert Cowell*

MAYGOLD 2 b.f. (Apr 26) Mayson 124 – Spanish Gold 82 (Vettori (IRE) 119) [2017 6g **76** 5v^3 5.1d^4 5s^2 p5g* Sep 26] rather unfurnished filly: half-sister to several winners, including useful winner up to 7f Spanish Bounty (2-y-o 5.7f/6f winner, by Bahamian Bounty) and useful 6f winner King Ferdinand (by Tobougg): dam 8.5f winner: fair performer: won nursery at Lingfield in September: best form at 5f: acts on polytrack: in hood last 2 starts. *Ed Walker*

MAYHEM MAYBE (IRE) 2 b.f. (Apr 15) Art Connoisseur (IRE) 121 – Altalena (ITY) – (Marju (IRE) 127) [2017 7d 6v Sep 28] €3,400Y: second foal: half-sister to Italian 2-y-o 9f winner Viso d'Angelo (by Verglas): dam, Italian 8.5f-10.5f winner, half-sister to useful 2-y-o 1m/9f winner Deynawari: well held in maiden/minor event. *Gay Kelleway*

MAYLEAF SHINE (IRE) 3 b.f. Mayson 124 – Let Me Shine (USA) 79 (Dixie Union **104** (USA) 121) [2017 89: 5.1s^4 5g 5.1d 5d^2 5m^5 5s* 5v^6 5v^3 Oct 16] rather lightly-built filly: fourth foal: half-sister to 6f-8.6f winner Makhfar (by Bushranger) and 5f (including at 2 yrs) winner Coto (by Fast Company): dam 2-y-o 5f winner who stayed 1m: useful handicapper: won at Haydock (by length from Soie d'Leau) in September: best form at 5f: acts on soft and good to firm going: in hood last 5 starts: usually races towards rear. *Iain Jardine*

MAYLEEN (IRE) 3 br.f. Big Bad Bob (IRE) 118 – Miss Megs (IRE) 81 (Croco Rouge – (IRE) 126) [2017 67: 7m t8s Sep 19] fair form at 2 yrs, little show in 2017: stays 1m: acts on good to firm and good to soft going: sometimes slowly away, often races in rear: sold £800, sent to Greece. *Ann Duffield*

MAY MIST 5 b.m. Nayef (USA) 129 – Midnight Mist (IRE) 87 (Green Desert (USA) 127) – [2017 62: t9.5m^6 t9.5g 9s 12m 10d t7.2g^6 t9.5g Oct 21] modest form in 2016, little impact (mostly in handicaps) in 2017: in blinkers last 2 starts. *Trevor Wall*

MAYPOLE 2 ch.c. (Mar 15) Mayson 124 – Constitute (USA) 85 (Gone West (USA)) **75**
[2017 6s^{4} 7m^{6} p6d^{2} Nov 9] sturdy colt: fair form: best effort when sixth in minor event at Newmarket (8 lengths behind Key Victory) in October. *Richard Hannon*

MAY REMAIN 2 b.c. (Mar 12) Mayson 124 – Ultimate Best 64 (King's Best (USA) 132) **87**
[2017 5m^{5} 5.1d^{2} 5m* 6g^{2} 5.1m^{2} 5d* 5v^{5} t5.1m^{4} Oct 28] 14,000F, £26,000Y: good-topped colt: third foal: half-brother to 8.6f winner Ultimate Star (by Starspangledbanner): dam, maiden (placed at 1½m), half-sister to smart 5.4f-7f winner Barney McGrew: fairly useful performer: won minor events at Goodwood in May and Nottingham (by 1¼ lengths from Ginbar) in July: stays 6f: acts on good to firm and good to soft going. *Paul Cole*

MAY SKY 3 b.f. Mayson 124 – Millinsky (USA) 85 (Stravinsky (USA) 133) [2017 7g^{2} 6d^{4} **69**
6m^{5} May 24] £9,000Y, 140,000 2-y-o: sturdy filly: sixth foal: half-sister to 5f/6f winner Moiety (by Myboycharlie) and a winner in Italy by Aqlaam: dam, 5f winner, half-sister to smart sprinter Mirza: fair form: best effort when second in maiden at Newbury in April: sold 21,000 gns in July, sent to Greece. *John Gosden*

MAYSONRI 3 b.g. Mayson 124 – Roshina (IRE) 79 (Chevalier (IRE) 115) [2017 51: **–**
10.1m 9.9d 11.9s 8v Oct 19] maiden: no form in 2017: often wears cheekpieces: sometimes slowly away. *Mark Hoad*

MAY SPIRIT 2 b.f. (Mar 29) Mayson 124 – World Spirit 97 (Agnes World (USA) 123) **–**
[2017 6m 7d p5g Nov 17] 10,000Y: fifth foal: half-sister to 1½m winner Authorized Spirit (by Authorized): dam, 1m winner (including at 2 yrs) who probably stayed 1¼m, half-sister to useful French performer up to 1m Espirita: well held in minor events/maiden. *Michael Blanshard*

MAYTHEORSEBEWITHU (IRE) 2 b.f. (Mar 10) Shirocco (GER) 129 – Amoya **49**
(GER) 88 (Royal Dragon (USA) 118) [2017 p8g Dec 23] 10,000Y: first foal: dam, 7f-1¼m winner, out of Preis der Diana winner Arkona: 33/1, seventh in minor event at Lingfield (6¾ lengths behind Lawn Ranger) in December. *Pat Phelan*

MAYYASAH (USA) 2 b.f. (Apr 21) More Than Ready (USA) 120 – Whipsaw City (FR) **88**
(Elusive City (USA) 117) [2017 6g* 7g^{6} 6.1g^{2} Sep 2] €160,000Y: useful-looking filly: second foal: dam, French 1m winner, half-sister to useful French/US winner up to 1m My Year Is A Day: fairly useful form: won minor event at Newbury (by 2½ lengths from Mushahadaat) in July: stays 6f. *Richard Hannon*

MAZAAHER 7 b.g. Elnadim (USA) 128 – Elutrah (Darshaan 133) [2017 –: t12.2g t8.6m **79**
t10.2g* t12.4d^{2} t12.2g^{2} 12.1m^{2} 10.2f 12v^{5} Jun 10] lengthy gelding: fair handicapper: won at Newcastle (apprentice) in March: stays 12.5f: acts on polytrack, tapeta and good to firm going: tried in cheekpieces: often races towards rear: sold 800 gns, sent Italy. *David Evans*

MAZALTO (IRE) 4 b.f. Teofilo (IRE) 126 – Mazaaya (USA) 95 (Cozzene (USA)) [2017 **77**
80: p12g^{5} 14f^{6} 16g^{4} 16.3s^{4} Jul 29] angular filly: fair maiden: stays 16.5f: acts on polytrack, soft and good to firm going. *Pat Phelan*

MAZYOUN 3 br.g. Mayson 124 – Hypnotize 103 (Machiavellian (USA) 123) [2017 96: **102**
8g^{4} 6m^{5} 7s^{6} 7m^{5} 7m^{4} 7s^{3} 7d^{4} p7d* p8d^{5} p8g 8d* 8.2d^{4} Oct 30] well-made gelding: useful handicapper: won at Kempton in August and Yarmouth (by nose from Hugin) in September: stays 1m: acts on polytrack, tapeta, good to firm and good to soft going: wears headgear. *Hugo Palmer*

MAZZINI 4 ch.g. Exceed And Excel (AUS) 126 – Firenze 109 (Efisio 120) [2017 107p: **113**
6m^{6} 6m p6s^{2} t6s^{6} p6s* p5g^{3} p7s^{3} p7s^{2} p6g p6g^{6} Nov 29] strong, sprint type: smart handicapper: won at Chelmsford (by 4½ lengths from Sign of The Kodiac) in July: placed at same course on 4 other occasions in 2017: stays 7f: acts on polytrack, tapeta and good to firm going: wears cheekpieces. *James Fanshawe*

MCCOOLS GOLD 4 b.g. Yeats (IRE) 128 – Gold Reef (Double Trigger (IRE) 123) **76**
[2017 70: p14g 16d^{2} 16.3m^{6} Jun 13] good-topped gelding: fair handicapper: stays 17f: acts on good to firm and good to soft going: usually wears headgear. *Alan King*

MCDELTA 7 b.g. Delta Dancer – Mcnairobi 89 (Josr Algarhoud (IRE) 118) [2017 72: **65**
p11g^{3} p12g^{5} 10g p8d 8s^{3} 8g^{4} 8g^{3} p8g p11g^{4} p10s Nov 16] sturdy gelding: fair handicapper: stays 11f: acts on polytrack, soft and good to firm going: has worn cheekpieces, including in 2017. *Geoffrey Deacon*

MCELLIGOTT (IRE) 4 b.g. Dark Angel (IRE) 113 – Nina Blini 90 (Bertolini (USA) **–**
125) [2017 –: f7g t8.6m Jan 14] no form, including over hurdles. *Richard Price*

MCERIN (USA) 2 ch.c. (Mar 17) Trappe Shot (USA) 123 – Erin Rose (USA) (Purge (USA) 121) [2017 a4.5f* a5f^3 5m 5f 5f^4 Dec 17] good-topped colt: first foal: dam US 6f winner: useful performer: won maiden at Keeneland in April: best effort when seventh to Sioux Nation in Norfolk Stakes at Royal Ascot on third outing: raced only up to 5f: acts on dirt: usually wears blinkers. *Wesley A. Ward, USA* **98**

MCMUNIGAL (IRE) 2 b.g. (Feb 26) Epaulette (AUS) 126 – Picture of Lily 65 (Medicean 128) [2017 7s* 7v^2 Oct 22] €33,000F, 50,000 2-y-o: third foal: dam, maiden (stayed 1½m), half-sister to very smart 1¼m-1¾m winner Scott's View: useful form: won maiden at Naas in September by 4 lengths from James Cook: length second to Kenya in Killavullan Stakes at Leopardstown, never nearer: open to further improvement. *G. M. Lyons, Ireland* **104 p**

MCVICAR 8 b.g. Tobougg (IRE) 125 – Aries (GER) 79 (Big Shuffle (USA) 122) [2017 67, a60: f12g^5 16.1g^3 13.4d^6 17.1g^3 t16.3s 11.2v Sep 18] smallish, sturdy gelding: modest handicapper nowadays: stays 17f: acts on polytrack, fibresand, good to firm and heavy going: wears cheekpieces: winning hurdler. *John Davies* **63**

MEADOW CROSS (IRE) 5 b.m. Cape Cross (IRE) 129 – Hovering (IRE) 100 (In The Wings 128) [2017 61, a72: p12g p10.7g p16g 10.2m 13.1m p12g Nov 1] fair handicapper, below form in 2017: stays 1½m: acts on polytrack: often wears headgear: often races towards rear: winning hurdler. *Denis Hogan, Ireland* **62**

MEADWAY 6 b.g. Captain Gerrard (IRE) 113 – Tibesti (Machiavellian (USA) 123) [2017 100: f5g^2 f5g f5g^5 5m 5m Jun 17] sturdy gelding: useful handicapper: second at Southwell (½ length behind Razin' Hell) in January: stays 5.5f: acts on fibresand, good to firm and good to soft going: wears headgear: usually races close up: temperamental. *Bryan Smart* **97 §**

MEANDMYSHADOW 9 ch.m. Tobougg (IRE) 125 – Queen Jean 73 (Pivotal 124) [2017 81§: 6g^5 6m^3 6m^6 6.1g 6d 6g t6d^2 7m 6d^2 6g^2 t6g^4 t6.1g f6.1g^3 f6.1g^3 Dec 21] plain, leggy mare: fair handicapper: best at 6f: acts on fibresand, tapeta and any turf going: wears headgear: usually races close up. *Alan Brown* **73**

MEARING 2 b.g. (Feb 13) Aussie Rules (USA) 123 – Director's Dream (IRE) 59 (Act One 124) [2017 5.5s^2 p6g^6 6v^5 Oct 21] compact gelding: fair form in minor events: left Charlie Fellowes after second start. *Iain Jardine* **70**

ME BEFORE YOU (IRE) 2 gr.f. (May 14) Clodovil (IRE) 116 – Pinewoods Lily (IRE) 66 (Indian Ridge 123) [2017 6m^3 5d^3 5g 5d Sep 16] €14,000Y: sixth foal: sister to 2-y-o 6f winner Herewego and half-sister to 2-y-o 6.5f winner Dainty Dandy (by Dandy Man): dam maiden (stayed 1m): fair form: best effort at 6f: tried in hood. *David O'Meara* **66**

MECCABAH (FR) 3 gr.f. Makfi 130 – Mintly Fresh (USA) (Rubiano (USA)) [2017 –: p8g^2 10.3m^3 9.9d^2 10g^5 10g^4 p8g^4 t8.6g^2 p10g Dec 13] lengthy, rather unfurnished filly: fairly useful maiden: placed 4 times: stays 1¼m: acts on polytrack and good to soft going: in blinkers last 2 starts: races prominently. *Andrew Balding* **80**

MECCA'S MINSTREL (IRE) 2 b.f. (Jan 27) Poet's Voice 126 – Hairy Rocket 98 (Pivotal 124) [2017 5s May 20] €50,000Y: first foal: dam, 2-y-o 5f winner, half-sister to useful 2-y-o 7f winner Marsh Hawk: 11/1, green when well held in maiden at Thirsk: should do better. *Michael Dods* **– p**

MECCA'S SPIRIT (IRE) 2 gr.f. (Apr 19) Dark Angel (IRE) 113 – Wiltshire Life (IRE) 72 (Camacho 118) [2017 6g^6 5.9m^5 6s^4 t7.1g Oct 10] 120,000Y: second foal: closely related to 2-y-o 5f winner Queen Celeste (by Acclamation): dam, 6f winner, sister to smart sprinter Humidor and half-sister to smart performer up to 1m Alhebayeb and useful performer up to 1¼m Azmaam (both by Dark Angel): modest form: stays 6f: tried in cheekpieces. *Michael Dods* **60**

MEDAHIM (IRE) 3 b.g. Kodiac 112 – Novel Fun (IRE) (Noverre (USA) 125) [2017 100p: t7.1g^2 8.1d 7g^2 8m 8g* 7d^3 7.9g^4 Aug 25] useful-looking gelding: useful handicapper: won at Newmarket (by 1½ lengths from Masham Star) in July: stays 1m: acts on polytrack, tapeta, best turf form on good going: usually races towards rear. *Richard Hannon* **109**

MEDALLA DE ORO 3 b.g. Teofilo (IRE) 126 – Nyarhini 103 (Fantastic Light (USA) 134) [2017 73p: 9g 12g^5 12g^3 10m 11.4g* 10m* 11.8d^2 12.1s^6 12m^6 10g^6 Nov 3] tall gelding: has scope: fairly useful handicapper: won at Windsor (twice) in August: second at Leicester in September: stays 1½m: acts on good to firm and good to soft going: wears hood: front runner. *Peter Chapple-Hyam* **89**

MEDAL OF HONOUR 2 ch.c. (May 11) Lope de Vega (IRE) 125 – Rich Gift 99 (Cadeaux Genereux 131) [2017 5.8m 7m^3 7g^2 7f^2 7v^4 7d^2 8d^6 6.5g p8g^5 p7g^2 p7s* Dec 8] €340,000Y: half-brother to several winners in Italy, including smart sprinter Black **91**

Mambazo (by Statue of Liberty): dam 2-y-o 6f winner: fairly useful performer: won maiden at Dundalk in December: stays 1m: acts on polytrack, firm and good to soft going: wears tongue tie. *Joseph Patrick O'Brien, Ireland*

MEDBURN CUTLER 7 ch.g. Zafeen (FR) 123 – Tiegs (IRE) 55 (Desert Prince (IRE) **88**
130) [2017 83: 16m^{4} 16m^{2} 16g^{2} 21.6m 16s^{4} 16g^{2} 18d 16s^{3} 16g^{3} Nov 3] plain gelding: fairly useful handicapper: placed 5 times in 2017: left Paul Henderson after eighth start: stays 2¼m: acts on polytrack, good to firm and heavy going: wears headgear: often races prominently/travels strongly. *Peter Hedger*

MEDBURN DREAM 4 b.g. Showcasing 117 – Tiegs (IRE) 55 (Desert Prince (IRE) 130) **97**
[2017 91: 8.3g^{3} 7f^{6} 8s^{5} 7m^{4} 7g^{2} 7.6d* 8.1g^{6} 7v 8d 8g 8s^{5} 7d Nov 4] lengthy gelding: useful handicapper: won at Lingfield (by 9 lengths from Majestic Moon) in June: left Paul Henderson after eleventh start: stays 8.5f: acts on polytrack and heavy going: usually leads. *Peter Hedger*

MEDIA WORLD (IRE) 4 ch.g. Medicean 128 – Panoptic 89 (Dubawi (IRE) 129) [2017 **52**
8g^{5} 7.4d 7g p7s^{5} t6g Nov 24] modest maiden: stays 8.5f: acts on polytrack, best turf form on good going. *Julie Camacho*

MEDICEAN BALLET (IRE) 3 b.f. Medicean 128 – Ballet Dancer (IRE) 77 (Refuse To **80**
Bend (IRE) 128) [2017 77: 8m^{4} 8v^{2} 8.1s^{6} 8.1s p8g^{2} 8.3d^{4} p8g Oct 25] sturdy filly: fairly useful handicapper: second at Kempton in October: stays 1m: acts on polytrack and good to firm going: usually races towards rear: sold 5,000 gns in November. *Henry Candy*

MEDICEAN EL DIABLO 4 b.g. Medicean 128 – Al Joudha (FR) (Green Desert (USA) **83**
127) [2017 80: 7g^{3} p7g^{6} p7g^{2} p8g* p7s^{6} p8g Dec 20] fairly useful handicapper: won at Kempton in October: stays 1m: acts on polytrack: often races in rear. *Jimmy Fox*

MEDICEAN MAN 11 ch.g. Medicean 128 – Kalindi 102 (Efisio 120) [2017 113: 5g* 5g^{2} **115**
6g 6d 5f Jun 20] good-topped gelding: smart performer: won 13 races during career, including handicap at Meydan (by head from Sir Maximilian) in January: second in similar event there (nose behind Speed Hawk) in February: effective at 5f to 7f: acted on polytrack, tapeta, firm and soft going: wore headgear/tongue tie: often raced towards rear: retired. *Jeremy Gask*

MEDICEAN QUEEN (IRE) 6 b.m. Medicean 128 – Qui Moi (CAN) 88 (Swain (IRE) **57**
134) [2017 66: p12g p12d^{4} p15.8g^{5} Jan 27] modest maiden: stays 1½m: raced on polytrack since debut: wears tongue tie: often races prominently. *Phil McEntee*

MEDICI BANCHIERE 3 ch.g. Medicean 128 – Fairy Shoes 77 (Kyllachy 129) [2017 **92**
98: 6m 6m 7g^{3} 6.5g^{6} 7d^{4} 7d p6g Nov 21] good-quartered gelding: fairly useful handicapper: third at York (apprentice) in July: stays 7f: best form on good going: tried in visor: usually races prominently. *K. R. Burke*

MEDICI MOON 3 ch.g. Medicean 128 – Cockney Fire 84 (Cockney Rebel (IRE) 127) **74**
[2017 –: t10.2g f8g^{3} f8m^{2} 10.2v 9.8m^{3} p8d^{4} f8.1g* t9.5m^{2} f8.1g* f8.1g f8.1g Dec 19] fair handicapper: won at Southwell in October and November: best form at 1m: acts on all-weather and good to firm going: wears cheekpieces: usually leads. *Scott Dixon*

MEDICINE HAT 6 b.g. Multiplex 114 – Blushing Heart 62 (Observatory (USA) 131) **80**
[2017 83: t16.3g^{2} t12.4d^{4} t12.2g t16.3g* 18g^{3} Apr 11] fairly useful handicapper: won at Newcastle (by 1½ lengths from Stoneham) in March: stays 2¼m: acts on tapeta: tried in cheekpieces: usually races prominently, often travels strongly: winning hurdler. *Marjorie Fife*

MEDICINE JACK 3 ch.g. Equiano (FR) 127 – Agony Aunt 81 (Formidable (USA) 125) **91**
[2017 105: 6f^{5} May 27] sturdy gelding: useful performer at 2 yrs, below that level sole outing (wore blinkers) in 2017: stays 6f: best form on good going. *G. M. Lyons, Ireland*

MEDICI ORO 2 ch.g. (Mar 26) Medicean 128 – Anapola (GER) (Polish Precedent (USA) **69**
131) [2017 5g^{3} 6d 5f^{6} f5g^{4} t6g t7.2g^{3} f8.1g^{2} f8.1g^{4} Dec 29] fair maiden: stays 1m: acts on fibresand and tapeta: front runner/races prominently. *David Brown*

MEDIEVAL BISHOP (IRE) 8 b.g. Bachelor Duke (USA) 122 – On The Backfoot **53**
(IRE) 69 (Bob Back (USA) 124) [2017 65: t12.2g^{5} t12.2g^{5} t12.2g t16.5g^{6} Oct 21] fair performer, below form in 2017: stays 16.5f: acts on polytrack, tapeta, good to firm and good to soft going: usually wears headgear. *Tony Forbes*

MEDIEVAL (IRE) 3 b.g. Kodiac 112 – Quickstyx 72 (Night Shift (USA)) [2017 101: 8m **101**
8m 10m 7v^{4} 8s 7d* Sep 23] compact gelding: carries condition: useful handicapper: won at Newmarket (by 1¾ lengths from Noble Star) in September: stays 8.5f: acts on good to firm and good to soft going: usually wears headgear. *Paul Cole*

MEDINA SIDONIA (IRE) 5 b.g. Montjeu (IRE) 137 – Valdara (Darshaan 133) [2017 81: 16m5 17.2g6 16d6 17.1d5 Jun 12] fairly useful handicapper, below form in 2017: stays 17f: acts on firm and good to soft going: wears headgear. *Tim Easterby* **71**

MEETINGS MAN (IRE) 10 gr.g. Footstepsinthesand 120 – Missella (IRE) 63 (Danehill (USA) 126) [2017 76: 14g p12g5 p15.8g p15.8g Nov 21] leggy gelding: fair handicapper, below form in 2017: stays 2m: acts on polytrack, firm and good to soft going: wears cheekpieces: front runner/races prominently. *Ali Stronge* **64**

MEGALALA (IRE) 16 b.g. Petardia 113 – Avionne 59 (Derrylin 115) [2017 61: 10d6 9.9g 10m5 11.6d 11.6s6 8d 11.4d Oct 23] lengthy gelding: modest handicapper: stays 1½m: acts on polytrack and any turf going: has worn headgear: usually leads. *John Bridger* **54**

MEGAN LILY (IRE) 3 b.f. Dragon Pulse (IRE) 114 – Nebraas (Green Desert (USA) 127) [2017 91: 5g5 5.1d3 5s2 5.1s* 5m 5.1d 5v 6d3 6s 6v5 Sep 21] smallish filly: useful handicapper: won at Chester (by ½ length from Poet's Society) in June: placed at York (1½ lengths behind Coolfitch) in May and Ascot (1¼ lengths behind Golden Apollo) in August: stays 6f: acts on polytrack and soft going: has worn hood. *Richard Fahey* **96**

MEHDI (IRE) 8 b.g. Holy Roman Emperor (IRE) 125 – College Fund Girl (IRE) 76 (Kahyasi 130) [2017 81: t7.1m2 t7.1d* t7.1g3 t7.2g Aug 31] big, well-made gelding: fairly useful performer: won minor event at Newcastle in February: left Richard Fahey after third start: stays 1m: acts on polytrack, tapeta, good to firm and good to soft going: tried in blinkers: usually wears tongue tie. *Patrick Morris* **82**

MEKHTAAL 4 ch.c. Sea The Stars (IRE) 140 – Aiglonne (USA) 108 (Silver Hawk (USA) 123) [2017 115: 9.9m2 8.9g* 10m6 10f 12f Sep 30] €300,000Y: well-made colt: closely related to useful French/US 11f/1½m winner Aigue Marine (by Galileo) and half-brother to several winners, including smart French 11f (Prix Hocquart) winner Democrate (by Dalakhani): dam French 9f-1½m winner: very smart performer: won Prix d'Ispahan at Chantilly (by neck from Robin of Navan) in May: also ran creditably when neck second to Cloth of Stars in Prix d'Harcourt at same course and 3¼ lengths sixth to Highland Reel in Prince of Wales's Stakes at Royal Ascot: below best last 2 starts, in Arlington Million (left Jean-Claude Rouget after) and Joe Hirsch Turf Classic: best efforts at shorter than 1½m: acts on good to firm going, winner on soft. *H. Graham Motion, USA* **120**

MEKONG 2 b.c. (Mar 3) Frankel 147 – Ship's Biscuit 107 (Tiger Hill (IRE) 127) [2017 8g6 p8g4 Oct 26] fair form: better effort when fourth in minor event at Chelmsford (5¾ lengths behind Dukhan) in October: bred to stay 1¼m+. *Sir Michael Stoute* **70**

Prix d'Ispahan, Chantilly—
Mekhtaal gains a first Group 1 success, beating British raider Robin of Navan and Usherette

MELABI (IRE) 4 b.g. Oasis Dream 129 – Briolette (IRE) 112 (Sadler's Wells (USA) 132) **73**
[2017 84: p11g^{5} t10.2g^{4} 10g^{4} 12g* 11.9g^{2} 10.2d^{6} 11.6m 10.3s^{6} 12d 11.9g^{4} t12.4g Nov 23] attractive gelding: fair handicapper: won at Thirsk in April: stays 1½m: acts on polytrack, firm and good to soft going: has worn headgear, including in 2017. *Richard Ford*

MELANIEMILLIE 3 gr.f. Hellvelyn 118 – Real Diamond 74 (Bertolini (USA) 125) **66**
[2017 70: 6m 5g 5.9s 7g^{4} 7.2s 7g^{2} 7d^{2} 6v* 6g^{2} 6v^{2} 7s 7.2s^{2} Oct 9] fair handicapper: won at Catterick in August: left Ollie Pears after second start: stays 7f: acts on good to firm and heavy going: tried in cheekpieces. *Ruth Carr*

MELANNA (IRE) 6 b.m. Camacho 118 – Colour's Red (IRE) (Red Ransom (USA)) **58**
[2017 85: t9.5m t10.2d t10.2d 14.5s 12g^{4} 11.2v^{5} 11.9s Oct 10] fairly useful handicapper, below form in 2017: stays 1½m: acts on polytrack, tapeta and heavy going: has worn headgear, including final start. *Richard Ford*

MELCANO 3 b.f. Arcano (IRE) 122 – Sablonne (USA) 100 (Silver Hawk (USA) 123) **–**
[2017 47: f7.1g f8.1g p10s Dec 15] maiden: no form in 2017: tried in visor. *Shaun Harris*

MELESINA (IRE) 3 b.f. Dark Angel (IRE) 113 – Lastroseofsummer (IRE) 82 (Haafhd **102**
129) [2017 102: a8f a9.4f^{4} 8d* 10.4d 9.9d p8g 10.2s^{3} Nov 11] smallish filly: useful **a94**
performer: won listed race at Saint-Cloud (by ¾ length from Heuristique) in March: third in similar event at Doncaster (3¼ lengths behind Star Rock) in November: stays 9.5f: acts on soft and good to firm going: sold 400,000 gns in December. *Richard Fahey*

MELGATE MELODY 4 b.g. Royal Applause 124 – Maeander (FR) 101 (Nashwan **62**
(USA) 135) [2017 67: t8.6g^{3} Apr 22] fair handicapper: should stay 1½m: acts on tapeta and good to firm going: front runner/races prominently. *Michael Easterby*

MELINOE 3 b.f. Sea The Stars (IRE) 140 – Persefona (IRE) (Montjeu (IRE) 137) [2017 **96**
–p: t8.6g^{4} t10.2s^{3} 11.9m^{4} 13.3g^{3} 14g* 14m^{2} 14s^{2} 14d^{3} Oct 18] tall filly: useful handicapper: won at Nottingham (by 1¾ lengths from Master Archer) in August: placed on 5 other occasions in 2017: stays 1¾m: acts on tapeta, soft and good to firm going: usually responds generously to pressure. *Sir Mark Prescott Bt*

MELISSA JANE 3 b.f. Foxwedge (AUS) 128 – Queensgate 60 (Compton Place 125) **93**
[2017 67: p7.5g* p8g* 8d^{2} 8s p7.5f^{2} 7s^{2} 7d^{2} p7.5g* p7.5g* Nov 28] rather unfurnished filly: fairly useful performer: much improved, winning claimers at Chantilly in February (left Henry Spiller after) and April (only start for H. Grewe), handicap at Deauville in October and minor event at latter course (beat Rolando 2 lengths) in November: stays 1m: acts on polytrack and soft going. *Y. Barberot, France*

MELLOR BROOK (IRE) 3 b.c. Born To Sea (IRE) 117 – Prima 76 (Primo Dominie **74**
121) [2017 8g^{3} 8.3m 8m^{4} 7.8s Aug 23] fair form: left Bryan Smart after third start: stays 1m. *Michael Dods*

MELLOW 3 ch.f. Bahamian Bounty 116 – Tarqua (IRE) (King Charlemagne (USA) 120) **–**
[2017 –: p6g p7g p8g Nov 29] little form: sometimes in hood. *Hughie Morrison*

MELODIC MOTION (IRE) 3 b.f. Nathaniel (IRE) 129 – Quad's Melody (IRE) 107 **109**
(Spinning World (USA) 130) [2017 80: 10m* 12m* 12g* 14v^{3} 14.5d^{2} p13g^{2} Nov 2] lengthy filly: useful performer: won handicaps at Pontefract (by head from Celestation) and Goodwood (by neck from Jelly Monger) in May, and Newmarket (by 3¾ lengths from Gallifrey) in July: placed in Lillie Langtry Stakes at Goodwood (½ length behind Endless Time) in August and Park Hill Stakes at Doncaster (½ length behind Alyssa) in September: stays 14.5f: acts on good to firm and heavy going: usually races prominently. *Ralph Beckett*

MELODIES 2 ch.f. (Mar 17) Iffraaj 127 – Singersongwriter 85 (Raven's Pass (USA) 133) **79**
[2017 7g^{4} 7g^{2} p8g^{5} Oct 13] first foal: dam, winner up to 1¼m (2-y-o 7f winner), half-sister to Eclipse Stakes winner Mount Nelson and Great Voltigeur Stakes winner Monitor Closely: fair form: best effort when second in minor event at Newbury (3½ lengths behind Magnolia Springs) in September: should stay at least 1m. *Ed Dunlop*

MELODINE 3 ch.f. Archipenko (USA) 127 – Monda (USA) (Cozzene (USA)) [2017 p8d^{6} **71**
t8d^{4} t8.6g 10.2m^{4} 9.9g^{5} Jul 4] second foal: half-sister to a winner in Czech Republic by Sir Percy: dam French 9.5f-10.5f winner: fair maiden: stays 1¼m: acts on tapeta and good to firm going: in cheekpieces last 2 starts: sold 4,000 gns, sent to Poland. *Sir Mark Prescott Bt*

MELO MAGIC 3 b.f. Dick Turpin (IRE) 127 – Sakhacity 65 (Sakhee (USA) 136) [2017 **–**
–: f8g f8d^{5} p8g Apr 7] no form, including in handicap. *J. R. Jenkins*

MELONADE 3 b.f. Mayson 124 – Cambridge Duchess 56 (Singspiel (IRE) 133) [2017 **75**
t5g* 6g* 5m Sep 15] first foal: dam lightly-raced half-sister to useful 2-y-o 6f winner Dubai Builder: fair form: won maiden at Newcastle (by 1¼ lengths from Sheepscar Lad) in March and handicap at Leicester (by length from Seyasah) in July: stays 6f. *David Barron*

MELROSE GIRL 3 b.f. Monsieur Bond (IRE) 120 – Keyaki (IRE) 97 (Shinko Forest (IRE)) [2017 6g^{4} 6m^{5} 5g^{4} 6g^{3} 5.9s^{6} 6g^{4} 7.2s Oct 9] fourth foal: dam 6f/7f winner: modest maiden: should stay 7f: best form on good going. *Bryan Smart* **62**

MELTING DEW 3 b.c. Cacique (IRE) 124 – Winter Sunrise 103 (Pivotal 124) [2017 84p: p10s* 11.2s^{3} 12m^{2} 12g^{6} 12g^{2} 12s^{2} 12m Oct 13] sturdy colt: useful handicapper: won at Chelmsford (by short head from Alfarris) in May: second at Ascot (neck behind Duke of Bronte) in September: stays 1½m: acts on polytrack, soft and good to firm going: tried in headgear: sold 310,000 gns in November. *Sir Michael Stoute* **103**

MEMORIES GALORE (IRE) 5 b.g. Invincible Spirit (IRE) 121 – Persian Memories (IRE) 78 (Indian Ridge 123) [2017 101: p6g^{5} p6g 6d 5m 5g^{5} 5g* 5s^{4} 5g^{2} 5v^{2} 5s t5g^{4} Nov 23] rather leggy gelding: useful handicapper: won at Thirsk in August: second at York and Catterick in October: left Harry Dunlop after second start: stays 6f: acts on polytrack, tapeta and heavy going: wears cheekpieces: often travels strongly. *Roger Fell* **95**

MENDALI 2 b.g. (Apr 21) Multiplex 114 – Future Regime (IRE) 56 (Xaar 132) [2017 5g 5f^{4} Jul 18] modest form when fourth at Beverley (2¾ lengths behind Roundhay Park) on second of 2 starts in minor events. *David C. Griffiths* **56**

MENDELSSOHN (USA) 2 b.c. (May 17) Scat Daddy (USA) 120 – Leslie's Lady (USA) (Tricky Creek (USA)) [2017 7f 8m* 7g 7m^{2} 8f* Nov 3] **116**

The main aim for Aidan O'Brien's latest Breeders' Cup winner, Mendelssohn, is reportedly to win the Kentucky Derby, as it was for his very first winner at the meeting sixteen years earlier, Mendelssohn's grandsire Johannesburg. Mendelssohn's win at Del Mar in the Breeders' Cup Juvenile Turf was O'Brien's twelfth victory at America's 'World Championships', making him much the most successful European trainer at the Breeders' Cup. Indeed, only two American trainers have had more winners than O'Brien at the meeting, D. Wayne Lukas with twenty and Bob Baffert with fourteen. Lukas and Baffert have each trained four Kentucky Derby winners (Lukas has won a record fourteen Triple Crown races all told), but in contrast to the Breeders' Cup, where there are opportunities on turf, America's most prestigious race for three-year-olds is the preserve of dirt specialists and is still unconquered territory for O'Brien. Incidentally, the Kentucky Derby was also a race which eluded Bobby Frankel, the trainer whose record number of Group/Grade 1 wins in a year O'Brien surpassed in the latest season. In fact, neither O'Brien, nor Saeed bin Suroor, the only other trainer from outside the States to have made repeated bids, has ever come close to winning the Kentucky Derby. Godolphin's 2017 contender, bin Suroor's first Kentucky Derby runner for eight years, was the UAE Derby winner Thunder Snow, though any chance he might have had ended soon after the stalls opened when he had to be pulled up after giving a bizarre display of bucking and kicking more reminiscent of a rodeo performer. Bin Suroor sent five runners to Churchill Downs in four years around the millennium at a time when Godolphin's then racing manager Simon Crisford described the race as 'top of our shopping list', saying 'we'll throw everything we have at winning it.'

While Godolphin's enthusiasm for the Kentucky Derby has apparently waned in recent years, O'Brien has returned after an absence since Johannesburg (a non-staying eighth) and Castle Gandolfo took their chance in 2002. Master of Hounds (fifth), Daddy Long Legs (pulled up) and Lines of Battle (seventh) contested consecutive renewals between 2011 and 2013. Like Thunder Snow, the last two had won the UAE Derby beforehand, while Master of Hounds was beaten narrowly in the same race. Presumably, the UAE Derby at Meydan, nowadays run on dirt (formerly tapeta), will also be considered for Mendelssohn who has raced only on turf so far, despite, as will be revealed, having a dirt pedigree. The Juvenile Turf was, in fact, his second preference at the Breeders' Cup, to which he was switched when O'Brien decided that he wasn't quite ready for the experience of running on dirt in the Juvenile—'We didn't want to stop the progression so that's why we left him on the grass.' The stable's more battle-hardened Middle Park and Dewhurst winner U S Navy Flag represented Ballydoyle in the Juvenile instead and beat only two home after making much of the running. Johannesburg, who ended his two-year-old season unbeaten in seven starts, had raced exclusively over five and six furlongs on

Breeders' Cup Juvenile Turf, Del Mar—one of a six-strong European contingent, Mendelssohn provides Aidan O'Brien and Ryan Moore with a fourth victory in seven Grade 1 editions of this race, beating the US-trained duo Untamed Domain (not in picture) and Voting Control (left)

turf before winning the Juvenile and remains O'Brien's only Breeders' Cup winner on dirt, though Man of Iron won the short-lived Breeders' Cup Marathon at Santa Anita on the equally short-lived synthetic pro-ride surface.

A fourth winner in seven Grade 1 editions of the Breeders' Cup Juvenile Turf for both O'Brien and Ryan Moore, after Wrote, George Vancouver and Hit It A Bomb, Mendelssohn started favourite in a field which, on paper at least, featured a strong-looking Anglo-Irish contingent. In fact, Mendelssohn was the only one of the visitors without a pattern-race win to his name unlike Masar (Solario Stakes), James Garfield (Mill Reef Stakes), Beckford (Railway Stakes), Sands of Mali (Gimcrack Stakes) and Rajasinghe (Coventry Stakes). On the other hand, he was proven at a mile, which the others weren't, and, just as importantly, he was drawn in stall one and broke alertly enough, after some early hustling along from Moore, to take full advantage of his inside berth. The turf course in particular at Del Mar is a tight circuit, inside the main dirt course and less than a mile round, with a very short run to the first turn, and a home straight of just over a furlong. In contrast to most of the European two-year-olds in the two Juvenile Turf races, Mendelssohn enjoyed a remarkably trouble-free race. Moore had endured a torrid time on the favourite Happily in the earlier Juvenile Fillies' Turf, Happily finishing last after encountering all sorts of trouble in a race in which stable-companion September had finished strongly for third after having to come wide from a long way back following a slow start. By the time the field had sorted itself out running down the back straight in the Juvenile Turf, Mendelssohn had an ideal pitch behind leader Sands of Mali. The Gimcrack winner kicked on entering the very short straight but his stamina began to ebb soon afterwards and Mendelssohn edged ahead inside the final furlong, having enough in hand as the pack closed on him. Untamed Domain and Voting Control took the places, beaten a length and half a length, the runner-up, who got behind early on, ending up having to cover a lot more ground than the winner despite being drawn next to him. Beckford and Masar fared best of the other Europeans in fifth and sixth despite being the last pair approaching the home turn, while the weakening Sands of Mali lost several places close home to finish ninth, just in front of the never-dangerous James Garfield and Rajasinghe, the latter slowly away from the widest draw of all.

Mendelssohn's last couple of starts made him look worth a lot closer to the 3,000,000 dollars he had cost as a yearling than his first try in pattern company which had seen him finish tailed-off last in the Champagne Stakes at Doncaster won by stable-companion Seahenge. That run proved too bad to be true, however. Fitted with blinkers for the first time (which he wore again at Del Mar), Mendelssohn outran his odds of 50/1 to finish two and a half lengths second to U S Navy Flag in the Dewhurst Stakes, Seahenge behind him in third this time and Threeandfourpence completing Ballydoyle's domination of the finish. Mendelssohn had begun his career in what was fairly typical fashion for one of his stable's two-year-olds in the latest season, showing plenty of improvement from his debut (eighth to stable-companion The Pentagon) to win a maiden at the second time of asking at the Curragh in August despite still looking green.

Mendelssohn (USA) (b.c. 2015)	Scat Daddy (USA) (b or br 2004)	Johannesburg (b 1999)	Hennessy
			Myth
		Love Style (ch 1999)	Mr Prospector
			Likeable Style
	Leslie's Lady (USA) (b 1996)	Tricky Creek (br 1986)	Clever Trick
			Battle Creek Girl
		Crystal Lady (b 1990)	Stop The Music
			One Last Bird

If Mendelssohn is to be a serious Kentucky Derby contender, he'll need to fare a lot better than his sire, as well as his grandsire. His sire Scat Daddy finished tailed off in his attempt at Churchill Downs after sustaining what proved a career-ending tendon injury. Also sire of the aforementioned Daddy Long Legs and Seahenge, Scat Daddy stayed well enough to win the nine-furlong Florida Derby. Mendelssohn's huge price tag, which made him the most expensive yearling sold anywhere in the world in 2016, and the highest-priced lot at Keeneland's September Yearling Sale since 2010, is only partly accounted for by his very much in-vogue sire. In fact, there was little room on Mendelssohn's page in the sale catalogue for any of his more distant relatives, with his dam's own produce taking up most of the space, much of that occupied by the exploits of his champion half-sister Beholder—and that was before she won her second Breeders' Cup Distaff a few months later. The winner of eleven Grade 1 races in all, Beholder was champion

Mr D. Smith, Mrs John Magnier and Mr M. Tabor's "Mendelssohn"

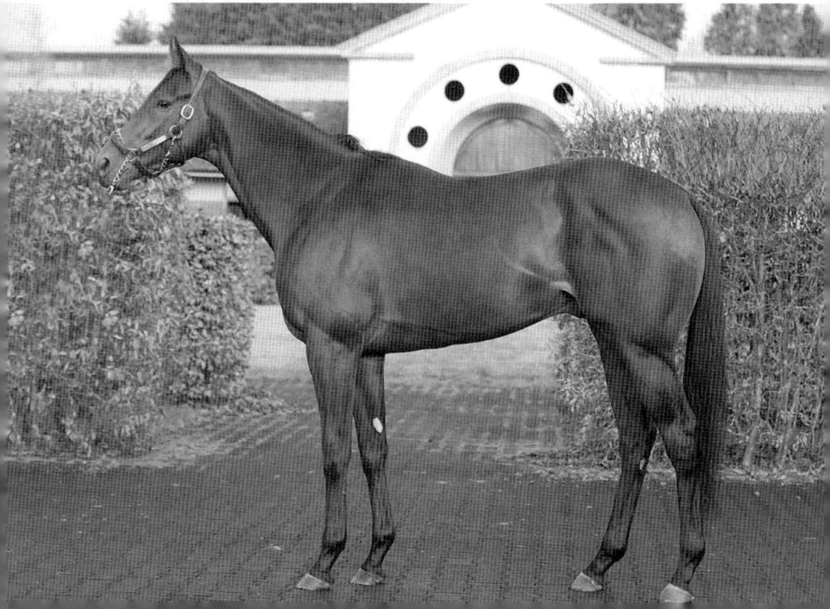

filly at two, when winning the Breeders' Cup Juvenile Fillies, and at three, when her wins included her first Distaff. Beholder's four-year-old season was interrupted by injury and illness, but she was champion older mare at five despite missing the Breeders' Cup for the second year running which was due to feature a clash with Triple Crown winner American Pharoah in the Classic. Beholder became the first of her sex to win the Pacific Classic that year, though, and was champion mare again at six when she ended her career by beating the hitherto unbeaten three-year-old filly Songbird by a nose to clinch her second Distaff after a memorable duel the length of the Santa Anita straight. The winner of the latest Distaff, Forever Unbridled, was back in third. Goldikova is the only other horse besides Beholder to have won three Breeders' Cup races, while Beholder's record of winning in Grade 1 company every year from two to six is unique. Beholder stayed further than her speedy sire Henny Hughes who was by Johannesburg's sire Hennessy. The other winner of note out of Mendelssohn's dam Leslie's Lady is Into Mischief, by Harlan's Holiday, another stallion from the Storm Cat line like Hennessy. Into Mischief is now a highly successful sire in his own right (dual Breeders' Cup Dirt Mile winner Goldencents being among his best horses), having been a Grade 1 winner at two in the Cashcall Futurity at Hollywood. Leslie's Lady, named Kentucky Broodmare of the Year in 2016 for Beholder's exploits, did all her winning on dirt and over sprint trips, with four of her five successes coming at two, including in a listed event at Hoosier Park, though later in her career she was placed at a mile on turf.

There's certainly encouragement to be taken from Beholder's record for Mendelssohn's staying further than either his sire or dam. However, even if he proves fully effective on the dirt, which shouldn't be a problem judged on his pedigree, taking on the very best American dirt performers in a big field for the Kentucky Derby would be a very different experience from anything he has encountered to date and, even after Del Mar, O'Brien stressed that the strong, well-made Mendelssohn was 'still learning'. The fitting of headgear for his last two starts clearly helped in that process and, in any case, however he fares at three, his pedigree, together with a Breeders' Cup win, has already assured him of a stallion career in due course. *Aidan O'Brien, Ireland*

MENELIK (IRE) 8 b.g. Oasis Dream 129 – Chica Roca (USA) 49 (Woodman (USA) 126) [2017 62: t7.1m^3 t9.5m^6 t6g^3 p6g* p7g^2 p6d* p5m* 5m p5g^2 p6s^4 p5g^5 p5g^3 p6g* Nov 10] attractive gelding: fairly useful handicapper: won at Chelmsford in February/March, Lingfield (by 3 lengths from Powerful Wind) later in March and Dundalk (claimer) in November: has form over 1½m, races mainly at 5f/6f nowadays: acts on polytrack and tapeta: wears headgear/tongue tie: front runner/races prominently. *Des Donovan, Ireland* **88**

MEN UNITED (FR) 4 b.g. Acclamation 118 – Moore's Melody (IRE) (Marju (IRE) 127) [2017 58: f6g^5 f5g t6g t7.2g 6g 5.2m f5g^2 5s t5.1m f5g f5g^5 Dec 21] modest handicapper: left Garry Moss after third start: stays 6f: acts on polytrack, fibresand, best turf form on good going: often wears headgear nowadays: has worn tongue tie, including final start: front runner/races prominently. *Roy Bowring* **57**

MERCERS 3 b.f. Piccolo 121 – Ivory's Joy 109 (Tina's Pet 121) [2017 62: p5g^2 p5g* p5g^3 5m^4 5.1m^5 p5g^5 5.1g^5 6g^6 5.3g^2 p5g^5 p5g^3 5.1d^4 p6g^4 p6g p5g^4 Dec 31] workmanlike filly: fair performer: won maiden at Lingfield in February: left Peter Crate after twelfth start: stays 6f: acts on polytrack and good to soft going: tried in headgear. *Paddy Butler* **69**

MERCERS ROW 10 b.g. Bahamian Bounty 116 – Invincible 76 (Slip Anchor 136) [2017 71: 6g 5.9g 5m 7.4m^6 6m^5 6s^5 t5g t7.1d Nov 4] leggy gelding: modest handicapper nowadays: left Michael Herrington after seventh start: stays 1m: acts on good to firm and heavy going: has worn headgear, including in 2017. *Martin Todhunter* **50**

MERCHANT MARINE (IRE) 2 b.g. (Feb 12) Epaulette (AUS) 126 – Chantilly Beauty (FR) 105 (Josr Algarhoud (IRE) 118) [2017 5.1m 6g^3 6.1m^3 7m 7g Sep 7] useful-looking gelding: fair maiden: best effort at 6f: acts on good to firm going: in visor last 4 starts: sent to Singapore. *Ralph Beckett* **71**

MERCHANT OF MEDICI 10 b.g. Medicean 128 – Regal Rose 110 (Danehill (USA) 126) [2017 69: 10.2d^5 12m^5 Jun 22] good-topped gelding: fairly useful handicapper at best: stayed 12.5f: acted on polytrack and any turf going: sometimes wore headgear: dead. *Micky Hammond* **54**

MERCURY 5 ch.g. Showcasing 117 – Miss Rimex (IRE) 84 (Ezzoud (IRE) 126) [2017 67: p7g p7g p8g p5g p6s* Dec 7] strong gelding: fair handicapper: won at Chelmsford in December: has won over 1¼m, raced at shorter nowadays: acts on polytrack, tapeta, soft and good to firm going: usually wears headgear: in tongue tie last 4 starts. *Adrian Brendan Joyce, Ireland* **66**

MERCURY RISING 2 b.c. (Feb 18) Henrythenavigator (USA) 131 – Millistar 88 (Galileo (IRE) 134) [2017 6v⁴ Sep 28] 8,000Y: half-brother to several winners, including 1½m winner (stays 1¾m) Hepplewhite (by Rail Link) and 1¼m-1½m winner Syncopate (by Oratorio): dam, 1¼m winner, out of top-class miler Milligram: 9/4, very green when well held in minor event at Pontefract: capable of better. *Andrew Balding* **– p**

MERCY ME 5 b.m. Mawatheeq (USA) 126 – Fantastic Santanyi (Fantastic Light (USA) 134) [2017 79: p10g³ p10g⁶ p10g² p10m⁵ p10g⁴ t10.2g² t9.5g³ Mar 30] tall mare: fair handicapper: stays 1½m: acts on polytrack, tapeta and good to firm going. *John Ryan* **79**

MERDON CASTLE (IRE) 5 b.g. Acclamation 118 – Siren's Gift 104 (Cadeaux Genereux 131) [2017 88: t7.1g⁴ t6g⁶ t7.1d t6g⁴ t7.1d 5.9g* 6g⁴ 7d⁶ 6s 7d 5.9s 7.4g⁵ 5g 5m³ 5g 5.3v⁵ p6g Dec 12] smallish, sturdy gelding: fairly useful handicapper: won at Carlisle (by ½ length from Penny Pot Lane) in May: left Ruth Carr after twelfth start: stays 6f: acts on polytrack and good to firm going: has worn eyeshields, including in 2017: races well off pace: inconsistent. *Jane Chapple-Hyam* **85**

MERE ANARCHY (IRE) 6 b.g. Yeats (IRE) 128 – Maracana (IRE) (Glacial Storm (USA) 127) [2017 68: t16.3g⁶ p16s* Sep 8] lengthy gelding: fair handicapper: won at Kempton in September: stays 2m: acts on polytrack: tried in tongue tie: carries head high. *Robert Stephens* **78**

MERKAVA 2 b.c. (Feb 2) Sayif (IRE) 122 – Dubawi's Spirit (IRE) (Dubawi (IRE) 129) [2017 6g³ t6d⁵ t7.2g² p7d² p8d* Oct 6] fair performer: won minor event at Chelmsford in October: stays 1m: acts on polytrack and tapeta: usually races close up. *Robyn Brisland* **72**

MERLIN 3 b.g. Oasis Dream 129 – Momentary 99 (Nayef (USA) 129) [2017 80: 8g² 6.1g* 7m* 7m² 6f* 6d³ 5.6g 6d Oct 6] lengthy, good-quartered gelding: useful performer: won maiden at Nottingham in May, and handicaps at Haydock in June and July (by 3½ lengths from Black Isle Boy): best up to 7f: acts on firm and good to soft going: usually leads. *Michael Bell* **103**

MERLIN MAGIC 2 b.c. (Mar 2) Camelot 128 – Seattle Ribbon (USA) 70 (Seattle Dancer (USA) 119) [2017 6d³ 7d² 7s⁵ 8.3d* 8d Oct 28] rather unfurnished colt: closely related to 3 winners, including smart 1¼m winner Snoqualmie Boy and useful winner up to 1½m Snoqualmie Girl (2-y-o 7f/1m winner) (both by Montjeu), and half-brother to several winners, including useful 1m-1¼m winner Snoqualmie Star (by Galileo): dam, maiden (stayed 1¼m), sister to Racing Post Trophy winner Seattle Rhyme: fairly useful performer: won maiden at Nottingham (by ¾ length from Sam Gold) in October: will stay at least 1¼m: acts on good to soft going. *David Elsworth* **91**

MERRIMENT 4 ch.f. Makfi 130 – Trianon 80 (Nayef (USA) 129) [2017 71: t16.3g⁶ f14g Jan 19] fair handicapper: stays 16.5f: acts on tapeta: wears cheekpieces. *Peter Niven* **66**

MERRY BANTER 3 b.f. Bated Breath 125 – Merry Diva 81 (Bahamian Bounty 116) [2017 90: t5g³ p5g² 5.1g⁴ 5m⁵ 5m² 5g 5f² 5g 5d⁵ 5.1g p5d Sep 28] fairly useful handicapper: second at Lingfield in March, Catterick in May and Haydock in July: raced only at 5f: acts on polytrack, tapeta and firm going: front runner/races prominently. *Paul Midgley* **93**

MESBAAR 3 b.g. Dalakhani (IRE) 133 – Wahylah (IRE) 87 (Shamardal (USA) 129) [2017 8.2d⁵ t9.5g² 10v Sep 21] sturdy, attractive gelding: fair form: best effort when second in maiden at Wolverhampton in August: should stay 1¼m. *Roger Varian* **77**

MESHARDAL (GER) 7 b.g. Shamardal (USA) 129 – Melody Fair (IRE) (Montjeu (IRE) 137) [2017 80: t6d³ f6d³ f6d² 6g 6m² 6m* 6g* 6m* 6m³ 6m³ 6m* 6d 6m 6s 7v Sep 30] well-made gelding: fairly useful handicapper: won at Catterick in May, Thirsk and York in June, and Catterick again (by ½ length from Love Oasis) in July: best at 6f: acts on fibresand, tapeta, soft and good to firm going: wears cheekpieces. *Ruth Carr* **84**

MESHAYKH (IRE) 3 b.f. Lope de Vega (IRE) 125 – French Lady (NZ) (Entrepreneur 123) [2017 73p: p8g⁵ 8.2d* 8.1m⁴ 10g⁶ Aug 2] good-topped filly: fairly useful handicapper: won at Leicester in May: best effort at 1m: acts on good to soft going: often races prominently. *Sir Michael Stoute* **86**

MESMERIC MOMENT 3 b.f. Showcasing 117 – Shared Moment (IRE) 73 (Tagula (IRE) 116) [2017 60: f5g⁴ f6g f5g f5g⁵ t7.1g p5d May 29] neat filly: modest at best: stayed 6f: acted on good to soft going: in headgear last 4 starts: front runner/raced prominently: dead. *Shaun Harris* **–**

MESOPHERE 3 ch.g. Exceed And Excel (AUS) 126 – Monturani (IRE) 112 (Indian Ridge 123) [2017 66p: t10.2g^5 p10g 8.1s^4 p11g Oct 24] fair maiden: left John Gosden after second start: stays 1¼m: acts on tapeta and soft going: tried in blinkers. *Harry Fry* **70**

MESQUITE 2 b.f. (Mar 23) High Chaparral (IRE) 132 – Puff (IRE) 107 (Camacho 118) [2017 p7g p7g Nov 6] first foal: dam, 6f (including at 2 yrs)/7f (Fred Darling Stakes) winner, half-sister to very smart winner up to 8.5f Sovereign Debt: modest form: better effort when eighth in maiden at Kempton (4 lengths behind George Villiers) in November. *Ralph Beckett* **63**

MESTI BOLEH 6 b.g. Cape Cross (IRE) 129 – Miss Meltemi (IRE) 100 (Miswaki Tern (USA) 120) [2017 f8.1g^5 12v Jun 10] modest form: stays 1¼m. *Michael Scudamore* **53**

METATRONS CUBE (IRE) 2 b.g. (Apr 3) Artie Schiller (USA) 124 – Quiet Down (USA) (Quiet American (USA)) [2017 7g^4 7g^4 7d p7g Oct 11] lengthy gelding: fair form: raced only at 7f. *Charles Hills* **71**

MET BY MOONLIGHT 3 b.f. Sakhee's Secret 128 – Starlight Walk 84 (Galileo (IRE) 134) [2017 57: p5g^2 p5g 5m^2 6.1m 5d^5 7.1d^6 p6g^6 p5g* Dec 31] workmanlike filly: fair handicapper: won at Lingfield in December: best form at 5f: acts on polytrack, good to firm and good to soft going: often races towards rear. *Ron Hodges* **77**

METEORIC RISER (USA) 3 b.c. More Than Ready (USA) 120 – Silimiss (Dansili 127) [2017 69p: p8g p7g^5 9.9f^6 10.2f p11s 8.1m Jun 26] modest maiden: stays 1¼m: acts on polytrack and firm going: in headgear last 2 starts. *Richard Hughes* **64**

METEOR LIGHT (IRE) 3 b.g. Clodovil (IRE) 116 – Nordkappe (GER) (High Chaparral (IRE) 132) [2017 68p: 8.3g* 10d* 10.3m Jul 1] sturdy gelding: fairly useful form: won maiden at Nottingham in May and handicap at Leicester (by ½ length from Cotinga) in June: will be suited by 1½m: wears hood: sent to Australia. *Ed Vaughan* **94**

METHAG (FR) 4 b.f. Pour Moi (IRE) 125 – Kyria (Grand Lodge (USA) 125) [2017 p12g^5 12s^2 p12g 14.2d p12g^6 Nov 7] seventh foal: half-sister to French 7.5f-8.5f winner Monte Napoleone (by Fol Parade) and French/Spanish 1¼m-1½m winner Kuttuna (by Sorcerous): dam French 1¼m winner: fairly useful handicapper: won twice in France for Francois Rohaut in 2016: second at Newbury in May: stays 1½m: acts on polytrack and soft going. *Alex Hales* **82**

METISIAN 3 b.g. Sleeping Indian 122 – Blushing Heart 62 (Observatory (USA) 131) [2017 63: t5s^4 6d* 6g^3 5s^4 5.9s^5 6s^2 6s^3 Oct 10] fair handicapper: won at Doncaster in June: will be suited by 7f: acts on tapeta and soft going: in cheekpieces last 2 starts: often races towards rear. *Jedd O'Keeffe* **77**

METKAIF 2 b.g. (Feb 18) Iffraaj 127 – Martagon Lily 80 (Manduro (GER) 135) [2017 p8g^6 p7g^6 p7g^4 Nov 2] 44,000F, 100,000Y: good-topped gelding: first foal: dam, maiden (stayed 1¼m), closely related to useful performer up to 2½m Mill Springs and half-sister to smart 1m-1¼m winner Monturani: fairly useful form: best effort when fourth in minor event at Lingfield (3¾ lengths behind Statehood) in November. *Richard Hannon* **80**

ME TOO NAGASAKI (IRE) 3 b.g. Iffraaj 127 – Distinguish (IRE) 68 (Refuse To Bend (IRE) 128) [2017 78p: p8g^4 8v* t8.6g^4 8g^2 9.9s^3 8v^2 Oct 9] useful handicapper: won at Doncaster (by head from Wahash) in May: placed at Sandown (½ length behind Surrey Hope) in June, Goodwood (4½ lengths behind Lunar Jet) in September and Pontefract (2¼ lengths behind The Grape Escape) in October: stays 8.5f: acts on polytrack, tapeta and heavy going: usually races towards rear: sold to join Stuart Williams 125,000 gns later in October. *Jeremy Noseda* **98**

METRONOMIC (IRE) 3 b.g. Roderic O'Connor (IRE) 119 – Meon Mix 61 (Kayf Tara 130) [2017 60: p7m^3 t7.1m^3 p7g^5 p8g^3 p8g* p8g^5 9.8m* 9.8d^4 9.9m* 10.3d t12.4s 8.5v 10v* Nov 7] fair performer: won handicap at Kempton in April, seller at Ripon in May, handicap at Beverley in June and claimer at Redcar in November: left Richard Hannon after seventh start: stays 1¼m: acts on polytrack, tapeta, good to firm and heavy going: has worn cheekpieces: front runner/races prominently. *Peter Niven* **74**

METROPOL (IRE) 6 b.h. Holy Roman Emperor (IRE) 125 – Monetary (GER) 107 (Winged Love (IRE) 121) [2017 109: p7.5g^2 p8.9g* p8g^3 p7g^5 p10g^6 8d p9.4g* p9.4f* p7.5g 9.9s^5 9.9g^4 Dec 1] useful performer: won minor event at Chantilly in January, and claimers at Deauville in July and August: 5¼ lengths sixth to Convey in Easter Classic AW Middle Distance Championships Stakes at Lingfield on fifth outing: left Mme Pia Brandt after eighth start: stays 1¼m: acts on polytrack and soft going: often in headgear. *Fabrice Vermeulen, Belgium* **98**

METTE 4 b.f. Virtual 122 – Regal Gallery (IRE) 76 (Royal Academy (USA) 130) [2017 –: p10g 10m p8g p7m f7.1g Dec 4] poor maiden: tried in hood: in tongue tie last 2 starts. *Mark Usher* **43**

MEWTOW 2 b.c. (Mar 5) Helmet (AUS) 127 – White Spirit (IRE) 64 (Invincible Spirit (IRE) 121) [2017 t7.2g^{6} p8g* Dec 20] 21,000Y, 80,000 2-y-o: second foal: dam, maiden (stayed 6f), half-sister to smart sprinter Face The Problem: fair form: won minor event at Lingfield (by 1½ lengths from Oskemen) in December: wears hood: open to further improvement. *George Scott* **78 p**

MEYANDI 3 ch.c. Mount Nelson 125 – Susi Wong (IRE) (Selkirk (USA) 129) [2017 61: f11.1g^{2} 13.3v^{2} 12g* 12s^{4} Sep 14] fairly useful handicapper: won at Chepstow (apprentice, by 3¼ lengths from Mirimar) in September: will be suited by 1¾m+: acts on heavy going: usually races close up: sold 20,000 gns in November. *Andrew Balding* **82**

MEYRICK 3 b.g. Helmet (AUS) 127 – Esteemed Lady (IRE) 96 (Mark of Esteem (IRE) 137) [2017 –p: 8.2d 6m^{5} Jun 17] well-made gelding: little impact in maidens. *William Haggas* **–**

MEZMAAR 8 b.g. Teofilo (IRE) 126 – Bay Tree (IRE) 100 (Daylami (IRE) 138) [2017 86: p7g p6g t7.1g p7d^{4} p7g t7.2g p8g^{3} p7g^{4} p7g Oct 4] useful-looking gelding: fair handicapper nowadays: stays 1m: acts on polytrack, good to firm and good to soft going: often wears hood: often races prominently. *Mark Usher* **76**

MEZYAN (IRE) 3 b.f. Acclamation 118 – Queen of Carthage (USA) (Cape Cross (IRE) 129) [2017 –: p6g^{4} p7d^{5} Feb 2] modest maiden: best effort at 6f: acts on polytrack: often races towards rear: sold 4,000 gns, sent to Italy. *John Butler* **50**

MEZZOTINT (IRE) 8 b.g. Diamond Green (FR) 121 – Aquatint (Dansili 127) [2017 80, a88: p7g p8m^{6} 7d p7d^{5} p10s 8.1m Jul 3] robust gelding: fairly useful handicapper, below form in 2017: stayed 1m: acted on polytrack and good to firm going: sometimes wore headgear: tried in tongue tie: dead. *Lee Carter* **75**

MIA CARA 3 b.f. Camacho 118 – Vita Mia 70 (Central Park (IRE) 123) [2017 67: t7.1m* f8s^{3} p7g* p7g^{6} t7.1g^{2} t7.1g^{4} 6m 7g^{6} 7.1v^{2} 6g 8.1d^{3} 7.6v^{2} Sep 15] compact filly: fair handicapper: won at Wolverhampton in January and Lingfield in February: stays 1m: acts on polytrack, tapeta and heavy going: usually wears visor. *David Evans* **75**

MIAMI SUNSET 3 b.f. Archipenko (USA) 127 – Laraib (IRE) (Invincible Spirit (IRE) 121) [2017 p8d^{2} 6m* p6s Sep 8] 5,500Y: first foal: dam unraced: fair form: won maiden at Yarmouth (by 2¾ lengths from Seyasah) in August: should stay beyond 6f. *Philip McBride* **73**

MIA TESORO (IRE) 4 b.f. Danehill Dancer (IRE) 117 – Souter's Sister (IRE) 103 (Desert Style (IRE) 121) [2017 87: p10g^{6} 9.9g^{6} 10g^{3} 10m p8g^{4} p10g^{3} p10g^{2} Dec 23] angular filly: useful performer: placed in listed races at Lingfield in November (2½ lengths behind Master The World) and December (neck behind Petite Jack): stays 10.5f: acts on polytrack, tapeta and firm going: wears hood. *Charlie Fellowes* **100**

MIA WALLACE (IRE) 3 b.f. Elzaam (AUS) 115 – Perfectly Clear (USA) (Woodman (USA) 126) [2017 t5d^{3} t6m Mar 14] half-sister to several winners, including useful 2-y-o 6f winner Madrinho (by Frozen Power) and winner up to 1¼m Safari Team (2-y-o 1m winner, by Pleasantly Perfect): dam US 1m/9f winner: poor form: better effort when third in maiden at Newcastle in February: should stay 6f+. *David O'Meara* **47**

MICA MIKA (IRE) 9 ch.g. Needwood Blade 117 – Happy Talk (IRE) 74 (Hamas (IRE) 125) [2017 90: p10g^{3} p12g^{3} t12.4d 10.3m Jun 16] fairly useful handicapper: third at Lingfield in January and February: stays 1¾m: acts on polytrack, tapeta, good to firm and heavy going: has worn headgear. *Richard Fahey* **91**

MI CAPRICHO (IRE) 2 b.c. (Mar 30) Elzaam (AUS) 115 – Mavemacullen (IRE) (Ad Valorem (USA) 125) [2017 7.2g^{5} 7.2d^{5} 7.2m^{2} 7.2m Sep 8] fair form when second in minor event at Musselburgh in August, standout effort: raced only at 7f. *Keith Dalgleish* **75**

MICHAEL'S MOUNT 4 ch.g. Mount Nelson 125 – Dumnoni 97 (Titus Livius (FR) 115) [2017 86: 12g 12.3d^{5} 16g 12.3d^{5} 10v* 10s^{2} 10.2s^{3} 12v* 12s^{3} Oct 15] sturdy gelding: fairly useful handicapper: won at Lingfield in July and Ripon (by ½ length from Indy) in September: stays 1¾m: acts on good to firm and heavy going: wears headgear: usually travels strongly: sold to join Ian Williams 62,000 gns in November. *Ed Dunlop* **92**

MICHELE STROGOFF 4 b.g. Aqlaam 125 – Maschera d'Oro (Mtoto 134) [2017 99: 7.6d^{5} 7.8g^{2} 7.2m p8s 7.6d* 6s 7.6s 10.1m t7.2g^{4} p8s^{3} t9.5g^{4} f7.1g Dec 11] useful performer: won claimer at Chester in June: second in handicap at Carlisle in May: best up to 1m: acts on polytrack, soft and good to firm going: usually wears headgear: usually races close up. *Tony Coyle* **94**

MICHIGAN (USA) 3 ch.c. Galileo (IRE) 134 – I'm So Excited (USA) (Street Cry (IRE) 130) [2017 10.4g4 10.4m3 12.4d t9.5g p12g p12g Dec 28] fair maiden: left Jean-Claude Rouget after third start: stays 10.5f: tried in cheekpieces: in tongue tie last 3 starts. *Mohamed Moubarak* **77**

MICKEY (IRE) 4 b.g. Zoffany (IRE) 121 – Enchantment 108 (Compton Place 125) [2017 98: p7g Dec 13] fairly useful handicapper: stays 7f: acts on tapeta and firm going: wears tongue tie. *Tom Dascombe* **86**

MICK THE POSER (IRE) 3 b.g. Art Connoisseur (IRE) 121 – Naked Poser (IRE) 83 (Night Shift (USA)) [2017 –: t8.6g 11.2d6 12.1s* 14.1v Sep 13] modest handicapper: won at Hamilton in August: stays 1½m: acts on soft going: in cheekpieces last 2 starts. *Jennie Candlish* **61**

MIDAS MAGGIE 2 b.f. (Feb 4) Archipenko (USA) 127 – Algarade 92 (Green Desert (USA) 127) [2017 7d6 p7d5 8d Oct 27] €40,000Y: third foal: sister to useful performer up to 1½m Alinstante (2-y-o 6f-1m winner) and half-sister to 13f-16.5f winner Alba Verde (by Verglas): dam winner up to 1¼m (2-y-o 1m winner): modest form on last of 3 starts in minor events: will stay at least 1¼m. *Charles Hills* **61**

MIDDLE CREEK 3 b.f. Poet's Voice 126 – Mezzogiorno 108 (Unfuwain (USA) 131) [2017 t8s5 t8.6g4 Dec 18] half-sister to numerous winners, including smart 1m-1¼m winner Monturani (by Indian Ridge) and useful 1½m-1¾m winner (stayed 2½m) Mill Springs (by Shirocco): dam winner up to 1¼m (2-y-o 7f winner) and third in Oaks: modest form: better effort when fourth in maiden at Wolverhampton in December: will stay 1¼m: open to further improvement. *John Gosden* **61 p**

MIDDLE KINGDOM (USA) 3 b.c. War Front (USA) 119 – River Belle 113 (Lahib (USA) 129) [2017 92p: 10m* p10d3 p10g4 Nov 21] good sort: useful form: won handicap at Newmarket (by neck from Euginio) in April: third in similar event at Chelmsford (½ length behind Plutonian) in November: stays 1¼m: in tongue tie last 2 starts. *John Gosden* **103**

MIDGE HALL (IRE) 3 ch.f. Helmet (AUS) 127 – Allegrissimo (IRE) 48 (Redback 116) [2017 –: t7.1g5 Jan 9] little impact in minor event/maiden. *Bryan Smart* **–**

MIDHMAAR 4 b.g. Iffraaj 127 – Merayaat (IRE) 80 (Darshaan 133) [2017 98: 8.3g4 8m4 8f3 8m3 Jul 7] well-made gelding: useful handicapper: third at Bath (3 lengths behind Realize) in June and Haydock (2 lengths behind Calder Prince) in July: stays 1¼m: acts on polytrack, firm and good to soft going: in headgear last 2 starts: sold 55,000 gns, sent to Bahrain. *Owen Burrows* **95**

MIDI 2 b.c. (Jan 28) Frankel 147 – Midday 126 (Oasis Dream 129) [2017 8g Sep 28] third foal: brother to useful 1¼m winner Mori and closely related to smart winner up to 1¼m Midterm (2-y-o 1m winner, by Galileo), both stay 1½m: dam multiple Group 1 winner at up to 1½m (2-y-o 1m winner): 8/1, badly needed experience when well held in maiden at Newmarket: will prove different proposition in time. *Sir Michael Stoute* **– P**

MIDLIGHT 5 b.g. Elusive City (USA) 117 – My Heart's Deelite (USA) (Afternoon Deelites (USA) 122) [2017 62: f7g 10g 8m* 8.5d5 8m4 8m Jul 10] tall gelding: fair handicapper: won at Ayr in May: stays 1¼m: acts on tapeta and good to firm going: tried in blinkers: usually wears tongue tie nowadays: front runner/races prominently. *Ruth Carr* **65**

MIDNIGHT BLUE 2 gr.f. (Mar 18) Pivotal 124 – Arabescatta (Monsun (GER) 124) [2017 t5.1g p7g p6d t6.1g Aug 10] neat filly: third foal: half-sister to 1¾m winner Plage Depampelonne (by Redoute's Choice) and a winner in Italy by Fastnet Rock: dam, 1m-1¼m winner, half-sister to St Leger runner-up Midas Touch and Ribblesdale Stakes winner Coronet: no form in minor events. *Sir Mark Prescott Bt* **–**

MIDNIGHT GUEST (IRE) 2 b.f. (Apr 18) Acclamation 118 – Midnight Martini 100 (Night Shift (USA)) [2017 p6s3 p6s6 Dec 1] 45,000Y: third foal: sister to winner around 6f (including at 2 yrs) Mr Pocket and half-sister to useful 5f (including at 2 yrs) winner Midnight Malibu (by Poet's Voice): dam 2-y-o 5f/6f winner: modest form when third at Chelmsford (5¾ lengths behind Red Cymbal) on first of 2 starts in minor events. *George Margarson* **62**

MIDNIGHTLY 3 b.f. Acclamation 118 – Midnight Shift (IRE) 73 (Night Shift (USA)) [2017 p5g2 p5g* 5g3 5m5 5.2m4 5.2g2 t5.1g* p5g Oct 13] half-sister to several winners, including useful 5f/6f winner Miss Anabaa (by Anabaa) and smart/ungenuine 5f/6f winner Out After Dark (by Cadeaux Genereux): dam, 6f winner, half-sister to July Cup winner Owington: fairly useful performer: won maiden at Chelmsford in March and handicap at Wolverhampton (by ½ length from Wild Approach) in August: raced only at 5f: acts on polytrack, tapeta, best turf form on good going: in tongue tie last 4 starts. *Rae Guest* **82**

MIDNIGHT MACCHIATO (IRE) 4 b.g. Dark Angel (IRE) 113 – Lathaat 72 (Dubai Destination (USA) 127) [2017 88: 8m 7s^3 8m^5 p8g^2 p7d f7.1g f5g Dec 29] rather leggy gelding: fairly useful handicapper: placed at Newmarket in May and Chelmsford in October: stays 1m: acts on polytrack and good to firm going: front runner/races prominently. *David Brown* **84**

MIDNIGHT MALIBU (IRE) 4 b.f. Poet's Voice 126 – Midnight Martini 100 (Night Shift (USA)) [2017 91: 5m^2 5m 5m^2 5f^6 5m^2 5m 5f^2 5d^3 5m* 5s 5v 5s^4 5v t5.1g^3 f5g* p5g^5 Dec 12] close-coupled filly: useful handicapper: won at Epsom in August and Southwell (by ½ length from Arzaak) in November: stays 5.5f: acts on polytrack, fibresand and any turf going: often races prominently. *Tim Easterby* **97**

MIDNIGHT MAN (FR) 3 ch.g. Evasive 116 – Moon Tree (FR) (Groom Dancer (USA) 128) [2017 66: f8g^3 10m^5 10m 8.3v t10.2s Sep 19] modest maiden: stays 1m: acts on fibresand and heavy going: tried in visor/tongue tie. *K. R. Burke* **62**

MIDNIGHT MOOD 4 b.f. Aqlaam 125 – Inflammable 76 (Montjeu (IRE) 137) [2017 66: 12m 10.1g 9.9m^6 10d 11.9d^3 p16g p11g^5 p12g^5 Nov 1] modest handicapper: stays 1½m: acts on polytrack, good to firm and good to soft going: tried in cheekpieces: in tongue tie last 2 starts. *Dominic Ffrench Davis* **59**

MIDNIGHT VIXEN 3 b.f. Foxwedge (AUS) 128 – Midnight Ransom (Red Ransom (USA)) [2017 68p: 10.2g 8m Jun 16] fair maiden: found little in handicaps in 2017: should prove suited by 1m+: acts on polytrack: front runner/races prominently. *Sir Michael Stoute* **68**

MIDNIGHT WARRIOR 7 b.g. Teofilo (IRE) 126 – Mauri Moon 104 (Green Desert (USA) 127) [2017 64: 12g 15.9m 14g^2 14m^5 12.1m^2 14g* 13d^3 14d 12.1g^4 12.1s 14d Oct 20] modest handicapper: won at Redcar (apprentice) in July: stays 2m: acts on soft and good to firm going: has worn hood: wears tongue tie. *Ron Barr* **64**

MIDNIGHT WHISTLER (USA) 5 b.g. Henrythenavigator (USA) 131 – Ball Gown (USA) (Silver Hawk (USA) 123) [2017 76: 8.5d* 8s^5 Jul 28] fairly useful handicapper: won at Epsom (apprentice, by neck from Chosen Character) in July: stays 1½m, effective over much shorter: acts on polytrack and good to soft going: in cheekpieces last 4 starts: races prominently: sold 1,000 gns in November, sent to Portugal. *Martyn Meade* **83**

MIDNIGHT WILDE 2 gr.g. (Feb 27) Poet's Voice 126 – Si Belle (IRE) 95 (Dalakhani (IRE) 133) [2017 7d^3 6m^2 7m* 7m^6 p7s^6 8d^2 8d^5 Sep 30] 8,000Y: fifth foal: half-brother to 1m-11.5f winner Betsalottie (by Aqlaam) and 7f/1m winner Golden Guest (by Bated Breath): dam 1½m-1¾m winner: fairly useful performer: won minor event at Yarmouth in August: second in similar event at York in July and nursery at Yarmouth in September: stays 1m: acts on good to firm and good to soft going: tried in blinkers: usually races prominently. *John Ryan* **82**

MIDNITEMUDCRABS (IRE) 4 ch.f. Arcano (IRE) 122 – Ma Nikitia (IRE) (Camacho 118) [2017 82, a69: 6d 7s^2 8m 7s 7.9g^6 6g^5 7d^5 7s 8s^5 8s^3 p7g^4 p7g p7g* p8g^2 p6g^4 p8s Dec 8] fairly useful performer: won claimer at Dundalk (by ¾ length from Maysonette) in October: stays 1m: acts on polytrack and soft going: sometimes wears cheekpieces: has worn tongue tie, including final start: front runner/races prominently. *J. J. Feane, Ireland* **80**

MIDSUMMER KNIGHT 2 b.g. (May 10) Dream Ahead (USA) 133 – High Spice (USA) 92 (Songandaprayer (USA) 118) [2017 5m^4 5.1m^2 t5.1g^2 5g^6 5.4g^2 t6.1m^2 t6g^3 t5.1g^2 t5.1d^2 Dec 26] lengthy gelding: fair maiden: left Mick Channon after fourth start: stays 6f: acts on tapeta and good to firm going: tried in cheekpieces/tongue tie: usually leads. *K. R. Burke* **78**

MIDTECH STAR (IRE) 5 b.g. Kodiac 112 – Royal Rival (IRE) (Marju (IRE) 127) [2017 88: t12.2m^6 p14d* p16d^3 t13.9g* p13g^3 t13.9g^2 13.1m* 14.6m* May 6] fairly useful handicapper: won at Chelmsford in February, Wolverhampton in March, Bath in April and Doncaster in May: stays 2m: acts on polytrack, tapeta, good to firm and good to soft going: wears headgear. *Ian Williams* **73 + a93**

MIDTERM 4 b.g. Galileo (IRE) 134 – Midday 126 (Oasis Dream 129) [2017 119: 12m^5 12s^3 12g^6 10.1m* p12g^6 12s^4 Oct 7] good-topped gelding: smart performer: won minor event at Epsom (by 2½ lengths from Mount Logan) in August: third in Aston Park Stakes at Newbury (4 lengths behind Hawkbill) in May: stays 1½m: acts on soft and good to firm going: tried in visor. *Sir Michael Stoute* **116**

MIGHTASWELLSMILE 3 b.f. Elnadim (USA) 128 – Intishaar (IRE) (Dubai Millennium 140) [2017 69: 5g^5 5g 6m Jul 10] fair at 2 yrs, no form in 2017. *Ron Barr* **–**

MIGHTY BOND 5 b.g. Misu Bond (IRE) 114 – Mighty Flyer (IRE) (Mujtahid (USA) 118) [2017 59: 5g 6d^6 t5g 6g^4 6g^2 6m 6s^3 5s 6d^4 7d 6v t7.1g Nov 15] modest maiden: stays 6f: acts on heavy going: wears cheekpieces: has suspect attitude. *Tracy Waggott* **54**

MIGHTY LADY 4 ch.f. Mighty 117 – Spia (USA) (Diesis 133) [2017 84: 11.4m^{6} p8g^{6} **78**
10v^{5} p16d t9.5g^{3} p10d^{5} p10g^{5} p8g Oct 25] rangy filly: fair handicapper: stays 10.5f: acts on polytrack, tapeta and good to soft going: tried in cheekpieces: sometimes slowly away, often races towards rear. *Robyn Brisland*

MIGHTY MAC (IRE) 2 b.g. (Apr 27) Dragon Pulse (IRE) 114 – Invincible Fire (IRE) **–**
66 (Invincible Spirit (IRE) 121) [2017 5m Sep 15] 10/1, green when well held in maiden at Sandown. *Ralph Beckett*

MIGHTY MISSILE (IRE) 6 ch.g. Majestic Missile (IRE) 118 – Magdalene (FR) **–**
(College Chapel 122) [2017 t13.9g 14.2g Aug 7] maiden, little impact in handicaps in 2017: usually in headgear nowadays: in tongue tie last 4 starts: quirky: winning hurdler. *Brian Barr*

MIGHTY ZIP (USA) 5 ch.g. City Zip (USA) 112 – Incredulous (FR) 95 (Indian Ridge **70**
123) [2017 54§, a68§: p6g t6g t5.1g p5d* p6g^{2} p6d^{3} p5g^{*d} p6g* p5g^{4} p5g^{5} 5g* 5m^{3} p5s* 5m^{3} 5.1d 5f p5s Dec 8] fair handicapper: won at Chelmsford in February (apprentice), April and May, and at Nottingham earlier in May: also first past post at former course in March, but disqualified after weighing in 6 lb light: stays 6f: acts on polytrack and tapeta: wears headgear. *Lisa Williamson*

MIGYAAS (USA) 3 b.g. Lonhro (AUS) 128 – Nasmatt 96 (Danehill (USA) 126) [2017 **72**
64p: 10m^{3} t12.2g^{3} 14f 10.2g a9.9f a9.7f Dec 15] fair maiden: left Saeed bin Suroor after fourth start: stays 1½m: acts on tapeta and good to firm going: in headgear last 5 starts, also tongue tied last 2: often races prominently/freely. *M. Ramadan, UAE*

MIKEY READY (USA) 3 b.g. Frankel 147 – Reaching (IRE) 71 (Dansili 127) [2017 61: **67**
p8m^{4} t9.5g^{6} Feb 13] fair form: stays 9.5f: wears tongue tie. *Ed Walker*

MIKMAK 4 b.g. Makfi 130 – Rakata (USA) 83 (Quiet American (USA)) [2017 93: t8.6g^{6} **88**
10s^{2} p10g^{5} 9.1g 9.9d^{5} 10.2s^{2} 10d 9.9g 10g 8.3d^{2} 8.1d Oct 23] tall, good-topped gelding: fairly useful handicapper: second at Leicester in May, Bath in August and Nottingham in October: stays 1¼m: acts on polytrack and heavy going: wears headgear: sometimes slowly away: inconsistent: sold to join Tim Easterby 27,000 gns in November. *William Muir*

MILAN REEF (IRE) 2 br.f. (Feb 4) Famous Name 124 – Jagapaw (IRE) (Manduro **68**
(GER) 135) [2017 6m 6m 7d 7s^{2} 8m 8.1s* 8g 8v^{2} 8.3v^{5} Nov 8] €800Y: small filly: second foal: sister to 1m/9f winner What Wonders Weave: dam once-raced half-sister to ungenuine winner up to 6f Rock Jock and 1m-1¼m winner Breden (both useful): fair performer: won nursery at Chepstow in September: stays 1m: best form on soft/heavy going: front runner/races prominently. *David Loughnane*

MILBURN JACK 3 br.g. Foxwedge (AUS) 128 – Tintac 53 (Intikhab (USA) 135) [2017 **74**
–p: p7g^{4} p7g^{5} 7m 8m^{5} 7g p7s Aug 9] fair maiden: stays 7f: acts on polytrack and good to firm going: in headgear last 3 starts: front runner/races prominently. *Clive Cox*

MILCHIK 2 b.f. (Apr 20) Lethal Force (IRE) 128 – Millsini 55 (Rossini (USA) 118) [2017 **48**
p5g^{6} 5m May 26] 15,000Y: sixth foal: half-sister to 2-y-o 5f winner Tribesman (by Equiano): dam, maiden (stayed 6f), half-sister to smart sprinter Mirza: last in minor events. *Michael Attwater*

MILDENBERGER 2 b.c. (Mar 14) Teofilo (IRE) 126 – Belle Josephine 80 (Dubawi **106 p**
(IRE) 129) [2017 7m* 7g* 7g^{3} 8g* 8d^{3} Sep 30] attractive colt, rather unfurnished at present: third foal: brother to 2-y-o 7f winner (stays 1¼m) Berengaria: dam, 1½m-2m winner, half-sister to smart performer up to 2m Yankee Doodle: useful performer: won minor events at Haydock and Newbury (by 5 lengths from Ode To Autumn) in July, and listed race at Salisbury (by nose from Albishr) in August: third in Vintage Stakes at Goodwood (5¼ lengths behind Expert Eye) earlier in August and Royal Lodge Stakes at Newmarket (2 lengths behind Roaring Lion) in September: will be suited by 1¼m+: acts on good to firm and good to soft going: front runner/races prominently, responds generously to pressure: remains with potential. *Mark Johnston*

MILITARY LAW 2 b.c. (Apr 4) Dubawi (IRE) 129 – Marine Bleue (IRE) 109 (Desert **85 p**
Prince (IRE) 130) [2017 8g 8d* Oct 27] attractive colt: brother to useful 2-y-o 6f winner Wednaan, closely related to 1¼m winner Adalene (by Makfi) and half-brother to 3 winners, including useful 9f-1½m winner Marina Piccola (by Halling): dam 7f/1m winner: fairly useful form: won minor event at Newbury (by ½ length from Blue Mist) in October: will stay further than 1m: open to further improvement. *John Gosden*

MILITARY MADAME (IRE) 2 b.f. (Apr 28) Epaulette (AUS) 126 – Sweet Kristeen **53**
(USA) 69 (Candy Stripes (USA) 115) [2017 t7.1g 7v t8g Nov 3] €20,000F, €47,000Y: strong filly: half-sister to several winners, including useful 1m winner Cliche (by Diktat)

and useful 6f/7f winner (including at 2 yrs) Al Shahaniya (by Zoffany), stayed 1¼m: dam 7f winner: modest form: best effort when eighth in maiden at Newcastle (7 lengths behind Chrisellaine) on debut. *John Quinn*

MILITARY PARADE 3 b.g. Dutch Art 126 – Bahia Emerald (IRE) 80 (Bahamian **78** Bounty 116) [2017 p10g^2 t9.5g^3 t12.4g Oct 10] fair form when placed on first 2 starts in maidens. *Saeed bin Suroor*

MILITIA 2 b.c. (Mar 9) Equiano (FR) 127 – Sweet As Honey 82 (Duke of Marmalade **84** (IRE) 132) [2017 5.4d^3 5v^4 5.4g^3 t5.1g^3 Nov 7] 14,000F, €45,000Y, 35,000 2-y-o: compact colt: first foal: dam, maiden (would have stayed 1¼m), half-sister to smart 11f-1¾m winner Tactician: fairly useful form: best form at 5f. *Richard Fahey*

MILKY WAY (IRE) 5 b.g. Galileo (IRE) 134 – Beauty Bright (IRE) 113 (Danehill (USA) **84** 126) [2017 11.2g 10g^2 11.4d^4 Sep 4] useful-looking gelding: fairly useful handicapper: second at Newbury (amateur) in July: stays 1¼m: acts on heavy going. *Gary Moore*

MILLADY PERCY 4 b.f. Sir Percy 129 – Steady Rain 68 (Zafonic (USA) 130) [2017 –: **–** t9.5g^5 Feb 20] no form: sometimes in hood. *Roy Brotherton*

MILLER AND COOK (IRE) 6 b.g. Oratorio (IRE) 128 – Canaan (IRE) 63 (Alhaarth **42** (IRE) 126) [2017 –: 13.1s 12.1s^6 Aug 24] maiden, poor form in 2017. *Mark McNiff, Ireland*

MILLE TANK 2 b.f. (Feb 13) Mastercraftsman (IRE) 129 – Millevini (IRE) (Hawk Wing **55** (USA) 136) [2017 8s t8.6g Nov 29] 60,000Y: first foal: dam, placed up to 1m in Scandinavia, half-sister to St Leger winner Kingston Hill (by Mastercraftsman): modest form when seventh at Wolverhampton on second of 2 starts in minor events. *William Muir*

MILLIE MAY 3 b.f. Sixties Icon 125 – Maydream 75 (Sea Freedom 84) [2017 –: 7m 8.1g **–** 8g Aug 7] well held in maidens. *Jimmy Fox*

MILLIE'S KISS 3 b.f. Aussie Rules (USA) 123 – Aliena (IRE) (Grand Lodge (USA) **78** 125) [2017 78: p7g* p8g^4 p8g 8g^6 9.1s^3 10.1g^3 10g^4 9.9g^5 9.9d^3 p10d^3 t8.6g^6 t8.6g^3 p10s Nov 17] workmanlike filly: fair performer: won maiden at Lingfield in March: stays 1¼m: acts on polytrack, tapeta, soft and good to firm going. *Philip McBride*

MILLYBOND 3 b.f. Misu Bond (IRE) 114 – Noble Attitude 60 (Best of The Bests (IRE) **–** 122) [2017 –: f8g Mar 9] no form, including in handicap. *David Brown*

MILORD (GER) 8 br.g. Monsun (GER) 124 – Montserrat (GER) (Zilzal (USA) 137) **–** [2017 16g Jun 11] useful performer in 2012 when trained in Germany, behind in handicap sole start on Flat since: stays 11f: best form on good going: in headgear last 2 starts: fairly useful hurdler. *Kim Bailey*

MILROW (IRE) 4 b.g. Tamayuz 126 – Cannikin (IRE) 82 (Lahib (USA) 129) [2017 78: **73** 11.6g May 24] fair maiden: stays 1½m: acts on polytrack: in cheekpieces last 4 starts: tried in tongue tie: sometimes slowly away, often travels strongly. *Dr Richard Newland*

MILTON ROAD 2 b.c. (Jun 8) Mazameer (IRE) 107 – Blakeshall Girl 64 (Piccolo 121) **78** [2017 5m^6 5.3m^2 5.3m^2 5.1m^3 5g^6 6m^6 5g* 6m^5 6g* 6.1g* 5v^6 p5g* 6d p7s^4 t6.1g^3 p6d^5 t5.1m^5 Oct 28] sturdy colt: fair performer: won sellers at Goodwood in June and Leicester in July, and nurseries at Nottingham later in July and Chelmsford in August: stays 7f: acts on polytrack, tapeta and good to firm going: usually races nearer last than first. *Mick Channon*

MIME DANCE 6 b.g. Notnowcato 128 – Encore My Love 68 (Royal Applause 124) **71** [2017 78: t7.1d^4 t7.1d^4 t7.1g^6 p8g p7g p7g p7s Jun 21] sturdy gelding: fair handicapper: left David O'Meara after third start: stays 8.5f: acts on tapeta, soft and good to firm going: wears headgear. *John Butler*

MIMIC'S MEMORY 3 b.f. Sayif (IRE) 122 – Blue Crest (FR) (Verglas (IRE) 118) **71** [2017 –: f6g^4 t6d^3 t6m 6g^5 6g^4 f7.1g* t8g^2 7.2v 6d^6 6v t8.6g^5 f8.1g^3 p8s^5 Dec 15] fair handicapper: won at Southwell in May: stays 8.5f: acts on fibresand, tapeta, best turf form on good going: tried in tongue tie. *Ann Duffield*

MIMRAM 2 b.f. (Feb 12) Kheleyf (USA) 116 – Tobaranama (IRE) 94 (Sadler's Wells **–** (USA) 132) [2017 p5g^4 p6d p7g p7g Sep 27] 8,000F: sturdy filly: half-sister to 2 winners by Fusaichi Pegasus, including 2-y-o 6f winner Winged Flight: dam, 9f winner who stayed 1¾m, closely related to Phoenix Stakes winner Pharoah's Delight: little impact in minor events/nursery: tried in tongue tie. *Dean Ivory*

MINDING (IRE) 4 b.f. Galileo (IRE) 134 – Lillie Langtry (IRE) 120 (Danehill Dancer **121** (IRE) 117) [2017 127: 10g* May 1] strong filly: high-class performer: won 7 Group 1 events, including 1000 Guineas and Oaks in 2016: also won Mooresbridge Stakes at Naas (by 3½ lengths from Moonlight Magic) on sole outing in 2017: stayed 1½m: acted on soft and good to firm going: retired after injurying pastern: visits Deep Impact. *Aidan O'Brien, Ireland*

MING DYNASTY (FR) 5 b.g. King's Best (USA) 132 – Memoire (FR) (Sadler's Wells (USA) 132) [2017 113: 10.9d* 11.9g^5 14.9d^5 p12g^5 Dec 23] one-time very smart performer, just useful nowadays: won minor event at Dieppe in June: left M. Delzangles after third start: stays 1½m: acts on soft going: has worn hood. *Marco Botti* **99**

MINIATURE DAFFODIL (IRE) 2 b.g. (Mar 14) Thewayyouare (USA) 117 – Queen of Stars (USA) (Green Desert (USA) 127) [2017 7.1s 6.5d Oct 27] well held in minor event/maiden. *Christian Williams* **–**

MINI MORUGA 3 b.f. Cockney Rebel (IRE) 127 – Artzola (IRE) 60 (Alzao (USA) 117) [2017 7d p8g Sep 27] fourth foal: half-sister to German 1m/9f winner Silvery Moon (by I Was Framed): dam 8.6f-1½m winner: well held in maidens. *Gary Moore* **–**

MININGGOLD 4 b.f. Piccolo 121 – Rosein 86 (Komaite (USA)) [2017 78: 5g 5m^3 5m 6d^3 5g* 5.9s^5 5g^3 5g* 5v^3 5s 5d^3 5g^6 Nov 1] good-topped filly: fairly useful handicapper: won at Pontefract in July and Beverley (by 1¼ lengths from Sandra's Secret) in September: stays 6f: acts on good to firm and heavy going: wears headgear: often races prominently. *Michael Dods* **86**

MININGROCKS (FR) 5 b.g. Lawman (FR) 121 – Fashion School (Shamardal (USA) 129) [2017 77: 10.3g 10m^4 10.2g* 9.9d* 10.2s* 10.2m^3 10s^3 12d 10m^4 9v^5 10.2d 10g* 10g 10d^2 f12.1g f7.1g f6.1g Dec 11] fairly useful handicapper: won at Nottingham in May/June, both apprentice events, Beverley earlier in June and Redcar (seller) in October: left Declan Carroll after fourteenth start: stays 1¼m: acts on good to firm and heavy going: has worn headgear, including sometimes in 2017: has worn tongue tie: usually leads. *Conor Dore* **83 a56**

MINMINWIN (IRE) 4 ch.f. Art Connoisseur (IRE) 121 – Anne-Lise 63 (Inchinor 119) [2017 75, a64: p8g^4 p8g p6.5g p6.5g 8s^6 Mar 27] leggy filly: modest performer: left Gay Kelleway before final outing: stays 7.5f: acts on polytrack and good to soft going: usually in headgear: has worn tongue tie: often starts slowly. *Mlle M. Henry, France* **57**

MINOTAUR (IRE) 5 b.g. Azamour (IRE) 130 – Mycenae (Inchinor 119) [2017 11.8s^4 18v^4 11.9s Nov 11] strong gelding: useful performer: won 4 times in France in 2016 for N. Clement, including listed race at Craon: below form after reappearance in 2017: stays 2m: acts on polytrack and soft going: tried in cheekpieces: fairly useful hurdler. *Jonjo O'Neill* **105**

MINTY JONES 8 b.g. Primo Valentino (IRE) 116 – Reveur 69 (Rossini (USA) 118) [2017 56§: t7.1m t6m 5g 5m^6 5m 6g^2 5s^2 5.1g^5 5.1v^5 5s^5 Oct 10] modest handicapper: raced mainly at sprint trips: acts on good to firm and heavy going: wears headgear: front runner/races prominently: temperamental. *Michael Mullineaux* **54 §**

MIO RAGAZZO 3 b.g. Mayson 124 – Mia Diletta 90 (Selkirk (USA) 129) [2017 t7.1g^5 7s^4 p7s p8g^3 t8.6d t9.5d Dec 26] fair maiden: stays 1m: acts on polytrack and soft going: tried in hood: usually races close up/freely, tends to find little. *Marco Botti* **71**

MIRACLE GARDEN 5 ch.g. Exceed And Excel (AUS) 126 – Sharp Terms (Kris 135) [2017 88: f6g t5.1g t5.1g^3 t5.1g 5d 5.7f^4 5.7f^6 t6.1g^3 t7.2g^5 p7g^3 t6.1g* p7d^3 p7d^2 p8s^5 t7.2g^3 Dec 5] workmanlike gelding: fair handicapper on turf, fairly useful on all-weather: won at Wolverhampton (by 1¼ lengths from Lord Cooper) in September: left Roy Brotherton after fourth start: stays 7f: acts on polytrack, tapeta and firm going: wears headgear: front runner/races prominently, usually travels strongly. *Ian Williams* **69 a87**

MIRACLE NINETYNINE (IRE) 5 b.g. Big Bad Bob (IRE) 118 – Scrumptious 69 (Sakhee (USA) 136) [2017 68, a80: p7g^3 p8d a7.5g^4 a7.5g^2 a7.5g* a7.5g^2 a7.5g^3 10.4g* 11.9m^6 10.9g 11.9g a10.4g* a10.4g^2 p9.4g^4 Dec 15] compact gelding: fairly useful performer: left Ed Vaughan after second start: won claimer at Mons-Ghlin in May, minor event at Ostend in July and handicap at Mons-Ghlin in October: stays 10.5f: acts on polytrack, soft and good to firm going: has worn headgear: tried in tongue tie: sometimes slowly away. *J. Goossens, Belgium* **82**

MIRACLE OF MEDINAH 6 ch.g. Milk It Mick 120 – Smart Ass (IRE) 91 (Shinko Forest (IRE)) [2017 103: 7g^4 7m 7m p6.5f* p7g Nov 2] neat gelding: useful performer: won minor event at Deauville (by ½ length from Absalon) in August: stays 7.5f: acts on polytrack and firm going: tried in cheekpieces. *Mark Usher* **99**

MIRAGE DANCER 3 b.c. Frankel 147 – Heat Haze 120 (Green Desert (USA) 127) [2017 95p: 10.3d4 10m3 11.9d3 10.2d4 Sep 13] tall, angular colt: very smart performer: third in Hampton Court Stakes at Royal Ascot (1¼ lengths behind Benbatl) in June and Great Voltigeur Stakes at York (12 lengths behind Cracksman) in August: stays 10.5f: acts on good to firm going: often races towards rear. *Sir Michael Stoute* **121**

MIRAMONTE DANCER (IRE) 4 b.f. Fast Company (IRE) 126 – Bonne 72 (Namid 128) [2017 68: p7m Jan 9] fair maiden, well held sole outing in 2017: stays 1m: acts on good to firm going: often in headgear nowadays: sent to Germany. *David C. Griffiths* **–**

MIREK (IRE) 2 gr.g. (Feb 20) Zebedee 113 – My Trust (IRE) 80 (Exceed And Excel (AUS) 126) [2017 5f t5.1g6 6g 6.1m6 t6.1g5 7s p6s Nov 16] poor maiden: left Jonathan Portman after fourth start: tried in hood: dead. *Patrick Chamings* **44**

MIRIAM VIOLET 3 b.f. Dick Turpin (IRE) 127 – Velvet Band 73 (Verglas (IRE) 118) [2017 –: 9.9m Jul 15] lengthy filly: no form: tried in tongue tie. *Paul Henderson* **–**

MIRIMAR (IRE) 3 br.g. Kalanisi (IRE) 132 – Peratus (IRE) 83 (Mujadil (USA) 119) [2017 58: f8g4 8.3m 10s* 12g2 12v2 12v4 Oct 9] fairly useful handicapper: won at Lingfield in August: second at Pontefract (apprentice) in September: stays 1½m: acts on heavy going: tried in hood. *Ed Vaughan* **81**

MIRROR MAGIC 2 br.f. (Feb 17) Nathaniel (IRE) 129 – Mirror Effect (IRE) (Shamardal (USA) 129) [2017 7d6 7g 7s6 Oct 10] lengthy filly: first foal: dam unraced half-sister to useful winner up to 7f Courageous: little impact in minor events/maidens. *Geoffrey Deacon* **–**

MIRROR MIRROR (IRE) 2 ch.f. (Feb 10) Intello (GER) 129 – Nouvelle Lune (Fantastic Light (USA) 134) [2017 7m 8s Oct 28] leggy filly, has scope: half-sister to several winners, including useful 7f-1¼m winner Maverik (by Iceman) and 13f/1¾m winner Pleasure Dome (by Makfi): dam unraced half-sister to smart dam of St Leger winner Kingston Hill: little impact in maiden/minor event. *Peter Chapple-Hyam* **–**

MIRSAALE 7 ch.g. Sir Percy 129 – String Quartet (IRE) 109 (Sadler's Wells (USA) 132) [2017 106: 18m 11.9s Nov 11] well-made gelding: useful handicapper, excuses both starts on Flat in 2017: stays 2m: acts on any turf going: usually wears headgear: has worn tongue tie: useful hurdler. *Keith Dalgleish* **–**

MIRZA 10 b.g. Oasis Dream 129 – Millyant 114 (Primo Dominie 121) [2017 115: 5m5 5m2 5d 5g5 5.2m5 5s4 5g5 Oct 17] good-topped gelding: smart performer: second in Sprint Stakes at Sandown (3¼ lengths behind Battaash) in July: best at 5f: acts on good to firm and heavy going: wears cheekpieces. *Rae Guest* **112**

MIRZAM (IRE) 3 gr.f. Mastercraftsman (IRE) 129 – Luxie (IRE) 77 (Acclamation 118) [2017 55p: 10g t12.2g4 12d* 12m2 10.2m3 t12.4g6 Jun 30] fair performer: won handicap at Chepstow in May: stays 1½m: acts on good to firm and good to soft going. *Mick Channon* **79**

MISCHIEF MANAGED (IRE) 3 ch.g. Tagula (IRE) 116 – Cape Clear 74 (Slip Anchor 136) [2017 6d4 8d4 7d4 5.9d6 7s4 8v Oct 12] rangy gelding: fair maiden: should stay 1m: acts on soft going: in eyeshields first 4 starts. *Tim Easterby* **71**

MISCHIEVOUS ROCK 2 b.f. (Feb 25) Society Rock (IRE) 126 – Twilight Pearl 63 (Pastoral Pursuits 127) [2017 f7.1g6 p6s4 p6g Dec 20] 5,500F, £600 2-y-o: first foal: dam 2-y-o 5f winner: modest form when fourth at Chelmsford (4 lengths behind Restless Rose) on second of 3 starts in minor events. *Michael Appleby* **64**

MISE EN ROSE (USA) 4 b.f. War Front (USA) 119 – Buy The Barrel (USA) (E Dubai (USA) 124) [2017 109: p7d3 Feb 8] useful-looking filly: useful performer: third in minor event at Chelmsford (2 lengths behind Ashadihan) on sole outing in 2017: stays 1m: acts on polytrack and firm going: in cheekpieces last 3 starts. *Charlie Appleby* **99**

MISHAAL (IRE) 7 ch.g. Kheleyf (USA) 116 – My Dubai (IRE) 76 (Dubai Millennium 140) [2017 94: t6g 7.1g 6m 6s 6m2 6d2 6g 6s 6g4 7.4m4 p6s2 p6g2 t6d4 p6g4 t7.2m Oct 28] fair handicapper nowadays: stays 1m, raced mainly at shorter: acts on polytrack, soft and good to firm going: has worn headgear: often races prominently. *Michael Herrington* **79**

MISHARI 3 b.c. Oasis Dream 129 – Nessina (USA) (Hennessy (USA) 122) [2017 –: 7d5 6g3 t7.2g4 Sep 23] fair form: stays 7f. *David Lanigan* **65**

MISHKO (IRE) 6 b.g. Amadeus Wolf 122 – Miss Shangri La 43 (Rainbow Quest (USA) 134) [2017 p13.3g* 14.5s6 14v3 p16spu Jul 25] tall gelding: fair handicapper: won at Chelmsford in May: stays 13.5f: acts on polytrack and good to firm going. *Steve Gollings* **73**

MISKIN 8 b.g. Motivator 131 – Castellina (USA) (Danzig Connection (USA)) [2017 12v3 12m2 12.5g 14.2g2 16s5 Sep 19] fairly useful handicapper at best, won 3 times in France for J. E. Hammond in 2014, modest nowadays: stays 1¾m: acts on good to firm and good to soft going: in hood last 2 starts: often travels strongly. *Robert Stephens* **64**

MISS ANTICIPATION (IRE) 3 b.f. Bated Breath 125 – Dusting (IRE) (Acclamation 118) [2017 68: 7d 6.1m² p7s t7.2g⁶ Sep 23] unfurnished filly: fair maiden: stays 6f: acts on good to firm going: has worn hood, including final start. *Roger Charlton* **71**

MISS BAR BEACH (IRE) 2 b.f. (Apr 3) Choisir (AUS) 126 – Whitegate Way 46 (Greensmith 121) [2017 5m² 6s* 6m 6d⁵ t7.1d* 7g³ 8g 7s⁴ Oct 28] €9,000Y: close-coupled filly: half-sister to 3 winners, including useful 1m/9f winner Brog Deas (by Arakan) and 9f/1¼m winner Oneofapear (by Pyrus): dam maiden sister to US Grade 2 1m/Grade 3 9f winner Lord Smith: fairly useful performer: won minor event at Hamilton in June and nursery at Newcastle (by 1¾ lengths from Seaella) in August: third in Prestige Stakes at Goodwood (1½ lengths behind Billesdon Brook) later in August: stays 7f: acts on tapeta, soft and good to firm going. *Keith Dalgleish* **94**

MISS BATES 3 b.f. Holy Roman Emperor (IRE) 125 – Jane Austen (IRE) 104 (Galileo (IRE) 134) [2017 74: 8m⁴ 9.9g 8.5v p8g t7.1s³ Nov 30] fair maiden: bred to be suited by at least 1¼m: acts on tapeta, soft and good to firm going: tried in hood/tongue tie: often races towards rear. *Ann Duffield* **67**

MISS BLONDELL 4 ch.f. Compton Place 125 – Where's Broughton 77 (Cadeaux Genereux 131) [2017 70: p8g⁶ p10g² Nov 2] rather leggy filly: fair handicapper, lightly raced: stays 1¼m: acts on polytrack. *Marcus Tregoning* **76**

MISSCARLETT (IRE) 3 b.f. Red Rocks (IRE) 124 – Coimbra (USA) (Trempolino (USA) 135) [2017 12g³ 10v* 10v Oct 23] €15,500F, €50,000Y: narrow, rather slightly-built filly: sixth foal: half-sister to 3 winners abroad, including useful French winner up to 1m Estoril City (2-y-o 6f winner, by Elusive City): dam, French 2-y-o 1m winner, half-sister to useful stayer Tarkheena Prince: fair form: won maiden at Pontefract (by 4½ lengths from Frankster) in September: stays 1½m. *Sally Haynes* **77**

MISS CONDI 2 b.f. (Mar 19) Most Improved (IRE) 119 – Mildenhall 56 (Compton Place 125) [2017 7.4d 5.1g 7.1s p8g p7d Nov 22] first foal: dam maiden (stayed 7f): no form: tried in hood. *Martin Keighley* **–**

MISS DANBY (IRE) 3 gr.f. Mastercraftsman (IRE) 129 – Dunbrody (FR) (Jeune Homme (USA) 120) [2017 71: 8m⁶ 9.9g 9.8m 12v p10s Nov 17] fair maiden: stays 1m: acts on tapeta and good to firm going: tried in blinkers. *Mark Johnston* **69**

MISS DD (IRE) 2 b.f. (Mar 28) Dandy Man (IRE) 123 – Dynaperformer (IRE) 78 (Dynaformer (USA)) [2017 6m² 6d* 6g 6d t5.1g⁵ Aug 11] €8,100Y, resold 16,000Y: good-topped filly: first foal: dam, 1¾m winner, half-sister to smart 5f-7f winner Roicead: fair performer: won minor event at Pontefract in June: stays 6f: acts on good to firm and good to soft going: in headgear last 3 starts: front runner/races prominently. *Tom Dascombe* **73**

MISS DUSKY DIVA (IRE) 5 gr.m. Verglas (IRE) 118 – Dispol Veleta 83 (Makbul 104) [2017 58: p15.8g* t16.5m* t16.5g t14g t16.5d t14dᵘʳ Dec 27] fair handicapper: won at Lingfield and Wolverhampton in January: stays 16.5f: acts on polytrack, tapeta and good to soft going: usually races towards rear. *David Drinkwater* **68**

MISS FAY (IRE) 3 br.f. Sayif (IRE) 122 – Lough Mewin (IRE) (Woodman (USA) 126) [2017 67p: p10s⁵ 8s⁵ Jul 28] fair form: stays 1¼m: in visor in 2017. *Michael Bell* **65**

MISS GERONIMO 5 b.m. Hellvelyn 118 – Churn Dat Butter (USA) (Unbridled (USA) 128) [2017 –: 6g Aug 17] angular mare: no form, including in handicap. *Ken Cunningham-Brown* **–**

MISS GOLDSMITH (IRE) 4 gr.f. Mastercraftsman (IRE) 129 – Golden Legacy (IRE) 107 (Rossini (USA) 118) [2017 69: t8g⁵ f8s p7g⁴ t7.1g t7.1g² p7g³ 8g⁵ 7.2m 7m² 9.2s⁶ 7.2d* 8g* 7.6v⁵ Sep 15] fair handicapper: won at Ayr in July and Thirsk in August: left Richard Fahey after ninth start, trained next start only by Lucinda Egerton: stays 1m: acts on polytrack, tapeta and good to soft going: has worn hood, including in 2017. *Rebecca Menzies* **69**

MISSGUIDED (IRE) 4 b.f. Rip Van Winkle (IRE) 134 – Foolish Ambition (GER) 95 (Danehill Dancer (IRE) 117) [2017 65: p8s⁵ 8s 8d⁵ 10d³ 10g 10.3m* 10d p12g p8g t9.5g Nov 25] second foal: sister to 1m/8.5f winner (stayed 1¼m) Bakht A Rawan: dam, 2-y-o 6f winner, sister to useful 6f winner True Verdict: fair handicapper: won at Down Royal in June: left Peter Fahey after sixth start: stays 10.5f: acts on good to firm and good to soft going: has worn blinkers, including final start: tried in tongue tie: sometimes slowly away, usually races towards rear. *Alex Hales* **69**

MISS ICON 3 b.f. Sixties Icon 125 – Pretty Miss 85 (Averti (IRE) 117) [2017 71: 7m³ p7s 7f⁶ 5.7f³ 6g⁵ 7s² p7g p6g Nov 17] fair handicapper: stays 7f: acts on polytrack and firm going. *Patrick Chamings* **74**

MISS INFINITY (IRE) 3 b.f. Rock of Gibraltar (IRE) 133 – Muravka (IRE) (High Chaparral (IRE) 132) [2017 101: 7m 10m^4 10.3s^5 8m 6.9s 7g 7m^4 Aug 26] sturdy filly: useful at 2 yrs, largely well below that level in 2017: stays 1¼m: acts on good to firm and good to soft going: tried in blinkers: usually races close up: sold 425,000 gns in December. *Mark Johnston* **94**

MISS INGA SOCK (IRE) 5 ch.m. Tagula (IRE) 116 – Support Fund (IRE) 83 (Intikhab (USA) 135) [2017 68: 9.9g* 10d* 10d^3 9.9d* 10g^3 9.9s^6 10.1d* 11.6d^4 Sep 16] close-coupled mare: fair handicapper: won at Brighton (apprentice) and Chepstow in May, Brighton again in June and Epsom (apprentice) in August: stays 1¼m: acts on polytrack, firm and soft going: has worn headgear. *Eve Johnson Houghton* **74**

MISSION IMPASSIBLE (IRE) 2 br.f. (Mar 17) Galileo (IRE) 134 – Margot Did (IRE) 122 (Exceed And Excel (AUS) 126) [2017 7g* 7d* 7g^4 8.2g* 8d^3 Oct 1] first foal: dam 5f (including Nunthorpe Stakes)/6f (at 2 yrs) winner: useful performer: won newcomers race at Toulouse in June, minor event at Clairefontaine in July and listed race at Craon (by 3 lengths from Altea) in September: 1½ lengths third to Wild Illusion in Prix Marcel Boussac at Chantilly final outing: stays 1m: acts on good to soft going. *Jean-Claude Rouget, France* **109**

MISS ISLAND RULER 3 b.f. Elzaam (AUS) 115 – Kodiac Island (Kodiac 112) [2017 45: 5m 8g^5 7g^6 Jul 20] compact filly: little form: has worn blinkers, including final start. *Shaun Harris* **–**

MISSISSIPPI MISS 3 ch.f. Equiano (FR) 127 – Junket 86 (Medicean 128) [2017 77p: 7d p7g p7g p7g^6 Oct 5] fair handicapper: stays 7f: acts on polytrack. *Dr Jon Scargill* **71**

MISS LAILA (IRE) 3 b.f. Dark Angel (IRE) 113 – Sister Red (IRE) 86 (Diamond Green (FR) 121) [2017 73: p7g^4 8s^5 May 18] fair handicapper: stays 7f: acts on polytrack, tapeta and good to soft going. *Tom Clover* **72**

MISS LIGURIA 3 b.f. Galileo (IRE) 134 – Miss Cap Ferrat 53 (Darshaan 133) [2017 10g 12s^5 p12g^3 12.3d^3 p12g p12g^2 t12.2d Dec 26] tall, shallow-girthed filly: half-sister to 1m-11f winner (including in Scandinavia) St Jean Cap Ferrat (by Domedriver) and 1m-1½m winner Miss Cap Estel (by Hernando), both useful: dam twice-raced half-sister to 1m winner Miss Riviera Golf and winner up to 1¼m Miss Corniche (both useful): fairly useful maiden: second in handicap at Lingfield in December: stays 12.5f: acts on polytrack and good to soft going: often races prominently. *Ed Walker* **81**

MISS MACCHIATO (IRE) 4 b.f. Holy Roman Emperor (IRE) 125 – Cafe Lassere (USA) (Giant's Causeway (USA) 132) [2017 50: f12g^2 f12s^5 t12.2g^5 Feb 20] modest maiden: stays 1½m: acts on fibresand: tried in cheekpieces: front runner/races prominently. *Keith Dalgleish* **54**

MISS MAYSON 3 b.f. Mayson 124 – High Class Girl (Royal Applause 124) [2017 64: 5m 5s 5s f5g Nov 13] modest maiden: best form at 5f: acts on polytrack and tapeta. *Karen Tutty* **50**

MISS MAZZIE 2 b.f. (Mar 13) Mazameer (IRE) 107 – Fizzy Lady 70 (Efisio 120) [2017 5d 6m 5m^6 7s^4 p8g t7.2g^5 7d Oct 20] 800F: sixth foal: dam unreliable 7f-1¼m winner: poor maiden: stays 7f: acts on soft going. *Michael Easterby* **46**

MISS MILLA B 2 b.f. (May 5) Sepoy (AUS) 129 – Dreamily (IRE) 65 (New Approach (IRE) 132) [2017 p7s^4 Dec 15] first foal: dam twice-raced half-sister to very smart winner up to 1m Calming Influence: 25/1, fourth in minor event at Chelmsford (6 lengths behind Crown Walk) in December. *Ed Vaughan* **64**

MISS MILLINER 2 ch.f. (Apr 11) Helmet (AUS) 127 – Elegant Pursuit (Pastoral Pursuits 127) [2017 5.5g 7g Aug 3] second foal: dam French 10.5f winner: well held in claimers in France. *Jo Hughes* **–**

MISS MINDING (IRE) 2 b.f. (Apr 25) Kodiac 112 – Lady Hawkfield (IRE) (Hawk Wing (USA) 136) [2017 6m 6d 7d Sep 30] fourth foal: closely related to winner up to 2m Royal Reserve (2-y-o 7f winner, by Duke of Marmalade) and half-sister to winner up to 1¼m Master Apprentice (2-y-o 1m winner, by Mastercraftsman), both useful: dam once-raced half-sister to Coronation Stakes winner Lillie Langtry, herself dam of 1000 Guineas/Oaks winner Minding: little impact in minor events/maiden: in hood last 2 starts. *Ed Dunlop* **–**

MISS MINUTY 5 gr.m. Verglas (IRE) 118 – Miss Provence 88 (Hernando (FR) 127) [2017 85: 9.9m 11.6d t9.5g p10g* Dec 13] fairly useful handicapper: won at Lingfield in December: stays 1½m: acts on polytrack, tapeta and firm going: has worn headgear: often races towards rear. *Jeremy Scott* **79**

MISS MIRABEAU 3 b.f. Oasis Dream 129 – Miss Corniche 104 (Hernando (FR) 127) [2017 p5g^4 p6f^3 p7g^6 7g^3 p7s^5 p10d p8g^3 p8g^5 p10s^5 t9.5g^2 p10s* p10.7g^{ur} Dec 21] half-sister to several winners, including smart 1m-1¾m winner Moyenne Corniche (by Selkirk) and winner up to 7f Miss Eze (2-y-o 6f winner, by Danehill Dancer): dam winner up to **73 §**

1¼m (2-y-o 7f winner): fair handicapper: won at Chelmsford in December: left Sir Mark Prescott Bt after eleventh start: stays 1¼m: acts on polytrack and tapeta: wears headgear: temperamental. *Keith Henry Clarke, Ireland*

MISS M (IRE) 3 b.f. Mastercraftsman (IRE) 129 – Tintern (Diktat 126) [2017 p7g^6 t8.6g^3 **63** t8.6g^6 8g 8d 10d^6 p10g* p10s Dec 1] sixth foal: half-sister to 3 winners, including untrustworthy 1m-9.5f winner Siouxperhero (by Sleeping Indian) and 2-y-o 1m winner York Minster (by Vale of York): dam unraced half-sister to smart 1¼m winner Solva: modest handicapper: won at Chelmsford in October: stays 1¼m: acts on polytrack and tapeta. *William Muir*

MISS MO BROWN BEAR (IRE) 2 b.f. (Apr 28) Kodiac 112 – Currentis (IRE) 51 **70** (Dylan Thomas (IRE) 132) [2017 p6g^4 6.1d^5 p7g^3 6d^3 6v^4 6g^2 7.4g 6s f7.1g Nov 28] 38,000F, £60,000Y: compact filly: second foal: half-sister to Swedish 11f winner Brocco (by Pour Moi): dam maiden half-sister to French 11f-12.5f winner Bernieres and Scandinavian 1m-1½m winner Hurricane Red (both smart): fair maiden: stays 7f: acts on polytrack and good to soft going: in headgear last 4 starts: front runner/races prominently. *Richard Hannon*

MISS MOLLIE 2 b.f. (Mar 28) Havana Gold (IRE) 118 – Erebis (Green Desert (USA) **–** 127) [2017 t6.1d^6 Dec 27] first foal: dam unraced close relative to very smart 5f performer Moorhouse Lad: 22/1, well held in minor event at Wolverhampton. *James Given*

MISS MONRO (IRE) 3 br.f. Intense Focus (USA) 117 – Runway Girl (IRE) 67 (Dansili **–** 127) [2017 60: t8g 8.2d 10m^5 Jun 17] neat filly: maiden: no form in 2017: tried in blinkers. *Brian Ellison*

MISS MUMTAZ (IRE) 2 ch.f. (Apr 5) Lope de Vega (IRE) 125 – Ispanka (Invincible **70** Spirit (IRE) 121) [2017 t8.6g^2 7g t8.6g^2 Sep 23] 55,000F: second foal: dam, French 10.5f winner, out of half-sister to very smart French 1m/9f winner Esoterique: fair form: best effort when second in minor event at Wolverhampton (2¼ lengths behind Kind Act) in September. *Tony Carroll*

MISS NOURIYA 3 b.f. Galileo (IRE) 134 – Nouriya 108 (Danehill Dancer (IRE) 117) **– p** [2017 10.2g Jul 21] second foal: half-sister to smart winner up to 1m Aljazzi (2-y-o 7f winner, by Shamardal): dam, 1¼m/10.4f winner, half-sister to smart 7f/1m winner Yuften: in tongue tie, 12/1, well held in maiden at Nottingham: should do better. *Marco Botti*

MISS OSIER 3 ch.f. Mastercraftsman (IRE) 129 – Lacy Sunday (USA) (King's Best **70** (USA) 132) [2017 60: f8g^3 8.3g^4 p10g^5 8.2g* 8d 8g^5 7g^3 p7d 8g^4 Oct 16] workmanlike filly: fair handicapper: won at Leicester in July: stays 8.5f: best form on good going: wears cheekpieces. *Rae Guest*

MISS PACIFIC 3 ch.f. Bated Breath 125 – Ocean View (USA) 109 (Gone West (USA)) **77** [2017 p7g 8m^5 8g^5 8s^2 8d^3 8g p8g^3 p10g Nov 2] 14,000F, €60,000Y: compact filly: half-sister to several winners, including US Grade 3 2-y-o 1m winner Officer Rocket (by Officer) and 1¼m winner Miss Lucy Jane (by Aqlaam): dam US winner up to 6.5f (2-y-o 5.5f winner): fair maiden: stays 1m: acts on polytrack and soft going: usually races nearer last than first. *William Jarvis*

MISS PARIS 2 b.f. (Apr 15) Champs Elysees 124 – Bantu 80 (Cape Cross (IRE) 129) **–** [2017 7v^6 7.6d Sep 16] well-made filly: third foal: closely related to a winner in Spain by Cacique and half-sister to smart winner up to 11f Banzari (2-y-o 1m winner, by Motivator): dam, maiden (stayed 1¼m), half-sister to Craven Stakes winner Adagio and US Grade 2 1½m winner Arvada: little impact in maiden/minor event. *Charles Hills*

MISS PATIENCE 3 b.f. Excelebration (IRE) 133 – Connote (Oasis Dream 129) [2017 **69** –p: t6g^4 7g^3 6g 6g Aug 5] fair maiden: stays 7f: in hood last 3 starts: usually races freely: sold £5,500, sent to Greece. *Peter Chapple-Hyam*

MISS PEPPER (IRE) 3 b.f. Acclamation 118 – Somerset Falls (UAE) 76 (Red Ransom **45** (USA)) [2017 –p: 5m 6g 5m 5d 5s^3 5f Jul 18] poor maiden: best effort at 5f: acts on soft going: usually in headgear. *Paul Midgley*

MISS PERCEPTION 2 b.f. (Feb 5) Vision d'Etat (FR) 127 – Monster Munchie (JPN) 76 **45** (Deep Impact (JPN) 134) [2017 6g 7d 8s^6 t7.2g^6 Oct 7] second foal: dam 9.5f winner out of Prix Saint-Alary winner Muncie: poor form: tried in cheekpieces. *Tom Dascombe*

MISS PUDDLES (IRE) 2 b.f. (Apr 21) Canford Cliffs (IRE) 133 – Puddles (FR) (Holy **85** Roman Emperor (IRE) 125) [2017 6m^4 5.1d* 8f t6f Nov 24] first foal: dam unraced half-sister to useful French performer up to 1¼m Restless Rixa: fairly useful form: won minor event at Chester (by 3 lengths from Charnock Richard) in July: left Richard Fahey after: best effort at 5f on good to soft going. *Doug F. O'Neill, USA*

MISS QUICK 3 b.f. Equiano (FR) 127 – Quixada (GER) (Konigstiger (GER) 112) [2017 –: 6m^5 May 9] well held in pair of maidens: in tongue tie on second occasion. *Ann Duffield* **–**

MISS QUOTED 5 b.m. Proclamation (IRE) 130 – Ambience Lady (Batshoof 122) [2017 7.1s Sep 19] fourth foal: half-sister to 7f/1m winner Zebrano (by Storming Home): dam bumper winner/winning chaser: well beaten in bumpers/Flat maiden. *Seamus Mullins* **–**

MISS RANGER (IRE) 5 gr.m. Bushranger (IRE) 119 – Remiss (IRE) (Indian Ridge 123) [2017 77: 8.5m 8.3g^6 10.2d^2 12.3s* Jun 10] compact mare: fair handicapper: won at Chester in June: stays 12.5f: acts on polytrack, soft and good to firm going: tried in cheekpieces/tongue tie: sometimes slowly away. *Brian Ellison* **79**

MISS RECYCLED 2 b.f. (Mar 10) Royal Applause 124 – Steel Free (IRE) 81 (Danehill Dancer (IRE) 117) [2017 7g 7.6d 6s^5 Oct 19] third foal: half-sister to 1¼m/11f winner Tommys Geal (by Halling): dam, 7f winner who stayed 9f, half-sister to useful 1¼m winner System Overload: little impact in minor events. *Michael Madgwick* **–**

MISS ROSINA (IRE) 3 ch.f. Choisir (AUS) 126 – Vera Lilley (IRE) 68 (Verglas (IRE) 118) [2017 68: 5m t6.1g^4 5.1m 5.2m^2 5.2g^4 5.3g 5.2m^2 p5g^6 p5g^4 t5.1m^5 Oct 28] compact filly: modest handicapper: stays 5.5f: acts on polytrack, good to firm and good to soft going: in cheekpieces last 4 starts: sold 4,000 gns, sent to Greece. *George Margarson* **63**

MISS SHERIDAN (IRE) 3 br.f. Lilbourne Lad (IRE) 111 – Sues Surprise (IRE) 98 (Montjeu (IRE) 137) [2017 67: 8m* 8m* 10.3g^6 6.9g* 8f^2 7v^6 p7g t7.1g 7s Oct 31] fairly useful handicapper: won at Redcar/Pontefract in April and Carlisle (by ¾ length from Contentment) in June: second at Haydock in July: stays 1m: acts on polytrack and firm going: front runner/races prominently. *Michael Easterby* **82**

MISS TEMPLE CITY (USA) 5 b.m. Temple City (USA) – Glittering Tax (USA) (Artax (USA) 126) [2017 120: 8f 9f^3 8f* 8f^6 Oct 7] well-made mare: smart performer: well held in Queen Anne Stakes at Royal Ascot on reappearance: won Grade 3 Kentucky Downs Ladies Turf Stakes in September by neck from Zipessa: stays 9f: acts on firm going: has worn tongue tie: usually races prominently: sold $2,500,000 in November. *H. Graham Motion, USA* **113**

MISS TENACITY 4 b.f. Rail Link 132 – Desert Secrets (IRE) 67 (Almutawakel 126) [2017 p13.3s Dec 14] 1,000Y: first foal: dam, maiden on Flat (stayed 11.6f), winning hurdler/chaser: 25/1, well held in maiden at Chelmsford. *Jane Chapple-Hyam* **–**

MISS TIGER LILY 7 b.m. Tiger Hill (IRE) 127 – Waitingonacloud (In The Wings 128) [2017 77: p15.8m^2 p16d^3 p15.8g^2 p12g^4 p15.8g^2 14f May 6] good-topped mare: fair handicapper: stays 2m: acts on polytrack, firm and soft going: tried in blinkers: front runner/races prominently. *Harry Dunlop* **79**

MISS TREE 6 b.m. Literato (FR) 127 – Tunguska (Silver Patriarch (IRE) 125) [2017 63: f12g^5 t12.4g^5 14g* 12m^3 12.1m^4 17.2s Aug 7] modest handicapper: won at Redcar in May: stays 1¾m: acts on viscoride, good to firm and heavy going: has worn cheekpieces: front runner/races prominently. *John Quinn* **63**

MISS UPPITY 4 ch.f. Notnowcato 128 – Instructress 66 (Diktat 126) [2017 –: t7.1d 6s^2 5d p6g^5 p7g^3 t6.1d Dec 16] modest maiden: stays 7f: acts on polytrack and soft going. *Ivan Furtado* **54**

MISS VAN GOGH 5 b.m. Dutch Art 126 – Accede 88 (Acclamation 118) [2017 93: 8g^5 9g^6 8s^6 8.3s Jun 29] workmanlike mare: fairly useful handicapper: stays 8.5f: acts on soft and good to firm going: tried in visor: usually races towards rear: sold 7,000 gns in December. *Richard Fahey* **86**

MISS VAN WINKLE 2 b.f. (Feb 12) Rip Van Winkle (IRE) 134 – Lasso 58 (Indian Ridge 123) [2017 6m 6d t7.1g p10s Dec 15] 8,500F: sixth foal: half-sister to winner up to 1m Gunner Lindley (2-y-o 7f winner, by Medicean) and winner up to 1½m Goldoni (2-y-o 7f winner, by Dylan Thomas), both useful: dam 7f winner: little impact in minor events/nursery. *Mark Johnston* **53**

MISS WOLVERINE 2 b.f. (Feb 13) Amadeus Wolf 122 – Mille Etoiles (USA) (Malibu Moon (USA)) [2017 5d^4 6v^6 7g Oct 7] 1,000F: fifth foal: half-sister to a winner abroad by Loup Breton: dam French 1m winner: modest form when fourth in minor event at Beverley (3¾ lengths behind Elnadim Star) on debut, standout effort. *Michael Easterby* **59**

MISSY MISCHIEF (USA) 2 b.f. (Feb 5) Into Mischief (USA) 115 – Ring True (USA) (Is It True (USA)) [2017 6g^5 5m Jun 21] $60,000Y, resold $195,000Y: good-quartered filly: sixth foal: half-sister to winners in USA by Ghostzapper and Gio Ponti: dam US 5f/6f winner: fairly useful form when ninth in Queen Mary Stakes at Royal Ascot (5 lengths behind Heartache) on second of 2 starts: open to further improvement. *Jeremy Noseda* **84 p**

MISSY WELLS 7 b.m. Misu Bond (IRE) 114 – Aqua 51 (Mister Baileys 123) [2017 13.9v Oct 21] fair maiden at best, well beaten sole outing in 2017 after long absence: stays 10.5f: acts on fibresand and heavy ground: often in headgear. *Marjorie Fife* **–**

MISTER BELVEDERE 3 b.g. Archipenko (USA) 127 – Diablerette 87 (Green Desert (USA) 127) [2017 91p: 8m^{6} 10.5d^{5} 12.1g^{4} 14.4g^{3} 11.9d^{2} 12s 10v Sep 21] fairly useful handicapper: placed at Chester in July and Doncaster in August: stays 14.5f: acts on soft going. *Michael Dods* **93**

MISTER BLUE SKY (IRE) 3 gr.g. Royal Applause 124 – Mujdeya 95 (Linamix (FR) 127) [2017 80: 8.1d 8.3g* 10.1m^{6} 10g* 12g 12d 9.9g* 9.9d^{3} Sep 20] well-made gelding: fairly useful handicapper: won at Nottingham in May, Windsor in July and Sandown (by 1¼ lengths from Know Your Limit) in September: should stay 1½m: acts on soft and good to firm going: sold 130,000 gns in October. *Sylvester Kirk* **93**

MISTER BOB (GER) 8 ch.g. Black Sam Bellamy (IRE) 121 – Mosquera (GER) 108 (Acatenango (GER) 127) [2017 84: t16.3g^{5} t16.3g^{4} f14d^{3} 14d^{4} p16g* t16.5g Sep 23] big gelding: fairly useful handicapper: won at Chelmsford (by neck from Piedita) in August: stays 16.5f: acts on all-weather and good to soft going: wears headgear: sometimes slowly away. *James Bethell* **85**

MISTER CHOW 3 ch.g. Nathaniel (IRE) 129 – Skimmia (Mark of Esteem (IRE) 137) [2017 p6g 7m 7d 7s p8d^{4} 10v^{3} p12g p16g^{2} p13.3s* Dec 1] big, strong gelding: fair handicapper: won at Chelmsford in December: stays 2m: acts on polytrack: in visor last 3 starts. *Gary Moore* **78**

MISTER FIZZ 9 b.g. Sulamani (IRE) 130 – Court Champagne (Batshoof 122) [2017 80: t16.3g t13.9g^{5} 12s t12.2g Dec 2] fairly useful at best, no form on Flat in 2017: has worn cheekpieces. *Miss Imogen Pickard* **–**

MISTER FLIP FLOP (IRE) 4 b.g. Danehill Dancer (IRE) 117 – Heavenly Bay (USA) 90 (Rahy (USA) 115) [2017 p8g p10g^{6} Apr 11] no form, including in bumper: in hood final start. *Adam West* **–**

MISTER FREEZE (IRE) 3 ch.g. Frozen Power (IRE) 108 – Beacon of Hope (IRE) (Barathea (IRE) 127) [2017 59: t6m^{4} f6s* 7v^{6} p7g p6g p6g^{2} p6g Dec 31] fair handicapper: won at Southwell in January: left Clive Cox after second start: stays 6f: acts on all-weather: tried in visor: wears tongue tie: usually races prominently. *Patrick Chamings* **76**

MISTER MAESTRO 2 b.g. (Apr 24) Showcasing 117 – Basque Beauty 96 (Nayef (USA) 129) [2017 6m 7.1s^{5} 7d^{6} t7.2g^{4} Nov 7] fair form: stays 7f. *Richard Hannon* **66**

MISTER MANDURO (FR) 3 ch.g. Manduro (GER) 135 – Semenova (FR) (Green Tune (USA) 125) [2017 84p: 11.7m^{2} 10m 14m^{4} 14m 14m 16d^{2} 14.4s 16s^{6} 18d 16d Oct 6] tall gelding: useful handicapper: second at Bath (head behind Hushood) in April and Ascot (4½ lengths behind Uae King) in July: stays 2m: acts on polytrack, tapeta, good to firm and good to soft going: tried in blinkers: sold to join Brian Ellison 30,000 gns in October. *Mark Johnston* **99**

MISTER MARCASITE 7 gr.g. Verglas (IRE) 118 – No Rehearsal (FR) (Baillamont (USA) 124) [2017 58: t12.2g^{4} Mar 27] modest handicapper, below form sole outing in 2017: stays 1½m: acts on polytrack, tapeta, good to firm and heavy going: tried in headgear: races prominently. *Antony Brittain* **–**

MISTER MOOSAH (IRE) 3 gr.g. Clodovil (IRE) 116 – Hendrina (IRE) 58 (Daylami (IRE) 138) [2017 68: 8m^{4} 8g^{6} 12d 9.8m 12.5m Sep 8] fair maiden: should stay 1¼m+: acts on good to firm going: often races towards rear. *Micky Hammond* **67**

MISTER MUSIC 8 b.g. Singspiel (IRE) 133 – Sierra 65 (Dr Fong (USA) 128) [2017 89: p8d^{4} p8d^{3} 7g 7g^{3} 8.2d 7g^{4} p8g^{4} p7d^{5} 8s^{5} 7g^{4} p8s Sep 8] attractive gelding: fairly useful handicapper: third at Leicester in April: stays 1¼m, raced mainly at shorter: acts on polytrack and any turf going: has worn headgear: usually races towards rear. *Tony Carroll* **87**

MISTER MUSICMASTER 8 b.g. Amadeus Wolf 122 – Misty Eyed (IRE) 112 (Paris House 123) [2017 84: t7.1g p8g^{5} p8f^{3} 7m 8f* 8m* 8f 8.1m 8g 8m 8d* 8.1g^{6} Sep 6] compact gelding: fair handicapper: won at Bath in May, June and August: stays 1¼m: acts on polytrack, tapeta, firm and soft going: has worn headgear: races towards rear. *Ron Hodges* **79 a67**

MISTER RAFFLES 3 b.g. Cockney Rebel (IRE) 127 – Shrewd Decision (Motivator 131) [2017 t7.1m p6g t9.5g Mar 6] well held in maidens: tried in headgear/tongue tie. *Mohamed Moubarak* **–**

MISTER SHOWMAN 4 b.g. Showcasing 117 – Theatre Royal 71 (Royal Applause 124) **75**
[2017 67: f12.1g* f12.1g^{5} f11.1g^{2} Dec 21] fair handicapper: won at Southwell in October: stays 13f: acts on fibresand, good to firm and good to soft going: in cheekpieces last 3 starts: often races prominently. *Keith Dalgleish*

MISTER SUNSHINE (IRE) 3 ch.g. Fast Company (IRE) 126 – Second Omen **–**
(Rainbow Quest (USA) 134) [2017 79: p7g Feb 8] good-topped gelding: fair form when won minor event on second start at 2 yrs, gone wrong way since: best effort at 6f. *Clive Cox*

MISTER TRADER 3 br.c. Hellvelyn 118 – Rehlaat (USA) (Swain (IRE) 134) [2017 106: **–**
6s 5s Oct 7] rather leggy colt: useful 5f winner at 2 yrs, well held both starts (tongue tied) in 2017: usually races close up. *Darren Bunyan, Ireland*

MISTIME (IRE) 3 b.f. Acclamation 118 – Out of Time (IRE) (Anabaa (USA) 130) [2017 **73**
87: 8d^{4} 6s 6m^{4} p7g Oct 5] unfurnished filly: fairly useful at 2 yrs, below that level in 2017: stays 7f: acts on polytrack, soft and good to firm going. *Mark Johnston*

MISTINESS (IRE) 6 b.g. Astronomer Royal (USA) 121 – Misty Daylight (USA) **67**
(Seeking Daylight (USA)) [2017 –: 11.3g^{5} 9.5d^{5} 10d* 13.1s* 11.1s^{6} 11.8v Aug 28] fair handicapper: won at Fairyhouse (apprentice) and Hamilton in June: stays 13f: acts on soft going: wears headgear: front runner/races prominently. *Keith Henry Clarke, Ireland*

MISTIROC 6 br.g. Rocamadour 116 – Mistinguett (IRE) 77 (Doyoun 124) [2017 102: **110**
t12.4g^{6} t12.2g^{4} t12.4s^{2} 10.3m^{3} 12m 10.3m^{3} Jul 15] good-topped gelding: smart handicapper: placed 3 times in 2017, including in John Smith's Cup at York (length behind Ballet Concerto) in July: stays 12.5f: acts on tapeta, good to firm and good to soft going: wears headgear: races prominently. *John Quinn*

MISTRESS OF VENICE 2 b.f. (Feb 24) Bated Breath 125 – Rohlindi 69 (Red Ransom **96**
(USA)) [2017 5m^{5} 5s^{3} 6m^{4} 6m^{4} 6d 6m^{2} Aug 26] £27,500Y: lengthy filly: second foal: half-sister to 8.5f winner War of Succession (by Casamento): dam, maiden (best effort at 5.7f), half-sister to useful French sprinter Tayseer: useful maiden: stays 6f: acts on soft and good to firm going: often leads. *James Given*

MISTRESS QUICKLY (IRE) 3 b.f. Mastercraftsman (IRE) 129 – In My Life (IRE) **97**
(Rainbow Quest (USA) 134) [2017 69p: 10m^{2} 9.9f^{3} 11.9d^{5} 12d* 14m^{5} 13.3g* 14s 15.4d Nov 10] workmanlike filly: useful handicapper: won at Newmarket in June and Newbury in July: stays 13f: acts on firm and good to soft going. *Ralph Beckett*

MISTRESS VIZ (IRE) 3 gr.f. Mastercraftsman (IRE) 129 – Vizean (IRE) 77 (Medicean **63**
128) [2017 65: 10.2g^{6} 10.2g 10d 8v t9.5g p12g^{3} p13.3s Dec 1] rather lightly-made filly: modest maiden: left John Mackie after second start, Daniel Loughnane after fourth: stays 1½m: acts on polytrack and good to soft going. *Sarah Hollinshead*

MISTRY 4 b.f. Mullionmileanhour (IRE) 116 – Smart Ass (IRE) 91 (Shinko Forest (IRE)) **55**
[2017 50: p6g^{5} p7d p6g^{2} p6g^{2} p5d^{5} t6.1m p6g* Nov 17] modest handicapper: won at Lingfield (apprentice) in November: best at 6f: acts on polytrack and tapeta: in headgear last 5 starts. *Mark Usher*

MISTY BREESE (IRE) 2 b.f. (Mar 20) Zebedee 113 – Geordie Iris (IRE) 99 (Elusive **44**
City (USA) 117) [2017 5g^{6} 6m p6s^{5} p7g p10g t9.5g Nov 20] 38,000Y: second foal: dam winner up to 1½m (2-y-o 8.6f winner), including in Scandinavia: poor maiden: in headgear last 3 starts: sometimes slowly away. *Paul D'Arcy*

MISTY SPIRIT 2 br.f. (Feb 8) Swiss Spirit 117 – Irrational 63 (Kyllachy 129) [2017 5.1m **80**
p6g^{2} 6g* 5.2s 6g 6g^{3} p6g^{4} Oct 24] 30,000Y: second foal: half-sister to 2-y-o 5f winner Whiteandgold (by Major Cadeaux): dam 2-y-o 5f winner: fairly useful performer: won minor event at Leicester in August: third in quite valuable sales race at Newmarket in October: stays 6f: best form on good going: front runner/races prominently, usually travels strongly. *David Elsworth*

MISU MAC 7 b.m. Misu Bond (IRE) 114 – Umbrian Gold (IRE) 83 (Perugino (USA) 84) **–**
[2017 50: t6g Jan 21] fair handicapper in 2015, little impact since: stays 6f: acts on fibresand. *Neville Bycroft*

MISU MONEYPENNY 4 b.f. Misu Bond (IRE) 114 – Watersilk (IRE) (Fasliyev (USA) **67**
120) [2017 72: p5g^{4} f5s f6g f5m f6g^{6} f5g^{4} 7m 6d^{2} 6m^{6} 5s^{5} 6s 6v^{4} f5g^{4} Aug 28] fair handicapper: stays 6f: acts on polytrack, fibresand and heavy going: wears headgear. *Scott Dixon*

MISU PETE 5 b.g. Misu Bond (IRE) 114 – Smart Ass (IRE) 91 (Shinko Forest (IRE)) **68**
[2017 66: t7.1m t6g^{4} t7.1g^{4} p8g t7.1g^{4} p7s^{2} t7.2g^{3} t8.6g^{ur} p7s* p7s 7.4g* p8s 7.4v^{5} 7s^{2} 8.1d^{5} t8.6g p7g^{2} Dec 21] fair handicapper: won at Chelmsford in June and Ffos Las in July: stays 1m: acts on polytrack, tapeta and soft going: often wears headgear. *Mark Usher*

MITCD (IRE) 6 gr.m. Mastercraftsman (IRE) 129 – Halicardia 104 (Halling (USA) 133) [2017 t16.3g^6 t12.4d^4 Dec 16] modest maiden: stays 16.5f: acts on tapeta and good to firm going: winning hurdler. *George Bewley* **54**

MITCHUM 8 b.g. Elnadim (USA) 128 – Maid To Matter (Pivotal 124) [2017 78: 5m^5 5g^5 6.9v^3 6d 5d t5g^3 6g^6 6g^4 6g^5 6d^5 5d^6 t5g 5s^4 6d Oct 30] close-coupled gelding: modest handicapper nowadays: stays 7f: acts on fibresand, tapeta, good to firm and heavy going: usually wears headgear. *Ron Barr* **63**

MITCHUM SWAGGER 5 b.g. Paco Boy (IRE) 129 – Dont Dili Dali 102 (Dansili 127) [2017 117: 8.1d^5 8s 7.2s^4 7d* 8.2s^5 7s Oct 7] useful-looking gelding: smart performer: below best in 2017, though did win minor event at Thirsk (by 2½ lengths from Lavetta) in August: stays 1m: acts on soft going: in cheekpieces last 3 starts: sold to join Ralph Beckett 75,000 gns in November. *David Lanigan* **109**

MITHQAAL (USA) 4 ch.g. Speightstown (USA) 124 – Bestowal (USA) (Unbridled's Song (USA) 125) [2017 105: f8g* a8f^6 8f a6f 6.5f 8f^6 Nov 12] useful performer: won handicap at Southwell (by 1¾ lengths from Showboating) in January on final start for Michael Appleby: below form in USA after: stays 9f: acts on polytrack, fibresand and good to firm going: often races prominently. *Doug F. O'Neill, USA* **102**

MITIGATE 3 b.f. Lawman (FR) 121 – Marika 103 (Marju (IRE) 127) [2017 72p: p5g^3 p7g* 7m^6 7m^6 8m p7s 8g^3 8s 8.1d Oct 23] fairly useful performer: won maiden at Lingfield (by 4 lengths from Havelock) in February: left David Elsworth after sixth start: stays 1m: acts on polytrack: tried in cheekpieces. *Jane Chapple-Hyam* **83**

MITTENS 3 b.f. New Approach (IRE) 132 – Warm Hands (Oasis Dream 129) [2017 79p: 10m^3 9.9d^3 8g* 8g* 8d^5 8.2d^6 8d^6 Sep 29] well-made filly: useful performer: won handicaps at Newmarket and Ascot (by 3¼ lengths from Havre de Paix) in July: stayed 1¼m: acted on polytrack and good to firm going: often raced towards rear: dead. *Sir Michael Stoute* **106**

MIX AND MINGLE (IRE) 4 ch.f. Exceed And Excel (AUS) 126 – Mango Lady 80 (Dalakhani (IRE) 133) [2017 105: 7m* 7d* 8m 7g 7m^6 Oct 13] useful-looking filly: smart performer: won handicap at Newmarket (by length from Tabarrak) in April and Chartwell Stakes at Lingfield (by 2¼ lengths from Qemah) in May: stays 1m: acts on soft and good to firm going. *Chris Wall* **110**

MIXBOY (FR) 7 gr.g. Fragrant Mix (IRE) 124 – Leston Girl (FR) (Lesotho (USA) 118) [2017 12v* 15v^5 12.1s* t12.2g^6 Dec 2] useful form: won maiden at Ripon in September and handicap at Catterick (by 6 lengths from Henry Smith) in October: will stay at least 1¾m: winning hurdler/useful chaser. *Keith Dalgleish* **95**

MIZEN MASTER (IRE) 4 b.g. Captain Rio 122 – Nilassiba (Daylami (IRE) 138) [2017 54: p16g Oct 4] lightly-raced maiden on Flat: tried in tongue tie: fairly useful hurdler. *Olly Murphy* **61**

MIZPAH (IRE) 5 b.m. Excellent Art 125 – Philosophers Guest (IRE) 67 (Desert Prince (IRE) 130) [2017 10d^6 May 29] first foal: dam 9f winner: little form: tried in cheekpieces/tongue tie. *Ken Wingrove* –

MJJACK (IRE) 3 gr.c. Elzaam (AUS) 115 – Docklands Grace (USA) 62 (Honour And Glory (USA) 122) [2017 82p: 6g 7v* 7.2s* 8g 7d^2 7s^2 7s^6 7s Oct 28] useful-looking colt: useful handicapper: won at Doncaster (by head from Musawaat) in May and Haydock (by 4½ lengths from Sir Reginald Brown) in June: second at Ascot in July (International Stakes, 1¼ lengths behind Stamp Hill) and September (½ length behind Remarkable): stays 7f: acts on good to firm and heavy going: front runner/races prominently. *K. R. Burke* **108**

MOABIT (GER) 5 b.g. Azamour (IRE) 130 – Moonlight Danceuse (IRE) (Bering 136) [2017 16m^5 14.2v* 14v^2 14.2s* f12.1g^6 Dec 21] fairly useful handicapper: won 3 times in France for E. Libaud in 2016: also won at Salisbury in July and October (by 4½ lengths from Champagne Champ): stays 15f: acts on heavy going: in tongue tie last 5 starts: useful hurdler. *Paul Nicholls* **91**

MOAKKAD 2 b.g. (Mar 31) Helmet (AUS) 127 – Generously Gifted (Sakhee (USA) 136) [2017 6g 6m 6.1g^5 Jul 21] big, strong gelding: fair form when fifth in maiden at Nottingham (3¼ lengths behind First Drive) on last of 3 starts. *Mark Johnston* **67**

MOAMAR 3 ch.g. Sepoy (AUS) 129 – Palitana (USA) 61 (Giant's Causeway (USA) 132) [2017 –: t8g* t8.6g^3 Jan 31] fair form: won maiden at Newcastle (by ½ length from Crindle Carr) in January: stays 8.5f: sent to Qatar: open to further improvement. *Ed Dunlop* **79 p**

MOANA 4 b.f. Kheleyf (USA) 116 – Torver 58 (Lake Coniston (IRE) 131) [2017 7g Oct 17] third foal: dam, maiden (stayed 7f), half-sister to smart winner up to 7f Tumbleweed Ridge: 50/1, well held in seller at Leicester. *Dr Jon Scargill* –

MOANS CROSS (USA) 3 ch.g. Spring At Last (USA) 122 – Playful Wink (USA) (Orientate (USA) 127) [2017 –p: 11.6m Jun 14] not knocked about when well held in 2 maidens: should do better. *Alan King* **– p**

MOAYADD (USA) 5 b.g. Street Cry (IRE) 130 – Aryaamm (IRE) 94 (Galileo (IRE) 134) [2017 –p: p7g³ t10.2d* p11d* p11g* p12m² 12.1m* May 5] fairly useful handicapper: won at Newcastle and Kempton in February, both apprentice events, Kempton (by 4½ lengths from Solveig's Song) in March and Chepstow (by 2 lengths from Mazaaher) in May: stays 1½m: acts on polytrack, tapeta and good to firm going: responds generously to pressure. *Neil Mulholland* **88**

MOBBHIJ 3 b.g. New Approach (IRE) 132 – Anaamil (IRE) 85 (Darshaan 133) [2017 p13.3g* t16.3g⁴ p12g t16.3g* Nov 15] half-brother to 3 winners, including very smart 1m-10.4f winner Sajjhaa (by King's Best) and useful 7f winner Momaris (by Dubai Destination): dam 10.5f winner out of Lancashire Oaks winner Noushkey: useful form: won maiden at Chelmsford in August and handicap at Newcastle (by ¾ length from Montanna) in November: stays 16.5f. *Saeed bin Suroor* **98**

MOBLEY CHAOS 7 b.g. Darnay 117 – Emmarander (Bob's Return (IRE) 123) [2017 p8d t7.1gF 8g 7m 5.7m p6g 5.7f Jul 12] poor maiden: wears headgear. *John Flint* **38**

MOBSTA (IRE) 5 b.h. Bushranger (IRE) 119 – Sweet Nicole 54 (Okawango (USA) 115) [2017 112: 6g 6s⁴ 6d⁵ 6m 6m⁵ 6g 6d 6d³ 6v 6d 7d Nov 11] tall, useful-looking horse: smart performer at best, below that level in 2017: stays 7f: acts on heavy going: tried in visor: usually races nearer last than first. *Mick Channon* **104**

MOCCASIN (FR) 8 b.g. Green Tune (USA) 125 – Museum Piece (Rainbow Quest (USA) 134) [2017 55: t10.2g 12g 12.1m⁵ 13.9m⁴ Jun 2] fairly useful at best, little form since 2015: stays 1½m: acts on tapeta, good to firm and heavy going: wears headgear. *Geoffrey Harker* **44**

MOCEAD CAPPALL 2 b.f. (Feb 18) Captain Gerrard (IRE) 113 – All Fur Coat 86 (Multiplex 114) [2017 5.1m⁶ 5g³ t5.1g⁶ f5g⁶ 5s⁵ p5g p5m Nov 25] £9,500Y: second foal: sister to 2-y-o 5f winner Gerrard's Fur Coat: dam 2-y-o 5f winner: modest form, standout effort on second outing: sometimes in hood: front runner/races prominently. *John Holt* **58**

MOCHALOV 2 b.g. (May 2) Denounce 89 – Awesome Asset (USA) (Awesome Again (CAN) 133) [2017 t9.5g Dec 18] 125/1, well held in minor event at Wolverhampton. *Jane Chapple-Hyam* **–**

MOD 3 b.f. Sixties Icon 125 – Panna 106 (Polish Precedent (USA) 131) [2017 10g 11.6d² p12g⁶ Jul 5] workmanlike filly: half-sister to several winners, including smart 1¾m winner The Twisler (by Motivator) and 1¼m winner Hot Diamond (by Desert Prince): dam 1¼m winner (stayed 1½m): fair form: best effort when second in maiden at Haydock in June. *James Fanshawe* **78**

MODEL (FR) 2 gr.f. (Feb 27) Mastercraftsman (IRE) 129 – Goddess of Love 81 (Galileo (IRE) 134) [2017 7d* 7g² 7g 7s Oct 28] €100,000Y, €320,000 2-y-o: leggy filly: first foal: dam, 1m winner, sister to smart winner up to 13f (in Australia) Marksmanship: fairly useful form: won minor event at Doncaster in July: second in listed race at Deauville (short neck behind Izzy Bizu) later same month: raced only at 7f. *Richard Hannon* **90**

MODERNISM 8 b.g. Monsun (GER) 124 – La Nuit Rose (FR) 109 (Rainbow Quest (USA) 134) [2017 92: p16g t12.2m* t9.5g⁶ t9.5g³ 12.3d³ 12.3s⁶ 10.3g 13.4d 10.3g⁵ 11.6g⁴ 12.1s⁶ t14g t12.4d Dec 16] sturdy gelding: fairly useful handicapper: won at Wolverhampton (by length from Clovelly Bay) in January: stays 12.5f: acts on polytrack, tapeta, firm and good to soft going: wears headgear: tried in tongue tie. *Ian Williams* **85**

MODERN LOVE (IRE) 2 b.f. (Mar 25) Dark Angel (IRE) 113 – The Hermitage (IRE) 83 (Kheleyf (USA) 116) [2017 6g² 7d³ p6g³ Oct 4] €200,000Y: fourth foal: sister to 6f winner Where's Sue and useful 2-y-o 6f winner Perfect Angel: dam 2-y-o 5f winner who stayed 7f: fairly useful form when placed in a trio of maidens. *M. D. O'Callaghan, Ireland* **84**

MODERN TUTOR 8 b.g. Selkirk (USA) 129 – Magical Romance (IRE) 110 (Barathea (IRE) 127) [2017 65: p7g⁶ p7g⁶ p8g 7d 6m 8d 9s³ 7d 7.8g a7g⁵ 8s p7s Dec 8] well-made gelding: fair handicapper, below form in 2017: stays 9f: acts on polytrack, soft and good to firm going: has worn headgear, including in 2017: has worn tongue tie. *Miss Nicole McKenna, Ireland* **50 a60**

MOGGY (USA) 2 b.f. (Apr 4) Kitten's Joy (USA) 128 – Day Glow (USA) (Dehere (USA) 121) [2017 p6s³ 7m p7s⁴ Sep 8] $25,000Y: first foal: dam US 1m winner: fair form: best effort when third in minor event at Lingfield (6¼ lengths behind Elizabeth Bennet) on debut. *Richard Hughes* **66**

MOHAB 4 b.g. Sir Percy 129 – Princess Aurora (USA) (Mr Greeley (USA) 122) [2017 89: 8g^{6} 7g^{5} 8.5g^{2} 7.9m 9.2g* 9.1g 7.8v^{3} 7.9g Oct 13] well-made gelding: fairly useful handicapper: won at Hamilton (by 2 lengths from Desert Ruler) in July: stays 9f: acts on good to firm going: has worn headgear, including often in 2017: usually races nearer last than first: sent to Saudi Arabia. *Kevin Ryan* **94**

MOHATEM (USA) 5 ch.g. Distorted Humor (USA) 117 – Soul Search (USA) 116 (A P Indy (USA) 131) [2017 98: 10.1g* 12m May 13] attractive gelding: useful handicapper, lightly raced: won at Yarmouth (by 3 lengths from Celebration Day) in April: stays 11f: acts on polytrack and good to firm going: sold 57,000 gns in July, sent to Saudi Arabia. *Owen Burrows* **96**

MO HENRY 5 b.g. Monsieur Bond (IRE) 120 – Mo Mhuirnin (IRE) 94 (Danetime (IRE) 121) [2017 76: p6g^{6} p6g p5g p5g^{2} 5m 5m 6m 6d^{4} 6g* 6g 6g* 7d 6m^{3} a6g^{6} p5g^{2} p7g^{2} 5.8v p6g p6g^{5} p5g Dec 15] fairly useful handicapper: won at Naas (twice) in July: second at Dundalk in September and October: best at 6f: acts on polytrack, tapeta, good to firm and heavy going: wears headgear. *A. P. Keatley, Ireland* **81**

MOHSEN 3 b.r. Bated Breath 125 – Harryana 79 (Efisio 120) [2017 6m^{4} 7s^{4} 6g^{2} p6g^{6} 7.1s^{2} 7s^{2} Oct 10] 80,000Y: half-brother to several winners, including smart 2-y-o 5f/6f (Mill Reef Stakes) winner Temple Meads (by Avonbridge) and useful 2-y-o 6f winner Sneak Preview (by Monsieur Bond): dam 2-y-o 5f winner: fairly useful maiden: runner-up 3 times: stays 7f: acts on soft going: sold 18,000 gns in October, sent to Qatar. *Marcus Tregoning* **80**

MOI AUSSIE 4 gr.f. Aussie Rules (USA) 123 – Oceana Blue 89 (Reel Buddy (USA) 118) [2017 64: t6g t9.5m^{3} p8g f8d t7.1g^{4} t8.6g 7m* 7m* 7.6s^{4} 8f^{3} 7g^{3} 7.4d 7s^{4} 7v p7g^{5} Dec 21] rather lightly-built filly: fair handicapper: won at Yarmouth (twice) in May: stays 1m: acts on tapeta and firm going: sometimes in cheekpieces in 2017: races prominently. *Michael Appleby* **71**

MOJITO (IRE) 3 b.c. Requinto (IRE) 109 – Narva (USA) (Grand Slam (USA) 120) [2017 87P: 7.2f^{3} 8d^{3} 7m* 7d* 7.9g* 7s Oct 7] strong, compact colt: smart handicapper: won at Sandown (by 1¾ lengths from Sultan Baybars) in July, and at Newmarket (by 2¼ lengths from Perfect Madge) and York (by 2¼ lengths from Battered) in August: stays 1m: acts on tapeta, firm and good to soft going: usually races prominently. *William Haggas* **112**

MOKAATIL 2 br.c. (Mar 30) Lethal Force (IRE) 128 – Moonlit Garden (IRE) 95 (Exceed And Excel (AUS) 126) [2017 5m^{2} 5f^{4} t5.1g^{2} 5m* 5m^{3} Oct 13] 100,000F: lengthy colt: second foal: half-brother to 2-y-o 5f winner Dream Dreamer (by Dream Ahead): dam 2-y-o 6f winner: useful performer: won maiden at Ripon in September: third in Cornwallis Stakes at Newmarket (¾ length behind Abel Handy) in October: raced only at 5f: acts on firm going: open to further improvement. *Owen Burrows* **101 p**

MOKARRIS (USA) 3 b.c. More Than Ready (USA) 120 – Limonar (IRE) 112 (Street Cry (IRE) 130) [2017 107: 6f May 3] useful-looking colt: useful at 2 yrs, well below form sole outing in 2017: bred to stay at least 7f: acts on good to firm going: usually races towards rear. *Simon Crisford* **–**

MOKHALAD 4 ch.g. Dubawi (IRE) 129 – Model Queen (USA) 76 (Kingmambo (USA) 125) [2017 –p: 7m^{4} 7m^{2} p12g 8s^{6} p8g^{4} p7g^{3} p10.7g p6g p7g* Dec 21] fairly useful performer: won handicap at Dundalk in December: left Sir Michael Stoute after second start: should stay 1m: acts on polytrack and good to firm going: tried in tongue tie. *Damian Joseph English, Ireland* **81**

MOLANS MARE (IRE) 7 ch.m. Shirocco (GER) 129 – Devious Diva (IRE) 94 (Dr Devious (IRE) 127) [2017 35: p6g 5.8g 5m^{6} 5g 5g 5s^{3} 5g^{5} 6g^{2} 5d 6m 5d 6.3s a7g^{5} Sep 5] modest maiden: left Emmet Michael Butterly after first start: stays 7f: acts on sand and good to firm going: tried in hood: often races towards rear. *Keith Henry Clarke, Ireland* **52**

MOLECULE (IRE) 3 ch.f. The Carbon Unit (USA) 106 – The Mighty Atom (USA) 78 (Sky Mesa (USA) 116) [2017 7d 9.5s 7g 6g^{6} Jul 3] third foal: sister to 5f-7f winner Split The Atom (2-y-o 6f winner) and 6f-7.6f winner Ionization, both useful: dam 6f winner: modest form when eighth in maiden at Naas in June, standout effort. *John Patrick Shanahan, Ireland* **60**

MOLLIANA 2 b.f. (Apr 18) Olden Times 121 – The Screamer (IRE) 53 (Insan (USA) 119) [2017 7s p8g f7.1g Nov 16] £2,600Y: half-sister to winner up to 7f Juventas (2-y-o 6f winner, by Sixties Icon) and a winner in Sweden by Imperial Dancer: dam, 1½m winner, also winning jumper: well held in minor events. *Neil Mulholland* **–**

MOLLY JONES 8 b.m. Three Valleys (USA) 119 – And Toto Too 79 (Averti (IRE) 117) [2017 55: p5m t5.1g p5f 5.1m^4 6g^4 5.7m 5.7f 5.7f^6 5m p5g Oct 13] compact mare: modest handicapper: stays 6f: acts on polytrack, fibresand, firm and good to soft going: has worn cheekpieces. *Matthew Salaman* **49**

MOLLY KAYE 4 b.f. Multiplex 114 – Persian Lass (IRE) 103 (Grand Lodge (USA) 125) [2017 9.5d 10.3v^4 12v^5 p12g p10.7g^6 t16.5g^5 p12g^6 p10.7g Dec 1] €2,000Y: seventh foal: half-sister to 11f winner Persian Patriot (by Bahamian Bounty): dam 1¼m winner: modest maiden: stays 1½m: acts on polytrack, tapeta and heavy going: tried in tongue tie. *S. M. Duffy, Ireland* **59**

MOLLY MAYHEM (IRE) 2 ch.f. (May 2) Casamento (IRE) 118 – Inez (Dai Jin 123) [2017 t7.1s 7m^4 p8g^6 Aug 8] €75,000Y: fourth foal: half-sister to French 1½m winner Stacey Sutton (by Tertullian) and smart German performer up to 1m (7f winner in France, including at 2 yrs) Spectre (by Siyouni): dam, German 1m winner, half-sister to very smart German/Hong Kong 1m-1¼m performer Irian: modest form when seventh at Newcastle (5¼ lengths behind Kit Marlowe) on first of 3 starts in minor events. *Richard Fahey* **54**

MOLTEN LAVA (IRE) 5 b.g. Rock of Gibraltar (IRE) 133 – Skehana (IRE) 69 (Mukaddamah (USA) 125) [2017 79: t8.6g p7g p7s t7.2g t8.6g^6 t12.4g t9.5g Oct 21] tall gelding: fair handicapper, well below form in 2017: left Christian Williams after fifth start: stays 8.5f: acts on polytrack, good to firm and good to soft going: often in headgear. *Philip Kirby* **54**

MOMENTARILY 2 b.f. (Jan 25) Cityscape 127 – Firebelly 86 (Nicolotte 118) [2017 8m^3 Aug 22] 30,000F, 68,000Y: sixth foal: half-sister to 1m (including at 2 yrs) winner Bombina (by Lomitas) and smart 6f/7f winner Firebeam (by Cadeaux Genereux): dam 2-y-o 6f-7.5f winner: 7/2, third in minor event at Yarmouth (6 lengths behind Wild Illusion) in August: will improve. *Hugo Palmer* **74 p**

MOMENTORI 4 ch.f. Observatory (USA) 131 – True Melody (IRE) (Grand Lodge (USA) 125) [2017 –: f7g Mar 15] well held in maidens. *Scott Dixon* **–**

MOMENT TO DREAM 5 b.m. Halling (USA) 133 – Pretty Majestic (IRE) 92 (Invincible Spirit (IRE) 121) [2017 –: f8g Jan 1] sturdy mare: little form: tried in cheekpieces. *Ken Wingrove* **–**

MOM SAID (IRE) 2 b.g. (Mar 13) Lawman (FR) 121 – Istishaara (USA) 90 (Kingmambo (USA) 125) [2017 p7g 7g^6 p8g Nov 7] fair form when sixth in maiden at Leicester (5¼ lengths behind Accessor) on second of 3 starts. *Ed Walker* **67**

MONAADHIL (IRE) 3 b.g. Dark Angel (IRE) 113 – Urban Daydream (IRE) 72 (Oasis Dream 129) [2017 8.2d* 8g^2 8.3g* Nov 1] 160,000Y: rather unfurnished gelding: first foal: dam, maiden (should have stayed beyond 1¼m), half-sister to very smart winner up to 1½m Rainbow Peak: fairly useful form: won maiden at Leicester (by ½ length from Wonderfillo) in June and handicap at Nottingham (by 2 lengths from Rosarno) in November: stays 8.5f: will go on improving. *Marcus Tregoning* **93 p**

MONACO ROSE 4 b.f. Sir Percy 129 – Pallas (Statue of Liberty (USA) 115) [2017 75: 10m^4 12g* 11.9v* 12m^4 12.3s^2 12.3d^3 13.1g^4 13.4d^3 t12.2g^5 14s^4 12.1s^6 10.3v Sep 30] fairly useful handicapper: won at Catterick in April and Doncaster (apprentice, by 2 lengths from Arrowtown) in May: placed at Chester in June and July: stays 1¾m: acts on polytrack, good to firm and heavy going: wears hood nowadays. *Richard Fahey* **84**

MONADEE 2 b.g. (May 19) Showcasing 117 – Messelina (Noverre (USA) 125) [2017 6d^6 p6g^3 p6d* Dec 13] 120,000Y: seventh foal: half-brother to 3 winners abroad, including useful French 1¼m winner Meliora (by Starspangledbanner): dam unraced half-sister to smart winner up to 7f Pan Jammer: fairly useful form: won minor event at Kempton (by 1½ lengths from Breathless Times) in December: will stay 7f: open to further improvement. *Roger Varian* **85 p**

MONARCH MAID 6 b.m. Captain Gerrard (IRE) 113 – Orange Lily (Royal Applause 124) [2017 80: p6g^5 6m 6.1g^5 6.1m 6g^4 6.1m^5 7m p6g t6.1m^4 t6.1g t6.1d Dec 16] compact mare: fair handicapper, on downgrade in 2017: stays 6f: acts on polytrack and firm going: tried in cheekpieces: front runner. *Peter Hiatt* **71 d**

MONARCHS GLEN 3 b.g. Frankel 147 – Mirabilis (USA) 114 (Lear Fan (USA) 130) [2017 89p: p11g* 10d^4 11.2m^4 9.9g^2 9.9s* 9m* Oct 14] tall, strong gelding: smart performer: won handicap at Kempton (by length from Big Challenge) in April, listed race at Goodwood (by short head from What About Carlo) in September and Darley Stakes at Newmarket (by 1¼ lengths from Robin of Navan) in October: stays 11f: acts on polytrack, soft and good to firm going: tried in cheekpieces: usually races freely. *John Gosden* **118**

MONAR LAD (IRE) 5 b.g. Mountain High (IRE) 124 – Cottage Lady (IRE) (Moscow Society (USA) 110) [2017 11.6v^5 9.9s^6 12v^4 12s^6 Sep 14] fair form: stays 1½m: unplaced in bumpers/over hurdles. *Dai Burchell* **65**

MON BEAU VISAGE (IRE) 4 br.g. Footstepsinthesand 120 – Hurricane Lily (IRE) 61 (Ali-Royal (IRE) 127) [2017 89: t7.1s^5 8.5f^4 8g^4 8g* 8m^3 8m^3 7.4m^3 8.5f^3 8d* 8m* 9d 8g^5 7.9g Oct 13] tall gelding: fairly useful handicapper: won at Pontefract in May, and at Thirsk and Redcar (by short head from Testa Rossa) in August: stays 8.5f: acts on tapeta, firm and soft going: usually wears cheekpieces. *David O'Meara* **94**

MONDAY CLUB 4 ch.g. Strategic Prince 114 – Support Fund (IRE) 83 (Intikhab (USA) 135) [2017 71: 9.9v^6 10.2g Nov 1] fair handicapper, below form in 2017: stays 1¼m: acts on tapeta, soft and good to firm going: has worn headgear: quirky sort. *Dominic Ffrench Davis* **56**

MONDIALISTE (IRE) 7 b.h. Galileo (IRE) 134 – Occupandiste (IRE) 123 (Kaldoun (FR) 122) [2017 123: 8.9d 8f^6 9.9m^4 7.9m^6 10.3g^2 8.8m^6 8f^4 8f^5 Oct 7] sturdy horse: smart performer: winner of 5 races, notably Woodbine Mile in 2015 (when also second in Breeders' Cup Mile at Keeneland) and Arlington Million in 2016: best efforts in 2017 when second in York Stakes (nose behind Success Days) and fourth in Woodbine Mile (beaten 3 lengths by World Approval): stayed 10.5f: acted on polytrack, firm and soft going: often raced towards rear: to stand at Elwick Stud, Hartlepool, fee £6,000. *David O'Meara* **119**

MONEY FOR LUCK (IRE) 2 br.g. (Mar 16) Arakan (USA) 123 – Invincible Wings (IRE) (Invincible Spirit (IRE) 121) [2017 5.5s 5m^6 Jun 21] well held in minor events. *Brian Ellison* **–**

MONEY IN MY POCKET (IRE) 3 b.f. Acclamation 118 – Azabara 106 (Pivotal 124) [2017 70: 9.7d 7.1s^5 8v 7v 8v p7g Nov 3] fair maiden at 2 yrs, has lost her way: left Harry Dunlop after second start: tried in cheekpieces: often races prominently. *G. Webb, Ireland* **48**

MONEYORYOURLIFE 3 b.c. Dick Turpin (IRE) 127 – Truly Pink (Mr Greeley (USA) 122) [2017 61: p7g^2 p10g^2 p10d* p12g^4 12m^3 9.9f^2 10.2f^4 p12g Dec 20] fair handicapper: won at Chelmsford (apprentice) in March: stays 1½m: acts on polytrack, firm and soft going. *Richard Hannon* **73**

MONEY TALKS 7 br.g. Motivator 131 – Movie Mogul 64 (Sakhee (USA) 136) [2017 p12g^4 p16d^4 p16g^4 11.6g^6 p16g 16.3d^5 Jul 12] good-topped gelding: modest maiden: stays 2m: acts on polytrack and good to firm going: tried in cheekpieces/tongue tie. *Michael Madgwick* **61**

MONEY TEAM (IRE) 6 b.g. Kodiac 112 – Coral Dawn (IRE) 67 (Trempolino (USA) 135) [2017 88: t6g^6 t5s^4 6v 6m 6v Sep 9] fairly useful handicapper: stays 6f: acts on polytrack, good to firm and heavy going: sometimes slowly away, usually races nearer last than first. *David Barron* **81**

MONJENI 4 b.g. Montjeu (IRE) 137 – Polly's Mark (IRE) 112 (Mark of Esteem (IRE) 137) [2017 70§: t13.9m* t13.9g* 13.1m^3 14m* 13.9m^3 Jun 16] fairly useful handicapper: won at Wolverhampton (twice) in March and Haydock (by 1¾ lengths from Jaameh) in May: stays 2m: acts on polytrack, tapeta and firm going: wears headgear: often travels strongly. *Ian Williams* **89**

MONKEY MAGIC 2 b.f. (May 2) Acclamation 118 – Happy (JPN) (Bago (FR) 130) [2017 5m 5m^6 6g^3 6d^5 6d^5 6g 5s t5g Nov 15] €20,000Y, resold €22,000Y: third foal: dam unraced granddaughter of Miesque: modest maiden: best effort at 6f: acts on good to soft going: tried in tongue tie: usually races close up. *Nigel Tinkler* **50**

MONKS STAND (USA) 3 b.g. More Than Ready (USA) 120 – Return The Jewel (USA) (Broken Vow (USA) 117) [2017 90: 6g 7.5m^6 7s 5m^3 5.6d^3 6.1g 6d 6m^5 Aug 28] smallish, lengthy gelding: fairly useful at 2 yrs, below form in 2017: stays 6f: acts on polytrack and good to firm going: wears headgear: not one to rely on. *Tim Easterby* **79 §**

MONNA VALLEY 5 ch.g. Exceed And Excel (AUS) 126 – Monnavanna (IRE) 109 (Machiavellian (USA) 123) [2017 69: t13.9m^5 t9.5g t9.5m t9.5g^4 p10g^6 Apr 26] strong, workmanlike gelding: fair handicapper, below form in Britain in first part of 2017: stays 10.5f: acts on polytrack, tapeta and good to firm going: tried in headgear: has worn tongue tie: often races prominently: sent to Italy, where won claimer at Varese in July. *Stuart Williams* **61**

MONOLOGUE (IRE) 4 ch.g. Manduro (GER) 135 – Homily (Singspiel (IRE) 133) [2017 57: p8g* t8.6g^4 p12g^5 t12.2g Jul 17] modest handicapper: won at Kempton in March: left Simon Hodgson after third start: stays 9.5f: acts on polytrack and tapeta: tried in tongue tie. *Neil Mulholland* **61**

188Bet Chester Cup Handicap, Chester—Montaly (white face, light colours) produces a career best to land this valuable prize, staying on strongly to beat Yorkidding and Fun Mac (armlets)

MONOSHKA (IRE) 3 b.g. Kodiac 112 – Coastal Waters 81 (Halling (USA) 133) [2017 79: t7.1f t6g6 t6m4 Mar 14] good-bodied gelding: fair at 2 yrs, last all 3 starts in 2017: stays 6f: acts on good to firm and good to soft going: sometimes slowly away. *James Given* **63**

MONSIEUR BAY 3 b.c. Sir Percy 129 – Pilcomayo (IRE) (Rahy (USA) 115) [2017 t9.5g5 p10g5 Dec 13] fair form in maidens: will be suited by 1½m. *Ismail Mohammed* **71**

MONSIEUR GLORY 4 ch.g. Monsieur Bond (IRE) 120 – Chushka 81 (Pivotal 124) [2017 80: 10.1m3 9.9m4 10m2 10m* 10.2g6 11.6m* t12.4s Sep 19] strong gelding: fairly useful handicapper: won at Newbury in July and Bath (by 1½ lengths from Pastoral Music) in August: stays 1½m: acts on tapeta and firm going: often wears headgear: temperament under suspicion: sold 27,000 gns in October, sent to Bahrain. *Tom Clover* **89**

MONSIEUR JAMIE 9 b.g. Monsieur Bond (IRE) 120 – Primula Bairn 77 (Bairn (USA) 126) [2017 70§: f5g f5g Dec 4] sturdy, good-bodied gelding: fair handicapper, well held both starts in 2017: stays 6f: acts on fibresand and heavy going: has worn headgear: has refused to race, and unreliable. *Clare Ellam* **– §**

MONSIEUR JIMMY 5 ch.g. Monsieur Bond (IRE) 120 – Artistic License (IRE) 94 (Chevalier (IRE) 115) [2017 51, a75: f7g f6m2 f6g5 f6d f7g4 f6.1g3 6g4 7g2 7m 7.2s 7.4d2 7.2d 8g f7.1g* 7s f8.1g2 f8.1g* Nov 16] compact gelding: modest handicapper on turf, fair on all-weather: won at Southwell in August and November: stays 1m: acts on fibresand, good to firm and heavy going: has worn headgear: often races towards rear. *Declan Carroll* **63 a78**

MONSIEUR JOE (IRE) 10 b.g. Choisir (AUS) 126 – Pascali 61 (Compton Place 125) [2017 117: 5g5 5g 5d4 5m5 5g 5d2 5d 5g5 5g 5s5 5s2 5g Oct 13] sturdy gelding: useful performer nowadays: second in minor event at Newmarket (4 lengths behind Ornate) in July and handicap at Naas (1½ lengths behind Tylery Wonder) in September: best at 5f: acts on polytrack, soft and good to firm going: has worn visor. *Paul Midgley* **96**

MONSIEUR MEL 3 b.g. Monsieur Bond (IRE) 120 – Melandre 74 (Lujain (USA) 119) [2017 t7.2g 7m 7d 6m Aug 26] modest form when seventh in maiden at Wolverhampton on debut, standout effort. *Antony Brittain* **52**

MONSIEUR PADDY 4 ch.g. Monsieur Bond (IRE) 120 – Minnina (IRE) (In The Wings 128) [2017 72: p6g5 t5g t5.1g 6d 5.5f2 5d4 5.7d Aug 19] lengthy, workmanlike gelding: modest handicapper: stays 5.5f: acts on tapeta and firm going: often races towards rear. *Tony Carroll* **63**

MONSIEUR RENARD 2 ch.g. (Feb 5) Monsieur Bond (IRE) 120 – Slightly Foxed (Royal Applause 124) [2017 p5g5 Jun 1] 100/1, well held in minor event at Chelmsford. *Charlie Wallis* **–**

MONSIEUR RIEUSSEC 7 bl.g. Halling (USA) 133 – Muscovado (USA) 71 (Mr 82
Greeley (USA) 122) [2017 p12g p10g* p11g Feb 1] good-topped gelding: fairly useful handicapper: won at Chelmsford (by nose from Bunbury) in January: stayed 1½m: acted on polytrack, soft and good to firm going: dead. *Jonathan Portman*

MONSIEUR ROYALE 7 ch.g. Monsieur Bond (IRE) 120 – Bond Royale 89 (Piccolo 55
121) [2017 p8d^5 p8d^6 7m^4 7m^3 p7s p7m^5 Nov 25] modest handicapper: stays 1m: acts on polytrack and good to firm going: has worn headgear. *Clive Drew*

MONTAGUE (IRE) 2 b.c. (Mar 16) Poet's Voice 126 – Silicon Star (FR) (Starborough 83
126) [2017 6m^5 6g^6 6s^4 p8g^6 p7g* 7d^3 t7.2m* p7g^5 f6.1g^2 p6g^3 Dec 30] half-brother to several winners, including 2-y-o 1m winner Pythius (by Lord Shanakill), later useful winner up to 1¼m in Italy, and 2-y-o 5f/6f winner Sterling Silva (by Sakhee's Secret), stays 1m: dam French maiden: fairly useful performer: won claimer at Chelmsford and minor event at Wolverhampton in October: stays 7f: acts on all-weather and good to soft going: usually leads. *Jamie Osborne*

MONTALY 6 b.g. Yeats (IRE) 128 – Le Badie (IRE) (Spectrum (IRE) 126) [2017 105: 116
18.6m* 16.2m^2 16.3g* 17.9g^6 15.4g Oct 22] sturdy gelding: smart performer: won Chester Cup Handicap (by neck from Yorkidding) in May and Lonsdale Cup at York (by nose from Dartmouth) in August: second in listed race at Sandown (¾ length behind Nearly Caught) in July: stays 2¼m: acts on any turf going: has worn hood: usually races towards rear. *Andrew Balding*

MONTANA DAWN (USA) 2 b.f. (May 9) Jimmy Creed (USA) 118 – Page Dancer –
(USA) (Hennessy (USA) 122) [2017 p7g Oct 5] $30,000Y, £38,000 2-y-o: half-sister to several winners abroad: dam unraced half-sister to US Grade 2 1m winner Dice Dancer: in tongue tie, 66/1, well held in minor event at Chelmsford. *Bryan Smart*

MONTANNA 3 ch.g. Notnowcato 128 – Asi (USA) (El Prado (IRE) 119) [2017 12m^5 9g^5 87
12.1m^2 t12.4g* 12d^4 t16.3g^6 14d^6 t16.3g^2 Nov 15] 10,000Y: sixth foal: half-brother to 3 winners, including French 9.5f winner Anabasis (by Anabaa) and 1m/8.5f winner California Rose (by Oratorio): dam, French 1¼m winner, sister to very smart US Grade 1 9f winner Asi Siempre: fairly useful performer: won minor event at Newcastle in June: second in handicap there in November: stays 16.5f: acts on tapeta: tried in blinkers. *Jedd O'Keeffe*

MONTATAIRE (IRE) 3 b.c. Cape Cross (IRE) 129 – Chantilly Pearl (USA) 74 (Smart 102
Strike (CAN) 121) [2017 105: 9m 7.9g 9.9g^4 8g Dec 3] good-topped colt: useful performer: left Mark Johnston after third start: stays 1¼m: acts on good to firm going: front runner/races prominently. *S. bin Ghadayer, UAE*

MONTEAMIATA (IRE) 3 b.f. Dream Ahead (USA) 133 – Tiger Spice 68 (Royal 83
Applause 124) [2017 67: p5g* 5g^2 5.7d^3 5g^2 p6g^5 6d* 6g^4 6d^2 p7g^4 p6g^6 Oct 18] lengthy filly: fairly useful performer: won maiden at Lingfield in January and handicap there (by length from Baby Gal) in July: stays 7f: acts on polytrack and good to soft going: tried in cheekpieces: sent to France. *Ed Walker*

MONTE CINQ (IRE) 3 b.g. Bushranger (IRE) 119 – Invincible Me (IRE) (Invincible 86
Spirit (IRE) 121) [2017 67, a90: p5g^2 t5.1m^5 p5g^3 5.4d^5 5.1g 5g^5 5g^4 7v p6s f5g^5 Dec 19] short-backed gelding: fairly useful handicapper: placed at Lingfield in January and March: stays 5.5f: acts on polytrack, tapeta and good to soft going: often in hood in 2017: tried in tongue tie: often races in rear. *Jason Ward*

Weatherbys Hamilton Lonsdale Cup Stakes, York—
16/1-shot Montaly causes a surprise, catching Dartmouth (dark cap) on the line; between them is St Michel, with Sheikhzayedroad (hood) and Dal Harraild (right) the others in shot

MONTEVERDI (FR) 4 b.g. Kyllachy 129 – West of Saturn (USA) (Gone West (USA)) [2017 98: 6.1d 7m 7d a7g* p7g^2 f7.1g^3 Dec 11] good-bodied gelding: fairly useful performer: won minor event at Laytown in September: placed after in handicaps at Kempton and Southwell: stays 7f: acts on polytrack, fibresand, sand and heavy going: sometimes wears headgear: often travels strongly: sent to France. *Jamie Osborne* **92**

MONTICELLO (IRE) 3 b.g. Teofilo (IRE) 126 – Towards (USA) (Fusaichi Pegasus (USA) 130) [2017 95: t7.1g^5 10.2s^3 10m^2 10d^2 10m 9.9v 9.8g 10d Sep 23] rangy gelding: fairly useful handicapper: second at Newmarket (twice) in June: stays 1¼m: acts on good to firm and good to soft going. *Mark Johnston* **94**

MONT KIARA (FR) 4 b.g. Kendargent (FR) 112 – Xaarienne (Xaar 132) [2017 102: p6g 6m^4 5s 5m 5g 6g* 5v^4 6d^2 t6s Nov 30] good-topped gelding: useful handicapper: won at Newmarket (by 1¼ lengths from Clear Spring) in August: second there (¾ length behind Glenamoy Lad) in September: stays 6f: acts on good to firm and good to soft going: tried in hood: unreliable. *Kevin Ryan* **97 §**

MONT KINABALU (IRE) 2 b.g. (Mar 31) Society Rock (IRE) 126 – Startori 86 (Vettori (IRE) 119) [2017 6m^4 6m^4 6d^2 7.4v^3 7g* 7d Oct 28] €49,000Y: half-brother to several winners, including useful winner up to 1m in Scandinavia Liber (2-y-o 5f/5.7f winner in Britain) and 2-y-o 5f winner Guru Girl (both by Ishiguru): dam 2-y-o 7f winner: fairly useful performer: won minor event at York (by ½ length from Chief Justice) in October: stays 7.5f: acts on good to firm and heavy going. *Kevin Ryan* **82**

MONT RAS (IRE) 10 ch.g. Indian Ridge 123 – Khayrat (IRE) (Polar Falcon (USA) 126) [2017 99: t8g^6 Jan 4] good-topped gelding: useful handicapper, below form sole outing in 2017: stays 9.5f: acts on polytrack, tapeta and good to firm going: tried in tongue tie: usually races close up. *Roger Fell* **80**

MONT ROYAL (FR) 3 gr.g. Naaqoos 117 – Take Blood (FR) (Take Risks (FR) 116) [2017 74: 6m^4 7d 7g^4 8.5f* 8.5d 9.8m^6 p8g Sep 25] strong, compact gelding: fair handicapper: won at Beverley in July: stays 8.5f: acts on firm going: often starts slowly, usually races in rear. *Ollie Pears* **76**

MONTYCRISTO 4 br.g. Motivator 131 – Water Gipsy 81 (Piccolo 121) [2017 –: p12g^5 9.9g 9.9m^4 11.6s 11.9g^3 16.3d Aug 21] strong gelding: modest maiden: best effort at 1¼m: acts on good to firm going: in blinkers last 4 starts: front runner/races prominently. *Philip Hide* **55**

MONUMENTAL MAN 8 b.g. Vital Equine (IRE) 121 – Spark Up 81 (Lahib (USA) 129) [2017 85: p6g* p5d^4 p5g^2 p5f^6 p5g^4 p5g* 5g p5g 6.1s 5.3m^3 6g 5.3d^2 5.1d^2 5m^5 p5d^6 p5s^5 Dec 14] big gelding: fairly useful performer: won claimer at Lingfield in January and handicap there (by neck from Sandfrankskipsgo) in March: stays 6f: acts on polytrack, firm and good to soft going: wears headgear: tried in tongue tie: front runner/races prominently. *Michael Attwater* **83** **a91**

MONZINO (USA) 9 b.g. More Than Ready (USA) 120 – Tasso's Magic Roo (USA) (Tasso (USA)) [2017 52§: f12g^3 f14g f14g^6 12.1s^4 8m f8.1g^4 f11.1g Dec 29] tall gelding: poor handicapper: has worn headgear/tongue tie: sometimes slowly away, often races towards rear: untrustworthy. *Michael Chapman* **– §**

MOOD FOR MISCHIEF 2 b.c. (Feb 15) Nathaniel (IRE) 129 – Tina's Spirit (IRE) 88 (Invincible Spirit (IRE) 121) [2017 p8g Dec 21] 12/1, very green when well held in maiden at Chelmsford. *Ed Walker* **–**

MOOJANED (IRE) 6 b.g. Raven's Pass (USA) 133 – Mufradat (IRE) 93 (Desert Prince (IRE) 130) [2017 a63: p11g f12s 10.3g 11.6m^6 11.4m^3 16m^6 14g^2 11.4g^5 14.2g^5 f12.1g^5 10d^5 9.9v^5 11.8v^6 11.4d^6 t12.2m Oct 28] sturdy gelding: fair handicapper on turf, modest on all-weather: left David Evans after fourth start: stays 1¾m: acts on fibresand, soft and good to firm going: in headgear last 3 starts: usually races close up. *John Flint* **66** **a58**

MOOLAZIM 3 b.c. Tamayuz 126 – Empire Rose (ARG) (Sunray Spirit (USA) 108) [2017 p7g* p7g^4 8g* 8s^5 p7g^4 p8g* Sep 25] second foal: half-brother to useful 2-y-o 1m winner Lazzam (by Archipenko), later 8.5f winner in USA: dam, South African 2-y-o 5f-7f winner, half-sister to Argentinian Group 2 1m winner Empire Aztec: useful performer: won maiden at Chelmsford in April, and handicaps at Yarmouth in June and Kempton (by neck from Ventura Blues) in September: stays 1m: acts on polytrack: tried in tongue tie: sold 120,000 gns in November, sent to Hong Kong. *Marco Botti* **99**

MOOLTAZEM (IRE) 3 b.g. Elzaam (AUS) 115 – Whisper Dance (USA) 64 (Stravinsky (USA) 133) [2017 8m^6 8m* p8s^3 8.3d^2 Oct 4] 90,000Y: fourth foal: half-brother to smart French 5.5f/6f winner Gold Vibe (by Dream Ahead): dam maiden (stayed 12.7f): fairly useful form: won maiden at Ripon in July: second in handicap at Nottingham in October: stays 8.5f: sold to join Michael Dods 26,000 gns in November. *John Gosden* **89**

MOON ARROW (IRE) 4 b.g. Authorized (IRE) 133 – Moon Sister (IRE) 100 (Cadeaux Genereux 131) [2017 61: 11.7f p10g^6 p13.3s Nov 17] modest maiden: stays 11f: acts on polytrack and tapeta: in headgear last 5 starts. *Michael Blake* **54**

MOONDUST (IRE) 3 b.f. Exceed And Excel (AUS) 126 – Lady Hawkfield (IRE) (Hawk Wing (USA) 136) [2017 65: f6s^2 p7d Feb 23] good-topped filly: fair maiden: stays 7f: acts on fibresand: tried in cheekpieces. *John Gosden* **65**

MOONDYNE JOE (IRE) 4 b.g. Bushranger (IRE) 119 – Golden Shine 80 (Royal Applause 124) [2017 87p: f5g^4 6m May 13] well-made gelding: fairly useful performer at best, lightly raced: left K. R. Burke after first start: best form at 5f on good going: sold 5,000 gns in July, sent to Bahrain. *Mark Pattinson* **58**

MOONLIGHT BAY 2 b.f. (Feb 14) Pivotal 124 – Naadrah (Muhtathir 126) [2017 5v* 6s^4 6s* 7s Oct 28] €36,000Y: third foal: sister to 2-y-o 6f/7f winner Martini Time: dam, French 2-y-o 9.5f winner, half-sister to smart French 1¼m winner Prince Mag: useful form: won maiden at Naas in March and nursery there (by neck from Guessthebill) in October: left Kevin Prendergast after second start: should stay 7f. *G. M. Lyons, Ireland* **97**

MOONLIGHT BLUE (IRE) 3 b.g. Approve (IRE) 112 – Nouvelle Reve (GER) (Acatenango (GER) 127) [2017 71: t10.2s^2 11.2g^6 9g^4 8.5d 14m Aug 26] fair maiden: should stay beyond 1¼m: acts on tapeta: in cheekpieces last 3 starts. *Michael Dods* **67**

MOONLIGHT MAGIC 4 b.c. Cape Cross (IRE) 129 – Melikah (IRE) 116 (Lammtarra (USA) 134) [2017 118: 10g^2 10.5d 10g^3 9d* 10d^4 Sep 9] sturdy colt: smart performer: won Meld Stakes at Leopardstown (by head from Deauville) in July: second in Mooresbridge Stakes at Naas (3½ lengths behind Minding) in May: stays 1¼m: acts on soft going: tried in cheekpieces: in tongue tie last 3 starts: races prominently: sent to Australia. *J. S. Bolger, Ireland* **119**

MOONLIGHTNAVIGATOR (USA) 5 br.g. Henrythenavigator (USA) 131 – Victorica (USA) (Exbourne (USA) 125) [2017 95: 8m 8s^2 t8s 7m 7.9m 8g 8d* Aug 5] good-topped gelding: fairly useful handicapper: won at Thirsk (dead-heated with Florenza) in August: stays 1m: acts on any turf going: tried in cheekpieces. *John Quinn* **94**

MOONLIGHT SILVER 3 gr.f. Makfi 130 – Moon Empress (FR) 84 (Rainbow Quest (USA) 134) [2017 65: t8.6g 8s 10d^6 9.9f^5 10v p12g* p12g Oct 9] fair handicapper: won at Kempton in August: stays 1½m: acts on polytrack, tapeta and firm going: tried in hood: sometimes slowly away. *William Muir* **67**

MOONLIT SANDS (IRE) 2 b.f. (Apr 13) Footstepsinthesand 120 – Dusty Moon 78 (Dr Fong (USA) 128) [2017 5m^5 5d^5 5m^3 6d^4 6.1g Aug 15] €11,000Y: sixth foal: half-sister to 3 winners, including 2-y-o 5f winner Athas An Bhean (by Royal Applause) and 7.5f winner (stayed 1½m) Mariners Moon (by Mount Nelson): dam, 2-y-o 7f winner, half-sister to dam of very smart miler Zoffany: fair maiden: stays 6f: acts on good to soft going. *Brian Ellison* **67**

MOONMEISTER (IRE) 6 b.g. Mastercraftsman (IRE) 129 – Moon Unit (IRE) 119 (Intikhab (USA) 135) [2017 96: 12m* 11.8m 12v 11.9g 12.8d p12g^6 Oct 20] lengthy, workmanlike gelding: useful handicapper: won at Cork (by neck from Spruce Meadows) in June: stays 15f: acts on polytrack, soft and good to firm going: has worn blinkers: wears tongue tie: sometimes slowly away. *A. J. Martin, Ireland* **95**

MOON OVER MOBAY 4 b.f. Archipenko (USA) 127 – Slew The Moon (ARG) (Kitwood (USA) 119) [2017 65: 17.2f^4 p15.8g p11d 12m Jul 4] fair maiden, below form in handicaps in 2017: stays 1m: acts on polytrack: tried in cheekpieces. *Michael Blanshard* **50**

MOON OVER RIO (IRE) 6 b.m. Captain Rio 122 – Moonchild (GER) (Acatenango (GER) 127) [2017 68: 12g 11.8s^2 12.1m^5 12.1s^5 12.1s Aug 24] compact mare: modest handicapper nowadays: stays 1½m: acts on soft and good to firm going: tried in cheekpieces. *Ben Haslam* **59**

MOONRAKER 5 ch.g. Starspangledbanner (AUS) 128 – Licence To Thrill 83 (Wolfhound (USA) 126) [2017 105: 5g 5g 5g 6m^3 6m^2 6m 6g t6s^3 6m 6g 6.1g^4 6d^4 7d 6d Oct 27] rangy gelding: useful handicapper: placed at Ascot (¾ length behind Normandy Barriere) in May and Newcastle (1¾ lengths behind Unabated) in July: stays 6f: acts on tapeta, good to firm and good to soft going: tried in visor: sold to join Michael Appleby 22,000 gns in October. *Mick Channon* **98**

MOONRISE LANDING (IRE) 6 gr.m. Dalakhani (IRE) 133 – Celtic Slipper (IRE) 102 (Anabaa (USA) 130) [2017 112: 14.1g^3 Apr 12] good-topped mare: smart performer: third in listed race at Nottingham (3 lengths behind Elidor) sole outing in 2017: stays 16.5f: acts on polytrack, tapeta, firm and good to soft going: tried in headgear. *Ralph Beckett* **104**

MOONSHINE DANCER 3 b.f. Dark Angel (IRE) 113 – Raggle Taggle (IRE) 95 (Tagula (IRE) 116) [2017 72p: t6f* 6.1g 6g^6 7g^4 7m^3 8g Aug 25] fair performer: won maiden at Wolverhampton in January: left David Simcock after: stays 7f: acts on tapeta: in hood last 4 starts. *Christian Williams* **69**

MOONSHINE RIDGE (IRE) 6 b.m. Duke of Marmalade (IRE) 132 – Dreams Come True (FR) 106 (Zafonic (USA) 130) [2017 77: f14g^5 Jan 30] fair handicapper, below form sole outing in 2017: stays 2m: acts on fibresand: sometimes slowly away. *Alan Swinbank* **–**

MOON SONG 2 gr.f. (Feb 7) Lethal Force (IRE) 128 – West of The Moon (Pivotal 124) [2017 p7g^5 p6s^2 p6g^6 Dec 20] 42,000F: small filly: first foal: dam twice-raced half-sister to smart performers Evasive (Horris Hill Stakes winner) and Autocratic (winner around 1¼m): fair form: best effort when second in minor event at Chelmsford (½ length behind Lady Willpower) in December. *Clive Cox* **68**

MOONSTONE ROCK 3 ch.f. Rock of Gibraltar (IRE) 133 – Komena 84 (Komaite (USA)) [2017 64: 8.3m^6 7m 8g^6 7m* 7d^4 8.5d 8g^6 8d p8g^5 p8g Oct 18] rather unfurnished filly: fair handicapper: won at Brighton in June: stays 1m: acts on polytrack and good to firm going: wears headgear: starts slowly, often races in rear. *Jim Boyle* **65**

MOONWISE (IRE) 3 ch.f. Exceed And Excel (AUS) 126 – Moonstone Magic 113 (Trade Fair 124) [2017 7m^3 6.9g* 6m^6 7.2m^4 p7g Sep 9] lengthy, good-quartered filly: first foal: dam 7f (including Fred Darling Stakes)/1m winner: fairly useful performer: won maiden at Carlisle (by head from Peach Melba) in May: stays 7f: acts on good to firm going: often races freely. *Ralph Beckett* **83**

MOOREA 3 ch.g. Medicean 128 – Priena (IRE) 95 (Priolo (USA) 127) [2017 p8g^6 p11g p10g 7s 10d 9.9s p6g p8g p10g p10g^5 Dec 20] workmanlike gelding: no form: tried in tongue tie. *John Bridger* **–**

MOOROVERTHEBRIDGE 3 b.f. Avonbridge 123 – Spennymoor (IRE) 71 (Exceed And Excel (AUS) 126) [2017 7.4d^5 6.1m^4 p7g^3 7s^6 Oct 9] second foal: sister to French 9.5f winner Tour: dam, 2-y-o 6f winner, half-sister to high-class sprinter Moss Vale: modest form: stays 7f. *Grace Harris* **62**

MOORSIDE 4 b.f. Champs Elysees 124 – Marching West (USA) 99 (Gone West (USA)) [2017 98: 12f^5 20f 14d^4 12d 14m^6 Aug 25] well-made filly: fairly useful performer: stays 1¾m: acts on polytrack, firm and good to soft going. *Charles Hills* **94**

MOOTAHARER (IRE) 4 b.c. Dubawi (IRE) 129 – Tahrir (IRE) 100 (Linamix (FR) 127) [2017 8f 10g 7m^6 Jun 30] rangy, good sort: fairly useful 7f winner at 2 yrs, last all 3 starts in 2017 after long absence. *Charles Hills* **–**

MOPS TANGO 2 b.f. (Feb 18) Piccolo 121 – Tanning 60 (Atraf 116) [2017 5g 5m 7d f8.1g Dec 11] leggy, close-coupled filly: fourth foal: sister to winner up to 6f Mops Angel (2-y-o 5f winner) and half-sister to 1m-1½m winner Tan Arabiq (by Arabian Gleam): dam, 1¼m winner, also won over hurdles: no form, including in nursery. *Michael Appleby* **–**

MOQARRAB (USA) 2 b.c. (May 1) Speightstown (USA) 124 – Grosse Pointe Anne (USA) (Silver Deputy (CAN)) [2017 7g^4 t7.2g* Dec 2] $400,000Y: third foal: half-brother to a winner in USA by Indian Charlie: dam, US 6f winner, half-sister to Breeders' Cup Juvenile winner Uncle Mo: fairly useful form: won minor event at Wolverhampton (by 4½ lengths from Epic Fantasy) in December: will go on improving. *Saeed bin Suroor* **87 p**

MOQARRAR (USA) 2 b.c. (Feb 11) Exchange Rate (USA) 111 – Time To Enjoy (USA) (Distorted Humor (USA) 117) [2017 6m^3 p7g^2 t7.1d* Oct 24] $47,000F, 120,000Y: half-brother to several winners in North America: dam ran 3 times in USA: fairly useful form: won minor event at Newcastle (by 1¾ lengths from Big Kitten) in October: will stay 1m. *Sir Michael Stoute* **85**

MORACHE MUSIC 9 b.g. Sleeping Indian 122 – Enchanted Princess 82 (Royal Applause 124) [2017 91: 6g^4 7d^3 6g^2 6d^4 6.1m* 6.1g^3 7v 6.1d^3 p7g Nov 21] sturdy gelding: fairly useful performer: won seller at Windsor in July: placed in handicaps at Goodwood in May and Chepstow in July: stays 7f: acts on good to firm and heavy going: wears headgear. *Patrick Chamings* **85**

MORANDO (FR) 4 gr.g. Kendargent (FR) 112 – Moranda (FR) (Indian Rocket 115) [2017 118p: 8.1g* 8g^4 8.2s^3 9.4g^2 Oct 10] useful-looking gelding: smart performer: won listed race at Windsor (by short head from Stormy Antarctic) in July: second in Prix Andre Baboin at Bordeaux (length behind Zafiro) in October: stays 9.5f: acts on soft and good to firm going: sold 290,000 gns in November, has joined Andrew Balding. *Roger Varian* **117**

MORDIN (IRE) 3 b.g. Invincible Spirit (IRE) 121 – Bryanstown (IRE) 69 (Galileo (IRE) 134) [2017 p8g* Dec 6] 88,000F, 200,000 2-y-o: second foal: half-brother to 1m winner La Celebs Ville (by Sea The Stars): dam, ran once, out of sister to Derby winner Commander In Chief and half-sister to Warning: 1/2, won maiden at Lingfield (by 2¼ lengths from Narjes with plenty in hand) in December: sure to progress. *Simon Crisford* **89 p**

MORDOREE (IRE) 3 ch.f. Mayson 124 – Lisieux Orchid (IRE) 88 (Sadler's Wells (USA) 132) [2017 –: 7d^3 9g^5 8g^2 8.3d* 8s^6 p8g Sep 13] workmanlike filly: fair handicapper: won at Nottingham in July: stays 9f: acts on polytrack and good to soft going: in cheekpieces last 3 starts: tried in tongue tie. *Clive Cox* **67**

MORE BEAU (USA) 6 b.g. More Than Ready (USA) 120 – Frontier Beauty (USA) (Gone West (USA)) [2017 80: t5s 6m^6 Jun 22] fair handicapper, well held both starts in 2017: stays 6f: acts on polytrack, tapeta, good to firm and heavy going: has worn headgear, including last 5 starts. *Noel Wilson* **–**

MORE HARRY 2 b.g. (Feb 13) Aussie Rules (USA) 123 – Native Ring (FR) (Bering 136) [2017 p7d f7.1g Nov 28] well held in minor events. *Neil Mulholland* **–**

MORELLO (IRE) 3 b.f. Medicean 128 – Mullein 110 (Oasis Dream 129) [2017 –: p8g 8.1d 6d^6 7s 6.1g^5 p6d^2 p7g^5 6s Sep 15] compact filly: modest maiden: best effort at 6f: acts on polytrack. *Henry Candy* **62**

MORE MISCHIEF 5 b.m. Azamour (IRE) 130 – Mischief Making (USA) 101 (Lemon Drop Kid (USA) 131) [2017 105: t10.2g* 12s^3 11.9d^2 Aug 24] strong, lengthy mare: useful performer: won listed race at Newcastle (by neck from Chain of Daisies) in June: placed in similar events at Newmarket (3 lengths behind God Given) in July and York (2¼ lengths behind Fleur Forsyte) in August: stays 1½m: acts on tapeta and heavy going: front runner/races prominently. *Jedd O'Keeffe* **106**

MOREMONEYMOREPARTY (IRE) 2 b.f. (Apr 1) Epaulette (AUS) 126 – Three Times (Bahamian Bounty 116) [2017 6s 6g^6 6v^3 6d p6s^4 Nov 16] €21,000F, £15,000Y: fifth foal: half-sister to Italian 6f/7.5f winner Nataconleali (by Approve): dam well beaten both starts: modest maiden: raced only at 6f: acts on polytrack and heavy going. *Richard Guest* **55**

MORE THAN MORE (USA) 2 b.f. (Mar 29) More Than Ready (USA) 120 – Donamour (USA) (Langfuhr (CAN) 124) [2017 7m Aug 25] $20,000Y, $55,000 2-y-o: fourth foal: half-sister to 3 winners in USA: dam, US 5.5f-1m winner, half-sister to US Grade 2 8.5f winner Luna Vega: 50/1, well held in minor event at Newmarket: sent to UAE. *George Peckham* **–**

MORETTI (IRE) 2 b.f. (Apr 9) Requinto (IRE) 109 – Hassaya (IRE) 77 (King's Best (USA) 132) [2017 6d^3 t6.1g Nov 18] €44,000 2-y-o: workmanlike filly: second foal: half-sister to smart Italian winner up to 1m Amore Hass (2-y-o 6f/7.5f winner, by Azamour): dam lightly-raced half-sister to smart 1¼m-1½m winner Glorious Protector: modest form: in hood, better effort when seventh in minor event at Wolverhampton (6¼ lengths behind Two Weeks) in November. *David O'Meara* **59**

MORI 3 b.f. Frankel 147 – Midday 126 (Oasis Dream 129) [2017 10g^5 10m* 9.9m* 12m^2 11.9d 12d^6 Sep 29] sturdy filly: type to carry condition: second foal: closely related to smart winner up to 1¼m (stays 1½m) Midterm (2-y-o 1m winner, by Galileo): dam multiple Group 1 winner at up to 1½m (2-y-o 1m winner): useful performer: won maiden at Ascot (by 1¾ lengths from Glittering Jewel) and listed race at Goodwood (by 1¾ lengths from Coconut Creme) in May: second in Ribblesdale Stakes at Royal Ascot (neck behind Coronet) in June: stays 1½m: acts on good to firm going: usually races prominently. *Sir Michael Stoute* **109**

MORITZBURG 3 ch.c. Dutch Art 126 – Providencia (Oasis Dream 129) [2017 79: 8m^2 8g* 8m 8m^6 Jul 13] strong colt: fairly useful performer: won maiden at Listowel (by 7 lengths from Allegio) in June: stays 1m: acts on good to firm going: in cheekpieces in 2017: usually leads. *M. Halford, Ireland* **90**

MORI YOSHINARI (IRE) 3 b.g. Helmet (AUS) 127 – Malyana 89 (Mtoto 134) [2017 p8m* 10.2g 10g 7g a8f a8f a9.7f Dec 15] 98,000F, 50,000Y, £55,000 2-y-o: lengthy gelding: fifth foal: half-brother to 2-y-o 7f winner Bint Malyana (by Bahamian Bounty) and a winner in Belgium by Rip Van Winkle: dam, winner up to 1¼m (2-y-o 1m winner), **81 d**

sister to smart winner up to 1¼m Tarfshi and half-sister to Cheveley Park Stakes winner Embassy: fairly useful form when winning maiden at Lingfield (by ½ length from Oud Metha Bridge) in February: failed to reproduce that, leaving Richard Hannon after fourth start: best effort at 1m: acts on polytrack: sometimes in headgear: tried in tongue tie. *A. bin Harmash, UAE*

MORLOCK (IRE) 2 b.c. (Mar 21) Epaulette (AUS) 126 – Mon Bijou (IRE) (Green Desert (USA) 127) [2017 p7s* 7g p8g³ Oct 12] €33,000F, £90,000 2-y-o: second foal: dam unraced half-sister to smart 1¼m-1½m winner Folk Opera: fairly useful form: won minor event at Kempton (by ½ length from Barton Mills) in September: stays 1m. *Charlie Appleby* **89**

MORNING BEAUTY 2 ch.f. (Apr 19) Dawn Approach (IRE) 132 – Extreme Beauty (USA) 89 (Rahy (USA) 115) [2017 t8.6g⁵ Nov 29] 70,000Y: half-sister to several winners, including 7f/1m winner Poet's Beauty (by Poet's Voice) and winner up to 1¼m Exceeding Power (2-y-o 6f winner, by Exceed And Excel): dam winner up to 7f (2-y-o 6f winner): 9/1, fifth in minor event at Wolverhampton (3¾ lengths behind West Palm Beach) on debut: better to come. *Hugo Palmer* **65 p**

MORNING CHIMES (IRE) 3 b.f. Shamardal (USA) 129 – Maidin Maith (IRE) 91 (Montjeu (IRE) 137) [2017 8g³ Aug 20] third foal: half-sister to 8.5f winner Mezajy (by Makfi) and 6f winner Dance Band (by Danehill Dancer): dam, 2-y-o 7f winner, half-sister to smart winner up to 7.5f Modeeroch and to useful dam of high-class miler Belardo: 9/1, third in maiden at Pontefract (2½ lengths behind Glassy Waters) in August: should progress. *Mark Johnston* **76 p**

MORNING HAS BROKEN (IRE) 2 ch.f. (Apr 10) Dawn Approach (IRE) 132 – Romie's Kastett (GER) 93 (Halling (USA) 133) [2017 p8d⁵ Dec 13] 32,000Y: fourth foal: half-sister to French 1m winner Al Dweha (by Invincible Spirit) and useful winner up to 1¼m (stays 1½m) Eagle Spirit (2-y-o 1m winner, by Holy Roman Emperor): dam, 9.5f winner, sister to high-class/temperamental performer up to 1½m Norse Dancer: 33/1, fifth in minor event at Kempton (7¼ lengths behind Highbrow) in December: open to improvement. *David Elsworth* **65 p**

MORNING SEQUEL 4 b.f. Revoque (IRE) 122 – Silver Sequel (Silver Patriarch (IRE) 125) [2017 10.2m 11.6d t7.2g Jun 7] third foal: half-sister to 9f-1½m winner Midnight Sequel (by Midnight Legend) and 2m winner Master Burbidge (by Pasternak): dam unraced: well held in maidens. *Neil Mulholland* **–**

MORNING SUIT (USA) 3 gr.g. Street Boss (USA) 124 – Blue Dress (USA) (Danzig (USA)) [2017 84: p8g* 8g* t7.1s 8m⁴ 8d² 9.1g³ 8g⁶ 9.9v 9.1d 8g⁶ p8s 8sᵖᵘ Sep 19] workmanlike gelding: fairly useful handicapper: won at Lingfield in January and Brighton (by 2¼ lengths from Munawer) in May: stayed 9f: acted on polytrack, tapeta and good to soft going: dead. *Mark Johnston* **94**

MORNINGTON 4 b.g. Aussie Rules (USA) 123 – Giusina Mia (USA) (Diesis 133) [2017 77p: 9.9g* 11.7f* 11.9g³ 9g³ 9g⁴ 9.9g⁴ 10.5g⁶ Dec 23] useful handicapper: won at Brighton in April and Bath (by 2¾ lengths from Plymouth Sound) in May: left Marcus Tregoning after third start: stays 1½m: acts on polytrack and firm going. *Chris Waller, Australia* **96**

MORNING WONDER (IRE) 2 ch.c. (Apr 1) Dawn Approach (IRE) 132 – Mount Elbrus 106 (Barathea (IRE) 127) [2017 7.4s² 8.2d* Sep 12] half-brother to several winners, including French 9.7f-11f winner Lava Flow (by Dalakhani) and winner up to 1½m Hunterview (2-y-o 7.5f winner, by Reset), both useful: dam 1¼m-13f winner: fairly useful form: won minor event at Leicester (by ¾ length from Setting Sail) in September: will stay 1¼m: will go on improving. *Kevin Ryan* **87 p**

MOSALIM (IRE) 2 b.g. (Apr 16) Arcano (IRE) 122 – Vision of Peace (IRE) (Invincible Spirit (IRE) 121) [2017 6m³ 7g⁶ Jul 21] useful-looking gelding: fair form when third at Yarmouth (4½ lengths behind Alba Power) on first of 2 starts in minor events. *William Haggas* **72**

MOSEEB (IRE) 2 b.g. (Feb 21) Invincible Spirit (IRE) 121 – Boastful (IRE) 110 (Clodovil (IRE) 116) [2017 6m* 5d⁶ t5.1g⁶ p6d³ 7s⁶ Oct 10] fair performer: won minor event at York in July: stays 6f: acts on polytrack and good to firm going: in hood last 3 starts. *Saeed bin Suroor* **79**

MOSMAN 7 b.g. Haafhd 129 – Last Dream (IRE) 80 (Alzao (USA) 117) [2017 –: p10.7g² p10.7g⁶ p8g⁵ p10.7gᵘʳ t9.5g⁶ p10.7g 10.2m 7g Jun 20] rather leggy gelding: modest handicapper: stays 10.5f: acts on polytrack and fibresand: wears headgear/tongue tie: often races prominently. *Paul W. Flynn, Ireland* **52**

MOSSEYB (IRE) 2 b.g. (Mar 29) Epaulette (AUS) 126 – Allegrissimo (IRE) 48 (Redback 116) [2017 p5g³ Nov 17] €95,000Y: third foal: half-brother to 1¼m/11.5f winner Skylark Lady (by Tamayuz): dam French 2-y-o 1m winner: 9/2, needed experience when third in minor event at Lingfield (3¼ lengths behind Drakefell) in November: should improve. *William Haggas* **66 p**

MOSSGO (IRE) 7 b.g. Moss Vale (IRE) 126 – Perovskia (USA) (Stravinsky (USA) 133) [2017 75: p5g⁴ p5g* p5m³ p5f⁴ p5g 5d p5s p5g p5g⁵ Dec 23] lengthy, angular gelding: fair handicapper: won at Lingfield in February: best at 5f: acts on polytrack, good to firm and good to soft going: tried in cheekpieces: wears tongue tie: usually races close up. *John Best* **74**

MOSSKETEER 2 b.g. (Apr 28) Moss Vale (IRE) 126 – Gracilia (FR) (Anabaa (USA) 130) [2017 6m 5m 5.1m p5g⁵ p6s* p7s³ p6g⁴ Dec 30] fair performer: won nursery at Chelmsford in November: stays 7f: acts on polytrack. *John Best* **73**

MOSS STREET 7 b.g. Moss Vale (IRE) 126 – Street Style (IRE) 83 (Rock of Gibraltar (IRE) 133) [2017 63: t12.2m t12.2g Jan 9] modest handicapper, well held both starts on Flat in 2017: stays 13f: acts on good to firm and good to soft going: wears blinkers: often in tongue tie: sometimes slowly away. *Conor Dore* **–**

MOSSY'S LODGE 4 b.f. Royal Applause 124 – Tee Cee 77 (Lion Cavern (USA) 117) [2017 73: p8g p8g 6d p7g t7.2g⁴ t6.1d³ Dec 16] modest handicapper: stays 7f: acts on polytrack and tapeta: tried in cheekpieces: often races prominently. *Anthony Carson* **61**

MOSTAHEL 3 b.c. Acclamation 118 – Entente Cordiale (IRE) 72 (Ela-Mana-Mou 132) [2017 –: 8.3g² t6g* 6m³ 6g Jul 13] strong, compact colt: useful performer: won maiden at Wolverhampton in April: third in handicap at Newmarket (2½ lengths behind Danielsflyer) in May: stays 6f: acts on tapeta and good to firm going. *Richard Hannon* **97**

MOSTASHREQAH 4 ch.f. Equiano (FR) 127 – China Cherub 94 (Inchinor 119) [2017 58d: t7.1g 5.7d⁶ p6d⁴ t5.1g³ 5.1m³ 5f 5.1g⁶ Jul 20] rather leggy filly: modest handicapper: stays 1m, raced mainly over shorter: acts on polytrack, tapeta and good to soft going: usually wears headgear: has worn tongue tie: front runner/races prominently: irresolute. *Milton Bradley* **53 §**

MOSTAWFEE (IRE) 4 b.g. Dandy Man (IRE) 123 – Grainne Mhaol (IRE) 59 (Spectrum (IRE) 126) [2017 64: 7.5s⁴ 8m 10d 7d 7.5d p7g 7.8g 6.3v p8g² p8g⁴ p8g p7g³ p7g Nov 10] modest maiden: stays 1m: acts on polytrack and soft going: usually wears headgear: in tongue tie last 2 starts. *J. J. Feane, Ireland* **60**

MOTABASSIM (IRE) 2 gr.c. (Feb 3) Zebedee 113 – Coastal Waters 81 (Halling (USA) 133) [2017 6.5g 6f 7d³ 8g² p8g* Oct 5] £75,000Y: good-topped colt: fourth foal: half-brother to 2-y-o 6f winner Monoshka and a winner in Italy (both by Kodiac): dam 7f winner: fairly useful performer: won nursery at Lingfield in October: stays 1m: acts on polytrack and good to soft going: in blinkers last 2 starts: usually races prominently: sold 30,000 gns later in October. *Brian Meehan* **82**

MOTHERLAND (IRE) 4 ch.g. Galileo (IRE) 134 – Pipalong (IRE) 121 (Pips Pride 117) [2017 114p: 12g² 14m³ 21.6m 14d⁶ 14.1v⁵ 14d Aug 24] useful performer: third in listed race at Leopardstown (6 lengths behind Order of St George) in May: stays 13f: best form on good going: front runner/races prominently. *Joseph Patrick O'Brien, Ireland* **106**

MOTHER OF DRAGONS (IRE) 2 ch.f. (Apr 26) Society Rock (IRE) 126 – Queen O'The Desert (IRE) 72 (Green Desert (USA) 127) [2017 5m² 5m² 5m 5.2v⁶ 5v 5.3g³ 5m p6d p5s² p6s² p5s³ p6g² Dec 12] €2,000Y: compact, sprint type: third foal: dam 6f winner: fair maiden: left Joseph Tuite after seventh start: stays 6f: acts on polytrack and good to firm going: tried in headgear/tongue tie: often races towards rear. *Phil McEntee* **70**

MOTLEY CREW 4 b.g. Mount Nelson 125 – Greensand 96 (Green Desert (USA) 127) [2017 t8.6g⁶ Dec 18] little show in various events, including Flat maiden. *Michael Easterby* **–**

MOTOWN MICK (IRE) 2 ch.g. (Mar 13) Intikhab (USA) 135 – Top Row 64 (Observatory (USA) 131) [2017 5.2g 7g⁵ 6.1d⁴ 6.1s* 8.1g* p7g² p7g³ p7g* Dec 20] 52,000Y: compact gelding: sixth foal: half-brother to useful 2-y-o 6f winner Crown Dependency (by Acclamation) and 2-y-o 7f winner (stayed 1¼m) Gold Top (by Teofilo): dam maiden half-sister to useful 2-y-o 5f-7f winner Rag Top: fairly useful performer: won nurseries at Chepstow in September, Windsor in October and Lingfield in December: stays 1m: acts on polytrack and soft going. *Richard Hannon* **92**

MOUCHEE (IRE) 2 b.c. (Apr 21) Zebedee 113 – Nashaat (Redoute's Choice (AUS)) [2017 6.1g⁵ 6s t5.1g 7g² p7g t8.6g⁵ p10g t9.5g* Nov 20] fair performer: won nursery at Wolverhampton in November: stays 1¼m: acts on polytrack and tapeta. *David Evans* **66**

MOUILLE POINT 3 b.f. Motivator 131 – Turning Leaf (IRE) 108 (Last Tycoon 131) **86** [2017 69p: 8m^6 10.2g* 10m^3 9.9g 8.1s^3 10.3v Sep 30] sturdy filly: fairly useful handicapper: won at Nottingham (by head from Plead) in May: stays 1¼m: acts on soft and good to firm going. *Richard Hannon*

MOUNTAIN ANGEL (IRE) 3 b.g. Dark Angel (IRE) 113 – Fanciful Dancer (Groom **94** Dancer (USA) 128) [2017 65p: t7.1m^2 7m^2 7.4g* 8d^2 8g 8m^2 8v^2 9d^5 Sep 29] fairly useful performer: won maiden at Beverley in May: second in handicaps at Doncaster in June, Yarmouth in August and Thirsk in September: stays 9f: acts on tapeta, good to firm and good to soft going. *Roger Varian*

MOUNTAIN APPROACH (IRE) 2 b.c. (May 17) Shamardal (USA) 129 – River **62** Mountain (Reset (AUS) 124) [2017 6f 7.2g^6 7s^4 7.2m 7s Sep 19] modest maiden: best effort at 7f: acts on soft going: in blinkers last 2 starts. *Richard Fahey*

MOUNTAIN BELL 4 b.f. Mount Nelson 125 – Shenir (Mark of Esteem (IRE) 137) [2017 **110** 108: 12s^4 p12g^4 t16.3d* Dec 16] smart performer: won minor event at Newcastle (by 2 lengths from Cape Cova) in December: stays 16.5f: acts on tapeta, best turf form on soft/heavy going: usually races nearer last than first. *Ralph Beckett*

MOUNTAIN BREATH 2 b.f. (Apr 14) Bated Breath 125 – Araminte (One Cool Cat **75 p** (USA) 123) [2017 t6s^3 t6g* Oct 19] first foal: dam unraced half-sister to smart winner up to 1¼m Mountain Song and useful performer up to 1m Please Sing: fair form: won minor event at Newcastle (by ¾ length from Royal Residence) in October: will be suited by at least 7f: open to further improvement. *Chris Fairhurst*

MOUNTAIN GUARD (IRE) 2 b.c. (Feb 5) Society Rock (IRE) 126 – Morinda 56 **82** (Selkirk (USA) 129) [2017 6.1g^2 6d^4 Sep 6] €95,000F, 120,000Y: neat colt: second foal: dam, ran twice, out of sister to very smart German 1½m performer Monsun: fairly useful form: better effort when second in maiden at Nottingham (2½ lengths behind Eqtidaar) in August, clear of rest: sold 7,000 gns in November, sent to Portugal. *Roger Varian*

MOUNTAIN HUNTER (USA) 3 b.g. Lonhro (AUS) 128 – Tamarillo 105 (Daylami **106 p** (IRE) 138) [2017 8g* 9.1g* p11s^4 Sep 8] sixth foal: half-brother to 3 winners, including useful 6f/7f winner (including at 2 yrs) Summer Fete and 1m winner Mulakim (both by Pivotal): dam winner up to 9f (2-y-o 1m winner): useful form: won maiden at Newmarket (by 1¾ lengths from Dawaaleeb) and handicap at Goodwood (by 2¾ lengths from Lawmaking) in August: stays 9f: remains with potential. *Saeed bin Suroor*

MOUNTAIN MEADOW 2 ch.f. (Apr 9) Dutch Art 126 – Romantic Settings 103 (Mount **44** Nelson 125) [2017 6.5d 7m 6.9g^6 8.3v t7.1g^6 8s^5 7d Oct 30] workmanlike filly: first foal: dam, winner up to 9f (2-y-o 1m winner), half-sister to useful 2-y-o 5f winner Miss Work of Art (by Dutch Art): poor maiden: should stay 1m: in cheekpieces last 3 starts. *Richard Fahey*

MOUNTAIN PEAK 2 b.g. (Apr 6) Swiss Spirit 117 – Nolas Lolly (IRE) 98 (Lomitas **71** 129) [2017 6.1m 6v 6s p7d* p7g* p6g^5 Oct 17] compact gelding: fair performer: won nurseries at Kempton in August and September: stays 7f: acts on polytrack: front runner/races prominently. *Ed Walker*

MOUNTAIN RESCUE (IRE) 5 b.g. High Chaparral (IRE) 132 – Amber Queen (IRE) **99** 92 (Cadeaux Genereux 131) [2017 95: 8m 8m 8m t8s^6 7s^2 7g* 7d 7d^2 Sep 21] close-coupled gelding: useful handicapper: won at Newmarket (by 2 lengths from Summer Chorus) in August: second at Yarmouth (2¼ lengths behind Big Tour) in September: stays 11f, at least as effective over much shorter: acts on polytrack and good to soft going: front runner/races prominently. *Chris Wall*

MOUNT CHEIRON (USA) 6 b.g. Henrythenavigator (USA) 131 – Chalamont (IRE) **54** 88 (Kris 135) [2017 63: t9.5m t8.6m^3 t8g t10.2d^3 t8.6g^5 t8.6g^5 t8.6g t8.6g^5 9.2g^4 9s^3 10g 11.2g^6 t10.2d 8.5d 10.9m^5 Aug 28] modest handicapper: stays 1¼m: acts on all-weather, soft and good to firm going: usually wears headgear. *Richard Ford*

MOUNT CLESHAR 3 b.g. Mount Nelson 125 – Resal (IRE) (Montjeu (IRE) 137) [2017 **–** p8g^5 t9.5g^6 f7g 12.1g May 16] no form, including in handicap. *John Butler*

MOUNT HELLVELYN 2 b.g. (May 2) Hellvelyn 118 – Sugar Mountain (IRE) (Lomitas **60** 129) [2017 5m^6 5f 6m 6g^5 6g Aug 15] modest maiden: stays 6f: acts on good to firm going. *Clive Mulhall*

MOUNT LOGAN (IRE) 6 ch.g. New Approach (IRE) 132 – Vistaria (USA) (Distant **116** View (USA) 126) [2017 118: 9.9g^3 12g^3 10.5d^2 10.1m^2 10.2d* Sep 13] small gelding: smart performer: won minor event at Doncaster (by length from Red Verdon) in September: placed in listed race at Newmarket (length behind Lord Yeats) in July and Rose of Lancaster Stakes at Haydock (¾ length behind Frankuus) in August: stays 1½m: acts on firm and good to soft going: in cheekpieces last 2 starts. *Roger Varian*

MOUNT MORIAH 3 b.g. Mount Nelson 125 – Rule Britannia 89 (Night Shift (USA)) [2017 85p: 11s* 14g* 12d³ 14s³ 14.2d⁵ 16s⁴ Oct 21] useful-looking gelding: smart performer: won handicaps at Newbury (by 3¾ lengths from Splash Around) in May and Ascot (by 4 lengths from Getback In Paris) in July: third in Irish St Leger at the Curragh (13½ lengths behind Order of St George) in September: stays 2m: acts on polytrack and heavy going: races handily. *Ralph Beckett* **118**

MOUNT ROCK 3 b.g. Mount Nelson 125 – Holamo (IRE) 75 (Montjeu (IRE) 137) [2017 67: 8g⁵ 9.8d⁶ 8.8g³ 8gF Aug 19] fair maiden: stayed 9f: best form on good going: dead. *Michael Easterby* **76**

MOUNT TAHAN (IRE) 5 b.g. Lope de Vega (IRE) 125 – Sorpresa (USA) (Pleasant Tap (USA)) [2017 99: 8g⁵ 7g³ p7g² 7d 7d⁴ 7gpu 7d t9.5g² t9.5d* Dec 26] big gelding: useful handicapper: won at Wolverhampton (by ½ length from Born To Be Alive) in December: stays 9.5f: acts on polytrack, tapeta, soft and good to firm going: tried in tongue tie: often starts slowly/races in rear: signs of temperament. *Kevin Ryan* **107**

MOUNT VESUVIUS (IRE) 9 b.g. Spartacus (IRE) 107 – Parker's Cove (USA) (Woodman (USA) 126) [2017 –: p8g⁶ Jan 4] in tongue tie, little impact in 2 Flat maidens: poor hurdler. *Paul Henderson* **–**

MOUNT VICTORIA (IRE) 2 b.f. (Jan 21) Arakan (USA) 123 – Salingers Star (IRE) 78 (Catcher In The Rye (IRE) 115) [2017 5m² 5s 5d⁶ Jun 10] second foal: dam 2-y-o 6f winner: fair form: best effort when second in minor event at Ripon (2¼ lengths behind Maggies Angel) on debut. *James Given* **67**

MOUNT WELLINGTON (IRE) 2 b.g. (Feb 10) Invincible Spirit (IRE) 121 – Marvada (IRE) 110 (Elusive City (USA) 117) [2017 p5g³ 6d 6s³ 5g³ 7v² 7d⁴ 7.2v⁵ t6.1g* Dec 22] €475,000Y: second foal: dam 6f-1m winner: fairly useful performer: won minor event at Wolverhampton (by ½ length from Epic Fantasy) in December: second in nursery at Galway in August: left Aidan O'Brien after seventh start: stays 7f: acts on tapeta and heavy going: wears headgear: usually races close up. *Henry Spiller* **90**

MOVE IN TIME 9 ch.g. Monsieur Bond (IRE) 120 – Tibesti (Machiavellian (USA) 123) [2017 107: 5s 5m 5m 5g⁵ 6g 5.4d 5.6g 5v⁶ 5g⁶ Oct 18] stocky gelding: useful handicapper, largely well below best in 2017: left David O'Meara after eighth start: stays 6f: acts on firm and soft going: sometimes in headgear. *Paul Midgley* **98**

MOVE IT MOVE IT 2 gr.c. (Mar 7) Lethal Force (IRE) 128 – Madam Valentine (Primo Valentino (IRE) 116) [2017 t6g³ 5s³ t6s² 6.9g³ 6g t7.1d² t6g⁴ Dec 6] £41,000Y: third foal: half-brother to smart 5f (including at 2 yrs)/6f winner Pipers Note (by Piccolo): dam unraced: fairly useful maiden: second in minor event at Newcastle in June and nursery there in November: stays 7f: acts on tapeta. *Keith Dalgleish* **84**

MOVE OVER 2 b.c. (Mar 9) Acclamation 118 – Framed (Elnadim (USA) 128) [2017 6g⁴ p6g p7s⁶ 7.4d² 7g* 7.4s* 8s⁴ 8.5v² 7.5g⁴ Oct 22] 44,000F, 110,000Y: second foal: closely related to 1m/1¼m winner Darkroom Angel (by Dark Angel): dam once-raced half-sister to Richmond Stakes winner Prolific: useful performer: won minor events at Salisbury and Ffos Las, both in August: creditable efforts last 2 starts, in minor event at Epsom (¾-length second to Dee Ex Bee) and Gran Criterium at Milan (3½ lengths fourth to Royal Youmzain): stays 8.5f: acts on heavy going: in blinkers last 6 starts: usually front runner: sold 85,000 gns, joined John W. Sadler in USA. *Richard Hannon* **96**

MOVE SWIFTLY 2 b.f. (Mar 24) Farhh 131 – Hurricane Harriet 81 (Bertolini (USA) 125) [2017 p7g* Dec 21] 30,000F, 70,000Y: second foal: closely related to French 7.5f-9f winner Kyllarney (by Kyllachy): dam, 6f winner, half-sister to smart 1m-1¼m winner Katy Nowaitee: 7/2, won minor event at Chelmsford (by head from Artieshow) on debut, finding plenty to lead dying strides after conceding first run: will stay 1m: sure to go on to better things. *William Haggas* **87 P**

MOVE TO THE FRONT (IRE) 2 b.g. (Feb 10) Lord Shanakill (USA) 121 – Dress Up (IRE) 77 (Noverre (USA) 125) [2017 5g 6g⁴ 6g⁴ 7s⁵ 7g* 7s* 7m Oct 25] neat gelding: fair performer: won nursery at Salisbury in September and minor event at Brighton in October: stays 7f: acts on soft going: wears headgear: front runner/races prominently. *Clive Cox* **76**

MOVE UP 4 b.c. Dubawi (IRE) 129 – Rosinka (IRE) 116 (Soviet Star (USA) 128) [2017 121: a9.9f⁴ a9.9g Mar 25] well-made colt: reportedly blind in one eye: very smart performer: 3¼ lengths fourth to Long River in Maktoum Challenge Round 3 at Meydan in March: well below form in Dubai World Cup there only subsequent outing: stays 1½m: acts on dirt, good to firm and good to soft going. *Saeed bin Suroor* **116**

MOVIE MAGIC 6 b.m. Multiplex 114 – Alucica 64 (Celtic Swing 138) [2017 50: p15.8g p15.8g^4 p12g p16g p12g^3 p15.8g 11.6g May 24] sturdy mare: poor maiden: probably stays 2m: acts on polytrack and good to soft going: wears headgear: front runner/races prominently. *Mark Hoad* **48**

MOVIESTA (USA) 7 b.g. Hard Spun (USA) 124 – Miss Brickyard (USA) (A P Indy (USA) 131) [2017 115: a6f^5 a6f^6 5g 6g^5 p5g* 6m^4 5.4d p6g^3 p5g^4 Oct 20] robust gelding: useful on turf, smart on all-weather: won handicap at Dundalk (by 2¾ lengths from Go Kart) in July: stays 6f: acts on polytrack, firm and good to soft going: wears headgear: tried in tongue tie. *Edward Lynam, Ireland* **109 a116**

MOVING ROBE (IRE) 4 b.f. Iffraaj 127 – Emma Dora (IRE) 64 (Medaglia d'Oro (USA) 129) [2017 49: p7g^2 p8d p7d^6 p10g^5 10.1m^6 8s t8.6g^3 8m^5 8m p10g 10.2d p7d^6 f8.1g* f8.1g^6 Dec 21] lengthy, angular filly: modest performer: won maiden at Southwell in November: stays 1m: acts on polytrack and fibresand: has worn headgear, including last 3 starts: wears tongue tie. *Conrad Allen* **54**

MOWHOOB 7 b.g. Medicean 128 – Pappas Ruby (USA) 63 (Red Ransom (USA)) [2017 56: p7d^4 t8.6g^5 p8d* p8d p8g^2 p8g^2 p8g^3 p8g^2 8f^2 8g^3 8g p7g p8g^6 p8s p7g^4 Dec 21] sturdy gelding: modest handicapper: awarded race at Chelmsford in February: stays 1m: acts on polytrack and any turf going: has worn headgear, including in 2017: tried in tongue tie: often races prominently. *Brian Barr* **61**

MOXY MARES 2 ch.g. (Jan 20) Motivator 131 – Privalova (IRE) (Alhaarth (IRE) 126) [2017 7g^3 t7.2g 7d^3 Oct 27] fair form: best effort when third in maiden at Doncaster (2 lengths behind Amplification) in October: will stay 1m+. *Daniel Loughnane* **74**

MR ANDROS 4 b.g. Phoenix Reach (IRE) 124 – Chocolada (Namid 128) [2017 71p: t7.1g 10m 7.4d 7m f7.1g 7d 8s p7g* p7m f8.1g^3 p8s p7g^3 Dec 21] modest handicapper: won at Chelmsford in November: stays 1m: acts on polytrack and fibresand: wears headgear/tongue tie. *Brendan Powell* **64**

MRASEEL (IRE) 2 b.f. (Mar 27) Sir Prancealot (IRE) 111 – Suffer Her (IRE) (Whipper (USA) 126) [2017 5m 5.1m^4 p6g^2 6m^2 5.7f* 6m^{ur} 6s^3 6m^2 p6d^6 t6.1m* Oct 28] £62,000Y: rather unfurnished filly: fifth foal: half-sister to 3 winners (all at 5f), including useful Tahoo (including at 2 yrs, by Zebedee): dam unraced: fairly useful performer: won minor events at Bath in June and Wolverhampton (by ½ length from Midsummer Knight) in October: stays 6f: acts on polytrack, tapeta, firm and soft going: wears cheekpieces: sold 27,000 gns, sent to USA. *James Tate* **82**

MR BOSSY BOOTS (IRE) 6 b.g. Teofilo (IRE) 126 – Zelding (IRE) 108 (Warning 136) [2017 93, a105: p8g^2 7g p7s 8g p8g p8g^5 p7g p8s p7g Dec 13] compact gelding: useful handicapper: second at Lingfield (1¼ lengths behind My Target) in January: stays 1m: acts on polytrack and tapeta: in cheekpieces last 4 starts: has worn tongue tie, including in 2017. *Amanda Perrett* **99**

MR BOYCIE QUEST 3 gr.c. Air Quest 105 – Salt Kettle (Royal Applause 124) [2017 p12g p12g Nov 17] little impact in maidens. *Gary Moore* **–**

MR BROWNSTONE 3 b.g. Sakhee (USA) 136 – Sweet Child O'Mine 98 (Singspiel (IRE) 133) [2017 p8d Dec 13] well held in bumpers: in tongue tie, 50/1, well held in maiden at Kempton. *Brendan Powell* **–**

MR CAFFREY 5 b.g. Duke of Marmalade (IRE) 132 – Quest For Eternity (IRE) (Sadler's Wells (USA) 132) [2017 71: 12s 12d Jun 6] fair maiden, little impact in handicaps in 2017: stays 1¼m: acts on soft going: in headgear last 3 starts: temperamental: won twice over hurdles in July for Dr Richard Newland. *John Flint* **– §**

MR CARBONATOR 2 b.g. (Mar 5) Bated Breath 125 – Diamond Lass (IRE) 72 (Rock of Gibraltar (IRE) 133) [2017 t6.1g 6m 7s^2 8.3v^2 7.4d^3 8v 8.2g 6d^3 t7.1g t8s^2 f8.1g* f8.1g^3 Dec 29] close-coupled gelding: fair performer: won nursery at Southwell in December: left Richard Fahey after third start: will stay 1¼m: acts on fibresand, tapeta and heavy going: usually races nearer last than first. *Philip Kirby* **66**

MR CHRISTOPHER (IRE) 5 b.g. Bahamian Bounty 116 – Embassy Pearl (IRE) 80 (Invincible Spirit (IRE) 121) [2017 86: p7g t7.1g t7.2g t7.2m f7.1g^2 t7.2g t7.2d^6 Dec 26] fairly useful handicapper: second at Southwell in December: stays 1m: acts on all-weather: wears headgear: usually races prominently. *Tom Dascombe* **86**

MR CHUCKLES (IRE) 4 b.g. Arcano (IRE) 122 – Caribbean Escape (Pivotal 124) [2017 63: t6m^2 p6g^3 t6g t6f^2 t6m^3 t6g^2 t6g^4 p6g^4 6g^2 t6.1g^3 5.1s^2 5.5g^5 8d^3 p9.4f p6.5g Dec 16] modest performer: placed 9 times in 2017: left Daniel Loughnane after eleventh start: stays 1m: acts on tapeta and soft going: usually wears headgear: usually races prominently. *Mme G. Rarick, France* **64**

MR C (IRE) 3 b.g. Fast Company (IRE) 126 – Vanitycase (IRE) 61 (Editor's Note (USA) 125) [2017 –: 9g 9.9m^3 10g* 10.2v^4 9.9m t9.5g^3 t10.2g^5 Oct 20] compact gelding: fair handicapper: won at Pontefract in July: will stay 1½m: acts on tapeta and good to firm going. *Ollie Pears* **65**

MR COCO BEAN (USA) 3 b.g. Gio Ponti (USA) 130 – Ing Ing (FR) 110 (Bering 136) [2017 74: 7m^6 7.1m^6 7.4d 5.9g t7.1s^4 t8s f8.1g^2 Dec 4] fair maiden: left Ann Duffield after sixth start: stays 1m: acts on fibresand and tapeta: tried in hood. *David Barron* **73**

MR CONUNDRUM 4 b.g. Paco Boy (IRE) 129 – Folly Drove 71 (Bahri (USA) 125) [2017 59: t6g 7f 5.9d 5.9g^6 t7.2g 6g 7g 6.9d^6 6v Sep 5] modest handicapper, below form in 2017: best at 6f: acts on tapeta and good to firm going: has worn headgear, including last 2 starts: often races towards rear. *Lynn Siddall* **45**

MR COOL CASH 5 b.g. Firebreak 125 – Cashleen (USA) 73 (Lemon Drop Kid (USA) 131) [2017 76: t7.1g t8.6g^5 f8.1g 8g 8.5d* 8.8m 8s^5 7.4s^5 7g^5 7.8d^5 8.3v^4 6.9v^4 8v^2 8.5v^4 8v Oct 9] fair handicapper: won at Beverley in June: stays 8.5f: acts on good to firm and heavy going: has worn tongue tie. *Richard Guest* **76**

MR CRIPPS 5 b.g. Sir Percy 129 – Pella 71 (Hector Protector (USA) 124) [2017 11.8g 16.3d May 18] compact gelding: fairly useful handicapper: should stay 2m: acts on polytrack and good to firm going. *Ralph Beckett* **84**

MR DAVIES 3 ch.g. Shirocco (GER) 129 – Pasithea (IRE) 101 (Celtic Swing 138) [2017 65: 10.3g 12m^4 11.8s 11.1g 10.1m 11.5m p13.3d^3 p16d^2 t16.3g^5 Oct 19] good-topped gelding: fair maiden: stays 16.5f: acts on polytrack and tapeta: tried in visor/tongue tie: front runner/races prominently. *David Brown* **70**

MR ENTHUSIASTIC 3 b.g. Assertive 121 – Selkirk Rose (IRE) 74 (Pips Pride 117) [2017 51: 7.2m^5 6m 5.5f 5g 5d^2 5g^4 5m 5s* t5.1m^6 f5g^5 t6s Nov 30] modest handicapper: won at Catterick (amateur) in October: best form at 5f: acts on soft going: tried in hood: front runner/races prominently. *Noel Wilson* **55**

MR FICKLE (IRE) 8 b.g. Jeremy (USA) 122 – Mamara Reef 71 (Salse (USA) 128) [2017 68: 11.4d Oct 23] sturdy, quite attractive gelding: fair handicapper, below form sole outing in 2017: stays 2m: acts on polytrack and soft going: has worn headgear: winning hurdler. *Gary Moore* **–**

MR FRANKIE 6 b.g. Sleeping Indian 122 – Shes Minnie 90 (Bertolini (USA) 125) [2017 64: p11g p11g^4 9.9d^2 12s t12.2g^2 10.1d t12.2g^5 t9.5d Dec 26] fair handicapper: left John Spearing after sixth start: stays 1½m: acts on tapeta, firm and soft going: has worn cheekpieces. *Adrian Wintle* **67**

MR GENT (IRE) 2 br.c. (Mar 23) Society Rock (IRE) 126 – Furnival (USA) (Street Cry (IRE) 130) [2017 7s^6 7v^3 6s^3 p7d^2 t7.2g Dec 22] 60,000F, 175,000Y: first foal: dam unraced daughter of Australian Group 3 6.5f/1m winner Wild Queen: fairly useful maiden: second in nursery at Kempton in December: best effort at 7f: acts on polytrack and heavy going: in blinkers last 2 starts. *Ed Dunlop* **83**

MR GLOBETROTTER (USA) 4 b.g. Henrythenavigator (USA) 131 – Sunshine For Life (USA) (Giant's Causeway (USA) 132) [2017 –: t16.3g^3 t16.5g* 16g^3 14m* 15.9s* 16m t16.5g 13.9s 14d Oct 20] fairly useful handicapper: won at Wolverhampton in March, and Musselburgh (apprentice) and Catterick (by 6 lengths from Question of Faith) in June: stays 16.5f: acts on tapeta, soft and good to firm going: tried in cheekpieces: sold only 800 gns in November. *Iain Jardine* **82**

MR GREENLIGHT 2 b.g. (Jan 20) Bahamian Bounty 116 – Nos Da (Cape Cross (IRE) 129) [2017 6m^5 5d^3 5m^4 6d 5.1v^6 5v^3 Sep 26] good-quartered gelding: fair maiden: best form at 5f: acts on good to soft going. *Tim Easterby* **68**

MR KHALID 4 b.g. Pour Moi (IRE) 125 – Island Dreams (USA) 71 (Giant's Causeway (USA) 132) [2017 11.6m* p11g^5 14d 11.9g Dec 17] good-topped gelding: fairly useful handicapper: won at Windsor (by neck from Jack of Diamonds) in April: left Roger Charlton after third start: stays 11.5f: acts on good to firm and good to soft going: tried in hood. *S. Seemar, UAE* **94**

MR LANDO 8 b.g. Shirocco (GER) 129 – Capitana (GER) 86 (Lando (GER) 128) [2017 65: p16s^5 13f^6 Jul 12] fair handicapper, below form both starts on Flat in 2017: stays 1½m: acts on polytrack, tapeta, good to firm and heavy going: has worn headgear: usually leads: winning hurdler. *Johnny Farrelly* **51**

MR LARGE (IRE) 2 b.c. (Apr 30) Footstepsinthesand 120 – Oh Happy Days (IRE) 83 (Galileo (IRE) 134) [2017 7.1m 7g 7.6s^3 8m^6 p10g t9.5g^5 p8m^2 Nov 25] close-coupled colt: fair maiden: stays 9.5f: acts on polytrack, tapeta, soft and good to firm going. *Jamie Osborne* **70**

MR LITTLE (IRE) 2 b.c. (Mar 11) Kodiac 112 – Shining Hour (USA) 104 (Red Ransom (USA)) [2017 p6s^{6} 6.1m^{pu} Jul 4] well held completed start in minor events: dead. *Jamie Osborne* –

MR LUPTON (IRE) 4 ch.g. Elnadim (USA) 128 – Chiloe Wigeon (IRE) 55 (Docksider (USA) 124) [2017 115: 5.7m^{2} 6m* 6.1m^{3} 6f 6g 6g^{2} 6m^{5} 6s^{6} 6v^{4} 6g Oct 14] rather leggy, good-topped gelding: smart performer: won handicap at Newmarket (by 1¼ lengths from Eastern Impact) in May: second in minor event at Bath (1¼ lengths behind Muthmir) in April: stays 6.5f: acts on good to firm going. *Richard Fahey* **117**

MR MAC 3 b.g. Makfi 130 – Veronica Franco 90 (Darshaan 133) [2017 –: p8g p8g^{3} p10g p8s p7d* p8g^{4} Dec 30] fair handicapper: won at Kempton in December: stays 1m: acts on polytrack: in hood last 5 starts: in tongue tie last 2. *Peter Hedger* **69**

MR MAGILL (FR) 5 b.g. Hamairi (IRE) 112 – Marie Cuddy (IRE) 66 (Galileo (IRE) 134) [2017 t9.5m^{6} p12g p16g Jun 28] compact ex-French gelding: maiden: no form in Britain in 2017: tried in hood. *Karen George* –

MR MICHAEL (IRE) 4 b.g. Big Bad Bob (IRE) 118 – Mastoora (IRE) 85 (Acclamation 118) [2017 –: p7g p6g t5.1g^{4} t6m p5g^{6} 8m 6g 7d 6g^{3} 5d* 6m 5g 5.8v^{4} 6d^{6} Oct 30] fair handicapper: won at Down Royal in July: stays 7f: acts on polytrack and good to soft going: has worn headgear/tongue tie: usually slowly away/races in rear: not one to trust. *Adrian Brendan Joyce, Ireland* **67**

MR MINERALS 3 ch.g. Poet's Voice 126 – River Song (USA) (Siphon (BRZ) 130) [2017 86p: 8m^{4} p8g* 8g^{2} Jul 13] good-bodied gelding: useful form: won handicap at Kempton (by 4½ lengths from Glorious Poet) in July: stays 1m: remains with potential. *Richard Hughes* **97 p**

MR MORSE 4 ro.g. Hellvelyn 118 – Songsheet 74 (Dominion 123) [2017 64: f7g t6d^{4} t6d Mar 1] fair handicapper: should stay 7f: acts on fibresand and good to firm going: tried in cheekpieces. *Brian Ellison* **67**

MR ORANGE (IRE) 4 b.g. Paco Boy (IRE) 129 – Shirley Blake (IRE) 101 (Acclamation 118) [2017 78: 7m 6m^{4} 5.9g^{4} 6d^{2} 5.9d* 6g* 6s^{3} 6g^{5} 6v t6g Oct 20] strong gelding: fairly useful handicapper: won at Carlisle (apprentice) and Pontefract (by 1½ lengths from Perfect Symphony) in July: stays 6f: acts on good to firm and heavy going: wears cheekpieces: often races prominently. *Paul Midgley* **80**

MR OWEN (USA) 5 b.h. Invincible Spirit (IRE) 121 – Mrs Lindsay (USA) 117 (Theatrical) [2017 113: 8.9g 7g 7d^{3} p8d^{3} p7.5g* Dec 16] good-topped horse: smart performer: won listed race at Deauville (by 1¾ lengths from City Light) in December: left Francois Rohaut after second start: stays 9.5f: acts on polytrack, good to firm and good to soft going: tried in cheekpieces/tongue tie: often races prominently. *David Simcock* **113**

MR POCKET (IRE) 3 b.c. Acclamation 118 – Midnight Martini 100 (Night Shift (USA)) [2017 80: 5.7f* 5.7m 5f^{2} 5.3m^{2} 5.7f^{6} 6.1g^{4} p6s p6g^{6} p5m^{6} p5s^{2} p5g Dec 23] useful-looking colt: fairly useful handicapper: won at Bath (dead-heated) in April: second at Salisbury/Brighton in June and Chelmsford in December: stays 6f: acts on polytrack, tapeta and firm going: usually wears headgear: tried in tongue tie: often races towards rear. *Paul Cole* **88**

MR POTTER 4 ch.g. Assertive 121 – Enclave (USA) (Woodman (USA) 126) [2017 64: t8g^{4} t7.1d^{4} p6g^{5} p7d* t7.1g^{4} t7.1g^{5} t7.1s p7g^{6} p7s* 7d t8d^{5} t7.1g t7.1s p7s^{4} p8s^{3} Dec 15] fair handicapper: won at Chelmsford in February and September: stays 1m: acts on polytrack, tapeta, good to firm and good to soft going: wears headgear: often races towards rear. *Richard Guest* **66**

MR RECKLESS (IRE) 2 gr.c. (Feb 16) Reckless Abandon 119 – Zarabaya (IRE) (Doyoun 124) [2017 p8g^{5} t8.6g t8.6d* Dec 9] €40,000 2-y-o: half-brother to 3 winners, including useful 1¼m-1½m winner (stayed 14.6f) Set To Music (by Danehill Dancer) and useful 1¼m winner Zarafsha (by Alzao): dam unraced: fairly useful form: won minor event at Wolverhampton (by 1½ lengths from Galactic Spirit) in December: stays 8.5f: will go on improving. *Jamie Osborne* **80 p**

MR RED CLUBS (IRE) 8 b.g. Red Clubs (IRE) 125 – Queen Cobra (IRE) 80 (Indian Rocket 115) [2017 80: t8.6g^{4} p8g^{2} t9.5g* t8.6g^{2} t8.6g* 10s^{3} p10g^{6} t9.5g^{3} t8.6g^{6} 9.1m* 7.6v^{3} 9.9s t9.5g Dec 18] rather leggy gelding: fairly useful performer: won sellers at Wolverhampton in March/April and handicap at Goodwood (amateur, by 2 lengths from City Ground) in August: left Michael Appleby after eighth start: stays 1¼m: acts on polytrack, tapeta, good to firm and heavy going: wears headgear. *Henry Tett* **82**

MR RITZ 2 b.c. (Jan 16) Oasis Dream 129 – Que Puntual (ARG) (Contested Bid (USA) 120) [2017 p7g* Dec 20] sixth foal: half-brother to 3 winners, including smart winner up to 12.5f Oceanographer (2-y-o 1¼m winner, by Sea The Stars): dam winner in Argentina/ North America, including Canadian Grade 2 8.5f event: 6/1, won minor event at Kempton (by length from La Maquina) on debut: will stay 1m: sure to progress. *Jeremy Noseda* **95 p**

MRS BENSON (IRE) 2 ch.f. (Feb 17) Rip Van Winkle (IRE) 134 – Ebble 77 (Oasis Dream 129) [2017 p7g^6 p7d^4 Nov 22] 22,000F, 10,000Y: second foal: closely related to useful winner up to 1¼m Ebbesbourne (2-y-o 7f winner, by Teofilo): dam, 6f winner, half-sister to smart UAE performer up to 9f Ibn Battuta out of smart performer up to 15.5f Sulk: fair form when fourth at Kempton (3½ lengths behind Qaysar) on second of 2 starts in minor events. *Michael Blanshard* **65**

MRS BIGGS 5 ch.m. Paco Boy (IRE) 129 – Hoh Chi Min 103 (Efisio 120) [2017 69: 12g 10g* 12.5g^3 12s^3 12.1m Jul 7] modest handicapper: won at Wetherby in May: stayed 12.5f: acted on tapeta, soft and good to firm going: tried in headgear/tongue tie: usually raced close up: dead. *Declan Carroll* **62**

MRS BURBIDGE 7 b.m. Pasternak 111 – Twin Time 77 (Syrtos 106) [2017 58: 10.2d^5 Aug 19] modest handicapper: stays 16.5f: acts on polytrack, tapeta, best turf form on good going: wears cheekpieces/tongue tie: often races prominently: winning hurdler. *Neil Mulholland* **53**

MR SCAFF (IRE) 3 br.g. Vocalised (USA) 114 – Nancy Rock (IRE) (Rock of Gibraltar (IRE) 133) [2017 59: 8.3m 9.9f 11.8s^3 11.6d^5 Jul 1] angular gelding: modest maiden: stays 1½m: acts on soft going. *Paul Henderson* **58**

MR SCARAMANGA 3 b.c. Sir Percy 129 – Lulla 87 (Oasis Dream 129) [2017 98: t8g^4 8g* p8g^2 7m 7m^4 8f 7d p8g 8g^6 p10g^4 p8g Dec 31] sturdy colt: useful performer: won Group 2 Al Biddah Mile at Doha (by ¾ length from Pazeer) in February: second in listed race at Lingfield (neck behind Law And Order) in April: stays 1m: acts on polytrack and good to firm going: often races prominently/freely. *Simon Dow* **106**

MR SCARLET 3 b.g. Dandy Man (IRE) 123 – Scarlet Buttons (IRE) (Marju (IRE) 127) [2017 88p: 5.8g^6 6s^3 6m^5 6m 5.8g^2 6s Sep 24] compact gelding: fifth foal: half-brother to 3 winners, including useful Italian 2-y-o 5f/6f winner Catalina Bay (by Pastoral Pursuits) and 11.6f winner Scarlet Sash (by Sir Percy): dam unraced: useful performer: won maiden at Naas in 2016: stays 6f: acts on soft and good to firm going. *Ms Sheila Lavery, Ireland* **105**

MRS DANVERS 3 gr.f. Hellvelyn 118 – Rebecca de Winter 83 (Kyllachy 129) [2017 109: 6m^6 Apr 9] good-quartered filly: useful performer at 2 yrs, unbeaten in 5 starts: well below form in Prix Sigy at Chantilly only outing in 2017: best form at 5f: acts on soft and good to firm going. *Jonathan Portman* **82**

MRS GALLAGHER 2 b.f. (Feb 8) Oasis Dream 129 – A Huge Dream (IRE) (Refuse To Bend (IRE) 128) [2017 5m* 5m 5g* 5.2s^3 6g 5m Oct 13] 140,000Y: compact filly: first foal: dam, useful French 6f winner, half-sister to very smart 1m/1¼m performer (including in Hong Kong) Xtension and to dam of top-class sprinter Harry Angel: useful performer: won maiden at Ascot in May and minor event at Nottingham (by neck from Princess Keira) in July: probably best at 5f: acts on good to firm going: usually races close up. *William Jarvis* **95**

MR SKINNYLEGS 3 b.g. Dream Win 82 – Impeccable Guest (IRE) 60 (Orpen (USA) 116) [2017 –: 7g 5g^2 5m^4 t5.1g^5 Jun 26] modest maiden: best form at 5f: acts on good to firm going. *Brian Ellison* **60**

MR SLICKER (FR) 3 b.g. Exceed And Excel (AUS) 126 – Glory Power (IRE) (Medicean 128) [2017 7g 8g^6 7.6v^3 t7.2g^6 Oct 27] modest form: best effort at 7f: tried in cheekpieces. *Tom Dascombe* **58**

MRS SIPPY (USA) 2 b.f. (Feb 11) Blame (USA) 129 – Qushchi 105 (Encosta de Lago (AUS)) [2017 p8g^4 8d* Oct 27] first foal: dam, winner up to 1½m (2-y-o 7f winner), out of smart half-sister to high-class performer up to 1¼m Grand Lodge: fairly useful form: won maiden at Doncaster (by 1¼ lengths from Ficanas) in October: will go on improving. *David Simcock* **89 p**

MR STANDFAST 4 b.g. Mullionmileanhour (IRE) 116 – Phantom Ridge (IRE) 72 (Indian Ridge 123) [2017 –: p12g^6 p10g 11.8s^3 14m 14d 10.2d Aug 23] sturdy gelding: little form: tried in tongue tie. *Alan Phillips* **47**

MRS TEASDALE 2 ch.f. (Feb 19) Harbour Watch (IRE) 121 – Ardessie (Bahamian Bounty 116) [2017 p6d 6g^3 7d^2 t7.2g* Jul 11] £16,000Y: fourth foal: half-sister to useful 5f (including at 2 yrs) winner Jebediah Shine (by Kyllachy) and 7f winner Lucky Louie (by Dutch Art): dam unraced half-sister to smart 5f winner Cathedral: fair form: in cheekpieces, won minor event at Wolverhampton in July: stays 7f. *Archie Watson* **74**

MR STRUTTER (IRE) 3 ch.g. Sir Prancealot (IRE) 111 – Khajool (IRE) (Haafhd 129) **74**
[2017 50: t6m^2 t6m t6d^4 p7g^4 t6g^6 6g* 5g* 6m 5m^2 6m^2 5g* t6.1g^6 t5g t6.1g t5.1g^6 Nov 29] fair performer: won handicap at Thirsk in April, seller at Beverley in May and another handicap at Thirsk in September: left John Quinn after eleventh start: stays 7f: acts on polytrack, tapeta and good to firm going: wears hood: usually races prominently. *Ronald Thompson*

MR STUNNING (AUS) 5 b.g. Exceed And Excel (AUS) 126 – With Fervour (USA) **126**
(Dayjur (USA) 137) [2017 6m^3 5g* 5m* 6m* 6m^2 6m 5d^6 6m* 6g* 6g* Dec 10] high-class performer: successful at Sha Tin in handicaps in January and March, Sprint Cup in April, Premier Bowl (Handicap) in October and Jockey Club Sprint in November, all Group 2, and Hong Kong Sprint (by neck from D B Pin) in December: stays 6f: acts on good to firm going. *J. Size, Hong Kong*

MR SUNDOWNER (USA) 5 b.g. Scat Daddy (USA) 120 – Bold Answer (USA) **81**
(Dynaformer (USA)) [2017 62: t8g^6 t8g^6 t8d^5 12g^2 10g* 12.5g^5 t10.2s 12m 10d^5 9m* 9s^3 12.5m* 12.1d^2 12.1s* 12.1v^6 12.1s^3 Oct 31] fairly useful handicapper: won at Wetherby (apprentice) in May, Redcar in July, Musselburgh in August and Catterick (by ½ length from Je Suis Charlie) in September: stays 12.5f: acts on polytrack, tapeta, good to firm and heavy going: tried in blinkers: wears tongue tie: often travels strongly. *Wilf Storey*

MR TOP HAT 2 b.c. (Apr 5) Helmet (AUS) 127 – Tut (IRE) 84 (Intikhab (USA) 135) **87**
[2017 6s 6.1m^2 6g^3 6v* 6s^2 Oct 28] £16,000Y: compact colt: third foal: closely related to 7f winner Exoplanet Blue (by Exceed And Excel): dam, 2-y-o 7f winner who stayed 1¼m, half-sister to smart 2-y-o 5f winner Electric Waves: fairly useful performer: won minor event at Salisbury in October: second in nursery at Newbury later same month: will be suited by at least 7f: acts on good to firm and heavy going: usually races close up. *David Evans*

MR TURNER 4 b.g. Nayef (USA) 129 – Seasonal Blossom (IRE) (Fairy King (USA)) **48**
[2017 –: p8d p7d p10g Mar 11] good-bodied gelding: poor maiden: tried in blinkers: sometimes slowly away, usually races nearer last than first: sold 1,500 gns, sent to Spain. *Mark H. Tompkins*

MR TYRRELL (IRE) 3 b.c. Helmet (AUS) 127 – Rocking 79 (Oasis Dream 129) [2017 **85**
76: p8g^3 p7g^2 7d^3 7.6g^2 8.2g^2 8.5d^4 8d 7m^5 p8g^2 Oct 5] fairly useful maiden: placed 6 times in 2017: stays 1m: acts on polytrack, best turf form on good going: tried in blinkers: front runner/races prominently. *Richard Hannon*

MR WAGYU (IRE) 2 ch.g. (Apr 2) Choisir (AUS) 126 – Lake Louise (IRE) 91 (Haatef **76**
(USA) 117) [2017 5m^6 6g^2 6m* 6m* 6d^6 t6.1g Sep 9] fair performer: won minor event at Ripon in June and nursery at York in July: stays 6f: acts on good to firm going. *John Quinn*

MSAIKAH (IRE) 2 b.f. (Apr 9) Galileo (IRE) 134 – Light Quest (USA) (Quest For Fame **52 p**
127) [2017 p8s^6 Nov 23] 300,000Y: sister to French 1¼m winner Orfeas, closely related to useful French 1¼m-1½m winner Diodoros (by High Chaparral) and half-sister to several winners, including useful French 9f-10.5f winner Skia (by Motivator): dam useful French 9f/1¼m winner: 12/1, green when sixth in minor event at Chelmsford (10¾ lengths behind Noble Expression) in November: will improve. *Luca Cumani*

MS ARSENAL 5 b.m. Mount Nelson 125 – Magical Dancer (IRE) 53 (Magical Wonder **–**
(USA) 125) [2017 51: p6d^6 p8g Mar 11] maiden: no form in 2017: usually leads, often races freely. *Giles Bravery*

MSAYYAN (IRE) 2 b.c. (Feb 1) Camelot 128 – Elusive Girl (IRE) 59 (Elusive City **87 p**
(USA) 117) [2017 p8g^2 8.3d* Oct 18] 150,000F, 200,000Y: first foal: dam once-raced half-sister to very smart winner up to 1m Aljamaaheer: fairly useful form: won maiden at Nottingham (by length from Corgi) in October: likely to stay beyond 1m: remains open to improvement. *John Gosden*

MS GILLARD 4 b.f. Aussie Rules (USA) 123 – Oval Office 99 (Pursuit of Love 124) **75**
[2017 69: t10.2g^3 t10.2d^2 t9.5g^2 t10.2d^2 p8g^4 t9.5g^2 9.9g^2 10.1m^4 10.2d^3 10.1g* Jun 13] compact filly: fair handicapper: won at Yarmouth in June: stayed 1¼m: acted on polytrack, tapeta and good to firm going: in headgear 4 of last 5 starts: in foal to Archipenko. *David Simcock*

MS TILLY 2 b.f. (Mar 28) Milk It Mick 120 – Clumber Pursuits (Pastoral Pursuits 127) **–**
[2017 6.1g 5v p7g t7.2m^6 Oct 31] third foal: dam ran twice: well held in maidens/minor events. *David Brown*

MT AUGUSTUS 2 b.g. (Feb 23) Champs Elysees 124 – In Secret 77 (Dalakhani (IRE) 133) [2017 8v⁴ 8d⁶ 9.9s² Sep 27] first foal: dam, ungenuine maiden (placed up to 1½m), half-sister to smart 7f winner Jedburgh and useful performers up to 1½m Warlu Way and In Disguise: fairly useful form: best effort when second in maiden at Goodwood (½ length behind Setting Sail) in September: open to further improvement. *Henry Candy* **82 p**

MUATADEL 4 b.g. Exceed And Excel (AUS) 126 – Rose Blossom 113 (Pastoral Pursuits 127) [2017 66: p6g⁵ 5s³ 5g² 5f⁶ 5d⁶ 5d* 6v* 5s² 5g* 5m² 5d³ 5v 6v⁴ t5g³ 5v⁵ Oct 23] fairly useful handicapper: won at Doncaster (twice) in July and Beverley (by head from Fujin) in August: left Ed Dunlop after first start: stays 6f: acts on polytrack, tapeta, good to firm and heavy going: tried in blinkers. *Roger Fell* **87**

MUBAJAL 4 br.g. Dubawi (IRE) 129 – Jadhwah (Nayef (USA) 129) [2017 96: 10.3g a8f a9.9f a8f⁵ Dec 1] fairly useful at 3 yrs, well below best in 2017: left Owen Burrows after first start: likely to stay 1½m: acts on polytrack: in headgear last 3 starts: front runner/races prominently. *A. bin Harmash, UAE* **71**

MUBTASIM (IRE) 3 b.g. Arcano (IRE) 122 – Start The Music (IRE) (King's Best (USA) 132) [2017 105: 6f³ 6f³ 7m³ 7m 7g Aug 25] well-made gelding: smart performer: third in Pavilion Stakes at Ascot (3 lengths behind Blue Point) in May, Sandy Lane Stakes at Haydock (6¼ lengths behind Harry Angel) later in May and Jersey Stakes at Royal Ascot (2½ lengths behind Le Brivido) in June: stays 7f: acts on firm going: in cheekpieces last 2 starts. *William Haggas* **111**

MUCHO APPLAUSE (IRE) 3 b.c. Acclamation 118 – Pediment 91 (Desert Prince (IRE) 130) [2017 79p: 8.1d² 10s² 10m Jun 22] big, rangy colt: has scope: useful handicapper: second at Sandown and Newbury (1¼ lengths behind Defoe): stays 1¼m: acts on soft going: front runner/races prominently: sent to Hong Kong, where renamed Fearless Fire. *Andrew Balding* **104**

MUDAARAB (USA) 3 ch.g. Distorted Humor (USA) 117 – Middle Club 107 (Fantastic Light (USA) 134) [2017 p8g⁴ 10m* 9.9m* 9.9g Sep 2] $450,000Y: first foal: dam, winner up to 9.5f (2-y-o 7f/1m winner), half-sister to Horris Hill Stakes winner Piping Rock: fairly useful form: won maiden at Pontefract in May and handicap at Goodwood (by length from Bear Valley) in June: will stay 1½m: sent to UAE. *Sir Michael Stoute* **94**

MUDAJAJ (USA) 3 b.g. Arch (USA) 127 – Checkered Flag (USA) (A P Indy (USA) 131) [2017 10g⁴ 11.6d⁶ 12d⁵ Jun 6] $425,000Y: half-brother to several winners abroad, including smart US Grade 2 8.5f/9f winner Zanjero (by Cherokee Run): dam unraced: fair form: best effort when fourth in maiden at Leicester on debut: remains capable of better. *Charles Hills* **78 p**

MUDALLEL (IRE) 3 b.g. Invincible Spirit (IRE) 121 – Lixirova (FR) 102 (Slickly (FR) 128) [2017 91p: 8d⁵ 6.1m⁴ 7.6d⁴ p7s⁴ p8d* p8g* p8g Sep 25] useful handicapper: won at Kempton (twice, by ½ length from Ventura Blues second occasion) in August: stays 1m: acts on polytrack and good to firm going: usually races towards rear. *Ed Dunlop* **96**

MUFFRI'HA (IRE) 5 b.m. Iffraaj 127 – Grecian Dancer 114 (Dansili 127) [2017 114: 8g³ 8.9g³ 8.9g³ p7g² 9m⁴ 8d* 8g 9m⁵ p8g* Nov 2] lengthy mare: smart performer: won listed races at Newmarket (by length from Permission) in September and Lingfield (by length from Zest) in November: third at Meydan first 3 starts, in Cape Verdi (¾ length behind Very Special), Balanchine (1½ lengths behind Opal Tiara) and Jebel Hatta (½ length behind Decorated Knight): effective at 1m to 1¼m: acts on polytrack, firm and good to soft going: tried in cheekpieces: front runner/races prominently, usually races freely. *William Haggas* **111**

MUHAJJAL 3 b.c. Cape Cross (IRE) 129 – Muqantara (USA) 57 (First Samurai (USA) 119) [2017 84: 7d p8g p7g p7s p7g⁶ p7g* Dec 28] compact colt: fair handicapper: won at Lingfield in December: left Owen Burrows after first start: stays 7f: acts on polytrack and good to firm going: in tongue tie last 4 starts. *George Peckham* **77**

MUIRIN (IRE) 2 b.f. (Apr 6) Born To Sea (IRE) 117 – Girouette (IRE) 108 (Pivotal 124) [2017 7m* 7s⁴ 8m Oct 13] €41,000Y: useful-looking filly: fifth foal: closely related to Japanese 7f winner Nouvelle Reine (by Sea The Stars): dam, 6f/7f winner, half-sister to smart French miler Prince d'Alienor: useful form: won minor event at the Curragh (by ¾ length from Sizzling) in August: best effort when fourth in Moyglare Stud Stakes at the Curragh (5¾ lengths behind Happily) in September: should stay 1m. *Edward Lynam, Ireland* **95**

MUIRSHEEN DURKIN 3 b.g. Fastnet Rock (AUS) 127 – Be My Queen (IRE) 104 (Sadler's Wells (USA) 132) [2017 82: t8.6g 7.8s² 7.4d⁶ 7d 8.5m⁶ Aug 27] fairly useful handicapper: second at Carlisle in June: stays 8.5f: acts on soft and good to firm going: usually wears cheekpieces. *Neville Bycroft* **87**

MUJASSAM 5 ch.g. Kyllachy 129 – Naizak 73 (Medicean 128) [2017 102§: 6g 6v^{2} 7g 7s^{6} f5g f6.1g* f6.1g^{6} Dec 19] good-topped gelding: fairly useful handicapper nowadays: won at Southwell (by length from Tricky Dicky) in December: stays 7f: acts on fibresand and heavy going: wears headgear: temperamental. *David O'Meara* **92 §**

MUKALAL 3 b.g. Mawatheeq (USA) 126 – Misdaqeya 106 (Red Ransom (USA)) [2017 80p: 7m^{5} p8g* t8.6g* p8s^{2} p8g^{4} 7g^{4} 7d* Oct 6] big, workmanlike gelding: useful performer: won maiden at Lingfield (by 3 lengths from Pillar of Society) in May, and handicaps at Wolverhampton (by head from Vantage Point) in June and Ascot (by nose from Tribute Act) in October: stays 8.5f: acts on polytrack, tapeta and good to soft going: has worn hood: usually leads: open to further improvement. *Marcus Tregoning* **107 p**

MUKHAATER 2 ch.g. (May 3) Bahamian Bounty 116 – Dame Shirley (Haafhd 129) [2017 7d^{5} Oct 27] 14/1, green when fifth in maiden at Doncaster (5¼ lengths behind Breath Caught) in October. *Charles Hills* **74**

MUKHAYYAM 5 b.g. Dark Angel (IRE) 113 – Caster Sugar (USA) 87 (Cozzene (USA)) [2017 97: 12m^{6} 12g 11.9s 9.8d^{2} 11.9m^{2} 11.2s 11.9g* 12d* 12d^{5} 11.9g 14s 12.1s^{3} 11.9d Oct 28] good-topped gelding: useful handicapper: won at York and Ripon (by 3½ lengths from Fleeting Visit) in July: stays 13f: acts on good to firm and heavy going: wears headgear: usually leads. *Tim Easterby* **101**

MULHIMATTY 3 b.f. Invincible Spirit (IRE) 121 – Raasekha 104 (Pivotal 124) [2017 7g* 7.9d^{5} 7g Sep 15] first foal: dam, 1m winner, half-sister to top-class winner up to 7f Muhaarar: fair form: won maiden at Newbury (by short head from May Sky) in April: stays 1m. *Charles Hills* **69**

MULLARKEY 3 b.g. Mullionmileanhour (IRE) 116 – Hannah's Dream (IRE) 69 (King's Best (USA) 132) [2017 73: p10g^{2} p7g^{3} 10.2g* 11s^{5} 9.9m^{5} 10.3g 11.9m^{5} p12g p10s^{3} p10s* Dec 14] compact gelding: fairly useful handicapper: won at Nottingham (by 1¼ lengths from Hertford Dancer) in April and Chelmsford (by length from Pinnata) in December: effective at 7f to 1¼m: acts on polytrack, best turf form on good going. *John Best* **80**

MULLED WINE 4 b.g. Mullionmileanhour (IRE) 116 – Numanthia (IRE) 56 (Barathea (IRE) 127) [2017 57: p12d p8d^{2} p8g p8g^{5} p8d May 29] modest maiden: stays 1m: acts on polytrack. *John Best* **56**

MULLIGATAWNY (IRE) 4 b.g. Lope de Vega (IRE) 125 – Wild Whim (IRE) (Whipper (USA) 126) [2017 97: 9.8m^{6} 7m^{4} 8s^{3} t8s 10.3m^{6} 9m^{2} 10d^{5} 9.8m^{2} 9.8d* 10d^{4} 8g^{4} 9.8g^{2} 9d Sep 30] useful handicapper: won maiden at Dundalk for Mrs J. Harrington in 2016: also won at Ripon (by 1¼ lengths from Jacbequick) in July: second at latter course on 3 other occasions in 2017: stays 10.5f: acts on polytrack, soft and good to firm going: in cheekpieces last 5 starts: front runner/races prominently. *Roger Fell* **99**

MULLIONHEIR 5 b.g. Mullionmileanhour (IRE) 116 – Peyto Princess 85 (Bold Arrangement 127) [2017 –: p6g^{4} p7d 8g 7g 7d 6s* Sep 8] lengthy gelding: fairly useful handicapper: won at Ascot (by ½ length from Alaadel) in September: stays 7f: acts on polytrack, soft and good to firm going: often races prominently. *John Best* **91**

MULLION STAR 2 b.g. (Apr 27) Mullionmileanhour (IRE) 116 – Leading Star 47 (Motivator 131) [2017 5m 5.1m 7m 5s Jul 29] lengthy gelding: well held in minor events: tried in visor. *Michael Madgwick* **–**

MULSANNE CHASE 3 b.g. Sixties Icon 125 – Hot Pursuits 89 (Pastoral Pursuits 127) [2017 7s 7m^{3} 8m 7v^{6} p6g p8g 7s^{5} 8v^{5} Oct 19] good-topped gelding: fair maiden: stays 7f: acts on soft going: in blinkers last 2 starts. *Brian Barr* **66**

MULTELLIE 5 b.g. Multiplex 114 – Bollin Nellie 98 (Rock Hopper 124) [2017 91: 13.9m 11.2s 11.9m^{4} 14.5d Oct 27] workmanlike gelding: fairly useful handicapper: stays 1¾m: acts on good to firm and heavy going. *Tim Easterby* **86**

MULTICULTURAL (IRE) 3 b.f. Fastnet Rock (AUS) 127 – Cochabamba (IRE) 102 (Hurricane Run (IRE) 134) [2017 75p: t8d^{2} 8m^{3} 7m* 7m^{3} 7m^{4} p7g^{6} 7d^{5} p8m^{5} t9.5g Dec 2] fairly useful handicapper: won at Yarmouth (by 2 lengths from Call Me Grumpy) in August: stays 1m: acts on polytrack, tapeta, good to firm and good to soft going: wears headgear: often races towards rear/travels strongly: sold 32,000 gns in December. *James Tate* **88**

MULTICURRENCY (USA) 2 gr.c. (Jan 19) Exchange Rate (USA) 111 – Istamara (Teofilo (IRE) 126) [2017 p8g Nov 7] 50/1, well held in minor event at Kempton:. *David Simcock* **–**

MULTIGIFTED 4 b.f. Multiplex 114 – Attlongglast (Groom Dancer (USA) 128) [2017 68: p13g^5 p12g^2 12s* 12v* p16g^6 12g^5 11.6d^5 Sep 16] workmanlike filly: fair handicapper: won at Newbury in May and Chepstow in June: stays 2m: acts on polytrack, good to firm and heavy going: has worn headgear, including in 2017: wears tongue tie: usually races prominently. *Michael Madgwick* **78 a71**

MULTI QUEST 5 b.m. Multiplex 114 – Ryan's Quest (IRE) 67 (Mukaddamah (USA) 125) [2017 60: p6g* p6d^6 p6d^5 f6m p6g^5 p6g^4 f6d 6.1g^5 6g 6m 6s^3 6g 6.1g^4 6.1g^6 t6.1m^5 p6g Nov 17] modest handicapper: won at Kempton in January: largely below form after: stays 6f: acts on polytrack, tapeta, firm and good to soft going: wears headgear: front runner/races prominently. *John E. Long* **60**

MULTITASK 7 b.g. Multiplex 114 – Attlongglast (Groom Dancer (USA) 128) [2017 77, a85: p7d p7s p8g 8s p8g t8.6g Sep 9] good-topped gelding: fairly useful at best, no form in 2017: has worn headgear. *Gary Moore* **–**

MULTIVIZ 4 b.f. Multiplex 114 – Vizean (IRE) 77 (Medicean 128) [2017 71: p12g^4 p12s p12g 8g^5 12g 10d 9.5g^3 9g 10v p12g^5 t9.5g p12g p10.7g^3 p12g Dec 6] first foal: dam, maiden (stayed 7f), half-sister to smart winner up to 7f Viztoria: modest maiden on turf, fair on all-weather: left Ms Sheila Lavery after ninth start: stays 1½m: acts on polytrack and good to soft going: has worn cheekpieces/tongue tie, including in 2017: often races towards rear. *S. M. Duffy, Ireland* **60 a66**

MULWITH (IRE) 3 b.g. Kodiac 112 – Crying Aloud (USA) 94 (Street Cry (IRE) 130) [2017 61: 8d 7g 6d 7m Jul 12] maiden: no form in 2017: has worn blinkers, including last 2 starts: front runner/races prominently. *Scott Dixon* **–**

MULZIM 3 b.c. Exceed And Excel (AUS) 126 – Samaah (IRE) (Cape Cross (IRE) 129) [2017 72: p7g^4 t7.1g* p7g^2 7d^5 6m^2 p7g p6g Oct 3] tall colt: fairly useful handicapper: won at Wolverhampton in April: second at Lingfield in May and Yarmouth in August: stays 7f: acts on polytrack and tapeta: tried in blinkers: sold 22,000 gns in November. *Ed Dunlop* **83**

MUMS THE WORD 3 b.f. Mayson 124 – Tell Mum (Marju (IRE) 127) [2017 76: t8.6g* p6g^4 t7.1f^3 p8d^3 Mar 13] fairly useful performer: won maiden at Wolverhampton in January: third in handicaps at same course in February and Chelmsford in March: stays 8.5f: acts on polytrack, tapeta, good to firm and heavy going: front runner/races prominently. *Richard Fahey* **80**

MUNAASHID (USA) 4 b.g. Lonhro (AUS) 128 – Freefourracing (USA) 108 (French Deputy (USA) 118) [2017 89: 8m 10g^6 7.6d^5 Jun 24] useful-looking gelding: fairly useful performer in 2016 for D. K. Weld, below that level in 2017: stays 11.5f: acts on heavy going: tried in headgear: often races towards rear: sold 22,000 gns in July, sent to Germany, where placed in 3 handicaps for M. F. Weissmeier. *Ed Dunlop* **71**

MUNAAWIB 9 b.g. Haafhd 129 – Mouwadh (USA) 64 (Nureyev (USA) 131) [2017 60: t8.6g^3 t8.6g 7d Jul 26] modest handicapper: stays 8.5f: acts on all-weather, soft and good to firm going: wears headgear/tongue tie. *Ray Peacock* **63**

MUNAWER 3 ch.g. Dutch Art 126 – Cantal 87 (Pivotal 124) [2017 81p: 8m^4 8g^2 8g^2 p9.4g^3 Dec 14] angular gelding: fairly useful performer: second in handicap at Brighton and minor event at Deauville: left Hugo Palmer after second start, Julien Phelippon after third: probably stays 9.5f: acts on polytrack and tapeta. *Mme G. Rarick, France* **84**

MUNDERSFIELD 3 b.f. Nathaniel (IRE) 129 – Captain's Paradise (IRE) (Rock of Gibraltar (IRE) 133) [2017 t8.6g^4 p10g^6 Dec 13] 3,000Y: third foal: dam twice-raced half-sister to very smart winner up to 1½m Kutub: fair form in maidens. *David Simcock* **66**

MUNFALLET (IRE) 6 b.g. Royal Applause 124 – Princess Mood (GER) (Muhtarram (USA) 125) [2017 99: 6g 6m 6s^5 6.1d^4 6s^6 6.1g^5 7m^3 7g^4 7v^4 p6g^4 Nov 2] well-made gelding: fairly useful handicapper nowadays: third at Epsom in August: raced mainly at 6f/7f: acts on polytrack, good to firm and heavy going: tried in headgear: usually leads. *David Brown* **84**

MUNGO MADNESS 3 gr.g. Sir Percy 129 – Emma's Gift (IRE) 96 (Aussie Rules (USA) 123) [2017 66: f8g^4 f8m 8g^6 8g^4 10g f12.1g^3 p13.3d 11.5g^3 Oct 16] rather leggy gelding: modest maiden: stays 1½m: acts on fibresand and good to firm going. *Julia Feilden* **56**

MUNRO 3 b.g. Kyllachy 129 – Meddle (Diktat 126) [2017 89p: p6d^5 p6g* 6.1m^2 6m Jun 17] useful handicapper: won at Lingfield (by ½ length from Marquee Club) in February: second at Chester (neck behind Zamjar) in May: will be suited by 7f: acts on polytrack and good to firm going: in cheekpieces last 3 starts: gelded, and sent to Hong Kong, where renamed Turin Redstar. *Ralph Beckett* **96**

MUNSARIM (IRE) 10 b.g. Shamardal (USA) 129 – Etizaaz (USA) 117 (Diesis 133) [2017 64: p12d p13g p11g^{5} p10g p12g Apr 24] lengthy, good-topped gelding: modest handicapper: stays 13f: acts on polytrack and good to firm going: wears headgear: often starts slowly/races towards rear: best treated with caution. *Lee Carter* **53 §**

MUNSTEAD GOLD 2 ch.c. (Apr 15) Sir Percy 129 – Royal Patron 78 (Royal Academy (USA) 130) [2017 8s p8g 9d^{5} Oct 30] little impact in minor events. *Andrew Balding* **–**

MUNSTEAD STAR 3 ch.f. Sir Percy 129 – Royal Patron 78 (Royal Academy (USA) 130) [2017 –: p13.3g^{3} 11.8d^{2} 12v^{4} 12.3d^{6} p12d* p16g* Sep 13] close-coupled filly: fairly useful performer: won maiden at Kempton in August and handicap there (by 1¼ lengths from Master Archer) in September: stays 2m: acts on polytrack and good to soft going. *Andrew Balding* **88**

MUNTADAB (IRE) 5 b.g. Invincible Spirit (IRE) 121 – Chibola (ARG) (Roy (USA)) [2017 102: 6g^{2} 6m^{2} 6s^{2} 6m 6g^{6} 6g 6g 6g 7s* 6.5g^{2} 8.2v^{5} 7.2v* 7d Nov 11] good-bodied gelding: smart handicapper: won at Haydock (by 1½ lengths from Explain) in September and Musselburgh (by 1¼ lengths from Right Touch) in October: best at 6f/7f: acts on polytrack, tapeta, good to firm and heavy going: tried in headgear: front runner. *Roger Fell* **111**

MUNTAHAA (IRE) 4 gr.g. Dansili 127 – Qertaas (IRE) 102 (Linamix (FR) 127) [2017 121: 12g^{3} 12m* 13.9d 12m 12g^{6} Jul 13] rangy gelding: smart performer: won John Porter Stakes at Newbury (by neck from Chemical Charge) in April: stays 13.5f: acts on polytrack, good to firm and good to soft going: has worn hood, including in 2017. *John Gosden* **118**

MUNTAZAH 4 b.g. Dubawi (IRE) 129 – Rumoush (USA) 114 (Rahy (USA) 115) [2017 107: 10d^{5} 12m 10m 8m^{3} p8g 8g Sep 16] well-made gelding: smart handicapper: third at Sandown (1½ lengths behind El Hayem) in July: stays 10.5f: acts on good to firm and good to soft going: tried in cheekpieces: often leads: gelded, and sent to UAE. *Owen Burrows* **113**

MUNTHANY (USA) 3 b.g. Raven's Pass (USA) 133 – Safarjal (IRE) 86 (Marju (IRE) 127) [2017 9.9m^{4} 10g^{5} 12d^{3} p10g^{3} 8v^{4} Oct 9] fair maiden: stays 1¼m: acts on good to firm going: usually leads. *Charles Hills* **79**

MUQAATIL (USA) 3 b.c. Lonhro (AUS) 128 – Lightning Lydia (USA) (Broad Brush (USA)) [2017 83: p7g^{2} t9.5g^{4} 8m^{5} 8.3s^{4} a8f^{5} a8f a8.9f a8f^{6} Dec 15] fair maiden: left Richard Hannon after fourth outing: stays 1m: acts on polytrack and good to firm going: often in headgear, tongue tied last 4 starts: usually leads. *A. bin Harmash, UAE* **79**

MUQARRED (USA) 5 b.g. Speightstown (USA) 124 – Bawaara (FR) (Quiet American (USA)) [2017 84: t10.2g t9.5g^{6} f8g* f12d^{4} f8g^{2} 8g f8.1g^{2} t10.2s t10.2s 9s f8.1g* t10.2d t8d f7.1g f8.1g^{2} f8.1g^{2} Dec 19] compact gelding: fairly useful performer: won claimer at Southwell in March and handicap there (by ½ length from Monsieur Jimmy) in October: stays 1¼m: acts on polytrack, fibresand and good to firm going: wears headgear: tried in tongue tie. *Roger Fell* **82**

MURAADEF 2 b.g. (Jan 24) Kodiac 112 – Dominatrix (Whipper (USA) 126) [2017 6.5m^{6} Jul 7] 65,000F, £130,000Y: second foal: dam, lightly raced in France (third at 7f), out of half-sister to smart performer up to 15f Bonny Scot: 25/1, sixth in minor event at Doncaster (7¾ lengths behind Wasim) in July: likely to improve. *Ed Dunlop* **62 p**

MURAD KHAN (FR) 4 b.g. Raven's Pass (USA) 133 – Lady Elgar (IRE) (Sadler's Wells (USA) 132) [2017 110: 7.9d 8.1g* 9.9g p8g 8d p10g^{5} Oct 12] useful-looking gelding: smart handicapper: won at Windsor (by 1½ lengths from Easy Tiger) in July: stays 1m: acts on polytrack, good to firm and heavy going: often in hood in 2017: sold 40,000 gns in October, sent to USA. *Hugo Palmer* **111**

MURASAKI 2 b.f. (Mar 24) Dubawi (IRE) 129 – Michita (USA) 113 (Dynaformer (USA)) [2017 p7g^{6} p8g Oct 13] fifth foal: half-sister to several winners, including smart 1m-1¼m winner Great Order (by Distorted Humor) and 1m-9.5f winner Thatchmaster (by Street Cry): dam, winner up to 1½m (Ribblesdale Stakes, also 2-y-o 1m winner), sister to very smart winner up to 1¾m Willing Foe: in need of experience when mid-division in minor event/maiden: remains with potential. *Charlie Appleby* **58 p**

MURCHISON RIVER 3 b.g. Medicean 128 – Free Offer 94 (Generous (IRE) 139) [2017 10m 10s 10g 14s^{4} 12g* 14.2v Oct 4] rather unfurnished gelding: fair performer: won handicap at Chepstow in August: best effort at 1½m. *Henry Candy* **78**

MURDANOVA (IRE) 4 gr.g. Zebedee 113 – Agnista (IRE) (Iffraaj 127) [2017 59: p7d* t7.1m* t7.1m^{6} 7g^{2} p7g^{3} t6.1g^{6} p8g^{5} t7.2m^{3} p7g Nov 7] lengthy gelding: fairly useful handicapper: won at Kempton and Wolverhampton (by 1¼ lengths from Tavener) in February: third at Chelmsford in August and Wolverhampton in October: left Daniel Loughnane after fourth start: stays 1m: acts on polytrack and tapeta: tried in cheekpieces. *Denis Quinn* **82**

MURGAN 5 b.g. Galileo (IRE) 134 – Approach 105 (Darshaan 133) [2017 –: p12g^5 14g^6 16g^6 12s^4 p12g Oct 9] tall, useful-looking gelding: fairly useful handicapper: stays 1½m: acts on soft and good to firm going: tried in cheekpieces: in tongue tie last 2 starts: sold 6,000 gns in October. *Stuart Kittow* **86**

MURILLO (USA) 2 b.c. (Mar 22) Scat Daddy (USA) 120 – Mostaqeleh (USA) 108 (Rahy (USA) 115) [2017 6g^6 5m* 6f^3 6g^3 Jul 1] $500,000F: well-made colt: half-brother to several winners, including smart 6f-1m winner Nawwaar (2-y-o 7f winner, by Distorted Humor): dam, 2-y-o 6f/7f winner, half-sister to very smart performer up to 1¼m Muqbil: useful form: won maiden at Tipperary (by 3 lengths from Wolfofbaggotstreet) in May: third in Coventry Stakes at Royal Ascot (neck behind Rajasinghe) in June and Railway Stakes at the Curragh (2¼ lengths behind Beckford) in July: will stay 7f: wears tongue tie. *Aidan O'Brien, Ireland* **107**

MURRAQIB (USA) 4 ch.g. Summer Bird (USA) 126 – Golden Party (USA) (Seeking The Gold (USA)) [2017 55: p15.8g Jan 27] modest maiden, well held sole outing in 2017: best effort at 13.5f: acts on polytrack: has worn headgear. *Brett Johnson* **–**

MUSAAHIM (USA) 3 b.g. Distorted Humor (USA) 117 – Lear's Princess (USA) 118 (Lear Fan (USA) 130) [2017 9.9m^2 11.9m^2 12s p12g^3 p13.3g^4 Oct 26] fourth foal: dam US Grade 1 9f winner: fairly useful maiden: placed 3 times: stays 1½m: acts on good to firm going: usually races prominently, often travels strongly: sold 28,000 gns in November. *Roger Varian* **84**

MUSAWAAT 3 b.c. Equiano (FR) 127 – Starry Sky 81 (Oasis Dream 129) [2017 82p: 7v^2 7m^6 7d^3 7m* 8s^5 Sep 8] tall, angular colt: useful handicapper: won at Newmarket (by 1¼ lengths from Plant Pot Power) in August: stays 7f: acts on good to firm and heavy going: sold 45,000 gns in November, sent to UAE. *Charles Hills* **96**

MUSBAQ (USA) 2 b.g. (Feb 2) Union Rags (USA) 124 – Eraada 76 (Medicean 128) [2017 6m^5 7m^5 Jun 16] fair form when fifth in maiden at Sandown (4¼ lengths behind Falmouth Light) on second of 2 starts. *Mark Johnston* **67**

MUSCIKA 3 b.g. Kyllachy 129 – Miss Villefranche 69 (Danehill Dancer (IRE) 117) [2017 73: 6g* 7s 6d* 6s^6 6g^2 6m^4 6d^3 Sep 10] workmanlike gelding: fairly useful performer: won maiden at Thirsk in April and handicap at Ayr (by ¾ length from Tatlisu) in June: should stay 7f: acts on good to soft going: tried in cheekpieces: often races prominently. *David O'Meara* **90**

MUSHAHADAAT (IRE) 2 b.f. (Mar 1) Invincible Spirit (IRE) 121 – Jamaayel 99 (Shamardal (USA) 129) [2017 6g^2 6v 5.1g^6 p6g* Oct 4] unfurnished filly: fourth foal: sister to 2-y-o 5f winner Fataawy, closely related to useful 5f and (including at 2 yrs) 5.7f winner Rathaath (by Oasis Dream) and half-sister to 2-y-o 6f winner Giennah (by Tamayuz): dam 2-y-o 6f/7f winner: fair form: won maiden at Kempton in October: likely to prove best at sprint trips: acts on polytrack: tried in cheekpieces: open to further improvement. *Brian Meehan* **79 p**

MUSHAIREB 3 b.g. Invincible Spirit (IRE) 121 – Hidden Brief 100 (Barathea (IRE) 127) [2017 85p: 10.3g 8v^4 8v* 8v^3 Oct 9] useful handicapper: won at Pontefract (by 1¾ lengths from Mr Cool Cash) in September: stays 1m: acts on tapeta and heavy going: often races towards rear/travels strongly: sold 60,000 gns in October. *Richard Fahey* **95**

MUSHAREEFA (IRE) 3 b.f. Makfi 130 – Winesong (IRE) 68 (Giant's Causeway (USA) 132) [2017 8.3g 8.3g 8.3g p12g Jun 3] €90,000Y: sixth foal: closely related to very smart 1¼m-1½m winner Universal and 9f/10.5f winner Windward Passage (both by Dubawi) and half-sister to 1½m winner Madam Mo (by Motivator): dam once-raced half-sister to Cheveley Park Stakes winner Seazun: no form: tried in cheekpieces. *Ed Dunlop* **–**

MUSHARRIF 5 b.g. Arcano (IRE) 122 – Cefira (USA) 66 (Distant View (USA) 126) [2017 89: 6g 5m 5m 5g^6 5d* 5s^4 5m^5 5v^5 t5g^3 f5g^5 5s^5 f5g^5 f7.1g^5 Dec 11] sturdy gelding: fairly useful handicapper: won at Beverley (by 2¼ lengths from Astrophysics) in July: raced mainly at 5f: acts on fibresand, tapeta, firm and good to soft going: tried in blinkers: usually races prominently. *Declan Carroll* **89**

MUSHTAQ (IRE) 2 b.g. (Mar 20) Zoffany (IRE) 121 – Iamfine (IRE) (Whipper (USA) 126) [2017 p7d^4 p6s* Dec 7] €150,000F, 210,000Y: third foal: dam unraced daughter of useful 6f/7f performer Cheyenne Spirit: fairly useful form: won minor event at Chelmsford (by ¾ length from Choice Encounter) in December: should be suited by 7f: likely to progress further. *Richard Hannon* **85 p**

MUSICAL ART (IRE) 2 ch.f. (Apr 18) Dutch Art 126 – Musical Bar (IRE) 93 (Barathea **90**
(IRE) 127) [2017 6m* 6d^3 7g^6 8m 7s Oct 28] €115,000Y: good-quartered filly: fifth foal: half-sister to 2-y-o 6f winner Chord Chart (by Acclamation) and 1m winner Lyric Harmony (by Teofilo): dam, 7f winner, half-sister to 1000 Guineas winner Finsceal Beo: fairly useful performer: won minor event at Newbury (by ¾ length from Your Choice) in July: third in Princess Margaret Stakes at Ascot (6¾ lengths behind Nyaleti) later same month: stays 1m: acts on good to firm and good to soft going: tried in tongue tie. *Paul Cole*

MUSICAL COMEDY 6 b.g. Royal Applause 124 – Spinning Top 105 (Alzao (USA) 117) **79**
[2017 92: 5m 5d^5 5.1m^6 6.1g^2 6m 7d f7.1g Dec 1] good-topped gelding: fair handicapper nowadays: stays 6f: acts on heavy going: tried in blinkers: often races towards rear. *Mike Murphy*

MUSICAL DREAM 2 ch.f. (Feb 18) Dream Ahead (USA) 133 – Gift of Music (IRE) 73 –
(Cadeaux Genereux 131) [2017 p6d Jul 12] first foal: dam 2-y-o 6f winner out of useful 5f winner Loch Verdi: 10/1, well held in minor event at Kempton. *Sylvester Kirk*

MUSICAL FIRE 3 b.f. Equiano (FR) 127 – Music In Exile (USA) 58 (Diesis 133) [2017 –
p7d^6 7d p7g Nov 1] 7,000Y: fourth foal: half-sister to 1½m-2m winner Bold Runner (by Mount Nelson) and useful 7f/1m winner Chestnut Fire (by Showcasing): dam ran twice: well held in maidens: tried in cheekpieces. *Peter Hedger*

MUSICAL MOON 7 b.g. Piccolo 121 – Lunasa (IRE) 82 (Don't Forget Me 127) [2017 –
t13.9f Feb 24] maiden: in cheekpieces, well held sole outing on Flat in 2017: dead. *Steve Flook*

MUSICAL TASTE 4 b.f. Makfi 130 – Blas Ceoil (USA) 97 (Mr Greeley (USA) 122) **54**
[2017 65: p7g^5 6g 8g^5 May 23] modest handicapper: stays 7f: acts on polytrack, tapeta and good to soft going: in headgear last 2 starts: has worn tongue tie. *Pat Phelan*

MUSICAL TERMS 3 b.g. Shamardal (USA) 129 – Dysphonia (AUS) 113 (Lonhro **87**
(AUS) 128) [2017 8m^2 7.6g^3 8s^4 8m* p8g* p8g^5 Oct 26] sturdy gelding: first foal: dam 6.5f-1m winner, mainly in Australia: fairly useful performer: won maiden at Ripon in August and handicap at Chelmsford (by short head from Toga Tiger) in October: will be suited by 1¼m: acts on polytrack and good to firm going: sold 120,000 gns later in October, sent to Qatar. *William Haggas*

MUSICAL THEATRE 2 b.f. (Feb 23) Exceed And Excel (AUS) 126 – Wise Melody 97 **70**
(Zamindar (USA) 116) [2017 6s^6 p6g^2 t6.1g^4 Nov 18] 35,000Y, 70,000 2-y-o: third foal: sister to useful French 6f (including at 2 yrs)/6.5f winner Sallal: dam 6f winner (including at 2 yrs): fair form when second in minor event at Chelmsford (3½ lengths behind Pretty Baby) on second of 3 starts: in hood last 2 starts. *David Simcock*

MUSIC BOX (IRE) 3 b.f. Invincible Spirit (IRE) 121 – Liscune (IRE) 73 (King's Best **108**
(USA) 132) [2017 p8g^3 8d^2 7d^2 7s* 6s 7g^2 6.7g^3 7g 7g^6 6g* 8.1g^2 6g^2 7s* 8g^2 7.5s^3 7g* Sep 15] 90,000F, 700,000Y: tall, close-coupled filly: sixth foal: sister to 3 winners, notably very smart winner up to 1½m Ektihaam (2-y-o 7f winner): dam 8.5f-1½m winner: useful performer: won maiden at Gowran in June, handicap at Naas (by ¾ length from Miss Power) in July, listed race at Galway (by 1½ lengths from Drumfad Bay) in August and Sceptre Stakes at Doncaster (by length from Eternally) in September: stayed 1m: acted on soft going: sometimes wore hood: usually travelled strongly: visits Galileo. *Aidan O'Brien, Ireland*

MUSIC LESSON 3 ch.f. Dutch Art 126 – Triple Sharp 80 (Selkirk (USA) 129) [2017 **81**
78p: 8.3g^4 7g^2 7d^4 p8s^2 p8d 10.1g^2 p10g Oct 5] strong, stocky filly: fairly useful maiden: second in handicaps at Chelmsford in July and Epsom in September: stays 1¼m: acts on polytrack, best turf form on good going: tried in blinkers. *Hughie Morrison*

MUSIC MAJOR 4 br.g. Bertolini (USA) 125 – Music Maid (IRE) 74 (Inzar (USA) 112) **78**
[2017 76: p10m* p10g^5 p8g^6 8g p8g p8g p10m* p10g^2 Dec 13] sturdy gelding: fair handicapper: won at Lingfield in February and November: stays 1¼m: acts on polytrack and tapeta. *Michael Attwater*

MUSICO (IRE) 3 b.g. Lilbourne Lad (IRE) 111 – Viola da Gamba (IRE) 76 (Alhaarth –
(IRE) 126) [2017 58: 8g Apr 30] little impact in maidens. *Patrick Holmes*

MUSIC SEEKER (IRE) 3 b.g. Henrythenavigator (USA) 131 – Danehill Music (IRE) **89 §**
106 (Danehill Dancer (IRE) 117) [2017 52p: 8s* 8d^6 10v^3 9.9d^6 8.3d Oct 4] fairly useful performer: won maiden at Newmarket (by 3 lengths from Tadween) in May: third in handicap at Newbury in July: should be suited by 1¼m: acts on soft going: tried in blinkers: sometimes slowly away: sold 9,000 gns in October: temperamental. *James Eustace*

MUSIC SOCIETY (IRE) 2 b.c. (Apr 29) Society Rock (IRE) 126 – Absolutely Cool (IRE) 74 (Indian Ridge 123) [2017 6.1g^{2} p7s* t6.1d^{2} Dec 9] €70,000Y: half-brother to several winners, including smart winner up to 1m Kool Kompany (2-y-o 5f/6f winner, by Jeremy) and useful French 6f-1¼m winner Ridge City (by Elusive City): dam maiden (stayed 1m): useful form: won minor event at Chelmsford (by 4½ lengths from Blue Candy) in November: best effort when second in similar event at Wolverhampton (length behind Never Back Down) in December: stays 7f: open to further improvement. *Sylvester Kirk* **101 p**

MUSIKEL (IRE) 3 ch.g. Frankel 147 – Musical Treat (IRE) 98 (Royal Academy (USA) 130) [2017 71: t8g* 8m 8.3d^{3} 9v^{3} 10.3d^{6} p12g Dec 13] lengthy, angular gelding: fair performer: won maiden at Newcastle in March: left K. R. Burke after fifth start: stays 9f: acts on tapeta and heavy going: in cheekpieces last 4 starts. *Chris Gordon* **76**

MUSTAAQEEM (USA) 5 b.g. Dynaformer (USA) – Wasseema (USA) 111 (Danzig (USA)) [2017 96: 12d t12.4g^{6} Dec 6] well-made gelding: fairly useful handicapper: stays 12.5f: acts on polytrack, tapeta, good to firm and good to soft going: tried in visor. *Richard Fahey* **92**

MUSTAJEER 4 b.g. Medicean 128 – Qelaan (USA) 93 (Dynaformer (USA)) [2017 105p: t12.4s 12m 11.6m^{4} 10s* 12s^{3} Nov 5] close-coupled gelding: useful handicapper: won at Naas (by 3¼ lengths from Espoir d'Soleil) in October: third in listed race there (3¼ lengths behind Tocco d'Amore) in November: left Owen Burrows after third start: stays 1½m: acts on polytrack and soft going. *G. M. Lyons, Ireland* **105**

MUSTAQBAL (IRE) 5 b.g. Invincible Spirit (IRE) 121 – Alshamatry (USA) (Seeking The Gold (USA)) [2017 81: 8m 8m^{6} 7.8v^{2} 7.8g^{4} 10g 7.8m 7.8s 7g^{3} 8d 8.5v^{3} 8s* 9v^{5} Oct 12] fair handicapper: won at Ayr (apprentice) in October: stays 8.5f: acts on good to firm and heavy going: wears cheekpieces: often races towards rear/travels strongly. *Michael Dods* **76**

MUSTARRID (IRE) 3 b.g. Elzaam (AUS) 115 – Symbol of Peace (IRE) 85 (Desert Sun 120) [2017 84p: p8g* 8m^{2} 8.2f^{5} 8s^{2} 8d 8.2d p8g Sep 9] compact gelding: useful handicapper: won at Chelmsford (by 1¼ lengths from Drochaid) in April: second at Doncaster in May (head behind City of Joy) and June (2¼ lengths behind Century Dream): stays 1m: acts on polytrack, tapeta, soft and good to firm going: sold 40,000 gns in November. *Richard Hannon* **102**

MUSTASHRY 4 b.c. Tamayuz 126 – Safwa (IRE) 85 (Green Desert (USA) 127) [2017 116: 8s p8g* 8.8m* 8d Sep 29] useful-looking colt: very smart performer: won handicap at Chelmsford (by ½ length from Masham Star) and Strensall Stakes at York (by ¾ length from Forest Ranger) in August: stays 9f: acts on polytrack, good to firm and good to soft going. *Sir Michael Stoute* **121**

MUST BE AMAZING 3 b.f. Foxwedge (AUS) 128 – Be Amazing (IRE) 71 (Refuse To Bend (IRE) 128) [2017 55: 6d^{6} 9.5g* 9.9g^{3} 12.9m* 11.9g^{3} a12.9g^{2} Dec 21] fairly useful performer: left Jeremy Gask after reappearance: won maiden and minor event at Nimes in October/November: stays 13f: acts on polytrack and good to firm going. *J. Reynier, France* **83**

MUST BE MAGIC (IRE) 2 b.f. (Feb 4) Camelot 128 – Saturn Girl (IRE) 78 (Danehill Dancer (IRE) 117) [2017 8d^{4} Sep 23] fourth foal: dam, 1m winner, half-sister to smart 1m-1¼m winner Livadiya and to dam of very smart performer up to 1¼m Linngari: 16/1, fourth in minor event at Newmarket (4¼ lengths behind Stream Song) in September: open to improvement. *Andrew Balding* **78 p**

MUSTN'T GRUMBLE (IRE) 4 ch.g. Intense Focus (USA) 117 – Lough Mist (IRE) 93 (Captain Rio 122) [2017 70: f7g^{3} f6g^{3} f6g f7g^{6} Jan 30] fair handicapper: stayed 7f: acted on polytrack, fibresand, soft and good to firm going: often wore headgear: often raced prominently: dead. *David Loughnane* **66**

MUTAAQEB 2 b.c. (Mar 26) Invincible Spirit (IRE) 121 – Mejala (IRE) 74 (Red Ransom (USA)) [2017 6d* 6d^{2} Oct 28] fourth foal: closely related to a winner in Hungary by Cape Cross: dam, 1¼m winner, half-sister to smart 7f/1m performer Muwaary: useful form: won minor event at Yarmouth (by neck from Rule of Honour) in September: second in listed race at Doncaster (½ length behind Speak In Colours) in October: will be suited by 7f: will go on improving. *Owen Burrows* **104 p**

MUTABAAHY (IRE) 2 b.g. (Apr 6) Oasis Dream 129 – Habaayib 108 (Royal Applause 124) [2017 5g 6d^{5} 6v^{4} 6d^{5} Oct 24] well-made gelding: modest form: likely to stay 7f: in hood last 3 starts. *Ed Dunlop* **60**

MUTADAFFEQ (IRE) 4 b.g. New Approach (IRE) 132 – Saajidah (USA) 101 (Dynaformer (USA)) [2017 81: 12g* 12g* 11.6m^{2} 13.1g^{5} 12v 12s* 12g^{6} 12s 10.3g Oct 14] useful handicapper: won at Thirsk and Pontefract in May, and at Pontefract again (by head **97**

from Sennockian Star) in August: stays 12.5f: acts on tapeta, soft and good to firm going: often races prominently. *David O'Meara*

MUTAFARRID (IRE) 2 gr.g. (Feb 18) Dark Angel (IRE) 113 – Margarita (IRE) 72 **84 p** (Marju (IRE) 127) [2017 6.5g p7s^4 t6.1g^5 7g* Oct 16] 250,000F: useful-looking gelding: fourth foal: half-brother to 2-y-o 6f winner Meetyouatthemoon (by Excelebration) and a winner in Italy by Cape Cross: dam, maiden (stayed 1m), sister to high-class miler Soviet Song and half-sister to grandam of top-class 5f performer Marsha: fairly useful form: won nursery at Yarmouth (by 3¾ lengths from Catapult) in October: stays 7f: open to further improvement. *Owen Burrows*

MUTAHAADY (IRE) 3 b.g. Elzaam (AUS) 115 – Midnight Oasis 49 (Oasis Dream 129) **92** [2017 94: 7m 7g 8g* 8d^3 Jul 5] fairly useful handicapper: won at Redcar (by ½ length from Ginger Jack) in June: stays 1m: acts on polytrack and soft going: sold 52,000 gns in July, sent to Bahrain. *K. R. Burke*

MUTAJAWEL (USA) 2 b.c. (Apr 14) Lonhro (AUS) 128 – How Cheeky (USA) (Mr **–** Greeley (USA) 122) [2017 p7g Sep 27] 9/1, very green when well held in minor event at Kempton. *Charles Hills*

MUTAKATIF (IRE) 2 b.c. (Apr 29) Acclamation 118 – Gorband (USA) 59 (Woodman **93** (USA) 126) [2017 6f^2 6.5g^2 6.5m^3 7g* Sep 2] €600,000Y: lengthy colt: brother to very smart 2-y-o 6f (including Richmond Stakes) winner Harbour Watch and half-brother to 3 winners, including useful 6f-1m winner Ghalib (by Lope de Vega): dam maiden in UAE (best effort at 1¼m): fairly useful form: won minor event at Chester (by neck from Spud) in September: stays 7f. *Charles Hills*

MUTAKAYYEF 6 ch.g. Sea The Stars (IRE) 140 – Infallible 114 (Pivotal 124) [2017 125: **125** 8.9d^5 8f^2 8g* Jul 15] lengthy gelding: high-class performer: won Summer Mile Stakes at Ascot (by 3 lengths from Kaspersky) in July (returned lame): second in Queen Anne Stakes at Royal Ascot (1¼ lengths behind Ribchester) in June: stays 10.5f: acts on firm and soft going: has worn headgear, including in 2017: often travels strongly. *William Haggas*

MUTAMADED (IRE) 4 b.g. Arcano (IRE) 122 – Sahaayeb (IRE) 77 (Indian Haven 119) **97** [2017 7m 10d 9.8g* 10.3v Sep 30] useful handicapper: won newcomers race in France for Jean-Claude Rouget at 2 yrs: also won at Ripon (by ½ length from Mulligatawny) in August: left Brian Meehan after first start: stays 1¼m: has worn headgear. *Ruth Carr*

MUTAMID 5 b.g. Medicean 128 – Inchberry 110 (Barathea (IRE) 127) [2017 90: t7.1g^2 **90** t7.1s p6g^6 p7d^2 p8g^6 8.3g Jul 21] sturdy gelding: fairly useful handicapper: second at Newcastle in March and Kempton in May: stays 8.5f: acts on all-weather: sold 5,000 gns in October. *Ismail Mohammed*

MUTANAASEQ (IRE) 2 ch.c. (Mar 26) Red Jazz (USA) 125 – Indaba (IRE) 98 (Indian **85** Ridge 123) [2017 5f* 5m* 7g^4 Aug 12] 70,000F, 125,000Y: strong, compact colt: half-brother to useful 2-y-o 5f winner Ahlan Emarati (by Holy Roman Emperor) and a winner in South Africa by Cape Cross: dam, 6f/7f winner, half-sister to useful dam of high-class 1½m performer Shirocco: fairly useful form: won minor events at Bath (by short head from Big Time Maybe) in April and Doncaster (by head from Bengali Boys) in May: best form at 5f. *Richard Hannon*

MUTANAQEL 2 b.g. (Feb 11) Havana Gold (IRE) 118 – Audaz (Oasis Dream 129) [2017 **74 p** 8g^5 p8g^3 Oct 26] 40,000F: fourth foal: half-brother to 11.5f-2m winner Authorized Too (by Authorized): dam useful French 9f/1¼m winner: fair form: better effort when fifth in maiden at Newmarket (9 lengths behind Ghaiyyath) on debut: remains with potential. *Owen Burrows*

MUTARABBY (IRE) 3 ch.c. Tamayuz 126 – Shaarfa (USA) (Dynaformer (USA)) [2017 **106 p** 81p: 10g^2 10d^3 8m^2 p8s* p8g^2 Aug 8] useful performer: won handicap at Chelmsford (by ½ length from Mukalal) in July: stays 1¼m: acts on polytrack, good to firm and good to soft going: tried in cheekpieces: sometimes slowly away: remains open to improvement. *Saeed bin Suroor*

MUTARAKEZ (IRE) 5 ch.g. Fast Company (IRE) 126 – Nightswimmer (IRE) 75 **95 §** (Noverre (USA) 125) [2017 80: p8f^5 8g 8m 8m 8s^3 8.5m p8s^3 9.9m^3 10g 9.9g 10.2d^6 10s^6 Oct 28] sturdy gelding: useful handicapper: third at Newbury (1½ lengths behind Withernsea) in May, Chelmsford (¾ length behind Wealth Tax) in June and Sandown (length behind Euginio) in July: stays 1¼m: acts on polytrack and soft going: tried in headgear: often races in rear: sold to join Ruth Carr £22,000 in November: temperamental. *Brian Meehan*

MUTAWAKKED (IRE) 3 b.g. Kodiac 112 – Your Opinion (IRE) (Xaar 132) [2017 91: 5.7f³ 6d⁵ 7g 8m² 8g⁶ 8.2d⁴ Aug 12] useful-looking gelding: fairly useful handicapper: placed at Bath in May and Haydock in June: stays 1m: acts on good to firm going: sent to UAE. *Brian Meehan* **86**

MUTAWATHEA 6 b.g. Exceed And Excel (AUS) 126 – Esteemed Lady (IRE) 96 (Mark of Esteem (IRE) 137) [2017 109: 7g⁴ a8f 7g⁶ 7m⁶ 7m² 7g 7s² 7s p7g p8s* p8g⁶ Dec 31] strong gelding: useful handicapper: won at Chelmsford (by 1¾ lengths from London) in December: second at York (¾ length behind Viscount Barfield) in June: stays 1m: acts on polytrack and good to firm going: wears cheekpieces: usually races close up. *Simon Crisford* **109**

MUTAWATHEB (IRE) 3 gr.c. Dark Angel (IRE) 113 – Queen Myrine (IRE) (Oratorio (IRE) 128) [2017 97: p8g² 7.6m* May 11] tall colt: useful handicapper: won at Chester (by 1¼ lengths from Masham Star) in May: stayed 1m: acted on polytrack, good to firm and good to soft going: front runner/raced prominently: dead. *Richard Hannon* **104**

MUTHMIRA 3 ch.f. Arcano (IRE) 122 – Carding (USA) (Street Cry (IRE) 130) [2017 89p: p7gᵖᵘ Apr 20] fairly useful 6f winner at 2 yrs: dead. *Simon Crisford* **–**

MUTHMIR (IRE) 7 b.g. Invincible Spirit (IRE) 121 – Fairy of The Night (IRE) 107 (Danehill (USA) 126) [2017 118: 5.7m* 5m 5g* 5f⁴ 5m⁴ 5.2m³ Sep 23] good-topped gelding: very smart performer: won minor event at Bath (by 1¼ lengths from Mr Lupton) in April and Prix du Gros-Chene at Chantilly (by length from Finsbury Square) in June: third in World Trophy at Newbury (1½ lengths behind Take Cover) in September: has won at 6f, probably best at 5f: acts on firm going: has worn cheekpieces, including last 4 starts: usually races towards rear. *William Haggas* **121**

MUTHRAAB ALDAAR (IRE) 4 b.g. Baltic King 120 – Vertigo On Course (IRE) 69 (Anabaa (USA) 130) [2017 77: p7d² p7m⁵ t8.6g* p8s⁴ 8.5f p8g 8.1d p8s⁶ Nov 16] fair handicapper: won at Wolverhampton in June: stays 9.5f: acts on polytrack and tapeta. *Jim Boyle* **70**

MUTINEER 3 ch.g. Sepoy (AUS) 129 – Violet (IRE) 77 (Mukaddamah (USA) 125) [2017 68: 8f⁶ 6.9g⁶ 7d⁶ p8d⁵ t8.6g² p8s* t8.6g* 8g p10d⁶ p8g p8g³ p8s⁵ Dec 8] fairly useful handicapper: won at Kempton and Wolverhampton (by 5 lengths from Top Offer) in August: stays 8.5f: acts on polytrack and tapeta. *Daniel Kubler* **84**

MUTOONDRESDASHORSE 3 ch.g. Harbour Watch (IRE) 121 – Mutoon (IRE) 64 (Erhaab (USA) 127) [2017 73p: 7s* p7d 6d⁶ 7gᵖᵘ Jul 21] strong gelding: fairly useful performer: won maiden at Newbury (by ¾ length from Alqalsar) in May: stays 7f: acts on soft going: tried in blinkers/tongue tie: often races towards rear: sold to join Nigel Hawke £1,500 in September. *Paul Cole* **81**

MUZAAHIM (IRE) 6 ch.g. Tamayuz 126 – Elizabeth Swann 95 (Bahamian Bounty 116) [2017 61: p10g² p8g t8.6g³ t8s⁶ t8.6g 10.2g Jul 8] modest maiden: stays 1¼m: acts on polytrack, tapeta and good to soft going: wears headgear. *Laura Morgan* **63**

MUZAAWEL 2 ch.c. (Jan 30) New Approach (IRE) 132 – Jilnaar (IRE) (Dansili 127) [2017 7g⁵ Sep 27] first foal: dam, French 9f winner, half-sister to very smart stayer Honolulu: 5/2, well held in maiden at Redcar: should do better. *Saeed bin Suroor* **– p**

Prix du Gros-Chene, Chantilly—Muthmir is driven out to win this race for the second time in three years, with Finsbury Square and the grey Plusquemavie filling the places

MY AMIGO 4 gr.g. Stimulation (IRE) 121 – Blue Crest (FR) (Verglas (IRE) 118) [2017 96: 6g 7s^5 8.2v^4 7d t8d t7.1g^3 t7.2d Dec 26] fairly useful handicapper: third at Newcastle in December: stays 7f: acts on good to firm and good to soft going: in cheekpieces last 4 starts: sometimes slowly away. *K. R. Burke* **83**

MY ANGEL 3 gr.f. Dark Angel (IRE) 113 – Tanda Tula (IRE) (Alhaarth (IRE) 126) [2017 6m^5 7g 7d 7s Sep 23] £50,000Y: fourth foal: sister to useful 6f and (including at 2 yrs) 7f winner My Sharona: dam twice-raced half-sister to smart 6f winner Stormont: little impact in maidens/handicap. *Ollie Pears* **–**

MYBOYHENRY (IRE) 2 b.g. (Jan 29) Footstepsinthesand 120 – Renaissance Rio (IRE) (Captain Rio 122) [2017 6m^5 7.2m* 7.2d* 8g 7g^2 7g Sep 28] €38,000F, €68,000Y: first foal: dam, ran once, closely related to smart sprinter Artistic Jewel: fairly useful performer: won minor events at Musselburgh in July and August (by ¾ length from Phoenix Lightning): stays 7f: acts on good to firm and good to soft going: front runner/races prominently. *K. R. Burke* **87**

MY BOY SEPOY 2 ch.c. (Mar 16) Sepoy (AUS) 129 – Emily Carr (IRE) 75 (Teofilo (IRE) 126) [2017 p7g^3 Dec 20] second foal: dam, second from 3 starts at 1m, out of half-sister to Prix de la Foret winner Septieme Ciel and Prix Marcel Boussac winner Macoumba: 50/1, third in minor event at Kempton (11 lengths behind Mr Ritz) in December: capable of better. *Stuart Williams* **61 p**

MY BROTHER (IRE) 4 b.g. Roderic O'Connor (IRE) 119 – Victory Peak (Shirley Heights 130) [2017 79: 11.1g^2 12.1g^6 14d 11.8g 10v Sep 20] fairly useful handicapper: second at Hamilton in June: stays 11f: acts on heavy going: wears cheekpieces: usually races close up: sold 21,000 gns in October. *L. Smyth, Ireland* **91**

MYBROTHERJOHNNY 6 b.g. Tiger Hill (IRE) 127 – Montjeu's Melody (IRE) 74 (Montjeu (IRE) 137) [2017 –: t16.5g p12d Jan 17] workmanlike gelding: no form: tried in hood: in tongue tie last 2 starts. *Fergal O'Brien* **–**

MY BROTHER MIKE (IRE) 3 b.g. Bated Breath 125 – Coming Back 89 (Fantastic Light (USA) 134) [2017 –: p8g^6 p10g^5 12d t9.5g^2 11.6m^5 t10.2s* p10g^4 t10.2g^2 t9.5m t12.2g^6 p12g^4 Dec 20] fair handicapper: won at Newcastle in September: left Daniel Loughnane after second start: stays 1½m: acts on polytrack and tapeta. *Kevin Frost* **79**

MY BRUNETTE (IRE) 3 br.f. Arcano (IRE) 122 – Holda (IRE) 81 (Docksider (USA) 124) [2017 8.1m^4 t8.6g Dec 5] tall filly: fifth foal: half-sister to 3 winners, including smart 1m-1¼m winner Blond Me (by Tamayuz) and 6f (including at 2 yrs) winner Red Larkspur (by Red Clubs): dam, 2-y-o 7f winner, half-sister to winner up to 11f Glass Harmonium and 1¼m-1½m winner Arab Spring (both very smart): fair form when fourth at Windsor on first of 2 starts in maidens: remains with potential. *Geoffrey Deacon* **68 p**

MY CHEROKEE 3 b.f. Sleeping Indian 122 – Another Paris (Paris House 123) [2017 6m Jul 13] third foal: half-sister to 11f-17f winner Another Lincolnday (by Desideratum): dam unraced sister to smart 7f-9f winner My Paris: 14/1, well held in maiden at Doncaster. *Michael Dods* **–**

MY CHERRY BLOSSOM 3 b.f. Kyllachy 129 – Echo River (USA) 101 (Irish River (FR) 131) [2017 68: 5g^6 6g Jun 5] fair form at 2 yrs, behind in handicaps in 2017: best effort at 5f: acts on good to soft going: sometimes slowly away. *Tim Easterby* **–**

MYDADSARED 2 b.g. (Feb 12) Captain Gerrard (IRE) 113 – Hoppy's Flyer (FR) 75 (Country Reel (USA) 113) [2017 7m 7g Aug 26] well beaten in minor events: tried in tongue tie. *Tony Coyle* **–**

MY DAD SYD (USA) 5 b.g. Acclamation 118 – Weekend Fling (USA) 68 (Forest Wildcat (USA) 120) [2017 83: 6m^5 6m^3 7g^2 7g 7g t6g Oct 20] angular gelding: fairly useful handicapper: placed at York in June and Ascot in July: stays 7f: acts on polytrack, tapeta, soft and good to firm going: usually wears headgear: usually races prominently: sold 10,000 gns in October. *Ian Williams* **85**

MY DISTANT MURPHY 3 b.g. Distant Peak (IRE) – So Cannie (Sakhee (USA) 136) [2017 12.1g t8g^5 f12.1g Nov 28] well held in maidens: in tongue tie last 2 starts. *Jacqueline Coward* **–**

MY DREAM BOAT (IRE) 5 b.h. Lord Shanakill (USA) 121 – Betty Burke 65 (Choisir (AUS) 126) [2017 124: 10d^3 12s^2 11.9g^4 12s 10.3d 11m Sep 23] sturdy horse: very smart performer: won 6 times, notably Gordon Richards Stakes at Sandown and Prince of Wales's Stakes at Royal Ascot in 2016: best efforts in 2017 when second in Aston Park Stakes at Newbury (2 lengths behind Hawkbill) in May and fourth in Grand Prix de Saint- **120**

Cloud (2¼ lengths behind Zarak) in July: stayed 1½m: acted on soft and good to firm going: in headgear last 4 starts: often raced towards rear: to stand at Bridge House Stud, Mullingar, Co. Westmeath, fee €4,000. *Clive Cox*

MY FANTASEA (IRE) 4 b.g. Sea The Stars (IRE) 140 – Speed Song 92 (Fasliyev (USA) 120) [2017 88: f12g 13.4d 8d⁴ t8.6g p8d Oct 6] fairly useful at 3 yrs, below that level in 2017: stays 10.5f: acts on polytrack and good to soft going: tried in visor. *David Evans* **67**

MY GIRL JO (FR) 5 b.m. Whipper (USA) 126 – Prairie Moon 47 (Halling (USA) 133) [2017 f7.1g⁴ Dec 29] maiden: well held sole outing in 2017: stays 9f. *John Balding* **–**

MY GIRL MAISIE (IRE) 3 b.f. Fast Company (IRE) 126 – Queen Al Andalous (IRE) (King's Best (USA) 132) [2017 –: t7.1g³ t6.1g³ 5.9s* 6d⁵ 6g⁶ t7.2g 6m² 7.2m* 6v² p7d⁵ 7.2s* 7d² t7.1d⁴ Nov 10] fair handicapper: won at Carlisle in June and Musselburgh in August/October: stays 7f: acts on good to firm and heavy going. *Richard Guest* **73**

MY GUY (IRE) 2 b.g. (Feb 17) Lilbourne Lad (IRE) 111 – Royale Life (FR) (Anabaa (USA) 130) [2017 5m 5.3m⁶ t7.2g p7d p7g Sep 6] poor maiden: in cheekpieces last 2 starts. *J. S. Moore* **37**

MY HEART 2 b.f. (Apr 17) Universal (IRE) 121 – Mazuna (IRE) 110 (Cape Cross (IRE) 129) [2017 p7d Nov 22] half-sister to 3 winners, including smart winner up to 1¾m (stays 2m) Beautiful Romance (2-y-o 1m winner, by New Approach) and useful 2-y-o 6f winner (stays 9f) Executive Force (by Sepoy): dam 11.5f/1½m winner who stayed 14.6f: 50/1, well held in minor event at Kempton. *Ismail Mohammed* **–**

MYHORSEWITHNONAME (IRE) 3 gr.g. Lilbourne Lad (IRE) 111 – Colleville 97 (Pharly (FR) 130) [2017 –: 10s p16d Oct 6] no form: tried in visor/tongue tie. *Mark Hoad* **–**

MY ILLUSIONIST 3 b.g. Kheleyf (USA) 116 – Shimoni 90 (Mark of Esteem (IRE) 137) [2017 p8g⁶ p7g⁴ p7g t7.2g² 8d⁵ p8g p8g³ p11g² t14g⁴ p12g Dec 13] sturdy gelding: fair maiden: stays 1½m: acts on polytrack and tapeta: tried in cheekpieces: often races prominently. *Harry Dunlop* **76**

MY LADY MARIE 3 b.f. Bated Breath 125 – Poppo's Song (CAN) (Polish Navy (USA)) [2017 67: p8d Jan 18] fair form at best in Britain: sold 5,000 gns, sent to Spain, where won 9.7f minor event at Madrid in April. *Amanda Perrett* **?**

MYLLACHY 3 b.f. Kyllachy 129 – Enchanted Princess 82 (Royal Applause 124) [2017 54: 6g 7.2m 6d Jun 30] maiden: no form in 2017: in blinkers last 2 starts. *Tim Easterby* **–**

MY LORD 9 br.g. Ishiguru (USA) 114 – Lady Smith (Greensmith 121) [2017 79, a73: p12g p10g p8d³ p12g 9.9s p15.8g p12g p12g⁶ Dec 28] workmanlike gelding: fairly useful at best, little form in 2017: has worn headgear, including last 2 starts: tried in tongue tie. *Paddy Butler* **–**

MY LORD AND MASTER (IRE) 2 ch.c. (Mar 28) Mastercraftsman (IRE) 129 – Affability (IRE) (Dalakhani (IRE) 133) [2017 8.3d⁶ 8.3v* Nov 8] 65,000Y: second foal: dam unraced half-sister to smart performers Al Khaleej (at 7f/1m) and Grand Ducal (winner up to 1¼m): fairly useful form: won maiden at Nottingham (by 6 lengths from Young Rascal, unchallenged) in November: will be suited by 1¼m+: will go on improving. *William Haggas* **92 p**

MY LUCILLE (IRE) 4 b.f. Lawman (FR) 121 – Stroke of Six (IRE) 84 (Woodborough (USA) 112) [2017 84: 7g 8.1d⁵ 8d⁶ 8d⁵ Jun 30] fairly useful at 3 yrs, below that level in 2017: stays 8.5f: acts on good to firm and good to soft going: sold £4,000, sent to Greece. *Chris Wall* **71**

MY MATADOR (IRE) 6 b.g. Kandahar Run 115 – My Special (IRE) (Peintre Celebre (USA) 137) [2017 75: p12d t8d Feb 10] fair handicapper, below form in 2017: stays 12.5f: acts on polytrack: has worn cheekpieces, including in 2017: in tongue tie last 3 starts. *Victor Dartnall* **62**

MY METEOR 10 b.g. Bahamian Bounty 116 – Emerald Peace (IRE) 103 (Green Desert (USA) 127) [2017 7f 5.5g 5.7d t5.1g⁶ 5.1m⁴ Jun 26] small gelding: poor handicapper nowadays: stays 6f: acts on polytrack, tapeta, firm and soft going. *Natalie Lloyd-Beavis* **44**

MY MISTRESS (IRE) 5 ch.m. Mastercraftsman (IRE) 129 – Majestic Eviction (IRE) 94 (King's Theatre (IRE) 128) [2017 58§: t9.5m t9.5m Jan 7] modest handicapper, well held both outings in Britain in 2017: stays 11.5f: acts on polytrack, tapeta and firm going: has worn headgear/tongue tie: travels well, but no battler: sold 2,000 gns in February, sent to Italy, where won 10.4f handicap at Syracuse in May. *Phil McEntee* **?**

MY MO (FR) 5 b.g. Silver Frost (IRE) 122 – Anna Ivanovna (FR) (Fasliyev (USA) 120) **62**
[2017 74: p10g 16d^2 14m^5 Jun 15] angular gelding: modest handicapper: stays 2m: acts on polytrack, tapeta, soft and good to firm going: wears headgear: usually races prominently. *David Dennis*

MY NAME IS JEFF 3 b.g. Mount Nelson 125 – Vale of Belvoir (IRE) 96 (Mull of **61**
Kintyre (USA) 114) [2017 9.9m^6 10g^5 10s 10.1g^6 Oct 16] modest form: raced only at 1¼m. *Julia Feilden*

MY NAME IS RIO (IRE) 7 ch.g. Captain Rio 122 – Walk In My Shadow (IRE) 71 **93**
(Orpen (USA) 116) [2017 97: 6g 6m 6s 5d^2 5s* 5g^6 5s 6d^5 5s 5v Oct 23] fairly useful handicapper: won at Ayr (by 1½ lengths from Dark Defender) in June: stays 6f: acts on fibresand, soft and good to firm going: has worn cheekpieces. *Michael Dods*

MYREDBUSH (IRE) 3 b.f. Bushranger (IRE) 119 – Damask (IRE) 66 (Red Clubs (IRE) **–**
125) [2017 –: p8g Apr 7] no form: tried in blinkers. *Simon Dow*

MY RENAISSANCE 7 b.g. Medicean 128 – Lebenstanz 66 (Singspiel (IRE) 133) [2017 **71**
63: t12.2g^2 f12s* f12g* f12m^5 12g^6 9.9v^5 f12.1g Oct 22] rather leggy gelding: fair handicapper: won at Southwell in January and February: stays 12.5f: acts on all-weather and good to firm going: tried in cheekpieces: has worn tongue tie. *Sam England*

MY REWARD 5 b.g. Rail Link 132 – Tarot Card 100 (Fasliyev (USA) 120) [2017 102: **107**
14g 16g* t16.3s^5 14d^4 16.3d^2 13.4g* 12.3v^4 11.8s^3 Oct 10] workmanlike gelding: useful handicapper: won at Ripon (by length from Sir Chauvelin) in April and Chester (listed event, by ¾ length from Cape Coast) in September: placed at York (length behind Magic Circle) in August and Leicester (2¾ lengths behind Blakeney Point) in October: stays 16.5f: acts on polytrack, tapeta, good to firm and heavy going: front runner. *Tim Easterby*

MY ROCK (IRE) 2 b.g. (Feb 16) Rock of Gibraltar (IRE) 133 – Laureldean Lady (IRE) **–**
(Statue of Liberty (USA) 115) [2017 7.1s 6.1d t6g Oct 19] well held in minor events: in tongue tie last 2 starts. *David Dennis*

MY ROSIE (IRE) 3 b.f. Redoute's Choice (AUS) – My Branch 111 (Distant Relative **70**
128) [2017 –: p10m^2 t9.5g t10.2d Mar 1] fair maiden: stays 1¼m: acts on polytrack: in blinkers last 4 starts. *John Gosden*

MYSAAN (IRE) 2 ch.c. (Mar 17) Havana Gold (IRE) 118 – Oblique (IRE) 102 (Giant's **63**
Causeway (USA) 132) [2017 5.2g 6d 6.1m 6g 7.4v^3 9.7g Oct 27] modest maiden: left Brian Meehan before final outing: should stay 7f: in headgear last 4 starts. *P. & F. Monfort, France*

MY SOCIETY (IRE) 2 b.g. (May 2) Society Rock (IRE) 126 – Greek Easter (IRE) 85 **–**
(Namid 128) [2017 6d Nov 11] 66/1, well held in maiden at Doncaster. *David Dennis*

MYSTERIAL 7 b.g. Invincible Spirit (IRE) 121 – Diamond Dilemma (IRE) (Sinndar **77**
(IRE) 134) [2017 86: 10.3g 12.1m^4 14.6m^4 16m^4 12g 11.9m^6 12.1m^5 10s* 12g^6 10m^5 12s^5 12d^3 9.9g^6 12.1m 16.3d t10.2s Sep 19] smallish gelding: fair handicapper: won at Pontefract (apprentice) in July: stays 2m: acts on polytrack, soft and good to firm going: has worn headgear, including in 2017: usually leads. *Declan Carroll*

MYSTERIOUS GLANCE 4 b.f. Cacique (IRE) 124 – Largo (IRE) 94 (Selkirk (USA) **44**
129) [2017 77: 5g 5g t6.1g t5.1g^6 t5.1g t6.1d Dec 9] fair handicapper, out of sorts in 2017: stays 6f: acts on tapeta and good to firm going. *Sarah Hollinshead*

MYSTERIOUS LOOK 4 ch.f. Sakhee's Secret 128 – Look Here's Carol (IRE) 102 **80 d**
(Safawan 118) [2017 84: f5s^3 f5g 5g t5.1g^5 t5.1g Nov 25] fairly useful handicapper: third at Southwell in January: left Ed McMahon/well below form after: stays 6f: acts on all-weather and heavy going: in cheekpieces last 2 starts. *Sarah Hollinshead*

MYSTERY OF WAR (IRE) 3 b.g. Canford Cliffs (IRE) 133 – Mystiara (IRE) (Orpen **50**
(USA) 116) [2017 p8d^4 t7.2g 8m^6 11.2g 10g^5 Aug 2] modest maiden: tried in cheekpieces. *George Scott*

MYSTICAL MAC (IRE) 2 b.c. (Apr 17) Clodovil (IRE) 116 – Long Lost Love 79 **57**
(Langfuhr (CAN) 124) [2017 5v t6g^5 Oct 19] modest form when fifth in minor event at Newcastle on second of 2 starts. *Iain Jardine*

MYSTICAL NELLY 3 b.f. Sakhee's Secret 128 – Dancing Nelly 52 (Shareef Dancer **56**
(USA) 135) [2017 –: p12m^3 12d 9g^4 9.9m Jun 20] modest maiden: best effort at 9f. *Jonathan Portman*

MYSTICAL SPIRIT (FR) 5 ch.g. Spirit One (FR) 122 – Miss Maguilove (FR) (Dyhim **78**
Diamond (IRE) 117) [2017 90: p7g^6 Feb 1] fairly useful handicapper, below form sole outing in 2017: stays 8.5f: acts on polytrack, soft and good to firm going. *Martyn Meade*

MYSTIC DAWN (IRE) 3 b.f. Oasis Dream 129 – Frivolity (Pivotal 124) [2017 94: 7m^6 6.1g 6f^5 6g* Jul 14] smallish filly: useful performer: won Summer Stakes at York (by short head from Queen Kindly) in July: stays 7f: acts on good to firm going. *David Simcock* **108**

MYSTIC MAEVE (IRE) 3 b.f. Tagula (IRE) 116 – Celtic Lynn (IRE) 83 (Celtic Swing 138) [2017 –: t10.2g 14m 12g Jul 3] rather lightly-made filly: little form: often in headgear. *Roger Fell* **–**

MYSTIC MEG 2 b.f. (Feb 8) Camelot 128 – Hypnology (USA) (Gone West (USA)) [2017 8d^2 Sep 23] 67,000Y: fifth foal: half-sister to 1m winner Trust The Wind (by Dansili): dam, unraced, closely related to smart performer up to 1¼m Hathal out of 1000 Guineas winner Sleepytime: in hood, 5/2, second in minor event at Newmarket (8 lengths behind Magic Lily) in September: open to improvement. *Hugo Palmer* **77 p**

MYSTIKANA 4 ch.f. Sir Percy 129 – Peintre d'Argent (IRE) 84 (Peintre Celebre (USA) 137) [2017 78: p12g p12d^5 p12g* p13.3d^2 11.5d Oct 24] leggy filly: fairly useful handicapper: won at Lingfield (by 3 lengths from The Ginger Berry) in February: second at Chelmsford (apprentice) in March: stays 13.5f: acts on polytrack and soft going: wears headgear: in tongue tie last 3 starts: often races towards rear: sold to join Keith Dalgleish 8,000 gns in November. *Marcus Tregoning* **80**

MYSTIQUE 2 b.f. (Apr 3) Oasis Dream 129 – Hidden Brief 100 (Barathea (IRE) 127) [2017 6m p7g Nov 8] 55,000Y: fourth foal: closely related to useful winner up to 1m Mushaireb (2-y-o 7f winner, by Invincible Spirit): dam, 1¼m winner, sister to smart performer up to 1½m Hazarista and half-sister to useful dam of Derby winner Harzand: little impact in minor events. *Charles Hills* **–**

MYSTIQUE MOON 3 ch.g. Shamardal (USA) 129 – Celestial Girl 84 (Dubai Destination (USA) 127) [2017 t7.1g* t8d* p8g^2 p8g^4 Dec 31] 450,000Y: second foal: dam 1¼m winner who stayed 1½m: useful form: won maiden at Wolverhampton in January and handicap at Newcastle (by ¾ length from Indian Dandy) in February: second in handicap at Chelmsford (length behind Arabian Hope) in April: stays 1m: remains capable of better. *Charlie Appleby* **102 p**

MY TARGET (IRE) 6 b.g. Cape Cross (IRE) 129 – Chercheuse (USA) 110 (Seeking The Gold (USA)) [2017 92, a102: p8g* p8g* p8f* t7.1g^6 p8g 7.6g 8m p8g Dec 31] smart handicapper: won at Lingfield in January (by 1¼ lengths from Mr Bossy Boots), February (by 1¼ lengths from Intransigent) and March (by ½ length from Franco's Secret): stays 1m: acts on polytrack, tapeta and good to soft going. *Michael Wigham* **111**

MYTHICAL MADNESS 6 b.g. Dubawi (IRE) 129 – Miss Delila (USA) (Malibu Moon (USA)) [2017 105: t9.5g^2 t8.6m* p10g^5 t8.6g^2 p10m p8g 8m 10.3d 8.5m^2 8m* 10m 8m 8s 7.9d t9.5g^6 p8s^5 t9.5d^5 Dec 26] sturdy gelding: useful handicapper: won at Wolverhampton (by length from Supersta) in January and Haydock (by 1¾ lengths from Calder Prince) in June: second at Epsom (length behind G K Chesterton) earlier in June: stays 1¼m: acts on polytrack, tapeta, good to firm and good to soft going: wears headgear. *David O'Meara* **108**

MYTHICAL MAGIC (IRE) 2 b.c. (Feb 7) Iffraaj 127 – Mythie (FR) (Octagonal (NZ) 126) [2017 6d* 7d* 7g^3 8d^5 7s^3 Oct 28] 140,000F: strong, good sort: half-brother to several winners, including 7f-8.5f winners Yojimbo (by Aussie Rules) and Esentepe (2-y-o 1m winner, by Oratorio), latter useful: dam French 10.5f winner: useful performer: won newcomers race at Ascot (by 2¼ lengths from No I'm Easy) in July and listed race at Deauville (by ¾ length from Cascadian) in August: third in Champagne Stakes at Doncaster (½ length behind Seahenge) in September and Horris Hill Stakes at Newbury (1¼ lengths behind Nebo) in October: should stay 1m: acts on soft going: front runner/races prominently. *Charlie Appleby* **108**

MYTHICAL SPIRIT (IRE) 3 b.f. Dragon Pulse (IRE) 114 – Call This Cat (IRE) 66 (One Cool Cat (USA) 123) [2017 –: t7.1g^5 p7g^4 p7s^6 t6.1g^3 Jul 11] fair maiden: stays 7f: acts on polytrack and tapeta: often races prominently: has joined Julie Camacho. *James Tate* **66**

MYTHMAKER 5 b.g. Major Cadeaux 121 – Mythicism 80 (Oasis Dream 129) [2017 108: t5g^6 p6g^2 p6g^5 6m* 6f^2 6m p6g^2 t6.1d^3 Dec 26] sturdy gelding: smart performer: won minor event at Haydock (by neck from Aeolus) in May: second in listed races at Lingfield (nose behind Lancelot du Lac) in February, Salisbury (neck behind Eqtiraan) in June and Lingfield again (1½ lengths behind Gifted Master) in November: best at 6f: acts on polytrack, tapeta, soft and good to firm going: front runner/races prominently. *Bryan Smart* **112**

MYTHOLOGICAL (IRE) 2 gr.c. (Feb 23) Galileo (IRE) 134 – Pembina (IRE) (Dalakhani (IRE) 133) [2017 8.1g 10m p8g Dec 21] rangy colt: little impact in minor events/maiden: left John Gosden after second start. *Peter Chapple-Hyam* **–**

MY TIME 8 b.g. Mind Games 121 – Tick Tock 68 (Timeless Times (USA) 99) [2017 51: 7d Jun 5] modest handicapper, well held sole outing in 2017: stays 7f: acts on polytrack, fibresand and good to firm going: wears headgear: usually races nearer last than first. *Michael Mullineaux* –

MY VALENTINO (IRE) 4 ch.g. Duke of Marmalade (IRE) 132 – Nadwah (USA) 107 (Shadeed (USA) 135) [2017 63: t10.2g 11.2s Aug 7] modest maiden, well held both starts in 2017: stays 1m: best form on good going: has worn cheekpieces, including final start: tried in tongue tie: often races in rear. *Dianne Sayer* –

MYWAYISTHEONLYWAY (IRE) 4 b.g. Tamayuz 126 – Soul Custody (CAN) 100 (Perfect Soul (IRE) 122) [2017 83: 6m t8s^{6} 7.2s 7.4m^{5} 7.4f* 7v^{6} 7d t7.1d^{3} Sep 29] fairly useful handicapper: won at Beverley in July: third at Newcastle in September: stays 7.5f: acts on polytrack, firm and soft going: tried in headgear/tongue tie. *Grant Tuer* **83**

MZOON (IRE) 2 b.f. (Feb 14) Dark Angel (IRE) 113 – Lethal Lena (IRE) (Thousand Words 113) [2017 6s^{5} p6g^{5} Oct 9] 125,000F, 110,000 2-y-o: first foal: dam unraced half-sister to high-class 6f/7f performer Lethal Force (by Dark Angel): modest form: better effort when fifth in minor event at Haydock (2¼ lengths behind Pulitzer) on debut: remains with potential. *Charlie Fellowes* **63 p**

N

NAAB (FR) 3 ch.c. Siyouni (FR) 122 – Magdala (FR) (Hawk Wing (USA) 136) [2017 t7.1g^{2} p7g 7d^{5} 6g 6g^{3} 6g^{5} 5.5g* 6d* 5.5d^{4} 5g 6g* 6d^{2} 6s 6.5d^{4} 6d^{2} p6.5f Nov 29] €40,000F, €70,000Y, €100,000 2-y-o: fourth foal: half-brother to 9.2f/1¼m winner Mega Bowl and 1¼m-1½m winner Lady Ionela (both by Turtle Bowl): dam, 9.5f/1¼m winner, half-sister to useful 7f/1m winner Kite Hunter: fairly useful performer: won claimer at Le Croise-Laroche in June, and handicaps at Deauville in July and Fontainebleau in September: left John Gosden after first start, Francis-Henri Graffard after seventh: stays 7f: acts on tapeta and good to soft going: tried in hood. *Mlle C. Fey, France* **91**

NAADIRR (IRE) 6 b.g. Oasis Dream 129 – Beach Bunny (IRE) 114 (High Chaparral (IRE) 132) [2017 113§: 6g 6g^{6} 6g^{5} t7.1g 6m 5g 6g p6g 6d^{3} p6g^{6} Dec 15] robust gelding: useful handicapper: third at Doncaster (½ length behind Perfect Pasture) in October: left Marco Botti after fourth start: best at 6f: acts on polytrack, good to firm and good to soft going: usually wears headgear: usually races nearer last than first, often travels strongly: temperamental. *Kevin Ryan* **103 §**

NAAEEBB (USA) 3 b.c. Lonhro (AUS) 128 – My Dubai (IRE) 76 (Dubai Millennium 140) [2017 8m^{5} 7d^{3} t8s^{5} a8f* a8f Nov 23] seventh foal: half-brother to 3 winners, including 7f winner Mizwaaj (by Invincible Spirit) and 6f-1m winner Mishaal (by Kheleyf), both useful: dam once-raced half-sister to winner up to 7f Iffraaj and winner up to 10.4f Farraaj (both high-class): fairly useful performer: won handicap at Meydan (by 1¼ lengths from Conquerant) in November: stays 1m: acts on dirt: tried in cheekpieces. *Saeed bin Suroor* **86**

NABHAN 5 b.g. Youmzain (IRE) 131 – Danidh Dubai (IRE) 93 (Noverre (USA) 125) [2017 89: 12.3d 13.4g^{6} 12v^{4} 14g* 16d^{2} 16g 14.4v Sep 16] lengthy gelding: fairly useful handicapper: won at Ffos Las (by 2¼ lengths from Moojaned) in July: stays 2m: acts on good to firm and good to soft going: wears cheekpieces: often wears tongue tie: usually races towards rear. *Bernard Llewellyn* **81**

NACHI FALLS 4 ch.g. New Approach (IRE) 132 – Lakuta (IRE) (Pivotal 124) [2017 t12.2g^{5} t12.2g^{4} t16.3s^{2} 16m^{2} Jun 16] fair maiden: stays 16.5f: acts on tapeta and good to firm going: wears tongue tie: fairly useful hurdler/chaser. *Nigel Hawke* **79**

NADAITAK 3 b.g. Teofilo (IRE) 126 – Tanfidh 93 (Marju (IRE) 127) [2017 12m^{2} p12d^{3} 11.2d* 14d^{2} 14.4s p16g^{2} 14.1d^{6} Sep 21] fourth foal: half-brother to 7f-1m winner Kestrel Dot Com (by Oasis Dream): dam, 1¼m winner, half-sister to smart 7f-1¼m winner Makderah: fairly useful performer: won maiden at Carlisle in July: second in handicaps at Sandown later in July and Kempton in August: stays 2m: acts on polytrack, good to firm and good to soft going: in headgear last 3 starts: sold to join Ben Pauling £80,000 in November: one to treat with caution. *Sir Michael Stoute* **94 §**

NADIA PROMISE 3 ch.f. Galileo (IRE) 134 – Majestic Sakeena (IRE) (King's Best (USA) 132) [2017 8f^{3} Jul 12] closely related to useful 2-y-o 7f winner (stayed 10.5f) Lady Nouf (by Teofilo) and half-sister to several winners, including smart 7f/1m winner Yuften (by Invincible Spirit) and useful 1¼m/10.4f winner Nouriya (by Danehill Dancer): dam unraced: 8/13, last of 3 in maiden at Bath (3¾ lengths behind Unified) in July: should do better. *William Haggas* **66 p**

NAFAATH (IRE) 11 ch.g. Nayef (USA) 129 – Alshakr 108 (Bahri (USA) 125) [2017 71: f16g^4 12g^2 13.1m^5 14v^6 Jun 8] good-bodied gelding: modest handicapper nowadays: stays 2½m: acts on good to firm and heavy going: wears headgear. *Donald McCain* **64**

NAFAAYES (IRE) 3 ch.f. Sea The Stars (IRE) 140 – Shamtari (IRE) (Alhaarth (IRE) 126) [2017 10g Apr 21] third foal: half-sister to useful 6f (including at 2 yrs) winner Greeb (by Oasis Dream): dam unraced sister to high-class winner up to 1¼m Haafhd out of Irish 1000 Guineas winner Al Bahathri: 20/1, never a threat in maiden at Newbury: has joined Jean-Rene Auvray. *Charles Hills* **–**

NAGAMAAT (IRE) 3 b.f. Raven's Pass (USA) 133 – Shawka 70 (Oasis Dream 129) [2017 10.2f^6 p12g t9.5g t8.6g Dec 13] first foal: dam lightly-raced sister to smart 7f winner Muwaary: no form: left Brian Meehan after first start: tried in tongue tie. *Nikki Evans* **–**

NAGGERS (IRE) 6 ch.g. Excellent Art 125 – Trika (First Trump 118) [2017 93: 6g^4 6s* 6m^2 5g 6g 6v 6d Oct 27] useful handicapper: won at Thirsk (by 3½ lengths from Handsome Dude) in May: stays 6f: acts on soft going. *Paul Midgley* **106**

NAG'S WAG (IRE) 4 b.f. Approve (IRE) 112 – Street Kitty (IRE) (Tiger Hill (IRE) 127) [2017 80: f7g p6g p6g p6g^2 p6g^5 p6s* p5g* 6.1m^3 6g^5 5g* 5.2m^4 5g^4 f6.1g p6d^6 p6g t5.1g Nov 20] rather leggy filly: fair performer: won sellers at Lingfield (twice) in June and Thirsk in July: left George Baker after eighth start: stays 6f: acts on polytrack and firm going. *Conor Dore* **79**

NAILED ON NINA (IRE) 2 b.f. (Mar 21) Tough As Nails (IRE) 108 – Anne-Lise 63 (Inchinor 119) [2017 p6g^5 6.3s 7v Sep 30] €10,500Y: half-sister to 7f-1¼m winner Rustic Deacon (by Pastoral Pursuits) and 5.7f winner Minminwin (by Art Connoisseur): dam 7f winner: modest form: best effort when fifth in maiden at Dundalk (5¼ lengths behind Freescape) in August. *P. M. Mooney, Ireland* **61**

NAJASHEE (IRE) 3 gr.g. Invincible Spirit (IRE) 121 – Tonnara (IRE) (Linamix (FR) 127) [2017 8m p8s^3 8m* 8g Sep 2] €700,000Y: good-topped gelding: sixth foal: closely related to smart winner up to 1m Most Improved (2-y-o 7f winner, by Lawman) and half-brother to 10.5f/11f winner Merville (by Montjeu) and very smart winner up to 1½m Ectot (2-y-o 7f/1m winner, by Hurricane Run): dam ran twice: fairly useful form: won maiden at Haydock in June: raced only at 1m. *Owen Burrows* **86**

NAJMAH (IRE) 2 br.f. (Mar 10) Dawn Approach (IRE) 132 – Dream of The Hill (IRE) (Tiger Hill (IRE) 127) [2017 p7s^6 Aug 9] 28,000Y: third foal: dam, ran twice, closely related to smart winner up to 1¼m Dream Peace out of smart 1¼m-1½m winner Truly A Dream: 12/1, sixth in minor event at Kempton (5¾ lengths behind Verandah) in August: should improve. *Ismail Mohammed* **65 p**

NAKEETA 6 b.g. Sixties Icon 125 – Easy Red (IRE) (Hunting Lion (IRE) 115) [2017 111: 18.6m 13.9g^2 14g^4 13.9m* 15.9g^5 Nov 7] rather leggy gelding: smart handicapper: won Ebor at York (by head from Flymetothestars) in August: 6½ lengths fifth to Rekindling in Melbourne Cup at Flemington: stays 2¼m: acts on soft and good to firm going: wears hood: consistent. *Iain Jardine* **114**

Betfred Ebor (Heritage Handicap), York—Nakeeta records the most notable success yet for his trainer Iain Jardine, holding on gamely from Flymetothestars (right) and Natural Scenery (cheekpieces); Nakeeta is also the third winner in the last four years to have been ridden by an apprentice, 5-lb claimer Callum Rodriguez doing the steering

NALAINI (IRE) 2 b.f. (Mar 3) Holy Roman Emperor (IRE) 125 – Lanark Belle (Selkirk (USA) 129) [2017 t6.1d^5 Dec 27] half-sister to several winners, including useful 2-y-o 7f winner Sharaakah (by Roderic O'Connor) and winner up to 1m Diamond Geezah (2-y-o 7f winner, by Diamond Green): dam lightly-raced half-sister to smart 8.3f-1¼m winner Adiemus: 22/1, well held in minor event at Wolverhampton. *Declan Carroll* –

NAMEITWHATYOULIKE 8 b.g. Trade Fair 124 – Emma Peel 113 (Emarati (USA) 74) [2017 115: 6g^5 6s t6s 6g 6g 6v^2 6g Oct 14] lengthy, good-topped gelding: useful handicapper: second at Ripon (½ length behind Flying Pursuit) in September: races at 6f nowadays: acts on good to firm and heavy going: has worn blinkers: front runner/races prominently. *Bryan Smart* **104**

NAME THAT TOON 4 b.f. Paco Boy (IRE) 129 – Saktoon (USA) 60 (El Prado (IRE) 119) [2017 39: p5g^4 f6m t5g p5g Mar 16] poor handicapper: stays 6f: acts on polytrack: wears headgear: usually races prominently. *Derek Shaw* **45**

NAMIRAH 3 b.f. Sepoy (AUS) 129 – Fairy Efisio 100 (Efisio 120) [2017 p7g Jan 11] 20,000F, 60,000Y: fourth foal: half-sister to 7f-1¼m winner Fata Birichina (by Dylan Thomas) and 9f/1¼m winner Flipper (by Cape Cross): dam, 1m-1¼m winner, half-sister to very smart 9f-11f winner Fair Nashwan: 25/1, well held in maiden at Kempton. *Michael Bell* –

NAMPARA 2 b.f. (Apr 4) Kyllachy 129 – Nurai 62 (Danehill Dancer (IRE) 117) [2017 5g^5 6d p6g^4 6g t5.1g^2 Nov 11] second foal: dam 1m winner who stayed 1¼m out of useful 2-y-o 7f winner (stayed 1¼m) Lady High Havens: fair maiden: best effort at 5f: acts on tapeta: usually races prominently. *Paul D'Arcy* **72**

NANCY HART 3 b.f. Sepoy (AUS) 129 – Lucky Token (IRE) 77 (Key of Luck (USA) 126) [2017 74: 8m^4 8.3g 7m 8g Jul 23] fair maiden: stays 1m: acts on good to firm going: tried in headgear: front runner/races prominently: has joined John Quinn. *Tom Dascombe* **67**

NANNY MAKFI 4 b.f. Makfi 130 – Pan Galactic (USA) 105 (Lear Fan (USA) 130) [2017 64: 11.1m^6 May 7] sturdy filly: modest maiden, well held sole start in 2017: stays 1½m: acts on soft going: tried in cheekpieces: has joined Brian Barr. *Keith Dalgleish* –

NAPLES BAY 3 b.g. Kodiac 112 – Trombe (FR) (Bering 136) [2017 81: 6d^5 6s 5v^6 t6d t5g Nov 24] good-quartered gelding: fairly useful at 2 yrs, below that level in 2017: stays 6f: acts on good to soft going. *John Quinn* **62**

NAPOLEON (IRE) 4 b.c. Jeremy (USA) 122 – Desert Drama (IRE) 106 (Green Desert (USA) 127) [2017 p8g p10g Dec 30] well held in 2 maidens. *Laura Mongan* –

NAPOLEON SOLO 5 b.g. Cockney Rebel (IRE) 127 – Trump Street 77 (First Trump 118) [2017 72: t7.1g t6d f7g Mar 9] fair performer, well below that level in 2017: has worn headgear: often leads. *David Barron* –

NAPPING 4 b.f. Sleeping Indian 122 – Vax Rapide 80 (Sharpo 132) [2017 p6g^5 p6f^3 6d^5 p6g^3 p6g^5 Dec 20] sister to 7.6f/1m winner Doctor Bong and half-sister to several winners, including useful 5f/6f winner Equuleus Pictor (by Piccolo) and 6f winner Volito (by Bertolini): dam 2-y-o 5f winner: modest maiden: raced only at 6f: acts on polytrack: in hood last 2 starts: often races prominently. *Anabel K. Murphy* **62**

NAQAAWA (IRE) 2 b.f. (Apr 8) Shamardal (USA) 129 – Hammiya (IRE) 103 (Darshaan 133) [2017 6v^6 7g 8.3d^3 Oct 18] seventh foal: sister to useful 1¼m winner Mafaaheem and half-sister to 3 winners, including smart 7f winner Masaalek (by Green Desert) and useful 1m-1¼m winner (stayed 1½m) Shaqira (by Redoute's Choice): dam 8.4f-11.4f winner: fair form: best effort when third in maiden at Nottingham (6¼ lengths behind Hadith) in October. *Owen Burrows* **79**

NARALSAIF (IRE) 3 b.f. Arcano (IRE) 122 – Mejala (IRE) 74 (Red Ransom (USA)) [2017 8.3d p10s 6d 6g^3 6d^6 5.1d t5g^6 t6s^2 p6g^3 Dec 21] good-quartered filly: third foal: half-sister to 6f/7f winner Hajeer (by Cape Cross): dam, 1¼m winner, half-sister to smart 7f winner Muwaary: modest maiden: should stay beyond 6f: acts on polytrack and tapeta: usually in visor. *Derek Shaw* **58**

NARCOS (IRE) 2 bl.g. (Mar 20) Lethal Force (IRE) 128 – Western Eyes (IRE) 57 (Rock of Gibraltar (IRE) 133) [2017 7g* 8.2v^6 Sep 30] €60,000F, 45,000Y: fourth foal: half-brother to 1¼m-1½m winner (stays 14.5f) Hubertas (by Lord of England) and winner up to 1m Ma Petite Folie (by Cockney Rebel), both useful: dam, maiden (best effort at 9.5f), half-sister to Australian Group 2 6f winner Newquay: fairly useful form: won minor event at Doncaster (by 1¼ lengths from Make Good) in August. *Richard Fahey* **82**

NARELLA (IRE) 2 gr.f. (Feb 23) Reliable Man 128 – Naomia (GER) (Monsun (GER) 124) [2017 7g* 7g* 8d Oct 1] half-sister to 2 winners, including German 8.7f-1½m winner Nelke (by Kallisto): dam German 1m (at 2 yrs) and 9f winner: useful form: won maiden at Cologne in July and Zukunfts-Rennen at Baden-Baden (by 2 lengths from Auenperle) in September: 7 lengths last of 7 behind Wild Illusion in Prix Marcel Boussac at Chantilly final outing: should stay 1m+. *Markus Klug, Germany* **103**

NARGIZA (USA) 3 ch.f. Elusive Quality (USA) – Any For Love (ARG) (Southern Halo (USA)) [2017 62: t8.6g 9.9d t8s Sep 19] modest maiden: best effort at 1m. *Chris Wall* **54**

NARJES 3 b.f. Sepoy (AUS) 129 – Dubai Sea (USA) (Street Sense (USA) 128) [2017 66p: t7.2g^2 t7.2g p7s^3 p8g^2 p8g^3 p7g^6 p8g^2 p8s^3 Dec 17] useful-looking filly: fairly useful maiden: placed in handicaps at Kempton in August and September: left James Fanshawe after sixth start: stays 1m: acts on polytrack, tapeta and good to soft going: wears hood: temperament under suspicion. *Laura Mongan* **82**

NARNIA DAWN (IRE) 4 b.f. Roderic O'Connor (IRE) 119 – Nordkappe (GER) (High Chaparral (IRE) 132) [2017 8g 7d 8g* p6.5g 7s Sep 16] €29,000F: sturdy filly: first foal: dam lightly-raced half-sister to useful German 1¼m/11f winner North Mum out of useful 11f winner North Queen: useful performer: won minor event at Lyon Parilly in May: stays 1m: acts on soft going: has worn tongue tie. *Francis-Henri Graffard, France* **98**

NARODOWA 2 ch.f. (Mar 20) Iffraaj 127 – Zacheta (Polish Precedent (USA) 131) [2017 7m 7g^5 8d Sep 23] half-sister to several winners, including very smart winner up to 9f Ransom Note (2-y-o 7f winner, by Red Ransom) and useful 1m-1¼m winner Shargiah (by New Approach): dam unraced half-sister to Prix de l'Arc de Triomphe winner Marienbard: fair form: best effort when fifth in maiden at Salisbury (7 lengths behind Herecomesthesun) in September: should stay 1m+. *David Lanigan* **65**

NASEE 2 b.c. (Mar 28) Intello (GER) 129 – Mischief Making (USA) 101 (Lemon Drop Kid (USA) 131) [2017 p7d Oct 6] 280,000Y: closely related to 16.5f winner Social Media (by New Approach) and half-brother to 3 winners, including winner up to 1¼m (stays 1½m) Horseplay (2-y-o 8.3f winner, by Cape Cross) and 8.3f-1½m winner More Mischief (by Azamour), both useful: dam, 9.5f-13f winner who stayed 2m, half-sister to smart 7f winner That Is The Spirit: 5/1, well held in minor event at Chelmsford: capable of better. *Sir Michael Stoute* **– p**

NASEEM (IRE) 3 br.g. Sea The Stars (IRE) 140 – Chiosina (IRE) (Danehill Dancer (IRE) 117) [2017 101p: 10d^4 8m^3 Jun 30] useful form: third in handicap at Yarmouth (1½ lengths behind Auberge du Lac) in June: stays 1m: tried in cheekpieces. *John Gosden* **101**

NASHVILLE (IRE) 8 b.g. Galileo (IRE) 134 – Brown Eyes 86 (Danehill (USA) 126) [2017 62: t16.3s 15.9s^6 17.2s Aug 7] fairly useful at best, regressive nowadays: has worn headgear. *Andrew Crook* **–**

NASRI 11 b.g. Kyllachy 129 – Triple Sharp 80 (Selkirk (USA) 129) [2017 70: p6g^6 p6g^2 p7g p6d^2 p7d^4 p6d^4 p6g* p6g^3 p6g 6m Apr 24] well-made gelding: modest handicapper nowadays: won at Kempton in March: stays 7f: acts on polytrack, firm and soft going: wears headgear. *Emma Owen* **64**

NASSYA 2 b.f. (Mar 27) Dubawi (IRE) 129 – Gemstone (IRE) 108 (Galileo (IRE) 134) [2017 8d^5 Oct 27] 525,000Y: third foal: half-sister to winner up to 1m (stays 1¼m) Bedrock (2-y-o 6.5f winner, by Fastnet Rock): dam 2-y-o 7f/1m winner who stayed 1½m: 11/1, plenty of promise when fifth in maiden at Doncaster (9 lengths behind Mrs Sippy) on debut: sort to improve markedly. *John Gosden* **65 P**

NASTENKA 3 b.f. Aussie Rules (USA) 123 – Nezhenka 99 (With Approval (CAN)) [2017 71: t9.5g* p10g^5 10.2g^6 9.9d^6 8g* 8d^6 p9.4g 14.9v a11.9g p13.4g Dec 19] fairly useful handicapper: won at Wolverhampton in January and Brighton (by neck from Al Nafoorah) in June (left Ed Walker after): stays 9.5f: acts on tapeta and good to soft going: tried in hood. *N. Caullery, France* **81**

NATAJACK 3 ch.g. Showcasing 117 – Douro (Manduro (GER) 135) [2017 82p: 7g t7.2g 8m 7.8d* 8.3d^4 8s^6 8.5g^5 Sep 14] tall gelding: fair handicapper: won at Carlisle in July: stays 1m: acts on soft going: has joined Rebecca Bastiman. *Richard Fahey* **77**

NATALIA 8 ch.m. Dutch Art 126 – Pintle 103 (Pivotal 124) [2017 50: f8d Apr 4] sturdy mare: modest maiden, well held sole start in 2017: stays 8.5f: acts on tapeta, good to firm and good to soft going: usually wears headgear: in tongue tie last 2 starts. *Sarah Hollinshead* **–**

NATALIE EXPRESS (FR) 3 b.f. Excelebration (IRE) 133 – Miss Emma May (IRE) 84 (Hawk Wing (USA) 136) [2017 7d 5.5g 7d 6g^5 p6g^6 Dec 20] fairly useful 5.5f winner on debut at 2 yrs, below that level in 2017: left H-A. Pantall after fourth start: has worn hood. *Henry Spiller* **66**

NATAVIA 3 ch.f. Nathaniel (IRE) 129 – Our Queen of Kings (Arazi (USA) 135) [2017 8m^{2} 10s* 12m 10m 12s Oct 28] 300,000F, 600,000Y: good-topped filly: half-sister to numerous winners, including smart winner up to 1m Spinning Queen (2-y-o 6f winner, by Spinning World) and useful 1¼m-1½m winner Shannon Springs (by Darshaan): dam unraced: useful performer: won listed race at Newbury (by 3¾ lengths from Flood Warning) in May: best effort at 1¼m: acts on soft going: in tongue tie last 2 starts. *Roger Charlton* **106**

NATCH 2 b.c. (Apr 10) Nathaniel (IRE) 129 – Angara 119 (Alzao (USA) 117) [2017 p8g^{4} Dec 21] closely related to useful 10.3f winner Space Ship and winner up to 1¼m Pleiades (2-y-o 7.4f winner) (both by Galileo) and half-brother to 3 winners, including winner up to 9f Sky Ship (2-y-o 7f winner, by Raven's Pass): dam 9f-1½m winner: 5/1, encouragement when fourth in maiden at Chelmsford (length behind Best Blue) in December: will improve. *John Gosden* **77 p**

NATHALIE 3 b.f. Nathaniel (IRE) 129 – Deirdre 101 (Dubawi (IRE) 129) [2017 9.9f^{4} 9.9f^{5} 11.6d^{2} 12g* 11.9d^{5} Sep 14] third foal: closely related to useful 1¼m-1½m winner Nigel (by New Approach) and half-sister to 1½m winner Stanley (by Sea The Stars): dam, 2-y-o 1m winner, half-sister to Irish St Leger winner Duncan and smart stayer Samuel: fairly useful performer: won maiden at Thirsk in August: stays 1½m: acts on good to soft going. *James Fanshawe* **86**

NATHAN 3 b.g. Nathaniel (IRE) 129 – Maid To Treasure (IRE) 77 (Rainbow Quest (USA) 134) [2017 10.2m^{3} 10s 10g^{2} 10.2d* 10d* 10.3v^{3} Sep 15] sturdy gelding: seventh foal: closely related to smart 1½m-16.4f winner King of Wands (by Galileo) and half-brother to 8.5f winner Queen of Wands (by Sakhee) and 1½m winner Knight of Wands (by Azamour): dam maiden: useful performer: won handicaps at Bath and Newbury in August: left Simon Crisford after second start: stays 1¼m: acts on good to firm and good to soft going: tried in hood: remains capable of better. *Alan King* **103 p**

NATHANIA 3 ch.f. Nathaniel (IRE) 129 – Glen Rosie (IRE) 102 (Mujtahid (USA) 118) [2017 83: p10g^{4} 11.6d* 9.9d^{2} 12g^{3} 12g^{3} 12g^{2} 12m^{4} 14s Sep 27] good-topped filly: fairly useful performer: won maiden at Bath in May: second at Salisbury in August: stays 1½m: acts on good to soft going: sometimes slowly away: sold 45,000 gns, sent to Saudi Arabia. *Richard Hughes* **91**

NATHAN MAYER 3 b.g. Nathaniel (IRE) 129 – Rosacara 71 (Green Desert (USA) 127) [2017 64: 10g^{6} 10.2g* p11g^{6} 11.4m^{4} Jun 26] smallish gelding: fair handicapper: won at Nottingham in May: stays 11.5f: acts on good to firm going. *Sir Michael Stoute* **79**

NATHEER (USA) 3 gr.f. Exchange Rate (USA) 111 – Ishraak (USA) (Sahm (USA) 112) [2017 p7d^{2} 7.1s^{3} t7.2g^{4} Oct 7] closely related to useful 7.4f (including at 2 yrs) winner (stayed 1¼m) Jabhaat and 2-y-o 7f winner Mahsooba (both by Hard Spun) and half-sister to 3 winners, including winner up to 1m Kafeel (2-y-o 7f winner, by First Samurai): dam unraced: fair form: best effort when second in maiden at Kempton in August. *Roger Varian* **71**

NATHRA (IRE) 4 b.f. Iffraaj 127 – Rada (IRE) 52 (Danehill (USA) 126) [2017 113: 8d^{6} 7d^{3} 8g^{2} 7g^{2} 8g^{3} 8s^{4} Oct 21] strong filly: smart performer: third in Hungerford Stakes at Newbury (2¼ lengths behind Massaat) in August, second in Park Stakes at Doncaster (¾ length behind Aclaim) in September, third in Sun Chariot Stakes at Newmarket (2½ lengths behind Roly Poly) and fourth in Queen Elizabeth II Stakes at Ascot (1¾ lengths behind Persuasive), last 2 in October: stays 1m: acts on soft going. *John Gosden* **116**

NATIONAL ANTHEM 2 ch.c. (Apr 13) Intikhab (USA) 135 – Song of Passion (IRE) 104 (Orpen (USA) 116) [2017 5d^{4} Oct 4] in hood, 20/1, fourth in maiden at Nottingham (2¼ lengths behind Kodiac Express) in October. *John Butler* **70**

NATIONAL DEFENSE 3 b.c. Invincible Spirit (IRE) 121 – Angel Falls (Kingmambo (USA) 125) [2017 118p: 7g^{2} 8d May 14] smart performer: won Prix Jean-Luc Lagadere at Chantilly at 2 yrs: second in Prix Djebel at Maisons-Laffitte (length behind Al Wukair) in April: tailed-off last in Poule d'Essai des Poulains at Deauville and not seen out again: stayed 1m: acted on good to firm going: to stand at Irish National Stud, fee €12,000. *Mme C. Head-Maarek, France* **110**

NATIONAL SERVICE (USA) 6 b.g. War Chant (USA) 126 – Cotton Club Ballet (USA) (Street Cry (IRE) 130) [2017 75d: t6m p6g^{6} p6g t6f^{3} p6g t6g^{4} t7.1g 7f^{2} 6m 5.5g^{3} 6g t7.2g 7.4g 5.5g* 7g^{2} 5.5f* p7g 6v Oct 19] strong gelding: modest handicapper: won at Les Landes in July and August: left Richard Ford after fifth start: stays 7f: acts on polytrack, tapeta and firm going: wears headgear/tongue tie. *Clare Ellam* **63** **a54**

NATIVE APPEAL (IRE) 2 b.c. (Apr 5) Exceed And Excel (AUS) 126 – Picture Hat (USA) (El Prado (IRE) 119) [2017 t7.2g^{3} p8g* Dec 20] third foal: dam, 7.5f winner, half-sister to very smart winner up to 2¼m Penglai Pavilion out of smart 1m (including at 2 yrs) winner Maiden Tower: fairly useful form: won minor event at Kempton (by ¾ length from Albishr) in December: wears tongue tie: will go on improving. *Charlie Appleby* **84 p**

NATIVE FALLS (IRE) 6 ch.g. Elnadim (USA) 128 – Sagrada (GER) (Primo Dominie 121) [2017 69: 6m Apr 12] neat gelding: fairly useful at best, well held sole start in 2017: stays 7f, usually races over shorter: acts on soft and good to firm going: front runner/races prominently. *Alan Swinbank* **–**

NATIVE PROSPECT 3 ch.c. Bated Breath 125 – Jakarta Jade (IRE) 103 (Royal Abjar (USA) 121) [2017 83p: f8m* 10.3g 8.5g^{2} 9.1m^{4} 8.5g^{2} 10s^{2} 10.3v^{2} 10.1v* Oct 1] tall, useful-looking colt: fairly useful performer: won maiden at Southwell in February and handicap at Epsom (by 2¼ lengths from Sparte Quercus) in October: stays 10.5f: acts on fibresand, good to firm and heavy going: front runner/races prominently: sold 80,000 gns, sent to Saudi Arabia. *Andrew Balding* **94**

NATIVE SOLDIER (IRE) 3 b.g. Sepoy (AUS) 129 – Electra Star 99 (Shamardal (USA) 129) [2017 84p: p8g^{6} 8s 7m 8m* 10d^{4} 8.1s 8d p8g Dec 20] fairly useful handicapper: won at Newbury (by length from Fastnet Spin) in July on final start for William Haggas: stays 1¼m: acts on tapeta, good to firm and good to soft going: usually in headgear: often races towards rear: temperament under suspicion. *John Flint* **84**

NATURAL HISTORY 2 b.c. (Feb 28) Nathaniel (IRE) 129 – Film Script 105 (Unfuwain (USA) 131) [2017 8.2g^{3} Oct 17] half-brother to 3 winners, including smart winner up to 1¾m Free Agent (2-y-o 6f-7f winner) and ungenuine 1½m winner Criterion (both stayed 2m, by Dr Fong): dam 1¼m-1½m winner who stayed 14.6f: 12/1, third in minor event at Leicester (3 lengths behind Bombyx) in October: will improve. *Andrew Balding* **76 p**

NATURAL (IRE) 2 b.f. (Feb 16) Kodiac 112 – Catch The Sea (IRE) 64 (Barathea (IRE) 127) [2017 6.5d* 6m 6g^{2} 6d Aug 24] €305,000Y: compact filly: closely related to very smart winner up to 7f My Catch (2-y-o 5.5f/6f winner, by Camacho) and half-sister to 3 winners, including useful 2-y-o 6f winner Pearl Sea (by Elusive City): dam maiden (stayed 1¼m): useful form: won minor event at Doncaster in June: second in listed race at Newbury (2¼ lengths behind Madeline) in July: stays 6.5f. *Richard Hannon* **97**

NATURAL SCENERY 4 b.f. Dubawi (IRE) 129 – Argentina (IRE) 116 (Sadler's Wells (USA) 132) [2017 101: t12.4g* t16.3g* p15.8g^{6} t16.3s^{2} 14v^{4} 13.9m^{3} 14.5d Sep 14] well-made filly: smart handicapper: won at Newcastle in January (by ½ length from Masterpaver) and February (by 2½ lengths from London Prize): second in Northumberland Plate at same course (½ length behind Higher Power) in July and third in Ebor at York (2 lengths behind Nakeeta) in August: stays 16.5f: acts on polytrack, tapeta, firm and good to soft going: has worn cheekpieces, including last 3 starts: often travels strongly. *Saeed bin Suroor* **112**

NATURE BOY (IRE) 3 ch.c. Intikhab (USA) 135 – Miss Latina (IRE) 74 (Mozart (IRE) 131) [2017 69: 7m^{5} Apr 10] fair form: fifth in maiden at Redcar (2½ lengths behind Sir Reginald Brown) on sole outing in 2017: has joined Robyn Brisland. *Peter Chapple-Hyam* **69**

NAUGHTY OR NICE (IRE) 3 b.f. Fastnet Rock (AUS) 127 – Monty's Girl (IRE) (High Chaparral (IRE) 132) [2017 9.5s* 13m* 12m 12f Jul 15] good-topped filly: fourth foal: closely related to useful 1¼m-13f winner Cailini Alainn (by Danehill Dancer) and half-sister to useful 11f-1¾m winner Dark Crusader (by Cape Cross): dam unraced half-sister to smart winner up to 9f Mutahadee: useful form: won maiden at Gowran in April and listed race at Navan (by head from Grandee) in May: last next 2 starts, in Ribblesdale Stakes at Royal Ascot (saddle slipped) and Irish Oaks at the Curragh: stays 13f: tried in blinkers. *John M. Oxx, Ireland* **102**

NAUPAKA 3 b.f. Haafhd 129 – Lily Lenor (IRE) 50 (Bertolini (USA) 125) [2017 67p: p8g t8d^{3} t8d^{5} t8g^{6} t7.1g 10.2m 14g^{5} 8s 10d 7.2s 7g^{5} t12.4d^{4} t8d p13.3s Dec 1] modest maiden: should stay beyond 1m: acts on tapeta: has worn headgear: sometimes slowly away, usually races nearer last than first. *Brian Ellison* **59**

NAUTICA (IRE) 2 ch.f. (Feb 19) Born To Sea (IRE) 117 – Moynsha Lady (IRE) (Namid 128) [2017 t7.2g^{5} Dec 5] €11,000Y: fourth foal: closely related to 1m winner Hutton (by Lawman) and half-sister to 5f winner Hamidans Girl (by Bahamian Bounty): dam, unraced, **60 p**

closely related to smart winner up to 1m Luck Money: 66/1, fifth in minor event at Wolverhampton (4¼ lengths behind American Endeavour) in December: should improve. *Jonathan Portman*

NAUTICAL HAVEN 3 b.g. Harbour Watch (IRE) 121 – Mania (IRE) (Danehill (USA) **94**
126) [2017 92: 6d p6s^{2} Dec 15] rather leggy gelding: fairly useful handicapper: second at Chelmsford in December: stays 6f: acts on polytrack and good to firm going: front runner/races prominently. *Kevin Ryan*

NAVAJO GREY (IRE) 3 gr.f. Dark Angel (IRE) 113 – Spring View (Fantastic Light **57**
(USA) 134) [2017 t8d 10.2m t12.2g^{6} 12.1m^{6} 11.8g Jul 8] 26,000Y: fifth foal: sister to 7f/1m winner Dark Light and half-sister to 5f-1m winner Spreadable (by Duke of Marmalade): dam unraced half-sister to very smart 7f-8.3f winner Sleeping Indian: modest maiden: sometimes slowly away: temperament under suspicion (has flashed tail). *Michael Appleby*

NAVAJO SQUAW 2 ch.f. (Feb 17) Sir Percy 129 – Navajo Charm 67 (Authorized (IRE) **58**
133) [2017 8.3d 8d^{6} Oct 24] 8,500Y: first foal: dam, 11f winner, half-sister to very smart winner up to 1¼m (stayed 1½m) Jammaal: modest form in maiden/minor event: in hood first start. *Ed Dunlop*

NAVAJO STAR (IRE) 3 b.f. Mastercraftsman (IRE) 129 – Champagne Aerial (IRE) **66**
(Night Shift (USA)) [2017 p7d t8.6g^{4} p10g^{6} p10d 10.2m 12.1g 14v p13.3d^{4} p16g* t16.3g* t16.5g^{4} p16g^{4} p16g Dec 20] 22,000F, 30,000Y: first foal: dam twice-raced half-sister to smart winner up to 7f Ishvana: fair handicapper: won at Chelmsford and Newcastle in October: stays 16.5f: acts on polytrack and tapeta: wears visor: front runner/races prominently: has joined Robyn Brisland. *Michael Appleby*

NAVAJO STORM (IRE) 4 gr.f. Dark Angel (IRE) 113 – Strike Lightly (Rainbow Quest **60**
(USA) 134) [2017 –: 10.1g^{5} 10.2g^{5} 9.1m^{4} 10d 8.2v Sep 25] modest maiden: stays 1¼m: acts on good to firm going: tried in cheekpieces: usually races prominently. *Michael Appleby*

NAVAJO THUNDER (IRE) 3 b.f. High Chaparral (IRE) 132 – Evening Dress 65 **60**
(Medicean 128) [2017 –: 10g^{5} 10.1g^{6} 9m^{pu} Jul 23] modest maiden: best effort at 1¼m. *Michael Appleby*

NAVAJO WAR DANCE 4 b.g. Makfi 130 – Navajo Rainbow (Rainbow Quest (USA) **88 §**
134) [2017 90: 10.3g^{4} 10m t10.2g^{3} 11.1g 11.4g Jul 2] useful-looking gelding: fairly useful handicapper: third at Newcastle in May: stays 10.5f: acts on tapeta and heavy going: tried in headgear: sold to join Ali Stronge 9,000 gns in July: unreliable. *K. R. Burke*

NAVAL OFFICER 2 b.c. (Apr 3) Helmet (AUS) 127 – Ariyfa (IRE) 89 (Cape Cross **65**
(IRE) 129) [2017 7v t6g^{4} Nov 23] fair form: better effort when fourth in minor event at Newcastle (3 lengths behind Gowanbuster) in November: should stay 7f. *Nigel Tinkler*

NAVAL WARFARE (IRE) 3 b.c. Born To Sea (IRE) 117 – Three Days In May 70 **107**
(Cadeaux Genereux 131) [2017 88p: 8.2g* 8m 8d 8g* 8d^{4} 9d Sep 30] sturdy colt: useful handicapper: won at Leicester (by 1¼ lengths from Sabador) in May and Newmarket (by 2½ lengths from Night Circus) in August: stays 1m: acts on soft going: front runner/races prominently: sold 160,000 gns in November. *Andrew Balding*

NAVARONE (IRE) 3 b.g. Casamento (IRE) 118 – Flash And Dazzle (IRE) 64 (Bertolini **84**
(USA) 125) [2017 78: 8g^{5} 7g^{3} t7.1g^{3} 7.4d* 7.2g^{2} 7.4d^{4} 7.6s 7s 7.4v^{5} t7.1g Oct 10] fairly useful performer: won maiden at Beverley in June: stays 7.5f: acts on good to soft going: tried in hood: in tongue tie last 2 starts: often races towards rear/freely: sold 7,000 gns in October. *Richard Fahey*

NAVARRA PRINCESS (IRE) 2 b.f. (Feb 16) Intense Focus (USA) 117 – Navarra **51**
Queen 107 (Singspiel (IRE) 133) [2017 5d 5d 5g^{5} 5m t7.1g f6.1g^{6} Dec 19] €6,500Y: second foal: half-sister to useful German 2-y-o 7f winner Navarra King (by Lope de Vega): dam winner up to 1¼m (2-y-o 6.5f winner): modest maiden: will stay 7f: acts on fibresand: often races in rear. *Don Cantillon*

NAWASSI 2 b.f. (Jan 26) Dubawi (IRE) 129 – Maqaasid 112 (Green Desert (USA) 127) **81 p**
[2017 7g 7d* Nov 4] sturdy, attractive filly: third foal: dam 2-y-o 5f winner (including Queen Mary Stakes) and third in 1000 Guineas: fairly useful form: won minor event at Newmarket (by 2¾ lengths from Revalue) in November, showing good attitude: will go on improving. *John Gosden*

NAYEL (IRE) 5 b.h. Acclamation 118 – Soliza (IRE) 93 (Intikhab (USA) 135) [2017 96: **97**
10.2f* 10g 9.1g 10.2d Oct 18] good-topped horse: useful handicapper: won at Nottingham (by 2½ lengths from Rotherwick) in June: stays 10.5f: acts on firm and good to soft going: wears headgear: front runner/races prominently. *Richard Hannon*

NAYYAR 3 ch.c. Exceed And Excel (AUS) 126 – Miss Queen (USA) (Miswaki (USA) 124) [2017 89: t5.1g^{3} 5g 5.1m^{5} Jun 12] sturdy colt: fairly useful handicapper: third at Wolverhampton in April: raced mainly around 5f: acts on tapeta and good to firm going: tried in tongue tie: often races prominently: sent to Bahrain. *Charles Hills* **91**

NAZZAA (IRE) 4 b.g. Shamardal (USA) 129 – Multicolour Wave (IRE) (Rainbow Quest (USA) 134) [2017 t8.6g 11.6d p12d 10.2g* 10.5v Sep 29] fair performer: won handicap at Nottingham (apprentice) in August: stays 1¼m. *Steve Flook* **77**

NEAR KETTERING 3 ch.c. Medicean 128 – Where's Broughton 77 (Cadeaux Genereux 131) [2017 8.1m^{4} 10m* 10m^{5} 10s 10m^{4} 11.8d^{6} Sep 12] 27,000F, 48,000 2-y-o: lengthy colt: fifth foal: half-brother to 3 winners, including 7f winner Colourfilly (by Compton Place) and 1¼m winner Where's Tiger (by Tiger Hill): dam, 9.5f winner, sister to very smart 1m-1¼m winner Desert Deer: fairly useful performer: won maiden at Redcar in May: stays 1¼m: acts on good to firm going: sold 45,000 gns in November. *Luca Cumani* **89**

NEARLY CAUGHT (IRE) 7 b.g. New Approach (IRE) 132 – Katch Me Katie 77 (Danehill (USA) 126) [2017 117: 16f^{3} 16.4g^{2} 20m 16.2m* 14.9g^{4} 14.9d^{6} 16g^{2} 16s Oct 21] strong gelding: smart performer: won listed race at Sandown (by ¾ length from Montaly) in July: second in Oleander-Rennen at Hoppegarten (1¼ lengths behind Red Cardinal) in May, fourth in Prix Kergorlay at Deauville (2¾ lengths behind Marmelo) in August and second in listed race at Newmarket (length behind Face The Facts) in September: stays 2½m: acts on polytrack, tapeta, good to firm and heavy going. *Hughie Morrison* **115**

NEBO (IRE) 2 b.c. (May 2) Kodiac 112 – Kindling 105 (Dr Fong (USA) 128) [2017 6s* 6f 7g^{2} 6v^{2} 6m^{6} 6m^{3} 6d^{2} 7s* Oct 28] 75,000Y: sturdy colt: sixth foal: closely related to useful 10.7f-1¾m winner Bayan (by Danehill Dancer) and half-brother to 1m/8.3f winner Investment Expert (by Tamayuz) and 1½m winner Dry Your Eyes (by Shamardal): dam, winner up to 2m (2-y-o 9f winner), half-sister to smart 9f/1¼m winner Thattinger: useful performer: won maiden at Newbury in May and Horris Hill Stakes there (by ½ length from Tangled) in October: placed in Superlative Stakes at Newmarket (head behind Gustav Klimt), Richmond Stakes at Goodwood (1¼ lengths behind Barraquero), Mill Reef Stakes at Newbury (1¼ lengths behind James Garfield) and Criterium de Maisons-Laffitte (head behind Fighting Irish): stays 7f: acts on any turf going. *Charles Hills* **107**

NEBUCHADNEZZAR (FR) 2 b.g. (Mar 12) Planteur (IRE) 124 – Trexana (Kaldoun (FR) 122) [2017 7g^{5} 8d^{4} 9.9s^{4} Sep 27] €10,000Y, 20,000 2-y-o: good-topped gelding: closely related to 7f winner Striking (by Danehill Dancer) and half-brother to several winners, including useful 1¼m/11f winner Biens Nanti (by Montjeu) and 2-y-o 6f winner Craggy Cat (by Statue of Liberty): dam ran twice: fair form: best effort when fourth in maiden at Goodwood (6¼ lengths behind Setting Sail) in September: should improve further. *Alan King* **70 p**

NEEDLESS SHOUTING (IRE) 6 b.g. Footstepsinthesand 120 – Ring The Relatives 75 (Bering 136) [2017 21.6m Apr 24] useful-looking gelding: fairly useful at best, well held sole start on Flat in 2017: stays 2m: acts on polytrack, soft and good to firm going: tried in visor: has joined Alexandra Dunn. *Joanne Foster* **–**

NEERAAN (USA) 2 gr.c. (Feb 7) Mizzen Mast (USA) 121 – Ishraak (USA) (Sahm (USA) 112) [2017 8g^{4} p8g^{5} 10m^{4} Oct 25] useful-looking colt: half-brother to several winners, including useful 7.4f (including at 2 yrs) winner (stayed 1¼m) Jabhaat (by Hard Spun) and winner up to 1m Kafeel (2-y-o 7f winner, by First Samurai): dam unraced: fairly useful form: best effort when fifth in minor event at Kempton (1¾ lengths behind Kassar) in October. *Roger Varian* **80**

NEFETARI 4 b.f. Kodiac 112 – Town And Gown 72 (Oasis Dream 129) [2017 53: t5g^{5} t6f 5.5f^{5} 5m 5g t5g 6g Aug 15] poor maiden: stays 6f: acts on tapeta: usually wears headgear: often leads. *Alan Brown* **39**

NELLIE DEEN (IRE) 4 b.f. Dream Ahead (USA) 133 – Dorothy Dene (Red Ransom (USA)) [2017 66: p8g^{5} 7g 6s^{6} 6d^{5} 6g^{6} 6m f7.1g^{5} f6.1g t7.1d t8d f7.1g^{4} Dec 1] poor maiden: left David Elsworth after first start, Roger Fell after seventh: stays 7f: acts on polytrack: wears headgear. *Simon West* **45**

NELLIE'S DANCER 3 b.f. Mount Nelson 125 – Xaphania (Sakhee (USA) 136) [2017 62: f7.1g 7.2d 6d 7g^{2} 7v 7m^{3} p6g^{2} f7.1g^{2} 6v^{2} f5g^{3} f7.1g Nov 16] fair maiden: stays 1m: acts on all-weather and heavy going: wears cheekpieces. *Scott Dixon* **65**

NELSON (IRE) 2 b.c. (Apr 11) Frankel 147 – Moonstone 119 (Dalakhani (IRE) 133) [2017 8g^{6} 7m^{2} 8g* 8d* 8d^{2} Sep 30] closely related to very smart 1¼m-12.3f winner US Army Ranger (by Galileo) and half-brother to 3 winners, including useful winner up to 1½m Words (2-y-o 7f winner) and smart winner up to 11.5f Nevis (2-y-o 1m winner) (both **112 p**

by Dansili): dam 1½m winner: smart performer: won maiden in August (by 3 lengths from Christopher Robin) and Willis Champions Juvenile Stakes in September (by 3 lengths from Kew Gardens), both at Leopardstown: second in Royal Lodge Stakes at Newmarket (neck behind Roaring Lion) in September: will be suited by 1¼m+: acts on good to firm and good to soft going: front runner/races prominently: remains capable of better. *Aidan O'Brien, Ireland*

NELSON RIVER 2 b.g. (Feb 21) Mount Nelson 125 – I Say (IRE) 86 (Oratorio (IRE) 128) [2017 7s 8g 8.3d Oct 11] first foal: dam, 9.3f winner, closely related to useful 2-y-o 6f/7f winner Tigrilla: modest form: will be suited by at least 1¼m: has joined Wilf Storey. *Clive Cox* **61**

NELSON'S BAY 8 b.g. Needwood Blade 117 – In Good Faith (USA) 74 (Dynaformer (USA)) [2017 63: t8g t7.1d t8g* t8d 7g 9m^6 t8s 8g t8s 8m 9m^6 8.9m t7.1d t8d^5 Nov 10] tall gelding: poor handicapper on turf, modest on all-weather: won at Newcastle in March: stays 1¼m: acts on tapeta, firm and soft going: has worn tongue tie: sometimes slowly away, often races in rear. *Wilf Storey* **47 a62**

NELSON'S HILL 7 b.g. Mount Nelson 125 – Regal Step 85 (Royal Applause 124) [2017 p8g Dec 28] no form. *William de Best-Turner* **–**

NELSON'S TOUCH 4 gr.g. Mount Nelson 125 – Lady Friend 85 (Environment Friend 128) [2017 t12.2g^3 p13.3g^4 11.8v^3 16g Nov 3] first foal: dam 1¼m winner who stayed 1½m: fairly useful form: best effort at 13.5f: has joined Seamus Mullins. *Denis Coakley* **83**

NEOLA 2 b.f. (Feb 6) Foxwedge (AUS) 128 – Effie B 98 (Sixties Icon 125) [2017 5.1m^5 5g* 5s^2 5m^5 6d^6 6d^6 6d 6d* 6.5g 5m 6d 6g^5 Nov 3] small filly: first foal: dam 5f/6f winner (including at 2 yrs): useful performer: won minor event at Nottingham in May and nursery at Goodwood (by ¾ length from Golden Salute) in September: second in listed race at York (½ length behind Main Desire) in May: stays 6f: acts on soft going: often races towards rear. *Mick Channon* **95**

NEPETA (USA) 3 ch.f. Kitten's Joy (USA) 128 – La Coruna (USA) (Thunder Gulch (USA) 129) [2017 72: 8.5d 11.2d^4 t12.4g^5 p16g Oct 12] fair handicapper: stays 12.5f: acts on tapeta, good to firm and good to soft going. *Mark Johnston* **75**

NEPTUNE STAR 3 b.f. Born To Sea (IRE) 117 – Nimbus Star (Nayef (USA) 129) [2017 t6f p5g p5g^4 7.5f^6 7g 7.1d 10m 9.9d 12g 9.9m^4 p10d Sep 21] 5,000Y, £32,000 2-y-o: first foal: dam twice-raced half-sister to smart 1m winner Glaswegian out of useful 6f winner (stayed 1m) Starfan: modest maiden: left Jeremy Gask after sixth start: stays 1¼m: acts on good to firm going: has worn hood: sometimes slowly away, usually races nearer last than first. *Michael Easterby* **54**

NESHMEYA 3 b.f. Lawman (FR) 121 – High Heeled (IRE) 122 (High Chaparral (IRE) 132) [2017 83: 10d 9.9f* 10.2g^3 10g* 10d Nov 4] lengthy filly: useful performer: won maiden at Salisbury in June and handicap at Newmarket in October: stays 1¼m: acts on firm going. *Charles Hills* **97**

NESS OF BRODGAR 2 b.f. (Mar 23) Harbour Watch (IRE) 121 – Missouri 86 (Charnwood Forest (IRE) 125) [2017 7d Nov 4] half-sister to several winners, including useful winner up to 1m Captain Cullen (2-y-o 7f winner, by Strategic Prince) and winner up to 1½m Battery Power (2-y-o 1m winner, by Royal Applause): dam 15f winner: 100/1, well held in minor event at Newmarket. *Mark H. Tompkins* **–**

NETLEY ABBEY 3 b.g. Myboycharlie (IRE) 118 – Ana Style (FR) (Anabaa Blue 122) [2017 –: p11g^5 p12f^6 9.9g p12g t14g^6 t14g^3 p13.3s t12.2g Dec 13] sturdy gelding: modest maiden: left Harry Dunlop after third start: stays 1¾m: acts on polytrack and tapeta: usually wears headgear. *Karen George* **57**

NEVALYASHKA 3 b.f. Sir Percy 129 – Ninotchka (USA) 110 (Nijinsky (CAN) 138) [2017 10.1v^5 p12g^6 t9.5g^4 p10s p13.3s^5 Dec 14] half-sister to several winners, including useful 2-y-o 6f winner (stayed 1m) Nataliya (by Green Desert) and 1¼m-1½m winner Nadeszhda (by Nashwan): dam 1½m winner: fair maiden: best effort at 9.5f: acts on tapeta: tried in headgear: often races towards rear. *Marcus Tregoning* **67**

NEVASCA (IRE) 3 gr.g. Invincible Spirit (IRE) 121 – Snowdrops (Gulch (USA)) [2017 p7g 8s 8g Aug 4] well held in maidens: tried in hood. *Lydia Pearce* **–**

NEVER A WORD (USA) 3 br.g. Lonhro (AUS) 128 – Janetstickettocats (USA) (Storm Cat (USA)) [2017 76p: 8g 8.5v t8g t9.5m^4 p10s p12g t12.2d^6 Dec 16] fair maiden: stays 9.5f: acts on tapeta: usually wears headgear: wears tongue tie: usually races close up. *Oliver Greenall* **73**

Willis Towers Watson Champions Juvenile Stakes, Leopardstown—Nelson storms to an emphatic success over stablemates Kew Gardens (far left) and Delano Roosevelt (second left)

NEVER BACK DOWN (IRE) 2 b.c. (Feb 2) Kodiac 112 – Steer By The Stars (IRE) 97 (Pivotal 124) [2017 5m^2 5g* 6g^6 6d^5 t6.1d* Dec 9] £100,000Y: first foal: dam, 2-y-o 6f/7f winner who stayed 1¼m, half-sister to very smart winner up to 1m (stays 1¼m) Consort: useful performer: won minor events at Leicester (by neck from Haddaf) in April and Wolverhampton (by length from Music Society) in December: will be suited by 7f+: acts on tapeta and good to firm going: remains with potential. *Hugo Palmer* **105 p**

NEVERBEEN TO PARIS (IRE) 2 b.g. (Apr 20) Champs Elysees 124 – Island Paradise (IRE) 96 (Trans Island 119) [2017 p7s 7s^2 7.1s^3 Aug 17] fair form: placed in 2 minor events: will be suited by at least 1m. *Michael Bell* **72**

NEVER FOLDING (IRE) 3 b.f. Requinto (IRE) 109 – Sarella Loren (USA) 69 (Theatrical) [2017 t7.1g^4 p7g^2 t8.6g p8g^5 8d 9d^4 p12d p8d^6 p7g p8g^2 p10s^2 Nov 16] €5,500Y, resold €15,000Y: leggy filly: third foal: dam, maiden (stayed 1¼m), out of useful winner up to 7f Miss Zafonic: modest maiden: stays 1¼m: acts on polytrack, tapeta and good to soft going: tried in hood/tongue tie. *Seamus Durack* **64**

NEVER GIVE IN 4 b.g. Alfred Nobel (IRE) 110 – Mad Annie (USA) (Anabaa (USA) 130) [2017 –: 10f 7m 6d Jul 5] fair form when fourth in maiden at 2 yrs, standout effort: in tongue tie last 2 starts. *John Weymes* **–**

NEVER SAY (IRE) 4 b.f. Monsieur Bond (IRE) 120 – Wong Again 62 (Araafa (IRE) 128) [2017 52: t9.5g t10.2d^5 t7.1d 9.8m^6 9s^5 12.1s^2 10d^2 t12.2g f11.1g f11.1g Dec 22] modest maiden on turf, poor on all-weather: left Jason Ward after sixth start: stays 1½m: acts on fibresand, tapeta and good to soft going: wears headgear. *Sam England* **52 a37**

NEVER SURRENDER (IRE) 3 b.g. High Chaparral (IRE) 132 – Meiosis (USA) 98 (Danzig (USA)) [2017 86: 10.3g^2 10.1g^5 10.3m* 12m 14m 12v 9.9m Aug 27] lengthy, rather unfurnished gelding: fairly useful performer: won maiden at Chester in May: stays 10.5f: acts on good to firm going: in cheekpieces last 2 starts. *Charles Hills* **93**

NEVER TO BE (USA) 6 b.g. Thewayyouare (USA) 117 – Kitty Foille (USA) (Black Minnaloushe (USA) 123) [2017 65: t7.1m p8g^6 p8g Mar 22] modest handicapper: stays 1m: acts on polytrack, good to firm and good to soft going: wears headgear/tongue tie. *Nikki Evans* **51**

NEVER YOU MIND (IRE) 3 b.g. Bated Breath 125 – Bimini (Sadler's Wells (USA) 132) [2017 7g 8.3g 7m 7d Jul 1] lengthy gelding: modest form: sold 5,000 gns, sent to Sweden. *Charles Hills* **52**

NEW ABBEY ANGEL (IRE) 4 gr.g. Dark Angel (IRE) 113 – Alinda (IRE) 86 (Revoque (IRE) 122) [2017 69: t8g 7.1m^2 8m^2 8m^6 9s^6 9.2m^4 12.5g^5 8.9m^6 10d^2 12.1s 9.2d^3 t10.2g t9.5g^2 t12.2g^2 Dec 13] workmanlike gelding: fair handicapper on turf, modest on all-weather: stays 1½m: acts on polytrack, tapeta, firm and good to soft going: has worn headgear: ungenuine (carries head high). *Keith Dalgleish* **67 § a60 §**

NEW AGENDA 5 b.g. New Approach (IRE) 132 – Prove 109 (Danehill (USA) 126) [2017 89: p8g^{3} 10m^{2} 9.9g^{3} Sep 2] tall gelding: fairly useful handicapper: second at Windsor in August: stays 1¼m: acts on polytrack, tapeta and good to firm going: wears hood: front runner/races prominently: fairly useful hurdler. *Paul Webber* **92**

NEW BIDDER 6 b.g. Auction House (USA) 120 – Noble Nova 69 (Fraam 114) [2017 103: 6g 6.1g Jul 2] sturdy gelding: useful handicapper, last both starts in 2017: stays 6f: acts on heavy going: usually wears headgear: usually races towards rear. *David Barron* –

NEWBOROUGH 2 b.g. (Mar 27) Farhh 131 – Comeraincomeshine (IRE) 67 (Night Shift (USA)) [2017 7g 8d p8g Oct 25] little impact in maiden/minor events. *Charles Hills* –

NEW DECADE 8 ch.g. Pivotal 124 – Irresistible 98 (Cadeaux Genereux 131) [2017 6g 6m 6m^{5} 8m 7.2d 6g 7.2s^{4} 8g 7.2d 7.2d Aug 14] strong, good-topped gelding: poor handicapper nowadays: stays 8.5f: acts on polytrack, fibresand, good to firm and heavy going: has worn headgear, including last 2 starts: has worn tongue tie: often races towards rear. *Jim Goldie* **46**

NEW DELHI (IRE) 3 ch.f. Sepoy (AUS) 129 – Crossover 105 (Cape Cross (IRE) 129) [2017 7m t6.1g^{5} 7.4m^{3} 8.3s^{6} 7.2s Jul 10] seventh foal: half-sister to 3 winners, including useful winner up to 7f Enlace (2-y-o 5f winner, by Shamardal) and 2-y-o 6f winner Overstep (by Exceed And Excel): dam, 6f winner, half-sister to 5f-7f winner Snaadee and 2-y-o 6f winner Russian Bond (both smart): modest maiden: best effort at 7.5f. *Mark Johnston* **62**

NEW EMPIRE 2 b.g. (May 3) Kodiac 112 – Quantum (IRE) 89 (Alhaarth (IRE) 126) [2017 6s 5m^{4} 5m 6f 6s^{2} 6d^{3} 6s t7.2g^{5} Nov 20] 45,000Y: compact, good-quartered gelding: seventh foal: half-brother to 3 winners, including useful 11f-16.6f winner Captain Navarre (by Excellent Art) and 7f-8.3f winner Salt Whistle Bay (by Royal Applause): dam, 1¼m winner who stayed 1¾m, half-sister to Irish 2000 Guineas winner Power and closely related/half-sister to Ribblesdale Stakes winners Thakafaat and Curvy: fairly useful maiden: second in nursery at Goodwood in August: should stay 7f: acts on soft going: tried in blinkers: often races towards rear: temperamental. *Peter Chapple-Hyam* **80 §**

NEWGATE DUCHESS 3 b.f. Haafhd 129 – Arctic Queen (Linamix (FR) 127) [2017 12g^{6} 12v 10d^{6} 8v^{6} Nov 7] closely related to 1½m winner Newgate Queen (by Phoenix Reach): dam, of little account, half-sister to useful 7f-8.6f winner Arctic Desert: no form. *Tony Coyle* –

NEWGATE SIOUX 3 b.f. Sleeping Indian 122 – Rio's Girl 66 (Captain Rio 122) [2017 59: 5f 5m^{6} 5m 5m 5m t5g Nov 3] modest form when winning claimer at 2 yrs, standout effort: raced mainly at 5f: acts on firm going: in tongue tie last 2 starts: often races prominently. *Tony Coyle* **47**

NEW IDENTITY (IRE) 6 b.g. Rock of Gibraltar (IRE) 133 – Zaafran 86 (Singspiel (IRE) 133) [2017 62: 5g 6.7m 5v* 6.3v 7v^{6} Oct 11] modest handicapper: won at Ffos Las in August: stays 1m: acts on good to firm and heavy going: often wears cheekpieces. *W. J. Martin, Ireland* **62**

NEWMARKET WARRIOR (IRE) 6 b.g. Dalakhani (IRE) 133 – Heavens Peak 64 (Pivotal 124) [2017 76: t8g^{4} t8d^{3} t8d* 8m^{3} 8m 7.2g 8d t8d^{2} 8v^{4} t8g* t8g^{3} t8g^{4} Dec 6] leggy gelding: fair handicapper on turf, fairly useful on all-weather: won at Newcastle in March (apprentice) and October (by 1¾ lengths from Thello): stays 1m: acts on tapeta, good to firm and good to soft going: wears headgear: quirky sort. *Iain Jardine* **76 a82**

NEW RICH 7 b.g. Bahamian Bounty 116 – Bling Bling (IRE) 70 (Indian Ridge 123) [2017 73: p6g^{2} p6g p6g^{4} p6g p6g p6g^{3} 6m^{5} 6g^{5} p7g^{4} p7g^{4} p7m^{4} Nov 25] fair handicapper: stays 7f: acts on polytrack, firm and soft going: wears headgear: temperamental. *Eve Johnson Houghton* **70 §**

NEW ROAD SIDE 4 b.f. Paco Boy (IRE) 129 – Spring Green 86 (Bahamian Bounty 116) [2017 87: t5d f5g^{2} t5s t6s^{3} 6s 5d 5g p5s 5g Jul 14] fair handicapper on turf, fairly useful on all-weather: second at Southwell in March: best form at 5f: acts on fibresand, tapeta, good to firm and good to soft going: sometimes wears visor: front runner/races prominently. *Richard Guest* **69 a83**

NEW SHOW (IRE) 2 ch.c. (Apr 28) New Approach (IRE) 132 – Music Show (IRE) 121 (Noverre (USA) 125) [2017 7.2d* Jul 31] second foal: dam winner up to 1m (2-y-o 5.7f-7f winner): 7/1, won minor event at Ayr (comfortably by 1½ lengths from Cosa Nostra) on debut: will be suited by at least 1m: sure to progress. *Kevin Ryan* **84 p**

NEW SOCIETY (IRE) 3 b.g. Rock of Gibraltar (IRE) 133 – Ajiaal 72 (Cape Cross (IRE) **84**
129) [2017 –: 12m^6 14m* 14m^4 12g^2 t12.4d^2 t12.4g^4 Sep 12] fairly useful handicapper: won at Redcar in May: second at Newcastle in August: stays 1¾m: acts on tapeta and good to firm going: usually races prominently. *James Bethell*

NEWSPEAK (IRE) 5 b.g. New Approach (IRE) 132 – Horatia (IRE) 106 (Machiavellian **58**
(USA) 123) [2017 50: 10m 8g^2 7.2d Jul 31] tall gelding: modest maiden: best effort at 1m: usually wears headgear. *Fred Watson*

NEWSTEAD ABBEY 7 b.g. Byron 117 – Oatcake 68 (Selkirk (USA) 129) [2017 77: t6g **76**
t7.1d t6g t7.1g^6 p7g^6 5.9g 6m t6.1g* t6.1g^2 p6g* t6.1g^4 p7g t7.2m t6.1g f6.1g* Dec 11] well-made gelding: fair performer nowadays: won handicaps at Wolverhampton in August and Chelmsford in September, and claimer at Southwell in December: stays 1m: acts on all-weather and any turf going: wears headgear. *Michael Herrington*

NEWT 3 b.f. Sixties Icon 125 – Froglet 83 (Shaamit (IRE) 127) [2017 61p: 14g 13m* 13f^3 **74**
14.1g^2 15.9s f14.1g Dec 11] fair handicapper: won at Bath in June: left Sir Mark Prescott Bt after fourth start: stays 1¾m: acts on good to firm going: tried in cheekpieces: often leads. *Chris Wall*

NEW TALE 3 b.g. Harbour Watch (IRE) 121 – Perfect Story (IRE) 95 (Desert Story (IRE) **52**
115) [2017 7g 7g^5 7g t6.1g^3 t6.1g t6.1g f8.1g^4 f7.1g^3 Dec 22] modest maiden: stays 7f: acts on fibresand and tapeta: in headgear last 3 starts. *Olly Williams*

NEW TARABELA 6 ch.g. New Approach (IRE) 132 – Tarabela (CHI) (Hussonet (USA)) **45**
[2017 –: p13g t13.9m Mar 14] strong, short-backed gelding: fairly useful handicapper at best, lightly raced and little form since 2014: stays 1¾m: acts on polytrack, soft and good to firm going: has worn headgear: tried in tongue tie. *Tony Carroll*

NEWTON HEATH (IRE) 3 b.g. Casamento (IRE) 118 – Carpet Lover (IRE) 46 (Fayruz **–**
116) [2017 t8.6m t7.1g f7g t7.1g t9.5g 7g May 9] little form: tried in cheekpieces. *Daniel Loughnane*

NEWTOWN CROSS (IRE) 7 ch.g. Kheleyf (USA) 116 – Sacred Pearl (IRE) (Daylami **50**
(IRE) 138) [2017 56: p15.8g^3 p16d^5 p16g Mar 22] strong, lengthy gelding: modest handicapper: stays 2m: acts on polytrack: has worn headgear: often races towards rear. *Jimmy Fox*

NEW WORLD POWER (JPN) 4 b.c. Deep Impact (JPN) 134 – Listen (IRE) 117 **92**
(Sadler's Wells (USA) 132) [2017 87: 14.6m^5 12g^2 11.9d^2 11.8d^6 13.3s^5 p14g^3 Sep 7] angular colt: fairly useful maiden: second at Brighton in July: stays 13.5f: acts on soft and good to firm going: sometimes slowly away, races well off pace. *David Simcock*

NEW YOUMZAIN (FR) 8 b.g. Sinndar (IRE) 134 – Luna Sacra (FR) 107 (Sadler's **72**
Wells (USA) 132) [2017 15d 14.1v^3 15s^4 15v Oct 12] tall, good-topped gelding: fair handicapper: stays 21.5f: acts on heavy going: has worn headgear. *Lucy Normile*

NEWZ WATCH 3 ch.f. Harbour Watch (IRE) 121 – Angus Newz 103 (Compton Place **–**
125) [2017 –: 6g Apr 7] little form: often races prominently. *Mick Quinn*

NEXIUS (IRE) 8 b.g. Catcher In The Rye (IRE) 115 – Nicolaia (GER) (Alkalde (GER)) **–**
[2017 p12g Jan 28] useful in Germany for W. Hickst in 2013, well held sole start on Flat since: stays 12.5f: winning hurdler/chaser. *Emma Lavelle*

NEXT CHALLENGE (GER) 3 ch.g. Shamardal (USA) 129 – Next Holy (IRE) (Holy **86**
Roman Emperor (IRE) 125) [2017 80p: 10m^3 Apr 24] well-made gelding: fairly useful form: third in maiden at Windsor (1½ lengths behind Wasatch Range) on sole outing in 2017. *Saeed bin Suroor*

NEXT EDITION (IRE) 9 b.g. Antonius Pius (USA) 123 – Starfish (IRE) (Galileo (IRE) **56**
134) [2017 69: t16.3g 16g Apr 17] fair handicapper: below best both starts in 2017: stayed 16.5f: acted on tapeta and any turf going: usually wore cheekpieces: often raced towards rear: dead. *Philip Kirby*

NEXT STAGE 4 ch.c. Dubawi (IRE) 129 – Dash To The Front 105 (Diktat 126) [2017 **105**
102p: 8m* 9m^2 May 6] lightly-raced useful handicapper: won at Newmarket (by 1½ lengths from Shaiyem) in April: stayed 9f: acted on polytrack and good to firm going: tried in hood: dead. *Saeed bin Suroor*

NEXT TRAIN'S GONE 4 b.g. Rail Link 132 – Coh Sho No 59 (Old Vic 136) [2017 76p: **97 p**
p16g* p16d* May 29] useful handicapper: won at Kempton in April and Chelmsford (by 9 lengths from Taper Tantrum) in May: stays 2m: acts on polytrack: open to further improvement. *James Eustace*

NEZAR (IRE) 6 ch.g. Mastercraftsman (IRE) 129 – Teddy Bears Picnic (Oasis Dream 129) **89**
[2017 78: p6g t6g^{6} p6g^{2} t6g* 6m^{4} 6d^{2} p6g^{4} 6s^{2} t6d p6g^{2} p7g^{2} p6s^{5} p6g^{5} Dec 21] angular gelding: fairly useful handicapper: won at Wolverhampton in April: runner-up on 5 occasions: stays 7f: acts on polytrack, tapeta, firm and soft going: has worn headgear: usually races towards rear. *Dean Ivory*

NEZWAAH 4 b.f. Dubawi (IRE) 129 – Ferdoos 122 (Dansili 127) [2017 113: 10m* **120**
10g* 11.9d^{4} 10s^{5} 9f Nov 4]

Roger Varian took over the licence at Kremlin House Stables in Newmarket in 2011 due to the poor health of his long-time boss Michael Jarvis. 'I've learned plenty. Michael's always been the guv'nor, but he became a friend, ally and mentor. It's maybe my name after the winners, but it's the same team,' Varian said at the time. Varian had joined as assistant trainer at Kremlin House in May 2001, around the time that the Sheikh Ahmed Al Maktoum-owned Ameerat gave Jarvis a first British classic winner in the One Thousand Guineas. Jarvis' career already spanned more than three decades at that stage—his first top-level winner was Tudor Music in the 1969 renewal of the Haydock Sprint Cup—while Sheikh Ahmed's own involvement in racing was kick-started by Mtoto, the winner of the Coral-Eclipse and King George VI and Queen Elizabeth Stakes in 1988. The first pattern-race successes for Jarvis with horses owned by Sheikh Ahmed came with Noushkey in the Lancashire Oaks and Alrassaam in the Prix Daphnis, both in 1999, while Morshdi won the Italian Derby just three weeks after Ameerat's One Thousand Guineas victory, before also finishing second to Galileo in the Irish Derby. Some of Sheikh Ahmed's best horses were switched to Godolphin in later years, including the 2005 Park Stakes winner Iffraaj and the 2010 Lonsdale Cup winner Opinion Poll, but there have been few more loyal supporters of the yard, and it was perhaps only fitting that Roger Varian's first Group 1 winner came in the yellow silks with black epaulets. Varian joined a select band who have won a Group 1 in their first season with a licence when Nahrain won the Prix de l'Opera at Longchamp, just twelve days after Michael Jarvis had passed away. Nahrain was one of two individual 'black-type' winners Varian had that season for Sheikh Ahmed, the other being the four-year-old filly Ferdoos, a smart performer who won her first start for Varian (having raced three times for Jarvis at two) in the listed Pinnacle Stakes at Haydock. She reportedly bled when well held behind Dancing Rain on her only subsequent start in the British Champions Fillies' And Mares' Stakes at Ascot and was retired to stud. Dubawi was selected for her first covering and, in a year of change for Varian, the resulting offspring ensured that Sheikh Ahmed's famous colours were still to the fore in 2017.

Already the winner of a listed race at Newcastle as a three-year-old, Nezwaah was due to make her seasonal reappearance in the Dahlia Stakes at Newmarket in May. She had other ideas, however, bursting out of the stalls and having to be withdrawn, a misdemeanour that Varian described as 'a freak occurrence'. After passing a stalls test, Nezwaah lined up in a listed race at Ayr later that month, and never looked in any danger, not needing to be at her very best in justifying odds of 2/1-on but still impressive in the way she quickened three and three quarter lengths clear. It was to Ireland next for the Pretty Polly Stakes, a race Varian and jockey Andrea Atzeni had won four years earlier with Ambivalent. In a really competitive renewal at the Curragh, the market was dominated by a pair of five-year-olds, the 2016 British Champions Fillies' And Mares' Stakes winner Journey (15/8) and last-time-out Man o' War Stakes winner Zhukova (7/2). Neither was at her best on the day, but both would have had their work cut out anyway against Nezwaah, who made the breakthrough at Group 1 level in taking style, storming clear after being produced to lead a furlong out. The official winning margin was three and a quarter lengths over Rain Goddess, with Turret Rocks a length and a half further back in third. Nezwaah was due to make her next start in the Nassau Stakes at Goodwood but was a late absentee on account of the heavy ground. Stepped up to a mile and a half in the Yorkshire Oaks, Nezwaah ran respectably to finish five and three quarter lengths fourth behind Enable, though she left the impression that slightly softer ground than she had faced before didn't suit her ideally. She was below form on her last two starts, in the E.P. Taylor Stakes at Woodbine and the Breeders' Cup Filly & Mare Turf at Del Mar.

Pretty Polly Stakes, the Curragh—British challenger Nezwaah quickens clear to make the breakthrough at Group 1 level, beating Rain Goddess (white face) and Turret Rocks (quartered cap)

Nezwaah's Pretty Polly victory was one of two Group 1 victories for Roger Varian in his first year at Carlburg Stables, Clive Brittain's former yard, a move he made in January after six seasons as trainer at Kremlin House ('I was naturally sad to leave but Carlburg is a wonderful yard with a peerless history and I am delighted to be training out of here. I hope the move will allow us to continue to grow as a training operation'). Ajman Princess registered the stable's other Group 1 when making most under Andrea Atzeni in the Prix Jean Romanet at Deauville, the only Group 1 victory of 2017 for her owner Sheikh Mohammed Obaid Al Maktoum. Sheikh Obaid, who removed his string from Luca Cumani in the autumn of 2015, is now one of the chief patrons of Roger Varian's yard that had over two hundred horses in the latest season. Among the horses switched from Luca Cumani was the King George winner Postponed, who went on to win the Dubai Sheema Classic, Coronation Cup and Juddmonte International in 2016, and was the best horse of any age trained in Britain that year. Postponed was below form in two starts in Dubai in early-2017, however, the second of which proved to be his swansong as he suffered a stress fracture in May. He will be standing alongside his sire Dubawi at Dalham Hall Stud in Newmarket in 2018, at a fee of £20,000. Sheikh Obaid has already set about finding his replacement, with Varian going to 2,600,000 guineas for a Dubawi colt out of the dual Group 1-winning filly Izzi Top at the Newmarket October Sales Book 1. Varian bought three Dubawi colts at the sale, the others being a 650,000 guineas colt out of the dual Guineas winner Finsceal Beo and a 400,000 guineas colt out of the listed winner and Group 3 placed Gemstone, both of whom also have Sheikh Obaid now listed as their owner. Though he failed to record a Group 1 winner in Britain in the latest season, Varian clearly has plenty to look forward to in 2018 with the backing of owners such as Sheikh Ahmed and Sheikh Obaid. The Geoffrey Freer Stakes winner Defoe and the Cheveley Park Stakes third Madeline are among those that could make their presence felt in Group 1 company for the yard in the next season.

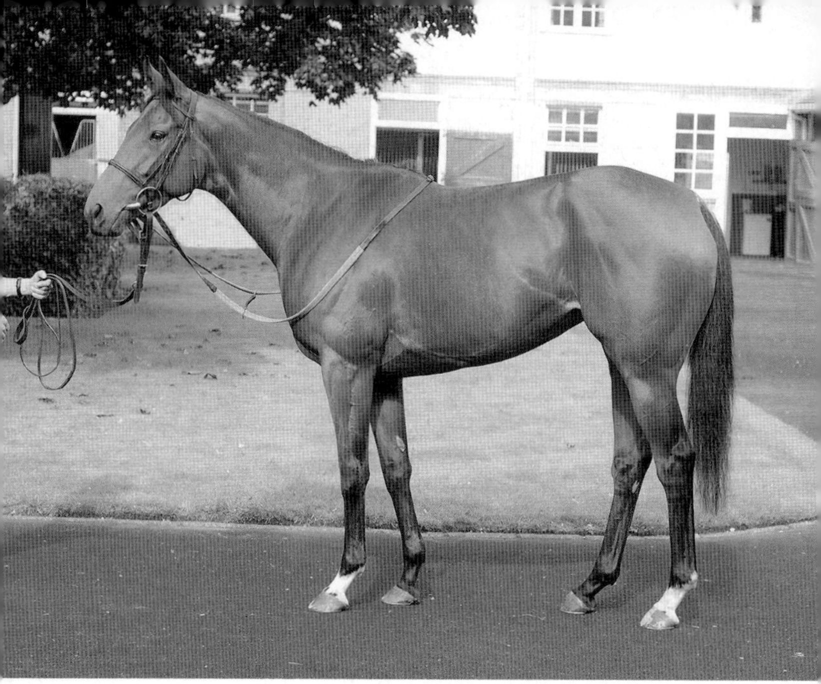

Mr Ahmed Al Maktoum's "Nezwaah"

Nezwaah (b.f. 2013)	Dubawi (IRE) (b 2002)	Dubai Millennium (b 1996)	Seeking The Gold
			Colorado Dancer
		Zomaradah (b 1995)	Deploy
			Jawaher
	Ferdoos (b 2007)	Dansili (b 1996)	Danehill
			Hasili
		Blaze of Colour (ch 2001)	Rainbow Quest
			Hawait Al Barr

The second foal out of the Dansili mare Ferdoos, Madjbor (by Pivotal), finished well held on his first start at Jebel Ali in early-November, while the two-year-old Monteja (by Shamardal), also trained by Varian, was withdrawn ahead of her intended racecourse debut at Wolverhampton later that month after proving unruly in the stalls. Ferdoos is out of the Rainbow Quest mare Blaze of Colour and was bought as a yearling by Michael Jarvis for 200,000 guineas. Blaze of Colour won a couple of handicaps over a mile and a half and improved at three and at four, finishing third in a listed race at Newmarket over the same trip on her final start. A half-brother to Ferdoos named Brusco won four races at three and four in Germany and Italy for Andreas Wohler, including a pair of listed events, and he was also placed in the German St Leger. Nezwaah's great grandam Hawait Al Barr was a winner at up to two miles. This is also the family of Real Quiet, a multiple Grade 1 winner in the States including the Kentucky Derby and Preakness Stakes in 1998. A compact filly, Nezwaah stayed a mile and a quarter and acted on polytrack, tapeta and good to firm going. She was possibly not at her best on going softer than good. She could sometimes be slowly away in her races, but was a strong travelling sort and often raced towards the rear. *Roger Varian*

NIBLAWI (IRE) 5 b.g. Vale of York (IRE) 117 – Finnmark (Halling (USA) 133) [2017 **103** 96: 10g^{5} 12v^{2} 12d^{4} 11.6g^{5} 11.9s Nov 11] tall gelding: useful handicapper: second at Ascot (length behind Royal Associate) in July: stays 1½m: acts on polytrack, good to firm and heavy going: has worn headgear. *Neil Mulholland*

NIBRAS AGAIN 3 b.g. Kyllachy 129 – Regina 97 (Green Desert (USA) 127) [2017 77: **79** 6m^{5} 6f^{5} 6.1m^{4} 7g^{2} 6g p8d Aug 16] sturdy gelding: fair maiden: stays 7f: acts on good to firm going: tried in cheekpieces. *Ismail Mohammed*

NIBRAS GALAXY (IRE) 2 b.c. (Feb 27) Nathaniel (IRE) 129 – Galaxy Dancer (USA) **77** (Kingmambo (USA) 125) [2017 8.2g^{6} 8.3v p8s^{3} Nov 23] fair form: best effort when third in minor event at Chelmsford (3 lengths behind Noble Expression) in November. *Ismail Mohammed*

NICE SHOT (IRE) 2 b.c. (Apr 8) Kodiac 112 – Emma Dora (IRE) 64 (Medaglia d'Oro **88 p** (USA) 129) [2017 p6g t6g^{3} p7s* Dec 8] €160,000Y: fourth foal: half-brother to 2 winners, including 1m winner Moving Robe (by Iffraaj): dam 2-y-o 6f winner: fairly useful form: won minor event at Chelmsford (by 2¾ lengths from Court House) in December: stays 7f: tried in hood: likely to progress further. *David Simcock*

NICE VINTAGE (IRE) 5 b.m. Big Bad Bob (IRE) 118 – High Vintage (IRE) 97 (High **–** Chaparral (IRE) 132) [2017 85: t8g t8g Dec 6] fairly useful handicapper, tailed-off last both starts in 2017: stays 10.5f: acts on soft and good to firm going: usually wears visor, not in 2017. *Katie Scott*

NICHOLAS T 5 b.g. Rail Link 132 – Thorntoun Piccolo 64 (Groom Dancer (USA) 128) **99** [2017 89: t8g 8m 8m* 8m^{2} 8.3m^{3} 8m* 8g* 8.3s 8g^{3} 7d 8d^{2} 10.3m 9d 7.9g Oct 13] strong gelding: useful handicapper: won at Doncaster in April, and Ayr in May and June: second at Ascot (2 lengths behind Raising Sand) in August: stays 1¼m: acts on soft and good to firm going. *Jim Goldie*

NICKLAUS 2 ch.g. (Mar 28) Exceed And Excel (AUS) 126 – Nianga (GER) 106 (Lomitas **75 p** 129) [2017 6d^{6} p7g^{5} 6d* Oct 20] €180,000Y: fourth foal: half-brother to German 2-y-o 6f winner Nossa (by Areion): dam, German winner up to 1½m (2-y-o 1m winner), half-sister to useful German winner up to 8.5f winner Nadelwald: fair form: won minor event at Redcar (by head from Wrenthorpe) in October: open to further improvement. *William Haggas*

NICK VEDDER 3 b.g. Rip Van Winkle (IRE) 134 – Devotion (IRE) 102 (Dylan Thomas **81** (IRE) 132) [2017 58: t8g^{3} t8d* 10.3m 8d t8g^{3} p8g^{3} Dec 31] fairly useful handicapper: won at Newcastle in March: left K. R. Burke after fifth start: stays 1m: acts on polytrack and tapeta: tried in cheekpieces: often races prominently. *Michael Wigham*

NICKY BABY (IRE) 3 gr.g. Dark Angel (IRE) 113 – Moon Club (IRE) (Red Clubs (IRE) **65** 125) [2017 61: t7.1m^{6} p7g^{4} p7d^{5} p8g 6g^{4} 6d t7.2g p7m p10s p12g Dec 23] good-topped gelding: fair maiden: stays 7f: acts on polytrack and tapeta: wears headgear: sometimes slowly away, usually races nearer last than first. *Dean Ivory*

NIDNOD 4 b.f. Myboycharlie (IRE) 118 – Littlemisstutti (IRE) (Noverre (USA) 125) **43** [2017 56: p6g p5m p6g^{5} p8d p7g Feb 22] smallish, angular filly: poor handicapper: stays 1m: acts on polytrack, best turf form on good going: tried in cheekpieces: often races in rear. *John Bridger*

NIETZSCHE 4 ch.g. Poet's Voice 126 – Ganga (IRE) 94 (Generous (IRE) 139) [2017 92: **–** 11.9g^{5} 16v Oct 8] fairly useful handicapper, below best both starts on Flat in 2017: should stay 2m: acts on polytrack, tapeta and heavy going: has worn hood, including last 2 starts: fairly useful hurdler. *Brian Ellison*

NIFTY NIECE (IRE) 3 gr.f. Zebedee 113 – Hasty Harriet (IRE) 63 (Choisir (AUS) 126) **38** [2017 55: 5m^{5} 5m 5.9s 6g t7.1d f8.1g Dec 4] poor maiden: best effort at 5f: acts on good to firm going: sometimes in cheekpieces. *Ann Duffield*

NIGH OR NEVER (IRE) 3 b.g. Excelebration (IRE) 133 – Nigh (IRE) (Galileo (IRE) **63** 134) [2017 –: 8.3g p7g 10m^{4} 10.2m 14s Aug 25] modest maiden: left Tom Dascombe after fourth start: tried in cheekpieces/tongue tie. *Rebecca Curtis*

NIGHT AIR 2 b.f. (Feb 24) Pastoral Pursuits 127 – Night Kiss (FR) 71 (Night Shift **–** (USA)) [2017 6g t5.1g 5d Oct 4] 2,000F: seventh foal: half-sister to useful winner up to 11f Avon River (2-y-o 5f-7f winner, by Avonbridge) and winner up to 9f Minal (2-y-o 7f winner, by Compton Place): dam 7f winner (including at 2 yrs): no form: in visor last 2 starts. *Derek Shaw*

NIGHT CIRCUS (IRE) 3 b.g. Invincible Spirit (IRE) 121 – Surrealism 93 (Pivotal 124) **99** [2017 8m* 10m^{5} 8d^{4} 8g^{2} 7d^{3} 8g^{6} Sep 28] strong, well-made gelding: fourth foal: half-brother to useful 1m/8.6f winner Momayyaz (by Elusive Quality): dam, 1¼m-15f winner, half-sister to Melbourne Cup runner-up Bauer: useful performer: won newcomers race at Newmarket in April: third in handicap at Doncaster (4½ lengths behind Lahore) in September: stays 1m: acts on good to firm and good to soft going: has joined Ismail Mohammed. *Charlie Appleby*

NIGHTDRESS (IRE) 3 b.f. Rip Van Winkle (IRE) 134 – Haute Volta (FR) (Grape Tree **–** Road 122) [2017 10m^{6} 12s 7.4m^{5} 7.4m 7d Jul 28] €40,000Y: half-sister to 3 winners, including 2-y-o 6f winner Attracted To You (by Hurricane Run) and winner up to 1m Super Motiva (by Motivator), both useful: dam unraced half-sister to useful winner up to 1m Heart of Darkness: no form: tried in visor: often starts slowly. *Tony Coyle*

NIGHT GENERATION (GER) 5 ch.g. Sholokhov (IRE) 121 – Night Woman (GER) **75** (Monsun (GER) 124) [2017 –: p15.8m^{5} p15.8g^{3} p16d^{2} p15.8g* 16.3m^{2} p16s^{3} p15.8g 16s p15.8g Dec 20] fair handicapper: won at Lingfield in May: stays 16.5f: acts on polytrack and good to firm going: wears cheekpieces: often wears tongue tie. *Chris Gordon*

NIGHTINGALE VALLEY 4 ch.f. Compton Place 125 – Dancing Storm 71 (Trans **86** Island 119) [2017 80: p6g* p7d^{5} p6g^{2} 7d^{2} p7d Aug 23] sturdy filly: fairly useful handicapper: won at Kempton in April: stays 7f: acts on polytrack and good to soft going. *Stuart Kittow*

NIGHT LAW 3 b.f. Lawman (FR) 121 – Night Carnation 116 (Sleeping Indian 122) [2017 **82** 79: 6d^{4} 5m^{4} 6g^{5} 5.4d 5.9s^{5} 6.3s 5.8g 5s p7g t6s p7s Dec 8] good-topped filly: fairly useful handicapper: left Richard Fahey after fifth start: stays 6f: acts on good to firm and good to soft going: has worn hood: often races towards rear. *Barry John Murphy, Ireland*

NIGHT MYTH (IRE) 2 b.f. (Jan 20) Epaulette (AUS) 126 – Angel Nights (IRE) (Night **–** Shift (USA)) [2017 7g 7d p7g Dec 22] £35,000Y: fifth foal: half-sister to winner up to 6f Monkey Bar Flies (2-y-o 5f winner, by Elusive City) and 6f winner Hepworth Marble (by Lilbourne Lad): dam unraced half-sister to winner up to 1m Sacred Nuts and winner up to 8.5f Them And Us (both useful): tailed-off last all 3 starts: left Richard Hannon after second one. *John Joseph Hanlon, Ireland*

NIGHT OF GLORY 3 b.g. Sea The Stars (IRE) 140 – Kesara (Sadler's Wells (USA) 132) **102** [2017 10m^{2} 10g* 12d^{4} 14m 11.9g 13.9m 11.8v^{2} 11.8s^{5} Oct 10] €50,000Y: fourth foal: half-brother to 3 winners, including 1¼m-1½m winner Apparatchika (by Archipenko) and 7f/1m winner Kirks Ryker (by Selkirk): dam, 7f/1m winner, half-sister to useful 8.6f-1¼m winner Persona Grata: useful performer: won maiden at the Curragh in May: second in handicap at Haydock (2¼ lengths behind Royal Line) in September: left M. D. O'Callaghan after fourth start: stays 1½m: acts on heavy going: tried in cheekpieces: often races prominently/lazily. *Andrew Balding*

NIGHT POETRY (IRE) 3 b.f. Sea The Stars (IRE) 140 – Aquila d'Oriente (ITY) **64** (Dubawi (IRE) 129) [2017 t8.6g^{3} p10g Mar 11] €230,000F: first foal: dam, winner up to 9f (2-y-o 7f/1m winner), half-sister to useful winner up to 1¾m Figli Fanesi: modest form: better effort when third in maiden at Wolverhampton in January. *Charlie Appleby*

NIGHT SHADOW 3 ch.g. Haafhd 129 – Totally Trusted 66 (Oasis Dream 129) [2017 –: **66** t8g t6g^{4} t5.1g^{4} t6m* 6m t7.1d t7.1g t6s t6.1d Dec 16] fair handicapper: won at Wolverhampton in March: stays 6f: acts on tapeta: tried in blinkers. *Alan Brown*

NIGHT SPARK (GER) 2 b.g. (Feb 26) Soldier Hollow 121 – Nocturna (GER) (Dai Jin **–** 123) [2017 7g t8.6d Dec 27] sturdy gelding: well held in maiden/minor event. *Ralph Beckett*

NIGHTSWIFT 5 b.g. Midnight Legend 118 – Sharbasia (IRE) (King's Best (USA) 132) **49** [2017 –: 7d^{4} 8g^{5} 10.2d^{6} Aug 23] poor maiden: stays 1m: acts on good to soft going. *James Evans*

NIKITA (IRE) 2 b.f. (Mar 4) Exceed And Excel (AUS) 126 – Rosinka (IRE) 116 (Soviet **–** Star (USA) 128) [2017 p6d^{6} Dec 13] fifth foal: closely related to 1½m winner (stayed 16.5f) Moshe (by Dansili) and 1m-1¼m winner Jam Jar (by Duke of Marmalade) and half-sister to very smart winner up to 1½m Move Up (2-y-o 7f/1m winner, by Dubawi): dam winner up to 11f (2-y-o 6f winner): in hood, 25/1, considerate introduction when well held in minor event at Kempton. *Hughie Morrison*

NIMR 4 b.g. Shamardal (USA) 129 – Riberac 110 (Efisio 120) [2017 101: t7.1g^{6} t7.1g* **81 +** t8.6g* 8g p8g^{2} 7g^{4} p9.9g^{2} p9.4g* a8.9g^{6} Sep 10] sturdy gelding: useful performer at best **a113** on turf, smart on all-weather: won handicaps at Wolverhampton in February and March (by 1¾ lengths from Forceful Appeal) and minor event at Deauville (by length from Allez Henri) in August: neck second to Sovereign Debt in All-Weather Mile Championships at Lingfield: left Richard Fahey after sixth start: stays 9.5f: acts on polytrack, tapeta, soft and good to firm going: has worn tongue tie. *Julien Phelippon, France*

NINE BELOW ZERO 2 b.g. (Mar 8) Showcasing 117 – Finesse 88 (Shamardal (USA) 129) [2017 5m* 5.1m* 5m 5g 6v^5 Oct 4] compact colt: first foal: dam 5f-7f winner: fairly useful performer: won minor events at Salisbury in May and Windsor (by 3¾ lengths from Midsummer Knight) in June: best form at 5f: acts on good to firm going: tried in blinkers: sometimes slowly away. *Ralph Beckett* **92**

NINEDARTER 3 b.g. Monsieur Bond (IRE) 120 – Caranbola 91 (Lucky Story (USA) 128) [2017 –: 7g^6 t7.2g^{pu} 6d t5g Nov 3] no form. *Antony Brittain* **–**

NINEPIN BOWLER 3 b.g. Rip Van Winkle (IRE) 134 – Smooth As Silk (IRE) 73 (Danehill Dancer (IRE) 117) [2017 t8g^3 8g^4 8g^6 t12.4d Sep 29] fair form in maidens/handicap. *Michael Dods* **73**

NINETY YEARS YOUNG 3 b.g. Paco Boy (IRE) 129 – Lady of Windsor (IRE) 73 (Woods of Windsor (USA)) [2017 72: t6g^3 p6g^5 Jan 28] neat gelding: fair at best at 2 yrs: stays 6f: acts on polytrack and good to soft going: wears blinkers. *David Elsworth* **63**

NINJAGO 7 b.g. Mount Nelson 125 – Fidelio's Miracle (USA) 108 (Mountain Cat (USA)) [2017 109: t6g^5 t6g 6g^3 6g^6 6s 6m^5 6g t6s 6d 6d^5 6m* 6d^3 6.1d^3 p6g Nov 7] good-topped gelding: useful handicapper: won at Newmarket in August: third at Doncaster (½ length behind Wentworth Falls) in April: stays 7f, raced mainly at shorter: acts on polytrack, tapeta, firm and soft going: has worn headgear. *Paul Midgley* **97**

NIP DOWN THE JUG 3 b.g. Piccolo 121 – The City Kid (IRE) 76 (Danetime (IRE) 121) [2017 –: 6g 8g 9d Jul 12] workmanlike gelding: no form. *Michael Attwater* **–**

NIQNAAQPAADIWAAQ 5 b.g. Aqlaam 125 – Aswaaq (IRE) 74 (Peintre Celebre (USA) 137) [2017 73: 7m 6d 6g 6.9v^6 8v t9.5g Nov 25] fair at best, out of form in 2017: tried in headgear: front runner/races prominently. *Eric Alston* **–**

NISEKO 3 b.g. Cacique (IRE) 124 – Snow Crystal (IRE) 87 (Kingmambo (USA) 125) [2017 –: 10m 8.2d^5 9.9m^2 9.9m^6 10m Jul 10] fair maiden: stayed 1¼m: acted on good to firm going: in headgear last 4 starts: dead. *William Muir* **67**

NITRO 3 b.g. Fight Club (GER) 115 – Come On Molly (Dreams End 93) [2017 6g 7.1g^6 10s^5 8.1m f5g t7.2g Nov 29] close-coupled gelding: no form. *Roy Brotherton* **–**

NOAH AMOR (IRE) 4 b.g. Kodiac 112 – Jumbo Romance (IRE) 69 (Tagula (IRE) 116) [2017 74: t5.1g t5g^3 6m* 5g* 5m^2 6g* 5g^4 6m^5 5.2m^3 5d* 5g^2 5m^2 5.1v^5 p5g^2 t5g f5g^4 Oct 22] fairly useful performer: won sellers at Redcar and Thirsk (twice) in April/May for Richard Fahey, and handicap at Beverley in August: left David Nicholls after second start: stays 6f: acts on polytrack, good to firm and good to soft going: front runner/races prominently: sold 11,000 gns in October. *David O'Meara* **81**

NOBLE ACT 4 b.f. Kyllachy 129 – Noble Desert (FR) (Green Desert (USA) 127) [2017 77: t6m p7g^4 p6g^5 p7g t7.2g^4 p7s p5s p7s t6.1g^6 Aug 18] fair handicapper: left Rae Guest after first start: probably stays 7f: acts on polytrack and good to firm going: tried in cheekpieces. *Phil McEntee* **71**

NOBLE ASSET 6 ch.g. Compton Place 125 – Chance For Romance 81 (Entrepreneur 123) [2017 77, a71: t5.1g^5 t5.1g^4 t5.1g^3 t5.1g p5g Mar 24] fair handicapper: usually raced at 5f: acted on polytrack, tapeta, good to firm and good to soft going: tried in headgear: dead. *Milton Bradley* **66**

NOBLE AUSSIE (IRE) 6 gr.g. Aussie Rules (USA) 123 – Nobilissima (IRE) 94 (Orpen (USA) 116) [2017 44: p8g^6 p8g 10g t12.4d Dec 16] modest maiden: left Patrick Martin after third start: stays 10.5f: acts on polytrack: tried in cheekpieces: sometimes in tongue tie. *Miss Nicole McKenna, Ireland* **52**

NOBLE BALLAD 3 b.g. Royal Applause 124 – Melody Maker 62 (Diktat 126) [2017 66p: p8g 8s f7.1g* 7d f8.1g^5 f7.1g Dec 19] smallish gelding: fair handicapper: won at Southwell in August: stays 7f: acts on polytrack and fibresand: often wears blinkers. *Ralph Beckett* **65**

NOBLE BEHEST 3 b.g. Sir Percy 129 – Lady Hestia (USA) 82 (Belong To Me (USA)) [2017 –: 8m 12m p16g* 16.1g* t16.5g* p15.8g* Dec 20] good-topped gelding: fairly useful handicapper: won at Chelmsford in August, Thirsk and Wolverhampton in September, and Lingfield in December: left Marcus Tregoning after fifth start: stays 16.5f: acts on polytrack and tapeta: often wears cheekpieces: often races prominently: remains with potential. *Robert Stephens* **88 p**

NOBLE CONQUEST (FR) 3 b.g. Siyouni (FR) 122 – Visualize 73 (Medicean 128) [2017 8.1m^3 p8s^5 8d^2 p7g Oct 25] €95,000Y, €150,000 2-y-o: tall gelding: third foal: dam 1¼m winner out of useful winner up to 1m Fantasize: fairly useful form: second in maiden at Thirsk in August: stays 1m: tried in hood: sold 3,500 gns in October. *Sir Michael Stoute* **91**

NOBLE DEED 7 ch.g. Kyllachy 129 – Noble One 107 (Primo Dominie 121) [2017 67, a80: p7g^{5} p6m p6g^{3} p6g^{6} p7m^{4} p6g^{2} p6g^{2} p6g^{6} 7d 6m^{3} 6m 7m p6g p7g p6g^{6} Dec 31] smallish, sturdy gelding: modest handicapper on turf, fair on all-weather: stays 6f: acts on polytrack and firm going: usually wears headgear. *Michael Attwater* **58 a70**

NOBLE EXPRESSION 2 b.c. (Feb 15) Sir Percy 129 – Disposition 83 (Selkirk (USA) 129) [2017 7s p8g^{6} p8s* Nov 23] 26,000F, 75,000Y: second foal: dam maiden (stayed 1½m): fairly useful form: won minor event at Chelmsford (by 1¼ lengths from Best Blue) in November: will stay 9f+: open to further improvement. *Roger Varian* **85 p**

NOBLE GIFT 7 ch.g. Cadeaux Genereux 131 – Noble Penny 64 (Pennekamp (USA) 130) [2017 107: p11g^{6} p10g* p10s^{2} 10d^{3} 12d 9.9g^{5} 9.9g p10s^{4} 11.8d^{3} Oct 30] workmanlike gelding: useful handicapper: won at Chelmsford (by ¾ length from Ickymasho) in May: second there (head behind Fanciful Angel) later in May and third at Newmarket (2 lengths behind Banditry) in June: stays 1½m: acts on polytrack, good to firm and heavy going: has worn hood: front runner. *William Knight* **107**

NOBLEMAN (GER) 3 b.g. Lord of England (GER) 119 – Naomia (GER) (Monsun (GER) 124) [2017 60: p12f 9.9f 11.6d 11.6d Jul 1] modest maiden: in headgear last 3 starts: often races freely: has joined Eamon Courtney, Ireland. *Hughie Morrison* **57**

NOBLE MANNERS (IRE) 2 b.f. (Apr 22) Myboycharlie (IRE) 118 – New Story (USA) 111 (Dynaformer (USA)) [2017 5m^{4} 5f^{2} 6m^{6} 6m^{3} 6d^{4} 7s* 8g^{5} 8d^{5} Sep 19] €14,000F, €30,000Y: big filly, has scope: half-sister to several winners, including smart winner up to 6f New Girlfriend (2-y-o 5f/5.5f winner, by Diesis) and 7.5f-1½m winner Wazn (by Whipper): dam winner up to 1¼m (2-y-o 5f winner): fairly useful performer: won nursery at Newmarket (by neck from Di Fede) in July: stays 7f: acts on firm and soft going: sometimes slowly away, often races in rear: sold £5,500 in November. *Mark Johnston* **82**

NOBLEMAN'S NEST 2 br.c. (Apr 12) Poet's Voice 126 – Tamzin (Hernando (FR) 127) [2017 6.5m^{2} 6s* 6m 7d* 7m Oct 14] tall colt: seventh foal: half-brother to smart winner up to 1m (stayed 12.5f) Lustrous (2-y-o 7f winner, by Champs Elysees), useful 2-y-o 6f winner Melody of Love (by Haafhd) and useful winner up to 7f Ustinov (2-y-o 6f winner, by Exceed And Excel): dam unraced: useful performer: won minor event at Newmarket in July and nursery at Doncaster (by 1½ lengths from Crownthorpe) in September: stays 7f: acts on soft going: often travels strongly. *Simon Crisford* **97**

NOBLE MASTERPIECE 3 ch.g. Dutch Art 126 – Elysian 79 (Galileo (IRE) 134) [2017 7d p6s^{3} 6s^{4} 7m* p8g^{2} 7d^{5} Sep 21] 170,000Y: first foal: dam, 1½m winner, half-sister to very smart 1m winner Integral out of very smart winner up to 9f Echelon: fairly useful performer: won handicap at Yarmouth in August: second in similar event at Kempton in September: stays 1m: acts on polytrack and good to firm going: sold 38,000 gns, sent to Qatar. *Sir Michael Stoute* **94**

NOBLE PEACE 4 b.g. Kyllachy 129 – Peace Concluded 72 (Bertolini (USA) 125) [2017 88: p8g^{5} 7m 7m* 7m^{3} 7f^{5} 7v^{2} 7d^{6} 7s^{4} 7d^{5} 8s* p10g^{6} Dec 12] good-topped gelding: useful handicapper: won at Goodwood in May and October (by 2½ lengths from Casement): left Henry Candy after tenth start: stays 1m: acts on polytrack, good to firm and heavy going. *Lydia Pearce* **97**

NOBLE STAR (IRE) 4 b.g. Acclamation 118 – Wrong Answer 102 (Verglas (IRE) 118) [2017 85p: p8d^{3} 7d^{2} p7g^{4} Oct 11] fairly useful handicapper: second at Newmarket in September: stays 1m: acts on polytrack, tapeta and good to soft going: remains with potential. *James Fanshawe* **86 p**

NOBLE SWORD 3 b.g. Sayif (IRE) 122 – Noble Nova 69 (Fraam 114) [2017 6m^{6} 6m t5s^{6} 6g^{F} 5m Jun 24] no form: tried in blinkers. *Jedd O'Keeffe* **–**

NOBLY BORN 3 ch.g. Mayson 124 – Noble One 107 (Primo Dominie 121) [2017 94p: 6.1g^{3} 6d^{4} 6d^{4} 6v^{6} 6d* Oct 6] smart handicapper: won at Ascot (by 2 lengths from Silent Echo) in October: raced only at 6f: acts on good to firm and good to soft going: tried in blinkers: sold 190,000 gns in October. *John Gosden* **110**

NOBRASSNOLASS (IRE) 2 b.f. (Apr 26) Kodiac 112 – Hams (USA) 67 (Dixie Union (USA) 121) [2017 5m^{4} 5m 5.1m^{6} 5g^{6} 5m Aug 31] €38,000Y: sixth foal: half-sister to 3 winners, including useful winner up to 1m Dixie's Dream (2-y-o 6f winner, by Hawk Wing) and 7f winner Tuff Love (by Casamento): dam lightly-raced half-sister to US Grade 2 2-y-o 6.5f winner Desert Digger: modest maiden: raced only at 5f: acts on good to firm going: in headgear last 3 starts: usually races prominently. *Tom Dascombe* **59**

NO CIVIL JUSTICE 2 b.g. (Mar 4) Milk It Mick 120 – Flashing Floozie 54 (Muhtarram (USA) 125) [2017 7v Nov 7] 150/1, well held in minor event at Redcar. *David Thompson* **–**

NOCTURN 8 b.g. Oasis Dream 129 – Pizzicato 64 (Statoblest 120) [2017 79: p6g Mar 8] good-bodied gelding: fair handicapper, well held sole start in 2017: stays 6f: acts on polytrack, tapeta, good to firm and good to soft going: wears headgear: often hangs, and hard to catch right. *Ronald Harris* **–**

NO DAMAGE (IRE) 3 ch.f. Roderic O'Connor (IRE) 119 – Flashing Blade 90 (Inchinor 119) [2017 7d p8g Oct 5] 5,500 2-y-o: seventh foal: half-sister to winner abroad by Cape Cross: dam, 8.2f winner, half-sister to smart 5f-9f winner Needwood Blade: tailed-off last in 2 maidens. *Michael Attwater* **–**

NOGUCHI (IRE) 12 ch.g. Pivotal 124 – Tuscania (USA) (Woodman (USA) 126) [2017 73: f14g² p12g f12m² f14m⁶ f14g⁵ p14g² p14g t12.2g⁴ Jun 26] fair handicapper: stays 2m, effective at shorter: acts on all-weather and good to firm going: wears headgear. *Chris Dwyer* **72**

NO I'M EASY (IRE) 2 b.c. (Mar 28) Zoffany (IRE) 121 – Caribbean Queen (IRE) (Celtic Swing 138) [2017 6d² 6g* 6m Sep 23] €130,000F, €70,000Y: tall, attractive colt: fourth foal: brother to 7f winner The Yellow Bus and half-brother to 2-y-o 7f winner Lady Pastrana (by Key of Luck): dam unraced: fairly useful form: won minor event at Thirsk (by neck from Harrogate) in August: best effort when second in newcomers race at Ascot (2¼ lengths behind Mythical Magic) 3 weeks earlier: raced only at 6f. *Tom Dascombe* **89**

NOMORECALLS (IRE) 2 b.g. (Feb 25) Dawn Approach (IRE) 132 – Semayyel (IRE) 108 (Green Desert (USA) 127) [2017 5d³ Jun 7] 26,000Y: first foal: dam winner up to 1¼m (2-y-o 7f winner) who stayed 1½m: 6/1, third in minor event at Ripon (6¼ lengths behind Another Batt) in June: should do better. *Robert Cowell* **64 p**

NO MORE COMMISERY (IRE) 2 b.f. (Apr 1) Dandy Man (IRE) 123 – Lady Bracknell (IRE) 68 (Definite Article 121) [2017 p5g⁴ p5g⁶ p5g⁵ Dec 12] €8,000Y, 22,000 2-y-o: third foal: half-sister to winner abroad by Refuse To Bend: dam, maiden (stayed 1m), half-sister to smart 2-y-o 5f winner Light The Rocket: modest form: best effort when fourth in minor event at Kempton (2¾ lengths behind Knockout Blow) in September. *Mick Quinn* **63**

NO MORE THRILLS 2 ch.f. (Feb 15) Dutch Art 126 – The Thrill Is Gone 98 (Bahamian Bounty 116) [2017 p6g³ 6.5d⁶ Oct 27] 160,000Y: second foal: dam, 2-y-o 5f winner, half-sister to high-class 6f/7f winner Muarrab: modest form: better effort when third in maiden at Kempton (5 lengths behind Mushahadaat) in October: should still improve. *Richard Hannon* **61 p**

NONCHALANT 6 gr.g. Oasis Dream 129 – Comeback Queen 91 (Nayef (USA) 129) [2017 a71: t9.5m* p8g⁶ p10g Feb 9] fair handicapper: won at Wolverhampton (apprentice, by 1¼ lengths from Frivolous Prince) in January: stayed 12.5f: acted on tapeta, good to firm and good to soft going: often wore headgear: usually led: dead. *Hugo Froud* **71**

NONEEDTOTELLME (IRE) 4 gr.f. Fast Company (IRE) 126 – Gemma's Delight (IRE) 71 (Clodovil (IRE) 116) [2017 44: 7m⁵ 6s t5.1g⁴ p6s t6.1d³ t6.1d⁴ Dec 27] modest maiden: stays 6f: acts on polytrack and tapeta: has worn visor. *James Unett* **51**

NONIOS (IRE) 5 b.g. Oasis Dream 129 – Young And Daring (USA) (Woodman (USA) 126) [2017 94: t9.5g³ 10g 8s t12.2g t9.5d⁵ Dec 16] fairly useful handicapper: third at Wolverhampton in February: stays 1½m: acts on polytrack and tapeta: wears hood: sometimes slowly away, often races in rear. *David Simcock* **89**

NONNIE AND NORNY 3 b.f. Frozen Power (IRE) 108 – Sophie'jo 73 (Agnes World (USA) 123) [2017 t8.6g⁶ t8d 6g 8g 6g 7d Sep 18] fifth foal: half-sister to winner abroad by Zebedee: dam, maiden (stayed 1m), half-sister to useful 6f-1m winner Alfresco: no form. *Shaun Harris* **–**

NONNO GIULIO (IRE) 6 ch.g. Halling (USA) 133 – Contrary (IRE) 79 (Mark of Esteem (IRE) 137) [2017 85: 8g 8g 8g⁴ 7m* 7.4m 7d 7g 8g³ t7.1d p7s⁴ 8d⁶ p7g p7s Sep 30] rather leggy gelding: fair on turf, modest on all-weather: won claimer at Redcar in June for Tony Coyle: stays 1m: acts on polytrack, good to firm and good to soft going: wears headgear: often races prominently: unreliable. *Conor Dore* **69 §** **a61 §**

NO NO CARDINAL (IRE) 8 ch.g. Touch of Land (FR) 122 – Four Moons (IRE) (Cardinal Flower 101) [2017 55: p10g p8d⁴ p8g⁶ Feb 28] lengthy gelding: poor handicapper: stays 1m: acts on firm going: tried in hood: often races prominently: winning chaser. *Mark Gillard* **47**

NO NOT AGAIN (IRE) 3 b.c. Roderic O'Connor (IRE) 119 – Bella Bella (IRE) 95 (Sri Pekan (USA) 117) [2017 70: p8g³ p8g⁶ p8g² p8g³ p6g² 7m⁴ 7.5f Jul 29] fair maiden: left Richard Hannon before final outing: stays 1m: acts on polytrack, soft and good to firm going: tried in cheekpieces: front runner/races prominently. *Saffie A. Joseph Jnr, USA* **71**

NOODLES BLUE BOY 11 b.g. Makbul 104 – Dee Dee Girl (IRE) 60 (Primo Dominie 121) [2017 74: 5m 5m⁴ May 4] neat gelding: fair handicapper, below best both starts in 2017: stays 6f: acts on polytrack, fibresand, soft and good to firm going: often wears headgear: often starts slowly. *Ollie Pears* **53**

NOOTKA SOUND (USA) 2 b.f. (Mar 13) Lonhro (AUS) 128 – Miss Red Delicious (USA) (Empire Maker (USA) 129) [2017 a4.5f* 5f Jun 20] $100,000Y: rather leggy filly: third foal: half-sister to winners in USA by Harlan's Holiday and Uncle Mo: dam US 7f minor stakes winner: fairly useful form: won maiden at Keeneland (by 5¼ lengths from C J S Suzie Byu) in April: down the field in listed Windsor Castle Stakes at Royal Ascot: wears blinkers. *Wesley A. Ward, USA* **84 +**

NORA BATT (IRE) 4 ch.f. Art Connoisseur (IRE) 121 – Mrs Batt (IRE) 66 (Medecis 119) [2017 76: f6g p6m p6g t5.1g t5g⁴ t5g 7.5d 5.8g 5d⁴ 5.8v³ 5v² p6g p5g Nov 24] modest handicapper on turf, poor on all-weather: left David Evans after sixth start: best form at 5f: acts on polytrack, good to firm and heavy going: front runner/races prominently. *John W. Nicholson, Ireland* **63 a48**

NORAB (GER) 6 b.g. Galileo (IRE) 134 – Night Woman (GER) (Monsun (GER) 124) [2017 81: 16d³ 16s 16g⁴ 16v⁵ t12.2g⁶ Oct 7] workmanlike gelding: fair handicapper: stays 2m: acts on polytrack, tapeta, good to firm and heavy going: wears headgear: usually races close up: winning hurdler. *Bernard Llewellyn* **79**

NORDENFELT (IRE) 4 b.g. Lilbourne Lad (IRE) 111 – There With Me (USA) 63 (Distant View (USA) 126) [2017 –: 8.1m 10.2d Aug 23] sturdy gelding: no form: left Tony Newcombe after first start. *Natalie Lloyd-Beavis* **–**

NORDIC COMBINED (IRE) 3 b.g. Haafhd 129 – Chilly Filly (IRE) 99 (Montjeu (IRE) 137) [2017 72: 11.9d⁵ 11.6d² 13.3g 12.1g 14s* 14v² 14d Oct 30] fairly useful handicapper: won at Haydock in September: stays 1¾m: acts on heavy going: tried in cheekpieces: sold to join Stuart Kittow 22,000 gns in November: one to treat with caution. *Brian Ellison* **84 §**

NOREENA 3 b.f. Medicean 128 – Nurai 62 (Danehill Dancer (IRE) 117) [2017 –: p7g p7g⁵ p8g Apr 7] modest form. *Paul D'Arcy* **51**

NO REFUND (IRE) 6 b.g. Invincible Spirit (IRE) 121 – Evangeline (Sadler's Wells (USA) 132) [2017 62, a53: p7g 7d p8g Dec 13] sturdy gelding: modest handicapper, no form in 2017: left David Loughnane after first start: often wears cheekpieces: tried in tongue tie: often starts slowly. *Martin Smith* **–**

NORMAL EQUILIBRIUM 7 b.g. Elnadim (USA) 128 – Acicula (IRE) 96 (Night Shift (USA)) [2017 94: f5g t5d t5.1g⁵ p5g² t5.1g 5g³ p5g 5f³ 5.1d* 5.1d 5.1g* 4d p5d 5g Oct 13] sturdy gelding: fairly useful handicapper: won at Chester in July and August (by 1½ lengths from Ballesteros): left Robert Cowell after first start: stays 6f: acts on polytrack, soft and good to firm going: has worn headgear. *Ivan Furtado* **92**

NORMANDIE ATTACK (FR) 3 gr.c. Kendargent (FR) 112 – Agenda (IRE) 102 (Sadler's Wells (USA) 132) [2017 12m⁴ 11.2d² 11.6v² p16s⁴ 14s Sep 8] €35,000F: sixth foal: half-brother to useful winner up to 1¼m (stayed 1½m) London Stripe (2-y-o 7f winner, by Rock of Gibraltar): dam 1¼m winner: fairly useful maiden: second at Lingfield in July: should stay further than 1½m: acts on heavy going: in visor last 2 starts: sometimes slowly away: sent to Qatar. *Charlie Fellowes* **82**

NORMANDIE LADY 4 b.f. Kheleyf (USA) 116 – Normandie Art (Rainbow Quest (USA) 134) [2017 85: 8.3g* p8g³ 8m⁶ 8d³ 8.3g⁵ p8g⁶ Oct 3] fairly useful handicapper: won at Nottingham (by 3¾ lengths from Lincoln Rocks) in May: stays 8.5f: acts on polytrack and soft going. *Richard Fahey* **88**

NORMANDY BARRIERE (IRE) 5 b.g. Rock of Gibraltar (IRE) 133 – Ma Paloma (FR) (Highest Honor (FR) 124) [2017 105: 6m² 6m* 6m 6.3f 7d⁵ 7g⁵ Aug 19] good-quartered gelding: useful handicapper: won at Ascot in May: effective at 6f/7f: acts on firm going. *Nigel Tinkler* **103**

NORMANDY BLUE 2 ch.g. (Feb 3) Le Havre (IRE) 124 – Ballerina Blue (IRE) (High Chaparral (IRE) 132) [2017 7g t8.6g⁶ 7g² 8v⁶ 8v³ Oct 23] lightly-built gelding: fair maiden: stays 1m: acts on heavy going: usually races towards rear. *Richard Fahey* **71**

NORSE CASTLE 4 b.g. Norse Dancer (IRE) 127 – Hursley Hope (IRE) (Barathea (IRE) 127) [2017 65: p13g Jan 18] modest maiden, well held sole start on Flat in 2017: best effort at 1¼m: acts on polytrack: often leads. *Martin Bosley* **–**

NORTH AMERICA 5 b.g. Dubawi (IRE) 129 – Northern Mischief (USA) (Yankee Victor (USA) 121) [2017 a8f* a8f* a8g Mar 25] very smart performer: successful at Meydan in handicap (by 1¼ lengths from Heavy Metal) in January and Firebreak Stakes **123**

(by 7 lengths from Ennobled Friend) in February: well held in Godolphin Mile there only subsequent outing: stays 1¼m: acts on dirt and good to firm going: has worn cheekpieces: in tongue tie last 4 starts. *S. Seemar, UAE*

NORTH ANGEL (IRE) 2 gr.f. (Apr 3) Dark Angel (IRE) 113 – Woodcock Moon (Kyllachy 129) [2017 5.9d Aug 29] €31,000Y: sixth foal: half-sister to smart 7f-8.3f winner Moonstone Magic (by Trade Fair) and 6f winner Van Velde (by Dutch Art): dam unraced: 16/1, well held in minor event at Carlisle: has joined Roger Varian. *David Brown* **–**

NORTH BAY SUNRISE (IRE) 2 b.f. (Apr 1) Kodiac 112 – Cat Fire (IRE) 87 (One Cool Cat (USA) 123) [2017 t7.1g p8g³ p8s Nov 16] €19,000Y, €38,000 2-y-o: second foal: dam 2-y-o 6f winner who stayed 9f: modest form: best effort when third in maiden at Lingfield (3½ lengths behind Connaught Ranger) in September: will stay beyond 1m. *Ed Vaughan* **60**

NORTH CREEK 4 b.g. Iffraaj 127 – Maine Rose (Red Ransom (USA)) [2017 91: p8g⁵ p8g⁶ p7s* p8s⁴ p7s⁴ 7m 6s⁶ 6d⁵ p7g⁶ Oct 25] sturdy gelding: fair handicapper on turf, fairly useful on all-weather: won at Kempton (by neck from Twin Point) in June: stays 1m: acts on polytrack: sold 14,000 gns in November. *Chris Wall* **67 a90**

NORTHDOWN 3 b.g. Paco Boy (IRE) 129 – Hazita (Singspiel (IRE) 133) [2017 77: 8.5g 8s 8.2g⁶ t7.2g⁵ 8.2g t9.5g⁴ t9.5g Sep 9] sturdy gelding: fair handicapper: stays 9.5f: acts on polytrack and tapeta: usually wears cheekpieces: often races freely. *David Lanigan* **76**

NORTHERN ANGEL (IRE) 2 b.f. (Feb 25) Dark Angel (IRE) 113 – Muzdaan (IRE) 55 (Exceed And Excel (AUS) 126) [2017 6s² 6.1g* Aug 18] €100,000Y: unfurnished filly: second foal: sister to 6f winner Parys Mountain: dam, ran twice, out of Moyglare Stud Stakes winner Belle Genius: fair form: won maiden at Nottingham (by short head from Bowler Hat) in August: open to further improvement. *John Quinn* **70 p**

NORTHERN FORCE 2 b.g. (Mar 28) Lethal Force (IRE) 128 – Border Minstral (IRE) 69 (Sri Pekan (USA) 117) [2017 7v Sep 9] 50/1, well held in minor event at Thirsk. *Roger Fell* **–**

NORTHERN LAW (IRE) 2 b.g. (Mar 15) Lawman (FR) 121 – Polly Perkins (IRE) 100 (Pivotal 124) [2017 6g⁵ 6m⁵ 7.2g⁴ 7s³ 7.4d Aug 17] fair maiden: best effort at 7f. *John Quinn* **70**

NORTHGATE LAD (IRE) 5 gr.g. Dark Angel (IRE) 113 – Canosa (IRE) 53 (Catrail (USA) 123) [2017 99: 6g⁶ 5m³ 6s⁴ 6d t6s² t7.1g* 7.9d 6.5g⁴ Sep 15] good-topped gelding: useful handicapper: won at Newcastle (by ½ length from Horroob) in July: stays 7f: acts on tapeta, good to firm and heavy going: tried in cheekpieces: front runner/races prominently. *Brian Ellison* **100**

NORTH ROAD REVUE 2 b.f. (Apr 17) Dick Turpin (IRE) 127 – Revue Princess (IRE) 80 (Mull of Kintyre (USA) 114) [2017 5.9m 6g t6d Aug 10] fourth foal: half-sister to 7f-1¼m winner Autumn Revue (by Monsieur Bond) and useful 5f winner East Street Revue (by Pastoral Pursuits): dam winner up to 7f (2-y-o 5f winner): modest form. *Tim Easterby* **51**

NORTHWEST FRONTIER (IRE) 3 b.g. Galileo (IRE) 134 – Francesca d'Gorgio (USA) 100 (Proud Citizen (USA) 122) [2017 9.8d³ 10g* 12.1d³ 12d² 13.9m 13s⁴ 12.1v p12d Nov 22] close-coupled gelding: third foal: half-brother to useful winner up to 1m Amazonas (2-y-o 6f winner, by Cape Cross): dam, 2-y-o 6f winner, half-sister to US Grade 1 8.5f winner Include Betty: fairly useful performer: won maiden at Redcar in June: best effort when second in handicap at Thirsk in August: stays 1½m: acts on good to soft going: tried in blinkers. *Richard Fahey* **88**

NORVILLE (IRE) 10 b.g. Elusive City (USA) 117 – Saraposa (IRE) 66 (Ahonoora 122) [2017 60: p10.7g 8m May 9] close-coupled gelding: useful at best, retains little ability: wears headgear: sometimes slowly away, often races towards rear. *L. Smyth, Ireland* **–**

NORWEGIAN HIGHNESS (FR) 3 ch.f. Kendargent (FR) 112 – Norwegian Princess (IRE) (Fairy King (USA)) [2017 79: 6g 6g⁶ 8g 7d² Oct 13] lengthy filly: fair performer: left Kevin Ryan after third start: stays 7f: acts on tapeta and soft going: often races freely. *H-A. Pantall, France* **78**

NOSTALGIE 3 gr.f. Archipenko (USA) 127 – Neige d'Antan 73 (Aussie Rules (USA) 123) [2017 70: t8.6g* 8s t8.6g³ t7.2g² p7d² p7d Sep 21] lengthy, rather unfurnished filly: fairly useful handicapper: won at Wolverhampton in May: second at same course in July and Kempton in August: stays 8.5f: acts on polytrack and tapeta: sold 13,000 gns, sent to Saudi Arabia. *James Tate* **88**

NOT A BAD OUL DAY (IRE) 5 ch.g. Captain Rio 122 – Woodville (Deploy 131) [2017 68: f6g 7.5s^{6} 8s* 8m* 7d^{2} 8m* 7g* 7s 7.3s* 7.4v^{4} 7v* 8v* 7s^{2} 8v Nov 24] useful performer: vastly improved in 2017, winning handicaps at Gowran in April, Ayr (apprentice) in May and Limerick/Gowran in June, minor event at Roscommon in August, and handicaps at Listowel in September and Limerick again (by ½ length from Stenographer) in October: 1¾ lengths second to Celebration in handicap at Cork next time: stays 1m: acts on polytrack, good to firm and heavy going: has worn headgear: tried in tongue tie: usually leads. *J. J. Feane, Ireland* **104**

NOT AFTER MIDNIGHT (IRE) 2 b.f. (Apr 8) Big Bad Bob (IRE) 118 – Zenella 95 (Kyllachy 129) [2017 6.1m^{3} 6m^{2} 7d p7g^{2} p7g t7.1s^{3} Nov 30] €10,000Y: third foal: half-sister to 2-y-o 7f winner Dark Crescent (by Elnadim) and 7f winner Art's Desire (by Dutch Art): dam 2-y-o 6f-1m winner: fair maiden: best effort at 7f: acts on polytrack: usually races prominently. *Daniel Kubler* **73**

NOTEWORTHY (IRE) 2 b.f. (Mar 3) Acclamation 118 – Church Melody (Oasis Dream 129) [2017 p7g^{6} Nov 2] 20,000F, 120,000Y: lengthy, rather unfurnished filly: fourth foal: sister to 2-y-o 5f winner Al Ghuwariyah and half-sister to winner up to 6f Indian Pursuit (by Compton Place): dam unraced half-sister to very smart 1¼m-1½m winner Gospel Choir: 50/1, sixth in minor event at Lingfield (6¼ lengths behind West Palm Beach) in November: should improve. *Richard Hughes* **61 p**

NOTHING COMPARES 3 b.f. Harbour Watch (IRE) 121 – Endorsement 107 (Warning 136) [2017 –: p12g^{4} t12.2g^{6} p12g^{6} p14g^{6} 12.1g^{3} 14m 16.1d^{3} 16v 14s Aug 9] modest maiden: stays 2m: acts on polytrack and good to soft going: tried in blinkers: temperament under suspicion. *Mark Johnston* **56**

NOTHING TO LOSE (IRE) 3 b.g. Fast Company (IRE) 126 – Invincible Woman (IRE) 87 (Invincible Spirit (IRE) 121) [2017 –: 6m 6g* 7d^{2} 7g^{2} 7.2d* 7.1d^{3} 7.4d* 7v Jul 31] fairly useful handicapper: won at Fairyhouse in June, and Ayr and Ffos Las (by ¾ length from Peach Melba) in July: stays 7.5f: acts on good to soft going. *John McConnell, Ireland* **87**

NOTICE (IRE) 4 ch.f. New Approach (IRE) 132 – Classic Remark (IRE) 101 (Dr Fong (USA) 128) [2017 86p: 12m^{3} p14s^{3} 13.3g^{2} 12g^{2} 14m^{4} 14s^{3} 14.1g Oct 16] tall, workmanlike filly: fairly useful handicapper: second at Salisbury in August and third at Goodwood in September: stays 1¾m: acts on polytrack, soft and good to firm going. *David Simcock* **93**

NOTNOWIVORHEADACHE 8 b.m. Notnowcato 128 – Inchcoonan 81 (Emperor Jones (USA) 119) [2017 p12g Jul 5] lengthy mare: runner-up on first of 2 starts in bumpers in 2013/14: 100/1, well held in maiden at Kempton. *Roger Ingram* **–**

NOT NOW NADIA (IRE) 3 b.f. Footstepsinthesand 120 – Lake Wanaka (IRE) 56 (Fasliyev (USA) 120) [2017 56: f6g^{2} t5.1g^{5} t6g Mar 10] modest maiden: stays 6f: acts on fibresand and soft going: tried in cheekpieces. *Michael Dods* **58**

NOTNOW SEAMUS 6 b.g. Notnowcato 128 – Special Beat 65 (Bustino 136) [2017 12.1m^{5} Jun 2] winning hurdler: 25/1, well held in maiden at Catterick, only outing on Flat: has joined Dan Skelton. *Marjorie Fife* **–**

NOT SO SLEEPY 5 ch.g. Beat Hollow 126 – Papillon de Bronze (IRE) (Marju (IRE) 127) [2017 108: 10.3d 10.1m* p12g^{5} p10g Dec 23] compact gelding: useful performer: won handicap at Epsom (by neck from Innocent Touch) in June: stays 1½m: acts on polytrack, good to firm and heavy going: wears hood/tongue tie: usually races freely. *Hughie Morrison* **105**

NOTTE ILLUMINATA (IRE) 4 b.f. Acclamation 118 – Sogno Verde (IRE) 82 (Green Desert (USA) 127) [2017 78p: p7m^{6} Jan 9] fair 1m winner at 3 yrs, down the field in handicap on sole start in 2017. *K. R. Burke* **–**

NOUVELLE ERE 6 b.g. Archipenko (USA) 127 – Sinister Ruckus (USA) (Trippi (USA) 121) [2017 56: t9.5m^{2} p10g p10d* t9.5g p12g^{4} 10.1m p11d^{4} 10.2m 10m^{4} 9.9m^{2} 10.2d 11.9d^{6} p10g p11g Oct 25] fair handicapper: won at Chelmsford in February: stays 1½m: acts on polytrack, tapeta, good to firm and good to soft going: has worn headgear: usually wears tongue tie: front runner/races prominently: unreliable. *Tony Carroll* **65 §**

NOUVELLI DANCER (IRE) 4 b.f. Lilbourne Lad (IRE) 111 – Kiralik 100 (Efisio 120) [2017 90: t7.1d t7.1g p6g 7d May 19] fairly useful handicapper at 3 yrs, below form in 2017: stays 8.5f: acts on polytrack, tapeta, soft and good to firm going: front runner/races prominently. *David C. Griffiths* **75**

NOVABRIDGE 9 ch.g. Avonbridge 123 – Petrovna (IRE) 78 (Petardia 113) [2017 68: t5d t5g^{4} t5g^{5} f5g^{2} f5d^{5} f5g 5g t5s^{6} t5g f5g^{2} f5g t5d^{4} t5.1g Dec 22] modest handicapper: stays 6f: acts on all-weather and any turf going: wears headgear. *Karen Tutty* **64**

N OVER J 2 b.g. (Apr 16) Kodiac 112 – Risk A Look (Observatory (USA) 131) [2017 7s* 74
p7g t8.6g^{6} Nov 11] rather unfurnished gelding: fair form: won minor event at Salisbury (by length from Bodes Well) in October: best effort at 7f. *William Knight*

NOVIS ADVENTUS (IRE) 5 b.g. New Approach (IRE) 132 – Tiffed (USA) (Seattle –
Slew (USA)) [2017 99: p12g Jan 28] useful at best, well held sole Flat start in 2017: stays 1¾m: acts on soft going: has worn headgear: has joined Neil Mulholland and won over hurdles in July/August. *Jeremy Noseda*

NOVOMAN (IRE) 3 ch.g. Sir Prancealot (IRE) 111 – Rublevka Star (USA) 77 (Elusive 106
Quality (USA)) [2017 93p: 8g 7g 8m^{6} 10.3g* 9.9m* 9d Sep 30] good-topped gelding: useful handicapper: won at York (by 4 lengths from Visitant) in July and Goodwood (by length from Anythingtoday) in August: likely to prove best up to 1¼m: acts on good to firm and good to soft going. *William Haggas*

NO WIN NO FEE 7 b.g. Firebreak 125 – Milliscent 49 (Primo Dominie 121) [2017 t8.6g^{4} –
10.2g 10.2f May 26] fairly useful at best, little impact on Flat in 2017: has worn cheekpieces: fair hurdler. *Barry Leavy*

NOW SAY YES (IRE) 2 b.f. (Mar 22) Elusive Quality (USA) – Say No Now (IRE) 103 54
(Refuse To Bend (IRE) 128) [2017 t8g p8g^{5} Dec 23] fourth foal: half-sister to 1¼m winner (stays 1½m) Spinning Melody (by Hard Spun): dam, 8.3f winner, half-sister to useful 2-y-o 6f winner Zumbi: modest form in maiden/minor event. *David Lanigan*

NOW YOU'RE TALKING (IRE) 2 b.f. (Feb 5) Zoffany (IRE) 121 – Granadilla 88 104
(Zafonic (USA) 130) [2017 6m^{5} 6d^{2} 5m^{4} 5m^{3} 6d^{4} 8f Nov 3] €185,000Y: compact filly: half-sister to several winners, including useful winner up to 1m Aktoria (2-y-o 7f winner, by Canford Cliffs) and 2-y-o 5f winner Galaktea (by Statue of Liberty), both in France: dam 7f winner: useful maiden: best effort when fourth in Cheveley Park Stakes at Newmarket (3¼ lengths behind Clemmie) in September: eighth in Breeders' Cup Juvenile Fillies Turf at Del Mar final start: stays 6f: acts on good to firm and good to soft going. *Joseph Patrick O'Brien, Ireland*

NSNAS ALWARD 2 b.f. (Feb 15) Poet's Voice 126 – Rosa Mundi (Alhaarth (IRE) 126) 64
[2017 t5s 5m^{3} 6m May 30] third foal: half-sister to German 9f/1¼m winner Arabian Dreamer (by Youmzain) and useful 7f winner Bint Arcano (by Arcano): dam, 1½m winner, half-sister to useful 1¼m winner Roscius out of smart 1¼m winner Rosefinch: modest form: best effort when third in minor event at Catterick (2¾ lengths behind Izzy Bizu) in May. *Kevin Ryan*

NUALA TAGULA (IRE) 4 b.f. Tagula (IRE) 116 – Dangle (IRE) 102 (Desert Style 66
(IRE) 121) [2017 68, a75: t6m^{4} t5d 6g 5m* 6m^{3} 5d^{4} 5g 5m^{4} t5g^{2} 5d^{2} 5g Aug 18] fair handicapper: won at Hamilton in May: stays 6f: acts on tapeta, good to firm and good to soft going: wears tongue tie. *John Quinn*

NUCKY THOMPSON 4 b.g. Cockney Rebel (IRE) 127 – Vino Veritas (USA) 72 –
(Chief's Crown (USA)) [2017 85: 9.9g 12d^{6} Jun 29] strong gelding: fairly useful at best, little impact in handicaps in 2017: stays 1½m: acts on polytrack and tapeta, best turf form on good going: wears headgear: tried in tongue tie. *Richard Spencer*

NUDGE 4 b.f. Dansili 127 – Take The Hint 107 (Montjeu (IRE) 137) [2017 66: 8g 7s 6.1g 71
8g Jun 4] fair maiden: best effort at 1m: acts on good to soft going: in blinkers last 3 starts: usually races close up. *Mrs A. M. O'Shea, Ireland*

NUITS ST GEORGES (IRE) 2 ch.c. (Feb 13) Mount Nelson 125 – Twelfth Night (IRE) 74
67 (Namid 128) [2017 8v^{2} 8d p8g^{3} Oct 14] fair form: best effort when third in minor event at Kempton (2 lengths behind Indiscretion) in October: will be suited by 1¼m+. *David Menuisier*

NUNCIO 3 b.g. Authorized (IRE) 133 – Sweet Pilgrim 74 (Talkin Man (CAN) 120) [2017 73
79p: 8m^{2} 7m^{2} 7g^{5} 7s^{3} 6m^{4} p8d^{6} p8g^{6} p8g Oct 26] fair maiden: stays 1m: acts on polytrack and good to firm going. *Daniel Kubler*

NUNNERY LANE 2 b.g. (May 2) Mazameer (IRE) 107 – Prices Lane 55 (Gentleman's –
Deal (IRE) 114) [2017 7m^{5} 7.4g Aug 16] well held in 2 minor events. *Michael Easterby*

NUNS WALK 3 ch.f. Sleeping Indian 122 – Dance Card 77 (Cape Cross (IRE) 129) [2017 78
5d^{2} 6g 7g^{2} t5s* 6g* 5g^{5} t6g^{2} t6d^{2} Nov 10] third foal: half-sister to 2-y-o 5f winner She Can Jig and 6f winner A Lovable Rogue (both by Dutch Art): dam 7f winner: fair performer: won maiden at Newcastle and handicap at Redcar in September: stays 7f: acts on tapeta, best turf form on good going: usually races prominently, often travels strongly. *Tim Easterby*

3 Batterhams and A. Reay's "Nyaleti"

NUOVA SCUOLA 4 b.f. Mount Nelson 125 – La Vecchia Scuola (IRE) 106 (Mull of Kintyre (USA) 114) [2017 10m^{6} 12s^{6} 10m^{5} 13.1g 12.5m 15g Aug 12] first foal: dam, 5f-1¾m winner who stayed 2¼m, also won over hurdles: no form on Flat/over hurdles: in visor last 3 starts. *Jim Goldie* –

NUPTIALS (USA) 3 b.f. Broken Vow (USA) 117 – European Union (USA) (Successful Appeal (USA) 118) [2017 52: t6f p6g Jan 28] compact filly: modest form on final 2016 start, standout effort: tried in blinkers. *Eve Johnson Houghton* –

NURSE NIGHTINGALE 3 b.f. Nathaniel (IRE) 129 – Whazzat 105 (Daylami (IRE) 138) [2017 78p: p10m^{3} 9.9d^{6} 10.2m^{5} t12.4g^{4} p14d^{2} t12.4g^{3} 12.1s^{4} p12g^{2} p12g^{6} Dec 20] fairly useful maiden: second in handicap at Chelmsford in September and maiden at Lingfield in November: left Hugo Palmer after third start: stays 1¾m: acts on polytrack, tapeta and soft going: usually wears hood: usually races close up. *Michael Bell* 82

NUTINI (IRE) 4 b.g. Lope de Vega (IRE) 125 – My Eurydice (Exceed And Excel (AUS) 126) [2017 75: 7s p8g^{4} 7g^{6} 8d^{4} 8d 7.1g 8.1s 5.7s^{2} 6.1g* t6.1m^{3} t6.1g^{3} Nov 11] fair handicapper: won at Windsor (amateur) in October: left Madeleine Tylicki after fourth start: best up to 1m: acts on tapeta, polytrack and soft going: often wears headgear: has worn tongue tie: front runner/races prominently. *Malcolm Saunders* 73

NUTZMA 4 b.f. Multiplex 114 – Nut (IRE) 65 (Fasliyev (USA) 120) [2017 42: f12g Jan 5] little form: usually in headgear. *Mike Murphy* –

NUZHA 3 ch.f. Mayson 124 – Always On My Mind 91 (Distant Relative 128) [2017 80: f5g^{5} f5g^{3} p6g^{2} p6g 6s 5s^{3} 5.1d t6.1g Nov 11] compact filly: fair handicapper: left David Evans after second start, Karen George after sixth: stays 6f: acts on all-weather and soft going: often in cheekpieces: sometimes slowly away. *Tony Newcombe* 72

NYALA 2 b.f. (Jan 30) Vale of York (IRE) 117 – Cio Cio San (IRE) 64 (Dalakhani (IRE) 133) [2017 7g Sep 7] first foal: dam, maiden (stayed 6f), half-sister to useful winner up to 1m Truth Or Dare: 100/1, well held in maiden at Salisbury. *Daniel Kubler* –

NYALETI (IRE) 2 ro.f. (May 5) Arch (USA) 127 – America Nova (FR) (Verglas (IRE) 118) [2017 6f* 7m^2 6m^2 6d* 6g^6 8g^3 7d^2 8m Oct 13] 40,000Y: leggy, quite attractive filly: sixth foal: half-sister to several winners, including useful winner up to 1m Stellar Path and useful 2-y-o 6f/7f winner Sir Patrick Moore (both by Astronomer Royal), latter later successful in Australia (where renamed Weary) in Group 2/3 6f/7.5f events: dam 2-y-o 1m winner: useful performer: won minor event at Salisbury (by ¾ length from Billesdon Brook) in June and Princess Margaret Stakes at Ascot (by 5 lengths from Dance Diva) in July: placed in Chesham Stakes at Royal Ascot in June, Duchess of Cambridge Stakes at Newmarket in July, and May Hill Stakes at Doncaster and Rockfel Stakes at Newmarket in September: stays 1m: acts on firm and good to soft going: front runner/races prominently. *Mark Johnston* **109**

NYX 3 ch.f. Harbour Watch (IRE) 121 – Fantastic Santanyi (Fantastic Light (USA) 134) [2017 –: 5m 5m 7g^6 Jun 23] no form: wore headgear in 2017. *Richard Guest* **–**

O

OAK BLUFFS (IRE) 6 b.g. Royal Applause 124 – Key Stage (IRE) (King's Best (USA) 132) [2017 71: t7.1g t7.1d Jan 27] smallish gelding: fair handicapper, well held both starts in Britain in 2017: tried in cheekpieces: often races prominently: sold 1,500 gns, sent to Italy, where won 2 sellers (both 11f) at Merano in July. *Richard Fahey* **?**

OAKLEY PRIDE (IRE) 3 b.g. Lilbourne Lad (IRE) 111 – There With Me (USA) 63 (Distant View (USA) 126) [2017 47: t7.1g^6 p7d^4 t7.1g* p8g p8g 7g 6d^3 t7.2g^3 7s^5 7d^3 8d^4 7v^3 7g^4 7d Oct 30] leggy gelding: modest performer: won seller at Wolverhampton in February: stays 1m: acts on tapeta and heavy going: wears headgear: usually wears tongue tie: sometimes slowly away. *Gay Kelleway* **63**

OASIS CHARM 3 b.g. Oasis Dream 129 – Albaraka 91 (Selkirk (USA) 129) [2017 10m^2 10g* 10m^6 12m 10m^2 Jul 14] 205,000F: good-quartered gelding: first foal: dam, 8.6f winner who stayed 11f, half-sister to smart winner up to 1¼m Algonquin out of dual Champion Stakes winner Alborada: useful performer: won maiden at Leicester in April: second in handicap at Newmarket (¾ length behind Marzouq) in July: stays 1¼m: acts on good to firm going: tried in cheekpieces: often races prominently/travels strongly. *Charlie Appleby* **99**

OASIS FANTASY (IRE) 6 br.g. Oasis Dream 129 – Cara Fantasy (IRE) 84 (Sadler's Wells (USA) 132) [2017 113: 9.9g 9.9g^5 10.3d^3 12m 11.9g^4 9.9g^6 12d^3 9.9g 10.1v^6 Oct 1] tall, attractive gelding: useful handicapper: third at Ascot (1¼ lengths behind Great Hall) in August: stays 1¾m, effective at shorter: acts on firm and good to soft going: has worn headgear, including last 4 starts: sold 24,000 gns in October. *David Simcock* **100**

OASIS SPEAR 5 b.g. Oasis Dream 129 – Sunspear (IRE) (Montjeu (IRE) 137) [2017 92: 8f t10.2s^4 10m 8d^5 9.1m p10g Sep 25] workmanlike gelding: fairly useful handicapper: stays 1¼m: acts on tapeta and good to firm going: usually races freely: temperamental: sold 1,500 gns, sent to Sweden. *Chris Wall* **82 §**

OBBOORR 8 b.g. Cape Cross (IRE) 129 – Felawnah (USA) 111 (Mr Prospector (USA)) [2017 81: f12g^5 t13.9m^5 f12g^5 t12.2g^3 p12d Feb 22] fairly useful handicapper, below best in 2017: stays 1¾m: acts on all-weather and good to firm going: has worn headgear. *James Given* **73**

OBERYN (IRE) 3 b.f. Holy Roman Emperor (IRE) 125 – Daraliya (IRE) (Kahyasi 130) [2017 54p: t7.1g* t7.1m^6 p8g* p10g^6 9.9f 12m 11.9d Jun 9] fair performer: won maiden at Wolverhampton and handicap at Lingfield in January: stays 1m: acts on polytrack and tapeta. *Sylvester Kirk* **70**

OBEYA 3 b.f. Oasis Dream 129 – Loulou (USA) 63 (El Prado (IRE) 119) [2017 7m^5 8d^4 7g^3 Aug 2] third foal: dam, 1¼m winner, half-sister to useful 1m winner Dubai Edition out of very smart 1m-1¼m winner (stayed 1½m) Hatoof: fair form: best effort when fourth in maiden at Newmarket in July. *Roger Varian* **70**

OBRIGADA 2 b.f. (Mar 4) Worthadd (IRE) 124 – Oblige 101 (Robellino (USA) 127) [2017 p7d 7.6d^6 p6g^5 t7.2g^5 p7d^3 t8s^6 Nov 30] half-sister to smart 1¼m-1½m winner Barye (by Archipenko) and winner up to 9.5f Herrbuga (by Hernando): dam 2-y-o 7f winner: modest maiden: should be suited by 1m: acts on polytrack and tapeta: sometimes slowly away. *Tom Clover* **64**

OCALA 2 ch.f. (Mar 22) Nathaniel (IRE) 129 – Night Carnation 116 (Sleeping Indian 122) [2017 6.1d^{2} p7g^{3} Nov 6] second foal: half-sister to 2-y-o 5f winner Night Law (by Lawman): dam 5f/6f winner (including at 2 yrs): fair form when placed in minor event/maiden, slowly away both times: remains capable of better. *Andrew Balding* **77 p**

OCCUPY (USA) 2 b.c. (Feb 17) Declaration of War (USA) 128 – Circumstances (IRE) 80 (Galileo (IRE) 134) [2017 p8g* Nov 7] $80,000Y: second foal: dam, 10.7f winner, sister to high-class winner up to 1½m Telescope: 25/1, won minor event at Kempton (by 2 lengths from Blame Culture) on debut: sure to progress. *Ralph Beckett* **87 p**

OCEAN AIR (FR) 3 b.c. Rio de La Plata (USA) 121 – Silver Miss (FR) (Numerous (USA)) [2017 80p: 7g* 8s 7d^{6} p8g p7g p8g Dec 22] fairly useful handicapper: won at Leicester (by length from Traveller) in April: left James Tate after third start: stays 7f: best form on good going: often races towards rear. *John McConnell, Ireland* **86**

OCEAN BENTLEY (IRE) 5 b.g. Amadeus Wolf 122 – Bentley's Bush (IRE) 96 (Barathea (IRE) 127) [2017 51: 11.6d Aug 30] poor maiden: stays 1¾m: acts on polytrack and tapeta: has worn headgear: modest maiden hurdler. *Tony Carroll* **–**

OCEAN DRIVE (IRE) 3 b.f. Sea The Stars (IRE) 140 – Cap Coz (IRE) 110 (Indian Ridge 123) [2017 p10m* p10g^{2} 10.2m^{4} 11.6d^{5} 9.9g^{2} p12.9g* Nov 24] 200,000Y: half-sister to winner up to 1½m Indian Days (2-y-o 7f winner, by Daylami), winner up to 6f Biniou (2-y-o 5f winner, by Mozart) and winner up to 7f Reply (2-y-o 6f/6.5f winner, by Oasis Dream), all smart: dam 2-y-o 5.5f-7f winner: fairly useful form: won maiden at Lingfield in January and minor event at Marseilles Vivaux in November: left William Haggas after fourth start: stays 13f: acts on polytrack. *N. Clement, France* **81**

OCEANE (FR) 5 b.g. Kentucky Dynamite (USA) 118 – Zahrana (FR) (Zamindar (USA) 116) [2017 100: t16.5g p13g^{5} 18g^{5} 16m^{2} 20f 16.3d 18d 18m Oct 14] compact gelding: useful handicapper: second at Ascot (apprentice, ¾ length behind Graceland) in May: stays 21f: acts on good to firm and good to soft going: wears headgear: usually races towards rear. *Alan King* **100**

OCEAN ELEVEN 4 b.g. Equiano (FR) 127 – Fittonia (FR) 66 (Ashkalani (IRE) 128) [2017 86: t9.5g Nov 25] lengthy gelding: fairly useful at best, well held sole start in 2017: stays 1¼m: acts on polytrack, good to firm and good to soft going: tried in cheekpieces. *Martin Keighley* **–**

OCEAN GALE 4 b.f. Shirocco (GER) 129 – Ocean Transit (IRE) 89 (Trans Island 119) [2017 –: 12d^{4} 11.8g^{3} 12g^{4} 14.2g* 14s^{3} 14.1v^{4} p16g^{3} t16.5g^{3} p16g Nov 7] modest handicapper: won at Salisbury in August: stays 16.5f: acts on polytrack, tapeta and soft going. *Richard Price* **59**

OCEAN LEGEND (IRE) 12 b.g. Night Shift (USA) – Rose of Mooncoin (IRE) 99 (Brief Truce (USA) 126) [2017 71: p6g^{6} Jan 11] workmanlike gelding: fair handicapper, below form on sole start in 2017: best up to 1m: acts on all-weather, good to firm and good to soft going: has worn visor: tried in tongue tie. *Tony Carroll* **58**

OCEAN OF LOVE 3 ch.f. Distorted Humor (USA) 117 – Michita (USA) 113 (Dynaformer (USA)) [2017 71p: p13.3g^{3} t14g^{2} t12.2d^{2} t12.2d* Dec 26] fairly useful performer: won handicap at Wolverhampton (by 8 lengths from Tan Arabiq) in December: stays 1¾m: acts on polytrack and tapeta: tried in hood: front runner/races prominently. *Saeed bin Suroor* **91**

OCEAN PRINCESS (IRE) 3 b.f. Acclamation 118 – Fathoming (USA) (Gulch (USA)) [2017 61p: t5d^{5} 7d Jun 2] modest maiden: stays 6f: acts on tapeta. *Michael Dods* **57**

OCEAN PROMISE (USA) 3 b.f. Quality Road (USA) 131 – I'm From Dixie (USA) (Dixieland Band (USA)) [2017 72: t9.5g^{6} p8d^{6} 8f^{5} p7g 6.1m^{4} Jul 3] lengthy filly: fair maiden: stays 1m: acts on polytrack and firm going: in headgear last 3 starts: front runner/races prominently. *Richard Hughes* **68**

OCEAN SIDE 2 gr.c. (Apr 13) Dark Angel (IRE) 113 – Mundus Novus (USA) (Unbridled's Song (USA) 125) [2017 6m 7g 8g 7s^{4} Oct 15] short-backed colt: fair form: should stay 1m. *Richard Hannon* **66**

OCEAN SPRAY 2 ch.f. (Mar 3) Showcasing 117 – Gibraltar Lass (USA) 49 (Concerto (USA) 114) [2017 p6g p7g p6s Dec 1] second foal: dam maiden: failed to beat a rival in 3 minor events. *Richard Hannon* **–**

OCEAN TEMPEST 8 gr.g. Act One 124 – Ipsa Loquitur 69 (Unfuwain (USA) 131) [2017 91: p8d Jan 17] plain, leggy gelding: smart at best, on downgrade nowadays: stays 9f: acts on polytrack, tapeta, good to firm and heavy going: has worn cheekpieces, including last 2 starts: often races lazily. *John Ryan* **–**

OCEAN TEMPTRESS 3 b.f. Equiano (FR) 127 – Ipsa Loquitur 69 (Unfuwain (USA) 131) [2017 65: p8g^5 8s^3 8g^2 7d^5 7g^6 7d^2 7d* 6d* p7s 6d* 6s^4 6s* 6g^4 Nov 3] fairly useful performer: won maiden at Brighton in August, and handicaps at Lingfield later in August, Yarmouth (by head from Quatrieme Ami) in September and Leicester (by ½ length from Bold Spirit) in October: stays 8.5f: acts on polytrack, soft and good to firm going: wears headgear: usually leads. *John Ryan* **82**

OCEANUS (IRE) 3 b.g. Born To Sea (IRE) 117 – Alkhawarah (USA) 60 (Intidab (USA) 115) [2017 74: p7m 10.1m^3 10m^5 9.9s^2 9.9d* 9.9s 10.1d^3 10.2v^6 Nov 8] sturdy gelding: fair handicapper: won at Brighton (apprentice) in September: left Ed Dunlop after first start: stays 1¼m: acts on soft going: has worn headgear. *Julia Feilden* **73**

OCEAN VOYAGE (IRE) 2 b.f. (Mar 9) Most Improved (IRE) 119 – Minshar 84 (Noverre (USA) 125) [2017 6.9v* t8.6g^4 t8.6g^2 Nov 11] €4,000Y: tall filly: has scope: fifth foal: half-sister to winner abroad by Kyllachy: dam, 2-y-o 6f winner, half-sister to smart 1m-1½m winner La Zona: fair form: won minor event at Carlisle (by nose from Book of Dreams) in September: will be suited by 9f+. *Richard Fahey* **75**

OCELOT 3 b.f. Poet's Voice 126 – Desert Lynx (IRE) 79 (Green Desert (USA) 127) [2017 69: 5.2m* 5g^5 5m* 5g* 5d^6 5v 5g^4 Oct 18] workmanlike filly: fairly useful performer: won maiden at Yarmouth in May, and handicaps at Leicester in June and Sandown (by 3½ lengths from Erissimus Maximus) in July: stays 5.5f: acts on good to firm and good to soft going. *Robert Cowell* **88**

OCHOS RIOS 4 b.g. Shirocco (GER) 129 – Society Rose 88 (Saddlers' Hall (IRE) 126) [2017 59: f11.1g* Dec 22] lengthy gelding: fair handicapper: won at Southwell on sole Flat start in 2017: stays 11.5f: acts on fibresand and good to firm going: often starts slowly, usually races nearer last than first: maiden hurdler. *Neil Mulholland* **65**

O'CONNOR (IRE) 4 ch.g. Roderic O'Connor (IRE) 119 – Fly By Magic (IRE) 92 (Indian Rocket 115) [2017 7m^6 Jul 15] 16/1, well held in maiden at Salisbury: sent to Sweden. *Rod Millman* **–**

OCOTILLO (IRE) 4 ch.g. Raven's Pass (USA) 133 – Meiosis (USA) 98 (Danzig (USA)) [2017 57: f6g p6g t6f^4 Feb 24] modest handicapper: stays 6f: acts on tapeta: has worn headgear: sold £3,000, sent to Belgium. *Kevin Frost* **57**

OCTOBER STORM 4 br.g. Shirocco (GER) 129 – Cyber Star 66 (King's Best (USA) 132) [2017 86: 14f* 16m^3 21.6m t16.3s 20.6v p16d 16.3g* Oct 14] angular gelding: fairly useful handicapper: won at Goodwood in May and York in October: stays 2m: acts on polytrack, firm and good to soft going: often races towards rear. *Mick Channon* **89**

ODDSOCKS (IRE) 5 b.m. Tagula (IRE) 116 – Datura 74 (Darshaan 133) [2017 44: p5g^6 p6g 7.1v 8m 7d^6 t6.1g 5d Sep 12] of little account: tried in blinkers. *Tony Carroll* **–**

ODDS ON OLI 2 b.g. (Apr 11) Camelot 128 – Red Blooded Woman (USA) 71 (Red Ransom (USA)) [2017 t6s^6 t7.2g 5d 8.3v^6 t7.2g^4 Nov 18] useful-looking gelding: modest maiden: best effort at 7f: acts on tapeta: tried in cheekpieces. *Richard Fahey* **54**

O DEE 5 ch.g. Iffraaj 127 – Queen's Grace 107 (Bahamian Bounty 116) [2017 68: t6.1g^4 6d* 5.5g* 5.5g^3 6g^2 4d^5 6d^5 5d^4 6.7d^5 Oct 22] fairly useful performer: won claimers at Argentan in June and Dieppe in July (left Jose Santos after): stays 7f: acts on polytrack: has worn headgear/tongue tie: often leads. *Julien Phelippon, France* **85**

ODELOUCA (IRE) 3 b.f. Elusive City (USA) 117 – Church Road (IRE) (Danehill Dancer (IRE) 117) [2017 67: 6.1m p7s 7d Jul 1] lengthy, plain filly: fair performer at 2 yrs, little impact in handicaps in 2017: tried in tongue tie. *Brendan Powell* **–**

ODEN 3 ch.g. Lope de Vega (IRE) 125 – Dashing (IRE) (Sadler's Wells (USA) 132) [2017 –: 10g 10.2d^3 9.8m^2 9.9d* Sep 11] fairly useful performer: won handicap at Brighton (by 5 lengths from Prerogative) in September: stays 1¼m: acts on good to firm and good to soft going: wore cheekpieces in 2017: front runner/races prominently: sold to join Nick Gifford 52,000 gns in November. *Roger Varian* **91**

ODE TO AUTUMN 2 br.g. (Mar 23) Showcasing 117 – Turning Leaf (IRE) 108 (Last Tycoon 131) [2017 7g^2 7g^2 7m^6 p7g^2 Dec 28] sturdy gelding: fair form in minor events: should stay 1m: tried in cheekpieces. *John Gosden* **79**

ODE TO GLORY 3 b.f. Poet's Voice 126 – Blue Lyric 81 (Refuse To Bend (IRE) 128) [2017 67: 9.9g 10.1m^6 10.1g^2 10.2g^3 10g^3 12m^2 t12.2g^6 p12g^4 p13.3s p12g^5 Dec 28] compact filly: fair handicapper: stays 1½m: acts on polytrack, tapeta and good to firm going: often starts slowly/races in rear. *Rae Guest* **72**

ODE TO PARIS 3 b.g. Poet's Voice 126 – Dream Belle (Oasis Dream 129) [2017 63p: t7.1f^4 p8g t7.1g Jan 25] modest maiden in Britain: stays 7f: acts on tapeta: often races freely: sold 6,000 gns, sent to Italy, where won maiden at Pisa in April, and handicaps at Milan in June and Florence in October. *Ed Dunlop* **63**

ODYSSA (IRE) 2 b.f. (Apr 23) Kodiac 112 – Deliziosa (IRE) (Iffraaj 127) [2017 t6.1g^3 6s* p7g^2 Sep 25] €33,000F, 43,000Y: first foal: dam lightly-raced half-sister to useful winner up to 9f Pleasant Day: fairly useful form: won minor event at Ascot (by 3¼ lengths from Last Enchantment) in September: best effort at 6f. *Richard Hughes* **88**

OEIL DE TIGRE (FR) 6 b.g. Footstepsinthesand 120 – Suerte 55 (Halling (USA) 133) [2017 77: p6g t7.1g 6g^3 6.1v 6.1g^4 6.1m* 6g^3 6.1s^6 5.7m* 5.7s^2 Oct 2] fair handicapper: won at Chepstow (amateur) in July and Bath (apprentice) in August: stays 6f: acts on soft and good to firm going. *Tony Carroll* **78**

OFF ART 7 ch.g. Dutch Art 126 – Off Camera (Efisio 120) [2017 100: 8g^5 8m 8s 8.5s^5 8d^6 8m^3 8d* 8g^3 8.3g^6 t8g^5 t8g^3 Dec 6] rather leggy gelding: fair performer nowadays: won minor event at Doncaster in September: stays 10.5f, usually races over shorter: acts on tapeta, soft and good to firm going: usually wears headgear. *Tim Easterby* **78**

OFFICER IN COMMAND (USA) 11 b.g. Officer (USA) 120 – Luv To Stay N Chat (USA) (Candi's Gold (USA)) [2017 48: t12.2g Jan 20] lengthy, angular gelding: poor handicapper nowadays: stays 1¼m: acts on polytrack, tapeta and good to firm going: wears headgear/tongue tie: sometimes slowly away, often races towards rear. *Alan Bailey* **–**

OFF THE SCALE (IRE) 5 b.g. Strategic Prince 114 – Vanilla Delight (IRE) 76 (Orpen (USA) 116) [2017 76: 6g 7.5f 6.9v Jun 8] fair at best, no form in 2017: tried in hood: usually races nearer last than first: has joined Sarah Robinson. *Rebecca Menzies* **–**

OGBOURNE DOWNS 7 b.g. Royal Applause 124 – Helen Sharp (Pivotal 124) [2017 8.1m^4 10m^4 8g p8g p8g Oct 13] lengthy, angular gelding: fair handicapper: barely stays 1¼m: acts on polytrack and good to firm going: tried in blinkers: usually slowly away. *Ben Pauling* **75**

OH GENO 3 b.g. Paco Boy (IRE) 129 – Key Light (IRE) 81 (Acclamation 118) [2017 65: t6m^4 Jan 16] modest maiden: stays 6f: acts on fibresand and tapeta: sold £4,000, sent to Greece. *Richard Spencer* **62**

OH IT'S SAUCEPOT 3 b.f. Sir Percy 129 – Oh So Saucy 90 (Imperial Ballet (IRE) 110) [2017 58: 8s^3 8s* 9.1d* 10d* Sep 4] sparely-made filly: fairly useful handicapper: won at Newmarket in July, Yarmouth in August and Windsor in September: likely to stay further than 1¼m: acts on soft going: likely to progress further. *Chris Wall* **89 p**

OH JAMES 4 b.g. Monsieur Bond (IRE) 120 – Sea Flower (IRE) 70 (Acclamation 118) [2017 78p: 6g 6v 6g Jun 5] fair 6f winner on debut at 3 yrs, no show in 2017: in hood last 2 starts. *Tim Easterby* **–**

OH SO DANDY (IRE) 3 ch.g. Dandy Man (IRE) 123 – Kelso Magic (USA) 98 (Distant View (USA) 126) [2017 60: t5g^5 6d f6.1g t5g^2 t5.1g Dec 13] modest maiden: best form at 5f: acts on tapeta: wears headgear: often starts slowly/races freely: temperamental. *Derek Shaw* **57 §**

OH SO SASSY 7 b.m. Pastoral Pursuits 127 – Almasi (IRE) 96 (Petorius 117) [2017 102: 5m^3 5d^5 5d 5g^6 5d^5 5m p5d^4 p5g^6 Oct 13] compact mare: useful handicapper: third at Newmarket (neck behind El Astronaute) in April: stays 6f: acts on polytrack and firm going: usually races towards rear. *Chris Wall* **97**

OH THIS IS US (IRE) 4 b.c. Acclamation 118 – Shamwari Lodge (IRE) 114 (Hawk Wing (USA) 136) [2017 113: 7g^3 7g^5 8g^2 8m* 7m^2 7m* 8.5m^3 8f 7g 8g^4 7s^3 8s 8d^5 Nov 4] lengthy colt: smart performer: won handicap at Bath (by neck from Hors de Combat) in April and listed race at Haydock (by neck from Absolutely So) in May: also second in Lincoln (Handicap) at Doncaster (neck behind Bravery) and handicap at Haydock (1¾ lengths behind Afjaan) in April: stays 8.5f: acts on polytrack, tapeta, good to firm and good to soft going. *Richard Hannon* **117**

OI THE CLUBB OI'S 2 gr.g. (Mar 30) Champs Elysees 124 – Red Boots (IRE) 66 (Verglas (IRE) 118) [2017 p8d t8.6d^6 Dec 27] 19,000F, £11,000Y, 42,000 2-y-o: fourth foal: brother to winner abroad and half-brother to useful 5f winner Stocking (by Acclamation): dam, maiden (stayed 7f), half-sister to smart 5f-7f winner Rose Bonheur out **64 p**

of smart winner up to 1m Red Feather: modest form: better effort when sixth in minor event at Wolverhampton (6½ lengths behind Antonian) in December: open to further improvement. *Ian Williams*

OJALA (IRE) 2 b.c. (Apr 18) Epaulette (AUS) 126 – Sonny Sunshine (Royal Applause 124) [2017 6m 6.1m³ t7.2g⁶ 7s* p7g* Dec 31] 20,000Y: lengthy colt: fourth foal: dam unraced half-sister to high-class 5f winner Sole Power: fairly useful performer: won nurseries at Salisbury in September and Lingfield in December: stays 7f: acts on polytrack, tapeta and soft going: front runner/races prominently: will go on improving. *Simon Dow* **83 p**

OK BY ME (IRE) 3 ch.f. Arcano (IRE) 122 – Kindest 92 (Cadeaux Genereux 131) [2017 67: t10.2d t7.1g t8.6g 8.1d May 29] workmanlike filly: maiden, no form in 2017: tried in visor: has joined Ian Williams. *David Evans* **–**

OKOOL (FR) 3 b.g. Cape Cross (IRE) 129 – Seschat (IRE) (Sinndar (IRE) 134) [2017 81p: 10.2m² 10.2g* 12.3g⁴ 9.9g³ 12d* 12m⁴ Sep 23] sturdy gelding: useful performer: won maiden at Nottingham in May and handicap at Newmarket (awarded race on demotion of Star of The East) in August: stays 1½m: acts on good to firm and good to soft going. *Owen Burrows* **96**

OLAUDAH 3 b.g. Equiano (FR) 127 – Bookiesindexdotnet 79 (Piccolo 121) [2017 –: 5m 5m 6d 5m⁶ 6m 5d⁵ 5g² 6.3v 5s p6s⁴ p6g² Dec 21] modest maiden: left A. P. Keatley after ninth start: stays 6f: acts on polytrack: sometimes in headgear: has worn tongue tie. *Henry Candy* **63**

OLD CHINA 4 b.g. Archipenko (USA) 127 – Porcelain (IRE) 82 (Peintre Celebre (USA) 137) [2017 65: 9s² 11.9d⁶ 8m⁴ 7.4d 7m² 7s* t8g Oct 20] fair performer: won maiden at Catterick in September: stays 9f: acts on soft and good to firm going: tried in tongue tie: often races prominently. *John Davies* **73**

OLD FASHIONED (CHI) 5 ch.g. Neko Bay (USA) 121 – Hebrides (CHI) (Schossberg (CAN) 117) [2017 102: t6g p5g 5m a6g⁴ t5g t5.1g Dec 5] useful performer at best: successful 3 times in Chile in 2015 and in minor event at Ovrevoll in 2016: little impact in handicaps in 2017: left Rune Haugen after third start, Fredrik Reuterskiold after fourth: stays 6f: acts on dirt and firm going: has worn headgear: often in tongue tie. *Luke McJannet* **79**

OLD PERSIAN 2 b.c. (Mar 14) Dubawi (IRE) 129 – Indian Petal 70 (Singspiel (IRE) 133) [2017 7d³ p8s* 8g* 8v Oct 23] strongly-built colt: first foal: dam twice-raced sister to 9.5f-1½m winner Silkwood and winner up to 1m Kavango (both smart): useful form: won minor events at Chelmsford in September and Newmarket (by 4½ lengths from Gronkowski) in October: will stay at least 1¼m. *Charlie Appleby* **100**

OLD TOWN BOY 6 b.g. Myboycharlie (IRE) 118 – Native Ring (FR) (Bering 136) [2017 91: t16.5m Jan 16] fairly useful performer, lightly raced: well held sole start in 2017: stays 12.5f: acts on polytrack, good to firm and heavy going. *Philip McBride* **–**

OLIMAR (FR) 3 gr.f. Kendargent (FR) 112 – Onega Lake (IRE) (Peintre Celebre (USA) 137) [2017 t8g Nov 3] fourth foal: half-sister to 3 winners, including useful 1½m-15.5f winner Oak Harbour (by Sinndar) and French 1m winner Osumi (by Zamindar): dam 2-y-o 1¼m winner: well held in 2 maidens, trained on debut in 2016 by N. Clement in France. *Marjorie Fife* **–**

OLIVE MABEL 2 b.f. (Feb 27) Captain Gerrard (IRE) 113 – Shembara (FR) (Dylan Thomas (IRE) 132) [2017 p6d⁶ 5g⁶ p7g Jul 5] smallish filly: second foal: dam, 2-y-o 9f winner, half-sister to smart 1¼m winner Shamkiyr: modest form: best effort when sixth in minor event at Chelmsford (6 lengths behind Joe's Spirit) in May. *Dean Ivory* **54**

OLIVER REED (IRE) 2 b.c. (Feb 20) Footstepsinthesand 120 – Montbretia 105 (Montjeu (IRE) 137) [2017 6m⁵ 6v² 6g⁵ Aug 1] €28,000F, £100,000Y: good-topped colt: third foal: half-brother to 6f-8.3f winner Specialv (by Big Bad Bob): dam 1¼m winner: fairly useful form: best effort when second in minor event at Newbury (½ length behind Alkhalifa) in July: will be suited by 7f: remains capable of better. *Richard Hannon* **81 p**

OLIVER'S BETTY 2 b.f. (Apr 30) Dick Turpin (IRE) 127 – Luck Will Come (IRE) 82 (Desert Style (IRE) 121) [2017 6.1v Aug 8] angular filly: fifth foal: half-sister to 1m/8.5f winner Lord Reason (by Sixties Icon) and winner up to 6f Lady Nayef (by Nayef): dam, 6f-1¼m winner, half-sister to useful winner up to 7f B Fifty Two: 20/1, well held in minor event at Nottingham. *Michael Appleby* **–**

OLIVER'S GOLD 9 b.g. Danehill Dancer (IRE) 117 – Gemini Gold (IRE) 97 (King's Best (USA) 132) [2017 52: 14d⁵ Aug 12] modest maiden: stays 2m: acts on polytrack and soft going: has worn headgear: tried in tongue tie: fairly useful hurdler/chaser. *Mark Walford* **50**

OLIVIA FALLOW (IRE) 5 b.m. Vale of York (IRE) 117 – Spinning Maid (USA) (Forestry (USA) 121) [2017 95: 5m^4 5m 5m^3 5m 5m 5g^6 5g^4 5s^4 5g 5m 5s^5 Oct 1] fairly useful handicapper: third at Redcar in May: best form at 5f: acts on firm and good to soft going: has worn headgear. *Paul Midgley* **92**

OLMEDO (FR) 2 b.c. (Apr 11) Declaration of War (USA) 128 – Super Pie (USA) (Pivotal 124) [2017 7.5g* 8d^2 8d^2 Oct 1] **116**

There were no Group 1 winners among the latest crop of French two-year-olds. It's far from rare for the top French two-year-old contests to be won by British or Irish yards at the expense of the locals, but opportunities were slimmer still in the latest season when protests over cuts to prize money and bonuses by a group uniting various professionals caused the abandonment of an important card at Saint-Cloud at the end of October which should have featured France's last two Group 1 races for two-year-olds, the Criterium International and the Criterium de Saint-Cloud. France Galop ruled out rescheduling the races, citing the betting revenue that had been lost and the costs of staging a replacement fixture. A classic case of the protesters, who included owners and trainers, shooting themselves in the foot, it would seem. Among the French two-year-olds deprived of the chance to bid for a Group 1 win at Saint-Cloud were the unbeaten pattern winners Sacred Life and Luminate who will now have to wait until the spring to get the chance to prove themselves at that level. As things stand, therefore, it is the Prix Jean-Luc Lagardere runner-up Olmedo who, on Timeform's reading of the form-book, can boast the best form among France's two-year-olds.

Olmedo made a big impression on his debut when readily beating fifteen other newcomers at Deauville in August, after which Jean-Claude Rouget described him as the stable's main hope for the rest of the year and the following season. There must have been a little disappointment, therefore, that he was beaten on his two remaining starts, though his trainer seemed unperturbed, after both defeats, about Olmedo's longer-term classic prospects. Olmedo's four-length win at Deauville meant he started odds on against four rivals in the Prix des Chenes at Chantilly the following month but he was unable to reel in the more experienced, and more enterprisingly-ridden, Godolphin colt Stage Magic and went down by just a short head without his rider asking him for everything. It was another Godolphin colt, Masar, who looked like proving Olmedo's biggest threat for much of the straight in the Jean-Luc Lagardere four weeks later. Olmedo loomed up on the bridle with two furlongs to run but, after narrowly getting the better of that argument in the closing stages after a lengthy duel, both colts were passed in the last fifty yards or so by the filly Happily who had a length and a quarter to spare at the line.

Olmedo (FR) (b.c. 2015)	Declaration of War (USA) (b 2009)	War Front (b 2002)	Danzig
			Starry Dreamer
		Tempo West (ch 1999)	Rahy
			Tempo
	Super Pie (USA) (ch 2008)	Pivotal (ch 1993)	Polar Falcon
			Fearless Revival
		Super Lina (gr 2001)	Linamix
			Supergirl

Olmedo carries the light blue, dark blue spots of part-owner Antonio Caro, colours made famous by Almanzor whose final start came at Deauville just a week after Olmedo made his debut there. Almanzor's other owner was Gerard Augustin-Normand, also part-owner of the latest season's Poule d'Essai des Poulains and Prix du Jockey Club winner Brametot, and Rouget envisages Olmedo attempting the same double. Qemah's essay in *Racehorses of 2016* referred to Rouget's limit of €100,000 on his auction purchases, a ceiling he had to go to secure Olmedo as a yearling at Deauville—Almanzor and Rouget's first Prix du Jockey Club winner Le Havre had cost the same amount. Another similarity between Olmedo and Almanzor (and Brametot, for that matter) is that they are all members of their respective sires' first crops. Olmedo's sire Declaration of War made his name as a tough and high-class performer for Aidan O'Brien, winning the Queen Anne Stakes and Juddmonte International in a busy campaign as a four-year-old which ended with his being beaten a nose and a head into third in the Breeders' Cup Classic.

Declaration of War had begun his career with Rouget for whom he won both his starts as a two-year-old. Another name in Olmedo's pedigree, albeit a rather distant relative in his dam's family, that probably struck a chord with his trainer is Stacelita, whom Rouget trained to win the Prix de Diane among other races. This is also the family of Arlington Million and Breeders' Cup Mile winner Steinlen who was a half-brother to Olmedo's unraced great grandam Supergirl. The Prix du Jockey Club runner-up Super Celebre was the pick of Supergirl's winners, though they also included Olmedo's useful grandam Super Lina, a nine-furlong winner at two who finished second in the Prix Penelope over ten and a half furlongs at three. Olmdo's lightly-raced dam, Super Pie, whose only win came on her debut over nine and a half furlongs on the all-weather at Deauville, is a half-sister to the useful French performer Art Contemporain who stayed eleven furlongs. Super Pie has only one other recorded foal, Super Mac (by Makfi), a winner in France at up to a mile and a quarter. Olmedo should stay a mile and a quarter himself in due course, though presumably he'll follow in the footsteps of Almanzor and Brametot by first reappearing over a mile in the Prix de Fontainebleau. *Jean-Claude Rouget, France*

OLYMPIC DUEL (IRE) 4 b.g. Acclamation 118 – Olympic Medal 66 (Nayef (USA) 129) [2017 63: p7g* 7g p7g 7s 8g^{pu} Aug 17] angular gelding: fair handicapper: won at Kempton (by 2½ lengths from Tidal's Baby) in April: stayed 7.5f: acted on polytrack and good to soft going: dead. *Peter Hiatt* **67**

OLYMPIC LEGEND (IRE) 3 ch.g. Choisir (AUS) 126 – Margaret's Dream (IRE) 61 (Muhtarram (USA) 125) [2017 74: p10g^4 p10g^5 t8.6g^5 10m 8m p10g p12g^4 p13.3s^2 Dec 1] small gelding: fair handicapper: stays 13.5f: acts on polytrack and soft: tried in cheekpieces: in tongue tie last 3 starts: front runner/races prominently. *Martin Bosley* **69**

OMEROS 3 ch.g. Poet's Voice 126 – Caribbean Pearl (USA) 86 (Silver Hawk (USA) 123) [2017 85p: 8m^5 9.1g^5 p8g^3 8s t8g Oct 10] fairly useful handicapper: third at Chelmsford in August: stays 1m: acts on polytrack and good to firm going: tried in hood: front runner/races prominently, often races freely: sold 24,000 gns, sent to Saudi Arabia. *Hugo Palmer* **90**

OMID 9 b.g. Dubawi (IRE) 129 – Mille Couleurs (FR) (Spectrum (IRE) 126) [2017 51§: 17.2g t16.3s Jun 3] big gelding: modest handicapper, well beaten in 2017: stays 21.5f: acts on fibresand, tapeta and heavy going: wears headgear/tongue tie: usually races close up: temperamental. *Kenneth Slack* **– §**

OMINOTAGO 5 ch.m. Aqlaam 125 – Sharp Dresser (USA) 80 (Diesis 133) [2017 71: f11g* t13.9m^4 f14d^2 11.5m^2 f12.1g^2 Nov 28] fairly useful performer: won maiden at Southwell in January: likely to stay 2m: acts on fibresand, tapeta, good to firm and good to soft going. *Michael Appleby* **80**

OMNEEYA 3 b.f. Frankel 147 – Amanee (AUS) (Pivotal 124) [2017 7g^3 p7g^4 7g^6 6.1m^3 6g^3 Jul 27] first foal: dam, South African 5f-1m (including Group 1) winner, out of close relative to Kingmambo: fair maiden: stays 7f: acts on good to firm going: tried in tongue tie. *Marco Botti* **70**

OMOTESANDO 7 b.g. Street Cry (IRE) 130 – Punctilious 117 (Danehill (USA) 126) [2017 81: t10.2s^6 9g^4 10.2m^4 9d^3 t12.2g^3 11.2s^2 11.6g* 10.2d^3 11.8v^6 t12.2g^2 12.1v t9.5m^5 t16.5g* t12.2g Nov 29] fair handicapper: won apprentice races at Haydock in August and Wolverhampton in November: stays 16.5f: acts on polytrack, tapeta, good to firm and heavy going: wears cheekpieces. *Oliver Greenall* **77**

OMRAN 3 ch.c. Choisir (AUS) 126 – Ruff Shod (USA) (Storm Boot (USA)) [2017 93p: 7g^4 t7.1s* 7g^6 8m 7s p7s p8g Oct 4] good-topped colt: useful handicapper: won at Newcastle in May: stays 7f: acts on polytrack and tapeta: tried in tongue tie: sold 40,000 gns in November. *Marco Botti* **104**

ON A ROLL 2 b.f. (Mar 5) Swiss Spirit 117 – Amary (IRE) 88 (Acclamation 118) [2017 5m^6 Apr 19] 6,800F: compact, good-quartered filly: second foal: dam, winner up to 7f (2-y-o 6f winner), sister to useful 1m-1¼m winner Wayfoong Express: 7/1, sixth in maiden at Newmarket (5¼ lengths behind Formidable Kitt) on debut: should improve. *Richard Hannon* **58 p**

ONE BIG SURPRISE 5 b.m. Kier Park (IRE) 114 – Cloridja (Indian Ridge 123) [2017 78: 6m* 7g^4 6m^6 5d^5 7d^2 7g^5 6g^3 p7g t6.1g Nov 20] lengthy mare: fair handicapper: won at Brighton in April: stays 7f: acts on good to firm and good to soft going: wears cheekpieces: in tongue tie last 2 starts. *Richard Hughes* **79**

ONE BOY (IRE) 6 ch.g. Captain Gerrard (IRE) 113 – Paris Song (IRE) 69 (Peintre Celebre (USA) 137) [2017 84: t5d^5 t5d 5g^3 5m^5 5g 5s^6 5f^6 5d^3 5s 5d 5s* 5m 5s* 5v Oct 16] sturdy gelding: fairly useful handicapper: won at Hamilton in August and Beverley (by 1¼ lengths from Flash City) in September: best at 5f: acts on good to firm and heavy going: has worn headgear. *Paul Midgley* **82**

ONE DRUNKEN NIGHT 2 ch.g. (Apr 1) Sakhee's Secret 128 – Amandian (IRE) 84 (Indian Ridge 123) [2017 5g^5 7s Jul 26] well held in sellers. *Gay Kelleway* –

ONEFOOTINFRONT 2 b.c. (Mar 4) Sir Percy 129 – Anaya 72 (Tobougg (IRE) 125) [2017 8g^5 t8.6g^5 8.2d 8.3d^4 t9.5g t8s Nov 30] modest maiden: stays 8.5f: acts on good to soft going: sometimes slowly away. *Daniel Loughnane* **59**

ONE FOOT IN HEAVEN (IRE) 5 b.h. Fastnet Rock (AUS) 127 – Pride (FR) 128 (Peintre Celebre (USA) 137) [2017 121: 9.9m 12m^2 9.9s^2 11.9d 11.9d^3 Oct 15] compact horse: very smart performer: second in Jockey Club Stakes at Newmarket (5 lengths behind Seventh Heaven) and La Coupe de Maisons-Laffitte (beaten ¾ length by Garlingari): 8¼ lengths eleventh to Enable in Prix de l'Arc de Triomphe at Chantilly next time: stays 1½m: acts on polytrack, soft and good to firm going: often races towards rear. *A. de Royer Dupre, France* **121**

ONEFOOTINPARADISE 2 b.f. (Mar 7) Footstepsinthesand 120 – Sancai (USA) (Elusive Quality (USA)) [2017 5g^5 5.2m^3 6d^2 5.2v 6d 5g^6 t6g^2 6g Oct 7] 2,000Y: compact filly: first foal: dam once-raced half-sister to smart winner up to 1¼m Prince Alzain: fair maiden: stays 6f: acts on tapeta, good to firm and good to soft going. *Philip McBride* **73**

ONE FOR JODIE (IRE) 6 ch.g. Majestic Missile (IRE) 118 – Tough Chic (IRE) 82 (Indian Ridge 123) [2017 –: t9.5g^5 p8g t8.6g^4 f6d^3 6g Apr 22] modest maiden: stays 8.5f: acts on tapeta and fibresand: in cheekpieces last 3 starts: often races prominently: has joined Steve Gollings. *Michael Appleby* **60**

ONE FOR JUNE (IRE) 2 b.f. (Feb 25) Arcano (IRE) 122 – Worthington (IRE) 84 (Kodiac 112) [2017 5g 6m^4 6d* 5.2v 7d p7g^3 7d* Oct 20] €30,000Y: lengthy filly: first foal: dam, 2-y-o 5f winner who stayed 7f, closely related to smart winner up to 1½m Come On Jonny: fair performer: won minor event at Lingfield in July and claimer at Redcar in October: stays 7f: acts on polytrack, good to firm and good to soft going: tried in cheekpieces. *William Haggas* **71**

ONEHELLUVATOUCH 4 gr.f. Hellvelyn 118 – Soft Touch (IRE) 78 (Petorius 117) [2017 69: 9.9g 9.9m 10m^6 11.4m Jul 3] angular filly: fair handicapper, no form in 2017: wears headgear. *Philip Hide* –

ONE LAST HUG 2 b.g. (Mar 14) Orientor 118 – Gargoyle Girl 75 (Be My Chief (USA) 122) [2017 5g Apr 1] 33/1, when well held in minor event at Doncaster. *Jim Goldie* –

ONE LINER 3 b.g. Delegator 125 – Quip (Green Desert (USA) 127) [2017 71: 10s 7g 8.2d^5 9.5s 6.7m 8g 12s 8.1d^4 10g^6 9s p8g t7.2g Dec 13] fair maiden: left Mrs J. Harrington after eleventh start: stays 1¼m: acts on good to soft going: has worn headgear. *John O'Shea* **68**

ONE MAN ARMY 5 b.g. Mount Nelson 125 – Hms Pinafore (IRE) (Singspiel (IRE) 133) [2017 –: f8s f7g Feb 10] fair handicapper at best: stayed 7f: acted on fibresand: tried in hood: dead. *Julia Brooke* **57**

ONE MASTER 3 b.f. Fastnet Rock (AUS) 127 – Enticing (IRE) 116 (Pivotal 124) [2017 6g^3 6d* 7s* Oct 7] sturdy filly: fifth foal: closely related to 6f/7f winner Triple Chocolate (by Danehill Dancer) and half-sister to 5f-6f winner Jacob's Pillow (by Oasis Dream): dam, 5f winner (including at 2 yrs), half-sister to smart 7f/1m winner Sentaril: useful form: won maiden at Yarmouth (by 2¾ lengths from Perfect Sense) in September and listed race at Ascot (by 1¼ lengths from Bletchley) in October: stays 7f: likely to progress further. *William Haggas* **107 p**

ONE MINUTE (IRE) 2 b.f. (Jan 28) Kodiac 112 – Amwaj (IRE) (Dubawi (IRE) 129) [2017 5d* 5.2m^2 5.4g* 5.2s 6g^4 7m 6g Nov 3] €39,000Y, £52,000 2-y-o: first foal: dam lightly raced: fairly useful performer: won minor events at Lingfield in May and York (by 1¼ lengths from Abel Handy) in July: stays 6f: acts on good to firm and good to soft going: tried in cheekpieces. *William Haggas* **93**

ONE MORE CHANCE (IRE) 2 b.f. (Mar 28) Epaulette (AUS) 126 – Hi Katriona (IRE) 63 (Second Empire (IRE) 124) [2017 f7.1g^4 Dec 11] €32,000Y: half-sister to several winners, including useful winner up to 7f Bayleyf (2-y-o 6f winner, by Kheleyf) and **71 p**

winner up to 1m Hard Yards (2-y-o 7f winner, by Moss Vale): dam maiden (stayed 8.6f): 50/1, fourth in minor event at Southwell (6½ lengths behind On The Warpath) in December: will improve. *David Brown*

ONE MORE DAWN 2 b.f. (Apr 8) Kheleyf (USA) 116 – Jocasta Dawn 87 (Kyllachy 129) [2017 p7d p6g Dec 20] first foal: dam 5f/6f winner: last in 2 minor events: in hood second start. *Mark Pattinson* –

ONE PEKAN (IRE) 7 b.g. Hard Spun (USA) 124 – Stormy Blessing (USA) (Storm Cat (USA)) [2017 91: p8g Jan 5] rangy gelding: fairly useful handicapper, below form sole start in 2017: stays 11f: acts on polytrack and any turf going: has worn headgear: tried in tongue tie. *Roger Varian* –

ONE PURSUIT (IRE) 9 br.g. Pastoral Pursuits 127 – Karinski (USA) (Palace Music (USA) 129) [2017 16m May 25] leggy, workmanlike gelding: useful handicapper for Brendan Powell in 2014: twice raced since, well held on sole start in 2017: stays 13f: acts on fibresand, good to firm and heavy going. *Charlie Mann* –

ONEROA (IRE) 2 b.f. (Apr 28) Dandy Man (IRE) 123 – Alexander Express (IRE) 102 (Sri Pekan (USA) 117) [2017 6.1f p6s^5 t6.1g^4 Dec 22] €10,000Y, £20,000 2-y-o: half-sister to several winners, including useful 6f-13f winner (stays 2m) Political Policy (by Bushranger) and 2-y-o 7f winner Andalacia (by Choisir): dam 1m winner: modest form: best effort when fourth in minor event at Wolverhampton (3¾ lengths behind Mount Wellington) in December: left Daniel Loughnane after first start: open to further improvement. *Ivan Furtado* **59 p**

ONESARNIESHORT (FR) 2 b.g. (Jan 20) Penny's Picnic (IRE) 111 – La Atomica (FR) (Silent Times (IRE) 108) [2017 6g^3 5d^5 5g^3 t6g 6d^4 p6.5g p9.4g Dec 26] modest maiden: left David O'Meara after fifth start: best form at 6f: tried in cheekpieces. *Mme G. Rarick, France* **64**

ONE SECOND 2 b.f. (Jan 31) Intello (GER) 129 – Albavilla 82 (Spectrum (IRE) 126) [2017 7m^4 7d^2 7g Jul 15] 42,000Y: sixth foal: half-sister to 9f-11f winner Antinori (by Fasliyev) and 2-y-o 5f-1m winner Pure Excellence (by Exceed And Excel), both useful: dam, 1¾m winner, half-sister to very smart 1¼m-1¾m winner Barolo: fair form: best effort when second in minor event at Doncaster (3½ lengths behind Learn By Heart) in June. *Mark Johnston* **75**

ONE TOO MANY (IRE) 3 gr.f. Zebedee 113 – Speckled Hen (IRE) 60 (Titus Livius (FR) 115) [2017 70: 8m 6d^4 6g^3 Jul 20] fair maiden: stays 6f: acts on good to soft going: sold 4,000 gns in November, sent to Belgium. *David Brown* **70**

ONE WORD MORE (IRE) 7 b.g. Thousand Words 113 – Somoushe (IRE) (Black Minnaloushe (USA) 123) [2017 108: 8.3g t8s^4 7.9m 8s^5 7.9d 8m^5 9d 8d^2 7.9g Oct 13] sturdy gelding: useful handicapper: second in minor event at Ascot (neck behind Zwayyan) in October: stays 1m: acts on polytrack and any turf going: wears headgear: sold 12,000 gns in October, sent to Italy. *Tim Easterby* **101**

ON FIRE 4 b.g. Olden Times 121 – La Notte 88 (Factual (USA) 108) [2017 63: p12d^2 p12d^2 t10.2d* t12.4g^2 14.1g* 16.3d^5 13.9m^4 14g^2 14g^3 16.1g^2 t16.3g^2 16.3g Oct 14] tall, lengthy gelding: fairly useful performer: won maiden at Newcastle in March and handicap at Nottingham in May: placed on 7 further occasions: stays 16.5f: acts on polytrack, tapeta and good to firm going: usually wears cheekpieces. *James Bethell* **86**

ON HER TOES (IRE) 3 b.f. Kodiac 112 – Dancing Jest (IRE) 71 (Averti (IRE) 117) [2017 94: 7.9d^2 8m 7g^3 8d* 7g^5 8d Sep 29] compact filly: useful performer: won listed race at Ascot (by ½ length from Pirouette) in July: second in similar event at York (¾ length behind Tomyris) in May and third in handicap at Newmarket (3¼ lengths behind Inshiraah) in July: stays 1m: acts on soft and good to firm going: often races prominently. *William Haggas* **104**

ONLY MINE (IRE) 4 b.f. Pour Moi (IRE) 125 – Truly Mine (IRE) 98 (Rock of Gibraltar (IRE) 133) [2017 107: 6v^3 6d^2 6s^2 6g* 6g* 6s Sep 24] workmanlike filly: useful performer: won listed races at the Curragh (by neck from Gordon Lord Byron) and Naas (by length from Music Box) in July: second at former course in Greenlands Stakes (1½ lengths behind Gordon Lord Byron) in May and Ballyogan Stakes (head behind Penny Pepper) in June: stays 7f: acts on good to firm and good to soft going: front runner/races prominently: sold 925,000 gns in December. *Joseph G. Murphy, Ireland* **106**

ONLY ORSENFOOLSIES 8 b.g. Trade Fair 124 – Desert Gold (IRE) 97 (Desert Prince (IRE) 130) [2017 79: 12.1s^6 12.1v^2 15.9s^4 Oct 31] lengthy gelding, shows traces of stringhalt: fair handicapper: stays 13f: acts on heavy going: fairly useful hurdler. *Micky Hammond* **78**

ONLY TEN PER CENT (IRE) 9 b.g. Kheleyf (USA) 116 – Cory Everson (IRE) (Brief Truce (USA) 126) [2017 71: p6g p7d p6g5 f5g 5.2m 5.2m f5g p6g Dec 21] fair handicapper, generally below best in 2017: stays 7f: acts on all-weather, good to firm and good to soft going: usually wears headgear: sometimes slowly away. *J. R. Jenkins* **61**

ONORINA (IRE) 5 b.m. Arcano (IRE) 122 – Miss Honorine (IRE) 109 (Highest Honor (FR) 124) [2017 77: p15.8g 14f 12m2 13.3g 14.2v p12g Oct 18] sturdy mare: fair handicapper: stays 1¾m: acts on polytrack and soft going: tried in hood. *Jim Boyle* **72**

ON THE HIGH TOPS (IRE) 9 b.g. Kheleyf (USA) 116 – Diplomats Daughter 81 (Unfuwain (USA) 131) [2017 –: 5g 5m3 5m May 25] fairly useful at best, no longer of much account: wears headgear: has worn tongue tie. *Colin Teague* **–**

ON THE WARPATH 2 ch.c. (Apr 1) Declaration of War (USA) 128 – Elusive Pearl (USA) (Medaglia d'Oro (USA) 129) [2017 p7d4 p7g2 f7.1g* f7.1g* Dec 11] $150,000Y: strong colt: first foal: dam minor US 1m stakes winner: useful form: won minor events at Southwell in November and December: will stay at least 1m: open to further improvement. *Sir Mark Prescott Bt* **99 p**

ON TO VICTORY 3 b.g. Rock of Gibraltar (IRE) 133 – Clouds of Magellan (USA) (Dynaformer (USA)) [2017 82: p7g2 8.2s* 9.9g2 12d* 12m3 12v2 13.9m4 14.2s* 14.2d4 Oct 6] tall gelding: smart performer: won handicaps at Leicester (by 2¼ lengths from Black Trilby) in May and Salisbury (by 8 lengths from Stone The Crows) in June, and minor event also at Salisbury (by 2½ lengths from Battersea) in September: stays 1¾m: acts on any turf going: usually wears hood: consistent. *Eve Johnson Houghton* **112**

OOR JOCK (IRE) 9 ch.g. Shamardal (USA) 129 – Katdogawn 114 (Bahhare (USA) 122) [2017 74: t7.1m* p7g5 t6g2 p6g* t6m2 p7g4 8s6 7g 6m6 6.7m 6.7g 8.1g6 7.5d5 6.3v p8g p7s p6g5 Dec 21] modest handicapper on turf, fair on all-weather: won at Wolverhampton in January and Dundalk in February: left Adrian McGuinness after sixth start, Albert Moriarty after fourteenth: stays 7.5f: acts on polytrack, tapeta, sand, soft and good to firm going: usually wears headgear. *D. P. Coakley, Ireland* **54 a66**

OOTY HILL 5 gr.g. Dubawi (IRE) 129 – Mussoorie (FR) 108 (Linamix (FR) 127) [2017 12g4 11.9d Oct 28] lengthy, well-made gelding: useful form at best, lightly raced: stays 1¼m: acts on good to firm and good to soft going: wore hood both starts in 2017. *Charlie Fellowes* **93**

OPAL TIARA (IRE) 4 b.f. Thousand Words 113 – Zarafa (Fraam 114) [2017 109: 8g2 8.9g* 8.9d 8.1d4 8d2 8m 8m 8g6 8g4 Sep 2] rather leggy filly: smart performer: won Balanchine at Meydan (by neck from Via Firenze) in February: second in Cape Verdi at same course (½ length behind Very Special) in January and Lanwades Stud Stakes at the Curragh (3¾ lengths behind Creggs Pipes) in May: stays 9f: acts on tapeta, firm and good to soft going: races prominently. *Mick Channon* **113**

OPENING TIME 3 b.g. Harbour Watch (IRE) 121 – Dozy (IRE) 90 (Exceed And Excel (AUS) 126) [2017 61: p8g 8d 7m2 7.1m Jun 26] modest maiden: stays 7f: acts on good to firm going: in blinkers last 3 starts: often races prominently: sold 4,000 gns, sent to Greece. *Richard Hannon* **63**

OPEN WIDE (USA) 3 b.g. Invincible Spirit (IRE) 121 – Nunavik (IRE) (Indian Ridge 123) [2017 82p: 6d6 6f3 5.1m2 6.1m2 5.7f* p7g5 6m3 Aug 25] fairly useful handicapper: won at Bath in July: stays 7f: acts on polytrack and firm going: usually wears headgear. *Amanda Perrett* **94**

OPERA BUFFA (IRE) 4 b.f. Exceed And Excel (AUS) 126 – Dubai Opera (USA) (Dubai Millennium 140) [2017 a59: 9.9g 11.9mur 10.2d Aug 23] maiden, no form in 2017: wears headgear: usually wears tongue tie: front runner/races prominently. *Steve Flook* **–**

OPERA QUEEN 3 b.f. Nathaniel (IRE) 129 – Opera Glass 88 (Barathea (IRE) 127) [2017 9.9g 9.9f 10g Jul 13] closely related to useful 1¼m-11.6f winner Opera Gal (by Galileo) and 1½m winner Opera Lad (by Teofilo) and half-sister to 1¾m winner (stays 2m) Opera Buff (by Oratorio): dam, 8.4f winner, sister to smart winner up to 7f Opera Cape: little impact in maidens: type to do better in handicaps. *Andrew Balding* **– p**

OPERATEUR (IRE) 9 b.g. Oratorio (IRE) 128 – Kassariya (IRE) (Be My Guest (USA) 126) [2017 –: t12.2g 13.1s5 Jun 7] fair handicapper at best, on downgrade: stays 1¾m: acts on polytrack, good to firm and heavy going: tried in cheekpieces/tongue tie. *Ben Haslam* **45**

OPERATIVE 4 ch.g. Pastoral Pursuits 127 – Gilt Linked 85 (Compton Place 125) [2017 81§: 7g 6s² 5g² 5m* 5d* 6.1d Oct 4] strong, compact gelding: fairly useful handicapper: won at Goodwood in August and Sandown (by ¾ length from African Friend) in September: stays 6f: acts on soft and good to firm going: has worn headgear: sometimes slowly away, often races towards rear: carries head awkwardly. *Ed de Giles* **89 §**

OPINIONATE 3 b.g. Cacique (IRE) 124 – Comment (Sadler's Wells (USA) 132) [2017 71p: p8g* 11.2s 12d³ 12g* 11.5d⁵ Sep 19] well-made gelding: useful performer: won maiden at Lingfield in January and handicap at Salisbury in September: stays 1½m: acts on polytrack and good to soft going: often races towards rear/travels strongly: sold 55,000 gns in November. *Amanda Perrett* **98**

OPPOSITION 4 gr.g. Dalakhani (IRE) 133 – Censored 79 (Pivotal 124) [2017 93: 12s⁶ 11.4d² 11.9m* 12g 12g⁴ t16.5g² 16.3g⁴ Oct 14] tall gelding: fairly useful handicapper: won at York (apprentice) in June: second at Wolverhampton in September: stays 16.5f: acts on tapeta, good to firm and good to soft going: sold 100,000 gns in November. *Ed Dunlop* **94**

OPTICAL HIGH 8 b.g. Rainbow High 121 – Forsweets (Forzando 122) [2017 11.8s⁶ May 22] strong gelding: winning hurdler: in cheekpieces, 33/1, well held in seller at Leicester. *Tony Forbes* **–**

OPTIMA PETAMUS 5 gr.g. Mastercraftsman (IRE) 129 – In A Silent Way (IRE) 102 (Desert Prince (IRE) 130) [2017 82: t10.2g 11.1g 12.1d 14s 10d p10s⁵ p10s⁶ Dec 7] lengthy gelding: fairly useful handicapper, well below best in 2017: stays 10.5f: acts on tapeta, good to firm and good to soft going: often wears headgear. *Patrick Holmes* **63**

OPTIMICKSTICKHILL 2 gr.f. (Mar 17) Milk It Mick 120 – Stylistickhill (IRE) 74 (Desert Style (IRE) 121) [2017 6d 6s⁴ 5d f6.1g⁴ f6.1g f8.1g Dec 29] first foal: dam 8.6f winner who stayed 1½m: modest maiden: stays 6f: acts on fibresand and soft going: front runner/races prominently. *Scott Dixon* **59**

OPTIMUM TIME (IRE) 2 b.g. (Mar 10) Manduro (GER) 135 – Mypreciousblue (Peintre Celebre (USA) 137) [2017 6.1d* 7m 6g 6.3s Sep 10] €10,000F, €18,000Y: rather unfurnished gelding: first foal: dam, 9f winner, half-sister to smart 1m-9.5f winner Sharpalo: fairly useful form: won minor event at Windsor in May: best effort at 6f. *Eve Johnson Houghton* **85**

ORACLE BOY 6 b.g. Mount Nelson 125 – Snow Princess (IRE) 111 (Ela-Mana-Mou 132) [2017 –: 11.5m 12m f16.5g 15.9s Oct 10] sturdy gelding: fair at best, of no account nowadays: has worn headgear: tried in tongue tie. *Michael Chapman* **–**

ORANGE SUIT (IRE) 2 b.c. (Feb 16) Declaration of War (USA) 128 – Guantanamera (IRE) (Sadler's Wells (USA) 132) [2017 6g* Sep 22] 90,000Y: half-brother to several winners, including very smart 1½m-14.6f (including St Leger) winner Simple Verse (by Duke of Marmalade), smart winner up to 1½m Even Song (2-y-o 1m winner, by Mastercraftsman) and useful winner up to 9f Maxentius (2-y-o 6f/7f winner, by Holy Roman Emperor): dam, unraced, out of useful performer up to 1½m Bluffing: 20/1, won maiden at Newbury (by neck from Jack Crow) on debut, showing willing attitude: will be suited by 7f+: sure to improve. *Richard Hannon* **94 p**

ORANGEY RED (IRE) 4 b.f. Lawman (FR) 121 – Triple Try (IRE) 89 (Sadler's Wells (USA) 132) [2017 86: 6d⁵ 7s 6.3g* 7g* 7g⁴ 7s 7m⁴ 7s Oct 7] leggy filly: fairly useful performer: won handicap at Listowel and minor event at Fairyhouse in June: stays 7f: acts on good to firm and heavy going: has worn headgear. *W. T. Farrell, Ireland* **94**

ORATORIO'S JOY (IRE) 7 b.m. Oratorio (IRE) 128 – Seeking The Fun (USA) (Alhaarth (IRE) 126) [2017 76, a83: p13m* t12.2g⁶ t13.9g⁵ p13.3d⁴ t13.9g³ t16.5g³ May 2] sturdy mare: fair performer: won claimer at Lingfield in January: left Jamie Osborne after fifth start: stays 17f: acts on polytrack, tapeta, firm and good to soft going: usually wore cheekpieces in 2017: sometimes slowly away. *Daniel Loughnane* **78**

ORCHID LILY 2 b.f. (Mar 29) Dansili 127 – Helleborine 111 (Observatory (USA) 131) [2017 8m⁴ 8d⁴ Oct 24] third foal: dam, 2-y-o 6f-1m winner, sister to smart winner up to 7f African Rose: fair form in 2 minor events. *John Gosden* **68**

ORDER OF SERVICE 7 ch.g. Medicean 128 – Choir Gallery (Pivotal 124) [2017 77§: t7.1g t7.1g⁵ f8g² f8g³ f7g⁵ 7g 7.2m 8.5g* 7g⁴ 8.5f⁶ 7d² Sep 10] fair handicapper: won at Les Landes in July: left Shaun Harris after eighth start: stays 8.5f: acts on all-weather, good to firm and good to soft going: has worn headgear/tongue tie: usually slowly away, often races in rear: unreliable. *K. Kukk, Jersey* **78 §**

ORDER OF ST GEORGE (IRE) 5 b.h. Galileo (IRE) 134 – Another Storm (USA) **128**
(Gone West (USA)) [2017 128: 14g^2 14m* 20m^2 14d* 14s* 11.9d^4 16s* Oct 21]

Royal Ascot's oldest race, the Gold Cup, seemed in terminal decline during the mid-'eighties because of the trend-shifting commercial breeders who had been shunning stayers for so long that it simply didn't seem viable to aim good horses at the Cup events because it would actually damage their stud prospects. When the game Gildoran landed his second successive Gold Cup for leading owner Robert Sangster in 1985, his Timeform rating of 117 contrasted sharply with the marks earned by some of the other top performers who carried Sangster's famous green and blue silks over shorter trips in the same era—El Gran Senor and Sadler's Wells, for example, were rated 136 and 132 respectively. This dip in quality of the Gold Cup winners continued for quite a while afterwards, prompting calls for the race distance to be reduced from two and a half miles to two miles to try to arrest the slide. The Ascot authorities thankfully resisted the calls and, happily, powerful connections began aiming choicely-bred types at the race again without the incentive of a shorter trip. Godolphin's dual Gold Cup winner Kayf Tara was a brother to top-class middle-distance performer Opera House, out of the 1986 Irish Oaks winner Colorspin, and Godolphin's 1996 Gold Cup winner Classic Cliche more than held his own when brought back a mile on his next start, finishing a fine second (a place ahead of that year's Derby winner Shaamit) in the King George VI and Queen Elizabeth Stakes. French-trained Westerner showed similar versatility, finishing runner-up in the Prix de l'Arc de Triomphe in the same season as his Gold Cup win (at York), before being snapped up by Coolmore to stand as a National Hunt stallion. Coolmore's lucrative National Hunt division is arguably the main reason behind the renewed demand for staying-bred sires and goes some way to explaining why Ballydoyle has targeted the Ascot showpiece in recent years, with Aidan O'Brien responsible for seven Gold Cup wins since Westerner's victory in 2005. They include four-times winner Yeats, who was a Group 1 winner over a mile and a half before his Ascot domination, while subsequent winners Fame And Glory and Leading Light had both tasted classic glory before being stepped up to the Gold Cup's marathon trip. Perhaps the best illustration of how times have changed is that O'Brien's most recent Gold Cup winner, Order of St George, fared best of the Ballydoyle quintet who lined

Comer Group International Irish St Leger, the Curragh—a demolition job by Order of St George, who emphatically makes amends for his shock reversal in this race in 2016, beating Torcedor (cheekpieces) by nine lengths, with Mount Moriah (right) back in third

Qipco British Champions Long Distance Cup, Ascot—much closer this time as Order of St George adds another major prize to his tally, coming from an unpromising position to catch Torcedor (cheekpieces) and the three-year-old Stradivarius (partially hidden by winner)

up in the latest Prix de l'Arc de Triomphe at Chantilly in October, his fine fourth to Enable being his second successive appearance in the frame (he was third in 2016) in Europe's most valuable and prestigious middle-distance race.

Order of St George may be a much better racehorse than Gildoran, but he was unable to emulate the latter's feat of winning successive Gold Cups, failing by just a short head to defend his crown when odds on for the latest renewal. The 2017 Gold Cup proved to be one of the highlights of the season, with front-running Big Orange just holding Order of St George's strong late surge in a thrilling grandstand finish to claim what was a hugely popular win with the Royal Ascot crowd. What tended to be overlooked in the immediate aftermath of the race, however, was that Order of St George had probably been an unlucky loser. He certainly didn't enjoy the run of things, as the enterprisingly-ridden winner had done, with Ryan Moore adopting even more patient tactics than usual on him. Order of St George was still only disputing twelfth on the home turn and was forced to challenge widest of all in the straight. Big Orange poached several lengths by kicking for home first and, given how rapidly Order of St George was reeling in Big Orange during the final furlong, the chances are that he would have won in a few more strides. This view seemed to be borne out by the respective odds of the pair—Order of St George at 5/4-on and Big Orange easy to back at 10/1—on their only subsequent meeting, in the British Champions Long Distance Cup back at Ascot in October. Big Orange flopped badly in the rain-softened ground, and the race proved far from plain sailing for the favourite either, with Moore again needing to be at his strongest in the closing stages. Order of St George got up late to deprive Torcedor by half a length, with the same distance back to main market rival the three-year-old Stradivarius in third, and a further length and a half back to fourth-placed Mount Moriah. Although he won, Order of St George didn't seem at his very best on the day, the fact he looked fourth best for much of the home straight perhaps an indication that his long season was beginning to catch up on him (he finished a below-par fourth in the 2016 renewal).

Apart from a race-rusty defeat conceding weight all around (second to Torcedor) in the Group 3 Vintage Crop Stakes at Navan on his reappearance, Order of St George's 2017 campaign was a carbon copy of 2016. Although he finished a place lower down in both the Gold Cup and the Arc, it was actually an even more successful season in terms of wins (four compared to three) the most spectacular highlight being his romp to a second victory in the Comer Group International Irish St Leger at the Curragh in September. Order of St George had been beaten at 7/1-on in a four-runner renewal in 2016, but favourite backers never had any worries in the latest edition. After being rushed up by Moore on the home turn, he demolished his rivals in the home straight to come home nine lengths in front (eleven lengths had been his winning margin in 2015!), with Mount Moriah a further four and a half lengths back in third and the 2016 winner Wicklow Brave another three quarters of a length away in fourth. This result was a more accurate reflection of Order of St George's superiority over those particular rivals than some of the other races already mentioned (he has a winning head-to-head record against all three). Order of St George's two other wins in 2017 were straightforward. He did no more than was necessary when claiming a second successive victory in the listed Seamus & Rosemary McGrath Memorial Saval Beg Stakes at Leopardstown in late-May, but was more impressive (both visually and in form terms) when completing a hat-trick of wins in the Group 3 Comer Group International Irish St Leger Trial Stakes at the Curragh in August, not having to be fully extended to beat subsequent Melbourne Cup winner Rekindling by four and three quarter lengths.

Order of St George (IRE) (b.h. 2012)	Galileo (IRE) (b 1998)	Sadler's Wells (b 1981)	Northern Dancer
			Fairy Bridge
		Urban Sea (ch 1989)	Miswaki
			Allegretta
	Another Storm (USA) (b 1999)	Gone West (b 1984)	Mr Prospector
			Secrettame
		Storm Song (b 1994)	Summer Squall
			Hum Along

The well-made Order of St George isn't without the odd quirk—he has been known to sweat before his races (a trait shared by others by Galileo, including the brothers Highland Reel and Idaho) and a tendency to hang right under pressure (and the fact that he has been beaten four times when odds on) has also led some to question his resolution in a finish. The overwhelming evidence from four full seasons, however, is that Order of St George is a genuine and durable performer. Versatility, of course, is another of Order of St George's assets, being fully effective at a mile and a half to two and a half miles, and he has also shown his form on every type of ground he has raced on to date (yet to encounter firm or heavy). Order of St George's pedigree has been discussed in detail in previous editions of *Racehorses* and there isn't a great deal to add. He is one of seven winners (from ten runners) out of Another Storm, the most recent being his three-year-old half-sister Arwa (by Holy Roman Emperor) who showed fairly useful form when winning over six furlongs at two for Charlie Hills. The early signs suggest Another Storm's most recent representative on the track Shakour (by Declaration of War) is unlikely to recoup much of the 250,000 guineas paid for him as a yearling, having shown just fair form when placed at a mile and ten furlongs on the all-weather for John Gosden. Hopefully better will emerge from Order of St George's latest sibling, Grenadier Guard (by Australia), who fetched 125,000 guineas as a yearling in the autumn and is in training with Mark Johnston. His five-year-old brother Kellstorm, who won only a maiden from five starts for Aidan O'Brien, enjoyed a good first year in Australia in 2017. He won over just seven furlongs on his debut Down Under but went on to complete a hat-trick in contests over an extended mile and a half and finished third in a Group 3 event over the same trip at Flemington in October.

Yeats, Fame And Glory and Leading Light have all joined Westerner on Coolmore's star-studded roster of National Hunt stallions which will presumably be the eventual destination for Order of St George once his racing days are over, though big-spending Australian owner Lloyd Williams owns a share in him and, for now, the plan for Order of St George is to race on and he again looks very much the stayer to beat, fully deserving his place at the head of the ante-post market for the Gold Cup, in which he will be aiming to become just the third horse (after Kayf Tara in 2000 and Anticipation in 1819) in the race's long history to regain the crown (he is already the first horse to regain the Irish St Leger after losing it). *Aidan O'Brien, Ireland*

ORDEROFTHEGARTER (IRE) 3 b.c. Galileo (IRE) 134 – Kitty Kiernan 111 (Pivotal 124) [2017 96p: 8v* 8d* 8d^5 10.4g^6 10m^2 11.9g Jul 14] small, workmanlike colt: very smart performer: won maiden at Naas in March and Leopardstown 2000 Guineas Trial (by 3¾ lengths from Taj Mahal) in April: ½-length second to Benbatl in Hampton Court Stakes at Royal Ascot in June: seventh in Grand Prix de Paris at Saint-Cloud final outing: stays 10.5f: acts on good to firm and heavy going: in cheekpieces last 3 starts: wears tongue tie: has joined Liam Howley in Australia. *Aidan O'Brien, Ireland* **120**

OREGON GIFT 5 b.g. Major Cadeaux 121 – Dayville (USA) 86 (Dayjur (USA) 137) [2017 71: 7m 7.8v^6 t9.5m^5 Oct 28] fair handicapper: stays 1¼m: acts on polytrack, tapeta and soft going: tried in blinkers: usually races close up: has joined Charlie Mann. *Brian Ellison* **64**

OREGON POINT (USA) 3 b.g. Cape Blanco (IRE) 130 – Dream The Blues (IRE) 75 (Oasis Dream 129) [2017 7g^{4} 7g 7g^{5} 9.8d 12g Jul 3] fair maiden: should stay beyond 7f: best form on good going: tried in blinkers: sometimes slowly away: races towards rear: temperamental. *Tim Easterby* **69 §**

OREWA (IRE) 3 ch.g. Helmet (AUS) 127 – Lucky (IRE) 95 (Sadler's Wells (USA) 132) [2017 92: 7m 7s May 17] good-quartered gelding: fairly useful performer at 2 yrs, below that level in 2017: stayed 6.5f: acted on good to firm and heavy going: dead. *Brian Ellison* **–**

ORIENTAL FOX (GER) 9 ch.g. Lomitas 129 – Oriental Pearl (GER) (Big Shuffle (USA) 122) [2017 107: 14s^{2} 14g^{5} 21.6m* 16.2m^{5} 16g 16.3d 18d^{4} Sep 23] leggy gelding: smart performer: won Queen Alexandra Stakes at Royal Ascot (by 1¼ lengths from Thomas Hobson) in June: second in handicap at Newmarket in May and fourth in similar event there in September: stays 21.5f: acts on any turf going: often races prominently. *Mark Johnston* **112**

ORIENTAL LILLY 3 ch.f. Orientor 118 – Eternal Instinct 77 (Exceed And Excel (AUS) 126) [2017 6m 6m^{3} 7g^{5} 5g^{2} 6d^{2} 5g^{5} 5m^{3} 5s t5g^{3} Nov 24] second foal: half-sister to 5f winner Eternalist (by Equiano): dam, 5f winner (including at 2 yrs), half-sister to very smart 5f-7f winner Jack Dexter (by Orientor): fair maiden: stays 6f: acts on tapeta and good to soft going: tried in hood: often races towards rear. *Jim Goldie* **74**

ORIENTAL POWER 2 b.g. (Apr 28) Orientor 118 – Star In The East 59 (Observatory (USA) 131) [2017 5m 6g 5m^{5} 7.2m 5d Sep 16] no form. *Jim Goldie* **–**

ORIENTAL RELATION (IRE) 6 gr.g. Tagula (IRE) 116 – Rofan (USA) (Cozzene (USA)) [2017 80, a93: f5g t5.1f^{3} t6m^{2} p6d^{5} p5d^{3} p6d t6g p6g^{3} 5m* 5m* 5m^{3} 5g 5m^{4} 5m 5g^{6} 5g 5v^{4} Oct 21] good-topped gelding: fairly useful handicapper: won at Pontefract in April (by 2¼ lengths from Henley) and May (apprentice): stays 6f: acts on all-weather, firm and soft going: wears headgear: often leads: sold to join John Balding 15,000 gns in November. *James Given* **87**

ORIENTAL SONG (IRE) 2 ch.f. (Mar 25) Shamardal (USA) 129 – Oriental Melody (IRE) 72 (Sakhee (USA) 136) [2017 6.1d^{2} 6d* 6g^{5} Sep 7] sixth foal: dam, 2-y-o 7f winner, half-sister to smart 7f winner Green Coast and useful 1m-1½m winner St Jean: fairly useful form: won minor event at Newmarket (by 6 lengths from Kareva) in June: raced only at 6f: remains with potential. *Owen Burrows* **94 p**

Mr Markus Graff's "Oriental Fox"

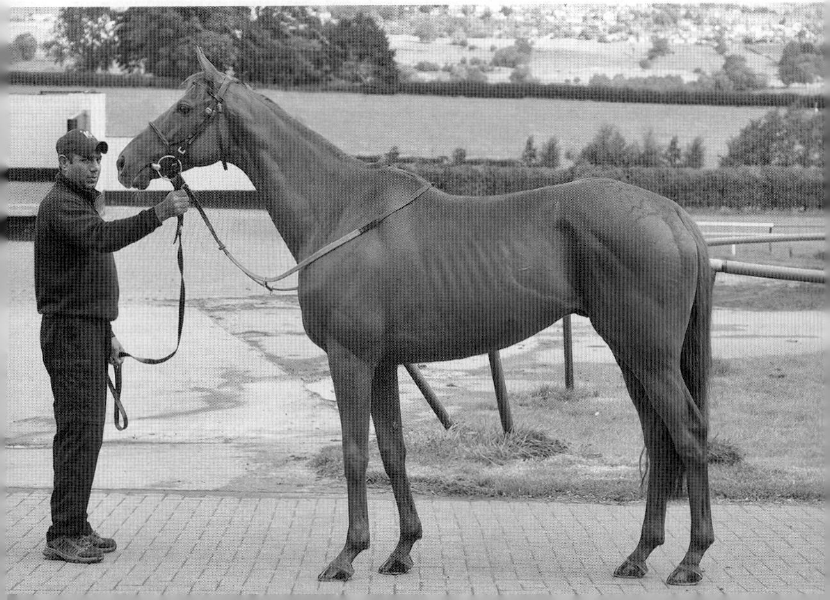

ORIENTAL SPLENDOUR (IRE) 5 br.g. Strategic Prince 114 – Asian Lady 68 (Kyllachy 129) [2017 79: 5m 5g t5s² 5d* 5m⁶ 5g⁴ 5d⁴ 5s³ 5d 5g 5v³ 5d⁶ t5d Oct 24] sturdy gelding: fair handicapper: won at Pontefract in June: stays 6f: acts on polytrack, tapeta and any turf going: has worn cheekpieces, including last 3 starts. *Ruth Carr* **79**

ORIENT CLASS 6 ch.g. Orientor 118 – Killer Class 72 (Kyllachy 129) [2017 91: f5g f5m t5d² t5s⁶ 5m² 5s⁴ 5s⁵ 5m* 5.1d⁴ 5.1d⁴ 5g 5m³ 5.2d⁶ Sep 20] compact gelding: useful handicapper on turf, fairly useful on all-weather: won at Musselburgh (by 1¼ lengths from Zac Brown) in June: best form at 5f: acts on tapeta, good to firm and heavy going: has worn visor: often races prominently. *Paul Midgley* **97 a88**

ORIENTELLE 3 ch.f. Compton Place 125 – Oriental Girl 79 (Dr Fong (USA) 128) [2017 –: 7g 7.4d³ 8f 8d 8s³ 8v f8.1g 8v³ p8s Nov 23] modest maiden: best effort at 7.5f: acts on good to soft going: usually wears headgear: usually leads. *Richard Whitaker* **60**

ORIENT PRINCESS 2 ch.f. (Apr 3) Orientor 118 – Killer Class 72 (Kyllachy 129) [2017 5m 5m⁶ 5.1d⁶ 5d Sep 16] £12,000Y: fifth foal: sister to 5f winner Orient Class: dam 5f winner: poor form: raced only at 5f. *Paul Midgley* **49**

ORIGINAL CHOICE (IRE) 3 ch.g. Dragon Pulse (IRE) 114 – Belle Watling (IRE) 67 (Street Cry (IRE) 130) [2017 81: t7.1g* 7m⁶ 8m² 8d* 7.6d² 8.2v² Sep 30] useful handicapper: won at Wolverhampton in April and Thirsk in July: best effort when second at Haydock (short head behind Century Dream) in September: stays 1m: acts on tapeta, good to firm and heavy going: usually races prominently, often travels strongly. *William Haggas* **104**

ORIN SWIFT (IRE) 3 b.g. Dragon Pulse (IRE) 114 – Hollow Green (IRE) 90 (Beat Hollow 126) [2017 10m 10g⁴ 11.6g³ 14.1d³ 11.5m⁶ 11.4m² Oct 16] 28,000Y: rangy, rather unfurnished gelding: second foal: half-brother to 5f-1m winner Limerick Lord (by Lord Shanakill): dam, winner up to 11.6f (2-y-o 7f winner): fairly useful maiden: second in handicap at Windsor in October: stays 11.5f: acts on good to firm going. *Jonathan Portman* **80**

ORION'S BOW 6 ch.g. Pivotal 124 – Heavenly Ray (USA) 97 (Rahy (USA) 115) [2017 116: 6m⁶ 6m⁴ 5m t5g³ 5g⁵ 5.4d 6v 6g 5v 5d Oct 28] big gelding: smart handicapper: third at Newcastle (1¼ lengths behind Line of Reason) in June: has won over 7f, best at shorter: acts on polytrack, tapeta, good to firm and heavy going: has worn blinkers/tongue tie: usually races prominently. *Tim Easterby* **111**

ORITHIA (USA) 3 b.f. More Than Ready (USA) 120 – Tiz My Time (USA) 95 (Sharp Humor (USA) 118) [2017 64: 8g⁵ p8g² p11s⁴ 10m* 11.4m⁶ 10g⁶ p8g⁴ p8g p10g Nov 2] sturdy filly: fair handicapper: won at Lingfield in June: stays 1¼m: acts on polytrack, tapeta and good to firm going: in blinkers last 3 starts: often wears tongue tie. *Seamus Durack* **73**

ORLANDO ROGUE (IRE) 5 b.g. Bushranger (IRE) 119 – Boston Ivy (USA) (Mark of Esteem (IRE) 137) [2017 66: t8g² t8g* t7.1g⁵ Mar 9] sturdy gelding: fair handicapper: won at Newcastle in January: stays 1m: acts on polytrack, tapeta and good to firm going: wears headgear: often races prominently/travels strongly. *Keith Dalgleish* **66**

ORMERING 4 b.f. Kyllachy 129 – Lihou Island 89 (Beveled (USA)) [2017 47: f6g t8.6g 8m Apr 25] maiden, well held all starts in 2017: wears cheekpieces. *Roger Teal* **–**

ORMESHER 2 b.g. (Mar 26) Sir Percy 129 – Marakabei 98 (Hernando (FR) 127) [2017 5.9s² 7.8v⁵ 6v³ Sep 28] fair form: best effort when second in maiden at Carlisle (½ length behind Canford's Joy) in August: should stay 7f+. *Donald McCain* **76**

ORNAMENTAL 2 b.c. (Apr 10) Iffraaj 127 – Tulipe Rose (FR) (Shamardal (USA) 129) [2017 6m⁵ 6d² Nov 11] €38,000F, 87,000 2-y-o: good-topped colt: fifth foal: half-brother to 9f-11f winner Takaran (by Teofilo) and 2-y-o 1m winner Tulipa Rosa (by Excelebration): dam lightly-raced half-sister to smart 2-y-o 6f winner (stayed 1m) Welcome Millenium: fairly useful form: better effort when second in maiden at Doncaster (1½ lengths behind Tallow) in November: will be suited by 7f: open to further improvement. *Henry Candy* **83 p**

ORNATE 4 b.g. Bahamian Bounty 116 – Adorn 105 (Kyllachy 129) [2017 113: 6m² 5m⁶ 5d⁶ t6s 5m⁵ 5d* 5g* 6m⁴ 5d⁴ 5v³ 5v² Oct 16] useful-looking gelding: smart performer: won minor events at Newmarket (by 4 lengths from Monsieur Joe) in July and Nottingham (by ¾ length from Kyllang Rock) in August: second in Abernant Stakes at Newmarket (length behind Brando) in April: stays 6f: acts on good to firm and good to soft going: wears hood: has worn tongue tie: front runner/races prominently: sold to join David C. Griffiths 110,000 gns in October. *Robert Cowell* **113**

ORSERA (IRE) 2 b.f. (Feb 23) Clodovil (IRE) 116 – Lally Mut (ITY) (Muhtathir 126) [2017 7d* 8d⁵ Nov 4] third foal: closely related to 7f-1¼m winner Mersi (by Kodiac) and half-sister to winner up to 9f Barbarigo (2-y-o 7f/7.5f winner, by Canford Cliffs): dam **86 p**

Italian 9f winner: fairly useful form: won minor event at Leicester (by length from Verve) in September: still green when fifth in listed race at Newmarket: wears hood: open to further improvement. *Peter Chapple-Hyam*

ORSINO (IRE) 3 b.g. Galileo (IRE) 134 – Birmanie (USA) (Aldebaran (USA) 126) [2017 t12.2g^2 11.5m^3 p12d^6 14m^4 14d^3 14.2g* 14s^5 14v^3 Sep 29] 75,000Y: rather unfurnished gelding: fourth foal: closely related to 1m-14.5f winner Solar Eclipse (by Montjeu) and winner up to 1¼m Aldar (2-y-o 7f winner, by New Approach) and half-brother to 1m winner Supersonic Dreamer (by Dream Ahead): dam, lightly raced, closely related to high-class performer up to 1½m English Channel: fairly useful handicapper: won at Salisbury in August: third at Haydock in September: stays 1¾m: acts on good to firm and heavy going: sold to join Seb Spencer 50,000 gns in November. *Andrew Balding* **84**

OR SO (USA) 5 ch.g. Rock Slide (USA) – Miss Santa Anita (CAN) (Ide (USA) 119) [2017 –: f6g Jan 10] modest 8.5f winner in US, no form in Britain: wears headgear. *Derek Shaw* **–**

ORTIZ 2 ch.f. (Mar 5) Havana Gold (IRE) 118 – Almatinka (IRE) (Indian Ridge 123) [2017 6.1g^5 p6g* p7g^2 Oct 9] 5,500F, £11,000Y: compact filly: sixth foal: half-sister to 3 winners, including useful 8.6f winner Dwight D (by Duke of Marmalade) and 2-y-o 5f winner At The Beach (by Harbour Watch): dam, 7f winner, half-sister to smart winner up to 1m Alanza: fairly useful form: won minor event at Kempton (by 2 lengths from Iconic Knight) in September: second in similar race there month later: best effort at 7f: likely to progress further. *Henry Candy* **83 p**

ORVAR (IRE) 4 b.g. Dandy Man (IRE) 123 – Roskeen (IRE) (Grand Lodge (USA) 125) [2017 92: 5d^2 5g^3 5g 5d^3 5s^6 p5g* Oct 13] good-quartered gelding: useful handicapper: won at Kempton (by neck from Thammin) in October: stays 6f: acts on polytrack, firm and good to soft going: tried in cheekpieces: front runner/races prominently: sold to join Paul Midgley 42,000 gns in October. *Robert Cowell* **99**

OSCAR RANGER (IRE) 3 b.g. Bushranger (IRE) 119 – Bruno Maris (IRE) (Bachelor Duke (USA) 122) [2017 6m^6 6d 8.2d^5 Jul 26] well held in maidens/seller: tried in blinkers. *Richard Fahey* **–**

OSCARS JOURNEY 7 ch.g. Dubai Destination (USA) 127 – Fruit of Glory 106 (Glory of Dancer 121) [2017 72: f6g^3 f5g^6 5.2m^3 Apr 25] quite good-topped gelding: fair handicapper, below form in 2017: stays 6f: acts on polytrack, fibresand, good to firm and heavy going: wears headgear: tried in tongue tie: usually races close up: inconsistent: sent to Belgium. *J. R. Jenkins* **57**

OSKEMEN 2 gr.g. (Feb 20) Mastercraftsman (IRE) 129 – Ollie Olga (USA) 101 (Stormy Atlantic (USA)) [2017 8d 8.3v^4 p8g^2 Dec 20] fair form: best effort when fourth in maiden at Nottingham (2½ lengths behind Kinaesthesia) in November: will be suited by 1¼m+. *Clive Cox* **75**

OSTATNIA (IRE) 5 b.m. Amadeus Wolf 122 – Ostrusa (AUT) (Rustan (HUN)) [2017 98: p6g^4 5f 5g^5 5m^4 5m^6 5g 5d^5 5s Aug 31] useful performer: stays 6f: acts on polytrack, firm and soft going: wears headgear: often races prominently. *W. McCreery, Ireland* **99**

OSTILIO 2 ch.c. (Apr 11) New Approach (IRE) 132 – Reem Three 103 (Mark of Esteem (IRE) 137) [2017 7g^2 t7.1g^2 Nov 15] sixth foal: closely related to smart 1¼m-1½m winner Ajman Princess (by Teofilo) and half-brother to 3 winners, including smart winner up to 1½m Naqshabban (2-y-o 7f winner, by Street Cry) and useful winner up to 1m Cape Byron (2-y-o 7f winner, by Shamardal): dam, 8.6f-10.4f winner, half-sister to very smart 1m-10.3f winner Afsare: fairly useful form: second in maiden at Leicester (½ length behind Accessor) in October and minor event at Newcastle (in hood, 1¼ lengths behind Kings Shield) in November: remains with potential. *Simon Crisford* **82 p**

OSWALD (IRE) 2 gr.c. (Mar 20) Mastercraftsman (IRE) 129 – Tough Chic (IRE) 82 (Indian Ridge 123) [2017 t7.2g^2 7d t7.2g^2 7.2m^3 p6g 7m^2 Oct 25] workmanlike colt: fair maiden: stays 7f: acts on tapeta and good to firm going: tried in blinkers. *Robyn Brisland* **77**

OTOMO 3 b.g. Equiano (FR) 127 – Akhira 90 (Emperor Jones (USA) 119) [2017 72: 6g* 6d^4 5d^6 5.3m^6 6g^3 6d^4 p6s p7g^6 Oct 9] fair handicapper: won at Brighton in May: stays 7f: acts on polytrack, fibresand, best turf form on good going: usually wears hood. *Philip Hide* **79**

OTTONIAN 3 ch.g. Dubawi (IRE) 129 – Evil Empire (GER) 108 (Acatenango (GER) 127) [2017 12s* 14m* Jun 14] brother to useful French 8.5f winner La Patria and half-brother to several winners, including smart 11f/1½m winner Counterpunch (by Halling) and useful 2-y-o 1m-1¼m winner Empire Day (by Lomitas): dam German winner up to 1½m (2-y-o 7f winner): fairly useful form: won both starts, maiden at Thirsk (by 1½ lengths from Kilowatt) in May and handicap at Haydock (by 2¼ lengths from Duke's Girl) in June: stays 1¾m: will go on improving. *Charlie Appleby* **90 p**

OUD METHA BRIDGE (IRE) 3 ch.g. Helmet (AUS) 127 – Central Force 82 (Pivotal 124) [2017 78p: p8m^2 t8g* 8.5g 8.2s 8s^4 7d t8d Sep 29] strong gelding: fairly useful performer: won maiden at Newcastle (by 6 lengths from Prancing Oscar) in March: stays 1m: acts on polytrack and tapeta: sold to join Julia Feilden 10,000 gns in November: temperamental. *Ed Dunlop* **81 §**

OUJA 3 b.f. Sea The Stars (IRE) 140 – Royale Danehill (IRE) (Danehill (USA) 126) [2017 –p: 10g^6 12s^4 p12s* 11.9d^4 10.1s 10m^6 p13g^5 p9.4g Nov 28] good-topped filly: useful performer: won maiden at Kempton in August: stays 13f: acts on polytrack and soft going: in blinkers last 3 starts: often races towards rear. *John Gosden* **97**

OUR BOY (IRE) 3 ch.g. Raven's Pass (USA) 133 – Burren Rose (USA) (Storm Cat (USA)) [2017 79: 9.9m^4 10d t12.2g^2 11.9d^5 12d^5 p11g^6 p12g Sep 13] sturdy gelding: fair handicapper: stays 1½m: acts on tapeta, soft and good to firm going: often races in rear, usually freely. *David Evans* **79**

OUR BOY JACK (IRE) 8 b.g. Camacho 118 – Jina (IRE) 36 (Petardia 113) [2017 84§, a72§: 7g 8m p8g 8s Jun 30] good-topped gelding: fairly useful performer, out of form in 2017: wears cheekpieces: carries head awkwardly. *Conor Dore* **– §**

OUR BOY JOHN (IRE) 3 b.c. Dandy Man (IRE) 123 – Jina (IRE) 36 (Petardia 113) [2017 61: t9.5g t7.1m 8g^3 8.7g* 10.7g^5 8g^3 8.6g^3 5.8g^3 5.8g^5 6.8g^4 8g* 8g* 8s^2 5.8s 10.7d^4 Oct 22] fairly useful performer: left Richard Fahey after second start: much improved after, successful at Ovrevoll in maiden in May and 2 minor events in August: stays 8.7f: acts on polytrack, tapeta, firm and soft going: blinkered nowadays. *Yvonne Durant, Norway* **83**

OUR CHANNEL (USA) 6 ch.g. English Channel (USA) 126 – Raw Gold (USA) 108 (Rahy (USA) 115) [2017 111: t9.5g^4 p10g p10g^5 p13g^5 8d 10g 10g Jul 2] angular gelding: smart handicapper, lost his way in 2017: left Jamie Osborne after fourth start: stays 1¼m: acts on polytrack, tapeta, firm and soft going: often wears headgear: often leads. *Miss Amanda Mooney, Ireland* **100**

OUR CHARLIE BROWN 3 b.g. American Post 121 – Cordoba 77 (Oasis Dream 129) [2017 76: 7.5m^5 7.5m^5 6.9g^2 7.2g* 7.2g^4 7m* 7.6d 7d 7.2m^2 7d* 7.2s^3 8v^5 7v 7s* Oct 31] leggy gelding: fairly useful handicapper: won at Musselburgh in May and Catterick in July, September and October (by ½ length from Boots And Spurs): stays 7.5f: acts on firm and soft going: often travels strongly. *Tim Easterby* **88**

OUR CILLA 3 gr.f. Sixties Icon 125 – Kinetix 78 (Linamix (FR) 127) [2017 –: p10g^4 f12g^5 12g^4 14v* 16v^3 14d* 13.9v Oct 21] lengthy filly: fair handicapper: won at Lingfield in July and September: stays 1¼m: acts on heavy going: wears headgear: often races in rear. *Julia Feilden* **69**

OUR FOLLY 9 b.g. Sakhee (USA) 136 – Regent's Folly (IRE) 101 (Touching Wood (USA) 127) [2017 71: 18g Apr 11] sturdy gelding: fair handicapper, little impact on sole Flat start in 2017: stays 2¼m: acts on any turf going: has worn headgear: often wears tongue tie: fair hurdler. *Stuart Kittow* **–**

OUR GRETA (IRE) 3 gr.f. Exchange Rate (USA) 111 – Academicienne (CAN) (Royal Academy (USA) 130) [2017 73: 6g 8f^3 8.8g^6 8g 7d* t6.1g^5 t7.1g Dec 6] workmanlike filly: fair handicapper: won at Yarmouth in October: stays 1m: acts on tapeta and firm going. *Michael Appleby* **73**

OUR KID (IRE) 2 b.g. (Mar 25) Elnadim (USA) 128 – Red Shoe (Selkirk (USA) 129) [2017 t5.1g* 5.9s^6 6g^6 6.1g p7g 5s f6.1g^3 t6.1g^3 f6.1g^4 Dec 21] fair performer: won minor event at Wolverhampton in May: stays 6f: acts on fibresand and tapeta: usually wears blinkers. *Richard Fahey* **65**

OUR KIM (IRE) 3 b.g. Lawman (FR) 121 – Kayd Kodaun (IRE) 98 (Traditionally (USA) 117) [2017 7g 6m p8s 11.4m^5 10.1m 10s p12g f8.1g p10s^2 Dec 17] modest maiden: left Mohamed Moubarak after sixth start: stays 1¼m: acts on polytrack. *John Butler* **55**

OUR KYLIE (IRE) 5 b.m. Jeremy (USA) 122 – Prakara (IRE) 53 (Indian Ridge 123) [2017 69: 11.9v^6 12m* 14.1g* Jul 13] fair handicapper: won at Ripon (amateur) in June and Carlisle in July: stays 1¾m: acts on good to firm and good to soft going. *Brian Ellison* **71**

OUR LITTLE PONY 2 b.f. (Apr 2) Bated Breath 125 – Cracking Lass (IRE) 106 (Whipper (USA) 126) [2017 5g^2 5m* 6m^3 5m^2 5g^3 5s^5 5d^3 5m^5 6g Oct 13] small filly: second foal: dam, temperamental winner up to 1½m (2-y-o 7f winner) who stayed 14.5f, half-sister to useful winner up to 7f Tagula Sunrise: fair performer: won claimer at Beverley in May for Richard Fahey: stays 6f: acts on good to firm and good to soft going. *Lawrence Mullaney* **66**

OUR LITTLE SISTER (IRE) 4 b.f. Big Bad Bob (IRE) 118 – Rehearsed (IRE) 81 (In The Wings 128) [2017 64: f16g t16.5m f12s Jan 26] modest maiden: below best in 2017 (disqualified all 3 starts due to positive sample): best effort at 8.5f: acts on polytrack and tapeta. *Hughie Morrison* –

OUR LOIS (IRE) 3 b.f. Bushranger (IRE) 119 – Atishoo (IRE) 70 (Revoque (IRE) 122) [2017 54: f8m t10.2d f8d Mar 21] modest form in maiden at 2 yrs, standout effort: in visor last 2 starts. *Keith Dalgleish* –

OUR LORD 5 gr.g. Proclamation (IRE) 130 – Lady Filly 92 (Atraf 116) [2017 65: 5m^4 5.1m^2 5.2m^2 5s* 5.7s* 5.7d* 5g^4 5.7s* 6v Oct 4] good-topped gelding: fairly useful handicapper: completed hat-trick at Salisbury and Bath (apprentice events, by 3¼ lengths from Field of Vision second occasion) in July/August, and won again at Bath (by neck from Storm Melody) in September: stays 5.5f: acts on soft and good to firm going. *Michael Attwater* 93

OUR MAN IN HAVANA 2 b.c. (Apr 6) Havana Gold (IRE) 118 – Auntie Kathryn (IRE) 64 (Acclamation 118) [2017 p5g^4 5v^6 t6.1g^2 5.9g^4 6f* 6g^2 6.1s 6.3s t6.1g* t5.1m^2 t7.2g* p7g^5 Dec 20] 11,000F, €16,000Y: second foal: half-brother to winner abroad by Excelebration: dam, 5f winner, closely related to useful winner up to 1¼m (stayed 1½m) Royal Intrigue: fairly useful performer: won nursery at Haydock in July, and seller in September and nursery in November, both at Wolverhampton: left Tom Dascombe after ninth start: stays 7f: acts on tapeta and firm going: front runner/races prominently. *Richard Price* 80

OURMULLION 3 b.g. Mullionmileanhour (IRE) 116 – Queen Ranavola (USA) (Medaglia d'Oro (USA) 129) [2017 63: p8g^2 p8g* p8d^2 p8s^3 p8s 10d^6 p10g* p10d* 10d p10s^4 p12g Dec 30] fairly useful handicapper: won at Lingfield in February and Chelmsford (twice, by neck from Corked second occasion) in September: stays 1¼m: acts on polytrack and tapeta: usually wears cheekpieces: front runner/races prominently. *John Best* 89

OUR OYSTERCATCHER 3 br.g. Pastoral Pursuits 127 – The Dark Eider (Superlative 118) [2017 6.1g* t7.2d Dec 26] sturdy gelding: fair form: won maiden at Windsor (by short head from Holiday Girl) in October for Henry Candy: last in handicap next time: wears hood. *Philip Hide* 75

OUR PLACE IN LOULE 4 ch.g. Compton Place 125 – Show Off 56 (Efisio 120) [2017 57: 6g^2 6m^3 6g^4 6m 5g^6 5g^3 5m^2 5s* 5.9s^5 5s^3 t5g^3 f5g Nov 13] modest handicapper: won lady riders event at Carlisle in August: also first past post at Musselburgh time before, but demoted after causing interference: stays 6f: acts on soft and good to firm going: tried in headgear: often races towards rear. *Noel Wilson* 63

OUR POWER (IRE) 2 b.g. (Mar 20) Power 117 – Scripture (IRE) (Sadler's Wells (USA) 132) [2017 7.4v^4 Sep 17] 12/1, well held in minor event at Ffos Las. *Christian Williams* –

OUR RUTH 4 ch.f. Assertive 121 – My Jeanie (IRE) 62 (King Charlemagne (USA) 120) [2017 p7g p7g 8g p7g^5 p7g p7g Oct 25] lengthy filly: first foal: dam 1m winner: no form: tried in cheekpieces. *Jimmy Fox* –

OUR TONY 2 b.f. (Feb 15) Rock of Gibraltar (IRE) 133 – Ecusson 52 (Singspiel (IRE) 133) [2017 t5.1g Dec 2] second foal: dam twice-raced half-sister to high-class winner up to 1m Delegator: 20/1, well held in minor event at Wolverhampton. *Keith Dalgleish* –

OUTBACK BLUE 4 gr.g. Aussie Rules (USA) 123 – Beautiful Lady (IRE) 77 (Peintre Celebre (USA) 137) [2017 85: 10m 10.3m^4 8.1m^4 10.2g^2 10.3s^3 10d^3 10s^4 10.3g 10.3v^6 10g^3 t9.5m 10v^3 Nov 7] close-coupled, workmanlike gelding: fairly useful handicapper: second at Haydock in July: stays 10.5f: acts on tapeta, soft and good to firm going: often in headgear in 2017: wears tongue tie: usually slowly away: not straightforward. *David Evans* 83

OUTBACK GUY (IRE) 4 b.g. Bushranger (IRE) 119 – Little Doll (Gulch (USA)) [2017 –: 12v Jun 10] little impact in maidens/handicaps. *Daniel Loughnane* –

OUTBACK TRAVELLER (IRE) 6 b.g. Bushranger (IRE) 119 – Blue Holly (IRE) 83 (Blues Traveller (IRE) 119) [2017 113: 7m 6m 6d 6v 6g^5 6d p6g Nov 29] compact gelding: useful handicapper: has won over 7f, probably better at shorter nowadays: acts on polytrack and firm going: often in headgear. *Robert Cowell* 105

OUTCROP (IRE) 3 b.g. Rock of Gibraltar (IRE) 133 – Desert Sage 91 (Selkirk (USA) 129) [2017 66: 10.2g* 11s^3 10g p11g 11.6d^2 10s* Sep 19] tall, useful-looking gelding: fair performer: won handicap at Nottingham in April and seller at Chepstow in September: stays 11f: acts on polytrack and soft going: usually leads: has joined Jennie Candlish. *Hughie Morrison* 79

Wokingham Stakes (Heritage Handicap), Royal Ascot—
the far side just have it as Out Do ends a near two-year losing run after getting the better of Steady Pace, with Projection (armlets) and Polybius (stars) first home on the stand side

OUT DO 8 ch.g. Exceed And Excel (AUS) 126 – Ludynosa (USA) 98 (Cadeaux Genereux 131) [2017 108: 6m^3 5g 6g^4 6m* 5m 6g p6g^5 p6g^3 p6g^5 Nov 29] strong gelding: smart handicapper: won Wokingham Stakes at Royal Ascot (by ½ length from Steady Pace) in June: third at Ripon (1¼ lengths behind Intisaab) in April and in listed race at Lingfield (1¾ lengths behind Gifted Master) in November: stays 6f: acts on polytrack, firm and soft going: wears headgear: often races towards rear/travels strongly. *David O'Meara* **110**

OUTER SPACE 6 b.g. Acclamation 118 – Venoge (IRE) (Green Desert (USA) 127) [2017 97: p7d p7g p7d* f7g^2 f7d^2 p7g^5 p7g 6g p6s 7.6d 7g p7s^6 7m^6 7g p7g p7d^5 p7g^5 t7.2g^6 t7.2d^3 Dec 26] strong, compact gelding: fairly useful handicapper: won at Chelmsford in February: stays 8.5f: acts on all-weather, good to firm and good to soft going: often races towards rear. *Jamie Osborne* **76 a98**

OUTFOX 3 b.f. Foxwedge (AUS) 128 – Spontaneity (IRE) 59 (Holy Roman Emperor (IRE) 125) [2017 69: 6m 7m^5 t7.2g^2 7m t7.1s^4 Sep 19] fair maiden: stays 7f: acts on tapeta and good to firm going. *Bryan Smart* **69**

OUTLANE 2 b.f. (Apr 8) Camelot 128 – Batik (IRE) 93 (Peintre Celebre (USA) 137) [2017 p8g Nov 21] sixth foal: half-sister to 3 winners, including winner up to 1m Bezique (2-y-o 7.5f winner, by Cape Cross) and 1¼m-15f winner Barkis (by Selkirk), both useful in Italy: dam, 1¼m-1½m winner who stayed 1¾m, half-sister to Melbourne Cup runner-up Bauer: 66/1, well held in minor event at Lingfield. *Luca Cumani* **–**

OUT LAST 2 b.f. (Mar 15) Lilbourne Lad (IRE) 111 – Ludynosa (USA) 98 (Cadeaux Genereux 131) [2017 7.2d^6 6g^5 5.9d t7.1g Nov 15] half-sister to several winners, including smart 5f-6f winner Out Do and useful 5f winner Outrage (both by Exceed And Excel): dam 6f/7f winner: little impact in minor events/nursery: tried in cheekpieces. *Keith Dalgleish* **–**

OUTLAW KATE (IRE) 5 b.m. Bushranger (IRE) 119 – Diosper (USA) 64 (Diesis 133) [2017 43: f6g f6g Jan 24] poor handicapper: stays 7.5f: acts on good to soft going: usually wears headgear. *Michael Mullineaux* **–**

OUTLAW TORN (IRE) 8 ch.g. Iffraaj 127 – Touch And Love (IRE) (Green Desert (USA) 127) [2017 64: t9.5m* t10.2g^5 t10.2d^6 t9.5g* p10g^4 p10g^5 t9.5g^3 p10g t8.6g^5 t8.6g^6 10g^3 t8.6g^4 10.2m^3 9.9d^6 10.1g* t9.5g^6 10.2d 9.9m^3 9.9g^2 p10d^4 9.9v p10g p10g t9.5g **61**

p10s^{4} p10s^{6} Dec 15] modest handicapper: won at Wolverhampton in January and February, and Yarmouth in July: stays 10.5f: acts on all-weather, firm and good to soft going: wears eyeshields: front runner/races prominently. *Richard Guest*

OUT OF MONEY 2 b.c. (Jan 28) Mazameer (IRE) 107 – Jane's Payoff (IRE) 72 (Danetime (IRE) 121) [2017 4.5d Mar 17] 22/1, eighth in claimer at Fontainebleau: dead. *Jo Hughes* –

OUT OF ORDER (IRE) 3 b.g. Holy Roman Emperor (IRE) 125 – Barring Order (IRE) 108 (Barathea (IRE) 127) [2017 66: t7.1g^{4} t8d^{2} t10.2d^{4} Mar 1] fair maiden: stays 1¼m: acts on tapeta: in tongue tie last 3 starts: sometimes slowly away, usually races nearer last than first. *Tim Easterby* **66**

OUT OF THE ASHES 4 ch.g. Phoenix Reach (IRE) 124 – Shrewd Decision (Motivator 131) [2017 85: p7g^{6} p8g t7.1g^{2} p7d^{5} 6m^{6} 6s^{6} 5g p7s^{2} p7s p8s Dec 7] strong gelding: fair handicapper: stays 7f: acts on polytrack and tapeta: tried in headgear: wears tongue tie: usually races close up. *Mohamed Moubarak* **73 a79**

OUT OF THE FLAMES 2 ch.f. (Feb 7) Showcasing 117 – Primo Lady 95 (Lucky Story (USA) 128) [2017 5m^{3} 5.1m* 5m^{3} 6m^{5} 5.2s 5m^{3} 5f^{3} Nov 4] 37,000Y, £190,000 2-y-o: good-quartered filly: first foal: dam 2-y-o 5f winner who stayed 7f: useful performer: won minor event at Windsor (by 3 lengths from Listen Alexander) in May: third after in Queen Mary Stakes at Royal Ascot (to Heartache), and in listed races at York (beaten ¾ length by Sound And Silence) and Del Mar (same distance behind Declarationofpeace): stays 6f: acts on firm going. *Richard Hannon* **101**

OUTOFTHEQUESTION 3 b.g. Delegator 125 – Why Dubai (USA) 93 (Kris S (USA)) [2017 10.2s^{5} 10g 10d^{6} 10.1g 11.4m^{5} Oct 16] good-topped gelding: fair maiden: will stay 1¾m: acts on good to firm going. *Alan King* **69**

OUTRAGE 5 ch.g. Exceed And Excel (AUS) 126 – Ludynosa (USA) 98 (Cadeaux Genereux 131) [2017 107: p6g Feb 9] strong gelding: useful handicapper, below best sole start in 2017: all wins at 5f: acts on polytrack, tapeta, firm and good to soft going: often wears blinkers: usually races nearer last than first. *Daniel Kubler* **80**

OVERHAUGH STREET 4 b.g. Bahri (USA) 125 – Bom Chicka Wah Wah (USA) (Dynaformer (USA)) [2017 –: t8d^{4} 8.1d t10.2s 8f^{4} p7s 7.4g 5.7g 9.9m* 11.9d^{3} 11.2s* 12.1s^{2} Sep 20] fair handicapper: won at Brighton in August and Goodwood in September: stays 1½m: acts on tapeta, soft and good to firm going: has worn headgear: usually leads. *Ed de Giles* **74**

OVERRIDER 7 b.g. Cockney Rebel (IRE) 127 – Fustaan (IRE) 71 (Royal Applause 124) [2017 59: t8.6g t12.2g t8.6g 10.1s t8.6g Jun 9] close-coupled gelding: modest handicapper, no form in 2017: wears headgear/tongue tie: usually races prominently. *Shaun Lycett* –

OVERTRUMPED 2 b.f. (May 12) Champs Elysees 124 – Perfect Hand (Barathea (IRE) 127) [2017 p10g t9.5g Dec 18] 20,000 2-y-o: sixth foal: closely related to French 10.5f winner Preempt (by Dansili) and half-sister to useful French 1¼m/11f winner (stays 1¾m) Tamelly: dam, French 9f winner, half-sister to smart winner up to 1m Price Tag: modest form: better effort when seventh in maiden at Kempton (9½ lengths behind Ispolini) in November. *Mike Murphy* **58**

OWEN THE LAW 2 b.c. (Mar 11) Equiano (FR) 127 – Ewenny 71 (Warrshan (USA) 117) [2017 5.2g 6g^{6} 5.1s^{4} 6.1g^{6} t6.1g 5.1s* 5s^{5} Oct 2] lengthy colt: modest performer: won nursery at Chepstow in September: best form at 5f: acts on soft going: in visor last 2 starts: front runner/races prominently. *David Evans* **59**

OWER FLY 4 b.g. Pastoral Pursuits 127 – Contrary Mary 85 (Mujadil (USA) 119) [2017 97: 6g p7g^{3} 7m 7.1v^{4} 7d 7s^{3} p7d^{2} 7s* 7d Sep 30] compact gelding: useful handicapper: won at Lingfield (by 4 lengths from Intense Style) in September: stays 7f: acts on polytrack and any turf going: often wears blinkers: often leads: sold to join Ruth Carr 20,000 gns in October. *Richard Hannon* **100**

OWNERS DAY 7 gr.m. Fair Mix (IRE) 123 – Charmeille (FR) (Exit To Nowhere (USA) 122) [2017 75: p10g Jan 7] fair handicapper, below form sole Flat start in 2017: stays 1¼m: acts on soft going. *Neil Mulholland* **62**

OXFORD BLU 3 b.g. Aqlaam 125 – Blue Zealot (IRE) 65 (Galileo (IRE) 134) [2017 71: t12.2g^{4} 14m^{3} 16.3d^{3} 16v^{5} p16g^{2} 18d* Aug 24] fair handicapper: won at Chepstow in August: stays 2¼m: acts on polytrack, tapeta and good to soft going: wears headgear: has since joined Olly Murphy and won on hurdling debut. *Sir Mark Prescott Bt* **78**

OXFORD DON 3 b.g. Archipenko (USA) 127 – Oval Office 99 (Pursuit of Love 124) [2017 t8.6g t9.5m^{2} t9.5g^{3} p12g Jul 26] fair form: best effort at 9.5f. *David Simcock* **70**

OXFORD THINKING (IRE) 3 b.g. Holy Roman Emperor (IRE) 125 – Larceny (IRE) **74**
(Cape Cross (IRE) 129) [2017 72: t8g^4 p7g^5 p7g 10.4d^2 10.9g^4 10.4s^5 May 19] fair maiden: left John Gosden after second start: stays 11f: acts on tapeta: sold €20,000 in July, gelded and joined Mohamed Moubarak. *J. E. Hammond, France*

OYSTER CARD 4 b.g. Rail Link 132 – Perle d'Or (IRE) 89 (Entrepreneur 123) [2017 56: **53**
t16.5m^5 p16g^5 p13.3d^3 t13.9m^4 t16.5g^5 p14g^3 f14g^6 p13.3g p13.3s Nov 17] modest maiden: stays 16.5f: acts on polytrack, tapeta and good to firm going: wears cheekpieces: front runner/races prominently. *Michael Appleby*

OYSTER PEARL (IRE) 4 gr.f. Thousand Words 113 – Rectify (IRE) (Mujadil (USA) **–**
119) [2017 –: t12.2g 12m Jul 4] maiden, no form since 2015: tried in visor: usually wears tongue tie. *Carroll Gray*

P

PACA PUNCH 4 b.f. Paco Boy (IRE) 129 – Plumage 70 (Royal Applause 124) [2017 –: **–**
8f 10.2f Jul 5] smallish filly: little sign of ability. *John Flint*

PACHARANA 4 b.f. Oasis Dream 129 – Cascata (IRE) 86 (Montjeu (IRE) 137) [2017 85: **100**
12.1m^5 12m^5 11.6m* 12g^4 11.9d* 11.6g* 12g^3 11.9d^2 14.1g^3 p13g^6 12.4s Nov 17] sturdy filly: useful handicapper: won at Lingfield in June, and Brighton and Bath (by 8 lengths from Silver Link) in July: stays 1¾m: acts on polytrack, firm and soft going: often races prominently. *Luca Cumani*

PACIFIC FLEET (USA) 2 b.c. (Apr 15) Elusive Quality (USA) – Coronado Rose **78**
(USA) (Coronado's Quest (USA) 130) [2017 6m^3 7d^3 Jul 28] fair form: better effort when third in minor event at York (2¾ lengths behind Wells Farhh Go) second start. *Archie Watson*

PACIFIC SALT (IRE) 4 gr.g. Zebedee 113 – Villa Nova (IRE) 55 (Petardia 113) [2017 **83**
76: 8.3g^6 7d^6 8m^2 8g^3 8.3g* 8.3v* 8d^3 8.5g^6 8.3d^3 8d Nov 4] lengthy gelding: fairly useful handicapper: won at Nottingham in July and August (by 3¾ lengths from Hijran): stays 8.5f: acts on polytrack, tapeta and heavy going: tried in hood: front runner/races prominently, often travels strongly. *Pam Sly*

PACIFY 5 b.g. Paco Boy (IRE) 129 – Supereva (IRE) (Sadler's Wells (USA) 132) [2017 **106**
109: 8m 10m 9.9m^5 10d^2 9.9g Sep 2] tall gelding: useful handicapper: second at Newmarket (½ length behind Anythingtoday) in July: stays 10.5f: acts on polytrack, soft and good to firm going: tried in visor. *Ralph Beckett*

PACK IT IN (IRE) 4 br.g. Big Bad Bob (IRE) 118 – Evening Dress 65 (Medicean 128) **77**
[2017 77: 9.9m^5 10.2f^4 10m^3 10g^5 9.9s 9.9m^5 10.2d^2 p12g Dec 13] strong gelding: fair handicapper: left Brian Meehan after seventh start: stays 11.5f: acts on soft and good to firm going: usually wears headgear. *Alexandra Dunn*

PACO BLEUE 2 b.f. (Feb 25) Paco Boy (IRE) 129 – Poulaine Bleue 44 (Bertolini (USA) **62**
125) [2017 6m^5 6d^5 6.1f Jun 19] 17,000F, £8,000Y: third foal: half-sister to 5f/6f winner Magical Daze (by Showcasing) and 2-y-o 6f winner Still On Top (by Royal Applause): dam, maiden (stayed 1m), half-sister to useful winner up to 9f Genre: modest form: best effort when fifth in minor event at Redcar (3¾ lengths behind Dance Diva) in May. *Tim Easterby*

PACO DAWN 3 ch.f. Paco Boy (IRE) 129 – First Dawn 68 (Dr Fong (USA) 128) [2017 –: **–**
t7.1m p8g Feb 1] little sign of ability: tried in blinkers: sometimes slowly away, usually races nearer last than first. *Philip Hide*

PACO ESCOSTAR 2 ch.f. (Mar 26) Paco Boy (IRE) 129 – Shesastar 96 (Bahamian **67**
Bounty 116) [2017 5g^2 5s 5s^2 Oct 10] 800F: first foal: dam 6f (including at 2 yrs)/7f winner: fair form when second in minor events. *Paul Midgley*

PACOFILHA 3 b.f. Paco Boy (IRE) 129 – Seradim 95 (Elnadim (USA) 128) [2017 71: 8f^4 **73**
8s^3 8d^6 9.9d^3 p12g^4 10s^2 Sep 19] compact filly: fair maiden: stays 1½m: acts on polytrack and soft going: tried in blinkers/tongue tie. *Paul Cole*

PACO FILLY 3 b.f. Paco Boy (IRE) 129 – Respectfilly (Mark of Esteem (IRE) 137) [2017 **–**
p11g t8.6g Nov 20] £1,400 3-y-o: third foal: half-sister to 8.6f winner Van Dyke (by Excellent Art): dam unraced half-sister to smart winner up to 1¾m Quiz Mistress: well held in maidens. *Nikki Evans*

PACO LADY 3 b.f. Paco Boy (IRE) 129 – Rosa Luxemburg (Needwood Blade 117) [2017 **–**
–: 7g 6m 6d p7g Oct 25] no form. *Ivan Furtado*

PACOLITA (IRE) 5 ch.m. Paco Boy (IRE) 129 – Clara (IRE) (In The Wings 128) [2017 **83**
82: p8g^3 t7.1d^2 t7.1g Mar 18] good-topped mare: fairly useful handicapper: second at Newcastle in March: has form at 1¼m, usually races over shorter: acts on polytrack, tapeta, soft and good to firm going: usually races towards rear, often freely. *Sylvester Kirk*

PACOMMAND 4 b.g. Paco Boy (IRE) 129 – Indian Story (IRE) (Indian Ridge 123) **57**
[2017 –: f8g t8d t8d Mar 31] fair maiden at 2 yrs: very lightly raced and little form after: stayed 1m: acted on polytrack and tapeta: often raced towards rear: dead. *David Barron*

PACO'S ANGEL 3 b.f. Paco Boy (IRE) 129 – Papabile (USA) 104 (Chief's Crown **101**
(USA)) [2017 95: p8g^4 8m^3 8m^5 Jul 8] lengthy filly: useful performer: third in listed Sandringham Handicap at Royal Ascot (2¼ lengths behind Con Te Partiro) in June: stays 1m: acts on good to firm going. *Richard Hughes*

PACO'S PRINCE 2 b.c. (Jan 17) Paco Boy (IRE) 129 – Equitissa (IRE) 78 (Chevalier **56 p**
(IRE) 115) [2017 6.1m Jun 26] 8,000F, £22,000Y, £35,000 2-y-o: first foal: dam 1m winner who stayed 1¼m: 25/1, eighth in maiden at Windsor (5¼ lengths behind Boomerang Betty) in June: should improve. *Martin Smith*

PACO STYLE 2 b.g. (Apr 9) Paco Boy (IRE) 129 – Al Aqabah (IRE) 82 (Redback 116) **–**
[2017 p7g Dec 20] 66/1, well held in minor event at Kempton. *Michael Attwater*

PACT OF STEEL 2 ch.c. (Jan 25) Declaration of War (USA) 128 – She's My Dandy **60**
(IRE) 80 (Holy Roman Emperor (IRE) 125) [2017 7m p7g Oct 5] little impact in pair of minor events. *Harry Dunlop*

PACTOLUS (IRE) 6 b.g. Footstepsinthesand 120 – Gold Marie (IRE) 92 (Green Desert **111**
(USA) 127) [2017 100: t7.1g t9.5g* t8.6g p10d^2 p10g^3 p10g^4 10g^4 8m p8g p8g^4 p10s^3 p10d^2 t9.5g* p8s^4 Dec 14] tall, useful-looking gelding: smart handicapper: won at Wolverhampton in February (by ½ length from Winterlude) and November (by neck from Mount Tahan): stays 1¼m: acts on polytrack, tapeta and good to firm going: wears headgear/tongue tie. *Stuart Williams*

PADDY A (IRE) 3 b.g. Holy Roman Emperor (IRE) 125 – Lilting (IRE) (Montjeu (IRE) **80**
137) [2017 71: p8g^4 p8g* 8s^4 10.1m^3 10m^6 12d 10d 10.2v t7.2d Dec 26] good-topped gelding: fairly useful handicapper: won at Chelmsford in May: third at Yarmouth in June: left Philip McBride after sixth start: stays 1¼m: acts on polytrack, tapeta and good to firm going. *Ian Williams*

PADDYPLEX 4 b.g. Multiplex 114 – Turtle Bay 64 (Dr Fong (USA) 128) [2017 10m* **93**
t10.2g* Nov 23] fourth foal: brother to 9f winner (stays 1½m) Starplex: dam lightly raced on Flat/maiden hurdler: unplaced in bumpers: fairly useful form on Flat: won both starts, maiden at Ayr (by length from Fiendish) in May and handicap at Newcastle (by head from Andok) in November: will stay 1½m. *Keith Dalgleish*

PADDY POWER (IRE) 4 ch.g. Pivotal 124 – Rag Top (IRE) 101 (Barathea (IRE) 127) **92**
[2017 92: t5s^2 5s* 6m 5m^{ur} 5m 5m^5 6g 6g^3 5v* 6.1m* 5d Oct 28] smallish, good-quartered gelding: fairly useful handicapper: won at Newmarket in May, Pontefract in September and Windsor (by ¾ length from Buccaneers Vault) in October: stays 6f: acts on polytrack, tapeta, good to firm and heavy going: tried in cheekpieces: often races towards rear. *Richard Fahey*

PADDY'S ROCK (IRE) 6 b.g. Whipper (USA) 126 – Hedera (USA) 90 (Woodman **67**
(USA) 126) [2017 64: t12.2g^5 f12s^3 t12.4g^4 t9.5m 11.1g^4 11.9d* 10s^5 14d 10.2g^5 12.1s^2 **a57**
12.1v^2 11.2v^4 11.8v^3 Sep 29] quite sparely-made gelding: fair handicapper: won at Doncaster in July: third at Haydock final start: stays 1½m: acts on fibresand, good to firm and heavy going: has worn headgear, including usually in 2017: sometimes slowly away, usually races towards rear. *Lynn Siddall*

PADDYS RUNNER 5 gr.g. Sir Percy 129 – Frosty Welcome (USA) 105 (With Approval **75**
(CAN)) [2017 77: t12.2g^2 Feb 11] good-topped gelding: fair maiden: barely stays 2m: acts on tapeta and good to firm going: fairly useful hurdler: has joined Graeme McPherson. *Alan King*

PADDY THE CHEF (IRE) 2 b.g. (Apr 11) Dandy Man (IRE) 123 – The Reek 67 (Tiger **77 p**
Hill (IRE) 127) [2017 p8d^4 p8s^2 Dec 15] 20,000F, €10,000Y: second foal: dam 1m winner: fair form in minor events: will be suited by 9f+: remains with potential. *Ian Williams*

PADLEYOUROWNCANOE 3 b.g. Nayef (USA) 129 – Pooka's Daughter (IRE) 63 **70**
(Eagle Eyed (USA) 111) [2017 52: f8g* f12g^4 t9.5g^5 t12.2g^3 t14g^2 t14g^5 f12.1g^{ur} t12.4s^2 t12.4g^2 Sep 22] rather leggy gelding: fair handicapper: won at Southwell in March: second at Newcastle in September: stays 1¾m: acts on fibresand and tapeta: wears headgear: fairly useful hurdler. *Daniel Loughnane*

PADRINHO (IRE) 3 b.g. High Chaparral (IRE) 132 – Belanoiva (IRE) (Motivator 131) **79**
[2017 66: p10g^{4} 10.2g 14g^{2} 14g* 14s^{3} 14.2g^{6} p14g Sep 7] smallish gelding: fair handicapper: won at Sandown in July: third at same course in August: stays 1¾m: acts on good to firm going: sold 2,000 gns, sent to Italy. *John Best*

PAGE OF WANDS 4 b.f. Multiplex 114 – No Page (IRE) 81 (Statue of Liberty (USA) **58**
115) [2017 69§, a61§: t10.2g^{4} t12.4g^{6} 9v t12.4g Oct 10] fair maiden, below best in 2017: left Karen McLintock after second start: stays 1¼m: acts on tapeta and good to soft going: has worn headgear, including in 2017: not one to trust. *George Bewley*

PAHENTE 9 br.g. Silver Patriarch (IRE) 125 – Miss Tehente (FR) (Tehente (FR)) [2017 **–**
f16.5g Aug 28] good-topped gelding: one-time fair handicapper: well held after long absence only start in 2017: stays 13f: acts on polytrack and good to firm going: has worn cheekpieces. *Tony Carroll*

PAINT 2 b.f. (Apr 17) Dutch Art 126 – Love Magic 89 (Dansili 127) [2017 6m 6s^{3} p7s^{4} 8m* **79**
8g^{3} 8.1g^{6} Oct 9] neat filly: first foal: dam, 2-y-o 7f winner who stayed 1¼m, out of Cheveley Park Stakes winner Magical Romance, herself closely related to Oaks winner Alexandrova: fair performer: won nursery at Bath in August: stays 1m: acts on polytrack, soft and good to firm going. *Richard Hannon*

PAK CHOI 2 ch.c. (Feb 4) Paco Boy (IRE) 129 – Spring Green 86 (Bahamian Bounty 116) **–**
[2017 p6g Dec 20] 25/1, well held in minor event at Kempton. *Andrew Balding*

PALACE BALL 3 ch.f. Choisir (AUS) 126 – Catherine Palace 60 (Grand Lodge (USA) **–**
125) [2017 7.2g^{4} 5.9g^{5} 9.2s Jun 29] fifth foal: half-sister to useful 2-y-o 5f winner (stayed 1¼m) Sleeper King (by Holy Roman Emperor): dam lightly-raced half-sister to useful winner up to 1½m Alessandria, herself dam of smart performer up to 1½m Saint Baudolino: little impact in maidens. *Stuart Coltherd*

PALACE MOON 12 b.g. Fantastic Light (USA) 134 – Palace Street (USA) 103 (Secreto **51 §**
(USA) 128) [2017 62§: p8g p8d^{6} p8m p8g p8g p8g Dec 30] tall, lengthy gelding: modest handicapper: stays 1m: acts on polytrack and good to firm going: wears tongue tie: unreliable. *Michael Attwater*

PALACE PRINCE (GER) 5 b.h. Areion (GER) 115 – Palace Princess (GER) (Tiger Hill **119**
(IRE) 127) [2017 115: 9.9d^{5} 9.9m^{5} 8g^{4} 8g* 8.7g 9.9g 9.9g* 8g^{2} 9.9s^{4} Oct 22] useful-looking horse: smart performer: won Badener Meile at Baden-Baden in May and Sparkassen-Finanzgruppe on same course (beat Devastar 2 lengths) in August: ¾-length second to Pas de Deux in Oettingen-Rennen there next time: effective at 1m to 1½m: acts on soft going: usually wears cheekpieces. *J-P. Carvalho, Germany*

PALADIN (IRE) 8 b.g. Dubawi (IRE) 129 – Palwina (FR) (Unfuwain (USA) 131) [2017 **74**
75: f12g* p12d Jan 18] quite attractive gelding: fair handicapper: won at Southwell in January: stayed 1½m: acted on all-weather and good to soft going: wore hood: dead. *Michael Blake*

PALAVICINI RUN (IRE) 4 ch.f. Palavicini (USA) 114 – Dawn's Sharp Shot (IRE) 73 **81**
(Son of Sharp Shot (IRE) 105) [2017 78: p8g^{3} p7g p6g^{4} p5g* 5m^{5} 6m 5g^{2} 6d 7g* 7.1d^{4} 6g^{2} 6m p6g 8s^{4} p7g p8g^{4} p10.7g^{6} p8s p8g^{5} Dec 21] fairly useful performer: won handicap at Dundalk in February and claimer at Fairyhouse in July: second in handicap at the Curragh in May: stays 10.5f: acts on polytrack, good to firm and good to soft going: usually wears headgear. *J. F. Levins, Ireland*

PALAWAN 4 b.g. Mount Nelson 125 – Apple Sauce 70 (Prince Sabo 123) [2017 99: 8.3g **88**
p8d 8f^{2} 7.6d 7s^{6} 7m^{4} a7g^{6} t8d Oct 24] lengthy gelding: fairly useful handicapper: second at Bath in June: stays 1m: acts on firm and soft going: tried in hood/tongue tie: inconsistent. *Jamie Osborne*

PALENVILLE (IRE) 4 ch.f. Rip Van Winkle (IRE) 134 – Faithful Duchess (IRE) 70 **81**
(Bachelor Duke (USA) 122) [2017 84: t7.1g^{3} t6d^{2} t7.1g^{4} t6s^{4} Jun 1] workmanlike filly: fairly useful handicapper: second at Newcastle (apprentice, ¾ length behind Burtonwood) in February: left Simon Crisford after second start: stays 7f: acts on polytrack, tapeta and good to firm going. *Grant Tuer*

PALERMO (IRE) 3 b.g. Intikhab (USA) 135 – La Spezia (IRE) 94 (Danehill Dancer **– p**
(IRE) 117) [2017 p8g Jan 7] 5/2, well held in maiden at Lingfield. *Michael Wigham*

PALINDROME (USA) 4 b.g. Poet's Voice 126 – Hi Dubai 112 (Rahy (USA) 115) [2017 **55**
–: t16.3g t12.4g f8g^{5} t9.5g p13.3g t8.6g^{3} 8.3d 9.2s^{5} 7.4g^{4} 9.9v^{3} t12.4d t8d^{2} Nov 10] modest maiden handicapper: left Ronald Thompson after ninth start: best up to 1¼m: acts on polytrack, tapeta and heavy going: usually wears headgear. *Marjorie Fife*

PALLASATOR 8 b.g. Motivator 131 – Ela Athena 119 (Ezzoud (IRE) 126) [2017 118: 16f^{5} 16g^{6} 14.9g^{6} 17.9g Sep 15] big gelding: smart performer: below best in 2017: stays 2¼m: acts on polytrack, soft and good to firm going: tried in cheekpieces: tends to prove troublesome in preliminaries/on way to post: has joined Gordon Elliott. *Sir Mark Prescott Bt* **109**

PALMER (IRE) 2 b.g. (Feb 20) Acclamation 118 – Aneedah (IRE) 101 (Invincible Spirit (IRE) 121) [2017 5m^{6} 5s^{3} 5m^{3} 5g^{2} 5.1g^{3} 5d^{3} 5s^{2} 5s Oct 10] rather leggy gelding: fair maiden: raced only at 5f: acts on soft and good to firm going: tried in cheekpieces. *Bryan Smart* **77**

PALMERSTON 4 b.g. Oasis Dream 129 – Marywell 87 (Selkirk (USA) 129) [2017 89: 10.3g 8g^{2} 8.5f^{2} 8.5m* 8m 8.3g^{6} t8.6g 8m^{5} 8g p8g Oct 26] fairly useful handicapper: won at Beverley (by ¾ length from Haraz) in May: second earlier at Redcar and Beverley: stays 8.5f: acts on polytrack and firm going: sold 7,000 gns in October to join Marjorie Fife. *Michael Appleby* **89**

PAMMI 2 b.f. (Feb 11) Poet's Voice 126 – Bright Girl (IRE) (Invincible Spirit (IRE) 121) [2017 7m 6d p6g^{6} p7s Dec 14] first foal: dam, of little account, half-sister to useful stayer Botany Bay: little sign of ability. *Anthony Carson* **–**

PAMPLEMOUSSE (IRE) 3 b.f. Siyouni (FR) 122 – Acatama (USA) (Efisio 120) [2017 p6.5g* 7m^{4} 7d* May 7] €250,000Y, €400,000 2-y-o: lengthy, rather unfurnished filly: closely related to smart 1m-10.5f winner Odeliz (by Falco) and half-sister to several winners, including 6f winner Acaster Malbis (by Arcano): dam unraced: useful form: won maiden at Chantilly (impressively) in April and listed race on same course (by ¾ length from Speed As) in May: 3¾ lengths fourth to Daban in Nell Gwyn Stakes at Newmarket in between: stays 7f: should continue to progress. *A. Fabre, France* **104 p**

PANCAKE DAY 5 b.g. Mullionmileanhour (IRE) 116 – Fangfoss Girls 68 (Monsieur Bond (IRE) 120) [2017 66: f6g^{3} f5g* p6d^{5} Jan 17] modest handicapper: won at Southwell (apprentice) in January: stays 6f: acts on all-weather and good to soft going: has worn headgear: tried in tongue tie: usually races prominently: sold £2,500, sent to Germany, and won at Mons in September. *David C. Griffiths* **62**

PANDINUS IMPERATOR (IRE) 4 b.g. Scorpion (IRE) 126 – Casiana (GER) (Acatenango (GER) 127) [2017 12v^{6} Oct 23] little impact in bumpers: 100/1, well held in maiden at Pontefract. *Martin Smith* **–**

PANKO (IRE) 4 b.g. Iffraaj 127 – Engraving (Sadler's Wells (USA) 132) [2017 88: 10.4m^{5} 10.2g^{3} 11.6g* 11.9m^{2} 11.2s^{6} 12g^{5} 12d^{6} 12v p12g^{6} Oct 9] tall, useful-looking gelding: fairly useful handicapper: won at Lingfield (by head from All My Love) in May: second at York (apprentice, ¾ length behind Opposition) in June: stays 1½m: acts on soft and good to firm going: tried in cheekpieces: front runner/races prominently: consistent: sold 16,000 gns in October to join Alex Hales. *Ed de Giles* **89**

PANOPHOBIA 2 br.g. (Apr 14) Bated Breath 125 – Methayel (IRE) 86 (Araafa (IRE) 128) [2017 6.1d^{6} 5d^{6} 5d 7.2m^{3} 7m^{6} p7g^{2} 8v^{5} 7d^{6} Oct 20] angular gelding: fair maiden: stays 7f: acts on polytrack and good to firm going. *Richard Fahey* **67**

PANOVA 3 b.f. Invincible Spirit (IRE) 121 – Safina 100 (Pivotal 124) [2017 85p: 8m^{2} 7m^{5} 8m^{4} 8d^{2} 8g^{2} 8d^{2} 8g Oct 7] useful handicapper: second at Goodwood (neck behind Dubara) in August: stays 1m: acts on polytrack, tapeta, good to firm and good to soft going: in cheekpieces last 2 starts. *Sir Michael Stoute* **96**

PANTERA 3 b.f. Dutch Art 126 – Plethora (Sadler's Wells (USA) 132) [2017 8s 12.1g^{4} Aug 18] fifth foal: half-sister to useful 1¾m-2m winner Dubawi Fifty (by Dubawi): dam unraced sister to St Leger winner Brian Boru and to dam of Derby/Prix de l'Arc de Triomphe winner Workforce: well held in maidens. *David O'Meara* **–**

PANTERA NEGRA (IRE) 3 b.f. Champs Elysees 124 – Penchee 107 (Grand Lodge (USA) 125) [2017 65: 7.4m^{2} 8g 8.9d* 8.5d* 8.3d^{3} Sep 2] fairly useful handicapper: won at Musselburgh and Beverley (by ¾ length from Tesko Fella) in August: third at Hamilton final start: stays 9f: acts on good to firm and good to soft going: often travels strongly. *David Barron* **81**

PANTHER IN PINK (IRE) 3 gr.f. Zebedee 113 – Annus Iucundus (IRE) 67 (Desert King (IRE) 129) [2017 51: t7.1m f8m^{3} t7.1g^{5} f8d 10m^{4} 8m^{2} 8.3g^{5} 8.3s 7d 10g^{6} 10d Oct 30] modest maiden: stays 1m: acts on fibresand, tapeta and good to firm going: has worn headgear, including often in 2017. *Ann Duffield* **52**

PANTHER PATROL (IRE) 7 b.g. Tagula (IRE) 116 – Quivala (USA) (Thunder Gulch (USA) 129) [2017 81: p6g^5 t6g^5 p6g 6g^3 6g^4 7d May 18] smallish gelding: fair handicapper: stays 7f: acts on polytrack, firm and good to soft going: usually wears headgear: often travels strongly. *Eve Johnson Houghton* **62 a75**

PANTOMIME (IRE) 5 gr.m. Mastercraftsman (IRE) 129 – Dama'a (IRE) 85 (Green Desert (USA) 127) [2017 14v^5 f11.1g^6 Dec 22] fifth foal: half-sister to 2-y-o 7f winner (stays 11f) Darkening (by Shamardal) and 2-y-o 6f/7f winner Art Official (by Excellent Art), both useful: dam 6f winner: maiden, fair form at best in Ireland at 2 yrs. *Rebecca Menzies* **53**

PAPA DELTA 3 b.g. Makfi 130 – Step Softly 95 (Golan (IRE) 129) [2017 –: 6.1m^5 5m Jun 17] good-topped gelding: little sign of ability. *Tony Carroll* **–**

PAPAGAYO (IRE) 5 b.g. Shirocco (GER) 129 – Jomana (IRE) 113 (Darshaan 133) [2017 –: 11.2v Sep 18] fair maiden at best: lightly raced and little impact since 2015: stays 11.5f: best form on good going: tried in tongue tie. *Barry Murtagh* **–**

PAPA STOUR (USA) 2 b.c. (Apr 12) Scat Daddy (USA) 120 – Illaunglass (IRE) 96 (Red Clubs (IRE) 125) [2017 5.8m 6v p8g^4 t8g Dec 6] 180,000Y: second foal: half-brother to useful 1m winner (including at 2 yrs) Illaunmore (by Shamardal): dam, 2-y-o 6f winner, half-sister to useful 1m/1¼m performer Redolent: fairly useful form: fourth in maiden at Dundalk in October: left A. P. Keatley after third start: stays 1m. *Andrew Balding* **80**

PAPER FACES (USA) 4 ch.f. Lemon Drop Kid (USA) 131 – Liffey Dancer (IRE) (Sadler's Wells (USA) 132) [2017 69: f11g^2 t12.2g^4 t9.5g^3 Jan 26] fair maiden: stays 1½m: acts on all-weather and good to firm going: usually in headgear: front runner/races prominently: sent to France. *Roger Varian* **69**

PAPOU TONY 4 b.g. Raven's Pass (USA) 133 – Lukrecia (IRE) 104 (Exceed And Excel (AUS) 126) [2017 76: p8g^4 t7.1g p8g* p7g* p7g^3 7g 8d^3 8d^4 7d^6 p7g Oct 11] useful-looking gelding: modest handicapper on turf, fairly useful on all-weather: won at Kempton in February and April (by 2¼ lengths from Higher Court): third at same course (2½ lengths behind Believe It) in June: stays 1m: acts on polytrack, tapeta and good to soft going: sometimes slowly away, often races towards rear: sold 5,000 gns in October. *George Baker* **64 a84**

PAQUITA BAILARINA 3 ch.f. Paco Boy (IRE) 129 – Prima Ballerina 73 (Pivotal 124) [2017 61: t6g^6 6g^4 6m t6.1g 8f 7d^5 Aug 10] modest maiden handicapper: stays 6f: acts on polytrack, best turf form on good going. *James Given* **58**

PARADISE COVE 3 ch.f. Harbour Watch (IRE) 121 – Peace Signal (USA) (Time For A Change (USA)) [2017 –p: 8.1m^4 10s* 9.9d^3 9s 10v^5 p10g Oct 5] rather unfurnished filly: fairly useful performer: won maiden at Ayr (by 5 lengths from Master Me) in June: third in handicap at Sandown (3¾ lengths behind Pondering) in July: left William Haggas after fourth start: stays 1¼m: acts on soft and good to firm going: usually leads. *Charlie Fellowes* **87**

PARADISE FOUND 6 b.m. Pastoral Pursuits 127 – Crochet (IRE) (Mark of Esteem (IRE) 137) [2017 5.1d p7g Jun 7] tall mare: little sign of ability. *Emma Owen* **–**

PARADISE LAKE (IRE) 3 b.g. Siyouni (FR) 122 – Kalandara (IRE) 72 (Rainbow Quest (USA) 134) [2017 60p: p8g^3 9.1m^6 8.1m^2 p8g^2 Dec 28] useful-looking gelding: fairly useful maiden: third in maiden at Chelmsford in May: left Sir Michael Stoute after third start: stays 1m: acts on polytrack and good to firm going: often races prominently. *Ed Walker* **85**

PARADWYS (IRE) 3 b.f. Exceed And Excel (AUS) 126 – First of Many 83 (Darshaan 133) [2017 77: t5g 6g* 6.1m^4 7m^4 p7g p8g Oct 5] lengthy filly: fair performer: won maiden at Ffos Las in July: stays 7f: acts on good to firm going: usually wears headgear. *Archie Watson* **76**

PARA MIO (IRE) 2 b.c. (Feb 17) Pour Moi (IRE) 125 – Malaspina (IRE) (Whipper (USA) 126) [2017 7s^4 8g Sep 28] fair form: better effort when fourth in maiden at Ascot (5¾ lengths behind Herculean) in September. *Seamus Durack* **77**

PARAMOUNT LOVE 2 b.f. (Mar 14) Pivotal 124 – Portraitofmylove (IRE) (Azamour (IRE) 130) [2017 6.5d^3 7m^3 6.9g^2 6d^5 8g^3 7v Oct 1] 52,000Y: rather leggy filly: second foal: dam once-raced half-sister to smart winner up to 11f Tha'ir: fair maiden: stays 7f: acts on good to firm going: tried in cheekpieces: often races towards rear. *Richard Fahey* **72**

PARASAIL 3 ch.f. New Approach (IRE) 132 – West Wind 118 (Machiavellian (USA) 123) [2017 t10.2s May 23] fourth foal: half-sister to useful 2-y-o 7f winner Zephuros (by Invincible Spirit): dam French 1¼m/10.5f (Prix de Diane) winner: 16/1, well held in maiden at Newcastle. *Mark Johnston* **–**

PARFAIT (IRE) 3 b.g. Invincible Spirit (IRE) 121 – Rakiza (IRE) (Elnadim (USA) 128) **115**
[2017 92: t7.1g^{3} 6d^{5} 7g* 7m^{4} 7m* Jul 14] smart handicapper: won at Newmarket in June (by 7 lengths from Six Strings) and July (by 2 lengths from Makzeem): stays 7f: acts on polytrack, tapeta, good to firm and good to soft going: in cheekpieces last 3 starts: front runner/races prominently. *John Gosden*

PARIS BOUND 4 b.g. Champs Elysees 124 – Averami 68 (Averti (IRE) 117) [2017 **70**
t12.2g^{5} p12g^{5} f12g^{2} f14g^{2} p16g^{2} Oct 4] fair maiden: stays 2m: acts on polytrack and fibresand: tried in cheekpieces: temperament under suspicion. *Andrew Balding*

PARISH BOY 5 gr.g. New Approach (IRE) 132 – Requesting (Rainbow Quest (USA) **93 §**
134) [2017 –: t8.6g 10.3m 11.6m^{5} 12.3d 10.2d^{2} 11.9s 10d^{3} 9.9g 10.3d^{6} 12v^{6} 10g Oct 17] fairly useful handicapper: stays 11.5f: acts on tapeta, good to firm and good to soft going: tried in headgear/tongue tie: usually slowly away/races in rear: sold 6,000 gns in November: temperamental. *David Loughnane*

PARISIAN CHIC (IRE) 3 b.f. Kodiac 112 – Divine Design (IRE) 77 (Barathea (IRE) **55**
127) [2017 61: p7g^{6} p8g p7g p7g 6.1m p7g p7g Nov 2] compact filly: modest maiden handicapper: stays 7f: acts on polytrack: sometimes in headgear in 2017: often starts slowly, usually races nearer last than first. *Lee Carter*

PARISIAN (IRE) 2 ch.g. (Feb 17) Champs Elysees 124 – La Persiana 112 (Daylami **–**
(IRE) 138) [2017 7m p8g t8.6g Nov 25] well held in maiden/minor events. *Ralph Beckett*

PARIS MAGIC 4 b.g. Champs Elysees 124 – Belgooree 51 (Haafhd 129) [2017 87: p14d^{6} **83**
Feb 2] fairly useful handicapper: stays 1¾m: acts on polytrack, tapeta and good to firm going: in headgear last 5 starts: sold 12,500 gns in February, sent to Italy. *Hugo Palmer*

PARIS PROTOCOL 4 b.g. Champs Elysees 124 – Island Vista 92 (Montjeu (IRE) 137) **96**
[2017 100: 14.1m^{3} 16.2f^{3} 16g^{5} 21.6m 13.3s^{3} 12m^{5} 14.2s^{5} t12.2g^{4} Oct 27] compact gelding: useful handicapper: third at Newbury (length behind Great Sound) in August: stays 2m: acts on firm and soft going: in cheekpieces last 5 starts: usually races prominently: sold £33,000 in November to join Mark Walford. *Richard Hannon*

PARIS ROOFTOPS (IRE) 3 b.f. Galileo (IRE) 134 – Daneleta (IRE) 101 (Danehill **74**
(USA) 126) [2017 9.9m^{6} 9.9g^{4} p12g 12.3d^{4} Jul 29] €300,000Y: angular filly: half-sister to several winners, including smart 2-y-o 6f/7f (Dewhurst Stakes) winner Intense Focus (by Giant's Causeway) and useful 1¼m winner Dane Street (by Street Cry): dam 7f winner (including at 2 yrs): fair form on first 2 starts in maidens: stays 1¼m. *Luca Cumani*

PARKOUR (IRE) 4 b.g. Holy Roman Emperor (IRE) 125 – School Holidays (USA) 90 **84**
(Harlan's Holiday (USA) 124) [2017 89: p6d^{4} t6g^{3} p6g^{5} May 8] fairly useful handicapper: third at Newcastle (1½ lengths behind Aprovado) in March: raced only at 6f: acts on polytrack and tapeta: has worn blinkers, including in 2017: often races prominently: temperament under suspicion: sold 16,000 gns, sent to Greece. *Marco Botti*

PARK PADDOCKS (IRE) 3 b.g. Sea The Stars (IRE) 140 – Dream of The Hill (IRE) **76**
(Tiger Hill (IRE) 127) [2017 10g^{5} 11.6d^{4} p12s 11.6f^{2} Jun 28] fair form: stays 11.5f: tried in cheekpieces. *William Haggas*

PARKWARDEN (IRE) 3 b.g. Bushranger (IRE) 119 – Honour And Obey (IRE) 79 **51**
(Hurricane Run (IRE) 134) [2017 49: 8g 11.2g^{3} 14s Sep 19] modest maiden: front runner/races prominently. *Chris Grant*

PARLANCE (IRE) 3 b.f. Invincible Spirit (IRE) 121 – Pleasantry (Johannesburg (USA) **92**
127) [2017 87p: p7s^{4} 6d^{3} 7g^{4} p7d 7g^{2} p7g Oct 18] fairly useful handicapper: second at Newmarket (neck behind Toy Theatre) in September: stays 7f: acts on polytrack. *Sir Michael Stoute*

PARLIAMENTARIAN (IRE) 4 b.g. Dubawi (IRE) 129 – Forum Floozie (NZ) **95**
(Danasinga (AUS)) [2017 99: 16.2f^{5} 14d^{4} 14g Jul 14] useful handicapper: stays 1¾m: acts on good to firm and good to soft going: in headgear last 2 starts: has joined S. Seemar in UAE. *Charlie Appleby*

PARMENTER 2 b.f. (May 7) Dick Turpin (IRE) 127 – Triple Cee (IRE) 73 (Cape Cross **65 p**
(IRE) 129) [2017 7g 7.1s^{4} t9.5g Oct 27] fourth foal: dam, maiden (stayed 1¼m), half-sister to smart 1¼m-1½m winner Campo Catino: fair form when fourth in minor event at Chepstow (2¾ lengths behind Zoraya) in September: remains with potential. *Alan King*

PARNASSIAN (IRE) 3 b.g. Elzaam (AUS) 115 – Adaptation 88 (Spectrum (IRE) 126) **94**
[2017 94: 7s 6d^{2} 6.1m* 6.9d^{4} 6.1s 6d p6s^{4} p6g p8g^{6} Nov 17] useful-looking gelding: fairly useful handicapper: won at Windsor (by ¾ length from Open Wide) in June: fourth at Carlisle (1¾ lengths behind Saint Equiano) in July: left K. R. Burke after fourth start: stays 1m: acts on all-weather, good to firm and good to soft going: often races lazily. *Amanda Perrett*

PAROLE (IRE) 5 ch.g. Mastercraftsman (IRE) 129 – Leniency (IRE) (Cape Cross (IRE) 129) [2017 11.9s 12d 9s* 8g^3 9v^4 10.2d^6 Oct 4] fair handicapper: won lady riders event at Carlisle in August: stays 1¼m: acts on soft and good to firm going: in tongue tie last 4 starts: front runner/races prominently. *Tim Easterby* **78**

PART EXCHANGE 3 b.f. Champs Elysees 124 – Market Forces 107 (Lomitas 129) [2017 p10g* p10g Nov 17] fifth foal: sister to useful 1¼m-1½m winner Distain, and half-sister to 1¼m winner Fast Pace (by Observatory) and 1½m winner Limousine (by Beat Hollow): dam, 1½m-15f winner, out of sister to Racing Post Trophy winner/St Leger runner-up Armiger: useful form: won maiden at Lingfield (by 6 lengths from Pretty Passe) in September: likely to stay beyond 1¼m. *Hugo Palmer* **96**

PAR THREE (IRE) 6 b.g. Azamour (IRE) 130 – Little Whisper (IRE) 95 (Be My Guest (USA) 126) [2017 59: p15.8g p13g p13.3g* t13.9g^2 p16g^6 p15.8g^6 14.1m^6 16.3d^4 11.9m^{pu} Aug 9] workmanlike gelding: modest handicapper: won at Chelmsford in March: stayed 16.5f: acted on polytrack, tapeta, soft and good to firm going: often wore headgear: tried in tongue tie: usually raced nearer last than first: dead. *Tony Carroll* **51** **a60**

PARTITIA 3 br.f. Bated Breath 125 – Palmette 81 (Oasis Dream 129) [2017 97p: 5g 5.1d^4 5.9s^3 6g^2 6d^6 Jul 21] sturdy filly: fairly useful handicapper: second at Pontefract in July: stays 6f: acts on good to firm going. *Sir Michael Stoute* **91**

PARTRY FLYER (IRE) 2 b.g. (Mar 30) Zoffany (IRE) 121 – Whitethorne Scent 70 (Monsieur Bond (IRE) 120) [2017 7m 6.1g 7g t7.1g t6g p8g t7.1g^5 Nov 15] small gelding: poor maiden: best effort at 7f: acts on tapeta: in headgear last 4 starts. *Oliver Greenall* **43**

PARTY FEARS TOO (IRE) 2 b.c. (Apr 1) Society Rock (IRE) 126 – Comedic Art (IRE) 86 (Dansili 127) [2017 7.2m Aug 30] 33/1, well held in minor event at Musselburgh. *Jim Goldie* **–**

PARTY ROYAL 7 b.g. Royal Applause 124 – Voliere 102 (Zafonic (USA) 130) [2017 57: p8g p12f^4 p12g^3 11.6m^3 11.6g* 10g^5 13.3v 11.4d^5 Oct 23] tall, angular gelding: fair handicapper: won at Lingfield in May: stays 1½m: acts on polytrack, good to firm and good to soft going: wears headgear: races towards rear. *Nick Gifford* **69**

PARTY TIGER 3 b.g. Excelebration (IRE) 133 – Poly Pomona 73 (Green Desert (USA) 127) [2017 77: t7.1f^2 t8.6g^5 t7.1g^4 7v 7v^6 7.2d^4 t6g 6m Jul 10] compact gelding: fair handicapper: stays 8.5f: acts on polytrack, tapeta, good to firm and heavy going: usually in headgear in 2017: sold 9,000 gns, sent to Greece. *Richard Fahey* **76**

PARYS MOUNTAIN (IRE) 3 gr.g. Dark Angel (IRE) 113 – Muzdaan (IRE) 55 (Exceed And Excel (AUS) 126) [2017 78: 6m 6m^2 6m* 6.1g 7d 6m^6 Aug 28] good-topped gelding: fairly useful handicapper: won at Hamilton (by 2½ lengths from Cosmic Chatter) in June: stays 7f: acts on good to firm going: has worn hood, including last 5 starts: sold 13,000 gns in November to join Tim Easterby. *David Brown* **86**

PAS DE BLANC 2 b.f. (Feb 28) Major Cadeaux 121 – Mancunian Way (Green Desert (USA) 127) [2017 6d p8g p6g^4 f6.1g Dec 19] £8,000Y: lengthy filly: fourth foal: sister to 5f winner Dancing Juice and 5f and (including at 2 yrs) 6f winner Savannah Beau: dam unraced: modest form: best effort at 6f. *Brian Barr* **59**

PAS DE DEUX (GER) 7 b.g. Saddex 124 – Palucca (GER) (Big Shuffle (USA) 122) [2017 118: 8g^5 8g* Aug 31] smart performer: won Oettingen-Rennen at Baden-Baden (for second successive year, by ¾ length from Palace Prince) in August: stays 10.4f: acts on good to soft going: races prominently. *Frau Yasmin Almenrader, Germany* **118**

PASSCODE 3 b.f. Camacho 118 – Passata (FR) (Polar Falcon (USA) 126) [2017 71p: f8g* 8s^5 8.1g^5 Jul 1] smallish filly: fair form: won maiden at Southwell in April: best effort at 1m. *Andrew Balding* **74**

PASSING CLOUDS 2 b.g. (Feb 2) Kheleyf (USA) 116 – Steppin Out 63 (First Trump 118) [2017 p8g^3 p8g Dec 20] fair form: better effort when third in minor event at Kempton (6½ lengths behind Tenedos) in October. *Michael Attwater* **70**

PASSING STAR 6 b.g. Royal Applause 124 – Passing Hour (USA) 80 (Red Ransom (USA)) [2017 92: p10g p8g t7.1g 8.3g^5 p6d* 6m^5 7f t6.1g 8g^4 7.1g^6 p8g^2 t8.6g p7g^5 Dec 6] angular gelding: fairly useful handicapper: won claimer at Chelmsford in May: left Charles Hills after first start: stays 1m: acts on polytrack and good to firm going: wears headgear/tongue tie. *Daniel Kubler* **74** **a83**

PASSIONATTA (IRE) 3 b.f. Intense Focus (USA) 117 – Hasanat 96 (Night Shift (USA)) [2017 –: p8g 8.5v 6m^6 5v 7g 5.1d* 5v* Sep 18] half-sister to several winners, including useful 2-y-o 7f winner Takrice (by Cadeaux Genereux) and 7.5f-9f winner Ela Enta (by **72**

Royal Applause): dam winner up to 9f (2-y-o 7f winner): fair handicapper: won at Chepstow in August and Carlisle (apprentice) in September: best form at 5f: acts on heavy going: in headgear last 4 starts: front runner/races prominently. *John Patrick Murtagh, Ireland*

PASS MARK 2 b.g. (Jan 30) Raven's Pass (USA) 133 – Examinee (GER) (Monsun (GER) **58**
124) [2017 7g p7g Nov 6] little impact in minor event/maiden. *Mrs Ilka Gansera-Leveque*

PASS THE CRISTAL (IRE) 3 b.g. Raven's Pass (USA) 133 – Crystal Melody (Nureyev **73**
(USA) 131) [2017 –p: t7.1g^{2} 7g* 7.4d* 7m^{6} 7g^{5} t7.1d^{4} 7m 7s^{3} p7d^{4} p8d* p8s^{5} p8s^{4} Dec 15] fair handicapper: won at Brighton in May, Beverley in June and Chelmsford in October: stays 1m: acts on polytrack, tapeta and good to soft going. *William Muir*

PASS THE TIME 8 b.m. Passing Glance 119 – Twin Time 77 (Syrtos 106) [2017 70: **67**
t16.3d^{3} Feb 7] fair handicapper: stays 16.5f: acts on fibresand, tapeta, good to firm and heavy going: wears cheekpieces: useful hurdler/chaser. *Neil Mulholland*

PASTAMAKESUFASTER 2 b.f. (Mar 2) Multiplex 114 – Sopran Cross (ITY) (Cape **75**
Cross (IRE) 129) [2017 6.1m^{6} 6.1s^{4} 7g^{6} 7s* 8s t8.6d^{5} Dec 26] sixth foal: sister to Italian 7.5f-11f winner Multicolours and half-sister to 5f (including at 2 yrs) winner Ivors Rebel (by Cockney Rebel): dam Italian 6.5f/7.5f winner: fair performer: won minor event at Goodwood in September: best effort at 7f: acts on soft going: front runner/races prominently. *David Evans*

PASTFACT 3 b.g. Pastoral Pursuits 127 – Matterofact (IRE) 83 (Bold Fact (USA) 116) **85**
[2017 66: 6g 5d^{4} 5.7f* 5.7f* 6.1s* 6m^{3} 5s^{4} 5.7s* 6.1m^{4} Oct 16] rather unfurnished gelding: fairly useful handicapper: won at Bath (twice) in June, Chepstow in August and Bath again (apprentice, by neck from Oeil de Tigre) in October: stays 6f: acts on firm and soft going. *Malcolm Saunders*

PASTIME 3 b.g. Pastoral Pursuits 127 – Piddies Pride (IRE) 75 (Indian Lodge (IRE) 127) **99**
[2017 7m^{6} 6m^{2} t8.6g* t7.1s* 8g^{3} 7s^{2} 7d^{2} 7d^{3} p7s t7.1d^{3} Dec 16] fourth foal: half-brother to 6f/6.5f winner Showtime Star (by Byron) and 1m winner Dusky Dawn (by Kheleyf): dam 5f/6f winner (including at 2 yrs): useful performer: won maiden at Wolverhampton and handicap at Newcastle (by 2¾ lengths from Savannah Moon) in June: placed most starts after, third in another handicap at Newcastle (½ length behind Charles Molson) final one: stays 8.5f: acts on tapeta and soft going. *Gay Kelleway*

PAST MASTER 4 gr.g. Mastercraftsman (IRE) 129 – Millestan (IRE) 91 (Invincible **78**
Spirit (IRE) 121) [2017 p10g^{2} Dec 13] compact gelding: fair form: second in maiden at Lingfield (3¾ lengths behind Dash of Spice) on sole outing in 2017. *Henry Candy*

PASTORAL DREAMS 2 b.c. (Mar 18) Pastoral Pursuits 127 – Engaging 62 (Oasis **–**
Dream 129) [2017 p8g Dec 20] 100/1, well held in minor event at Kempton. *Simon Dow*

PASTORAL MUSIC 4 b.g. Pastoral Pursuits 127 – Jasmeno 78 (Catcher In The Rye **80**
(IRE) 115) [2017 82: p16g^{3} 14.2d^{5} p16d^{3} 17.1d^{4} 11.6m^{2} 12v^{4} p12g* 12s^{5} Oct 28] smallish gelding: fairly useful handicapper: won at Kempton in October: third at same course in June: stays 17f: acts on polytrack, good to firm and good to soft going: usually in cheekpieces: usually races prominently. *Hughie Morrison*

PASTORAL PLAYER 10 b.g. Pastoral Pursuits 127 – Copy-Cat 60 (Lion Cavern (USA) **96 §**
117) [2017 94§: 7d^{2} 7m^{2} 7m^{6} 7f* 7d^{4} 8d^{6} 7d Nov 11] well-made gelding: useful handicapper: won at Epsom (by neck from Tavener) in July: stays 1m: acts on firm and soft going: often starts slowly/races in rear: tricky ride. *Hughie Morrison*

PATANJALI (IRE) 4 b.f. Poet's Voice 126 – Penang (IRE) 57 (Xaar 132) [2017 66: 10.2f **62**
p8s^{3} t7.2g Jun 26] modest handicapper: best at short of 1¼m: acts on polytrack, soft and good to firm going: has worn headgear. *Eve Johnson Houghton*

PATCHING 3 b.f. Foxwedge (AUS) 128 – Crinolette (IRE) (Sadler's Wells (USA) 132) **75**
[2017 67: t8.6g 10.2m^{4} 10.2g 8.3g^{4} 8g* 8.1m^{2} 8g 8m^{2} 7s^{2} 7d^{5} 7m^{3} 8d p8g Oct 3] leggy, close-coupled filly: fair performer: won minor event at Yarmouth in June: third in handicap at same course in August: best form up to 1m: acts on polytrack and good to firm going: wears headgear: front runner/races prominently. *Giles Bravery*

PATCHWORK 3 ch.g. Paco Boy (IRE) 129 – Medley 102 (Danehill Dancer (IRE) 117) **90**
[2017 p7g^{5} 7f^{2} 8m* 7d^{2} 6m 6d^{2} 5s p6s Oct 24] fourth foal: half-brother to 1m winner Sea Shanty and 2-y-o 7f winner Light Music (both useful and by Elusive Quality): dam, winner up to 1m (2-y-o 6f winner), half-sister to smart performer up to 8.5f in USA Green Line: fairly useful performer: won maiden at Redcar in May: second in handicaps at Newmarket in June and August (1¼ lengths behind Related): has won over 1m, may prove best at 6f: acts on firm and good to soft going: tried in cheekpieces: sold 22,000 gns, sent to Saudi Arabia. *Richard Hughes*

PATENT 4 b.g. Paco Boy (IRE) 129 – Film Script 105 (Unfuwain (USA) 131) [2017 72: **54**
t10.2g^{6} f12.1g^{6} 10.2m 9.9s 10.2g 12.1d^{6} 14s^{3} 15.9s 14v Nov 7] sturdy gelding: modest maiden handicapper nowadays: stays 1¾m: acts on good to firm and heavy going: wears headgear: usually races towards rear. *Peter Niven*

PATIENCEISAVIRTUE 2 b.f. (Apr 11) Libranno 119 – Patience (Kyllachy 129) [2017 –
6g^{6} 6d Oct 30] first foal: dam unraced: well held in minor events (hooded). *Christine Dunnett*

PATRON OF EXPLORES (USA) 6 b.g. Henrythenavigator (USA) 131 – India Halo – §
(ARG) (Halo Sunshine (USA) 118) [2017 49: t10.2g^{6} t8g t10.2d p8d p7d Feb 16] maiden, no form in 2017: tried in headgear: has worn tongue tie, including in 2017: usually slowly away, often races in rear: temperamental. *Patrick Holmes*

PATTIE 3 ch.f. Sixties Icon 125 – Excellent Day (IRE) 78 (Invincible Spirit (IRE) 121) **87**
[2017 74: p8g^{2} 9.9d^{3} 10m^{2} 10g^{6} 8g* 8f^{4} 8g^{5} 8d^{5} 8.1d* Aug 24] rather leggy filly: fairly useful handicapper: won at Pontefract in June and Chepstow (by ¾ length from Here's Two) in August: stays 1¼m: acts on polytrack, tapeta, good to firm and good to soft going: sometimes slowly away, usually races nearer last than first. *Mick Channon*

PATTY PATCH 2 b.f. (Apr 2) Big Bad Bob (IRE) 118 – Cockney Dancer 93 (Cockney **61**
Rebel (IRE) 127) [2017 6m^{6} p6s 6d^{5} Jun 29] 42,000Y: first foal: dam, winner up to 7f (2-y-o 6f winner), half-sister to winner up to 7f Gallagher and winner up to 1¼m Quick Wit (both smart): modest form: best effort when sixth in minor event at Redcar (4 lengths behind Dance Diva) in May: wears hood. *Richard Spencer*

PAULAMEY 2 gr.f. (Apr 18) Piccolo 121 – Tryptonic (FR) (Baryshnikov (AUS)) [2017 –
5m 5g^{6} 7g t7.2g Oct 7] £3,000Y: rather leggy filly: half-sister to 5f winner Ability N Delivery (by Kyllachy): dam French 1m winner: little sign of ability. *David Evans*

PAUVRE MOI (IRE) 2 b.f. (Mar 23) Pour Moi (IRE) 125 – Aitch (IRE) (Alhaarth (IRE) –
126) [2017 t6.1g t7.2g Oct 7] sixth foal: half-sister to 7f winner Sabratha (by Hawk Wing) and useful winner up to 1¼m Stellar Express (2-y-o 7f/1m winner, by Royal Applause): dam once-raced half-sister to smart 1¼m-17f winner Galileo's Choice: well held in sellers. *John Butler*

PAVARELLA SHOES 2 ch.f. (Mar 26) Lethal Force (IRE) 128 – Shena's Dream (IRE) **53 ?**
88 (Oasis Dream 129) [2017 5g 5m^{3} Aug 31] 4,000F, €7,500Y, €16,000 2-y-o: second foal: half-sister to 6f winner Scotch Myst (by Sepoy): dam 6f-1m winner: seemingly modest form on second of 2 starts in minor events. *Noel Wilson*

PAVED WITH GOLD (IRE) 4 b.g. Champs Elysees 124 – Luminous Gold 82 **61**
(Fantastic Light (USA) 134) [2017 75: 9.5d 8.6d 10g p8d^{2} p8g^{2} p8g^{6} Dec 21] fair **a72**
handicapper: stays 8.5f: acts on polytrack and good to soft going: tried in cheekpieces: usually races towards rear. *John Joseph Murphy, Ireland*

PAVERS PRIDE 3 ch.g. Bahamian Bounty 116 – Pride of Kinloch 80 (Dr Devious (IRE) **66**
127) [2017 53: t5s 5m 5.5f^{5} 6m 5d* 5m^{4} 5g^{4} 5s Oct 9] fair performer: won maiden at Thirsk in August: best form at 5f: acts on tapeta and good to soft going. *Noel Wilson*

PAVILLON 3 b.f. Showcasing 117 – Park Law (IRE) 94 (Fasliyev (USA) 120) [2017 84P: **91**
p8g* t8.6g^{3} 8m^{6} 8v^{3} Jul 22] lengthy filly: fairly useful handicapper: won at Chelmsford in May: third at Wolverhampton in June: stays 8.5f: acts on polytrack, tapeta and good to firm going. *Clive Cox*

PC DIXON 4 ch.g. Sixties Icon 125 – Lakaam 57 (Danzero (AUS)) [2017 72: p10m t8.6g **61**
7d May 18] fair maiden, below best in 2017: best effort at 1¼m: best form on good going: signs of temperament. *Mick Channon*

PEACE AND PLENTY 3 ch.c. Exceed And Excel (AUS) 126 – Putois Peace (Pivotal –
124) [2017 73p: t9.5g^{2} 10.2g 9.9g p8g^{3} p8g^{3} t9.5m^{2} p10d* p10s Dec 8] good-topped colt: **a90**
fairly useful handicapper: won at Kempton (by ½ length from Hairdryer) in November: stays 1¼m: acts on polytrack and tapeta: front runner/races prominently. *William Muir*

PEACE DREAMER (IRE) 3 b.f. Sir Prancealot (IRE) 111 – See Nuala (IRE) 73 **82**
(Kyllachy 129) [2017 60: 6m^{2} 6m* 6g 6m^{4} Aug 28] fairly useful performer: won maiden at Redcar (by 7 lengths from Granny Roz) in June: stays 6f: acts on good to firm going: has worn hood: usually races prominently. *Robert Cowell*

PEACE ENVOY (FR) 3 b.c. Power 117 – Hoh My Darling 71 (Dansili 127) [2017 111: **101**
7g^{4} 8d 8f 7m 7g Sep 16] compact colt: smart performer at 2 yrs, winning 3 times, including listed race at Naas and Anglesey Stakes at the Curragh, and good third in Prix Morny at Deauville: disappointing in 2017: should have stayed 7f: acted on polytrack and soft going: tried in headgear: tended to pull hard: to stand at Worsall Grange Farm, Yarm, North Yorkshire, fee £2,000. *Aidan O'Brien, Ireland*

PEACEFUL PASSAGE (USA) 3 b.f. War Front (USA) 119 – Flying Passage (USA) (A P Indy (USA) 131) [2017 73: p12d* a6.5f^5 8.5f Oct 15] fairly useful performer: won maiden at Kempton (by 3¼ lengths from Tomorrow Mystery) in February: left John Gosden after: stays 1½m: acts on polytrack and dirt. *Claude R. McGaughey III, USA* **81**

PEACE PREVAILS 2 ch.f. (Mar 5) Declaration of War (USA) 128 – Miss Mediator (USA) 77 (Consolidator (USA) 121) [2017 t5s^6 6d^3 6d^5 6s^6 6d^3 t7.1g Oct 10] second foal: half-sister to 2-y-o 1m winner Galahad (by Sir Prancealot): dam, 1m winner, half-sister to smart 2-y-o 6f winner Great White Eagle: fair maiden: bred to be suited by 7f+: acts on good to soft going: in cheekpieces last 2 starts: often races prominently. *Richard Fahey* **68**

PEACE TERMS (IRE) 3 b.f. Teofilo (IRE) 126 – Intapeace (IRE) 102 (Intikhab (USA) 135) [2017 p7g^3 t7.2d^2 Dec 16] €22,000F, 70,000Y: second foal: half-sister to temperamental 2-y-o 7f winner Gift Wrap (by Raven's Pass): dam, winner up to 7.5f (2-y-o 6f winner), sister to smart sprinter Hoh Mike: fairly useful form: better effort when second in maiden at Wolverhampton (neck behind Star Quality): will go on improving. *Ralph Beckett* **81 p**

PEACE TRAIL 2 b.f. (Mar 14) Kyllachy 129 – Path of Peace 86 (Rock of Gibraltar (IRE) 133) [2017 7g* 7g t6s* Sep 19] 120,000Y, 230,000 2-y-o: well-made filly: third foal: half-sister to smart 5f-1m winner (including at 2 yrs/in USA) Belvoir Bay (by Equiano): dam, 1m winner, half-sister to smart winner up to 1¼m Mountain Song: fairly useful form: won maiden at Newmarket (by ½ length from Altyn Orda) in August and minor event at Newcastle (by 1¼ lengths from Cirrus Minor) in September: stays 7f. *Charlie Appleby* **87**

PEACHEY CARNEHAN 3 ch.g. Foxwedge (AUS) 128 – Zubova 73 (Dubawi (IRE) 129) [2017 68: t7.1g* p7g^3 t7.1g^3 t6m* p6g^3 5.7f 6d^6 t6.1g^2 5m^4 6.1m^5 6d^4 5g* 6g^2 6d* 5d^5 5.1g 5s^6 6s 6s^6 t6.1g f6.1g^6 Dec 11] lengthy gelding: fair performer: won maiden at Wolverhampton in January, minor event at same course in March, and handicaps at Doncaster and Leicester in August: left Michael Attwater after eighth start: stays 7f, at least as effective over shorter: acts on polytrack, tapeta, good to firm and good to soft going: wears headgear: often races towards rear. *Michael Mullineaux* **79**

PEACH MELBA 3 b.f. Dream Ahead (USA) 133 – Nellie Melba 82 (Hurricane Sky (AUS)) [2017 6.9g^2 p7g^3 7s^2 8.3s^4 7g^3 7.4d^2 7.1v* 7s* 7.6d* 7.2m^2 8s 8s^2 8g* 8s* t7.2g^3 Nov 11] angular filly: sixth foal: half-sister to 3 winners, including useful/temperamental 6f winner (stays 1m) Major Crispies (by Pastoral Pursuits) and useful 5f (including at 2 yrs)/6f winner Bosun Breese (by Bahamian Bounty): dam 7f/1m winner: useful performer: won handicaps at Chepstow in July, Leicester and Lingfield in August, and Newmarket in October, and listed race at Hanover (by 1½ lengths from Vive Marie) later in October: stays 8.5f: acts on good to firm and heavy going: front runner/races prominently. *Mark Johnston* **104**

PEACH PAVLOVA (IRE) 3 b.f. Elzaam (AUS) 115 – Zvezda (USA) (Nureyev (USA) 131) [2017 74: 6.9g 6m 5m Jul 7] narrow filly: fair maiden at 2 yrs, no form in 2017: tried in cheekpieces. *Ann Duffield* **–**

PEAK HILL 4 ch.g. Bahamian Bounty 116 – River Naiad (Nayef (USA) 129) [2017 71: 10g p8g^3 t7.2g^3 t9.5g t9.5g^4 t8.6g Dec 5] modest handicapper nowadays: stays 1m: acts on polytrack, tapeta, good to firm and heavy going: has worn headgear: races prominently. *Adrian Wintle* **63**

PEAK PRINCESS (IRE) 3 b.f. Foxwedge (AUS) 128 – Foot of Pride (IRE) 65 (Footstepsinthesand 120) [2017 84: 7m^2 8d^4 7v^2 p7d* p7s^5 7g p7g^2 p8g Oct 27] good-topped filly: useful handicapper: won at Kempton (by length from Nostalgie) in August: second at same course (nose behind Yellowhammer) in October: stays 1m: acts on polytrack, good to firm and heavy going: usually in headgear in 2017: sometimes slowly away, usually races nearer last than first. *Richard Hannon* **97**

PEAK STORM 8 b.g. Sleeping Indian 122 – Jitterbug (IRE) (Marju (IRE) 127) [2017 87: 8.2d 8m 7.1v^6 10m^4 8m^5 8.1m 8.1v^4 10.5v 8.1d t8.6g Dec 13] compact gelding: fairly useful handicapper at best, has deteriorated: stays 1¼m: acts on polytrack, good to firm and heavy going: usually wears headgear: sometimes in tongue tie: usually races nearer last than first. *John O'Shea* **74**

PEALER (GER) 3 b.g. Campanologist (USA) 119 – Praia (GER) (Big Shuffle (USA) 122) [2017 86p: t12.2g^2 10m^4 f11.1g* 12m 8.5g* 8d^2 Jul 29] good-bodied gelding: useful performer: won maiden at Southwell (by 19 lengths) in May and handicap at Epsom (by 2½ lengths from Native Prospect) in July: second in handicap at Ascot (neck behind D'bai) final start: stays 11f: acts on fibresand and good to soft going: in tongue tie last 5 starts: gelded, and sent to Hong Kong, where renamed Go Go First. *John Gosden* **105**

PEARL ACCLAIM (IRE) 7 b.g. Acclamation 118 – With Colour (Rainbow Quest (USA) 134) [2017 87: 5m^5 5s^6 p6d^2 5d p5s^5 t5.1g^2 5m^2 5d^6 5m t5g p5s^3 f6.1g^5 f5g* f5g* f5g^2 Dec 21] compact gelding: fairly useful handicapper: won at Southwell (twice) in December: left David O'Meara after sixth start: stays 6f: acts on all-weather, firm and good to soft going: usually wears headgear: front runner/races prominently. *David C. Griffiths* **81**

PEARL CASTLE (IRE) 7 b.g. Montjeu (IRE) 137 – Ghurra (USA) 91 (War Chant (USA) 126) [2017 97: p16g^6 t12.4g^6 Nov 23] tall, attractive gelding: useful performer: below form both starts in 2017: stays 1¾m: acts on polytrack, soft and good to firm going: tried in cheekpieces. *K. R. Burke* **87**

PEARL NATION (USA) 8 b.g. Speightstown (USA) 124 – Happy Nation (USA) (Lear Fan (USA) 130) [2017 98: f8g^2 t9.5g f7.1g^2 f6.1g Dec 19] big, strong gelding: fairly useful performer nowadays: second in claimer at Southwell in January: stays 8.5f: acts on all-weather and firm going: usually hooded. *Michael Appleby* **92**

PEARL NOIR 7 b.g. Milk It Mick 120 – Cora Pearl (IRE) 51 (Montjeu (IRE) 137) [2017 **69**
71: f6g^4 f5g^3 t5.1g^2 t5.1g^6 p5d^4 t5g^2 t5.1g^5 5m 5g^4 5g^2 5m* 5m 5m 5m^3 5d^3 5m^5 5d f5g^3 **a62**
t5g^6 5.3d^5 Sep 18] strong gelding: fair handicapper on turf, modest on all-weather: won at Ripon (apprentice) in May: best at 5f: acts on all-weather and firm going: wears headgear: tried in tongue tie: front runner/races prominently. *Scott Dixon*

PEARL'S CALLING (IRE) 2 ch.f. (Apr 19) Dandy Man (IRE) 123 – Celtic Heroine (IRE) 111 (Hernando (FR) 127) [2017 7d^6 7.4m 7s^6 8.2g p10g Oct 26] good-topped filly: half-sister to smart 10.7f-12.5f winner Time For Action (by Dylan Thomas) and 1¼m winner (stayed 1½m) Mr Snagsby (by Duke of Marmalade): dam, 7f/1m winner (including at 2 yrs), sister to very smart winner up to 1½m Rainbow Peak: modest maiden: sometimes slowly away, usually races in rear. *David Barron* **54**

PEARL SPECTRE (USA) 6 ch.g. Street Cry (IRE) 130 – Dark Sky (USA) (Storm Cat (USA)) [2017 94: t6g^3 p7g^4 p7d p8d^3 p7g* p7g^4 p6g^3 p7g^6 p6g p7g 6m 7m p8g p7d^4 f7.1g^2 p7d* p7s^5 p7s p7g^3 p6s^4 p6g^5 Dec 30] rather leggy gelding: useful handicapper: won at Lingfield in March and Chelmsford in November: stays 1m: acts on all-weather, good to firm and good to soft going: tried in blinkers: usually races close up. *Phil McEntee* **98**

PEARLY PRINCE 5 b.g. Cockney Rebel (IRE) 127 – Princess Raya 58 (Act One 124) [2017 75: p12g^5 p12g^6 May 4] fair maiden handicapper: stays 1½m: acts on polytrack: wears headgear. *Martin Bosley* **75**

PEARLY QUEEN 4 b.f. Dutch Art 126 – Surprise (IRE) 67 (Anabaa Blue 122) [2017 60: t9.5g Jan 9] sturdy filly: modest maiden: down the field only start in 2017: stays 7f: acts on polytrack and firm going: usually hooded. *Dean Ivory* **–**

PEA SHOOTER 8 b.g. Piccolo 121 – Sparkling Eyes 80 (Lujain (USA) 119) [2017 89: f6g 5m 5m 5m^4 6m^5 5g^5 5g Aug 21] tall gelding: fairly useful handicapper: below form in 2017: stays 6f: acts on good to firm and good to soft going: has worn headgear: tried in tongue tie. *Brian Ellison* **77**

PEAS ON EARTH 2 ch.f. (Apr 27) Showcasing 117 – Meditation 88 (Inchinor 119) [2017 5g 5d^{ur} t5.1g^5 t5.1g t5.1g^4 Dec 18] sixth foal: half-sister to 5f winner Yisty (by Compton Place): dam 6f-1¼m winner (7f winner at 2 yrs): poor maiden: raced only at 5f: sometimes slowly away, usually races towards rear. *Derek Shaw* **46**

PECHEURS DE PERLES (IRE) 3 b.g. Pour Moi (IRE) 125 – Annacloy Pearl (IRE) (Mull of Kintyre (USA) 114) [2017 69p: 7v^2 7.5s* 7d 8.2d^3 8g 8d Nov 4] fairly useful performer: won maiden at Tipperary in April: third in handicap at Haydock in August: left Henry de Bromhead after second start: stays 1m: acts on polytrack and heavy going: usually races close up. *Iain Jardine* **85**

PEGGIE SUE 2 b.f. (Apr 22) Captain Gerrard (IRE) 113 – Aunt Minnie (Night Shift (USA)) [2017 7g 7g 7m 8s p6g^3 Nov 1] first foal: dam unraced: modest maiden: best effort at 6f: acts on polytrack: often races freely. *Adam West* **58**

PEGGY'S ANGEL 2 b.f. (Mar 17) Captain Gerrard (IRE) 113 – Dora's Sister (IRE) 69 (Dark Angel (IRE) 113) [2017 6s^5 6.1m* 6.1g* 6g Oct 14] workmanlike filly: second foal: dam, 7f winner, half-sister to useful 5f winner Duchess Dora: fairly useful form: won minor events at Windsor in July and Chester (by ½ length from Mayyasah) in September: raced only at 6f. *Jo Hughes* **85**

PEGI BROWNE (IRE) 4 ch.f. Fast Company (IRE) 126 – Alta Petens 90 (Mujadil (USA) 119) [2017 –: 11.3g 7d p7g Oct 17] fifth foal: half-sister to 2-y-o 5f winner Verus Decorus (by Titus Livius) and 1m winner Mordanmijobsworth (by Clodovil): dam 2-y-o 6f winner: modest maiden handicapper: left M. D. O'Callaghan after second start: best effort at 7f: acts on polytrack: often starts slowly. *Paul Midgley* **58**

PEKING FLYER (IRE) 3 b.g. Zoffany (IRE) 121 – Wing Diva (IRE) 65 (Hawk Wing (USA) 136) [2017 –: p7g t8.6g 9.9g[5] 9.9m Jun 27] modest maiden: best effort at 1¼m: in tongue tie last 3 starts: often races in rear. *Ed Walker* **52**

PELICE (IRE) 2 b.f. (Mar 12) Epaulette (AUS) 126 – Almansa (IRE) (Dr Devious (IRE) 127) [2017 7.2m[6] 7.4s 8.2v[4] 8.3d Oct 18] £16,000Y: half-sister to several winners, including smart winner up to 10.4f Tres Coronas (2-y-o 5f/1m winner, by Key of Luck) and useful winner around 1¼m Empress Ali (by Holy Roman Emperor): dam French 1½m winner: modest form: sold 3,500 gns, sent to Italy. *Mark Johnston* **60**

PELOTON 3 b.f. Mount Nelson 125 – Les Verguettes (IRE) 78 (Iffraaj 127) [2017 71: 8.5g 8.1d[2] 9g[5] 10d[3] 8.5d[4] Jul 20] sturdy filly: fair maiden: stayed 9f: acted on good to soft going: dead. *Pat Phelan* **71**

PENDO 6 b.g. Denounce 89 – Abundant 96 (Zafonic (USA) 130) [2017 82: p8g[3] p8d[2] p8g p8g* 8m 10m[5] p8s 8m[2] p8g[6] 9.9s Sep 27] workmanlike gelding: fairly useful handicapper: won at Chelmsford (by ½ length from Robero) in April: stays 8.5f: acts on polytrack, tapeta, soft and good to firm going: has worn headgear. *John Best* **86**

PENELOPE PITSTOP 5 b.m. Captain Gerrard (IRE) 113 – Obsessive Secret (IRE) (Grand Lodge (USA) 125) [2017 57: 9.1m[4] 9.2g 8.3g[4] 8m 10d 10d 7.8g[4] Aug 30] modest maiden handicapper: stays 10.5f: acts on good to firm and heavy going: tried in cheekpieces: front runner/races prominently. *L. Smyth, Ireland* **54**

PENGLAI PAVILION (USA) 7 b.g. Monsun (GER) 124 – Maiden Tower 116 (Groom Dancer (USA) 128) [2017 108: 16v 16.3d[4] 14.5g[6] Sep 15] good-topped gelding: useful handicapper nowadays: fourth at York (2¼ lengths behind Magic Circle) in August: stays 2¼m: acts on heavy going: tried in cheekpieces: front runner/races prominently. *Charlie Appleby* **107**

PENNERLEY 4 b.f. Aqlaam 125 – Penelewey 97 (Groom Dancer (USA) 128) [2017 74: 12s[6] 12m[6] 12.1m 12d[6] 15.9g[6] t12.4g 13.9v 10d Oct 30] smallish, lengthy filly: fair maiden handicapper: below form in 2017: stays 1¼m: acts on firm and good to soft going: tried in cheekpieces. *Micky Hammond* **61**

PENNINE WARRIOR 6 b.g. Lucky Story (USA) 128 – Discoed 38 (Distinctly North (USA) 115) [2017 66§: 7.4m 7g[4] 6s Jun 29] good-topped gelding: modest handicapper nowadays: stays 7f: acts on polytrack, fibresand, good to firm and good to soft going: wears headgear: ungenuine. *Scott Dixon* **60 §**

PENNINGTON 3 b.g. Poet's Voice 126 – Pryka (ARG) (Southern Halo (USA)) [2017 69: 8m 10.2f 8s 8.3d Jul 15] maiden, no form in 2017: in headgear last 2 starts: has joined Russell Ross. *Mark Johnston* **–**

PENNSYLVANIA DUTCH 3 b.g. Dutch Art 126 – Map of Heaven 82 (Pivotal 124) [2017 85p: 6d* 7g[5] 6d[3] 5m 6d Sep 10] good-quartered gelding: fairly useful handicapper: won at Haydock (by ½ length from Bellevarde) in June: stays 6f: acts on firm and good to soft going: often starts slowly/races in rear: sold 20,000 gns in October. *William Haggas* **91**

PENNY DREADFUL 5 b.m. Piccolo 121 – Trina's Pet 65 (Efisio 120) [2017 79: p6g[4] p6d[3] p6d[3] p6d[6] t5.1g[4] 6m[3] 6g[3] 6m[5] 5g[3] 6m[2] 5f* 5m[4] 5m[4] 5g[4] 5g* 5d t5g f5g[3] p5g[4] p5m[4] f6.1g p5s[4] p5s[4] f5g Dec 29] fairly useful handicapper: won at Nottingham (by 5 lengths from Sir Dudley) in June and Catterick (by 3¼ lengths from Landing Night) in August: stays 6f: acts on all-weather and firm going: wears headgear: front runner/races prominently. *Scott Dixon* **83**

PENNY PEPPER (IRE) 5 b.m. Fast Company (IRE) 126 – Evening Time (IRE) 117 (Keltos (FR) 132) [2017 93: 6v[2] 7s 6s* Jun 11] useful performer: won Ballyogan Stakes at the Curragh (by head from Only Mine) in June: stayed 1m: acted on good to firm and heavy going: sometimes slowly away, often raced towards rear: reportedly in foal to Dragon Pulse. *Kevin Prendergast, Ireland* **102**

PENNY POET (IRE) 4 b.f. Intikhab (USA) 135 – Mneme (FR) (Ocean of Wisdom (USA) 106) [2017 p8d p8g[6] t8.6g[5] t13.9g[3] 13d[4] Aug 23] 70,000Y, £1,500 3-y-o: second foal: half-sister to a winner in Czech Republic by Sir Percy: dam once-raced half-sister to smart French 1¼m/10.5f winner Sensible: modest maiden: stays 1¾m: acts on tapeta and good to soft going: often starts slowly/races towards rear. *Neil Mulholland* **60**

PENNY POT LANE 4 b.f. Misu Bond (IRE) 114 – Velvet Band 73 (Verglas (IRE) 118) **85**
[2017 79: 6m 5.9g^{2} 6g 6g^{2} 6.9d^{3} 6s* 6v* 6v^{3} 7v^{4} t6d^{4} Nov 10] leggy filly: fairly useful handicapper: won at Redcar and Pontefract (apprentice, by ¾ length from My Girl Maisie) in September: stays 6f: acts on good to firm and heavy going: usually races close up. *Richard Whitaker*

PENNY RED 3 ch.f. Medicean 128 – Peintre d'Argent (IRE) 84 (Peintre Celebre (USA) **69**
137) [2017 64: 10m p12g^{5} p11s 8g 12.3d^{su} 12v^{4} Aug 15] angular filly: fair maiden: left William Knight after fourth start: stays 1¼m: acts on polytrack and good to firm going: poor form over hurdles. *Nikki Evans*

PENSAX BOY 5 b.g. Rail Link 132 – Cyclone Connie 98 (Dr Devious (IRE) 127) [2017 **87**
88: 7.8g* 7.8s^{6} 10.2d^{5} t8.6g* 8g t9.5g t9.5d Dec 16] sturdy gelding: fairly useful **a93**
handicapper: won at Carlisle in May and Wolverhampton (by ¾ length from Ibazz) in August: stays 8.5f: acts on tapeta, firm and good to soft going: tried in cheekpieces. *Daniel Loughnane*

PENSAX LADY (IRE) 4 b.f. Fast Company (IRE) 126 – Aljafliyah (Halling (USA) 133) **66**
[2017 63: t9.5g^{2} t9.5g^{4} 10d^{6} 10.2g t8.6g^{2} t8s t9.5g t9.5g p10s^{5} t8.6g Dec 13] fair handicapper: stays 9.5f: acts on tapeta and firm going. *Daniel Loughnane*

PENSION MADNESS (IRE) 4 b.g. Vocalised (USA) 114 – Grinneas (IRE) 79 **–**
(Barathea (IRE) 127) [2017 68: p13.3g Mar 2] fair maiden handicapper: down the field only start on Flat in 2017: stays 13f: acts on good to firm going: tried in headgear: modest maiden hurdler. *Mark Usher*

PENTITO RAP (USA) 3 b.g. Smart Strike (CAN) 121 – Sing Like A Bird (USA) **50**
(Lawyer Ron (USA) 128) [2017 47: p8g^{6} p12g^{5} 10.2f 10m f8.1g^{3} Dec 4] modest maiden: stays 1½m: acts on polytrack and good to soft going. *Rod Millman*

PENTLAND HILLS (IRE) 2 b.g. (Feb 26) Motivator 131 – Elle Galante (GER) **– p**
(Galileo (IRE) 134) [2017 8g 8g 8m^{5} Oct 25] 40,000Y: good-topped gelding: half-brother to several winners, including smart winner up to 1½m (King Edward VII Stakes) Balios (2-y-o 1m winner, by Shamardal) and useful 6f/6.5f winner Cersei (by Invincible Spirit): dam German 10.5f-15f winner: little impact in minor events/maiden: type to do better in handicaps. *Chris Wall*

PENWORTHAM (IRE) 4 b.g. Dandy Man (IRE) 123 – Portofino Bay (IRE) 74 **97**
(Montjeu (IRE) 137) [2017 98: 7.1g 7m 7.6g^{2} 7m t7.1s 7s 7.6g^{5} 7.6g* 7v^{3} 7.2s f7.1g^{5} Oct 22] good-topped gelding: useful handicapper: won at Chester (by ½ length from War Glory) in September: stays 7.5f: acts on tapeta, good to firm and heavy going: wears hood: sold 27,000 gns in October. *Richard Fahey*

PENY ARCADE 3 b.f. Misu Bond (IRE) 114 – Bond Royale 89 (Piccolo 121) [2017 60: **55**
7.2m t8g^{6} 7.2m^{6} t8s 7.2s^{6} 7g^{6} t7.1s 7.2s^{3} t8.6g^{3} t7.1d t7.1s Nov 30] modest handicapper: stays 7f: acts on tapeta and good to firm going: tried in visor. *Alistair Whillans*

PEPITA (IRE) 3 ch.f. Sir Prancealot (IRE) 111 – Esterlina (IRE) 95 (Highest Honor (FR) **94**
124) [2017 77: p8g^{3} p7g* 7m^{3} p8g^{5} 6m^{2} 6d^{2} 6.1g^{6} 6.1m* 6m^{2} 6s^{5} t7.2g^{2} Nov 11] neat filly: fairly useful performer: won maiden at Kempton in February and handicap at Windsor (by neck from Angel of Darkness) in August: second in minor event at Wolverhampton (neck behind Bumptious) final start: stays 1m: acts on polytrack, tapeta, good to firm and good to soft going. *Richard Hannon*

PEPPER STREET (IRE) 2 b.f. (Feb 19) Born To Sea (IRE) 117 – Mindy (IRE) 89 **56**
(Zamindar (USA) 116) [2017 p8g^{6} p8g^{4} p8d Nov 22] £34,000Y: first foal: dam 11.7f winner: modest form: best effort when fourth in minor event at Kempton (7¼ lengths behind Blue Mist) in October: in hood last 2 starts. *Hugo Palmer*

PEPYS 3 b.g. Aqlaam 125 – Generously Gifted (Sakhee (USA) 136) [2017 66: 7.2g^{4} 7.4m^{5} **67**
7.2d^{4} t7.1g^{6} Oct 20] fair maiden handicapper: stays 8.5f: acts on heavy going. *Bryan Smart*

PEQUENINHA 3 b.f. Acclamation 118 – Choral 94 (Oratorio (IRE) 128) [2017 8.3d^{4} 9.9s **73 p**
p8g^{6} t8s^{3} Sep 8] 60,000Y: first foal: dam, 6f/7f winner, half-sister to smart winner up to 9f Mister Music: fair form: best effort when third in maiden at Newcastle final start: stays 8.5f: open to further improvement. *David Simcock*

PERAMBULATION 2 ch.f. (Apr 11) Stimulation (IRE) 121 – Love In The Park 78 **–**
(Pivotal 124) [2017 p5g Nov 17] second foal: dam 9f/1¼m winner: 33/1, well held in minor event at Lingfield. *Stuart Kittow*

PERCEIVED 5 ch.m. Sir Percy 129 – New Light 56 (Generous (IRE) 139) [2017 82: t10.2g^5 f11d^6 t9.5g^4 9.9d^2 t10.2s 9.9d^6 9.9g^4 9.9m t10.2s^2 10.2d t9.5g^5 Dec 5] lengthy mare: fair handicapper nowadays: stays 1¼m: acts on polytrack, tapeta, good to firm and heavy going. *Antony Brittain* **75**

PERCIPIO 3 b.f. Indian Haven 119 – Perception (IRE) 81 (Hawk Wing (USA) 136) [2017 8g^6 9.9f 11.6d 14d^4 p16g^5 p13.3s Dec 1] second foal: dam 2m/17f winner: modest maiden: stays 1¾m: acts on good to soft going: usually races towards rear. *Alan King* **54**

PERCY B SHELLEY 3 ch.g. Archipenko (USA) 127 – Oshiponga 72 (Barathea (IRE) 127) [2017 78p: 10m^4 11.9m^4 p12g Nov 17] fair form: left John Gosden after second start: stays 1¼m: tried in hood/tongue tie. *J. F. Levins, Ireland* **79**

PERCY PROSECCO 2 b.c. (Mar 23) Sir Percy 129 – Grapes Hill (Kingsalsa (USA) 118) [2017 p7g 7g 6.5d Oct 27] little impact in minor event/maidens. *Noel Williams* **–**

PERCYS PRINCESS 6 b.m. Sir Percy 129 – Enford Princess 89 (Pivotal 124) [2017 72: t12.2g^3 t12.2g* t12.2g^5 12.1m* 11.8d^3 11.9m* 10d 12d* 12.1s^5 f12.1g^3 Dec 4] fair performer: won handicap at Wolverhampton in April, claimer at Catterick in May, and more handicaps at Doncaster in July and Thirsk in August: stays 1¾m: acts on fibresand, tapeta, soft and good to firm going: tried in headgear/tongue tie: front runner/races prominently. *Michael Appleby* **79**

PERCY STREET 4 br.g. Sir Percy 129 – Star of Gibraltar 88 (Rock of Gibraltar (IRE) 133) [2017 105: 11.6g Sep 7] leggy gelding: useful performer: well below form only start on Flat in 2017: stays 1½m: acts on good to firm and heavy going: tried in visor: front runner/races prominently: fairly useful hurdler. *Nicky Henderson* **–**

PERCY'S WORD 3 b.g. Sir Percy 129 – Laverre (IRE) 81 (Noverre (USA) 125) [2017 79p: 11.8g^3 p16g* 13.9g^6 Oct 13] compact gelding: useful form: won handicap at Kempton in August: stays 2m. *Simon Crisford* **100**

PERCY THROWER (IRE) 3 ch.g. Sir Percy 129 – Dayrose 94 (Daylami (IRE) 138) [2017 73: f12d^3 9.9f 12m^5 t14g 14s^2 14d^3 p16g^5 14d^6 p12g^5 Oct 24] smallish gelding: fair maiden handicapper: stays 2m: acts on polytrack and soft going: tried in blinkers: usually races close up: has joined Sarah-Jayne Davies. *Charles Hills* **66**

PERCY TOPLIS 3 b.g. Kheleyf (USA) 116 – West Lorne (USA) 60 (Gone West (USA)) [2017 73: 5m 6m 6m p5d^2 t5.1g p5s 5.2d^4 6g 5.2g^5 5.2m 5d^5 p7g^5 6s Oct 10] rather leggy gelding: modest handicapper nowadays: stays 6f: acts on all-weather and heavy going: wears headgear: often races prominently. *Christine Dunnett* **53**

PERCY VEER 5 ch.g. Sir Percy 129 – Fandangerina 81 (Hernando (FR) 127) [2017 92: p16g^3 t16.5g^3 t16.5g p16d^5 18d Sep 23] compact gelding: fairly useful handicapper: third at Wolverhampton in January: stays 21f: acts on polytrack, tapeta, firm and good to soft going: often in headgear: often races prominently: has joined Eric McNamara, Ireland. *Sylvester Kirk* **89**

PERCY VERENCE 4 b.g. Sir Percy 129 – Bermondsey Girl 69 (Bertolini (USA) 125) [2017 67: t10.2d^3 p10d^3 14g^6 t10.2s 9s^5 14m^2 12.1m^4 12.5g 16.1g 14d 12.1d^5 9.8g^5 t12.4d t12.4d^5 Dec 16] modest maiden handicapper: left K. R. Burke after second start: stays 1¾m: acts on polytrack, tapeta and good to firm going: sometimes wears headgear/tongue tie: usually races prominently. *Tracy Waggott* **61**

PERFECT ANGEL (IRE) 3 br.f. Dark Angel (IRE) 113 – The Hermitage (IRE) 83 (Kheleyf (USA) 116) [2017 99: 6s^5 6m 6g 6s^2 7s 6d Nov 11] rather leggy filly: useful performer: second in Hackwood Stakes at Newbury (1¼ lengths behind Magical Memory) in July: stays 6f: acts on soft and good to firm going: often races prominently. *Andrew Balding* **107**

PERFECT ART 3 b.f. Archipenko (USA) 127 – Bassinet (USA) 84 (Stravinsky (USA) 133) [2017 p8g p12g Oct 18] fourth foal: half-sister to 1½m winner Perfect Rhythm (by Halling) and winner up to 7f Gun Case (2-y-o 6f winner, by Showcasing): dam, 1½m winner, half-sister to useful French winner up to 1m Birthplace: down the field in maidens. *Ralph Beckett* **–**

PERFECT BLUE (IRE) 2 b.c. (May 1) Pour Moi (IRE) 125 – Prairie Runner (IRE) 108 (Arazi (USA) 135) [2017 9.1s^6 t9.5g^3 t9.5g Nov 18] fair form: standout effort when third in minor event at Wolverhampton (3¾ lengths behind Deyaarna) in October. *Mark Johnston* **65**

PERFECT CLARITY 2 b.f. (Mar 19) Nathaniel (IRE) 129 – Clarietta 100 (Shamardal (USA) 129) [2017 8.3g* Aug 15] 30,000Y: third foal: half-sister to useful 1m winner Clarentine (by Dalakhani) and 2-y-o 7f winner Law Power (by Lawman), later winner up **83 p**

to 8.5f in Italy: dam, 2-y-o 7f winner who stayed 1¼m, half-sister to smart winner up to 11.5f Cassydora: 3/1, won minor event at Nottingham (by 1¼ lengths from Cosmopolitan Queen) in August: will be suited by 1¼m: sure to progress. *Clive Cox*

PERFECT CRACKER 9 ch.g. Dubai Destination (USA) 127 – Perfect Story (IRE) 95 (Desert Story (IRE) 115) [2017 98: t8.6m^3 t9.5g^6 t9.5g^3 t9.5g t9.5d Dec 16] sturdy gelding: useful handicapper: third at Wolverhampton (1¾ lengths behind Amazement) in March: stays 10.5f: acts on polytrack, tapeta and good to firm going: often races freely. *Clive Cox* **95**

PERFECT HUSTLER (USA) 2 ch.g. (Apr 27) Jimmy Creed (USA) 118 – Jacqui's Promise (USA) (Loup Sauvage (USA) 125) [2017 6.1g^5 7g p6g^2 p6g* Oct 24] $15,000Y, $60,000 2-y-o: seventh foal: half-brother to 3 winners in USA: dam, US winner up to 8.5f (2-y-o 6f winner), half-sister to smart US Grade 3 1m winner Corporate Jungle: fairly useful form: won minor event at Kempton in October: stays 7f. *Jeremy Noseda* **92**

PERFECT IN PINK 3 ch.f. Raven's Pass (USA) 133 – Fashion Rocks (IRE) 97 (Rock of Gibraltar (IRE) 133) [2017 70p: 10m^6 11.6d^4 11.8d* 14m^6 11.9m^6 11.8d^4 Aug 13] sturdy filly: fairly useful performer: won maiden at Leicester (by 1¼ lengths from Munstead Star) in May: stays 1½m: acts on good to soft going: sold 8,000 gns in October to join Mark McNiff, Ireland. *Mick Channon* **82**

PERFECTION 2 ch.f. (Feb 21) Dutch Art 126 – Cantal 87 (Pivotal 124) [2017 p8s^4 p7g^3 Dec 20] second foal: sister to 2-y-o 8.6f winner Munawer: dam, 2-y-o 7f winner, half-sister to smart 1¼m/10.4f winner Autocratic and Horris Hill Stakes winner Evasive: fair form when in frame in minor events. *John Gosden* **70**

PERFECT LADY 3 b.f. Excelebration (IRE) 133 – Theladyinquestion 89 (Dubawi (IRE) 129) [2017 t7.2d^4 Dec 16] first foal: dam, winner up to 7f (2-y-o 6f winner), half-sister to Mill Reef Stakes winner James Garfield and useful winner up to 1m The Shrew: 13/2, fourth in maiden at Wolverhampton (7¾ lengths behind Star Quality) in December: sure to progress. *Clive Cox* **59 p**

PERFECT MADGE (IRE) 3 b.f. Acclamation 118 – Soul Mountain (IRE) 88 (Rock of Gibraltar (IRE) 133) [2017 87?: p8g^5 6m^4 6d^3 7d^2 Aug 5] good-topped filly: useful performer: second in handicap at Newmarket (2¼ lengths behind Mojito) final start: stayed 1m: acted on polytrack, good to firm and good to soft going: tried in cheekpieces: dead. *Kevin Ryan* **96**

PERFECT PASTIME 9 ch.g. Pastoral Pursuits 127 – Puritanical (IRE) (Desert King (IRE) 129) [2017 73: p7g p6g 6g* 6m 6.1g^5 6d 6s 6g 5.7s* Oct 2] sturdy gelding: fair handicapper: won at Brighton in May and October: stays 7f: acts on polytrack and any turf going: usually wears headgear: usually races towards rear: temperamental. *Jim Boyle* **72 §**

PERFECT PASTURE 7 b.g. Pastoral Pursuits 127 – Word Perfect 87 (Diktat 126) [2017 115: 6.1m* t6s 6s^5 6d 7g 6v 6g 6d* 5s* 6d^2 Nov 11] strong gelding: smart performer: won listed race at Windsor (by neck from Dancing Star) in May, and handicaps at Doncaster (by neck from Flying Pursuit) in October and Nottingham (by 1¼ lengths from Clem Fandango) in November: best up to 6.5f: acts on polytrack, fibresand, good to firm and heavy going: wears headgear: often races prominently. *Michael Easterby* **115**

PERFECT QUEST 4 br.f. Bushranger (IRE) 119 – Love Quest (Pursuit of Love 124) [2017 76: 10m* 10.2m* 11.4m^2 9.9m^6 p11g 10g Nov 3] smallish filly: fairly useful handicapper: won at Windsor in April and Chepstow (by 2 lengths from Rum Swizzle) in May: stays 1¼m: acts on good to firm and heavy going: has worn headgear: wears tongue tie. *Clive Cox* **87**

PERFECT SENSE 3 b.g. Sepoy (AUS) 129 – Miss Chicane 77 (Refuse To Bend (IRE) 128) [2017 6d^3 8m^5 6d^2 p7d^2 a6f^3 a8f Dec 15] fair maiden: stays 7f: acts on polytrack, sand, and good to soft going: in headgear last 4 starts. *Saeed bin Suroor* **78**

PERFECT SOLDIER (IRE) 3 b.g. Kodiac 112 – Independent Girl (IRE) 85 (Bachelor Duke (USA) 122) [2017 80: 6g^5 7g^2 7g^5 8.6s* 7.3s^2 9v 8.1v^2 t9.5d^2 Dec 27] fairly useful performer: won maiden at Galway in August: second in handicap (1¾ lengths behind Lucky Mistake) at Leopardstown in October: stays 9.5f: acts on tapeta and heavy going: usually in cheekpieces. *M. D. O'Callaghan, Ireland* **89**

PERFECT SPY 3 b.f. Nathaniel (IRE) 129 – Heavenly Whisper (IRE) 105 (Halling (USA) 133) [2017 10m^3 p10g^3 t9.5g^4 11.6d^6 t9.5m Oct 28] 65,000Y: half-sister to several winners, including 1m winner River Tiber (by Danehill) and 2-y-o 1m/8.6f winner Premier Banker (by Cape Cross), later successful abroad, both useful: dam 1m winner (including at 2 yrs) who stayed 10.4f: fair maiden: stays 1¼m: acts on good to firm going: usually races prominently. *Luca Cumani* **72**

PERFECT SUMMER (IRE) 7 b.m. High Chaparral (IRE) 132 – Power of Future (GER) 104 (Definite Article 121) [2017 83: t12.2g 14f 11.4d* p14s 16.3m 15.9v^2 16d^3 Oct 6] good-topped mare: fairly useful handicapper: won at Windsor in May: second at Chester in September and third at Ascot final start: stays 2m: acts on polytrack, good to firm and heavy going: wears headgear: front runner/races prominently. *Ian Williams* **82**

PERFECT SYMPHONY (IRE) 3 b.g. Dandy Man (IRE) 123 – Fields of Joy (GER) 89 (Waky Nao 122) [2017 80: 5m 5g^3 6g^2 7d 6s 6s^5 t6d^5 t6g^4 t7.2g t6.1g t7.2d Dec 26] fair handicapper: left Kevin Ryan after eighth start: stays 6f: acts on tapeta, soft and good to firm going: wears headgear: usually races nearer last than first. *Sophie Leech* **79**

PERFECT THOUGHT 2 ch.f. (Mar 23) Dawn Approach (IRE) 132 – Masaya 101 (Dansili 127) [2017 6d^4 6d^2 6m^3 p7g^2 7v^4 7d* Nov 4] 70,000Y: rather lightly-built filly: third foal: half-sister to 2-y-o 5f/6f winner Shamsaya (by Shamardal) and a winner abroad by Halling: dam 2-y-o 5f-7f winner: fair performer: won minor event at Newmarket in November: stays 7f: acts on polytrack, good to firm and good to soft going: front runner/races prominently. *William Haggas* **79**

PERFECT WORDS (IRE) 7 ch.g. Thousand Words 113 – Zilayah (USA) 79 (Zilzal (USA) 137) [2017 70: 6m^5 6g 5s^5 5s^2 5d* 5d^4 5s^4 5s* 6g^5 5g* 5s^3 5g 5g t5g Nov 3] fair handicapper: won at Ayr (amateur) in July and Catterick (twice) in August: stays 7f: acts on polytrack, tapeta, good to firm and heavy going: wears headgear: usually races towards rear. *Marjorie Fife* **75**

PERFORMANCE ART (IRE) 3 b.f. Art Connoisseur (IRE) 121 – Heroic Performer (IRE) (Royal Applause 124) [2017 51: 9.9d 9.9m^4 9d 8s^5 10s^4 11.9s Oct 10] small filly: fifth foal: half-sister to 1½m winner MacNicholson (by Definite Article) and 9f winner Camile (by Captain Rio): dam unraced half-sister to winner up to 13f Banksters Bonus and winner up to 11f Backbench Blues (both smart): poor maiden: in cheekpieces last 2 starts. *Seamus Mullins* **45**

PERICLES (IRE) 4 ch.g. Danehill Dancer (IRE) 117 – Althea Rose (IRE) (Green Desert (USA) 127) [2017 58: 7g Oct 17] neat gelding: modest maiden: well beaten only start in 2017: stays 7f: acts on fibresand and good to soft going: sent to Belgium. *Denis Quinn* **–**

PERLA BLANCA (USA) 3 gr.f. Dalakhani (IRE) 133 – Trend Line (IRE) 83 (Holy Roman Emperor (IRE) 125) [2017 50p: p11g^4 12g^2 p12g^3 11.5m^5 14d^2 14.2v^4 p12g^6 Oct 24] fair maiden handicapper: stays 1¾m: acts on polytrack and good to soft going: races towards rear. *Marcus Tregoning* **72**

PERMANENT 3 b.g. Invincible Spirit (IRE) 121 – Love Everlasting 112 (Pursuit of Love 124) [2017 63: 10m^6 9g^2 8g 10m^5 t10.2d 10d 9.8g^6 5s t6.1g p10.7g Dec 15] sturdy gelding: modest maiden: left Daniel Kubler after seventh start, Eric Alston after ninth: stays 9f: best form on good going: has worn headgear: inconsistent. *Brian Francis Cawley, Ireland* **63**

PERMIAN (IRE) 3 b.c. Teofilo (IRE) 126 – Tessa Reef (IRE) (Mark of Esteem (IRE) 137) [2017 103: 11.7m^3 10.1g^2 10m* 10.3d* 12m 12m* 11.9g^2 10f^6 Aug 12] tall, good-topped colt: smart performer: won listed race at Newmarket (by 4½ lengths from Speedo **117**

Betfred Dante Stakes, York—
Permian progresses still further, keeping on well to beat Benbatl and Crystal Ocean (left)

King Edward VII Stakes, Royal Ascot—Permian (rail) resumes winning ways just three weeks on from the Derby, sticking on well to beat Khalidi (second right) and Crystal Ocean (centre)

Boy) and Dante Stakes at York (by ¾ length from Benbatl) in May, and King Edward VII Stakes at Royal Ascot (by ½ length from Khalidi) in June: second in Grand Prix de Paris at Saint-Cloud (nose behind Shakeel) in July: suffered fatal injury in Secretariat Stakes at Arlington: stayed 1½m: acted on polytrack, good to firm and heavy going: raced prominently, often travelled strongly. *Mark Johnston*

PERMISSION 4 b.f. Authorized (IRE) 133 – Continua (USA) (Elusive Quality (USA)) [2017 98: 8m² 10.2g⁴ 8d⁵ 8d² 10m² 10d* Nov 4] useful performer: won listed race at Newmarket (by neck from Air Pilot) in November: stays 1¼m: acts on firm and good to soft going: has worn hood: often starts slowly, usually races nearer last than first. *James Fanshawe* **106**

PERNICKETY 4 b.f. Sir Percy 129 – Nicola Bella (IRE) 98 (Sadler's Wells (USA) 132) [2017 69: 9.9g* 9.9g² 9.9g 9.8m⁴ 11.5m⁵ 9.9m⁵ 11.5d⁵ p10s Sep 30] leggy filly: fair handicapper: won at Brighton in April: stays 12.5f: acts on polytrack and good to firm going: usually wears hood: has worn tongue tie, including last 2 starts: sometimes slowly away, often races towards rear. *Lucy Wadham* **76**

PERPETRATOR (IRE) 2 b.c. (May 17) Shamardal (USA) 129 – Palmeraie (USA) (Lear Fan (USA) 130) [2017 p8g Nov 7] 25/1, well held in minor event at Kempton. *Roger Charlton* **–**

PERSAVERANCE 4 b.g. Sir Percy 129 – Marliana (IRE) (Mtoto 134) [2017 65: 10g Oct 9] lengthy gelding: fair maiden: well beaten in claimer only start in 2017: stays 1½m: acts on polytrack and good to firm going: in blinkers last 2 starts. *Gary Moore* **–**

PERSHING 6 gr.g. Mount Nelson 125 – La Gandilie (FR) 106 (Highest Honor (FR) 124) [2017 –: 12s t12.2g⁵ p11g Oct 25] workmanlike gelding: modest maiden handicapper nowadays: stays 1½m: acts on polytrack, tapeta and good to firm going: usually wears headgear: has worn tongue tie: temperament under suspicion. *Kevin Frost* **63**

PERSIAN STEEL (IRE) 5 ch.g. Lucarno (USA) 121 – Persian Walk (FR) (Persian Bold 123) [2017 62: t12.4g* t12.4d⁵ t13.9m⁵ Mar 17] fair performer: won maiden at Newcastle in January: stays 12.5f: raced only on tapeta. *Brian Ellison* **78**

PERSISTENCE (IRE) 3 b.f. Invincible Spirit (IRE) 121 – Lady Glinka (IRE) (Galileo (IRE) 134) [2017 p8d⁴ 9.9m⁴ 9.9s³ 10.3v⁵ 10d³ p12g* Nov 17] first foal: dam unraced sister to very smart winner up to 2m Mikhail Glinka out of sister to Derby winner Sir Percy: fairly useful performer: won maiden at Lingfield (by length from Nurse Nightingale) in November: stays 1½m: acts on polytrack, soft and good to firm going: often travels strongly: sold 52,000 gns in December. *Ralph Beckett* **84**

PERSPICACE 6 b.g. Sir Percy 129 – Cassique Lady (IRE) 105 (Langfuhr (CAN) 124) [2017 –: t13.9m p16d Feb 8] fairly useful maiden, lightly raced and below best on Flat since 2014: stays 1½m: acts on polytrack, tapeta and good to firm going: in cheekpieces last 3 starts. *David Pipe* **67**

PERSUASIVE (IRE) 4 gr.f. Dark Angel (IRE) 113 – Choose Me (IRE) 109 (Choisir (AUS) 126) [2017 117: 8g⁵ 8d³ 8g² 8s* Oct 21] **123**

'It never worries me late in a year with a filly taking on colts because I think they go through hell in the spring and summer coming in and out of season—hormonally they are a bit like a boy growing up. They come to the autumn and everything is settled and they can focus on racing,' explained trainer John Gosden after Persuasive had landed something of a gamble in the Queen Elizabeth II Stakes at Ascot in late-October. This long-standing championship event for milers was moved in 2011 from its original September date to the revamped British Champions' Day end-of-season fixture staged some four weeks later. The early signs suggest it is that change of date, rather than the track used (now run on the straight mile instead of the round course), which has had the most significant impact on the race. Fillies have now won the last two editions thanks to Minding and Persuasive, having drawn a blank in the twenty-eight previous renewals. Three of the first five places were filled by fillies in the latest Queen Elizabeth II Stakes, with the outsiders Nathra (a stable-companion of Persuasive) and Sea of Grace excelling themselves in fourth and fifth respectively. Admittedly that doesn't quite match the dominance shown back in 1987, when Milligram led home a one, two, three, with top-notch fillies Miesque and Sonic Lady completing that trio in the first Queen Elizabeth II Stakes since its upgrading to Group 1 status. The 1987 result has been very much the exception to the rule in the race's long history—until now possibly!

John Gosden has enjoyed an embarrassment of riches in recent seasons with his fillies, particularly in the latest one when they provided seven of the trainer's top eleven money-earners on British soil in 2017. Pride of place went to the brilliant Enable, who posted her own career-best effort with victory in the Prix de l'Arc de Triomphe earlier in October, as did Persuasive and Nathra at Ascot three weeks later. Persuasive had raced against her own sex on all nine previous career starts and, at first glance, had seemed to have her limitations exposed. After going unbeaten on her first five starts (which included the 2016 Sandringham Handicap over the same course and distance as the Queen Elizabeth II Stakes), Persuasive had had to settle for minor honours on her first four outings in Group 1 company. Those statistics don't reveal the full picture, however, as Persuasive endured her fair share of hard-luck stories along the way until Ascot. She wasn't seen out as a four-year-old until the Prix Rothschild at Deauville in July, when she showed that she retained all her ability after an eleven-month absence; although she managed only fifth to Roly Poly (her only ever finish outside the frame), Persuasive met trouble in running several times. If anything, Persuasive's next start in the Matron Stakes at Leopardstown (in which she'd finished runner-up twelve months earlier) must have been even more frustrating for her connections as she came from an impossible position on the home turn and was closing hand over fist in the later stages, finishing a close third to the

Queen Elizabeth II Stakes (Sponsored by Qipco), Ascot—Persuasive copes best with the conditions and lands a gamble on her final start, recording a smooth victory over leading older miler Ribchester (noseband) and dual Guineas winner Churchill (striped cap); Persuasive's stable-companion Nathra completes the frame

Aidan O'Brien-trained pair Hydrangea and Winter. Admittedly the excuses weren't quite so obvious when Persuasive failed to justify short-priced favouritism in the Sun Chariot Stakes at Newmarket in October, finishing runner-up to old rival Roly Poly (only sixth at Leopardstown), though Persuasive was forced to check briefly at a vital stage behind a weakening rival as she waited for a gap to emerge.

The chances are that, to spark a late gamble, Persuasive had been working impressively at home before her tilt at the Queen Elizabeth II Stakes a fortnight after the Sun Chariot, though the rain-softened conditions (it was her first run on soft) might also have been something that favoured her. Having been available at 33/1 on the morning of the race, she was backed down to 8/1 at the off, while 50/1-shot Nathra, who had finished just a length and a quarter behind Persuasive in third at Newmarket remained virtually friendless. Hot favourite, though, was 2016 runner-up Ribchester, with the progressive Beat The Bank and dual Guineas winner Churchill next in the betting. Beat The Bank failed to fire despite some pre-race divine intervention—his connections' decision to bless him with 'holy water' beforehand landed them in hot water with the BHA afterwards—but the other two market principals both figured prominently at the business end of the race (albeit neither was probably at his very best). It briefly looked as if Persuasive might be the subject of another hard-luck story when Frankie Dettori was forced to switch over two furlongs out after being trapped behind runners, though this particular interference was arguably a blessing in disguise as the other principals seemed guilty of making their challenges a shade too soon in the conditions (there was a strong headwind too). Persuasive kept on very strongly once in the clear and was always in command after overhauling the favourite a furlong out, with Dettori able to start celebrating several strides from the line—Persuasive won by a length from Ribchester, with a further half length back to Churchill in third and Nathra another neck away. It was a sixth Queen Elizabeth II Stakes win for Dettori and a third for Gosden, though it was the first one in which they had teamed up. It will be the only Queen Elizabeth II Stakes win for Persuasive, though, as she has been retired to stud.

Persuasive (IRE) (gr.f. 2013)	Dark Angel (IRE) (gr 2005)	Acclamation (b 1999)	Royal Applause
			Princess Athena
		Midnight Angel (gr 1994)	Machiavellian
			Night At Sea
	Choose Me (IRE) (ch 2006)	Choisir (ch 1999)	Danehill Dancer
			Great Selection
		Hecuba (ch 2000)	Hector Protector
			Ajuga

Persuasive isn't the only female member of her family to have beaten the colts in a prestigious late-season prize. The 1980 Champion Stakes winner Cairn Rouge (who had won the Irish One Thousand Guineas and Coronation Stakes earlier that year) is Persuasive's fourth dam, who has featured in plenty of 'black type' since then. The smart middle-distance performer Prolix, who tasted Group 3 success on British soil for Barry Hills before becoming a very prolific winner once exported to Saudi Arabia, was a half-brother to Persuasive's grandam Hecuba, who was a fairly useful ten-furlong winner for Hills but went on to achieve even greater success as a broodmare. The two highest-quality performers so far among Hecuba's winning offspring are the smart sprinter Shanghai Glory and the useful Irish mare Choose Me, who landed the very valuable Tattersalls Ireland Sale Stakes as a two-year-old before being placed in Group 2 company later in her career, proving herself effective at up to eleven furlongs. The early signs suggest that Choose Me is another member of the family who may do even better at stud. Persuasive is her second foal and her two other representatives to reach the track to date have also proved above-average performers and, tellingly, very durable ones too. Amazour (by Azamour) is a useful six- and seven-furlong performer for Ismail Mohammed who won at Doncaster in September and showed himself as good as ever, having just turned six, when winning on the all-weather early in 2018. Persuasive's year-younger half-sister Tisbutadream (by Dream Ahead) enjoyed a stellar campaign of her own in 2017, winning no fewer than five times over a mile , including a listed race at Sandown, and also finishing placed on a further five occasions (including three times in Group 3 company), progressing through the ranks so rapidly and changing hands for £400,000 midway through the season. Choose Me has since produced the 2015 filly Improve (by Iffraaj), as yet unraced, and the 2016 colt Songkran (by Slade Power), who fetched €150,000 and €100,000 respectively as yearlings.

The good-topped Persuasive was a strong-travelling sort who raced only at a mile, though her pedigree suggests she might have stayed a bit further if required, as did her Ascot performance in testing ground. She never raced on firmer than good, though won both of her races on polytrack and proved as consistent as her two siblings. She had looked an excellent broodmare prospect even prior to the Queen Elizabeth II Stakes and seems sure to do well in her new career as a member of the Cheveley Park broodmare band. *John Gosden*

PERSUN 5 ch.m. Sir Percy 129 – Sunley Shines (Komaite (USA)) [2017 92: t12.2m^{4} p11g* t16.3g^{5} Mar 3] sparely-made mare: fairly useful handicapper: won at Kempton (by head from Alcatraz) in February: stayed 1½m: acted on polytrack, tapeta, soft and good to firm going: dead. *Mick Channon* **87**

PERTUIS (IRE) 11 gr.g. Verglas (IRE) 118 – Lady Killeen (IRE) 60 (Marju (IRE) 127) [2017 69: 12g t12.4d 14v Nov 7] angular gelding: fair handicapper: below form in 2017: stayed 2m: acted on polytrack, viscoride, good to firm and heavy going: often wore headgear: sometimes slowly away, often raced towards rear: dead. *Micky Hammond* **55**

PESCEDORA (IRE) 2 b.f. (Jan 28) So You Think (NZ) 133 – Poisson d'Or 90 (Cape Cross (IRE) 129) [2017 8.3d 8.3d 8s p7g Nov 17] first foal: dam, 7f winner, out of smart winner up to 1¾m Lille Hammer: fair form: best effort at 8.5f. *Roger Charlton* **69**

PETERHOUSE (USA) 5 ch.g. Elusive Quality (USA) – Dynaire (USA) (Dynaformer (USA)) [2017 84, a78: 12.1m^{3} 12g^{4} 10g^{5} 11.9m^{3} 12d^{4} 14g^{5} 12.1g^{3} 10v^{2} 12.1v Oct 21] fairly useful handicapper: third at York (apprentice) in June and Beverley in August: stays 1½m: acts on polytrack, good to firm and heavy going: has worn headgear, including in 2017: sometimes slowly away, usually races towards rear, often travels strongly: sold 22,000 gns in November. *Jason Ward* **81**

PETER LEONARD 2 b.g. (Feb 25) Kyllachy 129 – Nardin 92 (Royal Applause 124) [2017 6g 5d^{4} 5.4g 6s Oct 10] little form: tried in blinkers. *Richard Fahey* **–**

PETER PARK 4 b.g. Kheleyf (USA) 116 – Go Go Girl 74 (Pivotal 124) [2017 78: 6s^{3} 5.7s^{4} p6g Oct 18] compact gelding: fair handicapper: stays 6.5f: acts on soft and good to firm going: often races towards rear. *Clive Cox* **78**

PETERPORT 3 b.c. Nathaniel (IRE) 129 – Spinning Queen 118 (Spinning World (USA) 130) [2017 10s^{6} p12d^{4} May 31] well-made colt: closely related to useful 11f/1½m winner (stayed 14.6f) Gallipot (by Galileo) and half-brother to several winners, including smart 1m-1¼m winner Trade Commissioner (by Montjeu): dam 6f (at 2 yrs) to 1m (Sun Chariot Stakes) winner: fairly useful form: fourth in maiden at Kempton (5¼ lengths behind Zubayr): open to further improvement. *John Gosden* **80 p**

PETERS FOLLY 4 ch.f. Captain Gerrard (IRE) 113 – Lipica (IRE) 99 (Night Shift (USA)) [2017 t8.6g^{5} p8d^{6} p8g Dec 28] £1,000Y: half-sister to 3 winners, including useful 9.5f/1¼m winner Colour Scheme (by Peintre Celebre) and winner up to 7f Chevise (2-y-o 5f/6f winner, by Holy Roman Emperor): dam 2-y-o 7f winner: mid-division at best in maidens: wears hood. *Peter Hiatt* **–**

PETER STUYVESANT (IRE) 3 b.g. Elusive City (USA) 117 – Dream For Life (FR) (Oasis Dream 129) [2017 p8g p8g^{6} 8.1m t9.5g p7g Dec 30] rather leggy gelding: modest maiden: stays 1m: acts on polytrack and good to firm going: tried in visor: usually races prominently. *Denis Coakley* **55**

PETE SO HIGH (GER) 3 b.g. High Chaparral (IRE) 132 – Paulaya (GER) (Peintre Celebre (USA) 137) [2017 82p: t9.5m* p14g^{4} 14g^{5} 13f^{2} 11.6d^{4} 11.6f^{3} 12d* 12.1g^{3} 11.6d* 11.9g* Sep 3] sturdy gelding: fairly useful performer: won maiden at Wolverhampton in January, and handicaps at Ripon and Lingfield in August, and Brighton (by 1¼ lengths from Inconceivable) in September: stays 1¾m: acts on polytrack, tapeta, firm and good to soft going: wears cheekpieces: has joined Gordon Elliott, Ireland. *Richard Hannon* **88**

PETICOATGOVERNMENT (IRE) 4 b.f. Holy Roman Emperor (IRE) 125 – Fotini (IRE) (King's Best (USA) 132) [2017 91: p7g^{5} 5d^{3} 5.8m* 6m* 6d^{2} 6s^{6} 6g^{3} 6g^{5} 6g^{5} 5.8v Oct 8] third foal: closely related to a winner in Sweden by Rock of Gibraltar: dam unraced half-sister to smart Italian miler Spirit of Desert: useful performer: won handicaps at Navan **99**

in April and Cork in May: second in similar event at the Curragh (¾ length behind Rattling Jewel) later in May: stays 7f: acts on polytrack, soft and good to firm going: tried in hood: often travels strongly. *W. McCreery, Ireland*

PETITE JACK 4 ch.g. Champs Elysees 124 – Pilcomayo (IRE) (Rahy (USA) 115) [2017 **102**
93: p12g* t12.4g^2 p12g* p15.8g 12m 10.1g^2 12d p10s* p10d^6 p10g^4 p10g^2 p10g* Dec 23] **a109**
sturdy gelding: useful performer: won handicaps at Lingfield in January (by 1½ lengths from Dolphin Village) and March (by 1½ lengths from Masterpaver), and Chelmsford (by ½ length from Abdon) in September, and listed race at Lingfield (by neck from Mia Tesoro) in December: left Neil King after fourth start: stays 12.5f: acts on polytrack and tapeta: wears headgear. *Archie Watson*

PETIT FILOUS 3 b.g. Equiano (FR) 127 – Haiti Dancer 64 (Josr Algarhoud (IRE) 118) **66**
[2017 63: p8g^4 8s^6 9.9m 9.9f t9.5g Nov 7] fair maiden handicapper: stays 1m: acts on polytrack and tapeta: tried in tongue tie: has joined Michael Wigham. *Giles Bravery*

PETITIONER (IRE) 3 b.g. Dansili 127 – Reflective (USA) (Seeking The Gold (USA)) **93 p**
[2017 t12.2g^3 p12s* 12s^2 Jul 28] fourth foal: half-brother to smart 1½m-1¾m winner (stayed 2¼m) Biographer (by Montjeu): dam unraced close relative to 1000 Guineas winner Bosra Sham and Poule d'Essai des Poulains winner Hector Protector: fairly useful form: won maiden at Kempton (by head from Qaviy Cash) in June: second in handicap at Newmarket (¾ length behind The Grand Visir) final start: raced only at 1½m: should still improve. *Roger Charlton*

PETIT PALAIS 2 ch.c. (Mar 10) Champs Elysees 124 – Galicuix (Galileo (IRE) 134) **64 p**
[2017 8.3g^6 Nov 1] 220,000Y: third foal: half-brother to 2000 Guineas winner Galileo Gold (6f/7f winner at 2 yrs) and 2-y-o 7f winner Choumicha (both by Paco Boy): dam twice-raced half-sister to very smart sprinter Goldream: 14/1, sixth in maiden at Nottingham (9½ lengths behind Come On Tier): should do better. *John Gosden*

PETRA'S PONY (IRE) 2 b.g. (Apr 2) Big Bad Bob (IRE) 118 – Gabriellina Klon (IRE) **–**
(Ashkalani (IRE) 128) [2017 7s 7d Aug 18] well held in maiden/minor event. *Brian Meehan*

PETRIFY 7 b.g. Rock of Gibraltar (IRE) 133 – Frigid (Indian Ridge 123) [2017 61: 11.7f* **63**
13f 11.6f^6 12g^4 12.1s^3 14.2g^6 16s Sep 19] modest handicapper: won at Bath in May: stays 13f: acts on polytrack, firm and good to soft going: wears cheekpieces/tongue tie: usually slowly away/races towards rear. *Bernard Llewellyn*

PETRUCCI (IRE) 5 b.g. Azamour (IRE) 130 – Spring Symphony (IRE) 94 (Darshaan **–**
133) [2017 87: t9.5m 11.9d Jul 1] fairly useful at best, has lost his way: stays 1¼m: acts on polytrack: sometimes in headgear: tried in tongue tie: sometimes slowly away: modest maiden hurdler. *Derek Shaw*

PETRUS (IRE) 2 b.c. (Apr 26) Zoffany (IRE) 121 – Ambrosine 81 (Nashwan (USA) 135) **99**
[2017 6.5g^4 7m* 8d^4 8m^4 Oct 14] €65,000F, £35,000Y: sturdy colt: seventh foal: half-brother to 2-y-o 6f winner Cat Patrol (by One Cool Cat): dam, 1¼m-1½m winner, half-sister to useful/ungenuine winner up to 1½m Camrose: useful form: won minor event at Sandown in July: fourth in Autumn Stakes (4½ lengths behind Ghaiyyath) at Newmarket final start: will stay 1¼m+. *Brian Meehan*

PETTOCHSIDE 8 b.g. Refuse To Bend (IRE) 128 – Clear Impression (IRE) 103 **99**
(Danehill (USA) 126) [2017 85: 6m^5 6m 6g^3 5g^2 5d* 6g^4 5.1g^3 5d^2 5g^6 6d 6.1s 5v* 5s 6s* 6d^3 p6g Nov 6] strong gelding: useful handicapper: won at Salisbury in June, Ascot in September and Goodwood (by neck from Baron Bolt) in October: effective at 5f/6f: acts on polytrack, good to firm and heavy going: has worn tongue tie: front runner/races prominently. *John Bridger*

PEVERIL POINT (IRE) 2 b.c. (Apr 11) Canford Cliffs (IRE) 133 – Galeaza (Galileo **–**
(IRE) 134) [2017 7d Jul 26] 200/1, well held in minor event at Lingfield. *Henry Tett*

PHALABORWA 3 b.f. Poet's Voice 126 – Sigurwana (USA) 78 (Arch (USA) 127) [2017 **91**
78: 7g 7f^5 t7.2g* p7d^3 p7g^6 p7s Dec 1] useful-looking filly: fairly useful handicapper: won at Wolverhampton (by 1¼ lengths from Nostalgie) in July: raced only at 7f: acts on polytrack, tapeta and firm going: front runner/races prominently: sold 35,000 gns in December. *Ed Vaughan*

PHANTASMIC 2 b.f. (Apr 29) Frankel 147 – Diary (IRE) (Green Desert (USA) 127) **– p**
[2017 p8s Nov 16] 675,000Y: half-sister to several winners, including very smart 5f/6f (including at 2 yrs) winner Total Gallery (by Namid) and useful 1½m/13f winner Tempest Fugit (by High Chaparral): dam 7f winner in Greece: 12/1, well held in minor event at Chelmsford: should do better. *Sir Michael Stoute*

PHAROH JAKE 9 ch.g. Piccolo 121 – Rose Amber (Double Trigger (IRE) 123) [2017 70: p5g^3 p5m^4 p6g^2 p5g^4 p5g^5 p5f^2 p5g^5 5g^4 p5g^6 p5g^6 p5g^6 Dec 31] smallish gelding: modest handicapper: stays 6f: acts on polytrack and heavy going: tried in visor. *John Bridger* **64**

PHEBES DREAM (IRE) 4 b.f. Roderic O'Connor (IRE) 119 – Alexander Family (IRE) 65 (Danetime (IRE) 121) [2017 59: 10d^3 Jul 25] third foal: half-sister to 2-y-o 6f winner Lucky Suit (by Red Clubs): dam 7f winner: modest maiden handicapper: stays 1¼m: acts on polytrack, good to firm and good to soft going: wears hood: races towards rear. *John McConnell, Ireland* **58**

PHEIDIPPIDES 2 ch.c. (Mar 3) Sepoy (AUS) 129 – Bounty Box 115 (Bahamian Bounty 116) [2017 6.1m 6.1g^3 Jul 21] strong colt: fair form: better effort when third in maiden at Nottingham (½ length behind First Drive) second start. *Tom Clover* **76**

PHIJEE 3 gr.c. Sepoy (AUS) 129 – Likeable (Dalakhani (IRE) 133) [2017 104p: 7m^6 Aug 27] angular colt: useful 6f winner at 2 yrs, stiff task only start in 2017. *William Muir* **–**

PHILAMUNDO (IRE) 2 b.g. (Mar 29) Sir Prancealot (IRE) 111 – Rublevka Star (USA) 77 (Elusive Quality (USA)) [2017 6m 6g p7g p6g t7.2g^4 Nov 29] fair maiden: stays 7f: acts on tapeta: usually races nearer last than first. *Richard Spencer* **65**

PHILBA 5 b.g. Cockney Rebel (IRE) 127 – Hisaronu (IRE) 75 (Stravinsky (USA) 133) [2017 103: f7g^3 7m 7m May 26] useful handicapper: third at Southwell (3¼ lengths behind Holiday Magic) in January: left Michael Appleby after: stays 1m: acts on fibresand and good to firm going: usually wears headgear/tongue tie: has joined David Evans. *David Lanigan* **96**

PHILLIMORE 2 b.f. (Apr 28) Invincible Spirit (IRE) 121 – Chibola (ARG) (Roy (USA)) [2017 p6s Jun 13] fourth foal: sister to smart 6f-1¼m winner Muntadab and half-sister to useful 1¼m winner Dubai Horizon (by Poet's Voice): dam Argentinian Group 3 7f winner: 14/1, well held in minor event at Lingfield. *Richard Hannon* **– p**

PHOENICIAN STAR (IRE) 2 ch.g. (May 3) Mastercraftsman (IRE) 129 – Place de L'Etoile (IRE) (Sadler's Wells (USA) 132) [2017 8d Oct 27] 33/1, well held in minor event at Newbury. *Brian Meehan* **–**

PHOENIX DAWN 3 b.g. Phoenix Reach (IRE) 124 – Comtesse Noire (CAN) 67 (Woodman (USA) 126) [2017 72: 10.2g 9.9m^2 12m^3 14.2g^2 11.8d Sep 12] workmanlike gelding: fair handicapper: likely to stay 2m: acts on good to firm going: has worn cheekpieces, including in 2017: front runner/races prominently: fairly useful hurdler. *Brendan Powell* **76**

PHOENIX LIGHTNING (IRE) 2 b.c. (Apr 20) Lawman (FR) 121 – Royal Fizz (IRE) (Royal Academy (USA) 130) [2017 6m^3 5.9m^3 7.2d^2 6.3s 7v t7.2g^6 Dec 22] fair maiden: left Richard Fahey after fifth start: stays 7f: acts on good to firm and good to soft going: in cheekpieces last 3 starts: sometimes slowly away. *Rebecca Menzies* **79**

PHOSPHORESCENCE (IRE) 7 b.g. Sakhee (USA) 136 – Eccentricity (USA) 75 (Kingmambo (USA) 125) [2017 77: 8m* p8s^2 8m Aug 1] fairly useful handicapper: won at Yarmouth (by short head from Harlequin Rock) in April: second at Kempton (apprentice, 1¼ lengths behind Believe It) in June: stays 1½m: acts on polytrack and good to firm going: usually in headgear. *George Scott* **83**

PHOTOGRAPHER 2 b.c. (Mar 27) New Approach (IRE) 132 – Approach 105 (Darshaan 133) [2017 p10d* Nov 9] closely related to very smart winner up to 1¼m/St Leger runner-up Midas Touch (2-y-o 7f winner) and useful 1¼m winner Murgan (both by Galileo) and half-brother to 3 winners, including smart winner up to 1½m (Ribblesdale Stakes) Coronet (2-y-o 1m/1¼m winner, by Dubawi): dam winner up to 1¼m (2-y-o 7.5f winner) who stayed 1½m: 7/4, won minor event at Chelmsford (by 1¼ lengths from Silverbook) in November: will stay 1½m: sure to progress. *John Gosden* **88 p**

PHOTONICS (IRE) 2 b.g. (Apr 9) Power 117 – Naval Affair (IRE) 101 (Last Tycoon 131) [2017 t8s^2 7.9g t8g^6 t8g Dec 6] good-topped gelding: fair form: raced only at 1m. *Hugo Palmer* **68**

PHYSICAL POWER (IRE) 2 b.f. (Apr 3) Power 117 – Street Shaana (FR) 111 (Darshaan 133) [2017 8s p8g t8.6g^3 Nov 29] £60,000Y: half-sister to 3 winners, including 11.6f winner Yeah Baby (by Danehill Dancer) and French 12.5f winner Sourabad (by Halling): dam, French 10.5f-15f winner, half-sister to smart 1½m-15.5f winner Stretarez: fair form: best effort when third in minor event at Wolverhampton (2¼ lengths behind Ghanimah) final start: will stay 1¼m. *Richard Hannon* **73**

PHYSICIST (IRE) 3 b.g. Galileo (IRE) 134 – Impressionist Art (USA) 70 (Giant's Causeway (USA) 132) [2017 70p: p12g^2 t12.2g Apr 29] fair form: much better effort in 2017 when second in maiden at Lingfield in April: tried in hood. *Paul Cole* **74**

PIAFFE (USA) 3 b.f. Successful Appeal (USA) 118 – Palisade (USA) 87 (Gone West (USA)) [2017 –: p10g^5 8m Apr 25] little impact in maidens: sent to Turkey. *Jane Chapple-Hyam* **–**

PIAZON 6 br.g. Striking Ambition 122 – Colonel's Daughter 61 (Colonel Collins (USA) 122) [2017 90§: f5g^2 f5g* f5g* 5d^5 f5g* f5g f5g^6 f5g^6 Dec 29] good-topped gelding: fairly useful performer: won 3 times at Southwell in 2017, claimer in February, seller in March and handicap (by ½ length from Treaty of Rome) in October: stays 6f: acts on polytrack, fibresand, soft and good to firm going: wears headgear: tried in tongue tie: not straightforward (tends to hang left). *John Butler* **89 §**

PICANSORT 10 b.g. Piccolo 121 – Running Glimpse (IRE) 84 (Runnett 125) [2017 62, a79: p6g p5g^2 p5m^5 p5f^3 p5g^2 6d^3 p5g^4 5.3g^2 p5g Oct 5] good-topped gelding: fair handicapper: stays 6f: acts on polytrack, good to firm and good to soft going: usually wears headgear: tried in tongue tie: often races in rear. *Peter Crate* **68**

PICC AND GO 4 b.f. Piccolo 121 – Just Down The Road (IRE) 71 (Night Shift (USA)) [2017 5.7m^6 5f^4 6.1m 5.1g 5.7s Sep 17] fourth foal: closely related to 6f winner Local Diktator (by Diktat) and half-sister to 2-y-o 5f winner Jawking (by Compton Place): dam 6f winner: modest maiden: best effort at 5f: acts on firm going. *Matthew Salaman* **52**

PICCOLA COLLINA (IRE) 2 b.f. (Jan 11) Dubawi (IRE) 129 – La Collina (IRE) 115 (Strategic Prince 114) [2017 7d Jul 20] 625,000F: first foal: dam winner up to 1m (2-y-o 6f/7f winner), including Phoenix Stakes and Matron Stakes: 9/4, seventh in maiden at Doncaster (9 lengths behind Laurens): will improve. *Charlie Appleby* **62 p**

PICCOLA POPPY 4 br.f. Piccolo 121 – Waraqa (USA) 76 (Red Ransom (USA)) [2017 –: 7d 8g May 23] little sign of ability: tried in visor. *John Bridger* **–**

PICCOLINO 3 b.f. Piccolo 121 – Miacarla 67 (Forzando 122) [2017 –: t8.6g 6d Jun 5] no form: tried in cheekpieces. *John David Riches* **–**

PICCOLORO 3 b.g. Piccolo 121 – Spanish Gold 82 (Vettori (IRE) 119) [2017 t12.2g^5 10m p8g May 4] good-topped gelding: no form, including in juvenile hurdle. *Jonathan Portman* **–**

PICHOLA DANCE (IRE) 3 ch.f. Distorted Humor (USA) 117 – Liffey Dancer (IRE) (Sadler's Wells (USA) 132) [2017 90: 7m 6.1g 6.9s^6 Jun 28] lengthy filly: fairly useful performer: stays 7f: acts on polytrack, soft and good to firm going: tried in blinkers: often races prominently: sent to France. *Roger Varian* **86**

PICK A LITTLE 9 b.g. Piccolo 121 – Little Caroline (IRE) (Great Commotion (USA) 123) [2017 77: 8.1d^5 7m^5 8.1m^4 8m^2 8g 8s^2 8v* p8g^6 Nov 7] close-coupled gelding: fair handicapper: won at Brighton in October: stays 1m: acts on polytrack, fibresand and any turf going: tried in cheekpieces: usually races close up. *Michael Blake* **73**

PICKET LINE 5 b.g. Multiplex 114 – Dockside Strike (Docksider (USA) 124) [2017 82: p6g t6g^6 p7g^3 p7g 6g* 6m 6.1v^4 6.1m p6g^6 5.7g^3 6.1s 6s Sep 8] good-topped gelding: fairly useful handicapper: won at Windsor (apprentice, by nose from Viva Verglas) in May: stays 7f: acts on polytrack, tapeta, good to firm and heavy going: in cheekpieces last 3 starts. *Geoffrey Deacon* **80**

PICKETT'S CHARGE 4 b.g. Clodovil (IRE) 116 – Chelsea Morning (USA) 80 (Giant's Causeway (USA) 132) [2017 76: t8g* t8g t8d 8g 8.3g t7.1d 8g^6 t8g^5 8.3g^4 Nov 1] fair handicapper: won at Newcastle in January: stays 1¼m: acts on tapeta and good to firm going: usually in headgear in 2017. *Richard Guest* **68 a77**

PICK OF ANY (IRE) 4 b.g. Zoffany (IRE) 121 – Choice Pickings (IRE) (Among Men (USA) 124) [2017 68: p7d^3 t6f* f6g^4 p6g^4 t6g^2 t7.1g^5 6g p6d^6 9.9g 6.3s Aug 20] modest handicapper: won at Wolverhampton (apprentice) in February: second at same course in March: had various trainers in 2017: stays 7f: acts on polytrack, tapeta and soft going: has worn hood, including usually in 2017: tried in tongue tie: usually races in rear. *Brian Francis Cawley, Ireland* **61**

PICKS PINTA 6 b.g. Piccolo 121 – Past 'N' Present (Cadeaux Genereux 131) [2017 73: 6m^5 6g 7f^3 5.9g^3 5g^2 7.2d 5.9s^4 6d t6.1g^4 Dec 18] fair handicapper: stays 7f: acts on polytrack, firm and soft going: often wears headgear. *John David Riches* **68**

PICTURE DEALER 8 b.g. Royal Applause 124 – Tychy 102 (Suave Dancer (USA) 136) [2017 78: t6m p6g 6m* 6g t6.1g 6m p6g p6g Oct 24] fair handicapper: won at Yarmouth in May: raced mainly over 6f: acts on polytrack, firm and soft going: has worn tongue tie: sometimes slowly away. *Lydia Pearce* **78 a68**

PICTURE NO SOUND (IRE) 2 b.c. (Mar 29) Dark Angel (IRE) 113 – Little Audio (IRE) (Shamardal (USA) 129) [2017 6.5m^{4} 6.1g^{4} 5.9s^{4} 7g^{5} 6.5d* Oct 27] second foal: dam unraced half-sister to smart winner up to 2m (Queen's Vase) Sword Fighter: fairly useful performer: won maiden at Newbury (by 2¾ lengths from George of Hearts) in October: should stay beyond 6.5f: acts on good to soft going: has joined D. Watson in UAE. *Richard Fahey* **88**

PICTURE PAINTER (IRE) 4 gr.g. Zoffany (IRE) 121 – Sisceal (Dalakhani (IRE) 133) [2017 75: 10m^{5} 13.1s^{3} 12.5g^{3} 14g^{5} 13d Aug 4] modest maiden handicapper: stays 1¾m: acts on heavy going: has worn headgear: fairly useful form over hurdles for Keith Dalgleish. *Jim Goldie* **60**

PIEDITA (IRE) 3 b.f. Authorized (IRE) 133 – Archina (IRE) 69 (Arch (USA) 127) [2017 62p: 12.1m^{3} 16.1d* 16.3d* p16g^{2} Aug 31] tall, good-topped filly: fairly useful handicapper: won at Beverley in July and Lingfield in August: stays 16.5f: acts on polytrack, good to firm and good to soft going: should still progress. *Sir Mark Prescott Bt* **92 p**

PILASTER 2 b.f. (Apr 19) Nathaniel (IRE) 129 – Portal 108 (Hernando (FR) 127) [2017 8d Oct 27] closely related to winner up to 11.5f Castellated (2-y-o 1¼m winner, by Teofilo) and half-sister to several winners, including smart winner up to 1½m Windshear (2-y-o 1m winner, by Hurricane Run) and useful 1¼m winner Palisade (by Fastnet Rock): dam winner up to 1¼m (2-y-o 7f winner): 10/1, seventh in maiden at Doncaster (9¾ lengths behind Mrs Sippy) in October: will do better. *Roger Varian* **63 p**

PILGRIM SOUL 2 b.f. (Jan 20) Yeats (IRE) 128 – Sabah 91 (Nashwan (USA) 135) [2017 p8d^{5} Nov 22] sixth foal: sister to 1½m-2m winner Rose Above and closely related to useful 1m winner Roserrow (by Beat Hollow): dam, 1m winner, half-sister to smart 6f-1m winner Vanderlin: 66/1, fifth in minor event at Kempton (8¾ lengths behind Tanseeq) in November: will stay 1¼m: sure to progress. *Andrew Balding* **59 p**

PILGRIM'S TREASURE (USA) 3 b.c. Dubawi (IRE) 129 – La Pelegrina (USA) (Redoute's Choice (AUS)) [2017 8m^{5} 10g^{3} 9v* 10m^{2} 10v^{6} a8f^{5} Dec 29] second foal: brother to useful 2-y-o 7f winner Albernathy: dam, placed up to 9.5f in France, sister to very smart Australian Group 1 6f-12.5f winner Miss Finland: useful performer: won maiden at Carlisle in June: left Charlie Appleby, appeared to run well at Jebel Ali final start: stays 1¼m: acts on sand, good to firm and heavy going: sometimes in cheekpieces. *S. Seemar, UAE* **100 ?**

PILKINGTON 2 ch.g. (Apr 28) Helmet (AUS) 127 – Aroundthebay 89 (Diktat 126) [2017 t5s* 5m 5.4g^{6} 6g Oct 7] good-topped gelding: has scope: second foal: dam, 6f winner (including at 2 yrs), half-sister to useful 2-y-o 5f/6f winner Bathwick Bear and to dam of July Cup winner Mayson: fairly useful form: won minor event at Newcastle (by neck from Sosian) in June: best effort at 5f. *David O'Meara* **82**

PILLAR 4 b.g. Rock of Gibraltar (IRE) 133 – Ceilidh House 107 (Selkirk (USA) 129) [2017 67: p7g t6g p6g^{5} p6g^{3} t6m^{2} p7g^{3} p5g^{2} 5m* 5m^{6} p6g^{3} 5g^{6} 6m^{3} 5m^{2} 5g^{2} 6g 5m 6g 5d^{2} 5d^{2} 5g^{4} a6g 5.8v^{5} 5v^{3} p5g^{2} Nov 3] fair handicapper: won at Navan in April: third at same course in October: races mainly at 5f/6f nowadays: acts on polytrack, tapeta, good to firm and heavy going: has worn headgear. *Adrian McGuinness, Ireland* **70**

PILLARD (FR) 5 b.g. Muhaymin (USA) 89 – Ultime Moment (IRE) (Anabaa (USA) 130) [2017 68: p11g^{3} p12g Dec 15] fair maiden: left Jonjo O'Neill after first start: stays 1½m: acts on polytrack: tried in headgear/tongue tie. *Paul Hennessy, Ireland* **75**

PILLAR OF SOCIETY (IRE) 3 b.g. Roderic O'Connor (IRE) 119 – Specific (IRE) 72 (Dubawi (IRE) 129) [2017 84: 8m^{6} p8g^{2} 8.1d* 8f^{2} 8d* 8g^{5} 7d Sep 13] useful-looking gelding: useful handicapper: won at Windsor in June and Newmarket (by ½ length from Don't Give Up) in July: stays 1m: acts on polytrack, firm and good to soft going: front runner: sold 26,000 gns, sent to UAE. *Richard Hannon* **97**

PINDARIC 3 ch.g. Poet's Voice 126 – Hunter's Fortune (USA) (Charismatic (USA) 127) [2017 65: 7.5m 9.9g 8s^{5} 9m t10.2d 8.5s 10d^{2} f8.1g f11.1g Dec 29] modest maiden handicapper: stays 1¼m: acts on good to soft going: often in cheekpieces. *Alan Lockwood* **59**

PINK PHANTOM 2 b.f. (Mar 11) Oasis Dream 129 – Pink Symphony 109 (Montjeu (IRE) 137) [2017 8s p8g^{5} Nov 8] second foal: half-sister to 1¼m winner African (by Dubawi): dam, 1¼m-1½m winner, closely related to smart winner up to 9.5f Fantasia: fair form: better effort when fifth in minor event at Kempton (3½ lengths behind Espadrille) second start: open to further improvement. *Paul Cole* **69 p**

PINK RIBBON (IRE) 5 gr.g. Dark Angel (IRE) 113 – My Funny Valentine (IRE) 105 (Mukaddamah (USA) 125) [2017 76: 10s 9.1g^{2} 10g 8s 9.9g^{4} 10.1m^{4} 9.9d^{5} p10g p10m^{2} t9.5g* p10g p10s^{6} p10g^{4} Dec 30] lengthy gelding: fair handicapper: won at Wolverhampton (apprentice) in December: stays 1¼m: acts on polytrack, tapeta, good to firm and heavy going: usually wears cheekpieces: often races prominently. *Sylvester Kirk* **73**

PINNATA (IRE) 3 b.g. Shamardal (USA) 129 – Lavande Violet (GER) (Hurricane Run (IRE) 134) [2017 p10g^{4} t12.2m^{4} 10g 8.1m* 8.5d p8g^{2} p8s* p10s^{2} Dec 14] €720,000Y, £8,000 2-y-o: second foal: dam, German 7.5f winner, half-sister to Prix du Jockey Club winner Lope de Vega (by Shamardal): fairly useful performer: won minor event at Chepstow in June and handicap at Chelmsford (by neck from Carnival King) in November: second in handicap at latter course final start: stays 1¼m: acts on polytrack and good to firm going: wears tongue tie. *Stuart Williams* **87**

PINWOOD (IRE) 4 b.g. Bushranger (IRE) 119 – Anne Bonney 58 (Jade Robbery (USA) 121) [2017 79: p13g* p16d^{3} p13g^{2} f14m^{5} p12g^{6} Apr 5] fairly useful handicapper: won at Lingfield in January: second at same course in February: stayed 2m, was effective at shorter: acted on polytrack and soft going: tried in cheekpieces: wore tongue tie: keen sort, often led: dead. *Adam West* **80**

PINZOLO 6 b.g. Monsun (GER) 124 – Pongee 110 (Barathea (IRE) 127) [2017 110: p12m* p10m^{2} p15.8g 12m^{3} May 6] strong, good-topped gelding: smart performer: won handicap at Lingfield (by ½ length from Rock Steady) in January: second in Winter Derby at same course (neck behind Convey) in February: stays 1¾m: acts on polytrack, good to firm and good to soft going: has worn headgear: usually leads. *Ismail Mohammed* **110**

PIONEERING (IRE) 3 b.g. Shamardal (USA) 129 – Oregon Trail (USA) (Gone West (USA)) [2017 66: 8g 8.2g^{4} 8.5m^{6} 8.3g^{2} 8d 9.9m* 8.5v* 8v* Oct 9] useful handicapper: won at Beverley in August/September and Pontefract (by 1½ lengths from Trinity Star) in October: stays 1¼m: acts on good to firm and heavy going. *David O'Meara* **95**

PIONEER SPIRIT 2 b.f. (Feb 3) Galileo (IRE) 134 – Ladys First 111 (Dutch Art 126) [2017 8.2v* 8d Nov 4] first foal: dam winner up to 1m (2-y-o 6f winner) who stayed 10.4f: fairly useful form: won minor event at Haydock (by 1¾ lengths from Endless Tangent) in September: last in listed race at Newmarket month later: will stay further than 1m: should still do better. *John Gosden* **83 p**

PIONEERTOWN (IRE) 3 b.g. High Chaparral (IRE) 132 – Tempura (GER) (Cape Cross (IRE) 129) [2017 p7g^{6} p7g 8.3m^{3} p12g^{4} 14.2g^{4} p11g^{2} 14s^{5} t12.4d* t12.4g* Oct 19] €60,000F, 200,000Y: lengthy gelding: first foal: dam, French 11.5f winner, out of smart French performer up to 12.5f Trumbaka: fairly useful handicapper: won at Newcastle in September and October (by ½ length from Eldritch): stays 12.5f: acts on polytrack, tapeta and good to firm going: often races towards rear: sold 130,000 gns later in October. *Sir Mark Prescott Bt* **93**

PIPE DREAMER 3 ch.g. Piccolo 121 – Card Games 89 (First Trump 118) [2017 –: t7.1m t7.1g 7.2d^{4} 7.2d 7.2s Oct 9] poor maiden: best effort at 7f: acts on good to soft going: in headgear last 4 starts: usually races towards rear. *Kevin Ryan* **47**

PIPERS NOTE 7 ch.g. Piccolo 121 – Madam Valentine (Primo Valentino (IRE) 116) [2017 108: 6g^{3} 6m 5s^{3} 5g 6d* 6m* 6m^{3} 5g^{3} 5d^{4} 6g^{2} 5g 5.6g^{5} 6g 5g Oct 17] strong gelding: useful handicapper: won at Ripon (by head from Snap Shots) and Doncaster (by head from Dougan) in June: stays 6f: acts on polytrack, soft and good to firm going. *Ruth Carr* **108**

PIPERS PIPING (IRE) 11 b.g. Noverre (USA) 125 – Monarchy (IRE) (Common Grounds 118) [2017 58: t9.5g^{4} p8g t8.6g^{3} t8.6g t8.6g^{5} t8.6g May 3] leggy gelding: modest handicapper: stays 9.5f: acts on all-weather, good to firm and good to soft going: has worn headgear: tried in tongue tie. *Mandy Rowland* **52**

PIPERS WAY 3 b.c. Piccolo 121 – Emmone (First Trump 118) [2017 6g 6s 7.8g^{5} Jul 13] modest form: best effort when fifth in maiden at Carlisle final start. *Richard Fahey* **60**

PIPPIN 2 ch.g. (Feb 16) Intello (GER) 129 – Golden Delicious 93 (Cadeaux Genereux 131) [2017 8d 8g 8.3d Oct 18] fair form: best effort when eighth in maiden at Nottingham (6¾ lengths behind Msayyan) final start. *Hughie Morrison* **65**

PIQUE SOUS (FR) 10 gr.g. Martaline 118 – Six Fois Sept (FR) (Epervier Bleu 131) [2017 98: p12g p16g^{3} p10.7g^{6} Mar 24] well-made gelding: useful performer: third in minor event at Chelmsford (5¼ lengths behind Watersmeet) in March: stays 21.5f: acts on polytrack, soft and good to firm going: wears tongue tie: useful hurdler. *W. P. Mullins, Ireland* **102**

PIRATE LOOK (IRE) 3 b.g. Canford Cliffs (IRE) 133 – Gerika (FR) (Galileo (IRE) 134) [2017 78: 10.3m^5 p10s^4 10.5d^2 10.2m^3 10d^3 10v Oct 23] rather lightly-made gelding: fairly useful handicapper: third at Lingfield in September: stays 10.5f: acts on polytrack, tapeta, good to firm and good to soft going: in cheekpieces last 3 starts: sold 35,000 gns in November to join Martin Keighley. *Marco Botti* **86**

PIRATE'S TREASURE 4 b.g. Iffraaj 127 – Musical Sands (Green Desert (USA) 127) [2017 84: 8.3g t7.2g p10s^6 11.8v Aug 5] fairly useful handicapper: below form in 2017: left Jennie Candlish after third start: stays 1¼m: acts on all-weather: tried in hood: sometimes slowly away, often races towards rear: quirky sort. *Ian O'Connor, Ireland* **73**

PIROUETTE 4 ch.f. Pivotal 124 – Passiflora 75 (Night Shift (USA)) [2017 102: 7d^3 7.2m^2 8m 8d^3 8d^2 7s* 7g^6 7s^5 p8g^5 Nov 2] lengthy filly: useful performer: won listed race at Dusseldorf (by 5 lengths from Wild Approach) in August: stays 8.5f: acts on polytrack, firm and soft going: in blinkers last 5 starts: usually races prominently. *Hughie Morrison* **105**

PITCH HIGH (IRE) 3 br.g. Requinto (IRE) 109 – Distant Skies (Tiger Hill (IRE) 127) [2017 64: f7d^5 7m^5 9.9g 9.9f^6 8.2g^2 8.1d^4 8.5s^5 t7.1g* t8.6g^5 p7g Dec 21] useful-looking gelding: modest handicapper: won at Newcastle in November: stays 1m: acts on tapeta, good to firm and good to soft going: front runner/races prominently. *Julia Feilden* **59**

PIVOINE (IRE) 3 b.g. Redoute's Choice (AUS) – Fleur de Cactus (IRE) 92 (Montjeu (IRE) 137) [2017 85p: 7g 8g 10.2d^4 p11g* 10.2g* Sep 15] lengthy, good-topped gelding: useful performer: won handicap at Kempton in August and minor event at Doncaster (by ½ length from Lawless Secret) in September: will stay 1½m: acts on polytrack, best turf form on good going: in visor last 2 starts: sold 340,000 gns in October to join Andrew Balding. *Sir Michael Stoute* **102**

PIVOTAL DREAM (IRE) 4 br.f. Excellent Art 125 – Oasis Fire (IRE) 85 (Oasis Dream 129) [2017 53: t9.5m^4 t9.5g^6 t8.6m^3 t8.6g* t8.6g t8.6g^5 p8d t8.6g^5 8g^6 t8.6g t8.6g^2 8m^4 Aug 22] modest handicapper: won at Wolverhampton in January: stays 9.5f: acts on tapeta and good to firm going. *Mark Brisbourne* **53**

PIVOTAL FLAME (IRE) 4 b.f. Pivotal 124 – Saadiah (IRE) (Dubai Destination (USA) 127) [2017 76: p12d p15.8g^6 p11g 9.9g^4 10d^6 Aug 30] fair handicapper: stays 1½m: acts on polytrack, tapeta and good to soft going: has worn cheekpieces. *Pat Phelan* **68**

PIVOT BRIDGE 9 ch.g. Pivotal 124 – Specifically (USA) (Sky Classic (CAN)) [2017 77: t13.9f* t13.9m* p16g 11.8g 18v p12g p12g p12g Nov 10] tall, good-topped gelding: fairly useful handicapper: won at Wolverhampton (twice) in January: stays 1¾m: acts on polytrack, tapeta and any turf going: has worn headgear: often races towards rear. *Adrian McGuinness, Ireland* **82**

PIVOTMAN 9 ch.g. Pivotal 124 – Grandalea 85 (Grand Lodge (USA) 125) [2017 72, a81: f8g^3 t7.1m^3 t9.5m* p10d^4 t9.5g t10.2d 8.3g* 8m 8g 8.5m 8.8m t8.6g p10s Dec 14] rangy gelding: fair handicapper on turf, fairly useful on all-weather: won at Wolverhampton (by 4½ lengths from Roman de Brut) in January and Leicester in April: stays 1½m, usually races over shorter: acts on polytrack, tapeta, good to firm and heavy going: usually blinkered: wears tongue tie. *Michael Easterby* **75 a83**

PIXELEEN 5 b.m. Pastoral Pursuits 127 – Ballyalla 90 (Mind Games 121) [2017 94: 5.7m^5 5g^4 6.1g^4 6f^3 5.7f* 6.1g 6g^5 5.7s^3 6g* 6m^3 Oct 14] lengthy, rather sparely-made mare: useful handicapper: won at Bath in June and Newmarket (by head from Magical Dreamer) in October: third in listed race at latter course (¾ length behind Eartha Kitt) final start: stays 6f: acts on firm and good to soft going: usually races close up: sold 140,000 gns in December. *Malcolm Saunders* **99**

PIXIE CUT (IRE) 7 b.m. Chineur (FR) 123 – Fantastic Cee (IRE) 71 (Noverre (USA) 125) [2017 t8g Jan 21] lengthy mare: fair handicapper at best, well held only start since 2015: stays 14.5f: acts on polytrack and any turf going: has worn headgear. *Alistair Whillans* **–**

PLACEBO EFFECT (IRE) 2 b.g. (Feb 22) Lilbourne Lad (IRE) 111 – Hawaiian Dream (IRE) 63 (Catcher In The Rye (IRE) 115) [2017 5m 5g^3 6m 5m^3 6d* 7s* 6g^3 7.2m* 7d^3 7s^3 Sep 19] fair performer: won sellers at Ripon and Catterick in July, and nursery at Musselburgh in August: stays 7f: acts on soft and good to firm going. *Ollie Pears* **75**

PLACE DES VOSGES (IRE) 2 b.f. (Mar 4) Rip Van Winkle (IRE) 134 – Red Blossom (USA) (Silver Hawk (USA) 123) [2017 p8.9g Nov 8] half-sister to several winners, including useful French 2-y-o 7f/1m winner Hannouma (by Anabaa) and French 11f-15f winner Red Hurricane (by Hurricane Run): dam lightly-raced half-sister to smart winner up to 10.4f Hataab: 207/10, well held in newcomers race at Chantilly. *David Menuisier* **–**

PLAGE DEPAMPELONNE 3 gr.f. Redoute's Choice (AUS) – Arabescatta (Monsun **76**
(GER) 124) [2017 –: t12.2g^{2} 14g^{2} 14f^{6} t12.2g 14m* p16g Sep 13] fair handicapper: won at Redcar in August: stays 1¾m: acts on tapeta and good to firm going: in cheekpieces last 2 starts: often races prominently. *James Bethell*

PLANETARIA (IRE) 4 b.g. Lilbourne Lad (IRE) 111 – Red Planet (Pivotal 124) [2017 **80**
90: 7.8s 8d 8d t8d t8g^{2} t8g^{6} Dec 6] fairly useful handicapper: second at Newcastle in November: left John Weymes after third start: stays 8.5f: acts on fibresand, tapeta and good to firm going: tried in blinkers. *Julie Camacho*

PLANET SUITE (FR) 4 b.f. Astronomer Royal (USA) 121 – Happy Clapper 70 (Royal **52**
Applause 124) [2017 f11g^{3} Jan 2] third foal: sister to winner up to 1¼m Jebril (2-y-o 1m winner) and closely related to 2-y-o 1m winner Barn Dance (by Country Reel), later successful in Scandinavia: dam lightly raced: 6/1, third in maiden at Southwell (17 lengths behind Ominotago). *Jonathan Portman*

PLANSINA 2 b.f. (Mar 24) Planteur (IRE) 124 – Sina (GER) (Trans Island 119) [2017 5m^{6} **51**
6m 6d 7.2m^{6} 6m^{3} 6.9v 6.1d Oct 4] 5,500F, £3,000Y: fourth foal: half-sister to French 2-y-o 7f winner Stateira (by Evasive): dam German/French 9f-10.5f winner: modest maiden: stays 7f: acts on good to firm and good to soft going: tried in cheekpieces: usually races close up. *Tim Easterby*

PLANT POT POWER (IRE) 3 b.g. Lawman (FR) 121 – Featherweight (IRE) 89 **91**
(Fantastic Light (USA) 134) [2017 92: p10g 7m^{5} p8s 7.6g^{2} 7.6d^{3} p7d^{5} 7m^{2} p7g^{5} 7.1s^{4} 7d 8d^{3} 8d^{5} Nov 4] strong gelding: fairly useful handicapper: second at Chester (apprentice) in July: stays 1m: acts on polytrack, good to firm and good to soft going: tried in cheekpieces: often starts slowly: sold £13,000 in November to join Richard Hughes. *Richard Hannon*

PLATA O PLOMO 3 ch.g. Paco Boy (IRE) 129 – Branston Gem 59 (So Factual (USA) **91**
120) [2017 87: 5.1g^{3} 5g 5m^{4} 5v Sep 9] strong, compact gelding: fairly useful performer: third in minor event at Nottingham (1½ lengths behind Kyllang Rock) in April: left Tony Coyle after third start: raced only at 5f: acted on good to soft going: front runner/raced prominently: dead. *David O'Meara*

PLATITUDE 4 b.g. Dansili 127 – Modesta (IRE) 105 (Sadler's Wells (USA) 132) [2017 **111**
112: 12g^{5} 13.9m^{4} 14d^{6} 16.3d^{5} 16g^{5} Sep 28] strong, compact gelding: smart performer: fifth in handicap at York (2¾ lengths behind Magic Circle) in August: stays 2m: acts on good to firm and good to soft going: tried in cheekpieces: usually races nearer last than first: sold 12,000 gns in November to join Amanda Perrett. *Sir Michael Stoute*

PLATO'S KODE (IRE) 3 b.g. Kodiac 112 – Speedy Sonata (USA) (Stravinsky (USA) **73**
133) [2017 63: p7g^{4} p8g^{6} 12d^{4} 13m^{3} 13f^{2} 11.6f* 11.6f^{2} p14d^{5} Sep 21] sturdy gelding: fair handicapper: won at Bath in July: stays 13f: acts on polytrack, tapeta, firm and good to soft going: wears headgear/tongue tie: often races towards rear, usually travels strongly: fairly useful hurdler. *Seamus Durack*

PLAYFUL DUDE (USA) 4 b.g. Drosselmeyer (USA) 126 – Choice Play (USA) **73**
(Vindication (USA) 122) [2017 65: f8g^{2} f8g* f8g^{2} f8g^{4} Jan 30] fair handicapper: won at Southwell in January: acts on fibresand and tapeta: wears hood: front runner/races prominently: sold 7,000 gns, sent to Italy, where successful at Syracuse in seller in July, handicap in September and minor event in November (from 7.5f to 10.5f). *Phil McEntee*

PLAYFUL SOUND 4 b.f. Street Cry (IRE) 130 – Giants Play (USA) 111 (Giant's **105**
Causeway (USA) 132) [2017 102p: 9m* 10.2g 10.3d^{3} 9.9m^{6} 12f^{6} 9.5f Dec 30] good-topped filly: useful performer: won handicap at Newmarket (by 1¼ lengths from Next Stage) in May: left Sir Michael Stoute after fourth start: stays 10.5f: acts on good to firm and good to soft going. *Christophe Clement, USA*

PLAY THE BLUES (IRE) 10 gr.m. Refuse To Bend (IRE) 128 – Paldouna (IRE) **–**
(Kaldoun (FR) 122) [2017 52: 8m 8d^{5} Aug 22] lengthy, angular mare: modest handicapper: well beaten both starts in 2017: stays 1m: acts on polytrack and good to firm going: has worn headgear, including final start: wears tongue tie: usually races freely. *Roger Ingram*

PLAYTOTHEWHISTLE 6 b.g. Sakhee's Secret 128 – Prima Ballerina 73 (Pivotal 124) **70**
[2017 74: t7.1g^{6} f8g^{3} f7g f8m t12.2g^{3} t8.6g^{5} 10g^{6} 10.2d Jun 11] fair handicapper: stays 1m: acts on fibresand, soft and good to firm going: wears headgear. *Michael Appleby*

PLAY WITH ME 3 ch.f. Captain Gerrard (IRE) 113 – Plead (FR) (Bering 136) [2017 **55**
t7.1g^{5} t8g^{4} t6g^{5} 7.2m^{3} May 8] half-sister to several winners, including 2-y-o 6f winner Adele Blanc Sec (by Marchand de Sable) and 2-y-o 9f winner (stayed 11.4f) Play Gal (by Multiplex): dam French 11f winner: modest form: best effort at 7f. *Keith Dalgleish*

PLAYWRITER (IRE) 3 b.g. New Approach (IRE) 132 – The Shrew 108 (Dansili 127) **84 p** [2017 8g^3 10m^2 Jun 23] second foal: half-brother to 6f winner Caitie (by Canford Cliffs): dam, winner up to 1m (2-y-o 7.5f winner), half-sister to Mill Reef Stakes winner James Garfield: fairly useful form: better effort when second in maiden at Newmarket (neck behind Yaarmen) second start: likely to progress further. *Charlie Appleby*

PLEAD 3 ch.f. Dutch Art 126 – Entreat 87 (Pivotal 124) [2017 83: t9.5m^4 10.2g^3 10.2g^2 **87 §** 10s^5 8m 10m^4 10.2m^5 t9.5g p10d^{rr} Nov 22] sturdy filly: fairly useful handicapper: second at Nottingham in May: stays 1¼m: acts on polytrack, tapeta, best turf form on good going: tried in blinkers: sometimes slowly away, often races towards rear: temperamental (refused to race final start). *Archie Watson*

PLEADINGS (USA) 4 ch.g. Street Cry (IRE) 130 – Say No Now (IRE) 103 (Refuse To **54** Bend (IRE) 128) [2017 47: p6g^5 p6g^3 p7d p6g 5.7f 6m^6 6m p6g^4 Jun 22] modest maiden handicapper: stays 6f: acts on polytrack and good to firm going: wears headgear: usually tongue tied: usually races towards rear. *Charlie Wallis*

PLEASANT SURPRISE (IRE) 3 b.f. Mastercraftsman (IRE) 129 – Ibiza Dream **107** (Night Shift (USA)) [2017 9.9m^3 t12.2g* 10g^5 11.9m* 12d^2 11.9g^2 12d^2 10.4g Oct 22] 25,000F, 52,000Y: rather unfurnished filly: third foal: half-sister to 2 winners abroad by Tertullian, including German/French 1m/1¼m winner Ice Man Star: dam lightly raced in Germany (second at 9.5f): useful performer: won maiden at Wolverhampton in May and handicap at Doncaster (by length from Di Alta) in July: second on next 3 starts, in Princess Royal Stakes at Newmarket (½ length behind Apphia) on last occasion: stays 1½m: acts on tapeta, good to firm and good to soft going: often travels strongly: consistent. *Luca Cumani*

PLEASURE DOME 4 b.f. Makfi 130 – Nouvelle Lune (Fantastic Light (USA) 134) **71** [2017 94: 14.2d Jun 28] good-topped filly: fairly useful handicapper: well below form only start on Flat in 2017: stays 1¾m: acts on polytrack and good to firm going: front runner/races prominently. *Jonjo O'Neill*

PLUCKY DIP 6 b.g. Nayef (USA) 129 – Plucky 93 (Kyllachy 129) [2017 92: t6m p7g **79** p7d^4 p6d^3 t7.1g^6 p6g^6 p6g* 7m 7.6d^6 7f 6g 7g 6m^4 p6g^5 p7g p7d p7g p7s^3 p7s t6.1g Dec **a85** 18] angular gelding: fairly useful handicapper: won at Chelmsford (by head from Dark Side Dream) in May: has form at 1m, usually races over shorter: acts on polytrack, tapeta and firm going: has worn cheekpieces. *John Ryan*

PLUMATIC 3 b.c. Dubawi (IRE) 129 – Plumania 117 (Anabaa (USA) 130) [2017 10.4d* **115** 8.9d^2 10.4g 9.9s^2 11.9d Oct 1] third foal: half-brother to French 1½m winners Maniaco (smart) and Solilea (useful) (both by Galileo): dam 1m (at 2 yrs) to 1½m (Grand Prix de Saint-Cloud) winner: smart performer: won maiden at Saint-Cloud in March: second in Prix de Guiche at Chantilly and Prix du Prince d'Orange at Maisons-Laffitte (nose behind Recoletos): thirteenth to Enable in Prix de l'Arc de Triomphe at Chantilly final outing: stays 1½m: acts on soft going. *A. Fabre, France*

PLUNDERED (IRE) 2 b.g. (Apr 15) Camacho 118 – Jouel (FR) (Machiavellian (USA) **54** 123) [2017 5g^5 t6s^5 6m^4 6g t6g Oct 19] modest maiden: best effort at 6f: acts on tapeta and good to firm going: tried in cheekpieces: sold 800 gns, sent to Spain. *David Brown*

PLUNGER 2 ch.c. (Mar 31) Helmet (AUS) 127 – Percolator 106 (Kheleyf (USA) 116) **90 p** [2017 p5g* 7g^2 Nov 3] lengthy colt: has scope: fourth foal: half-brother to 5f (including at 2 yrs) winner Cajmere (by Kyllachy): dam 2-y-o 5f winner: fairly useful form: won minor event at Kempton (by 1½ lengths from Dragon's Teeth) in April: second in similar event at Newmarket (length behind Maghaweer) when next seen 7 months later: open to further improvement. *Paul Cole*

PLUTOCRACY (IRE) 7 b.g. Dansili 127 – Private Life (FR) (Bering 136) [2017 98: **97** t12.2m^2 t12.2g^{pu} 11.4g^5 12g^4 t12.2g^3 12s^5 Oct 15] useful-looking gelding: useful handicapper: second at Wolverhampton (¾ length behind Hot Beat) in January: stays 1¾m: acts on polytrack, tapeta, soft and good to firm going: wears headgear. *Gary Moore*

PLUTONIAN (IRE) 3 b.c. Raven's Pass (USA) 133 – Ripalong (IRE) 68 (Revoque **100** (IRE) 122) [2017 t7.2g^5 7m^6 8.1m* 8g^3 p8g^6 p10d* Nov 9] 95,000Y: good-topped colt: closely related to a winner abroad by Elusive Quality and half-brother to several winners, including smart 6f (including at 2 yrs)/1m winner Shamwari Lodge (by Hawk Wing), herself dam of smart 7f/1m winner Oh This Is Us: dam, sprint maiden, half-sister to very smart sprinter Pipalong: useful performer: won maiden at Windsor in June and handicap at Chelmsford (by head from Pactolus) in November: stays 1¼m: acts on polytrack and good to firm going: front runner/races prominently. *Charles Hills*

PLY 3 b.g. Dubawi (IRE) 129 – Polygon (USA) 106 (Dynaformer (USA)) [2017 p8g^{2} 10m^{5} 10s p11g^{5} 10m^{3} p10g* p11g* p11g* Nov 6] lengthy gelding: first foal: dam 1¼m-1½m winner: useful handicapper: won at Kempton in September (by 4½ lengths from Exceeding Power), October (by 3 lengths from Desert Ruler) and November (by length from Royal Reserve): stays 11f: acts on polytrack and good to firm going: usually races towards rear: sent to UAE: will go on improving. *Roger Charlton* **108 p**

PLYMOUTH SOUND 5 b.g. Fastnet Rock (AUS) 127 – Shardette (IRE) (Darshaan 133) [2017 87: 14.1m^{4} 11.7f^{2} 14.2m^{4} p16g^{6} 11.6d* 10.2d 14.4v^{4} 14.4v^{2} Sep 30] leggy gelding: fairly useful handicapper: won at Lingfield (by 5 lengths from Hepplewhite) in June: left Eve Johnson Houghton after fifth start: stays 2m: acts on polytrack, firm and good to soft going: wears headgear: sometimes slowly away. *Bernard Llewellyn* **86**

POANA (FR) 3 ch.f. New Approach (IRE) 132 – Porlezza (FR) 117 (Sicyos (USA) 126) [2017 7g Apr 21] €80,000 2-y-o: seventh foal: half-sister to 3 winners in France, including useful 2-y-o 6f winners Pontenuovo (by Green Tune) and Ponte Vespucci (by Anabaa): dam French 5f (including at 2 yrs) to 6.5f (Prix Maurice de Gheest) winner: 3/1, well held in maiden at Newbury. *John Gosden* **–**

POBBLES 3 b.f. Medicean 128 – Oystermouth 74 (Averti (IRE) 117) [2017 70: p8d^{2} p8g^{6} 8.3g 7g* 7m^{6} Jun 24] fair performer: successful in seller at Redcar in May: left Roger Charlton after second start: stays 1m: acts on polytrack: in headgear in 2017: often races towards rear: sold 16,000 gns in July, sent to Spain, where won at Dos Hermanas in December. *George Scott* **70**

POCKETFULLOFDREAMS (FR) 3 b.f. Invincible Spirit (IRE) 121 – Dubai Rose 102 (Dubai Destination (USA) 127) [2017 84p: 8v^{4} 10d^{2} 10g^{2} 11.6d^{2} 12m 10v^{4} 8d* 10g 9m^{5} 9.5d^{5} 8.2s 9.5s 8s p8g Oct 27] €550,000Y: well-made filly: third foal: half-sister to 2 winners in France, including smart winner up to 1½m The Juliet Rose (2-y-o 1m winner, by Monsun): dam French 11f/1½m winner: useful performer: won maiden at Naas in June: second in listed Oaks Trial at Lingfield (1½ lengths behind Hertford Dancer) in May: stays 11.5f: acts on polytrack and good to soft going: usually hooded: in tongue tie last 2 starts: front runner/races prominently. *Aidan O'Brien, Ireland* **98**

POCKET WARRIOR 6 b.g. Tobougg (IRE) 125 – Navene (IRE) 74 (Desert Style (IRE) 121) [2017 p8m p6f^{6} p6g^{6} p6g Apr 12] modest form: best effort at 6f. *Martin Bosley* **59**

PODEMOS (GER) 2 b.c. (Feb 8) Shamardal (USA) 129 – Pearls Or Passion (FR) (Monsun (GER) 124) [2017 p8g^{2} Nov 7] first foal: dam, useful French 1½m winner, out of Prix Vermeille winner Pearly Shells: 8/1, second in minor event at Kempton (2¾ lengths behind Bow Street): sure to progress. *Ralph Beckett* **84 p**

POETA DILETTO 4 ch.c. Poet's Voice 126 – Mia Diletta 90 (Selkirk (USA) 129) [2017 110: p10g 8m^{6} 8.3g^{6} 7m^{2} 7s* Nov 11] second foal: half-brother to Italian 2-y-o 7.5f winner Mia Eccellenza (by Exceed And Excel): dam, Italian winner up to 1m (2-y-o 7.5f winner), half-sister to useful Italian winner up to 1m Mi Raccomando (by Poet's Voice): smart performer: won Premio Parioli at Rome in 2016: just respectable efforts for Marco Botti in Britain first 3 starts in 2017, then returned to former trainer: won listed race at Milan in November by 3 lengths from Zapel: effective at 7f to 9f: acts on soft and good to firm going. *A. & S. Botti, Italy* **110**

POETIC AFFAIR 2 ch.g. (Jan 23) Poet's Voice 126 – Wendylina (IRE) (In The Wings 128) [2017 7d^{6} Sep 18] 8/1, well held in maiden at Brighton. *Mark Johnston* **–**

POETIC CHARM 2 b.f. (Mar 31) Dubawi (IRE) 129 – Speirbhean (IRE) 111 (Danehill (USA) 126) [2017 7g* 7g^{5} p7s* Sep 8] sturdy filly: sister to useful 1m winner Bean Feasa and half-sister to 3 winners by Galileo, including high-class 2-y-o 7f winner (including Dewhurst Stakes) Teofilo and useful 1¼m winner Senora Galilei: dam 1m winner: fairly useful form: won maiden at Newmarket (by length from Sizzling) in July and minor event at Kempton (by length from Jousi) in September: best effort when fifth in Sweet Solera Stakes at Newmarket (2¼ lengths behind Tajaanus) in August: will stay 1m: remains with potential. *Charlie Appleby* **94 p**

POETIC CHOICE 6 b.m. Byron 117 – Ennobling 62 (Mark of Esteem (IRE) 137) [2017 86: p10.7g p8s^{2} p8g^{6} p7g 7s 8g p8g^{4} 9.2s^{5} 9.7s^{4} 7.9g^{4} 8m^{2} 8g p7g^{2} p8g p8g p8s p8g Dec 22] lengthy mare: fairly useful handicapper: second at Dundalk in February: stays 9f: acts on polytrack, good to firm and heavy going: has worn headgear, including in 2017. *Keith Henry Clarke, Ireland* **82 a88**

POETIC FORCE (IRE) 3 ch.g. Lope de Vega (IRE) 125 – Obligada (IRE) 100 (Beat Hollow 126) [2017 80: p10g* t8.6g* t8.6m* p8g^3 11.7m 8m 8m^6 7.6d^4 8g^5 7m 8g^2 7v^5 Oct 1] compact, well-made gelding: fairly useful handicapper: won at Lingfield and Wolverhampton in January, and at latter course (by head from Shamrokh) in February: stays 1¼m, effective at shorter: acts on polytrack, tapeta, good to firm and good to soft going: usually tongue tied. *Tony Carroll* **83**

POETIC IMAGINATION 2 b.f. (Feb 19) Exceed And Excel (AUS) 126 – Portrayal (USA) 114 (Saint Ballado (CAN)) [2017 7d p8g^2 t7.2g^4 t7.2g^5 Dec 22] closely related to useful French 7f and (including at 2 yrs) 1m winner Come Alive (by Dansili) and half-sister to 3 winners, including useful 1m winner Belle Boyd (by Oasis Dream) and useful 1½m-1¾m winner Street Artist (by Street Cry): dam winner up to 1¼m (2-y-o 6f winner): fair form: best effort at 1m: tried in visor. *John Gosden* **77**

POETIC QUEEN (IRE) 4 b.f. Dylan Thomas (IRE) 132 – Jubilant Lady (USA) (Aptitude (USA) 128) [2017 64: t6g^2 t6g* t5g Mar 15] fair performer: won maiden at Wolverhampton in February: stays 6f: acts on tapeta: front runner/races prominently. *Eric Alston* **74**

POETIC STEPS (FR) 2 ch.f. (Mar 9) Poet's Voice 126 – Step This Way (USA) 93 (Giant's Causeway (USA) 132) [2017 6s* 6.9g* 7v 6d 6.5g^5 6g Oct 7] angular filly: fourth foal: half-sister to 1½m winner Regal Ways (by Royal Applause): dam winner up to 1½m (2-y-o 8.6f winner) who stayed 1¾m: fair performer: won minor events at Hamilton and Carlisle in July: stays 7f: acts on soft going: front runner/races prominently. *Mark Johnston* **79**

POETIC VOICE 3 b.g. Poet's Voice 126 – Perfect Flight 101 (Hawk Wing (USA) 136) [2017 –p: 10.3m May 10] good-topped gelding: no form: burst blood vessel only start in 2017. *Eric Alston* **–**

POET'S BEAUTY (IRE) 4 ch.g. Poet's Voice 126 – Extreme Beauty (USA) 89 (Rahy (USA) 115) [2017 89: 8s t8g p7g Oct 25] good-topped gelding: fairly useful handicapper: stays 8.5f: acts on soft and good to firm going: wears headgear: front runner/races prominently: sold 4,000 gns in November. *Ismail Mohammed* **83**

POET'S CHARM (IRE) 3 b.g. Poet's Voice 126 – Antillia 82 (Red Ransom (USA)) [2017 65: p8g^6 10s^5 7.1g p12g t12.2g Dec 22] well-made gelding: modest maiden: left Simon Crisford after first start: stays 8.5f: acts on polytrack and tapeta: often in headgear: front runner/races prominently. *Martin Hill* **59**

POET'S DAWN 2 ch.g. (Feb 7) Poet's Voice 126 – Dudley Queen (IRE) (Excellent Art 125) [2017 5m^5 5f 6m 7.4m* 7.4m^3 7.4s^6 7.4d^5 8g^2 t8s^5 7s^2 8v^2 7s^4 Oct 10] 4,000Y: first foal: dam unraced half-sister to smart 1m winner Harvest Queen: fairly useful performer: won minor event at Beverley in June: second in nursery at Ripon in September: stays 1m: acts on any turf going. *Tim Easterby* **85**

POETS DREAM (IRE) 2 b.c. (Feb 19) Poet's Voice 126 – Sparkling Smile (IRE) 98 (Cape Cross (IRE) 129) [2017 6m^4 7d^4 7v* 7g^2 8v 7g^3 Dec 29] 55,000Y: compact colt: second foal: dam, 1¼m-1½m winner, half-sister to dam of Irish Oaks winner Covert Love: fairly useful performer: won minor event at Thirsk (by 3½ lengths from Barefoot Baby) in September: placed in similar races at Redcar (head behind Shuhood) and Doha (third to Tip Two Win): left Mohamed Moubarak after fifth start: should stay at least 1m: acts on heavy going: tongue tied on debut: usually races close up. *Mohammed Hussain Afroz, Qatar* **84**

POET'S PRIDE 2 b.g. (Mar 1) Arcano (IRE) 122 – Amber Heights 71 (Kyllachy 129) [2017 5.9s^3 6d^4 Sep 2] 50,000Y: first foal: dam, 5.7f/6f winner, half-sister to smart performers Millennium Force (winner around 7f) and Chrysander (stayed 1¼m): fair form: better effort when third in maiden at Carlisle (neck behind Highest Rank) in August: will stay 7f: should still improve. *David Barron* **71 p**

POET'S PRINCE 2 b.g. (Mar 30) Poet's Voice 126 – Palace Affair 113 (Pursuit of Love 124) [2017 6d^2 6m^2 7.2g* 7v 6d t7.1d^5 Nov 4] big gelding: has scope: fair performer: won minor event at Ayr in July: stays 7f: acts on good to firm and good to soft going: races prominently. *Mark Johnston* **76**

POET'S PRINCESS 3 ch.f. Poet's Voice 126 – Palace Affair 113 (Pursuit of Love 124) [2017 86: 7m 6d^2 6s 6d 7d 6g 6v^3 6s^4 Oct 15] lengthy filly: useful handicapper: second at Newmarket (head behind Ekhtiyaar) in May: stays 6f: acts on heavy going: front runner/races prominently: unreliable. *Hughie Morrison* **98 §**

Betfred Glorious Stakes, Goodwood—Poet's Word secures a first win in pattern company, beating Second Step and Scarlet Dragon (quartered cap)

POET'S QUEST 3 b.f. Poet's Voice 126 – Quest For Freedom (Falbrav (IRE) 133) [2017 p8g 8g 8.3g p8g p8s f8.1g Dec 4] fourth foal: half-sister to winner up to 1¼m Frantical (2-y-o 1m winner, by Observatory): dam unraced half-sister to very smart performer up to 14.6f Mikado: little sign of ability: left Dean Ivory after fourth start: tried in visor. *Michael Appleby* –

POET'S REWARD 3 b.g. Hellvelyn 118 – Oceanico Dot Com (IRE) 75 (Hernando (FR) 127) [2017 t5g² t5s² 6m³ 5g May 29] 6,000F, €75,000 2-y-o: fourth foal: half-brother to 2-y-o 5f winner Champagne Babe (by Captain Rio): dam 2-y-o 5f winner: fairly useful form: second in maidens at Newcastle in March: best effort at 5f. *David Barron* **83**

POET'S SOCIETY 3 ch.g. Poet's Voice 126 – Rahiyah (USA) 113 (Rahy (USA) 115) [2017 93: t5.1m² 5.7f⁴ 6.1m⁴ 5m 6d³ 5.1s² 6m⁴ 5d* 6g 5g 5v⁵ 6d⁶ 6m³ 5.5g 6v 5.2d* 5v t6.1g 5v Oct 21] strong gelding: useful handicapper: won at Newmarket (by neck from Compas Scoobie) in June and Yarmouth (by ¾ length from Magical Dreamer) in September: stays 6f: acts on polytrack, tapeta, firm and soft going: sold 18,000 gns in November. *Mark Johnston* **96**

POET'S TIME 3 ch.f. Poet's Voice 126 – Sandtime (IRE) 92 (Green Desert (USA) 127) [2017 –: 6m⁵ 7m 5m³ 5g⁵ t5g⁶ 5d³ 6g⁶ t6d⁵ Sep 29] modest maiden: best effort at 5f: acts on good to firm going. *Tim Easterby* **51**

POET'S VANITY 3 b.f. Poet's Voice 126 – Vanity (IRE) 75 (Thatching 131) [2017 103p: 7m³ 8m 6f⁴ 7d Aug 19] useful performer: third in Nell Gwyn Stakes at Newmarket (2 lengths behind Daban) in April: stays 7f: acts on good to firm going: front runner/races prominently. *Andrew Balding* **101**

POET'S WORD (IRE) 4 b.c. Poet's Voice 126 – Whirly Bird 101 (Nashwan (USA) 135) [2017 109p: p10g* 10.3m² 12s* 10d² 10s² 9.9g⁶ Dec 10] lengthy colt: progressed into a very smart performer, winning handicap at Chelmsford in April and Glorious Stakes at Goodwood (by 1½ lengths from Second Step) in August: also second in Huxley Stakes at Chester, Irish Champion Stakes at Leopardstown (beaten ½ length by Decorated Knight) and Champion Stakes at Ascot (7 lengths behind Cracksman): sixth to Time Warp in Hong Kong Cup at Sha Tin final outing: stays 1½m: acts on polytrack, soft and good to firm going: usually responds generously to pressure. *Sir Michael Stoute* **124**

POIGNANT 2 ch.c. (Apr 15) Sepoy (AUS) 129 – Brigh (IRE) 90 (Galileo (IRE) 134) [2017 5g 5.1m³ p5g² 6s 6m³ a6f a7f Dec 29] fair maiden: left Archie Watson after fifth start: best form at 5f: acts on polytrack and good to firm going: tried in visor. *D. Watson, UAE* **77**

POINT HOPE (IRE) 2 b.f. (Apr 10) Kodiac 112 – Frosted 65 (Dr Fong (USA) 128) **72 p** [2017 6m³ t7.2g* Dec 5] €125,000Y: compact filly: fourth foal: dam twice-raced sister to smart/untrustworthy sprinter Andronikos: fair form: won minor event at Wolverhampton (by neck from Allante) in December: open to further improvement. *Richard Hannon*

POINT IN TIME (IRE) 2 b.f. (Mar 26) Champs Elysees 124 – Creme Anglaise 101 **68** (Motivator 131) [2017 p8g p8g⁶ t8.6g⁵ Nov 29] 75,000Y: first foal: dam, 1¼m winner who stayed 1½m, half-sister to useful Scandinavian performer up to 1½m Grafitti: fair form: best effort when sixth in minor event at Kempton (4¼ lengths behind Espadrille) in November. *Mark Usher*

POINT NORTH (IRE) 10 b.g. Danehill Dancer (IRE) 117 – Briolette (IRE) 112 **74** (Sadler's Wells (USA) 132) [2017 81: t6m t5.1g² t5.1g* t6.1g⁵ t5.1g t5.1g t5.1d⁴ Dec 27] well-made gelding: fair performer: won claimer at Wolverhampton in June: has won at 8.5f, usually races over much shorter nowadays: acts on polytrack, tapeta and soft going: wears headgear: has worn tongue tie: sometimes slowly away, usually races nearer last than first. *John Balding*

POINT OF DISCOVERY 3 b.c. Exceed And Excel (AUS) 126 – Saggiatore 84 (Galileo **–** (IRE) 134) [2017 t10.2s May 23] 8/1, well held in maiden at Newcastle. *Marco Botti*

POINT OF WOODS 4 b.g. Showcasing 117 – Romantic Myth 105 (Mind Games 121) **74** [2017 78: 5g 6m 6d 5d² 5d² 6d² 5g 5g³ 6s⁴ 6g⁶ 6v* 6d² 7v Nov 7] sturdy gelding: fair handicapper: won at Ripon (apprentice) in September: stays 6f: acts on tapeta, good to firm and heavy going: wears headgear. *Tina Jackson*

POLAR FOREST 7 br.g. Kyllachy 129 – Woodbeck 90 (Terimon 124) [2017 86: t10.2g⁴ **77** t8g p8g t10.2s 9d⁶ 9.9s* 10.1d³ 11.2d⁶ 9v³ 10g⁵ 10.2d 10.2d 10d 10.1d Oct 24] fair **a71** handicapper: won at Beverley (amateur) in August: stays 1½m: acts on polytrack, tapeta, good to firm and heavy going: usually in headgear. *Richard Guest*

POLARISATION 5 b.g. Echo of Light 125 – Concordia (Pivotal 124) [2017 110: 16v* **110** Apr 22] tall, angular gelding: smart handicapper: won at Randwick (by head from Who Shot Thebarman) in April, only outing in 2017: stays 2m: acts on heavy and good to firm going: in cheekpieces last 2 starts: front runner/races prominently. *Charlie Appleby*

POLAR KITE (IRE) 9 b.g. Marju (IRE) 127 – Irina (IRE) 91 (Polar Falcon (USA) 126) **75 §** [2017 72§: p8g⁴ p7g* p8g² p8d p7g Apr 20] tall, lengthy gelding: fair handicapper: won at Lingfield in February: stays 1m: acts on polytrack and good to firm going: wears hood: often races towards rear/travels strongly: temperamental. *Michael Attwater*

POLAR LIGHT 2 b.f. (Mar 4) Norse Dancer (IRE) 127 – Dimelight 74 (Fantastic Light **69** (USA) 134) [2017 6g p7g⁶ 7d⁴ 6.1g 8.3d⁶ p7s Dec 1] tall, useful-looking filly: sister to 7f-1¾m winner Odin and 11.6f winner Norse Light, and half-sister to useful winner up to 7f Elusive Flame (2-y-o 6f/6.5f winner, by Elusive City): dam, maiden (stayed 1¼m), half-sister to smart performers Guys And Dolls (up to 1¼m) and Pawn Broker (up to 1½m): fair maiden: should stay 1m: acts on good to soft going: tried in blinkers. *David Elsworth*

POLITICAL SLOT 2 ch.f. (Feb 23) Helmet (AUS) 127 – Lady Elalmadol (IRE) **–** (Shamardal (USA) 129) [2017 6d⁶ 7d t8.6g Nov 29] first foal: dam unraced: little impact in minor events (hooded). *Derek Shaw*

POLKADOT PRINCESS (IRE) 3 b.f. Sir Prancealot (IRE) 111 – Miriam's Song 67 **49** (Royal Applause 124) [2017 54: 5.7f 6.1s t8.6g Dec 5] close-coupled filly: poor maiden: best effort at 6f: acts on soft going. *Nikki Evans*

POLKARENIX (FR) 5 b.g. Policy Maker (IRE) 119 – Arenix (FR) (Fragrant Mix (IRE) **–** 124) [2017 14g Aug 15] fairly useful handicapper at best in France: last only start on Flat in 2017: stayed 1¼m: acted on good to soft going: tried in tongue tie: dead. *Brendan Powell*

POLLY DOUGLAS (IRE) 4 b.f. Le Cadre Noir (IRE) 113 – Isabella Rose (IRE) (City **78** On A Hill (USA) 114) [2017 56: 6m* 6d* 6g 5m* 6m 5d² 6d² 5s⁶ 5v 6v⁶ Oct 24] second foal: dam unraced half-sister to useful 1m-1¼m winner Rose Hip: fair handicapper: won at Ayr in May, Naas in June and Navan in July: best at 5f/6f: acts on polytrack, good to firm and good to soft going. *Kieran Patrick Cotter, Ireland*

POLLY GLIDE (IRE) 3 ch.f. Nathaniel (IRE) 129 – Majestic Dancer (IRE) 92 (Danehill **84** Dancer (IRE) 117) [2017 65p: 8m⁵ 8f⁴ 10.2f⁴ Jun 23] compact filly: fairly useful form: saddle slipped final start: should stay beyond 1m: sold 6,000 gns in November. *Luca Cumani*

POLLYISSIMO 2 ch.f. (Jan 23) Nathaniel (IRE) 129 – Fleurissimo 79 (Dr Fong (USA) **–** 128) [2017 p6d 6s 7.1s Sep 19] 40,000Y: third foal: closely related to useful 1¼m-1½m winner Fleur Forsyte (by Teofilo): dam, maiden (stayed 1¼m), half-sister to smart 1m winner Dolores, herself dam of smart winners at 1¾m+ Duncan, Samuel and Gretchen: mid-division at best in minor events. *Richard Hughes*

POLLY'S GOLD (IRE) 2 ch.f. (Feb 3) Havana Gold (IRE) 118 – Keyta Bonita (IRE) 66 (Denon (USA) 121) [2017 5.1m⁴ 6g⁶ 6.1v² 6.1m² 6g³ 7.1s³ Sep 14] €40,000Y: first foal: dam, 1m winner in Czech Republic, half-sister to smart winners up to 9f Sandiva and Wentworth: fair maiden: stays 6f: acts on good to firm and heavy going: often travels strongly: has joined Karen George. *Richard Hughes* **75**

POLYBIUS 6 b.g. Oasis Dream 129 – Freedonia 117 (Selkirk (USA) 129) [2017 96: 6g⁴ 5g 6g³ 6m⁴ 5g² 6m t6.1d⁵ Dec 26] well-made gelding: smart handicapper: fourth (length behind Out Do) in Wokingham Stakes at Royal Ascot in June: stays 6f: acts on polytrack, tapeta and good to firm going: often races towards rear. *David Simcock* **112**

POLYDREAM (IRE) 2 b.f. (Apr 8) Oasis Dream 129 – Polygreen (FR) 109 (Green Tune (USA) 125) [2017 6g* 7g* 8d² Oct 1] **109 p**

The two most recent home-trained winners of France's top race for two-year-old fillies, the Prix Marcel Boussac, carried the colours of the Wertheimer brothers. Those victories of Silasol in 2012 and Indonesienne in 2013 had been followed by wins for the Aidan O'Brien-trained pair Found and Ballydoyle and then Wuheida's success for Charlie Appleby and Godolphin. Although both those visiting trainers were represented again in the latest edition, there were high hopes that Polydream, another Wertheimer-owned filly, this one trained by Freddie Head, would keep the prize at home. Head's sister Criquette, whose five Marcel Boussac winners is a joint record for the race, trained a couple more winners in the famous royal blue, white seams, sleeves and cap during the 'nineties with Gold Splash (owned by Jacques Wertheimer, father of Alain and Gerard) and Juvenia. The Wertheimers were doubly represented in the latest Marcel Boussac, with the Prix d'Aumale winner Soustraction also in the field, but it was the unbeaten Polydream who challenged Ballydoyle's Moyglare Stud Stakes runner-up Magical for favouritism. Polydream was held up off the pace set by Soustraction and was left with ground to make up in the straight when the more prominently-ridden Godolphin filly Wild Illusion was sent for home. With only two behind her over a furlong out, Polydream began to find her stride in the last hundred yards or so and finished well to come out best in a three-way photo for the runner-up spot, ahead of Mission Impassible and Magical, but a length and a half behind winner Wild Illusion. Magical didn't enjoy the run of the race as much as the winner, either, after having to switch, but Polydream might have gone closer still had she been ridden nearer to the pace.

Shadwell Prix du Calvados, Deauville—British-trained fillies outnumber French ones, but the Freddie Head-trained Polydream keeps the prize at home, producing a performance verging on smart to beat Laurens (star on cap) and Bonita Fransisca (left)

The Marcel Boussac at least proved that Polydream stays a mile and does so thoroughly, after her two wins had come at shorter trips. She had started out winning a newcomers race over six furlongs at Deauville at the end of July in good style, showing speed throughout, while an entry in the Cheveley Park Stakes suggested that connections might not have been in too much of a hurry to step her up in trip. But there was plenty of encouragement for Polydream's prospects at a mile when she followed up, again in taking fashion, at Deauville three weeks later, this time over seven furlongs, in the Shadwell Prix du Calvados. Ridden with restraint this time in a field of eleven, no fewer than seven of whom were trained in Britain, Polydream improved down the centre of the track to lead over a furlong out and was comfortably on top, her rider only having to glance at the big screen several times inside the final furlong to be certain the race was his before patting Polydream down the neck approaching the line. By the time Polydream was turned out again for the Marcel Boussac, the Calvados runner-up Laurens, beaten a length and three quarters, had paid her a big compliment by winning the May Hill Stakes. Laurens went on to win the Fillies' Mile as well in which Magical, sent off favourite, finished fourth and Polydream's stable-companion Efaadah seventh; Efaadah had earlier split Soustraction and Wild Illusion when runner-up in the Prix d'Aumale.

Polydream (IRE) (b.f. 2015)	Oasis Dream (b 2000)	Green Desert (b 1983)	Danzig
			Foreign Courier
		Hope (b 1991)	Dancing Brave
			Bahamian
	Polygreen (FR) (b 1999)	Green Tune (ch 1991)	Green Dancer
			Soundings
		Yxenery (b 1994)	Sillery
			Polyxena

Polydream is her dam's ninth foal and fourth winner. Pick of the others was the smart filly Evaporation (by Red Ransom) whose wins included listed events in France at seven furlongs and a mile, while Ankle (by Shamardal) has won at up to eleven furlongs, including in the latest season, and Your Game (by Montjeu) won at a mile and a half. Their useful dam Polygreen, by Jacques Wertheimer's Poule d'Essai des Poulains winner Green Tune, won a nine-furlong newcomers race but did all her subsequent racing at up to a mile, winning a listed race at that trip at Saint-Cloud and gaining her two other wins in the States at four, one of those over six and a half furlongs at Santa Anita where she was beaten a nose in a Grade 3 contest over the same trip. Grandam Yxenery and great grandam Polyxena were also useful fillies who won two listed races apiece, the former winning both of hers at a mile and the latter successful at a mile and a mile and a quarter. Like Polydream, her fourth dam, Minstrel Girl, was runner-up in the Marcel Boussac (or Criterium des Pouliches as it still was in 1978), trained by Freddie Head's father Alec. Like Goldikova, Polydream comes from a family that has been associated with the Wertheimers and the Heads over many generations and decades; this is also the family of Ma Biche who in 1982 became the third winner of the Cheveley Park Stakes from her immediate family before going on to win the One Thousand Guineas. Polydream is a best-priced 20/1 at the time of writing for the Guineas in a market dominated by fillies from Ballydoyle and she makes each-way appeal at those odds with further improvement to come. She would have the speed to strengthen her claims in the Prix Imprudence beforehand, a race she will almost certainly take in first if coming to Newmarket. Incidentally, Polydream's win in the Prix du Calvados proved a timely boost for her yearling half-sister by Invincible Spirit who was sold days later at Deauville for €400,000; Polygreen had been sold for €200,000 carrying the same foal in December 2015. *F. Head, France*

POLYMNIA 4 br.f. Poet's Voice 126 – Lucky Token (IRE) 77 (Key of Luck (USA) 126) **80**
[2017 76: p8g* 10m 10.1s 8.1g p7g p8g p7s^4 Dec 8] sturdy filly: fairly useful handicapper: won at Lingfield (by 1¾ lengths from Lucky Louie) in January: left Richard Hannon after: stays 1¼m: acts on polytrack, tapeta and good to firm going: has worn headgear: tried in tongue tie. *E. U. Hales, Ireland*

POMME DE TERRE (IRE) 5 ch.g. Sakhee's Secret 128 – Suzie Quw 83 (Bahamian **89**
Bounty 116) [2017 89: 6g 6g^{3} 6d^{3} 6g^{2} 5g^{3} 5s 6v^{4} 6v^{5} t5d t6d Nov 10] fairly useful
handicapper: second at York in July: stays 6f: acts on good to firm and heavy going: usually
wears headgear. *Michael Dods*

POMPEY CHIMES (IRE) 2 b.g. (Mar 9) Big Bad Bob (IRE) 118 – Zamarelle 65 **78 p**
(Zamindar (USA) 116) [2017 7g^{5} 7d^{2} p8g* Nov 1] fair form: won minor event at Kempton
(by 3¼ lengths from Sky Rocket) in November: will stay beyond 1m: likely to progress
further. *Gary Moore*

PONDERING 3 br.f. So You Think (NZ) 133 – Lebenstanz 66 (Singspiel (IRE) 133) **78**
[2017 71p: t12.2g^{3} 10.2m^{6} 11.8s^{4} 11.6g^{2} 10d* 11.6f^{4} 9.9d* 10s^{4} 10v^{4} Sep 17] angular filly:
fair performer: won maiden at Lingfield and handicap at Sandown in July: stays 1¼m: acts
on soft going: in visor last 5 starts: often races towards rear. *Eve Johnson Houghton*

PONTECARLO BOY 3 ch.g. Piccolo 121 – Dahshah 77 (Mujtahid (USA) 118) [2017 **49**
51: 7g 8g 7.4d^{6} 6d 9.9m^{4} 8.5s 12v t8d Nov 10] modest maiden: stays 1¼m: acts on firm
going: has worn headgear, including last 4 starts: often races prominently. *Richard Whitaker*

POOL HOUSE 6 b.g. Sakhee's Secret 128 – Gitane (FR) (Grand Lodge (USA) 125) [2017 **66**
77: t8.6m^{2} t8g^{6} t7.1g t8.6g f8g^{2} t9.5g^{3} p8g p8g^{5} May 8] fair performer: stays 8.5f: acts on
polytrack, tapeta and soft going: has worn headgear, including final start. *Mike Murphy*

POORAULDJOSEPHINE 2 ch.f. (Feb 17) Piccolo 121 – Moment In The Sun 69 **–**
(Dubai Destination (USA) 127) [2017 5m p6g p6s Dec 1] smallish, close-coupled filly: first
foal: dam 1m-1¼m winner: little sign of ability: left David Flood after first start: tried in
blinkers. *J. R. Jenkins*

POOR DUKE (IRE) 7 b.g. Bachelor Duke (USA) 122 – Graze On Too (IRE) 54 **61**
(Rainbow Quest (USA) 134) [2017 63: t8.6m t8.6g 6m 7d* 8.2g t7.2g 8.1d^{6} 8d 7v Sep 25] **a52**
sparely-made gelding: modest handicapper: won at Leicester in June: best up to 1m: acts
on polytrack, tapeta, firm and good to soft going: has worn headgear, including in 2017.
Michael Mullineaux

POPESWOOD (IRE) 5 b.g. Haatef (USA) 117 – Binfield (IRE) 77 (Officer (USA) 120) **– §**
[2017 79d: 7g^{5} p8d 7s 7s^{6} Aug 5] angular gelding: fairly useful handicapper at best, has lost
his form completely: has worn headgear, including last 2 starts: usually slowly away, often
races in rear. *Lee Carter*

POPPYINTHEPARK 4 b.f. Bahri (USA) 125 – Lark In The Park (IRE) 57 (Grand **61**
Lodge (USA) 125) [2017 11.2d 12g^{4} 12.3g^{5} 12.1v^{5} t14g Nov 25] fifth foal: half-sister to 3
winners, including useful 5f to (at 2 yrs) 7f winner Secretinthepark (by Sakhee's Secret)
and 7f-1¼m winner Dolphin Rock (by Mark of Esteem): dam 1m winner: modest maiden:
left Richard Ford after fourth start: best effort at 1½m: tried in hood: sometimes slowly
away. *Michael Mullineaux*

POPPY IN THE WIND 5 b.m. Piccolo 121 – Vintage Steps (IRE) 76 (Bahamian Bounty **81**
116) [2017 79: t5g^{2} t5g* t6d^{2} t6g^{3} t5d 5m^{6} 5g^{2} t5s^{4} 6m t5d^{6} t6d^{6} t5g^{6} t6.1g* Dec 18] fairly
useful handicapper: won at Newcastle in January and Wolverhampton in December: stays
6f: acts on tapeta, good to firm and good to soft going: wears headgear: races towards rear.
Alan Brown

POPPY JAG (IRE) 2 b.f. (Apr 25) Kodiac 112 – Jacquelin Jag (IRE) (Fayruz 116) [2017 **50**
6d t5.1g p5g^{5} p6g p6g t5g^{6} t6.1g^{6} Nov 29] €19,000Y, £18,000 2-y-o: fifth foal: closely
related to 5f to (at 2 yrs) 6f winner Jaganory (by Dylan Thomas): dam unraced sister to
smart sprinter Fayr Jag: poor maiden: stays 6f: acts on polytrack and tapeta: in cheekpieces
last 2 starts. *Kevin Frost*

POPPY LINE 2 b.f. (Feb 14) Equiano (FR) 127 – Ming Meng (IRE) 85 (Intikhab (USA) **–**
135) [2017 6d^{5} 6d Nov 11] third foal: half-sister to 6f winner Manipura (by Sleeping
Indian): dam, 6f winner, sister to useful winner up to 9f Fine Silver: well held in minor
event/maiden. *Derek Shaw*

POPPY MAY (IRE) 3 b.f. Zoffany (IRE) 121 – Lara Amelia (IRE) (Ishiguru (USA) 114) **51**
[2017 55: t6m^{3} t7.1m f8.1g Dec 4] modest maiden handicapper: stays 7f: acts on polytrack,
tapeta and good to firm going: tried in cheekpieces: usually races close up. *James Given*

POPPY PIVOT (IRE) 3 b.f. Pivotal 124 – Havin' A Good Time (IRE) 88 (Jeremy (USA) **–**
122) [2017 67: t6m t5g Jan 25] maiden, well beaten in handicaps in 2017: tried in visor/
tongue tie. *Michael Appleby*

POPPY TIME 4 b.f. Pour Moi (IRE) 125 – Shamandar (FR) 106 (Exceed And Excel **70**
(AUS) 126) [2017 64: 8.3g 10d^{2} 10.1m^{4} 10.1g^{4} Jul 12] sturdy filly: fair maiden handicapper:
stays 1½m: acts on good to firm and good to soft going. *James Eustace*

POPPY WALTON (IRE) 2 ch.f. (Apr 12) Society Rock (IRE) 126 – Bellacoola (GER) (Lomitas 129) [2017 6g^4 6m^6 7.4g^4 7.4m^4 6s Oct 10] 11,000F, £17,000Y: half-sister to several winners, including French 7f winner Manticore (by Dark Angel) and useful French 5f/6f winner Prinzde Glas (by Verglas): dam German 7f winner: modest maiden: best effort at 7.5f: best form on good going. *Ollie Pears* **64**

POPSI 2 b.f. (Jan 18) Captain Gerrard (IRE) 113 – Deslaya (IRE) 63 (Green Desert (USA) 127) [2017 4.5d 4.5g^5 5.5g^5 5g* 5m^2 5d t5.1g Aug 18] third foal: dam maiden who stayed 8.6f: modest performer: won seller at Redcar in May: left Jo Hughes after fifth start: stays 5.5f: probably acts on good to firm going: sometimes in cheekpieces: front runner/races prominently. *Marjorie Fife* **57**

POPSICLE (IRE) 2 b.f. (Jan 17) Acclamation 118 – Katchy Lady 84 (Kyllachy 129) [2017 6.1g^2 t6.1g p6s Dec 1] 60,000Y: first foal: dam 5f winner (including at 2 yrs): fair form: standout effort when second in minor event at Windsor (3¾ lengths behind Grand Koonta) in July. *Richard Hannon* **68**

POPSIES JOY (IRE) 4 b.f. Alfred Nobel (IRE) 110 – Senzate (Lujain (USA) 119) [2017 76: 8m 7.4m^5 6.9v^6 7.2m^6 7.4m^6 7.4s Aug 1] fair handicapper: stays 1m: acts on soft and good to firm going: has worn headgear, including in 2017: sometimes slowly away, often races towards rear: temperament under suspicion. *Tim Easterby* **65**

POPSILCA 3 b.f. Captain Gerrard (IRE) 113 – Silca Destination 65 (Dubai Destination (USA) 127) [2017 –: p5m* p6d^2 p5g^4 p5g 6m 5.1m^6 5.2d^5 p5g^6 p5g^3 Oct 13] lengthy, angular filly: modest handicapper: won at Lingfield in January: stays 6f: acts on polytrack: usually leads. *Mick Quinn* **58**

PORCHY PARTY (IRE) 2 ch.g. (Mar 15) Dragon Pulse (IRE) 114 – Shawaaty (IRE) (Monsun (GER) 124) [2017 5f^4 5g^2 6d^3 6.1g t5.1g^2 5d* 5m^5 5.1v* 5v^5 Sep 29] €18,000F, 18,000Y: well-grown gelding: third foal: half-brother to a winner abroad by Lilbourne Lad: dam lightly-raced half-sister to useful French 11f/1½m winner Mahaatheer: fairly useful performer: won nurseries at Carlisle in August and Chester (by 1¾ lengths from Mable Lee) in September: best form at 5f: acts on tapeta and heavy going: in cheekpieces last 5 starts: front runner/races prominently. *Tom Dascombe* **84**

PORRIMA (IRE) 2 gr.f. (Jan 11) Kodiac 112 – El Morocco (USA) (El Prado (IRE) 119) [2017 6g^3 Jun 20] €23,000 2-y-o: fifth foal: half-sister to 2-y-o 6f winners Cardmaster (by Red Clubs) and Arranger (by Bushranger): dam unraced: 33/1, third in minor event at Thirsk (2½ lengths behind Silca Mistress) in June: should improve. *Ben Haslam* **63 p**

PORTA ROSA (USA) 4 b.f. Street Cry (IRE) 130 – Sander Camillo (USA) 116 (Dixie Union (USA) 121) [2017 p7d^F p7s^6 p6s Jun 21] attractive filly: fairly useful at 2 yrs, below best only 2 completed starts since: stays 7f: acts on polytrack: sold 14,000 gns, sent to Greece. *Mohamed Moubarak* **78**

PORTH SWTAN (IRE) 2 b.c. (Mar 20) Invincible Spirit (IRE) 121 – Propaganda (IRE) 76 (Sadler's Wells (USA) 132) [2017 7d^3 7d^2 7g 7v^2 7m^2 7g^2 Nov 3] €110,000Y: lengthy, useful-looking colt: seventh foal: brother to useful 2-y-o 7f winner Shagah and half-brother to useful 1½m-13.4f winner (stayed 2m) Swnymor (by Dylan Thomas): dam 11f winner: fairly useful maiden: second 4 times, including in nursery at Newmarket in October minor event at same course (length behind Maghaweer) in November: raced only at 7f: acts on good to firm and good to soft going. *Charles Hills* **84**

PORT ISAAC (IRE) 4 b.g. Sakhee's Secret 128 – Dombeya (IRE) 66 (Danehill (USA) 126) [2017 78: 6m^5 p6g Nov 18] lengthy gelding: fair maiden: well below form both starts in 2017: stays 7f: acts on polytrack and good to firm going: tried in headgear. *Marcus Tregoning* **58**

PORT LAIRGE 7 b.g. Pastoral Pursuits 127 – Stylish Clare (IRE) 77 (Desert Style (IRE) 121) [2017 69: f12g f14g f12m f8d^6 8g^5 9.9s 10.2g 8d^3 9.9d 8v^4 f8.1g f11.1g f11.1g Dec 22] poor handicapper: stays 11f: acts on polytrack, fibresand, good to firm and heavy going: often in headgear: thoroughly ungenuine. *Michael Chapman* **§§**

PORTLAND STREET (IRE) 4 b.g. Dream Ahead (USA) 133 – Danaskaya (IRE) 106 (Danehill (USA) 126) [2017 77: 6g 6m^2 6m^2 5.9g 6d t6d Aug 10] fair handicapper: stays 6f: best form on good going: wears headgear. *Bryan Smart* **72**

PORTLEDGE (IRE) 3 b.g. Acclamation 118 – Off Chance 106 (Olden Times 121) [2017 76: t8d^3 8g^3 8.5d 8g^3 t8s^4 t7.1d t7.1g* p7g^3 Nov 6] fairly useful handicapper: won at Newcastle in October: third at Kempton (neck behind Dourado) final start: stays 1m: acts on polytrack, tapeta and good to firm going: sometimes in blinkers in 2017. *James Bethell* **86**

PORT MASTER 3 b.g. Harbour Watch (IRE) 121 – Gentle Guru 98 (Ishiguru (USA) 114) **58**
[2017 –: t6g^3 t5d 6m 5s 7.8d Aug 29] modest maiden: best effort at 6f: acts on tapeta: often races in rear. *Ann Duffield*

PORT OF CALL 2 b.g. (Mar 26) Harbour Watch (IRE) 121 – Valiantly 103 (Anabaa **71**
(USA) 130) [2017 7g^6 7g p7g^4 Sep 27] rather unfurnished gelding: fair form: best effort when sixth in maiden at Sandown (5 lengths behind Bathsheba Bay) in September. *Amanda Perrett*

PORTO FERRO (IRE) 3 b.f. Arcano (IRE) 122 – Sassari (IRE) 76 (Darshaan 133) **70**
[2017 80: p6g^5 p6g* p6g^5 7m 7m^4 p7g 7d p7g Aug 31] rather leggy filly: fair performer: won maiden at Lingfield in February: stays 7f: acts on polytrack, soft and good to firm going: usually in headgear in 2017: often races towards rear. *Dr Jon Scargill*

PORT PARADISE 4 gr.g. Paco Boy (IRE) 129 – Yacht Woman (USA) (Mizzen Mast **–**
(USA) 121) [2017 75: t9.5g 10d^4 Jul 12] leggy gelding: fair handicapper: well below form in sellers in 2017: stays 1¼m: acts on polytrack, firm and good to soft going: wears hood. *William Jarvis*

PORTRUSH STORM 12 ch.m. Observatory (USA) 131 – Overcast (IRE) 72 (Caerleon **–**
(USA) 132) [2017 –: t6g t7.1g 6s^5 t6.1g Nov 11] workmanlike mare: one-time fair handicapper: little impact since 2013: has worn headgear: often starts slowly. *Ray Peacock*

PORT SOIF 3 b.f. Foxwedge (AUS) 128 – Positivity 79 (Monsieur Bond (IRE) 120) [2017 **–**
t6d t8g^6 t6d^6 Nov 10] 20,000Y: second foal: half-sister to 2-y-o 6f winner Cumbrianna (by Hellvelyn): dam, 7.5f/1m winner, half-sister to useful 1m winner Peculiarity: mid-division at best in maidens. *David O'Meara*

POSEIDON (IRE) 3 ch.g. Born To Sea (IRE) 117 – Maskaya (IRE) 92 (Machiavellian **81**
(USA) 123) [2017 70p: 10.1m^6 12d^5 10d^2 9.9s* 10d^5 Oct 23] angular gelding: fairly useful handicapper: won at Salisbury (by head from Haulani) in October: stays 1¼m: acts on soft and good to firm going: sold 75,000 gns in November. *Ed Walker*

POSH BOUNTY 6 ch.m. Bahamian Bounty 116 – Fission 77 (Efisio 120) [2017 81: p7d **56**
6.1v p7g 6d^6 7.1v 6d^5 6g p7g 5.7s Sep 17] plain mare: fairly useful handicapper: well below form in 2017: stays 7.5f: acts on heavy going: sometimes in hood in 2017. *Paul Burgoyne*

POSTPONED (IRE) 6 b.h. Dubawi (IRE) 129 – Ever Rigg 83 (Dubai Destination (USA) **121**
127) [2017 130: 12g^2 12d^3 Mar 25] strong, close-coupled, attractive horse: top-class performer: winner of Great Voltigeur Stakes at York in 2014, and King George VI and Queen Elizabeth Stakes at Ascot and Prix Foy at Longchamp in 2015 when trained by Luca Cumani: better still at 5 yrs, winning 4 times, including Coronation Cup at Epsom and Juddmonte International at York: below best at Meydan in 2017 when second in Dubai City of Gold (neck behind Prize Money) and third in Dubai Sheema Classic (4 lengths behind Jack Hobbs) (had won both races in 2016): stayed 1½m: acted on soft and good to firm going: often raced prominently, usually travelled strongly: genuine and reliable: retired in May after suffering stress fracture: to stand at Dalham Hall Stud, Newmarket, fee £20,000. *Roger Varian*

POUCOR 2 b.g. (May 9) Pour Moi (IRE) 125 – Corinium (IRE) 116 (Turtle Island (IRE) **53**
123) [2017 7.1s^4 8d Sep 5] modest form on first of 2 starts. *Mick Channon*

POUND NOTE 5 b.g. Top Line Dancer (IRE) 72 – Avondale Girl (IRE) 73 (Case Law **–**
113) [2017 7s 6g 5.7s f6.1g Oct 22] little form: in headgear last 2 starts. *Michael Mullineaux*

POUR L'AMOUR (IRE) 4 b.f. Aqlaam 125 – Passion Fruit 91 (Pursuit of Love 124) **73**
[2017 t9.5m^3 t12.4g^2 t9.5g^4 t12.2g t12.2g^2 t12.2g^3 t12.2g* 12s t12.2g^4 12.1m^3 12g^3 t12.2g^5 t12.2d Dec 16] fair handicapper: won at Wolverhampton (dead-heated) in May: likely to stay beyond 1½m: acts on tapeta and good to firm going. *Daniel Loughnane*

POUR LA VICTOIRE (IRE) 7 b.g. Antonius Pius (USA) 123 – Lady Lucia (IRE) 51 **74**
(Royal Applause 124) [2017 85: 5.1m 6m 6m^6 6g^6 8m 6g^2 6g 5m 7v Oct 19] workmanlike gelding: fair handicapper: stays 1m: acts on polytrack, tapeta, good to firm and heavy going: wears headgear: usually slowly away, races well off pace. *Tony Carroll*

POURQUOI MOI 4 b.f. Multiplex 114 – Sweet Applause (IRE) 84 (Acclamation 118) **53**
[2017 p12g^4 Mar 22] second foal: half-sister to 1m-1¼m winner Captain Felix (by Captain Gerrard): dam 6f winner: well beaten in bumper: 14/1, fourth in maiden at Kempton (hooded, 14 lengths behind Villette). *George Scott*

POUVOIR MAGIQUE (FR) 3 b.c. Le Havre (IRE) 124 – Barmaid (FR) (Cape Cross (IRE) 129) [2017 9.9g^3 10d* 12s^4 10.2d t8d* Nov 10] €12,000Y, 300,000 2-y-o: first foal: dam, French 2-y-o 7.5f winner, half-sister to useful performer up to 13f Pivotal Answer: useful performer: won maiden at Ayr in July and handicap at Newcastle (by ¾ length from Alexandrakollontai) in November: stays 1¼m: acts on tapeta and good to soft going: often races prominently: will go on improving. *John Gosden* **101 p**

POWDERHOUSE (IRE) 3 b.g. Raven's Pass (USA) 133 – Monday Show (USA) 99 (Maria's Mon (USA) 121) [2017 10g^6 8.2d^3 8.3g^4 Aug 18] strong gelding: fair form: best effort when fourth in maiden at Nottingham final start: in cheekpieces last 2 starts: tried in tongue tie. *Charlie Appleby* **76**

POWDERONTHEBONNET (IRE) 9 b.g. Definite Article 121 – Zuhal 67 (Busted 134) [2017 56: 16.2m^3 May 5] modest maiden handicapper: stays 16.5f: acts on tapeta, good to firm and heavy going: tried in cheekpieces: modest hurdler. *Sam Thomas* **54**

POWERALLIED (IRE) 4 b.g. Camacho 118 – Kaplinsky (IRE) 75 (Fath (USA) 116) [2017 96: 5m 6.1s^6 5.1d^2 5g^2 5.1d 5.5g 5.5g* 5v Sep 30] stocky gelding: fairly useful handicapper: won at Chester (by 1¼ lengths from El Astronaute) in September: stays 6f: acts on heavy going. *Richard Fahey* **94**

POWER AND PEACE (IRE) 2 b.f. (Mar 30) Arcano (IRE) 122 – Dubai Power 89 (Cadeaux Genereux 131) [2017 6m^4 7f^2 p7g^3 Sep 25] €6,000F, €3,000Y, £32,000 2-y-o: fifth foal: half-sister to 2-y-o 1m winner Power of Light (by Echo of Light) and winner up to 1m Escrick (2-y-o 5f winner, by Vale of York): dam, 6f-1m winner, half-sister to useful 7f/1m performer Vanguard Dream: fair form: best effort when third in minor event at Kempton (length behind Homeopathic) final start: should be suited by 1m. *David Simcock* **75**

POWERCELL (IRE) 3 b.f. Power 117 – Celtic Heroine (IRE) 111 (Hernando (FR) 127) [2017 7g^6 8s 8g^4 7.4m Jul 8] 3,000Y: seventh foal: half-sister to smart 10.7f-12.5f winner Time For Action (by Dylan Thomas) and 1¼m winner (stayed 1½m) Mr Snagsby (by Duke of Marmalade): dam, 7f/1m winner (including at 2 yrs), sister to very smart winner up to 1½m winner Rainbow Peak: modest form: will be suited by 1¼m. *Tim Easterby* **52**

POWERED (IRE) 4 b.g. Frozen Power (IRE) 108 – Confirm (IRE) 62 (In The Wings 128) [2017 59: f8g^4 f8g^5 f8g t8.6g^6 p10g t9.5g^5 p12g^2 f12g^4 t9.5g^2 p12g^4 11.6g^3 10d^2 11.6g^2 11.6f^4 11.4m* 11.9g^5 11.6f t12.2g 11.4m^2 p12d^3 13d^3 12g^5 t12.2g^2 Sep 9] lengthy gelding: fair handicapper: won at Windsor (apprentice) in June: second at same course in August: stays 13f: acts on all-weather, firm and good to soft going: has worn headgear: often races towards rear. *David Evans* **67**

POWERFUL DREAM (IRE) 4 b.f. Frozen Power (IRE) 108 – Noble View (USA) 68 (Distant View (USA) 126) [2017 76: t5.1g^4 t5.1g* t5.1g^2 t5.1g^3 t5.1g 5f^{ur} 5.7f* 5.7d^6 5.7f* 5.7f^2 5m 5d^4 5m t5.1g^3 t5.1g^6 p5g^6 p6g^5 Dec 20] lengthy filly: fair handicapper: won at Wolverhampton in February and Bath (twice) in May: stays 5.5f: acts on polytrack, tapeta and firm going: wears headgear. *Ronald Harris* **78**

POWERFUL LOVE (IRE) 3 b.g. Clodovil (IRE) 116 – Ruby Ridge (IRE) (Acatenango (GER) 127) [2017 75: 9.8g^5 9.8d 11.2g^2 11.1g^5 10g 11.8s Aug 8] fair maiden handicapper: stays 11f: best form on good going: in headgear last 4 starts: usually races close up. *Mark Johnston* **74**

POWERFUL ROSE 2 b.f. (Mar 4) Power 117 – Fenella Rose 73 (Compton Place 125) [2017 6m 6d^5 p6g Nov 29] 12,000Y: rather unfurnished filly: first foal: dam 2-y-o 6f winner: little impact in minor events. *Michael Blanshard* **–**

POWERFUL SOCIETY (IRE) 2 b.f. (Apr 10) Power 117 – Society Gal (IRE) (Galileo (IRE) 134) [2017 6g 6.1v^4 7m^3 6.9v* 9d^5 f7.1g* Nov 28] €25,000Y: leggy, close-coupled filly: fifth foal: half-sister to 3 winners, including 1¼m-1½m winner Goldenfield (by Footstepsinthesand) and 2-y-o 1m winner Bleeding Hearts (by Peintre Celebre): dam unraced half-sister to US Grade 3 9f winner Good Mood: fair performer: won nursery at Carlisle in September and claimer at Southwell in November: should stay at least 1m: acts on fibresand, good to firm and heavy going: usually slowly away. *Richard Fahey* **73**

POWERFUL WIND (IRE) 8 ch.g. Titus Livius (FR) 115 – Queen of Fools (IRE) (Xaar 132) [2017 81: f5g t5.1g f5m^4 p5m^2 f5g^3 5.1m 5g^5 p5g^4 5.2m^5 Aug 1] stocky gelding: fair handicapper: stays 5.5f: acts on polytrack, fibresand, firm and good to soft going: tried in cheekpieces: wears tongue tie: front runner: temperamental. *Charlie Wallis* **61 §** **a70 §**

POWER GAME 5 ch.g. Shamardal (USA) 129 – Counterclaim 98 (Pivotal 124) [2017 101: 10.3m 7.9m Jul 1] good-topped gelding: useful handicapper: below form both starts in 2017: stays 11f: acts on polytrack: sent to Germany. *David O'Meara* **83**

POWER HOME (IRE) 3 ch.f. Power 117 – Ascendancy (Sadler's Wells (USA) 132) [2017 59: p8g5 p10g3 p12g6 t9.5m* t9.5g2 p12g Nov 29] fair performer: won minor event at Wolverhampton in October: stays 1¼m: acts on polytrack and tapeta. *Denis Coakley* **71**

POWER OF DARKNESS 2 b.c. (Mar 29) Power 117 – Summers Lease 92 (Pivotal 124) [2017 7d6 7m3 Aug 25] 52,000Y: fourth foal: half-brother to 5f winner Summer Isles (by Exceed And Excel) and 1m winner Nancy Astor (by Shamardal): dam, 1m winner, sister to smart sprinter/US Grade 3 9f winner Needwood Blade: fairly useful form: better effort when third in minor event at Newmarket (3¼ lengths behind Fortune's Pearl) second start: will stay 1m: open to further improvement. *Marcus Tregoning* **80 p**

POWER POWER (IRE) 3 ch.g. Power 117 – Charmingly (USA) 62 (King of Kings (IRE) 125) [2017 –: p8g5 p8g2 p8g3 May 2] fair maiden: stays 1m: acts on polytrack. *Marco Botti* **74**

POWER SAIL 2 gr.g. (Mar 18) Frozen Power (IRE) 108 – Gone Sailing (Mizzen Mast (USA) 121) [2017 7v 7.9g 8d4 t7.1g6 t9.5g Nov 20] modest maiden: may prove best at short of 1m: acts on good to soft going: tried in blinkers. *Tim Easterby* **60**

POWER SURGE (IRE) 3 ch.g. Power 117 – Silver Skates (IRE) 89 (Slip Anchor 136) [2017 t9.5g* Aug 31] €50,000Y: seventh foal: half-brother to 3 winners, including useful/ungenuine stayer Icon Dream (2-y-o 7.5f winner, by Sadler's Wells) and to dam of Phoenix/Matron Stakes winner La Collina: dam maiden (stayed 1¼m): 12/1, won maiden at Wolverhampton (by 2¾ lengths from Mesbaar) on debut: sure to progress. *Ralph Beckett* **83 p**

POWER UP 6 b.m. Rail Link 132 – Melpomene 95 (Peintre Celebre (USA) 137) [2017 68: p10dpu p11g p10s Nov 16] fair handicapper: no form in 2017: left Roger Ingram after second start: has worn headgear: tried in tongue tie. *Luke McJannet* **–**

POW WOW 3 b.g. Medicean 128 – Ship's Biscuit 107 (Tiger Hill (IRE) 127) [2017 57p: 12m* 12f* 13f* p12g3 Sep 27] fairly useful handicapper: won at Salisbury in May/June and Bath (by 9 lengths from Pete So High) later in June: third at Kempton final start: left Roger Charlton after third start: will stay at least 1¾m: acts on polytrack and firm going: often leads. *Martyn Meade* **92**

POYLE CHARLOTTE 2 b.f. (Apr 6) Farhh 131 – Poyle Caitlin (IRE) 62 (Bachir (IRE) 118) [2017 p7g5 Sep 25] half-sister to 3 winners, including 2-y-o 5f/6f winner Puddle Duck (by Pastoral Pursuits) and winner up to 1¼m Marhaba Malayeen (2-y-o 7f winner, by Dutch Art): dam, maiden (stayed 1m), half-sister to Lowther Stakes winner Jemima: 8/1, fifth in minor event at Kempton (2¾ lengths behind Homeopathic) in September: should improve. *Ralph Beckett* **70 p**

POYLE EMILY 4 b.f. Compton Place 125 – Poyle Dee Dee 72 (Oasis Dream 129) [2017 66p: 8g 7g p8g Sep 13] fair form on debut at 3 yrs, disappointing since: tried in visor. *Michael Madgwick* **–**

POYLE THOMAS 8 b.g. Rail Link 132 – Lost In Lucca 72 (Inchinor 119) [2017 100: 13.3s 12s6 18m p16g4 p16d p15.8g6 Dec 28] sturdy gelding: useful handicapper: largely well below form in 2017: stays 21f: acts on polytrack and firm going: has worn headgear: often races towards rear. *Michael Madgwick* **93 d**

POYLE VINNIE 7 b.g. Piccolo 121 – Poyle Dee Dee 72 (Oasis Dream 129) [2017 109: t6g3 f5g* p6g5 5.2g 6m 5s3 5g 6m 5g4 6d 6s 5v Sep 30] sturdy gelding: useful handicapper: won at Southwell (by 2½ lengths from Razin' Hell) in January: stays 6f: acts on all-weather, soft and good to firm going: has worn cheekpieces, including in 2017: often races in rear. *Michael Appleby* **108**

PRAECEPS (IRE) 2 b.g. (Jan 26) Canford Cliffs (IRE) 133 – Sliding Scale (Sadler's Wells (USA) 132) [2017 p8g p8g5 t8g p8d Nov 9] mid-division at best in minor events: raced only at 1m. *Sir Mark Prescott Bt* **54**

PRAIRIE IMPULSE 4 b.f. Major Cadeaux 121 – Prairie Sun (GER) 81 (Law Society (USA) 130) [2017 56: t12.4g5 Feb 14] maiden, well held only start in 2017. *Rebecca Menzies* **–**

PRANCEABOOTTHETOON (IRE) 2 ch.c. (Apr 14) Sir Prancealot (IRE) 111 – Cabopino (IRE) 58 (Captain Rio 122) [2017 6m* t5.1g6 6g4 6g3 Oct 16] fair form: won minor event at Brighton in June: stays 6f. *John Ryan* **75**

PRANCELINA (IRE) 3 ch.f. Sir Prancealot (IRE) 111 – Fingal Nights (IRE) 81 (Night Shift (USA)) [2017 64: p5g 5m^6 5.3g^3 5f^3 t6.1g 6d^4 Jul 11] smallish, sturdy filly: modest handicapper: stays 6f: acts on tapeta, best turf form on good going: tried in cheekpieces/ tongue tie: front runner/races prominently. *Phil McEntee* **63**

PRANCING OSCAR (IRE) 3 b.g. Sir Prancealot (IRE) 111 – Beguiler (Refuse To Bend (IRE) 128) [2017 54: t8g^2 7m 8d 8.3s^4 t8.6g* 8.9m^3 Aug 30] fair handicapper: won at Wolverhampton in July: stays 9f: acts on tapeta and good to firm going: tried in cheekpieces. *Ben Haslam* **72**

PRAXEDIS 2 b.f. (Mar 28) Dutch Art 126 – Angel Song 68 (Dansili 127) [2017 p6g Oct 17] 40,000Y: fourth foal: half-sister to 6f winner Hart Stopper (by Compton Place) and a winner in Italy by Kyllachy: dam, 6f winner, half-sister to smart sprinter Mood Music: 20/1, well held in minor event at Kempton: should do better. *James Fanshawe* **– p**

PRAZERES 3 b.g. Sepoy (AUS) 129 – Sewards Folly 70 (Rudimentary (USA) 118) [2017 82: t6g^3 t6g^3 t5d 6m^5 5m 5m^6 6g^3 6d 6d 7g* 7m^5 6v t6g Nov 3] compact gelding: fair handicapper: won at Catterick in August: stays 7f: acts on tapeta and good to firm going: has worn cheekpieces: tried in tongue tie: usually leads: temperamental. *Les Eyre* **70 §**

PREACHER MAN (IRE) 2 b.c. (Mar 18) Lope de Vega (IRE) 125 – Daniysha (IRE) 76 (Doyoun 124) [2017 7d^4 7g^2 7d^5 Aug 5] good-quartered colt: fair form: best effort when second in minor event at Ascot (½ length behind Curiosity) in July. *Jamie Osborne* **74**

PRECIEUSE (IRE) 3 ch.f. Tamayuz 126 – Zut Alors (IRE) 105 (Pivotal 124) [2017 6d* 6m^2 8d* 8m Jun 23] **116**

The Poule d'Essai des Pouliches was contested by one of the season's top miling fillies Roly Poly and the future Prix de Diane winner Senga but, on the day, neither managed to reach the frame behind outsider Precieuse, a filly with a family history of ambitious tilts at the French version of the One Thousand Guineas. Precieuse herself had only a maiden win to her name beforehand and had little opportunity to raise her profile subsequently, being unraced in the second half of the year following her export to the States. Precieuse had raced only over sprint trips prior to the Pouliches and had found one too good for her on all three of her starts the previous autumn, the last two of those being listed races in which she was beaten by British-trained opponents, going down to Private Matter at Maisons-Laffitte and then Simmie at Chantilly. Precieuse returned with a comfortable three-length win in a maiden at Fontainebleau in March and, kept to six furlongs, followed that with her best effort before Deauville when finishing three and a half lengths second to the colt Fas in the Prix Sigy at Chantilly. Apart from having her stamina to prove the following month, Precieuse had more to find than most on form in an eighteen-runner Poule d'Essai des Pouliches sponsored by Abu Dhabi. Roly Poly and Senga had shown the most at two, but the Cheveley Park runner-up had made a lacklustre return in the Nell Gwyn Stakes while Senga had confirmed the promise of her fourth in the Prix Marcel Boussac by winning the main Pouliches trial, the Prix de la Grotte, on her reappearance at Chantilly. It was Senga who shaded favouritism from the Andre Fabre-trained filly Via Ravenna who had won both her starts, notably the Prix Imprudence at Maisons-Laffitte from Senga's stable-companion Thais. Precieuse, bidding to give her jockey Olivier Peslier his third win in the race, was a 28/1 chance.

Approaching the final furlong, several were still in with a chance after Roly Poly had taken it up two out in the centre of the track, but Precieuse, delivered nearer the stand rail, quickened ahead in the final furlong and saw out the longer trip really well. Sea of Grace, fifth in the Nell Gwyn on her first start for William Haggas, was another who showed plenty of improvement to take second, a length and three quarters behind after challenging much wider out, while third-placed Heuristique, a listed winner at two and beaten just another three quarters of a length, had also shown only useful form beforehand. Roly Poly gave little indication of the progress she was to make later in the year in finishing sixth, just behind stable-companion Rain Goddess, with Via Ravenna seventh and a disappointing Senga further back, seemingly unsuited by the softer conditions, which, by contrast, Precieuse appeared to relish. Conditions were firmer at Royal Ascot where Precieuse made her only subsequent reappearance when supplemented in a bid to become the third consecutive French-trained winner of the Coronation Stakes. She and Roly Poly had something of a set-to from halfway and, while Roly Poly kept going to

Abu Dhabi Poule d'Essai des Pouliches, Deauville—28/1-shot Precieuse is much improved and pulls clear of British raider Sea of Grace (star on cap) and Heuristique (white cap)

chase home stable-companion Winter, Precieuse was already a spent force when squeezed against the rail under a furlong out and came home last of the seven. She was reported to have been exported to the States the following month but hadn't raced there by the end of the year.

Precieuse carried new colours at Ascot following a change of ownership, two-tone green silks which might have been vaguely familiar to older racegoers if perhaps a little hard to place. The reason was that they had last been carried on a British racecourse the best part of thirty years earlier, including by those excellent racemares Triptych and Roseate Tern. The colours are those of American Peter Brant who has made a big impact in the sale-ring on both sides of the Atlantic since resurrecting his racing and bloodstock interests under the name of White Birch Farm. Brant was used to his spending making headlines in former times as he had purchased Triptych for 3,400,000 dollars at the start of her six-year-old season in 1988, the final year of her remarkable career during which she won her second Coronation Cup, while a year later he paid 1,100,000 guineas for Yorkshire Oaks winner Roseate Tern as a three-year-old before she won the following season's Jockey Club Stakes. White Birch had its first winner in France early in June with one of a number of horses acquired from the dispersal of the Wildenstein bloodstock empire the previous autumn. Chief among them was the 2012 Poule d'Essai des Pouliches winner Beauty Parlour bought for €1,600,000. Besides Precieuse, another leading French filly to be snapped up was Sistercharlie who carried the White Birch colours into second behind Senga in the Prix de Diane and filled the same position in the Belmont Oaks, while Thais, who finished down the field in the Pouliches before winning a listed race, was another acquisition to join White Birch's US trainer Chad Brown. In partnership with Coolmore, Brant also paid 1,500,000 guineas for the Albany Stakes winner Different League when she came up for auction at Newmarket in December.

Precieuse (IRE) (ch.f. 2014)	Tamayuz (ch 2005)	Nayef (b 1998)	Gulch
			Height of Fashion
		Al Ishq (ch 1997)	Nureyev
			Allez Les Trois
	Zut Alors (IRE) (b 2004)	Pivotal (ch 1993)	Polar Falcon
			Fearless Revival
		Zeiting (b 1997)	Zieten
			Belle de Cadix

Precieuse's sire Tamayuz was a high-class miler, winning the Prix Jean Prat and Jacques le Marois, though his best progeny have been a very mixed bag distance-wise, ranging from the Sprint Cup winner G Force to the latest season's Doncaster Cup winner Desert Skyline. The Andrew Balding-trained E. P. Taylor Stakes winner Blond Me and the Strensall Stakes winner Mustashry were other good winners in the latest season for Tamayuz, a grandson, incidentally, of Breeders' Cup Sprint winner Gulch whom Brant bred and raced in the 'eighties. Precieuse's useful dam Zut Alors also contested the Pouliches, though she was even more of a long-shot (over 100/1 on the pari-mutuel) than her daughter and ran accordingly. A mile was too far for Zut Alors, in any case, and having won a newcomers race at two over seven furlongs, she ended up over sprint distances, running her best race when a narrowly-beaten third in a listed race at Chantilly over five and a half furlongs. Zut Alors' highest-rated foal is a sprinter too. Baccarat (by Dutch Art) won the Wokingham in 2014 when trained by Richard Fahey and retained plenty of ability for Godolphin in the latest season, winning a handicap at the Dubai Carnival. Her other two winners have stayed further, with the useful French filly Peut Etre (by Whipper) winning at around a mile and a quarter and Grey Blue (by Verglas) successful at up to a mile and a half. Precieuse's two-year-old half-brother Delph Crescent (by Dark Angel) showed fair form at best for Richard Fahey. Grandam Zeiting was another useful filly and, like her daughter and granddaughter, she too contested the Pouliches as a long shot, finishing a close sixth in a blanket finish. Zeiting's three wins at two included a six-furlong listed event, and she won another three races later in the States, including a couple more listed contests, one of them over an extended mile. Zeiting has been a fine broodmare, with most of her winners proving at least useful, including Scottish, fifth in the Prince of Wales's Stakes on his only start in the latest season, Geoffrey Freer Stakes winner Royal Empire and the smart German-trained miler Combat Zone. Zeiting's useful half-sister Dolled Up was yet another family member to try her luck at long odds in the Pouliches but she had been best as a sprinter at two, although their dam Belle de Cadix won over thirteen furlongs in Ireland. Dolled Up's two-year-old daughter Fou Rire showed enough in the latest season to suggest she might be the family's next Pouliches contender. Another of Zeiting's half-sisters is the dam of the latest Hungerford Stakes winner Massaat, also runner-up in the 2016 Two Thousand Guineas. Precieuse, an attractive filly, stays a mile and acts on heavy and good to firm ground and, along with her new owner's other acquisitions from France, has joined Chad Brown. Precieuse's French trainer Fabrice Chappet was formerly assistant to Robert Collet who trained both her dam and grandam for Precieuse's breeders Brendan and Anne-Marie Hayes in whose pink and brown colours she began her career. *F. Chappet, France*

PRECIOUS ANGEL (IRE) 3 b.f. Excelebration (IRE) 133 – Evangeline (Sadler's Wells (USA) 132) [2017 –: 10d 9.9d³ p8d² 9.9g⁵ 9.9d⁴ p8g Oct 9] well-made filly: fair maiden: stays 1¼m: acts on polytrack and good to soft going: sometimes slowly away. *Richard Hannon* **77**

PRECIOUS EQUITY (FR) 3 b.f. Equiano (FR) 127 – Anasy (USA) (Gone West (USA)) [2017 –: t6m Mar 14] well held in maidens. *David Menuisier* **–**

PRECIOUS RAMOTSWE 3 b.f. Nathaniel (IRE) 129 – Miss Pinkerton 104 (Danehill (USA) 126) [2017 84p: 10d* 12.4s Nov 17] fairly useful form: won handicap at Newbury (by head from Lorelina) in October: well held in listed race at Saint-Cloud next time: best effort at 1¼m. *John Gosden* **94**

PRECIOUS ROCK (IRE) 3 b.g. Fastnet Rock (AUS) 127 – Attasliyah (IRE) (Marju (IRE) 127) [2017 9.2s 7g 7d Aug 21] little impact in maidens/juvenile hurdle: tried in hood. *Jedd O'Keeffe* **–**

PRECIOUS SILK (IRE) 2 ch.f. (Mar 27) Harbour Watch (IRE) 121 – Fine Silk (USA) 69 (Rahy (USA) 115) [2017 p7s³ p7g⁵ Dec 31] €4,000Y: third foal: half-sister to 2-y-o 7f winner Silk Gem (by Roderic O'Connor) and a winner in Italy by Intense Focus: dam, maiden (stayed 7f), sister to smart performer up to 1m Rahiyah: modest form in minor events. *Jose Santos* **61**

PRECIOUS SKYE (IRE) 3 b.f. Born To Sea (IRE) 117 – Secret Flame 78 (Machiavellian (USA) 123) [2017 48: 5g 5g 5g Sep 1] poor maiden at 2 yrs, no form in 2017. *Ronald Thompson* **–**

PRECISION 3 b.c. Galileo (IRE) 134 – Pearl Earrine (FR) (Kaldounevees (FR) 118) [2017 10m 9.9g 10d³ 14s* 14g⁴ Aug 18] €250,000Y: useful-looking colt: fourth foal: half-brother to smart French 2-y-o 7f/1m winner Topaze Blanche (by Zamindar): dam French **90 p**

12.5f winner: fairly useful performer: won handicap at Sandown in August: fourth in handicap at Nottingham (2 lengths behind Dubawi Fifty) final start: stays 1¾m: acts on soft going: often races prominently: remains capable of better. *Sir Michael Stoute*

PRECISION FIVE 8 b.m. Proclamation (IRE) 130 – Sashay 72 (Bishop of Cashel 122) **77**
[2017 89: p12m^{pu} t12.2g Mar 30] fairly useful handicapper, below form only completed start in 2017 (bled on return): stays 13.5f: acts on polytrack, tapeta and firm going: usually wears cheekpieces. *Nick Lampard*

PREDICTION (IRE) 2 b.g. (Jan 13) Dream Ahead (USA) 133 – Sho Girl (IRE) 88 **–**
(Lawman (FR) 121) [2017 5m 7d Jul 28] well held in minor events. *Kevin Ryan*

PREENING 2 b.f. (Mar 6) Dutch Art 126 – Striving (IRE) 66 (Danehill Dancer (IRE) 117) **90 p**
[2017 7d p8g* Oct 13] closely related to 2 winners by Medicean, including winner up to 7f Best Endeavour (2-y-o 6f winner), and half-sister to 2-y-o 6f winner (stayed 1m) Showpiece (by Kyllachy) and 2-y-o 1m winner Staunch (by Pivotal), later successful abroad: dam, maiden (stayed 1¼m), closely related to Cheveley Park Stakes winner/1000 Guineas runner-up Wannabe Grand: fairly useful form: won maiden at Kempton (by ½ length from Beckton) in October: will go on improving. *James Fanshawe*

PREMIER CURRENCY (IRE) 4 b.g. Elusive Pimpernel (USA) 117 – Zeena 61 **–**
(Unfuwain (USA) 131) [2017 71: t9.5g Nov 25] good-topped gelding: fair handicapper: well below form only start on Flat in 2017: stays 8.5f: acts on polytrack, good to firm and heavy going: sometimes in headgear: in tongue tie last 2 starts: usually leads. *Mike Murphy*

PRENDERGAST HILL (IRE) 5 b.g. Raven's Pass (USA) 133 – Daraliya (IRE) **90**
(Kahyasi 130) [2017 95: p11g^2 10m^3 10.2f^2 9.9m^3 11.9s^2 11.9m^4 Aug 10] compact gelding: fairly useful handicapper: second at Doncaster in July: stays 1½m: acts on polytrack, firm and soft going: has worn cheekpieces, including in 2017. *Ed de Giles*

PREOBRAJENSKA 3 b.f. Paco Boy (IRE) 129 – Unex Mona Lisa (Shamardal (USA) **72**
129) [2017 70: t6f^3 p7g* p7g^6 Apr 5] fair performer: won maiden at Kempton in March: left Michael Bell after first start: stays 7f: acts on polytrack and good to soft going: wears hood: tricky ride. *William Jarvis*

PREROGATIVE (IRE) 3 b.g. Rock of Gibraltar (IRE) 133 – Tedarshana (Darshaan **81**
133) [2017 83: p8g^5 10.2m^2 10m^3 9.9d^2 12m^5 11.6d^3 9.9d^2 10g^2 p13.3s^2 Dec 14] neat gelding: fairly useful maiden: third at Windsor in June: left Richard Hannon after eighth start: stays 13.5f: acts on polytrack, good to firm and good to soft going: wears cheekpieces: usually races close up. *Tony Carroll*

PRESENCE PROCESS 3 b.g. Dansili 127 – Loulwa (IRE) 103 (Montjeu (IRE) 137) **68**
[2017 72: p8g^4 p11g p8d^6 10m^6 p12g Dec 23] sturdy gelding: fair maiden handicapper: stays 1m: acts on polytrack, best turf form on good going: usually races towards rear. *Pat Phelan*

PRESENTING JULIO (IRE) 9 b.g. Presenting 120 – Ouro Preto (Definite Article 121) **58**
[2017 70: 12m 18v^6 Sep 8] fair handicapper: below form both starts in 2017: stays 1½m: acts on polytrack: wears headgear: usually tongue tied: fair hurdler/chaser. *Gordon Elliott, Ireland*

PRESENT TENSE 3 b.f. Bated Breath 125 – Zenda 115 (Zamindar (USA) 116) [2017 **90**
8.3g 8m* 7d^3 8m Jun 21] close-coupled filly: closely related to 7f winner Panzanella and smart 1m-1¼m winner Remote (both by Dansili) and half-sister to top-class miler Kingman (2-y-o 7f winner, by Invincible Spirit): dam, 1m winner (including Poule d'Essai des Pouliches), half-sister to high-class sprinter Oasis Dream: fairly useful form: won maiden at Yarmouth in May: third in minor event at Leicester in June: stays 1m. *John Gosden*

PRESTBURY PARK (USA) 2 br.g. (Mar 20) Shamardal (USA) 129 – Sutra (USA) 111 **94**
(Meadowlake (USA)) [2017 6m 6f* 6.1d* 7m^3 6s^4 p7g^4 Nov 8] strong gelding: sixth foal: dam US 2-y-o Grade 1 1m winner: fairly useful performer: won minor events at Haydock in July and Chester (by short head from Regulator) in August: stays 7f: acts on firm and good to soft going: usually leads, often travels strongly. *Mark Johnston*

PRESTO BOY 5 b.g. Compton Place 125 – Presto Levanter 69 (Rock of Gibraltar (IRE) **53**
133) [2017 57: p5m p5g^4 t6f t6s May 23] modest maiden handicapper: left Richard Hughes after third start: stays 6f: acts on polytrack, tapeta and good to soft going: often wears headgear: has worn tongue tie. *John Balding*

PRESUMIDO (IRE) 7 b.g. Iffraaj 127 – Miss Megs (IRE) 81 (Croco Rouge (IRE) 126) **91**
[2017 95: p7g p8g^4 p8m^5 p8g p8d p8g p8g p8g p7g Nov 6] workmanlike gelding: fairly useful handicapper: stays 1m: acts on polytrack: has worn hood. *Simon Dow*

PRETEND (IRE) 6 b.g. Invincible Spirit (IRE) 121 – Fafinta (IRE) (Indian Ridge 123) [2017 117: p6g* p6g^5 p5m^5 p6g Apr 14] smart performer: won minor event at Kempton (by 1½ lengths from Gentlemen) in January: has won at 7f, but best at 5f/6f: acts on polytrack and tapeta: has worn hood: sometimes slowly away, often races in rear. *Charlie Appleby* **113**

PRETTY ASSET (IRE) 3 b.f. Shamardal (USA) 129 – What A Picture (FR) (Peintre Celebre (USA) 137) [2017 8d* 8g^5 Aug 1] 160,000F: half-sister to several winners, including very smart winner up to 9.5f Mufarrh (2-y-o 7f winner) and useful 10.7f-1½m winner (stayed 2m) Majenta (both by Marju): dam, well held in France, out of half-sister to Irish Derby winner Grey Swallow: fairly useful form: won maiden at Newmarket (by 2¼ lengths from Awfaa) in July: fifth in handicap at Goodwood (3½ lengths behind Shenanigans) soon after: still unexposed. *Charlie Appleby* **91 p**

PRETTY BABY (IRE) 2 b.f. (Apr 4) Orpen (USA) 116 – Premiere Danseuse (Gold Away (IRE) 125) [2017 5.4d^2 p6g* Oct 12] €50,000Y, €190,000 2-y-o: third foal: half-sister to French winners around 10.5f Puelo (by Sinndar) and Prime Suspect (by Silver Frost): dam unraced half-sister to smart French performers Pacific Rim (1½m winner) and Prairie Star (stayed 15.5f): fairly useful form: won minor event at Chelmsford (by 3½ lengths from Musical Theatre) in October: will go on improving: has joined Daniel Kubler. *William Haggas* **84 p**

PRETTY BUBBLES 8 b.m. Sleeping Indian 122 – Willmar (IRE) 53 (Zafonic (USA) 130) [2017 93: p6g^2 t6d^2 p6g^5 6m^3 6g^5 6.1g^6 6.1m 6v^3 6.1m^6 6d^5 6s^6 p7g^4 p6g^2 p6g^6 p6g^5 p6g^2 Dec 20] angular mare: fairly useful handicapper: second at Kempton in January and Newcastle in February: not same force later in year: races mainly at sprint trips nowadays: acts on all-weather, firm and good to soft going: wears headgear: usually races towards rear. *J. R. Jenkins* **91**

PRETTY JEWEL 4 b.f. Aqlaam 125 – Highland Jewel (IRE) 58 (Azamour (IRE) 130) [2017 63: t8.6g^6 11.6m t12.2g^4 10g 10g 8s* 10.2g^4 7.8d^2 Aug 29] rather leggy filly: fair handicapper: won at Salisbury (amateur) in July: left Sarah Hollinshead after second start: stays 8.5f: acts on tapeta and soft going: sometimes in hood: usually slowly away, often races in rear. *Kevin Frost* **68**

PRETTY OBVIOUS (FR) 4 b.g. Montmartre (FR) 126 – Societe (FR) (Panis (USA) 112) [2017 10m 8.3s^6 8.1m^6 10g Aug 7] angular gelding: fair form: best effort at 1¼m. *Jonjo O'Neill* **73**

PRETTY PASSE 3 b.f. Exceed And Excel (AUS) 126 – Passe Passe (USA) 78 (Lear Fan (USA) 130) [2017 7m^2 7g^4 t9.5g^2 p10g^2 p10g^3 Oct 12] half-sister to numerous winners, including useful winner up to 1¼m Cabinet (2-y-o 7f winner, by Grand Lodge) and ungenuine 7f-1½m winner Magic Instinct (by Entrepreneur), later smart in Australia: dam maiden (stayed 1½m): fairly useful maiden: second at Wolverhampton in August and Lingfield in September: stays 1¼m: acts on polytrack and tapeta: sold 30,000 gns in October to join Martin Todhunter. *William Haggas* **80**

PRETTY PEARL 2 b.f. (Mar 12) Canford Cliffs (IRE) 133 – Hijab (King's Best (USA) 132) [2017 p8d 7m p7s Dec 14] 2,000Y: rather unfurnished filly: fourth foal: half-sister to 6f winner Jimmy Elder (by Invincible Spirit) and a winner in Sweden by High Chaparral: dam unraced daughter of smart 1¼m winner Hi Dubai, herself sister to top-class 1¼m/1½m performer Fantastic Light: down the field in minor events. *Robert Eddery* –

PRETTY RISKY 2 b.f. (Feb 23) Royal Applause 124 – Pretty Miss 85 (Averti (IRE) 117) [2017 5.3g^5 p5g Sep 25] sixth foal: half-sister to 5.7f-7f winner Wild Dancer (by Mawatheeq) and 2-y-o 7f winner Miss Icon (by Sixties Icon): dam, 5f winner, half-sister to high-class 5f performer Kyllachy: modest form: better effort when fifth in maiden at Brighton (4¼ lengths behind Ghepardo) in September. *Patrick Chamings* **56**

PREZZIE 2 b.f. (Feb 15) Major Cadeaux 121 – Yearbook 56 (Byron 117) [2017 6m^4 5m t6.1g^6 p7g Sep 27] 45,000Y: second foal: sister to 2-y-o 6f winner Mr Wizard: dam, maiden (best at 5f), half-sister to useful 2-y-o 7f/1m winner Day of Conquest (by Major Cadeaux): modest form: best effort at 6f. *William Muir* **58**

PRICELESS 4 b.f. Exceed And Excel (AUS) 126 – Molly Brown 95 (Rudimentary (USA) 118) [2017 112: 5f* 5m^5 5f* 5f 5s 5g^5 5.2m Sep 23] rather leggy filly: smart performer: won listed race at Bath (by 5 lengths from Futoon) in April and Temple Stakes at Haydock (by ½ length from Goldream) in May: best form at 5f: acts on firm and good to soft going: tried in hood. *Clive Cox* **116**

PRIDE OF ANGELS 4 gr.f. Dark Angel (IRE) 113 – Openness (Grand Lodge (USA) 125) [2017 7d^5 5.1d^4 6.1m^3 5.1g^4 5s 5.3s^3 p6g* Dec 31] 65,000Y, 3,000 3-y-o: workmanlike filly: fifth foal: half-sister to useful winner up to 8.6f Almanack (2-y-o 5f winner, by Haatef) and a winner abroad by Motivator: dam unraced half-sister to Coronation Stakes winner Balisada: fair performer: won handicap at Lingfield in December: stays 6f: acts on polytrack and good to firm going: often races prominently. *Gary Moore* **75**

PRIMADONIA 3 b.f. Bated Breath 125 – Pretty Primo (IRE) 85 (Kyllachy 129) [2017 –p: p7g^4 6.1g^6 t8.6g 7m^6 p7g Jun 28] smallish filly: modest maiden: tried in blinkers. *Richard Hughes* **57**

PRIMANORA 4 ch.f. First Trump 118 – Danzanora (Groom Dancer (USA) 128) [2017 66p: 5m^4 6.1g^4 6.1g^4 5d^6 5g 8.3g Nov 1] workmanlike filly: fair maiden: best effort at 6f: best form on good going: in cheekpieces last 2 starts. *Michael Appleby* **67**

PRIME CHIEF (IRE) 2 b.c. (Feb 7) Air Chief Marshal (IRE) 115 – La Dame de Fer (IRE) (Mr Greeley (USA) 122) [2017 6m^6 5d p6g^6 t7.2g^6 Nov 7] €52,000Y: first foal: dam lightly-raced half-sister to useful French 1¼m-1½m winner Pretorio out of very smart US Grade 1 9.5f winner England's Legend: modest form: stays 7f: open to further improvement. *George Baker* **63 p**

PRIME MINISTER (IRE) 2 b.c. (Feb 22) Dream Ahead (USA) 133 – Logica (IRE) 81 (Priolo (USA) 127) [2017 7s^2 7g^5 Oct 17] fair form: better effort when second in maiden at Yarmouth (¾ length behind Imperial Past) in September: likely to stay 1m. *Ed Vaughan* **73**

PRIMERO (FR) 4 b.g. Cape Cross (IRE) 129 – Flamenba (USA) (Kingmambo (USA) 125) [2017 p11.9g* p9.9g* 9.9d 9.4g^2 p9.9g^3 t9.5g^5 p12g^2 Dec 23] brother to 1½m-1¾m winner Flambeuse and half-brother to 3 winners, including French 1½m winner Flamenko (by Green Tune): dam French 1½m winner: useful performer: won minor events at Cagnes-sur-Mer in January and February: second in handicap at Lingfield (¾ length behind Hajaam) final start: left C. Ferland after fifth start: stays 1½m: acts on all-weather. *David O'Meara* **109**

PRIMOGENITURE (IRE) 6 b.g. Glory of Dancer 121 – Jacqueline (IND) (King Charlemagne (USA) 120) [2017 96: 11.8g 11.6m^5 10g^4 10m^4 Jun 29] sturdy gelding: fairly useful handicapper: stays 2m, races mainly at shorter: acts on polytrack, good to firm and good to soft going: has worn headgear: tried in tongue tie: front runner/races prominently. *Mary Hambro* **87**

PRIMO'S COMET 2 b.g. (May 17) Orientor 118 – Primo Heights 87 (Primo Valentino (IRE) 116) [2017 5g 6m May 24] well held in minor events: tried in cheekpieces. *Jim Goldie* **–**

PRIMROSE PLACE 3 ch.f. Compton Place 125 – Pretty Girl (IRE) 103 (Polish Precedent (USA) 131) [2017 67, a56: 9g 8.1m^5 10d Jul 25] fair maiden at 2 yrs, no form in 2017: often in tongue tie. *David Evans* **–**

PRINCE AHWAHNEE 2 b.c. (Feb 27) Harbour Watch (IRE) 121 – Ahwahnee (Compton Place 125) [2017 6g^2 6.1m^4 6m^3 6d 6g^3 Sep 22] £43,000Y: useful-looking colt: third foal: half-brother to 5f winners Clouds Rest (at 2 yrs, by Showcasing) and Glacier Point (by Foxwedge): dam twice-raced half-sister to Prix de l'Abbaye winner Gilt Edge Girl: fairly useful maiden: third at Newbury final start: raced only at 6f: acts on good to firm going: tried in cheekpieces. *Clive Cox* **87**

PRINCE CONSORT (IRE) 2 b.g. (Apr 16) Most Improved (IRE) 119 – Fame And Fortune (IRE) (In The Wings 128) [2017 7m 7g^6 7v^6 7.9g 7m p10s^5 Dec 15] leggy gelding: modest maiden: stays 1m: acts on good to firm going: tried in cheekpieces. *Brian Meehan* **58**

PRINCE JAI 4 ch.g. Showcasing 117 – Play Around (IRE) 105 (Niniski (USA) 125) [2017 a9.4f a6f a7f 8.3g t7.2g^4 t8.6g^3 p8d^2 p7g* p7d* p7g t7.2g^2 p8s Dec 15] angular gelding: fair handicapper: won at Chelmsford (twice, first an apprentice event) in September: left S. Seemar after third start: stays 8.5f: acts on polytrack, tapeta and dirt: wears headgear: front runner/races prominently. *Ian Williams* **66**

PRINCELY 2 b.c. (Feb 23) Compton Place 125 – Royal Award 90 (Cadeaux Genereux 131) [2017 6g Aug 1] 12/1, well held in maiden at Goodwood. *Richard Hannon* **–**

PRINCE MAURICE (USA) 2 gr.c. (Apr 13) The Factor (USA) 126 – Ramblin Rosie (USA) (Roar (USA) 116) [2017 6.1m Aug 26] 14/1, well held in minor event at Windsor. *Jeremy Noseda* **–**

PRINCE OF ARRAN 4 b.g. Shirocco (GER) 129 – Storming Sioux 79 (Storming Home 128) [2017 105: p11g³ p15.8g⁵ 16f² 20m 16g 16.3g 14.2s⁵ Sep 15] close-coupled gelding: smart performer: placed in handicap at Kempton (3¾ lengths third to Big Country) in April and Sagaro Stakes at Ascot (1½ lengths second to Sweet Selection) in May: stays 2m: acts on polytrack, firm and soft going: has worn headgear. *Charlie Fellowes* **113**

PRINCE OF CARDAMOM (IRE) 5 b.g. Nayef (USA) 129 – Tiger Spice 68 (Royal Applause 124) [2017 65: p8f⁶ p10g⁵ 7.1g⁵ 7s⁶ 8g Aug 7] sturdy gelding: modest handicapper: stays 1½m: acts on polytrack, soft and good to firm going: wears cheekpieces: often carries head/tail awkwardly. *Jonathan Geake* **57**

PRINCE OF CLAPPERS 3 b.g. Royal Applause 124 – Blodwen (USA) 52 (Mister Baileys 123) [2017 62: 8.2g 7m Jul 23] maiden, well held in handicaps in 2017: best effort at 7f: sometimes slowly away, usually races towards rear. *Tim Easterby* **–**

PRINCE OF THE DARK 2 gr.c. (Feb 23) Lethal Force (IRE) 128 – Fanrouge (IRE) 93 (Red Clubs (IRE) 125) [2017 5.7f* 6f⁶ Jun 20] good-topped colt: first foal: dam, 5f (including at 2 yrs)/6f winner, half-sister to useful 2-y-o 5f/6f winner Haikbidiac: useful form: won minor event at Bath (by 2¼ lengths from Last Page) in May: sixth in Coventry Stakes at Royal Ascot (in cheekpieces, 1¾ lengths behind Rajasinghe) next time: will go on improving. *Clive Cox* **101 p**

PRINCEOFTHEQUEEN (USA) 3 br.c. Lonhro (AUS) 128 – Catch The Queen (USA) (Miswaki (USA) 124) [2017 72: 5g 6d Jul 5] fair maiden at 2 yrs, well held in handicaps in 2017: stays 6f: best form on good going: in hood last 2 starts. *David O'Meara* **–**

PRINCE OF TIME 5 ch.g. Bahamian Bounty 116 – Touching (IRE) 89 (Kheleyf (USA) 116) [2017 46: t7.1m² p7g⁴ p7d² p7gʳʳ f6m³ t7.1d³ t7.1g² f7d* f7g² t7.1g* t7.1g* p7g 7g p7g t7.1g Nov 3] angular gelding: fair handicapper: won at Southwell in April, and Wolverhampton later in April and in May: stays 7.5f: acts on all-weather and good to soft going: has worn headgear: tried in tongue tie: refused to race fourth start. *Richard Ford* **74**

PRINCE ROCK (IRE) 2 ch.g. (Apr 23) Society Rock (IRE) 126 – She's A Queen (IRE) 77 (Peintre Celebre (USA) 137) [2017 p7g p6g Oct 9] well held in pair of minor events. *Simon Dow* **–**

PRINCESS DE LUNE (IRE) 3 gr.f. Shamardal (USA) 129 – Princess Serena (USA) 48 (Unbridled's Song (USA) 125) [2017 7g* 7g 7s Oct 7] workmanlike filly: sister to 2 winners, including very smart French/Australian 7f-13f winner Puissance de Lune, and closely related/half-sister to several winners, including smart winner around 1m Zabeel Prince (by Lope de Vega): dam US 1m winner: useful form: won maiden at Newbury (by 4 lengths from Alnaas) in April: raced only at 7f. *Roger Charlton* **98**

PRINCESS HARLEY (IRE) 2 gr.f. (Feb 17) Dark Angel (IRE) 113 – Tonle Sap (IRE) 74 (Manduro (GER) 135) [2017 6s³ 7d³ Sep 30] €50,000Y, 85,000 2-y-o: second foal: dam lightly-raced half-sister to very smart 6f/7f winner Leahurst and smart performers Interception (at 6f), Dunelight and Sperry (both up to 1m): fair form: better effort when third in maiden at Newmarket (7 lengths behind Bye Bye Baby) in September: should improve further. *Mick Quinn* **76 p**

PRINCESS JESSICA (FR) 2 gr.f. (Mar 31) Style Vendome (FR) 116 – Scoutingaround (USA) (Deputy Minister (CAN)) [2017 6.1s⁵ 7d 8g⁶ Aug 14] €10,000F: half-sister to French 11f winner Reconnaissance (by Cockney Rebel) and a winner in USA by Forestry: dam unraced daughter of US Grade 1 9f winner Fit To Scout: well held in minor events/maiden: sold £3,000, sent to Norway. *Richard Fahey* **–**

PRINCESS KEIRA (IRE) 2 b.f. (Mar 3) Acclamation 118 – La Reine de Pearls (IRE) (Dubawi (IRE) 129) [2017 5g² 5d⁵ 6m 5d⁶ Oct 4] €24,000F, 110,000 2-y-o: second foal: dam French winner up to 1m (2-y-o 7f winner): fair form: best effort when second in minor event at Nottingham in July. *Mick Quinn* **74**

PRINCESS LYLA (IRE) 2 ch.f. (Apr 10) Arakan (USA) 123 – Hi Lyla (IRE) (Lahib (USA) 129) [2017 p5g³ 6g⁵ 5g⁵ 6d* t5.1g* 6s⁶ 6.1s⁶ t7.2g⁴ Oct 7] £3,000 2-y-o: fifth foal: half-sister to 3 winners, including 1m winner Carrigeen Prince (by Strategic Prince) and 7f-8.5f winner Empress Lyla (by Holy Roman Emperor): dam unraced: fair performer: won nurseries at Lingfield and Wolverhampton in August: stays 6f: acts on tapeta and good to soft going: front runner/races prominently, often freely. *Richard Hughes* **66**

PRINCESS NEARCO (IRE) 3 b.f. Elzaam (AUS) 115 – Royal Jubilee (IRE) 81 (King's Theatre (IRE) 128) [2017 –: 7.4m⁴ 8.3g⁵ 8.3g⁴ 12d⁴ 12g⁵ 11.2d³ 14s⁵ 12.1v⁴ Sep 26] fair maiden: stays 1¾m: acts on soft going: in headgear last 4 starts: sometimes slowly away. *Patrick Holmes* **68**

PRINCESS NIA (IRE) 4 b.f. Acclamation 118 – Shirley A Star (USA) 85 (Cozzene **84**
(USA)) [2017 76: 10.2f* 10d^{3} May 12] fairly useful handicapper: won at Bath (by ¾ length from Star of Lombardy) in April: stays 1¼m: acts on polytrack, tapeta and firm going: tried in blinkers. *Brian Meehan*

PRINCESS OPHELIA 3 b.f. Notnowcato 128 – Royal Bloom (IRE) 52 (Royal Applause **57**
124) [2017 7d^{6} 8.3s^{5} t9.5g^{4} t8.6g p8d Sep 21] £600Y: third foal: dam, maiden (seemed to stay 1m), half-sister to very smart winner up to 7f (best at shorter) Masamah: modest maiden: stays 8.5f: acts on tapeta and soft going. *Michael Appleby*

PRINCESS PEGGY (USA) 2 b.f. (Feb 4) Scat Daddy (USA) 120 – Peggy Jane (USA) **85**
(Kafwain (USA) 118) [2017 a5s* 6m a5.5s^{4} Jul 24] sturdy filly: first foal: dam US 6f (including at 2 yrs) winner: fairly useful form: won maiden at Belmont in May: 8 lengths tenth in Albany Stakes at Royal Ascot next time: wears blinkers. *Wesley A. Ward, USA*

PRINCESS RAIHANA 4 br.f. Cape Cross (IRE) 129 – Raihana (AUS) 117 (Elusive **–**
Quality (USA)) [2017 78: p12g^{5} Jan 13] tall filly: fair handicapper: well held only start in 2017: stays 11.5f: acts on polytrack, good to firm and good to soft going: in cheekpieces last 2 starts: usually races close up. *Marco Botti*

PRINCESS ROANIA (IRE) 6 b.m. Dubai Destination (USA) 127 – Lady Roania (IRE) **72**
(Saddlers' Hall (IRE) 126) [2017 79: 14.1g^{6} May 2] fair handicapper: stays 17f: acts on heavy going: in cheekpieces/tongue tie last 3 starts: usually races nearer last than first: modest maiden hurdler. *Peter Bowen*

PRINCESS WAY (IRE) 3 gr.f. Zebedee 113 – Stef's Girl (IRE) 73 (Petardia 113) [2017 **65**
62: t7.1f^{5} p7g t7.1g t7.1g t7.2g^{3} 7m^{5} p6d^{6} 7.1d^{4} 6.1g^{4} 7g^{3} t6.1g^{4} t6.1d f7.1g* Dec 22] fair handicapper: won at Southwell in December: stays 7f: acts on fibresand, tapeta and good to firm going: wears headgear. *David Evans*

PRIORS BROOK 6 b.g. Champs Elysees 124 – Dyanita 76 (Singspiel (IRE) 133) [2017 **85**
88: p12g^{4} f11g^{2} p12g 11.4d^{5} 10m* p10g^{3} 10g^{4} Sep 6] useful-looking gelding: fairly useful handicapper: won at Chepstow in June: second at Southwell (apprentice) in March: stays 1½m: acts on polytrack, fibresand and good to firm going: tried in cheekpieces: often races prominently. *Andrew Balding*

PRISCILLA'S DREAM 2 ch.f. (Apr 15) Bated Breath 125 – Be Free 60 (Selkirk (USA) **64 p**
129) [2017 6d^{4} p6g^{3} 6g Oct 7] 3,500Y: fifth foal: half-sister to 9f winner Freedom Rock (by Rock of Gibraltar) and 2-y-o 7f winner Aqua Libre (by Aqlaam): dam US 1m winner: modest form: best effort when tenth in quite valuable sales race at Newmarket (5 lengths behind Elysium Dream) final start: will be suited by 7f: better to come. *Philip McBride*

PRISOM (IRE) 4 gr.f. Zebedee 113 – Crystal Theatre (IRE) 72 (King's Theatre (IRE) **66**
128) [2017 72: f7g^{2} t7.1m^{2} p8g 7.5g p7g^{6} f7g 7m^{6} f6.1g^{6} t7.1g Nov 15] fair handicapper: stays 7f: acts on tapeta: often in cheekpieces in 2017: often races in rear. *Gay Kelleway*

PRIVATE DONALD 4 ch.g. Sakhee's Secret 128 – Excello 94 (Exceed And Excel **61**
(AUS) 126) [2017 61: f5g^{3} Jan 1] modest form: in cheekpieces last 2 starts: sent to Macau. *Robert Cowell*

PRIVATE MATTER 3 b.g. Mayson 124 – Privacy Order (Azamour (IRE) 130) [2017 **100**
102: 7m^{4} 6s 6m 6g 6d 6d 6d Sep 10] close-coupled gelding: useful handicapper: stays 6f: acts on soft and good to firm going: in hood last 2 starts: usually races prominently. *Richard Fahey*

PRIVATE MISSION 3 ch.g. Sepoy (AUS) 129 – Pivotal Drive (IRE) (Pivotal 124) [2017 **95**
78p: 7g* 8.2f 8m* Jul 14] useful handicapper: won at Leicester in May and Newmarket (by length from Dr Julius No) in July: stays 1m: acts on polytrack and good to firm going: usually races close up: sent to Hong Kong, where renamed Mickey Rich. *Hughie Morrison*

PRIVATE VIEW 2 b.f. (Apr 7) Exceed And Excel (AUS) 126 – Confidential Lady 116 **60 p**
(Singspiel (IRE) 133) [2017 p7g^{4} Oct 18] seventh foal: sister to useful 6f-1m winner Red Box and half-sister to useful French 1¼m winner Untold Secret (by Shamardal): dam won Prix de Diane (also 2-y-o 7f/7.5f winner): 4/1, fourth in minor event at Kempton (5¼ lengths behind Fille de Reve) in October: open to improvement. *Sir Michael Stoute*

PRIZE DIVA 3 b.f. Motivator 131 – Premier Prize 106 (Selkirk (USA) 129) [2017 57: **76**
p8g^{4} 10.2d 9g^{3} 10.2m* 11.5m^{4} 8s Jul 28] stocky filly: fair handicapper: won at Nottingham in June: stays 1¼m: acts on polytrack and good to firm going: in cheekpieces last 4 starts: usually races prominently. *David Elsworth*

PRIZE MONEY 4 b.g. Authorized (IRE) 133 – Dresden Doll (USA) 78 (Elusive Quality **121** (USA)) [2017 117: 12g^{2} 12.1g* 12g* 12d^{4} 12m 12m 9.9g^{6} 11.9g^{6} Sep 3] good-topped gelding: very smart performer: won handicap at Meydan (by neck from Rembrandt Van Rijn) in February and Dubai City of Gold at same course (by neck from Postponed) in March: fourth to Jack Hobbs in Dubai Sheema Classic there next time: stays 1½m: acts on good to firm and good to soft going: usually wears headgear. *Saeed bin Suroor*

PROCEDURE 2 gr.f. (Feb 19) Invincible Spirit (IRE) 121 – Clinical 109 (Motivator 131) **81** [2017 6g^{2} p6g^{5} p6g^{2} p6d^{4} Nov 9] neat filly: second foal: half-sister to smart 2-y-o 7f winner Lockheed (by Exceed And Excel): dam, winner up to 8.5f (2-y-o 7f winner), half-sister to smart winner up to 1¼m Cupid's Glory: fairly useful form: second in minor event at Kempton in October: will stay 7f. *Sir Michael Stoute*

PROCTOR 4 b.g. Makfi 130 – Super Motiva 99 (Motivator 131) [2017 90: 9.9m p12g^{5} Jul **73** 5] strong gelding: fairly useful handicapper: below form both starts in 2017: stays 1¼m: acts on soft going: tried in blinkers. *Stuart Kittow*

PROCURATOR (IRE) 3 b.c. Canford Cliffs (IRE) 133 – Lulawin (Kyllachy 129) [2017 **87** 84: 8.5g 8m^{5} 8m 8.1m^{2} 6m^{5} p7d 7v* p7g Nov 6] good-topped colt: fairly useful handicapper: won at Brighton (by head from Black Caesar) in October: stays 1m: acts on any turf going: sold £10,500 in November. *Richard Hannon*

PROFESSOR 7 ch.g. Byron 117 – Jubilee 66 (Selkirk (USA) 129) [2017 p7g^{5} t6g p6g 6g^{3} **93** 7m 7g^{3} 7d^{6} p7d 7s^{3} 7v^{6} p7g Sep 9] strong gelding: fairly useful handicapper: third at Goodwood in June: stays 1m: acts on firm going: has worn headgear, including last 3 starts. *Michael Attwater*

PROFITABLE (IRE) 5 b.h. Invincible Spirit (IRE) 121 – Dani Ridge (IRE) 92 (Indian **123** Ridge 123) [2017 125: 5d^{2} 5f^{2} 5s^{2} 5g^{6} 5d^{3} Oct 1] well-made horse: high-class performer at best: won Palace House Stakes at Newmarket, Temple Stakes at Haydock and King's Stand Stakes at Royal Ascot in 2016: close to best when second in King's Stand Stakes at Royal Ascot (3 lengths behind Lady Aurelia) and King George Stakes at Goodwood (2¼ lengths behind Battaash) in 2017: in cheekpieces, 4¼ lengths third to Battaash in Prix de l'Abbaye at Chantilly final start: best at 5f: acted on firm and soft going: often raced prominently/travelled strongly: to stand at Kildangan Stud, Co. Kildare, fee €12,000. *Clive Cox*

PROFOUND (IRE) 2 b.c. (Apr 5) Intello (GER) 129 – Bahama Spirit (IRE) 84 **80 p** (Invincible Spirit (IRE) 121) [2017 8.1g 8d^{5} t8.6g^{2} Nov 25] 54,000F, 70,000Y, €340,000 2-y-o: rather unfurnished colt: second foal: closely related to Italian 7.5f winner Hartswell (by Nathaniel): dam, 2-y-o 6f winner, half-sister to smart performer up to 15f Rio Tigre: fairly useful form: best effort when second in minor event at Wolverhampton (head behind Hipster Boy) final start: open to further improvement. *Roger Varian*

PROGRESSIVE JAZZ (IRE) 2 b.g. (Mar 12) Red Jazz (USA) 125 – Kind Regards **59** (IRE) 113 (Unfuwain (USA) 131) [2017 5m 5m 7.4m 7s 8v 8g^{3} 7g^{3} p8g^{2} t9.5g^{2} p10s^{3} f8.1g^{5} Dec 29] modest maiden handicapper: stays 9.5f: acts on polytrack, tapeta, best turf form on good going: wears visor: front runner/races prominently. *K. R. Burke*

PROJECT BLUEBOOK (FR) 4 bl.g. Sinndar (IRE) 134 – Apperella (Rainbow Quest **91** (USA) 134) [2017 86: 15.9m^{2} 16s^{2} Aug 17] compact gelding: fairly useful handicapper: second at Chepstow in August: stays 2m: acts on polytrack, tapeta and any turf going: useful hurdler. *John Quinn*

PROJECTION 4 b.g. Acclamation 118 – Spotlight 110 (Dr Fong (USA) 128) [2017 113p: **118** 6m^{6} 6m^{3} 6d 6s^{2} Oct 7] lengthy gelding: smart performer: third in Wokingham Stakes (Handicap) at Royal Ascot (¾ length behind Out Do) in June and second in Bengough Stakes at Ascot (½ length behind Blue Point) final start: stays 6.5f: acts on soft and good to firm going. *Roger Charlton*

PROMINNA 7 ch.g. Proclamation (IRE) 130 – Minnina (IRE) (In The Wings 128) [2017 **65** 70: 5g^{3} 5.2m^{6} 6d^{3} 5v^{4} 5d^{3} 5m^{6} 5.7s p5g* p5g^{4} Oct 17] lengthy, plain gelding: fair handicapper: won at Lingfield in September: best up to 6f: acts on polytrack, tapeta and soft going. *Tony Carroll*

PROMISING (IRE) 3 b.f. Invincible Spirit (IRE) 121 – Lethal Quality (USA) (Elusive **94** Quality (USA)) [2017 98: 7m^{3} Apr 22] good-bodied filly: useful form: third in Fred Darling Stakes at Newbury (2 lengths behind Dabyah) only start in 2017: stays 7f. *Richard Hannon*

PROMISING RUN (USA) 4 b.f. Hard Spun (USA) 124 – Aviacion (BRZ) (Know **112**
Heights (IRE) 118) [2017 112: 8.9g* 9.9g^3 8.9g 9.9s^4 p8g^3 Nov 2] rangy filly: smart performer: won Al Rashidiya at Meydan (by ½ length from Light The Lights) in January: third in Dubai Millennium Stakes at same course (3¼ lengths behind Zarak) in February: stays 10.5f: acts on good to soft going: has worn headgear, including in 2017: usually races close up. *Saeed bin Suroor*

PRONOUNCED (IRE) 3 b.g. Power 117 – Le Montrachet (Nashwan (USA) 135) [2017 **60**
75: p7g p7g 8s p8g^5 8.7m^5 9.7s^2 10g^5 8.3d p10.7g Nov 8] modest maiden handicapper: stays 8.5f: acts on polytrack and good to firm going: wears blinkers: winning hurdler. *Joseph Patrick O'Brien, Ireland*

PROSCHEMA (IRE) 2 ch.c. (Apr 2) Declaration of War (USA) 128 – Notable (Zafonic **85 p**
(USA) 130) [2017 8g^2 8d^3 Oct 27] 65,000Y: big, good-topped colt: has scope: seventh foal: half-brother to French 1¼m-12.5f winner (stayed 2½m) Maria Royal and 11.5f-2m winner Red Cardinal (both by Montjeu), both smart: dam unraced: fairly useful form: better effort when second in maiden at Newmarket (5 lengths behind Ghaiyyath) in September: will be suited by 1¼m+: remains open to improvement. *Tom Dascombe*

PROSECUTE (FR) 4 b.g. Lawman (FR) 121 – Dissitation (IRE) 77 (Spectrum (IRE) **–**
126) [2017 83: 10m 7d p12g p8g Oct 17] strong, compact gelding: fairly useful handicapper: well below form in 2017: tried in hood/tongue tie: often starts slowly. *Ali Stronge*

PROSECUTION 3 b.c. Lawman (FR) 121 – Convention 79 (Encosta de Lago (AUS)) **76 §**
[2017 63p: 10d^4 10m^2 11.8g^3 8.3v^2 9.9d^2 10d^4 p12g Oct 13] rather leggy colt: fair maiden handicapper: stays 1½m: acts on polytrack, good to firm and heavy going: tried in blinkers: often races prominently: weak finisher. *Hughie Morrison*

PROSPER 3 gr.f. Exceed And Excel (AUS) 126 – Ela Athena 119 (Ezzoud (IRE) 126) **90**
[2017 79p: p8g^2 8f* 10s^6 8m 9.9m^6 p10g^4 p10s^5 Sep 2] tall filly: fairly useful performer: won minor event at Ascot (by short head from Icespire) in May: stays 1¼m: acts on polytrack and firm going: in headgear last 4 starts. *Roger Varian*

PROST (GER) 3 b.g. Tin Horse (IRE) 120 – Plebeya (IRE) (Dubawi (IRE) 129) [2017 **99**
85p: 8d^4 7m 8.1g^2 7d^6 t8g* p9.4f Nov 29] good-topped gelding: useful handicapper: won at Newcastle (by length from Waarif) in October: stays 1m: acts on polytrack, tapeta and good to soft going. *Ed Vaughan*

PROTECTED GUEST 2 b.g. (Feb 17) Helmet (AUS) 127 – Reem Star 94 (Green Tune **72**
(USA) 125) [2017 7g 6d p8g^2 Sep 26] lengthy gelding: fair form: best effort when second in maiden at Lingfield (1¾ lengths behind Connaught Ranger) final start. *George Margarson*

PROUD ARCHI (IRE) 3 b.g. Archipenko (USA) 127 – Baharah (USA) 114 (Elusive **88**
Quality (USA)) [2017 82: 7.5m* 7.1m^3 8f^5 8m 7.4m^4 7.6g^3 7d 7d* 7.4g 7v 7s Oct 31] fairly useful handicapper: won at Beverley (by short head from Areen Heart) in April and Thirsk (by neck from Lady In Question) in August: stays 1m: acts on good to firm and good to soft going: often races towards rear. *Michael Dods*

PROUD KATE 3 b.f. Proud Citizen (USA) 122 – Oceans Apart 90 (Desert Prince (IRE) **49**
130) [2017 –: 7m 6m 5.2d^2 6g 6d f5g^6 Aug 28] poor maiden: best effort at 5f: acts on good to soft going: has worn headgear, including last 4 starts. *Christine Dunnett*

PROVOKING (USA) 4 b.g. Any Given Saturday (USA) 128 – Fair And Lively (USA) **56**
(Lively One (USA)) [2017 –: 8g^3 9.9g 8g^5 6g t7.2g^4 7.1g Jul 20] workmanlike gelding: modest maiden handicapper: stays 8.5f: acts on good to soft going: tried in headgear. *David Evans*

PRUFROCK (IRE) 3 ch.f. Roderic O'Connor (IRE) 119 – Indaba (IRE) 98 (Indian **56**
Ridge 123) [2017 71: t6f^5 p6g^6 t6g^6 Jan 31] modest maiden: stays 7f: acts on good to firm going: often races towards rear. *David Simcock*

PRUSSIAN EAGLE (IRE) 6 br.g. Jeremy (USA) 122 – Absolutely Cool (IRE) 74 **74**
(Indian Ridge 123) [2017 78: 8v^4 12v^5 Sep 17] fair handicapper: stays 13f: acts on heavy going: tried in hood: fair hurdler. *Evan Williams*

PRYING PANDORA (FR) 4 b.f. Dark Angel (IRE) 113 – Leniency (IRE) (Cape Cross **87**
(IRE) 129) [2017 85: 7g^5 t8g* t8s^5 9.9d^2 9.8m^6 9.8d^6 8d^2 8v^5 10d t8d Nov 10] sturdy filly: fairly useful handicapper: won at Newcastle (by 2½ lengths from Alexandrakollontai) in May: second at Newmarket (neck behind Titi Makfi) in August: stays 1¼m: acts on tapeta and soft going. *Richard Fahey*

PSYCHEDELIC FUNK 3 ch.c. Choisir (AUS) 126 – Parabola 72 (Galileo (IRE) 134) **112**
[2017 106: 5.8g 6s^{2} 7g^{3} 8g* 8.2s^{4} 8d^{3} 7.5v* Oct 1] smart performer: won minor event at Naas (by 4 lengths from Panama Hat) in July and Concorde Stakes at Tipperary (by ½ length from Downforce) in October: stays 1m: acts on heavy going: in blinkers last 2 starts. *G. M. Lyons, Ireland*

PSYCHOLOGY 4 b.g. Shamardal (USA) 129 – Emotion Parade (ARG) (Parade Marshal **61**
(USA)) [2017 59: t10.2g^{6} t8d t7.1d t16.3g^{4} t12.4d^{5} 16g t16.3s 11.9m^{6} Jun 18] modest maiden: stays 1¼m: acts on tapeta: tried in tongue tie: usually slowly away/races in rear. *Kenny Johnson*

PSYCHOTIC 4 b.g. Nayef (USA) 129 – Palatial 101 (Green Desert (USA) 127) [2017 7g^{5} **88**
9.9d^{5} p8g* p8g Oct 13] 50,000Y: good-bodied gelding: brother to smart 7f/1m winner (including at 2 yrs) Spacious and 2m winner Tower, and half-brother to several winners, including smart 6.5f-1m winner Dimension (by Medicean): dam 7f winner (including at 2 yrs): fairly useful form: won maiden at Kempton in September: stays 1¼m. *David Menuisier*

PTARMIGAN RIDGE 3 b.g. Kyllachy 129 – Joshua's Princess 92 (Danehill (USA) **88 p**
126) [2017 6v^{2} 6d^{3} 6d^{2} p6g^{3} 7s* Oct 10] well-made gelding: half-brother to several winners, including 7f/1m winner Floriss (by Medicean) and 1m/1¼m winner Don't Stare (by Zamindar), both useful: dam 1m winner: fairly useful performer: won maiden at Leicester (by 1¼ lengths from Mohsen) in October: stays 7f: acts on soft going: often races prominently: open to further improvement. *James Fanshawe*

PUCHITA (IRE) 2 b.f. (Mar 19) Acclamation 118 – Violet Ballerina (IRE) 85 (Namid **69**
128) [2017 6m^{6} 7g 6v 8.1m^{3} 7g^{2} p7g^{6} Oct 18] €68,000Y: rather unfurnished filly: half-sister to several winners, including 7f winner Fab Lolly (by Rock of Gibraltar) and 7f-2m winner Woofie (by Duke of Marmalade): dam, 6f and (at 2 yrs) 7f winner, half-sister to Richmond Stakes winner Carrizo Creek: fair maiden: stays 1m: acts on good to firm going. *Richard Hannon*

PUCON 8 b.m. Kyllachy 129 – The Fugative 94 (Nicholas (USA) 111) [2017 82: 5.1m^{5} **–**
Aug 13] fairly useful handicapper: well beaten only start in 2017: stays 6f: acts on polytrack, good to firm and good to soft going: has worn cheekpieces: usually leads. *Simon Dow*

PUDDING CHARE (IRE) 3 b.g. Arcano (IRE) 122 – Rosy Dudley (IRE) 72 (Grand **75**
Lodge (USA) 125) [2017 67: t6d^{3} 7d t6g^{5} t7.2g^{4} Dec 13] fair maiden: stays 6f: acts on tapeta. *Richard Fahey*

PUDS 2 br.f. (Mar 27) Bated Breath 125 – Missy Wassie Gal (USA) (High Chaparral (IRE) **75**
132) [2017 6d 6d^{2} t6.1g^{2} Nov 18] third foal: half-sister to 7f winner Polydus (by Rock of Gibraltar): dam unraced half-sister to smart winner up to 8.6f Dream Lodge: fair form: best effort when second in minor event at Wolverhampton (neck behind Gold Filigree) final start. *Charles Hills*

PULITZER 2 b.f. (Mar 16) Kodiac 112 – Solola (GER) (Black Sam Bellamy (IRE) 121) **89**
[2017 6g 6v^{3} 6s* 6g^{5} 7s Oct 28] 130,000Y: fourth foal: half-sister to useful 2-y-o 6f/7f winner (stayed 1¼m) Smaih (by Paco Boy): dam, German 11f/11.5f winner, half-sister to high-class/very smart German middle-distance performers Silvano and Sabiango: fairly useful performer: won minor event at Haydock in September: fifth in listed race at York (3¼ lengths behind Rebel Assault) in October: best effort at 6f: acts on soft going. *Hugo Palmer*

PULLMAN BROWN (USA) 5 b.g. Big Brown (USA) 132 – Touch Too Much (USA) **78**
(Holy Bull (USA) 134) [2017 93, a82: p8g f7m^{6} 8m^{5} 10m^{6} 8d^{4} Aug 12] fair handicapper nowadays: left David Marnane after first start: stays 1¼m: acts on good to firm and heavy going: has worn headgear/tongue tie: often leads. *Philip Kirby*

PULL THE PIN (IRE) 8 b.g. Kheleyf (USA) 116 – Inscribed (IRE) 55 (Fasliyev (USA) **40**
120) [2017 56: f5g f6g t5.1g^{5} t6f Feb 24] modest handicapper: below form in 2017: stays 1m: acts on polytrack, fibresand, good to firm and heavy going: usually wears headgear: wears tongue tie: usually races close up. *Mandy Rowland*

PULSATING (IRE) 3 b.f. Dragon Pulse (IRE) 114 – Safqa 91 (Singspiel (IRE) 133) **71**
[2017 69: f6g^{3} f6g^{2} p5m^{4} p6g t6g^{4} p6g^{5} t6m* p5g^{5} f5d 5.3g^{5} p7g 6g^{5} 8s 7d p7g p7g p6s^{2} t6.1d* p6g^{4} Dec 21] fair performer: won seller at Wolverhampton in February and handicap at same course in December: left Ali Stronge after second start, Daniel Steele after sixteenth: stays 6f: acts on all-weather: often in headgear in 2017. *Archie Watson*

PUMAFLOR (IRE) 5 b.g. Aussie Rules (USA) 123 – Krasotka (IRE) (Soviet Star (USA) 128) [2017 88: 8g 8m^5 8.3g^2 7.8g^5 8.5f^2 8.5d^2 t8.6g 8.5m^{pu} 8g 10.3v Sep 30] plain, rather leggy gelding: fairly useful handicapper: second at Nottingham in May: left Richard Whitaker after fourth start, David O'Meara after ninth: stays 9f: acts on firm and soft going: has worn cheekpieces, including usually in 2017: temperamental. *Philip Kirby* **89 §**

PUMBLECHOOK 4 b.g. Dalakhani (IRE) 133 – Chiang Mai (IRE) 113 (Sadler's Wells (USA) 132) [2017 87: 12g^3 16d^3 11.8m* 13m* p12g 18g^4 13.9v* 12.1s 14s 12v^5 Sep 30] angular gelding: useful handicapper: won at Leicester and Newmarket (by 10 lengths from Amanto) in June, and Catterick (by 2½ lengths from Ingleby Hollow) in August: stays 2m: acts on good to firm and heavy going. *Mark Johnston* **95**

PUNKAWALLAH 3 b.g. Sepoy (AUS) 129 – Max One Two Three (IRE) 102 (Princely Heir (IRE) 111) [2017 59p: p7g 10.2m* 10.2g* Aug 10] fairly useful handicapper: won at Haydock in July and August (by ½ length from Indian Chief): stays 1¼m: acts on good to firm going: in cheekpieces last 2 starts: sometimes slowly away. *Tom Dascombe* **85**

PURAMENTE 2 ch.g. (Apr 9) Pastoral Pursuits 127 – Sahend (IRE) (Danehill Dancer (IRE) 117) [2017 t6.1g 7m 5.7d 8.1s^4 p7g^2 8.2g^5 t7.2g^6 Nov 18] fair maiden: stays 1m: acts on polytrack and soft going: waited with. *Jo Hughes* **66**

PURANA 6 ch.m. Pastoral Pursuits 127 – Arruhan (IRE) 87 (Mujtahid (USA) 118) [2017 41: 7d Jun 5] maiden, well beaten only start in 2017: tried in hood/tongue tie. *Ms N. M. Hugo* **–**

PURE ACTION (IRE) 4 ch.g. Haatef (USA) 117 – Pure Jazz (IRE) 69 (Marju (IRE) 127) [2017 79: p10.7g^3 7g^5 7.5g^3 7.9g^2 7d^3 7s^2 p8g* 8.3g^4 Nov 1] fairly useful performer: won maiden claimer at Dundalk (by ¾ length from Smugglers Creek) in September: second in handicap at Cork (apprentice) in August: stays 10.5f: acts on polytrack and soft going: in cheekpieces last 4 starts: tried in tongue tie: front runner/races prominently: sold 20,000 gns in November. *J. J. Feane, Ireland* **84**

PURE ART 4 b.f. Dutch Art 126 – Pure Song 75 (Singspiel (IRE) 133) [2017 100: 10m^4 12g^4 10.3d Jul 28] angular filly: useful performer: fourth in listed race at Ayr (4½ lengths behind Nezwaah) in May: stays 1¼m: acts on polytrack and good to firm going. *Ralph Beckett* **95**

PURE SHORES 3 b.f. Dubawi (IRE) 129 – Polly's Mark (IRE) 112 (Mark of Esteem (IRE) 137) [2017 68p: p10g^2 10d^6 8s p8d^3 t8.6g* t8.6d^6 Dec 27] sturdy filly: fair performer: won maiden at Wolverhampton in December: left Charlie Appleby after third start: stays 1¼m: acts on polytrack, tapeta and good to soft going. *Ian Williams* **75**

PURPLE JAZZ (IRE) 2 b.g. (Jan 18) Red Jazz (USA) 125 – Breakmeheart (IRE) (Galileo (IRE) 134) [2017 p7g p7d t9.5g Dec 18] sturdy gelding: little impact in minor events. *George Baker* **–**

PURPLE ROCK (IRE) 5 b.g. Fastnet Rock (AUS) 127 – Amethyst (IRE) 111 (Sadler's Wells (USA) 132) [2017 90: 11.9s^2 14g 11.9m 11.2s 16.3m^6 12d^4 10v^6 t10.2g t9.5g^5 Dec 18] strong gelding: fairly useful handicapper: second at York in May: stays 1½m: acts on tapeta, good to firm and heavy going: has worn blinkers: wears tongue tie. *Michael Easterby* **88**

PURSER (USA) 2 b.c. (Mar 18) Mizzen Mast (USA) 121 – Solo Piano (USA) (Empire Maker (USA) 129) [2017 7d* 7g^4 p7g* 8m^3 Oct 14] lengthy, rather unfurnished colt: third foal: half-brother to a winner in USA by More Than Ready: dam, US 7f-8.5f winner, half-sister to smart US Grade 2 1m winner Filimbi (by Mizzen Mast) out of very smart US Grade 1 9f/1¼m winner Flute: useful form: won maiden at Newbury (by head from Merlin Magic) in August and minor event at Lingfield (by 9 lengths from Key Player) in October: should stay 1m. *John Gosden* **108**

PURSUING STEED 3 b.g. Pastoral Pursuits 127 – Emma Peel 113 (Emarati (USA) 74) [2017 –: p7g 7g* 7d* 7m* 7d* 8d 7m p8g Oct 13] fairly useful handicapper: won at Leicester in May, Doncaster and Newbury in June, and Leicester again (by short head from Flyboy) in July: stays 1m: acts on polytrack, good to firm and good to soft going: often races in rear. *Hughie Morrison* **87**

PURSUING THE DREAM (IRE) 2 b.f. (Apr 22) Dream Ahead (USA) 133 – Crimson Lass (IRE) (Dubawi (IRE) 129) [2017 5g 5m^4 5m^2 5m^6 5f^4 5.2v^5 5g* 5g^4 5m Oct 13] €30,000Y: compact filly: fourth foal: half-sister to 2-y-o 5f winner Dancing Zafeen (by Zafeen) and French winner up to 8.5f Akaroa (2-y-o 7.5f winner, by Intikhab): dam once-raced half-sister to smart winner up to 1¼m Foodbroker Fancy: useful performer: won listed race at Deauville (by neck from Coeur de Beaute) in August: raced only at 5f: acts on good to firm going: races towards rear, often travels strongly. *Jamie Osborne* **96**

PUSHAQ (IRE) 4 b.g. Roderic O'Connor (IRE) 119 – Et Dona Ferentes 61 (Green Desert (USA) 127) [2017 81: 10s t9.5g* t10.2s^2 10s 10m^3 t8.6g^2 8v p8g^6 p8g Nov 10] rather leggy gelding: fairly useful handicapper: won at Wolverhampton in April: second at Newcastle in May: stays 1¼m: acts on polytrack, tapeta and good to firm going: has worn headgear, including in 2017. *Anthony McCann, Ireland* **82 a88**

PUSHJOCKEYPUSH 3 gr.g. Silver Frost (IRE) 122 – Daraiyna (FR) (Refuse To Bend (IRE) 128) [2017 –: p8g p7g 9.9g 14g 10.1g Jul 27] big gelding: little form: in tongue tie in 2017. *Stuart Williams* –

PUSHKIN MUSEUM (IRE) 6 gr.g. Soviet Star (USA) 128 – Chaste 60 (Groom Dancer (USA) 128) [2017 73: t6f t6g^3 t6g* t6g* t6g^3 t6g^5 t6g^2 t6g^2 t5s^3 6m^2 5.1d^3 t6.1g^3 6g^4 p5s^5 t6.1g^5 t5.1g^5 Nov 18] good-topped gelding: fair handicapper: won at Wolverhampton in January (amateur) and February: stays 6f: acts on polytrack, tapeta, good to firm and good to soft going: has worn headgear, including last 2 starts. *Patrick Morris* **76**

PUSH N'PULL (IRE) 2 b.c. (Apr 10) Epaulette (AUS) 126 – Zoudie 79 (Ezzoud (IRE) 126) [2017 6m 6g^4 t6.1g Aug 10] modest form: best effort when fourth in minor event at York (10¾ lengths behind Hey Jonesy) in July: likely to stay 7f: sold 5,000 gns in November, sent to Spain. *Richard Fahey* **58**

PUT THE BOOT IN (IRE) 5 ch.g. Duke of Marmalade (IRE) 132 – Mubkera (IRE) 100 (Nashwan (USA) 135) [2017 63: t12.2g^6 p12g 16v Jul 28] modest maiden: no form in 2017: left Barry Brennan after second start: tried in cheekpieces. *Nikki Evans* –

PYJAMARAMA 3 b.f. Exceed And Excel (AUS) 126 – Dylanesque 91 (Royal Applause 124) [2017 69p: p7g 8.3g t7.2g^2 7g^2 Jun 15] good-topped filly: fair maiden handicapper: stays 7f: acts on polytrack and tapeta: tried in hood: sold 13,000 gns, sent to Greece. *Roger Varian* **71**

PYROCLASTIC (IRE) 5 b.g. Tagula (IRE) 116 – Gypsy Royal (IRE) 54 (Desert Prince (IRE) 130) [2017 67: f6g 6g 6.1m 8.3f 8.2g Jul 8] fair handicapper, out of form in 2017: stays 1m: acts on polytrack, tapeta and good to firm going: has worn headgear: in tongue tie last 4 starts. *Nick Kent* –

PYTHON 5 b.g. Dansili 127 – Imbabala (Zafonic (USA) 130) [2017 –: t10.2s 11.1g^6 12.1m t16.3g 15.9v 12.1d Aug 17] poor maiden handicapper: best effort at 16.5f: acts on tapeta. *Andrew Crook* **43**

Q

QAARAAT 2 b.g. (Feb 20) Acclamation 118 – Ladyship 109 (Oasis Dream 129) [2017 5.2g^4 5m^3 5.7f^3 t5.1g^3 5.1d^3 5m^2 Sep 4] 200,000Y: strong gelding: first foal: dam 6f-7f winner out of very smart 7f-1m winner Peeress: fairly useful maiden: second in nursery at Ripon final start: best form at 5f: acts on good to firm going: tried in blinkers. *Ed Dunlop* **80**

QADIRIYYAH 2 b.g. (May 4) Harbour Watch (IRE) 121 – Quadri (Polish Precedent (USA) 131) [2017 7.9g^4 8s^6 t9.5g^6 Oct 27] fair form: best effort when fourth in maiden at Bellewstown (1¾ lengths behind Tamboureen) in July: left R. P. McNamara after. *Mohamed Moubarak* **71**

QAFFAAL (USA) 6 b.g. Street Cry (IRE) 130 – Wasseema (USA) 111 (Danzig (USA)) [2017 81, a99: t7.1g p10g^2 p8d* p10d^3 p10g^6 p10s^3 t8s^3 7.9m 10v p7s^3 t7.1d^4 Dec 16] useful handicapper: won at Chelmsford in March: best effort when fourth at Newcastle (length behind Charles Molson) in December: effective at 7f to 1¼m: acts on polytrack, tapeta, good to firm and good to soft going: tried in blinkers: often races towards rear: consistent. *Michael Easterby* **102**

QAFILAH (IRE) 2 ch.f. (Mar 15) Arcano (IRE) 122 – Janina 96 (Namid 128) [2017 7g^3 t6s Sep 19] fourth foal: sister to 1m winner Mutadhamen and half-sister to 5f winner Suwaan (by Exceed And Excel): dam, 2-y-o 5f winner, half-sister to useful 5f winner Mattamia out of smart sprinter Lady Dominatrix: fair form: better effort when third in minor event at Lingfield (6½ lengths behind Gavota) in August. *Charles Hills* **65**

QAROUN 2 b.c. (Jan 6) Dark Angel (IRE) 113 – Exotic Isle 89 (Exceed And Excel (AUS) 126) [2017 7s^2 7d* Aug 18] 220,000Y: first foal: dam, 5f winner (including at 2 yrs), half-sister to useful 7f winner Meeting Waters out of smart winner up to 6f (including at 2 yrs) Paradise Isle: fairly useful form: won maiden at Newbury (by length from He's Amazing) in August: will stay 1m: will go on improving. *Sir Michael Stoute* **84 p**

QASR 3 b.c. Excelebration (IRE) 133 – Blur 62 (Oasis Dream 129) [2017 f12.1g^4 Nov 28] placed in 2 bumpers: in hood, 8/1, well held in maiden at Southwell. *Keith Dalgleish* –

QASSEM (IRE) 4 b.g. Lope de Vega (IRE) 125 – Biswa (USA) 48 (Kafwain (USA) 118) [2017 98: 10.3d5 p8g* 7.9d2 9d 8s Oct 21] lengthy gelding: useful handicapper: won at Chelmsford (by 1½ lengths from Mutarabby) in August: second at York (1¾ lengths behind Flaming Spear) later in month: stays 1m: acts on polytrack, good to firm and heavy going: tried in cheekpieces: races prominently: sold 55,000 gns in October to join Jamie Osborne. *Hugo Palmer* **106**

QASWARAH (IRE) 2 b.f. (May 7) Nayef (USA) 129 – Katoom (IRE) 75 (Soviet Star (USA) 128) [2017 8d p8s Nov 16] fifth foal: half-sister to 3 winners, including smart 6f/7f winner Intisaab (by Elnadim) and 2-y-o 7f winner (stays 1¼m) Mouteab (by Marju): dam, maiden (stayed 7f), half-sister to useful 2-y-o 7f winner Luminous Eyes: little impact in maiden/minor event. *Ed Dunlop* **–**

QATARI RIYALS (IRE) 3 b.f. Kodiac 112 – Mary Frith 61 (Acclamation 118) [2017 67p: t6g* 6d 7m4 5g4 6g4 t6.1g* Sep 23] fairly useful performer: won maiden in April and handicap (by short head from Logi) in September, both at Wolverhampton: stays 7f: acts on tapeta and good to firm going: usually races close up. *Richard Hannon* **82**

QATAR MAN (IRE) 3 b.g. Archarcharch (USA) 121 – Dough On The Go (USA) (Bernardini (USA) 132) [2017 84: a8f4 a9.4f2 a9.4g6 Mar 25] useful performer: second in listed race at Meydan (length behind Cosmo Charlie) in March: stays 9.5f: acts on polytrack and dirt: in blinkers last 3 starts: sold 150,000 gns in July, sent to Singapore. *Marco Botti* **108**

QAVIY CASH 3 b.g. Oasis Dream 129 – Neartica (FR) (Sadler's Wells (USA) 132) [2017 10m6 10s p12s2 11.1g* 13.9m Aug 26] €220,000Y: useful-looking gelding: sixth foal: half-brother to 1½m winner Sona (by Dansili): dam, 10.5f winner, closely related to very smart winner up to 1½m Galikova and half-sister to top-class miler Goldikova: fairly useful performer: won handicap at Hamilton (sole outing in cheekpieces, by neck from Archi's Affaire) in July: left Hugo Palmer after fourth start: stays 1½m: acts on polytrack: wears tongue tie. *Dan Skelton* **91**

QAWAMEES (IRE) 2 b.c. (Feb 13) Exceed And Excel (AUS) 126 – Jabhaat (USA) 98 (Hard Spun (USA) 124) [2017 8.3v2 Nov 8] first foal: dam 7.4f winner (including at 2 yrs) who stayed 1¼m: 33/1, second in maiden at Nottingham (short head behind Kinaesthesia) in November: should progress. *Ed Dunlop* **89 p**

QAYED (CAN) 2 b.c. (Mar 22) Blame (USA) 129 – Endless Journey (USA) (A P Indy (USA) 131) [2017 p8g4 Dec 20] $250,000Y: fourth foal: half-brother to 3 winners in North America: dam once-raced sister to US Grade 2 2-y-o 6.5f winner Jump Start: 12/1, promise when fourth in minor event at Kempton (2¾ lengths behind Native Appeal) in December: sure to improve. *David Simcock* **77 p**

QAYES 2 b.c. (Mar 20) Exceed And Excel (AUS) 126 – Time Control 78 (Sadler's Wells (USA) 132) [2017 6g 6v2 Jul 27] 400,000Y: sixth foal: half-brother to smart 2-y-o 6f/7f (Moyglare Stud Stakes) winner Cursory Glance (by Distorted Humor): dam temperamental 10.3f winner: fair form: better effort when second in minor event at Newbury (6 lengths behind Tathmeen) in July: should improve further. *John Gosden* **65 p**

QAYSAR (FR) 2 b.c. (Mar 10) Choisir (AUS) 126 – Coco Demure (IRE) (Titus Livius (FR) 115) [2017 7m2 p7d* Nov 22] €27,000Y, €200,000 2-y-o: compact colt: third foal: closely related to winner up to 1¼m (stays 1½m) White Chocolate (2-y-o 7f winner, by Mastercraftsman) and half-brother to French winner up to 8.5f Cajula (by Rock of Gibraltar): dam 7.5f/1m winner (including at 2 yrs): useful form: won minor event at Kempton (by length from Crack On Crack On) in November: likely to stay 1m: remains open to improvement. *Richard Hannon* **97 p**

QAZYNA (IRE) 2 b.f. (Mar 11) Frankel 147 – First 103 (Highest Honor (FR) 124) [2017 8d3 Oct 24] half-sister to several winners, including 1½m winner (including Group 2 in Australia) Au Revoir (by Singspiel), winner up to 1¼m Perfect Stride (2-y-o 7f winner, by Oasis Dream) and 2-y-o 6f winner (stayed 1m) Law Lord (by Diktat), all smart: dam, French 1m winner, half-sister to smart performers up to 7f Bluebook and Myself: 15/8, promise when third in minor event at Yarmouth (2 lengths behind Dramatic Queen) in October: open to improvement. *Roger Varian* **76 p**

Q CEE 4 b.g. Denounce 89 – Gibraltar Lass (USA) 49 (Concerto (USA) 114) [2017 70: p6g 7m 6g5 p6d 5.7s6 p7g3 Oct 25] modest maiden: stays 6f: acts on tapeta and polytrack: tried in blinkers: often races towards rear. *Eugene Stanford* **62**

QELMIM (IRE) 3 gr.f. Dark Angel (IRE) 113 – Bun Penny (Bertolini (USA) 125) [2017 8g Jun 15] 30,000F, £180,000Y: third foal: dam, of little account, half-sister to useful/ungenuine winner up to 9f La Neige: 16/1, well held in maiden at Newbury. *Richard Hannon* **–**

Duke of Cambridge Stakes, Royal Ascot—French raider Qemah scores at the Royal meeting for the second year running, getting the better of Aljazzi (hood) and Usherette (second right); Smart Call (spots on cap) comes fourth

QEMAH (IRE) 4 b.f. Danehill Dancer (IRE) 117 – Kartica 108 (Rainbow Quest (USA) 134) [2017 121: 7d² 8m* 8g⁴ 8d⁵ 8g⁶ Oct 7] tall filly: smart performer: won Duke of Cambridge Stakes at Royal Ascot (by ¾ length from Aljazzi) in June: fourth in Prix Rothschild at Deauville (¼ length behind Roly Poly) in July: stays 8.5f: acts on good to firm and good to soft going: usually races nearer last than first. *Jean-Claude Rouget, France* **116**

QEWY (IRE) 7 b.g. Street Cry (IRE) 130 – Princess Nada 108 (Barathea (IRE) 127) [2017 116: 21.6m⁴ 16g 11.9g* 12.9g⁶ Nov 11] sturdy gelding: smart performer: third success in Australia when winning Group 3 Bendigo Cup (Handicap) in November by head from Kiwiam: effective at 1½m to 2½m: acted on heavy and good to firm going: front runner/raced prominently: tried in cheekpieces: reportedly retired. *Charlie Appleby* **115**

QEYAADAH (IRE) 4 b.g. Acclamation 118 – Effervesce (IRE) 84 (Galileo (IRE) 134) [2017 96: 7m⁶ 6m⁶ 8m⁵ 8d⁵ 7m* 7f³ 7s⁴ 7g⁴ 7g² 7d³ 7d 7g Oct 13] good-topped gelding: fairly useful handicapper: won at Redcar (by ½ length from Horsted Keynes) in June: stays 7f: acts on firm and soft going: tried in cheekpieces: races prominently. *Michael Appleby* **94**

QIANLONG 2 b.c. (Mar 31) Dragon Pulse (IRE) 114 – Dream Day (FR) (Spectrum (IRE) 126) [2017 6.1v² 6.1s³ 7v² 7.9g² t7.1d³ Oct 24] 20,000F, 42,000Y: sturdy colt: fifth foal: half-brother to 1m winner Sooqaan (by Naaqoos) and a winner in Hong Kong by Dark Angel: dam French winner up to 1¼m (2-y-o 5.5f winner): fairly useful maiden: best effort when second in minor event at York in October: stays 1m: acts on heavy going: front runner/races prominently: sold 30,000 gns, sent to Qatar. *Roger Varian* **80**

QIBTEE (FR) 7 b.g. Antonius Pius (USA) 123 – Embers of Fame (IRE) (Sadler's Wells (USA) 132) [2017 67§: t9.5m t13.9m Jan 13] quite attractive gelding: fair handicapper, below best both Flat starts in 2017: stays 1½m: acts on polytrack, good to firm and heavy going: has worn headgear: often races prominently: quirky sort (often races freely) and is one to be wary of. *Les Eyre* **– §**

QORTAAJ 4 b.g. Kyllachy 129 – Cardrona 66 (Selkirk (USA) 129) [2017 75: p12g p11g p7g 8m⁴ 8.3g 8g 7d Jun 5] fair maiden: below form in 2017: stays 9.5f: acts on polytrack, tapeta and good to firm going: has worn headgear, including last 2 starts: tried in tongue tie: sometimes slowly away. *David Loughnane* **55**

Q TEN GIRL (IRE) 4 ch.f. Zebedee 113 – Regresa A Mi (IRE) 84 (Spartacus (IRE) 107) [2017 58: t7.1g Jan 9] compact filly: modest performer, well held sole start in 2017: stays 8.5f: acts on polytrack and tapeta: wears headgear. *James Unett* **–**

QUADRIGA (IRE) 7 b.g. Acclamation 118 – Turning Light (GER) 108 (Fantastic Light (USA) 134) [2017 60: f8g f12s f12g⁴ f8d⁴ f7g³ t8.6g⁴ t8.6g⁶ 8g f6.1g³ f7.1g f11.1g Dec 22] strong, lengthy gelding: modest handicapper: stays 1¾m, usually races over much shorter: acts on all-weather and good to firm going: often wears headgear: has worn tongue tie. *Chris Grant* **51**

QUALITY ART (USA) 9 b.g. Elusive Quality (USA) – Katherine Seymour 107 (Green **66**
Desert (USA) 127) [2017 69: p5g^{5} t5.1g* p5g^{pu} Apr 13] strong, attractive gelding: fair handicapper: won at Wolverhampton in March: fatally injured next time: stayed 6f: acted on all-weather, firm and soft going: tried in headgear/tongue tie: often raced prominently. *Simon Hodgson*

QUALITY SEEKER (USA) 2 b.c. (Feb 3) Quality Road (USA) 131 – Arravale (USA) **62 p**
116 (Arch (USA) 127) [2017 p8d^{5} Nov 9] €260,000Y: third living foal: half-brother to useful Canadian 7f winner Nancy O (by Pivotal): dam North American Grade 1 9f/1¼m winner: 33/1, fifth in minor event at Chelmsford (11½ lengths behind Gronkowski) in November: should do better. *Ed Walker*

QUANDARY PEAK 3 b.f. Mount Nelson 125 – Sahariri (IRE) (Red Ransom (USA)) **80**
[2017 62+: 8.1m^{4} May 5] close-coupled filly: fairly useful handicapper: stays 1m: acts on polytrack and good to firm going. *J. S. Moore*

QUANTATMENTAL (IRE) 2 ch.c. (Mar 10) New Approach (IRE) 132 – Anayid **61**
(A P Indy (USA) 131) [2017 8g 8.2g t9.5g^{5} Oct 27] well-made colt: modest form in maiden/minor events. *Tom Dascombe*

QUANTUM DOT (IRE) 6 ch.g. Exceed And Excel (AUS) 126 – Jeed (IRE) 86 **69 §**
(Mujtahid (USA) 118) [2017 69§: 5.1m^{5} 5g 5m 5.1m* 5.1m^{3} 5.3d^{3} 5.1g^{6} Sep 6] fair handicapper: won at Chepstow in June: best at 5f: acts on polytrack, tapeta and good to firm going: wears headgear: tried in tongue tie: usually leads: unreliable. *Ed de Giles*

QUARGENT (USA) 2 b.f. (Feb 6) War Front (USA) 119 – Naples Bay (USA) (Giant's **82 p**
Causeway (USA) 132) [2017 7g p7d* Aug 16] $585,000Y: first foal: dam, US Grade 3 1m/8.5f winner, half-sister to high-class 9f-1½m performer Medaglia d'Oro: fairly useful form: won minor event at Kempton (by 1¾ lengths from Amandine) in August: will go on improving. *Jeremy Noseda*

QUARTERBACK (GER) 5 b.h. American Post 121 – Quebra (GER) 106 (Surumu **108**
(GER)) [2017 116: p10g^{6} 12m Apr 22] big horse: smart performer: down the field in listed race at Kempton and John Porter Stakes at Newbury in 2017: stays 1¾m: acts on soft going: wears headgear: has worn tongue tie, including last 2 starts. *Rune Haugen*

QUATRIEME AMI 4 b.g. Equiano (FR) 127 – Hundred Year Flood (USA) (Giant's **84**
Causeway (USA) 132) [2017 93: p6g p6g 5m^{5} p6g^{3} 5g 6d^{2} 5g* 6.1d Oct 4] fairly useful handicapper: won at Redcar (by head from See The Sun) in September: stays 6f: acts on tapeta and good to soft going: has worn tongue tie: usually races prominently: sold 10,000 gns, sent to Sweden. *Philip McBride*

QUAY POINT (IRE) 4 b.f. Royal Applause 124 – Merle (Selkirk (USA) 129) [2017 10m **62**
11.8d^{5} p12g 14d* 14.2g 13d Aug 23] good-topped filly: seventh foal: half-sister to useful French 1¼m-1½m winner Ominous (by Oasis Dream) and 1m winner Equleus (by Equiano): dam unraced half-sister to very smart stayer Solo Mio: modest performer: won handicap at Nottingham in July: stays 1¾m: acts on good to soft going: front runner/races prominently. *Laura Mongan*

QUAYSIDE 2 ch.c. (Feb 17) Harbour Watch (IRE) 121 – Fantacise 83 (Pivotal 124) [2017 **77**
5g 6.1s^{3} 6s* 6f^{6} 6s^{6} 6g^{5} 6d^{6} Sep 2] strong colt: fair performer: won maiden at Hamilton in June: stays 6f: acts on soft going: tried in blinkers: often leads. *Richard Fahey*

QUEBEC 6 b.g. Dansili 127 – Milford Sound (Barathea (IRE) 127) [2017 p12g Dec 20] **71**
fairly useful for A. Fabre in 2014, below that level on sole Flat start since: stays 15f: acts on viscoride and good to soft going: modest hurdler. *Roger Ingram*

QUEEN ADELAIDE 2 b.f. (Mar 10) Helmet (AUS) 127 – Spunger 73 (Fraam 114) **63**
[2017 7g^{5} 7g p8g^{3} 6g Oct 7] 10,000Y: rather unfurnished filly: half-sister to several winners, including 2-y-o 6f-9.5f winner (stayed 1½m) Guava (by Kyllachy): dam, winner up to 1¼m (including at 2 yrs), half-sister to useful winner up to 9f Mafaaz: modest form: stays 1m. *John Ryan*

QUEEN BEATRICE 3 b.f. Iffraaj 127 – Skirrid (Halling (USA) 133) [2017 8.1m 9.9g **57**
8.1g 10d^{6} 7d^{2} 7v Sep 25] compact filly: second foal: half-sister to winner up to 1m Easy Code (2-y-o 6f winner, by Bahamian Bounty): dam unraced half-sister to smart 9f-1½m winner Spice Route out of Oaks d'Italia winner Zanzibar: modest maiden: best effort at 1¼m: acts on good to soft going. *William Muir*

QUEEN IN WAITING (IRE) 3 gr.f. Exceed And Excel (AUS) 126 – Princess Taise **98**
(USA) 100 (Cozzene (USA)) [2017 81p: t5.1g* 5g^{2} 6m^{4} 6m^{4} 6m^{5} 5m* 5.1d^{5} 5m^{5} 6.1g 5d 5m Aug 26] strong filly: useful handicapper: won at Wolverhampton in April and

Newmarket (by neck from Jumira Bridge) in June: best form at 5f: acts on polytrack, tapeta and good to firm going: often races prominently: sold to join David Barron 55,000 gns in November. *Mark Johnston*

QUEEN KINDLY 3 ch.f. Frankel 147 – Lady of The Desert (USA) 124 (Rahy (USA) **108** 115) [2017 113: 7m^5 8m 5g^3 6g^2 6g* 6s 5d^5 6m^4 Oct 14] lengthy filly: useful performer: won listed race at Pontefract (by head from Eartha Kitt) in August: second in Summer Stakes at York (short head behind Mystic Dawn) in July: stays 6f: acts on good to firm and good to soft going. *Richard Fahey*

QUEEN MAUREEN (USA) 2 b.f. (Apr 15) Elusive Quality (USA) – Star of Paris – (USA) (Dayjur (USA) 137) [2017 p7g 7d^6 Nov 4] $85,000Y: sister to 3 winners, including Prix Morny winner Elusive City and 2-y-o 6f winner Terhaab, and closely related to 5f (minor US stakes) winner Parisian Affair (by Mr Greeley): dam unraced: little show in 2 minor events: wears tongue tie. *Hugo Palmer*

QUEEN MOON (IRE) 3 b.f. Lawman (FR) 121 – Movie Queen (Danehill (USA) 126) **54** [2017 8.1d^5 7m 8m^4 9s^4 10d^5 f8.1g^3 f8.1g^4 Dec 4] €8,000Y: lengthy, angular filly: half-sister to 9f winner (stayed 1½m) Arte Del Calcio (by Manduro): dam unraced half-sister to smart performer up to 1¼m Two-Twenty-Two: modest maiden: stays 1m: acts on fibresand: often races towards rear. *Andrew Balding*

QUEEN OF DESIRE (IRE) 2 b.f. (Apr 22) Dubawi (IRE) 129 – Beyond Desire 112 **61 p** (Invincible Spirit (IRE) 121) [2017 p6s^5 Dec 1] second foal: half-sister to 5f winner Wishing Time (by Frankel): dam 5f/6f winner (including at 2 yrs): 11/1, fifth in minor event at Chelmsford (2½ lengths behind Lady Willpower) in December: will improve. *Roger Varian*

QUEEN OF DREAMS (IRE) 2 b.f. (Feb 26) Epaulette (AUS) 126 – Celestial Dream – (IRE) 69 (Oasis Dream 129) [2017 7m t6.1g p6s Dec 1] €45,000F, £52,000Y: smallish, angular filly: fourth foal: half-sister to 3 winners, including 5f winner Justice Lady (by Dream Ahead) and 1m winner (stayed 1¼m) Hesbaan (by Acclamation): dam 5f winner out of smart sprinter Lochangel: no form in minor events. *William Knight*

QUEEN OF KALAHARI 2 b.f. (Feb 25) Lethal Force (IRE) 128 – Aromatherapy 96 **77** (Oasis Dream 129) [2017 5m^5 5g^3 5s* p5g^2 6m* 6m^6 6s^5 6s^2 6v^2 p6g^2 Oct 17] £15,000Y: lengthy filly: fourth foal: half-sister to 3 winners, including 5f winner Pieman's Girl (by Henrythenavigator), later successful abroad, and 1¼m winner Scent of Power (by Authorized): dam 1m winner: fair performer: won minor events at Leicester in May and Newbury in June: stays 6f: acts on polytrack, good to firm and heavy going: sold 22,000 gns to join Les Eyre. *Charles Hills*

QUEEN OF TIME 3 b.f. Harbour Watch (IRE) 121 – Black Belt Shopper (IRE) 82 **99** (Desert Prince (IRE) 130) [2017 86p: 7f* 8m* 8m^4 8m^2 Jul 8] sturdy filly: useful performer: won maiden and handicap at Goodwood in May: best effort when second in listed race at Sandown (½ length behind Tisbutadream) in July: stays 1m: acts on firm going. *Henry Candy*

QUEEN PENN 2 gr.f. (Mar 29) Dark Angel (IRE) 113 – The Manx Touch (IRE) 70 **83** (Petardia 113) [2017 5.1m 6s^2 6m^3 6d^3 6s* Aug 24] 67,000Y: good-topped filly: half-sister to several winners, including useful winner up to 6f Baby Strange (2-y-o 5f/6f winner, by Superior Premium), smart 7f-8.3f winner Moone's My Name and useful winner up to 1m Frog Hollow (2-y-o 7f winner) (both by Intikhab): dam 7f/1m winner who stayed 11f: fairly useful performer: won maiden at Hamilton (by 3½ lengths from Grise Lightning) in August: stays 6f: acts on soft going: usually races prominently. *Richard Fahey*

QUEENSBRYDGE 3 ch.f. Dutch Art 126 – Meydan Princess (IRE) 109 (Choisir (AUS) **88** 126) [2017 89: 7.2m^6 8g p7d p8g^4 p8g^4 p8g* p8g Nov 17] fairly useful handicapper: won at Kempton (by 1½ lengths from Medicean Ballet) in October: left Robyn Brisland after sixth start: stays 1m: acts on polytrack. *K. J. Condon, Ireland*

QUEENS GALLERY 2 b.c. (Mar 19) Dutch Art 126 – Raymi Coya (CAN) 100 (Van **61** Nistelrooy (USA) 108) [2017 6.1m^4 7g^5 p7g Sep 27] close-coupled colt: modest form first 2 starts in minor events: sold 6,000 gns, sent to Spain. *Richard Hannon*

QUEENS ROYALE 3 b.f. Stimulation (IRE) 121 – Sofia Royale 61 (Royal Applause **85** 124) [2017 63: p6s^5 6g^6 8.3d^4 7.6d^3 7d^4 p7g* t7.2g f7.1g* p7s f7.1g* f7.1g* Dec 22] compact filly: fairly useful handicapper: won at Kempton in September and Southwell (3) in November/December: stays 8.5f: acts on polytrack, fibresand and good to soft going: often wears visor. *Michael Appleby*

QUEEN'S SARGENT (FR) 2 gr.g. (Feb 26) Kendargent (FR) 112 – Queen's Conquer (King's Best (USA) 132) [2017 5m $6g^{3}$ $7.2g^{2}$ $7g^{4}$ $6d^{2}$ 6.5g Sep 14] €42,000Y: sturdy gelding: seventh foal: half-brother to 3 winners, including useful winner up to 1m Queen's Daughter (by American Post) and winner up to 1¼m Espero (2-y-o 9f winner, by Verglas), both in France: dam French winner up to 9f (2-y-o 1m winner): fairly useful maiden: second in nursery at York in August: stays 7f: acts on good to soft going. *Kevin Ryan* **87**

QUEEN'S TRUST 4 b.f. Dansili 127 – Queen's Best 110 (King's Best (USA) 132) [2017 122: $10.3d^{4}$ $10m^{4}$ $9.9v^{6}$ $11.9d^{3}$ 9.9d $9f^{5}$ Nov 4] good-topped, attractive filly: very smart performer: best effort in 2017 when fourth in Prince of Wales's Stakes at Royal Ascot (2 lengths behind Highland Reel) in June: third in Yorkshire Oaks at York (5¾ lengths behind Enable) and fifth in Breeders' Cup Filly & Mare Turf at Del Mar (2 lengths behind Wuheida, had won race when held at Santa Anita in 2016): stays 1½m: has form on polytrack and good to soft going, but very best efforts on firm/good to firm. *Sir Michael Stoute* **120**

QUENCH DOLLY 3 gr.f. Hellvelyn 118 – Hollybell 87 (Beveled (USA)) [2017 78: $p6g^{6}$ 5.1g 6g* 6d* $6d^{3}$ 5m $6.1g^{2}$ $6d^{4}$ 5v* 5v 6m Oct 14] compact filly: useful handicapper: won at Leicester (by 8 lengths from The Stalking Moon) and Lingfield (by 6 lengths from Father McKenzie) in May, and Goodwood (by 3 lengths from Fair Cop) in August: stays 6f: acts on polytrack and any turf going: usually leads, often travels strongly. *John Gallagher* **106**

QUEST FOR MORE (IRE) 7 b.g. Teofilo (IRE) 126 – No Quest (IRE) (Rainbow Quest (USA) 134) [2017 118: 15.9d 16.2m 20m Jun 22] tall, useful-looking gelding: smart performer, won Lonsdale Cup at York and Prix du Cadran at Chantilly in 2016: well below best in 2017, shaping as if amiss on last 2 starts: wears blinkers. *Roger Charlton* **–**

QUESTION OF FAITH 6 b.m. Yeats (IRE) 128 – Anastasia Storm (Mozart (IRE) 131) [2017 61: $16g^{5}$ 14g $15.9s^{2}$ 13.1g* $12.5m^{2}$ 11.2s $15g^{2}$ 15.9g* 14.1v* 15s* Oct 3] fair handicapper: won at Ayr (apprentice) in July, Catterick in August, Carlisle in September and again at Ayr in October: stays 16.5f: acts on tapeta, good to firm and heavy going: tried in hood: often starts slowly, usually races nearer last than first. *Martin Todhunter* **77**

QUESTO 5 ch.g. Monsieur Bond (IRE) 120 – Ex Gracia (Efisio 120) [2017 73, a60: $6g^{3}$ $6g^{5}$ $5.9g^{5}$ 6d* $6d^{3}$ Aug 12] fair handicapper: won at Thirsk (by 4½ lengths from Sea of Green) in July: stayed 6f: acted on good to firm and good to soft going: often raced prominently: dead. *Tracy Waggott* **79**

QUICK BREATH 2 b.g. (Apr 8) Bated Breath 125 – Shy Appeal (IRE) 71 (Barathea (IRE) 127) [2017 7g $6m^{6}$ 6g 7g Oct 16] strong, compact gelding: fair form: best effort at 6f. *Jonathan Portman* **72**

QUICK LOOK 4 b.g. Kheleyf (USA) 116 – Weqaar (USA) 83 (Red Ransom (USA)) [2017 88: p6g 6m $5s^{4}$ $5.1g^{3}$ $6v^{2}$ 7d $5v^{6}$ 6s* 5s* Nov 8] tall gelding: useful handicapper: won at Catterick (by 6 lengths from Economic Crisis) in October and Nottingham in November: stays 6f: acts on good to firm and heavy going: tried in cheekpieces: sometimes slowly away, often travels strongly. *Michael Easterby* **97**

QUICK MONET (IRE) 4 b.g. Excellent Art 125 – Clinging Vine (USA) 60 (Fusaichi Pegasus (USA) 130) [2017 $t5.1g^{5}$ 5m 7s $p7s^{6}$ f6.1g $p7g^{5}$ $f8.1g^{3}$ t8.6g f8.1g Dec 21] poor maiden: best effort at 7f: tried in headgear. *Shaun Harris* **47**

QUICK N QUIRKY (IRE) 4 b.f. Lilbourne Lad (IRE) 111 – Beseech (IRE) (Danehill (USA) 126) [2017 87: 7m $7.8g^{6}$ 7m 8.8m $6.9s^{2}$ $5.9d^{4}$ Jul 8] fair handicapper: stays 1m: acts on soft and good to firm going: wears headgear: has worn tongue tie. *Tim Easterby* **77**

QUICK RECOVERY 2 gr.f. (Mar 2) Lethal Force (IRE) 128 – Lisiere (IRE) 87 (Excellent Art 125) [2017 $6g^{6}$ 7g 7g Sep 14] 92,000F, 43,000Y: lengthy filly: first foal: dam, 6f winner who stayed 1m, half-sister to smart winner up to 7f Dick Whittington: well held in minor events/maiden: tried in hood. *Jim Boyle* **–**

QUICK SKIPS LAD (IRE) 2 b.g. (Apr 4) Lilbourne Lad (IRE) 111 – Tallawalla (IRE) 66 (Oratorio (IRE) 128) [2017 5g $4.5g^{4}$ $p5g^{3}$ $5g^{6}$ $5d^{4}$ $5g^{2}$ $6.1m^{4}$ 5.5g* $7s^{3}$ $7d^{6}$ $7g^{5}$ Aug 3] sturdy gelding: modest performer: won claimer at Le Croise-Laroche in June (left J. S. Moore after): stays 7f: acts on polytrack and soft going: wears headgear. *D. Windrif, France* **64**

QUIDS IN (IRE) 4 b.g. Pour Moi (IRE) 125 – Quixotic (Pivotal 124) [2017 80: $10.2d^{6}$ Oct 11] fair maiden: stays 8.5f: acts on good to firm and good to soft going: tried in cheekpieces: in tongue tie last 3 starts: fairly useful hurdler. *Oliver Greenall* **68**

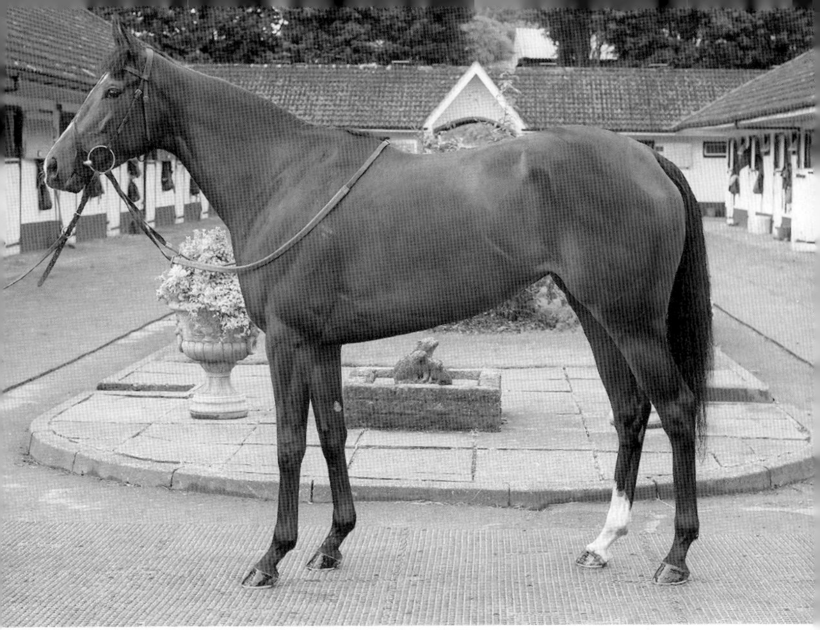

Ontoawinner, Strecker and Burke's "Quiet Reflection"

QUIET COMPANY 3 ch.g. Showcasing 117 – Kameruka 98 (Auction House (USA) 120) [2017 –: p7g 7g 8g^5 9g 10d p8g* p10.7g p8g Dec 6] modest handicapper: won at Dundalk in September: stays 1m: acts on polytrack: tried in cheekpieces. *A. P. Keatley, Ireland* **56**

QUIET MOMENT (IRE) 3 b.f. Dandy Man (IRE) 123 – Easee On (IRE) (Hawk Wing (USA) 136) [2017 64: 6m 6d^6 5d^5 7.2m^6 7.2s^2 7.2s^3 8v* f8.1g^2 f8.1g Nov 16] modest handicapper: won at Ayr in October: left Ben Haslam after third start: stays 1m: acts on fibresand, best turf form on soft/heavy going: has worn headgear. *Keith Dalgleish* **63**

QUIET REFLECTION 4 b.f. Showcasing 117 – My Delirium 83 (Haafhd 129) [2017 126: 5f 6s* 6s Oct 21] workmanlike filly: very smart performer: successful 4 times at 3 yrs, including in Commonwealth Cup at Royal Ascot and Sprint Cup at Haydock: lightly raced in 2017, standout effort when won Renaissance Stakes at Naas (by 2¾ lengths from Alphabet) in September: raced at 5f/6f: acts on soft and good to firm going: strong traveller: sold 2,100,000 gns in December. *K. R. Burke* **122**

QUIET WARRIOR (IRE) 6 b.g. Kodiac 112 – Pretty Woman (IRE) 45 (Night Shift (USA)) [2017 71: p7g^4 7m^2 t6g 6g^6 5d t7.2g Oct 27] smallish, good-quartered gelding: fair handicapper: left David Loughnane/below form after second start: stays 7f: acts on polytrack, tapeta and good to firm going: has worn headgear: tried in tongue tie: often leads: sold 1,500 gns, sent to Portugal. *Michael Easterby* **67**

QUIET WEEKEND 3 b.g. Mawatheeq (USA) 126 – Maid of Perth (Mark of Esteem (IRE) 137) [2017 –: 10.2d t12.4s Sep 8] no form: in tongue tie both 2017 starts. *James Bethell* **–**

QUINA BROOK (IRE) 4 b.f. Peintre Celebre (USA) 137 – Barconey (IRE) (Danehill Dancer (IRE) 117) [2017 –: 12g p8g Nov 3] little form: left Daniel Loughnane after first start. *Christian Delcros, Ireland* **–**

QUINQUEREME 3 b.f. Elusive Quality (USA) – Finding Neverland (FR) (Green Desert (USA) 127) [2017 7s^6 8d 7g Jun 10] first foal: dam 2-y-o 1m winner: well held in 3 maidens. *Michael Bell* **–**

QUINTEO (IRE) 3 b.g. Requinto (IRE) 109 – Haraplata (GER) (Platini (GER) 126) [2017 81: t8.6g t12.2g^{3} 14.4g^{5} p12.4f t9.5g p8g Sep 25] fair handicapper: stays 1½m: acts on tapeta: usually wears headgear: sold 3,000 gns, sent to Greece. *Jo Hughes* **78**

QUINTESSENTIAL 3 b.f. Dick Turpin (IRE) 127 – Quiquillo (USA) 73 (Cape Canaveral (USA) 115) [2017 –: t7.1m Jan 14] no form. *Richard Fahey* **–**

QUINTUS CERIALIS (IRE) 5 b.g. Vale of York (IRE) 117 – Red Fox (IRE) (Spectrum (IRE) 126) [2017 79: p7g^{4} p7g^{6} p7d^{4} p7g t7.1g^{6} 7m^{4} 7d 7m 6.1m^{4} 6g^{2} 6g p6s Dec 7] close-coupled gelding: modest handicapper: stays 7f: acts on polytrack: wears headgear/tongue tie: starts slowly, usually races nearer last than first: untrustworthy. *Karen George* **58 §**

QUITE A STORY 5 ch.m. Equiano (FR) 127 – Perfect Story (IRE) 95 (Desert Story (IRE) 115) [2017 73: 6m^{3} 6m^{4} 6.1m^{6} t7.2g^{5} t6.1g p6g^{4} t6.1m p6g Nov 17] leggy mare: fair handicapper on turf, modest on all-weather: left Patrick Chamings after sixth start: stays 6f: acts on polytrack and good to firm going: tried in cheekpieces: signs of temperament. *Archie Watson* **69 a62**

QUITE SHARP 3 ch.f. New Approach (IRE) 132 – Balisada 115 (Kris 135) [2017 10.2s 12s Jul 28] closely related to very smart 1¼m-1½m winner Galactic Star and smart 1½m-2m winner (stayed 21.5f) El Salvador (both by Galileo) and half-sister to several winners, including useful 7f-9f winner Blues Ballad (by Singspiel): dam 7f (at 2 yrs) and 1m (Coronation Stakes) winner: well held in 2 maidens. *Charlie Fellowes* **–**

QUIVERY (USA) 2 b.f. (Apr 22) Violence (USA) 125 – Passion du Coeur (USA) (Distorted Humor (USA) 117) [2017 7m* 7d* 7g^{4} 8m Oct 13] $30,000Y, $360,000 2-y-o: sturdy filly: fifth foal: half-sister to 3 minor US/Japanese winners by First Samurai, Tiznow and To Honor And Serve: dam US 2-y-o 7f winner: fairly useful form: won minor events at Doncaster in June and Newmarket in July: fourth in Prestige Stakes at Goodwood (2 lengths behind Billesdon Brook) in August: stays 7f. *Jeremy Noseda* **92**

QUIXOTE (GER) 7 b.h. Pivotal 124 – Quebrada (IRE) 109 (Devil's Bag (USA)) [2017 98: p7d^{4} f7d^{5} 8m* 7.9d 8.2v 7.9g Oct 13] sturdy horse: useful handicapper: won at Haydock (by 3¾ lengths from Early Morning) in April for David Loughnane: left Tony Carroll after first start: stays 8.5f: acts on polytrack, tapeta, soft and good to firm going: in tongue tie last 2 starts: usually races nearer last than first: has joined James Unett. *Michael Easterby* **100**

QULOOB 3 b.c. New Approach (IRE) 132 – Jadhwah (Nayef (USA) 129) [2017 70p: 10.2f* 11.9d* 12g* 14g^{2} Aug 18] smart/highly progressive handicapper: won at Bath (by neck from I'vegotthepower) in May, Brighton (by 8 lengths from Chaparrachik) in June and Newmarket (by 1¾ lengths from Batts Rock) in July: stays 1¾m: acts on tapeta, firm and good to soft going: often races towards rear. *Owen Burrows* **112**

QUOTELINE DIRECT 4 ch.g. Sir Percy 129 – Queen's Pudding (IRE) 84 (Royal Applause 124) [2017 74: 8m 10f^{3} 10g 10g^{2} 9s^{4} 11.2v^{6} 10.2d^{5} 10.2g* t9.5g^{2} Dec 18] fair handicapper: won at Nottingham (amateur) in November: stays 1¼m: acts on tapeta, firm and soft going: wears hood. *Micky Hammond* **73**

QUOTHQUAN (FR) 3 b.g. Myboycharlie (IRE) 118 – Lonestar Spirit (IRE) (Invincible Spirit (IRE) 121) [2017 79: p10g^{3} 8.5g^{6} 9.1m p11s^{2} p8g 10.1g^{5} 14.2v* p12g^{3} Nov 1] fairly useful handicapper: won at Salisbury (by length from Fields of Fortune) in October: stays 1¾m: acts on polytrack and heavy going: often races towards rear. *Michael Madgwick* **87**

QURBAAN (USA) 4 ch.c. Speightstown (USA) 124 – Flip Flop (FR) 114 (Zieten (USA) 118) [2017 112: p8g* p8g^{5} 9.4g^{4} 9.9g^{3} a9.9g^{4} 9.4g^{5} Oct 10] smart performer: won listed race at Cagnes-sur-Mer (by 1½ lengths from Cersei) in February: third in Grand Prix de Vichy (1¼ lengths behind Best Fouad) in July: stays 1¼m: acts on polytrack: tried in cheekpieces. *Francois Rohaut, France* **112**

R

RAASHDY (IRE) 4 b.g. Intikhab (USA) 135 – Maghya (IRE) 96 (Mujahid (USA) 125) [2017 65: t9.5m p10m f8g^{6} 8.1d^{6} 10.2d 10.2m t8.6g 8.1d p10g p10g* p11g* t12.2m* p12g* t14g^{3} t12.2d^{2} t14d^{3} Dec 27] fair handicapper: completed 4-timer at Chelmsford, Kempton, Wolverhampton and Lingfield in October/November: stays 1¾m: acts on polytrack and tapeta: often wears headgear: often races prominently. *Peter Hiatt* **72**

RAAWY 3 b.g. Dutch Art 126 – Age of Chivalry (IRE) 110 (Invincible Spirit (IRE) 121) [2017 7d^2 7s^3 7g Aug 17] good-bodied gelding: fair form: best effort when third in maiden at Doncaster in July. *Simon Crisford* **74**

RACEHORSE 2 ch.f. (Apr 22) Equiano (FR) 127 – Lovely Dream (IRE) 69 (Elnadim (USA) 128) [2017 p7s^4 t7.2g^5 Dec 22] fifth foal: half-sister to 2-y-o 5f winner Mosstang (by Moss Vale) and 1m-11.6f winner Ejayteekay (by Big Bad Bob): dam, maiden (seemed best at 7f), closely related to very smart 1m-11f winner Janet: modest form: better effort when fourth in minor event at Chelmsford (2½ lengths behind I'm Yer Man) in December. *Hughie Morrison* **57**

RACEMAKER 3 b.g. Stimulation (IRE) 121 – Sophies Heart (Hurricane Run (IRE) 134) [2017 70: 8g^4 9.8g^3 9.8d^3 8m* 9.8d^5 7.8s 8g^4 t8g Sep 12] fairly useful handicapper: won at Ripon (by neck from Hernando Torres) in July: stays 1¼m: acts on soft and good to firm going: front runner/races prominently. *Andrew Crook* **80**

RACE TIME (USA) 4 b.f. Street Sense (USA) 128 – Well At The Top (IRE) (Sadler's Wells (USA) 132) [2017 –: p11d t12.2g^6 f8g 11.6g^{pu} p10g Oct 12] poor maiden: left Seamus Durack after third start: best effort at 1½m: usually wears headgear: tried in tongue tie. *Zoe Davison* **45**

RACHAEL'S ROCKET (IRE) 2 ch.f. (Feb 16) Sir Prancealot (IRE) 111 – Red Blanche (IRE) (Red Clubs (IRE) 125) [2017 5d^6 6g^2 7d^4 6g p6.5g^5 8g^4 8s^2 6d^2 6d p7.5g* Nov 21] second foal: dam unraced half-sister to smart 7f-10.4f winner Middlemarch: fair performer: raced only in France after debut: left J. S. Moore after seventh start: won claimer at Marseilles Vivaux in November: stays 1m: acts on polytrack and soft going: in cheekpieces last 3 starts. *Cedric Boutin, France* **76**

RACING ANGEL (IRE) 5 b.m. Dark Angel (IRE) 113 – Roclette (USA) 76 (Rock of Gibraltar (IRE) 133) [2017 77: p6g^6 5s^4 6m 5m^5 5.2m^2 5d^4 5g 6v^6 5g t5g^4 t6g f5g^5 f6.1g^4 Dec 29] rather leggy mare: fair handicapper on turf, modest on all-weather: left Mick Quinn after sixth start: stays 6f: acts on tapeta, soft and good to firm going: tried in blinkers. *Adrian Nicholls* **69** **a61**

RACING COUNTRY (IRE) 2 b.c. (Feb 10) Dubawi (IRE) 129 – Movin' Out (AUS) (Encosta de Lago (AUS)) [2017 9.1s^5 p8g^4 Nov 7] fair form: better effort when fifth in minor event at Goodwood (3½ lengths behind dead-heaters Istanbul Sultan and Loxley) in October: may prove best at around 1m. *Saeed bin Suroor* **72**

RACING HISTORY (IRE) 5 b.h. Pivotal 124 – Gonbarda (GER) 117 (Lando (GER) 128) [2017 120: 11.9g^3 Aug 13] well-made horse: smart performer, lightly raced: in cheekpieces, third in Grosser Preis von Berlin at Hoppegarten (4½ lengths behind Dschingis Secret) on sole start in 2017: stays 1½m: acts on soft and good to firm going. *Saeed bin Suroor* **117**

RACING RADIO (IRE) 2 b.g. (Feb 15) Dandy Man (IRE) 123 – Vale of Avoca (IRE) (Azamour (IRE) 130) [2017 5s 6d^6 6m^4 t7.1g^5 8g Sep 27] modest maiden: stayed 6f: acted on good to firm going: usually raced nearer last than first: dead. *David Barron* **54**

RACING SPIRIT 5 ch.g. Sir Percy 129 – Suertuda (Domedriver (IRE) 128) [2017 40: 16s^6 Sep 19] poor maiden: tried in blinkers: modest maiden hurdler. *Dave Roberts* **–**

RACQUET 4 br.g. Pastoral Pursuits 127 – Billie Jean 65 (Bertolini (USA) 125) [2017 82: 6g 6m^3 6v 6m^6 6d t6g^6 6s* 6g^5 6g* 5.9s^3 6v 6s 5g 5g^6 5s^2 6v Nov 7] smallish gelding: fair handicapper: won at Ayr in July and August: stays 6f: acts on soft and good to firm going: has worn blinkers. *Ruth Carr* **74**

RADIO SOURCE (IRE) 2 ch.c. (Mar 13) Raven's Pass (USA) 133 – Roshanak (IRE) 91 (Spinning World (USA) 130) [2017 7g^2 7d* Aug 21] €110,000F, 120,000Y: well-made colt: half-brother to several winners, including smart 1m-10.7f winner Tom Melbourne (by Dylan Thomas) and useful French 1m-1¼m winner Araaja (by Iffraaj): dam 2-y-o 6f winner: fairly useful form: won minor event at Lingfield (by 5 lengths from Staunch) in August: sure to improve further. *Sir Michael Stoute* **87 p**

RADJASH 3 b.g. Shamardal (USA) 129 – White Moonstone (USA) 115 (Dynaformer (USA)) [2017 83p: 10m^4 8g^4 May 15] sturdy gelding: fairly useful form: stays 1¼m: wore cheekpieces in 2017: sold to join Ruth Carr £5,000 in September. *Charlie Appleby* **83**

RAFAAF (IRE) 9 b.g. Royal Applause 124 – Sciunfona (IRE) (Danehill (USA) 126) [2017 58: p8d^3 p8g^3 t8.6g^5 7d^6 7d^6 7v 6.1g^4 f6.1g Oct 22] strong gelding: modest handicapper: stays 8.5f: acts on polytrack, tapeta, good to firm and heavy going: has worn headgear. *Peter Hiatt* **59**

RAFFLE KING (IRE) 3 b.g. Kodiac 112 – Tap The Dot (IRE) (Sharp Humor (USA) 118) [2017 73: p6g^3 6g^2 6d 6m 6m t5g^2 p5g^2 t5.1g^3 Oct 21] close-coupled gelding: fair maiden: stays 6f: acts on polytrack, tapeta and good to soft going: has joined Ruth Carr. *Mick Channon* **79**

RAGSTONE RIDGE (FR) 2 ch.g. (Apr 1) Choisir (AUS) 126 – Almogia (USA) (Gone West (USA)) [2017 p7d p8d Dec 13] little impact in 2 minor events: has joined Murty McGrath. *Richard Hughes* –

RAGSTONE ROAD (IRE) 2 b.g. (Mar 19) Kodiac 112 – Greenflash 80 (Green Desert (USA) 127) [2017 6m^2 6d* 7d^4 Sep 20] €48,000F, £28,000Y, 240,000 2-y-o: close-coupled gelding: third foal: dam 7f winner: fairly useful form: won maiden at Lingfield (by ½ length from City Gent) in September: should stay 7f: has joined Murty McGrath. *Richard Hughes* **80**

RAGSTONE SAND (IRE) 2 b.g. (Mar 31) Footstepsinthesand 120 – Speedy Storm (IRE) (Invincible Spirit (IRE) 121) [2017 p6g 7s p8g Dec 23] little impact in minor events: left Murty McGrath after second start. *Gary Moore* –

RAGSTONE VIEW (IRE) 2 b.g. (Apr 2) Requinto (IRE) 109 – Highland Miss (USA) 71 (Theatrical) [2017 6f^5 6d^4 6.1g^3 5s* p6d^5 7s^5 Sep 15] fair performer: won minor event at Lingfield in July: stays 6f: acts on soft going: front runner/races prominently, usually freely: has joined Rod Millman. *Richard Hughes* **77**

RAGTAG RASCAL (IRE) 3 b.g. Tagula (IRE) 116 – Trebles (IRE) (Kenmare (FR) 125) [2017 p10g^6 Apr 1] €19,000F, 16,000Y, 26,000 2-y-o: half-brother to 2 winners by Titus Livius, notably smart German winner up to 1m Sehrezad (2-y-o 5f winner): dam 1¼m winner: 40/1, sixth in maiden at Kempton (7½ lengths behind Wefait) in April. *Amanda Perrett* **68**

RAG TATTER 3 b.g. Kheleyf (USA) 116 – Golden Nun 108 (Bishop of Cashel 122) [2017 75: p5m^2 p6d^2 6m 7g^5 7g^5 p5g p7g p7g^6 p7g p6g p6g^4 Dec 1] lengthy gelding: fair maiden: left Kevin Ryan after fifth start: stays 7f: acts on polytrack, good to firm and heavy going: has worn cheekpieces: usually races prominently. *Anthony Mulholland, Ireland* **71**

RAHAABA (IRE) 2 b.f. (May 13) Dubawi (IRE) 129 – Muthabara (IRE) 111 (Red Ransom (USA)) [2017 p7g p8g Nov 8] fourth foal: half-sister to 7f winner Jadaayil (by Oasis Dream): dam, 7f winner (including at 2 yrs) who barely stayed 1¼m, half-sister to smart 2-y-o 7f winner (stays 1¼m) Mustadeem: little show in 2 minor events. *Owen Burrows* –

RAHEEN HOUSE (IRE) 3 b.c. Sea The Stars (IRE) 140 – Jumooh (Monsun (GER) 124) [2017 107: 10g^2 11.2m^3 12m^4 13g* 14.5g 14.2d* 12s^2 Oct 28] well-made colt: smart performer: won Bahrain Trophy at Newmarket (by length from Desert Skyline) in July and listed race at Ascot (awarded race) in October: fourth in King Edward VII Stakes at Royal Ascot (2¾ lengths behind Permian) in June and second in St Simon Stakes at Newbury (1¾ lengths behind Best Solution) in October: stays 1¾m: acts on soft and good to firm going. *Brian Meehan* **119**

Bahrain Trophy Stakes, Newmarket—the consistent Raheen House is driven out to register a deserved first win at pattern level, beating Desert Skyline (star on cap) and Sofia's Rock

RAHMAH (IRE) 5 b.g. Vale of York (IRE) 117 – Sweet Home Alabama (IRE) 56 (Desert 78
Prince (IRE) 130) [2017 79: p11g^{4} 12g^{5} 12s^{6} 12d^{2} 10m* 14.2v^{4} 12s^{3} Aug 17] sturdy gelding: fair handicapper: won at Chepstow (dead-heated) in July: stays 1½m: acts on polytrack, tapeta, firm and good to soft going: has worn cheekpieces: often starts slowly. *Geoffrey Deacon*

RAID (IRE) 2 b.c. (Mar 13) Havana Gold (IRE) 118 – Remarkable Story (Mark of Esteem 92 p
(IRE) 137) [2017 6d* Nov 11] 22,000Y, £135,000 2-y-o: half-brother to several winners, including smart 1¼m-1½m winner Grendisar (by Invincible Spirit) and 5f/6f winner Alnoomaas (by Oasis Dream): dam ran once: 9/2, won maiden at Doncaster (by 2¼ lengths from Lady Willpower) on debut: better to come. *David Simcock*

RAIL DANCER 5 b.g. Rail Link 132 – Mara Dancer (Shareef Dancer (USA) 135) [2017 81
57: p11d* p12g^{3} p12d p12g^{3} p12g* p12g* p11g* 12d^{6} Aug 3] sturdy gelding: fairly useful handicapper: won at Kempton in January, April (2) and May (apprentice): stays 1½m: acts on polytrack and good to firm going: wears headgear: often travels strongly. *Richard Rowe*

RAILPORT DOLLY 2 b.f. (Mar 29) Rail Link 132 – Polly Adler 56 (Fantastic Light 67
(USA) 134) [2017 8.3g 7d^{6} 7g^{6} Sep 27] first foal: dam, maiden (best effort at 11f), half-sister to smart 6f-1m winner Lucky Strike: fair form: best effort when sixth in minor event at Leicester (6¾ lengths behind Aim of Artemis) in September: left Steph Hollinshead after first start: bred to stay at least 1m: in hood last 2 starts. *Michael Appleby*

RAINBOW CHIMES (IRE) 3 b.f. Galileo (IRE) 134 – Chiming (IRE) 110 (Danehill –
(USA) 126) [2017 56: t10.2g 9.9m 5.9g Jul 13] little form: often races prominently. *Ann Duffield*

RAINBOW DREAMER 4 b.g. Aqlaam 125 – Zamhrear 73 (Singspiel (IRE) 133) [2017 100
94: 11.8g^{3} 18g* 20f^{4} Jun 20] lengthy gelding: useful handicapper: won at Newbury in April: stays 2¼m: acts on good to firm and soft going: wore visor in 2017. *Alan King*

RAINBOW JAZZ (IRE) 2 b.g. (Mar 7) Red Jazz (USA) 125 – Let's Pretend 69 (Rainbow 72
Quest (USA) 134) [2017 6g^{3} 6g^{4} 7d 7m^{4} 7g p8g 7s^{3} 7d^{2} p7g^{5} Nov 8] sturdy gelding: fair maiden: stays 7f: acts on soft and good to firm going: wears headgear. *Mark Usher*

RAINBOW LAD (IRE) 4 b.g. Lilbourne Lad (IRE) 111 – Carmona 65 (Rainbow Quest 78
(USA) 134) [2017 61: t12.2g^{3} f14g* 12f* 12g^{2} May 14] fair handicapper: won at Southwell (amateur) in March and Les Landes in April: stays 1¾m: acts on all-weather, firm and good to soft going. *Michael Appleby*

RAINBOW ORSE 5 b.g. Zebedee 113 – Khafayif (USA) 62 (Swain (IRE) 134) [2017 79: 86
5d* 5s* 5v Aug 3] good-topped gelding: fairly useful handicapper: won at Nottingham in May and June (by length from Flash City): best at 5f: acts on soft and good to firm going: wears cheekpieces: front runner/races prominently: sold £12,000 in August. *Robert Cowell*

RAINBOW REBEL (IRE) 4 b.g. Acclamation 118 – Imperial Quest 61 (Rainbow Quest 97
(USA) 134) [2017 96: 9.8m^{6} 9g^{4} 10g^{2} 11.2v^{2} 10.3m^{5} 10g^{5} 11.9d^{3} p10d^{4} t12.4g^{2} t9.5g t9.5d^{4} p12g^{3} Dec 31] small gelding: useful handicapper: second at Carlisle (head behind Swaheen) in June: stays 12.5f: acts on tapeta, good to firm and heavy going. *Mark Johnston*

RAINBOW RISING (FR) 3 b.f. Henrythenavigator (USA) 131 – Rainbow Goddess 80
(Rainbow Quest (USA) 134) [2017 10g 10.2g 10d^{2} p12g^{2} 11.6d^{3} p11g^{3} p13.9g^{4} Nov 8] €32,000Y: half-sister to 3 winners, including smart 1¼m-2m winner Mahler (by Galileo) and 7f/1m winner Compton Rainbow (by Exceed And Excel): dam 1¼m winner: fairly useful maiden: third in handicap at Lingfield in September: stays 1½m: acts on polytrack and good to soft going. *David Menuisier*

RAINFORD GLORY (IRE) 7 ch.g. Rock of Gibraltar (IRE) 133 – My Dolly Madison –
77 (In The Wings 128) [2017 62: t12.2g Feb 20] fair at best, little show sole start in 2017: stays 13f: acts on polytrack, tapeta, soft and good to firm going: often wears headgear. *Tim Fitzgerald*

RAIN GODDESS (IRE) 3 b.f. Galileo (IRE) 134 – Where (IRE) 75 (Danehill Dancer 112
(IRE) 117) [2017 87p: 7d 7m^{4} 8d^{5} 8m^{2} 10g^{2} 12f^{2} 9.5f 9d* 10s^{3} 10s Oct 15] small, good-bodied filly: smart performer: won Dance Design Stakes at the Curragh (by ½ length from Intimation) in August: runner-up 3 times earlier, in listed Sandringham Handicap at Royal Ascot (1¼ lengths behind Con Te Partiro), Pretty Polly Stakes at the Curragh (beaten 3¼ lengths by Nezwaah) and Irish Oaks at latter course (5½ lengths behind Enable): 3¼ lengths third to Shamreen in Blandford Stakes there on penultimate start: effective at 1m to 1½m: acted on firm and soft going: often wore tongue tie: usually raced prominently: visits Caravaggio. *Aidan O'Brien, Ireland*

Coventry Stakes, Royal Ascot—Rajasinghe prevails in a tight finish, giving trainer Richard Spencer and jockey Stevie Donohoe their first winner at Royal Ascot; Headway (armlets) and Murillo (striped sleeves) fill the places

RAINING STARS 3 b.g. Sea The Stars (IRE) 140 – Sayyedati Symphony (USA) 90 (Gone West (USA)) [2017 p12d 10g 10.2v² Aug 8] sturdy gelding: fourth foal: half-brother to UAE 6f winner Daar Rashid (by Exceed And Excel): dam, maiden (stayed 1¼m), out of 1000 Guineas winner Sayyedati: fair form: best effort when second in maiden at Nottingham in August: has joined Keith Dalgleish: open to further improvement. *James Fanshawe* **78 p**

RAIN IN THE FACE 4 b.g. Naaqoos 117 – Makaaseb (USA) 100 (Pulpit (USA) 117) [2017 75: f8g Jan 1] fair maiden at best for Ralph Beckett, has lost way: stays 1m: acts on polytrack and fibresand: tried in cheekpieces/tongue tie: sometimes slowly away, often races lazily: has joined Sam England. *Karen Tutty* **–**

RAIN WIND AND FIRE (USA) 5 ch.g. Eskendereya (USA) 126 – Call Mariah (USA) (Dixie Union (USA) 121) [2017 t7.1g p6s⁶ Jun 13] lengthy, angular gelding: fairly useful for Jeremy Noseda at 3 yrs, missed following season and last both starts in 2017: seems to stay 1m: acts on polytrack: tried in headgear. *Ronald Harris* **–**

RAISE A LITTLE JOY 2 b.f. (May 5) Pastoral Pursuits 127 – Ray of Joy 94 (Tobougg (IRE) 125) [2017 5.1m 6g 6m Aug 27] first foal: dam 5.7f/6f winner (including at 2 yrs): well held in minor events. *J. R. Jenkins* **–**

RAISE THE GAME (IRE) 4 b.g. Bushranger (IRE) 119 – Fancy Feathers (IRE) 79 (Redback 116) [2017 70: t7.1m t7.1g³ p7g t9.5m f7g 7mᵖᵘ Aug 10] modest maiden: stayed 7f: acted on tapeta: usually raced close up: dead. *Bill Turner* **64**

RAISING SAND 5 b.g. Oasis Dream 129 – Balalaika 108 (Sadler's Wells (USA) 132) [2017 105: 8gᵖᵘ 8s 8s⁶ 8d* 7s⁴ 7s³ Oct 7] big, strong gelding: useful handicapper: won at Ascot (by 2 lengths from Nicholas T) in August: third in Challenge Cup at same course (1¼ lengths behind Accidental Agent) in October: stays 8.5f: acts on soft and good to firm going: often starts slowly. *Jamie Osborne* **109**

RAJAAM (IRE) 2 b.c. (Mar 17) Invincible Spirit (IRE) 121 – Midnight Partner (IRE) (Marju (IRE) 127) [2017 p8g* Nov 21] 375,000Y: closely related to French winner up to 1½m Desert Nights (2-y-o 1m winner, by Desert Style) and half-brother to several winners, including 2-y-o 7f winner Lilbourne Eliza (later useful 8.5f minor stakes winner in USA, by Elusive City): dam unraced: 7/1, created good impression when winning minor event at Lingfield (by ¾ length from Key Player) on debut: sure to progress. *Richard Hannon* **81 p**

RAJAPUR 4 gr.g. Dalakhani (IRE) 133 – A Beautiful Mind (GER) (Winged Love (IRE) 121) [2017 55: t12.4d t13.9g 8m 16g 14v* f12.1g^{4} Dec 4] modest handicapper: won at Redcar in November: left Philip Kirby after fourth start: stays 1¾m: acts on tapeta, good to firm and heavy going: has worn headgear, including last 3 starts. *David Thompson* **58**

RAJAR 3 b.f. Archipenko (USA) 127 – Barnezet (GR) 73 (Invincible Spirit (IRE) 121) [2017 93: a7f^{3} a8f^{3} a9.4f^{6} 7.2m^{3} 7v^{6} 6g^{2} t7.2g^{4} p7s t6.1d^{2} Dec 16] angular filly: useful performer: placed 5 times in 2017, including in listed UAE 1000 Guineas at Meydan (1¼ lengths third to Nashmiah), and handicaps at Musselburgh and Wolverhampton (1½ lengths second to Tropics) on second/fourth/final starts: stays 1m: acts on polytrack, tapeta, dirt and good to firm going: wears hood: usually front runner/races prominently. *Richard Fahey* **96**

RAJASINGHE (IRE) 2 b.c. (Mar 31) Choisir (AUS) 126 – Bunditten (IRE) 92 (Soviet Star (USA) 128) [2017 t6g* 6f* 6g^{3} 6d 8f Nov 3] €65,000F, £85,000Y: strong, good-quartered colt: half-brother to several winners, including 5f/6f winner Star Fire (by Dark Angel) and 2-y-o 5f winner Kurland (by Kheleyf): dam ungenuine 2-y-o 5f winner: useful performer: won minor event at Newcastle in May and Coventry Stakes at Royal Ascot (by head from Headway) in June: third in July Stakes at Newmarket (2½ lengths behind Cardsharp) next time: blinkered, eleventh behind Mendelssohn in Breeders' Cup Juvenile Turf at Del Mar final outing: bred to prove best at 5f/6f: acts on tapeta, best turf form on firm going: sometimes slowly away. *Richard Spencer* **107**

RAJ BALARAAJ (GER) 3 b.g. Kyllachy 129 – Ragazza Mio (IRE) (Generous (IRE) 139) [2017 71: 8f^{2} 8.1d 8m 10g^{3} 10g* Aug 7] fair handicapper: won at Windsor (by short head from Funky Footsteps) in August: stayed 1¼m: acted on firm going: tried in cheekpieces: dead. *George Baker* **80**

RAKEMATIZ 3 ch.g. Pivotal 124 – Regal Velvet 81 (Halling (USA) 133) [2017 56p: 7g 9g* 9.9g^{6} p10g p10g^{5} p8g^{2} Dec 30] rangy gelding: fair handicapper: won at Lingfield in June: stays 1¼m: acts on polytrack: often races towards rear. *Brett Johnson* **72**

RAKE'S PROGRESS 3 b.g. Sir Percy 129 – Cartoon 81 (Danehill Dancer (IRE) 117) [2017 65: 8s* 10d^{3} p11d^{5} 10v* 12d^{4} 12s Sep 9] sturdy gelding: fairly useful handicapper: won at Newmarket in May and Newbury in July: stays 1½m: acts on polytrack and heavy going: front runner/races prominently. *Heather Main* **90**

RAKTIMAN (IRE) 10 ch.g. Rakti 130 – Wish List (IRE) 98 (Mujadil (USA) 119) [2017 18v^{4} Oct 9] fair handicapper: fourth at Pontefract on only start on Flat since 2012: probably stays 2¼m: acts on polytrack and any turf going: usually wears headgear: tried in tongue tie: fairly useful chaser. *Sam England* **65**

RALPHY BOY (IRE) 8 b.g. Acclamation 118 – Silcasue (Selkirk (USA) 129) [2017 84: t7.1s 8m^{4} 6.9g^{6} 7.2g^{6} 7.2m^{3} 7.8g 7d^{6} 7.2d^{6} 8m^{6} Aug 11] fair handicapper: stays 8.5f: acts on good to firm and good to soft going: has worn cheekpieces: usually races close up. *Alistair Whillans* **75**

RALPHY LAD (IRE) 6 b.g. Iffraaj 127 – Hawattef (IRE) (Mujtahid (USA) 118) [2017 82d: t12.4g f14g^{4} f12g^{2} f12m Feb 21] fair handicapper: second at Southwell (1¾ lengths behind Thou Swell) in February: probably stayed 1¾m: acted on fibresand, soft and good to firm going: tried in blinkers: dead. *Alan Swinbank* **66**

RAMBLING QUEEN (IRE) 4 gr.f. Mastercraftsman (IRE) 129 – Dos Lunas (IRE) (Galileo (IRE) 134) [2017 10g 7m Jul 7] £11,000Y: first foal: dam ran twice in France: no form in bumpers and Flat maidens: wears tongue tie. *Brian Rothwell* **–**

RAMBLOW 4 b.f. Notnowcato 128 – Nsx 74 (Roi Danzig (USA)) [2017 54, a68: f8g^{2} f8g f12m Mar 7] fair maiden: stays 1¼m: acts on polytrack and fibresand: often in cheekpieces: in tongue tie last 3 starts: usually leads. *Michael Appleby* **67**

RAMPANT LION (IRE) 2 ch.g. (Apr 7) Bahamian Bounty 116 – Mamma Morton (IRE) 79 (Elnadim (USA) 128) [2017 6.1d^{6} 5.5s^{5} Jun 6] 52,000F, 26,000Y: tall, unfurnished gelding: brother to useful 6f (including at 2 yrs) winner Muaamara and half-brother to several winners, including smart winner up to 1m Master of War (2-y-o 6f winner, by Compton Place) and 1m winner Subhaan (by Dutch Art): dam maiden (stayed 1¼m): modest form: better effort when fifth in minor event at Wetherby (3 lengths behind Jedi Master) in June: should be suited by 6f+: open to further improvement. *Mark Johnston* **63 p**

RANDALL'S ALANNAH (IRE) 7 b.m. High Chaparral (IRE) 132 – Randall's Diana (IRE) 63 (Monashee Mountain (USA) 115) [2017 54: p8d^{2} p8g^{6} 8s p8g Apr 21] modest handicapper: first past post at Chelmsford in February, but demoted after barging way through: stays 1m: acts on polytrack and heavy going: has worn headgear, including final start. *Seamus Fahey, Ireland* **59**

RANTAN (IRE) 4 b.g. Kodiac 112 – Peace Talks (Pivotal 124) [2017 89: 6m 6s^2 6.1m 6.1s^5 Jun 29] fairly useful handicapper: second at Haydock in June: stays 6f: acts on soft going: tried in tongue tie: sold £8,000 in September. *David Barron* **82**

RAPID RANGER 3 b.g. Kyllachy 129 – Director's Dream (IRE) 59 (Act One 124) [2017 76: 5m^3 6d^5 5d^4 t6.1g^4 5m^3 6d^2 6g^3 6s* t6.1m t6.1g* t6.1d* t7.2d Dec 26] close-coupled gelding: fairly useful handicapper: won at Leicester in October, and Wolverhampton in November and December: stays 6f: acts on polytrack, tapeta and soft going: wears hood: usually races in rear/travels strongly. *David O'Meara* **86**

RAPID RISE (IRE) 3 b.g. Fast Company (IRE) 126 – French Doll (IRE) 66 (Titus Livius (FR) 115) [2017 78: p7g^5 p7g^6 7g^6 8.3d t5.1g^5 p6g 5.7s p6g p7g t6.1g p6g^6 p7m t6.1d^4 p7g^6 Dec 30] leggy, lengthy gelding: fair maiden: left David Brown after fourth start: stays 7f: acts on polytrack, tapeta and good to firm going: often wears visor. *Milton Bradley* **72**

RAPIER (USA) 2 ch.g. (Apr 19) Animal Kingdom (USA) 129 – Shadow Cast (USA) 117 (Smart Strike (CAN) 121) [2017 p8g Oct 4] $50,000Y, 60,000 2-y-o: seventh foal: half-brother to 3 minor US winners by Bernardini, Storm Cat and A P Indy: dam US Grade 1 1¼m winner: 33/1, better than result when ninth in minor event at Kempton (6½ lengths behind Kassar) in October, meeting trouble and considerately handled: open to significant improvement. *Sir Michael Stoute* **68 P**

RARE GROOVE (IRE) 2 ch.c. (Apr 30) Lope de Vega (IRE) 125 – Ascot Lady (IRE) 85 (Spinning World (USA) 130) [2017 7g^4 7g^3 t8g^2 Nov 15] fair form: best effort when third in maiden at Leicester (1½ lengths behind Accessor) in October. *Jedd O'Keeffe* **79**

RARE RHYTHM 5 b.g. Dubawi (IRE) 129 – Demisemiquaver 82 (Singspiel (IRE) 133) [2017 90: 12m* 13.9m* Jul 15] robust gelding: smart performer: won Duke of Edinburgh Stakes (Handicap) at Royal Ascot (by 2¼ lengths from Appeared) in June and listed race at York (by 2¾ lengths from Barsanti) in July: stays 1¾m: acts on good to firm and good to soft going. *Charlie Appleby* **117**

RASASEE (IRE) 4 gr.g. Rip Van Winkle (IRE) 134 – Gleaming Silver (IRE) 86 (Dalakhani (IRE) 133) [2017 82: t12.4g^6 Feb 17] sturdy gelding: fairly useful maiden, too free sole Flat start in 2017: stays 1¾m: acts on polytrack, tapeta and firm going: won novice hurdle in June. *Tim Vaughan* **–**

RASELASAD (IRE) 3 b.g. Acclamation 118 – Wajaha (IRE) 94 (Haafhd 129) [2017 6.9g^3 7g* 6.9d^2 8g^5 7d^5 7.2m* 7.2s^2 Oct 1] £3,200 3-y-o: fourth foal: dam, 1m winner (including at 2 yrs), half-sister to 1000 Guineas winner Lahan: useful performer: won maiden at Thirsk in June and handicap at Musselburgh in August: stays 1m: acts on soft and good to firm going: front runner/races prominently: likely to progress still further. *Tracy Waggott* **98 p**

RASHDAN (FR) 2 b.c. (Feb 27) Big Bad Bob (IRE) 118 – On Fair Stage (IRE) 103 (Sadler's Wells (USA) 132) [2017 8s^4 Sep 15] €120,000Y: half-brother to several winners, including high-class 1¼m-1½m winner Reliable Man (by Dalakhani) and very smart winner up to 10.4f (2-y-o 1m winner) Imposing (by Danehill Dancer): dam 1m-1½m winner: 7/2, fourth in minor event at Salisbury (9 lengths behind Alternative Fact) in September: sure to improve. *Hugo Palmer* **69 p**

John Smith's Silver Cup Stakes, York—Rare Rhythm improves again to follow up his win at Royal Ascot, outstaying favourite Barsanti (spots on cap) with Clever Cookie (cheekpieces) back in third

RASHEEQ (IRE) 4 b.g. Vale of York (IRE) 117 – Limber Up (IRE) (Dansili 127) [2017 **99**
5m 6m 5s^2 5g^2 5m^5 t5g 5g 6g^3 6d 6g 5s^3 5v^2 5g 5d Oct 28] good-topped gelding: useful handicapper: second at York (twice) in May: stays 6f: acts on all-weather, good to firm and heavy going: often races prominently. *Tim Easterby*

RASHFORD'S DOUBLE (IRE) 3 b.g. Zoffany (IRE) 121 – Ardent Lady 79 (Alhaarth **90**
(IRE) 126) [2017 86p: 8g 8s^6 9.2g^3 8d 8d^2 8g^5 8g^4 t8d^2 8g t8g 10v^3 Oct 23] tall gelding: fairly useful handicapper: second at Redcar in August and Newcastle in September: stays 1¼m: acts on tapeta, good to firm and heavy going: usually wears cheekpieces: sold 50,000 gns, sent to USA. *Richard Fahey*

RASIMA 2 gr.f. (Feb 11) Iffraaj 127 – Raushan (IRE) 86 (Dalakhani (IRE) 133) [2017 p7d^5 **68**
7d^3 Sep 5] first foal: dam, 1¼m winner, sister to smart winner up to 1¼m Chinese White out of smart performer up to 15.5f Chiang Mai: fair form in 2 minor events. *Roger Varian*

RASMEE 4 b.g. Fastnet Rock (AUS) 127 – Reem (AUS) 105 (Galileo (IRE) 134) [2017 **92**
88: t12.4s^3 Sep 19] fairly useful handicapper: third at Newcastle only start in 2017: stays 12.5f: acts on polytrack and tapeta: tried in headgear: sold £4,000 in November. *Roger Charlton*

RASPBERRY PRINCESS 3 b.f. Royal Applause 124 – Eraadaat (IRE) 59 (Intikhab **–**
(USA) 135) [2017 –: t6m p6d^4 p6d p6g p7g Apr 24] compact filly: no form: left Stuart Williams after second start: tried in blinkers: sometimes in tongue tie: often starts slowly. *Phil McEntee*

RASTACAP 2 ch.f. (Feb 27) Helmet (AUS) 127 – Caribbean Dancer (USA) 76 (Theatrical) **75**
[2017 5g^4 t6s* 6v^2 6v^3 p6g^4 Nov 2] half-sister to several winners, including smart winner up to 2m Notarised (2-y-o 1¼m winner, by Authorized) and 7f/7.4f winner Dasheen (by Bahamian Bounty): dam 1¼m winner who stayed 1½m: fair performer: won minor event at Newcastle in September: bred to be suited by 7f+: acts on tapeta and heavy going: usually leads. *Mark Johnston*

RASTRELLI (FR) 2 b.c. (Feb 19) Siyouni (FR) 122 – Ponte di Legno (FR) (Sinndar **93**
(IRE) 134) [2017 7d^5 8g^4 7d* 8g* 10m^4 Oct 14] €125,000Y, €550,000 2-y-o: well-made colt: third foal: dam, 2-y-o 6f winner, half-sister to useful 2-y-o 6f winner Pontenuovo out of smart winner up to 6.5f Porlezza: fairly useful performer: won minor event at Brighton and nursery at Newmarket (by ¾ length from Global Conqueror) in September: best effort at 1m: acts on good to soft going. *Charlie Appleby*

RAT CATCHER (IRE) 7 b.g. One Cool Cat (USA) 123 – Molly Marie (IRE) 75 **44**
(Fasliyev (USA) 120) [2017 57: t5.1g t6f p5g t5.1g 5g 6m^5 t5.1g 5.3m^3 6g 5f 5g t6.1g 5.2m Aug 22] leggy gelding: poor handicapper: stays 6f: acts on tapeta and good to firm going: wears headgear: often races towards rear. *Lisa Williamson*

RATHEALY (IRE) 6 b.g. Baltic King 120 – Baltic Belle (IRE) 86 (Redback 116) [2017 **–**
f12g^4 11.5d Sep 19] angular gelding: fairly useful at best, lightly raced and no form on Flat since 2014: stays 1¼m: acts on polytrack and heavy going: sometimes in headgear: fair hurdler. *Christine Dunnett*

RATTLE ON 4 ch.g. Pivotal 124 – Sabreon 85 (Caerleon (USA) 132) [2017 71: p8g^3 p8f* **69**
10d^4 p8g^4 t8.6g 8m^4 8.5d^5 7.6s^2 8m^4 7.6s Sep 16] rangy gelding: fair handicapper: won at Lingfield in April: stays 1¼m: acts on polytrack and soft going: wears cheekpieces. *Jim Boyle*

RAUCOUS 4 b.g. Dream Ahead (USA) 133 – Shyrl 98 (Acclamation 118) [2017 112: p6g* **108**
6.1m^4 6m 6s^4 6d 7g 6s 6g Oct 14] well-made gelding: useful performer: won minor event at Chelmsford (by 1¾ lengths from Kadrizzi) in April: fourth in listed race at Windsor (2 lengths behind Perfect Pasture) in May: stays 6f: acts on polytrack, good to firm and good to soft going: usually wears headgear: has worn tongue tie: sold to join Robert Cowell 110,000 gns in October. *William Haggas*

RAVENHOE (IRE) 4 ch.g. Bahamian Bounty 116 – Breathless Kiss (USA) 101 (Roman **80**
Ruler (USA) 122) [2017 81: t9.5m^2 p10g t8d p8d^4 p8g^5 p10g^3 10g t9.5g^3 9.9m^6 10g^2 8m* 8.1d 7.8g p10g^6 7.8g^6 7.8m^3 8.5d^4 8v 7.6d^4 t8.6g 8.5v 8v p8g f8.1g^5 p8g^6 Dec 13] angular gelding: fairly useful handicapper: won at Pontefract in May: stays 1¼m: acts on all-weather, good to firm and good to soft going: tried in blinkers: often races towards rear. *Mark Johnston*

RAVENOUS 6 b.g. Raven's Pass (USA) 133 – Supereva (IRE) (Sadler's Wells (USA) 132) **88**
[2017 85: 7.6d^4 11.4d 11.4g^3 12v^4 14g^3 14s p11g p16g Nov 1] compact, attractive gelding: fairly useful handicapper: third at Nottingham in August: stays 1¾m: acts on polytrack, good to firm and heavy going: tried in headgear: usually leads/travels strongly. *Luke Dace*

RAVEN'S GIRL 2 b.f. (Apr 8) Raven's Pass (USA) 133 – Ravenel (GER) 109 (Touch Down (GER) 116) [2017 6g 5.1s⁵ 7d 6.1g p7g Dec 6] €26,000Y, £10,000 2-y-o: neat filly: second foal: dam 7.5f/1m winner out of half-sister to high-class French 1½m performer Califet: no form in varied events. *Michael Madgwick* –

RAVEN'S LADY 3 ch.f. Raven's Pass (USA) 133 – Pivotal Lady (Pivotal 124) [2017 84: p8g² 8m⁵ p7s³ 6d* 6d* 6g³ p7g⁴ Aug 31] useful-looking filly: useful performer: won minor event in June and handicap in July (by neck from Clon Coulis), both at Newmarket: third in listed race at Pontefract (½ length behind Queen Kindly) in August: stays 7f: acts on polytrack and good to soft going. *Marco Botti* **104**

RAVENS QUEST 4 ch.g. Raven's Pass (USA) 133 – Seradim 95 (Elnadim (USA) 128) [2017 83: t12.2m³ p12d p10d t12.2g* t13.9g⁴ t12.2g³ p11g t12.2g⁵ Apr 29] fairly useful handicapper: won at Wolverhampton (by 2½ lengths from Heart Locket) in February: stays 1½m: acts on polytrack, tapeta and heavy going: usually races prominently: sold only 800 gns in October. *John Ryan* **83**

RAVEN'S RAFT (IRE) 2 gr.f. (Feb 18) Raven's Pass (USA) 133 – Sea Drift (FR) 72 (Warning 136) [2017 6.1f³ 6d³ 6.1v⁶ p6g⁶ f7.1g f8.1g Dec 29] €13,000F, €6,000Y, 22,000 2-y-o: half-sister to several winners, including useful 2-y-o 7f/1m winner (stays 1½m) Monsea (by Manduro) and winner up to 6f Drift And Dream (2-y-o 5f winner, by Exceed And Excel): dam 7f winner: modest maiden: best efforts at 6f: acts on firm and good to soft going: in headgear last 2 starts: usually leads. *Michael Appleby* **62**

RAVEN'S SONG (IRE) 2 b.f. (Mar 3) Raven's Pass (USA) 133 – Lyric of Fife (IRE) (Strategic Prince 114) [2017 7m 7.6d⁴ 8.5m Aug 29] €20,000F, €30,000Y: first foal: dam unraced: modest form: best effort when fourth in minor event at Lingfield (8½ lengths behind Yaafour) in August. *Harry Dunlop* **53**

RAVENSWOOD 4 b.g. Lawman (FR) 121 – Whatami 69 (Daylami (IRE) 138) [2017 –: 11.6m 11.6s³ 11.6d² 14d³ 11.9s p12g Nov 1] modest maiden: left Jonathan Portman after first start: stays 11.5f: acts on soft going: tried in cheekpieces. *Patrick Chamings* **62**

RAWEEYA 3 b.f. Oasis Dream 129 – Raihana (AUS) 117 (Elusive Quality (USA)) [2017 p8d Jan 18] second foal: closely related to 1¼m winner (stays 11.5f) Princess Raihana (by Cape Cross): dam 7f-9.5f winner, including UAE Oaks: 16/1, seventh in maiden at Kempton (7¼ lengths behind Dreaming of Paris). *Marco Botti* **57**

RAYAA 4 b.f. Virtual 122 – Winsa (USA) 80 (Riverman (USA) 131) [2017 77: p8g³ 8g p7g⁶ p8g⁶ 10g 10d² 10g⁴ p10g² 10g⁴ p10s* Nov 17] well-made filly: fairly useful handicapper: won at Chelmsford in November: left John Butler after seventh start: stays 1¼m: acts on polytrack, good to firm and good to soft going: wears tongue tie: often races prominently/travels strongly. *Michael Appleby* **80**

RAYDIANCE 2 b.c. (Feb 2) Mayson 124 – Iridescence 83 (Dutch Art 126) [2017 6.1d² 6d* 7d* Jul 29] £7,500Y: compact, good-quartered colt: first foal: dam, 8.6f-1¼m winner, sister to useful winner up to 1m (2-y-o 6f winner) Princess of Orange: useful form: won minor event at Haydock (by 2½ lengths from Poet's Prince) in June and listed race at Ascot (by neck from Another Batt) in July: stays 7f: remains with potential. *K. R. Burke* **101 p**

RAY DONOVAN (IRE) 3 b.g. Acclamation 118 – Always The Lady 89 (Halling (USA) 133) [2017 63: 8m 9g 9.8m 7g⁵ May 29] modest form when winning nursery at 2 yrs, standout effort: in visor last 2 starts. *David O'Meara* –

RAYNA'S WORLD (IRE) 2 b.f. (Apr 1) Poet's Voice 126 – Salmon Rose (IRE) (Iffraaj 127) [2017 7d⁶ 8g³ 8s⁵ 8d* Sep 19] 22,000Y: second foal: half-sister to useful winner up to 1m Ventura Blues (2-y-o 6f winner, by Bated Breath): dam unraced half-sister to Dubai World Cup winner Prince Bishop: fairly useful form: won nursery at Yarmouth (by 4½ lengths from Midnight Wilde) in September: will stay beyond 1m. *Philip Kirby* **83**

RAY PURCHASE 2 b.g. (May 2) Lethal Force (IRE) 128 – Raggle Taggle (IRE) 95 (Tagula (IRE) 116) [2017 5.9g 6s 5d 7.2m⁴ 7.2m² p7g³ 6g t6g Oct 19] modest maiden: stays 7f: acts on polytrack and good to firm going: tried in cheekpieces: front runner/races prominently. *Keith Dalgleish* **54**

RAY'S THE MONEY (IRE) 3 b.g. Dragon Pulse (IRE) 114 – Riymaisa (IRE) (Traditionally (USA) 117) [2017 81: t7.1g* p8g⁴ 8m⁵ 8f⁴ 8m* 10s² 9.9v⁶ 10d 9.8g⁵ p11g⁵ 12.1v Oct 21] fairly useful performer: won maiden at Newcastle in March and handicap at Haydock (by ¾ length from Mutawakked) in June: stays 11f: acts on polytrack, tapeta and firm going: wears headgear: sometimes slowly away, usually races nearer last than first: sold to join Charlie Mann 13,000 gns in October: one to treat with caution. *Michael Bell* **87 §**

RAZIN' HELL 6 b.g. Byron 117 – Loose Caboose (IRE) 82 (Tagula (IRE) 116) [2017 75, a91: f5g* f5g^{2} f5g 5f^{2} 5f p6g f5g^{4} f6.1g f5g^{2} Dec 22] fairly useful handicapper: won at Southwell (by ½ length from Meadway) in January: stays 6f: acts on fibresand, tapeta and firm going: wears headgear: usually leads. *John Balding* **92**

RAZZMATAZZ 3 b.f. Monsieur Bond (IRE) 120 – Tibesti (Machiavellian (USA) 123) [2017 6.1g^{3} 6.1m^{5} p6g* 5d^{2} 5s Oct 7] £21,000Y, resold 30,000Y: lengthy filly: sister to several winners, including smart winner up to 6f Move In Time and 7f winner Sciarra, and half-sister to winner abroad by Rock of Gibraltar: dam unraced: fairly useful performer: won maiden at Kempton in September: best effort when second in listed race at Doncaster (length behind Encore d'Or) later in month: stays 6f: acts on polytrack and good to soft going: sometimes slowly away: has joined Martyn Meade. *Clive Cox* **86**

REACHFORTHESTARS (IRE) 3 b.f. Sea The Stars (IRE) 140 – Behkiyra (IRE) 104 (Entrepreneur 123) [2017 89: 8f^{6} 8m^{4} 10.5d* 12m 10.3d 12d Aug 12] lengthy filly: useful handicapper: won at Haydock (by length from Pirate Look) in June: stays 10.5f: acts on heavy going: usually races close up. *David O'Meara* **96**

REACH HIGH 3 ch.c. Distorted Humor (USA) 117 – Silent Moment (USA) 94 (Giant's Causeway (USA) 132) [2017 92p: p8g* Oct 14] well-made colt: useful form: won handicap at Kempton (by head from The Warrior) on sole start in 2017: stays 1m: will go on improving. *Saeed bin Suroor* **103 p**

READY (IRE) 7 ch.g. Elnadim (USA) 128 – Fusili (IRE) 100 (Silvano (GER) 126) [2017 99: p10g^{6} t8.6m t9.5g^{6} 8.1m 8g t9.5m p8s Dec 7] lengthy gelding: useful handicapper at best, regressive during 2017: left Clare Ellam after fourth start: stays 1¼m: acts on polytrack, tapeta, good to firm and heavy going: usually wears headgear. *Mark Pattinson* **89**

READY TO IMPRESS (USA) 2 b.g. (Mar 21) More Than Ready (USA) 120 – Menekineko (USA) (Kingmambo (USA) 125) [2017 p8g t8.6g^{3} Oct 21] £38,000 2-y-o: brother to 2 winners, including smart US 7f winner Ready's Echo, runner-up in Breeders' Cup Dirt Mile/third in Belmont Stakes, and half-brother to several winners, including smart US Grade 3 1m/8.5f winner General Election (by Harlan's Holiday): dam lightly raced: fair form: better effort when third in minor event at Wolverhampton (length behind Wissahickon) in October: will stay 1¼m: open to further improvement. *Mark Johnston* **76 p**

REAL ESTATE (IRE) 2 b.c. (Apr 1) Dansili 127 – Maskunah (IRE) (Sadler's Wells (USA) 132) [2017 7m p8s^{5} t8.6g Nov 25] little impact in minor events. *James Tate* **–**

REAL GENT 2 gr.c. (Mar 9) Kendargent (FR) 112 – Ebatana (IRE) 88 (Rainbow Quest (USA) 134) [2017 7.4g^{5} 8.2v* Sep 30] 50,000F, 90,000 2-y-o: half-brother to several winners, including winner up to 1½m Ebasani (2-y-o 1m winner, by Manduro) and 1½m winner Ebadiyan (by Daylami), both useful: dam lightly-raced daughter of Irish Oaks winner Ebadiyla: fairly useful form: won minor event at Haydock (by ½ length from Bold Reason) in September, battling well: sold 130,000 gns in October: likely to progress further. *Kevin Ryan* **90 p**

REALITY SHOW (IRE) 10 b.g. Cape Cross (IRE) 129 – Really (IRE) 97 (Entrepreneur 123) [2017 p11g p12g p11g Oct 25] fairly useful at best, little show in 2017 after long absence: stays 1¾m: acts on polytrack and good to firm going. *Shaun Harris* **52**

REALIZE 7 b.g. Zafeen (FR) 123 – Relkida 76 (Bertolini (USA) 125) [2017 95, a109: p8g^{2} t7.1g t7.1g p6g^{6} 7m^{4} 7m* 8f* 7s Jul 22] lengthy gelding: useful handicapper: won at Yarmouth in May and Bath in June: left Stuart Williams after fifth start: stays 1m: acts on all-weather, firm and good to soft going: has worn cheekpieces: wears tongue tie. *David Simcock* **104**

REALLY SPECIAL 3 b.f. Shamardal (USA) 129 – Rumh (GER) 104 (Monsun (GER) 124) [2017 101p: a7f* a8f^{5} 7g^{3} 8m Jun 21] useful-looking filly: useful performer: won minor event at Meydan (by 3¼ lengths from Complimenti) in January: third in listed race at same course (½ length behind Top Score) in February: stays 1m: acts on polytrack, dirt and good to firm going: front runner/races prominently, usually freely. *Saeed bin Suroor* **100**

REALLY SUPER 3 b.f. Cacique (IRE) 124 – Sensationally 77 (Montjeu (IRE) 137) [2017 71p: 11m^{4} 12s^{3} 12g^{4} 14f^{4} 12d^{2} 11.6g^{3} 14.2g^{2} Aug 25] strong filly: fairly useful maiden: third in maiden at Newmarket in May and second in handicap at Salisbury in August: stays 1¾m: acts on firm and soft going: often wears headgear: often travels strongly: sold to join Amy Murphy £21,000 in September. *Ralph Beckett* **86**

REALPOLITIK (IRE) 2 b.f. (Jan 21) So You Think (NZ) 133 – Mare Imbrium (USA) (Mr Greeley (USA) 122) [2017 t8.6g t9.5g^4 Dec 18] 22,000Y: first foal: dam once-raced daughter of US Grade 3 8.5f winner Sea of Showers: fair form: better effort when fourth in minor event at Wolverhampton (½ length behind Jackfinbar) in December: will go on improving. *Roger Varian* **76 p**

REALTRA (IRE) 5 gr.m. Dark Angel (IRE) 113 – Devious Diva (IRE) 94 (Dr Devious (IRE) 127) [2017 110: 8g 8.9g^6 p7g* 7d^4 7.2m^5 7g* 8g 7.5s* 7d Oct 1] lengthy mare: smart performer: won valuable event at Lingfield (by neck from Muffri'ha) in April, Brownstown Stakes at Fairyhouse (by 1¼ lengths from Golden Stunner) in July and Fairy Bridge Stakes at Tipperary (by 1¾ lengths from Drumfad Bay) in August: stays 1m: acts on polytrack, soft and good to firm going: has worn blinkers: often races prominently. *Roger Varian* **110**

REASON TO BELIEVE (FR) 3 b.f. Rip Van Winkle (IRE) 134 – Showcall (USA) 70 (Kingmambo (USA) 125) [2017 a8.9g 6.5g 8g^3 p7.5g 8s 8.9s^4 7d p8g t7.1g p10s^4 Dec 17] modest maiden: left E. J. O'Neill after seventh start: stays 1¼m: acts on polytrack and heavy going: often in headgear. *David Bridgwater* **59**

REAVER (IRE) 4 b.g. Sabiango (GER) 120 – Mattinata (Tiger Hill (IRE) 127) [2017 84, a93: 8.3m* 8m p8d^4 8f^5 10g^3 10d^4 9.1g p8g^5 10m 8.1g^3 Oct 9] rangy gelding: fairly useful handicapper: won at Nottingham (by ½ length from Wannabe Friends) in April: stays 1¼m: acts on polytrack and good to firm going: in headgear last 3 starts: sold 20,000 gns in November. *Eve Johnson Houghton* **90**

REBECCA ROCKS 3 b.f. Exceed And Excel (AUS) 126 – Rebecca Rolfe 109 (Pivotal 124) [2017 73: 5m^3 5m* May 26] fairly useful form: won handicap at Goodwood (by length from Lightoller) in May: best form at 5f: should go on improving. *Henry Candy* **82 p**

REBEL ASSAULT (IRE) 2 b.f. (Apr 13) Excelebration (IRE) 133 – Naomh Geileis (USA) 95 (Grand Slam (USA) 120) [2017 5m* 5m^2 5d^4 5.1g* 5m 6d^5 5s^6 6g* 6d^4 Oct 28] well-grown filly: fifth foal: half-sister to 3 winners, including useful winner around 1¼m Alexander M (by Mastercraftsman) and winner up to 1m Assault On Rome (2-y-o 6.5f winner, by Holy Roman Emperor): dam winner up to 7f (2-y-o 6f winner): useful performer: won minor events at Catterick in May and Windsor in July, and listed race at York (by 1¼ lengths from It Dont Come Easy) in October: stays 6f: acts on good to firm going: often leads. *Mark Johnston* **101**

REBEL CAUSE (IRE) 4 b.g. Cockney Rebel (IRE) 127 – Happy Go Lily 89 (In The Wings 128) [2017 91p: t8.6g 10.2g^5 p8g 10.2d Oct 27] workmanlike gelding: fairly useful handicapper: stays 8.5f: acts on tapeta and soft going: in cheekpieces last 2 starts: often races prominently. *Richard Spencer* **83**

REBEL DE LOPE 3 b.g. Lope de Vega (IRE) 125 – Rivabella (FR) (Iron Mask (USA) 117) [2017 93: 8.1d 7.6m 7g^5 8d^5 8f^3 7g^2 p7g Oct 25] rather leggy gelding: fairly useful handicapper: third at Bath in July: stays 1m: acts on firm going: often races freely: sold to join Luke McJannet 43,000 gns in October. *Charles Hills* **89**

REBEL FLAME 3 b.c. Firebreak 125 – Spirit of Dixie 59 (Kheleyf (USA) 116) [2017 –: t7.1g^5 8.5s 7s Sep 23] no form: left Garry Moss after first start: often races prominently. *John Weymes* **–**

REBEL HEART 3 b.f. Kyllachy 129 – Just Like A Woman 96 (Observatory (USA) 131) [2017 60: t5.1g^6 6d^6 7.1d 5m^6 5.1g^4 t6.1g 6s^4 6s 6v* Oct 19] fair handicapper: won at Brighton in October: stays 6f: acts on tapeta and heavy going: usually wears visor. *Bill Turner* **66**

REBEL LIGHTNING (IRE) 4 gr.g. Zebedee 113 – Bellechance 56 (Acclamation 118) [2017 82: t7.1m^3 t7.1m t7.1g^2 t7.1m^2 a8.4g^6 p7.5f 6.7s^2 8d p6.5g^6 p8g^2 Nov 9] short-coupled gelding: fairly useful performer: placed in 3 handicaps at Wolverhampton, then left Richard Spencer: stays 1¼m: acts on polytrack, tapeta and heavy going: wears headgear. *P. & F. Monfort, France* **82**

REBEL STATE (IRE) 4 b.g. Zoffany (IRE) 121 – Stately Princess 70 (Robellino (USA) 127) [2017 73: p8g* t8.6m^4 p8d 8m^3 8g 10g 8g^2 8g^6 8.5d^4 8.5s^4 t8d^2 f8.1g Nov 13] lengthy gelding: modest on turf, fair on all-weather: won maiden at Lingfield in January: left Richard Spencer after third start: stays 1m: acts on polytrack, tapeta and good to soft going: wears headgear: tried in tongue tie: often races towards rear. *Jedd O'Keeffe* **60** **a72**

REBEL STREAK 2 b.g. (Feb 21) Dark Angel (IRE) 113 – Siren's Gift 104 (Cadeaux Genereux 131) [2017 p6g^4 6m^2 6g^2 6d^3 6m Sep 23] lengthy gelding: third foal: closely related to useful winner up to 6f Merdon Castle (2-y-o 5f winner, by Acclamation): dam, 5f winner (including at 2 yrs), sister to useful 5f winner Speed Cop: fairly useful maiden: second at Goodwood in August: raced only at 6f: acts on good to firm going. *Andrew Balding* **84**

REBEL SURGE (IRE) 4 b.f. Kodiac 112 – Face The Storm (IRE) 72 (Barathea (IRE) **94**
127) [2017 92: p7m^4 p8d^3 p7g^4 t7.1g^5 p7g 8m^2 7d* 7d^2 7m^4 8d 7.6d^4 6g^6 7g^4 p7g Oct 18] angular filly: fairly useful handicapper: won at Leicester in May: stays 1m: acts on polytrack, tapeta, firm and soft going: wears cheekpieces: usually races nearer last than first. *Richard Spencer*

REBEL WOODS (FR) 4 br.g. Cockney Rebel (IRE) 127 – In The Woods 101 (You And **–**
I (USA) 118) [2017 –: p12g 8m^4 Apr 25] little form. *Geoffrey Deacon*

REBOUNDED 3 ch.g. Mayson 124 – Winter Dress 67 (Haafhd 129) [2017 56: 8m Apr 10] **–**
maiden, well held sole start in 2017: best effort at 5f: dead. *Mark Walford*

RECKLESS ENDEAVOUR (IRE) 4 b.g. Kodiac 112 – Red Fanfare 62 (First Trump **107**
118) [2017 104: 8g^3 7s 8d 7s p6g* 6s p6g* p6g^3 t7.1d^5 p6g^3 Dec 30] useful performer: won handicap in August (by ½ length from Sharp Defence) and minor event in September (by 1¾ lengths from Geological), both at Dundalk: left G. M. Lyons after seventh start: stays 1m: acts on polytrack, tapeta, good to firm and good to soft going. *Jamie Osborne*

RECKLESS SERENADE (IRE) 3 b.f. Bushranger (IRE) 119 – Tomintoul Singer **64**
(IRE) 98 (Johannesburg (USA) 127) [2017 75: f5d^4 5g^6 6g^6 6d^6 6v^6 5s 5s Oct 31] fair handicapper: best form at 5f: acts on soft going: tried in visor: front runner/races prominently. *Keith Dalgleish*

RECKLESS WAVE (IRE) 4 b.f. Cape Cross (IRE) 129 – Fairybook (USA) (El Prado **76**
(IRE) 119) [2017 73p: t12.2g* 12s 10.2d^4 11m* Jun 29] good-topped filly: fair handicapper: won at Wolverhampton (dead-heated) in May and Newbury (apprentice) in June: stays 1½m: acts on polytrack, tapeta and good to firm going. *Ed Walker*

RECKLESS WOMAN (IRE) 3 b.f. Helmet (AUS) 127 – Paint The Town (IRE) 74 **–**
(Sadler's Wells (USA) 132) [2017 p7g 8s Jun 6] €13,000F, 50,000Y: fourth foal: half-sister to 1½m winner Great Ormond (by Zamindar) and 2-y-o 7f/1m winner Olympian Gold (by Holy Roman Emperor): dam, maiden, closely related to very smart winner up to 1½m Kutub: no form in maidens: tried in hood. *Jeremy Noseda*

RECKS (IRE) 2 ch.c. (Jan 28) Reckless Abandon 119 – Welsh Diva 112 (Selkirk (USA) **–**
129) [2017 7g Sep 27] 16/1, well held in maiden at Redcar. *K. R. Burke*

RECOGNITION (IRE) 4 gr.g. Rip Van Winkle (IRE) 134 – Bali Breeze (IRE) 85 **–**
(Common Grounds 118) [2017 76: 11.1m t12.4d Aug 10] good-bodied gelding: fair handicapper for Roger Varian at 3 yrs, no form in 2017: stays 1½m: acts on polytrack, tapeta, good to firm and heavy going: has worn headgear, including last 2 starts: tried in tongue tie. *Barry Murtagh*

RECOLETOS (FR) 3 b.c. Whipper (USA) 126 – Highphar (FR) (Highest Honor (FR) **118**
124) [2017 10.9s* 10.4g* 9.9s* 10.4g^3 9.9g 9.9s* 10s^4 Oct 21] good-bodied colt: half-brother to 3 winners in France, including 2-y-o 7.5f winner Tharsis (by Gold Away) and 1½m winner Maracena (by Marju): dam unraced: smart performer: won maiden at Fontainebleau in March, minor event at Saint-Cloud in April, Prix Greffulhe at Saint-Cloud (by 2½ lengths from Waldgeist) in May and Prix du Prince d'Orange at Maisons-Laffitte (by nose from Plumatic) in September: third in Prix du Jockey Club at Chantilly (length behind Brametot) in June and fourth in Champion Stakes at Ascot (8¼ lengths behind Cracksman) in October: stays 11f: acts on soft going. *C. Laffon-Parias, France*

RECOLLECT 2 b.c. (Apr 15) Invincible Spirit (IRE) 121 – Forgotten Dreams (IRE) 44 **82 p**
(Olden Times 121) [2017 7d^5 p7g^2 Oct 18] fifth foal: half-brother to 3 winners, including useful winner up to 7f Remember (by Selkirk) and useful 1¼m-1½m winner Fiesole (by Montjeu): dam twice-raced half-sister to Oaks d'Italia winner Zomaradah, herself dam of high-class miler Dubawi: fairly useful form: better effort when second in minor event at Kempton (1¼ lengths behind Archie McKellar) in October: will go on improving. *Luca Cumani*

RED ALERT 3 b.g. Sleeping Indian 122 – Red Sovereign 81 (Danzig Connection (USA)) **84**
[2017 73: p5g^2 p6d* 6d^5 5m^2 t5.1g^6 5g^3 5s^3 p6g p6g* Oct 18] lengthy gelding: fairly useful performer: first past post in maiden at Chelmsford in February, and handicaps at Salisbury (demoted for causing interference) in June and Lingfield (head in front of Desert Grey) in October: left Joseph Tuite after fifth start: stays 6f: acts on polytrack, soft and good to firm going: tried in cheekpieces: usually races close up. *William Muir*

REDARNA 3 ch.g. Aqlaam 125 – Curtains 96 (Dubawi (IRE) 129) [2017 –: t8g^4 t10.2g 5d^5 **69**
7.2d* 5.9s^3 7.8s^3 6.9v^3 6.9v^3 Sep 18] fair handicapper: won at Ayr in July: stays 1m: acts on heavy going: often starts slowly. *Dianne Sayer*

RED BARON (IRE) 8 b.g. Moss Vale (IRE) 126 – Twinberry (IRE) (Tagula (IRE) 116) [2017 105: t5.1g f5g 5g^{6} Apr 15] useful handicapper: no form in 2017: best at 5f: acted on polytrack, tapeta, soft and good to firm going: tried in headgear: front runner/raced prominently: dead. *Eric Alston* –

RED BORDEAUX (FR) 3 b.g. Myboycharlie (IRE) 118 – Blue Sail (USA) (Kingmambo (USA) 125) [2017 –: 8.3m 8.3s 7g Jul 20] failed to beat a rival in 4 starts: sent to France. *Tony Carroll* –

RED CARAVEL (IRE) 3 b.g. Henrythenavigator (USA) 131 – Red Fantasy (IRE) 98 (High Chaparral (IRE) 132) [2017 64p: p12g^{2} t12.2g^{5} 14g^{5} 11.6d Jul 1] fair maiden: stays 1½m: acts on polytrack: in headgear last 3 starts: has joined David Thompson: temperament under suspicion. *Richard Hughes* **73**

RED CARDINAL (IRE) 5 b.g. Montjeu (IRE) 137 – Notable (Zafonic (USA) 130) [2017 116: 16.4g* 16f* 14.9g^{5} 15.9g Nov 7] good-topped gelding: smart performer: won Oleander-Rennen at Hoppegarten (beat Nearly Caught by 1¼ lengths) in May and Grade 3 Belmont Gold Cup (by neck from St Michel) in June: bit below best after, in Prix Kergorlay at Deauville (fifth to Marmelo) and Melbourne Cup (Handicap) at Flemington (eleventh to Rekindling): stays 2m: acts on tapeta, firm and good to soft going. *Andreas Wohler, Germany* **117**

RED CHARMER (IRE) 7 b.g. Red Clubs (IRE) 125 – Golden Charm (IRE) 63 (Common Grounds 118) [2017 76: 8g 7.5f May 1] strong, close-coupled gelding: fair handicapper, below best both starts in 2017: best around 1m: acts on firm and good to soft going: tried in cheekpieces. *Ann Duffield* **59**

RED COSSACK (CAN) 6 ch.g. Rebellion 117 – Locata (USA) (Stravinsky (USA) 133) [2017 78: p10m p8g 10m 8m p8g Nov 1] lengthy, rather sparely-made gelding: fair handicapper, below best in 2017: stays 1¼m: acts on polytrack and soft going: wears headgear/tongue tie. *Paul Webber* **61**

RED CYMBAL 2 b.c. (Apr 24) Pivotal 124 – Red Baton (Exceed And Excel (AUS) 126) [2017 6d^{3} p6s* p6s^{4} Dec 7] lengthy colt: first foal: dam unraced half-sister to very smart sprinter Maarek (by Pivotal): fairly useful form: won minor event at Chelmsford (by ¾ length from Fakhoor) in November: raced only at 6f. *William Haggas* **88**

RED DOUGLAS 3 ch.c. Sakhee (USA) 136 – Chrystal Venture (IRE) 71 (Barathea (IRE) 127) [2017 –: 8g f8.1g f8.1g^{6} f7.1g^{6} Dec 22] no form: in cheekpieces last 2 starts. *Scott Dixon* –

RED DRAGON (IRE) 7 b.g. Acclamation 118 – Delphie Queen (IRE) 104 (Desert Sun 120) [2017 65: 10g 12v 8g* 8g p8g Sep 13] smallish gelding: modest handicapper nowadays: won at Salisbury in August: has form at 2m, usually races over much shorter: acts on polytrack, soft and good to firm going. *Michael Blanshard* **60**

REDEEMING 3 b.g. Exceed And Excel (AUS) 126 – Quiet Elegance 96 (Fantastic Light (USA) 134) [2017 5d 6g Aug 19] well held in 2 maidens. *Eric Alston* –

RED EMPEROR (IRE) 3 b.g. Holy Roman Emperor (IRE) 125 – Rougette 86 (Red Ransom (USA)) [2017 –p: 8.1m^{5} 7s^{6} 10m 8m Jul 6] good-topped gelding: fair maiden: best effort at 1m: acts on good to firm going: tried in cheekpieces. *Amanda Perrett* **66**

RED ENSIGN (IRE) 3 b.g. Dark Angel (IRE) 113 – Rayon Rouge (IRE) 72 (Manduro (GER) 135) [2017 94: p8g^{4} p10g^{6} May 10] useful-looking gelding: fairly useful performer: stays 1m: acts on polytrack: often races prominently. *Simon Crisford* **88**

RED FLUTE 5 ch.g. Piccolo 121 – Fee Faw Fum (IRE) (Great Commotion (USA) 123) [2017 59: p5g p5g^{6} p5g^{6} p5f^{3} f5g^{3} f5g^{2} f5g^{6} t5.1g^{6} f5g f5g Dec 11] well-made gelding: modest handicapper: left Denis Quinn after ninth start: best form at 5f: acts on polytrack and fibresand: wore headgear for previous yard: has worn tongue tie: usually races close up. *Michael Appleby* **53**

RED FORCE ONE 2 ro.g. (Apr 25) Lethal Force (IRE) 128 – Dusty Red 72 (Teofilo (IRE) 126) [2017 6s^{2} 6d^{4} 6f^{4} 7d^{4} 8g^{5} Aug 25] workmanlike gelding: fair maiden: stays 6f: acts on firm and soft going: tried in tongue tie: front runner/races prominently. *Tom Dascombe* **77**

RED FOR DANGER 2 b.f. (Apr 18) Equiano (FR) 127 – Red Shareef (Marju (IRE) 127) [2017 5g 5f 6m^{4} p6g 5m^{5} 5.1s^{6} 5s^{4} t6.1g^{4} p8g Nov 7] £11,000Y: closely related to 6f-9f winner Red Majesty (by Acclamation) and half-sister to numerous winners, including smart winner up to 7f Caesar Beware (2-y-o 6f winner, by Daggers Drawn) and useful winner up to 10.3f Collaboration (2-y-o 1m winner, by Halling): dam winner up to 11f (2-y-o 9f winner): poor maiden: stays 6f: acts on tapeta, soft and good to firm going: usually wears hood: front runner/races prominently. *Eve Johnson Houghton* **49**

RED FOREVER 6 ch.g. Major Cadeaux 121 – Spindara (IRE) 64 (Spinning World (USA) 130) [2017 48: 5d² 5s 5m³ 5s³ 5s Oct 10] modest handicapper: races at 5f: acts on soft and good to firm going: in hood last 2 starts. *Thomas Cuthbert* **56**

RED GALILEO 6 b.g. Dubawi (IRE) 129 – Ivory Gala (FR) 101 (Galileo (IRE) 134) [2017 14g* 15.9g³ 14g 12m 12d² 11.9g² 12d² Sep 29] useful-looking gelding: smart handicapper: won at Meydan (by neck from Carbon Dating) in January: second at Ascot (1¼ lengths behind Gawdawpalin) in July, York (½ length behind Fidaawy) in August and in listed race at Newmarket (½ length behind Frontiersman) in September: stays 2m: acts on polytrack, good to firm and heavy going: tried in tongue tie: front runner/races prominently. *Saeed bin Suroor* **115**

REDGRAVE (IRE) 3 b.g. Lope de Vega (IRE) 125 – Olympic Medal 66 (Nayef (USA) 129) [2017 73: p8g⁵ 8d* 7d³ 7v² 7d 8.1g² 7.1s⁵ 8d² Oct 27] rather unfurnished gelding: fairly useful handicapper: won at Newmarket in June: second at Chepstow in September and Newbury in October: stays 1m: acts on polytrack and heavy going: often wears hood: sold 35,000 gns in October. *Charles Hills* **88**

RED GUNNER 3 b.g. Oasis Dream 129 – Blue Maiden 113 (Medicean 128) [2017 80: t6g² 6m 6m t7.2g⁶ p7s p7g p6g⁵ t7.1g⁶ Oct 10] compact gelding: fair handicapper: left William Haggas after first start: stays 7f: acts on polytrack, tapeta and good to firm going: tried in cheekpieces: has joined Daniel Loughnane. *David O'Meara* **79**

RED HOT CHILLY (IRE) 4 ch.g. Frozen Power (IRE) 108 – She's Got The Look (Sulamani (IRE) 130) [2017 78: t12.2g³ Feb 11] fair maiden: stays 1½m: acts on polytrack and good to firm going: has joined Fergal O'Brien. *Dai Burchell* **71**

REDICEAN 3 b.g. Medicean 128 – Red Halo (IRE) 59 (Galileo (IRE) 134) [2017 80: 10m* 12d⁶ 10.2g⁴ 13.9m 12m³ t12.4g⁶ 14d* Oct 30] good-topped gelding: useful performer: won maiden in April and handicap in October, both at Redcar: left Peter Chapple-Hyam after second start: stays 1¾m: acts on tapeta, good to firm and good to soft going: sold to join Alan King 85,000 gns in October, and has made highly promising start over hurdles. *David O'Meara* **99**

RED INVADER (IRE) 7 b.g. Red Clubs (IRE) 125 – Tifariti (USA) (Elusive Quality (USA)) [2017 75: p6g p6g p6g⁶ f5m p5g* 5g p5g* 5.1g p5g p6g t5.1g p5g Dec 12] angular gelding: fair handicapper: won at Lingfield in March and July: races over 5f/6f nowadays: acts on polytrack, fibresand, good to firm and good to soft going: has worn headgear: often races in rear. *John Butler* **74**

RED MASTER (IRE) 3 ch.c. Mastercraftsman (IRE) 129 – Yaqootah (USA) 72 (Gone West (USA)) [2017 t12.2g p10g p8s 11.4m 12g Jul 3] no form: in headgear last 2 starts. *Ed Dunlop* **–**

RED MIRACLE 2 b.f. (Apr 12) Dylan Thomas (IRE) 132 – Under Milk Wood (Montjeu (IRE) 137) [2017 8d⁵ 8v⁶ 8.3d Oct 18] first foal: dam unraced sister to smart 1¼m-1½m winner Clowance: modest form: remains with potential. *Rod Millman* **58 p**

RED MIST 2 b.c. (Feb 8) Frankel 147 – Red Dune (IRE) 102 (Red Ransom (USA)) [2017 7s* 7d² 7g⁴ Sep 16] third foal: half-brother to useful 2-y-o 7f/1m winner Feedyah (by Street Cry): dam 7f/1m winner: useful form: won maiden at Sandown (by short head from Bathsheba Bay) in July: best effort when second in listed race at Newbury (short head behind Hey Gaman) in August: raced at 7f. *Simon Crisford* **106**

RED MOHICAN 3 ch.f. Harbour Watch (IRE) 121 – Magical Cliche (USA) 86 (Affirmed (USA)) [2017 57: t6f⁶ Jan 5] modest maiden: stays 6f: acts on fibresand and tapeta: in tongue tie last 3 starts: front runner/races prominently. *Phil McEntee* **50**

RED OCHRE 4 b.g. Virtual 122 – Red Hibiscus (Manduro (GER) 135) [2017 12m May 6] 22/1, well held in maiden at Thirsk: modest form over hurdles for Chris Grant. *John Quinn* **–**

RED PIKE (IRE) 6 ch.g. Kheleyf (USA) 116 – Fancy Feathers (IRE) 79 (Redback 116) [2017 104: t6g 6m 6m³ 6g 6d⁴ 6g² 6g³ 6v⁶ 6d Oct 27] good-topped gelding: useful handicapper: second at Ripon (neck behind Teruntum Star) in August and third at Thirsk (¾ length behind El Hombre) in September: best at 6f: acts on tapeta, soft and good to firm going: tried in visor: often races prominently. *Bryan Smart* **101**

RED RANNAGH (IRE) 4 b.g. Teofilo (IRE) 126 – Red Top (IRE) 85 (Fasliyev (USA) 120) [2017 97: 11.9s 9g³ 10.2f³ 11.4g⁴ 20.6v Aug 2] fairly useful handicapper: third at Nottingham in June: stays 1½m: acts on polytrack and firm going: sometimes in hood: has worn tongue tie: usually slowly away, races well off pace: has joined Nicky Henderson: one to treat with caution. *David Simcock* **87 §**

RED RIVERMAN 9 b.g. Haafhd 129 – Mocca (IRE) 99 (Sri Pekan (USA) 117) [2017 14s5 Aug 25] fair at best, laboured effort sole Flat start since 2015: stays 1½m: acts on good to firm and good to soft going: often in headgear: fairly useful chaser. *Nigel Twiston-Davies* **62**

RED ROMAN 2 b.c. (Mar 8) Holy Roman Emperor (IRE) 125 – Domitia (Pivotal 124) [2017 5m4 6d* 6f 7m 6s* 6d5 7g2 6g4 6d Oct 28] 30,000Y: compact colt: second foal: dam unraced half-sister to useful 2-y-o 6f winner Elronaq out of smart 6f winner Cartimandua: useful performer: won minor event at Newmarket in May and nursery at Goodwood in August: best effort when second in nursery at Newbury (short head behind Rogue) in September: stays 7f: acts on soft going: front runner/races prominently. *Charles Hills* **97**

REDROSEZORRO 3 b.g. Foxwedge (AUS) 128 – Garter Star 56 (Mark of Esteem (IRE) 137) [2017 62: 5m 9.2g 7f 7m3 7m 7v2 7.8d 7s3 6s* Oct 31] fair handicapper: won at Catterick in October: stays 7f: acts on heavy going: wears headgear: usually races towards rear. *Eric Alston* **66**

RED ROYALIST 3 b.g. Royal Applause 124 – Scarlet Royal 43 (Red Ransom (USA)) [2017 92p: 8m3 7g4 8m3 9.9d* 10g6 8s3 Oct 15] good-topped gelding: fairly useful performer: won maiden at Goodwood in September: stays 1¼m: acts on good to soft going: in cheekpieces last 4 starts: sold 38,000 gns in November. *Marcus Tregoning* **85**

RED SEEKER 2 ch.g. (Apr 9) Red Jazz (USA) 125 – Purepleasureseeker (IRE) (Grand Lodge (USA) 125) [2017 7g Oct 7] 100/1, well held in minor event at Redcar. *Andrew Crook* **–**

RED SHADOW 8 b.m. Royal Applause 124 – Just A Glimmer 93 (Bishop of Cashel 122) [2017 44: 6d 5s6 7.2s5 7.2d3 7.2d 8.3s4 9.2d6 7.2s 8s Oct 3] close-coupled mare: modest handicapper: stays 7f: acts on all-weather, good to firm and heavy going: wears headgear. *Alistair Whillans* **52**

RED SHANGHAI (IRE) 3 ch.f. Tamayuz 126 – Rouge Noir (USA) (Saint Ballado (CAN)) [2017 –: f6g6 f8g f8d 6g 7g f7.1g4 t6.1g 7.6d 7.6v5 f7.1g 6d f5g5 f8.1g Nov 28] poor maiden: has worn headgear, including last 2 starts. *Charles Smith* **43**

RED SNAPPER 2 b.f. (Feb 1) Kheleyf (USA) 116 – Amistress 82 (Kalanisi (IRE) 132) [2017 5.3m6 6d6 7d 7d2 7g 7d p6g p5s6 p5g2 Dec 23] first foal: dam, winner up to 11.5f (2-y-o 1m winner), also won over hurdles, half-sister to useful 2-y-o 6f/6.5f winner Twin Sails: modest maiden: stays 7f: acts on polytrack and good to soft going: in cheekpieces last 2 starts: front runner/races prominently. *William Stone* **50**

RED STAR DANCER (IRE) 3 b.g. Tamayuz 126 – Red Planet (Pivotal 124) [2017 8d5 9.2s 10d3 8.3g6 10g6 10d 11.2v 13.1v4 13.9v6 t12.4d Oct 24] modest maiden: left Linda Perratt after sixth start: stays 13f: acts on heavy going: tried in blinkers: usually races in rear, often lazily. *David Barron* **58**

RED STARLIGHT 2 br.f. (Jan 26) Pivotal 124 – Star Chart (IRE) 54 (Dubawi (IRE) 129) [2017 7s6 8s* Oct 28] strong filly: first foal: dam ran once: fairly useful form: won minor event at Newbury (by length from Expensive Liaison) in October: will go on improving. *Richard Hannon* **80 p**

RED STRIKER (IRE) 2 b.c. (Jan 31) Sea The Stars (IRE) 140 – Coolree Marj (IRE) (Marju (IRE) 127) [2017 p8g6 Oct 12] 190,000Y: first foal: dam unraced half-sister to smart stayer Far Cry: 10/3, 7¾ lengths sixth of 8 to Main Street in minor event at Chelmsford: will prove different proposition in time. *Sir Michael Stoute* **63 p**

RED STRIPES (USA) 5 b.g. Leroidesanimaux (BRZ) 127 – Kaleidoscopic (USA) (Fortunate Prospect (USA)) [2017 83, a77: t5g6 t5.1g6 f5s6 t5.1g f5m6 5.1d 6g5 5f5 5s6 5d2 t6.1g4 6g p5g p5s* p6g5 p5s5 t5.1g3 p5s3 p6s6 f5g2 f5g3 Dec 29] workmanlike gelding: fair handicapper: won at Chelmsford in September: stays 8.5f, usually races over shorter: acts on all-weather, firm and soft going: wears headgear: usually races close up. *Lisa Williamson* **71**

RED TEA 4 ch.f. Sakhee (USA) 136 – Maimoona (IRE) 96 (Pivotal 124) [2017 94: t8.6g5 8m* 8.2s 8g2 8d4 8m6 9d 8g3 p10g Nov 21] useful handicapper: won at Pontefract in April: second at same course (1¼ lengths behind Crowning Glory) in July: stays 8.5f: acts on polytrack, tapeta, soft and good to firm going. *Peter Hiatt* **98**

REDTEDD 2 ch.g. (Apr 17) Mazameer (IRE) 107 – Mermaid Melody (Machiavellian (USA) 123) [2017 6.1g t6.1g 5.7d Aug 23] well held in minor events: has joined Eric Alston. *Tom Dascombe* **–**

RED TORNADO (FR) 5 ch.g. Dr Fong (USA) 128 – Encircle (USA) (Spinning World (USA) 130) [2017 t12.2g Mar 6] sturdy gelding: useful at best, down the field in handicap on sole Flat start since 2015: stays 9f: acts on heavy going: fairly useful hurdler. *Dan Skelton* **–**

RED TOUCH (USA) 5 b.g. Bluegrass Cat (USA) 120 – Touchnow (CAN) (Pleasant Tap (USA)) [2017 90: f7g t7.1d^5 f8m^5 f6d^2 f7g^4 8s t7.2g^6 p7d t8.6g^6 f8.1g^2 f8.1g Dec 19] strong, compact gelding: fair handicapper: stays 1¼m: acts on fibresand and tapeta: usually wears headgear: usually races in rear. *Michael Appleby* **79**

RED TROOPER (FR) 4 ch.g. Shamardal (USA) 129 – Solar Midnight (USA) (Lemon Drop Kid (USA) 131) [2017 87: p7g^5 7d^6 6g^2 p6g* Sep 13] lengthy gelding: fair performer: won claimer at Kempton in September: stays 1m: acts on polytrack: tried in hood. *George Baker* **79**

RED TURTLE (FR) 6 ch.g. Turtle Bowl (IRE) 121 – Morlane (IRE) (Entrepreneur 123) [2017 91: t12.2m p11g^6 Apr 1] fairly useful performer: won 3 minor events at Ovrevoll in 2016: well held both starts in 2017: stayed 1½m: acted on polytrack and soft going: dead. *Rune Haugen* **–**

RED TYCOON (IRE) 5 b.g. Acclamation 118 – Rugged Up (IRE) (Marju (IRE) 127) [2017 90: p6g^6 p6g^5 6m^2 6.1s 6d 6d 7m^2 t7.1d p6s^3 p6g Dec 21] neat gelding: fairly useful handicapper on turf, fair on all-weather: second at Ascot in May and Epsom in August: stays 7f: acts on polytrack, good to firm and heavy going: tried in blinkers/tongue tie. *Ken Cunningham-Brown* **87 a78**

RED VERDON (USA) 4 ch.c. Lemon Drop Kid (USA) 131 – Porto Marmay (IRE) 92 (Choisir (AUS) 126) [2017 117: 13.4d^6 9.9m^5 12m 12g^4 10.2d^2 12d^6 p10g^3 p12g^2 p12g* Nov 29] sturdy colt: smart performer: won listed race at Kempton (by ½ length from Master The World) in November: placed in minor events at Doncaster in September and Chelmsford in October, and in listed race at Kempton (head behind Titi Makfi) in November: stays 12.5f: acts on polytrack, tapeta, good to firm and good to soft going: often wears headgear: often races towards rear. *Ed Dunlop* **116**

REDVERS (IRE) 9 br.g. Ishiguru (USA) 114 – Cradle Brief (IRE) (Brief Truce (USA) 126) [2017 73: 7g 7g 8d Jul 9] good-topped gelding: useful at best, no form in 2017: usually wears headgear: often starts slowly. *Noel Wilson* **–**

REEDANJAS (IRE) 3 b.f. Sir Prancealot (IRE) 111 – Blue Holly (IRE) 83 (Blues Traveller (IRE) 119) [2017 78+: 5.1g 6m^4 5.7f^3 t5g^6 6d 5d t5.1g 6d^3 t6.1g^3 p6g Dec 20] fairly useful handicapper: stays 6f: acts on tapeta, firm and good to soft going: sometimes wears cheekpieces. *Gay Kelleway* **80**

REEL LEISURE (GR) 4 ch.f. Reel Buddy (USA) 118 – Leisurely Way 71 (Kris 135) [2017 p11g^5 p12g 10g 11.9m Aug 9] workmanlike filly: second foal: dam, 8.3f winner, half-sister to smart winner up to 1½m (stayed 2m) Midas Way: runner-up once from 3 starts in bumpers: modest form on Flat, standout effort on first outing: has worn headgear: sent to Greece. *Amanda Perrett* **52**

REEL MR BOND 2 ch.c. (Mar 9) Monsieur Bond (IRE) 120 – Reel Cool (Reel Buddy (USA) 118) [2017 6m^6 7d^2 Jul 5] modest form: better effort when second in seller at Thirsk (½ length behind Give Em A Clump) in July. *Kevin Ryan* **57**

REFLATION 5 b.g. Stimulation (IRE) 121 – Miss Poppy 68 (Averti (IRE) 117) [2017 76: 6s 5s^6 6g 5.9d 6d 5s 5s 6d 6v^3 5v^6 7.2s Oct 9] fair handicapper, well below best in 2017: stays 7f: acts on polytrack, tapeta, good to firm and heavy going: usually wears headgear. *Patrick Holmes* **46**

REFLECT ALEXANDER (IRE) 2 b.f. (Apr 1) Kodiac 112 – Moon Club (IRE) (Red Clubs (IRE) 125) [2017 6.1m^4 6.1d^3 6g^4 6m^3 5m* 5g^5 5.2s 6.1g^4 6g Sep 7] 37,000F, £60,000Y: compact filly: third foal: dam, unraced, closely related to smart winner up to 6f Moon Unit: fairly useful performer: won minor event at Catterick (by 1½ lengths from May Girl) in July: stays 6f: acts on good to firm and good to soft going. *David Evans* **85**

REFLEKTOR (IRE) 4 ch.g. Bahamian Bounty 116 – Baby Bunting 63 (Wolfhound (USA) 126) [2017 104: 5.1d^6 6d 5.1d* 5.1d^3 5.5g 5s t6.1d Dec 16] useful handicapper: won at Chester in July: third at same course (length behind Confessional) later in month: stays 6f: acts on heavy going: often races prominently. *Tom Dascombe* **102**

REFRAIN (IRE) 2 b.c. (Feb 27) Dubawi (IRE) 129 – Folk Opera (IRE) 117 (Singspiel (IRE) 133) [2017 t7.2g Dec 2] 9/2, well held in minor event at Wolverhampton. *Sir Michael Stoute* **–**

REFUSE COLETTE (IRE) 8 ch.m. Refuse To Bend (IRE) 128 – Roclette (USA) 76 (Rock of Gibraltar (IRE) 133) [2017 68: p6g^4 6g 6m 7m 7s Sep 23] rather leggy mare: modest handicapper: left Mick Quinn after fourth start: best at 6f/7f: acts on polytrack, fibresand, soft and good to firm going: has worn headgear. *Adrian Nicholls* **61**

REGAL DECREE 3 b.g. Lawman (FR) 121 – Regal Riband 79 (Fantastic Light (USA) 134) [2017 53: 6g³ 6g³ 6m⁴ 7m³ 6m⁵ t7.1s 7s Sep 23] modest maiden: stays 7f: acts on good to firm going: usually wears headgear: tried in tongue tie. *Jedd O'Keeffe* **63**

REGAL DIRECTOR (IRE) 2 b.c. (Feb 28) New Approach (IRE) 132 – Dubai Queen (USA) 103 (Kingmambo (USA) 125) [2017 8.2d⁴ 8.3d⁵ Oct 11] third foal: half-brother to smart winner up to 1¼m Sharja Queen (2-y-o 7.4f winner, by Pivotal): dam, 1m winner, half-sister to high-class winner up to 1m Dubawi out of smart 1¼m-11f winner Zomaradah: fair form in minor event/maiden: likely to stay beyond 1m: remains open to improvement. *Simon Crisford* **71 p**

REGAL GAIT (IRE) 4 b.g. Tagula (IRE) 116 – Babylonian 66 (Shamardal (USA) 129) [2017 69p: p14g* p14d Sep 21] fair handicapper: won at Chelmsford in April: stays 1¾m: acts on polytrack: has joined Simon Dow. *Harry Whittington* **77**

REGAL MIRAGE (IRE) 3 ch.g. Aqlaam 125 – Alzaroof (USA) 72 (Kingmambo (USA) 125) [2017 –: 7m 10m³ 9.2m* 10d* 11.1g* 12s* 12.1g⁵ 11.8v 10g⁶ Oct 7] fair handicapper: completed 4-timer at Hamilton (2), Ayr and Pontefract in June/July: stays 1½m: acts on soft and good to firm going. *Tim Easterby* **79**

REGAL MISS 5 b.m. Royal Applause 124 – Pretty Miss 85 (Averti (IRE) 117) [2017 67: p5g⁵ p5g² 5.3g t5.1m p5g⁵ Dec 31] smallish mare: fair maiden, below best in 2017: stays 6f: acts on polytrack, good to firm and good to soft going. *Patrick Chamings* **59**

REGAL REALITY 2 b.c. (Feb 20) Intello (GER) 129 – Regal Realm 104 (Medicean 128) [2017 7s* Sep 20] second foal: dam 7f winner (including at 2 yrs): 9/4, won maiden at Yarmouth (by ½ length from Rich Identity) in September, dictating: will improve. *Sir Michael Stoute* **83 p**

REGARDE MOI 9 b.g. King's Best (USA) 132 – Life At Night (IRE) (Night Shift (USA)) [2017 f8g³ p8g³ f8g* t9.5g⁴ p8d⁶ 7.6g May 24] fairly useful performer: won claimer at Southwell in January: stays 1m: acts on all-weather, soft and good to firm going: has worn tongue tie: often races prominently. *Marco Botti* **89**

REGICIDE (IRE) 4 b.g. Archipenko (USA) 127 – Armoise 82 (Sadler's Wells (USA) 132) [2017 85: p10g* p11g² p12g⁶ 9.9g p12g⁵ Sep 27] neat gelding: fairly useful performer: won maiden at Lingfield in April: second in handicap at Kempton in May: stays 11f: acts on polytrack: often travels strongly. *James Fanshawe* **93**

REGIMENTED (IRE) 2 b.c. (Mar 13) Epaulette (AUS) 126 – Colour Coordinated (IRE) 70 (Spectrum (IRE) 126) [2017 7d* 8.1m³ 8.1g* 8g² 8.5v⁶ 8d² Oct 27] £18,000Y: sixth foal: half-brother to 10.7f winner Empress of Tara (by Holy Roman Emperor) and 11f/1½m winner Rabbit Thomas (by Dylan Thomas): dam maiden half-sister to winner up to 1½m (stayed 15f) Bonny Scot and 9f-1½m winner Mary Stuart (both smart): useful performer: won minor events at Lingfield in July and Chepstow in August: best effort when second in nursery at Doncaster (neck behind Ventura Knight) in October: stays 1m: acts on good to firm and good to soft going: has flashed tail/looked less than straightforward. *Richard Hannon* **97**

REGULAR INCOME (IRE) 2 b.c. (Mar 23) Fast Company (IRE) 126 – Max Almabrouka (USA) (Hennessy (USA) 122) [2017 7.6v³ p7g⁵ 8v³ 9m⁴ 8.3v* Nov 8] compact colt: fair performer: won nursery at Nottingham in November: stays 8.5f: acts on polytrack, best turf form on heavy going: often wears cheekpieces: sometimes slowly away, often races towards rear. *Adam West* **78**

REGULATOR (IRE) 2 b.g. (Mar 30) Acclamation 118 – Rasana 74 (Royal Academy (USA) 130) [2017 5m² 6g* 6.1d² 6m⁵ 6g Oct 7] 50,000Y, 105,000 2-y-o: half-brother to several winners, including useful 1m winner Aldovrandi (by Cape Cross) and useful 5f-7f winner Rasaman (by Namid): dam maiden (stayed 9f): fairly useful performer: won minor event at Ayr in July: will stay 7f: acts on good to soft going. *Richard Fahey* **92**

REHANA (IRE) 3 b.f. Dark Angel (IRE) 113 – Rayka (IRE) 72 (Selkirk (USA) 129) [2017 101: 7d³ 7g* 8d⁶ 6g³ 7m⁴ Oct 13] sturdy filly: third foal: half-sister to useful 2-y-o 1m winner Rayisa (by Holy Roman Emperor): dam twice-raced half-sister to smart 6f/7f winner Rayeni: useful performer: won Athasi Stakes at Naas (by 2¾ lengths from Rose de Pierre) in May: third in Leopardstown 1000 Guineas Trial in April (¾ length behind Hydrangea) and fourth in Challenge Stakes at Newmarket in October: stays 7f: acts on soft and good to firm going: front runner/races prominently. *M. Halford, Ireland* **106**

REIFFA (IRE) 2 b.f. (Feb 19) Epaulette (AUS) 126 – Phi Phi (IRE) 66 (Fasliyev (USA) 120) [2017 t5.1d* Dec 26] €20,000Y, 115,000 2-y-o: half-sister to several winners, including 1¼m/11f winner Parmeenion (by Beat Hollow) and 9.5f winner (stayed 1½m) **76 p**

Exning Halt (by Rail Link): dam 1m winner: 15/2, overcame greenness when won minor event at Wolverhampton (by length from Midsummer Knight) on debut: will stay 6f+: sure to progress. *William Haggas*

REINAS QUEEN (IRE) 4 b.f. Tagula (IRE) 116 – Darling Smile (IRE) (Darshaan 133) **66** [2017 –: 10s^2 9.5d 10d 10s^2 10g* 10d p12g 10.5d^4 9g Aug 10] fair handicapper: won at Naas (apprentice) in June: stays 1½m: acts on polytrack and soft going: usually wears headgear: has worn tongue tie. *Mrs Sarah Dawson, Ireland*

REINBEAU PRINCE 2 br.c. (Mar 12) Rip Van Winkle (IRE) 134 – Bridle Belle 98 **70** (Dansili 127) [2017 5g 6d^5 7.4m^4 6d^2 7.4d^6 7s 7.9g^4 7m^6 Oct 25] workmanlike colt: fair maiden: stays 1m: acts on good to firm and good to soft going. *Richard Fahey*

REINFORCED 4 ch.g. Equiano (FR) 127 – Fonnie (IRE) 58 (Barathea (IRE) 127) [2017 **75** 73: 7m 6s 6.9v* 7.2g 8g^5 7.2d 6.9d^2 6.9v^2 7s^4 Oct 10] fair handicapper: won at Carlisle in June: stays 7f: acts on good to firm and heavy going: wears cheekpieces/tongue tie: usually leads. *Michael Dods*

REINSTORM 3 b.g. Canford Cliffs (IRE) 133 – Bridle Belle 98 (Dansili 127) [2017 61: **69** 8m^5 9.9g* 9.8d 11.1g^4 11.1d 10s Jul 30] fair handicapper: won at Beverley in May: stays 1¼m: acts on good to firm and heavy going. *Richard Fahey*

REKINDLING 3 b.c. High Chaparral (IRE) 132 – Sitara 74 (Salse (USA) 128) **123** [2017 89: 10d* 10.3d^4 12m 14g* 14d^2 14.5g^4 15.9g* Nov 7]

'Robert and Vincent were stunned and when the result of the photograph came up it was Jacqueline O'Brien who rushed across to congratulate her son—Vincent was almost ripped apart by his divided loyalties, uncertain whether his genuine delight at David's triumph had entirely overshadowed the savage blow of The Senor's defeat.' This is how *Horsetrader*, the authorised biography of multiple champion owner Robert Sangster, described the immediate aftermath to the 1984 Derby, which had seen Vincent O'Brien's unbeaten 11/8-on favourite El Gran Senor touched off in Sangster's colours in one of Epsom's most famous finishes, edged out by a short head on the line by the 14/1-shot Secreto trained by O'Brien's twenty-seven-year-old son David. The post-race tension wasn't confined to the photo finish either, as a lengthy stewards' inquiry (losing jockey Pat Eddery also lodged an objection) ramped nerves to an even greater level before the 'result stands' announcement some ten minutes later. This very narrow defeat (the margin was measured at four inches) proved especially costly for O'Brien senior, who was also a partner in El Gran Senor (reportedly his favourite horse during his reign at Ballydoyle) as well as being his trainer. The defeat deprived him of a record-equalling seventh Derby win and, more tellingly at the height of the 'eighties boom, the defeat also slashed an estimated forty million dollars off El Gran Senor's stud value—a deal had been in place beforehand valuing him at a scarcely believable eighty million on the proviso that he won at Epsom. 'The money simply doesn't matter—I'm absolutely thrilled for my son,' O'Brien told the TV interviewer later on, before adding: 'I'm so glad the objection went the way it did. I'd have never got over it if the race had been taken from my son …'

Happily, there were no such divided loyalties after the Emirates Melbourne Cup at Flemington in November, the finish of which was dominated by the modern-day version of O'Brien father and son, with Joseph O'Brien's Rekindling swooping late to deprive the Aidan O'Brien-trained Johannes Vermeer of victory. 'It's absolutely marvellous and I couldn't be happier,' explained Aidan O'Brien, who watched the race on television in the middle of the night with other family members whilst on a rare holiday away from Ballydoyle, the iconic County Tipperary training establishment initially developed and made famous by Vincent O'Brien (no relation). 'It's the perfect result. I was hoping and praying we'd finish second all the way up the home straight. There was a lot of cheering and roaring for Joseph—we now know who is the most popular member of the family!' Similar sentiments had been expressed by O'Brien senior after the 2016 Moyglare Stud Stakes in which Intricately provided Joseph O'Brien with his first Group 1 winner as a trainer at the chief expense of the Ballydoyle fillies Hydrangea and Rhododendron. Such magnanimity after the Melbourne Cup was arguably helped by the fact Rekindling and Johannes Vermeer both ran in the colours of big-spending Australian owner Lloyd Williams (winning the race for a record sixth time), though the proud father has been consistently supportive of his son's fledgling training career—even directing all of the praise to him after Ivanovich Gorbatov had won the 2016 Triumph Hurdle when 'officially' still under the Ballydoyle banner (Joseph was in the process of qualifying for his licence at the time having quit the saddle because of his weight). Joseph O'Brien, who is based at his father's former Owning Hill stables (some twenty-eight miles away from Ballydoyle), finished sixth in the 2017 Irish trainers' table with fifty-two wins in his first full season with a licence, though Rekindling's Melbourne Cup success rather dwarfed any of the stable's achievements on home soil. For a start, the winner's pot of £2.25million is nearly three times the total O'Brien junior had accrued at home during the season. The Melbourne Cup was an eye-catching win for a variety of reasons with twenty-four-year-old O'Brien becoming the youngest winning trainer in the race's 156-year history, whilst northern-hemisphere foaled Rekindling was the first three-year-old to win since 1941 and just the third Irish-trained winner (following Vintage Crop in 1993 and Media Puzzle in 2002, both trained by Dermot Weld). A record six Irish-trained horses lined up for the latest Melbourne Cup and they dominated in a race in which the home-trained challenge struggled against European raiders, who accounted for nine of the first eleven home.

Rekindling was sent off a 14/1-shot in the Melbourne Cup (sixth choice in a field of twenty-three) after a relatively busy three-year-old campaign, his connections reportedly only making the decision to send him Down Under in mid-autumn. The step up to two miles seemed certain to suit and Australian jockey Corey Brown (who also rode 2009 Melbourne Cup winner Shocking) was booked for the lightly-weighted Rekindling who had 8-2 and went on to post a career-best effort. 'The race that stops a nation'—Melbourne Cup day is a public holiday in the state of Victoria—can often be a rough and tumble affair with hard-luck stories aplenty, yet it was remarkably smooth sailing for Rekindling, who travelled sweetly hugging the inner in mid-division before being switched to challenge early in the straight. The strong-travelling Johannes Vermeer (who was conceding 6 lb) got first run, but Rekindling stayed on strongly to overhaul him inside the final fifty yards to win by half a length, with a further two and a half lengths back to the 2015 Melbourne Cup runner-up Max Dynamite in third for Willie Mullins. Williams was effusive in his

Comer Group International Curragh Cup, the Curragh—the three-year-old Rekindling finds plenty to catch the favourite Wicklow Brave (star on cap) in the shadow of the post

Emirates Melbourne Cup Handicap, Flemington—Irish trainers dominate as Rekindling puts up a high-class performance to beat Johannes Vermeer (left) and Max Dynamite (pale colours, right), trainer Joseph O'Brien just foiling father Aidan's attempt to extend his record Group/Grade 1 haul; aged 24, Joseph O'Brien is the youngest trainer to win the race, while it is a record sixth win in the race for owner Lloyd Williams who has first and second

praise for the winning trainer when embracing him afterwards and he cited the Gold Cup at Royal Ascot (which O'Brien won aboard Leading Light in 2014 while still a jockey) as a possible target for Rekindling in 2018. A best price of 14/1 at the time of writing makes plenty of each-way appeal in an ante-post market which is headed by Order of St George (whom Williams part-owns) and Capri—who are both trained by Aidan O'Brien.

The Melbourne Cup wasn't the only time in 2017 that Rekindling lowered the colours of better-fancied runners from Ballydoyle. He began the campaign by springing a 16/1 surprise in the P. W. McGrath Memorial Ballysax Stakes at Leopardstown in April, a Group 3 ten-furlong event for three-year-olds in which O'Brien senior has endured an uncharacteristically lean spell of late (Fame And Glory in 2009 was his last winner). The Ballydoyle trio of Douglas Macarthur, Yucatan and Capri had to settle for second, third and fourth respectively as Rekindling was produced with a well-timed challenge to win by half a length. Rekindling matched that form when a never-nearer fourth to the ill-fated Permian in the Dante Stakes at York, but failed to give his running when an outsider for the Derby at Epsom, beating only two home in sixteenth. His limitations seemed exposed at this stage, but Rekindling took his form to another level (even prior to the Melbourne Cup) thanks to running in races with more emphasis on stamina during the second half of the season. Taking on older opposition for the first time, Rekindling flew home late to beat 2016 Irish St Leger winner Wicklow Brave (only tenth at Melbourne) in the Group 2 Comer Group International Curragh Cup in July, doing very well to get up after still having plenty to do two furlongs out. He then ran well on his next two starts when making the frame in the Irish St Leger Trial at the Curragh (runner-up to Order of St George) and the St Leger at Doncaster (fourth to Capri), though arguably he wasn't seen to full effect in either—again doing his best work late on in a strong renewal of the latter, beaten just over two lengths in the end having conceded first run under a patient ride from Donnacha O'Brien (Joseph's younger brother).

A son of High Chaparral, the good-topped Rekindling changed hands for 60,000 guineas as a foal, which clearly looks a bargain with the benefit of hindsight, though it looked on the cheap side even then considering his pedigree. He is the eighth foal out of the mile and a half winner Sitara and her fifth winner to date, the most notable one before Rekindling being his brother the Chester Vase winner Golden Sword, who was runner-up in the 2009 Irish Derby for Ballydoyle before enjoying success for Mike de Kock in the UAE later in his career. Another brother, All Body And Soul, isn't quite so good, but he has won three times over a mile and a half for Tracey Collins and has proved effective over further, as has their close relative Harrison's Cove (by Galileo), who was a useful performer when with Aidan O'Brien at the beginning of his career. Sitara's other winner Bitooh, a daughter of Diktat, was a mile and a quarter winner in France. There is plenty of stamina to be found elsewhere in this pedigree. Sitara is a half-sister to the 1997 Park Hill Stakes third Puce, who has produced several smart middle-distance stayers since retiring to the paddocks, notably the dual listed winner Lion Sands and 2004 Lancashire Oaks heroine Pongee. Another of Sitara's half-sisters was Shouk, who enjoyed an even more decorated broodmare career, her best representative being Ballydoyle's 2006 Oaks and Irish Oaks winner Alexandrova, herself the dam of smart pattern-winning performers Alex My Boy and Somehow, ill-fated winner of the Dahlia Stakes in the latest season. Shouk also produced the Cheveley Park winner Magical Romance. Third dam Soumana was an unraced daughter of Faizebad, the grandam of 1988 Two Thousand Guineas winner Doyoun and from a good Aga Khan family. Rekindling certainly shapes as if he'll stay beyond two miles and it is not out of the question that the Gold Cup trip could produce even more improvement in him. Bar that blip in the Derby (when the idiosyncratic course possibly didn't suit), Rekindling has proved an admirably consistent sort who seems versatile with regards to ground, characteristics which should continue to stand him in good stead in 2018 when he will continue to be trained in Ireland. By contrast, Douglas Macarthur is one of a quintet of Ballydoyle three-year-olds—Exemplar, Orderofthegarter, Spanish Steps and Venice Beach are the others—who have been sold to race in Australia as Lloyd Williams bolsters his team for another tilt at Melbourne Cup glory.

Rekindling (b.c. 2014)	High Chaparral (IRE) (b 1999)	Sadler's Wells (b 1981)	Northern Dancer
			Fairy Bridge
		Kasora (b 1993)	Darshaan
			Kozana
	Sitara (ch 1998)	Salse (b 1985)	Topsider
			Carnival Princess
		Souk (b 1988)	Ahonoora
			Soumana

David O'Brien lost his mantle as the youngest winning Derby trainer to Saeed bin Suroor eleven years after Secreto's win (Joseph O'Brien has until 2020 to beat this), though by that time he had already relocated to France (where he ran a successful vineyard until emigrating to Australia in 2009). He had shocked the racing world by retiring from training in the late-'eighties, having trained other notable performers during his brief training career including the 1982 Prix du Jockey Club/Irish Derby winner Assert and the remarkable filly Triptych, who won the 1985 Irish 2000 Guineas when trained by O'Brien at three. Rekindling's trainer as a two-year-old, David Wachman, caused a similar stir when surprisingly handing in his licence at the end of 2016, but the early signs suggest that Joseph O'Brien is in it for the long haul. 'I always intended to train and, from when I was young, training was always something that I'd really wanted to do,' he explained when reflecting on his Australian success. 'I do not miss the race-riding one bit—not one bit!' *Joseph Patrick O'Brien, Ireland*

RELATED 7 b.g. Kheleyf (USA) 116 – Balladonia 103 (Primo Dominie 121) [2017 102: p6g^5 6m 6s 7m 7m 6.1g* 6d* 6g 6g 6g^4 6d^5 p6s* Oct 24] lengthy gelding: useful handicapper: won at Nottingham in July, Newmarket in August and Kempton (by ¾ length from Show Stealer) in October: generally races at 6f nowadays: acts on polytrack, tapeta, firm and soft going: wears headgear: front runner/races prominently. *Paul Midgley* **95**

RELEVANT (IRE) 3 b.f. So You Think (NZ) 133 – Germane 100 (Distant Relative 128) **73**
[2017 12s^3 11.6d^4 p10g^4 9v^2 10d^5 t12.4d^2 p12g p10g^3 p10g^2 Dec 30] €90,000Y: closely related to smart 2-y-o 7f winner Lucky Chappy (by High Chaparral) and half-sister to several winners, including useful 1m/8.3f winner Granted and 7.4f/1m winner Robema (both by Cadeaux Genereux): dam 2-y-o 7f winner: fair maiden: left K. R. Burke after seventh start: stays 12.5f: acts on polytrack, tapeta and heavy going: tried in cheekpieces: in tongue tie last 2 starts: front runner/races prominently. *Stuart Williams*

RELIGHT MY FIRE 7 ch.g. Firebreak 125 – Making Music 72 (Makbul 104) [2017 76: 7.4m 7d 7.4f 7.4d^3 7.4s^2 8m* 8.5d^3 8m^3 7.4v^3 7d^6 Oct 20] strong gelding: fair handicapper: won at Musselburgh in August: stays 1m: acts on polytrack, fibresand and any turf going: wears headgear: has worn tongue tie. *Tim Easterby* **74**

RELY ON ME (IRE) 3 br.f. Kyllachy 129 – Life Rely (USA) (Maria's Mon (USA) 121) [2017 78p: p8g^4 7g^2 7m^6 5.9g^2 7v^5 6m* 6g^3 6g Oct 7] workmanlike filly: fairly useful handicapper: won at Newmarket (by ¾ length from Stanhope) in August: stays 1m: acts on polytrack and good to firm going: in cheekpieces last 3 starts: front runner/races prominently. *Andrew Balding* **92**

REMA AL KUWAIT (IRE) 2 b.f. (Feb 20) Kodiac 112 – Relinquished 80 (Royal Applause 124) [2017 5m^6 5m^4 5d^6 6g Sep 27] £100,000Y: fifth foal: half-sister to 6f winner Renounce (by Elnadim): dam, 2-y-o 7f/7.4f winner, half-sister to smart 7f/1m winner Green Line: modest form: best effort at 5f. *David O'Meara* **55**

REMARKABLE 4 b.g. Pivotal 124 – Irresistible 98 (Cadeaux Genereux 131) [2017 114: 7m 8.5m 8m^6 7s^2 7d 7s* Sep 9] good-topped gelding: smart handicapper: won at Ascot (by ½ length from Mjjack) in September: second at Newbury (neck behind Rusumaat) in July: stays 1m: acts on fibresand, soft and good to firm going: wears blinkers: usually races towards rear. *John Gosden* **118**

REMBRANDT 5 b.g. Dutch Art 126 – Authoritative (Diktat 126) [2017 a15.4g p15.9g t12.2g^3 16g^2 12g^3 16m^2 May 12] heavy-topped gelding: fair maiden: left E. J. O'Neill after second start: stays 2m: acts on good to firm going: often wears headgear: tried in tongue tie: often travels strongly. *Rebecca Menzies* **72**

REMEMBER ME 4 b.f. Acclamation 118 – Forgotten Me (IRE) (Holy Roman Emperor (IRE) 125) [2017 80: p8g^2 p8g* p8g^3 t9.5g^4 p8g^6 Apr 20] strong, compact filly: fairly useful handicapper: won at Lingfield in February: stays 1m: acts on polytrack: has worn headgear. *Hughie Morrison* **82**

REMEMBER NERJA (IRE) 3 ch.f. Lord Shanakill (USA) 121 – Tequise (IRE) 97 (Victory Note (USA) 120) [2017 –: 9.5s 10m 9.7s 10g^3 10g 12.9v t9.5g^3 t12.2g Dec 13] modest maiden: left Jarlath P. Fahey after sixth start: best effort at 1¼m: sometimes in headgear: often races towards rear. *Barry Leavy* **56**

REMEMBER ROCKY 8 ch.g. Haafhd 129 – Flower Market 68 (Cadeaux Genereux 131) [2017 68: 10m 9.1m^3 9s^6 10d^3 8g^2 8g* 8d 8m^6 7.8v Sep 13] fair handicapper: won at Ayr (amateur) in August: stays 1¼m: acts on soft and good to firm going: wears headgear. *Lucy Normile* **68**

REMEMBER THE MAN (IRE) 4 b.g. Dalakhani (IRE) 133 – Perfect Hedge 111 (Unfuwain (USA) 131) [2017 83: t13.9f^3 p12g^2 p15.8g* Feb 22] fairly useful handicapper: trained by A. de Royer Dupre in France in 2016: won (for first time) at Lingfield in February: stays 2m: acts on polytrack: tried in blinkers. *Ralph Beckett* **90**

REMNANT (IRE) 2 b.g. (Mar 18) Dawn Approach (IRE) 132 – Arbaah (USA) 90 (Invasor (ARG) 133) [2017 6s Jul 10] €75,000Y: first foal: dam, 1¼m-13f winner, half-sister to very smart 7f-9f winner Haatheq out of useful 2-y-o 6f winner Alshadiyah: 33/1, well held in minor event at Ayr. *K. R. Burke* **–**

RENE MATHIS (GER) 7 ch.g. Monsieur Bond (IRE) 120 – Remina (GER) (Erminius (GER) 111) [2017 105: 7g^2 7g t7.1g^5 6g 7g* 6v 7g^5 t7.1d Dec 16] workmanlike gelding: useful performer: won minor event at Thirsk (by 1½ lengths from Custom Cut) in April: second in handicap at Meydan (2½ lengths behind Flash Fire) in January: stays 7.5f: acts on polytrack and any turf going. *Richard Fahey* **102**

RENFREW STREET 4 br.f. Iffraaj 127 – Malpas Missile (IRE) 78 (Elusive City (USA) 117) [2017 90: t12.2g t12.2g* 13.1m^5 13.3g 14g^2 14.1s* p14g^2 11.9d^6 14s* 14.9s* Oct 15] lengthy, angular filly: useful performer: won handicaps at Wolverhampton in April, Carlisle in August and Goodwood (by neck from Melinoe) in September, and listed race at Cologne (by ¾ length from Adler) in October: stays 15f: acts on polytrack, tapeta and soft going: front runner/races prominently, usually responds generously to pressure: sold 80,000 gns, sent to Saudi Arabia. *Mark Johnston* **106**

RENNETI (FR) 8 b.g. Irish Wells (FR) 122 – Caprice Meill (FR) (French Glory 118) [2017 113: 11.6d^5 14.1v* 14d^5 12.8d 16s* 15.4g^4 Oct 22] strong gelding: smart performer: won minor event at Galway (by 13 lengths from Ted Veale) in August and Loughbrown Stakes at Naas (by 5 lengths from Stars Over The Sea) in September: fourth to Ice Breeze in Prix Royal-Oak at Saint-Cloud final start: stays 2¼m: acts on heavy going: tried in blinkers: usually races prominently: smart hurdler. *W. P. Mullins, Ireland* **115**

RENNY'S LADY (IRE) 2 ch.f. (Apr 1) Excelebration (IRE) 133 – Moriches (IRE) 68 (Alhaarth (IRE) 126) [2017 p7g^4 p7g Dec 31] €58,000F: fourth foal: half-sister to 3 winners, including 1m/9f winner Raj To Riches (by Iffraaj) and winner up to 11f Steevo (2-y-o 7f winner, by Dark Angel): dam lightly-raced half-sister to high-class Hong Kong 1m-1¼m winner Military Attack and to dams of Big Orange and Red Cadeaux: fair form: better effort when fourth in minor event at Lingfield (4 lengths behind Dancing Brave Bear) on debut. *David Evans* **66**

RENTON 2 ch.g. (Jan 24) Dandy Man (IRE) 123 – Private Equity (IRE) 65 (Haafhd 129) [2017 6.1g 6.1s 5.1d 9d^6 Oct 30] sturdy gelding: well held in maiden/minor events: tried in cheekpieces. *Tony Coyle* **–**

REPERCUSSION 4 b.g. Manduro (GER) 135 – Summertime Legacy 109 (Darshaan 133) [2017 93: 8m^6 10.3d p10s 10g^6 8.1m^2 8m^4 8g* Sep 28] lengthy gelding: trained by A. Fabre at 3 yrs, successful in maiden at Clairefontaine: useful handicapper in Britain, winning at Newmarket (by 5 lengths from Knight Owl) in September: stays 1¼m: acts on good to firm and good to soft going: has worn hood: tried in tongue tie. *Charlie Fellowes* **105**

REPLENISH (FR) 4 ch.g. Le Havre (IRE) 124 – Brambleberry 79 (Cape Cross (IRE) 129) [2017 103: p8g^3 8s^6 t8s p8g p8g p9.4f^3 Nov 29] sturdy gelding: useful performer: third in listed race at Deauville (¾ length behind Astral Merit) in November: left James Fanshawe after fifth start: stays 1¼m: acts on polytrack, tapeta and good to soft going: often races towards rear. *S. Cerulis, France* **106**

REPTON (IRE) 3 b.g. Zebedee 113 – African Moonlight (UAE) (Halling (USA) 133) [2017 99: 6d^6 7g 6v 6d 7s^3 6d^4 Oct 27] good-topped gelding: useful handicapper: third in minor event at Salisbury (2 lengths behind George William) in October: stays 7f: acts on soft and good to firm going: often races in rear. *Richard Hannon* **100**

REPUTATION (IRE) 4 b.g. Royal Applause 124 – Semaphore (Zamindar (USA) 116) [2017 100: 6m^5 6m 6s 6m* 7m 6f^4 6d^4 6g 6m Aug 29] strong, compact gelding: useful handicapper: won at Epsom (by ½ length from Naggers) in June: best at 6f: acts on soft and good to firm going: wears headgear. *John Quinn* **99**

REQUINTO DAWN (IRE) 2 br.g. (Apr 19) Requinto (IRE) 109 – Till Dawn (IRE) 63 (Kheleyf (USA) 116) [2017 5g* 5g^2 5.1m 5.2v 5g^6 5m^2 6.5g 5v^2 6g Oct 7] €7,000F, €24,000Y: first foal: dam, maiden (stayed 6f), half-sister to useful 2-y-o 5f/6f winner Rosabee: fairly useful performer: won minor event at Doncaster in April: also first past post (nose ahead of Weeton) in similar event at Beverley in September, but demoted for causing interference: may prove best at 5f: acts on good to firm and heavy going. *Richard Fahey* **87**

RE RUN (IRE) 3 b.g. Harbour Watch (IRE) 121 – Encore View 61 (Oasis Dream 129) [2017 76: t7.1d^4 Feb 1] fair maiden: raced only at 7f: acts on tapeta: tried in headgear: usually races towards rear. *Richard Fahey* **69**

RESHAAN (IRE) 2 b.c. (Jan 16) Dark Angel (IRE) 113 – Bluebell (IRE) 87 (Mastercraftsman (IRE) 129) [2017 p7s^4 7m Sep 23] fair form: better effort when fourth in minor event at Kempton (3½ lengths behind Morlock) in September. *Richard Hannon* **74**

RESHOUN (FR) 3 b.g. Shamardal (USA) 129 – Radiyya (IRE) (Sinndar (IRE) 134) [2017 10.9g* 12.4g^6 11.9g^2 11.2s^6 14m 11.8s^2 t12.4g^3 11.9d* Oct 28] rangy gelding: second foal: dam, 1½m winner, half-sister to very smart winner up to 1m Rajsaman: useful performer: won maiden at Angouleme in April and handicap at Doncaster (by 3¾ lengths from Lawless Secret) in October: left A. de Royer Dupre after third start: stays 12.5f: acts on tapeta and soft going: waited with. *Ian Williams* **103**

RESPECTABILITY 5 b.m. Echo of Light 125 – Respectfilly (Mark of Esteem (IRE) 137) [2017 –: p12g^6 Jan 18] tall mare: no form: in headgear last 2 starts. *David C. Griffiths* **–**

RESPECTABLE 2 b.f. (Feb 25) Champs Elysees 124 – Dalandra 68 (Montjeu (IRE) 137) [2017 8s^4 Sep 9] 65,000F: first foal: dam, maiden (stayed 1½m), closely related to useful 7f/1m winner Dalkova: 20/1, fourth in minor event at Ascot (2 lengths behind Soliloquy) in September: should do better. *Ralph Beckett* **78 p**

RESTIVE (IRE) 4 b.g. Rip Van Winkle (IRE) 134 – I Hearyou Knocking (IRE) 62 (Danehill Dancer (IRE) 117) [2017 86: f8g t7.1g t10.2g^2 t10.2d 11.1m^3 8.3m^4 10m 9g t10.2s^3 8s^6 t12.4g^2 10d* t10.2d^6 10v^2 f12.1g* f12.1g* f12.1g Dec 21] fair handicapper on turf, fairly useful on all-weather: won at Redcar (amateur) in October and Southwell (twice) in December: probably stays 13f: acts on fibresand, tapeta and heavy going: has worn headgear. *Iain Jardine* **76 a92**

RESTLESS ROSE 2 ch.f. (Feb 9) Power 117 – Albany Rose (IRE) 94 (Noverre (USA) 125) [2017 6s^{6} p6s* Dec 1] 40,000Y: second foal: dam, winner up to 5.7f (including at 2 yrs), half-sister to useful winner up to 1m Ayaar: fair form: won minor event at Chelmsford (by 2½ lengths from Ghepardo) in December: open to further improvement. *Stuart Williams* **78 p**

RESTORER 5 gr.g. Mastercraftsman (IRE) 129 – Moon Empress (FR) 84 (Rainbow Quest (USA) 134) [2017 108: 9.9d 10d 12m^{3} 12g^{5} 10m 10s^{5} 10.5d 11.9g^{3} 12s 10s Oct 28] good-topped gelding: useful performer: third in listed race at Ascot (2¾ lengths behind Desert Encounter) in May: stays 1½m: acts on polytrack, soft and good to firm going: sold to join Patrick Morris 33,000 gns in November. *William Muir* **108**

RETAINED (FR) 2 b.f. (Mar 12) Kentucky Dynamite (USA) 118 – Retainage (USA) (Polish Numbers (USA)) [2017 6s^{6} p6g^{3} p7g^{3} 6d p7g^{4} p7g Oct 18] lengthy filly: has scope: half-sister to several winners, including 1m-1½m winner Charlies Mate (by Myboycharlie) and 6f/7f winner Ballylare (by Mullionmileanhour): dam 6f-8.5f winner: fair maiden: stays 7f: acts on polytrack. *John Best* **67**

RETIREMENT BECKONS 2 b.g. (Apr 3) Epaulette (AUS) 126 – Mystical Ayr (IRE) 76 (Namid 128) [2017 6g^{5} 7.2g^{6} 6s 8s^{6} Oct 3] poor form: stays 1m. *Linda Perratt* **42**

RETRIBUTION 3 b.g. Iffraaj 127 – The Giving Tree (IRE) 92 (Rock of Gibraltar (IRE) 133) [2017 –p: 10d^{2} 10.1m^{4} 8.3v^{6} Sep 5] fair maiden: stays 1¼m: acts on good to firm and good to soft going: usually races nearer last than first. *David Lanigan* **74**

RETRIEVE (AUS) 10 b.g. Rahy (USA) 115 – Hold To Ransom (USA) 111 (Red Ransom (USA)) [2017 f8g^{5} p12g^{4} t9.5g* p16g^{4} p12g 12.1m^{3} 11.8s* 13.9m^{2} t12.2g^{3} t9.5g* p10s^{6} t12.2g^{rr} 9.1d 10.2d^{6} 14.2v p16s Dec 15] strong gelding: has reportedly had breathing operation: fair on turf, useful on all-weather: won claimer at Wolverhampton in February, seller at Leicester in May and another claimer at Wolverhampton in June, all for Jamie Osborne: left Carroll Gray after fifteenth start: probably stays 2m: acts on polytrack, tapeta, dirt and heavy going: has worn cheekpieces: has worn tongue tie, including in 2017. *Johnny Farrelly* **73** **a102**

RETURN ACE 5 b.m. Zamindar (USA) 116 – Match Point (Unfuwain (USA) 131) [2017 104: 11.8s^{5} 12s 16s^{4} 14d Oct 18] rather leggy mare: useful performer, below best in 2017: stays 15.5f: acts on polytrack and heavy going. *James Fanshawe* **83**

RETURNING GLORY 2 b.c. (Apr 1) Exceed And Excel (AUS) 126 – Tanzania (USA) (Darshaan 133) [2017 p8d^{2} Dec 13] half-brother to several winners, including very smart winner up to 9f True Story (2-y-o 7f winner, by Manduro), smart 1¼m-16.2f winner Winning Story (by New Approach) and smart 1½m winner Gold Star (by Nathaniel): dam unraced: 7/2, second in minor event at Kempton (4½ lengths behind Highbrow) in December: open to improvement. *Saeed bin Suroor* **78 p**

REVALUE 2 b.f. (Feb 25) Dansili 127 – Take The Hint 107 (Montjeu (IRE) 137) [2017 7d p7g* 7d^{2} Nov 4] fifth foal: sister to useful French 9.5f/1¼m winner Orienteer: dam, winner up to 1¼m (2-y-o 1m winner), half-sister to very smart 7f-1m winner Stronghold and smart winner up to 1¼m Convey (by Dansili): fair form: won minor event at Kempton (by 1¼ lengths from Bubble And Squeak) in October: raced only at 7f. *Charles Hills* **79**

REVEL 3 b.g. Makfi 130 – Cecily 88 (Oasis Dream 129) [2017 68: p7g^{4} p8d* t7.1g^{3} 8.2s^{6} 7m^{4} 8m Jul 6] compact gelding: fairly useful handicapper: won at Kempton in January: third at Wolverhampton in March: stays 1m: acts on polytrack, tapeta and good to firm going: wears tongue tie: sometimes slowly away: sold 10,000 gns in July. *Stuart Williams* **80**

REVELEON 2 ch.c. (Apr 3) Exceed And Excel (AUS) 126 – Rosika 112 (Sakhee (USA) 136) [2017 p8g p8g p8g Nov 18] fourth foal: half-brother to fairly useful 8.3f winner Desert Dream (by Oasis Dream) and useful 1½m winner (stays 1¾m) Dubka (by Dubawi): dam, 1¼m-1½m winner, half-sister to smart winner up to 1½m Rambling Rose: little impact in minor events: type to do better in handicaps. *Sir Michael Stoute* **– p**

REVENGE 2 b.g. (Feb 12) Arcano (IRE) 122 – Queens Revenge 87 (Multiplex 114) [2017 5g^{6} 5m^{4} 5s t6.1g^{5} p7g^{3} t6g^{6} 6.1d Oct 4] good-quartered gelding: modest maiden: stays 7f: acts on polytrack and tapeta: in blinkers last 4 starts. *Tim Easterby* **57**

REVERBERATION 2 ch.g. (Mar 29) Excelebration (IRE) 133 – Echo Ridge (IRE) 78 (Oratorio (IRE) 128) [2017 5d^{6} 6v^{5} 7m^{4} 7g 7v^{3} Oct 1] fair maiden: stays 7f: acts on good to firm and heavy going. *Sylvester Kirk* **68**

REVEREND JACOBS 3 b.g. Nathaniel (IRE) 129 – Light Impact (IRE) (Fantastic Light (USA) 134) [2017 64: 8m^{2} 10.3d^{2} 12d^{2} 12s* Sep 8] fairly useful performer: won maiden at Ascot in September: will be suited by 1¾m+: acts on soft and good to firm going: front runner/races prominently: remains open to improvement. *William Haggas* **89 p**

REVIVED 2 b.f. (Feb 23) Dark Angel (IRE) 113 – Tan Tan (King's Best (USA) 132) [2017 6v5 5g* 6g Nov 3] £42,000Y, €130,000 2-y-o: fourth foal: half-sister to 2-y-o 6f winner Music Stop (by Iffraaj) and 7f/1m winner German Whip (by Zoffany): dam, 6.5f winner, half-sister to smart winner up to 6f Land of Dreams, dam of Dream Ahead: fairly useful form: won minor event at Ripon (by 1¼ lengths from Deviate) in August: best effort at 5f: tried in hood. *Michael Bell* **81**

REVOLUTIONARY MAN (IRE) 2 b.c. (Feb 19) Exceed And Excel (AUS) 126 – Bint Almukhtar (IRE) (Halling (USA) 133) [2017 7m p8g5 p8d3 Nov 9] fair form: best effort when fifth in minor event at Chelmsford (4¾ lengths behind Main Street) in October. *Simon Crisford* **71**

REVOLUTIONARY WAR (USA) 4 b.c. War Front (USA) 119 – My Annette (USA) 78 (Red Ransom (USA)) [2017 80: t8.6m2 p8m* p8g5 t7.1d Feb 4] fairly useful performer: trained by A. Fabre at 3 yrs: won maiden at Lingfield (by head from Al Yarmouk) in January: stays 8.5f: acts on polytrack, tapeta and good to soft going. *Jamie Osborne* **86**

REWAAYAT 2 br.c. (Feb 23) Pivotal 124 – Rufoof 87 (Zamindar (USA) 116) [2017 6g Sep 22] first foal: dam, 7f winner, half-sister to top-class winner up to 7f Muhaarar: 11/2, needed experience when well held in maiden at Newbury: should do better. *Charles Hills* **– p**

REY LOOPY (IRE) 3 b.g. Lope de Vega (IRE) 125 – Al Basar (USA) (Sahm (USA) 112) [2017 –: t7.1g4 p8g4 t7.1g* t7.1s6 8.3g t7.1d2 t8d* t8g2 Nov 24] fairly useful performer: won minor event at Newcastle in May and handicap at same course (by 2¼ lengths from Rebel State) in November: stays 1m: acts on polytrack and tapeta: often races towards rear. *Ben Haslam* **80**

REZWAAN 10 b.g. Alhaarth (IRE) 126 – Nasij (USA) 101 (Elusive Quality (USA)) [2017 58: p11d3 p11d3 p12g4 p10g6 11.6g6 p13.3s Nov 17] good-bodied gelding: modest handicapper nowadays: stays 11f: acts on polytrack, good to firm and good to soft going: usually wears headgear. *Murty McGrath* **56**

RHIGOLTER ROSE (IRE) 2 ch.f. (Apr 15) Leroidesanimaux (BRZ) 127 – Landela 64 (Alhaarth (IRE) 126) [2017 7m Oct 25] €25,000Y: smallish filly: half-sister to several winners, including 6f winner Gravity Flow (by Exceed And Excel) and 1m/8.6f winner Trumpington Street (by Noverre), both useful: dam twice-raced half-sister to very smart 1¼m-1½m winner Zambezi Sun: 16/1, well held in minor event at Newmarket: has joined Daniel Kubler. *William Haggas* **–**

RHODE ISLAND (IRE) 2 ch.c. (May 9) Galileo (IRE) 134 – Native Force (IRE) 82 (Indian Ridge 123) [2017 8.3v5 p8g5 Nov 21] half-brother to several winners, including winners up to 6f Kingsgate Native (very smart, by Mujadil) and Vanishing Grey (by Verglas), both 2-y-o 5f winners: dam 1m winner: fair form: better effort when fifth in maiden at Nottingham (9¾ lengths behind My Lord And Master) on debut: will stay at least 1¼m: remains with potential. *John Gosden* **67 p**

RHODES HOUSE 3 b.c. Frankel 147 – Intrigued 105 (Darshaan 133) [2017 11m Apr 22] tall colt: in tongue tie, 22/1, well held in maiden at Newbury: sold £2,000 in September, sent to UAE. *Paul Cole* **–**

RHODODENDRON (IRE) 3 b.f. Galileo (IRE) 134 – Halfway To Heaven (IRE) 118 (Pivotal 124) [2017 118: 8m2 12m2 10.4mpu 8d 9.9d* 9f2 Nov 4] **118**

Rhododendron's essay in *Racehorses of 2016* began with an assessment of the pecking order among the fillies at the all-conquering Ballydoyle stables of Aidan O'Brien. Rhododendron began her three-year-old campaign firmly at the top of that pecking order but, with things not going to plan in the interim, her lofty pre-season reputation had faded by the time she lined up for the Group 1 Prix de l'Opera at Chantilly in early-October. Rhododendron was looking for her first win of the campaign and, in a role reversal from the spring, was the Ballydoyle second string, with both Ryan Moore and punters preferring her old rival Hydrangea, although Rhododendron led their head-to-head record by three to two. Hydrangea (who represents the same connections) had come out on top when springing a 20/1 surprise in the Matron Stakes at Leopardstown on their most recent meeting when seventh-placed Rhododendron was on the comeback trail and received a considerate ride, having burst a blood vessel when pulled up in the Prix de Diane almost three months earlier. There was no kid glove treatment at Chantilly, with Seamus Heffernan needing to get very serious on Rhododendron after producing her to lead over a furlong out, having tracked her better-fancied stable-companion. Heffernan found a willing partner in Rhododendron, who responded gamely under

Prix de l'Opera Longines, Chantilly—Rhododendron leads home a one, two for trainer Aidan O'Brien, beating Hydrangea (rail) with Lady Frankel (pale star on cap) back in third

pressure to hold off the rallying Hydrangea by a head, with a further neck back to the fast-finishing French-trained outsider Lady Frankel (the favourite Shamreen, another Irish raider, dropped away to finish last). Less than a length covered the first five home, partly as a result of a steady early gallop, and the latest Prix de l'Opera will hardly go down as a vintage renewal, though Rhododendron's win was some consolation for earlier misfortunes.

Rhododendron was certainly due a change of luck after a frustrating campaign. It might be stretching things to describe her as an unlucky loser when runner-up to another stable-companion Winter in the One Thousand Guineas at Newmarket (Hydrangea was only tenth), but she would certainly have gone closer with a clearer run. A well-backed 5/4 favourite, Rhododendron conceded first run to Winter when Ryan Moore was forced to switch her in the Dip after briefly being trapped behind two other runners (one of them Hydrangea). Rhododendron flew home once in the clear (she was still only fifth entering the final furlong), but was two lengths adrift of Winter at the line. Winter went on to prove herself a much improved filly in the remainder of the season, comments which also very much apply to Rhododendron's conqueror in the Oaks, Enable. At the time, Rhododendron's five-length defeat when 11/8-on at Epsom might have been viewed as disappointing by some, but it soon became clear that she had been beaten by an exceptional filly in Enable after finding the mile and a half trip stretching her stamina at the end of a strongly-run race. There is an argument for saying that Rhododendron would have won the Breeders' Cup Filly & Mare Turf at Del Mar on her final start had it been run over its more usual trip—it is usually run over ten furlongs but was cut back to nine furlongs (the shortest trip in the race's history) due to the configuration of Del Mar's turf track. As it was, Rhododendron again had to settle for the runner-up spot after enduring a troubled passage at a vital stage. In fairness to Moore, he had little option but to ride Rhododendron patiently as a result of a poor draw but, having managed to get across to the inner in the back straight, he found himself left with plenty to do after suffering interference on the home turn. As at Newmarket, Rhododendron finished with a flourish once in the clear, but British raider Wuheida (fourth in the Prix de l'Opera) had got first run and was still a length up by the line.

Rhododendron (IRE) (b.f. 2014)	Galileo (IRE) (b 1998)	Sadler's Wells (b 1981)	Northern Dancer
			Fairy Bridge
		Urban Sea (ch 1989)	Miswaki
			Allegretta
	Halfway To Heaven (IRE) (gr 2005)	Pivotal (ch 1993)	Polar Falcon
			Fearless Revival
		Cassandra Go (gr 1996)	Indian Ridge
			Rahaam

The lengthy, good-topped Rhododendron is an attractive filly who looks a top-notch broodmare prospect. She is the fourth of six foals (all by Galileo) produced so far by Halfway To Heaven, who ended her racing days rated the same as Rhododendron, though she achieved more in terms of wins at three, taking the Irish

Mrs John Magnier, Mr M. Tabor and Mr D. Smith's "Rhododendron"

One Thousand Guineas, the Nassau Stakes and the Sun Chariot—the first two of those successes coming in bunched finishes with just over half a length covering the first four home. All five of Halfway To Heaven's offspring to reach the racecourse so far are winners (four of them for O'Brien), the most recent being Rhododendron's year-younger sister Magical, who showed smart form when winning the Debutante Stakes at the Curragh in August, before a narrow defeat in the Moyglare Stud Stakes there and fourth-place finishes when sent off favourite for the Prix Marcel Boussac and Fillies' Mile. First foal Flying The Flag was also smart, and successful at up to a mile and a quarter. Grandam Cassandra Go was a very smart sprinter who and has done well since retiring to the paddocks—her yearling filly by Invincible Spirit was bought by Coolmore for 1,600,000 guineas in October. Cassandra Go's two best representatives other than Halfway To Heaven were the Group 3 winning sprinters Tickled Pink and Theann (the latter dam of Photo Call, a dual Grade 1 winner in the States at up to a mile and a quarter who was also by Galileo), though there is stamina elsewhere in this pedigree, as discussed in detail in Rhododendron's essay in *Racehorses of 2016*. Rhododendron clearly stays ten furlongs well and, although unlikely to be tried over a mile and a half again, may well last out the trip a little better away from Epsom. A consistent sort, she is a strong traveller who acts on soft and good to firm going and she should continue to pay her way in 2018. *Aidan O'Brien, Ireland*

RHOSNEIGR (IRE) 2 ch.c. (Feb 20) Iffraaj 127 – Sadinga (IRE) 85 (Sadler's Wells (USA) 132) [2017 6g^6 7g^2 7.4d* 7g* 8g^5 8g^6 Sep 28] 40,000F, 100,000Y: well-made colt: half-brother to several winners, including useful winner up to 11f (stayed 1¾m) Cool Judgement (2-y-o 9f winner, by Peintre Celebre) and useful 5f-1m winner Showboating (by Shamardal): dam 1½m winner: fairly useful performer: won minor event at Ffos Las in July and nursery at Haydock (by head from Veejay) in August: should stay 1m: acts on good to soft going. *Charles Hills* **85**

RIANNA STAR 4 b.f. Haafhd 129 – Sayrianna 46 (Sayaarr (USA)) [2017 64: p12d p13g^2 9.9g p12d^2 11.9d^2 p12g 11.9s Oct 10] modest maiden: stays 1½m: acts on polytrack and good to soft going: usually races prominently. *Gary Moore* **63**

RIBBING (USA) 4 ch.f. Distorted Humor (USA) 117 – Contentious (USA) 107 (Giant's Causeway (USA) 132) [2017 66: p8g^2 p12m^4 Jan 21] maiden, fair form at best: stays 1m: acts on polytrack and tapeta: tried in hood: sent to USA. *David Simcock* **58**

RIBCHESTER (IRE) 4 b.c. Iffraaj 127 – Mujarah (IRE) 59 (Marju (IRE) 127) [2017 129: 8.9d^3 8s* 8f* 8v^2 8d* 8s^2 8f^5 Nov 4] **129**

One notable absentee from Sheikh Mohammed's entourage at Royal Ascot was John Ferguson, Godolphin's erstwhile chief executive who had been one of the mainstays of the Sheikh's worldwide racing and breeding empire in one form or another for over a quarter of a century. Ferguson's resignation arose from a breakdown in his relationship with the Sheikh's long-standing private trainer Saeed bin Suroor, the reason for their differences dealt with in a little more detail in the essay on Thunder Snow. When bin Suroor made the rift public, Ferguson regarded his position as having become untenable. His immediate departure was met with surprise in the sport's corridors of power—dissent was unheard of in the Godolphin ranks—and must have been the cause of acute embarrassment to the Godolphin operation itself. Ferguson had been the public face of Godolphin and its breeding arm Darley at the world's major yearling sales over the years, one of the biggest spenders at public auction, and he also ran Godolphin's acquisitive cherry-picking of good horses in training, a policy that has paid off by providing the operation with so many of the horses that have kept it in the limelight in the big races.

The three Godolphin-owned Group 1 winners in Britain in the latest season, Ribchester, Barney Roy and Harry Angel (who won five of Britain's thirty-six Group 1s between them), were all bought privately while on their way up, all remaining with their original trainers (in-training acquisitions used to be automatically transferred at one time to Sheikh Mohammed's in-house trainers). Ferguson and his team could have had Ribchester, Barney Roy and Harry Angel for very much less than they eventually paid—all three were purchased for their original owners at auction as yearlings with £200,000 enough to secure the lot—but all three enhanced their value considerably after they were bought, leaving, it could be said, a sizeable legacy to Godolphin from the Ferguson era. While Harry Angel was already a lesser pattern winner before Godolphin acquired him for a rumoured £4m just before Royal Ascot, Barney Roy and Ribchester were both purchased from their original owners for considerably less as two-year-olds, Barney Roy after winning a maiden at Haydock on his only start and Ribchester after finishing second on each of his first two starts, the second of them in the Gimcrack Stakes at York (he won the Mill Reef at Newbury in the Godolphin royal blue on the last of his three outings in his first season).

Just days after John Ferguson's resignation, Ribchester, Barney Roy and Harry Angel all played their part in a memorable Royal Ascot for Godolphin. Ribchester and Barney Roy won the Queen Anne Stakes and the St James's Palace Stakes respectively on the opening day when the Godolphin private stable of Charlie Appleby had a one, two in the Windsor Castle Stakes with home-bred Sound And Silence and £360,000 Doncaster Breeze-Up purchase Roussel. The treble coincided with the fortieth anniversary of Sheikh Mohammed's very first winner in Britain, the two-year-old filly Hatta (a 6,200-guineas yearling) who was successful in a small race at Brighton. The famous maroon, white sleeves, maroon cap with white star dominated British racing from the mid-'eighties to the late-'nineties, with Sheikh Mohammed being leading owner in Britain on nine occasions, represented by the likes of Old Vic, Singspiel, Pebbles, Oh So Sharp and Indian Skimmer, among many others. The maroon silks hadn't been seen on Britain's racecourses for a decade but made a comeback in the latest season on horses owned by a partnership linked to his young daughter Sheikha Al Jalila (the blue and white colours carried by Hatta have been registered to Sheikh Mohammed's son Sheikh Zayad). Godolphin had six winners in all at the Royal meeting—where Harry Angel came second in the Commonwealth Cup—and ended the week as the leading owner. Another

Al Shaqab Lockinge Stakes, Newbury—Ribchester produces a high-class performance to secure his second win at Group 1 level, beating Lightning Spear; Breton Rock (quartered cap) gets up for third, ahead of the ill-fated Somehow (striped cap) and 2016 Two Thousand Guineas winner Galileo Gold (No.4), who is retired after being found to have sustained a soft-tissue injury

private, horse-in-training purchase Atty Persse won the King George V Stakes for Roger Charlton's stable, 650,000-guinea yearling Rare Rhythm won the Duke of Edinburgh Stakes to give Charlie Appleby a second winner and Saeed bin Suroor saddled home-bred Derby fifth Benbatl to win the Hampton Court Stakes.

'This is Royal Ascot, it is very difficult to win here because everyone comes,' Sheikh Mohammed said, adding one of his maxims—'In life there is no winning post, you have to keep going or others will catch you up.' Coolmore, for one, might argue that it has more than 'caught up' with the ruler of Dubai over the last twenty years and it was interesting that the end of John Ferguson's tenure coincided with a major shift in Sheikh Mohammed's buying policy at the yearling sales in the autumn. The new buying team, centred on trainer John Gosden, Anthony Stroud and David Loder, began to loosen what had been, for a number of years, an apparent embargo on buying the offspring of Coolmore sires (touched on in the entry on Barney Roy), the latest move perhaps an acknowledgement summed up in the more prosaic old saying 'If you can't beat 'em, join 'em'. The Godolphin team didn't acknowledge that any of its yearling transactions represented a shift in policy, merely saying that it was 'on a mission to find good horses'. John Gosden added 'The stud needs to be regenerated with new bloodlines … if we see nice fillies by any stallion we'll be very interested, just as we will with a nice colt.'

Ribchester did well as a three-year-old for Godolphin, finishing third at 33/1 in the Two Thousand Guineas before winning the Jersey Stakes at Royal Ascot and making his breakthrough as a Group 1 winner in the Prix Jacques le Marois at Deauville after a fine third in a very close finish to the Sussex Stakes. The Lockinge and the Queen Anne Stakes—both races in which Godolphin has enjoyed plenty of success over the years—were earmarked as targets for Ribchester as a four-year-old after he had ended his three-year-old season with a good second to the filly Minding in the Queen Elizabeth II Stakes on British Champions' Day at Ascot. Ribchester justified favouritism in fine style in a soft-ground Al Shaqab Lockinge after reappearing at Meydan on Dubai World Cup night when he seemed to find a mile and a furlong a shade too far in the Dubai Turf, quickening to lead again two furlongs out but headed in the last half furlong by Japanese-trained Vivlos and French-trained Heshem. Ribchester made much of the running at Meydan, a change of tactics from his three-year-old days, and similar tactics had to be employed at Newbury when his presumed pacemaker, 50/1-shot Toscanini, was very slowly away. Ribchester travelled well all the way and kept on strongly, after coming under pressure over a furlong out as he began to hang to his right, to win by three and three quarter lengths from the Queen Elizabeth II Stakes third Lightning Spear, with Breton Rock and the ill-fated Somehow completing the frame ahead of the previous year's Two Thousand Guineas winner Galileo Gold who had been kept in training but found his four-year-old career quickly curtailed when a soft-tissue injury was diagnosed after the Lockinge. Ribchester's victory was the eighth in the race for a Godolphin-owned runner, a sequence that began with 20/1-shot Cape Cross in 1998. Illustrating the different times, Saeed bin Suroor trained the first five of Godolphin's Lockinge winners but Ribchester completed a hat-trick for Godolphin runners that had been bought privately in training and left with their original handlers, Ribchester's win following those of Belardo (Roger Varian) in 2016 and Night of Thunder (Richard Hannon) in 2015.

There was a field of sixteen for the Queen Anne Stakes, the largest since the same number lined up in 2004 when Refuse To Bend gave Godolphin and trainer Saeed bin Suroor the sixth of their seven victories in the race. Seven of the twelve editions since Refuse To Bend's had been won by overseas-trained challengers, the most recent of them by the high-class North American mare Tepin who held the late thrust of Belardo who had been seeking to follow up his victory in the Lockinge. Ribchester started at 11/10 to go one better than Belardo in a field that included three who had won Grade 1s in North America, 20/1-shots American Patriot and Miss Temple City (making her third visit to Royal Ascot) and Aidan O'Brien-trained Deauville (winner of the Belmont Derby as a three-year-old) who was supplemented for the Queen Anne although holding entries at the meeting later in the week. Deauville started at 12/1, fourth favourite behind Ribchester, the 5/1-shot Mutakayyef, a high-class performer who had finished two places behind Ribchester in the Dubai Turf and hadn't been seen since, and 11/2-shot Lightning Spear who was expected to come on for his reappearance in the Lockinge. Toscanini managed to fulfil his pacemaking duties on this occasion, tearing off with 200/1-shot Dutch Uncle and essentially being ignored by the rest of the field. The Royal Ascot going was very firm—the track record for the period since the course was redeveloped was broken in the Queen Anne—and Ribchester demonstrated his versatility, reproducing his high-class effort on soft in the Lockinge by beating Mutakayyef and Deauville with something to spare by a length and a quarter and a neck, making good headway to lead over a furlong out as the pacemaker dropped away and then idling in front (as well as edging both left and right before finding more when Mutakayyef

Queen Anne Stakes, Royal Ascot—
in the largest field for this race since 2004, Ribchester follows up his Lockinge success in course-record time, proving too strong for Mutakayyef (striped cap) and Deauville

briefly drew up to his quarters). The French-trained filly Spectre was the first of the finishers from outside Britain and Ireland, coming a very good fourth at 50/1, but American Patriot and Miss Temple City both dropped away to finish among the backmarkers (Lightning Spear managed only ninth).

One interesting feature of both Ribchester's win in the Queen Anne and of Barney Roy's later in the afternoon was that Sheikh Mohammed himself did not go up to receive either of the Group 1 trophies, which were accepted by his wife Princess Haya and his son Sheikh Hamdan, who has a large string trained by Mark Johnston. It might simply have been Sheikh Mohammed's wish to see the moments enjoyed by members of his family, though there was some speculation that he might have been reluctant to be seen receiving trophies on a podium with a background liberally branded with the logos of Qatar, an 'official partner' of the Royal meeting. As ruler and prime minister of Dubai, Sheikh Mohammed played a part earlier in the year in forming an alliance of neighbouring Gulf states to cut travel ties and trade with Qatar which has been accused of covert support for Islamic terrorism. Qatar and its various investment businesses have been gradually extending the oil- and gas-rich state's worldwide influence, with sport a major area for investment. The country is controversially set to host the 2022 football World Cup, Qatar Airways has a shirt deal worth nearly £50m a year with Barcelona football club, while Qatari interests own another of Europe's top clubs Paris Saint Germain. Qatar's bountiful largesse—which some fear might give it undue influence—has manifested itself in British racing, not just at Ascot but also in a ten-year sponsorship deal with Goodwood's July meeting which is now branded as the Qatar Goodwood Festival (Qatar is already the source of the vast prize money on offer over Prix de l'Arc weekend and began sponsorship of the Prix du Jockey Club in the latest season through Qipco). Goodwood's five-day meeting has had an injection of around an extra £2m a year in prize money since 2015, the biggest slice going to the Sussex Stakes which was Ribchester's next target after Royal Ascot. Contrary to some speculation at the time, Sheikh Mohammed never considered boycotting Goodwood with his horses because of Dubai's political disagreement with Qatar, but Dubai TV, which normally has a team at Britain's major race meetings, did not cover Goodwood, and it did not take the world feed of the racing either (Qatar's prominent on-course branding is difficult for the cameras to avoid).

Goodwood's July meeting has long been known as 'Glorious Goodwood' but there was nothing glorious about conditions on Sussex Stakes day when torrential rain turned the track into a morass, leading to the eleventh-hour withdrawal of dual Two Thousand Guineas winner Churchill. Ribchester was left with just six opponents and was sent off at 13/8-on, but, in ground which deteriorated almost to the point of becoming unraceable, he was beaten a neck by 20/1-shot Here Comes When. Ribchester made the running but the pace was muddling and less than five lengths covered the seven runners at the post, where Ribchester was rallying, after being headed approaching the final furlong as the Frankie Dettori-ridden Zelzal found a gap between Ribchester and the running rail, a manoeuvre which seemed to contribute to Ribchester's lugging to the right a furlong out (possibly shying away from Dettori's whip). Ribchester's jockey William Buick stopped riding for a few strides but Ribchester picked up again—all too late—and might have got back up in another fifty yards. The stewards held an inquiry to consider why Buick had appeared to ease off—a full transcript of their findings appears in the essay on Here Comes When—and they 'noted' his explanation that he stopped riding because he thought Ribchester was going to run onto the heels of Here Comes When. The stewards also inquired into why Ribchester and 66/1 stablemate Toscanini (who was never dangerous) had failed to parade in the correct order. To crown what must have been a most frustrating afternoon all round for Ribchester's trainer Richard Fahey, the stewards fined him £1,000, a large sum for an offence that can hardly have been said to have inconvenienced racegoers or resulted in them suffering any monetary loss.

Twelve months earlier, Ribchester had gone on after the Sussex Stakes to Deauville for the Prix Jacques le Marois. There is usually two and a half weeks between the two races, as there had been in 2016 (and in 2014 when Kingman completed the double), but there was a gap of just eleven days in the latest season,

Qatar Prix du Moulin de Longchamp, Chantilly—
Ribchester bounces back from a surprise defeat at Goodwood, always doing enough to hold off the improving Taareef; Massaat (striped cap) leads home the others

as a result of most of the summer festivals in Britain falling a week later than usual. Ribchester waited instead for the Qatar Prix du Moulin at Chantilly on 'the day of trials' for the Arc in September. As at Goodwood, he faced six opponents—starting at evens this time—and, with James Doyle deputising for the injured William Buick, Ribchester made no mistakes. Without being as impressive as he had been in either the Lockinge or the Queen Anne, he quickened into the lead over a furlong out and held off the high-class French miler Taareef by three quarters of a length. Ribchester briefly hung left into Taareef's path near the finish but he survived a stewards' inquiry and was clearly the winner on merit, the first two stretching clear of the rest, with the Hungerford Stakes winner Massaat taking third, three and a half lengths behind Taareef.

Ribchester's slight waywardness at the end of his races—he wore a sheepskin noseband throughout his career—was again in evidence when he was beaten a length by the filly Persuasive (with Churchill half a length behind in third) when sent off 2/1 favourite for the Queen Elizabeth II Stakes on British Champions' Day. Reunited with William Buick, Ribchester shaped for a long way as if he was clearly the best and was almost certainly sent to the front too early, taking over on the bridle with more than two furlongs left in a race run in testing conditions and into a strong headwind. Ascot's straight mile is stiff (the raced used to be run on the round course before it became part of Champions' Day) and Ribchester edged right soon after taking the lead and couldn't respond when tackled and headed by the winner a furlong out. Ribchester had been on the go since March but connections decided on one final throw of the dice in the Breeders' Cup Mile at Del Mar only a fortnight after British Champions' Day. Ribchester ran below form and finished out of the first three for only the second time in his career (he'd been demoted after finishing second in the Prix Djebel on the other occasion), beaten a length and three quarters into fifth behind the favourite World Approval after Buick appeared to lose an iron rounding the home turn. Ribchester won three Group 1s as a four-year-old and showed himself the best miler in Europe, but he managed to leave the impression that, but for misfortune (to which his own slight idiosyncrasies made some contribution), he could have ended up with an even better record to take with him to stud. He will stand at Kildangan Stud in County Kildare, Ireland as the winner of four Group 1 races in all, each of them over a mile, and as a dual Royal Ascot winner. His fee in 2018 will be €30,000.

The lengthy, angular Ribchester, who usually took the eye in the preliminaries (looked really well before the Queen Elizabeth), is by Iffraaj who, like Cape Cross (a son of Iffraaj's grandam Park Appeal), looks like developing into an important stallion for Godolphin/Darley. Like Cape Cross (sire of Sea The Stars and Golden Horn), the six- and seven-furlong performer Iffraaj began his stud career at Kildangan

Godolphin's "Ribchester"

at a relatively modest fee (his original fee had been halved to €6,000 by his fourth season) but he has risen through the ranks, helped also by success with his New Zealand-sired crops which have included a New Zealand Derby winner Gingernuts and an Australian Derby winner in Jon Snow, and his fee at Dalham Hall Stud in 2018 will be £40,000, up from £27,500 in the latest season. One of Iffraaj's sons Wootton Bassett, who won the Prix Jean-Luc Lagardere for Ribchester's trainer, sired the 2016 Horse of the Year in Europe, Almanzor. Conditions were not ideal for Ribchester's posed portrait, incidentally, which was taken at Del Mar while he was still in quarantine.

Ribchester (IRE) (b.c. 2013)	Iffraaj (b 2001)	Zafonic (b 1990)	Gone West
			Zaizafon
		Pastorale (ch 1988)	Nureyev
			Park Appeal
	Mujarah (IRE) (b 2008)	Marju (br 1988)	Last Tycoon
			Flame of Tara
		Tanaghum (b 2000)	Darshaan
			Mehthaaf

Ribchester is the first foal out of the Marju mare Mujarah who showed only modest form and was culled by Sheikh Hamdan's Shadwell Stud, making only 18,000 guineas at the December Sales at the end of her three-year-old days (since the success of Ribchester she has been resold to Godolphin and has a colt foal by Dubawi). Mujarah's second foal, the three-year-old Golconda Prince (by Arcano), has run eleven times on the Flat for Ribchester's trainer without winning and has also been tried without success over hurdles. Mujarah may not have shown much on the racecourse but she is a half-sister to several winners over middle distances, including the Curragh Cup winner Tactic and the smart eleven-furlong winner Yaazy, and is out of a useful ten-furlong winner in Tanaghum. Mujarah's grandam Mehthaaf won the Irish One Thousand Guineas for Sheikh Hamdan and was closely related to one of Sheikh Hamdan's July Cup winners Elnadim. Mehthaaf entered Shadwell when her dam Elle Seule was bought, carrying her, for 1,500,000 dollars at the Keeneland November Sale in 1990. Elle Seule was a daughter of Fall Aspen who had compiled an outstanding record as a broodmare. Fall Aspen went on to breed eight pattern or graded winners, a modern record, and had twelve winners in all. She found further fame as the grandam of the short-lived Dubai Millennium (Dubawi's sire) who is the best horse to have carried the Godolphin colours. Ribchester was best at a mile and he acted on firm and soft going (his puzzling defeat in the Sussex came on his only start on heavy). He raced prominently and sometimes made the running. *Richard Fahey*

RICH AGAIN (IRE) 8 b.g. Amadeus Wolf 122 – Fully Fashioned (IRE) 75 (Brief Truce (USA) 126) [2017 81, a90: t5g* t5d* t6g 5g 5g t5.1g t5g^6 t5.1g Dec 5] fairly useful handicapper: won at Newcastle (twice, by length from Foxy Forever second occasion) in January: best at 5f nowadays: acts on polytrack, tapeta and good to firm going: wears headgear: usually races in rear. *James Bethell* **94**

RICH AND FAMOUS (USA) 3 b.g. Bernardini (USA) 132 – Enrichment (USA) (Ghostzapper (USA) 137) [2017 93: 6m^2 6m* 5.1d 5g 6g 6d Jul 29] useful-looking gelding: useful handicapper: won at Doncaster (by 1½ lengths from Ekhtiyaar) in April: stays 6f: acts on good to firm going: front runner/races prominently: sent to USA. *Mark Johnston* **97**

RICHARD PANKHURST 5 ch.h. Raven's Pass (USA) 133 – Mainstay 86 (Elmaamul (USA) 125) [2017 117: 7g 8g^5 8d p7s Sep 30] sturdy horse: smart performer, won Hungerford Stakes in 2016: below best in 2017: stays 1m: acts on good to firm and good to soft going: has worn headgear, including last 2 starts: often races towards rear: has joined S. bin Ghadayer in UAE. *John Gosden* **101**

RICHENZA (FR) 2 b.f. (Apr 22) Holy Roman Emperor (IRE) 125 – Nantha (IRE) 98 (King's Best (USA) 132) [2017 7m 7s^6 7d^2 Sep 5] 42,000Y: first foal: dam 2-y-o 1m winner: fair form: best effort when second in minor event at Goodwood (7 lengths behind Juliet Foxtrot) in September. *Ralph Beckett* **71**

RICH IDENTITY 2 gr.c. (Apr 16) Dubawi (IRE) 129 – Rose Diamond (IRE) 103 (Daylami (IRE) 138) [2017 7s^2 7g^3 8.3g^2 Nov 1] third foal: brother to useful 7f winner (stays 9f) To Dibba and half-brother to smart 1¼m winner Real Smart (by Smart Strike): dam 6f winner (including at 2 yrs) who stayed 1m out of high-class winner up to 7f (2-y-o 6f winner) Tante Rose: fairly useful form: best effort when second in maiden at Yarmouth (½ length behind Regal Reality) in September. *Roger Varian* **81**

RICHIE MCCAW 4 b.g. Zamindar (USA) 116 – Cochin (USA) (Swain (IRE) 134) [2017 85p: 9.9m^5 11.9m^5 Jul 1] fairly useful handicapper, below best both starts in 2017 (reportedly lame second occasion): stays 10.5f: acts on polytrack and good to firm going. *Ian Williams* **77**

RICH LEGACY (IRE) 3 b.f. Holy Roman Emperor (IRE) 125 – Borghesa (GER) (Galileo (IRE) 134) [2017 102: 11.3m^4 12m^4 11.8m^5 14v 12.3v^3 Sep 16] workmanlike filly: useful performer: fourth in Ribblesdale Stakes at Royal Ascot (2¾ lengths behind Coronet) in June: stays 12.5f: acts on good to firm and heavy going: often races towards rear. *Ralph Beckett* **103**

RICHTER SCALE (IRE) 4 gr.f. Lilbourne Lad (IRE) 111 – Danamight (IRE) 72 (Danetime (IRE) 121) [2017 79: f5g^4 t5g^4 Jan 4] fair handicapper: best form at 5f: acts on tapeta and good to firm going: often races prominently. *Iain Jardine* **76**

RICKYROADBOY 2 b.g. (Mar 28) Mazameer (IRE) 107 – Black Baccara 78 (Superior Premium 122) [2017 6g 5.9g Jun 19] well held in 2 minor events. *Mark Walford* **–**

RIDE LIKE THE WIND (IRE) 5 b.g. Lope de Vega (IRE) 125 – Biswa (USA) 48 (Kafwain (USA) 118) [2017 110: p5m 6g 6s May 17] sturdy gelding: smart performer, below best in 2017: stayed 7.5f: acted on polytrack, soft and good to firm going: in hood last 2 starts: tried in tongue tie: dead. *Kevin Ryan* **93**

RIDE THE LIGHTNING 4 b.g. Dalakhani (IRE) 133 – Bright Halo (IRE) (Bigstone (IRE) 126) [2017 89: t12.2m* p14d^2 Feb 2] attractive gelding: fairly useful handicapper: won at Wolverhampton in January: stays 1¾m: acts on polytrack, tapeta and good to soft going: front runner/races prominently: sold to join N. W. Alexander £10,000 in May. *Archie Watson* **90**

RIEN QUE POUR TOI (FR) 4 b.f. Orpen (USA) 116 – Ilinka (FR) (Gentlewave (IRE) 120) [2017 97: 7g^2 7d 8g^6 6d^5 6g^6 Jul 28] €18,000Y: well-made filly: first foal: dam once-raced half-sister to smart French winner up to 10.5f Handsome Maestro: useful performer: won maiden at Fontainebleau and minor event at Chantilly in 2016: second in minor event **97**

at Compiegne in April: not at best after, in Chartwell Fillies' Stakes at Lingfield first occasion: stays 1m: acts on polytrack and soft going: tried in cheekpieces. *T. Castanheira, France*

RIGHT ABOUT NOW (IRE) 3 b.c. Famous Name 124 – Right Reason (IRE) (Manduro (GER) 135) [2017 7s p7g^{2} t7.2g^{4} 8g^{5} 7s^{2} 8.1s p10s Nov 17] tall colt: fair maiden: left Ismail Mohammed after sixth start: best effort at 7f: acts on polytrack: tried in cheekpieces. *Chris Dwyer* **77**

RIGHT ACTION 3 b.g. Dandy Man (IRE) 123 – Rockaby Baby (IRE) 55 (Beckett (IRE) 116) [2017 75: t6g* p6g^{4} 6m^{6} 6m^{4} 6.9g* 7s^{2} 7.6d^{2} 7.6g^{5} 7d^{3} 7d 7m^{2} 7d t7.2d* Dec 26] fairly useful performer: won maiden at Wolverhampton in February, and handicaps at Carlisle in May and again at Wolverhampton (by head from Steal The Scene) in December: stays 7.5f: acts on tapeta, soft and good to firm going: sometimes slowly away, often races prominently. *Richard Fahey* **87**

RIGHT MADAM (IRE) 5 b.m. Jeremy (USA) 122 – Mawaared 61 (Machiavellian (USA) 123) [2017 54: t12.2g 9.9s^{2} 8.9g Jul 9] fair maiden: left Sarah Hollinshead after first start: stays 1½m: acts on tapeta, soft and good to firm going: often wears headgear: usually races in rear. *Andrew Hollinshead, France* **79**

RIGHT REBEL 5 b.m. Cockney Rebel (IRE) 127 – Right Rave (IRE) 84 (Soviet Star (USA) 128) [2017 76: t9.5m p8g^{6} t7.1m 8m^{4} Apr 25] fair handicapper: stays 1m: acts on polytrack, tapeta and good to firm going: front runner/races prominently. *Alan Bailey* **74**

RIGHT TOUCH 7 b.g. Royal Applause 124 – Amira 70 (Efisio 120) [2017 110: 6m^{5} 7g^{5} t7.1s^{6} 7g^{6} 6g 7v 6v^{4} 7.2v^{2} 7d^{4} t6s p7g^{2} Dec 13] lengthy gelding: useful handicapper: fifth at Ripon (1¾ lengths behind Swift Approval) in April: stays 7.5f: acts on polytrack, tapeta, good to firm and heavy going. *Richard Fahey* **103**

RIGHTWAY (IRE) 6 b.g. Cockney Rebel (IRE) 127 – Caeribland (IRE) 90 (Namaqualand (USA)) [2017 76: p8g^{3} f11g^{6} p8g p11g^{5} 11.2g p8d p8g Sep 13] leggy gelding: fair handicapper: stays 8.5f: acts on polytrack, tapeta and good to firm going: usually races prominently. *Tony Carroll* **71**

RIGID ROCK (IRE) 10 b.g. Refuse To Bend (IRE) 128 – Delia (IRE) (Darshaan 133) [2017 64, a54: t7.1m^{6} p7g p7g^{3} p8g p7g 7.5s 5.8g p7s Dec 8] good-topped gelding: modest handicapper: stays 1m: acts on polytrack, good to firm and heavy going: wears headgear: inconsistent. *Adrian McGuinness, Ireland* **54**

RIGOLETTO (SWI) 3 b.c. Zoffany (IRE) 121 – Rumina (FR) (Dashing Blade 117) [2017 7s^{5} 8s* 8d* 8d^{4} 8m^{3} 8.1g* 8g Sep 28] €40,000Y, 170,000 2-y-o: attractive colt: second foal: half-brother to 2-y-o 1m winner Ruanda (by Yeats): dam, Swiss 9f winner, half-sister to smart winner up to 7f Beckermet: useful performer: won maiden at Yarmouth (by length from Mabrook) in June, and handicaps at Newmarket (by ½ length from Endless Gold) later in June and Chepstow (by 4 lengths from Redgrave) in September: stays 1m: acts on soft and good to firm going: sometimes slowly away, often travels strongly: sold 140,000 gns in November, sent to USA. *Luca Cumani* **106**

RIGOLLETO (IRE) 9 b.g. Ad Valorem (USA) 125 – Jallaissine (IRE) (College Chapel 122) [2017 75: p6g^{4} p6m p6g p6g p6g^{4} p6g May 5] lengthy gelding: fair handicapper: races at 6f nowadays: acts on polytrack, good to firm and heavy going: wears headgear: inconsistent. *Anabel K. Murphy* **70**

RINARIA (IRE) 3 b.f. Tamayuz 126 – Riynaaz (IRE) 86 (Cape Cross (IRE) 129) [2017 t8.6g^{2} 8.5m* 8s 8f^{4} 8g^{2} 8.8g^{4} 8d^{2} 8.5m* t8g t8.6g* p8g^{6} Nov 2] €20,000F: lengthy filly: second foal: dam, 9f winner, half-sister to useful 1¼m winner (should have stayed 1½m) Riyalma out of smart 1½m winner Riyafa: fairly useful performer: won maiden at Beverley in April, and handicaps at same course in August and Wolverhampton (by nose from Song Maker) in October: stays 8.5f: acts on polytrack, tapeta, firm and good to soft going: usually wears headgear: tried in tongue tie: often races prominently. *K. R. Burke* **86**

RING EYE (IRE) 9 b.g. Definite Article 121 – Erins Lass (IRE) (Erins Isle 121) [2017 67, a57: 12.1m^{6} 13f 12v 12m^{5} 12m^{5} 16v 11.9m Aug 9] modest handicapper: stays 2m: acts on tapeta and any turf going: has worn headgear: often races in rear: has joined Sarah-Jayne Davies. *John O'Shea* **56**

RIOJA DAY (IRE) 7 b.g. Red Clubs (IRE) 125 – Dai E Dai (USA) (Seattle Dancer (USA) 119) [2017 61§: 8m^{4} 9.1m 8m 7.2d* 7.2s 10g 8.3g^{6} 8g 7.2d^{3} 8.3s* 9.2d 8s^{2} 8v Oct 12] sturdy gelding: fair handicapper: won at Ayr in June and Hamilton (apprentice) in August: stays 8.5f: acts on any turf going: wears headgear: temperamental. *Jim Goldie* **65 §**

RIO RONALDO (IRE) 5 b.g. Footstepsinthesand 120 – Flanders (IRE) 110 (Common Grounds 118) [2017 94: 7g 6m^6 6m 6.1d^3 5m* 5d^4 Jun 29] good-topped gelding: fairly useful handicapper: won at Sandown (by neck from Royal Mezyan) in June: stays 6f: acts on tapeta, soft and good to firm going: tried in blinkers: often starts slowly/races in rear: needs things to go his way. *Mike Murphy* **86**

RIO SANTOS 2 ch.g. (Mar 24) Casamento (IRE) 118 – Midnight Flower (IRE) 102 (Haafhd 129) [2017 5s 6m 6g 7.4v^4 7g 5.1s 6v^5 Sep 17] neat gelding: poor maiden: best effort at 6f. *Rod Millman* **45**

RIO'S CLIFFS 4 b.f. Canford Cliffs (IRE) 133 – What's Up Pussycat (IRE) 100 (Danehill Dancer (IRE) 117) [2017 87: p8d^5 Jan 17] good-topped filly: fairly useful handicapper: stays 9f: acts on polytrack, tapeta, soft and good to firm going: in blinkers last 2 starts. *Martyn Meade* **83**

RIOTICISM (FR) 2 b.f. (Jan 31) Rio de La Plata (USA) 121 – Romanticism (IRE) (Cape Cross (IRE) 129) [2017 4.5d^6 5g* 5g* 5.5g^3 5g^4 5m 5d* 5d^4 5s^4 6s^2 5.5s Nov 13] €8,000Y: rather unfurnished filly: fifth foal: half-sister to 3 winners, including 10.5f-1½m winner Rodyana (by Muhtathir) and 1¼m winner Romanne (by Dr Fong): dam, ran once, closely related to useful performer up to 1m Adventurous and half-sister to useful performer up to 1½m Crimson And Gold: useful performer: won maiden at Bordeaux in March, minor event at Maisons-Laffitte in April and listed race at Vichy (by ½ length from Rimini) in July: second in listed race at Maisons-Laffitte (2 lengths behind Coeur de Beaute) in October: behind in Queen Mary Stakes at Royal Ascot on sixth outing: stays 6f: acts on soft and good to firm going. *M. Palussiere, France* **98**

RIPLEY (IRE) 2 b.f. (Feb 11) Declaration of War (USA) 128 – La Conquerante 110 (Hurricane Run (IRE) 134) [2017 7v^2 7d^6 Aug 19] €90,000Y: useful-looking filly: first foal: dam 1¼m-12.5f winner: fairly useful form: second in maiden at Goodwood (neck behind Roulette) in August: last in listed event 2 weeks later: bred to be suited by 1m+: should still do better. *Charles Hills* **80 p**

RIP N ROAR (IRE) 5 b.g. Rip Van Winkle (IRE) 134 – Aine (IRE) 105 (Danehill Dancer (IRE) 117) [2017 7d 9.8d^{pu} Jun 7] lightly-raced maiden, modest form on debut in 2015: dead. *Tom Clover* **–**

RIPOLL (IRE) 4 b.g. Alfred Nobel (IRE) 110 – Lahu Lady (Red Ransom (USA)) [2017 91: 10m^4 p7g 10m^4 p8d* 8g 8m 7m 8.1g^4 p8g Sep 9] lengthy gelding: fairly useful handicapper on turf, useful on all-weather: won at Kempton in May: stays 1¼m: acts on polytrack, tapeta and good to soft going: wears tongue tie: sold 8,000 gns in October. *Sylvester Kirk* **84 a95**

RIPONIAN 7 ch.g. Trade Fair 124 – Dispol Katie 90 (Komaite (USA)) [2017 59: 7g 7.2d 13.1s 9.2s* 9.2d 7.2s* 8.3g Nov 1] fair handicapper: won at Hamilton in August and Musselburgh in September: effective from 7f to 1¼m: acts on soft and good to firm going: tried in blinkers: wears tongue tie: front runner. *Susan Corbett* **65**

RIPPED (IRE) 5 b.g. Rip Van Winkle (IRE) 134 – State Crystal (IRE) 114 (High Estate 127) [2017 56: 11.3g^3 12m^4 10.2m^5 13.1m May 31] modest maiden: stays 1½m: acts on soft and good to firm going: has worn headgear, including last 2 starts: wears tongue tie: usually races prominently. *Gavin Patrick Cromwell, Ireland* **57**

RIPPER STREET (IRE) 3 b.g. Big Bad Bob (IRE) 118 – Caster Sugar (USA) 87 (Cozzene (USA)) [2017 68: 7m 9g 8g^4 8g 8.2g 10.1g^6 9.1d^3 p10g p10g 10.1g^4 p8g p12g Nov 21] modest maiden: stays 1¼m: acts on good to soft going: usually wears hood. *Christine Dunnett* **55**

RIPTIDE 11 b.g. Val Royal (FR) 127 – Glittering Image (IRE) (Sadler's Wells (USA) 132) [2017 73§: 18g 21.6m^3 16.2m^2 17.2g^4 17.1d 16m 16v^3 18d^2 18v^6 16d Oct 27] good-bodied gelding: fair handicapper: stays 21.5f: acts on good to firm and heavy going: has worn headgear: moody and one to be wary of. *Michael Scudamore* **67 §**

RIP VAN GO 3 b.g. Rip Van Winkle (IRE) 134 – Thousandkissesdeep (IRE) 79 (Night Shift (USA)) [2017 t10.2s May 23] 50/1, well held in maiden at Newcastle: has joined Mike Sowersby. *Sally Haynes* **–**

RIP VAN SUZY (IRE) 4 br.f. Rip Van Winkle (IRE) 134 – Suzy Bliss 105 (Spinning World (USA) 130) [2017 80: p7.5g Dec 19] fairly useful performer at 3 yrs: well held in claimer at Chantilly, only outing in 2017: stays 1m: acts on polytrack, tapeta and good to soft going: tried in visor. *Jo Hughes* **–**

RISING (IRE) 3 b.g. Rip Van Winkle (IRE) 134 – Cause Celebre (IRE) 80 (Peintre Celebre (USA) 137) [2017 72p: 10m 8.3g^{2} 9.9g^{4} 11.4g p12g p8s p12g Dec 21] good-topped gelding: fairly useful maiden: second at Nottingham in August: left Brian Meehan after fifth start: stays 1¼m: acts on good to firm going: tried in tongue tie. *Noel C. Kelly, Ireland* **85**

RISING SUNSHINE (IRE) 4 b.g. Dark Angel (IRE) 113 – Little Audio (IRE) (Shamardal (USA) 129) [2017 57: t8.6g t7.1g p8g^{5} p8g^{5} t7.1g^{4} t7.1g 7m p8d^{4} 8f^{6} t8.6g 7.1g p7g p8g Dec 30] modest maiden: stays 7f: acts on tapeta: usually in headgear in 2017: has worn tongue tie: usually races prominently. *Milton Bradley* **54**

RISTRETTO (USA) 3 b.f. Medaglia d'Oro (USA) 129 – Visit 116 (Oasis Dream 129) [2017 7m^{5} Jul 15] third foal: half-sister to smart 1m (also minor US 8.5f stakes) winner Western Reserve (by Indian Charlie): dam, winner up to 7f (2-y-o 6f winner) who stayed 1¼m, half-sister to very smart 7f-10.4f winner Promising Lead: 9/2, fifth in maiden at Salisbury (4 lengths behind Robin Weathers) in July: will stay 1m: open to improvement. *Ralph Beckett* **68 p**

RITA'S GIRL 3 b.f. Harbour Watch (IRE) 121 – Brazilian Breeze (IRE) 87 (Invincible Spirit (IRE) 121) [2017 59: t7.1g p7g 7.7g^{4} 9.9g 7m^{2} 7g^{5} 8g* 7.7g^{6} 8d* 7.7s Oct 21] modest performer: left K. R. Burke after second start: won maiden at Klampenborg in July and minor event at Gothenburg in October: stays 1m: acts on good to firm and good to soft going: usually wears headgear. *T. Christensen, Denmark* **59**

RITAS LEGACY 3 b.g. Passing Glance 119 – Rita's Rock Ape 87 (Mon Tresor 113) [2017 7s^{6} f7.1g Nov 16] well held in 2 maidens. *Roy Brotherton* **–**

RITA'S MAN (IRE) 3 b.c. Lawman (FR) 121 – French Fern (IRE) 81 (Royal Applause 124) [2017 68: p5g^{5} t7.1g^{4} 8g* 9.8g* 8.1d^{3} 10m 9.9g^{6} 9s p7g p11g 10g^{3} 10s* 11.9g^{3} f12.1g Nov 28] rather leggy colt: fair performer: won handicaps at Redcar and Ripon in May, and seller at Leicester in October: left Richard Hannon after thirteenth start: stays 1½m: acts on tapeta and soft going: tried in cheekpieces: front runner/races prominently. *Keith Dalgleish* **76**

RITASUN (FR) 4 b.g. Monsun (GER) 124 – Baselga (GER) (Second Set (IRE) 127) [2017 80: 9.1m 10g 15.9v p9.4g Dec 15] neat gelding: fairly useful at best, no form in 2017: left Harry Whittington after second start: sometimes wears cheekpieces. *Frau M. Rotering, Germany* **–**

RITE TO REIGN 6 b.g. Tiger Hill (IRE) 127 – Magical Cliche (USA) 86 (Affirmed (USA)) [2017 97: 15.9g t16.3g 16d t12.2g f16.5g^{3} f12.1g^{6} t12.2d^{6} Dec 26] rangy, useful-looking gelding: fairly useful handicapper: stays 16.5f: acts on polytrack, fibresand, good to firm and good to soft going: has worn headgear, including last 4 starts: often races towards rear. *Philip McBride* **87**

RITHA 2 b.f. (Apr 14) Poet's Voice 126 – Danat Al Atheer 99 (Shamardal (USA) 129) [2017 6m 7d 7d Aug 18] useful-looking filly: first foal: dam, winner up to 1¼m (2-y-o 6f winner) who stayed 1½m, half-sister to useful winner up to 1¼m Speedy Approach: no form in minor events/maiden. *Richard Hannon* **–**

RIVAS ROB ROY 2 ch.g. (Mar 13) Archipenko (USA) 127 – Rivas Rhapsody (IRE) 99 (Hawk Wing (USA) 136) [2017 5.1s^{ur} 6m^{2} 7m 7d^{5} 6g^{5} Aug 11] workmanlike gelding: fair maiden: bucked and unseated rider soon after start on debut: best effort at 6f: acts on good to firm going: often races towards rear. *John Gallagher* **67**

RIVENDICATO 2 b.f. (Mar 6) Showcasing 117 – Carsulae (IRE) (Marju (IRE) 127) [2017 6.1m^{pu} 5d Oct 4] 70,000F, 120,000Y: third foal: sister to 7f winner Strada di Carsoli and half-sister to temperamental 1m winner Itsakindamagic (by Mount Nelson): dam unraced half-sister to useful 6f winner Blhadawa: no form. *Joseph Tuite* **–**

RIVEN LIGHT (IRE) 5 b.g. Raven's Pass (USA) 133 – Vivacity (Trempolino (USA) 135) [2017 12d^{3} 8.6d* 7s^{5} 9s* 9v* 9.9g Oct 14] smart performer: won handicap at Galway and minor event at Tipperary, both in August, and listed race at Listowel (by ¾ length from Zawraq) in September: 4½ lengths seventh to Gailo Chop in Ladbrokes Stakes at Caulfield final start (reportedly fractured a joint in off-fore): stays 1½m: acts on heavy going: strong traveller. *W. P. Mullins, Ireland* **112**

RIVER BOYNE (IRE) 2 b.c. (Apr 29) Dandy Man (IRE) 123 – Clytha 57 (Mark of Esteem (IRE) 137) [2017 6g^{6} p7g^{4} t6d^{2} 8f^{2} 9f* Dec 26] €20,000F, €65,000Y: half-brother to several winners, including 5f and (at 2 yrs) 6f winner Harome (by Bahamian Bounty) and 10.7f winner Brosnan (by Champs Elysees): dam maiden half-sister to smart winner up to 1m Ventiquattrofogli: fairly useful performer: won maiden at Santa Anita in December: left Gordon Elliott after third start: stays 9f: acts on tapeta and firm going. *Jeff Mullins, USA* **85**

RIVER CAFE (IRE) 2 b.f. (Feb 9) High Chaparral (IRE) 132 – Dingle View (IRE) 104 (Mujadil (USA) 119) [2017 7.6d^4 7s t8.6g Nov 29] first foal: dam winner up to 1m (2-y-o 5f/6f winner): modest form in minor events. *Sylvester Kirk* **64**

RIVER DART (IRE) 5 ch.g. Dutch Art 126 – Sky Galaxy (USA) 84 (Sky Classic (CAN)) [2017 88: p12g t16.3g^3 p15.8g^3 p15.8g^6 12g 12g^6 Jul 13] tall gelding: fairly useful handicapper: third at Newcastle in January: stays 16.5f: acts on polytrack, tapeta, firm and good to soft going: has worn headgear: often races towards rear. *Tony Carroll* **85**

RIVER ICON 5 b.m. Sixties Icon 125 – River Alder (Alderbrook 120) [2017 10.3v^3 12.1v* 16.3g Oct 14] quite well-made mare: fairly useful form: won maiden at Beverley (by short head from Kohinur) in September: best effort at 1½m: fairly useful hurdler. *Iain Jardine* **88**

RIVER OF GOLD (IRE) 2 ch.c. (Mar 13) New Approach (IRE) 132 – Nahoodh (IRE) 119 (Clodovil (IRE) 116) [2017 t9.5g Nov 18] sixth foal: half-brother to 2-y-o 5f winner Fire Blaze (by Dubawi) and smart/ungenuine winner up to 7f Hawkesbury (by Shamardal): dam won Lowther and Falmouth Stakes: 20/1, very green when well held in minor event at Wolverhampton: should do better. *John Gosden* **– p**

RIVER ROQUETTE (IRE) 3 b.f. Fastnet Rock (AUS) 127 – On The Nile (IRE) 103 (Sadler's Wells (USA) 132) [2017 12d Jun 6] sister to 9f-11.6f winner Storm Rider and closely related to 3 winners, including useful 2-y-o 8.4f winner Pussycat Lips (by Holy Roman Emperor) and 1m-1¼m winner Tommy Toogood (by Danehill): dam 2-y-o 9f winner: 66/1, well held in maiden at Chepstow. *J. S. Moore* **–**

RIVER RULE 2 b.f. (Feb 12) Bated Breath 125 – Ocean Countess (IRE) 78 (Storming Home 128) [2017 6.1g^6 6d 7m^5 Oct 25] rather unfurnished filly: second foal: dam 7f-1m winner who stayed 11f: well held in minor events/maiden. *Stuart Williams* **–**

RIVERSIDE BRIDGE (IRE) 5 gr.g. Rugby (USA) – Sahara Gold (IRE) 47 (Desert Prince (IRE) 130) [2017 f7.1g^2 Dec 29] little form over hurdles: 12/1, well held in maiden at Southwell. *Brian Ellison* **–**

RIVERSIDE WALK 2 b.f. (Jan 29) Showcasing 117 – Distant Waters 66 (Lomitas 129) [2017 t6g^4 t7.1g^2 t7.1g^4 Nov 23] 20,000Y: third foal: sister to winner abroad: dam 11.5f winner: fair form: best effort when second in minor event at Newcastle (2 lengths behind Augenblick) in November. *Keith Dalgleish* **65**

RIVERS OF ASIA 4 ch.g. Medicean 128 – Aliena (IRE) (Grand Lodge (USA) 125) [2017 79: p8d t8.6m 10.3g p8g^5 p8g p7g^4 p8s Nov 23] fair maiden: left Philip McBride after second start: stays 1¼m: acts on polytrack: has worn tongue tie: temperament under suspicion. *Martin Smith* **64**

RIVER WARRIOR 3 b.c. Majestic Warrior (USA) 116 – Triveni (FR) (Lando (GER) 128) [2017 t7.1g t8d t8g f8d^5 10m May 22] no form: in blinkers last 2 starts. *Richard Fahey* **–**

RIVET (IRE) 3 b.c. Fastnet Rock (AUS) 127 – Starship (IRE) 89 (Galileo (IRE) 134) [2017 113: 8m^2 8d^3 10.4g 8f^6 7g 8g Dec 10] sturdy colt: smart performer: won Racing Post Trophy at Doncaster at 2 yrs: placed in 2017 in Craven Stakes at Newmarket (1¾ lengths second to Eminent) and Poule d'Essai des Poulains at Deauville (3 lengths third to Brametot): left William Haggas after fourth start: should stay 1¼m (eighth in Prix du Jockey Club at Chantilly when tried): acts on good to firm and good to soft going: usually leads. *J. Moore, Hong Kong* **113**

RIVIERE ARGENTEE (FR) 3 gr.f. Hurricane Cat (USA) 111 – River Trebor (USA) (Myrakalu (FR)) [2017 83: 10.2m 10g 11.9d^6 14.9g 13.9g 13.9d^6 12.1s* 11.9g^6 Oct 29] fair handicapper: won at Catterick in October: stays 1½m: acts on soft going: wears headgear. *K. R. Burke* **72**

RIZZLE DIZZLE 2 b.f. (Mar 8) Foxwedge (AUS) 128 – Greensand 96 (Green Desert (USA) 127) [2017 6v^4 t6.1g^2 t6.1d^4 Dec 27] €20,000Y: quite attractive filly: half-sister to 3 winners, including 9f-11f winner Fongs Gazelle (by Dr Fong) and 5f (including at 2 yrs) winner Twizzell (by Equiano): dam 2-y-o 6f winner: fair form: best effort when second in minor event at Wolverhampton (¾ length behind Two Weeks) in November. *K. R. Burke* **79**

ROAD TO DUBAI (IRE) 3 ch.c. Aqlaam 125 – Fragrancy (IRE) 106 (Singspiel (IRE) 133) [2017 79p: p7g^4 10.2g^5 9.9f* 11.9d^3 9.9d* 12m^2 10g^4 9.9v^5 12g^4 9.9s^4 10g* 10d* Oct 23] lengthy colt: useful handicapper: won at Goodwood in May and June (apprentice), and Redcar and Windsor (by ¾ length from Bazooka) in October: stays 1½m: acts on tapeta, firm and soft going: tried in cheekpieces. *George Scott* **95**

ROARING FORTIES (IRE) 4 b.g. Invincible Spirit (IRE) 121 – Growling (IRE) (Celtic Swing 138) [2017 6s 7m 6s 7.4d^5 7.2d^2 7m^5 7.2m^2 7v^6 7.2v* 7v^5 7s^4 7d Nov 11] fairly useful handicapper: won at Musselburgh in October: stays 7f: acts on polytrack, good to firm and heavy going: in cheekpieces last 4 starts. *Rebecca Bastiman* **93**

ROARING LION (USA) 2 gr.c. (Mar 11) Kitten's Joy (USA) 128 – Vionnet (USA) (Street Sense (USA) 128) [2017 8d* p8s* 8d* 8d^2 Oct 28] **120 p**

Roaring Lion only lost his unbeaten record when succumbing narrowly in the dramatic late stages of the Racing Post Trophy when putting up an eye-catching performance which marks him down as one of the best three-year-old prospects for 2018. He had spent most of the race covered up last of all, as the field raced into a strong headwind up the Doncaster straight, before making smooth headway to tackle the favourite Saxon Warrior approaching the final furlong. Roaring Lion edged to his left when doing so before the pair were briefly upsides, but when Saxon Warrior himself went left towards the far rail entering the final furlong, Roaring Lion followed suit whilst initially looking like getting the better of the argument. Roaring Lion was never much more than a neck in front, however, and when the two colts were back on an even keel it was Saxon Warrior, with the rail to race against, who proved the stronger, rallying on Roaring Lion's inside to get up by a neck. All things considered, Roaring Lion emerged with plenty of credit against a rival who was also defending an unbeaten record.

The wind was clearly a factor in Roaring Lion's performance at Doncaster, but Roaring Lion's own tendency to hang left had almost cost his unbeaten record a race earlier in the Juddmonte Royal Lodge Stakes at Newmarket. Once again, it was a Ryan Moore-ridden and Aidan O'Brien-trained favourite who proved Roaring Lion's toughest rival, but on this occasion the neck verdict went the way of Roaring Lion. Nelson had won his last two starts at Leopardstown, including a Group 3 contest on Irish Champions' Weekend, and was sent off at 6/5-on, while Roaring Lion had won both his starts in minor events, following a successful debut on the July course with a six-length win under a penalty at Kempton earlier in September and he started at 11/4 at Newmarket. The Salisbury listed winner Mildenberger looked Nelson's other chief rival, while the two others, Petrus and Midnight Wilde, faced far stiffer tasks. Roaring Lion seemed to have the most potential among Nelson's rivals, but his inexperience almost caught him out. As at Doncaster, he made a rapid move to get into the race but, having hit the front, he forfeited his advantage when hanging going into the Dip before knuckling down well on meeting the rising ground and, in the end, having more in hand than the final margin. Nelson and Mildenberger disputed much of the running, the favourite regaining the lead briefly before Roaring Lion came back at him in the dying strides. Mildenberger was a length and a quarter back in third, ahead of Petrus who stuck to his task after coming off the bridle a good way out and Midnight Wilde who was left behind from two out.

Juddmonte Royal Lodge Stakes, Newmarket—
having hung left heading into the Dip, Roaring Lion knuckles down once meeting the rising ground to pull the race out of the fire, beating Nelson (No.4) and Mildenberger

Roaring Lion was a fifth winner of the Royal Lodge for John Gosden, none of his previous winners having been better than the first one, Benny The Dip in 1996. Defeat in the Racing Post Trophy afterwards (he was beaten into third by the Royal Lodge fifth Medaaly) clearly didn't do Benny The Dip's longer-term prospects any harm as he went on to win the Derby, becoming the last winner of the Royal Lodge to do so. Like Benny The Dip, Roaring Lion was bred in North America. His sire Kitten's Joy had already provided his trainer with a couple of earlier smart performers in Cymric, who went close in the Prix Jean-Luc Lagardere, and the stayer Marzocco. Kitten's Joy had Grade 1 winners on turf in the States with Oscar Performance, Sadler's Joy and Divisidero in the latest season, but he was well represented in Europe too by the likes of Princess of Wales's Stakes winner Hawkbill, the previous season's Eclipse winner, and high-class French miler Taareef. In fact, it looked likely at one stage in the latest season that Kitten's Joy, a dual Grade 1 winner on turf himself (also runner-up in the Breeders' Cup Turf and Arlington Million) who was once talked of as an Arc possible, might be coming to Europe to continue his stallion career. 'Disgusted' by the prices his latest crop of yearlings made at Keeneland, Kitten's Joy's owner Ken Ramsey felt the stallion and his progeny would be better received on the other side of the Atlantic. 'I want to see this horse become a Galileo in Europe, and right now he's Rodney Dangerfield,' claimed Ramsey, in a reference to the late American comedian famed for the catch-phrase 'I don't get no respect.' 'He is underappreciated here [in the USA], and I don't think things will get any better.' American breeders certainly haven't been shy about using Kitten's Joy, as he covered more than two hundred mares in 2016 alone, though many of those were Ramsey's own mares. Kitten's Joy will be staying put in Kentucky after all, though; having been based at Ramsey's own farm at a fee of 100,000 dollars, he will be relocating to Hill 'n' Dale Farms, who have bought a fifty per cent interest. He will be standing at a reduced fee of 60,000 dollars in 2018.

Roaring Lion (USA) (gr.c. 2015)	Kitten's Joy (USA) (ch 2001)	El Prado (gr 1989)	Sadler's Wells
			Lady Capulet
		Kitten's First (b 1991)	Lear Fan
			That's My Hon
	Vionnet (USA) (gr or ro 2009)	Street Sense (b or br 2004)	Street Cry
			Bedazzle
		Cambiocorsa (gr or ro 2002)	Avenue of Flags
			Ultrafleet

Qatar Racing's "Roaring Lion"

Roaring Lion was bought for 160,000 dollars at Keeneland as a yearling and is the first foal out of Vionnet, a daughter of Kentucky Derby winner Street Sense. All three of Vionnet's wins, from six and a half to eight and a half furlongs, came on turf. None of those successes came above allowance company, and there is a good chance she was flattered by her close third in the Grade 1 Rodeo Drive Stakes over a mile and a quarter at Santa Anita on her final start when she only just failed to make all after enjoying an uncontested lead. Nonetheless, a couple of Vionnet's half-sisters were Grade 2 winners in California, Schiaparelli at a mile and Moulin de Mougin at nine furlongs, while their dam Cambiocorsa numbered a couple of Grade 3 wins among her nine successes from eighteen starts, both over Santa Anita's downhill six and a half furlong course. Even more adept over the same idiosyncratic turf course was Cambiocorsa's full brother, the very speedy California Flag, whose wins included the Breeders' Cup Turf Sprint the second time it was held there—he actually contested the first five renewals of that event. California Flag also won three editions of the Grade 3 Morvich Handicap over the same course and distance, breaking the track record on the first occasion. The presence of such all-out speed relatively close up in Roaring Lion's pedigree raises doubts about how far he might stay in due course, though he has already shown that he stays a mile well, the emphasis being put on stamina at Doncaster thanks to the headwind, even if the good to soft going was no worse than for Roaring Lion's two other starts on turf. A strong colt who looks sure to train on, Roaring Lion could come up against Saxon Warrior again in the Derby, as well as in the Two Thousand Guineas, though Newmarket rather than Epsom probably offers him the better chance to avenge his Racing Post defeat, his only one to date. *John Gosden*

ROARING RORY 4 ch.g. Sakhee's Secret 128 – Barbieri (IRE) 91 (Encosta de Lago (AUS)) [2017 71: t5d^4 t5.1g* t5.1f^6 5m 5g^3 6g^3 5m^3 5g^5 5m^3 5f* 5d^3 5g f5g* t5g f5g Dec 19] fair performer: won handicaps at Wolverhampton in February and Beverley in July, and claimer at Southwell in November: best form at 5f: acts on fibresand, tapeta, firm and good to soft going: wears cheekpieces. *Ollie Pears* **74**

ROAR (IRE) 3 b.g. Pour Moi (IRE) 125 – Evening Rushour (IRE) 95 (Mull of Kintyre (USA) 114) [2017 81: 7.6s^6 10g* 12d^4 12s^3 12g^6 Sep 28] strong, good-topped gelding: fairly useful handicapper: won at Newmarket in July: stays 1½m: acts on soft and good to firm going: front runner/races prominently: sold to join Roger Charlton 30,000 gns in November. *Brian Ellison* **89**

ROBANNE 4 b.f. Paco Boy (IRE) 129 – Arctic Song (Charnwood Forest (IRE) 125) [2017 103: p8g^4 7d 7m May 25] lengthy filly: useful performer: stays 1m: acts on soft going. *William Knight* **96**

ROBBEN 5 b.g. Dutch Art 126 – Little Greenbird 39 (Ardkinglass 114) [2017 65: p15.8g^6 Jan 4] modest maiden: stays 1¾m: acts on polytrack, tapeta, good to firm and good to soft going: wears headgear: often starts slowly: sold £800, sent to Germany. *Alexandra Dunn* **55**

ROBBEN RAINBOW 3 b.g. Delegator 125 – Sally Can Wait (Sakhee (USA) 136) [2017 83: 6g 5m 6m^6 5s^6 Aug 1] fairly useful 6f winner at 2 yrs, disappointing since: races in rear. *David Barron* **–**

ROBBIAN 6 b.g. Bertolini (USA) 125 – Crathes 53 (Zilzal (USA) 137) [2017 59: f6g f5g 5d 6v^6 6.1g^3 6d^5 6d^4 6d 6s^3 6v^6 Nov 7] modest handicapper: stays 6f: acts on heavy going. *Charles Smith* **55**

ROBBIE ROO ROO 4 br.f. Kheleyf (USA) 116 – Haiti Dancer 64 (Josr Algarhoud (IRE) 118) [2017 66: 6m^5 p6g^3 6m^2 p7g* 7d^3 t7.2g^2 p6s* 7s t6.1g p7s Dec 8] tall filly: modest handicapper on turf, fair on all-weather: won at Kempton in June and September: stays 7f: acts on polytrack, tapeta, soft and good to firm going: wears headgear/tongue tie. *Mrs Ilka Gansera-Leveque* **63** **a70**

ROBERO 5 b.g. Piccolo 121 – Ceilidh Band (Celtic Swing 138) [2017 83: f7g^2 p8g^2 6m* t6s^5 6d* 7g^5 6g 7d 7.2v^3 6d 7d Nov 11] lengthy gelding: useful handicapper: won at Ascot in May and Pontefract (by 2 lengths from Mishaal) in July: best at 6f/7f nowadays: acts on all-weather, good to firm and good to soft going: usually races prominently. *Michael Easterby* **101**

ROBIN OF NAVAN (FR) 4 ch.c. American Post 121 – Cloghran (FR) (Muhtathir 126) [2017 116: 9.9m^4 8.9g^2 9.9m* 11.9g 8d^4 9.9d^5 9m^2 9.9g Dec 10] rangy colt: smart performer: won La Coupe at Chantilly (by ½ length from Garlingari) in June: second in **117**

Prix d'Ispahan on same course (beaten neck by Mekhtaal) and Darley Stakes at Newmarket (1¼ lengths behind Monarchs Glen): refused to settle when eighth in Hong Kong Cup at Sha Tin final outing: stays 1½m: acts on polytrack, soft and good to firm going: usually races close up. *Harry Dunlop*

ROBINSON CRUSOE (IRE) 2 b.c. (Apr 7) Footstepsinthesand 120 – Corrozal (GER) (Cape Cross (IRE) 129) [2017 6m⁵ 7d⁶ 7s⁶ 7d⁵ Oct 30] useful-looking colt: fair form: best effort at 7f. *Richard Hannon* **71**

ROBIN'S PURSE 3 b.f. Sir Percy 129 – Morant Bay (IRE) 80 (Montjeu (IRE) 137) [2017 66: p7g 7m 7d⁵ Jul 11] modest maiden at 2 yrs, no form in 2017. *Charles Hills* **–**

ROBIN WEATHERS (USA) 3 ch.g. Elusive Quality (USA) – Sharnberry 107 (Shamardal (USA) 129) [2017 7m* 8g⁶ 7d 7d 7d p7s⁴ Dec 1] good-topped gelding: first foal: dam winner up to 1m (2-y-o 6f winner): fairly useful performer: won maiden at Salisbury (by nose from Killay) in July: should stay 1m: acts on polytrack and good to firm going. *William Haggas* **84**

ROBOT BOY (IRE) 7 ch.g. Shamardal (USA) 129 – Pivotal's Princess (IRE) 107 (Pivotal 124) [2017 105: p6m t5.1g* p5f³ p5g² 5s 5m⁶ t5g⁵ 5g 5d 5.4d 5v² Sep 9] strong gelding: useful handicapper: won at Wolverhampton (by 1¼ lengths from Bowson Fred) in February: third at Lingfield (½ length behind Encore d'Or) in March and second at Kempton (¾ length behind A Momentofmadness) in April: best at 5f: acts on polytrack, tapeta and any turf going: has worn headgear. *David Barron* **107**

ROB'S LEGACY 4 ch.g. Phoenix Reach (IRE) 124 – Clumber Pursuits (Pastoral Pursuits 127) [2017 –: 16g 16.2m⁶ 11.5g⁵ 14d f16.5g⁵ 16s 13.1v⁶ Oct 12] modest maiden: best effort at 13f: has worn headgear. *Shaun Harris* **51**

ROC ASTRALE (IRE) 3 ch.g. Teofilo (IRE) 126 – Lumiere Astrale (FR) (Trempolino (USA) 135) [2017 p10g³ Apr 8] €110,000Y: fourth foal: half-brother to 3 winners, including useful 13.5f winner Theme Astral (by Cape Cross) and useful 7f-1m winner Feed The Goater (by Fastnet Rock): dam, 12.5f winner, half-sister to smart 6.5f-1¼m winner Desert Blanc: 7/1, third in maiden at Lingfield (3¼ lengths behind Dubai Horizon) in April: will be suited by 1½m: capable of better. *Amanda Perrett* **86 p**

ROCKABILLY RIOT (IRE) 7 br.g. Footstepsinthesand 120 – Zawariq (IRE) 62 (Marju (IRE) 127) [2017 67: 11.2g Jul 14] modest handicapper: below form sole start on Flat in 2017: stays 14.5f: acts on polytrack, tapeta, soft and good to firm going: has worn headgear: tried in tongue tie. *Martin Todhunter* **–**

ROCK A DOODLE DOO (IRE) 10 b.g. Oratorio (IRE) 128 – Nousaiyra (IRE) (Be My Guest (USA) 126) [2017 t12.4g⁴ 14d t12.4s Sep 8] good-bodied gelding: modest handicapper nowadays: stays 1¾m: acts on polytrack, soft and good to firm going: has worn headgear. *Sean Regan* **51**

ROCKALATER 3 b.f. Delegator 125 – Rock Candy (IRE) (Rock of Gibraltar (IRE) 133) [2017 –: t7.1g t6m⁶ p7g⁴ p7g f8d 5.1s 6.1g Oct 9] sturdy filly: poor maiden: left Sylvester Kirk after fifth start: stays 7f: acts on polytrack. *John Spearing* **48**

ROCK CHIC 2 ch.f. (Feb 20) Pastoral Pursuits 127 – Glittering Prize (UAE) 72 (Cadeaux Genereux 131) [2017 6.1m 7v⁶ Oct 4] well held in minor events: dead. *Rod Millman* **–**

ROCKESBURY 2 b.g. (Feb 28) Foxwedge (AUS) 128 – Nellie Ellis (IRE) 63 (Compton Place 125) [2017 5g 5m t5.1g⁶ Nov 7] well held in minor events: tried in blinkers. *Kevin Frost* **–**

ROCKET MAN DAN (IRE) 2 b.g. (Mar 28) Dandy Man (IRE) 123 – Manalisa (IRE) (Manduro (GER) 135) [2017 5g 5m² 5s⁶ 5m³ 5m 5d 5d 5s⁵ t7.1g t5.1m Oct 28] useful-looking gelding: fair maiden in Britain: sometimes in headgear: in tongue tie last 3 starts: sometimes slowly away: sold 4,500 gns, sent to Spain, where won over 6.5f at Dos Hermanas in December. *Keith Dalgleish* **65**

ROCKET RONNIE (IRE) 7 b.g. Antonius Pius (USA) 123 – Ctesiphon (USA) 55 (Arch (USA) 127) [2017 79d: t8.6m f8g⁶ p8d⁵ p10g⁴ 8f t8.6g⁵ 8g⁵ t8.6g³ 8g⁶ Aug 17] strong, good-bodied gelding: poor on turf, modest on all-weather nowadays: stays 1¼m: acts on polytrack and any turf going: sometimes wears headgear: tried in tongue tie: usually slowly away: modest maiden over hurdles. *Brian Barr* **45 a57**

ROCK HILL (IRE) 2 br.g. (Mar 17) Rock of Gibraltar (IRE) 133 – Pascali 61 (Compton Place 125) [2017 5m 5d⁵ 5d⁶ 5v⁶ 6d Oct 30] fair maiden: best effort at 5f: acts on good to soft going. *Paul Midgley* **65**

ROCK ICON 4 b.g. Sixties Icon 125 – Monashee Rock (IRE) 78 (Monashee Mountain (USA) 115) [2017 67: 8d* 10d^{3} p8g^{5} Dec 13] rather leggy gelding: fair handicapper: won at Brighton (apprentice) in August: left Jo Hughes after but rejoined yard after final start: stays 1¼m: acts on firm and good to soft going: in hood last 3 starts: front runner/races prominently, often freely. *J. S. Moore* **66**

ROCKIES SPIRIT 2 br.c. (Mar 10) Swiss Spirit 117 – Red Mischief (IRE) 72 (Red Clubs (IRE) 125) [2017 6m^{4} 6d* 6m^{2} Aug 26] 10,000F: second foal: half-brother to useful 2-y-o 6f winner Waqaas (by Showcasing): dam, 2-y-o 6f winner, half-sister to useful 5f winner Guto: fairly useful form: won minor event at Thirsk (by 1¾ lengths from Super Major) in July: best effort when second in similar event at Newmarket (¾ length behind Betty F) in August: raced only at 6f. *Denis Quinn* **82**

ROCKIN FELLA (IRE) 2 b.c. (Apr 9) Society Rock (IRE) 126 – Dearest Daisy 84 (Forzando 122) [2017 5m^{3} 5g^{3} 5f^{2} 5s 5g^{4} 6g* 7g Dec 29] £56,000Y: half-brother to several winners, including useful 2-y-o 5f winner Excel Bolt (by Exceed And Excel) and 1m winner Clive Clifton (by Wootton Bassett): dam 2-y-o 5f winner: fairly useful performer: left K. R. Burke, won minor event at Doha in December: stays 6f: acts on firm going: tried in cheekpieces: often races prominently. *H. Al Ramzani, Qatar* **85**

ROCKING RUDOLPH (USA) 4 b.f. Discreetly Mine (USA) 120 – Empire Spring (USA) (Empire Maker (USA) 129) [2017 –: f5s t5.1g Nov 25] fairly useful form when winning on debut in 2015, lightly raced and no show since: raced only at 5f: acts on fibresand: tried in hood. *Robert Cowell* **–**

ROCK ISLAND LINE 3 b.g. Haafhd 129 – Diablo Dancer 78 (Zafeen (FR) 123) [2017 7g^{6} 8g 8g 9.8d^{6} 10d^{4} t12.4g^{6} 10d^{6} t9.5g* Nov 7] fair handicapper: won at Wolverhampton in November: stays 1¼m: acts on tapeta and good to soft going: sometimes in headgear. *Mark Walford* **68**

ROCKLEY POINT 4 b.g. Canford Cliffs (IRE) 133 – Statua (IRE) 98 (Statoblest 120) [2017 86: f7g p6g^{2} p7g^{3} t7.1g^{5} 6m 6s 7m^{6} 6m t6.1g^{6} t6.1g 10.1d t6.1g^{2} t6.1g^{6} p7g p7s^{3} Dec 8] workmanlike gelding: fair handicapper on turf, fairly useful on all-weather: third at Chelmsford in March: stays 1m: acts on polytrack, tapeta and firm going: has worn headgear, including last 4 starts. *Paul D'Arcy* **76 a83**

ROCKLIFFE 4 b.g. Notnowcato 128 – Hope Island (IRE) 69 (Titus Livius (FR) 115) [2017 68: 8g^{6} 9.9m 12d^{4} 9.9m 8m^{6} 8.3g 8s^{3} 9.8g^{2} Aug 29] modest handicapper: stays 11.5f: acts on polytrack and soft going: in cheekpieces last 2 starts. *Micky Hammond* **56**

ROCK'N GOLD 4 b.g. Fastnet Rock (AUS) 127 – La Concorde (FR) 79 (Sadler's Wells (USA) 132) [2017 80: t7.1g p8g 8v 10d 10.2d 10.2g p12g^{2} Dec 6] modest handicapper nowadays: stays 1½m: acts on polytrack and good to soft going: tried in blinkers: often races in rear. *Adrian Wintle* **64**

ROCK N ROLLA (IRE) 3 ch.g. Intikhab (USA) 135 – Fantastic Opinion (IRE) 60 (Fantastic Light (USA) 134) [2017 86: 8m 10.3d 8s^{4} 7d^{6} 7.2d^{6} 8.9s^{2} t8d 7.2s 8v^{6} t7.2m^{5} t8.6g^{4} Nov 11] fairly useful handicapper: second at Musselburgh in September: stays 9f: acts on tapeta, best turf form on soft/heavy going: has worn headgear, including last 2 starts. *Keith Dalgleish* **85**

ROCK N ROLL GLOBAL (IRE) 3 ch.g. Power 117 – Laughter (IRE) 87 (Sadler's Wells (USA) 132) [2017 67p: p8g^{4} p7d^{3} 8m 9.9f 13m^{4} p8d^{3} 10d^{2} Aug 21] workmanlike gelding: fair maiden: stays 1¼m: acts on polytrack and good to soft going: tried in blinkers: usually races towards rear. *Richard Hughes* **74**

ROCK OF AMERICA (USA) 3 b.g. Arch (USA) 127 – Elusive Noise (USA) (Elusive Quality (USA)) [2017 t5g* p5g^{2} t5.1g^{4} 5m^{5} 5f^{4} 5m^{4} p5d^{2} Sep 28] fairly useful performer: won maiden at Newcastle in March: best effort when second in handicap at Chelmsford (½ length behind Alsvinder) in September: raced only at 5f: acted on polytrack and tapeta: often raced prominently: dead. *David O'Meara* **94**

ROCK OF ESTONIA (IRE) 2 ch.c. (Feb 19) Society Rock (IRE) 126 – Estonia 82 (Exceed And Excel (AUS) 126) [2017 5m* 5f* May 1] 68,000F, 90,000Y: close-coupled colt: second foal: half-brother to 5f winner Tallinski (by Mayson): dam 5f winner: fairly useful form: won minor events at Windsor (by neck from Angel of The South) in April and Bath (by ¾ length from Joe's Spirit) in May: should still improve. *Charles Hills* **80 p**

ROCK OF MONACO 4 b.f. Monsieur Bond (IRE) 120 – Melandre 74 (Lujain (USA) 119) [2017 –: t8.6g t7.2g t8s t8.6g^{6} 9.9d f7.1g Aug 28] poor handicapper: stays 7f: acts on tapeta: often wears headgear. *Antony Brittain* **47**

ROCK ON BAILEYS 2 ch.f. (Apr 16) Rock of Gibraltar (IRE) 133 – Ring For Baileys 88 (Kyllachy 129) [2017 6g 5d^4 p6g^6 6d t5g^2 p5s* Nov 23] first foal: dam, 5f winner, half-sister to useful winner up to 1m (stayed 10.5f) Bahia Breeze: fair performer: won nursery at Chelmsford in November: may prove best at 5f: acts on polytrack and tapeta: in headgear last 4 starts. *Chris Dwyer* **66**

ROCK ON BERTIE (IRE) 2 b.g. (Feb 23) Rock of Gibraltar (IRE) 133 – Princess Banu 74 (Oasis Dream 129) [2017 5m 5f t6g 6g 6m^5 7d 6.1g^2 6d^3 7g^3 t7.1g^5 6g^5 t7.1g^2 t8s^3 f8.1g Dec 11] modest maiden: stays 1m: acts on tapeta and good to soft going: usually wears cheekpieces. *Nigel Tinkler* **63**

ROCK ON BOLLINSKI 7 b.g. Bollin Eric 125 – Bred For Pleasure (Niniski (USA) 125) [2017 81§: 21.6m 16d 17.1d^6 18g 18v^5 15.9s Oct 31] workmanlike gelding: fair handicapper: stays 2m: acts on heavy going: wears cheekpieces: usually slowly away: temperamental. *Brian Ellison* **69 §**

ROCK ON DANDY (FR) 3 gr.g. Rajsaman (FR) 121 – Minnie's Mystery (FR) (Highest Honor (FR) 124) [2017 62: 8.2g^5 10m^2 11.4m^6 p12g 10.1g^2 p12g* p12g* p12g^5 Dec 21] fairly useful handicapper: won at Dundalk (twice) in December: left Harry Dunlop after fifth start: stays 1½m: acts on polytrack and good to firm going: wears headgear: in tongue tie last 3 starts: often races prominently. *F. Birrane, Ireland* **83**

ROCK ON ROSIE (IRE) 8 b.m. Gamut (IRE) 124 – Macs Goose (Kayf Tara 130) [2017 69: t9.5m^4 t12.2g^6 12s 12s p12g p10.7g^5 p10.7g Nov 8] fair handicapper: stays 1½m: acts on polytrack, tapeta and good to soft going: usually wears headgear: usually races close up. *Adrian Brendan Joyce, Ireland* **66**

ROCK PALM (IRE) 4 b.f. Rock of Gibraltar (IRE) 133 – Palm Pilot (IRE) 92 (Oasis Dream 129) [2017 68: 11.8g Jun 27] tall filly: fair maiden, well held sole start in 2017: stays 9f: acts on good to firm going: tried in cheekpieces. *Laura Morgan* **–**

ROCKSETTE 3 b.f. Mount Nelson 125 – Native Nickel (IRE) (Be My Native (USA) 122) [2017 p7g p7g^5 7g^5 7.6d^2 10d^4 p10g^5 9.9s^2 9.9v^2 Oct 19] rather leggy filly: half-sister to several winners, including smart winner up to 9f Five Cents (2-y-o 7f winner by Exceed And Excel): dam unraced: modest maiden: stays 1¼m: acts on heavy going. *Philip Hide* **62**

ROCKSHINE 3 b.f. Fastnet Rock (AUS) 127 – Shine Like A Star 60 (Fantastic Light (USA) 134) [2017 72: 7.1s^5 10.1d t8.6g^6 Nov 7] fair maiden at 2 yrs, below form in 2017: stays 8.5f: acts on good to firm going. *Richard Hannon* **54**

ROCK SONG 8 b.g. Rock of Gibraltar (IRE) 133 – Jackie's Opera (FR) (Indian Ridge 123) [2017 82: t8.6g^6 Apr 5] tall gelding: fairly useful handicapper, below best sole start in 2017: stays 1½m: acts on polytrack, tapeta, firm and good to soft going: usually races prominently. *John Mackie* **71**

ROCKSPIRIT (IRE) 4 b.g. Fastnet Rock (AUS) 127 – Phillippa (IRE) (Galileo (IRE) 134) [2017 112: p10g^4 Apr 13] rangy, useful-looking gelding: smart performer: fourth in handicap at Chelmsford only start in 2017: stays 1½m: acts on polytrack, soft and good to firm going: sent to Hong Kong. *Marco Botti* **109**

ROCK STEADY (IRE) 4 ch.g. Intikhab (USA) 135 – Mannsara (IRE) (Royal Academy (USA) 130) [2017 106: p12m^2 p12g^5 11.8d p16d Nov 22] leggy gelding: useful handicapper: second at Lingfield (½ length behind Pinzolo) in January: below best last 2 starts: stays 1¾m: acts on polytrack, tapeta, good to firm and heavy going: tried in cheekpieces. *Roger Charlton* **104**

ROCK WARBLER (IRE) 4 ch.g. Raven's Pass (USA) 133 – Rare Tern (IRE) 96 (Pivotal 124) [2017 76: t8g* t8g^2 t7.1d^2 7g 7f^6 8d t8g^5 t7.1d* p8g^6 t7.1g^6 t8.6g^3 t8g t7.2g^4 t7.2d Dec 26] fair handicapper on turf, fairly useful on all-weather: won at Newcastle in January and September: stays 8.5f: acts on polytrack and tapeta: usually wears hood: wears tongue tie. *Oliver Greenall* **74 a87**

ROCKWELL LLOYD (IRE) 2 b.c. (Apr 6) Fast Company (IRE) 126 – Lucy Liu (IRE) 59 (Grand Lodge (USA) 125) [2017 7g 7.6s 7d^5 8m Aug 27] close-coupled colt: little form: tried in visor: sold £1,000, sent to Germany. *Mick Channon* **–**

ROCKWOOD 6 b.g. Rock of Gibraltar (IRE) 133 – Hannah Frank (IRE) (High Chaparral (IRE) 132) [2017 81: 8g* 8m^5 8.3m* t8s^4 8.8m^5 t10.2s^4 10.3g^5 8d^4 t8g Dec 6] fairly useful handicapper on turf, fair on all-weather: won at Pontefract in April and Hamilton (by neck from Ionization) in May: stays 1¼m: acts on fibresand, tapeta, good to firm and heavy going: wears headgear: tried in tongue tie: often races in rear. *Karen McLintock* **84 a78**

ROCKY ELSOM (USA) 10 b.g. Rock of Gibraltar (IRE) 133 – Bowstring (IRE) 105 (Sadler's Wells (USA) 132) [2017 p15.8g⁶ 12s 18d t14g Oct 27] sturdy gelding: fair handicapper in 2014, little impact in 2017, including over hurdles: left Sophie Leech after second start: stays 1½m: acts on polytrack and soft going: tried in cheekpieces: sometimes in tongue tie. *Adrian Wintle* **59**

ROCKY SHORES (IRE) 2 b.c. (Feb 9) Canford Cliffs (IRE) 133 – Josphiel (IRE) 71 (Okawango (USA) 115) [2017 8d 8.3v⁶ Nov 8] fair form in minor event/maiden. *Mick Channon* **68**

ROCKY TWO (IRE) 7 ch.g. Rock of Gibraltar (IRE) 133 – Toorah Laura La (USA) (Black Minnaloushe (USA) 123) [2017 45: t16.3g Jan 3] poor handicapper nowadays: stays 1¾m: acts on soft and good to firm going: often wears cheekpieces: modest hurdler. *Philip Kirby* **–**

ROCOCO 2 b.f. (Mar 18) Dubawi (IRE) 129 – Intrigued 105 (Darshaan 133) [2017 7d⁵ Nov 4] sister to 8.6f winner (stays 1½m) All The Rage and half-sister to several winners, including smart 1¼m/11f winner Michelangelo and useful 1½m-18.7f winner No Heretic (both by Galileo): dam 2-y-o 8.5f winner who stayed 1½m: 4/1, fifth in minor event at Newmarket (7¾ lengths behind Nawassi) in November, not knocked about: will be suited by 1m+: sure to improve. *John Gosden* **57 p**

ROCUS (IRE) 2 b.g. (Mar 18) Rock of Gibraltar (IRE) 133 – Mythologie (FR) (Bering 136) [2017 7d t7.2g Aug 10] well held in 2 minor events. *Mark Usher* **–**

RODAINI (USA) 3 ch.g. Exchange Rate (USA) 111 – Blessings Count (USA) 63 (Pulpit (USA) 117) [2017 104p: 7m² 8m⁵ 10m 8g* Aug 29] good-bodied gelding: useful performer: won minor event at Ripon in August: second in listed Free Handicap at Newmarket (2¾ lengths behind Whitecliffsofdover) in April: stays 1m: acts on good to firm going: wore headgear in 2017. *Simon Crisford* **101**

RODDY (IRE) 3 ch.g. Roderic O'Connor (IRE) 119 – Sweet Chilli (IRE) 87 (Intikhab (USA) 135) [2017 10g⁵ 10d² 10.2d² Aug 5] £20,000Y: first foal: dam 2-y-o 5f winner: fairly useful form: second in maidens at Pontefract in July and Doncaster in August: remains open to improvement. *Tom Tate* **82 p**

ROD OF IRON 4 br.g. Alkaased (USA) 127 – Leading Star 47 (Motivator 131) [2017 46: 11.6s⁵ 11.9g⁵ 11.6d⁴ Aug 30] good-topped gelding: poor maiden: best effort at 11.5f: tried in visor. *Michael Madgwick* **47**

ROGER THORPE 8 b.g. Firebreak 125 – Nunthorpe 79 (Mystiko (USA) 124) [2017 69: 8.2g 7g f7.1g f5g f8.1g Dec 21] fair handicapper, no form in 2017: tried in cheekpieces. *John Balding* **–**

ROGUE 2 b.g. (Feb 25) Epaulette (AUS) 126 – Miskin Diamond (IRE) 53 (Diamond Green (FR) 121) [2017 6s⁴ 6.5g⁴ 7d⁴ 6m* 7g* 7d⁴ Oct 28] 24,000F, 45,000Y: sturdy gelding: second foal: half-brother to winner abroad by Intikhab: dam, unreliable 1¼m winner, half-sister to useful 6f winner Catch A Glimpse: fairly useful performer: won minor event at Salisbury in August and nursery at Newbury (by short head from Red Roman) in September: stays 7f: acts on good to firm going: front runner/races prominently. *Richard Hannon* **86**

ROGUE HERO (IRE) 2 b.g. (Feb 24) Oasis Dream 129 – Pink Damsel (IRE) 86 (Galileo (IRE) 134) [2017 6g t7.2g⁴ t8.6d⁴ Dec 9] fair form: best effort when fourth in minor event at Wolverhampton (5¼ lengths behind Mr Reckless) in December: in tongue tie last 2 starts. *Paul Cole* **68**

ROJINA (IRE) 4 ch.f. Intense Focus (USA) 117 – Hurricane Havoc (IRE) 106 (Hurricane Run (IRE) 134) [2017 52: p5g⁵ p5m⁵ t5.1g p5g t5.1g 5.3g⁵ 5.2m⁶ t7.1g⁶ 6g 7.6g May 27] poor maiden: best effort at 6f: acts on polytrack: has worn blinkers. *Lisa Williamson* **45**

ROLAND ROCKS (IRE) 2 b.c. (Apr 10) Red Jazz (USA) 125 – Toy Show (IRE) 86 (Danehill (USA) 126) [2017 5m* 6d³ 6g 7g 5g⁵ Sep 15] €10,000Y, 26,000 2-y-o: compact colt: half-brother to several winners, including useful winner up to 1¼m Wing Play (2-y-o 8.6f winner, by Hawk Wing) and winner up to 1m Cleveland Street (2-y-o 5f winner, by Windsor Knot): dam 1¼m winner (including at 2 yrs): fairly useful performer: won maiden at Musselburgh in June: stays 6f: acts on good to firm and good to soft going: tried in cheekpieces: usually races nearer last than first. *John Ryan* **89**

ROLANNA (IRE) 5 b.m. Strategic Prince 114 – Dalaika (CAN) (Rhythm (USA)) [2017 59: 12s³ 11.3g⁶ 17.1d 11.8v Aug 28] modest handicapper: stays 17f: acts on soft going: wears headgear: often races prominently. *W. J. Martin, Ireland* **56**

ROLLER 4 b.g. Rail Link 132 – Buffering 101 (Beat Hollow 126) [2017 81p: t7.1g² t8g⁶ 8g* 8.3m³ 8d² 8m⁶ Jun 15] useful handicapper: won at Redcar in April: stays 8.5f: acts on tapeta, good to firm and good to soft going: remains open to improvement. *Michael Easterby* **96 p**

ROLLING DICE 6 b.g. Rail Link 132 – Breathing Space (USA) (Expelled (USA) 116) [2017 f12.1g 10m 8g 8d⁵ 7.4v³ 7s⁴ 8v⁵ Oct 19] good-quartered gelding: fair handicapper: stays 8.5f: acts on heavy going: usually wears headgear. *Dominic Ffrench Davis* **66**

ROLLING MAUL (IRE) 9 b.g. Oscar (IRE) 122 – Water Sports (IRE) 79 (Marju (IRE) 127) [2017 11.6f* 16v* 16g* 16v⁴ 18m Oct 14] sturdy gelding: fairly useful performer: won maiden at Bath in June, and handicaps at Ffos Las and Newmarket (by head from Addicted To You) in August: stays 2m: acts on any turf going: tried in blinkers: usually races towards rear: fairly useful hurdler: best treated with caution. *Peter Bowen* **93 §**

ROLL ON RORY 4 b.g. Mullionmileanhour (IRE) 116 – Fangfoss Girls 68 (Monsieur Bond (IRE) 120) [2017 101: 7.1g 7f 6s 7m 7d 7g⁶ 8.3g⁴ 7d⁴ 7.4g³ 7d² t8d⁴ 8d* t9.5g Nov 29] compact gelding: useful handicapper: won at Newmarket (by 2 lengths from Shamrokh) in November: stays 8.5f: acts on tapeta, soft and good to firm going: wears headgear: front runner/races prominently. *Jason Ward* **96**

ROLY POLY (USA) 3 b.f. War Front (USA) 119 – Misty For Me (IRE) 122 (Galileo (IRE) 134) [2017 115: 7m 8d⁶ 8d² 8m² 8m* 8g* 8d⁶ 8g* 8f 8g Dec 10] **121**

The regularity with which Ballydoyle turns out big race winners might convey the misleading impression that everything there generally goes smoothly. Odd as it may seem, in a season in which Aidan O'Brien broke the world record for the number of Group/Grade 1 wins on the Flat in a calendar year, an awful lot didn't go to plan. Dual Guineas winner Churchill looked a banker to pick up further Group 1s after his victories at Newmarket and the Curragh, for example, and his contemporary Caravaggio—who had also been a leading two-year-old—looked the sprint champion-elect after winning the Commonwealth Cup at Royal Ascot. In fact, Churchill didn't win again in five starts after completing his Guineas double and Caravaggio, unbeaten up to the Commonwealth Cup, won only one of his four subsequent races. Ballydoyle looked to have a very strong hand with its fillies at the start of the season too. The outstanding Minding, a tough and versatile performer who had won five Group 1s as a three-year-old, stayed in training and looked to have the world at her feet, while the latest crop of classic fillies were a good bunch too, headed by Rhododendron whose victory in the Fillies' Mile at Newmarket represented the best form in the division and rightly earned her ante-post favouritism over the winter for the One Thousand Guineas and Oaks (both of which Minding had won). Minding accounted for three rivals on her reappearance in the Mooresbridge Stakes at Naas at the beginning of May, but that turned out to be her last appearance on a racecourse. A pastern injury proved more serious than originally thought and her trainer first revealed that her racing future was 'uncertain' in early-July, on the day he had to announce that Derby winner Wings of Eagles had suffered a career-ending injury when finishing third in the Irish Derby, and also that another of the

Tattersalls Falmouth Stakes, Newmarket—
Roly Poly makes all under Ryan Moore to gain a deserved first Group 1 victory, finding plenty to repel the Godolphin pair Wuheida and Arabian Hope (hood)

Prix Rothschild, Deauville—
Roly Poly again demonstrates all her battling qualities as she comes out on top in a bunched finish, with Via Ravenna (left), Siyoushake (spots on cap) and Qemah (right) just behind

stable's four-year-old fillies, the Dahlia Stakes winner Somehow, had had to be put down after suffering an inoperable fracture to a hind leg on the Ballydoyle gallops. Rhododendron meanwhile had been beaten in both the One Thousand Guineas and the Oaks, and also in the Prix de Diane during which she bled, and, in fact, she didn't open her three-year-old account until October when she finally got her head in front in the Prix de l'Opera on Arc weekend.

Stablemate Winter (who had been 33/1 in places a week before the race) unexpectedly defeated Rhododendron in the One Thousand Guineas and went on to add the Irish One Thousand Guineas and Royal Ascot's Coronation Stakes on her next two starts, her splendid performances putting her in pole position among the Ballydoyle fillies, after Rhododendron's defeats and the unfortunate injury to Minding. That Ballydoyle was still able to remain a major influence in the Group 1 mile races for fillies, after Winter was stepped up in trip in the second half of the season, illustrated the strength in depth that it had at its disposal. Roly Poly finished second to Winter, though she was no match for her, in the Irish One Thousand Guineas and the Coronation Stakes (in both of which Ballydoyle fillies filled the first three places) and it was she who stepped up—thriving on a busy campaign—to win three of the Group 1s for fillies and mares over a mile in the second half of the year.

That wasn't a scenario that many outside Ballydoyle could have envisaged at the start of the season. Roly Poly had run eight times as a two-year-old, her three wins including the Duchess of Cambridge Stakes (formerly the Cherry Hinton) at Newmarket, after which she finished second in both the Lowther and the Cheveley Park (to another stablemate Brave Anna who was well held in the Nell Gwyn Stakes at Newmarket on her only start in the latest season). As well as having had plenty of racing, Roly Poly also seemed to lack the physical scope of the best of her contemporaries, raising the possibility that she might not train on well from two to three, something which happened to her Lowther conqueror Queen Kindly. Roly Poly had reversed the Lowther form with fourth-placed Queen Kindly in the Cheveley Park and their paths didn't cross as three-year-olds. Interestingly, both started in a One Thousand Guineas trial, Queen Kindly finishing fifth in the Fred Darling at Newbury and Roly Poly coming a lacklustre seventh in the Nell Gwyn. Queen Kindly took her chance in the One Thousand Guineas, starting at 33/1 and finishing ninth of fourteen behind Winter before being returned to sprinting with limited success. Roly Poly joined the Ballydoyle 'second eleven'—trio to be more precise—in the Poule d'Essai des Pouliches at Deauville six days after the Newmarket Guineas, fitted with cheekpieces for the first time. She stepped up on her

Nell Gwyn effort, managing sixth of eighteen behind Precieuse, one position behind her best-placed stablemate, lightly-raced Rain Goddess, who had won her only race as a two-year-old.

Back in the 'first team' in the Irish One Thousand Guineas next time, 14/1-shot Roly Poly finished best of the rest behind Winter who won by four and three quarter lengths. Roly Poly kept stablemate Hydrangea, who started at half Roly Poly's odds, out of the runner's-up spot by a head, with fourth going to Intricately, who had beaten Hydrangea and Rhododendron in the Moyglare Stud Stakes as a two-year-old. Roly Poly and Hydrangea filled the same positions—separated by a neck this time—behind Winter in the Coronation Stakes at Royal Ascot, with the Fred Darling winner Dabyah in fourth after being forced to miss her shot at the One Thousand Guineas. The Poule d'Essai des Pouliches winner Precieuse also ran in the Coronation Stakes and, significantly, came off worst in a set-to with front-running Roly Poly from halfway. That Roly Poly saw off Precieuse and then kept on so well for second spoke volumes for the progress she was now making, the form on a par with the best she had shown at two.

The Tattersalls Falmouth Stakes at Newmarket's July meeting often pitches the classic generation against some of the leading older fillies who have stayed in training. However, the latest edition attracted only two four-year-olds, both of whom had finished down the field in the Duke of Cambridge Stakes at Royal Ascot last time. The betting was dominated by the three-year-olds with Roly Poly sent off 6/4 favourite, ahead of the Prix Marcel Boussac winner Wuheida, making a belated reappearance after recovering from a stress fracture to a hind leg, and the Poule d'Essai des Pouliches runner-up Sea of Grace. Those three filled three of the first four places, with Roly Poly producing a career-best up to that time under an enterprising ride and winning by a length and a quarter from Wuheida, with York listed winner Arabian Hope half a length further away in third and Sea of Grace fourth. Roly Poly was kept busy and followed up in the Prix Rothschild at Deauville sixteen days later, her never-say-die attitude very much in evidence as she got the better of outsiders Via Ravenna and Siyoushake, and the 2016 winner Qemah in a four-way photo finish. Roly Poly was, by now, a completely different proposition to the filly who had finished sixth in the Pouliches over the same straight mile four races earlier, and it was no surprise to see her start at considerably shorter odds than Rhododendron and Hydrangea in the Matron Stakes at Leopardstown on Irish Champions' Weekend. Winter headed Ballydoyle's four-pronged attack, dropped back to a mile after extending her winning sequence to four in the Nassau Stakes over a mile and a quarter at Goodwood. The outsider of the Ballydoyle quartet, 20/1-

Kingdom of Bahrain Sun Chariot Stakes, Newmarket—Roly Poly bounces straight back from a below-par run on Irish Champions' Weekend, producing a career-best effort to beat the grey Persuasive; Nathra (No.4) completes the places and is a final ride for Jimmy Fortune following a career in the saddle spanning almost thirty years

shot Hydrangea, pulled off a narrow victory over Winter who had reportedly missed some work in the lead-up to the race, but there was no obvious explanation for the rare below-par effort of Roly Poly who weakened into sixth after making the running as usual (she was also beaten by Persuasive, Wuheida and Qemah, all of whom had finished behind her in either the Falmouth or the Rothschild).

Roly Poly showed her Leopardstown running all wrong a month later when recording her best performance with another typically gutsy display to win the Kingdom of Bahrain Sun Chariot Stakes at Newmarket. Breaking well from stall one, Roly Poly was taken across to race on the favoured stand side where she led until 66/1-shot Dawn of Hope edged ahead two furlongs out. Already under pressure at that stage, Roly Poly battled back to lead again inside the final furlong and stayed on strongly to win going away by a length and a quarter and the same from the Gosden-trained four-year-olds Persuasive and Nathra (Qemah, who raced wide, came sixth). Persuasive went on to more than frank the Sun Chariot form when winning the Queen Elizabeth II Stakes on British Champions' Day, but Roly Poly bypassed Ascot to wait for an ambitious tilt against the top colts in the Breeders' Cup Mile at Del Mar. The only filly in the fourteen-strong line-up, she would have found it well-nigh impossible to take up her usual front-running role from her outside draw on such a tight track and she beat only three home after being dropped out. On her only subsequent start, in the Hong Kong Mile at Sha Tin in December, Roly Poly had an even worse draw (fourteen of fourteen) and was trapped out wide most of the way before weakening from two furlongs out, eventually trailing in last.

Roly Poly (USA) (b.f. 2014)	War Front (USA) (b 2002)	Danzig (b 1977)	Northern Dancer
			Pas de Nom
		Starry Dreamer (gr or ro 1994)	Rubiano
			Lara's Star
	Misty For Me (IRE) (b 2008)	Galileo (b 1998)	Sadler's Wells
			Urban Sea
		Butterfly Cove (b or br 2001)	Storm Cat
			Mr P's Princess

Mr M. Tabor, Mr D. Smith & Mrs John Magnier's "Roly Poly"

Roly Poly, a lengthy if not particularly prepossessing individual, was the first Group 1 winner in Europe over the age of two for her American sire, the Danzig stallion War Front, since Declaration of War won the 2013 International at York. War Front's two-year-olds had kept him in the limelight in the intervening years, but questions had started to be asked after a number of his leading juveniles had failed to train on from two to three. Early fears that Roly Poly might be another one to enter in the debit column were dispelled in the clearest manner by her three Group 1 wins, while Homesman, Spirit of Valor and War Decree were other pattern-winning three-year-olds for War Front in Europe in the latest season, all improving on their two-year-old form. The Dewhurst runner-up Lancaster Bomber didn't let War Front down either, finishing in the frame in the Two Thousand Guineas and runner-up in three Group 1s, the St James's Palace Stakes, the Woodbine Mile and the Breeders' Cup Mile. Apart from Roly Poly, though, War Front's star performer in the latest season was Roly Poly's equally tough younger brother U S Navy Flag, a front runner who completed the Middle Park/Dewhurst double to establish himself as the leading two-year-old in Europe.

Roly Poly and U S Navy Flag are the product of a growing number of matings of War Front with Galileo and Sadler's Wells mares. Thirteen of War Front's latest crop of two-year-olds were out of mares by Misty For Me's sire Galileo; the dam of Roly Poly and U S Navy Flag also has a yearling filly and a colt foal by War Front. Like her offspring, the small, workmanlike Misty For Me (whose first foal the Fastnet Rock filly Cover Song won in pattern company over a mile in the States) was a hardy type, winning twice at Group 1 level at two (Moyglare Stud Stakes and Marcel Boussac) and twice at three (Irish One Thousand Guineas and Pretty Polly Stakes). Misty For Me's younger sister Ballydoyle was also precocious and emulated Misty For Me by winning the Prix Marcel Boussac. She trained on to finish runner-up to Minding in the One Thousand Guineas before coming a creditable sixth in the Prix de Diane. Misty For Me and Ballydoyle may be by Galileo but there is plenty of speed on the distaff side of their pedigree, Roly Poly's unraced grandam Butterfly Cove being a half-sister to the very smart sprinting two-year-old Fasliyev who was also trained by Aidan O'Brien. Roly Poly's fourth dam Anne Campbell, who was successful in the States, was the great grandam of the Golden Jubilee and July Cup winner Les Arcs. Front-running Roly Poly stayed a mile and acted on firm and good to soft going. She wore cheekpieces but was as game and genuine as they come and there will be few, if any, better fillies in the first book of mares covered by stablemae Caravaggio in 2018. *Aidan O'Brien, Ireland*

ROMAANA 2 b.f. (Jan 23) Iffraaj 127 – Baheeja 100 (Dubawi (IRE) 129) [2017 7d^4 Sep 12] second foal: half-sister to useful winner up to 8.3f Dowayla (by Sepoy): dam 7f winner: 8/1, fourth in minor event at Leicester (3½ lengths behind Orsera) in September: should do better. *Simon Crisford* **70 p**

ROMAN DE BRUT (IRE) 5 ch.g. Rock of Gibraltar (IRE) 133 – Nesmeh (USA) (More Than Ready (USA) 120) [2017 75: t9.5m^3 t9.5m^2 t10.2g^5 t8.6m^5 t8.6g^4 p10g^3 t8.6g* 8.1d* 8.2d^3 t8g 8.3d^3 8v 8d Nov 4] lengthy gelding: fairly useful handicapper: won at Wolverhampton in April and Chepstow (by 3¼ lengths from Tripartite) in May: left Daniel Loughnane after eleventh start: stays 1¼m: acts on polytrack, tapeta and good to soft going: tried in cheekpieces: races prominently: has joined Ivan Furtado. *Denis Quinn* **82**

ROMAN HOLIDAY (IRE) 4 b.f. Holy Roman Emperor (IRE) 125 – Burn The Breeze (IRE) 115 (Beat Hollow 126) [2017 87: 6.1g^3 7m* 7.2m p8g^6 Sep 26] fairly useful handicapper: won at Newmarket (by neck from Angel of Darkness) in June: stays 1m: acts on polytrack and good to firm going: wears cheekpieces: sometimes slowly away. *Ed Vaughan* **86**

ROMANISED (IRE) 2 b.c. (Feb 5) Holy Roman Emperor (IRE) 125 – Romantic Venture (IRE) 88 (Indian Ridge 123) [2017 5.8m* 6f 6m^6 7g^2 Sep 2] good-quartered colt: closely related to smart 1½m-2m winner Rock of Romance (by Rock of Gibraltar) and half-brother to several winners, including useful 1m-17f winner Fictional Account (by Stravinsky) and useful 1m-1¼m winner Timely Production (by Peintre Celebre): dam 8.4f/9f winner: useful form: won maiden at Navan in April: second in Solario Stakes at Sandown (2 lengths behind Masar) in September: stays 7f: in tongue tie last 3 starts. *K. J. Condon, Ireland* **104**

ROMAN LEGION (IRE) 3 b.g. Holy Roman Emperor (IRE) 125 – Kibini (Galileo (IRE) 134) [2017 60: p8g $7d^5$ 7m Aug 17] plain gelding: modest maiden: stays 6f: acts on good to firm going. *Dean Ivory* **50**

ROMANN ANGEL 8 b.m. Sir Harry Lewis (USA) 127 – Roman Gospel (Roi de Rome (USA) 112) [2017 12.3d Jul 29] little form in bumpers/over hurdles: well held in maiden on Flat debut. *Michael Mullineaux* **–**

ROMAN NAVIGATOR (IRE) 3 b.c. Henrythenavigator (USA) 131 – Lollina Paulina 83 (Holy Roman Emperor (IRE) 125) [2017 –p: $p6g^3$ p6g* a6g Nov 30] fairly useful form: won maiden at Chelmsford (by ½ length from Al Sail) in January, then left Marco Botti: likely to stay at least 7f: in cheekpieces final start, tongue tied first 2. *Majed Seifeddine, Qatar* **80**

ROMANOR 3 b.g. Holy Roman Emperor (IRE) 125 – Salinia (IRE) (Rainbow Quest (USA) 134) [2017 75p: $8.5g^2$ $10g^5$ $9.9m^4$ $12m^5$ $8.5d^5$ 11.4d* $p11g^3$ t12.2g Oct 27] sturdy gelding: fairly useful handicapper: won at Windsor in September: stays 11.5f: acts on polytrack, good to firm and good to soft going: usually wears headgear: tried in tongue tie: sometimes slowly away: sold to join Seamus Mullins 35,000 gns in November. *Ed Walker* **88**

ROMAN RIVER 2 b.c. (Apr 8) Holy Roman Emperor (IRE) 125 – Inagh River 71 (Fasliyev (USA) 120) [2017 $5d^2$ 5m Jul 8] fair form: better effort when second in maiden at Nottingham (2½ lengths behind Abel Handy) in June. *Martin Smith* **68**

ROMAN SPINNER 2 ch.f. (Feb 23) Intikhab (USA) 135 – Pompeia 88 (Singspiel (IRE) 133) [2017 6d $6d^4$ $7m^5$ $t5.1g^6$ p6g* $p7g^2$ $6.1d^2$ p7d* $p7g^3$ Dec 31] 7,500Y: compact filly: first foal: dam, 2-y-o 7f winner who stayed 1½m, half-sister to smart 1¼m-1½m winner Corriolanus: fair performer: won nurseries at Kempton in September and November: stays 7f: acts on polytrack and good to soft going: wears tongue tie: often races towards rear, usually responds generously to pressure. *Rae Guest* **76**

ROMANTIC (IRE) 8 b.g. Holy Roman Emperor (IRE) 125 – Welsh Love (Ela-Mana-Mou 132) [2017 68: 9.5d 7d $t9.5g^5$ Dec 2] sturdy gelding: fair handicapper, below best in 2017: left Matthew J. Smith after second start: stays 10.5f: acts on polytrack, tapeta and any turf going: has worn headgear. *Noel C. Kelly, Ireland* **60**

ROMANTIC STORY 3 ch.f. Poet's Voice 126 – Scallywag (IRE) (Raven's Pass (USA) 133) [2017 f6.1g Dec 4] 29,000F: first foal: dam unraced half-sister to smart winner up to 9f City Style: 5/1, well held in maiden at Southwell. *Robert Cowell* **–**

ROMAN TIMES (IRE) 4 b.f. Holy Roman Emperor (IRE) 125 – Timeless Dream 79 (Oasis Dream 129) [2017 65: 6m 5m $5s^6$ 6m $t5g^5$ 6g 5s t5g Nov 3] modest handicapper, below form in 2017: left Colin Teague after sixth start: stays 6f: acts on tapeta and good to firm going: usually wears cheekpieces. *Alan Berry* **45**

ROMAN WARRIOR 2 b.c. (Mar 5) Holy Roman Emperor (IRE) 125 – Meet Marhaba (IRE) 63 (Marju (IRE) 127) [2017 p7s p7g Sep 27] fair form on first of 2 starts in minor events: will stay 1m+. *Harry Dunlop* **67**

ROMINA 3 b.f. Raven's Pass (USA) 133 – Dolores 111 (Danehill (USA) 126) [2017 $7m^4$ $10g^4$ p12g* Sep 13] tall, rather unfurnished filly: half-sister to several winners, including very smart 1¼m-1¾m winner (stayed 2m) Duncan (by Dalakhani), smart 1¾m-2¼m winner Samuel (by Sakhee) and smart 1½m-14.6f winner Gretchen (by Galileo): dam 1m winner: fairly useful form: won maiden at Kempton (in hood, by 1¼ lengths from Symbol) in September: stays 1½m: likely to progress further. *Richard Hughes* **86 p**

RONALDINHO (IRE) 7 b.g. Jeremy (USA) 122 – Spring Glory 73 (Dr Fong (USA) 128) [2017 62: 10g Jun 23] angular gelding: fairly useful handicapper at best, has deteriorated markedly: stays 12.5f: acts on polytrack and any turf going: has worn headgear, including last 3 starts: wears tongue tie. *Dianne Sayer* **–**

RONALD R (IRE) 3 ch.g. Nathaniel (IRE) 129 – Amazon Beauty (IRE) 105 (Wolfhound (USA) 126) [2017 90p: 8m* $8m^2$ $8g^6$ 7.9d Aug 24] useful-looking gelding: smart handicapper: won at Newmarket (by head from Son of The Stars) in May: second in Britannia Stakes at Royal Ascot (½ length behind Bless Him) in June: stays 1m: acts on good to firm going: races towards rear: has joined Simon Callaghan, USA. *Michael Bell* **113**

RONNIE THE ROOSTER 3 b.g. Captain Gerrard (IRE) 113 – Piranha (IRE) 82 (Exceed And Excel (AUS) 126) [2017 69p: $t8d^4$ $t8g^3$ $8m^2$ $9g^2$ 9.9g May 16] fair handicapper: stays 9f: acts on tapeta and good to firm going. *David Barron* **76**

RONNI LAYNE 3 b.f. Native Ruler 119 – Cindy Incidentally 49 (Shinko Forest (IRE)) [2017 –: 8m 9g p8g $9d^2$ $8.3d^5$ $10.2v^3$ 8d $p7d^3$ $p7g^5$ p8g $p7m^4$ $p8s^4$ $f7.1g^2$ Dec 22] sturdy filly: modest maiden: stays 9f: acts on polytrack and good to soft going: in blinkers last 3 starts: often races prominently. *Louise Allan* **60**

RONYA (IRE) 6 b.m. Bushranger (IRE) 119 – Beenablaw (IRE) 76 (Alzao (USA) 117) [2017 67: 10m^{2} Apr 10] fair performer: second in handicap at Redcar (nose behind Kerry Icon) on sole start in 2017: stayed 10.5f: acted on soft and good to firm going: tried in blinkers: front runner/raced prominently: dead. *Tracy Waggott* **70**

ROOF GARDEN 2 ch.c. (May 12) Cityscape 127 – Celebrity 90 (Pivotal 124) [2017 p6g 7s p8d^{5} p8g Oct 24] modest form. *Mark H. Tompkins* **55**

RORYSLITTLESISTER (IRE) 7 ch.m. Captain Rio 122 – Teacher Preacher (IRE) 37 (Taufan (USA) 119) [2017 43: p6g 5m t5.1g 5d 5g 5s Sep 26] poor handicapper: best form at 5f: acts on polytrack and good to soft going: tried in headgear: wears tongue tie. *S. M. Duffy, Ireland* **37**

ROSABELLE 3 b.f. Mayson 124 – Kirk 79 (Selkirk (USA) 129) [2017 98: 5.1d^{6} 5.1s^{6} 6d^{4} 6m 6s* 6g 5s p6g Dec 12] good-topped filly: fairly useful handicapper: won at Lingfield (by 2 lengths from Beck And Call) in September: stays 6f: acts on soft going: usually wears headgear. *Alan Bailey* **93**

ROSA DAMASCENA (FR) 4 b.f. Kalanisi (IRE) 132 – Rosewater (GER) (Winged Love (IRE) 121) [2017 p10g* 11.6g^{3} 14.2d^{4} Jun 28] sixth foal: half-sister to 1¼m winner Matavia Bay (by Bahamian Bounty), later winner abroad: dam, French maiden (stayed 1½m), half-sister to high-class/temperamental performer up to 1½m Norse Dancer: fairly useful performer: won maiden at Chelmsford (by ¾ length from Zehrah) in March: stays 11.5f: acts on polytrack. *Alan King* **84**

ROSAMARIA (IRE) 4 gr.f. Rip Van Winkle (IRE) 134 – Rosa Grace 106 (Lomitas 129) [2017 73: 8.5m 7m^{6} 8m^{4} 8.5d Jun 10] fair maiden, generally below best in 2017: stays 8.5f: acts on good to firm and heavy going. *Julie Camacho* **65**

ROSARNO (IRE) 3 b.c. Fastnet Rock (AUS) 127 – Jouet 71 (Reprimand 122) [2017 86p: 10g 9.9g^{4} 12m^{6} 9.9g^{pu} 9.9d^{5} 8.3d* 8.3g^{2} Nov 1] good-bodied colt: fairly useful handicapper: won at Nottingham (by neck from Mikmak) in October: stays 1¼m: acts on good to soft going: wears blinkers/tongue tie. *Charles Hills* **87**

ROSEALEE (IRE) 4 gr.f. Zebedee 113 – Why Now 81 (Dansili 127) [2017 86: t5.1f p5g^{6} p6g^{2} t5.1g^{4} 5m^{3} p5g^{4} 5.7m^{4} 5d^{2} 5.1d Jul 1] compact filly: fairly useful handicapper: second at Lingfield in March: stays 6f: acts on polytrack, tapeta, good to firm and good to soft going: in cheekpieces last 2 starts: sold 30,000 gns in July. *Jeremy Gask* **79** **a85**

ROSEAU CITY 2 ch.f. (May 1) Cityscape 127 – Dominica 115 (Alhaarth (IRE) 126) [2017 6s^{6} 6d^{5} 7.6d 6d p6s^{5} p6s^{6} p7s* p7g^{2} Dec 20] half-sister to several winners, including 2-y-o 5f winner (stayed 1m) Percy Alleline (by Sir Percy) and winner up to 7f Jungle Bay (by Oasis Dream): dam 5f winner (including at 2 yrs): fair performer: won nursery at Chelmsford in December: stays 7f: acts on polytrack: often wears blinkers: often starts slowly. *David Elsworth* **66**

ROSE BERRY 3 b.f. Archipenko (USA) 127 – Desert Berry 74 (Green Desert (USA) 127) [2017 85: t5.1g^{6} 5m* 6.1g^{3} 5f* 6.1g^{4} 5d 6m^{5} 6d^{3} 6g^{6} 7d^{5} p6g^{5} p6g^{2} Nov 21] sturdy filly: useful handicapper: won at Thirsk in May and Nottingham in June: second at Lingfield (½ length behind Gorgeous Noora) in November: stays 6f: acts on polytrack, tapeta, firm and good to soft going: wears hood: often races towards rear. *Chris Dwyer* **96**

ROSEDALE TOPPING (IRE) 2 b.f. (Feb 4) Zebedee 113 – Callmeakhab (IRE) 78 (Intikhab (USA) 135) [2017 7.6s^{5} 7g^{4} 6.1m 7d Oct 30] £15,000Y, £20,000 2-y-o: workmanlike filly: first foal: dam, 7f winner, half-sister to smart winner up to 1½m Meleagros: modest form when fourth in minor event at Epsom in September, standout effort: tried in blinkers. *Ed Vaughan* **56**

ROSE ECLAIR 4 b.f. Major Cadeaux 121 – Katie Boo (IRE) 92 (Namid 128) [2017 79: 5g^{4} 6m 5g^{4} 5s^{6} t5g^{5} 5d^{3} 5g^{6} 6g^{2} 6v 6g^{3} 6g^{6} t7.1s^{5} 7s* 7.4v t7.1d 7d Oct 20] fair handicapper on turf, modest on all-weather: won at Redcar (apprentice) in September: stays 7f: acts on tapeta and any turf going: usually wears headgear: often leads: no battler. *Tim Easterby* **71 §** **a62 §**

ROSE MARMARA 4 ch.f. Exceed And Excel (AUS) 126 – Show Rainbow 97 (Haafhd 129) [2017 87: 6g^{3} 5.5g^{6} 6m 6g 5m^{2} 5g^{4} 6g 6m^{3} Sep 4] fair handicapper: stays 6f: acts on good to firm going: tried in cheekpieces: wears tongue tie. *Brian Rothwell* **79**

ROSEMAY (FR) 3 b.f. Mayson 124 – Maine Rose (Red Ransom (USA)) [2017 69: t8g t7.1g^{3} 7m t8.6g 9.2g^{4} 9.9m^{2} 9.9m^{3} 11.1s 10d^{5} 8.9m^{2} 12.5m^{3} 10.3v^{3} 12.5v^{5} Oct 16] fair maiden: stays 12.5f: acts on tapeta, good to firm and heavy going: tried in cheekpieces. *Iain Jardine* **74**

ROSENBORG RIDER (IRE) 4 b.g. Kodiac 112 – Miss Sundance (IRE) 74 (Desert Sun 120) [2017 83: p6g 6d p7g^2 p8g 7s 8d 7g 7g 9.9g^4 8.6d 6m^4 6d^6 a6g^4 p5g p7g 7v p6g p7g p7g t7.2g p7s* p8g^2 Dec 21] fair handicapper on turf, fairly useful on all-weather: won at Dundalk (apprentice) in December: second at same course in April: stays 1m: acts on polytrack, tapeta, sand and good to firm going: often wears headgear: has worn tongue tie, including last 2 starts. *Adrian McGuinness, Ireland* **70 a84**

ROSENTAL 5 b.m. Pivotal 124 – Rose Trail (USA) (Kingmambo (USA) 125) [2017 109: 10.4g^4 10.3d^5 9.9m^3 10s^5 9.9s* 10.4d^4 Nov 11] tall mare: useful performer: won listed race at Saint-Cloud (for second successive year, by 2½ lengths from Company Asset) in October: fourth to Haggle in Prix Fille de l'Air at Toulouse final start: stayed 10.5f: acted on polytrack, tapeta, soft and good to firm going: usually raced mid-division: reportedly in foal by Frankel to Southern Hemisphere time. *Luca Cumani* **109**

ROSE OF SHIRAZ 2 b.f. (Mar 26) Mazameer (IRE) 107 – Redeemed 73 (Red Ransom (USA)) [2017 5m 5.7s^5 5.5d^5 p8m^4 p7s Dec 14] first foal: dam maiden out of useful 2-y-o 5f winner Pastel: modest maiden: best effort at 5.5f: tried in cheekpieces: often races towards rear. *J. S. Moore* **52**

ROSES IN JUNE (IRE) 2 ch.f. (Mar 24) Society Rock (IRE) 126 – Majestic South 56 (Bertolini (USA) 125) [2017 5.1m t6.1g^6 6m 6.1m^2 6g^4 6d^3 p7d p6g^4 5.1s p7g^6 p8g Oct 24] second foal: dam maiden half-sister to useful 2-y-o 5.7f/6f winner Majestic Dubawi: poor maiden: has worn headgear. *J. S. Moore* **48**

ROSE TINTED SPIRIT 2 b.c. (Apr 3) Swiss Spirit 117 – Woolfall Rose 66 (Generous (IRE) 139) [2017 6.5d p6d^5 t6.1g^3 Dec 22] 12,000F, €11,500Y, £20,000 2-y-o: first foal: dam, maiden (stayed 1½m), half-sister to winner up to 1½m Dower House and winner up to 7f Dowager (both useful): fair form: best effort when third in minor event at Wolverhampton (3¾ lengths behind Mount Wellington) in December: will stay 7f: open to further improvement. *Ralph Beckett* **65 p**

ROSIE BRIAR 3 ch.f. Mayson 124 – Lighted Way 66 (Kris 135) [2017 97p: 6f 5d^3 5.2m 6s Oct 7] smallish, angular filly: useful performer: third in listed race at Haydock (3¼ lengths behind Final Venture) in June: stays 6f: acts on good to soft and good to firm going: often races prominently. *Andrew Balding* **96**

ROSIE CROWE (IRE) 5 b.m. Approve (IRE) 112 – Tolzey (USA) 94 (Rahy (USA) 115) [2017 57: p7d^3 p7g^5 7m^2 7.2m^4 p7s^3 7.4d 7m^6 8m p7s p8s Dec 8] modest handicapper: stays 8.5f: acts on polytrack, tapeta and firm going: wears headgear: front runner/races prominently. *Shaun Harris* **59**

ROSIE HALL (IRE) 7 ch.m. Lion Heart (USA) 124 – Baltic Dip (IRE) 95 (Benny The Dip (USA) 127) [2017 47: t8d Nov 10] maiden, no longer of any account: wears headgear. *John Wainwright* **–**

ROSIE LEA (FR) 4 b.f. Manduro (GER) 135 – Saralea (FR) 103 (Sillery (USA) 122) [2017 p12g p12g^6 t12.2d Dec 9] half-sister to several winners, including useful German/US winner up to 1½m Hasay (by Lomitas) and French 7.5f winner Upside Down Cake (by Encosta de Lago): dam French/US winner up to 9f (2-y-o 5.5f-1m winner): bumper winner: well held in Flat maidens. *Stuart Kittow* **–**

ROSIE ROYALE (IRE) 5 gr.m. Verglas (IRE) 118 – Fearn Royal (IRE) 103 (Ali-Royal (IRE) 127) [2017 79: 12.1m^3 13d^2 11.6m^3 Jun 13] sturdy mare: fair handicapper: stays 13f: acts on polytrack, good to firm and heavy going: tried in headgear. *Roger Teal* **79**

ROSINA 4 b.f. Showcasing 117 – Mondovi 97 (Kyllachy 129) [2017 92: 5m 5g 5g* 5m t5.1g t5g p5s* Dec 14] fairly useful handicapper: won at Ayr in August and Chelmsford (by 1½ lengths from Mr Pocket) in December: mainly races at 5f: acts on polytrack, tapeta, soft and good to firm going: usually in cheekpieces in 2017: usually races in rear. *Ann Duffield* **93**

ROSSALL 2 b.g. (Feb 8) Mayson 124 – Medina (IRE) 97 (Pennekamp (USA) 130) [2017 5m^5 6g^3 5d^2 5d^4 5v^5 Sep 21] fair maiden: best effort at 5f: acts on good to soft going: often races prominently. *Michael Dods* **78**

ROSSETTI 9 gr.g. Dansili 127 – Snowdrops (Gulch (USA)) [2017 12g Sep 14] fairly useful at best, well held sole Flat outing since 2015: stays 1¾m: acts on polytrack, soft and good to firm going: often wears headgear: useful hurdler: quirky sort. *Neil Mulholland* **–**

ROSS (IRE) 5 b.h. Acclamation 118 – Ronja (USA) (El Corredor (USA) 123) [2017 a111: a8f^5 a7f^2 a8f^2 a8g^2 p6.5g* a7f a8f^5 p7.5g Dec 16] smart performer: won minor event at Deauville (by 2 lengths from Gold Vibe) in August: best effort when second in Godolphin Mile at Meydan (neck behind Second Summer) on fourth start: stays 1m: acts on polytrack, dirt, soft and good to firm going. *P. Schiergen, Germany* **115**

ROSS RAITH ROVER 4 b.g. Oasis Dream 129 – Baqah (IRE) 112 (Bahhare (USA) 122) [2017 66: p7m* p7g 8.3g^3 8m^3 8m* 8m^6 8.1m^3 7g^3 8d p8s^2 Dec 15] angular gelding: fair handicapper: won at Lingfield in January and Yarmouth in May: stays 8.5f: acts on polytrack and good to firm going: usually wears headgear. *Robert Eddery* **75**

ROSY RYAN (IRE) 7 b.m. Tagula (IRE) 116 – Khaydariya (IRE) (Akarad (FR) 130) [2017 61: 7f^2 8s^2 7g* 7.4s* 8g 8g* 7d Oct 20] fair handicapper: won at Thirsk in July, and Beverley and Ripon in August: best up to 1m: acts on tapeta, firm and soft going. *Tina Jackson* **75**

ROTHERHITHE 2 b.f. (Apr 2) Finjaan 122 – Reeling N' Rocking (IRE) 82 (Mr Greeley (USA) 122) [2017 7m^2 p7g^2 6s^2 Oct 19] 3,500Y: sixth foal: half-sister to 3 winners, including 1m winner Conan's Rock (by Shamardal) and 1¼m winner Rock Lobster (by Bahamian Bounty): dam, 7f winner who should have stayed 9f, half-sister to useful 6f winner Entrap: fair form: runner-up all 3 starts in minor events: stays 7f: has joined Richard Fahey. *Robyn Brisland* **73**

ROTHERWICK (IRE) 5 ch.g. Starspangledbanner (AUS) 128 – Pivotalia (IRE) 74 (Pivotal 124) [2017 92: 8.2g^4 9g* 10.2f^2 9.1g* 9.1d^6 9.9g^3 10.1s^2 9d 10.2d Oct 18] sturdy gelding: useful handicapper: won at Lingfield in June and Yarmouth in July: stays 1¼m: acts on tapeta, firm and soft going: has worn blinkers: wears tongue tie: often races towards rear. *Paul Cole* **97**

ROUBLES (USA) 3 b.f. Speightstown (USA) 124 – Soviet Song (IRE) 126 (Marju (IRE) 127) [2017 6m^5 6m t5g^6 t5.1m t5.1g^6 Dec 22] second foal: dam high-class miler (6f-1m winner at 2 yrs): modest maiden: left James Fanshawe after second start: best effort at 6f: tried in hood: often races freely. *Julie Camacho* **54**

ROUGE NUAGE (IRE) 7 ch.g. Indian Haven 119 – Nom Francais 39 (First Trump 118) [2017 82: t7.2g^4 p7s 7m^4 t7.2g* p7d^2 p7d p7d p7s t7.2g* Dec 13] lengthy gelding: fairly useful handicapper: won at Wolverhampton in August and December (by head from Inaam): best at 7f/1m: acts on polytrack, tapeta and good to firm going: has worn headgear. *Conrad Allen* **85**

ROULETTE 2 ch.f. (Feb 15) Poet's Voice 126 – Unex Mona Lisa (Shamardal (USA) 129) [2017 7g^6 7v* 7d Sep 29] good-topped filly: fifth foal: second foal: half-sister to 7f winner Preobrajenska (by Paco Boy): dam unraced half-sister to useful winner up to 9f Gender Agenda: fairly useful form: won maiden at Goodwood (by neck from Ripley) in August: raced only at 7f. *Michael Bell* **83**

ROUNDABOUT KITTEN (USA) 2 ch.g. (Feb 18) Kitten's Joy (USA) 128 – Shining Jewel (USA) (Gulch (USA)) [2017 t8.6d^6 t8.6d^4 Dec 27] fair form: better effort when fourth in minor event at Wolverhampton (5¼ lengths behind Antonian) in December. *David Lanigan* **67**

ROUNDABOUT MAGIC (IRE) 3 ch.c. Zebedee 113 – Cayo Largo (IRE) (Captain Rio 122) [2017 70: p5m t5.1m^3 p5g^4 p5g* p5g* 5.3g^4 5g 5m^4 5s^4 p5g^5 p5s p5g^2 p5g* Dec 23] neat colt: fair handicapper: won at Lingfield in February, March and December: best form at 5f: acts on polytrack, soft and good to firm going. *Simon Dow* **74**

ROUNDABOUT TIME (IRE) 4 gr.g. Zebedee 113 – Brosna Time (IRE) 61 (Danetime (IRE) 121) [2017 t8d Feb 4] no form in maidens 16 months apart. *Ann Duffield* **–**

ROUNDHAY PARK 2 ch.g. (Mar 28) Mayson 124 – Brave Mave 83 (Daylami (IRE) 138) [2017 5.9s 5m^2 5f* 5m^3 5s* 6g Oct 13] 25,000Y: strong gelding: fifth foal: half-brother to winner up to 12.4f Ryeolliean (2-y-o 1m winner, by Haafhd) and 1¾m winner Transpennine Star (by Mount Nelson): dam winner up to 1½m (2-y-o 7f winner): fairly useful performer: won minor event at Beverley in July and nursery at Bath (by 1¾ lengths from Maygold) in September: should stay 6f: acts on firm and soft going: often travels strongly. *Nigel Tinkler* **90**

ROUNDHEAD 2 ch.c. (Jan 29) Helmet (AUS) 127 – Blue Mistral (IRE) 69 (Spinning World (USA) 130) [2017 7s 7v^5 Oct 4] fair form: better effort when fifth in minor event at Salisbury (6 lengths behind Jamil) in October. *Richard Hannon* **66**

ROUND THE ISLAND 4 b.g. Royal Applause 124 – Luanshya 78 (First Trump 118) [2017 67§: 6g^2 6d* 6g^3 6m 7g^5 6s t6d t6.1m p7s^4 Nov 23] rather lightly-made gelding: fair handicapper on turf, modest on all-weather: won at Pontefract in June: stays 7f: acts on tapeta and good to soft going: has worn headgear: usually races prominently. *Richard Whitaker* **74 a62**

ROUSAYAN (IRE) 6 b.g. Invincible Spirit (IRE) 121 – Rose Quartz 85 (Lammtarra (USA) 134) [2017 96: 8g^4 8m^5 8.5g 7.8s 8d^3 8d^6 8g^3 7.4m* 7.4g* 7.2s^2 Oct 9] useful performer: won claimer at Beverley in August and handicap at same course in September: stays 8.5f: acts on tapeta, soft and good to firm going: wears headgear. *David O'Meara* **99**

ROUSSEL (IRE) 2 b.c. (Mar 28) Kodiac 112 – Sodashy (IRE) 71 (Noverre (USA) 125) [2017 5g* 5f^2 5m^2 6d^2 Jul 29] €68,000F, £360,000 2-y-o: good-quartered colt: third foal: half-brother to winner up to 7f Ponty Royale (2-y-o 6f winner, by Royal Applause): dam, maiden (stayed 1m), half-sister to useful 2-y-o 5f winner Ponty Acclaim: useful form: won minor event at Leicester in May: second in Windsor Castle Stakes at Royal Ascot (neck behind Sound And Silence) in June and another listed event at Sandown (1¼ lengths behind Havana Grey) in July: best form at 5f. *Charlie Appleby* **100**

ROWLESTONE LASS 7 b.m. Hernando (FR) 127 – Charmante Femme 53 (Bin Ajwaad (IRE) 119) [2017 t12.2m t12.2g^{pu} p13.3d* t16.5g^5 t12.2g 14.1g^4 13.4g^2 May 27] rather leggy mare: fairly useful handicapper: won at Chelmsford (apprentice, by length from Mystikana) in March: stays 16.5f: acts on polytrack, tapeta, firm and good to soft going: has worn hood. *Richard Price* **82**

ROWLESTONERENDEZVU 4 b.f. Rail Link 132 – Charmante Femme 53 (Bin Ajwaad (IRE) 119) [2017 55: 11.8g^5 12g* 12g^2 11.6d^6 10g^6 p12g^4 10.1d t9.5g t12.2g^5 Dec 13] lengthy filly: fair handicapper on turf, modest on all-weather: won at Ffos Las in July: stays 1½m. *Tony Carroll* **67** **a60**

ROWNAK (IRE) 4 ch.g. Rip Van Winkle (IRE) 134 – Apache Dream (IRE) 80 (Indian Ridge 123) [2017 8g Jul 18] modest form on first of 2 starts in bumpers: 28/1, well held in maiden at Thirsk. *Brian Ellison* **–**

ROYAL ACCLAIM (IRE) 5 b.g. Acclamation 118 – Top Row 64 (Observatory (USA) 131) [2017 54: t9.5m t8g Jan 21] modest maiden at best: last in 2 handicaps in 2017: tried in blinkers: often races prominently. *Rebecca Bastiman* **–**

ROYAL ARTILLERY (USA) 4 b.c. War Front (USA) 119 – Masseuse (USA) (Dynaformer (USA)) [2017 119: 10d^4 10.3m^6 May 11] big, strong colt: smart performer: won Rose of Lancaster Stakes at Haydock in 2016: fourth in Gordon Richards Stakes at Sandown (5¾ lengths behind Ulysses) in April, much better effort in 2017: stays 10.5f: acts on firm and good to soft going: tried in cheekpieces: usually in tongue tie: front runner/races prominently: sent to USA. *John Gosden* **113**

ROYAL ASSOCIATE 3 b.g. Cape Cross (IRE) 129 – Queen Consort (USA) (Kingmambo (USA) 125) [2017 11.9m* 12v* 14.9d 14v^5 Sep 29] good-topped gelding: third foal: half-brother to 11f winner (stays 1¾m) Come Back King (by Pivotal): dam maiden half-sister to smart 9.5f-2m winner Winterlude out of smart 1¼m-1½m winner New Morning: useful form: won maiden at Doncaster and handicap at Ascot (by length from Niblawi) in July: should stay beyond 1½m: tried in blinkers. *Charlie Appleby* **101**

ROYAL BATTALION 6 b.g. Sea The Stars (IRE) 140 – Yummy Mummy 86 (Montjeu (IRE) 137) [2017 63: p16g^5 Oct 4] fair maiden: stays 2m: acts on polytrack and tapeta: in cheekpieces last 3 starts: winning hurdler. *Gary Moore* **66**

ROYAL BIRTH 6 b.g. Exceed And Excel (AUS) 126 – Princess Georgina 78 (Royal Applause 124) [2017 102, a112: t5g t5.1g^3 p5m* p6g 5m p5s^2 5g p5g^5 p7s^6 p6g p5g^2 Dec 12] strong gelding: smart performer: won listed race at Lingfield (by ½ length from Lancelot du Lac) in February: second in handicaps at Chelmsford (neck behind Encore d'Or) in June and Lingfield (length behind Gracious John) in December: best at 5f/6f: acts on polytrack, tapeta and firm going: wears tongue tie: often races towards rear. *Stuart Williams* **111**

ROYAL BLESSING 5 b.g. Royal Applause 124 – Zuleika Dobson 106 (Cadeaux Genereux 131) [2017 62: p10.7g^3 t9.5g* t9.5g p10.7g Dec 22] fair handicapper: won at Wolverhampton in January: stays 1¼m: acts on polytrack, tapeta and good to soft going: often wears headgear. *Peter Fahey, Ireland* **68**

ROYAL BRAVE (IRE) 6 b.g. Acclamation 118 – Daqtora 70 (Dr Devious (IRE) 127) [2017 82: t5d^4 t5d 5g* 5m* 5m* 5m^3 5s^4 5g^3 5m* 6d^4 5g^4 5m^2 5v 5g^6 5v^6 Oct 23] lengthy gelding: useful handicapper: completed hat-trick at Musselburgh (2) and Ayr in April/May, and won again at Musselburgh in July: best effort of season when second there (short head behind Kinloch Pride) in August: stays 6f: acts on polytrack, tapeta, firm and good to soft going: tried in cheekpieces: most consistent. *Rebecca Bastiman* **95**

ROYAL CAPER 7 b.g. Royal Applause 124 – Ukraine (IRE) (Cape Cross (IRE) 129) [2017 52: p7g^3 7m p7g^4 p7s p7g^6 Oct 17] angular gelding: modest handicapper: stays 1m: acts on polytrack and good to firm going: has worn headgear: tried in tongue tie: none too consistent. *Miss Joey Ellis* **56**

ROYAL CELEBRATION 3 b.g. Excelebration (IRE) 133 – Auntie Kathryn (IRE) 64 (Acclamation 118) [2017 55: t5g^4 t5g* t5d^3 t5.1g^3 5m^6 May 5] modest handicapper: won at Newcastle in January: best form at 5f: acts on tapeta: often races towards rear: sold £800 in November, sent to Sweden. *Bryan Smart* **61**

ROYAL CONNOISSEUR (IRE) 6 b.g. Art Connoisseur (IRE) 121 – Valferno (IRE) 76 (Val Royal (FR) 127) [2017 88: 7g 6m 7g^4 6s^5 6d 6g^5 6s 6s^2 7.2m^3 6v^4 7s^5 Oct 31] smallish, rather lightly-built gelding: fairly useful handicapper: fourth at Wetherby in May: stays 7f: acts on tapeta, good to firm and heavy going: has worn headgear. *Richard Fahey* **82**

ROYAL COSMIC 3 b.f. Wootton Bassett 119 – Cosmic Case 66 (Casteddu 111) [2017 58: 9.2g^3 11.2g^5 12g^6 13.1g 9.9v^2 12.5s* 12.5v* 10.2g^3 Nov 1] fair handicapper: won at Musselburgh (twice) in October: stays 12.5f: acts on tapeta and heavy going: tried in blinkers. *Richard Fahey* **69**

ROYAL CROWN (IRE) 2 b.f. (May 2) Kodiac 112 – Lear's Crown (USA) 82 (Lear Fan (USA) 130) [2017 5m^3 5m^6 5g^6 5d p6s Nov 16] €25,000Y: closely related to 5f/6f winner Danesford (by Danetime) and half-sister to numerous winners, including useful winner up to 1m Howya Now Kid (2-y-o 5f/6f winner, by Daggers Drawn) and useful 2-y-o 6f winner Byronic (by Byron): dam 1½m winner: modest form when third in minor event on debut, standout effort: often races prominently. *David O'Meara* **61**

ROYAL DIPLOMAT (IRE) 2 b.c. (Mar 20) Zebedee 113 – Pretty Priceless (IRE) (Pearl of Love (IRE) 112) [2017 5v^2 p5g^4 5d^5 6s f5g* t5.1g 5v Sep 29] €27,000F, €78,000Y: third foal: dam unraced half-sister to useful 5f/6f winner Drawnfromthepast: fairly useful performer: won minor event at Southwell (by 6 lengths from Jim Rockford) in August: left A. P. Keatley after second start: best form at 5f: acts on fibresand and heavy going: usually races close up: sold 18,000 gns, sent to France. *Richard Fahey* **88**

ROYAL DUCHESS 7 b.m. Dutch Art 126 – Royal Citadel (IRE) 75 (City On A Hill (USA) 114) [2017 80: 7.2m^6 7.2s^5 7.2g^4 7.2d^3 7.2g^4 8v Oct 12] fair handicapper: stays 7f: acts on soft and good to firm going: sometimes slowly away. *Lucy Normile* **76**

ROYAL ETIQUETTE (IRE) 10 b.g. Royal Applause 124 – Alpine Gold (IRE) 86 (Montjeu (IRE) 137) [2017 47§: 11.9g^4 11.4m Aug 13] angular gelding: poor handicapper nowadays: stays 1½m: acts on polytrack, good to firm and good to soft going: usually wears headgear: wears tongue tie: sometimes slowly away: unreliable. *Lawney Hill* **– §**

ROYAL FLAG 7 b.g. New Approach (IRE) 132 – Gonbarda (GER) 117 (Lando (GER) 128) [2017 70: t16.3g^4 t16.3g* t16.3d^2 12g* 14.6m^6 12.3s^5 15.9d^3 14g^3 13.8s 16.1d^3 Aug 17] strong, deep-girthed gelding: fair handicapper: won at Newcastle in January and Doncaster (amateur) in April: stays 16.5f: acts on polytrack, tapeta, good to firm and good to soft going: has worn headgear. *Brian Ellison* **75**

ROYAL FLUTE 3 b.f. Piccolo 121 – Princess Almora 88 (Pivotal 124) [2017 –: t8d 8g t10.2s Sep 19] no form: tried in cheekpieces. *Mark Walford* **–**

ROYAL GOLDIE (IRE) 2 b.f. (Jan 24) Havana Gold (IRE) 118 – Dream Maker (IRE) 90 (Bahamian Bounty 116) [2017 8.3d^6 8s^3 Oct 19] 18,000F, £26,000Y: first foal: dam, 2-y-o 5.7f/6f winner, half-sister to useful winner up to 1½m Farquhar: fair form: better effort when sixth in maiden at Nottingham (3½ lengths behind Fayrouz Rose) in October: should still do better. *Mick Channon* **71 p**

ROYAL HALL (FR) 5 b.g. Halling (USA) 133 – Royal Fantasy (IRE) 87 (King's Best (USA) 132) [2017 11.6v^6 9.9s p10g^5 10.1m p13.3g Sep 26] modest maiden: best effort at 11.5f: often wears cheekpieces: races towards rear. *Gary Moore* **62**

ROYAL HEADLEY (IRE) 3 b.g. Nathaniel (IRE) 129 – Fearless Flyer (IRE) 100 (Brave Act 119) [2017 10m^4 11.9m^4 9.8m^4 14s t12.2g Oct 7] fair maiden: best effort at 1½m. *David O'Meara* **69**

ROYAL HOLIDAY (IRE) 10 ch.g. Captain Rio 122 – Sunny Slope 77 (Mujtahid (USA) 118) [2017 79: f8s^2 f8g^3 8g 9.9f 9s f7.1g 9.9v^6 8v f7.1g Dec 4] fair handicapper, regressed in 2017: best up to 1m: acts on polytrack, fibresand and heavy going: wears headgear: often leads. *Marjorie Fife* **64 d**

ROYAL HOUSEHOLD 2 b.g. (Apr 22) Camacho 118 – Dusting (IRE) (Acclamation 118) [2017 6g^2 6g* 6m^4 7v 7g^4 6d^2 7s^5 6s^6 Oct 28] good-topped gelding: fair performer: won minor event at Goodwood in June: stays 6f: acts on good to firm and good to soft going. *Richard Hannon* **78**

ROYAL ICON 3 b.f. Sixties Icon 125 – Gillstown Great (Royal Applause 124) [2017 64: 7m^3 t8.6g^6 8.3g 8g t8.6g 7m 11.2v^2 12.5s^5 t12.4g Oct 20] fair maiden: stays 11f: acts on fibresand, tapeta, good to firm and heavy going: sometimes in cheekpieces. *Kevin Ryan* **66**

ROYALISTIC (IRE) 3 ch.g. New Approach (IRE) 132 – Do The Honours (IRE) 121 (Highest Honor (FR) 124) [2017 p8g^3 p10g^{ro} Mar 16] fair form: challenging when hung right and ran out final 1f in maiden at Chelmsford: dead. *John Gosden* **80**

ROYAL LIBERTY 2 b.c. (Apr 8) Acclamation 118 – Anadolu (IRE) 93 (Statue of Liberty (USA) 115) [2017 5g^4 6g* 6g^4 5d p7g^6 6g 7d Oct 30] tall, good-topped colt: fair performer: won minor event at Brighton in June: best effort at 6f. *Mark Johnston* **70**

ROYAL LINE 3 ch.c. Dubawi (IRE) 129 – Melikah (IRE) 116 (Lammtarra (USA) 134) [2017 11.4d* 11.8v* 13.3d^3 11.9s Nov 11] well-made colt: half-brother to numerous winners, including winner up to 12.5f Masterstroke (2-y-o 1m winner, by Monsun), winner up to 1¼m Moonlight Magic (2-y-o 7f-9f winner, by Cape Cross) and 1¼m-16.5f winner Hidden Gold (by Shamardal), all smart: dam 1¼m winner: useful form: won maiden at Windsor (by 2¾ lengths from Lazarus) and handicap at Haydock (by 2¼ lengths from Night of Glory) in September: stays 1½m. *John Gosden* **108**

ROYAL MARSKELL 8 b.g. Multiplex 114 – Socialise 69 (Groom Dancer (USA) 128) [2017 96: t12.4g^4 f12g^5 p12g^{rr} p15.8f^3 p13g* 12g 16m t16.3s p16d f12.1g^{rr} Dec 21] workmanlike gelding: fairly useful handicapper: won at Lingfield in March: stays 16.5f: acts on all-weather, soft and good to firm going: often wears headgear: often races in rear: one to treat with caution (refused to race twice in 2017). *Gay Kelleway* **93 §**

ROYAL MELODY 3 b.f. Royal Applause 124 – Wannabe Free 76 (Red Ransom (USA)) [2017 54: 8d^4 7m t7.2g^5 7.1g 7.6d* 8.1d^2 8.2v^3 t9.5m Oct 31] modest handicapper: won at Lingfield in August: stays 8.5f: acts on tapeta and good to soft going: usually wears headgear. *Heather Main* **63**

ROYAL MEZYAN (IRE) 6 b.g. Royal Applause 124 – Rice Mother (IRE) 69 (Indian Ridge 123) [2017 92: 5s 5m^2 5.7f^6 5.1g^6 p5d^3 5g f5g Oct 22] sturdy gelding: fairly useful handicapper: second at Sandown in June: stays 6f: acts on polytrack, tapeta and good to firm going: has worn headgear, including final start: tried in tongue tie: sold 8,000 gns in October. *Henry Spiller* **87**

ROYAL NORMANDY 5 b.g. Royal Applause 124 – Border Minstral (IRE) 69 (Sri Pekan (USA) 117) [2017 69, a76: p6d^4 p7g p6g p8d 5.7d 6m 6.1m 5.1m 5d^3 6.1m 7.1d 6.1g 5.7s Oct 2] good-topped gelding: poor handicapper nowadays: stays 7f: acts on polytrack, tapeta and firm going: wears headgear. *Grace Harris* **43** **a51**

ROYAL OPERA HOUSE (IRE) 3 b.c. Royal Applause 124 – Jackie's Opera (FR) (Indian Ridge 123) [2017 84: t6g 9f^6 11f 8f^5 8.5f^3 t6f^2 8f^4 Dec 29] fairly useful performer: left Jamie Osborne after first start: best effort at 1m: acts on polytrack, raced only on firm going on turf. *Robert B. Hess Jr, USA* **91**

ROYAL PARKS 2 b.f. (Feb 20) Bated Breath 125 – Kensington Gardens 61 (Oasis Dream 129) [2017 6g^5 7f* 7d p7d^3 Aug 16] 50,000Y: first foal: dam, maiden (stayed 9f), sister to very smart/ungenuine winner up to 10.4f Sri Putra: fairly useful form: won minor event at Haydock (by 3¼ lengths from Akvavera) in July: stays 7f. *James Tate* **80**

ROYAL PEACE (IRE) 3 b.f. Royal Applause 124 – Trianon 80 (Nayef (USA) 129) [2017 63p: p8d^2 t7.1g^6 p7g^4 6d^4 7.1m^3 7d p7s Jul 25] fair maiden: stays 7f: acts on polytrack and good to firm going: in cheekpieces last 2 starts: front runner/races prominently. *Richard Hannon* **67**

ROYAL PROSPECT (IRE) 2 b.g. (Feb 27) Thewayyouare (USA) 117 – Jillian (USA) (Royal Academy (USA) 130) [2017 6.1d^6 6d^4 t6g* Nov 23] €10,500F: fourth foal: half-brother to winner up to 6f Slipstick (2-y-o 5.5f winner, by Slickly): dam 9f winner: fairly useful form: won minor event at Newcastle (by 1¼ lengths from Midsummer Knight) in November: will stay 7f. *Julie Camacho* **82**

ROYAL PURSUIT (USA) 2 br.c. (May 22) Lonhro (AUS) 128 – Catch The Queen (USA) (Miswaki (USA) 124) [2017 t6s^5 t5.1d Dec 26] modest form: better effort when fifth in minor event at Newcastle (5¼ lengths behind Rastacap) in September. *Kevin Ryan* **62**

ROYAL REGENT 5 b.g. Urgent Request (IRE) 120 – Royal Citadel (IRE) 75 (City On A Hill (USA) 114) [2017 81: 10m^2 10m^3 9.1s* 10g^3 10d^3 10g^3 10d^2 8s^3 10.3g^6 Oct 14] fairly useful handicapper: won at Ayr in June: placed all other starts there in 2017: stays 1¼m: acts on soft and good to firm going. *Lucy Normile* **91**

ROYAL REQUEST (IRE) 3 b.f. Royal Applause 124 – Garbah (IRE) 116 (Kodiac 112) [2017 t6m^2 t5g^4 5.5g 5.5d^6 p6.5f Aug 8] first foal: dam 6f/7f winner: fair maiden: left James Tate after second start: stays 6.5f: acts on polytrack. *Filip Caenepeel-Legrand, Belgium* **73**

ROYAL RESERVE 4 b.g. Duke of Marmalade (IRE) 132 – Lady Hawkfield (IRE) (Hawk Wing (USA) 136) [2017 90: p8g 8.3m 8m 10.2f t12.2g* 9.9f^2 t10.2g^3 12d^5 10.2g^2 12.1m^2 p12g* p11g p11g^2 p16d^3 t12.4g p15.8g* Dec 28] tall gelding: fairly useful handicapper on turf, useful on all-weather: won at Wolverhampton in July, Kempton in September and Lingfield in December: left Ian Williams after fourth start: stays 2m: acts on polytrack, tapeta and good to firm going: tried in tongue tie: often races in rear. *David O'Meara* **89 a98**

ROYAL RESIDENCE 2 b.c. (Feb 12) Epaulette (AUS) 126 – Jubilant Queen 81 (Kyllachy 129) [2017 6g^6 t6g^2 p7g^4 Dec 20] fair form: best effort when second in minor event at Newcastle (¾ length behind Mountain Breath) in October: tried in visor. *James Tate* **77**

ROYAL RETTIE 5 b.m. Royal Applause 124 – Bended Knee 83 (Refuse To Bend (IRE) 128) [2017 66: p6d p7g p6g f8.1g p7s Dec 14] fair maiden: below best in 2017: stays 7f: acts on polytrack, fibresand and good to soft going: wears hood: often races prominently. *Paddy Butler* **52**

ROYAL SENTIMENT (IRE) 3 b.g. So You Think (NZ) 133 – Rose Parade (Machiavellian (USA) 123) [2017 52: 9.9g 12m p10g Jun 3] maiden, no form in 2017: tried in visor: dead. *Mark Usher* **–**

ROYAL SHAHEEN (FR) 4 b.g. Myboycharlie (IRE) 118 – Viola Royale (IRE) 90 (Royal Academy (USA) 130) [2017 92: 8m^3 9.1s^5 8m^6 8d^3 8g* 8d^6 10d^3 10.3g^3 12v^5 10v* 10v^4 10v 10v Nov 7] fairly useful handicapper: won at Ayr in July and Pontefract (by 2¼ lengths from Peterhouse) in September: stays 1¼m: acts on good to firm and heavy going: wears headgear: usually races close up. *Alistair Whillans* **90**

ROYAL SUNDAY (FR) 3 gr.g. Never On Sunday (FR) 125 – Royale Malaisie (FR) (Villez (USA)) [2017 73: 10s 12d^6 Jun 6] tall gelding: fair form on debut in 2016, standout effort: tried in hood. *Alan King* **–**

ROYAL WAVE 2 b.f. (Mar 10) Royal Applause 124 – Air Biscuit (IRE) 84 (Galileo (IRE) 134) [2017 6m 6v 7g p6s p7g^5 Dec 28] £35,000Y: rather unfurnished filly: fifth foal: sister to useful winner up to 1m Warbird (2-y-o 7f winner) and half-sister to smart winner up to 7f Solar Flair (by Equiano): dam 1m-1¼m winner: poor maiden. *William Knight* **37**

ROYBOY 4 b.g. Equiano (FR) 127 – Pretty Bonnie 94 (Kyllachy 129) [2017 –: 6g Aug 2] no form. *Bryan Smart* **–**

ROY ROCKET (FR) 7 gr.g. Layman (USA) 121 – Minnie's Mystery (FR) (Highest Honor (FR) 124) [2017 78: 9.9m* 9.9g^5 11.9g^5 11m 9.9s^5 10.1d^3 9.9g^5 12m^5 14.2v 16d^6 Oct 27] workmanlike gelding: fair handicapper: won at Brighton in April: best form at up to 1¾m: acts on polytrack, good to firm and good to soft going: usually races freely. *John Berry* **77**

ROYS DREAM 3 b.f. Monsieur Bond (IRE) 120 – Velvet Jaguar (Hurricane Run (IRE) 134) [2017 73: t5s^5 6g^3 5.9g^2 7m 5.9s^4 6v^5 t6.1g^4 t6g Nov 3] fair handicapper: stays 6f: acts on polytrack, tapeta, soft and good to firm going: often races prominently. *Paul Collins* **75**

ROY'S LEGACY 8 b.h. Phoenix Reach (IRE) 124 – Chocolada (Namid 128) [2017 73: t5.1m^3 p5m^3 f5g^5 p5f^4 p5g^2 f5g* p5g* 5.1m^2 p5g^2 5.1m* 5m^4 5s^4 p5s 5d^3 5d 5v^6 5g f5g t5.1g^5 5s f5g^6 t5.1g* t5d f5g Dec 21] smallish horse: fair handicapper: won at Southwell in March, Chelmsford in April, Chepstow in May and Wolverhampton in December: stays 6f: acts on all-weather, good to firm and heavy going: has worn headgear/tongue tie: often races prominently. *Shaun Harris* **72**

ROYSTONIA (IRE) 2 b.f. (Feb 23) Redoute's Choice (AUS) – Waterlilly (IRE) (Galileo (IRE) 134) [2017 8d Oct 27] first foal: dam unraced sister to Irish 2000 Guineas winner Roderic O'Connor: 12/1, green when well held in maiden at Doncaster: likely to do better. *Hugo Palmer* **– p**

ROZANNE (IRE) 2 b.f. (Feb 26) Canford Cliffs (IRE) 133 – Spinning Lucy (IRE) 101 (Spinning World (USA) 130) [2017 7d 7g 6d^4 5d^3 p6.5g^2 Dec 5] compact filly: fourth foal: half-sister to 1¼m-1½m winner Villette (by Sixties Icon): dam, 2-y-o 6f winner, half-sister to useful 6f winner Midris: fair maiden: left Jeremy Noseda after fourth start: best effort at 6.5f: acts on polytrack. *P. & F. Monfort, France* **78**

ROZY BOYS 3 b.g. Kyllachy 129 – Responsive 91 (Dutch Art 126) [2017 87p: 5d 5m Aug 26] fairly useful form at 2 yrs, behind in handicaps in 2017: raced only at 5f: has joined Ruth Carr. *David Barron* **–**

RUA AUGUSTA (USA) 2 b.c. (May 11) Arch (USA) 127 – Wend (USA) 118 (Pulpit (USA) 117) [2017 8g^2 p8g^3 p8g^2 Oct 12] £65,000 2-y-o: sixth foal: half-brother to winners in USA by Empire Maker and War Front: dam US Grade 2 8.5f-1¼m winner: fairly useful form: best effort when third in minor event at Chelmsford (2½ lengths behind Chilean) in August: sold 52,000 gns in October, sent to UAE. *Kevin Ryan* **80**

RUBENS DREAM 3 ch.c. Dutch Art 126 – Apace (IRE) 94 (Oasis Dream 129) [2017 7m 7s* 8.1m^5 8d 8d Nov 4] £140,000Y: second foal: half-brother to 5f (including at 2 yrs) winner Curtain Call (by Acclamation): dam, 5f and (at 2 yrs) 7f winner, half-sister to smart winner up to 1¼m High Twelve: fairly useful performer: won maiden at Haydock (by short head from Peach Melba) in June: stays 7f: acts on soft going. *Charles Hills* **81**

RUBENSIAN 4 ch.g. Medicean 128 – Hymnsheet 93 (Pivotal 124) [2017 92p: 9.9g^4 11.9g^4 p12s^5 9.1m^6 p12g Sep 6] fairly useful handicapper: below form after reappearance: stays 1½m: acts on polytrack and tapeta: tried in cheekpieces: often races in rear. *David Simcock* **83**

RUBHEIRA 5 ch.m. Arkadian Hero (USA) 123 – Devon Ruby 51 (Zilzal (USA) 137) [2017 –: t6g p6g p5g p8g^6 p10g p10s p10s Dec 7] no form: left Paul Burgoyne after fourth start: wore headgear for him. *Neil Mulholland* **–**

RUBIS 4 ch.f. Monsieur Bond (IRE) 120 – Princess Cocoa (IRE) 86 (Desert Sun 120) [2017 65: 10g^3 10s* 12m^6 10g^3 9.9s 11.2v^2 9s* 10.1d^5 p10d Nov 22] fair handicapper: won at Ayr in June and October: stays 11f: acts on all-weather, good to firm and heavy going: tried in headgear. *Richard Fahey* **70**

RUBY LOOKER 6 b.g. Bertolini (USA) 125 – Ellcon (IRE) 71 (Royal Applause 124) [2017 f5g Jan 2] fair form when winning on debut in 2014, well beaten only 2 starts since: raced only at 5f. *J. R. Jenkins* **–**

RUBY'S GEM 2 b.f. (Feb 9) Havana Gold (IRE) 118 – News Desk 73 (Cape Cross (IRE) 129) [2017 7g 7d^4 7d^5 7d t8.6m^6 Oct 31] 3,000Y: compact filly: second foal: half-sister to 8.4f-1¼m winner Broughtons Story (by Royal Applause): dam 1¼m winner out of useful 2-y-o 6f winner La Presse: fair maiden: best effort at 7f: acts on good to soft going: tried in tongue tie: often races towards rear. *Philip McBride* **67**

RUBY SOUND 2 b.f. (May 1) Assertive 121 – Vermilion Creek 68 (Makbul 104) [2017 6.1g t6.1g t6.1g^6 Sep 23] seventh foal: half-sister to 3 winners, including 6f-7f winner Cadmium Loch (by Needwood Blade) and winner up to 6f (stayed 8.3f) Magenta Strait (by Sampower Star): dam winner up to 1¼m (2-y-o 8.4f winner) who stayed 1½m: little impact in minor event/sellers. *Steph Hollinshead* **–**

RUBY TAYLOR 5 b.m. Passing Glance 119 – Bold Rose 69 (Bold Edge 123) [2017 11.6g 12m Jun 16] tailed-off last both starts in maidens: wears hood. *Nick Lampard* **–**

RUBY WEDNESDAY 4 b.f. Mullionmileanhour (IRE) 116 – Cheap N Chic 79 (Primo Valentino (IRE) 116) [2017 74: p15.8g^5 p12d* p10g^6 Apr 8] fair handicapper: won at Kempton in February: stays 1¾m: acts on polytrack: often races towards rear. *John Best* **72**

RUDE AWAKENING 2 b.g. (Mar 12) Rip Van Winkle (IRE) 134 – First Exhibit (Machiavellian (USA) 123) [2017 p6g^5 p7s 6.1g^6 Jul 20] 50,000Y: closely related to 1½m winner Slide Show (by Galileo) and half-brother to several winners, including useful winner up to 8.6f Prime Exhibit (2-y-o 7f winner, by Selkirk) and 7f winner Figment (by Acclamation): dam unraced: fair form: best effort when fifth in minor event at Lingfield (1¼ lengths behind Tunes of Glory) in June: should be suited by 7f+: remains capable of better. *Sir Mark Prescott Bt* **67 p**

RUE CAMBON (IRE) 2 ch.f. (Mar 27) Exceed And Excel (AUS) 126 – Exciting Times (FR) (Jeune Homme (USA) 120) [2017 5.1m t5.1g 5m p6g p7g Oct 13] €150,000Y: half-sister to numerous winners, including very smart miler Gorella (2-y-o 7f winner, by Grape Tree Road), winner up to 1m Porto Santo (2-y-o 5f/5.5f winner, by Kingsalsa) and winner up to 1½m Stars Over The Sea (2-y-o 7f/1m winner, by Sea The Stars), latter 2 smart: dam maiden: no form: tried in blinkers. *George Peckham* **–**

RUFFINA (USA) 2 b.f. (May 2) Street Cry (IRE) 130 – Rubina (IRE) 99 (Invincible Spirit (IRE) 121) [2017 p7g p8g^{2} t8g^{3} Dec 6] second foal: half-sister to smart US 6f/1m winner Rubilinda (by Frankel): dam, 2-y-o 6f winner, out of smart 1½m winner Riyafa: fair form: best effort when second in minor event at Kempton (1½ lengths behind Espadrille) in November. *John Gosden* **74**

RUFUS KING 2 ch.g. (Mar 24) Iffraaj 127 – Mosqueras Romance 109 (Rock of Gibraltar (IRE) 133) [2017 t6g^{4} 6g* 5d^{2} 7g^{4} 6m* 6s 6d 6g^{5} 6.1v^{6} 7m* Oct 14] £42,000Y: sturdy gelding: third foal: dam 1m winner: useful performer: won minor event at Pontefract in May, and nurseries at Ascot in July and Newmarket (by ½ length from Porth Swtan) in October: stays 7f: acts on good to firm and good to soft going: tried in blinkers. *Mark Johnston* **104**

RULED BY THE MOON 3 b.g. Mawatheeq (USA) 126 – Hallingdal (UAE) 88 (Halling (USA) 133) [2017 7m 6m 8.2d p6g Nov 2] 2,000Y: compact gelding: first foal: dam, winner up to 9.7f (2-y-o 7f winner), half-sister to useful 7f/1m winner Akira: little impact in maidens/handicap: tried in cheekpieces. *Ivan Furtado* **–**

RULE OF HONOUR 2 ch.c. (Mar 30) New Approach (IRE) 132 – Our Queen of Kings (Arazi (USA) 135) [2017 6d^{2} Sep 19] 35,000Y: closely related to useful 1¼m winner Natavia (by Nathaniel) and half-brother to numerous winners, including smart winner up to 1m Spinning Queen (2-y-o 6f winner, by Spinning World) and useful 1¼m-1½m winner Shannon Springs (by Darshaan): dam unraced: 6/1, second in minor event at Yarmouth (neck behind Mutaaqeb) in September: will stay 7f: should improve. *Ismail Mohammed* **83 p**

RULER OF THE NILE 5 b.g. Exceed And Excel (AUS) 126 – Dinka Raja (USA) (Woodman (USA) 126) [2017 79: p16g^{4} t16.5g^{2} 16.3m t16.5g^{6} f16.5g^{4} t16.5g^{4} p16s^{4} f16.5g^{2} Dec 29] fair handicapper: stays 16.5f: acts on all-weather: has worn cheekpieces: tried in tongue tie. *Robert Stephens* **76**

R U MINE (IRE) 3 b.f. Elzaam (AUS) 115 – Imco Career (FR) (Barathea (IRE) 127) [2017 t8g t7.1g^{5} t8g^{6} Mar 15] well held in maidens: dead. *Keith Dalgleish* **–**

RUMPOLE 3 b.g. Lawman (FR) 121 – Complexion 92 (Hurricane Run (IRE) 134) [2017 8m^{4} 8.1m* 8d 8.1m^{2} 9.9v 8m^{3} 10g^{4} p11g^{5} Oct 11] 130,000Y: sturdy gelding: second foal: half-brother to 1¼m winner King of Dreams (by Dream Ahead): dam, 1m winner who stayed 1¼m, half-sister to high-class winner up to 1m Zacinto: fairly useful performer: won maiden at Windsor in May: best effort when fifth in handicap at Kempton (2¼ lengths behind Seniority) in October: stays 11f: acts on polytrack and good to firm going: sold 75,000 gns, sent to Saudi Arabia. *Hughie Morrison* **92**

RUM RATION 2 b.g. (Mar 1) Mount Nelson 125 – Myriades d'Etoiles (IRE) (Green Tune (USA) 125) [2017 t7.2g 7d Jul 26] tailed-off last in 2 minor events. *Mark H. Tompkins* **–**

RUM RUNNER 2 b.c. (Mar 12) Havana Gold (IRE) 118 – Thermopylae 81 (Tenby 125) [2017 6g 7d^{4} 7g* 7d Sep 13] 15,000F, €50,000Y: rather unfurnished colt: half-brother to several winners, including very smart 1¼m-1½m winner Unsung Heroine (by High Chaparral), runner-up in St Leger, and 7f/1m winner Ghostmilk (by Golan): dam maiden: fairly useful form: won maiden at Sandown (by 1¼ lengths from Enzemble) in September: stays 7f. *Richard Hannon* **85**

RUMSHAK (IRE) 2 ch.g. (Feb 24) Arcano (IRE) 122 – Scarlet Rosefinch (Cockney Rebel (IRE) 127) [2017 5m^{4} 5d* 5d^{2} 5m^{2} 5m 6g Oct 7] €2,500F, €15,000Y, £26,000 2-y-o: first foal: dam unraced half-sister to 6f winner So Will I and 5f/6f winner Sand Vixen (both smart): fairly useful performer: won minor event at Carlisle (by 5 lengths from Magic Jazz) in July: best form at 5f: acts on good to firm and good to soft going: often travels strongly. *Michael Dods* **81**

RUM SWIZZLE 5 b.m. Mawatheeq (USA) 126 – Port Providence (Red Ransom (USA)) [2017 76: t12.2g^{3} p10f* 10.2m^{2} 11.6d^{4} 10g 9.9d p12g^{5} p10g t12.2g Dec 2] lengthy mare: fair handicapper: won at Lingfield in April: stays 13f: acts on polytrack, tapeta and firm going: has worn headgear, including final start. *Harry Dunlop* **78**

RUNAIOCHT (IRE) 7 ch.g. Teofilo (IRE) 126 – Julie Girl (USA) (Jules (USA) 110) [2017 68: p10g^{5} p10m^{3} p12d^{4} t9.5g* p10m^{6} p11g p10g^{5} 10d 10s^{6} p11d p8s^{6} p8g^{6} p12g p10g p8g Dec 30] stocky gelding: fair handicapper: won at Wolverhampton in February: stays 1½m, effective at shorter: acts on polytrack, tapeta and firm going: has worn headgear: often races towards rear/freely. *Paul Burgoyne* **71**

RUN FOR EVA 4 b.f. Westerner 130 – Glorybe (GER) (Monsun (GER) 124) [2017 f12.1g Nov 28] first foal: dam, 11f winner, also won over hurdles, half-sister to useful 1¼m/11f winner Gentle Tiger: little impact in bumpers/Flat maiden (hooded): has joined Laura Morgan. *Olly Williams* **–**

RUNNING CLOUD (IRE) 2 b.g. (Feb 2) Cacique (IRE) 124 – Nimbus Star (Nayef (USA) 129) [2017 t6.1g* 6d5 6.1m3 7g5 Sep 22] 42,000F, €40,000Y: second foal: dam twice-raced half-sister to smart French performer up to 1¼m Glaswegian: fairly useful form: won minor event at Wolverhampton (by 4 lengths from Makanah) in June: best effort at 6f. *Eve Johnson Houghton* **83**

RUNTHATBYMEAGAIN (IRE) 2 b.f. (Apr 29) Sir Prancealot (IRE) 111 – Romanylei (IRE) 106 (Blues Traveller (IRE) 119) [2017 5m 6.1d 6.1m5 Jun 19] €5,000Y: sister to winner up to 7f Letmestopyouthere (2-y-o 5f winner) and half-sister to several winners, including useful 7f/1m winner Den's Gift (by City On A Hill) and 2-y-o 6f winner Carnaby Haggerston (by Invincible Spirit): dam 6f winner (including at 2 yrs): no form in minor events/seller: has joined Ian Williams. *David Evans* **–**

RUN TO THE HILLS (USA) 4 b.g. Quality Road (USA) 131 – Masada (USA) (Pleasant Tap (USA)) [2017 98: 8s p8d p8s4 Sep 8] fairly useful handicapper: stays 1m: acts on polytrack and soft going: usually races towards rear: sold 8,000 gns in October. *George Peckham* **86**

RUN WITH PRIDE (IRE) 7 b.g. Invincible Spirit (IRE) 121 – Zibilene 101 (Rainbow Quest (USA) 134) [2017 75: 6v p6g* t6.1g t5.1d2 Dec 27] sturdy gelding: fair handicapper: won at Kempton in October: stays 6f: acts on polytrack, tapeta and good to firm going. *Derek Shaw* **76**

RUPERT BOY (IRE) 4 ch.g. Frozen Power (IRE) 108 – Curious Lashes (IRE) (Footstepsinthesand 120) [2017 61: f7m3 f7g5 f7d5 8.5d f12.1g Oct 22] modest handicapper: stays 1m: acts on polytrack and fibresand: usually wears headgear. *Scott Dixon* **53**

RUPERTCAMBELLBLACK (IRE) 3 b.g. Canford Cliffs (IRE) 133 – Negotiate 102 (Red Ransom (USA)) [2017 –: t9.5m Jan 23] tailed-off last in 2 maidens. *Ronald Harris* **–**

RUPERT'S LASS 2 b.f. (Jan 17) Myboycharlie (IRE) 118 – Elusive Flash (USA) 98 (Freud (USA) 113) [2017 6.1g 6d 7s5 Oct 10] £10,000Y: rather unfurnished filly: fourth foal: half-sister to French 1½m winner Edda (by Dubawi) and German 9f-11f winner Emerald Fury (by Kheleyf): dam 2-y-o 7f winner: modest form: best effort when seventh in minor event at Yarmouth (5¼ lengths behind Beauty Filly) in September: will be suited by 1m+: type to do better in handicaps. *Michael Bell* **59 p**

RURAL CELEBRATION 6 b.m. Pastoral Pursuits 127 – Queens Jubilee 71 (Cayman Kai (IRE) 114) [2017 94: 6.1g 5g2 5s 5d* Aug 4] useful performer: won handicap at Musselburgh (by head from Mayleaf Shine) in August: second in listed race at Ayr (1¼ lengths behind Spring Fling) in June: stays 6f: acts on tapeta, good to firm and heavy going: wears headgear: usually travels strongly. *Kevin Ryan* **99**

RUSPER (IRE) 2 b.g. (Mar 16) Holy Roman Emperor (IRE) 125 – Sweet Dreams Baby (IRE) (Montjeu (IRE) 137) [2017 t8.6g4 p8g* p8d* Dec 13] €62,000Y: third foal: closely related to 2 winners by Fastnet Rock, including useful winner up to 8.3f (stayed 10.5f) Roxy Star (2-y-o 7f winner): dam unraced out of Oaks winner Shahtoush: fairly useful form: won minor events at Lingfield (by short head from Gaudi) in November and Kempton (by short head from Sod's Law) in December: stays 1m: open to further improvement. *Jamie Osborne* **87 p**

RUSSIAN RADIANCE 5 ch.m. Paco Boy (IRE) 129 – Russian Ruby (FR) 85 (Vettori (IRE) 119) [2017 93: p8g p7m2 p8d4 t8f3 t8.5f3 8f3 8.5f* 8f3 a8.3f5 9g3 t8.5f Nov 17] sturdy mare: fairly useful performer: second in handicap at Lingfield in January: left Jonathan Portman after next start: won allowance race at Golden Gate Fields in May: stays 9f: acts on polytrack, tapeta, dirt and firm going: wears headgear. *Manuel Badilla, USA* **91**

RUSSIAN RANGER (IRE) 4 b.g. Bushranger (IRE) 119 – Pink Sovietstaia (FR) (Soviet Star (USA) 128) [2017 74: t8.6g4 p8s t8.6g p10g4 t8.6g5 9.9d p8g Oct 14] sturdy gelding: fair handicapper: stays 1¼m: acts on polytrack, tapeta and good to soft going: wears headgear: usually races prominently. *Jonathan Portman* **65**

RUSSIAN REALM 7 b.g. Dansili 127 – Russian Rhythm (USA) 123 (Kingmambo (USA) 125) [2017 98: 7.1g 7m6 7m5 7.2m 6.1s2 6d 6d 6s4 6d* 6s5 6v Sep 30] compact gelding: fairly useful handicapper: won at Haydock in August: best up to 7f nowadays: acts on soft and good to firm going: has worn hood. *Paul Midgley* **91**

RUSSIAN REGARD (IRE) 3 ch.g. Intense Focus (USA) 117 – Russian Rave 97 (Danehill Dancer (IRE) 117) [2017 56: p12g4 12m 10m 10m 12v6 11.2m Aug 27] lengthy, angular gelding: modest maiden: stays 1½m: acts on polytrack. *Jonathan Portman* **63**

RUSSIAN REWARD (IRE) 5 b.g. Iffraaj 127 – Forever Times 98 (So Factual (USA) 120) [2017 81: p8d p10g6 p10g* p10g2 p8g6 9.9m2 p10g5 10.2f3 10m* Jul 10] good-topped gelding: fairly useful performer: won claimer at Lingfield in March and handicap at **87**

Windsor (by head from Marie Josephe) in July: stays 1¼m: acts on polytrack, tapeta and firm going: wears cheekpieces: has worn tongue tie: front runner/races prominently: sold 22,000 gns in July. *Amanda Perrett*

RUSSIAN ROYALE 7 b.m. Royal Applause 124 – Russian Ruby (FR) 85 (Vettori (IRE) 119) [2017 81: 13.8m 12g^{6} 14g 12.1m^{5} 16g^{6} 14m^{rr} Sep 8] fairly useful handicapper at best, has lost her way: stays 1¾m: acts on firm and soft going: has worn cheekpieces: temperamental (refused to race final start). *Micky Hammond* **64 §**

RUSSIAN SOUL (IRE) 9 b.g. Invincible Spirit (IRE) 121 – Russian Hill 116 (Indian Ridge 123) [2017 99, a106: t7.1g^{2} t7.1g^{4} t6g^{6} t6g^{4} 7m* 7m^{6} 7f^{4} p6s 6d p6g^{5} p7g^{4} Dec 22] fairly useful handicapper on turf, useful on all-weather: won at Chester in May: second at Wolverhampton (½ length behind Nimr) in February: left Jamie Osborne after ninth start: has form at 1m, races over shorter nowadays: acts on polytrack, tapeta and firm going: usually wears headgear: usually slowly away. *M. Halford, Ireland* **93 a100**

RUSTANG (FR) 2 b.g. (May 7) Holy Roman Emperor (IRE) 125 – Oppamattox (FR) (Munir 118) [2017 6.1m^{5} 7d 7d 8.1d^{4} p7g^{4} p10g* p10g^{2} Nov 2] compact gelding: fair performer: won nursery at Chelmsford in October: stays 1¼m: acts on polytrack: often wears hood. *Richard Hughes* **74**

RUSTIQUE 5 ch.m. Pastoral Pursuits 127 – Nihal (IRE) 94 (Singspiel (IRE) 133) [2017 71: p8g p8g^{5} t8.6g 8m^{4} 8m^{2} 8m^{2} 8g^{4} Jul 4] fair handicapper on turf, modest on all-weather: stays 1¼m: acts on polytrack, tapeta and firm going: often wears headgear: usually races close up: sold 5,000 gns, sent to Poland. *Ed Walker* **70 a62**

RUSTY BLADE (IRE) 2 ch.g. (Apr 15) Zebedee 113 – Flashing Blade 90 (Inchinor 119) [2017 5.1m 5m^{6} t5.1d Dec 26] little show in maiden/minor events. *Daniel Loughnane* **–**

RUSUMAAT (IRE) 3 b.g. Arcano (IRE) 122 – Queen Wasp (IRE) (Shamardal (USA) 129) [2017 96: 8g p7g^{2} 7m^{2} 8.2f* 8m 8m 7s* 7g 8.2s Sep 9] compact gelding: smart handicapper: won at Haydock (by 2½ lengths from Indian Dandy) in May and Newbury (by neck from Remarkable) in July: stays 1m: acts on polytrack, firm and soft going. *Mark Johnston* **115**

RUTHERFORD (IRE) 3 ch.f. Dutch Art 126 – Carraigoona (IRE) 76 (Rock of Gibraltar (IRE) 133) [2017 78: t7.1g^{2} t7.1g* 7g^{4} 6.9d^{3} 7.6d* 6s^{2} 6v^{4} 7g Oct 7] sturdy filly: fairly useful performer: won maiden at Newcastle in March and handicap at Chester (by ½ length from Shaaqaaf) in July: stays 7.5f: acts on tapeta and soft going: front runner/races prominently. *Kevin Ryan* **91**

RUTH MELODY (IRE) 5 b.m. Intikhab (USA) 135 – Mermaid Melody (Machiavellian (USA) 123) [2017 68: 11.1g^{3} 12g 13.1g 11.8g Aug 30] fair maiden: stays 1½m: acts on polytrack. *L. Smyth, Ireland* **66**

RUWASI 6 b.g. Authorized (IRE) 133 – Circle of Love 86 (Sakhee (USA) 136) [2017 97: 12g Apr 26] useful handicapper, well held on sole Flat start in 2017: stayed 1½m: acted on soft and good to firm going: often raced in rear/travelled strongly: dead. *Gary Moore* **–**

RUXLEYS STAR (USA) 3 b.f. Artie Schiller (USA) 124 – Ladue (USA) (Demons Begone (USA)) [2017 7g Apr 21] $65,000Y, resold 50,000Y: half-sister to several winners, including US Grade 1 9f winner Lucifer's Stone (by Horse Chestnut): dam US 6.5f-9f winner: 16/1, eighth in maiden at Newbury (3¼ lengths behind Mulhimatty) in April. *Richard Hannon* **61**

RUX RUXX (IRE) 2 b.f. (Mar 3) Dark Angel (IRE) 113 – Lady Duxyana 54 (Most Welcome 131) [2017 6d p7d Nov 22] €120,000Y, 230,000 2-y-o: fifth foal: half-sister to 2 winners by Multiplex, including 12.4f winner The Resdev Way: dam maiden (stayed 1m): modest form: better effort when seventh in minor event at Kempton (5¼ lengths behind Qaysar) in November. *Andrew Balding* **59**

RUYSCH (IRE) 2 b.f. (Apr 22) Dutch Art 126 – Convention 79 (Encosta de Lago (AUS)) [2017 7d^{4} 7d^{3} 7d^{6} 7m^{5} 7.4s^{5} 8.3d* Oct 18] close-coupled filly: third foal: dam, 9.5f winner who stayed 1½m, half-sister to very smart 6f/7f winner Regal Parade: fair performer: won nursery at Nottingham in October: stays 8.5f: acts on good to firm and good to soft going: tried in blinkers: sold 35,000 gns, sent to Saudi Arabia. *Ed Dunlop* **78**

RUZEIZ (USA) 8 b.g. Muhtathir 126 – Saraama (USA) (Bahri (USA) 125) [2017 63: p12g^{3} p13g 11.6g Jun 1] workmanlike gelding: modest handicapper nowadays: stays 1½m: acts on polytrack and soft going: has worn headgear: has worn tongue tie, including final start. *Peter Hedger* **57**

RYAN THE GIANT 4 b.g. Fastnet Rock (AUS) 127 – Comeraincomeshine (IRE) 67 **60**
(Night Shift (USA)) [2017 58§: t12.2m p15.8g^{2} t16.3d* t16.3d^{3} t16.3g^{2} t16.5g^{3} Mar 25]
modest handicapper: won at Newcastle (by length from Jan Smuts) in February: stayed
16.5f: acted on polytrack, tapeta, good to firm and good to soft going: wore headgear: often
raced prominently: dead. *Keith Dalgleish*

RYDAN (IRE) 6 ch.g. Intense Focus (USA) 117 – Lough Mewin (IRE) (Woodman (USA) **96 §**
126) [2017 97: p12g^{2} p12m^{3} 14d^{2} 14g^{5} 12d^{4} 13.3s 14.2s^{3} 14g^{5} p12g^{5} p16d^{2} p15.8g^{2} Dec
28] tall gelding: useful handicapper: placed 6 times in 2017: stays 2m: acts on polytrack,
soft and good to firm going: wears headgear: irresolute. *Gary Moore*

RYEDALE ENCORE 2 b.f. (Apr 16) Canford Cliffs (IRE) 133 – Jackie's Opera (FR) **59**
(Indian Ridge 123) [2017 7f^{4} 7d^{5} 8g^{4} 7.2m^{6} 5.9v Sep 13] half-sister to several winners,
including 2-y-o 7f winners Glisten (useful, by Oasis Dream) and Royal Opera House (by
Royal Applause): dam unraced daughter of Prix de Diane winner Escaline: modest maiden.
Tim Easterby

RYEDALE RIO (IRE) 4 b.g. Captain Rio 122 – Hallucination (IRE) 75 (Last Tycoon **52**
131) [2017 65: f5m^{5} t5.1g^{5} 6m f5g^{6} 5g^{6} 6m^{5} 7.2m t8.6g 6d Jul 22] modest maiden on turf, **a68**
fair on all-weather: best form at 5f: acts on fibresand, tapeta and soft going: usually wears
blinkers: often races prominently. *Tim Easterby*

S

SA'ADA (USA) 2 b.f. (Feb 18) Bellamy Road (USA) 123 – Hey Seattle (USA) (Seattle **72**
Slew (USA)) [2017 7m p7s a7f^{2} Dec 7] $53,000F, $85,000 2-y-o: eighth foal: half-sister to
several winners in North America: dam unraced daughter of US Grade 2 8.5f winner Hey
Hazel: fair form: best effort when second in maiden at Meydan (in hood, 9¾ lengths behind
Rayya) in December: left George Peckham after second start. *A. bin Harmash, UAE*

SAAHEQ 3 b.g. Invincible Spirit (IRE) 121 – Brevity (USA) 108 (Street Cry (IRE) 130) **71**
[2017 8m p7g^{4} 7m^{4} 7d^{3} Aug 19] well-made gelding: fair form: stays 7f: tried in blinkers.
Brian Meehan

SABADOR (FR) 3 gr.g. Kendargent (FR) 112 – Sabadora (FR) (Anabaa (USA) 130) **99 p**
[2017 56p: p8g* 8.2g^{2} 7.2m* 8m Jun 22] useful performer: won maiden at Kempton in
March and handicap at Ayr (by 3¼ lengths from Jay Kay) in May: met trouble in Britannia
Handicap at Royal Ascot final start: stays 1m: acts on polytrack and good to firm going:
often races towards rear: remains capable of better. *Ed Walker*

SABATO (IRE) 4 ch.g. Shamardal (USA) 129 – Mondalay (Monsun (GER) 124) [2017 **42**
58: 5.7d 5.7m 7g 8g Jun 27] modest maiden at best, below form in 2017: stays 7f: acts on
polytrack and tapeta: tried in visor/tongue tie: sometimes slowly away. *Fergal O'Brien*

SABELLUM (IRE) 2 b.f. (Apr 25) Iffraaj 127 – Startarette (USA) (Dixieland Band **–**
(USA)) [2017 5s^{6} 5d 5m Sep 4] €58,000Y: half-sister to several winners, including useful
winner up to 1¼m Star Links (2-y-o 7f winner, by Bernstein) and 2-y-o 6f winner Angels
Wings (by Dark Angel): dam twice-raced half-sister to useful dam of Dewhurst Stakes
winner Mujahid: little impact in minor events/maiden. *Richard Fahey*

SABHA (IRE) 5 b.m. Thewayyouare (USA) 117 – Genipabu (IRE) (Danetime (IRE) 121) **–**
[2017 –: f16g^{5} Jan 2] lengthy mare: maiden: lightly raced and no form since 2015: best
effort at 1½m: acts on firm going. *K. R. Burke*

SABLE ISLAND (IRE) 3 b.g. New Approach (IRE) 132 – Ratukidul (FR) 79 (Danehill **87**
(USA) 126) [2017 71p: 9.9m^{2} t12.2g^{4} 12s^{3} 14.2g^{3} 12.3g* 12s^{3} Sep 19] good-topped
gelding: fairly useful performer: won maiden at Chester in August: third in handicap at
Chepstow in September: stays 1¾m: acts on tapeta, soft and good to firm going: sold to join
Olly Murphy 30,000 gns in October. *Sir Michael Stoute*

SABORIDO (USA) 11 gr.g. Dixie Union (USA) 121 – Alexine (ARG) (Runaway Groom **79**
(CAN)) [2017 87: p16d^{5} p15.8g^{5} Feb 4] big, useful-looking gelding: fairly useful
handicapper: stays 17f: acts on polytrack and any turf going: often wears headgear: usually
races prominently. *Amanda Perrett*

SABRE SQUADRON (IRE) 4 b.g. Lope de Vega (IRE) 125 – Caravan of Dreams (IRE) **–**
74 (Anabaa (USA) 130) [2017 89p: 12g Sep 7] fairly useful 1m winner at 3 yrs, well held
sole outing in 2017. *Alan King*

SACKEB 2 b.c. (Mar 21) Invincible Spirit (IRE) 121 – Qilaada (USA) (Bernardini (USA) 132) [2017 7d 8d Aug 18] well held in minor events: tried in tongue tie. *Hugo Palmer* –

SACRED ACT 6 b.g. Oasis Dream 129 – Stage Presence (IRE) 95 (Selkirk (USA) 129) [2017 108: 8g 8m^3 8s^6 p7g^2 p8g^2 Nov 18] rangy gelding: smart handicapper, lightly raced: second at Lingfield (twice) in November: left John Gosden after second start: stays 8.5f: acts on polytrack, good to firm and good to soft going: often races prominently, usually travels strongly. *Michael Bell* **112**

SACRED LIFE (FR) 2 b.c. (Feb 27) Siyouni (FR) 122 – Knyazhna (IRE) (Montjeu (IRE) 137) [2017 8g* 7.5d* 7s* Oct 4] €10,000Y (privately): first foal: dam unraced half-sister to very smart French performer up to 1½m Migwar out of sister to St Leger winner Rule of Law: smart form: unbeaten in 3 starts, winning maiden at Saint-Malo and minor event at Deauville (by 5 lengths), both in August, and Prix Thomas Bryon at Saint-Cloud (impressively by 6 lengths from Alba Power) in October: will stay 1¼m: capable of better still. *S. Wattel, France* **113 p**

SACRED WAY 3 b.g. Oasis Dream 129 – Heronetta 78 (Halling (USA) 133) [2017 7d^2 p10d^4 8.1m^3 Oct 16] leggy gelding: fair form when in frame in maidens: sold 25,000 gns, sent to Qatar. *Kevin Ryan* **73**

SACRIFICE MY SOUL (IRE) 5 b.m. Nayef (USA) 129 – Via Saleria (IRE) 77 (Arazi (USA) 135) [2017 10.4g^6 11.9g^4 14.9d 14.9g^4 13.9s^5 p13g Nov 2] good-topped mare: half-sister to numerous winners, including very smart French/Australian 7f-1½m winner I'm Your Man (raced as He's Your Man in Australia, by Cape Cross) and smart winner up to 11f Perfect Hedge (2-y-o 9f winner, by Unfuwain): dam 9f winner: useful performer: won maiden at Cologne and handicap at Baden-Baden in 2016: best effort in 2017 when fifth in listed race at Saint-Cloud in October: blinkered, behind in similar event at Lingfield final start: stays 1¾m: acts on soft going: has worn tongue tie. *Mme Pia Brandt, France* **102**

SADHBH (IRE) 3 b.f. Lilbourne Lad (IRE) 111 – Stoney Cove (IRE) (Needwood Blade 117) [2017 65: p10g^6 t9.5g Dec 18] fair handicapper: left Richard Hannon after first start: seems to stay 1¼m: acts on polytrack. *John Flint* **66**

SADIEROSECLIFFORD (IRE) 3 b.f. Poet's Voice 126 – Voltairine (Selkirk (USA) 129) [2017 62: 6m^4 p5d^3 6g* 6d 6g^5 6g 7m 6d Aug 18] modest handicapper: won at Yarmouth in June: stays 7f: acts on polytrack. *Giles Bravery* **59**

SAFARHI 2 b.g. (Apr 5) Farhh 131 – Swarm (IRE) (Hurricane Run (IRE) 134) [2017 p8g 8.3d p8g Oct 25] little show in minor events/maiden. *Alan King* –

SAFE VOYAGE (IRE) 4 b.g. Fast Company (IRE) 126 – Shishangaan (IRE) (Mujadil (USA) 119) [2017 82: t7.1g* t7.1d* t7.1d t7.1d^2 8.3m^4 7.2d* t7.1s^4 Jun 29] fairly useful handicapper: won at Newcastle (twice) in January and Ayr (by 1½ lengths from Chaplin Bay) in June: stays 8.5f: acts on tapeta, good to firm and good to soft going. *John Quinn* **94**

SAFE WATERS 2 ch.f. (Mar 1) Helmet (AUS) 127 – Golden Waters 80 (Dubai Destination (USA) 127) [2017 6g^6 6m^5 7d^6 Jun 24] 5,000Y: second foal: half-sister to 6f winner Golden Opportunity (by Kheleyf): dam, 1¼m winner, half-sister to Oaks runner-up Something Exciting: fair form when fifth in minor event at Salisbury (2¼ lengths behind Simply Breathless) on second of 3 starts: should stay 7f. *Eve Johnson Houghton* **67**

SAFFAH (USA) 2 br.f. (Jan 31) More Than Ready (USA) 120 – Elghayoor (USA) (Ghostzapper (USA) 137) [2017 p7g p7g Oct 13] first foal: dam, US 6f winner, out of half-sister to Dewhurst Stakes winner Mujahid: modest form when eighth at Kempton on second of 2 starts in minor events. *Charles Hills* **62**

SAFIRA MENINA 5 b.m. Paco Boy (IRE) 129 – Isla Azul (IRE) 74 (Machiavellian (USA) 123) [2017 82: p12g^6 p12d^3 p12g^2 11.6m^2 10d^3 12d^4 12m^4 14.2v Oct 4] rather leggy mare: fairly useful handicapper: placed 4 times in 2017: stays 1¾m: acts on polytrack, fibresand, soft and good to firm going: tried in headgear: has worn tongue tie. *Martin Smith* **82**

SAFRANI (IRE) 2 b.g. (Apr 16) Lope de Vega (IRE) 125 – Wadjeka (USA) (Oasis Dream 129) [2017 6s^4 7g Aug 25] useful-looking gelding: modest form when fourth in minor event at Ayr (4¾ lengths behind Jackontherocks) on first of 2 starts. *David O'Meara* **52**

SAGA SPRINT (IRE) 4 b.f. Excellent Art 125 – Queen of Malta (IRE) (Exceed And Excel (AUS) 126) [2017 76: p10g 10d 11.5s^3 10.2s^3 11.5s^4 10.2g 11.5g p11g^6 f11.1g p10s^6 Dec 17] rather leggy filly: modest handicapper nowadays: stays 1½m: acts on polytrack, tapeta, good to firm and heavy going: in headgear last 4 starts. *J. R. Jenkins* **62**

SAGELY (IRE) 4 b.f. Frozen Power (IRE) 108 – Saga Celebre (FR) 104 (Peintre Celebre (USA) 137) [2017 98: 8m 9.9d4 p10s3 9.9m3 p10g 12d Sep 23] useful handicapper: third at Salisbury (length behind Standing Rock) in July: stays 1½m: acts on tapeta and good to firm going: sold 42,000 gns in December. *Ed Dunlop* **97**

SAGENESS (IRE) 2 b.f. (Mar 12) Most Improved (IRE) 119 – Saga Celebre (FR) 104 (Peintre Celebre (USA) 137) [2017 8.3d 8d Oct 27] fourth foal: closely related to winner up to 1¼m Sagaciously (2-y-o 1m winner, by Lawman) and half-sister to 8.6f-1¼m winner (stays 1½m) Sagely (by Frozen Power), both useful: dam, 9f/1¼m winner who stayed 1½m, out of sister to Prix de l'Arc de Triomphe winner Sagacity: well held in maidens. *Ed Dunlop* **–**

SAHALIN 4 b.f. Red Rocks (IRE) 124 – Tamathea (IRE) (Barathea (IRE) 127) [2017 68: p7g Dec 6] fair performer, well held sole outing on Flat in 2017: stays 8.5f: acts on polytrack and tapeta: little form over hurdles. *John Flint* **–**

SAHARAN STAR 3 br.f. Winker Watson 118 – Saharan Royal 70 (Val Royal (FR) 127) [2017 p8g 8.1m4 p8g Nov 6] angular filly: second foal: dam maiden (second at 7f at 2 yrs): modest form when fourth at Windsor on second of 3 starts in maidens. *Patrick Chamings* **57**

SAHREEJ (IRE) 4 gr.g. Zebedee 113 – Petite Boulangere (IRE) (Namid 128) [2017 94: 6v 5d 5s3 6d2 5g 5d2 6d 5s 5s 5v Oct 8] well-grown gelding: fairly useful handicapper: second at the Curragh in June and Tipperary in August: stays 6f: acts on polytrack, good to firm and heavy going: has worn headgear, including last 3 starts: tried in tongue tie. *A. P. Keatley, Ireland* **82**

SAIGON CITY 7 b.g. Mount Nelson 125 – Hoh Chi Min 103 (Efisio 120) [2017 99: 12g2 14s* 14d 16.3d6 Aug 23] well-made gelding: useful handicapper: won at Newmarket (by 2¼ lengths from Oriental Fox) in May: stays 16.5f: acts on tapeta and any turf going: has worn headgear: usually races prominently. *Declan Carroll* **104**

SAI KUNG STAR 3 ch.f. Harbour Watch (IRE) 121 – Warden Rose 61 (Compton Place 125) [2017 –: 8m 10m 10g Jun 23] no form. *Nigel Tinkler* **–**

SAILING HOME 2 b.f. (Mar 22) Shamardal (USA) 129 – Tidespring (IRE) 108 (Monsun (GER) 124) [2017 8.3d4 8d4 Oct 27] second foal: dam French 12.5f-14.5f winner (stayed 2m) out of Prix Vermeille winner Sweet Stream: fair form: better effort when fourth in maiden at Doncaster (6½ lengths behind Mrs Sippy) in October. *Michael Bell* **71**

SAILOR MALAN 5 b.g. Mount Nelson 125 – Flying Hi (Kyllachy 129) [2017 –: t12.2g t8.6g Jun 26] workmanlike gelding: maiden: no form in 2017: best effort at 1¼m: acts on polytrack: in hood last 2 starts. *Suzy Smith* **–**

SAILORS WARN (IRE) 10 b.g. Redback 116 – Coral Dawn (IRE) 67 (Trempolino (USA) 135) [2017 –: t12.2g 7d Oct 30] fairly useful at best, lightly raced on Flat nowadays: stays 15f: acts on polytrack, soft and good to firm going: has worn cheekpieces, including in 2017: tried in tongue tie: fairly useful hurdler. *Ian Williams* **63**

SAIL WITH SULTANA 6 ch.m. Black Sam Bellamy (IRE) 121 – Strathtay 60 (Pivotal 124) [2017 55: 16.2m6 16d5 16d Jun 7] sturdy mare: modest handicapper, little impact in 2017: sometimes slowly away. *Mark Rimell* **–**

SAINT ANTHONY 2 ch.g. (Apr 29) Pastoral Pursuits 127 – Mega (IRE) 66 (Petardia 113) [2017 7s p7d p8g Nov 7] well held in maiden/minor events. *Mark H. Tompkins* **–**

SAINT CONTEST (FR) 4 b.g. Air Chief Marshal (IRE) 115 – Sainte Adresse (Elusive City (USA) 117) [2017 82: 12g 11.4g Jul 2] fairly useful at best, little impression in pair of handicaps in 2017: stays 12.5f: acts on tapeta, raced only on good going on turf: tried in hood. *Alan King* **–**

SAINT CUTHBERTS 3 b.g. Shirocco (GER) 129 – Gladys' Gal 96 (Tobougg (IRE) 125) [2017 –: t10.2s Jun 3] well held in maidens. *David Brown* **–**

SAINTED 4 ch.f. Dutch Art 126 – Blithe 91 (Pivotal 124) [2017 94p: 7m* 7s6 6g* 6v 6d Nov 11] useful handicapper: won at York (by 3 lengths from Alpine Dream) in July and Haydock (by 1½ lengths from Clear Water) in August: stays 7f: acts on good to firm and heavy going: often races towards rear/travels strongly. *William Haggas* **106**

SAINT EQUIANO 3 b.g. Equiano (FR) 127 – St Athan (Authorized (IRE) 133) [2017 92p: 6m5 7.2d 6.9d* 7.4d2 7d4 7.8v 7.2s Oct 1] fairly useful handicapper: won at Carlisle (by neck from Raselasad) in July: stays 7.5f: acts on soft going: has worn hood, including final start: races freely. *Keith Dalgleish* **92**

SAINT HELENA (IRE) 9 b.m. Holy Roman Emperor (IRE) 125 – Tafseer (IRE) (Grand **69**
Lodge (USA) 125) [2017 78: 10.2d^4 8m^6 10.2f^6 10.2s^2 9.9d^5 9.9v p12g Dec 6] rather leggy mare: fair handicapper: stays 13f, usually raced at shorter: acts on polytrack, soft and good to firm going: wears headgear: often races prominently. *Mark Gillard*

SAINT HONORE 5 b.m. Champs Elysees 124 – Gwyneth 62 (Zafonic (USA) 130) [2017 **70**
80: p12g^6 p15.8g^5 Feb 22] lengthy mare: fair handicapper: stays 1½m: acts on polytrack, good to firm and good to soft going: tried in cheekpieces: often races towards rear. *Pat Phelan*

SAINTMONT (FR) 3 b.g. Monitor Closely (IRE) 122 – Saintheze (FR) (Saint des Saints **–**
(FR)) [2017 12d Jun 6] 40/1, well held in maiden at Chepstow. *Christian Williams*

SAINT THOMAS (IRE) 10 b.g. Alhaarth (IRE) 126 – Aguilas Perla (IRE) (Indian Ridge **63**
123) [2017 64: t12.2g^5 Apr 8] close-coupled gelding: modest handicapper: stays 1¾m: acts on polytrack, tapeta, firm and soft going: tried in blinkers. *John Mackie*

SAISONS D'OR (IRE) 2 ro.g. (Mar 20) Havana Gold (IRE) 118 – Deux Saisons **68**
(Chineur (FR) 123) [2017 6f^5 6g^5 t6s^3 6d^4 Oct 20] fair form in minor events: will stay 7f. *Jedd O'Keeffe*

SAKHALIN STAR (IRE) 6 ch.g. Footstepsinthesand 120 – Quela (GER) (Acatenango **67**
(GER) 127) [2017 77: t8.6g^4 10g^3 t8.6g^2 8.3g t8s t8.6g^6 10d^3 10d* 9.9s^6 t10.2d^5 12.1d* 10.2d^2 12.5m^5 11.2v 9.9v^F 12.5s^4 10.2g Nov 1] fair handicapper: won at Ffos Las in July and Beverley in August: stays 1½m: acts on tapeta, good to firm and heavy going: wears headgear. *Richard Guest*

SAKHEE'S JEM 4 ch.f. Sakhee's Secret 128 – Amandian (IRE) 84 (Indian Ridge 123) **60**
[2017 73: 7m 6g t7.2g 7g 5.2d^3 6g^3 7m 5.2m p7s^3 6d p7g Nov 8] rather leggy filly: modest handicapper nowadays: stays 7f: acts on polytrack, good to firm and good to soft going: has worn headgear, including in 2017. *Gay Kelleway*

SAKHEE'S RETURN 5 b.g. Sakhee's Secret 128 – Sofia Royale 61 (Royal Applause **87**
124) [2017 91: 7g^3 7s 7m 7m^5 7d^4 7d 7g* 7.2m^4 p7d 7.2s^4 Oct 9] quite good-topped gelding: fairly useful handicapper: won at Catterick (by neck from Lagenda) in August: stays 1m: acts on firm and good to soft going: wears tongue tie. *Tim Easterby*

SAKHRA 6 b.g. Nayef (USA) 129 – Noble Desert (FR) (Green Desert (USA) 127) [2017 **52**
51: t16.5g^5 t16.5m^2 Jan 14] modest maiden: stays 16.5f: acts on polytrack and tapeta: has worn headgear. *Mark Brisbourne*

SAKURAJIMA (IRE) 3 ch.g. Helmet (AUS) 127 – Park Approach (IRE) 77 (Indian **73**
Ridge 123) [2017 68: 8.3m^3 8m 8.1d 8m^5 10.2m^4 11.5m 12g p12g Oct 18] rangy gelding: fair maiden: stays 8.5f: acts on good to firm going: has worn hood, including final start: wears tongue tie: usually races nearer last than first. *Charles Hills*

SALAMAH (IRE) 3 b.f. Shamardal (USA) 129 – Spirit of Dubai (IRE) 103 (Cape Cross **87**
(IRE) 129) [2017 74: p8g^2 8m 8v^5 Jul 27] good-topped filly: fairly useful handicapper: second at Chelmsford (nose behind Pavillon) in May: left Simon Crisford after first start: stays 1m: acts on polytrack: often races prominently. *Michael Bell*

SALATEEN 5 ch.h. Dutch Art 126 – Amanda Carter 92 (Tobougg (IRE) 125) [2017 110: **113**
7g 7g* 7g t7.1g* p8g^3 7m^4 7m^3 7g^5 7d^2 7m^2 t6.1d^6 Dec 26] tall horse: smart performer: won handicap at Meydan (by nose from Flash Fire) in February and listed race at Wolverhampton (by nose from Keystroke) in March: placed in valuable event at Lingfield in April, handicaps at York in June and Newmarket (¾ length behind Swift Approval) in August, and Supreme Stakes at Goodwood (2 lengths behind Dutch Connection) later in August: stays 1m: acts on polytrack, tapeta, soft and good to firm going: front runner. *David O'Meara*

SALAZAR (IRE) 2 ch.g. (Feb 9) Raven's Pass (USA) 133 – Queen Padme (IRE) (Halling **79**
(USA) 133) [2017 7.2g* 7.9g^5 Oct 13] compact gelding: fair form: won minor event at Ayr (by ½ length from Weellan) in August. *Kevin Ryan*

SALEH (IRE) 4 b.g. Iffraaj 127 – Pellinore (USA) (Giant's Causeway (USA) 132) [2017 **84**
77: p8g* p8g^3 p8g^2 p7g* p8g^4 p7g^5 p7d 7d^6 p7s^6 Sep 2] lengthy gelding: fairly useful handicapper: won at Kempton in January and March (by 1½ lengths from Until Midnight): stays 1m: acts on polytrack and good to firm going: tried in eyeshields: often travels strongly. *Lee Carter*

SALIENT 13 b.g. Fasliyev (USA) 120 – Savannah Belle 84 (Green Desert (USA) 127) **–**
[2017 63: p12d p13g^6 p12g Feb 18] sturdy, compact gelding: useful at best, no form in 2017: has worn headgear: tried in tongue tie. *Michael Attwater*

SALIERI (FR) 3 b.g. Paco Boy (IRE) 129 – Ticklestone (IRE) (Mark of Esteem (IRE) 137) [2017 66: 8.3d 8m Jun 29] fair maiden at best: often raced freely: dead. *Alan King* –

SALIRE (IRE) 2 b.f. (Apr 22) Intense Focus (USA) 117 – Gariepa (GER) (Black Sam Bellamy (IRE) 121) [2017 6d 7v^3 7.4v^5 7v t7.2g^5 f8.1g f8.1g Dec 29] small, lightly-made filly: third foal: dam, placed all 3 starts at 11.5f in Germany, sister to useful German 11f winner Goathemala: modest maiden: stays 7f: acts on tapeta and heavy going. *Ann Duffield* **59**

SALLAB (IRE) 2 b.c. (Apr 16) Havana Gold (IRE) 118 – Waveband 102 (Exceed And Excel (AUS) 126) [2017 7m^6 7f* 7g 8.1g^2 8g^3 Sep 22] 90,000F, 200,000Y: well-made colt: fourth foal: half-brother to 5f (including at 2 yrs) winner Archimedes (by Invincible Spirit): dam, winner up to 7f (2-y-o 5f winner), half-sister to high-class UAE sprinter (7f winner in Britain) Muarrab: fairly useful performer: won minor event at Epsom in July: placed in similar events at Chepstow in August and Newbury in September: stays 1m: acts on firm going: front runner/races prominently. *Richard Hannon* **86**

SALLEE 3 b.f. Sakhee's Secret 128 – Rabshih (IRE) 62 (Green Desert (USA) 127) [2017 –: p6d^5 p8g t7.1g Mar 25] no form. *Adrian Wintle* –

SALMON SUSHI 6 ch.g. Dalakhani (IRE) 133 – Salsa Steps (USA) 103 (Giant's Causeway (USA) 132) [2017 93§: 9.8d^6 9m t10.2s^5 10d Jul 9] strong, close-coupled gelding: fairly useful handicapper, below form in 2017: stays 1½m: acts on polytrack, tapeta, good to firm and heavy going: has worn hood, including last 3 starts: usually races nearer last than first: not one to rely on. *Tim Easterby* **71 §**

SALOUEN (IRE) 3 b.c. Canford Cliffs (IRE) 133 – Gali Gal (IRE) 79 (Galileo (IRE) 134) [2017 108: 9m^2 12m 12m 9.9m 9.9g^2 9.9d^3 Sep 30] good-topped colt: smart performer: placed in listed race at Newmarket, Prix Guillaume d'Ornano at Deauville (3 lengths second to Eminent) and Prix Dollar at Chantilly (1½ lengths third to Garlingari): probably stays 1½m: acts on good to firm and good to soft going: often races towards rear. *Sylvester Kirk* **116**

SALSABEEL (IRE) 3 b.g. Exceed And Excel (AUS) 126 – Tokyo Rose (UAE) (Jade Robbery (USA) 121) [2017 104p: 7m^2 8d May 14] big, rangy gelding: useful form: second in minor event at Newmarket (neck behind Beat The Bank) in April: well held in Poule d'Essai des Poulains at Deauville only subsequent outing: stays 7f. *Charlie Appleby* **105**

SALSA VERDE (IRE) 2 b.g. (Feb 18) Canford Cliffs (IRE) 133 – Bridal Dance (IRE) 62 (Danehill Dancer (IRE) 117) [2017 6m 6v Jul 22] good-quartered gelding: well held in minor events. *Ed de Giles* –

SALT WHISTLE BAY (IRE) 3 b.c. Royal Applause 124 – Quantum (IRE) 89 (Alhaarth (IRE) 126) [2017 –: p8g^4 p12d^5 8g 8.2g^4 7s* 8d* 7.1s^3 8.3d* 8g^2 Nov 3] fairly useful handicapper: won at Lingfield in July, Newmarket in August and Nottingham (by head from Mooltazem) in October: second at Newmarket in November: stays 8.5f: acts on polytrack and soft going: front runner/races prominently: has good attitude. *Rae Guest* **89**

SALTY SUGAR 2 b.f. (Mar 6) Oasis Dream 129 – Shamandar (FR) 106 (Exceed And Excel (AUS) 126) [2017 6g 7d p6g p6g^4 t7.1g Nov 15] 120,000Y: sturdy filly: second foal: dam 2-y-o 6f/6.5f winner: modest maiden: left John Gosden after second start: best effort at 6f: acts on polytrack: tried in cheekpieces/tongue tie: often races in rear. *Paul Cole* **60**

SALUTE THE SOLDIER (GER) 2 br.c. (Mar 14) Sepoy (AUS) 129 – Street Fire (IRE) (Street Cry (IRE) 130) [2017 6.5d^3 p7d^2 Nov 22] sixth foal: half-brother to 3 winners, including 6f winner (including at 2 yrs) Storm Cry (by Poet's Voice) and 2-y-o 7f winner Way Too Hot (by King's Best): dam, unraced, out of half-sister to smart US Grade 1 9f winner Monzante: fairly useful form: better effort when second in minor event at Kempton (length behind Flavius Titus) in November: open to further improvement. *Clive Cox* **87 p**

SALUTI (IRE) 3 b.g. Acclamation 118 – Greek Easter (IRE) 85 (Namid 128) [2017 82p: 7d* 7g 7v* 7v p8g Aug 30] fairly useful performer: won maiden at Newmarket in June and handicap at Salisbury (by neck from Sans Souci Bay) in July: stays 7f: acts on polytrack and heavy going: often races prominently. *Amanda Perrett* **86**

SALVATORE FURY (IRE) 7 b.g. Strategic Prince 114 – Nocturnal (FR) 71 (Night Shift (USA)) [2017 81§, a90§: t6g^5 t5g t6g^4 p6d^6 p6d p6g^6 p6g^2 6m 5m^6 6m 5.9g 6m^6 5s^6 5g^6 5.9g 5d 6g t6d Sep 29] sturdy gelding: fairly useful handicapper: second at Lingfield in April: below form after: stays 6f: acts on polytrack, tapeta and firm going: wears headgear: often races towards rear: not one to rely on. *Keith Dalgleish* **85 d**

SAMARMADI 3 ch.g. Sepoy (AUS) 129 – Sweet Folly (IRE) 109 (Singspiel (IRE) 133) [2017 6d* t6.1g^2 7v 6d 6s t6g^2 t6d^5 Nov 10] strong gelding: half-brother to 3 winners, including useful 1¼m winner Fort Belvedere (by King's Best) and 7f winner Frivolous (by **84**

Green Desert): dam, French 10.5f winner, closely related to smart winner up to 9f Apprehension and half-sister to Coronation Stakes winner Kissing Cousin: fairly useful performer: won maiden at Doncaster (by ½ length from Dirchill) in July: second in handicaps at Wolverhampton in July and Newcastle in October: stays 6f: acts on tapeta and good to soft going: in cheekpieces last 2 starts. *Hugo Palmer*

SAMBUCA NERA 3 b.f. Black Sam Bellamy (IRE) 121 – Bebe de Cham 75 (Tragic Role (USA)) [2017 12g 12s^{5} 11.6d 16.1d 14m^{6} Aug 26] closely related to 2 winners by Beat Hollow, including 2-y-o 7f winner (stayed 10.4f) Punch Drunk, and half-sister to 2 winners, including ungenuine 2-y-o 1m winner (stayed 2m) Cava Bien (by Bien Bien): dam ungenuine 2-y-o 5f/6f winner: modest maiden: stays 1¾m: front runner/races prominently. *James Given* **50**

SAME JURISDICTION (SAF) 6 b.m. Mambo In Seattle (USA) 121 – Diana de Carlo (SAF) (Captain Al (SAF)) [2017 114: 7d^{2} 8m 7s^{5} 7.5s Aug 31] tall mare: useful performer: second in minor event at Leicester (1¾ lengths behind Bletchley) in June: stays 9f: acts on soft going: tried in tongue tie. *Ed Dunlop* **102**

SAM GOLD (IRE) 2 b.c. (Feb 21) Iffraaj 127 – Samdaniya 79 (Machiavellian (USA) 123) [2017 7g 7m^{2} 8.3d^{2} Oct 11] 120,000Y: lengthy colt: has scope: sixth foal: half-brother to 1½m-14.6f winner Samtu (by Teofilo) and smart 7f (including at 2 yrs) winner Dabyah (by Sepoy): dam, 9.7f winner, half-sister to smart dam of Breeders' Cup Filly & Mare Turf winner Queen's Trust: fairly useful form: second in maiden at Nottingham (¾ length behind Merlin Magic) in October: will stay beyond 1m: sure to progress further. *Roger Varian* **89 p**

SAMHARRY 3 b.g. Exceed And Excel (AUS) 126 – Ballymore Celebre (IRE) (Peintre Celebre (USA) 137) [2017 89p: p8s Dec 1] fairly useful 7f winner on debut at 2 yrs, little impression in handicap on sole outing in 2017. *John Gosden* **–**

SAM JAMES (IRE) 2 b.g. (Mar 30) Camacho 118 – Breathless Kiss (USA) 101 (Roman Ruler (USA) 122) [2017 5m 6m t6s^{4} 6s 6.9g^{6} 6m Aug 28] modest maiden: best effort at 6f: acts on tapeta: tried in cheekpieces. *Iain Jardine* **60**

SAM MISSILE (IRE) 4 b.g. Smart Strike (CAN) 121 – Kitty Matcham (IRE) 102 (Rock of Gibraltar (IRE) 133) [2017 102: 10.3m^{2} 12.1m^{4} 14d^{5} t16.3s^{6} 14g p11s Sep 8] useful handicapper: second at Doncaster (½ length behind Fidaawy) in April: stays 16.5f: acts on polytrack, tapeta and good to firm going: has worn headgear, including in 2017: sold to join Jamie Osborne 30,000 gns in November: one to treat with caution. *James Fanshawe* **99 §**

SAMMY'S CHOICE 5 ch.g. Pastoral Pursuits 127 – Diane's Choice 95 (Komaite (USA)) [2017 –: p8s Dec 17] little form: tried in blinkers. *J. R. Jenkins* **–**

SAMOVAR 2 b.g. (Apr 19) Finjaan 122 – Chrystal Venture (IRE) 71 (Barathea (IRE) 127) [2017 t6.1m f7.1g^{4} f7.1g^{6} Dec 11] fair form when sixth at Southwell on last of 3 starts in minor events. *Scott Dixon* **66**

SAMPAQUITA (FR) 3 b.f. Poet's Voice 126 – Forest Fire (SWE) 88 (Never So Bold 135) [2017 9.9m 9m 10s^{6} 11.9d^{5} 8.9v 12.4v Dec 9] half-sister to several winners, notably high-class 9f/1¼m winner Presvis (by Sakhee): dam 1m-1½m winner: modest maiden: left Gary Moore after fourth start: best effort at 1¼m: acts on heavy going. *J. M. G. Lefebvre, France* **59**

SAMPHIRE COAST 4 b.g. Fastnet Rock (AUS) 127 – Faslen (USA) 92 (Fasliyev (USA) 120) [2017 59: f7g^{4} f8g* f8g^{3} f11g^{4} p8g p8g p8g* 8m^{4} p8s 7s 7d^{4} p8g^{4} f8.1g^{3} p7s^{2} p8s^{2} p8s* Dec 15] fair handicapper: won at Southwell in January, and at Chelmsford in April and December (by 1¾ lengths from Ross Raith Rover): stays 1m: acts on polytrack, fibresand and good to soft going: wears headgear. *Derek Shaw* **65 a77**

SAMSON'S REACH 4 b.g. Phoenix Reach (IRE) 124 – Court Wing (IRE) 60 (Hawk Wing (USA) 136) [2017 t14g^{5} Nov 11] bumper/hurdle winner: 66/1, well held in maiden at Wolverhampton sole start on Flat. *Richard Price* **–**

SAM THE REBEL 3 b.g. Cockney Rebel (IRE) 127 – Casablanca Minx (IRE) 81 (Desert Story (IRE) 115) [2017 –: 10s^{6} Sep 19] no form. *Mike Hammond* **–**

SAMTU (IRE) 6 b.g. Teofilo (IRE) 126 – Samdaniya 79 (Machiavellian (USA) 123) [2017 85: f14m* f12g* 11.9s 11.9m 18g 12.1m p12g t12.4g t16.3g f14.1g^{3} f14.1g^{2} Dec 22] fairly useful handicapper: won at Southwell (twice, by 1½ lengths from Busy Street second occasion) in March: stays 14.5f: acts on polytrack, fibresand and good to firm going: tried in hood. *Marjorie Fife* **91**

SANAM 3 b.c. Oasis Dream 129 – Seta 113 (Pivotal 124) [2017 t9.5g p8g p8d Dec 13] little impact in maidens. *Ed Dunlop* **–**

Al Basti Equiworld Gimcrack Stakes, York—Sands of Mali takes the step up in class in his stride as he makes all to beat Invincible Army (striped cap) and Cardsharp (second left)

SANCERRE (IRE) 2 b.f. (Feb 18) Canford Cliffs (IRE) 133 – Kawaha (IRE) (Danehill Dancer (IRE) 117) [2017 t6.1g³ 5s* Aug 9] £5,000Y: sixth foal: half-sister to useful 2-y-o 7f/1m winner Seolan (by Alhaarth): dam Italian 5f/6f winner (including at 2 yrs): fair form: won maiden at Bath (by 3¾ lengths from Zapateado) in August. *Sylvester Kirk* **69**

SANCHES 3 b.g. Delegator 125 – Flamenco Dancer (Mark of Esteem (IRE) 137) [2017 t7.1m p6g t8.6g⁶ p12g* Dec 23] modest form: won handicap at Lingfield in December: left Simon Crisford after first start: best effort at 1½m. *Dr Jeremy Naylor* **61**

SANDACRES 4 b.g. Frozen Power (IRE) 108 – Lady Golan (IRE) (Golan (IRE) 129) [2017 66: 7d p8s 5.7d p6g p8g Oct 18] maiden: no form in 2017: in cheekpieces last 2 starts. *Laura Mongan* **–**

SANDAMA (IRE) 2 b.f. (Jan 1) Footstepsinthesand 120 – Nurama (Daylami (IRE) 138) [2017 6d 6s⁶ 6g 6d³ t5.1g³ t7.1g Sep 12] €16,000Y: sixth foal: half-sister to winner up to 9.5f Carlton Blue (2-y-o 6f/6.5f winner, by Aussie Rules): dam unraced: modest maiden: should stay 7f: acts on tapeta and good to soft going: sold 3,000 gns, sent to Denmark. *Richard Fahey* **52**

SANDFRANKSKIPSGO 8 ch.g. Piccolo 121 – Alhufoof (USA) 100 (Dayjur (USA) 137) [2017 94: p6g p5d⁵ p5g p5g² 5g⁶ 5.3g² p5g³ 5.3m⁴ 5.3m⁴ 5.1s⁴ 5.3d p5g⁵ p5g Dec 23] rather leggy gelding: fairly useful handicapper: second at Lingfield in March and Brighton in May: stays 5.5f: acts on polytrack and firm going: tried in tongue tie. *Peter Crate* **83**

SANDGATE 5 ch.g. Compton Place 125 – Jump Ship 74 (Night Shift (USA)) [2017 t12.4d t10.2s t10.2s 8.3g Jun 14] fair at best, no form in 2017: has worn cheekpieces, including final start: tried in tongue tie. *Kenny Johnson* **–**

SANDIE GEM 2 ch.f. (Mar 23) Equiano (FR) 127 – Spirit Na Heireann (IRE) 67 (Dubawi (IRE) 129) [2017 5m t5.1g 5g Aug 29] second foal: half-sister to 2-y-o 6f winner Springforth (by Mayson): dam, maiden (stayed 1¼m), half-sister to smart winner up to 10.4f Barefoot Lady: behind in minor events. *Richard Fahey* **–**

SANDKISSED (IRE) 2 b.f. (Apr 14) Sir Prancealot (IRE) 111 – Hapipi (Bertolini (USA) 125) [2017 5g 6d p6d Nov 9] €14,000Y: fourth foal: sister to 2-y-o 6f/7f winner Notalot (later useful 7f winner in Qatar) and half-sister to 2-y-o 5f-7f winner Danot (by Zebedee): dam unraced sister to smart winner up to 7f Prime Defender: well held in minor events: in hood last 2 starts. *Amy Murphy* **–**

SANDRA'S SECRET (IRE) 4 gr.f. Zebedee 113 – Good For Her 72 (Rock of Gibraltar (IRE) 133) [2017 88: t5.1g 5m p6g* 6m⁶ 6.1g⁵ 5m 5m 5g⁴ 5s⁶ 6g* 5g² 6v⁶ t5g* Oct 10] close-coupled filly: fairly useful handicapper: won at Lingfield in May, Pontefract in August and Newcastle (by short head from Liquid) in October: stays 6f: acts on polytrack, tapeta and good to firm going: tried in headgear: usually leads. *Les Eyre* **89**

SANDRO BOTTICELLI (IRE) 5 b.g. Galileo (IRE) 134 – Ask For The Moon (FR) 110 (Dr Fong (USA) 128) [2017 113: t16.5m^4 p16d^5 Feb 22] sturdy gelding: useful performer: stays 16.5f: acts on polytrack, good to firm and heavy going: wears cheekpieces: sold to join Alexandra Dunn £28,000 in June. *John Ryan* **108**

SANDS CHORUS 5 b.g. Footstepsinthesand 120 – Wood Chorus 97 (Singspiel (IRE) 133) [2017 88: f7g^4 t8.6m* p8d p8d f8g^4 8m^2 9.8m* 10.3g^6 9.8d* 9m^4 9.8m* 8g^5 8.6d 8g^2 9.8g^6 9d^2 10d^5 p10g t9.5g Nov 29] finely-made gelding: useful handicapper: won at Wolverhampton in January, and at Ripon in May, June and July (by 2¼ lengths from Mulligatawny): second in Cambridgeshire Handicap at Newmarket (1½ lengths behind Dolphin Vista) in September: stays 1¼m: acts on tapeta, good to firm and heavy going: front runner/races prominently. *James Given* **103**

SANDS OF MALI (FR) 2 b.c. (Apr 10) Panis (USA) 112 – Kadiania (FR) (Indian Rocket 115) [2017 6m 6.1v* 6m* 6d 8f Nov 3] €20,000Y, £75,000 2-y-o: third foal: half-brother to smart 5f and (including at 2 yrs) 6f winner Kadrizzi (by Hurricane Cat): dam unraced: smart performer: won minor event at Nottingham (by 3¾ lengths from Eirene) in August and Gimcrack Stakes at York (by 2¾ lengths from Invincible Army) in August: 3¼ lengths ninth to Mendelssohn in Breeders' Cup Juvenile Turf at Del Mar final start: likely to prove best short of 1m: acts on heavy and good to firm going: often travels strongly. *Richard Fahey* **116**

SANDSTREAM 4 ch.g. Paco Boy (IRE) 129 – Descriptive (IRE) 83 (Desert King (IRE) 129) [2017 –: t8g t7.1d^3 t7.1d 8g 7g^5 t6s Jun 1] modest maiden: stays 1m: acts on tapeta, best turf form on good going: wears hood/tongue tie. *Tracy Waggott* **57**

SANDWOOD BAY 3 b.f. Footstepsinthesand 120 – Diverting 99 (Nayef (USA) 129) [2017 69: 8.2d 7d Jul 1] maiden, little impact in handicaps in 2017: stays 1m: acts on good to firm and good to soft going: in eyeshields last 2 starts: often races towards rear. *Mark H. Tompkins* –

Cool Silk Partnership's "Sands of Mali"

SANDY COVE 6 br.g. Oasis Dream 129 – Maganda (IRE) 84 (Sadler's Wells (USA) 132) **77 §** [2017 77: p12d^6 p13.3d^4 p12d^6 12g 11.5m^{rr} Aug 1] compact gelding: fair handicapper: stays 1¾m: acts on polytrack, tapeta and good to firm going: has worn headgear: sometimes slowly away, often races in rear: temperamental (refused to race final outing). *James Eustace*

SANDY SHORES 3 b.f. Sixties Icon 125 – Salim Toto 107 (Mtoto 134) [2017 –: p8g^5 **79** p7g^3 p8g^5 10m 8.2g^2 8.5d^2 8s^4 8.1m* 10d^5 p8g^2 8.1m^4 Oct 16] lengthy filly: fair handicapper: won at Windsor in August: should stay 1¼m: acts on polytrack, good to firm and good to soft going: wears headgear: often races prominently. *Brian Meehan*

SANDYTOWN (IRE) 2 b.g. (Jan 18) Tamayuz 126 – Wild Ways (Green Desert (USA) **–** 127) [2017 5m 6.5m Jul 7] little impact in minor events. *Kevin Ryan*

SANGUINE 3 ch.f. Tamayuz 126 – Dubai Media (CAN) 98 (Songandaprayer (USA) 118) **–** [2017 8.3m Jun 15] second foal: dam, 6f winner, half-sister to smart US Grade 1 2-y-o 8.5f winner Square Eddie: in hood, 50/1, well held in maiden at Nottingham. *George Peckham*

SANIYAAT 3 b.f. Galileo (IRE) 134 – Starlit Sands 104 (Oasis Dream 129) [2017 8m **78** 10.2s^5 10.2g^4 12g^2 11.4d^3 p10g^6 Sep 26] €1,050,000Y: well-made filly: third foal: half-sister to 1m winner Scottish Strand (by Selkirk) and useful 6f/7f winner Seychelloise (by Pivotal): dam 2-y-o 5f/5.5f winner: fair maiden: stays 1½m: acts on good to soft going: in visor last 5 starts: usually races close up. *George Peckham*

SANKARI ROYALE (IRE) 2 b.f. (Feb 14) Epaulette (AUS) 126 – Amethystos (IRE) **90** (Danehill Dancer (IRE) 117) [2017 6g^5 6g^2 5m^2 5d* 5.2s^2 6d^4 5m 6d Oct 28] €4,500Y: neat filly: second foal: half-sister to 2-y-o 7f winner Jose Echegaray (by Lope de Vega): dam unraced daughter of smart performer up to 1m Amethyst, herself sister to 2000 Guineas winner King of Kings: fairly useful performer: won minor event (by 2 lengths from Treasuring) at Down Royal in July: second in listed race at Newbury (1¾ lengths behind Eirene) in August: stays 6f: acts on soft and good to firm going: tried in cheekpieces: often races towards rear. *John Patrick Murtagh, Ireland*

SAN QUENTIN (IRE) 6 gr.g. Lawman (FR) 121 – In The Soup (USA) (Alphabet Soup **68** (USA) 126) [2017 82: 12.1m^2 11.8m^6 p10g^5 Aug 8] good-topped gelding: fairly useful handicapper, below form in 2017: trained on reappearance only by Tony Coyle: stays 13.5f: acts on polytrack, tapeta, good to firm and good to soft going: often wears headgear: tried in tongue tie: sometimes slowly away, usually races in rear. *Dr Richard Newland*

SANS SOUCI BAY 3 b.c. Medicean 128 – Cumana Bay 90 (Dansili 127) [2017 82: t7.1g^6 **89** t7.1g p7g^2 p7g^4 p7g* 7d* p7s^5 7f 7v^2 p7s 7s 7g* 7d^2 7d Nov 11] compact colt: fairly useful performer: won claimers at Lingfield in April and Salisbury (by 8 lengths from Madam Prancealot) in May, and seller at Leicester in October: left Richard Hannon after twelfth start: stays 7f: acts on polytrack, good to firm and heavy going: wears blinkers: often starts slowly/races in rear. *Scott Dixon*

SANTA ANNA (IRE) 2 b.f. (Apr 29) Canford Cliffs (IRE) 133 – Ardent Lady 79 **–** (Alhaarth (IRE) 126) [2017 t8g Oct 10] €4,000Y, €12,500 2-y-o: half-sister to several winners, including 2-y-o 1m winner (stays 1¼m) Rashford's Double (by Zoffany) and 9f/1¼m winner Livella Fella (by Strategic Prince): dam 9f winner: 50/1, well held in minor event at Newcastle. *Mrs Caroline McCaldin, Ireland*

SANTADELACRUZE 8 b.g. Pastoral Pursuits 127 – Jupiters Princess 54 (Jupiter Island **58** 126) [2017 58: p12g^2 p13g^3 p12g^5 p12g^3 Mar 8] workmanlike gelding: modest handicapper: stays 13f: acts on polytrack, tapeta, good to firm and good to soft going: has worn headgear. *Mark Hoad*

SANTAFIORA 3 b.f. Poet's Voice 126 – Acquifer 75 (Oasis Dream 129) [2017 75: 6g **63** p7g^5 8.1m^5 t6.1m t6s Nov 30] fair winner on debut at 2 yrs, disappointing since: left Roger Charlton after fourth start: should be suited by at least 7f: acts on soft going: tried in hood: often races towards rear. *Julie Camacho*

SANTA MONICA 4 b.f. Mastercraftsman (IRE) 129 – Zacchera 82 (Zamindar (USA) **104** 116) [2017 102: 9.5s 12g^4 12m* 10g 12g^5 10s p10.7g^4 p10.7g^5 p13g Nov 2] lengthy, angular filly: half-sister to 1m-1¼m winner Oriental Girl (by Dr Fong) and a winner abroad by Sakhee: dam, 6f winner, half-sister to July Cup winner Sakhee's Secret: useful performer: won Munster Oaks at Cork (by neck from Butterflies) in June: stays 1½m: acts on polytrack, soft and good to firm going: tried in cheekpieces: sold 375,000 gns in December. *Charles O'Brien, Ireland*

SANTE (IRE) 4 b.f. Dream Ahead (USA) 133 – Zeiting (IRE) 105 (Zieten (USA) 118) **99** [2017 90: 7d^2 8m^2 7g^3 6.5s^4 7s^6 Oct 3] lengthy filly: useful performer: in frame in handicaps at Doncaster and Haydock (1¾ lengths second to Captain Courageous, left Charles Hills after), and listed races at Baden-Baden (1½ lengths third to Celebrity) and Munich (3¼ lengths fourth to Princess Asta): will prove best up to 7f: acts on soft and good to firm going: often races towards rear/travels strongly. *J-P. Carvalho, Germany*

SANTIAGO ROCK (IRE) 2 b.g. (Apr 12) Rock of Gibraltar (IRE) 133 – Snowpalm (Halling (USA) 133) [2017 p8g 8v 8.3v Nov 8] well held in maidens/minor event: in cheekpieces last 2 starts. *Noel Williams* **–**

SANTIBURI SPRING 4 b.f. Mullionmileanhour (IRE) 116 – Santiburi Girl 77 (Casteddu 111) [2017 76: p12g^{2} Jan 6] plain filly: fair handicapper: stays 2m: acts on polytrack, tapeta and good to firm going. *John Best* **79**

SANTORINI SUN (IRE) 2 b.f. (Apr 3) Born To Sea (IRE) 117 – Trentini (IRE) (Singspiel (IRE) 133) [2017 5v* 7g p7s^{5} Sep 8] €9,000Y: smallish filly: fourth foal: half-sister to useful winner up to 1¼m Speed Company (2-y-o 7f/1m winner, by Fast Company) and a winner in Italy by Clodovil: dam French 1¼m winner: fair form: won minor event at Sandown (by short head from Time For Wine) in August: should stay 7f. *Mick Channon* **78**

SANTRY (IRE) 2 b.c. (Feb 5) Harbour Watch (IRE) 121 – Babylonian 66 (Shamardal (USA) 129) [2017 5g* 5s* 5m^{2} Jun 22] compact, good-quartered colt: smart form: won minor events at Doncaster (by head from Last Page) in April and York (by 2¼ lengths from Consequences) in May: second in Norfolk Stakes at Royal Ascot (½ length behind Sioux Nation) in June: raced only at 5f: dead. *Declan Carroll* **112**

SAPHIL (IRE) 2 b.g. (Mar 1) Holy Roman Emperor (IRE) 125 – Lafite 100 (Robellino (USA) 127) [2017 6s Sep 8] 25/1, well held in minor event at Ascot. *John Ryan* **–**

SAPPER 2 b.c. (Jan 24) Sepoy (AUS) 129 – Green Poppy 68 (Green Desert (USA) 127) [2017 6g^{6} 7m p7g p8g^{6} Oct 24] modest form: best effort at 1m: sold 5,000 gns, sent to Denmark. *Ed Walker* **59**

SARABI 4 b.f. Rip Van Winkle (IRE) 134 – Xaphania (Sakhee (USA) 136) [2017 75: f5g^{6} f6g^{2} p6g 5m^{6} 5g 6d 5m^{2} 5g^{6} f6.1g^{5} 6d f6.1g^{4} 5s^{6} f6.1g^{3} f5g f6.1g Dec 11] sturdy filly: fair handicapper: stays 6f: acts on all-weather, soft and good to firm going: wears headgear: has worn tongue tie, including last 2 starts. *Scott Dixon* **70**

SARADANI BAY 3 b.g. Mawatheeq (USA) 126 – Sadaharu (FR) (Dansili 127) [2017 8.3v p8d t8g^{pu} Oct 19] fair form: went wrong final start. *Rae Guest* **66**

SARAKOVA (IRE) 4 b.g. Iffraaj 127 – Mary Pickford (USA) 61 (Speightstown (USA) 124) [2017 57: t9.5m t9.5g^{5} t8.6g t8.6g^{4} t8.6g 8.3g^{5} 10.1s t12.2g^{6} Jun 26] modest maiden: stays 8.5f: acts on tapeta and good to firm going: wears headgear: usually races nearer last than first. *Kevin Frost* **50**

SARANGOO 9 b.m. Piccolo 121 – Craic Sa Ceili (IRE) 83 (Danehill Dancer (IRE) 117) [2017 83: 7g^{4} 8.1d 7f^{3} 7m p7d^{4} 7d^{3} 7g 7d^{4} 7.1s Sep 19] workmanlike mare: fairly useful handicapper: third at Salisbury in June and Epsom in July: stays 1m, usually races over shorter: acts on polytrack and any turf going: has worn cheekpieces. *Malcolm Saunders* **80**

SARASOTA (IRE) 2 b.f. (Apr 17) Zoffany (IRE) 121 – Saldenaera (GER) (Areion (GER) 115) [2017 p7d Aug 16] 95,000Y: third foal: half-sister to 2-y-o 5f winner Strands of Silk (by Kodiac): dam German 5f winner: 50/1, seventh in minor event at Kempton (5½ lengths behind Quargent) in August. *Jamie Osborne* **65**

SARDENYA (IRE) 2 b.f. (Mar 27) Kodiac 112 – Pitrizza (IRE) (Machiavellian (USA) 123) [2017 6g^{6} p6s^{2} 6d^{3} p7g^{3} 8g p7g* Oct 18] 55,000F, 80,000Y: close-coupled filly: half-sister to several winners, including 2-y-o 7f/7.5f winner Snow Watch (by Verglas) and winner up to 1½m Winston C (2-y-o 7f winner, by Rip Van Winkle), both useful: dam French 11.5f winner: fairly useful performer: won nursery at Lingfield (by 1¾ lengths from Not After Midnight) in October: stays 7f: acts on polytrack and good to soft going: in headgear last 3 starts: sold 20,000 gns later in October. *Roger Charlton* **80**

SARIA 2 b.f. (Feb 28) Stimulation (IRE) 121 – Dijarvo 97 (Iceman 117) [2017 5.1m 5g 6.1s p6g^{5} 6.1s^{2} 6.1d^{6} p6g^{5} Oct 14] compact filly: first foal: dam, 2-y-o 5f winner, later 5.5f winner in USA: modest maiden: left Daniel Loughnane after third start: stays 6f: acts on soft going: often races towards rear. *Tony Carroll* **54**

SARK (IRE) 4 b.g. Zoffany (IRE) 121 – Breezeway (IRE) 70 (Grand Lodge (USA) 125) [2017 82: 10m^{6} 12s 10m^{3} 12v^{6} Jul 28] close-coupled gelding: fair handicapper: stays 1½m: acts on polytrack, tapeta and good to firm going: tried in visor/tongue tie. *David Evans* **73**

SAROOG 3 b.g. Nathaniel (IRE) 129 – Bahama Bay (GER) (Dansili 127) [2017 10g^{3} 9.9s^{4} Jul 29] 45,000Y: third foal: half-brother to winner up to 1¼m Bahama Moon (2-y-o 7f winner, by Lope de Vega): dam, French 1½m winner, out of very smart 1½m performer Borgia: fairly useful form: better effort when fourth in maiden at Salisbury (2¾ lengths behind Torcello) in July: will be suited by 1½m: capable of better again. *Simon Crisford* **84 p**

SAROOKH (USA) 2 b.c. (May 1) Speightstown (USA) 124 – Yaqeen 107 (Green Desert (USA) 127) [2017 t6s4 p6g* t6d5 Oct 24] sixth foal: half-brother to 3 winners, including 8.6f winner Istinfaar (by Street Cry) and 1¼m winner (stayed 1½m) Tafawuk (by Nayef): dam, 7f-1¼m winner, half-sister to very smart French/US winner up to 1½m Grand Couturier: fairly useful form: won minor event at Kempton (by 3 lengths from Fakhoor) in September: raced only at 6f: sold 47,000 gns, sent to Sweden. *Roger Varian* **88**

SARRAB (IRE) 3 b.f. Footstepsinthesand 120 – Credibility 65 (Komaite (USA)) [2017 p6d4 6g 8g 6g3 6g6 8g3 7g2 6g* 7g 9.2g4 6g6 Dec 7] 24,000 2-y-o: half-sister to 3 winners, including 1m-1¼m winner Edgeworth (by Pyrus) and 5f winner Colombia (by Art Connoisseur): dam maiden (best at 5f): modest performer: left Conrad Allen after debut: won maiden at Doha in May: stays 1m: has worn hood. *Osama Omer Al-Dafea, Qatar* **56**

SARROCCHI (IRE) 2 b.f. (Feb 15) Galileo (IRE) 134 – Thai Haku (IRE) 113 (Oasis Dream 129) [2017 7s* Oct 28] third foal: dam, French/US 7.5f and (including at 2 yrs) 1m winner, sister to smart French 1m/9f winner Albaraah: well-backed 7/2, overcame inexperience when won maiden at Leopardstown on debut by 1¼ lengths from New To Town, leading close home: sure to progress. *Aidan O'Brien, Ireland* **88 p**

SARSHAMPLA (IRE) 2 b.f. (Mar 23) Elzaam (AUS) 115 – Red Riddle (IRE) 66 (Verglas (IRE) 118) [2017 6m 5s* 5.2s6 Aug 18] €7,000F, €3,500Y, €60,000 2-y-o: second foal: dam, maiden (best form at 5f/6f), half-sister to smart winner up to 1¼m Elleval: fairly useful form: won minor event at Lingfield (by 1½ lengths from Zalshah) in August: should stay 6f: should still improve. *David Simcock* **81 p**

SARSTEDT 2 b.g. (Mar 6) Sixties Icon 125 – Saluem 82 (Salse (USA) 128) [2017 6.1m5 7d2 7d4 7v 6d5 Oct 30] sturdy gelding: fair maiden: best effort at 7f: acts on good to soft going. *Henry Candy* **73**

SARY ARQA 2 ch.f. (Mar 21) Dubawi (IRE) 129 – Rock Salt (Selkirk (USA) 129) [2017 7d5 Nov 4] half-sister to several winners, including smart 2-y-o 7f (including Moyglare Stud Stakes) winner Termagant (by Powerscourt) and useful winner up to 1½m Splinter Cell (2-y-o 1m winner, by Johannesburg): dam placed up to 11f in France: 8/1, shaped much better than result when fifth in minor event at Newmarket (4¾ lengths behind Perfect Thought) on debut, travelling well but not handling the Dip: open to significant progress. *Roger Varian* **60 P**

SASINI 3 b.f. Fastnet Rock (AUS) 127 – Eva's Request (IRE) 115 (Soviet Star (USA) 128) [2017 60p: 8.3g2 8f2 8.3d5 8f4 8.5f* 8f3 Nov 26] attractive filly: fairly useful performer: won maiden at Del Mar in November: left Charles Hills after third start: stays 8.5f: acts on firm going: in blinkers last 3 starts. *Simon Callaghan, USA* **88**

SASSIE (IRE) 2 b.f. (Mar 30) Rip Van Winkle (IRE) 134 – Star of Gibraltar 88 (Rock of Gibraltar (IRE) 133) [2017 8.1g4 t8g3 t9.5g2 t8.6g3 Nov 11] 2,000Y: fourth foal: half-sister to useful winner up to 1¼m (stays 1½m) Percy Street (2-y-o 1m winner, by Sir Percy) and German 1m winner Star of Malta (by Kyllachy): dam, 1½m winner, closely related to Coronation Stakes winner Fallen For You: fair form: will be suited by 1¼m. *Sylvester Kirk* **68**

SATCHVILLE FLYER 6 ch.g. Compton Place 125 – Palinisa (FR) 106 (Night Shift (USA)) [2017 83§, a56§: f6g f6g6 f7g3 t7.1d t5g f5g5 6m 8.1d4 6.1d* 6.1v5 7.1m3 5d5 7d4 t7.2g3 5g6 7.4d5 p8s2 p8g 6s5 6v2 p7g4 t8.6g3 f8.1g2 f6.1g5 Dec 29] lengthy, dipped-backed gelding: fairly useful handicapper on turf, modest on all-weather: won at Chepstow in June: stays 8.5f: acts on all-weather and any turf going: tried in visor: often races towards rear: temperamental. *David Evans* **83 § a63 §**

SATELLITE EXPRESS (IRE) 6 ch.m. Observatory (USA) 131 – Composition 82 (Wolfhound (USA) 126) [2017 5.7f 5.3g5 f5g p7s Sep 30] smallish, angular mare: modest performer in 2014, lightly raced and little form since: stays 7f: acts on all-weather: usually in headgear: in tongue tie last 4 starts. *Tim Pinfield* **42**

SATIN RIBBON 3 ch.f. Shamardal (USA) 129 – Seattle Ribbon (USA) 70 (Seattle Dancer (USA) 119) [2017 p8d Jan 18] half-sister to numerous winners, including smart 1¼m winner Snoqualmie Boy and useful winner up to 1½m Snoqualmie Girl (2-y-o 7f/1m winner) (both by Montjeu): dam, maiden (stayed 1¼m), sister to Racing Post Trophy winner Seattle Rhyme: 15/2, well held in maiden at Kempton. *David Elsworth* **–**

SATISFY (IRE) 3 b.f. New Approach (IRE) 132 – Venturi 103 (Danehill Dancer (IRE) 117) [2017 9.5d4 10v 9.9d4 11.8d* 11.6d5 12v3 14d Oct 18] 60,000Y: half-sister to several winners, including useful 1m-11f winner Cilium (by War Chant) and 1m winner Call To Reason (by Pivotal): dam 2-y-o 6f/7f winner: fairly useful handicapper: won at Leicester in August: third at Pontefract (apprentice) in September: left Joseph Patrick O'Brien after third start: stays 1½m: acts on heavy going: often races prominently. *K. R. Burke* **86**

SATISH 4 b.g. Dansili 127 – Maycocks Bay 100 (Muhtarram (USA) 125) [2017 80§: 13.8m t16.5g^4 10.2f^5 11.9m t10.2s^5 10g^4 10g^3 t12.4d^6 9.2s^3 Aug 24] fair maiden: stays 13.5f: acts on polytrack, tapeta and good to firm going: wears headgear: often starts slowly: irresolute: sent to USA. *David O'Meara* **75 §**

SATIS HOUSE 3 b.f. Bahri (USA) 125 – Ex Mill Lady 60 (Bishop of Cashel 122) [2017 –: t10.2s May 23] well held in maidens: modest form over hurdles. *Susan Corbett* **–**

SATONO DIAMOND (JPN) 4 b.c. Deep Impact (JPN) 134 – Malpensa (ARG) (Orpen (USA) 116) [2017 127: 14.9m* 15.9g^3 11.9d^4 11.9d Oct 1] high-class performer: won Group 2 Hanshin Daishoten (by 1½ lengths from Cheval Grand) in March: in frame in Tenno Sho (Spring) at Kyoto (1½ lengths third to Kitasan Black) and Prix Foy at Chantilly (3½ lengths fourth to Dschingis Secret): behind in Prix de l'Arc de Triomphe at last-named course final outing: stays 2m: acts on firm going. *Yasutoshi Ikee, Japan* **127**

SATPURA 3 b.f. Indian Haven 119 – Selinda 53 (Piccolo 121) [2017 69: t6f p8g Jan 27] maiden, no form in 2017: usually races nearer last than first. *Mick Channon* **–**

SATTAR (IRE) 3 b.g. Zebedee 113 – Patroller (USA) 59 (Grand Slam (USA) 120) [2017 56: p7g^5 6m May 17] modest form: stays 7f: tried in blinkers. *Luke McJannet* **53**

SATTELAC 4 b.f. Kodiac 112 – Sattelight (Fraam 114) [2017 72: t9.5g f12m^3 f12m^2 Mar 7] fair handicapper: stays 1½m: acts on fibresand, good to firm and heavy going: tried in cheekpieces. *Keith Dalgleish* **76**

SAUCHIEHALL STREET (IRE) 2 b.g. (Apr 25) Mastercraftsman (IRE) 129 – Top Trail (USA) 67 (Exchange Rate (USA) 111) [2017 t7.2g^5 7.4g^5 t7.2g^6 p8g* p8g^4 t9.5g^6 Nov 20] modest performer: won nursery at Kempton in October: stays 9.5f: acts on polytrack and tapeta: sometimes slowly away. *Sylvester Kirk* **63**

SAUMUR 5 b.m. Mawatheeq (USA) 126 – Sparkling Montjeu (IRE) 63 (Montjeu (IRE) 137) [2017 84: t12.2g^4 12s^4 11.6m^2 11.4m^5 p12g^3 p12g^6 12g^4 10d^4 Oct 27] good-topped mare: fair handicapper: stays 1½m: acts on polytrack, soft and good to firm going. *Denis Coakley* **79**

SAUNTER (FR) 4 gr.g. Myboycharlie (IRE) 118 – Marie des Fleurs (FR) (Smart Strike (CAN) 121) [2017 107: 8.9g^6 10.3d 10g 12d^4 14g 12g^2 11.9s* Nov 11] workmanlike gelding: useful handicapper: won November Handicap at Doncaster (by 1¼ lengths from Chelsea Lad): left David Menuisier after fifth start: stays 1½m: acts on polytrack, soft and good to firm going: tried in cheekpieces: usually races nearer last than first. *Ian Williams* **109**

SAUSAGE FINGERS 2 b.c. (Mar 6) Red Jazz (USA) 125 – Italian Affair 62 (Fumo di Londra (IRE) 108) [2017 6m 7d^5 6.1g^6 6d^5 6d Aug 12] little form: in cheekpieces last 2 starts: front runner/races prominently. *Tom Dascombe* **–**

SAVAANAH (IRE) 2 b.f. (Feb 27) Olden Times 121 – Tanouma (USA) (Mr Greeley (USA) 122) [2017 7d^6 7s^2 p8d^2 Nov 22] third foal: half-sister to 6f winner Tundra (by Bated Breath): dam unraced half-sister to US Grade 3 8.5f winner Silent Roar: fair form: best effort when second in minor event at Kempton (1½ lengths behind Tanseeq) in November. *Roger Varian* **79**

SAVALAS (IRE) 2 gr.g. (Apr 12) Zebedee 113 – Tap The Dot (IRE) (Sharp Humor (USA) 118) [2017 5s^5 5m^3 5d* 6d 5.4d^5 6g Oct 13] £100,000 2-y-o: good-topped gelding: second foal: dam unraced half-sister to useful 2-y-o 6f/7f winner Wildcat Wizard: fairly useful performer: won minor event at Thirsk in July: best form at 5f: acts on good to firm and good to soft going. *Kevin Ryan* **81**

Betfred November Handicap, Doncaster—Saunter proves better than ever on just his second start for the Ian Williams yard as he beats Chelsea Lad (No.9), Eddystone Rock and Storm King

SAVANNAH BEAU 5 b.m. Major Cadeaux 121 – Mancunian Way (Green Desert (USA) 127) [2017 78: t6m^{6} t6d^{5} t5g 5m^{3} 5g 5d^{2} 5d 5s p5g^{4} t5d^{6} t5g Nov 3] fair handicapper: left Iain Jardine after second start: stays 6f: acts on tapeta, good to firm and good to soft going: wears headgear: usually slowly away: temperament under suspicion. *Derek Shaw* **75**

SAVANNAH DUSK (IRE) 2 b.f. (Mar 14) Dream Ahead (USA) 133 – First Class Favour (IRE) 89 (Exceed And Excel (AUS) 126) [2017 p7g Sep 25] €25,000F: first foal: dam, winner up to 1m (2-y-o 5f-7f winner), half-sister to useful performer up to 9f Mister Brightside: 33/1, well held in minor event at Kempton: should do better. *Eve Johnson Houghton* **– p**

SAVANNAH MOON (IRE) 3 b.f. Canford Cliffs (IRE) 133 – Tennessee Moon 73 (Darshaan 133) [2017 67: 6m^{5} 8.2d t7.1s^{2} 7.8g^{3} 10.2v^{4} 11.1s 9s* t10.2s Sep 19] fair handicapper: won at Carlisle in August: stays 9f: acts on tapeta, firm and soft going: tried in hood. *Kevin Ryan* **73**

SAVANNAH'S DREAM 3 b.f. Showcasing 117 – Grandmas Dream 86 (Kyllachy 129) [2017 85: 5m* 5s^{6} 5.9s^{5} 5.4d 6.1v^{5} Aug 8] sturdy filly: fairly useful performer: won maiden at Thirsk in May: best form at 5f: acts on soft and good to firm going: tried in cheekpieces. *David O'Meara* **83**

SAVANNAH SLEW 3 b.f. Kheleyf (USA) 116 – Saratoga Slew (IRE) 79 (Footstepsinthesand 120) [2017 84: 5.1g 6m 5.9s* 6.9s^{5} 7v^{3} 6g 6v^{3} 6v^{4} 6m Oct 14] sturdy filly: fairly useful handicapper: won at Carlisle in June: third at Doncaster in July and Hamilton in September: stays 7f: acts on good to firm and heavy going: wears headgear: usually slowly away/races towards rear: suspect temperament: sold 11,000 gns, sent to USA. *James Given* **93**

SAVANNAH'S SHOW 2 b.f. (Apr 26) Showcasing 117 – Grandmas Dream 86 (Kyllachy 129) [2017 5m 5d^{5} 5d^{5} t5.1g 5d^{2} 5s* 6g Oct 14] £21,000Y: close-coupled filly: third foal: sister to 5f winner Savannah's Dream: dam, 5f/6f winner, half-sister to useful 6f/7f performer Tremar: fair performer: won nursery at Musselburgh in October: stays 6f: acts on soft going. *Richard Guest* **65**

SAVED BY THE BELL (IRE) 7 b.g. Teofilo (IRE) 126 – Eyrecourt (IRE) 64 (Efisio 120) [2017 96: 12g 16.3d 14.1s 18g 14.1g^{2} 16.3g 16.1d 17.1v 14d^{3} 14g^{4} 16g^{4} t16.3g Nov 15] lengthy gelding: fairly useful handicapper nowadays: second at Yarmouth in July and Redcar in October: left David O'Meara after seventh start: stays 16.5f: acts on polytrack, soft and good to firm going: has worn headgear, including in 2017. *Lawrence Mullaney* **81**

SAVED MY BACON (IRE) 6 b.m. Camacho 118 – Sally Green (IRE) 79 (Common Grounds 118) [2017 87: p5d f5g^{6} p6g^{4} p5g^{4} p5g^{3} p5s* p5s* p5s^{6} p5g p5g Nov 2] fairly useful handicapper: won at Chelmsford in June (by 1¼ lengths from Vale of Flight) and July (by head from Alsvinder): stays 6f: acts on all-weather and good to firm going: wears headgear: usually races in rear. *Chris Dwyer* **85**

SAVE THE BEES 9 b.g. Royal Applause 124 – Rock Concert 71 (Bishop of Cashel 122) [2017 88: 10.3g 8g 9.9f 8.5g^{6} 10g^{3} 10.2m^{5} 9.9m^{2} 10.3g^{5} 10g* 9.8d^{2} 9.9g* 10.3m 10.3d^{2} 10v^{4} 10.3g 10v Oct 23] workmanlike gelding: fairly useful handicapper: won at Redcar and Beverley in August: second at Ripon in between and York in September: raced mainly around 1¼m nowadays: acts on polytrack, good to firm and heavy going: has worn headgear, including in 2017: front runner/races prominently. *Declan Carroll* **93**

SAVILE ROW (FR) 3 b.c. Ransom O'War (USA) 117 – Shikoku (Green Desert (USA) 127) [2017 8d^{6} 8.4g^{3} 8g^{5} 10m p8.9g Nov 21] close-coupled colt: half-brother to several winners abroad, including useful German winner up to 1m Smokejumper (2-y-o 7f winner, by Big Shuffle): dam unraced daughter of Lancashire Oaks winner Sandy Island: useful maiden: third in Dr Busch-Memorial at Krefeld (3¾ lengths behind Dragon Lips) in April: stays 8.5f: acts on soft going: in cheekpieces in 2017: usually races in rear. *Frau E. Mader, Germany* **104**

SAVING GRACE 2 b.f. (Mar 28) Mastercraftsman (IRE) 129 – Lady of Everest (IRE) (Montjeu (IRE) 137) [2017 8.3d Oct 18] fifth foal: half-sister to 3 winners, including smart winner up to 1¼m (stayed 1½m) Lady of Dubai (2-y-o 1m winner) and useful French 1¼m/10.5f winner Indian Skies (both by Dubawi): dam, unraced, closely related to smart performer up to 1¾m Roses For The Lady: 33/1, eighth in maiden at Nottingham (11 lengths behind Hadith) in October: should do better. *Luca Cumani* **67 p**

SAWLAAT (IRE) 3 gr.c. Clodovil (IRE) 116 – Jaywick (UAE) (Jade Robbery (USA) 121) [2017 p6d Mar 13] 7/1, well held in maiden at Chelmsford. *Richard Hannon* **–**

SAXO JACK (FR) 7 b.g. King's Best (USA) 132 – Gamma (FR) (Sadler's Wells (USA) 132) [2017 –: 8.3g 10.2f3 11.9m 10.2g3 Jul 22] smallish, sparely-made gelding: fairly useful handicapper nowadays: stays 1½m: acts on polytrack, firm and good to soft going: often in headgear nowadays: wears tongue tie: often starts slowly, usually races in rear: irresolute. *Sophie Leech* **81 §**

SAXON FLAMES (GER) 3 b.c. Shamardal (USA) 129 – Saphira's Fire (IRE) 111 (Cape Cross (IRE) 129) [2017 p7g2 t8gur Feb 17] fair form when second to Abatement in maiden at Lingfield on completed start: dead. *William Muir* **75**

SAXON GOLD (IRE) 4 ch.f. Zoffany (IRE) 121 – Apple Brandy (USA) (Cox's Ridge (USA)) [2017 56: 7g t8s Jun 29] maiden, well held in handicaps in 2017: best effort at 7f: acts on good to firm going: often in headgear. *John Davies* **–**

SAXONROAD BOY (USA) 2 b.g. (Apr 27) Mastercraftsman (IRE) 129 – Good Strike (USA) 63 (Smart Strike (CAN) 121) [2017 t6.1g 6g 7g6 7.2m t8s 8s3 Oct 3] modest maiden: best effort at 1m: acts on soft going: in cheekpieces last 2 starts: usually races towards rear. *Richard Fahey* **53**

SAXON WARRIOR (JPN) 2 b.c. (Jan 26) Deep Impact (JPN) 134 – Maybe (IRE) 117 (Galileo (IRE) 134) [2017 8d* 8s* 8d* Oct 28] **120 p**

Aidan O'Brien won the Racing Post Trophy for the eighth time when Saxon Warrior fought his way back on a windy Town Moor to claim a neck win in the last Group 1 of the season in Britain. It's unlikely, though, that any of the trainer's seven previous successes have taken up so much space in the sponsor's pages the next day. Saxon Warrior's win brought O'Brien's total of Group/Grade 1 victories for the year to twenty-six, passing a record set by Bobby Frankel in America fourteen years earlier. O'Brien handled the post-race attention, which inevitably focussed more on his own achievement than Saxon Warrior's, with his usual modesty, but his progress towards Frankel's tally, and his prospects of surpassing it, had been a hot topic for much of the autumn and there was, maybe, a hint of relief as much as satisfaction in the trainer's post-race quote 'I'm delighted we've got there', expressing a hope, perhaps, that attention would now switch elsewhere. 'I wasn't even thinking about it [the record] for a long time, but this last month it's been building up.'

Saxon Warrior's win at Doncaster took O'Brien's record in the Racing Post Trophy a step closer to a benchmark set by another great among the training ranks. If, as seems inevitable, O'Brien breaks that record too in due course, as a like-for-like achievement it might have a bit more resonance than beating a total set on another continent. Sir Henry Cecil trained ten winners of the race between Approval in 1969 (when it was the Observer Gold Cup) and King's Theatre in 1993. King's Theatre started favourite for the following year's Two Thousand Guineas in which he finished down the field but went much closer in his second attempt at a classic when runner-up in the Derby. Reference Point in 1986 was Cecil's only winner of the Doncaster Group 1 to go on to classic success with wins in the Derby and St Leger. A strong-galloping stayer, Reference Point had looked unlikely to be quick enough for the Guineas anyway, but a sinus operation in the spring put paid to any chances of a bid for the triple crown. Cecil's 1984 Doncaster winner Lanfranco did contest all three classics open to him the following season, much his best performance in them coming in the St Leger when third to his stable-companion Oh So Sharp who was herself completing the fillies' triple crown.

There hasn't been any mention yet of a triple crown bid for Saxon Warrior but a win at Newmarket in the spring would soon change that. He was, after all, already ante-post favourite for the Derby before the Racing Post Trophy and after Doncaster went into the winter disputing favouritism in many lists for the Two Thousand Guineas as well. O'Brien first won the Racing Post Trophy twenty years earlier with Saratoga Springs, since when his subsequent winners have included horses who, between them, have won all three classics open to colts. High Chaparral and Brian Boru, successful in 2001 and 2002, went on to win the Derby and St Leger respectively, while 2011 winner Camelot went closer than any colt since Nijinsky in 1970 to landing the triple crown, winning the first two legs before losing his unbeaten record when the shortest-priced favourite for the St Leger since Reference

Racing Post Trophy, Doncaster—
Saxon Warrior completes an unbeaten two-year-old season, rallying gamely once headed by Roaring Lion (left) to regain the advantage close home; the victory also sets a new world record as the 26th Group/Grade 1 win of the year for trainer Aidan O'Brien

Point. As a son of Montjeu, the Two Thousand Guineas had looked the classic in which Camelot might prove most vulnerable—'he may just get away with it'—said *Racehorses of 2011*, anticipating, correctly as it turned out, a substandard renewal of the Guineas, while soft ground at Newmarket made the Guineas more of a test than usual. Camelot's Racing Post Trophy, in which he had faced only four rivals, hadn't been a vintage edition either, but the same couldn't be said of the latest edition which featured much more strength in depth.

For a start, Saxon Warrior couldn't boast the best form in the book although he was sent off the 13/8 favourite under Ryan Moore in a twelve-strong field. The standard was set instead by 5/2-chance Verbal Dexterity who had shown himself very much at home in soft conditions when staying on strongly to win the National Stakes at the Curragh by three and a half lengths. Next in the betting came the unbeaten Royal Lodge Stakes winner Roaring Lion, who had narrowly beaten Saxon Warrior's stable-companion Nelson at Newmarket, while two more Ballydoyle colts, Seahenge and The Pentagon, completed the first five in the betting at 9/1 and 10/1. The Champagne Stakes winner Seahenge had since finished third in a Dewhurst which had demonstrated his stable's formidable strength in the two-year-old department, while The Pentagon had been ante-post Derby favourite in the summer before Saxon Warrior supplanted him, though he hadn't been out for three months since winning the Tyros Stakes at Leopardstown. Of the remainder, Haydock listed winner Chilean was bidding to be a fifth consecutive winner of the race for his rider Andrea Atzeni. While underfoot conditions were not that extreme for the time of year, it turned into a searching test of character, with the field running into a headwind and being taken along at a strong pace by outsiders Coat of Arms (the fourth Ballydoyle representative) and Verbal Dexterity's stable-companion Theobald. With that pair soon clear of the rest, Saxon Warrior travelled strongly at the head of the main bunch before moving easily into the lead over two furlongs out, accompanied at first by Verbal Dexterity, trying to cover the move on his inner. However, Saxon Warrior's main threat came on the outside when Roaring Lion, who had been last of all for most of the way, moved into a narrow lead approaching the final furlong. Saxon Warrior shifted left soon afterwards which looked to give Roaring Lion the upper hand but, when he too came off a true line in the blustery conditions, it was Saxon Warrior who proved the stronger as the pair fought it out against the far rail, Moore driving him back up to get the verdict by a neck. The Pentagon stayed on best of the rest, gaining a little on the first two in the closing stages, to be beaten another two and a half lengths into third, while Verbal Dexterity, never going with much fluency, ran below his National Stakes form in a one-paced fourth.

Saxon Warrior had won both his starts prior to the Racing Post Trophy. Odds of 8/1 for his debut in a maiden at the Curragh at the end of August, when he was ridden by Donnacha O'Brien, suggested that not that much was expected of Saxon Warrior first time (the stable ran two others, with Moore on the odds-on Christopher Robin who'd had the benefit of a run), but he made a big impression, coming from an unpromising position to be well on top at the finish and winning by three and a quarter lengths. Two of O'Brien's earlier Racing Post Trophy winners, Saratoga Springs and St Nicholas Abbey, had won the Beresford Stakes beforehand and, four weeks on from his debut, Saxon Warrior became the third to do so. He was Moore's mount this time and the favourite among three from his stable in a field of five for the Group 2 contest sponsored by Juddmonte which was moved to Naas from its usual home of the Curragh. Whilst still showing signs of greenness, Saxon Warrior quickened well from just off the pace under the softest conditions he encountered in his three races and was again well on top, with one of his stable-companions Delano Roosevelt two and a half lengths back in second.

Saxon Warrior had the headlines largely to himself after the Beresford as he moved to the head of the Derby betting, but the race marked another noteworthy achievement at the very least—maybe even another record—for O'Brien, albeit one that this time seemed to go practically unnoticed. Saxon Warrior was not only O'Brien's seventh consecutive winner of the Beresford (future St Leger and Irish Derby winner Capri had won it twelve months earlier), he was the trainer's *seventeenth* winner in twenty-two runnings of a race he first won in 1996. Some Australian sources credit Sydney trainer Tommy Smith with setting a world record with his sixteen wins in the Chelmsford Stakes, though strictly speaking the majority of those wins came before Australia introduced its pattern race classification in 1979/80 (the latest running of the Group 2 Chelmsford was won by Winx). O'Brien himself won his sixteenth Phoenix Stakes with Sioux Nation earlier in the year before going one better in the Beresford.

Saxon Warrior certainly lived up to the second part of his name with his hard-fought win at Doncaster but on breeding he's arguably as much 'Samurai' as 'Saxon'. His sire Deep Impact was a top-class winner of the Japanese version of the triple crown, a feat that doesn't demand quite so much versatility as it does in Britain as the first leg is run over a mile and a quarter. Deep Impact's success at stud in Japan, where he has assumed the mantle of his outstanding sire Sunday Silence in much the same way Galileo succeeded Sadler's Wells in Ireland, has not gone unnoticed by some of Europe's leading bloodstock operations. The Wildensteins were the first to benefit in a major way from using Deep Impact when his daughter Beauty Parlour won the Poule d'Essai des Pouliches in 2012. Others to have had success sending mares to Japan to be covered by Deep Impact are the Niarchos and Wertheimer families, the latter being the breeders of the smart colt Akihiro who had an essay in *Racehorses of 2016*. Coolmore sent its first mares to Deep Impact in 2013, resulting in a couple of useful three-year-old winners in the latest season, Wisconsin and Pavlenko. However, repeating the experiment a year later yielded still better results as the full siblings to that pair are the Fillies' Mile runner-up September and Saxon Warrior. Wisconsin and September are out of the Irish Oaks, Nassau Stakes and Yorkshire Oaks winner Peeping Fawn who would have been a tricky mare to find a suitable mate for in Europe, being by Danehill out of a daughter of Sadler's Wells. A similar lack of options meant that Deep Impact was a suitable match for Maybe, the dam of Pavlenko and Saxon Warrior, as she is by Galileo out of a Danehill mare. These successes have encouraged Coolmore to send its classic-winning daughters of Galileo, Minding and Winter, to Deep Impact for the start of their broodmare careers in 2018.

Saxon Warrior (JPN) (b.c. 2015)	Deep Impact (JPN) (b 2002)	Sunday Silence (b or br 1986)	Halo
			Wishing Well
		Wind In Her Hair (b 1991)	Alzao
			Burghclere
	Maybe (IRE) (b 2009)	Galileo (b 1998)	Sadler's Wells
			Urban Sea
		Sumora (b 2002)	Danehill
			Rain Flower

Unusually for a daughter of Galileo, Maybe's three-year-old season was an anti-climax after a faultless two-year-old campaign. She was unbeaten in five starts in her first season, making a winning debut over six furlongs before reeling off the Chesham Stakes, Silver Flash Stakes, Debutante Stakes and Moyglare Stud Stakes, all over seven. Smart, progressive and looking just the type to train on well, Maybe was well fancied for both the One Thousand Guineas and the Oaks which went instead to stable companions. She finished third to Homecoming Queen when 13/8 favourite at Newmarket, and was then fifth to Was at Epsom, not beaten so far as in the Guineas but giving the impression a mile and a half stretched her stamina. However, back at a mile, disappointing efforts in the Falmouth and Matron Stakes suggested Maybe hadn't trained on. Maybe's sisters Fluff and Promise To Be True didn't build on initial promise either. Fluff won her only start at three impressively over a mile but failed to add to that success in three outings the following year, while Promise To Be True, who emulated Maybe by winning the Silver Flash and was runner-up in the Prix Marcel Boussac, made only one appearance in the latest season, finishing sixth when favourite for the One Thousand Guineas Trial at Leopardstown, the finish of which was fought out by stable-companions Hydrangea and Winter. But there's much more encouragement for Saxon Warrior's three-year-old prospects a bit further back in his family. His grandam Sumora, although a useful sprinter herself, was a close relative of Oaks winner Dancing Rain (dam of Magic Lily, third in the latest Fillies' Mile), while his unraced great grandam Rain Flower was a half-sister, among others, to the 1992 Derby winner Dr Devious. It is worth mentioning also that Saxon Warrior's sire comes from a family of classic performers; Deep Impact's dam Wind In Her Hair was second in the Oaks and out of a half-sister to the dam of Two Thousand Guineas and Derby winner Nashwan. Saxon Warrior's three-year-old sister Pavlenko ran ten times in the latest season but her best trip isn't the easiest to discern from all those starts. When she got off the mark in a seven-furlong maiden at the Curragh in July she was dropping back from eleven furlongs on her previous outing. She picked up some 'black type' from third place in a listed event at a mile later in the year, though that trip looked inadequate for her on her final start having been tried over as far as a mile and a half (respectable fourth in another listed contest) in the interim. Saxon Warrior, a tall colt with a powerful action, will stay at least a mile and a quarter, which isn't to say the Guineas will be too short for him as he is by no means short of speed. He looks sure to make up into a high-class three-year-old and as such is as good a classic prospect as any in a stable that, even by its usual high standards, was brimming with two-year-old talent in another memorable year for all at Ballydoyle. *Aidan O'Brien, Ireland*

SAXONY 6 b.m. Bertolini (USA) 125 – Just Down The Road (IRE) 71 (Night Shift (USA)) **–**
[2017 42: f6g t6g 8f 8v Sep 17] little form: tried in tongue tie. *Matthew Salaman*

SAY ABOUT IT 2 b.g. (Mar 1) Sayif (IRE) 122 – Manaaber (USA) 80 (Medicean 128) **54**
[2017 7.5g 8g p7.5g p8g Oct 14] modest form: stays 1m. *J. S. Moore*

SAYEDAATI SAADATI (IRE) 4 b.g. Montjeu (IRE) 137 – Guessing (USA) 52 **–**
(Kingmambo (USA) 125) [2017 64: f8g p12d p13.3g Mar 2] maiden: no form in 2017: has worn headgear/tongue tie, including in 2017: often races prominently/lazily. *John Butler*

SAYEM 3 b.f. Sayif (IRE) 122 – Usem (Bahamian Bounty 116) [2017 81p: p7g 7g^5 6m^6 **90**
8.1g* 8.1m* 8g 7g^3 8.1d^4 Oct 23] fairly useful handicapper: won at Windsor (twice, by 2¾ lengths from High On Love second occasion) in July: third at Newmarket in September: stays 1m: acts on polytrack, good to firm and good to soft going. *Ed Walker*

SAYESSE 3 b.g. Sayif (IRE) 122 – Pesse (IRE) (Eagle Eyed (USA) 111) [2017 88: p6g^{4} 5.7f^{3} 6.1m^{3} 6d 6m 6.1m^{6} 5.7g^{5} Jul 26] good-topped gelding: fairly useful handicapper: third at Bath in April and Chester in May: stays 6f: acts on polytrack, firm and soft going: tried in visor: sometimes slowly away, usually races in rear. *Mick Channon* **91**

SCALA REGIA (FR) 3 b.f. Kyllachy 129 – Caprarola (USA) 84 (Rahy (USA) 115) [2017 p5g^{6} p6g^{3} t6d^{3} t7.1g* t7.1g^{4} 8f^{5} p8d* p8s^{6} t9.5g p8g^{3} 8d p8g^{2} p7.5g^{5} p7.5g^{5} Dec 26] fifth foal: half-sister to French 5.5f-11f winner Rudyard (2-y-o 1m winner, by Iffraaj) and French 7.5f winner Boyissime (by Exceed And Excel): dam, 7f winner (including at 2 yrs), out of smart close relative to Halling: fairly useful performer: won handicaps at Newcastle in March and Kempton in July: second in minor event at Chantilly in November: left Sir Mark Prescott Bt after tenth start: stays 1m: acts on polytrack and tapeta: has worn headgear. *S. Wattel, France* **94**

SCALES OF JUSTICE (IRE) 3 b.g. Galileo (IRE) 134 – Half Queen (USA) (Deputy Minister (CAN)) [2017 66p: 10.2m^{3} p12d May 31] fair form: best effort when third in maiden at Chepstow in May: remains with potential. *Charles Hills* **76 p**

SCANDALEUSE (USA) 2 b.f. (Jan 31) War Front (USA) 119 – Aruna (USA) (Mr Greeley (USA) 122) [2017 p6g p6g^{2} p7g^{2} p7g^{3} Nov 2] sturdy filly: second foal: dam smart Grade 1 9f winner in USA (earlier 2-y-o 1m winner in France): fairly useful form: placed 3 times: stays 7f. *Sir Michael Stoute* **80**

SCANNERMANDANGO 4 b.f. Bahamian Bounty 116 – Regal Asset (USA) (Regal Classic (CAN)) [2017 –: t8g t8g^{6} t8d^{6} t8d 10m 8m 10s^{5} Jun 12] little form: tried in tongue tie: sometimes slowly away, usually races nearer last than first. *Jim Goldie* **–**

SCAPUSC 2 b.c. (Jan 23) Bated Breath 125 – Fularmada (Manduro (GER) 135) [2017 6d Sep 19] in tongue tie, 9/1, tenth in minor event at Yarmouth (6¼ lengths behind Mutaaqeb) in September. *Marco Botti* **61**

SCARLET DRAGON 4 b.g. Sir Percy 129 – Welsh Angel (Dubai Destination (USA) 127) [2017 118: 10m^{6} 10.3m 12s^{3} 13.9m p12g^{2} 11m Sep 23] sturdy gelding: smart performer: placed in Glorious Stakes at Goodwood (1¾ lengths behind Poet's Word) in August and September Stakes at Kempton (head behind Chemical Charge): stays 1½m: acts on polytrack, soft and good to firm going: usually wears hood: often races towards rear. *Eve Johnson Houghton* **116**

SCARLET THRUSH (IRE) 3 b.f. Kodiac 112 – Reveal The Star (USA) (Aptitude (USA) 128) [2017 69: t9.5g^{5} t9.5m 8g^{6} 8.2d^{3} 7.6s p16g^{6} p12g Nov 8] fair maiden: left Marco Botti after fourth start: best effort at 9.5f: acts on tapeta: often in headgear in 2017. *Luke McJannet* **67**

SCEALTARA (IRE) 3 b.f. Holy Roman Emperor (IRE) 125 – Sceal Nua (IRE) 92 (Iffraaj 127) [2017 t6d^{4} p5g p6g^{3} t7.1g t7.1g Apr 5] second foal: dam winner up to 1¼m (2-y-o 7f winner): modest maiden: stays 6f: acts on polytrack and tapeta: sometimes slowly away. *David O'Meara* **52**

SCENERY 2 ch.g. (Apr 7) Elnadim (USA) 128 – Widescreen (USA) (Distant View (USA) 126) [2017 6g^{4} 6s^{3} 6g Oct 7] fair form when third in minor event at Ascot (2½ lengths behind Speak In Colours) on second of 3 starts: will stay 7f. *Eve Johnson Houghton* **76**

SCENIC RIVER 2 ch.f. (Mar 30) Dutch Art 126 – Camp Riverside (USA) (Forest Camp (USA) 114) [2017 6s 6v^{6} 6d^{2} 6d^{4} Nov 11] £20,000Y: sixth foal: half-sister to 3 winners, including 7f winner Admiralty (by Iffraaj) and 1m winner Bluff Crag (by Canford Cliffs): dam, US 5.5f-6.5f winner, out of half-sister to dual Breeders' Cup Mile winner Da Hoss: fair form: raced only at 6f: will go on improving. *Tim Easterby* **71 p**

SCENT OF POWER 5 b.m. Authorized (IRE) 133 – Aromatherapy 96 (Oasis Dream 129) [2017 62: t8.6g 10g 10d^{3} 10.2m^{6} 8.2g^{4} 8.2g^{5} 10d 10d^{4} f8.1g Nov 16] modest handicapper: stays 1¼m: acts on polytrack, tapeta and soft going: tried in hood: often in tongue tie in 2017: often races prominently. *Barry Leavy* **54**

SCHMOOZE (IRE) 8 b.m. One Cool Cat (USA) 123 – If Dubai (USA) (Stephen Got Even (USA) 125) [2017 57: 14m^{2} 11.1g 12.1m^{6} 13.1s^{6} 12.5g^{4} 13.1g 11.1g^{2} 12.5m^{3} 15g^{6} 12.1s 14m^{5} 14s^{3} 12.5s Oct 9] modest handicapper: stays 1¾m: acts on polytrack, soft and good to firm going: has worn headgear: usually races in rear. *Linda Perratt* **57**

SCHOOL RUN (IRE) 3 b.f. Invincible Spirit (IRE) 121 – By Invitation (USA) 75 (Van Nistelrooy (USA) 108) [2017 67p: t6f^{4} t5g^{2} t5.1g* Feb 17] fair form: won handicap at Wolverhampton in February: best form at 5f. *David O'Meara* **70**

SCHOTTISCHE 7 ch.m. Pastoral Pursuits 127 – Calligraphy 79 (Kris 135) [2017 60: f8g* t8.6g4 t8.6g5 t9.5g 8m t8.6g4 p10g 8g Aug 12] fair handicapper: won at Southwell in January: stays 9.5f: acts on all-weather and good to soft going: wears headgear: sometimes slowly away, usually races nearer last than first: inconsistent. *Alan Bailey* **66**

SCOFFLAW 3 b.g. Foxwedge (AUS) 128 – Belle des Airs (IRE) 92 (Dr Fong (USA) 128) [2017 82: 6m4 6g* 6d 6m6 6m2 6m4 6d3 6d4 6m6 7g* 7d 7d Oct 28] lengthy gelding: useful handicapper: won at Thirsk in May and Epsom (by 1¼ lengths from Bumptious) in September: second at Haydock (head behind Hart Stopper) in July: stays 7f: acts on good to firm and good to soft going. *Richard Fahey* **95**

SCOONES 3 ch.g. Sepoy (AUS) 129 – Hannda (IRE) 74 (Dr Devious (IRE) 127) [2017 –p: 8g p8s5 p8d4 p10g* 10g Oct 17] fairly useful handicapper: won at Lingfield in September: stays 1¼m: acts on polytrack. *James Fanshawe* **81**

SCORCHING HEAT 3 b.g. Acclamation 118 – Pink Flames (IRE) (Redback 116) [2017 81: 6d* 6d2 6g2 6g3 6d2 6d* Aug 5] useful-looking gelding: useful handicapper: won at Salisbury in May and Goodwood (by ¾ length from Tommy G) in August: should stay 7f: acts on soft going: races prominently, often travels strongly. *Andrew Balding* **97**

SCOTCH MYST 3 gr.g. Sepoy (AUS) 129 – Shena's Dream (IRE) 88 (Oasis Dream 129) [2017 61: f6g* t6m5 t6f4 f5g2 6g 6g3 6m 6d t6.1g4 f6.1g3 Dec 29] leggy gelding: modest handicapper: won at Southwell in January: stays 6f: acts on all-weather and good to soft going: often races prominently. *Richard Fahey* **63**

SCOTS PIPER 3 b.g. Shamardal (USA) 129 – Miss Jean Brodie (USA) 106 (Maria's Mon (USA) 121) [2017 72p: 8s 8d5 10.2g6 Jul 8] fair form: should be suited by further than 1m: sold £10,000, sent to Denmark. *Mark Johnston* **71**

SCOTS SNAP (IRE) 2 b.f. (Mar 3) Kyllachy 129 – Sensational Samba (IRE) (Exceed And Excel (AUS) 126) [2017 6d 6d Nov 11] rather unfurnished filly: first foal: dam unraced half-sister to useful winners Gwaihir (at 1m) and Mombassa (up to 9.6f): well held in minor event/maiden. *Marcus Tregoning* **–**

SCOTTISH GLEN 11 ch.g. Kyllachy 129 – Dance For Fun 74 (Anabaa (USA) 130) [2017 102: 7s 7g6 7g4 7s4 7d 7d p8g p8g4 Dec 13] sturdy gelding: useful handicapper: stays 1m: acts on polytrack, firm and good to soft going: tried in cheekpieces. *Patrick Chamings* **94**

SCOTTISH (IRE) 5 b.g. Teofilo (IRE) 126 – Zeiting (IRE) 105 (Zieten (USA) 118) [2017 119: 10m5 Jun 21] rangy gelding: very smart performer: 3 lengths fifth to Highland Reel in Prince of Wales's Stakes at Royal Ascot only outing of 2017: effective at 9f to 1½m: acts on firm and good to soft going: front runner/races prominently: sent to USA. *Charlie Appleby* **122**

SCOTTISH JIG (USA) 2 ch.f. (Feb 7) Speightstown (USA) 124 – Light Jig 121 (Danehill (USA) 126) [2017 p8g Dec 20] sister to very smart winner up to 1¼m (US Grade 1) Seek Again (2-y-o 7f winner), closely related to smart winner up to 1½m Treble Jig (2-y-o 7f winner, by Gone West) and half-sister to 2 winners: dam 1m-1¼m (including US Grade 1) winner who stayed 1½m: 11/2, shaped well when seventh in minor event at Kempton (5½ lengths behind Native Appeal) in December, having hopeless task from position: sort to improve markedly. *John Gosden* **64 P**

SCOTTISH SUMMIT (IRE) 4 b.g. Shamardal (USA) 129 – Scottish Stage (IRE) 112 (Selkirk (USA) 129) [2017 75: 12g 10f2 10.2g4 8d6 10g3 Sep 27] lengthy gelding: fair maiden: stays 1¼m: acts on firm and good to soft going: usually races prominently. *Geoffrey Harker* **77**

SCOTTSDALE 4 b.g. Cape Cross (IRE) 129 – High Praise (USA) 111 (Quest For Fame 127) [2017 12.3g6 Aug 26] 15,000 3-y-o: close-coupled, rather leggy gelding: half-brother to several winners, including smart 1¼m-1½m winner Eagles Peak (by Galileo) and useful 11f/1½m winner Sight Unseen (by Sadler's Wells): dam, winner up to 1½m (2-y-o 7f/1m winner), half-sister to top-class winner up to 9f Observatory: dual bumper winner: 9/4, when well held in maiden at Chester: should do better. *Brian Ellison* **– p**

SCRAFTON 6 b.g. Leporello (IRE) 118 – Some Diva 75 (Dr Fong (USA) 128) [2017 71§: t13.9f5 f14g3 t13.9g* t13.9f6 p15.8f f14g* p10g f12.1g Nov 28] workmanlike gelding: fair handicapper: won apprentice events at Wolverhampton in February and Southwell in April: stays 2m: acts on all-weather and good to firm going: carries head high. *Tony Carroll* **73**

SCREAMING GEMINI (IRE) 3 b.g. Shamardal (USA) 129 – Littlefeather (IRE) 107 (Indian Ridge 123) [2017 70: 6g2 7g5 7d Aug 21] fair maiden: stays 7f: in headgear in 2017. *Roger Varian* **73**

SCRIBBLER 3 b.f. Excelebration (IRE) 133 – Ja One (IRE) 74 (Acclamation 118) [2017 7g^3 8g p8g Aug 22] fourth foal: closely related to 5f/6f winner You're Cool (by Exceed And Excel): dam, 2m winner, half-sister to Nunthorpe Stakes winner Margot Did: modest form when third at Lingfield on first of 3 starts in maidens. *Rae Guest* **63**

SCRIBNER CREEK (IRE) 4 b.g. Roderic O'Connor (IRE) 119 – Nebraska Lady (IRE) 87 (Lujain (USA) 119) [2017 72: t8.6m^3 p8g^6 p8g* 8.3g^2 t8.6g* 8.3g^4 p8s^6 p10d p8g t8.6g^5 p8g^5 Nov 7] fair handicapper: won at Chelmsford in March and Wolverhampton in April: left Daniel Loughnane after seventh start: stays 8.5f: acts on polytrack and tapeta: often races towards rear. *Denis Quinn* **74**

SCRUFFY MCGUFFY 4 b.g. Firebreak 125 – Eloquent Isle (IRE) (Mull of Kintyre (USA) 114) [2017 69: t8.6g 9m 9.1m 9s 12.1d Aug 17] fair performer at 3 yrs, no form in 2017: tried in cheekpieces. *Ann Duffield* **–**

SCRUTINEER (IRE) 4 b.g. Intense Focus (USA) 117 – Royal Esteem (Mark of Esteem (IRE) 137) [2017 109: 6g 6g 6s 6d a6f^2 a7f^2 a6f^5 Dec 1] rather leggy gelding: useful handicapper: twice second at Meydan in November: left Mick Channon after fourth start: stays 7f: acts on dirt, heavy and good to firm going: front runner/races prominently. *A. Al Rayhi, UAE* **101**

SCRUTINY 6 b.g. Aqlaam 125 – Aunty Mary 82 (Common Grounds 118) [2017 –: t8g f11.1g Dec 21] lengthy gelding: fairly useful at best, lightly raced and no form since 2015 (including over hurdles): stays 1¼m: acts on good to firm and heavy going: has worn headgear. *Kevin Ryan* **–**

SCUZEME 3 ch.g. Kheleyf (USA) 116 – Barbieri (IRE) 91 (Encosta de Lago (AUS)) [2017 –: t5g* 5.1g^2 5g^6 5m t5g Oct 10] fairly useful performer: won maiden at Newcastle (by 3 lengths from School Run) in January: raced mainly around 5f: acts on tapeta: sometimes slowly away, usually races towards rear. *David Barron* **89**

SEABORN (IRE) 3 b.g. Born To Sea (IRE) 117 – Next To The Top (Hurricane Run (IRE) 134) [2017 –: p12g p10g* 11.5d Sep 19] modest handicapper: won at Chelmsford in February, standout effort: left Simon Hodgson after. *Tim Vaughan* **64**

SEABOROUGH (IRE) 2 b.g. (Mar 19) Born To Sea (IRE) 117 – Nobilissima (IRE) 94 (Orpen (USA) 116) [2017 t8.6g^6 t8.6g 8.3g Nov 1] modest form: raced around 1m. *Alan King* **64**

SEA DWELLER 4 b.f. High Chaparral (IRE) 132 – Langoustine (AUS) 117 (Danehill (USA) 126) [2017 75p: t8.6g^3 t9.5g^3 12.1v^5 p10s Dec 14] fair maiden: stays 1¼m: acts on polytrack and tapeta. *Anthony Carson* **71**

SEAELLA (IRE) 2 b.f. (Mar 18) Canford Cliffs (IRE) 133 – Gems 73 (Haafhd 129) [2017 5m^4 6m 6m* 6.9g^3 7s^4 t7.1d^2 7m^2 6s* 7s* 7d^2 Nov 1] €18,000F, €14,000Y: second foal: half-sister to useful winner up to 1¼m Fayez (2-y-o 6f winner, by Zoffany): dam, 1½m/13f winner, half-sister to smart performer up to 2m Frank Sonata: useful performer: won seller at York in June, claimer at Fontainebleau in September (left John Quinn after) and minor event at Maisons-Laffitte in October: second in Prix Miesque at Maisons-Laffitte (short neck behind Sweety Dream) in November: stays 7f: acts on soft and good to firm going: front runner/races prominently. *Fabrice Vermeulen, Belgium* **99**

SEA ESS SEAS (IRE) 2 b.c. (Apr 18) Swiss Spirit 117 – Rabshih (IRE) 62 (Green Desert (USA) 127) [2017 p6g^6 p6g^5 p7g Dec 31] modest form in minor events: should stay at least 7f: wears tongue tie. *Jamie Osborne* **62**

SEAFARER (IRE) 3 br.g. Henrythenavigator (USA) 131 – Rose of Petra (IRE) 91 (Golan (IRE) 129) [2017 74: 10.1m^2 9.9m^2 10.2d^2 12d* 12s 12m^6 Sep 23] useful handicapper: won at Chepstow (by 2¼ lengths from Star of The East) in August: stays 1½m: acts on good to firm and good to soft going. *Marcus Tregoning* **105**

SEA FOX (IRE) 3 b.g. Kodiac 112 – City Maiden (USA) (Carson City (USA)) [2017 104: 8g^4 7m^6 8m^6 7d^6 9.9g 12m 7d^3 10s^5 7d Nov 11] tall, good-quartered gelding: useful handicapper: third at Ascot (¾ length behind Mukalal) in October: stays 1¼m: acts on good to firm and good to soft going: wears tongue tie. *David Evans* **98**

SEAHENGE (USA) 2 b.c. (Apr 10) Scat Daddy (USA) 120 – Fools In Love (USA) (Not For Love (USA)) [2017 6g* 7g^5 7g* 7m^3 8d Oct 28] $750,000Y: tall, attractive colt: third foal: half-brother to winners in USA by Mineshaft and City Zip: dam, US winner up to 8.5f (2-y-o 5f winner), closely related to smart US Grade 2 8.5f/9f winner International Star: **112**

Howcroft Industrial Supplies Champagne Stakes, Doncaster—Seahenge passes the whole field, edging out the consistent Hey Gaman (star on cap) and Mythical Magic (left)

smart performer: won maiden at Naas (by neck from Yulong Warrior) in July and Champagne Stakes at Doncaster (by neck from Hey Gaman) in September: third in Dewhurst Stakes at Newmarket (5 lengths behind U S Navy Flag) in October: stays 7f: best form on good going: usually races nearer last than first. *Aidan O'Brien, Ireland*

SEAMOOR SECRET 5 b.m. Sakhee's Secret 128 – Labaqa (USA) 92 (Rahy (USA) 115) [2017 40: p7d p8d Feb 15] poor maiden: stays 6f: acts on good to firm and good to soft going: has worn headgear: wears tongue tie. *Alex Hales* –

SEAMOUR (IRE) 6 b.g. Azamour (IRE) 130 – Chifney Rush (IRE) (Grand Lodge (USA) 125) [2017 114: 13.9g³ t16.3s 13.9m 14.5g⁴ Sep 15] lengthy gelding: useful performer: third in listed race at York (5 lengths behind Dal Harraild) in May: stays 16.5f: acts on polytrack, tapeta, soft and good to firm going: has worn cheekpieces, including final start. *Brian Ellison* **107**

SEAMSTER 10 ch.g. Pivotal 124 – Needles And Pins (IRE) 104 (Fasliyev (USA) 120) [2017 91: f5g p5g³ p6g³ p5g⁴ 5m² 5m 5m⁴ 5.1m⁶ 5s⁵ 6m⁴ 5g³ 5g³ 6g 5m 6.1g⁵ t6.1g 5.7g² 5.1v² 5d² 5s⁴ 6d* 5m 5d² 5.7d⁵ 6g 5.7s 5.7s³ 6s 5g* t5.1g Nov 11] compact gelding: fairly useful handicapper: won at Lingfield in August and Nottingham (by ¾ length from Lydiate Lady) in November: best at 5f/6f: acts on polytrack, fibresand, sand, good to firm and heavy going: has worn headgear: wears tongue tie. *David Loughnane* **89**

SEA MY DIAMOND (IRE) 3 b.f. Born To Sea (IRE) 117 – She's My Rock (IRE) 55 (Rock of Gibraltar (IRE) 133) [2017 –: 6.1m p5g 7.6d Aug 12] no form. *Mark Hoad* –

SEAN O'CASEY (IRE) 4 b.g. Galileo (IRE) 134 – Lahinch (IRE) 104 (Danehill Dancer (IRE) 117) [2017 82: 11.5m* 11.9g⁵ 12.3s p11g 10.2d³ 11.8d⁵ Sep 12] lengthy gelding: fairly useful handicapper: placed in maidens for Aidan O'Brien in Ireland in 2016: won at Yarmouth (by 3¼ lengths from Stoney Broke) in May: stays 1½m: acts on soft and good to firm going: has worn tongue tie: front runner/races prominently. *Michael Appleby* **86**

SEA OF FLAMES 4 ch.g. Aqlaam 125 – Hidden Fire 82 (Alhaarth (IRE) 126) [2017 96, a105: a8f a9.9f p8f Mar 4] sturdy gelding: useful performer at 3 yrs, below that level in 2017: stays 1m: acts on polytrack: sold to join Richard Spencer 35,000 gns in July. *David Elsworth* **90**

SEA OF GRACE (IRE) 3 ch.f. Born To Sea (IRE) 117 – Lady Dettoria (FR) (Vettori (IRE) 119) [2017 106p: 7m⁵ 8d² 8m⁴ 8.2d* 10s⁴ 8s⁵ Oct 21] lengthy, rather unfurnished filly: smart performer: won listed race at Haydock (by 4½ lengths from Lincoln Rocks) in August: second in Poule d'Essai des Pouliches at Deauville (1¾ lengths behind Precieuse) in May: stays 1m: acts on soft and good to firm going: often races towards rear/travels strongly. *William Haggas* **114**

SEA OF GREEN 5 b.m. Iffraaj 127 – Sea of Leaves (USA) 103 (Stormy Atlantic (USA)) [2017 54§: t5d³ t6d⁵ t5g⁵ t5g* 6g 6m² 5m⁵ 6m³ t6s⁵ 6d* 7.2m² 7.2g⁶ t6g⁵ 6d² 7.2d⁶ 5.9g³ 6g* 6g⁴ 6d⁴ 6d 7.2m⁴ Aug 11] fair handicapper: won at Newcastle in March and Ayr in June/July: stays 7f: acts on tapeta, firm and good to soft going: wears headgear: often races in rear. *Jim Goldie* **66**

SEA OF HEAVEN (IRE) 5 b.g. Sea The Stars (IRE) 140 – Maid of Killeen (IRE) 97 (Darshaan 133) [2017 105: 18.6m May 10] good-topped gelding: useful handicapper at best: had little go right when last of 17 to Montaly in Chester Cup on sole outing in 2017: stayed 2¼m: acted on polytrack, soft and good to firm going: dead. *Sir Mark Prescott Bt* –

SEA OF HOPE (IRE) 4 b.f. Rock of Gibraltar (IRE) 133 – Labrusca 58 (Grand Lodge (USA) 125) [2017 63: 8s 7.5s^3 7v p7g Dec 28] fair maiden: left A. P. Keatley after third start: stays 7.5f: acts on soft and good to firm going. *Henry Candy* **67**

SEAPORT 6 ch.g. Champs Elysees 124 – Cochin (USA) (Swain (IRE) 134) [2017 12d 18d Sep 23] workmanlike gelding: useful at best in France for A. Fabre, lightly raced and no form since 2015: stays 1¾m: acts on viscoride and soft going: tried in tongue tie. *Seamus Durack* **–**

SEAQUINN 2 b.f. (Apr 17) Equiano (FR) 127 – Marine Girl 73 (Shamardal (USA) 129) [2017 6d p6g Oct 4] second foal: sister to 6f winner Black Salt: dam 1m winner: little impact in maidens. *John Best* **–**

SEARANGER (USA) 4 b.g. U S Ranger (USA) 124 – Baby Lets Cruise (USA) (Tale of The Cat (USA) 113) [2017 72: 5m^6 5g^5 5g 6m* 6m^3 6m^4 5.9g^5 6m* 6g 6g^4 6g^3 t6g t7.1d t6.1g* Nov 11] fair performer: won sellers at Catterick in May and July, and handicap at Wolverhampton in November: stays 6f: acts on tapeta, soft and good to firm going: has worn cheekpieces, including in 2017: tried in tongue tie. *Rebecca Menzies* **68**

SEA'S ARIA (IRE) 6 b.g. Sea The Stars (IRE) 140 – Speed Song 92 (Fasliyev (USA) 120) [2017 61: p12g p12g^5 16.8m^4 p16g Dec 20] modest handicapper: left Denis Hogan after third start: stays 2m: acts on polytrack, soft and good to firm going: tried in cheekpieces: wears tongue tie: fair hurdler/maiden chaser. *Mark Hoad* **64**

SEASEARCH 2 b.g. (Feb 17) Passing Glance 119 – Seaflower Reef (IRE) 68 (Robellino (USA) 127) [2017 p8g p8g t8.6d Dec 9] little show in minor events. *Andrew Balding* **–**

SEA SHACK 3 b.g. Equiano (FR) 127 – Folly Bridge 106 (Avonbridge 123) [2017 81: p7g^2 p7g^2 p7d^6 7m^6 7d^6 p7d^4 8g^6 Sep 15] sturdy gelding: fairly useful handicapper: second at Kempton in April and Lingfield in May: stays 7f: acts on polytrack and good to firm going: races prominently. *William Knight* **85**

SEASIDE DREAMER 3 b.g. Pivotal 124 – Striving (IRE) 66 (Danehill Dancer (IRE) 117) [2017 8d 10g^4 Jul 20] well held in 2 maidens: sold £7,000, sent to Greece. *Michael Bell* **–**

SEA SKIMMER 3 ch.g. Dubawi (IRE) 129 – Portmanteau 96 (Barathea (IRE) 127) [2017 69p: 10m a6f* a8f* Dec 21] rather unfurnished gelding: fairly useful form: won maiden at Jebel Ali in November and handicap at Meydan (by ¾ length from Flashy Snapper) in December: left Saeed bin Suroor after first start: best form at up to 1m: acts on sand and dirt: tried in visor. *H. Al Alawi, UAE* **93**

SEA SOVEREIGN (IRE) 4 b.g. Sea The Stars (IRE) 140 – Lidakiya (IRE) 105 (Kahyasi 130) [2017 10m^3 11.6g^5 11.9m^4 10g Jul 24] €150,000F, 500,000Y, 6,000 3-y-o: tall gelding: half-brother to several winners, including very smart 6f-1¼m winner Linngari (2-y-o 7f winner, by Indian Ridge) and useful 7f/1m winner Lingapour (by Gulch): dam 1¼m-1½m winner: in frame twice in bumpers: fairly useful form: third in maiden at Windsor in May: stays 1½m. *Mark Pitman* **87**

SEA TEA DEA 3 b.f. Archipenko (USA) 127 – Half Sister (IRE) 63 (Oratorio (IRE) 128) [2017 63: p7m* p7g 7s^5 p8g^6 8.2v p8s p7g^6 Dec 28] fair handicapper: won at Lingfield in January: stays 7f: acts on polytrack. *Anthony Carson* **72**

SEA THE SUNRISE 2 ro.f. (Feb 16) Sea The Stars (IRE) 140 – Tequila Sunrise 60 (Dansili 127) [2017 7g Sep 7] 90,000F: first foal: dam, ran twice, closely related to very smart French 1m-1¼m winner Grey Lilas, herself dam of Poule d'Essai des Pouliches/Prix de Diane winner Golden Lilac: 20/1, needed experience when well held in maiden at Salisbury: sure to do better. *David Menuisier* **– p**

SEA TIDE 3 b.f. Champs Elysees 124 – Change Course 67 (Sadler's Wells (USA) 132) [2017 79p: 10.2g^2 10g^3 t9.5g^3 9d* 11.5d^2 10g Oct 7] sturdy filly: fairly useful performer: won maiden at Carlisle in August: second in handicap at Yarmouth in September: stays 11.5f: acts on polytrack and good to soft going: in cheekpieces last 4 starts: wears tongue tie: often races prominently: sold to join Laura Mongan 16,000 gns in December. *Hugo Palmer* **90**

SEAVIEW 3 b.f. Harbour Watch (IRE) 121 – Welanga (Dansili 127) [2017 52: f7g* t7.1m^2 f8g^2 p8g 7.5m^4 6.1d^2 6d^2 8g^5 6.1d 7.2v^4 7v^6 f8.1g f7.1g Dec 19] compact filly: fair handicapper: won at Southwell in January: stays 1m: acts on fibresand and good to soft going: tried in headgear: temperament under suspicion. *David Brown* **73**

SEA WOLF (IRE) 5 b.g. Amadeus Wolf 122 – Rose de France (IRE) (Diktat 126) [2017 108: 8v^3 8d* 8g^2 8g Aug 17] smart performer: won handicap at the Curragh (by 1¼ lengths from Windsor Beach) in May: second in listed race there (½ length behind True Valour) in **115**

July: stays 1m: acts on good to firm and heavy going: tried in cheekpieces: often races towards rear/travels strongly: sent to Australia. *G. M. Lyons, Ireland*

SEA YOUMZAIN (IRE) 2 b.f. (Feb 23) Sea The Stars (IRE) 140 – Chantilly Pearl **74 p**
(USA) 74 (Smart Strike (CAN) 121) [2017 8.2g^2 9d^2 Oct 30] €90,000Y: fourth foal: closely related to useful 2-y-o 6f-1m winner (stays 1¼m) Montataire (by Cape Cross): dam 2-y-o 6f winner who stayed 10.5f: fair form: better effort when second in minor event at Leicester (1¾ lengths behind Bombyx) on debut: remains with potential. *Mark Johnston*

SEBASTIANO RICCI (IRE) 2 b.g. (Feb 13) Lope de Vega (IRE) 125 – Dear Dream **84**
(IRE) (Montjeu (IRE) 137) [2017 5d^5 6.4m 7v^2 7g 7v^3 6d^4 7.4v* 6.5g 8.5s^2 8.1v 7s^6 Nov 5] 60,000F, 80,000Y: first foal: dam, French maiden (second at 11f), out of half-sister to smart stayer Darasim: fairly useful performer: won maiden at Roscommon in September: placed in nurseries at Galway in August and Cork in October: stays 8.5f: acts on heavy going. *Joseph Patrick O'Brien, Ireland*

SEBASTIAN'S WISH (IRE) 4 b.g. Aqlaam 125 – Swish (GER) (Monsun (GER) 124) **93**
[2017 58: t12.2g* 14m* 12.5g* 16m^3 16m* 14m^3 13s Oct 3] fairly useful handicapper: won at Wolverhampton in January, Musselburgh (twice) in May and Musselburgh again (by 1½ lengths from Stormin Tom) in July: stays 2m: acts on tapeta and good to firm going: tried in blinkers: front runner/races prominently. *Keith Dalgleish*

SECONDO (FR) 7 b.g. Sakhee's Secret 128 – Royal Jade 82 (Last Tycoon 131) [2017 **93**
6.1g 5.1g^5 6.1s p6g^2 p6s Oct 24] attractive gelding: fairly useful handicapper nowadays: second at Kempton in September: stays 6f: acts on polytrack, tapeta and firm going: has worn headgear: usually races nearer last than first: sold 8,000 gns in October. *Joseph Tuite*

SECOND PAGE 3 b.c. Harbour Watch (IRE) 121 – Almunia (IRE) (Mujadil (USA) 119) **82**
[2017 76: 7g^4 p11g^4 10.2m^3 t12.4g^3 11.8s^6 p13.3g^6 p11g^4 f11.1g* Nov 13] compact colt: fairly useful performer: won maiden at Southwell (by 3 lengths from Epitaph) in November: stays 12.5f: acts on all-weather: sometimes in headgear in 2017. *Richard Hannon*

SECOND STEP (IRE) 6 b.g. Dalakhani (IRE) 133 – My Dark Rosaleen 84 (Sadler's **118**
Wells (USA) 132) [2017 116: 12m^3 12g* 12g^2 12s^2 11.4m* 11m^2 Sep 23] useful-looking gelding: smart performer: won listed races at Goodwood (by ½ length from Desert Encounter) in May and Windsor (by 2½ lengths from Law And Order) in August: placed other 4 starts, in John Porter Stakes at Newbury, listed race at Newmarket, Glorious Stakes at Goodwood and Legacy Cup at Newbury: stays 1½m: acts on any turf going: tried in blinkers: often travels strongly. *Roger Charlton*

SECOND SUMMER (USA) 5 ch.g. Summer Bird (USA) 126 – Greenstreet (USA) **117**
(Street Cry (IRE) 130) [2017 a9.4f^2 a9.9f a8g* a9.9f Dec 21] smart performer: trained in USA prior to 2017 (Grade 2 9f winner at Santa Anita): won Godolphin Mile at Meydan (by neck from Ross) in March: second in Maktoum Challenge Round 2 there (nose behind Furia Cruzada) in February: stays 1¼m: acts on dirt and firm going: in visor last 2 starts: wears tongue tie: often races towards rear. *D. Watson, UAE*

SECOND THOUGHT (IRE) 3 b.c. Kodiac 112 – Bobby Jane 72 (Diktat 126) [2017 **116**
87p: p6d* p7f* p6g* 6f^2 7g^6 6s^5 p8d* Nov 22] compact colt: smart performer: won minor event at Kempton in January, listed race at Lingfield in March, minor event at Lingfield in April and listed race at Kempton (by ½ length from Keystroke) in November: second in Sandy Lane Stakes at Haydock (4½ lengths behind Harry Angel) in May: stays 1m: acts on polytrack, tapeta and firm going. *William Haggas*

SECOND WAVE (IRE) 5 b.g. New Approach (IRE) 132 – Tessa Reef (IRE) (Mark of **–**
Esteem (IRE) 137) [2017 115: 12d^5 Aug 19] angular gelding: smart handicapper at best: well held sole outing in 2017: should have stayed 1½m: acted on polytrack, tapeta, soft and good to firm going: in hood last 4 starts: dead. *Charlie Appleby*

SECRATARIO (FR) 2 ch.g. (Mar 25) Kendargent (FR) 112 – Amoa (USA) (Ghostzapper **68**
(USA) 137) [2017 7g 7d^5 8m^2 p7g^4 p8g^3 p8g* p7d^6 Nov 22] fair performer: won nursery at Kempton in November: will stay beyond 1m: acts on polytrack: in headgear last 4 starts: often travels strongly. *Richard Hughes*

SECRET ADVISOR (FR) 3 b.c. Dubawi (IRE) 129 – Sub Rose (IRE) 119 (Galileo (IRE) **110 p**
134) [2017 8g* 10g^2 9.1m^2 14m^3 12v^5 13.9m* Aug 26] tall colt: fourth foal: half-brother to smart winner in France around 1¼m Subway Dancer (by Shamardal): dam French 11f/1½m (Prix de Royaumont) winner: smart performer: won maiden at Thirsk (by ½ length from Materialist) in April and Melrose Stakes (Handicap) at York (by neck from Bin

Battuta) in August: third in Queen's Vase at Royal Ascot (2¼ lengths behind Stradivarius) in June: will stay 2m: acts on good to firm going: open to further improvement. *Charlie Appleby*

SECRET AGENT 3 b.g. Equiano (FR) 127 – Varnish 91 (Choisir (AUS) 126) [2017 74, a64: 5d^2 5m* 5.7f^2 5f^2 5d^5 5d^4 Aug 23] lengthy gelding: fair handicapper: awarded race at Salisbury in June: stays 6f: acts on firm and good to soft going: in headgear last 3 starts. *William Muir* **74**

SECRET ART (IRE) 7 ch.g. Excellent Art 125 – Ivy Queen (IRE) (Green Desert (USA) 127) [2017 102: 8m 8.3g* 8m 8s p8g^5 8.1m^3 8s 8g^4 9d p8g Oct 14] tall, rangy gelding: useful handicapper: won at Windsor (by 1¼ lengths from Breden) in May: stays 8.5f: acts on polytrack, soft and good to firm going: tried in cheekpieces: usually races prominently. *William Knight* **99**

SECRET ASSET (IRE) 12 gr.g. Clodovil (IRE) 116 – Skerray 71 (Soviet Star (USA) 128) [2017 88: p5g t5d p5g^6 p5g^6 t5.1g^5 5.1d 5.7f^4 5m 5m 5d 6.1g 5g Sep 1] sturdy gelding: one-time useful performer, on downgrade in 2017: stays 6f: acts on polytrack, tapeta, good to firm and good to soft going: wears headgear: usually races close up. *Lisa Williamson* **72 d**

SECRET BIRD (IRE) 5 br.g. Arcano (IRE) 122 – Asfurah (USA) 108 (Dayjur (USA) 137) [2017 71: p5g^3 p6g^2 t5.1g Feb 6] fair handicapper: stays 6f: acts on polytrack, tapeta and heavy going: tried in tongue tie: often leads. *Dean Ivory* **71**

SECRET CITY (IRE) 11 b.g. City On A Hill (USA) 114 – Secret Combe (IRE) 81 (Mujadil (USA) 119) [2017 60§: 6m^5 6g 6m^4 6m^4 7.2m^2 7.2s 7.1g 6g 8.3v Sep 5] good-bodied gelding: modest handicapper: stays 7f: acts on good to firm and heavy going: wears headgear: often races towards rear/lazily: untrustworthy. *Rebecca Bastiman* **51 §**

SECRET CLAUSE 4 b.g. Sakhee's Secret 128 – Claws 63 (Marju (IRE) 127) [2017 71: f6g p5g t6g Apr 22] fair handicapper, out of form in 2017: left Michael Appleby after first start: often races towards rear. *Derek Shaw* **–**

SECRET EYE (IRE) 2 ch.f. (Mar 27) Street Cry (IRE) 130 – What A Treasure (IRE) 78 (Cadeaux Genereux 131) [2017 p8g p7g^6 Nov 8] 90,000Y: fifth foal: sister to 7f winner Strada Facendo and half-sister to useful winner up to 1¼m Hoarding (2-y-o 7f/1m winner, by Elusive Quality): dam, 7f winner, sister to very smart 6f-1m winner Toylsome: modest form: better effort when sixth in minor event at Kempton (4¾ lengths behind Lush Life) in November: should stay 1m: wears headgear. *Paul Cole* **64**

SECRETFACT 4 br.g. Sakhee's Secret 128 – Matterofact (IRE) 83 (Bold Fact (USA) 116) [2017 77: 5m^6 5f* May 1] lengthy gelding: fairly useful handicapper: won at Bath (by 1¾ lengths from Swendab) in May: stays 5.5f: acts on firm and good to soft going: tried in cheekpieces: often travels strongly: has looked quirky. *Malcolm Saunders* **82**

SECRET GLANCE 5 b.g. Sakhee's Secret 128 – Look Here's Dee (Dansili 127) [2017 88, a71: f7g^3 f7g^2 7m^6 f8.1g^3 p8s p8d t8.6g f8.1g Nov 16] sturdy gelding: fair handicapper nowadays: left Richard Rowe after second start, Philip Kirby after third: stays 7f: acts on all-weather, good to firm and good to soft going: tried in visor: often races in rear. *Adrian Wintle* **74**

SECRET ICON 3 b.f. Sixties Icon 125 – Stan's Smarty Girl (USA) (Smarty Jones (USA) 134) [2017 –: p6d^6 Feb 3] leggy filly: no form. *Jamie Osborne* **–**

SECRET INTERLUDE (IRE) 4 b.f. Clodovil (IRE) 116 – Elouges (IRE) (Dalakhani (IRE) 133) [2017 57: f8g Jan 5] modest handicapper, well held sole outing in 2017: stays 7f: acts on tapeta: often races in rear. *Roger Fell* **–**

SECRET LIGHTNING (FR) 5 ch.m. Sakhee's Secret 128 – Dimelight 74 (Fantastic Light (USA) 134) [2017 61: t7.1g^{ur} p8g* t8.6g^6 p7g p8s^5 t8.6g* p8s^4 Dec 17] tall mare: modest handicapper: won at Kempton in March and Wolverhampton in December: stays 9f: acts on polytrack, tapeta, soft and good to firm going: often wears headgear. *Michael Appleby* **63**

SECRET LOOK 7 ch.g. Sakhee's Secret 128 – Look Here's Carol (IRE) 102 (Safawan 118) [2017 75: p7g 6m t6.1g 10s 8.1d Aug 24] fair handicapper, below form in 2017: stays 6f: acts on tapeta, good to firm and heavy going: often wears headgear: often races towards rear. *Richard Phillips* **54**

SECRET MEMORIES (IRE) 3 ch.f. Rip Van Winkle (IRE) 134 – Persian Memories (IRE) 78 (Indian Ridge 123) [2017 p8g^5 p7g p8g^2 p8g 5.8g 9.5s^4 8d^2 8f* 9.5g 10g^6 8.2d p8g^6 p7g^6 t7.2g^6 p7s* Dec 8] €1,200 2-y-o: fourth foal: half-sister to 5f/6f winners Persian Caliph (at 2 yrs, by Intikhab) and Memories Galore (useful, by Invincible Spirit): dam, **68**

maiden (stayed 1½m), half-sister to smart winner up to 1½m Persian Lightning: fair handicapper: won at Wetherby in June and Dundalk (apprentice) in December: stays 1m: acts on polytrack, tapeta, firm and good to soft going: has worn headgear, including last 2 starts: has worn tongue tie: sometimes slowly away. *Miss Katy Brown, Ireland*

SECRET MILLIONAIRE (IRE) 10 b.g. Kyllachy 129 – Mithl Al Hawa 99 (Salse (USA) 128) [2017 68: t6f t5.1m Jan 16] quite attractive gelding: fair handicapper, below form both starts in 2017: stays 6f: acts on polytrack, tapeta, good to firm and heavy going: usually wears headgear. *Shaun Harris* **47**

SECRET MISSILE 7 b.g. Sakhee's Secret 128 – Malelane (IRE) 48 (Prince Sabo 123) [2017 –: t5s 5m 6m 6s^4 6m^5 6g^4 7.2m^5 6v 8d t7.1d 6s 7d t7.2g p7g Nov 2] rangy gelding: one-time useful handicapper, deteriorated further in 2017: stays 6f: acts on polytrack, tapeta, good to firm and heavy going: often wears headgear: often races towards rear. *David C. Griffiths* **74 d**

SECRET NUMBER 7 b.g. Raven's Pass (USA) 133 – Mysterial (USA) (Alleged (USA) 138) [2017 116: 11.9g* 11m^3 12s^3 Oct 7] well-made gelding: smart performer: won Bosphorus Cup at Veliefendi (by 2 lengths from Elbereth) in September: third after in Legacy Cup at Newbury (length behind Desert Encounter) and Cumberland Lodge Stakes at Ascot (2 lengths behind Danehill Kodiac): stays 14.5f: acts on polytrack, tapeta, firm and soft going. *Saeed bin Suroor* **119**

SECRET POET (IRE) 3 b.f. Poet's Voice 126 – Nawaashi 86 (Green Desert (USA) 127) [2017 –: t9.5g Jan 9] no form. *Jamie Osborne* **–**

SECRET POTION 3 b.g. Stimulation (IRE) 121 – Fiancee (IRE) 59 (Pivotal 124) [2017 77: 5.1d^3 6.1m 5.7f^5 5.7g* 5d^4 5.7s^3 6.1s^3 5d^2 5s^6 Sep 17] fair handicapper: won at Bath in July: stays 6f: acts on soft going: front runner/races prominently. *Ronald Harris* **79**

SECRET RETURN (IRE) 4 ch.f. Roderic O'Connor (IRE) 119 – Quick Return (Polish Precedent (USA) 131) [2017 t7.2g^2 t7.2g^3 Nov 29] 26,000F: half-sister to 3 winners, including 2-y-o 5f winner Hilltown Gal (by Holy Roman Empire) and 7f winner Doc Jones (by Docksider): dam unraced: fair form when placed in maidens at Wolverhampton. *Karen George* **72**

SECRET SALVAGE (IRE) 3 b.f. Roderic O'Connor (IRE) 119 – Violet Flame (IRE) 60 (Kalanisi (IRE) 132) [2017 t8.6g^3 f8g^3 p7g^4 Mar 20] €16,000Y: third foal: half-sister to 1m winner Kubali (by Approve) and a winner in Italy by Intense Focus: dam twice-raced half-sister to Breeders' Cup Juvenile winner Vale of York: modest form when in frame in all-weather maidens. *Jamie Osborne* **63**

SECRET SANDS (IRE) 3 b.f. Cacique (IRE) 124 – Katy Nowaitee 112 (Komaite (USA)) [2017 p7g p11d p7g^4 Mar 3] 180,000Y, £11,000 2-y-o: half-sister to 3 useful winners, including winner up to 2m (in Australia) Mister Impatience (2-y-o 1m winner) and 1¼m-11f winner Harry Tricker (both by Hernando): dam 1m-1¼m winner: little impact in maidens. *Pat Phelan* **–**

SECRET SOUL 3 b.f. Street Cry (IRE) 130 – Shastye (IRE) 108 (Danehill (USA) 126) [2017 65: p10g^4 10.2g p11s 11.4m^3 10m^3 p12g^3 Oct 9] fair maiden: stays 1½m: acts on polytrack and good to firm going: in headgear last 5 starts. *Ralph Beckett* **70**

SECRET STRATEGY (IRE) 3 b.g. Kodiac 112 – Shall We Tell (Intikhab (USA) 135) [2017 t5.1g^2 5.3g^2 p6g^4 5.3g* 6.1m 5.3m^5 5.2g^6 t5.1g 5.3d* Aug 22] fair performer: won maiden at Brighton in May and handicap there in August: stays 6f: acts on polytrack and good to soft going: tried in cheekpieces: often races towards rear. *Julia Feilden* **78**

SECRET STRIKER 5 ch.m. Sakhee's Secret 128 – Silver Purse 67 (Interrex (CAN)) [2017 –: 6s^6 f5g Dec 21] no form. *Ken Cunningham-Brown* **–**

SECRET WILLOW 3 ch.g. Sakhee's Secret 128 – Willow Beauty 55 (Val Royal (FR) 127) [2017 –: p7d p8g p7g p7g 7s^6 p6g Oct 25] workmanlike gelding: no form: tried in blinkers. *John E. Long* **–**

SECTION D'OR 3 ch.g. New Approach (IRE) 132 – Junia Tepzia (IRE) 103 (Rock of Gibraltar (IRE) 133) [2017 10g p8s^6 p8s Aug 9] fair form: best effort when seventh in maiden at Kempton in August. *David Menuisier* **74**

SECTION ONESIXSIX (IRE) 2 b.f. (Mar 7) Dandy Man (IRE) 123 – The Last Laugh 78 (Kyllachy 129) [2017 5.3g^6 5m^5 6s Oct 15] €5,800F, €22,000Y: third foal: half-sister to 6f and (at 2 yrs) 7f winner Laughing Rock (by Rock of Gibraltar): dam, 2-y-o 5f winner, half-sister to smart winner up to 1¼m Kal Barg: modest form: best effort when fifth in maiden at Sandown (2¾ lengths behind Swing Out Sister) in September. *Mick Channon* **64**

SEDUCE ME 3 b.f. Dutch Art 126 – Deep Bleu (Kyllachy 129) [2017 83: 6g^4 7.1m^4 8.3g^2 **95**
6.9g^5 8v* 8.5d* 8d^3 8s^4 8g^6 Oct 7] compact filly: useful handicapper: won at Newbury in July and Epsom (by 3¼ lengths from Pumaflor) in August: stays 8.5f: acts on heavy going: wears cheekpieces: often races towards rear. *K. R. Burke*

SEE AND BE SEEN 7 b.g. Sakhee's Secret 128 – Anthea 66 (Tobougg (IRE) 125) [2017 **72 §**
83§: t16.5g^3 p16g^5 t16.5g^5 16m^5 p16d^4 p16g 16m^3 p16s^2 p16g^2 p16d 16.3d^4 t16.5g^4 18d p16g p15.8g p16g Oct 4] good-bodied gelding: fair handicapper nowadays: stays 2¼m: acts on polytrack, tapeta and any turf going: wears cheekpieces: not straightforward and is one to treat with caution. *Sylvester Kirk*

SEEBRING (IRE) 3 b.g. Tagula (IRE) 116 – Sunlit Romance (IRE) (Hernando (FR) 127) **62**
[2017 62: 7.4d^5 t7.1s 9.9f 8.5d t5s^3 t5g 7v t6.1g* Oct 27] modest performer: won minor event at Wolverhampton in October: stays 7f: acts on tapeta and good to soft going: sometimes in cheekpieces in 2017. *Brian Ellison*

SEEING THINGS (IRE) 3 b.g. Poet's Voice 126 – Sonning Rose (IRE) 96 (Hawk Wing **–**
(USA) 136) [2017 –: p8m p7g t9.5g t8.6g 8s^6 9.9m^6 p10g Oct 12] no form: in tongue tie last 5 starts. *Philip McBride*

SEEKING ATTENTION (USA) 3 b.f. Elusive Quality (USA) – Love of Dubai (USA) **56**
106 (More Than Ready (USA) 120) [2017 p8d f7g^5 t7.1g f8g 10.1m t8.6g^6 May 30] fourth foal: half-sister to a winner abroad by Bernardini: dam winner up to 1m (2-y-o 7f winner): modest maiden: best effort at 7f: acts on fibresand: tried in headgear: sometimes slowly away. *George Scott*

SEEKING MAGIC 9 b.g. Haafhd 129 – Atnab (USA) 64 (Riverman (USA) 131) [2017 **99**
104: 5m^5 6m 6m 6.1m^3 5m 6.1g* 6.1g^4 p6g^2 t6.1g^5 t6.1d Dec 16] stocky, close-coupled gelding: useful handicapper: won at Nottingham (by neck from Lexington Times) in July: second at Kempton (head behind Jaywalker) in September: raced at sprint trips: acts on polytrack, tapeta, firm and good to soft going: wears hood/tongue tie: front runner/races prominently. *Clive Cox*

SEEK THE FAIR LAND 11 b.g. Noverre (USA) 125 – Duchcov 101 (Caerleon (USA) **63**
132) [2017 72: p7g^6 p7g p8g Nov 7] workmanlike gelding: fair performer, below form in 2017: left Lee Carter after second start: stays 1m: acts on polytrack, fibresand, good to firm and heavy going: usually wears headgear: often races towards rear. *Daniel Steele*

SEEK THE MOON (USA) 2 b.f. (Mar 18) Giant's Causeway (USA) 132 – Crescent **–**
Moon (USA) (Seeking The Gold (USA)) [2017 p6s Dec 1] €80,000 2-y-o: half-sister to 3 winners, including 2-y-o 7f winner Marston Moor (by War Front): dam, ran once in USA, half-sister to very smart 2-y-o 6f/7f winner (including Coventry/Dewhurst Stakes) War Command: 28/1, well held in minor event at Chelmsford. *David O'Meara*

SEEN THE LYTE (IRE) 2 b.f. (Apr 12) Kodiac 112 – Highest Praise 62 (Acclamation **70**
118) [2017 5m^3 5m 5s^4 5m^2 5g^6 t5.1g^4 5d^2 6g^3 5m^6 5s* 5s^4 t5d^5 Nov 4] €24,000Y: first foal: dam maiden (stayed 7f) out of useful winner up to 1¼m Yarastar: fair performer: won claimer at Beverley in September: best at 5f: acts on tapeta, soft and good to firm going. *John Quinn*

SEE OF ROME 3 gr.g. Pour Moi (IRE) 125 – Balandra 79 (Medicean 128) [2017 76p: **91**
10g^3 9.9d* 12m 11.2s^3 13.4g^4 12s^6 Sep 19] rather leggy gelding: fairly useful performer: won maiden at Salisbury (by 5 lengths from Prerogative) in June: third in handicap at Goodwood in August: should stay beyond 1½m: acts on soft going: tried in cheekpieces. *Richard Hughes*

SEE THE CITY (IRE) 3 b.g. Lawman (FR) 121 – Cedar Sea (IRE) (Persian Bold 123) **79**
[2017 78: 10.2g 10.2g^4 10.1m 9.9g p12g 12v^5 Oct 9] fair handicapper: stays 1¼m: acts on tapeta and good to firm going: in blinkers last 2 starts. *James Eustace*

SEE THE MASTER (IRE) 3 b.c. Dutch Art 126 – See Emily Play (IRE) 63 (Galileo **87**
(IRE) 134) [2017 –p: 7m^2 7s 8.1d^4 8.1m* 8.3g* 8s^2 9.1g^5 8g^5 Sep 15] sturdy colt: fairly useful handicapper: won at Chepstow (by 1½ lengths from Procurator) and Nottingham (by 1¼ lengths from Ehtiraas) in July: stays 9f: acts on good to firm going: sold 60,000 gns in November. *Clive Cox*

SEE THE ROCK (IRE) 7 b.g. Shirocco (GER) 129 – Samara (IRE) 108 (Polish Patriot **81**
(USA) 128) [2017 88: 9g^2 10d^5 Aug 19] lengthy gelding: fairly useful handicapper: second at Lingfield in June: stays 1½m: acts on soft going: tried in hood. *Jonjo O'Neill*

SEE THE SEA (IRE) 3 b.f. Born To Sea (IRE) 117 – Shahmina (IRE) 78 (Danehill (USA) 126) [2017 70: t8.6g^5 8s 12f 10m^2 10.2g* 10s* Aug 9] close-coupled filly: fairly useful handicapper: won at Bath in July and Pontefract (amateur, by 1¼ lengths from Hawridge Glory) in August: should stay beyond 1¼m: acts on tapeta and soft going: in cheekpieces last 2 starts. *Richard Hannon* **81**

SEE THE SUN 6 ch.g. Assertive 121 – Cocabana 69 (Captain Rio 122) [2017 97: 6g 6s 6m 5m 6g 5s 6s 5g^2 5s^2 t5d^3 6s Oct 31] sturdy, close-coupled gelding: fairly useful handicapper nowadays: placed at Redcar in September, and at Musselburgh and Newcastle in October: stays 6f: acts on any turf going: has worn headgear, including often in 2017: tried in tongue tie: usually leads. *Tim Easterby* **81**

SEE THE TAR (IRE) 2 b.g. (May 5) Born To Sea (IRE) 117 – Image of Truce (IRE) (Brief Truce (USA) 126) [2017 6.1m p10g p10g t7.2g Nov 29] compact gelding: no form, including in nursery. *Jo Hughes* **–**

SEE VERMONT 9 b.g. Kyllachy 129 – Orange Lily (Royal Applause 124) [2017 72: t6m t5d^5 t5.1g^3 t5g^4 t5.1g^2 5m^5 5m^4 5g 5m^6 5m^3 5g^3 5m* 5s 5.2m 5m* 5s t5g^6 t5d^4 Sep 29] fair handicapper: won at Musselburgh in July (awarded race) and August: raced mainly at 5f nowadays: acts on tapeta, firm and soft going: wears headgear. *Rebecca Bastiman* **68**

SEE YOU IN MALTA (IRE) 4 b.g. Holy Roman Emperor (IRE) 125 – Ice Box (IRE) 75 (Pivotal 124) [2017 50: p7g 5d^5 t7.2g 7d^4 6.1m Jul 4] modest maiden: left Sean P. Hennessy after second start: stays 1m: acts on polytrack and heavy going: has worn cheekpieces/tongue tie, including in 2017. *Jennie Candlish* **55**

SEE YOU MUSH 3 b.g. Archipenko (USA) 127 – Snow Shoes 84 (Sri Pekan (USA) 117) [2017 55: p6g* 6g p7s^4 t6.1g^5 p6g^2 p6g^2 t7.1g^2 Oct 20] fair handicapper: won at Chelmsford in April: stays 7f: acts on polytrack and tapeta: wears headgear: tried in tongue tie. *Mrs Ilka Gansera-Leveque* **72**

SEHAIL (USA) 4 b.g. Giant's Causeway (USA) 132 – Persist (USA) (Tiznow (USA) 133) [2017 –: p11g^4 t12.2g 10.1m t10.2s^4 p16g 12.1m Jul 7] workmanlike gelding: modest maiden: stays 11f: acts on polytrack and tapeta: in headgear last 4 starts: often races prominently. *George Peckham* **58**

SEHAYLI (IRE) 4 b.g. Iffraaj 127 – Quaich 79 (Danehill (USA) 126) [2017 80§: p6g p7g Feb 22] good-topped gelding: fairly useful form first 2 starts at 3 yrs, has gone wrong way: tried in cheekpieces/tongue tie: often starts slowly/races towards rear: ungenuine. *Lee Carter* **– §**

SEINESATIONAL 2 b.g. (May 17) Champs Elysees 124 – Kibara 88 (Sadler's Wells (USA) 132) [2017 10m p8g Nov 7] good-topped gelding: well held in maiden/minor event. *William Knight* **–**

SEINFELD 3 b.g. Medicean 128 – Despatch 52 (Nayef (USA) 129) [2017 9.9g^4 10g 12d 11.8v p16g^6 Nov 8] rather unfurnished gelding: fair maiden: stays 1½m: acts on good to soft going: tried in headgear. *David Simcock* **70**

SEIRIOS (IRE) 3 b.g. Frankel 147 – Drifting (IRE) 85 (Sadler's Wells (USA) 132) [2017 12g^4 f12.1g Nov 28] soundly beaten in maidens. *Jane Chapple-Hyam* **–**

SELECTION (FR) 4 ch.g. Siyouni (FR) 122 – Perspective (FR) (Funambule (USA) 118) [2017 75p: p8g* 8f^3 10s^5 8m* 8g^2 Jul 19] lengthy gelding: fairly useful handicapper: won at Kempton in April and Yarmouth (by 2 lengths from Chiefofchiefs) in June: stays 1m: acts on polytrack, good to firm and good to soft going: tried in cheekpieces: front runner/races prominently: sold to join Michael Easterby 5,000 gns in October. *William Haggas* **93**

SELENA ROSE 4 b.f. Stimulation (IRE) 121 – Dot Hill (Refuse To Bend (IRE) 128) [2017 –: p12g 11.9g^6 10.2d^4 12g Aug 28] poor maiden: best effort at 1¼m: acts on good to soft going: often in headgear: sometimes slowly away. *Ronald Harris* **42**

SELLINGALLTHETIME (IRE) 6 ch.g. Tamayuz 126 – Anthyllis (GER) (Lycius (USA) 124) [2017 86: 12m^2 11.7f^3 11.9m^3 11.9m^3 10.2d^5 12.1g^2 12m^5 12.1s^4 12.1s^2 Oct 10] lengthy gelding: fairly useful handicapper: second at Catterick in April and August (amateur): stays 1½m: acts on fibresand and any turf going: wears headgear: often races prominently. *Michael Appleby* **80**

SEMANA SANTA 4 b.f. Arabian Gleam 122 – La Zamora 93 (Lujain (USA) 119) [2017 82: f6g^6 t6d t6g^5 t6g^2 t6g^6 5g^2 6g^4 5.9d^3 6g^5 Sep 27] fair handicapper: stays 6f: acts on tapeta, good to firm and good to soft going: usually races prominently. *David Barron* **73**

SEMPRE PRESTO (IRE) 2 b.f. (Mar 18) Nathaniel (IRE) 129 – Flandre (USA) (Elusive Quality (USA)) [2017 8g^{4} 7.4s^{4} 7g Oct 14] €50,000F: second foal: half-sister to a winner in Greece by Excelebration: dam ran twice in France: modest form: best effort when fourth in minor event at Thirsk (2½ lengths behind Exhort) on debut: will be suited by 1¼m+: remains with potential. *Richard Fahey* **62 p**

SENATOR 3 ch.g. Frankel 147 – Red Bloom 117 (Selkirk (USA) 129) [2017 83: 7s^{5} 8m^{6} Jun 22] lengthy gelding: fairly useful handicapper: stays 1m: acts on soft and good to firm going: races prominently, often freely: sent to Hong Kong, where renamed Simply Brilliant, second at Happy Valley and Sha Tin late in year. *Richard Fahey* **93**

SENATUS (FR) 5 b.g. Early March 118 – Winter Brook (FR) (Al Nasr (FR) 126) [2017 8g^{6} 8.3m^{6} 6.9g^{4} 10s t12.4g^{5} t16.3d^{4} Dec 16] bumper winner: fair maiden on Flat: stays 16.5f: acts on tapeta and good to firm going: wears hood: often starts slowly. *Karen McLintock* **71**

SEND UP (IRE) 3 b.f. Fastnet Rock (AUS) 127 – Briolette (IRE) 112 (Sadler's Wells (USA) 132) [2017 –: p8g 11.9d* p13.3g* t12.2g^{4} p13.3s^{5} Dec 1] fair handicapper: won at Brighton and Chelmsford in September: stays 13.5f: acts on polytrack and good to soft going: in headgear last 3 starts. *Sir Mark Prescott Bt* **77**

SENECA CHIEF 3 b.g. Invincible Spirit (IRE) 121 – Albertine Rose 89 (Namid 128) [2017 p5g^{5} t6g^{5} t5.1g^{5} t7.1g p5d* t5.1g^{2} 5.1m^{4} Jun 26] good-topped gelding: fair performer: won handicap at Chelmsford in May: best form at 5f: acts on polytrack and good to firm going: in hood last 4 starts. *Daniel Kubler* **71**

SENGA (USA) 3 b.f. Blame (USA) 129 – Beta Leo (USA) (A P Indy (USA) 131) [2017 111p: 8g* 8d 8g^{3} 10.4m* 9.9g^{3} 9.9d 9f Nov 4] **114**

It's not often that France fails to come up with a really good middle-distance three-year-old filly but 2017 wasn't a vintage year. There was nothing remotely in Enable's class across the Channel and there was no French-trained filly or mare of any age, let alone a three-year-old, deemed worthy of taking her on in the Arc. The classic generation didn't get a look-in in a Prix Vermeille dominated by mares and older fillies, while the Prix de Diane was a substandard affair, though against the odds it did result in a one, two, three for the home team despite the two visitors in the field, Shutter Speed and Rhododendron, looking to have the strongest claims beforehand. The winner, Senga, was sent off at odds of almost 22/1, which was something of a surprise for a filly who had been Timeform's top-rated two-year-old filly in France the year before. She had earned that rating from her fourth place in the Prix Marcel Boussac (behind fillies trained in Britain and Ireland) on her final two-year-old start in which she had shaped particularly well against more prominently-ridden rivals, coming from last in the straight to finish less than two lengths behind the winner Wuheida. Senga confirmed that promise when making a winning return back at Chantilly in the Prix de la Grotte in April, but two defeats prior to the Diane apparently did little to advertise her chances as a potential classic winner. She was reckoned to have a much better chance in the Poule d'Essai des Pouliches at Deauville (she also had the option of a One Thousand Guineas entry) but found

Prix de Diane Longines, Chantilly—Senga wins an eventful race in which Onthemoonagain comes down after clipping heels in the straight and Rhododendron is pulled up after suffering a bleed; Sistercharlie (centre) and Terrakova (second right) fill the places, with British raider Shutter Speed (left) only fourth just ahead of 69/1-shot Turf Laurel (right)

little and failed to make the first ten on softer ground than she had encountered thus far. Kept to a mile, Senga could finish only third of five to the Grotte runner-up La Sardane in the Prix de Sandringham at Chantilly a fortnight before the Diane, when once again she stayed on well from last place.

Sixteen fillies went to post for the Prix de Diane Longines and, despite her odds, on her best form Senga still looked the pick of the home team, even though the likes of Sistercharlie and Goldikova's daughter Terrakova had advanced their claims by winning a couple of the main trials, the Prix Penelope and Prix Cleopatre respectively. However, the unbeaten Musidora Stakes winner Shutter Speed, representing John Gosden who had won the Diane two years earlier with another Musidora winner, Star of Seville, could also boast a win at Newbury earlier in the season over the same connections' subsequent Oaks winner Enable. Shutter Speed started favourite but the pick on form was Ballydoyle's Rhododendron after her second places behind stable-companion Winter in the One Thousand Guineas and Enable in the Oaks. However, Rhododendron was out of the race soon after halfway, Ryan Moore pulling her up after she evidently bled badly (indeed, a close-up head-on photograph of Senga at the finish showed both her and her jockey spattered with blood—presumably Rhododendron's!). More drama followed in the straight when Christophe Soumillon's mount Onthemoonagain clipped heels and fell (a similar incident had occurred the year before, resulting in William Buick ending up in hot water, though no blame was apportioned this time), leaving Sistercharlie poorly placed in the scrimmaging which followed. Senga missed the trouble down the outside of the field, held up again but not so far back on this occasion, and quickened into the lead over a furlong out. She had a length to spare at the line over Sistercharlie who stayed on strongly from being only fifth a furlong out. Terrakova was just a nose behind in third, the same position in which her famous dam had finished nine years earlier; whereas the extended mile and a quarter was further than ideal for Goldikova, it looked barely enough of a test for Terrakova. Shutter Speed had looked Senga's main threat, challenging a furlong out after going well early in the straight, but she didn't last home, only just scraping into the frame a nose ahead of one of the rank outsiders Turf Laurel, after whom there was a break of four lengths to the remainder.

Another of the long shots, Yellow Storm, who finished eighth, attracted attention beforehand as the mount of Maryline Eon, the first female jockey to ride in the race, though she was unable to benefit from the two kilogram allowance for female jockeys which was introduced in France, outside the best races, in March. The new allowance prompted Britain's most successful female jockey Hayley Turner, who retired in 2015, to return to the saddle, basing herself in France, and she rode ten winners there from September onwards until starting a three-month ban in December imposed by the BHA for still having an active betting account when resuming riding. There were three female jockeys among the top forty riders in France in 2017, Eon's forty-three winners putting her behind Delphine Santiago whose fifty-nine victories made her the leading female jockey and placed her seventeenth overall. That represented a big difference from the year before when there were no female riders at all in the top forty, and Eon and Santiago's totals had been just twenty-four and nineteen respectively. The allowance will be reduced slightly, to a kilo and a half, for Flat races from March 2018 with a cap of four kilos in allowances for female riders also entitled to a claim as apprentices.

Senga provided her trainer Pascal Bary with his second Prix de Diane winner after Divine Proportions in 2005, and was the fourth American-bred filly to carry the Niarchos family colours to victory in the race. Divine Proportions won the Poule d'Essai des Pouliches beforehand, as did East of The Moon (a half-sister to Divine Proportions' sire Kingmambo) who won it for Stavros Niarchos in 1994. Miesque, the dam of East of The Moon and Kingmambo, also had a crack at the Diane but, like Goldikova, she proved best as a brilliant miler after she finished second to Indian Skimmer at Chantilly. The Niarchos colours were also carried to victory in 1984 by Northern Trick, the great grandam of both Cloth of Stars and Ulysses, the pair who chased home Enable in the Arc. Northern Trick had gone on to finish second in the Arc herself, but the Diane was as good as it got for Senga. She ran creditably to finish third in the Prix de la Nonette at Deauville next time behind Godolphin's Prix Saint-Alary winner Sobetsu and Onthemoonagain but softer conditions seemed her undoing once more when she finished in rear behind a fully recovered Rhododendron in the Prix de l'Opera. Senga's final appearance before being retired to the paddocks came at the Breeders' Cup where she finished a respectable eighth in the Filly & Mare Turf at Del Mar behind her old rivals Wuheida and Rhododendron after briefly taking third a furlong out.

Senga (USA) (b.f. 2014)	Blame (USA) (b 2006)	Arch (b or br 1995)	Kris S
			Aurora
		Liable (b 1995)	Seeking The Gold
			Bound
	Beta Leo (USA) (b or br 2007)	A P Indy (b 1989)	Seattle Slew
			Weekend Surprise
		Denebola (br 2001)	Storm Cat
			Coup de Genie

A far more memorable performance at the Breeders' Cup had been put up by Senga's sire Blame in the 2010 Classic at Churchill Downs, a race that will long be remembered because Blame, who held on by a head, ended Zenyatta's unbeaten record on the twentieth and final start of her career. Blame was retired afterwards too, to stand at Claiborne Farm in Kentucky, and Senga comes from his third crop. He has sired several graded stakes winners across the Atlantic, going closest to a Grade 1 winner there with the 2015 Hollywood Derby runner-up March. Senga comes from another of the top Niarchos families, this one originating with the purchase of Senga's great great grandam Coup de Folie who was out of a half-sister to Northern Dancer. She proved a smart two-year-old, winning the Prix d'Aumale and finishing third in the Marcel Boussac, but her daughter Coup de Genie and granddaughter Denebola, Senga's grandam, were the top two-year-old fillies of their respective crops in France. Both won the Prix de Cabourg, with Coup de Genie, a sister to the Two Thousand Guineas runner-up Machiavellian, going on to win the Prix Morny and Prix de la Salamandre (later third in the One Thousand Guineas, too) and Denebola the Prix Marcel Boussac. Coup de Genie produced a Prix de Cabourg winner of her own in Loving Kindness but her most notable descendant is her grandson Bago, winner of the Prix de l'Arc de Triomphe in 2004. Bago's siblings include another Group 1 winner Maxios, successful in the Prix d'Ispahan and Prix du Moulin. While Senga's dam Beta Leo didn't live up to the achievements of her predecessors on the track (no better than fairly useful), she too was successful at two, in a newcomers race at Maisons-Laffitte over five and a half furlongs. Senga is Beta Leo's second foal after the useful French winner at up to seven furlongs Bolting (by War Front) whose wins included a listed contest at Chantilly in 2016. Senga stayed ten and a half furlongs and was suited by good ground or firmer. She also won a minor event over a mile at Saint-Cloud prior to contesting the Marcel Boussac. *P. Bary, France*

SENIORITY 3 ch.g. Dubawi (IRE) 129 – Anna Palariva (IRE) 108 (Caerleon (USA) 132) **100**
[2017 85: 8m 8f^5 10m^3 p11g* p11g^3 t9.5g Nov 29] sturdy gelding: useful handicapper: won at Kempton (by nose from Ennjaaz) in October: third there (1¼ lengths behind Ply) in November: stays 11f: acts on polytrack and good to firm going: often races freely. *William Haggas*

SENNOCKIAN SONG 4 ch.g. New Approach (IRE) 132 – Chorist 120 (Pivotal 124) **52**
[2017 71: t12.4g^6 f12m Feb 21] angular gelding: fair maiden, below form in handicaps in 2017: stays 12.5f: acts on polytrack and tapeta: front runner. *Mark Johnston*

SENNOCKIAN STAR 7 ch.g. Rock of Gibraltar (IRE) 133 – Chorist 120 (Pivotal 124) **99**
[2017 95: p12g* p12m^3 p12g* t9.5g^4 t12.4g^3 p12m* p10g^5 p12g^5 p12g^3 p11g 13.1m^6 10.3m^5 12m^5 13.1g^4 12.1g^3 12d^3 12d 12s^2 14g^6 12.1s 11.6g^6 14.4v p12g p12g 12.1v^4 t12.2g Oct 27] workmanlike gelding: useful handicapper: won at Kempton (amateur) and Lingfield in January, and Lingfield again (by 2 lengths from Blue Surf) in February: stays 1½m: acts on polytrack, tapeta and any turf going: has worn headgear: sold 8,500 gns in November. *Mark Johnston*

SENOR GEORGE (IRE) 10 b.g. Traditionally (USA) 117 – Mrs St George (IRE) 87 (Orpen (USA) 116) [2017 66: t12.2g^4 f12s t12.2g p8g t12.2g^2 t12.2g^3 t12.2g^2 May 2] compact gelding: modest handicapper nowadays: stays 13f: acts on tapeta and good to firm going: sometimes wears headgear: tried in tongue tie. *Simon Hodgson* **58**

SENSORY (IRE) 2 gr.f. (Apr 23) Dream Ahead (USA) 133 – Dookus (IRE) (Linamix (FR) 127) [2017 p6g 6.5d 6m Jun 17] 170,000Y: rather unfurnished filly: half-sister to several winners, including smart winner up to 10.5f Frankuus (2-y-o 7f-9f winner, by Frankel) and useful French 2-y-o 1m winner US Law (by Lawman): dam, ran 3 times in France, half-sister to useful sprinter Pharmacist, herself dam of Breeders' Cup Turf winner Red Rocks: modest form on first of 3 starts in minor events: tried in blinkers. *John Gosden* **55**

SENTIMENTAL GENT (FR) 2 b.g. (Apr 1) Kendargent (FR) 112 – Sentimental Union (USA) (Dixie Union (USA) 121) [2017 6g 6.9v^6 Sep 18] well held in minor events. *Kevin Ryan* **–**

SENTINEL 3 b.g. Sepoy (AUS) 129 – Baralinka (IRE) 93 (Barathea (IRE) 127) [2017 54: t7.1m^2 p7g^5 7.6s^5 6d* t7.2g* Oct 27] fair handicapper: won at Yarmouth and Wolverhampton in October: stays 7f: acts on tapeta and good to soft going: sometimes slowly away. *Charlie Fellowes* **73**

SEPAL (USA) 4 b.f. Afleet Alex (USA) 128 – Faraway Flower (USA) 98 (Distant View (USA) 126) [2017 78: 8f^6 8.3s^6 13.1g 11.1s^3 10d* 12d* 12.1s* 14s* 14v^2 14d^6 11.9s Nov 11] good-topped filly: useful handicapper: won at Ayr, Thirsk and Hamilton in August, and Haydock (by 3 lengths from Graceland) in September: stays 1¾m: acts on heavy going: has worn hood. *Iain Jardine* **100**

SEPRANI 3 b.f. Sepoy (AUS) 129 – King's Guest (IRE) 68 (King's Best (USA) 132) [2017 66: p7m^3 p7g^3 6m^3 p6g* p7s^5 6m* p6g^3 Oct 3] fairly useful handicapper: won at Lingfield in July and Epsom in August: third at Kempton in October: stays 7f: acts on polytrack, tapeta and good to firm going: wears hood: often races prominently. *Marco Botti* **81**

SEPTEMBER (IRE) 2 b.f. (Feb 21) Deep Impact (JPN) 134 – Peeping Fawn (USA) 126 (Danehill (USA) 126) [2017 7d* 7m* 7s^4 7s^3 8m^2 8f^3 Nov 3] neat filly: fifth foal: sister to useful 12.5f winner Wisconsin, and half-sister to French 1¼m-12.5f winner Purely Priceless (by Galileo) and useful 2-y-o 6f winner Sir John Hawkins (by Henrythenavigator): dam 1m-1½m (including Irish/Yorkshire Oaks) winner: smart performer: won maiden at Leopardstown (by 5½ lengths) and Chesham Stakes at Royal Ascot (by 2¼ lengths from Nyaleti), both in June: placed in Moyglare Stud Stakes at the Curragh (3¾ lengths third to Happily), Fillies' Mile at Newmarket (nose second to Laurens) and Breeders' Cup Juvenile Fillies Turf at Del Mar (1¾ lengths third behind Rushing Fall): will be suited by 1¼m+: acts on firm and good to soft going: sometimes slowly away: capable of better still. *Aidan O'Brien, Ireland* **114 p**

SEPTEMBER ISSUE 4 b.g. Dutch Art 126 – Alexander Ballet 86 (Mind Games 121) [2017 85: p6g^2 t5g^4 p6d^4 f6g^3 6g^4 5.7f^4 t6.1g^5 5d* Aug 4] fairly useful handicapper: won at Bath (by neck from Seamster) in August: stays 6f: acts on all-weather and good to soft going: wears headgear. *Gay Kelleway* **89**

SERABRINA (IRE) 2 b.f. (Feb 17) Iffraaj 127 – Evening Frost (IRE) (Invincible Spirit (IRE) 121) [2017 5g^2 5d^2 p6g 5s^4 f7.1g Dec 11] second foal: half-sister to French 6f winner Top Chain (by Acclamation): dam, French 2-y-o 5.5f winner on only start, out of smart 6f winner Evening Time: fairly useful form when twice second at Bordeaux for C. Ferland, below that level in Britain after: tried in hood/tongue tie. *David Menuisier* **81**

SERANGOON 4 b.f. Authorized (IRE) 133 – Sharp Dresser (USA) 80 (Diesis 133) [2017 –: 10.2d^6 11.5m Jun 14] no form. *Michael Appleby* **–**

SERAPHIMA 7 b.m. Fusaichi Pegasus (USA) 130 – Millestan (IRE) 91 (Invincible Spirit (IRE) 121) [2017 52: t7.2g t6.1d p6s Dec 17] modest at best, no form in 2017: wears headgear. *Lisa Williamson* **–**

SERENADA 3 b.f. Azamour (IRE) 130 – Serres (IRE) (Daylami (IRE) 138) [2017 82p: 10d* 10.3s^3 12m 12s 9.9m^5 11.9d^5 Aug 24] good-topped filly: useful performer: won maiden at Sandown (by short head from Apphia) in April: third in Musidora Stakes at York (2¾ lengths behind Shutter Speed) in May: best up to 1¼m: acts on soft and good to firm going. *Roger Varian* **103**

SERENADE THE STARS (IRE) 3 b.g. Sea The Stars (IRE) 140 – Silent Serenade (Bertolini (USA) 125) [2017 –: t9.5g^2 p10g* p12g* 10.2g^4 8g* 10.1g^5 10.2g^3 12g 11.9g* Dec 26] fairly useful performer: won handicaps at Chelmsford in January and Kempton in **93**

February, and minor events at Bendigo in November and Caulfield (tongue tied) in December: left James Tate after fourth start: stays 1½m: acts on polytrack and tapeta: wears headgear: front runner/races prominently. *Peter Gelagotis, Australia*

SERENITY NOW (IRE) 9 b.g. Key of Luck (USA) 126 – Imdina (IRE) 70 (Soviet Star (USA) 128) [2017 76: f12g^{2} f12.1g^{2} 17.1d 14g 12.1g 12.1s^{4} f12.1g^{4} f16.5g* Dec 29] fair handicapper on turf, fairly useful on all-weather: won at Southwell in December: stays 16.5f: acts on fibresand, soft and good to firm going: tried in cheekpieces: often starts slowly, usually races towards rear. *Brian Ellison* **71 a81**

SERGEANT PINK (IRE) 11 b.g. Fasliyev (USA) 120 – Ring Pink (USA) 111 (Bering 136) [2017 12g 13.1m^{6} 11.2s Aug 7] tall, lengthy gelding: modest handicapper: stays 16.5f: acts on polytrack, good to firm and heavy going: has worn headgear, including in 2017: modest/unreliable chaser nowadays. *Dianne Sayer* **52**

SERGIO LEONE (IRE) 2 b.c. (Apr 27) Acclamation 118 – Elizabelle (IRE) 63 (Westerner 130) [2017 7d^{6} 6.1d^{2} p6g* Oct 9] 65,000F, 125,000Y: rather unfurnished colt: fourth foal: closely related to useful winner up to 1½m Southdown Lad (2-y-o 6f-9f winner, by Lilbourne Lad) and half-brother to 2 winners by Zebedee, including 2-y-o 6f-1m winner Power Play (later successful in Qatar): dam lightly raced (third at 7f at 2 yrs): fair form: won minor event at Kempton (by neck from Go Roo) in October: stays 6f: remains with potential. *Richard Hannon* **77 p**

SERJEANT PAINTER 2 b.g. (Apr 21) Royal Applause 124 – Szabo's Art 59 (Excellent Art 125) [2017 6.1m^{4} 7g^{5} Jul 15] tall, rather unfurnished gelding: fair form: better effort when fourth in maiden at Windsor (1½ lengths behind Boomerang Betty) on debut: should stay 7f. *Marcus Tregoning* **68**

SERVO (IRE) 3 b.g. Power 117 – Parade Scene (USA) (Parade Ground (USA) 124) [2017 61: t8d^{5} 7v t8s^{3} Nov 30] modest maiden: left Alan Swinbank after first start: stays 1m: acts on tapeta: sometimes slowly away, usually races freely: temperament under suspicion. *Lynn Siddall* **62**

SET IN STONE (IRE) 3 b.f. Famous Name 124 – Storminateacup (IRE) 74 (Galileo (IRE) 134) [2017 71: 8.5v^{3} 9.9m^{5} 7d^{4} 10.3g 9.2s* 9.2g^{6} 8.3s* 8d* 8s* 8s^{6} Oct 1] useful performer: won maiden at Hamilton in June, and handicaps at same course in August, Newbury later in August and Musselburgh (by 2 lengths from Invermere) in September: stays 1¼m: acts on heavy going: often races prominently. *John Patrick Shanahan, Ireland* **101**

SETTING SAIL 2 b.c. (Apr 7) Dansili 127 – West Wind 118 (Machiavellian (USA) 123) [2017 8.2d^{2} 9.9s* Sep 27] fifth foal: half-brother to useful 2-y-o 7f winner Zephuros (by Invincible Spirit): dam 1¼m/10.5f (Prix de Diane) winner: fairly useful form: won maiden at Goodwood (by ½ length from Mt Augustus) in September: remains with potential. *Charlie Appleby* **85 p**

SETTLE PETAL 3 b.f. Peintre Celebre (USA) 137 – Shall We Dance 83 (Rambo Dancer (CAN) 107) [2017 66: p8d^{3} p12g p8d 7d^{6} Aug 3] modest maiden: stays 1m: acts on polytrack. *Pat Phelan* **64**

SEVE 5 ch.g. Exceed And Excel (AUS) 126 – Flamenco Dancer (Mark of Esteem (IRE) 137) [2017 94: t5.1f f5g p5g^{6} 5s^{ur} 6.7s 7g p6.5g^{4} Dec 15] useful at best, well below that level in 2017: left Tom Dascombe after second start, Karen George after fourth: best at 5f: acts on polytrack, tapeta and good to firm going: has worn headgear/tongue tie: reared leaving stalls and unseated fourth outing. *P. & F. Monfort, France* **75**

SEVEN CLANS (IRE) 5 b.g. Cape Cross (IRE) 129 – Cherokee Rose (IRE) 122 (Dancing Brave (USA) 140) [2017 61: t9.5g* p10m^{2} 10.1m^{3} 10d* 10g^{3} Sep 6] fairly useful handicapper: won at Wolverhampton in January and Newmarket in August: will stay 1½m: acts on polytrack, tapeta, good to firm and good to soft going: wears blinkers: tried in tongue tie: often travels strongly. *Neil Mulholland* **81**

SEVEN HEAVENS 3 b.g. Frankel 147 – Heaven Sent 116 (Pivotal 124) [2017 107p: 7m^{3} 6f 7d^{3} 7m^{2} Jun 2] good sort: useful performer: placed in listed Free Handicap at Newmarket (3¼ lengths behind Whitecliffsofdover) in April, and listed races at same course (½ length behind Taamol) in May and Epsom (¾ length behind Solomon's Bay) in June: stays 7f: acts on good to firm and good to soft going: tried in hood: often races freely: gelded and sent to Hong Kong. *John Gosden* **104**

SEVENNA STAR (IRE) 2 b.c. (Mar 6) Redoute's Choice (AUS) – Sevenna (FR) 107 (Galileo (IRE) 134) [2017 8d^{2} 8.3d^{3} Oct 11] fifth foal: closely related to smart French 10.5f-1½m winner Savanne (by Rock of Gibraltar) and half-brother to French 1½m/12.5f winner Sassella (by Lope de Vega) and German 10.5f-1½m winner Samurai (by Shamardal), both useful: dam 1¼m-1¾m winner: fairly useful form when placed in minor event/maiden: will be suited by 1¼m: remains capable of better. *John Gosden* **89 p**

*Dunaden Jockey Club Stakes, Newmarket—
the well-backed Seventh Heaven proves different class to her four rivals, streaking clear of One Foot In Heaven (right) with Pinzolo (rail) back in third*

SEVENTH HEAVEN (IRE) 4 b.f. Galileo (IRE) 134 – La Traviata (USA) 112 (Johannesburg (USA) 127) [2017 126: 12d² 12m* 10s 11.9d 12f⁵ Nov 4] big, rangy filly: very smart performer: successful in Irish Oaks at the Curragh and Yorkshire Oaks at York in 2016: also won Jockey Club Stakes at Newmarket (by 5 lengths from One Foot In Heaven) in May: second in Dubai Sheema Classic at Meydan (2¼ lengths behind Jack Hobbs) in March and fifth in Breeders' Cup Turf at Del Mar (3¾ lengths behind Talismanic) in November: stayed 1½m: acted on polytrack, good to firm and good to soft going: often raced towards rear: stud. *Aidan O'Brien, Ireland* **121**

SEVENTII 3 b.f. Medicean 128 – Lowndes (Rail Link 132) [2017 –: 10.3g 10m 7m 8g 11.9m⁴ p10g 11.5d* 11.9s³ 11.4d² Oct 23] unfurnished filly: fair handicapper: won at Yarmouth in September: stays 1½m: acts on soft going. *Robert Eddery* **70**

SEVERUS (GER) 7 b.g. Shirocco (GER) 129 – Shikoku (Green Desert (USA) 127) [2017 85: 7s⁶ 6d⁵ 7m⁴ 8g 6.7m* 7g² 7f* 8d 7d Aug 19] fairly useful handicapper: won at Limerick in June and the Curragh (by ½ length from Have A Nice Day) in July: stays 1m: acts on polytrack, tapeta, firm and soft going: in cheekpieces last 2 starts. *Des Donovan, Ireland* **94**

SEVILLA 4 b.f. Duke of Marmalade (IRE) 132 – Glittering Prize (UAE) 72 (Cadeaux Genereux 131) [2017 72: t9.5m p12g p11g t12.2g⁴ p10g² 12.1d 11.9d⁴ Aug 22] angular filly: third foal: half-sister to winner up to 7f Echion (2-y-o 6f winner, by Ishiguru) and French 9f winner True Reflection (by Mastercraftsman): dam 2-y-o 7f winner: fair maiden: stays 11.5f: acts on good to soft going: in headgear last 2 starts. *Olly Murphy* **65**

SEXTON BLAKE (IRE) 4 b.g. Rip Van Winkle (IRE) 134 – Soviet Treat (IRE) 92 (Ashkalani (IRE) 128) [2017 68: p7g p8g⁴ 7m 8g Aug 2] lengthy gelding: modest maiden: left Gary Moore after third start: stays 7f: acts on polytrack: wears headgear. *John Norton* **62**

SEXY LEGS 5 b.m. Dutch Art 126 – Classic Lass 68 (Dr Fong (USA) 128) [2017 7m⁶ 6g⁴ t6d* 7.2v t6g t7.2g⁶ Nov 11] leggy mare: fair performer: won maiden at Newcastle in September: left Lucinda Egerton after second start: stays 7f: acts on tapeta and heavy going: wears headgear/tongue tie nowadays. *Rebecca Menzies* **70**

SEXY SECRET 6 b.g. Sakhee's Secret 128 – Orange Walk (IRE) 88 (Alzao (USA) 117) [2017 64: p10g p10d 11.5m⁵ 10.1m⁵ 10.1s³ 10.1m⁵ 11.5d⁵ p10g⁵ 11.5g² Oct 16] leggy, plain gelding: modest handicapper: stays 1½m: acts on all-weather and any turf going: wears headgear: front runner/races prominently. *Lydia Pearce* **55**

SEYAADY 2 b.c. (Apr 11) Exceed And Excel (AUS) 126 – Muwakaba (USA) 97 (Elusive Quality (USA)) [2017 5g² 5s³ 5m⁶ t5.1g* Jul 31] fourth foal: half-brother to 7.5f-11f winner Just Because (by Mawatheeq) and a winner abroad by Aqlaam: dam, 2-y-o 7f **80**

winner who stayed 1¼m, out of half-sister to Prix de l'Arc de Triomphe winner Urban Sea (dam of Galileo and Sea The Stars): fairly useful form: won nursery at Wolverhampton (by neck from Porchy Party) in July: raced only at 5f: sold £22,000 in August. *Mark Johnston*

SEYASAH (IRE) 3 b.f. Casamento (IRE) 118 – Defensive Boast (USA) (El Gran Senor (USA) 136) [2017 69: 7m 6g^2 6g^2 6m^2 6s p7g^4 Oct 4] fair maiden: stays 7f: acts on polytrack, best turf form on good going. *Chris Wall* **74**

SE YOU 2 b.g. (Apr 11) Sepoy (AUS) 129 – Lady Hestia (USA) 82 (Belong To Me (USA)) [2017 5.9d^5 6v^2 6g 8d^6 Oct 20] fair form: best effort at 6f. *Tim Easterby* **77**

SFUMATO 3 br.g. Bated Breath 125 – Modern Look 111 (Zamindar (USA) 116) [2017 81: 5.7f^6 6d^6 5.7f^3 6m^2 7m^6 t6d Oct 24] lengthy, attractive gelding: fairly useful handicapper: placed at Bath in July and Ripon in August: left Roger Charlton after third start: stays 6f: acts on firm going: has worn hood, including in 2017. *Iain Jardine* **86**

SGT RECKLESS 10 b.g. Imperial Dancer 123 – Lakaam 57 (Danzero (AUS)) [2017 p12g^3 p16g 11.9s* 10g Jun 10] fairly useful handicapper: won at Doncaster (by 2 lengths from Hermann) in June: trained by Simon Hodgson first 2 starts before rejoining former yard: stayed 1½m: acted on polytrack and soft going: useful hurdler/chaser at best: dead. *Mick Channon* **92**

SHAAQAAF (IRE) 3 b.f. Sepoy (AUS) 129 – Burke's Rock 104 (Cape Cross (IRE) 129) [2017 72: 7s^2 8g* 8g^2 7.6d^2 8g^6 Aug 25] useful performer: won maiden at Goodwood in June: second in handicaps at Newmarket and Chester (½ length behind Rutherford) in July: stays 1m: acts on soft going. *John Gosden* **102**

SHABAABY 2 br.c. (Feb 7) Kyllachy 129 – On The Brink 88 (Mind Games 121) [2017 6f^3 6d* 6d* 6g^4 Oct 14] 35,000F, 270,000Y: useful-looking colt: half-brother to several winners, including smart 5f-7f winner Aetna (by Indesatchel) and winner up to 11f Dubai Crest (2-y-o 1m winner, by Dubai Destination): dam 2-y-o 5f winner: smart form: won minor events at Newmarket (by 3¾ lengths from Travelcard) in August and Doncaster (by 7 lengths from John Kirkup) in September: raced only at 6f. *Owen Burrows* **111**

SHABBAH (IRE) 4 br.g. Sea The Stars (IRE) 140 – Alizaya (IRE) (Highest Honor (FR) 124) [2017 97: 10.1m^4 9.9g 10m 12s^2 Oct 15] useful handicapper, below best in 2017: stays 1½m: acts on good to firm going: sold to join Joseph Tuite 78,000 gns in October. *Sir Michael Stoute* **92**

SHABEEB (USA) 4 b.g. Smart Strike (CAN) 121 – Sortita (GER) 98 (Monsun (GER) 124) [2017 106: 10.3d 12m 14g^3 Jul 14] useful-looking gelding: useful handicapper: third at Ascot (4¼ lengths behind Mount Moriah) in July: stays 1¾m: acts on good to firm going: in cheekpieces last 2 starts: sometimes slowly away. *Roger Varian* **105**

SHABEEH (IRE) 3 b.g. Raven's Pass (USA) 133 – Mid Mon Lady (IRE) 110 (Danetime (IRE) 121) [2017 76: t7.1f^3 t7.1m^4 t8g^2 t8.6g^4 Jan 31] fair maiden: stays 1m: acts on tapeta. *Mark Johnston* **74**

SHACKLED N DRAWN (USA) 5 b.g. Candy Ride (ARG) 133 – Cajun Flash (USA) (Bertrando (USA) 127) [2017 84: 5f^3 5f^6 5.1s 5.1d^5 p5g^5 t5.1g p5g^3 p5g^2 p5g^2 Dec 31] strong gelding: fairly useful handicapper on all-weather, fair on turf: best form at 5f: acts on polytrack, tapeta and firm going: has worn headgear, including last 5 starts: has worn tongue tie, including last 2 starts: front runner/races prominently. *Peter Hedger* **80** **a70**

SHACKLES 3 b.g. Equiano (FR) 127 – Silent Waters (Polish Precedent (USA) 131) [2017 –: t8.6g Dec 5] no form. *Nicky Richards* –

SHADELE (IRE) 4 b.f. Rip Van Winkle (IRE) 134 – Zadalla 68 (Zaha (CAN) 106) [2017 66: p10m Jan 9] useful-looking filly: lightly-raced maiden, fair at best. *Jeremy Noseda* –

SHADES OF MIST 2 b.g. (Feb 12) Lilbourne Lad (IRE) 111 – Talqaa 74 (Exceed And Excel (AUS) 126) [2017 6m 5m^4 5d^6 f6.1g* Dec 19] fair form: won nursery at Southwell in December: left Ann Duffield after third start: best effort at 6f. *Tony Coyle* **68**

SHADES OF SILVER 7 b.g. Dansili 127 – Silver Pivotal (IRE) 113 (Pivotal 124) [2017 93: p16g^6 16v^6 p16g Nov 1] well-made, attractive gelding: fairly useful handicapper: stays 2m: acts on polytrack, soft and good to firm going. *Ed de Giles* **82**

SHADOW BEAUTY 3 b.c. Pivotal 124 – Rivara (Red Ransom (USA)) [2017 64p: p8s 9d^4 p8g Sep 13] modest form: stays 1m: tried in cheekpieces. *Marco Botti* **61**

SHADOW OF HERCULES (IRE) 3 ch.g. Roderic O'Connor (IRE) 119 – Baltic Princess (FR) 81 (Peintre Celebre (USA) 137) [2017 –: f8g p12g t14g p10.7g p12g Dec 15] poor maiden: left Michael Mullineaux after third start: usually wears headgear. *E. G. Barry, Ireland* **50**

Juddmonte Grand Prix de Paris, Saint-Cloud—
Shakeel registers a first success at pattern level, getting the verdict over the ill-fated Permian (right) in the tightest of finishes but sustaining a career-ending injury

SHADOW SEEKER (IRE) 2 b.f. (Apr 3) Arcano (IRE) 122 – New Atalanta (IRE) 59 (Xaar 132) [2017 6g p6g⁵ p5g⁶ 7d p6s t7.2g f6.1g Dec 19] 23,000 2-y-o: rather leggy filly: second foal: dam, irresolute maiden, half-sister to smart US Grade 1 9.5f winner Watsdachances: modest maiden: best effort at 6f: acts on polytrack: tried in blinkers. *Paul D'Arcy* **55**

SHADOW'S GIRL 5 gr.m. Fair Mix (IRE) 123 – Special Beat 65 (Bustino 136) [2017 p8g t9.5g⁵ t7.2g t8.6g Dec 13] half-sister to several winners, including useful winner up to 2m Gee Dee Nen (2-y-o 1m winner, by Mister Baileys): dam, 17f winner, also won over hurdles: placed in bumper: no form in Flat maidens/handicap. *Bernard Llewellyn* **–**

SHADOW SPIRIT 4 b.f. Makfi 130 – Highland Shot 91 (Selkirk (USA) 129) [2017 80: t12.2g t10.2g⁶ t9.5g⁶ Feb 27] fair maiden: stays 1¼m: acts on tapeta and good to firm going: sometimes slowly away, often races towards rear. *Iain Jardine* **69**

SHADOW WARRIOR 3 b.g. Born To Sea (IRE) 117 – Dolcetto (IRE) 83 (Danehill Dancer (IRE) 117) [2017 73p: 10.2g³ t12.2g² 10g* 10.2g⁵ p8g* Dec 31] rather unfurnished gelding: fairly useful performer: won maiden at Windsor in June and handicap at Lingfield (by length from Dark Magic) in December: effective at 1m to 1½m: acts on polytrack and tapeta. *Paul D'Arcy* **85**

SHADY MCCOY (USA) 7 b.g. English Channel (USA) 126 – Raw Gold (USA) 108 (Rahy (USA) 115) [2017 98: 8.3g 7m⁴ 7m⁴ 7m 7d⁴ 7m 7d 7g 7s 7d* 7g* 7d² p8g p7s⁴ Nov 23] sturdy gelding: smart handicapper: won at Ascot (by 1½ lengths from Hajjam) and York (by 2 lengths from Echo of Lightning) in October: second at Doncaster (neck behind Speculative Bid) in November: stays 1m: acts on polytrack, firm and soft going: tried in hood: often races in rear/travels strongly, usually responds generously to pressure. *Ian Williams* **110**

SHAELLA (IRE) 3 ch.f. Casamento (IRE) 118 – Mouriyana (IRE) (Akarad (FR) 130) [2017 p13.3s⁴ p10g Dec 30] closely related to 1½m winner Cerutty (by Shamardal) and half-sister to several winners, including smart French winner up to 9.5f Skins Game (2-y-o 1m winner, by Diktat): dam French 2-y-o 1m winner: placed in bumper: modest form when fourth at Chelmsford on first of 2 starts in Flat maidens. *Jane Chapple-Hyam* **60**

SHAHEEN (IRE) 2 b.g. (Feb 5) Society Rock (IRE) 126 – La Chicana (IRE) (Invincible Spirit (IRE) 121) [2017 t6g 6d³ 6m* 7g³ p6d³ 5m* p5d⁴ Sep 21] 120,000Y: third foal: half-brother to very smart 11f-1¾m winner Desert Encounter (by Halling) and useful 6f (including at 2 yrs) winner Fast Enough (by Kodiac): dam lightly-raced sister to smart **83**

1¼m-1½m winner Allied Powers: fairly useful performer: won minor event at Redcar in June and nursery at Beverley (by head from Requinto Dawn) in August: stays 6f: acts on polytrack, good to firm and good to soft going: in tongue tie last 5 starts: front runner/races prominently. *John Quinn*

SHAHEREZADA (IRE) 2 b.f. (Feb 16) Dutch Art 126 – Shabyt (Sadler's Wells (USA) 132) [2017 7d⁵ p7s 7g³ 8.1g² 9m³ 9d* Nov 4] small filly: third foal: half-sister to useful 1¼m/11f winner Shymkent (by Pivotal): dam, unraced, closely related to smart performers up to 1½m Sir Isaac Newton and Secret Gesture: fairly useful performer: won nursery at Newmarket (by 5 lengths from Galactic) in November: will stay at least 1¼m: acts on polytrack, good to firm and good to soft going: often races towards rear. *Clive Cox* **88**

SHAH OF ARMAAN (IRE) 4 b.g. Fastnet Rock (AUS) 127 – Queen of Tara (IRE) (Sadler's Wells (USA) 132) [2017 79: t8.6m* t8g³ f8m t8.6g³ t9.5g 8g 8d 7.4m Aug 27] fair performer: won maiden at Wolverhampton (by 2¼ lengths from Revolutionary War) in January: stays 9.5f: acts on tapeta and soft going: in cheekpieces last 3 starts: sold £800 in November. *Kevin Ryan* **79**

SHAIYEM (IRE) 4 b.g. Starspangledbanner (AUS) 128 – Shaanbar (IRE) 53 (Darshaan 133) [2017 95: 8m² p8g 7.6d* May 13] smallish gelding: useful handicapper: won at Lingfield (by 1¼ lengths from Ghalib) in May: stays 1m: acts on polytrack, good to firm and good to soft going: often races prominently/freely: sold £32,000 in August, sent to Greece. *Richard Hannon* **99**

SHAKABULA (IRE) 3 b.g. Kheleyf (USA) 116 – Tinaar (USA) 99 (Giant's Causeway (USA) 132) [2017 56: 7g 10g 12d⁵ Aug 4] modest maiden: stays 1¼m: acts on tapeta: usually races nearer last than first. *Brian Ellison* **56**

SHAKEEL (FR) 3 b.c. Dalakhani (IRE) 133 – Shamiyra (FR) (Medicean 128) [2017 10.4d³ 9.9g* 11.9g³ 11.9m² 11.9g* Jul 14] first foal: dam unraced half-sister to smart French 1¼m/10.5f winner Shemiyla: smart performer: won maiden at Chantilly in April and Grand Prix de Paris at Saint-Cloud (by nose from Permian, though reportedly injured in race) in July: stayed 1½m: acted on good to firm and good to soft going: to stand at Clongiffen Stud, Co. Meath, Ireland. *A. de Royer Dupre, France* **117**

SHAKIAH (IRE) 2 b.f. (Apr 18) Farhh 131 – Dubai Sea (USA) (Street Sense (USA) 128) [2017 6.9v⁶ 6v 6d⁵ Oct 20] 36,000Y: third foal: dam unraced half-sister to smart winner up to 7f Racer Forever: modest form when fifth in minor event at Redcar (4¾ lengths behind Nicklaus) on last of 3 starts. *Sharon Watt* **51**

SHAKOUR (IRE) 2 b.c. (May 9) Declaration of War (USA) 128 – Another Storm (USA) (Gone West (USA)) [2017 t8.6g⁶ p8d³ Dec 13] fair form when third at Kempton (4½ lengths behind Highbrow) on second of 2 starts in minor events: will be suited by 1¼m+: wears tongue tie. *John Gosden* **77**

SHALAILAH (IRE) 2 b.f. (Feb 7) Showcasing 117 – Perfect Venture 76 (Bahamian Bounty 116) [2017 6g 7d² 7g² p6g p7g² p7g* 8d Nov 4] £48,000Y: first foal: dam 6f winner: fairly useful performer: won maiden at Dundalk in October: second in Silver Flash Stakes at Leopardstown (5 lengths behind Happily) in July: left G. M. Lyons after third start: stays 7f: acts on polytrack and good to soft going: tried in tongue tie. *Joseph Patrick O'Brien, Ireland* **86**

SHA LA LA LA LEE 2 b.c. (Apr 14) Helmet (AUS) 127 – Shamara (IRE) 99 (Spectrum (IRE) 126) [2017 7g⁶ 8g² Sep 15] fair form: better effort when second in maiden at Doncaster (4½ lengths behind Blue Laureate) in September. *Tom Dascombe* **76**

SHALAMZAR (FR) 8 ch.g. Selkirk (USA) 129 – Shamalana (IRE) (Sinndar (IRE) 134) [2017 72: 14v Nov 7] fair handicapper, well held sole outing on Flat in 2017: stays 1½m: acts on good to firm and heavy going: tried in cheekpieces/tongue tie: often races towards rear: winning hurdler. *Micky Hammond* **–**

SHALIANZI (IRE) 7 b.g. Azamour (IRE) 130 – Shalama (IRE) 91 (Kahyasi 130) [2017 54: p16d³ p16g Mar 22] modest handicapper: stays 2m: acts on polytrack, best turf form on good going: wears blinkers: winning hurdler. *Chris Gordon* **63**

SHALIMAH (IRE) 5 br.g. Dark Angel (IRE) 113 – Jemima's Art 61 (Fantastic Light (USA) 134) [2017 75: p15.8m⁴ Jan 9] smallish gelding: fair handicapper: stays 2m: acts on polytrack, good to firm and good to soft going: wears visor. *Clive Cox* **70**

SHAMAHEART (IRE) 7 b.g. Shamardal (USA) 129 – Encouragement 76 (Royal Applause 124) [2017 90: t7.1d t7.1d⁵ t7.1g t7.1d⁵ 8m 7g 8.8m 7.4m 7v Aug 8] strong gelding: fairly useful handicapper: stays 1½m, raced mainly at shorter: acts on polytrack, firm and good to soft going: wears headgear: often starts slowly, races towards rear. *Geoffrey Harker* **83**

SHAMAR (FR) 9 b.g. Dr Fong (USA) 128 – Shamalana (IRE) (Sinndar (IRE) 134) [2017 82: 12m 12d 13.1s^3 10.5d^2 12s 13.8s^{pu} 10g 12.1d^5 p12g p10.7g p10.7g Dec 1] fair handicapper: stays 13f: acts on good to firm and heavy going: usually wears headgear/tongue tie: usually races nearer last than first: temperamental. *R. K. Watson, Ireland* **72 §**

SHAMASH (IRE) 5 b.g. Oasis Dream 129 – Shareen (IRE) 110 (Bahri (USA) 125) [2017 72: p12s^6 t12.2g* t13.9g^2 t12.2g* Mar 30] fairly useful handicapper: won at Wolverhampton (twice) in March: stays 1¾m: acts on polytrack, tapeta and soft going: has worn cheekpieces: wears tongue tie. *John McConnell, Ireland* **83**

SHAMBRA (IRE) 3 b.f. Clodovil (IRE) 116 – Shambodia (IRE) (Petardia 113) [2017 55p: f8g^4 f8g^5 10m* 9.9f^3 12.1m^3 t9.5g 9.2v^4 11.2v* Sep 18] fair handicapper: won at Redcar in May and Carlisle in September: stays 11f: acts on any turf going: in hood last 2 starts: front runner/races prominently. *Roger Fell* **73**

SHAMLAN (IRE) 5 br.g. Shamardal (USA) 129 – Atamana (IRE) 82 (Lahib (USA) 129) [2017 77: t9.5g t8.6g p7s t8.6g^2 Dec 5] fair handicapper: left Johnny Farrelly after third start: stays 8.5f: acts on tapeta: often wears headgear/tongue tie: sometimes slowly away, usually races in rear, often lazily. *Kevin Frost* **66**

SHAMONIX (IRE) 3 b.f. Elusive Pimpernel (USA) 117 – Shamora (FR) 79 (Oratorio (IRE) 128) [2017 p8g 8.1m t8.6g^5 p7g^6 p8d 8.3d 8s 5.1m 7d^5 p10g Sep 26] €5,000Y: sturdy filly: first foal: dam 7f winner: poor maiden. *Mark Usher* **42**

SHAMREEN (IRE) 4 b.f. Dubawi (IRE) 129 – Shareen (IRE) 110 (Bahri (USA) 125) [2017 110: 10g^6 10s* 10s* 9.9d Oct 1] smart performer: won Royal Whip Stakes at the Curragh (by 3¼ lengths from Massif Central) in August and Blandford Stakes at same course (for second successive year, by 3 lengths from Beautiful Morning) in September: best at 1¼m: acts on good to firm and heavy going: sometimes wears headgear: usually races close up. *D. K. Weld, Ireland* **112**

SHAMROCK EMMA (IRE) 2 ch.f. (May 11) Mizzen Mast (USA) 121 – Lisselan Diva (IRE) 109 (Barathea (IRE) 127) [2017 p6g^4 p5g 5.1d p6s Dec 1] second foal: dam French 5f/5.5f winner: modest form when fourth in minor event at Kempton on debut, best effort. *John Best* **52**

SHAMROKH (IRE) 3 b.g. Invincible Spirit (IRE) 121 – Alshakr 108 (Bahri (USA) 125) [2017 70: t8g* t8.6m^2 p8g^4 8m 9m^6 8g 12v^6 11.8d 8v^6 8d^2 p8s^4 f8.1g Dec 11] rangy gelding: fairly useful performer: won maiden at Newcastle in January: second in handicaps at Wolverhampton in February and Newmarket in November: left John Gosden after fourth start: stays 9f: acts on polytrack, tapeta, good to firm and good to soft going: sometimes in headgear/tongue tie. *Michael Appleby* **90**

SHAMSAYA (IRE) 3 b.f. Shamardal (USA) 129 – Masaya 101 (Dansili 127) [2017 93: 6m 6.1g^3 6g^4 6d^6 p6g^5 p6g^2 Dec 12] fairly useful handicapper: placed at Nottingham in July and Lingfield in December: stays 6f: acts on polytrack, good to firm and heavy going. *Simon Crisford* **93**

Moyglare Jewels Blandford Stakes, the Curragh—
Shamreen produces a smart performance to win this race for the second year running, with Beautiful Morning (striped sleeves) heading the chasing pack

SHAMSHON (IRE) 6 b.g. Invincible Spirit (IRE) 121 – Greenisland (IRE) 100 (Fasliyev (USA) 120) [2017 103: p6g^5 t5.1g t6g 5g^5 6s 5m^3 5g* 5d^6 5.4d 5g^4 5v 5s^6 p5g^3 p5g^4 t5.1g Dec 22] strong, attractive gelding: useful handicapper: won at Newmarket (by ½ length from Top Boy) in July: stays 6f: acts on polytrack, tapeta, soft and good to firm going: wears tongue tie: usually races towards rear. *Stuart Williams* **98**

SHANAKILL STAR (IRE) 3 b.f. Lord Shanakill (USA) 121 – Lola Rosa (IRE) (Peintre Celebre (USA) 137) [2017 8m May 3] 5,000F, 7,000Y: fourth foal: half-sister to 2-y-o 1m winner Taskeen (by Lilbourne Lad): dam unraced out of smart US Grade 1 9.5f winner Snow Polina: 50/1, well held in maiden at Yarmouth. *Miss Joey Ellis* **–**

SHANANDOA 6 b.m. Shamardal (USA) 129 – Divisa (GER) 107 (Lomitas 129) [2017 9.9d^6 9.9g p12g 10d Jul 19] sturdy mare: sister to 1½m winner Danisa and half-sister to 3 winners abroad: dam German 9f-1½m winner: modest form: stays 1¼m: tried in hood: bumper winner/poor hurdler. *Brian Barr* **62**

SHAN DUN NA NGALL (IRE) 6 b.g. Shantou (USA) 125 – Omanah (USA) (Kayrawan (USA) 91) [2017 64: p15.8g* p16d p15.8g^6 p15.8g^6 t16.3d Dec 16] modest handicapper: won at Lingfield in January: stays 16.5f: acts on polytrack, tapeta and soft going: usually wears headgear/tongue tie: usually races towards rear. *Amy Murphy* **64**

SHANGHAI ELASTIC 2 b.f. (Feb 8) Swiss Spirit 117 – Reveille 67 (Sakhee's Secret 128) [2017 5m^3 May 5] 5,000Y: first foal: dam, maiden (stayed 1m), half-sister to smart US Grade 2 1m winner Up In Time: 11/1, hinted at ability when third in maiden at Musselburgh: open to improvement. *David Barron* **47 p**

SHANGHAI GLORY (IRE) 4 ch.g. Exceed And Excel (AUS) 126 – Hecuba 93 (Hector Protector (USA) 124) [2017 113: 6m 6d^5 6g^3 6v 6d Oct 27] lengthy, good-quartered gelding: smart handicapper: third in Great St Wilfrid Stakes at Ripon (¾ length behind Mattmu) in August: best at 6f: acts on soft going. *Charles Hills* **112**

SHANGHAI SHANE (IRE) 3 b.g. Lord Shanakill (USA) 121 – Lamassu (IRE) (Entrepreneur 123) [2017 t9.5g 8.1m^{ro} p7g t9.5g^6 Nov 18] lengthy gelding: no form in maidens. *Brian Barr* **–**

SHANIA SAYS (IRE) 2 b.f. (Mar 23) Red Jazz (USA) 125 – Vexatious (IRE) (Shamardal (USA) 129) [2017 5g^4 t6.1g^6 p6g^3 6.1g^3 5v^3 t6.1g* 6d^3 6.1d Oct 4] 5,000F, €45,000Y: rather unfurnished filly: second foal: half-sister to useful winner up to 8.6f Shawaahid (2-y-o 5f-7f winner, by Elnadim): dam unraced half-sister to smart 1m-1¼m winner Mango Diva: fair performer: won minor event at Wolverhampton in August: stays 6f: acts on polytrack, tapeta and good to soft going: front runner/races prominently. *Tony Carroll* **72**

SHANKARA (IRE) 3 gr.f. Mastercraftsman (IRE) 129 – White And Red (IRE) 93 (Orpen (USA) 116) [2017 t8.6g^2 p10g^3 p8s^5 7g^5 8d^{rr} Aug 10] 42,000F, €52,000 2-y-o: third foal: half-sister to 2-y-o 5f winner (stayed 7f) Fashionable Spirit (by Invincible Spirit): dam 6.5f winner: fair maiden: stays 1¼m: acts on polytrack and tapeta: temperamental (refused to race final outing). *David Simcock* **71 §**

SHANNAH BINT ERIC 3 ch.f. Poet's Voice 126 – Crystal Mountain (USA) (Monashee Mountain (USA) 115) [2017 –: 7m May 22] well held in maidens. *Kevin Ryan* **–**

SHAQOOS (FR) 3 ch.f. Naaqoos 117 – Shemrana (USA) (Woodman (USA) 126) [2017 –: f7g^6 p10g Jan 19] no form. *Jo Hughes* **–**

SHARED EQUITY 6 b.g. Elnadim (USA) 128 – Pelican Key (IRE) 80 (Mujadil (USA) 119) [2017 100: 6s 6d Jun 7] lengthy gelding: useful handicapper, well below form in 2017: effective at 6f/7f: acts on soft and good to firm going. *Jedd O'Keeffe* **73**

SHARGIAH (IRE) 4 ch.g. New Approach (IRE) 132 – Zacheta (Polish Precedent (USA) 131) [2017 84: p8f^4 10m* t10.2s* 9.9m* Jun 16] tall gelding: useful handicapper: won at Windsor (by length from Eskendash) and Newcastle (by 1½ lengths from Pushaq) in May, and Sandown (by 2½ lengths from Artful Rogue) in June: will stay 1½m: acts on polytrack, tapeta, good to firm and good to soft going: usually races prominently: open to further improvement. *Roger Varian* **106 p**

SHARJA BRIDGE 3 b.c. Oasis Dream 129 – Quetena (GER) (Acatenango (GER) 127) [2017 8m^3 8s^2 8.3g* 8g^2 Sep 15] 500,000Y: brother to very smart German winner up to 1¼m Querari (2-y-o 7f winner) and half-brother to 3 winners, including Canadian Grade 2 9f winner Quidura (2-y-o 7.5f winner in Germany, by Dubawi) and German 1¼m/11f winner Quasillo (by Sea The Stars), both smart: dam useful German 1¼m/10.5f winner: smart form: won maiden at Nottingham (by 4 lengths from Rising) in August: second in handicap at Sandown (head behind The Grape Escape) in September: stays 8.5f: will go on improving. *Roger Varian* **113 p**

SHARJAH (IRE) 7 b.g. Shamardal (USA) 129 – Lunar Lustre (IRE) (Desert Prince (IRE) 130) [2017 82: p16g^4 p10.7g p12g p16g^5 p10.7g* 12.5m^3 9.7m 10.2f^2 10g 12g^3 p12g^6 p10.7g^6 p10.7g p16s p10.7g* p12g^6 Dec 21] sturdy gelding: fairly useful handicapper: won at Dundalk in April and December: stays 2m, effective at much shorter: acts on polytrack, firm and good to soft going: ofter wears blinkers: has worn tongue tie. *A. Slattery, Ireland* **85**

SHARJA SILK 2 b.c. (May 1) Dubawi (IRE) 129 – So Silk (Rainbow Quest (USA) 134) [2017 8d^5 Oct 27] 850,000Y: tall, close-coupled, good-topped colt: half-brother to several winners, including smart 1½m-14.6f (Park Hill Stakes) winner Silk Sari (by Dalakhani) and winner around 1½m So Sleek (by Lawman): dam unraced half-sister to Racing Post Trophy winner Ibn Khaldun out of Fillies' Mile and Irish 1000 Guineas winner Gossamer, herself sister to Barathea: 8/1, promise when fifth in minor event at Newbury (4¾ lengths behind Extra Elusive) in October: capable of better. *Roger Varian* **74 p**

SHARP DEFENCE (USA) 3 b.c. First Defence (USA) 119 – Jazz Drummer (USA) (Dixieland Band (USA)) [2017 82: 7.1g^2 7m* 7.6m^5 6m^4 6s* 6g p6g^2 7.6g 8g a7f^6 a8f Dec 7] brother to smart winner up to 8.5f Dancetrack (2-y-o 7f winner) and closely related/half-brother to 3 winners abroad, including French 2-y-o 8.5f winner Fairwater (by Empire Maker): dam, placed up to 8.5f in France, half-sister to smart French 7f-1¼m performer Mizzen Mast: useful performer: won maiden at Salisbury in April and handicap at Hamilton (by 3¼ lengths from Harwoods Volante) in July: second in handicap at Dundalk (½ length behind Reckless Endeavour) in August: left John Patrick Shanahan after eighth start: stays 7.5f: acts on polytrack, soft and good to firm going: in cheekpieces last 2 starts. *S. Seemar, UAE* **105**

SHARP OPERATOR 4 ch.g. Medicean 128 – Helen Sharp (Pivotal 124) [2017 59: 9.5d^4 10d 12d p7s Dec 14] modest maiden: left Charles O'Brien after third start: stays 1¼m: acts on polytrack: often in hood: sometimes slowly away. *Charlie Wallis* **51**

SHARP REMINDER 2 b.f. (Mar 3) Kyllachy 129 – Sharp Relief (IRE) 78 (Galileo (IRE) 134) [2017 p7d^6 t7.1g^2 p8g^4 t8g^3 Dec 6] 42,000Y: third foal: half-sister to useful winner up to 1¾m Calvinist (2-y-o 1¼m winner, by Holy Roman Emperor) and a winner abroad by Makfi: dam 11.5f-1¾m winner: fair form: stays 1m. *James Tate* **76**

SHAWWAL 2 b.g. (Jan 27) Harbour Watch (IRE) 121 – Orton Park (IRE) 80 (Moss Vale (IRE) 126) [2017 p6d^5 7f^2 6g^3 7g^5 Dec 29] fair form: left John Gosden after second start: stays 7f. *S. Ibido, Qatar* **78**

SHAYA (IRE) 2 b.f. (May 18) Invincible Spirit (IRE) 121 – Nidhaal (IRE) 107 (Observatory (USA) 131) [2017 5.1m^4 5.1g^2 6.1v* p6d 5s t6d Oct 24] closely related to 2-y-o 5f/6f winner Sadafiya and 5f and (at 2 yrs) 6f winner Sharaarah (both by Oasis Dream) and half-sister to 3 winners, including useful 2-y-o 5f winner Burwaaz (by Exceed And Excel): dam 2-y-o 6f winner: fairly useful performer: won minor event at Chester (by ½ length from Gabrial The Saint) in September: stays 6f: acts on heavy going: often races prominently: sold 27,000 gns, sent to Spain. *Roger Fell* **83**

SHAY C 2 b.c. (Apr 3) Foxwedge (AUS) 128 – Sirenuse (IRE) 91 (Exceed And Excel (AUS) 126) [2017 5m 5m^2 5g^5 5m^3 5g^5 5d 5d Sep 16] fair maiden: raced only at 5f: acts on good to firm going: front runner/races prominently. *Declan Carroll* **66**

SHAZZAB (IRE) 2 b.f. (Mar 10) Elzaam (AUS) 115 – Ceylon Round (FR) (Royal Applause 124) [2017 5m^4 6m^5 6d* 6.9g^4 7g^6 8.1d^3 8v* 7.9g Oct 14] €6,000Y, resold €10,000Y: good-quartered filly: half-sister to several winners, including 2-y-o 7f winner Todd's Forge (by Daggers Drawn) and 5.7f-7f winner Chester'slittlegem (2-y-o 6f winner, by Atraf): dam of little account: fairly useful performer: won maiden at Leicester in June and nursery at Pontefract (by 2¼ lengths from Dathanna) in September: stays 1m: acts on good to firm and heavy going: in cheekpieces last 3 starts: often races towards rear. *Richard Fahey* **80**

SHEARIAN 7 b.g. Royal Applause 124 – Regal Asset (USA) (Regal Classic (CAN)) [2017 67: f8g* f8g* f8m 8g^4 8m f8.1g^6 p8s 8.5d 8.2g^2 8.3g 7.4s 8d 9.9g f8.1g^6 f8.1g^5 f8.1g* f8.1g^6 f8.1g^3 Dec 22] strong gelding, has only one eye: fair handicapper: won at Southwell in January, February and December: raced mainly around 1m: acts on polytrack, fibresand, good to firm and good to soft going: has worn headgear, including in 2017. *Declan Carroll* **70 a80**

SHEARLING 4 b.f. Rail Link 132 – Casual 102 (Nayef (USA) 129) [2017 12g^3 12.5g^5 12.3d^2 11.9d 16.3d^2 Sep 10] 25,000 3-y-o: well-made filly: third foal: half-sister to smart French 1½m winner Harlem (by Champs Elysees): dam winner up to 1½m (2-y-o 7f **92**

winner): multiple bumper winner: fairly useful maiden on Flat: placed in listed race at Pontefract (10¾ lengths behind Abingdon) in June and handicap at York in September: stays 16.5f: acts on good to soft going: sold 22,000 gns in December. *Brian Ellison*

SHE BELIEVES (IRE) 2 ch.f. (Feb 8) Arcano (IRE) 122 – African Moonlight (UAE) **96** (Halling (USA) 133) [2017 5.1m^{2} 6m^{5} 7m^{6} 6.1g* 6s* 7g* 8g^{6} 6g Oct 7] €33,000F, 45,000Y: third foal: half-sister to 3 winners, including useful 2-y-o 5f winner (stays 7f) Repton (by Zebedee) and smart US Grade 3 9f winner Syntax (by Haatef): dam twice-raced sister to smart 1¼m-1¾m winner Mkuzi: useful performer: won minor event at Chepstow in July, and nurseries at Leicester and Goodwood (by 6 lengths from Simply Breathless) in August: stays 7f: acts on soft going. *Sylvester Kirk*

SHEEPSCAR LAD (IRE) 3 b.g. Arcano (IRE) 122 – Piccadilly Filly (IRE) 111 (Exceed **91** And Excel (AUS) 126) [2017 71: t5g^{2} f5d^{3} 6m^{4} 5f^{5} 6g^{2} 6g^{2} 5d* 5.4d^{4} 6.1v^{3} 5g* 5v* Sep 9] robust gelding: fairly useful handicapper: won at Pontefract in July, and at Beverley and Thirsk (dead-heated with Erissimus Maximus) in September: stays 6f: acts on fibresand, tapeta, good to firm and heavy going: has worn visor. *Nigel Tinkler*

SHEER INTENSITY (IRE) 4 ch.f. Dutch Art 126 – Sheer Elegance (IRE) (Pivotal 124) **60** [2017 66: t7.1m t8.6m p10m t9.5g^{ur} t10.2d^{6} t9.5g p8g t8g^{2} p8g^{2} p8g^{2} t8.6g^{6} p8d^{3} t7.1g^{3} 8.3g^{4} 8g* t8.6g 8.1m^{4} p8g 10.2f^{5} 10d^{4} 10s^{6} p10s^{4} t8.6g^{2} Dec 13] modest handicapper: won at Brighton in May: stays 8.5f: acts on polytrack, tapeta and heavy going: has worn headgear, including in 2017: sometimes slowly away. *David Evans*

SHEE'S LUCKY 3 b.f. Yorgunnabelucky (USA) 102 – She's The Lady 64 (Unfuwain **–** (USA) 131) [2017 67: t9.5g p8g Nov 1] modest maiden at 2 yrs, behind in handicaps in 2017: left Mark Johnston after first start: stays 8.5f: acts on tapeta. *Neil Mulholland*

SHEF WEDSNEIGH (IRE) 2 ch.f. (Mar 11) Choisir (AUS) 126 – Tullawadgeen (IRE) **–** (Sinndar (IRE) 134) [2017 7g 7m 7.4v^{6} Sep 26] €3,000Y: half-sister to several winners, including useful 1m-1¼m winner Weapon of Choice (2-y-o 9f winner, by Iffraaj) and 6f/7f winner Eager To Bow (by Acclamation): dam twice-raced half-sister to Poule d'Essai des Pouliches winner Tie Black: little impact in minor events. *Roger Fell*

SHEIKHA REIKA (FR) 2 b.f. (Mar 14) Shamardal (USA) 129 – Screen Star (IRE) 110 **89** (Tobougg (IRE) 125) [2017 8s^{2} 8d^{2} 8.3d^{2} Oct 18] 550,000Y: sixth foal: sister to smart winner up to 1m Lumiere (2-y-o 6f winner, including Cheveley Park Stakes) and half-sister to 1½m winner Silent Movie (by Cape Cross) and winner up to 1¼m X Rated (2-y-o 8.6f winner, by Exceed And Excel): dam 2-y-o 7f winner on only start: fairly useful form when runner-up in minor events/maiden. *Roger Varian*

SHEIKHZAYEDROAD 8 b.g. Dubawi (IRE) 129 – Royal Secrets (IRE) 78 (Highest **119** Honor (FR) 124) [2017 119: 14g^{3} 15.9d^{3} 20m^{6} 16g 16.3g^{4} 17.9g^{3} 16s Oct 21] deep-girthed gelding: smart performer: third in Dubai Gold Cup at Meydan (1½ lengths behind Vazirabad) in March and Doncaster Cup (1½ lengths behind Desert Skyline) in September: stays 2½m: acts on any turf going: wears hood. *David Simcock*

SHEIKSPEAR 3 b.c. Bahamian Bounty 116 – Crinkle (IRE) (Distant Relative 128) [2017 **85** 84: 6.1m 6.1m* 7g^{3} p7s* 7g^{2} p7g^{5} Oct 11] fairly useful handicapper: won at Chepstow in July and Kempton (by neck from Tobrave) in August: stays 7f: acts on polytrack and good to firm going: front runner/races prominently: sold 24,000 gns, sent to Qatar. *Ed de Giles*

SHEILA ROSE (IRE) 2 b.f. (May 24) Rip Van Winkle (IRE) 134 – Al Ihsas (IRE) 99 **–** (Danehill (USA) 126) [2017 p7d p7g Dec 20] closely related to 1m winner (stayed 11f) Jinsha Lake (by Galileo) and half-sister to 3 winners abroad: dam 7f winner: well held in minor events. *Denis Coakley*

SHEILA'S FANCY (IRE) 3 ch.g. Casamento (IRE) 118 – Fancy Vivid (IRE) 69 (Galileo **68** (IRE) 134) [2017 52: p12g^{3} 12d^{6} 13.3g^{6} 14s^{5} p10m t16.5d^{2} p15.8g^{5} Dec 20] fair maiden: stays 16.5f: acts on polytrack and tapeta. *J. S. Moore*

SHEILA'S PALACE 3 ch.f. Sakhee's Secret 128 – Loreto Rose 76 (Lahib (USA) 129) **65** [2017 64: p5g^{3} t6m^{3} p7m^{6} t6.1g^{pu} Aug 10] fair maiden: stays 6f: acts on polytrack and tapeta: front runner/races prominently. *J. S. Moore*

SHEILA'S RETURN 3 ch.f. Bated Breath 125 – Deora De (Night Shift (USA)) [2017 **50** 56: t7.1g f6g^{5} t5.1g Feb 27] modest maiden: stays 7f: acts on tapeta and good to firm going: front runner/races prominently. *John Balding*

SHEILA'S ROCK (IRE) 3 b.f. Fastnet Rock (AUS) 127 – Crystal Curling (IRE) 100 **77 p** (Peintre Celebre (USA) 137) [2017 8.3g^{3} p8g^{3} Nov 6] 17,000Y: sixth foal: closely related to 1m winner Sparkling Crystal (by Danehill Dancer) and a winner in Greece by Oratorio: dam, 2-y-o 7f winner (stayed 11f), out of Lancashire Oaks winner State Crystal: fair form when third in maidens at Kempton and Windsor: remains capable of better. *Denis Coakley*

SHE IS NO LADY 5 b.m. Lope de Vega (IRE) 125 – Capestar (IRE) 78 (Cape Cross (IRE) 129) [2017 108: 16.2m^{3} 20m^{4} 16g^{5} 17.9g Sep 15] sturdy mare: smart performer: third in Henry II Stakes at Sandown (7 lengths behind Big Orange) in May: stays 2½m: acts on polytrack, good to firm and heavy going. *Ralph Beckett* **112**

SHELNEVERWALKALONE 3 b.f. Captain Gerrard (IRE) 113 – Rabarama (Xaar 132) [2017 –: 6m^{5} 6v^{4} 5v^{6} 5.2m^{4} 5.3s Oct 10] modest maiden: stays 6f: acts on good to firm going: tried in blinkers: usually leads. *Ivan Furtado* **60**

SHELTERED WATERS 3 b.f. Aqlaam 125 – Velvet Waters 80 (Unfuwain (USA) 131) [2017 –: p12m^{5} Mar 29] well held in maidens. *Eve Johnson Houghton* **–**

SHENANIGANS (IRE) 3 b.f. Arcano (IRE) 122 – Ladylishandra (IRE) 82 (Mujadil (USA) 119) [2017 88p: 7v^{3} p7s^{6} 8m^{2} 8g* 8d* 8g^{2} Oct 7] useful handicapper: won at Goodwood in August and Newmarket (by 1¼ lengths from Panova) in September: second at latter course (1½ lengths behind Peach Melba) in October: stays 1m: acts on polytrack, tapeta, good to firm and heavy going. *Roger Varian* **102**

SHEPHERD MARKET (IRE) 2 b.f. (Jan 31) Reckless Abandon 119 – Shepherdia (IRE) (Pivotal 124) [2017 7s^{4} 7.1s* 7d^{2} 7s^{2} Oct 28] 22,000Y: second foal: half-sister to winner up to 7f Experto Crede (2-y-o 6f winner, by Exceed And Excel): dam, French maiden (third at 9f at 2 yrs), half-sister to US Grade 3 1m winner Chattahoochee War out of US Grade 3 8.5f winner Buffalo Berry: useful form: won minor event at Chepstow (by 4½ lengths from Great Vizier) in August: second in listed race at Newbury (¾ length behind Hikmaa) in October: raced only at 7f. *Clive Cox* **96**

SHEPHERD'S PURSE 5 b.g. Pastoral Pursuits 127 – Neyraan 53 (Lujain (USA) 119) [2017 99: p7g p6g^{3} p6g^{2} 5.8m 7s 7g^{3} 6.3f 6m p6g^{4} a7g^{4} t7.2d^{2} Dec 16] big gelding: fairly useful handicapper: placed at Dundalk (twice) in February and Wolverhampton in December left Joseph G. Murphy after tenth start: stays 7f: acts on polytrack, tapeta, good to firm and good to soft going: has worn headgear: front runner/races prominently. *David Loughnane* **90**

SHERBERT 3 b.f. Power 117 – Original (Caerleon (USA) 132) [2017 –: t7.1g^{4} 9.5s 7v Oct 11] modest form when fourth in maiden at Wolverhampton in March, standout effort: left Richard Hannon after first start: should be suited by 1m+. *Jonathan Fogarty, Ireland* **59**

SHERIFF 2 br.g. (Feb 22) Lawman (FR) 121 – Chatline (IRE) 90 (One Cool Cat (USA) 123) [2017 7s^{6} 7g p7g^{6} p7s^{5} Nov 16] unfurnished gelding: fourth foal: half-brother to winner up to 1¼m Ay Ay (2-y-o 7f winner, by Pour Moi) and a winner abroad by Iffraaj: dam, 6f winner, half-sister to smart 6f-1m winner Mugharreb out of very smart winner up to 1m Marling: fair form: raced only at 7f: remains with potential. *Michael Bell* **70 p**

SHERIFF GARRETT (IRE) 3 b.g. Lawman (FR) 121 – Few Are Chosen (IRE) 97 (Sulamani (IRE) 130) [2017 63: 12m^{6} 14g^{4} 14m^{2} t14g* 12d^{2} t14g* 13.4g^{5} 13.9d^{4} 13.9s^{5} 14s^{4} 14d^{2} 14d^{2} Oct 30] fairly useful handicapper: won at Wolverhampton in July and August: second at Redcar (twice) in October: stays 1¾m: acts on tapeta, soft and good to firm going: often wears cheekpieces: often races towards rear. *Tim Easterby* **80**

SHERIFF OF NAWTON (IRE) 6 b.g. Lawman (FR) 121 – Pivotal Role 66 (Pivotal 124) [2017 12g 11.1d 12g^{4} 11.9s^{3} 11.2s^{5} 11.2d* 12v^{6} t16.5g^{6} Nov 20] fairly useful handicapper: won at Carlisle in August: stays 1½m: acts on tapeta, good to firm and heavy going: often travels strongly. *Roger Fell* **80**

SHERMAN MCCOY 11 ch.g. Reset (AUS) 124 – Naomi Wildman (USA) (Kingmambo (USA) 125) [2017 74: t12.4g 13.1s^{4} 12.1m^{6} 12.1s 11.2s Aug 7] lengthy gelding: fairly useful handicapper at best, little form in 2017: stayed 2m: acted on polytrack, fibresand and any turf going: sometimes wore cheekpieces: dead. *Marjorie Fife* **51**

SHERZY BOY 2 b.c. (Feb 16) Champs Elysees 124 – Sherzam 89 (Exceed And Excel (AUS) 126) [2017 8d^{4} 8g^{6} 8g^{4} 8s Oct 19] useful-looking colt: fair form: raced only at 1m. *Richard Hannon* **76**

SHESAIDYES (IRE) 2 b.f. (Apr 14) Kodiac 112 – Bluebell Park (USA) 60 (Gulch (USA)) [2017 6m t7.1g Sep 12] €10,000Y, €85,000 2-y-o: closely related to 11f/1½m winner Captain Teemo (by Oratorio) and half-sister to several winners, including 10.5f winner Manhattan Swing (by Invincible Spirit) and 1m-1½m winner Apparition (by Dream Ahead), both useful: dam lightly raced: modest form on first of 2 outings: sent to UAE. *Henry Spiller* **62**

SHE'SASTORM (IRE) 2 b.f. (Apr 23) Footstepsinthesand 120 – Snap Alam (IRE) 88 (Alamshar (IRE) 133) [2017 6g 7s a7f Dec 21] €35,000 2-y-o: third foal: dam 6.5f-9f winner: no form: left Henry Spiller after second start: tried in hood/tongue tie. *A. bin Harmash, UAE* **–**

SHE'S DIFFERENT (IRE) 2 b.f. (Apr 29) Epaulette (AUS) 126 – Quickstyx 72 (Night **71**
Shift (USA)) [2017 6.5m 6d^6 6g^4 6s* 6.5g^3 Sep 14] €30,000Y: half-sister to numerous winners, including useful 6f-8.5f winner (including at 2 yrs) Medieval (by Kodiac) and 6f (including at 2 yrs) winner Hairspray (by Bahamian Bounty): dam 1m winner who stayed 1¼m: fair performer: won nursery at Hamilton in August: will stay at least 7f: acts on soft going. *Nigel Tinkler*

SHESGOTTHELOT 2 b.f. (Feb 24) Finjaan 122 – Noble Nova 69 (Fraam 114) [2017 **65**
p5g^3 t5.1g^3 p6g^3 6d^4 p6.5g^3 6g 7d p7.5g^5 6s^6 t6.1g^3 t7.2g^3 Oct 7] seventh foal: half-sister to 3 winners, including useful 6f (including at 2 yrs) winner New Bidder (by Auction House): dam winner up to 1m (2-y-o 6f winner): fair maiden: stays 7f: acts on polytrack and good to soft going: in cheekpieces last 2 starts. *J. S. Moore*

SHE'S PUKKA 3 ch.f. Makfi 130 – Chieftess (IRE) 87 (Mr Greeley (USA) 122) [2017 **76**
9v* t8g^6 Oct 19] €65,000Y: second foal: dam lightly-raced daughter of useful 2-y-o 6f winner Cherokee: fair form: won maiden at Carlisle (by 1½ lengths from Relevant) in September: will be suited by 1¼m+. *Iain Jardine*

SHE'S ROSANNA 3 b.f. Poet's Voice 126 – She Storm (IRE) (Rainbow Quest (USA) **35 §**
134) [2017 –§: 7g 6.1m 5.7f 5.1g Jul 20] small filly: poor maiden: tried in hood/tongue tie: temperamental. *Steph Hollinshead*

SHE'S ROYAL 2 b.f. (Apr 29) Delegator 125 – Sukuma (IRE) 55 (Highest Honor (FR) **66**
124) [2017 7v t8g^6 t8g^3 f7.1g t8g^6 Nov 24] £800Y: half-sister to several winners, including 1m winners Geordan Murphy (by Firebreak) and Flaming Miracle (at 2 yrs) (both by Firebreak): dam maiden (stayed 1m): fair maiden: best effort at 1m: acts on tapeta. *Bryan Smart*

SHESTHEDREAM (IRE) 4 b.f. Dream Ahead (USA) 133 – Tatiana Romanova (USA) **72**
81 (Mr Greeley (USA) 122) [2017 65: 6m* t6d t6.1g t6g Nov 3] fair handicapper: won at Doncaster in April: stays 6f: acts on good to firm and good to soft going: has worn hood: sometimes slowly away, usually races towards rear. *David Barron*

SHE'S ZOFF (IRE) 3 b.f. Zoffany (IRE) 121 – Vindication People (USA) (Vindication **48**
(USA) 122) [2017 –: 8.3m 7.1g^4 7d^4 6m t7.1s Nov 30] poor maiden: stays 7f: acts on good to soft going. *John Quinn*

SHEVINGTON MOOR 3 b.f. Equiano (FR) 127 – Soapy Delight (Dansili 127) [2017 **–**
7g May 4] £1,000Y: first foal: dam once-raced half-sister to very smart 9.5f-2m (Queen's Vase) winner Soapy Danger out of US Grade 1 1½m winner On A Soapbox: 16/1, well held in maiden at Redcar. *Bryan Smart*

SHIFT CROSS 3 br.f. Cape Cross (IRE) 129 – Rose Shift (IRE) (Night Shift (USA)) **67**
[2017 t8.6g^5 Mar 23] sixth foal: half-sister to 3 winners in Italy, including useful 2-y-o 6f/7.5f winner (stayed 11f) Rosa Eglanteria (by Nayef): dam, useful Italian winner up to 1m (2-y-o 7f winner), half-sister to smart US Grade 2 1¼m winner Whilly: 11/4, fifth in maiden at Wolverhampton (3 lengths behind Hidden Charms) in March. *Marco Botti*

SHIFTING STAR (IRE) 12 ch.g. Night Shift (USA) – Ahshado 70 (Bin Ajwaad (IRE) **78**
119) [2017 78: p8g p8g* 8.3m^3 8m* 8g^3 8d^4 8.1m* 8.1m^4 8.1m^2 8.1g^5 8.5m^3 8.5g p8g^6 8.1d p10g^6 Nov 2] strong, sturdy gelding: fair handicapper: won at Lingfield in March, Brighton in May and Windsor in June: stays 8.5f: acts on polytrack, good to firm and heavy going: wears headgear/tongue tie: front runner/races prominently. *John Bridger*

SHIFT ON SHEILA 4 b.f. Aussie Rules (USA) 123 – Black Salix (USA) 54 (More Than **–**
Ready (USA) 120) [2017 64: 10g 11.5s^5 Jun 6] modest maiden, little impact in handicaps in 2017: stays 1¼m: acts on polytrack and tapeta. *Pam Sly*

SHIKOBA (IRE) 2 b.f. (Feb 19) Kodiac 112 – Shoshoni Wind 100 (Sleeping Indian 122) **–**
[2017 7g Sep 7] 85,000Y: first foal: dam 5f and (at 2 yrs) 6f winner: 20/1, well held in maiden at Salisbury. *Simon Crisford*

SHILLBOURNE LAD (IRE) 3 b.g. Lilbourne Lad (IRE) 111 – Gemma's Delight (IRE) **–**
71 (Clodovil (IRE) 116) [2017 –: p6s^5 Jun 13] no form: tried in tongue tie. *Bill Turner*

SHILOH 3 b.f. Poet's Voice 126 – Loveable (Oasis Dream 129) [2017 –: p7g p8g Feb 1] **48**
poor form: sold 2,000 gns, sent hurdling in Italy. *Simon Crisford*

SHIMMERING LIGHT 3 ch.f. Dubawi (IRE) 129 – Summertime Legacy 109 **77**
(Darshaan 133) [2017 8g^5 10.2s 8d^6 10g 9.9d^2 10g^3 t9.5m^6 p10s Dec 1] useful-looking filly: half-sister to numerous winners, including 1m-1¼m (Criterium de Saint-Cloud) winner Mandaean (by Manduro) and French 1¼m winner (including Prix Saint-Alary) Wavering (by Refuse To Bend), both smart: dam French 2-y-o 1m winner: fair maiden: stays 1¼m: acts on tapeta and good to soft going: in visor last 4 starts: temperament under suspicion. *Michael Bell*

SHIMMY SHOES (IRE) 2 b.f. (Mar 2) Reckless Abandon 119 – Silver Shoon (IRE) 94 (Fasliyev (USA) 120) [2017 6g 5v p5g Dec 12] rather leggy filly: third foal: dam, 7f winner, half-sister to very smart sprinter Pipalong: no form for various trainers. *Jamie Osborne* –

SHINE BABY SHINE 3 b.f. Aqlaam 125 – Rosewood Belle (USA) 70 (Woodman (USA) 126) [2017 11.6d 9.2s 7.8g^6 10.2v t10.2d^6 f16.5g* t16.3s^2 Sep 8] 5,000Y: half-sister to several winners, including 1½m-2m winner Ermyn Lodge (by Singspiel) and 11.6f/16.5f winner Flemish School (by Dutch Art), both useful: dam maiden (best effort at 10.5f): fair handicapper: won at Southwell in August: stays 16.5f: acts on fibresand and tapeta: often races in rear. *Philip Kirby* **66**

SHINE THROUGH (IRE) 3 b.f. Poet's Voice 126 – She Wolf (Medicean 128) [2017 p12d p10g Mar 11] 55,000Y: second foal: dam twice-raced half-sister to useful performers Oh Goodness Me (1m winner) and Eradicate (stayed 1½m): well held in maidens. *Hugo Palmer* –

SHINING ROMEO 5 b.g. Royal Applause 124 – Silver Pivotal (IRE) 113 (Pivotal 124) [2017 73: p10g^4 p12g* p13g^6 p11g^5 p12g 11.8g* 11.5s* 10.2v Nov 8] rather leggy gelding: fair handicapper: won at Kempton in January, Leicester in June and Yarmouth (apprentice) in July: stays 1½m: acts on polytrack, tapeta and soft going: has worn headgear, including in 2017: tried in tongue tie: sometimes slowly away. *Denis Quinn* **77**

SHIP OF THE FEN 2 b.c. (Feb 24) Champs Elysees 124 – Ruffled 77 (Harlan's Holiday (USA) 124) [2017 7g^3 8v^5 8d^2 9d* 9m^6 Oct 25] sturdy colt: first foal: dam, 9.5f winner, half-sister to smart 9f-11f winner Monarchs Glen: fairly useful performer: won nursery at Nottingham (by 2 lengths from Baileys Excelerate) in October: stays 9f: acts on heavy going: often races prominently. *Martyn Meade* **82**

SHIRATAKI (IRE) 9 b.g. Cape Cross (IRE) 129 – Noodle Soup (USA) (Alphabet Soup (USA) 126) [2017 62: 11.5m 11.8d^2 10.2g^4 11.4m^6 10.2f^6 Jul 12] modest handicapper: stays 13f: acts on polytrack, tapeta, firm and good to soft going: often wears hood: tried in tongue tie: sometimes slowly away, usually races nearer last than first. *Peter Hiatt* **54**

SHOBROM (IRE) 2 b.g. (Mar 10) Acclamation 118 – Strasbourg Place 48 (Compton Place 125) [2017 5m^6 5m^2 5m^6 6f^6 Jul 6] small, workmanlike gelding: fair form: best efforts at 5f: sent to Qatar. *Richard Fahey* **71**

SHOOFLY (IRE) 4 b.f. Azamour (IRE) 130 – Natural Flair (USA) 90 (Giant's Causeway (USA) 132) [2017 78: p10.7g t12.2g^2 12.5d^2 11.8v 12v p12g p10.7g t14g Nov 25] fair handicapper: left Miss Natalia Lupini after first start: stays 12.5f: acts on polytrack, tapeta and good to soft going. *David Harry Kelly, Ireland* **72**

SHOOTINGSTA (IRE) 5 b.g. Fast Company (IRE) 126 – Kiva (Indian Ridge 123) [2017 84: t7.1g 7.1m 5.9g^6 May 22] tall gelding: fairly useful at best, no form in 2017: wears headgear: often races prominently. *Bryan Smart* –

SHOOTINGTHE BREEZE 2 b.g. (Apr 13) Dutch Art 126 – Clinet (IRE) 110 (Docksider (USA) 124) [2017 7m^4 6d^5 t6.1g t6.1g^5 t8.6g Oct 7] modest maiden: stays 6f: acts on tapeta and good to soft going: in cheekpieces last 2 starts: usually races close up: sold 11,000 gns, sent to Belgium. *Tom Dascombe* **63**

SHORT CALL (IRE) 2 b.f. (Mar 6) Kodiac 112 – Wiwilia (Konigstiger (GER) 112) [2017 5g* 5f^3 Jun 17] €45,000Y: first foal: dam, Swiss 2-y-o 5.5f/1m winner, half-sister to very smart US Grade 1 11f winner Wake Forest: fair form: won minor event at Goodwood (by 2¾ lengths from Looks A Million) in June: remains capable of better. *Mick Channon* **77 p**

SHORT WORK 4 ch.g. Kyllachy 129 – Agony Aunt 81 (Formidable (USA) 125) [2017 87: t7.1s 7.1m^5 7g^6 8d^5 8.8m 5.9d^3 7v^4 6g* 7d^3 6s* 6s* 7g^3 6s* p6g Nov 21] fairly useful handicapper: won at Pontefract in August, Redcar in September and Catterick (twice, by ¾ length from Adam's Ale second occasion) in October: likely to prove best at 6f: acts on soft and good to firm going: wears headgear: front runner/races prominently. *David O'Meara* **91**

SHOT IN THE DARK (IRE) 8 ch.g. Dr Fong (USA) 128 – Highland Shot 91 (Selkirk (USA) 129) [2017 14g^6 13d Aug 23] good-topped gelding: fair maiden at best, behind in handicaps in 2017: stays 11.5f: acts on soft going: has worn headgear, including final start: tried in tongue tie: winning hurdler. *Jonathan Geake* –

SHOULDERTOSHOULDER 3 ch.g. Paco Boy (IRE) 129 – Miss Bond (IRE) (Danehill Dancer (IRE) 117) [2017 –: p6f^5 p6g 7g 6g^5 Jun 13] poor maiden: stays 6f: acts on polytrack: usually races nearer last than first. *Stuart Williams* **48**

SHOURANOUR (IRE) 7 b.g. Lawman (FR) 121 – Sharesha (IRE) 93 (Ashkalani (IRE) 128) [2017 92, a79: 8g³ 8s 7s² 7m⁶ 7.8s 8d* 7d³ 8g 7g 7.6v 7g 7s Oct 31] fairly useful handicapper: won at Ripon (by ½ length from Areen Heart) in July: best up to 1m: acts on good to firm and heavy going: wears headgear: front runner/races prominently. *Alan Brown* **93**

SHOVEL IT ON (IRE) 2 br.c. (Jan 17) Elusive Pimpernel (USA) 117 – Fitrah (IRE) 72 (Tamayuz 126) [2017 5g⁴ 5m⁵ t6.1g 6f⁵ 7s³ 7s* 6.1g* 7g⁴ 6.3s Sep 10] fair performer: won nurseries at Leicester and Nottingham in August: stays 7f: acts on firm and soft going: usually races nearer last than first. *David Evans* **74**

SHOWBOATING (IRE) 9 b.g. Shamardal (USA) 129 – Sadinga (IRE) 85 (Sadler's Wells (USA) 132) [2017 83, a93: f7g⁶ f8g² t8g f8m* f7g³ 8.2d⁶ 7s* 7.8s* 8d⁵ 8d 8s⁴ 7v 7v⁶ 7d Nov 11] fairly useful handicapper: won at Southwell in March, and at Catterick and Carlisle in June: stays 1m: acts on polytrack, fibresand, good to firm and heavy going: has worn headgear, including in 2017: has worn tongue tie. *John Balding* **91**

SHOWDAISY 4 ch.f. Showcasing 117 – Darling Daisy (Komaite (USA)) [2017 101: f5g f5g⁶ f5g 5m⁵ 5m³ 5m⁶ 5s* Jul 10] angular filly: fairly useful handicapper: won at Ayr (by head from Foxtrot Knight) in July: stays 6f: acts on fibresand, tapeta, firm and soft going: wears headgear: tried in tongue tie: sometimes slowly away: sold 36,000 gns, sent to Bahrain. *Keith Dalgleish* **94**

SHOWDANCE KID 3 b.g. Showcasing 117 – Maid To Dance 62 (Pyramus (USA) 78) [2017 71p: 8m⁶ 7d 10.2m 8g³ 7m³ t7.2g² 7s² 7d f8.1g Dec 11] fair handicapper: left K. R. Burke after fourth start, Neville Bycroft after eighth: stays 7f: acts on tapeta, soft and good to firm going: tried in headgear. *Kevin Frost* **74**

SHOWDANCING 2 b.f. (Feb 13) Showcasing 117 – Lady Vermeer 76 (Dutch Art 126) [2017 5m⁶ p7g Oct 18] 42,000Y: first foal: dam maiden (best effort on debut at 6f): little impact in minor events. *James Tate* **–**

SHOWING OFF (IRE) 4 ch.g. Notnowcato 128 – Walk On Water 99 (Exceed And Excel (AUS) 126) [2017 79: f7g f8s f7g f7m Feb 21] fair at best, no form in 2017: usually slowly away/races in rear. *Michael Wigham* **–**

SHOWMETHEDOUGH 2 ch.g. (Apr 4) Showcasing 117 – Silver Purse 67 (Interrex (CAN)) [2017 t5.1g³ 5g² 6v* Sep 30] 7,000F, €25,000Y: half-brother to 2-y-o 5f winner Only In Jest (by Averti) and several winners abroad: dam 2-y-o 5.7f winner: fairly useful form: won minor event at Ripon (by 2¼ lengths from Rastacap) in September: stays 6f: sold 85,000 gns in October. *Richard Fahey* **81**

SHOWMETHEWAYAVRILO 4 ch.g. Showcasing 117 – Avrilo 78 (Piccolo 121) [2017 80: t5.1g⁶ 5.3g⁵ 6.1d 6d³ 6.1m* 6m p6d³ 6.1g⁶ 6v⁵ 5.7s⁴ 5.7d³ 5.7m² p6s⁴ 5.7s⁶ 6s* 6.1d p7g Oct 11] fairly useful handicapper: won at Chepstow in June and Goodwood (by neck from Nezar) in September: stays 6f: acts on polytrack, tapeta and any turf going. *Malcolm Saunders* **80**

SHOW OF FORCE 2 gr.f. (Mar 21) Lethal Force (IRE) 128 – Craighall 66 (Dubawi (IRE) 129) [2017 p6d 6m 7.4g⁴ 7s 8g² 8.1g* 8.3d⁵ Oct 18] 20,000Y, £18,000 2-y-o: fourth foal: half-sister to 7f/1m winner Kylla Instinct (by Kyllachy): dam maiden half-sister to smart performer up to 1¾m Connecticut: fair performer: won minor event at Chepstow in August: stays 1m: best form on good going: front runner/races prominently. *Jonathan Portman* **68**

SHOW PALACE 4 ch.g. Showcasing 117 – Palais Polaire 65 (Polar Falcon (USA) 126) [2017 73: 5.1m 6s² p5s⁴ 5d* 5d³ 5v* 5d* 5s 5.1v* 5v* 5g Oct 13] sturdy gelding: useful handicapper: most progressive in 2017, winning at Carlisle in July, Nottingham/Haydock in August and Chester/Ripon (by ½ length from Ballesteros) in September: all wins at 5f: acts on polytrack, good to firm and heavy going: often travels strongly. *Jennie Candlish* **100**

SHOW PRINCESS 2 b.f. (Apr 14) Showcasing 117 – Irina Princess (Selkirk (USA) 129) [2017 5d⁴ 5d 7m⁴ 6.9v³ 8.3d f6.1g⁵ Nov 16] £4,000Y: second foal: half-sister to useful 2-y-o 6f winner Mirdif (by Kodiac): dam, unraced, out of half-sister to Derby Italiano winner Hailsham: fair maiden: stays 7f: acts on heavy going. *Michael Appleby* **65**

SHOWROOM (FR) 2 b.c. (Apr 12) Motivator 131 – Lemon Twist (IRE) (Marju (IRE) 127) [2017 8d* Sep 5] €30,000Y: fourth foal: half-brother to smart French 10.5f-1½m (Prix de Malleret) winner Al Wathna (by Nayef): dam unraced half-sister to useful French winner up to 1½m Hebah: 7/2, won maiden at Goodwood (by 5 lengths from Ship of The Fen) on debut: will stay 1¼m: will improve. *Mark Johnston* **88 p**

SHOW STEALER 4 ch.f. Showcasing 117 – Winifred Jo 52 (Bahamian Bounty 116) **99**
[2017 103: 7f 6g 6g 5g p5s^{3} p6s^{2} p7s^{6} p6g* Dec 12] sturdy filly: useful handicapper: won at Lingfield (by 1½ lengths from Shamsaya) in December: best at 6f: acts on polytrack, good to firm and good to soft going: wears cheekpieces. *Rae Guest*

SHOWTIME BLUES 5 b.g. Showcasing 117 – Night Symphonie (Cloudings (IRE) 112) **64**
[2017 67: t7.1g^{3} t7.1g^{5} p7g Nov 2] tall gelding: modest handicapper: stays 7f: acts on polytrack and tapeta: usually wears headgear: often races prominently: has looked awkward. *Jim Boyle*

SHOYD 2 ch.f. (Apr 13) Showcasing 117 – Yding (IRE) (Danehill (USA) 126) [2017 6.1d **65**
6m 6g p7d^{2} 7g p7g^{4} Sep 6] small, compact filly: sister to 6f (including at 2 yrs) and 7f winner Danecase: dam unraced: fair maiden: stays 7f: acts on polytrack. *Richard Hannon*

SHRAAOH (IRE) 4 b.g. Sea The Stars (IRE) 140 – Jumooh (Monsun (GER) 124) [2017 **99**
104: 12m^{4} 11.8m^{3} 14d 13.4g Sep 2] lengthy, attractive gelding: useful handicapper: third in Old Newton Cup at Haydock (3½ lengths behind Dylan Mouth) in July: stays 1¾m: acts on tapeta and good to firm going: tried in cheekpieces: often races prominently: sold to join Harry Fry 30,000 gns in October. *Sir Michael Stoute*

SHREWD 7 b.g. Street Sense (USA) 128 – Cala (FR) 98 (Desert Prince (IRE) 130) [2017 **106**
110: 14g 20f 16.3d 14.5g^{3} 18d^{3} 18m Oct 14] sturdy gelding: useful handicapper: third at Newmarket (3½ lengths behind Who Dares Wins) in September: stays 2¼m: acts on tapeta, good to firm and heavy going: tried in cheekpieces. *Iain Jardine*

SHREWD APPROACH (IRE) 2 ch.f. (Mar 25) Dawn Approach (IRE) 132 – Al **73**
Sharood 108 (Shamardal (USA) 129) [2017 p7g^{5} 7.4d^{3} 7s* 7d^{6} 7v* 7s Nov 21] angular filly: first foal: dam winner up to 7.5f (2-y-o 6f winner): fair performer: won minor event at Catterick in August and nursery at Epsom in October: stays 7.5f: acts on heavy going: front runner/races prominently. *Simon Crisford*

SHRILL 4 b.f. Shamardal (USA) 129 – Wood Vine (USA) (Woodman (USA) 126) [2017 –
90: 5f 5g Jun 24] useful at best, stiff tasks in 2017: best form at 5f: acts on firm going: tried in headgear: usually races prominently. *Robert Cowell*

SHRUBLAND 4 b.g. High Chaparral (IRE) 132 – Ratukidul (FR) 79 (Danehill (USA) –
126) [2017 62: p15.8g Apr 11] good-topped gelding: modest maiden, well beaten sole outing on Flat in 2017: stays 2m: acts on polytrack and good to soft going: usually in blinkers: fair hurdler. *Alexandra Dunn*

SHUDBEME 4 ch.g. Monsieur Bond (IRE) 120 – Oomph 83 (Shareef Dancer (USA) 135) **44**
[2017 –: 6m^{6} 9.9g t7.1s^{5} Nov 30] poor maiden: stays 7f: acts on tapeta and good to firm going: in cheekpieces last 4 starts: often races in rear. *Neville Bycroft*

SHUHOOD (IRE) 2 b.g. (May 16) Tamayuz 126 – Walayef (USA) 105 (Danzig (USA)) **76 p**
[2017 6m 7g* Oct 7] half-brother to several winners, including useful 2-y-o 6f/7f winner Jamaayel (by Shamardal) and 2-y-o 7f winner (stayed 1½m) Reyaada (by Daylami): dam winner up to 7f (2-y-o 6f winner): fair form: won minor event at Redcar (by head from Poets Dream) in October: open to further improvement. *Richard Hannon*

SHUJAHA (AUS) 5 b.m. New Approach (IRE) 132 – Umoya (Nashwan (USA) 135) –
[2017 8.1m May 22] fourth foal: half-sister to 3 winners in Australia: dam unraced half-sister to E. P. Taylor Stakes winner Miss Keller: in hood, 100/1, well held in maiden at Windsor. *Pat Murphy*

SHULAMMITE MAN (IRE) 4 ch.g. Arcano (IRE) 122 – Shulammite Woman (IRE) **50**
(Desert Sun 120) [2017 55: f12g^{6} t16.3g^{5} t16.3d Dec 16] well-grown, angular gelding: modest maiden: probably stays 2m: acts on tapeta. *Sally Haynes*

SHUROOQ 2 gr.f. (Apr 13) Dubawi (IRE) 129 – Natagora (FR) 116 (Divine Light (JPN)) **65**
[2017 p7g 7d^{4} Nov 4] sixth foal: sister to 2-y-o 6.5f winner Raaqy, and half-sister to 2-y-o 6f winner Rayaheen (by Nayef) and useful French 1m (including at 2 yrs) winner Mankib (by Tamayuz): dam won 1000 Guineas (also 2-y-o 5f/6f winner, including Cheveley Park Stakes): fair form when fourth at Newmarket (3 lengths behind Perfect Thought) on second of 2 starts in minor events. *Owen Burrows*

SHUTTER SPEED 3 br.f. Dansili 127 – Photographic 99 (Oasis Dream 129) [2017 85p: **111**
10g* 10.3s* 10.4m^{4} 10.3d^{6} Aug 23] tall, good sort: smart performer: won minor event at Newbury (by 2½ lengths from Raheen House) in April and Musidora Stakes at York (by 1¾ lengths from Vintage Folly) in May: best effort when 1½ lengths fourth to Senga in Prix de Diane at Chantilly: stays 10.4f: acts on soft and good to firm going: tried in tongue tie: usually travels strongly: sent to USA. *John Gosden*

SHYARCH 3 b.g. Archipenko (USA) 127 – Coconut Shy 88 (Bahamian Bounty 116) [2017 8m 6m^4 6m^6 6g^4 6g^2 7d* p7g^6 Sep 26] fair handicapper: won at Yarmouth in August: left George Margarson after sixth start: should stay 1m: acts on good to soft going. *Christine Dunnett* **68**

SHYJACK 2 ch.g. (May 2) Archipenko (USA) 127 – Coconut Shy 88 (Bahamian Bounty 116) [2017 p7s f7.1g^6 p7g Dec 21] little impact in minor events. *George Margarson* **–**

SHYMKENT 3 b.g. Pivotal 124 – Shabyt (Sadler's Wells (USA) 132) [2017 –: 10g* 11.2m^5 11.2s* 12m 11.2s^4 Aug 4] useful performer: won maiden at Wetherby in May and handicap at Carlisle in June: will stay beyond 1½m: acts on soft going. *David O'Meara* **96**

SHYPEN 4 b.f. Archipenko (USA) 127 – Coconut Shy 88 (Bahamian Bounty 116) [2017 91: p7g t7.1d^3 p7g^6 t7.1g* p7g^5 7d 6m t6f* Oct 21] fairly useful performer: won handicap at Wolverhampton in March and allowance race at Golden Gate Fields (first outing after leaving Richard Fahey, awarded race) in October: stays 1m: acts on polytrack, tapeta, dirt and firm going: front runner/races prominently. *Manuel Badilla, USA* **92**

SHYRON 6 b.g. Byron 117 – Coconut Shy 88 (Bahamian Bounty 116) [2017 100: f7g t7.1g t7.1g^5 p7g p7g^2 7g^3 7g 7m^3 7d p7g^3 p7s p7s p7g* Dec 13] useful-looking gelding: fair handicapper on turf, useful on all-weather: won at Lingfield (by ½ length from Right Touch) in December: stays 7f: acts on polytrack, tapeta and good to firm going: tried in headgear: sometimes slowly away. *George Margarson* **79 a98**

SIBILANCE 3 gr.f. Bated Breath 125 – Santa Sophia (IRE) 106 (Linamix (FR) 127) [2017 80p: p8g* 7.9d^3 8m 7g 8d^3 p8s^3 Dec 7] compact filly: useful performer: won minor event at Kempton (by 2¼ lengths from Raven's Lady) in April: third in listed race at York (3¼ lengths behind Tomyris) in May, minor event at Ascot (1½ lengths behind Zwayyan) in October and handicap at Chelmsford (2¾ lengths behind Bowerman) in December: stays 1m: acts on polytrack and good to soft going. *Ralph Beckett* **98**

SICARIO (IRE) 2 b.g. (Apr 23) Thewayyouare (USA) 117 – Blessed Beauty (IRE) (Alhaarth (IRE) 126) [2017 p8g^4 Aug 22] in blinkers, 14/1, fourth in minor event at Kempton (5¾ lengths behind We Are The World) in August. *Jamie Osborne* **61**

SIDEWINDER (IRE) 3 b.g. Majestic Missile (IRE) 118 – Ron's Secret 92 (Efisio 120) [2017 77: t7.1m^2 t6g^5 t7.1g^3 t7.1g^2 8m* 8f* 8m 8m^4 7.6d^5 8d p8g^3 Oct 13] fairly useful handicapper: won at Haydock in April and May (by neck from Inner Circle): third at Kempton in October: stays 1m: acts on polytrack, tapeta and firm going: has worn headgear: sold 20,000 gns in November. *Tom Dascombe* **88**

SIEGE OF BOSTON (IRE) 4 ch.g. Starspangledbanner (AUS) 128 – Milton of Campsie 83 (Medicean 128) [2017 74: t7.1m^5 p7d* t7.1g^2 6d^4 7g^3 p7g* p7g* p7g^3 7d t7.2g^4 p6s^6 Dec 15] fair handicapper on turf, fairly useful on all-weather: won at Chelmsford in February/August and Kempton (by 3¼ lengths from Ubla) in September: left Gordon Elliott after first start, John Butler after eighth: stays 1m: acts on polytrack, tapeta, good to firm and good to soft going: wears tongue tie. *David C. Griffiths* **78 a92**

SIEMPRE AMIGOS (IRE) 4 gr.f. Fast Company (IRE) 126 – Zamiyla (IRE) 86 (Daylami (IRE) 138) [2017 58: 9.5s^6 12.5g 12s^2 11.8v^3 p12g 12v^5 f11.1g^{ur} Dec 4] third foal: half-sister to 1m-1¼m winner Trinity Star (by Kheleyf): dam, 1½m winner, half-sister to smart 1¼m-1½m winner Zanughan: fair maiden: stays 1½m: best form on soft/heavy going: often races in rear. *Gavin Patrick Cromwell, Ireland* **71**

Tattersalls Musidora Stakes, York—odds-on Shutter Speed overcomes concerns about the soft going to maintain her unbeaten record, well on top of Vintage Folly (hooped cap) at the line

SIENA FLYER (IRE) 2 b.f. (Mar 21) Big Bad Bob (IRE) 118 – Raggiante (IRE) (Rock of Gibraltar (IRE) 133) [2017 5d 5d 5m^6 t5d Nov 4] third foal: half-sister to a winner abroad by Aqlaam: dam, Italian 6f winner, half-sister to very smart 1m-1¼m winner Arod: no form. *Jedd O'Keeffe* –

SIENNA DREAM 2 b.f. (Apr 7) Swiss Spirit 117 – Angry Bark (USA) 62 (Woodman (USA) 126) [2017 8.9s^5 t7.1g^4 t6d Nov 4] 8,500F, €6,000Y: half-sister to several winners, including winner up to 2m Arthurs Secret (2-y-o 7.5f winner, by Sakhee's Secret) and 11.6f winner Ablaze (by Arcano): dam maiden (stayed 1¼m): modest form: best effort when fifth in minor event at Musselburgh (10¾ lengths behind House Edge) on debut. *Alistair Whillans* **58**

SIENNA SAYS 2 b.f. (Feb 3) Bated Breath 125 – Broughtons Charm (IRE) 86 (Invincible Spirit (IRE) 121) [2017 5g^6 6m^3 6g^5 5.3m^3 t6.1g^6 6s Oct 10] £20,000Y: close-coupled filly: first foal: dam, winner up to 7f (2-y-o 6f winner), out of half-sister to smart sprinter Majestic Missile: fair maiden: stays 6f: acts on good to firm going: front runner/races prominently. *Tony Carroll* **65**

SIGNE (IRE) 4 b.f. Sea The Stars (IRE) 140 – Green Room (USA) (Theatrical) [2017 t8d* t10.2g* 10m* 12g 9d p10.7g Sep 29] €1,100,000Y: sturdy, good-topped filly: closely related to smart 2-y-o 1m winner (including Fillies' Mile) Together Forever (by Galileo) and half-sister to several winners, including very smart winner up to 1m Lord Shanakill (2-y-o 6f winner, by Speightstown): dam unraced: fairly useful performer: won maiden at Newcastle in February, and handicaps at same course in March and Newbury in April: left William Haggas after fourth start: should be suited by 1½m: acts on tapeta and good to firm going: sometimes slowly away. *Mrs J. Harrington, Ireland* **94**

SIGN OF THE KODIAC (IRE) 4 b.c. Kodiac 112 – Summer Magic (IRE) 90 (Desert Sun 120) [2017 99, a105: p6g^3 p6m t5.1g p5m^6 p6g* p6g 6m^5 5m p6s^2 p5g^6 5.5g^6 p6g^5 t6.1g^2 t5.1g^6 Dec 22] strong colt: fairly useful on turf, useful on all-weather: won minor event at Dundalk (by ½ length from Gordon Lord Byron) in March: placed in handicaps at Lingfield (2¼ lengths behind Jordan Sport) in January, Chelmsford (4½ lengths behind Mazzini) in July and Wolverhampton (neck behind Gulliver) in October: left James Given after thirteenth start: stays 6f: acts on polytrack, tapeta, good to firm and good to soft going: has worn headgear, including in 2017: races prominently. *Tony Newcombe* **86** **a102**

SIGNORE PICCOLO 6 b.g. Piccolo 121 – Piccolo Cativo 67 (Komaite (USA)) [2017 87: 6v^4 5g^2 6s^4 5m* 5.1d^6 5m^2 5.1d^6 6d^4 5g 6.1s^6 5s 5g^3 Oct 18] workmanlike gelding: fairly useful handicapper: won at Haydock (by 1½ lengths from Coolfitch) in June: stays 7f: acts on good to firm and heavy going: wears headgear. *David Loughnane* **92**

SIGNS OF BLESSING (IRE) 6 b.g. Invincible Spirit (IRE) 121 – Sun Bittern (USA) (Seeking The Gold (USA)) [2017 121: 5d* 5f 6.5g^5 6g* 5d 6g Dec 10] big, good-topped gelding: very smart performer: better than ever when winning Prix de Saint-Georges at Deauville (by 2 lengths from Profitable) in May and Prix de Meautry on same course (beat Finsbury Square 2 lengths) in August: below form otherwise in 2017, including in King's Stand Stakes at Royal Ascot on second outing: effective at 5f to 6.5f: acts on polytrack and soft going: has worn headgear: often leads. *Francois Rohaut, France* **124**

Prix de Saint-Georges, Deauville—
Signs of Blessing produces a very smart performance conceding plenty of weight to most, with Profitable (partially hidden by winner) and Finsbury Square (blinkers) filling the places

SIGRID NANSEN 2 b.f. (Feb 25) Cityscape 127 – Hail Shower (IRE) 82 (Red Clubs (IRE) 125) [2017 8m^6 7.4g^4 7d 7m 8.3v t9.5g^4 Nov 20] sturdy filly: first foal: dam 6f and (at 2 yrs) 7f winner: fair maiden: stays 9.5f: acts on tapeta: often races towards rear. *George Scott* **70**

SIGURD (GER) 5 ch.g. Sholokhov (IRE) 121 – Sky News (GER) (Highest Honor (FR) 124) [2017 –: 16.2m^5 14m^3 Jun 15] modest maiden: stays 1¾m: acts on good to firm and good to soft going: sometimes in cheekpieces: often travels strongly: fairly useful hurdler. *Jonjo O'Neill* **53**

SIKANDAR (IRE) 5 ch.g. Medicean 128 – Siniyya (IRE) 70 (Grand Lodge (USA) 125) [2017 83§: 10.3g 12g 12g t10.2s 8g^6 t10.2g^2 9s^5 Aug 7] fair handicapper: stays 1½m: acts on tapeta and good to firm going: often in cheekpieces: wears tongue tie: usually races in rear: temperamental (has carried head awkwardly): winning hurdler. *Brian Ellison* **70 §**

SILCA MISTRESS 2 ch.f. (Mar 2) Dutch Art 126 – Strictly Silca 89 (Danehill Dancer (IRE) 117) [2017 6g^4 6.5d^5 6g* 6g 6d^2 6d p6d^6 Aug 16] rather unfurnished filly: first foal: dam 6f-1m winner out of useful half-sister to Prix Morny winner Silca's Sister and smart winner up to 9f Golden Silca: fair performer: won minor event at Thirsk in June: stays 6.5f: acts on good to soft going. *Mick Channon* **71**

SILCA STAR 4 ch.g. Medicean 128 – Silca Chiave 106 (Pivotal 124) [2017 –: 10m 11.5m^3 p11g 11.8d Jul 26] big, lengthy gelding: fairly useful maiden: third in handicap at Yarmouth in May: stays 11.5f: acts on soft and good to firm going: sometimes slowly away: sold £12,000, sent to Greece. *Alan King* **80**

SILEEL (USA) 3 b.f. War Front (USA) 119 – Gilt (USA) (Bernardini (USA) 132) [2017 p8g 9.9g^2 p12g^2 10.2g^6 12d^4 p13.3g^2 t12.4g* Sep 12] $425,000Y: lengthy filly: second foal: sister to a winner in USA: dam maiden half-sister to smart winner around 1¼m Sabre d'Argent and US Grade 2 7f winner Exchange Rate: fairly useful performer: won handicap at Newcastle (by ¾ length from Henpecked) in September: stays 13.5f: acts on polytrack and tapeta: usually in visor. *Ed Dunlop* **82**

SILENT ECHO 3 b.g. Oasis Dream 129 – Quiet 91 (Observatory (USA) 131) [2017 –p: p7g* 7.2f* 7g^6 6d^4 6d^2 Oct 6] good-topped gelding: useful performer: won maiden at Lingfield and handicap at Haydock (by neck from Chessman) in May: second in handicap at Ascot (2 lengths behind Nobly Born) in October: stays 7f: acts on polytrack, firm and good to soft going: in hood last 2 starts: front runner/races prominently: sold to join Peter Hedger 120,000 gns in November. *Roger Charlton* **97**

SILENTLY 4 b.f. Zamindar (USA) 116 – Quiet Elegance 96 (Fantastic Light (USA) 134) [2017 53: 5.1m^2 6m^5 Aug 22] angular filly: modest form: best effort when second in maiden at Windsor in August. *Daniel Kubler* **59**

SILHUETTE (IRE) 4 b.f. Canford Cliffs (IRE) 133 – Lisfannon 68 (Bahamian Bounty 116) [2017 80: t6d t6d t6g f8g^6 f6d^5 5g^4 6m 5d 6g Jun 14] fairly useful at 2 yrs, has deteriorated considerably: stays 6f: acts on good to firm and heavy going: wears headgear: sometimes slowly away. *Colin Teague* **61**

SILKEN DANCER 3 b.g. Dubawi (IRE) 129 – Silkwood 116 (Singspiel (IRE) 133) [2017 10m* 12g^6 Jul 15] smallish gelding: fifth foal: half-brother to French 8.5f winner Ghostflower (by Dansili) and 2-y-o 6f winner Next Life (by Oasis Dream): dam 9.5f-1½m (Ribblesdale Stakes) winner: fairly useful form: won maiden at Windsor (by 2 lengths from Cross Step) in May. *Charlie Appleby* **85**

SILKEN MOONLIGHT 3 b.f. Aqlaam 125 – Silk (IRE) (Machiavellian (USA) 123) [2017 7.4d 8g 8d Aug 5] seventh foal: half-sister to 3 winners, including 7f winner Apple Blossom (by Danehill Dancer) and 1¼m-2m winner Herrera (by High Chaparral): dam unraced: well held in maidens. *Scott Dixon* **–**

SILK MILL BLUE 3 b.g. Piccolo 121 – Marysienka 78 (Primo Dominie 121) [2017 62: 6m^4 5.9g^6 t7.2g 7m 8.5s Sep 20] modest maiden: stays 7f: acts on tapeta and good to firm going: in headgear last 2 starts: front runner/races prominently. *Richard Whitaker* **52**

SILK TRADER (IRE) 3 b.f. Tagula (IRE) 116 – Silk Affair (IRE) 95 (Barathea (IRE) 127) [2017 10m 10m^4 10g 9.2g t16.3s Sep 8] €8,000Y: third foal: half-sister to 9.5f winner Wider World (by Dubai Destination): dam, 2-y-o 1m winner, also useful over hurdles, half-sister to smart performer up to 2m Lochbuie: no form: tried in tongue tie. *Sharon Watt* **–**

SILVA ECLIPSE 4 gr.g. Multiplex 114 – Linen Line (Double Eclipse (IRE) 122) [2017 85: t16.3g^6 16.3d^4 14.1s^4 14.5s^5 15d^6 Jul 31] good-topped gelding: fairly useful handicapper: stays 16.5f: acts on tapeta, good to firm and good to soft going: tried in headgear: often races prominently: won over hurdles in September. *Jedd O'Keeffe* **87**

SILVANUS (IRE) 12 b.g. Danehill Dancer (IRE) 117 – Mala Mala (IRE) 104 (Brief Truce **88**
(USA) 126) [2017 98: t5.1f^4 t5g p5d^6 p5g 5m^6 5m^2 5m^2 5g^2 5g 5.1d 5g* 5m^3 5.1g^5 5m^5 5.2d^4 Sep 19] angular, useful-looking gelding: fairly useful handicapper nowadays: won at Musselburgh in July: second at same course and Pontefract in May: stays 6f: acts on polytrack, soft and good to firm going: has worn headgear. *Paul Midgley*

SILVER ALLIANCE 9 gr.g. Proclamation (IRE) 130 – Aimee Vibert 76 (Zilzal (USA) **61**
137) [2017 75: t9.5m p11g 10g 10.1m^5 10.1m p10g 9.9g^4 9.9m Aug 9] good-topped gelding: fair handicapper, below form in 2017: stays 1¼m: acts on polytrack, soft and good to firm going: wears headgear. *Julia Feilden*

SILVER BID (USA) 5 gr.g. Exchange Rate (USA) 111 – Micaela's Moon (USA) (Malibu **55**
Moon (USA)) [2017 75?: f6g f5g^5 f5g^5 6g^5 t6s Jun 1] workmanlike gelding: maiden, modest form in 2017: stays 6f: acts on fibresand and polytrack: often starts slowly/races in rear. *Karen Tutty*

SILVERBOOK 2 b.c. (Apr 23) New Approach (IRE) 132 – Sahraah (USA) (Kingmambo **85 p**
(USA) 125) [2017 p10d^2 Nov 9] third foal: half-brother to 2-y-o 1¼m winner Hamada (by Cape Cross): dam unraced sister to smart stayer Ley Hunter out of Irish Oaks winner Lailani: 3/1, second in minor event at Chelmsford (1¼ lengths behind Photographer) in November: sure to progress. *Charlie Appleby*

SILVER BULLET (IRE) 2 gr.f. (Apr 28) Camacho 118 – Sixfields Flyer (IRE) 66 **61**
(Desert Style (IRE) 121) [2017 5.1m^5 p6s 5.1m^6 p6g^4 t6.1g p7g Sep 27] €55,000Y: sister to 2 winners, including winner up to 1¼m (in Germany) Rich Forever (2-y-o 6f winner) and half-sister to 3 winners by Dark Angel, including useful 6f winner (including at 2 yrs) Dark Power: dam maiden (stayed 1m): modest maiden: stays 6f: acts on polytrack and good to firm going: in headgear last 4 starts. *Tom Dascombe*

SILVER CHARACTER (IRE) 2 gr.c. (Jan 25) Camelot 128 – Convocate (USA) 91 **67 p**
(Exchange Rate (USA) 111) [2017 t9.5g^4 Nov 18] 65,000Y: first foal: dam, 1¼m winner who stayed 12.5f, half-sister to smart French winner up to 10.5f Dance Dress: 66/1, fourth in minor event at Wolverhampton (6¼ lengths behind Corelli) in November: should progress. *Tom Dascombe*

SILVER CONCORDE 9 b.g. Dansili 127 – Sacred Pearl (IRE) (Daylami (IRE) 138) **92**
[2017 110: 17d^3 Aug 24] lengthy gelding: useful performer, below form sole outing on Flat in 2017: stays 2¼m: acts on soft going: tried in visor: sold to join Keith Dalgleish €33,000 in October: useful hurdler. *D. K. Weld, Ireland*

SILVER CRESCENT 2 b.g. (Jan 29) Champs Elysees 124 – Winter Solstice 104 **69 p**
(Unfuwain (USA) 131) [2017 8d 8g t8.6g^5 Nov 25] brother to French 10.5f winner Low Sun, closely related to 2 winners by Dansili, including smart French 1¼m/11f winner Ice Blue, and half-brother to several winners, including 1¼m winner Winter Sunrise (by Pivotal), herself dam of Nassau Stakes winner Winsili: dam French 2-y-o 1m winner: fair form: best effort when fifth in minor event at Wolverhampton (6 lengths behind Hipster Boy) in November: will be suited by 1¼m+: open to further improvement. *Ralph Beckett*

SILVER DIXIE (USA) 7 br.g. Dixie Union (USA) 121 – More Silver (USA) 90 (Silver **70**
Hawk (USA) 123) [2017 75: 10g 10m^5 11.6d^5 10.2d^2 10d^2 p10g^5 10.2d p10g^3 p10m^5 p12g^{pu} Dec 6] useful-looking gelding: fair handicapper: stays 1½m: acts on polytrack, firm and good to soft going: wears headgear: often races towards rear. *Peter Hedger*

SILVER DUKE (IRE) 6 gr.g. Papal Bull 128 – Dumaani's Dream (USA) (Dumaani **–**
(USA) 115) [2017 71: t8g 8g 10d 8.9m Jul 25] sturdy gelding: fair maiden, little show in handicaps in 2017: usually wears blinkers. *Jim Goldie*

SILVER GHOST (IRE) 4 gr.g. Dark Angel (IRE) 113 – Aqualina (IRE) 104 (King's **104**
Theatre (IRE) 128) [2017 75: p10g^4 9.9g^2 11.2g* 10.1f* 9.9d* 9.9g^4 10m^4 10.2d^3 Oct 4] lengthy gelding: useful handicapper: won at Goodwood in June, and at Epsom and Sandown (by 3 lengths from Eynhallow) in July: stayed 11f: acted on firm and good to soft going: raced prominently, usually travelled strongly: dead. *Eve Johnson Houghton*

SILVER GLEAM (IRE) 3 gr.f. Zoffany (IRE) 121 – Gleaming Silver (IRE) 86 **57**
(Dalakhani (IRE) 133) [2017 53: 12.1g^6 14m 11.6d 12.1m^4 12d^6 12d^4 16g 14s^4 12v^4 Sep 30] modest maiden: stays 1¾m: acts on good to firm and heavy going: often races in rear. *Chris Fairhurst*

SILVERLIGHT (IRE) 2 gr.f. (Feb 5) Fast Company (IRE) 126 – Rangooned 76 **51**
(Bahamian Bounty 116) [2017 6d^2 6d^4 6m^6 Aug 28] €3,000F, €3,500Y: first foal: dam 5f winner: modest form when second at Thirsk (2 lengths behind Tie Em Up Tel) on first of 3 starts in sellers. *Philip Kirby*

SILVER LINING (IRE) 5 gr.g. Dark Angel (IRE) 113 – Out of Woods (USA) (Woodman (USA) 126) [2017 66: t9.5m p11d p10g t12.2g 9.9m p10g Jul 26] useful-looking gelding: maiden: no form in 2017: has worn headgear, including in 2017: often wears tongue tie: usually races towards rear. *Mark Hoad* **–**

SILVER LINK (IRE) 3 b.f. Arcano (IRE) 122 – Miss Bellbird (IRE) (Danehill (USA) 126) [2017 84: t12.2g^{2} 11.6g^{2} 14d^{4} 14d^{6} t14g* t16.5g Dec 5] useful-looking filly: fairly useful performer: won maiden at Wolverhampton (by 6 lengths from Ocean of Love) in November: stays 1¾m: acts on tapeta and heavy going: in cheekpieces last 2 starts. *Marcus Tregoning* **85**

SILVER MEADOW (IRE) 4 b.f. Teofilo (IRE) 126 – Silver Bark 68 (Royal Applause 124) [2017 7s* 8d^{3} 8.5m^{4} 8d^{4} 8.4s^{5} Oct 1] rather leggy filly: fifth foal: half-sister to 3 winners, including smart 2-y-o 6f winner Toofi (by Henrythenavigator): dam, 2-y-o 7f winner, half-sister to high-class sprinter Brando and smart US Grade 1 9f/1¼m winner Ticker Tape: useful performer: won handicap at Compiegne in March: in frame in listed race at Chantilly, Princess Elizabeth Stakes at Epsom (5¾ lengths fourth to Laugh Aloud) and listed race at Maisons-Laffitte (¾-length fourth to Usherette): stays 8.5f: acts on heavy and good to firm going: has worn tongue tie. *Francis-Henri Graffard, France* **106**

SILVER MIST 3 gr.f. Kyllachy 129 – Mundus Novus (USA) (Unbridled's Song (USA) 125) [2017 –: p6g^{6} 7s^{6} 7m 8.1d Aug 24] no form: tried in blinkers. *Sylvester Kirk* **–**

SILVER PENNY 3 gr.f. Hellvelyn 118 – Pennyspider (IRE) 74 (Redback 116) [2017 70: 5g 5.7d p6g^{5} p6g 6d p6d p6g^{6} 5.7s 5s^{4} p5g^{2} 5.1d^{3} f5g^{3} p6s^{3} Dec 7] rather leggy filly: modest handicapper: stays 6f: acts on polytrack and good to soft going: wears headgear: front runner/races prominently. *Jim Boyle* **59**

SILVER QUARTZ 2 gr.c. (Feb 5) Frankel 147 – Rosamixa (FR) (Linamix (FR) 127) [2017 8g^{2} Oct 7] sixth foal: half-brother to 3 winners, including smart winner up to 1m Pearl Mix (2-y-o 7f winner, by Oratorio) and winner up to 1½m Cartier (2-y-o 1m winner, by Montjeu): dam, French 2-y-o 7f winner, sister to very smart French winner up to 1m Rajsaman: in tongue tie, 11/4, second in minor event at Newmarket (length behind Just Brilliant) in October: will improve. *Hugo Palmer* **81 p**

SILVER QUAY (IRE) 5 gr.g. Dark Angel (IRE) 113 – She Runs (FR) (Sheyrann) [2017 90, a101: t12.2m p12g^{4} p12g^{2} p16d^{5} t13.9g f16d^{2} 12g^{3} 16g Aug 28] rangy gelding: useful handicapper: second at Lingfield in February and Southwell in April: left Jamie Osborne after sixth start: stays 2m: acts on all-weather and good to firm going: tried in cheekpieces: sometimes slowly away. *Jimmy Frost* **94**

SILVERRICA (IRE) 7 gr.m. Ad Valorem (USA) 125 – Allegorica (IRE) (Alzao (USA) 117) [2017 82: 5.1m^{2} 5g 5.7f^{2} 5m^{5} 5f 5.7f 5d^{6} 5.7d^{6} Aug 23] sturdy mare: fairly useful handicapper: second at Chepstow and Bath in May: stays 5.5f: acts on firm and soft going: usually races prominently. *Malcolm Saunders* **81**

SILVER SEA 4 b.g. Sholokhov (IRE) 121 – Sword Roche (GER) 101 (Laroche (GER) 123) [2017 p16d^{6} 14.2v Jul 29] fairly useful at 3 yrs for P. Schiergen, below that level in handicaps in 2017: stays 1½m. *Seamus Mullins* **66**

SILVER SHUFFLE (IRE) 10 ch.g. Big Shuffle (USA) 122 – Silvetta (Lando (GER) 128) [2017 65: 12g Apr 2] fair handicapper, well held sole outing on Flat in 2017: stays 2m: acts on polytrack, soft and good to firm going: has worn headgear/tongue tie. *Dianne Sayer* **–**

SILVER SPRINGS (IRE) 4 gr.f. Zebedee 113 – Charming Vista (Josr Algarhoud (IRE) 118) [2017 50, a71: t5.1g p6g t6g^{5} p7g p6g^{4} 5.7f 5.7f 6m 5.7f p6g p6g Dec 21] quite attractive filly: poor handicapper on turf, modest on all-weather: left David Evans after fifth start: stays 7f: acts on polytrack and good to firm going. *Roger Ingram* **43 a58**

SILVER STARLIGHT 2 gr.f. (Mar 19) Showcasing 117 – Pendulum 82 (Pursuit of Love 124) [2017 5m^{6} 5v^{3} 5m* 5g^{2} 6d* 5d^{2} 6d^{6} 6.5g^{4} 6g Oct 7] £19,000Y: good-topped filly: half-sister to several winners, including 5f (including at 2 yrs) to 7.5f winner My Son Max (by Avonbridge) and 5f/6f winner Medici Time (by Medicean), both useful: dam 7f winner: fairly useful performer: won minor event at Ripon in June and nursery at Thirsk in July: second in nursery at latter course in August: stays 6f: acts on good to firm and heavy going. *Tim Easterby* **81**

SILVER STEP (FR) 4 gr.f. Silver Frost (IRE) 122 – Negra Del Oro (GER) (Danehill Dancer (IRE) 117) [2017 8g^{4} 8.9g^{4} 9m^{6} 8.5m^{6} 9.9g* 8d^{6} Sep 5] good-topped filly: third foal: half-sister to winners in Scandinavia by Whipper and High Chaparral: dam Norwegian winner up to 1½m (2-y-o 6f winner): useful performer: successful twice at 3 yrs, including in Premio Elena E Sergio Cumani at Milan: also won listed race at Maisons-Laffitte in July **109**

by short neck from Avenue Dargent: below best in Britain third/fourth outings: stays 1¼m: acts on polytrack, heavy and good to firm going: often in headgear: races towards rear. *Mme Pia Brandt, France*

SILVER SWIFT 2 b.f. (Apr 16) Dutch Art 126 – Silver Kestrel (USA) (Silver Hawk (USA) 123) [2017 p6g Oct 4] £42,000Y: half-sister to useful 2-y-o 5f/6f (Albany Stakes) winner Habaayib and 5f (including at 2 yrs) winner Golden Flower (both by Royal Applause): dam, US 7f winner, out of US Grade 2 2-y-o 6.5f winner Salty Perfume: 7/1, very green when well held in maiden at Kempton: should do better. *Andrew Balding* **– p**

SILVERTURNSTOGOLD 2 ch.c. (May 18) Equiano (FR) 127 – Saharan Song (IRE) 64 (Singspiel (IRE) 133) [2017 p6d p7g⁶ Dec 20] modest form when sixth at Kempton on second of 2 starts in minor events. *Neil Mulholland* **57**

SILVERWAVE (FR) 5 b.h. Silver Frost (IRE) 122 – Miss Bio (FR) (River Mist (USA) 119) [2017 125: 10.4g³ 11.9g* 11.9g² 11.9d⁵ 11.9d Oct 1] very smart performer: third in Prix Ganay at Saint-Cloud (length behind Cloth of Stars) prior to winning Grand Prix de Chantilly (by neck from Talismanic) in June: attempted to repeat 2016 successes in Grand Prix de Saint-Cloud and Prix Foy at Chantilly on next 2 starts, ¾-length second to Zarak in former, then fifth to Dschingis Secret in latter: sold €500,000 on eve of race, last of 18 in Prix de l'Arc de Triomphe at Chantilly final outing: stays 1½m: acts on viscoride, soft and good to firm going: wears hood: races nearer last than first: send to USA. *P. Bary, France* **123**

SILVER WINGS (IRE) 4 gr.g. Zebedee 113 – Daisy Hill (Indian Ridge 123) [2017 64: p6g⁵ 5.7f⁶ May 10] sturdy gelding: modest handicapper: stays 5.5f: acts on good to soft going: has worn headgear. *David Evans* **55**

SILVERY MOON (IRE) 10 gr.g. Verglas (IRE) 118 – Starry Night 89 (Sheikh Albadou 128) [2017 97: 9.8m⁵ 8g 8m 9g 7.8s⁴ 7.9m⁶ 8s⁵ 8.2v² 8g 10.3g 10v* 10v⁴ Nov 7] big, lengthy gelding: fairly useful handicapper nowadays: won at Pontefract (by 1¼ lengths from Tuff Rock) in October: stays 10.5f: acts on good to firm and heavy going. *Tim Easterby* **92**

SILVINGTON 2 b.c. (Apr 4) Firebreak 125 – Millinsky (USA) 85 (Stravinsky (USA) 133) [2017 6m³ 6.1s³ 6v⁵ p7g t7.2g Nov 7] modest maiden: left Daniel Loughnane after third start: best effort at 6f: acts on soft going. *Tony Carroll* **63**

SIMMIE (IRE) 3 b.f. Fast Company (IRE) 126 – Kathy Sun (IRE) (Intikhab (USA) 135) [2017 100: 6s² 6.5g⁵ 6s 6d Nov 1] neat filly: useful performer: second in listed race at Newbury (head behind Visionary) in May: below form after: stays 6f: acts on tapeta, good to firm and heavy going: has joined A. P. Keatley. *K. R. Burke* **103**

SIMMO'S PARTYTRICK (IRE) 4 b.c. Baltic King 120 – Goose Island (IRE) 85 (Kahyasi 130) [2017 10g 8d 8m⁵ t7.1s Sep 8] modest form. *Geoffrey Harker* **51**

SIMMY'S COPSHOP 2 ch.c. (Mar 28) Bahamian Bounty 116 – Conversational (IRE) 81 (Thousand Words 113) [2017 5.1m* 5s³ 5f 6g² 6g⁴ 6g² 5.1v³ 5v³ 6g Oct 7] 15,500F, €45,000Y: sturdy colt: first foal: dam, 7f/1m winner, half-sister to smart winner up to 1¼m Road To Love: fairly useful performer: won minor event at Nottingham (by ½ length from Havana Grey) in April: third in listed race at Naas (1¼ lengths behind True Blue Moon) in May stays 6f: acts on good to firm and heavy going: sold 25,000 gns, sent to Norway. *Richard Fahey* **91**

SIMPLE THOUGHT (IRE) 2 b.f. (Apr 24) Teofilo (IRE) 126 – Punita (USA) 91 (Distorted Humor (USA) 117) [2017 7g Aug 12] 210,000Y: well-made filly: second foal: dam, winner up to 1m (2-y-o 7f winner), half-sister to smart 7f winner Ecliptic out of smart US Grade 1 9f winner Indy Five Hundred: 15/2, well held in maiden at Newmarket: should do better. *Simon Crisford* **– p**

SIMPLE VERSE (IRE) 5 b.m. Duke of Marmalade (IRE) 132 – Guantanamera (IRE) (Sadler's Wells (USA) 132) [2017 121: 13.9d² 20m Jun 22] strong, lengthy mare: very smart performer: won St Leger at Doncaster and Fillies' And Mares' Stakes at Ascot in 2015: second in Yorkshire Cup at York (neck behind Dartmouth) in May: stayed 2m: acted on polytrack, good to firm and good to soft going: stud. *Ralph Beckett* **114**

SIMPLY BREATHLESS 2 b.f. (Mar 31) Bated Breath 125 – Darling Grace 71 (Nayef (USA) 129) [2017 6d⁶ 6m* 7g³ 7g² p8g³ Oct 5] £10,000Y: second foal: half-sister to French 9f winner Fruit Spirit (by Dutch Art): dam, 1m winner, half-sister to smart performer up to 1½m Glencadam Glory: fair performer: won minor event at Salisbury in June: stays 1m: acts on polytrack and good to firm going: front runner/races prominently. *Clive Cox* **73**

SIMPLY CLEVER 4 ch.f. Stimulation (IRE) 121 – Well of Echoes 68 (Diktat 126) [2017 66: t8.6g^2 t8.6g^2 f8d^2 t8.6g p10g 11.5g t9.5m Oct 31] modest handicapper: stays 1¼m: acts on all-weather and good to soft going: tried in visor: usually races prominently. *David Brown* **64**

SIMPLY ME 4 b.f. New Approach (IRE) 132 – Ego 107 (Green Desert (USA) 127) [2017 77: p7g* p8g* p8g* t7.1g^3 t8.6g^6 t7.2g* p7d^5 p8g p8g Nov 2] good-topped filly: fairly useful handicapper: won at Lingfield in January, February and March, and Wolverhampton in June: stays 1m: acts on polytrack, tapeta and good to firm going: wears cheekpieces. *Tom Dascombe* **88**

SIMPSON (IRE) 2 ch.g. (May 12) Dragon Pulse (IRE) 114 – Salydora (FR) (Peintre Celebre (USA) 137) [2017 6d^2 p6s^3 6g^5 8.1d* 8d^3 8.1g^3 9m^2 Oct 25] €8,500F, €22,000Y: smallish gelding: brother to useful 7f-1¼m winner Komodo and half-brother to several winners abroad: dam useful French 9f-10.5f winner: fairly useful performer: won nursery at Windsor in September: second in similar event at Newmarket in October: stays 9f: acts on good to firm and good to soft going: often travels strongly. *Ed Walker* **89**

SINALOA (IRE) 2 ch.g. (Mar 22) Camacho 118 – Rose of Battle 80 (Averti (IRE) 117) [2017 5m^3 5m^5 6g^5 6s^2 6d^5 t6g 8v Oct 23] quite good-topped gelding: fair maiden: stays 6f: acts on soft and good to firm going: sold 4,000 gns, sent to Spain. *Richard Fahey* **72**

SINCERELY RESDEV 2 br.g. (Jan 31) Rock of Gibraltar (IRE) 133 – Sincerely 74 (Singspiel (IRE) 133) [2017 8g^6 8v^5 8v^4 Oct 12] modest form: best effort when sixth in minor event at Thirsk (5 lengths behind Trumps Up) on debut: left David O'Meara after. *Philip Kirby* **58**

SINDARBAN (IRE) 6 ch.g. Teofilo (IRE) 126 – Sinndiya (IRE) 84 (Pharly (FR) 130) [2017 98: 14g^5 12g^5 11.6m^6 t9.5d Dec 16] useful handicapper: stays 1¾m: acts on soft and good to firm going: has worn tongue tie, including final start: sometimes slowly away, often races towards rear. *Keith Dalgleish* **96**

SINDARIN 4 b.g. Sulamani (IRE) 130 – Aunt Rita (IRE) 81 (Grand Lodge (USA) 125) [2017 8.3m 12s May 20] no form, including in bumper: in hood final start. *Jim Goldie* **–**

SINFONIETTA (FR) 5 b.g. Sinndar (IRE) 134 – Final Whistle (IRE) (Rossini (USA) 118) [2017 98: 8g^2 8s 10g^4 7v 8d^3 8g 9d 8g^4 p9.4f Nov 29] stocky gelding: useful handicapper: placed at Doncaster (¾-length second to Ballet Concerto) in April and the Curragh (3¾ lengths third to Elusive Time in Irish Cambridgeshire) in August: stays 1¼m: acts on polytrack and heavy going. *David Menuisier* **99**

SINGAPORE SLING 4 b.g. Paco Boy (IRE) 129 – Buena Notte (IRE) (Halling (USA) 133) [2017 77: 8s^3 8m^3 10v^2 12d p10s^3 Sep 30] tall gelding: fairly useful maiden handicapper: best efforts when second at Lingfield in July and third at Chelmsford in September: stays 1¼m: acts on polytrack, tapeta, good to firm and heavy going: in hood in 2017: sold 9,000 gns, sent to Saudi Arabia. *James Fanshawe* **85**

SINGER IN THE SAND (IRE) 2 b.f. (May 4) Footstepsinthesand 120 – Village Singer (USA) (Rahy (USA) 115) [2017 p10g p8d Dec 13] €4,500F, €2,200Y: fifth foal: half-sister to Italian winner around 1¼m Tender Fantasy (by High Chaparral): dam US 1m winner out of Moyglare Stud Stakes winner Preseli: little impact in maiden/minor event: in hood first start. *Pat Phelan* **–**

SINGEUR (IRE) 10 b.g. Chineur (FR) 123 – Singitta (Singspiel (IRE) 133) [2017 94: 5m 5m^5 6d^4 6g^5 5d t5g^5 Oct 10] lengthy gelding: fairly useful handicapper: stays 6f: acts on fibresand, firm and soft going: has worn headgear. *Rebecca Bastiman* **88**

SINGING SANDS (IRE) 3 b.f. Harbour Watch (IRE) 121 – Elektra Marino (Mount Nelson 125) [2017 78: 8.3m^4 8.3g^4 8.2d^6 8.2g 7g 10.2g p6g^6 Aug 8] fair maiden: stays 8.5f: acts on polytrack and good to firm going: tried in cheekpieces/tongue tie. *Seamus Durack* **73**

SINGLE ESTATE 3 b.g. Tamayuz 126 – Duo de Choc (IRE) (Manduro (GER) 135) [2017 –: 10m^2 12.1m^6 9.2m t16.3s 9.9v Sep 26] rangy gelding: modest maiden: best effort at 1¼m: acts on good to firm going: has worn headgear. *Simon Waugh* **51**

SING OUT LOUD (IRE) 2 b.g. (Mar 15) Vocalised (USA) 114 – Tus Maith (IRE) 88 (Entrepreneur 123) [2017 7d 6d* p6g^3 7s^2 6s* Oct 19] €5,000F, €20,000 2-y-o: compact gelding: brother to 2-y-o 6f winner Leath Na Hoibre and half-brother to several winners, including useful 2-y-o 6f winner Suntan (by Bachelor Duke) and winner up to 7.5f Focussed (2-y-o 6.5f/7f winner, by Intense Focus): dam maiden (stayed 1m): fairly useful performer: won minor events at Lingfield in August and Brighton (by ½ length from Rotherhithe) in October: stays 7f: acts on polytrack and soft going: often races prominently. *Gary Moore* **83**

SINGULA 3 b.g. Mayson 124 – Tagula Sunrise (IRE) 101 (Tagula (IRE) 116) [2017 63p: 7m t5.1g t6.1g Nov 11] modest form at 2 yrs, none in 2017: dead. *Alan King* **–**

SINGULAR QUEST 5 ch.g. Dalakhani (IRE) 133 – Singuliere (IRE) (Singspiel (IRE) **70**
133) [2017 64: t12.2g^3 t12.2g^3 t14g^3 t14g^4 t14d^6 Dec 27] angular gelding: fair maiden: stays 16.5f: acts on polytrack, tapeta and good to firm going: has worn headgear. *Daniel Loughnane*

SINGYOURSONG (IRE) 4 b.f. Aqlaam 125 – Dhan Dhana (IRE) 79 (Dubawi (IRE) **102**
129) [2017 88: 9.9g* 8m^3 10.2g^2 12d p8g^2 Dec 23] sturdy filly: useful performer: won handicap at Brighton in May: second in listed race at Nottingham (length behind Wilamina) later in month: stays 1¼m: acts on polytrack, firm and good to soft going: in hood last 3 starts: usually races in rear. *David Simcock*

SINOUR (IRE) 7 b.g. Observatory (USA) 131 – Siniyya (IRE) 70 (Grand Lodge (USA) –
125) [2017 f16g^6 Jan 2] maiden, lightly raced on Flat and no form since return in 2014: tried in hood: wears tongue tie: maiden jumper. *Robert Stephens*

SIOUX FRONTIER (IRE) 2 b.g. (Apr 4) Excelebration (IRE) 133 – Sioux Rising (IRE) **69**
104 (Danetime (IRE) 121) [2017 7g^5 6v t7.1d^2 t8g Dec 6] quite good-topped gelding: fair form: should stay 1m. *Richard Fahey*

SIOUX NATION (USA) 2 b.c. (Jan 25) Scat Daddy (USA) 120 – Dream The Blues **115**
(IRE) 75 (Oasis Dream 129) [2017 5d^3 6.4m^2 6m* 6d^6 5m* 6m* 6d^6 Sep 30]

Vincent O'Brien won the National Stakes at the Curragh fifteen times, a record which prompted the proposal in the essay on the last of his winners, Fatherland in 1992, that the race should be named in the trainer's honour on his retirement. The suggestion was taken up in 2009, the year of O'Brien's death at the age of ninety-two. Maybe future generations will be referring to the Aidan O'Brien Phoenix Stakes because Ballydoyle's current trainer sent out his sixteenth winner of Ireland's other Group 1 contest open to two-year-old colts in August. Aidan O'Brien first won the Phoenix Stakes in 1998 when the race was still run at Leopardstown and since then David Wachman (twice), Jim Bolger and Kevin Prendergast have been the only other trainers to break O'Brien's stranglehold. Both of Wachman's winners, Damson and Sudirman, were owned or part-owned by Coolmore interests like all the Ballydoyle winners. The Phoenix is Europe's first Group 1 for two-year-olds and its winner often proves best at that age, but there's every reason to think its latest winner Sioux Nation will take after the likes of the same stable's George Washington, Mastercraftsman and Caravaggio and enjoy further success at a high level as a three-year-old.

O'Brien accounted for half of the field of eight for the latest Keeneland-sponsored Phoenix Stakes, with the Ryan Moore-ridden Sioux Nation the shortest-priced of the quartet at 2/1 after winning the Norfolk Stakes. His stable-companions Actress, U S Navy Flag and Declarationofpeace had all been beaten in other races at Royal Ascot, though Actress had since won the Anglesey Stakes at the Curragh and she looked the second string at 5/1.The 15/8 favourite, though, was the Gordon Elliott-trained Beckford after winning both his races over course and distance, notably the Railway Stakes with a smart effort that made him the one to beat, while the Norfolk fourth Frozen Angel and the Bath maiden winner Helvetian represented British stables which used to have a good record in the Phoenix before O'Brien's domination began. U S Navy Flag and Actress were the leading pair most of the way before the first two in the betting made their move on either side of them and it was Sioux Nation who quickened the better initially to lead a furlong out, though he only had a diminishing lead of half a length at the line from the strong-finishing Beckford. Actress and U S Navy Flag completed the frame for Ballydoyle, beaten a further length and a half and half a length. The first two, along with U S Navy Flag, the fifth Frozen Angel and the seventh Declarationofpeace, all met again in the Middle Park Stakes at Newmarket the following month when Beckford again started favourite despite his reverse in the Phoenix. However, this time, neither he nor Sioux Nation were a match for the improving U S Navy Flag who beat another stable-companion Fleet Review by half a length. Sioux Nation had excuses, though, back in sixth, a head behind Beckford. A slow start meant he was always on the back foot, while meeting some trouble two furlongs out didn't help his cause. There's a good chance, too, that the softer conditions at Newmarket didn't suit Sioux Nation who had accounted for sixteen rivals on good to firm ground when putting up a much improved performance to win the Norfolk by half a length from the ill-fated

Keeneland Phoenix Stakes, the Curragh—
Aidan O'Brien maintains his strangehold on this race, recording his 16th victory since 1998 as Sioux Nation beats Beckford (star on cap) to follow up his Norfolk Stakes win at Royal Ascot

Santry, with Cardsharp, who filled the same position in the Middle Park, third. Sioux Nation had already run four times before Royal Ascot, easily landing the odds in an uncompetitive five-runner maiden at Cork in May after being placed in similar events at Naas and Leopardstown. He beat only one home after another slow start in the listed Marble Hill Stakes at the Curragh on his last outing before Ascot, though that was again on softer ground, and the winner Brother Bear had already beaten him into second at Leopardstown.

The Norfolk-Phoenix double was also completed by Sioux Nation's grandsire Johannesburg who was unbeaten in seven starts for O'Brien at two, which also included the Prix Morny, the Middle Park and the Breeders' Cup Juvenile. Johannesburg's son Scat Daddy was responsible for the Phoenix Stakes winner for the second year running, following Caravaggio who had won the Coventry Stakes instead at Royal Ascot beforehand in 2016. Caravaggio won the Commonwealth Cup at the latest Royal meeting, where he and Sioux Nation were among four winners for their late sire, along with Lady Aurelia in the King's Stand (she too successful at the meeting for the second year running after her spectacular success in the Queen Mary) and her stable-companion Con Te Partiro in the Sandringham Handicap. Wesley Ward had been successful in the past with Scat Daddy two-year-olds at Royal Ascot, No Nay Never also winning the Norfolk, in 2013, and Acapulco giving him another Queen Mary in 2015.

Sioux Nation (USA) (b.c. 2015)	Scat Daddy (USA) (b or br 2004)	Johannesburg (b 1999)	Hennessy
			Myth
		Love Style (ch 1999)	Mr Prospector
			Likeable Style
	Dream The Blues (IRE) (b 2008)	Oasis Dream (b 2000)	Green Desert
			Hope
		Catch The Blues (b 1992)	Bluebird
			Dear Lorraine

Aidan O'Brien trained Sioux Nation's grandam, as well as his grandsire. The smart sprinter Catch The Blues was one of the trainer's first good Flat horses at a time when he was still best known for his jumpers. Although she made a winning debut at three over seven furlongs, Catch The Blues proved best at shorter trips in headgear, with her biggest win coming over five in the Ballyogan Stakes as a five-year-old. She was also placed twice at Royal Ascot in the Cork And Orrery Stakes and her other placings included a third in the Sprint Cup at Haydock. Catch The Blues, a daughter of the French mile and a quarter winner Dear Lorraine, had her seventh winner in the latest season when The Blues Master won a mile and a half maiden at Kempton early in the year. She has also produced a useful winner in

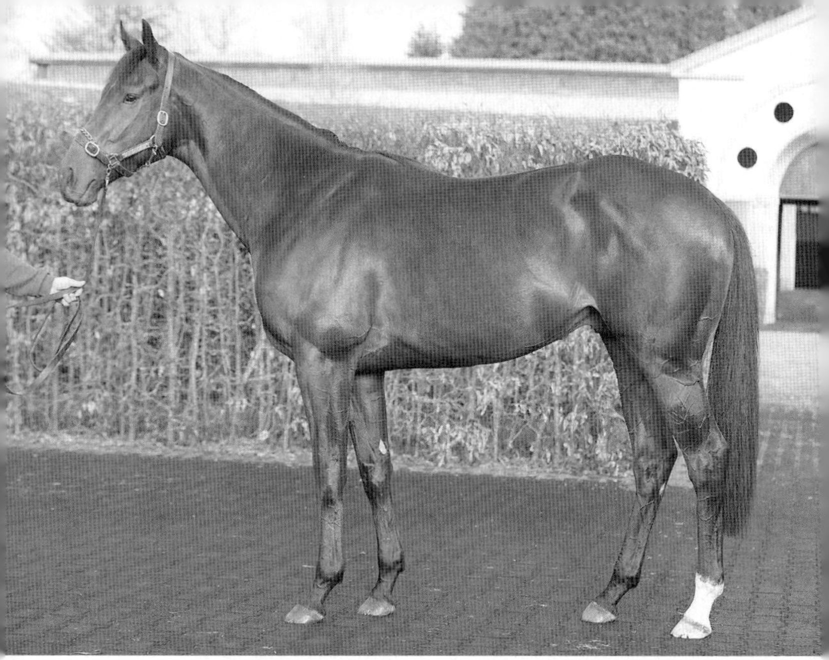

Mr M. Tabor, Mr D. Smith & Mrs John Magnier's "Sioux Nation"

Ireland at around seven furlongs and a mile, Colour Blue, and is grandam of My Catch who was a useful two-year-old for David Brown in Britain before becoming a smart sprinter in Dubai. Catch The Blues' other winners included Sioux Nation's dam Dream The Blues who won her only start, a six-furlong maiden at Redcar as a three-year-old for Kevin Ryan. Sioux Nation is his dam's second foal after the ungenuine maiden Oregon Point (by Cape Blanco). Sioux Nation might not have the reputation of Caravaggio, or the price tag and flashy pedigree of another of his stable's Scat Daddy colts Mendelssohn, but he is a fine sprinting type on looks, big and good-bodied, the sort to carry condition. With his stable looking very well armed for the Two Thousand Guineas, there may well not be much of a temptation to try Sioux Nation over a mile and it would be no surprise if he was campaigned similarly to Caravaggio with the Commonwealth Cup as his target. All three of his wins came on good to firm ground which looked to suit him much better than softer conditions. Incidentally, as recorded in the essay on its latest winner Saxon Warrior, O'Brien has an even better record in another important two-year-old contest in Ireland, the Beresford Stakes, as he won that race for the seventeenth time in September. *Aidan O'Brien, Ireland*

SIOUXPERHERO (IRE) 8 b.g. Sleeping Indian 122 – Tintern (Diktat 126) [2017 69§: t8.6m t9.5g^2 p10g t9.5g^2 t9.5g* t8.6g t9.5g^5 9.9m^4 9.9d^5 Jun 9] compact gelding: fair handicapper: won at Wolverhampton in March: stays 1¼m: acts on polytrack, tapeta, firm and good to soft going: wears headgear: tried in tongue tie: not one to trust. *William Muir* **69 §**

SIR BILLY WRIGHT (IRE) 6 b.g. High Chaparral (IRE) 132 – Lure of The Moon (USA) (Lure (USA) 131) [2017 94: f5g* f5g^3 f7d^4 6g 7m 6.1d 6.1d^2 6d* 6.1g^4 6d^5 6s^3 6v^6 6v^4 Oct 4] lengthy gelding: fairly useful handicapper: won at Southwell in February and Thirsk (by ¾ length from Bossipop) in July: second at Chepstow in June: stays 7f: acts on all-weather, good to firm and heavy going: tried in visor: usually races prominently. *David Evans* **93**

SIR CHAUVELIN 5 b.g. Authorized (IRE) 133 – Jabbara (IRE) 65 (Kingmambo (USA) 125) [2017 102: 14g^{6} 16g^{2} 18.6m 12.1m* t16.3s^{6} 12.5g^{2} 14d 9d 11.9s t12.4g* Nov 23] useful handicapper: won at Hamilton (by short head from Kensington Star) in May and Newcastle (by length from Rainbow Rebel) in November: stays 16.5f: acts on tapeta, firm and soft going: tried in hood: often races towards rear. *Jim Goldie* **105**

SIR COMMANDER (IRE) 2 b.c. (Apr 15) Lethal Force (IRE) 128 – Ronja (USA) (El Corredor (USA) 123) [2017 p6g^{3} Nov 29] 65,000F, €130,000Y: fourth foal: half-brother to 3 winners abroad, including smart German 6.5f/7.5f winner Ross (by Acclamation): dam German winner up to 1m (2-y-o 7f winner): 11/4, third in minor event at Kempton (1¾ lengths behind Desert Doctor) in November: likely to stay 7f: sure to improve. *William Haggas* **71 p**

SIR COMPTON 4 b.g. Compton Place 125 – Dilys 84 (Efisio 120) [2017 63: p7g 7m p8d^{3} 8.1v^{6} p8s Aug 9] workmanlike gelding: modest maiden: stays 1m: acts on polytrack: in headgear last 2 starts. *Stuart Kittow* **64**

SIR DANCEALOT (IRE) 3 b.g. Sir Prancealot (IRE) 111 – Majesty's Dancer (IRE) (Danehill Dancer (IRE) 117) [2017 110p: 7m^{5} 6f^{6} 7m 7g^{2} 6d 7d^{5} 7g^{6} 7g^{2} 7d* 6d^{5} Nov 11] big well-made gelding: very smart performer: won minor event at Doncaster (by 1¾ lengths from Jallota) in October: second in Bunbury Cup (Handicap) at Newmarket in July and handicap at Leicester (nose behind Emmaus) in October: stays 7f: acts on polytrack, good to firm and good to soft going: often races towards rear. *David Elsworth* **120**

SIR DERRICK (IRE) 2 ch.g. (May 2) Sir Prancealot (IRE) 111 – Alexander Confranc (IRE) 73 (Magical Wonder (USA) 125) [2017 5g^{6} 6m 6d^{6} Sep 12] modest form when sixth at Beverley (5½ lengths behind Equitant) on first of 3 starts in minor events: should stay 6f+. *Tim Easterby* **60**

SIR DOMINO (FR) 5 b.g. Evasive 116 – Domino Queen (IRE) 68 (Primo Dominie 121) [2017 80: 5m 6g 5.9d 6v 5s^{6} 6v^{6} 5v 5g Oct 7] fairly useful handicapper for Kevin Ryan, well below form in 2017: stays 6f: acts on tapeta and soft going: has worn headgear, including in 2017. *Patrick Holmes* **50**

SIR DUDLEY (IRE) 4 b.g. Arcano (IRE) 122 – Rosy Dudley (IRE) 72 (Grand Lodge (USA) 125) [2017 74, a94: 5f^{2} Jun 19] fair handicapper on turf: second at Nottingham sole outing in 2017: stays 7f: acts on polytrack, tapeta and firm going: wears blinkers: often races prominently. *James Given* **76**

SIR DYLAN 8 b.g. Dylan Thomas (IRE) 132 – Monteleone (IRE) (Montjeu (IRE) 137) [2017 –§: t12.2g^{2} 14.2g 13d 11.6d^{6} t12.2m^{6} Oct 28] modest handicapper: stays 1½m: acts on polytrack, tapeta and good to soft going: wears headgear: irresolute. *Polly Gundry* **55 §**

SIREN'S COVE 5 b.m. Sir Percy 129 – Siren Sound 80 (Singspiel (IRE) 133) [2017 83: t10.2g^{2} Jan 4] angular mare: fairly useful performer, second in minor event at Newcastle sole outing in 2017: stays 16.5f: acts on polytrack, tapeta and good to firm going: has worn headgear, including last 4 starts. *Kenneth Slack* **79**

SIRENS ROCK (IRE) 4 b.f. Fastnet Rock (AUS) 127 – Foolish Act (IRE) (Sadler's Wells (USA) 132) [2017 p10m^{pu} Jan 9] 62,000Y: closely related to 3 winners by Danehill Dancer, including useful winners around 6f True Verdict and Foolish Ambition (latter at 2 yrs), and half-sister to 1m winner Lone Star (by Sea The Stars): dam unraced half-sister to smart winner up to 9f Circle of Gold: 50/1, pulled up lame in maiden at Lingfield. *Eve Johnson Houghton* **–**

SIR GEOFFREY (IRE) 11 b.g. Captain Rio 122 – Disarm (IRE) (Bahamian Bounty 116) [2017 67: 5g^{6} 6m* f5g^{3} 5m^{2} 6m* 5d^{5} 6.1m 6s 5s 5g^{2} f5g Aug 28] sturdy gelding: modest handicapper nowadays: won at Brighton in May and Catterick in June: stays 6f: acts on all-weather, firm and soft going: wears headgear: has worn tongue tie: front runner/races prominently. *Scott Dixon* **60**

SIR GNET (IRE) 3 b.c. Galileo (IRE) 134 – Ecoutila (USA) (Rahy (USA) 115) [2017 t8.6g^{5} 10s 8d^{6} 8m^{2} 8g^{2} 10g^{5} t9.5g^{3} t9.5g^{2} t12.4d^{6} t12.2g^{5} p10g^{4} t9.5g Dec 22] sturdy colt: fair maiden: stays 1½m: acts on polytrack, tapeta and good to firm going: usually wears hood. *Ed Dunlop* **75**

SIR HAMILTON (IRE) 2 b.c. (Feb 14) Canford Cliffs (IRE) 133 – Cawett (IRE) (Danehill Dancer (IRE) 117) [2017 7g p8s* Dec 15] €57,000F: fourth foal: dam unraced half-sister to smart performers Sasanuma (French 10.5f-11.5f winner) and Asawer (stayed 1½m): fairly useful form: won minor event at Chelmsford (by 3 lengths from Paddy The Chef) in December: will stay beyond 1m: open to further improvement. *Denis Quinn* **84 p**

SIR HARRY COLLINS (IRE) 3 gr.g. Zebedee 113 – Unreal 79 (Dansili 127) [2017 –: p6g^2 p6g t7.1g p5d 6g f6.1g f8.1g^5 t6g^4 t6.1g^4 f5g Dec 21] modest maiden: left Richard Spencer after fifth start: best effort at 6f: acts on all-weather: often wears headgear. *Michael Appleby* **57**

SIR HECTOR (IRE) 2 ch.g. (Mar 24) Sir Prancealot (IRE) 111 – Awwal Malika (USA) 73 (Kingmambo (USA) 125) [2017 5d p6s p6d^5 Dec 13] modest form when fifth at Kempton on last of 3 starts in minor events. *Charlie Wallis* **60**

SIRICI (IRE) 2 ch.f. (Feb 1) Choisir (AUS) 126 – Mironica (IRE) 89 (Excellent Art 125) [2017 p5g^2 p5g* p5g* 5s^6 5m 5m* 5s^3 5g^5 Sep 2] smallish filly: first foal: dam 2-y-o 6f winner: fairly useful performer: won maiden and minor event at Dundalk in April, and listed race at Tipperary (by neck from Actress) in July: third in Curragh Stakes (length behind Treasuring) in August: raced only at 5f: acts on polytrack, soft and good to firm going. *J. A. Stack, Ireland* **92**

SIR JACK 4 b.g. Sir Percy 129 – Play Bouzouki 70 (Halling (USA) 133) [2017 58: p12d^3 f12g^4 p12g t12.2g 9.9g^2 11.9m^6 9.9g^3 10d* 10.2d^2 10m^2 9.9s^3 9s^2 11.9m^2 10.2g^5 10d 10.2d p12g Oct 17] rather leggy gelding: fair on turf, modest on all-weather: won seller at Leicester in May: stays 1½m: acts on polytrack, soft and good to firm going: tried in headgear. *Tony Carroll* **72** **a57**

SIR JAMIE 4 ch.g. Monsieur Bond (IRE) 120 – First Dawn 68 (Dr Fong (USA) 128) [2017 44: p7g^5 t8.6g^3 p10g p8m^2 t8.6g* 8g 7m^6 8.5f^5 p8g^5 p8g t8.6g p7g Dec 30] modest handicapper: won at Wolverhampton in April: stays 8.5f: acts on polytrack and tapeta: in cheekpieces last 2 starts: often races towards rear. *Tony Carroll* **56**

SIR JOHN LAVERY (IRE) 3 b.c. Galileo (IRE) 134 – Race For The Stars (USA) 113 (Fusaichi Pegasus (USA) 130) [2017 94p: 11.6d^6 12m 8s* 8d^4 8d^2 8s Oct 21] attractive colt: smart performer: won listed race at Cork (by 3 lengths from Rose de Pierre) in August: second in Joel Stakes at Newmarket (5 lengths behind Beat The Bank) in September: best at 1m: acts on heavy going: tried in tongue tie: usually races nearer last than first, often travels strongly: quirky. *Aidan O'Brien, Ireland* **114**

SIR LANCELOTT 5 b.g. Piccolo 121 – Selkirk Rose (IRE) 74 (Pips Pride 117) [2017 –: t8.6m* t9.5g^5 t9.5g t8.6m p8g t8.6g^4 t8.6g^5 10.2d t8.6g f7.1g f8.1g Dec 21] workmanlike gelding: fair handicapper: won at Wolverhampton (apprentice) in January: left David O'Meara after fourth start, Brian Barr after fifth: stays 9.5f: acts on tapeta and good to firm going: usually wears headgear: usually races prominently. *Adrian Nicholls* **66**

SIR LEONARD KITTER (IRE) 2 b.c. (Jan 19) Mastercraftsman (IRE) 129 – Trail of Tears (IRE) 69 (Exceed And Excel (AUS) 126) [2017 7v p10g Oct 18] well held in minor events. *Richard Hannon* **–**

SIR MAXIMILIAN (IRE) 8 b.g. Royal Applause 124 – Nebraska Lady (IRE) 87 (Lujain (USA) 119) [2017 115: 5g 5g^2 5g 6g^3 p5g Dec 12] good-topped gelding: useful handicapper: placed at Meydan in January (1½ lengths behind Medicean Man) and February (1½ lengths behind Krypton Factor): stays 6f, races mainly at 5f: acts on polytrack, good to firm and heavy going: often in cheekpieces. *Ian Williams* **107**

SIR OTTOMAN (FR) 4 b.g. Excellent Art 125 – Hali Layali (Green Desert (USA) 127) [2017 p6.5g^2 p6.5g^6 p7.5g^4 5m 6m t6.1g p6g^6 p6s Dec 15] fairly useful handicapper: won 3 times in France in 2016: second in minor event at Cagnes-sur-Mer in January: left C. Ferland after third start, Mohamed Moubarak after fifth: stays 7f: acts on polytrack, tapeta and heavy going: often wears cheekpieces: tried in tongue tie. *Ivan Furtado* **93**

SIR PASS I AM 4 b.g. Passing Glance 119 – Orbital Orchid 63 (Mujahid (USA) 125) [2017 68: p12g 16d* 14g 16s^6 Aug 17] fair handicapper: won at Chepstow (dead-heated) in May: stays 2m: acts on good to soft and good to firm going: tried in hood: not straightforward. *Andrew Balding* **77**

SIR PLATO (IRE) 3 b.g. Sir Prancealot (IRE) 111 – Dessert Flower (IRE) (Intikhab (USA) 135) [2017 60: p8g* 8.3m* 9.9m^6 8.1d* 8.1m* 9.9g^5 8.1g* 8.5m 8g 8.1g^6 Oct 9] rather leggy gelding: fairly useful handicapper: won at Kempton in March and 4 times at Windsor between April and August: stays 8.5f: acts on polytrack, good to firm and good to soft going: front runner/races prominently. *Rod Millman* **84**

SIR REGINALD BROWN 3 b.g. Archipenko (USA) 127 – Elusive Sue (USA) 83 (Elusive Quality (USA)) [2017 7m* 7s 7.2s^2 7g 8g^6 10.2d Oct 27] tall gelding: third foal: dam winner up to 7f (2-y-o 6f winner): fairly useful performer: won maiden at Redcar in April: second in handicap at Haydock in June: stays 1m: acts on soft and good to firm going. *Richard Fahey* **80**

SIR ROBERT CHEVAL 6 b.g. Green Desert (USA) 127 – Aunt Ruby (USA) 67 **112** (Rubiano (USA)) [2017 106: 5.2g* $5g^6$ 5g $5d^2$ $5s^2$ Oct 7] compact gelding: smart performer: won handicap at Newbury (by 1¼ lengths from Bowson Fred) in April: second in similar event (neck behind Stake Acclaim) in August and listed race (¾ length behind Just Glamorous) in October, both at Ascot: has won over 1m, raced at 5f/6f nowadays: acts on polytrack, soft and good to firm going: sometimes slowly away, usually races towards rear. *Robert Cowell*

SIR RODERIC (IRE) 4 b.g. Roderic O'Connor (IRE) 119 – Begin The Beguine (IRE) **100** 72 (Peintre Celebre (USA) 137) [2017 104: 8g 8m $8m^3$ 8m $8d^5$ 7.9m 7d 8s $7d^3$ 7.6g 8g 8.1d Oct 23] rather leggy gelding: useful handicapper: third at Sandown (1¼ lengths behind Laidback Romeo) in May: raced mainly around 1m: acts on good to firm and heavy going: tried in cheekpieces/tongue tie. *Rod Millman*

SIR RUNS A LOT 5 b.g. Sir Percy 129 – Monjouet (IRE) (Montjeu (IRE) 137) [2017 **63** 75p: 8g 9.8d 9g 10d $12g^3$ 14d t12.4s* t12.4g Oct 10] lengthy gelding: modest handicapper: won at Newcastle in September: stays 12.5f: acts on tapeta: in blinkers last 2 starts. *David Barron*

SIR THEODORE (IRE) 4 b.g. Arcano (IRE) 122 – Key Rose (IRE) 88 (Key of Luck **59** (USA) 126) [2017 81: t6m p5d $6d^3$ $7.5s^2$ $7g^4$ a6s $a4.7g^6$ Dec 10] compact gelding: fairly useful at best, has deteriorated: left Richard Spencer after second outing: probably stays 7.5f: acts on heavy and good to firm going: tried in cheekpieces. *S. Richter, Germany*

SIR TITAN 3 b.g. Aqlaam 125 – Femme de Fer 79 (Hamas (IRE) 125) [2017 72: t7.2g* **95** 8.1m* $7d^2$ p7g 7d p10g Nov 21] sturdy gelding: useful performer: won maiden at Wolverhampton in June and handicap at Windsor (by head from Shifting Star) in July: second in handicap at Goodwood (head behind Battered) in August: stays 1m: acts on tapeta, good to firm and good to soft going: front runner/races prominently. *Marcus Tregoning*

SIR VALENTINE (GER) 4 b.g. Cacique (IRE) 124 – Singuna (GER) (Black Sam **95** Bellamy (IRE) 121) [2017 91: $13.4g^5$ May 27] well-made gelding: useful handicapper: stays 13.5f: acts on polytrack, best turf form on good going: usually races prominently. *Alan King*

SIR WALTER (IRE) 2 b.g. (Apr 23) Camacho 118 – Damalis (IRE) 106 (Mukaddamah **–** (USA) 125) [2017 5.1m 6m $5s^6$ 6g 5s 6d Oct 30] no form: in headgear last 2 starts: tried in tongue tie. *Eric Alston*

SISTER CELINE (IRE) 2 b.f. (Feb 18) Al Kazeem 128 – Quan Yin (IRE) (Sadler's **– p** Wells (USA) 132) [2017 7m p8g 8s Oct 28] 130,000Y: fifth foal: half-sister to useful 1½m winner Ode To Psyche (by Dansili) and 6f winner Oasis Moon (by Oasis Dream): dam unraced daughter of Poule d'Essai des Pouliches/Prix de Diane winner East of The Moon: little impact in minor events/maiden: type to do better in handicaps. *Roger Charlton*

SISTER DUDE 4 ch.f. Notnowcato 128 – Inaminute (IRE) 86 (Spectrum (IRE) 126) **68** [2017 75: $7m^3$ 8.2d 7d $10m^5$ 10d Jul 26] smallish filly: fair handicapper: stays 1m: acts on soft and good to firm going: tried in tongue tie. *Jonathan Portman*

SISYPHUS 5 b.g. Halling (USA) 133 – Cape Dancer (IRE) 66 (Cape Cross (IRE) 129) **88** [2017 85: f14d* Apr 4] rather leggy gelding: fairly useful handicapper: won at Southwell (by 4½ lengths from Ominotago) only outing in 2017: stays 2m: acts on fibresand, good to firm and good to soft going: front runner/races prominently: temperament under suspicion. *Ollie Pears*

SITAR 3 b.f. Aqlaam 125 – Soundwave (Prince Sabo 123) [2017 70: 6m $5.7d^5$ 5d* $5.2m^3$ **80** 5d* $5g^6$ 6s $6s^5$ Sep 20] lengthy filly: fairly useful handicapper: won at Nottingham in June and July (by 1¼ lengths from Glacier Point): best form at 5f: acts on good to soft going: often in hood in 2017. *James Fanshawe*

SITSI 2 ch.f. (Feb 4) Captain Gerrard (IRE) 113 – Ayasha 76 (Indesatchel (IRE) 120) [2017 **–** 5d $6g^4$ $5m^4$ t5g Nov 15] £800Y: first foal: dam 6f winner (including at 2 yrs): no form. *Bryan Smart*

SITUATION 2 ch.g. (Apr 4) Lethal Force (IRE) 128 – Russian Dance (USA) 93 (Nureyev **65** (USA) 131) [2017 $6g^4$ $6d^4$ 5d $7s^5$ 7s $7s^4$ 7.2m 8g Sep 27] fair maiden: stays 7f: acts on soft going: tried in cheekpieces: front runner/races prominently: temperament under suspicion. *Richard Guest*

SIX OF THE BEST 5 b.m. Monsieur Bond (IRE) 120 – Bond Casino 69 (Kyllachy 129) **44** [2017 t7.1d t6g $t5g^5$ $5s^6$ $5f^6$ 6g 6g $t6d^5$ Nov 4] poor maiden: left Ollie Pears after third start: best effort at 5f: acts on firm going: tried in cheekpieces. *Bryan Smart*

SIX SILVER LANE 9 gr.g. Aussie Rules (USA) 123 – Aurelia 80 (Rainbow Quest (USA) 134) [2017 72: p10.7g^{3} p8g^{6} p10.7g^{6} p10.7g^{3} p10.7g* p10.7g^{2} p12g^{3} 10m^{4} p8g* 9.9g^{2} 9d 12d^{2} p10.7g* p12g^{3} p10.7g^{4} p12g^{5} p10.7g^{2} p8s^{3} Dec 8] fair on turf, fairly useful on all-weather: won handicap in March, claimer in July and handicap in September, all at Dundalk: stays 1½m: acts on polytrack, sand, good to firm and good to soft going: wears headgear: has worn tongue tie: usually leads. *J. J. Feane, Ireland* **73 a80**

SIX STRINGS 3 b.g. Requinto (IRE) 109 – Island Music (IRE) 74 (Mujahid (USA) 125) [2017 92p: 7g^{2} 6g^{3} 6d 7g^{3} 7d Sep 13] useful handicapper: third at Hamilton (2 lengths behind Classic Seniority) in July and Doncaster (neck behind Bertiewhittle) in August: stays 7f: acts on tapeta, best turf form on good going. *Richard Fahey* **95**

SIXTH OF JUNE 3 b.f. Crosspeace (IRE) 118 – Eccentricity (Emarati (USA) 74) [2017 –: 7s p7g^{6} p10s Dec 15] no form. *Rod Millman* **–**

SIXTIES GROOVE (IRE) 4 b.g. Sixties Icon 125 – Gift Dancer (Imperial Dancer 123) [2017 112: 8.5m 12m^{5} 10.3m Jul 15] sturdy gelding: useful handicapper: stays 1½m: acts on polytrack, soft and good to firm going: wears cheekpieces: often races towards rear: sent to Germany. *Jeremy Noseda* **106**

SIXTIES HABANA 3 b.g. Sixties Icon 125 – Vilnius 67 (Imperial Dancer 123) [2017 65: p7m p7g^{6} 7g 6g^{3} p7g p6g^{3} 7s^{3} Jul 29] lengthy gelding: modest handicapper: stays 7f: acts on polytrack and any turf going. *Pat Phelan* **57**

SIXTIES IDOL 4 b.f. Sixties Icon 125 – Fading Away (Fraam 114) [2017 57: p12d^{5} p12g^{5} p10g p12g Mar 8] smallish filly: poor maiden: stays 1½m: acts on polytrack and heavy going: often races towards rear. *Sheena West* **47**

SIXTIES SECRET 2 b.f. (May 9) Sixties Icon 125 – Jollyhockeysticks 72 (Fantastic Light (USA) 134) [2017 6m 7m 6d^{4} 8.3v^{3} p8g^{3} 7.4s^{6} Aug 25] rather unfurnished filly: fourth foal: half-sister to Italian 5f and (including at 2 yrs) 6f winner Grand Bounty (by Bahamian Bounty): dam, 1m winner who stayed 1¼m, half-sister to useful sprinter Pic Up Sticks: poor maiden: stays 8.5f: acts on polytrack and heavy going. *Mick Channon* **47**

SIXTIES SONG (ARG) 4 b.c. Sixties Icon 125 – Blissful Song (USA) (Unbridled's Song (USA) 125) [2017 12g* 11.9v^{3} 12s a11.9f^{6} 11.9s Dec 16] sturdy colt: third foal: half-brother to 2 winners in Argentina, including Group 2 1m winner Celestial Candy (by Candy Ride): dam, North American 8.5f/1¼m winner, out of half-sister to Arlington Million winner Paradise Creek: smart performer: successful 3 times in 2016, notably in Gran Premio Carlos Pellegrini at San Isidro: also won Gran Premio Latinoamericano at Valparaiso (by 2¼ lengths from Tinku) in March: third in Gran Premio 25 de Mayo at San Isidro (3¼ lengths behind Ordak Dan) in May: well below form after, including in King George VI and Queen Elizabeth Stakes at Ascot: stays 1½m: acts on any turf going. *Alfredo F. Gaitan Dassie, Argentina* **115**

SIXTIES SYMPHONY 3 b.f. Sixties Icon 125 – Moyoko (IRE) 64 (Mozart (IRE) 131) [2017 –: 7s 5.7m 6.1m Jun 15] good-bodied filly: no form. *John Flint* **–**

SIYAHAMBA (IRE) 3 ch.g. Helmet (AUS) 127 – Kalabunga (IRE) 71 (Val Royal (FR) 127) [2017 54: 10.2m^{3} 9g^{3} 12d^{4} 12g 8.5s^{6} 10g^{5} 8v^{2} f8.1g^{3} t12.2g Dec 13] modest maiden: stays 1¼m: acts on tapeta, good to firm and heavy going. *Bryan Smart* **60**

SIYOUSHAKE (IRE) 5 b.m. Siyouni (FR) 122 – Shakeyourbody (USA) (Giant's Causeway (USA) 132) [2017 115: 8g 8m^{3} 8g^{3} 9.9g^{2} 8g Oct 7] sturdy mare: smart performer: placed in Prix Bertrand du Breuil at Chantilly (2¼ lengths behind Taareef), Prix Rothschild at Deauville (beaten neck by Roly Poly) and Prix Jean Romanet at Deauville (1¼ lengths behind Ajman Princess): behind in Sun Chariot Stakes at Newmarket final start: stays 1¼m: acts on soft and good to firm going. *F. Head, France* **116**

SIZE MATTERS 3 b.g. Captain Gerrard (IRE) 113 – Icky Woo (Mark of Esteem (IRE) 137) [2017 –: t9.5g 9.9g^{2} 10.2m^{5} 8s^{3} 8.3g^{4} 8d^{3} 7.2d* f7.1g^{5} 7s^{5} Oct 10] fair handicapper: won at Ayr in August: stays 1¼m: acts on soft going: tried in tongue tie: front runner/races prominently. *Mark Walford* **67**

SIZZLING (IRE) 2 ch.f. (Mar 16) Galileo (IRE) 134 – Weekend Strike (USA) (Smart Strike (CAN) 121) [2017 7d^{3} 7g^{2} 7d^{3} 7m^{2} 7.5s* 8g^{4} 7s^{2} 8v^{4} Oct 8] fourth foal: sister to 12.5f winner Squire's Tale and half-sister to a winner in USA by Malibu Moon: dam, US winner around 1m, (including at 2 yrs), closely related to Breeders' Cup Mile winner Court Vision: useful performer: won maiden at Tipperary in August: second in C. L. & M. F. Weld Park Stakes at Naas (2¾ lengths behind Ellthea) in September: stays 1m: acts on soft and good to firm going: usually races prominently. *Aidan O'Brien, Ireland* **101**

SKEAPING 4 b.g. Excellent Art 125 – Gale Green 78 (Galileo (IRE) 134) [2017 86: p10.7g 7m May 10] strong gelding: fairly useful handicapper, below form in 2017: stays 1½m: acts on good to firm and heavy going: in blinkers last 3 starts: maiden hurdler. *Gordon Elliott, Ireland* **74**

SKELLIG MICHAEL 3 b.g. Arakan (USA) 123 – Ambonnay 89 (Ashkalani (IRE) 128) [2017 57: t6g^5 p6d* t6g^2 6g Apr 30] modest handicapper: won at Kempton in February: stays 6f: acts on polytrack and tapeta: in cheekpieces last 3 starts. *Ben Haslam* **63**

SKETCH BOOK VENUE (IRE) 3 b.g. Rip Van Winkle (IRE) 134 – Parvenue (FR) 79 (Ezzoud (IRE) 126) [2017 10m^2 10.2v^{pu} Aug 8] fair form when second in maiden at Redcar in April: suffered fatal injury only other start. *Sally Haynes* **73**

SKI BLAST 6 ch.g. Three Valleys (USA) 119 – Chasing Stars 103 (Observatory (USA) 131) [2017 81: 8.2g^5 8s 8s^6 9.1g^2 10.2g* Aug 19] fairly useful handicapper: won at Doncaster (apprentice, by length from Royal Reserve) in August: stays 1¼m: acts on good to firm going. *Ivan Furtado* **80**

SKIDBY MILL (IRE) 7 b.m. Ramonti (FR) 126 – Glasnas Giant 60 (Giant's Causeway (USA) 132) [2017 82: p8g* p8g^2 p8g^4 p8g^4 p8d^2 p8g^4 p8g p8g p8g p8g p10g Nov 2] workmanlike mare: fairly useful handicapper: won at Lingfield (by ½ length from Remember Me) in January: stays 8.5f: acts on polytrack, good to firm and heavy going: has worn headgear: usually races prominently. *Laura Mongan* **81**

SKIDDAW VALLEYS 5 ch.g. Three Valleys (USA) 119 – Skiddaw Wolf 74 (Wolfhound (USA) 126) [2017 79: 12d^6 Aug 7] strong gelding: fairly useful handicapper, below form sole outing in 2017: stays 1¾m: acts on tapeta, firm and good to soft going. *Sally Haynes* **66**

SKIFFLE 4 b.f. Dubawi (IRE) 129 – Princesse Dansante (IRE) 109 (King's Best (USA) 132) [2017 104: 9m 12s^6 9.9v^5 9.9m Aug 16] sturdy filly: useful performer: best effort at 1¼m: acts on good to soft going: in cheekpieces last 2 starts. *Charlie Appleby* **98**

SKILFUL LORD (IRE) 3 ch.g. Lord Shanakill (USA) 121 – Monsusu (IRE) 86 (Montjeu (IRE) 137) [2017 51: p8g t9.5g^6 p12g Nov 8] poor maiden: left Stuart Kittow after second start: stays 9.5f: acts on tapeta: in headgear last 3 starts: tried in tongue tie. *David Pipe* **47**

SKILLED 6 b.g. Mastercraftsman (IRE) 129 – Treacle (USA) (Seeking The Gold (USA)) [2017 68: t13.9f Jan 5] fair maiden, well held sole outing on Flat in 2017: stays 15f: acts on good to firm and heavy going: tried in cheekpieces: winning hurdler/chaser. *Anabel K. Murphy* **–**

SKITO SOLDIER 2 b.g. (Feb 3) Sepoy (AUS) 129 – Kotsi (IRE) 103 (Nayef (USA) 129) [2017 7g^3 7.4m^3 8.2v t7.1d Oct 24] fair form: best effort at 7f. *K. R. Burke* **66**

SKY BALLERINA 3 b.f. Makfi 130 – Maid In Heaven (IRE) 99 (Clodovil (IRE) 116) [2017 70p: t7.1m* p8g^2 t7.1d^3 Feb 1] fair handicapper: won at Wolverhampton in January: likely to stay beyond 1m: acts on polytrack and tapeta: often races prominently: sold 16,000 gns, sent to Greece. *Simon Crisford* **78**

SKY BANDIT 2 gr.f. (Feb 24) Dick Turpin (IRE) 127 – Aurora Sky (IRE) 81 (Hawk Wing (USA) 136) [2017 7s^5 Sep 27] second foal: dam 1¼m winner: 16/1, well held in minor event at Goodwood. *Gary Moore* **–**

SKY CAPE 5 b.g. Cape Cross (IRE) 129 – Green Swallow (FR) 107 (Green Tune (USA) 125) [2017 p11g^5 10s^4 May 19] useful handicapper at 3 yrs, little impact either start in 2017 after long absence: stayed 11f: acted on polytrack, tapeta and good to firm going: dead. *Heather Main* **–**

SKY EAGLE (IRE) 3 ch.c. Lope de Vega (IRE) 125 – Penelope Star (GER) (Acatenango (GER) 127) [2017 10g 12v^3 11.6g^4 p12g^2 p12g* Nov 29] very big colt: fair performer: won handicap at Kempton in November: stays 1½m: acts on polytrack. *Ed Walker* **79**

SKY GYPSY 3 gr.f. Dandy Man (IRE) 123 – Gypsy Style 63 (Desert Style (IRE) 121) [2017 69: f5g^5 5g Sep 27] fair form at 2 yrs, little impact in 2017: raced only at 5f: acts on good to firm going. *David Brown* **–**

SKYLARK LADY (IRE) 4 ch.f. Tamayuz 126 – Allegrissimo (IRE) 48 (Redback 116) [2017 67: p12g^5 13f 16m^5 13f Jul 12] fair handicapper, below form in 2017: left Michael Wigham after first start: stays 13f: acts on polytrack, fibresand, good to firm and good to soft going: in headgear last 4 starts: usually races prominently. *Nikki Evans* **59**

SKY MARSHAL (IRE) 3 b.g. Lawman (FR) 121 – Evensong (GER) (Waky Nao 122) [2017 7g p8g 7.1s^4 8.1d t8.6g p12g* Dec 6] well-made gelding: fair performer: won handicap at Lingfield in December: best effort at 1½m: acts on polytrack. *Ed Walker* **68**

SKY ROCKET 2 b.g. (Mar 29) Azamour (IRE) 130 – Roseum 102 (Lahib (USA) 129) [2017 8s p8d^{3} p8g^{2} Nov 1] fair form when placed in minor events at Chelmsford and Kempton. *Sylvester Kirk* **68**

SKYVA 2 b.g. (Feb 5) Dick Turpin (IRE) 127 – Skylla 96 (Kyllachy 129) [2017 5g^{6} 6d^{5} f5g^{3} 5.9v^{6} t6g t5d^{3} t6.1g* Nov 29] fair performer: won nursery at Wolverhampton in November: stays 6f: acts on tapeta and heavy going: tried in hood. *Brian Ellison* **66**

SLAVE TO FREEDOM 3 b.f. Equiano (FR) 127 – Fontegiusta (IRE) 69 (Desert Prince (IRE) 130) [2017 –: t5d 7m 7g May 29] no form: tried in cheekpieces. *Ann Duffield* **–**

SLAYING THE DRAGON (IRE) 4 ch.g. Notnowcato 128 – Empress Charlotte 77 (Holy Roman Emperor (IRE) 125) [2017 t7.1g^{3} t10.2d^{6} 7m 7g 9.8m^{4} t14d^{5} Dec 27] modest maiden: left Nigel Tinkler after fifth start: probably stays 1¼m: acts on tapeta: tried in blinkers: usually races towards rear. *Martin Hill* **54**

SLEEP EASY 5 b.g. Rip Van Winkle (IRE) 134 – Strictly Lambada 77 (Red Ransom (USA)) [2017 16s^{5} 12g p11g 16d f16.5g^{6} f14.1g Dec 11] useful-looking gelding: fairly useful handicapper: below form after reappearance: stays 2m: acts on polytrack, fibresand, soft and good to firm going: usually wears headgear: often in tongue tie in 2017: useful hurdler. *Neil Mulholland* **85**

SLEEPING LION (USA) 2 ch.c. (Apr 9) Teofilo (IRE) 126 – Flame of Hestia (IRE) 79 (Giant's Causeway (USA) 132) [2017 p8g^{4} Nov 7] third foal: half-brother to useful 9.5f-1½m winner Colonial Classic (by Dansili): dam maiden (stayed 11.5f): 16/1, fourth in minor event at Kempton (6¼ lengths behind Bow Street) in November: sure to progress. *James Fanshawe* **74 p**

SLEMY (IRE) 6 b.g. Raven's Pass (USA) 133 – Wolf Cleugh (IRE) 65 (Last Tycoon 131) [2017 87: t7.1d 7m 7g 7g 7.2s 7.4m 7.2g 7.2g t6d 7g Aug 19] fairly useful at best, out of sorts in 2017: in cheekpieces last 2 starts: sent to Germany. *Ruth Carr* **–**

SLICEOFLIFE 3 b.g. Sayif (IRE) 122 – Cherrego (USA) (Borrego (USA) 126) [2017 65: p8g^{2} p8g^{2} a7.5g* a6g* a7.5g^{2} a8g* 8g^{2} a10.9g^{2} 10.4g^{5} 9g* 9g* 7g 14.1s^{6} Sep 27] fairly useful performer: left Marco Botti after second start: successful at Bro Park in maiden and minor events in March/April, and at Klampenborg in minor events in July/August: stays 11f: acts on dirt, polytrack and tapeta: tried in cheekpieces. *Bent Olsen, Denmark* **85**

SLIM CHANCE (IRE) 8 b.m. Clodovil (IRE) 116 – Valluga (IRE) (Ashkalani (IRE) 128) [2017 67: f5g^{6} Jan 10] fair handicapper, below form sole outing in 2017: raced mainly at sprint trips: acts on polytrack, tapeta, good to firm and heavy going: wears headgear: has worn tongue tie. *Simon West* **–**

SLINGSBY 6 b.g. Dutch Art 126 – Ballet Fame (USA) 79 (Quest For Fame 127) [2017 79: t6d* t6d^{5} t7.1g t6g^{6} t5s^{6} Jun 1] fairly useful handicapper: won at Newcastle (by 1¼ lengths from Pretty Bubbles) in February: stays 1m, raced mainly at shorter: acts on tapeta, best turf form on good going: wears headgear: often races prominently: sold 3,000 gns in July. *Michael Easterby* **81**

SLIPALONGTREVASKIS 4 b.g. Kheleyf (USA) 116 – Tilly's Dream 87 (Arkadian Hero (USA) 123) [2017 p6d p6d f5d f5g p7g f8.1g^{6} Nov 28] no form. *J. R. Jenkins* **–**

SLIPPER SATIN (IRE) 7 b.m. Excellent Art 125 – In The Ribbons 88 (In The Wings 128) [2017 57: 14d Aug 12] fair handicapper at best, well held sole outing in 2017: stays 1¾m: acts on good to firm and good to soft going: has worn headgear: wears tongue tie: front runner/races prominently. *Simon West* **–**

SLIPSTREAM (IRE) 2 b.c. (Feb 16) Invincible Spirit (IRE) 121 – Kiltubber (IRE) 104 (Sadler's Wells (USA) 132) [2017 7d Jul 29] 16/1, eighth in minor event at Newmarket (6¾ lengths behind Anna Nerium) in July. *George Scott* **66**

SLOW TO HAND 3 ch.g. Sepoy (AUS) 129 – One Giant Leap (IRE) 73 (Pivotal 124) [2017 7d^{6} p7s^{4} 8g 7m* 8m^{2} p8g^{5} p8d^{5} 10.1d Oct 24] fair handicapper: won at Yarmouth in August: should stay 1¼m: acts on good to firm going: in blinkers last 5 starts. *William Jarvis* **71**

SLUNOVRAT (FR) 6 b.g. Astronomer Royal (USA) 121 – Slewmamba (FR) (Kingsalsa (USA) 118) [2017 93: 14s^{2} 16g^{6} 16.3g Oct 14] workmanlike gelding: fairly useful handicapper: second at Sandown in July: stays 16.5f: acts on any turf going: front runner/races prominently. *David Menuisier* **94**

SMART CALL (SAF) 6 b.m. Ideal World (USA) 118 – Good Judgement (USA) (Horse Chestnut (SAF) 119) [2017 119: 10.3d^{3} 8m^{4} 10g 9.9g^{4} 10s^{6} 11.9g Dec 10] well-made mare: half-sister to winners in South Africa by Strike Smartly: dam unraced half-sister to very smart South African winner up to 1½m Greys Inn: smart performer: won 2 Grade 1 events (Paddock Stakes and J & B Met), both at Kenilworth, in early-2016 for A. G. Laird: in **114**

frame in 2017 in Middleton Stakes at York (1½ lengths third to Blond Me), Duke of Cambridge Stakes at Royal Ascot (1¾ lengths fourth to Qemah) and Prix Jean Romanet at Deauville (1¼ lengths fourth to Ajman Princess): stays 1¼m, possibly not 1½m: acts on good to firm going, possibly unsuited by soft. *Sir Michael Stoute*

SMART CHAMPION 2 b.c. (Apr 5) Teofilo (IRE) 126 – Soryah (IRE) 97 (Shamardal **72**
(USA) 129) [2017 p10d^{6} Nov 9] 16/1, sixth in minor event at Chelmsford (8 lengths behind Photographer) in November. *Simon Crisford*

SMART DART 2 b.f. (May 6) Mastercraftsman (IRE) 129 – Dark Missile 114 (Night Shift **54 p**
(USA)) [2017 t7.2g^{6} Dec 5] third foal: closely related to 6f winner Midnight Dance (by Danehill Dancer) and half-sister to useful 5f winner Dark Shot (by Acclamation): dam 6f winner (including at 2 yrs): 17/2, sixth in minor event at Wolverhampton (6¼ lengths behind American Endeavour) in December: open to improvement. *Ralph Beckett*

SMART DJ 6 ch.g. Major Cadeaux 121 – Katy-Q (IRE) 58 (Taufan (USA) 119) [2017 54: **–**
t6m Jan 13] modest handicapper, well held sole outing in 2017: stays 6f: acts on tapeta and good to firm going: sometimes slowly away. *Sarah Hollinshead*

SMART MOVER (IRE) 4 b.f. Fast Company (IRE) 126 – Alltherightmoves (IRE) 45 **60 §**
(Namid 128) [2017 76§: p8g^{6} t12.2g^{6} 10.2m^{5} 8.1d 8.1m^{3} 8g 8g^{4} p7g^{5} Dec 28] modest handicapper nowadays: stays 1m: acts on soft and good to firm going: has worn headgear: irresolute. *Nikki Evans*

SMART TOGETHER (USA) 3 b.f. Smart Strike (CAN) 121 – Forever Together (USA) **96 p**
120 (Belong To Me (USA)) [2017 –p: 8f* 10g^{3} Jun 15] useful-looking filly: useful form: won maiden at Haydock (by head from Sasini) in May: third in listed race at Newbury (3¾ lengths behind Elas Ruby) in June: stays 1¼m: sent to USA: open to further improvement. *John Gosden*

SMILEY BAGEL (IRE) 4 b.g. Kyllachy 129 – Epistoliere (IRE) (Alzao (USA) 117) **78**
[2017 61: t12.2g^{6} p10g* p12g* p12g* t12.2g* t12.2g^{6} 11.9v 10m t12.2g Jul 11] fair handicapper: won at Kempton/Lingfield in February, Kempton again in March and Wolverhampton in April: stays 1½m: acts on polytrack, tapeta, best turf form on good going: usually races prominently. *Ed Walker*

SMILEY RILEY (IRE) 3 b.g. Fast Company (IRE) 126 – Betty Fontaine (IRE) 88 **–**
(Mujadil (USA) 119) [2017 47: f7.1g 8.3s Jul 4] maiden, no form in 2017: tried in cheekpieces. *Tony Coyle*

SMOKETHATTHUNDERS (IRE) 7 gr.g. Elusive City (USA) 117 – Zinstar (IRE) **78**
(Sinndar (IRE) 134) [2017 75, a82: t7.1m f8g^{4} t7.2d Dec 26] fair performer: stays 1m: acts on all-weather and soft going: has worn headgear: tried in tongue tie. *James Unett*

SMOKEY LANE (IRE) 3 ch.g. Zebedee 113 – Masela (IRE) 71 (Medicean 128) [2017 **102**
100: 5.1g^{5} 5g^{5} 6m 6d* 6m 7d 6d 6d 6s^{4} 7d^{5} 5v^{2} 6d 6d Oct 27] good-topped gelding: useful handicapper: won at Leicester (by 2¾ lengths from Scorching Heat) in May: second there (1½ lengths behind Soie d'Leau) in September: left David Evans after sixth start: stays 6f: acts on good to firm and heavy going. *Christian Williams*

SMOKY HILL (IRE) 8 gr.g. Galileo (IRE) 134 – Danaskaya (IRE) 106 (Danehill (USA) **54**
126) [2017 69: t12.2m^{5} p12d^{4} p12g^{5} 11.5m 14.1m May 24] strong, close-coupled gelding: modest handicapper nowadays: stays 15.5f: acts on polytrack and soft going: has worn headgear, including in 2017. *Tony Carroll*

SMOOTH OPERATOR 5 b.g. Azamour (IRE) 130 – Teggiano (IRE) 108 (Mujtahid **70**
(USA) 118) [2017 56: 14g^{4} 12d^{5} Aug 3] fair maiden: stays 1¾m: best form on good going: has worn tongue tie. *Mark Pitman*

SMOOTH SAILING 2 b.f. (Feb 11) Bated Breath 125 – Royal Confidence 108 (Royal **–**
Applause 124) [2017 5.1m 6.1m Aug 14] sturdy filly: fourth foal: dam, winner up to 7f (5f/6.5f winner at 2 yrs), half-sister to smart 5f-7f winner Doctor Sardonicus: little impact in minor events. *Charles Hills*

SMOULDER 3 b.f. Redoute's Choice (AUS) – Yummy Mummy 86 (Montjeu (IRE) 137) **96**
[2017 6d^{6} 7g^{3} p7g* 8d 6d^{6} 6s 6g^{4} 7s 7.5s^{5} 7g 8s p8g Oct 27] 725,000Y: lengthy filly: fourth foal: closely related to very smart winner (including 1000 Guineas) up to 1¼m Legatissimo (2-y-o 7f winner, by Danehill Dancer) and half-sister to useful 1½m winner (stayed 2½m) Another Cocktail (by Dalakhani): dam, 1¼m winner who probably stayed 1½m, sister to Irish Derby/Gold Cup winner Fame And Glory: useful performer: won maiden at Dundalk in May: stays 7f: acts on polytrack and soft going: wears hood: sometimes slowly away, often races towards rear. *Aidan O'Brien, Ireland*

SMUGGLERS CREEK (IRE) 3 b.g. Medicean 128 – Crystany (IRE) 98 (Green Desert **80**
(USA) 127) [2017 6m p8g^2 p7g* t7.2d^5 Dec 26] fourth foal: half-brother to 7f winner Cosquillas (by Selkirk) and 1m winner Sapphirine (by Shamardal): dam, 2-y-o 6f winner, half-sister to smart performer up to 11.5f High End out of Fillies' Mile winner Crystal Music: fairly useful form: won claimer at Dundalk (by neck from Delegating) in October: left M. Halford after third start: stays 1m. *Iain Jardine*

SMUGGLERS TOP 2 ch.g. (Jan 31) Kendargent (FR) 112 – Penny's Gift 108 (Tobougg **66**
(IRE) 125) [2017 6d 6g 7.1s^4 p7g^4 7m Oct 25] sturdy gelding: fair maiden: stays 7f: acts on polytrack and soft going: in cheekpieces last 2 starts: sold 5,500 gns, sent to Italy. *Tom Dascombe*

SNAFFLED (IRE) 2 b.c. (Apr 30) Camacho 118 – Little Oz (IRE) 71 (Red Ransom **52**
(USA)) [2017 5.1m 6g^5 8d^5 p8g t7.1g^4 Nov 15] modest maiden: should stay 1m: acts on tapeta. *David Brown*

SNAPPYDRESSER 4 b.f. Medicean 128 – Dand Nee (USA) 86 (Kabool 119) [2017 –: **–**
9m t10.2d Aug 10] no form. *Chris Grant*

SNAP SHOTS (IRE) 5 b.g. Kodiac 112 – Refuse To Give Up (IRE) (Refuse To Bend **101 §**
(IRE) 128) [2017 103: 5s 6d^2 6d^3 6.3f^2 6g 6d^{rr} 6g^4 6s 6v^{rr} Sep 30] compact, quite attractive gelding: useful handicapper: placed at Ripon (head behind Pipers Note) and Haydock (head behind Handsome Dude) in June, and the Curragh (½ length behind Tithonus) in July: stays 6.5f: acts on firm and good to soft going: usually wears headgear: has worn tongue tie: sometimes slowly away: one to treat with plenty of caution (twice refused to race). *Tony Coyle*

SNATTY DANCER 2 ch.f. (Mar 29) Nathaniel (IRE) 129 – Spicy Dal 96 (Dalakhani **–**
(IRE) 133) [2017 8s p8s Nov 16] first foal: dam 1m winner who stayed 1½m: little show in minor events. *Hughie Morrison*

SNAX 2 b.f. (May 3) High Chaparral (IRE) 132 – Cosmodrome (USA) 108 (Bahri (USA) **65**
125) [2017 7g^6 t8g^6 Sep 22] 17,000Y: sixth foal: half-sister to useful performer up to 1¼m Lovell (2-y-o 7f winner, by Dubawi): dam, 9.5f/1¼m winner, half-sister to useful winners up to 1¼m Splashdown and Boogie Shoes: fair form when sixth at Salisbury (7¼ lengths behind Herecomesthesun) on first of 2 starts in maidens. *Mark Johnston*

SNAZZY JAZZY (IRE) 2 b.c. (Mar 23) Red Jazz (USA) 125 – Bulrushes (Byron 117) **96 p**
[2017 6g* 6.1s* 6.3s* Sep 10] €65,000Y: third foal: half-brother to useful French 5.5f/6.5f winner Ross Castle (by Bushranger) and a winner in Scandinavia by Fast Company: dam unraced half-sister to very smart winner up to 7f Tariq: useful form: won minor events at Goodwood (by 1¼ lengths from Alrahaal) in June and Windsor (by ½ length from Society Power) in August, and valuable sales race at the Curragh (by 3 lengths from Pretty Boy Floyd) in September: stays 6.5f: will go on improving. *Clive Cox*

SNIPER VIPER 3 ch.f. Paco Boy (IRE) 129 – Brilliance 74 (Cadeaux Genereux 131) **–**
[2017 –: 5m^4 8g 7.4g Jul 17] no form, including in handicap: wears blinkers. *Daniel Kubler*

SNOANO 5 b.g. Nayef (USA) 129 – White Dress (IRE) (Pivotal 124) [2017 104: 10g* **110**
10.3m^5 9g 10m* 10.3m 12s^4 10.3m 10m Sep 23] close-coupled gelding: smart handicapper: won at Pontefract (by 2¼ lengths from Final) in April and Royal Ascot (Wolferton Handicap, by neck from Majeed) in June: stays 1½m: acts on soft and good to firm going: sold 82,000 gns in October. *Tim Easterby*

SNOBBERY (IRE) 4 b.g. Duke of Marmalade (IRE) 132 – Boast 99 (Most Welcome 131) **85**
[2017 79p: p12g t12.2m^4 Jan 23] big, strong gelding: fairly useful form: raced only at 1½m: tried in tongue tie: sold to join Nigel Twiston-Davies 31,000 gns in February: little show over hurdles. *Roger Charlton*

SNOOKERED (IRE) 3 b.g. Born To Sea (IRE) 117 – Secret Quest 85 (Pivotal 124) **75**
[2017 62: 10.2g 9g^4 t8.6g^3 8s^2 8.3g^3 9.9d* 10g 10.1g^3 12v^6 Oct 9] fair handicapper: won at Beverley in July: stays 1¼m: acts on tapeta and soft going: front runner/races prominently: has joined Brian Ellison. *Richard Fahey*

SNOOKER JIM 2 b.c. (Mar 7) Holy Roman Emperor (IRE) 125 – Lucia de Medici **70**
(Medicean 128) [2017 7d 7g^4 7d^3 Aug 6] sturdy colt: fair form: best effort when fourth in minor event at Ascot (2 lengths behind Curiosity) in July. *Steph Hollinshead*

SNOOP 2 b.f. (Mar 2) Paco Boy (IRE) 129 – Carafe 85 (Selkirk (USA) 129) [2017 6f 6s **–**
Jun 8] £4,000Y: half-sister to useful 1¼m winner Next Approach (by New Approach) and a winner in Qatar by Oasis Dream: dam 7f winner out of Falmouth/Nassau Stakes winner Caramba: well held in minor event/maiden. *David Loughnane*

SNOOZY SIOUX (IRE) 3 b.f. Sleeping Indian 122 – Castalian Spring (IRE) 45 (Oasis Dream 129) [2017 62: p5g^6 p5g* 5m 5.1d p5g f5g^4 Nov 13] sturdy filly: modest handicapper: won at Lingfield in March: best form at 5f: acts on polytrack and good to firm going: tried in headgear: sent to Belgium. *Martin Smith* **63**

SNORING 3 b.g. Sleeping Indian 122 – Porcelain (IRE) 82 (Peintre Celebre (USA) 137) [2017 6s^5 6m^6 8m Jul 10] well held in maidens. *John Davies* **–**

SNOW BLAZE 3 b.f. Proclamation (IRE) 130 – Dancealot Lady (USA) (Theatrical) [2017 7.4m^6 May 31] first foal: dam of little account: 33/1, well held in maiden at Beverley. *Michael Appleby* **–**

SNOWDON 2 b.f. (Apr 2) Iffraaj 127 – Solva 110 (Singspiel (IRE) 133) [2017 7v Sep 9] 40,000F: fifth foal: sister to 7f winner Able Jack and half-sister to 1¼m winner Solvanna (by Haafhd): dam 1¼m winner: 9/1, well held in minor event at Thirsk. *Michael Dods* **–**

SNOW EXCUSE 3 gr.g. Hellvelyn 118 – Satin Doll 68 (Diktat 126) [2017 6m 6m 5d^6 p6g^4 6s^{pu} t6.1g^2 t6.1d Dec 27] modest maiden: will stay 7f: acts on tapeta: usually wears tongue tie: often races towards rear. *Bryan Smart* **56**

SNOW FALCON (IRE) 7 b.g. Presenting 120 – Flocon de Neige (IRE) (Kahyasi 130) [2017 94p: 14d* 12.8d 16v^2 18m Oct 14] well-made gelding: useful handicapper: won at Killarney (by 2¾ lengths from Bayan) in August: second in Irish Cesarewitch at Navan (2½ lengths behind Lord Erskine) in October: stays 2m: acts on heavy going: smart hurdler/chaser. *Noel Meade, Ireland* **108**

SNOWFLAKES (IRE) 2 br.f. (Feb 20) Galileo (IRE) 134 – Laddies Poker Two (IRE) 117 (Choisir (AUS) 126) [2017 6d 6m Jun 23] compact filly: third foal: sister to very smart winner (including 1000 Guineas) up to 1¼m Winter (2-y-o 7f winner): dam 6f/7f winner: fairly useful form: better effort when eighth in Albany Stakes at Royal Ascot (5 lengths behind Different League) in June: should go on improving. *Aidan O'Brien, Ireland* **91 p**

SNOW SQUAW 3 ch.f. Excelebration (IRE) 133 – Snoqualmie Girl (IRE) 103 (Montjeu (IRE) 137) [2017 73: p5g^4 7m* 8s 8.1g^2 8.1g^4 8.1s^4 7g^3 p7g^5 Oct 18] rather unfurnished filly: fair performer: won maiden at Salisbury in April: stays 1m: acts on polytrack and good to firm going: sometimes in cheekpieces: races freely. *David Elsworth* **79**

SNOWY DAWN 7 gr.g. Notnowcato 128 – Tereyna 58 (Terimon 124) [2017 78: p14g* 13.4g May 27] good-topped gelding: fair handicapper: won at Chelmsford in April: stays 17f: acts on polytrack, tapeta, good to firm and heavy going: has worn cheekpieces: often races prominently: consistent. *Steph Hollinshead* **76**

SNOWY WINTER (USA) 3 b.f. Elusive Quality (USA) – Pamona Ball (USA) (Pleasantly Perfect (USA) 130) [2017 p8s 8.3g* 8.9d^4 10.2g^3 11.6m^2 14d p13.3d* p16d^5 t12.4g* p12g* p12d^5 f12.1g* Dec 21] €7,500 3-y-o: third foal: sister to UAE 6f winner Ticket Holder and half-sister to a winner in USA by Hard Spun: dam, US 1m and (at 2 yrs) 8.5f winner, runner-up in Grade 2 7f event: useful handicapper: progressed really well, winning at Hamilton (maiden) in July, Chelmsford in September, Newcastle in October, Kempton (amateur) in November and Southwell (by 4 lengths from Good Time Ahead) in December: stays 13.5f: acts on all-weather and good to firm going: wears tongue tie. *Archie Watson* **99**

SNUGGY (IRE) 3 b.f. Elzaam (AUS) 115 – Mandhooma 77 (Oasis Dream 129) [2017 67: t5g^2 p5m^3 Jan 20] fair handicapper: stayed 6f: acted on polytrack, tapeta and good to firm going: often raced prominently: dead. *David Barron* **66**

SOARING SPIRITS (IRE) 7 ch.g. Tamayuz 126 – Follow My Lead 72 (Night Shift (USA)) [2017 83, a64: p5g^5 8.3m 6m 6g^4 6.1m* 7m^3 7g 6s^6 p6g^6 p6g 7v^3 t7.2g^4 p7s p7g^2 Dec 30] good-topped gelding: fair handicapper: won at Nottingham in June: raced mainly at 6f/7f: acts on polytrack, tapeta and any turf going: usually wears headgear: tried in tongue tie. *Dean Ivory* **74** **a66**

SO BELOVED 7 b.g. Dansili 127 – Valencia 79 (Kenmare (FR) 125) [2017 118: 7g^5 7m^3 7.2s^3 8.1g^4 7m^2 7g^5 7g^5 7g^4 7d^2 7s^4 p8d Nov 22] big, well-made gelding: smart performer: placed in listed race at Haydock (1¼ lengths behind Oh This Is Us) in May, John of Gaunt Stakes at same course (¾ length behind Absolutely So) in June, Minstrel Stakes at the Curragh (1¾ lengths behind Spirit of Valor) in July and Prix de la Foret at Chantilly (¾ length behind Aclaim) in October: stays 1m: acts on polytrack, firm and soft going: has worn headgear, including in 2017. *David O'Meara* **113**

SOBER UP 5 b.m. Kheleyf (USA) 116 – Morning After 84 (Emperor Jones (USA) 119) [2017 62: p7g^5 f7m Mar 7] compact mare: modest handicapper at best, has lost her way: stays 7f: acts on polytrack: usually wears headgear: often races in rear/lazily. *Ivan Furtado* **45**

The Gurkha Coolmore Prix Saint-Alary, Deauville—
Sobetsu resumes her progress after seven months off to beat Vue Fantastique and the grey Coronet

SOBETSU 3 b.f. Dubawi (IRE) 129 – Lake Toya (USA) 110 (Darshaan 133) [2017 103: 9.9d* 12m 9.9v³ 9.9g* Aug 19] strong filly: smart performer: won Prix Saint-Alary at Deauville (by 3 lengths from Vue Fantastique) in May and Prix de la Nonette at same course (by 2½ lengths from Onthemoonagain) in August: third in Nassau Stakes at Goodwood (1¾ lengths behind Winter) in August: stays 1¼m (well held in Oaks at Epsom at 1½m): acts on heavy going: front runner/races prominently. *Charlie Appleby* **118**

SO CELEBRE (GER) 4 ch.g. Peintre Celebre (USA) 137 – Saldennahe (GER) 105 (Next Desert (IRE) 122) [2017 86: 10.2m 10d 9.9g⁶ p12g² p12g² p12g Nov 7] workmanlike gelding: fairly useful handicapper: second at Kempton and Lingfield in October: stays 1½m: acts on polytrack, soft and good to firm going: tried in cheekpieces: fairly useful hurdler. *Ian Williams* **82**

SOCIALITES RED 4 ch.f. Sakhee's Secret 128 – Tipsy Girl 79 (Haafhd 129) [2017 74, a67: f5g t6m⁵ p6g³ t6g t5.1g⁶ t5g⁵ t5g⁴ t6g³ 6m⁴ 6m⁵ 6.1g* 5g³ 6.1g² 6.1g* 5f² 6.1s³ 6.1g Jul 8] compact filly: fair handicapper on turf, modest on all-weather: won at Nottingham (twice) in May: stays 6f: acts on polytrack, tapeta, firm and soft going: wears cheekpieces. *Scott Dixon* **77 a63**

SOCIETY LILLY (IRE) 2 b.f. (Feb 20) Society Rock (IRE) 126 – Lilly Be (IRE) 81 (Titus Livius (FR) 115) [2017 6s⁶ p6g Oct 4] £32,000Y: second foal: half-sister to a winner in Greece by Tagula: dam 5f/6f winner: well backed, well held in minor event/maiden, hampered/bumped in latter: clearly thought capable of better. *Hugo Palmer* **– p**

SOCIETY POWER (IRE) 2 b.c. (Feb 14) Society Rock (IRE) 126 – Yajala (Fasliyev (USA) 120) [2017 6.1s² 6d* p7d* Oct 6] €160,000 2-y-o: second foal: half-brother to useful Italian 5f (including at 2 yrs)/6f winner Evil Spell (by Dutch Art): dam, Italian 6f-7.5f winner, half-sister to useful Italian sprinter Dasami: fairly useful form: won maiden at Lingfield (by ½ length from Manthoor) in September and minor event at Chelmsford (by ¾ length from Barig Al Thumama) in October: stays 7f: open to further improvement. *William Haggas* **88 p**

SOCIETY PRINCE (IRE) 2 br.g. (Mar 1) Society Rock (IRE) 126 – Princess Atoosa (USA) (Gone West (USA)) [2017 6d⁴ p6g³ t6.1m⁵ Oct 28] £40,000Y: half-brother to numerous winners, including useful 2-y-o 7f winner Princess Sinead (by Jeremy) and 1m winner (stayed 11f) Elmfield Giant (by Giant's Causeway): dam unraced: fair form in minor events: remains with potential. *James Fanshawe* **70 p**

SOCIETY RANGER (IRE) 4 b.g. Bushranger (IRE) 119 – High Society Girl (IRE) (Key of Luck (USA) 126) [2017 46, a60: p10.7g p12g⁶ p12s⁶ p8g⁴ p10.7g t8.6g* 8m t8.6g* t8.6g⁴ 8.2s⁶ p8g p7g⁵ p7g⁵ p8g p10.7g⁴ p8g⁵ Dec 21] fair handicapper: won at Wolverhampton in March and June (apprentice): left Adrian McGuinness after second start: stays 10.5f: acts on polytrack, tapeta and good to soft going: wears headgear: tried in tongue tie. *S. M. Duffy, Ireland* **72**

SOCIETY RED 3 ch.g. Arcano (IRE) 122 – Idonea (CAN) (Swain (IRE) 134) [2017 82: 8g⁶ 10m³ 8.2f 10.5d⁴ 10.3m² 12g 9.9v 10.2g 9.9g* 10.3g 10.2d² Oct 27] plain gelding: fairly useful handicapper: won at Beverley (by neck from The Statesman) in September: second at York in July and Doncaster in October: stays 10.5f: acts on good to firm and good to soft going: front runner/races prominently. *Richard Fahey* **92**

SOCIETY'S DREAM (IRE) 2 ch.f. (Feb 28) Society Rock (IRE) 126 – Majestic Eviction (IRE) 94 (King's Theatre (IRE) 128) [2017 5m⁶ 5g⁴ 5m³ 7sᵖᵘ 6d* 7.2m⁵ t7.1g 6g⁴ 5s Oct 10] €12,000Y: fifth foal: half-sister to 3 winners, including winner up to 9.5f My Mistress (2-y-o 7f winner, by Mastercraftsman) and 2-y-o 5f winner Majestic Red (by Red **53**

Clubs): dam, untrustworthy 2-y-o 1m winner who stayed 1¼m, half-sister to smart 6f-7.5f winner Miss Sally: modest performer: won seller at Redcar in August: stays 6f: acts on good to firm and good to soft going. *K. R. Burke*

SOCIETY SECRET (IRE) 2 ch.c. (Apr 16) Society Rock (IRE) 126 – Bond Deal (IRE) **–**
104 (Pivotal 124) [2017 t6.1g t8.6g^{5} 7d Oct 27] well held in minor events/maiden. *Tom Dascombe*

SOCKS AND SHARES (IRE) 4 b.g. Elnadim (USA) 128 – Al Andalyya (USA) 65 **–**
(Kingmambo (USA) 125) [2017 t7.1g p6g 6m May 17] little impact in maidens. *Derek Shaw*

SO CRAFTY 2 ch.f. (Mar 27) Mastercraftsman (IRE) 129 – Mea Parvitas (IRE) 71 (Oasis **64 p**
Dream 129) [2017 7m Jun 29] 32,000Y: second foal: dam, maiden (stayed 1m), half-sister to smart winner up to 1¼m Foodbroker Fancy: 25/1, seventh in minor event at Newbury (4¼ lengths behind Time Change) in June: likely to improve. *Eve Johnson Houghton*

SOCRATES 3 b.g. Dick Turpin (IRE) 127 – Lisathedaddy 94 (Darnay 117) [2017 64: 8.1d **58**
8f^{6} 9.9m^{5} 8g p6d^{3} p7g Sep 26] leggy gelding: modest maiden: stays 7f: acts on polytrack: in blinkers last 2 starts: sometimes slowly away: sold 800 gns, sent to Spain. *Daniel Kubler*

SOD'S LAW 2 b.g. (Feb 6) Mayson 124 – Lawyers Choice 86 (Namid 128) [2017 p8d^{2} **80 p**
Dec 13] sixth foal: half-brother to 3 winners, including 7f/1m winner Dutch Law and ungenuine winner up to 7f Dutch Art Dealer (2-y-o 6f winner) (both by Dutch Art): dam 7f/1m winner: 50/1, second in minor event at Kempton (short head behind Rusper) in December, finishing strongly: better to come. *Hughie Morrison*

SOFIA'S ROCK (FR) 3 b.g. Rock of Gibraltar (IRE) 133 – Princess Sofia (UAE) **108**
(Pennekamp (USA) 130) [2017 92p: 11.7m^{4} 11.8g* 11.6d 11.9f* 12m 13g^{3} 12v 12d^{2} 13.9m Aug 26] good-topped gelding: useful handicapper: won at Leicester (by 10 lengths from Wefait) in April and Haydock (by 3 lengths from Stone The Crows) in May: third in Bahrain Trophy at Newmarket (1½ lengths behind Raheen House) in July: stays 13f: acts on firm and good to soft going: usually races close up. *Mark Johnston*

SOFT SAND 2 b.c. (Apr 8) Piccolo 121 – Ivory's Joy 109 (Tina's Pet 121) [2017 p6g Sep **–**
6] 50/1, well held in minor event at Kempton. *Peter Crate*

SOGHAN (IRE) 3 br.g. Cape Cross (IRE) 129 – Quiet Dream (USA) (Seattle Slew **95 p**
(USA)) [2017 56p: p12g^{4} p12g^{4} p12g^{3} t12.2d* Dec 9] useful performer: won maiden at Wolverhampton (by 2¾ lengths from Ocean of Love) in December: left John Gosden after second start: likely to stay beyond 1½m: acts on polytrack and tapeta: in tongue tie last 4 starts: likely to progress further. *Richard Hughes*

SO HI SOCIETY (IRE) 2 b.f. (Feb 15) Society Rock (IRE) 126 – Lilac Mist 81 **98**
(Spectrum (IRE) 126) [2017 5f^{3} 6.1d* 6g^{3} 6m^{6} 7d^{4} 6d^{4} 6.5d^{4} Sep 11] €5,000Y, £62,000 2-y-o: close-coupled filly: sixth foal: half-sister to useful 7f (including at 2 yrs)/1m winner Lilac Lace (by Captain Marvelous) and a winner in Italy by Red Clubs: dam, 1¼m winner, half-sister to smart performer up to 1½m Shagraan: useful performer: won minor event at Chepstow in June: fourth in Lowther Stakes at York (3¼ lengths behind Threading) on sixth outing: stays 7f: acts on good to firm and good to soft going: often races prominently. *Archie Watson*

SO HOITY TOITY 3 ch.f. Harbour Watch (IRE) 121 – Dignify (IRE) 105 (Rainbow **78**
Quest (USA) 134) [2017 80: 8m^{4} 8m 9.9d^{4} Jul 27] half-sister to 3 winners, including winner up to 1¼m Personify (2-y-o 6f winner, by Zafonic) and 6f-8.5f winner Declamation (by Shamardal): dam French 2-y-o 7f/1m winner: fair maiden: runner-up once at Deauville in 2016 for E. J. O'Neill: stays 1m: acts on good to firm going: often races prominently. *Hughie Morrison*

SOIE D'LEAU 5 b.g. Monsieur Bond (IRE) 120 – Silky Silence (High Chaparral (IRE) **103**
132) [2017 108: 5.2g^{4} 5s 5g^{5} 5d^{5} 5m^{2} t5g^{6} 5g^{4} 5d^{3} 5g^{3} 5.4d 5.5g 5s^{2} 5v* 5v^{5} 5g 5d^{2} Oct 28] strong gelding: useful handicapper: won at Leicester (by 1½ lengths from Smokey Lane) in September: also placed 5 times, including at Ascot (1½ lengths behind Jack Dexter) in July, Haydock (length behind Mayleaf Shine) in September and Doncaster (½ length behind Tomily) in October: stays 6f: acts on tapeta, good to firm and heavy going: tried in cheekpieces: usually leads. *Kristin Stubbs*

SOIESAUVAGE (FR) 6 b.m. Lauro (GER) 112 – Taffetas (FR) (Nikos 124) [2017 p13g^{4} **76 §**
21.6m t12.2g^{rr} Jul 11] second foal: half-sister to French 13f winner Sultan Silk (by Sulamani): dam winning chaser in France: fair performer: won minor event at Fontainebleau for Francois Doumen in 2016: left Gary Moore after first start: refused to race final outing: stays 15f: acts on soft going: in hood/tongue tie last 2 starts: one to treat with caution: modest hurdler. *Sophie Leech*

SO IT'S WAR (FR) 6 b.g. Orpen (USA) 116 – Impulsive Decision (IRE) 71 (Nomination 125) [2017 77: f8g^{5} t8g^{5} t7.1d^{6} t7.1g t8g^{3} t8.6g^{3} 7.5f 8.3m^{3} 7.2m^{5} 7.8g^{2} 8m 7.4d 9.9g^{5} 7.2v^{2} Oct 16] fair handicapper: stays 9f: acts on tapeta, good to firm and heavy going: wears headgear: sometimes slowly away, often races in rear: temperamental. *Keith Dalgleish* **74 §**

SOLAJAN (IRE) 3 ch.g. Lope de Vega (IRE) 125 – Undercover Glamour (USA) 75 (Kingmambo (USA) 125) [2017 t8.6g^{2} p10g* p10g p11g 10g Jul 24] rangy gelding: fair performer: won maiden at Lingfield in March: stays 1¼m: acts on polytrack: often in hood: usually races freely: sold £13,000, sent to Greece. *Ed Dunlop* **78**

SOLAR CROSS 3 b.g. Sea The Stars (IRE) 140 – Nantyglo 101 (Mark of Esteem (IRE) 137) [2017 76: 10.3m^{4} 11.9d* 13d^{4} 10.2g^{5} 11.4g* Oct 9] good-topped gelding: fairly useful handicapper: won at Doncaster in June and Windsor (by ¾ length from Zamperini) in October: stays 1½m: acts on good to firm and good to soft going: usually races close up, often travels strongly: sold 75,000 gns later in October. *Roger Charlton* **90**

SOLAR DEITY (IRE) 8 b.h. Exceed And Excel (AUS) 126 – Dawn Raid (IRE) 94 (Docksider (USA) 124) [2017 94, a109: p10g^{6} p10m^{pu} Feb 25] good-topped horse: smart performer at best: stayed 1¼m: acted on polytrack, tapeta and good to firm going: often wore headgear: dead. *Jane Chapple-Hyam* **105**

SOLAR FLAIR 5 b.g. Equiano (FR) 127 – Air Biscuit (IRE) 84 (Galileo (IRE) 134) [2017 109: 6g 6g p6g^{2} p6g* p6g^{5} t6s^{6} 6d Aug 5] sturdy gelding: useful handicapper: won at Kempton (by nose from Stellarta) in April: best at 6f: acts on polytrack, good to firm and good to soft going: has worn headgear: front runner/races prominently. *William Knight* **109**

SOLDIER BLUE (FR) 3 ch.g. Sepoy (AUS) 129 – Kocooning (IRE) (King's Best (USA) 132) [2017 8m t7.1g^{6} 8s^{3} 8d 8v^{6} Oct 9] fair maiden: left Charlie Appleby after first start: best effort at 1m: acts on soft going: tried in hood. *Brian Ellison* **76**

SOLDIER IN ACTION (FR) 4 ch.g. Soldier of Fortune (IRE) 131 – Ripley (GER) (Platini (GER) 126) [2017 111: 14g 11.9d^{6} 12m* 12m 11.8m^{2} 12.5g^{3} 14d* 13.9m 12.3v^{5} 11.8s^{6} p12g^{4} p16d* Nov 22] sturdy gelding: smart handicapper: won at Epsom (by 2 lengths from Eddystone Rock) in June, Goodwood (by head from Blakeney Point) in August and Kempton (by ½ length from Lord George) in November: second in Old Newton Cup at Haydock (2¼ lengths behind Dylan Mouth) in July: stays 2m: acts on polytrack, tapeta, good to firm and heavy going: front runner/races prominently: winning hurdler for Nicky Henderson. *Mark Johnston* **117**

SOLDIERS BAY (IRE) 2 b.c. (Feb 20) Acclamation 118 – Viletta (GER) 102 (Doyen (IRE) 132) [2017 7d^{6} 7s^{5} 8g^{4} Oct 7] fair form: in cheekpieces, best effort when fourth in minor event at Newmarket (2¼ lengths behind Just Brilliant) in October. *Brian Meehan* **78**

Qatar Summer Handicap, Goodwood—
the hardy Soldier In Action defies top weight, staying on strongly to collar Blakeney Point (diamonds on cap) and Getback In Paris in the final strides

SOLDIER'S GIRL (IRE) 3 br.f. Sepoy (AUS) 129 – Crystal Bull (USA) (Holy Bull **87**
(USA) 134) [2017 86: 8f^3 8g t8.6g 8g Aug 25] good-topped filly: fairly useful handicapper: third in minor event at Ascot in May: stays 1m: acts on polytrack, firm and good to soft going: tried in blinkers: sometimes slowly away: sold 6,000 gns, sent to Saudi Arabia. *Richard Hannon*

SOLDIER'S MINUTE 2 b.c. (May 15) Raven's Pass (USA) 133 – Hadba (IRE) 95 **90**
(Cape Cross (IRE) 129) [2017 6g^4 7.2m* 7g^4 Sep 15] 5,000Y, €85,000 2-y-o: sturdy colt: second foal: half-brother to 5f winner Little Kingdom (by Royal Applause): dam, UAE 9.5f winner, half-sister to useful 8.5f-1¼m winner Alive Alive Oh: fairly useful form: won minor event at Musselburgh (by 2½ lengths from Mi Capricho) in August: best effort when fourth in listed race at Doncaster (4 lengths behind Tip Two Win) in September: stays 7f. *Keith Dalgleish*

SOLDIER TO FOLLOW 2 b.c. (Apr 8) Soldier Hollow 121 – Nota Bene (GER) **80**
(Slickly (FR) 128) [2017 8.1m^2 7.8v^2 Sep 13] €25,000Y: fourth foal: half-brother to useful French 1¼m-1½m winner Not After Hours (by Wiener Walzer): dam, French 1½m/12.5f winner, half-sister to smart French performer up to 2m Now We Can: fairly useful form: better effort when second in maiden at Carlisle (¾ length behind Wax And Wane) in September. *Andrew Balding*

SOLENT MEADS (IRE) 3 ch.g. Intense Focus (USA) 117 – No Trimmings (IRE) 83 **79**
(Medecis 119) [2017 74: 10.2g 10.2f^6 8.1d 10d^4 11.4g^4 10d^6 t8.6g^2 p8g* p8g^4 p8g^6 t8.6g^4 Oct 27] tall gelding: fair handicapper: won at Kempton in September: stays 9.5f: acts on polytrack and tapeta: wears headgear: front runner/races prominently. *Daniel Kubler*

SOLE POWER 10 br.g. Kyllachy 129 – Demerger (USA) (Distant View (USA) 126) **110**
[2017 116: 6g 5g^4 5g^6 Feb 16] small, close-coupled gelding: high-class performer at best, winner of 5 Group 1 races, including King's Stand Stakes at Royal Ascot and Nunthorpe Stakes at York (both for second time) at 7 yrs: still showed smart form in 2017, raced only at Meydan: ¾-length fourth to Speed Hawk in handicap on second outing: best at 5f: acted on polytrack and any turf going: usually raced towards rear: retired. *Edward Lynam, Ireland*

SOLID JUSTICE (IRE) 6 b.g. Rock of Gibraltar (IRE) 133 – Burnin' Memories (USA) **43**
(Lit de Justice (USA) 125) [2017 57: 9.9m 9.9g p10g^5 10.2d Aug 23] good-topped gelding: modest handicapper, below form in 2017: stays 13.5f: acts on polytrack, fibresand, soft and good to firm going: has worn headgear, including in 2017. *Mark Pattinson*

SOLID MAN (JPN) 2 b.g. (Apr 17) Lord Kanaloa (JPN) 133 – Maruka Sawayaka (JPN) **51**
(Sunday Silence (USA)) [2017 5m^6 6g^5 6m Aug 16] good-quartered gelding: modest form when fifth in maiden at Leicester on second of 3 starts: left Ralph Beckett after. *David Simcock*

SOLILOQUY 2 b.f. (Apr 19) Dubawi (IRE) 129 – Dysphonia (AUS) 113 (Lonhro (AUS) **83 p**
128) [2017 7m^2 8s* Sep 9] second foal: half-sister to 1m winner Musical Terms (by Shamardal): dam 6.5f-1m winner, mainly in Australia: fairly useful form: won minor event at Ascot (by ½ length from Sheikha Reika) in September: likely to progress further. *Charlie Appleby*

SOLITARY SISTER (IRE) 3 br.f. Cockney Rebel (IRE) 127 – Sweet Afton (IRE) 98 **55 §**
(Mujadil (USA) 119) [2017 58p: 7m^6 p8s 7m 6s^5 8d^3 7d^4 7v^5 p7g^6 Oct 11] modest maiden: stays 1m: acts on soft going: wears headgear: has worn tongue tie: often races towards rear: temperamental. *Richard Spencer*

SOLO HUNTER 6 b.g. Sleeping Indian 122 – Night Owl 73 (Night Shift (USA)) [2017 **96**
96: 10g* 9.9m^6 10.1s^4 Sep 20] compact gelding: useful handicapper: won at Windsor (by neck from Getback In Paris) in May: stays 1¼m: acts on polytrack, good to firm and heavy going: wears headgear. *Martyn Meade*

SOLO MISSION 3 b.g. Sea The Stars (IRE) 140 – Lonely Ahead (USA) 97 (Rahy (USA) **94**
115) [2017 62: 10.1m^2 11.2g* 12m^4 12g* p12g^2 14s^3 Sep 16] fairly useful handicapper: won at Carlisle in June and Ripon (by 2½ lengths from Chocolate Box) in August: placed at Kempton and Musselburgh in September: stays 1¾m: acts on polytrack, soft and good to firm going: in headgear last 5 starts: sold 60,000 gns in October. *William Haggas*

SOLOMON'S BAY (IRE) 3 ch.g. Exceed And Excel (AUS) 126 – Gentle On My Mind **112**
(IRE) 100 (Sadler's Wells (USA) 132) [2017 91p: 7g 7d^4 7m* 7m 8s^4 7g^3 p6g* Oct 11] good-topped gelding: smart performer: won listed race at Epsom (by ¾ length from Seven Heavens) in June and minor event at Kempton (by neck from Blue de Vega) in October: stays 1m, effective at shorter: acts on polytrack, soft and good to firm going: tried in blinkers: sold 390,000 gns in November. *Roger Varian*

SOLVEIG'S SONG 5 b.m. Norse Dancer (IRE) 127 – Ivory Lace 96 (Atraf 116) [2017 **71**
80: p10g p12d p10m p11g^{2} 9.9g^{6} 9.9m^{6} 9.9g^{6} 10d p11g^{4} 9.1g^{5} 9.9d p10g p10g Dec 13]
lengthy, workmanlike mare: fair handicapper: stays 1½m: acts on polytrack, good to firm
and good to soft going: wears headgear. *Steve Woodman*

SOMEHOW (IRE) 4 b.f. Fastnet Rock (AUS) 127 – Alexandrova (IRE) 123 (Sadler's **120**
Wells (USA) 132) [2017 114: 8v^{2} 9.5s* 9m* 8s^{4} 10.5d^{2} May 28] compact filly: smart
performer: won listed race at Gowran in April and Dahlia Stakes at Newmarket (by 3¼
lengths from Elbereth) in May: 1¼ lengths second to Decorated Knight in Tattersalls Gold
Cup at the Curragh final start: stayed 1½m: acted on heavy and good to firm going: wore
headgear: waited with: reported in July to have been put down after suffering fractured leg.
Aidan O'Brien, Ireland

SOMEONE EXCITING 4 b.f. Notnowcato 128 – Quite Something 69 (Footstepsinthesand **67**
120) [2017 76: 7m^{4} 8m 6g 7.8v^{4} 7.8g^{3} 6.9s^{6} 8g^{4} 7g^{3} 6m^{3} 7s* 8v^{4} t7.1d Nov 4] fair
handicapper: won at Catterick in September: stays 7f: acts on polytrack, good to firm and
heavy going. *David Thompson*

SOMEPINK (IRE) 4 b.f. Lilbourne Lad (IRE) 111 – Cloonkeary (In The Wings 128) **39**
[2017 –: t9.5g t13.9f p10g f11.1g Nov 13] little form: tried in headgear. *Daniel Loughnane*

SOMES SOUND (IRE) 3 b.g. Big Bad Bob (IRE) 118 – Zapping (IRE) (Lycius (USA) **–**
124) [2017 p8g 8.3g 10g 12.1m May 31] no form, including in handicap. *Jane Chapple-Hyam*

SOMETHING BREWING (FR) 3 gr.g. Clodovil (IRE) 116 – Talwin (IRE) 99 **75**
(Alhaarth (IRE) 126) [2017 11.2s^{6} 7.2g^{5} 7.9m 7.6d 9s 8v Oct 9] fairly useful in France for
M. Palussiere at 2 yrs, largely well below that level in 2017: should stay beyond 1m: acts
on good to firm and good to soft going: often wears blinkers. *Iain Jardine*

SOMETHING LUCKY (IRE) 5 gr.g. Clodovil (IRE) 116 – Lucky Leigh 96 (Piccolo **65**
121) [2017 83: t5g p6g p6g p6g 6s^{5} t5.1g^{5} p6g 5.3d p6g 5.3s^{5} f5g^{2} t5.1g^{2} t5d^{5} Dec 16]
fairly useful handicapper, below form in 2017: left Kristin Stubbs after first start, Daniel
Steele after tenth: stays 6.5f: acts on all-weather and soft going: wears headgear: tried in
tongue tie. *Michael Appleby*

SOMETHINGTHRILLING 5 b.m. Makfi 130 – Something Exciting 114 (Halling **92**
(USA) 133) [2017 100: t8.6g^{3} p8g 8s 10.1s 8d p8g Nov 2] sturdy mare: useful performer,
below form in 2017: stays 1¼m: acts on polytrack, good to firm and good to soft going:
tried in tongue tie. *David Elsworth*

SOMEWHERE SECRET 3 ch.g. Sakhee's Secret 128 – Lark In The Park (IRE) 57 **85 §**
(Grand Lodge (USA) 125) [2017 80p: 5.6d^{5} 6.1g 6v^{4} 6d 6s^{3} 5d* 5v^{6} 5g 5g Nov 1] strong
gelding: fairly useful handicapper: won at Doncaster (by head from Suwaan) in September:
stays 6f: acts on good to firm and heavy going: wears headgear: temperamental.
Michael Mullineaux

SO MI DAR 4 b.f. Dubawi (IRE) 129 – Dar Re Mi 124 (Singspiel (IRE) 133) [2017 120: **111**
9.9v^{5} 9.9g^{5} Aug 20] rangy filly: smart performer: reportedly suffered from muscle enzyme
problem and not seen out in 2017 until August: fifth in Nassau Stakes at Goodwood (beaten
3½ lengths by Winter) and Prix Jean Romanet at Deauville (3¾ lengths behind Ajman
Princess): stays 10.5f: acts on soft going: often races freely. *John Gosden*

SOMNAMBULIST 3 b.g. Rip Van Winkle (IRE) 134 – Sister Moonshine 65 (Averti **76**
(IRE) 117) [2017 81: 8g 8.3m^{3} 9.2s^{2} 9.2s^{5} 8.3g^{3} 10g^{3} 12g^{5} 14s^{6} t12.4d^{4} t10.2g Oct 20] fair
maiden: stays 12.5f: acts on tapeta, soft and good to firm going: usually wears hood: often
starts slowly. *Keith Dalgleish*

SO MUCH FUN (IRE) 4 b.f. Iffraaj 127 – Seminole Lass (USA) (Indian Charlie (USA) **73**
126) [2017 75: p7g^{2} Jan 25] rather leggy filly: fair maiden: stays 1m: acts on polytrack, tapeta
and good to firm going: has worn headgear: often races prominently. *Ismail Mohammed*

SO MUCH WATER (FR) 5 gr.m. Le Havre (IRE) 124 – Minnie's Mystery (FR) **–**
(Highest Honor (FR) 124) [2017 –: 7g^{6} 10m Jun 19] well held in maidens. *John Berry*

SON CASTELLO (IRE) 3 b.g. Lilbourne Lad (IRE) 111 – Dancing Lauren (IRE) **–**
(Oratorio (IRE) 128) [2017 –: t7.1m p10g^{6} Feb 9] workmanlike gelding: little form: tried
in blinkers: often races freely. *Gary Moore*

SO NEAR SO FARHH 2 ch.f. (Feb 24) Farhh 131 – Protectress 110 (Hector Protector **56**
(USA) 124) [2017 8.1g 7v^{5} 7.9g Oct 13] 10,000Y: half-sister to several winners, including
useful 8.6f-1¾m winner Stand Guard (by Danehill) and 1½m winner (stays 2m) Arrowtown
(by Rail Link): dam 2-y-o 7f winner who stayed 1¼m: modest form when fifth at Chester
on second of 3 starts in minor events: should stay 1m. *Mick Channon*

SONG LIGHT 7 b.g. Echo of Light 125 – Blue Lullaby (IRE) 82 (Fasliyev (USA) 120) **89 §** [2017 81: 16s* p16d^{rr} Dec 13] tall, lengthy gelding: fairly useful handicapper: won at Goodwood (by 8 lengths from Taper Tantrum) in October: stays 2m: acts on polytrack and heavy going: temperamental (refused to race final start, as well as twice over hurdles in 2017). *Seamus Mullins*

SONG MAKER 3 b.f. Oasis Dream 129 – Please Sing 103 (Royal Applause 124) [2017 **96** 84: 8d^3 10.3v* p8g^3 t8.6g^2 8m^6 Oct 25] rather tall, well-made filly: useful performer: won maiden at Chester (by neck from Gakku) in September: second in handicap at Wolverhampton (nose behind Rinaria) in October: stays 10.5f: acts on polytrack, tapeta and heavy going: in headgear last 5 starts: often travels strongly. *Charlie Appleby*

SONG OF LOVE (IRE) 5 b.g. Fastnet Rock (AUS) 127 – Delicate Charm (IRE) (High **84** Chaparral (IRE) 132) [2017 82: p12g^3 p10.7g^3 p10.7g^2 p12g* p12g 11.9d 11.9m 12g^4 p12s^6 11.9g p12d f11.1g^4 f16.5g Dec 29] fairly useful handicapper: won at Dundalk (by neck from Duchessofflorence) in February: left Joseph Patrick O'Brien after fifth start: stays 1½m: acts on polytrack, fibresand and good to firm going: often wears cheekpieces: has worn tongue tie, including in 2017: sometimes slowly away. *Shaun Harris*

SONG OF SHADOWS 4 b.g. Invincible Spirit (IRE) 121 – Lyrique (IRE) (Iffraaj 127) **71** [2017 83p: 7m^5 p6s Jun 21] lengthy gelding: fair handicapper, lightly raced: stays 6f: acts on tapeta and good to firm going: tried in hood: in tongue tie last 3 starts. *Michael Wigham*

SONG OF SUMMER 2 ch.f. (Mar 25) Choisir (AUS) 126 – Height of Summer (IRE) 85 **70** (Alhaarth (IRE) 126) [2017 p6g 6m^6 6d^6 6d* 6s^2 6d^6 p7g^3 Oct 18] rather unfurnished filly: second foal: dam, 1¼m winner, half-sister to smart performer up to 1¼m I'm A Dreamer: fair performer: won nursery at Doncaster in July: stays 6f: acts on soft and good to firm going. *Archie Watson*

SONNETIST 3 b.g. Poet's Voice 126 – Society Rose 88 (Saddlers' Hall (IRE) 126) [2017 **83** 8.1d^4 11.6g^4 9.9g^4 9.9d^6 p11g^5 10g 10.2v^4 t12.2d^6 f11.1g* Dec 22] half-brother to several winners, including 9f winner Society Venue (by Where Or When) and 11f winner Ochos Rios (by Shirocco): dam 2-y-o 7f winner: fairly useful performer: won handicap at Southwell in December: left Richard Hannon after sixth start: stays 11f: acts on polytrack and fibresand, best turf form on good going. *David Evans*

SONNET ROSE (IRE) 3 ch.f. Poet's Voice 126 – Arabian Pearl (IRE) 83 (Refuse To **65** Bend (IRE) 128) [2017 p12g 12s p12g^3 p10g 10.1g p8g^6 p8g^3 f8.1g* f8.1g Dec 11] good-bodied filly: first foal: dam 7f/7.5f winner: fair handicapper: won at Southwell in December: stays 1½m: acts on polytrack and fibresand: in blinkers last 3 starts: usually in tongue tie: usually races close up. *Conrad Allen*

SON OF AFRICA 5 b.g. Equiano (FR) 127 – Generously Gifted (Sakhee (USA) 136) **100** [2017 105: 6m 5g^5 5g 6d^3 Aug 5] strong gelding: useful handicapper: third at Goodwood (1¾ lengths behind Scorching Heat) in August: stays 6f: acts on good to firm and good to soft going: tried in hood: often races in rear. *Henry Candy*

SON OF REST 3 b.c. Pivotal 124 – Hightime Heroine (IRE) 89 (Danetime (IRE) 121) **118** [2017 81p: 5v* 7g 5v* 5s^5 5s^3 5.8v^2 Oct 8] fourth foal: brother to a winner abroad: dam, 6f winner, half-sister to useful winner up to 1m Redolent: smart performer: won maiden at Cork (by 6½ lengths from Florida Times) in April and handicap at the Curragh (by 1¾ lengths from Patuano) in June: third in Flying Five Stakes at latter course (2¼ lengths behind Caravaggio) in September: best at 5f: acts on heavy going. *J. A. Stack, Ireland*

SON OF THE STARS 3 b.g. Delegator 125 – Michelle Shift (Night Shift (USA)) [2017 **104** 79p: p8g* 8m^2 8m Jun 22] strong, compact gelding: useful form: won handicap at Chelmsford (by 2 lengths from Prosper) in April: second in similar event at Newmarket (head behind Ronald R) in May: raced only at 1m: sent to Hong Kong, where renamed Beauty Energy. *Richard Hannon*

SOODA (USA) 2 b.f. (Mar 14) Street Cry (IRE) 130 – Nayarra (IRE) 105 (Cape Cross **60 p** (IRE) 129) [2017 t6.1g^5 Nov 18] second foal: half-sister to useful 5f-7f winner Lahore (by Elusive Quality): dam, 2-y-o 1m (Gran Criterium) winner, half-sister to very smart performer up to 1¼m Mars and Superlative Stakes winner Gustav Klimt: 11/4, fifth in minor event at Wolverhampton (6 lengths behind Two Weeks) in November: will improve. *Roger Varian*

SOOQAAN 6 bl.g. Naaqoos 117 – Dream Day (FR) (Spectrum (IRE) 126) [2017 67: f7g **56** t8.6g^3 t9.5g^4 t8s^5 8.5m^4 9m^5 8s^5 8.5d 8.5v t9.5g^4 t9.5g t8.6g* Dec 13] modest handicapper: **a63** won at Wolverhampton in December: stays 9.5f: acts on fibresand, tapeta, good to firm and heavy going. *Antony Brittain*

SOPHIE GRAY (IRE) 2 b.f. (Feb 7) Dansili 127 – Susan Stroman 83 (Monsun (GER) 124) [2017 p8g Dec 20] second foal: dam, 1¾m-2m winner, half-sister to high-class performer up to 1½m The Fugue (by Dansili): 9/2, very green when seventh in minor event at Lingfield (6¾ lengths behind Mewtow) in December: open to improvement. *John Gosden* **55 p**

SOPHIE P 4 b.f. Bushranger (IRE) 119 – Fountains Abbey (USA) 86 (Giant's Causeway (USA) 132) [2017 90: 8m* 10m^{2} 8g^{2} 8g 10.3d 10.5s 8s* 7.2s* Oct 9] useful handicapper: won at Ayr (by short head from Nicholas T) in May and Musselburgh (twice, by ½ length from Rousayan second occasion) in October: stays 1¼m: acts on good to firm and heavy going: sold 160,000 gns in December. *R. Mike Smith* **109**

SOPHISTICATED HEIR (IRE) 7 b.g. New Approach (IRE) 132 – My Girl Sophie (USA) 99 (Danzig (USA)) [2017 92: t6m^{5} f6g^{2} p7g^{3} p6g 5.5g 7m^{5} t7.2g^{2} 7d 7g t7.2g 6v^{4} p7g t6.1m t6.1g Nov 11] fairly useful handicapper: placed at Southwell in January and Lingfield (claimer) in February: below form after: left Michael Herrington after seventh start: stays 1¼m, raced mainly at shorter: acts on all-weather, good to firm and heavy going: has worn headgear, including in 2017. *Kevin Frost* **85 d**

SOQRAT 3 b.g. Paco Boy (IRE) 129 – Tamara Moon (IRE) 75 (Acclamation 118) [2017 8.2d 8s Oct 28] useful-looking gelding: behind in maidens: left Ed Dunlop after first start: in blinkers second one. *E. U. Hales, Ireland* **–**

SORORITY 2 ch.f. (Feb 16) Exceed And Excel (AUS) 126 – Belonging (Raven's Pass (USA) 133) [2017 p6g 6m^{3} 6g^{3} 7.2m^{2} 6g^{6} 7s p7g^{6} a8.5g^{2} a8.5g^{3} Dec 28] well-made filly: first foal: dam, useful French 10.5f winner, half-sister to very smart French performers around 1½m Poet Laureate and Desideratum: fair maiden: left Mark Johnston after seventh start: stays 7f: acts on viscoride and good to firm going. *Mlle L. Kneip, France* **69**

SO SHE THINKS (IRE) 2 b.f. (Mar 15) So You Think (NZ) 133 – Spice It Up (Authorized (IRE) 133) [2017 8s^{3} Oct 20] second foal: dam unraced half-sister to Oaks d'Italia winner Zanzibar: 13/1, third in claimer at Clairefontaine (3¼ lengths behind Tosen Hardi) in October, finishing strongly: should improve. *J. S. Moore* **74 p**

SOSIAN 2 b.f. (Mar 8) Showcasing 117 – Leonica 92 (Lion Cavern (USA) 117) [2017 t5s^{2} 5m^{2} 5s^{4} t6g Sep 22] half-sister to several winners, including useful 6f (including at 2 yrs) to 1m winner Rodrigo de Torres (by Bahamian Bounty) and 1¼m winner Dune Dancer (by Footstepsinthesand): dam, 1m winner, half-sister to smart winner up to 1½m Greek Envoy: fair form: should be suited by 6f. *Richard Fahey* **76**

SO SLEEK 3 b.f. Lawman (FR) 121 – So Silk (Rainbow Quest (USA) 134) [2017 72p: 10d^{3} 11.8d^{3} 12m^{2} 11.6d* 12g* 11.5d* Sep 21] compact filly: fairly useful performer: won maiden at Lingfield in July, and handicaps at Salisbury in August and Yarmouth (by ½ length from Sea Tide) in September: stays 1½m: acts on polytrack and good to soft going: usually responds generously to pressure. *Luca Cumani* **92**

SOTOMAYOR 2 b.c. (Mar 8) Havana Gold (IRE) 118 – No Frills (IRE) 62 (Darshaan 133) [2017 7g 7s^{5} 8v 7g t8.6g p8g^{2} p7d Nov 22] compact colt: fair maiden: stays 1m: acts on polytrack and soft going: tried in tongue tie: sometimes slowly away. *Richard Hannon* **68**

SOUL SILVER (IRE) 3 ch.f. Dragon Pulse (IRE) 114 – Free Lance (IRE) 69 (Grand Lodge (USA) 125) [2017 88: 8m 8v* 8g^{6} 8s 8d^{4} 8g t8.6d^{4} Dec 27] sturdy filly: useful handicapper: won at Newbury (by ¾ length from Lincoln Rocks) in July: stays 1m: acts on polytrack and any turf going: usually races nearer last than first. *David Simcock* **97**

SOULS IN THE WIND (IRE) 3 b.f. Fastnet Rock (AUS) 127 – Enchanted Evening (IRE) 105 (High Chaparral (IRE) 132) [2017 7g^{2} 7g^{4} 7g 5v^{6} 5.8g 6s* 8.3s 6s^{5} 6.1m 6v* Sep 5] second foal: half-sister to useful 2-y-o 5f winner Taexali (by Raven's Pass): dam, 7f/1m winner, half-sister to smart 5f-1m winner King Jock: fair performer: won maiden at Hamilton in June and handicap there in September: left S. Seemar after third start: stays 7f: acts on heavy going: tried in blinkers: temperamental: returned to UAE. *John Patrick Shanahan, Ireland* **77 §**

SOUND ADVICE 8 b.g. Echo of Light 125 – Flylowflylong (IRE) 74 (Danetime (IRE) 121) [2017 107: 8m 7.6d* 7.6g 7g 7d^{5} 7.6g Sep 2] good-topped gelding: useful handicapper: won at Chester (by 1¼ lengths from El Hayem) in May: best up to 1m: acts on polytrack, fibresand, firm and soft going: tried in blinkers/tongue tie. *Keith Dalgleish* **109**

SOUND AND SILENCE 2 b.c. (Mar 29) Exceed And Excel (AUS) 126 – Veil of Silence (IRE) (Elusive Quality (USA)) [2017 5m* 5m^{4} 5f* 6g 5m* 5d^{2} 6d* 5m^{2} 5f^{2} t6.1d^{4} Dec 9] strong, well-made colt: sixth foal: brother to useful 2-y-o 7f winner Silent Bullet, and half-brother to 5f winner Hushing (by Pivotal) and 2-y-o 8.6f winner Stay Silent (by Cape Cross): dam unraced half-sister to Racing Post Trophy winner Ibn Khaldun out of Irish **107**

1000 Guineas winner Gossamer: useful performer: won minor event at Newmarket in April, Windsor Castle Stakes at Royal Ascot (by neck from Roussel) in June, another listed race at York (by ½ length from Abel Handy) in August and Prix Eclipse at Maisons-Laffitte (by 3 lengths from Coeur de Beaute) in September: second in Prix d'Arenberg at Chantilly (½ length behind Rimini), Cornwallis Stakes at Newmarket (beaten neck by Abel Handy) and listed race at Del Mar (head behind Declarationofpeace): stays 6f: acts on firm and good to soft going: wears cheekpieces: often in tongue tie. *Charlie Appleby*

SOUND BAR 3 b.g. Oasis Dream 129 – Milford Sound (Barathea (IRE) 127) [2017 85p: 8d 10g² 10.3g⁶ 10.3d⁴ 10.1m Aug 28] good-topped, attractive gelding: fairly useful handicapper: second at Pontefract in June: stays 10.5f: acts on good to soft going: tried in headgear: not straightforward: sold 12,000 gns in November, sent to Saudi Arabia. *Ralph Beckett* **85**

SOUNDBYTE 12 b.g. Beat All (USA) 120 – Gloaming 74 (Celtic Swing 138) [2017 –: p12g p13.3g⁴ p14g⁵ Apr 6] angular gelding: modest handicapper: stays 2m: acts on polytrack, good to firm and heavy going: wears visor. *John Gallagher* **50**

SOURIYAN (FR) 6 b.g. Alhaarth (IRE) 126 – Serasana (Red Ransom (USA)) [2017 14v⁶ Aug 15] fairly useful in France for Jean-Claude Rouget in 2014, well held only start on Flat since: stays 1½m: acts on viscoride and soft going: tried in blinkers: fairly useful hurdler/chaser. *Peter Bowen* **–**

SOUTHDOWN LAD (IRE) 4 b.g. Lilbourne Lad (IRE) 111 – Elizabelle (IRE) 63 (Westerner 130) [2017 104: p11g 11.9d⁴ 14g⁶ Jun 10] good-topped gelding: useful handicapper: stays 1½m: acts on soft going: often races towards rear: sold £28,000 in September, sent to Greece. *William Knight* **101**

SOUTHERN BELLE (IRE) 4 b.f. Aqlaam 125 – Areyaam (USA) 75 (Elusive Quality (USA)) [2017 99: p5g⁴ 5m⁴ 6m* 6g⁴ 6m² 6.1g⁵ 6g³ 6v² 6v Sep 21] tall filly: useful handicapper: won at Ripon (by ½ length from The Feathered Nest) in May: second at York (½ length behind Eartha Kitt) in June and Hamilton (neck behind Guishan) in September: stays 6f: acts on good to firm and heavy going: often starts slowly/races freely. *Robert Cowell* **103**

SOUTHERN STATES 4 b.g. Medaglia d'Oro (USA) 129 – Little Belle (USA) 116 (A P Indy (USA) 131) [2017 74: p15.8g⁵ p16g⁴ p16s⁴ p16g⁴ p16d⁵ 16.3s³ 14.2v p16g Nov 7] good-topped gelding: fair maiden: stays 2m: acts on polytrack and viscoride: often in headgear in 2017: usually races prominently. *Lydia Richards* **69**

SOUTHPARK 2 b.g. (Apr 2) Epaulette (AUS) 126 – Spirit of Success 68 (Invincible Spirit (IRE) 121) [2017 7.2m 6.9v³ 7.2s² Oct 9] modest form: best effort when second in minor event at Musselburgh (3¼ lengths behind Han Solo Berger) in October: sold 16,000 gns, sent to Italy. *Richard Fahey* **64**

SOUTH SEA BELLE (IRE) 3 ch.f. New Approach (IRE) 132 – South Atlantic (USA) (Stormy Atlantic (USA)) [2017 65p: 7m⁴ 7m⁴ 6g p8g p8g 11.4m Oct 16] rather unfurnished filly: fair maiden: best effort at 7f: acts on good to firm going: tried in cheekpieces/tongue tie: sometimes slowly away: sold 6,000 gns, sent to Greece. *David Menuisier* **70**

SOUTH SEAS (IRE) 3 ch.g. Lope de Vega (IRE) 125 – Let It Be Me (USA) (Mizzen Mast (USA) 121) [2017 108: t8s⁵ 8d May 14] tall gelding: useful performer at 2 yrs: below best in 2017, in Poule d'Essai des Poulains at Deauville second outing: subsequently gelded: stays 7f: acts on soft and good to firm going. *Andrew Balding* **91**

SOUTHVIEW LADY 5 b.m. Misu Bond (IRE) 114 – Salalah 62 (Lion Cavern (USA) 117) [2017 –: t10.2g 8.3g 8g 10d Oct 20] maiden: no form since 2015: has worn headgear. *Sean Regan* **–**

SOVEREIGN BOUNTY 5 ch.g. Bahamian Bounty 116 – Sovereign Abbey (IRE) 68 (Royal Academy (USA) 130) [2017 87: 8m 8.5g⁵ 8m* 8m⁵ 7.4d³ 8d 8d 7.4m Aug 27] fairly useful handicapper: awarded race at Doncaster in June: stayed 8.5f: acted on good to firm and good to soft going: tried in hood: often raced prominently: dead. *Jedd O'Keeffe* **88**

SOVEREIGN DEBT (IRE) 8 gr.g. Dark Angel (IRE) 113 – Kelsey Rose 97 (Most Welcome 131) [2017 118: 8g* p10g³ p8g* 8.1d* 8.5m* 8g⁵ 8.8m³ 8.2s⁴ 8d⁴ 9m⁴ Oct 14] **117**

Good Friday has long been a contentious day when it comes to betting or horse racing. Church groups were up in arms when High Street betting shops opened on Good Friday for the first time in 2008 (following a tweak to the UK's gambling laws), and there was also plenty of resistance within racing itself to the BHA's move in 2014 to finally allow racing to be staged on Good Friday. Lambourn and Middleham both had long-established Open Days and jockeys and stable staff bemoaned losing an increasingly rare day off. The centre-piece to Good Friday racing is All-Weather Championships Finals Day at Lingfield (there are also meetings elsewhere). Finals Day has been a qualified success, going some way to achieving its stated aim to 'improve the quality of and reputation of all-weather racing.' Could the All-Weather Championships be improved, though? The polytrack at Lingfield, for example, isn't everyone's favourite track and, given the different surfaces used elsewhere, it is perhaps worth changing the venue for Finals Day from year to year—as with the Open Golf championship, for example. The relatively remote Southwell (fibresand) probably isn't equipped to host a bumper crowd, but there would be no such qualms at either Kempton (polytrack) or Newcastle (tapeta), whilst Chelmsford (polytrack) is arguably the fairest track of them all for the horses. It is Good Friday itself which remains the most fundamental issue, however, and the criticism is not based on religious grounds. Because of the vagaries of the calendar, All-Weather Championships Finals Day is a movable feast which often falls after the turf season has started. The 2016 Finals Day, for example, took place four weeks earlier than that inaugural 2014 meeting, and the 2017 renewal fell a fortnight after the turf season's traditional curtain-raiser, the Lincoln meeting at Doncaster. Ideally, All-Weather Championships Finals Day should take place the weekend before Doncaster's Lincoln fixture (which should always start the turf season as it traditionally has done).

In many ways, Sovereign Debt has been the poster horse for the All-Weather Championships, being a smart performer who ordinarily would have been kept for the turf, in the days before opportunities arose for better horses through the BHA's all-weather initiative. His win in the Sunbets All-Weather Mile Championships Conditions Stakes at Lingfield in April (worth £93,375 to the winner) certainly wasn't coming out of turn either, as he had been an unlucky loser when runner-up in the last two renewals of the same race. In the latest season, Sovereign Debut got his bad luck out of the way on his prep run, when he was hampered before coming third in the listed Magnolia Stakes at Kempton a fortnight earlier. Sent off 8/1 fourth choice in a field of twelve at Lingfield, Sovereign Debt got first run on runner-up Nimr thanks to a good tactical ride from James Sullivan (who retained the mount for the remainder of 2017), though he was eventually all out to hold off that fast-finishing rival by a neck. Another Richard Fahey-trained runner pushed him closest on his next two starts too, with Gabrial chasing home Sovereign Debt in both the bet365 Mile Stakes at Sandown (where the winner received another good ride) later in April and the Investec Diomed Stakes at Epsom in June. Although the winning margin was narrower in the latter (a neck instead of half a length), Sovereign Debt's hat-trick-winning performance in the Group 3 at Epsom actually represented stronger form than his Group 2 success at Sandown. He was conceding weight all round because of his Group 2 penalty and kept on gamely after being produced to lead over a furlong out, again enjoying the run of things compared to some of his beaten rivals (third-placed Oh This Is Us was arguably an unlucky

Sunbets All-Weather Mile Championships Conditions Stakes, Lingfield— the grey Sovereign Debt beats the fast-finishing Nimr (dark cap/breastgirth, left) and Salateen (right) to make it third time lucky in this race

bet365 Mile Stakes, Sandown—a pair of eight-year-olds dominate the finish, Sovereign Debt holding Gabrial to follow up his Lingfield success, with Jallota (quartered cap) back in third

loser). That proved to be the end of Sovereign Debt's winning in 2017 but he largely acquitted himself well during the remainder of the campaign, making the frame four more times in Group 3 or Group 2 company, finishing a good fourth to Monarchs Glen in the Darley Club Stakes at Newmarket on the final occasion.

It reflected very well on Sovereign Debt that he could still run up to his best at Newmarket in mid-October in another busy season which had begun way back in February, with victory in the Group 2 Irish Thoroughbred Marketing Cup at Doha, where he overcame interference a furlong and a half out to land the £92,000 first prize. On this trip to Qatar, Sovereign Debt proved to be the final runner sent out by his former trainer David 'Dandy' Nicholls, who relinquished his licence under a cloud in early-March and then passed away, aged just sixty-one, in June (just twenty-four hours after Sovereign Debt's Diomed win) following a lengthy illness. Nicholls saddled over 1,200 winners and earned the tag 'sprint king', his record including numerous wins in valuable handicaps such as the Ayr Gold Cup (six) and Stewards' Cup (three). Nicholls once ran a record twelve horses in a Stewards' Cup consolation handicap, but he enjoyed plenty of success at pattern level too, the highlight probably being his one, two in the 2002 July Cup with Continent (who also won that year's Prix de l'Abbaye) and Bahamian Pirate. Both Continent and Bahamian Pirate were themselves former Ayr Gold Cup winners, the latter becoming the oldest winner of a Group 1 in Britain when successful in the 2004 Nunthorpe at the age of nine. Sovereign Debt had been the stable star at the Tall Trees yard near Thirsk in recent years, Nicholls having bought the gelding out of Michael Bell's stable for 145,000 guineas after his four-year-old campaign, though he missed the whole of the following season before finally making his debut for Nicholls early in 2015. Nicholls rode horses with vastly lower price tags than that when a hard-grafting jockey, notching up over 400 wins in a career best known for his association with the prolific winners Soba and Chaplins Club. Both of those were trained by the late David Chapman (another renowned for his prowess with sprinters), so it was fitting that Chapman's granddaughter Ruth Carr took over the care of Sovereign Debt after his Qatar win—'It's great for a small yard like ours to have the chance to train a horse like him,' was her immediate reaction. Carr made good use of her new inmate, Sovereign Debt's lucrative trips to Sandown and Epsom (Carr's first successes at pattern level) helping the yard to its best season, both in terms of prize money and number of wins.

Sovereign Debt (IRE) (gr.g. 2009)	Dark Angel (IRE) (gr 2005)	Acclamation (b 1999)	Royal Applause
			Princess Athena
		Midnight Angel (gr 1994)	Machiavellian
			Night At Sea
	Kelsey Rose (b 1999)	Most Welcome (ch 1984)	Be My Guest
			Topsy
		Duxyana (b 1990)	Cyrano de Bergerac
			Sarong

A compact gelding, Sovereign Debt is the sixth foal out of the useful winning sprinter Kelsey Rose and much her best representative to date. The David Evans-trained Kelsey Rose, who had form at up to a mile, ran thirty-one times at two and three, so it perhaps isn't surprising that such durability has been passed on to her offspring. Sovereign Debt isn't the only one who has stood up well to a very busy workload, as his half-brother With Approval (by Approve) has raced thirty-seven times during the past three seasons, winning four times at seven furlongs or a mile. Kelsey Rose has visited Dark Angel three more times, producing three sisters to Sovereign Debt, including her latest as-yet-unnamed foal. The oldest of this trio, Angelic Guest, was unplaced in five starts for Mick Channon before fetching 150,000 guineas in December when sold as a broodmare prospect (in foal to Zoffany). Her year-younger sister Sorelle Delle Rose (a €350,000 yearling) had already done her bit for the family name, having won twice (at six and seven furlongs) for Dermot Weld earlier in 2017, showing useful form. The best of Sovereign Debt's siblings, however, was the 2010 Fred Darling Stakes winner Puff (by Camacho), herself now a broodmare. The next one likely to see a racecourse is the 2016 colt Lyndon B (by Charm Spirit), who was sold for €70,000 as a yearling in the autumn. Speed tends to be the overriding theme further back in this family tree—grandam Duxyana, for example, was an unraced half-sister to the dam of smart sprinter Indian Rocket—so Sovereign Debt clearly stays better than might have been expected, having placed form at up to ten furlongs. An admirably consistent sort, Sovereign Debt is versatile with regards to ground (acts on polytrack, tapeta, soft and good to firm) and is a credit to his connections, past and present. *Ruth Carr*

SOVEREIGN DUKE (GER) 2 b.c. (Mar 30) Jukebox Jury (IRE) 123 – Shadow Queen (GER) (Lando (GER) 128) [2017 p8d Dec 13] 50,000Y: fifth foal: half-brother to useful German winner up to 1m Survey (2-y-o 6f winner, by Big Shuffle) and smart German 1¼m-1½m winner Shadow Sadness (by Soldier Hollow): dam German 1½m winner: 7/1, seventh in minor event at Kempton (5 lengths behind Rusper) in December: will be suited by 1¼m+: should improve. *Henry Candy* **72 p**

SOVEREIGN KATIE (IRE) 2 b.f. (Feb 24) Society Rock (IRE) 126 – Dane Thyme (IRE) (Danetime (IRE) 121) [2017 6g 5m 6v Oct 21] €10,000F, £10,000Y: compact filly: fifth foal: half-sister to 3 winners, including 1m/8.6f winner High Time Too (by High Chaparral): dam unraced half-sister to useful winner up to 7f Compton Arrow: no form. *Ollie Pears* **–**

SOVEREIGN STATE 2 b.g. (Mar 21) Compton Place 125 – One Night In May (IRE) 50 (Choisir (AUS) 126) [2017 5.2m⁵ 5v³ 5v 5.1d⁵ Oct 23] modest form: raced only at 5f. *Robert Cowell* **64**

SOVRANO DOLCE (IRE) 4 b.f. Roderic O'Connor (IRE) 119 – Tartufo Dolce (IRE) 73 (Key of Luck (USA) 126) [2017 64: p7d⁵ p8g⁶ Sep 7] modest form only start on turf at 3 yrs, standout effort: best effort at 8.5f: acts on good to firm going. *Mike Murphy* **–**

SPACE ARTIST (IRE) 7 b.g. Captain Marvelous (IRE) 114 – Dame Laura (IRE) 100 (Royal Academy (USA) 130) [2017 65: 5m Apr 27] sturdy gelding: fairly useful at best, well held sole outing in 2017: stays 6f: acts on all-weather, firm and good to soft going: has worn visor/tongue tie: usually races nearer last than first. *Nigel Tinkler* **–**

SPACE WAR 10 b.g. Elusive City (USA) 117 – Princess Luna (GER) (Grand Lodge (USA) 125) [2017 76: f6g f8s t8d⁵ p6g* p6g³ p7d⁴ p7g⁴ t6g* 5m³ 6m⁵ 5.9g 5g 7.8m 5s⁵ p6d⁴ Sep 21] useful-looking gelding: fair handicapper: won at Lingfield in February and Wolverhampton (apprentice) in April: best up to 7.5f nowadays: acts on all-weather, soft and good to firm going: has worn blinkers: usually wears tongue tie: sometimes slowly away: inconsistent. *Michael Easterby* **70 a76**

SPAIN BURG (FR) 3 b.f. Sageburg (IRE) 123 – Spain Blues (FR) (Anabaa Blue 122) [2017 110: 7d⁵ 6g Aug 20] useful performer, won 4 times at 2 yrs: ran in listed races in 2017, fifth at Maisons-Laffitte then well held at Pontefract (reportedly struck into on left hind): stays 7f: acts on soft and good to firm going: sold 650,000 gns in December. *N. Clement, France* **99**

SPANGLED 5 ch.m. Starspangledbanner (AUS) 128 – Zykina (Pivotal 124) [2017 110: 7g 8g Oct 7] tall mare: smart performer, well below best both starts in 2017: stays 7f: acts on good to firm going. *Roger Varian* **–**

SPANISH BEAUTY 3 b.f. Paco Boy (IRE) 129 – Basque Beauty 96 (Nayef (USA) 129) [2017 48: 9.9m⁵ 9.9m⁵ 12d Aug 4] modest maiden: best effort at 1¼m: acts on good to firm going: sometimes slowly away, often races towards rear. *Ollie Pears* **51**

SPANISH CITY 4 ch.g. Exceed And Excel (AUS) 126 – Annabelle's Charm (IRE) 107 (Indian Ridge 123) [2017 99p: 6m⁴ Jun 24] useful handicapper, below best only start in 2017: stays 6f: acts on tapeta, best turf form on good going. *Roger Varian* **83**

SPANISH HISTORY (USA) 3 b.g. Street Cry (IRE) 130 – Infanta (IRE) 65 (Cape Cross (IRE) 129) [2017 8s² 8.1m* Oct 16] good-bodied gelding: third foal: brother to a winner in Belgium: dam, maiden who stayed 1¼m, half-sister to smart French 9f/9.5f winner Utrecht: fairly useful form: won maiden at Windsor (by neck from Paradise Lake) in October. *Seamus Durack* **84**

SPANISH MANE (IRE) 2 b.f. (Jan 21) Havana Gold (IRE) 118 – Kiva (Indian Ridge 123) [2017 6d t6.1g⁶ t5.1g⁶ Dec 2] €30,000F: half-sister to numerous winners, including useful 5f (including at 2 yrs) winner Annie Beach (by Redback) and 6f/7f winner Shootingsta (by Fast Company): dam unraced: modest form when sixth at Wolverhampton on second of 3 starts in minor events. *Richard Fahey* **50**

SPANISH STAR (IRE) 2 b.g. (May 9) Requinto (IRE) 109 – Rancho Star (IRE) (Soviet Star (USA) 128) [2017 6g⁴ 6d² 5.7d³ 5s³ p5g³ Sep 26] good-bodied gelding: fair maiden: best effort at 5f: acts on polytrack and good to soft going: usually races freely. *Patrick Chamings* **71**

SPANISH STEPS (IRE) 3 b.c. Galileo (IRE) 134 – Turbulent Descent (USA) 122 (Congrats (USA) 118) [2017 69: 10m³ 10.1m² 9.5g* 11.9g 12g* 11.9d⁵ 12d⁵ Sep 9] rather leggy colt: first foal: dam US Grade 1 7f and (including at 2 yrs) 8.5f winner: smart performer: won maiden at Gowran (by 10 lengths from Dawn Choir) in June and Ballyroan Stakes at Leopardstown (by ½ length from Johannes Vermeer) in August: stays 1½m: acts on good to firm and good to soft going: front runner/races prominently: has joined Liam Howley in Australia. *Aidan O'Brien, Ireland* **112**

SPANISH TENOR (IRE) 3 ch.c. Lope de Vega (IRE) 125 – Devious Soprano (IRE) 64 (Orpen (USA) 116) [2017 98: 8d⁶ 8g⁴ 7d* 7.5v³ 8.5s⁵ 7s³ Oct 28] third foal: dam maiden half-sister to smart 9.5f-1¾m winner Midnight Soprano: useful performer: won minor event at Leopardstown (by length from Oh Grace) in June: third in Concorde Stakes at Tipperary (2¼ lengths behind Psychedelic Funk) and listed race at Leopardstown (2 lengths behind Larchmont Lad) in October: stays 7.5f: acts on heavy going. *Timothy Doyle, Ireland* **106**

SPARE PARTS (IRE) 3 b.g. Choisir (AUS) 126 – Grandel (Owington 123) [2017 p6g p6g p6g 6.1m⁴ 6d⁴ 7m 6g⁴ 7.4g² 7.1g 7m⁴ 8g p8g³ Dec 30] modest maiden: left Charles Hills after eleventh start: stays 1m: acts on polytrack, good to firm and good to soft going: front runner/races prominently. *Phil McEntee* **60**

SPARKALOT 3 br.c. Bated Breath 125 – Three Wrens (IRE) 99 (Second Empire (IRE) 124) [2017 p6g⁴ p6g* 6.1g⁶ p6s* Jun 14] 30,000F, 47,000Y, 120,000 2-y-o: well-made colt: half-brother to several winners, including useful 11f-2m winner Courtesy Call (by Manduro) and 1m-1¼m winner You'reagoat (by Notnowcato): dam 1m winner (including at 2 yrs): fairly useful form: won maiden at Kempton in April and handicap there (by 1¾ lengths from Cajmere) in June: raced only at 6f. *Simon Dow* **89**

SPARKLE 3 b.f. Oasis Dream 129 – Gemstone (IRE) 108 (Galileo (IRE) 134) [2017 77: 6m p7g 7d⁴ Jul 11] compact filly: fair maiden: stays 7f: acts on polytrack and good to firm going: tried in hood. *Ed Dunlop* **66**

SPARKLING COSSACK 3 ch.f. Famous Name 124 – Eleanor Eloise (USA) 61 (Minardi (USA) 119) [2017 –: p6g³ p6f⁴ t6m p7g 7d⁴ t7.1g t7.2g⁶ Jun 26] modest maiden: stays 7f: acts on polytrack and good to soft going: in cheekpieces last 3 starts. *Jeremy Gask* **50**

SPARK OF WAR (IRE) 2 b.c. (May 5) Declaration of War (USA) 128 – Acts of Grace (USA) 109 (Bahri (USA) 125) [2017 8.2v⁴ 8v³ t7.1d⁶ Oct 24] fair form when third at Ayr on second of 3 starts in minor events: will stay further than 1m. *Keith Dalgleish* **67**

SPARK PLUG (IRE) 6 b.g. Dylan Thomas (IRE) 132 – Kournikova (SAF) (Sportsworld (USA) 121) [2017 120: 9m³ 9.9g² 7.9m⁵ 9.9m* 10m² 9m³ 10d⁶ Nov 4] smallish gelding: smart performer: won listed race at Sandown (by 1¾ lengths from Kidmenever) in July: placed in similar race at Goodwood (nose behind First Sitting) in May, Winter Hill Stakes at Windsor (1¼ lengths behind Fabricate) in August and Darley Stakes at Newmarket (2¼ lengths behind Monarchs Glen) in October: stays 1¼m: acts on good to firm and good to soft going: usually wears headgear. *Brian Meehan* **116**

SPARTE QUERCUS (IRE) 4 b.g. Canford Cliffs (IRE) 133 – Khaizarana 90 (Alhaarth (IRE) 126) [2017 10g t10.2s⁵ 10m⁵ 11.9m* 13.4d 12d³ 10g* 9.9g² 10.1v² 10m³ t12.2g⁵ Oct 27] €65,000Y, 300,000 2-y-o: lengthy gelding: half-brother to several winners, including French winner up to 12.5f Eos Quercus (2-y-o 1¼m winner, by Arcano) and 1m winner Maghya (by Mujahid), both useful: dam 7f winner who stayed 1¼m: fairly useful handicapper: won at Doncaster in July and Chepstow (by 4½ lengths from Angelical) in September: placed after at Sandown, Epsom and Windsor: stays 1½m: acts on tapeta and good to firm going. *Ed Dunlop* **91**

SPATIAL 3 b.f. New Approach (IRE) 132 – Spacious 119 (Nayef (USA) 129) [2017 99: p8g^{5} Jun 1] well-made filly: useful 7f winner at 2 yrs, last in handicap sole outing in 2017. *Sir Michael Stoute* **88**

SPEAK IN COLOURS 2 gr.c. (Mar 11) Excelebration (IRE) 133 – Maglietta Fina (IRE) 95 (Verglas (IRE) 118) [2017 6.1v^{3} 6s* 6d* Oct 28] close-coupled colt: first foal: dam, 5f and (in Italy at 2 yrs) 7f winner, half-sister to very smart winner up to 10.4f Tullius: useful form: won minor event at Ascot (by 1½ lengths from Lady Dancealot) in September and listed race at Doncaster (by ½ length from Mutaaqeb) in October: raced only at 6f: has joined Joseph Patrick O'Brien: will go on improving. *Marco Botti* **108 p**

SPECIAL CODE (IRE) 5 b.g. Iffraaj 127 – Najmati (Green Desert (USA) 127) [2017 49: 6s p5g 5.1d Oct 23] modest performer, lightly raced and below form since 2015: often wears tongue tie. *Paddy Butler* **–**

SPECIALIST (IRE) 3 b.g. Mastercraftsman (IRE) 129 – My Lass 91 (Elmaamul (USA) 125) [2017 p8d^{5} t12.2m^{2} t9.5g^{2} p10g* 10m 12d^{3} Jun 12] €26,000Y: angular gelding: half-brother to several winners, including very smart winner up to 1¼m Mac Love (2-y-o 5f winner, by Cape Cross) and useful winner up to 10.4f Donny Rover (2-y-o 6f winner, by Excellent Art): dam 1½m winner: fairly useful performer: won maiden at Chelmsford (by 6 lengths from Gee Sixty Six) in March: third in handicap at Pontefract in June: stays 1½m: acts on polytrack, tapeta and good to soft going: front runner/races prominently: sold only £800 in November. *Mark Johnston* **82**

SPECIALITY (FR) 3 b.f. Lawman (FR) 121 – Pride (FR) 128 (Peintre Celebre (USA) 137) [2017 8g^{2} 10.4s^{5} 9.9g^{5} p12.4f 14.9s 10.2v^{5} f12.1g^{3} Nov 28] half-sister to several winners, notably very smart French 9.5f-1½m winner One Foot In Heaven (by Fastnet Rock): dam 1¼m-1½m winner, including Champion Stakes: fair maiden: left A. de Royer Dupre after fifth start: stays 1½m: acts on soft going: in blinkers last 2 starts. *Ralph Beckett* **79**

SPECIAL MISSION 2 b.f. (Feb 25) Declaration of War (USA) 128 – Soft Morning 108 (Pivotal 124) [2017 p6g May 24] well-grown filly: fifth foal: half-sister to 3 winners, including useful performer up to 1½m Savanna La Mar (2-y-o 7f winner, by Curlin) and useful French performer up to 1m So In Love (2-y-o 6f winner, by Smart Strike): dam 7f-1¼m winner: 20/1, seventh in minor event at Kempton (3¾ lengths behind Di Fede) in May, finishing with running left: will stay 7f: should improve. *Sir Mark Prescott Bt* **57 p**

SPECIAL PURPOSE (IRE) 2 b.f. (Mar 29) Scat Daddy (USA) 120 – Pussycat Lips (IRE) 101 (Holy Roman Emperor (IRE) 125) [2017 5d* 5d* 6d^{5} 6g^{3} 7m Oct 13] £90,000Y: small, close-coupled filly: first foal: dam 2-y-o 8.5f winner: useful performer: won minor events at Lingfield and Beverley in July: third in Dick Poole Fillies' Stakes at Salisbury (neck behind Anna Nerium) in September: stays 6f: acts on good to soft going: sent to USA. *William Haggas* **98**

SPECIAL RELATION (IRE) 3 b.g. Casamento (IRE) 118 – Sindiyma (IRE) 98 (Kalanisi (IRE) 132) [2017 77p: t8.6m^{2} p8g^{2} 12d* Jun 12] good-topped gelding: useful performer: won handicap at Pontefract (by 2 lengths from Tor) in June: stays 1½m: acts on polytrack and good to soft going: should progress further. *Hughie Morrison* **95 p**

SPECIAL SEASON 4 ch.g. Lope de Vega (IRE) 125 – Keep Dancing (IRE) 77 (Distant Music (USA) 126) [2017 97: p8g a6.5g^{2} f7g^{4} p8g^{5} 8.5f a7f 6.5f 8f 8.5g^{5} Dec 30] well-made gelding: useful performer: second in minor event at Saint Moritz (neck behind Footprintinthesand) in February: left Jamie Osborne after fourth start, Tim Yakteen after eighth: stays 1¼m: acts on polytrack, snow and soft going: sometimes wears headgear. *Steve Specht, USA* **95**

SPECIALV (IRE) 4 br.f. Big Bad Bob (IRE) 118 – Montbretia 105 (Montjeu (IRE) 137) [2017 80: f6d 6g^{4} 7g 7.4m 6.1g 6s^{3} 6g^{5} 6d^{3} 6g* 6.1g^{6} 6.9v 6.1d Oct 4] fair handicapper: won at Haydock in August: stays 8.5f, effective at shorter: acts on fibresand and soft going: wears headgear: usually races towards rear. *Brian Ellison* **76**

SPECTRE (FR) 4 ch.f. Siyouni (FR) 122 – Inez (Dai Jin 123) [2017 118: 8g 7s^{4} 8f^{4} Jun 20] well-made filly: smart performer: best effort in 2017 when 2½ lengths fourth to Ribchester in Queen Anne Stakes at Royal Ascot on final start: stayed 1m: acted on firm and soft going: often raced towards rear: visits Galileo. *M. Munch, France* **117**

SPECULATIVE BID (IRE) 6 b.g. Excellent Art 125 – Barzah (IRE) 98 (Darshaan 133) [2017 7s 8s 7d* p7.5g^{6} Dec 16] angular gelding: smart handicapper: won at Doncaster (by neck from Shady McCoy) in November: stays 1m: acts on polytrack and any turf going. *David Elsworth* **117**

SPECULATOR 5 gr.g. Bahamian Bounty 116 – Swift Dispersal 87 (Shareef Dancer (USA) 135) [2017 76: p11g f8g t9.5g t12.2g May 30] fair at best, no form in 2017: wears cheekpieces: tends to find little. *John Butler* –

SPEED COMPANY (IRE) 4 b.g. Fast Company (IRE) 126 – Trentini (IRE) (Singspiel (IRE) 133) [2017 108: 10.1g^{5} 10.3d 10.1m 10g* 10m^{5} 9.9g 10.3m^{5} 10.3g Oct 14] close-coupled gelding: useful handicapper: won at Ayr (by nose from Testa Rossa) in June: stays 10.5f: acts on soft and good to firm going: usually wears hood. *John Quinn* **107**

SPEED CRAFT 2 ch.f. (Apr 27) Mastercraftsman (IRE) 129 – Exorcet (FR) 78 (Selkirk (USA) 129) [2017 p8g 8d p7g p10g Oct 26] half-sister to several winners, including smart 6f (including at 2 yrs) winner Dark Missile (by Night Shift) and useful 1m-1¼m winner Breakheart (by Sakhee): dam 6f winner: little form: wears cheekpieces. *James Eustace* –

SPEED FREAK 3 b.f. Fastnet Rock (AUS) 127 – The Thrill Is Gone 98 (Bahamian Bounty 116) [2017 70: p5g^{2} f5s^{4} Jan 26] useful-looking filly: fair maiden: best form at 5f: acts on polytrack, tapeta and good to firm going: wears headgear: often races prominently. *Ralph Beckett* **69**

SPEEDO BOY (FR) 3 ch.g. Vision d'Etat (FR) 127 – Shamardanse (IRE) (Shamardal (USA) 129) [2017 75p: p10g* p8.9g^{2} 8.9s* 10m^{2} 10m^{6} 10m 11.9g 12s Sep 9] good-topped gelding: useful performer: won maiden at Chelmsford (by ½ length from Draw Swords) in January and listed race at Fontainebleau (by ½ length from Phoceen) in March: second in listed race at Newmarket (4½ lengths behind Permian) in May: stays 1½m: acts on polytrack, tapeta, soft and good to firm going. *Ian Williams* **106**

SPEIGHTOWNS KID (USA) 9 gr.g. Speightstown (USA) 124 – Seize The Wind (USA) (Maria's Mon (USA) 121) [2017 73: f6g^{pu} Jan 2] well-made gelding: fair handicapper: stayed 6f: acted on polytrack, fibresand and good to soft going: wore headgear: dead. *Ann Stokell* –

SPELLMAKER 8 b.g. Kheleyf (USA) 116 – Midnight Spell 79 (Night Shift (USA)) [2017 73: t5.1g p6g^{3} 6.1g 5.7m^{4} 6.1m Jun 26] fair handicapper: stays 6f: acts on polytrack, tapeta and good to firm going: tried in eyeshields. *Tony Newcombe* **66**

SPENNY'S LASS 2 b.f. (Jan 16) Bated Breath 125 – Midnight Hush (FR) (Anabaa (USA) 130) [2017 5d^{5} 6.1m^{3} 6d^{3} Oct 24] 13,500F, £90,000Y, 15,000 2-y-o: sturdy filly: first foal: dam unraced half-sister to smart/ungenuine sprinter Out After Dark: fair form: best effort when third in minor event at Yarmouth (3½ lengths behind Talaaqy) in October. *John Ryan* **66**

SPES NOSTRA 9 b.g. Ad Valorem (USA) 125 – Millagros (IRE) 86 (Pennekamp (USA) 130) [2017 94: t12.2m t9.5g^{4} t12.2g t10.2d^{3} t9.5g^{3} 10m t10.2g* 10m 9.1s 11.1g 10d 10g 11.1v 9v t12.2g Oct 27] fairly useful handicapper: won at Newcastle in May: below form after, mainly back on turf: stays 1½m: acts on polytrack, tapeta, good to firm and heavy going: wears blinkers: has worn tongue tie, including in 2017. *Iain Jardine* **71** **a82**

SPEY SECRET (IRE) 4 br.g. Kyllachy 129 – Chiarezza (AUS) (Fantastic Light (USA) 134) [2017 –: t7.1m f8g Jan 30] no form. *Tom Dascombe* –

SPICE BOAT 5 ch.g. Shamardal (USA) 129 – Frizzante 121 (Efisio 120) [2017 –: p8m Mar 29] compact gelding: maiden, no form since 2015: has worn cheekpieces: tried in tongue tie. *Paddy Butler* –

SPICE FAIR 10 ch.g. Trade Fair 124 – Focosa (ITY) (In The Wings 128) [2017 86: 16d^{4} 16v^{3} p16s 16s Oct 15] sturdy gelding: fair handicapper nowadays: stays 2m: acts on polytrack, good to firm and heavy going: usually races nearer last than first: fairly useful hurdler. *Mark Usher* **78**

SPICE MILL (IRE) 4 b.g. Dream Ahead (USA) 133 – High Spice (USA) 92 (Songandaprayer (USA) 118) [2017 74: t7.1g t6m^{5} f6m^{5} f7g Mar 14] fair maiden at 3 yrs, below that level in 2017: stays 6f: acts on polytrack and fibresand: wears headgear/tongue tie: often starts slowly. *Michael Appleby* **61**

SPICE WAR 2 b.g. (May 6) Declaration of War (USA) 128 – Blast Furnace (IRE) 74 (Sadler's Wells (USA) 132) [2017 8g p10g^{6} Sep 25] little impact in minor events. *Brian Meehan* –

SPIKE (IRE) 4 b.g. Lilbourne Lad (IRE) 111 – Vintage Allure (IRE) (Barathea (IRE) 127) [2017 68: t6g^{6} 5m 6m^{4} 5.5f 6m^{4} 6s t6.1g 5g^{6} Sep 1] modest handicapper: stays 6f: acts on good to firm and good to soft going: wears blinkers: tried in tongue tie: front runner/races prominently. *Donald McCain* **56**

SPIKE'S PRINCESS (IRE) 3 b.f. Bushranger (IRE) 119 – Deportment 90 (Barathea (IRE) 127) [2017 t6d t5d^4 7d^6 p7d^5 p10s Dec 15] £6,000Y: third foal: half-sister to useful winner up to 7f Commodore (2-y-o 5f winner) and 1m winner Protocol (both by Kodiac): dam, 1¼m winner who stayed 1¾m, half-sister to smart performer up to 1½m Summitville: no form: left Adrian Nicholls after third start. *Brian Barr* –

SPINART 4 ch.g. Dutch Art 126 – Spinneret 62 (Pivotal 124) [2017 73: 10m 10m 10.2d^3 10.2g^3 9.9f^6 8s^2 p8g^6 8v^6 t8.6g Oct 27] lengthy gelding: fair maiden: stays 1¼m: acts on tapeta and soft going: in headgear last 5 starts: front runner/races prominently. *Pam Sly* **76**

SPIN DOCTOR 3 gr.f. Mayson 124 – Doctor's Glory (USA) 91 (Elmaamul (USA) 125) [2017 85: 5.9s^6 6g^6 Jul 3] rather leggy filly: fairly useful at 2 yrs, below that level in 2017: stays 6f: acts on fibresand, tapeta and good to firm going. *Richard Fahey* **78**

SPINNAKA (IRE) 3 b.f. Invincible Spirit (IRE) 121 – Spinning Well (IRE) 83 (Pivotal 124) [2017 82p: 7m^2 t8.6g^5 7m^2 8g^2 7.9m^2 8g^2 7g^3 7.1s* 7v^5 t7.2m^2 p7g^6 Nov 7] compact filly: fairly useful performer: won maiden at Chepstow (by head from Diagnostic) in September: second in handicap at Wolverhampton in October: stays 1m: acts on tapeta, soft and good to firm going: in headgear last 5 starts: sold 36,000 gns in December. *Luca Cumani* **85**

SPINNAKER BAY (IRE) 3 b.f. Lawman (FR) 121 – Wizz Kid (IRE) 122 (Whipper (USA) 126) [2017 76: t6g^6 6d^5 Aug 10] modest maiden: stays 6f: acts on good to firm going: usually races close up. *William Jarvis* **63**

SPINNERS BALL (IRE) 4 b.g. Excellent Art 125 – Meek Appeal (USA) (Woodman (USA) 126) [2017 84: 11.6m^3 11.4m* 12m p11g* 12v 11.9m Aug 10] tall, angular gelding: fairly useful handicapper: won at Windsor in May and Kempton (by head from Tom's Rock) in June: stays 12.5f: acts on polytrack, tapeta and good to firm going: often races prominently: sold 8,000 gns in October, sent to Saudi Arabia. *Sylvester Kirk* **87**

SPINNING MELODY (USA) 3 b.f. Hard Spun (USA) 124 – Say No Now (IRE) 103 (Refuse To Bend (IRE) 128) [2017 p10g* t12.2g^3 f12.1g^4 Dec 21] third foal: dam, 1m winner, half-sister to smart Hong Kong performer up to 1¼m Poetic Justice (2-y-o 6f winner in Britain as Zumbi): fairly useful form: won maiden at Chelmsford (by neck from Footman) in October: best effort when third in handicap at Wolverhampton (1¾ lengths behind Island Brave) in November: stays 1½m: tried in cheekpieces. *Simon Crisford* **91**

SPIN POINT (IRE) 5 b.g. Pivotal 124 – Daneleta (IRE) 101 (Danehill (USA) 126) [2017 74: p12g t9.5g^6 12m^6 t12.4g^6 t16.5d^5 Dec 9] fair handicapper: stays 1½m: acts on soft going: often in headgear in 2017: tried in tongue tie. *Ian Williams* **70**

SPIN TOP 3 b.g. Acclamation 118 – Miss Work of Art 100 (Dutch Art 126) [2017 65: p5m^5 t5d^4 p6g p6g^3 p5s^2 t5.1g Nov 29] fair handicapper: left Joseph Tuite after third start: stays 6f: acts on polytrack, tapeta and good to firm going: has worn visor, including in 2017. *William Muir* **71**

SPINWHEEL 3 ch.f. Pivotal 124 – Angel's Tears (Seeking The Gold (USA)) [2017 65: t6f^4 p8g^4 t7.1g* t7.1g* t8.6m^3 t7.1g t7.1g Dec 6] fair handicapper: won at Newcastle in January and February: left Mark Johnston after sixth start: stays 1m: acts on polytrack and tapeta: usually races close up. *John Davies* **77**

SPIRAEA 7 ch.m. Bahamian Bounty 116 – Salvia (Pivotal 124) [2017 71: f6g f5g^2 t5g^2 p6d^2 t6g f6d^6 6m^4 Apr 24] sturdy mare: fair handicapper: stays 6f: acts on all-weather, good to firm and heavy going: tried in cheekpieces: often races prominently. *Ivan Furtado* **74**

SPIRIT BE WITH YOU (IRE) 4 b.f. Dandy Man (IRE) 123 – Mar Sin De (IRE) (Danetime (IRE) 121) [2017 61: 6.8m 7.2d 7v 7v Oct 24] maiden: no form in 2017: tried in headgear. *L. Smyth, Ireland* –

SPIRITED BOSS 2 b.g. (Feb 22) Swiss Spirit 117 – Bossy Kitty 81 (Avonbridge 123) [2017 t5.1g^4 Jun 26] 20/1, well held in minor event at Wolverhampton. *David Evans* –

SPIRIT OF APPIN 2 b.f. (Jan 27) Champs Elysees 124 – Oshiponga 72 (Barathea (IRE) 127) [2017 8s^2 Oct 28] closely related to temperamental 6f/7f winner Caramack (by Danehill Dancer) and half-sister to several winners, including smart 5f-7f winner (including at 2 yrs) Hatta Fort (by Cape Cross) and useful 2-y-o 6f/7f winner Blue Bayou (by Bahamian Bounty): dam 9f winner: 16/1, second in minor event at Newbury (2¼ lengths behind Highgarden) in October: will probably stay 1¼m: sure to progress. *Brian Meehan* **80 p**

SPIRIT OF BELLE 3 b.g. Sir Percy 129 – Yensi 86 (Doyen (IRE) 132) [2017 74: t12.2g^5 8.1d^2 10.2m 8g^2 8g 8v^3 8.1s 7v* p7g* Nov 7] fairly useful performer: won seller at Leicester in September and handicap at Kempton (by 2 lengths from Wicker) in November: left David Evans after eighth start: stays 8.5f: acts on polytrack and heavy going: has worn headgear (blinkered both wins): front runner/races prominently. *Paul Cole* **88**

SPIRITOFEDINBURGH (IRE) 3 b.g. Lilbourne Lad (IRE) 111 – Xema (Danehill (USA) 126) [2017 72: p7m^3 8f 8.1d 6d 7d p6g p12g^6 p11g^3 p12g^4 Nov 8] rather leggy gelding: fair maiden: stays 1½m: acts on polytrack: tried in headgear: in tongue tie last 3 starts: often races towards rear. *Brendan Powell* **70**

SPIRIT OF GONDREE (IRE) 9 b.g. Invincible Spirit (IRE) 121 – Kristal's Paradise (IRE) 100 (Bluebird (USA) 125) [2017 69: t8.6m^5 t7.1g^2 t7.1g^4 p8d p8g p6g^5 t8.6g p7g t6.1g t7.2g^6 p7g p8g Dec 30] sturdy, lengthy gelding: modest handicapper nowadays: stays 1¼m: acts on polytrack, tapeta and soft going: wears headgear: quirky sort. *Milton Bradley* **61**

SPIRITOFHAYTON (IRE) 3 br.g. Big Bad Bob (IRE) 118 – Teodelight (IRE) (Teofilo (IRE) 126) [2017 t8g^2 t8g^3 t8d^4 8.3s 10d 11.1d^6 Sep 2] fair maiden: best effort at 1m: acts on tapeta: sold £800, sent to Italy. *David Barron* **74**

SPIRIT OF ISHY 2 b.f. (Apr 7) Hellvelyn 118 – Our Piccadilly (IRE) 84 (Piccolo 121) [2017 p6g 6g 6.1m Oct 16] lengthy, angular filly: second foal: dam 5f and (at 2 yrs) 6f winner: well held in minor events/maiden. *Stuart Kittow* **–**

SPIRIT OF ROME (IRE) 3 ch.f. Mastercraftsman (IRE) 129 – Zagreb Flyer (Old Vic 136) [2017 53: t12.2g^3 t12.2g^3 12.1m^5 12.1g 12s^5 t14g 12g Aug 15] modest maiden: stays 1½m: acts on tapeta: in cheekpieces last 2 starts. *James Bethell* **63**

SPIRIT OF ROSANNA 5 gr.m. Hellvelyn 118 – Tharwa (IRE) 63 (Last Tycoon 131) [2017 65: 6m 6.1d^2 6.1v^2 5.1v^3 6g^6 5g^5 5s* 5.3v* Oct 19] rather leggy mare: fair handicapper: won at Bath and Brighton in October: stays 6f: acts on heavy going: usually in headgear: wears tongue tie: usually leads. *Steph Hollinshead* **75**

SPIRIT OF SARWAN (IRE) 3 b.g. Elzaam (AUS) 115 – Hidden Heart (USA) 62 (Kingmambo (USA) 125) [2017 76: p7g* t7.1f^5 p8g^2 7m^2 8.3g 7m 8d^6 7m^6 p7g^2 p8g^6 Dec 31] unfurnished gelding: fairly useful handicapper: won at Lingfield (apprentice) in February: second at Brighton in May and Lingfield in December: stays 1m: acts on polytrack and good to firm going: tried in cheekpieces: often starts slowly/races towards rear. *Julia Feilden* **82**

SPIRIT OF THE VALE (IRE) 4 b.f. Royal Applause 124 – Nesmeh (USA) (More Than Ready (USA) 120) [2017 54: t12.2m^6 t10.2g* p11d^4 t10.2g* t10.2g^2 10m^5 11.7f^4 11.9g^5 t10.2d^2 10.2d^5 9.9m^2 t12.4s t10.2s^6 p11g^{ur} Oct 4] fair handicapper: won at Newcastle in January and March: stays 11.5f: acts on polytrack, tapeta, firm and soft going: wears headgear/tongue tie: temperamental. *Oliver Greenall* **66 §**

SPIRITOFTOMINTOUL 8 gr.g. Authorized (IRE) 133 – Diamond Line (FR) (Linamix (FR) 127) [2017 84: t13.9f^4 t16.3g^4 t13.9g^6 f14m 12g^4 14f 14.5s^3 14d^2 13.1s 17.1d^5 p16s^5 14.1d^5 16d p16g^3 Dec 20] good-topped gelding: fair handicapper nowadays: stays 17f: acts on all-weather, soft and good to firm going: in headgear last 3 starts: often wears tongue tie: often races towards rear: one to treat with caution. *Tony Carroll* **74 §**

SPIRIT OF VALOR (USA) 3 br.c. War Front (USA) 119 – Stone Hope (USA) (Grindstone (USA) 124) [2017 101p: a9.4g 8m 8d^6 7m^2 7m* 7g 7g^4 Sep 16] strong colt: smart performer: won Minstrel Stakes at the Curragh (by 1¾ lengths from So Beloved) in July: second in Jersey Stakes at Royal Ascot (neck behind Le Brivido) in June: best at 7f: acts on good to firm and heavy going: wears blinkers/tongue tie: races prominently. *Aidan O'Brien, Ireland* **117**

SPIRIT OF WEDZA (IRE) 5 b.g. Footstepsinthesand 120 – Sampers (IRE) 94 (Exceed And Excel (AUS) 126) [2017 73: t5g^6 p6g^2 t6d^6 t6g* t6g^2 5m* 5g^5 t6.1g^4 5g^6 Sep 2] rather lightly-made gelding: fair handicapper: won at Wolverhampton in February and Hamilton in May: stays 6.5f: acts on polytrack, tapeta, good to firm and good to soft going: has worn headgear: front runner/races prominently. *Julie Camacho* **77**

SPIRIT OF ZEBEDEE (IRE) 4 gr.g. Zebedee 113 – Sampers (IRE) 94 (Exceed And Excel (AUS) 126) [2017 69: t6g^2 t6d* p6g* t6g^2 p6g^3 t6g 5m 5f 5f 6g^2 6g* 6d^3 6g 6s^3 Oct 31] fair handicapper: won at Newcastle/Lingfield in February and Catterick in August: stays 6f: acts on polytrack, tapeta, soft and good to firm going: usually wears headgear: front runner/races prominently. *John Quinn* **74**

SPIRIT POWER 2 b.g. (Mar 5) Swiss Spirit 117 – Verasina (USA) 83 (Woodman (USA) 126) [2017 p5g^2 p5g^2 5m^4 6d^4 7g 5d^6 p6g^4 5g^4 p5g^4 Dec 22] fair maiden: stays 6f: acts on polytrack: tried in tongue tie. *Joseph Patrick O'Brien, Ireland* **75**

SPIRITUAL LADY 3 b.f. Pastoral Pursuits 127 – Rouge Dancer (Elusive City (USA) 117) [2017 105p: 6d 6m 5s^5 Nov 8] compact filly: useful at 2 yrs, below best in 2017: stays 6f: acts on polytrack, soft and good to firm going: usually travels strongly: sold 100,000 gns in December. *Philip McBride* **94**

SPIRITUAL STAR (IRE) 8 b.g. Soviet Star (USA) 128 – Million Spirits (IRE) 90 (Invincible Spirit (IRE) 121) [2017 88d: p8g p8g p8g^3 t8.6g* p8g^2 t8.6g^2 t8.6g^2 p8s^{pu} 8g p8g^3 t8.6g p7g Dec 6] rather leggy gelding: fair handicapper nowadays: won at Wolverhampton (apprentice) in March: stays 9.5f: acts on polytrack, tapeta and good to firm going: has worn blinkers/tongue tie: often races in rear. *Lee Carter* **78**

SPITFIRE LIMITED 3 b.f. Excelebration (IRE) 133 – First Bloom (USA) 71 (Fusaichi Pegasus (USA) 130) [2017 6s 5.1m^6 6.1g t5.1m^2 p6g^4 p6s^5 Dec 7] lengthy filly: fifth foal: half-sister to 6f winner At A Clip (by Green Desert): dam lightly-raced half-sister to very smart performer (best at 6f/7f) Diffident: modest maiden: likely to stay 7f: acts on polytrack and tapeta: in hood after debut: often races towards rear. *George Baker* **62**

SPIX'S MACAW 2 ch.f. (Feb 21) Footstepsinthesand 120 – Featherweight (IRE) 89 (Fantastic Light (USA) 134) [2017 5.1m t6.1g^5 7g 6s^6 Oct 19] fourth foal: half-sister to 2-y-o 5f winner War Whisper (by Royal Applause) and 2-y-o 7f/1m winner Plant Pot Power (by Lawman): dam, 1¼m winner (best up to 1½m), half-sister to useful 7f winner Carniolan: poor form: best effort at 6f. *Bill Turner* **47**

SPLASH AROUND 3 ch.c. Nathaniel (IRE) 129 – Splashdown 105 (Falbrav (IRE) 133) [2017 75p: 10g^3 11s^2 14g^3 p14s^4 Jun 22] fairly useful maiden: placed in handicaps at Newbury in May and Sandown in June: stays 1¾m: acts on soft and good to firm going: sold to join Michael Appleby £17,000 in August. *Sir Michael Stoute* **87**

SPOKEN WORDS 8 b.m. Fruits of Love (USA) 127 – Jerre Jo Glanville (USA) (Skywalker (USA)) [2017 53: 6m 6m^6 5.5f^2 5.9g 5m^5 t6.1d Dec 27] modest handicapper: stays 1m, usually raced over shorter: acts on tapeta and firm going: usually wears headgear. *John David Riches* **53**

SPOKESPERSON (USA) 9 b.g. Henny Hughes (USA) 125 – Verbal (USA) (Kingmambo (USA) 125) [2017 –: t12.4d 12.5m Jul 25] fair at best, no form since 2015: stays 1½m: acts on tapeta and good to firm going: has worn headgear, including in 2017. *Fred Watson* **–**

SPOOF 2 b.g. (Jan 26) Poet's Voice 126 – Filona (IRE) (Motivator 131) [2017 5.2g^5 5.1m^2 5g^3 5.3d 5v^5 5.1d* 5g* 5g 5m^5 Oct 13] 20,000F, €50,000Y: lengthy gelding: first foal: dam, Italian sprint maiden, half-sister to useful performer up to 1½m Fanoulpifer: fairly useful performer: won minor event at Chepstow in August and nursery at Sandown (by neck from Kodiac Express) in September: best form at 5f: acts on good to firm and good to soft going: usually in hood: temperamental. *Charles Hills* **94 §**

SPORTING BILL (IRE) 2 br.c. (Feb 15) Society Rock (IRE) 126 – Pandoras Secret (IRE) (Monashee Mountain (USA) 115) [2017 p6g 6d^2 Oct 30] €26,000F, 110,000Y: tall, useful-looking colt: fourth foal: half-brother to Italian 10.5f winner Thinkandlink (by Ivan Denisovich): dam unraced half-sister to smart winner up to 1m Diamond Max: fair form: better effort when second in minor event at Leicester (1¼ lengths behind Zumurud) in October: will stay 7f: open to further improvement. *James Fanshawe* **77 p**

SPORTING TIMES 3 ch.g. Sir Percy 129 – Queen of Iceni 81 (Erhaab (USA) 127) [2017 89p: 8.3d^4 9m* 10m^6 12g^3 14m^6 p12g^2 11.8s^5 Oct 10] sturdy gelding: fairly useful performer: won maiden at Lingfield in June: placed in handicaps at Newmarket in July and Kempton in September: should be suited by 1¾m+: acts on polytrack and good to firm going. *Ed Dunlop* **91**

SPORTY YANKEE (USA) 4 gr.g. Paddy O'Prado (USA) 121 – I Insist (USA) (Green Dancer (USA) 132) [2017 84: 16d p16d Aug 23] workmanlike gelding: fairly useful handicapper, little impact either start on Flat in 2017: stays 1¾m: acts on heavy going: tried in headgear/tongue tie: winning hurdler. *Martin Keighley* **–**

SPOT LITE 2 b.g. (Feb 16) Compton Place 125 – High Class Girl (Royal Applause 124) [2017 6m 6.1m^6 6s 6d Aug 12] compact gelding: little show, including in nursery. *Rod Millman* **–**

SPOWARTICUS 8 ch.g. Shamardal (USA) 129 – Helen Bradley (IRE) 85 (Indian Ridge 123) [2017 70: f6g^6 f6g^4 f6g f7g f6m f6g^2 f6g^5 t6g 6m May 3] modest handicapper nowadays: stays 6f: acts on all-weather, good to firm and good to soft going: wears headgear. *Scott Dixon* **63**

SPRAY THE SEA (IRE) 2 b.g. (Mar 4) Intikhab (USA) 135 – Ramamara (IRE) 81 (Trans Island 119) [2017 t6s^5 6m^3 7.2m^2 6.9v^5 Sep 18] fair form: stays 7f. *Bryan Smart* **74**

SPRING ABILITY (IRE) 2 b.g. (Apr 6) Oasis Dream 129 – Because (IRE) 87 (Sadler's Wells (USA) 132) [2017 p8g p8g^4 p8g Nov 21] modest form when fourth in minor event at Kempton on second of 3 starts. *Laura Mongan* **64**

SPRING BEAUTY 3 b.f. Equiano (FR) 127 – Spring Goddess (IRE) 89 (Daggers Drawn (USA) 114) [2017 7d 6s⁵ t6d⁴ t8.6g Dec 13] third foal: half-sister to 1m winner Straight Arrow (by Refuse To Bend): dam, winner up to 1¼m (2-y-o 7.5f winner), half-sister to useful 6f-1m winner Mac's Power: poor form. *John Weymes* **33**

SPRING COSMOS (IRE) 2 b.f. (Feb 12) Acclamation 118 – Sister Red (IRE) 86 (Diamond Green (FR) 121) [2017 6g* 6d⁴ 7g⁵ p6g⁶ Oct 17] €46,000Y, £100,000 2-y-o: neat filly: third foal: closely related to 2-y-o 7f winner Miss Laila (by Dark Angel): dam, 2-y-o 7f winner, half-sister to smart winner up to 1¼m Red Badge: fairly useful form: won maiden at Newmarket (by 1¼ lengths from Indicia) in July: stays 7f. *Charlie Appleby* **86**

SPRING ETERNAL 3 b.f. Oasis Dream 129 – Short Dance (USA) 105 (Hennessy (USA) 122) [2017 –: 6d⁴ 6m² 6m² 5m 6g 6.5d³ Nov 30] maiden: left Charles Hills after first start: stays 6f: acts on good to firm going: has been tongue tied. *Luciano Vitabile, Italy* **?**

SPRING FLING 6 b.m. Assertive 121 – Twilight Mistress 84 (Bin Ajwaad (IRE) 119) [2017 104: 6.1g 6f⁴ 6f⁶ 5g* 5m Jul 8] strong mare: useful performer: won listed race at Ayr (by 1¼ lengths from Rural Celebration) in June: best at 5f/6f: acts on tapeta and any turf going. *Henry Candy* **102**

SPRINGFORTH 3 ch.g. Mayson 124 – Spirit Na Heireann (IRE) 67 (Dubawi (IRE) 129) [2017 67: 6m² 6m² 6d 6g³ 6m⁵ 7d Jul 28] fair handicapper: stays 7f: acts on good to firm and good to soft going. *Richard Fahey* **71**

SPRING LOADED (IRE) 5 gr.g. Zebedee 113 – Nisriyna (IRE) (Intikhab (USA) 135) [2017 100, a115: p6g³ 5.1m⁴ 6g 5.1m² 6.1s⁵ 5.5g³ 5.6g* 6g² 5d p6g⁶ Nov 18] good-topped gelding: smart handicapper: won Portland at Doncaster (by 3½ lengths from Vibrant Chords) in September: best at 5f/6f: acts on polytrack, tapeta, soft and good to firm going: usually responds generously to pressure. *Paul D'Arcy* **116**

SPRING OFFENSIVE (IRE) 5 b.g. Iffraaj 127 – Night Sphere (IRE) 74 (Night Shift (USA)) [2017 101: 8v⁵ 8m³ 8.5m⁶ 8g⁴ 8g³ 9.1d 10.3m 8.2v Sep 29] good-topped gelding: useful handicapper: third at Thirsk (2½ lengths behind Cote d'Azur) in May and Pontefract (2¼ lengths behind Crowning Glory) in July: stays 9f: acts on any turf going: tried in cheekpieces: sold 20,000 gns in October. *Richard Fahey* **96**

SPRING PRAISE (IRE) 2 b.c. (Mar 23) Oasis Dream 129 – Applauded (IRE) 83 (Royal Applause 124) [2017 7g 7d t8.6g Nov 25] little impact in minor events/maiden: in tongue tie last 2 starts. *Marco Botti* **–**

SPRING ROMANCE (IRE) 2 b.g. (Apr 14) Zebedee 113 – Love And Devotion 64 (Shamardal (USA) 129) [2017 5.1m 6.1m 5.1g⁵ Jul 31] good-topped gelding: well held in minor events/maiden. *Dean Ivory* **–**

SPRING WATERFALL (IRE) 2 b.f. (Feb 4) Exceed And Excel (AUS) 126 – Forest Pearl (USA) (Woodman (USA) 126) [2017 p7g t8.6g² Nov 29] sister to a winner in Australia, closely related to very smart Australian winner up to 12.5f Miss Finland (2-y-o 5f/6f winner, by Redoute's Choice) and half-sister to 11f winner Turnbuckle (by Teofilo): dam unraced daughter of Oaks winner Moonshell: fair form when second at Wolverhampton (1¼ lengths behind Ghanimah) on second of 2 starts in minor events. *Saeed bin Suroor* **75**

William Hill Portland Handicap, Doncaster—Spring Loaded belatedly reproduces his smart all-weather form on turf, quickening sharply to leave a big field for dead; Vibrant Chords and Justanotherbottle (No.16) head the chasing pack

SPRITZIG 2 ch.f. (Apr 20) Exceed And Excel (AUS) 126 – Generous Lady 98 (Generous –
(IRE) 139) [2017 p7g p8g Oct 13] closely related to 1½m winner Summer Wine (by Desert King) and half-sister to several winners, including very smart winner up to 1½m High Accolade (2-y-o 7f winner, by Mark of Esteem), also runner-up in St Leger: dam 1½m-1¾m winner who stayed 2m: well held in minor event/maiden. *Chris Wall*

SPRUCE LODGE 3 b.g. Compton Place 125 – Beautiful Lady (IRE) 77 (Peintre Celebre –
(USA) 137) [2017 68p: t5g Sep 22] fair form on debut at 2 yrs, little impact either start since: should be suited by 6f. *David Barron*

SPRYT (IRE) 5 b.g. Invincible Spirit (IRE) 121 – Out of Thanks (IRE) 89 (Sadler's Wells **57**
(USA) 132) [2017 88d: f8g p10g^4 f7d p8s* Jun 13] modest handicapper nowadays: in tongue tie, won at Lingfield in June: left Conor Dore after first start: stays 8.5f: acts on polytrack, tapeta, good to firm and good to soft going: wears headgear: front runner/races prominently. *John Butler*

SPUD (IRE) 2 b.c. (May 2) Fast Company (IRE) 126 – Nightswimmer (IRE) 75 (Noverre **105 p**
(USA) 125) [2017 7g^2 7.6v* Sep 15] 36,000F, 75,000Y: leggy colt: fourth foal: brother to useful/temperamental winner up to 1m (stays 1¼m) Mutarakez (2-y-o 7f winner) and half-brother to 5f winner Bashiba (by Iffraaj) and 1m winner Casina di Notte (by Casamento): dam lightly raced: useful form: won minor event at Chester (by 15 lengths from Manor Park) in September, making all: will stay 1m: sent to Hong Kong, where renamed Super Giant: open to further improvement. *Tom Dascombe*

SPUN GOLD 3 ch.g. Exceed And Excel (AUS) 126 – Victoire Celebre (USA) (Stravinsky **78**
(USA) 133) [2017 67: p8g 7g 7.6s^2 p8g p8g^5 t7.1g p10s^6 f8.1g* Dec 22] fair handicapper: won at Southwell in December: left Luca Cumani after second start: stays 1m: acts on polytrack, fibresand and soft going: tried in headgear/tongue tie. *Charlie Fellowes*

SPUTNIK PLANUM (USA) 3 b.g. Quality Road (USA) 131 – Shiva (JPN) 127 (Hector **80**
Protector (USA) 124) [2017 10.2g 9.9g 9.9d^5 12d^5 p12g^4 p12g^2 p14d^4 p15.8g^6 Oct 5] big, heavy-topped gelding: closely related to useful French 9f-10.5f winner That Which Is Not (by Elusive Quality) and half-brother to 3 winners: dam, 8.5f-10.5f (Tattersalls Gold Cup) winner, half-sister to Oaks winner Light Shift, herself dam of top-class 1¼m/1½m performer Ulysses: fairly useful maiden: second in handicap at Kempton in September: best up to 1½m: acts on polytrack: in tongue tie last 4 starts: sometimes slowly away: sold to join Michael Appleby 40,000 gns in November. *David Lanigan*

SQUATS (IRE) 5 b.g. Dandy Man (IRE) 123 – Light Sea (IRE) 59 (King's Best (USA) **108**
132) [2017 113: 7m 6m 5g 7d 7d* p7s 7s Sep 9] close-coupled gelding: useful handicapper: won at Newbury (by ¾ length from Graphite Storm) in August: stays 7f: acts on firm and good to soft going: has worn cheekpieces, including in 2017: tried in tongue tie: often races towards rear. *William Haggas*

SQUIGGLEY 4 b.f. Sir Percy 129 – Oat Cuisine 92 (Mujahid (USA) 125) [2017 78: 10m^2 **82**
10g^6 10g^2 12g 8.5g^3 10g^6 Oct 17] angular filly: fairly useful handicapper: placed at Windsor in July and Epsom in September: stays 1¼m: acts on good to firm going: sold 2,500 gns in November. *Henry Candy*

SQUIRE 6 b.g. Teofilo (IRE) 126 – Most Charming (FR) (Darshaan 133) [2017 85: p8g^2 **77**
p8d^4 p8d 8.5f^4 8m 10.1m^6 p8g p10g^2 Dec 13] sturdy gelding: fairly useful handicapper: **a83**
second at Chelmsford in January and Lingfield in December: stays 10.5f: acts on polytrack and firm going: wears tongue tie. *Michael Attwater*

SQUIRRELHEED 2 b.g. (Apr 19) Finjaan 122 – Valjarv (IRE) 97 (Bluebird (USA) 125) –
[2017 6g^6 6m 6g t8g Dec 6] no form, including in nursery. *Richard Guest*

SS VEGA 4 b.f. Kheleyf (USA) 116 – Annie Gee (Primo Valentino (IRE) 116) [2017 52: **54**
5m^5 6m^2 7.2m^3 7.2d^5 6s^3 7.2d 6g^5 6g Aug 21] modest maiden: stays 7f: acts on soft and good to firm going: sometimes wears headgear: usually races towards rear. *Jim Goldie*

STAFFA (IRE) 4 b.f. Rock of Gibraltar (IRE) 133 – Gabriellina Klon (IRE) (Ashkalani **69**
(IRE) 128) [2017 –: p6g^5 p6g^4 5g^3 p5g* 5f p5g^6 5s^2 5.7d t5.1g* p5s^4 p5g^5 5.1d^5 Oct 23] fair handicapper: won at Lingfield in June and Wolverhampton in September: stays 6f: acts on polytrack, tapeta and soft going: races towards rear. *Denis Coakley*

STAFF COLLEGE (FR) 3 b.g. Slickly (FR) 128 – School of Music (FR) (Green Tune **74**
(USA) 125) [2017 84?: 8d 10d^4 10.3v Sep 16] fair maiden: stays 1¼m: acts on good to soft going: front runner/races prominently: placed in juvenile hurdles. *Henry Spiller*

STAGE MAGIC (IRE) 2 b.c. (Mar 11) Dark Angel (IRE) 113 – Witnessed 94 **107**
(Authorized (IRE) 133) [2017 7m^2 7g* 8g^2 8d* 8.9s^6 Oct 7] 160,000F: compact colt: second foal: dam, 2-y-o 7.5f winner, half-sister to Breeders' Cup Turf winner Talismanic: useful performer: won minor event at Newbury in July and Prix des Chenes at Chantilly

(by short head from Olmedo) in September: short-head second to Francesco Bere in listed race at Deauville in between: well held in Prix de Conde at Chantilly final start: stays 1m: acts on good to soft going: made running last 2 outings. *Charlie Appleby*

STAGE NAME 3 ch.f. Famous Name 124 – Striking Choice (USA) (Smart Strike (CAN) 121) [2017 8m² Aug 25] second foal: half-sister to French 1m winner Classification (by Three Valleys): dam, ran once, closely related to dam of smart French 1¼m-12.5f winner Announce: 6/1, second in maiden at Newmarket (3¾ lengths behind Dynamic) in August: sold 3,000 gns in November: should improve. *Hugo Palmer* **80 p**

STAG PARTY (IRE) 3 b.g. Thewayyouare (USA) 117 – Betrothed (IRE) 84 (Oratorio (IRE) 128) [2017 58: f7g⁴ f8g⁶ f8m⁴ t9.5g 12.1g 10g Jul 3] poor maiden: left Andrew Balding after second start: often in headgear: in tongue tie last 4 starts. *Julia Brooke* **48**

STAINTONDALE LASS (IRE) 4 b.f. Bushranger (IRE) 119 – Siphon Melody (USA) (Siphon (BRZ) 130) [2017 94: p7g p6g t7.1g² p7g 7g* 6m* 6d⁵ 6g t6f⁵ Dec 31] angular filly: useful handicapper: won at Brighton in May and Newbury (by 2¾ lengths from Carolinae) in July: left Ed Vaughan before final outing: stays 7f: acts on polytrack, tapeta and good to firm going: sometimes slowly away. *Manuel Badilla, USA* **99**

STAKE ACCLAIM (IRE) 5 b.g. Acclamation 118 – Golden Legacy (IRE) 107 (Rossini (USA) 118) [2017 96, a84: 5m³ 5m⁶ 5s² 6.1d* 5d² 6.1g⁶ 6d 5d* 6.1s³ 5.6g 6v² 6g 6d Nov 11] rather leggy gelding: smart handicapper: won at Windsor (by 4 lengths from Upstaging) in June and Ascot (by neck from Sir Robert Cheval) in August: second in Gold Cup at Haydock (short head behind Donjuan Triumphant) in September: stays 6f: acts on heavy going: has worn cheekpieces, including in 2017: front runner/races prominently. *Dean Ivory* **111**

STAMFORD RAFFLES 4 b.g. Champs Elysees 124 – Romantic Retreat 63 (Rainbow Quest (USA) 134) [2017 87: 10g² 14g* 12d² 14g 13.9d Sep 17] lengthy gelding: useful handicapper: won at Haydock (by 1¼ lengths from On Fire) in July: second at Newmarket later same month (½ length behind Roar) and in August (beaten ¾ length by Amazing Red): stays 16.5f: acts on polytrack, tapeta and good to soft going: usually races prominently. *Jane Chapple-Hyam* **95**

STAMP DUTY (IRE) 9 b.g. Ad Valorem (USA) 125 – Lothian Lass (IRE) 67 (Daylami (IRE) 138) [2017 49: t10.2d⁴ t8.6g² t8.6g² t8.6g² Dec 13] workmanlike gelding: modest handicapper: stays 12.5f, effective at shorter: acts on polytrack, tapeta, good to firm and heavy going: has worn cheekpieces. *Suzzanne France* **57**

STAMP HILL (IRE) 4 b.g. Zoffany (IRE) 121 – Edelfa (IRE) (Fasliyev (USA) 120) [2017 99: 7m 7m 8d 7m 7d* 7g Oct 7] lengthy gelding: useful handicapper: won International Stakes at Ascot (by 1¼ lengths from Mjjack) in July: stays 7f: acts on heavy going: in headgear last 3 starts. *Richard Fahey* **106**

STANARLEY PIC 6 b.g. Piccolo 121 – Harlestone Lady (Shaamit (IRE) 127) [2017 73: 16g 14.1g t16.3s³ 14m t16.3g⁴ 14d* 14s² 14s⁶ 14d Oct 20] fair handicapper: won at Redcar in August: stays 16.5f: acts on tapeta, good to firm and heavy going: tried in cheekpieces: front runner/races prominently. *Sally Haynes* **71**

Gigaset International Stakes (Heritage Handicap), Ascot—
big-priced runners fill the frame with 50/1-shot Stamp Hill proving too strong for the grey Mjjack, stablemate Withernsea (diamonds) and Johnny Barnes (dark colours)

STANDER (IRE) 3 b.c. Famous Name 124 – Coill Cri (IRE) 51 (Shinko Forest (IRE)) [2017 p7g 6v 7g 12v^2 f16.5g^4 14g Sep 2] little form, including in handicaps. *John McConnell, Ireland* **–**

STAND GUARD 13 b.g. Danehill (USA) 126 – Protectress 110 (Hector Protector (USA) 124) [2017 66: p12g* p12d f12.1g p12g p12g Dec 6] lengthy gelding: fair handicapper: won at Kempton (28th win on the all-weather) in January: barely stays 2m: acts on polytrack and fibresand. *John Butler* **67**

STANDING ROCK (IRE) 3 b.f. Fastnet Rock (AUS) 127 – Great Hope (IRE) 87 (Halling (USA) 133) [2017 8g* 9.9m* 12.4d^6 Aug 13] 50,000Y: lengthy filly: closely related to 2 winners, including useful 2-y-o 1m winner (stayed 1½m) Reckoning (by Danehill Dancer), and half-sister to 2 winners, including useful 2-y-o 7f winner Stylish One (by Invincible Spirit): dam 1m winner: useful form: won maiden at Newbury in June and handicap at Salisbury (by neck from Billesdon Bess) in July: improved again when sixth in Prix Minerve at Deauville (4¾ lengths behind God Given) in August: stays 12.5f: sold 35,000 gns in December. *John Gosden* **103**

ST ANDREWS (IRE) 4 ch.g. Rip Van Winkle (IRE) 134 – Stellavera (FR) (Anabaa (USA) 130) [2017 –: f8s t7.1g p7g 10.2f^2 11.5g^4 12g^2 11.4g^5 12g p15.8g^2 p16g* Oct 4] fair handicapper: won at Kempton in October: stays 2m: acts on polytrack, best turf form on good going: wears headgear: often in tongue tie: sold £8,000 in November. *Ian Williams* **66**

STANGHOW 5 b.g. Monsieur Bond (IRE) 120 – Melandre 74 (Lujain (USA) 119) [2017 94: t5s 5m 5g^4 6m^2 5m^4 5.1d^3 5m* 5g^4 p6s 6g 5.5g^5 5m^4 p5s t5.1g Nov 7] fairly useful handicapper: won at Beverley (by nose from Signore Piccolo) in July: stayed 6f: acted on polytrack, good to firm and good to soft going: tried in cheekpieces: dead. *Antony Brittain* **93**

STANHOPE 3 b.g. Equiano (FR) 127 – Nicoise (IRE) (Lear Spear (USA) 124) [2017 81: 6m^4 6.1g^5 6d* 6s 6d^2 6m^2 6d^2 Sep 20] sturdy gelding: fairly useful handicapper: won at Newmarket (by 3 lengths from Hart Stopper) in June: second at same course in August and Yarmouth in September: stays 6f: acts on good to firm and good to soft going: tried in headgear: usually races prominently: sold to join Simon Crisford 50,000 gns in October. *Mick Quinn* **93**

STANLEY 4 ch.g. Sea The Stars (IRE) 140 – Deirdre 101 (Dubawi (IRE) 129) [2017 84: p13.3g^3 p12g^2 p12g* Oct 18] strong, round-barrelled gelding: fairly useful performer: won maiden at Kempton (by ½ length from Warm Oasis) in October: stays 13.5f: acts on polytrack and tapeta: usually races close up. *Richard Hughes* **84**

STANLEY (GER) 6 bl.g. Pivotal 124 – Sky Dancing (IRE) (Exit To Nowhere (USA) 122) [2017 84: 8g 8m^4 8s^4 8.1g^2 8s^2 9.1m^3 Aug 27] sturdy gelding: fair handicapper: stays 1¼m: acts on soft and good to firm going: tried in cheekpieces. *Jonjo O'Neill* **79**

STANLOW 7 b.g. Invincible Spirit (IRE) 121 – Ghazal (USA) 103 (Gone West (USA)) [2017 55§: t10.2g t8.6g 8.2g 8.5d Aug 17] modest handicapper, no form in 2017: often wears headgear: tried in tongue tie: sometimes slowly away, usually races towards rear: one to treat with caution. *Michael Mullineaux* **– §**

STAPLEHURST (IRE) 4 b.f. Beat Hollow 126 – Kelpie (IRE) 86 (Kahyasi 130) [2017 61: p12d* p12g 12m^6 11.8g^6 12m Jul 4] modest handicapper: won at Kempton in January: stays 1½m: acts on polytrack: tried in cheekpieces: wears tongue tie: covered by Requinto, sent to France. *Geoffrey Deacon* **59**

STARARCHITECTURE (IRE) 3 b.c. Mastercraftsman (IRE) 129 – City of Cities (IRE) 71 (In The Wings 128) [2017 p8d^3 8.3d^3 9v^4 8m^4 Jul 6] €72,000F, 120,000Y: well-made colt: fourth foal: half-brother to 2-y-o 5f winner Stinky Socks (by Footstepsinthesand): dam, maiden (stayed 1¼m), half-sister to useful performer up to 1¼m Ahlaain: fairly useful form: should be suited by further than 1m: tried in blinkers: wears tongue tie: sold 16,000 gns in July. *William Haggas* **80**

STAR ASCENDING (IRE) 5 ch.g. Thousand Words 113 – Sakaka (Tobougg (IRE) 125) [2017 71: f8g^5 t9.5m^3 f8d t12.2g* t12.2g^3 12.5g^6 11.8g^4 11.8g t12.2g^6 f12.1g^4 t12.2g^5 f12.1g^5 t12.2m^4 f11.1g* f11.1g^2 f11.1g^2 Dec 29] fair handicapper: won at Wolverhampton in April and Southwell in December: stays 1½m: acts on fibresand, tapeta and good to firm going: wears headgear: tried in tongue tie: sometimes slowly away, usually races freely. *Jennie Candlish* **57 a66**

STAR ATTRACTION (FR) 2 b.f. (Mar 19) Orpen (USA) 116 – Heaven 84 (Reel Buddy (USA) 118) [2017 6d^4 Oct 30] lengthy filly: third foal: half-sister to 6f winner Wedgewood Estates (by Assertive): dam 5f winner (including at 2 yrs): 9/1, well held in minor event at Leicester: should improve. *David Menuisier* **– p**

STARBOARD 8 b.g. Zamindar (USA) 116 – Summer Shower (Sadler's Wells (USA) 132) [2017 87: p8d^{6} p8d* p10g^{2} Feb 9] fairly useful handicapper: won at Chelmsford (apprentice, by 2¾ lengths from Zorba The Greek) in February: stays 11f, raced at shorter nowadays: acts on polytrack, tapeta and soft going: wears headgear nowadays. *David Simcock* **89**

STARBOARD WATCH 3 b.f. Harbour Watch (IRE) 121 – Makhsusah (IRE) (Darshaan 133) [2017 7g 8.3d 8v 7d^{2} 7m t7.1g^{3} p8g^{4} 10.1g Oct 16] tall filly: half-sister to several winners, including winner up to 1m Market Day (2-y-o 6f/7f winner, by Tobougg) and winner up to 1½m Wild Rose (2-y-o 1m/8.6f winner, by Doyen), both useful: dam unraced: fair maiden: best effort at 7f: acts on good to soft going. *James Given* **66**

STARBOY (IRE) 2 br.g. (Feb 16) Camacho 118 – New Magic (IRE) 101 (Statue of Liberty (USA) 115) [2017 5.1m^{5} p6d 6g 6s^{5} t8s^{5} 7s* Oct 10] stocky gelding: fair performer: won nursery at Brighton in October: stays 1m: acts on tapeta and soft going: tried in cheekpieces: races towards rear. *George Scott* **73**

STARCASTER 2 b.c. (Feb 4) Dansili 127 – Shirocco Star 116 (Shirocco (GER) 129) [2017 8.2d^{3} 9.1s^{3} Oct 15] first foal: dam 2-y-o 1m winner who stayed 12.5f (second in Oaks): fair form: third in minor events at Leicester and Goodwood: remains open to improvement. *Hughie Morrison* **77 p**

STAR CATCH 3 b.f. Cacique (IRE) 124 – Jolie Etoile (USA) (Diesis 133) [2017 80p: 6m p6s^{4} Jun 21] fair form: stays 6f. *Charles Hills* **74**

STAR CITIZEN 5 b.g. New Approach (IRE) 132 – Faslen (USA) 92 (Fasliyev (USA) 120) [2017 72: 6v 5d^{6} 5s^{3} Jun 29] fair handicapper: stays 6f: acts on good to soft going. *Fred Watson* **68**

STAR CRACKER (IRE) 5 ch.g. Starspangledbanner (AUS) 128 – Champagne Cracker 74 (Up And At 'Em 109) [2017 75: 5g 5m^{6} 6s 5d^{6} 5g^{6} 5d^{3} 5d* 5s^{6} 5s 5s^{6} 6d t6g* Dec 6] fair handicapper: won at Ayr in August and Newcastle in December: stays 6f: acts on tapeta, soft and good to firm going: wears cheekpieces. *Jim Goldie* **69**

STARDRIFTER 5 b.g. Rock of Gibraltar (IRE) 133 – Alchemilla (Dubai Destination (USA) 127) [2017 83: 8.3m 10m 8.3s^{5} 9.2m 7.2g 10d 8.3d^{6} 8.3g^{3} 9.2g^{4} 7.2d 8g^{5} 10d^{4} 12.1s 9.2d^{5} 8s^{5} 8v t7.1d^{2} t7.1g^{2} Nov 15] modest handicapper nowadays: stays 1¼m: acts on tapeta, firm and soft going: tried in cheekpieces: often starts slowly/races towards rear. *Linda Perratt* **61**

STARFALL 4 b.g. Misu Bond (IRE) 114 – Davana 62 (Primo Valentino (IRE) 116) [2017 7m 6s^{4} 6m Jun 24] little impact in bumpers/Flat maidens. *Christopher Wilson* **–**

STARFIELD 8 b.g. Marju (IRE) 127 – Sister Moonshine (FR) 99 (Piccolo 121) [2017 74: f8g f8g^{6} p8d Mar 30] well-made gelding: fair handicapper, below form in 2017: stays 1¼m: acts on all-weather: wears headgear: tried in tongue tie: usually leads: temperament under suspicion. *Mandy Rowland* **60**

STAR GENERAL 3 b.c. Galileo (IRE) 134 – Sweet Cecily (IRE) 99 (Kodiac 112) [2017 p10g^{6} Jan 5] 14/1, well held in maiden at Chelmsford: sold 13,000 gns in February, sent to UAE. *Marco Botti* **–**

STAR GLITTER (FR) 4 ch.g. Sea The Stars (IRE) 140 – Gadalka (USA) (Giant's Causeway (USA) 132) [2017 70p: 12g^{4} 11.1m^{4} 13.1m^{4} t12.2g 10m Jun 17] smallish gelding: fair maiden: should stay beyond 1½m: acts on heavy going: in headgear last 2 starts: hurdling in USA. *David O'Meara* **73**

STAR GUIDE 3 b.f. Henrythenavigator (USA) 131 – Exorcet (FR) 78 (Selkirk (USA) 129) [2017 10d^{5} p12d^{2} 11.6d* 14s Sep 27] half-sister to several winners, including smart 6f (including at 2 yrs) winner Dark Missile (by Night Shift) and useful 1m-1¼m winner Breakheart (by Sakhee): dam 6f winner: fair form: won maiden at Lingfield in September: stays 1½m. *Sylvester Kirk* **77**

STAR GYPSY (FR) 3 br.g. Myboycharlie (IRE) 118 – Melandia (IRE) (One Cool Cat (USA) 123) [2017 10g p8s^{4} 8v* 9.1s^{5} Jul 6] €30,000Y, €120,000 2-y-o: well-made gelding: first foal: dam, Greek 6f winner, half-sister to high-class 6f winner Society Rock: fairly useful form: won maiden at Wetherby (by 3¼ lengths from Thornton) in June: stays 1m: sold to join Harry Dunlop 50,000 gns in November. *Luca Cumani* **86**

STARK REALITY (IRE) 2 b.f. (Apr 4) Arcano (IRE) 122 – Eliza Doolittle 67 (Royal Applause 124) [2017 6d 5g^{6} 6m t7.1g Sep 12] €3,000Y: fourth foal: half-sister to 6f-9f winner Adventure Zone (by Elnadim): dam, 7f winner, half-sister to smart sprinters Strike Up The Band, Fire Up The Band and Sampower Star: no form, including in nursery. *Nigel Tinkler* **–**

STARLIGHT CIRCUS (IRE) 3 b.f. High Chaparral (IRE) 132 – Mountain Law (USA) (Mountain Cat (USA)) [2017 60: 9g 11.5m^3 10.1g^5 10.1d^4 14m^3 p12g Oct 3] fair maiden: stays 1¾m: acts on polytrack and good to firm going: tried in headgear: front runner/races prominently. *Marco Botti* **69**

STARLIGHT MYSTERY (IRE) 2 b.f. (Feb 13) Iffraaj 127 – Electra Star 99 (Shamardal (USA) 129) [2017 5m^3 5.3g* 5m* 6s^2 6m 7m 7v^6 7g^6 6g Oct 7] 14,000Y: tall, rather unfurnished filly: third foal: half-sister to winners up to 1m Electra Voice (by Poet's Voice) and Native Soldier (by Sepoy), both 7f winners at 2 yrs: dam 1m winner: fairly useful performer: won minor events at Brighton and Ripon in May: stays 7f: acts on good to firm and heavy going: sometimes slowly away. *Mark Johnston* **86**

STARLIGHT ROMANCE (IRE) 3 b.f. Excelebration (IRE) 133 – Takizada (IRE) 71 (Sendawar (IRE) 129) [2017 74: 7.5m* 7s^3 7.6s* 7d^2 7g 7.9g 8g Nov 3] angular filly: useful handicapper: won at Beverley in April and Chester (by short head from Vona) in June: second at latter course (¾ length behind Lualiwa) in July: stays 7.5f: acts on soft and good to firm going. *Richard Fahey* **99**

STAR LINKS (USA) 11 b.g. Bernstein (USA) 115 – Startarette (USA) (Dixieland Band (USA)) [2017 58: p8d t8.6g^2 t8.6g p10g p12g Sep 5] leggy gelding: poor handicapper nowadays: stays 1¼m: acts on polytrack, tapeta and any turf going: wears headgear: has worn tongue tie. *John Butler* **49**

STARLIT CANTATA 6 b.m. Oratorio (IRE) 128 – Starlit Sky (Galileo (IRE) 134) [2017 87: p10g^5 Jan 4] sturdy mare: fairly useful handicapper, below form sole outing in 2017: stays 1¼m: acts on polytrack, tapeta, firm and good to soft going: has worn cheekpieces, including last 2 starts. *Eve Johnson Houghton* **77**

STARLITE SIENNA (IRE) 3 b.f. Elusive Pimpernel (USA) 117 – Devious Diva (IRE) 94 (Dr Devious (IRE) 127) [2017 71: 7.5m 9.9g 9.9m^4 p12g Dec 6] fair maiden: left Richard Fahey after third start: stays 1¼m: acts on good to firm going: tried in cheekpieces. *Eamon O'Connell, Ireland* **66**

STAR MAKER 3 ch.g. Mastercraftsman (IRE) 129 – Snoqualmie Star 98 (Galileo (IRE) 134) [2017 72: 8.5g^3 9.9f 11.8s^2 p12g^3 12g 11.6d* 12v^5 11.6d* 12g p12g 12v Oct 1] lengthy gelding: fairly useful handicapper: won at Lingfield in July and August (by ¾ length from Falcon Cliffs): stays 1½m: acts on polytrack and soft going: tried in blinkers. *Sylvester Kirk* **84**

STAR OF ASSISI (USA) 2 b.f. (Feb 8) Arch (USA) 127 – Charming Tale (USA) 62 (Kingmambo (USA) 125) [2017 7m Oct 13] $55,000Y: sturdy filly: third foal: sister/half-sister to 2 winners in USA, latter by Quality Road: dam, maiden (stayed 1m), sister to St Leger winner Rule of Law: 66/1, well held in maiden at Newmarket. *John Ryan* **–**

STAR OF BRISTOL (USA) 3 ch.f. Speightstown (USA) 124 – Starlight Dreams (USA) (Black Tie Affair 128) [2017 67: p7g^5 t8.6g^3 8m p12g Jun 22] fair maiden: stays 8.5f: acts on polytrack and tapeta: in headgear last 2 starts. *Richard Hughes* **74**

STAR OF DOHA 3 b.f. Lawman (FR) 121 – Smart Step 75 (Montjeu (IRE) 137) [2017 69: 9.9d^4 10d^5 12g Aug 4] modest maiden: best effort at 1m: acts on polytrack. *Ralph Beckett* **62**

STAR OF LOMBARDY (IRE) 4 b.f. Cape Cross (IRE) 129 – Million Waves (IRE) 92 (Mull of Kintyre (USA) 114) [2017 51: t10.2g^3 t9.5g* f11d* 10.2f^2 p10f^5 12m^2 13d^3 14g^4 t12.4s 12m^3 12f* 12d^3 t12.4g 11.9m^6 12.1g^4 12m 13.9s^4 t12.2g* p12g* Oct 18] fairly useful handicapper: won at Wolverhampton in March, Southwell in April, Epsom in July, and at Wolverhampton again and Lingfield (by ½ length from So Celebre) in October: stays 1½m: acts on all-weather and firm going: front runner/races prominently: sold 16,000 gns later in October. *Mark Johnston* **83**

STAR OF RORY (IRE) 3 b.g. Born To Sea (IRE) 117 – Dame Alicia (IRE) 94 (Sadler's Wells (USA) 132) [2017 99: 10.3d^6 10.2f^4 10.3m 9.9v^3 10.2s^2 10v 10.3g Oct 14] useful handicapper: placed at Sandown (4¼ lengths behind Time Chaser) in August and Haydock (½ length behind Awake My Soul) in September: stays 1¼m: acts on firm and soft going: in headgear last 3 starts. *Tom Dascombe* **96**

STAR OF SIENA 2 ch.f. (Apr 1) Exceed And Excel (AUS) 126 – Blagueuse (IRE) (Statue of Liberty (USA) 115) [2017 5g 8d 6g^3 Nov 3] €17,000Y, €30,000 2-y-o: third foal: half-sister to French 6f winner Bohemien (by Acclamation): dam, French 6f and (at 2 yrs) 7f winner, out of Prix de Diane winner Bright Sky: fair form when third at Newmarket (7½ lengths behind Consequences) on last of 3 starts in minor events: tried in hood. *John Ryan* **67**

STAR OF SPRING (IRE) 5 b.m. Iffraaj 127 – Gift of Spring (USA) (Gilded Time (USA)) [2017 77: t8g^3 t8d^5 Jan 27] fair handicapper: stays 8.5f: acts on tapeta, good to firm and good to soft going: wears hood. *Iain Jardine* **74**

STAR OF THE EAST (IRE) 3 b.g. Cape Cross (IRE) 129 – Serenity Star 89 (Monsun (GER) 124) [2017 85: 11.2s 12d^{2} 12d^{2} 12s^{5} 14s^{4} 14.1d^{4} 14v* 13.9g^{4} Oct 13] unfurnished gelding: useful handicapper: won at Haydock in September: also first past post at Newmarket in August, but demoted for causing interference: stays 1¾m: acts on heavy going: front runner/races prominently. *Mark Johnston* **96**

STAR OF THE STAGE 5 b.g. Invincible Spirit (IRE) 121 – Enact 104 (Kyllachy 129) [2017 76: p7g p7g p7g f7g Apr 18] sturdy gelding: fair handicapper, no form in 2017: often wears cheekpieces. *John Butler* **–**

STAR OF VENDOME (FR) 2 gr.f. (Mar 13) Style Vendome (FR) 116 – Celestina Agostino (USA) (Street Cry (IRE) 130) [2017 p6g^{6} p6g 7d 6g 8g^{3} 8.2s^{3} 8.9s Oct 11] €70,000Y: fifth foal: half-sister to 3 winners in France, including smart 10.5f winner Toruk (later 1m winner in Hong Kong, by Arcano) and useful 1m winner Calvin (by Whipper): dam French 9f winner: fair maiden: stays 1m: acts on soft going: has worn tongue tie. *Harry Dunlop* **79**

STAR OF ZAAM (IRE) 2 br.g. (Mar 30) Elzaam (AUS) 115 – Golconda (IRE) 92 (Lahib (USA) 129) [2017 5m^{3} 5g^{5} 5.9s^{2} 6.9g^{2} 6s* 6s^{3} t7.2g^{3} t8s 7s^{3} 7s^{3} Oct 10] fair performer: won minor event at Catterick in July: stays 7f: acts on tapeta and soft going: wears cheekpieces. *K. R. Burke* **77**

STARPLEX 7 b.g. Multiplex 114 – Turtle Bay 64 (Dr Fong (USA) 128) [2017 9.1g^{4} 9.2s* 12d^{3} 11.6g^{2} Aug 10] fairly useful form: won maiden at Hamilton (by 1¼ lengths from Broadway Dreams) in July: placed in handicaps at Ripon later in July and Haydock in August: will be suited by 1¾m: winning hurdler. *Keith Dalgleish* **87**

STAR QUALITY 3 b.f. Champs Elysees 124 – Starfan (USA) 101 (Lear Fan (USA) 130) [2017 p9.4g 10.4d t7.2d* t8.6d^{2} Dec 27] half-sister to 3 winners, including smart French/Hong Kong 1m winner (including at 2 yrs) Glaswegian (by Selkirk): dam, 6f winner, half-sister to smart French/US performer up to 8.5f Etoile Montante: fairly useful form: won maiden at Wolverhampton in December: second in handicap there later same month: left P. Bary after second start: stays 8.5f. *David Loughnane* **83**

STAR RIDER 5 gr.m. Cape Cross (IRE) 129 – Starfala 108 (Galileo (IRE) 134) [2017 103: 18g^{6} 20f^{6} 20.6v 16.3d 18m Oct 14] angular mare: useful handicapper: stays 21f: acts on polytrack, firm and good to soft going: wears cheekpieces: tried in tongue tie: sold 70,000 gns in December. *Hughie Morrison* **99**

STAR ROCK 3 b.f. Fastnet Rock (AUS) 127 – Starfala 108 (Galileo (IRE) 134) [2017 68p: 10g^{2} 12s* 12d* 13.9g^{3} 10.2s* Nov 11] sparely-made filly: useful performer: won maiden at Newmarket (by ½ length from God Given) in May, handicap at same course (by 1½ lengths from Cribbs Causeway) in September and listed race at Doncaster (by ¾ length from Vintage Folly) in November: should stay 1¾m: acts on polytrack and soft going: usually races prominently. *Hughie Morrison* **107**

STARSHELL (IRE) 3 b.g. Sea The Stars (IRE) 140 – Aquarelle Bleue (Sadler's Wells (USA) 132) [2017 56p: p12g^{2} p12g^{2} 12g^{3} 14.1v^{4} p13.3d^{6} p16g^{5} Oct 12] fair maiden: stays 1½m: acts on polytrack: in headgear last 2 starts: best treated with caution. *Sir Mark Prescott Bt* **73 §**

STARSOVERTHERIVER (IRE) 3 b.f. Kodiac 112 – River Style (IRE) 53 (Desert Style (IRE) 121) [2017 6.1m* Jul 3] 16,000F, 40,000Y: fourth foal: sister to 6f winner Monashka Bay: dam, maiden (stayed 6f), half-sister to useful winner up to 1m Withernsea: 4/1, won maiden at Windsor (by neck from Charleston Belle) in July: should improve. *Ismail Mohammed* **71 p**

STARS OVER THE SEA (USA) 6 b.g. Sea The Stars (IRE) 140 – Exciting Times (FR) (Jeune Homme (USA) 120) [2017 111: 14m^{4} 14g* 16s^{2} 16s Oct 21] leggy gelding: useful performer: won minor event at Killarney (by 5 lengths from Ancient Sands) in July: second in Loughbrown Stakes at Naas (5 lengths behind Renneti) in September: stays 2m: acts on soft and good to firm going: usually races close up. *Henry de Bromhead, Ireland* **109**

STAR STORM (IRE) 5 b.h. Sea The Stars (IRE) 140 – Sayyedati Storm (USA) 52 (Storm Cat (USA)) [2017 112: 12m^{2} 12m^{3} 13.9m^{pu} Aug 26] useful-looking horse: smart handicapper: placed in listed race at Ascot (2¾ lengths behind Desert Encounter) in May and Duke of Edinburgh Stakes at Royal Ascot (3¼ lengths behind Rare Rhythm) in June: went as if amiss in Ebor: stays 1½m: acts on polytrack, soft and good to firm going: waited with. *James Fanshawe* **111**

STAR STORY 3 b.f. Sea The Stars (IRE) 140 – Stylish One (IRE) 101 (Invincible Spirit **86**
(IRE) 121) [2017 –p: 9.9s^2 10.1v^4 12g^3 t12.2g^2 t12.4d^3 Dec 16] fairly useful maiden: second in handicap at Wolverhampton in November: likely to stay 1¾m: acts on tapeta and soft going. *Ralph Beckett*

START SEVEN 5 br.g. Dilum (USA) 115 – Dancingintheclouds (IRE) 67 (Rainbow **98**
Quest (USA) 134) [2017 69: t13.9m* t13.9m* f14g* f16g^2 p13g^4 9.9d 11.9m 14.2g^6 t12.2g^5 t16.5g^3 f12.1g^5 Dec 21] useful handicapper: won at Wolverhampton (twice) and Southwell in January: placed at latter course in February and former course in December: stays 16.5f: acts on all-weather: sometimes slowly away. *Jamie Osborne*

START TIME (IRE) 4 b.g. Invincible Spirit (IRE) 121 – Silca's Sister 112 (Inchinor 119) **80**
[2017 7g 7d 6g 6v t6d 5g^3 t6d Nov 10] fairly useful handicapper nowadays: third at Nottingham in November: stays 8.5f: acts on heavy going: has worn headgear, including in 2017: quirky sort. *Paul Midgley*

STATEHOOD (IRE) 2 b.c. (Mar 12) Kodiac 112 – Analysis (Dubai Destination (USA) **94**
127) [2017 p7g* p8g^4 Dec 20] 200,000F: rather unfurnished colt: second foal: dam, unraced, closely related to smart French 7f-1¼m winner Runaway: fairly useful form: won minor event at Lingfield (by neck from On The Warpath) in November. *Charlie Appleby*

STATE RESIDENCE (IRE) 3 b.g. Arcano (IRE) 122 – Sugar Blossom (IRE) (Marju **65**
(IRE) 127) [2017 p8g t7.1m^4 f8g^4 p8g^6 f8d 8g t8g 7g^4 t8s^5 t7.2g^3 6m* 6g^5 t7.1s^3 7.2s^3 p6g^4 Sep 26] fair handicapper: won at Redcar in August: stayed 1m: acted on all-weather and good to firm going: wore headgear/tongue tie: dead. *David O'Meara*

STATE SOVEREIGNTY 5 b.m. Authorized (IRE) 133 – Sovereign's Honour (USA) 96 **85**
(Kingmambo (USA) 125) [2017 p12g^4 12d^2 12.1g* 11.1v^4 12v Oct 1] sturdy mare: third foal: dam, maiden (seemed to stay 1½m), half-sister to useful sprinter Jamaican Bolt out of smart performer up to 1½m Chiming: fairly useful performer: won maiden at Catterick (by 19 lengths from Bumble Bay) in August: stays 1½m: acts on good to soft going: placed in bumpers. *Michael Scudamore*

STATUARIO 2 b.g. (Mar 17) Helmet (AUS) 127 – Cat Hunter 77 (One Cool Cat (USA) **80**
123) [2017 7.1s* 7g 7s Oct 10] third foal: half-brother to 2m winner General Allenby (by Medicean): dam winner up to 1m (2-y-o 7f winner): fairly useful form when won minor event at Chepstow (by 2½ lengths from Beyond Equal) on debut in September: behind both starts after, including in Group 3: raced only at 7f. *Eve Johnson Houghton*

STAUNCH (USA) 2 b.g. (Apr 1) Union Rags (USA) 124 – Stylish Storm (USA) 63 **74**
(Storm Bird (CAN) 134) [2017 7d^2 t8.6g^3 Sep 23] rather unfurnished gelding: fair form when placed in minor events. *Jeremy Noseda*

STAXTON 2 b.c. (Feb 1) Equiano (FR) 127 – Snake's Head 81 (Golden Snake (USA) 127) **100**
[2017 6f* 6g^2 6g* 6m^5 6m^6 6g^3 6d^3 Oct 28] £19,000Y, £24,000 2-y-o: fifth foal: half-brother to 2-y-o 7f winner Lazarus Bell (by Bahamian Bounty) and 5f and (including at 2 yrs) 6f winner Classic Pursuit (by Pastoral Pursuits): dam, 12.4f winner, half-sister to useful 6f/7f performer Flyman: useful performer: won minor events at Haydock in July and August (by ¾ length from Humble Gratitude): third in listed races at York (2 lengths behind Rebel Assault) and Doncaster (1½ lengths behind Speak In Colours) in October: likely to stay 7f: acts on firm going. *Tim Easterby*

ST DUNSTAN (IRE) 4 b.g. Zoffany (IRE) 121 – Box of Frogs (IRE) 50 (One Cool Cat **62**
(USA) 123) [2017 57: 10.2m* 10m 9.9d Jul 24] modest handicapper: won at Nottingham in June: stays 1¼m: acts on good to firm going: in visor last 4 starts. *John Quinn*

STEADY (IRE) 3 b.f. Tagula (IRE) 116 – First Rains (Green Desert (USA) 127) [2017 –
8.3v p8g p7g^6 5.3s Oct 10] first foal: dam, French maiden (third at 9f), half-sister to useful French 1m winner Turning For Home: no form, including in handicap: tried in tongue tie. *Dan Skelton*

STEADY MAJOR (IRE) 5 b.g. Invincible Spirit (IRE) 121 – Combust (USA) (Aptitude **55**
(USA) 128) [2017 –: t8.6m t12.2g t8.6g p10g t12.2g t12.2g^4 t9.5g^6 t12.2g t12.2g 10.2d Aug 23] good-topped gelding: modest handicapper: stays 1½m: acts on all-weather and good to firm going: has worn headgear, including in 2017: tried in tongue tie. *Mark Brisbourne*

STEADY PACE 4 b.g. Dark Angel (IRE) 113 – Cool Kitten (IRE) 65 (One Cool Cat **117**
(USA) 123) [2017 100: 6g^2 6g^4 6g^4 7g^4 6m^2 7g^3 6m^2 6d^4 p7s* Sep 30] compact, attractive gelding: smart performer: won minor event at Chelmsford (by length from Mazzini) in September: placed in handicap at Meydan, Wokingham Stakes (Handicap) at Royal Ascot (½ length behind Out Do), Bunbury Cup (Handicap) at Newmarket (¾ length behind

Above The Rest) and listed race at Newmarket (beaten short head by Gifted Master): stays 7f: acts on polytrack, dirt and firm going: has worn headgear, including in 2017: often travels strongly. *Saeed bin Suroor*

STEALTH 2 b.c. (May 30) Kodiac 112 – White Dress (IRE) (Pivotal 124) [2017 p7g^5 Dec 20] 38,000F, 150,000 2-y-o: fifth foal: half-brother to smart winner up to 1½m Snoano (2-y-o 1m winner, by Nayef) and 6f/7f winner (stays 9.5f) Tulip Dress (by Dutch Art): dam unraced half-sister to smart French winner up to 1¼m Sparkling Beam: 4/1, fifth in minor event at Kempton (11 lengths behind Mr Ritz) in December, having hopeless task from position: capable of better. *John Gosden* **61 p**

STEAL THE SCENE (IRE) 5 b.g. Lord Shanakill (USA) 121 – Namoos (USA) 74 (Sahm (USA) 112) [2017 83, a93: 7g 7g 7.4m 7g^3 7f p7d p7g t7.2m t7.2d^2 Dec 26] well-made gelding: fair handicapper nowadays: stays 1m: acts on polytrack, tapeta, firm and good to soft going: tried in headgear: sometimes slowly away, usually races nearer last than first. *Kevin Frost* **71 a77**

STEAMING (IRE) 3 ch.g. Rail Link 132 – Dazzling Day 103 (Hernando (FR) 127) [2017 77p: t12.2g^2 12s^2 10g^4 12v^3 11.4d^5 p13.3g* t16.5g Dec 5] tall gelding: fairly useful performer: won maiden at Chelmsford (by 1½ lengths from Marine One) in October: stays 13.5f: acts on polytrack, tapeta and soft going: in cheekpieces last 2 starts. *Ralph Beckett* **84**

STECCANDO (IRE) 4 b.g. Lawman (FR) 121 – Second Act (Sadler's Wells (USA) 132) [2017 78: 7m 12g^6 12g^3 12s 12.5m^4 12d^2 12.1d^3 t12.4g t10.2g^6 Oct 20] fair maiden: stays 1½m: acts on heavy going. *Sally Haynes* **67**

STEEL HELMET (IRE) 3 ch.g. Helmet (AUS) 127 – Marine City (JPN) 77 (Carnegie (IRE) 129) [2017 65: 9.9m^5 10m 12.1m t8s^2 t10.2g t7.1s 10d^5 Oct 30] fair maiden: stays 1m: acts on tapeta and soft going: tried in headgear. *Brian Ellison* **67**

STEEL OF MADRID (IRE) 4 b.c. Lope de Vega (IRE) 125 – Bibury 80 (Royal Applause 124) [2017 116: 9m* 9.9m^3 8.1g^5 Jul 1] good-topped colt: smart performer: won Earl of Sefton Stakes at Newmarket (by ½ length from Folkswood) in April: third in Brigadier Gerard Stakes at Sandown (2¼ lengths behind Autocratic) in May: stays 1¼m: acts on polytrack and good to firm going: usually races prominently: sent to Australia. *Richard Hannon* **118**

STEELRIVER (IRE) 7 b.g. Iffraaj 127 – Numerus Clausus (FR) (Numerous (USA)) [2017 79, a99: t5.1f^2 p6g^3 p6d^5 t6g p6g^2 6g 5g^6 6m^3 6m p5g Nov 17] close-coupled gelding: fair handicapper on turf, fairly useful on all-weather: second at Wolverhampton in January and Kempton in March: left David Barron after eighth start: raced over sprint trips nowadays: acts on polytrack, tapeta and good to firm going: has worn headgear: usually races nearer last than first: hard to win with. *J. F. Levins, Ireland* **74 a91**

STEEL TRAIN (FR) 6 b.g. Zafeen (FR) 123 – Silent Sunday (IRE) (Testa Rossa (AUS) 128) [2017 110: t7.1g t7.1g t8.6g 8g p8g 7m 7m 7.9g 7d p7s* p8s Dec 14] rather leggy gelding: useful handicapper: won at Chelmsford (by length from Swift Approval) in November: stays 8.5f: acts on polytrack, tapeta, soft and good to firm going: tried in cheekpieces: often races towards rear/travels strongly. *David O'Meara* **107**

STELLAR MASS (IRE) 4 b.c. Sea The Stars (IRE) 140 – Juno Marlowe (IRE) 100 (Danehill (USA) 126) [2017 114: 10d^4 12m 14g^4 12g^3 Aug 10] good-topped colt: smart performer: third in Ballyroan Stakes at Leopardstown (3 lengths behind Spanish Steps) in August: stays 1¾m: acts on soft and good to firm going: tried in cheekpieces. *J. S. Bolger, Ireland* **113**

STELLAR SURPRISE 3 b.f. Notnowcato 128 – Crystal Etoile 76 (Dansili 127) [2017 79: 8m^3 8g^3 8d^6 8d* 8s^5 8g 7g^5 p10g^2 t8.6d* Dec 27] fairly useful handicapper: won at Yarmouth in August and Wolverhampton (by short head from Star Quality) in December: also first past post at Lingfield in November, but demoted for causing interference: stays 1¼m: acts on polytrack, tapeta, good to firm and good to soft going: usually wears tongue tie. *Stuart Williams* **92**

STELLARTA 6 b.m. Sakhee's Secret 128 – Torgau (IRE) 109 (Zieten (USA) 118) [2017 100: p6g^3 p6g^2 6m^5 6g^5 6f 6.1g^3 6m 6d^5 5.5g 6g p6g^3 6s p6g p6g Dec 30] angular mare: useful handicapper: placed at Kempton (twice) in April and Windsor (½ length behind Upstaging) in July: stays 6f: acts on polytrack and any turf going. *Michael Blanshard* **101**

STELLEKAYA (IRE) 3 gr.f. Mastercraftsman (IRE) 129 – Delitme (IRE) (Val Royal (FR) 127) [2017 10g 12g Aug 15] 20,000F, 32,000Y: sixth foal: half-sister to 6f/7f winner Art Dzeko (by Acclamation) and 6f (including at 2 yrs) winner Irish Eclare (by Equiano): dam, Italian 6.5f-1m winner (including at 2 yrs), half-sister to Nell Gwyn Stakes winner Reunion: well held in maidens. *Mark H. Tompkins* **–**

STEPHENSONS ROCKET (IRE) 2 gr.c. (Feb 4) Teofilo (IRE) 126 – Tipperary Honor (FR) 67 (Highest Honor (FR) 124) [2017 8g^{2} 8d* Oct 20] €235,000Y: seventh foal: brother to useful French winner up to 1m Vaunoise (2-y-o 7.5f winner) and half-brother to smart French 7.5f and (at 2 yrs) 1m winner Beauvoir (by Footstepsinthesand): dam, ran 3 times, sister to useful 9.5f-1½m winner Tipperary All Star: fairly useful form: won minor event at Redcar (by 3½ lengths from Hazarfan) in October: sure to go on to better things. *Ed Walker* **91 p**

STEPNEY 3 b.f. Mount Nelson 125 – Fancy Rose (USA) (Joyeux Danseur (USA) 123) [2017 p12m^{2} t12.2g* t12.2g^{5} t12.2g^{3} 10d^{5} t12.2g^{2} p12g^{3} t12.4g^{5} Oct 20] 1,500Y: seventh foal: half-sister to French 6.5f winner Magical Flower (by Oasis Dream) and 2-y-o 7f winner (stayed 11.6f) Lady Charlie (by Myboycharlie): dam, US 6.5f winner, half-sister to smart winner up to 1m Dijeerr: fair performer: won maiden at Wolverhampton in April: stays 1½m: acts on polytrack, tapeta and good to soft going: often races prominently. *Robyn Brisland* **79**

STEPPER POINT 8 b.g. Kyllachy 129 – Sacre Coeur 90 (Compton Place 125) [2017 105: p5g^{2} p5g^{4} 5m* 5f 5d^{4} p5g* 5m 5g 5.1m Jul 17] sturdy, good-quartered gelding: very smart at best, winner of 10 races, including handicaps at Windsor in April and Chelmsford (by 1¼ lengths from Excellent George) in June: stayed 5.5f: acted on polytrack, good to firm and good to soft going: wore headgear: usually led: retired. *William Muir* **102**

STERLING SILVA (IRE) 3 ch.g. Sakhee's Secret 128 – Silicon Star (FR) (Starborough 126) [2017 83: 6m 8s^{5} 8d^{2} 7v^{4} 8s^{3} 8.2d^{6} p8g p8g^{4} Oct 25] strong gelding: fairly useful handicapper: second at Newmarket in July: stays 1m: acts on polytrack and heavy going: in headgear last 3 starts. *Richard Hannon* **85**

STERNRUBIN (GER) 6 b.g. Authorized (IRE) 133 – Sworn Mum (GER) (Samum (GER) 126) [2017 11.6g* 16g^{3} 14.2d^{2} 14m^{3} 14v* 18d Sep 23] lengthy gelding: useful handicapper: won at Windsor in May and Ffos Las (by 9 lengths from Moabit) in August: stays 1¾m: acts on good to firm and heavy going: tried in hood: front runner/races prominently. *Philip Hobbs* **99**

STEVE PRESCOTT 5 gr.g. Dutch Art 126 – Toy Top (USA) 86 (Tactical Cat (USA) 116) [2017 t6g Mar 30] useful handicapper, well held after long absence sole outing in 2017: stays 6f: acts on firm and good to soft going: tried in blinkers. *Patrick Morris* **–**

STEVE ROGERS (IRE) 6 b.g. Montjeu (IRE) 137 – Three Owls (IRE) 79 (Warning 136) [2017 106: t16.5m^{3} p15.8g^{3} Apr 14] good-topped gelding: smart performer: third in minor event at Wolverhampton (6¼ lengths behind Antiquarium) in January and valuable event at Lingfield (2½ lengths behind Winning Story) in April: stays 16.5f: acts on polytrack, tapeta and firm going: often races prominently: sold to join Michael Bell 105,000 gns in May. *Roger Varian* **110**

STEVIE BROWN 3 b.g. Bushranger (IRE) 119 – Oriental Romance (IRE) 52 (Elusive City (USA) 117) [2017 64: f7d^{3} 8g 7g May 30] good-topped gelding: modest maiden: stays 7f: acts on fibresand and good to firm going: tried in cheekpieces. *David Brown* **64**

ST HELENS GATE (IRE) 2 b.f. (Jan 31) Lilbourne Lad (IRE) 111 – Lyca Ballerina 76 (Marju (IRE) 127) [2017 5m 5f 6d Jul 22] €3,000Y: closely related to 3 winners by Acclamation, including useful 6f/7f winner Purcell, and half-sister to 7f/1m winner Quite Smart (by Arcano): dam 7.5f winner: no form. *Rebecca Menzies* **–**

STICKLEBACK 8 ch.m. Manduro (GER) 135 – The Stick 61 (Singspiel (IRE) 133) [2017 14v Jun 6] maiden: well held in handicap after long absence sole outing in 2017: stays 21.5f: acts on heavy going: often in headgear: temperamental. *Micky Hammond* **– §**

STILL BELIEVING (IRE) 9 ch.m. Blueprint (IRE) 120 – Im A Believer (IRE) (Erins Isle 121) [2017 12v^{6} Aug 15] fairly useful hurdler/chaser: 7/2, well held in maiden at Ffos Las sole outing on Flat. *Evan Williams* **–**

STILL GOT IT 2 b.f. (Mar 28) Captain Gerrard (IRE) 113 – Petaluma 83 (Teofilo (IRE) 126) [2017 6s^{6} 7g^{5} 7d^{4} 7d^{2} t8.6m t7.2g f6.1g Dec 19] first foal: dam 17f winner: modest maiden: left Mick Channon after fourth start: stays 7f: acts on soft going: often races towards rear. *Daniel Loughnane* **61**

STILL ON TOP 4 b.g. Royal Applause 124 – Poulaine Bleue 44 (Bertolini (USA) 125) [2017 –: 6m^{5} 6m^{6} 8d Jun 9] strong gelding: fair handicapper nowadays: stays 6f: acts on good to firm going: wears hood. *Tim Easterby* **73**

STILL WAITING 3 b.g. Kheleyf (USA) 116 – First Approval 78 (Royal Applause 124) [2017 67: p8g^{2} p8g^{3} 8s^{6} 7m^{2} 7g 7g^{2} 7g^{2} 7m^{6} 7d^{6} Oct 24] fair maiden: stays 1m: acts on polytrack and good to firm going: tried in headgear: sometimes slowly away. *William Jarvis* **72**

STIMULATOR 4 b.g. Motivator 131 – Fleeting Echo 99 (Beat Hollow 126) [2017 –: p12g Jan 28] no form: in hood last 3 starts. *Andi Brown* **–**

STIPULATE 8 b.g. Dansili 127 – Indication 76 (Sadler's Wells (USA) 132) [2017 106: 14g 8m^3 8.5m 10.3m 8.6d 7s Aug 6] strong gelding: useful handicapper: third at Thirsk (2½ lengths behind Cote d'Azur) in May: probably stays 1½m: acts on good to firm and good to soft going: has worn headgear: sometimes slowly away, usually races in rear: sold 800 gns in November: not one to trust. *Brian Ellison* **96 §**

STIRLING VALUE 2 b.c. (Mar 21) Pour Moi (IRE) 125 – Celebre Vadala (FR) (Peintre Celebre (USA) 137) [2017 t9.5g Dec 18] €80,000Y: half-brother to several winners in France, including high-class miler (also won up to 1½m) Vadamos (by Monsun) and useful 1¼m winner Volfango (by Dutch Art): dam, French 1¼m-1½m winner, half-sister to high-class winner up to 1½m Valixir: 50/1, well held in minor event at Wolverhampton. *David Simcock* **–**

ST JAMES'S PARK (IRE) 4 br.g. Invincible Spirit (IRE) 121 – Rakiza (IRE) (Elnadim (USA) 128) [2017 p7g^5 p7s^5 p8s p8g p10g 8.3g Nov 1] sturdy gelding: fair maiden: should stay 1m: acts on polytrack: tried in headgear. *Luke McJannet* **70**

ST MALO (USA) 4 b.g. Street Cry (IRE) 130 – Arkadina (IRE) 102 (Danehill (USA) 126) [2017 90p: 11.9g^6 p11d^2 10d p12g^2 p12g Nov 10] useful handicapper: second at Kempton (¾ length behind Golden Birthday) in October: left Roger Varian after fourth start: stays 12.5f: acts on polytrack and tapeta: tried in headgear. *Denis Hogan, Ireland* **100**

ST MARY'S 4 b.f. Siyouni (FR) 122 – Once Over (Sakhee (USA) 136) [2017 85: 12.3d* 12.3s 13.3g^6 16v^2 15.9g* 14.4v^2 14s^5 14d^2 14g* 15.4d^6 p16d^4 Nov 22] rather leggy filly: useful handicapper: won at Chester in May/September and Nottingham (by ½ length from Master Archer) in November: stays 2m: acts on polytrack, good to firm and heavy going. *Andrew Balding* **96**

ST MICHEL 4 b.c. Sea The Stars (IRE) 140 – Miss Provence 88 (Hernando (FR) 127) [2017 113p: p14g^2 16f^2 16.3g^3 Aug 25] compact colt: smart performer: placed in minor event at Chelmsford (2¼ lengths behind Harrison) in May, Grade 3 Belmont Gold Cup (neck behind Red Cardinal) in June and Lonsdale Cup at York (½ length behind Montaly) in August: stays 2¼m: acts on polytrack and any turf going: in headgear last 5 starts: often races towards rear/travels strongly. *Sir Mark Prescott Bt* **116**

STOCKHILL DIVA 7 ch.m. Haafhd 129 – April Stock 97 (Beveled (USA)) [2017 96: 11.6g^4 11.4m* 11.4g^6 11.6g^5 Jul 26] workmanlike mare: fairly useful handicapper nowadays: won at Windsor (by head from Jacob Cats) in June: stays 1½m: acts on good to firm and heavy going: often races towards rear. *Brendan Powell* **88**

STOCK HILL FAIR 9 b.g. Sakhee (USA) 136 – April Stock 97 (Beveled (USA)) [2017 14.2m^{pu} 12g Sep 7] tall gelding: fairly useful handicapper at best, shaped as if amiss both starts in 2017 after long absence: stays 1¾m: acts on polytrack and heavy going: usually wears tongue tie nowadays. *Brendan Powell* **–**

STOCKHILL STAR 3 b.f. Aqlaam 125 – April Stock 97 (Beveled (USA)) [2017 7.1s p7g Nov 1] seventh foal: half-sister to 1½m-1¾m winner Stock Hill Fair (by Sakhee) and useful 1¼m-1½m winner Stockhill Diva (by Haafhd): dam 11.6f/1½m winner: well held in pair of maidens, in hood on second occasion. *Brendan Powell* **–**

STOCKINGS LANE (IRE) 2 ch.c. (Jan 12) Excelebration (IRE) 133 – Mubkera (IRE) 100 (Nashwan (USA) 135) [2017 6.1m 7s Aug 2] sturdy colt: behind in minor events. *Steph Hollinshead* **–**

STOCKTON (IRE) 3 b.g. Galileo (IRE) 134 – Walklikeanegyptian (IRE) 77 (Danehill (USA) 126) [2017 11.5m 11.6g p12d May 31] well held in maidens. *David Simcock* **–**

STOIC BOY 5 ch.g. Paco Boy (IRE) 129 – Dramatic Turn 87 (Pivotal 124) [2017 p6g^3 Dec 31] fair form, off over 2 years before only outing in 2017: stays 6f. *Henry Candy* **65**

STOLEN ANGEL (IRE) 3 b.g. Dark Angel (IRE) 113 – Tamarisk (GER) (Selkirk (USA) 129) [2017 8g^5 7g 8.3g t10.2s 8g Sep 27] modest form when fifth in maiden on debut, standout effort: tried in hood: often races freely. *Antony Brittain* **57**

STOMACHION (IRE) 7 b.g. Duke of Marmalade (IRE) 132 – Insight (FR) 115 (Sadler's Wells (USA) 132) [2017 –: f12g^5 Mar 9] lengthy gelding: useful at best, very lightly raced and no form since 2014. *John Butler* **–**

STONEBOAT BILL 5 ch.g. Virtual 122 – Applauding (IRE) (Royal Applause 124) [2017 74: 8.3g 10g^3 10m^2 9.1m^2 12g^2 10.2d^5 16.1g^5 10.2g 10d^4 10.5v^2 f8.1g Dec 22] leggy, close-coupled gelding: fair handicapper: stays 2m: acts on tapeta, good to firm and heavy going: tried in blinkers: often starts slowly, usually races in rear. *Declan Carroll* **70**

STONECOLDSOBA 4 b.g. Aqlaam 125 – Aswaaq (IRE) 74 (Peintre Celebre (USA) **67** 137) [2017 67: f12g^3 t13.9m^3 p12g^4 f12g^3 t12.2m^3 t13.9g t12.2g t12.2g Sep 9] fair handicapper: left David Evans after fourth start: stays 1¾m: acts on all-weather and soft going: tried in visor: winning hurdler. *Denis Quinn*

STONEHAM 6 b.m. Sixties Icon 125 – Cibenze 74 (Owington 123) [2017 75: t16.3d* **76** t16.3g^2 15d^3 16m^4 16g^3 16m^4 14m^4 t16.3g Sep 22] rather leggy mare: fair handicapper: won at Newcastle in March: stays 17f: acts on polytrack, tapeta, firm and soft going: wears headgear: often races in rear. *Iain Jardine*

STONE OF FOLCA 9 b.g. Kodiac 112 – Soyalang (FR) (Alydeed (CAN) 120) [2017 6g^6 – Jul 23] leggy gelding: useful at best, folded tamely after long absence sole outing in 2017: best form at 5f: acts on firm going: usually in hood. *Lucinda Egerton*

STONE THE CROWS 3 b.g. Cape Cross (IRE) 129 – Stars In Your Eyes 75 (Galileo **92** (IRE) 134) [2017 79p: 12m* 11.9f^2 12d^2 12d^6 p11g^6 Sep 27] good-bodied gelding: fairly useful performer: won maiden at Salisbury in April: second in handicaps at Haydock in May and former course in June: stays 1½m: acts on polytrack, firm and good to soft going: in cheekpieces last 2 starts: sold to join Iain Jardine 75,000 gns in October. *Roger Charlton*

STONEY BROKE 4 b.f. Dansili 127 – Alvee (IRE) 75 (Key of Luck (USA) 126) [2017 **92** –: 11.5m^2 t12.4s* 12g^5 t12.4g^2 11.9d^3 14d^5 Oct 18] fairly useful handicapper: won at Newcastle in June: placed at same course in July and Doncaster in September: stays 12.5f: acts on tapeta, good to firm and good to soft going. *James Fanshawe*

STONEYFORD LANE (IRE) 3 b.g. Bushranger (IRE) 119 – Peace Talks (Pivotal 124) **87** [2017 80: 5s^5 6d 5f* 5g 5s^3 5d* 6d^6 Aug 13] compact gelding: fairly useful handicapper: won at Haydock in July and Bath (by length from Jashma) in August: should be suited by 6f: acts on any turf going: in cheekpieces last 5 starts: often races towards rear. *Steph Hollinshead*

STOPDWORLDNLETMEOF 3 b.g. Piccolo 121 – Dilli Dancer 69 (Dansili 127) **48** [2017 –: f5g^4 f5d^6 6m^6 5.1s^3 7m^6 7.6d^4 5.1d Aug 24] poor maiden: best form at 5f: acts on soft going: tried in headgear: usually leads. *David Flood*

STOPWATCH 2 b.g. (Feb 10) Harbour Watch (IRE) 121 – Almond Branches 85 (Dutch – Art 126) [2017 5s^6 5g^5 5d 7.2m t7.1g Oct 10] little impact in minor events/nurseries: in cheekpieces last 2 starts. *Karen McLintock*

STORM AGAIN 2 ch.c. (Feb 25) Nathaniel (IRE) 129 – Triveni (FR) (Lando (GER) 128) – [2017 p8d Dec 13] 66/1, well held in minor event at Kempton. *Philip Hide*

STORM AHEAD (IRE) 4 b.g. Iffraaj 127 – Loose Julie (IRE) (Cape Cross (IRE) 129) **99** [2017 100: 8m 8s^4 8.1g^5 9.1d 8s^2 8d Oct 6] useful handicapper: second at Ascot (2¼ lengths behind Leader Writer) in September: stays 1m: acts on polytrack, soft and good to firm going: in cheekpieces last 2 starts: sold to join Tim Easterby 24,000 gns in November. *Marcus Tregoning*

STORMBOUND (IRE) 8 b.g. Galileo (IRE) 134 – A Footstep Away (USA) (Giant's **74** Causeway (USA) 132) [2017 74: p8g t8.6g^6 8m* 8m^2 8f^4 p7.5f^5 t8.6g Sep 9] strong, lengthy gelding: fair handicapper: won at Brighton in April: raced mainly around 1m: acts on polytrack, tapeta and firm going: usually wears headgear: tried in tongue tie: often races towards rear. *Paul Cole*

STORMBRINGER 2 b.c. (Mar 20) Dutch Art 126 – Riva Royale 93 (Royal Applause **94** 124) [2017 6s^3 6g* 6m Aug 26] 50,000Y, 190,000 2-y-o: sixth foal: half-brother to 3 winners, including very smart Hong Kong 7f winner Let Me Fight (2-y-o 6f winner in Britain as Ask Frank, by Hawk Wing) and useful Hong Kong 6f/7f winner Exciting Dream (2-y-o 6f winner in Britain as Bertie Royale, by Bertolini): dam winner up to 7f (2-y-o 5f winner): fairly useful form: in cheekpieces, won minor event at Redcar (by 2 lengths from Miss Mo Brown Bear) in August: improved again when seventh in Gimcrack Stakes at York: raced only at 6f. *Kevin Ryan*

STORM CRY 3 b.f. Poet's Voice 126 – Street Fire (IRE) (Street Cry (IRE) 130) [2017 91: **87** 6m^5 p8g 7.2g^4 5.9s^2 7m^3 6d^2 6f^2 5.9g^6 6.1d^6 p6g^4 6d* 7v^3 7.2s^5 6d Oct 27] lengthy filly: fairly useful handicapper: won at Brighton (by 1½ lengths from Monteamiata) in September: placed on 5 other occasions in 2017: stays 7f: acts on firm and soft going: usually races prominently: sold 16,000 gns, sent to Saudi Arabia. *Mark Johnston*

STORM DORIS (IRE) 2 br.f. (Feb 16) Lilbourne Lad (IRE) 111 – Big Sylv (IRE) 72 **53** (Clodovil (IRE) 116) [2017 5f^6 t5.1g^2 5.1m t6.1g 7g Aug 30] first foal: dam 7f-8.6f winner: modest form when second in minor event at Wolverhampton, standout effort: tried in visor. *James Unett*

STORMFLOWER 4 gr.f. Arcano (IRE) 122 – Someone's Angel (USA) (Runaway Groom (CAN)) [2017 78: 5m^5 p5g^5 May 5] rather leggy filly: fair handicapper: stayed 6f: acted on polytrack, good to firm and heavy going: front runner/raced prominently: dead. *John Bridger* **73**

STORM HAWK (IRE) 10 b.g. Hawk Wing (USA) 136 – Stormy Larissa (IRE) 79 (Royal Applause 124) [2017 59§: p16g Sep 6] compact gelding: fairly useful handicapper at best, lightly raced and little form since 2012: wears headgear. *Emma Owen* **–**

STORMING AMBITION 4 b.g. Captain Gerrard (IRE) 113 – Lady Roxanne 65 (Cyrano de Bergerac 120) [2017 –: p11d p6g^6 p6g f6d f7g 5.2m^5 May 2] no form: has worn blinkers, including in 2017: in tongue tie last 5 starts. *Conrad Allen* **–**

STORMING HARRY 5 ch.g. Assertive 121 – Miss Pebbles (IRE) 82 (Lake Coniston (IRE) 131) [2017 p16g 16v p12d t16.5g Oct 21] sturdy gelding: poor handicapper nowadays: stays 2m: acts on polytrack: tried in tongue tie. *Robin Dickin* **49**

STORMIN TOM (IRE) 5 b.g. Dylan Thomas (IRE) 132 – She Storm (IRE) (Rainbow Quest (USA) 134) [2017 85: 14.6m 14g 16d^4 16m 16.5m^2 16m^2 17.2s^6 14g* 16.1g^3 12v 16.3g^6 14g^3 t16.3g^4 Nov 15] fairly useful handicapper: won at Ripon in August: stays 16.5f: acts on tapeta, good to firm and good to soft going: tried in cheekpieces: front runner/races prominently. *Tim Easterby* **80**

STORM JAZZ (IRE) 2 b.f. (Apr 9) Red Jazz (USA) 125 – Singitta (Singspiel (IRE) 133) [2017 6.1m^3 7g^4 p6g 7d Oct 30] 15,000F, 28,000Y: rather leggy filly: half-sister to several winners, including useful 5f (including at 2 yrs) winner Singeur (by Chineur) and 1m winner Sighora (by Royal Applause): dam of little account: fair form: best effort at 7f. *Ed Dunlop* **72**

STORM KING 8 b.g. Shamardal (USA) 129 – Tarandot (IRE) 104 (Singspiel (IRE) 133) [2017 85: t10.2g^6 f11g^2 p12g^4 t10.2d^6 f11g* f12g^3 f11d^2 10.3m* 10.1m 10.3m 10.1f 10.3g* 9.1d* 10.3m 11.9s^4 p10g p12g Dec 23] sturdy gelding: useful handicapper on turf, fairly useful on all-weather: won at Southwell (apprentice) in March, Chester in May/July and Goodwood (apprentice, by ½ length from Born To Be Alive) in August: stays 1½m: acts on all-weather, soft and good to firm going: has worn headgear, including in 2017: front runner/races prominently. *David C. Griffiths* **100 a87**

STORM LIGHTNING 8 b.g. Exceed And Excel (AUS) 126 – All For Laura 99 (Cadeaux Genereux 131) [2017 68: p6g^6 t6.1m t5.1g t6.1d t5.1g^3 t6.1d Dec 27] workmanlike gelding: modest handicapper nowadays: raced at sprint trips: acts on polytrack, tapeta, good to firm and heavy going: has worn headgear: often races towards rear. *Mark Brisbourne* **55**

STORM MELODY 4 b.g. Royal Applause 124 – Plume 88 (Pastoral Pursuits 127) [2017 87: 6m^5 6m 6.1g^4 5.7g^4 7s^5 5.7s^2 6s Oct 10] compact, good-quartered gelding: fairly useful handicapper: stays 5.5f: acts on heavy going: has worn headgear: races towards rear. *Jonjo O'Neill* **79**

STORM OVER (IRE) 3 b.c. Elnadim (USA) 128 – Stormy View (USA) 77 (Cozzene (USA)) [2017 69p: 5g* 5.2s^3 5v^5 5v* Oct 21] attractive colt: useful handicapper: won at Redcar in May and Catterick (by ¾ length from Memories Galore) in October: raced only at 5f: acts on tapeta and heavy going: sometimes slowly away. *Robert Cowell* **103**

STORM ROCK 5 b.g. Rock of Gibraltar (IRE) 133 – Seasonal Cross 80 (Cape Cross (IRE) 129) [2017 100: p11g p11g^6 8d^4 10d 10.2s^4 10.2s 9.9v^3 10.2d^3 10s p11d Dec 13] fairly useful handicapper nowadays: third at Nottingham in October: stays 10.5f: acts on soft going: tried in cheekpieces. *Harry Dunlop* **88**

STORM RUNNER (IRE) 9 b.g. Rakti 130 – Saibhreas (IRE) 83 (Last Tycoon 131) [2017 62: 9.9g^5 p11g Oct 25] good-topped gelding: has stringhalt: modest handicapper: stays 1¼m: acts on polytrack and good to soft going: has worn headgear: usually races nearer last than first. *George Margarson* **54**

STORM TROOPER (IRE) 6 b.g. Acclamation 118 – Maid To Order (IRE) 83 (Zafonic (USA) 130) [2017 72, a59: t6f^5 t5.1g^3 6g 5g^4 t5.1g^3 5m 5g t5d t6.1d Dec 27] quite good-topped gelding: modest handicapper: left David Nicholls after second start, Marjorie Fife after seventh: stays 6f: acts on tapeta, good to firm and good to soft going: tried in cheekpieces/tongue tie. *Adam West* **62**

STORMY ANTARCTIC 4 ch.g. Stormy Atlantic (USA) – Bea Remembered 105 (Doyen (IRE) 132) [2017 119: 8g^2 8m^5 8.1g^2 7m^3 7g 8d* p8d^6 Nov 22] well-made gelding: smart performer: won listed race at Chantilly (by 4 lengths from Blessed Silence) in October: placed in similar races at Doncaster (short head behind Kool Kompany) in April **117**

and Windsor (short head behind Morando) in July, and in Minstrel Stakes at the Curragh (1¾ lengths behind Spirit of Valor) later in July: stays 1m: acts on any turf going: tried in blinkers. *Ed Walker*

STORMY BLUES 3 b.g. Sepoy (AUS) 129 – Miss Brown To You (IRE) 84 (Fasliyev (USA) 120) [2017 8m 10.2s^2 10g Jul 24] 160,000Y: sturdy gelding: fifth foal: half-brother to 3 winners, including very smart 1¼m-2½m (Gold Cup) winner Big Orange (by Duke of Marmalade) and 1½m winner The Paris Shrug (by Manduro): dam, 1m winner, half-sister to high-class Hong Kong 1m-1¼m winner Military Attack: fairly useful form when second at Nottingham (¾ length behind Intellect) on second of 3 starts in maidens, standout effort: in tongue tie last 2 starts: sold £7,000 in September. *Charlie Appleby* **85**

STORMY SAND (IRE) 2 br.g. (Mar 6) Footstepsinthesand 120 – Think Again (Dubawi (IRE) 129) [2017 p7s 6s^5 6.1g^4 6d p8g^6 7g Oct 16] fair maiden: should stay 7f: acts on soft going: tried in tongue tie. *Marco Botti* **66**

STORY MINISTER (IRE) 2 ch.g. (Mar 9) Camacho 118 – Hartstown House (IRE) 83 (Primo Dominie 121) [2017 5m^3 5m^4 t5.1g^3 6v^3 6.1g^6 p6d^5 t6.1g* Oct 27] fair performer: won seller at Wolverhampton in October: stays 6f: acts on tapeta, good to firm and heavy going: in headgear last 3 starts: front runner/races prominently: sold 13,000 gns, sent to Norway. *Tom Dascombe* **71**

STOSUR (IRE) 6 b.m. Mount Nelson 125 – Jules (IRE) 76 (Danehill (USA) 126) [2017 84: t8.6g^2 p8d 8.3g^3 8m^3 t7.2g^3 p8g^2 8.5d^3 8d^2 7m^5 9.1m^2 p8g^2 t8.6g f7.1g p8g^4 Dec 21] sturdy mare: fairly useful handicapper: placed 9 times in 2017: raced mainly around 1m: acts on all-weather, good to firm and heavy going: wears headgear: usually leads. *Gay Kelleway* **82**

ST PATRICK'S DAY (IRE) 5 b.g. Fastnet Rock (AUS) 127 – Race For The Stars (USA) 113 (Fusaichi Pegasus (USA) 130) [2017 86: p8g^6 t9.5m p8g p8d f11.1g^6 f8.1g^3 Dec 21] sturdy gelding: fairly useful handicapper, well below best in 2017: stays 8.5f: acts on fibresand, tapeta and good to firm going: wears visor: sometimes slowly away. *J. R. Jenkins* **62**

STRADA DI CARSOLI 4 br.g. Showcasing 117 – Carsulae (IRE) (Marju (IRE) 127) [2017 86: t6g Mar 24] fairly useful handicapper in Ireland for G. M. Lyons at 3 yrs, below that level sole outing in 2017: stays 7f: acts on polytrack. *Henry Spiller* **72**

STRADIVARIUS (IRE) 3 ch.c. Sea The Stars (IRE) 140 – Private Life (FR) (Bering 136) [2017 83p: 9.9m* 12.3m^2 14m* 16g* 14.5g^3 16s^3 Oct 21] **123**

Staying events have always been an attractive feature of British racing which offers a rich variety in the distances of its races. Its North American cousin, for example, stages hardly any races over long distances and regards a mile and a half as a marathon. Much has been written in these pages over the years about the need to protect the programme of staying races in Britain, and to enhance it, and it has taken far too long for the issue to be taken as seriously as it should be. The announcement made in February 2017 of a raft of measures, including raising the Goodwood Cup to Group 1 and restoring the Queen's Vase to the pattern, came as a surprise and caused some hasty, late revision to *Racehorses of 2016*, particularly to the essay on Big Orange which had been the latest vehicle for urging the British Horseracing Authority to tackle the plight of the stayers (the essay took as an example the long-established Phil Bull Trophy, a conditions race for stayers at Pontefract, which the BHA had set out to dismantle but which, after a campaign supported by the Thoroughbred Breeders' Association and others, earned a temporary reprieve). The Thoroughbred Breeders' Association, which celebrated its hundredth year in the latest season, had produced a report in 2015 urging improvements in the staying programme and, given its ambivalent attitude over the years, the BHA made what appeared at the time to be a most surprising concession in a review of the pattern-race programme which it published in 2016. The review concluded that there was no need for the pattern system as a whole to be overhauled (many are concerned about the erosion of the quality of 'black type' as more pattern races are promoted and new ones created). However, the authors of the BHA's pattern review declared that the stayers' programme in Britain was 'worthy of further constructive debate,' the kind of phrase often found in reviews and reports that are then left to gather dust (the problems had been virtually ignored for so long, why should anyone have felt they were now going to be dealt with?).

Queen's Vase, Royal Ascot—the first edition of this race as a Group 2, also staged over a trip two furlongs shorter than in previous years; Stradivarius (blaze) wins after a sustained battle with Count Octave, the pair two lengths clear of Secret Advisor (right) at the line

The popularity of long distance races among punters and racegoers was illustrated in the latest season by betting turnover figures at Royal Ascot released by one of the big bookmakers, Coral, which had the Gold Cup at number one on its list (as it has been for many years), the Queen Alexandra Stakes at number five and the Queen's Vase at seventh. Before its power to make decisions was eroded, the old Flat Pattern Committee, whose independent members acted solely 'for the good of the sport', recognised the need to transform the pattern for staying horses but, largely because of the intransigence of the French authorities and complacency on the English side of the Channel, little was done in the years after the opening of the Irish St Leger to older horses in 1983, four years after its French equivalent the Prix Royal-Oak had led the way (these moves in themselves a blow to the stayers of each subsequent classic generation). Until the Goodwood Cup was elevated in the latest season, the Gold Cup at Royal Ascot and the St Leger (for three-year-olds) were the only Group 1s in Britain run over a mile and three quarters or more, a scandalous situation given the Group 1 opportunities for other specialist groups (there are seven Group 1 sprints in Britain for three-year-olds and upwards, for example). The Goodwood Cup—which had already had a sizeable hike in prize money from a new sponsor—was perfectly placed in the calendar to follow on from the Gold Cup but, until it relented, the BHA (through its Race Planning Committee) had refused even to permit the Goodwood executive to waive penalties in the race, which would at least have allowed it to attract the best field available and made it a Group 1 in all but name. The BHA had allowed Ascot to tinker with the conditions of the Long Distance Cup on British Champions' Day, but refused to let Goodwood do the same.

The raising of the Goodwood Cup to Group 1 status was achieved through the auspices of the recently introduced sub committee of the European Pattern Committee which was set up to consider 'possible enhancements' to the staying programme in Britain, Ireland and France. Much against expectations, the sub committee came out in favour of quite wide-ranging proposals for the staying programme. So far as Britain is concerned, the majority of racehorses are nowadays by sires who never won beyond a mile; fewer than one in six are by stallions who won at a mile and a half or further, and those numbers continue to decline. To try to redress this headlong rush for speed, the authorities have agreed that no pattern races in Europe will be downgraded over the next five years and that there will be higher minimum prize money for any such contests that are promoted (the first prize for the Goodwood Cup in its first year as a Group 1 was £296,593, making it the most valuable of the Cup races—the Gold Cup first prize was £226,850—and the Queen's

Qatar Goodwood Cup, Goodwood—Stradivarius lands the first running of this race as a Group 1, in the process becoming the first three-year-old winner since Lucky Moon in 1990; dual winner Big Orange comes up a little short in his hat-trick bid, with Desert Skyline back in third

Vase prize money is set to rise significantly over the next three years). The staying programme for fillies and mares has been enhanced too, the changes including the promotion of Goodwood's Lillie Langtry Stakes from Group 3 to Group 2. The Long Distance Cup, which is also already more valuable than the Gold Cup, meets the rating parameters for it to qualify for promotion to Group 1 and it seems sure to be upgraded in the next year or so to provide a third Group 1 in Britain for the out-and-out stayers. France stages the Prix du Cadran and the Prix Royal-Oak either side of the Long Distance Cup, both of them Group 1s, but the days when that would have been an obstacle to the upgrading of the Long Distance Cup seem to be over. Ascot's director of racing Nick Smith talked openly in the latest season about the prospect of 'an agreement with France that will require some kind of quid pro quo somewhere in the calendar to make it happen.' What price France might put on such agreement isn't clear—and it might also result in the Cadran returning to its original place in the spring—but the very idea that a race's status in the pattern race system is seemingly open to bartering is another source of worry for purists concerned about the erosion of the prestige of some pattern races. Away from the pattern races, the new measures announced to encourage stayers include more maiden and novice events for two-year-olds over nine and ten furlongs in the autumn, the introduction of a number of valuable new staying handicaps for three-year-olds, and increased grants for sixty races in the staying programme from the BHA's Development Fund (money that comes from the leasing of BHA-owned fixtures to racecourses).

It was perhaps a sign of the times that the stoutly-bred Stradivarius, a son of Sea The Stars out of a Bering mare who won at up to eleven furlongs, failed to make his reserve when sent to the Newmarket yearling sales. His owner-breeder, the New York-based Swede Bjorn Nielsen, sent Stradivarius to John Gosden. Stradivarius ran three times as a two-year-old—all three of his outings over a mile—and showed fairly useful form when winning his maiden at Newcastle in November, rallying strongly to lead again after making the running, and looking an interesting prospect over longer trips as a three-year-old. He quickly graduated from handicaps in the latest season—after winning by six lengths at Beverley and finishing second at Chester (looking as if he needed a more galloping track)—and was stepped up further in trip in the Queen's Vase at Royal Ascot on his third start. The decision to reduce the distance of the Queen's Vase by two furlongs was as surprising as the decision to elevate it to Group 2 just two years after it had been removed from the pattern and downgraded to listed status. Although two miles is an extreme trip for a horse mid-way through its three-year-old campaign, two of the most recent Queen's Vase winners, Estimate and St Leger winner Leading Light, had gone on to win the following year's Gold Cup. Dropping the distance to a mile and three quarters does not make sufficient distinction between the Queen's Vase and another of Royal Ascot's races for three-year-olds, 'the Ascot Derby', the King Edward VII Stakes over a mile and a half which is also a Group 2 (there was some interference in the early stages of the latest Queen's Vase, in which the runners had to negotiate a bend shortly after leaving the stalls, and it might be better if the distance was extended and the stalls were moved back closer to the old two-mile start). Stradivarius showed further improvement over the extra distance of the Queen's Vase, leading in the last half furlong and winning by a neck and two lengths from Count Octave and Secret Advisor, the form nowhere near Group 2 standard it must be said, though Stradivarius was certainly going the right way to consider him an eventual candidate for the St Leger.

The appearance in the Qatar Goodwood Cup line-up of Stradivarius and the Queen's Vase sixth Desert Skyline (who had since finished runner-up in the Bahrain Trophy at Newmarket) was something of a surprise at the time, but might well have provided a glimpse of the future. Not many three-year-olds have contested the two-mile Goodwood Cup in the last decade or so, with Lucky Moon (in 1990 before the distance of the race was reduced—at the Jockey Club's insistence—from two miles five furlongs) being the last of that age to win. The performances of Stradivarius and Desert Skyline in the latest edition should encourage owners of other staying three-year-olds to target the race, particularly now that it is so valuable. The latest Goodwood Cup took place on August 1st but the race has now been moved from the traditional Thursday to the opening day on Tuesday which makes it more likely to be run in July when the three-year-olds receive more weight for age from the older horses. The promotion of the Queen's Vase to Group 2 also influenced the connections of Stradivarius to run him at Goodwood as the new larger penalty for winning the Royal Ascot race would have meant him conceding weight in more traditional St Leger trials such as the Gordon Stakes and York's Great Voltigeur Stakes.

Most interest before the Goodwood Cup was in whether the six-year-old Big Orange could make history by becoming the first horse to win three successive runnings of the race (Double Trigger had won it three times, but not successively). The Gold Cup winner Big Orange (not penalised with the Goodwood Cup being Group 1) started 6/4 favourite, with Stradivarius second favourite at 6/1, ahead of the previous year's Irish St Leger winner Wicklow Brave and his compatriot US Army Ranger (both 8/1), and the previous year's Doncaster Cup and Long Distance Cup winner Sheikhzayedroad (at 10/1). Desert Skyline, who was supplemented at a cost of £25,000, started at 14/1. Front-running Big Orange wasn't far below his best on the day, though he found himself forced into setting a stronger pace than in the Gold Cup, and he came up against a most progressive type in Stradivarius who travelled well throughout and stayed on well to win by a length and three quarters, with Desert Skyline three and a half lengths behind Big Orange in third, and Wicklow Brave completing the frame.

Stradivarius was a best-priced 5/1 for the St Leger immediately after the Goodwood Cup and he started 9/2 second favourite on the day at Doncaster behind the Irish Derby winner Capri. Back against his own age group, Stradivarius ran another excellent race to finish third in a good renewal of the St Leger, sticking to his task to be beaten half a length and a short head by Capri and the Gordon Stakes winner Crystal Ocean, with subsequent Melbourne Cup winner Rekindling fourth and Count Octave, upholding the Queen's Vase form, a creditable sixth (Desert Skyline was barred from the race because he is a gelding). Stradivarius had one more run, finishing a creditable third to Order of St George in the Long Distance Cup on British Champions' Day, running almost up to his Goodwood Cup and St Leger form on the softest ground he has encountered (the state of the going provided an obvious excuse for Big Orange's poor performance at Ascot).

Stradivarius (IRE) (ch.c. 2014)	Sea The Stars (IRE) (b 2006)	Cape Cross (b 1994)	Green Desert
			Park Appeal
		Urban Sea (ch 1989)	Miswaki
			Allegretta
	Private Life (FR) (b 1997)	Bering (ch 1983)	Arctic Tern
			Beaune
		Poughkeepsie (b 1992)	Sadler's Wells
			Pawneese

A strong, attractive individual of medium size, and a good walker as well as being a fluent mover in his faster paces, Stradivarius kept his condition well and really took the eye in the preliminaries before the Long Distance Cup. His sire Sea The Stars, whose other Group 1 winners in the latest season were the Ganay

Mr B. E. Nielsen's "Stradivarius"

winner Cloth of Stars and the Prix d'Ispahan winner Mekhtaal, is generally proving an influence for stamina at stud (the average distance of races won by his three-year-olds and upwards is about the same as that of his half-brother Galileo, around eleven furlongs). Stradivarius is the sixth winner produced by the useful Private Life who is a granddaughter of one of the Wildenstein studs' champion fillies Pawneese, winner of the Oaks, Prix de Diane and King George VI and Queen Elizabeth Stakes in 1976. Pawneese didn't set the world on fire as a broodmare but her winning daughter Poughkeepsie, the grandam of Stradivarius, has made an impression and is also the great grandam of another very good stayer, the 2014 Melbourne Cup winner Protectionist. The best of Private Life's previous winners include the smart pair Persian Storm (by Monsun), who won twice in pattern company in Germany over a mile and a quarter, and Rembrandt Van Rijn (by Peintre Celebre), a winner at a mile and a half who stayed a mile and three quarters. Stradivarius stays two miles and acts on good to firm going and, judged on the Long Distance Cup, also on soft, although his participation in the St Leger (in which Frankie Dettori rode the Ribblesdale winner Coronet instead) was only confirmed after the ground dried out to good, connections saying they would not risk him that day if the going was soft. The genuine Stradivarius, who finds plenty under pressure, is sure to be a major force again in the Cup races as a four-year-old. It is intended that he will tackle a new £1m bonus offered by Weatherbys Hamilton, sponsors of the Lonsdale Cup at York's Ebor meeting. It will be a tall order as he will have to win four races, starting with one of four nominated preparatory events (the Sagaro, Ormonde, Yorkshire Cup or Henry II) and then add the Gold Cup, the Goodwood Cup and the Lonsdale. The connections of Big Orange, who completed the equivalent of the first two legs in the latest season, have also announced that the Gold Cup winner will follow the same schedule. *John Gosden*

STRAFFAN (IRE) 2 b.f. (Apr 28) Clodovil (IRE) 116 – Laureldean Spirit (IRE) 71 (Whipper (USA) 126) [2017 5m t5.1g^5 t5.1d^5 Dec 16] third foal: sister to 2-y-o 7f/7.5f winner Drifting Spirit: dam, maiden (raced only at 7f), half-sister to Lowther/Falmouth Stakes winner Nahoodh (by Clodovil): modest form: best effort when seventh in maiden at Beverley (6 lengths behind Ghayadh) on debut. *David O'Meara* **53**

STRAGAR 3 br.g. Delegator 125 – Roccabella (FR) (Rock of Gibraltar (IRE) 133) [2017 f8g^6 t7.1g^4 10g 14g p10g p7g p7g f8.1g^5 Dec 1] little form, including in handicaps: in headgear last 2 starts. *Michael Appleby* **–**

STRAIGHT ASH (IRE) 2 gr.c. (May 5) Zebedee 113 – Blackangelheart (IRE) (Danehill Dancer (IRE) 117) [2017 5g^5 5.1g^4 5.1s* p6g 7m p7g^6 Nov 17] sturdy colt: fair performer: won minor event at Chepstow in June: will probably stay 1m: acts on soft and good to firm going: often races towards rear. *Richard Hannon* **73**

STRAIGHT AWAY 3 b.f. Dubawi (IRE) 129 – Ihsas (USA) 89 (Rahy (USA) 115) [2017 7d* f8.1g^6 p6g Nov 29] 50,000 3-y-o: first foal: dam, 2-y-o 7f winner, sister to very smart winner up to 1¼m Rio de La Plata: fair form: won maiden at Redcar (by neck from Vive La Difference) in October: best effort at 7f. *Andrew Balding* **76**

STRAIGHTOTHEPOINT 5 b.g. Kyllachy 129 – Choisette 75 (Choisir (AUS) 126) [2017 93: 6m^2 6m^2 5m^6 5m^6 5m^3 6m^3 t5g 5v 5s^6 Nov 8] small gelding: fairly useful handicapper: second at Ripon in April and May: stays 6f: acts on soft and good to firm going: sometimes wears headgear. *Bryan Smart* **92**

STRAIGHT RIGHT (FR) 3 b.c. Siyouni (FR) 122 – Sailor Moon (IRE) (Tiger Hill (IRE) 127) [2017 p8g* p8g* 7g^4 5.5g^3 6m 7s^5 7g^3 7s p6g^4 Nov 29] good-topped colt: third foal: half-brother to useful French 1m-1¼m winner Stone Roses (by Rip Van Winkle) and French 1½m winner Silentium (by Soldier of Fortune): dam, French 2-y-o 7.5f winner, half-sister to smart sprinter Teruntum Star: smart performer: won minor event at Cagnes-sur-Mer in January and listed race there (by short head from Markazi) in February: third in handicap at Goodwood (3 lengths behind Johnny Barnes) in August: left C. Ferland after fifth start: stays 1m: acts on polytrack and good to firm going: tried in hood: races towards rear. *Andrew Balding* **110**

STRANGE SOCIETY (IRE) 2 br.c. (Feb 13) Society Rock (IRE) 126 – Strange Magic (IRE) 94 (Diamond Green (FR) 121) [2017 p7s^3 t7.1s* Nov 30] 210,000Y: first foal: dam 2-y-o 5f/6f winner: fairly useful form: won minor event at Newcastle (by neck from Ambient) in November: likely to progress further. *Hugo Palmer* **80 p**

STRATEGIC HEIGHTS (IRE) 8 b.g. Strategic Prince 114 – Shot of Redemption (Shirley Heights 130) [2017 58, a74: p5g^4 p6g^2 p5g^2 p6g* p6g^3 p7g^6 p6g^5 p6g^2 6.7g 6g^3 6g 6.3s^3 a6g f5g^2 t6.1g^5 f6.1g p6g^2 Dec 31] fair handicapper: won at Dundalk in March: left J. J. Feane after twelfth start: stays 6.5f: acts on polytrack, soft and good to firm going: usually wears headgear. *Jamie Osborne* **74**

STRATEGIC (IRE) 2 b.g. (Feb 12) Kodiac 112 – Run To Jane (IRE) (Doyoun 124) [2017 6.1m 7m^5 7m^3 8g 7d p7s^5 Dec 1] well-made gelding: fair maiden: stays 7f: acts on good to firm going: tried in blinkers: temperamental. *Richard Hannon* **65 §**

STRATEGIST (IRE) 2 ch.g. (Jan 31) Shamardal (USA) 129 – Snow Powder (IRE) 84 (Raven's Pass (USA) 133) [2017 6d^4 6m^4 Aug 16] strong, compact gelding: first foal: dam, maiden (best at 1¼m), closely related to very smart French miler Elusive Wave: fairly useful form when fourth in newcomers race at Ascot (3¾ lengths behind Mythical Magic): went as if amiss next time. *William Haggas* **83**

STRAWBERRYANDCREAM 2 ch.f. (Apr 24) Cityscape 127 – Miss Apricot 48 (Indian Ridge 123) [2017 t7.1g^5 t7.1g^3 Nov 23] half-sister to several winners, including 5f/6f winner Apricot Sky (by Pastoral Pursuits) and 5f (including at 2 yrs) winner Fruit Salad (by Monsieur Bond): dam ran twice: modest form: better effort when third in minor event at Newcastle (1¾ lengths behind Great Shot Sam) in November. *James Bethell* **62**

STREAM SONG 2 gr.f. (Mar 6) Mastercraftsman (IRE) 129 – Montare (IRE) 116 (Montjeu (IRE) 137) [2017 7d 8g^4 8d* Sep 23] well-made filly: sixth foal: half-sister to very smart 1¼m-1½m winner Journey (by Dubawi) and smart French 1½m winner (stays 15.5f) Travelling Man (by Oasis Dream): dam French winner up to 15.5f (2-y-o 1¼m winner), including Prix Royal-Oak: useful form: won minor event at Newmarket (by neck from Sheikha Reika) in September: will be suited by 1¼m+: will go on improving. *John Gosden* **95 p**

STREET ART (IRE) 5 ch.g. Excellent Art 125 – Via Aurelia (IRE) 66 (Antonius Pius **58**
(USA) 123) [2017 53: p12d p11d^{2} p12g p10g* 10.1m* 10.1s^{5} 10.2s^{5} 10d^{6} 9.9m p10g Aug 31] modest handicapper: won at Chelmsford in March and Yarmouth in May: stays 1½m: acts on polytrack, tapeta and good to firm going: wears blinkers/tongue tie: often starts slowly. *Mike Murphy*

STREET JAZZ 3 b.f. Acclamation 118 – Wake Up Call 103 (Noverre (USA) 125) [2017 **67**
71: t5.1m^{4} t5.1m^{2} p5g^{5} Feb 24] fair handicapper: stays 6f: acts on polytrack, tapeta and good to firm going: sometimes wears blinkers. *James Given*

STREET JESTER 3 b.g. Avonbridge 123 – Street Diva (USA) 69 (Street Cry (IRE) 130) **–**
[2017 –: t7.1g p7g 11.6m p16d Oct 6] no form. *Robert Stephens*

STREET MARIE (USA) 3 b.f. Street Cry (IRE) 130 – Real Sense (IRE) (Galileo (IRE) **63**
134) [2017 8.3g 9.9m 8.1m^{3} 8s Jul 28] $300,000 2-y-o: second foal: dam, French maiden (third at 1½m), closely related to very smart German performer up to 1½m Saddex: modest form: best effort at 1m. *John Gosden*

STREET POET (IRE) 4 b.g. Poet's Voice 126 – Street Star (USA) 91 (Street Cry (IRE) **66**
130) [2017 83: t9.5g 11.9v t10.2s 10.2g^{6} t8d^{2} f8.1g^{5} Dec 22] rather leggy gelding: fairly useful at 3 yrs, below that level in 2017: stays 11f: acts on tapeta and soft going: tried in visor: front runner/races prominently. *Michael Herrington*

STREET SENSATION (IRE) 2 b.c. (Mar 18) Street Cry (IRE) 130 – Sweet Hope **–**
(USA) 106 (Lemon Drop Kid (USA) 131) [2017 t5.1d f5g^{6} Dec 29] little impact in minor events. *Richard Fahey*

STREETS OF JOY 2 b.f. (Jun 6) Champs Elysees 124 – Nellie Gwyn (King's Best **–**
(USA) 132) [2017 t8g Dec 6] half-sister to several winners in France, including 2-y-o 6.5f winner Special Reward (by Bahamian Bounty) and 1m winner Special Favour (by Royal Applause): dam of little account: 33/1, well held in maiden at Newcastle. *Henry Spiller*

STRETEWISE (IRE) 3 b.f. Tagula (IRE) 116 – Leglen Wood (IRE) (High Chaparral **64**
(IRE) 132) [2017 –: t8d^{5} t8d t7.1g^{2} f7d^{4} 8g May 4] modest maiden: stays 1m: acts on tapeta. *Jason Ward*

STRICTLY ART (IRE) 4 b.g. Excellent Art 125 – Sadinga (IRE) 85 (Sadler's Wells **73**
(USA) 132) [2017 63: p8d^{2} p10g^{6} p8g 9.1g* 9.9d^{3} 12m^{2} 11.9g^{2} 11.5m^{4} 11.4m^{6} 10.9m* p11g^{2} t14g^{2} p15.8g* t16.3d^{2} Dec 16] angular gelding: fair handicapper: won amateur events at Goodwood in June, Ripon in August and Lingfield in December: stays 16.5f: acts on all-weather, soft and good to firm going: has worn cheekpieces, including in 2017: usually races prominently. *Alan Bailey*

STRICTLY CARTER 4 b.g. Multiplex 114 – Compolina (Compton Place 125) [2017 **68**
65: t6g* t6g^{4} 5.2m^{2} t6g^{3} t6.1g^{2} 6m* 7d t6.1g 6s 6d p6g^{3} p6g^{2} Dec 20] sturdy gelding: fair handicapper: won at Wolverhampton in February and Brighton in June: stays 6f: acts on polytrack, tapeta and good to firm going: has worn headgear, including in 2017: in tongue tie last 2 starts. *Alan Bailey*

STRIKEMASTER (IRE) 11 b.g. Xaar 132 – Mas A Fuera (IRE) (Alzao (USA) 117) **–**
[2017 –: t16.3d t16.3g 12.1s 16g Aug 29] leggy gelding: fair at best, no form since 2015: has worn headgear, including final start: usually wears tongue tie: races towards rear. *Lee James*

STRIKER (IRE) 3 b.g. Nathaniel (IRE) 129 – Walk On Bye (IRE) 105 (Danehill Dancer **–**
(IRE) 117) [2017 11.9m^{5} 12d Jun 6] well held in 2 maidens: sold £2,500, sent to Sweden. *Tom Dascombe*

STRIKING FOR GOLD 3 b.g. Equiano (FR) 127 – Crossbow (Mount Nelson 125) **42**
[2017 t7.1g^{4} f7g t8.6g^{6} 10.2g 8s 6.1g 5.7s Sep 17] poor maiden: in headgear last 4 starts. *Sarah Hollinshead*

STRINGYBARK CREEK 3 b.g. Bushranger (IRE) 119 – Money Note 68 (Librettist **67**
(USA) 124) [2017 77: p6g 5m 5.1m^{2} 5f^{6} 6d 6g 6.1g^{3} 6d^{6} 6.1v^{2} 5.1s 5.7d^{4} 5g^{5} 5.3d^{6} p7g^{5} 8.1d p8g* f7.1g Dec 22] compact gelding: fair handicapper: won at Lingfield (apprentice) in December: left Mick Channon after twelfth start: stays 1m: acts on polytrack, good to firm and heavy going: in cheekpieces last 2 starts: sometimes slowly away. *Daniel Steele*

STRIPEY 2 ch.f. (Mar 27) Sepoy (AUS) 129 – Birthday Suit (IRE) 94 (Daylami (IRE) **–**
138) [2017 7d 7.4g Sep 2] half-sister to 3 winners, including 6f (including at 2 yrs) winner Bimbo (by Iffraaj) and 1½m-1¾m winner Excelsior Academy (by Montjeu): dam, 2-y-o 5f winner, half-sister to Irish 1000 Guineas winner Classic Park: well held in minor events. *Richard Fahey*

STRONGARM CHASER (IRE) 2 b.c. (Mar 19) Footstepsinthesand 120 – Sarawati (IRE) 69 (Haafhd 129) [2017 8.3d 10m Oct 25] rather unfurnished colt: fair form when seventh at Nottingham on first of 2 starts in maidens: bred to be suited by 1¼m+. *Richard Hannon* **66**

STRONG BELIEF (IRE) 3 b.g. Cape Cross (IRE) 129 – Opinionated (IRE) (Dubai Destination (USA) 127) [2017 9.8d* Jun 7] 6/1, won maiden at Ripon (by 7 lengths from Kilowatt) only start: dead. *Charlie Appleby* **99**

STRONG CHALLENGE (IRE) 4 ch.g. Exceed And Excel (AUS) 126 – Miss Brief (IRE) 72 (Brief Truce (USA) 126) [2017 –: p7g^4 p7g a7f a5f^6 a6f Dec 29] good sort: fairly useful handicapper: left Saeed bin Suroor after second start: stays 7f: acts on polytrack: sometimes wears headgear/tongue tie. *A. bin Harmash, UAE* **90**

STRONG STEPS 5 br.g. Aqlaam 125 – Wunders Dream (IRE) 107 (Averti (IRE) 117) [2017 100: 8g^6 8m 7.9d 9g t9.5g^2 8.2s^5 7.8s 7.6d^2 7.2g^2 t7.1g 8d* 8d^4 9.2s 8s Oct 3] good-topped gelding: fairly useful handicapper: won at Ayr (by ¾ length from Crazy Tornado) in July: left Roger Fell after eighth start: stays 1¼m: acts on polytrack, tapeta and soft going: has worn headgear, including in 2017. *Jim Goldie* **92**

STRUCK BY THE MOON 3 b.f. Fastnet Rock (AUS) 127 – Ho Hi The Moon (IRE) (Be My Guest (USA) 126) [2017 –p: 10g 12.3g^4 t12.4g t9.5g Nov 7] rather unfurnished filly: modest maiden: stays 12.5f: raced only on good going on turf. *Charles Hills* **62**

STRUMMER (IRE) 4 b.g. Frozen Power (IRE) 108 – Question (USA) 56 (Coronado's Quest (USA) 130) [2017 71§: t10.2g^4 9.9m^2 10m 10m t10.2s^3 9.9d^2 10.2g^4 Aug 10] fair handicapper: stays 12.5f: acts on tapeta, good to firm and good to soft going: wears headgear: not one to trust. *Kevin Ryan* **74 §**

STUBYTUESDAY 3 b.g. Dick Turpin (IRE) 127 – Just Dreams 85 (Salse (USA) 128) [2017 57: 6g* 5f^2 6g^6 6g 6m^6 7v* t7.2g^5 8g^5 7d^4 7v Nov 7] fair handicapper: won at Redcar in April and Catterick in August: stays 1m: acts on tapeta and any turf going. *Michael Easterby* **77**

STUN GUN 7 b.g. Medicean 128 – Tapas En Bal (FR) (Mille Balles (FR) 124) [2017 61§, a74§: f8g^4 f8s^3 f8g^4 f7m f8g 8m^6 p8g 10.1m^3 11.5s^6 10.2m^5 12.1m t10.2s t7.1d Sep 29] modest handicapper on turf, fair on all-weather: stays 1¼m: acts on polytrack, fibresand, good to firm and good to soft going: wears headgear: unreliable. *Derek Shaw* **55 § a68 §**

STURDY DAWN 7 br.m. Striking Ambition 122 – Lucky Find (IRE) 50 (Key of Luck (USA) 126) [2017 12.3d Jul 29] no form, including in Flat maiden (wore hood): dead. *Michael Mullineaux* **–**

STYLEHUNTER 2 ch.c. (Feb 13) Raven's Pass (USA) 133 – Sunday Bess (JPN) 88 (Deep Impact (JPN) 134) [2017 7m p8d^3 Dec 13] 55,000Y: well-made, attractive colt: second foal: half-brother to 6f (including at 2 yrs) winner Turanga Leela (by Paco Boy): dam 1¼m winner: fairly useful form when third at Kempton (in blinkers, length behind Rusper) on second of 2 starts in minor events: open to further improvement. *John Gosden* **80 p**

STYLISH DANCER 3 b.f. Nathaniel (IRE) 129 – Hazy Dancer 81 (Oasis Dream 129) [2017 10m^6 p12s 12v^2 p15.8g^2 t14g^3 p16s Dec 15] 150,000Y: third foal: half-sister to 1¼m-1½m winner Bollihope (by Medicean) and useful 1¼m winner Burguillos (by Lope de Vega): dam, 2-y-o 1m winner who stayed 1½m, out of smart performer up to 13.5f Shadow Dancing: fair maiden: stays 2m: acts on polytrack and heavy going. *Luca Cumani* **79**

STYLISH GRACE (FR) 2 gr.f. (May 8) Style Vendome (FR) 116 – Conciliatory 96 (Medicean 128) [2017 5m 6g Sep 22] €30,000Y: third foal: half-sister to French 12.5f winner Flexible (by Kyllachy): dam 1m winner: well held in maidens. *J. S. Moore* **–**

SUANAS (IRE) 2 br.f. (Mar 10) Society Rock (IRE) 126 – Penny Serenade (IRE) 78 (Lawman (FR) 121) [2017 5m 5m May 11] £12,000Y: first foal: dam 6f/6.7f winner: well held in minor events. *Richard Fahey* **–**

SUBATOMIC 3 b.f. Makfi 130 – Miss Universe (IRE) 99 (Warning 136) [2017 80: 8.2s^4 7.6s Jun 10] close-coupled filly: fairly useful 7f winner at 2 yrs, standout effort: sometimes slowly away, often races towards rear. *Ralph Beckett* **65**

SUBCONTINENT (IRE) 5 b.g. Dubawi (IRE) 129 – Saree 95 (Barathea (IRE) 127) [2017 12.3d May 12] useful-looking gelding: useful handicapper, well held sole outing on Flat since 2015: stays 10.5f: acts on tapeta and firm going. *Venetia Williams* **–**

SUBHAAN 3 ch.g. Dutch Art 126 – Mamma Morton (IRE) 79 (Elnadim (USA) 128) [2017 p7s^2 p8s^4 7g^4 t8s^2 t8d* Oct 24] 150,000F, £205,000Y: angular gelding: half-brother to several winners, including smart 6f (including at 2 yrs)/1m winner Master of War (by **89**

Compton Place) and useful 6f (including at 2 yrs) winner Muaamara (by Bahamian Bounty): dam maiden (stayed 10.7f): fairly useful performer: won minor event at Newcastle (by neck from Breanski) in October: stays 1m: acts on polytrack and tapeta: sold 27,000 gns, sent to Qatar. *Roger Varian*

SUBJECTIVE 3 ch.g. Equiano (FR) 127 – Hope Island (IRE) 69 (Titus Livius (FR) 115) [2017 81: 6m 5f² 6m³ Jun 24] fair maiden: stays 7f: acts on tapeta, firm and soft going: in blinkers last 2 starts: sold 20,000 gns in July: courage under suspicion. *David Simcock* **72**

SUBJECTIVITY (USA) 3 ch.g. Girolamo (USA) 122 – Always Loyal (USA) 113 (Zilzal (USA) 137) [2017 f7.1g⁵ Oct 22] £3,200 3-y-o: half-brother to several winners, including 7f winner Yaroslav and 2-y-o 6f winner Loyal Love (both by Danzig): dam, won Poule d'Essai des Pouliches and stayed 10.5f, half-sister to top-class French sprinter Anabaa and high-class performer up to 1¼m Key of Luck: 4/1, fifth in maiden at Southwell (11 lengths behind Mama Africa) in October: open to improvement. *Michael Appleby* **60 p**

SUBLIMATION (IRE) 7 ch.g. Manduro (GER) 135 – Meon Mix 61 (Kayf Tara 130) [2017 67: t8.6g p10g³ t8.6g² t8.6g² Apr 22] small gelding: fair handicapper: stays 1¼m: acts on polytrack, tapeta, soft and good to firm going: often races prominently. *Steve Gollings* **65**

SUBLIME 3 b.f. Exceed And Excel (AUS) 126 – Singuliere (IRE) (Singspiel (IRE) 133) [2017 54: p8d p8g f8m 10.2f⁴ 10.2f² 9.9g 10.2f² Jul 5] modest maiden: stays 1¼m: acts on polytrack, best turf form on firm going: in cheekpieces last 3 starts: front runner/races prominently. *Rod Millman* **55**

SUBOTAL (IRE) 4 ch.g. Pivotal 124 – Suba (USA) 85 (Seeking The Gold (USA)) [2017 8g 6s p7d⁴ t8.6g⁴ t9.5m p8g t8d p10s Nov 16] poor maiden: best effort at 8.5f: acts on tapeta: in eyeshields last 2 starts: sometimes slowly away, often races freely. *Richard Guest* **47**

SUBWAY DANCER (IRE) 5 b.g. Shamardal (USA) 129 – Sub Rose (IRE) 119 (Galileo (IRE) 134) [2017 114: p9.4g⁴ 9.9d⁶ 9.9g 9.9g⁵ 9.9g⁴ 9.9s⁶ 9.9d² 9.9g³ p9.4f⁶ Nov 29] third foal: dam French 11f/1½m (Prix de Royaumont) winner: smart performer: won 3 times at 4 yrs, including in Prix Andre Baboin at Lyon Parilly: placed in 2017 in Prix Dollar at Chantilly (short-neck second to Garlingari) and listed race at Marseilles Borely (¾-length third to Soleil d'Octobre): stays 1¼m: acts on good to soft going: none too consistent. *Z. Koplik, Czech Republic* **117**

SUCCESS DAYS (IRE) 5 gr.h. Jeremy (USA) 122 – Malaica (FR) 103 (Roi Gironde (IRE) 104) [2017 118: 10d² 10.5d⁴ 10g² 10.3g* 10d 10s Oct 21] good-topped horse: smart performer: won York Stakes (by nose from Mondialiste) in July: second in Alleged Stakes at Naas (head behind Air Pilot) in April and International Stakes at the Curragh (½ length behind Johannes Vermeer) in July: stays 10.5f: acts on heavy going: tried in blinkers: in tongue tie last 4 starts: usually leads. *K. J. Condon, Ireland* **119**

SUDDEN WISH (IRE) 8 b.m. Jeremy (USA) 122 – Fun Time 64 (Fraam 114) [2017 61: p13g Feb 9] good-bodied mare: modest handicapper: held when hampered sole outing on Flat in 2017: stays 13.5f: acts on polytrack, soft and good to firm going: has worn headgear. *Gary Moore* **–**

SUDONA 2 b.f. (Mar 10) Zoffany (IRE) 121 – Vickers Vimy 52 (Montjeu (IRE) 137) [2017 8s Oct 28] £34,000Y: first foal: dam, lightly raced, out of half-sister to very smart performer (best at 6f/7f) Diffident: 5/1, eighth in minor event at Newbury (10¼ lengths behind Highgarden) in October: capable of better. *Hugo Palmer* **58 p**

SUEDOIS (FR) 6 b.g. Le Havre (IRE) 124 – Cup Cake (IRE) (Singspiel (IRE) 133) [2017 121: 6s 6d³ 6m 7g³ 7g³ 8d* 8f* 8f⁴ Nov 4] **121**

David O'Meara comfortably topped the hundred-winner mark in Britain for the fifth successive year, though his total again fell below that in his final season at his former base at Arthington Barn Stables in Nawton, North Yorkshire. Leaving a yard that had provided him with his first Group 1 winner (G Force in the 2014 Sprint Cup) and given him another excellent season in 2015 when Amazing Maria won the Duke of Cambridge and the Falmouth Stakes (as well as a Prix Rothschild) has proved tough. Amazing Maria's win in the Falmouth remains the yard's last domestic Group 1 win. That said, the operation has enjoyed plenty of big-race domestic success since relocating to Willow Farm, winning the Lincoln in the latest season with Ballydoyle cast-off Bravery and enjoying further Royal Ascot success with Out Do in the Wokingham Stakes, while Balmoral Handicap winner Lord Glitters looks a good prospect for pattern races in the next season. Although it took €270,000 to secure the already-gelded Lord Glitters from France in July, he looks another typically shrewd buy for O'Meara, having won £150,000 of his purchase price back in the Balmoral, and looks the sort who has even more to offer (he lost little in defeat when second in a tactical listed race at Newmarket on his final start). Lord Glitters' owners the Turnbulls will be hoping he proves as good a buy as their Mondialiste, who was also purchased by O'Meara from France and became a huge success story for the O'Meara stable, winning the Woodbine Mile in 2015 and the Arlington Million in 2016 (the horse will be at the Turnbulls' Elwick Stud in County Durham in 2018, standing at a fee of £6,000). Stable jockey Daniel Tudhope won the Arlington Million on Mondialiste but deserted him in the latest Turf Mile at Keeneland in favour of Suedois, who was having his first start on American soil (Fergal Lynch, who had ridden Mondialiste to success in the Woodbine Mile in 2015, re-took the ride).

Suedois was having only his second start at a mile at Keeneland since joining O'Meara, having won the Boomerang Stakes at Leopardstown over the same trip a month earlier. Though it has Group 2 status, the Boomerang was not a strong race, but Suedois, who had been keeping stronger company since joining O'Meara for €165,000 at the end of 2015, gained a deserved first win for the yard, not needing to be at his best to prevail by half a length from True Valour. Suedois' last victory had come in the Group 3 Prix de Meautry at Deauville in August 2015 (when in the care of French trainer Christian Baillet) and he had gone twelve starts without a win for O'Meara over the following two seasons. That said, Suedois still more than paid his way with placed efforts in the July Cup, Sprint Cup and Prix de la Foret in 2016 (bumping into Limato on two of those occasions). He had finished a good third in the Lennox Stakes at Goodwood (without the smoothest of passages) in the latest season and filled the same spot (beaten only a neck and a short head) in a highly competitive City of York Stakes. As has been said, he didn't have to reproduce his best form to win at Leopardstown, and reached a new level on his final two runs of the season in America, qualifying for the Breeders' Cup Mile with his win in the Shadwell Turf Mile at Keeneland, getting on top to lead in the last fifty yards to win by a length

Clipper Logistics Boomerang Stakes, Leopardstown—Suedois gains reward for a series of consistent efforts in pattern company, beating True Valour (No.6) and Psychedelic Funk (spots)

Shadwell Turf Mile Stakes, Keeneland—
Suedois beats Heart To Heart (far side) and Ballagh Rocks to provide trainer David O'Meara with a third Grade 1 victory in North America in the last three years

and a half from Heart To Heart with Mondialiste back in fifth. Suedois went to Del Mar and made the frame behind World Approval, running a career best, beaten just a length and a half into fourth and faring better than all the European challengers with the exception of runner-up Lancaster Bomber.

Suedois (FR) (b.g. 2011)	Le Havre (IRE) (b 2006)	Noverre (b 1998)	Rahy
			Danseur Fabuleux
		Marie Rheinberg (b 2002)	Surako
			Marie d'Argonne
	Cup Cake (IRE) (ch 2006)	Singspiel (b 1992)	In The Wings
			Glorious Song
		Gold Mark (ch 2001)	Mark of Esteem
			Gold Script

Despite being primarily campaigned over six and seven furlongs (the Meautry was the most important of his six wins in France) there is stamina in Suedois' pedigree. He is a lengthy individual by Prix du Jockey Club winner Le Havre out of the Singspiel mare Cup Cake who won over a mile and a mile and a quarter in Sweden. The grandam Gold Mark, who showed only a little ability in France, is a half-sister to the likes of Railway Stakes winner Honours List and the fairly useful handicapper Shahdaroba (who won a mile handicap for the O'Meara yard in 2015). Le Havre's best progeny to date have been fillies (headed by French classic winners Avenir Certain and La Cressonniere) and Suedois is now his best male representative. Suedois will be seven in the next season but is still relatively unexposed at a mile, and may do better yet. He acts on polytrack, firm and good to soft going and usually races prominently. He has been tried in a visor. *David O'Meara*

SUEGIOO (FR) 8 ch.g. Manduro (GER) 135 – Mantesera (IRE) (In The Wings 128) **105 §** [2017 115: 14g 18.6m 16.2f^2 20f^5 t16.3s 20.6v 16.3d 15.9v^5 14v^3 18v^2 p16d Nov 22] angular gelding: useful handicapper: second at Haydock (head behind Yorkidding) in May: stays 2½m: acts on polytrack and any turf going: usually wears headgear: usually races towards rear: not one to trust. *Richard Fahey*

SUE'S ANGEL (IRE) 3 gr.f. Dark Angel (IRE) 113 – La Chassotte (FR) 103 (Until **74** Sundown (USA)) [2017 64: 8.3g 7g^5 11.9d^3 May 19] fair maiden: stays 1½m: acts on good to soft going: often starts slowly, usually races nearer last than first. *Richard Fahey*

SUFFRAGETTE CITY (IRE) 3 b.f. Dragon Pulse (IRE) 114 – Queen of Stars (USA) (Green Desert (USA) 127) [2017 74: t7.1m f6s³ Jan 26] rather leggy filly: fair maiden at 2 yrs, below that level in 2017: stayed 1m: acted on polytrack and good to firm going: in headgear last 3 starts: often raced prominently: covered by Fascinating Rock. *Richard Hannon* **63**

SUFI 3 ch.g. Pivotal 124 – Basanti (USA) 80 (Galileo (IRE) 134) [2017 83p: t8.6g³ 11.8g⁴ 11.6d³ 12g 12d p10d⁴ p12g Dec 13] fairly useful maiden: left Richard Hannon after fifth start: stays 1½m: acts on polytrack, tapeta and good to soft going. *Ken Cunningham-Brown* **82**

SUGAR BEACH (FR) 3 b.f. Canford Cliffs (IRE) 133 – Aktia (IRE) 96 (Danehill Dancer (IRE) 117) [2017 71: 6g⁴ 6m 7s t10.2g t7.1d p8s⁴ t8.6g⁴ Dec 5] fair maiden: stays 8.5f: acts on polytrack, tapeta and good to firm going: in headgear last 5 starts: tried in tongue tie. *Ann Duffield* **69**

SUGAR COATING 2 b.f. (Mar 18) Dutch Art 126 – Muscovado (USA) 71 (Mr Greeley (USA) 122) [2017 t6.1d² Dec 27] 60,000F, 90,000Y: fifth foal: half-sister to 3 winners, including useful 1¼m winner Maybelater (by Mount Nelson) and 1m-1¼m winner (stayed 1½m) Monsieur Rieussec (by Halling): dam twice-raced daughter of dual Yorkshire Oaks winner Only Royale: 13/8, second in minor event at Wolverhampton (4 lengths behind Hello Brigette) in December: will stay 7f: sure to progress. *Richard Fahey* **68 p**

SUGARDROP 3 br.f. Cacique (IRE) 124 – Tates Creek (USA) 118 (Rahy (USA) 115) [2017 9.9m³ 10.2s p10g³ 9.9s² p10s² Nov 17] sixth foal: half-sister to a winner in USA by Storm Cat: dam, US Grade 1 9f/1¼m winner, half-sister to US Grade 1 7f-9f winner Sightseek and to dam of 1000 Guineas winner Special Duty: fair maiden: raced only at 1¼m: acts on polytrack and good to firm going: tried in tongue tie. *Amanda Perrett* **79**

SUGAR FREE (GER) 4 b.f. Exceed And Excel (AUS) 126 – Sugar Baby Love (GER) 99 (Second Empire (IRE) 124) [2017 7s⁵ 6g² 6f⁶ 6g 6g⁶ 7g⁵ 6.5s³ Oct 29] third foal: half-sister to German 7f winner Sugar Love (by Elusive City) and 7f/1m winner Sugar Boy (by Areion): dam, German 2-y-o 6.5f winner, half-sister to smart German winner up to 7f Smooth Operator: useful performer: won maiden at Mulheim and handicap at Baden-Baden in 2016: best effort when second in listed race at Hanover (½ length behind Schang) in May: well held in Summer Stakes at York fourth outing: stays 6.5f: acts on soft going: blinkered final start: sold 32,000 gns in December. *D. Moser, Germany* **100**

SUGARLOAF MOUNTAIN (IRE) 4 b.g. Fastnet Rock (AUS) 127 – Cherry Hinton 103 (Green Desert (USA) 127) [2017 –: t10.2g³ t12.4g⁴ t12.4g² f14g² f12.1g³ t12.4d⁴ Dec 16] fairly useful maiden: placed in handicaps at Southwell in April (apprentice) and December: stays 1¾m: acts on fibresand and tapeta: tried in hood: has worn tongue tie, including final start: front runner/races prominently. *Brian Ellison* **81**

SUGAR PLUM FAIRY 2 ch.f. (Feb 25) Halling (USA) 133 – Atyaab 78 (Green Desert (USA) 127) [2017 6g 7m Sep 23] second foal: dam, untrustworthy maiden (barely stayed 1m), out of sister to Breeders' Cup Juvenile winner Timber Country and half-sister to July Cup winner Hamas: well held in minor events. *Tony Carroll* **–**

SUGAR TOWN 7 b.m. Elusive City (USA) 117 – Sweetsformysweet (USA) 63 (Forest Wildcat (USA) 120) [2017 67: t5d² t6d⁴ t6g Feb 20] fair handicapper: best at 5f/6f: acts on tapeta and good to firm going: tried in cheekpieces: usually leads. *Peter Niven* **67**

SUHAYL MOON (IRE) 2 b.f. (Apr 11) Invincible Spirit (IRE) 121 – Sander Camillo (USA) 116 (Dixie Union (USA) 121) [2017 p7g⁵ Dec 20] seventh foal: half-sister to winner up to 8.5f Vociferous (2-y-o 1m winner) and 2-y-o 6f winner Porta Rosa (both by Street Cry): dam 2-y-o 6f (Albany/Cherry Hinton Stakes) winner: 11/8, fifth in minor event at Lingfield (4 lengths behind Dancing Brave Bear) in December, short of room early in straight and not knocked about: better to come. *Charlie Appleby* **65 p**

SUITCASE 'N' TAXI 3 br.g. Major Cadeaux 121 – Finalize (Firebreak 125) [2017 67: 6m² 6m* 6f 6d⁶ 6g 5.9s* 6m 6v⁵ 6s Oct 10] fairly useful handicapper: won at Pontefract in May and Carlisle (lady riders event, by length from Castle Hill Cassie) in August: stays 6f: acts on soft and good to firm going: inconsistent. *Tim Easterby* **82**

SUITED 3 b.f. Paco Boy (IRE) 129 – Birthday Suit (IRE) 94 (Daylami (IRE) 138) [2017 67p: 6g 6g t7.1g⁶ May 19] modest form sole outing at 2 yrs, standout effort. *Tim Easterby* **–**

SUIT OF LIGHTS (IRE) 3 b.g. Approve (IRE) 112 – Lindoras Grace (Galileo (IRE) 134) [2017 6s⁵ 7g Aug 17] rather unfurnished gelding: modest form: better effort when fifth in maiden at Salisbury on debut. *Henry Tett* **53**

SUITOR 5 ch.g. Dutch Art 126 – Entreat 87 (Pivotal 124) [2017 86: 10.3g 8m 10s^4 11.6m^2 t12.4s^3 10.3g p10.7g Dec 22] tall gelding: fairly useful handicapper: third at Newcastle in July: left Brian Ellison after sixth start: stays 12.5f: acts on tapeta and good to firm going: in cheekpieces last 5 starts: often races prominently: won over hurdles in December. *Gordon Elliott, Ireland* **87**

SUITSUS 6 b.g. Virtual 122 – Point Perfect (Dansili 127) [2017 63: p10g^3 t9.5g^3 t9.5g p8g 8g* 8f* 8g^3 p8g^2 p10m Nov 25] good-bodied gelding: fair handicapper: won at Brighton in May and Bath in June: stays 1¼m: acts on polytrack, tapeta, firm and soft going: has worn cheekpieces: wears tongue tie: sometimes slowly away, often races in rear. *Geoffrey Deacon* **77**

SUKHOVEY (USA) 2 b.f. (Mar 26) Lookin At Lucky (USA) 127 – Allencat (USA) (Storm Cat (USA)) [2017 7m^5 7g 8g Aug 25] $35,000F, 27,000Y: closely related to 2 winners, including smart performer up to 11f Prizefighting (2-y-o 7f winner, by Smart Strike), and half-sister to several winners in USA: dam unraced daughter of US Grade 1 9f winner Pharma: fair form when fifth in minor event at Newbury (3¾ lengths behind Time Change) on first of 3 starts: tried in tongue tie. *Michael Attwater* **66**

SUKOOT (IRE) 3 ch.g. Sir Prancealot (IRE) 111 – Yandina (IRE) 89 (Danehill (USA) 126) [2017 8.3m^5 t7.1g Jun 30] fair form: better effort when fifth in maiden at Nottingham on debut. *Ed Dunlop* **67**

SULAFAAT (IRE) 2 ch.f. (Mar 21) Haatef (USA) 117 – Elraabeya (CAN) 77 (Seeking The Gold (USA)) [2017 5.5s^5 6d^5 6s^4 t7.1g* p7g Oct 18] third foal: closely related to Italian winner around 1¼m Ektifaa (by Mawatheeq): dam 1m winner who stayed 1¼m: fair performer: won nursery at Newcastle in September: best effort at 7f: acts on tapeta. *Mark Johnston* **75**

SULAFAH (IRE) 3 b.f. Mawatheeq (USA) 126 – Maany (USA) 62 (Mr Greeley (USA) 122) [2017 73: t8g^2 t7.1g^3 t8d 5.9s t7.1g Oct 20] good-topped filly: fair maiden: stays 1m: acts on tapeta: wears headgear: tried in tongue tie: front runner/races prominently: sold 800 gns, sent to Germany. *Simon West* **68**

SULA ISLAND 3 ch.f. Sulamani (IRE) 130 – Cosmea 87 (Compton Place 125) [2017 11.6d^5 10g^6 11.6d^2 p12g t12.2d^5 Dec 9] lengthy filly: third foal: half-sister to useful winner up to 1½m Cosmeapolitan (2-y-o 7f winner) and 11.6f/1½m winner William Hunter (both stay 1¾m, both by Mawatheeq): dam, 1¼m-11.6f winner, also won over hurdles: fairly useful maiden: likely to stay beyond 1½m: acts on good to soft going. *Alan King* **81**

SULTANAA 2 gr.f. (Jan 24) Acclamation 118 – Pink Opaque (Nayef (USA) 129) [2017 6s^4 7d^2 7d^3 7d a7f^5 Dec 7] 18,000F, 55,000Y: good-topped filly: first foal: dam, French 1¼m winner, half-sister to Breeders' Cup Juvenile Turf winner Donativum: fair maiden: best effort at 7f: acts on good to soft going. *Ismail Mohammed* **78**

SULTAN BAYBARS 3 b.g. Invincible Spirit (IRE) 121 – Rock Salt (Selkirk (USA) 129) [2017 93: p8g 8m 7m^2 7s^2 7m^6 p8g 10.2d Oct 27] small gelding: useful handicapper: second at Sandown (twice, head behind Fox Trotter second occasion) in July: stays 1m: acts on polytrack, soft and good to firm going: sometimes in headgear: sold to join David O'Meara 30,000 gns in November. *Roger Varian* **98**

SUMBAL (IRE) 5 gr.h. Danehill Dancer (IRE) 117 – Alix Road (FR) 112 (Linamix (FR) 127) [2017 117: 10.2d^3 11.8s Oct 10] good-topped horse: smart performer: below best only 2 starts in 2017: should stay 1½m: acts on soft and good to firm going. *David Simcock* **108**

SUMMER CHORUS 4 b.f. Exceed And Excel (AUS) 126 – Soviet Terms (Soviet Star (USA) 128) [2017 94: 6.1d 6m 6d^3 7g^2 p7s^2 7g Sep 28] useful handicapper: second at Newmarket (2 lengths behind Mountain Rescue) in August and Chelmsford (½ length behind Big Tour) in September: stays 7f: acts on polytrack, good to firm and good to soft going: has worn hood, including in 2017: sometimes slowly away. *Andrew Balding* **96**

SUMMER COLLECTION (IRE) 4 b.f. Teofilo (IRE) 126 – Towards (USA) (Fusaichi Pegasus (USA) 130) [2017 73: t12.4g Jan 12] fair maiden, well held sole outing in 2017: stays 12.5f: acts on polytrack, tapeta and soft going. *K. R. Burke* **–**

SUMMER DOVE (USA) 4 gr.f. Super Saver (USA) 121 – No Foul Play (CAN) (Great Gladiator (USA)) [2017 p10g^6 p8g Dec 6] modest maiden: left George Peckham after first start: best effort at 7f: acts on polytrack. *G. M. Lyons, Ireland* **56**

SUMMER FALLS (IRE) 4 b.f. Iffraaj 127 – Encouragement 76 (Royal Applause 124) [2017 68: p8d^5 t7.2g^4 8f^6 p7f^6 p8.5f^2 p7f^5 Dec 8] fair maiden: left Rae Guest after second start: stays 8.5f: acts on polytrack and dirt: tried in blinkers. *Rachel Halden, USA* **69**

SUMMERGHAND (IRE) 3 b.g. Lope de Vega (IRE) 125 – Kate The Great 79 (Xaar **87**
132) [2017 6m^4 p6s* 6m^5 6v 6s* 6m^2 6s^5 p6g^2 t6d Oct 24] 250,000Y: fourth foal: half-brother to 3 winners, including smart winner up to 6f Eastern Impact (2-y-o 5f winner, by Bahamian Bounty) and useful 6f (at 2 yrs) and 6.5f (in Canada) winner Miss Katie Mae (by Dark Angel): dam 2-y-o 5f winner: fairly useful performer: won maiden at Chelmsford in June and handicap at Yarmouth (by head from Abiento) in August: second in handicaps at Epsom in August and Kempton in October: raced only at 6f: acts on polytrack, soft and good to firm going. *David O'Meara*

SUMMER ICON 4 b.f. Sixties Icon 125 – Summer Cry (USA) (Street Cry (IRE) 130) **98**
[2017 96: p7m* t8.6g^3 p7g^3 t7.1g p8g 7g^3 7d^6 7.2m^6 8m 7m^5 8d 7s 7s^4 8d^5 7s^4 p7d^3 p7s^3 **a104**
p7g^4 p8g^3 Dec 23] rather leggy filly: useful performer: won handicap at Lingfield in January: placed on 6 other occasions in 2017: stays 8.5f: acts on polytrack, tapeta, good to firm and good to soft going: often races towards rear. *Mick Channon*

SUMMERINTHECITY (IRE) 10 ch.g. Indian Ridge 123 – Miss Assertive 88 (Zafonic **48**
(USA) 130) [2017 78: t6m^3 t5.1g Mar 11] sturdy gelding: fair performer, well below best in 2017: stays 7f: acts on polytrack, tapeta, soft and good to firm going: has worn cheekpieces, including final start. *Patrick Morris*

SUMMERLING (IRE) 6 br.m. Excellent Art 125 – Sun Seasons (IRE) 99 (Salse (USA) **–**
128) [2017 –: p10s Dec 17] maiden: lightly raced and no form since 2015: stays 1m: acts on good to soft going: tried in headgear. *Rae Guest*

SUMMER NAME (IRE) 5 b.g. Duke of Marmalade (IRE) 132 – Summer's Eve 104 **82**
(Singspiel (IRE) 133) [2017 f12.1g* Nov 28] second foal: half-brother to useful 7f/1m winner Early Morning (by New Approach): dam, 9f winner who stayed 1½m, sister to Gold Cup winner Papineau and half-sister to St Leger winner Silver Patriarch: in tongue tie, 33/1, won maiden at Southwell (by 4½ lengths from Epitaph) in November. *Rebecca Curtis*

SUMMER SHAMAL (FR) 2 b.f. (Mar 21) Wootton Bassett 119 – Chinook Wind (IRE) **90**
79 (Encosta de Lago (AUS)) [2017 p5g* 5.5g^2 6m 5f Nov 24] €20,000F: good-topped filly: third foal: half-sister to French 2-y-o 6f winner Madame Mistral (by Exchange Rate): dam, maiden (placed up to 9.5f in USA), closely related to Ribblesdale Stakes winner Fairy Queen and half-sister to Falmouth Stakes winner Tashawak: fairly useful form: won newcomers race at Chantilly in April (left M. Palussiere after): too free when well held in Albany Stakes at Royal Ascot on third outing, then left Francis-Henri Graffard: stays 5.5f: blinkered final start. *Peter Miller, USA*

SUMMER THUNDER (USA) 2 b.f. (May 5) Street Cry (IRE) 130 – Satulagi (USA) 98 **–**
(Officer (USA) 120) [2017 6g p7g^6 5.1m Jul 17] lengthy filly: sixth foal: half-sister to 6f/7f winner (including at 2 yrs) One More Roman (by Holy Roman Emperor), later successful in Qatar, and winner up to 11f Teolagi (2-y-o 1m winner, by Teofilo): dam 2-y-o 5f-7f winner: little impact in minor events/maiden. *Paul Cole*

SUMNER BEACH 3 ch.g. Aqlaam 125 – Cosmic Song 58 (Cosmonaut) [2017 83p: 6f **81**
6d^4 7s t5g t6d t8g^4 t8g f8.1g^5 t9.5d^6 Dec 27] fairly useful handicapper: stays 1m: acts on fibresand, tapeta and good to soft going: tried in cheekpieces: has worn tongue tie, including last 4 starts. *Brian Ellison*

SUMOU (IRE) 4 b.g. Arcano (IRE) 122 – Three Times (Bahamian Bounty 116) [2017 84: **78**
5.7m^3 6g 5s 6.1d 5.7m^3 7.1m^5 Jun 16] fair maiden: stayed 1m: acted on soft and good to firm going: dead. *Milton Bradley*

SUN AND SHADOW 2 b.c. (Feb 28) Royal Applause 124 – Sonko (IRE) 90 (Red Clubs **62**
(IRE) 125) [2017 p6g Jun 22] 8/1, ninth in minor event at Lingfield (2¾ lengths behind Tunes of Glory) in June: sent to USA. *Ed Walker*

SUN ANGEL (IRE) 3 ch.f. Sir Prancealot (IRE) 111 – Fuerta Ventura (IRE) 102 (Desert **67**
Sun 120) [2017 73: f8g^3 9.9g 7s Aug 8] fair maiden: left Henry Candy after first start: stays 1m: acts on polytrack and good to firm going: tried in cheekpieces: often races prominently. *Timothy Doyle, Ireland*

SUNBLAZER (IRE) 7 gr.g. Dark Angel (IRE) 113 – Damask Rose (IRE) 100 (Dr **96**
Devious (IRE) 127) [2017 103: 14.1m^2 13.4g p12g^4 20.6v 12m p11g^3 16g* p12d^3 p16d* Dec 13] angular gelding: useful handicapper: won at Newmarket in November and Kempton (by length from Rydan) in December: stays 16.5f: acts on polytrack, tapeta and firm going: has worn headgear: wears tongue tie. *Kim Bailey*

SUNBREAK (IRE) 2 b.g. (Feb 11) Dawn Approach (IRE) 132 – Carry On Katie (USA) **74**
109 (Fasliyev (USA) 120) [2017 5.7f^5 6s^3 6g^5 p8g* p7g* 7.9g t8g Dec 6] fair performer: won nurseries at Chelmsford and Kempton in September: stays 1m: acts on polytrack and soft going: front runner. *Mark Johnston*

SUNCHISETAGIOO 3 b.f. Exceed And Excel (AUS) 126 – Sunsemperchi 92 (Montjeu (IRE) 137) [2017 9.9g^{2} 9.9f^{3} 8d^{4} 7.6d^{5} t8.6g^{3} Oct 7] good-topped filly: closely related to 3 winners in Italy, including useful winner up to 11f Finidaprest (2-y-o 1m winner, by Dylan Thomas), and half-sister to Italian 1½m-1¾m winner Fastidigrass (by Shirocco): dam Italian 1¼m/11f winner: fairly useful performer: won both starts at 2 yrs, newcomers race at Milan and minor event at Rome: placed in 2017 in minor events at Rome and Milan (left A. & S. Botti after) and handicap at Wolverhampton: stays 1¼m: acts on tapeta and firm going: in hood last 3 starts: sold 38,000 gns in December. *Marco Botti* **93**

SUNDANCE BOY 8 gr.g. Proclamation (IRE) 130 – Just Beth (Carlingford Castle 126) [2017 t12.2g Aug 11] little sign of ability, including in Flat maiden. *Giuseppe Fierro* **–**

SUNDAY BEST 2 ch.f. (Apr 17) Nathaniel (IRE) 129 – Lacy Sunday (USA) (King's Best (USA) 132) [2017 7m p7s 7d Sep 5] £4,000Y: fifth foal: half-sister to 1m winner Miss Osier (by Mastercraftsman) and German 2-y-o 6f winner Sanandaj (by Soldier Hollow): dam German 7f winner: little impact in minor events. *Jonathan Portman* **–**

SUNDAY PROSPECT (FR) 3 ch.g. Sunday Break (JPN) 121 – Green Shadow (FR) (Green Tune (USA) 125) [2017 51p: 7s^{2} Jul 27] fair form: better effort when second in maiden at Doncaster (1¼ lengths behind Wasm) on sole outing in 2017: will stay at least 1m: has joined John Weymes. *K. R. Burke* **76**

SUNDAY SMART (IRE) 2 b.f. (Mar 10) Dandy Man (IRE) 123 – Sharp And Smart (IRE) 88 (Dark Angel (IRE) 113) [2017 5m^{4} 6s^{2} 6.7v* 7s Oct 28] €7,000Y, resold €13,500Y, €27,000 2-y-o: first foal: dam 7.5f/1m winner: fairly useful form: won maiden at Limerick in October: best effort at 7f: remains with potential. *P. J. Prendergast, Ireland* **88 p**

SUND CITY (FR) 4 b.f. Turtle Bowl (IRE) 121 – Calithea (IRE) 55 (Marju (IRE) 127) [2017 63: t12.2m^{3} Jan 7] modest maiden handicapper: stays 2m: acts on polytrack, soft and good to firm going: usually leads. *Harry Dunlop* **49**

SUNGLIDER (IRE) 4 br.g. High Chaparral (IRE) 132 – Desert Ease (IRE) 94 (Green Desert (USA) 127) [2017 85: 9.9f* 10.2g^{5} 10g 8.8m 9.9m* 9.8m^{3} 9.9g^{4} p10g Sep 7] fairly useful handicapper: won at Beverley in May (by ¾ length from Kingthistle) and June (by 1¼ lengths from Save The Bees): stays 12.5f: acts on tapeta, firm and good to soft going: often wears headgear: has worn tongue tie, including last 5 starts. *David O'Meara* **85**

SUN HAT (IRE) 2 ch.f. (Mar 8) Helmet (AUS) 127 – Bright Water (Refuse To Bend (IRE) 128) [2017 t7.2g^{5} Dec 2] first foal: dam unraced half-sister to useful French 7f/1m winner Emboss: 25/1, fifth in minor event at Wolverhampton (7¼ lengths behind Jellmood) in December. *Simon Crisford* **57**

SUNHILL LAD (IRE) 2 gr.g. (Mar 4) Lilbourne Lad (IRE) 111 – Gris Ladera (IRE) 78 (Verglas (IRE) 118) [2017 t8g^{3} 8v^{2} t7.1s^{4} t8d^{6} f8.1g^{6} Dec 29] fair maiden: best effort at 1m: acts on tapeta: sometimes slowly away. *Ann Duffield* **65**

SUNI DANCER 6 b.m. Captain Gerrard (IRE) 113 – Sunisa (IRE) 87 (Daggers Drawn (USA) 114) [2017 60: p6d p6g 7.1v^{4} 7m^{5} 7d p8g Nov 29] modest handicapper: stays 10.5f: acts on polytrack, tapeta, good to firm and heavy going: has worn cheekpieces/tongue tie: often starts slowly/races towards rear. *Tony Carroll* **55**

SUNLIT WATERS 4 ch.f. New Approach (IRE) 132 – Faraway Waters 102 (Pharly (FR) 130) [2017 62: p8g^{6} 11.5m^{6} 10.2f^{6} 12g^{6} Jul 17] lengthy, useful-looking filly: modest maiden: left Eve Johnson Houghton after second start: should stay beyond 1¼m: acts on polytrack: tried in visor. *Tony Carroll* **54**

SUN LOVER 4 b.g. Oasis Dream 129 – Come Touch The Sun (IRE) (Fusaichi Pegasus (USA) 130) [2017 92: 7m^{2} 7m^{2} 7.6g^{2} 8g Sep 28] good-topped gelding: useful handicapper: second at York (1¾ lengths behind Be Kool) in June, Doncaster (minor event, head behind Classic Seniority) in July and Chester (3½ lengths behind Kenstone) in August: should stay 1m: acts on tapeta and good to firm going: sold 32,000 gns, sent to USA. *Roger Varian* **96**

SUN MAIDEN 2 b.f. (Apr 25) Frankel 147 – Midsummer 99 (Kingmambo (USA) 125) [2017 t7.2g^{4} Dec 5] half-sister to several winners, notably high-class winner up to 1½m Midday (2-y-o 1m winner, by Oasis Dream), herself dam of useful performer up to 1½m Mori (by Frankel) and smart performer up to 1½m Midterm: dam 11f winner: 7/2, needed experience when fourth in minor event at Wolverhampton (3¾ lengths behind American Endeavour) in December, nearest finish: open to significant improvement. *Sir Michael Stoute* **61 P**

SUNNUA (IRE) 4 gr.f. Dark Angel (IRE) 113 – Island Sunset (IRE) 98 (Trans Island 119) [2017 86: 8g^{5} 8m 8m 8g 9.2g^{5} 7.2m^{6} 7g^{4} 7s^{4} t7.1g 8.3g* f8.1g Nov 13] compact filly: fair handicapper: won at Nottingham in November: stays 8.5f: acts on good to firm and heavy going: tried in cheekpieces. *Richard Fahey* **72**

SUNNY FUTURE (IRE) 11 b.g. Masterful (USA) 119 – Be Magic 57 (Persian Bold 123) [2017 82: 11.7f^4 14.2m 14g 17.1d Aug 4] big, rangy gelding: fairly useful handicapper, below form in 2017: stays 17f: acts on any turf going: usually wears hood: usually races nearer last than first. *Malcolm Saunders* **66**

SUNNY LANE (IRE) 2 b.f. (Feb 18) Arakan (USA) 123 – Four Kicks (IRE) 64 (Pyrus (USA) 106) [2017 8s Sep 15] first foal: dam 1m-1¼m winner: 66/1, well held in minor event at Salisbury. *J. S. Moore* **–**

SUNNYSIDE BOB (IRE) 4 b.g. Big Bad Bob (IRE) 118 – Jinxy Jill (Royal Applause 124) [2017 70: t6d 5m t5g t8.6g t7.2g Dec 2] fair maiden, below form in 2017: stays 6f: acts on tapeta and good to firm going: has worn headgear, including in 2017. *Neville Bycroft* **60**

SUN OR SHADE (IRE) 3 b.c. Galileo (IRE) 134 – Desert Classic 63 (Green Desert (USA) 127) [2017 p11d Feb 22] in blinkers, 7/1, well held in maiden at Kempton. *John Gosden* **–**

SUNOVAREBEL 3 b.g. Cockney Rebel (IRE) 127 – Atacama Sunrise 74 (Desert Sun 120) [2017 59: p7d f8g^5 Mar 9] modest form at 2 yrs, none in 2017. *Alan Bailey* **–**

SUNRISE DANCE 8 ch.m. Monsieur Bond (IRE) 120 – Wachiwi (IRE) 67 (Namid 128) [2017 44: t5s 6g 5s Jun 29] lengthy mare: fairly useful at best, no form in 2017: has worn headgear: in tongue tie last 4 starts: quirky. *Kenny Johnson* **–**

SUNRIZE (IRE) 3 b.g. Azamour (IRE) 130 – Valmari (IRE) 91 (Kalanisi (IRE) 132) [2017 9.9m^5 12m^3 12s^6 May 20] modest form: best effort when third in maiden at Thirsk in May: likely to stay beyond 1½m. *David O'Meara* **62**

SUNSET BOUNTY 3 b.f. Bahamian Bounty 116 – Sunset Kitty (USA) 95 (Gone West (USA)) [2017 8m 8.1m p7g t8.6g Dec 13] angular filly: first foal: dam 7f/1m winner: no form, including in handicap. *Julia Feilden* **–**

SUNSET FLYER 2 b.f. (Feb 17) Arabian Gleam 122 – King's Guest (IRE) 68 (King's Best (USA) 132) [2017 5.1m 5.7f^6 7d p8g^{pu} Oct 24] no form: dead. *Amy Murphy* **–**

SUNSHINEANDBUBBLES 4 b.f. Multiplex 114 – Dockside Strike (Docksider (USA) 124) [2017 66: p10g^6 p10m^6 f8g^5 p10g^2 10.1g 10.1m^5 t8.6g^3 t9.5g^4 t9.5g^4 t8.6g^6 f8.1g* Dec 21] modest handicapper: won at Southwell in December: left Daniel Loughnane after seventh start: stays 1½m: acts on all-weather, good to firm and good to soft going: usually wears cheekpieces: front runner/races prominently. *Jennie Candlish* **64**

SUNSTORM 2 ch.c. (Mar 10) Medicean 128 – Crimson Cloud 87 (Kyllachy 129) [2017 6.5m 7d 7g^2 7g t8g t6g Nov 23] useful-looking colt: fair maiden: best effort at 7f. *David Brown* **69**

SUPER FLORENCE (IRE) 2 gr.f. (Apr 17) Zebedee 113 – Top of The Ridge (IRE) (Celtic Swing 138) [2017 5.3g^2 5.1d 6g p7d^3 7g^4 p7g^6 p6g^2 Oct 14] €9,000Y: fourth foal: half-sister to 3 winners, including 6f winner Kody Ridge (by Kodiac) and 7f winner You Gotta Move (by Bushranger): dam unraced half-sister to useful sprinter Exhibition: fair maiden: stays 7f: acts on polytrack. *Eve Johnson Houghton* **70**

SUPERIORITYCOMPLEX (IRE) 3 ch.f. Hard Spun (USA) 124 – Justlookdontouch (IRE) (Galileo (IRE) 134) [2017 7g 9.9f^2 10.2s^2 10g^2 p10g* Aug 15] rangy filly: second foal: half-sister to smart 1¼m-1½m winner Abingdon (by Street Cry): dam unraced close relative/half-sister to very smart 1¼m-1½m performers Islington and Mountain High: fairly useful performer: won maiden at Chelmsford in August: stays 1¼m: acts on polytrack, firm and soft going: sold 400,000 gns in December, sent to USA. *Sir Michael Stoute* **86**

SUPER JULIUS 3 ch.g. Bated Breath 125 – Paradise Isle 112 (Bahamian Bounty 116) [2017 90: 5.7f^5 5g 5f^4 t5.1g* 5.3g* 5.1m^5 5g^2 p5g p6g^6 Nov 21] good-quartered gelding: useful handicapper: won at Wolverhampton in June and Brighton (by ½ length from Come On Dave) in July: second at Sandown (1¼ lengths behind Justice Lady) in September: stays 5.5f: acts on tapeta, good to firm and good to soft going: wears cheekpieces. *Eve Johnson Houghton* **95**

SUPER MAJOR (IRE) 2 b.g. (Feb 9) Sir Prancealot (IRE) 111 – Majestic Alexander (IRE) 93 (Bushranger (IRE) 119) [2017 5m^6 5g 6d^2 6g^4 7s^6 Sep 19] fair maiden: stays 6f: acts on good to soft going. *Michael Dods* **75**

SUPERMOSS 2 b.f. (May 5) Cacique (IRE) 124 – Fairy Moss (IRE) 43 (Amadeus Wolf 122) [2017 7.1s p7g t7.2g Dec 5] 12,500F, €13,000 2-y-o: second foal: half-sister to Spanish 1m winner Jannia (by Iffraaj): dam maiden half-sister to smart winner up to 1¼m Nashmiah: little impact in minor events. *Heather Main* **–**

SUPERNOVA 2 b.c. (Feb 26) Intello (GER) 129 – Carding (USA) (Street Cry (IRE) 130) **81 p** [2017 8g^5 p10d^3 Nov 9] €24,000Y, 135,000 2-y-o: second foal: half-brother to 2-y-o 6f winner Muthmira (by Arcano): dam unraced daughter of Lowther Stakes winner Silk Blossom: fairly useful form: better effort when third in minor event at Chelmsford (3½ lengths behind Photographer) in November: open to further improvement. *David Simcock*

SUPER RUBY 3 b.f. Equiano (FR) 127 – Danehill Dazzler (IRE) 85 (Danehill Dancer **46** (IRE) 117) [2017 7.4g^6 8s^6 7s^6 8d t9.5g f8.1g^6 Oct 22] first foal: dam 7f-1½m winner: poor maiden. *K. R. Burke*

SUPERSTA 6 ch.g. Pivotal 124 – Resort 97 (Oasis Dream 129) [2017 90, a103: p8g^5 **95** t8.6m^2 p8g t7.1g t8.6g^6 f7d* p8g a8.6g 7d^2 8m^4 7s p8g p7s f7.1g Oct 22] lengthy gelding: **a105** useful handicapper: won at Southwell (by 3¾ lengths from Outer Space) in March: stays 8.5f: acts on all-weather, good to firm and good to soft going: wears headgear: tends to start slowly: sold 20,000 gns, sent to Saudi Arabia. *Michael Appleby*

SUPERSYMMETRY (IRE) 2 br.f. (Mar 22) Kyllachy 129 – Duniatty (Green Desert **69** (USA) 127) [2017 6s^4 6v 6.1g p7g Oct 18] 48,000F, 60,000Y: second foal: dam, French 2-y-o 7f winner, half-sister to very smart winner up to 7f Tariq: fair form when fourth in maiden on debut, standout effort. *Tom Dascombe*

SUPREMATISM (USA) 2 b.c. (May 25) More Than Ready (USA) 120 – Exotic **–** Behavior (USA) (Giant's Causeway (USA) 132) [2017 p7s^6 Dec 8] 16/1, well held in minor event at Chelmsford. *Marco Botti*

SUPREME POWER (IRE) 3 b.g. Power 117 – Supreme Spirit (IRE) 86 (Invincible **69** Spirit (IRE) 121) [2017 70: 7g^2 7g t7.1d^3 7.8s^6 7.8d^4 8.9s t8d t8d^3 t8s^6 Nov 30] fair maiden: left Philip McBride after first start: stays 1m: acts on polytrack, tapeta and good to soft going: in cheekpieces last 2 starts: usually races prominently. *Tracy Waggott*

SUQOOR 4 b.g. Equiano (FR) 127 – Ukraine (IRE) (Cape Cross (IRE) 129) [2017 89, **86** a100: t7.1g p6g^3 p7g^4 p7g^3 6m^6 6m^4 7m^4 8m^3 7.6d^3 Jun 24] tall gelding: fairly useful **a95** handicapper on turf, useful on all-weather: third at Lingfield in February (1¼ lengths behind Zac Brown) and April (1¾ lengths behind Take The Helm): stays 1m: acts on polytrack and good to firm going: wears headgear: sold 27,000 gns in July, sent to Saudi Arabia. *Chris Dwyer*

SURAAT (IRE) 3 b.f. Kodiac 112 – Baltic Belle (IRE) 86 (Redback 116) [2017 –: 6g t5g **–** Sep 12] no form, including in handicap. *Robert Cowell*

SURE TO EXPLORE (IRE) 3 b.f. Henrythenavigator (USA) 131 – Shibina (IRE) 95 **83 §** (Kalanisi (IRE) 132) [2017 11.8d^4 12m* 11.6g^4 t12.2g^6 p16g^4 p15.8g Oct 5] good-topped filly: fifth foal: closely related to useful 7f winner (stayed 1¼m) Shebella (by Dubai Destination) and half-sister to smart French/Australian 1m-11f winner Shikarpour (by Dr Fong) and 1¼m winner (stayed 13f) Shalabina (by Nayef): dam 1¼m-1½m winner: fairly useful performer: won maiden at Chepstow in June: stays 2m: acts on polytrack and good to firm going: tried in cheekpieces: sometimes slowly away: temperamental: sold 1,000 gns in December. *William Muir*

SUREYOUTOLDME (IRE) 3 ch.g. Tamayuz 126 – Place de Moscou (IRE) (Rock of **57** Gibraltar (IRE) 133) [2017 76p: 7g^4 Aug 2] fair form when second in maiden at 2 yrs, standout effort: will stay at least 1m. *Ruth Carr*

SURFA ROSA 2 b.c. (Jan 31) Delegator 125 – Beechnut (IRE) (Mujadil (USA) 119) [2017 **74** 6.1g^5 7s 6g^5 6d^6 t7.2g* Nov 7] fair performer: won nursery at Wolverhampton in November: stays 7f: acts on tapeta. *Richard Hannon*

SURFSIDE 3 b.f. Sixties Icon 125 – Altona (IRE) 73 (Redback 116) [2017 p8g p8m p10g **55** p8g May 12] first foal: dam, maiden (stayed 1m), half-sister to useful performer up to 11f Duke of Tuscany: modest form: left Mick Channon after third start: stays 1m: tried in hood. *Denis W. Cullen, Ireland*

SURRENDER 2 b.g. (Apr 10) Sixties Icon 125 – Mango Music 93 (Distant Music (USA) **–** 126) [2017 7.4m 7d 7g 8g Sep 27] little show in minor events/nursery. *Tim Easterby*

SURREY BLAZE (IRE) 2 b.g. (May 7) Thewayyouare (USA) 117 – Catadalya (IRE) 53 **– p** (One Cool Cat (USA) 123) [2017 7s 7d 7d Aug 21] €1,000F, €2,800Y, 45,000 2-y-o: workmanlike gelding: first foal: dam lightly-raced half-sister to useful winner up to 1½m Adjaliya: little impact in minor events/maiden: type to do better in handicaps. *Joseph Tuite*

SURREY HOPE (USA) 3 b.c. Lemon Drop Kid (USA) 131 – She Be Classy (USA) **102 p** (Toccet (USA) 118) [2017 68p: p8g* 8g* 8d^3 8m* Aug 16] good-topped colt: useful performer: won maiden at Kempton in March, and handicaps at Sandown in June and Salisbury (by neck from Kryptos) in August: raced only at 1m: acts on polytrack, good to firm and good to soft going: usually races prominently: will go on improving. *Joseph Tuite*

SURROUND SOUND 7 b.g. Multiplex 114 – Tintera (IRE) (King's Theatre (IRE) 128) [2017 62: t12.4g³ t13.9m² t12.2g² t12.2g* 13.8m⁴ p14g⁴ 12.5g² 12g 14m⁴ 11.9m³ 11.8g⁶ 13d⁴ 12d t12.4s⁵ t14g Oct 27] workmanlike gelding: fair handicapper: won at Wolverhampton in March: stays 1¾m: acts on tapeta, good to firm and heavy going: wears headgear: usually in tongue tie: usually slowly away, races well off pace. *Tim Easterby* **72**

SUSPECT PACKAGE (USA) 3 b.g. Lonhro (AUS) 128 – Pretty Meadow (USA) (Meadowlake (USA)) [2017 75p: 8.3g³ 8.1d³ 10.2m³ 10.2g³ Jul 8] fairly useful maiden: third all 4 starts in 2017: barely stays 1¼m: best turf form on good going: in hood last 4 starts: tried in tongue tie: sold 28,000 gns, sent to Bahrain. *James Fanshawe* **81**

SUSSEX GIRL 3 ch.f. Compton Place 125 – Palinisa (FR) 106 (Night Shift (USA)) [2017 –: 5.2m⁴ 7g⁴ 8s 8g⁶ p10d 9.9s³ 9.9v* 10.1d* Oct 24] lengthy filly: fair handicapper: won at Brighton and Yarmouth in October: stays 1¼m: acts on heavy going. *John Berry* **75**

SUSSEX RANGER (USA) 3 b.g. Hat Trick (JPN) 121 – Purple (USA) (Royal Academy (USA) 130) [2017 80p: p11g 11.4m³ 14g² 14s* 16g³ p16g³ Sep 13] tall gelding: fairly useful handicapper: won at Lingfield (by 1¼ lengths from Leapt) in July: third at Goodwood in August and Kempton in September: stays 2m: acts on polytrack, soft and good to firm going: in cheekpieces last 2 starts: often races towards rear, usually responds generously to pressure: useful form over hurdles, won first 2 starts. *Gary Moore* **86**

SUTOOR (IRE) 3 b.g. Cape Cross (IRE) 129 – Yanabeeaa (USA) 84 (Street Cry (IRE) 130) [2017 t12.2d t8.6g⁵ Dec 18] no form, including in bumpers. *Mark Brisbourne* **–**

SUTTER COUNTY 3 b.c. Invincible Spirit (IRE) 121 – Rio Osa (AUS) (Canny Lad (AUS)) [2017 106: p6d² p6g² t5g* p7f² p6g⁵ 5m³ 7g* 7m 7m 6m⁴ 7g p8g⁴ 7g p7s² Sep 2] strong, compact colt: smart performer: won minor event at Newcastle (by 2¼ lengths from Dazacam) in February and handicap at Goodwood (by ½ length from Medahim) in May: second in handicap at Chelmsford (head behind Masham Star) in September: stays 7f: acts on polytrack, tapeta and good to soft going: tried in blinkers: often races prominently: sent to UAE. *Mark Johnston* **113**

SUWAAN (IRE) 3 ch.g. Exceed And Excel (AUS) 126 – Janina 96 (Namid 128) [2017 61: t5d* 5.1m³ 5g 5s⁵ 5g⁵ t5d² t5.1g³ 5m* 5d² 5s t5g Oct 10] fairly useful handicapper: won at Newcastle in March and Musselburgh (by 1½ lengths from Jeany) in August: second at Doncaster in September: best form at 5f: acts on tapeta, good to firm and good to soft going: tried in eyeshields: front runner/races prominently, often travels strongly: ungenuine. *Ruth Carr* **84 §**

SUZI ICON 5 ch.m. Sixties Icon 125 – Suzi Spends (IRE) 94 (Royal Applause 124) [2017 –: 9.9g p7s* t8.6g⁶ 6g Jul 4] modest handicapper: won at Chelmsford in May: stays 1½m: acts on polytrack and good to firm going: has worn headgear, including last 4 starts: temperament under suspicion. *Michael Appleby* **56**

SUZI'S CONNOISSEUR 6 b.g. Art Connoisseur (IRE) 121 – Suzi Spends (IRE) 94 (Royal Applause 124) [2017 108: t7.1g⁵ t7.1g* p7g⁶ 7f 6m 7m 7g³ 7g p7s 7d t6.1d³ Dec 16] angular gelding: fairly useful handicapper on turf, useful on all-weather: won at Newcastle (by head from Holiday Magic) in February: third at Wolverhampton (1½ lengths behind Tropics) in December: stays 7f: acts on polytrack, tapeta and any turf going: usually wears headgear: has worn tongue tie, including last 5 starts. *Stuart Williams* **92 a103**

SWAFFHAM BULBECK (IRE) 3 b.g. Jeremy (USA) 122 – Ballygologue (IRE) 90 (Montjeu (IRE) 137) [2017 8.3m⁶ t9.5g⁵ 8.3v* 10.1g⁶ 9.9s⁶ Oct 9] fair performer: won maiden at Nottingham in August: best effort at 8.5f: acts on heavy going: tried in cheekpieces. *Ed Vaughan* **78**

SWAG (IRE) 3 b.g. Bahamian Bounty 116 – Tahtheeb (IRE) 105 (Muhtarram (USA) 125) [2017 74: p7s⁴ 6d⁵ 6.1g Jul 8] fair maiden: likely to have stayed at least 1m: acted on firm and good to soft going: wore tongue tie: dead. *Michael Easterby* **69**

SWAHEEN 5 b.g. Lawman (FR) 121 – Whole Grain 72 (Polish Precedent (USA) 131) [2017 91: 12g⁶ 10s 11.2v* 11.2s 11.8d⁵ 11.8d⁴ 12v³ 11.8v⁴ 14g Nov 1] sturdy gelding: fairly useful handicapper: won at Carlisle (by head from Rainbow Rebel) in June: third at Thirsk in September: stays 1¾m: acts on good to firm and heavy going: has worn headgear, including last 4 starts: often races prominently. *Julie Camacho* **88**

SWALLOW DANCER 3 b.f. Danehill Dancer (IRE) 117 – Bay Swallow (IRE) 77 (Daylami (IRE) 138) [2017 p12d t9.5g^{5} t9.5g^{6} 12m p10g Jun 3] second foal: dam 1½m winner who stayed 1¾m: modest maiden: should stay at least 1½m: acts on tapeta: tried in tongue tie. *Harry Dunlop* **51**

SWAMP FOX (IRE) 5 br.g. Windsor Knot (IRE) 118 – Brogella (IRE) 92 (King's Theatre (IRE) 128) [2017 98: 16.8v^{2} 18m^{6} 14s* Nov 5] good-bodied gelding: useful handicapper: won at Naas (by short head from Highland Fling) in November: stays 17f: acts on good to firm and heavy going: wears blinkers: smart hurdler. *Joseph G. Murphy, Ireland* **102**

SWAN SERENADE 3 b.f. Paco Boy (IRE) 129 – Accede 88 (Acclamation 118) [2017 57: p8g 5.7f^{5} 7.4g Jul 17] small filly: modest form at 2 yrs, little impact in handicaps in 2017: best effort at 5.5f: acts on polytrack and good to soft going. *Jonathan Portman* **40**

SWANSWAY 4 ch.g. Showcasing 117 – Spring Stroll (USA) (Skywalker (USA)) [2017 72: t8g^{2} t8d^{2} t8.6g^{4} f8.1g t10.2s^{6} 12m^{3} 10.2g^{2} 12.1m* 12.1s 12.1g Aug 18] fair handicapper: won at Catterick (amateur) in July: stays 1½m: acts on fibresand, tapeta and good to firm: tried in headgear. *Michael Easterby* **76**

SWANTON BLUE (IRE) 4 b.g. Kodiac 112 – Cabopino (IRE) 58 (Captain Rio 122) [2017 75: 6m* 6m^{3} 6m^{2} 5.2m 6m^{6} 6g^{6} 5.7m^{6} p7g p6g^{3} t6.1g^{6} Nov 11] fairly useful handicapper: won at Salisbury in May: second at Newbury in June: stays 6f: acts on polytrack, tapeta and firm going: usually leads. *Ed de Giles* **80**

SWASHBUCKLE 4 b.g. Dashing Blade 117 – Inhibition 96 (Nayef (USA) 129) [2017 89: t16.3g^{3} 18g^{3} 16m^{3} 16.2f 14.2d* 16d 16g^{6} 18m Oct 14] rangy gelding: useful handicapper: won at Salisbury (by ½ length from Sternrubin) in June: stays 2¼m: acts on tapeta, soft and good to firm going: tried in cheekpieces: front runner/races prominently: sold to join Donald McCain 40,000 gns in November. *Andrew Balding* **100**

SWEEPING ROCK (IRE) 7 b.g. Rock of Gibraltar (IRE) 133 – Sweeping Story (USA) (End Sweep (USA)) [2017 –: t12.2g p13g^{4} t12.2g Feb 20] workmanlike gelding: modest handicapper: stays 2m: acts on polytrack and any turf going: has worn cheekpieces, including last 3 starts: often wears tongue tie. *John Spearing* **50**

SWEET AMAZEMENT 3 ch.f. Kheleyf (USA) 116 – Sweetest Revenge (IRE) 78 (Daggers Drawn (USA) 114) [2017 –: t6g t6g^{6} p5d^{5} 5m Jun 17] unfurnished filly: no form: tried in hood. *Mark Usher* **–**

SWEET AND DANDY (IRE) 2 b.f. (May 2) Dandy Man (IRE) 123 – Translator (IRE) 65 (Choisir (AUS) 126) [2017 p6g Nov 29] €7,000Y: second foal: dam maiden (stayed 1m): 5/1, seventh in minor event at Kempton (5 lengths behind Desert Doctor) in November. *Jimmy Fox* **54**

SWEETASEVER (IRE) 3 br.f. Power 117 – In My Dreams (IRE) 52 (Sadler's Wells (USA) 132) [2017 76: p7g^{3} p8g^{3} p8g^{4} p7g 10d 8.5d^{5} 8g* 7.9g 8.3d^{2} 8g Jul 27] fifth foal: half-sister to French/Belgian 1¼m-11f winner Dylans Verse (by Dylan Thomas): dam twice-raced half-sister to top-class miler Rock of Gibraltar: fair handicapper: won at Navan in June: should stay 1¼m: acts on polytrack and good to soft going: usually races nearer last than first. *Joseph Patrick O'Brien, Ireland* **76**

SWEET CHARITY 2 b.f. (Jan 24) Mount Nelson 125 – Fanny May 96 (Nayef (USA) 129) [2017 p8g^{3} p8g^{3} Dec 20] first foal: dam 2-y-o 6f winner who stayed 1¼m: fair form: third in minor events at Lingfield: will be suited by 1¼m: remains with potential. *Denis Coakley* **67 p**

SWEET LADY ROSE (IRE) 2 ch.f. (Mar 28) Shamardal (USA) 129 – Sweet Rose (New Approach (IRE) 132) [2017 p8g^{6} Nov 8] first foal: dam unraced half-sister to smart winner up to 1½m Elite Army: 40/1, sixth in minor event at Kempton (11½ lengths behind Cecchini) in November: will stay at least 1¼m: should do better. *Andrew Balding* **54 p**

SWEET PICCOLO 7 ch.g. Piccolo 121 – Quality Street 86 (Fraam 114) [2017 –: p7s Dec 14] little form: has worn headgear. *Paddy Butler* **–**

SWEET PURSUIT 3 b.f. Pastoral Pursuits 127 – Sugar Beet 98 (Beat Hollow 126) [2017 –: p7g^{3} 7g^{4} 6d^{2} 6.1m^{3} 6s* 6s* 6g^{3} 7.1g 6.1g Oct 9] compact filly: fair handicapper: won at Lingfield in July (amateur) and August: stays 7f: acts on polytrack, soft and good to firm going. *Rod Millman* **74**

SWEET SELECTION 5 b.m. Stimulation (IRE) 121 – Sweet Coincidence 69 (Mujahid (USA) 125) [2017 107: 16f* 20m 13.9g^{6} 16g 14.5d Sep 14] sturdy mare: useful performer: **109**

won Sagaro Stakes at Ascot (by 1½ lengths from Prince of Arran) in May: stays 2¼m: acts on polytrack and any turf going: has worn blinkers, including in 2017. *Hughie Morrison*

SWEET SIENNA 3 ch.f. Harbour Watch (IRE) 121 – Look Busy (IRE) 113 (Danetime (IRE) 121) [2017 53: 6g 5.1d 6s Sep 4] modest maiden at 2 yrs, little impact in handicaps in 2017. *Dean Ivory* **–**

SWEET SYMPHONY 2 ch.f. (Feb 16) Helmet (AUS) 127 – Solfilia 91 (Teofilo (IRE) 126) [2017 p7g^5 Oct 26] 32,000Y: second foal: dam 2-y-o 6f winner who stayed 1½m: 50/1, fifth in minor event at Chelmsford (2¼ lengths behind Bath And Tennis) in October: will stay 1m: should improve. *Marco Botti* **69 p**

SWEET VIXEN 2 b.f. (Apr 21) Foxwedge (AUS) 128 – Sugar Beet 98 (Beat Hollow 126) [2017 p5g^6 6.1s^2 6.1g^3 6g Oct 7] sturdy filly: second foal: half-sister to 6f winner Sweet Pursuit (by Pastoral Pursuits): dam, 5f/6f winner (including at 2 yrs), half-sister to useful 6f/7f performer Flyman: fair form: stays 6f. *Tom Clover* **74**

SWEET ZAIN (IRE) 3 b.f. Requinto (IRE) 109 – Pillars of Society (IRE) 96 (Caerleon (USA) 132) [2017 56: 5m* Jun 23] fair form: won handicap at Newmarket on sole outing in 2017: should be suited by 6f: sold 30,000 gns in July, sent to Norway. *John Butler* **75**

SWENDAB (IRE) 9 b.g. Trans Island 119 – Lavish Spirit (USA) 80 (Southern Halo (USA)) [2017 73§, a64§: f5g t5.1m t6g^2 p5g* t5.1g p5g^4 t6m^5 p6g* p6g^5 5f^2 5.1m^6 5.7f^3 5.7m^2 t5.1g^5 5d* 5g^4 5.1m 5g 5.1v^6 5.1s^5 5s^5 5m^3 t5.1g^3 p5s^2 p5g^5 t5.1m* t5.1g* p5s^2 t5.1d* Dec 27] good-topped gelding: fair handicapper: won at Kempton in February and March, Lingfield in June, and Wolverhampton in October, November and December: stays 6f: acts on polytrack, tapeta, firm and soft going: wears headgear: usually races close up: tough. *John O'Shea* **76**

SWIFT APPROVAL (IRE) 5 ch.g. Approve (IRE) 112 – Tiltili (IRE) 51 (Spectrum (IRE) 126) [2017 108: t7.1g 6g 6m 7m^4 7d 7d* p8g^6 7g p7s p8g p7s^2 t7.1d Dec 16] strong gelding: useful handicapper: won at Newmarket (by ¾ length from Salateen) in August: second at Chelmsford (length behind Steel Train) in November: stays 7f: acts on polytrack, firm and soft going: wears headgear: often in tongue tie in 2017: usually races close up. *Stuart Williams* **102**

SWIFT CEDAR (IRE) 7 ch.g. Excellent Art 125 – Ravish 58 (Efisio 120) [2017 81, a87: 7.6v^6 12v 10g^3 f12.1g^5 f11.1g^2 Dec 22] rather leggy gelding: fairly useful handicapper: second at Southwell in December: stays 1½m: acts on polytrack, fibresand, firm and soft going: has worn headgear: often races towards rear. *David Evans* **81**

SWIFTEE (IRE) 4 ch.g. Camacho 118 – Algaira (USA) (Irish River (FR) 131) [2017 73: f8g^2 f8g t10.2d 8.3g 7m 8g t8s^4 8g 7m^5 7.2s^5 p8g Oct 24] tall, good-topped gelding: disappointing maiden: stays 8.5f: acts on fibresand, tapeta and good to firm going: wears headgear: tried in tongue tie. *Ivan Furtado* **64 d**

SWIFT EMPEROR (IRE) 5 b.g. Holy Roman Emperor (IRE) 125 – Big Swifty (IRE) (Intikhab (USA) 135) [2017 98: t8g^4 t8g* 8g^4 9.8m^3 10g 8d t8s 10.3g^2 10v^5 t9.5g t9.5d* Dec 16] useful handicapper: won at Newcastle in March and Wolverhampton (by 1¼ lengths from Andok) in December: stays 10.5f: acts on tapeta, firm and soft going: sometimes slowly away. *David Barron* **99**

SWIFT FOX 2 b.g. (Apr 13) Foxwedge (AUS) 128 – Amontillado (IRE) 60 (Pastoral Pursuits 127) [2017 5m 7d 7d^5 p6g p6g^4 p5s^4 Nov 16] poor maiden: in blinkers last 2 starts. *Gary Moore* **44**

SWIFTSURE (IRE) 3 b.g. Dubawi (IRE) 129 – La Sylphide (SWI) 110 (Barathea (IRE) 127) [2017 77p: 10m 11.9d 10g* 10g^3 11.2s 10.1s* Sep 20] good-topped gelding: useful handicapper: won at Pontefract in June and Yarmouth (by ½ length from Rotherwick) in September: should stay 1½m: acts on soft and good to firm going: sold 180,000 gns, sent to Saudi Arabia. *Sir Michael Stoute* **97**

SWILLY BAY (IRE) 3 gr.g. Mastercraftsman (IRE) 129 – Eastern Appeal (IRE) 110 (Shinko Forest (IRE)) [2017 p7d^6 p7g^5 p10g^3 Mar 16] 75,000F, €100,000Y: fourth foal: half-brother to winner around 1m (including at 2 yrs) Lord Kelvin (by Iffraaj): dam 6f-1m winner: modest form: best effort when third in maiden at Chelmsford in March. *Charles Hills* **61**

SWILLY SUNSET 4 b.g. Kyllachy 129 – Spanish Springs (IRE) 69 (Xaar 132) [2017 f7g p8d 7m^2 7m^4 7m^3 8s* 8g* 8.1m* 10d* 9.9g^2 10.2g Sep 15] lengthy gelding: fairly useful handicapper: won at Yarmouth in June, Brighton/Chepstow in July and Newmarket (by ½ **94**

length from Ghinia) in August: second at Sandown (head behind Glorious Forever) in September: stays 1¼m: acts on tapeta, soft and good to firm going: tried in hood. *Anthony Carson*

SWINFORD LASS 5 b.m. Dutch Art 126 – Tidal 94 (Bin Ajwaad (IRE) 119) [2017 p8d p10g Mar 23] no form, including in handicap. *Tony Carroll* –

SWING OUT SISTER (IRE) 2 b.f. (Apr 8) Kodiac 112 – Dance Club (IRE) 71 (Fasliyev (USA) 120) [2017 5g^{5} 5.7d^{2} 5d^{2} 5m* t5.1m^{3} p6d^{6} Nov 9] 28,000Y: fifth foal: half-sister to 3 winners, including useful 5f (including at 2 yrs) winner Online Alexander (by Acclamation) and winner up to 10.4f Bnedel (2-y-o 1m winner, by Teofilo): dam, 7f winner, half-sister to high-class 6f/7f performer Red Clubs: fair performer: won maiden at Sandown in September: stays 5.5f: acts on tapeta, good to firm and good to soft going: usually races prominently. *Clive Cox* **75**

SWING TIME (IRE) 3 b.g. Choisir (AUS) 126 – Damalis (IRE) 106 (Mukaddamah (USA) 125) [2017 5d^{4} 6g t5s 7d Oct 30] well held in maidens: dead. *Eric Alston* –

SWIRRAL EDGE 4 b.f. Hellvelyn 118 – Pizzarra 62 (Shamardal (USA) 129) [2017 84: t5d^{5} 5g 5s May 20] fairly useful handicapper: stays 6.5f: acts on tapeta, soft and good to firm going: usually races nearer last than first. *David Brown* **81**

SWISH (IRE) 3 gr.f. Lilbourne Lad (IRE) 111 – Maidservant (USA) (Seeking The Gold (USA)) [2017 86: p7g* 5f 6g^{6} 6d^{5} 5.8m^{4} 6d 5.8g^{3} 6s^{5} p7g^{5} p8g Oct 27] fairly useful performer: won minor event at Dundalk in March: stays 7f: acts on polytrack, soft and good to firm going: tried in cheekpieces: sold 50,000 gns in December. *J. J. Feane, Ireland* **92**

SWISSAL (IRE) 2 b.g. (Mar 15) Swiss Spirit 117 – Al Gharrafa 70 (Dutch Art 126) [2017 6.1m^{6} 6.1g 6.1s 6.1s t6g^{4} p6g^{2} p6s* t7.2g^{2} Dec 22] good-bodied gelding: fair performer: won nursery at Chelmsford in December: stays 7f: acts on polytrack and tapeta: usually races nearer last than first. *David Dennis* **72**

SWISS CHOCOLATE (IRE) 2 b.f. (Apr 2) Swiss Spirit 117 – Aqua Vitae (IRE) 63 (Camacho 118) [2017 t5.1g^{4} t6s 5s^{6} 6d Oct 30] modest form: best effort at 5f: dead. *William Haggas* **60**

SWISS CROSS 10 b.g. Cape Cross (IRE) 129 – Swiss Lake (USA) 115 (Indian Ridge 123) [2017 71, a98: t7.1g p7g^{6} t7.1g p7g p6g p6g^{4} p6g^{4} p6g 7m^{3} 5.3g^{3} 5.5f* 6m^{4} 7m^{4} 5.5f* 6g 7m^{5} a6g Sep 5] useful-looking gelding: fairly useful handicapper: won at Les Landes in June and July: stays 1m: acts on polytrack, tapeta and firm going: usually in headgear: wears tongue tie. *Phil McEntee* **84**

SWISSIE 2 br.g. (Mar 7) Swiss Spirit 117 – Princess Pivotal 63 (Pivotal 124) [2017 6d t7.1g Nov 15] well held in minor events. *Ivan Furtado* –

SWISS KNIGHT 2 b.c. (Jan 25) Oasis Dream 129 – Swiss Diva 119 (Pivotal 124) [2017 t7.2g^{2} Dec 2] 475,000Y: first foal: dam, 5f and (including at 2 yrs) 6f winner, half-sister to smart sprinter Swiss Spirit: 15/8, second in minor event at Wolverhampton (neck behind Jellmood) in December: will improve. *Charlie Appleby* **91 p**

SWISS LAIT 6 b.m. Milk It Mick 120 – Matilda Peace (Namaqualand (USA)) [2017 61: t12.4g t10.2d^{5} p11d p8d^{6} 8.5m 9.9d 9.2s 9s 8.3s 12.1v 9.9v 8s Oct 3] lengthy mare: modest handicapper: stays 9f: acts on tapeta, soft and good to firm going: sometimes wears headgear: usually slowly away, often races in rear: signs of temperament (carries head awkwardly). *Patrick Holmes* **53**

SWISS MARLIN 2 b.f. (Apr 13) Swiss Spirit 117 – Piranha (IRE) 82 (Exceed And Excel (AUS) 126) [2017 t6s 6s^{6} t7.1d Nov 10] 6,000F: third foal: half-sister to useful 5f and (at 2 yrs) 6f winner Go On Go On Go On (by Medicean) and 2-y-o 7f/1m winner Ronnie The Rooster (by Captain Gerrard): dam 2-y-o 5f winner: well held in minor events. *John Quinn* –

SWISS PSALM 2 b.f. (Apr 26) Swiss Spirit 117 – Athwaab 74 (Cadeaux Genereux 131) [2017 p5g^{6} 8d p7g p5m p6g^{4} Dec 12] first foal: dam 5f and (including at 2 yrs) 6f winner: poor maiden: left Simon Hodgson after first start. *Mark Gillard* **36**

SWISS STORM 3 b.c. Frankel 147 – Swiss Lake (USA) 115 (Indian Ridge 123) [2017 92P: 10.3d 8.5v^{3} 8g Nov 3] big, strong colt: useful winner at 2 yrs, disappointing in 2017: should stay 1m: acts on good to soft going. *David Elsworth* **69**

SWISS VINNARE 3 b.g. Arabian Gleam 122 – Matilda Peace (Namaqualand (USA)) [2017 p8d^{2} p8s^{4} f11.1g^{5} p10g^{3} p8g* Dec 28] seventh foal: half-brother to winner up to 9.5f Poppy Bond (2-y-o 5f winner, by Misu Bond) and 9f winner Swiss Lait (by Milk It Mick): **84**

dam unraced half-sister to useful sprinter Blue Iris: fairly useful performer: won maiden at Lingfield (by 3¼ lengths from Paradise Lake) in December: stays 1¼m: acts on polytrack: in hood last 2 starts. *Phil McEntee*

SWORD EXCEED (GER) 3 b.g. Exceed And Excel (AUS) 126 – Sword Roche (GER) 101 (Laroche (GER) 123) [2017 72: p6g* p7g³ 6.1g 6m⁴ 6m⁴ p6g* t7.2d Dec 16] good-topped gelding: useful handicapper: won at Lingfield in March and November (by 1½ lengths from Pretty Bubbles): stays 6f: acts on polytrack and good to firm going. *Ivan Furtado* **95**

SWOT 5 b.g. Exceed And Excel (AUS) 126 – House Point 59 (Pivotal 124) [2017 69: p8g⁴ 8g⁵ 7.4v⁴ 7s³ t7.2g³ f8.1g³ Dec 1] quite attractive gelding: fair handicapper: stays 1m: acts on all-weather, good to firm and heavy going: wears headgear: consistent. *Roger Teal* **66**

SYMBOL 3 ch.f. Nathaniel (IRE) 129 – Succinct 104 (Hector Protector (USA) 124) [2017 10d⁴ p12g² p12g⁶ Oct 3] rangy filly: half-sister to several winners, including 2-y-o 7f winner Starry Sky (by Oasis Dream) and 13f/2m winner Aumerle (by Authorized): dam 1¼m winner: fairly useful form: best effort when second in maiden at Kempton (1¼ lengths behind Romina) in September. *James Fanshawe* **84**

SYMBOLIC STAR (IRE) 5 b.g. New Approach (IRE) 132 – Epitome (IRE) 71 (Nashwan (USA) 135) [2017 74: t7.1d* t7.1g⁶ 7g⁵ t8s* 8.3g t8s* 8.9m t7.1d Aug 10] good-topped gelding: modest handicapper on turf, fair on all-weather: won at Newcastle in March, May and June: stays 1¼m: acts on tapeta and good to firm going: wears headgear: starts slowly. *Barry Murtagh* **55 a71**

SYMBOL IN THE SAND (NOR) 3 b.f. Giant Sandman (IRE) 115 – Symbol of Arch (USA) 107 (Arch (USA) 127) [2017 p7g 9s 5.8s* 5.8g Jun 29] modest form: left Rune Haugen after first start: won minor event at Ovrevoll in June: stays 6f: acts on soft going. *Are Hyldmo, Norway* **56**

SYMBOLIZATION (IRE) 2 b.c. (Mar 1) Cape Cross (IRE) 129 – Yorkshire Lass (IRE) (Pivotal 124) [2017 7d² p7s* Sep 8] good-topped, attractive colt: first foal: dam, 1½m-17f winner, half-sister to smart winner up to 1½m Elite Army: useful form: won minor event at Kempton (by 1½ lengths from Glendevon) in September: will stay 1m: will improve further. *Charlie Appleby* **100 p**

SYMPHONIC 2 b.f. (May 5) Mayson 124 – Musical Moonlight (Observatory (USA) 131) [2017 7v 6d t6g Nov 23] €16,000 2-y-o: leggy filly: sixth foal: closely related to 1m winner Zabdi (by Zebedee) and half-sister to a winner in Italy by Red Clubs: dam unraced half-sister to Dewhurst Stakes runner-up Musical Pursuit: well held in minor events. *Ann Duffield* **–**

SYNCOPATE 8 b.g. Oratorio (IRE) 128 – Millistar 88 (Galileo (IRE) 134) [2017 88: 12m⁵ 11.4m May 8] angular gelding: fairly useful handicapper: stayed 1½m: acted on polytrack and heavy going: dead. *Pam Sly* **79**

SYNDEX (IRE) 4 b.f. Frozen Power (IRE) 108 – Zankara (FR) (Linamix (FR) 127) [2017 70: p8g p7s Nov 16] half-sister to several winners, including useful winner up to 1½m Ballybacka Queen (2-y-o 7.5f winner, by Hurricane Run) and 1¾m-16.5f winner Zakatal (by Kalanisi): dam French 1m winner: fair maiden at best, well held in handicaps in 2017: left Miss Natalia Lupini after first start: best effort at 9f: acts on polytrack and good to soft going: has worn hood. *Johnny Farrelly* **–**

SYNDICATE 3 b.f. Dansili 127 – Indication 76 (Sadler's Wells (USA) 132) [2017 81: 8m⁶ p7s Jun 14] good-topped filly: fair at 2 yrs, looked awkward both starts in 2017: stays 1m: acts on polytrack and fibresand. *Ralph Beckett* **68**

SYNODIC (USA) 5 br.g. Henrythenavigator (USA) 131 – Seven Moons (JPN) (Sunday Silence (USA)) [2017 68: t9.5m⁵ t9.5g³ p10g* p12f* p12g* p12g³ p10g³ May 4] tall gelding: fairly useful handicapper: won at Lingfield in February (amateur) and March (twice): stays 1½m: acts on polytrack, tapeta and good to soft going: tried in blinkers: wears tongue tie: waited with: sold £12,000 in May. *Seamus Durack* **80**

SYPHAX (USA) 3 b.c. Arch (USA) 127 – Much Obliged (USA) (Kingmambo (USA) 125) [2017 110p: t8s² 10.3d 8g 7.9g 10.3g² 11.9s Nov 11] well-made colt: useful performer: second in minor event at Newcastle (2¾ lengths behind Forest Ranger) in April and handicap at York (2¼ lengths behind Dark Red) in October: stays 10.5f: acts on good to firm and good to soft going: tried in cheekpieces: temperamental. *Kevin Ryan* **107 §**

SYRIAN PEARL 6 gr.m. Clodovil (IRE) 116 – Syrian Queen 82 (Slip Anchor 136) [2017 93: 6m 6.1m 6g⁶ 6m⁶ 6d⁵ 6m⁴ 6.1d* Oct 4] sturdy mare: fairly useful handicapper: won at **92**

Nottingham (by ½ length from Fantasy Keeper) in October: stays 7f, usually raced at 6f: acts on polytrack, good to firm and good to soft going: sometimes slowly away, often races towards rear. *Chris Wall*

T

TAAJUB (IRE) 10 b.g. Exceed And Excel (AUS) 126 – Purple Tiger (IRE) (Rainbow Quest (USA) 134) [2017 90: p5g^5 p5m^6 6m^6 5.3g* 5g^2 5m^5 6f^6 5.3d^4 5m^2 5d^3 5.3s^4 Oct 10] good-bodied gelding: fair handicapper: won at Brighton in May: stays 6f: acts on polytrack, tapeta, firm and soft going: has worn headgear. *Peter Crate* **79**

TAAMOL (IRE) 3 b.g. Helmet (AUS) 127 – Supreme Seductress (IRE) 66 (Montjeu (IRE) 137) [2017 100: t8s^4 7d* 7m 7d Aug 5] lengthy gelding: useful performer: won listed race at Newmarket (by head from Larchmont Lad) in May: stays 7f: acts on heavy going: tried in cheekpieces: has joined A. Al Rayhi, UAE. *Sir Michael Stoute* **106**

TAAREEF (USA) 4 ch.c. Kitten's Joy (USA) 128 – Sacred Feather (USA) (Carson City (USA)) [2017 118: 8m* 8g* 8d^5 8d^2 8d* Sep 30] high-class performer: won Prix Bertrand du Breuil at Chantilly (by 1¾ lengths from Zelzal) in June, Prix Messidor at Maisons-Laffitte (by 2 lengths from Al Wukair) in July and Prix Daniel Wildenstein at Chantilly (for second successive year, beat Buthela 1¼ lengths) in September: ¾-length second to Ribchester in Prix du Moulin de Longchamp at Chantilly: suited by 1m: acts on polytrack, good to firm and good to soft going. *Jean-Claude Rouget, France* **125**

TABARRAK (IRE) 4 b.g. Acclamation 118 – Bahati (IRE) 99 (Intikhab (USA) 135) [2017 112: 7m^2 8f* 8m^5 7g 8g^2 7g* Sep 22] strong gelding: smart performer: won listed races at Ascot (by neck from Ennaadd) in May and Newbury (by neck from Accidental Agent) in September: stays 1m: acts on firm and soft going: usually races prominently. *Richard Hannon* **117**

TABDEED 2 ch.c. (Jan 26) Havana Gold (IRE) 118 – Puzzled (IRE) 91 (Peintre Celebre (USA) 137) [2017 6g* Aug 2] 42,000F: second foal: dam, maiden (stayed 1½m), half-sister to Derby runner-up Walk In The Park out of Irish 1000 Guineas winner Classic Park: 14/1, won minor event at Leicester (by 2¼ lengths from Yafta) in August: will stay 7f+: will improve. *Owen Burrows* **98 p**

TABERNAS (IRE) 2 ch.c. (Apr 16) Dawn Approach (IRE) 132 – Simonetta (IRE) 82 (Lil's Boy (USA) 109) [2017 p8s t8s^4 Sep 19] fair form: better effort when fourth in minor event at Newcastle (2 lengths behind Tansheet) second start. *Charlie Appleby* **67**

TABIKAT ELLE (IRE) 4 ch.f. Showcasing 117 – Mansiya 65 (Vettori (IRE) 119) [2017 t5g Mar 15] fair maiden at 2 yrs: well held in handicap after long absence only start in 2017. *Ollie Pears* **–**

TABLA 5 b.m. Rail Link 132 – Questa Nova (Rainbow Quest (USA) 134) [2017 76: p7g^6 p8g^3 p8g Feb 11] well-made mare: fair handicapper: stays 1¼m: acts on polytrack: tried in visor: often races prominently: temperamental. *Lee Carter* **69 §**

TABLE MANNERS 5 b.m. Dutch Art 126 – Nine Red 63 (Royal Applause 124) [2017 64: t7.1d* t8d^5 t6g t8s* 9d t8g t8g^2 t8d^6 Nov 4] fair handicapper: won at Newcastle in February (apprentice) and May: stays 1¼m: acts on tapeta and good to firm going. *Wilf Storey* **71**

TADAANY (IRE) 5 b.g. Acclamation 118 – Park Haven (IRE) 79 (Marju (IRE) 127) [2017 87: 7g 8s 7d 7v^5 7s^3 8.3d p8g^3 p7d t9.5g^5 p8s^4 Dec 8] fairly useful handicapper: third at Chelmsford in October: left David O'Meara after fourth start: stays 8.5f: acts on polytrack and soft going: has worn headgear: front runner/races prominently: inconsistent. *Ruth Carr* **80**

Qatar Prix Daniel Wildenstein, Chantilly—Taareef is driven out to repeat his 2016 victory in this race, beating the improving Buthela (No.8) and German challenger Noor Al Hawa (No.4)

TADAAWOL 4 b.g. Kyllachy 129 – Bright Edge 102 (Danehill Dancer (IRE) 117) [2017 **86**
74: t6g t6d^4 t7.1g^5 t7.1d^3 7m^2 7m^2 7.1m^2 8g 8g 7m^3 7.4f^5 7s^4 7.4s^4 7v* 7g^4 7d 7.6v^4 6.9v^5 **a76**
Sep 18] fairly useful handicapper: won at Catterick (by 7 lengths from Mango Chutney) in
August: stays 7.5f: acts on tapeta, good to firm and heavy going: wears cheekpieces: often
leads. *Roger Fell*

TADBIR (IRE) 2 b.g. (Mar 1) Kodiac 112 – Queen Wasp (IRE) (Shamardal (USA) 129) **52 p**
[2017 5d^5 May 12] £150,000Y: third foal: half-brother to smart winner up to 1m Rusumaat
(2-y-o 6f winner, by Arcano): dam unraced half-sister to smart winner up to 11.6f Naheef:
5/2, fifth in minor event at Lingfield (9 lengths behind One Minute) in May: should
progress. *Brian Meehan*

TADLEEL 2 b.c. (Feb 13) Dark Angel (IRE) 113 – Quelle Affaire 47 (Bahamian Bounty **92**
116) [2017 6s 7g* 7m^2 7m^2 p8g* 8g Sep 28] £130,000Y: close-coupled colt: first foal: dam
lightly-raced half-sister to smart sprinter Justice Good: fairly useful performer: won minor
event at Newmarket in July and nursery at Kempton (by length from Jazeel) in September:
stays 1m: acts on polytrack and good to firm going. *Ed Dunlop*

TADWEEN (IRE) 3 b.g. Tagula (IRE) 116 – Stained Glass (Dansili 127) [2017 p7g^6 p7g^3 **77**
8s^2 t8.6g^4 7d a6f a9.9f Dec 21] fair maiden: left Richard Hannon after fifth start: stays 8.5f:
acts on polytrack, tapeta and soft going: tried in visor. *Fawzi Abdulla Nass, Bahrain*

TAEL O' GOLD 3 ch.f. Zoffany (IRE) 121 – Wedding Dream 81 (Oasis Dream 129) **–**
[2017 56: t8g 5.9s 7.2m 7.2s 8g 5d Jul 31] workmanlike filly: modest maiden at 2 yrs, no
form in 2017: left Iain Jardine after third start: in headgear last 5 starts. *R. Mike Smith*

TAEXALI (IRE) 4 ch.g. Raven's Pass (USA) 133 – Enchanted Evening (IRE) 105 (High **103 §**
Chaparral (IRE) 132) [2017 104: 5g 5g 7g 6g^6 5g^4 5m^6 5.1m^2 5.1d 5g 6d^6 5s^4 5.5g^5 5v^4 5g^6
5.8v p5g Nov 17] stocky gelding: useful handicapper: second at Chester (neck behind El
Astronaute) in May: left S. Seemar after fourth start (then returned to former trainer): stays
7f: acts on good to firm and heavy going: has worn headgear, including in 2017:
temperamental. *John Patrick Shanahan, Ireland*

TAFAAKHOR (IRE) 3 gr.g. Dark Angel (IRE) 113 – Tellelle (IRE) 91 (Trans Island 119) **92**
[2017 86: t7.1g^2 t7.1g^2 7g* p7g^5 p7d^5 8m^3 p8s^5 8d* 8g^6 a7f Dec 7] sturdy gelding: fairly
useful performer: won maiden at Brighton in April and handicap at Newmarket (by 1½
lengths from Sterling Silva) in July: left Richard Hannon after ninth start: stays 1m: acts on
polytrack, tapeta, good to firm and good to soft going: in blinkers last 4 starts: often travels
strongly. *A. Al Rayhi, UAE*

TAFTEESH (IRE) 4 b.g. Kodiac 112 – Mudalalah (IRE) 70 (Singspiel (IRE) 133) [2017 **69**
–: t6g^4 t7.1g^5 7.5f 6s^4 6m^4 t8g 7.2v t7.1g t7.2g 6d^4 Oct 30] fair handicapper: stays 7f: acts
on tapeta and good to soft going: tried in tongue tie: often races prominently: sold 3,500
gns, sent to the Netherlands. *Michael Easterby*

TAGHEE 2 b.c. (Feb 20) Acclamation 118 – Umneeyatee (AUS) (Encosta de Lago (AUS)) **71**
[2017 7s^3 7d t7.2g t8.6g^5 Dec 18] fair form: stays 8.5f. *Marco Botti*

TAGUR (IRE) 3 ch.g. Tagula (IRE) 116 – Westcote (USA) 78 (Gone West (USA)) [2017 **72**
72: t7.1g^6 8.3g 6.9g^3 6d 6d 7v 7.2m^2 6.9v* 7.2v^4 t7.1g f6.1g^4 Dec 21] sturdy gelding: fair
handicapper: won at Carlisle in September: stays 1m: acts on polytrack, tapeta, good to
firm and heavy going: usually wears headgear: front runner/races prominently. *Kevin Ryan*

TAHITI ONE 4 b.f. Bertolini (USA) 125 – Club Tahiti 92 (Hernando (FR) 127) [2017 58: **–**
t7.1m^6 p6g Feb 9] modest handicapper: well below form both starts in 2017: stays 7f: acts
on polytrack, tapeta and heavy going: in headgear last 3 starts: often leads. *Tony Carroll*

TAHOO (IRE) 3 b.f. Zebedee 113 – Suffer Her (IRE) (Whipper (USA) 126) [2017 89: 6m **97**
5g^4 5m^4 5.1m^3 5.1g* 5g^4 5m 5g* Oct 18] workmanlike filly: useful handicapper: won at
Windsor in July and Nottingham (by neck from Bahamian Sunrise) in October: best form
at 5f: acts on good to firm going: front runner/races prominently: sold 30,000 gns later in
October. *K. R. Burke*

TAHREEK 2 b.c. (Apr 12) Dansili 127 – Rifqah (USA) (Elusive Quality (USA)) [2017 7d^5 **70 P**
Sep 29] sixth foal: half-brother to 3 winners, including very smart 6f-1m winner Mustajeeb
(2-y-o 7f winner, by Nayef) and smart 6f and (including at 2 yrs) 7f winner Muaanid (by
Kheleyf): dam, French maiden, out of half-sister to Prix du Jockey Club winner Anabaa
Blue: 28/1, green when fifth in maiden at Newmarket (8 lengths behind Thrave) in
September, finishing with running left: open to significant improvement. *Sir Michael Stoute*

TAIFBALADY (IRE) 2 b.g. (Apr 5) Dark Angel (IRE) 113 – Tartiflette 99 (Dr Fong **–**
(USA) 128) [2017 6s 6f 7v Sep 9] well-grown gelding: little impact in maiden/minor
events. *Mark Johnston*

TAI HANG DRAGON (IRE) 3 b.f. Tamayuz 126 – Give A Whistle (IRE) 100 (Mujadil (USA) 119) [2017 –p: p6g4 t7.1g3 p7g* p7g* 6g4 6d2 7f4 7d* 8m4 8g 8m p8g5 Nov 6] rather leggy filly: useful handicapper: won at Kempton in February, and Lingfield in April and July (by 4½ lengths from Bassmah): stays 1m: acts on polytrack, tapeta, firm and good to soft going. *Richard Hannon* **97**

TAILOR'S ROW (USA) 3 ch.c. Street Cry (IRE) 130 – Raw Silk (USA) (Malibu Moon (USA)) [2017 82: t7.1g2 t7.1d2 p8g6 t7.1f2 7g4 7.2d6 p8g 7.6g 7.4d 8g2 7g4 p7g6 t8g p8g p8g t9.5m* Oct 28] workmanlike colt: fairly useful handicapper: won at Wolverhampton (by length from Barnaby Brook) in October: second at Redcar in August: stays 9.5f: acts on polytrack, tapeta, best turf form on good going: temperamental: sold 8,000 gns, sent to UAE. *Mark Johnston* **83 §**

TAILWIND 4 b.g. Dubawi (IRE) 129 – Time Saved 89 (Green Desert (USA) 127) [2017 83: t5g 6g p5g* 5d3 Jun 24] fairly useful handicapper: won at Lingfield (by short head from Menelik) in May: left Roger Varian after first start: stays 6f: acts on polytrack and good to soft going: in blinkers last 2 starts: front runner/races prominently: sold 12,000 gns in July. *Richard Hannon* **81**

TAI SING YEH (IRE) 3 b.g. Exceed And Excel (AUS) 126 – Cherry Orchard (IRE) (King's Best (USA) 132) [2017 78p: 7g2 7.2f5 7g 7m 7d3 p7g p7d Nov 9] useful-looking gelding: fairly useful handicapper: second at Redcar in May and third at Catterick in September: raced only at 7f: acts on polytrack and good to soft going: wears tongue tie: often races prominently. *Charles Hills* **83**

TAJAANUS (IRE) 2 b.f. (Mar 3) Arcano (IRE) 122 – Rayaheen 84 (Nayef (USA) 129) [2017 6s* 6g6 7d* 7g* 8g Sep 14] sturdy filly: first foal: dam 2-y-o 6f winner out of 1000 Guineas winner Natagora: useful performer: won minor event at Newmarket in May, listed race at Sandown (by nose from Capomento) in July and Sweet Solera Stakes at Newmarket (by length from Juliet Capulet) in August: stays 7f: acts on soft going. *Richard Hannon* **101**

TAJARROB (IRE) 2 b.f. (Apr 2) Intikhab (USA) 135 – Maany (USA) 62 (Mr Greeley (USA) 122) [2017 p7g Nov 2] tall filly: third foal: half-sister to useful 2-y-o 7f winner Majdool (by Acclamation): dam lightly-raced half-sister to smart US Grade 2 9f winner Adonis: 50/1, considerately handled when seventh in minor event at Lingfield (6½ lengths behind West Palm Beach) on debut, finishing with running left: likely to improve markedly. *Ed Dunlop* **60 P**

TAJ MAHAL (IRE) 3 b.c. Galileo (IRE) 134 – You'resothrilling (USA) 117 (Storm Cat (USA)) [2017 106: 8d2 9.5s2 10.4g4 10m4 12g6 9.9m 10f2 10d5 9.9g 9.9g4 12g* Nov 18] strong, good-bodied colt: type to carry condition: smart performer: fourth in Prix du Jockey Club at Chantilly (1½ lengths behind Brametot) and Hampton Court Stakes at Royal Ascot (beaten 2 lengths by Benbatl) in June, second in Secretariat Stakes at Arlington (2¼ lengths behind Oscar Performance) in August and fourth in Emirates Stakes at Flemington (beaten 1¾ lengths by Tosen Stardom) in November, then left Aidan O'Brien: won Group 2 Zipping Classic at Sandown (Australia) in November by 3½ lengths from Almandin: stays 1½m: acts on polytrack, soft and good to firm going: usually in headgear: has worn tongue tie: ran under the name of The Taj Mahal last 3 starts. *Robert Hickmott, Australia* **119**

TAKATUL (USA) 4 b.g. Smart Strike (CAN) 121 – Torrestrella (IRE) 117 (Orpen (USA) 116) [2017 96p: p7g4 p8g* 8s5 7m4 8m5 Aug 27] strong gelding: fairly useful handicapper: won at Lingfield (by ½ length from Take The Helm) in April: stays 1m: acts on polytrack and good to firm going: in blinkers last 2 starts: gelded, and sent to UAE. *Charles Hills* **94**

TAKBEER (IRE) 5 b.g. Aqlaam 125 – Precious Secret (IRE) 63 (Fusaichi Pegasus (USA) 130) [2017 –: t9.5g t13.9m2 11.6g6 12g 13.3g* 14g2 14s t16.5g6 Dec 5] fairly useful handicapper: won at Newbury (by ½ length from Flight of Fantasy) in July: stays 1¾m: acts on polytrack, tapeta and good to soft going: wears headgear: usually races close up. *Nikki Evans* **83**

TAKE A DROP (IRE) 4 b.f. Bushranger (IRE) 119 – Brogan's Well (IRE) (Caerleon (USA) 132) [2017 54: p8g p7g p6g 8m2 8g 8.1d 6s Sep 4] half-sister to several winners, including winner up to 1½m Liquid Form (2-y-o 1m winner, by Bahhare) and 1¼m winner (stayed 1½m) Etain (by Alhaarth): dam unraced: modest maiden handicapper: left Patrick Martin after third start: stays 1m: acts on good to firm and good to soft going: sometimes in headgear: has worn tongue tie. *Seamus Mullins* **53**

TAKE A NOTE 8 b.g. Singspiel (IRE) 133 – Ela Paparouna 85 (Vettori (IRE) 119) [2017 79: p6d5 May 29] sturdy gelding: one-time useful handicapper, on the downgrade: stays 1m: acts on polytrack and firm going: wears headgear: usually races towards rear. *Patrick Chamings* **43**

TAKE A TURN (IRE) 3 b.g. Henrythenavigator (USA) 131 – Satwa Pearl 91 (Rock of Gibraltar (IRE) 133) [2017 60: p10g 10m4 10d* 12d6 10d* 8.9m4 9.9s5 Oct 9] compact gelding: fair handicapper: won at Ayr in July and Lingfield in August: stays 1¼m: acts on polytrack, soft and good to firm going: sometimes slowly away. *David Lanigan* **75**

TAKE COVER 10 b.g. Singspiel (IRE) 133 – Enchanted 99 (Magic Ring (IRE) 115) [2017 120: 5f 5f5 5m* 5s4 5g 5g* 5.2m* p5g* Oct 20] **120**

Highland Reel's career earnings of £7,920,350 are testament to his racing character and to his constitution. In that respect, there are similarities between Highland Reel and another horse who was once the leading European-trained money earner, Singspiel, who was one of the first to contribute to the increased internationalisation of modern racing through his globe-trotting achievements. Singspiel retired with total prize money won of over £3.6m, a figure that took him past Lando, the leading European-trained money earner at the time. Both Singspiel and Lando now sit well outside the top ten for reasons explained in Singspiel's essay in *Racehorses of 1996*: 'such [prize money] statistics, though interesting, are of limited significance with the level of prize money rising over the years as the value of money falls'. That caveat is as true today as it was then and, allowing that the increased level of global competition is also a factor, each of the current top ten started their careers in 2006 or later and owe their places largely to the continued rises in prize money. The 2017 Dubai World Cup, for example, was worth £4,838,710 to the winner Arrogate, who in winning at Meydan became the highest-earning racehorse in history. Compare the Dubai World Cup first prize to the £1,568,627 won by Singspiel in the same race at Nad Al Sheba twenty years earlier, and it emphasises the point. The 1996 Japan Cup, also won by Singspiel, was worth £946,040 to the winner compared to £2,025,658 in the latest season, while the prize money for the Juddmonte International winner has more than doubled since 1997 (when Singspiel won it) from £202,152 to £567,100. Singspiel went on to excel as a stallion, siring thirteen individual Group 1 winners before his death in 2010, those winners including the Dubai World Cup winner Moon Ballad and the Yorkshire Oaks and Dubai Sheema Classic winner Dar Re Mi as he generally established himself as a source of middle-distance performers. There have been a few notable exceptions, though. Rewaaya beat subsequent King's Stand winner Miss Andretti when winning the Group 1 Sir Rupert Clarke Stakes over seven furlongs in Australia in 2006, and Solow won five Group 1 races at around a mile/nine furlongs in 2015 (he had to be retired in May after failing to recover from a leg injury sustained after his comeback run the previous year). In Solow's absence, the very speedy Take Cover was the flagbearer for his sire in the latest season when he proved as good as ever at the age of ten, winning four times, all at the minimum trip, hardly a typical profile for a son of Singspiel.

Dubai International Airport World Trophy Stakes, Newbury—at the ripe old age of ten, making him the joint-oldest winner of a pattern race since the official pattern began in 1971, Take Cover shows trademark speed from the stalls before making all to beat Cotai Glory (centre) and Muthmir (striped cap)

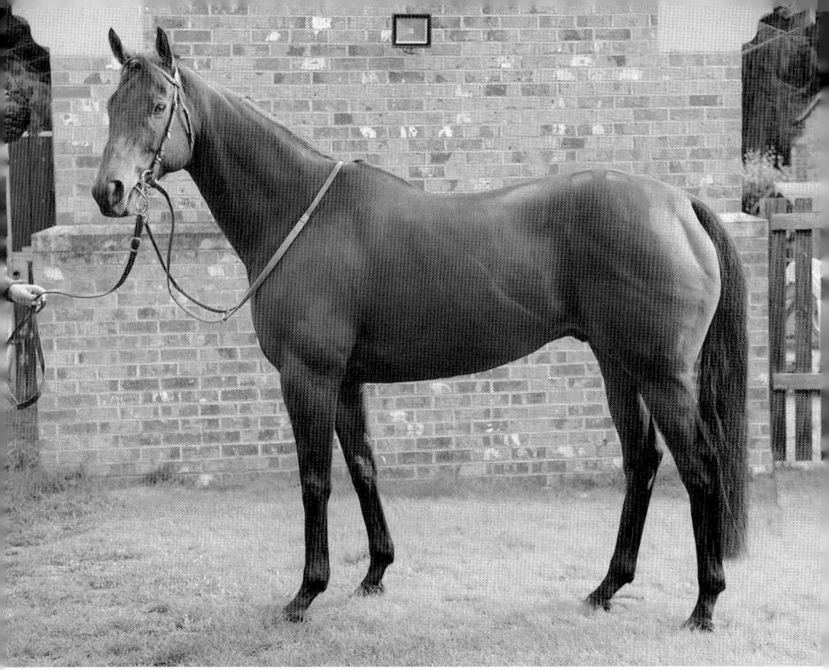

Norcroft Park Stud's "Take Cover"

Take Cover shaped as if retaining all his ability on his first two starts before taking advantage of a drop in grade to resume winning ways in a listed event at York in July, making all and holding on gamely to repeat his victory in the race three years earlier. Take Cover had won the King George Stakes at Goodwood on his next start in 2014—and again in 2016—but could not repeat the feat in a red-hot renewal in the latest season, finishing three and three quarter lengths fourth behind Battaash. After then running well below form in the Nunthorpe Stakes, Take Cover returned to his best to win again at listed level at Beverley just eight days later, showing all his trademark speed to beat Final Venture in a race in which only a length and three quarters covered the first seven past the post. Take Cover was ridden by Tom Queally for the first time at Beverley, with regular jockey David Allan riding at Chester, but Allan was back in the saddle for the Group 3 Dubai International Airport World Trophy Stakes at Newbury, for which there was a much bigger field than usual and a strong one, too, containing some of the fastest horses around. Take Cover left them all standing leaving the stalls and battled on well to beat Cotai Glory by three quarters of a length, with Muthmir the same distance back in third. Take Cover hadn't managed to trouble the judge in three previous attempts at the Prix de l'Abbaye and connections opted to bypass the latest renewal in favour of a listed race at Dundalk, a contest Take Cover had won 2015. Sent off at 11/8-on in a thirteen-strong field, Take Cover was headed entering the final furlong, but responded gamely to regain the lead near the line and complete the hat-trick, beating Hit The Bid by a neck, with another length and a half back to the two-year-old Declarationofpeace, who on his next start won the Juvenile Turf Sprint Stakes on the undercard at Del Mar, a race set to become a fully-fledged part of the Breeders' Cup programme in 2018. Take Cover didn't take up a possible overseas engagement of his own in the Hong Kong Sprint at Sha Tin in December, but he is set to return to action as an eleven-year-old. After showing himself as good as ever in the latest season, it would be no surprise if more good races came his way. His win in the World Trophy made him the joint-oldest winner of a European pattern race on the Flat and if he adds another to his already commendable record it will put him out on his own.

Take Cover (b.g. 2007)	Singspiel (IRE) (b 1992)	In The Wings (b 1986)	Sadler's Wells
			High Hawk
		Glorious Song (b 1976)	Halo
			Ballade
	Enchanted (b 1999)	Magic Ring (b 1989)	Green Desert
			Emaline
		Snugfit Annie (b 1991)	Midyan
			Great Aim

With Singspiel considered more of an influence for stamina, the speed in Take Cover's pedigree has presumably been supplied by his useful dam Enchanted. By Magic Ring, who won the Norfolk Stakes and the Cornwallis Stakes as well as finishing a close third in the Prix de l'Abbaye as a two-year-old, Enchanted won five races at five to seven furlongs and was third in the listed Chartwell Fillies' Stakes at Lingfield. Enchanted is a half-sister to a couple of winning sprinters, the useful Golden Asha and the fair handicapper Excellent Aim. The trio all started their racing careers in the colours of their breeder Norcroft Park Stud and Enchanted joined her dam among the stud's broodmare band after her retirement from the track. Norcroft Park Stud have retained each of her four progeny to have raced to date, including the useful six/seven-furlong handicapper Arteus (by Fantastic Light), who is the only other offspring of Enchanted to have won a race. Norcroft Park Stud bought a yearling Sepoy half-brother to Take Cover for 29,000 guineas at the 2016 December Sales. A big, strong, lengthy gelding, Take Cover is best at five furlongs and acts on polytrack, fibresand, firm and soft going. He is a catch-me-if-you-can runner and is often taken to post early, though he has never shown any signs of temperament in his races. He is a credit to his trainer. *David C. Griffiths*

TAKE ME WITH YOU (USA) 2 b.f. (Mar 1) Scat Daddy (USA) 120 – Me And Miss **105**
Jones (USA) (Smarty Jones (USA) 134) [2017 $6g^3$ $6m^3$ 6.1d* Sep 4] $205,000F, $285,000Y, $800,000 2-y-o: sturdy filly: fourth foal: half-sister to a winner in USA by Yes It's True: dam unraced daughter of smart US 2-y-o Grade 3 6f winner Forest Heiress: useful form: won minor event at Windsor (by 9 lengths from Sergio Leone) in September: raced only at 6f. *Jeremy Noseda*

TAKEONEFORTHETEAM 2 b.g. (Feb 16) Bahamian Bounty 116 – Miss Bond (IRE) **65**
(Danehill Dancer (IRE) 117) [2017 $6d^4$ $t6g^5$ $f5g^5$ Dec 29] smallish, lengthy gelding: mid-division in minor events. *Daniel Loughnane*

TAKE SHELTER 2 b.f. (Feb 11) Harbour Watch (IRE) 121 – Secret Night 99 (Dansili **76**
127) [2017 $5m^2$ $5m^2$ $6s^6$ $5m^4$ $6g^2$ 6g Aug 14] 21,000Y: compact filly: fifth foal: sister to 7f winner Bassmah and half-sister to 7f winner On The Tiles (by Royal Applause): dam, winner up to 7f (2-y-o 5f/6f winner), half-sister to useful winner up to 1¼m Rosa Grace: fair maiden: best form at 5f: acts on good to firm going: usually races prominently. *James Tate*

TAKE THE HELM 4 ch.g. Monsieur Bond (IRE) 120 – Oasis Breeze 88 (Oasis Dream **100**
129) [2017 90, a98: p7g $p7g^2$ p7g* $p8d^2$ p7g* $p7g^4$ $p8g^2$ Apr 26] strong, compact gelding: useful handicapper: won at Lingfield in February and April (by head from War Glory): stays 8.5f: acts on polytrack, tapeta, soft and good to firm going: tried in cheekpieces: front runner/races prominently. *Brian Meehan*

TAKE THE HIGH ROAD 3 b.g. Kyllachy 129 – China Tea (USA) (High Chaparral **84**
(IRE) 132) [2017 $9.5s^3$ $9.5v^3$ $f7.1g^5$ Nov 16] 26,000Y: fourth foal: half-brother to smart hurdler Elgin (by Duke of Marmalade): dam unraced sister to smart French 1¼m-1½m winner Magadan: fairly useful form: best effort when third in maiden at Gowran (2 lengths behind World War) in October: left John M. Oxx after: tried in cheekpieces. *Keith Dalgleish*

TAKE THIS WALTZ 3 b.f. Royal Applause 124 – Constant Craving 82 (Pastoral **–**
Pursuits 127) [2017 –: f8.1g $f6.1g^6$ Dec 4] little sign of ability. *Bill Turner*

TAKE TWO 8 b.g. Act One 124 – Lac Marmot (FR) (Marju (IRE) 127) [2017 80: $p12g^3$ **90**
$p12g^6$ $p12d^4$ $t10.2d^4$ $10.3g^4$ $p11g^4$ $10s^3$ $13.3v^3$ 11.4m* 11.6g* $11.4g^4$ $12s^2$ $p12g^2$ $t12.2g^5$ p12g* Dec 13] fairly useful handicapper: won at Windsor in August and Haydock in

September, both amateur events, and Lingfield in December: stays 13.5f: acts on polytrack, tapeta, good to firm and heavy going: sometimes slowly away, often races towards rear. *Alex Hales*

TAKIAH 2 b.f. (Feb 19) Arcano (IRE) 122 – Elmaam 86 (Nayef (USA) 129) [2017 7m^5 **– p**
Aug 25] third foal: half-sister to German 9f winner Laquyood (by Medicean): dam, 7.5f/1m winner, half-sister to smart/ungenuine winner up to 7f Dafeef: 20/1, well held in minor event at Newmarket: should do better. *Brian Meehan*

TALAAQY (IRE) 2 b.f. (Apr 11) Dansili 127 – Shabiba (USA) 103 (Seeking The Gold **78 p**
(USA)) [2017 6d* Oct 24] sister to useful 8.6f-1¼m winner Muzdawaj and half-sister to several winners, notably high-class 5f-7f winner Ertijaal (2-y-o 6f winner, by Oasis Dream): dam winner up to 1m (2-y-o 6f winner): 2/5, won minor event at Yarmouth (by 1½ lengths from Puds) in October: better to come. *William Haggas*

TALAAYEB 3 b.f. Dansili 127 – Rumoush (USA) 114 (Rahy (USA) 115) [2017 99p: 8m^4 **112**
10g 7g* 7g^4 Sep 15] tall, rather unfurnished filly: smart performer: won City of York Stakes (by neck from Toscanini) in August: likely to prove best at 7f/1m: acts on good to firm going: often travels strongly. *Owen Burrows*

TALAS (IRE) 2 b.g. (Mar 7) Dansili 127 – Tamarind (IRE) 107 (Sadler's Wells (USA) **78**
132) [2017 8m^4 t9.5g^3 p8g^3 Dec 20] rather leggy gelding: fifth foal: brother to 2-y-o 1m winner (stays 15f) Tansholpan and half-brother to 1¼m winners Taraz (by Oasis Dream) and Tamasha (useful, by Sea The Stars), latter stayed 13f: dam, 1½m winner, sister to smart winner up to 1½m Crimson Tide: fair form: best effort when third in minor event at Kempton (2¼ lengths behind Native Appeal) final start: will stay at least 1¼m: open to further improvement. *Roger Varian*

TALENT SCOUT (IRE) 11 b.g. Exceed And Excel (AUS) 126 – Taalluf (USA) 82 **80**
(Hansel (USA)) [2017 75: 7.5f 8g^6 7.4m* 8.8m 7.4m* 8.5m* 7.4f^4 7.4d 7.4g* 7.4m 7.4v Sep 26] sturdy gelding: fairly useful performer: won 4 times at Beverley in 2017, handicaps in May, June and July (by ¾ length from Ingleby Angel) and claimer in August: stays 8.5f: acts on polytrack, good to firm and good to soft going: wears headgear: usually races close up. *Karen Tutty*

TALE OF TAILS (IRE) 2 b.g. (Feb 25) Rip Van Winkle (IRE) 134 – Salute To Seville **77**
(IRE) 66 (Duke of Marmalade (IRE) 132) [2017 6.1m^2 t7.1s^5 Jun 29] fair form: better effort when second in minor event at Nottingham (2 lengths behind Great Prospector) in June: should stay 7f. *Brian Ellison*

TALISMANIC 4 b.c. Medaglia d'Oro (USA) 129 – Magic Mission 117 (Machiavellian **125**
(USA) 123) [2017 114: 11.9d^2 11.9g* 11.9s^2 11.9g^2 13.9g* 11.9d^3 12f* 11.9g^2 Dec 10]

Sport is losing its battle with drugs. Eyebrows are raised when journalists raise the subject and ask athletes awkward questions. Take the press conference with the medallists after the 100m final at the World Athletics Championships at London in 2017, when Justin Gatlin, who has served two drug bans, inflicted an unexpected defeat on three-times Olympic champion Usain Bolt. 'The winning time today was the slowest for a gold medallist since 2003 and the marks in general were much slower than the last World Championships,' began the journalist. 'I would like to know from you guys whether you think there is any kind of relationship with a stronger anti-doping control?' Bolt, used to being indulged, with journalists fawning over him, didn't like it. 'Whoa, whoa, whoa, what?' Bolt looked astonished, though the factually-based question demanded a considered answer. Bolt cut off the journalist when she began to ask the question again—'I heard you but I'm saying "What?"' Bolt added 'I'm sure everybody up here takes that very disrespectful … Justin has done his time and he has proved himself over and over again.' Gatlin then took over, at least addressing the question by talking about the effect on times of injuries and loss of form (the World Championships were 'at the end of a long season'). Gatlin, though, seemed astonished to be asked by another journalist whether he enjoyed being 'the bad boy' of athletics (he had been booed by a section of the London crowd). 'What do I do that makes me the bad boy?' was an answer that showed a reluctance to acknowledge the facts in the immediate aftermath of victory—that he was caught cheating with drugs twice in a period when his times were getting faster as he got older, and that he was then welcomed back into the sport by his sponsors Nike and by those guardians of athletics, the governing bodies, who seem happy for everyone to skim over the transgressions of drugs cheats when they return after serving their ban.

The same happened in tennis when Maria Sharapova, caught still using meldonium after it was outlawed, was welcomed back after a fifteen-month doping suspension with a wildcard straight into the main draw for the US Open (her world ranking had slipped to 146 and she could have been made to qualify). Sharapova's star quality, like that of Gatlin, ensured that her bandwagon was quickly rolling again, with most of those involved in tennis eagerly clambering aboard. The year ended with one of Britain's sporting icons, four-times Tour de France winner Chris Froome, facing a ban from cycling after being found competing in an event with twice the permitted dose of asthma medication in his system. This left seemingly ultra-professional Team Sky, already reeling from investigations involving one of its former stars Sir Bradley Wiggins, with yet more awkward questions to answer.

In the minds of the more general sporting public, cycling and athletics are among the sports that can no longer be trusted, sports in which outstanding performances and world records demand too much of a leap of faith by the spectators. Having had its fingers burned so often in the past, the sporting public now tends to stand further back from the flames, regarding exceptional events with understandably more scepticism than it used to do. The reasons for such scepticism are not hard to find, with many historical world records in athletics, for example, standing as testimony to the power of drugs (it is not possible to prove that the record times of such as Florence Griffith Joyner, Marita Koch and Jarmila Kratochvilova were achieved through doping, but the authorities know that many of that era were). The depth of institutionalised doping in Russia is still being revealed, with 'thousands more cheats' to be named according to the World Anti-Doping Agency ('vital information' is still to come out about the extent of doping in Russian football, for example, which will be an embarrassment to the host country of the 2018 World Cup as well as to governing body FIFA which has so far outwardly shown little concern).

In horse racing, efforts are still being made by a vocal minority in North American racing to prohibit the use of raceday medication on that continent, the single biggest stumbling block to racing becoming a truly global sport. Drugs that are banned in nearly every other major racing jurisdiction are still freely injected, the ubiquitous use of the diuretic furosemide on racedays continuing to undermine confidence around the world in the integrity of racing in North America (the world's largest producer of thoroughbreds) where outstanding performances continue to raise questions in many quarters about whether they might be too good to be true. Any sport which is a betting medium has to be particularly mindful of not allowing anything to undermine public confidence. Seeing is believing, or it should be, in such sports. But can the racegoers and punters really believe everything they see in North American racing? What difference does furosemide (lasix) make? Well, on the evidence of the 2018 running of the Pegasus World Cup, it would seem that American trainers think it is worth more than 7 lb, seeing that was the allowance in the race conditions for running without lasix (it had been 5 lb the year before). None of the connections took it up!

Congressmen reintroduced legislation in the latest season that would give the United States Anti-Doping Agency oversight of medication issues and drug testing in horse racing. 'The time has come for uniform medication rules in American horse racing to ensure integrity, competitiveness and the safety of horse racing,' said Congressman Andy Barr when introducing the bill in May. Inconsistent and conflicting rules on medication in different states of North America have long been a problem and attempts to at least impose some sort of uniformity on medication among the thirty-two individual state authorities have signally failed. At the time the Horseracing Integrity Act was introduced in the House of Representatives, only eleven of the state jurisdictions, for example, had a rule insisting on third-party furosemide administration (vets employed by individual trainers are still allowed by most state authorities to inject on racedays, even though furosemide—ostensibly

Longines Breeders' Cup Turf, Del Mar—the late withdrawal of Ulysses robs the race of one of its classiest entrants, paving the way for Talismanic to make the breakthrough at Group/Grade 1 level; Arlington Million winner Beach Patrol (blinkers) is second for the home team ahead of Highland Reel (left), who goes close in defence of his 2016 title

given to prevent bleeding—is a masking agent and additional supplements can be administered with little prospect of being detected). The same eleven states are the only ones signed up to using fully-accredited labs for their testing.

The Horseracing Integrity Act, if it is passed, will specifically prohibit raceday medication and has the outside support of the International Federation of Horseracing Authorities which ought to be using its own limited powers more effectively. The IFHA has responsibility for the official racehorse rankings and has announced that any horse disqualified for a drugs violation will not appear in the final rankings for the year (Masochistic, runner-up in the 2016 Breeders' Cup Sprint, was disqualified from that race when a banned substance was found in a sample taken after the race; the horse appeared in the final official rankings on a mark of 115 that year but would not have been included in 2017). The IFHA also has responsibility for Group/Graded races worldwide and its executive council, which meets two or three times a year, should flex its muscles by threatening to remove international pattern status from drug-associated races. If that is seen as too big a threat to make, it should at least adopt the suggestion made in *Racehorses* in recent years that the published results of such races—including those at the Breeders' Cup—should be accompanied by some sort of symbol to distinguish them from 'clean' races.

Almost without exception, the domestic runners in the thirteen Breeders' Cup races at Del Mar in November were on furosemide (lasix), with the European challengers divided between those adopting the 'When in Rome' stance (headed by Ballydoyle's sizeable team) and those electing to race 'clean', which were Madeline (Roger Varian) and Juliet Capulet (John Gosden) in the Juvenile Fillies Turf, Nezwaah (Roger Varian) in the Filly & Mare Turf, Ribchester (Richard Fahey) in the Mile and Talismanic (Andre Fabre) and Decorated Knight (Roger Charlton) in the Turf (late-withdrawal Ulysses, owned by the Niarchos family and trained by Sir Michael Stoute, was not declared to run on lasix). Talismanic's trainer Andre Fabre has been a long-term opponent of raceday medication and none of his five Breeders' Cup winners have run on lasix. Talismanic is Fabre's third Breeders' Cup Turf winner, following In The Wings in 1990 and Shirocco in 2005, and Talismanic started at longer odds than either of those two, both of whom had finished fourth in the Prix de l'Arc de Triomphe on their most recent start. Talismanic had finished fourth in the Prix du Jockey Club and had also run in the Prix de l'Arc as a three-year-old (finishing eleventh), but connections had to wait until he was four for his first win in pattern company. After adding a third listed win to his record in the Prix Lord Seymour at Maisons-Laffitte in April, Talismanic was runner-up in pattern company at Saint-Cloud (to Tiberian) and Chantilly (to Silverwave) before finally getting his name on the honours board in the Prix Maurice de Nieuil over a mile and three quarters at Saint-Cloud in July, winning by a length and a quarter from British challenger Marmelo.

Talismanic followed in the footsteps of In The Wings (first) and Shirocco (third) when contesting the Prix Foy on the 'day of trials' in September, run in the latest season at Chantilly because of Longchamp's redevelopment. Talismanic was apparently earmarked for a tilt at the Breeders' Cup Turf straight after winning the Prix Maurice de Nieuil but a reconnaissance trip to North America for the Sword Dancer Stakes at Saratoga (a race Fabre had won with Flintshire in 2015) had to be abandoned when he suffered a minor setback. Talismanic lined up for the Prix Foy with stablemate Cloth of Stars who was having the final touches put to his preparation for the Arc (both horses are trained by Andre Fabre for Godolphin). They were beaten into the places by German challenger Dschingis Secret but the Foy served its purpose well for both, Cloth of Stars going on to finish a good second to Enable in the Arc and Talismanic justifying the faith shown in him when landing the Longines Breeders' Cup Turf.

The Turf has been the most successful of the Breeders' Cup races for the European-trained challengers and Talismanic was joined in the field of thirteen at Del Mar by Decorated Knight from Britain and by the previous year's winner Highland Reel, Seventh Heaven and Cliffs of Moher from Ireland (all representing Ballydoyle). Talismanic was a 141/10-shot in a field that was weakened by the late withdrawal of the Eclipse and International winner Ulysses after he was found to have heat in a foreleg. Mickael Barzalona, riding at his first Breeders' Cup, was always in the right place on the sharp, turning Del Mar track and he never left the inside on Talismanic until the home straight where he challenged between the Arlington Million and Joe Hirsch Turf Classic winner Beach Patrol and Highland Reel to win by half a length and a neck, getting on top under pressure only in the final hundred yards. Seventh Heaven came fifth, with Cliffs of Moher and Decorated Knight eighth and tenth, split by the previous year's Juvenile Turf winner Oscar Performance who again ran without lasix (he had been the only one of the previous year's Breeders' Cup winners to race 'clean', that distinction belonging to Talismanic at the latest self-styled 'Breeders' Cup World Championships').

European trainers saddled thirty-four runners in the thirteen Breeders' Cup races and Ireland was successful with the two-year-old Mendelssohn in the Juvenile Turf and Britain with the three-year-old Wuheida in the Filly & Mare Turf to make it Europe's most successful Breeders' Cup since Santa Anita in 2013 when European stables had five winners (the record is six in 2009, also at Santa Anita, but in a year when the dirt races were run on pro-ride). For the record, the European visitors now lead their North American counterparts as a group in the Breeders' Cup Turf by twenty and a half victories to thirteen and a half (the 'half' being the dead heat in 2003). Talismanic and Highland Reel went on to meet again in the Hong Kong Vase in December when Highland Reel reversed the Breeders' Cup form on the more galloping Sha Tin track, though Talismanic, who was beaten a length and a half after travelling smoothly and looking the likely winner early in the final straight, lost little in defeat up against the winner at his most tenacious.

Talismanic (b.c. 2013)	Medaglia d'Oro (USA) (b or br 1999)	El Prado (gr 1989)	Sadler's Wells
			Lady Capulet
		Cappucino Bay (b 1989)	Bailjumper
			Dubbed In
	Magic Mission (b 1998)	Machiavellian (b 1987)	Mr Prospector
			Coup de Folie
		Dream Ticket (b 1992)	Danzig
			Capo di Monte

The strongly-built Talismanic, easily distinguished by his four white stockings and big white face, is by Medaglia d'Oro, the winner of the Travers Stakes who was twice second in the Breeders' Cup Classic. Medaglia d'Oro is the sire of two outstanding American fillies in Rachel Alexandra and Songbird, among others.

Talismanic is a brother to Harriet Tubman, who was awarded a nine-furlong event in the States, and is also a half-brother to three other winners including the very lightly-raced two-year-old mile winner Witnessed (by Authorized) who is the dam of the useful two-year-old Stage Magic. Witnessed was culled from Darley at the end of her three-year-old days when she made only €7,000. Talismanic's dam Magic Mission was raced in France (trained by Andre Fabre) and in the States and won at a mile and nine furlongs, her successes including the Grade 3 Royal Heroine Stakes at Hollywood Park. Further back, Talismanic's great grandam Capo di Monte, who won the Pretty Polly Stakes at Newmarket and was beaten a short head in the Sun Chariot, is a daughter of Burghclere, who was sold by the Royal Studs and became the grandam of Japanese champion racehorse and outstanding sire Deep Impact. Talismanic stays a mile and three quarters and acts on any turf going, though he seemed to particularly relish the firm conditions at Del Mar. A strong traveller, he has made the running but usually tracks the leaders. He stays in training. *A. Fabre, France*

TALKSALOT (IRE) 6 b.g. Thousand Words 113 – Lady Piste (IRE) 67 (Ali-Royal (IRE) 127) [2017 p7d^3 p7g^6 Apr 7] fair handicapper nowadays: stays 7f: acts on polytrack, viscoride and good to firm going: has worn headgear: tried in tongue tie. *Mark Bradstock* **68**

TALLINSKI (IRE) 3 ch.g. Mayson 124 – Estonia 82 (Exceed And Excel (AUS) 126) [2017 81: 5.1m* 5.1s 6.1g^5 t6g^5 5m^3 5g^3 t5g Oct 10] strong, compact gelding: fairly useful handicapper: won at Nottingham (by short head from Stringybark Creek) in April: third at Beverley in September: stays 6f: acts on good to firm going: usually races close up. *Brian Ellison* **84**

TALLOW (IRE) 2 b.f. (Apr 19) Kodiac 112 – Flames (Blushing Flame (USA) 109) [2017 6d^5 6d* f7.1g* Nov 28] €100,000Y: half-sister to several winners, including very smart winner up to 1¼m Lahaleeb (2-y-o 7f winner, by Redback) and winner up to 1m Precocious Star (2-y-o 6f winner, by Bold Fact): dam unraced: fairly useful form: won maiden at Doncaster (by 1½ lengths from Ornamental) and minor event at Southwell (by length from Magnetic Boundary) in November: will go on improving. *William Haggas* **85 p**

TALLULAH FLEUR 4 b.f. Royal Applause 124 – Topflightcoolracer 89 (Lujain (USA) 119) [2017 –: p8d f7m Mar 7] little form: in cheekpieces last 3 starts. *David Loughnane* **–**

TALLULAH ROSE 3 b.f. Exceed And Excel (AUS) 126 – Blinking (Marju (IRE) 127) [2017 87: 7m 6m Jun 16] good-topped filly: fairly useful at 2 yrs, well held both starts in 2017: stays 6f: acts on firm going. *K. R. Burke* **–**

TALLULAH'S QUEST (IRE) 3 b.f. Tagula (IRE) 116 – Sarin Dubhe (IRE) (Catcher In The Rye (IRE) 115) [2017 8m 8s 8.2d 7.4g^2 7s 7m^2 7.1d^5 p7g^5 Sep 26] €4,200F, €6,500Y, 8,000 2-y-o: workmanlike filly: third foal: sister to a winner abroad: dam unraced half-sister to useful French 7.5f winner Double Vie (by Tagula): fair maiden handicapper: stays 7.5f: acts on good to firm going: often races towards rear/travels strongly. *Julia Feilden* **67**

TALLY'S SON 3 b.g. Assertive 121 – Talamahana 66 (Kyllachy 129) [2017 –: 7s^4 7.1d 7.4g^4 8g^6 8.1d^5 7.4v 8.3g Nov 1] modest maiden handicapper: stays 1m: acts on good to soft going: tried in cheekpieces. *Grace Harris* **56**

TALLY'S SONG 4 b.f. Piccolo 121 – Talamahana 66 (Kyllachy 129) [2017 44: 5.1s 5.7f 6.1m^4 5.7f^4 5.1g 5v^5 5s^5 6.1s 7.1g 5.7m 5.7s 5.7s t6.1m^3 t6.1g^3 Dec 13] modest maiden handicapper: stays 6f: acts on tapeta, good to firm and heavy going: wears cheekpieces: often races prominently. *Grace Harris* **54**

TAMARIN 5 ch.m. Paco Boy (IRE) 129 – Les Hurlants (IRE) (Barathea (IRE) 127) [2017 35: 8.3g 7.6g t6.1g 11.6m 8m^6 7.6d Jun 30] has no near-side eye: maiden, no form in 2017: wears headgear. *Lisa Williamson* **–**

TAMAYEF (IRE) 3 b.g. Sir Prancealot (IRE) 111 – Miss Glitters (IRE) 91 (Chevalier (IRE) 115) [2017 83: 10g^4 10.1m^4 9.1s^2 10.3d 10d^5 p8g* p8g^3 8d Oct 27] good-topped gelding: fairly useful handicapper: won at Kempton in September: stays 1¼m: acts on polytrack, tapeta, soft and good to firm going: tried in cheekpieces: sold 22,000 gns in October to join Matt Sheppard. *Hugo Palmer* **91**

TAMAYUZ MAGIC (IRE) 6 b.g. Tamayuz 126 – Anne Tudor (IRE) 79 (Anabaa (USA) 130) [2017 90: 10.3g 12g 11.2s 12d^2 12d^3 12m 12.1v^5 Oct 21] fairly useful handicapper: second at Ripon in July: stays 13f: acts on any turf going: usually wears headgear: sold 6,000 gns in October. *Michael Easterby* **88**

TAMBOUR 4 b.g. Notnowcato 128 – Tamso (USA) (Seeking The Gold (USA)) [2017 p12g[6] t10.2d 7.1g[6] 9m[4] 9.2g[6] 10s[4] 12.1s[3] 12.5m[3] Aug 30] modest maiden: left Roger Charlton after first start: stays 12.5f: acts on polytrack, soft and good to firm going: tried in tongue tie. *Keith Dalgleish* **64**

TAMIH (IRE) 3 b.c. Dark Angel (IRE) 113 – Mairead Anne (USA) (Elusive Quality (USA)) [2017 t7.2g[4] t7.1g[2] p8g[2] 7.6v* 8g 7g[6] Dec 16] 30,000Y, 38,000 2-y-o: fourth foal: half-brother to 6f winner Tigserin (by Approve) and a winner in Italy by Verglas: dam, US 1m winner, half-sister to useful French 7f-9f winner Quittance: fairly useful form: won maiden at Chester (by 1½ lengths from Ebqaa) in September: left Roger Varian after: stays 1m: acts on polytrack, tapeta and on heavy going. *M. Hamad Al Attiya, Qatar* **88**

TAMKEEN 2 ch.c. (Mar 31) Kyllachy 129 – Regatta (USA) (Giant's Causeway (USA) 132) [2017 7s[5] 7g[2] 8.3g[2] Nov 1] £58,000Y: fifth foal: dam unraced half-sister to smart US Grade 2 9f winner Sightseeing: fairly useful form: best effort when second in maiden at Nottingham (1¼ lengths behind King's Proctor) final start. *Owen Burrows* **84**

TAMLEEK (USA) 3 b.c. Hard Spun (USA) 124 – Tafaneen (USA) 74 (Dynaformer (USA)) [2017 70p: 10m* 12.3m[4] 10m 13g[4] 12v Aug 2] big, deep-girthed colt: useful performer: won maiden at Newmarket (by 4 lengths from dead-heaters Mafaaheem and Oasis Charm) in April: fourth in Chester Vase (2¼ lengths behind Venice Beach) next time: stays 12.5f: acts on good to firm going: tried in cheekpieces: often races prominently/ travels strongly. *Saeed bin Suroor* **107**

TAN 3 b.g. Aqlaam 125 – Sunburnt (Haafhd 129) [2017 6g[5] 6g[4] 6d 6g* 6g 5.5g* 6d[3] 5.9s 5m[6] 5g 5s 5g[6] 5v 5s t6g f5g[4] t7.1s Nov 30] fairly useful performer: won handicap at Maisons-Laffitte in May and claimer at same course in June: left E. J. O'Neill/well below form after seventh start: stays 6.5f: acts on polytrack and soft going: usually in headgear/ tongue tie for current yard. *Tony Coyle* **86 d**

TAN ARABIQ 4 b.g. Arabian Gleam 122 – Tanning 60 (Atraf 116) [2017 70, a76: t9.5m* 8g[5] 8d[5] p10g[5] p10s[5] 8g t12.2g* t12.2d[2] Dec 26] fair handicapper: won at Wolverhampton in January and December: stays 1½m: acts on tapeta and good to firm going. *Michael Appleby* **70 a77**

TANASOQ (IRE) 4 b.g. Acclamation 118 – Alexander Youth (IRE) 98 (Exceed And Excel (AUS) 126) [2017 82: 6g[2] 6g[3] 6.1g[6] Aug 28] fairly useful handicapper: second at Leicester in April: stays 6.5f: acts on soft going: tried in headgear: sold 15,000 gns in November to join Paul Midgley. *Owen Burrows* **83**

TANAWAR (IRE) 7 b.g. Elusive City (USA) 117 – Parakopi (IRE) 53 (Green Desert (USA) 127) [2017 72: 7g* 7.1m[5] 7.2m[4] 7g* 7d 7.4f 7.2d[6] 7g[6] 7.8d 6d[4] 7s[2] t7.1d 7.2s[6] 6d Oct 30] fair handicapper: won at Catterick (apprentice) in April and Thirsk (by neck from Kirkham) in June: stayed 1¼m: acted on polytrack, soft and good to firm going: wore headgear: dead. *Ruth Carr* **72**

TANAYA 2 b.c. (Mar 8) Kodiac 112 – Serena's Pride 85 (Danbird (AUS)) [2017 5.9v[4] 6s 7d 7g 8m* Dec 26] modest form: left Richard Fahey after second start: won minor event at Syracuse in December: stays 1m: acts on good to firm going. *S. Cannavo, Italy* **64**

TANGLED (IRE) 2 b.c. (Feb 5) Society Rock (IRE) 126 – Open Verse (USA) 69 (Black Minnaloushe (USA) 123) [2017 5f[5] p6d[2] 6g[4] 7m* 6d* 6.5g 7g[3] 7s[2] Oct 28] £67,000Y: good-topped colt: seventh foal: half-brother to 2-y-o 5f winner Peter Mac (by Kodiac), later successful in Qatar, and winner up to 1½m Faithful Creek (2-y-o 7f winner, by Bushranger), both useful: dam, maiden (stayed 1m), half-sister to smart performer up to 1½m Polaris Flight: useful performer: won nursery at Newmarket in July and valuable sales race at York **105**

Goffs Premier Yearling Stakes, York—
the cream rises to the top with four of the five horses at single-figure odds comfortably clear, Tangled getting the better of a sustained duel with Great Prospector (hooped cap) close home; favourite Hey Jonesy (white sleeves) isn't helped by being isolated on the stand side

(by neck from Great Prospector) in August: placed in Somerville Tattersall Stakes at Newmarket (2¼ lengths third to Elarqam) and Horris Hill Stakes at Newbury (½-length second to Nebo) last 2 starts: stays 7f: acts on polytrack, soft and good to firm going. *Richard Hannon*

TANGO FIRE (USA) 3 b.c. Frankel 147 – Latin Love (IRE) 112 (Danehill Dancer (IRE) 117) [2017 8.3g 8m p8g Oct 5] sturdy colt: little impact in maidens. *Richard Hannon* **–**

TANGO SKY (IRE) 8 b.g. Namid 128 – Sky Galaxy (USA) 84 (Sky Classic (CAN)) [2017 68: p6g^{3} t6d 6s t6s^{4} 6g^{5} 6g^{3} 6.1g t7.1s Sep 8] lengthy, useful-looking gelding: fair handicapper: stays 7f: acts on polytrack, tapeta, good to firm and heavy going: has worn headgear. *Paul Midgley* **61 a67**

TANGRAMM 5 b.g. Sakhee's Secret 128 – Tripti (IRE) 72 (Sesaro (USA) 81) [2017 92: t12.2m^{4} t12.2m^{5} t9.5g^{3} p12g p11d p11g^{4} p10g 10d t12.2g p10s* Dec 8] compact gelding: fairly useful handicapper: won at Chelmsford (by ¾ length from Eltezam) in December: stays 1½m: acts on polytrack and tapeta: usually in cheekpieces. *Dean Ivory* **90**

TANKSALOT (IRE) 3 b.f. Sir Prancealot (IRE) 111 – Pearly Brooks 77 (Efisio 120) [2017 53: t6m^{5} t7.1m p6g^{6} Jan 28] poor maiden: stays 6f: acts on tapeta and soft going: tried in visor: sold 3,000 gns, sent to Spain, where third once from 11 starts. *Harry Dunlop* **47**

TANSEEQ 2 b.c. (Feb 2) Havana Gold (IRE) 118 – Roslea Lady (IRE) 63 (Alhaarth (IRE) 126) [2017 7m^{2} p7s^{3} p8d* Nov 22] £160,000Y: sturdy colt: seventh foal: half-brother to 3 winners, including 2-y-o 6f winner Hoot (by Invincible Spirit) and 1¼m-1½m winner Royal Roslea (by Royal Applause): dam maiden half-sister to smart/unreliable sprinter Conquest: fairly useful form: won minor event at Kempton (by 1½ lengths from Savaanah) in November: stays 1m. *William Haggas* **88**

TANSHEET (IRE) 2 ch.c. (Feb 22) Shamardal (USA) 129 – Sharedah (IRE) 94 (Pivotal 124) [2017 7d t8s* p8g^{4} Oct 4] third foal: half-brother to smart 1m-1½m winner Tawdeea (by Intikhab) and French 1¼m winner (stays 1½m) Alward (by Aqlaam): dam, 1¼m winner, half-sister to high-class winner up to 1½m Maraahel: fairly useful form: won minor event at Newcastle (by 1½ lengths from Photonics) in September: improved again when fourth in similar event at Kempton (1½ lengths behind Kassar) final start: bred to stay 1¼m+: sold 110,000 gns in November. *William Haggas* **87**

TANSHOLPAN 3 b.f. Dansili 127 – Tamarind (IRE) 107 (Sadler's Wells (USA) 132) [2017 92p: 11.3m^{3} 14.9d Aug 13] tall, leggy filly: fairly useful form: third in listed Cheshire Oaks at Chester (10¾ lengths behind Enable) in May: eighth in similar race at Deauville 3 months later: probably stays 15f. *Roger Varian* **90**

TANTHEEM 2 b.f. (Mar 25) Teofilo (IRE) 126 – Riqa 102 (Dubawi (IRE) 129) [2017 6m^{2} p6.5g* 6g* 6g Aug 20] third foal: half-sister to French 12.5f winner Murafrif (by Sea The Stars): dam, useful French winner up to 1m (2-y-o 7.5f winner), out of half-sister to high-class miler Tamayuz: useful form: successful at Deauville in July in maiden and Prix de Cabourg (by 3½ lengths from Darkanna): only seventh in Prix Morny there: will stay 7f. *F. Head, France* **103**

TANZEEL (IRE) 6 b.g. Elusive City (USA) 117 – Royal Fizz (IRE) (Royal Academy (USA) 130) [2017 98: 7m Jun 17] sturdy gelding: useful handicapper: well below form only start in 2017: stays 6f: acts on good to firm going: usually tongue tied. *Charles Hills* **–**

TAOISEACH 2 b.c. (Mar 7) Roderic O'Connor (IRE) 119 – Munaa's Dream (Oasis Dream 129) [2017 p6g^{5} Nov 2] 28,000F, 85,000Y: third foal: half-brother to 6f (including at 2 yrs) winner Happy Call (by Kodiac): dam, little form, out of half-sister to useful performers Anna Karenina (stayed 9.5f) and Windsor Palace (stayed 10.5f): 4/1, fifth in minor event at Chelmsford (4¼ lengths behind Etisalat): open to improvement. *Hugo Palmer* **65 p**

TAOPIX 5 b.g. Rip Van Winkle (IRE) 134 – Sinister Ruckus (USA) (Trippi (USA) 121) [2017 75: t12.4d* t10.2g^{3} Feb 14] fair performer: won handicap at Newcastle in February: third in minor event at same course later that month: stays 12.5f: acts on tapeta and good to soft going: tried in blinkers. *Karen McLintock* **76**

TAPDANCEALLTHEWAY 3 b.f. Nathaniel (IRE) 129 – Tap Dance Way (IRE) 77 (Azamour (IRE) 130) [2017 p10g^{2} p12g^{4} 11.6g 12g^{3} p12g p15.8g Oct 5] second foal: half-sister to 1¼m winner Lady Rocka (by Rock of Gibraltar): dam, 1m winner, half-sister to smart Japanese miler Live Concert: fair maiden: stays 1½m. *Amanda Perrett* **72**

TAPER TANTRUM (IRE) 5 b.g. Azamour (IRE) 130 – Maramba (USA) 97 (Hussonet (USA)) [2017 89: p10g^5 t10.2g p16d^2 14m^2 16.1d^2 p16g^3 16s^2 Oct 15] sturdy gelding: fairly useful handicapper: placed last 5 starts: stays 2m: acts on polytrack, soft and good to firm going: wears headgear: usually races close up: sold 30,000 gns, sent to USA. *Michael Bell* **86**

TAPIS LIBRE 9 b.g. Librettist (USA) 124 – Stella Manuela (FR) (Galileo (IRE) 134) [2017 89: 11.9s^3 10g^6 11.9m* 12g* 11.8d^6 14.1s^3 12m 12.1s Sep 20] workmanlike gelding: fairly useful handicapper: won lady amateur events at York (by 1¼ lengths from Mukhayyam) in June and Epsom (by short head from Whinging Willie) in July: stays 2m: acts on polytrack, tapeta, good to firm and heavy going: has worn headgear. *Jacqueline Coward* **87**

TAP ON THE BAR 3 b.g. Sayif (IRE) 122 – Peneia (USA) (Nureyev (USA) 131) [2017 6m Jun 24] 50/1, well held in maiden at Redcar (hooded). *John Wainwright* **–**

TAP TAP BOOM 3 ro.g. Foxwedge (AUS) 128 – Exclusive Approval (USA) (With Approval (CAN)) [2017 77: 7d^5 8d* 8d* 8.9g^5 8g 8d* 8d 8g 8s p7.5g 8.2s^3 8s Nov 7] sturdy gelding: fairly useful performer: won claimers at Saint-Cloud in May and June (left George Baker after), and Compiegne in July: stays 1m: acts on soft and good to firm going: in cheekpieces final start. *Butel & Beaunez, France* **90**

TARA CELEB 3 b.f. Excelebration (IRE) 133 – Tara Moon (Pivotal 124) [2017 82: 8m May 12] compact filly: fairly useful at 2 yrs, below form in handicap only start in 2017: stays 6f. *Mick Channon* **–**

TARAKKOM (FR) 5 ch.g. Naaqoos 117 – Sahabah (USA) (Swain (IRE) 134) [2017 66: p16d p12g 16d 14.5s p16s 16s Sep 19] fair handicapper: below form in 2017: stays 2m: acts on polytrack, tapeta and soft going: has worn headgear: front runner/races prominently. *Peter Hiatt* **54**

TARA RIVER (FR) 8 b.g. Stormy River (FR) 123 – Tarabela (FR) (Johann Quatz (FR) 120) [2017 t12.2g^6 Apr 29] one-time smart performer in France: last in handicap only outing on Flat in 2017: stays 15f: acts on soft going: has worn cheekpieces: useful hurdler. *Brian Barr* **–**

TARBOOSH 4 b.g. Bahamian Bounty 116 – Mullein 110 (Oasis Dream 129) [2017 88§: t6d^6 t5d^6 t5.1g 5m 5m* 5m 5s* 5s^5 5s* 5m* 5v^3 Sep 30] has reportedly had breathing operation: useful handicapper: won at Ripon in June, Beverley/Carlisle in August and Ripon again (by ½ length from Muatadel) in September: third at Haydock (neck behind Boundsy) final start: has won over 7f, usually raced at shorter: acts on polytrack, good to firm and heavy going: tried in headgear/tongue tie: usually races prominently. *Paul Midgley* **101** **a77**

TARNEMAH (IRE) 2 b.f. (May 8) Lope de Vega (IRE) 125 – Ice Rock (IRE) (Rock of Gibraltar (IRE) 133) [2017 6m^5 7d 7d 7g p7g^5 a7f^6 a7f Dec 7] 21,000Y, €30,000 2-y-o: strong filly: sixth foal: half-sister to useful 7.5f/1m winner Ice Slice (by Dark Angel) and 2-y-o 9f winner Shadow Rock (by Verglas): dam, French maiden (stayed 1¼m), lightly-raced half-sister to 1m winner Khateeb and winner up to 1½m Chock A Block (both smart): poor maiden: left George Peckham after fifth start: best effort at 7f: acts on polytrack: tried in hood. *A. bin Harmash, UAE* **47**

TARNHELM 2 b.f. (Apr 9) Helmet (AUS) 127 – Anosti 92 (Act One 124) [2017 6g^2 p5s^4 5v^4 t7.1d f6.1g^{ur} t6.1g^4 Nov 25] £20,000Y: third foal: half-sister to 1m winner Akeed Dubawi (by Dubawi): dam ungenuine 2-y-o 5f winner: fair maiden: best effort at 6f. *Mark Johnston* **71**

TAROUM (IRE) 10 b.g. Refuse To Bend (IRE) 128 – Taraza (IRE) 109 (Darshaan 133) [2017 16.2m 12d^4 11.6f Jun 17] fair handicapper at best: lightly raced and little impact on Flat since 2012: stays 15f: acts on heavy going: blinkered/tongue tied in 2017: poor hurdler. *John Flint* **57**

TARSEEKH 4 b.g. Kyllachy 129 – Constitute (USA) 85 (Gone West (USA)) [2017 70: 8.3m 8m^5 9.1g 8.1m 8.1m p8g^2 p8g p10s^6 p8g^4 Dec 13] tall gelding: fair maiden handicapper: stays 8.5f: acts on polytrack and good to firm going: in headgear last 4 starts: front runner/races prominently. *Chris Gordon* **66** **a60**

TARTAN BUTE 4 b.g. Azamour (IRE) 130 – On A Soapbox (USA) 119 (Mi Cielo (USA)) [2017 80: t13.9g* p15.8f* t13.9g^3 p15.8g* Mar 31] useful handicapper: won at Wolverhampton in February and Lingfield (twice) in March: stays 2m: acts on polytrack, tapeta and firm going: has worn headgear, including last 5 starts. *Mark Johnston* **96**

TARTE TROPEZIENNE (IRE) 3 b.f. Nathaniel (IRE) 129 – High Heel Sneakers 111 (Dansili 127) [2017 9.9g^5 11.6d^3 12d* 11.6d^2 12d^5 Sep 23] fifth foal: half-sister to useful winner up to 11.5f Toujours L'Amour (2-y-o 1m winner, by Authorized): dam winner up to **91**

13f (2-y-o 6f winner): fairly useful performer: won maiden at Ripon (by 1¼ lengths from State Sovereignty) in August: second in handicap at Bath later that month: will stay 1¾m: acts on good to soft going. *William Haggas*

TARTINI (USA) 3 ch.c. Giant's Causeway (USA) 132 – Vignette (USA) 93 (Diesis 133) [2017 103P: 10.1g⁴ 11.6d³ 10.1m⁴ 12m 12s⁴ Oct 15] sturdy colt: useful performer: third in Derby Trial at Lingfield (6¼ lengths behind Best Solution) in May: will stay beyond 1½m: acts on good to firm and good to soft going: tried in hood: sold 50,000 gns, sent to USA. *John Gosden* **100**

TARTUFO CLASSICO 4 b.g. Paco Boy (IRE) 129 – Tartatartufata 94 (Tagula (IRE) 116) [2017 p5g⁶ f5d 5m⁶ f5g⁶ t5.1m Oct 28] little form. *Derek Shaw* **36**

TASAABOQ 6 b.g. Aqlaam 125 – Seldemosa 67 (Selkirk (USA) 129) [2017 63: f7g p6g p6g⁶ p6g⁴ f7m⁴ t6m* t6g* p7d⁴ p6g² p5g⁵ t6g 7m t5.1g² p6g⁵ p7s⁵ f6.1g² t6.1m⁶ f6.1g⁴ p8s⁶ f6.1g⁶ p7s³ p7s⁶ t6.1d² Dec 27] modest handicapper: won at Wolverhampton (twice) in March: stays 1m: acts on all-weather: sometimes in headgear: wears tongue tie: temperament under suspicion. *Phil McEntee* **62**

TASHAABOH (IRE) 2 gr.c. (Feb 20) Lethal Force (IRE) 128 – Rush 59 (Compton Place 125) [2017 6v⁶ p6g* Oct 24] €120,000F: first foal: dam, maiden (stayed 6f), half-sister to Fred Darling Stakes winner Rimth: fair form: won minor event at Kempton (by neck from Masked Defender) in October. *Owen Burrows* **78**

TASHWEEQ (IRE) 4 b.g. Big Bad Bob (IRE) 118 – Dance Hall Girl (IRE) 81 (Dansili 127) [2017 8.1d 8m³ 7g 8s⁴ Jul 30] well-made gelding: smart performer: third in Royal Hunt Cup (Handicap) at Royal Ascot (¾ length behind Zhui Feng) in June: stays 1m: acts on good to firm going: sent to UAE. *John Gosden* **118**

TASKEEN (IRE) 4 b.g. Lilbourne Lad (IRE) 111 – Lola Rosa (IRE) (Peintre Celebre (USA) 137) [2017 –: 6m 6m³ 6m⁵ 7d 7g 7.4m 6v 7v t7.1s Nov 30] strong gelding: fairly useful handicapper: third at Thirsk in May: stays 1m: acts on soft and good to firm going: tried in cheekpieces. *Roger Fell* **80**

TASLEET 4 b.c. Showcasing 117 – Bird Key (Cadeaux Genereux 131) [2017 110: 7g² 6s* 6m² 6g 6s² 6s² Oct 21] good-topped colt: very smart performer: won Duke of York Stakes at York (by 2½ lengths from Magical Memory) in May: second after in Diamond Jubilee Stakes at Royal Ascot (neck behind The Tin Man), Sprint Cup at Haydock (beaten 4 lengths by Harry Angel) and Champions Sprint Stakes at Ascot (1¼ lengths behind Librisa Breeze): has won at 7f, but best over 6f: acts on polytrack, soft and good to firm going: in cheekpieces last 5 starts. *William Haggas* **124**

TASTE THE WINE (IRE) 11 gr.g. Verglas (IRE) 118 – Azia (IRE) 71 (Desert Story (IRE) 115) [2017 57: 16.2m⁴ 16d⁵ 12.1s⁴ 14.2g 16s Sep 19] rather leggy gelding: modest handicapper: stays 2m: acts on polytrack and any turf going: sometimes in cheekpieces: has worn tongue tie, including last 3 starts: modest hurdler. *Bernard Llewellyn* **56**

TASTY GINGER (IRE) 4 ch.g. Tamayuz 126 – Secret Fashion (King's Best (USA) 132) [2017 66: p12g³ p16d² p12d⁴ f12m⁴ p16g² p16g³ Apr 1] fair handicapper: stays 2m: acts on polytrack, good to firm and heavy going: has worn headgear: often races in rear. *J. R. Jenkins* **72**

TATAWU (IRE) 5 b.g. Mawatheeq (USA) 126 – Mooteeah (IRE) 77 (Sakhee (USA) 136) [2017 71: 8.3g p11g 11.4g 11.6d⁵ 14d Sep 16] close-coupled, rather sparely-made gelding: fair handicapper, below form in 2017: stays 1¼m: acts on polytrack, tapeta, good to firm and good to soft going: in blinkers last 2 starts: sometimes slowly away. *Peter Hiatt* **54**

Duke of York Clipper Logistics Stakes, York—Tasleet proves a revelation in first-time cheekpieces, beating 2016 winner the grey Magical Memory and Comicas (blinkers)

TATHMEEN (IRE) 2 b.c. (Feb 2) Exceed And Excel (AUS) 126 – Deyaar (USA) (Storm Cat (USA)) [2017 6m 6m^3 6v* 6d 6s^3 6d Nov 11] good-topped colt: third foal: half-brother to 2-y-o 6f winner Khobaraa (by Invincible Spirit) and winner up to 1¼m Jufn (2-y-o 7f winner, by Nayef): dam, unraced, out of very smart US Grade 1 9f/1¼m winner Golden Apples: fairly useful performer: won minor event at Newbury (by 6 lengths from Qayes) in July: raced only at 6f: acts on heavy going. *Richard Hannon* **87**

TATLISU (IRE) 7 b.g. Red Clubs (IRE) 125 – Zwadi (IRE) 74 (Docksider (USA) 124) [2017 96: t6g* t5g^3 t7.1g t6g^3 6v 6m 6d^2 6m* 6s 6d^2 6d^3 7.4m^6 t7.2g^2 7s p6s^3 t7.2g* Dec 5] compact gelding: useful performer: won handicap at Newcastle (by 1¾ lengths from Doc Sportello) in January, and claimers at Ripon in June and Wolverhampton in December: stays 7f: acts on tapeta and any turf going: has worn headgear. *Richard Fahey* **95**

TATTING 8 ch.g. Street Cry (IRE) 130 – Needlecraft (IRE) 113 (Mark of Esteem (IRE) 137) [2017 88: f12g* f12g f12d* f11g* 16.3d May 18] tall gelding: fairly useful performer: won 3 times at Southwell, claimer in January, handicap in March and another claimer in April (by head from Luv U Whatever): stays 1½m: acts on all-weather, firm and good to soft going: tried in blinkers: has worn tongue tie: usually races towards rear. *Lawrence Mullaney* **88**

TAUREAN DANCER (IRE) 2 b.g. (Apr 26) Intello (GER) 129 – Traou Mad (IRE) 107 (Barathea (IRE) 127) [2017 7m 7d^4 7g Sep 1] €35,000F, 100,000Y: good-topped gelding: half-brother to several winners, including useful French 7.5f winner Roscoff (by Daylami) and 1¼m-1½m winner Honoured (by Mark of Esteem): dam, 2-y-o 5f winner, half-sister to smart performers Sainte Marine (suited by 5f) and Josr Algarhoud (stayed 1m): fair form: best effort when fourth in minor event at Yarmouth (3¼ lengths behind Barford) in August: remains open to improvement. *Michael Bell* **70 p**

TAUREAN GOLD 3 b.g. Piccolo 121 – Elsie's Orphan 81 (Pastoral Pursuits 127) [2017 p7g^6 p8g p6g 5g 7g 5m p6g p6g Dec 31] little form. *John Bridger* **–**

TAUREAN STAR (IRE) 4 b.g. Elnadim (USA) 128 – Marhaba 73 (Nayef (USA) 129) [2017 99: 7m* 7m 8m 7d^6 8d Oct 6] sturdy gelding: useful handicapper: won at Yarmouth (by neck from Horsted Keynes) in May: stays 1m: acts on firm and good to soft going: often races towards rear: sold 16,000 gns in October to join Ralph Beckett. *Michael Bell* **97**

TAURIAN 6 b.m. Central Park (IRE) 123 – Emma-Lyne 65 (Emarati (USA) 74) [2017 74: p10g t12.2g^3 Feb 17] lengthy mare: fair handicapper: below form both starts on Flat in 2017: stays 1½m: acts on polytrack and good to soft going: in cheekpieces last 2 starts: often races in rear: sent to Germany. *Ian Williams* **58**

TAVENER 5 b.g. Exceed And Excel (AUS) 126 – Sea Chorus 82 (Singspiel (IRE) 133) [2017 69: f6g^3 f6g^5 f7g p7d^3 p6g^4 t7.1m^2 p8g^5 t7.1g* 7m t7.1g^3 p7g* t7.1g^3 7.1m* p7g^2 7d^5 7.2m^5 t7.2g^5 6.1s^3 7.2m^5 7f^2 6g 6g t6d p7d 5v t7.2m^2 Oct 28] fairly useful handicapper: won at Wolverhampton in March, Lingfield in April and Musselburgh in May: second at Epsom (neck behind Pastoral Player) in July: stays 1m: acts on all-weather, firm and soft going: wears headgear: tried in tongue tie: usually leads. *David C. Griffiths* **84**

TAWAAFOQ 3 b.g. Showcasing 117 – Gilt Linked 85 (Compton Place 125) [2017 77: p6g^4 7m 6m^4 5d^3 6d^3 5.3g^5 6d Sep 19] fair maiden: left Richard Hannon after third start: stays 6f: acts on polytrack, good to firm and good to soft going: has worn hood: sometimes slowly away. *Mick Quinn* **74**

TAWDEEA 5 b.g. Intikhab (USA) 135 – Sharedah (IRE) 94 (Pivotal 124) [2017 110: 12g^6 t12.4s 12g^2 11.9g^4 14g 11.8m^5 12d^6 11.6g^3 11.9g^6 11.8v^5 18m Oct 14] well-made gelding: useful handicapper: second at Ripon (5 lengths behind Knights Table) in April: stays 12.5f: acts on tapeta, firm and soft going: has worn headgear, including usually in 2017: usually races nearer last than first: temperamental. *David O'Meara* **108 §**

TAWFEER 3 b.g. Lawman (FR) 121 – Wild Gardenia 58 (Alhaarth (IRE) 126) [2017 t7.1g f8.1g t6.1g^6 6g t8.6g t8.6g p10d 8g 8v^2 7d^4 p8s Nov 23] modest maiden: left James Unett after seventh start: should stay 1¼m: acts on heavy going: usually in cheekpieces: often races towards rear. *Phil McEntee* **56**

TAWNY PORT 3 ch.g. Arcano (IRE) 122 – Tawaasul 83 (Haafhd 129) [2017 87: 7s May 17] angular gelding: fairly useful handicapper: well below form only start in 2017: stays 6f: acts on tapeta, good to firm and heavy going. *James Given* **–**

TAWS 6 b.m. Hernando (FR) 127 – Reaf (In The Wings 128) [2017 p16g 20.6v^4 16s* 16g* 18d^6 18m Oct 14] sparely-made mare: useful handicapper: won at Chepstow (twice) in August: stays 21.5f: acts on polytrack, tapeta and any turf going: in cheekpieces last 5 starts: usually races prominently. *Rod Millman* **100**

TAWSEEF (IRE) 9 b.g. Monsun (GER) 124 – Sahool 109 (Unfuwain (USA) 131) [2017 68: 12.1m 17.2s* 16v* 12s⁴ Oct 28] rather leggy gelding: fair handicapper: won lady riders event at Carlisle in August and amateur race at Musselburgh in October: stays 17f: acts on polytrack, good to firm and heavy going: has worn headgear: useful hurdler. *Donald McCain* **79**

TAXMEIFYOUCAN (IRE) 3 b.g. Beat Hollow 126 – Accounting (Sillery (USA) 122) [2017 73: f12d* 11.9d 14m t12.4g⁵ 11.1s* 11.1d* 14s* 14v⁶ Sep 29] useful handicapper: won at Southwell in April, Hamilton in August/September and Haydock (by ½ length from Face The Facts) later in September: stays 1¾m: acts on fibresand and soft going: wears headgear: often races towards rear: won on hurdling debut in July. *Keith Dalgleish* **98**

TAYAAR (IRE) 4 b.g. High Chaparral (IRE) 132 – Ursula Minor (IRE) (Footstepsinthesand 120) [2017 60: 12g p16s⁵ 14.1d⁴ 11.5m p13.3s Nov 17] modest maiden: stays 2m: acts on polytrack and tapeta: tried in cheekpieces. *John Ryan* **60**

TAZMANIA (IRE) 3 b.f. Helmet (AUS) 127 – Red Fuschia (Polish Precedent (USA) 131) [2017 58: 7.1s⁴ p8g Oct 14] lightly-raced maiden, modest form at best. *Clive Cox* **–**

TEA EL TEE (IRE) 3 b.g. Holy Roman Emperor (IRE) 125 – Mayenne (USA) (Nureyev (USA) 131) [2017 54: p6g³ 5m f7.1g⁵ 6m⁶ 6g⁵ 5d² 5.2s* 5.7d t5g 5s f5g p6g Dec 21] rather leggy gelding: fair handicapper: won at Yarmouth in August: stays 6f: acts on polytrack and soft going: wears headgear: sometimes slowly away. *Gay Kelleway* **65**

TEAK (IRE) 10 b.g. Barathea (IRE) 127 – Szabo (IRE) 88 (Anabaa (USA) 130) [2017 78: t12.2g⁶ t12.2g t12.2g⁶ 17.2g² p16d³ 17.1d⁴ 18g t16.3d Dec 16] smallish, good-bodied gelding: fair handicapper nowadays: stays 21.5f: acts on polytrack, firm and good to soft going: wears headgear: has worn tongue tie: front runner/races prominently. *Ian Williams* **67**

TEAM MEETING (USA) 3 b.c. Exceed And Excel (AUS) 126 – Sylvan Song (USA) 103 (Street Cry (IRE) 130) [2017 78p: p6g³ 5g p7g* p6s⁶ a6f Dec 29] fairly useful handicapper: won at Lingfield (by nose from Mulzim) in May: left Saeed bin Suroor after fourth start: stays 7f: acts on polytrack: tried in hood: front runner/races prominently. *D. Watson, UAE* **81**

TEAM SHOWME 2 b.f. (Jan 16) Harbour Watch (IRE) 121 – Straitjacket 73 (Refuse To Bend (IRE) 128) [2017 f7.1g Dec 11] second foal: dam temperamental 7f winner: 66/1, well held in minor event at Southwell. *Michael Dods* **–**

TEA RATTLE 2 b.f. (Apr 25) Finjaan 122 – Scrooby Baby 66 (Mind Games 121) [2017 5.1m 5m 5m f7.1g⁴ f8.1g f6.1g Dec 19] fifth foal: half-sister to 5f winner (stayed 7f) Sandy Toes (by Footstepsinthesand) and temperamental 2-y-o 6f winner Scrooby Doo (by Kheleyf): dam, maiden (stayed 6f), half-sister to Dewhurst Stakes/US Grade 1 1m winner Milk It Mick: little form: often leads. *Scott Dixon* **–**

TEASER 2 b.c. (Apr 17) Dansili 127 – Tottie 96 (Fantastic Light (USA) 134) [2017 p8d Dec 13] fourth foal: half-brother to winner up to 1m Column (2-y-o 7.5f winner, by Mount Nelson): dam, 2-y-o 1m winner (later winner up to 11f in USA, including Grade 3 9f event), half-sister to useful winner up to 2m Mister Impatience: 20/1, needed experience when well held in minor event at Kempton (hooded): should do better. *James Fanshawe* **– p**

TEATRO (IRE) 2 b.c. (Mar 4) Shamardal (USA) 129 – Airline Hostess (IRE) (Sadler's Wells (USA) 132) [2017 8d 8.3g Nov 1] well held in minor event/maiden. *James Given* **–**

TEBAY (IRE) 2 b.g. (Mar 7) Elzaam (AUS) 115 – Maid of Ale (IRE) 61 (Barathea (IRE) 127) [2017 5.9s⁵ 7m⁵ 6s³ Aug 9] €12,000Y, resold £40,000Y: third foal: dam maiden half-sister to useful winner up to 9.5f Huzzah: fair form: best effort when fifth in minor event at Redcar (6¼ lengths behind Arbalet) in July: remains with potential. *Michael Dods* **71 p**

TECHNOLOGICAL 2 gr.c. (Apr 14) Universal (IRE) 121 – Qeethaara (USA) 91 (Aljabr (USA) 125) [2017 6m⁶ 7g 7d⁶ Oct 27] 1,500F: rather unfurnished colt: first foal: dam 7f/1m winner: fair form: best effort when sixth in maiden at Doncaster (5½ lengths behind Breath Caught) final start: better to come. *George Margarson* **74 p**

TECTONIC (IRE) 8 b.g. Dylan Thomas (IRE) 132 – Pine Chip (USA) (Nureyev (USA) 131) [2017 73§: 10m⁴ 9.2s 7.8s 11.1d 12.5m³ 16m² 15g³ 16m² 14m 16v t12.4g Nov 23] fair handicapper: stays 2m: acts on polytrack, tapeta, soft and good to firm going: wears headgear: often races towards rear: irresolute. *Keith Dalgleish* **70 §**

TED'S BROTHER (IRE) 9 b.g. Fath (USA) 116 – Estertide (IRE) (Tagula (IRE) 116) [2017 64§: t12.2g³ p12g⁵ t12.2g² p14g³ t16.3s 13.1s² 10g² 10.2g⁵ t12.2m p10s* t12.2g³ Dec 22] modest handicapper: won at Chelmsford (apprentice) in December: stays 1¾m: acts on polytrack, tapeta, good to firm and heavy going: has worn headgear, including last 2 starts: tried in tongue tie: usually races towards rear: not straightforward. *Laura Morgan* **55 a61**

TEE IT UP TOMMO (IRE) 8 gr.g. Clodovil (IRE) 116 – Lamh Eile (IRE) 93 (Lend A Hand 124) [2017 65§: p8g^4 p8g* p8g^2 p8g^3 8m p8g^4 p8s* p10g^4 p8g p10d p8g Dec 13] long-backed gelding: fairly useful handicapper: won at Kempton in February and Chelmsford (by ¾ length from Andalusite) in May: stays 8.5f: acts on polytrack and good to firm going: has worn cheekpieces/tongue tie: often starts slowly/races towards rear: not one to trust. *Daniel Steele* **80 §**

TEENAGE GAL (IRE) 2 b.f. (Jan 29) Acclamation 118 – Bobbie Soxer (IRE) 90 (Pivotal 124) [2017 p7g 7s^2 Oct 9] fourth foal: sister to smart 1m winner Mittersill: dam, 6f and (at 2 yrs) 7f winner, half-sister to smart winner up to 10.6f Big Bad Bob: fair form when second in minor event at Salisbury (neck behind Caiya) on second of 2 starts. *Ed Dunlop* **73**

TEEPEE TIME 4 b.f. Compton Place 125 – Deora De (Night Shift (USA)) [2017 –: t5.1m^2 p6g t5.1g* t5.1g^5 5g^3 5m^6 5.1s t5.1g^3 5g* 5g* 5g^5 t5.1m t5.1g t5.1g Dec 22] modest handicapper: won at Wolverhampton in February, and Haydock in July and August: stays 6f: acts on tapeta, best turf form on good going: wears headgear nowadays: usually races prominently. *Michael Mullineaux* **64 a56**

TEGARA 4 ch.f. Hard Spun (USA) 124 – Damaniyat Girl (USA) 108 (Elusive Quality (USA)) [2017 80: p8g* 8m p8g^4 p8g* t10.2g^5 Jun 30] fairly useful handicapper: won at Lingfield in April and Kempton (by 1¾ lengths from Karisma) in June: stays 1m: acts on polytrack, best turf form on good going: often races freely. *David Simcock* **83**

TE KOOP 2 ch.g. (Feb 2) Mastercraftsman (IRE) 129 – Miss You Too 105§ (Montjeu (IRE) 137) [2017 t8g^2 p8g^5 Nov 1] fair form: second in maiden at Newcastle (2¾ lengths behind Champarisi) in September: sold 8,000 gns, sent to Spain. *David Simcock* **68**

TELL A STORY 4 b.f. Dutch Art 126 – Ghenwah (FR) (Selkirk (USA) 129) [2017 66: p8g^3 p6g^3 p7g^5 Jan 25] fair maiden: best effort at 6f: acts on polytrack: sometimes slowly away: tail flasher: sold 8,500 gns, sent to Greece. *David Simcock* **71 §**

TELL ME (IRE) 2 b.f. (Apr 14) Kodiac 112 – Fearn Royal (IRE) 103 (Ali-Royal (IRE) 127) [2017 6g 7d^4 p7s Aug 9] €50,000F, €80,000Y: closely related to 2-y-o 7f winner Our Way Only (by Oratorio) and 7f-10.7f winner Shabra Emperor (by Holy Roman Emperor) and half-sister to 3 winners, including 1m-13f winner Rosie Royale (by Verglas): dam 7f and (at 2 yrs) 1m winner: mid-division at best in minor events: in visor last 2 starts. *Simon Crisford* **64**

TELLOVOI (IRE) 9 b.g. Indian Haven 119 – Kloonlara (IRE) 73 (Green Desert (USA) 127) [2017 81: 8g^5 p8g 8m^2 7g^5 6.9g 7g 7s^4 8.5m^4 7d 8.3g 7g^5 8g^{rr} 7m 7s^6 7.2s 6d 6s^5 t7.1g^2 f8.1g^6 p7s^6 p7s^3 Dec 17] fair handicapper: stays 8.5f: acts on all-weather, soft and good to firm going: wears headgear: sometimes slowly away: needs treating with caution (has refused to race). *Richard Guest* **78 §**

TELLTALE 2 ch.g. (Mar 1) Monsieur Bond (IRE) 120 – Yarn 72 (Dutch Art 126) [2017 6.5d Oct 27] 66/1, well held in maiden at Newbury. *Mick Channon* **–**

TEMASEK STAR (IRE) 6 b.g. Soviet Star (USA) 128 – Crazy About You (IRE) 75 (Montjeu (IRE) 137) [2017 73: t12.4g^2 p12s^5 p12g^4 p12g^3 p10.7g^4 t13.9g* 15g^5 p12g^2 15g* Jul 27] fair handicapper: won at Wolverhampton in April and Leopardstown in July: stays 15f: acts on polytrack, tapeta and good to soft going: wears headgear: often travels strongly. *Anthony McCann, Ireland* **74**

TEMBER 2 b.g. (Jan 30) Sayif (IRE) 122 – Tranquil Flight (Oasis Dream 129) [2017 5m^2 5s^6 5f^3 6g 6d Oct 24] fair maiden: best form at 5f: acts on firm going: tried in blinkers. *David Barron* **70**

TEMERAIRE (FR) 3 gr.f. Mount Nelson 125 – Tadorne (FR) (Inchinor 119) [2017 p9.4g^3 9.9d 8g^4 8g^2 p6g* p7g^2 Dec 6] half-sister to several winners in France, including smart 1m-1¼m (Prix Guillaume d'Ornano) winner Pinson and useful 9.5f winner Mimosa (both by Halling): dam useful French 5.5f/1m winner (including at 2 yrs): fairly useful performer: won maiden at Lingfield (by 4½ lengths from Trotter) in November: left H-A. Pantall after fourth start: effective at 6f to 9.5f: acts on polytrack. *Hugo Palmer* **83**

TEMIR KAZYK 3 b.g. Oasis Dream 129 – Tingling (USA) 81 (Storm Cat (USA)) [2017 t8d^5 p12g^3 p11g^3 11.9d^6 10g Aug 2] fair maiden: stays 1½m: acts on polytrack and tapeta: often races towards rear. *David Simcock* **66**

TEMPLE CHURCH (IRE) 3 b.g. Lawman (FR) 121 – All Hallows (IRE) (Dalakhani (IRE) 133) [2017 97p: 10g^4 8.9g^3 9.9g^5 10.3m^4 8s^4 12g^5 Sep 22] well-made gelding: useful performer: fourth in handicap at York (3 lengths behind Defoe) in July: should stay 1½m: acts on soft and good to firm going: tried in tongue tie. *Hughie Morrison* **106**

TEMPLEMARY BOY (IRE) 4 b.g. Vocalised (USA) 114 – Marino Lil (IRE) 72 (Lil's **54**
Boy (USA) 109) [2017 8s 10.3g^{6} 6d 8.7m 8.3d^{4} p8g^{2} 8.5s Oct 14] modest maiden: stays 1m: acts on polytrack: tried in cheekpieces: often races in rear. *Paul W. Flynn, Ireland*

TEMPLE ROAD (IRE) 9 b.g. Street Cry (IRE) 130 – Sugarhoneybaby (IRE) 104 **77**
(Docksider (USA) 124) [2017 78: t5.1g^{2} p5g^{2} t5.1g^{5} t5.1g^{4} t5.1g^{4} p5g^{3} p5m^{4} t5.1g t5.1g t5.1g p5g* p5g^{3} Dec 23] fair handicapper: won at Lingfield in December: stays 6f: acts on polytrack, tapeta and good to firm going: wears headgear/tongue tie: sometimes slowly away, often races towards rear. *Milton Bradley*

TEMPURAN 8 b.g. Unbridled's Song (USA) 125 – Tenderly (IRE) (Danehill (USA) 126) **72**
[2017 78: p11g p12g p15.8g^{3} f14m^{4} t16.5g 11.9g^{3} 11.9g* 16.5m Jul 13] tall gelding: fair handicapper: won at Brighton (amateur) in June: stays 17f: acts on polytrack, tapeta and good to soft going: has worn headgear, including last 3 starts: tried in tongue tie: front runner/races prominently: fair hurdler. *David Bridgwater*

TEMUR KHAN 2 br.c. (Mar 19) Dansili 127 – Slink (Selkirk (USA) 129) [2017 p8g Nov **61 P**
18] 230,000F: seventh foal: half-brother to useful 5f/6f (including at 2 yrs) winner Bye Bye Birdie and 7f winner Sleek (both by Oasis Dream): dam unraced half-sister to high-class performer up to 1½m Eagle Mountain and Breeders' Cup Filly & Mare Turf winner Dank (by Dansili): 5/1, needed experience when eighth in minor event at Lingfield (5¾ lengths behind Rusper) in November: sure to improve plenty. *Hugo Palmer*

TENBY TWO 3 gr.f. Rip Van Winkle (IRE) 134 – Ayla (IRE) 101 (Daylami (IRE) 138) **66**
[2017 7g^{5} 7f^{4} 9.9d^{5} 14m 12m^{6} 13f^{4} 10.2f^{3} 13f^{4} 8.2d^{2} 10g^{2} Aug 2] fifth foal: half-sister to 1¼m-11.6f winner Ayla's Emperor (by Holy Roman Emperor): dam, 1½m winner who stayed 1¾m, half-sister to very smart 1½m-2½m (Prix du Cadran) winner Alandi: fair maiden: stays 1½m: acts on firm going: tried in eyeshields. *Mick Channon*

TENEDOS 2 b.c. (Mar 10) High Chaparral (IRE) 132 – Garanciere (FR) (Anabaa (USA) **88 p**
130) [2017 p8g* Oct 25] 65,000F: seventh foal: half-brother to 3 winners, including smart performer up to 1m I Love Me (2-y-o 7f winner, by Cape Cross) and useful winner up to 1¼m Ningara (2-y-o 1m winner, by Singspiel): dam, French 9.5f winner, half-sister to Fillies' Mile winner Glorosia: 10/1 and tongue tied, won minor event at Kempton (by 2 lengths from Maaward) on debut: will stay further than 1m: sure to progress. *Hugo Palmer*

TENEREZZA (IRE) 4 b.f. Shamardal (USA) 129 – Geminiani (IRE) 106 (King of Kings **75**
(IRE) 125) [2017 76: t10.2d^{4} t9.5g^{2} t8.6g* p10.7g^{3} 8m May 6] fair handicapper: won at Wolverhampton in February: left Iain Jardine after fourth start: stays 10.5f: acts on polytrack and tapeta: usually races freely: has carried head awkwardly. *Joseph G. Murphy, Ireland*

TENERIFE SONG 4 b.f. Fastnet Rock (AUS) 127 – Dancingintheclouds (IRE) 67 **–**
(Rainbow Quest (USA) 134) [2017 p12g Nov 29] ex-Turkish filly: sixth foal: closely related to 1m winner On My Own (by Rock of Gibraltar) and half-sister to 2 winners by Dilum, including useful 1¾m winner (stays 2m) Start Seven: dam lightly-raced sister to St Leger winner Millenary: successful at Veliefendi in 2016 in maiden, handicap, Kisrak Kosusu (local Group 1) and Nene Hatun Kosusu (local Group 2): well held in listed race at Kempton only start in 2017: stays 1½m: acts on polytrack. *Jamie Osborne*

TENHOO 11 b.g. Reset (AUS) 124 – Bella Bambina 45 (Turtle Island (IRE) 123) [2017 **45**
t10.2g^{4} f12s^{6} p13g Feb 9] fairly useful handicapper at best, has deteriorated: stays 13f: acts on all-weather, soft and good to firm going: has worn headgear. *Richard Ford*

TEN IN THE HAT (IRE) 3 b.g. Sir Prancealot (IRE) 111 – Vampire Queen (IRE) 54 **–**
(General Monash (USA) 107) [2017 46: 8.3g 8.3s f8.1g Oct 22] poor maiden: left Shaun Harris after second start: tried in cheekpieces. *Tom Gretton*

TENNESSEE BELLE 3 b.f. Teofilo (IRE) 126 – Dixie Belle 113 (Diktat 126) [2017 p8g **60**
p8g Sep 26] 36,000Y: fifth foal: half-sister to 3 winners, including useful 6f (including at 2 yrs) winner Blanche Dubawi (by Dubawi) and 7f winner Diamond Belle (by Rock of Gibraltar): dam 5f and (at 2 yrs) 6f winner: modest form: better effort when seventh in maiden at Chelmsford second start. *James Tate*

TENNESSEE ROSE (IRE) 3 b.f. Tagula (IRE) 116 – Bonny Rose 79 (Zaha (CAN) 106) **69**
[2017 65: 7m^{2} 8.1d^{4} t7.2g^{6} 7d^{2} 7.5s p7g Oct 3] tall filly: fair handicapper: left Luke McJannet after fourth start: stays 8.5f: acts on polytrack, tapeta, good to firm and good to soft going: has worn tongue tie: front runner/races prominently. *A. P. Keatley, Ireland*

TENZING NORGAY 4 gr.g. Aussie Rules (USA) 123 – Miss Katmandu (IRE) (Rainbow Quest (USA) 134) [2017 87p: 15.9m^3 14s^3 13.9v^4 Aug 8] fairly useful handicapper: third at Sandown (2 lengths behind West Drive) in July: stays 1¾m: acts on polytrack, tapeta and heavy going: wears headgear: usually races nearer last than first: sold 7,000 gns, sent to Greece. *Sir Mark Prescott Bt* **91**

TEODORO (IRE) 3 ch.g. Teofilo (IRE) 126 – Altesse Imperiale (IRE) (Rock of Gibraltar (IRE) 133) [2017 70: t7.1m^5 9g* 12.3m^4 11.9d 10.2m* 10.2m* 10.1m* 10m Sep 23] useful handicapper: won at Redcar (dead-heated) in May, Haydock in June/July and Yarmouth (by 2½ lengths from Mafaaheem) in August: stays 12.5f: acts on tapeta and good to firm going: in hood last 4 starts: usually leads. *Tom Dascombe* **102**

TEOFONIC (IRE) 3 b.f. Teofilo (IRE) 126 – Dusty Answer 97 (Zafonic (USA) 130) [2017 92: 10m^5 10.3m 12g^2 12s* 11.9d^5 Oct 28] tall filly: useful performer: won handicap at Goodwood (by 7 lengths from Shabbah) in October: likely to stay further than 1½m: acts on soft and good to firm going: often races prominently: sold 95,000 gns later in October. *Mark Johnston* **105**

TEOMARIA 3 b.f. Teofilo (IRE) 126 – Sylvestris (IRE) 96 (Arch (USA) 127) [2017 7g^5 8g^5 8v^3 p8g 7d 8.3g* t8g Nov 24] 60,000F: first foal: dam, 7f winner, out of half-sister to 1000 Guineas runner-up Arch Swing: fair handicapper: won at Nottingham in November: stays 8.5f: acts on heavy going. *K. R. Burke* **74**

TEPPAL (FR) 2 b.f. (May 10) Camacho 118 – Jummana (FR) 96 (Cadeaux Genereux 131) [2017 7g* p7g* Sep 25] €60,000Y, €105,000 2-y-o: half-sister to several winners in France, including smart winner up to 6.5f Another Party (2-y-o 5f/6f winner, by Pomellato) and 1¼m winner Jevousvoisencore (by American Post): dam 2-y-o 7f winner: fairly useful form: won both starts, minor events at Lingfield (by neck from Awesometank) in August and Kempton (by 4 lengths from Gather) in September: will go on improving. *David Simcock* **93 p**

TEQANY (IRE) 3 gr.g. Dark Angel (IRE) 113 – Capulet Monteque (IRE) 84 (Camacho 118) [2017 74: 8.3g^6 7m^6 7m^6 8.3s^5 p10.7g^5 p10.7g Dec 15] good-topped gelding: fair maiden: left Owen Burrows after fourth start: stays 10.5f: acts on polytrack and good to firm going. *G. M. Lyons, Ireland* **75**

TERMSNCONDITIONS (IRE) 3 b.g. Kodiac 112 – Sweet'n Sassy (IRE) 69 (Grand Lodge (USA) 125) [2017 57: p6g* p6g* 6m^5 6g 5.7s t6g^5 p6g^2 p7g^6 Dec 28] fair handicapper: won at Lingfield in March and April: stays 7f: acts on polytrack and tapeta: in visor last 4 starts. *Tim Vaughan* **67**

TERRIFIC FEELING (IRE) 3 b.g. Sir Prancealot (IRE) 111 – Easy Feeling (IRE) 84 (Night Shift (USA)) [2017 82: 6g 5.5g 5.2g^6 Jul 27] fairly useful form at 2 yrs, successful in minor event at Vichy: little impact in 2017: left M. Palussiere after second start: best form at 5f: tried in blinkers. *Dominic Ffrench Davis* **–**

TERRI RULES (IRE) 2 b.f. (Mar 5) Camacho 118 – Hawaiian Storm 65 (Jeremy (USA) 122) [2017 5g 6d 5g^3 6g^5 5d^2 t5.1g^5 5.3m^5 t5.1g^3 t6.1g 6v 5s^6 Oct 2] €4,500F, €7,000Y, £16,000 2-y-o: compact filly: first foal: dam 1m winner: modest maiden handicapper: best form at 5f: acts on tapeta and good to soft going. *Julia Feilden* **58**

TERUNTUM STAR (FR) 5 ch.g. Dutch Art 126 – Seralia 95 (Royal Academy (USA) 130) [2017 105: t6s 6g^4 6g* 6g* 6d^4 Nov 11] quite attractive gelding: smart handicapper: won at Ripon (by neck from Red Pike) in August and Coral Sprint Trophy at York (by 1¾ lengths from Spring Loaded) in October: stays 6f: acts on good to firm and good to soft going: has worn headgear, including cheekpieces last 4 starts in 2017: front runner/races prominently. *Kevin Ryan* **113**

TESKO FELLA (IRE) 3 b.g. Myboycharlie (IRE) 118 – Foundation Filly (Lando (GER) 128) [2017 72: 6m 7m^4 8.1m^4 p7s^3 8g^6 8d 8.5d^2 8.3s^2 Aug 25] angular gelding: fair maiden: left Luke McJannet after fourth start: stayed 8.5f: acted on firm and good to soft going: tried in headgear: usually raced prominently: dead. *Ruth Carr* **72**

TESORINA (IRE) 2 b.f. (Feb 21) Lilbourne Lad (IRE) 111 – Insieme (IRE) 68 (Barathea (IRE) 127) [2017 7d^5 7d^4 Sep 18] €6,500Y: third foal: half-sister to useful winner up to 1¼m Goodwood Zodiac (2-y-o 7f winner, by Kodiac): dam, 1m winner, half-sister to useful 1m winner Aldovrandi: modest form: better effort when fifth in maiden at Lingfield (1¼ lengths behind Claudine) in September. *William Knight* **62**

TESS GRAHAM 3 b.f. Pastoral Pursuits 127 – Zartwyda (IRE) (Mozart (IRE) 131) [2017 –: 5g^4 t6.1g 5m^5 5m 5f^6 5m Aug 27] poor maiden handicapper: best effort at 5f: acts on good to firm going: wears cheekpieces. *Sarah Hollinshead* **42**

TESTA ROSSA (IRE) 7 b.g. Oratorio (IRE) 128 – Red Rita (IRE) 97 (Kefaah (USA) **89**
124) [2017 69+, a85: t8g* t8g^4 t7.1d^5 t7.1g t8g^3 t7.1d 8m* 8.3m^6 t8s 10g^6 10g^2 t10.2s^3 8g^6
10g^4 t10.2g 10d^6 8m^2 t8g^6 t8d^3 t10.2g^5 Nov 23] fairly useful handicapper: won at Newcastle
in January and Ayr (amateur) in May: stays 12.5f: acts on polytrack, tapeta, soft and good
to firm going: wears headgear: usually races nearer last than first. *Jim Goldie*

TESTBOURNE (IRE) 3 b.g. Big Bad Bob (IRE) 118 – Magnificent Bell (IRE) **73**
(Octagonal (NZ) 126) [2017 f8d^3 10m^2 11.5g^2 9.9m 9.2s 8d^4 Jul 27] fair maiden: best effort
at 1¼m: acts on good to firm going: tried in tongue tie: front runner/races prominently. *K.
R. Burke*

TETRADRACHM 4 b.g. Holy Roman Emperor (IRE) 125 – Dahlia's Krissy (USA) **88**
(Kris S (USA)) [2017 83: p14d^3 t16.3g t13.9m^3 p16d^6 t16.3s^6 p14g t16.3g p16g^3 Nov 1]
fairly useful handicapper: third at Chelmsford in February: stays 16.5f: acts on polytrack,
tapeta and soft going: in cheekpieces last 4 starts: sold £4,200 in November. *David Simcock*

TEWAFEEDJ 3 b.g. Mawatheeq (USA) 126 – It's The War (USA) (Consolidator (USA) **67**
121) [2017 69p: f8m^4 t12.4g^4 10.2m 9.9g^6 9.9m^3 12d* 12g^4 p13.3d Sep 28] fair
handicapper: won at Thirsk in August: stays 1½m: acts on good to firm and good to soft
going: tried in cheekpieces: front runner/races prominently. *Kevin Ryan*

TEXAS ROCK (IRE) 6 b.g. Rock of Gibraltar (IRE) 133 – Vestavia (IRE) (Alhaarth **112**
(IRE) 126) [2017 102: p8g^3 7m^4 7s* 8g^5 7d^2 7d^5 5.8v* 7s Oct 28] smart performer: won
listed races at Naas (by head from Drumfad Bay) in May and Navan (by neck from Son of
Rest) in October: stays 1m: acts on polytrack, good to firm and heavy going: wears
headgear: usually races close up. *M. C. Grassick, Ireland*

TEXAS WEDGE 3 b.g. Foxwedge (AUS) 128 – Sacre Coeur 90 (Compton Place 125) **–**
[2017 5.1d 5d^6 5f^5 t6.1g p6g 5v Aug 3] sturdy gelding: little sign of ability: in headgear last
5 starts. *William Muir*

TEXTURED (IRE) 3 b.f. Dark Angel (IRE) 113 – Timbre (Dubai Destination (USA) **79**
127) [2017 84: p8g 7m^5 Jun 24] sturdy filly: fairly useful handicapper: best effort at 7f: acts
on tapeta. *Sir Michael Stoute*

T FOR TANGO (IRE) 2 b.g. (Mar 2) Zoffany (IRE) 121 – Diminish (IRE) (Raven's Pass **89**
(USA) 133) [2017 5d* 5s^4 5f 6d^6 6s p5g Oct 27] €80,000Y: lengthy gelding: second foal:
half-brother to Italian 5f winner (including at 2 yrs) Divine Tenerife (by Bushranger): dam
unraced half-sister to smart performer up to 1m Rahiyah: fairly useful performer: won
maiden at Naas in April: fourth in listed race at same course in May: best form at 5f: acts
on soft going: in blinkers last 2 starts. *James A. Nash, Ireland*

THAAQIB 3 gr.g. Invincible Spirit (IRE) 121 – Light Shine 82 (Dansili 127) [2017 79: **82**
p7g^6 8f 7m^5 a8.4f Dec 23] fairly useful handicapper: left Charles Hills after third start:
stays 8.5f: acts on dirt, polytrack, good to firm and good to soft going: tried in blinkers:
usually races prominently. *E. Charpy, UAE*

THACKERAY 10 b.g. Fasliyev (USA) 120 – Chinon (IRE) (Entrepreneur 123) [2017 55: **51**
f16g^3 f14g^3 t16.3d f14g^4 f14g^3 14g 13.1s^2 13.1g 17.2s Aug 7] modest handicapper: stays
1¾m: acts on polytrack, fibresand and soft going: often races in rear. *Chris Fairhurst*

THAFEERA (USA) 3 b.f. War Front (USA) 119 – Aqsaam (USA) (Dynaformer (USA)) **105**
[2017 72p: p8g^3 8s^3 p8s^4 6g* 6.1g* 6g* 6m Oct 14] good-topped filly: useful performer:
won maiden at Yarmouth (by 3½ lengths from Dream of Joy) in July, and handicaps at
Nottingham (by 1¼ lengths from Maid In India) in August and Salisbury (by 3 lengths
from Kassia) in September: best at 6f: acts on polytrack, best turf form on good going: has
worn hood: front runner/races prominently. *Charles Hills*

THAHAB IFRAJ (IRE) 4 ch.g. Frozen Power (IRE) 108 – Penny Rouge (IRE) 59 **76**
(Pennekamp (USA) 130) [2017 78: p11g^2 p12d^3 11.4m^3 Aug 13] fair maiden handicapper:
left Ismail Mohammed after second start: should stay 1½m: acts on polytrack, fibresand,
soft and good to firm going: tried in cheekpieces. *Alexandra Dunn*

THA'IR (IRE) 7 b.g. New Approach (IRE) 132 – Flashing Green (Green Desert (USA) **91**
127) [2017 9.9g 9d 7.9g t10.2d^5 p10d t9.5g^2 p10s^6 Dec 8] compact gelding: fairly useful
handicapper: second in claimer at Wolverhampton in November: stays 11f: acts on
polytrack, tapeta, firm and good to soft going: has worn headgear, including last 5 starts.
Michael Appleby

THAMA 2 b.f. (Mar 25) Finjaan 122 – It's The War (USA) (Consolidator (USA) 121) **–**
[2017 p8g Dec 20] third foal: half-sister to 1½m winner Tewafeedj (by Mawatheeq): dam
unraced: 100/1, well held in minor event at Kempton (hooded). *Mrs Ilka Gansera-Leveque*

THAMES KNIGHT 5 b.g. Sir Percy 129 – Bermondsey Girl 69 (Bertolini (USA) 125) [2017 88: 12g^6 11.9s 12g* 11.2g^2 12m^2 Aug 28] sturdy gelding: fairly useful handicapper: won at Goodwood in June: second at Epsom (amateur) in August: stays 1½m: acts on polytrack, soft and good to firm going: has worn headgear: sold 42,000 gns in November to join Jim Boyle, well held over hurdles. *Marcus Tregoning* **90**

THAMMIN 3 gr.c. Dark Angel (IRE) 113 – Gimme Some Lovin (IRE) 70 (Desert Style (IRE) 121) [2017 87p: 6d p5g^2 Oct 13] useful handicapper: second at Kempton (neck behind Orvar) in October: stays 6f: acts on polytrack, soft and good to firm going: tried in hood: often starts slowly. *Owen Burrows* **97**

THANE OF CAWDOR (IRE) 8 b.g. Danehill Dancer (IRE) 117 – Holy Nola (USA) (Silver Deputy (CAN)) [2017 68: t9.5m p11g Jan 11] big, rangy gelding: fair handicapper: well below form both starts in 2017: stays 1½m: acts on polytrack, tapeta, good to firm and heavy going: has worn headgear, including final start. *Joseph Tuite* **–**

THANKYOU STARS 4 b.f. Exceed And Excel (AUS) 126 – Magic Music (IRE) 82 (Magic Ring (IRE) 115) [2017 71: 6m^6 t6.1g Sep 23] leggy filly: fair form at 3 yrs, last in handicaps in 2017: raced only at 6f: front runner/races prominently, tends to find little. *Jonathan Portman* **–**

THANKYOU VERY MUCH 7 b.m. Lucky Story (USA) 128 – Maid of Perth (Mark of Esteem (IRE) 137) [2017 63: t16.3g^2 p16g Nov 7] modest handicapper: stays 16.5f: acts on all-weather, firm and good to soft going: wears headgear: in tongue tie last 2 starts: usually races towards rear: fair chaser. *James Bethell* **63**

THAQAFFA (IRE) 4 b.g. Kodiac 112 – Incense 73 (Unfuwain (USA) 131) [2017 88: p7d p8g^5 8g^6 8.3g* 8s^5 7g 7m^6 8v 8.3d^5 t7.2m p7s p10s^3 p10g^5 Dec 21] compact gelding: fairly useful handicapper: won at Nottingham (by 1½ lengths from Therthaar) in May: stays 1¼m: acts on polytrack, good to firm and good to soft going: has worn headgear. *Amy Murphy* **86 a76**

THATCHERITE (IRE) 9 gr.g. Verglas (IRE) 118 – Damiana (IRE) (Thatching 131) [2017 5m 5g^5 5m 5.5f* 5m^5 5d Jul 24] angular gelding: fair handicapper: won at Wetherby in June: has won over 8.5f, best at sprint trips nowadays: acts on polytrack, firm and good to soft going: has worn headgear: wears tongue tie: often races in rear: quirky. *Tony Coyle* **72**

THAT IS THE SPIRIT 6 b.g. Invincible Spirit (IRE) 121 – Fraulein 117 (Acatenango (GER) 127) [2017 103: p7g* p7g^3 7.2s^6 t7.1s^5 7g^3 7d^3 7g^5 p7s 7d^6 7.2s^3 Oct 9] tall, good-topped gelding: useful handicapper: won at Chelmsford (by neck from Rusumaat) in April: stays 7f: acts on polytrack, soft and good to firm going: front runner. *David O'Meara* **106**

THAT'S A SURPRISE (IRE) 2 ch.c. (Mar 29) Zoffany (IRE) 121 – Sweet Surprise (IRE) 69 (Danetime (IRE) 121) [2017 5m* 6g 6m Aug 26] fair form: won maiden at Beverley (by ¾ length from Roundhay Park) in July: best effort at 5f. *Tony Coyle* **73**

THAT'S MY GIRL (IRE) 2 b.f. (Feb 11) Mastercraftsman (IRE) 129 – Caribbean Ace (IRE) (Red Clubs (IRE) 125) [2017 6.1m^5 5.1m p6d^5 6v* 7d^5 p8g^5 p7g^5 p8g^5 p7g Dec 6] €23,000F, £50,000Y: sturdy filly: first foal: dam, unraced, out of half-sister to smart sprinter Splice: modest performer: won nursery at Newbury in July, suited by way race developed: stays 6f: acts on polytrack and heavy going: tried in blinkers. *Richard Hannon* **64**

THAT'S SO COOL (IRE) 2 b.g. (Apr 5) Born To Sea (IRE) 117 – Bibury 80 (Royal Applause 124) [2017 t9.5g^5 Dec 18] 52,000Y: third foal: half-brother to smart winner up to 1¼m Steel of Madrid (2-y-o 6f winner, by Lope de Vega) and a winner abroad by Duke of Marmalade: dam, 7f winner who stayed 10.7f, half-sister to Gold Cup winner Rite of Passage: 28/1, fifth in minor event at Wolverhampton (¾ length behind Jackfinbar). *David Simcock* **81**

THATSTHEWAYTODOIT (IRE) 4 ch.f. Lord Shanakill (USA) 121 – Van de Cappelle (IRE) (Pivotal 124) [2017 59: t10.2g p8d^5 9s t7.2g Jun 26] modest maiden at best, out of form in 2017: tried in blinkers: often races freely. *Daniel Loughnane* **–**

THE ABSENT MARE 9 gr.m. Fair Mix (IRE) 123 – Precious Lucy (FR) (Kadrou (FR) 126) [2017 t16.5g Aug 11] angular mare: one-time fair handicapper: last only start on Flat since 2014: has worn headgear/tongue tie. *Sarah-Jayne Davies* **–**

THE AMBER FORT (USA) 3 b.g. Elusive Quality (USA) – Unreachable (USA) 61 (Giant's Causeway (USA) 132) [2017 80: 6.1m 6f 7.6s t6.1g^2 6.1g^3 t7.2g^3 6g^2 t6.1g^5 t6g^6 t7.2m^5 f6.1g^2 Dec 21] strong, close-coupled gelding: fairly useful handicapper: stays 7f: acts on fibresand, tapeta, best turf form on good going: consistent. *David O'Meara* **81**

THE ANVIL (IRE) 3 b.c. Galileo (IRE) 134 – Brightest (Rainbow Quest (USA) 134) **109**
[2017 105: p10.7g* 12.3m³ 12m 12g 14.5g Sep 16] tall, rather lightly-made colt: useful performer: second in Royal Lodge Stakes at Newmarket at 2 yrs: won maiden at Dundalk (by 5½ lengths from Mauricio) in March: third in Chester Vase (1¼ lengths behind Venice Beach) in May: acted as pacemaker in Derby, Irish Derby and St Leger last 3 starts: stayed 12.5f: acted on polytrack and good to firm going: to stand at Haras du Grand Chesnaie, France, fee €2,300. *Aidan O'Brien, Ireland*

THE ARMED MAN 4 b.g. Misu Bond (IRE) 114 – Accamelia 67 (Shinko Forest (IRE)) **84**
[2017 65: 5m⁴ 5g² 6g* t6s* 5m² 6g* 6m⁶ 6d* 6g 6g Sep 1] fairly useful handicapper: won at Thirsk/Newcastle in May, and again at Thirsk in June and August (by neck from Bogart): stays 6f: acts on tapeta, soft and good to firm going: tried in cheekpieces: front runner/races prominently. *Chris Fairhurst*

THEATRE ROYALE 5 ch.m. Sulamani (IRE) 130 – Theatre Belle 57 (King's Theatre **–**
(IRE) 128) [2017 p12d Aug 23] third foal: dam, maiden on Flat, winning hurdler: 100/1, well held in maiden at Kempton: failed to complete both starts over hurdles. *Brian Barr*

THE AULD HOOSE (IRE) 2 gr.c. (Apr 15) Zebedee 113 – Merry Moon (IRE) 58 **54**
(Night Shift (USA)) [2017 6s t6d 5g⁵ 5.9v 5s⁶ Sep 23] modest maiden: best effort at 6f: acts on soft going: tried in blinkers: front runner/races prominently. *Richard Fahey*

THE BARD'S ADVICE 3 ch.f. Poet's Voice 126 – Flylowflylong (IRE) 74 (Danetime **64**
(IRE) 121) [2017 59p: t8g⁴ t7.1d⁵ t6g⁵ 7.1m 8.3g Jul 20] modest maiden: best effort at 7f: acts on tapeta: tried in cheekpieces. *Keith Dalgleish*

THE BATHAM BOY (IRE) 3 b.g. Thewayyouare (USA) 117 – Margaux Dancer (IRE) **–**
(Danehill Dancer (IRE) 117) [2017 –: t9.5g t12.2g 14d Aug 19] little form, including over hurdles: tried in cheekpieces. *Daniel Loughnane*

THE BEAR CAN FLY 3 b.f. Pastoral Pursuits 127 – Torrecilla 68 (General Monash **69**
(USA) 107) [2017 7d⁴ 7s² 7d³ 8v³ p8g Oct 26] rather unfurnished filly: fourth foal: dam 2-y-o 6f winner: fair maiden: stays 1m: acts on heavy going: tried in cheekpieces: sometimes slowly away. *David Menuisier*

THE BEARFIGHTER (IRE) 2 b.c. (Mar 18) Society Rock (IRE) 126 – Absolute Fun **60 p**
(IRE) 62 (Lawman (FR) 121) [2017 t8.6g Nov 25] €47,000F, 25,000Y: second foal: dam maiden (best efforts around 7f at 2 yrs): 33/1, seventh in minor event at Wolverhampton (8 lengths behind Hipster Boy): capable of better. *Charlie Fellowes*

THE BIG DAY (IRE) 4 gr.f. Le Cadre Noir (IRE) 113 – Grey Galava 64 (Generous (IRE) **–**
139) [2017 60: t10.2g Jan 11] modest maiden: well held only start in 2017: stays 7f: acts on good to firm and good to soft going: tried in hood. *Nigel Tinkler*

THE BIG LAD 5 ch.g. Kheleyf (USA) 116 – Cultured Pride (IRE) 81 (King's Best (USA) **84**
132) [2017 82: f5g* p5d⁶ f5g⁴ t5.1g² p5g³ 5.3g² 5m² 5m⁶ 5.1g⁶ 5.3m³ f6.1g p6g 6.1d² f5g³ Nov 13] fairly useful handicapper: won at Southwell (by ½ length from Dungannon) in January: second at Wolverhampton in April and Bath in June: stays 6f: acts on all-weather, good to firm and good to soft going: usually wears headgear: temperament under suspicion (has looked awkward). *Richard Hughes*

THE BIG SHORT 3 ch.g. Bahamian Bounty 116 – Royal Punch (Royal Applause 124) **77**
[2017 64: 5.1m⁵ t6g 5m* 5d⁵ 5g³ 5m² 5.3d² 5s⁵ t5d Oct 24] sturdy gelding: fair handicapper: won at Leicester in June: second at Brighton in September: stays 6f: acts on polytrack, good to firm and good to soft going: front runner/races prominently: temperament under suspicion: sold 10,000 gns in October to join Milton Bradley. *Charles Hills*

THE BLACK PRINCESS (FR) 4 b.f. Iffraaj 127 – Larceny (IRE) (Cape Cross (IRE) **112**
129) [2017 107p: 9.9g* 10.3d² 11.8m* 11.9d 9.9d 12s⁵ Oct 21] lengthy filly: smart performer: won Prix Allez France at Chantilly (by 1¼ lengths from Armande) in April and Lancashire Oaks at Haydock (by ½ length from Abingdon) in July: stays 1½m: acts on polytrack, soft and good to firm going. *John Gosden*

THE BLUE BOMBER 5 b.g. Stimulation (IRE) 121 – Mar Blue (FR) 75 (Marju (IRE) **65**
127) [2017 p12g³ Feb 24] placed in bumpers/over hurdles: 9/4, third in maiden at Lingfield (7¾ lengths behind Casablanca). *Mick Channon*

THE BLUES MASTER (IRE) 3 gr.g. Mastercraftsman (IRE) 129 – Catch The Blues **80**
(IRE) 115 (Bluebird (USA) 125) [2017 83: p12g* 12.1m² 12.3m 14m 14m³ p14s³ t12.4g 16.1f⁵ p16s⁶ 12g³ Aug 19] fairly useful performer: won maiden at Kempton in January: second in handicap at Beverley (¾ length behind Global Revival) in April: stays 2m: acts on polytrack and good to firm going: has worn headgear: fair form over hurdles for Alan King. *Mark Johnston*

THE BRITISH LION (IRE) 2 b.c. (Apr 26) Power 117 – Mala Mala (IRE) 104 (Brief Truce (USA) 126) [2017 6d t6g^2 p7g^3 Dec 21] fair form: best effort when second in minor event at Newcastle (2 lengths behind Royal Prospect) in November. *Mark Johnston* **77**

THE BURNHAM MARE (IRE) 4 b.f. Kodiac 112 – Courte Paille (IRE) (Common Grounds 118) [2017 72: p5g p6g p5g p6g t5g Mar 10] angular filly: fair handicapper: below form in 2017: stays 6f: acts on polytrack, tapeta and good to soft going: usually wears cheekpieces: usually races close up. *Barry John Murphy, Ireland* **58**

THE CASHEL MAN (IRE) 5 b.g. High Chaparral (IRE) 132 – Hadarama (IRE) 86 (Sinndar (IRE) 134) [2017 102: 18.6m 14g^3 May 27] attractive, good-topped gelding: useful handicapper: third at Goodwood (2 lengths behind Top Tug) in May: stays 2¼m: acts on good to firm and good to soft going: wears headgear: often races in rear: not straightforward. *David Simcock* **99**

THECHAMPAGNESONICE 4 b.f. Compton Place 125 – Extremely Rare (IRE) 82 (Mark of Esteem (IRE) 137) [2017 7.4d 7.1g^4 7.1s^5 p7g t8.6g Nov 20] fifth foal: sister to 5f winner Miss Complex, and half-sister to 8.6f-1¼m winner Heezararity (by Librettist) and 7f (including at 2 yrs) winner Easy Tiger (by Refuse To Bend): dam 5f/6f winner: well held in bumpers: little form on Flat: left Ed de Giles after first start: tried in cheekpieces. *Malcolm Saunders* **–**

THECHILDREN'STRUST (IRE) 2 br.g. (Mar 29) Society Rock (IRE) 126 – Estemaala (IRE) 80 (Cape Cross (IRE) 129) [2017 6g* 6v^3 Oct 4] 37,000F, €24,000 2-y-o: first foal: dam 1¼m-2m winner: fairly useful form: won maiden at Goodwood (by short head from Rebel Streak) in August. *Gary Moore* **84**

THE CLIFF HORSE (IRE) 2 b.f. (Mar 6) Canford Cliffs (IRE) 133 – Ballet School (IRE) (Sadler's Wells (USA) 132) [2017 7m^6 6.9v^2 7g Oct 7] 4,000 2-y-o: sixth foal: half-sister to a winner abroad by Street Sense: dam unraced sister to smart 1¼m winner Musha Merr and closely related to very smart Australian Group 1 2m winner The Offer: fair form: best effort when seventh in minor event at Redcar (3¼ lengths behind Three Saints Bay) final start: will be suited by 1m+: open to further improvement. *Donald McCain* **65 p**

THE COMMENDATORE 4 b.g. Starspangledbanner (AUS) 128 – Donna Giovanna 74 (Mozart (IRE) 131) [2017 87: 6m* t6s 6d^6 6m 7g^4 Oct 13] fairly useful handicapper: won at Doncaster (by ½ length from Jaywalker) in May: stays 7f: acts on polytrack and good to firm going: has worn headgear: front runner/races prominently: temperament under suspicion. *David Barron* **89**

THECORNISHBARRON (IRE) 5 b.g. Bushranger (IRE) 119 – Tripudium (IRE) (Night Shift (USA)) [2017 82: t8g^4 p8g 8.3m 9.1d^5 9.1m^3 p8g 10.1d Oct 24] workmanlike gelding: fair handicapper: stays 1¼m: acts on polytrack, tapeta and firm going: has joined Aytach Sadik. *John Ryan* **71**

THE DALEY EXPRESS (IRE) 3 b.g. Elzaam (AUS) 115 – Seraphina (IRE) 99 (Pips Pride 117) [2017 76: t5.1g^4 5g^2 6d* 6v^6 6s* 6.1s^4 6v^6 5g Oct 18] fairly useful handicapper: won at Ffos Las in July and Goodwood (by ½ length from Jashma) in September: stays 6f: acts on tapeta and soft going. *Ronald Harris* **93**

THE DANCING LORD 8 br.g. Imperial Dancer 123 – Miss Brookie 70 (The West (USA) 107) [2017 68: p10.7g p8g p12g p8g t9.5g^5 7m p10g p12g^{pu} Dec 28] sturdy gelding: fairly useful handicapper at best, lost his way in 2017: left Liam P. Cusack after second start: stayed 1¼m: acted on polytrack, tapeta and good to firm going: often in headgear: wore tongue tie: dead. *Adam West* **61**

THE DETAINEE 4 b.g. Aqlaam 125 – Jakarta Jade (IRE) 103 (Royal Abjar (USA) 121) [2017 60: p12g^3 p11g p12g^2 14m^5 12s 12m* 11.5m* 12s^2 Aug 17] well-made gelding: fair handicapper: won at Chepstow in July and Yarmouth in August: left Jeremy Gask after fifth start: stays 1½m: acts on polytrack, soft and good to firm going: has worn headgear, including last 4 starts: fair form over hurdles. *Neil Mulholland* **71**

THE DUKKERER (IRE) 6 b.m. Footstepsinthesand 120 – Saffron Crocus 83 (Shareef Dancer (USA) 135) [2017 68: f8g t8.6m^6 f8g p10g^4 p10d t8.6g^2 t8.6g* 10g^6 t8.6g^2 10.2m^2 8.2g^3 8.5m 9m^4 t8.6g^6 p10g^5 p10g Oct 12] fair handicapper: won at Wolverhampton (apprentice) in May: stays 1¼m: acts on all-weather, good to firm and good to soft going. *James Given* **67**

THE EAGLE'S NEST (IRE) 3 ch.g. Lope de Vega (IRE) 125 – Follow My Lead 72 (Night Shift (USA)) [2017 t7.1g^3 8v 7m^3 8m^2 8m 8g^4 8v^4 t10.2g* p8s* Dec 17] €130,000F: half-brother to several winners, including smart winner up to 8.6f Graphic (2-y-o 7f winner, by Excellent Art) and 2-y-o 7f winner Ms Brinkleys (by Arcano): dam 1m winner: **84**

fairly useful handicapper: won at Newcastle in October and Chelmsford (by ¾ length from Lagenda) in December: left Richard Fahey after eighth start: stays 1¼m: acts on polytrack, tapeta and good to firm going. *Rae Guest*

THE EMPEROR WITHIN (FR) 2 b.c. (Feb 21) Holy Roman Emperor (IRE) 125 – **58** Watchful (IRE) 94 (Galileo (IRE) 134) [2017 7d p8g Oct 25] modest form: better effort when eighth in minor event at Kempton. *Martin Smith*

THE FEATHERED NEST (IRE) 3 b.f. Dragon Pulse (IRE) 114 – Jorum 76 (Dansili **94** 127) [2017 82p: 6m^{4} 6m^{2} 6m^{3} 6g^{3} 6d* 6d t7.2d Dec 16] fairly useful handicapper: won at Newmarket (by neck from Scorching Heat) in July: stays 7f: acts on all-weather, good to firm and good to soft going: tried in cheekpieces: usually races towards rear. *Richard Fahey*

THE FETTLER (IRE) 2 ch.g. (Apr 6) Rock of Gibraltar (IRE) 133 – Green Empire **–** (IRE) (Second Empire (IRE) 124) [2017 7d^{6} 7s^{5} 7d t8.6g Oct 7] stocky gelding: little form: tried in cheekpieces. *Kevin Frost*

THE FIDDLER 2 b.g. (Mar 18) Big Bad Bob (IRE) 118 – Strings (Unfuwain (USA) 131) **60** [2017 8.2d 8v 8s Oct 19] little impact in minor events. *Chris Wall*

THE FIRM (IRE) 8 b.g. Acclamation 118 – Aspen Falls (IRE) 78 (Elnadim (USA) 128) **60** [2017 74: p7g p7g t8.6g p7s 8m 7d^{3} 8m^{6} 8d Sep 11] modest handicapper: stays 10.5f: acts **a52** on all-weather, good to firm and good to soft going: wears headgear: usually races prominently. *J. R. Jenkins*

THE FOOZLER 4 ch.g. Haafhd 129 – Blades Baby (Bertolini (USA) 125) [2017 12.1g^{6} **–** 9.8m^{5} 10v t12.4d^{6} Dec 16] little impact in maidens. *Peter Niven*

THE GAY CAVALIER 6 b.g. Henrythenavigator (USA) 131 – Dear Daughter 111 **76 §** (Polish Precedent (USA) 131) [2017 85: p10g p12g t12.2g^{4} p10g^{4} t12.2g p10g^{4} 10m 10.1g^{5} 10s p10g* p10s^{4} 8m^{3} 10g 10.1f 7d^{6} 9.9s^{2} 10.1d^{4} 10d^{4} 9.1m^{5} 10.1m^{3} p10g 8d^{6} p10d 10.2d 10.2d p10g^{6} p12g^{3} p10s t9.5g^{6} p10g t9.5d Dec 26] lengthy gelding: fair handicapper: won at Lingfield (amateur) in June: stays 11f: acts on polytrack, tapeta, soft and good to firm going: tried in cheekpieces: wears tongue tie: sometimes slowly away, usually races nearer last than first: unreliable. *John Ryan*

THE GINGER BERRY 7 ch.g. First Trump 118 – Dolly Coughdrop (IRE) 72 (Titus **71** Livius (FR) 115) [2017 72: p12d^{6} p12g^{2} p10g p11d 11.5m^{6} p12g* Sep 5] fair handicapper: won at Kempton in September: stays 1½m: acts on polytrack: wears hood: often races towards rear, usually travels strongly. *Dr Jon Scargill*

THE GINGERBREADMAN 2 b.g. (Mar 10) Misu Bond (IRE) 114 – Accamelia 67 **–** (Shinko Forest (IRE)) [2017 6m t6d 7v 6g Sep 27] little sign of ability. *Chris Fairhurst*

THEGLASGOWWARRIOR 3 b.g. Sir Percy 129 – Sweet Cando (IRE) 72 (Royal **73** Applause 124) [2017 10.3g 10.2m 10g 12f^{2} 12d^{2} 11.6d^{3} 12g^{2} 16g 12.5v^{4} 14d^{5} t12.4d* Dec 16] rather unfurnished gelding: fair handicapper: won at Newcastle in December: left Michael Bell after eighth start: stays 12.5f: acts on tapeta, firm and good to soft going: tried in cheekpieces. *Jim Goldie*

THE GOLDEN CUE 2 ch.g. (Mar 26) Zebedee 113 – Khafayif (USA) 62 (Swain (IRE) **74** 134) [2017 5.1m^{6} 5s^{4} 5.1m^{5} 5d^{3} 5v* 5g 5d Oct 11] angular gelding: fair performer: won nursery at Sandown in August: raced only at 5f: acts on heavy going: front runner/races prominently. *Steph Hollinshead*

THE GRADUATE (IRE) 4 gr.g. Mastercraftsman (IRE) 129 – Ballyvarra (IRE) **83** (Sadler's Wells (USA) 132) [2017 99: 18d 14s Nov 5] good-topped gelding: useful handicapper: below form both starts in 2017: stays 1¾m: acts on good to firm and heavy going: tried in cheekpieces. *A. J. Martin, Ireland*

THE GRAND VISIR 3 b.c. Frankel 147 – Piping (IRE) (Montjeu (IRE) 137) [2017 **101** 11.5m* 11.2m^{6} 12m^{4} 12s* 13.9m^{5} 13.9g Oct 13] €750,000Y: good-topped colt: third foal: half-brother to French 11f/12.5f winner Phedre (by Rock of Gibraltar): dam unraced half-sister to Prix de l'Arc de Triomphe winner Sagamix: useful performer: won maiden at Yarmouth in May and handicap at Newmarket (by ¾ length from Petitioner) in July: stays 1¾m: acts on soft and good to firm going: sometimes in cheekpieces: usually races prominently. *William Haggas*

THE GRAPE ESCAPE (IRE) 3 b.c. Arakan (USA) 123 – Bessichka 70 (Exceed And **115** Excel (AUS) 126) [2017 82p: 8.1d^{3} 8m^{2} 8m 8g* 8v* 8s Oct 21] tall, attractive colt: smart handicapper: won at Sandown (by head from Sharja Bridge) in September and Pontefract (by 2¼ lengths from Me Too Nagasaki) in October: stays 1m: acts on good to firm and heavy going: usually races prominently: sold 42,000 gns, sent to Qatar. *Richard Hannon*

THE GREAT DANDINI (IRE) 2 b.c. (Feb 22) Dandy Man (IRE) 123 – Monivea (IRE) 98 (Fasliyev (USA) 120) [2017 6g 6m^3 6d^4 Sep 12] strong colt: fair form: best effort when third in minor event at Salisbury (½ length behind Rogue) in August: tried in tongue tie. *Seamus Durack* **77**

THE GREAT WALL (USA) 3 b.g. Bernardini (USA) 132 – Music Room (USA) (Unbridled's Song (USA) 125) [2017 7d 6m^2 p7g^4 f7.1g* Dec 29] $17,000Y, €18,000 2-y-o: tall, rather unfurnished gelding: fourth foal: half-brother to winners in USA by Smart Strike and Distorted Humor: dam unraced half-sister to very smart US Grade 1 7f-1¼m winner Music Note and Poule d'Essai des Pouliches winner Musical Chimes: useful form: won maiden at Southwell (by 19 lengths from Riverside Bridge) in December: left M. D. O'Callaghan after third start: stays 7f: open to further improvement. *Michael Appleby* **96 p**

THE GREEDY BOY 4 b.g. Atlantic Sport (USA) 115 – Indian Girl 59 (Erhaab (USA) 127) [2017 55: t9.5m^4 t8.6g t8.6g^4 11.8s^4 12v t12.2g Jun 26] compact gelding: poor maiden: stays 1½m: acts on tapeta and soft going: wears headgear: in tongue tie last 4 starts: front runner/races prominently. *Steve Flook* **49**

THE GREY GATSBY (IRE) 6 gr.h. Mastercraftsman (IRE) 129 – Marie Vison (IRE) 103 (Entrepreneur 123) [2017 122: 10g^4 9d^5 12g^4 10d 12f 9g Oct 9] strong, compact horse: type to carry plenty of condition: high-class performer at best: won Prix du Jockey Club at Chantilly and Irish Champion Stakes at Leopardstown at 3 yrs: just useful form in 2017, fourth in International Stakes at the Curragh and Ballyroan Stakes at Leopardstown: best around 1¼m: acted on firm and good to soft going: often wore headgear later in career: to stand at Haras du Petit Tellier, France, fee €7,000. *D. K. Weld, Ireland* **108**

THE GREY HOBBIT 4 gr.f. Shirocco (GER) 129 – Princess Pivotal 63 (Pivotal 124) [2017 –: f11g^4 Jan 2] well held in 2 maidens. *Ed de Giles* **–**

THE GREY WARRIOR (IRE) 3 gr.g. Mastercraftsman (IRE) 129 – Cranky Spanky (IRE) (Spectrum (IRE) 126) [2017 75p: t8g^3 10m^3 12m^4 May 6] fair form: third in maiden at Redcar in April: stayed 1¼m: dead. *Kevin Ryan* **72**

THE GROOVE 4 b.g. Azamour (IRE) 130 – Dance East 101 (Shamardal (USA) 129) [2017 8.1m^5 10g 10.2v^4 8g* 7.4v^2 7v^2 6s^3 p8g^5 Oct 17] well-made gelding: fair handicapper: won at Salisbury (apprentice) in September: second at Leicester later that month: stays 1m: acts on polytrack and heavy going: tried in tongue tie: races prominently. *Fergal O'Brien* **76**

THE HAPPY HAMMER (IRE) 11 b.g. Acclamation 118 – Emma's Star (ITY) (Darshaan 133) [2017 70: p7g 7m^5 7g^2 7m^4 p7s p8d p8g Oct 5] workmanlike gelding: modest handicapper nowadays: stays 1m: acts on polytrack and good to firm going: has worn headgear: usually races towards rear. *Eugene Stanford* **55**

THE HOODED CLAW (IRE) 6 ch.g. Dandy Man (IRE) 123 – Changari (USA) 90 (Gulch (USA)) [2017 81: t6d 7s^5 5.9d 5d^5 6.1g t6.1g^5 t5.1g t6.1d^5 Dec 16] fairly useful handicapper: well below form in 2017: left Tim Easterby after first start: stays 6f: acts on tapeta, good to firm and heavy going: has worn headgear, including in 2017. *Patrick Morris* **61**

THE HOPPINGS 2 b.f. (Jan 26) Kyllachy 129 – Rosa Bud (Cape Cross (IRE) 129) [2017 6v t6g^6 Oct 19] first foal: dam unraced: modest form: better effort when sixth in minor event at Newcastle (6½ lengths behind Mountain Breath) second start. *John Davies* **51**

THE IRON FACTOR (USA) 3 b.c. The Factor (USA) 126 – I Am Iron Woman (USA) (Any Given Saturday (USA) 128) [2017 9.9m 12s p10g^6 Aug 8] little show in maidens: left David Lanigan after first start: wears tongue tie. *Phil McEntee* **–**

THE JEAN GENIE 3 b.f. Lawman (FR) 121 – Miracle Seeker 104 (Rainbow Quest (USA) 134) [2017 85p: 10g 9.9f^6 10g Jul 8] fairly useful form when second in maiden on debut at 2 yrs, best effort. *Clive Cox* **71**

THE JUGGLER 4 b.g. Archipenko (USA) 127 – Oblige 101 (Robellino (USA) 127) [2017 63: p14g^4 p13.3g^4 p11d^5 12v 11.8g^5 t12.2g^2 p10g* p10g^2 p11g Oct 25] fair handicapper: won at Chelmsford in August: stays 1½m: acts on polytrack, tapeta and heavy going: has worn headgear, including last 4 starts: front runner/races prominently. *William Knight* **66**

THE JULIET ROSE (FR) 4 b.f. Monsun (GER) 124 – Dubai Rose 102 (Dubai Destination (USA) 127) [2017 116: 12.4g^4 11.9d* 12s^4 Oct 21] rangy filly: smart performer: won Prix de Royallieu at Chantilly (for second year running, by short neck from Listen In) in September: in hood, 8¾ lengths fourth to Hydrangea in Fillies' And Mares' Stakes at Ascot final outing: stays 12.5f: acts on heavy going: usually races close up. *N. Clement, France* **109**

THE JUNGLE VIP 2 b.c. (Apr 25) Leroidesanimaux (BRZ) 127 – Alakananda 92 (Hernando (FR) 127) [2017 f7.1g^2 p8g Dec 21] fair form: better effort when second in minor event at Southwell (¾ length behind German Bight) in November: should stay 1m+. *Mark Johnston* **69**

THE KIDDIE KID 2 b.c. (Jun 7) Mazameer (IRE) 107 – Hi Hoh (IRE) (Fayruz 116) [2017 6m 6g 6.1m Jun 19] little sign of ability. *Mick Channon* **–**

THE KING (IRE) 2 ch.c. (Apr 29) Mastercraftsman (IRE) 129 – Catch The Moon (IRE) (Peintre Celebre (USA) 137) [2017 8m^5 8s* Sep 16] 120,000F, 140,000Y: half-brother to several winners, including very smart 6f winner Lightning Moon (by Shamardal) and useful 2-y-o 6f winners Song of My Heart (by Footstepsinthesand) and Catskill Mountain (by One Cool Cat): dam 9f winner: useful form: won maiden at Gowran (by 3¼ lengths from Imaging) in September: will stay further than 1m: will go on improving. *Mrs J. Harrington, Ireland* **97 p**

THE KING'S STEED 4 b.g. Equiano (FR) 127 – King's Siren (IRE) 77 (King's Best (USA) 132) [2017 72: t8s 8g 8.3f^6 8.3g^4 9.9v 8v* t8.6g^2 p10s^3 Dec 15] sturdy gelding: modest handicapper nowadays: won at Ayr in October: left Micky Hammond after seventh start: stays 8.5f: acts on tapeta and heavy going: tried in cheekpieces/tongue tie. *Shaun Lycett* **58**

THE KNOT IS TIED (IRE) 2 b.g. (Mar 13) Casamento (IRE) 118 – Really Polish (USA) (Polish Numbers (USA)) [2017 8g 7d^5 8v Sep 28] lengthy gelding: little impact in minor events. *Tim Easterby* **55**

THE LACEMAKER 3 b.f. Dutch Art 126 – Sospel (Kendor (FR) 122) [2017 74: p7g^3 8.3g 7g^4 6v^5 t7.1s Sep 19] fair maiden: stays 7f: acts on polytrack and good to firm going: tried in blinkers. *Ed Dunlop* **77**

THE LADY RULES 3 ch.f. Native Ruler 119 – Lady Author 39 (Authorized (IRE) 133) [2017 8.3v p12g^4 p10g Sep 26] first foal: dam maiden daughter of useful 1m winner Kelucia: little impact in maidens: modest form over hurdles. *Mrs Ilka Gansera-Leveque* **56**

THE LAMPLIGHTER (FR) 2 b.g. (May 8) Elusive City (USA) 117 – Plume Rouge 104 (Pivotal 124) [2017 7d 6.5d^3 p6.5g^3 8d Oct 28] €20,000Y: half-brother to 3 winners, including useful 7f winner Mean Lae (by Johannesburg), herself dam of Irish 1000 Guineas winner Jet Setting: dam winner up to 7.5f (2-y-o 6f winner): fairly useful form: third in maidens at Maisons-Laffitte and Chantilly: stays 6.5f. *George Baker* **81**

THE LAMPO GENIE 5 b.g. Champs Elysees 124 – Samar Qand 59 (Selkirk (USA) 129) [2017 66§: t13.9m p14g^2 16d May 16] modest handicapper nowadays: stays 2¼m: acts on polytrack, tapeta, good to firm and good to soft going: has worn headgear, including last 4 starts: temperamental. *Johnny Farrelly* **64 §**

THE LAST DEBUTANTE 3 b.f. Henrythenavigator (USA) 131 – Lady Eclair (IRE) 104 (Danehill Dancer (IRE) 117) [2017 65p: t9.5g^5 t9.5m^2 p12g^2 t12.2g^5 12m* Apr 29] fair handicapper: won at Doncaster in April: stays 1½m: acts on polytrack, tapeta and good to firm going. *Mark Johnston* **70**

THE LAST EMPEROR 2 b.c. (Feb 19) Azamour (IRE) 130 – Raskutani (Dansili 127) [2017 7g* 7d^2 8g^5 Aug 25] 230,000Y: fifth foal: half-brother to 3 winners, including smart 1m-13f winner Agent Murphy (by Cape Cross): dam unraced: fairly useful form: won minor event at Yarmouth (by ½ length from Radio Source) in July: best effort when second in similar event at same course (length behind Barford) in August: stays 7f. *Roger Varian* **84**

THE LAST MELON 5 ch.g. Sir Percy 129 – Step Fast (USA) (Giant's Causeway (USA) 132) [2017 10m 12v^6 t12.2g^5 t12.2g^3 p16g t16.5g t14g^6 p13.3s Nov 17] fair maiden: stays 1¾m: acts on tapeta: tried in hood: often races prominently. *James Bennett* **65**

THE LINCOLN LAWYER 2 b.g. (Apr 10) Lawman (FR) 121 – Adventure Seeker (FR) 115 (Bering 136) [2017 8.3g^3 t8g^3 t8.6g^4 Nov 25] fair form: best effort when third in maiden at Nottingham (3¾ lengths behind Come On Tier) on debut. *Mark Johnston* **77**

THELLO 5 b.g. Arcano (IRE) 122 – Silca Destination 65 (Dubai Destination (USA) 127) [2017 76: t10.2g* 10.2m^2 10m^4 t10.2g^5 t8d^6 t8g^2 t8g^6 t8g* Dec 6] fairly useful performer: won minor event at Newcastle in February and handicap at same course (by 3 lengths from Enigmatic) in December: left Garry Moss after first start, Jo Hughes after fourth: stays 1¼m: acts on all-weather and good to firm going: strong traveller. *Jim Goldie* **83**

THE LOCK MASTER (IRE) 10 b.g. Key of Luck (USA) 126 – Pitrizza (IRE) (Machiavellian (USA) 123) [2017 71, a88: f12g^6 f11g^3 t12.2g^6 f12m* f11g^3 f12d^6 f11d^3 12g^5 f12.1g* 11.8d^6 10.2m^6 11.8g 11.5g f12.1g f12.1g^6 f11.1g f11.1g^6 Dec 29] fair handicapper: won at Southwell in February and May: stays 1¾m: acts on polytrack, fibresand and any turf going: wears headgear: often races lazily. *Michael Appleby* **62 a79**

THE LOVE DOCTOR (IRE) 2 b.c. (Mar 11) Elnadim (USA) 128 – Street Kitty (IRE) (Tiger Hill (IRE) 127) [2017 5g^2 5m^4 5.1m^3 6s^6 6m^2 6d^2 6v^5 p7g^5 8.1d^6 t6.1g^2 Sep 23] angular colt: fair maiden: stays 6f: acts on good to firm and good to soft going: tried in visor. *David Evans* **72**

THE LYNCH MAN 4 b.g. Sakhee's Secret 128 – Diliza 65 (Dilum (USA) 115) [2017 73: 8.3m May 19] fair handicapper: well below form only start in 2017: stays 1¼m: acts on tapeta and soft going: wears headgear. *John Quinn* **–**

THE MAGIC PENCIL (IRE) 4 b.g. Dream Ahead (USA) 133 – Kylemore (IRE) (Sadler's Wells (USA) 132) [2017 75: t8.6m t8g^5 t7.1g^5 6m^2 t6g^3 6s Jun 29] fair handicapper: has form at 1¼m, races over much shorter nowadays: acts on polytrack and tapeta: wears headgear: usually leads. *Kevin Ryan* **72**

THE MAJOR 4 b.g. Major Cadeaux 121 – Ballerina Suprema (IRE) 87 (Sadler's Wells (USA) 132) [2017 77: 9.9g^4 10.2d* 10g* Jun 15] fairly useful handicapper: won at Haydock (apprentice) and Newbury (amateur, by ½ length from Zephyros) in June: stays 1¼m: acts on polytrack, good to firm and good to soft going: often races prominently: ran over hurdles later in year for Richard Woollacott. *Michael Bell* **83**

THE MCGREGORNATOR (IRE) 3 b.g. Bushranger (IRE) 119 – Bridal Path 75 (Groom Dancer (USA) 128) [2017 76: 6d^3 6m^2 6d^4 7d* 7g 7v 8.2s Aug 23] fairly useful handicapper: won at Naas (apprentice, by neck from Nothing To Lose) in June: stays 7f: acts on good to firm and heavy going: wears headgear: has worn tongue tie: pulled up on hurdling debut. *A. P. Keatley, Ireland* **85**

THE MUMS 2 b.f. (Apr 23) Holy Roman Emperor (IRE) 125 – Ballyalla 90 (Mind Games 121) [2017 7m 7g 6s* 6.5g^6 p7g p6s^3 p7g^3 Dec 20] 65,000Y: fourth foal: half-sister to useful 5f and (including at 2 yrs) 6f winner Pixeleen (by Pastoral Pursuits): dam, 2-y-o 6f winner, half-sister to smart sprinter (best at 5f) Priceless: fairly useful performer: won minor event at Newbury in August: third in nursery at Lingfield final start: stays 7f: acts on polytrack and soft going: in headgear last 3 starts: front runner/races prominently. *John Gosden* **83**

THE NAME'S PAVER 4 ch.g. Monsieur Bond (IRE) 120 – Pride of Kinloch 80 (Dr Devious (IRE) 127) [2017 68: 7m 7g* t8s 7.2m^2 7f 7d 7.2g^5 Jul 24] fair handicapper: won at Thirsk in April: second at Ayr in May: stays 7f: acts on good to firm and heavy going: has worn headgear. *Noel Wilson* **71**

THE NAUGHTY STEP (IRE) 2 b.g. (Jan 13) Camacho 118 – Echad (IRE) (Kris Kin (USA) 126) [2017 7f 7d 7m 8d Sep 20] well held in minor events: tried in cheekpieces. *Jim Boyle* **–**

THE NAVIGATOR 2 br.g. (Apr 29) Mastercraftsman (IRE) 129 – Blessing (USA) 79 (Pulpit (USA) 117) [2017 8d^3 Oct 20] fifth foal: closely related to 2-y-o 6f winner Mustique (by Danehill Dancer): dam, maiden (stayed 1¼m), half-sister to dam of very smart US Grade 2 1½m winner Redeemed: 14/1, third in minor event at Redcar (4½ lengths behind Stephensons Rocket) in October: open to improvement. *Richard Fahey* **74 p**

THE NAZCA LINES (IRE) 3 ch.g. Fast Company (IRE) 126 – Princess Banu 74 (Oasis Dream 129) [2017 83: 5m^3 6d 5m^2 5m^2 5m* 5d t5d^5 5d^3 5g^5 t6d Sep 29] smallish, lengthy gelding: fairly useful handicapper: won at Carlisle (by head from Intense Romance) in July: stays 6f: acts on good to firm going: wears headgear: sold 7,000 gns in November. *John Quinn* **82**

THE NEW MASTER 4 br.g. New Approach (IRE) 132 – Maziona 89 (Dansili 127) [2017 76: 10g 12d Jun 29] fair form when second in maiden at 3 yrs, standout effort. *David Elsworth* **–**

THE NEW PHARAOH (IRE) 6 b.g. Montjeu (IRE) 137 – Out West (USA) 103 (Gone West (USA)) [2017 86: p11g^6 14g 11.9d^2 11.9s* 11.6g^5 11.8d^4 12.1s^3 16d^2 Oct 27] tall gelding: fairly useful handicapper: won at Doncaster (by ½ length from Prendergast Hill) in July: stays 2m: acts on soft going: usually races nearer last than first: sold 22,000 gns in November to join Laura Morgan. *Chris Wall* **86**

THE NIGHT BEFORE 3 b.g. Equiano (FR) 127 – Morning After 84 (Emperor Jones (USA) 119) [2017 53: 6g^5 5g^6 5m^2 5m^2 Sep 8] fair maiden: best form at 5f: acts on good to firm going: front runner/races prominently. *Robert Cowell* **67**

THE NIGHT KING 2 b.g. (Feb 2) Arcano (IRE) 122 – Semplicita (IRE) (In The Wings 128) [2017 7.4s 8.1g^5 8d t8.6g Oct 7] modest form: best effort at 1m. *Mick Channon* **65**

THEOBALD (IRE) 2 ch.c. (May 19) Teofilo (IRE) 126 – Sanaara (USA) (Anabaa (USA) 130) [2017 8g* 6.3f^2 7g^2 8d 7m 8d p8g* Dec 22] sturdy colt: fourth foal: dam unraced: useful performer: won maiden at Leopardstown in June and minor event at Dundalk in December: second in Tyros Stakes at Leopardstown (1¾ lengths behind The Pentagon) in July: stays 1m: acts on polytrack and firm going: tried in cheekpieces: front runner/races prominently. *J. S. Bolger, Ireland* **100**

THEODORICO (IRE) 4 b.g. Teofilo (IRE) 126 – Yes Oh Yes (USA) (Gone West (USA)) [2017 88: p8g 10.4m 7g* 7g* 7m 7m^4 8m 7s^6 7d* 7d^5 7s^6 7d^3 7d 7.2v^4 Oct 16] useful handicapper: won at Wetherby/York (amateur) in May and Thirsk (by neck from Burnt Sugar) in August: stays 1m: acts on soft going: tried in cheekpieces: usually races prominently. *David Loughnane* **97**

THEOS LOLLY (IRE) 4 b.g. Kodiac 112 – Aluana (IRE) 67 (Alzao (USA) 117) [2017 87: 10g^5 p10g t10.2g^2 12m* t12.4s 10.3g^2 13.4d^5 12g^5 12m^4 Sep 4] angular gelding: fairly useful handicapper: won at Ripon (by 2 lengths from Chant) in June: second at Chester (¾ length behind Storm King) in July: barely stays 13f: acts on polytrack, tapeta, soft and good to firm going: sold 11,000 gns in October. *Richard Fahey* **88** **a78**

THE OTMOOR POET 4 b.g. Yeats (IRE) 128 – Kristalette (IRE) 95 (Leporello (IRE) 118) [2017 85: 11.4m^2 13.4g p11g^5 Jun 28] lengthy gelding: fairly useful maiden handicapper: second at Windsor (short head behind Spinners Ball) in May: stays 1½m: acts on polytrack, good to firm and good to soft going: in cheekpieces in 2017: modest maiden hurdler. *Alex Hales* **84**

THE PENTAGON (IRE) 2 b.c. (Apr 2) Galileo (IRE) 134 – Vadawina (IRE) 118 (Unfuwain (USA) 131) [2017 7v^6 7f* 7g* 8d^3 Oct 28] **114 p**

Maidens are not normally won with the quality of performance The Pentagon put up to win the opener on Irish Oaks day at the Curragh in July. He simply routed his dozen rivals from the front, storming clear to win by eight and a half lengths. It was a visually striking display but there was much more to it than that. More impressive still was that he ran to a smart level of form, exceptional by maiden standards and one that wouldn't have been out of place in pattern company. What gave The Pentagon's performance substance was that both placed horses had shown fairly useful form already. Runner-up Medal of Honor had finished second to The Pentagon's stable-companion Rostropovich at Gowran on his previous start, while the third, Bond Street, sent off favourite and also trained by Aidan O'Brien, had finished fifth last time out to yet another Ballydoyle colt, Gustav Klimt, who had himself shown useful form to win an above-average maiden over the same course and distance. Gustav Klimt followed up in the Superlative Stakes at Newmarket later on Irish Oaks day under Ryan Moore. In the absence of Ballydoyle's number one jockey at the Curragh, Bond Street was ridden by Seamus Heffernan and, with Donnacha O'Brien partnering Medal of Honor for his brother Joseph, it was their sister Ana who was in the saddle on The Pentagon (Wayne Lordan took the ride on the stable's third runner, newcomer Mendelssohn, who finished down the field but was to make much more of a name for himself later in the year). The Pentagon was Miss O'Brien's twenty-second winner of the year during which the 3-lb claimer had had rides in the Derby and Irish Derby on The Anvil. But just three days after The Pentagon's win, her season was brought to an abrupt end when she suffered serious injuries in a fall at Killarney from Druids Cross, trained by her brother Joseph. Sustaining fractured vertebrae in her back and neck, it was not until October that she was released from hospital to continue her recuperation at home.

Like a number of his stable companions, The Pentagon improved from his debut to win at the second time of asking, though in his case the progress he made was huge, the vastly different conditions he encountered in his two maidens a possible factor. Along with Bond Street, who started favourite on that first occasion too, The Pentagon made his debut over the same course and distance the previous month on heavy ground but was beaten nearly twenty lengths into sixth (Bond Street was next) by Verbal Dexterity whose winning margin was even wider than The Pentagon's, though that horse's win came on firm going. Twelve days after getting off the mark, The Pentagon became his stable's fourth consecutive winner of the Japan Racing Association Tyros Stakes at Leopardstown, following in the footsteps of Gleneagles, Deauville and, most recently, Churchill. Without needing to run up to the same form as in his maiden, The Pentagon won by a length and three quarters under Moore, looking better the further he went in beating Verbal Dexterity's stable-companion Theobald. The Pentagon was ante-post favourite for the Derby by now, and at single figures in places, though by the time he was next seen out, fully three months later, he had lost that position to stable-companion Saxon Warrior, winner of both his starts in the interim, including the Beresford Stakes. When the pair lined up for the Racing Post Trophy, Saxon Warrior was the only Ballydoyle runner the market wanted to know, sent off the 13/8 favourite as Moore's chosen mount, with Heffernan taking over on 10/1-shot The Pentagon. The Pentagon proved no match for Saxon Warrior, or for the neck runner-up Roaring Lion, but he shaped nicely behind them under a patient ride and was gaining on both in the closing stages, finishing two and a half lengths behind the runner-up and giving the firm impression that he is a first-rate Derby prospect. This time, he had Verbal Dexterity behind him in fourth.

The Pentagon (IRE) (b.c. 2015)	Galileo (IRE) (b 1998)	Sadler's Wells (b 1981)	Northern Dancer
			Fairy Bridge
		Urban Sea (ch 1989)	Miswaki
			Allegretta
	Vadawina (IRE) (b 2002)	Unfuwain (b 1985)	Northern Dancer
			Height of Fashion
		Vadaza (b 1997)	Zafonic
			Vadlamixa

Talk of the Derby is backed up by The Pentagon's pedigree. Unlike many by Galileo, who is more often mated with mares from speedier backgrounds nowadays, The Pentagon comes from a family of middle-distance performers and smart ones at that. His dam Vadawina, by stamina influence Unfuwain, started favourite for the Prix de Diane after winning all three of her previous starts, successful on her debut over a mile and a half before following up in the Prix Cleopatre and Prix Saint-Alary.

Mr D. Smith, Mrs John Magnier and Mr M. Tabor's "The Pentagon"

However, at Chantilly she could manage only fourth behind Divine Proportions, after which she was found to have fractured her near-hind pastern which ended her racing career. Vadawina produced four winners for the Aga Khan at stud, three of whom proved at least useful, though, being from a family with numerous representatives in the Aga's broodmare band, she was moved on as an eleven-year-old at Deauville at the end of 2013 when she made €600,000. Vadawina's earlier winners were: Vadamar (by Dalakhani), who proved a smart stayer in France after finishing seventh in Pour Moi's Derby; Vaderana (by Monsun), who won a maiden over eleven and a half furlongs; the lightly-raced but useful filly Vedouma (also by Dalakhani), who won a listed race at Chantilly at two before being placed on both her starts in pattern races at three without getting the chance to run over trips that should have suited; and Vedevani (by Dubawi), whose only win came in a newcomers race at two, although he made into a smart colt, finishing third to Talismanic in a mile and a half listed race before acting as pacemaker for his owner's Derby winner Harzand in the 2016 Arc. Vadawina had been sold in foal to Redoute's Choice; the colt she was carrying, named Valcartier, was an impressive winner of a maiden at Nottingham in April for John Gosden and Godolphin, and showed useful form when second in a handicap at Windsor over a mile and a quarter on his next start.

Vadawina, a daughter of the useful French mile and a quarter winner Vadaza, had been among the horses acquired when the Aga Khan purchased the bloodstock empire of the late Jean-Luc Lagardere in 2005. The same year, Valixir, a four-year-old half-brother to Vadawina's useful dam Vadaza, a mile and a quarter winner in France, became one of Europe's top milers, winning the Queen Anne Stakes after an earlier Group 1 success in the Prix d'Ispahan. However, Valixir had been campaigned as a mile and a half performer at three, finishing third in the Prix du Jockey Club (the final running of the race over that trip) and winning the Prix Niel. Other recent Group 1 winners from the family include Vadawina's half-sister Vazira, who was awarded the Prix Saint-Alary, and Prix du Moulin winner Vadamos, who was out of a half-sister to Valixir and whose essay in last year's Annual gives further details of this prolific family. Buying into it through the purchase of Vadawina has already paid dividends for Barronstown Stud which is owned by close associates of Coolmore, David and Diane Nagle; Valcartier had been sold for €950,000 as a yearling, and they sold a yearling sister to The Pentagon at Newmarket in October for 1,550,000 guineas.

The Pentagon is a rangy colt who looks just the sort to do better at three over middle distances. As such, he seems much more likely to be campaigned in a Derby trial or two in the spring rather than take in the Guineas which looks to be the route being mapped out for ante-post Epsom favourite Saxon Warrior. The Pentagon will stay at least a mile and a half in due course and he acts on firm and good to soft going—it would be harsh to judge his effectiveness on heavy ground on the evidence of his debut effort, though it is something to bear in mind if he does encounter similar conditions again (his dam won on soft ground on her debut but ran her best race on good to firm). *Aidan O'Brien, Ireland*

THE PERFECT SHOW 4 ch.g. Showcasing 117 – Nizhoni (USA) 65 (Mineshaft (USA) 132) [2017 60: 6g p6g t5.1g t6.1g 6.1m 7.1g 5s 7g Oct 17] maiden, no form in 2017: has worn headgear, including last 5 starts: often starts slowly. *Milton Bradley* **–**

THE QUARTERJACK 8 b.g. Haafhd 129 – Caressed 92 (Medicean 128) [2017 61: t16.5g p15.8g^6 11.7f^4 16d 13f^6 May 26] leggy gelding: modest handicapper: stays 17f: acts on polytrack, fibresand and any turf going: has worn cheekpieces. *Ron Hodges* **56**

THE RAVEN MASTER (IRE) 3 b.g. Raven's Pass (USA) 133 – Rainbow Desert (USA) 86 (Dynaformer (USA)) [2017 p8g^5 p8g^6 p8g p12g^3 9.9g^3 May 16] fair maiden: best effort at 1½m: acts on polytrack: sometimes in hood: winner over hurdles for Dan Skelton. *Michael Bell* **69**

THE REEL WAY (GR) 6 br.m. Reel Buddy (USA) 118 – Nephetriti Way (IRE) 92 (Docksider (USA) 124) [2017 53: p7d p6g Feb 9] tall, narrow mare: modest maiden: below form both starts in 2017: stays 7f: best form on good going. *Patrick Chamings* **–**

THE RESDEV WAY 4 b.g. Multiplex 114 – Lady Duxyana 54 (Most Welcome 131) [2017 52+, a86: 12g t10.2g 12.1g^{6} 12.1s Oct 10] fairly useful handicapper at best, out of form in 2017: left Richard Whitaker after first start, David O'Meara after third: often races freely. *Philip Kirby* **–**

THE REVENANT 2 ch.c. (Apr 20) Dubawi (IRE) 129 – Hazel Lavery (IRE) 113 (Excellent Art 125) [2017 8g* 8.5v^{3} Oct 1] second foal: dam winner up to 1½m (2-y-o 7f winner) who stayed 14.6f: fairly useful form: won minor event at Haydock (by ¾ length from Global Conqueror) in September: third in similar event at Epsom (2 lengths behind Dee Ex Bee) 3 weeks later: bred to be suited by at least 1¼m: remains open to improvement. *Hugo Palmer* **92 p**

THE RIGHT CHOICE (IRE) 2 ch.g. (Mar 24) Choisir (AUS) 126 – Expedience (USA) 74 (With Approval (CAN)) [2017 5g^{4} 6d^{3} 6f 6m^{3} Jul 15] fair form: stays 6f: temperament under suspicion. *Richard Fahey* **69**

THE RIGHT MAN 5 br.g. Lope de Vega (IRE) 125 – Three Owls (IRE) 79 (Warning 136) [2017 116: 6g^{3} 6d* 6m 6.5g 6d* 6g Dec 10] useful-looking gelding: smart performer: won Al Quoz Sprint at Meydan (by nose from Long On Value) in March and Prix de Seine-et-Oise at Maisons-Laffitte (for second successive year, beat Gold Vibe 1¾ lengths) in November: below form otherwise, including in Diamond Jubilee Stakes at Royal Ascot and Hong Kong Sprint at Sha Tin: stays 6.5f: acts on good to soft going. *D. Guillemin, France* **119**

THERTHAAR 4 b.g. Kyllachy 129 – Red Tiara (USA) 60 (Mr Prospector (USA)) [2017 80p: t9.5g^{2} 8.3g^{2} 10.2f^{2} t10.2s* 11.9m p11g* Sep 9] workmanlike gelding: fairly useful handicapper: won at Newcastle in June and Kempton (by head from Pioneertown) in September: stays 11f: acts on polytrack, tapeta and firm going: front runner/races prominently. *Ismail Mohammed* **81 a89**

THE SALMON MAN 5 b.g. Showcasing 117 – Donna Vita 85 (Vettori (IRE) 119) [2017 83: 8.1m^{6} 12f^{5} 11.5m 11.6m^{5} p10s^{pu} Nov 17] compact gelding: fairly useful maiden handicapper at best: largely out of sorts in 2017: stays 1¼m: acts on polytrack and good to soft going: has worn headgear: usually slowly away: ungenuine. *Brendan Powell* **72 §**

THE SECRETS OUT 3 bl.g. Sakhee's Secret 128 – Brooksby 77 (Diktat 126) [2017 56: p8g p7g 7m^{6} 11.4m* 11.6d^{2} 11.4m^{2} 14s^{4} 14d^{2} 11.4m^{4} Aug 26] rather leggy gelding: modest handicapper: won at Windsor in June: stays 1¾m: acts on polytrack, good to firm and good to soft going: wears hood: front runner/races prominently. *Luke Dace* **64**

THE SKY IS BLAZING (IRE) 3 b.f. Sea The Stars (IRE) 140 – Mamonta 65 (Fantastic Light (USA) 134) [2017 t8d* 11.6d^{3} 10.3g^{4} 12m Jun 22] €160,000F, 240,000Y: leggy filly: sixth foal: sister to smart winner up to 1¾m Endless Time (2-y-o 1m winner) and half-sister to winner up to 1¾m Marhaba Malyoon (2-y-o 1¼m winner, by Tiger Hill): dam maiden (stayed 2m): useful form: won maiden at Newcastle in March: in cheekpieces, 6¾ lengths eighth to Coronet in Ribblesdale Stakes at Royal Ascot final start: should be suited by 1½m+: sent to France. *William Haggas* **95**

THESME 5 b.m. Exceed And Excel (AUS) 126 – Final Dynasty 104 (Komaite (USA)) [2017 109: 5m 5f 5m^{3} 5.4d^{3} 5d^{5} 5.2m 5s Oct 9] lengthy mare: useful performer: standout 2017 effort when third in handicap at York (1½ lengths behind Desert Law) in August: stays 5.5f: acts on good to firm and good to soft going: usually leads, tends to find little. *Nigel Tinkler* **108**

THE SPECIAL ONE (IRE) 4 br.f. Cape Cross (IRE) 129 – Capote West (USA) (Capote (USA)) [2017 64: t8.6g p8g^{3} p8m 7m^{4} 7m^{6} 7.4g* 7m* 8s^{6} 7d* 8s^{4} p7g^{3} p7g^{3} Dec 28] fair handicapper: won at Ffos Las in July, and Brighton in August and September: stays 1m: acts on polytrack, good to firm and good to soft going: has worn hood: usually tongue tied in 2017: usually races nearer last than first. *Ali Stronge* **70**

THE STALKING MOON (IRE) 3 b.f. Arcano (IRE) 122 – Cornakill (USA) 97 (Stormin Fever (USA) 116) [2017 77: 6g^{2} 6g^{4} 7.4d^{3} 6.9s^{4} 7m* 7g 7.2d* 7.2m^{6} 7.2m^{4} 7.4v t8g Oct 19] angular filly: fairly useful handicapper: won at Catterick in July and Musselburgh (by 1¼ lengths from Roaring Forties) in August: stays 7.5f: acts on good to firm and good to soft going. *John Quinn* **84**

THE STATESMAN 3 b.g. Zoffany (IRE) 121 – Chelsey Jayne (IRE) 57 (Galileo (IRE) 134) [2017 83: 8d^{3} 9m* 10.3m 8g^{6} 10.2g^{3} 9.9g^{2} 9.9d* 10d* Sep 23] useful handicapper: won at Sandown in June and September, and Newmarket (by 2½ lengths from First Nation) later in September: stays 10.5f: acts on polytrack, tapeta, good to firm and heavy going: sold 310,000 gns in October. *Ian Williams* **103**

THE TAJ MAHAL see Taj Mahal

Diamond Jubilee Stakes, Royal Ascot—
The Tin Man gains a second Group 1 win at the track, staying on strongly under firm driving to beat Tasleet (striped cap) and Limato (white cap); the winner hangs left and hampers the placed horses close home, but the placings remain unaltered after a stewards' inquiry

THE TARTAN SPARTAN (IRE) 4 ch.c. The Carbon Unit (USA) 106 – The Real Thing (IRE) 84 (Traditionally (USA) 117) [2017 100: 14g^{3} 14.1m* 13.9g^{5} 14.9d^{5} 14d* 13.3d 13.4g 14s Sep 10] good-topped colt: useful performer: won handicap at Salisbury (by 1½ lengths from Sunblazer) in April and listed race at Down Royal (by 1½ lengths from Twilight Payment) in July: stays 2m: acts on good to firm and heavy going: has joined S. Seemar in UAE. *John Patrick Shanahan, Ireland* **107**

THE THROSTLES 2 b.g. (Feb 8) Poet's Voice 126 – Stylish Dream (USA) 66 (Elusive Quality (USA)) [2017 t7.2g^{4} 6g^{3} t7.2g* 7v t8.6g^{6} Oct 21] tall gelding: fair performer: won minor event at Wolverhampton in August: stays 8.5f: acts on tapeta: usually races prominently. *Kevin Frost* **74**

THE TICHBORNE (IRE) 9 b.g. Shinko Forest (IRE) – Brunswick (Warning 136) [2017 74: t7.1g Jan 21] strong gelding: fair handicapper: below form only outing in 2017: stays 8.5f: acts on polytrack, tapeta, soft and good to firm going: wears headgear. *Patrick Morris* **61**

THE TIN MAN 5 b.g. Equiano (FR) 127 – Persario 96 (Bishop of Cashel 122) [2017 126: 6s^{5} 6m* 6g 6s^{3} 6s^{5} Oct 21] robust gelding: high-class performer: won Diamond Jubilee Stakes at Royal Ascot (by neck from Tasleet) in June: third in Sprint Cup at Haydock (5½ lengths behind Harry Angel) in September: raced only at 6f: acts on soft and good to firm going: waited with: sent to Hong Kong to contest Sprint, but missed race after developing a fever. *James Fanshawe* **125**

THETRIOANDME (IRE) 3 b.g. Tagula (IRE) 116 – Peninsula Girl (IRE) 76 (Cape Cross (IRE) 129) [2017 71: p7g^{4} Jan 28] fair form when third in maiden at 2 yrs, best effort. *John Best* **58**

THE TWISLER 5 b.g. Motivator 131 – Panna 106 (Polish Precedent (USA) 131) [2017 108d: p12g p14d 12d^{6} 14g^{3} 14.2g^{3} Aug 25] rather leggy gelding: fairly useful handicapper nowadays: third at Nottingham (3¾ lengths behind Melinoe) in August: left Roger Ingram after second start: stays 2m: acts on polytrack and any turf going: in cheekpieces last 2 starts: fair form over hurdles. *Neil Mulholland* **85**

THE WAGON WHEEL (IRE) 3 b.f. Acclamation 118 – Bahati (IRE) 99 (Intikhab (USA) 135) [2017 95p: 6m^{6} 7g 6m^{2} 6.1g* 6d 6g 5g^{3} 5s^{6} 6m Oct 14] angular filly: useful handicapper: won at Chester (by 3 lengths from Avon Breeze) in July: third in listed race at Beverley (length behind Take Cover) in September: stays 6f: acts on firm going: wears blinkers. *Richard Fahey* **104**

THE WARRIOR (IRE) 5 b.g. Exceed And Excel (AUS) 126 – Aymara 85 (Darshaan 133) [2017 98: p7g^{3} p8g^{2} p8g* 8m^{4} p8f^{5} 7f^{3} 7m 7m^{2} 7g^{5} 8m 7v 7g^{4} p8d^{4} p8g^{2} 8g^{4} p8g^{2} Oct 14] strong gelding: useful handicapper: won at Kempton (by ½ length from Ballard Down) **99**

in March: second at same course (head behind Reach High) final start: stays 1m: acts on polytrack and any turf going: has worn headgear, including in 2017: tried in tongue tie: races towards rear: hard to win with. *Amanda Perrett*

THE WAY YOU DANCE (IRE) 5 b.g. Thewayyouare (USA) 117 – Beautiful Dancer (IRE) 50 (Danehill Dancer (IRE) 117) [2017 74: p12g 11.2s³ t12.2g p16g p16g⁴ Oct 12] compact gelding: fair handicapper: stays 2m: acts on polytrack, tapeta and good to firm going: wears headgear: quirky: fair hurdler. *Neil Mulholland* **70**

THE WEE CHIEF (IRE) 11 ch.g. King Charlemagne (USA) 120 – La Belle Clare (IRE) 61 (Paris House 123) [2017 63§: p5f⁶ Mar 4] lengthy, rather sparely-made gelding: modest handicapper: stays 6f: acts on polytrack and good to firm going: has worn headgear/tongue tie: often races towards rear: one to treat with caution (finds little/carries head high). *Jimmy Fox* **49 §**

THEWESTWALIAN (USA) 9 b.g. Stormy Atlantic (USA) – Skies of Blue (USA) (Ogygian (USA)) [2017 6m 5.7m² 6m 5.7f Jun 17] modest handicapper: usually races over sprint trips nowadays: acts on polytrack and good to firm going: has worn hood. *Peter Hiatt* **61**

THE WIRE FLYER 2 b.g. (Feb 19) Champs Elysees 124 – Good Morning Star (IRE) 105 (Shirocco (GER) 129) [2017 t9.5g Dec 18] 100/1, well held in minor event at Wolverhampton. *Amy Murphy* **–**

THE YANK 8 b.g. Trade Fair 124 – Silver Gyre (IRE) 65 (Silver Hawk (USA) 123) [2017 –: 12g Apr 2] tall gelding: fair handicapper at best: very lightly raced and little impact on Flat since 2015: stays 16.5f: acts on polytrack and tapeta: tried in hood/tongue tie: fair chaser. *David Bridgwater* **–**

THEYDON GIRLS 4 b.f. Poet's Voice 126 – Match Point (Unfuwain (USA) 131) [2017 –: p13.3g 10.1s* 10.1g³ 11.8g Jul 20] modest handicapper: won at Yarmouth in June: best effort at 1¼m: acts on soft going: often races freely. *Peter Charalambous* **60**

THEYDON GREY 4 gr.g. Champs Elysees 124 – Cheerfully 67 (Sadler's Wells (USA) 132) [2017 96: 10.1g⁴ 11.9s⁴ 11.9g* 13.9m* 16.3m* 14m⁵ 14.1d Sep 21] lengthy gelding: useful handicapper: won at York in May, June and July (by neck from Byron Flyer): stays 16.5f: acts on polytrack, tapeta and good to firm going: front runner/races prominently: has bled: sold 23,000 gns, sent to USA. *William Haggas* **98**

THE YELLOW BUS 4 b.f. Zoffany (IRE) 121 – Caribbean Queen (IRE) (Celtic Swing 138) [2017 77: t7.1g⁵ p7g⁵ 7m⁴ t7.2g* 8m⁴ p8g⁵ p8g 10d p10d⁶ p7g f8.1g Dec 22] third foal: half-sister to 2-y-o 7f winner Lady Pastrana (by Key of Luck): dam unraced: fairly useful handicapper: won at Wolverhampton (by ¾ length from Energia Flavio) in July: left Michael Wigham after third start, John Butler after sixth: stays 1m: acts on polytrack, tapeta and good to firm going: tried in cheekpieces. *Daniel Steele* **80**

THIKRIYAAT (IRE) 4 b.g. Azamour (IRE) 130 – Malaspina (IRE) (Whipper (USA) 126) [2017 117: 7.9d 7.9m³ 7g 10s⁴ Jul 22] lengthy, attractive gelding: smart performer: standout 2017 effort when third in listed race at York (¾ length behind Arabian Hope) in June: stays 1m: acts on polytrack, good to firm and good to soft going: tried in cheekpieces: usually races towards rear. *Sir Michael Stoute* **111**

THINGS HAPPEN 3 ch.g. Captain Gerrard (IRE) 113 – Aquasulis (IRE) 76 (Titus Livius (FR) 115) [2017 73: f6g² f6g² t7.1m⁵ t6d⁵ t9.5g* p8g⁵ 8.3m Apr 10] fair handicapper: won at Wolverhampton in February: stays 9.5f: acts on all-weather and good to soft going: has worn visor, including last 3 starts: front runner/races prominently. *David Evans* **73**

THINK FASHION (IRE) 3 b.f. So You Think (NZ) 133 – Passionforfashion (IRE) 60 (Fasliyev (USA) 120) [2017 84p: 7m 6d³ 5.1d³ 6.1m* 6v 5.1s⁵ Aug 17] useful-looking filly: fairly useful performer: won maiden at Windsor in June: stays 7f: acts on good to firm going: tried in cheekpieces: often races freely. *Brian Meehan* **83**

THINK SO (IRE) 3 b.g. So You Think (NZ) 133 – Mabalane (IRE) (Danehill (USA) 126) [2017 –: 11.6g 9.9g 12g Jul 17] little form. *Mark Johnston* **–**

THIRD TIME LUCKY (IRE) 5 gr.g. Clodovil (IRE) 116 – Speckled Hen (IRE) 60 (Titus Livius (FR) 115) [2017 111: p8g⁴ t8.6g* p8f³ 8g p10g⁵ p8g t9.5g p8g³ Dec 31] workmanlike gelding: useful performer: won minor event at Wolverhampton (by neck from Mythical Madness) in February: third in handicap at Lingfield (1½ lengths behind My Target) in March: stays 9.5f: acts on polytrack, tapeta, firm and soft going: sometimes in hood in 2017: often races towards rear/travels strongly. *Richard Fahey* **106**

THIS GIRL 2 b.f. (May 9) Nathaniel (IRE) 129 – Fibou (USA) (Seeking The Gold (USA)) **88 p**
[2017 6v* Sep 29] 12,000Y: half-sister to several winners, including smart UAE 6f-9.5f winner Faulkner and 2-y-o 6f winner Finoon (both by Pivotal): dam ran once: 20/1, won maiden at Haydock (by 1¾ lengths from Maybride) on debut: will be suited by 7f+: should progress. *Tom Dascombe*

THISTIMELASTYEAR 2 b.f. (Feb 19) Cacique (IRE) 124 – Despatch 52 (Nayef (USA) 129) [2017 p7g^{6} t7.2g p8g^{3} Dec 20] second foal: dam lightly-raced half-sister to smart performer up to 11f Lay Time and King Edward VII Stakes winner Plea Bargain: modest form: best effort when third in minor event at Lingfield (7¾ lengths behind Three Weeks) final start. *Philip Hide* **54**

THISTIMENEXTYEAR 3 gr.g. New Approach (IRE) 132 – Scarlet Empire (IRE) (Red Ransom (USA)) [2017 9.8g^{4} p12d 11.6v* 14v^{4} t12.2g Nov 29] 95,000F, 70,000Y: fourth foal: half-brother to useful 9f-10.4f winner Danchai (by Authorized): dam unraced close relative to 1000 Guineas winner Sky Lantern: fairly useful performer: won maiden at Lingfield (by 1¾ lengths from Normandie Attack) in July: best effort at 11.5f: acts on heavy going: sometimes slowly away. *Richard Spencer* **84**

THOMAS BLOSSOM (IRE) 7 b.g. Dylan Thomas (IRE) 132 – Woman Secret (IRE) (Sadler's Wells (USA) 132) [2017 71: p13g^{3} p16g^{2} 16.2m^{4} 14.1m May 24] fair handicapper: stays 2m: acts on polytrack, tapeta and soft going: sometimes wears headgear: wears tongue tie. *Ali Stronge* **74**

THOMAS CRANMER (USA) 3 b.g. Hard Spun (USA) 124 – House of Grace (USA) (Limehouse (USA) 119) [2017 88p: f7d^{3} 7.1m* 7.2g^{5} 8m* 7g 8m 8d^{6} 7s^{5} p8g 7m^{6} 7.2m^{6} 7.1s^{6} t8g 7d Oct 28] close-coupled gelding: fairly useful handicapper: won at Musselburgh in May (by neck from Atteq) and June (by 1½ lengths from The Eagle's Nest): stays 1m: acts on tapeta and good to firm going: often races prominently: sold 16,000 gns in October to join Tina Jackson. *Mark Johnston* **94**

THOMAS CROWN (IRE) 3 b.g. Helmet (AUS) 127 – Picture of Lily 65 (Medicean 128) [2017 –: 8.5m^{5} 7g^{6} 8d 8f 9.9m^{5} 11.2g 16.1d 12.1s 12d 16g^{5} Aug 29] modest maiden handicapper: stays 8.5f: acts on good to firm going: sometimes in cheekpieces. *Roger Fell* **56**

THOMAS HOBSON 7 b.g. Halling (USA) 133 – La Spezia (IRE) 94 (Danehill Dancer (IRE) 117) [2017 20f* 21.6m^{2} 16.3g 17.9g^{2} 15.9g^{6} Nov 7] lengthy gelding: smart performer: won Ascot Stakes (Handicap) at Royal Ascot (by 6 lengths from Endless Acres) in June: second in Queen Alexandra Stakes on same course (beaten 1¼ lengths by Oriental **117**

Ascot Stakes (Handicap), Royal Ascot—Thomas Hobson wins well on his first start on the Flat since October 2013, defying a BHA mark of 100 as he beats Endless Acres and Who Dares Wins

Fox) 4 days later and Doncaster Cup (1½ lengths behind Desert Skyline) in September: sixth to Rekindling in Melbourne Cup (Handicap) at Flemington final outing: stays 2½m: acts on any turf going: smart hurdler. *W. P. Mullins, Ireland*

THORNABY NASH 6 br.g. Kheleyf (USA) 116 – Mistress Twister 83 (Pivotal 124) **68**
[2017 70: t8s^5 8m^2 8.5d^4 8m 7.4d^6 8g 7g^5 7.8d* 7.8v^4 t8s^4 t8d t8d^4 Nov 10] fair handicapper: won at Carlisle in August: stays 1m: acts on tapeta, soft and good to firm going: wears headgear: tried in tongue tie: races prominently: temperament under suspicion. *Karen Tutty*

THORNABY PRINCESS 6 b.m. Camacho 118 – Ingleby Princess 78 (Bold Edge 123) **52**
[2017 59: 5m^3 5g^5 5m 5g^4 5m 5m 5m^3 t5g^4 t5d Sep 29] modest handicapper: stays 6f: acts on tapeta, firm and good to soft going: wears cheekpieces: often races close up. *Colin Teague*

THORNTON 3 b.g. Mayson 124 – Cardrona 66 (Selkirk (USA) 129) [2017 62p: 8v^2 t7.1g **77**
8g^5 8d Aug 5] fair maiden: stays 1m: acts on heavy going: usually races prominently. *Michael Dods*

THORNTON FRANK 3 b.g. Misu Bond (IRE) 114 – Byton 82 (Byron 117) [2017 –: t8g **–**
f6.1g Dec 19] little sign of ability. *Brian Rothwell*

THORNTON MARY 3 b.f. Mawatheeq (USA) 126 – Bezant (IRE) 51 (Zamindar (USA) **–**
116) [2017 –: 7g 10m 9.9m 7m 12d 12g Aug 15] little form. *Brian Rothwell*

THORNTOUN CARE 6 b.g. Rail Link 132 – Thorntoun Piccolo 64 (Groom Dancer **80**
(USA) 128) [2017 t12.4d^6 t12.4g^6 t16.3d^6 t12.2g t12.2g t12.2g* t12.2g^4 14m^4 12.5g 13.1m^4 12.1m^2 11.2g* 12s^2 11.2s^4 12.5m* 11.2d^2 11.6g^2 11.8v Sep 29] fairly useful handicapper: won at Wolverhampton in April, Carlisle in July and Musselburgh in August: second at Haydock (amateur, nose behind Take Two) in September: stays 1¾m: acts on tapeta, soft and good to firm going: wears headgear: races towards rear, often travels strongly. *Iain Jardine*

THORNTOUN LADY (USA) 7 b.m. Henrythenavigator (USA) 131 – Valery Lady **63**
(ARG) (Roy (USA)) [2017 72: t5g t6g^5 t6d^5 t5g 6m^4 5m^6 7.2s t7.2g t6.1m* Oct 31] modest handicapper: won at Wolverhampton in October: stays 1m, effective at much shorter: acts on tapeta, firm and good to soft going: tried in cheekpieces: usually races in rear. *Jim Goldie*

THOU SWELL (IRE) 5 b.g. Tiznow (USA) 133 – Kamarinskaya (USA) 105 (Storm Cat **62**
(USA)) [2017 67: f14g p15.8g^6 f12g* f12g^3 t12.2g^6 f11g t8.6g 11.9v 11.5m 10.2g f12.1g Aug 28] modest handicapper: won at Southwell in February: stays 1½m: acts on polytrack and fibresand: has worn headgear, including last 5 starts. *Shaun Harris*

THRAVE 2 b.c. (Mar 28) Sir Percy 129 – Feis Ceoil (IRE) 86 (Key of Luck (USA) 126) **95 p**
[2017 7m^2 7d* Sep 29] £88,000Y: third foal: half-brother to a winner in Greece by Jeremy: dam, 7f winner, half-sister to smart 1½m-15.5f winner Stretarez: useful form: won maiden at Newmarket (by 1¾ lengths from Elwazir) in September: will be suited by 1m: sure to progress further. *Henry Candy*

THREADING (IRE) 2 b.f. (Apr 30) Exceed And Excel (AUS) 126 – Chaquiras (USA) **110**
(Seeking The Gold (USA)) [2017 6v* 6d* 6d Sep 30] rangy filly: sixth foal: half-sister to 3 winners, including useful UAE 7f winner Beachy Head (by Shamardal) and 2-y-o 5f winner Camargue (by Invincible Spirit): dam unraced sister to Dubai Millennium: smart

Sky Bet Lowther Stakes, York—Threading lands this Group 2 on just her second start, beating Madeline (spotted cap) and Irish raider Mamba Noire (striped cap)

Mr Hamdan Bin Mohammed Al Maktoum's "Threading"

form: won maiden at Goodwood (by 6 lengths from Your Choice) and Lowther Stakes at York (by 1¾ lengths from Madeline) in August: looked ill-at-ease on track when only seventh in Cheveley Park Stakes at Newmarket: raced only at 6f. *Mark Johnston*

THREAT ASSESSED (IRE) 4 b.g. Holy Roman Emperor (IRE) 125 – High Reserve 95 (Dr Fong (USA) 128) [2017 93: 10m 10.2d Oct 18] good-topped gelding: fairly useful handicapper: below form both starts in 2017: stays 10.5f: acts on soft and good to firm going: sold 6,000 gns, sent to Saudi Arabia. *Clive Cox* –

THREEANDFOURPENCE (USA) 2 b.c. (May 12) War Front (USA) 119 – Liscanna (IRE) 105 (Sadler's Wells (USA) 132) [2017 7s^2 6v* 7m^4 Oct 14] good-bodied colt: sixth foal: brother to 2-y-o 7f/1m (Breeders' Cup Juvenile Turf) winner Hit It A Bomb and 2-y-o 6f winner (including Cheveley Park Stakes) Brave Anna, both smart, and half-brother to a winner abroad by Kingmambo: dam 6f winner (including at 2 yrs): useful form: won maiden at Fairyhouse (by short head from Miss Zizi) in September: best effort when fourth in Dewhurst Stakes at Newmarket (5 lengths behind U S Navy Flag) final start: stays 7f. *Aidan O'Brien, Ireland* **107**

THREEBAGSUE (IRE) 4 ch.f. Lord Shanakill (USA) 121 – Feet of Flame (USA) 59 (Theatrical) [2017 76: t8.6g^5 p8g* p7g^2 Feb 18] workmanlike filly: fairly useful performer: won claimer at Chelmsford in January: second in handicap at Kempton (½ length behind Jacquotte Delahaye) final start: stays 9f: acts on polytrack, tapeta and good to firm going: wears blinkers: usually races close up. *J. S. Moore* **85**

THREE COLOURS RED (IRE) 5 b.g. Camacho 118 – Colour's Red (IRE) (Red Ransom (USA)) [2017 53: f14g^4 t16.5g* 16.5m^3 Jul 13] fair handicapper: won at Wolverhampton (amateur) in April: stays 16.5f: acts on tapeta, soft and good to firm going: sometimes in cheekpieces: tried in tongue tie: fair hurdler. *Robert Stephens* **71**

THREE C'S (IRE) 3 b.g. Kodiac 112 – Ms Mary C (IRE) 68 (Dolphin Street (FR) 125) [2017 78: p5g^4 5.7m^{pu} 6.1m t6.1g^5 5.7f^3 6d 5f t5g 5d^6 6g Aug 21] compact gelding: fair maiden handicapper: stays 6f: acts on firm and good to soft going: wears headgear/tongue tie. *David Dennis* **65**

THREEDIAMONDRINGS 4 ch.g. Geordieland (FR) 122 – Five Gold Rings (IRE) 68 (Captain Rio 122) [2017 74: t12.2m p14g 12d 10d p11g t9.5g Nov 7] fair handicapper: below form in 2017: left Brendan Powell after second start: stays 1½m: acts on polytrack and tapeta: tried in visor: wears tongue tie: often starts slowly. *Mark Usher* **62**

THREE DUCHESSES 3 b.f. Dutch Art 126 – Three Ducks 89 (Diktat 126) [2017 71p: t8.6g 10.2d^{4} 10.2m^{4} 10.1g* 12.1m* 9.9v^{6} 12m^{3} 10.2g^{3} Sep 15] sturdy filly: fairly useful handicapper: won at Yarmouth and Catterick (by 5 lengths from Cool Music) in July: stays 1½m: acts on polytrack, tapeta and good to firm going: usually races towards rear, often travels strongly: sent to Saudi Arabia. *Michael Bell* **90**

THREE LITTLE BIRDS 2 b.f. (Mar 22) Dandy Man (IRE) 123 – Oilinda 78 (Nayef (USA) 129) [2017 p5g^{2} 5m^{2} p5g^{3} 5m^{2} 6d^{3} 5.2v 5v^{6} 5.3g^{4} p5g^{2} p5g* Oct 18] 8,500F: first foal: dam 2-y-o 7f winner: fair performer: won minor event at Lingfield in October: stays 6f: acts on polytrack, good to firm and good to soft going: usually leads. *Sylvester Kirk* **78**

THREE LOVES (IRE) 4 b.f. Duke of Marmalade (IRE) 132 – Three Moons (IRE) 104 (Montjeu (IRE) 137) [2017 –: 11.5m^{4} 12m^{6} 11.5m^{6} Aug 1] modest maiden: best effort at 11.5f: acts on good to firm going: tried in headgear/tongue tie. *Stuart Williams* **58**

THREE MAJORS (IRE) 4 b.g. Lilbourne Lad (IRE) 111 – Saricana (IRE) 76 (Invincible Spirit (IRE) 121) [2017 68: p7g^{2} p8g^{5} p8g p8g^{5} t8.6g^{6} t8s p7g^{6} p8g^{6} p8g Dec 21] fair handicapper: left P. D. Deegan after second start: stays 9.5f: acts on polytrack, good to firm and heavy going: wears headgear: has worn tongue tie. *Anthony McCann, Ireland* **69**

THREE'S A CROWD (IRE) 3 br.g. Vocalised (USA) 114 – Tense (IRE) 69 (Invincible Spirit (IRE) 121) [2017 p7g 8.3d t7.2g p8d f8.1g t6.1d^{6} p7g Dec 30] compact gelding: poor maiden handicapper: in blinkers last 2 starts: usually races nearer last than first. *Ed de Giles* **45**

THREE SAINTS BAY (IRE) 2 b.g. (Apr 2) Kodiac 112 – Fiuise (IRE) (Montjeu (IRE) 137) [2017 7s^{2} 7.2m^{4} 6s^{2} 7g* t6d^{4} Oct 24] £40,000Y: first foal: dam unraced half-sister to useful 1m winner El Hayem: fairly useful performer: won minor event at Redcar (by 1¼ lengths from Tamkeen) in October: stays 7f: acts on tapeta and soft going: sold 50,000 gns later in October. *David O'Meara* **81**

THREE STAR GENERAL 4 b.g. Montjeu (IRE) 137 – Honorlina (FR) (Linamix (FR) 127) [2017 80: 14f May 6] fair maiden: below form only start on Flat in 2017: stays 1¾m: acts on heavy going: wears headgear: front runner/races prominently: won over hurdles in June: temperament under suspicion. *David Pipe* **–**

THREE WEEKS (USA) 2 gr.c. (Feb 6) Tapit (USA) 118 – Midnight Thoughts (USA) (Henrythenavigator (USA) 131) [2017 p7d p8g* Dec 20] first foal: dam unraced half-sister to smart performers Mad About You (stayed 1¼m), Princess Highway (stayed 1½m) and Royal Diamond (stayed 2m): fairly useful form: won minor event at Lingfield (by ¾ length from Brigham Young) in December: will go on improving. *William Haggas* **84 p**

THRESHOLDOFADREAM (IRE) 2 b.f. (Mar 2) Camelot 128 – Signella 66 (Selkirk (USA) 129) [2017 8s Oct 28] 60,000Y: fifth foal: half-sister to 3 winners, including winner up to 7.5f Harley's Harley (2-y-o 6.5f/7f winner, by Cockney Rebel) and 1¼m winner Beijing Star (by Dylan Thomas): dam, 1¼m winner, half-sister to smart dam of St Leger winner Kingston Hill: 40/1, down the field in minor event at Newbury. *Amanda Perrett* **–**

THRIFTY 2 b.f. (Feb 22) Harbour Watch (IRE) 121 – Isobel Rose (IRE) 73 (Royal Applause 124) [2017 t5s^{2} 5f^{4} 5m^{6} 6f Jul 6] fifth foal: half-sister to 3 winners, including 6f (including at 2 yrs)/7f winner Sakhee's Rose (by Sakhee's Secret) and 6f/1m winner Tifl (by Approve): dam ungenuine 6f winner: modest form: best effort at 5f: sold 7,000 gns, sent to Spain. *Tim Easterby* **61**

THROCKLEY 6 b.g. Passing Glance 119 – Porcelain (IRE) 82 (Peintre Celebre (USA) 137) [2017 88: 12g^{2} 8.8m^{2} 10d 8d 8m 10.3v^{5} 10g f12.1g* t12.2g f11.1g* Dec 19] fairly useful performer: won handicap at Southwell in November and claimer at same course (by 2 lengths from Every Chance) in December: left John Davies after seventh start: stays 1½m: acts on fibresand, good to firm and heavy going: often tongue tied in 2017. *Conor Dore* **90**

THRTYPOINTSTOTHREE (IRE) 6 b.g. Kodiac 112 – Miss Taken (IRE) 58 (Dubai Destination (USA) 127) [2017 48: p10g^{6} f7m Mar 7] small, close-coupled gelding: maiden, little impact either start in 2017: stays 9.5f: acts on tapeta: often blinkered/tongue tied nowadays. *Nikki Evans* **–**

THUNDERBELL 3 ch.f. Haafhd 129 – Trustthunder 87 (Selkirk (USA) 129) [2017 56: f6.1g Dec 4] twice-raced maiden, well held only start in 2017 (in headgear). *Scott Dixon* **–**

THUNDERBOLT ROCKS 2 b.c. (Mar 17) Farhh 131 – Coquette Noire (IRE) 85 (Holy Roman Emperor (IRE) 125) [2017 8d t8.6g* Nov 25] 57,000Y: first foal: dam, 7f winner, closely related to smart/ungenuine 2-y-o 7f winner (also first past post in 1000 Guineas) Jacqueline Quest: fair form: won minor event at Wolverhampton (by ¾ length from Dance Me) in November. *Hugo Palmer* **75**

THUNDERCLOUD 2 gr.f. (Apr 20) Aussie Rules (USA) 123 – Trustthunder 87 (Selkirk (USA) 129) [2017 6.5d 7m^6 6.5m f7.1g f8.1g^5 f8.1g Dec 29] half-sister to 3 winners, including useful 6f to (including at 2 yrs) 1m winner Thunderball (by Haafhd) and 7.6f winner Thunderousapplause (by Royal Applause): dam 6f winner (including at 2 yrs): modest maiden: best effort at 7f: tried in cheekpieces: front runner/races prominently. *Scott Dixon* **53**

THUNDERHOOVES 2 ro.c. (Apr 23) Raven's Pass (USA) 133 – Regrette Rien (USA) (Unbridled's Song (USA) 125) [2017 8g 7d Sep 29] tall colt: down the field in maidens. *John Ryan* –

THUNDERING BLUE (USA) 4 gr.g. Exchange Rate (USA) 111 – Relampago Azul (USA) (Forestry (USA) 121) [2017 82: p8g^3 8.3m p8g^3 10.1f^3 10.1d* 10g* 9.9g* 9d Sep 30] workmanlike gelding: useful handicapper: won at Epsom (by 4½ lengths from First Up) in July, Newmarket (by length from Atkinson Grimshaw) in August and Sandown (by 1½ lengths from Monarchs Glen) in September: stays 1¼m: acts on polytrack, firm and good to soft going: tried in visor: usually races nearer last than first/responds generously to pressure. *David Menuisier* **108**

THUNDER NORTH (IRE) 2 b.c. (May 11) Dansili 127 – Maidin Maith (IRE) 91 (Montjeu (IRE) 137) [2017 6m 7m t8s Sep 19] 90,000Y: fourth foal: closely related to 6f winner Dance Band (by Danehill Dancer) and half-brother to 8.5f winner Mezajy (by Makfi): dam, 2-y-o 7f winner, half-sister to smart winner up to 7.5f Modeeroch and to useful dam of high-class miler Belardo: little impact in minor events: type to do better in handicaps. *David Lanigan* **58 p**

THUNDER SNOW (IRE) 3 b.c. Helmet (AUS) 127 – Eastern Joy (Dubai Destination (USA) 127) [2017 119: a8f* a9.4g* a10s 8d^2 8f^3 8g* 8d^3 8s Oct 21] **122**

Saeed bin Suroor has been champion trainer in Britain four times, has saddled winners of all five British classics and has had thirty-six Royal Ascot successes. His claim that his stable is 'the main Godolphin stable' has plenty of substance and his evident frustration at his yard's 2017 two-year-old intake, relative to the collection allocated to Godolphin's other private trainer Charlie Appleby, boiled over into a public outburst which led to the resignation in June of Godolphin's chief executive John Ferguson. 'They are a disaster, some of them only came this month and I can't train them, have no chance to run them, it is very hard to do my job properly,' said bin Suroor who revealed that he had been bypassing Ferguson—whose son James was working as Appleby's assistant—and dealing directly with Sheikh Mohammed. The claim that bin Suroor had been given something of a rough deal is backed up by a look at the two-year-old intake, compared to that at Appleby's yard.

In terms of numbers, Appleby certainly got the lion's share and he got the bulk of the expensive purchases too, as well as nearly all the home breds by Darley's top stallion Dubawi. Appleby had sixty-three wins with his two-year-olds (at a strike rate of 36%) and bin Suroor had just six (strike rate 16%). The bin Suroor stable's two-year-olds were more likely to be found having an introduction to racing on the all-weather at Chelmsford or Wolverhampton than running in good company at Ascot or Newmarket. Wolverhampton was where the Dubawi colt Laieth got off the mark (at 550,000 guineas he was the most expensive yearling to run for the bin Suroor stable) while the other Dubawi to race for bin Suroor was home-bred Racing Country who was unplaced on both his starts. Charlie Appleby's string included the Prix Marcel Boussac winner Wild Illusion (a home bred by Dubawi), the Jean-Luc Lagardere third Masar, the Autumn Stakes winner Ghaiyyath (€1,100,000 foal by Dubawi), the Fillies' Mile third Magic Lily, the Champagne Stakes third Mythical Magic, the Prix des Chenes winner Stage Magic, the Prix Eclipse winner Sound And Silence (also successful at Royal Ascot) and the Prix La Rochette winner Glorious Journey (at 2,600,000 guineas the most expensive yearling to race for Godolphin in 2017).

UAE Derby Sponsored By The Saeed Mohammed Al Naboodah Group, Meydan—
Japan narrowly fails to land a second successive renewal of this race, Epicharis (rail) just losing out to Thunder Snow; the victory is a first in this race for Godolphin since 2011

One of the more promising of Saeed bin Suroor's two-year-olds is once-raced Winter Lightning, a Shamardal half-sister to the stable's torch bearer Thunder Snow. Winter Lightning didn't make her introduction at Chelmsford or Wolverhampton, but in a maiden at Newmarket in October where she fared easily the best of the newcomers when second to the promising, Stoute-trained Frankel filly Veracious, showing plenty and not being knocked about once the winner had gone. If Winter Lightning trains on to be anything like so good or tough as Thunder Snow, she will certainly be an asset to the bin Suroor stable in the next season. Thunder Snow himself was the leading Godolphin two-year-old in 2017 when his five-length victory in the Criterium International at Saint-Cloud gave Saeed bin Suroor his first Group 1 win since Prince Bishop's Dubai World Cup victory (bin Suroor's seventh in that race) in 2015, and his first outside Dubai since Farhh's victory in the 2013 Champion Stakes.

Thunder Snow kept up the good work as a three-year-old, adding a further Group 1 victory in the Prix Jean Prat at Chantilly in July and generally running well in a busy campaign that began at the Dubai Carnival at Meydan in February and ended, eight races later, on British Champions' Day at Ascot in October. The Queen Elizabeth II Stakes on British Champions' Day was one of only two races during the season in which Thunder Snow failed to reach the first three (he ran no sort of race, visored for the first time). The other was the Kentucky Derby in which Thunder Snow effectively took no part, pulled up after becoming unrideable as he gave an inexplicable bucking bronco display almost straight after leaving the stalls. Those two performances excepted, Thunder Snow was a model of consistency. He landed the UAE Two Thousand Guineas/Derby double on the dirt at Meydan in February and March, getting up on the line to win by a short head on the second occasion after a particularly strong ride by regular jockey Christophe Soumillon who struck his mount more than a dozen times in the final furlong, getting him unbalanced at one point as Thunder Snow flinched and jinked into the whip. Whether Thunder Snow's unfortunate UAE Derby experience had any bearing on his extraordinary antics next time at Churchill Downs is impossible to say, but, in any event, Thunder Snow was right back to his best, returned to turf, three weeks after the Kentucky Derby when finishing second to Churchill in the Irish Two Thousand Guineas, in which he was the only overseas challenger and kept on well to go down by two and a half lengths—clear of the rest—after leading briefly just under two furlongs out.

Thunder Snow turned the tables on a below-form Churchill in the St James's Palace Stakes at Royal Ascot where a strong, last-furlong challenge earned him a good third behind Barney Roy and Churchill's stablemate Lancaster Bomber (odds-

Prix Jean Prat, Chantilly—with just five runners going to post, the smallest field for this race since 2001, Thunder Snow is able to dictate and registers his second Group 1 success, beating Trais Fluors (second right) and Gold Luck

on Churchill finished over three lengths behind Thunder Snow in fourth). Thunder Snow faced only four opponents—three of them fillies—in the Prix Jean Prat on his next appearance just under three weeks later, and he made all to win by a length and a quarter, with a bit in hand, from the other colt in the line-up, the previously undefeated favourite Trais Fluors. Thunder Snow confirmed the form with Trais Fluors when the pair finished third and fourth in the Prix Jacques le Marois at Deauville in August, Thunder Snow trying to repeat his all-the-way win in the Jean Prat but being caught well inside the last furlong and beaten in a three-way photo finish by Al Wukair and his stablemate Inns of Court. Thunder Snow was given by far the longest break between races of his three-year-old campaign after the Jacques le Marois, but his performance in the Queen Elizabeth II Stakes more than two months later came on the softest going he has so far encountered and he trailed in last of fifteen behind Persuasive, Godolphin's best miler Ribchester and Churchill after coming under pressure some way out.

Thunder Snow (IRE) (b.c. 2014)	Helmet (AUS) (ch 2008)	Exceed And Excel (b 2000)	Danehill
			Patrona
		Accessories (b 2003)	Singspiel
			Anna Matrushka
	Eastern Joy (b 2006)	Dubai Destination (b 1999)	Kingmambo
			Mysterial
		Red Slippers (ch 1989)	Nureyev
			Morning Devotion

The well-made Thunder Snow (who looked in superb shape, belying his long season, before the Queen Elizabeth II Stakes) is by the Australian-bred miler Helmet, a son of Exceed And Excel. Thunder Snow's dam Eastern Joy won a nine-furlong race at Vichy on the first of four starts as a three-year-old for Sheikh Mohammed, and she has done well at stud, Thunder Snow being her fourth 'black type' winner from her first four foals, all of whom have been trained by Saeed bin Suroor and shown at least useful form. Eastern Joy's first foal Ihtimal, a sister to the two-year-old Winter Lightning, won the Sweet Solera Stakes and the May Hill Stakes as a two-year-old before completing the UAE One Thousand Guineas/Oaks double (on tapeta) on her first two starts at three; back in Britain, Ihtimal came third in the One Thousand Guineas and fifth in the Oaks. The ill-fated Always Smile (by Cape Cross) was Eastern Joy's second foal and she was at least as good as Ihtimal, winning four times at up to a mile and also reaching a place in Group 1 company in the Falmouth Stakes and the Sun Chariot Stakes as a four-year-old. Eastern Joy's third foal was also a filly, First Victory (by Teofilo), and she won the Oh So Sharp Stakes at Newmarket as a two-year-old. Eastern Joy was trained by Henri-Alex Pantall who trained her half-sister West Wind, whom he also had for Sheikh Mohammed. Eastern Joy and West Wind are among no fewer than eleven winners bred by the Sun

Godolphin's "Thunder Snow"

Chariot Stakes winner Red Slippers who ran in Sheikh Mohammed's colours too. The family has been with the Maktoums since the earliest days of Godolphin, Red Slippers being a close relative of Balanchine (both by sons of Northern Dancer out of Morning Devotion) who became the Godolphin operation's first important winner (carrying the colours of part-owner Maktoum Al Maktoum and trained—officially in Dubai—by Hilal Ibrahim) when successful in the 1994 Oaks before she beat the colts in the Irish Derby. A brother to Red Slippers, Romanov, was placed in the Irish Two Thousand Guineas and the Derby at Epsom. Thunder Snow stays nine and a half furlongs (the distance of the UAE Derby) but has raced mainly at a mile to date. He acts on dirt, and on firm and good to firm going on turf. He wore headgear on his last four starts (cheekpieces on the first three of them) and usually races close up or makes the running. He stays in training. *Saeed bin Suroor*

TIARA GOLD 2 ch.f. (Mar 25) Poet's Voice 126 – Dress Code (IRE) 83 (Barathea (IRE) 127) [2017 7.4s³ Sep 20] €6,000Y: half-sister to several winners, including smart 2-y-o 6f winner Lucky General (by Hawk Wing): dam 2-y-o 5f winner who stayed 7f: 20/1, third in minor event at Beverley (4½ lengths behind Bee Ina Bonnet). *Rae Guest* **60**

TIAR NA NOG (IRE) 5 b.m. Ask 126 – Carmencita (Rock of Gibraltar (IRE) 133) [2017 p12d³ p11g p13.3s³ Dec 14] third foal: half-sister to 1¼m winners Banreenahreenkah and Steppe Daughter (both by Steppe Dancer): dam unraced: unplaced in bumpers: fair form in Flat maidens: best effort when third at Kempton in August. *Denis Coakley* **71**

TIBERIAN (FR) 5 b.h. Tiberius Caesar (FR) 116 – Toamasina (FR) (Marju (IRE) 127) [2017 115: 11.9d* 11.9s* 11.9g 12.4g* 12.4g* 15.9g 11.9g Dec 10] strong, lengthy horse: smart performer: won listed race at Saint-Cloud (by 3 lengths from Talismanic) in March, Prix d'Hedouville on same course (by length from same rival) in May, then Prix de Reux at Deauville and Grand Prix de Deauville (beat Doha Dream by short neck), both in August: below form in Melbourne Cup at Flemington and Hong Kong Vase at Sha Tin last 2 starts: stays 15f: acts on soft and good to firm going. *Alain Couetil, France* **119**

TIBIBIT 4 b.f. Kyllachy 129 – Cat Hunter 77 (One Cool Cat (USA) 123) [2017 60: p7g⁵ p8g² p7g² p8g 8d⁵ p7g Sep 5] fair maiden: stays 1m: acts on polytrack. *Henry Tett* **74**

TICKS THE BOXES (IRE) 5 ch.g. Fast Company (IRE) 126 – Swan Sea (USA) (Sea Hero (USA) 124) [2017 88: f6g^4 t7.1g^2 p7g f7m t6d^6 t7.1g^4 t6g* f6d^2 5m^5 5g^6 t6s 6d^6 7d^5 6d^3 5.9s^3 7g^2 7d 6v 6d^3 f6.1g^5 f7.1g Dec 19] workmanlike gelding: fairly useful performer: won claimer at Newcastle in March: second in handicap at same course (apprentice, 2 lengths behind Safe Voyage) in January: left Michael Herrington after eighth start: stays 7f: acts on fibresand, tapeta, soft and good to firm going: wears headgear: temperamental. *John Wainwright* **83 §**

TIDAL'S BABY 8 b.g. Dutch Art 126 – Tidal 94 (Bin Ajwaad (IRE) 119) [2017 62: p6d^2 p6g^2 p7g^2 7m^2 7d^2 5s^2 7m^3 a7g^4 5.8v^6 t5.1m^2 p6g^3 p6g Dec 6] workmanlike gelding: fair handicapper: left Tony Carroll after seventh start, Jamie Osborne after eighth: stays 7f: acts on polytrack, tapeta, firm and soft going: has worn headgear, including last 3 starts: sometimes slowly away: ungenuine. *Adrian Brendan Joyce, Ireland* **69 §**

TIDAL WATCH (IRE) 3 b.g. Harbour Watch (IRE) 121 – Najmati (Green Desert (USA) 127) [2017 8.1m 7s^3 8v^4 8m Jul 6] tall gelding: fair form: best effort at 7f: placed over hurdles. *Jonjo O'Neill* **75**

TIE EM UP TEL (IRE) 2 b.c. (Apr 12) Sir Prancealot (IRE) 111 – Cinarosa (IRE) 71 (Kodiac 112) [2017 p5g 5g^5 5g^3 6.1m* 5m^4 6d^4 6d* Aug 4] fair performer: won sellers at Windsor in June and Thirsk in August: stays 6f: acts on good to firm and good to soft going: front runner/races prominently: sent to Austria. *David Evans* **68**

TIEPOLO (IRE) 2 gr.g. (Mar 8) Dark Angel (IRE) 113 – Trempjane 71 (Lujain (USA) 119) [2017 6.1m 6g^2 6.1m^3 7g^3 7s p6g^6 Oct 17] good-topped gelding: fair maiden: stays 6f: acts on polytrack, best turf form on good going: sold 25,000 gns, sent to USA. *Gary Moore* **74**

TIERCEL 4 b.c. Olden Times 121 – Sharp Mode (USA) (Diesis 133) [2017 98p: t8g p8g^3 Nov 17] sturdy colt: fairly useful handicapper: stays 8.5f: acts on polytrack and soft going: often races prominently, usually travels strongly. *Roger Varian* **91**

TIFFIN TOP 2 gr.c. (Feb 28) Oasis Dream 129 – Mussoorie (FR) 108 (Linamix (FR) 127) [2017 8g^4 8g Sep 28] sturdy colt: fair form: better effort when fourth in maiden at Doncaster (6½ lengths behind Blue Laureate) in September. *John Gosden* **71**

TIFL 4 ch.g. Approve (IRE) 112 – Isobel Rose (IRE) 73 (Royal Applause 124) [2017 73: p8m^5 t10.2g p8g 7g p8s 6.1g* 7d^3 p6g p7g 7d^3 t8d* Nov 10] sturdy gelding: modest performer: won seller at Chepstow in August and handicap at Newcastle in November: stays 1m: acts on polytrack, tapeta and good to soft going: wears blinkers/tongue tie. *Heather Main* **63**

TIGERFILLY 2 ch.f. (Feb 2) Equiano (FR) 127 – Bestfootforward 64 (Motivator 131) [2017 7s^6 6g^4 Oct 16] 1,500F: first foal: dam, 7f winner, half-sister to useful winner up to 1¼m Azmeel: modest form: better effort when fourth in minor event at Yarmouth (6 lengths behind Foreseeable Future) second start: sold £600, sent to Germany. *John Ryan* **55**

TIGERFISH (IRE) 3 b.f. Lilbourne Lad (IRE) 111 – Nisriyna (IRE) (Intikhab (USA) 135) [2017 48: p8g^4 t7.1m^5 p7g^3 p7g* p7g* p7d^5 7g^5 7m 7g* 7d* 7m^2 t7.2g^6 7d p7m p7g^4 Dec 30] modest handicapper: won at Lingfield (twice) in February, and Brighton in June (apprentice) and July: stays 1m: acts on polytrack, tapeta, good to firm and good to soft going: wears cheekpieces. *William Stone* **64**

TIGER JIM 7 b.g. Tiger Hill (IRE) 127 – Quintrell 92 (Royal Applause 124) [2017 95, a82: 7g 6g^2 Apr 17] fairly useful handicapper: second at Redcar second start: stays 7f: acts on polytrack, soft and good to firm going: sometimes slowly away. *Jim Goldie* **91**

TIGER KHAN 3 b.g. Zamindar (USA) 116 – Waitingonacloud (In The Wings 128) [2017 10g 11.6g^4 Jun 1] little impact in maiden/seller. *Harry Dunlop* **47**

TIGER LYON (USA) 2 b.c. (May 1) Kitten's Joy (USA) 128 – Hold It (USA) (Discreet Cat (USA) 127) [2017 5.4g p7g p8d p6s^3 t5.1g* Dec 18] fair performer: won nursery at Wolverhampton in December: may prove best at 5f: acts on polytrack and tapeta: in hood last 4 starts: usually leads. *John Butler* **65**

TIGERSHARK (IRE) 2 gr.c. (Mar 13) Lethal Force (IRE) 128 – Fearless Flyer (IRE) 100 (Brave Act 119) [2017 7g^6 Oct 7] 50/1, sixth in minor event at Redcar (6¼ lengths behind Shuhood). *Bryan Smart* **56**

TIGERWOLF (IRE) 4 br.g. Dream Ahead (USA) 133 – Singing Field (IRE) (Singspiel (IRE) 133) [2017 92: 7m^5 6d 7v^5 7g^6 7m^4 7.6s^6 p7g^4 p8g^6 t9.5g f8.1g^6 Dec 19] good-topped gelding: fair handicapper: left Mick Channon after eighth start: stays 7f: acts on good to firm going: tried in visor: temperament under suspicion. *Daniel Loughnane* **77**

TIGHT LINES 2 b.f. (Apr 20) Fastnet Rock (AUS) 127 – Dusty Answer 97 (Zafonic (USA) 130) [2017 6s⁵ 7m* Jul 23] closely related to useful 7f-1¼m winner Grand Inquisitor (by Dansili) and half-sister to several winners, including useful winner up to 1½m Teofonic (2-y-o 6f/7f winner, by Teofilo): dam 2-y-o 7f winner: fair form: won minor event at Redcar (by 3¾ lengths from Glacier Fox) in July: open to further improvement. *Mark Johnston* **78 p**

TIGRE DU TERRE (FR) 2 b.c. (Jan 26) Le Havre (IRE) 124 – Allmia (FR) (Johann Quatz (FR) 120) [2017 7g* 7d⁴ 8g³ 7g² Sep 15] €55,000Y: tall colt: third foal: half-brother to French 2-y-o 1m winner Alicenora (by Astronomer Royal) and French 9.5f-12.5f winner Altesse Thais (by Myboycharlie): dam, French 1½m-15f winner, also won over hurdles: useful form: won minor event at Ascot in July: second in listed race at Doncaster (2 lengths behind Tip Two Win) final start: stays 1m. *Richard Hannon* **98**

TIGSERIN (IRE) 4 ch.f. Approve (IRE) 112 – Mairead Anne (USA) (Elusive Quality (USA)) [2017 78: p6g 6m⁴ 8m⁵ p7d³ 7g p7s⁶ 7s⁶ p6g⁵ Sep 27] lengthy filly: modest handicapper: stays 1m: acts on polytrack: has worn headgear. *Giles Bravery* **64**

TIG TOG (IRE) 2 b.f. (Mar 20) Dark Angel (IRE) 113 – Deira Dubai 75 (Green Desert (USA) 127) [2017 7m⁵ 7m² 7d⁴ 6d 7g³ p7g³ Sep 9] 48,000F, 90,000Y: angular filly: fifth foal: half-sister to 6f (including at 2 yrs) winner Centre Haafhd (by Haafhd) and a winner in USA by Iffraaj: dam, 7f winner, half-sister to useful 1¼m winner Agenda: fair maiden: stays 7f: acts on polytrack and good to firm going. *Richard Hannon* **76**

TIHANA 4 b.f. Lawman (FR) 121 – La Bocca (USA) 70 (Latent Heat (USA) 118) [2017 t5.1g⁴ t6m Jan 13] modest maiden: best form at 5f: acts on tapeta and good to firm going: tried in blinkers. *John Murray* **50**

TILLY DEVINE 3 gr.f. Aussie Rules (USA) 123 – Cora Pearl (IRE) 51 (Montjeu (IRE) 137) [2017 –: 6d 6g p10g p8g f8.1g f8.1g* f8.1g⁵ f7.1g⁵ Dec 22] modest handicapper: won at Southwell in December: best effort at 1m: acts on fibresand: in headgear last 4 starts. *Scott Dixon* **61**

TILLY'S BRIDGE 4 b.f. Avonbridge 123 – Ivory Lace 96 (Atraf 116) [2017 p7g p7g p6g p8g 7m 6.1m Jul 10] second foal: half-sister to 1¼m winner Solveig's Song (by Norse Dancer): dam winner up to 7f (2-y-o 5f winner) who stayed 9f: little form: in headgear last 2 starts. *Steve Woodman* **–**

TILLY TINKER 3 ch.f. Doncaster Rover (USA) 114 – Lawless Bridget 62 (Alnasr Alwasheek 117) [2017 7m 8g 6g⁶ 6s³ 6.9s t7.1g Oct 20] £1,800Y: half-sister to numerous winners, including 5f/6f winner Bondesire (by Misu Bond) and 2-y-o 5f winner Fred's Lad (by Warningford), both useful: dam maiden: modest maiden: stays 6f: acts on soft going: tried in blinkers. *Michael Easterby* **59**

TILLY TROTTER (IRE) 3 b.f. Kodiac 112 – Inourthoughts (IRE) 106 (Desert Style (IRE) 121) [2017 89: p5g⁵ 5.8g 6g⁵ 6d 5d 6v⁶ t5g⁴ t6d* t6s t5.1g² f5g* Dec 22] good-topped filly: fourth foal: half-sister to 2-y-o 6f winner Focusofourthoughts (by Intense Focus): dam, 2-y-o 5f winner, half-sister to smart 5f winner Green Door: useful handicapper: won at Newcastle in November and Southwell (by head from dead-heaters Razin' Hell and Kickboxer) in December: left D. K. Weld after second start: stays 6f: acts on all-weather and soft going: front runner/races prominently, often travels strongly. *Declan Carroll* **95**

TILSWORTH LUKEY 4 b.g. Sixties Icon 125 – Chara 72 (Deploy 131) [2017 p7g p7g 8s 7d 6d⁶ p6s⁵ f6.1g⁵ Dec 19] little sign of ability. *J. R. Jenkins* **–**

TILSWORTH MICKY 5 br.g. Kheleyf (USA) 116 – Tilsworth Charlie 70 (Dansili 127) [2017 57, a67: f6g p6d* t6gpu p6d p6gpu 8s 6.1mpu Jun 26] fair handicapper: won at Kempton in January: stays 6f: acts on polytrack: sometimes slowly away, often races in rear: often bleeds, and one to treat with plenty of caution. *J. R. Jenkins* **67 §**

TIME CHANGE 2 ch.f. (Apr 2) Dutch Art 126 – Time Honoured 83 (Sadler's Wells (USA) 132) [2017 6.5d² 7m* 8g⁴ 7d Sep 30] half-sister to several winners, including 1¼m winner Huge Future (by Shamardal) and UAE 7f-9.5f winner Baroot (by Dubawi), both useful: dam, 2-y-o 1m winner, sister to smart 1½m winner Time Allowed: fair form: won minor event at Newbury in June: best effort at 7f. *Ralph Beckett* **76**

TIME CHASER 3 b.f. Dubawi (IRE) 129 – Passage of Time 115 (Dansili 127) [2017 p8g* 8m* 9.9v* 10.5s³ 10.2s Nov 11] fifth foal: sister to high-class winner up to 10.4f Time Test (2-y-o 7f winner) and half-sister to smart 11f-2m winner Retirement Plan (by Monsun): dam winner up to 10.4f (2-y-o 7f-1¼m winner, including Criterium de Saint- **100**

Cloud): useful performer: won maiden at Kempton in April, and handicaps at Sandown in June and August (by ½ length from Glenys The Menace): stays 1¼m: acts on polytrack, good to firm and heavy going: usually races prominently. *Roger Charlton*

TIME CONSTRAINTS (USA) 3 b.g. Gio Ponti (USA) 130 – Escape To Victory (Salse (USA) 128) [2017 79p: p8g* p8g^5 p8g^5 6d Sep 20] fair performer: won maiden at Dundalk in January: left M. Halford after third start: stays 1m: acts on polytrack: wore headgear for former yard: usually leads. *Anthony Carson* **78**

TIME CONTINUUM 5 b.m. Monsieur Bond (IRE) 120 – Primum Tempus 49 (Primo Dominie 121) [2017 5m 5s f7.1g Aug 28] poor/lightly-raced maiden. *Eric Alston* **–**

TIME EXPOSED (IRE) 2 b.f. (Apr 4) High Chaparral (IRE) 132 – Palace of Winds (IRE) 76 (Monsun (GER) 124) [2017 6g Aug 2] first foal: dam, 1m winner who stayed 1½m, half-sister to very smart French/US 1m-9.5f performer Gorella: 33/1, well held in minor event at Redcar. *K. R. Burke* **–**

TIME FOR TREACLE 2 b.f. (Mar 13) Sayif (IRE) 122 – Fiancee (IRE) 59 (Pivotal 124) [2017 t5s 5s^3 6s^2 7g^3 6d^6 6g Sep 27] smallish filly: third foal: half-sister to winner up to 5.7f Secret Potion (2-y-o 5f winner, by Stimulation): dam, maiden (stayed 7f), out of Rockfel Stakes winner Name of Love: modest maiden: stays 6f: acts on soft going: usually races close up. *Ben Haslam* **53**

TIME FOR WINE (IRE) 2 b.f. (Mar 22) Equiano (FR) 127 – Steam Cuisine 104 (Mark of Esteem (IRE) 137) [2017 5.1m^6 6.1g 6.1g^2 5v^2 5.1d^2 5m^3 5.7s^3 Oct 2] €20,000Y: fifth foal: half-sister to German 9f winner Genax (by Green Desert) and winner up to 1¼m Juste Pour Nous (2-y-o 1m winner, by Pour Moi): dam 7f/1m winner (including at 2 yrs): fair maiden: stays 6f: acts on good to firm and heavy going: front runner/races prominently. *David Evans* **76**

TIMELESS ART (IRE) 4 b.g. Medicean 128 – Bellona (IRE) 105 (Bering 136) [2017 94p: 7g^3 8m 8m^5 9.1s^4 8s^3 8d p8d* p8g t8g Oct 10] tall gelding: fairly useful handicapper: won at Kempton (by 2½ lengths from Golden Wedding) in August: stays 1m: acts on polytrack, soft and good to firm going: has worn headgear, including last 4 starts: sold 13,000 gns in October. *K. R. Burke* **93**

TIMELY ARRIVAL 3 b.c. Cacique (IRE) 124 – Winter Bloom (USA) 89 (Aptitude (USA) 128) [2017 8g p10d^3 Sep 28] fair form: better effort when third in maiden at Chelmsford: sold 7,000 gns, sent to Italy. *Amanda Perrett* **72**

TIME MEDICEAN 11 gr.g. Medicean 128 – Ribbons And Bows (IRE) 91 (Dr Devious (IRE) 127) [2017 69: 5.7f 6s^2 7m^4 6d 6s^3 5.7s^2 5s^2 6.1g Oct 9] lightly-made gelding: fair handicapper: stays 7f: acts on polytrack, tapeta, good to firm and heavy going: tried in blinkers: has worn tongue tie, including in 2017. *Tony Carroll* **66**

TIME OF MY LIFE (GER) 6 ch.g. Nayef (USA) 129 – Tamaja (GER) (Tiger Hill (IRE) 127) [2017 93: t16.3g^5 t12.4d^4 Mar 2] fairly useful handicapper: stays 16.5f: acts on tapeta and soft going: wears headgear: usually races towards rear: little impact in novice hurdles. *Patrick Holmes* **89**

TIME'S ARROW (IRE) 3 b.c. Redoute's Choice (AUS) – Gilt Edge Girl 122 (Monsieur Bond (IRE) 120) [2017 p7g p7g^2 p7g^2 7.4m^2 8g* 8d 8s 8g^2 8s^4 p8g* Nov 21] second foal: dam 5f/6f winner, including Prix de l'Abbaye: useful performer: won maiden at Thirsk in June (left Sir Michael Stoute after next start) and handicap at Chantilly (by 1½ lengths from Highest Rockeur) in November: stays 1m: acts on polytrack and soft going: usually races prominently. *P. Sogorb, France* **97**

TIMES IN ANATEFKA (IRE) 7 b.m. Pyrus (USA) 106 – Brooklands Time (IRE) 63 (Danetime (IRE) 121) [2017 59: p5g^3 p5g^5 t5.1g* t5.1g* 5g May 14] fair handicapper: won at Wolverhampton (twice) in February: stays 6f: acts on polytrack and tapeta: usually wears headgear: wears tongue tie: front runner/races prominently. *Adrian Brendan Joyce, Ireland* **71**

TIME TEST 5 b.h. Dubawi (IRE) 129 – Passage of Time 115 (Dansili 127) [2017 125: 9d^2 10f^2 8d^2 Aug 12] well-made horse: high-class performer at best, successful 6 times, including in Joel Stakes at Newmarket at 3 yrs, and Brigadier Gerard Stakes at Sandown and York Stakes in 2016: left Roger Charlton, runner-up all 3 starts in USA in 2017, including in Manhattan Stakes at Belmont (1¼ lengths behind Ascend) and Fourstardave Handicap at Saratoga (beaten 2¼ lengths by World Approval): stayed 10.5f: best efforts on good or firmer going: often travelled strongly: to stand at National Stud, Newmarket, fee £8,500. *Chad C. Brown, USA* **119**

TIME TO BLOSSOM 4 b.f. Cape Cross (IRE) 129 – Time Over 76 (Mark of Esteem (IRE) 137) [2017 73: 10m* 12s Sep 19] fairly useful handicapper: won at Redcar (amateur, by length from Broadway Dreams) in August: should be suited by 1½m+: acts on polytrack and good to firm going. *Simon Crisford* **88**

TIME TO EXCEED (IRE) 4 b.f. Exceed And Excel (AUS) 126 – In Your Time (Dalakhani (IRE) 133) [2017 82p: 6g* 6.1g^{2} 7g Jun 11] rather leggy filly: fairly useful handicapper: won at Leicester (by 1½ lengths from Tanasoq) in April: second at Windsor (short head behind Englishman) in May: stays 6f: acts on good to firm going. *Henry Candy* **91**

TIME TO PERFECTION (IRE) 2 gr.f. (Apr 12) Mastercraftsman (IRE) 129 – Time Ahead 112 (Spectrum (IRE) 126) [2017 t8g t9.5g^{4} t9.5g Nov 18] 25,000Y: half-sister to 11.5f winner World Time (by Dalakhani): dam 1¼m winner and second in Prix de Diane: modest form: best effort when fourth in minor event at Wolverhampton (4¼ lengths behind Deyaarna) in October: will stay 1¼m+: remains open to progress. *Sylvester Kirk* **59 p**

TIME TO SEA (IRE) 3 b.g. Born To Sea (IRE) 117 – Eastern Glow (Cape Cross (IRE) 129) [2017 –: f8g 8.3g 8.3d^{5} 8.3d^{4} 10.1m^{5} 8.2g^{3} 10d^{3} 10d^{3} p12g^{4} Oct 3] good-topped gelding: fair maiden handicapper: stays 1½m: acts on polytrack, good to firm and good to soft going. *John Butler* **74**

TIME TO STUDY (FR) 3 ch.c. Motivator 131 – Dissertation (FR) 104 (Sillery (USA) 122) [2017 86p: 10s^{3} 14m* 14m^{5} 14s^{3} 14.5g* 18m 13.3d* Oct 27] strong colt: smart performer: won handicap at Musselburgh (by head from Alabaster) in June, Mallard Stakes (Handicap) at Doncaster (by head from Byron Flyer) in September and minor event at Newbury (by 2¼ lengths from Duke of Bronte) in October: stays 14.5f: acts on polytrack, soft and good to firm going. *Mark Johnston* **114**

TIME TRAIL 2 b.f. (Apr 2) Swiss Spirit 117 – Starbeck (IRE) 94 (Spectrum (IRE) 126) [2017 5f* 5m* 5.2v 5d^{5} 5d^{4} 5v^{rr} Oct 16] £38,000Y: half-sister to several winners, including temperamental 6f (including at 2 yrs) winner Byronic Hero (by Byron) and 7f winner Loveatfirstsight (by Bertolini): dam 2-y-o 6f winner: fairly useful performer: won minor events at Beverley and Catterick (by head from Lady Anjorica) in May: raced only at 5f: acts on firm going: one to treat with caution (refused to race final outing): sold 6,000 gns, sent to Spain. *Michael Dods* **80 §**

TIME WARP 4 ch.g. Archipenko (USA) 127 – Here To Eternity (USA) 74 (Stormy Atlantic (USA)) [2017 112: 7g 7g 6m^{3} 6m^{3} 6g^{6} 7m^{4} 8.2g 8.9m* 8.2m* 8d* 7d^{3} 8.9m^{2} 9.9g^{2} 9.9g* Dec 10] big, strong gelding: very smart performer: trained by Sir Mark Prescott Bt at 2/3 yrs: improved in second half of 2017, winning handicaps at Happy Valley (twice) in June and Sha Tin in July, and Hong Kong Cup on latter course (by 2¼ lengths from Werther, dictating) in December: stays 1¼m: acts on polytrack, fibresand, heavy and good to firm going: wears tongue tie. *A. S. Cruz, Hong Kong* **124**

TIME ZONE 3 b.g. Kheleyf (USA) 116 – Be Joyful (IRE) (Teofilo (IRE) 126) [2017 85: 7m^{5} 8m 8s^{5} Aug 2] rangy gelding: fairly useful 7f winner on debut at 2 yrs, little impact in minor event/handicaps in 2017. *Peter Chapple-Hyam* **83**

TIMIA 4 b.f. Cape Cross (IRE) 129 – Cinerama (IRE) 68 (Machiavellian (USA) 123) [2017 67: p8g^{2} 8.3s^{4} 8.2s^{4} p8g^{4} 7v p7g^{2} p7g* p8g* p7g^{4} Dec 21] useful-looking filly: fairly useful handicapper: won at Dundalk (twice, by length from Paved With Gold second occasion) in November: stays 1m: acts on polytrack and soft going: has worn headgear: often races prominently. *Keith Henry Clarke, Ireland* **85**

TIMOSHENKO 2 ch.g. (Mar 18) Archipenko (USA) 127 – Nezhenka 99 (With Approval (CAN)) [2017 7s p8g 7g t9.5g Oct 27] down the field in maiden/minor events. *Sir Mark Prescott Bt* **–**

TIMPANI (IRE) 2 ch.f. (Feb 20) Raven's Pass (USA) 133 – Fanny Cerrito (USA) (Gulch (USA)) [2017 p7g p8g^{6} 7m* Oct 25] 170,000Y: tall filly: half-sister to several winners, including smart winner up to 1¾m Poseidon Adventure (2-y-o 1m winner) and useful performer up to 1½m Kisses For Me (2-y-o 1m winner) (both by Sadler's Wells): dam unraced: fairly useful form: won minor event at Newmarket (by nose from Left Alone) in October: should stay at least 1m. *John Gosden* **87**

TINA TEASPOON 3 b.f. Kheleyf (USA) 116 – Button Moon (IRE) 91 (Compton Place 125) [2017 5d^{5} Jul 26] first foal: dam, 6f winner, half-sister to Etlaala and to dam of Tasleet (both very smart 6f/7f performers) and to dam of top-class 5f performer Battaash: 50/1, well held in maiden at Leicester. *Derek Shaw* **–**

TINDARO (FR) 10 gr.g. Kingsalsa (USA) 118 – Star's Mixa (FR) (Linamix (FR) 127) [2017 83: 12s Oct 28] big gelding: fairly useful handicapper: well below form only start on Flat in 2017: stays 2m: acts on firm going: tried in headgear: often tongue tied. *Paul Webber* **–**

TINGO IN THE TALE (IRE) 8 b.g. Oratorio (IRE) 128 – Sunlit Skies 65 (Selkirk (USA) 129) [2017 65: t9.5g t8.6m t13.9g^{3} t13.9f^{2} t13.9m^{3} p12g t16.5g^{3} 16d 10.2g^{4} 14d 10.2g* t12.2g 10.2g Nov 1] compact gelding: modest handicapper: won at Nottingham (amateur) in August: left Sophie Leech after eighth start: stays 1¾m: acts on polytrack, tapeta and any turf going: wears cheekpieces: sometimes tongue tied in 2017. *Tony Forbes* **64**

TINK 3 ch.f. Captain Gerrard (IRE) 113 – Ensign's Trick 72 (Cayman Kai (IRE) 114) [2017 –: t6f t6m p6g t6m^{6} t7.1g^{2} t7.1g t7.1g t6.1g t6.1g^{6} p7g t6.1d f7.1g Dec 22] modest maiden handicapper: best effort at 7f: acts on tapeta: has worn headgear. *Mark Brisbourne* **53**

TINKER TAILOR (IRE) 4 ch.f. Intikhab (USA) 135 – Luanas Pearl (IRE) (Bahri (USA) 125) [2017 8g^{3} 12s^{5} 12d 11.6d^{6} Aug 21] 27,000Y: lengthy filly: third foal: half-sister to 11.6f-2m winner Cosette (by Champs Elysees): dam unraced half-sister to smart 8.6f-12.3f winner Hattan and smart performer up to 2¼m Tastahil: fair form: likely to stay beyond 1½m: sometimes in tongue tie. *Denis Quinn* **78**

TINOS (GER) 3 b.g. Soldier Hollow 121 – Ticinella (GER) 105 (Hernando (FR) 127) [2017 8m^{6} Apr 22] €67,000Y: compact gelding: half-brother to several winners abroad by Lord of England, including smart German winner up to 11f Theo Danon (2-y-o 1m winner): dam, 1½m winner in France, half-sister to smart French/US 9.5f-1½m winner Sea Calisi: 50/1, sixth in maiden at Newbury (5¾ lengths behind Call To Mind): will stay 1¼m: should improve. *Ed Walker* **72 p**

TIN PAN ALLEY 9 b.g. Singspiel (IRE) 133 – Tazmeen (Darshaan 133) [2017 9.9f^{4} 9.9m 9.9m 12.1m 12.1d Aug 17] fair handicapper, below form in 2017 after long absence: stays 1¼m: acts on polytrack, good to firm and good to soft going: has worn cheekpieces, including final start: usually leads. *David C. Griffiths* **59**

TINSILL 6 ch.g. Firebreak 125 – Concentration (IRE) (Mind Games 121) [2017 58: 6g 5g 5m 5s^{2} 5g 5m 5s^{4} 5f^{3} 5d t5g 5s 5d 5s 5g Oct 7] modest handicapper: best form at 5f: acts on good to firm and heavy going: has worn headgear, including in 2017. *Nigel Tinkler* **53**

TINTED (IRE) 3 b.f. Galileo (IRE) 134 – Regal Rose 110 (Danehill (USA) 126) [2017 p12g Oct 3] half-sister to several winners, including useful winner up to 1m Bobby Wheeler (2-y-o 7f winner, by Pivotal) and 7f-1½m winner Merchant of Medici (by Medicean): dam 2-y-o 6f winner (including Cheveley Park Stakes): 7/1, well held in maiden at Kempton: should do better. *John Gosden* **– p**

Coral Distaff, Sandown—fifth win of the campaign for the progressive Tisbutadream who makes all to beat Queen of Time (spots on sleeves) and Dancing Breeze (checks)

TINY TEMPEST (IRE) 2 b.f. (Apr 2) Rip Van Winkle (IRE) 134 – Mahaazen (IRE) 86 (Cape Cross (IRE) 129) [2017 7f⁴ 6g⁵ 8d⁵ 7g⁵ t8.6g* Oct 7] second foal: dam 2-y-o 9f winner: fair performer: won nursery at Wolverhampton in October: stays 8.5f: acts on tapeta. *Eve Johnson Houghton* **73**

TIOGA PASS 6 b.m. High Chaparral (IRE) 132 – Seren Devious (Dr Devious (IRE) 127) [2017 103: 12g⁶ Jun 25] good-topped mare: useful performer: well below form only start in 2017: stays 1¾m: acts on polytrack, good to firm and heavy going: wears headgear: tried in tongue tie: usually races in rear. *Paul Cole* **–**

TIPI 2 b.g. (Jan 31) Sleeping Indian 122 – Jazan (IRE) 94 (Danehill (USA) 126) [2017 t7.2gpu p6g p6g Sep 26] no form. *Charlie Wallis* **–**

TIP TWO WIN 2 gr.c. (May 12) Dark Angel (IRE) 113 – Freddie's Girl (USA) 85 (More Than Ready (USA) 120) [2017 6.1m* 6.1g³ 6m² 7g* 7g² 7g* Dec 29] compact colt: first foal: dam 5f/6f winner: useful performer: won minor event at Windsor in July, listed race at Doncaster (by 2 lengths from Tigre du Terre) in September and minor event at Doha (by 4½ lengths from Anima Rock) in December: second in Somerville Tattersall Stakes at Newmarket (2¼ lengths behind Elarqam) on penultimate start: stays 7f: acts on good to firm going: often races towards rear. *Roger Teal* **105**

TIRANIA 3 b.f. Pivotal 124 – Tiriana (Common Grounds 118) [2017 7g³ 8.1m* 8m² 8g⁴ 7.2m* 6v² 6m⁵ Oct 14] 62,000F, €370,000Y: lengthy, rather unfurnished filly: sister to smart 6f/7f winner (including at 2 yrs, and Fred Darling Stakes) Penkenna Princess, closely related to 6f/7f winner Divine Power (by Kyllachy) and half-sister to several winners: dam French maiden (stayed 1m): useful performer: won maiden at Windsor in May and handicap at Musselburgh (by ¾ length from Peach Melba) in August: stays 1m: acts on good to firm going. *William Haggas* **97**

TISA RIVER (IRE) 3 b.f. Equiano (FR) 127 – Senta's Dream (Danehill (USA) 126) [2017 t6g 5.7m t7.2g t6.1g 6.1m 5.7s⁴ Sep 17] €92,000Y, £3,000 2-y-o: close-coupled filly: fifth foal: half-sister to 9.7f winner Caterina (by Medicean) and 7f winner Dream And Hope (by Royal Applause): dam unraced out of Breeders' Cup Filly & Mare Turf winner Starine: modest maiden: stays 7f: acts on tapeta and soft going: tried in tongue tie: front runner/races prominently. *Milton Bradley* **50**

TISBUTADREAM (IRE) 3 ch.f. Dream Ahead (USA) 133 – Choose Me (IRE) 109 (Choisir (AUS) 126) [2017 74p: p8g* p8g* p8g* p7f 8m* 8.5m³ 8m 8m* 8d³ 8g² 8g³ 8d³ Sep 29] rather leggy filly: useful performer: progressed really well, winning handicaps at Lingfield (twice) in January, Kempton in February and Ascot in May, and listed race at Sandown (by ½ length from Queen of Time) in July: third in Atalanta Stakes at Sandown (4½ lengths behind Aljazzi) in September: stays 8.5f: acts on polytrack, good to firm and good to soft going: usually races close up: tough and reliable. *David Elsworth* **108**

TIS MARVELLOUS 3 b.g. Harbour Watch (IRE) 121 – Mythicism 80 (Oasis Dream 129) [2017 116: 6f⁴ 6m⁶ 5m⁵ 5s Sep 10] useful-looking gelding: smart performer at 2 yrs: below best in 2017: stays 6f: acts on good to firm going: wears tongue tie: usually races prominently. *Clive Cox* **104**

TIS WONDERFUL (IRE) 3 b.g. Casamento (IRE) 118 – Cosenza 71 (Bahri (USA) 125) [2017 –p: 7.1d⁴ 8f⁴ p8g p12g⁴ t12.2g² Dec 22] well-made gelding: fair maiden handicapper: left Clive Cox after second start: stays 1½m: acts on polytrack, tapeta and good to soft going. *Carroll Gray* **69**

TITAN 3 b.g. Lawman (FR) 121 – Dragonera 99 (Doyen (IRE) 132) [2017 8m 10.2s⁴ 11.9m 14v⁵ p12g Aug 22] has scope: fair maiden: best effort at 1¼m: acts on soft going. *Ed Dunlop* **66**

TITAN GODDESS 5 b.m. Equiano (FR) 127 – Phoebe Woodstock (IRE) 76 (Grand Lodge (USA) 125) [2017 82: 7g⁵ 7s 8d 8g³ 8g² p8g* 8d³ p8s p8s* p8g² Dec 21] workmanlike mare: fairly useful performer: won handicap at Chelmsford in October and seller at same course in December: second in handicap there final start: stays 8.5f: acts on polytrack, tapeta, good to firm and good to soft going: usually responds generously to pressure. *Mike Murphy* **80**

TITCHY DIGITS 2 ch.f. (Apr 18) Helmet (AUS) 127 – Sarah Park (IRE) 100 (Redback 116) [2017 6g 7v⁵ 7g⁴ 6d 6v* 6g Oct 7] 9,000Y: rather unfurnished filly: third foal: half-sister to 7f winner Delilah Park (by Delegator): dam, 7f-8.5f winner, sister to useful winner up to 7f Gouray Girl: fair performer: won nursery at Leicester in September: best effort at 6f: acts on heavy going: sold 7,000 gns, sent to Denmark. *Michael Attwater* **74**

TITHONUS (IRE) 6 b.g. Glory of Dancer 121 – Aurora Aurealis (IND) (Indictment (IND)) [2017 99: 8v 5d^{4} 5.8m 5g* 6.3f* 7s 5.4d^{5} 6s^{4} 5s^{5} Sep 24] lengthy gelding: useful handicapper: won at the Curragh (twice, by ½ length from Snap Shots second occasion) in July: best up to 7f: acts on polytrack, sand, firm and soft going: wears headgear/tongue tie: front runner/races prominently. *Denis Hogan, Ireland* **106**

TITI MAKFI 3 b.f. Makfi 130 – Titivation 83 (Montjeu (IRE) 137) [2017 72: 8.3g* 9g* 8.3m* 10.3d* 10m^{5} 9.9v^{2} 8d* 10.3m^{2} 10.1s^{6} 10.9s^{3} p12g* Nov 6] smart/progressive performer: won handicaps at Hamilton (2), Sandown and Chester in June, and Newmarket (by neck from Prying Pandora) in August, and listed race at Kempton (by head from Red Verdon) in November: stays 1½m: acts on polytrack, good to firm and heavy going. *Mark Johnston* **110**

TITUS BOLT (IRE) 8 b.g. Titus Livius (FR) 115 – Megan's Bay 82 (Muhtarram (USA) 125) [2017 12.5s t12.4d Oct 24] fair handicapper: below form both starts on Flat in 2017: stays 13f: acts on polytrack, good to firm and heavy going: has worn visor. *Jim Goldie* **–**

TITUS SECRET 5 ch.g. Sakhee's Secret 128 – Crimson Fern (IRE) 104 (Titus Livius (FR) 115) [2017 74p: 6m^{2} 6.1g^{6} 6m^{3} t6.1g* 6.1m^{2} Jul 4] fair handicapper: won at Wolverhampton in June: second at Chepstow final start: stays 6f: acts on tapeta, good to firm and good to soft going: has worn headgear: front runner/races prominently: quirky. *Malcolm Saunders* **79**

TIVOLI (IRE) 2 b.f. (Jan 22) Dark Angel (IRE) 113 – Fluvial (IRE) 75 (Exceed And Excel (AUS) 126) [2017 7d^{4} 7m^{2} 7d^{3} p6g* Oct 4] 180,000Y: well-made filly: second foal: dam, 2-y-o 7f winner who stayed 9.5f, half-sister to useful sprinter Elletelle: fairly useful form: won maiden at Kempton (by 1¼ lengths from Left Alone) in October: stays 7f. *John Gosden* **87**

TO ARMS (USA) 2 b.c. (May 2) War Front (USA) 119 – Moon Safari (USA) 101 (Mr Prospector (USA)) [2017 7m p8g^{4} Aug 31] half-brother to several winners, including smart 1m winner (stayed 1½m) Just Pretending (by Giant's Causeway): dam, 2-y-o 7f winner, sister to US Grade 1 1m/9f winner Scan: fair form: better effort when fourth in minor event at Chelmsford (5¾ lengths behind Chilean). *John Gosden* **71**

TOAST OF LONDON 4 ch.f. Haafhd 129 – First Harmony (First Trump 118) [2017 f8g^{5} 12s^{4} t12.2g^{5} t16.3g^{5} f16.5g Aug 28] seventh foal: half-sister to 3 winners, including 2m winner Generous Dream (by Generous) and 1¼m winner Harmonic Lady (by Trade Fair): dam bumper winner: modest maiden: stays 16.5f: acts on tapeta and soft going. *Antony Brittain* **54**

TOAST OF NEW YORK (USA) 6 b.h. Thewayyouare (USA) 117 – Claire Soleil (USA) (Syncline (USA)) [2017 p10g* Dec 6] strong horse: high-class performer at best: returned from long absence (had been at stud in Qatar) to win minor event at Lingfield (hooded, by length from Petite Jack) in December: stays 1¼m: acts on polytrack, tapeta and dirt. *Jamie Osborne* **110**

TOBACCO ROAD (IRE) 7 b.g. Westerner 130 – Virginias Best (King's Best (USA) 132) [2017 11.8g 12.3d^{6} p10g^{2} 10.3s^{5} p11g 13.3g Jul 13] compact gelding: fairly useful handicapper: second at Chelmsford (½ length behind Celebration Day) in June: stays 12.5f: acts on polytrack, soft and good to firm going: wears headgear: in tongue tie last 4 starts: won over hurdles in November. *David Pipe* **84**

TO BE WILD (IRE) 4 br.g. Big Bad Bob (IRE) 118 – Fire Up (Motivator 131) [2017 110p: t12.4s 12s^{4} May 20] lengthy gelding: smart performer: fourth in Aston Park Stakes at Newbury (4½ lengths behind Hawkbill) in May: stays 1½m: acts on soft and good to firm going. *Hugo Palmer* **115**

TOBOGGAN'S FIRE 4 b.f. Firebreak 125 – Toboggan Lady 75 (Tobougg (IRE) 125) [2017 88: t8.6g* t8g^{4} 9.8d 7.8s^{4} 9.2s 9v^{6} 12.1s t10.2d Oct 24] leggy filly: fairly useful handicapper: won at Wolverhampton (by head from Auntie Barber) in March: stays 8.5f: acts on tapeta, good to firm and heavy going. *Ann Duffield* **86**

TOBOGGAN'S GIFT 5 b.m. Major Cadeaux 121 – Toboggan Lady 75 (Tobougg (IRE) 125) [2017 61: f12g f14g Mar 29] modest handicapper: well held both starts in 2017: stays 1½m: acts on fibresand, tapeta and good to soft going. *Ann Duffield* **–**

TOBOUGGALOO 6 ch.m. Tobougg (IRE) 125 – Let Alone 78 (Warning 136) [2017 76: 14f 12d^{5} 12m* 12g* 12s^{ur} 11.6m^{3} Aug 31] fair handicapper: won apprentice events at Chepstow in July: stays 1½m: acts on good to firm and good to soft going: often races towards rear, usually travels strongly. *Stuart Kittow* **76**

TOBRAVE (IRE) 3 b.g. Invincible Spirit (IRE) 121 – Qasirah (IRE) 97 (Machiavellian (USA) 123) [2017 74: p7s^2 p7d Sep 21] rather unfurnished gelding: fairly useful maiden: second in handicap at Kempton (neck behind Sheikspear) in August: raced only at 7f: acts on polytrack: in hood last 3 starts: often races prominently, usually freely: sent to UAE. *Roger Varian* **84**

TO DIBBA 3 gr.c. Dubawi (IRE) 129 – Rose Diamond (IRE) 103 (Daylami (IRE) 138) [2017 72p: 7g^2 7s* 8m^2 8d^3 9.2s^2 12s Sep 9] good-bodied colt: useful performer: won maiden at Leicester (by 2½ lengths from Loujain) in May: second in handicap at Hamilton (head behind Whatsthemessage) in August: stays 9f: acts on soft and good to firm going: often races prominently. *Roger Varian* **105**

TO ETERNITY 4 b.f. Galileo (IRE) 134 – All's Forgotten (USA) 81 (Darshaan 133) [2017 103: 12d* 13.3d 12d^3 Sep 29] tall, attractive filly: useful performer: won listed race at Newmarket (by 6 lengths from Pleasant Surprise) in August: stays 1½m: acts on tapeta, good to firm and good to soft going: front runner/races prominently. *John Gosden* **108**

TOGA TIGER (IRE) 10 b.g. Antonius Pius (USA) 123 – Minerwa (GER) (Protektor (GER) 120) [2017 88§: t9.5g^3 t9.5g^4 9.9m^4 t8.6g^3 t8.6g^3 p8g^2 t9.5d^5 Dec 27] rather leggy gelding: fairly useful handicapper: third at Wolverhampton (1½ lengths behind Dutch Uncle) in February: stays 10.5f: acts on polytrack, tapeta, firm and good to soft going. *Daniel Loughnane* **86**

TOGETHERNESS (IRE) 4 b.g. Pour Moi (IRE) 125 – Madeira Mist (IRE) 80 (Grand Lodge (USA) 125) [2017 84: 13.1m^6 14m 10.2f^3 12s^3 Oct 28] fairly useful maiden handicapper: left Harry Dunlop after third start: stays 1½m: acts on soft and good to firm going: tried in cheekpieces. *Patrick Chamings* **79**

TOGETHERWECAN (IRE) 5 b.m. Danehill Dancer (IRE) 117 – Crystal Bull (USA) (Holy Bull (USA) 134) [2017 60§: 12.5s Oct 9] modest handicapper: left Mark Johnston, well beaten only start in 2017: stays 1¼m: acts on polytrack, tapeta and good to firm going: wears headgear: sometimes slowly away, often races towards rear: temperamental. *Iain Jardine* **– §**

TOJOSIMBRE 3 gr.g. Dark Angel (IRE) 113 – Shes Heavy Lifting (USA) (Broken Vow (USA) 117) [2017 p6g^6 p6g 7g 9.9g 11.6d 11.9m* 14d 11.6d^6 9.9d^3 p15.8g^4 Sep 26] modest handicapper: won at Brighton in August: stays 2m: acts on polytrack, good to firm and good to soft going: has worn headgear, including last 2 starts: in tongue tie last 5 starts: often races in rear. *Richard Hughes* **58**

TOMAHAWK KID 4 b.g. Major Cadeaux 121 – Say A Prayer 48 (Indesatchel (IRE) 120) [2017 86: 8m 10.2g^2 10d^5 8g 8m^5 10m 10.2d^5 10.2d* 10g Nov 3] angular gelding: fairly useful handicapper: won at Doncaster (amateur, by 3½ lengths from England Expects) in October: stays 1¼m: acts on soft and good to firm going. *Ian Williams* **90**

TOMILY (IRE) 3 b.g. Canford Cliffs (IRE) 133 – Cake (IRE) 100 (Acclamation 118) [2017 100: p6d^3 p6g* t6g^3 p6g^3 5.1d^5 5.1d^5 6m 5.1g^4 5m^4 5.7f^5 6.1s 5d* 5s p6g t5.1g^2 Dec 22] sturdy gelding: useful performer: won minor event at Lingfield (by ½ length from Sutter County) in February and handicap at Doncaster (by ½ length from Soie d'Leau) in October: second in handicap at Wolverhampton (short head behind Gracious John) final start: stays 6f: acts on polytrack, tapeta, soft and good to firm going: often races towards rear. *Richard Hannon* **106**

TOMMY BOY 2 ch.c. (May 11) Camacho 118 – Jacaranda Ridge 83 (Indian Ridge 123) [2017 7m 7d t5.1d Dec 26] well held in minor events/maiden: left Tony Carroll after second start. *Ian Williams* **–**

TOMMY DOCC (IRE) 5 b.g. Thewayyouare (USA) 117 – Liturgy (IRE) 83 (Catcher In The Rye (IRE) 115) [2017 95: f12g^6 Jan 24] sturdy gelding: useful handicapper: stays 2m: acts on fibresand and firm going. *Keith Dalgleish* **90**

TOMMY G 4 ch.g. Makfi 130 – Primo Heights 87 (Primo Valentino (IRE) 116) [2017 80: 6g^4 7.2m* 5m^4 5m 6g^6 5g^4 6s^5 7m 7s^3 6d^2 6d 6s t6d t7.1g^5 Dec 6] fairly useful handicapper: won at Ayr in May: second at Goodwood (¾ length behind Scorching Heat) in August: stays 7f: acts on soft and good to firm going: often races towards rear. *Jim Goldie* **86**

TOMMYS GEAL 5 b.m. Halling (USA) 133 – Steel Free (IRE) 81 (Danehill Dancer (IRE) 117) [2017 70: p10g^5 p10m p11g* 9.9g^3 11.9m^5 9.9g^2 p11d^2 9.9v p12g p12g p16g Dec 20] compact mare: modest handicapper: won at Kempton in March: stays 1½m: acts on polytrack, good to firm and good to soft going. *Michael Madgwick* **64**

TOMMY SHELBY (FR) 2 b.g. (Mar 2) Dabirsim (FR) 120 – Interior (USA) (Fusaichi Pegasus (USA) 130) [2017 6s^5 t7.2g t8s 7.2s^3 Oct 9] modest form in minor events: should be suited by further than 7f. *Richard Fahey* **64**

TOMMY'S SECRET 7 gr.g. Sakhee's Secret 128 – La Gessa 69 (Largesse 112) [2017 71: 8m^6 8s^4 8m^4 7d^6 7m p10g^2 p10d^3 p10g^4 Oct 12] sturdy gelding: modest handicapper nowadays: stays 1¼m: acts on polytrack and good to firm going: wears cheekpieces. *Jane Chapple-Hyam* **56**

TOMMY TAYLOR (USA) 3 b.g. Mizzen Mast (USA) 121 – Sharp Apple (USA) (Diesis 133) [2017 97: 6m^3 6g^2 6d 6d 6d* 6s Oct 7] sturdy gelding: smart performer: won listed race at York (by nose from Downforce) in September: has won over 7f, best form at 6f: acts on good to firm and good to soft going: often travels strongly. *Kevin Ryan* **112**

TOMORROW MYSTERY 3 b.f. Nathaniel (IRE) 129 – Retake (Reset (AUS) 124) [2017 58p: p10m^5 p10m^2 p12d^2 9.9d^5 t12.2g* p12g^2 12g^2 Sep 7] fairly useful handicapper: won at Wolverhampton (by 6 lengths from La Vie En Rose) in August: second at Kempton and Salisbury last 2 starts: stays 1½m: acts on polytrack and tapeta: usually leads: has joined Paul Nicholls. *Jamie Osborne* **92**

TOM'S ANNA (IRE) 7 b.m. Antonius Pius (USA) 123 – Vanilla Delight (IRE) 76 (Orpen (USA) 116) [2017 48: t7.1d t7.1g 8.3g^3 8.3f^2 7m^3 8.3g 8g^5 t7.1s Nov 30] modest handicapper: stays 8.5f: acts on firm going. *Sean Regan* **51** **a41**

TOM'S ROCK (IRE) 4 gr.g. Rock of Gibraltar (IRE) 133 – Asheyana (IRE) (Soviet Star (USA) 128) [2017 80: 10m p10g* t10.2s^3 p11g^2 p11d^6 12d^6 p8g^4 p11g Oct 11] workmanlike gelding: fairly useful handicapper: won at Lingfield (by 2 lengths from Ataman) in May: second at Kempton (head behind Spinners Ball) in June: stays 11f: acts on polytrack, tapeta, best turf form on good going: sometimes slowly away, often races freely. *John Butler* **90**

TOMYRIS 3 b.f. Invincible Spirit (IRE) 121 – Totally Devoted (USA) 104 (Seeking The Gold (USA)) [2017 74P: 7m* 7.9d* 8m^6 7s^3 7g^3 8g Oct 7] rather unfurnished filly: useful performer: won maiden at Newmarket (by 1½ lengths from Spinnaka) in April and listed race at York (by ¾ length from On Her Toes) in May: will stay 1¼m: acts on soft and good to firm going: usually races towards rear, often travels strongly. *Roger Varian* **106**

TONAHUTU (IRE) 3 b.f. Sir Prancealot (IRE) 111 – Really Polish (USA) (Polish Numbers (USA)) [2017 74: 7m* 8.5f^2 Sep 2] useful performer: won handicap at Lingfield in June: left Ed Vaughan, nose second in optional claimer at Del Mar: stays 8.5f: acts on polytrack, tapeta and firm going: often travels strongly. *Dan Blacker, USA* **96**

TONI'S A STAR 5 b.m. Avonbridge 123 – Canina 70 (Foxhound (USA) 103) [2017 70: f5g t5.1g t5.1g^6 f5g^5 p6g 5f^3 5.1g* 5s t5.1g 5s^2 6.1g^3 Oct 9] fair handicapper: won at Chepstow in July: stays 6f: acts on tapeta, firm and soft going: has worn blinkers, including in 2017. *Tony Carroll* **65**

TONKIN (IRE) 2 b.c. (Jan 18) Camelot 128 – Anklet (IRE) 56 (Acclamation 118) [2017 8.2s^2 7v* Sep 12] second foal: dam twice-raced half-sister to very smart 12.5f/13f winner Sarah Lynx and smart performer up to 1½m Sugar Boy: useful form: won maiden at Listowel (by 8½ lengths from Harbour Approach) in September: open to further improvement. *P. J. Prendergast, Ireland* **96 p**

TONKOLILI (IRE) 2 b.f. (Mar 27) Kodiac 112 – Heart's Desire (IRE) 79 (Royal Applause 124) [2017 5f^2 5.1g^2 5g 5s^5 5.1m^6 t5.1g^5 p5s p5g^3 Dec 23] €54,000Y, £30,000 2-y-o: closely related to 6f-10.5f winner Hearts And Minds (2-y-o 7f/1m winner, by Clodovil) and half-sister to several winners, including winner up to 1½m Unsinkable (2-y-o 6f winner, by Verglas) and winner up to 1¾m Knight Eagle (2-y-o 1m winner, by Night Shift), both useful: dam maiden (best effort at 7f): fair maiden: raced only at 5f: acts on tapeta and firm going: in headgear last 4 starts. *William Muir* **74**

TONTO'S SPIRIT 5 b.g. Authorized (IRE) 133 – Desert Royalty (IRE) 96 (Alhaarth (IRE) 126) [2017 55: 12g* 13.1s* 12.1m^3 12.1m^3 11.2s 12.1g 13.9v* 15.9s* t16.3g Nov 15] fairly useful handicapper: won at Thirsk and Ayr (amateur) in June, and Catterick (twice, by 6 lengths from Attention Seaker second occasion) in October: stays 2m: acts on good to firm and heavy going: wears headgear: usually leads: fairly useful hurdler. *Kenneth Slack* **88**

TONY CURTIS 4 b.g. Rock of Gibraltar (IRE) 133 – Strawberry Lolly 89 (Lomitas 129) [2017 111: 9.9g 7g^4 8s^2 Aug 4] good-topped gelding: smart performer: second in Betfred Mile (Handicap) at Goodwood (¾ length behind Master The World) final start: stays 1m: acts on any turf going. *Richard Hannon* **114**

TONY SOPRANO (IRE) 2 b.g. (Mar 6) Lethal Force (IRE) 128 – Zarkalia (IRE) (Red Ransom (USA)) [2017 5.2g t6.1g 6s^5 8.3v^4 8.1s^3 p7g Sep 27] sturdy gelding: fair maiden: best effort at 1m: acts on soft going: tried in blinkers. *Martyn Meade* **67**

TOOFI (FR) 6 b.g. Henrythenavigator (USA) 131 – Silver Bark 68 (Royal Applause 124) [2017 101: 6g 6s 6m 6d⁴ 7m⁶ 7s 6d⁶ 6s² 6v 6s⁵ Oct 15] sturdy gelding: fairly useful handicapper: fourth at Haydock (1½ lengths behind Handsome Dude) in June: stays 7f: acts on soft and good to firm going: has worn headgear, including last 4 starts. *John Butler* **93**

TOOHOTTOTOUCH 2 b.g. (Mar 12) Hellvelyn 118 – Soft Touch (IRE) 78 (Petorius 117) [2017 7f 7.2g Jul 17] well held in minor events. *Michael Dods* **–**

TOOLA BOOLA 7 b.m. Tobougg (IRE) 125 – Forsythia 63 (Most Welcome 131) [2017 76: t12.4d³ 11.2v t12.4d Oct 24] fair maiden handicapper: should be suited by at least 1¾m: acts on tapeta and soft going: tried in visor. *Jedd O'Keeffe* **59**

TOOLATETODELEGATE 3 b.f. Delegator 125 – Little Caroline (IRE) (Great Commotion (USA) 123) [2017 t8.6g⁶ p7g⁴ p7g³ p8g 8d 10m 7.4g⁶ 8.1d t7.2g⁵ p6g² t5.1m* t6.1g t5.1g² t5.1g³ p6g³ Dec 20] seventh foal: half-sister to 5f (including at 2 yrs) to 1m winner Pick A Little (by Piccolo) and 5f/6f winner Sartori (by Elnadim): dam, US 1m winner, half-sister to smart German winner up to 1m Chagall: fair performer: won minor event at Wolverhampton in October: stays 7f: acts on polytrack and tapeta: in cheekpieces last 5 starts: wears tongue tie. *Brian Barr* **66**

TOO MANY SHOTS 3 b.g. Mullionmileanhour (IRE) 116 – Neissa (USA) (Three Wonders (USA)) [2017 65: p8g⁴ p8g⁴ f8m p12g² p12f² 12.1g⁵ p12g⁴ 11.6d³ p13.3g³ p12g² p12g p13.3s Dec 1] modest maiden handicapper: stays 13.5f: acts on polytrack and good to soft going: often races prominently. *John Best* **64**

TOOMER 2 ch.f. (Feb 27) Iffraaj 127 – Harlem Dancer (Dr Devious (IRE) 127) [2017 6g 6v 8g⁵ 6d⁴ 7d⁵ p7g Oct 18] 45,000F, 85,000Y: fifth foal: half-sister to smart 5f/6f winner (including at 2 yrs) Hototo (by Sleeping Indian): dam useful French 1¼m/10.5f winner who stayed 1½m: fair maiden: stays 1m: best form on good going. *Richard Hannon* **68**

TOOTY FRUITTI 3 b.f. Captain Gerrard (IRE) 113 – Littlemisstutti (IRE) (Noverre (USA) 125) [2017 t6m⁶ p5g³ f5d² t5.1g⁴ 5d 5.7f⁴ 5.7f⁴ t5.1g* t6.1g² p5g³ t6.1g² t6.1g⁵ Aug 31] third foal: half-sister to 2-y-o 6f winner Nidnod (by Myboycharlie): dam unraced half-sister to smart sprinter Guinea Hunter: fair performer: won seller at Wolverhampton in July: second in handicap at same course later that month: stays 6f: acts on fibresand, tapeta, best turf form on firm going: sometimes slowly away: sold 7,000 gns, sent to Greece. *Jo Hughes* **72**

TOPALING 6 ch.m. Halling (USA) 133 – Topatori (IRE) 89 (Topanoora 118) [2017 67: t13.9mʳʳ Jan 13] fair handicapper: refused to race only outing in 2017: stays 16.5f: acts on polytrack and tapeta: tried in cheekpieces: temperamental. *Mark H. Tompkins* **– §**

TOPALOVA 4 ch.f. Champs Elysees 124 – Topatori (IRE) 89 (Topanoora 118) [2017 59: p13.3d⁴ p13.3g³ t13.9m p16g² p15.8g⁵ p16s³ 16.3d p16g Sep 6] sturdy filly: modest maiden handicapper: stays 2m: acts on polytrack and tapeta: has worn headgear. *Mark H. Tompkins* **57**

TOPAMICHI 7 b.g. Beat Hollow 126 – Topatori (IRE) 89 (Topanoora 118) [2017 78: 9v p10s⁶ f12.1g³ 10.2v* f12.1g² f11.1g³ Dec 22] fair handicapper: won at Nottingham (amateur) in November: second at Southwell later that month: stays 1½m: acts on polytrack, fibresand, good to firm and heavy going: has worn headgear: often races freely. *Michael Appleby* **79**

TOPAPINION 2 b.c. (Apr 28) So You Think (NZ) 133 – Topatoo 109 (Bahamian Bounty 116) [2017 7d p8s⁶ p7d³ Oct 6] fourth foal: half-brother to 1½m winner Toptempo (by Halling): dam 1m-10.4f winner: fair form: best effort when third in minor event at Chelmsford (2½ lengths behind Society Power) final start: should stay 1m+: open to further improvement. *Mark H. Tompkins* **71 p**

TOP BEAK (IRE) 4 b.g. Lawman (FR) 121 – Tree Tops 77 (Grand Lodge (USA) 125) [2017 99: 10m³ 8s 10.1m 9.9m p12g³ 10d⁶ 9.9g 8g p8g⁴ p12g⁴ p12g⁶ Dec 30] good-topped gelding: useful handicapper: third at Newbury (1½ lengths behind Signe) in April: left Hughie Morrison/regressed after fifth start: stays 1½m: acts on polytrack, good to firm and good to soft going: in hood last 2 starts: wears tongue tie. *Michael Attwater* **96 d**

TOP BOY 7 b.g. Exceed And Excel (AUS) 126 – Injaaz 99 (Sheikh Albadou 128) [2017 94: p5g⁶ f5g p5d* p5g p5g⁶ p5g⁵ p6s⁵ 6d⁶ 5g² 5d⁵ 5s 5g p5g⁵ t5.1g⁶ Dec 5] tall, lengthy gelding: fairly useful handicapper: won at Chelmsford (by length from Dynamo Walt) in February: best form at 5f: acts on polytrack, tapeta, good to firm and heavy going: wears headgear: usually races nearer last than first. *Derek Shaw* **90**

TOP COP 8 b.g. Acclamation 118 – Speed Cop 104 (Cadeaux Genereux 131) [2017 61d: t6m Jan 13] big gelding: modest handicapper: lost form since first start in 2016: stays 7f: acts on polytrack, tapeta and good to firm going: wears headgear. *Ronald Harris* **36**

TOP DIKTAT 9 b.g. Diktat 126 – Top Romance (IRE) 105 (Entrepreneur 123) [2017 78: 9.9v^{6} 9.1m p10g 10.2g p10g^{3} Dec 20] good-topped gelding: fair performer: stays 11f: acts on polytrack, good to firm and heavy going: tried in visor: usually races towards rear. *Gary Moore* **68**

TOPMEUP 3 ch.f. Mayson 124 – Ambrix (IRE) 64 (Xaar 132) [2017 54: f8g^{3} f8d^{3} p7m^{2} 7.1d^{3} 7m^{3} p8g^{3} 7.1m^{4} 7g^{4} 8g^{4} 8.1d* 7.4v* 7s^{2} p8g^{5} 7d* p8g^{4} f8.1g^{6} p8g^{2} t9.5d^{4} Dec 26] leggy filly: fair performer: won handicaps at Chepstow in August and Ffos Las in September, and claimer at Leicester in October: left David Evans after fourteenth start: stays 1¼m, usually races over shorter: acts on all-weather, good to firm and heavy going: wears visor. *Gay Kelleway* **69**

TOP MISSION 3 b.g. Dubawi (IRE) 129 – Ever Love (BRZ) (Nedawi 126) [2017 79p: 7m^{2} 7s^{3} p7g* p8g^{2} Nov 17] strong gelding: useful performer: won maiden at Chelmsford (by neck from Buxted Dream) in June: second in handicap at Lingfield (length behind Al Galayel) final start: stays 1m: acts on polytrack and good to firm going: tried in cheekpieces: front runner/races prominently. *Saeed bin Suroor* **95**

TOP NOTCH TONTO (IRE) 7 ch.g. Thousand Words 113 – Elite Hope (USA) 84 (Moment of Hope (USA)) [2017 109: t8.6g 8g 8m^{4} 7.9d 10g t8s Jun 29] small gelding: very smart at best, on the downgrade nowadays: stays 10.5f: acts on soft and good to firm going: has worn headgear: often tongue tied in 2017: sometimes slowly away, often races towards rear. *Brian Ellison* **104**

TOP OFFER 8 b.g. Dansili 127 – Zante 108 (Zafonic (USA) 130) [2017 64, a73: t7.1g^{3} t7.1g t7.1m^{5} t7.1g^{6} t7.2g t8.6g^{3} t8.6g^{2} 8g^{5} t8.6g t8.6g^{4} t8.6g* t8.6g t9.5d Dec 26] well-made gelding: fair handicapper: won at Wolverhampton (apprentice) in November: stays 8.5f: acts on polytrack, tapeta and good to firm going: wears headgear. *Patrick Morris* **67**

TOP OF THE BANK 4 b.g. Piccolo 121 – America Lontana (FR) (King's Theatre (IRE) 128) [2017 72: t6m* t5g p6g* p6g* t6g^{5} 6g 5m^{2} 6m^{6} p6g^{3} 7.2m 6.1g 6g^{5} 6g t6.1g^{3} p6d p5g t6.1g^{6} t6.1g Nov 20] fair handicapper: won at Wolverhampton in January and Lingfield (twice) in March: stays 6f: acts on polytrack, tapeta and good to firm going: wears headgear: front runner/races prominently. *Kristin Stubbs* **79**

TOP OF THE GLAS (IRE) 6 gr.g. Verglas (IRE) 118 – Fury Dance (USA) (Cryptoclearance (USA)) [2017 88: t12.4g 10.3g 12g^{5} 12g^{6} t10.2s^{6} 11.2v^{3} Jun 8] tall gelding: fairly useful handicapper: stays 12.5f: acts on tapeta and good to firm going: tried in cheekpieces: sometimes slowly away. *Brian Ellison* **84**

TOPOLOGY 4 br.g. Passing Glance 119 – Bold Byzantium (Bold Arrangement 127) [2017 83: 8.3g 9.9g 7m 8.1g 7m^{6} 6g^{5} 7s^{3} p8g^{4} Oct 14] angular gelding: fair maiden handicapper: stays 1m: acts on polytrack and soft going: often in headgear in 2017. *Joseph Tuite* **71**

TOP SCORE 3 b.g. Hard Spun (USA) 124 – Windsor County (USA) (Elusive Quality (USA)) [2017 99: a7f^{3} 7g* 7g* a9.4g 8m 7g^{6} 7m 7d 7s p6g^{4} Oct 11] compact gelding: smart performer: won minor event (by nose from Nobelium) and listed race (by ½ length from Fly At Dawn), both at Meydan in February: seventh in 2000 Guineas at Newmarket (3½ lengths behind Churchill) in May: stays 1m: acts on polytrack, soft and good to firm going: has worn headgear, including in 2017: often starts slowly: temperament under suspicion. *Saeed bin Suroor* **116**

TOPSOIL 4 b.g. Kheleyf (USA) 116 – Edge of Gold 81 (Choisir (AUS) 126) [2017 56: p5g^{2} t5.1m* t5.1g p5d Feb 23] modest handicapper: won at Wolverhampton (by ½ length from Dandilion) in January: best form at 5f: acted on polytrack, tapeta and good to soft going: wore headgear: sometimes slowly away, but usually front runner/raced prominently: dead. *Ronald Harris* **61**

TOPTEMPO 8 ch.m. Halling (USA) 133 – Topatoo 109 (Bahamian Bounty 116) [2017 –: p16g 16.3d 16.3s^{2} f16.5g Aug 28] lengthy, angular mare: modest handicapper nowadays: stays 16.5f: acts on polytrack and soft going: has worn blinkers. *Ralph Smith* **56**

TOP TUG (IRE) 6 ch.g. Halling (USA) 133 – Top Romance (IRE) 105 (Entrepreneur 123) [2017 108: 12m^{2} 14g* 12m^{4} 13.9m 11.8d^{2} 11.9s Nov 11] good-topped gelding: smart handicapper: won at Goodwood (by 1¾ lengths from High Secret) in May: second at Leicester (1½ lengths behind Dance The Dream) in October: stays 1¾m: acts on polytrack, soft and good to firm going: tried in cheekpieces: usually races towards rear. *Alan King* **114**

TOP VILLE BEN (IRE) 5 b.g. Beneficial 117 – Great Decision (IRE) (Simply Great (FR) 122) [2017 14.2s^4 Sep 15] 40/1, possibly flattered when 5¾ lengths fourth of 6 to On To Victory in minor event at Salisbury: useful hurdler. *Philip Kirby* **102 ?**

TOR 3 ch.g. Orientor 118 – Dance In The Sun 94 (Halling (USA) 133) [2017 84: t7.1g t7.1g t7.1g t12.2g^4 t12.2g^6 12d^2 14f^3 12m^3 13.1g* 15d^2 14.4s* 13.9m 14s* 14v^4 Sep 29] useful handicapper: won at Hamilton in July, Chester in August and Musselburgh (by nose from Dominating) in September: stays 15f: acts on tapeta and any turf going: usually leads, often travels strongly. *Iain Jardine* **96**

TORCEDOR (IRE) 5 b.g. Fastnet Rock (AUS) 127 – Magnolia Lane (IRE) 87 (Sadler's Wells (USA) 132) [2017 108: 14s* 14g* 20m^5 14s^2 16s^2 Oct 21] lengthy gelding: smart performer: won minor event at Leopardstown (by 5½ lengths from Twilight Payment) and Vintage Crop Stakes at Navan (by 1½ lengths from Order of St George) in April: second in Long Distance Cup at Ascot (½ length behind Order of St George) in October: stays 2½m: acts on soft and good to firm going: usually wears headgear. *Mrs J. Harrington, Ireland* **118**

TORCELLO (IRE) 3 ch.g. Born To Sea (IRE) 117 – Islandagore (IRE) 97 (Indian Ridge 123) [2017 9v^2 9.2s^3 9.9s* 10m* 12s^6 12g* 12m Oct 13] 40,000Y: useful-looking gelding: half-brother to several winners, including useful 2-y-o 6f winner Iron Range and useful 6f (including at 2 yrs)/7f winner Alice's Dancer (both by Clodovil): dam 7f winner: useful performer: won maiden at Salisbury in July, and handicaps at Newmarket in August and September (by 3 lengths from Saunter): stays 1½m: acts on soft and good to firm going: has joined A. J. McNamara, Ireland. *Andrew Balding* **102**

TORCH 4 b.g. Paco Boy (IRE) 129 – Singed (Zamindar (USA) 116) [2017 89, a83: p8d p10g f8g t8s t8.6g Jun 26] rangy gelding: fairly useful handicapper at 3 yrs, has lost his way: has worn cheekpieces, including last 2 starts: sometimes slowly away. *John Butler* **–**

TORERO 8 b.g. Hernando (FR) 127 – After You 92 (Pursuit of Love 124) [2017 16v Jul 28] fair handicapper in 2013, well held only start on Flat since: has worn headgear: poor hurdler: one to treat with caution. *Alan Phillips* **– §**

TORIANO 4 ch.g. Equiano (FR) 127 – Ticki Tori (IRE) 80 (Vettori (IRE) 119) [2017 93p: p7d p8g p8g Dec 13] fairly useful form at 3 yrs, below that level in 2017: left James Eustace after first start: stays 7f: acts on polytrack. *Nick Littmoden* **76**

TORMENT 4 gr.g. Dark Angel (IRE) 113 – Selkirk Sky 65 (Selkirk (USA) 129) [2017 76: p8d p7g^5 p7g 6g^5 p6g 6g 6s^6 5.1g^6 8m Aug 22] useful-looking gelding: fair handicapper: left Richard Hannon/regressed after first start: should stay 1m: acts on good to firm going: usually in headgear nowadays: tried in tongue tie. *Charlie Wallis* **65 d**

TORNEQUETA MAY 2 b.f. (Mar 15) Style Vendome (FR) 116 – Alabastrine 56 (Green Desert (USA) 127) [2017 p7g Dec 20] half-sister to several winners, including useful winner up to 1½m Hail Caesar (2-y-o 7.5f winner, by Montjeu) and 1½m winner (stayed 2m) Alsacienne (by Dalakhani): dam lightly-raced half-sister to Nassau/Sun Chariot Stakes winner Last Second: 50/1, well held in minor event at Lingfield (in cheekpieces). *Adam West* **–**

TORONTO SOUND 3 b.g. Aussie Rules (USA) 123 – Caribana 77 (Hernando (FR) 127) [2017 p10g^6 p8s t10.2s 10.1m^3 Jun 30] 58,000Y: sixth foal: half-brother to smart winner up to 1½m Cubanita (2-y-o 1m winner, by Selkirk) and 2-y-o 1m winner Camagueyana (by Archipenko): dam 9.5f winner: modest form: will be suited by 1½m: remains capable of better. *Sir Mark Prescott Bt* **62 p**

TORREMAR (FR) 4 br.g. Excellent Art 125 – Sabela (IRE) (Sinndar (IRE) 134) [2017 82: f12d 12g^4 9.9m^3 13.1s 14g 14s Oct 1] fairly useful handicapper: stays 1¾m: acts on good to firm and heavy going: wears cheekpieces: usually races prominently. *Kevin Ryan* **78**

TORRID 6 ch.g. Three Valleys (USA) 119 – Western Appeal (USA) (Gone West (USA)) [2017 89: 8m* t8s^2 8d^5 8d t8d Sep 29] fairly useful handicapper: won at Redcar (by 1¾ lengths from Heir To A Throne) in April: stays 8.5f: acts on good to firm and heavy going: tried in hood. *Michael Easterby* **87**

TOSCANINI (IRE) 5 b.g. Shamardal (USA) 129 – Tuzla (FR) 121 (Panoramic 120) [2017 116: 8g^4 8g^5 8s 8f 8v^5 7g^2 7d 8s Oct 21] close-coupled gelding: smart performer: second in City of York Stakes (neck behind Talaayeb) in August: stays 1m: acts on polytrack and any turf going: has worn headgear. *Richard Fahey* **114**

TOTALLY MAGIC (IRE) 5 b.m. Captain Rio 122 – Hypocrisy 85 (Bertolini (USA) 125) [2017 75: 8g 7m^3 8f^2 7m^2 7g^3 8g^2 8g^2 8g t8g^4 t7.1s^5 8v Oct 9] fair handicapper: stays 1m: acts on tapeta, soft and good to firm going: has worn cheekpieces. *Richard Whitaker* **74**

TOTAL POWER 4 b.g. Sleeping Indian 122 – House of Frills 69 (Paris House 123) [2017 72: 5g t5.1g 6d 6s Jul 10] fair handicapper: stays 6.5f: acts on soft going: tried in hood/ tongue tie: sometimes slowly away, often races towards rear. *Brian Ellison* **66**

TOTAL STAR 3 gr.c. Pivotal 124 – Millennium Star (IRE) 60 (High Chaparral (IRE) 132) [2017 96: p10g³ 10.2f⁵ p11g Sep 27] useful-looking colt: useful handicapper: third at Chelmsford (4½ lengths behind Drochaid) in May: stays 1¼m: acts on polytrack and good to firm going: sold 25,000 gns, sent to Saudi Arabia. *Luca Cumani* **97**

TOUCHED BY LOVE (USA) 4 b.g. Street Sense (USA) 128 – Love of Dubai (USA) 106 (More Than Ready (USA) 120) [2017 –: 10.2f May 26] lightly-raced maiden, well beaten in handicap only start in 2017. *Ismail Mohammed* **–**

TOUCH ME (IRE) 3 b.f. Masterofthehorse (IRE) 122 – User Name (USA) (Mr Greeley (USA) 122) [2017 65: p8g p7g² t7.1g³ p7g⁵ 6g May 9] fair handicapper: stays 7f: acts on polytrack: wears hood: often races prominently: sent to Qatar. *K. R. Burke* **70**

TOUCH OF COLOR 4 b.f. Sixties Icon 125 – Shesells Seashells 83 (Tiger Hill (IRE) 127) [2017 64: 7d p7d p7g f8.1g Dec 4] close-coupled filly: fair maiden at best, no form in 2017: tried in cheekpieces. *Richard Fahey* **–**

TOUCH OF FAITH (IRE) 3 ch.g. Zoffany (IRE) 121 – Jusoor (USA) (El Prado (IRE) 119) [2017 p8d⁶ f8m⁶ t12.2m⁵ Feb 25] well beaten in maidens. *Michael Appleby* **–**

TOUCH OF PARADISE (IRE) 3 ch.f. Frankel 147 – Ramruma (USA) 123 (Diesis 133) [2017 t8g³ t8d Feb 4] half-sister to smart winner up to 1½m (stayed 1¾m) Flying Cross (2-y-o 1m winner, by Sadler's Wells) and Belgian 2½m winner Gunboat (by Danehill Dancer): dam won at around 1½m (including Oaks) and second in St Leger: fair form: better effort when third in maiden at Newcastle in January: bred to stay 1½m. *Richard Fahey* **66**

TOUCH THE CLOUDS 6 b.g. Sleeping Indian 122 – Aptina (USA) (Aptitude (USA) 128) [2017 42: f5g⁵ 10.2m⁴ 8g⁴ 11.8g⁴ 10.2d⁵ t12.2g p8g² p7g² p7g p8s p8s² Dec 17] rather leggy gelding: modest handicapper: stays 1½m: acts on polytrack, fibresand, good to firm and heavy going: has worn headgear/tongue tie: front runner/races prominently. *William Stone* **56**

TOUGH LASS (IRE) 2 b.f. (Mar 26) Kodiac 112 – Sagemacca (IRE) (Danehill Dancer (IRE) 117) [2017 p7g Dec 20] €80,000Y: fourth foal: closely related to Italian 2-y-o 1m winner Sagegrey (by Clodovil) and half-sister to 1¼m winner Chocolate Diamond (by Intense Focus): dam ran once: 66/1, well held in minor event at Lingfield. *George Peckham* **–**

TOUGH REMEDY (IRE) 2 b.g. (Apr 21) Tough As Nails (IRE) 108 – Remediate (USA) (Miswaki (USA) 124) [2017 5.5s² 5g³ 5s⁵ 6g² Jul 24] fair form: will be suited by 7f. *Keith Dalgleish* **77**

TOULSON 4 b.g. Champs Elysees 124 – Flower Market 68 (Cadeaux Genereux 131) [2017 87: 10.2g* 10d* 11.8m 10d⁴ 10m⁵ 10.2d⁴ Oct 18] useful-looking gelding: useful handicapper: won at Nottingham and Windsor (by short head from Getback In Paris) in May: stays 1¼m: acts on polytrack, good to firm and good to soft going: in cheekpieces last 2 starts: usually races prominently: has joined Charles Byrnes, Ireland. *Eve Johnson Houghton* **98**

TOUR DE PARIS (IRE) 2 b.g. (Apr 30) Champs Elysees 124 – Disco Lights 76 (Spectrum (IRE) 126) [2017 7m 8v p8g⁴ Nov 1] fair form: best effort when fourth in minor event at Kempton (neck behind Losingmyreligion) final start. *Eve Johnson Houghton* **68**

TOUWARI (IRE) 3 b.c. Teofilo (IRE) 126 – Luminaria (IRE) (Danehill (USA) 126) [2017 p12g⁵ 11.5m⁴ 9.9m³ 11.6f⁴ t12.2g Jul 11] fair maiden: stays 11.5f: acts on good to firm going: wears blinkers: usually leads. *John Gosden* **79**

TO WAFIJ (IRE) 2 b.c. (Mar 14) Kodiac 112 – Rajmahal (UAE) (Indian Ridge 123) [2017 5.2m* 5d² 5m³ 5v³ 5m⁶ 5m⁶ Oct 13] 130,000Y: compact colt: fifth foal: brother to useful 2-y-o 6f winner No Leaf Clover: dam unraced half-sister to smart winner up to 1m Furner's Green: useful performer: won maiden at Yarmouth in May: third in Molecomb Stakes at Goodwood (1¾ lengths behind Havana Grey) in August: will be suited by 6f: acts on good to firm and heavy going. *Roger Varian* **100**

TOWELRADS BOY (IRE) 2 b.c. (Apr 28) Red Jazz (USA) 125 – Mystery Hill (USA) 72 (Danehill (USA) 126) [2017 6d⁶ t5.1g* Nov 7] €10,500F, £20,000Y: good-topped colt: half-brother to several winners, including useful winner up to 1¾m (stayed 2¼m) Mystery Star (2-y-o 8.6f winner, by Kris Kin) and 5f/6f winner Lilly Be (by Titus Livius): dam UAE 7f winner: fairly useful form: won minor event at Wolverhampton (by length from Axe Cap) in November: open to further improvement. *Paul Cole* **82 p**

TOWERLANDS PARK (IRE) 4 b.g. Danehill Dancer (IRE) 117 – Strategy 92 **101**
(Machiavellian (USA) 123) [2017 100p: 10s^3 11.9s t9.5g^3 Dec 2] useful handicapper: third at Newbury (2 lengths behind Century Dream) in October: stays 11f: acts on polytrack, tapeta and soft going: tried in cheekpieces. *Michael Bell*

TOWER POWER 6 b.g. Nayef (USA) 129 – Voile (IRE) 102 (Barathea (IRE) 127) [2017 **74**
84: 9.9m 10.2d^4 p12g Dec 13] strong, good-topped gelding: fairly useful handicapper: below best in 2017 after long absence: stays 1½m: acts on polytrack, tapeta, good to firm and good to soft going: tried in cheekpieces/tongue tie: front runner/races prominently. *Phil McEntee*

TOWIE (IRE) 3 br.c. Sea The Stars (IRE) 140 – Epping 81 (Charnwood Forest (IRE) 125) **78**
[2017 12d 11.4d^4 11.8v^4 Sep 25] good-topped colt: fair form: best effort when fourth in maiden at Windsor in September: will be suited by 1¾m+: has joined Gary Moore. *Hughie Morrison*

TOWN CHARTER (USA) 3 gr.c. Lonhro (AUS) 128 – Summer Fete (IRE) 104 (Pivotal **88**
124) [2017 90: 7g 7g^3 8g^4 7d^4 8d^6 8d^4 t7.1g^6 8d 10g t8g Nov 24] tall colt: fairly useful handicapper: third at Newmarket in June: left Mark Johnston after eighth start: stays 7f: acts on good to firm and good to soft going: in tongue tie last 2 starts. *Tony Coyle*

TOY THEATRE 3 b.f. Lonhro (AUS) 128 – Puppet Queen (USA) (Kingmambo (USA) **88**
125) [2017 58: p7d* p7d^2 t7.1m* p8g^5 t7.1g^2 p8s p8s^5 7.6d^4 p7g 7g* 7d* t7.2g^5 f7.1g^6 Dec 11] fairly useful handicapper: won at Chelmsford in February, Wolverhampton in March, Newmarket in September and Doncaster (apprentice, by neck from Pastime) in October: all wins at around 7f: acts on polytrack, tapeta and good to soft going. *Michael Appleby*

TRACTIVE EFFORT 4 b.g. Rail Link 132 – Anastasia Venture 70 (Lion Cavern (USA) **53**
117) [2017 55: p12d p12d* p16s Jun 14] modest handicapper: won at Kempton in February: best effort at 1½m: acts on polytrack. *Michael Attwater*

TRADE ROUTE (IRE) 3 gr.g. Mastercraftsman (IRE) 129 – Shanghai Visit (IRE) **77**
(Peintre Celebre (USA) 137) [2017 p8g^5 p8g^5 p8m^3 8.3g 8m 10d^6 Jul 11] fair maiden: stays 1m: acts on polytrack: sometimes in cheekpieces. *David Elsworth*

TRADING POINT (FR) 3 b.c. Siyouni (FR) 122 – Zita Blues (IRE) (Zieten (USA) 118) **–**
[2017 85p: 10.3d 8d Oct 27] fairly useful 1m winner at 2 yrs, little impact in handicaps in 2017. *John Quinn*

TRADING PUNCHES (IRE) 3 b.g. Elzaam (AUS) 115 – Kiralik 100 (Efisio 120) **95**
[2017 84: 8s^2 9.9g^5 9.9d 8.3d 8d Oct 27] useful handicapper: second at Newmarket (½ length behind Fire Brigade) in May: went wrong way after: stays 1m: acts on soft and good to firm going: tried in cheekpieces: front runner/races prominently. *David Brown*

TRADITIONAL DANCER (IRE) 5 b.g. Danehill Dancer (IRE) 117 – Cote Quest **61 §**
(USA) 96 (Green Desert (USA) 127) [2017 –: 9.1g 12.5g^2 12.5m^6 t16.3s^3 14s^5 t16.3g t16.3d^5 Dec 16] modest maiden handicapper: stays 16.5f: acts on tapeta: often in headgear: ungenuine. *Iain Jardine*

TRAIS FLUORS 3 b.c. Dansili 127 – Trois Lunes (FR) 111 (Manduro (GER) 135) [2017 **119**
8d* 8g* 8m* 8g^2 8d^4 Aug 13] first foal: dam French 1m (at 2 yrs) and 9f (Prix Vanteaux) winner: smart form: won first 4 starts, newcomers race at Maisons-Laffitte at 2 yrs, minor event at Compiegne in April, listed race at Saint-Cloud in May and Prix Paul de Moussac at Chantilly (by length from Stunning Spirit) in June: in frame after in Prix Jean Prat at Chantilly (1¼ lengths second to Thunder Snow) and Prix Jacques le Marois at Deauville (1½ lengths fourth to Al Wukair): stays 1m: acts on good to firm and good to soft going: often races towards rear. *A. Fabre, France*

TRANQUIL DAZE (IRE) 3 ch.g. Sir Prancealot (IRE) 111 – Endless Peace (IRE) 62 **76**
(Russian Revival (USA) 125) [2017 56: t6f^3 f6g* p6g^3 t6g^4 t7.1g^4 6.1d 5m Jun 24] good-quartered gelding: fair handicapper: won at Southwell in February: stays 6f: acts on all-weather: tried in visor: sold 5,000 gns in July, sent to Sweden. *David Brown*

TRANQUIL SOUL 2 b.f. (May 7) Farhh 131 – Peaceful Soul (USA) 65 (Dynaformer **69**
(USA)) [2017 6.1f^6 t6.1g^2 t7.2g^3 7.4s^5 p7g p8d^4 p10g^3 Oct 26] third foal: half-sister to winners abroad by Poet's Voice and Mayson: dam maiden (best effort at 1¼m): fair maiden: probably stays 1¼m: acts on polytrack and tapeta: tried in blinkers. *David Lanigan*

TRANQUIL STAR (IRE) 3 b.f. Galileo (IRE) 134 – We Can Say It Now (AUS) 119 **98**
(Starcraft (NZ) 128) [2017 8m 10m^3 9.9s^3 p12g^5 12v^2 t10.2g* Nov 23] compact filly: second foal: closely related to smart 1m-1¼m winner Sky Kingdom (by Montjeu): dam New Zealand Group 1 1m winner: useful performer: won maiden at Newcastle in November: stays 1½m: acts on tapeta, good to firm and heavy going. *Jeremy Noseda*

TRANQUIL TRACY 3 b.f. Stimulation (IRE) 121 – Tranquil Flight (Oasis Dream 129) [2017 –: t7.1m^{4} t7.1m^{6} t7.1g^{6} p7g t7.2g t8s^{6} 10.2v^{6} 8.3s^{6} 8g t8.6g Oct 21] sturdy filly: poor maiden: stays 1m: acts on tapeta, soft and good to firm going. *John Norton* **48**

TRANSMITTING 4 b.g. Cacique (IRE) 124 – Shuttle Mission (Sadler's Wells (USA) 132) [2017 78: p11g^{6} 9.9d^{4} 10.1g^{2} 10.2d^{3} 10d* p12g Oct 3] good-topped gelding: fair handicapper: won at Lingfield in August: stays 1¼m: acts on good to firm and good to soft going: in headgear last 5 starts. *Ed Vaughan* **77**

TRANSPENNINE STAR 4 ch.g. Mount Nelson 125 – Brave Mave 83 (Daylami (IRE) 138) [2017 82: 12g 13.9m 13.1s^{4} 14.1g^{4} 17.2s^{2} 16.3d^{3} 17.1v^{2} 18v Oct 9] fairly useful handicapper: second at Pontefract (nose behind La Fritillaire) in September: stays 17f: acts on heavy going: in cheekpieces last 4 starts: usually races close up: has joined Jonjo O'Neill. *Michael Dods* **84**

TRAUMATISED 2 b.f. (Apr 11) Kheleyf (USA) 116 – Reveal The Light 52 (Fantastic Light (USA) 134) [2017 f7.1g Dec 11] first foal: dam, maiden on Flat, third in bumper: 100/1, well held in minor event at Southwell. *Michael Appleby* **–**

TRAUTMANN (IRE) 3 ch.g. Casamento (IRE) 118 – Klang (IRE) 59 (Night Shift (USA)) [2017 –: p8g p7d^{5} 9.9m 11.9d^{3} 12v^{5} 11.6m^{4} Aug 31] modest maiden: stays 1½m: acts on good to firm and good to soft going. *Daniel Loughnane* **60**

TRAVELCARD (USA) 2 b.f. (Mar 30) Iffraaj 127 – Central Line (USA) 52 (Redoute's Choice (AUS)) [2017 p6d^{3} p6g* 6d^{2} 7v^{3} 6s^{3} 7s^{2} Oct 15] rangy filly: second foal: half-sister to useful 5f winner Snowstar (by Raven's Pass): dam twice-raced half-sister to useful performer up to 1m Good Place: fairly useful performer: won minor event at Lingfield in July: second in nursery at Goodwood (¾ length behind Zoraya) final start: stays 7f: acts on polytrack and soft going: usually races close up. *Mark Johnston* **83**

TRAVELLER (FR) 3 b.g. Henrythenavigator (USA) 131 – Nantes (GER) (Night Shift (USA)) [2017 66p: p8g^{5} p8d^{3} p7g* 7g^{2} 8g^{4} 7s^{4} 7m^{3} 8.5g^{2} p8g^{2} p8g Oct 25] fairly useful performer: won maiden at Lingfield in February: second in handicap at Kempton (½ length behind Cool Team) in October: stays 1m: acts on polytrack and good to firm going: wears tongue tie: sold 20,000 gns later in October. *Charles Hills* **86**

TRAVELLERS JOY 2 b.f. (Mar 11) Equiano (FR) 127 – Travelling 81 (Dubai Destination (USA) 127) [2017 7.1m Jul 4] first foal: dam, winner up to 9.5f (2-y-o 7f winner), half-sister to useful winner up to 1¼m Bonfire Knight: 33/1, well held in minor event at Chepstow. *Richard Hughes* **–**

TRAVEL LIGHTLY 2 b.f. (Feb 14) Showcasing 117 – Upton Seas 83 (Josr Algarhoud (IRE) 118) [2017 6g 6d 7d Jul 28] third foal: dam, 1¼m-1½m winner, half-sister to useful winner around 1¼m Sound Hearts: well held in minor events. *Tim Easterby* **–**

TRAVELTALK (IRE) 3 b.g. Fast Company (IRE) 126 – Laheen (IRE) 60 (Bluebird (USA) 125) [2017 72: t6g 7.4f 7s^{5} 6d 7v 10s^{3} t10.2g^{3} 10d* t12.4g Nov 23] fair performer: won seller at Redcar in October: stays 1¼m: acts on tapeta and soft going: has worn cheekpieces: usually races prominently. *Brian Ellison* **69**

TREACHEROUS 3 b.g. Paco Boy (IRE) 129 – Black Baroness (Ishiguru (USA) 114) [2017 7g 8s p6g p6g* p7g p7g^{4} Nov 7] lengthy gelding: fair performer: won handicap at Kempton in September: best effort at 6f: acts on polytrack: often starts slowly/races towards rear. *Ed de Giles* **78**

TREAD LIGHTLY 3 b.g. Canford Cliffs (IRE) 133 – Step Lightly (IRE) 65 (Danehill Dancer (IRE) 117) [2017 55: 8m 8g 10m^{2} 9.2g^{2} 10.2m 9.2s^{3} 14.4g^{6} 9.8m 12v 8.3g Nov 1] fair maiden: stays 1¼m: acts on good to firm going. *Tim Easterby* **73**

TREAGUS 3 b.g. Mayson 124 – Danceatdusk (Desert Prince (IRE) 130) [2017 –: f7.1g^{3} 8s^{4} 9.9m^{4} 10m^{6} f7.1g p7g^{2} 6v^{2} t6.1g^{3} Oct 27] rather unfurnished gelding: modest maiden: left Charlie Fellowes after fifth start: stays 7f: acts on polytrack, fibresand and heavy going: tried in cheekpieces. *Anthony Carson* **64**

TREASURE THE RIDGE (IRE) 8 b.g. Galileo (IRE) 134 – Treasure The Lady (IRE) 95 (Indian Ridge 123) [2017 85: t16.5g p16g^{4} 14.2s Oct 9] sturdy gelding: fairly useful handicapper: fourth at Kempton (2 lengths behind Next Train's Gone) in April: stays 2m: acts on polytrack and any turf going: often in headgear: tried in tongue tie: won over hurdles in July. *Martin Hill* **81**

TREASURING 2 ch.f. (Feb 6) Havana Gold (IRE) 118 – You Look So Good 68 (Excellent Art 125) [2017 p5g^{2} 5g* 5m 5d^{2} 5d* 5s* 6d 5f Nov 4] 32,000F: compact filly: first foal: dam, 7f winner, half-sister to smart German 6f/7f performer Electric Beat: useful **96**

performer: won maiden at Navan in June, and nursery at Tipperary and Curragh Stakes (by ½ length from Goodthingstaketime, flashing tail), both in August: left G. M. Lyons before final outing: should stay 6f: acts on soft going: usually leads. *Simon Callaghan, USA*

TREATY OF ROME (USA) 5 b.g. War Front (USA) 119 – Blading Gold Ring (USA) (During (USA)) [2017 –: f6g^2 f6g^2 f6g^4 f5g* f5m^2 f6g* f6g* p6g 5d 6d f6.1g^3 t6d f5g^2 f5g f6.1g^3 Dec 4] fairly useful handicapper: won at Southwell in February, March and April (by 1½ lengths from Vroom): usually races at 5f/6f: acts on polytrack and fibresand: wears headgear: tried in tongue tie. *Derek Shaw* **83**

TREBLE STRIKE (USA) 4 b.g. Hat Trick (JPN) 121 – Lady Simpson (Yankee Victor (USA) 121) [2017 p12g^2 p12g^6 p12d^6 p15.8g^3 p16g^6 p16g t16.3s^5 17.1v p16g f12.1g Oct 22] sturdy gelding: fair maiden handicapper: left Dean Ivory after sixth start: best effort at 2m: acts on polytrack: often in headgear in 2017: often races lazily: sold £2,500, sent to Germany. *David C. Griffiths* **69**

TRED SOFTLY (IRE) 4 b.g. Yeats (IRE) 128 – Elayoon (USA) 76 (Danzig (USA)) [2017 62: t12.2g* p12d t13.9f^4 t12.4d^4 12g^3 12.5g^4 12.1m^2 t12.4s 15.9s f11.1g Dec 22] fair handicapper: won at Wolverhampton in January: stays 1¾m: acts on fibresand, tapeta and good to firm going: wears blinkers: has hung/carried head awkwardly. *John Quinn* **66**

TREMENDOUS (IRE) 3 b.f. Kodiac 112 – Clockwise (Pivotal 124) [2017 51: p8g 6d^6 7d^3 p7g Oct 27] modest maiden: left Richard Hannon after third start: should be suited by at least 1m: acts on polytrack and good to soft going. *Liam Lennon, Ireland* **55**

TRENCHARD (USA) 3 b.c. Elusive Quality (USA) – Temporada (USA) (Summer Squall (USA)) [2017 f7g^4 t8d^2 t7.1m^2 p8g^6 p7g* Apr 12] $285,000Y: closely related/half-brother to numerous winners abroad: dam, US 6.5f winner, out of US Grade 2 1½m winner Lemhi Go: fairly useful performer: won minor event at Kempton (by 1½ lengths from On To Victory) in April: stays 1m: acts on polytrack and tapeta: in headgear last 2 starts: sent to UAE. *John Gosden* **80**

TRENDING (IRE) 8 gr.g. Dark Angel (IRE) 113 – Call Later (USA) (Gone West (USA)) [2017 73: t9.5m* t12.2g^2 p10d^5 t8.6m t12.2g^3 Mar 18] plain gelding: fair handicapper: won at Wolverhampton in January: stays 13f: acts on polytrack, tapeta, firm and good to soft going: wears headgear/tongue tie. *Jeremy Gask* **74**

TRENDSETTER (IRE) 6 b.g. Mastercraftsman (IRE) 129 – Fashion Trade (Dansili 127) [2017 94: t8.6m^5 10.3d 11.8v^6 10.3g 10v 12.1s p10.7g Dec 15] strong gelding: fairly useful handicapper: left Micky Hammond after sixth start: stays 16.5f: acts on tapeta, good to firm and heavy going: usually wears cheekpieces nowadays: tried in tongue tie. *Brian Francis Cawley, Ireland* **89**

TREVITHICK 2 b.c. (May 12) Champs Elysees 124 – New Choice (IRE) (Barathea (IRE) 127) [2017 8.3g t8g* t8d^2 Dec 16] 13,000Y: fifth foal: half-brother to 6f-7.5f winner Dasho (by Dubawi): dam, unraced, closely related to useful performer up to 1½m The Anvil and half-sister to smart performer up to 15.5f Glaring (by Champs Elysees): fairly useful form: won minor event at Newcastle (by 3½ lengths from Rare Groove) in November: stays 1m. *Bryan Smart* **84**

TRIANGULATE 5 b.g. Zamindar (USA) 116 – Heart of Hearts 86 (Oasis Dream 129) [2017 8g^4 8g^6 May 13] well beaten in bumpers: fair form on Flat: would have stayed 1¼m+: dead. *Micky Hammond* **70**

TRIBAL CONQUEST (IRE) 3 b.g. Shamardal (USA) 129 – Assabiyya (IRE) 91 (Cape Cross (IRE) 129) [2017 8g^2 8d^3 10.2d* 9.9m Aug 27] 550,000Y: useful-looking gelding: third foal: half-brother to smart winner up to 11.6f Solidarity (2-y-o 8.5f winner, by Dubawi) and useful 6f winner Brave Leader (by Pivotal): dam 1¼m winner: useful form: won maiden at Doncaster (by 4½ lengths from Roddy) in August: stays 1¼m: has joined Ismail Mohammed. *Charlie Appleby* **95**

TRIBAL PATH (IRE) 7 b.g. Giant's Causeway (USA) 132 – Navajo Moon (IRE) 111 (Danehill (USA) 126) [2017 94, a85: p8g^4 8v^4 p7g^2 6d 7.6d^6 8d 7s 7.9g 8g^2 8.4s^3 6m^5 6g^3 8d 7.4v^2 7v^2 p7g^5 7s p7g Oct 20] lengthy gelding: fairly useful handicapper: second at Dundalk (¾ length behind Split The Atom) in March: stays 1m: acts on polytrack and heavy going: tried in cheekpieces: wears tongue tie: front runner/races prominently: sold €20,000 in October. *Damian Joseph English, Ireland* **92**

TRIBAL QUEST (USA) 2 b.g. (Mar 27) War Front (USA) 119 – Haka (USA) (Dynaformer (USA)) [2017 6m^2 7m^2 6g Aug 1] $575,000Y: third foal: half-brother to winners in USA by Malibu Moon and Awesome Again: dam US Grade 3 8.5f winner: fairly useful form: best effort when second in maiden at Newmarket (short head behind Global Giant) in July. *Charlie Appleby* **90**

TRIBAL WARRIOR 2 b.c. (Apr 28) New Approach (IRE) 132 – Lunda (IRE) 60 (Soviet Star (USA) 128) [2017 p7d^6 p8d Dec 13] fair form: better effort when sixth in minor event at Kempton (4 lengths behind Qaysar) in November: should stay 1m. *James Tate* **69**

TRIBESMAN 4 ch.g. Equiano (FR) 127 – Millsini 55 (Rossini (USA) 118) [2017 66: t5.1m^3 t6g^4 5g Jun 14] fair handicapper at best: often in headgear: wears tongue tie: often races prominently: sent to Germany, where placed 5 times at up to 8.5f. *Marjorie Fife* **56**

TRIBUTE ACT 3 b.f. Exceed And Excel (AUS) 126 – Sister Act 85 (Marju (IRE) 127) [2017 83p: 8s^4 p7s* 8m* 8g 7d^2 Oct 6] useful handicapper: won at Kempton in June and Doncaster in July: second at Ascot (nose behind Mukalal) final start: stays 1m: acts on polytrack, good to firm and good to soft going: sometimes slowly away, usually races nearer last than first. *James Fanshawe* **98**

TRICK OF THE LIGHT (IRE) 3 ch.g. Dragon Pulse (IRE) 114 – Galistic (IRE) 104 (Galileo (IRE) 134) [2017 77p: 6m^3 6d^3 5.7m* 5f^2 t6g^3 5m^2 5m Aug 26] workmanlike gelding: fairly useful handicapper: won at Bath (by 1½ lengths from Swendab) in June: second at Salisbury (head behind Waseem Faris) in August: stays 6f: acts on tapeta and firm going: tried in blinkers: often races prominently: sold 25,000 gns in November. *Roger Varian* **92**

TRICK OF THE LYTE (IRE) 3 b.c. Kodiac 112 – Alpine River (IRE) (Redback 116) [2017 68: t6d t6g^6 6m 6g 6d 6m^6 6s^6 7.2m^4 6d^5 t5g Sep 22] fair at 2 yrs, below form in 2017: stays 6f: tried in cheekpieces: often races prominently. *John Quinn* **55**

TRICK SHOT JENNY 2 b.f. (Apr 22) Acclamation 118 – Chincoteague (IRE) 75 (Daylami (IRE) 138) [2017 p7d^6 p8g t8.6g t8s* p10s^6 t8.6g Dec 18] 20,000Y: fourth foal: closely related to 1m and (at 2 yrs) 9f winner Maftoon (by Dark Angel): dam, maiden (stayed 13f), half-sister to smart performer up to 1½m Indian Creek and to dam of Irish Derby winner Treasure Beach: modest performer: won nursery at Newcastle in November: stays 1m: acts on tapeta. *Jamie Osborne* **61**

TRICKSY SPIRIT 2 b.f. (Mar 3) Lethal Force (IRE) 128 – Spritzeria 81 (Bigstone (IRE) 126) [2017 7g 7s 6g* 6g Sep 7] 24,000Y: half-sister to 3 winners, including useful 6f/7f winner Esprit de Midas (by Namid) and 5f/6f winner Be Lucky (by Kyllachy): dam winner up to 1m (2-y-o 6f winner): fair form: won minor event at Goodwood in August: best effort at 6f. *Mick Channon* **76**

TRICKY DICKY 4 b.g. Holy Roman Emperor (IRE) 125 – Tricky Situation 78 (Mark of Esteem (IRE) 137) [2017 76: 6g f6.1g* 6m 6m^2 6d 6s^4 6d^2 f6.1g* 6.1d t6d^3 6s^5 f6.1g^2 f6.1g^2 Dec 19] strong, close-coupled gelding: fairly useful handicapper: won at Southwell in May and August (by 1¾ lengths from Interlink): second at same course last 2 starts: all wins at 6f: acts on fibresand, tapeta, good to firm and heavy going: front runner/races prominently. *Olly Williams* **82** **a92**

TRICORN (IRE) 3 b.g. Helmet (AUS) 127 – Special Dancer (Shareef Dancer (USA) 135) [2017 p7d^2 t7.1g* t8g* 8m* p8g^2 8m^3 8g Jul 13] 100,000 2-y-o: big, strong, rangy gelding: closely related to very smart 5f (including Nunthorpe Stakes) and (at 2 yrs) 6f winner Margot Did (by Exceed And Excel) and half-brother to French 10.5f-15f winner Special Reggae (by Xaar) and 2m winner Ja One (by Acclamation): dam Italian 1¼m-1½m winner: smart performer: won maiden at Wolverhampton in February, and handicaps at Newcastle (by 4 lengths from Marzouq) in March and Newmarket (by ½ length from same horse) in April: third in Britannia Stakes (Handicap) at Royal Ascot (2 lengths behind Bless Him) in June: stays 1m: acts on polytrack, tapeta and good to firm going. *John Gosden* **112**

TRILLIANT (IRE) 3 b.f. Dansili 127 – Priceless Jewel 94 (Selkirk (USA) 129) [2017 63p: 7m^6 9.9d^3 9.9g^6 8f* 8g^2 8f^3 Nov 18] tall, lengthy filly: has scope: fairly useful performer: won handicap at Haydock (by 2¼ lengths from Miss Sheridan) in July: placed after in similar event on same course (½-length second to Heaven's Rock, left Ed Walker after) and optional claimer at Aqueduct: best form at 1m: acts on firm going. *H. Graham Motion, USA* **94**

TRINITY STAR (IRE) 6 gr.g. Kheleyf (USA) 116 – Zamiyla (IRE) 86 (Daylami (IRE) 138) [2017 83: t8g^5 t8g^6 t7.1d 8g 8m^5 10m^2 10m^5 10f^5 8g^3 9.9m^6 8v^4 8v^2 Oct 9] fair handicapper: best up to 1¼m: acts on good to firm and heavy going: wears headgear: often starts slowly/races towards rear/travels strongly: not straightforward. *Michael Dods* **78** **a68**

TRIPARTITE (IRE) 4 b.g. Zebedee 113 – Baltic Belle (IRE) 86 (Redback 116) [2017 81: t7.1g* p7g^5 7g 7m 8.1d^2 8.1d^3 10m* 10.1f^4 Jul 6] fairly useful handicapper: won at Wolverhampton in February and Lingfield (by 1½ lengths from Monsieur Glory) in June: stays 1¼m: acts on polytrack, tapeta, firm and good to soft going: sold 45,000 gns in July, joined Alan Bailey. *Jeremy Gask* **82**

TRIPLE DREAM 12 ch.g. Vision of Night 115 – Triple Joy 104 (Most Welcome 131) **66** [2017 54, a73: p6g^{3} 6d^{5} t6.1g^{2} t6.1g 5.7s p6g^{3} t6.1m^{5} Oct 31] well-made gelding: fair handicapper: usually races up to 6f: acts on polytrack, tapeta and any turf going: has worn headgear/tongue tie: usually races prominently. *Milton Bradley*

TRIPLE FIRST 3 b.f. Dick Turpin (IRE) 127 – Orphina (IRE) 63 (Orpen (USA) 116) **62** [2017 8m^{6} p12g Oct 3] third foal: dam 1½m winner: modest form: better effort when sixth in maiden at Bath in August. *Seamus Mullins*

TRIP TO PARIS (IRE) 6 b.g. Champs Elysees 124 – La Grande Zoa (IRE) 50 (Fantastic **107** Light (USA) 134) [2017 109: 15.9d 14.1g^{4} 20m Jun 22] well-made gelding: very smart performer at best, winner of Gold Cup at Royal Ascot in 2015: just useful in last 2 years: fourth in listed race at Nottingham (4 lengths behind Elidor) in April: stayed 2½m: acted on polytrack, firm and good to soft going: sometimes wore headgear: retired. *Ed Dunlop*

TRISTRAM 3 b.g. Sinndar (IRE) 134 – Treasured Dream 68 (Oasis Dream 129) [2017 **74** p8g^{3} p12g^{3} 10.2m^{4} 11.9d 13f^{4} 12v f12.1g Nov 16] fair maiden: left Richard Hughes after fifth start: best effort at 1½m: acts on polytrack. *John Mackie*

TROGON (IRE) 2 ch.g. (Feb 11) Leroidesanimaux (BRZ) 127 – Savanna Days (IRE) 86 **70** (Danehill Dancer (IRE) 117) [2017 7m^{3} 7d 8d^{2} 7g^{6} p10g^{3} p8g^{5} 8.3d^{3} Oct 18] sturdy gelding: fair maiden: stays 1¼m: acts on polytrack, good to firm and good to soft going. *Mick Channon*

TROIS BON AMIS (IRE) 3 b.g. Lilbourne Lad (IRE) 111 – Vanozza (FR) (Dylan **52** Thomas (IRE) 132) [2017 59: 6g t8g 10v t8g^{6} f8.1g^{2} Dec 4] modest maiden: left Tim Easterby after second start: stays 1m: acts on fibresand and good to firm going: in tongue tie last 3 starts. *Mark Campion*

TROIS POINTS (FR) 5 b.g. Motivator 131 – Trading (FR) (Anabaa (USA) 130) [2017 **–** 55: p11.9g p9.9g Feb 1] maiden, raced only in France: well held both starts in 2017: tried in cheekpieces. *Gay Kelleway*

TROOP 2 gr.g. (Mar 14) Lethal Force (IRE) 128 – Bendis (GER) (Danehill (USA) 126) **54** [2017 7.4s 7g 7.4m^{6} t8s Sep 19] modest form: tried in cheekpieces. *Ann Duffield*

TROOPER'S GOLD 3 ch.g. Sepoy (AUS) 129 – Samira Gold (FR) 107 (Gold Away **70** (IRE) 125) [2017 83: 6m 7v May 20] fairly useful at 2 yrs, disappointing both starts in 2017: stays 1m: acts on tapeta. *Kevin Ryan*

TROPICAL BACHELOR (IRE) 11 b.g. Bachelor Duke (USA) 122 – Tropical Coral **49** (IRE) 82 (Pennekamp (USA) 130) [2017 11.9d^{4} 12.5g 12.1g Aug 18] smallish gelding: modest handicapper: stays 14.5f: acts on polytrack, firm and soft going: has worn headgear. *Ruth Carr*

TROPICAL ROCK 3 b.f. Fastnet Rock (AUS) 127 – Tropical Treat 112 (Bahamian **91** Bounty 116) [2017 88p: 6.1g 7g^{5} p6s^{3} p7d Nov 9] good-quartered filly: fairly useful handicapper: third at Kempton (1¼ lengths behind Related) in October: stays 6f: acts on polytrack and good to firm going. *Ralph Beckett*

TROPICAL WATERS (IRE) 2 b.f. (Mar 29) Acclamation 118 – Hurricane Havoc **–** (IRE) 106 (Hurricane Run (IRE) 134) [2017 6d^{4} Oct 24] 30,000Y: third foal: dam winner up to 1¼m (2-y-o 7f winner): 10/1, well held in minor event at Yarmouth (hooded). *Robert Cowell*

TROPICS (USA) 9 ch.g. Speightstown (USA) 124 – Taj Aire (USA) (Taj Alriyadh **102** (USA)) [2017 6.1m^{6} 6f 5d^{4} 5d 6.5g p6g p6g^{4} t6s^{2} t6.1d* p6g^{4} Dec 30] strong gelding: useful handicapper nowadays: won at Wolverhampton (by 1½ lengths from Rajar) in December: best at sprint trips: acts on polytrack, tapeta, firm and soft going: usually wears hood: usually races close up. *Dean Ivory*

TROTTER 3 b.g. Piccolo 121 – Vintage Steps (IRE) 76 (Bahamian Bounty 116) [2017 –: **80** t6g^{6} t6g^{2} t6g^{2} 5.7m^{4} t6.1g p6g^{2} p6g^{2} t6.1d^{3} Dec 9] fairly useful maiden: placed 5 times in 2017: stays 6f: acts on polytrack and tapeta: in blinkers last 3 starts. *Stuart Kittow*

TROUBLE AND STRIFE (IRE) 2 br.f. (May 10) Declaration of War (USA) 128 – **52 p** Rare Tern (IRE) 96 (Pivotal 124) [2017 p7g 8d p8g^{5} Nov 1] €25,000Y: third foal: half-sister to 6f-1m winner Rock Warbler (by Raven's Pass): dam, 8.5f winner, out of half-sister to very smart miler Marling: mid-division at best in minor events: type to do better in handicaps. *Sir Mark Prescott Bt*

TROY BOY 7 b.g. Choisir (AUS) 126 – Love Thing 68 (Phountzi (USA) 104) [2017 51: **–** t10.2g Jan 11] modest maiden handicapper: well beaten only start in 2017: stays 11.5f: acts on polytrack, soft and good to firm going: usually wears headgear. *Rebecca Bastiman*

TRUE BLUE MOON (IRE) 2 gr.c. (Feb 8) Holy Roman Emperor (IRE) 125 – Fancy Intense (Peintre Celebre (USA) 137) [2017 p5g* 5s* 5m^{6} 6g^{6} p6g^{6} Sep 9] small colt: closely related to 7f/1m winner Unscripted (by Oratorio) and half-brother to several winners, including 1m (including at 2 yrs) winner Kid Suitor (by Choisir) and 1¼m-1½m winner Refractor (by Refuse To Bend): dam, ran twice in France, half-sister to Poule d'Essai des Poulains winner Tin Horse: useful performer: won maiden at Dundalk in April and listed race at Naas (by ½ length from Verhoyen) in May: sixth in Norfolk Stakes at Royal Ascot (3¾ lengths behind Sioux Nation) in June: best form at 5f: acts on polytrack, soft and good to firm going. *Joseph Patrick O'Brien, Ireland* **100**

TRUE COLORS 3 b.g. Sir Percy 129 – Shesells Seashells 83 (Tiger Hill (IRE) 127) [2017 7.8g^{3} 8.3v^{6} 8g p8g^{3} p10d 10d f8.1g f8.1g Dec 1] fair maiden: stays 8.5f: acts on polytrack and heavy going: tried in cheekpieces. *Richard Fahey* **69**

TRUE COMPANION (IRE) 4 b.g. Fast Company (IRE) 126 – Panglossian (IRE) 72 (Barathea (IRE) 127) [2017 69: 7d p7g 7.8g^{6} 7s* 6.3v^{3} 7v^{5} 7v^{3} 7d^{5} p8g Nov 17] fair handicapper: won at Gowran (apprentice) in September: stays 8.5f: acts on polytrack and heavy going: wears headgear. *Adrian Brendan Joyce, Ireland* **70**

TRUE DESTINY 2 ch.g. (Jan 31) Mastercraftsman (IRE) 129 – Holy Dazzle (Sunday Break (JPN) 121) [2017 8.3v p8g Nov 18] well held in maiden/minor event. *Roger Charlton* **–**

TRUE GENTLEMAN 3 b.g. Bahamian Bounty 116 – Kampai 71 (Sakhee (USA) 136) [2017 p7g p7g May 24] angular gelding: tailed off in maidens. *Sylvester Kirk* **–**

TRUE NORTH (IRE) 2 b.g. (Feb 1) Henrythenavigator (USA) 131 – Cosmic Fire (FR) (Dalakhani (IRE) 133) [2017 t6d f5g t6s 6d Sep 19] 50,000Y: fourth foal: half-brother to French 1½m-14.5f winner Cosmic City (by Elusive City) and 2-y-o 7f winner Ray's The Bar (by Exceed And Excel), later useful 9.5f winner in USA: dam, French 11.5f winner, half-sister to very smart French performer around 1¼m Smoking Sun and to dam of Breeders' Cup Turf winner Main Sequence: fair form: will be suited by 1m+: likely to improve further. *Sir Mark Prescott Bt* **65 p**

TRUE ROMANCE (IRE) 3 gr.g. Mastercraftsman (IRE) 129 – Full of Love (IRE) 88 (Hawk Wing (USA) 136) [2017 66: 8g^{5} 9.9g^{3} t12.2g* 12d^{4} 9g^{2} 10g^{4} 10.2g^{6} Aug 19] fair handicapper: won at Wolverhampton in June: stays 1½m: acts on tapeta, best turf form on good going: usually travels strongly. *James Given* **79**

TRUE VALOUR (IRE) 3 b.c. Kodiac 112 – Sutton Veny (IRE) 98 (Acclamation 118) [2017 93: 7g* 7g^{3} 7m^{3} 7m 8g* 8g 8d^{2} 7m Oct 13] smallish colt: first foal: dam 6f winner: smart performer: won maiden at Limerick (by ½ length from Yulong Xionghu) in April and listed race at the Curragh (by ½ length from Sea Wolf) in July: second in Boomerang Stakes at Leopardstown (½ length behind Suedois) in September: stays 1m: acts on soft going. *John Patrick Murtagh, Ireland* **111**

TRULEE SCRUMPTIOUS 8 b.m. Strategic Prince 114 – Morning Rise (GER) (Acatenango (GER) 127) [2017 74: 8m* 8d^{2} 10d^{6} Jul 21] lengthy, angular mare: fairly useful handicapper: won at Newmarket (apprentice, by 7 lengths from Pacific Salt) in June: stays 1¼m: acts on polytrack, soft and good to firm going: wears headgear: usually leads. *Peter Charalambous* **80**

TRULOVE 4 b.f. Piccolo 121 – Snow Dancer (IRE) 88 (Desert Style (IRE) 121) [2017 –: t8.6g 6m^{6} 9.2m 5g 5d Jul 31] poor maiden handicapper: has worn headgear, including last 2 starts. *John David Riches* **33**

TRULY 6 b.m. Archipenko (USA) 127 – Sincerely 74 (Singspiel (IRE) 133) [2017 69: t7.1d 7g Aug 18] fair maiden at best, well held in handicaps in 2017: best effort at 1m: acts on good to firm going: in hood last 2 starts. *Paul Collins* **–**

TRUMP ALEXANDER (IRE) 2 b.f. (Jan 16) Iffraaj 127 – Obama Rule (IRE) 108 (Danehill Dancer (IRE) 117) [2017 8s^{5} 8d Sep 23] third foal: half-sister to 7f winner Yamarhaba Malayeen (by Rip Van Winkle): dam, 9f winner, sister to smart winner up to 1m Osaila: fair form: better effort when fifth in minor event at Ascot (3¼ lengths behind Soliloquy) in September. *Richard Hannon* **75**

TRUMPS UP 2 b.c. (Apr 3) Cape Blanco (IRE) 130 – Zeva 78 (Zamindar (USA) 116) [2017 7s* 8g* 8v^{4} Sep 30] 3,000Y: first foal: dam, 1m winner, half-sister to smart winner up to 1m Osaila: fair form: won minor events at Leicester (by ¾ length from Neverbeen To Paris) in August and Thirsk (by ¾ length from French Flyer) in September: stays 1m. *Mick Channon* **77**

TRUSTING FRIEND (USA) 2 b.c. (Feb 22) The Factor (USA) 126 – She's Justa Friend (USA) (Hussonet (USA)) [2017 5m^2 t6.1g 6d* 6f^4 8f 5f^6 Nov 24] fair performer: won minor event at Thirsk in July: left Kevin Ryan after third start, Brendan P. Walsh after fourth: should stay 1m: acts on firm and good to soft going: tried in blinkers. *Doug F. O'Neill, USA* **79**

TRUST ME BOY 9 gr.g. Avonbridge 123 – Eastern Lyric 93 (Petong 126) [2017 46§, a66§: f8g f7g^4 f7d^2 f7g^5 f7.1g f7.1g Dec 4] compact gelding: modest handicapper: stays 1m: acts on fibresand and heavy going: has worn headgear, including final start: temperamental. *John E. Long* **60 §**

TRUST THE INDIAN 3 ch.g. Sleeping Indian 122 – Trust Fund Babe (IRE) 67 (Captain Rio 122) [2017 50: t6m t7.1m^5 t7.1m 7g May 30] workmanlike gelding: poor maiden: stays 7f: acts on soft going: often in headgear. *Bill Turner* **46**

TRUST THE MAN (IRE) 4 br.g. Manduro (GER) 135 – Saree 95 (Barathea (IRE) 127) [2017 58: p15.8m 11.9d p11g Oct 11] stocky gelding: modest maiden at best, little show in 2017: left Simon Dow after first start: stays 1½m: acts on polytrack and soft going: has worn headgear, including last 2 starts when also in tongue tie. *Adam West* **47**

TRUTH OR DARE 6 b.g. Invincible Spirit (IRE) 121 – Unreachable Star 81 (Halling (USA) 133) [2017 98: 7m^4 8s^3 7d^6 7s^4 7m^3 7.9m^2 8g^2 7v* 7g 8s^5 7.9g Oct 13] well-made gelding: useful handicapper: won at Goodwood (by 1½ lengths from Noble Peace) in August: best at 7f/1m: acts on polytrack, good to firm and heavy going. *James Bethell* **98**

TRY AGAIN (IRE) 4 b.g. Dubai Destination (USA) 127 – Diamond Katie (IRE) 75 (Night Shift (USA)) [2017 55: p8g* p8g* p8g* 8s^2 8.3m* 8m^2 9.7s^3 9g^5 8s^3 8v^6 p7g^6 p7g p8s^4 p10.7g^3 Dec 15] fair handicapper: won at Dundalk in January, February and March (apprentice), and Hamilton in May: stays 10.5f: acts on polytrack, tapeta, soft and good to firm going: has worn headgear/tongue tie: often races prominently. *Paul W. Flynn, Ireland* **79**

TSARGLAS 6 gr.g. Verglas (IRE) 118 – Russian Empress (IRE) 101 (Trans Island 119) [2017 –: t8g^5 Jan 21] modest handicapper at best, no form since early-2015: usually wears headgear/tongue tie. *Christopher Wilson* **–**

TSUNDOKU (IRE) 6 ch.m. Medicean 128 – Toberanthawn (IRE) 87 (Danehill Dancer (IRE) 117) [2017 p8g p11g p12g 12v 16v* 16s Sep 19] modest handicapper: won at Chepstow in July: stays 2m: acts on polytrack and heavy going: tried in headgear: often starts slowly/races in rear (more forcefully ridden last 2 starts): fair hurdler. *Alexandra Dunn* **61**

TTMAB 2 b.c. (Mar 4) Mawatheeq (USA) 126 – Astrodiva 78 (Where Or When (IRE) 124) [2017 8m p8g^6 Dec 21] tall colt: modest form: better effort when sixth in maiden at Chelmsford. *Mark H. Tompkins* **59**

TUFF ROCK (USA) 3 b.g. Fastnet Rock (AUS) 127 – Wonder of Wonders (USA) 116 (Kingmambo (USA) 125) [2017 –p: 10s^4 9.9d* 11.2s p11g^2 10v^2 Oct 23] well-made gelding: useful performer: won maiden at Goodwood in June: second in handicap at Pontefract (1¼ lengths behind Silvery Moon) final start: stays 11f: acts on polytrack and heavy going: tried in blinkers. *Ed Walker* **96**

TUKHOOM (IRE) 4 b.g. Acclamation 118 – Carioca (IRE) 107 (Rakti 130) [2017 87: 7g 7d 7d^5 8d Aug 5] strong, good-bodied gelding: fairly useful handicapper: below form in 2017: stays 1m: acts on soft and good to firm going: tried in hood. *Michael Herrington* **75**

TULANE (IRE) 2 br.g. (May 4) Arcano (IRE) 122 – Jeunesse Doree (IRE) 68 (Rock of Gibraltar (IRE) 133) [2017 6.1g 7s^3 8s 7d Oct 30] sturdy gelding: fair form: best effort at 7f. *Richard Phillips* **68**

TULIP DRESS 4 ch.f. Dutch Art 126 – White Dress (IRE) (Pivotal 124) [2017 67: t9.5g^2 p11g 7m* 8.3g p7d^4 8d^3 8m^6 7d 8s^4 7.1d^2 7s^5 p7d^6 p7s^5 Dec 17] fair handicapper: won at Brighton in April: stays 9.5f: acts on tapeta, firm and good to soft going: usually races nearer last than first. *Anthony Carson* **70**

TULIP FEVER 2 ch.f. (Mar 8) Dutch Art 126 – Cara Gina 75 (Bahamian Bounty 116) [2017 5g^3 5m* 5.7f^3 6s* 5d^3 6m* 6g Oct 13] leggy filly: first foal: dam, 5.7f winner, half-sister to smart 5f winner Royal Birth: fairly useful performer: won minor event at York in June, and nurseries at Lingfield in July and Yarmouth (by ½ length from Mraseel) in August: stays 6f: acts on soft and good to firm going: often races freely. *William Haggas* **83**

TULLINAHOO (IRE) 3 b.g. Elzaam (AUS) 115 – Pitullie (USA) (Rockport Harbor (USA) 114) [2017 63: t7.2g Jul 17] leggy gelding: modest maiden at 2 yrs, shaped as if amiss only start in 2017: stays 6f: acts on tapeta: tried in tongue tie: sometimes slowly away, often races in rear. *Denis Coakley* **–**

TULLIUS (IRE) 9 ch.g. Le Vie dei Colori 126 – Whipped Queen (USA) (Kingmambo **108**
(USA) 125) [2017 115: 8g^5 9.9g^4 May 27] good-bodied gelding: very smart performer at best: won 11 races during career, including Mile at Sandown, York Stakes and Diomed Stakes at Epsom: better effort in 2017 when fourth in listed race at Goodwood (4 lengths behind First Sitting, sustaining injury): stayed 10.5f: acted on polytrack, heavy and good to firm going: wore visor in later races: retired. *Andrew Balding*

TULLYALLEN (IRE) 2 b.c. (Mar 18) Arcano (IRE) 122 – Come April 77 (Singspiel **72**
(IRE) 133) [2017 6d^4 p8g^5 p8g^3 Oct 25] good sort: fair form: best effort when third in minor event at Kempton (3½ lengths behind King And Empire) final start. *Richard Hannon*

TUMBAGA (USA) 6 b.g. E Dubai (USA) 124 – Brushed Gold (USA) (Touch Gold **100**
(USA) 127) [2017 a8f^6 8g 10m 10.3m p8g Aug 8] smart performer at 4 yrs, below best in 2017 after long absence: stays 1¼m: acts on polytrack and good to firm going: tried in hood: front runner/races prominently. *Saeed bin Suroor*

TUMBLEWIND 7 ch.m. Captain Rio 122 – African Breeze 79 (Atraf 116) [2017 91: 5s^6 **106**
6m^3 5g* 5d* 5d^5 Jun 11] workmanlike mare: useful handicapper: won at Pontefract (by length from Silvanus) in May and Doncaster (by 1¾ lengths from My Name Is Rio) in June: best at 5f: acts on soft and good to firm going: races prominently. *Richard Whitaker*

TUM TUM 2 ch.c. (Feb 6) Dawn Approach (IRE) 132 – Lalectra (King Charlemagne **83**
(USA) 120) [2017 7g^5 p8d^4 p8g^2 Dec 20] 62,000Y: half-brother to several winners, including smart winner up to 1m (stayed 1¼m) Van Der Neer (2-y-o 6f/7f winner, by Dutch Art) and useful 2-y-o 5f winner Showing Character (by Showcasing), both later successful in Hong Kong: dam unraced: fairly useful form: best effort when second in minor event at Kempton (1¾ lengths behind Glencadam Master) final start. *Martyn Meade*

TUNDRA 3 b.f. Bated Breath 125 – Tanouma (USA) (Mr Greeley (USA) 122) [2017 73p: **92**
6m* 7s 6g 6g Oct 7] fairly useful performer: won maiden at Lingfield in June: stays 7f: acts on polytrack, soft and good to firm going: races prominently: sold 45,000 gns in November. *Roger Varian*

TUNES OF GLORY 2 b.c. (Apr 15) Lope de Vega (IRE) 125 – Bay Tree (IRE) 100 **78**
(Daylami (IRE) 138) [2017 p6g* t7.2g^6 p6s^3 7.4s^2 p7g^5 7s^6 Sep 23] sturdy colt: fair performer: won minor event at Lingfield in June: second in similar event at Ffos Las in August: stays 7.5f: acts on polytrack, tapeta and soft going: tried in cheekpieces: sold 25,000 gns, sent to Italy. *Sir Mark Prescott Bt*

TUOLUMNE MEADOWS 4 b.f. High Chaparral (IRE) 132 – Seren Devious (Dr **72**
Devious (IRE) 127) [2017 85: 10.2f^4 p13.3g^5 11.6m^5 11.6d^5 11.6d^2 p12d^4 p12g p12g f11.1g Dec 4] good-topped filly: fair maiden: left Paul Cole after fifth start: stays 1½m: acts on polytrack: sometimes in headgear in 2017: tried in tongue tie. *Tony Newcombe*

TUPI (IRE) 5 b.g. Tamayuz 126 – Carioca (IRE) 107 (Rakti 130) [2017 111: 8g 8g 6g^4 6g* **116**
6s^6 6m^6 6s 6.5g^3 6m 7g Sep 22] strong, useful-looking gelding: smart performer: won listed race at Doncaster (by 4 lengths from Captain Colby) in April: third in Prix Maurice de Gheest at Deauville (2¼ lengths behind Brando) in August: effective at 6f to 1m: acts on firm and soft going: tried in blinkers: usually races towards rear. *Richard Hannon*

TURAATHY (IRE) 4 b.f. Lilbourne Lad (IRE) 111 – Key Girl (IRE) 48 (Key of Luck **–**
(USA) 126) [2017 64: p7d t8.6g 8g 8s Sep 4] modest handicapper at 3 yrs: well below form in 2017: tried in cheekpieces: often starts slowly, usually races in rear. *Tony Newcombe*

TURANGA LEELA 3 ch.f. Paco Boy (IRE) 129 – Sunday Bess (JPN) 88 (Deep Impact **89**
(JPN) 134) [2017 84: 6.1m 6.1g* 6m^4 6.1g^3 5v^6 6g 6s^4 p7g t6.1d^6 p6g Dec 30] leggy filly: fairly useful handicapper: won at Chester (by 1½ lengths from Socialites Red) in May: fourth at York (2¼ lengths behind Eartha Kitt) in June: stays 6f: acts on polytrack, tapeta and any turf going: wears headgear. *Ian Williams*

TURNBURY 6 b.g. Azamour (IRE) 130 – Scottish Heights (IRE) (Selkirk (USA) 129) **62**
[2017 69: t12.2g p10g t9.5g^6 t9.5m^5 p12g^3 12g 10d^4 12s^3 11.4d^4 10.2v Nov 8] sturdy gelding: modest handicapper: stays 1½m: acts on polytrack and heavy going: wears headgear: has worn tongue tie: often races prominently. *Nikki Evans*

TURNING GOLD 3 ch.g. Pivotal 124 – Illusion 98 (Anabaa (USA) 130) [2017 –p: 9g **90**
t8g^3 8m^2 8g* 8g* 8d 10.2g 10g^2 Sep 28] big, workmanlike gelding: fairly useful handicapper: won at Yarmouth (twice, by 8 lengths from Ice Alert second occasion) in July: should stay 1¼m: acts on good to firm going: wears headgear: usually leads: sold 30,000 gns in October to join Nigel Twiston-Davies. *Sir Mark Prescott Bt*

TURNING THE TABLE (IRE) 4 gr.f. Mastercraftsman (IRE) 129 – Duchess Dee (IRE) (Bachelor Duke (USA) 122) [2017 89: 12m^3 11.4m* 11.4d^4 9.9m^5 9.9v Aug 2] good-topped filly: fairly useful handicapper: won at Windsor (by 4½ lengths from Perfect Quest) in May: stays 1½m: acts on good to firm and heavy going: sometimes slowly away, often races in rear. *David Simcock* **92**

TURNPIKE TRIP 3 b.g. Champs Elysees 124 – Neqaawi 72 (Alhaarth (IRE) 126) [2017 p10m^4 12m^4 p12d^2 12d^4 12s^6 10s* 10d* 9.9s^5 Sep 27] fifth foal: half-brother to French 1¼m winner Bouquetot Liberty (by Statue of Liberty): dam, 7f-10.5f winner, half-sister to smart sprinter Indian Maiden: fairly useful performer: won maiden at Windsor in August and handicap at Lingfield (by ½ length from Harbour Rock) in September: stays 1½m: acts on polytrack, soft and good to firm going: usually races prominently. *Henry Candy* **91**

TURQUOISE BAY (USA) 2 b.c. (Mar 24) Lonhro (AUS) 128 – Torre di Pisa (USA) (Tiznow (USA) 133) [2017 7m^5 6d Sep 19] $60,000F, €100,000 2-y-o: first foal: dam unraced half-sister to US Grade 1 1m winner Karelian: modest form in minor events: remains with potential. *Chris Dwyer* **64 p**

TURRET ROCKS (IRE) 4 b.f. Fastnet Rock (AUS) 127 – Beyond Compare (IRE) 76 (Galileo (IRE) 134) [2017 109: 9.5s^6 10g* 8d^3 8m^6 10g^3 9m^4 Jul 16] strong, well-made filly: smart performer: won Blue Wind Stakes at the Curragh (by ¾ length from Laganore) in May: third in Pretty Polly Stakes at same course (4¾ lengths behind Nezwaah) in July: stays 1½m: acts on good to firm and good to soft going: has worn hood: tried in tongue tie. *J. S. Bolger, Ireland* **110**

TUSCAN GOLD 10 ch.g. Medicean 128 – Louella (USA) (El Gran Senor (USA) 136) [2017 75: 18g^2 21.6m* 17.1d 18g^5 17.1g 17.1v^4 18v^2 18v^5 Oct 23] well-made gelding: fair handicapper: won at Pontefract in April: second at same course in October: stays 21.5f: acts on polytrack, good to firm and heavy going: wears headgear: sometimes slowly away, often races towards rear. *Micky Hammond* **71**

TUSCAN PEARL 2 b.f. (Feb 25) Medicean 128 – Western Pearl 104 (High Chaparral (IRE) 132) [2017 8s^6 Oct 28] second foal: dam 1½m winner who stayed 2½m: 66/1, sixth in minor event at Newbury (9¼ lengths behind Highgarden): capable of better. *William Knight* **61 p**

TUSCANY (IRE) 3 ch.g. Poet's Voice 126 – Avril Rose (IRE) (Xaar 132) [2017 71p: 7m^5 8s p12g p7g* t7.2g* Nov 25] fairly useful handicapper: won at Kempton in October and Wolverhampton (by neck from Baltic Prince) in November: should stay 1m: acts on polytrack and tapeta: tried in blinkers. *Paul Cole* **86**

TWADDLE 3 b.f. Paco Boy (IRE) 129 – Blue Dream (IRE) 100 (Cadeaux Genereux 131) [2017 –: 9.9g Jun 12] little sign of ability. *Rae Guest* **–**

TWEETHEART 4 ch.f. Dutch Art 126 – Strictly (USA) (Fusaichi Pegasus (USA) 130) [2017 51: 7m 6m May 30] modest maiden at best, has lost her way: usually wears headgear: sometimes slowly away, often races towards rear. *Ron Barr* **–**

TWEETING 2 ch.f. (Feb 17) Sleeping Indian 122 – Lady Sledmere (IRE) 72 (Barathea (IRE) 127) [2017 6m 7g^5 Jun 23] first foal: dam 7f winner: little impact in minor event/seller. *John Quinn* **–**

TWELVE A 2 ch.c. (Apr 10) Piccolo 121 – Nihal (IRE) 94 (Singspiel (IRE) 133) [2017 5.9s 5v Sep 21] well held in maidens. *David O'Meara* **–**

TWENTYSVNTHLANCERS 4 b.g. Hellvelyn 118 – Subtle Move (USA) 60 (Known Fact (USA) 135) [2017 77: 5g 5m 5g^4 5m 5d^3 5m 5m 5g^3 5s^4 5s^5 5g Oct 18] fair handicapper: raced only at 5f: acts on soft and good to firm going: has worn headgear: temperamental. *Paul Midgley* **70 §**

TWENTY TIMES (IRE) 3 b.f. Dream Ahead (USA) 133 – Mad Existence (IRE) 74 (Val Royal (FR) 127) [2017 71p: 7m^5 10d* 12m^5 10d^2 14.4s^5 10s* 10g^4 Oct 7] fairly useful handicapper: won at Chepstow in June and Ffos Las (by 1¼ lengths from Brief Visit) in August: fourth at Newmarket final start: stays 1¼m: acts on soft going: in cheekpieces last 2 starts. *Richard Hughes* **93**

TWENTYTWOWONTDO (IRE) 2 ch.f. (Feb 17) Dandy Man (IRE) 123 – Balladiene (IRE) 95 (Noverre (USA) 125) [2017 5s^4 5.5s^3 5d* 5.8g* 6g* 5.8d^4 6.8s^6 a6s^5 Oct 25] €34,000Y: second foal: dam 7f and (including at 2 yrs) 1m winner: fair performer: won minor events at Catterick in June (left David O'Meara after), and Ovrevoll and Bro Park in August: stays 6f: acts on good to soft going. *Pia Hoiom, Norway* **67**

TWICKENHAM (IRE) 2 b.c. (Apr 16) Champs Elysees 124 – Morinqua (IRE) 99 **53** (Cadeaux Genereux 131) [2017 p7g 5.8v^6 p8g Oct 26] modest form: best effort when sixth in maiden at Navan (10¼ lengths behind Krispen) in October. *John Joseph Murphy, Ireland*

TWIGGY 3 b.f. Sixties Icon 125 – Queen's Pudding (IRE) 84 (Royal Applause 124) [2017 **71** 68: 7m 8.2d^2 8.9d 8m 9.9m t8.6g 8s^3 7d^4 p7g Dec 21] fair maiden handicapper: left Jane Chapple-Hyam after second start: stays 1m: acts on polytrack and good to soft going: often hooded. *Iain Jardine*

TWILIGHT ANGEL 9 ch.m. Compton Place 125 – Leaping Flame (USA) (Trempolino **–** (USA) 135) [2017 –: p7g f14g^6 p15.8g t9.5g Feb 15] maiden, little form since 2014: wears headgear: tried in tongue tie. *Emma Owen*

TWILIGHT PAYMENT (IRE) 4 b.g. Teofilo (IRE) 126 – Dream On Buddy (IRE) 84 **114** (Oasis Dream 129) [2017 110: 14s^2 14g^3 14m^2 14d^2 14d^3 14s^6 Sep 10] smart performer: third in Vintage Crop Stakes at Navan (2 lengths behind Torcedor) in April and second in listed race at Leopardstown (2¼ lengths behind Order of St George) in May: stays 2m: acts on soft and good to firm going: usually wears cheekpieces: in tongue tie last 5 starts: front runner/races prominently. *J. S. Bolger, Ireland*

TWILIGHT SPIRIT 3 b.f. Assertive 121 – Twilight Mistress 84 (Bin Ajwaad (IRE) 119) **71** [2017 63p: 6g 6d 6d^2 6g^4 7g^4 6s* 7d Oct 24] lengthy filly: fair handicapper: won at Salisbury in September: stays 6f: acts on soft going: in blinkers last 2 starts. *Tony Carroll*

TWIN APPEAL (IRE) 6 b.g. Oratorio (IRE) 128 – Velvet Appeal (IRE) 101 (Petorius **100** 117) [2017 101: t7.1g^3 f7d^3 7.1g* 7m^5 7m t7.1s^6 7m^6 7d^3 7g^2 7.9m 7g^4 8d 7.6g^6 7s 7g 7d^5 t7.2g^2 t7.2d* Dec 16] heavy-topped gelding: useful handicapper: won at Musselburgh (by 1¾ lengths from Lat Hawill) in April and Wolverhampton (by ¾ length from Shepherd's Purse) in December: stays 7f: acts on tapeta, good to firm and heavy going: wears blinkers. *David Barron*

TWIN POINT 6 br.g. Invincible Spirit (IRE) 121 – Gemini Joan (Montjeu (IRE) 137) **92** [2017 86: p7g* p7g 7m^5 p7s^2 Jun 14] tall, useful-looking gelding: fairly useful handicapper: won at Kempton (by ½ length from Lexington Times) in February: second at same course (neck behind North Creek) final start: stays 1m: acts on polytrack and good to firm going: has worn hood: wears tongue tie: front runner/races prominently: sold 16,000 gns in July. *Charlie Fellowes*

TWIN STAR (IRE) 3 ch.g. Tagula (IRE) 116 – Chronicle (Observatory (USA) 131) **101** [2017 –: 8.5d^6 10m* 10d^4 12m 11.1g^5 9.9m^5 Aug 27] smallish gelding: fifth foal: half-brother to winner up to 11.6f Diletta Tommasa (2-y-o 8.6f winner, by Dylan Thomas) and useful winner up to 1m Another Story (2-y-o 6f winner, by Rip Van Winkle): dam unraced: useful performer: won maiden at Navan in May: fourth in Gallinule Stakes at the Curragh (2¼ lengths behind Homesman) later in month: left Ms Sheila Lavery after fourth start: stays 1¼m: acts on good to firm and good to soft going: tried in tongue tie. *Andrew Balding*

TWISTED LOGIC (IRE) 2 b.c. (Apr 30) Shamardal (USA) 129 – Myrine (IRE) 103 **–** (Sadler's Wells (USA) 132) [2017 8g 8.3d Oct 11] well held in minor event/maiden: sold 9,000 gns, sent to Hungary. *Keith Dalgleish*

TWISTER (IRE) 2 ch.g. (Apr 27) Hurricane Run (IRE) 134 – Arizona Sun (IRE) **66 p** (Spinning World (USA) 130) [2017 7s t8.6g 8.3g Nov 1] €50,000Y: seventh foal: brother to useful French 1m-13f winner Arizona Run (2-y-o 9f/1¼m winner) and French 1½m/14.5f winner Arizona Air, and half-brother to German 1m-10.5f winner Arizona Star (by Anabaa): dam, useful French 5.5f winner (including at 2 yrs), half-sister to useful French winner up to 1½m Aristote: fair form: best effort when eighth in minor event at Wolverhampton (5¾ lengths behind Wissahickon) in October: remains capable of better. *Sir Mark Prescott Bt*

TWIST OF MAGIC (IRE) 3 b.f. Arcano (IRE) 122 – Walayef (USA) 105 (Danzig **78** (USA)) [2017 74: 5m 7g^6 7v^2 7.3s^4 5.8g 7s 7v 5g Nov 1] half-sister to several winners, including useful 2-y-o 6f/7f winner Jamaayel (by Shamardal) and 2-y-o 7f winner (stayed 1½m) Reyaada (by Daylami): dam winner up to 7f (2-y-o 6f winner): fair handicapper: stays 1m: acts on polytrack, good to firm and heavy going: has worn headgear, including in 2017: often leads. *J. J. Feane, Ireland*

TWISTON SHOUT (IRE) 3 b.g. Lawman (FR) 121 – Minkova (IRE) (Sadler's Wells **51** (USA) 132) [2017 –: f12g^3 Apr 16] modest form: best effort at 1½m. *Richard Spencer*

TWISTSANDTURNS (IRE) 6 b.g. Acclamation 118 – Shesthebiscuit 76 (Diktat 126) **62 d** [2017 63: p7g^{3} p7g 10.2m 9m t7.2g 6m p7g^{4} Oct 17] modest handicapper: below form after first start: left Patrick J. Flynn after second one: stays 8.5f: acts on polytrack, good to firm and good to soft going: has worn headgear: has joined Adrian Wintle. *Declan Carroll*

TWIZZELL 3 b.f. Equiano (FR) 127 – Greensand 96 (Green Desert (USA) 127) [2017 80: **88** 5.1g 5f* 5s^{4} 5.1s^{3} 5m 5m^{3} 5.4d^{3} 5s^{4} t5g Oct 10] close-coupled filly: fairly useful handicapper: won at Beverley (by ¾ length from Stubytuesday) in May: best form at 5f: acts on firm and soft going. *K. R. Burke*

TWO DOLLARS (IRE) 3 ch.g. Casamento (IRE) 118 – Two Marks (USA) 73 **72** (Woodman (USA) 126) [2017 –: t10.2s^{4} 9.9g 14f 11.9d^{4} 14s^{6} 11.5m p13.3g^{5} Oct 26] fair maiden: stays 13.5f: acts on good to soft going: tried in hood/tongue tie: often races towards rear. *William Jarvis*

TWO FOR TWO (IRE) 9 b.g. Danehill Dancer (IRE) 117 – D'articleshore (IRE) **95** (Definite Article 121) [2017 100: 8.3g^{6} 8g^{2} 8m^{2} 10.3d 8d 8d* 7.9d 8d^{4} 8.2d^{3} 8g 8m 7.9g Oct 13] close-coupled gelding: useful handicapper: won at Ayr (by head from Finn Class) in July: stays 9f: acts on good to firm and heavy going: wears cheekpieces: sometimes slowly away, usually races in rear. *Roger Fell*

TWO IN THE PINK (IRE) 7 gr.m. Clodovil (IRE) 116 – Secret Circle (Magic Ring **53** (IRE) 115) [2017 70: p10g f8g p10g Feb 22] workmanlike mare: fair handicapper: below form in 2017: stays 1¼m: acts on polytrack, tapeta and good to firm going: tried in headgear/tongue tie. *Ralph Smith*

TWO SEAS 2 b.g. (Mar 15) Sepoy (AUS) 129 – Fifty (IRE) 86 (Fasliyev (USA) 120) **59 p** [2017 6.1m 5m 6.1g Aug 18] 13,000F, €24,000Y, 140,000 2-y-o: well-made gelding: fifth foal: dam, ungenuine 6f winner, out of Irish 1000 Guineas runner-up Amethyst, herself sister to 2000 Guineas winner King of Kings: mid-division at best in maidens: should do better. *George Peckham*

TWO WEEKS 2 ch.f. (Mar 2) Mayson 124 – Laurena (GER) (Acatenango (GER) 127) **82 p** [2017 6s^{5} t6.1g* Nov 18] £10,000Y, 75,000 2-y-o: fifth foal: half-sister to German 2-y-o 6f winner Boliche (by Key of Luck) and UAE 1m winner Expert Answer (by Dubawi): dam, 1¼m/11f winner in France, half-sister to smart German 10.5f-1½m winner Lauro: fairly useful form: won minor event at Wolverhampton (by ¾ length from Rizzle Dizzle) in November: open to further improvement. *Clive Cox*

TYLERY WONDER (IRE) 7 ch.g. Choisir (AUS) 126 – Over The Tylery (IRE) 78 **95** (Swallow Flight (IRE) 124) [2017 91: t5s 5m^{3} 5.5g^{2} 5m^{5} 5d^{4} 5m 5m* 5g 5d 5g 5d 5s* 5g^{4} 5v p5g^{6} Nov 2] sturdy gelding: useful handicapper: won at York in July and Naas (by 1½ lengths from Monsieur Joe) in September: best up to 6f: acts on polytrack, soft and good to firm going: wears headgear: usually races close up. *Paul Midgley*

TYNECASTLE PARK 4 b.g. Sea The Stars (IRE) 140 – So Silk (Rainbow Quest (USA) **60** 134) [2017 66: f8g^{6} p16g f16.5g^{2} p16s^{5} Dec 15] tall gelding: modest maiden handicapper: stays 16.5f: acts on polytrack, fibresand and good to soft going: tried in cheekpieces: sometimes slowly away: fair form over hurdles. *Robert Eddery*

TYRELL (IRE) 4 b.g. Teofilo (IRE) 126 – Sleeveless (USA) 76 (Fusaichi Pegasus (USA) **81** 130) [2017 79: p16d^{3} 14f^{3} 16m^{4} 17.1d^{2} 17.1v Sep 21] tall gelding: fairly useful handicapper: third at Kempton (2½ lengths behind King Calypso) in May: left Alan King after fourth start: stays 17f: acts on polytrack, firm and good to soft going: wears headgear: front runner/races prominently: fairly useful hurdler. *Micky Hammond*

TY ROCK BRANDY (IRE) 2 b.f. (Apr 1) Dandy Man (IRE) 123 – Britain's Pride **64** (Royal Applause 124) [2017 5g^{5} 5g^{4} 5m^{5} 5d^{5} 5d^{6} 5g^{3} 5d^{6} 6v p6s t5.1d* Dec 16] first foal: dam of little account: modest performer: won minor event at Wolverhampton in December: best form at 5f: acts on tapeta, good to firm and good to soft going: tried in cheekpieces: signs of temperament. *L. Smyth, Ireland*

TYROLEAN 4 b.g. Raven's Pass (USA) 133 – Alessandria 100 (Sunday Silence (USA)) **72** [2017 74: p7g 9m^{6} 14.2v 14s^{2} 14.1v^{3} t14g Oct 27] good-topped gelding: fair maiden: trained only start at 3 yrs by A. Fabre: stays 1¾m: acts on heavy going: in cheekpieces last 2 starts. *Seamus Durack*

TYRSAL (IRE) 6 b.g. Jeremy (USA) 122 – Blanchelande (IRE) (Subotica (FR) 131) **73** [2017 70: p11g^{3} p12g p10g 8m 10.1m^{2} 11.5m^{2} 11.5m^{5} 10g^{4} 11.8g* 10.1g^{2} 10d 10.1d^{2} **a63** 11.5m 9d^{6} 10g 11.5d^{6} p12g^{6} Nov 29] sturdy gelding: fair handicapper: won at Leicester in July: stays 1½m: acts on polytrack, firm and good to soft going: has worn headgear, including in 2017: usually races in rear. *Clifford Lines*

U

UAE KING 3 b.c. Frankel 147 – Zomaradah 118 (Deploy 131) [2017 67P: 11m^5 11.6d^2 11.6m* 14m* 16d* 14g^3 16g^3 Sep 28] well-made colt: smart performer: improved with nearly every run, winning maiden at Haydock (by length from Festival of Ages) in June, and handicaps at Sandown (by ¾ length from Machine Learner) and Ascot (by 4½ lengths from Mister Manduro) in July: third in listed races at Goodwood (4¼ lengths behind Call To Mind) in August and Newmarket (4 lengths behind Face The Facts) in September: stays 2m: acts on good to firm and good to soft going. *Roger Varian* **111**

UAE PRINCE (IRE) 4 b.g. Sea The Stars (IRE) 140 – By Request 64 (Giant's Causeway (USA) 132) [2017 97p: 9.8m* 12m^5 10.3m^4 9.9g^4 10.3m Aug 26] useful handicapper: won at Ripon (by ¾ length from Final) in April: fourth in John Smith's Cup at York (length behind Ballet Concerto) in July: stays 1½m: acts on good to firm going: usually races prominently, often travels strongly. *Roger Varian* **108**

UAE QUEEN 3 b.f. Oasis Dream 129 – Pongee 110 (Barathea (IRE) 127) [2017 7m^3 8.3d 7g* 8.1s^2 8d* 10m Oct 13] 450,000Y: good-topped filly: sister to useful winner up to 8.3f Materialistic (2-y-o 7f winner) and half-sister to several winners, including smart winner up to 1¾m Pinzolo (2-y-o 1m winner, by Monsun) and useful 2-y-o 1m winner Poplin (by Medicean): dam 1¼m-1½m winner who stayed 1¾m: fairly useful performer: won maiden at Yarmouth in July and handicap at Sandown (by ½ length from Finale) in September: should be suited by 1¼m: acts on soft going. *Roger Varian* **90**

UAE SOLDIER (USA) 2 b.g. (Feb 12) Dansili 127 – Time On 114 (Sadler's Wells (USA) 132) [2017 8.3g Nov 1] 160,000Y: fourth foal: half-brother to 2-y-o 1m winner Moontime (by Sea The Stars) and 1½m winner (stays 2m) Balancing Time (by Pivotal): dam 9.7f-1½m winner: 15/2, very green when well held in maiden at Nottingham: should do better. *Roger Varian* **– p**

UBER COOL (IRE) 3 b.g. Born To Sea (IRE) 117 – My Uptown Girl (Dubai Destination (USA) 127) [2017 10g^5 11.6m^5 12.1m* 12d* 12g^3 14v* Sep 29] €50,000Y: fourth foal: closely related to 1m-9.5f winner Max's Spirit (by Invincible Spirit) and half-brother to 1½m-1¾m winner (stays 16.5f) Crakehall Lad (by Manduro): dam unraced half-sister to smart 2-y-o 6f/7f winner Piping Rock: fairly useful performer: won maiden at Catterick in July, and handicaps at Thirsk in August and Haydock in September: stays 1¾m: acts on good to firm and heavy going. *Jane Chapple-Hyam* **91**

UBLA (IRE) 4 ch.g. Arcano (IRE) 122 – Manuelita Rose (ITY) (Desert Style (IRE) 121) [2017 61, a76: f8g p7g 7g 8s^3 7d^6 p8g p7g^2 p7g^6 7d^3 f8.1g^4 t7.2g^3 f7.1g^5 p7g* Dec 28] strong gelding: modest handicapper on turf, fair on all-weather: won at Lingfield in December: trained by Jane Chapple-Hyam third to eighth starts: stays 1m: acts on all-weather and soft going: often wears headgear: has worn tongue tie: often races prominently. *Gay Kelleway* **64 a71**

UDOGO 6 b.g. Lucky Story (USA) 128 – Welanga (Dansili 127) [2017 87: p12g* p10.7g p10.7g^3 p12g^5 p12g^3 p12g^6 8.1m 10m^6 10m^5 11.4g 9s^6 p8g t12.2d p10g Dec 30] fairly useful handicapper: won at Dundalk (by ½ length from Specific Gravity) in January: left Joseph Patrick O'Brien/below form after sixth start: stays 13f: acts on polytrack, good to firm and good to soft going: has worn cheekpieces: often races towards rear. *Brendan Powell* **84 d**

UDONTDODOU 4 b.g. Fastnet Rock (AUS) 127 – Forever Times 98 (So Factual (USA) 120) [2017 95: p6g* 6s 6.1d p6s* p6s^3 p5s* Sep 30] good-topped gelding: useful handicapper: won at Chelmsford in April (by length from Zac Brown), June (by 1¾ lengths from Mazzini) and September (by 1¾ lengths from Foxy Forever): stays 6f: acts on polytrack, good to firm and heavy going. *Richard Guest* **109**

UDZUNGWA FOREST 3 ch.f. Power 117 – Uvinza 100 (Bertolini (USA) 125) [2017 10.2g Jul 21] third foal: half-sister to 1¼m winner Isamol (by Intikhab): dam, 2-y-o 1m winner who stayed 1½m, sister to useful winner up to 7f Baddilini: 50/1, well held in maiden at Nottingham. *Henry Candy* **–**

UELE RIVER 5 b.m. Refuse To Bend (IRE) 128 – Baddi Heights (FR) (Shirley Heights 130) [2017 8f 9.9m^4 9.9m 11.4m^4 9.9g* 12d Sep 29] quite attractive mare: useful performer: won listed race at Saint-Cloud (by head from Kourkan) in September: stays 11.5f: acts on good to firm going. *Henry Candy* **106**

ULSHAW BRIDGE (IRE) 2 b.c. (Feb 10) High Chaparral (IRE) 132 – Sharaarah (IRE) 98 (Oasis Dream 129) [2017 t6s^4 6m* 6.1d^3 7d 6d^6 Oct 28] €30,000Y: rather unfurnished colt: first foal: dam, 5f/6f winner (including at 2 yrs), half-sister to useful 2-y-o 5f winner Burwaaz: fairly useful performer: won minor event at York in July: third in similar event at Chester in August: stays 6f: acts on good to firm and good to soft going. *James Bethell* **94**

ULSTER (IRE) 2 gr.c. (Apr 2) Intello (GER) 129 – Ronaldsay 108 (Kirkwall 118) [2017 p10d^4 Nov 9] 120,000F: sixth foal: closely related to useful 9f/1¼m winner (stays 1½m) Eynhallow (by Nathaniel) and half-brother to smart winner up to 7f (stayed 9f) Gale Force Ten (2-y-o 6f winner, by Oasis Dream) and winner up to 1¼m Offshore (2-y-o 1m winner, by Iffraaj): dam winner up to 11f (2-y-o 7f winner): 7/1, some encouragement when fourth in minor event at Chelmsford (3¾ lengths behind Photographer) in November: should progress. *Saeed bin Suroor* **80 p**

ULTIMATE AVENUE (IRE) 3 b.g. Excelebration (IRE) 133 – Dance Avenue (IRE) (Sadler's Wells (USA) 132) [2017 95p: p8g^3 6g^3 7g 6d^6 Oct 6] good sort: smart handicapper: third at Newmarket (½ length behind Ekhtiyaar) in July: stays 7f: acts on good to firm going: in tongue tie last 3 starts. *Ed Walker* **110**

ULYSSES (GER) 3 b.g. Sinndar (IRE) 134 – Ungarin (GER) (Goofalik (USA) 118) [2017 p12g^2 p12g^2 10m 14m^6 16.3d^5 16v^6 Aug 3] good-topped gelding: fair maiden: stays 1½m: acts on polytrack: in blinkers last 3 starts: usually races prominently: temperamental. *Ralph Beckett* **73 §**

ULYSSES (IRE) 4 ch.c. Galileo (IRE) 134 – Light Shift (USA) 121 (Kingmambo (USA) 125) [2017 121: 10d* 10m^3 9.9m* 12s^2 10.3d* 11.9d^3 Oct 1] **130**

'I won't be champion trainer again, I don't have the fire-power or the numbers … I would love to have fifteen or twenty Galileos but we only get the occasional one.' Sir Michael Stoute, whose training career spans five decades, has been champion in Britain on ten occasions, a record bettered since the beginning of the twentieth century only by Alec Taylor with twelve titles during his tenure at Manton between 1902 and 1927. Henry Cecil is the only other trainer to have been champion ten times since 1900. The power nowadays, however, is very much held by Coolmore (Galileo is among its stallions) and its racing arm Ballydoyle. Acknowledging that he is 'better off than most' and still 'hanging in there', Stoute did particularly well with the latest of his 'occasional Galileos', the four-year-old Ulysses who, coincidentally, is a son of the Oaks winner Light Shift whose success at Epsom helped to spark a renaissance in Sir Henry Cecil's faltering training career which went on to be adorned by the achievements of Frankel. It was eight years since Sir Michael Stoute's last trainers' championship and seven years since his last British classic victory, but the performances of Ulysses in winning two of Britain's most prestigious races, the Eclipse and the International, helped him into fourth in the championship in the latest season with record earnings for the stable of £3,856,639 (he hadn't finished in the top four since being runner-up in 2010, the year Workforce gave him his fifth Derby winner). The latest season wasn't without its disappointments for the master of Freemason Lodge, though, with the biggest probably being the failure of his strong team (which included Ulysses) to win a race at Royal Ascot where Stoute remains on seventy-five winners, still needing one more to go clear at the top of the all-time list (he is currently level with Sir Henry Cecil).

Ulysses showed himself in the latest season to be the horse his trainer had always believed him to be. Bred by his owners the Niarchos family (he raced for Flaxman Stables Ireland), Ulysses was brought along patiently, considerately handled when finishing sixth of fifteen to Algometer in a mile maiden at Newbury on his only outing as a two-year-old. It took Ulysses three races in all to get off the mark, romping home in a maiden over a mile and a quarter, again at Newbury, after going down narrowly to Imperial Aviator in a similar event at Leicester on his reappearance at three. With his trainer notably bullish—not a characteristic usually associated with him—Ulysses started at only 8/1 for the Derby on his fourth outing, just three weeks after that maiden win at Newbury. Ulysses managed only twelfth of sixteen behind Harzand, the race almost certainly coming too soon for him at his stage of development (though the trainer claimed Ulysses had been 'knocked over twice in the race so had no chance'). The rest of Ulysses' three-year-old campaign was rather a mixed bag. He got back on track after the Derby when winning the Gordon Stakes at Goodwood on his next start, but he then suffered a surprising defeat at the hands of the smart older filly Chain of Daisies in the Winter Hill

Stakes at Windsor (the last race for which he started favourite) before finishing a respectable fourth behind Highland Reel in the Breeders' Cup Turf on his last outing, the entry and trip to Santa Anita confirming that connections still had plenty of faith in Ulysses breaking through at Group 1 level.

Ulysses opened his four-year-old campaign with the second pattern win of his career, winning the bet365 Gordon Richards Stakes at Sandown in good style from Deauville (who had finished a place ahead of him in the Derby), held up and produced to lead a furlong out. Ulysses repeated that form when third to Highland Reel and Decorated Knight in the Prince of Wales's Stakes at the Royal meeting, though he looked to be making a winning move when leading briefly a furlong out, only for his chance to evaporate, giving the impression he might have done better being held up for a little longer. Jim Crowley, who partnered Ulysses for the first time at Royal Ascot, retained the ride in the Coral-Eclipse at Sandown (after he lost the mount on the Craven Stakes winner Eminent whom he had ridden into sixth in the Two Thousand Guineas and fourth in the Derby).

The latest Eclipse was an above-average renewal with three-year-olds Cliffs of Moher (runner-up in the Derby), Barney Roy (second in the Two Thousand Guineas before winning the St James's Palace) and Eminent filling the first three places in the betting, ahead of 8/1-shot Ulysses, the shortest-priced of the four older horses in the nine-strong line-up. The race itself was full of incident, with significant trouble in the back straight affecting the favourite Cliffs of Moher. In a muddling race, Ulysses was given a confident ride, travelling strongly before making smooth headway to saunter into the lead entering the final furlong and then knuckling down really well to hold off the strong-challenging Barney Roy by a nose, the minimum distance (fortunately for Ulysses, the official weight-for-age scale had been revised for 2017, requiring three-year-olds in the Eclipse to carry 1 lb more!). The pair flashed past the post together and connections of Ulysses—including jockey Jim Crowley—weren't sure at first that he had won. Ulysses and Barney Roy finished three and a half lengths clear of third-placed 50/1-shot Desert Encounter. Cliffs of Moher, who was shuffled back through the field after three furlongs, was not quite able to repeat his Derby form in fourth, while Eminent and Decorated Knight finished fifth and sixth. The stewards were busy afterwards, imposing an eight-

Coral-Eclipse, Sandown—
the strong-travelling Ulysses knuckles down well to get the better of Barney Roy in a thrilling finish, with favourite Cliffs of Moher only fourth behind the hooded Desert Encounter after meeting trouble early on; the jockeys of Eminent and Taj Mahal earn careless riding bans, while James Doyle on the runner-up is referred to the BHA under totting-up rules for his use of the whip

Juddmonte International Stakes, York—
Ulysses proves better than ever, more emphatic than in the Eclipse as three-year-olds Barney Roy and Churchill (striped cap) are decisively beaten, with the first three clear

day ban for careless riding on Derby-winning jockey Padraig Beggy, the rider of Cliffs of Moher's pacemaker Taj Mahal, who caused interference on the first bend to Decorated Knight, leaving Cliffs of Moher with no place to go and causing him to stumble and collide with the running rail. Decorated Knight was also involved in a later incident when Eminent attempted to bite him while causing interference, for which Eminent's jockey Silvestre de Sousa picked up a two-day careless riding ban. James Doyle, the rider of Barney Roy, was found guilty of using his whip above the permitted level and, as it was his fifth such ban within six months, he was referred to the BHA under the totting-up procedure. There was also a sting in the tail for Sir Michael Stoute, whose victory with Ulysses was a record-equalling sixth in the race (the aforementioned Alec Taylor saddled the winner six times between 1909 and 1923). Ulysses was very late into the paddock and the fact that he was still not there, after the signal to mount was given, resulted in the stewards imposing a £1,000 fine on Stoute.

Sir Michael Stoute's most recent Eclipse winner before Ulysses had been Notnowcato ten years earlier, but he had won the King George VI and Queen Elizabeth Stakes more recently than that, the victories of Conduit in 2009 and Harbinger in 2010 bringing him level at the top of the table on five King George winners with Dick Hern and Saeed bin Suroor. Ulysses was sent next to Ascot to try to become the first winner of the Eclipse to go on to success in the King George in the same season since the Stoute-trained Opera House won both races in 1993 (Daylami had won both races since then, but in different years). Ulysses did his best against a top-class younger filly in dual Oaks winner Enable, momentarily looking a threat as he quickened in eye-catching style early in the straight but ultimately not proving good enough and going down by four and a half lengths, clear second best in a most representative field that lacked only a top-class three-year-old colt (not many of which contest the King George nowadays anyway).

Ulysses did face three of the best colts from the classic generation in his next race, the Juddmonte International at York, which had prize money of £1m for the first time, placing it behind only the Derby, the Champion Stakes, the King George VI and Queen Elizabeth Stakes and the Queen Elizabeth II Stakes among the most valuable races in Britain (the Sussex Stakes also has £1m in prize money). The changes to the official weight-for-age scale in Europe, which were introduced in 2017, were mostly fashioned around three-year-olds requiring less of an advantage over longer distances in the second half of the season (the BHA's racing department had conducted extensive research of six seasons' results and their findings were adopted unanimously by the European Pattern Committee). The difference in the Juddmonte International was 1 lb, as it had been in the Eclipse, but Ulysses didn't need any assistance from the new scale this time. Up against dual Two Thousand Guineas winner Churchill (who started favourite), as well as Barney Roy and Cliffs of Moher, in a field of seven, Ulysses could hardly have won more impressively. He looked better than ever, travelling very strongly and looming up two furlongs out before dealing the knock-out blow to the duelling pair Churchill and Barney Roy who had pressed on from three furlongs out. Ulysses moved past the pair entering the final furlong and was driven out to beat them by two lengths and a neck, Cliffs of Moher finishing four and a half lengths further back in fourth, with Decorated Knight, Shutter Speed and My Dream Boat completing the field.

Ulysses put up a top-class performance in the International in which his timefigure backed up the form assessment, his 1.09 fast (equivalent to a timerating of 127) placing him third among the season's 'fast-timers', behind only Battaash (1.18 fast in the King George at Goodwood) and Cracksman (1.11 fast in the Champion Stakes at Ascot). For Sir Michael Stoute, the performance of Ulysses was another landmark, providing him with a record sixth winner of the International, a race he hadn't won since Notnowcato's victory eleven years before, and in which he had shared the record with Aidan O'Brien. All the Stoute-trained International winners have been older horses, the age group which has dominated the race in recent times. Only five three-year-olds have won the race in the last quarter of a century, two of them, Giant's Causeway and Derby winner Australia, being among O'Brien's quintet, the others being the Derby winners Authorized and Sea The Stars, and 50/1-shot Arabian Queen (who upset Derby winner Golden Horn in 2015). The International, incidentally, was inaugurated (as the Benson & Hedges Gold Cup) in 1972, the year that Ulysses' trainer first took out a licence.

Ulysses was earmarked for another tilt at the Breeders' Cup Turf after the International, but he didn't make it in the end, eventually withdrawn on veterinary advice after suffering a minor injury at Del Mar (where Frankie Dettori had been set to replace Jim Crowley, Sir Michael Stoute saying 'It was my decision, we've been delighted with what Jim has done on him but we're in America now, and Frankie rode him in the race last year'). Ulysses ran once more after the International, running another good race to finish third to Enable and Cloth of Stars in the Prix de l'Arc de Triomphe at Chantilly, before which Cheveley Park Stud bought a majority share in him (he has been retired there and will stand at a fee of £30,000 in 2018). Ulysses ran in the colours of the Flaxman operation in the Arc, in which he finished a little closer to Enable than he had at Ascot, never far away but unable to go with the winner when she burst clear in the home straight, eventually beaten two and a half lengths and a length and a quarter. It looked at one time as if Ulysses would take on Cracksman and company in the Champion Stakes at Ascot on the way to the Breeders' Cup a fortnight later—there was a three-week gap in the latest season between Arc weekend and British Champions' Day—but there was a change of plan when the going came up very soft (which contributed to some disappointing performances from good horses on the day).

Ulysses (IRE) (ch.c. 2013)	Galileo (IRE) (b 1998)	Sadler's Wells (b 1981)	Northern Dancer
			Fairy Bridge
		Urban Sea (ch 1989)	Miswaki
			Allegretta
	Light Shift (USA) (b 2004)	Kingmambo (b 1990)	Mr Prospector
			Miesque
		Lingerie (b 1988)	Shirley Heights
			Northern Trick

The good-topped Ulysses, named after a mythical Greek hero, is from a family that has done well for the Niarchos family since Greek shipping magnate Stavros Niarchos bought Ulysses' great grandam Northern Trick for 530,000 dollars at the 1982 Keeneland July Sale. Northern Trick's sale price wasn't that extravagant for a Northern Dancer yearling at the time, especially as her dam had already produced four winners from four runners. The legendary Keeneland July Sale was targeted by Europe's richest owners and the demand for American bloodlines was going through the roof (thirty-three yearlings made a million dollars or more at the July Sale the following year and when the bidding reached ten million for Snaafi

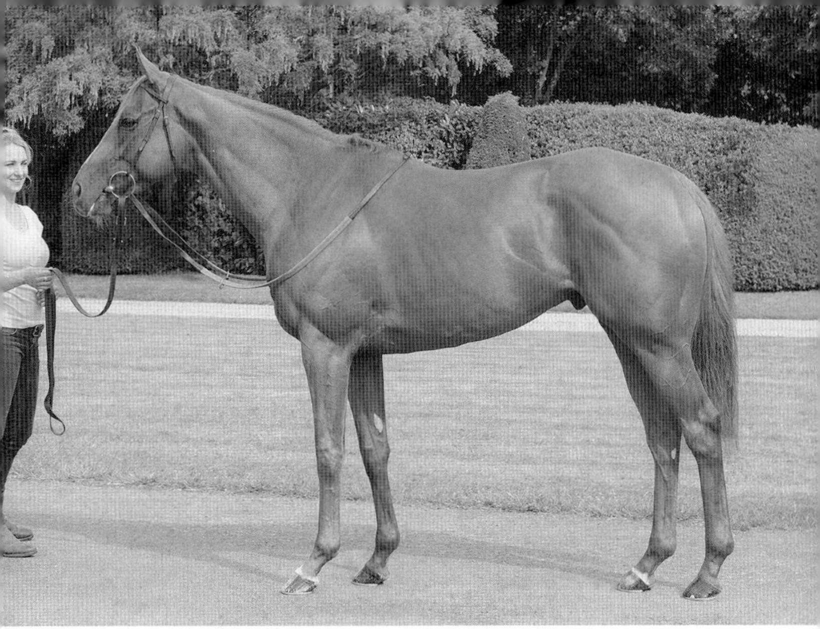

Flaxman Stables and Cheveley Park Stud's "Ulysses"

Dancer the auctioneers' electronic display couldn't cope, having been designed to show no more than seven digits!). Northern Trick was trained in France by Francois Boutin and trained on into the best middle-distance filly in Europe in 1984 when she won the Prix de Diane and the Prix Vermeille and finished second in the Prix de l'Arc. Northern Trick wasn't a typical Northern Dancer in appearance—she was tall, narrow and sparely made—and she bred nothing of note for the Niarchos family until she was twenty when she produced the Prix Imprudence winner Onda Nova.

Light Shift's dam Lingerie was a maiden but she made up for Northern Trick's shortcomings as a broodmare by breeding two others, apart from Light Shift, who made their mark in pattern company. They were the brother and sister Limnos and Shiva, the former a very smart middle-distance performer and the latter winner of the Tattersalls Gold Cup for Light Shift's trainer, as well as finishing third to Giant's Causeway in the Eclipse. Another of Lingerie's winners was the useful mile- to mile-and-a-quarter filly Burning Sunset who is the grandam of Main Sequence, second in Camelot's Derby before going on to carry the Niarchos silks with distinction in North America where he won four Grade 1s in a row as a five-year-old, including the Breeders' Cup Turf. 'Put the best to the best, and hope for the best'—or, more particularly, mate a Derby winner with an Oaks winner—is a strategy that has certainly paid off with Ulysses for the Niarchos family, but Light Shift is not the only Oaks winner in recent times to have produced the goods at stud. Two other Oaks winners this century have produced classic winners by Derby winner Galileo, Love Divine being the dam of St Leger winner Sixties Icon and Ouija Board being the dam of dual Derby winner Australia. The Arc runner-up Cloth of Stars is by Galileo's half-brother Sea The Stars and, like Ulysses, is out of a Niarchos-bred daughter (in her case Strawberry Fledge) of the outstanding sire Kingmambo and Lingerie. Unfortunately, Ulysses is the last of just three foals out of Light Shift who died in 2014 while delivering a foal (which also died) by Frankel. Ulysses stayed a mile and a half and acted on firm and soft going. He travelled strongly in his races and was best held up. *Sir Michael Stoute*

UMAIMAH (USA) 2 b.f. (Mar 21) Speightstown (USA) 124 – Soohaad (USA) 75 (Hard Spun (USA) 124) [2017 7d⁶ p7g Oct 26] second foal: half-sister to useful 2-y-o 6f winner Gheedaa (by Tamayuz): dam, 7f winner, closely related to smart winner up to 7f Haatef: modest form in maiden on first of 2 starts. *William Haggas* **56**

UNABATED (IRE) 3 b.c. Bated Breath 125 – Elhareer (IRE) 71 (Selkirk (USA) 129) [2017 93: t6g* t6s* 6g 6.1s³ Aug 6] smart handicapper: won at Newcastle in March (by neck from Letmestopyouthere) and July (by neck from Northgate Lad): raced only at 6f: acts on polytrack, tapeta, soft and good to firm going: often in tongue tie. *Marco Botti* **111**

UNBLINKING 4 b.g. Cacique (IRE) 124 – Deliberate (King's Best (USA) 132) [2017 78: 12s 10.2d p16g⁵ Dec 20] fair maiden: stays 2m: acts on polytrack: sometimes slowly away: placed over hurdles. *Nigel Twiston-Davies* **65**

UNBRIDLED SPIRIT 2 b.g. (Mar 12) Passing Glance 119 – Sweet Mandolin (Soviet Star (USA) 128) [2017 8d 8s⁵ 8d Oct 27] fair form: best effort when seventh in minor event at Sandown (8¾ lengths behind Kitaabaat) on debut: bred to be suited by 1¼m+. *Andrew Balding* **69**

UNCHAINING MELODY 2 b.f. (Mar 15) Excelebration (IRE) 133 – Sky To Sky (USA) (Sky Classic (CAN)) [2017 7g² Aug 30] third foal: half-sister to 2 winners abroad by Kingsfort: dam lightly-raced half-sister to smart 2-y-o 7f winner No Jet Lag (later US Grade 2 1m winner): 14/1, second in minor event at Lingfield (6 lengths behind Gavota): sent to USA: should improve. *Marco Botti* **66 p**

UNCLE BERNIE (IRE) 7 gr.g. Aussie Rules (USA) 123 – Alwiyda (USA) (Trempolino (USA) 135) [2017 t13.9f² t13.9m⁴ t13.9g⁶ 18g* t16.3g⁶ 17.1d 18g⁶ Jun 25] leggy, close-coupled gelding: fairly useful handicapper: won at Pontefract in April: stays 2¼m: acts on polytrack, tapeta and good to firm going: has worn headgear, including last 4 starts: usually races in rear. *Sarah Hollinshead* **80**

UNCLE CHARLIE (IRE) 3 b.g. Vale of York (IRE) 117 – Velvet Kiss (IRE) (Danehill Dancer (IRE) 117) [2017 68: 6.9g 6g* 5.9g 6d 5.9s³ 6d⁴ 6g 6d⁴ Oct 30] fair handicapper: won at Thirsk in June: stays 6f: acts on soft going: tried in tongue tie. *Ann Duffield* **74**

UNCOVERED 2 b.g. (Mar 3) Helmet (AUS) 127 – Caritas (Generous (IRE) 139) [2017 t7.2g⁶ 7d 7s p6g⁶ Sep 5] little impact in minor events/nursery: has joined Marjorie Fife. *Tom Dascombe* **–**

UNDER APPROVAL 6 b.g. Captain Gerrard (IRE) 113 – Dockside Strike (Docksider (USA) 124) [2017 58: f5g³ 5m 5g 5m⁶ 5g 5m⁴ 5g 5.5f Jun 19] poor handicapper: stays 6f: acts on polytrack, fibresand, good to firm and good to soft going: wears headgear: sometimes slowly away: one to treat with caution. *Karen Tutty* **46 §**

UNDER ATTACK (IRE) 4 b.g. Dubawi (IRE) 129 – Ship's Biscuit 107 (Tiger Hill (IRE) 127) [2017 80p: 10m⁶ 11.6g 12g⁵ 11.9m 8.3d⁵ Jul 25] close-coupled gelding: fairly useful maiden: left Roger Charlton after second start: stays 1¼m: acts on polytrack, soft and good to firm going: wore headgear in 2017: often races towards rear: sold £13,000 in August. *Ruth Carr* **85**

UNDER CONTROL (IRE) 3 b.g. Power 117 – High Figurine (IRE) 88 (High Chaparral (IRE) 132) [2017 79p: p8g³ 8.9s p8g³ Oct 13] fairly useful handicapper: third at Kempton in August and October: stays 1m: acts on polytrack and good to firm going: tried in blinkers: usually races freely: sold 16,000 gns, sent to Qatar. *William Haggas* **89**

UNDERCOVER BROTHER 2 ch.g. (Mar 14) Captain Gerrard (IRE) 113 – Socceroo 65 (Choisir (AUS) 126) [2017 5d³ 5m* 5d² 5g 5g³ 5m⁴ 5s² p5g Oct 3] fair performer: won minor event at Hamilton in June: raced only at 5f: acts on soft and good to firm going: tried in visor: races prominently: has joined John Balding. *David O'Meara* **73**

UNDER OFFER (IRE) 2 ch.f. (Mar 17) Bated Breath 125 – Bailonguera (ARG) (Southern Halo (USA)) [2017 5m³ 5g⁵ May 12] €40,000F, 52,000Y: half-sister to several winners, including useful winner up to 9.5f Bayargal (2-y-o 7.5f winner, by Bernstein) and 2-y-o 7f winner Bandidazo (by Van Nistelrooy), both in France: dam Argentinian Grade 2 1m winner: fair form: better effort when third in minor event at Ripon (2½ lengths behind Maggies Angel) in April. *James Tate* **66**

UNDER SIEGE (IRE) 5 b.g. Invincible Spirit (IRE) 121 – Interpose (Indian Ridge 123) [2017 90: p6d p6d² p6g³ 6m Apr 24] fairly useful handicapper: third at Kempton (length behind Bouclier) in March: stayed 6f: acted on polytrack and good to soft going: tried in cheekpieces: wore tongue tie: dead. *Stuart Williams* **90**

UNDERSTORY (USA) 10 b.g. Forestry (USA) 121 – Sha Tha (USA) 118 (Mr Prospector (USA)) [2017 59: p10g p12g p10g^4 p10g^4 p10g p10s Dec 15] big, workmanlike gelding: poor handicapper nowadays: stays 1¼m: acts on polytrack and good to firm going: has worn headgear: front runner/races prominently. *Tim McCarthy* **44**

UNDER THE COVERS 4 b.f. Stimulation (IRE) 121 – Sakha 109 (Wolfhound (USA) 126) [2017 t7.1g^5 5.7f^4 p7d 5.7m* 5.7f^2 6g 5.2s* 6s* 6g^6 5.6g 6g Oct 7] useful performer: won maiden at Bath in June, and handicaps at Newbury and Ffos Las (by 3 lengths from Go Far) in August: best at 5f/6f: acts on firm and soft going: front runner/races prominently. *Ronald Harris* **98**

UNDISCOVERED ANGEL (FR) 3 b.f. Wootton Bassett 119 – Angel Voices (IRE) 81 (Tagula (IRE) 116) [2017 73p: 6m^3 7.2g^3 7.4d^4 p6.5g 8d^4 8d 8d 7v^4 t6d^5 5.5v^6 Nov 25] fair maiden: stays 1m: acts on soft going: tried in cheekpieces: front runner/races prominently. *K. R. Burke* **77**

UNFORGETABLE FILLY 3 b.f. Sepoy (AUS) 129 – Beautiful Filly 78 (Oasis Dream 129) [2017 97: 7m^2 8m^6 7.2m* 8g* 7g 9f Oct 14] rather unfurnished filly: useful performer: won listed race at Musselburgh (by 1¾ lengths from Pirouette) and German 1000 Guineas at Dusseldorf (by length from Peace In Motion), both in June: second in Nell Gwyn Stakes at Newmarket (¾ length behind Daban) in April: stays 1m: acts on good to firm going. *Hugo Palmer* **107**

UNFORGIVING MINUTE 6 b.g. Cape Cross (IRE) 129 – Ada River 102 (Dansili 127) [2017 99: p8d p8s t7.2g* p7g* t7.2g^2 Dec 5] good-topped gelding: useful performer: won claimers at Wolverhampton in September and Lingfield in November: stays 8.5f: acts on polytrack and tapeta. *John Butler* **96**

UNFORTUNATELY (IRE) 2 b.c. (Mar 16) Society Rock (IRE) 126 – Unfortunate 55 (Komaite (USA)) [2017 5m^5 5m* 5g^2 6g^2 5.5g* 6g* 6d Sep 30] **117**

Finally, after years of French intransigence, there will be uniform rules across Europe governing interference in races. If a horse does not improve its position, relative to the horse to which it has caused interference, the placings in a race will remain unaltered. That has been the position for many years in Britain, Ireland and most other major racing countries outside North America, while, in France, interference has been liable to result in demotion behind the horse suffering the interference. The belated introduction of unanimity is a feather in the cap of the International Federation of Horseracing Authorities which has adopted a universal rule as part of its international agreement with members. The IFHA chairman Louis Romanet, a former director general of France Galop, also revealed that the new Article 32 also covers the types of whip—padded or shock absorbing only—that may be carried in a race. 'Achieving greater uniformity in raceday rules is important to the development of an international fan base, and is essential to simulcasting and co-mingling [betting] arrangements which are increasingly significant for the revenues of the sport.' A common approach to permissible whip use and to penalties for various disciplinary offences could perhaps be other areas the IFHA's

Prix Robert Papin, Maisons-Laffitte—
visored Unfortunately leads home a one, two, three for British stables, beating the grey Frozen Angel and Queen Mary winner Heartache (braces); fourth High Dream Milena (second right) is hampered by the winner, but the placings remain unaltered after a stewards' inquiry

Darley Prix Morny, Deauville—a notable one, two for trainer Karl Burke, Unfortunately and Havana Grey showing further improvement to finish ahead of two fillies, Different League (rail) and Zonza (not in picture), who suffer their first defeats

harmonisation of raceday rules committee could look into, as well as trying to bring about uniformity in the way equipment is declared (France, for example, does not distinguish between blinkers and a visor and still does not require tongue straps to be declared). From a global perspective, rather than just a European one, North America's permissive approach to raceday medication—allowing the use of drugs banned in every other major jurisdiction—remains by far the greatest barrier to horse racing becoming a truly global sport. Racegoers need to be able to believe in what they are seeing, and to have trust in the integrity of the sport, if it is to become a worldwide betting medium (there is more on this particular topic in the essay on Talismanic).

On a traditionally strict reading of the old French rules on interference—which were still in force at the time—it was perhaps surprising that British-trained Unfortunately survived a stewards' inquiry after finishing first past the post in the Prix Robert Papin at Maisons-Laffitte in July. The race was dominated by British-trained runners, with Unfortunately (the longest-priced of the four British challengers in the field of six) leading home a one, two, three and scoring by half a length and a short head from Frozen Angel and odds-on Heartache, who had won the Queen Mary at Royal Ascot. Unfortunately hung left when making his challenge and hampered fourth-placed High Dream Milena, the only home-trained runner, whose rider was forced to snatch up. Finishing with running left, once-raced High Dream Milena recovered to finish three quarters of a length behind Heartache in fourth and it was rather surprising that the Maisons-Laffitte stewards did not find in her favour. While the same incident in Britain would certainly have seen the result unchanged (Unfortunately was the winner on merit), it was possible to argue that High Dream Milena would at least have finished in the first three with a clear run, which, under the French rules, provided grounds for disqualifying Unfortunately and placing him behind High Dream Milena. The stewards, however, decided that High Dream Milena 'lacked the resources to advance' at the time of the interference and they left the placings unaltered (an appeal by High Dream Milena's owners was unsuccessful). Unfortunately's jockey Tony Piccone was given a two-day suspension for careless riding.

The Prix Robert Papin was the speedily-bred Unfortunately's fifth appearance, after he had been on the go since mid-April, gaining his only victory in a minor event at Hamilton on his second start before failing narrowly in a listed event at Maisons-Laffitte in June and the Spindrifter Conditions Stakes at Pontefract in early-July, hanging left and collared on the post by Zaman in the last-named. Unfortunately was tried in a visor for the first time in the Robert Papin and showed improved form, which led to his return to France a month later for the Group 1 Prix Morny in which his stablemate Havana Grey, winner of the Molecomb Stakes at Goodwood, was also a runner (as was High Dream Milena and the French-trained winner of the Albany Stakes at Royal Ascot, Different League, who started second favourite behind the Prix de Cabourg winner Tantheem). Unfortunately and Havana Grey pulled off a notable one, two for Middleham trainer Karl Burke, both showing further improvement to finish ahead of Different League and another pattern-winning filly who was suffering her first defeat, Zonza (High Dream Milena was fifth). Unfortunately had too many guns for his stablemate, taking over from him inside the final furlong and being driven out to win by a length and a quarter, with the third and fourth just held by the keeping-on Havana Grey. Havana Grey was a creditable second to Heartache in the Flying Childers Stakes at Doncaster on his only subsequent start and Unfortunately—acquired by Cheveley Park Stud after his win in the Morny—can probably be excused his below-par ninth in the Middle Park on his only other start, as he was slowly away and the effort he had to make to try to get into the firing line, which he did two furlongs out, perhaps took its toll (the going at Newmarket was also the softest he had encountered).

Unfortunately (IRE) (b.c. 2015)	Society Rock (IRE) (b 2007)	Rock of Gibraltar (b 1999)	Danehill
			Offshore Boom
		High Society (b 1999)	Key of Luck
			Ela's Gold
	Unfortunate (ch 1997)	Komaite (b 1983)	Nureyev
			Brown Berry
		Honour And Glory (ch 1990)	Hotfoot
			Cheb's Honour

The strong-quartered Unfortunately cost €24,000 as a yearling and is a fine advertisement for his sadly-deceased sire Society Rock who had to be put down with laminitis in 2016 after only three seasons at stud. Unfortunately's family on the distaff side is certainly nothing to write home about, the three mares on the bottom

Cheveley Park Stud's "Unfortunately"

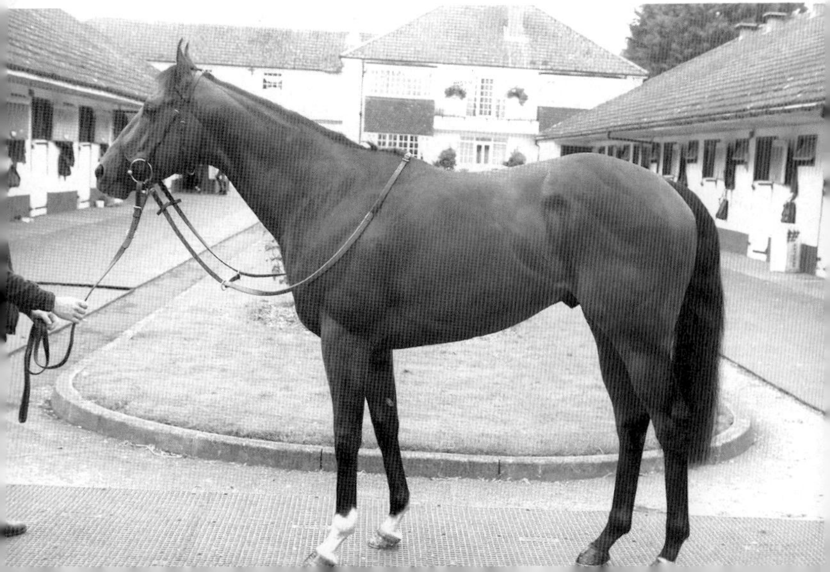

line of his pedigree managing Timeform ratings of 55§, 46 and 70 in their racing careers. Unfortunately's great grandam Cheb's Honour showed the best form of the three but she lost her way after being placed over five furlongs at two; the grandam Honour And Glory was a poor maiden; and Unfortunately's dam Unfortunate, a 1,000-guinea yearling, was a poor sprinter who won a seller at Southwell as a two-year-old from eight starts and a selling handicap at Leicester from twelve starts at three (she picked up her Timeform squiggle for a propensity to start slowly and wander in her races). Unfortunately is the sixth winner bred by Unfortunate who, remarkably, has produced another smart sprinter in Look Busy (by Danetime), her third foal, who won twelve times, gaining her most important successes in the Temple Stakes and the Flying Five at the Curragh. Both of those wins came while Look Busy was trained in Britain, but she ran for new connections in Ireland as a six-year-old (winning once, though she did not appear in *Racehorses* that year). The wider family was also represented by another smart sprinter in the 'eighties, Honour And Glory's half-brother Singing Steven winning the Cornwallis at two and the King George Stakes at Goodwood at three. Like most in the family, Singing Steven was purchased comparatively cheaply as a yearling, making only 3,000 guineas. Unfortunately's dam herself was bought at Goffs November Sale by her present owners Tally-Ho Stud (who stood Society Rock) for only €5,000 as an eight-year-old, having delivered Look Busy earlier that year. Unfortunate has a yearling filly by Sir Prancealot and a filly foal by Morpheus. Unfortunately stays six furlongs and acts on good to firm going. He wore a visor on his last three starts. *K. R. Burke*

UNIFIED 3 b.f. Oasis Dream 129 – Ensemble (FR) (Iron Mask (USA) 117) [2017 7g^2 8g^4 8.1m^4 8f* p8g Sep 26] 145,000Y: quite attractive filly: second foal: half-sister to useful 1m winner Desert Haze (by New Approach): dam, 9f winner, half-sister to very smart winner up to 1m Occupandiste: fair performer: won maiden at Bath in July: stays 1m: acts on firm going. *Clive Cox* **75**

UNION ROSE 5 b.g. Stimulation (IRE) 121 – Dot Hill (Refuse To Bend (IRE) 128) [2017 104: 5d^6 5s^5 5g 5m 5m 5f* 5.1g^4 5g 5.2s^4 5v^5 5s 5g t5.1g* p5s^6 Dec 14] rangy gelding: fairly useful handicapper: won at Bath (by 2 lengths from Trick of The Light) in July and Wolverhampton in December: best form at 5f: acts on tapeta, firm and soft going: has worn headgear, including last 3 starts. *Ronald Harris* **94**

UNISON (IRE) 7 b.g. Jeremy (USA) 122 – Easter Song (USA) (Rubiano (USA)) [2017 87: 10m 9.9v^4 9.9g 8.1s^6 Sep 14] good-topped gelding: fairly useful handicapper: stays 1¼m: acts on polytrack, good to firm and heavy going: usually races prominently: useful hurdler. *Jeremy Scott* **83**

UNITED KINGDOM 2 b.g. (Jan 31) Equiano (FR) 127 – Lucky Legs (IRE) 89 (Danehill Dancer (IRE) 117) [2017 6s p6g^5 Oct 14] fair form: better effort when fifth in minor event at Kempton (2¼ lengths behind Lansky) in October. *Paul Cole* **65**

UNITE THE CLANS (IRE) 3 b.g. Danehill Dancer (IRE) 117 – Janna's Jewel (IRE) (Traditionally (USA) 117) [2017 12m^3 10.3m^5 9.2s^5 9.2s 11.4m* a8.9f Nov 17] closely related to useful 1m-1¼m winner (stayed 1½m) Hold The Line (by Ivan Denisovich) and half-brother to 3 winners, including useful 7f winner Rominintheglomin (by Whipper) and useful 1m winner (stayed 1½m) Dolce N Karama (by The Carbon Unit): dam maiden: fairly useful performer: won handicap at Windsor (by head from Love Conquers) in August: left John Patrick Shanahan after fifth start: stays 11.5f: acts on good to firm going: often races prominently. *S. Seemar, UAE* **84**

UNIT OF ASSESSMENT (IRE) 3 b.g. Dragon Pulse (IRE) 114 – Before The Storm 78 (Sadler's Wells (USA) 132) [2017 8m 10s 8.2d^2 8g^3 10.2d^6 8d 8.5g^3 9.9s^4 p10g p10g^3 p10g^2 Dec 30] compact gelding: fair maiden: stays 1¼m: acts on polytrack and soft going: sometimes in visor: usually wears tongue tie. *William Knight* **76**

UNIVERSAL COMMAND 2 b.g. (Apr 6) Delegator 125 – Telescopic (Galileo (IRE) 134) [2017 7g 7d p8g^4 Oct 14] good-topped gelding: second foal: half-brother to useful 1¼m winner Imperial Aviator (by Paco Boy): dam of little account: fair form: best effort when fourth in minor event at Kempton (2½ lengths behind Indiscretion) in October: open to further improvement. *Roger Charlton* **72 p**

UNNOTICED 5 b.g. Observatory (USA) 131 – Celestial Empire (USA) (Empire Maker (USA) 129) [2017 74: f7g^2 t7.1g^5 f7g^2 f7m f6.1g f7.1g^4 Dec 19] fair handicapper: stays 7.5f: acts on fibresand, tapeta, best turf form on good going: has worn headgear: usually wears tongue tie: usually travels strongly. *Ollie Pears* **72**

UNONOTHINJONSNOW 3 b.g. Arakan (USA) 123 – Kleio 73 (Sadler's Wells (USA) 132) [2017 –: 8.2g^{6} f7.1g 11.2v^{3} p10d 8.3g 14v^{6} p13.3s Dec 1] modest maiden: stays 11f: acts on heavy going: tried in cheekpieces: sometimes slowly away, often races towards rear. *Richard Guest* **54**

UNSUSPECTED GIRL (IRE) 4 b.f. Rip Van Winkle (IRE) 134 – Sweet Sioux 59 (Halling (USA) 133) [2017 79: 11.6d p14d 10g* p11g t9.5g t9.5g Nov 25] lengthy filly: fair performer: won claimer at Windsor in October for Graeme McPherson: trained on reappearance only by Brian Barr: stays 1¾m: acts on polytrack and firm going: usually in tongue tie in 2017: often races towards rear. *Milton Bradley* **65**

UNTIL MIDNIGHT (IRE) 7 b.g. Moss Vale (IRE) 126 – Emma's Star (ITY) (Darshaan 133) [2017 90: p7d^{3} p7g^{2} p7g^{5} 6m^{2} 7m^{6} p7s^{5} 7g p7s^{2} Jul 25] fair handicapper on turf, fairly useful on all-weather: second at Chelmsford in July: stays 1m: acts on polytrack, tapeta, good to firm and good to soft going: in blinkers last 2 starts: tried in tongue tie. *Eugene Stanford* **71** **a88**

UNVEILING 2 b.f. (Feb 6) Mayson 124 – Silkenveil (IRE) 55 (Indian Ridge 123) [2017 t7.2g* Dec 22] £7,000Y: third foal: half-sister to winner up to 1¼m Brown Velvet (2-y-o 5.7f winner) and 7.4f-1¼m winner Jawaayiz (both by Kodiac): dam lightly-raced half-sister to smart 1¼m winner (stays 16.5f) Excellent Result: 12/1, won minor event at Wolverhampton (by ½ length from Golden Image) on debut. *Jonathan Portman* **66**

UNWRITTEN 2 b.g. (May 28) Poet's Voice 126 – Passata (FR) (Polar Falcon (USA) 126) [2017 8.3s^{4} 8v* 8v^{5} Oct 23] 25,000Y: half-brother to numerous winners, including useful German/Italian 11f-2m winner Parivash (by Singspiel) and smart French/German 2-y-o 6f/7f winner Pomellato (by Big Shuffle): dam 1m winner: fairly useful form: won minor event at Pontefract (by 9 lengths from Sunhill Lad) in September: stays 1m. *K. R. Burke* **85**

UNZIPPED 3 ch.f. Captain Gerrard (IRE) 113 – Justazippy 66 (Where Or When (IRE) 124) [2017 65: 8.3m 10.2m 7g May 9] angular filly: modest form first 2 starts in 2016, little impact since. *Stuart Edmunds* **–**

UPAVON 7 b.g. Avonbridge 123 – Blaina 76 (Compton Place 125) [2017 87, a99: p5g^{3} p6m t6g^{2} t6g^{2} p5g 5d^{6} p6s 5.3m* 6g^{4} 6g^{3} t5.1g^{5} t5.1g p6g^{3} Dec 21] tall, workmanlike gelding: fairly useful handicapper on turf, useful on all-weather: won at Brighton in August: second at Wolverhampton in February and March: stays 7f: acts on polytrack, tapeta and good to firm going: wears headgear/tongue tie: temperamental. *Stuart Williams* **83 §** **a96 §**

UPENDED 3 b.g. Paco Boy (IRE) 129 – Upskittled (Diktat 126) [2017 8.1m 8s^{6} 8.2d 10.2g^{5} 10.2v^{2} t8.6g^{5} Sep 9] angular gelding: fair maiden: stays 1¼m: acts on heavy going: usually races towards rear. *Chris Wall* **65**

UPGRADE 3 gr.c. Excelebration (IRE) 133 – Pinch of Posh (IRE) 75 (Pivotal 124) [2017 72: p10g^{4} f8s* Jan 26] fair performer: won handicap at Southwell in January: stays 8.5f: acts on tapeta, fibresand and firm going: sometimes in cheekpieces: front runner/races prominently: sold 26,000 gns in February, sent Greece. *K. R. Burke* **79**

UPHOLD 10 b.g. Oasis Dream 129 – Allegro Viva (USA) (Distant View (USA) 126) [2017 60: p11.9g p11.9g^{3} p11.9g t12.2g t12.2g^{3} t12.2g Jun 26] well-made gelding: modest performer nowadays: stays 1½m: acts on all-weather, good to firm and heavy going: wears headgear: has worn tongue tie. *Gay Kelleway* **60**

UPPER LAMBOURN (IRE) 9 b.g. Exceed And Excel (AUS) 126 – In The Fashion (IRE) 88 (In The Wings 128) [2017 43: f6g^{5} p6g^{3} p7d^{5} p6g p7s Sep 30] good-bodied gelding: modest handicapper: left John Holt after third start: stays 6f: acts on polytrack and fibresand: has worn headgear: usually wears tongue tie. *Denis Quinn* **51**

UPSTAGING 5 b.g. Mount Nelson 125 – Corndavon (USA) 95 (Sheikh Albadou 128) [2017 103: 6m 6.1d^{2} 6.1g* 6d^{3} 6.1s^{2} 6g Oct 14] good-topped gelding: useful handicapper: won at Windsor (by ½ length from Englishman) in July: third in Stewards' Cup at Goodwood (¾ length behind Lancelot du Lac) and second at Windsor (length behind Ice Age) in August: best at 5f/6f: acts on polytrack, tapeta and soft going: has worn headgear, including last 4 starts. *Paul Cole* **108**

UP STICKS AND GO 2 gr.c. (Mar 22) Equiano (FR) 127 – Reaching Ahead (USA) (Mizzen Mast (USA) 121) [2017 6g^{2} 6s^{4} 6d^{2} 5v^{2} 7v* Nov 7] £20,000Y: half-brother to several winners, including winner up to 1¼m Grey Britain (2-y-o 6f winner, by Arcano) and 1¼m/11f winner Full of Beauty (by Motivator), both useful: dam French 6.5f and (at 2 yrs) 1m winner: fairly useful performer: won minor event at Redcar in November: stays 7f: acts on heavy going: front runner/races prominently. *Keith Dalgleish* **82**

UP TEN DOWN TWO (IRE) 8 b.g. Hurricane Run (IRE) 134 – Darabela (IRE) 84 (Desert King (IRE) 129) [2017 67: t16.3g* t12.4d* 11.6m 11.6g 12m 13.9s^{6} 12.1s f12.1g f11.1g^{3} Dec 21] fair handicapper: won at Newcastle (twice) in March: stays 16.5f: acts on all-weather, firm and good to soft going: has worn tongue tie. *Michael Easterby* **69 a75**

UPTOWN FUNK (IRE) 3 b.g. Galileo (IRE) 134 – All's Forgotten (USA) 81 (Darshaan 133) [2017 –p: 10.2g^{5} p12s^{6} 11.8g^{2} 12s^{5} p14d^{3} 11.4m^{6} t16.3d^{3} Dec 16] good-bodied gelding: fairly useful maiden: third in handicap at Newcastle in December: left John Gosden after sixth start: stays 16.5f: acts on polytrack and tapeta: wears headgear: sometimes in tongue tie. *Keith Dalgleish* **82**

UPTOWN GIRL 3 b.f. Doncaster Rover (USA) 114 – Mon Petit Diamant 54 (Hector Protector (USA) 124) [2017 p8g Dec 28] fifth foal: half-sister to 6f winner Force To Spend (by Reset): dam maiden: 33/1, well held in maiden at Lingfield. *Lydia Pearce* **–**

URBAN FOX 3 b.f. Foxwedge (AUS) 128 – Lomapamar 76 (Nashwan (USA) 135) [2017 97: 7m^{2} 8m 8.5m 8d^{4} 8g 7g^{4} 7s^{4} Oct 7] rather leggy filly: useful performer: fourth in listed race at Newbury (1¼ lengths behind Tabarrak) in September: stays 1m: acts on polytrack, firm and good to soft going: in headgear last 4 starts: sold to join William Haggas 425,000 gns in December. *James Tate* **104**

URBAN SOUL (IRE) 2 b.g. (Mar 5) Worthadd (IRE) 124 – Capsaicin (IRE) (Invincible Spirit (IRE) 121) [2017 7m 7d 7g^{3} t7.1d t8.6g^{4} p10s^{2} Dec 15] fair maiden: stays 1¼m: acts on polytrack and tapeta: in cheekpieces last 2 starts. *James Bethell* **72**

URBAN SPACE 11 ch.g. Sulamani (IRE) 130 – Rasmalai 71 (Sadler's Wells (USA) 132) [2017 75: 13.1m^{5} 16.2m^{5} 16m^{6} Jun 16] small gelding: fair handicapper, below form in 2017: stays 17f: acts on any turf going: wears tongue tie. *John Flint* **61**

URBAN SPIRIT (IRE) 3 b.g. Born To Sea (IRE) 117 – Rose of Mooncoin (IRE) 99 (Brief Truce (USA) 126) [2017 –: 7g^{5} 6m^{4} 7g^{6} 6v 10v^{5} 10g^{4} t8d t8s^{4} Nov 30] modest maiden: left Jedd O'Keeffe after third start: stays 1m: acts on tapeta and good to firm going: tried in cheekpieces. *Roger Fell* **58**

URBINO 2 b.c. (May 7) Dansili 127 – Novellara 107 (Sadler's Wells (USA) 132) [2017 p8g^{4} Oct 25] fifth foal: brother to smart winner up to 11f Disclaimer (2-y-o 9f winner) and half-brother to 1¼m winner (stayed 1½m) Word Power (by Oasis Dream): dam, 1¼m/1¾m winner, closely related to Oaks winner Reams of Verse and half-sister to high-class 1¼m performer Elmaamul: 12/1, needed experience when fourth in minor event at Kempton (10 lengths behind Tenedos) on debut, late headway: sort to improve markedly. *Sir Michael Stoute* **61 P**

URIAH HEEP (FR) 8 b.g. Danehill Dancer (IRE) 117 – Canasita 107 (Zafonic (USA) 130) [2017 12.1m^{4} 10d 13.1s Jul 10] tall gelding: fairly useful at best, just modest form in 2017: stays 1½m: acts on polytrack, soft and good to firm going: often in cheekpieces: winning hurdler/chaser. *R. Mike Smith* **63**

URSUS BELLE (IRE) 2 b.f. (Apr 7) Kodiac 112 – Switcher (IRE) 105 (Whipper (USA) 126) [2017 5m^{3} 6m^{4} Jun 20] 75,000Y: first foal: dam, 2-y-o 6f winner, half-sister to useful 2-y-o 6f winner Marine Boy: modest form in minor event/maiden: has joined William Durkan: remains with potential. *Richard Hannon* **56 p**

US ARMY RANGER (IRE) 4 b.c. Galileo (IRE) 134 – Moonstone 119 (Dalakhani (IRE) 133) [2017 123: 10d^{3} 13.4d^{2} 12m 21.6m^{3} 16g 12d^{6} 15.9g Nov 7] well-made colt: very smart performer at best, mostly disappointing since second in Derby at Epsom: placed in 2017 in Alleged Stakes at Naas (3¼ lengths third behind Air Pilot), Ormonde Stakes at Chester (short-head second to Western Hymn) and Queen Alexandra Stakes at Royal Ascot (3 lengths third to Oriental Fox): left Aidan O'Brien before final start: best effort at 1½m: acts on heavy going: tried in hood. *Joseph Patrick O'Brien, Ireland* **112**

USED TO BE 3 ch.g. Kyllachy 129 – Polly Floyer 66 (Halling (USA) 133) [2017 74: 7m 7m 9.2s^{6} 7.1v^{3} 8g^{4} t7.1g^{5} 7d Oct 24] fair maiden: stays 7f: best form on good going: tried in cheekpieces: sold 4,000 gns, sent to Hungary. *K. R. Burke* **65**

USHER 2 b.g. (Mar 3) Oasis Dream 129 – Nimble Thimble (USA) 76 (Mizzen Mast (USA) 121) [2017 6.1g 7d Aug 21] compact gelding: last in minor events. *Roger Charlton* **–**

USHERETTE (IRE) 5 b.m. Shamardal (USA) 129 – Monday Show (USA) 99 (Maria's Mon (USA) 121) [2017 123: 8g^{3} 8.9g^{3} 8m^{3} 8g^{6} 8d* 8g^{4} Oct 7] attractive mare: smart performer: won listed race at Maisons-Laffitte (by short neck from Game Theory) in September: also in frame in Prix du Muguet at Saint-Cloud (1¾ lengths third behind Jimmy Two Times), Prix d'Ispahan at Chantilly (¾-length third to Mekhtaal), Duke of Cambridge **116**

Stakes at Royal Ascot (length third to Qemah) and Sun Chariot Stakes at Newmarket (2½ lengths fourth to Roly Poly): stays 9.5f: acts on polytrack, good to firm and good to soft going. *A. Fabre, France*

U S NAVY FLAG (USA) 2 b.c. (Feb 6) War Front (USA) 119 – Misty For Me (IRE) 122 (Galileo (IRE) 134) [2017 5m4 6g3 6d3 6f 6g* 6g2 6m4 6d* 6d* 7m* a8.5f Nov 4] **123**

There may only be a furlong in distance between the Middle Park Stakes and the Dewhurst but Newmarket's two big juvenile contests of the autumn for colts normally cater for two very distinct types of two-year-old. On the one hand, the six-furlong Middle Park almost has the status of a sprint championship for speedy and precocious colts who have been thoroughly tried and tested at two. As such, it has often proved a career highlight for its winners and has even been the final destination for some of its participants who have been packed off to stud without being tried at all at three. That was the fate of the 2016 winner The Last Lion, as well as the third, Mehmas, following the example set by the 2007 winner Dark Angel who did at least attempt the Dewhurst, albeit beating just one home a fortnight later when a 25/1-shot, thereby ending any remaining ambitions to persevere with him (there was no Commonwealth Cup at Royal Ascot at that time). Dream Ahead, successful in 2010, was the last Middle Park winner to win in Group 1 company again at three when he was a top-class winner of the July Cup, Sprint Cup and Prix de la Foret. Oasis Dream, another July Cup winner who also won the Nunthorpe, is the only other Middle Park winner this century to cover himself in glory in the same way at three. The last time the Middle Park had a bearing on any of the classics was in 1991 when its winner Rodrigo de Triano went on to land the Two Thousand Guineas for Robert Sangster and Peter Chapple-Hyam. But Rodrigo de Triano was an untypical Middle Park winner, having already won twice over seven furlongs, and it is likely that he would have been aimed at the Dewhurst had the same connections not had Dr Devious (who actually changed ownership shortly beforehand) for that race.

Dr Devious became the second consecutive Dewhurst winner, after Generous, to win the Derby the following year, something also achieved this century by Dewhurst winners Sir Percy and New Approach. The Dewhurst has served as an even better guide to the Two Thousand Guineas, with Churchill just the latest since 2000 to win both races, following Rock of Gibraltar, Frankel and Dawn Approach. All are good examples of the very different types of colts that tend to win the Dewhurst, compared to Middle Park winners. The Dewhurst winners are more likely to be later-maturing types with classic aspirations, for whom the race is a stepping stone towards better things, and longer trips, at three. It was no doubt thought that not much harm would be done if the Middle Park and Dewhurst were run on the same card when Future Champions' Day was created as part of the Racing for Change initiative in 2011. After all, Diesis in 1982 had been the only colt to win both races since the future classic winners Bayardo and Lemberg in the first decade of the twentieth century. It therefore looked as though Dream Ahead, who had won the Middle Park by nine lengths to make him Frankel's chief rival in the Dewhurst, would be the last colt with the opportunity to do the double. But, as Dream Ahead's essay in *Racehorses* that year pointed out, 'holding the two races on the same day poses a real risk of reducing the competitiveness of one or both' and was 'a move that will weaken the British programme.'

The controversial change to the two-year-old programme lasted only five seasons and, lo and behold, just a year after Blue Point was placed in both races in the first year that the double became possible again, the latest Middle Park winner U S Navy Flag became the first since Diesis to follow up a fortnight later in the Dewhurst. In the case of the Henry Cecil-trained Diesis, he didn't fit the archetypal profile of the Middle Park winner described above. He had had only two starts beforehand, getting off the mark by seven lengths on the second occasion and, despite his immaturity, he took his chance in the Middle Park as a substitute for his stable-companion Salieri who had had less time to recover after winning the Mill Reef Stakes. Diesis landed the odds in game fashion in the Middle Park, but what looked a stiffer task on form in the Dewhurst actually resulted in a far easier victory as he doubled his winning margin to five lengths in the latter contest. It rewarded his connections' decision to stand their ground as one of only three opponents for the hot favourite Gorytus who, as recounted in the essay on the disappointing favourite for the latest Dewhurst, Expert Eye, was an even bigger flop in his year.

U S Navy Flag, on the other hand, very much fits the mould of the typical Middle Park winner rather than a Dewhurst winner, which makes his Guineas prospects harder to evaluate. However, now that he's won a Dewhurst as well, he deserves more serious consideration as a potential classic winner, something which probably wouldn't have happened if connections had decided to draw stumps after the Middle Park. Few would have blamed them if they had. The Middle Park was U S Navy Flag's ninth race of a campaign that had begun on the first of May, and he had had only one race fewer than The Last Lion the year before. It wasn't as if U S Navy Flag's stable was lacking other Dewhurst candidates, either. But there were at least two good reasons for U S Navy Flag to take his chance. Firstly, his overall, most progressive profile belied his record of just two wins in eight starts. Secondly, his sister Roly Poly, who herself was kept busy at two, winning the Duchess of Cambridge Stakes before being beaten a short head in the Cheveley Park, made further unheralded improvement in the latest season, clearly thriving on her racing, and collected her third Group 1 of the season in the Sun Chariot Stakes just a week after U S Navy Flag won the Middle Park. Roly Poly wore cheekpieces for much of the year and the fitting of headgear likewise seemed to benefit U S Navy Flag.

U S Navy Flag's early-season form was nothing to write home about, though third place in the listed Marble Hill Stakes at the Curragh on his third start earned him a crack at the Coventry Stakes. Sent off at 33/1 at Royal Ascot, he gave no indication of the heights he was to reach in the autumn, never getting on terms in a field of eighteen and beating only four home. However, just eleven days later, fitted with blinkers for the first time, and with his sights lowered, U S Navy Flag made all the running for a ready success by three and a half lengths in a maiden at the Curragh. It was a useful performance, with the combination of blinkers and forcing tactics clearly suiting U S Navy Flag perfectly. Back in pattern company, U S Navy Flag went from strength to strength through the remainder of the season. He finished a place in front of the Coventry winner Rajasinghe when runner-up in the July Stakes at Newmarket next time, beaten a length and three quarters by Cardsharp, and a month later finished two and a half lengths fourth to stable-companion Sioux Nation in the Phoenix Stakes at the Curragh. On his last start before the Middle Park, U S Navy Flag registered his second win at the Curragh, later in August, with a six-length success over Landshark in the Plusvital Round Tower Stakes, the opposition not amounting to much by Group 3 standards, but the margin of his success indicating that U S Navy Flag was still on the way up.

Juddmonte Middle Park Stakes, Newmarket—a representative field including the winners of the Coventry, July Stakes, Phoenix, Gimcrack and Morny, but it is 10/1-shot U S Navy Flag who takes a significant step forward on his ninth start of the season; stablemate Fleet Review (right) and Cardsharp (second left in the pale colours) fill the places

Darley Dewhurst Stakes, Newmarket—U S Navy Flag leads home a remarkable one, two, three, four for trainer Aidan O'Brien, in the process becoming the first horse since Diesis in 1982 to complete the Middle Park/Dewhurst double; Mendelssohn (No.5), Seahenge (No.6) and Threeandfourpence (No.8) complete the Ballydoyle quartet, with odds-on Expert Eye trailing in last of nine

Even so, Ryan Moore, who had ridden U S Navy Flag in the Round Tower, preferred Sioux Nation (winner of the Norfolk Stakes at Royal Ascot prior to the Phoenix) when the pair took their chance in the Juddmonte Middle Park Stakes at the end of September. U S Navy Flag started at 10/1 under Seamus Heffernan, with Sioux Nation at 11/2, while a couple of outsiders, Fleet Review and Declarationofpeace completed a quartet from Ballydoyle; Fleet Review had won twice since finishing third in the maiden won by U S Navy Flag. The twelve-runner Middle Park looked an open contest, with the Phoenix Stakes runner-up Beckford sent off the 7/2 favourite back at six furlongs after finishing second in the National Stakes over seven on his most recent start. Cardsharp, representing The Last Lion's trainer Mark Johnston, and Rajasinghe were also in the field, along with the Gimcrack Stakes winner Sands of Mali and Unfortunately who had gained his big wins in France, in the Prix Robert Papin and Prix Morny. The field raced in two distinct groups until halfway, with U S Navy Flag helping force the pace widest of all towards the centre of the track. Edging ahead over a furlong out, he responded well to hold off the challenge of his 25/1 stablemate Fleet Review who had chased him on the same part of the track before challenging in the final furlong. There was half a length between the pair at the line, both of them putting up smart performances to finish two and a half lengths clear of Cardsharp in third. Beckford was fifth, just in front of the slow-starting Sioux Nation, who then met some trouble two furlongs out, while Unfortunately, Rajasinghe and Sands of Mali all ran well below their best.

U S Navy Flag gave his trainer a record fifth win in the Middle Park. Several other trainers have won it four times, the last to do so before O'Brien being Fred Darling and Frank Butters who won their fourth Middle Parks just after World War II. However, none of O'Brien's earlier winners, Minardi, Johannesburg, Ad Valorem or Crusade, had been asked to tackle the Dewhurst afterwards. Crusade, who had also been ridden by Heffernan, couldn't have done so anyway as he won the first running of the Middle Park on the inaugural Future Champions' card in 2011, when it featured the Dewhurst as well. As in the Middle Park, U S Navy Flag was one of a quartet of Ballydoyle colts sent for the Darley Dewhurst Stakes, though this time he was the stable's leading hope under Ryan Moore. Interestingly, Ballydoyle had given entries to several of its fillies in the Dewhurst and one of them, Happily, who had already beaten colts in the Prix Jean-Luc Lagardere, was among a total of seven possibles from her stable still engaged in the race at the six-day stage. In the end, she took her chance more conventionally in the Fillies' Mile twenty-four hours earlier, and, as it turned out, any fears that Ballydoyle's team of colts for the Dewhurst might be a little under strength were well and truly dispelled. The Ballydoyle team did lack the Superlative Stakes winner Gustav Klimt who had been on course for the race until a late setback caused him to miss the previous month's National Stakes at the Curragh. The National Stakes winner Verbal Dexterity was also an important absentee, his trainer Jim Bolger having won the Dewhurst five times in a seven-year period earlier in the century. More recently, it has been O'Brien who has dominated the race, winning three of the last four runnings with odds-on shots War Command, Air Force Blue and Churchill. The Sir Michael Stoute-trained Expert Eye, another who had had to miss an intended run in the National Stakes, started at odds on for the latest Dewhurst, though he had not been seen since a most impressive win in the Vintage Stakes at Goodwood, form which had worked out really well in the meantime. Among those from the Vintage to have won since was Seahenge, fifth at Goodwood, who lined up as Ballydoyle's apparent second string in the Dewhurst, following a win in the Champagne Stakes at Doncaster in which stable-companion Mendelssohn ran as though amiss. Mendelssohn, wearing blinkers for the first time, was the outsider of Ballydoyle's Dewhurst runners at 50/1, with Threeandfourpence, a maiden winner at Fairyhouse, completing the quartet. Besides U S Navy Flag, Expert Eye's other chief rival—according to the betting—was the dark horse in the line-up Emaraaty, an impressive winner of a minor event at Newbury.

Emaraaty didn't live up to expectations in the Dewhurst, undone by a lack of experience, but a still greater disappointment was Expert Eye, the only horse he managed to beat in the end, who pulled even harder and was beaten with over two furlongs to run. U S Navy Flag, on the other hand, was always prominent, seen to good advantage racing against the stand rail. Travelling well in front, he went clear over a furlong out and kept on well over the extra furlong to put up his best effort on his tenth start of the year. Beethoven was also having his tenth outing when successful for the same stable in 2009, though Beethoven's win, in a first-time visor, came out of the blue, representing a big improvement on his previous efforts. The 2003 winner Milk It Mick, incidentally, won the Dewhurst on his twelfth start. U S Navy Flag was O'Brien's sixth winner of the Dewhurst all told. He had first won it in 2001 with Rock of Gibraltar who gained a narrow victory over stable-companions Landseer and Tendulkar. Saddling the first three home in a Group 1 is not such a rare feat (see the essay on Winter) so far as O'Brien is concerned (he also had the third and fourth in Beethoven's Dewhurst), but he went one better than that in the latest Dewhurst, with Mendelssohn, Seahenge and Threeandfourpence completing the frame. U S Navy Flag had two and a half lengths to spare at the line, with the same distance back to Seahenge who took third by a head. Cardsharp fared best of the rest in fifth. While U S Navy Flag was the first to complete the Middle Park-Dewhurst double for thirty-five years, the O'Brien-trained Tomahawk finished runner-up in both races in 2002 and Brahms was placed in both in 1999. Both of those ended their two-year-old seasons in the Breeders' Cup Juvenile, as did U S Navy Flag. However, he failed to emulate the 2001 Middle Park winner Johannesburg and finished well beaten at Del Mar after being taken on for the lead in the back straight. It was U S Navy Flag's greater experience which prompted connections to take up the dirt option with him and, although it didn't pay off with him, Mendelssohn's win in the Juvenile Turf made it a successful Breeders' Cup for the Ballydoyle two-year-old team.

U S Navy Flag (USA) (b.c. 2015)	War Front (USA) (b 2002)	Danzig (b 1977)	Northern Dancer
			Pas de Nom
		Starry Dreamer (gr or ro 1994)	Rubiano
			Lara's Star
	Misty For Me (IRE) (b 2008)	Galileo (b 1998)	Sadler's Wells
			Urban Sea
		Butterfly Cove (b or br 2001)	Storm Cat
			Mr P's Princess

U S Navy Flag and Roly Poly are out of the very smart Misty For Me who was Timeform's top-rated two-year-old filly in Europe in 2010 when she won the Moyglare Stud Stakes and Prix Marcel Boussac. Her lack of size tempered enthusiasm about her classic prospects, however, and those doubts seemed justified when she finished well beaten in the One Thousand Guineas, but, in the end, she trained on well, winning the Irish One Thousand Guineas and the Pretty Polly Stakes (after failing to stay in the Oaks in between) and ended her career being beaten less than a length into third in the Breeders' Cup Filly & Mare Turf. Further details about the dam's side of U S Navy Flag's pedigree can be found in the essay on Roly Poly. Certainly, the records of both his dam and his sister are encouraging for U S Navy Flag's three-year-old prospects and he has a little more substance to him than his dam, being a strong colt of around medium size. His sire War Front, though, who had a one, two in the Middle Park (he is also the sire of Fleet Review) might set alarm bells ringing for some. War Front was responsible for two of Ballydoyle's recent Dewhurst winners, War Command and Air Force Blue, who each met with just one defeat in five starts apiece as two-year-olds. However, both were beaten in the Two Thousand Guineas and neither won another race, the highly regarded Air Force Blue in particular being a bitter disappointment at three (odds on for the Guineas) after looking inferior only to Frankel among Dewhurst winners of the last twenty years. Hit It A Bomb, who won the Breeders' Cup Juvenile Turf, and the 2016 Cheveley Park winner Brave Anna—both full siblings of the latest Dewhurst fourth Threeandfourpence—are others by War Front who have failed to win again after big wins at two. Lancaster Bomber, runner-up to Churchill in the 2016 Dewhurst, didn't add to his sole success in a two-year-old maiden in the latest season, though, given he finished second in the St James's Palace Stakes and Breeders' Cup Mile, it could hardly be said of him that he didn't train on. U S Navy Flag achieved more at two than either Gustav Klimt or the Racing Post Trophy winner Saxon Warrior, the two stable companions with whom he ended the year vying for favouritism for the Two Thousand Guineas, though that pair undoubtedly have the more scope to progress as three-year-olds. A line can be put through U S Navy Flag's run on dirt at the Breeders' Cup—he should stay a mile on his pedigree—and he acts on good to firm and good to soft going. He wears a tongue tie as well as blinkers and has made the running since being fitted with headgear. *Aidan O'Brien, Ireland*

U S S MISSOURI (USA) 2 b.g. (Feb 28) War Front (USA) 119 – I'm So Excited (USA) (Street Cry (IRE) 130) [2017 p7g^4 p7g^3 p8g^3 Nov 7] second foal: dam twice-raced daughter of smart French/US winner up to 1½m Volga: fairly useful form: best effort when third in minor event at Kempton (1¼ lengths behind Archie McKellar) in October. *Ed Walker* **82**

USTINOV 5 b.g. Exceed And Excel (AUS) 126 – Tamzin (Hernando (FR) 127) [2017 98: t6s Nov 30] smallish gelding: useful handicapper, below form sole start in 2017: stays 7f: acts on tapeta and good to firm going: in hood last 5 starts: often races towards rear. *David O'Meara* **85**

UTAH (IRE) 3 b.c. Galileo (IRE) 134 – Healing Music (FR) (Bering 136) [2017 93: 10d^6 12m^6 12.8d Sep 9] strong, good-bodied colt: useful handicapper: probably stays 13f: acts on good to firm and good to soft going: tried in tongue tie. *Aidan O'Brien, Ireland* **102**

UTHER PENDRAGON (IRE) 2 b.g. (Mar 26) Dragon Pulse (IRE) 114 – Unreal 79 (Dansili 127) [2017 5m^6 5f^4 p7s^3 p6.5g^3 7m^2 7.5g^2 7g^2 7g^2 8g^6 p6.5g^5 p7.5g^6 8d^4 Oct 28] €21,000F, £15,000Y: half-brother to 2-y-o 5f winner Britain (by Manduro): dam, 2-y-o 5f winner, half-sister to smart 1¼m/11f winner Illustrator: fairly useful maiden: stays 1m: acts on polytrack and firm going: usually wears cheekpieces. *J. S. Moore* **88**

UTMOST (USA) 3 ch.c. Giant's Causeway (USA) 132 – Fugitive Angel (USA) (Alphabet Soup (USA) 126) [2017 93p: t8s^3 p8g^4 p9.4f p10g^3 Dec 23] smart performer: fourth in handicap at Lingfield (1¾ lengths behind Arcanada) in November: stays 1¼m: acts on polytrack and tapeta. *John Gosden* **110**

UTOPIAN DREAM 3 b.f. High Chaparral (IRE) 132 – You Too 74 (Monsun (GER) 124) [2017 p10m^4 p10g^4 t12.2g^2 p13.3g* May 10] sister to 2-y-o 1m/9f winner Your So High and half-sister to several winners, including 1¼m-1¾m winner (stays 2½m) Totalize (by Authorized) and 1m/8.6f winner Carolinae (by Makfi), both useful: dam 1¾m winner: fairly useful form: won maiden at Chelmsford (by 5 lengths from Inconceivable) in May: stays 13.5f: in blinkers last 2 starts. *John Gosden* **86**

UTTERLY CHARMING (IRE) 2 b.f. (Mar 2) Dandy Man (IRE) 123 – Dream Date (IRE) 78 (Oasis Dream 129) [2017 5g^4 5m* Jun 17] 120,000F: fourth foal: sister to very smart 5f (including at 2 yrs) winner Extortionist and half-sister to 1m winner Knight's Dream (by Sir Prancealot): dam 7f winner: fair form: won minor event at Lingfield (by neck from Three Little Birds) in June: will stay 6f: open to further improvement. *Clive Cox* **74 p**

V

VALANTINO OYSTER (IRE) 10 b.g. Pearl of Love (IRE) 112 – Mishor 83 (Slip Anchor 136) [2017 p11g t9.5g p10g Mar 11] fairly useful performer at best, no form in 2017 after long absence: wears headgear: tried in tongue tie. *Ali Stronge* **–**

VALBCHEK (IRE) 8 b.g. Acclamation 118 – Spectacular Show (IRE) 79 (Spectrum (IRE) 126) [2017 100: p7d^4 p7g^4 p7g Feb 24] strong, sturdy gelding: useful handicapper: stays 7f: acts on polytrack and good to soft going: wears headgear: has suspect attitude (virtually refused to race final start). *Jane Chapple-Hyam* **96**

VALCARTIER (IRE) 3 b.g. Redoute's Choice (AUS) – Vadawina (IRE) 118 (Unfuwain (USA) 131) [2017 –P: 8.3g* 10g^2 10s^3 Jul 22] useful form: won maiden at Nottingham in April: second in handicap at Windsor (head behind Mister Blue Sky) in July: stays 1¼m. *John Gosden* **98**

VAL DE MARNE 3 b.f. Invincible Spirit (IRE) 121 – Vallericca (USA) (Dynaformer (USA)) [2017 8g^3 8g 9.7d^3 p9.4f* 10.4d^4 a8.9g* p13g Nov 2] lengthy filly: third foal: half-sister to useful 1m-1½m winner Newmarch (by New Approach): dam unraced half-sister to smart Japanese Group 1m winner World Ace out of useful half-sister to top-class 1m-1½m performer Manduro: useful performer: won maiden at Deauville in August and minor event at Lyon La Soie in September: fourth in listed race at Chantilly (2¾ lengths behind Golden Legend) in between: stays 10.5f (didn't settle at Lingfield over 13f): acts on polytrack, viscoride and good to soft going. *A. Fabre, France* **100**

VALDOLOBO (IRE) 2 b.g. (Feb 23) Lope de Vega (IRE) 125 – Eucharist (IRE) 101 (Acclamation 118) [2017 8g^3 7g^4 Sep 27] fair form: better effort when third in minor event at Haydock (head behind White Mocha) in August. *K. R. Burke* **70**

VALENTINO BOY (IRE) 3 b.g. Bated Breath 125 – Capistrano Day (USA) 110 (Diesis 133) [2017 80: 5g 7.1m^2 7.4d^2 7.6d* 7.6g^4 8.9d^5 t7.1d^2 Sep 29] fairly useful handicapper: won at Chester (apprentice) in June: stays 7.5f: acts on tapeta and good to soft going: usually leads: sold to join Harriet Bethell £15,000 in November. *Brian Ellison* **83**

VALENTINO DANCER 2 ch.c. (Feb 14) Mastercraftsman (IRE) 129 – Bertie's Best (King's Best (USA) 132) [2017 p7g^5 t7.2g Dec 2] modest form in minor events: left Robyn Brisland after first start. *David O'Meara* **62**

VALE OF FLIGHT (IRE) 4 b.f. Vale of York (IRE) 117 – Barbera (GER) (Night Shift (USA)) [2017 74: t6g^5 p6g t5.1g^2 t5.1g^6 p5g^3 t5.1g^5 p5s^2 5d Jul 1] fair handicapper: best form at 5f: acts on polytrack and tapeta: has worn headgear, including last 2 starts. *Luke McJannet* **66**

VALERIE'S MEMORY 2 b.f. (Apr 20) Sixties Icon 125 – Nadinska 70 (Doyen (IRE) 132) [2017 7d Aug 21] £1,200Y: lengthy filly: fourth foal: half-sister to winner up to 1m Wink Oliver (by Winker Watson) and winner up to 7.3f Texas Katie (by Clodovil), both 2-y-o 7f winners: dam, 5.7f winner who stayed 9.5f, half-sister to smart 1m winner Laugh Out Loud: 66/1, well held in minor event at Lingfield. *Philip Hide* **–**

VALIDATOR 2 b.f. (Apr 11) Kodiac 112 – Enact 104 (Kyllachy 129) [2017 5.2m^3 5s* 5g^2 5g^2 5.2s 6s^2 Sep 15] fourth foal: closely related to winner up to 1m Star of The Stage (2-y-o 7f winner, by Invincible Spirit) and half-sister to 7f winner Dubai Art (by Dutch Art): dam, 6f winner (including at 2 yrs), closely related to useful 6f-7f winner Enrol: fairly useful performer: won maiden at Thirsk in May: best form at 5f: acts on soft going: often leads, usually travels strongly. *William Haggas* **88**

VALLARTA (IRE) 7 b.g. Footstepsinthesand 120 – Mexican Miss (IRE) 75 (Tagula (IRE) 116) [2017 86: f6g^6 f6g^3 p6g^3 7.1m^3 6m* 6m^4 7.2s^3 6g^5 7.2d t6d 6s^5 t5d t6d t6.1g Nov 20] lengthy gelding: fairly useful handicapper: won at Catterick (by ¾ length from Meshardal) in May: stays 7f: acts on all-weather and any turf going: has worn visor. *Ruth Carr* **81**

VALLESA (IRE) 2 b.f. (Mar 8) Elzaam (AUS) 115 – Rousing Applause (USA) (Candy Ride (ARG) 133) [2017 6d 6.1f 7d^5 Jul 5] €3,500Y: unfurnished filly: second foal: dam unraced half-sister to useful 7f-8.4f winner Sharp Focus: poor form. *David Brown* **39**

VALLEY LODGE 3 ch.c. Mayson 124 – Beat As One (Medicean 128) [2017 60: t7.1m t7.1g^6 p7g^6 Feb 24] strong, compact colt: modest maiden at 2 yrs, no form in 2017: often wears cheekpieces. *Julia Feilden* **–**

VALLEY OF FIRE 5 b.g. Firebreak 125 – Charlie Girl 70 (Puissance 110) [2017 95: f6g Mar 14] compact gelding: fairly useful handicapper, well held sole start in 2017: stays 7f: acts on firm and good to soft going: has worn headgear. *Les Eyre* **–**

VALLEY OF LIGHT 3 b.f. Dubawi (IRE) 129 – Elusive Sparkle (USA) (Elusive Quality **72**
(USA)) [2017 p10g^{3} p10g^{5} t8s^{2} Nov 30] 400,000F: fourth foal: half-sister to 6f/7f winner Camdus (by Street Cry) and 7f/1m winner Sea The Sparkle (by Sea The Stars): dam, US 6f (minor stakes)/6.5f winner, half-sister to Breeders' Cup Juvenile and Kentucky Derby winner Street Sense: fair form: best effort when third in maiden at Lingfield in September: tried in visor. *Saeed bin Suroor*

VALLEY OF ROCKS (IRE) 3 b.g. Big Bad Bob (IRE) 118 – Arctic Hunt (IRE) (Bering **72**
136) [2017 76: 8.1d^{2} 6g^{5} 7s^{5} 7m^{4} 8.2g^{3} 8.2g* 8.5f 8.5s 9.1m^{6} t10.2g Oct 20] lengthy gelding: fair handicapper: won at Leicester in July: stays 1m: acts on tapeta and good to soft going: often races towards rear. *Mark Johnston*

VAL'S MAGIC TOUCH 3 b.f. Captain Gerrard (IRE) 113 – Under My Spell 80 (Wizard **–**
King 122) [2017 5.1m p6g 6.1g Oct 9] compact filly: sixth foal: half-sister to 5f/6f winner Major Valentine (by Major Cadeaux): dam, winner up to 6f (2-y-o 5f winner) who stayed 1m, half-sister to useful winner up to 1m Ardbrae Lady: little impact in maidens. *John O'Shea*

VALYRIAN 2 b.c. (May 5) Dansili 127 – Victoire Finale (Peintre Celebre (USA) 137) **66 p**
[2017 p8g^{5} Dec 20] closely related to 2-y-o 8.3f winner (stays 10.5f) Vanity Queen (by Fastnet Rock) and 1½m/12.4f winner Vuela (by Duke of Marmalade) and half-brother to 3 winners, including smart winner up to 1¼m (stayed 1½m) Volume (2-y-o 1m/9f winner, by Mount Nelson): dam 1m winner: 20/1, fifth in minor event at Kempton (7¾ lengths behind Glencadam Master) in December: will stay 1¼m: capable of better. *Luca Cumani*

VAN GERWEN 4 ch.g. Bahamian Bounty 116 – Disco Ball 75 (Fantastic Light (USA) **89**
134) [2017 87: t5.1g^{3} t5s 6v 6s 5s^{5} 5v^{2} 5v* 5s Nov 8] fairly useful handicapper: won at Pontefract (by 1¼ lengths from Henley) in October: stays 6f: acts on tapeta, good to firm and heavy going: has worn hood. *Les Eyre*

VAN HUYSEN (IRE) 5 br.g. Excellent Art 125 – Tara Too (IRE) 97 (Danetime (IRE) **93**
121) [2017 93: p10g^{2} p10g^{4} p10g^{3} p10g^{3} p10g 10.1g p10s p8g p10g Dec 12] useful-looking gelding: fairly useful handicapper: placed at Lingfield in January and February (twice): stays 1¼m: acts on polytrack and good to firm going: has worn headgear. *Dominic Ffrench Davis*

VANITY QUEEN 3 b.f. Fastnet Rock (AUS) 127 – Victoire Finale (Peintre Celebre **84**
(USA) 137) [2017 76p: 10.3m^{6} 9.9d 8d t8g^{3} 8g^{5} Oct 16] fairly useful handicapper: third at Newcastle in September: stays 1m: acts on tapeta and good to firm going: sold 125,000 gns in December. *Luca Cumani*

VANTAGE POINT (IRE) 3 b.c. Galileo (IRE) 134 – Adoration (USA) 124 (Honor **90**
Grades (USA)) [2017 76: t10.2g^{4} f8g* f8g* 8.5g^{5} 10g t8.6g^{2} 8g p8g Jun 28] well-made colt: fairly useful performer: won maiden at Southwell in January and handicap there in March: second in handicap at Wolverhampton in June: left John Gosden after second start: stays 1¼m: acts on fibresand, tapeta, best turf form on good going: wears cheekpieces: sold 52,000 gns in July, sent to Singapore, where renamed Yulong Honor. *Gary Moore*

VANTASY 2 b.g. (Mar 22) Rip Van Winkle (IRE) 134 – Tesary 98 (Danehill (USA) 126) **–**
[2017 7g p8g Nov 7] well held in 2 minor events. *Chris Wall*

VAN VELDE (IRE) 3 ch.g. Dutch Art 126 – Woodcock Moon (Kyllachy 129) [2017 t6d^{2} **76**
7.4g^{2} 6s* 7d Oct 20] fair form: won maiden at Redcar in September: stays 7.5f: in cheekpieces last 3 starts. *John Quinn*

VARSOVIAN 7 ch.g. Refuse To Bend (IRE) 128 – Queen of Poland 109 (Halling (USA) **83**
133) [2017 88: p6g* p6g^{4} p7g^{4} p6g^{4} p6g^{4} p7d^{4} p6g t6.1g p7d p7g* p6g^{4} Dec 28] lengthy gelding: fairly useful handicapper: won at Lingfield in February (by ¾ length from Rockley Point) and December: stays 7f: acts on polytrack: has worn headgear. *Dean Ivory*

VARUN'S BRIDE (IRE) 3 b.f. Lawman (FR) 121 – Belgique (IRE) 87 (Compton Place **65**
125) [2017 56: p7g^{4} 9.9g t8.6g^{2} p8g* t8.6g Jul 3] compact filly: fair handicapper: won at Lingfield in June: stays 8.5f: acts on polytrack, tapeta and good to soft going: front runner/races prominently. *Richard Hannon*

VASTLY (USA) 8 gr.g. Mizzen Mast (USA) 121 – Valentine Band (USA) 104 (Dixieland **–**
Band (USA)) [2017 81: t9.5g t6.1g Sep 23] sturdy gelding: fairly useful handicapper, no form in 2017: stays 1¼m: acts on polytrack, tapeta and good to firm going: has worn headgear, including final start: wears tongue tie. *Sophie Leech*

VATICAN HILL (IRE) 3 b.c. Canford Cliffs (IRE) 133 – Empress Ella (IRE) (Holy **92**
Roman Emperor (IRE) 125) [2017 84: t7.1g* t7.1d^{5} t7.1g t7.1g p7g^{2} 8g^{6} 8g* 9.9g* 11.9g^{3} 9.9g^{5} 10.7g^{6} 9.9g^{6} Sep 29] fairly useful performer: won handicap at Wolverhampton in

January then, having left Jamie Osborne after fifth start, women jockeys claimer at Saint-Cloud and minor event at Le Lion d'Angers, both in June: stays 1½m: acts on polytrack, tapeta and good to firm going: has worn headgear. *P. & F. Monfort, France*

VAUDIEU 3 ch.f. Bated Breath 125 – Gretna 77 (Groom Dancer (USA) 128) [2017 p8g t12.2g^{5} p13.3g^{4} 11.9d^{5} Sep 11] £16,000Y: half-sister to several winners, including useful winner up to 12.3f (stayed 15f) Red Runaway (2-y-o 1m winner, by Medicean) and 11.5f winner Reconcilliation (by Aqlaam): dam, 9.7f winner, half-sister to Irish St Leger winner Sans Frontieres: modest form: wears headgear. *Dean Ivory* **57**

VAULTED 3 b.f. Kyllachy 129 – Palatial 101 (Green Desert (USA) 127) [2017 68: 7.2g^{2} 7m^{4} 8.5m* 8g^{5} 8d 8d^{5} 8.3d^{6} Sep 2] fair handicapper: won at Beverley in July: stays 8.5f: acts on soft and good to firm going: has worn cheekpieces, including final start. *Richard Fahey* **75**

VAUX (IRE) 3 b.g. Sir Prancealot (IRE) 111 – Greenflash 80 (Green Desert (USA) 127) [2017 66: t6f^{3} t6m 6g 6g 5g^{3} 5g^{4} t5g 6m Aug 26] modest maiden: stays 6f: acts on tapeta and good to firm going: has worn cheekpieces: usually races towards rear. *Ben Haslam* **60**

VAZIRABAD (FR) 5 b.g. Manduro (GER) 135 – Visorama (IRE) 114 (Linamix (FR) 127) [2017 123: 14g^{2} 15.9d* 14.9g* 14.9d* 20.4d* 15.4g^{2} Oct 22] very smart performer: won Dubai Gold Cup at Meydan (by neck from Beautiful Romance) in March, Prix Vicomtesse Vigier at Chantilly in May, Prix Gladiateur at Chantilly in September (all for second year running) and Prix du Cadran at Chantilly again (unimpressive in landing odds by ½ length from Mille Et Mille) in September: attempting third successive win in Prix Royal-Oak at Saint-Cloud final outing, but went down by 1¼ lengths to Ice Breeze: stays 2½m: acts on soft and good to firm going: tried in headgear: often races towards rear, usually travels strongly. *A. de Royer Dupre, France* **123**

VECHEKA (IRE) 6 b.g. Lawman (FR) 121 – Lidanski (IRE) 100 (Soviet Star (USA) 128) [2017 56: t6s^{2} t5g 6g t7.1s 5s^{5} 5s 5s^{6} t5g^{2} t6g t7.1s^{6} t5d Dec 16] fair at best: left Chris Grant/below form after first start: stays 6f: acts on tapeta and good to firm going: usually wears headgear: has worn tongue tie: sometimes slowly away. *Kenny Johnson* **62 d**

VEDANI (IRE) 8 b.g. Dalakhani (IRE) 133 – Velandia (IRE) (Sadler's Wells (USA) 132) [2017 60: p16g^{3} p13.3g Mar 2] modest handicapper: stays 16.5f: acts on polytrack, tapeta, soft and good to firm going: has worn cheekpieces/tongue tie. *Tony Carroll* **52**

VEEJAY (IRE) 2 b.c. (Mar 10) Approve (IRE) 112 – Regresa A Mi (IRE) 84 (Spartacus (IRE) 107) [2017 6d* 7g* 7v 7g^{2} 8g* 8.2s 8.5v 7.9g^{3} 8v^{6} Oct 23] €5,500Y, £14,000 2-y-o: smallish, leggy colt: second foal: half-brother to 2-y-o 7f winner Q Ten Girl (by Zebedee): dam 1½m-2m winner: fairly useful performer: won minor events at Salisbury in June and Haydock in July, and nursery at Ripon in August: stays 1m: acts on good to soft going: often races towards rear: sold 34,000 gns, sent to Saudi Arabia. *Mick Channon* **93**

VEENA (FR) 4 b.f. Elusive City (USA) 117 – Kensita (FR) (Soviet Star (USA) 128) [2017 83: t7.1g^{4} t6d* p6d* t6g^{4} 6f t6d^{5} p7g p7g* Dec 20] fairly useful handicapper: won at Newcastle and Chelmsford (by head from Beau Mistral) in February, and Kempton in December: stays 7f: acts on polytrack and tapeta: tried in cheekpieces. *David Simcock* **83**

Dubai Gold Cup Sponsored By Al Tayer Motors, Meydan—Vazirabad repeats his 2016 victory in this race, beating Beautiful Romance (right), Sheikhzayedroad (hood) and Big Orange

Qatar Prix du Cadran, Chantilly—the absence of Gold Cup winner Big Orange leaves Vazirabad with an apparently simple task but 2015 winner Mille Et Mille (rail) pushes him close

VEERAYA 7 b.g. Rail Link 132 – Follow Flanders 92 (Pursuit of Love 124) [2017 71: t7.1g^{6} f8g 7d May 12] lengthy gelding: fair handicapper, below form in 2017: races up to 1m nowadays: acts on polytrack, tapeta, good to firm and good to soft going: has worn headgear: wears tongue tie. *Julia Feilden* **63**

VEGAS BOY (IRE) 2 ch.c. (Apr 30) Society Rock (IRE) 126 – Consensus (IRE) 91 (Common Grounds 118) [2017 5.3m^{5} t6.1g^{5} 6.1g p6g^{3} 7g^{6} p6g^{2} p6g* p6d* t6.1g^{3} Nov 25] €48,000Y: half-brother to several winners, including useful 5f (including at 2 yrs) winner (stayed 8.5f) Cloneylass (by Verglas) and useful winner up to 1m Al's Memory (2-y-o 6f winner, by Red Clubs): dam, 5f winner (including at 2 yrs), half-sister to smart winner up to 7.4f Fathsta: fairly useful performer: won nurseries at Chelmsford in October and November (by ½ length from Blackheath): stays 6f: acts on polytrack and tapeta: wears tongue tie. *Jamie Osborne* **80**

VEILED SECRET (IRE) 3 b.g. Teofilo (IRE) 126 – Seven Veils (IRE) 87 (Danehill Dancer (IRE) 117) [2017 62p: 12.1m^{5} 14g^{2} 14g^{6} 14.1d* 14v^{3} 16g^{6} p16g^{5} p15.8g^{3} Oct 5] fairly useful handicapper: won at Yarmouth in August: third at Lingfield in October: stays 2m: acts on polytrack and good to soft going: tried in cheekpieces: usually leads: sold to join David Dennis 35,000 gns in October. *Sir Mark Prescott Bt* **87**

VELVET CHARM 3 b.f. Excelebration (IRE) 133 – Velvet Star (IRE) 54 (Galileo (IRE) 134) [2017 7s^{4} 8.3d 7m 8.3d 7.6d Aug 12] 18,000Y: tall filly: first foal: dam maiden half-sister to Dubai World Cup winner Moon Ballad: modest maiden: sometimes in hood: usually races in rear. *Rae Guest* **54**

VELVET REVOLUTION 4 ch.g. Pivotal 124 – Gino's Spirits 98 (Perugino (USA) 84) [2017 93p: p16g^{4} p14g^{2} 16.2f t16.3s p16d* p16g^{2} t14d* Dec 9] good-topped gelding: useful handicapper: won at Kempton in August and Wolverhampton (by short head from Cohesion) in December: stays 2m: acts on polytrack, tapeta and good to firm going: has worn cheekpieces: usually races towards rear. *Marco Botti* **97**

VELVET VOICE 3 b.f. Azamour (IRE) 130 – Battery Power 89 (Royal Applause 124) [2017 64: 11.8g 10s^{2} 12g p10g^{5} Sep 7] fair maiden: stays 1¼m: acts on soft going. *Mark H. Tompkins* **68**

VENETIAN PROPOSAL (IRE) 3 b.f. Fast Company (IRE) 126 – Ide Say (IRE) (Grand Lodge (USA) 125) [2017 59: t7.1f^{6} p7g 7g 7m^{3} 8.2g 9d* 9.9d 10s^{3} 10d^{3} p10s^{3} Dec 7] close-coupled filly: modest handicapper: won at Lingfield in July: stays 1¼m: acts on polytrack, soft and good to firm going: wears cheekpieces. *Zoe Davison* **64**

VENICE BEACH (IRE) 3 b.c. Galileo (IRE) 134 – Danedrop (IRE) (Danehill (USA) 126) [2017 90P: 10s^{3} 12g* 12.3m* 12m 11.9g^{3} 11.9d^{2} 14.5g Sep 16] well-made colt: smart performer: won maiden at Tipperary (by 5½ lengths from Clongowes) in April and Chester Vase (by 1¼ lengths from Wings of Eagles) in May: third in Grand Prix de Paris at Saint-Cloud (length behind Shakeel) in July and second in Great Voltigeur Stakes at York (6 **117**

lengths behind Cracksman) in August: stays 12.5f (eighth in St Leger at 14.5f): acts on soft and good to firm going: wears cheekpieces/tongue tie: races prominently: has joined Liam Howley in Australia. *Aidan O'Brien, Ireland*

VENTDANSLESARBRES 3 b.f. Aqlaam 125 – Velma Kelly 63 (Vettori (IRE) 119) **–** [2017 7d Jul 12] €16,000Y: sturdy filly: fifth foal: half-sister to 2 winners abroad, including French 1¼m winner Kitty Baxter (by Leporello): dam 9.5f winner: 33/1, well held in maiden at Lingfield. *George Baker*

VENT DE FORCE 6 b.g. Hurricane Run (IRE) 134 – Capriolla 55 (In The Wings 128) **106** [2017 95: 16.2m^{4} 15.4g^{2} 14.9d Sep 10] strong gelding: useful performer: second in listed race at Maisons-Laffitte (nose behind Fun Mac) in July: stays 16.5f: acts on firm and soft going. *Hughie Morrison*

VENTURA BLUES (IRE) 3 b.f. Bated Breath 125 – Salmon Rose (IRE) (Iffraaj 127) **96** [2017 88p: p6g^{5} 6g^{3} p7s^{2} 7g 6s^{6} 8d^{4} p8g^{2} p8g* p8g^{4} p8g^{2} 6.1d Oct 4] sturdy filly: useful handicapper: won at Kempton in September: second there (neck behind Moolazim) later in month: stays 1m: acts on polytrack and soft going: wears cheekpieces. *Richard Hannon*

VENTURA CREST (IRE) 2 b.g. (Apr 20) Elzaam (AUS) 115 – Ms Cromby (IRE) **63** (Arakan (USA) 123) [2017 5m^{6} 6m^{4} 5.9g^{6} 6f 7.4d 8g^{2} 8v Oct 23] tall gelding: modest maiden: best effort at 1m: front runner/races prominently. *Tim Easterby*

VENTURA DRAGON (IRE) 2 ch.g. (Apr 19) Dragon Pulse (IRE) 114 – Dancing **78** Duchess (IRE) 93 (Danehill Dancer (IRE) 117) [2017 5m^{3} 5g* 6m^{5} 7g^{5} 7.4v* 6d 8g^{6} 9d^{3} Oct 11] sturdy gelding: fair performer: won minor event at Carlisle in May and nursery at Ffos Las in August: stays 9f: acts on heavy going. *Richard Fahey*

VENTURA GOLD (IRE) 2 b.g. (Mar 27) Red Jazz (USA) 125 – Desert Shine (IRE) 78 **73** (Green Desert (USA) 127) [2017 5m^{6} 5f^{6} 5g^{5} 6s^{4} 7.2m^{2} 6.3s 7g^{6} Oct 16] fair maiden: stays 7f: acts on good to firm going. *Richard Fahey*

VENTURA JAZZ 3 b.f. Dandy Man (IRE) 123 – Aljafliyah (Halling (USA) 133) [2017 **–** –: t6g^{5} p7m Jan 20] no form. *Richard Fahey*

VENTURA KNIGHT (IRE) 2 b.c. (Mar 22) Casamento (IRE) 118 – Alltherightmoves **98** (IRE) 45 (Namid 128) [2017 f5d^{3} 5m^{4} 6m^{3} 7.4m* 6.9g* 7g* 7d p7s^{5} 8g^{3} 7s^{5} 8d* Oct 27] €36,000F, £40,000Y: well-made colt: second foal: half-brother to winner up to 7f (stays 1m) Smart Mover (by Fast Company): dam, maiden (stayed 5f), half-sister to smart winner up to 11.5f Crown of Light: useful performer: won minor event at Beverley in June, and nurseries at Carlisle and Leicester in July, and Doncaster (by neck from dead-heaters Regimented and Che Bella) in October: stays 1m: acts on good to firm and good to soft going. *Mark Johnston*

VENTURA MAGIC 2 b.c. (Mar 5) Mount Nelson 125 – Elle Desert (GER) (Next Desert **62** (IRE) 122) [2017 p8g p8g Dec 20] modest form in 2 minor events: will be suited by 1¼m. *Richard Hannon*

VENTURA ROYAL (IRE) 2 ch.f. (Jan 26) Teofilo (IRE) 126 – Ermine And Velvet 87 **68** (Nayef (USA) 129) [2017 7d 7.2d^{5} 8g^{3} 7g* Sep 27] 52,000Y: fifth foal: half-sister to useful 7f-8.3f winner Sir Guy Porteous (by Shamardal) and 2-y-o 6f winner Velveteen (by Exceed And Excel): dam, maiden (stayed 1m), sister to smart 11f winner Top Lock: fair form: won maiden at Redcar in September: stays 1m. *David O'Meara*

VENTURA SECRET (IRE) 3 ch.g. Roderic O'Connor (IRE) 119 – Bajan Belle (IRE) **82** 72 (Efisio 120) [2017 72: 5g^{4} 5g^{6} 6g^{5} 6g 7.8g* 7d^{4} 8s* 8d 8g^{3} 7.8v* 8g^{4} t8d Oct 24] leggy gelding: fairly useful handicapper: won at Carlisle in July, Pontefract in August and again at Carlisle (by ½ length from Jay Kay) in September: stays 1m: acts on good to firm and heavy going: front runner/races prominently: sold 12,000 gns in October. *Tim Easterby*

VENTUROUS (IRE) 4 ch.g. Raven's Pass (USA) 133 – Bold Desire 58 (Cadeaux **88** Genereux 131) [2017 103: 6m 6m 5g 5g^{6} 5d^{6} 5v^{3} 5g^{5} Oct 13] well-made gelding: fairly useful handicapper: third at Ripon in September: stays 6f: acts on good to firm and heavy going: often races in rear. *David Barron*

VENUTIUS 10 b.g. Doyen (IRE) 132 – Boadicea's Chariot (Commanche Run 133) [2017 **71** 82: 7s^{5} 8.1m^{5} 10m 8g t9.5g Dec 18] stocky gelding: fairly useful handicapper, below form in 2017: stays 8.5f: acts on polytrack, good to firm and good to soft going: often races prominently. *Charles Hills*

VERACIOUS 2 b.f. (Feb 17) Frankel 147 – Infallible 114 (Pivotal 124) [2017 7g^{3} 7m* **97 p** Oct 13] lengthy filly: half-sister to several winners, including high-class 1m-1¼m winner Mutakayyef (by Sea The Stars), smart 6f winner Intrinsic (by Oasis Dream) and smart

8.3f-1¼m winner Intimation (by Dubawi): dam 7f winner (including at 2 yrs): useful form: won maiden at Newmarket (by 4 lengths from Winter Lightning) in October, storming clear: open to further improvement. *Sir Michael Stoute*

VERA DRAKE (FR) 2 ch.f. (Apr 26) Footstepsinthesand 120 – Venetian Beauty (USA) (Lear Fan (USA) 130) [2017 7g^4 7d^2 7.4s^2 t8g^4 Oct 10] €25,000Y: half-sister to several winners, including Australian/French 1½m-13f (Group 3) winner Vengeur Masque (by Monsun) and 9.5f-12.5f winner Vermont (by Muhtathir), both useful: dam unraced half-sister to very smart 1m winner Vetheuil: fair form: bred to be suited by at least 1m. *Richard Fahey* **70**

VERANDAH 2 b.f. (Mar 28) Medicean 128 – Palatial 101 (Green Desert (USA) 127) [2017 p7s* 7g^5 Aug 26] sister to useful winner up to 1m Artimino (2-y-o 7f winner) and smart 6f-1m winner Dimension, and half-sister to several winners, including smart winner up to 1m Spacious (by Nayef): dam 7f winner (including at 2 yrs): fairly useful form: won minor event at Kempton (by 2 lengths from Fille de Reve) in August: fifth in Prestige Stakes at Goodwood (2¼ lengths behind Billesdon Brook) later in month: should improve further. *John Gosden* **92 p**

VERBAL DEXTERITY (IRE) 2 b.c. (Feb 8) Vocalised (USA) 114 – Lonrach (IRE) 80 (Holy Roman Emperor (IRE) 125) [2017 7v* 6g^2 7s* 8d^4 Oct 28] **119**

'Breeders pin their faith in stallions from the most familiar pedigree backgrounds, and their neglect of lines that thrived in former times means that they are throwing away the precious diversity that their predecessors cherished and sustained.' Writing in the December issue of *Thoroughbred Owner & Breeder*, that doyen of bloodstock writers Tony Morris went on to lament 'breeders' insane concentration on the same elements in pedigrees and their wanton neglect of almost everything else.' One influential breeder not afraid to plough a lone furrow is Jim Bolger whose latest star two-year-old, Verbal Dexterity, comes from just the sort of unfashionable sire line—at least in Europe—that Morris was presumably referring to. Bold Ruler was America's Horse of the Year in 1957 when his eleven wins from sixteen starts that season included the Preakness Stakes. He went on to make an immediate impact as a stallion, becoming champion sire in the States in 1963 when his first crop were still only three-year-olds, and it was a title he held for the remainder of that decade. Bold Ruler was champion sire again in 1973 thanks to the triple crown exploits of his outstanding son Secretariat, America's 'Horse of the Century' in *A Century of Champions* which Morris co-wrote with John Randall, assessing the world's best horses of the twentieth century. Bold Ruler's sire line exerted remarkable influence on the Kentucky Derby in the 'seventies when it was responsible for no fewer than seven of the winners that decade; besides Secretariat, they included five of Bold Ruler's grandsons and a great grandson, Seattle Slew, who also completed the triple crown in 1977. What's more, with Secretariat, Spectacular Bid (the 1979 Kentucky Derby winner) and Seattle Slew, a son, a grandson and a great grandson of Bold Ruler accounted for three of the top four American horses of the twentieth century according to Morris and Randall's classification.

Bold Ruler proved nothing like so dominant in the decades that followed, as the Northern Dancer and Mr Prospector sire lines began to proliferate, and it was Seattle Slew who came up with the sire who was chiefly responsible for sustaining the Bold Ruler line into the twenty-first century. That was 1992 Horse of The Year A. P. Indy, winner of that year's Belmont Stakes and Breeders' Cup Classic. Bold Ruler also featured in the bottom half of his pedigree, as well as on the top line, as A. P. Indy was out of a Secretariat mare. A. P. Indy was leading sire in North America in 2003 and 2006, a title that his grandson Tapit, currently America's most expensive sire at 300,000 dollars, took for the third year running in 2016. Another of Seattle Slew's sons to go to stud was Vindication who won all four of his starts at two, notably the Breeders' Cup Juvenile which earned him the title of champion two-year-old of 2002. Vindication never raced again after picking up a suspensory injury and his stallion career was likewise cut short when he died from colic aged just eight. Vindication was bred by Virginia Kraft Payson who is best known in Europe as the owner and breeder of St Jovite, a very smart Jim Bolger-trained two-year-old who became an outstanding three-year-old, winning the Irish Derby by twelve lengths and the King George VI and Queen Elizabeth Stakes by six. St Jovite's essay

Goffs Vincent O'Brien National Stakes, the Curragh—
Verbal Dexterity reverses Railway Stakes form with Beckford to give trainer Jim Bolger and jockey Kevin Manning a fourth victory in this race

in *Racehorses of 1991* as a two-year-old had also quoted Morris, this time on the subject of American dirt stallions and the effectiveness of their progeny on turf in Europe. Hailing from another sire line that had become unfashionable, that of Ribot, St Jovite was a rare example of a son of Pleasant Colony, America's champion three-year-old of 1981 (winner of the Kentucky Derby and Preakness Stakes), to excel on this side of the Atlantic.

Given that the success of the Bold Ruler line was confined largely to America and to racing on dirt, there was little to suggest that Vindication's stock would thrive in Europe either, but Bolger was prepared to take the risk, paying 560,000 dollars for a well-bred yearling (whose grandam was the champion three-year-old filly Serena's Song, dam of the Coronation Stakes winner Sophisticat) from Vindication's second crop. Named Vocalised, he proved a smart three-year-old in the spring of 2009 after winning a maiden at Leopardstown over seven furlongs at two, running up a quick hat-trick in a listed race at the Curragh, the Greenham Stakes at Newbury and the Tetrarch Stakes back at the Curragh, all three on soft or heavy ground. Bolger won the Tetrarch again a year later with another son of Vindication, Free Judgement, who finished second in the Irish Two Thousand Guineas on his next start. The gelded Free Judgement ended up in Hong Kong but, with little interest in his stallion prospects from elsewhere and as just a Group 3 winner after all, Vocalised was retired by Bolger to his own Redmondstown Stud—'nobody was beating a path to my door in this part of the world because the Bold Ruler line doesn't go down well in Europe'. For what it's worth, Vocalised's pedigree subsequently received a boost when Honor Code, bred on similar lines, became champion older horse in America in 2015. Honor Code is by A. P. Indy out of a half-sister to Vocalised.

If nothing else, Verbal Dexterity showed straight away that, just like his sire, he goes very well in the mud. He made a winning debut when storming away on heavy ground to win by almost ten lengths in a maiden at the Curragh in June and he was a clear-cut winner again at the Curragh three months later on soft ground when becoming his trainer's fourth winner of the Goffs Vincent O'Brien National Stakes which is now an integral part of Irish Champions' Weekend. In between, Verbal Dexterity was beaten a length by Beckford in the Railway Stakes, also at the Curragh, though that race was more of a test of speed, being over six furlongs and on good ground. Runner-up since in the Phoenix Stakes, Beckford was favourite to beat Verbal Dexterity for a second time in the National Stakes, the pair starting at 6/4 and 5/2 respectively in a field of seven. Morning favourite Gustav Klimt was a late absentee with a stone bruise, the race already having lost another leading contender when the very impressive British-trained Vintage Stakes winner Expert Eye was ruled out after an unsatisfactory scope. With conditions putting the emphasis on stamina, Verbal Dexterity turned the tables on Beckford after his rival had travelled best and led briefly over a furlong out, only to be outstayed by the always-prominent Verbal Dexterity who had gained an early advantage (not that it made any difference to the result) when his stall appeared to open a fraction early. Beckford was beaten three and a half lengths in second, with two and three quarters back to the Futurity Stakes winner Rostropovich who had become Ballydoyle's first string in the absence of Gustav Klimt. Bolger's earlier National Stakes winners Teofilo, New Approach and Dawn Approach all followed up in the Dewhurst Stakes, but Verbal Dexterity didn't take his chance at Newmarket after an unsatisfactory scope and he ended his season instead in the Racing Post Trophy at Doncaster two weeks after the Dewhurst. The step up to a mile should have suited Verbal Dexterity but he was never travelling comfortably, after being rousted along soon after the start, and ran below his best, managing only a one-paced fourth, left behind by the first two, Saxon Warrior and Roaring Lion, and losing out on third to the winner's stable-companion The Pentagon.

Verbal Dexterity (IRE) (b.c. 2015)	Vocalised (USA) (b 2006)	Vindication (b 2000)	Seattle Slew
			Strawberry Reason
		Serena's Tune (b 1998)	Mr Prospector
			Serena's Song
	Lonrach (IRE) (b 2009)	Holy Roman Emperor (b 2004)	Danehill
			L'On Vite
		Luminous One (b 2004)	Galileo
			Smaoineamh

Descendants of the daughters of Verbal Dexterity's fourth dam Fanghorn, a smart filly (third in the Poule d'Essai des Pouliches) who also produced the top-class sprinter of the late-'seventies Double Form, have been supplying the Bolgers (many carrying the colours of Bolger's wife Jackie) with good winners for years. Verbal Dexterity's dam Lonrach wasn't one of them as she was a maiden, albeit a fairly useful one in handicap company who was placed several times at up to a mile and a half. Verbal Dexterity's grandam Luminous One is yet to produce a

Mrs J. S. Bolger's "Verbal Dexterity"

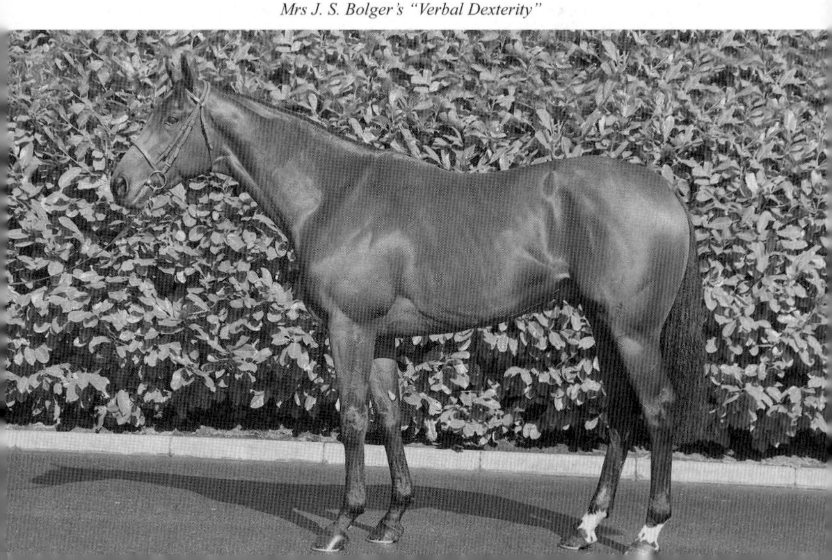

winner at all from three foals to race, but she was successful herself, in a heavy-ground maiden at Tipperary over nine furlongs. Although no better than fairly useful either, Luminous One picked up some 'black type' from third place in a listed race at Leopardstown at two over the same trip. There is more 'black type' among the descendants of great grandam Smaoineamh who was herself a useful listed winner at a mile and a quarter and a mile and three quarters. Among them are the useful sprinter Aretha and Luminata who was placed in the Moyglare Stud Stakes and the Prix Marcel Boussac, while Smaoineamh's unraced daughter Scribonia has become one of the Bolgers' best broodmares, producing several smart performers by Galileo. They include the fillies Cuis Ghaire and Gile Na Greine who were both placed in the One Thousand Guineas (the former also won the Albany Stakes, while the latter was second in the Coronation Stakes) and more recently The Major General who finished second to Ulysses in the Gordon Stakes in 2016. Other Group 1-winning Bolger two-year-olds who trace back to Fanghorn are the 1994 Phoenix Stakes winner Eva Luna, the 2008 Dewhurst winner Intense Focus (also sire of Lonrach's unraced first foal Renewed Focus) and the 2012 Criterium International winner Loch Garman. Another descendant is Irish Derby and Coronation Cup winner Soldier of Fortune who raced for Aidan O'Brien but was bred by Bolger who recounted in a *Racing Post* interview in the latest season how Coolmore chose the son of Galileo from a trio of yearlings, of which they had been given the pick to settle an outstanding debt; one of the others, also by Galileo, turned out to be none other than Teofilo whose unbeaten two-year-old season for Bolger in 2006 was a vital boost to his sire's early stallion career. It is easily forgotten, given the reputation he has now, that the nine-times champion wasn't an immediate success at stud and Bolger's faith in Galileo, whom he supported heavily with his own broodmares (Verbal Dexterity's grandam was another by Galileo from the same crop as Soldier of Fortune and Teofilo) proved crucial in those early days. 'John Magnier freely admits things might have been different if it hadn't been for me,' says Bolger. 'I'd say there was every danger Galileo might have got sold to Japan or whoever would have him. They can move things on fairly quickly there [at Coolmore], and he definitely wasn't going well when they reduced him to €37,500.'

Vocalised won't be another Galileo, but, as Teofilo did, Verbal Dexterity has raised his own sire's profile no end. Another above-average two-year-old in Vocalised's latest crop of juveniles is Warm The Voice (trained by Bolger's former assistant Brendan Duke) who completed a hat-trick before finishing third to Saxon Warrior in the Beresford Stakes. Injury prevented Teofilo from racing after the age of two, but hopefully Verbal Dexterity, a big colt, will enjoy a full campaign at three. 'He is the real deal and he is as good as any of the two-year-olds I have trained,' said Bolger after the National Stakes. There's enough stamina on the dam's side of his pedigree to suggest he will stay at least a mile and a quarter, though he would need supplementing for Epsom if the Derby becomes a possibility (he holds an entry in the Irish version). One thing we do know is that Verbal Dexterity handles heavy going, though he has yet to encounter ground firmer than good. *J. S. Bolger, Ireland*

VERCINGETORIX (IRE) 6 b.g. Dylan Thomas (IRE) 132 – Great Artist (FR) (Desert Prince (IRE) 130) [2017 82: f12g^4 p13m^3 f12.1g^5 12.1m^4 15d* 16.1g* 16.3g^6 f16.5g^5 Dec 29] fair handicapper: won at Ayr in June and Thirsk in July: left Harriet Bethell after fourth start: stays 2m: acts on polytrack, soft and good to firm going: wears headgear: usually races close up: fairly useful hurdler/maiden chaser, though not straightforward. *Iain Jardine* **79**

VERDI (IRE) 3 b.g. Invincible Spirit (IRE) 121 – Leopard Hunt (USA) 89 (Diesis 133) [2017 –: p6g^5 7.2m^5 5.1m 6d^6 6d 5.2m 6g^5 5d Sep 12] smallish gelding: modest maiden: stays 7f: acts on good to firm going: usually wears headgear: sometimes slowly away. *John Ryan* **55**

VERHOYEN 2 b.c. (Mar 29) Piccolo 121 – Memory Lane 84 (With Approval (CAN)) [2017 5v^3 6g^5 5s^2 5v^3 5m^3 5m^3 6.3s 5d^3 5.8v^6 7s Oct 15] €9,000Y: third foal: half-brother to 2-y-o 7f winner Henshaw (by Archipenko): dam 1½m winner who stayed 1¾m: fairly useful maiden: second in listed race at Naas (½ length behind True Blue Moon) in May: stays 6f: acts on good to firm and heavy going: has worn headgear. *M. C. Grassick, Ireland* **82**

VERITY 3 b.f. Redoute's Choice (AUS) – Virtuous 92 (Exit To Nowhere (USA) 122) [2017 8.2d^4 p8s^2 Jul 7] strong filly: closely related to 1½m winner Honour (by Dansili) and half-sister to several winners, including very smart 7f-9f winner Virtual (by Pivotal) and smart 2-y-o 6f winner (stayed 1m) Iceman (by Polar Falcon): dam 2-y-o 8.2f winner: fair form: better effort when second in maiden at Chelmsford in July: should improve further. *Sir Michael Stoute* **76 p**

VERNATTI 4 b.f. Teofilo (IRE) 126 – Speciosa (IRE) 115 (Danehill Dancer (IRE) 117) [2017 62: f8g^2 10.1m* 10g* 10.2d 9.9g 11.5d^3 12.1v Oct 21] angular filly: fairly useful handicapper: won at Yarmouth and Leicester in May: stays 11.5f: acts on fibresand, good to firm and good to soft going: usually leads. *Pam Sly* **86**

VERNE CASTLE 4 ch.g. Sakhee's Secret 128 – Lochangel 119 (Night Shift (USA)) [2017 94: t5.1f^5 p5g* p5g* p5m^3 p5g^6 p6g 5d p5g^4 5.5g p6g^6 Oct 11] lengthy gelding: useful handicapper: won at Lingfield (twice, by ¾ length from Monumental Man second occasion) in February: third in listed race there (½ length behind Royal Birth) later in month: best at 5f: acts on polytrack and firm going: wears hood: sold to join Michael Wigham 20,000 gns in November. *Andrew Balding* **107**

VERSTAPPEN (IRE) 2 b.c. (Mar 24) Dark Angel (IRE) 113 – Hugs 'N Kisses (IRE) 82 (Noverre (USA) 125) [2017 7g 7d^4 p8s^4 Sep 8] lengthy colt: fair form: best effort when fourth in minor event at Kempton (6¾ lengths behind Roaring Lion) in September. *Marco Botti* **66**

VERVE (IRE) 2 b.f. (Feb 24) Epaulette (AUS) 126 – Onomatomania (USA) (Mr Greeley (USA) 122) [2017 7d^2 Sep 12] €150,000Y: second foal: half-sister to 2-y-o 5f winner Miss Cogent (by Clodovil): dam unraced: 6/4, second in minor event at Leicester (length behind Orsera) in September: has joined Henry Candy: sure to improve. *Hugo Palmer* **78 p**

VERY DASHING 4 br.f. Dansili 127 – Dash To The Top 116 (Montjeu (IRE) 137) [2017 100: p10g^4 10.2g^6 t10.2g^3 10.3d^4 Jul 28] useful performer: third in listed race at Newcastle (½ length behind More Mischief) in June: stays 10.5f: acts on polytrack, tapeta, good to firm and good to soft going: often races freely. *Ralph Beckett* **107**

VERY FIRST BLADE 8 b.g. Needwood Blade 117 – Dispol Verity 60 (Averti (IRE) 117) [2017 62: f5g^2 t6g^5 f6m f5g 5m^4 5g^3 5.1m 5s 5s 5g 6g f6.1g f5g^3 f5g Dec 21] modest handicapper: races at 5f/6f nowadays: acts on all-weather, soft and good to firm going: wears headgear: usually races nearer last than first. *Michael Mullineaux* **60**

VERY HONEST (IRE) 4 b.f. Poet's Voice 126 – Cercle d'Amour (USA) (Storm Cat (USA)) [2017 87: p6g p6d p6g p6g^3 6m 5m 5.3g^3 7d^4 5g^5 p6g^5 p6g^3 p6g^3 p6g^3 p6g^5 Dec 28] fairly useful handicapper: third at Brighton in July and Kempton in November: stays 6f: acts on polytrack and good to firm going: has worn visor: front runner/races prominently. *Brett Johnson* **81**

VERY SPECIAL (IRE) 5 ch.m. Lope de Vega (IRE) 125 – Danielli (IRE) 79 (Danehill (USA) 126) [2017 116: 8g* 8.9g^5 8.9d Mar 25] lengthy mare: useful performer: won Cape Verdi at Meydan (for second successive year, by ½ length from Opal Tiara) in January: disappointing there in Balanchine and Dubai Turf after: stays 9f: acts on polytrack and firm going: wears hood: front runner/races prominently. *Saeed bin Suroor* **109**

VETTORI RULES 4 gr.g. Aussie Rules (USA) 123 – Vettori Loose (IRE) (Vettori (IRE) 119) [2017 99: t9.5g^5 p16d^2 p15.8g^3 p15.8g 12g^4 10g 10g 11.8d 10.1m 10.3v 12v p10g p16d^3 Dec 13] good-topped gelding: fairly useful handicapper on turf, useful on all-weather: trained in 2016 by A. & S. Botti, Italy: second in minor event at Kempton (1¾ lengths behind Winterlude) in February: stays 2m: acts on polytrack, tapeta and good to firm going: has worn headgear: often races towards rear. *Gay Kelleway* **91** **a102**

VEXILLUM (IRE) 8 br.g. Mujadil (USA) 119 – Common Cause 87 (Polish Patriot (USA) 128) [2017 13f 11.6f^3 11.6f^4 13d^5 p12g^6 14.1d p12g Oct 17] sturdy gelding: modest handicapper nowadays: stays 2m: acts on polytrack and any turf going: wears headgear: has worn tongue tie, including final start: often races towards rear: winning hurdler/chaser. *Neil Mulholland* **53**

VIA EGNATIA (USA) 3 b.c. Distorted Humor (USA) 117 – Honest Lady (USA) 119 (Seattle Slew (USA)) [2017 104p: 7m^3 7.6m^4 a6f 8.5f^3 8g^2 a7f Dec 1] strong, good-bodied colt: useful performer: left John Gosden after second start: second in optional claimer at Belmont in October: stays 1m: acts on good to firm going: tried in hood. *William I. Mott, USA* **98**

VIA SERENDIPITY 3 b.g. Invincible Spirit (IRE) 121 – Mambo Light (USA) 105 (Kingmambo (USA) 125) [2017 93p: 7m^5 8m 8m p8s^6 p7g^3 8g^5 8g* Nov 3] compact gelding: useful handicapper: won at Newmarket (by 1¼ lengths from Salt Whistle Bay) in November: left Hugo Palmer after fourth start: stays 1m: acts on polytrack and good to firm going: wears tongue tie. *Stuart Williams* **96**

VIA VIA (IRE) 5 b.h. Lope de Vega (IRE) 125 – Atalina (FR) (Linamix (FR) 127) [2017 94p: t7.1g* 7g^4 8d^3 p8d Nov 22] good-bodied horse: smart performer: won handicap at Newcastle (by ½ length from War Department) in March: third in listed race at Newmarket (1½ lengths behind Bravo Zolo) in November: stays 1m: acts on tapeta, good to firm and good to soft going. *James Tate* **110**

VIBES (IRE) 3 ch.g. Helmet (AUS) 127 – Smoken Rosa (USA) (Smoke Glacken (USA) 120) [2017 68: 8.1d 7s^2 7s* 8.2d^5 7d^6 Oct 30] lengthy gelding: fairly useful handicapper: won at Lingfield (by 8 lengths from Right About Now) in August: stays 7f: acts on polytrack and soft going: front runner/races prominently. *Jamie Osborne* **87**

VIBRANT CHORDS 4 b.g. Poet's Voice 126 – Lovely Thought 92 (Dubai Destination (USA) 127) [2017 102: 5m^6 5f* 6m^2 5g 5g^2 5.6g^2 5g Oct 17] good-quartered gelding: useful handicapper: won at Goodwood (by ¾ length from A Momentofmadness) in May: second at Doncaster (length behind Desert Law) in August and in Portland at same course (3½ lengths behind Spring Loaded) in September: stays 7f, usually races at 5f/6f: acts on polytrack and any turf going. *Henry Candy* **108**

VICE MARSHAL (IRE) 2 b.c. (Jan 12) Wootton Bassett 119 – Celsius Degre (IRE) (Verglas (IRE) 118) [2017 6g 7m p8g Dec 20] sturdy colt: little impact in maidens/minor event. *Charlie Fellowes* **–**

VICEROY MAC 2 b.g. (Feb 9) Sepoy (AUS) 129 – Tebee's Oasis 70 (Oasis Dream 129) [2017 6d 6f^3 6g^5 7m^3 p8g Oct 5] fair maiden: should stay at least 1m: acts on firm going: often races towards rear. *David Loughnane* **71**

VICE VERSA 3 b.f. Oasis Dream 129 – Mascarene (USA) 82 (Empire Maker (USA) 129) [2017 –p: 8m t8.6g* 8.3g^5 7.6d^5 Jul 29] well-made filly: fair performer: won maiden at Wolverhampton in May: stays 8.5f: acts on tapeta: tried in visor: usually races close up. *Sir Michael Stoute* **76**

VICKY PARK 3 b.f. Compton Place 125 – Sonko (IRE) 90 (Red Clubs (IRE) 125) [2017 –: p5g^5 f5g^4 Apr 16] no form. *George Margarson* **–**

VICTOIRE DE LYPHAR (IRE) 10 b.g. Bertolini (USA) 125 – Victory Peak (Shirley Heights 130) [2017 88§: 7m^2 Apr 12] compact gelding: fairly useful performer: second in claimer at Catterick on sole start in 2017: stayed 8.5f: acted on good to firm and heavy going: wore headgear: not straightforward: dead. *Ruth Carr* **80 §**

VICTORIA POLLARD 5 b.m. Sir Percy 129 – Victoria Montoya 104 (High Chaparral (IRE) 132) [2017 86: t10.2d^3 t10.2g^4 p15.8f^4 Mar 4] rather leggy mare: fairly useful handicapper: third at Newcastle in February: stays 1½m: acts on polytrack, tapeta and good to firm going: usually wears cheekpieces: often races towards rear. *Andrew Balding* **81**

VICTORIOUSLY 5 b.g. Azamour (IRE) 130 – Ambria (GER) (Monsun (GER) 124) [2017 63: p10g* p10s t9.5d^2 Dec 26] good-topped gelding: fair handicapper: won at Lingfield in April: stays 1¼m: acts on polytrack, tapeta and firm going: wears headgear: tried in tongue tie. *Andi Brown* **67**

VICTOR'S BET (SPA) 8 b.g. Leadership 124 – Marmaria (SPA) (Limpid 119) [2017 75: t9.5g t9.5m^2 p12g* 9.9g^5 p11d* t12.2g 9.9v 9.1m p12g p15.8g p16g p15.8g p15.8g Dec 6] close-coupled gelding: fair handicapper: won apprentice races at Lingfield in April and Kempton in May: stays 1½m: acts on polytrack, soft and good to firm going: tried in tongue tie: usually races in rear. *Ralph Smith* **75**

VICTORY ANGEL (IRE) 3 b.c. Acclamation 118 – Golden Shadow (IRE) 77 (Selkirk (USA) 129) [2017 94p: 6m* 6m 6m 6g 6m* 6d Oct 6] well-made colt: useful handicapper: won at Newmarket (by 2¼ lengths from Rich And Famous) in April and Yarmouth (by 2½ lengths from Gulliver) in August: best form at 6f: acts on good to firm going: tried in visor: often races towards rear. *Roger Varian* **107**

VICTORY BOND 4 b.g. Medicean 128 – Antebellum (FR) (Anabaa (USA) 130) [2017 107: 7.9d^3 10.3m 10.3g^4 7.9d 8.2s p10g* p10g^2 Nov 18] smart performer: won minor event at Chelmsford (by ½ length from Boynton) in October: fourth in York Stakes (3 lengths behind Success Days) in July: stays 10.5f: acts on polytrack, soft and good to firm going: tried in blinkers. *William Haggas* **115**

VICTORY CHIME (IRE) 2 b.g. (Jan 21) Campanologist (USA) 119 – Patuca (Teofilo (IRE) 126) [2017 8.3d^5 8.3v^4 p8d Nov 22] 48,000Y: first foal: dam, 1m winner, closely related to very smart German 1m-1¼m winner Potemkin and useful 8.5f-11f winner Pealer (by Campanologist): fair form: best effort when fifth in maiden at Nottingham (3 lengths behind Msayyan) on debut: will be suited by 1¼m+: remains with potential. *Ralph Beckett* **74 p**

VIEWPOINT (IRE) 8 b.g. Exceed And Excel (AUS) 126 – Lady's View (USA) 85 (Distant View (USA) 126) [2017 91: t12.2g^5 p10g* p10g^3 a8.6g^4 13.9m* t12.2g^2 t12.2g* 11.9m^5 Jul 13] strong gelding: fairly useful performer: won sellers at Lingfield in April, and Catterick and Wolverhampton (by 1¼ lengths from Luv U Whatever) in June: left Michael Appleby after seventh start: stays 1¾m: acts on polytrack, tapeta, good to firm and good to soft going: often races prominently. *Harriet Bethell* **90**

VIGEE LE BRUN (IRE) 3 gr.f. Dark Angel (IRE) 113 – Wonderful Town (USA) (Bernstein (USA) 115) [2017 74: p7g^3 8m^5 9g 10.2g^2 f11.1g^5 Dec 22] sturdy filly: fair maiden: left Brian Meehan after fourth start: stays 1¼m: acts on soft and good to firm going: tried in cheekpieces. *Olly Williams* **77**

VIKING HOARD (IRE) 3 b.g. Vale of York (IRE) 117 – Tibouchina (IRE) 77 (Daylami (IRE) 138) [2017 81: 9.9m^4 9.9g 8.1m^5 9.9m* 9.9g p12g Oct 9] good-topped gelding: fairly useful handicapper: won at Salisbury in August: stays 1¼m: acts on good to firm going: in headgear last 3 starts: often races in rear: has joined Charles Byrne, Ireland. *Harry Dunlop* **83**

VIKING WAY (IRE) 2 ch.g. (Apr 5) Society Rock (IRE) 126 – Patrimony (Cadeaux Genereux 131) [2017 6.1s^6 7g 6m Aug 26] little show in minor events. *Olly Williams* **–**

VIKTORIYA TARABAN (IRE) 2 b.f. (Jan 24) Lilbourne Lad (IRE) 111 – Fritta Mista (IRE) (Linamix (FR) 127) [2017 7g^5 8.1g^6 Aug 28] rather leggy filly: closely related to 2 winners by Acclamation, including smart Hong Kong 7f winner Sparkling Power (2-y-o 7f winner in Ireland as Montecchio) and half-sister to 2 winners, including useful 2-y-o 6f-7f winner Sans Reward (by Barathea): dam maiden: little impact in maiden/minor event. *Joseph Tuite* **–**

VILLA MARIA 2 b.f. (Mar 8) Makfi 130 – An Ghalanta (IRE) 97 (Holy Roman Emperor (IRE) 125) [2017 p8g Nov 21] 52,000Y, 70,000 2-y-o: third foal: sister to useful winner up to 7f Bletchley (2-y-o 5f winner) and half-sister to 1m winner Elegant Annie (by Lawman): dam, 2-y-o 5f winner, closely related to smart 1m/9f winner Bancnuanaheireann: 33/1, well held in minor event at Lingfield. *K. R. Burke* **–**

VILLA SAVINA (IRE) 2 b.f. (Apr 5) Elusive Pimpernel (USA) 117 – Swan Sea (USA) (Sea Hero (USA) 124) [2017 6.1g* 6.3s p6g^3 Oct 9] €800Y: leggy, close-coupled filly: half-sister to several winners, including useful/ungenuine winner up to 6f Titus Alone (2-y-o 5f winner, by Titus Livius) and useful 6f (including at 2 yrs) winner Ticks The Boxes (by Fast Company): dam unraced: fair form: won minor event at Windsor (by neck from demoted Sweet Vixen) in July: stays 6f: sold 30,000 gns, sent to USA. *Clive Cox* **76**

VILLA TORA 2 ch.f. (Feb 12) Excelebration (IRE) 133 – Tatora (Selkirk (USA) 129) [2017 5f^4 6s^3 5g* 5d^2 5m^5 5d^4 5d^4 6s^6 6.3s t5.1g^4 Nov 11] 11,000F: half-sister to several winners, including very smart winner up to 7f Tariq (2-y-o 6f winner) and smart 6.5f/7f winner Tariq Too (both by Kyllachy): dam unraced: fair performer: won minor event at Hamilton in June: best form at 5f: acts on soft going: front runner/races prominently. *Mark Johnston* **70**

VILLETTE (IRE) 3 b.f. Sixties Icon 125 – Spinning Lucy (IRE) 101 (Spinning World (USA) 130) [2017 p12g* p11g^6 p10s 10g* p10g^6 t12.2g Nov 29] 5,500 2-y-o: third foal: dam, 2-y-o 6f winner, half-sister to useful 6f winner Midris: fairly useful performer: won maiden at Kempton in March and handicap at Leicester (awarded race having dead-heated with Entangling) in October: stays 1½m: acts on polytrack. *Dean Ivory* **88**

VIMY RIDGE 5 ch.g. American Post 121 – Fairy Shoes 77 (Kyllachy 129) [2017 85: p5g^2 p6g^5 t5d^3 p6g^4 p5g 5g^2 5g* 6g^4 5.1m* 5.1d* 6g 5s^5 p6g Nov 6] stocky gelding: fairly useful handicapper: won at Leicester (amateur) in June, and Windsor in August and September (by 2 lengths from Monumental Man): best at 5f/6f: acts on polytrack, good to firm and good to soft going: has worn headgear: wears tongue tie: usually races towards rear. *Alan Bailey* **88**

VINCENT'S FOREVER 4 b.g. Pour Moi (IRE) 125 – Glen Rosie (IRE) 102 (Mujtahid (USA) 118) [2017 90: p11d Jul 12] sturdy gelding: fairly useful handicapper, well held sole start on Flat in 2017: stays 11f: acts on polytrack and soft going: often wears headgear: tried in tongue tie. *David Pipe* **–**

VINCENTTI (IRE) 7 b.g. Invincible Spirit (IRE) 121 – Bint Al Balad (IRE) 63 (Ahonoora 122) [2017 85§: 5.7f^{5} p6d 6.1d 6.1v 6.1m 6.1m^{2} 6.1g 6g Aug 7] sturdy gelding: fair handicapper nowadays: stays 6f: acts on polytrack, good to firm and heavy going: wears headgear: tried in tongue tie: ungenuine. *Ronald Harris* **73 §**

VINCENZO COCCOTTI (USA) 5 gr.g. Speightstown (USA) 124 – Ocean Colors (USA) (Orientate (USA) 127) [2017 79: 7d^{6} 6g^{6} 6m^{3} 6d^{3} 7g Sep 1] good-topped gelding: fair handicapper: stays 7f: acts on polytrack, tapeta, good to firm and good to soft going: has worn cheekpieces. *Ken Cunningham-Brown* **74**

VINDICATOR (IRE) 3 b.g. Delegator 125 – Monroe (Tomba 119) [2017 9.8g^{6} t10.2s^{4} 9.1g^{6} 13.1g^{4} 12d* 14d^{2} 13.9d* 13s^{2} Oct 3] first foal: dam unraced sister to smart winner up to 6f Chief Editor: fairly useful handicapper: won at Thirsk in August and Catterick (by 1¾ lengths from Wolfcatcherjack) in September: stays 1¾m: acts on tapeta and good to soft going: usually wears cheekpieces: sold 60,000 gns, sent to Saudi Arabia. *Michael Dods* **89**

VINTAGE DREAM (IRE) 3 b.g. Dream Ahead (USA) 133 – Stella Del Mattino (USA) (Golden Gear (USA) 116) [2017 68: 8m 6.1d 7.2d 6d^{3} 6d 5g^{2} 6m^{2} 5s 6d^{2} 5d^{2} 5s^{4} t6g 7d^{6} Oct 30] leggy gelding: fair maiden: stays 6f: acts on good to firm and good to soft going: usually wears headgear: usually leads. *Noel Wilson* **70**

VINTAGE FOLLY 3 b.f. Makfi 130 – Katimont (IRE) 90 (Montjeu (IRE) 137) [2017 84p: 10.3s^{2} 11.9g 10.1s^{2} 10.2s^{2} p9.4g^{2} Nov 28] sturdy filly: useful performer: second in Musidora Stakes at York (beaten 1¾ lengths by Shutter Speed) and in listed races at Yarmouth, Doncaster and Deauville (2 lengths behind Indian Blessing): should be suited by 1½m: acts on polytrack, tapeta and soft going: often races prominently. *Hugo Palmer* **104**

VINTAGER 2 ro.c. (Apr 4) Mastercraftsman (IRE) 129 – White And Red (IRE) 93 (Orpen (USA) 116) [2017 7d* 7g^{5} 7s^{5} Oct 28] 25,000F, 65,000Y: lengthy colt: fourth foal: half-brother to 2-y-o 5f winner (stays 7f) Fashionable Spirit (by Invincible Spirit): dam, 6.5f winner, half-sister to useful 10.5f-1½m winner Wild Passion: useful form: won maiden at Newmarket (by 1½ lengths from Symbolization) in August: will be suited by 1m: remains open to improvement. *David Menuisier* **97 p**

VIOLA PARK 3 b.g. Aqlaam 125 – Violette 106 (Observatory (USA) 131) [2017 53: p8g t7.1m^{4} p7d* f8g^{4} t7.1g^{4} t7.1g^{2} t7.1g^{5} 6.1m 8d^{3} 7.1d^{5} t7.2g* t7.2g^{5} 8g 8s^{5} p7d^{2} t7.2g^{6} p7s^{2} p7d^{2} Dec 13] fair handicapper: won at Chelmsford in February and Wolverhampton in June: stays 1m: acts on polytrack, tapeta and good to soft going: wears headgear: front runner/races prominently. *Ronald Harris* **68**

VIOLET BEAUREGARDE 2 b.f. (Apr 12) Captain Gerrard (IRE) 113 – Style Award 88 (Acclamation 118) [2017 5d t5.1g^{5} t6.1g Sep 23] fourth foal: half-sister to 2-y-o 5f winner Kuramathi (by Paco Boy): dam, winner up to 6f (2-y-o 5f winner), half-sister to useful 8.6f winner Eloquently: little show in varied events: in hood last 2 starts. *Harry Dunlop* **–**

VIOLET MIST (IRE) 3 gr.f. Clodovil (IRE) 116 – Vision of Peace (IRE) (Invincible Spirit (IRE) 121) [2017 –: t5g^{5} t5d 5m^{6} 5g^{5} Apr 22] no form: tried in cheekpieces/tongue tie. *Ben Haslam* **–**

VIOLET'S LADS (IRE) 3 b.f. Myboycharlie (IRE) 118 – Cape Violet (IRE) 70 (Cape Cross (IRE) 129) [2017 7g 8.1m^{2} 7s^{4} 7g^{6} 6s^{3} p7g^{3} p7d p7g^{4} Dec 28] €20,000Y: lengthy filly: first foal: dam 7f-9f winner: fair maiden: stays 7f: acts on polytrack and soft going: temperament under suspicion. *Brett Johnson* **70**

VIREN'S ARMY (IRE) 4 b.g. Twirling Candy (USA) 124 – Blue Angel (IRE) 107 (Oratorio (IRE) 128) [2017 110: 12.1g 9.9g* 9m^{5} Apr 19] strong, lengthy gelding: smart handicapper: won at Meydan (by 1½ lengths from Kidmenever) in February: stays 10.5f: acts on polytrack and heavy going: in cheekpieces last 2 starts. *Charlie Appleby* **114**

VIRILE (IRE) 6 ch.g. Exceed And Excel (AUS) 126 – Winding (USA) (Irish River (FR) 131) [2017 73: p6g t7.1g t6g^{6} p6g^{3} t6m^{4} p6g^{2} p7g^{2} 7m^{3} 6m^{2} 6.1g 7d 6m^{5} 7m Aug 16] sturdy gelding: fair handicapper: stays 7f: acts on polytrack, tapeta, good to firm and good to soft going: usually wears headgear/tongue tie. *Sylvester Kirk* **65**

VIRNON 6 b.g. Virtual 122 – Freedom Song 74 (Singspiel (IRE) 133) [2017 85: f16g^{4} f14g^{3} f16d* f14g^{3} Apr 18] fair handicapper: won at Southwell in April: stays 2m: acts on fibresand, soft and good to firm going: fair chaser. *Alan Swinbank* **78**

VISANDI (FR) 5 b.g. Azamour (IRE) 130 – Vadaza (FR) (Zafonic (USA) 130) [2017 14m^{6} 11.8d Jul 26] rangy gelding: fairly useful performer for Jean-Claude Rouget in 2015, winner of newcomers race at Senonnes-Pouance: well held both starts on Flat in 2017: stays 15f: acts on good to soft going: tried in tongue tie. *Jonjo O'Neill* **–**

VISCOUNT BARFIELD 4 b.g. Raven's Pass (USA) 133 – Madonna Dell'orto 83 **108**
(Montjeu (IRE) 137) [2017 102: p7g^6 p7g^4 p7g^4 7.6g^6 7m* 7g* 7d 7m^3 7g Sep 16] good-topped gelding: useful performer: won handicap at York (by ¾ length from Mutawathea) in June and listed race at Chester (by head from Jungle Cat) in July: third in Supreme Stakes at Goodwood (3 lengths behind Dutch Connection) in August: stays 7.5f: acts on polytrack, firm and good to soft going: wears hood: has joined Niels Petersen, Norway. *Andrew Balding*

VISCOUNT LOFTUS (IRE) 2 b.g. (Feb 27) Clodovil (IRE) 116 – Melpomene 95 **85**
(Peintre Celebre (USA) 137) [2017 5.2m* 5m 5g* 5.1v^4 5d Oct 11] sixth foal: half-brother to 3 winners, including 2-y-o 5f winner Rogues' Gallery (by Fast Company) and 1¼m-1½m winner Triple Dip (by Three Valleys): dam 1½m-1¾m winner who stayed 2m: fairly useful performer: won minor events at Yarmouth in June and Pontefract (by 1½ lengths from Showmethedough) in August: raced only at 5f: acts on good to firm and heavy going: front runner/races prominently. *Mark Johnston*

VISIONARY (IRE) 3 b.g. Dream Ahead (USA) 133 – Avodale (IRE) (Lawman (FR) 121) **106**
[2017 91: t5.1m* p6g^3 p7g* p6g^2 6s* 6m 6s 6s Oct 7] lengthy gelding: useful performer: won minor events at Wolverhampton (by ¾ length from Poet's Society) in January and Dundalk (by 1¼ lengths from Rock In Peace) in March, and listed race at Newbury (by head from Simmie) in May: stays 7f: acts on polytrack, tapeta, soft and good to firm going. *Robert Cowell*

VISION CLEAR (GER) 2 b.g. (Apr 26) Soldier Hollow 121 – Vive Madame (GER) **64 p**
(Big Shuffle (USA) 122) [2017 p8s t8s^6 7d Sep 29] €52,000Y: half-brother to several winners, including smart German 1m-1½m winner Vif Monsieur and useful 1½m winner (stays 16.5f) Vive Ma Fille (both by Doyen): dam 7f/1m winner: modest form in minor events/maiden: bred to be suited by 1¼m: remains open to improvement. *Ed Dunlop*

VISION OF BEAUTY (FR) 4 b.f. Vision d'Etat (FR) 127 – Belle Dame (GER) **68**
(Pilsudski (IRE) 134) [2017 63: f11g^5 t9.5g^3 t9.5g Feb 11] fair maiden: stayed 9.5f: acted on tapeta: usually raced close up: dead. *Keith Dalgleish*

VISITANT 4 ch.g. Pivotal 124 – Invitee 74 (Medicean 128) [2017 72: 10m* 10g^4 8.8m* **92**
10.3g^2 10g^3 10.3d Sep 10] fairly useful handicapper: won at Ayr in May and York in June: stays 10.5f: acts on tapeta and good to firm going. *David Thompson*

VISOR 2 b.g. (Apr 3) Helmet (AUS) 127 – Entitlement 68 (Authorized (IRE) 133) [2017 **– p**
p8g Nov 21] first foal: dam, 2m winner, half-sister to very smart winner up to 14.6f Craigsteel and Prix du Cadran winner Invermark: in hood, 66/1, eighth in minor event at Lingfield: capable of better. *James Fanshawe*

VITAMIN (IRE) 2 b.f. (Jan 15) Camelot 128 – True Verdict (IRE) 101 (Danehill Dancer **84 p**
(IRE) 117) [2017 7g^3 7m* Aug 25] €95,000Y: lengthy filly: has scope: first foal: dam 6f winner: fairly useful form: won minor event at Newmarket (by 2 lengths from Soliloquy) in August: will stay 1m: remains open to improvement. *Richard Hannon*

VIVARDIA (IRE) 3 ch.f. Rip Van Winkle (IRE) 134 – Raggiante (IRE) (Rock of Gibraltar **–**
(IRE) 133) [2017 61: 6g Apr 30] modest form at 2 yrs, well held sole start in 2017. *Ben Haslam*

VIVAT REX (IRE) 6 b.g. Fastnet Rock (AUS) 127 – Strawberry Roan (IRE) 113 **89**
(Sadler's Wells (USA) 132) [2017 86: f8g* f8g^3 p10g f8g^3 f11.1g^4 Dec 19] fairly useful performer: won claimer at Southwell in January: third in handicap at same course next time: left J. J. Feane after first start: stays 1½m: acts on all-weather and heavy going: wears headgear/tongue tie. *Conor Dore*

VIVA VERGLAS (IRE) 6 gr.g. Verglas (IRE) 118 – Yellow Trumpet 75 (Petong 126) **79**
[2017 64, a72: t6m f6m* f6g* f6g^4 t6g^4 6g^2 f6.1g 6g^6 5d^5 t7.2m p7g f6.1g t6.1g^2 f6.1g^5 Dec 21] strong gelding: fair handicapper: won at Southwell (twice) in March: stays 6f: acts on all-weather, good to firm and heavy going: has worn headgear: often races towards rear. *Daniel Loughnane*

VIVE LA DIFFERENCE (IRE) 3 b.g. Holy Roman Emperor (IRE) 125 – Galaxie Sud **80**
(USA) (El Prado (IRE) 119) [2017 8d 8g 7s^2 6d^3 7d^2 7v^4 Nov 7] fairly useful maiden: second in maiden at Redcar in October: left A. Fabre after second start: stays 7f: acts on good to soft going. *Tim Easterby*

VIVIAN WARD 3 b.f. Kyllachy 129 – Al Joudha (FR) (Green Desert (USA) 127) [2017 **50**
–: p6g^6 Jan 25] little show in 2 maidens in Britain: sold 3,000 gns, sent to Italy, where third once (at 5f) from 11 starts. *John Gosden*

VIVLOS (JPN) 4 bl.f. Deep Impact (JPN) 134 – Halwa Sweet (JPN) (Machiavellian (USA) 123) [2017 115: 8.9f^{5} 8.9d* 8.9g^{2} 10.9f^{5} Nov 12] fifth foal: sister to smart Japanese 1m-1¼m winner Verxina and closely related to 3 winners, notably Japan Cup winner Cheval Grand (by Heart's Cry): dam Japanese 5f-9f winner: very smart performer: successful twice in 2016, including in Shuka Sho at Kyoto: also won Dubai Turf at Meydan (by ½ length from Heshem) in March: neck second to Crocosmia in Group 2 Fuchu Himba Stakes at Tokyo in October: 2¼ lengths fifth to Mozu Katchan in Queen Elizabeth II Cup at Kyoto final outing: stays 1¼m: acts on firm and good to soft going: often wears hood. *Yasuo Tomomichi, Japan* **120**

VIVRE LA REVE 5 b.m. Assertive 121 – Noor El Houdah (IRE) 61 (Fayruz 116) [2017 55: f6g t7.1g^{2} f6m^{6} t8.6g* t8.6g t8.6g^{3} t8.6g t9.5m Oct 31] modest handicapper: won at Wolverhampton in March: stays 9.5f: acts on fibresand and tapeta: wears headgear. *James Unett* **61**

VIXEN (IRE) 3 b.f. Kodiac 112 – Radio Wave 78 (Dalakhani (IRE) 133) [2017 7m^{5} 7s^{5} 8g 6g^{4} 6s^{2} 7s* p7d^{6} Dec 13] 41,000Y: rather unfurnished filly: third foal: dam, maiden (probably stayed 1½m), half-sister to smart 10.6f winner Tuning Fork out of smart 1¾m winner Tuning: fair handicapper: won at Salisbury in October: left Geoffrey Deacon after third start: stays 7f: acts on soft going: often wears hood: front runner/races prominently. *Eve Johnson Houghton* **68**

VIZIER 4 b.g. Pivotal 124 – Rare Ransom 97 (Oasis Dream 129) [2017 85: 8m^{6} 10g^{5} p10s 11.1g^{6} Jul 3] compact gelding: fairly useful at best, below that level in 2017: has worn headgear, including last 2 starts. *David O'Meara* **67**

VJ DAY (USA) 2 b.g. (Apr 20) War Front (USA) 119 – Sassy Image (USA) 121 (Broken Vow (USA) 117) [2017 6s^{5} 6f^{6} 7.2m^{3} Aug 30] $250,000Y: big, attractive gelding: second foal: half-brother to a winner in USA by Distorted Humor: dam US Grade 1 6f/7f winner: fair form: third in minor event at Musselburgh (4 lengths behind Soldier's Minute) in August: remains with potential. *Kevin Ryan* **71 p**

VOCALISATION (IRE) 3 ch.f. Poet's Voice 126 – Mi Rubina (IRE) (Rock of Gibraltar (IRE) 133) [2017 –: t6f^{5} t6m^{4} t5d t5.1g t6m^{4} t6g 5m Apr 12] poor maiden: stayed 6f: acted on tapeta: tried in cheekpieces: front runner/raced prominently: covered by Dylan Thomas, sent to Pakistan. *John Weymes* **47**

VOCIFEROUS MARINA (IRE) 3 b.f. Vocalised (USA) 114 – Marina of Venice (IRE) 94 (Galileo (IRE) 134) [2017 90p: 7v 10g* 10.3s^{4} 10d 10d Jun 28] well-made filly: useful performer: won listed race at Navan (by 1½ lengths from Pocketfullofdreams) in April: stays 1¼m: acts on soft going: often wears tongue tie: usually races nearer last than first. *J. S. Bolger, Ireland* **100**

VODKA PIGEON 2 ch.f. (Mar 2) Sepoy (AUS) 129 – Hanging On 94 (Spinning World (USA) 130) [2017 6m^{2} 6d^{3} 7d t6.1d^{3} Dec 27] 60,000Y: well-made filly: fourth foal: half-sister to winners abroad by Barathea and Leporello: dam, 2-y-o 7f winner, half-sister to very smart 1¼m-1¾m winner Barolo: fair form: left Tom Dascombe after third start: should stay at least 7f. *Adam West* **71**

VODKA WELLS (FR) 7 b.g. Irish Wells (FR) 122 – Kahipiroska (FR) (Mansonnien (FR) 122) [2017 10g Jul 21] maiden on Flat: stays 1½m: acts on good to firm going: sometimes in headgear: tried in tongue tie: fairly useful chaser, won in May: sold £9,500 in September, hurdling in Italy. *Rebecca Menzies* **–**

VOGUEATTI (USA) 4 b.f. Arch (USA) 127 – Not Here (USA) (Gone West (USA)) [2017 76p: t9.5g^{3} t10.2g* 10.2v^{6} t12.4s^{4} p10g^{2} p10s^{4} p12d p10s Dec 8] fairly useful handicapper: won at Newcastle (by 2 lengths from Mariee) in February: stays 1¼m: acts on polytrack and tapeta. *Marco Botti* **86**

VOGUELA (IRE) 2 b.f. (Apr 12) Arcano (IRE) 122 – Trading Places (Dansili 127) [2017 6v 5.4g 6v Oct 23] €25,000Y: rather slightly-built filly: half-sister to several winners, including winner up to 6f Vona (2-y-o 5f winner, by Dark Angel) and 1¼m winner (stays 16.5f) Glan Y Gors (by High Chaparral), both useful: dam unraced half-sister to smart winner up to 9f Wharf: well held in maiden/minor events. *Tim Easterby* **–**

VOI 3 b.f. Holy Roman Emperor (IRE) 125 – Bride Unbridled (IRE) (Hurricane Run (IRE) 134) [2017 t7.1d^{3} 7d^{5} p10s 9.1s* 9.9d^{6} 9.1m^{2} 10g^{6} 10g^{3} p10g^{4} Nov 17] workmanlike filly: first foal: dam unraced half-sister to useful 2-y-o 6f winner French Emperor (by Holy Roman Emperor): fairly useful handicapper: won at Yarmouth in July: third at Newmarket in November: left Hugo Palmer after first start: stays 1¼m: acts on polytrack, soft and good to firm going: wears tongue tie: sometimes slowly away. *Conrad Allen* **83**

VOICEMAIL 2 b.f. (Feb 5) Poet's Voice 126 – Dame Helen (Royal Applause 124) [2017 7d^{3} 8g* p8g^{3} t8.6g Nov 18] 27,000Y: first foal: dam, French 2-y-o 1m winner, half-sister to useful 9f-1½m winner Demolition: fair form: won minor event at Ripon in August: stays 1m. *James Tate* **75**

VOICE OF A LEADER (IRE) 6 b.g. Danehill Dancer (IRE) 117 – Thewaytosanjose (IRE) 58 (Fasliyev (USA) 120) [2017 –: t9.5g* Mar 27] lengthy, rather dipped-backed gelding: fair handicapper nowadays: won at Wolverhampton on sole start in 2017: stays 10.5f: acts on polytrack, tapeta and good to soft going: wears hood. *Andi Brown* **69**

VOICE OF THE NORTH 2 b.c. (May 10) Mount Nelson 125 – Darakshaana (IRE) (Barathea (IRE) 127) [2017 7m^{4} 7.8v^{4} 9.9s 8v Oct 23] strong colt: fair form: stays 1m. *Mark Johnston* **68**

VOLATILE 3 b.g. Poet's Voice 126 – Neshla 49 (Singspiel (IRE) 133) [2017 83p: p7f^{3} t8s^{6} 7g 6.1m^{4} 8g^{5} p7g Aug 15] well-made gelding: useful handicapper: third in listed race at Lingfield (3 lengths behind Second Thought) in March: stays 7f: acts on polytrack and good to firm going: tried in cheekpieces: front runner/races prominently: sold to join Jamie Osborne 32,000 gns in October. *James Tate* **97**

VOLCANIC JACK (IRE) 9 b.g. Kodiac 112 – Rosaria Panatta (IRE) (Mujtahid (USA) 118) [2017 12.1m Jul 19] angular gelding: fair at best, retains little ability. *Michael Chapman* **–**

VOLEVO LUI 2 b.c. (Apr 14) Farhh 131 – Veronica Franco (ITY) (Lomitas 129) [2017 8d^{6} p10g^{6} Nov 29] modest form. *Marco Botti* **64**

VOLPONE JELOIS (FR) 4 gr.g. Vol de Nuit 114 – Jenne Jelois (FR) (My Risk (FR) 120) [2017 10.3g^{3} 14.2m^{2} p12g^{3} p15.8g^{3} Dec 20] fairly useful handicapper: placed all 4 starts on Flat in 2017: stays 2m: acts on polytrack, good to firm and good to soft going: in headgear in 2017: fair hurdler. *Paul Nicholls* **83**

VOLTURNUS 3 b.g. Azamour (IRE) 130 – Daffydowndilly 82 (Oasis Dream 129) [2017 10.2g 10.2s 11.6v t14g^{4} 14d p13.3d p16g* p13.3s^{3} p13.3s^{4} t16.5d Dec 9] modest handicapper: won at Kempton in November: stays 2m: acts on polytrack: wears headgear: often wears tongue tie: sometimes slowly away. *Jamie Osborne* **63**

VOLUMINOUS 2 b.f. (Feb 22) Nathaniel (IRE) 129 – Capacious 76 (Nayef (USA) 129) [2017 8.3d Oct 18] second foal: dam lightly-raced sister to winner up to 1m Spacious (second in 1000 Guineas) and 7f/1m winner Dimension (both smart): 16/1, considerate introduction when well held in maiden at Nottingham: should do better. *James Fanshawe* **– p**

VOLUNTEER POINT (IRE) 5 b.m. Footstepsinthesand 120 – Piffling (Pivotal 124) [2017 99, a106: t7.1g p7d^{2} t7.1d^{6} p7g Apr 14] rather leggy mare: useful performer: second in minor event at Chelmsford (1½ lengths behind Ashadihan) in February: stays 1m: acts on polytrack, tapeta, good to firm and good to soft going: often races towards rear: sold 240,000 gns in December. *Mick Channon* **99**

VONA (IRE) 3 b.f. Dark Angel (IRE) 113 – Trading Places (Dansili 127) [2017 87: 7m^{4} 7.6s^{2} 7d^{3} 6g* 7g^{3} 9.9g^{6} Dec 29] smallish, close-coupled filly: useful performer: second in handicap at Chester (short head behind Starlight Romance) in June: left Richard Fahey 140,000 gns after next start: won minor event at Doha in December: stays 7.5f: acts on soft and good to firm going. *Jassim Mohammed G. Jahromi, Qatar* **98**

VON BLUCHER (IRE) 4 ch.g. Zoffany (IRE) 121 – Tropical Lady (IRE) 117 (Sri Pekan (USA) 117) [2017 108: 7m^{5} 8m 7g^{6} 7g^{3} 7s 7g^{2} 7.2v 7d Nov 11] strong, lengthy gelding: useful handicapper: third at York (2¼ lengths behind Get Knotted) in July and second in listed race at Redcar (4½ lengths behind Jallota) in October: stays 1m: acts on polytrack and good to firm going: in cheekpieces last 3 starts: usually wears tongue tie. *Rebecca Menzies* **101**

VOSKI (USA) 3 b.c. Medaglia d'Oro (USA) 129 – Say You Will (IRE) (A P Indy (USA) 131) [2017 p12g* 12.3g^{3} 11.2s^{5} t12.2g^{6} p12s 12.1g^{5} t12.4g^{5} t12.2g p11g Oct 24] third foal: half-brother to 7f/1m winner World's Greatest (by Discreet Cat): dam, useful US 6.5f-9f winner, out of smart half-sister to Lammtarra: fairly useful performer: won maiden at Lingfield in March: stays 1½m: acts on polytrack: tried in blinkers: sometimes slowly away: sold 25,000 gns in October. *Mark Johnston* **84**

VOSNE ROMANEE 6 ch.g. Arakan (USA) 123 – Vento Del Oreno (FR) 67 (Lando (GER) 128) [2017 t13.9g* Feb 17] fairly useful handicapper: won at Wolverhampton (by length from Marshall Aid) on sole Flat start in 2017: stays 1¾m: acts on polytrack, tapeta, soft and good to firm going: wears headgear: tried in tongue tie: useful hurdler/chaser. *Dr Richard Newland* **80**

VOTE 3 b.f. Aqlaam 125 – Bidding Time (Rock of Gibraltar (IRE) 133) [2017 66: 6g p6g^3 **72**
Aug 30] smallish filly: fair maiden: stays 6f: acts on polytrack and good to firm going.
James Eustace

VOYAGER BLUE 2 br.c. (Jan 29) Footstepsinthesand 120 – Bristol Fashion (Dansili **82 p**
127) [2017 t8.6g^3 t9.5g^2 Dec 18] 92,000F, 60,000Y: second foal: half-brother to useful
11f-1½m winner Cribbs Causeway (by Rip Van Winkle): dam unraced half-sister to Irish
Derby/St Leger runner-up Midas Touch: fairly useful form: better effort when second in
minor event at Wolverhampton (neck behind Jackfinbar) in December: open to further
improvement. *Jamie Osborne*

VRIKA BAY 3 b.f. Mastercraftsman (IRE) 129 – Fascination Street (IRE) 69 (Mujadil **–**
(USA) 119) [2017 59: p10g p8g p8g Mar 2] modest form when fourth in maiden at 2 yrs,
standout effort: tried in cheekpieces. *Robert Eddery*

VROOM (IRE) 4 ch.g. Poet's Voice 126 – Shivaree 88 (Rahy (USA) 115) [2017 81: f6g^3 **85**
f7g* f7m^2 f6g^4 f6d* f6g^2 t7.2g 7s^5 p7.5f p7.5f 6.1d^6 p6g^5 f5g^5 f6.1g^6 t6.1g* f6.1g Dec 21]
useful-looking gelding: fairly useful performer: won handicap at Southwell (apprentice) in
February, claimer at same course in April and handicap at Wolverhampton in December:
stays 7f: acts on all-weather: wears headgear: usually races prominently. *Gay Kelleway*

VUELA 4 ch.f. Duke of Marmalade (IRE) 132 – Victoire Finale (Peintre Celebre (USA) **92**
137) [2017 78p: 12m* 14m^4 11.8d^2 12d Sep 23] lengthy filly: fairly useful handicapper:
won at Doncaster in May: stays 1¾m: acts on tapeta, good to firm and good to soft going:
usually races close up. *Luca Cumani*

W

WAADY (IRE) 5 b.g. Approve (IRE) 112 – Anne Bonney 58 (Jade Robbery (USA) 121) **113**
[2017 114: 6m^6 5f 5d* 5.2m^4 5s^3 Oct 7] rangy gelding: smart performer: won minor event
at Leicester (by 1½ lengths from Kachy) in September: best form at 5f: acts on good to firm
and good to soft going: wears hood: has joined D. Watson, UAE. *John Gosden*

WAARIF (IRE) 4 b.g. Arcano (IRE) 122 – Indian Belle (IRE) 83 (Indian Ridge 123) **90**
[2017 85p: t8g^2 t8d^5 t10.2g^3 p8s^5 p10s t9.5d^4 Dec 27] fairly useful handicapper: won
maiden at Dundalk for Kevin Prendergast in 2016: placed at Newcastle in October and
November: stays 1¼m: acts on polytrack, tapeta and good to soft going: in cheekpieces last
3 starts: often wears tongue tie. *David O'Meara*

WADIGOR 4 b.c. Champs Elysees 124 – Haven's Wave (IRE) (Whipper (USA) 126) **113**
[2017 106p: p11g* 12m Jun 23] good-topped colt: smart form: won handicap at Kempton
(by 1½ lengths from Regicide) in May: excuses only other start in 2017: stays 11f: has
joined G. Selvaratnam in UAE. *Roger Varian*

WADILSAFA 2 b.c. (Feb 28) Frankel 147 – Rumoush (USA) 114 (Rahy (USA) 115) [2017 **91 p**
7s^2 Sep 8] fourth foal: half-brother to 2-y-o 7f winner (stays 10.5f) Muntazah (by Dubawi)
and 7f (including at 2 yrs) winner Talaayeb (by Dansili), both smart: dam, winner up to 9f
(2-y-o 1m winner) who stayed 14.6f, half-sister to high-class 1m-1½m winner Mawatheeq
and 1000 Guineas winner Ghanaati: 9/2, shaped well when second in maiden at Ascot (1¾
lengths behind Herculean) on debut: sure to progress. *Owen Burrows*

WADOOD (IRE) 3 b.c. Kodiac 112 – Cakestown Lady (IRE) 100 (Petorius 117) [2017 **81**
75: 5m^5 5.2m* 5m^4 t5g Oct 10] fairly useful handicapper: won at Yarmouth (by ½ length
from Miss Rosina) in June: raced only at 5f: acts on soft and good to firm going: tried in
hood: usually races close up: sold 3,500 gns in October. *Robert Cowell*

WAFEER (IRE) 2 b.c. (Feb 10) Equiano (FR) 127 – Star Approval (IRE) (Hawk Wing **77**
(USA) 136) [2017 6f^5 7s^4 5m^2 6.1d^4 Oct 11] fair form in minor events/maiden: stays 6f.
Richard Hannon

WAFY (IRE) 2 br.c. (Feb 28) Dubawi (IRE) 129 – Ghanaati (USA) 122 (Giant's Causeway **94**
(USA) 132) [2017 7d 7d* 8m Oct 14] good-bodied colt: fourth foal: brother to useful 7f/1m
winner Alnashama and half-brother to 2 winners, including useful 1m winner Afaak (by
Oasis Dream): dam, won 1000 Guineas and Coronation Stakes (also 2-y-o 7f winner), half-
sister to high-class 1m-1½m winner Mawatheeq: fairly useful form: won minor event at
Sandown (by 1½ lengths from Il Primo Sole) in September: should be suited by at least 1m.
Charles Hills

WAGGLE (IRE) 4 b.g. Acclamation 118 – Week End (Selkirk (USA) 129) [2017 –: p6g **–**
p8d 8m^4 Jun 20] no form: tried in blinkers. *Michael Wigham*

WAHAAB (IRE) 6 ch.g. Tamayuz 126 – Indian Ink (IRE) 122 (Indian Ridge 123) [2017 76: t8g t7.1g4 t7.2g 5.1s4 7.1g3 7.1g* 8.1s5 7s* 7v4 p7s t7.2g Dec 5] well-made gelding: fairly useful handicapper on turf, fair on all-weather: won at Chepstow in September and Leicester (apprentice, by 3¼ lengths from Showdance Kid) in October: left Iain Jardine after second start: stays 7f: acts on tapeta, soft and good to firm going: has worn headgear, including in 2017: wears tongue tie nowadays. *Sophie Leech* **83 a66**

WAHASH (IRE) 3 gr.c. Dark Angel (IRE) 113 – Delira (IRE) 75 (Namid 128) [2017 93: 10m4 10m5 8v2 7m2 6m 7d 7.9g Aug 25] compact colt: useful handicapper: second at Doncaster (head behind Me Too Nagasaki) in May and Epsom (length behind Juanito Chico) in June: stays 1¼m: acts on polytrack, good to firm and heavy going. *Richard Hannon* **104**

WAHIBA (GER) 4 b.f. Poet's Voice 126 – Walayta (GER) (Oasis Dream 129) [2017 70: p11g p8g6 7m* 6.1g6 7g4 t7.1s6 Sep 19] fair handicapper: won at Yarmouth in May: best effort at 7f: acts on good to firm going: front runner/races prominently. *Marco Botti* **75**

WAHOO 2 b.g. (Feb 18) Stimulation (IRE) 121 – Shohrah (IRE) 103 (Giant's Causeway (USA) 132) [2017 5m2 5g3 6g4 7g* 6g6 Oct 7] fair performer: won minor event at Thirsk in August: stays 7f: acts on good to firm going. *Michael Dods* **78**

WAITING A LOT (IRE) 3 b.f. Iffraaj 127 – Love Intrigue (IRE) 107 (Marju (IRE) 127) [2017 7.4m4 9.2s t9.5g6 t8.6gpu Nov 7] modest form: dead. *David O'Meara* **64**

WAITINGFORACHANCE 3 b.f. Sayif (IRE) 122 – Alice's Girl (Galileo (IRE) 134) [2017 7s May 19] rather leggy filly: third foal: dam unraced: 50/1, well held in maiden at Newbury. *Mick Channon* **–**

WAITING FOR RICHIE 4 b.g. Rail Link 132 – Heart of Hearts 86 (Oasis Dream 129) [2017 68: 14.6m3 14.5s 13.9m2 16.5m5 t12.4d4 t16.3g* 16g2 t16.3g3 Nov 15] fairly useful handicapper: won at Newcastle in September: stays 16.5f: acts on tapeta and firm going: front runner/races prominently. *Tom Tate* **81**

WAITING ROOM 2 ch.c. (Feb 6) Bated Breath 125 – Lily In Pink 104 (Sakhee (USA) 136) [2017 p8g Nov 1] 9/2, well held in minor event at Kempton. *James Tate* **–**

WAITOMO 3 b.f. Equiano (FR) 127 – Lucky Legs (IRE) 89 (Danehill Dancer (IRE) 117) [2017 6g6 6m Aug 22] second foal: sister to useful US Grade 3 8.5f winner Baciami Piccola (also 2-y-o 5f winner in Italy): dam 1m-1¼m winner: well held in maidens. *Charles Hills* **–**

WAJAAHA (IRE) 2 b.c. (Apr 2) New Approach (IRE) 132 – Thaahira (USA) 89 (Dynaformer (USA)) [2017 p7g3 Oct 5] fourth foal: half-brother to French winner up to 10.5f Manaasek (2-y-o 1m winner, by Raven's Pass) and 1½m winner Maghfoor (by Cape Cross): dam, 1¼m winner, out of Irish 1000 Guineas winner Mehthaaf: 7/1, third in minor event at Lingfield (9½ lengths behind Purser) in October: will be suited by 1m+: open to improvement. *Saeed bin Suroor* **70 p**

WALDGEIST 3 ch.c. Galileo (IRE) 134 – Waldlerche 109 (Monsun (GER) 124) [2017 111p: 9.9s2 10.4g2 12g4 12s2 11.9s4 Nov 1] close-coupled colt: very smart performer: won Criterium de Saint-Cloud at 2 yrs: in frame all starts in 2017, including in Prix du Jockey Club at Chantilly (short-head second to Brametot), Irish Derby at the Curragh (fourth to Capri), Cumberland Lodge Stakes at Ascot (neck second to Danehill Kodiac, losing a shoe) and Grosser Preis von Bayern at Munich (2 lengths fourth to Guignol): stays 1½m: acts on soft going. *A. Fabre, France* **122**

WALKABOUT (IRE) 5 b.g. Papal Bull 128 – Dainty Steps (IRE) 78 (Xaar 132) [2017 66: p10.7g6 t12.2g 8m 10.2m 10g Sep 2] modest maiden on Flat nowadays: best effort at 10.5f: best form on good going: tried in cheekpieces: fairly useful hurdler. *Gordon Elliott, Ireland* **58**

WALKING IN RHYTHM (IRE) 4 b.f. Lord Shanakill (USA) 121 – So Sweet (IRE) 97 (Cape Cross (IRE) 129) [2017 69: 8.3g t8.6g 8.3g6 t12.2g Jul 17] leggy filly: fair performer at 3 yrs, below form in 2017: stays 7f: acts on soft and good to firm going. *Barry Leavy* **53**

WALK ON WALTER (IRE) 2 b.g. (Apr 8) Footstepsinthesand 120 – Hajmah (IRE) 85 (Singspiel (IRE) 133) [2017 7v6 p6g4 t6.1m4 Oct 28] €26,000F, 60,000 2-y-o: second foal: half-brother to French 6f winner Hurricane Vicky (by Sir Prancealot): dam, 11.6f winner, out of smart performer up to 1½m Midnight Line: fair form: best effort when fourth in minor event at Kempton (2 lengths behind Sergio Leone) in October: should stay at least 7f: tried in hood: remains with potential. *David Simcock* **76 p**

WALLFLOWER (IRE) 2 b.f. (Apr 3) Thewayyouare (USA) 117 – Gaselee (USA) 83 (Toccet (USA) 118) [2017 t7.2g Dec 5] third foal: half-sister to French 10.5f winner Millepassi (by Holy Roman Emperor): dam, 9f-2m winner, half-sister to smart 1½m winner Sayadaw: 50/1, well held in minor event at Wolverhampton. *Rae Guest* **–**

WALL OF FIRE (IRE) 4 b.c. Canford Cliffs (IRE) 133 – Bright Sapphire (IRE) 55 **117**
(Galileo (IRE) 134) [2017 114: 15.9d^{6} 14.1g^{2} 13.4d^{4} 16f 13.3d^{2} 12g^{2} 15.9g Nov 7] close-coupled colt: smart performer: second in listed race at Nottingham (nose behind Elidor), Geoffrey Freer Stakes at Newbury (beaten ¾ length by Defoe) and Group 2 Herbert Power Stakes at Caulfield (length behind Lord Fandango): behind in Melbourne Cup at Flemington final outing: stays 14.6f: acts on soft and good to firm going: wears headgear. *Hugo Palmer*

WALSINGHAM GRANGE (USA) 4 b.g. Paddy O'Prado (USA) 121 – Mambo Queen **80**
(USA) (Kingmambo (USA) 125) [2017 82: 12v^{4} 12s^{6} Oct 28] strong gelding: fairly useful handicapper: stays 1½m: acts on heavy going: tried in cheekpieces. *Pam Sly*

WALTON STREET 3 b.g. Cape Cross (IRE) 129 – Brom Felinity (AUS) (Encosta de **110 p**
Lago (AUS)) [2017 10d* 11.2s* 14g^{4} Aug 26] fifth foal: half-brother to 5f/6f winner Iriomote (by Exceed And Excel) and 6f-9f winner Macavity (by Street Cry), both in Australia: dam, Australian 5f/1¼m winner, sister to Australian Group 1 1m winner Delago Brom: smart form: won maiden at Pontefract (by 1¾ lengths from Roddy) in July and handicap at Goodwood (by 2 lengths from Londinium) in August: fourth in listed race at Goodwood (4¾ lengths behind Call To Mind) final start: stays 1¾m: likely to progress further. *Charlie Appleby*

WANEEN (IRE) 4 b.g. Approve (IRE) 112 – Million All Day (IRE) 57 (Daylami (IRE) **72**
138) [2017 83: f5s p6g^{4} t5.1g f5m p6g f5g p6g t5.1g Nov 20] fairly useful handicapper, below form in 2017: stays 7f: acts on polytrack, tapeta, best turf form on heavy going. *John Butler*

WANNABE FRIENDS 4 ch.g. Dubawi (IRE) 129 – Wannabe Posh (IRE) 107 (Grand **87**
Lodge (USA) 125) [2017 74p: 8.3m^{2} 10.2g^{4} 10m 8m^{3} 7s^{4} 7g* p8s 7d^{3} 8s^{6} Oct 15] sturdy gelding: fairly useful handicapper: won at Goodwood (by 2¼ lengths from Sheikspear) in August: placed at Nottingham in April and Newmarket in September: left Luca Cumani after second start: stays 8.5f: acts on good to firm and good to soft going: sometimes slowly away. *Richard Hughes*

WANNABE LIKE YOU 3 b.g. Sepoy (AUS) 129 – Wannabe Posh (IRE) 107 (Grand **65**
Lodge (USA) 125) [2017 8m^{4} 8g p7g^{4} p10s^{3} p8g^{5} f8.1g Dec 22] compact gelding: fair maiden: left William Haggas after second start: stays 1m: acts on polytrack: in cheekpieces last 2 starts. *Archie Watson*

WANT THE FAIRYTALE 4 b.f. Mount Nelson 125 – Tattercoats (FR) (Whywhywhy **57**
(USA) 115) [2017 66: t13.9g^{5} Apr 29] fair handicapper: stays 1½m: acts on polytrack and tapeta: usually races towards rear: fair form over hurdles. *Alan King*

WAPPING (USA) 4 b.g. Smart Strike (CAN) 121 – Exciting Times (FR) (Jeune Homme **95**
(USA) 120) [2017 96p: 10.1g^{3} 10g^{2} 10.2f* 11.9g* Jun 12] stocky gelding: useful handicapper: won at Bath (by ¾ length from Prendergast Hill) in May and Brighton (by neck from Impressive Day) in June: stays 1½m: acts on firm going: in blinkers last 3 starts: sold to join Jamie Osborne 16,000 gns in November: quirky sort. *David Lanigan*

WAQAAS 3 b.g. Showcasing 117 – Red Mischief (IRE) 72 (Red Clubs (IRE) 125) [2017 **97**
93: 6d 6d^{5} 6d^{3} Oct 6] useful handicapper: third at Ascot (2 lengths behind Nobly Born) in October: will stay 7f: acts on good to firm and good to soft going. *Charles Hills*

WAQT (IRE) 3 b.g. Acclamation 118 – Needles And Pins (IRE) 104 (Fasliyev (USA) 120) **76**
[2017 69p: 6g^{2} 7g 7.1g 6d^{5} p7g^{2} p8g p7g Dec 28] lengthy gelding: fair maiden: stays 7f: acts on polytrack and good to soft going. *Marcus Tregoning*

WAR AT SEA (IRE) 3 gr.g. Mastercraftsman (IRE) 129 – Swirling (IRE) (Galileo (IRE) **83**
134) [2017 67p: t8d^{2} t9.5g^{2} 12m 10g^{4} 10.1d^{3} 9.1m^{3} 11.6d^{4} p12g^{5} Oct 18] fairly useful maiden: placed 4 times in 2017: stays 1½m: acts on polytrack, tapeta and good to firm going: in hood last 5 starts: sold to join Ali Stronge 35,000 gns in October. *David Simcock*

WARBA (IRE) 3 ch.f. Intense Focus (USA) 117 – Have A Heart (IRE) 87 (Daggers Drawn **62**
(USA) 114) [2017 63: t7.1m p6g p5g p7g^{2} p7g^{3} p7m^{2} t6.1d Dec 16] modest maiden: stays 7f: acts on polytrack: tried in cheekpieces: wears tongue tie: usually races prominently. *Mohamed Moubarak*

WAR BRIGADE (FR) 3 b.g. Manduro (GER) 135 – Adjudicate (Dansili 127) [2017 **80**
11.6m^{pu} 10.2d 12v^{2} 12s^{4} 12v^{4} Oct 23] €140,000Y: neat gelding: first foal: dam unraced sister to useful French/Australian 11f-1¾m winner Permit: fair maiden: stays 1½m: acts on heavy going: sometimes in hood: usually races towards rear: sold to join Ian Williams 40,000 gns in November. *David Simcock*

WAR CHIEF 3 ch.g. Aqlaam 125 – My Colleen (USA) (Discreet Cat (USA) 127) [2017 83p: 8.1m^{2} 9.1m^{3} 9m Jun 17] useful-looking gelding: fairly useful handicapper: placed at Chepstow and Goodwood in May: stays 9f: acts on good to firm and good to soft going: in hood last 2 starts: tends to start slowly/race freely. *Alan King* **88**

WAR DECREE (USA) 3 b.c. War Front (USA) 119 – Royal Decree (USA) (Street Cry (IRE) 130) [2017 115p: 8m^{6} 10.4g^{5} p10.7g* a10f 9.9g Dec 10] well-made colt: very smart performer: won Diamond Stakes at Dundalk (easily by 2¼ lengths from Absolute Blast) in September: 2½ lengths fifth to Brametot in Prix du Jockey Club at Chantilly on second outing: below form in Breeders' Cup Classic at Del Mar and Hong Kong Cup at Sha Tin last 2 starts: stays 10.7f: acts on polytrack and good to firm going: often races prominently. *Aidan O'Brien, Ireland* **120**

WAR DEPARTMENT (IRE) 4 b.g. Frozen Power (IRE) 108 – On My Kness (FR) (Fasliyev (USA) 120) [2017 93: f7g^{2} p7d t7.1d^{4} t7.1d* t7.1g^{2} f7d^{6} 7m^{4} 8g^{3} t7.1s* 6g p8g f7.1g Oct 22] strong gelding: useful handicapper: won at Newcastle in March and June (by 1½ lengths from Florencio): stays 1m: acts on tapeta and good to firm going: wears headgear. *Keith Dalgleish* **100**

WAR DRUMS 3 b.g. Authorized (IRE) 133 – Crystal Swan (IRE) 88 (Dalakhani (IRE) 133) [2017 11.6g May 24] third foal: half-brother to 1½m winner (stays 1¾m) Blenheim Warrior (by Galileo): dam, 1¼m winner who stayed 1½m, half-sister to useful US Grade 2 8.5f winner Grande Melody: 33/1, seventh in maiden at Lingfield (6 lengths behind Cross Step) in May: should progress. *Luca Cumani* **79 p**

WARDY (IRE) 3 b.c. Dandy Man (IRE) 123 – Why Now 81 (Dansili 127) [2017 6d^{5} 7d^{6} p7g^{6} f8.1g Nov 16] close-coupled colt: fair form: best effort at 6f. *Peter Chapple-Hyam* **68**

WARFARE 8 b.g. Soviet Star (USA) 128 – Fluffy 67 (Efisio 120) [2017 83: t8g^{3} p10g^{6} t8g t8g^{2} f8.1g^{4} t10.2g^{6} 10.2d 9.9s^{5} 9s^{5} t12.4s t10.2s 9.9v Sep 26] deep-girthed gelding: type to carry condition: fair handicapper: stays 10.5f: acts on all-weather and soft going: has worn headgear, including last 4 starts: sometimes slowly away. *Tim Fitzgerald* **75**

WAR GLORY (IRE) 4 b.g. Canford Cliffs (IRE) 133 – Attracted To You (IRE) 92 (Hurricane Run (IRE) 134) [2017 97: p7g^{2} p7g^{2} 8m^{5} 7g^{4} 7m^{5} 7v^{3} 7g^{2} 7.6g^{2} 7d^{4} 7g Oct 17] sturdy gelding: useful handicapper: second at Lingfield (twice) in April, Newmarket in August and Chester (½ length behind Penwortham) in September: stays 1m: acts on polytrack, tapeta and good to firm going: usually races prominently. *Richard Hannon* **103**

WARLEGGAN (FR) 3 gr.g. Rajsaman (FR) 121 – Nostalchia (FR) (Genereux Genie 111) [2017 45: 7.2m 6m 8m 6d 5s 5s^{5} 6s 6g 6s^{4} Aug 5] poor maiden: stays 6f: often wears headgear. *Linda Perratt* **32**

WARM LOVE 3 ch.f. Dutch Art 126 – Irish Song (FR) (Singspiel (IRE) 133) [2017 71: 10m^{3} 9.8g 9.8d^{5} 10.9g* 12.4g^{6} 10.9s^{5} 12.4g 11.4d^{2} 10.4g* Nov 29] fair performer: left David O'Meara after third start: won maiden at Gramat in August and handicap at Toulouse in November: stays 11.5f: acts on good to firm and good to soft going: in headgear 3 of last 4 starts: usually races close up. *S. Brogi, France* **76**

WARM OASIS 3 gr.g. Oasis Dream 129 – Warling (IRE) 101 (Montjeu (IRE) 137) [2017 10g^{6} p12g^{2} p12g^{4} t12.4d* Dec 16] 200,000Y: second foal: brother to useful 2-y-o 7f winner Hayadh: dam, 11f winner who stayed 14.6f, closely related to smart French performer up to 1½m War Is War: fairly useful form: won maiden at Newcastle in December: stays 12.5f. *James Fanshawe* **86**

WARM ORDER 6 b.m. Assertive 121 – Even Hotter 63 (Desert Style (IRE) 121) [2017 54: t5.1m t5.1g p5g^{5} Mar 16] modest handicapper, below form in 2017: stays 5.5f: acts on polytrack, tapeta and good to firm going: sometimes wears headgear: tried in tongue tie. *Tony Carroll* **34**

WARM THE VOICE (IRE) 2 b.g. (Mar 30) Vocalised (USA) 114 – Heir Today (IRE) 69 (Princely Heir (IRE) 111) [2017 8g^{3} 7v* 7d* 8v* 8s^{3} Sep 24] brother to 1m winner Vocal Heir: dam 2-y-o 6f winner: useful performer: won maiden at Galway (by 2¾ lengths from Shifted Strategy) in August, and nurseries at the Curragh (by ½ length from Medal of Honour) later same month and Listowel (by ½ length from Drombeg Dream) in September: third in Beresford Stakes at Naas (2½ lengths behind Saxon Warrior) final start: stays 1m: acts on heavy going: gelded, and sent to Hong Kong. *Brendan Duke, Ireland* **108**

WARM WORDS 3 b.f. Poet's Voice 126 – Limber Up (IRE) (Dansili 127) [2017 80: f8g^{4} f8g^{3} Jan 30] compact filly: maiden, fair form at best: best effort at 1m: acts on fibresand: tried in blinkers: usually races prominently: sold 12,000 gns in February, sent to Greece. *Ralph Beckett* **63**

WAROFINDEPENDENCE (USA) 5 b.g. War Front (USA) 119 – My Dear Annie (USA) (Smart Strike (CAN) 121) [2017 82: 8s^5 Aug 25] lengthy gelding: fairly useful maiden, well below best sole outing in 2017: stays 1m: acts on polytrack: has worn headgear: tried in tongue tie. *John O'Shea* **54**

WAR OF SUCCESSION 3 b.g. Casamento (IRE) 118 – Rohlindi 69 (Red Ransom (USA)) [2017 93p: 7.1g^3 8v^5 8.5m* p8d 9.9d p8g p7g^6 t9.5g Dec 22] fairly useful performer: won maiden at Beverley (by 2 lengths from Luminous) in June: left Andrew Balding after third start: stays 8.5f: acts on polytrack and firm going: tried in blinkers: temperament under suspicion. *Tony Newcombe* **84**

WARP FACTOR (IRE) 4 b.g. The Carbon Unit (USA) 106 – Storminateacup (IRE) 74 (Galileo (IRE) 134) [2017 89: 8.5v 8g^5 10m^3 12.3d^2 11.9g^3 12.1g^5 13.1g^3 10d^6 15.9g 8v* Oct 8] useful handicapper: won at Navan (apprentice, by 3½ lengths from Bigger And Better) in October: stays 13f: acts on good to firm and heavy going: has worn blinkers, including final start: sold 50,000 gns, sent to USA. *John Patrick Shanahan, Ireland* **95**

WARRIOR OF LIGHT (IRE) 6 b.g. High Chaparral (IRE) 132 – Strawberry Fledge (USA) (Kingmambo (USA) 125) [2017 14g^4 15.9g^6 18g 12m 11.4g 14s^6 Jul 26] attractive gelding: useful handicapper: stayed 1½m: acted on polytrack and firm going: tried in headgear: dead. *Brendan Powell* **100**

WARRIOR PRINCE 4 ch.g. Sakhee (USA) 136 – Queen of Iceni 81 (Erhaab (USA) 127) [2017 81p: p10s^5 11.9s 11.4d^5 p14d Sep 21] sturdy, workmanlike gelding: fair maiden: should stay at least 1¼m: best form on good going: tried in tongue tie. *Ed Dunlop* **72**

WARRIOR'S SPIRIT (IRE) 3 b.g. Requinto (IRE) 109 – Sandbox Two (IRE) (Foxhound (USA) 103) [2017 83p: 7g 8s^4 7.2s^6 7g p8g^6 p8g Sep 26] tall gelding: has scope: fairly useful handicapper: stays 7f: acts on good to soft going: usually races nearer last than first: sold to join David O'Meara 6,000 gns in November. *Richard Hannon* **86**

WARRIOR'S VALLEY 2 b.c. (Apr 11) Mayson 124 – Sand And Deliver 67 (Royal Applause 124) [2017 5s 5s t5.1g Nov 7] first foal: dam, maiden (raced only at 5f), sister to very smart 7f/1m performer Finjaan: little impact in minor events: capable of better. *David C. Griffiths* **– p**

WARSAAN 2 b.g. (Apr 16) Oasis Dream 129 – Tanfidh 93 (Marju (IRE) 127) [2017 6m^2 6g^3 p7s^6 7s^5 Oct 10] fifth foal: brother to 7f/1m winner Kestrel Dot Com and half-brother to ungenuine 11f winner (stays 2m) Nadaitak (by Teofilo): dam, 1¼m winner, out of useful close relative/half-sister to Nayef, Nashwan and Unfuwain: fair form: stays 7f: remains open to improvement. *Owen Burrows* **78 p**

WARSAW ROAD (IRE) 3 ch.g. Zebedee 113 – Warda (Pivotal 124) [2017 8s^4 8d 7m* 7d 7m* 7m* Sep 23] 45,000Y: first foal: dam unraced half-sister to useful French winner up to 1¾m Galiteo out of useful 2-y-o 7f winner Queen of Poland: fairly useful performer: won maiden at Lingfield in June, and handicaps at Yarmouth in August and Newbury (by ½ length from Esprit de Corps) in September: stays 7f: acts on good to firm going. *Luca Cumani* **93**

WAR SECRETARY (USA) 3 b.c. War Front (USA) 119 – Upperline (USA) (Maria's Mon (USA) 121) [2017 91p: p7g* 7m Apr 22] rangy colt: useful form: won listed race at Dundalk (by neck from Noivado) in April: last in Greenham Stakes at Newbury 10 days later: stays 7f: in tongue tie last 3 starts. *Aidan O'Brien, Ireland* **104**

WAR WHISPER (IRE) 4 b.c. Royal Applause 124 – Featherweight (IRE) 89 (Fantastic Light (USA) 134) [2017 85: 6m^3 7m 6.1m 6.1m p6g Oct 3] sturdy colt: fairly useful handicapper: third at Ascot in May: stays 6f: acts on good to firm going: usually races in rear: sold to join Paul Midgley 4,000 gns in October. *Richard Hannon* **86**

WASATCH RANGE 3 b.c. High Chaparral (IRE) 132 – Pearl City (IRE) (Zamindar (USA) 116) [2017 82p: 10.3g^4 10m* 11s 11.4m^3 Jul 10] strong, attractive colt: useful performer: won maiden at Windsor (by short head from Janszoon) in April: third in handicap there (2¼ lengths behind Harebell) in July: stays 11.5f: acts on good to firm going: tried in blinkers: sold 21,000 gns later in July: remains with potential. *John Gosden* **95 p**

WASEEM FARIS (IRE) 8 b.g. Exceed And Excel (AUS) 126 – Kissing Time 79 (Lugana Beach 116) [2017 92: 5m^2 5f^6 5g^6 5f^6 5d^4 5d 5m* 5.1d^4 6.1m Oct 16] lengthy gelding: fairly useful handicapper: won at Salisbury (by head from Trick of The Light) in August: stays 6f: acts on polytrack and any turf going: has worn headgear. *Ken Cunningham-Brown* **89**

WASHEEK (IRE) 2 b.c. (Apr 25) Kodiac 112 – Starring (FR) 74 (Ashkalani (IRE) 128) [2017 5g^4 Apr 15] 7/2, fourth in minor event at Musselburgh: dead. *Mark Johnston* **53**

WASHINGTON BLUE 3 b.f. Rip Van Winkle (IRE) 134 – Powder Blue 64 (Daylami (IRE) 138) [2017 77: p8g Jan 25] fair at 2 yrs, below form sole outing in 2017: stays 1m: acts on polytrack and good to soft going: in headgear last 2 starts. *Clive Cox* **–**

WASHINGTON DC (IRE) 4 b.c. Zoffany (IRE) 121 – How's She Cuttin' (IRE) 99 (Shinko Forest (IRE)) [2017 121: 6d 5m* 5m^2 5f^6 5f 5s^5 6m* 5g 6s 5f Nov 4] small, well-made colt: smart performer: won listed race at Navan (by neck from Ardhoomey) in April and Phoenix Sprint Stakes at the Curragh (by ½ length from Cougar Mountain) in August: neck second to Marsha in Palace House Stakes at Newmarket on third start, but struggled in better company most other outings: has won over 7f, best form at 5f/6f: acts on polytrack, firm and good to soft going: wears tongue tie, also blinkered last 5 starts: races off pace. *Aidan O'Brien, Ireland* **118**

WASIM (IRE) 2 b.c. (Apr 1) Acclamation 118 – Quiet Protest (USA) (Kingmambo (USA) 125) [2017 6.5m* 7g^3 7g 6s^4 a7f^3 Dec 7] 55,000Y, 38,000 2-y-o: tall colt: has scope: fifth foal: half-brother to 3 winners, including 9.5f/10.4f winner Demonstration (by Cape Cross) and 1¼m winner Just For You (by Fastnet Rock): dam US 1m winner: fairly useful performer: won minor event at Doncaster in July: third in similar event at Haydock in July and nursery at Meydan in December: best effort at 7f: acts on dirt and good to firm going: tried in hood. *Ismail Mohammed* **89**

WASM 3 ch.g. Exceed And Excel (AUS) 126 – Finchley (Machiavellian (USA) 123) [2017 8.3g 10.2g 7s* 8.3v^4 8g 9s^3 t8g^6 8.3g Nov 1] 130,000Y: good-topped gelding: fourth foal: dam unraced half-sister to smart winner up to 1¾m Songcraft: fairly useful performer: won maiden at Doncaster (by 1¼ lengths from Sunday Prospect) in July: third in handicap at Ayr in October: left Simon Crisford after second start: stays 9f: acts on soft going: tried in tongue tie: often starts slowly, usually races in rear: sold to join Ruth Carr 14,000 gns in November: temperamental. *Roger Fell* **80 §**

WASSAIL 4 b.f. Shamardal (USA) 129 – Gower Song 114 (Singspiel (IRE) 133) [2017 46: 13f^3 14m* 13f^5 13d^2 p12g 14.1d p16g Oct 12] useful-looking filly: modest handicapper: won at Nottingham in June: stays 1¾m: acts on good to firm and good to soft going: tried in headgear: usually races prominently. *Ed de Giles* **59**

WASSEEM (IRE) 4 ch.g. Approve (IRE) 112 – Vintage Escape (IRE) 84 (Cyrano de Bergerac 120) [2017 67: p7m^5 Jan 9] modest maiden in Britain: stays 8.5f: acts on polytrack and tapeta: wears headgear/tongue tie: sold 8,500 gns in February, sent to be trained in the Netherlands, won handicap at Dusseldorf in September. *Simon Crisford* **61**

WASTED SUNSETS (FR) 3 b.f. Myboycharlie (IRE) 118 – Freezing (USA) (Bering 136) [2017 p7g^4 p10d^6 Sep 28] €32,000Y: half-sister to several winners in France, including 7.5f-1¼m winner (including at 2 yrs) Polarix (by Linamix) and 11f-12.5f winner Lando Blue (by Lando), both useful: dam French 1m winner: well held in maidens: wears tongue tie. *John Berry* **–**

WATAR DAY 3 b.f. Watar (IRE) 117 – Hopeshedoes (USA) 53 (Johannesburg (USA) 127) [2017 p7g^5 p8g p8g Dec 6] first foal: dam maiden: well held in maidens. *Linda Jewell* **–**

WATCHABLE 7 ch.g. Pivotal 124 – Irresistible 98 (Cadeaux Genereux 131) [2017 112: 6g 6g 6g^4 5g^5 6g p5g^4 p5g^5 6m^4 5g^3 6m^4 p6s^6 5.4d t6.1g^4 Oct 7] workmanlike gelding: useful handicapper: third at York (2 lengths behind Copper Knight) in May: stays 6.5f: acts on polytrack, tapeta, soft and good to firm going: wears headgear: usually races prominently. *David O'Meara* **103**

WATCHING SPIRITS 2 br.g. (Feb 24) Harbour Watch (IRE) 121 – Naayla (IRE) 85 (Invincible Spirit (IRE) 121) [2017 5m 6v^5 6d t6.1m^3 p6s^3 Nov 16] modest maiden: left Ann Duffield after fourth start: stays 6f: acts on polytrack and tapeta: often races prominently. *Michael Appleby* **58**

WATCH TAN 2 gr.f. (Mar 22) Harbour Watch (IRE) 121 – High Tan (High Chaparral (IRE) 132) [2017 p6s 5.1m 5s^5 t6.1g^2 p6g 7d^4 Sep 12] third foal: half-sister to 7f (including at 2 yrs) to 1¼m winner Boutan (by Tobougg): dam unraced: modest maiden: best effort at 6f: acts on tapeta: in hood last 3 starts. *George Baker* **54**

WATERCLOCK (IRE) 8 ch.g. Notnowcato 128 – Waterfall One 62 (Nashwan (USA) 135) [2017 82§: 21.6m^4 16.1f^{pu} Jul 18] rather leggy gelding: fairly useful handicapper, below form in 2017: stayed 2¼m: acted on good to firm going: wore headgear: temperamental: dead. *Micky Hammond* **66 §**

WATERSMEET 6 gr.g. Dansili 127 – Under The Rainbow 107 (Fantastic Light (USA) 134) [2017 110: t12.4g^3 p12g* p16g* p15.8g^2 18.6m^6 18m p14g^2 t16.3d^3 Dec 16] good-topped gelding: smart performer: won minor events at Lingfield (by 2 lengths from Calling Out) in February and Chelmsford (by 3 lengths from Winning Story) in March: placed on **112**

4 other occasions, including in handicap at Chelmsford in November: stays 2¼m: acts on polytrack, tapeta and firm going: front runner/races prominently, usually travels strongly. *Mark Johnston*

WATERVILLE DANCER (IRE) 3 b.g. Nathaniel (IRE) 129 – Tobiano (USA) (Mt **87**
Livermore (USA)) [2017 t9.5g^{3} p10g^{2} 11.8g^{5} t12.2g^{3} 14.2v^{2} 12v^{2} p16g^{5} 14.2s^{4} Oct 9] €50,000Y: half-brother to several winners abroad, including French 11f-13.5f winner Aioros (by Hernando) and French 1m-10.5f winner Tau (2-y-o 9f/9.5f winner, by Lemon Drop Kid): dam, French maiden, out of sister to Sadler's Wells: fairly useful maiden: second in handicap at Salisbury in July and maiden at Ffos Las in August: stays 1¾m: acts on polytrack, tapeta, best turf form on heavy going: tried in cheekpieces. *Richard Hughes*

WATHEEQA (USA) 2 b.f. (Mar 2) More Than Ready (USA) 120 – Tafaneen (USA) 74 **67 p**
(Dynaformer (USA)) [2017 p7g^{5} Oct 18] second foal: half-sister to useful 1¼m winner (stays 1½m) Tamleek (by Hard Spun): dam, maiden (stayed 1½m), out of US Grade 3 8.5f winner Cozzy Corner: 5/1, looked unlucky not to finish closer when fifth in minor event at Kempton (3¾ lengths behind Revalue) in October, hampered start: will stay 1m+: sure to progress. *Roger Varian*

WATHEER 2 ch.g. (Jan 30) Leroidesanimaux (BRZ) 127 – Sunset Shore 84 (Oasis Dream **81**
129) [2017 6f^{4} p7s* 8g Aug 25] 15,000F: first foal: dam, 2-y-o 5.7f winner, half-sister to smart performers Songerie (up to 14.6f) and Souvenance (stayed 2¼m): fairly useful form: won minor event at Chelmsford (by ¾ length from Barbarianatthegate) in July: stays 7f. *Marcus Tregoning*

WATTABOUTSTEVE 6 b.g. Araafa (IRE) 128 – Angel Kate (IRE) 81 (Invincible Spirit **49**
(IRE) 121) [2017 55: p5m p6g^{3} p5g May 5] sturdy gelding: poor maiden: stays 6f: acts on polytrack and fibresand. *Ralph Smith*

WAVES (IRE) 3 b.f. Born To Sea (IRE) 117 – Johannesburg Cat (USA) 88 (Johannesburg **75**
(USA) 127) [2017 61: f6g^{5} 8d* 8.2d^{5} 10.2m^{6} 8g 8v^{3} 8.2v^{4} Sep 25] fair handicapper: won at Bath in May: stays 1m: acts on good to firm and heavy going: tried in hood. *Eve Johnson Houghton*

WAX AND WANE 2 b.c. (Mar 7) Maxios 123 – Moonavvara (IRE) (Sadler's Wells (USA) **90**
132) [2017 7s^{6} 7.8v* 8v* Oct 12] 20,000Y: half-brother to several winners, including useful 2-y-o 6f winner Moon Pearl (by Johannesburg) and French 1m winner Beret (by Sageburg): dam unraced half-sister to Moyglare Stud Stakes/Prix Marcel Boussac winner Rumplestiltskin (herself dam of Yorkshire Oaks winner Tapestry) and to dam of Dubai Turf winner Real Steel: fairly useful form: won maiden at Carlisle (by ¾ length from Soldier To Follow) in September and minor event at Ayr (by 1¾ lengths from Lynwood Gold) in October: stays 1m. *K. R. Burke*

WAY OF WISDOM 2 b.g. (Mar 26) Lonhro (AUS) 128 – La Pelegrina (USA) (Redoute's **83**
Choice (AUS)) [2017 5m* 6m^{2} 6g t6.1g^{2} Aug 10] useful-looking gelding: third foal: half-brother to 2-y-o 7f winner Albernathy and 9f winner Pilgrim's Treasure (both useful and by Dubawi): dam, placed up to 9.5f in France, sister to very smart Australian Group 1 6f-12.5f winner Miss Finland: fairly useful form: won maiden at Newmarket (by neck from Kit Marlowe) in May: stays 6f. *Charlie Appleby*

WAYSIDE MAGIC 4 b.g. Thewayyouare (USA) 117 – Poppy's Rose 85 (Diktat 126) **–**
[2017 58: t10.2d f12g 15.9m May 11] maiden, behind in handicaps in 2017: often wears headgear: tried in tongue tie: front runner/races prominently. *Neville Bycroft*

WAY UP HIGH 5 b.m. Getaway (GER) 127 – High Life (Kayf Tara 130) [2017 t7.1g f8g **–**
t9.5g p8g^{4} t8.6g p8m Mar 29] third foal: dam ungenuine winning hurdler: no form, including in bumpers: in headgear last 2 starts. *Steve Flook*

WAZIN 2 b.f. (Apr 30) Dutch Art 126 – Azameera (IRE) 96 (Azamour (IRE) 130) [2017 **71**
p6g^{3} t6.1g^{4} Nov 18] 20,000Y: second foal: dam, 7f (including at 2 yrs) and 1m winner, sister to US Grade 3 8.5f winner No Explaining: fair form: better effort when third in minor event at Chelmsford (1¼ lengths behind Etisalat) in November. *Simon Crisford*

WEALTH TAX 4 gr.g. Canford Cliffs (IRE) 133 – Firoza (FR) (King's Best (USA) 132) **89**
[2017 76: p11g^{5} 10s t7.1s^{3} p8s* p8s 8.3v* 8v* 9.2s^{6} 8s^{6} 9d 8.1d^{5} Oct 23] fairly useful handicapper: won at Chelmsford in June, and at Nottingham and Sandown (by length from High Draw) in August: stays 8.5f: acts on polytrack and tapeta, best turf form on heavy going: sold 18,000 gns, sent to Spain. *Ed Dunlop*

WEAPON OF CHOICE (IRE) 9 b.g. Iffraaj 127 – Tullawadgeen (IRE) (Sinndar (IRE) **–**
134) [2017 77: 9s Aug 7] lengthy gelding: fair handicapper, well held sole outing on Flat in 2017: stays 10.5f: acts on polytrack and any turf going: has worn headgear, including last 3 starts: has worn tongue tie, including last 4 starts: winning hurdler. *Dianne Sayer*

WEARDIDITALLGORONG 5 b.m. Fast Company (IRE) 126 – Little Oz (IRE) 71 **67**
(Red Ransom (USA)) [2017 67: t12.2m^4 9.9g 10d^3 10d^2 10.2g t9.5g^3 Dec 2] sparely-made mare: fair handicapper: stays 1¼m: acts on tapeta and soft going: wears headgear. *Des Donovan, Ireland*

WE ARE THE WORLD 2 b.g. (Feb 27) Sir Percy 129 – Emerald Sea 73 (Green Desert **80**
(USA) 127) [2017 6m^3 7m 7.4g^3 p8g* p8g^6 Sep 9] 13,500F, €22,000Y: angular gelding: first foal: dam maiden (raced at 6f/7f): fairly useful performer: won minor event at Kempton in August: stays 1m: acts on polytrack: in cheekpieces last 2 starts: front runner/races prominently. *Archie Watson*

WEAR IT WELL 2 b.f. (Feb 19) Kodiac 112 – Choosey Girl (IRE) (Choisir (AUS) 126) **75**
[2017 6m 6.1g^4 6s* 5d^5 Oct 11] £32,000Y: fifth foal: half-sister to 6f winner Bay Mirage (by Kheleyf): dam, of little account, half-sister to smart/ungenuine winner up to 1½m Halicarnassus: fair form: won maiden at Brighton in September: stays 6f. *Henry Candy*

WEATHER FRONT (USA) 4 ch.g. Stormy Atlantic (USA) – Kiswahili 105 (Selkirk **67**
(USA) 129) [2017 84: t8d^6 10g t8g t8d Nov 4] tall gelding: fairly useful at 3 yrs, below that level in 2017: stays 1m: acts on polytrack and good to soft going: usually in headgear nowadays: sometimes slowly away: temperament under suspicion. *Karen McLintock*

WEDDING BREAKFAST (IRE) 3 ch.f. Casamento (IRE) 118 – Fair Countenance **68**
(IRE) 72 (Almutawakel 126) [2017 t8.6g^2 p10g^5 t9.5g^2 t8.6g 8g Aug 15] €11,000F, £26,000Y: third foal: dam, 9f winner, half-sister to useful winner up to 1m Icesolator: fair maiden: left Hugo Palmer after fourth start: stays 9.5f: acts on tapeta: tried in hood. *Richard Ford*

WEDDING PHOTO (USA) 3 b.f. Lonhro (AUS) 128 – Well At The Top (IRE) (Sadler's **61 p**
Wells (USA) 132) [2017 p8g^6 Sep 26] $230,000Y: half-sister to several winners in North/South America, including US 1m/8.5f winner Top Surprize (by Pure Prize): dam, US maiden (third at 1m), half-sister to smart winner up to 9f Tiger Shark: 2/1, sixth in maiden at Chelmsford (7 lengths behind Kitty Boo) in September: should do better. *Saeed bin Suroor*

WEDGEWOOD ESTATES 6 ch.m. Assertive 121 – Heaven 84 (Reel Buddy (USA) **63**
118) [2017 65: p6d^3 t6g p6g^{pu} p6g^6 6m^4 6g^3 5.7f^3 5.7f^2 7m 6v p7m Nov 25] modest **a52**
handicapper: stays 7f: acts on polytrack, tapeta and firm going. *Tony Carroll*

WEDGEWOOD WONDER 3 b.f. Medicean 128 – Katya Kabanova (Sadler's Wells **–**
(USA) 132) [2017 –: 5.7m^5 Jun 2] well held in maidens. *Tony Carroll*

WEE BOGUS 4 b.g. Multiplex 114 – Silver Gyre (IRE) 65 (Silver Hawk (USA) 123) **48**
[2017 9.2s 10d^4 10g^5 12.5m t16.3s^6 14s t12.4d^5 Oct 24] poor maiden: in cheekpieces last 3 starts. *Alistair Whillans*

WEE JOCK (IRE) 3 b.c. Pour Moi (IRE) 125 – Wee Mad Snout (IRE) (Soviet Star **69**
(USA) 128) [2017 7v^{ro} 7.5s 8m 6m 5.8m 5s* 5s* 5s Jul 29] fair performer: won handicaps at Hamilton in June and July: best form at 5f: acted on soft going: tried in headgear: front runner: dead. *John Patrick Shanahan, Ireland*

WEEKENDER 3 b.c. Frankel 147 – Very Good News (USA) (Empire Maker (USA) 129) **114 p**
[2017 74P: p10g* 10.2f^3 10m* 12m^2 14.2d^2 Oct 6] smart performer: won maiden at Chelmsford in April and handicap at Newmarket (by neck from Monticello) in June: also first past post in listed race at Ascot in October, but demoted for causing interference: stays 1¾m: acts on polytrack, firm and good to soft going: usually responds generously to pressure: open to further improvement. *John Gosden*

WEEKEND OFFENDER (FR) 4 ch.g. Lope de Vega (IRE) 125 – Huroof (IRE) 87 **105**
(Pivotal 124) [2017 98: 8.3g^3 8.3s^{pu} 7.9m^6 10d^2 10d* 10.3m 9d 10.3g 10s Oct 28] useful handicapper: won at Ayr (by 1¾ lengths from Royal Regent) in August: second there (½ length behind Euro Nightmare) in July: stays 1¼m: acts on firm and soft going: sold 44,000 gns in October. *Kevin Ryan*

WEELLAN 2 ch.g. (Jan 24) Mayson 124 – Regal Salute 91 (Medicean 128) [2017 6m^3 6s^2 **78**
t7.1s^2 7m 7.4s^3 7.2g^2 t8s^2 7.4v^4 t8g^4 Oct 20] fair maiden: stays 1m: acts on tapeta and soft going: tried in cheekpieces: often leads. *John Quinn*

WEETON (IRE) 2 br.c. (Apr 20) Society Rock (IRE) 126 – Petite Boulangere (IRE) **80**
(Namid 128) [2017 5s^2 5d 5g^4 p6g^4 5v* Sep 26] £18,000 2-y-o: sixth foal: half-brother to 3 winning sprinters, including 2-y-o 5f winners Sahreej (useful, by Zebedee) and She's A

Worldie (by Kodiac): dam, of little account, half-sister to smart sprinter Guinea Hunter: fairly useful performer: awarded minor event at Beverley in September: left Bryan Smart after second start: best form at 5f on soft/heavy going: sold 15,000 gns, sent to Italy. *Julie Camacho*

WEFAIT (IRE) 3 br.c. Harbour Watch (IRE) 121 – Night Club 60 (Mozart (IRE) 131) [2017 75: t10.2g^2 p10g* 11.8g^2 11.9f^3 14g^4 11.4m* 12v^3 11.9d^4 12d^4 p14g^4 Sep 7] useful-looking colt: fairly useful performer: won maiden at Kempton in April and handicap at Windsor (by length from The Secrets Out) in June: probably stays 1¾m: acts on polytrack, tapeta, firm and good to soft going: sold 40,000 gns, sent to Saudi Arabia. *Richard Hannon* **88**

WEINBERG 2 b.g. (Mar 6) Cityscape 127 – Willmar (IRE) 53 (Zafonic (USA) 130) [2017 8g 7.6v^4 Sep 15] compact gelding: little impact in minor events. *Donald McCain* **53**

WE KNOW (IRE) 2 b.c. (Mar 23) Teofilo (IRE) 126 – Yellow Rosebud (IRE) 117 (Jeremy (USA) 122) [2017 8.5m^6 9.1s^4 9d^4 Oct 30] fair form when fourth in minor event at Goodwood (2¾ lengths behind dead-heaters Istanbul Sultan and Loxley) on second of 3 starts: wears tongue tie. *Simon Crisford* **74**

WELD AL EMARAT 5 b.g. Dubawi (IRE) 129 – Spirit of Dubai (IRE) 103 (Cape Cross (IRE) 129) [2017 94: 12.1s 7d Nov 11] sturdy gelding: fairly useful handicapper, below form in 2017: stays 1m: acts on fibresand and good to firm going. *Michael Easterby* **73**

WELD ARAB (IRE) 6 b.g. Shamardal (USA) 129 – Itqaan (USA) 83 (Danzig (USA)) [2017 72: p12g^6 Apr 24] fair handicapper: stays 1½m: acts on polytrack, tapeta and good to firm going: has worn headgear: usually races close up: modest maiden hurdler. *Michael Blake* **68**

WELEASE BWIAN (IRE) 8 b.g. Kheleyf (USA) 116 – Urbanize (USA) 68 (Chester House (USA) 123) [2017 74, a84: t6m p5d Feb 2] strong gelding: fairly useful handicapper, below best in 2017: stays 6f: acts on polytrack, good to firm and good to soft going: has worn headgear/tongue tie: sometimes slowly away, often races towards rear. *Stuart Williams* **59**

WELLIESINTHEWATER (IRE) 7 b.g. Footstepsinthesand 120 – Shadow Ash (IRE) 75 (Ashkalani (IRE) 128) [2017 87: p7d p7g* p8g* p8g p7g* 7d t7.1s^3 7g^5 t7.1g 7d p7s p7s^6 Dec 1] fairly useful handicapper on turf, useful on all-weather: won at Chelmsford in March (twice) and May (by ¾ length from Mount Tahan): third at Newcastle (2 lengths behind War Department) in June: stays 1m: acts on all-weather, best turf form on good going: wears headgear. *Derek Shaw* **85 a95**

WELL PAINTED (IRE) 8 ch.g. Excellent Art 125 – Aoife (IRE) 83 (Thatching 131) [2017 p11g Feb 18] rangy gelding: useful at best, behind in handicap on sole outing on Flat since 2015: stays 11.5f: acts on polytrack, soft and good to firm going: has worn headgear: wears tongue tie. *Daniel Steele* **–**

WELLS FARHH GO (IRE) 2 b.c. (Mar 21) Farhh 131 – Mowazana (IRE) 74 (Galileo (IRE) 134) [2017 7d* 7d* Aug 23] €16,000F, 16,000Y: tall colt: sixth foal: half-brother to 3 winners, including 7f winner Yulong Xionghu and 1m winner Red Raven (both by Raven's Pass): dam 1¼m winner: smart form: won minor event (by 2¼ lengths from Laugh A Minute) in July and Acomb Stakes (by nose from James Garfield) in August, both at York: will be suited by at least 1m: open to further improvement. *Tim Easterby* **111 p**

Tattersalls Acomb Stakes, York—Wells Farhh Go (left) beats James Garfield and Lansky (star on cap) to maintain his unbeaten record

WE'LL SHAKE HANDS (FR) 6 b.g. Excellent Art 125 – Amou Daria (FR) (Kendor –
(FR) 122) [2017 71: 10.3g 10g Apr 11] rather slightly-built gelding: fair handicapper, little
impact either start in 2017: stays 10.5f: acts on soft and good to firm going: has worn visor.
K. R. Burke

WELL SUITED (IRE) 2 ch.c. (Feb 11) Dandy Man (IRE) 123 – Dame d'Honneur (IRE) **74 p**
(Teofilo (IRE) 126) [2017 6.1m^2 Jul 10] €26,000F, 160,000 2-y-o: close-coupled colt: third
foal: half-brother to 1¼m winner Mystery Gal (by Big Bad Bob): dam unraced: 7/4, second
in minor event at Windsor (nose behind Peggy's Angel) in July: sure to improve.
Simon Crisford

WELOOF (FR) 3 b.g. Redoute's Choice (AUS) – Peinted Song (USA) (Unbridled's Song **88**
(USA) 125) [2017 –: t8.6g* t8.6g 8m t8.6g^6 8m p8g t7.2g p7s p6g^4 Dec 31] fairly useful
performer: won maiden at Wolverhampton in March: left Ed Dunlop after sixth start: stays
8.5f: acts on tapeta: tried in blinkers/tongue tie. *John Butler*

WELSH INLET (IRE) 9 br.m. Kheleyf (USA) 116 – Ervedya (IRE) (Doyoun 124) [2017 **65**
56: p7g p7g^4 p7d* p7g^2 p7g p8g^3 p8m^4 p7g^5 7g^2 7m^6 8g^6 7.6s^4 7m p7g 8s^6 p8g Oct 24]
compact mare: fair handicapper: won at Kempton in February: stays 8.5f: acts on polytrack,
good to firm and heavy going: tried in tongue tie. *John Bridger*

WELSH LORD 2 gr.c. (Mar 24) Dark Angel (IRE) 113 – Welsh Angel (Dubai Destination **74 p**
(USA) 127) [2017 p8g^4 Oct 12] 170,000F, 250,000Y: fourth foal: half-brother to smart
winner up to 1½m Scarlet Dragon (2-y-o 7f winner, by Sir Percy) and useful 2-y-o 7f-8.6f
winner Commander Cole (by Kyllachy): dam unraced: 4/1, fourth in minor event at
Chelmsford (3¾ lengths behind Main Street) in October: will improve. *Saeed bin Suroor*

WELSH ROSE 4 b.f. Exceed And Excel (AUS) 126 – Nantyglo 101 (Mark of Esteem **68**
(IRE) 137) [2017 81: p6g^3 5.7f^5 t7.2g p6g Sep 7] useful-looking filly: fair maiden: left Ed
de Giles after third start: stays 6f: acts on tapeta: in hood last 5 starts: front runner/races
prominently. *Archie Watson*

WEMYSS POINT 5 b.g. Champs Elysees 124 – Wemyss Bay (Sadler's Wells (USA) 132) –
[2017 t12.2g 10m May 9] placed in bumpers/winning hurdler: no form in Flat maidens.
Philip Kirby

WENSARA DREAM 4 b.f. Lilbourne Lad (IRE) 111 – Emerald Fire 86 (Pivotal 124) –
[2017 52: t7.1m Jan 4] maiden, well held sole outing in 2017: best effort at 6f: often raced
towards rear: dead. *Andrew Balding*

WENSLEY 2 b.c. (Mar 14) Poet's Voice 126 – Keladora (USA) (Crafty Prospector (USA)) **77**
[2017 6s^5 5f^2 5s* 5g^3 6d^4 6g 7d^5 Oct 28] fair performer: won minor event at Pontefract in
July: should stay 7f: acts on firm and soft going. *James Bethell*

WENTWELL YESTERDAY (IRE) 3 b.c. Kodiac 112 – Roisin's Star (IRE) 96 **68**
(Accordion) [2017 77: t7.1m t6g^2 Jan 31] fair performer: stays 7f: acts on polytrack and
tapeta: front runner/races prominently: sold 8,500 gns in February, sent to Greece.
Jamie Osborne

WENTWORTH FALLS 5 gr.g. Dansili 127 – Strawberry Morn (CAN) (Travelling **102**
Victor (CAN)) [2017 98: f5m 6g* 6g* 6s 6m^4 6d 6d Aug 7] useful-looking gelding: useful
handicapper: won at Doncaster and Redcar (by ½ length from Tiger Jim) in April: stays 7f:
acts on polytrack, tapeta and good to firm going: has worn headgear, including final start:
usually races towards rear. *Geoffrey Harker*

WESTBROOK BERTIE 2 b.c. (Feb 21) Sixties Icon 125 – Evanesce 72 (Lujain (USA) **69**
119) [2017 7g 8s^3 8s^F 8.3g^4 Nov 1] useful-looking colt: fair form: stays 8.5f. *Mick Channon*

WEST COAST (USA) 3 b.c. Flatter (USA) – Caressing (USA) 115 (Honour And Glory **128**
(USA) 122) [2017 a8f^2 a8.5f* a8.5f^2 a8.5f* a8.5f* a9f* a10f* a9f* a10f^3 Nov 4]
$425,000Y: half-brother to 8.6f winner Fun Affair (by Distorted Humor) and several
winners in USA: dam won Breeders' Cup Juvenile Fillies: unraced at 2 yrs: developed into
a high-class performer in 2017, winning maiden at Santa Anita in March, optional claimer
at same track in May, listed race at Belmont in June, Grade 3 Los Alamitos Derby in July,
Travers Stakes at Saratoga (by 3¼ lengths from Gunnevera) in August and Pennsylvania
Derby at Parx (beat Irap by 7¼ lengths) in September: 3½ lengths third to Gun Runner in
Breeders' Cup Classic at Del Mar final outing: stays 1¼m: raced only on dirt: usually wears
blinkers. *Bob Baffert, USA*

WEST DRIVE (IRE) 4 ch.g. Sea The Stars (IRE) 140 – Fair Sailing (IRE) 62 (Docksider **95**
(USA) 124) [2017 87: 11.6g^4 11.4d* 11.2s^5 14s* 14g^5 14.4v Sep 16] useful handicapper:
won at Windsor in June and Sandown (by length from Slunovrat) in July: stays 1¾m: acts
on firm and soft going: often wears headgear: sold to join Gary Moore 11,000 gns in
November. *Roger Varian*

WESTERLAND 2 b.c. (Apr 17) Frankel 147 – Arabesque 100 (Zafonic (USA) 130) **92**
[2017 6s^2 6g* 7m 7s^2 p7s^2 8g* 10m^5 Oct 14] strong, well-grown colt: closely related to useful 1¼m-2m winner Almagest (by Galileo) and half-brother to several winners, including 6f (including at 2 yrs) winner Camacho (by Danehill) and 2-y-o 6f (including Gimcrack Stakes) winner Showcasing (by Oasis Dream), both smart: dam 6f winner: fairly useful performer: won maiden at Leicester in May and nursery at Doncaster (by short head from Regimented) in September: stays 1m: acts on polytrack and soft going: in cheekpieces last 3 starts: sent to USA. *John Gosden*

WESTERN DUKE (IRE) 3 b.g. High Chaparral (IRE) 132 – Witch of Fife (USA) 91 **100**
(Lear Fan (USA) 130) [2017 93p: 10.3g 10m 10g^3 10g^4 p11s* p11g^5 Nov 6] good-topped gelding: useful handicapper: won at Kempton (by ½ length from Arab Moon) in September: stays 11f: acts on polytrack and good to firm going: usually races prominently. *Ralph Beckett*

WESTERN DYNAMISME (FR) 2 b.f. (Apr 14) Manduro (GER) 135 – Western Hope **–**
(IRE) (High Chaparral (IRE) 132) [2017 5.7d 8.1g t6.1g Sep 23] first foal: dam, of little account, half-sister to smart performer up to 1½m Saphira's Fire: no form. *Harry Dunlop*

WESTERN HYMN 6 b.g. High Chaparral (IRE) 132 – Blue Rhapsody 79 (Cape Cross **110**
(IRE) 129) [2017 116: 13.4d* 12m 12g^4 14s 12s p12g^5 p12g Nov 29] well-made gelding: smart performer: won Ormonde Stakes at Chester (by short head from US Army Ranger) in May: stays 13.5f: acts on polytrack and any turf going: wears headgear: often races towards rear: not straightforward (carries head awkwardly). *John Gosden*

WESTERN PRESENCE 3 ch.c. Sleeping Indian 122 – Mawjoodah 80 (Cadeaux **69**
Genereux 131) [2017 62, a69: f6g* f6s Jan 26] fair performer: won seller at Southwell in January: stays 6f: acts on fibresand, tapeta and good to firm going: sold 5,000 gns in February, sent to Greece. *Richard Fahey*

WESTERN PRINCE 4 b.g. Cape Cross (IRE) 129 – Vigee Le Brun (USA) (Pulpit **82 §**
(USA) 117) [2017 85: p16g^5 f12g^4 12g^5 13.9m 14m^5 Jul 7] fairly useful handicapper: stays 1¾m: acts on fibresand and good to soft going: wears hood: often starts slowly, races in rear/freely: sold 23,000 gns in July: temperamental. *Michael Appleby*

WESTERN SAFARI (IRE) 3 b.f. High Chaparral (IRE) 132 – Shamwari Lodge (IRE) **63**
114 (Hawk Wing (USA) 136) [2017 p7g^3 8m^5 p8g 7.6s p7d Sep 28] €65,000Y: third foal: half-sister to smart 7f/1m winner Oh This Is Us (by Acclamation): dam 6f (including at 2 yrs) and 1m winner: modest maiden: stays 1m: acts on polytrack and good to firm going. *Richard Hannon*

WESTERN WAY (IRE) 8 b.g. Westerner 130 – Faucon (Polar Falcon (USA) 126) [2017 **69**
77§: t7.1s^2 t12.4d Dec 16] fair maiden: should be suited by 1½m+: acts on tapeta and soft going: often in cheekpieces: often races in rear: bumper/hurdle winner. *Don Cantillon*

WESTFIELD WONDER 2 b.c. (Feb 17) Captain Gerrard (IRE) 113 – Flying Highest **54**
(Spectrum (IRE) 126) [2017 5d 6.1m 5d 5s^3 6g t7.2g^6 p7s^5 Dec 14] modest maiden: stays 7f: acts on tapeta and soft going. *Ronald Thompson*

WEST LEAKE (IRE) 11 b.g. Acclamation 118 – Kilshanny 70 (Groom Dancer (USA) **52**
128) [2017 61: p8d^6 p7d^3 p8d^4 p8g p8m^3 t8.6g^4 Apr 5] compact, attractive gelding: modest handicapper: stays 1m: acts on polytrack, fibresand and soft going: has worn headgear: usually races towards rear. *Paul Burgoyne*

WEST PALM BEACH (IRE) 2 br.f. (Jan 26) Scat Daddy (USA) 120 – Shelley Beach **81**
(IRE) 79 (Danehill Dancer (IRE) 117) [2017 p7s^3 p7g^5 p7g* t8.6g* Nov 29] 260,000Y: leggy, close-coupled filly: second foal: dam maiden (placed up to 1m in USA): fairly useful form: won minor events at Lingfield (by neck from Bubble And Squeak) and Wolverhampton (by head from Heeyaam) in November: stays 8.5f: sent to USA. *John Gosden*

WESTWARD HO (IRE) 4 b.g. Fastnet Rock (AUS) 127 – Thought Is Free 88 (Cadeaux **73**
Genereux 131) [2017 89: 8m 10.2g^6 May 13] fairly useful 1m winner on tapeta at 3 yrs, mid-division at best in handicaps in 2017: often starts slowly/races towards rear. *James Bethell*

WE WIN 3 b.f. Hellvelyn 118 – Pink Champagne (Cosmonaut) [2017 p6g Nov 18] half- **–**
sister to several winners, including 5f/6f winner George The Second (by Josr Algarhoud) and 11f/1½m winner Crimson Mitre (by Bishop of Cashel): dam of little account: 100/1, well held in maiden at Lingfield. *J. R. Jenkins*

W G GRACE (IRE) 2 b.c. (Mar 24) Exceed And Excel (AUS) 126 – Ownwan (USA) **67**
(Kingmambo (USA) 125) [2017 5m^4 5d^5 5.1g^5 p6g* 6d^4 6.1s^3 6.1d 6s t6g 6d Oct 30] fair performer: won nursery at Kempton in August: stays 6f: acts on polytrack and soft going. *Mark Johnston*

WHALEWEIGH STATION 6 b.g. Zamindar (USA) 116 – Looby Loo 71 (Kyllachy 129) [2017 68§: p7d* p6g* p6d^3 p7d^6 p6g^6 f6m p6g^6 p6g p7s p7g p6g p7g^3 p7g^6 p6s Dec 7] angular gelding: fair handicapper: won at Kempton (twice) in January: raced mainly at 6f/7f: acts on polytrack, fibresand and good to firm going: usually wears headgear: unreliable. *J. R. Jenkins* **67 §**

WHAT ABOUT CARLO (FR) 6 b.g. Creachadoir (IRE) 126 – Boccatenera (GER) (Artan (IRE) 119) [2017 108: p10s 10.1m^3 11.4g^2 10s* 9.9g 11m 9.9s^2 12s^5 Oct 28] tall gelding: smart performer: won listed race at Newbury (by 2¾ lengths from Arthenus) in July: second in similar event at Goodwood (short head behind Monarchs Glen) in September: stays 11.5f: acts on good to firm and heavy going: tried in headgear. *Eve Johnson Houghton* **115**

WHAT A HOME (IRE) 3 b.f. Lope de Vega (IRE) 125 – Inchmahome 72 (Galileo (IRE) 134) [2017 8g^3 10.2s^3 12.3d* 11.9d* Sep 14] €300,000F, 300,000Y: lengthy, attractive filly: sixth foal: closely related to 1¼m winner Earl of Menteith (by Shamardal) and half-sister to 2m winner Wayne Manor (by Cape Cross) and smart 1¼m-1½m winner Venus de Milo (by Duke of Marmalade): dam 11.5f winner: useful form: won maiden at Chester in July and handicap at Doncaster (by 1½ lengths from Pacharana) in September: stays 12.5f: open to further improvement. *William Haggas* **95 p**

WHATALOVE 3 ch.f. Arcano (IRE) 122 – Secret Happiness (Cape Cross (IRE) 129) [2017 –: p7d^3 p8g^5 p8g^2 p8g^6 7g 7.1d^2 7.1m^2 9d 6.1g^3 Oct 9] good-topped filly: modest maiden: stays 1m: acts on polytrack, good to firm and good to soft going: tried in hood. *Martin Keighley* **54**

WHAT A SCORCHER 6 b.m. Authorized (IRE) 133 – Street Fire (IRE) (Street Cry (IRE) 130) [2017 75: 12.1m^5 12m^4 12m^2 12s^4 Aug 17] rather leggy mare: fair maiden: stays 1½m: acts on good to firm and heavy going: front runner/races prominently. *Nikki Evans* **79**

WHAT A WELCOME 3 ch.g. Nathaniel (IRE) 129 – Hometime (Dubai Destination (USA) 127) [2017 9.9s 10s p8g^5 p10g* p12g* Nov 21] second foal: half-brother to 10.7f winner Share The Honour (by Shamardal): dam, French 1¼m winner, sister to dam of very smart winner up to 9.5f Thunder Snow and half-sister to Prix de Diane winner West Wind: fairly useful performer: won handicaps at Lingfield (twice, by ¾ length from Kohinoor Diamond second occasion) in November: left Eric Wheeler after second start: will stay further than 1½m: acts on polytrack: open to further improvement. *Patrick Chamings* **83 p**

WHAT DO YOU THINK (IRE) 2 b.f. (Feb 4) Excelebration (IRE) 133 – Dama'a (IRE) 85 (Green Desert (USA) 127) [2017 6g^6 5m^6 6g t7.1g^3 Sep 12] 19,000F: half-sister to 3 winners, including 2-y-o 7f winner (stays 11f) Darkening (by Shamardal) and 2-y-o 6f/7f winner Art Official (by Excellent Art), both useful: dam, 6f winner, half-sister to smart 6f/7f performer Himalya: modest form: stays 7f. *Michael Dods* **55**

WHATELSEABOUTYOU (IRE) 3 b.f. Canford Cliffs (IRE) 133 – Brigids Cross (IRE) (Sadler's Wells (USA) 132) [2017 62: p10g^5 p10g^4 t10.2d^3 Mar 1] modest maiden: stays 1¼m: acts on polytrack and tapeta: tried in cheekpieces. *Richard Fahey* **62**

WHATSTHEMESSAGE (IRE) 3 b.f. Bushranger (IRE) 119 – Fatwa (IRE) 95 (Lahib (USA) 129) [2017 79: t7.1g^6 f8s^4 t8.6g^6 t6g^5 6.9g^4 6.9s* 7.8g^2 7.2m^3 8d* 7.2m* 9.2s* 8.3d* 7g 8s^4 Oct 1] useful handicapper: had excellent season, winning at Carlisle in June, Thirsk, Musselburgh and Hamilton in August, and again at Hamilton (by neck from Isabella) in September: stays 9f: acts on soft and good to firm going: front runner/races prominently. *Keith Dalgleish* **100**

WHAT'S THE STORY 3 b.c. Harbour Watch (IRE) 121 – Spring Fashion (IRE) 54 (Galileo (IRE) 134) [2017 88p: 7.1g* 7d* Nov 11] useful performer: won maiden at Musselburgh in April and handicap at Doncaster (apprentice, by 2½ lengths from Hajjam) when next seen out in November: will be suited by 1m+: acts on soft and good to firm going: usually races prominently/responds generously to pressure: will go on improving. *Keith Dalgleish* **103 p**

WHAT'S UP WALTER 3 ch.g. Stimulation (IRE) 121 – Pose (IRE) 85 (Acclamation 118) [2017 t8g t7.1g t9.5m^6 8.3g 12d Aug 4] no form, including in handicaps. *Philip Kirby* **–**

WHAT USAIN 5 b.g. Misu Bond (IRE) 114 – Bond Shakira 54 (Daggers Drawn (USA) 114) [2017 67: t8.6m^2 f8s^5 f12g^3 p11g* t8.6m^4 f8g^5 t12.2g^2 p12g* t9.5g^3 f12.1g 11.5m^6 May 24] fairly useful handicapper: won at Kempton in February and April: stays 1½m: acts on polytrack and tapeta: wears headgear: front runner/races prominently. *Michael Appleby* **80**

WHAT WONDERS WEAVE (IRE) 3 b.f. Famous Name 124 – Jagapaw (IRE) (Manduro (GER) 135) [2017 p10.7g^3 8.3m* 11.3m^5 11.1g^3 14.2v 12d^5 9.2v* 8.9s^3 10g^4 8v p10.7g^5 Nov 24] first foal: dam once-raced half-sister to useful/ungenuine performer up to **84**

7f Rock Jock: fairly useful performer: won maiden at Hamilton in May and seller there in September: third in handicap at Musselburgh later in September: stays 11.5f: acts on good to firm and heavy going. *John Patrick Shanahan, Ireland*

WHATWOULDYOUKNOW (IRE) 2 b.g. (Mar 3) Lope de Vega (IRE) 125 – Holamo (IRE) 75 (Montjeu (IRE) 137) [2017 6d t7.1g Nov 15] little impact in minor events. *Richard Guest* **–**

WHERERAINBOWSEND (IRE) 2 br.f. (Feb 17) Roderic O'Connor (IRE) 119 – Mikes Baby (IRE) 72 (Key of Luck (USA) 126) [2017 t7.1g^{5} t7.2g^{6} Dec 22] €3,000Y: seventh foal: half-sister to winners abroad by Antonius Pius and Indian Haven: dam, 6f winner, half-sister to useful winner up to 1½m Palace Royale: modest form when fifth at Newcastle on first of 2 starts in minor events: wears hood. *Bryan Smart* **57**

WHERE'S JEFF 2 b.g. (Apr 16) Haafhd 129 – Piece of Magic (Alflora (IRE) 120) [2017 6m^{6} t5s^{6} 5.4g 6g 5s^{2} t7.2g Nov 29] modest maiden: bred to stay 7f: acts on soft going. *Michael Easterby* **64**

WHERE'S STEWART 3 ch.g. Firebreak 125 – Sukuma (IRE) 55 (Highest Honor (FR) 124) [2017 –: 8g 6m May 25] no form: tried in headgear/tongue tie. *Nigel Tinkler* **–**

WHIGWHAM 3 ch.f. Sleeping Indian 122 – Normandy Maid 75 (American Post 121) [2017 70: 5f 5g^{2} 6m^{5} 5d Aug 17] fair form at 2 yrs, below that level in 2017: left Richard Fahey after third start: should prove suited by 6f: acts on good to firm going. *Gary Sanderson* **49**

WHINGING WILLIE (IRE) 8 b.g. Cape Cross (IRE) 129 – Pacific Grove 89 (Persian Bold 123) [2017 87: 12g^{2} 12m^{6} 12g^{2} p12s^{2} 12d^{6} 12m 12v* 14g^{6} Nov 1] sturdy gelding: fairly useful handicapper: won at Epsom (apprentice, by ½ length from Golden Wolf) in October: stays 1½m: acts on polytrack, good to firm and heavy going: wears headgear. *Gary Moore* **91**

WHINMOOR 2 gr.g. (Apr 8) Havana Gold (IRE) 118 – Makhsusah (IRE) (Darshaan 133) [2017 6v 5.4g Oct 13] big, plain gelding: little impact in minor events. *Nigel Tinkler* **–**

WHIPCRACKAWAY (IRE) 8 b.g. Whipper (USA) 126 – Former Drama (USA) (Dynaformer (USA)) [2017 12v^{3} 11.4g^{6} p12d Aug 16] tall gelding: modest handicapper nowadays: stays 1½m: acts on polytrack and heavy going: often in headgear. *Peter Hedger* **60**

WHIP NAE NAE (IRE) 3 ch.c. Dragon Pulse (IRE) 114 – Love In May (IRE) 80 (City On A Hill (USA) 114) [2017 83: 10.3m^{3} 12.3m^{6} 11s^{6} 8d 8m^{4} 8m* 8.1g Oct 9] strong colt: fairly useful handicapper: won at Newmarket (by 1¼ lengths from Slow To Hand) in August: stays 10.5f: acts on tapeta and good to firm going: tried in cheekpieces: sold 40,000 gns, sent to Saudi Arabia. *Richard Hannon* **91**

WHIPPHOUND 9 b.g. Whipper (USA) 126 – Golden Symbol 54 (Wolfhound (USA) 126) [2017 62: t6f 6g 6m^{5} 6g^{3} 5.9g 6s^{3} 6g 6v^{3} 6g 6g* 6d^{4} 5d 5v 5s 6s Oct 31] lengthy gelding: modest handicapper: won at Thirsk (amateur) in August: stays 7f: acts on polytrack, tapeta, good to firm and heavy going: wears headgear: sometimes slowly away, usually races nearer last than first, often lazily: unreliable. *Ruth Carr* **59 §**

WHIP UP A FRENZY (IRE) 5 b.g. Vale of York (IRE) 117 – Answer Do (Groom Dancer (USA) 128) [2017 59: p11d^{6} p10g^{6} p10d 7g 7.2s 10g t8.6g^{5} p10s Nov 16] modest handicapper, below form in 2017: left Richard Rowe after third start: stays 1¼m: acts on polytrack and soft going: has worn headgear, including last 2 starts. *David O'Meara* **46**

WHIRLING DERVISH 2 b.c. (Feb 13) Camelot 128 – Synergy (FR) 108 (Victory Note (USA) 120) [2017 8.4s^{3} 9v* Oct 1] 62,000Y: third foal: half-brother to 1m-1¼m winner Kaskarau (by Zamindar) and 2-y-o 1¼m winner Gaillefontaine (by Myboycharlie): dam 10.5f-1½m winner: fairly useful form: won maiden at Tipperary (by 6 lengths from Tashman) in October: will stay further than 9f: likely to progress further. *Mrs J. Harrington, Ireland* **90 p**

WHIRL ME ROUND 3 ch.g. Piccolo 121 – Give Her A Whirl 63 (Pursuit of Love 124) [2017 90: t7.2g p6s p6g Dec 28] fairly useful form at 2 yrs, behind in handicaps in 2017: tried in headgear: usually races nearer last than first. *George Peckham* **–**

WHIRLWIND ROMANCE (IRE) 3 b.f. Canford Cliffs (IRE) 133 – Tencarola (IRE) (Night Shift (USA)) [2017 t8.6m p10m p8g Feb 1] 36,000Y: half-sister to 3 winners, including 6f winner Impel (by Excellent Art), later successful abroad, and French 6f winner Master Rookie (by Mastercraftsman): dam French 1m winner: little impact in all-weather maidens: in blinkers last 2 starts. *Hugo Palmer* **–**

WHISKY BARON (AUS) 5 b.g. Manhattan Rain (AUS) 122 – Tazkara (FR) (Sinndar (IRE) 134) [2017 8.9g* 9.9g* 8d^{6} Sep 29] brother to Australian 6f winner Downtown Manhattan and half-brother to 2 winners in Australia by Flying Spur, including 6f-1m winner Rowie: dam unraced half-sister to smart French 1m-10.5f winner Tashelka: smart **118**

performer: won Grade 2 handicap at Kenilworth and Grade 1 Sun Met at same course (by 1½ lengths from Legal Eagle) in January: shaped as if needing run when sixth to Beat The Bank in Joel Stakes at Newmarket: stays 1¼m: best form on good going: sent to UAE. *B. Crawford, South Africa*

WHISPER A WORD (IRE) 3 ch.f. Bated Breath 125 – Affability (IRE) (Dalakhani (IRE) 133) [2017 –: 6g 7.2m 9.9m 11.8g Jul 8] poor maiden. *Tim Easterby* **40**

WHISPERED KISS 4 b.f. Medicean 128 – Desert Kiss 100 (Cape Cross (IRE) 129) [2017 59: p8g* t8.6g^{2} p8g* 8.1m 7d* 8d* 7s* 7d 8s^{3} Sep 9] tall filly: fairly useful/ progressive handicapper: won at Lingfield in April/May, Newmarket in July/August and Yarmouth (by 5 lengths from Patching) later in August: stays 8.5f: acts on polytrack, tapeta and soft going: has worn hood: usually races close up. *Mike Murphy* **94**

WHISPERING BELL (IRE) 3 b.f. Galileo (IRE) 134 – Red Avis 74 (Exceed And Excel (AUS) 126) [2017 75p: 8.1g* 8d Jul 28] rather unfurnished filly: fairly useful form: won maiden at Windsor (by 4½ lengths from Euqranian) in July: last in listed race at Ascot next time: best effort at 1m: in hood last 2 starts: sold 58,000 gns in December. *John Gosden* **90**

WHISPERING SOUL (IRE) 4 b.f. Majestic Missile (IRE) 118 – Belle of The Blues (IRE) (Blues Traveller (IRE) 119) [2017 61: t5.1g t5.1m^{5} t6f t6.1d^{6} t5.1g Dec 22] modest handicapper, below form in 2017: stays 6f: acts on tapeta, good to firm and good to soft going: usually wears headgear. *Brian Baugh* **48**

WHISPERING WOLF 4 b.f. Amadeus Wolf 122 – Ashover Amber 81 (Green Desert (USA) 127) [2017 54: t5.1m^{6} t5d t5.1g^{6} t5g 5g^{6} 5m 5f 6g Aug 15] poor handicapper: stays 6f: acts on tapeta and good to firm going: tried in cheekpieces. *Suzzanne France* **47**

WHITCHURCH 5 b.g. Mawatheeq (USA) 126 – Silvereine (FR) (Bering 136) [2017 62: t10.2g t8.6g 11.8s^{5} 10s^{6} 10g 10d Jul 9] workmanlike gelding: fair at best, no form in 2017: left Philip Kirby after third start: has worn headgear, including last 5 starts: has worn tongue tie: often races towards rear. *Iain Jardine* **–**

WHITEANDGOLD 3 b.f. Major Cadeaux 121 – Irrational 63 (Kyllachy 129) [2017 72: 5d^{5} 5d 5m^{5} Aug 30] fair at 2 yrs, below form in handicaps in 2017: best form at 5f: acts on good to firm going: tried in blinkers. *Bryan Smart* **57**

WHITE CHOCOLATE (IRE) 3 gr.f. Mastercraftsman (IRE) 129 – Coco Demure (IRE) (Titus Livius (FR) 115) [2017 75p: 9.9d* 9.9d* 10.3d^{2} 9.9v^{4} 12m^{2} 9.9g^{4} 12g Oct 7] good-topped filly: fairly useful handicapper: won at Salisbury in May and Goodwood in June: second at Chester later in June and Goodwood in August: stays 1½m: acts on good to firm and good to soft going: often races towards rear. *David Simcock* **93**

WHITECLIFF PARK (IRE) 4 b.g. Canford Cliffs (IRE) 133 – Venetian Rhapsody (IRE) (Galileo (IRE) 134) [2017 68: 12g^{6} t9.5g^{4} 12g 10g^{4} t12.2g^{6} t16.3s* 13.1s 14d t16.5g* p16d^{4} p16s^{4} t16.3g Sep 22] good-quartered gelding: modest handicapper on turf, fairly useful on all-weather: won at Newcastle in June and Wolverhampton in August: stays 16.5f: acts on polytrack and tapeta: wears headgear: usually slowly away/races nearer last than first: sold 5,000 gns in November: temperamental. *Brian Ellison* **58 §** **a80 §**

WHITECLIFFSOFDOVER (USA) 3 b.c. War Front (USA) 119 – Orate (USA) (A P Indy (USA) 131) [2017 107: 7m* 7s^{3} 7m 10f 8s^{4} 8d^{5} 8d Sep 29] big, strong colt: smart performer: won listed Free Handicap at Newmarket (by 2¾ lengths from Rodaini) in April: third in listed race at Naas (½ length behind Texas Rock) in May: stayed 1m: acted on good to firm and good to soft going: in blinkers last 5 starts: usually wore tongue tie: usually led: to stand at Haras de la Haie Neuve, France, fee €3,000. *Aidan O'Brien, Ireland* **111**

WHITECREST 9 ch.m. Ishiguru (USA) 114 – Risky Valentine 68 (Risk Me (FR) 127) [2017 75: 5.1m t6g* 6g* 6g* p6g 6.1m^{5} 6.1s^{4} p6g^{5} 6m^{2} 6d^{4} 6g^{2} 6d^{2} 6g^{5} 6d^{2} 6d^{4} 6d^{2} t6.1g^{5} 6s^{6} t6.1g p6g^{3} Oct 24] leggy mare: fairly useful handicapper: completed hat-trick at Wolverhampton, Brighton and Lingfield in May: stays 7f: acts on polytrack, tapeta and any turf going. *John Spearing* **80**

WHITE DESERT (IRE) 3 ch.g. Teofilo (IRE) 126 – Artisia (IRE) (Peintre Celebre (USA) 137) [2017 10g* 12g^{5} Aug 26] 220,000F: brother to useful 1¼m/1½m winner Amazing Red and half-brother to 3 winners, notably high-class 1½m-1¾m winner (stayed 2m) Red Cadeaux (by Cadeaux Genereux): dam, well held all 3 starts, half-sister to high-class Hong Kong 1m-1¼m performer Military Attack and to dam of Gold Cup winner Big Orange: fairly useful form: won maiden at Newbury (in hood, by head from Love Conquers) in July: fifth in handicap at Goodwood (5¼ lengths behind Just In Time) in August, left poorly placed: should be suited by 1½m: remains with potential. *Charlie Appleby* **82 p**

WHITE DOG (IRE) 5 b.g. Le Cadre Noir (IRE) 113 – Little Annie 43 (Compton Place **–**
125) [2017 56: p11d Jan 18] modest maiden, behind in handicap sole outing in 2017: stays 13.5f: acts on polytrack: has worn headgear: in tongue tie last 3 starts. *Sarah Humphrey*

WHITE FEATHER 2 ch.g. (Feb 11) Bated Breath 125 – Just Wood (FR) (Highest Honor **79**
(FR) 124) [2017 5g^3 5d^2 5.5g^5 5g^3 8.1g^5 Oct 9] 10,000Y: close-coupled gelding: half-brother to 3 winners abroad, including useful French winner up to 9f (Prix Vanteaux) Just Little (2-y-o 7.5f/1m winner, by Grand Slam): dam, French 9f/1¼m winner, sister to useful 1¼m performer Katchina Quest: fair maiden: best form at 5f: acts on good to soft going: tried in cheekpieces: front runner/races prominently. *Jo Hughes*

WHITEFOUNTAINFAIRY (IRE) 2 ch.f. (Apr 13) Casamento (IRE) 118 – Groupetime **96**
(USA) 69 (Gilded Time (USA)) [2017 6g 6d* 6m 7d^5 7g^2 Aug 26] €3,000Y: rather unfurnished filly: half-sister to several winners, including useful winner up to 1¼m Swing Alone (2-y-o 8.6f winner, by Celtic Swing): dam maiden (stayed 1¼m): useful performer: won maiden at Fairyhouse in June: second in Prestige Stakes at Goodwood (¾ length behind Billesdon Brook) in August: left Mrs J. Harrington after third start: stays 7f: acts on good to soft going. *Andrew Balding*

WHITE GUARD 2 b.c. (Mar 23) Frankel 147 – Arbella 106 (Primo Dominie 121) [2017 **63 p**
7v^3 Sep 25] half-brother to several winners, including winner up to 9.5f Lat Hawill (2-y-o 7f winner, by Invincible Spirit) and 1¾m-2m winner Chocala (by Rock of Gibraltar), both useful: dam, 1½m winner, half-sister to smart stayer/high-class hurdler Overturn: 8/1, third in minor event at Leicester (7½ lengths behind Alkhawaneej Boy) in September: will be suited by 1m+: sure to progress. *Sir Mark Prescott Bt*

WHITEHALL 2 b.g. (Mar 31) Dansili 127 – Majestic Roi (USA) 122 (Street Cry (IRE) **61 p**
130) [2017 7m 7v^4 8.2g Oct 17] 200,000Y: half-brother to several winners, including smart German winner up to 1¼m Noor Al Hawa (2-y-o 1m winner, by Makfi) and useful 9f/1¼m winner Majestic Jasmine (by New Approach): dam winner up to 1m (2-y-o 6f winner), including Fred Darling/Sun Chariot Stakes: modest form in minor events: should stay at least 1m: remains with potential. *Sir Michael Stoute*

WHITE LAKE 5 b.g. Pivotal 124 – White Palace 80 (Shirley Heights 130) [2017 106: **106**
7.9d 8s^6 Oct 21] rangy, attractive gelding: useful handicapper: stays 1m: acts on soft and good to firm going: tried in headgear. *Roger Varian*

WHITELEY (IRE) 3 b.f. Dark Angel (IRE) 113 – Carallia (IRE) 101 (Common Grounds **68**
118) [2017 65: 8.3m^5 8.3g^6 8.2d^4 8g^4 7m^5 t6.1g^6 6d^3 6g^5 7m* 5.1d^3 5.3g^4 5.7s p6g^4 p5g Oct 18] close-coupled filly: fair handicapper: won at Brighton in August: stays 8.5f: acts on good to firm and good to soft going. *Mick Channon*

WHITE MOCHA (USA) 2 ch.c. (Mar 11) Lope de Vega (IRE) 125 – Lastroseofsummer **98 p**
(IRE) 82 (Haafhd 129) [2017 8g* 8d^2 8g* Sep 22] 90,000Y: third foal: half-brother to 7f winner Lastmanlastround (by Azamour) and useful 7.5f/1m winner (including at 2 yrs) Melesina (by Dark Angel): dam, 13f-17f winner, also won over hurdles, half-sister to smart stayer Romantic Affair: useful form: won minor events at Haydock (by head from Rua Augusta) in August and Newbury (by nose from Knight To Behold) in September: raced only at 1m: open to further improvement. *Hugo Palmer*

WHITE NILE (IRE) 8 b.h. Galileo (IRE) 134 – Super Gift (IRE) 96 (Darshaan 133) **–**
[2017 11.9m 10.2s^5 Aug 9] good-topped horse: useful at best, behind in handicaps in 2017 after long absence: stays 2m: acts on polytrack and heavy going: has worn tongue tie, including last 2 starts. *Laura Young*

WHITE ROSA (IRE) 3 b.f. Galileo (IRE) 134 – Dhanyata (IRE) 109 (Danetime (IRE) **80**
121) [2017 8s^2 7.9m^3 9.2s* 10.9s p9.4g Nov 28] 150,000Y: fourth foal: dam, 2-y-o 6f winner, half-sister to smart sprinter Guinea Hunter: fairly useful performer: won maiden at Hamilton (by 3 lengths from Haroon) in August: well held in listed races after: stays 9f: acts on soft going: in hood last 3 outings. *Hugo Palmer*

WHITE ROYALE (USA) 3 b.f. Speightstown (USA) 124 – Sweet Hope (USA) 106 **78**
(Lemon Drop Kid (USA) 131) [2017 77: t5g^3 f5g^2 p6g Jan 28] fair handicapper: stays 6f: acts on fibresand and tapeta: in cheekpieces last 2 starts. *Kevin Ryan*

WHITE TOWER (IRE) 3 b.g. Cape Cross (IRE) 129 – Star Blossom (USA) (Good **78**
Reward (USA) 120) [2017 87: 8m^4 8d^6 10.1d^4 8d^6 8.3v^6 Aug 8] sturdy gelding: fairly useful form at 2 yrs, below that level in 2017: stays 7f: acts on good to firm going: has joined Tim McCarthy. *Mark Johnston*

WHITKIRK 4 b.g. Iffraaj 127 – Bedouin Bride (USA) (Chester House (USA) 123) [2017 72: 8m^2 8g^4 8.3f* 8d^3 8g^5 t7.1d 7d t8d Nov 4] fair handicapper: won at Nottingham in June: stays 8.5f: acts on firm and good to soft going: usually races prominently. *Jedd O'Keeffe* **76**

WHITLOCK 2 ch.c. (Feb 26) Dutch Art 126 – Barynya 77 (Pivotal 124) [2017 p8d Nov 9] fourth foal: brother to smart winner up to 1m Zonderland (2-y-o 7f winner) and half-brother to useful 1½m winner Osipova (by Makfi): dam, maiden (stayed 1m), out of 1000 Guineas/Nassau Stakes winner Russian Rhythm: 4/1, very green when well held in minor event at Chelmsford: should do better. *John Gosden* **– p**

WHITMEL 4 b.g. Sulamani (IRE) 130 – My Valentina 84 (Royal Academy (USA) 130) [2017 p13.3s^6 Dec 14] placed in bumper: 33/1, well held in maiden at Chelmsford only outing on Flat. *Michael Appleby* **–**

WHITSTABLE PEARL (IRE) 4 b.f. Kodiac 112 – Amber's Bluff 80 (Mind Games 121) [2017 60: 10.2f 8.1m^5 t8.6g Jul 17] good-topped filly: modest handicapper at best, little impact in 2017: tried in cheekpieces: sometimes slowly away. *Sophie Leech* **–**

WHO DARES WINS (IRE) 5 b.g. Jeremy (USA) 122 – Savignano (Polish Precedent (USA) 131) [2017 102: 18.6m^4 20f^3 13.4g 18d* 18m Oct 14] compact gelding: useful handicapper: won at Newmarket (by 1¾ lengths from Coeur de Lion) in September: stays 2½m: acts on tapeta, firm and soft going: has worn cheekpieces, including last 5 starts: smart hurdler. *Alan King* **108**

WHO'S SHIRL 11 b.m. Shinko Forest (IRE) – Shirl 52 (Shirley Heights 130) [2017 62: t8g Jan 21] workmanlike mare: modest handicapper, well held sole outing in 2017: stays 8.5f: acts on polytrack, tapeta, good to firm and good to soft going: often races in rear: has looked hard ride. *Chris Fairhurst* **–**

WHOSYOURHOUSEMATE 3 ch.g. Bahamian Bounty 116 – Starlit Sky (Galileo (IRE) 134) [2017 p8g^3 f8d* 8d^3 9.1m^4 8d^3 p8g* Oct 26] 32,000Y: workmanlike gelding: half-brother to several winners, including useful 8.6f-1¼m winner (stayed 1½m) Sky Khan (by Cape Cross) and 1¼m winner Starlit Cantata (by Oratorio): dam unraced: fairly useful performer: won maiden at Southwell in March and handicap at Chelmsford (in blinkers, by ½ length from Midnight Macchiato) in October: stays 1m: acts on polytrack, fibresand, good to firm and good to soft going. *Ed Vaughan* **89**

WHO TOLD JO JO (IRE) 3 b.g. Bushranger (IRE) 119 – Shenkara (IRE) 79 (Night Shift (USA)) [2017 75: p5g^6 p5g^3 t6g 5m* 5g^6 p6s^4 5m 5s 6d^4 p6g^5 p6g Sep 27] workmanlike gelding: fair handicapper: won at Windsor in April: stays 6f: acts on polytrack, tapeta, soft and good to firm going: has worn headgear, including final start. *Joseph Tuite* **75**

WHY ME 7 b.g. Dubai Destination (USA) 127 – My Golly (Mozart (IRE) 131) [2017 –: 13d 13.1s 9v^4 7v 7v^3 f7.1g^2 f8.1g^4 Dec 21] modest maiden: stays 1½m: acts on heavy going: has worn hood, including in 2017: sometimes wears tongue tie. *Gavin Patrick Cromwell, Ireland* **59**

WHY WE DREAM (IRE) 2 b.f. (Feb 5) Al Kazeem 128 – Sandreamer (IRE) 98 (Oasis Dream 129) [2017 6.5d Oct 27] first foal: dam, 2-y-o 6f winner, half-sister to useful performer up to 9.5f Assume: 50/1, eighth in maiden at Newbury (7¾ lengths behind Picture No Sound) in October: will be suited by 7f+. *Mick Channon* **55**

WICKER 3 b.f. Myboycharlie (IRE) 118 – Lady Berta 65 (Bertolini (USA) 125) [2017 8.3g 8.1m 8s^3 p7g^2 p8s^3 p8s* Dec 17] £50,000Y, £20,000 2-y-o: third foal: closely related to French 11f winner Lady Pimm's (by Bushranger) and half-sister to 1m winner Goolagong Girl (by Avonbridge): dam maiden (stayed 7f), half-sister to smart/moody winner up to 1m Selinka: fairly useful performer: won maiden at Chelmsford in December: second in handicap at Kempton in November: stays 1m: acts on polytrack and soft going: tried in tongue tie. *Jane Chapple-Hyam* **80**

WICKLOW BRAVE 8 b.g. Beat Hollow 126 – Moraine 71 (Rainbow Quest (USA) 134) [2017 119: 16f^4 14g^2 16g^4 14d^4 14s^4 11.9g 15.9g Nov 7] strong, workmanlike gelding: smart performer: best efforts in 2017 when fourth in Grade 3 Belmont Gold Cup (2¼ lengths behind Red Cardinal) and second in Curragh Cup (½ length behind Rekindling) first 2 starts: mid-division in Caulfield Cup and Melbourne Cup last 2 outings: stays 16.5f: acts on any turf going: has worn headgear: high-class hurdler. *W. P. Mullins, Ireland* **116**

WICK POWELL 3 b.g. Sakhee's Secret 128 – London Welsh (Cape Cross (IRE) 129) [2017 88: f5g^3 t6g* t6g^4 p6g^4 6d May 20] sturdy gelding: useful handicapper: won at Newcastle (by 3¾ lengths from Hemingway) in March: stays 6f: acts on fibresand, tapeta and good to soft going: front runner/races prominently: sold 70,000 gns in July, sent to Singapore, where renamed Elite Power. *David Barron* **100**

WIDNES 3 b.g. Showcasing 117 – Largo (IRE) 94 (Selkirk (USA) 129) [2017 72: p7g^2 t7.1g^4 7m^4 7s 7g^6 p7g^4 p8g p8d 10.1d^4 p12g^5 p12g^6 p12g^2 Dec 23] workmanlike gelding: fair maiden: stays 1½m: acts on polytrack, good to firm and good to soft going: wears headgear: in tongue tie last 2 starts: usually races towards rear. *Alan Bailey* **75**

WIFF WAFF 2 b.g. (Feb 15) Poet's Voice 126 – Eraadaat (IRE) 59 (Intikhab (USA) 135) [2017 p6d 5m^5 6m p5g t5.1m^6 t5d^4 Nov 4] fair maiden: best effort at 5f: acts on good to firm going: often in tongue tie. *Stuart Williams* **64**

WIGAN WARRIOR 3 b.g. Doncaster Rover (USA) 114 – Rattleyurjewellery 38 (Royal Applause 124) [2017 74: p7g^2 7.2m* 8m^6 8g* 8.2d^5 8g p8g^4 8g p8g Oct 26] fairly useful handicapper: won at Musselburgh in June and Haydock (by ½ length from Jumira Prince) in July: stays 8.5f: acts on polytrack, soft and good to firm going: often starts slowly/races towards rear: temperamental: sold 9,000 gns, sent to Saudi Arabia. *David Brown* **84 §**

WILAMINA (IRE) 4 b.f. Zoffany (IRE) 121 – Tropical Lake (IRE) 100 (Lomond (USA) 128) [2017 104: 10.2g* 9m^2 9.9g 9.5s^3 10m^5 Oct 13] angular filly: useful performer: won listed race at Nottingham (by length from Singyoursong) in May: second in Kilboy Estate Stakes at the Curragh (1¾ lengths behind Elizabeth Browning) in July: stays 1¼m: acts on soft and good to firm going: often races prominently. *Martyn Meade* **102**

WILD ACCLAIM (IRE) 3 b.g. Acclamation 118 – Anam Allta (IRE) 117 (Invincible Spirit (IRE) 121) [2017 73: 6m^2 6m^3 5s p7s p7d t9.5g Dec 22] fair maiden: left Ann Duffield after third start: best effort at 6f: acts on good to firm and good to soft going. *Michael Appleby* **73**

WILD APPROACH (GER) 4 ch.f. New Approach (IRE) 132 – Wildfahrte (GER) 95 (Mark of Esteem (IRE) 137) [2017 9.9s 8.7g* 8g^5 8s^2 7s^4 7s^2 8g^6 Sep 17] second foal: half-sister to smart German 1m/9f winner Wildpark (by Shamardal): dam, German 1¼m winner, closely related to very smart German/US performer up to 1½m Wake Forest: useful performer: won minor event at Hanover (by 1¾ lengths from Parthenius) in May: in frame after in Group 3 at Hamburg (1¾ lengths second to Shy Witch), Oak Tree Stakes at Goodwood (2½ lengths fourth to Al Jazi) and listed race at Dusseldorf (5 lengths second to Pirouette): stays 8.5f: acts on soft going. *D. Moser, Germany* **107**

WILD APPROACH (IRE) 3 b.g. Approve (IRE) 112 – Mike's Wildcat (USA) (Forest Wildcat (USA) 120) [2017 59p: f5g* t5d* t5.1m^4 t5.1g^3 5.2g^3 5.2g^3 t5.1g^2 5g^{ur} Aug 30] fair handicapper: won at Southwell in January and Newcastle in February: raced only at 5f: acted on fibresand, tapeta, raced only on good going on turf: tried in headgear: front runner/raced prominently: dead. *Robert Cowell* **79**

WILD DANCER 4 b.f. Mawatheeq (USA) 126 – Pretty Miss 85 (Averti (IRE) 117) [2017 84: p6g^4 5.7m 6g p7g Oct 5] sturdy filly: fairly useful at 3 yrs, below form in 2017: stays 7f: acts on good to firm going: sometimes slowly away, usually races nearer last than first. *Patrick Chamings* **69**

WILD DUDE (USA) 7 b.h. Wildcat Heir (USA) 118 – Courtly Choice (USA) (Doneraile Court (USA)) [2017 115: a6f^3 a6f^3 a7f a6f^5 a6g a5f^4 a8f a8f^2 Dec 21] useful performer: placed at Meydan in listed race (4¾ lengths third to Reynaldothewizard), Al Shindagha Sprint (5 lengths third behind Cool Cowboy) and another listed race (4½ lengths second to Heavy Metal): left M. Halford after fifth start: stays 7f: acts on polytrack and dirt: often wears headgear: wears tongue tie. *A. bin Harmash, UAE* **109**

WILDE EXTRAVAGANCE (IRE) 4 ch.g. Dandy Man (IRE) 123 – Castanetta (IRE) 90 (Dancing Dissident (USA) 119) [2017 76: 6g^6 6m^6 t5s^4 5d 6d 6g^5 6d t6g Nov 24] fair handicapper, below form in 2017: stays 6f: acts on good to soft going: in headgear last 3 starts. *Julie Camacho* **64**

WILDE INSPIRATION (IRE) 6 ch.g. Dandy Man (IRE) 123 – Wishing Chair (USA) (Giant's Causeway (USA) 132) [2017 98: 8g 8s^5 May 20] workmanlike gelding: useful handicapper at best: stayed 8.5f: acted on heavy going: tried in hood: often raced prominently: dead. *Julie Camacho* **84**

WILD FLOWER (IRE) 5 b.m. Approve (IRE) 112 – Midsummernitedream (GER) 43 (Thatching 131) [2017 59: p7d^6 6m^2 6d* p6g^3 6.1m* 6g^6 5.7s^6 t6.1m^3 p6g* p6g^4 p6g^4 Dec 31] sturdy mare: fair handicapper: won at Brighton in July, Windsor (apprentice) in August and Lingfield (apprentice) in November: stays 1m: acts on polytrack, tapeta, good to firm and good to soft going: has worn headgear/tongue tie: usually leads. *Jimmy Fox* **66**

WILD HACKED (USA) 4 b.c. Lemon Drop Kid (USA) 131 – Dance Pass (IRE) 104 (Sadler's Wells (USA) 132) [2017 105: p11g^2 t12.4s* 12m^6 11.9m^5 13.9m p12g^3 12g^3 11.9s Nov 11] sturdy colt: useful performer on turf, smart on all-weather: won handicap at Newcastle (by ½ length from Mistiroc) in April: placed in handicap (1½ lengths behind Big **106 a114**

Country) in April and September Stakes (¾ length behind Chemical Charge), both at Kempton: stays 12.5f: acts on polytrack, tapeta, firm and soft going: usually races prominently. *Marco Botti*

WILD ILLUSION 2 b.f. (Feb 18) Dubawi (IRE) 129 – Rumh (GER) 104 (Monsun (GER) 124) [2017 8m* 8d³ 8d* Oct 1] **113 p**

There are lies, damned lies and owners' statistics. Not for the first time, Godolphin profited from the rather enigmatic way the 'official' stats are decided in Britain which treat the Coolmore partners as separate entities and thus divide up their share of prize money into smaller units. Combining the prize money won by the horses which carry one or other of the Magnier, Smith and Tabor colours, but in practice are owned by all three individuals, would make them the leading owners. However, in France, a similarly puzzling anomaly works against Godolphin. There, members of Godolphin's French string, most of them trained by Andre Fabre, are listed as 'Godolphin SNC' and treated separately in France Galop's statistics from British-trained runners in the royal blue listed simply as 'Godolphin.' As a result, Khalid Abdullah was champion owner in France in 2017, largely thanks to British-trained Enable's Arc victory (much of the Juddmonte string is also split between Britain and France, but their horses are not treated differently, according to which side of the Channel they are based). Godolphin SNC finished a close second, and the inclusion of earnings from Godolphin's British-trained winners in France would have made the difference. The Fabre-trained Prix Ganay winner (and Arc runner-up) Cloth of Stars was Godolphin SNC's only Group 1 winner of the year in France but, from across the Channel, Sobetsu (Prix Saint-Alary), Thunder Snow (Prix Jean Prat), Ribchester (Prix du Moulin) and Wild Illusion (Prix Marcel Boussac) won Group 1 contests on French soil.

Wild Illusion's trainer Charlie Appleby had another good season, winning over a hundred races in Britain and recording an excellent 28% strike rate of wins to runs (he finished ninth in the trainers' prize money table). Appleby also had fourteen wins overseas, spreading his net far and wide, with important successes in Australia giving him winners on four continents in 2017. He was second to John Gosden in the IRB's table of British trainers' overseas earnings, picking up £2,949,579. Appleby did particularly well with his runners in France, Sobetsu winning a second pattern race at Deauville, the Prix de la Nonette, while Wild Illusion was one of several from her stable to pick up two-year-old pattern races in the autumn, along with Stage Magic in the Prix des Chenes, Glorious Journey in the Prix La Rochette and Sound And Silence in the Prix Eclipse. Instead of the Godolphin blue, Glorious Journey, who made it two from two at Saint-Cloud, carried Sheikh Mohammed's former maroon and white colours which were revived in the latest season to represent the Sheikh's nine-year-old daughter under the name of HH Sheikha Al Jalila Racing.

Total Prix Marcel Boussac - Criterium des Pouliches, Chantilly—Wild Illusion improves again in first-time cheekpieces to give connections a second consecutive win in this race after Wuheida in 2016, beating Polydream (white cap), Mission Impassible and favourite Magical (striped sleeves)

The Marcel Boussac was Wild Illusion's second visit to France, though defeat on her first trip made her one of the outsiders, in spite of the fact she had been supplemented. Over the same course and distance at Chantilly in the Prix d'Aumale the previous month she was beaten a length and a head into third behind Soustraction and Efaadah in a field of five. That followed a winning debut in a minor event at Yarmouth in August in which she made all, justifying strong support in the process to beat second favourite Give And Take, the only runner with prior experience, by two and a half lengths. Wild Illusion was ridden more patiently in the Aumale, but in the Marcel Boussac, in which she was fitted with cheekpieces for the first time, James Doyle rode her more prominently again, a tactic which proved decisive. The betting was dominated by the Moyglare Stud Stakes runner-up Magical, bidding to become Ballydoyle's third consecutive winner of the race, and the Freddie Head-trained Polydream, a stable-companion of Efaadah, who had looked a good prospect in winning both her starts at Deauville, including the Prix du Calvados. Efaadah wasn't in the field, but Wild Illusion came up against Soustraction (on whom Olivier Peslier put up 1 lb overweight), with listed winner Mission Impassible (the first foal of Nunthorpe winner Margot Did), the German Group 3 winner Narella and the Prix Morny fourth Zonza, the last-named the only one to start at longer odds than Wild Illusion, completing the field of seven.

Soustraction set the pace, with Wild Illusion pressing her, but, after challenging early in the straight, Doyle sent Wild Illusion into the lead under two furlongs out and she kept on well for a length and a half victory. It was much tighter for the places with only a head and a short head separating Polydream, Mission Impassible and Magical who were clear of the remaining three. In contrast to the winner, the two most-fancied fillies didn't enjoy the run of the race. From much further back, Polydream was putting in her best work close home to snatch second on the line, while Magical, who had tracked the pace, found herself short of room over a furlong out and had to be switched to the rail before running on. Another meeting between the three of them might not produce the same outcome, but there is no doubting that Wild Illusion, who looked to have the most to find on form beforehand, showed plenty of improvement and is a smart filly who looks sure to make further progress at three. She has something to live up to as the same connections' Wuheida, winner of the Marcel Boussac the year before, made a splendid recovery from a stress fracture to a hind leg to make her mark in the second half of the latest season after missing the classics. She finished a close fourth to Magical's sister Rhododendron in the Prix de l'Opera later on Arc afternoon and went on to turn the tables on Rhododendron in the Breeders' Cup Filly & Mare Turf to give her trainer another big overseas winner, his second at the Breeders' Cup after Outstrip in 2013.

Wild Illusion (b.f. 2015)	Dubawi (IRE) (b 2002)	Dubai Millennium (b 1996)	Seeking The Gold
			Colorado Dancer
		Zomaradah (b 1995)	Deploy
			Jawaher
	Rumh (GER) (ch 2008)	Monsun (br 1990)	Konigsstuhl
			Mosella
		Royal Dubai (ch 2000)	Dashing Blade
			Reem Dubai

Wild Illusion is also by the same sire as Wuheida, Dubawi, who was also represented by Sobetsu and two other Group 1 winners in France in the latest season, Grand Prix de Saint-Cloud winner Zarak and Prix Vermeille winner Bateel. The latest season only served to underline the importance of Dubawi to Godolphin and the wider Maktoum bloodstock empire, a topic discussed in Wuheida's essay in last year's Annual. Incidentally, the 2,600,000-guinea yearling out of Coronation Stakes winner Fallen For You mentioned there turned out to be none other than Glorious Journey, while the other Dubawi yearling who fetched the same price was named Emaraaty and contested the Dewhurst Stakes after winning impressively at Newbury. Dubawi failed to stay in the Derby but stamina shouldn't be a problem for Wild Illusion as her dam Rumh had plenty of it as would be expected of a daughter of Monsun. Trained by Saeed bin Suroor, Rumh won a maiden at Wolverhampton over an extended mile at two and went on to listed success over a mile and a quarter at Newbury at three. However, her front-running style lent itself to pacemaking duties and she effectively carried out that role for Godolphin's One Thousand Guineas winner Blue Bunting in the Irish Oaks, Yorkshire Oaks (both of which Blue Bunting also won) and the St Leger. At four, however, Rumh was allowed to run on her own merits and she found her level in staying handicaps, winning two such races at Kempton and Goodwood, though she was also placed twice more in listed company at shorter distances. Wild Illusion is Rumh's second foal after the rather headstrong Really Special (by Shamardal) who proved useful, like her dam, and won her first three starts, including a listed race over a mile at Newmarket at two and a trial for the UAE One Thousand Guineas at Meydan early in the year. Rumh is the best of four winners out of another useful filly, Royal Dubai, whose two wins in Germany at two included that country's equivalent of the Marcel Boussac, the Preis der Winterkonigin. Royal Dubai had a still better half-sister in Royal Highness (another daughter of Monsun) who showed smart form in France, where she won the Prix de Malleret and was placed twice in the Prix Vermeille, before going on to gain her biggest success at four in the States in the Beverly D Stakes. Wild Illusion's lightly-raced great grandam Reem Dubai didn't have anything like the same ability but she was well bred, by Nashwan out of a half-sister to the dual Gold Cup winner Ardross, the smart Gesedeh whose wins included the Pretty Polly Stakes at Newmarket and the Prix de Flore. Reem Dubai was also closely related to the dam of Electrocutionist, who won a Dubai World Cup for Godolphin, and a half-sister to the dam of Deutsches Derby winner Robertico. A mile is likely to prove on the sharp side, therefore, for Wild Illusion at three, and middle distances should suit her ideally, with a mile and a half unlikely to prove a problem for her. She has yet to race on extremes of ground. *Charlie Appleby*

WILD IMPALA (FR) 2 b.f. (Jan 19) Monsieur Bond (IRE) 120 – Dilag (IRE) (Almutawakel 126) [2017 6g 6m 7m^5 7m* 8d^6 Nov 4] €145,000Y: good-topped filly: half-sister to several winners, including French 2-y-o 5f/6f winner Souvenir Delondres (by Siyouni) and winner up to 7f I'm So Glad (2-y-o 6f winner, by Clodovil), both useful: dam French 7f winner: fairly useful performer: won minor event at Newmarket (by 3¼ lengths from High Seas) in October: stays 1m: acts on good to firm and good to soft going: has joined Jean-Claude Rouget in France. *John Gosden* **84**

WILD IRISH ROSE (IRE) 3 b.f. Galileo (IRE) 134 – Sea Picture (IRE) 82 (Royal Academy (USA) 130) [2017 79: 10s^6 10g 12g^3 12g* 14d* 14v^5 12s^3 14.5d^5 16s^3 12s Oct 21] good-topped filly: half-sister to several winners, including smart 1¼m-12.5f winner Ruscello (by Cape Cross) and useful 1m-1¼m winner (stayed 2m) Cradle Mountain (by Mastercraftsman): dam, maiden (stayed 1¼m), half-sister to Yorkshire Oaks winner/excellent broodmare Hellenic: useful performer: won handicap at Fairyhouse (by ½ length from Bold Knight) and listed race at Leopardstown (by ½ length from Wingingit) in July: third in Give Thanks Stakes at Cork (3 lengths behind Eziyra) in August: stays 14.5f: acts on heavy going: races towards rear: consistent: sold 325,000 gns in December. *Aidan O'Brien, Ireland* **106**

WILDNIGHTINVEGAS (IRE) 2 b.g. (Mar 22) Kodiac 112 – Wild Whim (IRE) (Whipper (USA) 126) [2017 5.1g^5 t6.1g^3 7d* Jul 11] angular gelding: fair form: won minor event at Brighton (by ¾ length from Jazirat) in July: stays 7f: gelded, and sent to Singapore, where renamed Wilde Ryker. *Richard Hannon* **73**

WILD STATE (IRE) 2 ch.c. (Feb 24) Reckless Abandon 119 – Be Glad 105 (Selkirk (USA) 129) [2017 5m May 26] 24,000F, £15,000 2-y-o: half-brother to several winners, including 1¼m winner Positively (by Oasis Dream) and 13f winner Gratified (by Sadler's Wells): dam French 1¼m winner: 20/1, seventh in minor event at Goodwood (4 lengths behind May Remain) in May: open to improvement. *J. S. Moore* **58 p**

WILD WEST HERO 2 b.c. (Apr 5) Exceed And Excel (AUS) 126 – Hi Calypso (IRE) 114 (In The Wings 128) [2017 8m^6 p8d t8.6g Nov 25] good-bodied colt: sixth foal: closely related to useful 1¾m winner Yangtze (by Dansili) and half-brother to useful 7f-11.6f winner Evangelist (by Oasis Dream): dam winner up to 14.6f (2-y-o 7f winner), including Park Hill Stakes: little impact in minor events: type to do better in handicaps. *Sir Michael Stoute* **– p**

WILEY POST 4 b.g. Kyllachy 129 – Orange Pip 89 (Bold Edge 123) [2017 85: 6.1d 5s^3 5.1g^2 5.1m^3 5.1d^3 Sep 4] neat gelding: fair handicapper: stays 6.5f: acts on soft and good to firm going: wears blinkers. *Tony Carroll* **78**

WILFRED OWEN 2 br.c. (Apr 11) Poet's Voice 126 – Mini Mosa 73 (Indian Ridge 123) **46**
[2017 8g 8.3d p7s p7s^{4} Dec 14] poor form: best effort at 7f: in headgear last 2 starts. *John Gosden*

WILLBEME 9 b.m. Kyllachy 129 – Befriend (USA) 76 (Allied Forces (USA) 123) [2017 **72 d**
84: t5d^{6} t5d 6g^{2} 6m^{4} 7d^{3} 5.9g^{4} 6g^{5} 6v 6g^{3} 7.2s t5d^{5} t6g^{6} t7.1d t6g f6.1g Dec 1] one-time useful performer, on downgrade nowadays: left Neville Bycroft after fourth start: stays 7f: acts on good to firm and good to soft going: has worn headgear, including last 5 starts: usually wears tongue tie nowadays: often races prominently. *Simon West*

WILLIAM BOOTH (IRE) 3 b.g. Born To Sea (IRE) 117 – Chaguaramas (IRE) 93 **76**
(Mujadil (USA) 119) [2017 72: 10.2g^{4} 8.5m^{3} 10.2g 8.3d^{3} 8.1d^{4} p10s t9.5g^{3} Dec 22] fair maiden: left Daniel Loughnane after third start: stays 1¼m: acts on tapeta and good to soft going. *Ivan Furtado*

WILLIAM HUNTER 5 b.g. Mawatheeq (USA) 126 – Cosmea 87 (Compton Place 125) **94**
[2017 92: p11g 12g^{4} 12m^{5} 11.8d^{3} 11.8d^{3} 14.1d^{3} Sep 21] lengthy gelding: fairly useful handicapper: third at Leicester in July and Haydock (amateur) in August: stays 1¾m: acts on soft and good to firm going. *Alan King*

WILLIAM OF WYKEHAM (IRE) 2 ch.c. (Apr 15) Arcano (IRE) 122 – Highland **– p**
Gift (IRE) 95 (Generous (IRE) 139) [2017 p7s Sep 8] well-made colt: half-brother to numerous winners, notably 2000 Guineas and King George VI & Queen Elizabeth Stakes winner Golan (2-y-o 7f winner) and 1¼m winner/Derby runner-up Tartan Bearer (both by Spectrum): dam 1¼m winner: 16/1, very green when well held in minor event at Kempton: should do better. *Sir Michael Stoute*

WILLIAM SAYLE 3 ch.g. Bahamian Bounty 116 – Incarnation (IRE) 72 (Samum (GER) **80**
126) [2017 p8g t8.6g* 10.2d p8s t8g^{5} Dec 6] 28,000F, 100,000 2-y-o: fourth foal: half-brother to 1½m winners Impertinent and Al (both by Halling): dam, 1¼m winner who stayed 1½m, half-sister to high-class/temperamental performer up to 1½m Norse Dancer: fairly useful performer: won maiden at Wolverhampton (by 2 lengths from Golden Wolf) in March: stays 8.5f: acts on tapeta: in cheekpieces last 2 starts: usually races prominently. *John Gosden*

WILLIE JOHN 2 b.c. (Feb 13) Dansili 127 – Izzi Top 121 (Pivotal 124) [2017 7g* Oct **87 P**
16] 325,000Y: second foal: half-brother to useful 2-y-o 6f/7f winner Dreamfield (by Oasis Dream): dam, 9f-10.5f (including Pretty Polly Stakes/Prix Jean Romanet) winner, half-sister to very smart 1m/1¼m winner Jazzi Top: 15/2, looked good prospect when won minor event at Yarmouth (by 2½ lengths from Humbolt Current) on debut: will stay at least 1m: open to significant improvement (sold 1,900,000 gns in February 2018, joined Roger Varian). *William Haggas*

WILLIE'S ANNE (IRE) 3 b.f. Lilbourne Lad (IRE) 111 – Cape Sydney (IRE) 52 (Cape **54**
Cross (IRE) 129) [2017 51: t9.5g^{6} t12.2g^{5} Feb 23] modest maiden: stays 9.5f: acts on tapeta. *Daniel Loughnane*

WILLINGFORSHILLING (IRE) 2 br.f. (Mar 19) Dabirsim (FR) 120 – Anavera (GER) **–**
(Acatenango (GER) 127) [2017 7m Oct 25] €16,500Y, 38,000 2-y-o: close-coupled filly: seventh foal: half-sister to German 9.5f-15f winner Aloha Iwanaga (by Samum) and useful German performer up to 11f Auctorita (2-y-o 1m winner, by Authorized): dam, German 1¼m/11f winner, half-sister to Preis der Diana winner Amarette and to dam of Melbourne Cup winner Almandin: in hood, 66/1, well held in minor event at Newmarket. *Harry Dunlop*

WILLOW SPRING 5 b.m. Compton Place 125 – Upstream 79 (Prince Sabo 123) [2017 **53**
56: p5m^{3} p5g p5f p6g 5m 5.2d^{6} 5.2m Aug 17] rather leggy mare: modest handicapper: best form at 5f: acts on polytrack and good to firm going: has worn blinkers. *Denis Quinn*

WILLOW TIGER LILY 3 ch.f. Sakhee's Secret 128 – Tinkerbell Will 57 (Where Or **–**
When (IRE) 124) [2017 6m 6d 6.1m Jul 3] smallish, angular filly: first foal: dam 1m-11f winner: well held in maidens. *J. R. Jenkins*

WILLSY 4 b.g. Sakhee's Secret 128 – Blakeshall Rose 38 (Tobougg (IRE) 125) [2017 80: **70**
7m 7m^{5} 8g 8m^{6} 8g 5.9g^{2} 6v^{3} 5.9s^{2} 7g^{4} 7m 5.9d 6g t7.1g^{5} 8.3g^{5} Nov 1] fair handicapper: stays 7f: acts on polytrack, tapeta, good to firm and heavy going: has worn headgear, including often in 2017. *Karen Tutty*

WILLWAMS (IRE) 3 b.g. Duke of Marmalade (IRE) 132 – Aweebounce (IRE) (Dubawi **73**
(IRE) 129) [2017 p8g t8.6g^{5} p7g* p8g^{4} May 5] fair form: won claimer at Lingfield in March: likely to stay 1¼m. *Richard Hannon*

WILLYEGOLASSIEGO 4 br.f. Kheleyf (USA) 116 – Kryena 72 (Kris 135) [2017 –: p13g* p13.3d^{2} p12g* 13f^{2} t14d* Dec 27] fair handicapper: won at Lingfield in February and April (apprentice), and Wolverhampton in December: stays 1¾m: acts on polytrack, tapeta and firm going: winning hurdler. *Neil Mulholland* **77**

WILLYTHECONQUEROR (IRE) 4 b.g. Kodiac 112 – Jazzie (FR) (Zilzal (USA) 137) [2017 111: 5.7m^{3} 5g^{3} 5g 5f 5m^{6} 5d 5d^{5} 5.5g 5v^{4} 5s Oct 7] sturdy gelding: useful performer: third in minor event at Bath (2 lengths behind Muthmir) in April and listed race at the Curragh (length behind Acapulco) in May: stays 6f: acts on polytrack, good to firm and heavy going: tried in cheekpieces: sold to join David Barron 58,000 gns in November. *William Muir* **109**

WILSON (IRE) 2 b.c. (Apr 4) Born To Sea (IRE) 117 – Alkhawarah (USA) 60 (Intidab (USA) 115) [2017 7d 7g* 8s^{4} Oct 19] 25,000F, £36,000Y, resold 25,000Y: second foal: brother to 1¼m winner Oceanus: dam, maiden (stayed 7.5f), half-sister to smart winner up to 1¼m Tamhid and Middle Park Stakes winner Hayil: fairly useful form: won minor event at Brighton (by 3½ lengths from Myboyhenry) in September. *Luca Cumani* **80**

WILSPA'S MAGIC (IRE) 4 gr.f. Zebedee 113 – Triple Zero (IRE) 70 (Raise A Grand (IRE) 114) [2017 60: 5.7f 5.7d 8.1d 5.1g 7m^{5} 6.1g^{5} Aug 28] poor maiden: in blinkers last 2 starts: usually races close up. *Ron Hodges* **45**

WILTONS (FR) 2 b.c. (May 3) Thewayyouare (USA) 117 – Pink Sapphire (IRE) 83 (Danehill Dancer (IRE) 117) [2017 6g 7s t7.2g^{4} a7g^{3} a7g* a8g* Nov 8] fair form: left Harry Dunlop after third start: won minor events at Bro Park in October and November: stays 1m: acts on dirt: tried in cheekpieces. *Catharina Vang, Sweden* **69**

WILY RUMPUS (IRE) 3 b.g. Intense Focus (USA) 117 – Supercat (IRE) 68 (Indian Rocket 115) [2017 67: p8g^{5} p8g^{5} p7g^{3} 8g Apr 15] fair handicapper: stays 1m: acts on polytrack. *Ed Walker* **67**

WIMBOLDSLEY 6 ch.g. Milk It Mick 120 – Chrystal Venture (IRE) 71 (Barathea (IRE) 127) [2017 54: f6g^{5} f6g* f6g^{3} t6s 5m t6.1g^{3} f5g^{6} f6.1g Nov 13] big gelding: modest handicapper: won at Southwell in January: stays 7f: acts on fibresand, tapeta and good to firm going: has worn hood: usually races close up. *Scott Dixon* **56**

WIMPOLE HALL 4 b.g. Canford Cliffs (IRE) 133 – Sparkling Eyes 80 (Lujain (USA) 119) [2017 96: 8.1d p8g p10s^{3} Dec 8] fairly useful handicapper: third at Chelmsford in December: stays 1m: acts on polytrack and good to firm going: tried in cheekpieces. *William Jarvis* **89**

WINDFAST (IRE) 6 b.g. Exceed And Excel (AUS) 126 – Fair Sailing (IRE) 62 (Docksider (USA) 124) [2017 114: 6m^{3} 6m 6m Aug 26] quite attractive, good-bodied gelding: useful performer: third in Abernant Stakes at Newmarket (3 lengths behind Brando) in April: stays 7f: acts on good to firm and good to soft going: tried in cheekpieces. *Brian Meehan* **104**

WINDFORPOWER (IRE) 7 b.g. Red Clubs (IRE) 125 – Dubai Princess (IRE) 105 (Dubai Destination (USA) 127) [2017 67§: t6g t5d* t5g^{6} t5g^{4} t5g^{2} t5g* 6m^{2} 5m 6m^{5} 6m t5s^{3} 5g^{3} 5d^{6} 5s^{2} 5s^{5} 5d^{6} 5g^{5} 6g^{5} t7.1s 5s t5g^{2} t5g^{3} t5d* Dec 16] fair handicapper: won at Newcastle in January, March and December: stays 6f: acts on all-weather, good to firm and heavy going: wears headgear: unreliable. *Tracy Waggott* **70 §**

WIND IN MY SAILS 5 b.g. Footstepsinthesand 120 – Dylanesque 91 (Royal Applause 124) [2017 93: 8.3g p8g 8g^{3} t8.6g 9.1g p8g^{6} Sep 25] sturdy gelding: fairly useful handicapper: third at Newbury in June: stays 8.5f: acts on polytrack and firm going: usually wears hood nowadays: usually races in rear. *Ed de Giles* **90**

WIND PLACE AND SHO 5 b.g. Shirocco (GER) 129 – Coh Sho No 59 (Old Vic 136) [2017 95: 16g^{5} p16d 16.3d 16s^{6} Oct 15] compact gelding: useful handicapper, below form in 2017: stays 2¼m: acts on firm and soft going: has worn headgear, including final start. *James Eustace* **81**

WINDS OF FIRE (USA) 2 b.c. (Apr 3) Kitten's Joy (USA) 128 – Laureldean Gale (USA) 114 (Grand Slam (USA) 120) [2017 t8.6d p8g^{3} Dec 21] fourth foal: half-brother to French 6f winner Gentle Breeze (by Dubawi): dam, 2-y-o 6f winner (later 1m winner in USA), half-sister to Musidora Stakes winner Secret History: fair form when third in maiden at Chelmsford (neck behind Best Blue) on second of 2 starts: will stay 1¼m+. *Charlie Appleby* **79**

WINDSOR CROSS (IRE) 2 gr.g. (Mar 16) Camacho 118 – Lizzy's Township (USA) (Delaware Township (USA) 124) [2017 t7.1d^{4} t8g^{5} t7.1g* t8d^{3} t8.6d^{4} Dec 26] fair performer: won minor event at Newcastle in November: stays 8.5f: acts on tapeta: in blinkers last 3 starts: front runner/races prominently. *Richard Fahey* **78**

WINDSORLOT (IRE) 4 ch.g. Windsor Knot (IRE) 118 – Majestic Jenny (IRE) 64 (Zamindar (USA) 116) [2017 68: p8g p7g^{2} p7g p7g^{6} 6.1v 8m^{4} 8.2g^{6} 8g^{4} 10.2d* p12g^{5} t9.5g^{6} t9.5g^{6} t9.5g^{2} t9.5d^{3} Dec 26] fair handicapper: won at Bath in August: left Henry de Bromhead after fourth start: stays 1¼m: acts on polytrack, tapeta and good to soft going: has worn headgear/tongue tie, including in 2017. *Tony Carroll* **66**

WINDSOR WHIRLYBIRD (IRE) 2 ch.f. (Feb 15) Harbour Watch (IRE) 121 – Charaig (Rainbow Quest (USA) 134) [2017 6.1g 6d Oct 30] €6,500F, £8,500Y: workmanlike filly: closely related to winner up to 1m Lawyer (2-y-o 6f/7f winner, by Acclamation) and half-sister to 3 winners, including 2-y-o 7f winner Empiricist (by Holy Roman Emperor), later successful abroad: dam ran once in France: well held in maiden/minor event. *Ali Stronge* **–**

WINDSTOSS (GER) 3 b.c. Shirocco (GER) 129 – Wellenspiel (GER) (Sternkonig (GER)) [2017 10.9g* 10.9g^{bd} 10.9g^{2} 11.9s* 11.9g^{4} 11.9s* Sep 24] first foal: dam, German 10.5f/11f winner, half-sister to very smart German 1½m performer Well Made: very smart performer: won listed race at Dusseldorf in April, Deutsches Derby at Hamburg (by length from Enjoy Vijay) in July and Preis von Europa at Cologne (beat Son Macia 4 lengths) in September: 3½ lengths fourth to Guignol in Grosser Preis von Baden on fifth start: suited by 1½m: acts on soft going. *Markus Klug, Germany* **121**

WIND TURBINE (IRE) 3 b.g. Power 117 – First Breeze (USA) 87 (Woodman (USA) 126) [2017 6d 7d t8g^{6} t12.4d Dec 16] no form, including in handicap. *Tim Easterby* **–**

WINE LIST 3 ch.g. Champs Elysees 124 – Masandra (IRE) (Desert Prince (IRE) 130) [2017 68p: 12v^{4} 10.1v^{3} p11g* Oct 11] fairly useful form: won maiden at Kempton in October: stays 11f: sold to join Jamie Osborne 26,000 gns in November: open to further improvement. *Andrew Balding* **80 p**

WINGED SPUR (IRE) 2 ch.f. (Mar 13) Motivator 131 – Mark of An Angel (IRE) 86 (Mark of Esteem (IRE) 137) [2017 p8g^{3} t8d^{4} p8g^{3} Dec 23] €16,000Y: fourth foal: half-sister to useful 1m (including at 2 yrs) winner Queen Blossom (by Jeremy) and a winner in Spain by Duke of Marmalade: dam maiden (stayed 7f): fair form: best effort when third in minor event at Lingfield (5½ lengths behind Masaarr) on debut. *Mark Johnston* **68**

WINGINGIT (IRE) 3 ch.f. Helmet (AUS) 127 – Chirkova (USA) 97 (Sadler's Wells (USA) 132) [2017 57: p7g^{2} p8g^{2} 10g* 12m* 12.7m^{2} 14d^{2} 11m^{6} 14.1g Oct 16] fourth foal: dam, 11f winner, sister to smart winner up to 1¾m Poseidon Adventure: useful handicapper: won at Navan (by ¾ length from Pandagreen) in April and Leopardstown (by 1¾ lengths from Grey Waters) in May: left Noel Meade after sixth start: stays 1¾m: acts on polytrack, good to firm and good to soft going: often races towards rear. *Andrew Balding* **106**

WINGS OF DESIRE 4 ch.c. Pivotal 124 – Gull Wing (IRE) 108 (In The Wings 128) [2017 122: 12m^{5} 12g^{5} Jul 13] lengthy colt: very smart performer at 3 yrs, winning Dante Stakes at York before fourth in Derby and best effort when 1¼ lengths second to Highland Reel in King George VI and Queen Elizabeth Stakes at Ascot: below that level in 2017, fifth in Hardwicke Stakes at Royal Ascot (3½ lengths behind Idaho) and Princess of Wales's Stakes at Newmarket (wore cheekpieces): stayed 1½m: acted on tapeta and good to firm going: to stand at Heversham Park Farm, South Africa. *John Gosden* **114**

WINGS OF EAGLES (FR) 3 b.c. Pour Moi (IRE) 125 – Ysoldina (FR) 110 (Kendor (FR) 122) [2017 99: 12.3m^{2} 12m* 12g^{3} Jul 1] **124**

The Derby is proof that imitation is the sincerest form of flattery. Virtually every other country where horse racing takes place has an incarnation of the historic Epsom classic which, for the best part of two centuries, has been the race in Britain that owners, trainers, jockeys and breeders most want to win. Nothing in Flat racing can begin to match the sport's greatest invention which did not emerge from any marketing department, or as part of any grand design, but from the toss of a coin—so the story goes—at a 'roystering' party at Lord Derby's country house on the outskirts of Epsom at which Sir Charles Bunbury, the greatest racing man of his day, was a guest. Lord Derby and friends had founded the Oaks (named after his country home), a race for three-year-old fillies over a mile and a half, which was first run in 1779. It was considered a success—most other races were for older horses—and another three-year-old race, for colts and fillies over a mile (it became a mile and a half race from 1784), was proposed for the following year. The toss of the coin was used to decide whether that was named the Derby or the Bunbury, after Lord Derby's distinguished house guest (Lord Derby's archives contain no specific details about the founding and naming of the great race and it could equally have been that the guests that day at The Oaks insisted that their host should give his name to it). It would be wrong to pretend that the Derby is anything like so dominant as it once was. The latest edition languished at number 37 in the 2017 list of the world's richest races, as compiled by the International Racing Bureau. Those 'newcomers' the Pegasus World Cup and The Everest head the list of the world's richest races on dirt and turf respectively, with the Breeders' Cup Classic and three races on Dubai World Cup night, the World Cup itself, the Sheema Classic and the Dubai Turf making up the world's 'top six'. Whether the Derby can still claim to be 'the greatest race in the world' has to be a moot point, and it would be a bit rich to counsel being wary of 'cheap imitations' in a year when the Japanese Derby, the Hong Kong Derby, the Kentucky Derby and the UAE Derby were all worth more than the Epsom original.

Prize money isn't everything, however, and, judged on the richness of its history and its tradition, the status and prestige of the Derby is largely undiminished. It continues to draw the best middle-distance three-year-olds and regularly produces champions, as well as maintaining a high profile in the media and still being a special occasion in the wider sporting calendar. For any racing professional, winning it is a major accomplishment which usually only spurs a desire to try to win it again. It is a major objective each year, for example, for European racing's 'superpowers', none of which seems more in thrall of the Derby than the Coolmore operation and its racing arm Ballydoyle. For Coolmore supremo John Magnier, the Derby is 'what it's all about…the race where all the qualities of a colt are tested.' Magnier himself has never officially won the Derby—his name appears nowhere on the race's roll of honour—but he has been associated with the Robert Sangster and Coolmore partnerships that have owned nine winners of the race.

The concentration of many of the best 'Derby types' in the hands of Coolmore, with well-bred, potential staying performers flowing through in numbers each year to Ballydoyle, has been a feature of the Derby in the first part of the century when Aidan O'Brien has saddled six winners, matching the total of his legendary namesake Vincent (John Magnier's father-in-law) who was his predecessor at Ballydoyle. The interest that surrounds Ballydoyle's runners in the various Derby trials each year has become a feature of the build up to Epsom, never more so than in the Aidan O'Brien era when the stable has often been mob-handed in the race. At one point, after the last of the major trials had been run, O'Brien revealed that Ballydoyle might have no fewer than eight runners in the Derby. 'The lads [Coolmore partners] will decide. We've got the seven horses from the trials—the three from Leopardstown, the three from the Chester Vase and the Dee Stakes winner Cliffs of Moher…the eighth would be Churchill [Two Thousand Guineas winner who had also been winter favourite for the Derby] but there's a big chance the lads will keep him at a mile, he is very comfortable at a mile and you never know about a mile and a half.'

Churchill went on to complete the Anglo-Irish Two Thousand Guineas double and the runner-up in the Derrinstown Stud Derby Trial, Yucatan, fell by the wayside (not seen out again). That left Ballydoyle with six in the Derby line-up, headed by the joint second favourite, 5/1-shot Cliffs of Moher, the Chester Vase winner Venice Beach at 12/1, the Derrinstown third Capri at 16/1 and the surprise Derrinstown winner Douglas Macarthur at 25/1 (a brother to the stable's Oaks winner Was, he had been the top-priced colt of his year—1,250,000 guineas—at Newmarket October Sales, Book 1). The Ballydoyle sextet was completed by Chester Vase runner-up Wings of Eagles at 40/1 and Chester Vase third The Anvil at 66/1 (The Anvil's rider Ana O'Brien, a 3-lb claiming apprentice unable to claim because of the status of the race, became the third female jockey to ride in the race after Alex Greaves and Hayley Turner).

Ballydoyle wasn't the only stable with a multiple Derby entry. John Gosden saddled five runners, all in different ownership, including the 7/2 favourite Cracksman, representing the owner, trainer, jockey combination which had won the Derby two years earlier with Golden Horn. Cracksman, a late withdrawal from the Dante Stakes on account of the soft going and the closeness to the Derby, had won both his starts, a back-end maiden at two and the Derby Trial at Epsom in April. Backing him up were: Khalidi, a 20/1-shot supplemented for £85,000 after winning the Cocked Hat Stakes at Goodwood only eight days before the Derby (the Cocked

Investec Derby, Epsom—Ballydoyle pacemaker Douglas Macarthur leads stablemates The Anvil and Venice Beach around Tattenham Corner, with favourite Cracksman (white sleeves) in touch; Wings of Eagles has just one behind him as he tracks another Aidan O'Brien-trained runner, Cliffs of Moher (dark colours), Benbatl the one bringing up the rear ...

Hat took over some years ago from the Predominate Stakes, a race won by Troy before his Derby win in 1979); Crowned Eagle, a brother to the previous year's fourth Wings of Desire and winner of a class 4 handicap at Windsor last time, and the Lingfield Derby Trial runner-up Glencadam Glory were both 33/1-shots; the Gosden quintet was completed by 100/1 rank outsider Pealer who had run only in maidens, winning at the fourth time of asking, on the all-weather at Southwell by nineteen lengths. Saeed bin Suroor was the other Derby-winning trainer represented by a 'team', his trio for Godolphin headed by 9/1 fifth favourite Dubai Thunder, an impressive winner of a Newbury maiden on his only start (the last Derby winner to step up straight from winning a three-year-old maiden was Morston in 1973); bin Suroor's second string was the Lingfield Derby Trial winner Best Solution, a 12/1-shot, and his third runner was 20/1-shot Benbatl, third in the Craven Stakes to Eminent and runner-up to Permian in the Dante at York. Eminent and Permian were both in the Derby field, Eminent, who had gone on to finish sixth in the Two Thousand Guineas, starting joint second favourite with Cliffs of Moher, and Permian (another who was supplemented) being sent off fourth favourite at 8/1. The maximum permitted field in the Derby nowadays is twenty, and the fact that Churchill was being kept at a mile and that the Derby trials had proved largely inconclusive contributed to an unusually big field, one that hadn't been exceeded since twenty lined up in Kris Kin's year, 2003, when the limit was reduced from twenty-five (two were eliminated that year).

The latest Derby would have had nineteen runners instead of eighteen if 1000/1 'vanity runner' Diore Lia (who had been entered in the Derby as a yearling) had not been withdrawn on the morning of the race due to a pulled muscle. The hullabaloo over the participation of Diore Lia—beaten twenty lengths when fifth in a Lingfield maiden on her last start—made some of the biggest headlines in the run up to the Derby when the BHA (using little-known Rule 83) intervened to prevent twenty-five-year-old apprentice Gina Mangan, who had been a jockey for eight years and had ridden one winner, from taking the mount, the BHA citing a risk to the welfare of horses and riders and the need to 'preserve the reputation of racing's championship events.' There were plenty who agreed with and applauded the BHA's decision, but it did deny racing the sort of story that resonates with the wider public. That a no-hoper could take his or her chance on the biggest stage, against those representing racing's 'superpowers', made horse racing different (plenty of general interest had been created by Olympic cyclist Victoria Pendleton's bid to 'switch saddles' and ride at the 2016 Cheltenham Festival). Followers of sport love an underdog and, without such stories in future, some of the romance will be lost.

More pertinently, Gina Mangan had an apprentice jockey's licence and, on the face of it, that should have allowed her to ride in any race that an apprentice may ride in (although Mangan was banned from the Derby, presumably no objection would have been raised against her riding in the race after the Derby, a handicap over the identical course and distance?). When the ban was first implemented, Diore Lia's owner—ostensibly running the horse to publicise a charitable cause—announced that the filly would not run. In the end, he relented and another apprentice, Paddy Pilley, was booked before Diore Lia went lame.

Some weeks after the Derby, the BHA announced that all runners in Group 1 races on the Flat for three-year-olds and upwards would in future need to have attained a BHA mark of at least 80 (a similar rule came into force over jumps). There have been 1000/1-shots in the Derby before (Shergar's year and Teenoso's, for example) but Diore Lia would have been the longest-priced Derby runner since 250/1-shot Maidstone Mixture in 2008. A winner over hurdles in the French Provinces on his last start, and owned by the Wilson family, whose 'vanity runners' in some of the big Flat and jumps races raised eyebrows at the time, Maidstone Mixture actually led the Derby field in the early stage before eventually finishing last. Neither Maidstone Mixture, nor 150/1-shot Castlemorris King three years later, would have qualified for the race under the new requirements. The same would have applied to Portuguese Lil, the 500/1-shot who was the mount of Alex Greaves when she became the first woman to ride in the Derby (a big story in 1996).

The Coolmore partners have run outsiders in the Derby themselves—100/1-shot At First Sight was second in 2010, finishing in front of two stablemates who started favourite and joint third favourite respectively—and they take the view that, with the fire-power available to them, it makes sense to leave it to the race to sort out their runners. 'In the Derby, you don't really know what will happen until you run the race, it's vastly different from nearly anything the runners have contested before,' said Aidan O'Brien. 'Well-bred three-year-olds can make dramatic improvement too from race to race and it would be folly for the "lads" to ask me to make a smaller selection, I can't be sure'. The words proved prophetic in the latest Investec Derby with the race going to the horse who was ostensibly Ballydoyle's fifth choice. Wings of Eagles had run four times as a two-year-old and his only success had come in a Killarney maiden, his last run coming in the Criterium de Saint-Cloud on his only start in Group 1 company when he finished ninth to French-trained Waldgeist and behind three other challengers from his own stable, Capri (third), Douglas Macarthur (fourth) and Taj Mahal (fifth). Taj Mahal had been ridden that day by thirty-one-year-old Padraig Beggy, a little-known jockey who gets few rides and whose main role at Ballydoyle is that of work rider (he joined Ballydoyle after trying to make it in Australia, returning to Ireland after being suspended for a year in 2014 following a positive test for cocaine and giving false evidence about the sample).

Like his jockey, Wings of Eagles might be termed 'the Derby winner who came out of nowhere'—in more ways than one. Beggy had never ridden in the Derby and had never ridden Wings of Eagles in a race, with Seamus Heffernan (on Capri in the Derby) having given him a considerate ride (struck just once with the whip and finishing best of all) when runner-up, starting at longer odds than The Anvil, to Venice Beach (who started favourite) in the Chester Vase on his only outing as a three-year-old before the Derby. A fierce early gallop in the Derby was set by Douglas Macarthur and The Anvil, making the race a thorough test of stamina, something which, combined with the unique configuration of Epsom's mile and a half course, with its undulations and its pronounced camber in the home straight, illustrated perfectly why the Derby comes as such a revelation for most of the runners. Considering the large field, however, there was surprisingly little trouble in running in the latest edition, although Wings of Eagles, who was dropped out, encountered some when making his run in the home straight, coming out of Tattenham Corner in a near-impossible-looking position with just two behind him and not getting a clear run three furlongs out, and again two furlongs out, before staying on with gusto, after being switched to the outside, to win in similarly astonishing fashion to his own sire Pour Moi six years earlier. Wings of Eagles hit the front close home to win by three quarters of a length and a neck from Cliffs of Moher and Cracksman, both of whom had every chance and were beaten fairly and squarely on the day, with Cliffs of Moher also racing off the pace for a long way, coming from a position just in front of the winner at Tattenham Corner and having a clearer run before arriving on the scene to lead a furlong out. Fourth-placed Eminent was another to keep on well after being held up, with the staying-on Benbatl fifth, Capri sixth and Douglas Macarthur seventh after only giving best late in the race. Permian, having his fifth outing in seven weeks, came tenth, and Venice Beach and The Anvil finished twelfth and seventeenth respectively.

Wings of Eagles, the longest-priced Derby winner since 50/1-shot Snow Knight in 1974, carried the purple, white seams, striped sleeves which had also been worn by two of the other Aidan O'Brien-trained Derby winners, Camelot and Australia. The colours are those of Coolmore partner Derrick Smith who has now partly-owned five Derby winners, the others being Wings of Eagles' sire the Andre Fabre-trained Pour Moi (Smith's first) and Ruler of The World. That pair won the Derby in the colours of Mrs John (Sue) Magnier. Mrs Magnier and Michael Tabor were joint-owners of all those five winners and they were also part-owners of the two earlier Derby winners trained by Aidan O'Brien, Galileo (successful in Mrs Magnier's silks) and High Chaparral (who wore the Tabor colours). The victories of Galileo and High Chaparral were gained before Derrick Smith became involved in ownership in a large way and, even before the success of Wings of Eagles, Mrs Magnier and Michael Tabor already held the official owners' record for the most wins in the history of the race, Australia's victory having taken them past the record of five jointly held by the 3rd Earl of Egremont and the present Aga Khan's grandfather (the Aga Khan himself has since owned a fifth Derby winner in Harzand). Aidan O'Brien, who has trained the Derby winner four times in the last six years, now stands just one short of the trainers' record of seven victories in the race, set by Robert Robson in the first part of the nineteenth century and since equalled by John Porter in the last quarter of that century and by Fred Darling in the first half of the twentieth century (two of Darling's victories were achieved in World War II substitutes run at Newmarket).

The paying attendance on Derby Day at Epsom in the latest season was 29,732, the lowest since 1992, just before the race was moved from its traditional Wednesday running. However, the estimated non-paying attendance of 150,000 on the Hill (renamed Poundland Hill in a sponsorship deal) helped to put the Derby comfortably among the ten best attended events of the British sporting year, as it has always been. There will have been some relief that the TV viewing figures showed an increase of more than twenty per cent on the previous year which had been the

... Cliffs of Moher looks the likeliest winner after taking over from Cracksman and Eminent (quartered cap) a furlong out, but Wings of Eagles is only just hitting top gear and swoops late to score in a style reminiscent of his sire Pour Moi; the 40/1-winner is the sixth in the race for his trainer Aidan O'Brien and one of only a handful of winners since 2015 for Ballydoyle work rider Padraig Beggy

last covered by Channel 4 (the five-minute peak for the latest Derby, the first in a new deal with ITV, was 1.7m, representing a terrestrial TV audience share of 11.3 per cent, though that is well short of the average of just over 3m in the last years of the BBC era which attracted a fifteen-minute peak audience of 3.3m for its final Derby in 2012. Forty-two of the ninety-four days' racing shown by ITV in 2017 were on the main ITV channel (the rest were on ITV4) and, as a result, viewing figures for almost all the major Flat meetings and festivals were up. A total audience of 4,319,000 watched the five days of Royal Ascot, for example, up from 2,708,000 on Channel 4 the year before, though still well short of the audience in the BBC's days, the figure in 2012 being 6,913,000. The viewing figures on the occasions racing appeared on ITV4 were well below previous Channel 4 levels and, when taken together, ITV's audience figures were just six per cent up on Channel 4's overall numbers in 2016 (the average on the main ITV channel was over 700,000, a terrestrial audience share of nine per cent, compared to around 275,000 on ITV4). The Derby is still out on its own as Britain's most watched Flat race and more money is bet on it than any other Flat race too (the Grand National dwarfs all other events in British racing on both counts).

Four of Aidan O'Brien's five previous Derby winners had gone on to complete the Anglo-Irish Derby double but Wings of Eagles joined Ruler of The World as an exception. Ryan Moore took over from Padraig Beggy at the Curragh and Wings of Eagles did better than Ruler of The World in reaching a place. With Permian and Benbatl both going on to win at Royal Ascot after their efforts in the Derby, there was nothing to suggest that the unconsidered Wings of Eagles had triumphed in a substandard Derby and he started 2/1 favourite at the Curragh, where, in front of a crowd limited to 6,000 because of course redevelopment, Cracksman took him on again (Cliffs of Moher was in reserve for the following week's Eclipse) and was joined by Waldgeist who had been runner-up in the Prix du Jockey Club on his last start. Ballydoyle ran five in the Irish Derby, other Epsom runners Capri, Douglas Macarthur and The Anvil being joined by Taj Mahal in the field of nine. Aidan O'Brien duly won the race for the twelfth time, but with Capri who held off Cracksman and Wings of Eagles by a neck and a short head, with Waldgeist fourth. Unfortunately, Wings of Eagles—the twelfth Epsom Derby winner defeated in the Irish Derby since the latter became a race of international importance—suffered a career-ending injury, found to be 'fracture lame' the following morning, according to his trainer. A broken near-fore sesamoid joint was confirmed on closer investigation. Wings of Eagles had an operation to insert a pin into the leg and will begin his stud career—in association with Coolmore—at Haras de Montaigu in Normandy, his fee set at €12,000 for 2018.

A good-topped colt with plenty of size about him (he was on his toes and had two handlers in the paddock at Epsom), the grandly-named Wings of Eagles is the first Derby winner to have been bred in France for over half a century, since the mighty Sea-Bird in fact. He was bred at the Haras de Montaigu and purchased by the Coolmore partners as a yearling at the Deauville August Sale for €220,000. His sire Pour Moi was the third of four Derby winners for Montjeu in the eight years from 2005 to 2012. Pour Moi's last-gasp victory over Treasure Beach denied Galileo, Montjeu's stud companion at Coolmore, a Derby winner that, taken with New Approach, Ruler of The World and Australia, would, by now, have put him ahead of Montjeu (whose other Derby winners are Motivator, Authorized and Camelot). It was rubbing salt into the wounds that Pour Moi's son Wings of Eagles should also have denied Derby victory in the shadow of the post to a more fashionable son of Galileo who would almost certainly have had more appeal at stud (all the other Ballydoyle runners were by Galileo). Pour Moi didn't race again after winning the Derby, sustaining an injury in late-summer while being prepared for the Prix de l'Arc de Triomphe (for which he was 2/1 ante-post favourite at the time). In truth, he wasn't given the support that some Coolmore stallions have received (stallions need the numbers nowadays), his first crop numbering ninety-six and his second (which includes Wings of Eagles) only fifty-one. By the time Wings of Eagles contested the Derby, Pour Moi had already been dispatched to Coolmore's National Hunt division at Grange Stud, a decision probably also influenced by the impact that Montjeu's sons Walk In The Park and Scorpion were having on the jumping game.

Wings of Eagles (FR) (b.c. 2014)	Pour Moi (IRE) (b 2008)	Montjeu (b 1996)	Sadler's Wells
			Floripedes
		Gwynn (b 1997)	Darshaan
			Victoress
	Ysoldina (FR) (gr 2002)	Kendor (gr 1986)	Kenmare
			Belle Mecene
		Rotina (b 1988)	Crystal Glitters
			Rudolfina

Montjeu and Pour Moi both rose to stardom in France and the distaff side of Wings of Eagles' family is also largely French, his dam Ysoldina being a daughter of the consistent French sire Kendor (winner of the Poule d'Essai des Poulains) out of the prolific broodmare Rotina who has produced a number of 'black type' performers, most notably the Group 1 winner Belle Et Celebre who lost her maiden tag when pulling off a surprise victory in the Prix Saint-Alary at Longchamp. Other smart performers out of Rotina were the Prix Perth and Prix Edmond Blanc winner Valentino, the Prix Jean Romanet winner Whortleberry and the Scandinavian champion Appel Au Maitre who won the Swedish and Norwegian versions of the Derby after finishing fourth in the German equivalent. Ysoldina herself gained her only victory at a mile (as a two-year-old) but she ran well in defeat a number of times in pattern company, finishing second in the Prix de la Grotte and third in the Poule d'Essai des Pouliches, both times behind Divine Proportions, and she stayed ten and a half furlongs. Wings of Eagles is the fourth winner out of Ysoldina, the three others—all fillies—having won in France, Torentosa (by Oasis Dream) winning twice as a two-year-old when she was placed in listed company, Gyrella (a sister to Torentosa) winning over five furlongs as a two-year-old and at up to seven furlongs at three, and Sweet Electra (by Sea The Stars) being successful over nine furlongs as a two-year-old. A yearling filly by Kingman out of Ysoldina made €750,000 at Deauville in August, knocked down to David Redvers representing Qatar Racing and Chinese investors. Ysoldina has no foal and was covered in the latest season by Siyouni. The usually patiently-ridden Wings of Eagles would probably have stayed further than a mile and a half and he acted on good to firm going. He cannot be rated highly as Derby winners go but, then again, in common with his sire, he did not have the opportunity, afforded to most recent Derby winners, to enhance his Epsom reputation with significant victories later in the season against horses outside his own age group, in the prestigious open-aged championship events. *Aidan O'Brien, Ireland*

WINGS OF ESTEEM (IRE) 4 b.f. Sir Percy 129 – Wings of Fame (IRE) (Namid 128) **76**
[2017 73, a85: 8m^{3} 8m^{3} p7s^{4} 8d^{3} Jun 30] good-topped filly: fair handicapper: stays 1¼m: acts on all-weather, good to firm and good to soft going. *Luke McJannet*

WINGS OF GOLD (IRE) 2 ch.c. (Feb 14) Raven's Pass (USA) 133 – Rosa Clara (IRE) **– p**
(Peintre Celebre (USA) 137) [2017 7g Jul 21] 100,000F: well-made colt: second foal: dam unraced half-sister to smart 7f-1¼m winner Blythe Knight: 7/2, well held in minor event at Newbury: should do better. *Saeed bin Suroor*

WINGS OF THE ROCK (IRE) 2 ch.f. (Jan 28) Rock of Gibraltar (IRE) 133 – Bless **76**
You 90 (Bahamian Bounty 116) [2017 5g^{6} 5g* 5m 5v^{4} 5.2s 5g t5.1m Oct 28] €67,000Y: sturdy filly: second foal: half-sister to useful 2-y-o 5f winner Yulong Baobei (by Choisir): dam 6f winner: fair performer: won maiden at Nottingham in May: raced only at 5f: acts on heavy going: in headgear last 4 starts: front runner/races prominently. *Scott Dixon*

WINKLEMANN (IRE) 5 br.g. Rip Van Winkle (IRE) 134 – Kykuit (IRE) 103 (Green **78**
Desert (USA) 127) [2017 82: 8m 8.3g^{6} p8g 7.1v Jun 10] lengthy, angular gelding: useful at best, little impact in handicaps in Britain: stays 8.5f: acts on good to firm going: has worn headgear, including last 4 starts: has worn tongue tie, including in 2017: sometimes slowly away. *John Flint*

WINK OLIVER 5 b.g. Winker Watson 118 – Nadinska 70 (Doyen (IRE) 132) [2017 75: **89**
t7.1g^{4} p7g^{4} p7g^{2} p7d^{5} t7.1g^{5} t7.1g* t7.1m^{4} p8g* p8g^{2} p8g^{4} t7.1g^{2} 8m^{3} 8m* 7.4m t7.2g* 7m 8f^{6} p7.5f^{2} 7.6g^{5} p8g Sep 25] fairly useful handicapper: won at Wolverhampton (apprentice) in February, Lingfield in March, Redcar in May and Wolverhampton again in June: second in claimer at Deauville in August: stays 1m: acts on polytrack, tapeta and good to firm going: wears headgear: often races towards rear. *Jo Hughes*

WIN LOSE DRAW (IRE) 5 b.g. Dark Angel (IRE) 113 – Caherassdotcom 79 (Compton **65**
Place 125) [2017 75: t7.1g^{5} t7.1g p8g^{6} 7m t7.2g 7g p10s^{3} f8.1g^{4} Nov 28] fair handicapper: best form at 7f: acts on tapeta: often in headgear. *Michael Appleby*

WINNING STORY 4 b.g. New Approach (IRE) 132 – Tanzania (USA) (Darshaan 133) **114**
[2017 112: p16g^{2} p15.8g* 13.4d^{5} 21.6m 13.9m 16g^{pu} Sep 28] smart performer: won valuable event at Lingfield (by 1¾ lengths from Watersmeet) in April: stayed 16.5f: acted on polytrack, tapeta and good to soft going: wore headgear: dead. *Saeed bin Suroor*

WINNING WAYS (IRE) 3 b.g. Lope de Vega (IRE) 125 – Sahara Sky (IRE) (Danehill **110**
(USA) 126) [2017 74p: p6g* p6g^{4} 7g^{3} 7m* 7m 7g^{5} Jul 1] strong, attractive gelding: smart performer: won maiden at Lingfield (by 5 lengths from Edged In Blue) in January and handicap at Ascot (by 3¾ lengths from Rusumaat) in May: stays 7f: acts on polytrack, good to firm and good to soft going: wears hood/tongue tie: waited with: sold 250,000 gns in October. *Jeremy Noseda*

WINSTON C (IRE) 3 b.g. Rip Van Winkle (IRE) 134 – Pitrizza (IRE) (Machiavellian **98**
(USA) 123) [2017 82: p11g^{3} 10m^{3} t12.2g* 12v^{3} 13.9m^{6} 14s^{4} 12m Oct 13] well-made gelding: useful handicapper: won at Wolverhampton (by 3½ lengths from African Beat) in July: third at Goodwood (2¾ lengths behind Londinium) in August: stays 1¾m: acts on polytrack, tapeta, good to firm and heavy going. *Michael Bell*

WINTER (IRE) 3 gr.f. Galileo (IRE) 134 – Laddies Poker Two (IRE) 117 (Choisir **124**
(AUS) 126) [2017 92p: 7d^{2} 8m* 8d* 8m* 9.9v* 8d^{2} 11.9d Oct 1]

The grey filly Winter was one of three dual classic winners—all by Galileo—to come out of Ballydoyle in the latest season. However, while the colts Churchill (Anglo-Irish Two Thousand Guineas double) and Capri (Irish Derby and St Leger at Doncaster) managed two Group 1s for the season, Winter went a long way towards emulating their older stablemate Minding's splendid season in 2016 when that filly was the winner of five Group 1s. The latest Horse of the Year Enable was the only performer to win as many as five Group 1s in Europe in 2017, but Winter was only one behind her, completing the Anglo-Irish One Thousand Guineas double (succeeding where Minding had failed), then adding the Coronation Stakes at Royal Ascot (to become only the second filly to achieve what might be termed the 'fillies triple crown' for the three-year-old milers) before making history by adding the richly-endowed Nassau Stakes when stepped up to a mile and a quarter against older fillies at Goodwood. The enforced mid-season retirement of Minding, who had won the Nassau twelve months earlier, left Winter at the top of the fillies' pecking order at Ballydoyle. She looked a worthy successor but, after a good spring and summer, Winter's run came to an end in the autumn and she didn't win again after the Nassau. Her trainer had mooted a possible clash with Enable in the Yorkshire Oaks but

Winter bruised a foot at home which put her on the sidelines until September. The injury held her up in her work, which was widely accepted as an explanation for her narrow defeat when favourite for the Matron Stakes on Irish Champions' Weekend, but in the Prix de l'Arc de Triomphe on what proved her final start, Winter couldn't emulate Minding's rare achievement in the previous year's Queen Elizabeth II Stakes by showing herself capable of beating the very best of the colts in an open championship event. That is a rare enough distinction—though Enable achieved it in both the King George and the Arc—and, if Winter ultimately came up short in trying to fill Minding's shoes, and those of another recent Ballydoyle champion filly Found (who won the 2016 Arc), there is no disgrace in that. Fillies as good as Found and Minding—not to mention Enable—don't come along very often.

Handled by David Wachman as a two-year-old, when she won a Dundalk maiden over seven furlongs on the third of her three outings, Winter was transferred at the end of that season to Ballydoyle when Wachman decided to retire from training. Winter looked a useful sort in the making as a two-year-old and she showed much improved form in the One Thousand Guineas Trial at Leopardstown in April on her first start for Aidan O'Brien—and her first outside maiden company. Ballydoyle ran four in the Trial at Leopardstown in which four of the first five in the previous season's Moyglare Stud Stakes reappeared (among them the Ballydoyle pair Hydrangea and Promise To Be True who had come second and fifth respectively at the Curragh). Ryan Moore rode Promise To Be True who started favourite at Leopardstown but it was Hydrangea and Winter who fought out the finish, Winter just failing to catch her stablemate and going down by a head.

The One Thousand Guineas Trial was the first indication that Winter might be a classic contender and she duly took her chance in the Qipco One Thousand Guineas at Newmarket, where she joined Hydrangea and hot favourite Rhododendron in a three-strong Ballydoyle challenge. Rhododendron, the mount of Moore, had won the Fillies' Mile at Newmarket as a two-year-old and always seemed likely to go straight to the Guineas without a preparatory run, as Minding had done (as Group 1 winners at two, both would have had to carry a penalty in a Guineas trial, as the Moyglare winner Intricately did when fourth in the Leopardstown Trial). Second favourite at Newmarket behind 5/4-shot Rhododendron was the Nell Gwyn Stakes winner Daban, with another home-trained contender the Princess Margaret Stakes winner Fair Eva, who didn't have a preparatory race, next in the betting. Hydrangea and Winter (who had still been 33/1 in places a week before the race) were the only others to start at single-figure odds in the fourteen-strong line-up. Wayne Lordan, who had been stable jockey to David Wachman, maintained his partnership with Winter who carried the pale pink second colours of Mrs John (Sue) Magnier, with Rhododendron in the much more familiar dark blue. It was a representative Guineas field, with the Moyglare winner Intricately and the Lowther winner Queen Kindly among others who represented the best two-year-old form, and the trials form was also represented by the runner-up in both the Nell Gwyn (Unforgetable Filly) and the

Qipco 1000 Guineas Stakes, Newmarket—the grey Winter shows much improved form to lead home a one, two for Aidan O'Brien, looking a worthy winner despite Rhododendron (second right) meeting trouble; Nell Gwyn winner Daban (No.2) is third

Tattersalls Irish 1000 Guineas, the Curragh—
Winter becomes just the third filly to complete the Anglo-Irish One Thousand Guineas double, just as impressive as at Newmarket as she beats stablemates Roly Poly (not in picture) and Hydrangea (cheekpieces) in a one, two, three for Aidan O'Brien

Fred Darling (Urban Fox). The most notable absentees were the Fred Darling winner Dabyah and the Prix Marcel Boussac winner Wuheida, Godolphin's main hope, who missed the first half of the season after suffering a stress fracture in a hind leg.

A good gallop, set initially by Hydrangea, ensured that the One Thousand Guineas was truly run—in contrast to the previous day's Two Thousand Guineas—and the cream duly rose to the top. Winter was in front over two furlongs out, after travelling strongly from the outset, and she ran on well to win by two lengths and a neck from Rhododendron and Daban, with the promising once-raced maiden winner Talaayeb completing the frame, ahead of Fair Eva and Unforgetable Filly (Urban Fox was eighth, Queen Kindly ninth, a below-form Hydrangea tenth and Intricately twelfth). The patiently-ridden Rhododendron had her excuses on the day, denied a clear run two furlongs out, but whether she would have beaten Winter if she hadn't met trouble was hard to say (she kept on well inside the final furlong to take second in the last fifty yards). Winter's trainer had won a record eighth Two Thousand Guineas with Churchill and Winter gave him a fourth success in the One Thousand; O'Brien had completed the Guineas double twice before, with Footstepsinthesand and Virginia Waters in 2005 and with Camelot and Homecoming Queen in 2012. Winter was a first classic winner for Wayne Lordan who missed out on the David Wachman-trained 2015 One Thousand Guineas winner Legatissimo who was ridden by Ryan Moore.

The training record of Aidan O'Brien also includes completing the Irish Two Thousand Guineas/One Thousand Guineas double on no fewer than four occasions. Desert King and, twenty-four hours earlier, Classic Park, were his first two classic winners back in 1997, and the same double was then completed by Black Minnaloushe and Imagine in 2001, Henrythenavigator and Halfway To Heaven in 2008 and Roderic O'Connor and Misty For Me in 2011. Churchill and Winter made it five, with Winter (partnered by Ryan Moore and now sporting Mrs Magnier's first colours) also becoming the first of O'Brien's One Thousand Guineas winners to go on to complete the double at the Curragh, Virginia Waters and Homecoming Queen having both failed to reach a place when hot favourites, while Minding lost out to Jet Setting in a tight finish, after which Minding was found to be bleeding from a head wound suffered leaving the stalls. There were no worries with Winter who landed the odds at the Curragh in spectacular fashion, making headway on the bridle from three furlongs out and quickening clear after leading a furlong later to win by four and three quarter lengths and a head from stablemates Roly Poly (sixth in the Poule d'Essai des Pouliches) and Hydrangea, with Intricately close behind them in fourth. Underfoot conditions were different from Newmarket (where it was good to firm) but Winter was proven on softer ground and she put up an even better performance on the form-book at the Curragh where she gave the distinct impression there was even more to come if required.

Surprisingly, Winter was only the third filly to complete the Anglo-Irish One Thousand Guineas double, following Attraction in 2004 and Finsceal Beo (who was narrowly beaten in the Poule d'Essai des Pouliches in between) in 2007. Attraction went on to add victory in the Coronation Stakes at Royal Ascot to her two Guineas wins, a treble which Finsceal Beo also attempted, managing only eighth at Royal Ascot. Back on good to firm going, 9/4-on shot Winter won the Coronation Stakes every bit as authoritatively as she had won at the Curragh, settling well for Moore before picking up the leaders in the home straight and drawing clear in good style to win by two and a quarter lengths and a neck from Roly Poly and Hydrangea, with the Fred Darling winner Dabyah, recovered after missing her shot at the One Thousand Guineas, a creditable fourth, ahead of American challenger La Coronel, 33/1-shot Tomyris and the Poule d'Essai des Pouliches winner Precieuse who found herself drawn into a premature battle from halfway with front-running Roly Poly.

With Roly Poly and Hydrangea reproducing their placed efforts from the Curragh, the Coronation Stakes was the sixteenth occasion that Aidan O'Brien has had the one, two, three in a European Group 1 race. Later he achieved the same feat, stretching his record to eighteen, in the Moyglare Stud Stakes and the Dewhurst (in which he saddled the first four). Saeed bin Suroor, who saddled the first three in the Eclipse in 1998, and Sir Michael Stoute, with the first three in the King George VI and Queen Elizabeth Stakes in 2009, are the only other trainers responsible for the first three in a Group 1 Flat race in Britain since the official pattern was introduced in 1971. O'Brien has now achieved the feat twice at Royal Ascot, having had the one, two, three in the 2007 St James's Palace Stakes.

Attraction's winning run in 2004 came to an end in the first running of the Falmouth Stakes as a Group 1 at Newmarket's July meeting, when she was beaten by the year-older Soviet Song who went on to beat the colts in the Sussex Stakes on her next start, before recording another victory over Attraction in the Matron Stakes at the Curragh, also upgraded to Group 1 that year. Winter faced no opponent of the calibre of Soviet Song when she attempted her four-timer in the Qatar Nassau Stakes at Goodwood. Aidan O'Brien had mentioned the Falmouth as a possible next target for Winter after the Coronation Stakes but the lure of the Nassau's £340,260 first prize (three times that for the Falmouth), which made it the second richest race for fillies in Britain, behind only the Fillies' And Mares' Stakes on British Champions' Day in the latest season, tilted the scales in favour of Goodwood (Roly Poly took the Falmouth in Winter's absence). The weather-battered Qatar Goodwood Festival had seen Churchill pulled out of the Sussex Stakes twenty-four hours earlier (the Nassau was moved from Saturday's to Thursday's card in the latest season in a rearrangement of Goodwood's big races), but Winter took her chance, stepped up to a mile and a quarter for the first time with the added complication that the prevailing heavy going—Aidan O'Brien called it 'winter jumping ground'—would

Coronation Stakes, Royal Ascot—Winter lands a Group 1 treble that has been completed just once before, by Attraction in 2004, with the placed horses from the Curragh (Roly Poly, striped cap; Hydrangea, second right) filling the same positions in another clean sweep for Ballydoyle

Qatar Nassau Stakes, Goodwood—Winter copes well with the testing conditions and longer trip, and lands her fourth straight Group 1 win; Nezwaah, Shutter Speed and Wuheida are all non-runners on account of the ground, leaving Blond Me (seams), Sobetsu (second left) and Hydrangea (striped sleeves) to complete the frame

make the Nassau a severe test at the trip. The late withdrawal of Nezwaah, Wuheida and Shutter Speed reduced the Nassau field to six but the risk paid off with Winter who, sent off at a shade of odds on, coped with the conditions and kept on well after leading entering the final furlong to win by a length and a half and a neck from Blond Me, the 16/1 outsider of the party, and the Prix Saint-Alary winner Sobetsu, with Hydrangea—like Winter racing beyond a mile for the first time—fourth and the four-year-olds So Mi Dar and Queen's Trust completing the field which finished quite bunched, four lengths covering the runners at the line, after a steadily-run affair in which they didn't start racing in earnest until the final three furlongs.

Winter's bruised foot, which interrupted her training, also resulted in changes to her autumn schedule. After the possible meeting with Enable in the Yorkshire Oaks went by the wayside (the Juddmonte International had also been talked about as a York target), Winter was aimed at Irish Champions' Weekend. The Irish Champion Stakes itself had been the initial target, but Churchill's creditable run in the International at York and the hold-up to Winter's training led eventually to Churchill going for the Irish Champion and Winter for the Matron, in which her stablemates Roly Poly, Rhododendron and Hydrangea were also saddled in an excellent renewal. All the Ballydoyle stars usually turn up to support Irish Champions' Weekend but both Churchill and Winter were among a number of beaten short-priced favourites for the stable at the latest renewal (though Ballydoyle still won three of the five Group 1s). Winter, who started at evens, was just edged out late on by 20/1-shot Hydrangea (ridden by Wayne Lordan) after travelling like the best horse in the field for most of the journey and leading from a furlong out until worn down by her stablemate. Moore wasn't unduly hard on Winter and he chose to ride her in the Prix de l'Arc de Triomphe three weeks later, preferring her to the runaway Irish St Leger winner Order of St George (third in the Arc twelve months earlier), the Hardwicke winner Idaho, the St Leger winner Capri and the previous year's Irish Oaks and Yorkshire Oaks winner Seventh Heaven. Winter was taking on the colts for the first time and had to prove her stamina, and she didn't help her cause by racing keenly in mid-division early on. Moore produced her to make an effort behind the leaders two furlongs out but she found no extra in the final furlong, shaping as though the trip was too far for her. She wasn't disgraced in ninth, beaten just over seven lengths (Order of St George fared best of the Ballydoyle quintet in fourth).

Winter's sire, the phenomenal Galileo, topped the combined sires' table for Britain and Ireland for the ninth time in the last ten years—his run interrupted by Danehill Dancer in 2009—and he may eventually equal, or go very close to matching, his own sire's record fourteen championships. Galileo may be at the veteran stage but Sadler's Wells himself was still covering mares in his mid-twenties and his fertility did not finally fail him until he was twenty-seven. Whether or not Galileo eventually matches Sadler's Wells's number of championships, he will certainly surpass his number of pattern winners. According to records maintained—without a computer programme to help him—by bloodstock historian Tony Morris since the official pattern was inaugurated in 1971, Galileo had sired the winners of three hundred and seven pattern races in Europe up to the end of 2017. He is within twenty of the record held by Sadler's Wells and will take over at the top of the table some time during 2018. Galileo's tallies over the last six seasons, starting in 2012, have been 30, 25, 32, 29, 39 and a scarcely believable 46 (more than 11% of the entire pattern programme) in the latest campaign (when he was also the top pattern-race broodmare sire, his daughters producing the winners of eighteen pattern races).

Winter (IRE) (gr.f. 2014)	Galileo (IRE) (b 1998)	Sadler's Wells (b 1981)	Northern Dancer
			Fairy Bridge
		Urban Sea (ch 1989)	Miswaki
			Allegretta
	Laddies Poker Two (IRE) (gr 2005)	Choisir (ch 1999)	Danehill Dancer
			Great Selection
		Break of Day (gr or ro 2000)	Favorite Trick
			Quelle Affaire

Winter was Galileo's leading pattern scorer with her four wins (all Group 1s), while Ballydoyle stablemates Order of St George, Hydrangea and the two-year-olds Clemmie and Happily all recorded three pattern wins (as did the Sir Michael Stoute-trained Ulysses). The fact that thirty-eight of the forty-six pattern wins by Galileo's progeny were recorded by horses trained at Ballydoyle illustrates the part the stallion has played in consolidating Coolmore/Ballydoyle as the dominant force in European racing in the first part of the twenty-first century. The various Morris tables also illustrate the enormous influence that the great Canadian-bred stallion Northern Dancer has had on European racing. He never had a crop larger than thirty-six—smaller crops were the order of the day in the 'seventies and 'eighties—but his number of pattern wins in Europe reached three figures, his final pattern victory recorded by Wajd in the 1991 Grand Prix d'Evry which brought Northern Dancer's total to exactly a hundred. There will soon be fifteen stallions who have recorded a hundred pattern wins or more in Europe and only four of them, Monsun, Dubawi (runner-up to Galileo in the general sires' tables in Britain and Ireland four of the last five years), Habitat and Riverman, are not male-line descendants of Northern Dancer. Apart from Northern Dancer himself, the top fifteen comprise three of his sons, Sadler's Wells, Nureyev and Danzig, three of his grandsons, Galileo, Danehill and Montjeu, and four of his great-grandsons, Danehill Dancer, Dansili, Pivotal and Invincible Spirit (the last-named on 99 wins at the end of 2017 and certain to join the '100 club' early in 2018).

Galileo is a versatile sire but he generally proves to be a strong influence for stamina in pedigrees. Winter's pedigree on the distaff side, however, contains far more speed than stamina. Her dam Laddies Poker Two, who only ran five times and won the Wokingham at Royal Ascot as a five-year-old, was a daughter of Choisir who made his name with those Royal Ascot victories in the King's Stand and the Golden Jubilee in 2003 and has been an influence for speed at stud. Winter's grandam Break of Day never raced and was sold out of Criquette Head-Maarek's yard for 15,500 guineas as a three-year-old at the December Sales. Break of Day's pedigree was all speed, her sire Favorite Trick an unbeaten two-year-old, winner of the Breeders' Cup Juvenile, who was the first of his age to be voted Horse of the Year in the States since Secretariat won the first of his awards (Favorite Trick was a disappointing sire in the end and died in a barn fire after being moved from Kentucky to stand in New Mexico). Break of Day's dam Quelle Affaire was a maiden but made the frame in the Prix de Cabourg and the Prix du Calvados over six and seven furlongs as a two-year-old and was herself a daughter of Ancient Regime, the best French two-year-old filly of 1980 who showed smart form over sprint distances at three after finishing fourth in the Poule d'Essai des Pouliches. Ancient Regime's dam was the very fast Caterina whose blistering speed made her very difficult to catch; she led all the way when winning the Nunthorpe at three after failing only narrowly in the same race as a two-year-old. Caterina also foaled two brothers to Ancient Regime who also made their mark as sprinters, the tough and consistent Cricket Ball, who won the Prix de Meautry at Deauville four years in a row in the 'eighties, and Olden, who was a very useful sprint stakes winner in the States. One of Ancient Regime's offspring was the Prix de l'Abbaye runner-up La Grande Epoque. Winter's dam Laddies Poker Two is among a growing band of good sprinting mares being acquired by Coolmore as mates for Galileo (there is more in the essay on Marsha) and she has visited him each year so far. Winter is her second foal, and her third Snowflakes hasn't reached the frame yet but showed fairly useful form on the second of her two starts for Aidan O'Brien in the latest season (not seen out after Royal Ascot). The tall, good-topped Winter, a strong traveller in her races, was probably best at up to a mile and quarter, and she acted on polytrack, good to firm and heavy going. Along with Minding, Winter begins her broodmare career with a visit to Japanese champion Deep Impact. *Aidan O'Brien, Ireland*

WINTER LIGHTNING (IRE) 2 b.f. (Apr 16) Shamardal (USA) 129 – Eastern Joy (Dubai Destination (USA) 127) [2017 7m^2 Oct 13] rather unfurnished filly: sister to smart winner up to 9.5f Ihtimal (2-y-o 7f/1m winner) and half-sister to 3 winners, including very smart winner up to 9.5f Thunder Snow (2-y-o 6f/7f winner, by Helmet) and smart winner up to 8.6f Always Smile (2-y-o 6f winner, by Cape Cross): dam, French 9f winner, half-sister to Prix de Diane winner West Wind: 11/4, second in maiden at Newmarket (4 lengths behind Veracious) in October: sure to progress. *Saeed bin Suroor* **85 p**

WINTERLUDE (IRE) 7 b.g. Street Cry (IRE) 130 – New Morning (IRE) 115 (Sadler's Wells (USA) 132) [2017 92: t12.4g^6 p10g* t9.5g^2 p16d* t12.2g^2 p15.8g^5 p15.8g t16.3s Jul 1] useful performer: won handicap at Lingfield (by head from Kyllachy Gala) in January and minor event at Kempton (by 1¾ lengths from Vettori Rules) in February: second in handicaps at Wolverhampton in February (½ length behind Pactolus) and March (1¼ lengths behind Cohesion): stays 2m: acts on polytrack, tapeta, best turf form on good going: tried in cheekpieces: often races towards rear. *Jennie Candlish* **109**

WINTER SPICE (IRE) 6 gr.g. Verglas (IRE) 118 – Summer Spice (IRE) 88 (Key of Luck (USA) 126) [2017 84: p16d^6 p16g^6 Mar 16] good-topped gelding: fairly useful handicapper, last on both starts in 2017: left Clive Cox after first one: stays 2m: acts on polytrack and firm going: often wears headgear: sometimes slowly away, often races in rear. *Sam Thomas* **74**

WINTOUR LEAP 6 b.m. Nayef (USA) 129 – Mountain Leap (IRE) (Sadler's Wells (USA) 132) [2017 14g^6 p16s^3 p16s 16s p16g^3 p15.8g^3 t16.5d p16g Dec 20] fair maiden: stays 16.5f: acts on polytrack, tapeta and firm going: usually in cheekpieces: winning hurdler. *Robert Stephens* **65**

WINX (AUS) 6 b.m. Street Cry (IRE) 130 – Vegas Showgirl (NZ) (Al Akbar (AUS)) [2017 133: 7g* 8v* 7.5v* 9.9s* 7g* 8g* 8g* 9.9g* 10.1g* Oct 28] **134**

Will she or won't she? The connections of Australia's queen of the turf Winx have so far been reluctant to commit her to a Royal Ascot challenge in 2018, the most encouraging response to Ascot's overtures coming in a statement from the filly's owners—before she won her third Cox Plate in October—that a European trip is 'on the cards'. Subsequent deliberations seemed to focus just as much on the possibility of Winx being trained for a fourth Cox Plate, four wins in Australia's weight-for-age race never having been achieved before. 'The Cox Plate is a big part of Australian history, the weight-for-age grand final, so to win it four times would be quite an accolade for the horse,' said her trainer Chris Waller. Although the flow seems to be drying up, Australian challengers were very much part of the Royal Ascot scene for over a decade after pathfinding Choisir completed a famous King's Stand/Golden Jubilee double in 2003, and Black Caviar's appearance at the Royal meeting in 2012 was one of racing's biggest box-office events. Black Caviar's monumental achievements—she ended her career unbeaten in twenty-five races (including an Australian record fifteen Group 1s)—would have made her a legend anyway without all the attention she received when visiting Britain for the Diamond Jubilee Stakes. But her appearance did wonders for the cause of international competition and was widely viewed as having secured her place in racing history.

Whether or not Winx follows in Black Caviar's footsteps remains to be seen, but the thoughts of Sydney's top trainer Chris Waller, who has handled Winx's career so well, are interesting. 'You need to take the right horse to England, in my opinion that is a colt whose value you can significantly enhance by bringing him to the attention of northern hemisphere breeders [Waller trained 2015 Diamond Jubilee runner-up Brazen Beau, now a shuttle stallion] … the downside of travelling to another hemisphere from Australia is that they're going from winter to summer which has an unbelievable effect on them. There is normally a window of a couple of weeks where they show no effects, providing they cope well with the travelling, but then they start to train off a little and lose that edge. Furthermore, the horses then need to come back so they have to go through this process not once but twice. Bringing a horse back to Australia and expecting it to fit back into some of the strongest races in the world is unrealistic, you've almost lost six months. When you're racing for such big prize money in Australia it's a huge issue that needs considering.'

The first prize for the Cox Plate is over a million pounds, while the two races leading up to it that were used for Winx's preparation in the latest season both had a first prize of over £170,000. The Queen Anne Stakes, the likely target for Winx if she comes to Royal Ascot, is the second most valuable race at the fixture (behind the Prince of Wales's Stakes) and would have earned her connections £388,464 had she won the latest renewal. Black Caviar, incidentally, wasn't seen out again in 2012 after winning at Royal Ascot and she didn't resume her career until February 2013, eight months later, when she won the Lightning Stakes—named in her honour—at Flemington for the third time, breaking the track record as she stretched her sequence to twenty-three wins from twenty-three starts. She was retired in the April after adding further victories in the William Reid Stakes at Moonee Valley and the TJ Smith Stakes at Randwick. Black Caviar's lengthy absence after her run at Royal Ascot came after she was found to have suffered damage to a suspensory ligament and to some muscles in her back, but Winx's trainer has a point about the time it takes for some horses to get over the effects of racing in another hemisphere. Australian horses, who are offered financial incentives in Group 1 races at Royal Ascot, were absent altogether from the Royal meeting in the latest season when the leading sprinters had a lucrative new event, The Everest (the world's most valuable turf race at A$10m), to aim at in October at Randwick. Plans for Australia's best sprinter Chautauqua, who won his third successive TJ Smith Stakes, to come to Royal Ascot, after taking in the Chairman's Sprint in Hong Kong in May, were shelved in favour of staying at home for The Everest (in which he was fourth behind Redzel). Other leading Australian sprinters, including Spieth and Flying Artie, who were being talked about as Royal Ascot challengers, didn't come through their domestic programmes in February and March well enough. The Caulfield Cup winner Jameka had been pencilled in for the Hardwicke Stakes, and then for the King George VI and Queen Elizabeth Stakes, but illness put paid to plans for her international campaign and she wasn't seen out after winning the BMW at Rosehill in March.

There is not much doubt about Winx's constitution being able to stand up to the rigours of being flown halfway round the world to take up a Royal Ascot challenge. As well as being one of the best racemares seen anywhere since the end of World War II, she has proved herself as tough as old boots. After running eight times in 2016, she had nine races in 2017, running four times between February and April and then, after a break, having five races from the middle of August to the end of October, ending with that crowning third victory in the Cox Plate. Her programme in the first part of the year was pretty much a carbon copy of the previous year, except that she ran in the Queen Elizabeth Stakes, worth even more than the Cox Plate and Australia's richest Group 1 weight-for-age race, at 'The Championships', Sydney's two-meeting showpiece staged at Randwick in April. Winx ran there in preference to one of Australia's great handicaps the Doncaster Mile which she had won under top weight the year before (it had been intended then that Winx would also contest the Queen Elizabeth Stakes on the second Saturday of 'The Championships' but, in the end, connections decided against it). Winx gained her fourteenth, fifteenth and sixteenth successive wins in the Star Apollo Stakes over seven furlongs at Randwick (beating her old rival Hartnell by two and three quarter lengths), the Group 1 Chipping Norton Stakes over a mile at Randwick again (winning readily by two lengths from Lasqueti Spirit) and the Group 1 China Horse Club George Ryder Stakes over seven and a half furlongs at Rosehill.

Winx's performance in the George Ryder was arguably the best performance of her life so far, even better than her eight-length victory in her second Cox Plate. Conditions were very testing, as they had been for the Chipping Norton, and Winx

China Horse Club George Ryder Stakes, Rosehill—Winx repeats her 2016 victory in this race and makes it 16 wins on the trot, producing a truly outstanding performance in the testing conditions

was up against the first three from the Group 1 Canterbury Stakes earlier in March, Le Romain, the champion sprinter Chautauqua and the previous year's Epsom Handicap winner Hauraki, stronger opposition—collectively—than she had faced in the George Ryder twelve months earlier. Winx travelled smoothly all the way and stretched clear of her field after leading on the bridle in the home straight, having the race in safe keeping after accelerating away over the penultimate furlong and then being allowed to coast home in the closing stages. She won by seven and a quarter lengths from Le Romain with Chautauqua a further length and a quarter away in third and Hauraki fourth of the seven runners. The Longines Queen Elizabeth Stakes over a mile and a quarter, back at Randwick three weeks after the George Ryder, provided Winx with her seventeenth successive victory. Again patiently ridden early on, Winx moved through to lead a furlong and a half out and quickened clear to win comfortably by five and a quarter lengths from Hartnell, the form not quite so strong as the George Ryder (third-placed Sense of Occasion, only a neck behind Hartnell, appeared to show much improved form).

During her break over the Australian winter, Winx was named Australia's Horse of the Year for the second time and inducted into Australian racing's Hall of Fame, having become the fourth horse to have completed the Cox Plate/Queen Elizabeth Stakes double in the same season, joining Our Poetic Prince, Summer Regent and Tulloch. Lonhro, in 2003, was the only horse previously to have landed the George Ryder/Queen Elizabeth Stakes double in the same season in the past thirty years. No other horse has won the Cox Plate, the Chipping Norton and the George Ryder in the same season, something Winx has now achieved twice. Winx reappeared in the Australian spring, after four months off, but her first two races didn't quite go to plan. She gave plenty of ground away at the start of the Bob Ingham Warwick Stakes at Randwick in August and did well to snatch the seven-furlong race by a head in the last few strides from her stablemate Foxplay, after still having plenty to do when last into the home straight. Supporters of Winx suffered a further heart-in-the-mouth moment a fortnight later in another Group 2, the Tattersalls Club Chelmsford Stakes, over Randwick's mile course this time. Wearing a hood for the first time, Winx got away on terms on this occasion but was left with a lot to do when the Warwick Stakes fourth Red Excitement tried to slip the field shortly after halfway. Winx improved from fourth to second after the field turned into the short Randwick home straight but still had five lengths to make up in the final furlong. She finished very strongly to lead in the last fifty yards and win by a length in the end from Red Excitement, the pair clear. Winx had started at 11/1-on and even for her trainer ('with two furlongs to run I was concerned') and jockey Hugh Bowman ('I was worried and can't explain the feeling when she finally hit the afterburners') harboured thoughts at one stage that Winx might be beaten. On the other side of the coin, for Winx to win from the position she had been in, in both the Warwick and the Chelmsford, seemed to illustrate that she was back as good as ever.

Seppelt Turnbull Stakes, Flemington—
without the hood she had worn on her last two starts, Winx scores in effortless fashion, barely coming off the bridle to beat Ventura Storm (stripes)

Success in the Chelmsford took Winx to nineteen consecutive victories, level with Gloaming and Desert Gold, and behind only Black Caviar in the list of horses who have recorded the longest winning streaks in Australian racing (she had passed Mainbrace's seventeen and Ajax's eighteen on the way). Winx had one more race in Sydney, her trainer saying that 'a bit of extra racing will bring her on', and she was out on her own with twenty successive wins after a more straightforward victory, again wearing a hood, in the Group 1 Colgate Optic White Stakes (better known as the George Main Stakes) over a mile at Randwick. Winx again seemed to be left with plenty to do—niggled along in sixth at one point—but came with her customary run, after having only one behind her on the home turn, to get there for a comfortable victory in the end by a length and a quarter from the veteran Happy Clapper, with Foxplay a further four and a half lengths away in third.

Winx's victory in the George Main was her thirteenth Group 1 success which put her on course to equal Black Caviar's record for an Australian performer if she could win her two remaining races of the year, the Seppelt Turnbull Stakes and the Ladbrokes Cox Plate, both staged at the Melbourne Spring Carnival in October, the former at Flemington (her first start there) and the latter at Moonee Valley. Success in those two races would also take her past the 14,526,690 Australian dollars earned by three-times Melbourne Cup winner Makybe Diva, Australia's leading money-earner. The hood Winx had worn on her two previous starts was dispensed with in the Turnbull in which, faced by six opponents, she put up one of her best performances, making eye-catchingly easy progress before the home turn and hardly coming off the bridle as she moved into the lead with under two furlongs to run. Winx won most decisively, needing minimal assistance from the saddle to beat Ventura Storm (a good second in the St Leger at Doncaster before being sold to race in Australia) and Humidor by six and a half lengths and three quarters of a length (there was another ex-European in fifth, Sir Isaac Newton, a Royal Ascot winner who had finished in the frame in the King George VI and Queen Elizabeth Stakes and the Juddmonte International).

All was set for Winx's third Cox Plate and her attempt to become the first triple winner of the race for thirty-five years, since the history-making Kingston Town in 1982. Winx had started favourite for all twenty-one races that comprised her unblemished run, and she had been odds-on for her last sixteen, following the first of her Cox Plate wins in 2015, Winx's come-from-behind style of racing makes her exciting to watch and, as she moved through from fifth to lead rounding the home turn at Moonee Valley, the stage seemed set for another clear-cut victory to mark her third Cox Plate win. That was reckoning without 30/1-shot Humidor, however, who ran the race of his life to challenge 11/2-on Winx in the home straight. Winx never looked like being beaten but she had to be pushed out (Bowman resorted to the whip just once) to hold off Humidor by half a length, the pair pulling clear of the rest. The only overseas-trained challenger the very smart Folkswood, one of a group of Charlie Appleby-trained runners to enjoy a short Australian campaign in October and November, came a good third, disputing the lead over two furlongs out before finishing four and a quarter lengths behind Humidor, with Royal Symphony, front-running Gailo Chop and Happy Clapper completing the first six. There had been another British-trained entry, the smart Kaspersky, but he was a late absentee due to swelling in a foreleg, while the Aidan O'Brien-trained three-year-old (The) Taj Mahal was also an intended runner until a few days before the race (he went on to win the Zipping Classic in November after his permanent transfer to Australia). Winx's two previous Cox Plate victories had also come in fields containing European challengers, with Highland Reel, trying to emulate his stablemate Adelaide's ground-breaking victory the year before, finishing third behind Winx in 2015 (Arod and then-French-trained Gailo Chop also ran); the Prix du Moulin winner Vadamos came fourth in 2016 when Winx won by a record eight lengths. Winx broke her own course record in the latest Cox Plate, passing the post in a time of 2m 2.94sec. Her victory put the seal on her third year of racing at the highest level, during which she showed her form under all conditions, at virtually every distance from seven furlongs to a mile and a quarter, sometimes coming from seemingly-impossible positions to maintain her aura of invincibility. 'Every race is so big now,' says her trainer 'because of her winning sequence and the fact that she carries the expectations of so many people.'

Ladbrokes Cox Plate, Moonee Valley—Winx becomes the first triple winner of this race since Kingston Town in 1982, in the process recording her 22nd consecutive success and matching Black Caviar's tally of 15 wins at Group 1 level; Winx also becomes Australia's leading money earner, though Humidor (blinkers) makes her work for it in a race run in course-record time

Winx (AUS) (b.m. 2011)	Street Cry (IRE) (br 1998)	Machiavellian (b 1987)	Mr Prospector
			Coup de Folie
		Helen Street (b 1982)	Troy
			Waterway
	Vegas Showgirl (NZ) (b 2002)	Al Akbar (b 1990)	Success Express
			Gala Night
		Vegas Magic (b 1985)	Voodoo Rhythm
			Vegas Street

Winx's pedigree was covered in *Racehorses of 2016*. She was sired by the Dubai World Cup winner Street Cry (who did all his racing on dirt) on one of his shuttle trips to Australia. Street Cry's death in 2014 at the age of sixteen was a blow to Darley as he had established himself as a versatile sire who had produced a regular flow of good-class winners on both dirt and turf, as well as in both hemispheres (his best-known progeny also include another top racemare who achieved celebrity status, American Horse of the Year in 2010 Zenyatta who was beaten only once in twenty career starts). Winx's dam Vegas Showgirl, a listed-winning sprinter successful at up to seven furlongs, delivered her seventh foal (a filly by Exceed And Excel) on the day Winx won the George Main Stakes. Winx is the second foal of Vegas Showgirl whose other offspring include the very useful sprinter El Divino. El Divino is by champion Australian sire Snitzel who is also the sire of Vegas Showgirl's son—now named Boulder City—who topped the Inglis Easter Yearling Sale in 2016 when snapped up by leading trainer Gai Waterhouse. Vegas Showgirl produced a filly by Snitzel in 2016 who is being retained by her breeders. *Chris Waller, Australia*

WIRRAL GIRL (IRE) 2 b.f. (Apr 24) Kodiac 112 – Ursula (IRE) 87 (Namid 128) [2017 5v^6 5m* 5.2s 6.1g 5s^3 Oct 10] €21,000Y, £100,000 2-y-o: second foal: dam, winner up to 7f (2-y-o 5f winner), half-sister to smart performer up to 1m in Hong Kong Sparkling Power (2-y-o 7f winner in Ireland as Montecchio): fair performer: won minor event at Beverley in July: best effort at 5f: acts on good to firm going: front runner/races prominently. *Richard Fahey* **78**

WISCONSIN (JPN) 3 b.g. Deep Impact (JPN) 134 – Peeping Fawn (USA) 126 (Danehill (USA) 126) [2017 10g^2 12.5m* 14m 14g^5 13g Jul 13] tall gelding: fourth foal: half-brother to French 1¼m-12.5f winner Purely Priceless (by Galileo) and useful 2-y-o 6f winner Sir John Hawkins (by Henrythenavigator): dam 1m-1½m (including Irish/Yorkshire Oaks) winner: useful performer: won maiden at Tipperary (by ¾ length from Steel Prince) in May: 4¾ lengths fifth to Rekindling in Curragh Cup in July: stays 1¾m: acts on good to firm going: tried in cheekpieces: races prominently: gelded, and sent to Australia. *Aidan O'Brien, Ireland* **105**

WISHING TIME (IRE) 3 b.f. Frankel 147 – Beyond Desire 112 (Invincible Spirit (IRE) 121) [2017 –p: t5g^4 t5.1g^3 5m* Apr 12] fair form: won handicap at Catterick in April: raced only at 5f: should progress further. *David O'Meara* **66 p**

WISHING TREE 4 ch.f. Haafhd 129 – Ananda Kanda (USA) 76 (Hero's Tribute (USA)) [2017 49: t7.2g t8s Jun 29] modest maiden: stays 7f: acts on tapeta and good to soft going. *Brian Ellison* **51**

WISHING WELL 5 b.m. Bahri (USA) 125 – Amourallis (IRE) 101 (Dushyantor (USA) 123) [2017 80: 12m 16m^6 16d* t12.4g Dec 6] fairly useful handicapper: won at Ripon in June: stays 2m: acts on polytrack, tapeta, soft and good to firm going: has worn headgear. *Micky Hammond* **82**

WISSAHICKON (USA) 2 ch.c. (Feb 4) Tapit (USA) 118 – No Matter What (USA) 110 (Nureyev (USA) 131) [2017 t8.6g* p10s^2 Nov 23] half-brother to several winners, including very smart winner up to 8.5f Rainbow View (2-y-o 7f/1m winner, by Dynaformer) and smart US performer up to 1½m Just As Well (by A P Indy): dam, 1m (in France)/9f (US Grade 1) winner, half-sister to US Grade 1 1¼m winner E Dubai: fairly useful form: won minor event at Wolverhampton (by nose from Craving) in October: second in similar event at Chelmsford (2 lengths behind Lucky Deal) in November: remains with potential. *John Gosden* **88 p**

WITH APPROVAL (IRE) 5 b.g. Approve (IRE) 112 – Kelsey Rose 97 (Most Welcome 131) [2017 72: p8g p8g^5 p10m p10g^3 p8g^6 p8d^6 p10g^3 8g^2 7d^2 7m 8d^4 8s* 8d^3 8s 8v^5 p8s p8g^5 Dec 30] rather leggy gelding: fair handicapper: won at Brighton in September: stays 1¼m: acts on polytrack and heavy going: wears cheekpieces: often races prominently. *Laura Mongan* **66**

WITHERNSEA (IRE) 6 b.g. Dark Angel (IRE) 113 – Charlene Lacy (IRE) 77 (Pips **106** Pride 117) [2017 103: 8g 7m 8s* 8m 7g 7d^3 8s^4 7d^3 6v 7s 8s Oct 21] good-topped gelding: useful handicapper: won at Newbury (by neck from Brigliadoro) in May: third at Ascot (International Stakes, 2¼ lengths behind Stamp Hill) in July and Leopardstown (3 lengths behind Burnt Sugar) in September: stays 1m: acts on good to firm and heavy going. *Richard Fahey*

WITH HINDSIGHT (IRE) 9 b.g. Ad Valorem (USA) 125 – Lady From Limerick (IRE) **64** 61 (Rainbows For Life (CAN)) [2017 78: t12.2m f16g t12.2g f14d^4 t13.9g^2 14.1m^3 14v^2 14m Jun 24] rather leggy gelding: fair handicapper: stays 1¾m: acts on all-weather, good to firm and heavy going: front runner/races prominently. *Steve Gollings*

WITHHOLD 4 b.g. Champs Elysees 124 – Coming Back 89 (Fantastic Light (USA) 134) **108 p** [2017 90: 12m^3 18m* Oct 14] strong gelding: useful handicapper: won Cesarewitch Handicap at Newmarket (by 3¾ lengths from London Prize) in October: stays 2¼m: acts on polytrack, soft and good to firm going: tried in cheekpieces: races prominently: open to further improvement. *Roger Charlton*

WITH INTENT 3 gr.g. Monsieur Bond (IRE) 120 – Dim Ofan 80 (Petong 126) [2017 –: **–** 6.9g May 22] no form: tried in cheekpieces. *Ollie Pears*

WITHOUT PAROLE 2 b.c. (Mar 20) Frankel 147 – Without You Babe (USA) (Lemon **93 p** Drop Kid (USA) 131) [2017 t8d* Dec 16] fifth foal: half-brother to 3 winners, including high-class 1m winner (including Breeders' Cup Dirt Mile) Tamarkuz (also 2-y-o 7f winner, by Speightstown): dam unraced half-sister to very smart US Grade 1 1m/1¼m winner Stay Thirsty: 8/13, looked good prospect when won minor event at Newcastle (by 6 lengths from Trevithick) on debut: sure to improve. *John Gosden*

WITH PLEASURE 4 b.g. Poet's Voice 126 – With Fascination (USA) 111 (Dayjur **78** (USA) 137) [2017 83: t8.6m^4 p10g 10m^3 8g^3 17.1d* 12d^2 14.1d^4 16d Oct 6] fair handicapper: won at Bath in August: left David O'Meara after first start: stays 17f: acts on polytrack, tapeta and good to soft going: tried in cheekpieces. *John Flint*

WITH YOU 2 b.f. (Mar 3) Dansili 127 – In Clover 114 (Inchinor 119) [2017 8s* 8s* Oct **105 p** 18] sixth foal: sister to 2 winners, notably smart 1m-1¼m (Prix de l'Opera) winner We Are, and half-sister to 2 useful winners by Oasis Dream, including French 7f-9f winner Dream Clover: dam French 1m-10.5f (Prix de Flore) winner: useful form: won both starts, newcomers race at Saint-Cloud (by 6 lengths) in September and Prix des Reservoirs at Deauville (by 2½ lengths from Altea) in October: will stay 1¼m: likely to improve further. *F. Head, France*

WOGGLE (IRE) 2 ch.f. (Apr 3) Camacho 118 – Radio Wave 78 (Dalakhani (IRE) 133) **–** [2017 p6g Dec 20] €6,000Y: fourth foal: closely related to 7f winner Vixen (by Kodiac): dam, maiden (probably stayed 1½m), out of smart 1¾m winner Tuning: 100/1, well held in minor event at Kempton. *Geoffrey Deacon*

WOLFCATCHER (IRE) 5 b.g. King's Best (USA) 132 – Miss Particular (IRE) 86 **89** (Sadler's Wells (USA) 132) [2017 98: 20f 16d^5 16d 16g Aug 28] good-topped gelding: useful at best, below that level in 2017: stays 15f: wears headgear: in tongue tie last 4 starts: often races prominently. *Ian Williams*

Betfred Cesarewitch (Heritage Handicap), Newmarket—
Withhold beats London Prize and Lagostovegas to land a significant gamble, looking a pattern race performer in the making as he pulls clear in course-record time

WOLFCATCHERJACK (IRE) 3 b.g. Lawman (FR) 121 – Alleluia 117 (Caerleon (USA) 132) [2017 t7.2g p7g 8.3m p12d* p12g* t12.2g* 13.9d² Sep 12] €42,000Y: rather unfurnished gelding: half-brother to several winners, including smart 1½m-16.4f winner Allegretto (by Galileo) and useful 1½m winner (stays 2m) Altaayil (by Sea The Stars): dam 1¼m-2¼m winner, including Doncaster Cup: fairly useful handicapper: won at Kempton (twice) and Wolverhampton (amateur) in August: second at Catterick in September: stays 1¾m: acts on polytrack, tapeta and good to soft going. *Sir Mark Prescott Bt* **86**

WOLF COUNTRY 3 b.g. Dubawi (IRE) 129 – Goathemala (GER) 105 (Black Sam Bellamy (IRE) 121) [2017 99p: 11.9g* 10.3d⁵ 13g⁵ 12v Aug 2] sturdy, attractive gelding: useful performer: won listed race at Saint-Cloud (by ¾ length from Falcon Wings) in May: stays 1½m: acts on good to soft going: usually leads. *Charlie Appleby* **107**

WOLF HEART (IRE) 9 b.g. Dalakhani (IRE) 133 – Lisieux Orchid (IRE) 88 (Sadler's Wells (USA) 132) [2017 –: 10g 10d 8g 12.5m⁶ 11.2v Sep 18] fair at best, no form since 2015: tried in visor. *Lucy Normile* **–**

WONDERFILLO (IRE) 3 b.g. Teofilo (IRE) 126 – Wonderfilly (FR) 100 (Invincible Spirit (IRE) 121) [2017 p8g⁴ p8g² 8.2d² 8f² t8.6g² Dec 18] 95,000Y: lengthy gelding: second foal: dam, French 2-y-o 5.5f/6.5f winner, half-sister to smart sprinter Triple Aspect: fairly useful maiden: runner-up on 4 occasions: left Paul Cole after fourth start: raced around 1m: acts on polytrack and good to soft going: tried in tongue tie: often races prominently. *David O'Meara* **80**

WONDERFUL LIFE (IRE) 4 b.f. Canford Cliffs (IRE) 133 – Feeling Wonderful (IRE) 73 (Fruits of Love (USA) 127) [2017 73: t7.1g⁶ f8g p6d⁵ Feb 2] lengthy, angular filly: fair maiden at 3 yrs, no form in 2017: in headgear last 2 starts. *Richard Spencer* **–**

WONDER OF DUBAI (IRE) 3 b.g. So You Think (NZ) 133 – Ruby Suesday 79 (Refuse To Bend (IRE) 128) [2017 –: p7m² 7g² 8s² 7s⁴ 7g⁶ a8f a9.9f Dec 21] fair maiden: left Michael Bell after fifth start: stays 1m: acts on polytrack and soft going: tried in cheekpieces. *A. Al Rayhi, UAE* **77**

WOODACRE 10 b.g. Pyrus (USA) 106 – Fairy Ring (IRE) 69 (Fairy King (USA)) [2017 77: t12.4g⁵ t12.4dᵘʳ Feb 1] strong gelding: fair handicapper: stayed 12.5f: acted on tapeta, good to firm and good to soft going: tried in cheekpieces: often travelled strongly: dead. *Richard Whitaker* **76**

WOODMAX (GER) 2 b.c. (Feb 14) Maxios 123 – Waldtraut (GER) (Oasis Dream 129) [2017 7g⁴ 8.9g* 8d* 8d⁴ Oct 1] €240,000Y: second foal: dam, useful German winner up to 1m (2-y-o 7f winner), half-sister to smart German 1m-1¼m performer Wiesenpfad: smart form: won maiden at Evreux in August and minor event at Maisons-Laffitte (by length from Stella di Camelot) in September: 3¼ lengths fourth to Happily in Prix Jean-Luc Lagardere at Chantilly final outing: stays 9f. *N. Clement, France* **111**

WOODY BAY 7 b.g. New Approach (IRE) 132 – Dublino (USA) 116 (Lear Fan (USA) 130) [2017 87: 8.8m 7.8d⁶ 7g 8s³ 8g Oct 7] tall gelding: fairly useful handicapper: stays 10.5f: acts on polytrack, soft and good to firm going: tried in blinkers/tongue tie. *Mark Walford* **79**

WOOFIE (IRE) 5 b.g. Duke of Marmalade (IRE) 132 – Violet Ballerina (IRE) 85 (Namid 128) [2017 77§: p11g 10m 10d⁵ p16g³ p16s* p14d p16g Nov 7] lengthy, dipped-backed gelding: fair handicapper: won at Chelmsford in July: stays 2m: acts on polytrack and tapeta: often wears headgear: front runner/races prominently: untrustworthy. *Laura Mongan* **65 §**

WOOTTON (FR) 2 b.c. (Feb 6) Wootton Bassett 119 – American Nizzy (FR) 97 (American Post 121) [2017 8g* 8s* Oct 19] fourth foal: dam French 2-y-o 6f winner (stayed 9f): useful form: impressive winner of both starts, newcomers race at Deauville (by 6 lengths) in August and listed race on same course (by 5 lengths from Alternative Fact, quickening clear) in October: will improve further. *H-A. Pantall, France* **106 p**

WOOTYHOOT (FR) 3 b.g. Wootton Bassett 119 – Orlena (USA) (Gone West (USA)) [2017 66: 8.1m 8.3m p7g p10g² p8g p10s⁵ p12g Dec 23] close-coupled gelding: fair maiden: stays 1¼m: acts on polytrack: tried in hood: usually races towards rear. *James Fanshawe* **65**

WORDINESS 9 br.g. Dansili 127 – Verbose (USA) 97 (Storm Bird (CAN) 134) [2017 90: t16.3g t16.3g p16d⁴ p15.8g⁴ 13.1m³ 17.2f³ p13.3g⁵ 14g⁴ 14.5m² 16m² 16.5m* 14g⁴ t16.5g⁵ 17.1g* 16g⁵ t16.5g⁴ p15.8g t16.3g⁶ t16.5g t16.5d³ f16.5g⁴ Dec 29] smallish gelding: fair handicapper nowadays: won at Doncaster (amateur) in July and Pontefract in August: stays 17f: acts on polytrack, tapeta and firm going: tried in cheekpieces: has worn tongue tie: usually races towards rear. *David Evans* **77**

WORDISMYBOND 8 b.g. Monsieur Bond (IRE) 120 – La Gessa 69 (Largesse 112) **78**
[2017 79: 10g^6 10g 8s^6 8g^6 8s* 8v^4 7d^3 Oct 30] sturdy gelding: fair handicapper: won at Brighton in October: left Brendan Powell after fourth start: stays 9f: acts on polytrack, firm and soft going: has worn cheekpieces, including last 4 starts: often races towards rear. *Amanda Perrett*

WORDSEARCH (USA) 3 b.g. Pleasantly Perfect (USA) 130 – Jibe (USA) 107 (Danzig **73**
(USA)) [2017 77: p10g^5 13.1s Jul 4] fair maiden: should stay at least 1¼m: acts on polytrack and tapeta: usually races prominently. *Hugo Palmer*

WORKING CLASS 3 b.g. Bahri (USA) 125 – Louise d'Arzens 73 (Anabaa (USA) 130) **82**
[2017 60p: 9.9d^3 8g^2 7s* 8m^5 8d^4 8v 7d Nov 4] fairly useful performer: won maiden at Lingfield (by 4 lengths from The Bear Can Fly) in July: stays 1¼m: acts on soft and good to firm going: usually races prominently: sold to join Oliver Sherwood £16,000 in November. *Peter Chapple-Hyam*

WORKING TOGETHER 2 b.f. (May 4) Monsieur Bond (IRE) 120 – Melandre 74 **–**
(Lujain (USA) 119) [2017 t7.1s t6g Oct 19] sister to 5f winner Stanghow and 2-y-o 7f winner Rock of Monaco, and half-sister to 2 winners, including winner up to 7f Lucky Lodge (2-y-o 5f winner, by Lucky Story): dam 2-y-o 5f winner: little impact in minor events. *Antony Brittain*

WORK (IRE) 4 b.f. Mastercraftsman (IRE) 129 – Abbeyleix Lady (IRE) (Montjeu (IRE) **66 §**
137) [2017 69p: 16d^4 p16s 16s Sep 19] fair handicapper: stays 2m: acts on polytrack and soft going: in blinkers last 2 starts: wore tongue tie in 2017: often travels strongly: ungenuine. *David Pipe*

WOR LASS 9 br.m. And Beyond (IRE) 113 – Patience Please 59 (King of Spain 121) **83**
[2017 89: t12.4s^3 14.1s^6 16m t12.4s 16m^3 15d^3 14.1s^5 12.5m^2 t12.4g t16.3g 15s^2 16v^5 Oct 16] fairly useful handicapper: third at Musselburgh and Ayr in July: stays 16.5f: acts on tapeta, firm and soft going: tried in cheekpieces. *Donald Whillans*

WORLD APPROVAL (USA) 5 gr.g. Northern Afleet (USA) 117 – Win Approval (USA) **130**
(With Approval (CAN)) [2017 120: 9f* 8.5g* 10f^5 8d* 8f* 8f* Nov 4] top-class performer: won non-graded event at Tampa Bay in April, Grade 2 Dixie Stakes at Pimlico in May, Fourstardave Handicap at Saratoga (beat Time Test 2¼ lengths) in August, Woodbine Mile (by 2½ lengths from Lancaster Bomber) in September and Breeders' Cup Mile at Del Mar (beat Lancaster Bomber by 1¼ lengths) in November: fifth to Ascend in Manhattan Stakes at Belmont on other start: Grade 1 winner over 11f, but best at 1m: acts on firm and good to soft going: wears blinkers. *Mark E. Casse, North America*

WORLD BREAKER (ITY) 2 b.c. (Mar 17) Helmet (AUS) 127 – Serata di Gala (FR) **–**
75 (Footstepsinthesand 120) [2017 p8g Nov 7] 33/1, well held in minor event at Kempton. *Marco Botti*

WORLD OF GOOD 4 ch.f. Danehill Dancer (IRE) 117 – Edaraat (USA) (Rahy (USA) **72**
115) [2017 75: p8g* p8g^4 t7.1m^3 p7g p7g^6 p8g t8.6d Dec 9] first foal: dam, ran once, closely related to smart 1¼m winner Najah out of Irish 1000 Guineas winner Mehthaaf: fair performer: won maiden at Dundalk in January: left John Joseph Murphy after that: stays 1m: acts on polytrack, tapeta and soft going: usually in headgear. *Anabel K. Murphy*

WORLD POWER (IRE) 3 ch.f. Power 117 – Izzy Lou (IRE) 68 (Spinning World (USA) **86**
130) [2017 7g 6g^2 t6.1g^2 5.9g^2 7g* p6.5f 8d^4 8g 6.7g^5 8s 6s^6 7.7g^5 5.5s^5 p6.5g p7.5g* Dec 16] £27,000Y: third foal: half-sister to 2-y-o 7f winner Juan Alonso (by Rock of Gibraltar): dam lightly-raced half-sister to US Grade 2 1m winner Missit: fairly useful performer: won handicaps at Newbury (by ¾ length from Dance Teacher) in July and Deauville in December: left Paul Cole after sixth start and had various trainers after: stays 7.5f: acts on polytrack and tapeta: has worn cheekpieces, including last 4 starts. *H. Grewe, Germany*

WORLD RECORD (IRE) 7 b.g. Choisir (AUS) 126 – Dancing Debut 83 (Polar Falcon **65**
(USA) 126) [2017 67: 8g^2 8g 7.6d^2 8d^2 8v^3 8.3g^6 Nov 1] lengthy gelding: fair handicapper: stays 8.5f: acts on polytrack, good to firm and heavy going: races prominently: sold £2,200, sent to Germany. *Mick Quinn*

WORLDS HIS OYSTER 4 b.g. Pivotal 124 – Regal Salute 91 (Medicean 128) [2017 **94**
92: t8d* t8g^6 8m^5 8g 8m 10.3g^3 10.2f^4 7.8s 8.5f^4 7.8s^3 8d 7.4g^2 7v^3 7s^3 Oct 31] compact gelding: fairly useful handicapper: won at Newcastle in February: placed 5 times after: stays 10.5f: acts on tapeta and any turf going: sometimes in headgear: sold 38,000 gns, sent to Saudi Arabia. *John Quinn*

Breeders' Cup Filly & Mare Turf, Del Mar—
Wuheida records a second Group/Grade 1 success in first-time cheekpieces, beating Rhododendron in a one, two for the European raiders; the race is held over the shortest trip in its history due to the configuration of Del Mar's turf track

WORSHIP (IRE) 2 b.f. (Apr 20) Havana Gold (IRE) 118 – Up In Time 91 (Noverre (USA) 125) [2017 p6g* Dec 20] 16,000Y, €260,000 2-y-o: first foal: dam, 2-y-o 7f winner, later smart 6f-1m (Grade 2) winner in USA: 11/4, won minor event at Kempton (by ½ length from Desert Doctor) on debut: will stay 7f: sure to progress. *David Simcock* **80 p**

WORTH WAITING 2 b.f. (Apr 18) Bated Breath 125 – Salutare (IRE) (Sadler's Wells (USA) 132) [2017 7d^{2} Nov 4] 40,000Y: half-sister to several winners, including 1½m winners From Frost (useful, by Nayef) and She Will Call (in France, by Dalakhani): dam, useful French 12.5f-15f winner, closely related to smart French winner up to 15.5f Montare, herself dam of very smart 1½m performer Journey: 33/1, second in minor event at Newmarket (¾ length behind Perfect Thought) in November: will be suited by 1m+: sure to improve. *David Lanigan* **73 p**

WORTHY SPIRIT (GER) 6 b.g. Shirocco (GER) 129 – Wakytara (GER) (Danehill (USA) 126) [2017 p12g^{5} p8g^{ur} Feb 1] big gelding: no form, including in Flat maidens: temperamental. *Adrian Wintle* **– §**

WOTABOND 4 ch.g. Monsieur Bond (IRE) 120 – Wotatomboy 65 (Captain Rio 122) [2017 –: f6g f7g^{6} f7d Apr 6] no form: tried in blinkers. *Richard Whitaker* **–**

WOTABREEZE (IRE) 4 ch.g. Excellent Art 125 – Sparkling Crystal (IRE) 80 (Danehill Dancer (IRE) 117) [2017 91: 12m 12g 11.9s 12f^{2} 12m^{3} 13.4d 12.1g^{5} 12.1m 12.1d* 12.1s Sep 23] workmanlike gelding: fairly useful handicapper: won at Catterick in September: stays 1½m: acts on firm and soft going: in headgear last 3 starts. *John Quinn* **80**

WOTADOLL 3 b.f. Harbour Watch (IRE) 121 – Rhapsilian 68 (Dansili 127) [2017 –: 6m^{2} 6g^{3} p7g^{5} 6g* 5.2s^{4} 6s^{4} 5.3s* 5g^{3} t6.1g Nov 11] rather leggy filly: fair handicapper: won at Yarmouth in July and Brighton in October: stays 6f: acts on soft and good to firm going. *Dean Ivory* **73**

WOTAMADAM 2 gr.f. (Apr 23) Lethal Force (IRE) 128 – Rhapsilian 68 (Dansili 127) [2017 p6d 6.1g^{6} 6d p6g Oct 5] fifth foal: half-sister to 5f/6f winner Wotadoll (by Harbour Watch) and 6f winner He's Complete (by Royal Applause): dam, ungenuine 6f winner, half-sister to smart 2-y-o 6f/7f winner Peak To Creek: poor form: raced only at 6f. *Dean Ivory* **48**

WOWSHAM (IRE) 2 b.c. (Apr 30) Elzaam (AUS) 115 – Shams Wa Matar (Polish Precedent (USA) 131) [2017 8.9s t7.1d t8.6g Nov 11] little impact in minor events. *Keith Dalgleish* **–**

WRAP STAR (IRE) 6 b.g. Cape Cross (IRE) 129 – Twinkling (NZ) (Star Way 119) [2017 77: t16.3g^{6} p12g^{2} 17g^{2} p12g^{3} p12g^{6} Nov 17] fair maiden: stays 17f: acts on polytrack, tapeta, good to firm and good to soft going: wears headgear/tongue tie. *Anthony McCann, Ireland* **78**

WRENTHORPE 2 b.g. (Apr 4) Hellvelyn 118 – Milly-M (Cadeaux Genereux 131) [2017 6v^2 6d^2 6d^3 Oct 30] fair form: best effort when second in minor event at Redcar (head behind Nicklaus) in October. *Bryan Smart* **75**

WRIGHT PATTERSON (IRE) 4 b.g. Dream Ahead (USA) 133 – Anam Allta (IRE) 117 (Invincible Spirit (IRE) 121) [2017 –: t10.2d Feb 7] poor maiden. *John Quinn* **47**

WUHEIDA 3 ch.f. Dubawi (IRE) 129 – Hibaayeb 120 (Singspiel (IRE) 133) [2017 112p: 8m^2 10.9s^3 8d^4 9.9d^4 9f* Nov 4] sturdy filly: very smart performer: suffered stress fracture to off-hind in the spring and not seen out until July: in first-time cheekpieces, won Breeders' Cup Filly & Mare Turf at Del Mar in November by length from Rhododendron: earlier second in Falmouth Stakes at Newmarket (1¼ lengths behind Roly Poly) and fourth in Matron Stakes at Leopardstown (1½ lengths behind Hydrangea) and Prix de l'Opera at Chantilly (beaten ½ length by Rhododendron): stays 1¼m: acts on firm and good to soft going, below form on soft (in German Oaks): usually races prominently. *Charlie Appleby* **120**

WUROOD 3 gr.f. Dark Angel (IRE) 113 – Key Rose (IRE) 88 (Key of Luck (USA) 126) [2017 72: t7.1g* 7m^6 6g^5 May 30] sturdy filly: fair performer: won maiden at Wolverhampton in March: best effort at 7f: acts on tapeta: tried in tongue tie: often races prominently. *William Haggas* **75**

WYNFAUL THE WIZARD (USA) 2 b.g. (Mar 8) Bodemeister (USA) 129 – Red Dot (USA) (Diesis 133) [2017 7.2s^6 t7.1g t8g^6 t8g Dec 6] no form, including in nursery. *Richard Guest* **–**

WYNFORD (IRE) 4 ch.g. Dylan Thomas (IRE) 132 – Wishing Chair (USA) (Giant's Causeway (USA) 132) [2017 81: p15.8g^5 Mar 8] compact gelding: fairly useful handicapper, below form sole outing on Flat in 2017: stays 2m: acts on polytrack, soft and good to firm going: tried in hood: fairly useful hurdler. *David Loughnane* **71**

X

XAAR ISLAND 2 b.f. (Apr 3) Trans Island 119 – Nihil Petere (IRE) (Xaar 132) [2017 t5.1g t6.1g Jun 7] £2,000Y: first foal: dam of little account: poor form in minor events. *David Evans* **39**

XCLUSIVE 7 b.g. Pivotal 124 – Dance A Daydream 67 (Daylami (IRE) 138) [2017 –: p8g Mar 8] fair at best, lightly raced and no form on Flat since 2014: tried in cheekpieces. *Ronald Harris* **–**

XENOBIA (IRE) 3 ch.f. Falco (USA) 122 – Acago (USA) 115 (Royal Academy (USA) 130) [2017 82p: 7s^5 8g* 7d* 7s Oct 7] workmanlike filly: eighth foal: dam French winner up to 9f (2-y-o 5f winner): useful performer: won maiden at Leopardstown in June and handicap at the Curragh (by ¾ length from Texas Rock) in August: stays 1m: acts on soft going: sometimes in hood: usually races prominently. *W. T. Farrell, Ireland* **99**

X RATED (IRE) 3 gr.g. Exceed And Excel (AUS) 126 – Screen Star (IRE) 110 (Tobougg (IRE) 125) [2017 78: 8m^4 8m^6 10.1m 10.2f* 9.2g^5 10g^2 10.3s^5 p10g^6 p11g p11g^4 t10.2g t12.4g^3 t9.5g^4 Dec 18] fairly useful handicapper: won at Bath (by 2¼ lengths from High Wells) in July: second at Windsor later that month: stays 12.5f: acts on polytrack, tapeta and firm going: front runner/races prominently. *Mark Johnston* **85**

XYLOPHONE 3 ch.f. Medicean 128 – Piano 101 (Azamour (IRE) 130) [2017 8v p10s^6 t9.5g p12d Aug 16] 14,000F, €52,000Y: first foal: dam 1¼m/11f winner out of smart winner up to 10.5f Humouresque: modest form: best effort at 1¼m: tried in cheekpieces/tongue tie. *Archie Watson* **58**

Y

YAAFOUR 2 br.c. (Feb 28) Poet's Voice 126 – Whatizzit 88 (Galileo (IRE) 134) [2017 p6g 7m^3 6s^3 7.6d* 8d^3 6g^5 t8.6g^5 Oct 21] 42,000Y: good-topped colt: fourth foal: half-brother to 9.5f winner Dream Scape (by Oasis Dream): dam, 2-y-o 8.6f winner who stayed 1½m, half-sister to useful winner up to 1m Whazzis, herself dam of smart 6f/7f winner Culturati: fairly useful performer: won minor event at Lingfield (by ½ length from Blanchefleur) in August: stays 1m: acts on good to firm and good to soft going: usually leads: sold 70,000 gns, sent to USA. *Richard Hannon* **84**

YAARMEN (USA) 3 b.g. Nayef (USA) 129 – Haamaat (IRE) 98 (Shamardal (USA) 129) [2017 t8.6g² 10m* 10.2m⁴ Jul 7] first foal: dam 6f/7f winner: fairly useful form: won maiden at Newmarket (by neck from Playwriter) in June: stays 1¼m: sold 62,000 gns, sent to Qatar. *William Haggas* **85**

YABASS (IRE) 2 ch.c. (Jan 18) Lope de Vega (IRE) 125 – Fresh Mint (IRE) 86 (Sadler's Wells (USA) 132) [2017 8.1m* 8.2s⁶ p10g² Oct 18] 28,000Y: sixth foal: half-brother to 3 winners, including useful winner up to 1m Canary Row (2-y-o 5f winner, by Holy Roman Emperor) and 1½m winner Andratx (by Manduro): dam 11f/1½m winner: fairly useful form: won minor event at Windsor (by neck from Soldier To Follow) in August: second in similar event at Lingfield (2 lengths behind Bowditch) in October: stays 1¼m. *Archie Watson* **81**

YABRAVE 3 b.g. Bahamian Bounty 116 – Dare To Dream 89 (Exceed And Excel (AUS) 126) [2017 p7g³ 6s* p7g Sep 9] 130,000Y: rather leggy gelding: first foal: dam, 2-y-o 7f winner, half-sister to smart 1¼m-1½m winner Area Fifty One out of Musidora Stakes winner Secret History: fairly useful form: won maiden at Salisbury (by 1¼ lengths from Killay) in July: best effort at 6f: has joined G. Selvaratnam in UAE. *Roger Varian* **89**

YAFTA 2 gr.c. (Feb 5) Dark Angel (IRE) 113 – Swiss Dream 110 (Oasis Dream 129) [2017 6.1g⁴ 7m² 6g² 5.7d* p6d* Sep 28] £280,000Y: first foal: dam, winner up to 6f (2-y-o 5f winner), closely related/half-sister to smart sprinters Swiss Spirit and Swiss Diva: useful performer: won minor event at Bath in August and nursery at Chelmsford (by 2¼ lengths from Amazing Alice) in September: stays 7f: acts on polytrack, good to firm and good to soft going: front runner/races prominently. *Richard Hannon* **95**

YAIR HILL (IRE) 9 b.g. Selkirk (USA) 129 – Conspiracy 98 (Rudimentary (USA) 118) [2017 54§: 5.9s 8g 8.5d 6.9v Sep 13] big gelding: useful at best, retains little ability: usually wears headgear: ungenuine. *Thomas Cuthbert* **– §**

YA JAMMEEL 4 b.g. Dubawi (IRE) 129 – Silver Touch (IRE) 115 (Dansili 127) [2017 66: 8d³ 10m⁴ 10m* 12d* 12d* 15.9g 12s Sep 19] fairly useful handicapper: completed hat-trick at Chepstow (dead-heated) and Epsom (twice) in July/August: stays 1½m: acts on soft and good to firm going: front runner/races prominently: sold 45,000 gns, sent to Saudi Arabia. *Mick Channon* **86**

YAJOOLL 2 b.c. (May 3) Invincible Spirit (IRE) 121 – Tafiya 83 (Bahri (USA) 125) [2017 6d Nov 11] 100,000Y: fifth foal: half-brother to useful 2-y-o 6f/7f winner Overpowered (by Choisir) and 1¼m winner Sovereign Power (by Royal Applause): dam, maiden (stayed 1½m), half-sister to useful dam of 2000 Guineas/Derby winner Camelot: 11/2, shaped as if needing experience when seventh in maiden at Doncaster (9¼ lengths behind Raid) in November: open to improvement. *William Haggas* **52 p**

YALAWIN (IRE) 3 b.c. Lawman (FR) 121 – Urgele (FR) 102 (Zafonic (USA) 130) [2017 82: 6m* 5.1d² 5.7f⁴ Jul 18] good-quartered colt: useful performer: won maiden at Ripon in May: second in handicap at Windsor (length behind Evergate) later in month: stays 7f: acts on polytrack, good to firm and good to soft going: tried in hood: often travels strongly: has joined G. Selvaratnam in UAE. *Roger Varian* **98**

YALTA (IRE) 3 b.c. Exceed And Excel (AUS) 126 – Lacily (USA) 90 (Elusive Quality (USA)) [2017 110: 6f⁵ 6m p5g a6f² a6f⁴ Dec 21] good-topped colt: smart performer: second in handicap at Jebel Ali (nose behind Kasb) in December: left Mark Johnston after third start: stays 6f: acts on sand and good to firm going: seems best when able to dominate. *S. bin Ghadayer, UAE* **111**

YAMARHABA MALAYEEN (IRE) 3 ch.c. Rip Van Winkle (IRE) 134 – Obama Rule (IRE) 108 (Danehill Dancer (IRE) 117) [2017 p7g* 8m⁶ 8m³ p12g⁴ p12d⁴ Nov 22] fairly useful performer: won maiden at Kempton on debut in April: left Simon Crisford after third start: stayed 1m: acted on polytrack and good to firm going: dead. *Michael Bell* **88**

YAMUNA RIVER 2 b.f. (Mar 8) Foxwedge (AUS) 128 – Harryana To 57 (Compton Place 125) [2017 7d⁶ t7.1d⁶ t8.6g³ t9.5g Dec 18] 22,000Y: third foal: half-sister to a winner abroad by Sakhee's Secret: dam, maiden (stayed 7f), half-sister to smart 2-y-o 5f/6f winner Temple Meads: fair form: stays 8.5f. *James Tate* **72**

YARAKI 3 b.f. Frankel 147 – Superstar Leo (IRE) 114 (College Chapel 122) [2017 6d* p7s⁵ Jun 14] stocky filly: closely related to 1m winner Curriculum (by New Approach) and half-sister to several winners, including smart 5f (including at 2 yrs) winner Enticing (by Pivotal) and smart 7f/1m winner Sentaril (by Danehill Dancer): dam 2-y-o 5f (including Flying Childers Stakes) winner: fairly useful form: won maiden at Lingfield (by neck from Dealer's Choice) in May: sent to USA. *William Haggas* **80**

YARMOUK (FR) 3 ch.g. Siyouni (FR) 122 – Tassara (FR) 103 (Sendawar (IRE) 129) **78** [2017 73: 6m^5 6.9g t6g* 8d^6 p7.5f 7g Sep 27] fair handicapper: won at Newcastle in June: left Richard Fahey after third start: best effort at 6f: acts on tapeta and soft going: tried in visor. *Mme G. Rarick, France*

YASIR (USA) 9 b.g. Dynaformer (USA) – Khazayin (USA) 74 (Bahri (USA) 125) [2017 **69** 74: t16.5g* t16.5m^4 p16g t13.9g^3 t16.3d t9.5g^5 p13.3g^6 t12.2g^5 t8.6g^6 t12.2g^3 t12.2g 14d f16.5g^6 t12.2g^4 p10g t16.5g Oct 21] close-coupled gelding: fair handicapper: won at Wolverhampton in January: stays 16.5f: acts on all-weather, good to firm and heavy going: has worn headgear: tried in tongue tie: often races towards rear. *Conor Dore*

YASOOD (IRE) 4 b.g. Acclamation 118 – Lucina (Machiavellian (USA) 123) [2017 62: **67** t9.5m^3 t8g* p8d^4 Feb 2] rather sparely-made gelding: fair performer: won handicap at Newcastle (apprentice) in January: stays 9.5f: acts on polytrack and tapeta: has worn headgear: sent to Italy, won claimer at Syracuse in March. *Phil McEntee*

YATTWEE (USA) 4 b.g. Hard Spun (USA) 124 – Alzerra (UAE) 108 (Pivotal 124) [2017 **108** 108: 7g^2 7g^5 Oct 7] sturdy gelding: useful performer: second in minor event at Haydock (1¼ lengths behind Donjuan Triumphant) in September: stays 1m: acts on fibresand, good to firm and good to soft going: usually races prominently. *Saeed bin Suroor*

YEAH BABY YEAH (IRE) 4 b.f. Art Connoisseur (IRE) 121 – Royal Interlude (IRE) **88** 67 (King's Theatre (IRE) 128) [2017 98: 8.3g^4 7d^3 7m^6 7m^3 8g^6 7d^5 p6.5g^4 p7.5f p7.5g^4 6v^6 p7g^3 Dec 6] medium-sized filly: fairly useful handicapper: third at Doncaster, York and Lingfield: stays 1m: acts on polytrack, firm and good to soft going: often wears headgear. *Gay Kelleway*

YEEOOW (IRE) 8 b.g. Holy Roman Emperor (IRE) 125 – Taraya (IRE) (Doyoun 124) **81** [2017 89: p6g^4 f6d^4 6m^5 5.9g^5 6m^3 6.1s 6g p6g^4 p7g Nov 21] sturdy gelding: fairly useful handicapper: third at Ayr (1½ lengths behind Black Isle Boy) in May: stayed 6.5f: acted on polytrack, firm and good to soft going: wore headgear: front runner/raced prominently: dead. *K. R. Burke*

YELLOWHAMMER 3 b.f. Raven's Pass (USA) 133 – Magical Romance (IRE) 110 **98 p** (Barathea (IRE) 127) [2017 81p: 7s* p7g* 7d* Nov 4] useful handicapper: won all 3 starts in 2017, at Newmarket in July, Kempton in October and again at Newmarket (by ¾ length from Give It Some Teddy) in November: raced only at 7f: acts on polytrack, soft and good to firm going: responds generously to pressure: will go on improving. *Roger Charlton*

YEMNAAK (FR) 3 b.g. Medicean 128 – Aujiang (GER) (Royal Dragon (USA) 118) **–** [2017 p10g^4 10.3g p8g 11.6d Jul 1] well held in maidens/seller: tried in visor/tongue tie. *George Peckham*

YENSIR 4 ch.g. Sir Percy 129 – Yensi 86 (Doyen (IRE) 132) [2017 64: t10.2s^3 11.1g^2 7.8s^5 **76** 8m 12.1s^4 10d^2 9.9g^2 11.1v^5 t8g Sep 12] fair maiden: stays 11f: acts on tapeta and soft going: has worn headgear: has joined Olly Murphy. *Grant Tuer*

YES DADDY (IRE) 9 b.g. Golan (IRE) 129 – Hollygrove Samba (IRE) (Accordion) **78** [2017 79: 16g^2 16g p15.8g Oct 5] fair handicapper: stays 16.5f: acts on polytrack and tapeta: usually wears headgear: in tongue tie in 2017. *Robert Stephens*

YES YOU (IRE) 3 ch.f. Choisir (AUS) 126 – Mexican Milly (IRE) 60 (Noverre (USA) **76** 125) [2017 53: 6d^2 7.2s^3 6g* 6g* 7.2d^3 5.9s* 5.9d^5 5v^5 6d* 6d Nov 11] fair handicapper: won at Hamilton in July, Redcar and Carlisle in August, and again at Redcar (apprentice) in October: stays 7f: acts on soft going. *Iain Jardine*

Y FYN DUW A FYDD 2 b.f. (Mar 1) Nathaniel (IRE) 129 – Dignify (IRE) 105 (Rainbow **–** Quest (USA) 134) [2017 8.3v Nov 8] half-sister to 3 winners, including winner up to 1¼m Personify (2-y-o 6f winner, by Zafonic) and 6f-8.5f winner Declamation (by Shamardal): dam French 2-y-o 7f/1m winner: 100/1, well held in maiden at Nottingham. *John Gallagher*

YISTY 4 ch.f. Compton Place 125 – Meditation 88 (Inchinor 119) [2017 48: p5g p5d t5g **35** p5g Mar 16] poor handicapper: best form at 5f: acts on polytrack: wears headgear. *Derek Shaw*

YOGI'S GIRL (IRE) 2 ch.f. (Mar 26) Harbour Watch (IRE) 121 – Ayr Missile 76 **84** (Cadeaux Genereux 131) [2017 t5.1g 5m* 5.1m* 5.2s^4 6.1g^3 5g t6d t6.1d p5g^4 Dec 23] €8,000Y: lengthy, rather unfurnished filly: first foal: dam, maiden (stayed 6f), half-sister to useful winner up to 7f Outer Space: fairly useful performer: won minor events at Windsor in April and Chester (by nose from Black Orange) in May: third in similar event at Chester in September: stays 6f: acts on soft and good to firm going. *David Evans*

YOGIYOGIYOGI (IRE) 3 ch.f. Finsceal Fior (IRE) – Zelloof (IRE) 79 (Kheleyf (USA) 116) [2017 p8g^4 p8d^3 p8g^6 p10m p10g^6 Dec 13] second foal: half-sister to Italian 6f (including at 2 yrs) to 11f winner Irishman Mark (by Vocalised): dam 2-y-o 7f winner out of Moyglare Stud Stakes winner Belle Genius: fair maiden: stays 1¼m: acts on polytrack: tried in visor. *Denis Coakley* **71**

YOLO STAR (IRE) 2 br.f. (Apr 15) Society Rock (IRE) 126 – Pearly Brooks 77 (Efisio 120) [2017 6m 5g^2 5m* 5d* 5m^4 Oct 13] €17,000F, £10,000Y: sturdy filly: half-sister to several winners, including useful 5f (including at 2 yrs) winner Fine 'n Dandy (by Dandy Man) and 1m winner (including at 2 yrs) Classic Voice (by Oratorio): dam 6f winner: fairly useful performer: won maiden at Cork in May and nursery at Naas in October: fourth in Cornwallis at Newmarket: best at 5f: acts on good to firm and good to soft going: front runner/races prominently: sold to join Dean Ivory 100,000 gns in November. *John Patrick Murtagh, Ireland* **91**

YORBELUCKY 2 b.g. (Feb 27) Yorgunnabelucky (USA) 102 – Circle of Angels 73 (Royal Applause 124) [2017 6.1m^5 7g 7.4s^3 7.4v* Sep 17] workmanlike gelding: fair form: won minor event at Ffos Las in September: bred to be suited by 1m+. *David Evans* **75**

YORKEE MO SABEE (IRE) 4 ch.g. Teofilo (IRE) 126 – Pivotal's Princess (IRE) 107 (Pivotal 124) [2017 84: 8.5f 8.5g^4 6.9g 8.5m^2 7.4m^3 8g^4 6d p5s^6 Dec 8] close-coupled gelding: fairly useful handicapper: second at Beverley in June: left Mark Johnston after sixth start: stays 8.5f: acts on tapeta, good to firm and good to soft going: often wears hood: in tongue tie last 2 starts. *Stuart Williams* **81**

YORKIDDING 5 b.m. Dalakhani (IRE) 133 – Claxon 110 (Caerleon (USA) 132) [2017 104: 16g^3 18.6m^2 12.1m^3 16.2f* 20f 12g^5 t16.3s 14m* 16.3d Aug 23] useful-looking mare: useful handicapper: won at Haydock (by head from Suegioo) in May and Musselburgh (by 1½ lengths from Great Fighter) in August: second in Chester Cup (neck behind Montaly) in May: stays 2¼m, effective over shorter: acts on firm and soft going: often races towards rear: consistent. *Mark Johnston* **107**

YORKSHIREDEBUT (IRE) 3 ch.f. Sir Prancealot (IRE) 111 – Yasmeena (USA) 80 (Mr Greeley (USA) 122) [2017 72: 5.3g^2 5m^4 5g* 5g^5 5f^3 5m^6 5m* 5v^6 5m 5.1g^4 5v^3 5v Sep 30] fairly useful handicapper: won at Thirsk in May and Catterick (by 4½ lengths from Liberatum) in July: stays 5.5f: acts on any turf going: often in cheekpieces. *Paul Midgley* **86**

YORKSHIREMAN (IRE) 7 b.g. Red Clubs (IRE) 125 – Ossiana (IRE) 72 (Polish Precedent (USA) 131) [2017 53: t16.3d^4 t16.5g^6 Feb 13] neat gelding: poor handicapper: stays 16.5f: acts on tapeta and heavy going: wears headgear. *Lynn Siddall* **46**

YORKSHIRE MONARCH (IRE) 6 b.g. Montjeu (IRE) 137 – Inkling (USA) 104 (Seeking The Gold (USA)) [2017 t12.2g Aug 31] no form, including in novice hurdle. *Sarah Hollinshead* **–**

YORKSHIRE PUDDING 3 b.f. Sleeping Indian 122 – Cadeau Speciale 54 (Cadeaux Genereux 131) [2017 7g^4 7m^5 6g^2 6m^3 6g 7g^5 6d^4 8d^6 8g^6 Aug 15] sister to useful 5f and (at 2 yrs) 6f winner Shoshoni Wind, closely related to a winner in Sweden by Compton Place, and half-sister to 2 winners, including smart winner up to 7f Burnwynd Boy (2-y-o 6f winner, by Tobougg): dam maiden: modest maiden: stays 7f: acts on good to soft going: often wears headgear: often races prominently. *Tim Easterby* **64**

YORKSHIRE ROVER 3 b.g. Doncaster Rover (USA) 114 – Mother Jones 82 (Sleeping Indian 122) [2017 5m^3 t5s^5 6s^4 t6.1g^4 t6.1g^5 6g* Jul 19] modest performer: won handicap at Yarmouth in July: likely to stay 7f: acts on tapeta: tried in cheekpieces: has joined Colin Teague. *David Brown* **64**

YORKSHIRE STAR (IRE) 3 ch.g. Fast Company (IRE) 126 – March Star (IRE) 109 (Mac's Imp (USA) 116) [2017 50: 7m 8.1d^6 p10g Aug 31] poor maiden: best effort at 6f: acts on soft going: usually in headgear. *Bill Turner* **44**

YOUKAN (IRE) 2 b.g. (Feb 26) Choisir (AUS) 126 – Ellikan (IRE) 60 (Exceed And Excel (AUS) 126) [2017 5d* May 18] first foal: dam maiden (stayed 6f): 20/1, won minor event at Salisbury (by 2¼ lengths from Joegogo) on debut: should improve. *Stuart Kittow* **78 p**

YOU LOOK DIFFERENT 3 ch.f. Sleeping Indian 122 – First Harmony (First Trump 118) [2017 –: 8.5m^5 t14g Jul 17] no form. *Antony Brittain* **–**

YOUMKIN (USA) 3 ch.g. Street Cry (IRE) 130 – Aryaamm (IRE) 94 (Galileo (IRE) 134) [2017 85p: 10.1g^6 10.2s^4 Jun 3] fairly useful form: better effort at 3 yrs when sixth in Derby Trial at Epsom (in cheekpieces, 9¾ lengths behind Cracksman) in April: has joined G. Selvaratnam in UAE. *Saeed bin Suroor* **82**

YOUNG JOHN (IRE) 4 b.g. Acclamation 118 – Carpet Lady (IRE) 70 (Night Shift **89**
(USA)) [2017 94: f7g^{4} p7d t7.1d t7.1s^{5} 7s^{3} 7g 8d Aug 18] fairly useful handicapper: fourth
at Southwell in January: left Richard Fahey after fifth start: stays 7f: acts on tapeta, good to
firm and heavy going. *Mike Murphy*

YOUNG OFFICER (IRE) 3 b.g. Fast Company (IRE) 126 – Sara Mana Mou 41 **–**
(Medicean 128) [2017 –: t7.1m p8g p10g^{6} Feb 22] sturdy gelding: no form: in headgear in
2017. *Brian Meehan*

YOUNG RASCAL (FR) 2 b.c. (Feb 14) Intello (GER) 129 – Rock My Soul (IRE) 110 **83 p**
(Clodovil (IRE) 116) [2017 8.3v^{2} Nov 8] €215,000Y: first foal: dam German 1m-1¼m
winner: 9/1, caught eye when second in maiden at Nottingham (6 lengths behind My Lord
And Master) in November, having hopeless task from position: sure to progress.
William Haggas

YOUNG TIGER 4 b.g. Captain Gerrard (IRE) 113 – Blades Princess 92 (Needwood **60**
Blade 117) [2017 69: 6g^{6} 6g^{6} 5m 5g 5m t5g t5g^{2} t5g* t5g* t5g Nov 24] strong gelding: **a76**
modest handicapper on turf, fair on all-weather: won at Newcastle in September and
November: best form at 5f: acts on tapeta and good to firm going: often wears hood: often
races prominently. *Tom Tate*

YOUNG TOM 4 b.g. Sir Percy 129 – Enford Princess 89 (Pivotal 124) [2017 68: f11g^{2} **67**
10.1m 12d^{3} f12.1g Nov 16] fair handicapper: left Michael Appleby after third start: stays
1½m: acts on fibresand and heavy going: front runner/races prominently. *Sue Smith*

YOURARTISONFIRE 7 ch.g. Dutch Art 126 – Queens Jubilee 71 (Cayman Kai (IRE) **–**
114) [2017 86: f8g 7g May 13] sturdy gelding: fairly useful handicapper, well below form
both starts in 2017: left Lisa Williamson after first one: stays 8.5f: acts on polytrack, good
to firm and heavy going: often wears headgear: usually races nearer last than first. *M. D.
O'Callaghan, Ireland*

YOUR CHOICE 2 ch.f. (Feb 1) Foxwedge (AUS) 128 – Mildoura (FR) 96 (Sendawar **81**
(IRE) 129) [2017 6m^{2} 6v^{2} 7g p7g^{4} 6d^{2} Oct 30] tall filly: second foal: half-sister to 2-y-o 1m
winner Golden Nectar (by Sakhee's Secret): dam 11f/1½m winner who stayed 1¾m out of
useful French winner around 1¼m Miliana: fairly useful maiden: second at Goodwood in
August: best form at 6f: acts on good to firm and heavy going: front runner/races
prominently. *Laura Mongan*

YOU'RE COOL 5 b.g. Exceed And Excel (AUS) 126 – Ja One (IRE) 74 (Acclamation **76**
118) [2017 78: f5g^{5} t5.1g* p5d^{2} t5.1g* t5d t5.1g^{3} 5d^{6} 5m^{2} 5d^{4} p5g* p5g* p5s^{3} Dec 14] fair **a89**
handicapper on turf, fairly useful on all-weather: won at Wolverhampton in January and
February, and Chelmsford in September and November (by short head from Gorgeous
Noora): stays 6f: acts on polytrack, tapeta and good to firm going: tried in blinkers: front
runner/races prominently, often travels strongly. *John Balding*

YOU'RE FIRED (IRE) 6 b.g. Firebreak 125 – My Sweet Georgia (IRE) 79 (Royal **113**
Applause 124) [2017 112: p8g^{6} p10m 8g 8g^{3} 9d Sep 30] angular gelding: smart handicapper:
third at Doncaster (2½ lengths behind Kryptos) in September: stays 8.5f: acts on polytrack,
soft and good to firm going. *K. R. Burke*

YOU'RE HIRED 4 b.g. Dalakhani (IRE) 133 – Heaven Sent 116 (Pivotal 124) [2017 **–**
103p: 9.1d 12m Sep 23] useful form when winning 3 times at 3 yrs: well held both starts in
handicaps in 2017: stays 11.5f: acts on soft and good to firm going. *Amanda Perrett*

YOUR GIFTED (IRE) 10 b.m. Trans Island 119 – Dame Laura (IRE) 100 (Royal **55**
Academy (USA) 130) [2017 73: t5.1g t5.1g 5m 5d* 5g^{6} t5.1m^{5} t5.1g^{5} t5.1g^{2} t5.1d Dec 27]
modest handicapper nowadays: won at Ffos Las in July: races at 5f: acts on all-weather,
good to firm and heavy going: wears headgear. *Lisa Williamson*

YOURHOLIDAYISOVER (IRE) 10 ch.g. Sulamani (IRE) 130 – Whitehaven 116 **51**
(Top Ville 129) [2017 51: 12m^{4} Jul 4] modest maiden: stays 12.5f: acts on good to firm and
good to soft going: has worn headgear, including in 2017: tried in tongue tie: winning
hurdler/chaser. *Tom Gretton*

YOUR JUST DESSERTS (IRE) 2 b.f. (Feb 28) Requinto (IRE) 109 – Whats For **–**
Pudding (IRE) 62 (Kheleyf (USA) 116) [2017 5s 5d 5m t7.1g Sep 12] first foal: dam
winner up to 7f (2-y-o 6f winner): no form. *Micky Hammond*

YOUR LADYSHIP (IRE) 3 b.f. Lawman (FR) 121 – Bufera (IRE) 101 (King's Best **71 p**
(USA) 132) [2017 9.9g 8.1m^{3} 8g Aug 7] 230,000Y: fourth foal: sister to useful French 1m
(including at 2 yrs) winner Chartreuse and half-sister to a winner abroad by Acclamation:

dam, French 1m winner (including at 2 yrs), half-sister to smart winner up to 1m Johnny Barnes: fair form: best effort when third in maiden at Windsor in July: remains open to improvement. *Ralph Beckett*

YPRES 8 b.g. Byron 117 – Esligier (IRE) 87 (Sabrehill (USA) 120) [2017 69, a59: t6s 5.5f^3 **69**
6m^4 5.9g* 6g 6g^3 5.9d^4 6g t7.1g^6 f6.1g Nov 28] fair handicapper on turf, poor on all- **a40**
weather: won at Carlisle in July: stays 6f: acts on fibresand, tapeta, firm and good to soft going: wears headgear: often races in rear. *Jason Ward*

YUCATAN (IRE) 3 b.c. Galileo (IRE) 134 – Six Perfections (FR) 124 (Celtic Swing 138) **111**
[2017 109: 10d^3 10m^2 May 7] big colt: smart performer: third in Ballysax Stakes at Leopardstown (length behind Rekindling) in April and second in Derrinstown Stud Derby Trial at same course (head behind Douglas Macarthur) in May: will stay 1½m: acts on soft and good to firm going. *Aidan O'Brien, Ireland*

YUFTEN 6 b.g. Invincible Spirit (IRE) 121 – Majestic Sakeena (IRE) (King's Best (USA) **110**
132) [2017 114: t7.1g^3 8g 8m 7d 7g^5 Sep 7] rather leggy gelding: smart handicapper: third in listed race at Wolverhampton (head behind Salateen) in March: stays 1m: acts on polytrack, good to firm and good to soft going: tried in blinkers. *Roger Charlton*

YUL FINEGOLD (IRE) 7 b.g. Invincible Spirit (IRE) 121 – Mascara (Mtoto 134) [2017 **61**
76, a87d: p12g^6 t13.9m p15.8g^6 f12g^6 t12.2g^5 14v^5 11.8g^2 11.8g Jul 20] rather leggy gelding: modest handicapper nowadays: stays 1½m: acts on all-weather, good to firm and heavy going: has worn headgear: usually races close up. *Conor Dore*

YULONG XIONGBA (IRE) 5 b.g. Kodiac 112 – Moon Legend (USA) 70 (Gulch **–**
(USA)) [2017 73: t8d Mar 1] leggy, close-coupled gelding: fair handicapper, last on sole start in 2017: barely stays 1½m, effective at much shorter: acts on tapeta and soft going: wears headgear. *Julie Camacho*

Z

ZAAJER 2 b.c. (Mar 13) Shamardal (USA) 129 – Zahoo (IRE) 105 (Nayef (USA) 129) **77**
[2017 7g^3 8g^4 p7d^5 Oct 6] strong colt: fair form: best effort when third in maiden at Sandown (3 lengths behind Bathsheba Bay) in September: should stay 1m. *Owen Burrows*

ZAAKI 2 b.c. (Feb 15) Leroidesanimaux (BRZ) 127 – Kesara (Sadler's Wells (USA) 132) **96**
[2017 6s^2 7g^5 7d^4 7g^5 Sep 15] 40,000Y: well-made colt: half-brother to several winners, including useful 1¼m winner Night of Glory (by Sea The Stars) and 1¼m-1½m winner Apparatchika (by Archipenko): dam 7f/1m winner: useful form: fourth in Acomb Stakes at York (4¼ lengths behind Wells Farhh Go) in August: bred to be suited by at least 1m: has joined Sir Michael Stoute. *Mohamed Moubarak*

ZAATAR (IRE) 3 b.f. Fast Company (IRE) 126 – Amazing Win (IRE) 70 (Marju (IRE) **–**
127) [2017 54: t6f t7.1m Jan 23] modest maiden at 2 yrs, well held in handicaps in 2017: best effort at 5f: sometimes slowly away, usually races nearer last than first, often freely. *Mick Channon*

ZABALETASWANSONG (GER) 2 b.c. (Feb 18) Maxios 123 – Zavaala (IRE) (Rock **73**
of Gibraltar (IRE) 133) [2017 5m^5 5v^3 6.1d^2 p7s^4 7d^4 7s^5 7v 6d^2 f7.1g^5 p6g^5 Dec 30] compact colt: fair maiden: stays 7f: acts on heavy going: tried in cheekpieces: usually races prominently. *Richard Hannon*

ZABDI 4 b.c. Zebedee 113 – Musical Moonlight (Observatory (USA) 131) [2017 66: p7m^2 **70**
p7g^3 p7g^5 p8d* p8g p8f^4 6g^5 p7g^4 p7s^3 Jun 21] good-topped colt: fair handicapper: won at Kempton in February: stays 1m: acts on polytrack: tried in hood/tongue tie: usually leads. *Lee Carter*

ZABEEL PRINCE (IRE) 4 ch.g. Lope de Vega (IRE) 125 – Princess Serena (USA) 48 **115**
(Unbridled's Song (USA) 125) [2017 78p: 8.3s* 8s* 7.9g* 8s Oct 21] tall gelding: smart performer: won maiden at Nottingham (by 3 lengths from Cape To Cuba) in June, and handicaps at Yarmouth (by 3½ lengths from London) in September and York (by 2¾ lengths from Bravery) in October: stays 8.5f: acts on soft going: often travels strongly. *Roger Varian*

ZABEEL STAR (IRE) 5 ch.g. Arcano (IRE) 122 – Deep Winter 94 (Pivotal 124) [2017 **84**
81: t12.2m^2 p11g^4 p10g^3 t10.2d p8g t12.2g* t10.2d t8d^6 t10.2g^4 t12.4g^2 Dec 6] angular gelding: fairly useful handicapper: won at Wolverhampton (by neck from Mazaaher) in April: second at Newcastle (½ length behind Gallifrey) final start: left Graeme McPherson after sixth start: stays 12.5f: acts on polytrack, tapeta and firm going: often races towards rear. *Karen McLintock*

ZABRISKIE (IRE) 2 b.c. (Apr 22) Frankel 147 – Moonlight's Box (USA) (Nureyev **92**
(USA) 131) [2017 7s 7.5s* 8m Oct 14] €750,000Y: well-made colt: closely related to French 2-y-o 5.5f winner Malicieuse (by Galileo) and half-brother to several winners, including Prix de l'Arc de Triomphe winner Bago (2-y-o 1m winner, by Nashwan) and very smart winner up to 1¼m Maxios (2-y-o 1m winner, by Monsun): dam unraced: fairly useful form: won maiden at Tipperary (by head from Spanish Point) in September: last in Autumn Stakes at Newmarket: should prove suited by 1m+. *Aidan O'Brien, Ireland*

ZAC BROWN (IRE) 6 b.g. Kodiac 112 – Mildmay (USA) (Elusive Quality (USA)) **93**
[2017 67, a98: t5.1f* p6m^3 p6g^2 p6g* p5f^2 p5g^5 5m p6g^2 p5g* 5g^4 5g* 5m^2 5m^6 5d^6 p5g **a103**
p5g p6g Dec 30] good-quartered gelding: fairly useful handicapper on turf, useful on all-weather: won at Wolverhampton in January, Lingfield in February, Chelmsford (by head from Exceed The Limit) in May and Goodwood (by ½ length from Pettochside) in June: stays 6f: acts on polytrack, tapeta and good to firm going: has worn hood: wears tongue tie. *Charlie Wallis*

ZACCHETTO (USA) 3 b.g. Bernardini (USA) 132 – Minister's Melody (USA) 115 **59**
(Deputy Minister (CAN)) [2017 –: t8g^5 10g 10d 9.9d Jul 24] modest maiden: best effort at 1¼m: sold £2,500 in August, sent to UAE. *Mark Johnston*

ZACK MAYO 3 b.g. Air Chief Marshal (IRE) 115 – White Wedding (IRE) (Green Desert **97**
(USA) 127) [2017 8m p10g^3 11.6g^2 t12.2g* 12d^2 12m* 11.5d* Sep 19] third foal: half-brother to French 2-y-o 1m winner Navignies (by Le Havre): dam, unraced, closely related to smart winner up to 1m Simply Perfect: useful performer: won maiden at Wolverhampton in July, and handicaps at Ripon and Yarmouth (by ½ length from High End) in September: will stay further than 1½m: acts on polytrack, tapeta, good to firm and good to soft going: tried in cheekpieces: responds generously to pressure. *Philip McBride*

ZAEEM 8 b.g. Echo of Light 125 – Across (ARG) (Roy (USA)) [2017 95: f7g p8d 7d^6 8m^5 **80**
7m f8.1g^4 t7.2g^3 f7.1g* Dec 1] fairly useful performer: won seller at Southwell in December: stays 1¼m, usually races over shorter: acts on all-weather, firm and good to soft going: has worn headgear/tongue tie: usually races prominently. *Ivan Furtado*

ZAFARANAH (USA) 3 ch.f. Raven's Pass (USA) 133 – Jiwen (CAN) 95 (Singspiel **76**
(IRE) 133) [2017 56: p8s^3 10g p8g^5 p10g^5 p8g^2 p8s Nov 16] workmanlike filly: fair maiden: left Roger Varian after first start: stays 1¼m: acts on polytrack. *Pam Sly*

ZAHRAA 2 b.f. (Feb 17) Finjaan 122 – Alzahra (Exceed And Excel (AUS) 126) [2017 7s^4 **67**
p7g^5 7v^3 Oct 21] 20,000F: first foal: dam unraced out of half-sister to 1000 Guineas winner Attraction: fair form: best effort when third in minor event at Catterick (3 lengths behind Lady Anjorica) final start. *Robyn Brisland*

ZAIDIYN (FR) 7 b.g. Zamindar (USA) 116 – Zainta (IRE) 118 (Kahyasi 130) [2017 12v **92**
14.5d^2 t16.3g Nov 15] strong, good-topped gelding: fairly useful handicapper: second at Doncaster (2½ lengths behind Golden Birthday) in October: stays 14.5f: acts on good to firm and heavy going: tried in hood. *Brian Ellison*

ZAIN ARION (IRE) 4 b.f. Danehill Dancer (IRE) 117 – Shaanara (IRE) 82 (Darshaan **89**
133) [2017 80: p12g* 10.4m^2 11.9s* 11.8s 11.9d p16g 10d Oct 27] smallish filly: fairly useful handicapper: won at Lingfield in January and York (by 1½ lengths from Purple Rock) in May: stays 1½m: acts on polytrack, soft and good to firm going. *John Butler*

ZAIN EMPEROR (IRE) 4 b.g. Holy Roman Emperor (IRE) 125 – Love Thirty 93 **86**
(Mister Baileys 123) [2017 86: t8g p8g^2 p8g* Mar 31] fairly useful handicapper: won at Lingfield (by ½ length from Wink Oliver) in March: should stay 1¼m: acts on polytrack, firm and good to soft going: has worn visor: sold 30,000 gns in May, sent to Bahrain. *John Butler*

ZAIN FLASH 2 b.c. (Mar 15) Royal Applause 124 – Jade 87 (Cadeaux Genereux 131) **64**
[2017 5g^2 6.1d^4 6.1m^6 6d p5g t6g^5 Oct 19] sturdy colt: modest maiden: best effort at 5f: acts on good to soft going: usually races prominently. *David Evans*

ZAIN HANA 2 b.f. (Feb 16) Shamardal (USA) 129 – Lavender And Lace 55 (Barathea **87 p**
(IRE) 127) [2017 6m* Aug 27] €100,000Y, 320,000 2-y-o: second foal: half-sister to winner abroad by Oasis Dream: dam, maiden, closely related to Prix Saint-Alary winner Wavering and half-sister to Criterium de Saint-Cloud winner Mandaean: 7/1, won minor event at Yarmouth (by neck from Foxtrot Lady) on debut: sure to progress. *Jeremy Noseda*

ZAINHOM (USA) 3 ch.g. Street Cry (IRE) 130 – Kaseema (USA) 95 (Storm Cat (USA)) **101**
[2017 108p: 7m^3 8m^3 8s^6 Aug 4] strong gelding: useful performer: third in Greenham Stakes at Newbury (6 lengths behind Barney Roy) in April: likely to stay beyond 1m: acts on good to firm and good to soft going: often travels strongly. *Sir Michael Stoute*

ZAIN SMARTS (IRE) 2 b.f. (Mar 29) Kodiac 112 – Indian Navy (IRE) (Elusive City (USA) 117) [2017 5m 5m^4 5.1s^3 5.1m t5.1g^3 5m* 5s^6 p5g 5.1m Oct 16] 30,000F, £50,000Y: neat filly: first foal: dam French maiden sister to smart 2-y-o 7f winner Soul City, third in Irish 1000 Guineas and stayed 1¼m: fair performer: won nursery at Bath in August: raced only at 5f: acts on tapeta, soft and good to firm going: front runner/races prominently. *David Evans* **69**

ZAIN STAR (IRE) 3 b.c. Shamardal (USA) 129 – Astrologie (FR) 110 (Polish Precedent (USA) 131) [2017 8m p8s^2 p8g^4 8d Oct 6] 115,000Y: third foal: closely related to 1¼m/10.4f winner Barreesh (by Giant's Causeway) and half-brother to French 10.5f winner San Sicario (by Smart Strike): dam, 10.5f-1½m winner, half-sister to useful winner up to 1¼m Quest For Honor: fairly useful form: second in maiden at Kempton (head behind Jus Pires) in August: left Charlie Fellowes after first start: raced only at 1m. *John Butler* **88**

ZAKATAL 11 gr.g. Kalanisi (IRE) 132 – Zankara (FR) (Linamix (FR) 127) [2017 90: t16.3g^2 t16.5g^2 t16.3g^6 t16.3g* t16.3g^5 t16.5g^5 May 30] fairly useful handicapper: won at Newcastle (by neck from Fair Loch) in March: stays 16.5f: acts on polytrack, tapeta, good to firm and heavy going: tried in blinkers/tongue tie. *Rebecca Menzies* **92**

ZALAMEA (IRE) 4 b.c. Lope de Vega (IRE) 125 – Tanzania (IRE) 87 (Alzao (USA) 117) [2017 p7.5g* 7.5g^3 p7.5g* 8g^6 8m^5 8g 6.5g 7d^4 7d^5 6d^5 p7.5g Dec 16] good-topped colt: smart performer: won minor event at Marseilles Vivaux in January and claimer at Deauville in March: best efforts when sixth in Prix du Muguet at Saint-Cloud (2 lengths behind Jimmy Two Times) and fifth in Prix de la Foret at Chantilly (beaten 1½ lengths by Aclaim): below form in Summer Mile at Ascot on sixth outing: left K. Borgel after third start: stays 1m: acts on polytrack and good to soft going. *Mlle C. Fey, France* **111**

ZALSHAH 2 ch.c. (Feb 8) Mayson 124 – Regal Velvet 81 (Halling (USA) 133) [2017 5m 5.1m^3 5d^2 5d^3 5.2v 5s^2 p5g^6 5g 7s^2 7v^5 8d p7g^2 p7s* p7g^3 Dec 28] 40,000F, £40,000Y: good-quartered colt: seventh foal: half-brother to several winners, including useful 1m winner (stayed 10.5f) Robemaker (by Oasis Dream): dam, 1¼m winner, half-sister to smart stayer Regal Flush: fairly useful performer: won nursery at Chelmsford (by length from Dance Emperor) in December: stays 7f: acts on polytrack, soft and good to firm going: in cheekpieces last 5 starts. *Richard Hannon* **86**

ZAMADANCE 3 ch.g. Zamindar (USA) 116 – Opera Dancer 79 (Norse Dancer (IRE) 127) [2017 66: 10.2m^6 12.1m^3 11.6d^4 9.9m^3 11.8g 10.1g p12d^6 Aug 16] well-grown gelding: fair handicapper: stays 1½m: acts on polytrack, good to firm and good to soft going: tried in blinkers. *Ed Dunlop* **66**

ZAMALIGHT 3 ch.g. Zamindar (USA) 116 – Mountain Chain (USA) (Royal Academy (USA) 130) [2017 63p: p8g^5 p10g^3 9.9m^6 9.9g^3 8m^6 p8g 10m Oct 16] tall gelding: fair maiden: stays 1¼m: acts on polytrack and good to firm going: tried in hood. *Amanda Perrett* **79**

ZAMAN 2 b.c. (Jan 30) Dutch Art 126 – Wake Up Call 103 (Noverre (USA) 125) [2017 6g* 6f 6g* 7g^4 7g^2 Aug 1] 77,000F, 160,000 2-y-o: strong, attractive colt: second foal: half-brother to 2-y-o 5f winner Street Jazz (by Acclamation): dam, 6f-7f winner, half-sister to winner up to 9f Tamarillo and winner up to 1¼m Take It To The Max (both useful): useful performer: won minor events at York in May and Pontefract in July: second in Vintage Stakes at Goodwood (blinkered, 4½ lengths behind Expert Eye): stays 7f: usually races close up. *Charlie Appleby* **104**

ZAMANDAS (IRE) 2 b.c. (Feb 12) Pivotal 124 – Zimira (IRE) 86 (Invincible Spirit (IRE) 121) [2017 8.3v Nov 8] second foal: half-brother to 1m (including at 2 yrs) winner Zymyran (by Henrythenavigator): dam, 2-y-o 1m winner who stayed 1½m, half-sister to smart performer up to 1m Oracle: 20/1, tenth in maiden at Nottingham (6½ lengths behind Kinaesthesia): open to improvement. *Roger Varian* **66 p**

ZAMBEASY 6 b.g. Zamindar (USA) 116 – Hanella (IRE) 91 (Galileo (IRE) 134) [2017 90: p12g 11.4g^2 12v 9.9g^5 11.4g p12g^3 f12.1g p12g^3 Dec 20] workmanlike gelding: fairly useful handicapper: second at Windsor (1½ lengths behind C'est No Mour) in July: stays 1½m: acts on polytrack, soft and good to firm going: in cheekpieces last 2 starts: usually races close up. *Philip Hide* **86 a79**

ZAMBEZI QUEEN (IRE) 3 gr.f. Helmet (AUS) 127 – Lesotho (IRE) 80 (Excellent Art 125) [2017 50: 6.1m* 5.7f^3 6.1m^3 6v^5 p5g^6 Oct 5] fair handicapper: won at Chepstow in May: stays 6f: acts on polytrack and good to firm going: in cheekpieces last 2 starts. *Paul Cole* **75**

ZAMFIR 3 b.g. New Approach (IRE) 132 – Antara (GER) 119 (Platini (GER) 126) [2017 8.3g* 11.6dpu 11.4g Oct 9] lengthy, rather unfurnished gelding: second foal: dam winner up to 1¼m (twice Princess Elizabeth Stakes winner and 2-y-o 1m winner): fairly useful form: won maiden at Leicester (by 1½ lengths from Mostahel) in April: best effort at 8.5f: tried in blinkers: sold £11,000 in November. *Charlie Appleby* **86**

ZAMJAR 3 b.g. Exceed And Excel (AUS) 126 – Cloud's End 87 (Dubawi (IRE) 129) [2017 91: t6g3 t6g 7g5 6.1m* 7m 6m 6g 6g5 6d3 p8s6 t8d5 t7.1g4 Oct 10] good-topped gelding: fairly useful handicapper: won at Chester (by neck from Munro) in May: stays 1m: acts on polytrack, tapeta and good to firm going: has worn headgear, including in 2017: sold 35,000 gns, has joined Robert Cowell. *Ed Dunlop* **86**

ZAMPERINI (IRE) 5 ch.g. Fast Company (IRE) 126 – Lucky Date (IRE) 91 (Halling (USA) 133) [2017 94: p10g p12g6 11.8g6 12s 9.9m 9.9g4 9.9s2 11.4g2 10g2 10g Nov 3] good-topped gelding: fairly useful handicapper: second at Leicester (1¾ lengths behind Hajaam) in October: stays 11.5f: acts on tapeta, soft and good to firm going: has worn headgear, including in 2017: often starts slowly, usually races nearer last than first: quirky sort (has high head carriage). *Mike Murphy* **91**

ZANDRADEE (IRE) 3 br.f. Zebedee 113 – Annie Beach (IRE) 95 (Redback 116) [2017 f5g* t5d6 t5.1g f5g3 Mar 15] first foal: dam 5f winner (including at 2 yrs): modest form: won maiden at Southwell in January: raced only at 5f: sold £3,000 in August, sent to Sweden. *David Barron* **62**

ZANETTO 7 b.g. Medicean 128 – Play Bouzouki 70 (Halling (USA) 133) [2017 100§: 6g* 6m 6d 6m 5v Oct 21] attractive gelding: has reportedly had breathing operation: fairly useful handicapper: won at Thirsk (by length from Kalk Bay) in April: below form after: races up to 6f: acts on polytrack and any turf going: has worn headgear: unreliable. *John Quinn* **93 §**

ZAP 2 b.g. (Feb 10) Mayson 124 – Moonglow 65 (Nayef (USA) 129) [2017 6s* 6m2 6g4 6d6 6.5g5 6.1v5 6g6 7d2 Oct 28] 28,000F, 70,000Y: useful-looking gelding: has scope: second foal: half-brother to 1m winner (probably stays 1¾m) Crucial Moment (by Pivotal): dam, maiden (stayed 11f), half-sister to high-class 1m-1¼m winner Medicean: fairly useful performer: won maiden at York in May: second in nursery at Doncaster (3½ lengths behind Al Hajar) final start: stays 7f: acts on good to firm and heavy going. *Richard Fahey* **93**

ZAPATEADO 2 b.f. (May 20) Zoffany (IRE) 121 – Ziggy Zaggy (Diktat 126) [2017 6.1g 5s2 t5.1g4 5.1s 5s3 p5g4 p6g5 t7.2g* t7.2g t8.6g2 Dec 18] 4,000Y, €18,000 2-y-o: compact filly: half-sister to several winners, including winner up to 7f Ziggy's Secret (2-y-o 5f winner, by Sakhee's Secret) and 7f/1m winner Ziggys Star (by Compton Place): dam unraced half-sister to very smart winner up to 1½m Imperial Dancer: modest performer: won nursery at Wolverhampton in November: stays 8.5f: acts on polytrack, tapeta and soft going. *Richard Hughes* **64**

ZAPPA 2 b.g. (May 22) Sixties Icon 125 – Vilnius 67 (Imperial Dancer 123) [2017 8m Aug 27] angular gelding: 12/1, well held in minor event at Goodwood. *Mick Channon* **–**

ZAPPER CASS (FR) 4 b.g. Elusive City (USA) 117 – Moonlight Cass (IRE) 65 (Danehill Dancer (IRE) 117) [2017 91: 7m 6m 6.1s* 6s 6g4 7d6 6d t7.2g 5v4 f5g f6.1g t6.1d Dec 9] fairly useful handicapper: won at Nottingham (by head from Lexington Times) in June: below form after: stays 1m: acts on polytrack, fibresand and soft going: sometimes wears headgear/tongue tie. *Tony Coyle* **86 d**

ZARAK (FR) 4 b.c. Dubawi (IRE) 129 – Zarkava (IRE) 133 (Zamindar (USA) 116) [2017 121: 9.9g* 8.9d4 10.4g2 8.9g5 11.9g* 11.9d Oct 1] **124**

Like the other three-year-old fillies to have won the Prix de l'Arc de Triomphe this decade, Danedream and Treve, Enable will race on as a four-year-old. Hopefully, the welcome decision to postpone Enable's broodmare career will prove as rewarding for Enable's connections as it was for those of Danedream, who won a King George at four, and Treve, who won her second Arc. The Aga Khan's three-year-old Zarkava, on the other hand, was retired to the paddocks straight after taking her record to seven wins from as many starts with a top-class performance to win the Arc in 2009. Zarkava's retirement was regrettable as it meant the true extent of her ability would never be known for certain. From her owner's point of view, however, it was also understandable that he would want one of the best fillies ever to carry his colours to be integrated without further risk into his broodmare band, the lifeblood of his bloodstock operation. However, there are no certainties at stud, either, and it was not until the latest season, nine years later, when her fourth foal Zarak was in his fourth year, that Zarkava could be said to have finally come good as a broodmare. None of her first three foals even made it to the track and two of them are already dead. The first two were the results of matings with other Arc winners; the filly Zerkaza was by the Aga Khan's 2003 winner Dalakhani, while the colt Zarkash was by Sea The Stars who was retired to the Aga Khan's Gilltown Stud after winning the Arc a year after Zarkava. Zerkaza is herself now in the Aga Khan's stud-book (her oldest foal is an unraced two-year-old filly named Zerenda), while Zarkash broke a hind leg on the Chantilly gallops in the autumn of his three-year-old season and had to be put down. Zarkava's third foal, Zarkar, was by Galileo, breeding which earned him the opportunity of a stallion career, even though he never raced. However, Zarkar completed only one season at stud in Argentina before he had a paddock accident in May which proved fatal for him too.

Zarak has had better fortune than his siblings so far, though it has taken him a little longer than expected to fulfil early promise. Bred as he is, there was plenty of expectation when he finally became the first foal of his dam to reach the track as a two-year-old in the autumn of 2015. He won that newcomers race at Deauville and, after a winning reappearance at three in a minor event at Maisons-Laffitte, was sent off the 2/1 favourite for the Poule d'Essai des Poulains. He didn't have anything like the chance on form that his odds suggested but wasn't disgraced in fifth behind the easy winner The Gurkha and improved plenty over a longer trip when finding only Almanzor too good in the Prix du Jockey Club. Zarak didn't win again as a three-year-old but finished second to Almanzor again in the Prix Guillaume d'Ornano and made the frame on his last couple of starts, in the Prix du Moulin and Prix Dollar.

Zarak returned in the latest season with a couple of races at Meydan, following an impressive winning reappearance in the Dubai Millennium Stakes when just fourth behind the Japanese filly Vivlos when starting favourite for the Dubai Turf on World Cup night. Back in France, little went right for Zarak on his next two starts in the Prix Ganay and Prix d'Ispahan. In the Ganay at Saint-Cloud he lost out by a short neck to Cloth of Stars, meeting trouble in running before Christophe Soumillon dropped his whip in the closing stages and had to resort to using the flat of his hand for encouragement. Later in May, against just four rivals in the d'Ispahan at Chantilly, Zarak looked to have his best chance yet of an elusive Group 1 success but actually ran the worst race of his career, Soumillon easing him as he trailed home last.

Zarak still hadn't been tried at a mile and a half and his chance finally came in the Grand Prix de Saint-Cloud at the beginning of July. The Aga Khan had won the race three times before, including with the three-year-olds Shakapour and Akarad in

Grand Prix de Saint-Cloud, Saint-Cloud—
a first Group 1 winner for the unbeaten Arc winner Zarkava as Zarak sweeps through wide to beat Silverwave (hood) and Armande (dark colours and pale cap)

the early-'eighties. Another dropped whip didn't stop Shakapour earning a share of the spoils, though his rider Yves Saint-Martin believed he would have won outright but for that. By the time the Aga Khan won his next Grand Prix de Saint-Cloud in 2011 three-year-olds were ineligible and he won with his four-year-old filly Sarafina who had been kept in training in a bid to improve on her third place in the Arc as a three-year-old (she started favourite for her second Arc attempt, finishing fourth to Danedream). In an open-looking field of ten at Saint-Cloud, Zarak started second favourite behind the previous year's winner Silverwave who had won the Grand Prix de Chantilly since finishing just behind Zarak when third in the Ganay. The previous year's runner-up Erupt was also back again (after finishing fourth in the Ganay), while a three-strong challenge from Britain comprised the previous season's Prince of Wales's Stakes and Eclipse winners, My Dream Boat and Hawkbill, and Robin of Navan who had been second in the d'Ispahan. Held up in a well-run race, Zarak was last of all as the field turned into the straight but readily made up ground on the outside before getting the better of a brief tussle with Silverwave inside the final furlong. Zarak won by three quarters of a length, with a length and a quarter back to third-placed Armande, winner of the Prix Corrida. My Dream Boat fared much the best of the visitors in fourth after holding every chance a furlong out, though several of the others were eased and came home at wide intervals, after an incident on the rails under two furlongs out when outsider Doha Dream was tightened up and parted company with his rider.

Unusually for a French contender in the Arc, Zarak wasn't tuned up in a trial beforehand, Alain de Royer Dupre preferring instead to give him a racecourse gallop at Maisons-Laffitte and bring him fresh to the Arc after a three-month break. There were apparently some misgivings about running Zarak in the Prix Foy given his mixed record at Chantilly where he had been beaten on all his four starts. Even so, on the big day itself, at pari-mutuel odds of just over 15/1, Zarak actually started at the shortest odds of any of the home-trained Arc contenders. However, he never looked like joining his dam on the race's roll of honour, dropped out from a wide draw and making only a little ground early in the straight before not getting the clearest of runs up the rail and finishing a never-dangerous tenth, some eight lengths behind Enable. Arc-winning mares do have a good record, though, when it comes to producing other winners of the race. Sea The Stars was out of Urban Sea, the last filly before Zarkava to win the Arc when she was successful in 1993, while 1980 winner Detroit became the dam of Carnegie who was successful fourteen years later.

Zarak (FR) (b.c. 2013)	Dubawi (IRE) (b 2002)	Dubai Millennium (b 1996)	Seeking The Gold
			Colorado Dancer
		Zomaradah (b 1995)	Deploy
			Jawaher
	Zarkava (IRE) (b 2005)	Zamindar (b 1994)	Gone West
			Zaizafon
		Zarkasha (b 1999)	Kahyasi
			Zarkana

Zarkava's Arc win had come after earlier victories in the Poule d'Essai des Pouliches, Prix de Diane and Prix Vermeille, while she also won the Prix Marcel Boussac at two. With a dam as good as his, Zarak's pedigree hardly needs delving into any further back, though it is worth mentioning that Zarkava traces back to the Aga Khan's outstanding racemare Petite Etoile, her fifth dam, whose own record at stud was distinctly patchy. She was barren more often than not and her female line survives today in the Aga Khan's stud book only because of a single surviving daughter, Zahra, who failed to win in ten starts. This is a thriving family nowadays, though, and, as well as that first daughter Zerkaza, Zarkava's eighteen-year-old dam Zarkasha, who was unraced, is still active in the broodmare band. Her other winners include the top-class hurdler Zarkandar. Zarak remains the only one of Zarkava's foals to race, despite her having two more foals of racing age. Three-year-old colt Zarmitan (by Redoute's Choice) and two-year-old filly Zarkamiya (by Frankel) were both in training with Alain de Royer Dupre in the latest season but neither was seen out. They are followed by a yearling colt by Invincible Spirit and a filly foal by Siyouni. After visiting different stallions to date—common policy with the Aga

Khan's mares over the years—Zarkava is due to return in 2018 to Sea The Stars, sire of ill-fated Zarkash. Zarak will be at stud, too, and will stand at €12,000 at the Aga Khan's Haras de Bonneval in Normandy. He stayed a mile and a half and only ever encountered good or good to soft ground, except when winning on soft ground on his debut. He was usually held up, and, like his dam, was ridden in all his races by Christophe Soumillon. Soumillon regained his French jockeys' title outright in a record-breaking season in which he piled up a domestic total of 306 winners from 1,635 rides. That tally beat the previous European record of 301 wins in a year set twelve months earlier by Pierre-Charles Boudot, with whom Soumillon had shared the French title in 2015. *A. de Royer Dupre, France*

ZARIA 6 b.m. Tomba 119 – Princess Zara (Reprimand 122) [2017 69: 8.1d 8.1d 8.2g^5 8.1m^3 10.2d^4 8g 8.1d^3 10d^2 8.2v* 8g Oct 16] compact mare: modest handicapper: won at Leicester (dead-heated) in September: stays 1¼m: acts on good to firm and heavy going: wears headgear: often races prominently. *Richard Price* **64**

ZARKAVON 3 b.f. Avonbridge 123 – Zarkavean (Medicean 128) [2017 –: 7.4g 6d 7m 7d 7d 10.3v f7.1g f12.1g Nov 28] strong filly: of no account: wears headgear. *John Wainwright* **–**

ZARLIMAN (IRE) 7 ch.g. Zamindar (USA) 116 – Zarlana (IRE) (Darshaan 133) [2017 64: p12g p12g t14d Dec 27] fair handicapper: well below form in 2017: usually wears headgear: has worn tongue tie. *Roger Ingram* **–**

ZATORIUS (GER) 2 b.g. (Apr 16) Pastorius (GER) 124 – Zarah Top (GER) (Big Shuffle (USA) 122) [2017 7v^2 7.9g^4 Oct 13] €20,000Y: close-coupled gelding: second foal: half-brother to German 7f winner (Swiss 2-y-o 6f winner) Zazoulino (by Tiger Hill): dam, 6f winner, half-sister to useful winner up to 1¼m Zaza Top: fairly useful form: better effort when second in minor event at Chester (2¼ lengths behind Ayutthaya) in September: should stay 1m. *Andrew Balding* **85**

ZAVIKON 3 b.c. Compton Place 125 – Hakuraa (IRE) (Elnadim (USA) 128) [2017 65: t5.1f^5 t6g^5 6m^3 5.1m* p6g^5 6s^2 5.1s^3 7s^6 5.3s^6 t6.1m^4 Oct 28] lengthy, shallow-girthed colt: fair handicapper: won at Windsor in June: stays 6f: acts on tapeta, soft and good to firm going: has worn headgear: sometimes slowly away. *Richard Hughes* **73**

ZAYTOON (IRE) 4 b.g. Cape Cross (IRE) 129 – Megec Blis (IRE) 92 (Soviet Star (USA) 128) [2017 8g 7m 6m^6 8.3f 6m Jul 19] poor ex-French-trained maiden: tried in cheekpieces. *Micky Hammond* **–**

ZEALOUS (IRE) 4 br.g. Intense Focus (USA) 117 – Velvet Kiss (IRE) (Danehill Dancer (IRE) 117) [2017 89: 7g 8m 8m t8g 10g^2 10g^5 10.2g^4 10g Sep 27] workmanlike gelding: fairly useful handicapper: fourth in minor event at Doncaster (5½ lengths behind Pivoine) in September: stays 1¼m: acts on soft and good to firm going. *Sally Haynes* **84**

ZEBEDEE'S GIRL (IRE) 4 gr.f. Zebedee 113 – Rafelite 67 (Fraam 114) [2017 60: p6g^6 p8g^4 p10g t8.6g Mar 27] modest maiden handicapper: stays 1m: acts on polytrack and firm going: has worn headgear: often races towards rear. *David Evans* **51**

ZEBEDEE'S SON (IRE) 4 gr.g. Zebedee 113 – Lady Ginevra (IRE) (Touch of The Blues (FR) 125) [2017 58, a50: p8g p8g 8g May 23] tall gelding: modest handicapper: below form in 2017: stays 1¼m: acts on polytrack and any turf going: has worn headgear, including in 2017. *Roger Ingram* **44**

ZEBEDEE STAR 3 b.f. Zebedee 113 – Sonna Star (IRE) (Red Clubs (IRE) 125) [2017 58: 6g 6g 6m 7.4m^5 7d^3 7.4g f7.1g Aug 28] modest maiden: stays 7f: acts on good to firm and good to soft going: tried in blinkers: often races prominently. *Karen Tutty* **48**

ZEBELINI (IRE) 5 gr.m. Zebedee 113 – Ma Nikitia (IRE) (Camacho 118) [2017 55: f6g f5g f6g p5g^4 p7d 6g t7.1g^3 t7.2g* t7.2g p7g t7.1g^5 f8.1g Dec 21] modest handicapper: won at Wolverhampton in June: stays 7f: acts on all-weather and good to firm going: has worn headgear/tongue tie. *Roy Bowring* **54**

ZEBS LAD (IRE) 5 ro.g. Zebedee 113 – Dubai Princess (IRE) 105 (Dubai Destination (USA) 127) [2017 64: 6.1g 8g 7.4v 7v Sep 25] lengthy gelding: fair handicapper: out of form in 2017: usually wears headgear: tried in tongue tie. *Nikki Evans* **–**

ZEBSTAR (IRE) 4 b.g. Zebedee 113 – Zinstar (IRE) (Sinndar (IRE) 134) [2017 76: 6g 5m^{pu} Jun 17] sturdy gelding: useful at 2 yrs, lightly raced and little form since: broke down final start: stays 6f: acts on firm going: tried in cheekpieces. *Gay Kelleway* **–**

ZEBULON (IRE) 3 gr.g. Zebedee 113 – Novelina (IRE) 60 (Fusaichi Pegasus (USA) **87**
130) [2017 76p: 7g^5 5.7f* 6.1m^6 8m^3 8.1g^4 8.2d^6 6d^2 6.1d* 6s^6 Sep 27] medium-sized gelding: fairly useful performer: won maiden at Bath in May and handicap at Windsor (by 1¼ lengths from Kodicat) in September: stays 1m: acts on firm and good to soft going: sold 20,000 gns in October to join Ruth Carr. *Richard Hannon*

ZED CANDY GIRL 7 ch.m. Sakhee's Secret 128 – Musical Twist (USA) 97 (Woodman **41**
(USA) 126) [2017 65: t7.1m t8.6g Jan 26] lengthy mare: fair handicapper: below form both starts in 2017: stayed 8.5f: acted on polytrack, tapeta and soft going: wore headgear: dead. *Daniel Loughnane*

ZEELANDER 3 b.c. Dubawi (IRE) 129 – Zeeba (IRE) 82 (Barathea (IRE) 127) [2017 –p: **84 p**
10.2v^3 12d^5 11.4m* Oct 16] good-bodied colt: fairly useful form: won handicap at Windsor (by length from Orin Swift) in October: will stay beyond 1½m: open to further improvement. *Roger Varian*

ZEFFERINO 3 ch.g. Frankel 147 – Turama (Pivotal 124) [2017 84: 7d* 8m^6 7m p7d Aug **85**
16] good-topped gelding: fairly useful performer: won maiden at Lingfield (by 1½ lengths from Luna Bear) in May: stays 1m: acts on good to firm and good to soft going: often races towards rear: sold 17,000 gns, has joined Marco Botti. *Roger Charlton*

ZEHRAH (IRE) 3 b.f. Raven's Pass (USA) 133 – Ahla Wasahl 111 (Dubai Destination **75**
(USA) 127) [2017 t8.6g^6 p10g^2 10g 10.2g^6 10.2g^3 8.8g Jul 28] 65,000Y: third foal: half-sister to useful 1m winner Generalship (by New Approach), later successful abroad: dam winner up to 1m (2-y-o 6f winner): fair maiden: third in handicap at Nottingham (2½ lengths behind Aelius) in July: stays 1¼m: acts on polytrack, raced only on good going on turf: front runner/races prominently. *Simon Crisford*

ZELZAL (FR) 4 b.c. Sea The Stars (IRE) 140 – Olga Prekrasa (USA) (Kingmambo **120**
(USA) 125) [2017 122: 8m^2 8v^4 7d^6 8f^6 Nov 4] very smart performer: won Prix Jean Prat at Chantilly at 3 yrs: in frame in 2017 in Prix Bertrand du Breuil on same course (1¾ lengths second to Taareef) and Sussex Stakes at Goodwood (2½ lengths fourth to Here Comes When): 1¾ lengths sixth to World Approval in Breeders' Cup Mile at Del Mar final outing: stayed 1m: acted on polytrack and firm going: raced nearer last than first: to stand at Haras de Bouquetot, France, fee €8,000. *Jean-Claude Rouget, France*

ZENAFIRE 8 b.g. Firebreak 125 – Zen Garden (Alzao (USA) 117) [2017 74: 14m^3 14v* **79**
11.6m^3 15.9d* 14g^6 13.4d^4 15.9g^5 16.3d Sep 10] good-topped gelding: fair handicapper: won at Haydock (amateur) in June and Chester in July: stays 2m: acts on polytrack, good to firm and heavy going: wears cheekpieces. *Sarah Hollinshead*

ZENON (IRE) 3 b.c. Galileo (IRE) 134 – Jacqueline (IND) (King Charlemagne (USA) **106**
120) [2017 73p: 10d^2 12d* 14m* 14.4s^3 14g^5 14.1d^2 14.2d^6 Oct 6] sturdy colt: useful performer: won maiden at Chepstow (by 3 lengths from Dark Pearl) in June and handicap at Haydock (by 1½ lengths from Dominating) in July: second in handicap at Yarmouth (1½ lengths behind Great Hall) in September: stays 14.5f: acts on soft and good to firm going: in headgear last 3 starts. *John Gosden*

ZENOVIA (IRE) 3 b.f. Invincible Spirit (IRE) 121 – Zallerina (Zamindar (USA) 116) **67**
[2017 62: p8g^6 p10d p7d^5 t7.1g t6.1m* t6.1g^4 p6g^5 f6.1g t6.1g^5 p6g Dec 20] fair handicapper: won at Wolverhampton in October: left David Simcock after second start: best form at 6f: acts on polytrack and tapeta: wears headgear/tongue tie. *Archie Watson*

ZEPHYROS (GER) 6 br.g. Areion (GER) 115 – Zandra (GER) (Lagunas) [2017 74: **73**
p12g p10g^4 p10g^5 p11g p10g^3 10g^2 10v^3 8.5d 7.1g^6 p10g^3 Dec 30] lengthy gelding: fair handicapper: stays 1¼m: acts on polytrack, tapeta, soft and good to firm going: tried in cheekpieces. *David Bridgwater*

ZERAFINO (BEL) 4 b.g. Piccolo 121 – Semiramis (BEL) (Zeami (IRE)) [2017 p7g p6g **–**
p6g p8d 6.1m 10m Jul 17] little form: usually races towards rear, often lazily. *Jimmy Fox*

ZESHOV (IRE) 6 b.g. Acclamation 118 – Fathoming (USA) (Gulch (USA)) [2017 79: 8g **83**
8m* 7.8s 8s 8d^3 8m^6 t8d 8g^2 8g^3 8.3g^5 Nov 1] angular gelding: fairly useful handicapper: won at Musselburgh (by ¾ length from Crazy Tornado) in May: stays 8.5f: acts on polytrack, firm and soft going: has worn headgear, including last 3 starts. *Rebecca Bastiman*

ZEST (IRE) 4 b.f. Duke of Marmalade (IRE) 132 – Affinity 76 (Sadler's Wells (USA) 132) **100**
[2017 98: p8g^3 8f 8d^5 8v^4 p7g^3 p8g^2 p8g* Dec 23] sturdy filly: useful performer: won minor event at Lingfield (by neck from Singyoursong) in December: second in listed race at same course (length behind Muffri'ha) in November: stays 1¼m: acts on polytrack, firm and good to soft going: has worn headgear: races prominently: signs of temperament. *James Fanshawe*

Royal Hunt Cup (Heritage Handicap), Royal Ascot—Zhui Feng makes all and digs deep to beat Blair House, Tashweeq and Ballet Concerto (spotted cap)

ZETEAH 7 b.m. Passing Glance 119 – Ajeebah (IRE) (Mujtahid (USA) 118) [2017 52: f8g^6 p8d p11d p12g t13.9g Mar 18] good-topped mare: modest handicapper: below form in 2017: stays 1¼m: acts on tapeta, soft and good to firm going: tried in cheekpieces: has worn tongue tie: often races towards rear. *Tony Carroll* **42**

ZHUI FENG (IRE) 4 b.c. Invincible Spirit (IRE) 121 – Es Que (Inchinor 119) [2017 109: p10m^4 8g 8m 7m^3 8m* 8s Aug 4] good-bodied colt: smart handicapper: won Royal Hunt Cup at Royal Ascot (by ½ length from Blair House) in June: stays 1¼m: acts on polytrack, good to firm and good to soft going: in cheekpieces last 3 starts: usually leads. *Amanda Perrett* **114**

ZHUKOVA (IRE) 5 b.m. Fastnet Rock (AUS) 127 – Nightime (IRE) 113 (Galileo (IRE) 134) [2017 122: 12d* 11s* 10g^4 10d 10f^6 Oct 8] lengthy mare: very smart performer: won listed race at Cork in April and Man o'War Stakes at Belmont (by 6 lengths from Taghleeb) in May: below form after: stayed 1½m: raced mainly on good or softer ground (acted on heavy): tried in cheekpieces: usually raced prominently: sold 3,700,000 gns in December: retired. *D. K. Weld, Ireland* **119**

ZIARAH (IRE) 2 b.f. (Apr 23) Iffraaj 127 – Ashtown Girl (IRE) (Exceed And Excel (AUS) 126) [2017 5m^3 5m^6 7m^3 7d^4 7d^4 Sep 30] €140,000Y: well-grown filly: third foal: half-sister to 6f winner Brave Display (by Requinto): dam unraced half-sister to very smart winner up to 6f Hot Streak (by Iffraaj): fairly useful maiden: best effort at 7f: acts on good to firm and good to soft going: sometimes in hood. *James Tate* **80**

ZIGGY LEE 11 b.g. Lujain (USA) 119 – Mary O'Grady (USA) (Swain (IRE) 134) [2017 91: t5g Nov 23] lengthy gelding: fairly useful at best, well held sole start in 2017: races at 5f: acts on polytrack, tapeta, firm and good to soft going: tried in tongue tie: often races towards rear. *Lawrence Mullaney* –

ZIG ZAG GIRL 3 b.f. Sixties Icon 125 – Mistic Magic (IRE) 95 (Orpen (USA) 116) [2017 73: t5g^6 5m Jun 23] fair form when winning seller at 2 yrs, standout effort: left Scott Dixon after first start: stays 6f: acts on good to firm going: tried in blinkers: usually leads. *John Butler* –

ZIHAAM 3 ch.g. Dutch Art 126 – Hymnsheet 93 (Pivotal 124) [2017 10m 9.5s³ 8s 9s⁶ 12.1g⁴ 12g 14.1v⁶ Sep 13] fair maiden: left Kevin Prendergast after second start: best effort at 9.5f: acts on soft going: tried in cheekpieces. *Roger Fell* **70**

ZILARA (IRE) 2 b.f. (Jan 23) Big Bad Bob (IRE) 118 – Celtic Slipper (IRE) 102 (Anabaa (USA) 130) [2017 7v⁴ 7g Aug 25] rather unfurnished filly: fourth foal: half-sister to 9f winner Are You Mine (by Nayef) and smart 1¼m-16.5f winner Moonrise Landing (by Dalakhani): dam 2-y-o 7f/1m winner who stayed 1½m: fair form: better effort when fourth in maiden at Goodwood (1½ lengths behind Roulette) in August: will be suited by 1m+. *Ralph Beckett* **71**

ZILLION (IRE) 3 b.g. Zebedee 113 – Redelusion (IRE) 59 (Hernando (FR) 127) [2017 p8d⁴ t7.1g Apr 19] €25,000F, 34,000 2-y-o: third foal: half-brother to winner abroad by Haatef: dam maiden (stayed 7f) out of useful winner up to 7f (2-y-o 6f winner) Red Liason: modest form in maidens: tried in cheekpieces: has joined Susan Gardner. *John Gosden* **61**

ZILZA (IRE) 3 b.f. Paco Boy (IRE) 129 – Helen Glaz (IRE) (Giant's Causeway (USA) 132) [2017 68: p6g⁴ p6d² p7g⁴ t7.2g⁵ p7g⁵ 7g³ 8s⁶ 7d⁵ p6g⁴ t7.2g³ 6.1g³ t5.1g⁵ p6g* Oct 25] rather leggy filly: fair performer: won maiden at Kempton in October: stays 7f: acts on polytrack, tapeta, best turf form on good going: wears headgear/tongue tie: usually leads. *Conrad Allen* **72**

ZIP ALONG (IRE) 2 b.f. (Apr 24) Iffraaj 127 – Wizz Up (IRE) (Whipper (USA) 126) [2017 5d² t6s⁵ Sep 19] €32,000Y, 50,000 2-y-o: second foal: dam once-raced sister to smart winner up to 7.6f Yaa Wayl and half-sister to dam of very smart sprinter Wizz Kid: fair form: better effort when second in minor event at Beverley (1¼ lengths behind Elnadim Star) in August: remains capable of better. *Richard Fahey* **68 p**

ZIPEDEE 3 gr.f. Zebedee 113 – White Shift (IRE) 87 (Night Shift (USA)) [2017 46: p8g p12f 11.5g³ Apr 25] little form: tried in hood/tongue tie. *John Ryan* **–**

ZIPEDEEDODAH (IRE) 5 gr.g. Zebedee 113 – Beverley Macca 73 (Piccolo 121) [2017 67, a84: p5d* p5g⁶ t5.1g⁵ p5g³ 5m⁴ 5g* 5.3g² 5g p5s 5g³ 5.1g⁴ 5.1m⁴ 5m⁵ 5.1g² 5m⁶ 5.3d⁴ p5m⁵ p5s⁵ p6g Dec 28] compact gelding: fair handicapper on turf, fairly useful on all-weather: won at Chelmsford (by ¾ length from You're Cool) in February and Lingfield in May: best form at 5f: acts on polytrack, tapeta, best turf form on good going: wears tongue tie. *Joseph Tuite* **79 a85**

ZIZUM 2 ch.c. (May 18) Showcasing 117 – Proud Duchess (IRE) (Duke of Marmalade (IRE) 132) [2017 5m⁵ 6g 6d 6s² 6d Oct 24] fair maiden: left David Marnane after second start: stays 6f: acts on soft going: often in tongue tie. *George Scott* **68**

ZLATAN (IRE) 4 b.g. Dark Angel (IRE) 113 – Guard Hill (USA) 87 (Rahy (USA) 115) [2017 85: 8.3m 8.3g* 8s 8s⁵ 7.8s⁴ 8m⁴ 8g² 7.6s⁴ Aug 6] sturdy gelding: fairly useful handicapper: won at Nottingham (by neck from Pumaflor) in May: stays 8.5f: acts on polytrack, soft and good to firm going: wears headgear. *Ed de Giles* **87**

ZODIAKOS (IRE) 4 b.g. Kodiac 112 – Zonic 59 (Zafonic (USA) 130) [2017 94: 8m³ 7g 8m⁴ 8.5m⁴ 8.8m 8d* 8.5s* 8d⁵ 8d* 7.8v 8g⁶ 7.9g Oct 13] big gelding: fairly useful handicapper: won at Ayr in July, and Beverley and Redcar (by 1½ lengths from Rashford's Double) in August: stays 8.5f: acts on polytrack, soft and good to firm going: wears cheekpieces: often races prominently. *Roger Fell* **93**

ZOFFALEE (FR) 2 ch.c. (Mar 1) Zoffany (IRE) 121 – Senderlea (IRE) (Giant's Causeway (USA) 132) [2017 7m⁶ 7d* 7g Sep 15] 44,000F, €110,000Y: good-topped colt: half-brother to several winners, including smart 6f/7f (including at 2 yrs) winner Cheikeljack (by Myboycharlie) and 2-y-o 1m winner Salez (by Manduro), both in France: dam unraced: fairly useful form: won minor event at Chester (by head from Porth Swtan) in August: raced only at 7f. *Tom Dascombe* **81**

ZOFFANIST (IRE) 3 ch.g. Zoffany (IRE) 121 – Frynia (USA) (Cat Thief (USA) 126) [2017 60: 12f⁵ 13f³ 12m⁶ 9.9g⁴ p12g 11.2m³ 9d³ 8d 9.9v⁴ Oct 19] tall gelding: fair maiden: stays 1¼m: acts on heavy going: often wears headgear. *Amanda Perrett* **67**

ZOFFANY BAY (IRE) 3 b.g. Zoffany (IRE) 121 – Trois Graces (USA) (Alysheba (USA)) [2017 p8g 8.3g⁴ 10.1g 8.1d 8m p8g p8g 9.9s p10g⁵ p10s⁵ p10s* t9.5g⁵ p10g Dec 30] good-topped gelding: fair handicapper: won at Chelmsford in December: stays 1¼m: acts on polytrack: wears headgear. *George Peckham* **71**

ZOFFINIA (IRE) 2 b.f. (Apr 1) Zoffany (IRE) 121 – Princess Nala (IRE) 104 (In The Wings 128) [2017 7d⁵ 7d⁶ 8g⁶ 8v⁵ 8g Sep 27] €50,000F, €130,000Y: finely-made filly: fifth foal: half-sister to winners abroad by Sir Percy and Tamayuz: dam 1¼m-1½m winner who stayed 1¾m: modest maiden: races towards rear: sold 3,500 gns, sent to Hungary. *Richard Fahey* **56**

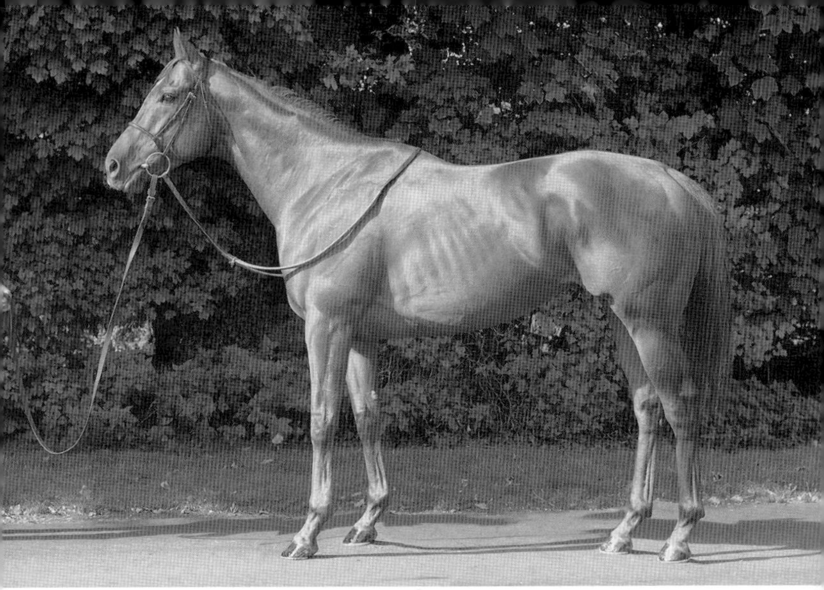

Cheveley Park Stud's "Zonderland"

ZONDERLAND 4 ch.c. Dutch Art 126 – Barynya 77 (Pivotal 124) [2017 118: 8g^{2} 8s Oct 21] well-made colt: smart performer: second in Celebration Mile at Goodwood (nose behind Lightning Spear) in August: well held in Queen Elizabeth II Stakes next time: stays 1m: acts on polytrack and good to firm going. *Clive Cox* **119**

ZONE IN 3 b.g. Equiano (FR) 127 – Donna Giovanna 74 (Mozart (IRE) 131) [2017 8g 6m^{6} 7.4g^{4} 5.9s^{5} 6d t6.1g 8.5d Aug 17] modest maiden: left Roger Fell after sixth start: tried in cheekpieces: front runner/races prominently: has joined Ivan Furtado. *David C. Griffiths* **63**

ZONZA (FR) 2 b.f. (Jan 19) Alex The Winner (USA) – Zanyeva (IRE) (Oasis Dream 129) [2017 5g* 5.5g* 5d* 6g^{4} 8d^{5} Oct 1] half-sister to French 2-y-o 7.5f winner Killing Joke (by Sageburg): dam won 3 times up to 6.5f in France at 2 yrs: useful form: won newcomers race at Bordeaux in April, minor event at Maisons-Laffitte in May and Prix du Bois at Deauville (by ¾ length from Elizabeth Darcy) in July: 1½ lengths fourth to Unfortunately in Prix Morny on last-named course: should stay 7f. *D. Guillemin, France* **108**

ZOPHILLY (IRE) 4 b.f. Zoffany (IRE) 121 – Extreme Pleasure (IRE) 72 (High Chaparral (IRE) 132) [2017 –: p6g 5.7f 5.7f 5.7d* 5.7m Jun 2] modest handicapper: won at Bath in May: stays 6f: acts on tapeta and good to soft going: wears hood/tongue tie: usually races nearer last than first. *Jeremy Gask* **57**

ZORAVAN (USA) 4 ch.g. More Than Ready (USA) 120 – Zaralanta (IRE) 100 (Danehill Dancer (IRE) 117) [2017 –: f8g* f8s f8m^{2} 7g* 7m 8m 7.2m^{6} 10.3s 7.8s 8.3s t7.1g Dec 6] fairly useful handicapper: won at Southwell in January and Doncaster (by 1¼ lengths from Invermere) in April: stays 1m: acts on polytrack and fibresand: wears visor: tried in tongue tie. *Keith Dalgleish* **90**

ZORAYA (FR) 2 b.f. (Jan 13) Zoffany (IRE) 121 – Aztec Queen (Holy Roman Emperor (IRE) 125) [2017 p6g p7g^{4} 8g 7.1s* 7s* Oct 15] lengthy, rather unfurnished filly: first foal: dam unraced: fairly useful performer: won minor event at Chepstow in September and nursery at Goodwood (by ¾ length from Travelcard) in October: should stay 1m: acts on soft going. *Paul Cole* **87**

ZORBA THE GREEK 5 b.g. Invincible Spirit (IRE) 121 – Mistress Greeley (USA) 83 (Mr Greeley (USA) 122) [2017 85: p8d^{2} p8g^{5} 10m 12d^{3} 11.6d^{2} p10g^{2} 10.1m^{6} 7.6s^{4} Sep 16] workmanlike gelding: fair handicapper: stays 1½m: acts on polytrack, good to firm and good to soft going: usually in headgear in 2017: often races prominently. *Ed Vaughan* **78**

ZORLU (IRE) 4 b.g. Invincible Spirit (IRE) 121 – Special Assignment (USA) (Lemon –
Drop Kid (USA) 131) [2017 55: t7.1g 5.7m 7.4g Jul 17] little form: has worn headgear, including in 2017: sometimes slowly away, usually races nearer last than first. *John O'Shea*

ZOUCH 2 b.g. (Apr 6) Sakhee's Secret 128 – Sabrina Brown 85 (Polar Falcon (USA) 126) 71
[2017 5d^{5} 5.5d^{4} p5m Nov 25] fair form: best effort when fourth in maiden at Le Croise-Laroche (2 lengths behind Historia) in October. *J. S. Moore*

ZUBAIDAH 5 b.m. Exceed And Excel (AUS) 126 – Bedouin Bride (USA) (Chester House 64
(USA) 123) [2017 45: t8.6g 11.5m* 11.6g* 11.5m^{2} Jun 14] lengthy mare: modest handicapper: won at Yarmouth in May and Lingfield in June: stays 11.5f: acts on polytrack, tapeta and firm going: wears headgear: often in tongue tie: usually races close up. *Jane Chapple-Hyam*

ZUBAYR (IRE) 5 b.g. Authorized (IRE) 133 – Zaziyra (IRE) 79 (Dalakhani (IRE) 133) 98
[2017 p12d* p12g^{2} 11.8d^{2} p12g^{2} Dec 30] sturdy gelding: useful performer: trained at 3 yrs by A. de Royer Dupre: won maiden at Kempton in May: best effort when second in handicap at Lingfield (½ length behind Lexington Law) in December: stays 1½m: acts on polytrack and good to soft going: useful hurdler. *Paul Nicholls*

ZULU 3 b.g. Cockney Rebel (IRE) 127 – Pantita 74 (Polish Precedent (USA) 131) [2017 –: 68
7m^{4} 8.1d^{3} p8s p10g Dec 30] fair maiden: stays 1m: acts on good to firm and good to soft going. *Rod Millman*

ZUMRAN 3 b.f. Rock of Gibraltar (IRE) 133 – Maid For Winning (USA) (Gone West 88
(USA)) [2017 62: p6s^{2} 6d* 6.1g* 6v^{4} Jul 27] compact filly: fairly useful handicapper: won at Doncaster in June and Nottingham (by 3 lengths from Fantasy Keeper) in July: stays 6f: acts on polytrack and good to soft going. *Philip McBride*

ZUMURUDEE (USA) 3 b.c. Stormy Atlantic (USA) – Voting Right (FR) (High 103
Chaparral (IRE) 132) [2017 91p: a9.4f p10g^{2} 10d^{5} 10.2d Oct 18] useful performer: second in handicap at Chelmsford (short head behind Drochaid) in May: stays 1¼m: acts on polytrack, tapeta and good to firm going: sold 70,000 gns, sent to USA. *Marco Botti*

ZUMURUD (IRE) 2 gr.g. (Jan 17) Zebedee 113 – Thaisy (USA) (Tabasco Cat (USA) 83 p
126) [2017 5g^{5} 6d* Oct 30] €6,000F, £62,000Y: sturdy gelding: sixth foal: half-brother to 8.3f winner Ice Box (by Pivotal) and winner up to 6f (including at 2 yrs) David's Beauty (by Kodiac): dam lightly-raced half-sister to high-class winner up to 1½m Fruits of Love: fairly useful form: won minor event at Leicester (by 1¼ lengths from Sporting Bill) in October: sold to join Rebecca Bastiman £33,000 in November: open to further improvement. *Charles Hills*

ZWAYYAN 4 ch.g. Pivotal 124 – Mail The Desert (IRE) 110 (Desert Prince (IRE) 130) 105
[2017 96p: 7f 8.2s* 8s^{3} 10.2d^{4} 10.2s^{4} 8d* 7.9g^{4} Oct 13] strong gelding: useful performer: won handicap at Haydock (by head from Ionization) in June and minor event at Ascot (by neck from One Word More) in October: stays 1m: acts on firm and soft going: sometimes in headgear: often races towards rear, usually travels strongly: sold to join Andrew Balding 100,000 gns in October. *William Haggas*

ZYLAN (IRE) 5 ch.g. Kyllachy 129 – Belgique (IRE) 87 (Compton Place 125) [2017 73: 88
f5d* 5m^{3} f5g* 6g^{2} 6m* 6s 6d 6g^{5} 6d 7g^{6} 6v Sep 9] fairly useful handicapper: won at Southwell (twice, by 6 lengths from Indian Tinker second occasion) in April and Hamilton (by 1¼ lengths from Portland Street) in May: has won over 1m, usually races at shorter: acts on polytrack, fibresand and good to firm going: has worn headgear. *Roger Fell*

ZYMYRAN 3 b.g. Henrythenavigator (USA) 131 – Zimira (IRE) 86 (Invincible Spirit 93
(IRE) 121) [2017 87: 8m^{3} 10s 9.9m^{5} 8d* 7.9g^{6} 8.1g^{4} t8g^{3} Oct 10] sturdy gelding: fairly useful handicapper: won at Newmarket in August: stays 8.5f: acts on tapeta, good to firm and good to soft going: often wears hood: often races towards rear: sold 42,000 gns in October. *David Simcock*

ZYZZYVA (FR) 2 b.c. (Mar 2) Siyouni (FR) 122 – Zanatiya (FR) (Sinndar (IRE) 134) 106
[2017 6.1m^{2} 7d* 8d^{3} Sep 3] €37,000F, €105,000Y: fifth foal: half-brother to 2-y-o 6.5f winner Zayev (by Diableneyev) and useful 1½m-2m winner Zadrak (by Dragon Dancer), both in France: dam unraced half-sister to smart 7f-1¼m winner (stayed 2m) Zanzamar: useful form: won maiden at Deauville in August: third in Prix des Chenes at Chantilly (neck behind Stage Magic) in September: stays 1m. *Robyn Brisland*

ZZORO (IRE) 4 b.g. Manduro (GER) 135 – Krynica (USA) 80 (Danzig (USA)) [2017 94: 96
10g^{5} 10s* p10s^{4} 10d^{5} 9.9g^{5} 9.9s^{6} 10.2d Oct 18] sturdy gelding: useful handicapper: won at Newmarket (by 2 lengths from Interconnection) in May: stays 1¼m: acts on tapeta and soft going: tried in cheekpieces: front runner/races prominently. *Amanda Perrett*

SELECTED BIG RACES 2017

Prize money for racing abroad has been converted to £ sterling at the exchange rate current at the time of the race. The figures are correct to the nearest £. The Timeform ratings (TR) recorded by the principals in each race appear on the last line.

MEYDAN Saturday, Mar 25 DIRT: Standard; TURF: Good to Soft

1	**Dubai Turf Sponsored By DP World (Gr 1) (4yo+)** £2,903,226			1m209y
	VIVLOS (JPN) *YasuoTomomichi,Japan* 4-8-10 (h) JoaoMoreira (9)	14/1		1
	HESHEM (IRE) *C.Ferland,France* 4-9-0 GregoryBenoist (3)	20/1	½	2
	RIBCHESTER (IRE) *RichardFahey,GB* 4-9-0 WilliamBuick (1)	11/4	½	3
	Zarak (FR) *A.deRoyerDupre,France* 4-9-0 ChristopheSoumillon (2)	2/1f	1¾	4
	Mutakayyef *WilliamHaggas,GB* 6-9-0 (s) JimCrowley (6)	6/1	3	5
	Decorated Knight *RogerCharlton,GB* 5-9-0 AndreaAtzeni (4)	15/2	1¼	6
	Deauville (IRE) *AidanO'Brien,Ireland* 4-9-0 (t) RyanMoore (12)	16/1	nk	7
	Cougar Mountain (IRE) *AidanO'Brien,Ireland* 6-9-0 (s+t) DonnachaO'Brien (11)	66/1	1¼	8
	Debt Collector (NZ) *CliffBrown,Singapore* 5-9-0 MichaelRodd (10)	50/1	1¼	9
	Very Special (IRE) *SaeedbinSuroor,GB* 5-8-10 (h) SilvestreDeSousa (8)	25/1	4½	10
	Mondialiste (IRE) *DavidO'Meara,GB* 7-9-0 DanielTudhope (7)	25/1	4¼	11
	Long Island Sound (USA) *AidanO'Brien,Ireland* 4-9-0 (v+t) SeamieHeffernan (13)	40/1	2	12
	Opal Tiara (IRE) *MickChannon,GB* 4-8-10 OisinMurphy (5)	66/1	18	13
	Kazuhiro Sasaki 13ran 1m50.20			120/123/121/117/108/105

2	**Longines Dubai Sheema Classic (Gr 1) (4yo+)** £2,903,226			1m3f216y
	JACK HOBBS *JohnGosden,GB* 5-9-0 (b) WilliamBuick (2)	4/1		1
	SEVENTH HEAVEN (IRE) *AidanO'Brien,Ireland* 4-8-8 SeamieHeffernan (6)	8/1	2¼	2
	POSTPONED (IRE) *RogerVarian,GB* 6-9-0 AndreaAtzeni (7)	7/4f	1¾	3
	Prize Money *SaeedbinSuroor,GB* 4-8-13 (h) AdriedeVries (5)	9/1	½	4
	Earnshaw (USA) *S.binGhadayer,UAE* 6-9-0 (t) MickaelBarzalona (1)	66/1	2¼	5
	Sounds of Earth (JPN) *KenichiFujioka,Japan* 6-9-0 Christophe-PatriceLemaire (4)	20/1	3¾	6
	Highland Reel (IRE) *AidanO'Brien,Ireland* 5-9-0 RyanMoore (3)	5/2	1½	7
	Godolphin & Partners 7ran 2m32.39			126/120/118/120/114/106

3	**Dubai World Cup Sponsored By Emirates Airline (Gr 1) (4yo+)** £4,838,710			1m1f207y (Dirt)
	ARROGATE (USA) *BobBaffert,USA* 4-9-0 (t) MikeE.Smith (9)	1/3f		1
	GUN RUNNER (USA) *StevenM.Asmussen,USA* 4-9-0 (t) FlorentGeroux (5)	7/1	2¼	2
	NEOLITHIC (USA) *ToddA.Pletcher,USA* 4-9-0 (b) JohnR.Velazquez (11)	25/1	5	3
	Mubtaahij (IRE) *M.F.deKock,SouthAfrica* 5-9-0 ChristopheSoumillon (14)	16/1	1¾	4
	Awardee (USA) *MikioMatsunaga,Japan* 7-9-0 (b) YutakaTake (7)	66/1	1½	5
	Hoppertunity (USA) *BobBaffert,USA* 6-9-0 (b+t) FlavienPrat (12)	16/1	nk	6
	Keen Ice (USA) *ToddA.Pletcher,USA* 5-9-0 JavierCastellano (10)	33/1	1	7
	Lani (USA) *MikioMatsunaga,Japan* 4-9-0 RyanMoore (4)	100/1	4	8
	Apollo Kentucky (USA) *KenjiYamauchi,Japan* 5-9-0 Christophe-PatriceLemaire (1)	66/1	5	9
	Move Up *SaeedbinSuroor,GB* 4-9-0 AdriedeVries (6)	16/1	2¾	10
	Long River (USA) *S.binGhadayer,UAE* 7-9-0 (b) MickaelBarzalona (2)	50/1	8	11
	Special Fighter (IRE) *MariaRitchie,UAE* 6-9-0 FernandoJara (13)	40/1	15	12
	Furia Cruzada (CHI) *E.Charpy,UAE* 6-8-10 AntonioFresu (8)	100/1	½	13
	Gold Dream (JPN) *OsamuHirata,Japan* 4-9-0 (h) JoaoMoreira (3)	50/1	13½	14
	Juddmonte Farms Inc 14ran 2m02.15			135/131/122/117/114/114

SAINT-CLOUD Monday, May 1 GOOD

4	**Prix Ganay (Gr 1) (4yo+)** £144,050			1¼m97y
	CLOTH OF STARS (IRE) *A.Fabre,France* 4-9-2 MickaelBarzalona	13/10f		1
1	ZARAK (FR) *A.deRoyerDupre,France* 4-9-2 ChristopheSoumillon	25/10	sn	2
	SILVERWAVE (FR) *P.Bary,France* 5-9-2 (h) Pierre-CharlesBoudot	85/10	¾	3
	Erupt (IRE) *Francis-HenriGraffard,France* 5-9-2 StephanePasquier	11/1	hd	4
	Hawkbill (USA) *CharlieAppleby,GB* 4-9-2 (s) WilliamBuick	26/1	2	5
	Guignol (GER) *J-P.Carvalho,Germany* 5-9-2 VincentCheminaud	28/1	1½	6
	Potemkin (GER) *AndreasWohler,Germany* 6-9-2 GeraldMosse	43/10	1	7
	Godolphin S.N.C. 7ran 2m11.70			125/124/121/121/118/114

NEWMARKET Saturday, May 6 GOOD to FIRM (Rowley Mile Course)

5	**Qipco 2000 Guineas Stakes (Gr 1) (1) (3yo c+f)** £283,550			1m
	CHURCHILL (IRE) *AidanO'Brien,Ireland* 3-9-0 RyanMoore (3)	6/4f		1
	BARNEY ROY *RichardHannon* 3-9-0 JamesDoyle (5)	7/2	1	2
	AL WUKAIR (IRE) *A.Fabre,France* 3-9-0 GregoryBenoist (7)	11/2	nk	3
	Lancaster Bomber (USA) *AidanO'Brien,Ireland* 3-9-0 DonnachaO'Brien (4)	14/1	hd	4

Dream Castle *SaeedbinSuroor* 3-9-0 (h) SilvestreDeSousa (10)..............................8/1 1¾ 5
Eminent (IRE) *MartynMeade* 3-9-0 JimCrowley (2) ....5/1 nk 6
Top Score *SaeedbinSuroor* 3-9-0 JoeFanning (9)...100/1 nk 7
Spirit of Valor (USA) *AidanO'Brien,Ireland* 3-9-0 (b+t) SeamieHeffernan (8).....33/1 1½ 8
Larchmont Lad (IRE) *RichardHannon* 3-9-0 WilliamBuick (6) 33/1 3¾ 9
Law And Order (IRE) *JamesTate* 3-9-0 MartinHarley (1) ....100/1 hd 10
Mr M. Tabor, D. Smith & Mrs John Magnier 10ran 1m36.61 125/122/122/121/117/116

NEWMARKET Sunday, May 7 GOOD to FIRM (Rowley Mile Course)

6 **Qipco 1000 Guineas Stakes (Gr 1) (1) (3yo f)** £283,550 1m

WINTER (IRE) *AidanO'Brien,Ireland* 3-9-0 W.M.Lordan (7)...............................9/1 1
RHODODENDRON (IRE) *AidanO'Brien,Ireland* 3-9-0 RyanMoore (9)............. 5/4f 2 2
DABAN (IRE) *JohnGosden* 3-9-0 FrankieDettori (1) ....5/1 nk 3
Talaayeb *OwenBurrows* 3-9-0 JimCrowley (11) 11/1 1¼ 4
Fair Eva *RogerCharlton* 3-9-0 JamesDoyle (3)..8/1 2¼ 5
Unforgetable Filly *HugoPalmer* 3-9-0 WilliamBuick (8) 25/1 5 6
Poet's Vanity *AndrewBalding* 3-9-0 DavidProbert (14)...20/1 1¼ 7
Urban Fox *JamesTate* 3-9-0 MartinHarley (4) ....50/1 ¾ 8
Queen Kindly *RichardFahey* 3-9-0 GeraldMosse (13)...33/1 1½ 9
Hydrangea (IRE) *AidanO'Brien,Ireland* 3-9-0 P.B.Beggy (6) ....9/1 ½ 10
Kilmah *MarkJohnston* 3-9-0 RichardKingscote (12) 100/1 2½ 11
Intricately (IRE) *JosephPatrickO'Brien,Ireland* 3-9-0 DonnachaO'Brien (5).......20/1 8 12
Ce La Vie *KeithDalgleish* 3-9-0 TomQueally (2)..150/1 2¼ 13
Dream Start *JohnRyan* 3-9-0 (t) JosephineGordon (10)..200/1 30 14
Mrs John Magnier,Mr M.Tabor & Mr D.Smith 14ran 1m35.66 120/115/114/111/104/91

DEAUVILLE Saturday, May 13 GOOD to SOFT

7 **Abu Dhabi Poule d'Essai des Pouliches (Gr 1) (3yo f)** £242,119 7f210y

PRECIEUSE (IRE) *F.Chappet,France* 3-9-0 OlivierPeslier 28/1 1
SEA OF GRACE (IRE) *WilliamHaggas,GB* 3-9-0 ChristopheSoumillon 84/10 1¾ 2
HEURISTIQUE (IRE) *Francis-HenriGraffard,France* 3-9-0
Pierre-CharlesBoudot ....153/10 ¾ 3
Wajnah (FR) *FrancoisRohaut,France* 3-9-0 GregoryBenoist ....94/10 sn 4
Rain Goddess (IRE) *AidanO'Brien,Ireland* 3-9-0 W.M.Lordan 248/10 1¼ 5
Roly Poly (USA) *AidanO'Brien,Ireland* 3-9-0 (s) DonnachaO'Brien ....172/10 ns 6
Via Ravenna (IRE) *A.Fabre,France* 3-9-0 VincentCheminaud ....43/10 ¾ 7
Cristal Fizz (IRE) *WilliamHaggas,GB* 3-9-0 GeraldMosse 22/1 1¾ 8
Gokena (FR) *P.Sogorb,France* 3-9-0 JulienAuge ....68/1 hd 9
Thais (FR) *P.Bary,France* 3-9-0 MaximeGuyon 25/1 1¾ 10
Senga (USA) *P.Bary,France* 3-9-0 StephanePasquier .... 42/10f ½ 11
Asidious Alexander (IRE) *SimonCrisford,GB* 3-9-0 (b) MickaelBarzalona 50/1 4 12
Amaani (FR) *G.E.Mikhalides,France* 3-9-0 TonyPiccone ....75/1 ¾ 13
Toulifaut (IRE) *Jean-ClaudeRouget,France* 3-9-0 CristianDemuro ....138/10 ¾ 14
Charm Appeal (FR) *H-F.Devin,France* 3-9-0 AlexBadel 169/10 3 15
Delectation *AndreasWohler,Germany* 3-9-0 EduardoPedroza 7/1 3½ 16
Festive (FR) *E.Saint-Martin,France* 3-9-0 (s) TheoBachelot 57/1 2 17
Smoulder *AidanO'Brien,Ireland* 3-9-0 (h) P.B.Beggy 67/1 7 18
Mme Anne-Marie Hayes 18ran 1m37.69 116/112/110/110/107/107

DEAUVILLE Sunday, May 14 GOOD to SOFT

8 **The Gurkha Coolmore Prix Saint-Alary (Gr 1) (3yo f)** £121,059 1m1f207y

SOBETSU *CharlieAppleby,GB* 3-9-0 WilliamBuick 202/10 1
VUE FANTASTIQUE (FR) *F.Chappet,France* 3-9-0 OlivierPeslier 27/1 3 2
CORONET *JohnGosden,GB* 3-9-0 FrankieDettori 35/10 1¾ 3
Hebah (IRE) *Jean-ClaudeRouget,France* 3-9-0 ChristopheSoumillon ....35/10 sh 4
Gold Luck (FR) *F.Head,France* 3-9-0 MaximeGuyon .... 3/1f sh 5
Lady Frankel *A.Fabre,France* 3-9-0 Pierre-CharlesBoudot ....55/10 ½ 6
Body Sculpt (FR) *S.Kobayashi,France* 3-9-0 GregoryBenoist 55/1 1¾ 7
Peace In Motion (USA) *W.Hickst,Germany* 3-9-0 MarcLerner ....28/1 sn 8
Asking (IRE) *AidanO'Brien,Ireland* 3-9-0 (s) RyanMoore 135/10 4 9
Estelle Ma Belle (FR) *T.Castanheira,France* 3-9-0 GeraldMosse 31/1 7 10
Monroe Bay (IRE) *P.Bary,France* 3-9-0 VincentCheminaud 88/10 8 11
Godolphin 11ran 2m05.92 114/108/105/105/105/104

9 **Abu Dhabi Poule d'Essai des Poulains (Gr 1) (3yo c)** £290,542 7f210y

BRAMETOT (IRE) *Jean-ClaudeRouget,France* 3-9-2 CristianDemuro 5/1 1
LE BRIVIDO (FR) *A.Fabre,France* 3-9-2 Pierre-CharlesBoudot ....128/10 sh 2
RIVET (IRE) *WilliamHaggas,GB* 3-9-2 FrankieDettori 57/10 3 3
Spotify (FR) *C.Ferland,France* 3-9-2 MaximeGuyon 201/10 6 4
Orderofthegarter (IRE) *AidanO'Brien,Ireland* 3-9-2 SeamieHeffernan ....43/10 ns 5

Inns of Court (IRE) *A.Fabre,France* 3-9-2 MickaelBarzalona ... 137/10 nk 6
African Ride *C.Laffon-Parias,France* 3-9-2 (h) OlivierPeslier ... 22/1 3 7
Mankib *F.Head,France* 3-9-2 AurelienLemaitre ... 15/1 1¾ 8
Kings Gift (IRE) *MichaelDods,GB* 3-9-2 PaulMulrennan ... 30/1 1 9
Peace Envoy (FR) *AidanO'Brien,Ireland* 3-9-2 RyanMoore ... 19/1 sh 10
South Seas (IRE) *AndrewBalding,GB* 3-9-2 OisinMurphy ... 198/10 sh 11
Salsabeel (IRE) *CharlieAppleby,GB* 3-9-2 WilliamBuick ... 179/10 ½ 12
National Defense *MmeC.Head-Maarek,France* 3-9-2 ChristopheSoumillon ... 4/1f 12 13
Al Shaqab Racing/Gerard Augustin Normand 13ran 1m36.82 120/120/113/99/99/99

NEWBURY Saturday, May 20 SOFT
10 Al Shaqab Lockinge Stakes (Gr 1) (1) (4yo+) £198,485 1m
1 RIBCHESTER (IRE) *RichardFahey* 4-9-0 WilliamBuick (5) ... 7/4f 1
LIGHTNING SPEAR *DavidSimcock* 6-9-0 OisinMurphy (4) ... 9/2 3¾ 2
BRETON ROCK (IRE) *DavidSimcock* 7-9-0 AndreaAtzeni (9) ... 25/1 2½ 3
Somehow (IRE) *AidanO'Brien,Ireland* 4-8-11 (v) RyanMoore (1) ... 10/3 ¾ 4
Galileo Gold *HugoPalmer* 4-9-0 FrankieDettori (7) ... 9/2 3 5
Aclaim (IRE) *MartynMeade* 4-9-0 (t) JamieSpencer (2) ... 9/1 3 6
Mitchum Swagger *DavidLanigan* 5-9-0 TomQueally (3) ... 25/1 ¾ 7
Toscanini (IRE) *RichardFahey* 5-9-0 PaulHanagan (8) ... 50/1 4½ 8
Godolphin 8ran 1m43.00 129/117/111/105/101/91

CURRAGH Saturday, May 27 GOOD to SOFT
11 Tattersalls Irish 2000 Guineas (Gr 1) (3yo c+f) £147,414 1m
5 CHURCHILL (IRE) *AidanO'Brien* 3-9-0 RyanMoore (6) ... 4/9f 1
THUNDER SNOW (IRE) *SaeedbinSuroor,GB* 3-9-0 ChristopheSoumillon (2) ... 5/1 2½ 2
IRISHCORRESPONDENT (IRE) *M.Halford* 3-9-0 ShaneFoley (5) ... 7/1 4½ 3
Glastonbury Song (IRE) *G.M.Lyons* 3-9-0 C.T.Keane (4) ... 20/1 4 4
5 Lancaster Bomber (USA) *AidanO'Brien* 3-9-0 DonnachaO'Brien (1) ... 11/1 1 5
5 Spirit of Valor (USA) *AidanO'Brien* 3-9-0 (b+t) SeamieHeffernan (3) ... 33/1 26 6
Mr M. Tabor, D. Smith & Mrs John Magnier 6ran 1m40.46 126/120/108/96/94/24

CHANTILLY Sunday, May 28 GOOD
12 Prix d'Ispahan (Gr 1) (4yo+) £123,147 1m209y
MEKHTAAL *Jean-ClaudeRouget,France* 4-9-2 GregoryBenoist ... 23/10 1
ROBIN OF NAVAN (FR) *HarryDunlop,GB* 4-9-2 CristianDemuro ... 17/1 nk 2
USHERETTE (IRE) *A.Fabre,France* 5-8-13 MickaelBarzalona ... 38/10 ½ 3
Dicton *GianlucaBietolini,France* 4-9-2 OlivierPeslier ... 116/10 5 4
4 Zarak (FR) *A.deRoyerDupre,France* 4-9-2 ChristopheSoumillon ... 8/10f 5 5
Al Shaqab Racing 5ran 1m49.92 118/117/113/105/95

CURRAGH Sunday, May 28 GOOD to SOFT
13 Tattersalls Gold Cup (Gr 1) (4yo+) £152,586 1¼m110y
1 DECORATED KNIGHT *RogerCharlton,GB* 5-9-3 AndreaAtzeni (1) ... 7/2f 1
10 SOMEHOW (IRE) *AidanO'Brien* 4-9-0 (v) SeamieHeffernan (3) ... 4/1 1¼ 2
1 DEAUVILLE (IRE) *AidanO'Brien* 4-9-3 RyanMoore (8) ... 4/1 2¼ 3
Success Days (IRE) *K.J.Condon* 5-9-3 ShaneFoley (5) ... 9/2 ¾ 4
Johannes Vermeer (IRE) *AidanO'Brien* 4-9-3 DonnachaO'Brien (7) ... 8/1 sh 5
Reckless Gold (IRE) *JosephPatrickO'Brien* 4-9-3 W.M.Lordan (2) ... 50/1 1¾ 6
Moonlight Magic *J.S.Bolger* 4-9-3 K.J.Manning (4) ... 11/2 hd 7
Gentil J (IRE) *HarryRogers* 4-9-0 (t) C.D.Hayes (6) ... 100/1 6 8
Saleh Al Homaizi & Imad Al Sagar 8ran 2m18.03 122/118/116/114/114/110

14 Tattersalls Irish 1000 Guineas (Gr 1) (3yo f) £147,414 1m
6 WINTER (IRE) *AidanO'Brien* 3-9-0 RyanMoore (4) ... 8/13f 1
7 ROLY POLY (USA) *AidanO'Brien* 3-9-0 (s) SeamieHeffernan (7) ... 14/1 4¾ 2
6 HYDRANGEA (IRE) *AidanO'Brien* 3-9-0 (s) P.B.Beggy (3) ... 7/1 hd 3
6 Intricately (IRE) *JosephPatrickO'Brien* 3-9-0 DonnachaO'Brien (5) ... 14/1 ns 4
Rehana (IRE) *M.Halford* 3-9-0 PatSmullen (6) ... 6/1 11 6
Bean Feasa *J.S.Bolger* 3-9-0 K.J.Manning (1) ... 20/1 1¼ 5
Aneen (IRE) *KevinPrendergast* 3-9-0 C.D.Hayes (8) ... 10/1 ½ 7
8 Asking (IRE) *AidanO'Brien* 3-9-0 (s+t) MissA.O'Brien (2) ... 50/1 2 8
Mrs John Magnier & M Tabor & D Smith 8ran 1m39.78 124/112/112/112/80/78

EPSOM DOWNS Friday, Jun 2 GOOD to FIRM
15 Investec Coronation Cup (Gr 1) (1) (4yo+) £238,182 1½m6y
2 HIGHLAND REEL (IRE) *AidanO'Brien,Ireland* 5-9-0 RyanMoore (3) ... 9/4f 1
FRONTIERSMAN *CharlieAppleby* 4-9-0 JamesDoyle (10) ... 9/1 1¾ 2
4 HAWKBILL (USA) *CharlieAppleby* 4-9-0 (s) WilliamBuick (4) ... 11/2 3½ 3
Elbereth *AndrewBalding* 6-8-11 OisinMurphy (6) ... 33/1 1 4

Journey *JohnGosden* 5-8-11 (h) FrankieDettori (2) .... 7/2 sh 5
Idaho (IRE) *AidanO'Brien,Ireland* 4-9-0 SeamieHeffernan (7) 11/1 1 6
Red Verdon (USA) *EdDunlop* 4-9-0 (s) PatSmullen (8) .... 33/1 ½ 7
Air Pilot *RalphBeckett* 8-9-0 FranBerry (9) 25/1 1¼ 8
2 Prize Money *SaeedbinSuroor* 4-9-0 (h) OlivierPeslier (1) .... 10/1 ¾ 9
Us Army Ranger (IRE) *AidanO'Brien,Ireland* 4-9-0 DonnachaO'Brien (5) 8/1 2 10
Mr D. Smith, Mrs J. Magnier, Mr M. Tabor 10ran 2m33.34 122/120/114/108/108/111

16 Investec Oaks (Gr 1) (1) (3yo f) £283,550 1½m6y
ENABLE *JohnGosden* 3-9-0 FrankieDettori (9) 6/1 1
6 RHODODENDRON (IRE) *AidanO'Brien,Ireland* 3-9-0 RyanMoore (5) 8/11f 5 2
ALLURINGLY (USA) *AidanO'Brien,Ireland* 3-9-0 SeamieHeffernan (7) 16/1 6 3
Horseplay *AndrewBalding* 3-9-0 OisinMurphy (3) 14/1 3¾ 4
8 Coronet *JohnGosden* 3-9-0 AndreaAtzeni (6) 12/1 1 5
Isabel de Urbina (IRE) *RalphBeckett* 3-9-0 FranBerry (8) 33/1 2¾ 6
Pocketfullofdreams (FR) *AidanO'Brien,Ireland* 3-9-0 (h) DonnachaO'Brien (1) .50/1 2¾ 7
8 Sobetsu *CharlieAppleby* 3-9-0 WilliamBuick (10) 6/1 1¾ 8
Natavia *RogerCharlton* 3-9-0 PatSmullen (2) 12/1 7 9
Mr K. Abdullah 9ran 2m34.13 125/117/106/100/98/94

EPSOM DOWNS Saturday, Jun 3 GOOD to FIRM
17 Investec Derby (Gr 1) (1) (3yo c+f) £921,538 1½m6y
WINGS OF EAGLES (FR) *AidanO'Brien,Ireland* 3-9-0 P.B.Beggy (14) 40/1 1
CLIFFS OF MOHER (IRE) *AidanO'Brien,Ireland* 3-9-0 (t) RyanMoore (13) .... 5/1 ¾ 2
CRACKSMAN *JohnGosden* 3-9-0 FrankieDettori (7) .... 7/2f nk 3
5 Eminent (IRE) *MartynMeade* 3-9-0 JimCrowley (4) .... 5/1 ¾ 4
Benbatl *SaeedbinSuroor* 3-9-0 (h+t) OisinMurphy (16) 20/1 1¾ 5
Capri (IRE) *AidanO'Brien,Ireland* 3-9-0 SeamieHeffernan (10) .... 16/1 nk 6
Douglas Macarthur (IRE) *AidanO'Brien,Ireland* 3-9-0 ColmO'Donoghue (19) ...25/1 1 7
Best Solution (IRE) *SaeedbinSuroor* 3-9-0 PatCosgrave (8) 12/1 1¾ 8
Glencadam Glory *JohnGosden* 3-9-0 (h) JamesDoyle (18) 33/1 1¼ 9
Permian (IRE) *MarkJohnston* 3-9-0 WilliamBuick (3) .... 8/1 nk 10
Dubai Thunder *SaeedbinSuroor* 3-9-0 AdamKirby (1) .... 9/1 nk 11
Venice Beach (IRE) *AidanO'Brien,Ireland* 3-9-0 (s+t) DonnachaO'Brien (9) 12/1 2½ 12
Salouen (IRE) *SylvesterKirk* 3-9-0 FranBerry (11) .... 33/1 ½ 13
Khalidi *JohnGosden* 3-9-0 PatSmullen (6) 20/1 2¼ 14
Crowned Eagle *JohnGosden* 3-9-0 (s) AndreaAtzeni (12) 33/1 2¼ 15
Rekindling *JosephPatrickO'Brien,Ireland* 3-9-0 W.M.Lordan (15) 25/1 2¼ 16
The Anvil (IRE) *AidanO'Brien,Ireland* 3-9-0 MissA.O'Brien (2) 66/1 5 17
Pealer (GER) *JohnGosden* 3-9-0 (t) SilvestreDeSousa (5) 100/1 10 18
Mr D. Smith, Mrs J. Magnier, Mr M. Tabor 18ran 2m33.02 124/123/122/121/118/118

CHANTILLY Sunday, Jun 4 GOOD
18 Qipco Prix du Jockey Club (Gr 1) (3yo c) £751,842 1¼m97y
9 BRAMETOT (IRE) *Jean-ClaudeRouget,France* 3-9-2 CristianDemuro 17/10f 1
WALDGEIST *A.Fabre,France* 3-9-2 Pierre-CharlesBoudot .... 74/10 sh 2
RECOLETOS (FR) *C.Laffon-Parias,France* 3-9-2 OlivierPeslier 41/10 1 3
Taj Mahal (IRE) *AidanO'Brien,Ireland* 3-9-2 (v) DonnachaO'Brien .... 47/1 ½ 4
War Decree (USA) *AidanO'Brien,Ireland* 3-9-2 RyanMoore 148/10 1 5
9 Orderofthegarter (IRE) *AidanO'Brien,Ireland* 3-9-2 (s) SeamieHeffernan ......208/10 nk 6
Bay of Poets (IRE) *CharlieAppleby,GB* 3-9-2 WilliamBuick .... 31/1 sh 7
9 Rivet (IRE) *WilliamHaggas,GB* 3-9-2 FrankieDettori 53/10 1¾ 8
Be My Sheriff (GER) *M.Rulec,Germany* 3-9-2 TheoBachelot .... 51/1 ¾ 9
D'bai (IRE) *CharlieAppleby,GB* 3-9-2 (s) JamesDoyle .... 89/1 sn 10
Soleil Marin (IRE) *A.Fabre,France* 3-9-2 MickaelBarzalona 123/10 1¼ 11
Plumatic *A.Fabre,France* 3-9-2 MaximeGuyon 143/10 3½ 12
Al Shaqab Racing/Gerard Augustin Normand 12ran 2m06.51 120/120/118/117/115/114

CHANTILLY Sunday, Jun 18 GOOD to FIRM
19 Prix de Diane Longines (Gr 1) (3yo f) £501,228 1¼m97y
7 SENGA (USA) *P.Bary,France* 3-9-0 StephanePasquier 218/10 1
SISTERCHARLIE (IRE) *H-A.Pantall,France* 3-9-0 Pierre-CharlesBoudot 121/10 1 2
TERRAKOVA (IRE) *F.Head,France* 3-9-0 MaximeGuyon .... 53/10 ns 3
Shutter Speed *JohnGosden,GB* 3-9-0 FrankieDettori .... 23/10f ½ 4
Turf Laurel (IRE) *S.Kobayashi,France* 3-9-0 CristianDemuro .... 69/1 ns 5
Mademoiselle Marie (FR) *K.Borgel,France* 3-9-0 TonyPiccone 56/1 4 6
Panthelia (FR) *P.Sogorb,France* 3-9-0 Jean-BernardEyquem .... 39/1 hd 7
Yellow Storm (FR) *AlainCouetil,France* 3-9-0 MarylineEon 51/1 4½ 8
8 Monroe Bay (IRE) *P.Bary,France* 3-9-0 (b) GeraldMosse .... 25/1 hd 9
Kitesurf *A.Fabre,France* 3-9-0 MickaelBarzalona .... 126/10 sn 10

8	Vue Fantastique (FR) *F.Chappet,France* 3-9-0 OlivierPeslier	183/10	4	11
	Haya of Fortune (FR) *N.Leenders,France* 3-9-0 TheoBachelot	74/1	2½	12
7	Festive (FR) *E.Saint-Martin,France* 3-9-0 JulienAuge	83/1	1¼	13
	Normandie (GER) *MmePiaBrandt,France* 3-9-0 GregoryBenoist	71/1	9	14
	Onthemoonagain (FR) *Jean-ClaudeRouget,France* 3-9-0 ChristopheSoumillon	104/10		F
16	Rhododendron (IRE) *AidanO'Brien,Ireland* 3-9-0 RyanMoore	34/10		pu
	Flaxman Stables Ireland Ltd 16ran 2m05.97	114/112/112/111/111/103		

ROYAL ASCOT Tuesday, Jun 20 FIRM

20	**Queen Anne Stakes (Gr 1) (1) (4yo+)** £388,464			1m
10	RIBCHESTER (IRE) *RichardFahey* 4-9-0 WilliamBuick (1)	11/10f		1
1	MUTAKAYYEF *WilliamHaggas* 6-9-0 JimCrowley (9)	5/1	1¼	2
13	DEAUVILLE (IRE) *AidanO'Brien,Ireland* 4-9-0 (s) RyanMoore (6)	12/1	nk	3
	Spectre (FR) *M.Munch,Germany* 4-8-11 StephanePasquier (13)	50/1	1	4
	Kaspersky (IRE) *JaneChapple-Hyam* 6-9-0 MichellePayne (3)	66/1	3¼	5
	Dutch Connection *CharlesHills* 5-9-0 JamesDoyle (2)	25/1	nk	6
1	Cougar Mountain (IRE) *AidanO'Brien,Ireland* 6-9-0 (s+t) DonnachaO'Brien (7)	33/1	nk	7
	Oh This Is Us (IRE) *RichardHannon* 4-9-0 PatDobbs (15)	33/1	1½	8
10	Lightning Spear *DavidSimcock* 6-9-0 JamieSpencer (14)	11/2	hd	9
	Jallota *CharlesHills* 6-9-0 SilvestreDeSousa (12)	40/1	5	10
	American Patriot (USA) *ToddA.Pletcher,USA* 4-9-0 (b) JohnR.Velazquez (16)	20/1	1	11
	Kool Kompany (IRE) *RichardHannon* 5-9-0 PatSmullen (8)	50/1	sh	12
	Miss Temple City (USA) *H.GrahamMotion,USA* 5-8-11 (t) EdgarS.Prado (4)	20/1	¾	13
10	Toscanini (IRE) *RichardFahey* 5-9-0 PaulHanagan (10)	150/1	1	14
	Ennaadd *RogerVarian* 4-9-0 AndreaAtzeni (11)	16/1	nk	15
	Dutch Uncle *RobertCowell* 5-9-0 (s) MartinHarley (5)	200/1	36	16
	Godolphin 16ran 1m36.60	127/125/123/117/113/111		

21	**King's Stand Stakes (Gr 1) (1) (3yo+)** £226,840			5f
	LADY AURELIA (USA) *WesleyA.Ward,USA* 3-8-9 JohnR.Velazquez (18)	7/2		1
	PROFITABLE (IRE) *CliveCox* 5-9-4 JamesDoyle (1)	14/1	3	2
	MARSHA (IRE) *SirMarkPrescottBt* 4-9-1 LukeMorris (9)	11/4f	hd	3
	Muthmir (IRE) *WilliamHaggas* 7-9-4 (s) JimCrowley (2)	16/1	½	4
	Take Cover *DavidC.Griffiths* 10-9-4 DavidAllan (11)	66/1	1¼	5
	Alpha Delphini *BryanSmart* 6-9-4 (v) ConnorBeasley (14)	20/1	sh	6
	Cotai Glory *CharlesHills* 5-9-4 SilvestreDeSousa (16)	28/1	nk	7
	Signs of Blessing (IRE) *FrancoisRohaut,France* 6-9-4 StephanePasquier (13)	5/1	nk	8
	Final Venture *PaulMidgley* 5-9-4 (h) PatDobbs (3)	40/1	1½	9
	Goldream *RobertCowell* 8-9-4 (s) MartinHarley (12)	12/1	1¼	10
	Ardhoomey (IRE) *G.M.Lyons,Ireland* 5-9-4 (t) ColinKeane (5)	20/1	nk	11
	Priceless *CliveCox* 4-9-1 AdamKirby (7)	11/1	ns	12
	Willytheconqueror (IRE) *WilliamMuir* 4-9-4 MartinDwyer (4)	125/1	ns	13
	Gracious John (IRE) *DavidEvans* 4-9-4 JohnEgan (10)	80/1	1¼	14
	Washington Dc (IRE) *AidanO'Brien,Ireland* 4-9-4 (t) RyanMoore (17)	8/1	2¾	15
	Medicean Man *JeremyGask* 11-9-4 (s+t) AndreaAtzeni (15)	66/1	½	16
	Just Glamorous (IRE) *RonaldHarris* 4-9-4 ShaneKelly (8)	100/1	25	17
	Stonestreet Stables/G Bolton/P Leidel 17ran 57.45secs	133/123/121/121/115/115		

22	**St James's Palace Stakes (Gr 1) (1) (3yo c)** £226,840			7f213y
5	BARNEY ROY *RichardHannon* 3-9-0 JamesDoyle (4)	5/2		1
11	LANCASTER BOMBER (USA) *AidanO'Brien,Ireland* 3-9-0 DonnachaO'Brien (1)	12/1	1	2
11	THUNDER SNOW (IRE) *SaeedbinSuroor* 3-9-0 (s) ChristopheSoumillon (2)	6/1	hd	3
11	Churchill (IRE) *AidanO'Brien,Ireland* 3-9-0 RyanMoore (5)	1/2f	3¼	4
	Forest Ranger (IRE) *RichardFahey* 3-9-0 TonyHamilton (6)	33/1	3½	5
18	Rivet (IRE) *WilliamHaggas* 3-9-0 AndreaAtzeni (7)	16/1	nk	6
	Mr Scaramanga *SimonDow* 3-9-0 HarryBentley (3)	66/1	2¼	7
9	Peace Envoy (FR) *AidanO'Brien,Ireland* 3-9-0 (h+b) SeamieHeffernan (8)	33/1	43	8
	Godolphin 8ran 1m37.22	124/121/121/112/103/103		

ROYAL ASCOT Wednesday, Jun 21 GOOD to FIRM

23	**Duke of Cambridge Stakes (Gr 2) (1) (4yo+ f+m)** £114,271			1m
	QEMAH (IRE) *Jean-ClaudeRouget,France* 4-9-0 GregoryBenoist (10)	5/2f		1
	ALJAZZI *MarcoBotti* 4-9-0 (h) AdamKirby (14)	40/1	¾	2
12	USHERETTE (IRE) *A.Fabre,France* 5-9-0 MickaelBarzalona (13)	11/4	nk	3
	Smart Call (SAF) *SirMichaelStoute* 6-9-0 RyanMoore (11)	9/2	¾	4
	Aim To Please (FR) *FrancoisDoumen,France* 4-9-0 P.J.McDonald (15)	40/1	2	5
	Turret Rocks (IRE) *J.S.Bolger,Ireland* 4-9-0 KevinManning (7)	16/1	½	6
	Dawn of Hope (IRE) *RogerVarian* 4-9-0 AndreaAtzeni (16)	33/1	hd	7
	Pirouette *HughieMorrison* 4-9-0 JimCrowley (9)	14/1	2¼	8
	Greta G (ARG) *JohnGosden* 4-8-13 OlivierPeslier (8)	14/1	nk	9

3 Furia Cruzada (CHI) *S.Kobayashi,France* 6-9-3 AurelienLemaitre (3)..................66/1 nk 10
Same Jurisdiction (SAF) *EdDunlop* 6-9-0 GavinLerena (4)................................125/1 5 11
Mix And Mingle (IRE) *ChrisWall* 4-9-0 WilliamBuick (1).....................................8/1 1 12
1 Opal Tiara (IRE) *MickChannon* 4-9-3 OisinMurphy (12)......................................33/1 3½ 13
Summer Icon *MickChannon* 4-9-0 GrahamLee (2)...150/1 1½ 14
Al Shaqab Racing 14ran 1m38.34 115/113/113/111/105/105

24 Prince of Wales's Stakes (Gr 1) (1) (4yo+) £425,325 1m1f212y
15 HIGHLAND REEL (IRE) *AidanO'Brien,Ireland* 5-9-0 RyanMoore (6).................9/4 1
13 DECORATED KNIGHT *RogerCharlton* 5-9-0 AndreaAtzeni (4)..........................10/1 1¼ 2
ULYSSES (IRE) *SirMichaelStoute* 4-9-0 JimCrowley (7)..9/2 sh 3
Queen's Trust *SirMichaelStoute* 4-8-11 OlivierPeslier (1)....................................16/1 ¾ 4
Scottish (IRE) *CharlieAppleby* 5-9-0 JamesDoyle (5)..20/1 1 5
12 Mekhtaal *Jean-ClaudeRouget,France* 4-9-0 GregoryBenoist (2)..........................17/2 nk 6
13 Johannes Vermeer (IRE) *AidanO'Brien,Ireland* 4-9-0 (t) DonnachaO'Brien (3)...50/1 1½ 7
2 Jack Hobbs *JohnGosden* 5-9-0 (b) WilliamBuick (8)..2/1f ½ 8
Mr D. Smith, Mrs J. Magnier, Mr M. Tabor 8ran 2m05.04 128/124/124/120/122/120

ROYAL ASCOT Thursday, Jun 22 GOOD to FIRM
25 Gold Cup (Gr 1) (1) (4yo+) £226,840 2m3f210y
BIG ORANGE *MichaelBell* 6-9-2 (s) JamesDoyle (7)..5/1 1
ORDER OF ST GEORGE (IRE) *AidanO'Brien,Ireland* 5-9-2 RyanMoore (13) .. 5/6f sh 2
HARBOUR LAW *LauraMongan* 4-9-0 JimCrowley (5)...33/1 6 3
She Is No Lady *RalphBeckett* 5-8-13 FranBerry (8)...50/1 ½ 4
Torcedor (IRE) *MrsJ.Harrington,Ireland* 5-9-2 ColmO'Donoghue (1).................20/1 2¾ 5
Sheikhzayedroad *DavidSimcock* 8-9-2 (h) MartinHarley (3).................................10/1 ½ 6
Sweet Selection *HughieMorrison* 5-8-13 SilvestreDeSousa (10)..........................14/1 1¼ 7
Prince of Arran *CharlieFellowes* 4-9-0 TomQueally (14).......................................66/1 hd 8
Nearly Caught (IRE) *HughieMorrison* 7-9-2 AdamKirby (12)..............................66/1 4 9
Endless Time (IRE) *CharlieAppleby* 5-8-13 WilliamBuick (6)..............................20/1 2¾ 10
Harrison *MickChannon* 4-9-0 GrahamLee (11)...66/1 10 11
Quest For More (IRE) *RogerCharlton* 7-9-2 (b) JamieSpencer (9)........................25/1 40 12
Trip To Paris (IRE) *EdDunlop* 6-9-2 AndreaAtzeni (2)...50/1 13 13
Simple Verse (IRE) *RalphBeckett* 5-8-13 OisinMurphy (4)....................................15/2 23 14
W. J. and T. C. O. Gredley 14ran 4m22.40 122/122/117/112/112/111

ROYAL ASCOT Friday, Jun 23 GOOD to FIRM
26 Commonwealth Cup (Gr 1) (1) (3yo) £226,840 6f
CARAVAGGIO (USA) *AidanO'Brien,Ireland* 3-9-3 RyanMoore (5).................... 5/6f 1
HARRY ANGEL (IRE) *CliveCox* 3-9-3 AdamKirby (7).......................................11/4 ¾ 2
BLUE POINT (IRE) *CharlieAppleby* 3-9-3 WilliamBuick (10)...............................9/2 ½ 3
Bound For Nowhere (USA) *WesleyA.Ward,USA* 3-9-3 DavidFlores (3)................10/1 3 4
Mr Scarlet *MsSheilaLavery,Ireland* 3-9-3 PatSmullen (9)......................................80/1 2 5
Tis Marvellous *CliveCox* 3-9-3 (t) GeraldMosse (4)...33/1 ½ 6
Straight Right (FR) *C.Ferland,France* 3-9-3 OlivierPeslier (8)..............................66/1 ¾ 7
Visionary (IRE) *RobertCowell* 3-9-3 JamieSpencer (2)..50/1 1¾ 8
Intelligence Cross (USA) *AidanO'Brien,Ireland* 3-9-3 (b+t) SeamieHeffernan (1).25/1 ¾ 9
Legendary Lunch (IRE) *RichardHannon* 3-9-3 TomMarquand (12).....................50/1 5 10
Victory Angel (IRE) *RogerVarian* 3-9-3 SilvestreDeSousa (11)............................66/1 4½ 11
Yalta (IRE) *MarkJohnston* 3-9-3 JamesDoyle (6)...50/1 6 12
Mrs John Magnier,Mr M.Tabor & Mr D.Smith 12ran 1m13.49 125/123/121/111/105/103

27 Coronation Stakes (Gr 1) (1) (3yo f) £243,853 7f213y
14 WINTER (IRE) *AidanO'Brien,Ireland* 3-9-0 RyanMoore (7)............................... 4/9f 1
14 ROLY POLY (USA) *AidanO'Brien,Ireland* 3-9-0 (s) SeamieHeffernan (2)..........12/1 2¼ 2
14 HYDRANGEA (IRE) *AidanO'Brien,Ireland* 3-9-0 (s) P.B.Beggy (5)...................16/1 nk 3
Dabyah (IRE) *JohnGosden* 3-9-0 JimCrowley (3)..13/2 1 4
La Coronel (USA) *MarkE.Casse,NorthAmerica* 3-9-0 FlorentGeroux (6)............25/1 1¾ 5
Tomyris *RogerVarian* 3-9-0 AndreaAtzeni (4)...33/1 ¾ 6
7 Precieuse (IRE) *F.Chappet,France* 3-9-0 OlivierPeslier (1)....................................8/1 nk 7
Mrs John Magnier,Mr M.Tabor & Mr D.Smith 7ran 1m39.39 121/115/115/112/108/106

28 Queen's Vase (Gr 2) (1) (3yo) £91,445 1m5f211y
STRADIVARIUS (IRE) *JohnGosden* 3-9-0 AndreaAtzeni (9)..............................11/2 1
COUNT OCTAVE *AndrewBalding* 3-9-0 OisinMurphy (3)...8/1 nk 2
SECRET ADVISOR (FR) *CharlieAppleby* 3-9-0 WilliamBuick (11)....................10/1 2 3
Belgravia (IRE) *AidanO'Brien,Ireland* 3-9-0 (b+t) RyanMoore (7)...................... 5/1f hd 4
Time To Study (FR) *MarkJohnston* 3-9-0 SilvestreDeSousa (2)..............................7/1 1 5
Desert Skyline (IRE) *DavidElsworth* 3-9-0 FranBerry (5)..8/1 nk 6
Mister Manduro (FR) *MarkJohnston* 3-9-0 JimCrowley (12).................................25/1 ¾ 7

Face The Facts (IRE) *JohnGosden* 3-9-0 AdamKirby (1) .... 33/1 ½ 8
Alqamar *CharlieAppleby* 3-9-0 (s) JamesDoyle (8) 14/1 2¼ 9
Night of Glory *M.D.O'Callaghan,Ireland* 3-9-0 (s) ShaneFoley (13) .... 16/1 hd 10
Haripour (IRE) *D.K.Weld,Ireland* 3-9-0 (b) PatSmullen (10) 11/1 3½ 11
Wisconsin (JPN) *AidanO'Brien,Ireland* 3-9-0 (s) SeamieHeffernan (4) 8/1 18 12
Fierce Impact (JPN) *DavidSimcock* 3-9-0 JamieSpencer (6) 14/1 5 13
Mr B. E. Nielsen 13ran 3m01.47 105/105/103/103/101/101

ROYAL ASCOT Saturday, Jun 24 GOOD to FIRM

29 **Hardwicke Stakes (Gr 2) (1) (4yo+)** £127,597 1m3f211y
15 IDAHO (IRE) *AidanO'Brien,Ireland* 4-9-1 SeamieHeffernan (7) 9/2 1
BARSANTI (IRE) *RogerVarian* 5-9-1 AndreaAtzeni (14) .... 20/1 ½ 2
CHEMICAL CHARGE (IRE) *RalphBeckett* 5-9-1 OisinMurphy (12) 25/1 1¼ 3
Dartmouth *SirMichaelStoute* 5-9-1 RyanMoore (4) 9/4f 1½ 4
Wings of Desire *JohnGosden* 4-9-1 WilliamBuick (2) .... 11/2 nk 5
Dal Harraild *WilliamHaggas* 4-9-1 PatCosgrave (6) .... 13/2 ½ 6
Western Hymn *JohnGosden* 6-9-1 (s) JamesDoyle (3) 12/1 4 7
Across The Stars (IRE) *SirMichaelStoute* 4-9-1 OlivierPeslier (9) 16/1 1¼ 8
Muntahaa (IRE) *JohnGosden* 4-9-1 JimCrowley (1) 14/1 1½ 9
Stellar Mass (IRE) *J.S.Bolger,Ireland* 4-9-1 KevinManning (8) 40/1 1¾ 10
15 Prize Money *SaeedbinSuroor* 4-9-1 PatSmullen (11) 10/1 1½ 11
Arthenus *JamesFanshawe* 5-9-1 (s) TomQueally (5) .... 66/1 hd 12
Mr M. Tabor, D. Smith & Mrs John Magnier 12ran 2m28.94 120/118/116/113/114/113

30 **Diamond Jubilee Stakes (Gr 1) (1) (4yo+)** £340,260 6f
THE TIN MAN *JamesFanshawe* 5-9-3 TomQueally (3) 9/2 1
TASLEET *WilliamHaggas* 4-9-3 (s) JimCrowley (12) .... 7/1 nk 2
LIMATO (IRE) *HenryCandy* 5-9-3 RyanMoore (15) .... 2/1f ¾ 3
Librisa Breeze *DeanIvory* 5-9-3 RobertWinston (10) 11/1 1¼ 4
Finsbury Square (IRE) *F.Chappet,France* 5-9-3 (b) OlivierPeslier (7) .... 40/1 ¾ 5
Tupi (IRE) *RichardHannon* 5-9-3 SeanLevey (1) .... 66/1 ½ 6
Suedois (FR) *DavidO'Meara* 6-9-3 (v) DanielTudhope (9) .... 25/1 ns 7
10 Aclaim (IRE) *MartynMeade* 4-9-3 JamieSpencer (11) .... 25/1 ½ 8
Al Jazi (IRE) *FrancoisRohaut,France* 4-9-0 GregoryBenoist (16) 33/1 1 9
Kachy *TomDascombe* 4-9-3 (t) RichardKingscote (8) .... 33/1 nk 10
The Right Man *D.Guillemin,France* 5-9-3 Francois-XavierBertras (2) .... 14/1 sh 11
Long On Value (USA) *WilliamI.Mott,USA* 6-9-3 (t) JoelRosario (14) 14/1 6 12
Comicas (USA) *CharlieAppleby* 4-9-3 (b) WilliamBuick (6) .... 33/1 hd 13
Dancing Star *AndrewBalding* 4-9-0 DavidProbert (5) .... 25/1 sh 14
Windfast (IRE) *BrianMeehan* 6-9-3 SilvestreDeSousa (4) 66/1 4½ 15
Mobsta (IRE) *MickChannon* 5-9-3 (v) PatSmullen (19) 100/1 12 16
Kassia (IRE) *MickChannon* 4-9-0 GrahamLee (13) 100/1 1½ 17
Magical Memory (IRE) *CharlesHills* 5-9-3 JamesDoyle (18) 8/1 4½ 18
Growl *RichardFahey* 5-9-3 (s) PaulHanagan (17) .... 40/1 ur
Fred Archer Racing - Ormonde 19ran 1m12.02 125/124/122/117/115/113

CURRAGH Saturday, Jul 1 GOOD

31 **Dubai Duty Free Irish Derby (Gr 1) (3yo c+f)** £750,000 1½m
17 CAPRI (IRE) *AidanO'Brien* 3-9-0 SeamieHeffernan (1) 6/1 1
17 CRACKSMAN *JohnGosden,GB* 3-9-0 PatSmullen (7) .... 3/1 nk 2
17 WINGS OF EAGLES (FR) *AidanO'Brien* 3-9-0 RyanMoore (3) .... 2/1f sh 3
18 Waldgeist *A.Fabre,France* 3-9-0 Pierre-CharlesBoudot (8) 3/1 1½ 4
17 Douglas Macarthur (IRE) *AidanO'Brien* 3-9-0 DonnachaO'Brien (6) 12/1 2¼ 5
18 Taj Mahal (IRE) *AidanO'Brien* 3-9-0 (b) W.M.Lordan (5) 20/1 3 6
Dubai Sand (IRE) *J.S.Bolger* 3-9-0 (s) K.J.Manning (9) 100/1 3½ 7
17 The Anvil (IRE) *AidanO'Brien* 3-9-0 MissA.O'Brien (2) 66/1 1 8
Grandee (IRE) *MrsJ.Harrington* 3-9-0 C.O'Donoghue (4) 33/1 1½ 9
Mr D. Smith, Mrs J. Magnier, Mr M. Tabor 9ran 2m35.45 124/124/124/120/116/110

CURRAGH Sunday, Jul 2 GOOD

32 **Pretty Polly Stakes (Gr 1) (3yo+ f+m)** £116,448 1¼m
NEZWAAH *RogerVarian,GB* 4-9-8 AndreaAtzeni (5) 13/2 1
7 RAIN GODDESS (IRE) *AidanO'Brien* 3-8-12 (t) RyanMoore (11) 6/1 3¼ 2
23 TURRET ROCKS (IRE) *J.S.Bolger* 4-9-8 R.P.Whelan (8) 25/1 1½ 3
Zhukova (IRE) *D.K.Weld* 5-9-8 PatSmullen (2) .... 7/2 hd 4
Laganore (IRE) *A.J.Martin* 5-9-8 C.T.Keane (4) 20/1 1½ 5
14 Intricately (IRE) *JosephPatrickO'Brien* 3-8-12 DonnachaO'Brien (1) .... 14/1 ½ 6
23 Smart Call (SAF) *SirMichaelStoute,GB* 6-9-8 JimCrowley (3) 13/2 1¾ 7
Santa Monica *CharlesO'Brien* 4-9-8 WilliamJamesLee (10) .... 66/1 nk 8
16 Pocketfullofdreams (FR) *AidanO'Brien* 3-8-12 (h) SeamieHeffernan (9) 33/1 2 9

15 Journey *JohnGosden,GB* 5-9-8 (h) K.J.Manning (6)........ 15/8f 2¾ 10
Creggs Pipes (IRE) *A.Slattery* 5-9-8 DeclanMcDonogh (7)........ 25/1 1¼ 11
Sheikh Ahmed Al Maktoum 11ran 2m06.19 120/111/110/110/107/104

SAINT-CLOUD Sunday, Jul 2 GOOD
33 Grand Prix de Saint-Cloud (Gr 1) (4yo+) £200,491 1m3f205y
12 ZARAK (FR) *A.deRoyerDupre,France* 4-9-2 ChristopheSoumillon 49/10 1
4 SILVERWAVE (FR) *P.Bary,France* 5-9-2 (h) GeraldMosse .... 33/10f ¾ 2
ARMANDE (IRE) *A.Fabre,France* 4-8-13 Pierre-CharlesBoudot 9/1 1¼ 3
My Dream Boat (IRE) *CliveCox,GB* 5-9-2 (s) AdamKirby .... 155/10 sn 4
Left Hand *C.Laffon-Parias,France* 4-8-13 (s) MaximeGuyon 188/10 2½ 5
15 Hawkbill (USA) *CharlieAppleby,GB* 4-9-2 (s) WilliamBuick 67/10 10 6
Tiberian (FR) *AlainCouetil,France* 5-9-2 OlivierPeslier 68/10 18 7
12 Robin of Navan (FR) *HarryDunlop,GB* 4-9-2 CristianDemuro 74/10 18 8
4 Erupt (IRE) *Francis-HenriGraffard,France* 5-9-2 StephanePasquier 57/10 6 9
Doha Dream (FR) *A.Fabre,France* 4-9-2 GregoryBenoist .... 25/1 ur
H.H. Aga Khan 10ran 2m27.76 124/122/118/120/113/98

SANDOWN Saturday, Jul 8 GOOD to FIRM
34 Coral-Eclipse (Gr 1) (1) (3yo+) £283,550 1m1f209y
24 ULYSSES (IRE) *SirMichaelStoute* 4-9-7 JimCrowley (6)........ 8/1 1
22 BARNEY ROY *RichardHannon* 3-8-11 JamesDoyle (4) .... 9/4 ns 2
DESERT ENCOUNTER (IRE) *DavidSimcock* 5-9-7 (h) SeanLevey (8) 50/1 3½ 3
17 Cliffs of Moher (IRE) *AidanO'Brien,Ireland* 3-8-11 (t) RyanMoore (1) 7/4f 1 4
17 Eminent (IRE) *MartynMeade* 3-8-11 SilvestreDeSousa (3)........ 4/1 sh 5
24 Decorated Knight *RogerCharlton* 5-9-7 OlivierPeslier (2) .... 10/1 ¾ 6
20 Lightning Spear *DavidSimcock* 6-9-7 OisinMurphy (5)........ 25/1 2¼ 7
17 Salouen (IRE) *SylvesterKirk* 3-8-11 WilliamBuick (7) .... 33/1 ½ 8
31 Taj Mahal (IRE) *AidanO'Brien,Ireland* 3-8-11 (b) P.B.Beggy (9) .... 50/1 ½ 9
Flaxman Stables Ireland Ltd 9ran 2m03.49 128/126/121/116/116/117

CHANTILLY Sunday, Jul 9 GOOD
35 Prix Jean Prat (Gr 1) (3yo) £200,491 7f210y
22 THUNDER SNOW (IRE) *SaeedbinSuroor,GB* 3-9-2 (s) ChristopheSoumillon . 14/10 1
TRAIS FLUORS *A.Fabre,France* 3-9-2 VincentCheminaud 11/10f 1¼ 2
8 GOLD LUCK (FR) *F.Head,France* 3-8-13 MaximeGuyon 5/1 1¼ 3
19 Turf Laurel (IRE) *S.Kobayashi,France* 3-8-13 CristianDemuro 145/10 3 4
Lightupthenight *Francis-HenriGraffard,France* 3-8-13 (h) Pierre-CharlesBoudot . 154/10 ds 5
Godolphin 5ran 1m38.78 121/118/112/104/

NEWMARKET Friday, Jul 14 GOOD to FIRM (July Course)
36 Tattersalls Falmouth Stakes (Gr 1) (1) (3yo+ f+m) £113,420 1m
27 ROLY POLY (USA) *AidanO'Brien,Ireland* 3-8-12 (s) RyanMoore (3)........ 6/4f 1
WUHEIDA *CharlieAppleby* 3-8-12 WilliamBuick (7) 3/1 1¼ 2
ARABIAN HOPE (USA) *SaeedbinSuroor* 3-8-12 (h) JosephineGordon (4)........ 13/2 ½ 3
7 Sea of Grace (IRE) *WilliamHaggas* 3-8-12 AndreaAtzeni (1) 9/2 1½ 4
7 Delectation *AndreasWohler,Germany* 3-8-12 EduardoPedroza (5) 16/1 1¼ 5
23 Greta G (ARG) *JohnGosden* 4-9-7 JimCrowley (6)........ 14/1 2½ 6
23 Opal Tiara (IRE) *MickChannon* 4-9-7 R.P.Whelan (2) 25/1 1¼ 7
Mr M. Tabor, D. Smith & Mrs John Magnier 7ran 1m36.01 116/114/112/108/104/100

SAINT-CLOUD Friday, Jul 14 GOOD
37 Juddmonte Grand Prix de Paris (Gr 1) (3yo) £303,398 1m3f205y
SHAKEEL (FR) *A.deRoyerDupre,France* 3-9-2 ChristopheSoumillon 57/10 1
17 PERMIAN (IRE) *MarkJohnston,GB* 3-9-2 WilliamBuick .... 3/1f ns 2
17 VENICE BEACH (IRE) *AidanO'Brien,Ireland* 3-9-2 (s) SeamieHeffernan 28/1 1 3
Ice Breeze *P.Bary,France* 3-9-2 VincentCheminaud 48/10 1 4
Falcon Wings *N.Clement,France* 3-9-2 (s) OlivierPeslier 22/1 1 5
Parabellum (IRE) *A.Fabre,France* 3-9-2 MickaelBarzalona .... 4/1 ¾ 6
18 Orderofthegarter (IRE) *AidanO'Brien,Ireland* 3-9-2 (s) RyanMoore .... 45/10 sn 7
Mac Mahon (ITY) *A.&S.Botti,Italy* 3-9-2 CristianDemuro 65/10 3 8
Spanish Steps (IRE) *AidanO'Brien,Ireland* 3-9-2 DonnachaO'Brien 54/1 1 9
S. A. Aga Khan 9ran 2m30.42 117/117/115/113/112/110

NEWMARKET Saturday, Jul 15 GOOD (July Course)
38 Bet365 Superlative Stakes (Gr 2) (1) (2yo) £45,368 7f
GUSTAV KLIMT (IRE) *AidanO'Brien,Ireland* 2-9-1 (t) RyanMoore (6) 5/6f 1
NEBO (IRE) *CharlesHills* 2-9-1 JimCrowley (4) .... 10/1 hd 2
GREAT PROSPECTOR (IRE) *RichardFahey* 2-9-1 PaulHanagan (7)........ 12/1 ½ 3
Zaman *CharlieAppleby* 2-9-1 AdamKirby (1)........ 14/1 ¾ 4

Zaaki *MohamedMoubarak* 2-9-1 TomQueally (5) ... 66/1 ¾ 5
Finniston Farm *TomDascombe* 2-9-1 RichardKingscote (8) ... 7/1 ½ 6
Bullington Bandit (IRE) *JaneChapple-Hyam* 2-9-1 (s) JosephineGordon (2) ... 20/1 ¾ 7
Etefaaq (IRE) *RichardHannon* 2-9-1 SeanLevey (10) ... 33/1 1½ 8
Aqabah (USA) *CharlieAppleby* 2-9-1 WilliamBuick (3) ... 5/1 2¾ 9
Maksab (IRE) *MickChannon* 2-9-1 P.J.McDonald (9) ... 33/1 ½ 10
Mrs John Magnier,Mr M.Tabor & Mr D.Smith 10ran 1m25.39 102/102/100/98/96/94

39 Darley July Cup Stakes (Gr 1) (1) (3yo+) £283,550 6f
26 HARRY ANGEL (IRE) *CliveCox* 3-9-0 AdamKirby (6) ... 9/2 1
30 LIMATO (IRE) *HenryCandy* 5-9-6 HarryBentley (1) ... 4/1 1¼ 2
BRANDO *KevinRyan* 5-9-6 TomEaves (4) ... 28/1 ½ 3
26 Caravaggio (USA) *AidanO'Brien,Ireland* 3-9-0 RyanMoore (2) ... 10/11f sh 4
26 Intelligence Cross (USA) *AidanO'Brien,Ireland* 3-9-0 (b+t) P.B.Beggy (3) ... 100/1 nk 5
30 Growl *RichardFahey* 5-9-6 PaulHanagan (9) ... 50/1 ½ 6
Intisaab *DavidO'Meara* 6-9-6 (s) WilliamBuick (7) ... 66/1 1¼ 7
30 The Tin Man *JamesFanshawe* 5-9-6 TomQueally (10) ... 7/1 1 8
Mr Lupton (IRE) *RichardFahey* 4-9-6 JamieSpencer (8) ... 66/1 ½ 9
30 Tasleet *WilliamHaggas* 4-9-6 (s) JimCrowley (5) ... 9/1 nk 10
Godolphin 10ran 1m11.25 119/115/115/113/113/111

CURRAGH Saturday, Jul 15 FIRM
40 Darley Irish Oaks (Gr 1) (3yo f) £201,770 1½m
16 ENABLE *JohnGosden,GB* 3-9-0 FrankieDettori (6) ... 2/5f 1
32 RAIN GODDESS (IRE) *AidanO'Brien* 3-9-0 (t) SeamieHeffernan (2) ... 7/1 5½ 2
EZIYRA (IRE) *D.K.Weld* 3-9-0 (h) PatSmullen (3) ... 20/1 2 3
16 Coronet *JohnGosden,GB* 3-9-0 OlivierPeslier (9) ... 6/1 1¼ 4
Aurora Butterfly (IRE) *W.McCreery* 3-9-0 (h) WilliamJamesLee (1) ... 66/1 2½ 5
16 Alluringly (USA) *AidanO'Brien* 3-9-0 W.M.Lordan (8) ... 16/1 1¼ 6
32 Intricately (IRE) *JosephPatrickO'Brien* 3-9-0 DonnachaO'Brien (5) ... 20/1 2 7
14 Bean Feasa *J.S.Bolger* 3-9-0 (t) K.J.Manning (10) ... 33/1 5 8
Bengala (FR) *JohnM.Oxx* 3-9-0 (h) DeclanMcDonogh (4) ... 33/1 ¾ 9
Naughty Or Nice (IRE) *JohnM.Oxx* 3-9-0 C.T.Keane (7) ... 16/1 7½ 10
Mr K. Abdullah 10ran 2m32.13 121/111/108/106/102/99

ASCOT Saturday, Jul 29 SOFT
41 King George VI and Queen Elizabeth Stakes (Sponsored By Qipco) (Gr 1) (1) (3yo+) £652,165 1m3f211y
40 ENABLE *JohnGosden* 3-8-7 FrankieDettori (7) ... 5/4f 1
34 ULYSSES (IRE) *SirMichaelStoute* 4-9-7 JimCrowley (8) ... 9/1 4½ 2
29 IDAHO (IRE) *AidanO'Brien,Ireland* 4-9-7 SeamieHeffernan (3) ... 8/1 ¾ 3
24 Highland Reel (IRE) *AidanO'Brien,Ireland* 5-9-7 RyanMoore (4) ... 9/2 4 4
17 Benbatl *SaeedbinSuroor* 3-8-10 (t) OisinMurphy (1) ... 14/1 2¼ 5
34 Desert Encounter (IRE) *DavidSimcock* 5-9-7 (h) SeanLevey (9) ... 33/1 6 6
33 My Dream Boat (IRE) *CliveCox* 5-9-7 (s) AdamKirby (6) ... 16/1 sh 7
Maverick Wave (USA) *JohnGosden* 6-9-7 GrahamLee (10) ... 100/1 2 8
24 Jack Hobbs *JohnGosden* 5-9-7 (b) WilliamBuick (2) ... 11/2 11 9
Sixties Song (ARG) *AlfredoF.GaitanDassie,Argentina* 4-9-3 GeraldMosse (5) ... 33/1 4½ 10
Mr K. Abdullah 10ran 2m36.22 130/127/126/117/112/103

DEAUVILLE Sunday, Jul 30 GOOD
42 Prix Rothschild (Gr 1) (3yo+ f+m) £154,432 7f210y
36 ROLY POLY (USA) *AidanO'Brien,Ireland* 3-8-9 (s) RyanMoore ... 32/10 1
7 VIA RAVENNA (IRE) *A.Fabre,France* 3-8-9 VincentCheminaud ... 155/10 sn 2
SIYOUSHAKE (IRE) *F.Head,France* 5-9-3 StephanePasquier ... 17/1 sh 3
23 Qemah (IRE) *Jean-ClaudeRouget,France* 4-9-3 CristianDemuro ... 19/10f sn 4
Persuasive (IRE) *JohnGosden,GB* 4-9-3 FrankieDettori ... 69/10 1¼ 5
23 Usherette (IRE) *A.Fabre,France* 5-9-3 MickaelBarzalona ... 38/10 1¼ 6
23 Furia Cruzada (CHI) *S.Kobayashi,France* 6-9-3 AlexBadel ... 75/1 ns 7
Dame du Roi (IRE) *F.Head,France* 3-8-9 MaximeGuyon ... 13/1 hd 8
Realtra (IRE) *RogerVarian,GB* 5-9-3 Pierre-CharlesBoudot ... 32/1 4 9
36 Arabian Hope (USA) *SaeedbinSuroor,GB* 3-8-10 (h) ChristopheSoumillon ... 26/1 2 10
Mr M. Tabor, D. Smith & Mrs John Magnier 10ran 1m36.45 116/115/116/116/113/109

GOODWOOD Tuesday, Aug 1 GOOD
43 Qatar Vintage Stakes (Gr 2) (1) (2yo) £113,420 7f
EXPERT EYE *SirMichaelStoute* 2-9-1 AndreaAtzeni (7) ... 7/4f 1
38 ZAMAN *CharlieAppleby* 2-9-1 (b) WilliamBuick (1) ... 8/1 4½ 2
MILDENBERGER *MarkJohnston* 2-9-1 JamesDoyle (5) ... 7/2 ¾ 3
James Garfield (IRE) *GeorgeScott* 2-9-1 OisinMurphy (4) ... 12/1 hd 4

Seahenge (USA) *AidanO'Brien,Ireland* 2-9-1 RyanMoore (3) 4/1 2½ 5
Curiosity (IRE) *HugoPalmer* 2-9-1 JosephineGordon (8) 33/1 4½ 6
Roland Rocks (IRE) *JohnRyan* 2-9-1 JamieSpencer (6) 66/1 3¼ 7
Finsbury Park *RobynBrisland* 2-9-1 LukeMorris (9) 100/1 4 8
Cold Stare (IRE) *E.J.O'Neill,France* 2-9-1 FabriceVeron (10) 16/1 1¼ 9
Sallab (IRE) *RichardHannon* 2-9-1 FrankieDettori (2) 25/1 8 10
Mr K. Abdullah 10ran 1m26.97 117/104/102/102/95/82

44 Qatar Lennox Stakes (Gr 2) (1) (3yo+) £170,130 7f

10 BRETON ROCK (IRE) *DavidSimcock* 7-9-3 AndreaAtzeni (15) 50/1 1
HOME OF THE BRAVE (IRE) *HugoPalmer* 5-9-3 (t) JamesDoyle (1) 4/1 ½ 2
30 SUEDOIS (FR) *DavidO'Meara* 6-9-3 DanielTudhope (6) 25/1 sh 3
39 Limato (IRE) *HenryCandy* 5-9-3 HarryBentley (8) 3/1f ns 4
So Beloved *DavidO'Meara* 7-9-3 (h) AdamKirby (3) 50/1 ½ 5
30 Aclaim (IRE) *MartynMeade* 4-9-3 FrankieDettori (2) 9/1 nk 6
5 Dream Castle *SaeedbinSuroor* 3-8-11 OisinMurphy (5) 5/1 ns 7
20 Jallota *CharlesHills* 6-9-3 FranBerry (12) 100/1 1¾ 8
30 Librisa Breeze *DeanIvory* 5-9-3 RobertWinston (14) 7/1 ½ 9
11 Spirit of Valor (USA) *AidanO'Brien,Ireland* 3-9-0 (b+t) RyanMoore (10) 7/1 1 10
20 Oh This Is Us (IRE) *RichardHannon* 4-9-3 SeanLevey (9) 33/1 ¾ 11
Jungle Cat (IRE) *CharlieAppleby* 5-9-3 (b) WilliamBuick (11) 20/1 ½ 12
Stormy Antarctic *EdWalker* 4-9-3 JamieSpencer (13) 20/1 2¼ 13
Mr John Cook 13ran 1m26.62 115/114/113/113/112/111

45 Qatar Goodwood Cup (Gr 1) (1) (3yo+) £296,593 2m

28 STRADIVARIUS (IRE) *JohnGosden* 3-8-8 AndreaAtzeni (5) 6/1 1
25 BIG ORANGE *MichaelBell* 6-9-7 (s) FrankieDettori (11) 6/4f 1¾ 2
28 DESERT SKYLINE (IRE) *DavidElsworth* 3-8-8 (s) DavidProbert (13) 14/1 3½ 3
Wicklow Brave *W.P.Mullins,Ireland* 8-9-7 JimCrowley (7) 8/1 3½ 4
25 She Is No Lady *RalphBeckett* 5-9-4 JamesDoyle (10) 33/1 ¾ 5
Pallasator *SirMarkPrescottBt* 8-9-7 OisinMurphy (9) 25/1 ¾ 6
25 Sheikhzayedroad *DavidSimcock* 8-9-7 (h) MartinHarley (12) 10/1 ½ 7
15 Us Army Ranger (IRE) *AidanO'Brien,Ireland* 4-9-7 (h) RyanMoore (16) 8/1 ½ 8
25 Sweet Selection *HughieMorrison* 5-9-4 (b) AdamKirby (8) 33/1 3¼ 9
25 Prince of Arran *CharlieFellowes* 4-9-7 StevieDonohoe (3) 33/1 1 10
Higher Power *JamesFanshawe* 5-9-7 TomQueally (14) 20/1 3¼ 11
High Jinx (IRE) *TimEasterby* 9-9-7 DavidAllan (1) 66/1 5 12
Qewy (IRE) *CharlieAppleby* 7-9-7 (s) WilliamBuick (4) 16/1 2 13
Oriental Fox (GER) *MarkJohnston* 9-9-7 JoeFanning (2) 50/1 30 14
Mr B. E. Nielsen 14ran 3m25.47 123/121/115/111/107/109

GOODWOOD Wednesday, Aug 2 HEAVY

46 Qatar Sussex Stakes (Gr 1) (1) (3yo+) £560,200 1m

HERE COMES WHEN (IRE) *AndrewBalding* 7-9-8 (h) JimCrowley (5) 20/1 1
20 RIBCHESTER (IRE) *RichardFahey* 4-9-8 WilliamBuick (6) 8/13f nk 2
34 LIGHTNING SPEAR *DavidSimcock* 6-9-8 OisinMurphy (1) 8/1 ¾ 3
Zelzal (FR) *Jean-ClaudeRouget,France* 4-9-8 FrankieDettori (7) 4/1 1½ 4
20 Toscanini (IRE) *RichardFahey* 5-9-8 JamesDoyle (2) 66/1 ½ 5
22 Lancaster Bomber (USA) *AidanO'Brien,Ireland* 3-9-1 RyanMoore (3) 8/1 1¼ 6
20 Kool Kompany (IRE) *RichardHannon* 5-9-8 AndreaAtzeni (9) 40/1 ½ 7
Mrs Fitri Hay 7ran 1m46.11 121/119/117/113/113/109

GOODWOOD Thursday, Aug 3 HEAVY

47 Qatar Richmond Stakes (Gr 2) (1) (2yo) £113,420 6f

BARRAQUERO (IRE) *BrianMeehan* 2-9-0 WilliamBuick (3) 4/1 1
38 NEBO (IRE) *CharlesHills* 2-9-0 JimCrowley (1) 3/1 1¼ 2
CARDSHARP *MarkJohnston* 2-9-3 JamesDoyle (2) 2/1f 2¼ 3
38 Etefaaq (IRE) *RichardHannon* 2-9-0 FrankieDettori (6) 16/1 2¼ 4
Green Power *JohnGallagher* 2-9-0 B.A.Curtis (4) 16/1 hd 5
Headway *WilliamHaggas* 2-9-0 PatCosgrave (9) 4/1 ns 6
38 Bullington Bandit (IRE) *JaneChapple-Hyam* 2-9-0 (s) StevieDonohoe (10) 22/1 2¾ 7
Manton Thoroughbreds II 7ran 1m15.42 110/106/100/88/88/88

48 Qatar Nassau Stakes (Gr 1) (1) (3yo+ f+m) £340,260 1m1f197y

27 WINTER (IRE) *AidanO'Brien,Ireland* 3-8-13 RyanMoore (6) 10/11f 1
BLOND ME (IRE) *AndrewBalding* 5-9-7 OisinMurphy (9) 16/1 1½ 2
16 SOBETSU *CharlieAppleby* 3-8-13 WilliamBuick (2) 6/1 nk 3
27 Hydrangea (IRE) *AidanO'Brien,Ireland* 3-8-13 (s) SeamieHeffernan (4) 10/1 1¼ 4
So Mi Dar *JohnGosden* 4-9-7 FrankieDettori (3) 4/1 ½ 5

24 Queen's Trust *SirMichaelStoute* 4-9-7 JimCrowley (7) ....8/1 ½ 6
Mrs John Magnier,Mr M.Tabor & Mr D.Smith 6ran 2m11.79 117/115/113/111/111/109

GOODWOOD Friday, Aug 4 SOFT

49 Qatar King George Stakes (Gr 2) (1) (3yo+) £176,992 5f
BATTAASH (IRE) *CharlesHills* 3-8-13 JimCrowley (1) 9/2 1
21 PROFITABLE (IRE) *CliveCox* 5-9-2 JamesDoyle (5).................... 9/4f 2¼ 2
21 MARSHA (IRE) *SirMarkPrescottBt* 4-8-13 LukeMorris (7)....................9/2 ¾ 3
21 Take Cover *DavidC.Griffiths* 10-9-2 DavidAllan (3)....................10/1 ¾ 4
21 Washington Dc (IRE) *AidanO'Brien,Ireland* 4-9-2 (b+t) RyanMoore (4)....................4/1 1¼ 5
Kyllang Rock (IRE) *JamesTate* 3-8-13 MartinHarley (2)....................33/1 ¾ 6
21 Final Venture *PaulMidgley* 5-9-2 OisinMurphy (11) 16/1 1 7
Glass Office *DavidSimcock* 7-9-2 JamieSpencer (9)....................40/1 2½ 8
21 Priceless *CliveCox* 4-9-2 AdamKirby (12)....................20/1 sh 9
30 Kachy *TomDascombe* 4-9-2 (t) RichardKingscote (8) ....25/1 ½ 10
Ardad (IRE) *JohnGosden* 3-8-13 FrankieDettori (10)....................20/1 ¾ 11
Mr Hamdan Al Maktoum 11ran 58.51secs 136/123/116/115/109/106

GOODWOOD Saturday, Aug 5 GOOD to SOFT

50 Qatar Gordon Stakes (Gr 3) (1) (3yo) £56,710 1m3f218y
CRYSTAL OCEAN *SirMichaelStoute* 3-9-1 RyanMoore (1).................... 6/4f 1
17 KHALIDI *JohnGosden* 3-9-1 FrankieDettori (4)....................9/4 3½ 2
MOUNT MORIAH *RalphBeckett* 3-9-1 HarryBentley (2)....................10/3 1 3
Jake's Hill *EveJohnsonHoughton* 3-9-1 CharlesBishop (3)....................16/1 1¼ 4
Across Dubai *WilliamHaggas* 3-9-1 PatCosgrave (5)....................9/1 1¾ 5
Sir Evelyn De Rothschild 5ran 2m42.94 119/113/111/109/105

DEAUVILLE Sunday, Aug 6 GOOD

51 LARC Prix Maurice de Gheest (Gr 1) (3yo+) £193,868 6f102y
39 BRANDO *KevinRyan,GB* 5-9-3 TomEaves 104/10 1
44 ACLAIM (IRE) *MartynMeade,GB* 4-9-3 OlivierPeslier ....37/1 ½ 2
30 TUPI (IRE) *RichardHannon,GB* 5-9-3 SeanLevey 153/1 1¾ 3
30 Magical Memory (IRE) *CharlesHills,GB* 5-9-3 AndreaAtzeni 24/1 2 4
21 Signs of Blessing (IRE) *FrancoisRohaut,France* 6-9-3 StephanePasquier ....43/10 ns 5
39 Caravaggio (USA) *AidanO'Brien,Ireland* 3-8-13 RyanMoore .... 15/10f hd 6
30 The Right Man *D.Guillemin,France* 5-9-3 Francois-XavierBertras 164/10 1 7
Zalamea (IRE) *MlleC.Fey,France* 4-9-3 AntoineCoutier ....148/1 ¾ 8
Rosa Imperial (IRE) *A.Fabre,France* 4-9-0 MickaelBarzalona 55/10 1 9
26 Bound For Nowhere (USA) *WesleyA.Ward,USA* 3-8-13 FrankieDettori ....75/10 sn 10
Black Max (FR) *H-A.Pantall,France* 4-9-3 Pierre-CharlesBoudot 42/1 2 11
39 Intelligence Cross (USA) *AidanO'Brien,Ireland* 3-8-13 (b) SeamieHeffernan ....83/1 nk 12
Fas (IRE) *MmePiaBrandt,France* 3-8-13 MaximeGuyon 13/1 12 13
Mrs Angie Bailey 13ran 1m15.61 124/122/116/110/110/109

CURRAGH Sunday, Aug 13 GOOD to FIRM

52 Keeneland Phoenix Stakes (Gr 1) (2yo) £128,378 6f
SIOUX NATION (USA) *AidanO'Brien* 2-9-3 RyanMoore (3)....................2/1 1
BECKFORD *GordonElliott* 2-9-3 DeclanMcDonogh (6).................... 15/8f ½ 2
ACTRESS (IRE) *AidanO'Brien* 2-9-0 SeamieHeffernan (2)....................5/1 1½ 3
U S Navy Flag (USA) *AidanO'Brien* 2-9-3 (b+t) DonnachaO'Brien (1)....................11/1 ½ 4
Frozen Angel (IRE) *TomDascombe,GB* 2-9-3 RichardKingscote (8)....................16/1 hd 5
Romanised (IRE) *K.J.Condon* 2-9-3 (t) PatSmullen (4)....................8/1 ½ 6
Declarationofpeace (USA) *AidanO'Brien* 2-9-3 (t) W.M.Lordan (7)....................16/1 sh 7
Helvetian *MickChannon,GB* 2-9-3 R.P.Whelan (5)....................66/1 1¾ 8
Mr M. Tabor, D. Smith & Mrs John Magnier 8ran 1m11.72 115/113/105/106/106/104

DEAUVILLE Sunday, Aug 13 GOOD to SOFT

53 Prix du Haras de Fresnay-le-Buffard - Jacques le Marois (Gr 1) (3yo+) £360,342 7f210y
5 AL WUKAIR (IRE) *A.Fabre,France* 3-8-13 FrankieDettori (6) 4/1 1
9 INNS OF COURT (IRE) *A.Fabre,France* 3-8-13 MickaelBarzalona (3) ....151/10 sh 2
35 THUNDER SNOW (IRE) *SaeedbinSuroor,GB* 3-8-13 (s) ChristopheSoumillon (4). 18/10f sn 3
35 Trais Fluors *A.Fabre,France* 3-8-13 VincentCheminaud (5)....................35/10 1¼ 4
Taareef (USA) *Jean-ClaudeRouget,France* 4-9-5 Jean-BernardEyquem (2).......29/10 1 5
35 Gold Luck (FR) *F.Head,France* 3-8-9 MaximeGuyon (1)....................124/10 1¼ 6
Al Shaqab Racing 6ran 1m38.51 123/123/122/119/117/109

DEAUVILLE Saturday, Aug 19 GOOD

54 Shadwell Prix du Calvados (Gr 3) (2yo) £36,364 6f211y
POLYDREAM (IRE) *F.Head,France* 2-8-11 MaximeGuyon (10) 16/10f 1
LAURENS (FR) *K.R.Burke,GB* 2-8-11 P.J.McDonald (7)....................75/10 1¾ 2

BONITA FRANSISCA (FR) *A.Marcialis,Italy* 2-8-11 CristianDemuro (5)...........38/1 2½ 3
Capomento (IRE) *TomDascombe,GB* 2-8-11 GeraldMosse (9) 9/1 2½ 4
Spring Cosmos (IRE) *CharlieAppleby,GB* 2-8-11 JamesDoyle (6)......................65/10 nk 5
Musical Art (IRE) *PaulCole,GB* 2-8-11 ChristopheSoumillon (3).......................55/10 sh 6
Fou Rire (IRE) *F.Chappet,France* 2-8-11 Pierre-CharlesBoudot (8) 13/1 3 7
Model (FR) *RichardHannon,GB* 2-8-11 MickaelBarzalona (11) 7/1 5 8
Ellthea (IRE) *K.R.Burke,GB* 2-8-11 (b) TonyPiccone (1) 42/1 2 9
Debutante's Ball (IRE) *J.S.Moore,GB* 2-8-11 (s) AlexBadel (2)............................36/1 4 10
Lili du Sud (FR) *Y.Gourraud,France* 2-8-11 MathieuPelletan (4) 30/1 3½ 11
Wertheimer et Frere 11ran 1m23.21 106/101/94/87/86/86

DEL MAR Saturday, Aug 19 FAST

55 $1 Million TVG Pacific Classic Stakes (Gr 1) (3yo+) £276,923 1¼m (Dirt)
COLLECTED (USA) *BobBaffert,USA* 4-8-12 MartinGarcia (2)..........................30/10 1
3 ARROGATE (USA) *BobBaffert,USA* 4-8-12 MikeE.Smith (7)............................ 7/10f ½ 2
ACCELERATE (USA) *JohnW.Sadler,USA* 4-8-12 (b) VictorEspinoza (3)..........32/10 3¾ 3
Curlin Road (USA) *DougF.O'Neill,USA* 4-8-12 FlavienPrat (6) 298/10 6½ 4
Hard Aces (USA) *JohnW.Sadler,USA* 7-8-12 (b) SantiagoGonzalez (4)............298/10 ½ 5
Royal Albert Hall *KristinMulhall,USA* 5-8-12 CoreyS.Nakatani (1) 863/10 21¼ 6
Donworth (USA) *DougF.O'Neill,USA* 5-8-12 MarioGutierrez (5) 208/10 2¾ 7
Speedway Stable LLC 7ran 2m00.70 130/129/124/114/113/80

DEAUVILLE Sunday, Aug 20 GOOD

56 Darley Prix Jean Romanet (Gr 1) (4yo+ f+m) £129,864 1m1f207y
AJMAN PRINCESS (IRE) *RogerVarian,GB* 4-9-0 (s) AndreaAtzeni 144/10 1
42 SIYOUSHAKE (IRE) *F.Head,France* 5-9-0 AurelienLemaitre 55/10 1¼ 2
33 LEFT HAND *C.Laffon-Parias,France* 4-9-0 (s) MaximeGuyon ....38/10 sh 3
32 Smart Call (SAF) *SirMichaelStoute,GB* 6-9-0 JimCrowley ....11/1 sh 4
48 So Mi Dar *JohnGosden,GB* 4-9-0 FrankieDettori 15/10f 2½ 5
That Which Is Not (USA) *Francis-HenriGraffard,France* 4-9-0 (h) StephanePasquier 14/1 3½ 6
Haggle *H-F.Devin,France* 4-9-0 AlexBadel ....11/1 sn 7
Syrita (FR) *M.&S.Nigge,France* 4-9-0 (s) VincentCheminaud 54/1 2 8
42 Furia Cruzada (CHI) *S.Kobayashi,France* 6-9-0 (h) GregoryBenoist ....36/1 ¾ 9
Wilamina (IRE) *MartynMeade,GB* 4-9-0 JamesDoyle 11/1 1¼ 10
Sheikh Mohammed Obaid Al Maktoum 10ran 2m04.13 117/114/114/114/109/102

57 Darley Prix Morny (Gr 1) (2yo c+f) £181,809 5f212y
UNFORTUNATELY (IRE) *K.R.Burke,GB* 2-9-0 (v) TonyPiccone 57/10 1
HAVANA GREY *K.R.Burke,GB* 2-9-0 P.J.McDonald 63/10 1¼ 2
DIFFERENT LEAGUE (FR) *M.Palussiere,France* 2-8-11 AntoineHamelin ....4/1 sh 3
Zonza (FR) *D.Guillemin,France* 2-8-11 CristianDemuro ....78/10 sn 4
High Dream Milena (FR) *MmeC.Head-Maarek,France* 2-8-11 Pierre-CharlesBoudot 8/1 2 5
Nyaleti (IRE) *MarkJohnston,GB* 2-8-11 JamesDoyle ....53/10 hd 6
Tantheem *F.Head,France* 2-8-11 AurelienLemaitre 25/10f 1¾ 7
Dameron (FR) *C.Ferland,France* 2-9-0 JulienAuge 37/1 5 8
Mr J Laughton & Mrs E Burke 8ran 1m08.92 117/112/109/108/101/101

YORK Wednesday, Aug 23 GOOD to SOFT

58 Tattersalls Acomb Stakes (Gr 3) (1) (2yo) £51,039 7f
WELLS FARHH GO (IRE) *TimEasterby* 2-9-1 DavidAllan (8)............................10/1 1
43 JAMES GARFIELD (IRE) *GeorgeScott* 2-9-1 FrankieDettori (6) ....10/1 ns 2
LANSKY (IRE) *JeremyNoseda* 2-9-1 GeraldMosse (11) 8/1 3¾ 3
38 Zaaki *MohamedMoubarak* 2-9-1 JimCrowley (5)...20/1 ½ 4
Danzan (IRE) *AndrewBalding* 2-9-1 DavidProbert (7) 25/1 1 5
Dee Ex Bee *MarkJohnston* 2-9-1 JamesDoyle (1) 6/5f 2¼ 6
Beatbox Rhythm (IRE) *K.R.Burke* 2-9-1 P.J.McDonald (9).................................25/1 3½ 7
Jazeel (IRE) *MickChannon* 2-9-1 AndreaAtzeni (3) ....50/1 ½ 8
Fleet Review (USA) *AidanO'Brien,Ireland* 2-9-1 (t) RyanMoore (10) 9/2 2¾ 9
Ulshaw Bridge (IRE) *JamesBethell* 2-9-1 DanielTudhope (4)...............................14/1 5 10
Chief Justice *RichardFahey* 2-9-1 PaulHanagan (2) ....33/1 ur
Mr S A Heley & Partner 11ran 1m26.32 110/110/98/96/92/86

59 Betway Great Voltigeur Stakes (Gr 2) (1) (3yo) £96,407 1m3f188y
31 CRACKSMAN *JohnGosden* 3-9-0 FrankieDettori (3) 4/6f 1
37 VENICE BEACH (IRE) *AidanO'Brien,Ireland* 3-9-0 (s+t) RyanMoore (5)...........9/2 6 2
MIRAGE DANCER *SirMichaelStoute* 3-9-0 AndreaAtzeni (2)..............................5/1 6 3
31 Douglas Macarthur (IRE) *AidanO'Brien,Ireland* 3-9-0 (h) W.M.Lordan (6).........14/1 ½ 4
37 Spanish Steps (IRE) *AidanO'Brien,Ireland* 3-9-0 SeamieHeffernan (7)................16/1 16 5

	Atty Persse (IRE) *RogerCharlton* 3-9-0 (s) JamesDoyle (4)	25/1	22	6
	Mr A. E. Oppenheimer 6ran 2m34.65	127/117/105/105/77/37		

60 Juddmonte International Stakes (Gr 1) (1) (3yo+) £567,100 — 1¼m56y

41	ULYSSES (IRE) *SirMichaelStoute* 4-9-6 JimCrowley (3)	4/1		1
22	CHURCHILL (IRE) *AidanO'Brien,Ireland* 3-8-13 RyanMoore (5)	5/2f	2	2
34	BARNEY ROY *RichardHannon* 3-8-13 JamesDoyle (7)	11/4	nk	3
34	Cliffs of Moher (IRE) *AidanO'Brien,Ireland* 3-8-13 (t) SeamieHeffernan (2)	9/2	4½	4
34	Decorated Knight *RogerCharlton* 5-9-6 AndreaAtzeni (1)	16/1	1¾	5
19	Shutter Speed *JohnGosden* 3-8-10 (t) FrankieDettori (6)	9/1	4½	6
41	My Dream Boat (IRE) *CliveCox* 5-9-6 (v) AdamKirby (4)	28/1	1	7
	Flaxman Stables Ireland Ltd 7ran 2m12.11	130/126/126/116/112/100		

YORK Thursday, Aug 24 GOOD to SOFT

61 Sky Bet Lowther Stakes (Gr 2) (1) (2yo f) £142,058 — 6f

	THREADING (IRE) *MarkJohnston* 2-9-0 JamesDoyle (7)	9/2		1
	MADELINE (IRE) *RogerVarian* 2-9-0 AndreaAtzeni (9)	7/2	1¾	2
	MAMBA NOIRE (FR) *K.J.Condon,Ireland* 2-9-0 (v) ShaneFoley (4)	25/1	¾	3
	So Hi Society (IRE) *ArchieWatson* 2-9-0 RichardKingscote (3)	16/1	¾	4
	Special Purpose (IRE) *WilliamHaggas* 2-9-0 OisinMurphy (5)	6/1	ns	5
	Happy Like A Fool (USA) *WesleyA.Ward,USA* 2-9-0 (b+t) FrankieDettori (6)	11/2	½	6
	Natural (IRE) *RichardHannon* 2-9-0 JamieSpencer (8)	12/1	3½	7
	Neola *MickChannon* 2-9-0 GrahamLee (2)	50/1	½	8
52	Actress (IRE) *AidanO'Brien,Ireland* 2-9-0 RyanMoore (1)	10/3f	12	9
	Sheikh Hamdan Bin Mohammed Al Maktoum 9ran 1m12.48	110/103/101/98/98/96		

62 Darley Yorkshire Oaks (Gr 1) (1) (3yo+ f+m) £198,485 — 1m3f188y

41	ENABLE *JohnGosden* 3-8-12 FrankieDettori (1)	1/4f		1
40	CORONET *JohnGosden* 3-8-12 OlivierPeslier (6)	16/1	5	2
48	QUEEN'S TRUST *SirMichaelStoute* 4-9-7 JimCrowley (2)	12/1	¾	3
32	Nezwaah *RogerVarian* 4-9-7 AndreaAtzeni (4)	7/1	hd	4
40	Alluringly (USA) *AidanO'Brien,Ireland* 3-8-12 RyanMoore (5)	16/1	9	5
	Abingdon (USA) *SirMichaelStoute* 4-9-7 RichardKingscote (3)	33/1	13	6
	Mr K. Abdullah 6ran 2m35.79	125/116/115/115/99/76		

YORK Friday, Aug 25 GOOD

63 Weatherbys Hamilton Lonsdale Cup (Gr 2) (1) (3yo+) £113,420 — 2m56y

	MONTALY *AndrewBalding* 6-9-3 P.J.McDonald (4)	16/1		1
29	DARTMOUTH *SirMichaelStoute* 5-9-6 RyanMoore (8)	11/4f	ns	2
	ST MICHEL *SirMarkPrescottBt* 4-9-3 (b) LukeMorris (7)	14/1	½	3
45	Sheikhzayedroad *DavidSimcock* 8-9-3 (h) MartinHarley (1)	15/2	2	4
45	High Jinx (IRE) *TimEasterby* 9-9-3 DavidAllan (9)	33/1	1	5
29	Dal Harraild *WilliamHaggas* 4-9-3 PatCosgrave (3)	7/2	sh	6
	Thomas Hobson *W.P.Mullins,Ireland* 7-9-3 JimCrowley (6)	4/1	1¼	7
45	Prince of Arran *CharlieFellowes* 4-9-3 (s) StevieDonohoe (5)	25/1	12	8
45	Higher Power *JamesFanshawe* 5-9-3 JamesDoyle (2)	7/1	2½	9
	Farleigh Racing 9ran 3m31.06	116/120/116/114/112/112		

64 Coolmore Nunthorpe Stakes (Gr 1) (1) (2yo+) £198,485 — 5f

49	MARSHA (IRE) *SirMarkPrescottBt* 4-9-8 LukeMorris (8)	8/1		1
21	LADY AURELIA (USA) *WesleyA.Ward,USA* 3-9-6 FrankieDettori (3)	10/11f	ns	2
21	COTAI GLORY *CharlesHills* 5-9-11 SilvestreDeSousa (4)	50/1	3¾	3
49	Battaash (IRE) *CharlesHills* 3-9-9 JimCrowley (9)	11/4	1½	4
49	Priceless *CliveCox* 4-9-8 AdamKirby (2)	33/1	sh	5
49	Profitable (IRE) *CliveCox* 5-9-11 JamesDoyle (1)	8/1	½	6
49	Final Venture *PaulMidgley* 5-9-11 PaulMulrennan (12)	40/1	1	7
21	Alpha Delphini *BryanSmart* 6-9-11 (s) GrahamLee (5)	50/1	sh	8
21	Goldream *RobertCowell* 8-9-11 (v) MartinHarley (10)	66/1	nk	9
49	Washington Dc (IRE) *AidanO'Brien,Ireland* 4-9-11 (b+t) RyanMoore (7)	20/1	3	10
49	Take Cover *DavidC.Griffiths* 10-9-11 DavidAllan (6)	25/1	ns	11
	Elite Racing Club 11ran 57.97secs	130/131/116/110/106/107		

YORK Saturday, Aug 26 GOOD to FIRM

65 Al Basti Equiworld Gimcrack Stakes (Gr 2) (1) (2yo c+g) £127,597 — 6f

	SANDS OF MALI (FR) *RichardFahey* 2-9-0 PaulHanagan (4)	14/1		1
	INVINCIBLE ARMY (IRE) *JamesTate* 2-9-0 MartinHarley (10)	9/2cf	2¾	2
47	CARDSHARP *MarkJohnston* 2-9-3 JamesDoyle (6)	5/1	1	3
47	HEADWAY *WilliamHaggas* 2-9-0 HarryBentley (7)	9/2cf	dh	3
	Staxton *TimEasterby* 2-9-0 DavidAllan (12)	10/1	1	5
47	Nebo (IRE) *CharlesHills* 2-9-0 JimCrowley (9)	9/2cf	1½	6

Stormbringer *KevinRyan* 2-9-0 TomEaves (3) .... 16/1 nk 7
52 Frozen Angel (IRE) *TomDascombe* 2-9-0 RichardKingscote (11) .... 6/1 ¾ 8
That's A Surprise (IRE) *TonyCoyle* 2-9-0 BarryMcHugh (1) 100/1 7 9
Nobleman's Nest *SimonCrisford* 2-9-0 DanielTudhope (8) 10/1 3¼ 10
The Cool Silk Partnership 10ran 1m11.16 116/106/106/102/100/94

HAYDOCK Saturday, Sep 9 SOFT

66 32Red Sprint Cup Stakes (Gr 1) (1) (3yo+) £147,446 6f
39 HARRY ANGEL (IRE) *CliveCox* 3-9-1 AdamKirby (8) 2/1f 1
39 TASLEET *WilliamHaggas* 4-9-3 (s) JimCrowley (5) 9/2 4 2
39 THE TIN MAN *JamesFanshawe* 5-9-3 TomQueally (9) 11/2 1½ 3
26 Blue Point (IRE) *CharlieAppleby* 3-9-1 JamesDoyle (1) 15/2 2½ 4
20 Cougar Mountain (IRE) *AidanO'Brien,Ireland* 6-9-3 (s+t) B.A.Curtis (10) 40/1 2 5
39 Mr Lupton (IRE) *RichardFahey* 4-9-3 RichardKingscote (11) .... 50/1 ½ 6
39 Growl *RichardFahey* 5-9-3 (s) GrahamLee (7) .... 25/1 ½ 7
Kimberella *RichardFahey* 7-9-3 PaulMulrennan (6) .... 40/1 ½ 8
51 Brando *KevinRyan* 5-9-3 TomEaves (4) .... 5/1 nk 9
6 Queen Kindly *RichardFahey* 3-8-12 PaulHanagan (3) .... 33/1 ¾ 10
51 Magical Memory (IRE) *CharlesHills* 5-9-3 SilvestreDeSousa (2) 12/1 3¾ 11
Godolphin 11ran 1m13.90 132/116/110/100/92/90

LEOPARDSTOWN Saturday, Sep 9 GOOD to SOFT

67 Coolmore Fastnet Rock Matron Stakes (Gr 1) (3yo+ f+m) £189,450 1m
48 HYDRANGEA (IRE) *AidanO'Brien* 3-9-0 (s) W.M.Lordan (9) 20/1 1
48 WINTER (IRE) *AidanO'Brien* 3-9-0 RyanMoore (3) .... evsf hd 2
42 PERSUASIVE (IRE) *JohnGosden,GB* 4-9-5 FrankieDettori (11) .... 6/1 ¾ 3
36 Wuheida *CharlieAppleby,GB* 3-9-0 JamesDoyle (6) .... 12/1 ¾ 4
42 Qemah (IRE) *Jean-ClaudeRouget,France* 4-9-5 GregoryBenoist (12) 5/1 2½ 5
42 Roly Poly (USA) *AidanO'Brien* 3-9-0 (s) SeamieHeffernan (8) .... 13/2 nk 6
19 Rhododendron (IRE) *AidanO'Brien* 3-9-0 P.B.Beggy (10) .... 12/1 hd 7
40 Intricately (IRE) *JosephPatrickO'Brien* 3-9-0 (b) DonnachaO'Brien (2) .... 50/1 ½ 8
Diamond Fields (IRE) *J.A.Stack* 4-9-5 C.D.Hayes (4) 100/1 4¼ 9
40 Bean Feasa *J.S.Bolger* 3-9-0 (t) K.J.Manning (1) 100/1 2¼ 10
Mr D. Smith, Mrs J. Magnier, Mr M. Tabor 10ran 1m41.89 118/118/116/114/108/108

68 Qipco Irish Champion Stakes (Gr 1) (3yo+) £653,670 1¼m
60 DECORATED KNIGHT *RogerCharlton,GB* 5-9-7 AndreaAtzeni (10) 25/1 1
POET'S WORD (IRE) *SirMichaelStoute,GB* 4-9-7 JamesDoyle (9) .... 10/1 ½ 2
34 EMINENT (IRE) *MartynMeade,GB* 3-9-1 FrankieDettori (1) 3/1 1¾ 3
13 Moonlight Magic *J.S.Bolger* 4-9-7 (t) K.J.Manning (5) .... 33/1 ¾ 4
34 Taj Mahal (IRE) *AidanO'Brien* 3-9-1 DonnachaO'Brien (4) .... 50/1 ¾ 5
60 Cliffs of Moher (IRE) *AidanO'Brien* 3-9-1 (t) SeamieHeffernan (6) .... 9/1 sh 6
60 Churchill (IRE) *AidanO'Brien* 3-9-1 RyanMoore (2) .... 8/11f ns 7
32 Zhukova (IRE) *D.K.Weld* 5-9-4 PatSmullen (3) 10/1 1 8
The Grey Gatsby (IRE) *D.K.Weld* 6-9-7 DeclanMcDonogh (7) 66/1 3½ 9
13 Success Days (IRE) *K.J.Condon* 5-9-7 (t) ShaneFoley (8) 40/1 4½ 10
Saleh Al Homaizi & Imad Al Sagar 10ran 2m08.36 125/124/120/119/117/117

CHANTILLY Sunday, Sep 10 GOOD to SOFT

69 Qatar Prix Vermeille (Gr 1) (3yo+ f+m) £183,477 1m3f205y
BATEEL (IRE) *Francis-HenriGraffard,France* 5-9-3 (h) Pierre-CharlesBoudot (4) .. 53/10 1
32 JOURNEY *JohnGosden,GB* 5-9-3 (h) FrankieDettori (2) 41/10f 2½ 2
56 LEFT HAND *C.Laffon-Parias,France* 4-9-3 (s) MaximeGuyon (5) 71/10 3 3
Traffic Jam (IRE) *N.Clement,France* 4-9-3 StephanePasquier (6) .... 103/10 ½ 4
Strathspey *A.Fabre,France* 3-8-9 MickaelBarzalona (11) .... 163/10 ½ 5
God Given *LucaCumani,GB* 3-8-9 JamieSpencer (10) 121/10 1¼ 6
56 Ajman Princess (IRE) *RogerVarian,GB* 4-9-3 (s) AndreaAtzeni (3) 132/10 10 7
The Black Princess (FR) *JohnGosden,GB* 4-9-3 JimCrowley (9) 53/10 2 8
Baiyouna (FR) *A.deRoyerDupre,France* 3-8-10 ChristopheSoumillon (1) 156/10 10 9
25 Endless Time (IRE) *CharlieAppleby,GB* 5-9-3 (s) JamesDoyle (8) .... 9/1 ds 10
48 Blond Me (IRE) *AndrewBalding,GB* 5-9-3 OisinMurphy (7) .... 9/1 ds 11
Al Asayl Bloodstock Ltd 11ran 2m32.90 122/118/114/113/112/110

70 Qatar Prix du Moulin de Longchamp (Gr 1) (3yo+ c+f) £235,899 7f210y
46 RIBCHESTER (IRE) *RichardFahey,GB* 4-9-3 JamesDoyle (8) .... evsf 1
53 TAAREEF (USA) *Jean-ClaudeRouget,France* 4-9-3 ChristopheSoumillon (7) ..... 4/1 ¾ 2
MASSAAT (IRE) *OwenBurrows,GB* 4-9-3 JimCrowley (4) 91/10 3½ 3
33 Robin of Navan (FR) *HarryDunlop,GB* 4-9-3 CristianDemuro (5) .... 148/10 nk 4
53 Inns of Court (IRE) *A.Fabre,France* 3-8-13 MickaelBarzalona (6) .... 8/1 nk 5
46 Lightning Spear *DavidSimcock,GB* 6-9-3 OisinMurphy (1) 9/1 1¼ 6

8 Lady Frankel *A.Fabre,France* 3-8-10 Pierre-CharlesBoudot (3) 76/10 1¾ 7
Godolphin 7ran 1m40.75 127/125/116/115/115/111

CURRAGH Sunday, Sep 10 SOFT

71 Moyglare Stud Stakes (Gr 1) (2yo f) £183,028 7f
HAPPILY (IRE) *AidanO'Brien* 2-9-0 (t) DonnachaO'Brien (10)..........................13/2 1
MAGICAL (IRE) *AidanO'Brien* 2-9-0 RyanMoore (2)..9/4 sh 2
SEPTEMBER (IRE) *AidanO'Brien* 2-9-0 SeamieHeffernan (9) 4/1 3¾ 3
Muirin (IRE) *EdwardLynam* 2-9-0 DeclanMcDonogh (7)....................................10/1 2 4
Alpha Centauri (IRE) *MrsJ.Harrington* 2-9-0 C.O'Donoghue (6) .... 2/1f ¾ 5
Gasta (IRE) *J.S.Bolger* 2-9-0 R.P.Whelan (4) 66/1 1½ 6
Ballet Shoes (IRE) *AidanO'Brien* 2-9-0 W.M.Lordan (8).......................................14/1 2¼ 7
Active Approach *J.S.Bolger* 2-9-0 K.J.Manning (5) ....33/1 ½ 8
Derrick Smith, Mrs J. Magnier & M. Tabor 8ran 1m26.93 115/115/102/95/92/87

72 Goffs Vincent O'Brien National Stakes (Gr 1) (2yo c+f) £183,028 7f
VERBAL DEXTERITY (IRE) *J.S.Bolger* 2-9-3 K.J.Manning (4) 5/2 1
52 BECKFORD *GordonElliott* 2-9-3 PatSmullen (6)... 6/4f 3½ 2
ROSTROPOVICH (IRE) *AidanO'Brien* 2-9-3 (t) RyanMoore (5)..........................7/1 2¾ 3
Coat of Arms (IRE) *AidanO'Brien* 2-9-3 DonnachaO'Brien (1)...............................8/1 4½ 4
Lethal Steps *G.M.Lyons* 2-9-3 C.T.Keane (7)...16/1 ½ 5
Brother Bear (IRE) *MrsJ.Harrington* 2-9-3 C.O'Donoghue (3) 7/1 2½ 6
Berkeley Square (IRE) *AidanO'Brien* 2-9-3 SeamieHeffernan (8)........................20/1 6 7
Mrs J. S. Bolger 7ran 1m27.32 119/107/98/82/81/73

73 Comer Group International Irish St Leger (Gr 1) (3yo+) £261,468 1¾m
25 ORDER OF ST GEORGE (IRE) *AidanO'Brien* 5-9-10 RyanMoore (5)............... 2/5f 1
25 TORCEDOR (IRE) *MrsJ.Harrington* 5-9-10 (s) C.O'Donoghue (3) 14/1 9 2
50 MOUNT MORIAH *RalphBeckett,GB* 3-9-1 HarryBentley (2).............................14/1 4½ 3
45 Wicklow Brave *W.P.Mullins* 8-9-10 C.D.Hayes (7) ....11/1 ¾ 4
Lord Yeats *JeddO'Keeffe,GB* 4-9-10 PaulMulrennan (1).......................................28/1 10 5
Twilight Payment (IRE) *J.S.Bolger* 4-9-10 (s+t) K.J.Manning (9) 20/1 2¾ 6
The Tartan Spartan (IRE) *JohnPatrickShanahan* 4-9-10 R.P.Whelan (10)............66/1 4½ 7
63 Dartmouth *SirMichaelStoute,GB* 5-9-10 SeamieHeffernan (6)................................5/1 1½ 8
Benkei (IRE) *HarryRogers* 7-9-10 C.T.Keane (8)...66/1 ½ 9
29 Western Hymn *JohnGosden,GB* 6-9-10 (s) PatSmullen (4) 14/1 35 10
M.Tabor,D.Smith,MrsJ Magnier,L Williams 10ran 3m07.82 128/112/106/104/88/84

DONCASTER Friday, Sep 15 GOOD

74 Wainwrights Flying Childers Stakes (Gr 2) (1) (2yo) £39,697 5f3y
HEARTACHE *CliveCox* 2-8-12 RyanMoore (1)...6/4 1
57 HAVANA GREY *K.R.Burke* 2-9-1 P.J.McDonald (8) .... evsf ½ 2
MAY GIRL *RobertCowell* 2-8-12 AndreaAtzeni (3)..10/1 4½ 3
Pursuing The Dream (IRE) *JamieOsborne* 2-8-12 DougieCostello (4) ....12/1 ½ 4
43 Roland Rocks (IRE) *JohnRyan* 2-9-1 GeraldMosse (9) 20/1 3 5
Midsummer Knight *MickChannon* 2-9-1 SilvestreDeSousa (6).............................40/1 2¼ 6
Spoof *CharlesHills* 2-9-1 (h) CallumShepherd (5)..28/1 nk 7
Yogi's Girl (IRE) *DavidEvans* 2-8-12 StevieDonohoe (7) ....25/1 ¾ 8
Wings of The Rock (IRE) *ScottDixon* 2-8-12 (h) LukeMorris (2) 50/1 3 9
The Hot to Trot Syndicate - Heartache 9ran 58.73sec 111/112/87/85/74/63

75 Doncaster Cup (Gr 2) (1) (3yo+) £56,710 2m1f197y
45 DESERT SKYLINE (IRE) *DavidElsworth* 3-8-5 (s) SilvestreDeSousa (6) 2/1f 1
63 THOMAS HOBSON *W.P.Mullins,Ireland* 7-9-3 RyanMoore (5)............................4/1 1½ 2
63 SHEIKHZAYEDROAD *DavidSimcock* 8-9-3 (h) MartinHarley (7) ....5/1 hd 3
Clever Cookie *PeterNiven* 9-9-3 (s) GrahamLee (3)...33/1 ½ 4
63 High Jinx (IRE) *TimEasterby* 9-9-3 DavidAllan (8) 20/1 8 5
63 Montaly *AndrewBalding* 6-9-6 OisinMurphy (9)..15/2 1¾ 6
45 She Is No Lady *RalphBeckett* 5-9-0 JamesDoyle (1) 7/1 6 7
45 Pallasator *SirMarkPrescottBt* 8-9-3 (s) RosieJessop (4)...16/1 20 8
Fun Mac (GER) *HughieMorrison* 6-9-3 (b+t) AdamKirby (2) 22/1 12 9
C Benham/ D Whitford/ L Quinn/ K Quinn 9ran 3m51.88 117/114/114/113/103/103

DONCASTER Saturday, Sep 16 GOOD

76 Howcroft Industrial Supplies Champagne Stakes (Gr 2) (1) (2yo) £42,532 7f6y
43 SEAHENGE (USA) *AidanO'Brien,Ireland* 2-9-0 DonnachaO'Brien (6)................8/1 1
HEY GAMAN *JamesTate* 2-9-0 MartinHarley (7) ....6/1 nk 2
MYTHICAL MAGIC (IRE) *CharlieAppleby* 2-9-0 JamesDoyle (8)..................... 9/4f nk 3
Red Mist *SimonCrisford* 2-9-0 AndreaAtzeni (5)..7/2 4 4
Dream Today (IRE) *MarkJohnston* 2-9-0 OisinMurphy (2)...................................10/3 4 5

	Island Sound *HeatherMain* 2-9-0 GeorgeWood (1) 100/1	3	6
	Mendelssohn (USA) *AidanO'Brien,Ireland* 2-9-0 RyanMoore (3) 9/1	22	7
	Mr M. Tabor, D. Smith & Mrs John Magnier 7ran 1m25.78	108/108/108/94/82/72	

77 William Hill St Leger Stakes (Gr 1) (1) (3yo c+f) £396,970 — 1¾m115y

31	CAPRI (IRE) *AidanO'Brien,Ireland* 3-9-1 RyanMoore (9) 3/1f		1
50	CRYSTAL OCEAN *SirMichaelStoute* 3-9-1 JimCrowley (1) 5/1	½	2
45	STRADIVARIUS (IRE) *JohnGosden* 3-9-1 JamesDoyle (6) 9/2	sh	3
17	Rekindling *JosephPatrickO'Brien,Ireland* 3-9-1 DonnachaO'Brien (10) 10/1	1½	4
62	Coronet *JohnGosden* 3-8-12 FrankieDettori (7) 8/1	1¼	5
28	Count Octave *AndrewBalding* 3-9-1 OisinMurphy (8) 20/1	2¼	6
	Raheen House (IRE) *BrianMeehan* 3-9-1 AdamKirby (11) 14/1	11	7
59	Venice Beach (IRE) *AidanO'Brien,Ireland* 3-9-1 (s+t) SeamieHeffernan (3) 12/1	9	8
59	Douglas Macarthur (IRE) *AidanO'Brien,Ireland* 3-9-1 EmmetMcNamara (5) 33/1	1½	9
	Defoe (IRE) *RogerVarian* 3-9-1 AndreaAtzeni (2) 6/1	1¾	10
31	The Anvil (IRE) *AidanO'Brien,Ireland* 3-9-1 MichaelC.Hussey (4) 66/1	31	11
	Mr D. Smith, Mrs J. Magnier, Mr M. Tabor 11ran 3m04.04	124/123/123/121/116/115	

NEWMARKET Friday, Sep 29 GOOD to SOFT (Rowley Mile Course)

78 Shadwell Joel Stakes (Gr 2) (1) (3yo+) £56,710 — 1m

	BEAT THE BANK *AndrewBalding* 3-9-0 OisinMurphy (6) 11/8f		1
	SIR JOHN LAVERY (IRE) *AidanO'Brien,Ireland* 3-9-0 RyanMoore (9) 3/1	5	2
44	JALLOTA *CharlesHills* 6-9-4 JamieSpencer (1) 20/1	2¼	3
	Sovereign Debt (IRE) *RuthCarr* 8-9-7 JamesSullivan (3) 14/1	1¼	4
	Custom Cut (IRE) *DavidO'Meara* 8-9-4 (s) DanielTudhope (7) 33/1	3½	5
	Whisky Baron (AUS) *B.Crawford,SouthAfrica* 5-9-4 GregCheyne (5) 20/1	2	6
	Whitecliffsofdover (USA) *AidanO'Brien,Ireland* 3-9-0 (b+t) SeanLevey (8) 20/1	3½	7
	Mustashry *SirMichaelStoute* 4-9-4 JimCrowley (4) 7/2	dh	7
	King Power Racing Co Ltd 8ran 1m38.67	125/111/104/103/90/85	

NEWMARKET Saturday, Sep 30 GOOD to SOFT (Rowley Mile Course)

79 Juddmonte Royal Lodge Stakes (Gr 2) (1) (2yo) £56,710 — 1m

	ROARING LION (USA) *JohnGosden* 2-9-0 OisinMurphy (6) 11/4		1
	NELSON (IRE) *AidanO'Brien,Ireland* 2-9-0 RyanMoore (1) 5/6f	nk	2
43	MILDENBERGER *MarkJohnston* 2-9-0 JamesDoyle (2) 7/2	1¾	3
	Petrus (IRE) *BrianMeehan* 2-9-0 JamieSpencer (4) 16/1	2¼	4
	Midnight Wilde *JohnRyan* 2-9-0 (b) JosephineGordon (3) 100/1	6	5
	Qatar Racing Limited 5ran 1m39.56	111/110/106/99/83	

80 Juddmonte Cheveley Park Stakes (Gr 1) (1) (2yo f) £121,076 — 6f

	CLEMMIE (IRE) *AidanO'Brien,Ireland* 2-9-0 (t) RyanMoore (3) 15/8f		1
57	DIFFERENT LEAGUE (FR) *M.Palussiere,France* 2-9-0 AntoineHamelin (13) 4/1	1¾	2
61	MADELINE (IRE) *RogerVarian* 2-9-0 AndreaAtzeni (2) 8/1	1½	3
	Now You're Talking (IRE) *JosephPatrickO'Brien,Ireland* 2-9-0 DonnachaO'Brien (4) 50/1	hd	4
	Darkanna (IRE) *RichardFahey* 2-9-0 BarryMcHugh (9) 66/1	½	5
	Eirene *DeanIvory* 2-9-0 RobertWinston (7) 14/1	1½	6
61	Threading (IRE) *MarkJohnston* 2-9-0 JamesDoyle (11) 5/2	nk	7
	Betty F *JeremyNoseda* 2-9-0 PatSmullen (6) 16/1	1	8
	Treasuring *G.M.Lyons,Ireland* 2-9-0 ColinKeane (1) 33/1	3¾	9
	Crossing The Line *AndrewBalding* 2-9-0 JimCrowley (10) 28/1	1½	10
	Chica La Habana (IRE) *RobertCowell* 2-9-0 SilvestreDeSousa (12) 66/1	10	11
	Mr M. Tabor, D. Smith & Mrs John Magnier 11ran 1m12.00	118/110/104/104/102/96	

81 Juddmonte Middle Park Stakes (Gr 1) (1) (2yo c) £121,076 — 6f

52	U S NAVY FLAG (USA) *AidanO'Brien,Ireland* 2-9-0 (b+t) SeamieHeffernan (11) .10/1		1
58	FLEET REVIEW (USA) *AidanO'Brien,Ireland* 2-9-0 (t) DonnachaO'Brien (12) ..25/1	½	2
65	CARDSHARP *MarkJohnston* 2-9-0 JamesDoyle (3) 14/1	2¼	3
	Hey Jonesy (IRE) *KevinRyan* 2-9-0 KevinStott (5) 8/1	hd	4
72	Beckford *GordonElliott,Ireland* 2-9-0 PatSmullen (10) 7/2f	½	5
52	Sioux Nation (USA) *AidanO'Brien,Ireland* 2-9-0 RyanMoore (1) 11/2	hd	6
52	Declarationofpeace (USA) *AidanO'Brien,Ireland* 2-9-0 (t) W.M.Lordan (4) 40/1	½	7
58	Danzan (IRE) *AndrewBalding* 2-9-0 DavidProbert (7) 20/1	nk	8
57	Unfortunately (IRE) *K.R.Burke* 2-9-0 (v) JimCrowley (6) 6/1	1	9
65	Frozen Angel (IRE) *TomDascombe* 2-9-0 RichardKingscote (2) 40/1	nk	10
	Rajasinghe (IRE) *RichardSpencer* 2-9-0 StevieDonohoe (8) 10/1	½	11
65	Sands of Mali (FR) *RichardFahey* 2-9-0 PaulHanagan (9) 9/2	3¾	12
	Mr D. Smith, Mrs J. Magnier, Mr M. Tabor 12ran 1m12.44	118/116/108/107/105/105	

CHANTILLY Saturday, Sep 30 GOOD to SOFT

82	**Qatar Prix du Cadran (Gr 1) (4yo+)** £151,699			2½m84y
	VAZIRABAD (FR) *A.deRoyerDupre,France* 5-9-2 ChristopheSoumillon (2)	2/10f		1
	MILLE ET MILLE *C.&Y.Lerner,France* 7-9-2 FranckBlondel (6)	85/10	½	2
	TRIP TO RHODOS (FR) *P.Tuma,CzechRepublic* 8-9-2 TheoBachelot (1)	133/10	7	3
75	High Jinx (IRE) *TimEasterby,GB* 9-9-2 (s) OlivierPeslier (4)	78/10	¾	4
	Pearl Dragon (FR) *M.Delzangles,France* 6-9-2 VincentCheminaud (3)	207/10	5	5
	Aussi Celebre (IRE) *C.Martinon,France* 8-9-2 DelphineSantiago (5)	188/10	sh	6
	H.H. Aga Khan 6ran 4m34.60	117/116/109/108/103/103		

CHANTILLY Sunday, Oct 1 GOOD to SOFT

83	**Total Prix Marcel Boussac - Criterium des Pouliches (Gr 1) (2yo f)** £151,699			7f210y
	WILD ILLUSION *CharlieAppleby,GB* 2-8-11 (s) JamesDoyle (6)	155/10		1
54	POLYDREAM (IRE) *F.Head,France* 2-8-11 MaximeGuyon (2)	18/10	1½	2
	MISSION IMPASSIBLE (IRE) *Jean-ClaudeRouget,France* 2-8-11 ChristopheSoumillon (4)	8/1	hd	3
71	Magical (IRE) *AidanO'Brien,Ireland* 2-8-11 RyanMoore (3)	15/10f	sh	4
57	Zonza (FR) *D.Guillemin,France* 2-8-11 CristianDemuro (7)	188/10	3½	5
	Soustraction (IRE) *C.Laffon-Parias,France* 2-8-11 OlivierPeslier (1)	85/10	1¾	6
	Narella (IRE) *MarkusKlug,Germany* 2-8-11 Christophe-PatriceLemaire (5)	118/10	sh	7
	Godolphin 7ran 1m37.47	113/109/109/109/99/96		

84	**Qatar Prix Jean-Luc Lagardere (Grand Criterium) Sponsored By Al Hazm (Gr 1) (2yo c+f)** £176,982			7f210y
71	HAPPILY (IRE) *AidanO'Brien,Ireland* 2-8-11 RyanMoore (4)	14/10f		1
	OLMEDO (FR) *Jean-ClaudeRouget,France* 2-9-0 CristianDemuro (1)	25/10	1¼	2
	MASAR (IRE) *CharlieAppleby,GB* 2-9-0 JamesDoyle (5)	31/10	sn	3
	Woodmax (GER) *N.Clement,France* 2-9-0 StephanePasquier (3)	17/1	1¾	4
76	Mythical Magic (IRE) *CharlieAppleby,GB* 2-9-0 JamieSpencer (2)	108/10	2½	5
	Francesco Bere (FR) *D.Guillemin,France* 2-9-0 AlexandreGavilan (6)	93/10	6½	6
	Mr D. Smith, Mrs J. Magnier, Mr M. Tabor 6ran 1m38.51	116/116/115/111/104/88		

85	**Qatar Prix de l'Arc de Triomphe (Gr 1) (3yo+)** £2,528,319			1m3f205y
62	ENABLE *JohnGosden,GB* 3-8-9 FrankieDettori (2)	8/10f		1
4	CLOTH OF STARS (IRE) *A.Fabre,France* 4-9-5 MickaelBarzalona (3)	209/10	2½	2
60	ULYSSES (IRE) *SirMichaelStoute,GB* 4-9-5 JimCrowley (1)	121/10	1¼	3
73	Order of St George (IRE) *AidanO'Brien,Ireland* 5-9-5 DonnachaO'Brien (9)	141/10	1½	4
18	Brametot (IRE) *Jean-ClaudeRouget,France* 3-8-12 CristianDemuro (4)	174/10	1¼	5
	Dschingis Secret (GER) *MarkusKlug,Germany* 4-9-5 AdriedeVries (10)	145/10	½	6
	Iquitos (GER) *H-J.Groschel,Germany* 5-9-5 AndraschStarke (6)	45/1	hd	7
41	Idaho (IRE) *AidanO'Brien,Ireland* 4-9-5 SeamieHeffernan (7)	35/1	ns	8
67	Winter (IRE) *AidanO'Brien,Ireland* 3-8-9 RyanMoore (8)	114/10	nk	9
33	Zarak (FR) *A.deRoyerDupre,France* 4-9-5 ChristopheSoumillon (18)	152/10	¾	10
	One Foot In Heaven (IRE) *A.deRoyerDupre,France* 5-9-5 JamesDoyle (11)	95/1	nk	11
33	Doha Dream (FR) *A.Fabre,France* 4-9-5 GregoryBenoist (12)	82/1	nk	12
18	Plumatic *A.Fabre,France* 3-8-12 MaximeGuyon (14)	45/1	1½	13
2	Seventh Heaven (IRE) *AidanO'Brien,Ireland* 4-9-2 PatSmullen (17)	86/1	½	14
	Satono Diamond (JPN) *YasutoshiIkee,Japan* 4-9-5 Christophe-PatriceLemaire (13)	217/10	hd	15
	Satono Noblesse (JPN) *YasutoshiIkee,Japan* 7-9-5 YugaKawada (5)	107/1	½	16
77	Capri (IRE) *AidanO'Brien,Ireland* 3-8-12 W.M.Lordan (15)	37/1	1	17
33	Silverwave (FR) *P.Bary,France* 5-9-5 (h) Pierre-CharlesBoudot (16)	87/1	20	18
	Mr K. Abdullah 18ran 2m28.69	133/132/130/127/124/123		

86	**Prix de l'Opera Longines (Gr 1) (3yo+ f+m)** £202,265			1m1f207y
67	RHODODENDRON (IRE) *AidanO'Brien,Ireland* 3-8-12 SeamieHeffernan (5)	92/10		1
67	HYDRANGEA (IRE) *AidanO'Brien,Ireland* 3-8-12 (s) RyanMoore (9)	43/10	hd	2
70	LADY FRANKEL *A.Fabre,France* 3-8-12 Pierre-CharlesBoudot (4)	38/1	nk	3
67	Wuheida *CharlieAppleby,GB* 3-8-12 JamesDoyle (3)	126/10	nk	4
69	Left Hand *C.Laffon-Parias,France* 4-9-2 (s) MaximeGuyon (13)	98/10	hd	5
	Ashiana (GER) *P.Schiergen,Germany* 3-8-12 AdriedeVries (8)	58/1	2½	6
69	The Black Princess (FR) *JohnGosden,GB* 4-9-2 FrankieDettori (10)	238/10	nk	7
62	Queen's Trust *SirMichaelStoute,GB* 4-9-2 OlivierPeslier (2)	81/10	½	8
	Lacazar (GER) *P.Schiergen,Germany* 3-8-12 AndraschStarke (14)	58/10	nk	9
19	Onthemoonagain (FR) *Jean-ClaudeRouget,France* 3-8-12 ChristopheSoumillon (11)	167/10	¾	10
19	Senga (USA) *P.Bary,France* 3-8-12 StephanePasquier (1)	75/10	5½	11
	Melesina (IRE) *RichardFahey,GB* 3-8-12 AlexBadel (12)	129/1	3½	12
	Shamreen (IRE) *D.K.Weld,Ireland* 4-9-2 PatSmullen (7)	4/1f	6	13
	Mrs John Magnier,Mr M.Tabor & Mr D.Smith 13ran 2m03.60	117/116/115/114/113/109		

87 Prix de l'Abbaye de Longchamp Longines (Gr 1) (2yo+) £176,982 4f214y
64 BATTAASH (IRE) *CharlesHills,GB* 3-9-11 JimCrowley (2) … 33/10 1
64 MARSHA (IRE) *SirMarkPrescottBt,GB* 4-9-8 LukeMorris (4) … 23/10f 4 2
64 PROFITABLE (IRE) *CliveCox,GB* 5-9-11 (s) JamesDoyle (12) … 78/10 nk 3
Duke of Firenze *DavidC.Griffiths,GB* 8-9-11 OisinMurphy (10) … 109/1 1 4
66 Queen Kindly *RichardFahey,GB* 3-9-8 PaulHanagan (9) … 45/1 ½ 5
Rimini (FR) *C.Ferland,France* 2-8-7 JulienAuge (13) … 187/10 hd 6
30 Finsbury Square (IRE) *F.Chappet,France* 5-9-11 (b) ChristopheSoumillon (8). 134/10 2½ 7
Largent du Bonheur (FR) *M.Delzangles,France* 4-9-11 (v) Christophe-PatriceLemaire (7) … 74/1 1 8
Fashion Queen *DavidO'Meara,GB* 3-9-8 DanielTudhope (6) … 50/1 2½ 9
Alphabet *AidanO'Brien,Ireland* 3-9-8 RyanMoore (11) … 181/10 ns 10
Son Cesio (FR) *H-A.Pantall,France* 6-9-11 Pierre-CharlesBoudot (5) … 207/10 2 11
51 Signs of Blessing (IRE) *FrancoisRohaut,France* 6-9-11 StephanePasquier (3) .. 35/10 5 12
Der Graue (IRE) *B.Mohamed,France* 6-9-11 AntoineHamelin (1) … 27/1 2½ 13
Mr Hamdan Al Maktoum 13ran 57.59secs 136/112/114/110/106/102

88 Qatar Prix de la Foret (Gr 1) (3yo+) £151,699 6f211y
51 ACLAIM (IRE) *MartynMeade,GB* 4-9-2 OisinMurphy (1) … 32/10 1
44 SO BELOVED *DavidO'Meara,GB* 7-9-2 DanielTudhope (2) … 31/1 ¾ 2
KARAR *Francis-HenriGraffard,France* 5-9-2 Pierre-CharlesBoudot (3) … 83/10 sh 3
42 Dame du Roi (IRE) *F.Head,France* 3-8-11 AurelienLemaitre (4) … 144/10 hd 4
51 Zalamea (IRE) *MlleC.Fey,France* 4-9-2 EddyHardouin (5) … 60/1 ½ 5
46 Zelzal (FR) *Jean-ClaudeRouget,France* 4-9-2 GregoryBenoist (7) … 19/10f sn 6
66 Brando *KevinRyan,GB* 5-9-2 TomEaves (6) … 45/10 1 7
46 Toscanini (IRE) *RichardFahey,GB* 5-9-2 JamesDoyle (9) … 133/10 1¼ 8
Attendu (FR) *C.Laffon-Parias,France* 4-9-2 MaximeGuyon (8) … 93/10 2 9
42 Realtra (IRE) *RogerVarian,GB* 5-8-13 YugaKawada (10) … 33/1 1 10
Canning Downs & Partner 10ran 1m25.75 115/113/113/111/111/111

NEWMARKET Saturday, Oct 7 GOOD (Rowley Mile Course)
89 Kingdom of Bahrain Sun Chariot Stakes (Gr 1) (1) (3yo+ f+m) £141,775 1m
67 ROLY POLY (USA) *AidanO'Brien,Ireland* 3-9-0 (s) RyanMoore (1) … 4/1 1
67 PERSUASIVE (IRE) *JohnGosden* 4-9-3 FrankieDettori (10) … 9/4f 1¼ 2
NATHRA (IRE) *JohnGosden* 4-9-3 JimmyFortune (13) … 20/1 1¼ 3
42 Usherette (IRE) *A.Fabre,France* 5-9-3 MickaelBarzalona (9) … 9/1 hd 4
23 Dawn of Hope (IRE) *RogerVarian* 4-9-3 ColmO'Donoghue (12) … 66/1 sh 5
67 Qemah (IRE) *Jean-ClaudeRouget,France* 4-9-3 GregoryBenoist (8) … 5/1 ¾ 6
Muffri'ha (IRE) *WilliamHaggas* 5-9-3 JoeFanning (4) … 18/1 ½ 7
62 Alluringly (USA) *AidanO'Brien,Ireland* 3-9-0 SeamieHeffernan (3) … 50/1 1 8
23 Aljazzi *MarcoBotti* 4-9-3 (h) AdamKirby (6) … 8/1 nk 9
56 Siyoushake (IRE) *F.Head,France* 5-9-3 StephanePasquier (5) … 9/1 2 10
27 Tomyris *RogerVarian* 3-9-0 JamieSpencer (7) … 50/1 1¾ 11
Spangled *RogerVarian* 5-9-3 HarryBentley (11) … 66/1 4 12
42 Arabian Hope (USA) *SaeedbinSuroor* 3-9-0 (h) JimmyQuinn (2) … 50/1 1¼ 13
Mr M. Tabor, D. Smith & Mrs John Magnier 13ran 1m34.88 121/117/113/113/113/109

NEWMARKET Friday, Oct 13 GOOD to FIRM (Rowley Mile Course)
90 Godolphin Stud And Stable Staff Awards Challenge Stakes (Gr 2) (1) (3yo+) £68,052 7f
44 LIMATO (IRE) *HenryCandy* 5-9-3 HarryBentley (9) … 6/4f 1
70 MASSAAT (IRE) *OwenBurrows* 4-9-6 JimCrowley (8) … 11/2 3½ 2
GORDON LORD BYRON (IRE) *T.Hogan,Ireland* 9-9-6 AndreaAtzeni (1) … 66/1 1½ 3
14 Rehana (IRE) *M.Halford,Ireland* 3-8-12 ColmO'Donoghue (4) … 33/1 1¼ 4
66 Cougar Mountain (IRE) *AidanO'Brien,Ireland* 6-9-3 (s+t) RyanMoore (10) … 16/1 hd 5
23 Mix And Mingle (IRE) *ChrisWall* 4-9-0 TedDurcan (6) … 25/1 ¾ 6
True Valour (IRE) *JohnPatrickMurtagh,Ireland* 3-9-1 OisinMurphy (2) … 25/1 ½ 7
Gifted Master (IRE) *HugoPalmer* 4-9-3 (b) WilliamBuick (3) … 9/1 10 8
Absolutely So (IRE) *AndrewBalding* 7-9-3 DavidProbert (5) … 33/1 10 9
27 Dabyah (IRE) *JohnGosden* 3-8-12 FrankieDettori (7) … 6/1 7 10
20 Dutch Connection *CharlesHills* 5-9-3 JamesDoyle (11) … 15/2 pu
Mr Paul G. Jacobs 11ran 1m22.24 127/119/115/105/107/101

91 Bet365 Fillies' Mile (Gr 1) (1) (2yo f) £321,829 1m
54 LAURENS (FR) *K.R.Burke* 2-9-0 P.J.McDonald (10) … 10/1 1
71 SEPTEMBER (IRE) *AidanO'Brien,Ireland* 2-9-0 SeamieHeffernan (7) … 9/2 ns 2
MAGIC LILY *CharlieAppleby* 2-9-0 (t) WilliamBuick (12) … 8/1 ¾ 3
83 Magical (IRE) *AidanO'Brien,Ireland* 2-9-0 RyanMoore (2) … 15/8f 3 4
54 Ellthea (IRE) *K.R.Burke* 2-9-0 ColmO'Donoghue (8) … 20/1 ¾ 5
Lubinka (IRE) *PeterChapple-Hyam* 2-9-0 JackMitchell (9) … 150/1 1¾ 6
54 Musical Art (IRE) *PaulCole* 2-9-0 (t) JimCrowley (11) … 33/1 1½ 7

	Efaadah (IRE) *F.Head,France* 2-9-0 AurelienLemaitre (3)	11/2	1	8
57	Nyaleti (IRE) *MarkJohnston* 2-9-0 JamesDoyle (6)	8/1	2¼	9
71	Muirin (IRE) *EdwardLynam,Ireland* 2-9-0 DeclanMcDonogh (1)	20/1	4½	10
	Quivery (USA) *JeremyNoseda* 2-9-0 FrankieDettori (5)	50/1	12	11
	Mr John Dance 11ran 1m36.15	112/112/110/102/100/94		

NEWMARKET Saturday, Oct 14 GOOD to FIRM (Rowley Mile Course)

92 Darley Dewhurst Stakes (Gr 1) (1) (2yo) £283,550 — 7f

81	U S NAVY FLAG (USA) *AidanO'Brien,Ireland* 2-9-1 (b+t) RyanMoore (1)	5/1		1
76	MENDELSSOHN (USA) *AidanO'Brien,Ireland* 2-9-1 (b) W.M.Lordan (7)	50/1	2½	2
76	SEAHENGE (USA) *AidanO'Brien,Ireland* 2-9-1 DonnachaO'Brien (9)	9/1	2½	3
	Threeandfourpence (USA) *AidanO'Brien,Ireland* 2-9-1 SeamieHeffernan (6)	20/1	hd	4
81	Cardsharp *MarkJohnston* 2-9-1 JamesDoyle (4)	20/1	1½	5
38	Great Prospector (IRE) *RichardFahey* 2-9-1 PaulHanagan (3)	50/1	¾	6
	Theobald (IRE) *J.S.Bolger,Ireland* 2-9-1 (s) KevinManning (8)	33/1	2	7
	Emaraaty *JohnGosden* 2-9-1 JimCrowley (2)	6/1	sh	8
43	Expert Eye *SirMichaelStoute* 2-9-1 AndreaAtzeni (5)	4/7f	1	9
	Mr D. Smith, Mrs J. Magnier, Mr M. Tabor 9ran 1m22.37	123/115/107/107/102/100		

ASCOT Saturday, Oct 21 SOFT

93 Qipco British Champions Long Distance Cup (Gr 2) (1) (3yo+) £263,418 — 1m7f209y

85	ORDER OF ST GEORGE (IRE) *AidanO'Brien,Ireland* 5-9-7 RyanMoore (12)	4/5f		1
73	TORCEDOR (IRE) *MrsJ.Harrington,Ireland* 5-9-7 (s) ColmO'Donoghue (7)	25/1	½	2
77	STRADIVARIUS (IRE) *JohnGosden* 3-8-13 FrankieDettori (5)	4/1	½	3
73	Mount Moriah *RalphBeckett* 3-8-13 HarryBentley (13)	66/1	1½	4
	Duretto *AndrewBalding* 5-9-7 GrahamLee (11)	16/1	4	5
75	Clever Cookie *PeterNiven* 9-9-7 (s) JamieSpencer (1)	33/1	8	6
75	Sheikhzayedroad *DavidSimcock* 8-9-7 (h) MartinHarley (8)	25/1	½	7
25	Nearly Caught (IRE) *HughieMorrison* 7-9-7 AdamKirby (10)	66/1	24	8
75	Desert Skyline (IRE) *DavidElsworth* 3-8-13 (s) SilvestreDeSousa (9)	9/1	14	9
73	Dartmouth *SirMichaelStoute* 5-9-7 JimCrowley (4)	20/1	2¾	10
45	Big Orange *MichaelBell* 6-9-7 (s) JamesDoyle (6)	10/1	½	11
	Stars Over The Sea (USA) *HenrydeBromhead,Ireland* 6-9-7 FranBerry (2)	100/1	sh	12
	Cap'n (IRE) *BrendanPowell* 6-9-7 MitchGodwin (3)	150/1	ds	13
	M.Tabor,D.Smith,MrsJ Magnier,L Williams 13ran 3m37.84	119/118/121/118/110/98		

94 Qipco British Champions Sprint Stakes (Gr 1) (1) (3yo+) £340,260 — 6f

44	LIBRISA BREEZE *DeanIvory* 5-9-2 RobertWinston (3)	10/1		1
66	TASLEET *WilliamHaggas* 4-9-2 (s) JimCrowley (5)	10/1	1¼	2
51	CARAVAGGIO (USA) *AidanO'Brien,Ireland* 3-9-1 RyanMoore (12)	9/2	¾	3
66	Harry Angel (IRE) *CliveCox* 3-9-1 AdamKirby (9)	5/4f	nk	4
66	The Tin Man *JamesFanshawe* 5-9-2 TomQueally (7)	9/1	1¼	5
88	Brando *KevinRyan* 5-9-2 TomEaves (2)	20/1	1	6
64	Washington Dc (IRE) *AidanO'Brien,Ireland* 4-9-2 (b+t) DonnachaO'Brien (4)	50/1	1	7
	Donjuan Triumphant (IRE) *AndrewBalding* 4-9-2 (h) P.J.McDonald (11)	20/1	¾	8
	Quiet Reflection *K.R.Burke* 4-8-13 MartinHarley (1)	6/1	nk	9
	Danzeno *MichaelAppleby* 6-9-2 FrankieDettori (6)	33/1	2	10
87	Alphabet *AidanO'Brien,Ireland* 3-8-12 (t) W.M.Lordan (8)	66/1	9	11
51	Intelligence Cross (USA) *AidanO'Brien,Ireland* 3-9-1 (b+t) SeamieHeffernan (13)	100/1	1¼	12
	Mr Tony Bloom 12ran 1m16.78	125/121/119/119/113/109		

95 Qipco British Champions Fillies' And Mares' Stakes (Gr 1) (1) (3yo+ f+m) £355,855 — 1m3f211y

86	HYDRANGEA (IRE) *AidanO'Brien,Ireland* 3-8-13 (s) RyanMoore (8)	4/1		1
69	BATEEL (IRE) *Francis-HenriGraffard,France* 5-9-5 (h) Pierre-CharlesBoudot (4)	7/4f	2	2
77	CORONET *JohnGosden* 3-8-13 OlivierPeslier (9)	11/2	1¾	3
	The Juliet Rose (FR) *N.Clement,France* 4-9-5 (h) StephanePasquier (1)	16/1	5	4
86	The Black Princess (FR) *JohnGosden* 4-9-5 RobertHavlin (10)	40/1	1½	5
69	Journey *JohnGosden* 5-9-5 (h) FrankieDettori (5)	7/2	2¼	6
	Alyssa *RalphBeckett* 4-9-5 PatDobbs (7)	28/1	3½	7
16	Horseplay *AndrewBalding* 3-8-13 DavidProbert (3)	20/1	1½	8
86	Left Hand *C.Laffon-Parias,France* 4-9-5 (b) MaximeGuyon (2)	16/1	3¾	9
	Wild Irish Rose (IRE) *AidanO'Brien,Ireland* 3-8-13 SeamieHeffernan (6)	66/1	ds	10
	Mr D. Smith, Mrs J. Magnier, Mr M. Tabor 10ran 2m40.82	123/118/116/106/103/99		

96 Queen Elizabeth II Stakes (Sponsored By Qipco) (Gr 1) (1) (3yo+) £623,810 — 1m

89	PERSUASIVE (IRE) *JohnGosden* 4-9-1 FrankieDettori (6)	8/1		1
70	RIBCHESTER (IRE) *RichardFahey* 4-9-4 WilliamBuick (13)	2/1f	1	2
68	CHURCHILL (IRE) *AidanO'Brien,Ireland* 3-9-1 RyanMoore (1)	9/2	½	3
89	Nathra (IRE) *JohnGosden* 4-9-1 RobertHavlin (9)	50/1	nk	4
36	Sea of Grace (IRE) *WilliamHaggas* 3-8-12 DanielTudhope (2)	33/1	4½	5

70 Lightning Spear *DavidSimcock* 6-9-4 OisinMurphy (14)..40/1 ½ 6
53 Al Wukair (IRE) *A.Fabre,France* 3-9-1 (s) GregoryBenoist (11)............................7/1 ¾ 7
Zonderland *CliveCox* 4-9-4 AdamKirby (8)..66/1 2¾ 8
46 Here Comes When (IRE) *AndrewBalding* 7-9-4 (h) JamieSpencer (7)..................20/1 sh 9
78 Beat The Bank *AndrewBalding* 3-9-1 JimCrowley (12)...4/1 1 10
78 Sir John Lavery (IRE) *AidanO'Brien,Ireland* 3-9-1 SeamieHeffernan (5)............33/1 6 11
44 Breton Rock (IRE) *DavidSimcock* 7-9-4 AndreaAtzeni (10)................................66/1 3¾ 12
88 Toscanini (IRE) *RichardFahey* 5-9-4 JamesDoyle (4)...100/1 9 13
46 Lancaster Bomber (USA) *AidanO'Brien,Ireland* 3-9-1 DonnachaO'Brien (3)......40/1 ½ 14
53 Thunder Snow (IRE) *SaeedbinSuroor* 3-9-1 (v) ChristopheSoumillon (15)..........16/1 2¼ 15
Cheveley Park Stud 15ran 1m46.13 122/122/122/116/106/106

97 Qipco Champion Stakes (Gr 1) (1) (3yo+) £737,230 1m1f212y
59 CRACKSMAN *JohnGosden* 3-9-1 FrankieDettori (4)..13/8f 1
68 POET'S WORD (IRE) *SirMichaelStoute* 4-9-5 AndreaAtzeni (7)..........................7/1 7 2
41 HIGHLAND REEL (IRE) *AidanO'Brien,Ireland* 5-9-5 RyanMoore (9)..............17/2 nk 3
18 Recoletos (FR) *C.Laffon-Parias,France* 3-9-1 OlivierPeslier (6)..........................14/1 1 4
41 Desert Encounter (IRE) *DavidSimcock* 5-9-5 (h) SeanLevey (8)...........................33/1 1½ 5
85 Brametot (IRE) *Jean-ClaudeRouget,France* 3-9-1 CristianDemuro (3)................11/2 5 6
68 Cliffs of Moher (IRE) *AidanO'Brien,Ireland* 3-9-1 (t) SeamieHeffernan (1)........10/1 sh 7
41 Maverick Wave (USA) *JohnGosden* 6-9-5 RobertHavlin (5)..............................100/1 1 8
60 Barney Roy *RichardHannon* 3-9-1 JamesDoyle (2)...9/2 1 9
68 Success Days (IRE) *K.J.Condon,Ireland* 5-9-5 (t) ShaneFoley (10)......................40/1 25 10
Mr A. E. Oppenheimer 10ran 2m11.75 136/119/119/118/113/103

SAINT-CLOUD Sunday, Oct 22 GOOD
98 Prix Royal-Oak (Gr 1) (3yo+) £178,563 1m7f90y
37 ICE BREEZE *P.Bary,France* 3-8-10 VincentCheminaud 51/10 1
82 VAZIRABAD (FR) *A.deRoyerDupre,France* 5-9-4 ChristopheSoumillon 8/10f 1¼ 2
HOLDTHASIGREEN (FR) *C.LeLay,France* 5-9-4 (s) TonyPiccone 45/10 2 3
Renneti (FR) *W.P.Mullins,Ireland* 8-9-4 Pierre-CharlesBoudot 246/10 8 4
19 Kitesurf *A.Fabre,France* 3-8-7 MickaelBarzalona ....128/10 sn 5
Oriental Eagle (GER) *J.Hirschberger,Germany* 3-8-10 JackMitchell 48/1 4 6
75 Montaly *AndrewBalding,GB* 6-9-4 OisinMurphy 29/1 1¾ 7
82 Mille Et Mille *C.&Y.Lerner,France* 7-9-4 FranckBlondel ....112/10 ds 8
Brandon Castle *ArchieWatson,GB* 5-9-4 (h) AndrewMullen 27/1 10 9
Khalid Abdullah 9ran 3m25.40 124/120/118/109/108/105

MOONEE VALLEY Saturday, Oct 28 GOOD
99 Ladbrokes Cox Plate (Gr 1) (3yo+) £1,065,089 1¼m31y
WINX (AUS) *ChrisWaller,Australia* 6-9-0 HughBowman (5)..............................2/11f 1
HUMIDOR (NZ) *DarrenWeir,Australia* 5-9-4 (b+t) BlakeShinn (7)......................30/1 ½ 2
FOLKSWOOD *CharlieAppleby,GB* 4-9-4 (s) KerrinMcEvoy (4)..........................25/1 4¼ 3
Royal Symphony (AUS) *T.McEvoy,Australia* 3-7-11 (s) DeanYendall (6)............18/1 1½ 4
Gailo Chop (FR) *DarrenWeir,Australia* 6-9-4 MarkZahra (3)...............................20/1 sh 5
Happy Clapper (AUS) *PatrickWebster,Australia* 7-9-4 (b) DamienOliver (8).......30/1 nk 6
Seaburge (AUS) *David&BHayes/TomDabernig,Australia* 4-9-1 (s) ReganBayliss (1) 100/1 7 7
Hardham (AUS) *D.Brideoake,Australia* 4-9-1 (b) LukeNolen (2).......................100/1 1¼ 8
Magic Bloodstock Racing 8ran 2m02.94 126/129/120/116/116/115

DONCASTER Saturday, Oct 28 GOOD to SOFT
100 Racing Post Trophy Stakes (Gr 1) (1) (2yo c+f) £122,210 1m
SAXON WARRIOR (JPN) *AidanO'Brien,Ireland* 2-9-1 RyanMoore (9)............ 13/8f 1
79 ROARING LION (USA) *JohnGosden* 2-9-1 OisinMurphy (12)...............................8/1 nk 2
THE PENTAGON (IRE) *AidanO'Brien,Ireland* 2-9-1 SeamieHeffernan (4)........10/1 2½ 3
72 Verbal Dexterity (IRE) *J.S.Bolger,Ireland* 2-9-1 KevinManning (1)........................5/2 ¾ 4
Gabr *SirMichaelStoute* 2-9-1 JimCrowley (10)...33/1 1¾ 5
Chilean *MartynMeade* 2-9-1 AndreaAtzeni (3)..12/1 ¾ 6
Loxley (IRE) *CharlieAppleby* 2-9-1 WilliamBuick (7)..25/1 2¼ 7
92 Seahenge (USA) *AidanO'Brien,Ireland* 2-9-1 DonnachaO'Brien (11)....................9/1 1¾ 8
Merlin Magic *DavidElsworth* 2-9-1 PaulMulrennan (8)...66/1 8 9
Alfa McGuire (IRE) *BryanSmart* 2-9-1 GrahamLee (5)..100/1 3¾ 10
72 Coat of Arms (IRE) *AidanO'Brien,Ireland* 2-9-1 W.M.Lordan (2)........................66/1 3 11
92 Theobald (IRE) *J.S.Bolger,Ireland* 2-9-1 (s) R.P.Whelan (6)...............................100/1 ¾ 12
Mr D. Smith, Mrs J. Magnier, Mr M. Tabor 12ran 1m40.12 120/120/114/112/108/106

SAINT-CLOUD Sunday, Oct 29
101 Criterium de Saint-Cloud (Gr 1) (2yo) 1m1f207y
ABANDONED – Paddock access blocked by protesters

102 Criterium International (Gr 1) (2yo) 6f211y

ABANDONED – Paddock access blocked by protesters

DEL MAR Friday, Nov 3 FIRM

103 Breeders' Cup Juvenile Turf (Gr 1) (2yo) £419,847 1m

92	MENDELSSOHN (USA) *AidanO'Brien,Ireland* 2-8-10 (b) RyanMoore (1).... 48/10f	1
	UNTAMED DOMAIN (USA) *H.GrahamMotion,USA* 2-8-10 (b) JoseL.Ortiz (2)..128/10	1 2
	VOTING CONTROL (USA) *ChadC.Brown,USA* 2-8-10 JavierCastellano (8)...93/10	½ 3
	Catholic Boy (USA) *JonathanThomas,USA* 2-8-10 (b) ManuelFranco (4) 64/10	hd 4
81	Beckford *GordonElliott,Ireland* 2-8-10 JoelRosario (5) 148/10	½ 5
84	Masar (IRE) *CharlieAppleby,GB* 2-8-10 WilliamBuick (6) 51/10	½ 6
	My Boy Jack (USA) *J.KeithDesormeaux,USA* 2-8-10 KentJ.Desormeaux (13).113/10	½ 7
	Flameaway (CAN) *MarkE.Casse,NorthAmerica* 2-8-10 JulienR.Leparoux (10).. 230/10	hd 8
81	Sands of Mali (FR) *RichardFahey,GB* 2-8-10 FlavienPrat (3)...........................204/10	ns 9
58	James Garfield (IRE) *GeorgeScott,GB* 2-8-10 FrankieDettori (7) 68/10	¾ 10
81	Rajasinghe (IRE) *RichardSpencer,GB* 2-8-10 (b) StevieDonohoe (14) 617/10	½ 11
	Snapper Sinclair (USA) *StevenM.Asmussen,USA* 2-8-10 RicardoSantana,Jnr (11)..207/10	5¾ 12
	Encumbered (USA) *SimonCallaghan,USA* 2-8-10 MarioGutierrez (9).............127/10	6¼ 13
	Hemp Hemp Hurray (CAN) *WesleyA.Ward,USA* 2-8-10 (b) JohnR.Velazquez (12).177/10	½ 14
	Mr D. Smith, Mrs J. Magnier, Mr M. Tabor 14ran 1m35.97	116/113/112/112/110/109

DEL MAR Saturday, Nov 4 Turf Course: FIRM Dirt Course: FAST

104 Breeders' Cup Filly & Mare Turf (Gr 1) (3yo+ f+m) £839,695 1m1f

86	WUHEIDA *CharlieAppleby,GB* 3-8-9 (s) WilliamBuick (5).............................112/10	1
86	RHODODENDRON (IRE) *AidanO'Brien,Ireland* 3-8-9 RyanMoore (14).........56/10	1 2
	CAMBODIA (USA) *ThomasF.Proctor,USA* 5-8-12 DraydenVanDyke (6) 114/10	¾ 3
	Dacita (CHI) *ChadC.Brown,USA* 6-8-12 (b) JoelRosario (7) 169/10	hd 4
86	Queen's Trust *SirMichaelStoute,GB* 4-8-12 FrankieDettori (10).......................153/10	ns 5
	War Flag (USA) *ClaudeR.McGaugheyIII,USA* 4-8-12 JoseL.Ortiz (1) 184/10	1¼ 6
	Lady Eli (USA) *ChadC.Brown,USA* 5-8-12 IradOrtiz,Jr (9).............................. 15/10f	½ 7
86	Senga (USA) *P.Bary,France* 3-8-9 StephanePasquier (2)..................................141/10	ns 8
	Grand Jete *ChadC.Brown,USA* 4-8-12 JavierCastellano (8) 116/10	ns 9
62	Nezwaah *RogerVarian,GB* 4-8-12 AndreaAtzeni (11) 444/10	1¼ 10
	Zipessa (USA) *MichaelStidham,USA* 5-8-12 JoeBravo (4)................................379/10	1½ 11
	Birdie Gold (USA) *GaryMandella,USA* 3-8-9 MikeE.Smith (3).......................318/10	1½ 12
	Goodyearforroses (IRE) *RichardBaltas,USA* 5-8-12 CoreyS.Nakatani (13)......306/10	1½ 13
	Avenge (USA) *RichardE.Mandella,USA* 5-8-12 FlavienPrat (12).....................197/10	8¼ 14
	Godolphin 14ran 1m47.91	120/118/115/115/115/112

105 Breeders' Cup Mile (Gr 1) (3yo+) £839,695 1m

	WORLD APPROVAL (USA) *MarkE.Casse,NorthAmerica* 5-9-0 (b) JohnR.Velazquez (5)... 27/10f	1
96	LANCASTER BOMBER (USA) *AidanO'Brien,Ireland* 3-8-11 SeamieHeffernan (4) 130/10	1¼ 2
	BLACKJACKCAT (USA) *MarkGlatt,USA* 4-9-0 (b) KentJ.Desormeaux (13).190/10	hd 3
44	Suedois (FR) *DavidO'Meara,GB* 6-9-0 DanielTudhope (8) 81/10	nk 4
96	Ribchester (IRE) *RichardFahey,GB* 4-9-0 WilliamBuick (10)..............................35/10	ns 5
88	Zelzal (FR) *Jean-ClaudeRouget,France* 4-9-0 GregoryBenoist (6).....................94/10	hd 6
88	Karar *Francis-HenriGraffard,France* 5-9-0 FrankieDettori (14).......................608/10	nk 7
	Om (USA) *DanL.Hendricks,USA* 5-9-0 (b) DraydenVanDyke (7) 245/10	½ 8
	Ballagh Rocks (USA) *WilliamI.Mott,USA* 4-9-0 (b) JoseLezcano (11) 169/10	½ 9
	Heart To Heart (CAN) *BrianA.Lynch,USA* 6-9-0 JulienR.Leparoux (2)............159/10	ns 10
89	Roly Poly (USA) *AidanO'Brien,Ireland* 3-8-8 (s) RyanMoore (12)....................84/10	ns 11
	Midnight Storm (USA) *Philipd'Amato,USA* 6-9-0 TylerBaze (1)......................235/10	4½ 12
	Mr. Roary (USA) *GeorgePapaprodromou,USA* 4-9-0 (b) TylerConner (3).......614/10	1¼ 13
44	Home of The Brave (IRE) *HugoPalmer,GB* 5-9-0 MikeE.Smith (9) 275/10	1½ 14
	Live Oak Plantation 14ran 1m34.55	125/122/121/121/121/120

106 Longines Breeders' Cup Turf (Gr 1) (3yo+) £1,679,389 1½m

	TALISMANIC *A.Fabre,France* 4-9-0 MickaelBarzalona (1)............................141/10	1
	BEACH PATROL (USA) *ChadC.Brown,USA* 4-9-0 (b) JoelRosario (11)...........34/10	½ 2
97	HIGHLAND REEL (IRE) *AidanO'Brien,Ireland* 5-9-0 RyanMoore (3)........... 14/10f	nk 3
	Sadler's Joy (USA) *ThomasAlbertrani,USA* 4-9-0 JulienR.Leparoux (12)........166/10	1½ 4
85	Seventh Heaven (IRE) *AidanO'Brien,Ireland* 4-8-11 SeamieHeffernan (8)......123/10	1½ 5
	Bullards Alley (USA) *TimGlyshaw,USA* 5-9-0 (b) JavierCastellano (2)............236/10	hd 6
	Itsinthepost (FR) *JeffMullins,USA* 5-9-0 (b) TylerBaze (6)................................257/10	1½ 7
97	Cliffs of Moher (IRE) *AidanO'Brien,Ireland* 3-8-10 W.M.Lordan (5) 164/10	1 8
	Oscar Performance (USA) *BrianA.Lynch,USA* 3-8-10 JoseL.Ortiz (13)............221/10	½ 9
68	Decorated Knight *RogerCharlton,GB* 5-9-0 AndreaAtzeni (4)..........................113/10	nk 10
	Fanciful Angel (IRE) *ChadC.Brown,USA* 5-9-0 IradOrtiz,Jr (9) 221/10	1 11

Bigger Picture (USA) *MichaelJ.Maker,USA* 6-9-0 (b) JohnR.Velazquez (7).....317/10 2¾ 12
Hunt (IRE) *Philipd'Amato,USA* 5-9-0 (b) FlavienPrat (10)..............380/10 9¾ 13
Godolphin S.N.C. 13ran 2m26.19 125/124/124/121/116/118

107 Breeders' Cup Classic (Gr 1) (3yo+) £2,519,084 1¼m (Dirt)
3 GUN RUNNER (USA) *StevenM.Asmussen,USA* 4-9-0 FlorentGeroux (5).........24/10 1
55 COLLECTED (USA) *BobBaffert,USA* 4-9-0 MartinGarcia (11)..............59/10 2¼ 2
WEST COAST (USA) *BobBaffert,USA* 3-8-10 (b) JavierCastellano (8)............42/10 1¼ 3
War Story (USA) *JorgeNavarro,USA* 5-9-0 JoseL.Ortiz (4)..............561/10 ½ 4
Gunnevera (USA) *AntonioSano,USA* 3-8-10 (b) EdgardJ.Zayas (9)..............150/10 2¼ 5
55 Arrogate (USA) *BobBaffert,USA* 4-9-0 MikeE.Smith (1).............. 21/10f dh 5
96 Churchill (IRE) *AidanO'Brien,Ireland* 3-8-10 RyanMoore (7)..............198/10 12¼ 7
3 Mubtaahij (IRE) *BobBaffert,USA* 5-9-0 (b) DraydenVanDyke (6)..............204/10 ½ 8
18 War Decree (USA) *AidanO'Brien,Ireland* 3-8-10 SeamieHeffernan (2)..........448/10 4¼ 9
Pavel (USA) *DougF.O'Neill,USA* 3-8-10 MarioGutierrez (10)..............280/10 10¾ 10
Win The Space (USA) *GeorgePapaprodromou,USA* 5-9-0 JosephTalamo (3)..787/10 7 11
WinchellThoroughbreds/ThreeChimneyFarms 11ran 2m01.29 128/125/123/122/119/119

FLEMINGTON Tuesday, Nov 7 GOOD
108 Emirates Melbourne Cup (Handicap) (Gr 1) (3yo+) £2,105,263 1m7f200y
77 REKINDLING *JosephPatrickO'Brien,Ireland* 3-8-2 CoreyBrown (4)..............14/1 1
24 JOHANNES VERMEER (IRE) *AidanO'Brien,Ireland* 4-8-8 (t) BenMelham (3).12/1 ½ 2
MAX DYNAMITE (FR) *W.P.Mullins,Ireland* 7-8-7 ZacPurton (2)..............19/1 2½ 3
Big Duke (IRE) *DarrenWeir,Australia* 5-8-6 BrentonAvdulla (5)..............20/1 2¾ 4
Nakeeta *IainJardine,GB* 6-8-5 (h) GlynSchofield (19)..............40/1 ¾ 5
75 Thomas Hobson *W.P.Mullins,Ireland* 7-8-3 BenAllen (20)..............20/1 2¼ 6
33 Tiberian (FR) *AlainCouetil,France* 5-8-10 OlivierPeslier (22)..............30/1 ½ 7
Libran (IRE) *ChrisWaller,Australia* 6-8-5 (t) DwayneDunn (7)..............60/1 ½ 8
Marmelo *HughieMorrison,GB* 4-8-9 HughBowman (16).............. 6/1jf sh 9
73 Wicklow Brave *W.P.Mullins,Ireland* 8-8-7 StephenBaster (8)..............70/1 ¾ 10
Red Cardinal (IRE) *AndreasWohler,Germany* 5-8-9 KerrinMcEvoy (23)..............15/1 ¾ 11
Almandin (GER) *RobertHickmott,Australia* 7-8-13 FrankieDettori (14).............. 6/1jf hd 12
Cismontane (NZ) *GaiWaterhouse&AdrianBott,Australia* 5-7-12 (b)
BeauMertens (17)..............40/1 ¾ 13
Amelie's Star (AUS) *DarrenWeir,Australia* 6-8-0 DeanYendall (10)..............20/1 ¾ 14
Boom Time (AUS) *David&BHayes/TomDabernig,Australia* 6-8-5 (b) CoryParish (9)..30/1 1 15
Wall of Fire (IRE) *HugoPalmer,GB* 4-8-5 (v) CraigWilliams (15)..............10/1 1½ 16
Single Gaze (AUS) *NickOlive,Australia* 5-8-5 KathyO'Hara (11)..............30/1 ½ 17
45 Us Army Ranger (IRE) *JosephPatrickO'Brien,Ireland* 4-8-6 JamieSpencer (21).70/1 nk 18
99 Humidor (NZ) *DarrenWeir,Australia* 5-8-11 (b+t) BlakeShinn (13)..............10/1 ½ 19
Hartnell *JamesCummings,Australia* 6-9-1 DamianLane (12)..............25/1 8 20
Ventura Storm (IRE) *David&BHayes/TomDabernig,Australia* 4-8-7 GlenBoss (6)..30/1 1½ 21
Bondi Beach (IRE) *RobertHickmott,Australia* 5-8-7 (b) MichaelWalker (1).........70/1 1¼ 22
Gallante (IRE) *RobertHickmott,Australia* 6-8-5 (t) MichaelDee (18)..............90/1 ds 23
N. C. Williams/Mr and Mrs L. J. Williams 23ran 3m21.19 123/118/114/110/108/103

SHA TIN Sunday, Dec 10 GOOD
109 Longines Hong Kong Vase (Gr 1) (3yo+) £975,285 1m3f205y
106 HIGHLAND REEL (IRE) *AidanO'Brien,Ireland* 5-9-0 RyanMoore (8)........... 43/20f 1
106 TALISMANIC *A.Fabre,France* 4-9-0 MaximeGuyon (1)..............43/10 1¾ 2
TOSEN BASIL (JPN) *HideakiFujiwara,Japan* 5-9-0 JoaoMoreira (7)..............84/10 ¾ 3
29 Chemical Charge (IRE) *RalphBeckett,GB* 5-9-0 OisinMurphy (4)..............87/1 nk 4
Gold Mount *A.S.Cruz,HongKong* 4-9-0 (t) ZacPurton (12)..............81/10 ¾ 5
108 Max Dynamite (FR) *W.P.Mullins,Ireland* 7-9-0 GlynSchofield (2)..............42/1 nk 6
56 Smart Call (SAF) *SirMichaelStoute,GB* 6-8-10 JimCrowley (11)..............155/1 3 7
Eagle Way (AUS) *J.Moore,HongKong* 5-9-0 (b) TommyBerry (5)..............13/1 2 8
Kiseki (JPN) *KatsuhikoSumii,Japan* 3-8-9 MircoDemuro (3)..............13/5 ¾ 9
Danehill Kodiac (IRE) *RichardHannon,GB* 4-9-0 SeanLevey (10)..............121/1 2 10
108 Tiberian (FR) *AlainCouetil,France* 5-9-0 OlivierPeslier (9)..............12/1 1¼ 11
Helene Charisma (FR) *J.Moore,HongKong* 4-9-0 (h+b+t) SamClipperton (6)......39/1 8½ 12
Mr D Smith, Mrs J Magnier & Mr M Tabor 12ran 2m26.23 125/122/120/120/119/118

110 Longines Hong Kong Cup (Gr 1) (3yo+) £1,354,563 1m1f207y
TIME WARP *A.S.Cruz,HongKong* 4-9-0 (t) ZacPurton (5)..............61/20 1
WERTHER (NZ) *J.Moore,HongKong* 6-9-0 TommyBerry (3).............. 6/5f 2¼ 2
NEOREALISM (JPN) *NoriyukiHori,Japan* 6-9-0 JoaoMoreira (1)..............63/10 1½ 3
Staphanos (JPN) *HideakiFujiwara,Japan* 6-9-0 (h) HughBowman (8)..............15/1 ½ 4
Smart Layer (JPN) *RyujiOkubo,Japan* 7-8-10 (h+t) YutakaTake (9)..............27/1 ½ 5
97 Poet's Word (IRE) *SirMichaelStoute,GB* 4-9-0 AndreaAtzeni (12)..............36/5 nk 6
Secret Weapon *C.H.Yip,HongKong* 7-9-0 (t) NashRawiller (11)..............37/1 2 7

70 Robin of Navan (FR) *HarryDunlop,GB* 4-9-0 SamClipperton (4)........................104/1 sh 8
Garlingari (FR) *MmeC.Barande-Barbe,France* 6-9-0 (s) StephanePasquier (6) ...94/1 ½ 9
107 War Decree (USA) *AidanO'Brien,Ireland* 3-8-11 SeamieHeffernan (7)................77/1 nk 10
20 Deauville (IRE) *AidanO'Brien,Ireland* 4-9-0 (b) RyanMoore (2)..........................10/1 1¼ 11
69 Blond Me (IRE) *AndrewBalding,GB* 5-8-10 OisinMurphy (10) 51/1 1 12
Martin Siu Kim Sun 12ran 2m01.63 124/119/116/115/110/113

INDEX TO SELECTED BIG RACES

ERRATA & ADDENDA

'Racehorses of 2001'

Spring Symphony — was **not** dead (she became the dam of Glass Harmonium and Arab Spring, and the grandam of Blond Me)

'Racehorses of 2015'

Air Force Blue — p49, 9 lines from the bottom ... went on to produce the **Grade**-1 winning filly Surfside

Gleneagles — p406, 6 lines down ... **Aidan** O'Brien

'Racehorses of 2016'

Churchill — p214, 4 lines from bottom, Churchill ... won the Tyros, the Futurity and the **National** Stakes

Log Out Island — tested positive for a metabolite of tramadol after his listed victory at Newbury (Carnarvon Stakes) in May and was disqualified (trainer fined £5,000) at an inquiry in June 2017; the race was awarded to runner-up Remarkable

Remarkable — won **three** times in 2016; awarded listed race at Newbury on third start after disqualification of Log Out Island

THE TIMEFORM 'TOP HORSES ABROAD'

FRANCE Anything you can do, I can do better. After Pierre-Charles Boudot had set a new European record by riding 300 winners in 2016, Christophe Soumillon topped that in 2017 with a total of 306, securing him a ninth jockeys' championship in France. Boudot was next best with 209 victories, but perhaps the most significant name amongst the top twenty French riders was Delphine Santiago, whose 59 winners placed her as high as seventeenth in the standings. The tally was more than double Santiago's previous best and, by her own admission, a direct consequence of the controversial initiative by France Galop to address a perceived gender imbalance by giving a two kilogram allowance to all female riders. By the end of the year, as many as twelve of the leading hundred jockeys in France were women, with a further four reaching double figures for wins, including Hayley Turner who came out of retirement to take advantage of a concession which, in light of the seasonal data, has been shaved to a kilo and a half, effective from 1st March 2018.

Four of Soumillon's 306 winners came in Group 1s, one for Godolphin (Thunder Snow in the Prix Jean Prat) and three for Alain de Royer Dupre and the Aga Khan. **Shakeel** narrowly held off the British and Irish challenge in the Grand Prix de Paris at Saint-Cloud in July (injured in the process and missed the rest of the season), shortly after **Zarak**'s breakthrough at the top level, on his first try over a mile and a half, in the Grand Prix de Saint-Cloud. **Vazirabad** plugged an important gap on his CV as he landed the Prix du Cadran, to add to his second successive Dubai Gold Cup earlier in 2017, but he failed in his bid for a third Prix Royal-Oak on his final start of the campaign, a length-and-a-quarter defeat behind three-year-old **Ice Breeze** having the whiff of a French staying revolution about it.

The clouds that gathered over Chantilly for Arc day—before the meeting returns to its renovated home of Longchamp for 2018—were foreboding for the home contingent, who drew a blank on their biggest stage, the six Group 1 events for thoroughbreds being shared between Britain and Ireland. Eighteen runners for the Prix de l'Arc de Triomphe included just seven French representatives, Zarak the shortest priced of them, but it was Prix Ganay winner **Cloth of Stars** who improved the most to chase home Enable, putting up comfortably the best performance by a French-trained horse in 2017.

The competition for that accolade wasn't what it might have been. Part of the reason Andre Fabre was able to regain the trainers' title—his twenty-eighth—was that Jean Claude-Rouget couldn't call upon his two biggest guns of 2016. La Cressonniere never made it to the racecourse due to a recurrence of the back problem that curtailed her defining season when ante-post favourite for the Arc, while **Almanzor**—Europe's top performer of 2016—was retired following a disappointing reappearance in the Prix Gontaut-Biron at Deauville, a return delayed until August after he was among those affected by the EHV-1 virus that struck Rouget's yard in the spring and caused the death of two horses.

The tonic that Rouget needed in the early part of the season was provided by **Brametot**, who became the first horse since Lope de Vega in 2010 to complete the double of the Poule d'Essai des Poulains and the Prix du Jockey Club, winning both races by a short head. No further success followed, but finishing fifth in the Arc made Brametot the joint-best three-year-old in France in 2017 alongside his Al Shaqab Racing team-mate, the Andre Fabre-trained **Al Wukair**, who scrambled home in the Prix Jacques le Marois from stable companion **Inns of Court** having earlier finished third in the Two Thousand Guineas. However, it might have been a different story if **Le Brivido**, pipped by Brametot in the Poulains, had been able to race after his highly promising win in the Jersey Stakes in which he overcame an apparent track bias towards the stand-side runners. Fabre reported that the colt had suffered a setback while being prepared for the Jacques le Marois in August and Le Brivido wasn't seen out again. Fabre's other three-year-old miler of note was the progressive **Buthela** who ended the year finishing second to France's top older miler **Taareef** in the Prix Daniel Wildenstein, the Rouget-trained winner repeating his 2016 success and landing his third pattern race of the year.

Le Brivido was one of three winners at Royal Ascot for France. Neither **Qemah** nor **Usherette** were quite the same force as in 2016, but the previous season's Coronation Stakes winner still managed to beat the luckless Usherette (into third) in the Duke of Cambridge Stakes. Thanks to **Different League**, who came from humble beginnings, successful in her first two races in the Provinces (like her sire Dabirsim in that regard), France won the Albany Stakes for the first time in the race's sixteen-year history. Her two subsequent performances showed she was more than an early-season type, finishing placed in the Prix Morny and Cheveley Park Stakes, and she continues her career with Aidan O'Brien after being bought for 1,500,000 guineas at the Newmarket December Sales.

Only three colts achieved a higher rating than Different League amongst the French two-year-old crop, namely **Sacred Life**, **Olmedo** and **Woodmax**, the last two finishing in the frame in the Prix Jean-Luc Lagardere behind Aidan O'Brien's Happily, who became the first filly to win that Group 1 since Danishkada in 1986. The unbeaten Sacred Life ran away with the Prix Thomas Bryon at Saint-Cloud, by six lengths, and was due to return there for the Criterium International later in October, only for a meeting which also included the Criterium de Saint-Cloud to be abandoned because of protesters blocking access from the pre-parade ring to the paddock. The demonstrators included members of the owners' and trainers' association as well as a group of professionals who were unhappy with plans being put forward by France Galop to cut prize money and bonuses. Run at Saint-Cloud since it was created in 2001, the seven-furlong Criterium International will move to a new home at Longchamp in 2018.

The British runner whom Sacred Life left for dead in second in the Prix Thomas Bryon, the Hugo Palmer-trained Alba Power, subsequently finished even further adrift of **Wootton** in the Prix Isonomy at Deauville. That was the second wide-margin win in as many starts for Wootton, who was bought privately by Godolphin in between but remained with Henri-Alex Pantall, a long-standing trainer for Sheikh Mohammed. The Prix Isonomy has a richer history than its listed status might suggest, providing a springboard for Montjeu, Domedriver and La Cressonniere amongst others, and Guineas possible Wootton (by Almanzor's sire Wootton Bassett) looks as good a prospect as France has got in the crop, at least amongst the colts.

Different League was one of as many as six fillies in the top ten French juveniles in the end-of-year ratings. **Polydream** made a big impression in winning her first two starts at Deauville, including inflicting the only defeat on Laurens, in the Prix du Calvados, and though beaten into second in the Prix Marcel Boussac, by Godolphin's Wild Illusion, Polydream still had some greenness about her that day and remains on course for a Guineas, either at home or at Newmarket. Freddie Head doesn't only have Polydream to look forward to, as he also trains the unbeaten pair **With You** and **Luminate**, both Group 3 winners and the former filly a sister to the same connections' Prix de l'Opera winner We Are.

The fillies' classics of 2017 in France went to surprise packages, **Precieuse** defying odds of 28/1 in the Poule d'Essai des Pouliches, a race in which **Senga** finished down the field prior to winning the Prix de Diane. It was a substandard Diane in which second favourite Rhododendron was pulled up, though she later returned to form with a bang in the Prix de l'Opera on Arc day. Precieuse ran only once more, last of seven in the Coronation Stakes at Ascot before her export to the States, but Senga raced right through until November and formed part of the French team for the Breeders' Cup. She could finish only eighth in the Filly & Mare Turf, but **Talismanic** struck a blow at the meeting for France in the Turf, a fifth Breeders' Cup success for Andre Fabre. Talismanic had Highland Reel back in third at Del Mar but the tables were turned in the Hong Kong Vase a month later.

Signs of Blessing trailed in last in the Hong Kong Sprint, his second lifeless display in a row following on from a Prix de l'Abbaye which was dominated by Battaash, but earlier wins in the Prix de Saint-Georges and Prix de Meautry, over five and six furlongs respectively at Deauville, were enough to make Signs of Blessing the highest-rated sprinter in France for a second year. The three-year-old **Fas** was shaping up to be a challenger in the spring, winning over six furlongs at Chantilly on his first two starts of the campaign, including the Group 2 Prix Sigy at Chantilly (from Precieuse), before he was beaten a long way in both the Prix Maurice de Gheest (won by Brando with Signs of Blessing the best of the home team in fifth) and Prix de Meautry.

One who did hold her form well through the season was **Bateel**. Following her transfer from David Simcock to Francis-Henri Graffard, Bateel went from strength to strength in her new surroundings as a five-year-old and completed a hat-trick in the Prix Vermeille at Chantilly which was dominated by mares and older fillies. With the rain-softened ground very much in her favour on British Champions' Day at Ascot, she was sent off 7/4 favourite for the Fillies' And Mares' Stakes but had to settle for second as Hydrangea proved too tough.

The retirement of Criquette Head-Maarek, whose last runners were on February 1st 2018, marked the end of an era. Numbers had dwindled for Head-Maarek in recent seasons—in 2016 she had eight winners from thirty-two individual horses, and twelve from forty-four in 2017—but her stable regularly housed in excess of two hundred inmates up until 2006.

Born into the Head racing dynasty that began with her great-grandfather, who is buried in the churchyard at Newmarket, she made history as the first female trainer to win the Arc, in 1979, with Three Troikas, who was ridden by her brother, Freddie, and owned by her mother, Ghislaine. **National Defense**, in the 2016 Prix Jean-Luc Lagardere, was the last of her sixty Group 1 wins in France, a haul that included twelve domestic classics. Her French Derby victory, in 1986, came courtesy of Bering, the best horse that Head-Maarek trained, though her crowning glory came with the back-to-back wins by Treve in the Prix de l'Arc. Treve was bred by Criquette Head-Maarek's father at Haras du Quesnay, which has been owned by the Head family since 1958, and where Head-Maarek will focus more of her time following her outstanding and pioneering training career. As well as top-level success in Germany, Canada, Singapore and the United States, Head-Maarek won fourteen Group 1 events in Britain, including the One Thousand Guineas on four occasions. As *Racehorses* was going to press, news came through of another important retirement, that of Elie Lellouche, long serving trainer to members of the Wildenstein family, for whom he won the Gold Cup with Westerner who also won numerous big races in France where Lellouche enjoyed classic success with the likes of Aquarelliste and Beauty Sky, both of whom won the Prix de Diane, and Beauty Parlour, his last Group 1 winner for the Wildensteins when she won the Poule d'Essai des Pouliches in 2012. Lellouche also trained an Arc winner, Hellissio, for Spanish owner Enrique Sarasola.

Two-Year-Olds

116	Olmedo
113p	Sacred Life
111	Woodmax
110	Different League (f)
109p	Polydream (f)
109	Mission Impassible (f)
108p	Luminate (f)
108	Zonza (f)
106p	Wootton
105p	With You (f)

Three-Year-Olds

124	Al Wukair
124	Brametot
124	Ice Breeze
123	Inns of Court
123	Le Brivido
122	Waldgeist
119	Trais Fluors
118p	Buthela
118	Recoletos
117	Fas
117	Shakeel
116	Avilius
116	Cox Bazar
116	Precieuse (f)
116	Soleil d'Octobre
115	Golden Legend (f)
115	La Sardane (f)
115	Lady Frankel (f)
115	Plumatic
115	Via Ravenna (f)
114p	*Sistercharlie (f)
114	Called To The Bar
114	Finche
114	Senga (f)
113	Akihiro
113	Onthemoonagain (f)
112	Afandem
112	African Ride
112	Falcon Wings
112	Gold Luck (f)
112	Graphite
112	Strathspey (f)
112	Terrakova (f)
111	Dame du Roi (f)
111	*Darbuzan
111	Listen In (f)
111	Phelps Win
111?	Turf Laurel (f)
110	Aladdine (f)
110	City Light
110	Gipoia (f)
110	Glen Shiel
110	Heuristique (f)
110	Liwanu
110	National Defense
110	Parabellum
110	Wajnah (f)

Older Horses

132	Cloth of Stars
125	Taareef
125	Talismanic
124	Signs of Blessing
124	Zarak
123	Heshem
123	Silverwave
123	Vazirabad
122	Bateel (f)
121	Erupt
121	One Foot In Heaven
120	Jimmy Two Times
120	Karar
120	*Mekhtaal
120	Zelzal
119	The Right Man

119 Tiberian
118 Armande (f)
118 Doha Dream
118 Garlingari
118 Holdthasigreen
117 Maniaco
117 Spectre (f)
116 Mille Et Mille
116 Qemah (f)
116 Rosa Imperial (f)
116 Siyoushake (f)
116 Ultra
116 Usherette (f)
115 Almorox
115 Attendu
115 Finsbury Square
115 Kourkan
115 Son Cesio
114 Best Fouad
114 Left Hand (f)
114 Smart Whip
114 Zafiro
113 Dicton
113 Haggle (f)
113 *Nimr
113 Royal Julius
113 Traffic Jam (f)
113 Travelling Man
112 Apilobar
112 Djiguite
112 Gold Vibe
112 Nordic Dream
112 Qurbaan
112 Via Firenze (f)
111 Cafe Royal
111 Game Theory (f)
111 Golden Wood
111 Love Spirit
111 Moon Trouble
111 Quatorze
111 Savoken
111 Zalamea
110 Al Jazi (f)
110 Blue Soave
110 Largent du Bonheur
110 Spiritfix (f)
110 Star Victory

GERMANY **Dschingis Secret** topped the ratings in 2017 as he continued the progress he had made in his four-year-old season which culminated in a win in the St Leger Italiano. Trained by Markus Klug, Dschingis Secret won the Gerling-Preis at Cologne on his reappearance in May and, after running below form dropped in trip at Baden-Baden later that month, proceeded to win his next three starts, upstaging his elders **Iquitos** and **Guignol** in the Grosser Hansa-Preis before confirming his status as Germany's top performer with a first Group 1 win in the Grosser Preis von Berlin at Hoppergarten in August. Despite the British-trained Hawkbill having the run of the race, Dschingis Secret led inside the final furlong for a length success. With the Prix de l'Arc de Triomphe in mind, Dschingis Secret then travelled to France to contest the Prix Foy at Chantilly in September and duly completed a fine hat-trick with another high-class performance. He was then the subject of support in anticipation of conditions being more testing than they actually proved to be but ran creditably in the Arc three weeks later, finishing sixth to Enable with Iquitos just a head behind him. The effects of that big effort perhaps lingered for Dschingis Secret's final run of the season in the Grosser Preis von Bayern at Munich, where he was a little below his very best when beaten a neck and the same by Guignol and Iquitos. Repeating his 2016 success at Munich, that win was Guignol's third of the campaign, having earlier triumphed at Baden-Baden in the Grosser Preis der Badischen Wirtschaft in May and the Grosser Preis von Baden in September, with Iquitos runner-up

Longines Grosser Preis von Berlin, Hoppegarten—a first Group 1 win for Dschingis Secret who proves too strong for the Godolphin pair Hawkbill (blaze) and Racing History (cheekpieces, centre)

on both those occasions as well. Despite the latter win qualifying Guignol for a berth in the Breeders' Cup Turf at Del Mar, connections decided instead to run him outside Europe for the first time in the Japan Cup at Tokyo in November, perhaps swayed by the lure of a bonus worth two million dollars to connections of any horse who could add the Japan Cup to a win in the Grosser Preis von Baden. However, Guignol could only manage a below-form ninth behind Cheval Grand. Iquitos, who was the German Horse of the Year in 2016, fared much worse than when seventh in the same race twelve months earlier as he only managed to beat two home, a lacklustre end to a campaign which saw him gain the second Group 1 of his career when beating the British-trained Best Solution by a length and a half in the Grosser Dallmayr-Preis Bayerisches Zuchtrennen at Munich in July. Iquitos was ridden on that occasion by Italian-born jockey Daniele Porcu who was diagnosed with cancer not long after riding Iquitos in Japan and died, aged just thirty-four, in early-January. Germany's top older stayer was the former David Simcock-trained gelding **Red Cardinal** who provided Andreas Wohler with a seventh success in the Oleander-Rennen at Hoppegarten in May, a race promoted to Group 2 as part of the European-wide strengthening of the stayers' programme. Whilst only mid-division in the Melbourne Cup late in the year, Red Cardinal gained a significant win overseas in the Belmont Gold Cup in June.

Although bred for the job, the two-year-old campaign of **Windstoss** didn't give too many indications that he would be following in the footsteps of his sire Deutsches Derby winner Shirocco. He won the listed Derby-Trial at Dusseldorf in April, but was then brought down in a similar contest at Hanover in an incident which led to his jockey Adrie de Vries spending several weeks on the sidelines through injury. However, with Maxim Pecheur taking over in the saddle, Windstoss proved the incident had left no scars on him when showing improved form to finish half a length second to stablemate **Colomano** in the Oppenheim-Union-Rennen at Cologne in June before going one better in the 148th renewal of the Deutsches Derby at Hamburg the following month. In a wholly domestic affair, Windstoss proved suited by the longer trip as he reversed the form with favourite Colomano, staying on best to beat the Peter Schiergen-trained pair **Enjoy Vijay** and **Rosenpurpur**. As well as providing Pecheur with easily the biggest win of his career, Windstoss' victory was a second in the race for his trainer Markus Klug, who first won it with Sea The Moon in 2014, and, surprisingly, a first win for the long-established stud Gestut Rottgen since Uomo prevailed in 1959. Both Colomano and Windstoss then ran in the Grosser Preis von Baden, finishing third and fourth respectively, but it was Windstoss who got the upper hand once more when storming clear to win the Preis von Europa at Cologne back on soft ground in September. Windstoss came home four lengths ahead of the year-older filly Son Macia (109), with a head back to Colomano in third, in the process following in the footsteps of his dam's half-brother Well Made who carried the same Gestut Rottgen silks to victory in 2002.

Poetic Dream beat the British-trained Lockheed by a neck in the Mehl-Mulhens-Rennen (German Two Thousand Guineas) in May and went on to run his best race when third behind the leading older milers **Pas de Deux** and **Palace Prince** in the Oettingen-Rennen at Baden-Baden. Pas de Deux won that contest for the second year running, while Palace Prince had two earlier wins at Baden-Baden in the Badener Meile and when conceding weight all round in the Preis der Sparkassen Finanzgruppe over a mile and a quarter. **Oriental Eagle** took nine races to get off the mark, but followed up a win at Baden-Baden with a length and a quarter victory in the Deutsches St Leger at Dortmund the following month. However, he could make no impression in sixth when stepped up in trip for the Prix Royal-Oak at Saint-Cloud in October. The leading three-year-old filly was the former Bryan Smart-trained **Delectation**, who was fourth behind British raider Unforgetable Filly in the German One Thousand Guineas before finishing fifth to Roly Poly in the Falmouth Stakes at Newmarket in July, one of eleven German-trained horses to run in Britain and Ireland in 2017. Incidentally, only one managed to win, with **Artistica** landing a six-furlong listed race at Nottingham in May. Delectation returned to more familiar surroundings to win the Grosse Europa Meile at Dusseldorf in September with much her best effort. **Lacazar** progressed well through the summer, the filly completing a four-timer when winning the Preis der Diana at Dusseldorf (by three quarters of a length from the Andreas Wohler-trained **Megera**) in August. The win not only provided her trainer Peter Schiergen with a fourth victory in the race, but denied Wohler a fourth consecutive success in the contest.

While Gestut Rottgen's Windstoss might not have announced himself as a future classic winner as a juvenile, it was a very different story for their **Erasmus** who emerged as the leading German two-year-old in 2017. He followed up his maiden win at Cologne with a dominant eight-length victory in the Preis der Winterfavoriten back there in October, the son of the Preis der Diana winner Enora looking very much the type to go on to better things, especially when stepped up in trip. Stablemate **Narella** was also successful in pattern company, winning the Zukunftsrennen at Baden-Baden in September, though she failed to fire when last of seven in the Prix Marcel Boussac at Chantilly the following month when sporting the silks of the Yoshida family for the first time. Indeed, Markus Klug had a glut of above average juveniles, with **Rock My Love** another to make a strong impression, winning all three starts, culminating with an all-the-way success in the Preis der Winterkonigin at Baden-Baden in October. Other performances of note included the win of **Poldi's Liebling** in the Herzog von Ratibor-Rennen, the winning margin of a neck not a true reflection of his superiority, and the victory of **Royal Youmzain** in the Gran Criterium at Milan in October.

Two-Year-Olds

112p	Erasmus
104p	Rock My Love (f)
103	Alounak
103	Narella (f)
103	Poldi's Liebling
102	Royal Youmzain
102	Suada (f)
101	Guiri
99	Angelita (f)
98	Binti Al Nar (f)
96	Julio
95	Salve del Rio

Three-Year-Olds

121	Windstoss
119	Colomano
116	Dragon Lips
116	Oriental Eagle
116	Poetic Dream
115	Delectation (f)
114	Empire of The Star
114	Khan
113	Enjoy Vijay
113	Navaro Girl (f)
112	Amigo
112	Lacazar (f)
112	Rosenpurpur
111	Artistica (f)
111	Instigator
111	Megera (f)
110	Adler
110	Parviz
110	Shanjo

Older Horses

125	Dschingis Secret
124	Guignol
123	Iquitos
119	Palace Prince
118	Pas de Deux
117	Red Cardinal
116	Matchwinner
116	Wild Chief
115	Daring Match
115	Moonshiner
115	Potemkin
115	Ross
115	San Salvador
115	Sarandia (f)
115	Savoir Vivre
115	Sirius
115	Veneto
115	Wai Key Star
115	Wonnemond
114	Devastar
114	Millowitsch
114	Noor Al Hawa
113	Degas
113	El Loco
112	Diplomat
112	Nepal (f)
112	Princess Asta (f)
112	Shutterbug
111	Cashman
111	Shy Witch (f)
111	Sound Check
110	Be Famous
110	Mighty Mouse
110	Shadow Sadness

ITALY The downgrading of three of Italy's four remaining Group 1 races in 2017 left Rome's Premio Lydia Tesio, for fillies in October, as the country's sole top-level contest. That race, won by the Irish-trained mare Laganore, was one of only four pattern races which went abroad during the year, the others including the top two-year-old race (itself a former Group 1 contest), the Gran Criterium, which was won by Germany's Royal Youmzain. How long the Lydia Tesio survives as a Group 1 contest must be open to doubt; it has never been Italy's best race, has lost its Group 1 status in the past and only four home-trained fillies contested the latest renewal which brought together just a useful field on balance. All four were from the stable of Alduino and Stefano Botti which was once again the overwhelmingly dominant force in Italian racing, winning more than three times as many races as the next most successful stable and more than five times as much prize money.

Italy's best horse was the Botti-trained four-year-old colt **Full Drago** whose only defeat all year in five starts was on his sole outing abroad when a creditable fifth in the Prix Maurice de Nieuil at Saint-Cloud. He was never headed in his four races at home, winning the Premio Carlo d'Alessio and Gran Premio di Milano in the first half of the year and the Premio Federico Tesio and the Gran Premio del Jockey Club in the autumn. Despite facing just three rivals in the Jockey Club, that rates as just about his best effort (won by three lengths from the smart German colt Savoir Vivre), though he unfortunately suffered a career-ending injury in the closing stages and retires with a record of nine wins from fourteen starts, with his third place in the 2016 Derby Italiano the only other time, apart from at Saint-Cloud, that he finished out of the first two. **Way To Paris** was Full Drago's closest rival over a mile and a half, chasing him home in the Gran Premio di Milano and Federico Tesio (he was a below-form third in the Jockey Club), and he too ran creditably in France, finishing third in the Prix d'Hedouville at Saint-Cloud. Full Drago's stable-companion **Time To Choose** was fourth behind him in the Gran Premio di Milano and was better suited by shorter trips, winning the nine-furlong Premio Presidente della Repubblica at Rome in May from the dual listed winner **Greg Pass** (the only one of the five runners not trained by the Bottis) and the Premio Ribot there in October. Third in the Presidente della Repubblica, **Voice of Love** gained both his pattern wins at Milan, in the Premio Ambrosiano in April (another race dominated by the Bottis, saddling the first four in a field of five) and the Premio del Giubileo in June. The consistent **Circus Couture** was placed in both those contests and had Greg Pass back in third when winning the Premio Carlo Vittadini at Milan in May in between. The 2016 Premio Parioli (2000 Guineas) winner **Poeta Diletto** returned to the Botti stable after an unsuccessful spell with Marco Botti in Britain and was back to his best when winning a listed race at Milan in November. **Presley** was an interesting colt from the Botti stable who hasn't looked back since finishing well held in the previous year's Derby Italiano. He won seven of his eight starts in minor events and handicaps before his winning streak was ended when finishing third behind the top two three-year-old colts in the Premio Roma.

Anda Muchacho and **Mac Mahon** were separated by half a length in the Roma which had to be run three weeks late at the end of November after a deluge had caused the original fixture to be abandoned midway through the card. Unraced at two, Anda Muchacho won six of his seven starts, his other victories including the Premio Parioli (2000 Guineas) in May and the Premio del Piazzale (from Voice of Love) in October. His only defeat came in the Derby Italiano in May when third to Mac Mahon, who made it four out of four with a five-length win in Italy's richest race. Another of the leading performers in the Botti stable, Mac Mahon was below form on his next two starts in the Grand Prix de Paris and Federico Tesio but returned to his best at Rome before landing a second Derby, the Qatar version in December, and he and Anda Muchacho should do well again in the top middle-distance races in 2018. The other leading three-year-olds included **Amore Hass** who beat older rivals Greg Pass and Time To Choose in the Premio Vittorio di Capua (one of the downgraded former Group 1 races) at Milan in September after making the frame in the Parioli and Derby. **Aethos** won three times in listed company, while two more Botti colts, **Together Again** and **Chasedown**, could make their mark in pattern company at four after ending the year with listed victories.

Both fillies' classics were weak affairs, though predictably enough both races were won by the Bottis. Premio Regina Elena winner Mi Raccomando (rated 104) finished well held in the Oaks d'Italia in which her stable-companions, headed by **Folega**, took the first three places. Those three, along with another stable-companion, fifth-placed **Candy Store**, failed to make an impact in the Lydia Tesio, though the last-named did gain a win over older fillies and mares in the Premio Elena e Sergio Cumani at Milan in September. Another leading three-year-old filly, **My Lea**, improved late in the year to register a couple of wins over some top older sprinters in the listed Premio Omenoni at Milan and the Premio Carlo e Francesco Aloisi at Rome. Omenoni runner-up **Trust You** hit top form earlier in the year, winning Italy's other Group 3 sprint, the Premio Tudini at Rome and following up in a listed race at Milan. **Plusquemavie** was fourth when bidding to win the Tudini for the second year, though he beat Trust You in two of their other meetings (including in a listed event at Milan beforehand) and was successful four times in all, as well as finishing a creditable third in the Prix du Gros-Chene at Chantilly.

Among the two-year-olds, **Wiesenbach** and **Wait For Ever** were separated by just a short head in the Premio Guido Berardelli at Rome over nine furlongs in November. Speedier types prominent in the two-year-old ratings included the filly **Atiam**, who ended her campaign with a seven-length win in a listed race at Rome, and the colt **Gold Tail** who was only a short head away from being unbeaten in six starts, he too ending his season winning a listed race at Rome. The filly **Sweet Gentle Kiss** completed a four-timer (won five times all told) in the Premio Dormello at Milan in October, while earlier in the season **Ipompieridiviggiu** won the Premio Primi Passi at Milan but wasn't seen out again after contesting the Prix Robert Papin in July.

Two-Year-Olds
105p Atiam (f)
104 Ipompieridiviggiu
104 Wait Forever
104 Wiesenbach
103 Gold Tail
99 Old Fox
99 Sweet Gentle Kiss (f)
98 Sopran Roccia
97 Beautiful Vintage
96 Captain Cirdan
96 Fundeghe (f)
96 Villabate

Three-Year-Olds
116 Anda Muchacho
115 Mac Mahon
112 Amore Hass
112 Together Again
110 Aethos
110 Chasedown
109 *Holy Water
108 Dirk
108 My Lea (f)
108 Patriot Hero
107 Aspettatemi
106 Candy Store (f)
106 Folega (f)
106 Paiardina (f)
106 Penalty

Older Horses
120 Full Drago
116 Greg Pass
115 Time To Choose
115 Voice of Love
114 Trust You
114 Way To Paris
113 Circus Couture
112 Presley
112§ Plusquemavie
110 Basileus
110 *Poeta Diletto
109 Per Un Dixir
109 Refuse To Bobbin
109 Zapel
108 Azzeccagarbugli
108 Troublemaker

SCANDINAVIA Denmark's lightly-raced five-year-old **Giuseppe Piazzi** improved to top the ratings in 2017 thanks to victories in the Oslo Cup and the Scandinavian Open Championship, though the first of those wins came in somewhat fortuitous circumstances. 2015 winner **Eye In The Sky** passed the post first again but was demoted to third for hampering **Hurricane Red** a furlong out, with the race awarded to Giuseppe Piazzi who was not involved in the incident. Giuseppe Piazzi's subsequent win at Klampenborg was more straightforward, going three places better than a year earlier and in the process recording his sixth win from only eight starts. Eye In The Sky was beaten fair and square in second, with Hurricane Red having to settle for fourth on this occasion, though the 2016 Oslo Cup winner had earlier beaten **Brownie** by two lengths in the Stockholms Stora Pris (a race he also won in 2015) in June before signing off with victory in a listed race on dirt at Jagersro in October, another contest he had won before and his the seventeenth success all told. Brownie, whose wins the previous season included the Polar Cup and Marit Sveaas Minnelop, had a consistent campaign with listed wins in the valuable Pramms Memorial at Jagersro and the Nickes Minneslopning at Bro Park. In between, as well as finishing second in the Stockholms Stora Pris, he was beaten a neck and a head into third behind **Vortex** in the listed Polar Mile Cup, before filling the same position behind **Trouble of Course** when attempting to defend his crown in the Marit Sveaas Minnelop, both at Ovrevoll. The Norwegian-trained Trouble of Course was Scandinavia's leading three-year-old colt, but the prolific Swedish filly **Dorcia** ended the season with a higher rating. She won the Svenskt Derby (at odds of 53/1 and the first filly to be successful since 2001 in what was the hundredth edition of Scandinavia's richest race) and Svenskt Oaks, before completing a memorable hat-trick in style when winning the Stockholm Cup International by five lengths, becoming the first three-year-old to win the race since Touch of Hawk in 2009.

Land's End took the top prize in the sprint division and completed a four-timer when landing the Zawawi Cup on the dirt at Jagersro. However, slightly better form was shown on turf by the Norwegian-trained sprinters **Captain America** and **Tinnitus**, with precious little between the pair. Captain America had Tinnitus back in fourth in a listed race at Bro Park in June, but the seven-year-old had to settle for second in the Polar Cup at Ovrevoll in August, as his three-year-younger rival Tinnitus recorded a nose success after a tremendous duel in the final furlong and the margin was the same when the pair met again in the listed Bro Park Sprint Championship a month later. Captain America was second again in another listed race at Ovrevoll in October, though this time was conceding 9 lb to the winner **Backcountry**.

Three-Year-Olds
114 Dorcia (f)
112 Trouble of Course
105 Stricker

Older Horses
115 Giuseppe Piazzi
114 Hurricane Red
113 Captain America
113 Tinnitus
112 Brownie
112 Eye In The Sky
112 Falconet
112 Guerre
112 Vortex
111 Jubilance
111 Karmastrikesback
111 Land's End
110 Ruler of Course
109 Backcountry
109 Bokan
109 No Comment
109 Pas de Secrets
108 Berling
108 Fearless Hunter
108 Red Hot Chili
107 Coprah
107 IKC Dragon Heart
107 Saving Kenny

The following European-trained horses also achieved significant ratings

Three-Year-Old
112 Cerastes (Turkey)

Older Horses
117 Subway Dancer (Czech Republic)
114 Wireless (Slovakia)
111 Quelindo (Hungary)
111 Victory Is Ours (Turkey)
110 Father Frost (Czech Republic)
110 Trip To Rhodos (Czech Republic)

UNITED ARAB EMIRATES For all that Arrogate's star may have waned in the latter half of the year, what isn't in dispute is the remarkable performance he put up in the 2017 Dubai World Cup. Fresh from his win in the inaugural running of the Pegasus World Cup (now the world's richest race, taking that mantle from Meydan's showpiece), Arrogate faced a truly international field, with representatives from the home nation, Japan and South Africa, as well as four of his compatriots, including stablemate Hoppertunity, and the horse who was to go on to be named North America's Horse of the Year, Gun Runner. Overcoming a poor start and wide passage, Arrogate stayed on strongly under a hands-and-heels ride for a very impressive victory. A more in-depth analysis of Arrogate's win and his season overall can be found in his individual essay earlier in the annual.

Prize Money, in the care of Saeed bin Suroor, was Godolphin's best performer at the Carnival, starting off in handicap company and posting a very smart performance on his second start to win off top weight. Prize Money followed up on Super Saturday, taking the Group 2 Dubai City of Gold, benefiting from a fine Adrie de Vries ride, and beating the previous year's Juddmonte International winner Postponed by a neck. Prize Money wasn't at all discredited on World Cup night itself, finishing fourth in the Dubai Sheema Classic. Over longer distances, the filly **Beautiful Romance**, who had finished a fine seventh in the 2016 Melbourne Cup, produced smart efforts on her two Carnival starts. The first of them, in the Group 3 Nad Al Sheba Trophy, saw her prevail by a length and a half from Vazirabad, before the French gelding turned the tables for a neck win in the Dubai Gold Cup on World Cup night, Vazirabad taking the race for a second successive year. On dirt, the three-year-old **Thunder Snow** was bin Suroor's flagbearer, for all that he wasn't obviously bred for the surface, winning the UAE 2000 Guineas, and sealing himself a place in the Kentucky Derby with a gutsy win in the UAE Derby despite jinking into the whip inside the final furlong under a very strong ride, but still prevailing over Japanese challenger Epicharis by a short head.

The top performer for Godolphin's other trainer Charlie Appleby was **Folkswood**, who graduated from a handicap win to finish a creditable second to Decorated Knight in the Jebel Hatta on Super Saturday, dictating matters before going down by a neck. Later in the year, Folkswood ran his best race when third to Winx in the Cox Plate. Other Appleby performers of note were **Emotionless** and **Bravo Zolo**. The former had a couple of runs on dirt before reverting to turf and finishing a good third to Prize Money in the Dubai City of Gold. Bravo Zolo was purchased by Godolphin for 170,000 guineas at the Autumn Horses in Training Sales at the end of his four-year-old season and made two Carnival appearances for his new connections, winning a mile handicap from **Suyoof** before going down by a neck to the same rival on worse terms over seven furlongs on his only other outing.

For the second year running, Mike de Kock's **Mubtaahij** reached the frame in the Dubai World Cup, albeit finishing two places worse than the previous year in fourth behind Arrogate. Having been transferred to Kiaran McLaughlin's stable following the

2016 World Cup, Mubtaahij was back with de Kock, and made only two Carnival starts, the first when runner-up to **Etijaah** in a listed handicap won in the past by World Cup winners Curlin (after whom the race is named) and California Chrome, giving over a stone away to the winner. Mubtaahij was returned to the States later in the year, joining Bob Baffert and recording a first win at the top level when taking the Awesome Again Stakes at Santa Anita in September. At the time of writing he was still in training with Baffert, a third tilt at the World Cup likely to be on his agenda.

On turf, de Kock's best performers were **Light The Lights** and **Sanshaawes**, who at the age of eight, was competing in his fourth Carnival. Light The Lights had Sanshaawes behind him in fourth when winning on the first day of the Carnival in the listed Singspiel Stakes. He then matched that effort when runner-up to the Godolphin filly **Promising Run** in the Group 2 Al Rashidiya. Sanshaawes came on for that first run, winning a handicap in February before three successive fourth-place finishes, including in the Jebel Hatta in which Light The Lights could manage only sixth.

The best locally-trained performer was once again Ali Al Rayhi's **Ertijaal**, who posted high-class efforts in winning a handicap and the Group 3 Meydan Sprint (beating **Jungle Cat** by nearly 3 lengths in record time). Having finished runner-up to Australian-trained Buffering in the Al Quoz Sprint the previous year, hopes were high that Ertijaal could go one better in 2017. However, the combination of softening ground and longer trip (the race reverted to its original six furlongs) seemed to find out the speedy Ertijaal who faded into third behind French raider The Right Man, who just edged out the US-trained Long On Value, both putting up career-best performances.

Other local performers worthy of mention are **North America**, trained by Satish Seemar and Ahmed bin Harmash's **Championship**. Ex-Godolphin performer North America completed a four-timer over a mile on dirt when winning the Group 3 Firebreak Stakes by seven lengths having only broken his maiden late in 2016. He subsequently disappointed behind Doug Watson's **Second Summer** in the Godolphin Mile, having been up with the frantic early pace which put paid to his chances, the ex-American winner coming from a long way back to record a first success in the UAE. Championship had won a handicap at the 2016 Carnival, but supplemented a listed success at Abu Dhabi late that year with a pair of Group 2s at the latest Carnival, the Al Fahidi Fort (by three and a half lengths from **Flash Fire**) and the Zabeel Mile. **Heavy Metal** was another who did too much too soon in the Godophin Mile but had made all for a wide-margin win in the Group 3 Burj Nahaar and landed a fourth win of the year over a mile on dirt at Meydan in a listed contest in December. Salem bin Ghadayer's other leading performer was **Long River** who made all at long odds in Round 3 of the Maktoum Challenge.

Europeans claimed three successes on World Cup night, including the aforementioned The Right Man in the Al Quoz Sprint and Vazirabad in the Dubai Gold Cup. The third European win came courtesy of John Gosden's Jack Hobbs in the Dubai Sheema Classic

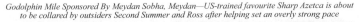

Godolphin Mile Sponsored By Meydan Sobha, Meydan—US-trained favourite Sharp Azetca is about to be collared by outsiders Second Summer and Ross after helping set an overly strong pace

Dubai Turf sponsored by DP World, Meydan—a third Japanese winner of this race in four years as the filly Vivlos (star on cap, centre) comes late to deny a strong European challenge headed by French colt Heshem and Ribchester (noseband)

who produced a high-class performance in first-time blinkers. Japan claimed a third Dubai Turf in four years with the success of Vivlos, the four-year-old filly seeing off a strong European challenge when beating French colt Heshem by a cosy half a length under Hong Kong's champion jockey Joao Moreira. Back on dirt, the USA supplemented Arrogate's Dubai World Cup victory when Mind Your Biscuits came from off the pace to land the Dubai Golden Shaheen (by three lengths from Godolphin's **Comicas**) under Joel Rosario. After heavy overnight rain, the outside part of the dirt track was possibly a little drier, and Mind Your Biscuits found that working to his advantage as he charted a wide course on the way to a convincing win. **Morawij** and **Cool Cowboy**, third and fifth respectively in the Golden Shaheen, were a couple of the leading dirt sprinters, with only a head between them in the Group 3 Mahab Al Shimaal beforehand, while veteran **Reynaldothewizard** showed he retains plenty of dash at the age of eleven, winning the listed Dubawi Stakes for the third year running when beating the 2016 Golden Shaheen winner **Muarrab**.

The performances reviewed here are those that took place in the calendar year 2017. Horses which were trained and raced in the UAE but showed significantly better form elsewhere are not included in the list below.

Three-Year-Olds

122	*Thunder Snow
111	*Yalta
110	Cosmo Charlie
110	Fly At Dawn
106	Fawree
105	Bee Jersey
105	Thegreatcollection

Older Horses

129	Ertijaal (IRE)
123	*Mubtaahij
122	North America
121	Championship
121	*Prize Money
120	*Folkswood
120	Long River
120	Reynaldothewizard
119	*Cool Cowboy
119	Emotionless
118	*Beautiful Romance (f)
118	*Bravo Zolo
118	Heavy Metal
118	Muarrab
118	Special Fighter
117	*Baccarat
117	Gold Trail
117	*Jungle Cat
117	Le Bernardin
117	Morawij
117	Second Summer
116	Flash Fire
116	Light The Lights
116	Move Up
116	Sanshaawes
115	*Comicas
115	Elhaame
115	Farrier
115	Suyoof
115§	Rembrandt Van Rijn
114	*Cymric
114	Earnshaw
114	Forjatt
114	Tahanee
114	*Viren's Army
113	Artigiano
113	Basateen
113	Etijaah
113	Fityaan
113	*Furia Cruzada (f)
113	Ghaamer
113	Lindo Amor
112	*Promising Run (f)
111	Gold City
111	Mushir
111	Shamaal Nibras
111	Zamaam
110	Hunting Ground
110	Noah From Goa
110	Sharpalo

NORTH AMERICA If 'Horse of The Year' voting in the United States had taken place covering the period June 2016 to May 2017 **Arrogate** would have had overwhelming claims. During that period he was unbeaten in seven races, inflicting the only defeat of the year on 2016 Horse of the Year, California Chrome, in that year's Breeders' Cup Classic, and winning the 2017 Dubai World Cup impressively from **Gun Runner** to become the world's leading money earner. By our reckoning, Arrogate was responsible for the best single performance in each year, but he was passed over for the Eclipse Awards top prize both times. The 2017 title was won by Gun Runner by the huge margin of 248 votes to 2 (for Arrogate), a reward for four consecutive Grade 1 victories, while Arrogate disappointed in his last three races, the last of which, the Breeders' Cup Classic, was won by Gun Runner.

Following the 2016 Breeders' Cup Classic, there was great anticipation when Arrogate and California Chrome met again at Gulfstream in January in the inaugural running of the world's richest race, the Pegasus World Cup, which automatically gained Grade 1 status by replacing the Donn Handicap—new races normally require at least two runnings before they are considered for graded status. The race was restricted to twelve horses whose connections were required to pay $1,000,000 each to buy a place in the starting gate. The entrant's owner could then race, lease, contract or share a starter. Shareholders could also share equally in the net income from the race.

It was to have been California Chrome's last race before retirement, but he failed to fire at all—a subsequently discovered knee problem the likely cause of his abject display. This left the 9/10 favourite Arrogate to beat **Shaman Ghost** by nearly five lengths.

Arrogate started even shorter, at 1/3 on the industry prices, for the Dubai World Cup at Meydan two months later. He put up another top-class performance, overcoming a dreadful start and wide passage, before effortlessly running down a very smart field that were far from stopping, finishing two and a quarter lengths ahead of Gun Runner.

However, by the time of the Breeders' Cup Classic in early-November, the gloss had come off. Given a four-month break after Meydan, Arrogate reappeared in the Grade 2 San Diego Handicap at Del Mar, but he was unable to get past the first three and trailed home fifteen lengths behind **Accelerate**. He finished ahead of that rival in the Pacific Classic on the same track in August, but failed by half a length to overcome his stable-companion **Collected**. Although Arrogate raced closer to the pace this time, it was again all rather laboured.

Breeders' Cup Classic, Del Mar—Florent Geroux celebrates after making all on Gun Runner, avenging his only defeat of the year behind Arrogate in Dubai; the 2016 winner is out of shot, and it's his stable-companions Collected and West Coast who fill the places for Bob Baffert

Whitney Stakes, Saratoga—another of Gun Runner's top-class performances as he strides clear of eventual third Breaking Lucky

Arrogate and Gun Runner were at the forefront of the betting for the Breeders' Cup Classic, the former starting at 21/10, with Gun Runner at 24/10, but they didn't have it all to themselves, the Travers Stakes and Pennsylvania Derby winner West Coast coming next at 42/10, with Collected at 59/10. Arrogate never looked as though he was going to launch a challenge and could manage only a share of fifth place, just over six lengths behind Gun Runner. Collected was second, West Coast third and **War Story** fourth.

Gun Runner had flourished after the Dubai World Cup, impressing with his constitution in winning the Stephen Foster Handicap at Churchill Downs (by 7 lengths), and the Whitney Stakes (by over five lengths from **Keen Ice**) and the Woodward Stakes (by 10¼ lengths), both at Saratoga, before the Breeders' Cup, in which he proved himself thoroughly at the trip for the first time, putting up an aggressive display of front-running and seeing off Collected by two and a quarter lengths. Collected had missed the second half of 2016, but had won his four races before the Breeders' Cup, and didn't get the recognition he deserved for his success in the Pacific Classic.

Among the also-rans in the Classic was **Mubtaahij**, who had earlier finished fourth in the Dubai World Cup and had won the Awesome Again Stakes at Santa Anita from **Midnight Storm** with the Gold Cup at Santa Anita winner **Cupid** back in fourth. Midnight Storm, who'll be at stud in 2018, had previously finished second to Shaman Ghost in the Santa Anita Handicap. **Neolithic** finished a place ahead of Mubtaahij in the Dubai World Cup, and had also occupied the same position in the Pegasus.

Keen Ice had caused a big upset in beating American Pharoah in the 2015 Travers Stakes and gained his first success since when beating Shaman Ghost (who gave 6 lb) in the Grade 2 Suburban Stakes at Belmont in July. Keen Ice went on to finish second in both the Whitney Stakes at Saratoga and the Jockey Club Gold Cup at Belmont in the latter to the improved **Diversify**. Keen Ice will be at stud in 2018, as will Shaman Ghost, who underwent throat surgery in August.

Cupid and Accelerate avoided the big two in the Classic by contesting the Dirt Mile at the Breeders' Cup, but they finished in the rear along with another to disappoint in that race, **Mor Spirit**, who started favourite despite a five-month absence since putting up a high-class performance in winning the Metropolitan Handicap at Belmont by over six lengths from **Sharp Azteca**. The last-named was second to the three-year-old **Battle of Midway** in the Dirt Mile and then improved again to give weight away all round in the Cigar Mile Handicap—one of only 11 of the 107 US Grade 1s still run as a handicap—albeit in a limited form compared to European handicaps. In the Cigar Mile, Sharp Azteca finished more than five lengths ahead of the Dubai Golden Shaheen winner **Mind Your Biscuits**. **Seeking The Soul** took advantage of the weight he received from all his closest rivals to win a competitive Clark Handicap at Churchill Downs towards the end of the season, beating a very smart trio in the three-year-old **Good Samaritan**, **Hoppertunity** (having only his second race since finishing sixth in the Dubai World Cup) and Diversify. **Connect**, winner of the Cigar Mile in 2016, showed himself to be as good as ever when winning the Grade 3 Westchester Stakes at Belmont in May, but suffered an injury later in the month and was retired to stud.

The much improved **Roy H** was the only horse to win two Grade 1s over sprint trips. After finishing an unlucky second behind **Ransom The Moon** in the Bing Crosby Stakes at Del Mar—he was carried wide by the riderless **Drefong**—Roy H won both the Santa Anita Sprint Championship and the Breeders' Cup Sprint, the latter at Del Mar by a length from **Imperial Hint** with Mind Your Biscuits third and Ransom The Moon fifth. The 2016 Sprint winner Drefong made only three appearances in 2017, swerving left and unseating soon after the start in the Bing Crosby, but bouncing back to gain a four-length success in the Forego Stakes at Saratoga before disappointing when favourite at the Breeders' Cup. Trainer Jorge Navarro found vast improvement from **El Deal**, who won three races, including the Alfred G. Vanderbilt Handicap at Saratoga by eight lengths, before going down by a length to **Takaful** in the Vosburgh Stakes at Belmont. **Practical Joke**, who was fourth in the Dirt Mile, had earlier beaten Takaful in the seven-furlong H. Allen Jerkens Stakes (previously the King's Bishop) at Saratoga. Roy H's trainer, Peter Miller, gained a notable sprint double at the Breeders' Cup as he also collected the Turf Sprint with **Stormy Liberal**, who caused a 30/1 upset, winning by a head from **Richard's Boy** with the likes of Marsha and Lady Aurelia further back. The Filly & Mare Sprint (7f) saw an even bigger surprise with **Bar of Gold** defying her odds of 667/10 to get up near the line and beat **Ami's Mesa** by a nose with dual Grade 1 winner **Paulassilverlining** (Madison Stakes and Humana Distaff Stakes) back in sixth.

The older fillies' races at 8f+ on dirt were dominated by three fillies, **Songbird**, **Forever Unbridled** and **Stellar Wind**. They ran only ten times between them but collected seven Grade 1s altogether. Songbird won the Ogden Phipps Stakes at Belmont (from **Paid Up Subscriber**) and the Delaware Handicap before suffering only her second defeat in fifteen races when beaten a neck by Forever Unbridled in the Personal Ensign Stakes at Saratoga. It was announced a few days later that Songbird had suffered an injury and she was later sold for $9,500,000 (the highest auction price worldwide in 2017).

Forever Unbridled and Stellar Wind, however, did make it to the Breeders' Cup with the former going two places better than in the previous year in the Distaff, in which the next five home were all three-year-olds. Stellar Wind disappointed when finishing last in that race, but had earlier won all three of her starts, the Apple Blossom Handicap

Breeders' Cup Turf Sprint, Del Mar—
an upset as the Peter Miller-trained pair Stormy Liberal and Richard's Boy finish 1, 2, while Nunthorpe winner Marsha (left) isn't beaten far in sixth on her final start

Kentucky Derby Presented by Yum! Brands, Churchill Downs—
Florida Derby winner Always Dreaming follows up with a dominant display in sloppy conditions from Lookin At Lee and Battle of Midway

at Oaklawn (from **Terra Promessa**), the Beholder Mile (previously the Vanity Mile) at Santa Anita and the Clement L. Hirsch Stakes at Del Mar, the last two both by a neck from the Santa Margarita Stakes winner **Vale Dori**.

There wasn't much between the top three-year-old fillies at 8f+, **Abel Tasman**, **Paradise Woods** and **Elate**, who filled the three places immediately behind Forever Unbridled in the Breeders' Cup Distaff. Abel Tasman achieved a notable treble, not achieved since Open Mind in 1989, winning the Kentucky Oaks, the Acorn Stakes and the Coaching Club American Oaks. Those last two races, along with the Alabama Stakes make up the Filly Triple Tiara, but, without the Kentucky Oaks being included, it doesn't have the same prestige as the colts' equivalent—all the races being held in New York—and no filly has been able to win them since the series was revamped in 2010. The Mother Goose Stakes was once part of the Triple Tiara, but was downgraded to Grade 2 for 2017.

The Kentucky Oaks at Churchill Downs was run at an overly strong pace and the principals all came from a long way back, Abel Tasman beating **Daddys Lil Darling** (who later switched to the turf, winning the American Oaks at the end of December, having had an abortive trip to Epsom for the Oaks, in which she bolted going to post and was

Preakness Stakes, Pimlico—Always Dreaming disappoints this time as Kentucky Derby fourth Classic Empire (right), winner of the previous season's Breeders' Cup Juvenile, goes down narrowly to Cloud Computing

Belmont Stakes, Belmont—sixth and tenth respectively at Churchill Downs, Tapwrit outstays Irish War Cry in the final leg of the Triple Crown from which the winners of the two other legs were both absent

withdrawn). Abel Tasman then won a modest Acorn Stakes at Belmont before holding on by a head from Elate in the CCA Oaks at Saratoga. Her mid-race exertions seemed to find her out when she went down by two lengths to **It Tiz Well** in the Cotillion Stakes at Parx. The last named missed the Breeders' Cup but stays in training for 2018.

Elate had beaten It Tiz Now by just over five lengths in the Alabama Stakes at Saratoga then followed up when landing the odds by an even bigger margin from her elders in the Beldame Stakes at Belmont. Paradise Woods had run away with the Santa Anita Oaks in April, beating Abel Tasman by nearly twelve lengths, but could finish only eleventh, going off far too quickly, behind that filly when favourite for the Kentucky Oaks, before redeeming herself by beating three older fillies in a modest renewal of the Zenyatta Stakes at Santa Anita. Paradise Woods found **Unique Bella** too strong in the closing stages when dropped back down in trip for the La Brea Stakes at Santa Anita on her final outing. Unique Bella had previously won four successive Grade 2/3 events, but was only seventh when a short-priced favourite in the Breeders' Cup Filly & Mare Sprint. **American Gal** won both her starts during the year, including the Test Stakes at Saratoga in August, but wasn't seen out again.

The three-year-old classic winners, **Always Dreaming**, **Cloud Computing** and **Tapwrit** were a relatively modest bunch, and all failed to win again after their major successes. Always Dreaming was a five-length winner of the Florida Derby—one of just three Kentucky Derby trials to hold Grade 1 status after The Blue Grass Stakes and the Wood Memorial were downgraded for 2017—and he started favourite at Churchill Downs, where he was up with the strong pace throughout on a sloppy track, coming home two and three quarter lengths ahead of **Lookin At Lee**, with Battle of Midway third, ahead of the previous year's Breeders' Cup Juvenile and Arkansas Derby winner **Classic Empire**, Practical Joke, Tapwrit and **Gunnevera**, with Godolphin's Thunder Snow pulled up very early on after inexplicably bucking and kicking leaving his stall.

Always Dreaming proved a disappointment in the Preakness Stakes, which went to Cloud Computing, who wore down Classic Empire to win by a head with Lookin At Lee and Gunnevera fourth and fifth. Neither of the winners of the first two legs of the Triple

Travers Stakes Presented by NYRA Bets, Saratoga—
further progress from West Coast who missed the Triple Crown races himself but accounted for all three winners here, though it's Gunnevera who chases him home

Crown contested the Belmont Stakes, those bred more for stamina coming to the fore in that race with Tapwrit, who had skipped the Preakness, outstaying another Kentucky Derby also-ran in **Irish War Cry**. Jockey Jose Ortiz rode his first classic winner aboard Tapwrit and he was also the leading rider for the year on prize money earnings, while, not to be outdone by his sibling, elder brother Irad was the country's top jockey judged on wins with 318 victories.

The Travers Stakes at Saratoga in August attracted all three classic winners, but it was **West Coast**, unraced as a two-year-old and having missed the Triple Crown races, who took himself to the head of the colts' list with a convincing front-running success, beating Gunnevera by over three lengths with **Irap** third and Tapwrit fourth; fifth was Good Samaritan, who had been successful in the Grade 2 Jim Dandy Stakes (in which Always Dreaming and Cloud Computing were both below form) on his previous start, and was later a good second to Seeking The Soul as the only three-year-old in the Clark Handicap at Churchill Downs. West Coast went on to put up another high-class performance to win the Pennsylvania Derby (upgraded to Grade 1 for the first time in 2017) by over seven lengths from Irap before being a creditable third in the Breeders' Cup Classic. While West Coast and Always Dreaming (treated for stomach ulcers after the Travers) stay in training in 2018, Battle of Midway, Classic Empire, Practical Joke, **Gormley** and **Mastery** will all be at stud. Mastery's career was all too short-lived, unbeaten in four races, including the Grade 2 San Felipe Stakes at Santa Anita in March by nearly seven lengths, but he suffered an injury in that race and wasn't seen again. Gormley beat Battle of Midway in the Santa Anita Derby but finished behind that rival in the Kentucky Derby and was again below form when fourth in the Belmont. Amongst others staying in training will be **Pavel**, who put his best performance when third in the Jockey Club Gold Cup at Belmont, and **Girvin**, who, after being well held in the Kentucky Derby, later won the Haskell Invitational at Monmouth by a nose from Kentucky Derby eighth **McCracken** with Practical Joke third, Irish War Cry fourth and Battle of Midway sixth.

Over on the turf, **Oscar Performance** dominated the three-year-olds, winning the Belmont Derby and the Secretariat Stakes, the latter at Arlington from the Aidan O'Brien-trained Taj Mahal, before finding it tougher against older horses in the Joe Hirsch Turf Classic at Belmont and the Breeders' Cup Turf at Del Mar.

Ahead of Oscar Performance in both those races was the four-year-old **Beach Patrol**, who won a muddling Arlington Million as well as the Joe Hirsch Turf Classic, both from Fanciful Angel, who had joined Beach Patrol's trainer, Chad Brown, from Marco Botti, in between. Beach Patrol had earlier been placed in the Turf Classic at Churchill Downs (second to **Divisidero**) and the United Nations Stakes at Monmouth (third behind **Bigger Picture**). Bigger Picture came out the best horse at the weights when third behind Sadler's Joy in the Sword Dancer Stakes before finishing in the rear in the Breeders' Cup Turf. The last-named race was won by Andre Fabre for a third time—with Talismanic, who beat Beach Patrol by half a length with Highland Reel third and Sadler's Joy fourth. **Sadler's Joy** had previously been third at Belmont in the Man o'War Stakes and the Manhattan Stakes, the latter won in an upset by Ascend (rated 115) with some notable scalps behind him, including Beach Patrol, **World Approval** and Divisidero. However, Ascend couldn't reproduce that effort, including when fifth in the Arlington Million and the Joe Hirsch Classic. World Approval returned to a mile after the Manhattan Stakes and won three Grade 1s in a row, showing himself to be the leading turf performer in North America when winning the Fourstardave Handicap at Saratoga (from the former Roger Charlton-trained **Time Test**), the Woodbine Mile and the Breeders' Cup Mile, the last two from the Aidan O'Brien-trained Lancaster Bomber. Third in the Breeders' Cup Mile was **Blackjackcat** (whose biggest success came in the Grade 2 Del Mar Mile Handicap), while Suedois, who had won the Shadwell Turf Mile for David O'Meara the previous month, was back in fourth. The former Brazilian triple crown winner **Bal A Bali**, winner of eleven of his twelve starts there, is one of the best horses to have been imported into the States in recent years, but he took time to acclimatize before eventually capturing two Grade 1s in the Frank E. Kilroe Mile and the Shoemaker Mile, both at Santa Anita, for Richard Mandella. Another import, **Almanaar**, missed more than twelve months

Breeders' Cup Mile, Del Mar—North America's top turf horse the grey World Approval asserts to land his third Grade 1 in a row but it's very tight behind with Lancaster Bomber (blaze, second right) for Ireland, Blackjackcat (left), the Yorkshire-trained pair Suedois (second left) and Ribchester (noseband), and French colt Zelzal (rail) next home

after first leaving France in 2015, but gained a Grade 1 success in the Gulfstream Park Turf Handicap (from the subsequently demoted Beach Patrol) in February before being sidelined for the rest of the year.

Both Almanaar and Beach Patrol were trained by Chad Brown, who was champion trainer on North American earnings for a second year in a row. Although his top-flight wins included the Breeders' Cup Juvenile and the Preakness Stakes, more than half his haul of sixteen Grade 1 wins were gained in turf races, five of them in the older fillies' category, with **Lady Eli** (twice), **Antonoe**, **Dacita** and **Off Limits**. Lady Eli won the Gamely Stakes at Santa Anita (with subsequent Rodeo Drive winner Avenge, who is rated 115, back in third), the Diana Stakes at Saratoga (Just A Game Stakes winner Antonoe in third) and the Grade 2 Ballston Spa Stakes (reversing Jenny Wiley Stakes form with **Dickinson** on more favourable terms) before finishing only seventh when favourite for the Breeders' Cup Filly & Mare Turf at Del Mar. That race resulted in a one, two for European trainers as Wuheida beat Rhododendron, with **Cambodia**, doing best of the home team, in third, Dacita fourth and War Flag (rated 114) sixth. Dacita had earlier got home by half a length from an unlucky **Grand Jete**, who dead-heated for second with Dona Bruja (rated 116) in the Beverly D Stakes at Arlington before failing by a head to concede 4 lb to War Flag in the Flower Bowl Stakes at Belmont (Grand Jete third). With no foreign challengers in the field Cambodia was sent off favourite for the Matriarch Stakes back at Del Mar later in November but could manage only fourth behind Off Limits. The Irish-trained Zhukova, in a good piece of placing by Dermot Weld, pitching his mare in against the males, won the Man o'War Stakes at Belmont in May by six lengths, one of seven North American Grade 1s won by European trainers during the year, which also included Blond Me's success in the E. P. Taylor Stakes at Woodbine for Andrew Balding and Capla Temptress' win in the Natalma Stakes at Woodbine for Marco Botti.

One who travelled in the opposite direction, of course, was the outstanding King's Stand Stakes winner **Lady Aurelia**, who, after finishing second in the Nunthorpe Stakes, disappointed back on home soil in the Breeders' Cup Turf Sprint. Lady Aurelia's trainer Wesley Ward saddled nine other runners at Royal Ascot, and also won the Sandringham Handicap with Con Te Partiro, who subsequently finished a creditable fourth in the Del Mar Oaks (behind Dream Dancing, rated 113) but only ninth in the Queen Elizabeth II Challenge Cup at Keeneland behind La Coronel, who had earlier finished fifth in the Coronation Stakes at Royal Ascot and became the fourth filly to come out of that race and go on to Grade 1 success.

Bolt d'Oro (a $630,000 yearling by Medaglia d'Oro and trained by former scaffolding businessman Mick Ruis) put up the best performance by a two-year-old when a most impressive winner of the FrontRunner Stakes at Santa Anita, where he beat **Solomini** by

Breeders' Cup Juvenile Fillies Turf, Del Mar—Rushing Fall keeps her unbeaten record for trainer Chad Brown who has an excellent record in this contest; Best Performance is next while the Aidan O'Brien-trained September (dark colours) finishes best of all for third

nearly eight lengths. Bolt d'Oro had earlier gained his first Grade 1 success in the Del Mar Futurity and he started at odds on for the Breeders' Cup Juvenile, also at Del Mar. However, from an unfavourable draw he raced wide throughout and finished only third behind **Good Magic** and Solomini, beaten four and a quarter lengths and a length with other Grade 1 winners **Firenze Fire** seventh, **Free Drop Billy** ninth and the Middle Park Stakes/Dewhurst winner U S Navy Flag tenth. That was an improvement for Good Magic (a $1,000,000 yearling by Curlin) after his second to Firenze Fire in the Champagne Stakes at Belmont. Firenze Fire had also progressed after finishing fourth to **Sporting Chance** in the Hopeful Stakes at Saratoga in September, but the latter missed the rest of the season after undergoing surgery for a knee chip. Free Drop Billy was second in the Hopeful and was a four-length winner of the Breeders' Futurity at Keeneland on his next outing before the Breeders' Cup. Solomini (another by Curlin) later gave the Del Mar form a boost when passing the post first in the Los Alamitos Cash Call Futurity but was harshly demoted to third behind **McKinzie** and **Instilled Regard**, the latter a $1,050,000 purchase at Ocala in March. Another one for Chad Brown to look forward to next year is Analyze It (rated 108p), who impressed in winning both his starts, including the Grade 3 Cecil B. DeMille Stakes at Del Mar in late-November.

The top two-year-old filly was **Caledonia Road**, trained by Ralph Nicks, a former assistant to Bill Mott. She showed improved form to give her trainer his biggest win in the Breeders' Cup Juvenile Fillies at Del Mar, where she beat **Alluring Star** by more than three lengths with **Separationofpowers** fourth, dual Grade 1 winner and favourite **Moonshine Memories** seventh and **Heavenly Love**, successful in the Alcibiades Stakes at Keeneland, eleventh. Caledonia Road had earlier finished second to Separationofpowers in the Frizette Stakes at Belmont, but it was Moonshine Memories who had looked the best filly before the Breeders' Cup, unbeaten in three races, including the Del Mar Debutante Stakes and the Chandelier Stakes, the latter by just under three lengths from Alluring Star. **Lady Ivanka** missed the Breeders' Cup with a bruised foot but had Separationofpowers back in third when winning the Spinaway Stakes at Saratoga by three quarters of a length from Maya Malibu. **Dream Tree** made it three wins from as many starts when an impressive winner of the four-runner Starlet Stakes at Los Alamitos late in the year. Meanwhile on the turf, **Rushing Fall** also extended her unbeaten record to three when beating **Best Performance** in the Breeders' Cup Juvenile Fillies Turf. In the colts' equivalent, Mendelssohn gave Aidan O'Brien and Ryan Moore a fourth win in seven Grade 1 editions of the Breeders' Cup Juvenile Turf when beating **Untamed Domain**, **Voting Control** and **Catholic Boy**, the last named subsequently switching to the dirt to record a near-five-length success in the Grade 2 Remsen Stakes at Aqueduct.

Two-Year-Olds

121p	†Bolt d'Oro
120p	†Good Magic
118	Solomini
117	McKinzie
116	Instilled Regard
115	Caledonia Road (f)
115	Catholic Boy
115	Firenze Fire
115	Sporting Chance
114p	Dream Tree (f)
114	Free Drop Billy
114	Moonshine Memories (f)
113p	Rushing Fall (f)
113	Separationofpowers (f)
113	Untamed Domain
112p	Alluring Star (f)
112p	Dream It Is (f)
112	Givemeaminit
112	Heavenly Love (f)
112	Voting Control
111p	Engage
111	Best Performance (f)
111	Greyvitos
111	Piedi Bianchi (f)
110p	Lady Ivanka (f)
110p	Road To Victory (f)
110	Monomoy Girl (f)
110	Spectator (f)
110	The Tabulator
110	Wonder Gadot (f)
110	Zatter

Three-Year-Olds

133	†Lady Aurelia (f)
128	†West Coast
125	Battle of Midway
124	†Always Dreaming
124	Mastery
124	Practical Joke
123	Abel Tasman (f)
123	Elate (f)
123	Good Samaritan
123	Takaful
123	Tapwrit
122	Irap
122	Paradise Woods (f)
122	Unique Bella (f)
121	Classic Empire
121	Cloud Computing
121	Gunnevera
121	Irish War Cry
121	Oscar Performance
121	Pavel
120	American Anthem
120	City of Light
120	Lookin At Lee
120	Mr. Hinx
119	Girvin
119	It Tiz Well (f)
119	McCraken
118	American Gal (f)
118	Timeline
117p	One Liner
117	Actress (f)
117	Bricks And Mortar
117	Coal Front
117	Conquest Mo Money
117	Daddys Lil Darling (f)
117	Gormley
117	Iliad
117	Mo Town

Older Horses

135	†Arrogate
133	†Gun Runner
130	†World Approval
129	†Collected
128	Mor Spirit
127	Sharp Azteca
126	Forever Unbridled (f)
126	Roy H
125	Drefong
125	Songbird (f)
124	Accelerate
124	Beach Patrol
124	Cupid
124	Mind Your Biscuits
124	Shaman Ghost
124	Stellar Wind (f)
123	Connect
123	Diversify
123	Imperial Hint
123	*Mubtaahij
122	Bigger Picture
122	El Deal
122	Hoppertunity
122	Keen Ice
122	Midnight Storm
122	Neolithic
122	Paid Up Subscriber (f)
122	Ransom The Moon
122	Vale Dori (f)
122	War Story
121	Blackjackcat
121	Danzing Candy
121	Lady Eli (f)
121	Paulassilverlining (f)
121	Sadler's Joy
121	Skye Diamonds (f)
121	Terra Promessa (f)
120	Ami's Mesa (f)
120	Bar of Gold (f)
120	Curlin's Approval (f)
120	Divisidero
120	Finest City (f)
120	Giant Expectations
120	Highway Star (f)
120	Send It In
120	St. Joe Bay
120	Unified
120	Win The Space
119	Almanaar
119	Bal A Bali
119	Bullards Alley
119	Constellation (f)
119	Green Mask
119	†Long On Value
119	Off Limits (f)
119	Sea Calisi (f)
119	Time Test
119	Vyjack
118	Antonoe (f)
118	Awesome Slew
118	By The Moon (f)
118	Cambodia (f)
118	Carina Mia (f)
118	Dacita (f)
118	Finley'sluckycharm (f)
118	Grand Jete (f)
118	Heart To Heart
118	Hunt
118	Kasaqui
118	Lewis Bay (f)
118	Money Multiplier
118	Om
118	Pure Sensation
118	Richard's Boy
118	Seeking The Soul
118	Stallwalkin' Dude
118	Stormy Liberal
118	Whitmore
117	A. P. Indian
117	Ballagh Rocks
117	Bird Song
117	Blacktype
117	Blue Prize (f)
117	Conquest Enforcer
117	Dickinson (f)
117	Farhaan
117	Honorable Duty
117	Hunter O'Riley
117	Limousine Liberal
117	Projected
117	Sunny Ridge
117	The Player
117	Tommy Macho
117	Tu Brutus
117§	Green Gratto

JAPAN Reigning Horse of the Year **Kitasan Black** might not have had the chance to shine abroad and nor did he manage to retain his Japan Cup crown, but the high-class five-year-old won another four top-level contests to become Japan's highest-rated horse in the latest season, retiring to stud with record domestic earnings and retaining his Horse of the Year title. He returned with a win in the upgraded Osaka Hai at Hanshin before a second consecutive success in the Tenno Sho (Spring) at Kyoto, but following a rare disappointing effort in the Takarazuka Kinen back at Hanshin in June, plans to aim him at the Prix de l'Arc de Triomphe in the autumn were changed in favour of what proved a lucrative domestic campaign again later in the year. Another Group 1 win in the Tenno Sho (Autumn), run in unusually testing conditions, made Kitasan Black only the fifth horse to win the two Tenno Sho or 'Emperor's Cup' races in the same year and the first since Meisho Samson ten years earlier. Kitasan Black's attempt to make all in the Japan Cup for the second year running looked like succeeding until the final hundred yards, though he was eventually beaten a length and a half into third behind **Cheval Grand**. Third the year before, Cheval Grand put up an improved effort to turn the tables, ridden for the first time by Australian jockey Hugh Bowman, best known for his association with Winx. Earlier in the year, Cheval Grand had been placed behind Kitasan Black in the Tenno Sho (Spring) for the second year running when runner-up, though he too disappointed in the Takarazuka Kinen. A final meeting between the pair in the Arima Kinen at Nakayama in December went the way of Kitasan Black, with Cheval Grand pipped for second by the mare **Queens Ring**. Placed in the two previous editions of the end-of-year championship contest, Kitasan Black's all-the-way win took his career total of JRA Group 1 victories to a record-equalling seven.

Japan was represented in the latest Arc but, like the year before, the challenge fell well short of some previous attempts. **Satono Diamond**, who had signed off his three-year-old season beating Kitasan Black in the Arima Kinen, began the year well, winning the Group 2 Hanshin Daishoten before finishing a good third at level weights in the Tenno Sho (Spring) – on Timeform's weight for age scale he would have been entitled to receive 5 lb at that time of year from his elders Kitasan Black and Cheval Grand over two miles.

Satono Diamond had been prominent in the Arc betting, but finishing only fourth in the Prix Foy beforehand did little to advance his claims and he ended up down the field, in company with his travelling companion **Satono Noblesse** who had come last in the Foy. The same owner's **Satono Crown**, who'd ended 2016 winning the Hong Kong Vase and had made a winning reappearance in the Group 2 Kyoto Kinen for the second year running, gained a first Group 1 win on home turf when successful in the Takarazuka Kinen from **Gold Actor** and he ran well in defeat when running a back-to-form Kitasan Black to a neck in the Tenno Sho (Autumn) before finishing down the field in both the Japan Cup and Arima Kinen.

After a Group 2 win at Nakayama early on, **Neorealism** provided one of Japan's biggest overseas successes of the year in Hong Kong when winning the Audemars Piguet Queen Elizabeth II Cup in April under an enterprising ride from local champion Joao Moreira. There were no Japanese winners at Sha Tin's International meeting in December, but Neorealism finished a respectable third in the Hong Kong Cup with **Staphanos** (third the year before, and runner-up to Kitasan Black in the Osaka Hai) and the seven-year-old mare **Smart Layer** taking the next two places. Smart Layer had beaten **Tosen Basil** and Cheval Grand in a Group 2 at Kyoto beforehand, with the runner-up going on to finish third in the Hong Kong Vase. Moreira was also in the saddle on another big Japanese winner abroad when Cheval Grand's younger half-sister **Vivlos** took the Dubai Turf. The 2016 Tokyo Yushun (Japanese Derby) winner **Makahiki**, who'd disappointed in the Arc that year, struggled to find his best form at four, though he finished fourth in the Japan Cup after reaching the frame behind Satono Crown at Kyoto and Kitasan Black at Hanshin earlier in the year. **Rainbow Line** finished sixth in the Japan Cup for the second successive year after running his best race of the year when third in the Tenno Sho (Autumn), while Group 2 winners **Yamakatsu Ace** and **Sciacchetra** were further down the Japan Cup field after good efforts in the first half of the year to finish third in the Osaka Hai and fourth in the Takarazuka Kinen respectively – Sciacchetra fared the better of that pair in the Arima Kinen when sixth. **Albert** finished a creditable fifth in the Tenno Sho (Spring) behind some top middle-distance performers but he's more of an out-and-out stayer who has made the Group 2 Stayers Stakes at Nakayama his own, winning the two and a quarter mile event for the third year running in December.

There was no standout performer among the milers as demonstrated by the result of the Yasuda Kinen at Tokyo in June when there was a neck between each of the first five home. The previous year's winner **Logotype** tried to make all again but just went down to **Satono Aladdin** who had been fourth behind him twelve months earlier. Satono Aladdin went on to be a good second to the previous year's Dubai Turf winner **Real Steel**

Japan Cup, Tokyo—third the year before, Cheval Grand (blaze) improves to turn the tables on 2016 winner Kitasan Black (right) who just loses out for second to Japanese Derby winner Rey de Oro (left)

Yushun Himba (Japanese Oaks), Tokyo—Soul Stirring (centre) gets the better of Mozu Katchan (other jockey in white cap, right) and provides one of the highlights of the year for Frenchman Christophe Lemaire who makes history as the first foreign jockey to become champion in Japan

in the Group 2 Mainichi Okan at Tokyo over nine furlongs before losing his form later in the autumn. **Air Spinel**, fifth in the Yasuda Kinen, fared best of the older milers in the Mile Championship at Kyoto in the autumn when second in a race that was otherwise dominated by three-year-olds. **Isla Bonita**, placed in the two previous runnings of the Mile Championship, was only fifth this time, though had made a winning return in the Group 2 Yomiuri Milers Cup at Kyoto in April giving weight to Air Spinel in second. **Red Falx** ran in both the Group 1 mile contests for older horses, running well when third in the Yasuda Kinen, but shorter trips suit him ideally as he showed when winning the Sprinters Stakes at Nakayama for the second year running earlier in the autumn. Red Falx had finished third to **Seiun Kosei** in the other Group 1 sprint, the Takamatsunomiya Kinen at Chukyo in March before conceding weight all round to win the Group 2 Keio Hai Spring Cup over seven furlongs at Tokyo. Seiun Kosei was down the field in the Sprinters Stakes, but the mare **Let's Go Donki**, a former Japanese 1000 Guineas winner, ran well to finish runner-up in both Group 1 sprints. The other sprinter of note was **Fine Needle**, winner of the Group 2 Centaur Stakes at Hanshin in September, though he failed to repeat that form in the Sprinters Stakes.

Three-year-olds haven't often made much impact against their elders in the Japan Cup this century and **Rey de Oro** was bidding to become the first since Jungle Pocket in 2001 to complete the Tokyo Yushun (Derby)-Japan Cup double (Derby runner-up Rose Kingdom was awarded the Japan Cup in 2010, while the other three-year-old winner since Jungle Pocket was the filly Gentildonna in 2012). Rey de Oro ran well in defeat in the Japan Cup, taking second from Kitasan Black close home after returning in the autumn to beat the subsequent Kikuka Sho (St Leger) winner **Kiseki** in the Group 2 Kobe Shimbun Hai at Hanshin. Kiseki's St Leger, incidentally, which he won from **Clincher**, was another autumn race run in unusually attritional conditions by Japanese standards resulting in a very slow time. Derby runner-up **Suave Richard** also ran well against older horses later in the year, winning the Group 2 Copa Republica Argentina at Tokyo on the way to finishing a good fourth behind Kitasan Black in the Arima Kinen. Rey de Oro's win in the Tokyo Yushun completed a Derby-Oaks double for both his trainer Kazuo Fujisawa and jockey Christophe Lemaire after **Soul Stirring**'s success the previous weekend in the Yushun Himba (Oaks). Lemaire was the first jockey to complete the classic double for forty-two years; he'd also ridden the filly's dam Stacelita to win the French equivalent, the Prix de Diane. The Frenchman, who along with Italian Mirco Demuro, became the first foreign jockey to be granted a permanent licence by the JRA in 2015, made history again in the latest season as the first overseas jockey to win the Japanese championship. Soul Stirring was campaigned ambitiously later in the year (and could be again in 2018, in Europe), though she was unable to reproduce her Oaks form, finishing sixth in the Tenno

Sho (Autumn) and seventh in the Japan Cup. Among Soul Stirring's Oaks victims were the pair who had beaten her in the Oka Sho (1000 Guineas), Reine Minoru (rated 114) and **Lys Gracieux**.

The highest-rated three-year-old filly, though, by the autumn was the Oaks runner-up **Mozu Katchan**. She finished third to **Deirdre** and Lys Gracieux in the final leg of the fillies' triple crown, the Shuka Sho, but fared much the best of that trio when winning the Queen Elizabeth II Cup at Kyoto against older fillies and mares. Mozu Katchan and Deirdre are both daughters of the King George VI & Queen Elizabeth Stakes winner Harbinger who had another Group 1 winner in the autumn when his son **Persian Knight** won the Mile Championship. As already noted, three-year-olds fared well in this contest, with the Group 2 Swan Stakes winner **Sungrazer** in third and Reine Minoru in fourth. Persian Knight had been beaten a neck by stable-companion **Al Ain** in the Satsuki Sho (2000 Guineas) in the spring, though Rey de Oro and Suave Richard (fifth and sixth respectively) turned the tables on that pair over the extra two furlongs of the Derby. After Lani the year before, Japan went close to a second win in the UAE Derby at Meydan when **Epicharis** lost his unbeaten record by a short head to Thunder Snow. Lani had gone on to finish third in the Belmont Stakes, though a hoof problem prevented Epicharis from tackling the same race.

Epicharis shares his sire Gold Allure with the leading older dirt performer **Gold Dream** who became the third horse (the first since Transcend in 2011) to win both of the JRA Group 1 races on dirt in the same year. His win in the February Stakes came just days after his sire's death (Gold Allure was himself a former February Stakes winner), while Ryan Moore was in the saddle when he won the Champions Cup at Chukyo in December in a finish of necks with **T M Jinsoku** and **Copano Rickey**, the latter another son of Gold Allure. Gold Dream had been among four Japanese-trained outsiders in the latest Dubai World Cup, though he finished last of all with the previous season's Champions Cup runner-up (fifth in the latest edition) **Awardee**, faring best of them in fifth.

The winners of both the Hanshin Juvenile Fillies, **Lucky Lilac** (from the first crop of dual Arc runner-up Orfevre), and the Asahi Hai Futurity **Danon Premium** took their records to three out of three in what have traditionally been Japan's top two-year-old contests. However, there is now a third Group 1 for two-year-olds with the upgrading of the Hopeful Stakes (which Rey de Oro won in 2016) run over a mile and a quarter at Nakayama at the end of December which went to favourite **Time Flyer**.

Two-Year-Olds

118p	Danon Premium
113p	Lucky Lilac (f)
112p	Wagnerian
112	Time Flyer
112	Tower of London
112	Grail
111	Lily Noble (f)
109	Gendarme
109	Mau Lea (f)
109	Stay Foolish
109	Stelvio
107	Beluga (f)
107	Frontier
107	Keiai Nautique
107	Le Vent Se Leve
106	Asakusa Genki
106	Cassius
106	Katsuji
106	K T Clever

Three-Year-Olds

125	Rey de Oro
124	Suave Richard
122	Kiseki
122	Persian Knight
121	Sungrazer
119	Clincher
119	Mozu Katchan (f)
119	Popocatepetl
119	Satono Chronicle
118	Deirdre (f)
118	Mikki Swallow
117	Al Ain
117	Epicharis
117	Soul Stirring (f)
116	Aerolithe (f)
116	Bless Journey
116	Meiner Wunsch
115	Admirable
115	Daiwa Cagney
115	Danburite
115	Lys Gracieux (f)
115	My Style
115	Rabbit Run (f)
115	Satono Arthur

Older Horses

128	†Kitasan Black
127	Satono Crown
127	†Satono Diamond
126	Cheval Grand
125	Gold Actor
124	Neorealism
123	Seiun Kosei
123	Staphanos
122	Admire Deus
122	Copano Rickey
122	Gold Dream
122	Logotype
122	Makahiki
122	Red Falx
122	Satono Aladdin
122	T M Jinsoku
122	Tanta Alegria
122	Yamakatsu Ace
121	Air Spinel
121	Dee Majesty
121	Rainbow Line
121	Real Steel
121	Sciacchetra
120	Albert
120	Apollo Kentucky
120	Fine Needle
120	Greater London
120	Isla Bonita
120	K T Brave
120	Mikki Rocket
120	Miraieno Tsubasa
120	Narita Hurricane
120	Sakura Empereur
120	Sound True
120	Sounds of Earth
120	Tosen Basil

120 Vivlos (f)
119 Ambitious
119 Best Warrior
119 Fame Game
119 Nero
119 Queens Ring (f)
119 Snow Dragon
118 Chrysolite
118 Crocosmia (f)
118 London Town
118 Meiner Milano
118 Mikki Queen (f)
118 Moanin
118 Rouge Buck (f)
118 Seewind
118 Shonan Bach
117 Admire Lead (f)
117 Awardee
117 Big Arthur
117 Black Moon
117 Decipher
117 Kafuji Take
117 Kazenoko
117 Let's Go Donki (f)
117 Satono Noblesse
117 Smart Layer (f)

HONG KONG The highest-rated horse in Hong Kong in 2017 was sprinter **Mr Stunning** who developed into a high-class performer by the end of the year, during which he won a total of six races, culminating in a neck win over stablemate **D B Pin** in the Hong Kong Sprint in December. John Size's other leading sprinter **Amazing Kids** ran below his best in fifth, though had played his part in a one, two, three for his trainer the previous month when he and D B Pin were placed behind Mr Stunning in the Jockey Club Sprint. Outsider **Blizzard** and the previous year's runner-up **Lucky Bubbles** completed the frame in the Hong Kong Sprint, though the latter wasn't at his best at the end of the year. However, in May Lucky Bubbles had accounted for a field of top sprinters in the Chairman's Sprint, beating Mr Stunning by a neck with **Not Listenin'tome**, **Thewizardofoz**, Centenary Sprint Cup winner **Peniaphobia** and Amazing Kids all close up, while Lucky Bubbles had run creditably on his return in October when splitting Mr Stunning and Amazing Kids to finish second in the Premier Bowl Handicap. Former Hong Kong Sprint winner Peniaphobia had accounted for Lucky Bubbles, Not Listenin'tome and Amazing Kids in January's Centenary Sprint Cup but his form rather tailed off after finishing second to Mr Stunning in the Sprint Cup in April.

A substandard edition of the Hong Kong Mile went to **Beauty Generation** who dictated a modest pace from the front to beat outsider **Western Express**, though it was hard to knock the record of a gelding who won five times in all during 2017 and showed unusual versatility in winning at distances from seven to eleven furlongs. 2016 Hong Kong Mile winner **Beauty Only** (only seventh in the latest edition) failed to get his head in front during the year but wasn't far off his best form on occasions, going close in the Chairman's Trophy and Champions Mile (the latter won by outsider **Contentment**) in the first half of the year. **Helene Paragon**, trained like Beauty Generation by John Moore, was another with claims to being the top miler, though was third to his stablemate in the latest edition of the Hong Kong Mile after being runner-up in 2016. He gained two Group 1 wins earlier in the year in the Stewards' Cup (from a field that included the last three winners) and the seven-furlong Queen's Silver Jubilee Cup from stablemates **Able Friend** (the former top-class winner of the same two races was subsequently retired) and **Joyful Trinity** who was second in the Stewards' Cup. Helene Paragon held his form well, conceding weight to the winner **Seasons Bloom** (subsequently fourth in the Hong Kong Mile) when runner-up in the Jockey Club Mile in November in which Beauty Generation and Beauty Only completed the frame.

Longines Hong Kong Mile, Sha Tin—another race won from the front, with a substandard renewal going to Beauty Generation from outsider Western Express and 2016 runner-up Helene Paragon, a stablemate of the winner

Longines Hong Kong Cup, Sha Tin—the much improved Time Warp, who began his career in Britain with Sir Mark Prescott, steals the race from the front under Zac Purton from favourite Werther and Japan's Neorealism (rail) who head the chasing pack

Hong Kong's 2015/16 Horse of the Year **Werther**—winner of the Hong Kong Derby and Queen Elizabeth II Cup—added two more Group 1 prizes to his record in 2017, and, though he was beaten by **Time Warp** when favourite for the Hong Kong Cup in December, he remained the top performer over middle distances. The Hong Kong Cup was run at a steady pace, and Time Warp, a dual listed winner for Sir Mark Prescott earlier in his career who had risen through the handicapping ranks in his first year in Hong Kong, benefited from an excellent front-running ride from Zac Purton. Werther had given weight and a neck beating to Time Warp the previous month in the Jockey Club Cup. Earlier in the year, Werther, who made a belated return in the latest season (having sustained a freak injury incurred when trying to kick another horse and slipping over during track work), did well to overhaul old rival **Blazing Speed** in the Hong Kong Gold Cup in February by a short head after being hampered. With a clearer run, Werther extended the winning margin to three lengths when the pair finished first and second again in the Champions & Chater Cup over a mile and a half in May (Werther had finished a close third to Blazing Speed the year before). In between, Werther was one of several not seen to best effect when attempting to win his second Audemars Piguet Queen Elizabeth II Cup, finishing third in a tactical race to the Japanese horse Neorealism.

In the same contest, the mercurial **Pakistan Star** put his best foot forward to finish second with a career-best effort. The four-year-old had first made a name for himself, even outside Hong Kong, when making a remarkable winning debut in July 2016, coming from a detached last and making a sweeping move around the whole field in the straight to win readily. However, he disgraced himself when pulling himself up on what proved his last appearance in a Group 3 handicap in June, resulting in a ban from racing until passing a trial satisfactorily, something he failed to do when misbehaving again whilst being put through his paces in October. For all his temperament, though, Pakistan Star was the main rival to **Rapper Dragon** who looked a potential new star on the Hong Kong racing scene in the early part of the year, though his Horse of the Year award in July sadly proved a posthumous one. Rapper Dragon became the first horse to complete the 'triple crown' for four-year-olds of the Classic Mile, nine-furlong Classic Cup and ten-furlong Derby. Pakistan Star finished runner-up in the last two contests, with Beauty Generation third in the Classic Mile and Derby and Seasons Bloom reaching the frame in all three. Rapper Dragon went on to complete his four-timer in the Chairman's Trophy back at a mile from the previous year's winner Beauty Only (with Werther fourth) but suffered fatal injuries when breaking down in the Champions Mile in May for which he was sent off at odds on.

Three locally-trained horses contested the Hong Kong Vase at the International meeting in December, with **Gold Mount** (down the field in the Derby and more recently fourth to Werther in the Jockey Club Cup) faring best of them in fifth behind Highland Reel who was winning the mile and a half contest for the second time and was the only overseas-trained winner of the four International races. Indigenous (1998) and Dominant (2013) are the only Hong Kong-trained horses to have kept the prize at home.

Older Horses

126	† Mr Stunning
125	Lucky Bubbles
125	Werther
124	Amazing Kids
124	Beauty Only
124	D B Pin
124	Helene Paragon
124	Not Listenin'tome
124	Peniaphobia
124	Rapper Dragon
124	† Time Warp
123	Able Friend
123	Contentment
123§	Pakistan Star
122	† Beauty Generation
122	Blazing Speed
122	Joyful Trinity
122	Seasons Bloom
122	Thewizardofoz
120	Blizzard
120	Secret Weapon
119	Eagle Way
119	Gold Mount
119	Western Express
118	Dashing Fellow
118	Dundonnell
118	Giant Treasure
118	Horse of Fortune
118	Romantic Touch
118	Sun Jewellery
117	Basic Trilogy
117	Circuit Land

AUSTRALIA AND NEW ZEALAND Australian challengers have become very much part and parcel of the Royal Ascot scene over the last decade or so. However, Holler was the only Australian sprinter to make the trip in 2016, when he failed to reach the first six in the Diamond Jubilee, and Australian horses were absent altogether in the latest season when the focus for the home sprinters was very much on the newest addition to the world's richest races. The Everest, with prize money of A$10m (slots were available in the race for A$600,000), became the world's most valuable turf race overnight. Run at Randwick over six furlongs in October as a counter-attraction to the Melbourne Spring Carnival, The Everest didn't provoke a rush of international challengers, but the prize money made consideration of any other targets irrelevant for Australia's top sprinters. The field was headed by **Chautauqua** who had become the first horse to win three successive editions of the TJ Smith Stakes over Randwick's six furlongs at 'The Championships' in April. Still last of the fifteen TJ Smith runners at the three-hundred-metre mark, Chautauqua unleashed a scintillating turn of foot once he got a split inside the final furlong to win in breathtaking style from the filly **English** and **Fell Swoop**, who had filled the placings (albeit in reverse order) behind Chautauqua the year before. Chautauqua, English and Fell Swoop were all prepared for The Everest, after the winter break, and ran in The Shorts, a Group 2 at Randwick in September in which they clashed with the progressive **Redzel**. Redzel continued his winning streak, which had included the Group 1 Doomben 10,000 in May, and started as one of the leading fancies for The Everest, for which the field also included the Golden Slipper winner **She Will Reign**, who had since won the Moir Stakes at Moonee Valley, and **Vega Magic**, formerly trained in Western Australia, who

Darley TJ Smith Stakes, Randwick—the grey Chautauqua puts up a memorable performance to come from last to first to win this prestigious sprint for the third time; the filly English and Fell Swoop are placed again, though in reverse order from the previous year

The TAB Everest, Randwick—a purely domestic field for the inaugural running of the world's richest turf race which is won by Redzel; he enjoys the run of the race much more than eventual third Brave Smash (checks, under Jamie Spencer) and top sprinter Chautauqua (grey) who completes the frame from a long way back, while eventual runner-up Vega Magic is out of shot out wide with just 100m to run

had made a big impression when winning the Group 1 Goodwood at Morphettville in May and had won the Group 1 Memsie Stakes over seven at Caulfield in September on his final run before The Everest. The established sprinters could not prevent Redzel continuing on his winning ways as he beat unlucky-in-running Vega Magic by three quarters of a length, with four-year-old **Brave Smash** third and Chautauqua fourth. Redzel went on to extend his unbeaten run to six when adding the Darley Classic to his tally at Flemington in November from veteran **Terravista** (Chautauqua fourth). **Hey Doc**, winner of the Australian Guineas at Flemington in March, was the top four-year-old sprinter—he led throughout to win the Manikato Stakes at Moonee Valley in October—with **Impending** (third in the Darley Classic) and **Russian Revolution** (sixth in the TJ Smith and fourth in the Doomben 10,000) among the other four-year-olds who made their mark in the sprinting division.

Australia's queen of the turf **Winx**, who has an essay in the main body of this edition, took on some of Australia's best sprinter-milers in the Group 1 George Ryder Stakes over seven and a half furlongs at Rosehill in March. Winx was up against the first three in the Group 1 Canterbury Stakes, **Le Romain**, Chautauqua and the previous year's Epsom Handicap winner **Hauraki**. Winx had the race in safe keeping some way from home and won by seven and a quarter lengths and a length and a quarter from Le Romain and Chautauqua. Australia's most valuable Group 1 weight-for-age event the Queen Elizabeth Stakes over a mile and a quarter at 'The Championships' was next for Winx

Longines Queen Elizabeth Stakes, Randwick—Australia's richest Group 1 weight-for-age race is won easily by Winx who records her seventeenth successive victory, chased home by Hartnell

BMW Caulfield Cup Handicap, Caulfield—an upset as 50/1-shot Boom Time (blinkers) takes this major spring prize from fellow outsider Single Gaze (blaze) and Irish-trained favourite Johannes Vermeer (white cap)

who recorded her seventeenth successive victory, beating old rival **Hartnell** by five and a quarter lengths. After a winter break, during which she won the Horse of the Year title for the second time and was inducted into the Australian Hall of Fame, Winx returned in the [southern hemisphere] spring to eventually stretch her unbeaten run to twenty-two, crowning her spring campaign with a third successive win in the Cox Plate at Moonee Valley in October. New Zealand import **Humidor**, who had won the Makybe Diva Stakes at Flemington the previous month, ran Winx close, recording a performance that made him the second highest-rated horse in Australia in 2017 (he had also won the Australian Cup at Flemington in March). Humidor's trainer Darren Weir, who is based in Victoria, did very well with the older horses in his yard, which also included **Black Heart Bart** (C. F. Orr Stakes/Futurity Stakes), **Gailo Chop** (Caulfield Stakes) and **Tosen Stardom** (Toorak Handicap/Emirates Stakes, formerly the Mackinnon). Weir broke his own record by training 449 winners, eight of them Group 1s, in the 2016/17 season. Two of Weir's fellow Victorian trainers, Mark Kavanagh and Danny O'Brien, successfully appealed in November when facing lengthy suspensions after being caught up in Australia's ongoing cobalt investigations which still seem to have some way to run. Australian racing is in danger of being besmirched by doping scandals, another mammoth investigation into seven years of alleged doping with alkalising agents ('milkshaking') resulting in a total of 271 charges being brought by Racing Victoria against five trainers, who face potentially explosive hearings in 2018 (leading Melbourne trainer Robert Smerdon, one of the accused, has agreed to stand down pending the inquiry, while another of the trainers involved Tony Vasil will be better known to European readers, as he handled Elvstroem, winner of the Dubai Duty Free in 2005 before running in Britain, and also had Haradasun who went on to win at Royal Ascot for Aidan O'Brien).

If Australia's sprinters are likely to have more pressing matters at home, there is still hope that Winx may appear at Royal Ascot in 2018, though the considerations outlined by her trainer Chris Waller (covered in Winx's essay) make a European trip far from certain, with a tilt at a fourth Cox Plate probably higher on the agenda (Kingston Town is the only other horse to have won three Cox Plates). Apart from Winx, the best older mare in Australia in 2017 was **Jameka**, second behind Humidor in the Australian Cup at Flemington before turning the tables on him in the BMW at Rosehill shortly afterwards. Jameka had been earmarked for the Hardwicke Stakes at Royal Ascot and the King George VI and Queen Elizabeth Stakes but she was prevented from making the trip to

Britain by pneumonia which kept her out of action in the [southern hemisphere] spring. Jameka had won the 2016 Caulfield Cup and the latest edition of that major spring event produced an upset when 50/1-shot **Boom Time** won from another outsider **Single Gaze** (the previous week's Caulfield Guineas had produced an even bigger surprise with the success of 100/1-shot **Mighty Boss**). Boom Time was invited to the Japan Cup in November and finished twelfth behind Cheval Grand.

The Caulfield Cup has had surprise winners before, including British challengers Taufan's Melody, at 66/1 in 1998, and Godolphin-raced All The Good, at 40/1 in 2008. Godolphin Australia underwent some key changes in personnel in 2017, among those to step down being trainer John O'Shea and managing director Henry Plumptre (both in trouble with the authorities over failing to report a strangles outbreak in 2016). O'Shea's last day featured **It's Somewhat** taking the Hollindale Stakes at the Gold Coast in May. The horse had earlier won the prestigious Group 1 Doncaster Mile at 'The Championships' at Randwick from the veteran **Happy Clapper** who finally got his head in front in Group 1 company when carrying top weight to victory later in the year in the Epsom Handicap over the same course. British-based Charlie Appleby made further successful raids with Godolphin horses during the year, though two of his runners, Polarisation and Penglai Pavilion, were involved in the abandoned Sydney Cup on the day that Winx won the Queen Elizabeth Stakes at 'The Championships'. The Godolphin pair passed the post in first and third but the stewards had declared a 'no race' after two of the runners fell (one of them fatally). Appleby eventually got his hands on the Sydney Cup when Polarisation won the event when it was rescheduled two weeks later. Appleby also had pattern wins with Qewy and Folkswood, the last-named going on to finish third to Winx in the Cox Plate. James Cummings, the grandson of the legendary Bart Cummings (who won twelve Melbourne Cups), took over as Godolphin's head Australian trainer in July and had his first Group 1 winner in his new role when **Alizee** won the Flight Stakes at Randwick in September.

New Zealand raiders were more than a match for Australia's leading four-year-olds, with New Zealand Derby winner **Gingernuts** successful in the Rosehill Guineas. After returning from the winter break and winning the Group 1 Horlicks Plate at Hastings in September, Gingernuts was returned to Australia for the Emirates Stakes in November but fractured a pastern and had to be withdrawn. New Zealand Oaks winner **Bonneval** was the pick of the four-year-old fillies and followed up in the Australian Oaks, adding a third Group 1 in the Underwood Stakes at Caufield after her winter break. A New Zealand raider, **Jon Snow**, also won the Australian Derby at Randwick in April. Australia's leading four-year-old **Extreme Choice** was retired to stud after only a short autumn campaign. The best of the Australian three-year-olds were the sprinters **Menari** and **Trapeze Artist**, the latter upstaging his stablemate (Menari was third) when winning the Golden Rose in September at 40/1 by a record winning margin of four and a quarter lengths. **Merchant Navy** won the Coolmore Stud Stakes at Flemington in November and was the pick of the Victorian sprinters. The fillies **Catchy** and **Houtzen** had won the Blue Diamond Stakes at

Schweppes Sydney Cup, Randwick—
a big win for Godolphin with British-trained Polarisation who narrowly holds the challenge of Who Shot Thebarman whose fall in the original running of the race was one of the reasons it was declared void; Polarisation had also been first past the post on that occasion

Caulfield in February and the Magic Millions 2-Y-O Classic on the Gold Coast in January before finishing down the field behind easy winner She Will Reign in the world's richest two-year-old race the Golden Slipper at Rosehill in March. **Aloisia**, the joint highest-rated filly with She Will Reign, won the Thousand Guineas at Caulfield in October and followed up when beating the colts on Cox Plate day in the Moonee Valley Vase. **Ace High** won the Victoria Derby at the Melbourne Spring Carnival but it was a northern hemisphere three-year-old, Irish-trained Rekindling, who made the biggest impression at Flemington when edging out fellow Irish challenger Johannes Vermeer to win the 2017 Melbourne Cup, 'the race that stops a nation'. Rekindling, fourth in the St Leger at Doncaster before making his Melbourne Cup challenge, has an extended entry in the A to Z, his essay covering the father and son story as Rekindling gave his trainer Joseph O'Brien a memorable triumph over his famous father Aidan. Rekindling and Johannes Vermeer both carried the colours of major Australian owner Lloyd Williams who had won the Melbourne Cup five times before, with Just A Dash (1981), What A Nuisance (1985), Efficient (2007), Green Moon (2012) and Almandin (2016). Rekindling, incidentally, maintained the run of overseas-trained or imported Melbourne Cup winners, 100/1-shot Prince of Penzance in 2016 being the only Australian-bred winner in the eight renewals this decade. Rekindling was returned to Ireland—with the Gold Cup at Royal Ascot his main target in 2018—but Johannes Vermeer had been transferred permanently to Australia where he is to be joined by a further batch of Ballydoyle imports (listed in the essay on Rekindling) which will be trained by Liam Howley who took over from Robert Hickmott at the Macedon Lodge stables of Lloyd Williams at the end of November.

On what was seen of the latest two-year-old crop up to the end of December, the Sydney juveniles hold the upper hand, headed by **Performer** and **Bondi**. Performer won the Breeders' Plate at Randwick at the end of September in a time over a second quicker than the winner of the Gimcrack on the same card. **Ef Troop** was a runaway winner in listed company at Doomben in December, while **Run Naan** looks the pick of the Melbourne juveniles so far.

Ratings and text for Australia and New Zealand are supplied courtesy of Gary Crispe (www.racingandsports.com.au) The ages listed below are as at 31st December 2017

Two-Year-Olds

115p	Performer
112	Bondi
108	Ef Troop
107	Run Naan
106p	Legend of Condor
106	Encryption
106	Jonker
106	Neutrality
105	Legislation
105	Ranier
105	Setsuna (f)
105	Spin

Three-Year-Olds

122	Menari
122	Trapeze Artist
120p	Merchant Navy
119	Aloisia (f)
119	Invader
119	Pariah
119	She Will Reign (f)
119	†(The) Taj Mahal
118	Ace High
118	Alizee (f)
117	Cliff's Edge
117	Summer Passage
117?	Mighty Boss
116p	Kementari
116	Catchy (f)
116	Houtzen (f)
116	Property
116	Royal Symphony
116?	The Mission
115	Chauffeur
115	Formality (f)
115	Gold Standard
115	Gunnison
115	Invincible Star (f)
115	Perast
115	Tangled
115	Astoria
114	Embellish
114	Shoals (f)
114	Sully
114	Veranillo
113p	Main Stage
113p	Viridine
113	Ever Loyal
113	Frolic (f)
113	Showtime
113	Tulip (f)
113?	Achernar Star
113?	Pissaro
112	Jukebox
112	Melody Belle (f)
112	Sircconi
111p	Villermont
111p	Peaceful State
111	Age of Fire
111	Champagne Cuddles (f)
111	Doubt I'm Dreaming
111	Eptimum
111	Jorda (f)
111	Limestone (f)
111	Pierata
111	Pinot (f)
111	Sanctioned
111	Weather With You
111?	Aberro
111?	Wolfe Tone
110	Black Sail
110	Dracarys
110	Eshtiraak
110	Hasahalo (f)
110	Nature Strip
110	Ocean's Fourteen
110	Wait For No One
110	Whypeeo
110?	Salubrious

Four-Year-Olds

123	Extreme Choice
123	Gingernuts
122	Hey Doc
122	Impending
121	*Brave Smash
120	Bonneval (f)
120	Jon Snow
120	Russian Revolution
120	Star Turn

119 Inference
119? Harper's Choice
119? Attention
118 Hardham
118 So Si Bon
118 Ventura Storm
117 Derryn
117 Foxplay (f)
117? Odeon
116 Prized Icon
116 Ruthven
116 Snitty Kitty (f)
116? Rising Red
116? Snitzson
115 I Am A Star (f)
115 Invincible Gem (f)
115 Man From Uncle
115 Savile Row
114 Anaheim
114 Divine Prophet
114 Eckstein (f)
114 Global Glamour (f)
114 Mr Sneaky
114? Echo Effect
114? Lasqueti Spirit (f)
113 Comin' Through
113 La Diosa (f)
113 Prompt Response (f)
113 Samovare (f)
113 Saracino
113 Seaburge
112 Beaumarchais
112 Great Honour
112 Heroic Valour
112 Montoya's Secret (f)
112 Sacred Elixir
112 Spectroscope
112 Theanswermyfriend
112 Thronum
111 Crack Me Up
111 El Divino
111 Flying Artie
111 Fuhryk (f)
111 Guard of Honour
111 *Hall of Fame
111 Impavido
111 Land of Plenty
111 Nurse Kitchen (f)
111 Oak Door
111 Perfect Rhyme (f)
111 Raiment (f)
111 Scarlet Rain (f)
110 Charles Road
110 Gatting
110 Harlow Gold (f)
110 Kiwia
110 Northwest Passage
110 Now Or Later (f)
110 Variation
110 Volatile Mix
110 Winning Rupert

Older Horses

134 †Winx (f)
129 Humidor
127 Chautauqua
126 Black Heart Bart
126 Redzel
126 Vega Magic
125 Happy Clapper
125 Le Romain
124 Hartnell
124 Jameka (f)
124 Palentino
123 Our Ivanhowe
123 Stratum Star
123 Terravista
123 Turn Me Loose
123? Sense of Occasion
122 Ecuador
122 Fell Swoop
122 Gailo Chop
122 It's Somewhat
122 Music Magnate
122 Redkirk Warrior
122 The United States
122 Tosen Stardom
122 Who Shot Thebarman
121 Almandin
121 Clearly Innocent
121 English (f)
121 Exospheric
121 Hellbent
121 Lucky Hussler
121 Malaguerra
121 Spieth
120 Flamberge
120 Red Excitement
120 Tivaci
119 Ball of Muscle
119 Counterattack
119 Kawi
119 Start Wondering
118 Antonio Giuseppe
118 Dothraki
118 In Her Time (f)
118 Rock Magic
118 Sheidel (f)
118 Single Gaze (f)
118 Tally
117 Awesome Rock
117 Boom Time
117 Harlem
117 Keen Array
117 Mighty Lucky
117 Mourinho
117 Sound Proposition
117 Supply And Demand
117 Takedown
116 Big Duke
116 Close Up
116 Deploy
116 He's Our Rokkii
116 Hooked
116 Jungle Edge
116 Kuro
116 Libran
116 Maurus
116 Religify
116 Rudy
116 Scales of Justice
116 Scapolo
116 Silent Sedition (f)
116 Star Exhibit
116 Tavago
116 Tom Melbourne
116 Viddora (f)
116 Voodoo Lad
115 Abbey Marie (f)
115 Allergic
115 Articus
115 Assign
115 Authentic Paddy
115 Burning Front
115 Charmed Harmony
115 Classic Uniform
115 Disposition
115 Guardini
115 High Church
115 Magic Hurricane
115 Material Man
115 McCreery
115 Pounamu
115 Real Love (f)
115 Santa Ana Lane
115 The Monstar
115 Volkstok'n'Barrell

*(f) fillies and mares; *horse trained in the country for only part of the season; † (sections outside Europe and UAE) horse has a commentary in main section*

INDEX TO PHOTOGRAPHS

PORTRAITS & SNAPSHOTS

RACE PHOTOGRAPHS

Prix de Saint-Georges (Deauville)	*John Crofts*	910
Prix d'Ispahan (Chantilly)	*Bertrand*	644
Prix du Gros-Chene (Chantilly)	*John Crofts*	693
Prix du Haras de Fresnay-le-Buffard - Jacques le Marois (Deauville)	*Bertrand*	56
Prix Ganay (Saint-Cloud)	*Bertrand*	231
Prix Gontaut-Biron Hong Kong Jockey Club (Deauville)	*George Selwyn*	381
Prix Jean Prat (Chantilly)	*Bertrand*	1020
Prix Robert Papin (Maisons-Laffitte)	*Bertrand*	1053
Prix Rothschild (Deauville)	*Bertrand*	848
Prix Royal-Oak (Saint-Cloud)	*Bertrand*	495
Qatar Goodwood Cup (Goodwood)	*John Crofts*	960
Qatar Gordon Stakes (Goodwood)	*Bill Selwyn*	261
Qatar King George Stakes (Goodwood)	*George Selwyn*	107
Qatar Lennox Stakes (Goodwood)	*George Selwyn*	164
Qatar Nassau Stakes (Goodwood)	*John Crofts*	1113
Qatar Prix Daniel Wildenstein (Chantilly)	*Frank Sorge*	980
Qatar Prix de la Foret (Chantilly)	*George Selwyn*	34
Qatar Prix de l'Abbaye de Longchamp (Chantilly)	*John Crofts*	109
Qatar Prix de l'Arc de Triomphe (Chantilly)	*Bill Selwyn*	341
Qatar Prix Dollar (Chantilly)	*Bill Selwyn*	406
Qatar Prix du Cadran (Chantilly)	*Frank Sorge*	1067
Qatar Prix du Moulin de Longchamp (Chantilly)	*John Crofts*	833
Qatar Prix Foy (Chantilly)	*John Crofts*	312
Qatar Prix Jean-Luc Lagardere (Chantilly)	*John Crofts*	448
Qatar Prix Vermeille (Chantilly)	*George Selwyn*	105
Qatar Richmond Stakes (Goodwood)	*Ed Byrne*	102
Qatar Stewards' Cup (Heritage Handicap) (Goodwood)	*Bill Selwyn*	568
Qatar Summer Handicap (Goodwood)	*Bill Selwyn*	930
Qatar Sussex Stakes (Goodwood)	*Bill Selwyn*	469
Qatar Vintage Stakes (Goodwood)	*John Crofts*	359
Qipco British Champions Fillies' And Mares' Stakes (Ascot)	*John Crofts*	492
Qipco British Champions Long Distance Cup (Ascot)	*John Crofts*	735
Qipco British Champions Sprint Stakes (Ascot)	*John Crofts*	583
Qipco Champion Stakes (Ascot)	*John Crofts*	254
Qipco Irish Champion Stakes (Leopardstown)	*Frank Sorge*	283
Qipco 1000 Guineas Stakes (Newmarket)	*John Crofts*	1110
Qipco Prix du Jockey Club (Chantilly)	*John Crofts*	157
Qipco 2000 Guineas Stakes (Newmarket)	*John Crofts*	217
Queen Anne Stakes (Royal Ascot)	*Ed Byrne*	831
Queen Elizabeth II Stakes (Sponsored by Qipco) (Ascot)	*John Crofts*	761
Queen Mary Stakes (Royal Ascot)	*John Crofts*	462
Queen's Vase (Royal Ascot)	*Ed Byrne*	959
Racing Post Trophy (Doncaster)	*Ed Byrne*	878
Ribblesdale Stakes (Royal Ascot)	*Ed Byrne*	246
Royal Hunt Cup (Heritage Handicap) (Royal Ascot)	*Bill Selwyn*	1138
Sandringham Handicap (Royal Ascot)	*Bill Selwyn*	242
Seppelt Turnbull Stakes (Flemington)	*Darren Tindale*	1118
Shadwell Joel Stakes (Newmarket)	*John Crofts*	114
Shadwell Prix du Calvados (Deauville)	*Bertrand*	776
Shadwell Turf Mile Stakes (Keeneland)	*Z Photos*	968
Sky Bet Lowther Stakes (York)	*John Crofts*	1015
St James's Palace Stakes (Royal Ascot)	*John Crofts*	99
Stobart Rail Northumberland Plate (Heritage Handicap) (Newcastle)	*John Grossick*	474
Sunbets All-Weather Mile Championships Conditions Stakes (Lingfield)	*Ed Byrne*	936
Tattersalls Acomb Stakes (York)	*John Crofts*	1088
Tattersalls Falmouth Stakes (Newmarket)	*Martin Lynch*	847
Tattersalls Gold Cup (the Curragh)	*Caroline Norris*	282
Tattersalls Irish 1000 Guineas (the Curragh)	*Peter Mooney*	1111
Tattersalls Irish 2000 Guineas (the Curragh)	*Peter Mooney*	218

ADDITIONAL PHOTOGRAPHS

The following photos appear in the Introduction:- Enable and Frankie Dettori after winning the Yorkshire Oaks (taken by Bill Selwyn), record-breaking Aidan O'Brien and Saxon Warrior (Ed Byrne), Wings of Eagles springs a surprise in the Derby (Ed Byrne), Silvestre de Sousa champion jockey (Bill Selwyn), John Ferguson and Fred Done (both George Selwyn), Steve Drowne and Jimmy Fortune (both George Selwyn), Ballymacoll-bred Troy wins the 1979 Derby (inset Peter Reynolds and Islington)

Credits for the photographs in 'Top Horses Abroad' are as follows:- Grosser Preis von Berlin (Frank Sorge), Godolphin Mile (Frank Sorge), Dubai Turf (Bill Selwyn), Breeders' Cup Classic (Bill Selwyn), Whitney Stakes, Kentucky Derby, Preakness Stakes and Belmont Stakes (all Z Photos), Travers Stakes (Mathea Kelley), Breeders' Cup Mile, Breeders' Cup Turf Sprint (both Bill Selwyn), Breeders' Cup Juvenile Fillies' Stakes (George Selwyn), Japan Cup, Japanese Oaks (both Frank Sorge), Hong Kong Cup, Hong Kong Mile (both Frank Sorge), Queen Elizabeth Stakes (Gary Crispe), Caulfield Cup (Bronwen Healy), The Everest, TJ Smith Stakes and Sydney Cup (all Gary Crispe)

BIG RACE WINNERS

The record includes the Timeform Ratings recorded by the winner in the race (not its Timeform Annual Rating), the weight carried (sometimes preceded by age), starting price, trainer, jockey and number of runners. Race conditions and sponsors' names in the race titles are for the 2017 runnings. An asterisk prior to a horse's name denotes that it was awarded the race.

British Classic Races

QIPCO 2000 GUINEAS STAKES (3-y-o colts and fillies) (Newmarket 1m)

1970	135+	Nijinsky 9-0: 4/7f	M V O'Brien	*L Piggott*	14
1971	141	Brigadier Gerard 9-0: 11/2	W R Hern	*J Mercer*	6
1972	129	High Top 9-0: 85/40f	B van Cutsem	*W Carson*	12
1973	124	Mon Fils 9-0: 50/1	R Hannon	*F Durr*	18
1974	130+	Nonoalco 9-0: 19/2	F Boutin	*Y Saint-Martin*	12
1975	131	Bolkonski 9-0: 33/1	H R A Cecil	*G Dettori*	24
1976	125	Wollow 9-0: 1/1f	H R A Cecil	*G Dettori*	17
1977	125	Nebbiolo 9-0: 20/1	K Prendergast	*G Curran*	18
1978	122	Roland Gardens 9-0: 28/1	D Sasse	*F Durr*	19
1979	130	Tap On Wood 9-0: 20/1	B W Hills	*S Cauthen*	20
1980	130	*Known Fact 9-0: 14/1	A J Tree	*W Carson*	14
1981	125	To-Agori-Mou 9-0: 5/2f	G Harwood	*G Starkey*	19
1982	127	Zino 9-0: 8/1	F Boutin	*F Head*	26
1983	128	Lomond 9-0: 9/1	M V O'Brien	*Pat Eddery*	16
1984	136	El Gran Senor 9-0: 15/8f	M V O'Brien	*Pat Eddery*	9
1985	126	Shadeed 9-0: 4/5f	M R Stoute	*L Piggott*	14
1986	134	Dancing Brave 9-0: 15/8f	G Harwood	*G Starkey*	15
1987	127	Don't Forget Me 9-0: 9/1	R Hannon	*W Carson*	13
1988	124	Doyoun 9-0: 4/5f	M R Stoute	*W R Swinburn*	9
1989	127	Nashwan 9-0: 3/1f	W R Hern	*W Carson*	14
1990	127	Tirol 9-0: 9/1	R Hannon	*M J Kinane*	14
1991	124	Mystiko 9-0: 13/2	C E Brittain	*M Roberts*	14
1992	121	Rodrigo de Triano 9-0: 6/1	P W Chapple-Hyam	*L Piggott*	16
1993	130	Zafonic 9-0: 5/6f	A Fabre	*Pat Eddery*	14
1994	123	Mister Baileys 9-0: 16/1	M Johnston	*J Weaver*	23
1995	130	Pennekamp 9-0: 9/2	A Fabre	*T Jarnet*	11
1996	127	Mark of Esteem 9-0: 8/1	Saeed bin Suroor	*L Dettori*	13
1997	123	Entrepreneur 9-0: 11/2	M R Stoute	*M J Kinane*	16
1998	125	King of Kings 9-0: 7/2	A P O'Brien	*M J Kinane*	18
1999	122	Island Sands 9-0: 10/1	Saeed bin Suroor	*L Dettori*	16
2000	130+	King's Best 9-0: 13/2	Sir Michael Stoute	*K Fallon*	27
2001	122+	Golan 9-0: 11/1	Sir Michael Stoute	*K Fallon*	18
2002	120+	Rock of Gibraltar 9-0: 9/1	A P O'Brien	*J Murtagh*	22
2003	118+	Refuse To Bend 9-0: 9/2	D K Weld	*P J Smullen*	20
2004	129	Haafhd 9-0: 11/2	B W Hills	*R Hills*	14
2005	120	Footstepsinthesand 9-0: 13/2	A P O'Brien	*K Fallon*	19
2006	129+	George Washington 9-0: 6/4f	A P O'Brien	*K Fallon*	14
2007	125+	Cockney Rebel 9-0: 25/1	G A Huffer	*O Peslier*	24
2008	124+	Henrythenavigator 9-0: 11/1	A P O'Brien	*J Murtagh*	15
2009	128+	Sea The Stars 9-0: 8/1	J Oxx	*M J Kinane*	15
2010	124+	Makfi 9-0: 33/1	M Delzangles	*C P Lemaire*	19
2011	135+	Frankel 9-0: 1/2f	Sir Henry Cecil	*Tom Queally*	13
2012	123+	Camelot 9-0: 15/8f	Aidan O'Brien	*Joseph O'Brien*	18
2013	130+	Dawn Approach 9-0: 11/8f	Jim Bolger	*Kevin Manning*	13
2014	126	Night of Thunder 9-0: 40/1	Richard Hannon	*Kieren Fallon*	14
2015	125	Gleneagles 9-0: 4/1f	Aidan O'Brien	*Ryan Moore*	18
2016	126	Galileo Gold 9-0: 14/1	Hugo Palmer	*Frankie Dettori*	13
2017	125	Churchill 9-0: 6/4	Aidan O'Brien	*Ryan Moore*	10

QIPCO 1000 GUINEAS STAKES (3-y-o fillies) (Newmarket 1m)

1970	127	Humble Duty 9-0: 3/1jf	P Walwyn	*L Piggott*	12
1971	121	Altesse Royale 9-0: 25/1	C F N Murless	*Y Saint-Martin*	10
1972	115	Waterloo 9-0: 8/1	J W Watts	*E Hide*	18
1973	116+	Mysterious 9-0: 11/1	C F N Murless	*G Lewis*	14
1974	118	Highclere 9-0: 12/1	W R Hern	*J Mercer*	15
1975	121	Nocturnal Spree 9-0: 14/1	H V S Murless	*J Roe*	16
1976	120	Flying Water 9-0: 2/1f	A Penna	*Y Saint-Martin*	25
1977	122+	Mrs McArdy 9-0: 16/1	M W Easterby	*E Hide*	18
1978	119	Enstone Spark 9-0: 35/1	B W Hills	*E Johnson*	16
1979	113	One In A Million 9-0: 1/1f	H R A Cecil	*J Mercer*	17
1980	116	Quick As Lightning 9-0: 12/1	J L Dunlop	*B Rouse*	23
1981	121	Fairy Footsteps 9-0: 6/4f	H R A Cecil	*L Piggott*	14
1982	125	On The House 9-0: 33/1	H Wragg	*J Reid*	15
1983	124+	Ma Biche 9-0: 5/2f	Mme C Head	*F Head*	18
1984	121	Pebbles 9-0: 8/1	C E Brittain	*P Robinson*	15
1985	119	Oh So Sharp 9-0: 2/1f	H R A Cecil	*S Cauthen*	17
1986	120	Midway Lady 9-0: 10/1	B Hanbury	*R Cochrane*	15
1987	123+	Miesque 9-0: 15/8f	F Boutin	*F Head*	14
1988	121	Ravinella 9-0: 4/5f	Mme C Head	*G W Moore*	12
1989	117	Musical Bliss 9-0: 7/2	M R Stoute	*W R Swinburn*	7
1990	122	Salsabil 9-0: 6/4f	J L Dunlop	*W Carson*	10
1991	120	Shadayid 9-0: 4/6f	J L Dunlop	*W Carson*	14
1992	117	Hatoof 9-0: 5/1	Mme C Head	*W R Swinburn*	14
1993	113	Sayyedati 9-0: 4/1	C E Brittain	*W R Swinburn*	12
1994	115	Las Meninas 9-0: 12/1	T Stack	*J Reid*	15
1995	119	Harayir 9-0: 5/1	W R Hern	*R Hills*	14
1996	112+	Bosra Sham 9-0: 10/11f	H R A Cecil	*Pat Eddery*	13
1997	121	Sleepytime 9-0: 5/1	H R A Cecil	*K Fallon*	15
1998	126	Cape Verdi 9-0: 10/3jf	Saeed bin Suroor	*L Dettori*	16
1999	117	Wince 9-0: 4/1f	H R A Cecil	*K Fallon*	22
2000	117	Lahan 9-0: 14/1	J H M Gosden	*R Hills*	18
2001	116	Ameerat 9-0: 11/1	M A Jarvis	*P Robinson*	15
2002	112	Kazzia 9-0: 14/1	Saeed bin Suroor	*L Dettori*	17
2003	117+	Russian Rhythm 9-0: 12/1	Sir Michael Stoute	*K Fallon*	19
2004	116	Attraction 9-0: 11/2	M Johnston	*K Darley*	16
2005	116	Virginia Waters 9-0: 12/1	A P O'Brien	*K Fallon*	20
2006	115	Speciosa 9-0: 10/1	Mrs P Sly	*M Fenton*	13
2007	123	Finsceal Beo 9-0: 5/4f	J S Bolger	*K J Manning*	21
2008	114	Natagora 9-0: 11/4f	P Bary	*C P Lemaire*	15
2009	117	Ghanaati 9-0: 20/1	B W Hills	*R Hills*	14
2010	113	*Special Duty 9-0: 9/2f	Mme C Head-Maarek	*S Pasquier*	17
2011	117	Blue Bunting 9-0: 16/1	Mahmood Al Zarooni	*Frankie Dettori*	18
2012	120	Homecoming Queen 9-0: 25/1	Aidan O'Brien	*Ryan Moore*	17
2013	115+	Sky Lantern 9-0: 9/1	Richard Hannon	*Richard Hughes*	15
2014	112	Miss France 9-0: 7/1	Andre Fabre	*Maxime Guyon*	17
2015	121	Legatissimo 9-0: 13/2	David Wachman	*Ryan Moore*	13
2016	121	Minding 9-0: 11/10f	Aidan O'Brien	*Ryan Moore*	16
2017	120	Winter 9-0: 9/1	Aidan O'Brien	*W. M. Lordan*	14

INVESTEC OAKS (3-y-o fillies) (Epsom 1½m10y)

1970	120	Lupe 9-0: 100/30f	C F N Murless	*A Barclay*	16
1971	123	Altesse Royale 9-0: 6/4f	C F N Murless	*G Lewis*	11
1972	122	Ginevra 9-0: 8/1	R Price	*A Murray*	17
1973	127	Mysterious 9-0: 13/8f	C F N Murless	*G Lewis*	10
1974	118	Polygamy 9-0: 3/1f	P Walwyn	*Pat Eddery*	15
1975	120+	Juiliette Marny 9-0: 12/1	A J Tree	*L Piggott*	12
1976	123+	Pawneese 9-0: 6/5f	A Penna	*Y Saint-Martin*	14
1977	119	Dunfermline 9-0: 6/1	W R Hern	*W Carson*	13
1978	117	Fair Salinia 9-0: 8/1	M R Stoute	*G Starkey*	15
1979	117+	Scintillate 9-0: 20/1	A J Tree	*Pat Eddery*	14
1980	127	Bireme 9-0: 9/2	W R Hern	*W Carson*	11
1981	127	Blue Wind 9-0: 3/1jf	D K Weld	*L Piggott*	12
1982	124	Time Charter 9-0: 12/1	H Candy	*W Newnes*	13
1983	130	Sun Princess 9-0: 6/1	W R Hern	*W Carson*	15

1984	120	Circus Plume 9-0: 4/1	J L Dunlop	*L Piggott*	15
1985	131	Oh So Sharp 9-0: 6/4f	H R A Cecil	*S Cauthen*	12
1986	124+	Midway Lady 9-0: 15/8f	B Hanbury	*R Cochrane*	15
1987	125+	Unite 9-0: 11/1	M R Stoute	*W R Swinburn*	11
1988	126	Diminuendo 9-0: 7/4f	H R A Cecil	*S Cauthen*	11
1989	121	*Snow Bride 9-0: 13/2	H R A Cecil	*S Cauthen*	9
1990	127	Salsabil 9-0: 2/1f	J L Dunlop	*W Carson*	8
1991	122	Jet Ski Lady 9-0: 50/1	J S Bolger	*C Roche*	9
1992	128	User Friendly 9-0: 5/1	C E Brittain	*G Duffield*	7
1993	118	Intrepidity 9-0: 5/1	A Fabre	*M Roberts*	14
1994	115	Balanchine 9-0: 6/1	H Ibrahim	*L Dettori*	10
1995	117	Moonshell 9-0: 3/1	Saeed bin Suroor	*L Dettori*	10
1996	122	Lady Carla 9-0: 10/3	H R A Cecil	*Pat Eddery*	11
1997	117+	Reams of Verse 9-0: 5/6f	H R A Cecil	*K Fallon*	12
1998	120	Shahtoush 9-0: 12/1	A P O'Brien	*M J Kinane*	8
1999	123	Ramruma 9-0: 3/1	H R A Cecil	*K Fallon*	10
2000	120	Love Divine 9-0: 9/4f	H R A Cecil	*T Quinn*	16
2001	115	Imagine 9-0: 3/1f	A P O'Brien	*M J Kinane*	14
2002	121	Kazzia 9-0: 10/3f	Saeed bin Suroor	*L Dettori*	14
2003	114	Casual Look 9-0: 10/1	A M Balding	*Martin Dwyer*	15
2004	124	Ouija Board 9-0: 7/2	E A L Dunlop	*K Fallon*	7
2005	117	Eswarah 9-0: 11/4jf	M A Jarvis	*R Hills*	12
2006	123	Alexandrova 9-0: 9/4f	A P O'Brien	*K Fallon*	10
2007	121	Light Shift 9-0: 13/2	H R A Cecil	*T Durcan*	14
2008	123	Look Here 9-0: 33/1	R M Beckett	*S Sanders*	16
2009	122+	Sariska 9-0: 9/4f	M L W Bell	*J P Spencer*	10
2010	115+	Snow Fairy 9-0: 9/1	E A L Dunlop	*R L Moore*	15
2011	117	Dancing Rain 9-0: 20/1	William Haggas	*Johnny Murtagh*	13
2012	115	Was 9-0: 20/1	Aidan O'Brien	*Seamus Heffernan*	12
2013	114+	Talent 9-0: 20/1	Ralph Beckett	*Richard Hughes*	11
2014	117+	Taghrooda 9-0: 5/1	John Gosden	*Paul Hanagan*	17
2015	114	Qualify 9-0: 50/1	Aidan O'Brien	*Colm O'Donoghue*	11
2016	117+	Minding 9-0: 10/11f	Aidan O'Brien	*Ryan Moore*	9
2017	125	Enable 9-0: 6/1	John Gosden	*Frankie Dettori*	9

INVESTEC DERBY (3-y-o colts and fillies) (Epsom 1½m10y)

1970	135+	Nijinsky 9-0: 11/8f	M V O'Brien	*L Piggott*	11
1971	130	Mill Reef 9-0: 100/30f	I Balding	*G Lewis*	21
1972	131	Roberto 9-0: 3/1f	M V O'Brien	*L Piggott*	22
1973	125	Morston 9-0: 25/1	A Budgett	*E Hide*	25
1974	125	Snow Knight 9-0: 50/1	P Nelson	*B Taylor*	18
1975	135	Grundy 9-0: 5/1	P Walwyn	*Pat Eddery*	18
1976	128	Empery 9-0: 10/1	M Zilber	*L Piggott*	23
1977	129	The Minstrel 9-0: 5/1	M V O'Brien	*L Piggott*	22
1978	130	Shirley Heights 9-0: 8/1	J L Dunlop	*G Starkey*	25
1979	137	Troy 9-0: 6/1	W R Hern	*W Carson*	23
1980	130	Henbit 9-0: 7/1	W R Hern	*W Carson*	24
1981	140	Shergar 9-0: 10/11f	M R Stoute	*W R Swinburn*	18
1982	133	Golden Fleece 9-0: 3/1f	M V O'Brien	*Pat Eddery*	18
1983	132	Teenoso 9-0: 9/2f	G Wragg	*L Piggott*	21
1984	128	Secreto 9-0: 14/1	D V O'Brien	*C Roche*	17
1985	136	Slip Anchor 9-0: 9/4f	H R A Cecil	*S Cauthen*	14
1986	127	Shahrastani 9-0: 11/2	M R Stoute	*W R Swinburn*	17
1987	134	Reference Point 9-0: 6/4f	H R A Cecil	*S Cauthen*	19
1988	130	Kahyasi 9-0: 11/1	L M Cumani	*R Cochrane*	14
1989	129	Nashwan 9-0: 5/4f	W R Hern	*W Carson*	12
1990	127	Quest For Fame 9-0: 7/1	R Charlton	*Pat Eddery*	18
1991	135	Generous 9-0: 9/1	P F I Cole	*A Munro*	13
1992	127	Dr Devious 9-0: 8/1	P W Chapple-Hyam	*J Reid*	18
1993	126	Commander In Chief 9-0: 15/2	H R A Cecil	*M J Kinane*	16
1994	127	Erhaab 9-0: 7/2f	J L Dunlop	*W Carson*	25
1995	123	Lammtarra 9-0: 14/1	Saeed bin Suroor	*W R Swinburn*	15
1996	125	Shaamit 9-0: 12/1	W J Haggas	*M Hills*	20
1997	125	Benny The Dip 9-0: 11/1	J H M Gosden	*W Ryan*	13
1998	125	High-Rise 9-0: 20/1	L M Cumani	*O Peslier*	15

1999	125	Oath 9-0: 13/2	H R A Cecil	*K Fallon*	16
2000	129	Sinndar 9-0: 7/1	J Oxx	*J Murtagh*	15
2001	132	Galileo 9-0: 11/4jf	A P O'Brien	*M J Kinane*	12
2002	130	High Chaparral 9-0: 7/2	A P O'Brien	*J Murtagh*	12
2003	122+	Kris Kin 9-0: 6/1	Sir Michael Stoute	*K Fallon*	20
2004	125+	North Light 9-0: 7/2jf	Sir Michael Stoute	*K Fallon*	14
2005	131	Motivator 9-0: 3/1f	M L W Bell	*J Murtagh*	13
2006	119+	Sir Percy 9-0: 6/1	M P Tregoning	*Martin Dwyer*	18
2007	132+	Authorized 9-0: 5/4f	P W Chapple-Hyam	*L Dettori*	17
2008	128+	New Approach 9-0: 5/1	J S Bolger	*K J Manning*	16
2009	126+	Sea The Stars 9-0: 11/4	J Oxx	*M J Kinane*	12
2010	133	Workforce 9-0: 6/1	Sir Michael Stoute	*R L Moore*	12
2011	120+	Pour Moi 9-0: 4/1	A Fabre	*Mikael Barzalona*	13
2012	128	Camelot 9-0: 8/13f	Aidan O'Brien	*Joseph O'Brien*	9
2013	120+	Ruler of The World 9-0: 7/1	Aidan O'Brien	*Ryan Moore*	12
2014	127+	Australia 9-0: 11/8f	Aidan O'Brien	*Joseph O'Brien*	16
2015	132	Golden Horn 9-0: 13/8f	John Gosden	*Frankie Dettori*	12
2016	126	Harzand 9-0: 13/2	D K Weld	*Pat Smullen*	16
2017	124	Wings of Eagles 9-0: 40/1	Aidan O'Brien	*P. B. Beggy*	18

LADBROKES ST LEGER STAKES (3-y-o colts and fillies)
(Doncaster 1¾m132y, 1¾m115y from 2017, Ayr in 1989 and York 1m5f197y in 2006)

1970	127+	Nijinsky 9-0: 2/7f	M V O'Brien	*L Piggott*	9
1971	126	Athens Wood 9-0: 5/2	H T Jones	*L Piggott*	8
1972	124	Boucher 9-0: 3/1	M V O'Brien	*L Piggott*	7
1973	125	Peleid 9-0: 28/1	C W C Elsey	*F Durr*	13
1974	127+	Bustino 9-0: 11/10f	W R Hern	*J Mercer*	10
1975	132	Bruni 9-0: 9/1	R Price	*A Murray*	12
1976	131+	Crow 9-0: 6/1cf	A Penna	*Y Saint-Martin*	15
1977	133	Dunfermline 8-11: 10/1	W R Hern	*W Carson*	13
1978	127	Julio Mariner 9-0: 28/1	C Brittain	*E Hide*	14
1979	126	Son of Love 9-0: 20/1	R Collet	*A Lequeux*	17
1980	128	Light Cavalry 9-0: 3/1	H R A Cecil	*J Mercer*	7
1981	130	Cut Above 9-0: 28/1	W R Hern	*J Mercer*	7
1982	126	Touching Wood 9-0: 7/1	H Thomson Jones	*P Cook*	15
1983	124	Sun Princess 8-11: 11/8f	W R Hern	*W Carson*	10
1984	129	Commanche Run 9-0: 7/4f	L M Cumani	*L Piggott*	11
1985	121	Oh So Sharp 8-11: 8/11f	H R A Cecil	*S Cauthen*	6
1986	128	Moon Madness 9-0: 9/2	J Dunlop	*Pat Eddery*	8
1987	127	Reference Point 9-0: 4/11f	H R A Cecil	*S Cauthen*	7
1988	130	Minster Son 9-0: 15/2	N A Graham	*W Carson*	6
1989	127	Michelozzo 9-0: 6/4f	H R A Cecil	*S Cauthen*	8
1990	130	Snurge 9-0: 7/2	P F I Cole	*T Quinn*	8
1991	125	Toulon 9-0: 5/2f	A Fabre	*Pat Eddery*	10
1992	122	User Friendly 8-11: 7/4f	C E Brittain	*G Duffield*	7
1993	121	Bob's Return 9-0: 3/1f	M H Tompkins	*P Robinson*	9
1994	121	Moonax 9-0: 40/1	B W Hills	*Pat Eddery*	8
1995	120	Classic Cliche 9-0: 10/3f	Saeed bin Suroor	*L Dettori*	10
1996	124	Shantou 9-0: 8/1	J H M Gosden	*L Dettori*	11
1997	124	Silver Patriarch 9-0: 5/4f	J L Dunlop	*Pat Eddery*	10
1998	124	Nedawi 9-0: 5/2f	Saeed bin Suroor	*J Reid*	9
1999	129	Mutafaweq 9-0: 11/2	Saeed bin Suroor	*R Hills*	9
2000	122	Millenary 9-0: 11/4f	J L Dunlop	*T Quinn*	11
2001	126+	Milan 9-0: 13/8f	A P O'Brien	*M J Kinane*	10
2002	125	Bollin Eric 9-0: 7/1	T D Easterby	*K Darley*	8
2003	124	Brian Boru 9-0: 5/4f	A P O'Brien	*J P Spencer*	12
2004	125	Rule of Law 9-0: 3/1jf	Saeed bin Suroor	*K McEvoy*	9
2005	123+	Scorpion 9-0: 10/11f	A P O'Brien	*L Dettori*	6
2006	123+	Sixties Icon 9-0: 11/8f	J Noseda	*L Dettori*	11
2007	120+	Lucarno 9-0: 7/2	J H M Gosden	*J Fortune*	10
2008	127+	Conduit 9-0: 8/1	Sir Michael Stoute	*L Dettori*	14
2009	122	Mastery 9-0: 14/1	Saeed bin Suroor	*T E Durcan*	8
2010	123	Arctic Cosmos 9-0: 12/1	J H M Gosden	*W Buick*	10
2011	126	Masked Marvel 9-0: 15/2	John Gosden	*William Buick*	9

2012	123	Encke 9-0: 25/1	Mahmood Al Zarooni	*Mikael Barzalona*	9
2013	120+	Leading Light 9-0: 7/2f	Aidan O'Brien	*Joseph O'Brien*	11
2014	123+	Kingston Hill 9-1: 9/4f	Roger Varian	*Andrea Atzeni*	12
2015	119	Simple Verse 8-12: 8/1	Ralph Beckett	*Andrea Atzeni*	7
2016	119	Harbour Law 9-1: 22/1	Laura Mongan	*George Baker*	9
2017	124	Capri 9-1: 3/1f	Aidan O'Brien	*Ryan Moore*	11

King George VI & Prix de l'Arc de Triomphe

KING GEORGE VI AND QUEEN ELIZABETH STAKES (SPONSORED BY QIPCO)

(3-y-o+) (Ascot 1½m; Newbury 1½m5y in 2005)

1970	131+	Nijinsky 3-8-7: 40/85f	M V O'Brien	*L Piggott*	6
1971	139+	Mill Reef 3-8-7: 8/13f	I Balding	*G Lewis*	10
1972	134	Brigadier Gerard 4-9-7: 8/13f	W R Hern	*J Mercer*	9
1973	132	Dahlia 3-8-4: 10/1	M Zilber	*W Pyers*	12
1974	131+	Dahlia 4-9-4: 15/8f	M Zilber	*L Piggott*	10
1975	137	Grundy 3-8-7: 4/5f	P Walwyn	*Pat Eddery*	11
1976	131	Pawneese 3-8-5: 9/4	A Penna	*Y Saint-Martin*	10
1977	135	The Minstrel 3-8-8: 7/4f	M V O'Brien	*L Piggott*	11
1978	133	Ile de Bourbon 3-8-8: 12/1	F J Houghton	*J Reid*	14
1979	133	Troy 3-8-8: 2/5f	W R Hern	*W Carson*	7
1980	129	Ela-Mana-Mou 4-9-7: 11/4	W R Hern	*W Carson*	10
1981	132+	Shergar 3-8-8: 2/5f	M R Stoute	*W R Swinburn*	7
1982	132	Kalaglow 4-9-7: 13/2	G Harwood	*G Starkey*	9
1983	129	Time Charter 4-9-4: 5/1	H Candy	*J Mercer*	9
1984	135	Teenoso 4-9-7: 13/2	G Wragg	*L Piggott*	13
1985	135	Petoski 3-8-8: 12/1	W R Hern	*W Carson*	12
1986	137	Dancing Brave 3-8-8: 6/4	G Harwood	*Pat Eddery*	9
1987	139	Reference Point 3-8-8: 11/10f	H R A Cecil	*S Cauthen*	9
1988	131	Mtoto 5-9-7: 4/1	A Stewart	*M Roberts*	10
1989	131	Nashwan 3-8-8: 2/9f	W R Hern	*W Carson*	7
1990	131	Belmez 3-8-9: 15/2	H R A Cecil	*M J Kinane*	11
1991	138+	Generous 3-8-9: 4/6f	P F I Cole	*A Munro*	9
1992	135	St Jovite 3-8-9: 4/5f	J S Bolger	*S Craine*	8
1993	131	Opera House 5-9-7: 8/1	M R Stoute	*M Roberts*	10
1994	128	King's Theatre 3-8-9: 12/1	H R A Cecil	*M J Kinane*	12
1995	125	Lammtarra 3-8-9: 9/4f	Saeed bin Suroor	*L Dettori*	7
1996	132	Pentire 4-9-7: 10/3	G Wragg	*M Hills*	8
1997	134	Swain 5-9-7: 16/1	Saeed bin Suroor	*J Reid*	8
1998	132	Swain 6-9-7: 11/2	Saeed bin Suroor	*L Dettori*	8
1999	135+	Daylami 5-9-7: 3/1	Saeed bin Suroor	*L Dettori*	8
2000	131+	Montjeu 4-9-7: 1/3f	J E Hammond	*M J Kinane*	7
2001	134	Galileo 3-8-9: 1/2f	A P O'Brien	*M J Kinane*	12
2002	129	Golan 4-9-7: 11/2	Sir Michael Stoute	*K Fallon*	9
2003	133	Alamshar 3-8-9: 13/2	J Oxx	*J Murtagh*	12
2004	132	Doyen 4-9-7: 11/10f	Saeed bin Suroor	*L Dettori*	11
2005	130	Azamour 4-9-7: 5/2f	J Oxx	*M J Kinane*	12
2006	128+	Hurricane Run 4-9-7: 5/6f	A Fabre	*C Soumillon*	6
2007	132	Dylan Thomas 4-9-7: 5/4f	A P O'Brien	*J Murtagh*	7
2008	129	Duke of Marmalade 4-9-7: 4/6f	A P O'Brien	*J Murtagh*	8
2009	130	Conduit 4-9-7: 13/8f	Sir Michael Stoute	*R L Moore*	9
2010	140	Harbinger 4-9-7: 4/1	Sir Michael Stoute	*O Peslier*	6
2011	127	Nathaniel 3-8-9: 11/2	John Gosden	*William Buick*	5
2012	124+	Danedream 4-9-4: 9/1	P Schiergen	*Andrasch Starke*	10
2013	132	Novellist 4-9-7: 13/2	Andreas Wohler	*Johnny Murtagh*	8
2014	127	Taghrooda 3-8-6: 7/2	John Gosden	*Paul Hanagan*	8
2015	125	Postponed 4-9-7: 6/1	Luca Cumani	*Andrea Atzeni*	7
2016	127	Highland Reel 4-9-7: 13/8f	Aidan O'Brien	*Ryan Moore*	7
2017	130	Enable 3-8-7: 5/4f	John Gosden	*Frankie Dettori*	10

QATAR PRIX DE L'ARC DE TRIOMPHE

(3-y-o+ colts and fillies) (Longchamp 1½m; Chantilly in 2016 & 2017)

1970	135	Sassafras 3-8-10: 19/1	F Mathet	*Y Saint-Martin*	15
1971	141	Mill Reef 3-8-10: 7/10f	I A Balding	*G Lewis*	18
1972	133	San San 3-8-7: 185/10	A Penna	*F Head*	19
1973	137	Rheingold 4-9-6: 77/10	B W Hills	*L Piggott*	27
1974	132+	Allez France 4-9-3: 1/2cpf	A Penna	*Y Saint-Martin*	20
1975	133	Star Appeal 5-9-6: 119/1	T Grieper	*G Starkey*	24
1976	132	Ivanjica 4-9-1: 71/10cp	A Head	*F Head*	20
1977	137	Alleged 3-8-11: 39/10f	V O'Brien	*L Piggott*	26
1978	138	Alleged 4-9-4: 14/10f	V O'Brien	*L Piggott*	18
1979	133	Three Troikas 3-8-8: 88/10	Mme C Head	*F Head*	22
1980	131	Detroit 3-8-8: 67/10	O Douieb	*Pat Eddery*	20
1981	132	Gold River 4-9-1: 53/1	A Head	*G W Moore*	24
1982	131	Akiyda 3-8-8: 11/1	F Mathet	*Y Saint-Martin*	17
1983	131	All Along 4-9-1: 173/10	P L Biancone	*W R Swinburn*	26
1984	135	Sagace 4-9-4: 39/10cp	P L Biancone	*Y Saint-Martin*	22
1985	134	*Rainbow Quest 4-9-4: 71/10	J Tree	*Pat Eddery*	15
1986	140	Dancing Brave 3-8-11: 11/10f	G Harwood	*Pat Eddery*	15
1987	135	Trempolino 3-8-11: 20/1	A Fabre	*Pat Eddery*	11
1988	134	Tony Bin 5-9-4: 14/1	L Camici	*J Reid*	24
1989	132	Carroll House 4-9-4: 19/1	M A Jarvis	*M J Kinane*	19
1990	132	Saumarez 3-8-11: 154/10	N Clement	*G Mosse*	21
1991	135	Suave Dancer 3-8-11: 37/10	J E Hammond	*C Asmussen*	14
1992	131	Subotica 4-9-4: 88/10	A Fabre	*T Jarnet*	18
1993	126	Urban Sea 4-9-1: 37/1	J Lesbordes	*E Saint-Martin*	23
1994	129	Carnegie 3-8-11: 3/1cpf	A Fabre	*T Jarnet*	20
1995	134	Lammtarra 3-8-11: 21/10f	Saeed bin Suroor	*L Dettori*	16
1996	136	Helissio 3-8-11: 18/10f	E Lellouche	*O Peslier*	16
1997	137	Peintre Celebre 3-8-11: 22/10f	A Fabre	*O Peslier*	18
1998	129	Sagamix 3-8-11: 5/2jf	A Fabre	*O Peslier*	14
1999	137	Montjeu 3-8-11: 6/4cpf	J E Hammond	*M J Kinane*	14
2000	134	Sinndar 3-8-11: 6/4cp	J Oxx	*J Murtagh*	10
2001	135+	Sakhee 4-9-5: 22/10f	Saeed bin Suroor	*L Dettori*	17
2002	129	Marienbard 5-9-5: 158/10	Saeed bin Suroor	*L Dettori*	16
2003	133	Dalakhani 3-8-11: 14/10cpf	A de Royer Dupre	*C Soumillon*	13
2004	130	Bago 3-8-11: 77/10	J E Pease	*T Gillet*	19
2005	134	Hurricane Run 3-8-11: 19/10cpjf	A Fabre	*K Fallon*	15
2006	132	Rail Link 3-8-11: 236/10	A Fabre	*S Pasquier*	8
2007	127+	Dylan Thomas 4-9-5: 6/1	A P O'Brien	*K Fallon*	12
2008	130+	Zarkava 3-8-8: 1/1f	A de Royer Dupre	*C Soumillon*	16
2009	129+	Sea The Stars 3-8-11: 8/10f	J Oxx	*M J Kinane*	19
2010	133	Workforce 3-8-11: 76/10	Sir Michael Stoute	*R L Moore*	19
2011	132	Danedream 3-8-8: 27/1	P Schiergen	*Andrasch Starke*	16
2012	124	Solemia 4-9-2: 33/1	C Laffon-Parias	*Olivier Peslier*	18
2013	134	Treve 8-8: 48/10	Mme C Head-Maarek	*Thierry Jarnet*	17
2014	129	Treve 4-9-2: 14/1	Mme C Head-Maarek	*Thierry Jarnet*	20
2015	132	Golden Horn 3-8-11: 52/10	John Gosden	*Frankie Dettori*	17
2016	129	Found 4-9-2: 96/10	Aidan O'Brien	*Ryan Moore*	16
2017	133+	Enable 3-8-9: 8/10f	John Gosden	*Frankie Dettori*	18

Other Selected Group 1s (3-y-o+)

GOLD CUP (4-y-o+) (Royal Ascot 2½m; York in 2005)

2000	117+	Kayf Tara 6-9-2: 11/8f	Saeed bin Suroor	*M J Kinane*	11
2001	123	Royal Rebel 5-9-2: 8/1	M Johnston	*J Murtagh*	12
2002	124	Royal Rebel 6-9-2: 16/1	M Johnston	*J Murtagh*	15
2003	123+	Mr Dinos 4-9-0: 3/1	P F I Cole	*K Fallon*	12
2004	123+	Papineau 4-9-0: 5/1	Saeed bin Suroor	*L Dettori*	13
2005	125+	Westerner 6-9-2: 7/4f	E Lellouche	*O Peslier*	17
2006	122+	Yeats 5-9-2: 7/1	A P O'Brien	*K Fallon*	12
2007	121+	Yeats 6-9-2: 8/13f	A P O'Brien	*M J Kinane*	14

2008	126+	Yeats 7-9-2: 11/8f	A P O'Brien	*J Murtagh*	10
2009	126	Yeats 8-9-2: 6/4f	A P O'Brien	*J Murtagh*	9
2010	124	Rite of Passage 6-9-2: 20/1	D K Weld	*P Smullen*	12
2011	123+	Fame And Glory 5-9-2: 11/8f	Aidan O'Brien	*Jamie Spencer*	15
2012	121	Colour Vision 4-9-0: 6/1	Saeed bin Suroor	*Frankie Dettori*	9
2013	118	Estimate 4-8-11: 7/2f	Sir Michael Stoute	*Ryan Moore*	14
2014	123+	Leading Light 4-9-0: 10/11f	Aidan O'Brien	*Joseph O'Brien*	13
2015	120	Trip To Paris 4-9-0: 12/1	Ed Dunlop	*Graham Lee*	12
2016	125+	Order of St George 4-9-0: 10/11f	Aidan O'Brien	*Ryan Moore*	17
2017	122	Big Orange 6-9-2: 5/1	Michael Bell	*James Doyle*	14

CORAL-ECLIPSE (3-y-o+) (Sandown 1¼m7y)

2000	130+	Giant's Causeway 3-8-10: 8/1	A P O'Brien	*G Duffield*	8
2001	123+	Medicean 4-9-7: 7/2	Sir Michael Stoute	*K Fallon*	8
2002	125+	Hawk Wing 3-8-10: 8/15f	A P O'Brien	*M J Kinane*	5
2003	126+	Falbrav 5-9-7: 8/1	L M Cumani	*D Holland*	15
2004	128	Refuse To Bend 4-9-7: 15/2	Saeed bin Suroor	*L Dettori*	12
2005	127+	Oratorio 3-8-10: 12/1	A P O'Brien	*K Fallon*	7
2006	124+	David Junior 4-9-7: 9/4	B J Meehan	*J P Spencer*	9
2007	128	Notnowcato 5-9-7: 7/1	Sir Michael Stoute	*R L Moore*	8
2008	124+	Mount Nelson 4-9-7: 7/2	A P O'Brien	*J Murtagh*	8
2009	136+	Sea The Stars 3-8-10: 4/7f	J Oxx	*M J Kinane*	10
2010	122+	Twice Over 5-9-7: 13/8f	H R A Cecil	*T P Queally*	5
2011	131	So You Think 5-9-7: 4/6f	Aidan O'Brien	*Seamus Heffernan*	5
2012	129	Nathaniel 4-9-7: 7/2	John Gosden	*William Buick*	9
2013	128	Al Kazeem 5-9-7: 15/8f	Roger Charlton	*James Doyle*	7
2014	126	Mukhadram 5-9-7: 14/1	William Haggas	*Paul Hanagan*	9
2015	134	Golden Horn 3-8-10: 4/9f	John Gosden	*Frankie Dettori*	5
2016	124+	Hawkbill 3-8-10: 6/1	Charlie Appleby	*William Buick*	7
2017	128	Ulysses 4-9-7: 8/1	Sir Michael Stoute	*Jim Crowley*	9

DARLEY JULY CUP (3-y-o+) (Newmarket 6f)

2000	121	Agnes World 5-9-5: 4/1f	Hideyuki Mori	*Y Take*	10
2001	131	Mozart 3-8-13: 4/1f	A P O'Brien	*M J Kinane*	18
2002	121	Continent 5-9-5: 12/1	D Nicholls	*D Holland*	14
2003	128	Oasis Dream 3-8-13: 9/2	J H M Gosden	*R Hughes*	16
2004	120+	Frizzante 5-9-2: 14/1	J R Fanshawe	*J Murtagh*	20
2005	127	Pastoral Pursuits 4-9-5: 22/1	H Morrison	*J F Egan*	19
2006	125+	Les Arcs 6-9-5: 10/1	T J Pitt	*J F Egan*	15
2007	128	Sakhee's Secret 3-8-13: 9/2	H Morrison	*S Drowne*	18
2008	124+	Marchand d'Or 5-9-5: 5/2f	F Head	*D Bonilla*	13
2009	124	Fleeting Spirit 4-9-2: 12/1	J Noseda	*T P Queally*	13
2010	128	Starspangledbanner 4-9-5: 2/1f	A P O'Brien	*J Murtagh*	14
2011	125+	Dream Ahead 3-8-13: 7/1	David Simcock	*Hayley Turner*	16
2012	124	Mayson 4-9-5: 20/1	Richard Fahey	*Paul Hanagan*	12
2013	128	Lethal Force 4-9-5: 9/2	Clive Cox	*Adam Kirby*	11
2014	125	Slade Power 5-9-6: 7/4f	Edward Lynam	*W M Lordan*	13
2015	121	Muhaarar 3-9-0: 2/1jf	Charlie Hills	*Paul Hanagan*	14
2016	128+	Limato 4-9-6: 9/2f	Henry Candy	*Harry Bentley*	18
2017	119	Harry Angel 3-9-0: 9/2	Clive Cox	*Adam Kirby*	10

QATAR SUSSEX STAKES (3-y-o+) (Goodwood 1m)

2000	126+	Giant's Causeway 3-9-0: 3/1jf	A P O'Brien	*M J Kinane*	10
2001	125	Noverre 3-9-0: 9/2	Saeed bin Suroor	*L Dettori*	10
2002	124+	Rock of Gibraltar 3-8-13: 8/13f	A P O'Brien	*M J Kinane*	5
2003	118	Reel Buddy 5-9-7: 20/1	R Hannon	*Pat Eddery*	9
2004	124	Soviet Song 4-9-4: 3/1	J R Fanshawe	*J Murtagh*	11
2005	124+	Proclamation 3-8-13: 3/1	J Noseda	*M J Kinane*	12
2006	126+	Court Masterpiece 6-9-7: 15/2	E A L Dunlop	*J Fortune*	7
2007	126	Ramonti 5-9-7: 9/2	Saeed bin Suroor	*L Dettori*	8
2008	128+	Henrythenavigator 3-8-13: 4/11f	A P O'Brien	*J Murtagh*	6
2009	134	Rip Van Winkle 3-8-13: 6/4f	A P O'Brien	*J Murtagh*	8
2010	128+	Canford Cliffs 3-8-13: 4/6f	R Hannon	*R Hughes*	7
2011	139+	Frankel 3-8-13: 8/13f	Sir Henry Cecil	*Tom Queally*	4
2012	136+	Frankel 4-9-7: 1/20f	Sir Henry Cecil	*Tom Queally*	4
2013	133	Toronado 3-8-13: 11/4	Richard Hannon	*Richard Hughes*	7

2014	123+	Kingman 3-9-0: 2/5f	John Gosden	*James Doyle*	4
2015	126	Solow 5-9-8: 2/5f	F Head	*Maxime Guyon*	8
2016	127	The Gurkha 3-9-0: 11/8f	Aidan O'Brien	*Ryan Moore*	10
2017	121	Here Comes When 7-9-8: 20/1	Andrew Balding	*Jim Crowley*	7

JUDDMONTE INTERNATIONAL STAKES

(3-y-o+) (York 1¼m88y; run at Newmarket 1¼m in 2008)

2000	131+	Giant's Causeway 3-8-11: 10/11f	A P O'Brien	*M J Kinane*	6
2001	136	Sakhee 4-9-5: 7/4f	Saeed bin Suroor	*L Dettori*	8
2002	127+	Nayef 4-9-5: 6/4f	M P Tregoning	*R Hills*	7
2003	129+	Falbrav 5-9-5: 5/2	L M Cumani	*D Holland*	8
2004	126+	Sulamani 5-9-5: 3/1	Saeed bin Suroor	*L Dettori*	9
2005	127	Electrocutionist 4-9-5: 9/2	V Valiani	*M J Kinane*	7
2006	126	Notnowcato 4-9-5: 8/1	Sir Michael Stoute	*R L Moore*	7
2007	133	Authorized 3-8-11: 6/4f	P W Chapple-Hyam	*L Dettori*	7
2008	127+	Duke of Marmalade 4-9-5: 4/6f	A P O'Brien	*J Murtagh*	9
2009	131+	Sea The Stars 3-8-11: 1/4f	J Oxx	*M J Kinane*	4
2010	129	Rip Van Winkle 4-9-5: 7/4f	A P O'Brien	*J Murtagh*	9
2011	128	Twice Over 6-9-5: 11/2	Sir Henry Cecil	*Ian Mongan*	5
2012	142+	Frankel 4-9-5: 1/10f	Sir Henry Cecil	*Tom Queally*	9
2013	127+	Declaration of War 4-9-5: 7/1	Aidan O'Brien	*Joseph O'Brien*	6
2014	131+	Australia 3-8-12: 8/13f	Aidan O'Brien	*Joseph O'Brien*	6
2015	117	Arabian Queen 3-8-9: 50/1	David Elsworth	*Silvestre de Sousa*	7
2016	130+	Postponed 5-9-6: 15/8f	Roger Varian	*Andrea Atzeni*	12
2017	130	Ulysses 4-9-6: 4/1	Sir Michael Stoute	*Jim Crowley*	7

QUEEN ELIZABETH II STAKES SPONSORED BY QIPCO

(3-y-o+) (Ascot 1m; Newmarket in 2005)

2000	131	Observatory 3-8-11: 14/1	J H M Gosden	*K Darley*	12
2001	118	Summoner 4-9-1: 33/1	Saeed bin Suroor	*R Hills*	8
2002	124	Where Or When 3-8-11: 7/1	T G Mills	*K Darley*	5
2003	131+	Falbrav 5-9-1: 6/4f	L M Cumani	*D Holland*	8
2004	129	Rakti 5-9-1: 9/2	M A Jarvis	*P Robinson*	11
2005	123+	Starcraft 5-9-1: 7/2	L M Cumani	*C P Lemaire*	6
2006	132+	George Washington 3-8-13: 13/8f	A P O'Brien	*M J Kinane*	8
2007	126	Ramonti 5-9-3: 5/1	Saeed bin Suroor	*L Dettori*	7
2008	133	Raven's Pass 3-8-13: 3/1	J H M Gosden	*J Fortune*	7
2009	129+	Rip Van Winkle 3-8-13: 8/13f	A P O'Brien	*J Murtagh*	4
2010	126	Poet's Voice 3-8-13: 9/2	Saeed bin Suroor	*L Dettori*	8
2011	143	Frankel 9-0: 4/11f	Sir Henry Cecil	*Tom Queally*	8
2012	133	Excelebration 4-9-3: 10/11f	Aidan O'Brien	*Joseph O'Brien*	8
2013	132	Olympic Glory 3-9-0: 11/2	Richard Hannon	*Richard Hughes*	12
2014	127	Charm Spirit 3-9-1: 5/1	F Head	*Olivier Peslier*	11
2015	125	Solow 5-9-4: 11/10f	F Head	*Maxime Guyon*	9
2016	127	Minding 3-8-12: 7/4f	Aidan O'Brien	*Ryan Moore*	13
2017	122+	Persuasive 4-9-1: 8/1	John Gosden	*Frankie Dettori*	15

QIPCO CHAMPION STAKES (3-y-o+) (Ascot 1¼m; Newmarket prior to 2011)

2000	132	Kalanisi 4-9-2: 5/1	Sir Michael Stoute	*J Murtagh*	15
2001	126+	Nayef 3-8-11: 3/1f	M P Tregoning	*R Hills*	12
2002	125	Storming Home 4-9-2: 8/1	B W Hills	*M Hills*	11
2003	126	Rakti 4-9-2: 11/1	M A Jarvis	*P Robinson*	12
2004	129	Haafhd 3-8-11: 12/1	B W Hills	*R Hills*	11
2005	127	David Junior 3-8-11: 25/1	B J Meehan	*J P Spencer*	15
2006	126+	Pride 6-9-0: 7/2	A de Royer Dupre	*C P Lemaire*	8
2007	126+	Literato 3-8-12: 7/2	J-C Rouget	*C P Lemaire*	12
2008	132	New Approach 3-8-12: 6/5f	J S Bolger	*K J Manning*	11
2009	125+	Twice Over 4-9-3: 14/1	H R A Cecil	*T P Queally*	14
2010	128	Twice Over 5-9-3: 7/2	H R A Cecil	*T P Queally*	10
2011	133	Cirrus des Aigles 5-9-3: 12/1	Mme C Barande-Barbe	*Christophe Soumillon*	12
2012	139+	Frankel 4-9-3: 2/11f	Sir Henry Cecil	*Tom Queally*	6
2013	130+	Farhh 5-9-3: 11/4	Saeed bin Suroor	*Silvestre de Sousa*	10
2014	128	Noble Mission 5-9-5: 7/1	Lady Cecil	*James Doyle*	9
2015	127	Fascinating Rock 4-9-5: 10/1	D K Weld	*Pat Smullen*	13
2016	132+	Almanzor 3-9-0: 11/8f	Jean-Claude Rouget	*Christophe Soumillon*	10
2017	136	Cracksman 3-9-1: 13/8f	John Gosden	*Frankie Dettori*	10

AGE WEIGHT & DISTANCE TABLE

TIMEFORM'S SCALE OF WEIGHT-FOR-AGE FOR THE FLAT: JANUARY-MARCH

Distance	Age	January				February				March			
		1-8	9-16	17-23	24-31	1-8	9-16	17-23	24-29	1-8	9-16	17-23	24-31
5f	4	10-0	10-0	10-0	10-0	10-0	10-0	10-0	10-0	10-0	10-0	10-0	10-0
	3	9-4	9-4	9-4	9-4	9-4	9-4	9-4	9-4	9-6	9-6	9-6	9-6
	2											8-3	8-3
6f	4	9-13	9-13	9-13	9-13	10-0	10-0	10-0	10-0	10-0	10-0	10-0	10-0
	3	9-3	9-3	9-3	9-3	9-3	9-3	9-3	9-3	9-5	9-5	9-5	9-5
	2												
7f	4	9-13	9-13	9-13	9-13	9-13	9-13	9-13	9-13	10-0	10-0	10-0	10-0
	3	9-2	9-2	9-2	9-2	9-2	9-2	9-2	9-2	9-4	9-4	9-4	9-4
	2												
1m	4	9-12	9-12	9-12	9-12	9-12	9-12	9-12	9-12	9-13	9-13	9-13	9-13
	3	9-1	9-1	9-1	9-1	9-1	9-1	9-1	9-1	9-3	9-3	9-3	9-3
	2												
1m1f	4	9-12	9-12	9-12	9-12	9-12	9-12	9-12	9-12	9-13	9-13	9-13	9-13
	3	8-13	8-13	8-13	8-13	9-0	9-0	9-0	9-0	9-2	9-2	9-2	9-2
	2												
1m2f	4	9-11	9-11	9-11	9-11	9-11	9-11	9-11	9-11	9-12	9-12	9-12	9-12
	3	8-11	8-11	8-11	8-11	8-12	8-12	8-12	8-12	9-0	9-0	9-0	9-0
	2												
1m3f	4	9-10	9-10	9-10	9-10	9-10	9-10	9-10	9-10	9-11	9-11	9-11	9-11
	3	8-10	8-10	8-10	8-10	8-11	8-11	8-11	8-11	8-13	8-13	8-13	8-13
1m4f	4	9-10	9-10	9-10	9-10	9-10	9-10	9-10	9-10	9-11	9-11	9-11	9-11
	3	8-9	8-9	8-9	8-9	8-10	8-10	8-10	8-10	8-11	8-11	8-12	8-12
1m5f	4	9-9	9-9	9-9	9-9	9-9	9-9	9-9	9-9	9-10	9-10	9-10	9-10
	3												
1m6f	4	9-8	9-8	9-8	9-8	9-8	9-8	9-8	9-8	9-9	9-9	9-9	9-9
	3												
1m7f	4	9-7	9-7	9-7	9-7	9-8	9-8	9-8	9-8	9-9	9-9	9-9	9-9
	3												
2m	4	9-6	9-6	9-6	9-6	9-7	9-7	9-7	9-7	9-8	9-8	9-8	9-8
	3												
2m1f	4	9-5	9-5	9-5	9-5	9-6	9-6	9-6	9-6	9-7	9-7	9-7	9-7
	3												
2m2f	4	9-5	9-5	9-5	9-5	9-6	9-6	9-6	9-6	9-7	9-7	9-7	9-7
	3												
2m3f	4	9-4	9-4	9-4	9-4	9-5	9-5	9-5	9-5	9-6	9-6	9-6	9-6
	3												
2m4f	4	9-4	9-4	9-4	9-4	9-5	9-5	9-5	9-5	9-6	9-6	9-6	9-6
	3												
2m5f	4	9-4	9-4	9-4	9-4	9-5	9-5	9-5	9-5	9-6	9-6	9-6	9-6
	3												
2m6f	4	9-4	9-4	9-4	9-4	9-5	9-5	9-5	9-5	9-6	9-6	9-6	9-6
	3												

For 5-y-o's and older, use 10-0 in all cases

Note: Race distances in the above table are shown only at 1f intervals. For races over odd distances, the nearest distance shown in the table should be used: thus for races of 1m to 1m 109 yards, use the table weight for 1m; for 1m 110 yards to 1m 219 yards use 9f table.

AGE WEIGHT & DISTANCE TABLE

TIMEFORM'S SCALE OF WEIGHT-FOR-AGE FOR THE FLAT: APRIL-JUNE

Distance	Age	April				May				June			
		1-8	9-16	17-23	24-30	1-8	9-16	17-23	24-31	1-8	9-16	17-23	24-30
5f	4	10-0	10-0	10-0	10-0	10-0	10-0	10-0	10-0	10-0	10-0	10-0	10-0
	3	9-7	9-7	9-7	9-7	9-8	9-8	9-8	9-8	9-9	9-9	9-9	9-9
	2	8-4	8-4	8-5	8-5	8-6	8-6	8-7	8-7	8-8	8-8	8-9	8-9
6f	4	10-0	10-0	10-0	10-0	10-0	10-0	10-0	10-0	10-0	10-0	10-0	10-0
	3	9-6	9-6	9-6	9-6	9-7	9-7	9-7	9-7	9-8	9-8	9-8	9-8
	2					8-3	8-3	8-4	8-4	8-5	8-5	8-6	8-6
7f	4	10-0	10-0	10-0	10-0	10-0	10-0	10-0	10-0	10-0	10-0	10-0	10-0
	3	9-5	9-5	9-5	9-5	9-6	9-6	9-6	9-6	9-7	9-7	9-7	9-7
	2									8-3	8-3	8-4	8-4
1m	4	10-0	10-0	10-0	10-0	10-0	10-0	10-0	10-0	10-0	10-0	10-0	10-0
	3	9-4	9-4	9-4	9-4	9-5	9-5	9-5	9-5	9-6	9-6	9-6	9-6
	2												
1m1f	4	9-13	9-13	9-13	9-13	10-0	10-0	10-0	10-0	10-0	10-0	10-0	10-0
	3	9-3	9-3	9-3	9-3	9-4	9-4	9-4	9-4	9-5	9-5	9-5	9-5
	2												
1m2f	4	9-13	9-13	9-13	9-13	9-13	9-13	9-13	9-13	10-0	10-0	10-0	10-0
	3	9-1	9-1	9-2	9-2	9-3	9-3	9-4	9-4	9-5	9-5	9-5	9-5
	2												
1m3f	4	9-12	9-12	9-12	9-12	9-12	9-12	9-12	9-12	9-13	9-13	9-13	9-13
	3	9-0	9-0	9-1	9-1	9-2	9-2	9-3	9-3	9-4	9-4	9-4	9-4
1m4f	4	9-12	9-12	9-12	9-12	9-12	9-12	9-12	9-12	9-13	9-13	9-13	9-13
	3	8-13	8-13	9-0	9-0	9-1	9-1	9-2	9-2	9-3	9-3	9-3	9-3
1m5f	4	9-11	9-11	9-11	9-11	9-11	9-11	9-11	9-12	9-12	9-12	9-12	9-12
	3					9-0	9-0	9-1	9-1	9-2	9-2	9-2	9-2
1m6f	4	9-10	9-10	9-10	9-10	9-11	9-11	9-11	9-11	9-12	9-12	9-12	9-12
	3					8-12	8-12	8-13	8-13	9-0	9-0	9-1	9-1
1m7f	4	9-10	9-10	9-10	9-10	9-11	9-11	9-11	9-11	9-12	9-12	9-12	9-12
	3	8-9	8-9	8-10	8-10	8-11	8-11	8-12	8-12	8-13	8-13	9-0	9-0
2m	4	9-9	9-9	9-9	9-9	9-10	9-10	9-10	9-10	9-11	9-11	9-11	9-11
	3									8-11	8-11	8-12	8-12
2m1f	4	9-8	9-8	9-9	9-9	9-9	9-9	9-10	9-10	9-10	9-10	9-10	9-10
	3									8-10	8-10	8-11	8-11
2m2f	4	9-8	9-8	9-9	9-9	9-9	9-9	9-10	9-10	9-10	9-10	9-10	9-10
	3									8-9	8-9	8-10	8-10
2m3f	4	9-7	9-7	9-8	9-8	9-9	9-9	9-9	9-9	9-10	9-10	9-10	9-10
	3									8-8	8-8	8-9	8-9
2m4f	4	9-7	9-7	9-8	9-8	9-9	9-9	9-9	9-9	9-10	9-10	9-10	9-10
	3									8-7	8-7	8-8	8-8
2m5f	4	9-7	9-7	9-8	9-8	9-9	9-9	9-9	9-9	9-10	9-10	9-10	9-10
	3									8-7	8-7	8-8	8-8
2m6f	4	9-7	9-7	9-8	9-8	9-9	9-9	9-9	9-9	9-10	9-10	9-10	9-10
	3									8-7	8-7	8-8	8-8

For 5-y-o's and older, use 10-0 in all cases

Note: Race distances in the above table are shown only at 1f intervals. For races over odd distances, the nearest distance shown in the table should be used: thus for races of 1m to 1m 109 yards, use the table weight for 1m; for 1m 110 yards to 1m 219 yards use 9f table.

AGE WEIGHT & DISTANCE TABLE

TIMEFORM'S SCALE OF WEIGHT-FOR-AGE FOR THE FLAT: JULY-AUGUST

Distance	Age	July				August				September			
		1-8	9-16	17-23	24-31	1-8	9-16	17-23	24-31	1-8	9-16	17-23	24-30
5f	4	10-0	10-0	10-0	10-0	10-0	10-0	10-0	10-0	10-0	10-0	10-0	10-0
	3	9-10	9-10	9-10	9-10	9-10	9-10	9-11	9-11	9-11	9-11	9-11	9-11
	2	8-10	8-10	8-10	8-10	8-11	8-11	8-12	8-12	8-13	8-13	9-0	9-0
6f	4	10-0	10-0	10-0	10-0	10-0	10-0	10-0	10-0	10-0	10-0	10-0	10-0
	3	9-9	9-9	9-9	9-9	9-10	9-10	9-10	9-10	9-11	9-11	9-11	9-11
	2	8-7	8-7	8-8	8-8	8-9	8-9	8-10	8-10	8-11	8-11	8-12	8-12
7f	4	10-0	10-0	10-0	10-0	10-0	10-0	10-0	10-0	10-0	10-0	10-0	10-0
	3	9-8	9-8	9-8	9-8	9-9	9-9	9-9	9-9	9-10	9-10	9-10	9-10
	2	8-5	8-5	8-6	8-6	8-7	8-7	8-8	8-8	8-9	8-9	8-10	8-10
1m	4	10-0	10-0	10-0	10-0	10-0	10-0	10-0	10-0	10-0	10-0	10-0	10-0
	3	9-7	9-7	9-7	9-7	9-8	9-8	9-8	9-8	9-9	9-9	9-9	9-9
	2					8-6	8-6	8-7	8-7	8-8	8-8	8-9	8-9
1m1f	4	10-0	10-0	10-0	10-0	10-0	10-0	10-0	10-0	10-0	10-0	10-0	10-0
	3	9-6	9-6	9-6	9-6	9-7	9-7	9-7	9-7	9-8	9-8	9-8	9-8
	2									8-6	8-6	8-7	8-7
1m2f	4	10-0	10-0	10-0	10-0	10-0	10-0	10-0	10-0	10-0	10-0	10-0	10-0
	3	9-6	9-6	9-6	9-6	9-7	9-7	9-7	9-7	9-8	9-8	9-8	9-8
	2											8-5	8-5
1m3f	4	10-0	10-0	10-0	10-0	10-0	10-0	10-0	10-0	10-0	10-0	10-0	10-0
	3	9-5	9-5	9-5	9-5	9-6	9-6	9-6	9-6	9-7	9-7	9-7	9-7
1m4f	4	9-13	9-13	9-13	9-13	10-0	10-0	10-0	10-0	10-0	10-0	10-0	10-0
	3	9-4	9-4	9-4	9-4	9-5	9-5	9-5	9-5	9-6	9-6	9-6	9-6
1m5f	4	9-13	9-13	9-13	9-13	9-13	9-13	9-13	9-13	10-0	10-0	10-0	10-0
	3	9-3	9-3	9-3	9-3	9-4	9-4	9-4	9-4	9-5	9-5	9-5	9-5
1m6f	4	9-13	9-13	9-13	9-13	9-13	9-13	9-13	9-13	9-13	9-13	10-0	10-0
	3	9-2	9-2	9-2	9-2	9-3	9-3	9-3	9-3	9-4	9-4	9-4	9-4
1m7f	4	9-12	9-12	9-13	9-13	9-13	9-13	9-13	9-13	9-13	9-13	9-13	9-13
	3	9-1	9-1	9-1	9-1	9-2	9-2	9-2	9-2	9-3	9-3	9-3	9-3
2m	4	9-12	9-12	9-12	9-12	9-13	9-13	9-13	9-13	9-13	9-13	9-13	9-13
	3	8-13	8-13	9-0	9-0	9-1	9-1	9-1	9-1	9-2	9-2	9-2	9-2
2m1f	4	9-11	9-11	9-12	9-12	9-12	9-12	9-12	9-12	9-12	9-12	9-13	9-13
	3	8-12	8-12	8-13	8-13	9-0	9-0	9-0	9-0	9-1	9-1	9-1	9-1
2m2f	4	9-11	9-11	9-12	9-12	9-12	9-12	9-12	9-12	9-12	9-12	9-13	9-13
	3	8-11	8-11	8-12	8-12	8-13	8-13	9-0	9-0	9-1	9-1	9-1	9-1
2m3f	4	9-10	9-10	9-11	9-11	9-11	9-11	9-12	9-12	9-12	9-12	9-12	9-12
	3	8-10	8-10	8-11	8-11	8-12	8-12	8-13	8-13	9-0	9-0	9-0	9-0
2m4f	4	9-10	9-10	9-11	9-11	9-11	9-11	9-12	9-12	9-12	9-12	9-12	9-12
	3	8-9	8-9	8-10	8-10	8-11	8-11	8-12	8-12	8-13	8-13	8-13	8-13
2m5f	4	9-10	9-10	9-11	9-11	9-11	9-11	9-12	9-12	9-12	9-12	9-12	9-12
	3	8-9	8-9	8-10	8-10	8-11	8-11	8-12	8-12	8-13	8-13	8-13	8-13
2m6f	4	9-10	9-10	9-11	9-11	9-11	9-11	9-12	9-12	9-12	9-12	9-12	9-12
	3	8-9	8-9	8-10	8-10	8-11	8-11	8-12	8-12	8-13	8-13	8-13	8-13

For 5-y-o's and older, use 10-0 in all cases

Note: Race distances in the above table are shown only at 1f intervals. For races over odd distances, the nearest distance shown in the table should be used: thus for races of 1m to 1m 109 yards, use the table weight for 1m; for 1m 110 yards to 1m 219 yards use 9f table.

AGE WEIGHT & DISTANCE TABLE

TIMEFORM'S SCALE OF WEIGHT-FOR-AGE FOR THE FLAT: OCTOBER-DECEMBER

Distance	Age	October				November				December			
		1-8	9-16	17-23	24-31	1-8	9-16	17-23	24-30	1-8	9-16	17-23	24-31
5f	4	10-0	10-0	10-0	10-0	10-0	10-0	10-0	10-0	10-0	10-0	10-0	10-0
	3	9-12	9-12	9-12	9-12	9-13	9-13	9-13	9-13	9-13	9-13	9-13	9-13
	2	9-1	9-1	9-2	9-2	9-2	9-2	9-2	9-2	9-3	9-3	9-3	9-3
6f	4	10-0	10-0	10-0	10-0	10-0	10-0	10-0	10-0	10-0	10-0	10-0	10-0
	3	9-12	9-12	9-12	9-12	9-13	9-13	9-13	9-13	9-13	9-13	9-13	9-13
	2	8-13	8-13	9-0	9-0	9-1	9-1	9-1	9-1	9-2	9-2	9-2	9-2
7f	4	10-0	10-0	10-0	10-0	10-0	10-0	10-0	10-0	10-0	10-0	10-0	10-0
	3	9-11	9-11	9-11	9-11	9-12	9-12	9-12	9-12	9-12	9-12	9-12	9-12
	2	8-11	8-11	8-12	8-12	8-13	8-13	9-0	9-0	9-1	9-1	9-1	9-1
1m	4	10-0	10-0	10-0	10-0	10-0	10-0	10-0	10-0	10-0	10-0	10-0	10-0
	3	9-10	9-10	9-10	9-10	9-11	9-11	9-11	9-11	9-11	9-11	9-11	9-11
	2	8-10	8-10	8-11	8-11	8-12	8-12	8-13	8-13	9-0	9-0	9-0	9-0
1m1f	4	10-0	10-0	10-0	10-0	10-0	10-0	10-0	10-0	10-0	10-0	10-0	10-0
	3	9-9	9-9	9-9	9-9	9-10	9-10	9-10	9-10	9-11	9-11	9-11	9-11
	2	8-8	8-8	8-9	8-9	8-10	8-10	8-11	8-11	8-12	8-12	8-12	8-12
1m2f	4	10-0	10-0	10-0	10-0	10-0	10-0	10-0	10-0	10-0	10-0	10-0	10-0
	3	9-9	9-9	9-9	9-9	9-10	9-10	9-10	9-10	9-11	9-11	9-11	9-11
	2	8-6	8-6	8-7	8-7	8-8	8-8	8-9	8-9	8-10	8-10	8-10	8-10
1m3f	4	10-0	10-0	10-0	10-0	10-0	10-0	10-0	10-0	10-0	10-0	10-0	10-0
	3	9-8	9-8	9-8	9-8	9-9	9-9	9-9	9-9	9-10	9-10	9-10	9-10
1m4f	4	10-0	10-0	10-0	10-0	10-0	10-0	10-0	10-0	10-0	10-0	10-0	10-0
	3	9-7	9-7	9-7	9-7	9-8	9-8	9-8	9-8	9-9	9-9	9-9	9-9
1m5f	4	10-0	10-0	10-0	10-0	10-0	10-0	10-0	10-0	10-0	10-0	10-0	10-0
	3	9-6	9-6	9-6	9-6	9-7	9-7	9-7	9-7	9-8	9-8	9-8	9-8
1m6f	4	10-0	10-0	10-0	10-0	10-0	10-0	10-0	10-0	10-0	10-0	10-0	10-0
	3	9-5	9-5	9-5	9-5	9-6	9-6	9-6	9-6	9-7	9-7	9-7	9-7
1m7f	4	10-0	10-0	10-0	10-0	10-0	10-0	10-0	10-0	10-0	10-0	10-0	10-0
	3	9-4	9-4	9-4	9-4	9-5	9-5	9-5	9-5	9-6	9-6	9-6	9-6
2m	4	9-13	9-13	10-0	10-0	10-0	10-0	10-0	10-0	10-0	10-0	10-0	10-0
	3	9-3	9-3	9-3	9-3	9-4	9-4	9-4	9-4	9-5	9-5	9-5	9-5
2m1f	4	9-13	9-13	9-13	9-13	9-13	9-13	10-0	10-0	10-0	10-0	10-0	10-0
	3	9-2	9-2	9-2	9-2	9-3	9-3	9-3	9-3	9-4	9-4	9-4	9-4
2m2f	4	9-13	9-13	9-13	9-13	9-13	9-13	10-0	10-0	10-0	10-0	10-0	10-0
	3	9-2	9-2	9-2	9-2	9-3	9-3	9-3	9-3	9-4	9-4	9-4	9-4
2m3f	4	9-13	9-13	9-13	9-13	9-13	9-13	9-13	9-13	10-0	10-0	10-0	10-0
	3	9-1	9-1	9-1	9-1	9-2	9-2	9-2	9-2	9-3	9-3	9-3	9-3
2m4f	4	9-13	9-13	9-13	9-13	9-13	9-13	9-13	9-13	10-0	10-0	10-0	10-0
	3	9-0	9-0	9-0	9-0	9-1	9-1	9-2	9-2	9-3	9-3	9-3	9-3
2m5f	4	9-13	9-13	9-13	9-13	9-13	9-13	9-13	9-13	10-0	10-0	10-0	10-0
	3	9-0	9-0	9-0	9-0	9-1	9-1	9-2	9-2	9-3	9-3	9-3	9-3
2m6f	4	9-13	9-13	9-13	9-13	9-13	9-13	9-13	9-13	10-0	10-0	10-0	10-0
	3	9-0	9-0	9-0	9-0	9-1	9-1	9-2	9-2	9-3	9-3	9-3	9-3

For 5-y-o's and older, use 10-0 in all cases

Note: Race distances in the above table are shown only at 1f intervals. For races over odd distances, the nearest distance shown in the table should be used: thus for races of 1m to 1m 109 yards, use the table weight for 1m; for 1m 110 yards to 1m 219 yards use 9f table.